סידור קורן שלם

The Koren Shalem Siddur

קורן ירושלים

ORTHODOX UNION
תורה ומצוות

THE LOBEL EDITION

סידור קורן שלם
THE KOREN SHALEM SIDDUR

WITH INTRODUCTION, TRANSLATION
AND COMMENTARY BY

Rabbi Lord Jonathan Sacks שליט״א

•

KOREN PUBLISHERS JERUSALEM

The Lobel Edition

of

The Koren Shalem Siddur

is dedicated

in loving memory of

Daniella Moffson, ז״ל

who prayed consistently, intently,

and with sincere commitment

May Daniella's dedication to prayer

inspire and guide us

whenever we use this siddur

The Lobel Family

New York, USA

The Koren Shalem Siddur
Nusaḥ Ashkenaz
First Hebrew/English Edition, 2019
Combined American/Canadian Edition

Koren Publishers Jerusalem Ltd.
POB 4044, Jerusalem 91040, ISRAEL
POB 8531, New Milford, CT 06776, USA

www.korenpub.com

The English translation and commentary in this edition are based on the English translation and commentary first published in Great Britain in 2006 in the Authorised Daily Prayer Book of the United Hebrew Congregations of the Commonwealth: New Translation and Commentary by Chief Rabbi Jonathan Sacks, (Fourth Edition, Compilation © United Synagogue) by Collins, a division of HarperCollins Publishers, London.

The creation of this Siddur was made possible with the generous support of Torah Education in Israel.

Printed in the PRC

Leader's Size, Hardcover, ISBN 978 965 301 945 4
Standard Size, Hardcover, ISBN 978 965 301 930 0
Compact Size, Hardcover, ISBN 978 965 301 932 4
Compact Size, Softcover, ISBN 978 965 301 931 7
Compact Size, Hardcover, Brown Leather, ISBN 978 965 301 933 1
Compact Size, Hardcover, artwork by Emanuel, ISBN 978 965 301 934 8
Compact Size, Flexible Cover, Pink, ISBN 978 965 301 953 9
Compact Size, Flexible Cover, Turquoise, ISBN 978 965 301 954 6
Compact Size, Flexible Cover, Purple, ISBN 978 965 301 955 3
Compact Size, Flexible Cover, Denim, ISBN 978 965 301 956 0
Compact Size, Flexible Cover, Green, ISBN 978 965 301 957 7
Compact Size, Flexible Cover, Light Blue, ISBN 978 965 776 503 6

KSMA04

CONTENTS

פסח PESAḤ

חול המועד ḤOL HAMO'ED

Table of Contents for Ḥol HaMo'ed and Shabbat Ḥol HaMo'ed is on the previous pages

PREFACE TO THE FIRST HEBREW EDITION

"My help comes from the Lord…"

"And their fear toward Me is as a commandment of men learned by rote" (Is. 29:13) laments the prophet, referring to those who turn prayer into routine habit. Even when they pray before the Lord, "With their mouth and with their lips do [they] honor Me, but have removed their heart far from Me." This is precisely as our sages cautioned, saying: "When you pray, do not do so as a fixed routine, but as a plea for mercy and grace before God" (*Avot* 2:18). Bartenura elaborates, "[Do not say] as a person who has a duty to fulfill says: I shall relieve myself from this burden." Thus is the nature of ritual duties: when they become routine habit, their original meaning is diminished.

The prayers in this Siddur – the same words, those same sentences we repeat daily and even several times each day – become routine verbiage, "a chirping of a starling" which lacks the deep concentration and the vital sense of "knowing before whom one stands."

This unfortunate situation – which is natural – became our inspiration to present worshipers with the means to connect to prayer, both to the words of the prayers and to the content and meaning our sages infused into the phrases. We resolved to bring the prayers before the worshiper not in a secular form, as a regular book, but in a more sacred manner, so as to enable the worldly structure to become a source of inspiration, reverence, sanctity and awe.

To achieve this, we created an original design of the printed font and the layout of the words in accordance with the meaning of the prayers, line-by-line, page-by-page. From a visual standpoint, the contents of the prayers are presented in a style that does not spur habit and hurry, but rather encourages the worshiper to engross his mind and heart in prayer.

One possible hazard that undermines the beauty and the purity of the prayers is carelessness of diction when pronouncing the words. Disregard for grammar and punctuation, disrespect, or lack of knowledge of the laws of the *dagesh*, the quiescent *sh'va* and the mobile *sh'va*, and so forth, that our sages – the authors of the *Mesora*, the scholars of the linguistic form of the language, the adjudicators of the laws and students of the Torah

◂ and Kabbala

and Kabbala – were so meticulous about perfecting. In parts of prayers (such as the Shema and the Blessing of the Kohanim), they viewed this meticulous pronunciation as obligatory.

In order to relieve the worshiper of these details – for the sake of his praying – we have presented him (excluding Biblical quotations) with a different notation between the two *sh'vas* (the mobile *sh'va* is more predominant, which is a sign for the worshiper to express the vowel as a brief *segol*, while the quiescent *sh'va* is smaller, as it is not pronounced), and a special form of the *kamatz* (the "small *kamatz*" has a longer foot).

"A window thou shalt make to the ark," says God to Noaḥ, and our sages took this also to mean that the correct pronunciation of the words is an embellishment to the prayers. It is fitting that our conversations with God be clear, pure and unblemished, open and lit as this window.

The Nusaḥ Ashkenaz edition of this Siddur is based upon that of the "first Ashkenazic scholars," incorporating the revisions that were accepted in the land of Israel by the pupils of the Vilna Ga'on, and are customary in synagogues in Israel and the Diaspora (with different customs indicated).

I am very grateful to the excellent proofreaders Shmuel Vexler and Abraham Frankel, for their diligent work, and to Esther Be'er, who skillfully prepared the difficult typesetting of this Siddur.

All this would not have been possible without the help and guidance of my friend Meir Medan, who helped us reach this goal. Using his vast knowledge and careful comparison between different versions, we strived together to make this Siddur as perfect as humanly possible.

And let the beauty of the Lord our God be upon us: and establish the work of our hands upon us; O prosper it, the work of our hands.

Eliyahu Koren

PREFACE TO THE KOREN SHALEM SIDDUR

"One generation will praise Your works to the next..."

Since its initial publication in Hebrew in 1981, the original Koren Siddur has been recognized for its textual accuracy and innovative graphic design, which led to nothing less than a transformation in the very way people pray and connect to God. It was the hope of master typographer Eliyahu Koren "to present to worshipers a means to draw and connect them not only to the words of the prayers, but also to the contents and meaning that were before our sages when engraving the phrases of the prayers, and our rabbis throughout the ages when compiling versions of the prayers." Koren typographic design aims to slow the reader down and help bring alive the meaning of the text to the user.

We have remained committed to these qualities in our Siddurim with English, and have enriched the Siddur with the eloquent English translation and insightful introduction and commentary of one of the most articulate and original Jewish thinkers of our time, Rabbi Lord Jonathan Sacks.

This is the most complete Siddur we have published. Building on the wonderful reception of the first Koren Sacks Siddur in 2008, we have responded to the various requests to create an edition which is more comprehensive and useful all year round, including the Ḥagim. To that purpose, in the Koren Shalem Siddur, we have introduced:

- All Torah readings for Sukkot, Pesaḥ, Shavuot, Ḥanukka, Purim and Yom HaAtzma'ut, with new English translations for the Shalosh Regalim, including Ḥol HaMo'ed
- The Five Megillot with new English translation
- Additional prayers for personal supplications.

We have maintained the same page numbers as the standard Koren Sacks Siddur for easy synagogue adoption.

In common with all our Siddurim and Maḥzorim, this Siddur presents several unique features:

- There are two distinct fonts, designed by Eliyahu Koren, used throughout the Siddur. The Koren Tanakh Font is used for Tanakh texts

◂ (except

(except when embedded in prayers), and the Koren Siddur Font is used for prayers, in keeping with Mr. Koren's belief that the presentation of Tanakh text should be distinctive.

- Reading aids, fully explained in the Guide to the Reader, facilitate correct reading.
- The graphic layout distinguishes poetry from prose, and provides space to allow pages to "breathe." We have developed a parallel style for the English text that balances the weight of the Hebrew letters to further Mr. Koren's intention of presenting the texts "in a style that does not spur habit and hurry, but rather encourages the worshiper to engross his mind and heart in prayer."
- There are concise instructions throughout the text and practical Halakha guides at the back of the Siddur.
- There are prayers for visitors to Israel, and for Yom HaZikaron and Yom HaAtzma'ut, to reflect the essential and integral connection between the Jewish people in Israel and around the world, and the centrality of Jerusalem to us all.

It is always a privilege to collaborate on a project with those who share our commitment and enthusiasm for bringing out the beauty of *Tefilla*. We are grateful to Judith and David Lobel for their support and are proud to have their name grace this edition. Mr. Lobel's eminently practical suggestions were particularly helpful during the conceptual process. On behalf of the scholars, editors and designers of this volume, we thank you; on behalf of the users of this Siddur, we are forever in your debt.

We wish to thank Rabbi Sacks, שליט״א, for his exceptional introduction, translation and commentary, and his dedicated involvement throughout the preparation of this Siddur; Rabbi Eli Clark for his extraordinarily helpful section on Halakha; and Rabbi Tzvi Hersh Weinreb, שליט״א, and his colleagues at the Orthodox Union for their support and appreciation.

My colleagues Rabbi David Fuchs, Dena Landowne Bailey, and Rachel Meghnagi were instrumental in the creation of this new edition.

We can only hope that we have extended the vision of Eliyahu Koren to a new generation and a larger audience, furthering *Avodat HaShem* for Jews everywhere.

Matthew Miller, Publisher
Jerusalem, 5777 (2017)

FOREWORD

Our sages encourage us to have very lofty expectations of ourselves with regard to our prayers. Maimonides, for example, considers the duty to pray to have a firm basis in the written Torah. Rabbi Judah HaLevi considers our moment of prayer to be the "heart of our daily routine." Rabbi Kook speaks of the "perennial prayer of the soul."

Most of us have occasionally experienced such moments of spirituality – perhaps during a particularly inspirational holiday service, or perhaps in a moment of exultant joy or poignant sorrow. But those rare moments depend on very special circumstances. The challenge is to achieve a sense of spirituality during routine prayer times, which are fixed and regular – three times a day, every day of the year – and even in mundane moments and dreary contexts.

We need external stimuli which can refresh our inner selves to help us capture, if not sublimity, then at least a sense of the sacred. A proper siddur, which is sensitive to the needs of he or she who prays, can be such a stimulus.

The Siddur which you have before you, produced by master publishers of Hebrew books, Koren of Jerusalem, attempts to relate to the spiritual needs of those who turn to prayer and need an aesthetic context which will raise them from their routine to a higher sphere. This Siddur accomplishes this mission in several ways. It affords us the beautiful, contemporary, impactful translation of a man who, perhaps more than anyone else of our generation, is in tune with the spiritual needs of the English-speaking Jew. In this prayer book, Rabbi Jonathan Sacks offers us words of introduction and explanation, commentary, and an exquisite grasp of the poetry of prayer. The conceptual richness of his thoughts, coupled with the artistic beauty of his choice of words, will stimulate a sense of the sacred in everyone who uses this Siddur.

The clear print, the spacing, and the punctilious attention to the grammar and syntax of the Hebrew are all part and parcel of what we have come to expect from Koren Publishers. Every page is a pleasure to the eye. The layout conveys dignity and depth, and the subtleties of text and design will move us, sometimes unconsciously, to feelings and intuitions that are novel, pleasing and uplifting.

◂ In our prayers

In our prayers, we are connected to the Almighty through the land of Israel, the city of Jerusalem and the site of the holy Temple. It is, therefore, especially valuable that this Siddur connects those who use it to the land of Israel in very contemporary ways. It contains, for example, the prayer for the welfare of Israel, as well as the prayer for the soldiers of the Israel Defense Forces. It reflects our celebration of Israel's independence and our sorrow for those who have fallen in its defense.

It is with great pride that the Orthodox Union joins in presenting this Siddur to the Jewish communities of North America. Numerous siddurim are available, but this one, through a variety of modalities – intellectual, aesthetic, poetic and visual – is designed and is destined to motivate prayers which are richer, more meaningful, and – yes – more effective.

For prayer to "fly heavenward," it must come from a heart full of contrition and sincerity. This Siddur will help bring forth that contrition and sincerity from the souls of those who use it.

May He who hears all of our prayers listen attentively to the prayers which this Siddur will evoke.

Rabbi Dr. Tzvi Hersh Weinreb
Executive Vice President, Orthodox Union
New York 5769 (2009)

UNDERSTANDING JEWISH PRAYER

1. Introduction

Prayer is the language of the soul in conversation with God. It is the most intimate gesture of the religious life, and the most transformative. The very fact that we can pray testifies to the deepest elements of Jewish faith: that the universe did not come into existence accidentally, nor are our lives destined to be bereft of meaning. The universe exists, and we exist, because someone – the One God, Author of all – brought us into existence with love. It is this belief more than any other that redeems life from solitude and fate from tragedy.

In prayer we speak to a presence vaster than the unfathomable universe, yet closer to us than we are to ourselves: the God beyond, who is also the Voice within. Though language must fail when we try to describe a Being beyond all parameters of speech, language is all we have, and it is enough. For God who made the world with creative words, and who revealed His will through holy words, listens to our prayerful words. Language is the bridge joining us to Infinity.

Judah HaLevi, the great eleventh-century poet, said that prayer is to the soul what food is to the body. Without prayer, something within us atrophies and dies. It is possible to have a life without prayer, just as it is possible to have a life without music, or love, or laughter, but it is a diminished thing, missing whole dimensions of experience. We need space within the soul to express our joy in being, our wonder at the universe, our hopes, our fears, our failures, our aspirations – bringing our deepest thoughts as offerings to the One who listens, and listening, in turn, to the One who calls. Those who pray breathe a more expansive air: "In the prison of his days / Teach the free man how to praise" (W. H. Auden).

The siddur is the choral symphony the covenantal people has sung to God across forty centuries, from the days of the patriarchs until the present day. In it we hear the voices of Israel's prophets, priests and kings, its sages and scholars, poets and philosophers, rationalists and mystics, singing in calibrated harmony. Its libretto weaves together texts from almost every part of the vast library of Jewish spirituality: Torah, the Prophets, the Writings, the classic compendia of the Oral Law – Mishna, Midrash

◂ and

and Talmud – together with philosophical passages like Maimonides' "Thirteen Principles of Faith" and extracts from the *Zohar*, the key text of Jewish mysticism.

There is space in Judaism for private meditation – the personal plea. But when we pray publicly, we do so as members of a people who have served, spoken to, and wrestled with God for longer and in more varied circumstances than any other in history. We use the words of the greatest of those who came before us to make our prayers articulate and to join them to the prayers of others throughout the world and throughout the centuries.

Almost every age and major Jewish community has added something of its own: new words, prayers, customs and melodies. There are many different liturgies: Ashkenazi, Sephardi, Oriental, Yemenite, Italian, those of Rabbi Isaac Luria and the Vilna Gaon and others, each with its own subdivisions. Each tradition has a character of its own, to which Jewish law applies the principle *nahara nahara ufashteh*: "Every river has its own course." Each of the historic traditions has its own integrity, its own channel through which words stream from earth to heaven.

This introduction tells of how prayer came to take its present form, the distinct spiritual strands of which it is woven, the structures it has, and the path it takes in the journey of the spirit.

2. *Two Sources of Prayer*

The best-known phrase about Jewish religious worship is: "If you serve the LORD your God with all your heart (Deut. 11:13) – what is [the sacrificial] service of the heart (*avoda shebalev*)? This is prayer" (*Sifrei* to Deuteronomy, 41). Behind these simple words lies a remarkable story.

Throughout the Hebrew Bible, we find two quite different forms of religious worship. One is prayer. Outside the book of Psalms there are some 140 references to people praying; in ninety-seven cases we are told the words they said. Abraham prays for the cities of the plain. Jacob prays for deliverance before confronting Esau. Hannah prays for a child. These prayers are direct, simple and spontaneous. They have no fixed formula, no set text. Some are very brief, like Moses' five-word prayer for his sister Miriam: "Please, God, heal her now." Others are long, like Moses' forty-day prayer for forgiveness of the people after the sin of the Golden

Calf. There are no general rules: these prayers have no fixed time, place or liturgy. They are improvised as circumstance demands.

The other form – generally known as *avoda*, "service" – is sacrifice. Sacrifice could not be less like prayer. As set out from Exodus to Deuteronomy, the sacrificial service is minutely specified. It has its prescribed order: which offerings should be made, when, and by whom. It has a designated place: the Tabernacle in the wilderness, and later, the Temple in Jerusalem. There is no room for spontaneity. When two of Aaron's sons, Nadav and Avihu, make a spontaneous offering of incense, they die (Lev. 10:1–2). The Mosaic books contain two set texts associated with the Temple: the Priestly Blessing (Num. 6:24–26) and the declaration made when bringing the first fruits (Deut. 26:5–10). Certain sacrifices, such as sin-offerings, involved verbal confession. Psalms were sung in the Temple, and the Mishna details the prayers said there. But the sacrificial act itself was wordless. It took place in silence.

So we have two quite different traditions, prayer and sacrifice: one spontaneous, the other rigorously legislated; one that could be undertaken anywhere, at any time, by anyone; the other which could only happen in a set place and time in accordance with detailed and inflexible procedures. How did these two forms of worship become one?

The answer lies in the national crisis and renewal that occurred after the destruction of the First Temple by Nebuchadnezzar in 586 BCE. Psalm 137 has preserved a vivid record of the mood of near-despair among the exiles: "By the rivers of Babylon we sat and wept as we remembered Zion… How can we sing the LORD's songs in a strange land?" In exile in Babylon, Jews began to gather to expound the Torah, articulate a collective hope of return, and recall the Temple and its service. These assemblies (*kinishtu* in Babylonian, *knesset* in Hebrew) were not substitutes for the Temple; rather, they were reminders of it. The book of Daniel, set in Babylon, speaks of threefold daily prayer facing Jerusalem (Dan. 6:11). The loss of the Temple and the experience of exile led to the emergence of regular gatherings for study and prayer.

The next chapter in this story was written by Ezra (fifth century BCE) who, together with the statesman Nehemiah, reorganized Jewish life in Israel after the return from Babylon. Ezra ("the scribe") was a new type in

history: the educator as hero. The book of Nehemiah (8:1–9) contains a detailed description of the national assembly Ezra convened in Jerusalem, where he read the Torah aloud, with the help of the Levites who explained it to the people.

Ezra and Nehemiah were disturbed by the high degree of assimilation among the Jews who had remained in Israel. They knew that without a strong religious identity, the people would eventually disappear through intermingling with other nations and cultures. To guard against this, they set in motion far-reaching initiatives, including a national reaffirmation of the nation's covenant with God (Nehemiah, chapter 10). One of the most important developments was the first formulation of prayers, attributed by the sages to Ezra and the Men of the Great Assembly. Maimonides suggests that one of their motives for so doing was to reestablish Hebrew as the national language: at that time, "Half of their children spoke the language of Ashdod, or the language of the other peoples, and did not know how to speak the language of Judah" (Neh. 13:24; Maimonides' "Laws of Prayer" 1:4).

One of the results of this religious renewal was the birth, or growth, of the synagogue. During the Second Temple period, priests were divided into twenty-four groups, *mishmarot*, each of which served in the Temple for a week in a rota. They were accompanied by groups of local laypeople, *ma'amadot*, some of whom accompanied them to the Temple, others of whom stayed in their towns but said prayers to coincide with the sacrifices. Whether the synagogue developed from these *ma'amadot*, or whether its origins were earlier, by the time the Second Temple was destroyed in 70 CE, it was a well-established institution.

The synagogue was "one of the greatest revolutions in the history of religion and society" (M. Stern). It was the first place of worship made holy, not because of any historic association, nor because sacrifices were offered, but simply because people gathered there to study and pray. It embodied one of the great truths of monotheism: that the God of everywhere could be worshiped anywhere. After the loss of the Second Temple it became the home-in-exile of a scattered people. Every synagogue was a fragment of Jerusalem. And though the destruction of the Temple meant that sacrifices could no longer be offered, in their place came an offering of words, namely prayer.

◂ The

The transition from sacrifice to prayer was not a sudden development. A thousand years earlier, in his speech at the dedication of the Temple, King Solomon had emphasized prayer rather than sacrifice (1 Kings 8:12–53). Through Isaiah, God had said "My House shall be called *a house of prayer* for all peoples" (Is. 56:7). The prophet Hosea had said: "Take words with you and return to the LORD… Instead of bulls we will pay [the offering of] our lips" (Hos. 14:3). Sacrifice was the external accompaniment of an inner act of heart and mind: thanksgiving, atonement, and so on. Therefore, though the outer act was no longer possible, the inner act remained. That is how sacrifice turned into prayer.

What had once been two quite different forms of worship now became one. Prayer took on the highly structured character of the sacrificial service, with fixed texts and times. The silence that had accompanied the sacrifice was transmuted into speech. Two traditions – prophetic prayer on the one hand, priestly sacrificial service on the other – merged and became one. That is the remarkable story behind the words, "What is the [sacrificial] service of the heart? This is prayer."

There is a series of arguments, spanning the centuries, about the nature of prayer. According to Maimonides, daily prayer is a biblical commandment; according to Nahmanides it is merely rabbinic. Two third-century teachers, Rabbi Yose son of Rabbi Ḥanina, and Rabbi Joshua ben Levi, disagreed as to the origin of the prayers, the former holding that they were instituted by the patriarchs – Abraham initiating the morning prayer, Isaac the afternoon, and Jacob the evening service – while the latter held that they corresponded to the sacrifices. Centuries earlier, Rabban Gamliel and the sages differed as to which was primary, the silent Amida or the Leader's Repetition. Each of these debates ultimately hinges on the question as to which of the two sources of prayer – the improvised prayers of the figures of the Bible or the sacrificial service of the Tabernacle and Temple – is the more fundamental.

In truth, there is no answer: prayer as we have known it for two millennia draws on both traditions. More remarkably, we honor both, because *each Amida is said twice*, once silently by individuals, a second time aloud and publicly by the Leader. The silent Amida recalls the prayers of individuals in the Bible, while the Leader's Repetition recalls the sacrifice: hence there is no Repetition of the evening Amida, since there was no

◂ sacrifice

sacrifice in the evening. In prayer, two great streams of Jewish spirituality met and became one.

3. Structures of Prayer

The Hebrew word for a prayer book, *siddur*, means "order." At its height, prayer is an intensely emotional experience. The wonder of praise, the joy of thanksgiving, the passion of love, the trembling of awe, the broken-heartedness of confession, the yearning of hope – all these are part of the tonality of prayer. Yet Judaism is also, and supremely, a religion of the mind – for untutored emotion, like a river that bursts its banks, can be anarchic and destructive. The opening chapter of Genesis, with its account of creation, evokes a sense of order. Each day has its task; each life-form has its place; and the result (until the birth of sin) was harmony. Jewish prayer, therefore, has an order. Like a choral symphony, it has movements, each with its moods, its unfolding themes, its developmental logic. In this section, I analyze some of these structures.

The siddur as it exists today is the result of some forty centuries of Jewish history. Yet the result is not mere bricolage, a patchwork of random additions. It is as if the composition of the prayer book has been shaped by an "invisible hand," a divine inspiration that transcends the intentions of any particular author. Specifically, form mirrors substance. The shape of the prayers reveals the basic shape of the Jewish spirit as it has been molded by its encounter with God. These are some of the structural features of the prayers:

A. FROM UNIVERSAL TO PARTICULAR

In general, sequences of Jewish prayer move from the universal to the particular. Grace after Meals, for example, begins with a blessing thanking God "who in His goodness feeds *the whole world*." The second blessing moves to particularities: Israel, liberation from slavery, "the covenant which You sealed in our flesh," Torah and the commandments. We thank God "for the land [of Israel] and for the food." The third is more narrowly focused still. It is about the holy city, Jerusalem.

The same pattern exists in the two blessings before the Shema in the morning and evening service. The first is about the universe (God gives light to the earth, creates day and night), and the second is about Torah,

◂ the specific

the specific bond of love between God and the Jewish people. Look and you will find many more examples in the siddur. (The one exception is *Aleinu*, whose first paragraph is about Jewish particularity and whose second is a universal hope. Regarding this, see section B. MIRROR-IMAGE SYMMETRY.)

This movement from universal to particular is distinctively Jewish. Western culture, under the influence of Plato, has tended to move in the opposite direction, from the concrete instance to the general rule, valuing universals above particularities. Judaism is the great counter-Platonic narrative in Western civilization.

Moving from the universal to the particular, the prayer book mirrors the structure of the Torah itself. Genesis begins, in its first eleven chapters, with a description of the universal condition of humankind. Only in its twelfth chapter is there a call to an individual, Abraham, to leave his land, family and father's house and lead a life of righteousness through which "all the families of the earth shall be blessed."

There are universals of human behavior: we call them the Noahide Laws. But we worship God in and through the particularity of our history, language and heritage. The highest love is not abstract but concrete. Those who truly love, cherish what makes the beloved different, unique, irreplaceable: that is the theme of the greatest of all books of religious love, *the* Song of Songs. That, we believe, is how God loves us.

B. MIRROR-IMAGE SYMMETRY

Many Torah passages are constructed in the form of a mirror-image symmetry, technically known as *chiasmus*: a sequence with the form ABCCBA, where the second half reverses the order of the first. A precise example is the six-word commandment that forms the central element of the Noahide covenant (Gen. 9:6):

> [A] Who sheds [B] the blood [C] of man [C] by man [B] shall his blood [A] be shed.

This is more than a stylistic device. It is the expression of one of the Torah's most profound beliefs; namely, the reciprocal nature of justice. Those who do good are blessed with good. Those who do evil, suffer evil. What happens to us is a mirror image of what we do. Thus, form

◂ mirrors

mirrors substance: mirror-image symmetry is the literary equivalent of a just world.

Some prayers have a mirror-image structure. Most of the paragraphs of the Amida, for example, finish the same way as they begin ("at the end of a blessing one should say something similar to its beginning," *Pesaḥim* 104a). So, for example, the sixteenth blessing begins, "Listen to our voice" and ends "who listens to prayer." The eighteenth begins, "We give thanks to You" and ends "to whom thanks are due." The Amida as a whole begins with a request to God to help us open our mouths in prayer. It ends with a request to God to help us close our mouths from deceitful speech.

According to Rabbi Joseph Soloveitchik, the first and last three blessings of the Amida stand in a mirror-image relationship. The last uses the same key words as the first: kindness (*ḥessed*) and love (*ahava*). The penultimate has the same subject as the second: the gift of life and the hidden miracles that surround us constantly. The seventeenth and third are both about holiness. Thus the end of the Amida is a mirror image of its beginning.

This explains why *Aleinu* – the prayer with which most services end – is constructed in a sequence opposite to all other prayers. Others move from the universal to the particular, but *Aleinu* reverses the order, beginning with a hymn to particularity ("Who has not made us like the nations of the lands") and ending with one of the great prayers for universality, when "*all* humanity will call on Your name." *Aleinu* gives each service a chiastic structure. Previous prayers have been A–B (universal–particular); *Aleinu* is B–A (particular–universal).

As we will see, many of the other structuring principles are three-part series of the form A–B–A.

C. PRAISE, REQUEST, THANKS

The sages ruled that the Amida – prayer par excellence – should follow a basic pattern of praise (*shevaḥ*), request (*bakasha*), and acknowledgment or thanks (*hodaya*). This is how Maimonides puts it: "The obligation of prayer is that every person should daily, according to his ability, offer up supplication and prayer, first uttering *praises* of God, then with humble *supplication and petition* asking for all that he needs, and finally offering praise and *thanksgiving* to the Eternal for the benefits already bestowed on him in rich measure" (Laws of Prayer 1:2).

◂ The Amida

The Amida is constructed on this template. Of its nineteen blessings, the first three express praise. The middle thirteen on weekdays are requests (we do not make requests in the Amida on Shabbat or Yom Tov, which are times dedicated to thanking God for what we have, as opposed to asking Him for what we lack). The final three are acknowledgments. The same pattern can be seen in the blessings over the Torah at the beginning of the morning service (see section G. FRACTALS).

D. PREPARATION, PRAYER, MEDITATION

Prayer requires intense concentration, and this takes time. It is impossible to move directly from the stresses and preoccupations of everyday life into the presence of eternity. Nor should prayer end abruptly. It must be internalized if it is to leave its trace within us as we move back into our worldly pursuits. Maimonides writes that because prayer needs mental focus,

> One should therefore sit awhile *before* beginning his prayers, so as to concentrate his mind. He should then pray in gentle tones, beseechingly, and not regard the service as a burden that he is carrying and which he will cast off before proceeding on his way. He should thus sit awhile *after* concluding the prayers, and only then leave. The ancient saints used to pause and meditate one hour before prayer and one hour after prayer, and spend an hour in prayer itself. (Laws of Prayer 4:16)

In the morning service, the Verses of Praise (*Pesukei deZimra*) are the preparation. In them, our thoughts gradually turn from the visible world to its invisible Creator. The Shema, Amida and their surrounding blessings are prayer as such. The remainder of the service is our meditation as we leave the orbit of heaven and reenter the gravitational field of earth.

E. DESCRIPTION, EXPERIENCE, RECOLLECTION

It is one thing to describe an experience, another to live it. One of the striking features of the weekday morning service is its threefold repetition of the *Kedusha* ("Holy, holy, holy"), once before the Shema (known as *Kedushat Yotzer*); a second time during the Leader's Repetition of the Amida; and a third time during the prayer "A redeemer will come to Zion" (known as *Kedusha deSidra*). The first and third are different from

◂ the second

the second in that, (1) they do not require a *minyan*, and (2) they do not need to be said standing.

The *Kedusha* – one of the supreme moments of holiness in Jewish prayer – is constructed around the mystical visions of Isaiah and Ezekiel, of God enthroned in majesty, surrounded by angels singing His praises. In the first and third *Kedushot*, we *describe* the angelic order; in the second, we *enact* it, using the same words, but this time in direct, not reported, speech (Geonim, Maimonides). The intensity of *Kedusha* is heightened by this three-movement form: first the anticipation and preparation, then the experience itself, and finally the recollection.

F. PRIVATE, PUBLIC, PRIVATE

The Amida itself – especially on weekday mornings and afternoons – is constructed on a triadic pattern. First it is said silently by the members of the congregation as individuals. Next it is repeated publicly out loud by the Leader. This is then usually followed by private supplications (*Taḥanun*), also said quietly. As I have suggested above, this is a way of reenacting the two modes of spirituality from which prayer derives. The silent Amida recalls the intensely personal prayers of the patriarchs and prophets. The public Repetition represents the daily sacrifices offered by the priests in the Temple on behalf of all Israel (there is no Repetition of the evening Amida because there were no sacrifices at night). Thus the prayers weave priestly and prophetic, individual and collective voices, into a single three-movement sonata of great depth and resonance.

G. FRACTALS

We owe to the scientist Benoit Mandelbrot the concept of fractals: the discovery that phenomena in nature often display the same pattern at different levels of magnitude. A single rock looks like a mountain. Crystals, snowflakes and ferns are made up of elements that have the same shape as the whole. Fractal geometry is the scientific equivalent of the mystical ability to sense the great in the small: "To see a world in a grain of sand / And a Heaven in a wild flower, / Hold Infinity in the palm of your hand, and Eternity in an hour" (William Blake).

◂ The first

The first of the "request" prayers in the daily Amida is a fractal. It replicates in miniature the structure of the Amida as a whole (Praise–Request–Thanks). It begins with praise: "You grace humanity with knowledge and teach mortals understanding," moves to request: "Grace us with the knowledge, understanding and discernment," and ends with thanksgiving: "Blessed are You, O Lord, who graciously grants knowledge." You will find many other fractals in the siddur.

The existence of fractals in the siddur shows us how profoundly the structures of Jewish spirituality feed back repeatedly into the architectonics of prayer.

H. MIDRASHIC EXPANSION

Midrash is the rabbinic investigation into the meaning of holy texts: the root *d-r-sh* means "to explore, enquire, explain, expound." It seeks out the inflections and innuendos of words, making explicit their implicit dimensions of meaning.

One example occurs in the *Nishmat* prayer on Shabbat morning (page 445). A key phrase in prayer, spoken by Moses and incorporated into the first paragraph of the Amida, is "God, great, mighty and awesome" (Deut. 10:17). *Nishmat* meditates on these four words, one by one:

God – in Your absolute power,
Great – in the glory of Your name,
Mighty – for ever,
Awesome – in Your awe-inspiring deeds.

Another is the passage on Shabbat morning following the phrase "who forms light and creates darkness, makes peace and creates all" (pages 455–457). A brief prayer takes the last word, "all," and builds around it a fivefold set of variations: "*All* will thank You. *All* will praise You. *All* will declare: Nothing is holy as is the Lord. *All* will exalt You, Selah, You who form *all*."

Always look for apparent repetition in prayer – like the tenfold "Blessed" in *Barukh SheAmar* ("Blessed is He who spoke"), the eightfold "True" after the Shema, or the fivefold "All" immediately after *Barekhu* ("Bless the Lord") on Shabbat morning. Reiteration is never mere repetition. The prayer is inviting us to meditate on the multiple layers of

◂ meaning

meaning that may exist in a single word or phrase, as if words were diamonds and we were turning them this way and that to catch their multiple refractions of light.

I. NUMERICAL STRUCTURES

As we have seen, many of the prayers have an obvious three-part structure, but in some cases this is repeated in great detail on a smaller scale, as in fractals.

The most striking example is the weekday Amida, which is composed of three parts: praise–request–acknowledgment. The first and last of these are each constructed in threes: three blessings of praise at the beginning, and three of acknowledgment at the end. Less obvious is the fact that the middle thirteen blessings – "requests" – *also* share this structure. There are six individual requests, followed by six collective ones, each divided into two groups of three. The individual requests begin with three spiritual needs (understanding, repentance, forgiveness) followed by three material ones (deliverance from oppression, healing, prosperity). The collective requests begin with three political-historical elements (ingathering of exiles, restoration of judges, and an end to internal strife – the "slanderers"), followed by the three spiritual bases of nationhood (the righteous, Jerusalem, and the restoration of the Davidic monarchy). The thirteenth, "Listen to our voice," stands outside this structure because it is not directed to any specific request but is, instead, a prayer that our prayers be heeded.

The number seven is also significant and always indicates holiness, as in the seventh day, Shabbat; the seventh month, Tishrei with its Days of Awe; the seventh year, the "year of release"; and the fiftieth year, the Jubilee, which follows seven cycles of seven years. Seven in Judaism is not a simple prime number. It is the *one-after-six*. Six represents the material, physical, secular. Ancient Mesopotamia, the birthplace of Abraham, originally used a numerical system based on the number six. Western civilization still bears traces of this in the twenty-four hour day (2 × 6 hours of light, plus 2 × 6 of darkness); the sixty (10 × 6) minutes in an hour, and seconds in a minute; and the 360 degrees in a circle (6 × 6 × 10). All of these originated in astronomy, at which the ancient Mesopotamians excelled. Judaism acknowledges the six-part structure of time and space,

◂ but adds

but adds that God exists *beyond* time and space. Hence seven – the one beyond six – became the symbol of the holy.

Six, too, is not a simple number in Judaism. This becomes evident when we read the story of creation in Genesis 1 carefully. The first six days fall into two groups. On the first three, God created and separated *domains* (1: light and darkness, 2: upper and lower waters, 3: sea and dry land). On the second three God *populated* these domains, each with its appropriate objects or life-forms (4: sun, moon and stars, 5: birds and fish, 6: land animals and man). The seventh day, Shabbat, is *holy* because it stands *outside* nature and its causal-scientific laws.

Mirroring this pattern, the morning service is structured around the number seven: the three paragraphs of the Shema, surrounded by three blessings, leading to the seventh, the Amida, which is the domain of the holy, where we stand directly in the presence of God. On holy days – Shabbat and Yom Tov – the Amida has a sevenfold structure: the three opening and closing paragraphs, plus a middle paragraph dedicated to "the holiness of the day."

It follows that sixfold structures in the siddur signal the universe and creation. Thus, on weekday mornings we say six psalms (145–150) in the Verses of Praise. *Kabbalat Shabbat* also contains six psalms, corresponding to the days of the week, before *Lekha Dodi*, which represents Shabbat itself. The blessing after the Shema repeats the keyword *Emet* ("true") six times to show how God's love is translated into redemptive activity in a this-worldly time and space.

Many prayers such as *El Adon* (page 461) and *Aleinu* are constructed in a pattern of fours: four-line verses, each of four words. Often these reflect Jewish mysticism with its four "worlds": *Asiyya* (Action), *Yetzira* (Formation), *Beri'a* (Creation) and *Atzilut* (Emanation). *Merkava* mysticism, based on Ezekiel's vision of the divine chariot, is an important strand of early rabbinic prayer.

The number ten represents the "ten utterances with which the world was created" (the ten places in Genesis 1 where an act of creation is preceded by the words "God said"). That is why *Barukh SheAmar*, the blessing before the creation section of the prayers, begins with a tenfold litany of phrases each beginning with the word "Blessed."

Fifteen represents the fifteen steps between the courtyards of the Temple, the fifteen psalms beginning "A song of ascents," and the numerical value of the first two letters of God's holiest name. Hence, there are fifteen expressions of praise in the paragraph *Yishtabaḥ* (page 451), fifteen adjectives following "the LORD Your God is true" at the end of the Shema in the morning service, fifteen psalms in the Verses of Praise on Shabbat and Yom Tov mornings, and so on. There are also more intricate numerical patterns.

These are not mere aesthetic conventions like, for example, the fourteen-line sonnet form or the four-movement structure of a symphony. As always in Judaism there is a matching of form to content, structure to substance. The sages understood – as did the ancient Greeks, amply confirmed by modern science – that *reality has a numerical structure.* Mirroring this structure in prayer, we evoke the sense of a world of order in which we are called upon to respect differences and honor boundaries, accepting graciously the integrity of natural and moral law.

J. FROM LOVE TO AWE

The supreme religious emotions are love and awe – in that order. We are commanded to "Love the LORD your God." We are also commanded to experience the feelings associated with the Hebrew word *yira,* which means "awe, fear, reverence." This is how Maimonides puts it: "When a person contemplates His great and wondrous works and creatures and from them obtains a glimpse of His wisdom, which is incomparable and infinite, he will immediately love Him, praise Him, glorify Him, and long with an exceeding longing to know His great name… And when he ponders these matters, he will recoil frightened, and realize that he is a small creature, lowly and obscure, endowed with slight and slender intelligence, standing in the presence of He who is perfect in knowledge" (*Yesodei HaTorah* 2:2).

The supreme expression of love in Judaism is the Shema with its injunction: "Love the LORD your God with all your heart, with all your soul, and with all your might." The supreme expression of awe is the Amida prayer, when we stand consciously in the presence of God. The basic movement of the morning and evening prayers is first, to climb to the peak of love, the Shema, and from there to the summit of awe, the Amida.

◂ 4. *Creation*

4. *Creation, Revelation, Redemption*

One structural principle of the prayers deserves special attention, since it touches on the fundamentals of Jewish faith. In the twelfth century, Moses Maimonides enumerated the Thirteen Principles of Jewish Faith. They appear in the siddur in two forms: the poem known as Yigdal (page 25) and a prose version after the end of the morning service (page 203).

Rabbi Shimon ben Tzemaḥ Duran (1361–1444) pointed out that Maimonides' principles could be analyzed and categorized into three themes: (1) the existence of God, the Creator (principles 1–5: God's existence, unity, incorporeality and eternity, and that He alone is to be worshiped); (2) Divine revelation (principles 6–9: prophecy, Moses' uniqueness, the God-given character of the Torah and its immutability), and (3) God's justice (principles 10–13: God knows all, repays us according to our deeds, and will bring the Messiah and the resurrection of the dead). The philosopher Franz Rosenzweig summarized these in three words: creation, revelation, redemption. Creation is the relationship between God and the universe. Revelation is the relationship between God and humanity. Redemption occurs when we apply revelation to creation.

The movement from creation to revelation to redemption is one of the great structural motifs of prayer. One example is the three blessings in the morning service, surrounding the Shema and leading up to the Amida (pages 89–107). The first is about the *creation* of the universe in space and time; the second is about the *revelation* of the Torah; and the third is about the miracles of history, ending with the words, "who *redeemed* Israel."

The three paragraphs of the Shema display the same pattern. The first is about creation (God's unity and sovereignty), the second about revelation (acceptance of the commandments), and the third about redemption ("I am the Lord your God, who brought you out of the land of Egypt").

The weekday morning service as a whole is constructed on this principle. First come the Verses of Praise, taken from the book of Psalms, with their majestic vision of creation. Then follows the central section – the Shema and its blessings, leading to the Amida – in which we sit, then stand, in the immediate presence of God (revelation). Finally we come to the concluding prayers with their central line, "A *redeemer* will come to Zion." The second paragraph of *Aleinu* is likewise a vision of redemption.

The pattern is repeated yet again in the Shabbat evening, morning

and afternoon prayers. On Friday evening, in the central blessing of the Amida, we speak of the Shabbat of creation ("the culmination of the creation of heaven and earth"). In the morning we refer to the Shabbat of revelation (when Moses "brought down in his hands two tablets of stone"). In the afternoon we anticipate future redemption (when "You are One, Your name is One" and the people Israel are again one "nation unique on earth").

Rabbi Joseph Soloveitchik suggested that the same sequence is the basis for the threefold structure of the weekday Amida: praise, request, thanks. Praise "emerges from an enraptured soul gazing at the *mysterium magnum* of creation," request "flows from an aching heart which finds itself in existential depths," and thanksgiving "is sung by the person who has attained, by the grace of God, redemption." Creation leads to praise, revelation to request, and redemption to thanksgiving.

In these multiple ways, prayer continually reiterates the basic principles of Jewish faith.

5. *Prayer and Study*

There is one spiritual activity that the sages regarded as even higher than prayer: namely, study of Torah, God's word to humanity and His covenant with our ancestors and us (*Shabbat* 10a). The entire *Pirkei Avot* (Ethics of the Fathers) is a set of variations on the theme of a life devoted to Torah study. In prayer, we speak to God. Through Torah, God speaks to us. Praying, we speak. Studying, we listen.

From earliest times, the synagogue was a house of study as well as a house of prayer. Gatherings for study (perhaps around the figure of the prophet; see II Kings 4:23 and the commentaries of Radak and Ralbag; *Sukka* 27b) may well have preceded formal prayer services by many centuries. Accordingly, interwoven with prayer are acts of study.

The most obvious is the public reading from the Torah, a central part of the Shabbat and Yom Tov services, and in an abridged form on Monday and Thursday mornings and Shabbat afternoons. There are other examples. In the morning blessings before the Verses of Praise, there are two cycles of study, each in three parts: (1) Torah, that is a passage from the Mosaic books; (2) Mishna, the key document of the Oral Law; and (3) Talmud in the broadest sense (pages 11 and 43–55).

◂ In the main

In the main section of prayer, the paragraph preceding the Shema is a form of blessing over the Torah (see *Berakhot* 11b), and the Shema itself represents Torah study (*Menaḥot* 99b). The last section of the weekday morning prayers (pages 175–177) was originally associated with the custom of studying ten verses from the prophetic books. Kaddish, which plays such a large part in the prayers, had its origin in the house of study as the conclusion of a *derasha*, a public exposition of biblical texts. The entire weekday morning service is thus an extended fugue between study and prayer.

This is dramatized in two key phrases: the first is *Shema Yisrael*, "Listen, Israel," God's word through Moses and the Torah, and the second is *Shema Koleinu*, "Listen to our voice," the paragraph within the Amida that summarizes all our requests (see above). These two phrases frame the great dialogue of study and prayer. Faith lives in these two acts of listening: ours to the call of God, God's to the cry of humankind.

6. Prayer and Mysticism

Jewish mysticism has played a major role in the prayer book. The most obvious examples are the passage from the *Zohar*, "Blessed is the name" (page 303), the Song of Glory (pages 571–573) written by one of the medieval north-European pietists, and the two songs written by the sixteenth-century Safed mystics associated with Rabbi Isaac Luria, "Beloved of the soul" (page 309) and "Come, my Beloved" (pages 319–323).

Less obviously, many of the early post-biblical prayers were deeply influenced by *Hekhalot* ("Palace") and *Merkava* ("Chariot") mysticism, two esoteric systems that charted the mysteries of creation, the angelic orders, and the innermost chambers of the divine glory.

Undoubtedly, though, the most significant mystical contribution to the prayers is the *Kedusha*, said in three different forms, most notably during the Leader's Repetition of the Amida. We have noted the two major tributaries of prayer: the spontaneous prayers said by figures in the Hebrew Bible, and the sacrificial service in the Temple. Mysticism is the third, and its most sublime expression is the *Kedusha*, based on the mystical visions of Isaiah (chapter 6) and Ezekiel (chapters 1–3). There are times in the prayers when we are like prophets, others when we are like priests, but there is no more daring leap of faith than during the

Kedusha, when we act out the role of angels singing praises to God in His innermost chambers.

Familiarity breeds inattention, and we can all too easily pass over the *Kedusha* without noticing its astonishing drama. "The ministering angels do not begin to sing praises in heaven until Israel sings praises down here on earth" (*Ḥullin* 91b). "You," said God through Isaiah, "are My witnesses" (Is. 43:10). Israel is "the people I formed for Myself that they might declare My praise" (ibid, 43:20). We are God's angels on earth, His emissaries and ambassadors. The Jewish people, always small and vulnerable, have nonetheless been singled out for the most exalted mission ever entrusted to humankind: to be witnesses, in ourselves, to something beyond ourselves: to be God's "signal of transcendence" in a world in which His presence is often hidden.

This is a mystical idea, and like all mysticism it hovers at the edge of intelligibility. Mysticism is the attempt to say the unsayable, know the unknowable, to reach out in language to a reality that lies beyond the scope of language. Often in the course of history, mysticism has tended to devalue the world of the senses in favor of a more exalted realm of disembodied spirituality. Jewish mysticism did not take this course. Instead it chose to bathe our life on earth in the dazzling light of the divine radiance (*Zohar*, the title of Judaism's most famous mystical text).

7. *Reliving History*

History, too, has left its mark on the siddur. There are passages, indicated in the Commentary, that were born in the aftermath of tragedy or miraculous redemption. This edition of the siddur also includes suggested orders of service for Yom HaAtzma'ut and Yom Yerushalayim, marking the birth of the State of Israel in 1948, and the Six Day War of 1967.

No less significantly, the synagogue service invites us at many points to reenact history. The Verses of Praise begin with the song of celebration sung by King David when he brought the Ark to Jerusalem. The verses we sing when we take the Torah scroll from the Ark and when we return it recall the Israelites' journeys through the wilderness, when they carried the Ark with them. In one of the most fascinating transitions in the service, as we move from private meditation to public prayer (pages 79–83), we recall three epic moments of nation-formation: when David gathered the

people to charge them with the task of building the Temple; when Ezra convened a national assembly to renew the covenant after the return from Babylonian exile; and when Moses led the Israelites through the Reed Sea. Even the three steps forward we take as we begin the Amida recall the three biblical episodes in which people stepped forward (*vayigash*) as a prelude to prayer: Abraham pleading for the cities of the plain, Judah pleading with Joseph for Benjamin to be set free, and Elijah invoking God against the prophets of Ba'al on Mount Carmel.

We are a people defined by history. We carry our past with us. We relive it in ritual and prayer. We are not lonely individuals, disconnected with past and present. We are characters in the world's oldest continuous story, charged with writing its next chapter and handing it on to those who come after us. The siddur is, among other things, a book of Jewish memory.

8. *Prayer and Faith*

The siddur is also the book of Jewish faith. Scholars of Judaism, noting that it contains little systematic theology, have sometimes concluded that it is a religion of deeds not creeds, acts not beliefs. They were wrong because they were searching in the wrong place. They were looking for a library of works like Moses Maimonides' *Guide for the Perplexed*. They should have looked instead at the prayer book. The home of Jewish belief is the siddur.

At several points, the prayers have been shaped in response to theological controversy. The opening statement in the morning service after *Barekhu*, "who forms light and creates darkness, makes peace and creates all," is a protest against dualism, which had a considerable following in the first four centuries CE in the form of Gnosticism and Manichaeism. Its presence can be traced in the ancient documents discovered in the 1940s, the Dead Sea Scrolls and the Nag Hammadi codices. Against dualism, with its vision of perpetual cosmic struggle, Judaism insists that all reality derives from a single source.

The second paragraph of the Amida, with its fivefold reference to the resurrection of the dead, reflects the ancient controversy between the Pharisees and Sadducees. The morning prayer, "My God, the soul You placed within me is pure" (page 7), may be directed against the Pauline doctrine of original sin. The Mishna chapter, "With what wicks may we

◂ light

light?" (pages 329–331), was probably inserted as part of the polemic against the Karaite sect. The Ten Commandments, said daily as part of the Temple service immediately after the Shema, was removed from the prayers when it was used by sectarians to argue that only these ten commandments were commanded by God.

The fact that Jewish faith was written into the prayers, rather than analyzed in works of theology, is of immense significance. We do not analyze our faith: we pray it. We do not philosophize about truth: we sing it. Even Maimonides' Thirteen Principles of Jewish Faith – the most famous creed in the history of Judaism – only entered the mainstream of Jewish consciousness when they were turned into a song and included in the siddur as the hymn known as Yigdal. For Judaism, theology becomes real when it becomes prayer. We do not talk *about* God. We talk *to* God.

I have known many atheists. My doctoral supervisor, the late Sir Bernard Williams, described as the most brilliant mind in Britain, was one. He was a good, caring, deeply moral human being, but he could not understand my faith at all. For him, life was ultimately tragic. The universe was blind to our presence, deaf to our prayers, indifferent to our hopes. There is no meaning beyond that which human beings construct for themselves. We are dust on the surface of infinity.

I understood that vision, yet in the end I could not share his belief that it is somehow more honest to despair than to trust, to see existence as an accident rather than as invested with a meaning we strive to discover. Sir Bernard loved ancient Greece; I loved biblical Israel. Greece gave the world tragedy; Israel taught it hope. A people, a person, who can pray is one who, even in the darkest night of the soul, can never ultimately lose hope.

9. Prayer and Sacrifice

The connection between prayer and sacrifice is deep. As we have seen, sacrifice is not the only forerunner of our prayers; many prayers were spoken by figures in the Bible. These were said without any accompanying offering. Yet the sacrificial system is a major tributary of the Jewish river of prayer. After the destruction of the Second Temple, prayer became a substitute for sacrifice. It is *avoda shebalev,* "the sacrificial service of the heart." Yet it is just this feature of the prayers that many find difficult to understand or find uplifting. What, then, was sacrifice?

◄ The Hebrew

The Hebrew word for sacrifice is *korban*, which comes from a root that means "to come, or bring, close." The essential problem to which sacrifice is an answer is: how can we come close to God? This is a profound question – perhaps *the* question of the religious life – not simply because of the utter disparity between God's infinity and our finitude, but also because the very circumstances of life tend to focus our gaze downward to our needs rather than upward to our source. The Hebrew word for universe, *olam*, is connected to the verb meaning "to hide" (see Lev. 4:13; Deut. 22:1). The physical world is a place in which the presence of God is real, yet hidden. Our horizon of consciousness is foreshortened. We focus on our own devices and desires. We walk in God's light, but often our mind is on other things.

How then do we come close to God? By *an act of renunciation*; by giving something away; specifically, by giving something *back*. The sacrifices of the biblical age were ways in which the individual, or the nation as a whole, in effect said: what we have, God, is really Yours. The world exists because of You. *We* exist because of You. Nothing we have is ultimately ours. The fundamental gesture of sacrifice is, on the face of it, absurd. What we give to God is something that already belongs to Him. As King David said: "Who am I and who are my people that we should be able to give as generously as this? Everything comes from You, and we have given You only what comes from Your hand" (1 Chr. 29:14). Yet to *give back* to God is one of the most profound instincts of the soul. Doing so, we acknowledge our dependency. We cast off the carapace of self-absorption. That is why, in one of its most striking phrases, the Torah speaks of sacrifice as being *rei'aḥ niḥo'aḥ*, "sweet savor" to God.

One of the sweetest savors of parenthood is when a child, by now grown to maturity, brings a parent a gift to express his or her thanks. This too seems absurd. What can a child give a parent that remotely approximates what a parent gives a child, namely life itself? Yet it is so, and the reverse is also true. The cruelest thing a child can do is *not* to acknowledge his or her parents. The Talmud attributes to Rabbi Akiva the phrase *Avinu Malkenu*, "Our Father, our King." Those two words encapsulate the essence of Jewish worship. God is King – Maker and Sovereign of the vast universe. Yet even before God is our King, He is our Father, our Parent, the One who brought us into being in love, who nurtured and sustained us, who taught us His ways, and who tenderly watches over our destiny.

Sacrifice – the gift we bring to God – is the gift of the made to its Maker, the owned to its Owner, the child to its Parent. If creation is an act of love, sacrifice is an acknowledgment of that love.

The late Rabbi Joseph Soloveitchik emphasized the difference between *ma'aseh mitzva,* the external act specified by a commandment, and *kiyum mitzva,* the actual fulfillment of a commandment. When the Temple stood, for example, a penitent would bring a guilt- or sin-offering to atone for his sin: that was the external act. The fulfillment of the commandment, though, lay in confession and contrition, acts of the mind and will. In biblical times, the sacrificial order was the external act, but the internal act – acknowledgment, dependency, recognition, thanks, praise – was essential to its fulfillment. That is why Judaism was able to survive the destruction of the Temple and the cessation of the sacrificial order. The external act could no longer be performed, but the internal act remained. That is the link between sacrifice and prayer.

The difference between prayer-as-request and prayer-as-sacrifice is that request *seeks,* sacrifice *gives.* The prophets asked, usually on behalf of the people as a whole, for forgiveness, deliverance, and blessing. The priests who offered sacrifices in the Temple asked for nothing. Sacrificial prayer is the giving back to God what God already owns: our lives, our days, our world. Prayer is creation's gift to its Creator.

The prophets were critical of the sacrificial system. They reserved for it some of their most lacerating prose. Yet none proposed its abolition, because what they opposed was not the sacrificial act, but the *ma'aseh* without the *kiyum,* the outer act without the inner acknowledgment that gives the act its meaning and significance. The idea that God can be worshiped through externalities alone is pagan, and there is nothing worse than the intrusion of paganism into the domain of holiness itself. Then as now, the sign of paganism is the coexistence of religious worship with injustice and a lack of compassion in the dealings between the worshiper and the world.

Sacrifice, like prayer, is a transformative act. We should leave the synagogue, as our ancestors once left the Temple, seeing ourselves and the universe differently, freshly conscious that the world is God's work, the Torah God's word, our fellow believers God's children, and our fellow human beings God's image. We emerge refocused and reenergized,

◂ for we

for we have made the journey back to our source, to the One who gives life to all. Distant, we have come close. That is prayer as sacrifice, *korban*, giving back to God a token of what He has given us, thereby coming to see existence itself as a gift, to be celebrated and sanctified.

10. Kavana: Directing the Mind

Prayer is more than saying certain words in the right order. It needs concentration, attention, engagement of mind and heart, and the left and right hemispheres of the brain. Without devotion, said Rabbi Baḥye ibn Pakuda, prayer is like a body without a soul. The key Hebrew word here is *kavana,* meaning mindfulness, intention, focus, direction of the mind. In the context of prayer, it means several different things.

The most basic level is *kavana le-shem mitzva,* which means, having the intention to fulfill a *mitzva*. This means that we do not act for social or aesthetic reasons. We pray because we are commanded to pray. Generally in Judaism there is a long-standing debate about whether the commandments require *kavana,* but certainly prayer does, because it is supremely an act of the mind.

At a second level, *kavana* means understanding the words (*perush hamilim*). At least the most important sections of prayer require *kavana* in this sense. Without it, the words we say would be mere sounds. Understanding the words is, of course, made much easier by the existence of translations and commentaries.

A third level relates to context. How do I understand my situation when I pray? Maimonides states this principle as follows: "The mind should be *freed from all extraneous thoughts* and the one who prays should *realize that he is standing before the Divine Presence.*" These are essential elements of at least the Amida, the prayer par excellence in which we are conscious of standing before God. That is why we take three steps forward at the beginning, and three back at the end – as if we were entering, then leaving, sacred space.

The fourth level of *kavana* is not merely saying the words but meaning them, affirming them. Thus, for example, while saying the first paragraph of the Shema, we "accept of the yoke of the kingdom of heaven" – declaring our allegiance to God as the supreme authority in our lives. In the second paragraph, we "accept of the yoke of the commandments." The

word *Amen* means roughly, "I affirm what has been said." In prayer we put ourselves into the words. We make a commitment. We declare our faith, our trust, and our dependency. We mean what we say.

There are, of course, higher reaches of *kavana*. Mystics and philosophers throughout the ages developed elaborate meditative practices before and during prayer. But at its simplest, *kavana* is the practiced harmony of word and thought, body and mind. This is how Judah HaLevi described it:

> The tongue agrees with the thought, and does not overstep its bounds, does not speak in prayer in a mere mechanical way as the starling and the parrot, but every word is uttered thoughtfully and attentively. This moment forms the heart and fruit of his time, while the other hours represent the way that leads to it. He looks forward to its approach, because while it lasts he resembles the spiritual beings, and is removed from merely animal existence. Those three times of daily prayer are the fruit of his day and night, and the Sabbath is the fruit of the week, because it has been appointed to establish the connection with the Divine Spirit and to serve God in joy, not in sadness… (*Kuzari*, III:5, as translated by Hartwig Hirschfeld)

Of course it does not always happen. It is told that on one occasion Rabbi Levi Yitzḥak of Berditchev went up to one of his followers after the prayers, held out his hand and said "Welcome home." "But I haven't been anywhere," said the disciple. "Your body hasn't been anywhere," said the Rebbe, "but your mind has been far away. That is why I wished it, 'Welcome home.'"

Rabbi Menaḥem Mendel of Kotzk once asked: "Why does it say in the Shema, 'These words shall be *on* your heart'? Should it not say, 'These words shall be *in* your heart'? The answer is that the heart is not always open. Therefore we should lay these words on our heart, so that when it opens, they will be there, ready to enter."

Prayer requires practice. That is implicit in defining prayer as *avoda shebalev*, "service of the heart." The word *avoda*, service, also means hard work, labor, strenuous activity. We have to work at prayer. But there are also times when the most inarticulate prayer, said from the heart, pierces the heavens. What matters is seriousness and honesty. "The Lord is close to all who call on Him, to all who call on Him in truth."

◂ 11. *Jacob's*

11. *Jacob's Ladder*

Prayer is a journey that has been described in many ways. According to the mystics, it is a journey through the four levels of being – Action, Formation, Creation and Emanation. Rabbi Jacob Emden worked out an elaborate scheme in which the prayers represent a movement from the outer courtyards to the Holy of Holies of the Temple in Jerusalem. According to everyone, the stages of prayer constitute an ascent and descent, reaching their highest level in the middle, in the Shema and Amida.

The metaphor that, to me, captures the spirit of prayer more than any other is Jacob's dream in which, alone at night, fleeing danger and far from home, he saw a ladder stretching from earth to heaven with angels ascending and descending. He woke and said, "How awesome is this place! This is none other than the House of God; this is the gate to heaven" (Gen. 28:10–17).

Our sages said that "this place" was Jerusalem. That is midrashic truth. But there is another meaning, the plain one, no less transfiguring. The verb the Torah uses, *vayifga*, means "to happen upon, as if by chance." "This place" was any place. Any place, any time, even the dark of a lonely night, can be a place and time for prayer. If we have the strength to dream and then, awakening, refuse to let go of the dream, then here, now, where I stand, can be the gate to heaven.

Prayer is a ladder and we are the angels. If there is one theme sounded throughout the prayers, it is creation–revelation–redemption, or ascent–summit–descent. In the Verses of Praise, we climb from earth to heaven by meditating on creation. Like a Turner or Monet landscape, the psalms let us see the universe bathed in light, but *this* light is not the light of beauty but of holiness – the light the sages say God made on the first day and "hid for the righteous in the life to come." Through some of the most magnificent poetry ever written, we see the world as God's masterpiece, suffused with His radiance, until we reach a crescendo in Psalm 150 with its thirteen-fold repetition of "Praise" in a mere thirty-five words.

By the time we reach *Barekhu* and the blessings of the Shema we have neared the summit. Now we are in heaven with the angels. We have reached revelation. The Divine Presence is close, almost tangible. We speak of love in one of the most hauntingly beautiful of blessings, "Great love" with its striking phrase: "Our Father, merciful Father, the Merciful,

◂ have

have mercy on us." Now comes the great declaration of faith at the heart of prayer, the Shema with its passionate profession of the unity of God and the highest of all expressions of love, "with all your heart, with all your soul, and with all your might." Ending with a reference to the exodus, the Shema gives way to the *Emet* blessing with its emphasis on redemption, the exodus and the division of the sea. Then comes the Amida, the supreme height of prayer. Three traditions fuse at this point: the silent Amida said by individuals, reminding us of prophetic prayer; the Leader's Repetition representing priestly worship and prayer as sacrifice; and then the *Kedusha*, prayer as a mystical experience.

From here, prayer begins its descent. First comes *Taḥanun* in which we speak privately and intimately to the King. At this point, with a mixture of anguish and plea, we speak not of God's love for Israel but of Israel's defiant love of God: "Yet despite all this we have not forgotten Your name. Please do not forget us." There is a direct reference back to the Shema: "Guardian of Israel, guard the remnant of Israel, and let not Israel perish who declare, *Shema Yisrael*."

Then comes *Ashrei* and the subsequent passages, similar to the Verses of Praise but this time with redemption, not creation, as their theme. The key verse is "A redeemer will come to Zion." The section closes with a prayer that we may become agents of redemption as we reengage with the world ("May it be Your will… that we keep Your laws in this world"). We are now back on earth, the service complete except for *Aleinu*, Kaddish and the Daily Psalm. We are ready to reenter life and its challenges.

What has prayer achieved? If we have truly prayed, we now know that the world did not materialize by chance. A single, guiding Will, directed its apparent randomness. We know too that this Will did not end there, but remains intimately involved with the universe, which He renews daily, and with humanity, over whose destinies He presides. We have climbed the high ladder and have seen, if only dimly, how small some of our worries are. Our emotional landscape has been expanded. We have given voice to a whole range of emotions: thanks, praise, love, awe, guilt, repentance, remembrance, hope. As we leave the synagogue for the world outside, we now know that we are not alone; that God is with us; that we need not fear failure, for God forgives; that our hopes are not vain; that we are here for a purpose and there is work to do.

We are not the same after we have stood in the Divine Presence as we were before. We have been transformed. We see the world in a different light. Perhaps we radiate a different light. We have spoken to and listened to God. We have aligned ourselves with the moral energies of the universe. We have become, in Lurianic terminology, vessels for God's blessing. We are changed by prayer.

12. *Is Prayer Answered?*

Is prayer answered? If God is changeless, how can we change Him by what we say? Even discounting this, why do we need to articulate our requests? Surely God, who sees the heart, knows our wishes even before we do, without our having to put them into words. What we wish to happen is either right or wrong in the eyes of God. If it is right, God will bring it about even if we do not pray. If it is wrong, God will not bring it about even if we do. So why pray?

The classic Jewish answer is simple but profound. Without a vessel to contain a blessing, there can be no blessing. If we have no receptacle to catch the rain, the rain may fall, but we will have none to drink. If we have no radio receiver, the sound waves will flow, but we will be unable to convert them into sound. God's blessings flow continuously, but unless we make ourselves into a vessel for them, they will flow elsewhere. *Prayer is the act of turning ourselves into a vehicle for the Divine.*

Speaking from personal experience, and from many encounters with people for whom prayer was a lifeline, I know that our prayers are answered: not always in the *way* we expected, not always as quickly as we hoped, but *prayer is never in vain.* Sometimes the answer is, "No." If granting a request would do us or others harm, God will not grant it. But "No" is also an answer, and when God decides that something I have prayed for should not come to pass, then I pray for the wisdom to understand why. That too is part of spiritual growth: to accept graciously what we cannot or should not change. Nor is prayer a substitute for human effort: on the contrary, prayer is one of the most powerful sources of energy for human effort. God gives us the strength to achieve what we need to achieve, and to do what we were placed on earth to do.

Prayer changes the world because it changes us. At its height, it is a profoundly transformative experience. If we have truly prayed, we come in

the course of time to know that the world was made, and we were made, for a purpose; that God, though immeasurably vast, is also intensely close; that "were my father and my mother to forsake me, the LORD would take me in"; that God is with us in our efforts, and that we do not labor in vain. We know, too, that we are part of the community of faith, and with us are four thousand years of history and the prayers and hopes of those who came before us. However far we feel from God, He is there behind us, and all we have to do is turn to face Him. Faith is born and lives in prayer, and faith is the antidote to fear: "The LORD is the stronghold of my life – of whom shall I be afraid?"

It makes a difference to be brushed by the wings of eternity. Regular thrice-daily prayer works on us in ways not immediately apparent. As the sea smoothes the stone, as the repeated hammer-blows of the sculptor shape the marble, so prayer – cyclical, tracking the rhythms of time itself – gradually wears away the jagged edges of our character, turning it into a work of devotional art. We begin to see the beauty of the created world. We locate ourselves as part of the story of our people. Slowly, we come to think less of the "I," more of the "We"; less of what we lack than of what we have; less of what we need from the world, more of what the world needs from us. Prayer is less about getting what we want than about learning what to want. Our priorities change; we become less angular; we learn the deep happiness that comes from learning to give praise and thanks. The world we build tomorrow is born in the prayers we say today.

When, at the end of his vision, Jacob opened his eyes, he said with a sense of awe: "Surely God is in this place and I did not know it." That is what prayer does. It opens our eyes to the wonder of the world. It opens our ears to the still, small voice of God. It opens our hearts to those who need our help. God exists where we pray. As Rabbi Menaḥem Mendel of Kotzk said: "God lives where we let Him in." And in that dialogue between the human soul and the Soul of the universe a momentous yet gentle strength is born.

Chief Rabbi Jonathan Sacks
London 5769 (2009)

KEYWORDS OF PRAYER

THE NAMES OF GOD

The two key names, in prayer as in the Torah, are (1) the Tetragrammaton, יהוה, the "four letter" name, and (2) אֱלֹהִים *Elohim.* They are different in meaning and tone. The sages understood the Tetragrammaton as God's compassion. *Elohim* is God's attribute of justice.

Judah HaLevi (*Kuzari*, IV:1) made a more fundamental distinction. The ancients used the word *El* or *Elo'ah* to designate a force of nature: the sun, the sea, the storm, and so on. These they personified as gods. Often, therefore, *el,* or *elil,* denotes an idol. In Hebrew, monotheism's mother tongue, *Elohim* in the plural means "the One who is the totality of powers, forces and causes in the universe." It refers to God as we experience Him in creation and its natural laws, as well as in justice and its moral laws (it sometimes also has a secular sense, meaning those who hold positions of power, usually judges).

The Tetragrammaton not only has a different meaning, it is also a word of a different grammatical type. It is God's *proper name,* standing in relation to Him as the names Abraham or Sarah attach to human beings (hence it is sometimes referred to as *HaShem,* "the name"). The use of a proper name in connection with God means that a direct relationship between us and heaven is possible. We can speak to God, and He listens. There is a direct connection between the Tetragrammaton and the word "You." Only a being that has a proper name can we address as "You." Hence, in prayer, "You" is always directed to the Tetragrammaton; *Elohim* goes with the third-person, "He." Thus, *Elohim* signifies God-as-law, natural or moral. The Tetragrammaton refers to God as we encounter Him in intimacy, compassion and love.

Though I have followed convention, rendering the Tetragrammaton as "Lord," it should be remembered that "Lord" is not a *translation* but a *substitution.* So holy was the divine name that it was used only in the Temple. In all other contexts, it was (and still is) pronounced as *Adonai,* which means "my Lord."

The use of the word *Eloheinu,* "*Our* God," signifies our acceptance of God as the sole object of our worship. Formal acknowledgment of this fact – in the first line of the Shema – is a pledge of loyalty and service, called by the sages, "Acceptance of the yoke of divine kingship."

◂ The word

The word מֶלֶךְ, "King," when applied to God means, first, that God is the sole ultimate Sovereign of the people Israel, who accepted His kingship and covenant at Mount Sinai. At that ceremony, God undertook to guide the Israelites' destiny, while the people accepted their vocation as "a kingdom of priests and a holy nation," bound by God's laws. The second and wider meaning is that God is Sovereign over the universe and all humanity – with whom, via Noah, He made a covenant after the Flood (Genesis, chapter 9). That covenant, with its seven laws, embodies the fundamental principles of human conduct under God. Though God's sovereignty is not yet recognized by all, it will be in the end of days. Hence our prayers often end with the prophecy of Zechariah (14:9), "Then the Lord shall be King over all the earth." The sovereignty of God is the ultimate sanction against tyranny. It implies that all human authority is delegated authority, to be exercised only within the constraints of the covenant.

Sometimes God is referred to as קוֹנֵה which, though I have followed convention by translating it as "Creator," literally means "Owner" of heaven and earth. This represents the idea that because God *created* the universe, He *owns* it. The world and its benefits do not belong to us. What we possess, we hold in trust from God. This is the legal basis of divine sovereignty of the universe – similar to the ancient concept of "eminent domain" by which all ownership of land within a country is ultimately vested in its head of state. As Sovereign of the universe, God rules by right, not power.

ATTRIBUTES OF GOD

Many of the key terms descriptive of God are not precisely translatable because they presuppose the concept of covenant: an open-ended pledge between two or more parties to join their destinies together in a reciprocal bond of loyalty and love. The nearest human equivalents are, (1) the bond of marriage, (2) peace treaties between nations. The unique idea of the Torah is that such a covenant can exist between God and humanity.

Thus אֱמֶת, often translated as "true," actually means "faithful, one who acts in accord with his word, one who honors commitments and promises." חֶסֶד, translated as "loving-kindness" or "love," refers to the emotions and actions that flow from a covenantal bond, such as between husband and wife, or between parents and children. It means *love translated into deed.*

◂ There is

There is no English word for צְדָקָה, which means both "justice" and "charity." צֶדֶק, often translated as "righteousness," means "distributive justice, equity" as opposed to מִשְׁפָּט, which means "legal or retributive justice." רַחֲמִים, which I have translated as "compassion," derives from the word *reḥem*, meaning "a womb." It signifies the unconditional love of a mother for her child. חֵן, "grace," means gratuitous kindness, which flows from the generosity of the giver, not the merits of the recipient.

קָדוֹשׁ *Holy*. In general, this means "separated, set apart, standing outside." Used of God, it means "He who stands outside nature" because He *made* nature. Used of the people of Israel (as in "a holy nation," Ex. 19:6) it means the people who stand outside the normal laws of nations – defined by land, language, race or political structure – because they are the sole nation whose constitutive *raison d'être* is to serve God as His witnesses to the world. Shabbat is holy time because it stands outside the normal concerns of the week. The Temple is holy space because it is dedicated to the service of God.

To stand in the presence of holiness, as in prayer, is to enter God's domain; that is, the place where His will rules, not ours. That is why prayer is like sacrifice, because both involve a psychological-spiritual act of renunciation. We renounce our will, accepting His. The Hebrew word for sacrifice, *korban*, means "coming, or bringing, close." Often, in non-Hebraic languages, the word "holy" implies distance and awe. In Judaism, the reverse is also true: Israel encounters holiness as a special closeness to God. This is experienced as both love and awe: love, because of our closeness to the Infinite; awe because of the exacting responsibilities this carries with it.

OTHER KEY TERMS

אָמֵן *Amen*. Saying "Amen" is what philosophers call a "performative utterance." It is a formal act of acceptance and affirmation, meaning, (1) we believe this to be true, or (2) we associate ourselves with what has been said. It functions in the Torah as an assent to an oath (for example, in Deuteronomy 27:15–26). The root *'-m-n* has a range of senses, including "to believe, to trust, to care, to be faithful." In general, liturgical responses – such as "Blessed is He and blessed is His name" – form an essential link between the Leader and congregation, turning a prayer *on behalf of* the

◂ community

community into one assented to *by* the community. Special significance was attached by the sages to the response during the recital of Kaddish, "May His great name be blessed for ever and all time." Indeed for them, the merit of saying Kaddish is precisely that it evokes this response from the community.

אַתָּה *You.* The gods of the ancient world were at best indifferent, at worst actively hostile, to human beings. The God of the philosophers – abstract, conceptual, the prime mover or necessary being – can be contemplated but not addressed. The difference between the God of the prophets and the God of the philosophers is that the former knows us, cares about us, and listens to us (Judah HaLevi, *Kuzari*). Without the word "You" there can be meditation, but not prayer. The central section of most forms of the Amida begins with the word "You."

בָּרוּךְ *Blessed.* When applied to God it means: He is the *source* of all blessings, not only spiritual but also physical: health, livelihood, safety and security. In prayer we learn to see our material enjoyments as God's blessing, belonging as they do to the world He created and pronounced good. The root *b-r-kh* also means (1) to bow, bend the knee; (2) a pool or reservoir of water. What connects these is *downward movement.* A blessing is what, metaphorically, flows down to earth from heaven.

There are several categories of blessings in the siddur: (1) blessings of acknowledgment, which are forms of praise and thanksgiving; (2) blessings over the performance of commandments, which are formal declarations of intent (*kavana*) that the act we are about to perform is done because God has commanded us to do so; (3) blessings over enjoyments (food, drink, and so on), which are acts of redemption in the technical sense of buying something back for secular use that would otherwise be holy, and thus not available for our personal benefit.

מִזְמוֹר *Mizmor* ("Psalm") is found 57 times as the heading of a psalm, and is used nowhere else in Tanakh. Many believe it refers to a song written to be accompanied by musical instruments. תְּהִלָּה *Tehilla,* "song of praise," is used only once as superscription to a psalm (Psalm 145); despite this, the book of Psalms as a whole is known to Jewish tradition as *Tehillim,* "Songs of Praise." Some psalms carry the name of the person who wrote it or to whom it was dedicated; others the occasion on which it was sung; yet others are musical directions. The term לַמְנַצֵּחַ, *lamenatze'aḥ,*

◂ means

means "for the conductor, director of music, choir-master," and usually signals a choral work.

סֶלָה *Selah.* A word of unknown meaning. Some hold that it means "for ever"; others understand it as an affirmation, similar to the word "Amen." Yet others see it as a musical notation, a signaled pause, or an indication of the end of a passage.

עוֹלָם *Olam.* The word *olam* means both "universe" and "eternity" – the outermost limits of space and time. It may come from the same root as *ne'elam*, "hidden." This was understood by Jewish mystics, especially of the Lurianic school, as meaning that to create a universe, the Infinite had to contract or limit Himself, otherwise Infinity would leave no space for finitude. God is present in the physical universe but in a hidden way. We are, explains Nahmanides, surrounded by miracles. The world is filled with the radiance of God, but to see it, we have to open our eyes. Part of the purpose of prayer is, in this sense, to open our eyes.

שֵׁם *Name*: How God is perceived by human beings. When He is recognized as the supreme Sovereign, this is a "sanctification of the name." When He is forced to exile His people – and thus seen by the nations as if powerless to protect them – this is a "desecration of the name." The opening words of Kaddish, "Magnified and sanctified may His great name be," mean "May the sovereignty of God be ever more widely recognized by human beings." The closing words of *Aleinu*, "On that day the Lord shall be One and His name One," refer to a time – the Messianic Age – when God will be recognized by all. God does not change; human recognition of God does. The use of the word "name" marks the distinction between God as He is and as He is humanly perceived.

Other terms are explained within the Commentary.

JS

GUIDE TO THE READER

This new edition of the Koren Siddur continues the Koren tradition of making the language of prayer more accessible, thus enhancing the prayer experience.

One of the unique features of the Siddur is the use of typesetting to break up a prayer phrase-by-phrase – rather than using a block paragraph format – so that the reader will naturally pause at the correct places. No commas appear in the Hebrew text at the end of lines, but in the English translation, where linguistic clarity requires, we have retained the use of commas at the end of lines. Unlike other bilingual siddurim, the Hebrew text is on the left-hand page and the English on the right. This arrangement preserves the distinctive "fanning out" effect of the Koren text and the beauty of the Koren layout.

PRONUNCIATION AIDS:

- Most Hebrew words are pronounced with a stress on the last syllable. For words where the stress is placed on the penultimate syllable, a short vertical line (the *meteg*) appears next to the vowel of that syllable, so readers know how to pronounce the word correctly [מֶֽלֶךְ]. However, this system is not used in the text of the Shema and the Torah readings because their pronunciation is indicated by the *ta'amei hamikra*.

- We have differentiated between the *kamatz katan* (the *oh* sound) and the *kamatz gadol* (the *ah* sound in Sephardi pronunciation) by using a larger symbol for the *kamatz katan*. See *Ḥokhma* [חׇכְמָה]. Similarly, we have differentiated between the *sh'va na* (a pronounced vowel) and the *sh'va naḥ* (an unpronounced vowel) by using a larger symbol for the *sh'va na*. See *Nafshekha* [נַפְשְׁךָ]. We have followed the rules of grammar for the placement of the *kamatz katan* and *sh'va na*.

- As is traditional in the Koren Tanakh, the furtive *pataḥ* is placed slightly to the right, rather than centered underneath the letter, to indicate to the reader that the vowel is pronounced before the consonant rather than after; for example, פּוֹתֵחַ is pronounced *pote'aḥ* and not *poteḥa*.

◂ A small

A small arrow (◂) indicates the suggested starting point for the *Shaliaḥ Tzibbur*. However, where the local custom differs, the *Shaliaḥ Tzibbur* should certainly follow that custom.

We have tried to provide concise instructions for prayer within the text. Expanded explanations and *halakhot* are provided in the Guides to Prayer at the end of the Siddur.

For those who are using the Siddur on a visit to Israel, changes in the prayers have been indicated throughout the text. In addition, a comprehensive "Halakhic Guide for Visitors to Israel" has been added at the end of the Siddur.

In transliterating Hebrew, we have followed modern Israeli pronunciation. We have transliterated the Hebrew ח with a *ḥ* and the כ with a *kh*. We have also compromised on strict consistency in favor of clarity and ease of use. For example, although we have generally omitted the *h* at the end of words like "Amida," we have retained it in the word "Torah," because that is the common spelling. In addition, the *sh'va na* is sometimes represented by an apostrophe and sometimes with an *e* (for example, *Barekhi*, *sh'va*). We have also used an apostrophe to separate syllables where the correct pronunciation is not readily apparent, as in *mo'ed*.

There are two Koren typefaces: one used exclusively for Tanakh, and one for the Siddur. Sections of the Siddur that reproduce complete paragraphs from the Tanakh, such as much of *Pesukei DeZimra*, have been set in the Tanakh typeface. However, where verses from the Tanakh are quoted within the prayers, we have in general used the Siddur typeface to maintain a consistent look and feel. Nevertheless all verses from Tanakh conclude with the *sof pasuk* (:), the double diamond that is the "period" of the Tanakh. This differs from the colon (:) which is used where appropriate in prayers that are not quotations from Tanakh.

We hope that these innovations will make praying with the Siddur a more profound and uplifting experience.

Raphaël Freeman, Editor
Jerusalem 5769 (2009)

סידור קורן
THE KOREN SIDDUR

ימי חול

WEEKDAYS

Shaḥarit

The following order of prayers and blessings, which departs from that of most prayer books, is based on the consensus of recent halakhic authorities. See laws 315–323.

ON WAKING

On waking, our first thought should be that we are in the presence of God. Since we are forbidden to speak God's name until we have washed our hands, the following prayer is said, which, without mentioning God's name, acknowledges His presence and gives thanks for a new day and for the gift of life. See laws 315–323.

מוֹדֶה I thank You, living and eternal King,
for giving me back my soul in mercy.
Great is Your faithfulness.

Wash hands and say the following blessings.
Some have the custom to say "Wisdom begins" on page 10 at this point.

בָּרוּךְ Blessed are You, Lord our God, King of the Universe,
who has made us holy through His commandments,
and has commanded us about washing hands.

בָּרוּךְ Blessed are You, Lord our God, King of the Universe,
who formed man in wisdom
and created in him many orifices and cavities.
It is revealed and known before the throne of Your glory
that were one of them to be ruptured or blocked,
it would be impossible to survive
and stand before You.
Blessed are You, Lord,
Healer of all flesh who does wondrous deeds.

אֲשֶׁר יָצַר *Who formed man in wisdom:* A blessing of thanks for the intricate wonders of the human body. *Were one of them to be ruptured or blocked* – even the smallest variation in the human genome can cause potentially fatal illness. The more we understand of the complexity of life, the more we appreciate "How numerous are Your works, Lord; You made them all in wisdom; the earth is full of Your creations" (Psalm 104:24). This blessing is a rejection of the idea that the spirit alone is holy, and physical life bereft of God.

שחרית

The following order of prayers and blessings, which departs from that of most prayer books, is based on the consensus of recent halakhic authorities. See laws 315–323.

השכמת הבוקר

On waking, our first thought should be that we are in the presence of God. Since we are forbidden to speak God's name until we have washed our hands, the following prayer is said, which, without mentioning God's name, acknowledges His presence and gives thanks for a new day and for the gift of life. See laws 315–323.

מוֹדֶה/women מוֹדָה/ אֲנִי לְפָנֶיךָ מֶלֶךְ חַי וְקַיָּם
שֶׁהֶחֱזַרְתָּ בִּי נִשְׁמָתִי בְּחֶמְלָה
רַבָּה אֱמוּנָתֶךָ.

Wash hands and say the following blessings.
Some have the custom to say רֵאשִׁית חָכְמָה *on page 11 at this point.*

בָּרוּךְ אַתָּה יהוה אֱלֹהֵינוּ מֶלֶךְ הָעוֹלָם
אֲשֶׁר קִדְּשָׁנוּ בְּמִצְוֹתָיו וְצִוָּנוּ עַל נְטִילַת יָדָיִם.

בָּרוּךְ אַתָּה יהוה אֱלֹהֵינוּ מֶלֶךְ הָעוֹלָם
אֲשֶׁר יָצַר אֶת הָאָדָם בְּחָכְמָה
וּבָרָא בוֹ נְקָבִים נְקָבִים, חֲלוּלִים חֲלוּלִים.
גָּלוּי וְיָדוּעַ לִפְנֵי כִסֵּא כְבוֹדֶךָ
שֶׁאִם יִפָּתֵחַ אֶחָד מֵהֶם אוֹ יִסָּתֵם אֶחָד מֵהֶם
אִי אֶפְשַׁר לְהִתְקַיֵּם וְלַעֲמֹד לְפָנֶיךָ.
בָּרוּךְ אַתָּה יהוה, רוֹפֵא כָל בָּשָׂר וּמַפְלִיא לַעֲשׂוֹת.

מוֹדֶה אֲנִי *I thank You:* These words are to be said immediately on waking from sleep. In them we thank God for life itself, renewed each day. Sleep, said the sages, is "one-sixtieth of death" (*Berakhot* 57b). Waking, therefore, is a miniature rebirth. Despite its brevity, this sentence articulates a transformative act of faith: the recognition that life is a gift from God. Expressing gratitude at the fact of being alive, we prepare ourselves to celebrate and sanctify the new day.

אֱלֹהַי My God,
the soul You placed within me is pure.
You created it, You formed it, You breathed it into me,
and You guard it while it is within me.
One day You will take it from me,
and restore it to me in the time to come.
As long as the soul is within me,
I will thank You,
LORD my God and God of my ancestors,
Master of all works, LORD of all souls.
Blessed are You, LORD,
who restores souls to lifeless bodies.

TZITZIT

The following blessing is said before putting on tzitzit. Neither it nor the subsequent prayer is said by those who wear a tallit. The blessing over the latter exempts the former. See laws 324–330.

בָּרוּךְ Blessed are You, LORD our God, King of the Universe,
who has made us holy through His commandments,
and has commanded us
about the command of tasseled garments.

After putting on tzitzit, say:

יְהִי רָצוֹן May it be Your will, LORD my God and God of my ancestors,
that the commandment of the tasseled garment be considered before You
as if I had fulfilled it in all its specifics,
details and intentions,
as well as the 613 commandments
dependent on it,
Amen, Selah.

---

them. The blessing ends with a reference to the resurrection of the dead, returning to the theme of the first words said in the morning.

אֱלֹהַי
נְשָׁמָה שֶׁנָּתַתָּ בִּי טְהוֹרָה הִיא.
אַתָּה בְרָאתָהּ, אַתָּה יְצַרְתָּהּ, אַתָּה נְפַחְתָּהּ בִּי
וְאַתָּה מְשַׁמְּרָהּ בְּקִרְבִּי, וְאַתָּה עָתִיד לִטְּלָהּ מִמֶּנִּי
וּלְהַחֲזִירָהּ בִּי לֶעָתִיד לָבוֹא.
כָּל זְמַן שֶׁהַנְּשָׁמָה בְקִרְבִּי, מוֹדֶה/*women* מוֹדָה/ אֲנִי לְפָנֶיךָ
יהוה אֱלֹהַי וֵאלֹהֵי אֲבוֹתַי
רִבּוֹן כָּל הַמַּעֲשִׂים, אֲדוֹן כָּל הַנְּשָׁמוֹת.
בָּרוּךְ אַתָּה יהוה, הַמַּחֲזִיר נְשָׁמוֹת לִפְגָרִים מֵתִים.

לבישת ציצית

The following blessing is said before putting on a טלית קטן*.*
Neither it nor יְהִי רָצוֹן *is said by those who wear a* טלית*. The blessing over the latter exempts the former. See laws 324–330.*

בָּרוּךְ אַתָּה יהוה אֱלֹהֵינוּ מֶלֶךְ הָעוֹלָם
אֲשֶׁר קִדְּשָׁנוּ בְּמִצְוֹתָיו וְצִוָּנוּ עַל מִצְוַת צִיצִית.

After putting on the טלית קטן*, say:*

יְהִי רָצוֹן מִלְּפָנֶיךָ, יהוה אֱלֹהַי וֵאלֹהֵי אֲבוֹתַי
שֶׁתְּהֵא חֲשׁוּבָה מִצְוַת צִיצִית לְפָנֶיךָ
כְּאִלּוּ קִיַּמְתִּיהָ בְּכָל פְּרָטֶיהָ וְדִקְדּוּקֶיהָ וְכַוָּנוֹתֶיהָ
וְתַרְיַ״ג מִצְוֹת הַתְּלוּיוֹת בָּהּ
אָמֵן סֶלָה.

אֱלֹהַי *My God, the soul You placed within me is pure:* An affirmation of Jewish belief in the freedom and responsibility of each human being. The soul as such is pure. We have good instincts and bad, and we must choose between

BLESSINGS OVER THE TORAH

In Judaism, study is greater even than prayer. So, before beginning to pray, we engage in a miniature act of study, preceded by the appropriate blessings. The blessings are followed by brief selections from Scripture, Mishna and Gemara, the three foundational texts of Judaism.

בָּרוּךְ Blessed are You, LORD our God, King of the Universe,
who has made us holy through His commandments,
and has commanded us to engage in study
of the words of Torah.
Please, LORD our God, make the words of Your Torah
sweet in our mouths and in the mouths of Your people,
the house of Israel,
so that we, our descendants (and their descendants)
and the descendants of Your people,
the house of Israel,
may all know Your name
and study Your Torah for its own sake.
Blessed are You, LORD,
who teaches Torah to His people Israel.

בָּרוּךְ Blessed are You, LORD our God, King of the Universe,
who has chosen us from all the peoples
and given us His Torah.
Blessed are You, LORD, Giver of the Torah.

---

chosenness means responsibility, and is inseparably linked to the study and practice of Torah.

So as to follow the blessings immediately with an act that fulfills the commandment, we read three texts whose recitation forms an act of study. The Talmud (*Kiddushin* 30a) rules that Torah study must be divided into three: study of (1) Torah, (2) Mishna, and (3) Gemara. Hence we read: (1) a biblical text – the priestly blessings, (2) a passage from the Mishna about commandments that have no fixed measure, and (3) a passage from the Gemara about the reward of good deeds in this world and the next.

ברכות התורה

In Judaism, study is greater even than prayer. So, before beginning to pray, we engage in a miniature act of study, preceded by the appropriate blessings. The blessings are followed by brief selections from תנ״ך, משנה and גמרא, the three foundational texts of Judaism.

בָּרוּךְ אַתָּה יהוה אֱלֹהֵינוּ מֶלֶךְ הָעוֹלָם
אֲשֶׁר קִדְּשָׁנוּ בְּמִצְוֹתָיו
וְצִוָּנוּ לַעֲסֹק בְּדִבְרֵי תוֹרָה.
וְהַעֲרֶב נָא יהוה אֱלֹהֵינוּ אֶת דִּבְרֵי תוֹרָתְךָ
בְּפִינוּ וּבְפִי עַמְּךָ בֵּית יִשְׂרָאֵל
וְנִהְיֶה אֲנַחְנוּ וְצֶאֱצָאֵינוּ (וְצֶאֱצָאֵי צֶאֱצָאֵינוּ)
וְצֶאֱצָאֵי עַמְּךָ בֵּית יִשְׂרָאֵל
כֻּלָּנוּ יוֹדְעֵי שְׁמֶךָ וְלוֹמְדֵי תוֹרָתְךָ לִשְׁמָהּ.
בָּרוּךְ אַתָּה יהוה, הַמְלַמֵּד תּוֹרָה לְעַמּוֹ יִשְׂרָאֵל.

בָּרוּךְ אַתָּה יהוה אֱלֹהֵינוּ מֶלֶךְ הָעוֹלָם
אֲשֶׁר בָּחַר בָּנוּ מִכָּל הָעַמִּים
וְנָתַן לָנוּ אֶת תּוֹרָתוֹ.
בָּרוּךְ אַתָּה יהוה, נוֹתֵן הַתּוֹרָה.

BLESSINGS OVER THE TORAH

The history of Judaism is a story of the love of a people for the Book of Books, the Torah. As a preliminary to study, we pronounce two blessings and a prayer. The first, "who has made us holy through His commandments," is a blessing over the commandment to engage in study of the Torah, a declaration that we do not simply study as an intellectual or cultural exercise but as the fulfillment of a divine commandment. This is followed by a prayer that God make Torah study sweet, and help us to hand it on to our children. The final blessing, "who has chosen us," is a blessing of acknowledgment that

יְבָרֶכְךָ May the LORD bless you and protect you. *Num. 6*
May the LORD make His face shine on you
and be gracious to you.
May the LORD turn His face toward you
and grant you peace.

אֵלּוּ These are the things *Mishna Pe'ah 1:1*
for which there is no fixed measure:
the corner of the field, first-fruits,
appearances before the LORD
[on festivals, with offerings],
acts of kindness and the study of Torah.

אֵלּוּ These are the things *Shabbat 127a*
whose fruits we eat in this world
but whose full reward awaits us
in the World to Come:

honoring parents; acts of kindness;
arriving early at the house of study
morning and evening;
hospitality to strangers; visiting the sick;
helping the needy bride; attending to the dead;
devotion in prayer;
and bringing peace between people –
but the study of Torah is equal to them all.

Some say:

רֵאשִׁית חָכְמָה Wisdom begins in awe of the LORD; *Ps. 111*
all who fulfill [His commandments] gain good understanding;
His praise is ever-lasting.
The Torah Moses commanded us *Deut. 33*
is the heritage of the congregation of Jacob.
Listen, my son, to your father's instruction, *Prov. 1*
and do not forsake your mother's teaching.
May the Torah be my faith and Almighty God my help.
Blessed be the name of His glorious kingdom for ever and all time.

במדבר ו

יְבָרֶכְךָ יהוה וְיִשְׁמְרֶךָ:
יָאֵר יהוה פָּנָיו אֵלֶיךָ וִיחֻנֶּךָּ:
יִשָּׂא יהוה פָּנָיו אֵלֶיךָ וְיָשֵׂם לְךָ שָׁלוֹם:

משנה, פאה א:א

אֵלּוּ דְבָרִים שֶׁאֵין לָהֶם שִׁעוּר
הַפֵּאָה וְהַבִּכּוּרִים וְהָרֵאָיוֹן
וּגְמִילוּת חֲסָדִים וְתַלְמוּד תּוֹרָה.

שבת קכז.

אֵלּוּ דְבָרִים שֶׁאָדָם אוֹכֵל פֵּרוֹתֵיהֶם בָּעוֹלָם הַזֶּה
וְהַקֶּרֶן קַיֶּמֶת לוֹ לָעוֹלָם הַבָּא
וְאֵלּוּ הֵן
כִּבּוּד אָב וָאֵם, וּגְמִילוּת חֲסָדִים
וְהַשְׁכָּמַת בֵּית הַמִּדְרָשׁ שַׁחֲרִית וְעַרְבִית
וְהַכְנָסַת אוֹרְחִים, וּבִקּוּר חוֹלִים
וְהַכְנָסַת כַּלָּה, וּלְוָיַת הַמֵּת
וְעִיּוּן תְּפִלָּה
וַהֲבָאַת שָׁלוֹם בֵּין אָדָם לַחֲבֵרוֹ
וְתַלְמוּד תּוֹרָה כְּנֶגֶד כֻּלָּם.

Some say:

תהלים קיא

רֵאשִׁית חָכְמָה יִרְאַת יהוה
שֵׂכֶל טוֹב לְכָל־עֹשֵׂיהֶם
תְּהִלָּתוֹ עֹמֶדֶת לָעַד:

דברים לג

תּוֹרָה צִוָּה־לָנוּ מֹשֶׁה, מוֹרָשָׁה קְהִלַּת יַעֲקֹב:

משלי א

שְׁמַע בְּנִי מוּסַר אָבִיךָ וְאַל־תִּטֹּשׁ תּוֹרַת אִמֶּךָ:
תּוֹרָה תְּהֵא אֱמוּנָתִי, וְאֵל שַׁדַּי בְּעֶזְרָתִי.
בָּרוּךְ שֵׁם כְּבוֹד מַלְכוּתוֹ לְעוֹלָם וָעֶד.

TALLIT

Say the following meditation before putting on the tallit. Meditations before the fulfillment of mitzvot are to ensure that we do so with the requisite intention (kavana). This particularly applies to mitzvot whose purpose is to induce in us certain states of mind, as is the case with tallit and tefillin, both of which are external symbols of inward commitment to the life of observance of the mitzvot.

בָּרְכִי נַפְשִׁי Bless the LORD, my soul. LORD, my God, You are very great, clothed in majesty and splendor, wrapped in a robe of light, spreading out the heavens like a tent. *Ps. 104*

Some say:

For the sake of the unification of the Holy One, blessed be He, and His Divine Presence, in reverence and love, to unify the name *Yod-Heh* with *Vav-Heh* in perfect unity in the name of all Israel.

I am about to wrap myself in this tasseled garment (tallit). So may my soul, my 248 limbs and 365 sinews be wrapped in the light of the tassel (*hatzitzit*) which amounts to 613 [commandments]. And just as I cover myself with a tasseled garment in this world, so may I be worthy of rabbinical dress and a fine garment in the World to Come in the Garden of Eden. Through the commandment of tassels may my life's-breath, spirit, soul and prayer be delivered from external impediments, and may the tallit spread its wings over them like an eagle stirring up its nest, hovering over its young. *Deut. 32* May the commandment of the tasseled garment be considered before the Holy One, blessed be He, as if I had fulfilled it in all its specifics, details and intentions, as well as the 613 commandments dependent on it, Amen, Selah.

Before wrapping oneself in the tallit, say:

בָּרוּךְ Blessed are You, LORD our God, King of the Universe,
who has made us holy through His commandments,
and has commanded us to wrap ourselves
in the tasseled garment.

According to the Shela (R. Isaiah Horowitz), one should say these verses after wrapping oneself in the tallit:

מַה־יָּקָר How precious is Your loving-kindness, O God, and the children of men find refuge under the shadow of Your wings. They are filled with the rich plenty of Your House. You give them drink from Your river of delights. For with You is the fountain of life; in Your light, we see light. Continue Your loving-kindness to those who know You, and Your righteousness to the upright in heart. *Ps. 36*

---

an undergarment *beneath* our outer clothes. Though they fulfill a single commandment, they were deemed so different as to warrant two different blessings.

עטיפת טלית

Say the following meditation before putting on the טלית. Meditations before the fulfillment of מצוות are to ensure that we do so with the requisite intention (כוונה). This particularly applies to מצוות whose purpose is to induce in us certain states of mind, as is the case with טלית and תפילין, both of which are external symbols of inward commitment to the life of observance of the מצוות.

תהלים קד בָּרְכִי נַפְשִׁי אֶת־יהוה, יהוה אֱלֹהַי גָּדַלְתָּ מְּאֹד, הוֹד וְהָדָר לָבָשְׁתָּ:
עֹטֶה־אוֹר כַּשַּׂלְמָה, נוֹטֶה שָׁמַיִם כַּיְרִיעָה:

Some say:

לְשֵׁם יִחוּד קֻדְשָׁא בְּרִיךְ הוּא וּשְׁכִינְתֵּהּ בִּדְחִילוּ וּרְחִימוּ, לְיַחֵד שֵׁם י״ה בו״ה בְּיִחוּדָא שְׁלִים בְּשֵׁם כָּל יִשְׂרָאֵל.

הֲרֵינִי מִתְעַטֵּף בַּצִּיצִית. כֵּן תִּתְעַטֵּף נִשְׁמָתִי וּרְמַ״ח אֵבָרַי וּשְׁסָ״ה גִידַי בְּאוֹר הַצִּיצִית
הָעוֹלָה תַּרְיַ״ג. וּכְשֵׁם שֶׁאֲנִי מִתְכַּסֶּה בְּטַלִּית בָּעוֹלָם הַזֶּה, כָּךְ אֶזְכֶּה לַחֲלוּקָא
דְרַבָּנָן וּלְטַלִּית נָאָה לָעוֹלָם הַבָּא בְּגַן עֵדֶן. וְעַל יְדֵי מִצְוַת צִיצִית תִּנָּצֵל נַפְשִׁי רוּחִי
דברים לב וְנִשְׁמָתִי וּתְפִלָּתִי מִן הַחִיצוֹנִים. וְהַטַּלִּית תִּפְרֹשׂ כְּנָפֶיהָ עֲלֵיהֶם וְתַצִּילֵם, כְּנֶשֶׁר יָעִיר
קִנּוֹ, עַל גּוֹזָלָיו יְרַחֵף: וּתְהֵא חֲשׁוּבָה מִצְוַת צִיצִית לִפְנֵי הַקָּדוֹשׁ בָּרוּךְ הוּא, כְּאִלּוּ
קִיַּמְתִּיהָ בְּכָל פְּרָטֶיהָ וְדִקְדּוּקֶיהָ וְכַוָּנוֹתֶיהָ וְתַרְיַ״ג מִצְוֹת הַתְּלוּיוֹת בָּהּ, אָמֵן סֶלָה.

Before wrapping oneself in the טלית, say:

בָּרוּךְ אַתָּה יהוה אֱלֹהֵינוּ מֶלֶךְ הָעוֹלָם
אֲשֶׁר קִדְּשָׁנוּ בְּמִצְוֹתָיו וְצִוָּנוּ לְהִתְעַטֵּף בַּצִּיצִית.

According to the Shela (R. Isaiah Horowitz), one should say these verses after wrapping oneself in the טלית:

תהלים לו מַה־יָּקָר חַסְדְּךָ אֱלֹהִים, וּבְנֵי אָדָם בְּצֵל כְּנָפֶיךָ יֶחֱסָיוּן: יִרְוְיֻן
מִדֶּשֶׁן בֵּיתֶךָ, וְנַחַל עֲדָנֶיךָ תַשְׁקֵם: כִּי־עִמְּךָ מְקוֹר חַיִּים, בְּאוֹרְךָ
נִרְאֶה־אוֹר: מְשֹׁךְ חַסְדְּךָ לְיֹדְעֶיךָ, וְצִדְקָתְךָ לְיִשְׁרֵי־לֵב:

TALLIT AND TEFILLIN

The mitzva of tzitzit, placing tassels on the corner of our garments, is to recall us constantly to our vocation: "Thus you will be reminded to keep all My commandments, and be holy to your God" (Num. 15:40). Over the course of time, the fulfillment of this commandment took two different forms: the tallit, worn as a robe during prayer, *over* our clothes, and the tallit katan, worn as

TEFILLIN

Some say the following meditation before putting on the tefillin.

For the sake of the unification of the Holy One, blessed be He, and His Divine Presence, in reverence and love, to unify the name *Yod-Heh* with *Vav-Heh* in perfect unity in the name of all Israel.

By putting on the tefillin I hereby intend to fulfill the commandment of my Creator who commanded us to wear tefillin, as it is written in His Torah: "Bind them as a sign on your hand, and they shall be an emblem on the center of your head." They contain these four sections of the Torah: one beginning with *Shema* [Deut. 6:4–9]; another with *Vehaya im shamo'a* [ibid. 11:13–21]; the third with *Kadesh Li* [Ex. 13:1–10]; and the fourth with *Vehaya ki yevi'akha* [ibid. 13:11–16]. These proclaim the uniqueness and unity of God, blessed be His name in the world. They also remind us of the miracles and wonders which He did for us when He brought us out of Egypt, and that He has the power and the dominion over the highest and the lowest to deal with them as He pleases. He commanded us to place one of the tefillin on the arm in memory of His "outstretched arm" (of redemption), setting it opposite the heart, to subject the desires and designs of our heart to His service, blessed be His name. The other is to be on the head, opposite the brain, so that my mind, whose seat is in the brain, together with my other senses and faculties, may be subjected to His service, blessed be His name. May the spiritual influence of the commandment of the tefillin be with me so that I may have a long life, a flow of holiness, and sacred thoughts, free from any suggestion of sin or iniquity. May the evil inclination neither incite nor entice us, but leave us to serve the LORD, as it is in our hearts to do.

Deut. 6

And may it be Your will, LORD our God and God of our ancestors, that the commandment of tefillin be considered before You as if I had fulfilled it in all its specifics, details and intentions, as well as the 613 commandments dependent on it, Amen, Selah.

Tefillin thus symbolize the love for God in emotion (heart), thought (head) and deed (hand).

הנחת תפילין

Some say the following meditation before putting on the תפילין.

לְשֵׁם יִחוּד קֻדְשָׁא בְּרִיךְ הוּא וּשְׁכִינְתֵּהּ בִּדְחִילוּ וּרְחִימוּ, לְיַחֵד שֵׁם י״ה בו״ה בְּיִחוּדָא שְׁלִים בְּשֵׁם כָּל יִשְׂרָאֵל.

הִנְנִי מְכַוֵּן בְּהֲנָחַת תְּפִלִּין לְקַיֵּם מִצְוַת בּוֹרְאִי, שֶׁצִּוָּנוּ לְהָנִיחַ תְּפִלִּין,
כַּכָּתוּב בְּתוֹרָתוֹ: וּקְשַׁרְתָּם לְאוֹת עַל־יָדֶךָ, וְהָיוּ לְטֹטָפֹת בֵּין עֵינֶיךָ: דברים ו
וְהֵן אַרְבַּע פָּרָשִׁיּוֹת אֵלּוּ, שְׁמַע, וְהָיָה אִם שָׁמֹעַ, קַדֶּשׁ לִי, וְהָיָה כִּי יְבִאֲךָ, שֶׁיֵּשׁ בָּהֶם יִחוּדוֹ וְאַחְדוּתוֹ יִתְבָּרַךְ שְׁמוֹ בָּעוֹלָם, וְשֶׁנִּזְכֹּר נִסִּים וְנִפְלָאוֹת שֶׁעָשָׂה עִמָּנוּ בְּהוֹצִיאוֹ אוֹתָנוּ מִמִּצְרַיִם, וַאֲשֶׁר לוֹ הַכֹּחַ וְהַמֶּמְשָׁלָה בָּעֶלְיוֹנִים וּבַתַּחְתּוֹנִים לַעֲשׂוֹת בָּהֶם כִּרְצוֹנוֹ. וְצִוָּנוּ לְהָנִיחַ עַל הַיָּד לְזִכְרוֹן זְרוֹעַ הַנְּטוּיָה, וְשֶׁהִיא נֶגֶד הַלֵּב, לְשַׁעְבֵּד בָּזֶה תַּאֲווֹת וּמַחְשְׁבוֹת לִבֵּנוּ לַעֲבוֹדָתוֹ יִתְבָּרַךְ שְׁמוֹ. וְעַל הָרֹאשׁ נֶגֶד הַמֹּחַ, שֶׁהַנְּשָׁמָה שֶׁבְּמֹחִי עִם שְׁאָר חוּשַׁי וְכֹחוֹתַי כֻּלָּם יִהְיוּ מְשֻׁעְבָּדִים לַעֲבוֹדָתוֹ, יִתְבָּרַךְ שְׁמוֹ. וּמִשֶּׁפַע מִצְוַת תְּפִלִּין יִתְמַשֵּׁךְ עָלַי לִהְיוֹת לִי חַיִּים אֲרוּכִים וְשֶׁפַע קֹדֶשׁ וּמַחְשָׁבוֹת קְדוֹשׁוֹת בְּלִי הִרְהוּר חֵטְא וְעָוֹן כְּלָל, וְשֶׁלֹּא יְפַתֵּנוּ וְלֹא יִתְגָּרֶה בָּנוּ יֵצֶר הָרָע, וְיַנִּיחֵנוּ לַעֲבֹד אֶת יהוה כַּאֲשֶׁר עִם לְבָבֵנוּ.

וִיהִי רָצוֹן מִלְּפָנֶיךָ, יהוה אֱלֹהֵינוּ וֵאלֹהֵי אֲבוֹתֵינוּ, שֶׁתְּהֵא חֲשׁוּבָה מִצְוַת הֲנָחַת תְּפִלִּין לִפְנֵי הַקָּדוֹשׁ בָּרוּךְ הוּא, כְּאִלּוּ קִיַּמְתִּיהָ בְּכָל פְּרָטֶיהָ וְדִקְדּוּקֶיהָ וְכַוָּנוֹתֶיהָ וְתַרְיַ״ג מִצְוֹת הַתְּלוּיוֹת בָּהּ, אָמֵן סֶלָה.

Tefillin: The word tefillin (called *totafot* in the Torah) means "emblem, sign, insignia," the visible symbol of an abstract idea. Tefillin are our reminder of the commandment of the Shema: "Love the Lord your God your with all your heart, with all your soul and with all your might" (Deut. 6:5). *All your heart:* this is the tefillin on the upper arm opposite the heart. *All your soul:* this is the head-tefillin opposite the seat of consciousness, the soul. *All your might:* this is the strap of the hand-tefillin, symbolizing action, power, might.

Stand and place the hand-tefillin on the biceps of the left arm (or right arm if you are left-handed), angled toward the heart, and before tightening the strap, say:

בָּרוּךְ Blessed are You, Lord our God,
King of the Universe,
who has made us holy through His commandments,
and has commanded us to put on tefillin.

Wrap the strap of the hand-tefillin seven times around the arm. Place the head-tefillin above the hairline, centered between the eyes, and say quietly:

בָּרוּךְ Blessed are You, Lord our God,
King of the Universe,
who has made us holy through His commandments,
and has commanded us about the commandment of tefillin.

Adjust the head-tefillin and say:

בָּרוּךְ Blessed be the name of His glorious kingdom for ever and all time.

Some say:

From Your wisdom, God most high, grant me [wisdom], and from Your understanding, give me understanding. May Your loving-kindness be greatly upon me, and in Your might may my enemies and those who rise against me be subdued. Pour Your goodly oil on the seven branches of the menora so that Your good flows down upon Your creatures. You open Your hand, and satisfy every living thing with favor. *Ps. 145*

Wind the strap of the hand-tefillin three times around the middle finger, saying:

וְאֵרַשְׂתִּיךְ I will betroth you to Me for ever; *Hos. 2*
I will betroth you to Me in righteousness and justice,
loving-kindness and compassion;
I will betroth you to Me in faithfulness;
and you shall know the Lord.

---

like a wedding ring, we remind ourselves of God's love for Israel, and Israel's love for God.

Stand and place the תפילין של יד *on the biceps of the left arm (or right arm if you are left-handed), angled toward the heart, and before tightening the strap, say:*

בָּרוּךְ אַתָּה יהוה אֱלֹהֵינוּ מֶלֶךְ הָעוֹלָם
אֲשֶׁר קִדְּשָׁנוּ בְּמִצְוֹתָיו
וְצִוָּנוּ לְהָנִיחַ תְּפִלִּין.

Wrap the strap of the תפילין של יד *seven times around the arm. Place the* תפילין של ראש *above the hairline, centered between the eyes, and say quietly:*

בָּרוּךְ אַתָּה יהוה אֱלֹהֵינוּ מֶלֶךְ הָעוֹלָם
אֲשֶׁר קִדְּשָׁנוּ בְּמִצְוֹתָיו
וְצִוָּנוּ עַל מִצְוַת תְּפִלִּין.

Adjust the תפילין של ראש *and say:*

בָּרוּךְ שֵׁם כְּבוֹד מַלְכוּתוֹ לְעוֹלָם וָעֶד

Some say:

וּמֵחָכְמָתְךָ אֵל עֶלְיוֹן תַּאֲצִיל עָלַי, וּמִבִּינָתְךָ תְּבִינֵנִי, וּבְחַסְדְּךָ תַּגְדִּיל עָלַי, וּבִגְבוּרָתְךָ תַּצְמִית אוֹיְבַי וְקָמַי. וְשֶׁמֶן הַטּוֹב תָּרִיק עַל
תהלים קמה שִׁבְעָה קְנֵי הַמְּנוֹרָה, לְהַשְׁפִּיעַ טוּבְךָ לִבְרִיּוֹתֶיךָ. פּוֹתֵחַ אֶת־יָדֶךָ וּמַשְׂבִּיעַ לְכָל־חַי רָצוֹן:

Wind the strap of the תפילין של יד *three times around the middle finger, saying:*

הושע ב וְאֵרַשְׂתִּיךְ לִי לְעוֹלָם
וְאֵרַשְׂתִּיךְ לִי בְּצֶדֶק וּבְמִשְׁפָּט וּבְחֶסֶד וּבְרַחֲמִים:
וְאֵרַשְׂתִּיךְ לִי בֶּאֱמוּנָה, וְיָדַעַתְּ אֶת־יהוה:

וְאֵרַשְׂתִּיךְ *I will betroth you to Me:* These exquisite lines from the book of Hosea speak of God's covenant with Israel as a marriage – a mutual pledge of faith, born of love. Wrapping the strap of the hand-tefillin around the middle finger

After putting on the tefillin, say the following:

וַיְדַבֵּר The Lord spoke to Moses, saying, "Consecrate to Me every firstborn male. The first offspring of every womb among the Israelites, whether man or beast, belongs to Me." Then Moses said to the people, "Remember this day on which you left Egypt, the slave-house, when the Lord brought you out of it with a mighty hand. No leaven shall be eaten. You are leaving on this day, in the month of Aviv. When the Lord brings you into the land of the Canaanites, Hittites, Amorites, Hivites and Jebusites, the land He swore to your ancestors to give you, a land flowing with milk and honey, you are to observe this service in this same month. For seven days you shall eat unleavened bread, and make the seventh day a festival to the Lord. Unleavened bread shall be eaten throughout the seven days. No leavened bread may be seen in your possession, and no leaven shall be seen anywhere within your borders. On that day you shall tell your son, 'This is because of what the Lord did for me when I left Egypt.' [These words] shall also be a sign on your hand, and a reminder above your forehead, so that the Lord's Torah may always be in your mouth, because with a mighty hand the Lord brought you out of Egypt. You shall therefore keep this statute at its appointed time from year to year." *Ex. 13*

וְהָיָה After the Lord has brought you into the land of the Canaanites, as He swore to you and your ancestors, and He has given it to you, you shall set apart for the Lord the first offspring of every womb. All the firstborn males of your cattle belong to the Lord. Every firstling donkey you shall redeem with a lamb. If you do not redeem it, you must break its neck. Every firstborn among your sons you must redeem. If, in time to come, your son asks you, "What does this mean?" you shall say to him, "With a mighty hand the Lord brought us out of Egypt, out of the slave-house. When Pharaoh stubbornly refused to let us leave, the Lord killed all the firstborn in the land of Egypt, both man and beast. That is why I sacrifice to the Lord the first male offspring of every womb, and redeem all the firstborn of my sons." [These words] shall be a sign on your hand and as an emblem above your forehead, that with a mighty hand the Lord brought us out of Egypt.

After putting on the תפילין, say the following:

שמות יג

וַיְדַבֵּר יְהוָה אֶל־מֹשֶׁה לֵּאמֹר: קַדֶּשׁ־לִי כָל־בְּכוֹר, פֶּטֶר כָּל־רֶחֶם
בִּבְנֵי יִשְׂרָאֵל, בָּאָדָם וּבַבְּהֵמָה, לִי הוּא: וַיֹּאמֶר מֹשֶׁה אֶל־הָעָם, זָכוֹר
אֶת־הַיּוֹם הַזֶּה, אֲשֶׁר יְצָאתֶם מִמִּצְרַיִם מִבֵּית עֲבָדִים, כִּי בְּחֹזֶק יָד
הוֹצִיא יְהוָה אֶתְכֶם מִזֶּה, וְלֹא יֵאָכֵל חָמֵץ: הַיּוֹם אַתֶּם יֹצְאִים, בְּחֹדֶשׁ
הָאָבִיב: וְהָיָה כִי־יְבִיאֲךָ יְהוָה אֶל־אֶרֶץ הַכְּנַעֲנִי וְהַחִתִּי וְהָאֱמֹרִי
וְהַחִוִּי וְהַיְבוּסִי, אֲשֶׁר נִשְׁבַּע לַאֲבֹתֶיךָ לָתֶת לָךְ, אֶרֶץ זָבַת חָלָב
וּדְבָשׁ, וְעָבַדְתָּ אֶת־הָעֲבֹדָה הַזֹּאת בַּחֹדֶשׁ הַזֶּה: שִׁבְעַת יָמִים תֹּאכַל
מַצֹּת, וּבַיּוֹם הַשְּׁבִיעִי חַג לַיהוָה: מַצּוֹת יֵאָכֵל אֵת שִׁבְעַת הַיָּמִים,
וְלֹא־יֵרָאֶה לְךָ חָמֵץ וְלֹא־יֵרָאֶה לְךָ שְׂאֹר, בְּכָל־גְּבֻלֶךָ: וְהִגַּדְתָּ לְבִנְךָ
בַּיּוֹם הַהוּא לֵאמֹר, בַּעֲבוּר זֶה עָשָׂה יְהוָה לִי בְּצֵאתִי מִמִּצְרָיִם: וְהָיָה
לְךָ לְאוֹת עַל־יָדְךָ וּלְזִכָּרוֹן בֵּין עֵינֶיךָ, לְמַעַן תִּהְיֶה תּוֹרַת יְהוָה בְּפִיךָ,
כִּי בְּיָד חֲזָקָה הוֹצִאֲךָ יְהוָה מִמִּצְרָיִם: וְשָׁמַרְתָּ אֶת־הַחֻקָּה הַזֹּאת
לְמוֹעֲדָהּ, מִיָּמִים יָמִימָה:

וְהָיָה כִּי־יְבִאֲךָ יְהוָה אֶל־אֶרֶץ הַכְּנַעֲנִי כַּאֲשֶׁר נִשְׁבַּע לְךָ וְלַאֲבֹתֶיךָ,
וּנְתָנָהּ לָךְ: וְהַעֲבַרְתָּ כָל־פֶּטֶר־רֶחֶם לַיהוָה, וְכָל־פֶּטֶר שֶׁגֶר בְּהֵמָה
אֲשֶׁר יִהְיֶה לְךָ הַזְּכָרִים, לַיהוָה: וְכָל־פֶּטֶר חֲמֹר תִּפְדֶּה בְשֶׂה, וְאִם־
לֹא תִפְדֶּה וַעֲרַפְתּוֹ, וְכֹל בְּכוֹר אָדָם בְּבָנֶיךָ תִּפְדֶּה: וְהָיָה כִּי־יִשְׁאָלְךָ
בִנְךָ מָחָר, לֵאמֹר מַה־זֹּאת, וְאָמַרְתָּ אֵלָיו, בְּחֹזֶק יָד הוֹצִיאָנוּ יְהוָה
מִמִּצְרַיִם מִבֵּית עֲבָדִים: וַיְהִי כִּי־הִקְשָׁה פַרְעֹה לְשַׁלְּחֵנוּ, וַיַּהֲרֹג יְהוָה
כָּל־בְּכוֹר בְּאֶרֶץ מִצְרַיִם, מִבְּכֹר אָדָם וְעַד־בְּכוֹר בְּהֵמָה, עַל־כֵּן אֲנִי
זֹבֵחַ לַיהוָה כָּל־פֶּטֶר רֶחֶם הַזְּכָרִים, וְכָל־בְּכוֹר בָּנַי אֶפְדֶּה: וְהָיָה
לְאוֹת עַל־יָדְכָה וּלְטוֹטָפֹת בֵּין עֵינֶיךָ, כִּי בְּחֹזֶק יָד הוֹצִיאָנוּ יְהוָה
מִמִּצְרָיִם:

PREPARATION FOR PRAYER

On entering the synagogue:

HOW GOODLY *Num. 24*

are your tents, Jacob, your dwelling places, Israel.
As for me, *Ps. 5*
in Your great loving-kindness,
I will come into Your House.
I will bow down to Your holy Temple
in awe of You.
Lord, I love the habitation of Your House, *Ps. 26*
the place where Your glory dwells.

As for me,
I will bow in worship;
I will bend the knee
before the Lord my Maker.

As for me, *Ps. 69*
may my prayer come to You, Lord,
at a time of favor.
God, in Your great loving-kindness,
answer me with Your faithful salvation.

הכנה לתפילה

On entering the בית כנסת*:*

מַה־טֹּבוּ במדבר כד

אֹהָלֶיךָ יַעֲקֹב, מִשְׁכְּנֹתֶיךָ יִשְׂרָאֵל:

וַאֲנִי בְּרֹב חַסְדְּךָ אָבוֹא בֵיתֶךָ תהלים ה

אֶשְׁתַּחֲוֶה אֶל־הֵיכַל־קָדְשְׁךָ

בְּיִרְאָתֶךָ:

יהוה אָהַבְתִּי מְעוֹן בֵּיתֶךָ תהלים כו

וּמְקוֹם מִשְׁכַּן כְּבוֹדֶךָ:

וַאֲנִי אֶשְׁתַּחֲוֶה

וְאֶכְרָעָה

אֶבְרְכָה לִפְנֵי יהוה עֹשִׂי.

וַאֲנִי תְפִלָּתִי־לְךָ יהוה תהלים סט

עֵת רָצוֹן

אֱלֹהִים בְּרָב־חַסְדֶּךָ

עֲנֵנִי בֶּאֱמֶת יִשְׁעֶךָ:

The following poems, on this page and the next, both from the Middle Ages, are summary statements of Jewish faith, orienting us to the spiritual contours of the world that we actualize in the mind by the act of prayer.

LORD OF THE UNIVERSE,
who reigned before the birth of any thing –

When by His will all things were made
then was His name proclaimed King.

And when all things shall cease to be
He alone will reign in awe.

He was, He is, and He shall be
glorious for evermore.

He is One, there is none else,
alone, unique, beyond compare;

Without beginning, without end,
His might, His rule are everywhere.

He is my God; my Redeemer lives.
He is the Rock on whom I rely –

My banner and my safe retreat,
my cup, my portion when I cry.

Into His hand my soul I place,
when I awake and when I sleep.

The LORD is with me, I shall not fear;
body and soul from harm will He keep.

The following poems, on this page and the next, both from the Middle Ages, are summary statements of Jewish faith, orienting us to the spiritual contours of the world that we actualize in the mind by the act of prayer.

אֲדוֹן עוֹלָם

אֲשֶׁר מָלַךְ בְּטֶרֶם כָּל־יְצִיר נִבְרָא.
לְעֵת נַעֲשָׂה בְחֶפְצוֹ כֹּל אֲזַי מֶלֶךְ שְׁמוֹ נִקְרָא.
וְאַחֲרֵי כִּכְלוֹת הַכֹּל לְבַדּוֹ יִמְלֹךְ נוֹרָא.
וְהוּא הָיָה וְהוּא הֹוֶה וְהוּא יִהְיֶה בְּתִפְאָרָה.
וְהוּא אֶחָד וְאֵין שֵׁנִי לְהַמְשִׁיל לוֹ לְהַחְבִּירָה.
בְּלִי רֵאשִׁית בְּלִי תַכְלִית וְלוֹ הָעֹז וְהַמִּשְׂרָה.
וְהוּא אֵלִי וְחַי גֹּאֲלִי וְצוּר חֶבְלִי בְּעֵת צָרָה.
וְהוּא נִסִּי וּמָנוֹס לִי מְנָת כּוֹסִי בְּיוֹם אֶקְרָא.
בְּיָדוֹ אַפְקִיד רוּחִי בְּעֵת אִישַׁן וְאָעִירָה.
וְעִם רוּחִי גְּוִיָּתִי יהוה לִי וְלֹא אִירָא.

GREAT
is the living God and praised.
He exists, and His existence is beyond time.

He is One, and there is no unity like His.
Unfathomable, His oneness is infinite.

He has neither bodily form nor substance;
His holiness is beyond compare.

He preceded all that was created.
He was first: there was no beginning to His beginning.

Behold He is Master of the Universe; and every creature
shows His greatness and majesty.

The rich flow of His prophecy He gave
to His treasured people in whom He gloried.

Never in Israel has there arisen another like Moses,
a prophet who beheld God's image.

God gave His people a Torah of truth
by the hand of His prophet, most faithful of His House.

God will not alter or change His law
for any other, for eternity.

He sees and knows our secret thoughts;
as soon as something is begun, He foresees its end.

He rewards people with loving-kindness according to their deeds;
He punishes the wicked according to his wickedness.

At the end of days He will send our Messiah
to redeem those who await His final salvation.

God will revive the dead in His great loving-kindness.
Blessed for evermore is His glorious name!

יִגְדַּל

אֱלֹהִים חַי וְיִשְׁתַּבַּח, נִמְצָא וְאֵין עֵת אֶל מְצִיאוּתוֹ.

אֶחָד וְאֵין יָחִיד כְּיִחוּדוֹ, נֶעְלָם וְגַם אֵין סוֹף לְאַחְדוּתוֹ.

אֵין לוֹ דְּמוּת הַגּוּף וְאֵינוֹ גוּף, לֹא נַעֲרֹךְ אֵלָיו קְדֻשָּׁתוֹ.

קַדְמוֹן לְכָל דָּבָר אֲשֶׁר נִבְרָא, רִאשׁוֹן וְאֵין רֵאשִׁית לְרֵאשִׁיתוֹ.

הִנּוֹ אֲדוֹן עוֹלָם, וְכָל נוֹצָר יוֹרֶה גְדֻלָּתוֹ וּמַלְכוּתוֹ.

שֶׁפַע נְבוּאָתוֹ נְתָנוֹ אֶל־אַנְשֵׁי סְגֻלָּתוֹ וְתִפְאַרְתּוֹ.

לֹא קָם בְּיִשְׂרָאֵל כְּמֹשֶׁה עוֹד נָבִיא וּמַבִּיט אֶת תְּמוּנָתוֹ.

תּוֹרַת אֱמֶת נָתַן לְעַמּוֹ אֵל עַל יַד נְבִיאוֹ נֶאֱמַן בֵּיתוֹ.

לֹא יַחֲלִיף הָאֵל וְלֹא יָמִיר דָּתוֹ לְעוֹלָמִים לְזוּלָתוֹ.

צוֹפֶה וְיוֹדֵעַ סְתָרֵינוּ, מַבִּיט לְסוֹף דָּבָר בְּקַדְמָתוֹ.

גּוֹמֵל לְאִישׁ חֶסֶד כְּמִפְעָלוֹ, נוֹתֵן לְרָשָׁע רָע כְּרִשְׁעָתוֹ.

יִשְׁלַח לְקֵץ יָמִין מְשִׁיחֵנוּ לִפְדּוֹת מְחַכֵּי קֵץ יְשׁוּעָתוֹ.

מֵתִים יְחַיֶּה אֵל בְּרֹב חַסְדּוֹ, בָּרוּךְ עֲדֵי עַד שֵׁם תְּהִלָּתוֹ.

MORNING BLESSINGS

The following blessings are said aloud by the Leader, but each individual should say them quietly as well. It is our custom to say them standing.

בָּרוּךְ Blessed are You, LORD our God,
King of the Universe,
who gives the heart understanding
to distinguish day from night.

Blessed are You, LORD our God,
King of the Universe,
who has not made me a heathen.

Blessed are You, LORD our God,
King of the Universe,
who has not made me a slave.

Blessed are You, LORD our God,
King of the Universe,
men: who has not made me a woman.
women: who has made me according to His will.

שֶׁלֹּא עָשַׂנִי *Who has not made me a heathen, a slave, a woman:* These three blessings are mentioned in the Talmud (*Menaḥot* 43b). Before we bless God for the universalities of human life, we bless Him for the particularities of our identity. We belong to the people of the covenant; we are free; and we have differentiated responsibilities as women and men. These blessings have nothing to do with hierarchies of dignity, for we believe that every human being is equally formed in the image of God. Rather, they are expressions of acknowledgment of the special duties of Jewish life. Heathens, slaves and women are exempt from certain commands which apply to Jewish men. By these blessings, we express our faith that the commandments are not a burden but a cherished vocation.

ברכות השחר

The following blessings are said aloud by the שליח ציבור*, but each individual should say them quietly as well. It is our custom to say them standing.*

בָּרוּךְ אַתָּה יהוה אֱלֹהֵינוּ מֶלֶךְ הָעוֹלָם
אֲשֶׁר נָתַן לַשֶּׂכְוִי בִינָה
לְהַבְחִין בֵּין יוֹם וּבֵין לָיְלָה.

בָּרוּךְ אַתָּה יהוה אֱלֹהֵינוּ מֶלֶךְ הָעוֹלָם
שֶׁלֹּא עָשַׂנִי גּוֹי.

בָּרוּךְ אַתָּה יהוה אֱלֹהֵינוּ מֶלֶךְ הָעוֹלָם
שֶׁלֹּא עָשַׂנִי עָבֶד.

בָּרוּךְ אַתָּה יהוה אֱלֹהֵינוּ מֶלֶךְ הָעוֹלָם
men שֶׁלֹּא עָשַׂנִי אִשָּׁה. / *women* שֶׁעָשַׂנִי כִּרְצוֹנוֹ.

בָּרוּךְ אַתָּה *Blessed are You:* These blessings, itemized in the Talmud (*Berakhot* 60b), were originally said at home to accompany the various stages of waking and rising. "Who gives sight to the blind" was said on opening one's eyes, "Who clothes the naked" on putting on clothes, and so on. Several medieval authorities, however, held that they should be said in the synagogue.

Their purpose is to make us conscious of what we might otherwise take for granted. Praise is an act of focused attention, foregrounding what is usually in the background of awareness. "The world is full of the light of God, but to see it we must learn to open our eyes" (Rabbi Naḥman of Bratslav).

אֲשֶׁר נָתַן לַשֶּׂכְוִי *Who gives the heart:* This is the translation according to Rabbeinu Asher (Rosh); Rashi and Abudarham read it, "who gives the cockerel." According to Rosh's reading, the first blessing mirrors the first request of the Amida, for human understanding, as well as the first act of creation in which God created light, separating it from darkness.

Blessed are You, LORD our God,
King of the Universe,
who gives sight to the blind.

Blessed are You, LORD our God,
King of the Universe,
who clothes the naked.

Blessed are You, LORD our God,
King of the Universe,
who sets captives free.

Blessed are You, LORD our God,
King of the Universe,
who raises those bowed down.

Blessed are You, LORD our God,
King of the Universe,
who spreads the earth above the waters.

Blessed are You, LORD our God,
King of the Universe,
who has provided me with all I need.

Blessed are You, LORD our God,
King of the Universe,
who makes firm the steps of man.

Blessed are You, LORD our God,
King of the Universe,
who girds Israel with strength.

Blessed are You, LORD our God,
King of the Universe,
who crowns Israel with glory.

Blessed are You, LORD our God,
King of the Universe,
who gives strength to the weary.

בָּרוּךְ אַתָּה יהוה אֱלֹהֵינוּ מֶלֶךְ הָעוֹלָם
פּוֹקֵחַ עִוְרִים.

בָּרוּךְ אַתָּה יהוה אֱלֹהֵינוּ מֶלֶךְ הָעוֹלָם
מַלְבִּישׁ עֲרֻמִּים.

בָּרוּךְ אַתָּה יהוה אֱלֹהֵינוּ מֶלֶךְ הָעוֹלָם
מַתִּיר אֲסוּרִים.

בָּרוּךְ אַתָּה יהוה אֱלֹהֵינוּ מֶלֶךְ הָעוֹלָם
זוֹקֵף כְּפוּפִים.

בָּרוּךְ אַתָּה יהוה אֱלֹהֵינוּ מֶלֶךְ הָעוֹלָם
רוֹקַע הָאָרֶץ עַל הַמָּיִם.

בָּרוּךְ אַתָּה יהוה אֱלֹהֵינוּ מֶלֶךְ הָעוֹלָם
שֶׁעָשָׂה לִי כָּל צָרְכִּי.

בָּרוּךְ אַתָּה יהוה אֱלֹהֵינוּ מֶלֶךְ הָעוֹלָם
הַמֵּכִין מִצְעֲדֵי גָבֶר.

בָּרוּךְ אַתָּה יהוה אֱלֹהֵינוּ מֶלֶךְ הָעוֹלָם
אוֹזֵר יִשְׂרָאֵל בִּגְבוּרָה.

בָּרוּךְ אַתָּה יהוה אֱלֹהֵינוּ מֶלֶךְ הָעוֹלָם
עוֹטֵר יִשְׂרָאֵל בְּתִפְאָרָה.

בָּרוּךְ אַתָּה יהוה אֱלֹהֵינוּ מֶלֶךְ הָעוֹלָם
הַנּוֹתֵן לַיָּעֵף כֹּחַ.

בָּרוּךְ Blessed are You, Lord our God, King of the Universe,
who removes sleep from my eyes
and slumber from my eyelids.
And may it be Your will, Lord our God
and God of our ancestors,
to accustom us to Your Torah,
and make us attached to Your commandments.
Lead us not into error, transgression,
iniquity, temptation or disgrace.
Do not let the evil instinct dominate us.
Keep us far from a bad man and a bad companion.
Help us attach ourselves to the good instinct and to good deeds
and bend our instincts to be subservient to You.
Grant us, this day and every day,
grace, loving-kindness and compassion in Your eyes
and in the eyes of all who see us,
and bestow loving-kindness upon us.
Blessed are You, Lord,
who bestows loving-kindness on His people Israel.

יְהִי רָצוֹן May it be Your will, Lord my God and God of my ancestors, to save me today and every day, from the arrogant and from arrogance itself, from a bad man, a bad friend, a bad neighbor, a bad mishap, a destructive adversary, a harsh trial and a harsh opponent, whether or not he is a son of the covenant. *Berakhot 16b*

---

us of the verse from Psalms (92:3): "To proclaim Your loving-kindness in the morning and Your faithfulness at night."

יְהִי רָצוֹן *May it be Your will:* A meditation composed by Rabbi Judah the Prince (late second–early third century), redactor of the Mishna and leader of the Jewish community in Israel. We are social beings, influenced by our environment (Maimonides); therefore, we pray to be protected from harmful people, events and temptations. The prayer reflects the "social fabric of faith" (Rabbi Lord Jakobovits).

בָּרוּךְ אַתָּה יהוה אֱלֹהֵינוּ מֶלֶךְ הָעוֹלָם
הַמַּעֲבִיר שֵׁנָה מֵעֵינַי וּתְנוּמָה מֵעַפְעַפָּי.
וִיהִי רָצוֹן מִלְּפָנֶיךָ יהוה אֱלֹהֵינוּ וֵאלֹהֵי אֲבוֹתֵינוּ
שֶׁתַּרְגִּילֵנוּ בְּתוֹרָתֶךָ
וְדַבְּקֵנוּ בְּמִצְוֹתֶיךָ
וְאַל תְּבִיאֵנוּ לֹא לִידֵי חֵטְא
וְלֹא לִידֵי עֲבֵרָה וְעָוֹן
וְלֹא לִידֵי נִסָּיוֹן וְלֹא לִידֵי בִזָּיוֹן
וְאַל תַּשְׁלֶט בָּנוּ יֵצֶר הָרָע
וְהַרְחִיקֵנוּ מֵאָדָם רָע וּמֵחָבֵר רָע
וְדַבְּקֵנוּ בְּיֵצֶר הַטּוֹב וּבְמַעֲשִׂים טוֹבִים
וְכֹף אֶת יִצְרֵנוּ לְהִשְׁתַּעְבֶּד לָךְ
וּתְנֵנוּ הַיּוֹם וּבְכָל יוֹם לְחֵן וּלְחֶסֶד וּלְרַחֲמִים
בְּעֵינֶיךָ, וּבְעֵינֵי כָל רוֹאֵינוּ
וְתִגְמְלֵנוּ חֲסָדִים טוֹבִים.
בָּרוּךְ אַתָּה יהוה, גּוֹמֵל חֲסָדִים טוֹבִים לְעַמּוֹ יִשְׂרָאֵל.

ברכות טז: **יְהִי רָצוֹן מִלְּפָנֶיךָ יהוה אֱלֹהַי וֵאלֹהֵי אֲבוֹתַי, שֶׁתַּצִּילֵנִי הַיּוֹם וּבְכָל יוֹם מֵעַזֵּי פָנִים וּמֵעַזּוּת פָּנִים, מֵאָדָם רָע, וּמֵחָבֵר רָע, וּמִשָּׁכֵן רָע, וּמִפֶּגַע רָע, וּמִשָּׂטָן הַמַּשְׁחִית, מִדִּין קָשֶׁה, וּמִבַּעַל דִּין קָשֶׁה בֵּין שֶׁהוּא בֶן בְּרִית וּבֵין שֶׁאֵינוֹ בֶן בְּרִית.**

הַמַּעֲבִיר *Who removes sleep from my eyes:* Having thanked God for the blessings with which we are surrounded, we conclude by asking for His help in dedicating our lives to His service, undeterred by obstacles that may stand in our way. The prayer ends with thanksgiving for God's kindness, reminding

THE BINDING OF ISAAC

On the basis of Jewish mystical tradition, some have the custom of saying daily the biblical passage recounting the Binding of Isaac, the supreme trial of faith in which Abraham demonstrated his love of God above all other loves. On Shabbat and Yom Tov, most omit the introductory and concluding prayers, "Our God and God of our ancestors" and "Master of the Universe." Others skip to "A person should" on the next page.

Our God and God of our ancestors, remember us with a favorable memory, and recall us with a remembrance of salvation and compassion from the highest of high heavens. Remember, LORD our God, on our behalf, the love of the ancients, Abraham, Isaac and Yisrael Your servants; the covenant, the loving-kindness, and the oath You swore to Abraham our father on Mount Moriah, and the Binding, when he bound Isaac his son on the altar, as is written in Your Torah:

It happened after these things that God tested Abraham. He said to him, "Abraham!" "Here I am," he replied. He said, "Take your son, your only son, Isaac, whom you love, and go to the land of Moriah and offer him there as a burnt-offering on one of the mountains which I shall say to you." Early the next morning Abraham rose and saddled his donkey and took his two lads with him, and Isaac his son, and he cut wood for the burnt-offering, and he set out for the place of which God had told him. On the third day Abraham looked up and saw the place from afar. Abraham said to his lads, "Stay here with the donkey while I and the boy go on ahead. We will worship and we will return to you." Abraham took the wood for the burnt-offering and placed it on Isaac his son, and he took in his hand the fire and the knife, and the two of them went together. Isaac said to Abraham his father, "Father?" and he said "Here I am, my son." And he said, "Here are the fire and the wood, but where is the sheep for the burnt-offering?" Abraham said, "God will see to the sheep for the burnt-offering, my son." And the two of them went together. They came to the place God had told him about, and Abraham built there an altar and arranged the wood and bound Isaac his son and laid him on the altar on top of the wood. He reached out his hand and took the knife to slay his son. Then an angel of the LORD called out to him from heaven, "Abraham! Abraham!" He said, "Here I am." He said, "Do not reach out your hand against the boy; do not do anything to him, for now I know that you fear God, because you have not held back your son, your only son, from Me." Abraham looked up and there he saw a ram caught in a thicket by its horns, and Abraham went and took the ram and offered it as a burnt-offering instead of his son. Abraham called that place "The LORD will see," as is said to this day, "On the mountain of the LORD He will be seen." The angel of the LORD called to Abraham a second time from heaven, and said, "By Myself I swear, declares the LORD, that because you have done this and have not held *Gen. 22*

פרשת העקדה

On the basis of Jewish mystical tradition, some have the custom of saying daily the biblical passage recounting the Binding of Isaac, the supreme trial of faith in which Abraham demonstrated his love of God above all other loves. On שבת *and* יום טוב*, most omit the introductory and concluding prayers,* אֱלֹהֵינוּ וֵאלֹהֵי אֲבוֹתֵינוּ *and* רִבּוֹנוֹ שֶׁל עוֹלָם*. Others skip to* לְעוֹלָם יְהֵא אָדָם *on the next page.*

אֱלֹהֵינוּ וֵאלֹהֵי אֲבוֹתֵינוּ, זָכְרֵנוּ בְּזִכְרוֹן טוֹב לְפָנֶיךָ, וּפָקְדֵנוּ בִּפְקֻדַּת יְשׁוּעָה וְרַחֲמִים
מִשְּׁמֵי שְׁמֵי קֶדֶם, וּזְכָר לָנוּ יהוה אֱלֹהֵינוּ, אַהֲבַת הַקַּדְמוֹנִים אַבְרָהָם יִצְחָק וְיִשְׂרָאֵל
עֲבָדֶיךָ, אֶת הַבְּרִית וְאֶת הַחֶסֶד וְאֶת הַשְּׁבוּעָה שֶׁנִּשְׁבַּעְתָּ לְאַבְרָהָם אָבִינוּ בְּהַר
הַמּוֹרִיָּה, וְאֶת הָעֲקֵדָה שֶׁעָקַד אֶת יִצְחָק בְּנוֹ עַל גַּבֵּי הַמִּזְבֵּחַ, כַּכָּתוּב בְּתוֹרָתֶךָ:

בראשית כב וַיְהִי אַחַר הַדְּבָרִים הָאֵלֶּה, וְהָאֱלֹהִים נִסָּה אֶת־אַבְרָהָם, וַיֹּאמֶר אֵלָיו אַבְרָהָם,
וַיֹּאמֶר הִנֵּנִי: וַיֹּאמֶר קַח־נָא אֶת־בִּנְךָ אֶת־יְחִידְךָ אֲשֶׁר־אָהַבְתָּ, אֶת־יִצְחָק,
וְלֶךְ־לְךָ אֶל־אֶרֶץ הַמֹּרִיָּה, וְהַעֲלֵהוּ שָׁם לְעֹלָה עַל אַחַד הֶהָרִים אֲשֶׁר אֹמַר
אֵלֶיךָ: וַיַּשְׁכֵּם אַבְרָהָם בַּבֹּקֶר, וַיַּחֲבֹשׁ אֶת־חֲמֹרוֹ, וַיִּקַּח אֶת־שְׁנֵי נְעָרָיו אִתּוֹ
וְאֵת יִצְחָק בְּנוֹ, וַיְבַקַּע עֲצֵי עֹלָה, וַיָּקָם וַיֵּלֶךְ אֶל־הַמָּקוֹם אֲשֶׁר־אָמַר־לוֹ
הָאֱלֹהִים: בַּיּוֹם הַשְּׁלִישִׁי וַיִּשָּׂא אַבְרָהָם אֶת־עֵינָיו וַיַּרְא אֶת־הַמָּקוֹם מֵרָחֹק:
וַיֹּאמֶר אַבְרָהָם אֶל־נְעָרָיו, שְׁבוּ־לָכֶם פֹּה עִם־הַחֲמוֹר, וַאֲנִי וְהַנַּעַר נֵלְכָה עַד־
כֹּה, וְנִשְׁתַּחֲוֶה וְנָשׁוּבָה אֲלֵיכֶם: וַיִּקַּח אַבְרָהָם אֶת־עֲצֵי הָעֹלָה וַיָּשֶׂם עַל־יִצְחָק
בְּנוֹ, וַיִּקַּח בְּיָדוֹ אֶת־הָאֵשׁ וְאֶת־הַמַּאֲכֶלֶת, וַיֵּלְכוּ שְׁנֵיהֶם יַחְדָּו: וַיֹּאמֶר יִצְחָק
אֶל־אַבְרָהָם אָבִיו, וַיֹּאמֶר אָבִי, וַיֹּאמֶר הִנֶּנִּי בְנִי, וַיֹּאמֶר, הִנֵּה הָאֵשׁ וְהָעֵצִים,
וְאַיֵּה הַשֶּׂה לְעֹלָה: וַיֹּאמֶר אַבְרָהָם, אֱלֹהִים יִרְאֶה־לּוֹ הַשֶּׂה לְעֹלָה, בְּנִי, וַיֵּלְכוּ
שְׁנֵיהֶם יַחְדָּו: וַיָּבֹאוּ אֶל־הַמָּקוֹם אֲשֶׁר אָמַר־לוֹ הָאֱלֹהִים, וַיִּבֶן שָׁם אַבְרָהָם
אֶת־הַמִּזְבֵּחַ וַיַּעֲרֹךְ אֶת־הָעֵצִים, וַיַּעֲקֹד אֶת־יִצְחָק בְּנוֹ, וַיָּשֶׂם אֹתוֹ עַל־הַמִּזְבֵּחַ
מִמַּעַל לָעֵצִים: וַיִּשְׁלַח אַבְרָהָם אֶת־יָדוֹ, וַיִּקַּח אֶת־הַמַּאֲכֶלֶת, לִשְׁחֹט אֶת־
בְּנוֹ: וַיִּקְרָא אֵלָיו מַלְאַךְ יהוה מִן־הַשָּׁמַיִם, וַיֹּאמֶר אַבְרָהָם אַבְרָהָם, וַיֹּאמֶר
הִנֵּנִי: וַיֹּאמֶר אַל־תִּשְׁלַח יָדְךָ אֶל־הַנַּעַר, וְאַל־תַּעַשׂ לוֹ מְאוּמָה, כִּי עַתָּה
יָדַעְתִּי כִּי־יְרֵא אֱלֹהִים אַתָּה, וְלֹא חָשַׂכְתָּ אֶת־בִּנְךָ אֶת־יְחִידְךָ מִמֶּנִּי: וַיִּשָּׂא
אַבְרָהָם אֶת־עֵינָיו, וַיַּרְא וְהִנֵּה־אַיִל, אַחַר נֶאֱחַז בַּסְּבַךְ בְּקַרְנָיו, וַיֵּלֶךְ אַבְרָהָם
וַיִּקַּח אֶת־הָאַיִל, וַיַּעֲלֵהוּ לְעֹלָה תַּחַת בְּנוֹ: וַיִּקְרָא אַבְרָהָם שֵׁם־הַמָּקוֹם
הַהוּא יהוה יִרְאֶה, אֲשֶׁר יֵאָמֵר הַיּוֹם בְּהַר יהוה יֵרָאֶה: וַיִּקְרָא מַלְאַךְ יהוה

back your son, your only son, I will greatly bless you and greatly multiply your descendants, as the stars of heaven and the sand of the seashore, and your descendants shall take possession of the gates of their enemies. Through your descendants, all the nations of the earth will be blessed, because you have heeded My voice." Then Abraham returned to his lads, and they rose and went together to Beersheba, and Abraham stayed in Beersheba.

Most omit this passage on Shabbat and Yom Tov.

Master of the Universe, just as Abraham our father suppressed his compassion to do Your will wholeheartedly, so may Your compassion suppress Your anger from us and may Your compassion prevail over Your other attributes. Deal with us, LORD our God, with the attributes of loving-kindness and compassion, and in Your great goodness may Your anger be turned away from Your people, Your city, Your land and Your inheritance. Fulfill in us, LORD our God, the promise You made in Your Torah through the hand of Moses Your servant, as it is said: "I will remember My covenant with Jacob, and also My covenant with Isaac, and also My covenant with Abraham I will remember, and the land I will remember." *Lev. 26*

ACCEPTING THE SOVEREIGNTY OF HEAVEN

לְעוֹלָם A person should always be God-fearing, privately and publicly, acknowledging the truth and speaking it in his heart. He should rise early and say: *Tanna DeVei Eliyahu, ch. 21*

Master of all worlds,
not because of our righteousness *Dan. 9*
do we lay our pleas before You,
but because of Your great compassion.

"privately" and "speaking it [truth] in his heart" (that is, the secret practice of Judaism) and the recitation here of the first lines of the Shema, which could not be said at the normal time. The final blessing, "Who sanctifies His name among the multitudes," refers to the martyrdom of those who went to their deaths rather than renounce their faith. Martyrdom is called *Kiddush HaShem,* "sanctifying [God's] name."

רִבּוֹן *Master of all worlds:* This passage also appears in the *Ne'ila* prayer on Yom

אֶל־אַבְרָהָם שֵׁנִית מִן־הַשָּׁמָיִם: וַיֹּאמֶר, בִּי נִשְׁבַּעְתִּי נְאֻם־יהוה, כִּי יַעַן אֲשֶׁר עָשִׂיתָ אֶת־הַדָּבָר הַזֶּה, וְלֹא חָשַׂכְתָּ אֶת־בִּנְךָ אֶת־יְחִידֶךָ: כִּי־בָרֵךְ אֲבָרֶכְךָ, וְהַרְבָּה אַרְבֶּה אֶת־זַרְעֲךָ כְּכוֹכְבֵי הַשָּׁמַיִם, וְכַחוֹל אֲשֶׁר עַל־שְׂפַת הַיָּם, וְיִרַשׁ זַרְעֲךָ אֵת שַׁעַר אֹיְבָיו: וְהִתְבָּרְכוּ בְזַרְעֲךָ כֹּל גּוֹיֵי הָאָרֶץ, עֵקֶב אֲשֶׁר שָׁמַעְתָּ בְּקֹלִי: וַיָּשָׁב אַבְרָהָם אֶל־נְעָרָיו, וַיָּקֻמוּ וַיֵּלְכוּ יַחְדָּו אֶל־בְּאֵר שָׁבַע, וַיֵּשֶׁב אַבְרָהָם בִּבְאֵר שָׁבַע:

Most omit this passage on שבת *and* יום טוב.

רִבּוֹנוֹ שֶׁל עוֹלָם, כְּמוֹ שֶׁכָּבַשׁ אַבְרָהָם אָבִינוּ אֶת רַחֲמָיו לַעֲשׂוֹת רְצוֹנְךָ בְּלֵבָב שָׁלֵם, כֵּן יִכְבְּשׁוּ רַחֲמֶיךָ אֶת כַּעַסְךָ מֵעָלֵינוּ וְיִגֹּלּוּ רַחֲמֶיךָ עַל מִדּוֹתֶיךָ. וְתִתְנַהֵג עִמָּנוּ יהוה אֱלֹהֵינוּ בְּמִדַּת הַחֶסֶד וּבְמִדַּת הָרַחֲמִים, וּבְטוּבְךָ הַגָּדוֹל יָשׁוּב חֲרוֹן אַפְּךָ מֵעַמְּךָ וּמֵעִירְךָ וּמֵאַרְצְךָ וּמִנַּחֲלָתֶךָ. וְקַיֶּם לָנוּ יהוה אֱלֹהֵינוּ אֶת הַדָּבָר שֶׁהִבְטַחְתָּנוּ בְּתוֹרָתֶךָ
ויקרא כו עַל יְדֵי מֹשֶׁה עַבְדֶּךָ, כָּאָמוּר: וְזָכַרְתִּי אֶת־בְּרִיתִי יַעֲקוֹב וְאַף אֶת־בְּרִיתִי יִצְחָק, וְאַף
אֶת־בְּרִיתִי אַבְרָהָם אֶזְכֹּר, וְהָאָרֶץ אֶזְכֹּר:

קבלת עול מלכות שמים

תנא דבי אליהו, פרק כא

לְעוֹלָם יְהֵא אָדָם יְרֵא שָׁמַיִם בְּסֵתֶר וּבְגָלוּי
וּמוֹדֶה עַל הָאֱמֶת, וְדוֹבֵר אֱמֶת בִּלְבָבוֹ
וְיַשְׁכֵּם וְיֹאמַר
רִבּוֹן כָּל הָעוֹלָמִים
דניאל ט לֹא עַל־צִדְקוֹתֵינוּ אֲנַחְנוּ מַפִּילִים תַּחֲנוּנֵינוּ לְפָנֶיךָ
כִּי עַל־רַחֲמֶיךָ הָרַבִּים:

לְעוֹלָם *A person should always:* This whole section until "Who sanctifies His name among the multitudes" appears in the tenth-century Midrash, *Tanna DeVei Eliyahu* (chapter 21). Some believe that it dates from a period of persecution under the Persian ruler Yazdegerd II who, in 456 CE, forbade the observance of Shabbat and the reading of the Torah. Jews continued to practice their faith in secret, saying prayers at times and in ways that would not be detected by their persecutors. This explains the reference to fearing God

What are we? What are our lives?
What is our loving-kindness? What is our righteousness?
What is our salvation? What is our strength?
What is our might? What shall we say before You,
Lord our God and God of our ancestors?
Are not all the mighty like nothing before You,
the men of renown as if they had never been,
the wise as if they know nothing,
and the understanding as if they lack intelligence?
For their many works are in vain,
and the days of their lives like a fleeting breath before You.
The pre-eminence of man over the animals is nothing, *Eccl. 3*
for all is but a fleeting breath.

אֲבָל Yet we are Your people, the children of Your covenant,
the children of Abraham, Your beloved,
to whom You made a promise on Mount Moriah;
the offspring of Isaac his only one who was bound on the altar;
the congregation of Jacob Your firstborn son
whom – because of the love with which You loved him
and the joy with which You rejoiced in him –
You called Yisrael and Yeshurun.

לְפִיכָךְ Therefore it is our duty
to thank You, and to praise, glorify, bless, sanctify
and give praise and thanks to Your name.
Happy are we, how good is our portion,
how lovely our fate, how beautiful our heritage.

---

empty, futile." However, it literally means "a short breath." It conveys a sense of the brevity and insubstantiality of life as a physical phenomenon. All that lives soon dies, and is as if it had never been. *Yet:* You created us, made us, chose us. We are infinitesimally small, yet brushed by the wings of Infinity. We are dust; yet *we are Your people, children of Your covenant,* descendants of those You singled out to be witnesses to the world of Your existence and majesty.

מָה אָנוּ, מֶה חַיֵּינוּ, מֶה חַסְדֵּנוּ, מַה צִּדְקוֹתֵינוּ
מַה יְשׁוּעָתֵנוּ, מַה כֹּחֵנוּ, מַה גְּבוּרָתֵנוּ
מַה נֹּאמַר לְפָנֶיךָ, יהוה אֱלֹהֵינוּ וֵאלֹהֵי אֲבוֹתֵינוּ
הֲלֹא כָּל הַגִּבּוֹרִים כְּאַיִן לְפָנֶיךָ
וְאַנְשֵׁי הַשֵּׁם כְּלֹא הָיוּ
וַחֲכָמִים כִּבְלִי מַדָּע, וּנְבוֹנִים כִּבְלִי הַשְׂכֵּל
כִּי רֹב מַעֲשֵׂיהֶם תֹּהוּ, וִימֵי חַיֵּיהֶם הֶבֶל לְפָנֶיךָ
וּמוֹתַר הָאָדָם מִן־הַבְּהֵמָה אָיִן קהלת ג
כִּי הַכֹּל הָבֶל:

אֲבָל אֲנַחְנוּ עַמְּךָ בְּנֵי בְרִיתֶךָ
בְּנֵי אַבְרָהָם אֹהַבְךָ שֶׁנִּשְׁבַּעְתָּ לּוֹ בְּהַר הַמּוֹרִיָּה
זֶרַע יִצְחָק יְחִידוֹ שֶׁנֶּעֱקַד עַל גַּבֵּי הַמִּזְבֵּחַ
עֲדַת יַעֲקֹב בִּנְךָ בְּכוֹרֶךָ
שֶׁמֵּאַהֲבָתְךָ שֶׁאָהַבְתָּ אוֹתוֹ, וּמִשִּׂמְחָתְךָ שֶׁשָּׂמַחְתָּ בּוֹ
קָרָאתָ אֶת שְׁמוֹ יִשְׂרָאֵל וִישֻׁרוּן.

לְפִיכָךְ אֲנַחְנוּ חַיָּבִים
לְהוֹדוֹת לְךָ וּלְשַׁבֵּחֲךָ וּלְפָאֶרְךָ
וּלְבָרֵךְ וּלְקַדֵּשׁ וְלָתֵת שֶׁבַח וְהוֹדָיָה לִשְׁמֶךָ.
אַשְׁרֵינוּ, מַה טּוֹב חֶלְקֵנוּ
וּמַה נָּעִים גּוֹרָלֵנוּ, וּמַה יָּפָה יְרֻשָּׁתֵנוּ.

Kippur. It expresses the paradox of the human condition in the presence of God. We know how small we are and how brief our lives. *Fleeting breath:* the Hebrew word *hevel* – the key word of the opening chapters of Ecclesiastes, from which this line is taken – has been translated as "vain, meaningless,

▸ Happy are we who, early and late,
evening and morning,
say twice each day –

Listen, Israel: the Lord is our God, the Lord is One. *Deut. 6*

Quietly: Blessed be the name of His glorious kingdom for ever and all time.

Some congregations say the entire first paragraph of the Shema (below) at this point. If there is a concern that the Shema will not be recited within the prescribed time, then all three paragraphs should be said. See law 340.

Love the Lord your God with all your heart, with all your soul, and with all your might. These words which I command you today shall be on your heart. Teach them repeatedly to your children, speaking of them when you sit at home and when you travel on the way, when you lie down and when you rise. Bind them as a sign on your hand, and they shall be an emblem between your eyes. Write them on the doorposts of your house and gates.

אַתָּה הוּא It was You who existed
before the world was created,
it is You now that the world has been created.
It is You in this world
and You in the World to Come.
▸ Sanctify Your name
through those who sanctify Your name,
and sanctify Your name
throughout Your world.
By Your salvation may our pride be exalted;
raise high our pride.
Blessed are You, Lord,
who sanctifies His name among the multitudes.

His covenant; therefore, we may not renounce our religion or identity: "I, God, do not change; so you, children of Jacob, are not destroyed" (Mal. 3:6).

◂ אַשְׁרֵינוּ, שֶׁאֲנַחְנוּ מַשְׁכִּימִים וּמַעֲרִיבִים עֶרֶב וָבֹקֶר
וְאוֹמְרִים פַּעֲמַיִם בְּכָל יוֹם

שְׁמַע יִשְׂרָאֵל, יהוה אֱלֹהֵינוּ, יהוה אֶחָד: דברים ו

Quietly בָּרוּךְ שֵׁם כְּבוֹד מַלְכוּתוֹ לְעוֹלָם וָעֶד.

Some congregations say the entire first paragraph of the שמע *(below) at this point. If there is a concern that the* שמע *will not be recited within the prescribed time, then all three paragraphs should be said. See law 340.*

וְאָהַבְתָּ אֵת יהוה אֱלֹהֶיךָ, בְּכָל־לְבָבְךָ, וּבְכָל־נַפְשְׁךָ, וּבְכָל־מְאֹדֶךָ: וְהָיוּ הַדְּבָרִים הָאֵלֶּה, אֲשֶׁר אָנֹכִי מְצַוְּךָ הַיּוֹם, עַל־לְבָבֶךָ: וְשִׁנַּנְתָּם לְבָנֶיךָ, וְדִבַּרְתָּ בָּם, בְּשִׁבְתְּךָ בְּבֵיתֶךָ, וּבְלֶכְתְּךָ בַדֶּרֶךְ, וּבְשָׁכְבְּךָ וּבְקוּמֶךָ: וּקְשַׁרְתָּם לְאוֹת עַל־יָדֶךָ וְהָיוּ לְטֹטָפֹת בֵּין עֵינֶיךָ: וּכְתַבְתָּם עַל־מְזֻזוֹת בֵּיתֶךָ וּבִשְׁעָרֶיךָ:

אַתָּה הוּא עַד שֶׁלֹּא נִבְרָא הָעוֹלָם
אַתָּה הוּא מִשֶּׁנִּבְרָא הָעוֹלָם.
אַתָּה הוּא בָּעוֹלָם הַזֶּה
וְאַתָּה הוּא לָעוֹלָם הַבָּא.
◂ קַדֵּשׁ אֶת שִׁמְךָ עַל מַקְדִּישֵׁי שְׁמֶךָ
וְקַדֵּשׁ אֶת שִׁמְךָ בְּעוֹלָמֶךָ
וּבִישׁוּעָתְךָ תָּרוּם וְתַגְבִּיהַּ קַרְנֵנוּ.
בָּרוּךְ אַתָּה יהוה
הַמְקַדֵּשׁ אֶת שִׁמְךָ בָּרַבִּים.

אַתָּה הוּא *It was You who existed:* This prayer, with its emphasis on the changelessness of God, may have been incorporated at a time of persecution, expressing the refusal of Jews to abandon their faith. God does not alter or revoke

אַתָּה הוּא You are the LORD our God
in heaven and on earth,
and in the highest heaven of heavens.
Truly, You are the first
and You are the last,
and besides You there is no god.
Gather those who hope in You
from the four quarters of the earth.
May all mankind recognize and know
that You alone are God
over all the kingdoms on earth.

You made the heavens and the earth,
the sea and all they contain.
Who among all the works of Your hands,
above and below,
can tell You what to do?

Heavenly Father,
deal kindly with us
for the sake of Your great name
by which we are called,
and fulfill for us,
LORD our God,
that which is written:

"At that time I will bring you home, and at that time I will gather you, for I will give you renown and praise among all the peoples of the earth when I bring back your exiles before your eyes, says the LORD." *Zeph. 3*

---

ingathering of Jews and of a time when "I will give you renown and praise among all the peoples of the earth." This entire sequence of prayers is eloquent testimony to how Jews sustained faith and hope, dignity and pride, during some of the most prolonged periods of persecution in history.

אַתָּה הוּא יהוה אֱלֹהֵינוּ
בַּשָּׁמַיִם וּבָאָרֶץ
וּבִשְׁמֵי הַשָּׁמַיִם הָעֶלְיוֹנִים.
אֱמֶת, אַתָּה הוּא רִאשׁוֹן
וְאַתָּה הוּא אַחֲרוֹן
וּמִבַּלְעָדֶיךָ אֵין אֱלֹהִים.
קַבֵּץ קוֶֹיךָ מֵאַרְבַּע כַּנְפוֹת הָאָרֶץ.
יַכִּירוּ וְיֵדְעוּ כָּל בָּאֵי עוֹלָם
כִּי אַתָּה הוּא הָאֱלֹהִים לְבַדְּךָ לְכֹל מַמְלְכוֹת הָאָרֶץ.

אַתָּה עָשִׂיתָ אֶת הַשָּׁמַיִם וְאֶת הָאָרֶץ
אֶת הַיָּם וְאֶת כָּל אֲשֶׁר בָּם
וּמִי בְּכָל מַעֲשֵׂי יָדֶיךָ בָּעֶלְיוֹנִים אוֹ בַתַּחְתּוֹנִים
שֶׁיֹּאמַר לְךָ מַה תַּעֲשֶׂה.
אָבִינוּ שֶׁבַּשָּׁמַיִם
עֲשֵׂה עִמָּנוּ חֶסֶד
בַּעֲבוּר שִׁמְךָ הַגָּדוֹל שֶׁנִּקְרָא עָלֵינוּ
וְקַיֶּם לָנוּ יהוה אֱלֹהֵינוּ
מַה שֶּׁכָּתוּב:
צפניה ג בָּעֵת הַהִיא אָבִיא אֶתְכֶם, וּבָעֵת קַבְּצִי אֶתְכֶם,
כִּי־אֶתֵּן אֶתְכֶם לְשֵׁם וְלִתְהִלָּה בְּכֹל עַמֵּי הָאָרֶץ,
בְּשׁוּבִי אֶת־שְׁבוּתֵיכֶם לְעֵינֵיכֶם, אָמַר יהוה:

אַתָּה הוּא *You are the* L*ORD* *our God:* This second prayer, for the end of exile, culminates with the verse from Zephania (3:20) which speaks of the

OFFERINGS

The sages held that, in the absence of the Temple, studying the laws of sacrifices is the equivalent of offering them. Hence the following texts. There are different customs as to how many passages are to be said, and one should follow the custom of one's congregation. The minimum requirement is to say the verses relating to The Daily Sacrifice on the next page.

THE BASIN

The Lord spoke to Moses, saying: Make a bronze basin, with its bronze stand for washing, and place it between the Tent of Meeting and the altar, and put water in it. From it, Aaron and his sons are to wash their hands and feet. When they enter the Tent of Meeting, they shall wash with water so that they will not die; likewise when they approach the altar to minister, presenting a fire-offering to the Lord. They must wash their hands and feet so that they will not die. This shall be an everlasting ordinance for Aaron and his descendants throughout their generations. *Ex. 30*

TAKING OF THE ASHES

The Lord spoke to Moses, saying: Instruct Aaron and his sons, saying, This is the law of the burnt-offering. The burnt-offering shall remain on the altar hearth throughout the night until morning, and the altar fire shall be kept burning on it. The priest shall then put on his linen garments, and linen breeches next to his body, and shall remove the ashes of the burnt-offering that the fire has consumed on the altar and place them beside the altar. Then he shall take off these clothes and put on others, and carry the ashes outside the camp to a clean place. The fire on the altar must be kept burning; it must not go out. Each morning the priest shall burn wood on it, and prepare on it the burnt-offering and burn the fat of the peace-offerings. A perpetual fire must be kept burning on the altar; it must not go out. *Lev. 6*

May it be Your will, Lord our God and God of our ancestors, that You have compassion on us and pardon us all our sins, grant atonement for all our iniquities and forgive all our transgressions. May You rebuild the Temple swiftly in our days so that we may offer You the continual-offering that it may atone for us as You have prescribed for us in Your Torah through Moses Your servant, from the mouthpiece of Your glory, as it is said:

---

about sacrifice was a substitute for sacrifice itself (*Ta'anit* 27b). The passage from the Mishna (*Zevaḥim* 5) is also about sacrifices, and was chosen because it does not contain any disagreement between the sages, and thus accords with the rule that one should pray "after a decided *halakha*," that is, an item of Jewish law about which there is no debate.

סדר הקרבנות

חז״ל held that, in the absence of the Temple, studying the laws of sacrifices is the equivalent of offering them. Hence the following texts. There are different customs as to how many passages are to be said, and one should follow the custom of one's congregation. The minimum requirement is to say the verses relating to the קרבן תמיד on the next page.

פרשת הכיור

וַיְדַבֵּר יהוה אֶל־מֹשֶׁה לֵּאמֹר: וְעָשִׂיתָ כִּיּוֹר נְחֹשֶׁת וְכַנּוֹ נְחֹשֶׁת לְרָחְצָה, שמות ל
וְנָתַתָּ אֹתוֹ בֵּין־אֹהֶל מוֹעֵד וּבֵין הַמִּזְבֵּחַ, וְנָתַתָּ שָׁמָּה מָיִם: וְרָחֲצוּ אַהֲרֹן
וּבָנָיו מִמֶּנּוּ אֶת־יְדֵיהֶם וְאֶת־רַגְלֵיהֶם: בְּבֹאָם אֶל־אֹהֶל מוֹעֵד יִרְחֲצוּ־מַיִם,
וְלֹא יָמֻתוּ, אוֹ בְגִשְׁתָּם אֶל־הַמִּזְבֵּחַ לְשָׁרֵת, לְהַקְטִיר אִשֶּׁה לַיהוה: וְרָחֲצוּ
יְדֵיהֶם וְרַגְלֵיהֶם וְלֹא יָמֻתוּ, וְהָיְתָה לָהֶם חָק־עוֹלָם, לוֹ וּלְזַרְעוֹ לְדֹרֹתָם:

פרשת תרומת הדשן

וַיְדַבֵּר יהוה אֶל־מֹשֶׁה לֵּאמֹר: צַו אֶת־אַהֲרֹן וְאֶת־בָּנָיו לֵאמֹר, זֹאת תּוֹרַת ויקרא ו
הָעֹלָה, הִוא הָעֹלָה עַל מוֹקְדָה עַל־הַמִּזְבֵּחַ כָּל־הַלַּיְלָה עַד־הַבֹּקֶר, וְאֵשׁ
הַמִּזְבֵּחַ תּוּקַד בּוֹ: וְלָבַשׁ הַכֹּהֵן מִדּוֹ בַד, וּמִכְנְסֵי־בַד יִלְבַּשׁ עַל־בְּשָׂרוֹ,
וְהֵרִים אֶת־הַדֶּשֶׁן אֲשֶׁר תֹּאכַל הָאֵשׁ אֶת־הָעֹלָה, עַל־הַמִּזְבֵּחַ, וְשָׂמוֹ אֵצֶל
הַמִּזְבֵּחַ: וּפָשַׁט אֶת־בְּגָדָיו, וְלָבַשׁ בְּגָדִים אֲחֵרִים, וְהוֹצִיא אֶת־הַדֶּשֶׁן אֶל־
מִחוּץ לַמַּחֲנֶה, אֶל־מָקוֹם טָהוֹר: וְהָאֵשׁ עַל־הַמִּזְבֵּחַ תּוּקַד־בּוֹ, לֹא תִכְבֶּה,
וּבִעֵר עָלֶיהָ הַכֹּהֵן עֵצִים בַּבֹּקֶר בַּבֹּקֶר, וְעָרַךְ עָלֶיהָ הָעֹלָה, וְהִקְטִיר עָלֶיהָ
חֶלְבֵי הַשְּׁלָמִים: אֵשׁ, תָּמִיד תּוּקַד עַל־הַמִּזְבֵּחַ, לֹא תִכְבֶּה:

יְהִי רָצוֹן מִלְּפָנֶיךָ יהוה אֱלֹהֵינוּ וֵאלֹהֵי אֲבוֹתֵינוּ, שֶׁתְּרַחֵם עָלֵינוּ, וְתִמְחֹל לָנוּ עַל כָּל חַטֹּאתֵינוּ וּתְכַפֵּר לָנוּ עַל כָּל עֲוֹנוֹתֵינוּ וְתִסְלַח לָנוּ עַל כָּל פְּשָׁעֵינוּ, וְתִבְנֶה בֵּית הַמִּקְדָּשׁ בִּמְהֵרָה בְיָמֵינוּ, וְנַקְרִיב לְפָנֶיךָ קָרְבַּן הַתָּמִיד שֶׁיְּכַפֵּר בַּעֲדֵנוּ, כְּמוֹ שֶׁכָּתַבְתָּ עָלֵינוּ בְּתוֹרָתֶךָ עַל יְדֵי מֹשֶׁה עַבְדֶּךָ מִפִּי כְבוֹדֶךָ, כָּאָמוּר

OFFERINGS

There now follows a second cycle of study, with the same structure as the first, with passages from (1) the Torah, (2) the Mishna, and (3) the Gemara. The passages from the Torah relate to the daily, weekly and monthly sacrifices because, in the absence of the Temple, the sages held that study of the laws

THE DAILY SACRIFICE

וַיְדַבֵּר The LORD said to Moses, "Command the Israelites and tell them: 'Be careful to offer to Me at the appointed time My food-offering consumed by fire, as an aroma pleasing to Me.' Tell them: 'This is the fire-offering you shall offer to the LORD – two lambs a year old without blemish, as a regular burnt-offering each day. Prepare one lamb in the morning and the other toward evening, together with a meal-offering of a tenth of an ephah of fine flour mixed with a quarter of a hin of oil from pressed olives. This is the regular burnt-offering instituted at Mount Sinai as a pleasing aroma, a fire-offering made to the LORD. Its libation is to be a quarter of a hin [of wine] with each lamb, poured in the Sanctuary as a libation of strong drink to the LORD. Prepare the second lamb in the afternoon, along with the same meal-offering and libation as in the morning. This is a fire-offering, an aroma pleasing to the LORD.'" *Num. 28*

וְשָׁחַט He shall slaughter it at the north side of the altar before the LORD, and Aaron's sons the priests shall sprinkle its blood against the altar on all sides. *Lev. 1*

May it be Your will, LORD our God and God of our ancestors,
that this recitation be considered accepted and favored before You
as if we had offered the daily sacrifice at its appointed time and place, according to its laws.

It is You, LORD our God, to whom our ancestors offered fragrant incense when the Temple stood, as You commanded them through Moses Your prophet, as is written in Your Torah:

THE INCENSE

The LORD said to Moses: Take fragrant spices – balsam, onycha, galbanum and pure frankincense, all in equal amounts – and make a fragrant blend of incense, the work of a perfumer, well mixed, pure and holy. Grind it very finely and place it in front of the [Ark of] Testimony in the Tent of Meeting, where I will meet with you. It shall be most holy to you. *Ex. 30*

And it is said:

Aaron shall burn fragrant incense on the altar every morning when he cleans the lamps. He shall burn incense again when he lights the lamps toward evening so that there will be incense before the LORD at all times, throughout your generations.

פרשת קרבן התמיד

בְּמִדְבַּר כח וַיְדַבֵּר יהוה אֶל־מֹשֶׁה לֵּאמֹר: צַו אֶת־בְּנֵי יִשְׂרָאֵל וְאָמַרְתָּ אֲלֵהֶם, אֶת־קָרְבָּנִי לַחְמִי לְאִשַּׁי, רֵיחַ נִיחֹחִי, תִּשְׁמְרוּ לְהַקְרִיב לִי בְּמוֹעֲדוֹ: וְאָמַרְתָּ לָהֶם, זֶה הָאִשֶּׁה אֲשֶׁר תַּקְרִיבוּ לַיהוה, כְּבָשִׂים בְּנֵי־שָׁנָה תְמִימִם שְׁנַיִם לַיּוֹם, עֹלָה תָמִיד: אֶת־הַכֶּבֶשׂ אֶחָד תַּעֲשֶׂה בַבֹּקֶר, וְאֵת הַכֶּבֶשׂ הַשֵּׁנִי תַּעֲשֶׂה בֵּין הָעַרְבָּיִם: וַעֲשִׂירִית הָאֵיפָה סֹלֶת לְמִנְחָה, בְּלוּלָה בְּשֶׁמֶן כָּתִית רְבִיעִת הַהִין: עֹלַת תָּמִיד, הָעֲשֻׂיָה בְּהַר סִינַי, לְרֵיחַ נִיחֹחַ אִשֶּׁה לַיהוה: וְנִסְכּוֹ רְבִיעִת הַהִין לַכֶּבֶשׂ הָאֶחָד, בַּקֹּדֶשׁ הַסֵּךְ נֶסֶךְ שֵׁכָר לַיהוה: וְאֵת הַכֶּבֶשׂ הַשֵּׁנִי תַּעֲשֶׂה בֵּין הָעַרְבָּיִם, כְּמִנְחַת הַבֹּקֶר וּכְנִסְכּוֹ תַּעֲשֶׂה, אִשֵּׁה רֵיחַ נִיחֹחַ לַיהוה:

וַיִּקְרָא א וְשָׁחַט אֹתוֹ עַל יֶרֶךְ הַמִּזְבֵּחַ צָפֹנָה לִפְנֵי יהוה, וְזָרְקוּ בְּנֵי אַהֲרֹן הַכֹּהֲנִים אֶת־דָּמוֹ עַל־הַמִּזְבֵּחַ, סָבִיב:

יְהִי רָצוֹן מִלְּפָנֶיךָ, יהוה אֱלֹהֵינוּ וֵאלֹהֵי אֲבוֹתֵינוּ
שֶׁתְּהֵא אֲמִירָה זוֹ חֲשׁוּבָה וּמְקֻבֶּלֶת וּמְרֻצָּה לְפָנֶיךָ
כְּאִלּוּ הִקְרַבְנוּ קָרְבַּן הַתָּמִיד בְּמוֹעֲדוֹ וּבִמְקוֹמוֹ וּכְהִלְכָתוֹ.

אַתָּה הוּא יהוה אֱלֹהֵינוּ שֶׁהִקְטִירוּ אֲבוֹתֵינוּ לְפָנֶיךָ אֶת קְטֹרֶת הַסַּמִּים בִּזְמַן שֶׁבֵּית הַמִּקְדָּשׁ הָיָה קַיָּם, כַּאֲשֶׁר צִוִּיתָ אוֹתָם עַל יְדֵי מֹשֶׁה נְבִיאֶךָ, כַּכָּתוּב בְּתוֹרָתֶךָ:

פרשת הקטורת

שְׁמוֹת ל וַיֹּאמֶר יהוה אֶל־מֹשֶׁה, קַח־לְךָ סַמִּים נָטָף וּשְׁחֵלֶת וְחֶלְבְּנָה, סַמִּים וּלְבֹנָה זַכָּה, בַּד בְּבַד יִהְיֶה: וְעָשִׂיתָ אֹתָהּ קְטֹרֶת, רֹקַח מַעֲשֵׂה רוֹקֵחַ, מְמֻלָּח, טָהוֹר קֹדֶשׁ: וְשָׁחַקְתָּ מִמֶּנָּה הָדֵק, וְנָתַתָּה מִמֶּנָּה לִפְנֵי הָעֵדֻת בְּאֹהֶל מוֹעֵד אֲשֶׁר אִוָּעֵד לְךָ שָׁמָּה, קֹדֶשׁ קָדָשִׁים תִּהְיֶה לָכֶם:

וְנֶאֱמַר
וְהִקְטִיר עָלָיו אַהֲרֹן קְטֹרֶת סַמִּים, בַּבֹּקֶר בַּבֹּקֶר בְּהֵיטִיבוֹ אֶת־הַנֵּרֹת יַקְטִירֶנָּה: וּבְהַעֲלֹת אַהֲרֹן אֶת־הַנֵּרֹת בֵּין הָעַרְבַּיִם יַקְטִירֶנָּה, קְטֹרֶת תָּמִיד לִפְנֵי יהוה לְדֹרֹתֵיכֶם:

The rabbis taught: How was the incense prepared? It weighed 368 manehs, 365 corresponding to the number of days in a solar year, a maneh for each day, half to be offered in the morning and half in the afternoon, and three additional manehs from which the High Priest took two handfuls on Yom Kippur. These were put back into the mortar on the day before Yom Kippur and ground again very thoroughly so as to be extremely fine. The incense contained eleven kinds of spices: balsam, onycha, galbanum and frankincense, each weighing seventy manehs; myrrh, cassia, spikenard and saffron, each weighing sixteen manehs; twelve manehs of costus, three of aromatic bark; nine of cinnamon; nine kabs of Carsina lye; three seahs and three kabs of Cyprus wine. If Cyprus wine was not available, old white wine might be used. A quarter of a kab of Sodom salt, and a minute amount of a smoke-raising herb. Rabbi Nathan the Babylonian says: also a minute amount of Jordan amber. If one added honey to the mixture, he rendered it unfit for sacred use. If he omitted any one of its ingredients, he is guilty of a capital offense. *Keritot 6a*

Rabban Simeon ben Gamliel says: "Balsam" refers to the sap that drips from the balsam tree. The Carsina lye was used for bleaching the onycha to improve it. The Cyprus wine was used to soak the onycha in it to make it pungent. Though urine is suitable for this purpose, it is not brought into the Temple out of respect.

It was taught, Rabbi Nathan says: While it was being ground, another would say, "Grind well, well grind," because the [rhythmic] sound is good for spices. If it was mixed in half-quantities, it is fit for use, but we have not heard whether this applies to a third or a quarter. Rabbi Judah said: The general rule is that if it was made in the correct proportions, it is fit for use even if made in half-quantity, but if he omitted any one of its ingredients, he is guilty of a capital offense.

It was taught, Bar Kappara says: Once every sixty or seventy years, the accumulated surpluses amounted to half the yearly quantity. Bar Kappara also taught: If a minute quantity of honey had been mixed into the incense, no one could have resisted the scent. Why did they not put honey into it? Because the Torah says, "For you are not to burn any leaven or honey in a fire-offering made to the LORD." *JT Yoma 4:5* *Lev. 2*

The following three verses are each said three times:

The LORD of hosts is with us; the God of Jacob is our stronghold, Selah. *Ps. 46*
LORD of hosts, happy is the one who trusts in You. *Ps. 84*
LORD, save! May the King answer us on the day we call. *Ps. 20*

כריתות ו. תָּנוּ רַבָּנָן: פִּטּוּם הַקְּטֹרֶת כֵּיצַד, שְׁלֹשׁ מֵאוֹת וְשִׁשִּׁים וּשְׁמוֹנָה מָנִים הָיוּ בָהּ. שְׁלֹשׁ מֵאוֹת וְשִׁשִּׁים וַחֲמִשָּׁה כְּמִנְיַן יְמוֹת הַחַמָּה, מָנֶה לְכָל יוֹם, פְּרַס בְּשַׁחֲרִית וּפְרַס בֵּין הָעַרְבָּיִם, וּשְׁלֹשָׁה מָנִים יְתֵרִים שֶׁמֵּהֶם מַכְנִיס כֹּהֵן גָּדוֹל מְלֹא חָפְנָיו בְּיוֹם הַכִּפּוּרִים, וּמַחֲזִירָן לְמַכְתֶּשֶׁת בְּעֶרֶב יוֹם הַכִּפּוּרִים וְשׁוֹחֲקָן יָפֶה יָפֶה, כְּדֵי שֶׁתְּהֵא דַקָּה מִן הַדַּקָּה. וְאַחַד עָשָׂר סַמָּנִים הָיוּ בָהּ, וְאֵלּוּ הֵן: הַצְּרִי, וְהַצִּפֹּרֶן, וְהַחֶלְבְּנָה, וְהַלְּבוֹנָה מִשְׁקַל שִׁבְעִים שִׁבְעִים מָנֶה, מֹר, וּקְצִיעָה, שִׁבֹּלֶת נֵרְדְּ, וְכַרְכֹּם מִשְׁקַל שִׁשָּׁה עָשָׂר שִׁשָּׁה עָשָׂר מָנֶה, הַקֹּשְׁטְ שְׁנֵים עָשָׂר, קִלּוּפָה שְׁלֹשָׁה, קִנָּמוֹן תִּשְׁעָה, בֹּרִית כַּרְשִׁינָה תִּשְׁעָה קַבִּין, יֵין קַפְרִיסִין סְאִין תְּלָת וְקַבִּין תְּלָתָא, וְאִם לֹא מָצָא יֵין קַפְרִיסִין, מֵבִיא חֲמַר חִוַּרְיָן עַתִּיק. מֶלַח סְדוֹמִית רֹבַע, מַעֲלֶה עָשָׁן כָּל שֶׁהוּא. רַבִּי נָתָן הַבַּבְלִי אוֹמֵר: אַף כִּפַּת הַיַּרְדֵּן כָּל שֶׁהוּא, וְאִם נָתַן בָּהּ דְּבַשׁ פְּסָלָהּ, וְאִם חִסַּר אֶחָד מִכָּל סַמָּנֶיהָ, חַיָּב מִיתָה.

רַבָּן שִׁמְעוֹן בֶּן גַּמְלִיאֵל אוֹמֵר: הַצְּרִי אֵינוֹ אֶלָּא שְׂרָף הַנּוֹטֵף מֵעֲצֵי הַקְּטָף. בֹּרִית כַּרְשִׁינָה שֶׁשָּׁפִין בָּהּ אֶת הַצִּפֹּרֶן כְּדֵי שֶׁתְּהֵא נָאָה, יֵין קַפְרִיסִין שֶׁשּׁוֹרִין בּוֹ אֶת הַצִּפֹּרֶן כְּדֵי שֶׁתְּהֵא עַזָּה, וַהֲלֹא מֵי רַגְלַיִם יָפִין לָהּ, אֶלָּא שֶׁאֵין מַכְנִיסִין מֵי רַגְלַיִם בַּמִּקְדָּשׁ מִפְּנֵי הַכָּבוֹד.

תַּנְיָא, רַבִּי נָתָן אוֹמֵר: כְּשֶׁהוּא שׁוֹחֵק אוֹמֵר, הָדֵק הֵיטֵב הֵיטֵב הָדֵק, מִפְּנֵי שֶׁהַקּוֹל יָפֶה לַבְּשָׂמִים. פִּטְּמָהּ לַחֲצָאִין כְּשֵׁרָה, לִשְׁלִישׁ וְלִרְבִיעַ לֹא שָׁמַעְנוּ. אָמַר רַבִּי יְהוּדָה: זֶה הַכְּלָל, אִם כְּמִדָּתָהּ כְּשֵׁרָה לַחֲצָאִין, וְאִם חִסַּר אֶחָד מִכָּל סַמָּנֶיהָ חַיָּב מִיתָה.

ירושלמי יומא ד, הלכה ה תַּנְיָא, בַּר קַפָּרָא אוֹמֵר: אַחַת לְשִׁשִּׁים אוֹ לְשִׁבְעִים שָׁנָה הָיְתָה בָאָה שֶׁל שִׁירַיִם לַחֲצָאִין. וְעוֹד תָּנֵי בַּר קַפָּרָא: אִלּוּ הָיָה נוֹתֵן בָּהּ קוֹרְטוֹב שֶׁל דְּבַשׁ אֵין אָדָם יָכוֹל לַעֲמֹד מִפְּנֵי רֵיחָהּ, וְלָמָּה אֵין מְעָרְבִין בָּהּ דְּבַשׁ, מִפְּנֵי שֶׁהַתּוֹרָה אָמְרָה: כִּי כָל־שְׂאֹר וְכָל־דְּבַשׁ לֹא־תַקְטִירוּ מִמֶּנּוּ אִשֶּׁה לַיהוה: ויקרא ב

The following three verses are each said three times:

תהלים מו יהוה צְבָאוֹת עִמָּנוּ, מִשְׂגָּב לָנוּ אֱלֹהֵי יַעֲקֹב סֶלָה:

תהלים פד יהוה צְבָאוֹת, אַשְׁרֵי אָדָם בֹּטֵחַ בָּךְ:

תהלים כ יהוה הוֹשִׁיעָה, הַמֶּלֶךְ יַעֲנֵנוּ בְיוֹם־קָרְאֵנוּ:

You are my hiding place; You will protect me from distress and surround me with songs of salvation, Selah. *Ps. 32*

Then the offering of Judah and Jerusalem will be pleasing to the LORD as in the days of old and as in former years. *Mal. 3*

THE ORDER OF THE PRIESTLY FUNCTIONS

Abaye related the order of the daily priestly functions in the name of tradition and in accordance with Abba Shaul: The large pile [of wood] comes before the second pile for the incense; the second pile for the incense precedes the laying in order of the two logs of wood; the laying in order of the two logs of wood comes before the removing of ashes from the inner altar; the removing of ashes from the inner altar precedes the cleaning of the five lamps; the cleaning of the five lamps comes before the blood of the daily offering; the blood of the daily offering precedes the cleaning of the [other] two lamps; the cleaning of the two lamps comes before the incense-offering; the incense-offering precedes the burning of the limbs; the burning of the limbs comes before the meal-offering; the meal-offering precedes the pancakes; the pancakes come before the wine-libations; the wine-libations precede the additional offerings; the additional offerings come before the [frankincense] censers; the censers precede the daily afternoon offering; as it is said, "On it he shall arrange burnt-offerings, and on it he shall burn the fat of the peace-offerings" – "on it" [the daily offering] all the offerings were completed. *Yoma 33a* *Lev. 6*

Please, by the power of Your great right hand, set the captive nation free.
Accept Your people's prayer. Strengthen us, purify us, You who are revered.
Please, Mighty One, guard like the pupil of the eye those who seek Your unity.
Bless them, cleanse them, have compassion on them,
grant them Your righteousness always.
Mighty One, Holy One, in Your great goodness guide Your congregation.
Only One, Exalted One, turn to Your people, who proclaim Your holiness.
Accept our plea and heed our cry, You who know all secret thoughts.
Blessed be the name of His glorious kingdom for ever and all time.

Master of the Universe, You have commanded us to offer the daily sacrifice at its appointed time with the priests at their service, the Levites on their platform, and the Israelites at their post. Now, because of our sins, the Temple is destroyed and the daily sacrifice discontinued, and we have no priest at his service, no Levite on his platform, no Israelite at his post. But You said: "We will offer in place of bullocks [the prayer of] our lips." Therefore may it be Your will, LORD our God and God of our ancestors, that the prayer of our lips be considered, accepted and favored before You as if we had offered the daily sacrifice at its appointed time and place, according to its laws. *Hos. 14*

אַתָּה סֵתֶר לִי, מִצַּר תִּצְּרֵנִי, רָנֵּי פַלֵּט תְּסוֹבְבֵנִי סֶלָה: תהלים לב
וְעָרְבָה לַיהוה מִנְחַת יְהוּדָה וִירוּשָׁלָםִ מלאכי ג
כִּימֵי עוֹלָם וּכְשָׁנִים קַדְמֹנִיּוֹת:

סדר המערכה

יומא לג. אַבַּיֵּי הֲוָה מְסַדֵּר סֵדֶר הַמַּעֲרָכָה מִשְּׁמָא דִגְמָרָא, וְאַלִּבָּא דְאַבָּא שָׁאוּל: מַעֲרָכָה גְדוֹלָה קוֹדֶמֶת לְמַעֲרָכָה שְׁנִיָּה שֶׁל קְטֹרֶת, וּמַעֲרָכָה שְׁנִיָּה שֶׁל קְטֹרֶת קוֹדֶמֶת לְסִדּוּר שְׁנֵי גִזְרֵי עֵצִים, וְסִדּוּר שְׁנֵי גִזְרֵי עֵצִים קוֹדֵם לְדִשּׁוּן מִזְבֵּחַ הַפְּנִימִי, וְדִשּׁוּן מִזְבֵּחַ הַפְּנִימִי קוֹדֵם לַהֲטָבַת חָמֵשׁ נֵרוֹת, וַהֲטָבַת חָמֵשׁ נֵרוֹת קוֹדֶמֶת לְדַם הַתָּמִיד, וְדַם הַתָּמִיד קוֹדֵם לַהֲטָבַת שְׁתֵּי נֵרוֹת, וַהֲטָבַת שְׁתֵּי נֵרוֹת קוֹדֶמֶת לִקְטֹרֶת, וּקְטֹרֶת קוֹדֶמֶת לְאֵבָרִים, וְאֵבָרִים לְמִנְחָה, וּמִנְחָה לַחֲבִתִּין, וַחֲבִתִּין לִנְסָכִין, וּנְסָכִין לְמוּסָפִין, וּמוּסָפִין לְבָזִיכִין, וּבָזִיכִין קוֹדְמִין לְתָמִיד שֶׁל בֵּין הָעַרְבָּיִם. שֶׁנֶּאֱמַר: וְעָרַךְ עָלֶיהָ הָעֹלָה, ויקרא ו
וְהִקְטִיר עָלֶיהָ חֶלְבֵי הַשְּׁלָמִים: עָלֶיהָ הַשְׁלֵם כָּל הַקָּרְבָּנוֹת כֻּלָּם.

אָנָּא, בְּכֹחַ גְּדֻלַּת יְמִינְךָ, תַּתִּיר צְרוּרָה.
קַבֵּל רִנַּת עַמְּךָ, שַׂגְּבֵנוּ, טַהֲרֵנוּ, נוֹרָא.
נָא גִבּוֹר, דּוֹרְשֵׁי יִחוּדְךָ כְּבָבַת שָׁמְרֵם.
בָּרְכֵם, טַהֲרֵם, רַחֲמֵם, צִדְקָתְךָ תָּמִיד גָּמְלֵם.
חֲסִין קָדוֹשׁ, בְּרֹב טוּבְךָ נַהֵל עֲדָתֶךָ.
יָחִיד גֵּאֶה, לְעַמְּךָ פְּנֵה, זוֹכְרֵי קְדֻשָּׁתֶךָ.
שַׁוְעָתֵנוּ קַבֵּל וּשְׁמַע צַעֲקָתֵנוּ, יוֹדֵעַ תַּעֲלוּמוֹת.
בָּרוּךְ שֵׁם כְּבוֹד מַלְכוּתוֹ לְעוֹלָם וָעֶד.

רִבּוֹן הָעוֹלָמִים, אַתָּה צִוִּיתָנוּ לְהַקְרִיב קָרְבַּן הַתָּמִיד בְּמוֹעֲדוֹ וְלִהְיוֹת כֹּהֲנִים בַּעֲבוֹדָתָם וּלְוִיִּם בְּדוּכָנָם וְיִשְׂרָאֵל בְּמַעֲמָדָם, וְעַתָּה בַּעֲוֹנוֹתֵינוּ חָרַב בֵּית הַמִּקְדָּשׁ וּבָטַל הַתָּמִיד וְאֵין לָנוּ לֹא כֹהֵן בַּעֲבוֹדָתוֹ וְלֹא לֵוִי בְּדוּכָנוֹ וְלֹא יִשְׂרָאֵל בְּמַעֲמָדוֹ, וְאַתָּה אָמַרְתָּ: וּנְשַׁלְּמָה פָרִים שְׂפָתֵינוּ: הושע יד
לָכֵן יְהִי רָצוֹן מִלְּפָנֶיךָ יהוה אֱלֹהֵינוּ וֵאלֹהֵי אֲבוֹתֵינוּ, שֶׁיְּהֵא שִׂיחַ שִׂפְתוֹתֵינוּ חָשׁוּב וּמְקֻבָּל וּמְרֻצֶּה לְפָנֶיךָ, כְּאִלּוּ הִקְרַבְנוּ קָרְבַּן הַתָּמִיד בְּמוֹעֲדוֹ וּבִמְקוֹמוֹ וּכְהִלְכָתוֹ.

On Shabbat:

וּבְיוֹם הַשַּׁבָּת On the Shabbat day, make an offering of two lambs a year old, without blemish, together with two-tenths of an ephah of fine flour mixed with oil as a meal-offering, and its appropriate libation. This is the burnt-offering for every Shabbat, in addition to the regular daily burnt-offering and its libation. *Num. 28*

On Rosh Ḥodesh:

וּבְרָאשֵׁי חָדְשֵׁיכֶם On your new moons, present as a burnt-offering to the Lord, two young bulls, one ram, and seven yearling lambs without blemish. There shall be a meal-offering of three-tenths of an ephah of fine flour mixed with oil for each bull, two-tenths of an ephah of fine flour mixed with oil for the ram, and one-tenth of an ephah of fine flour mixed with oil for each lamb. This is the burnt-offering – a fire-offering of pleasing aroma to the Lord. Their libations shall be: half a hin of wine for each bull, a third of a hin for the ram, and a quarter of a hin for each lamb. This is the monthly burnt-offering to be made at each new moon throughout the year. One male goat should be offered as a sin-offering to God, in addition to the regular daily burnt-offering and its libation. *Num. 28*

LAWS OF OFFERINGS, MISHNA ZEVAḤIM

אֵיזֶהוּ מְקוֹמָן What is the location for sacrifices? The holiest offerings were slaughtered on the north side. The bull and he-goat of Yom Kippur were slaughtered on the north side. Their blood was received in a sacred vessel on the north side, and had to be sprinkled between the poles [of the Ark], toward the veil [screening the Holy of Holies], and on the golden altar. [The omission of] one of these sprinklings invalidated [the atonement ceremony]. The leftover blood was to be poured onto the western base of the outer altar. If this was not done, however, the omission did not invalidate [the ceremony]. *Zevaḥim Ch. 5*

The bulls and he-goats that were completely burnt were slaughtered on the north side, their blood was received in a sacred vessel on the north side, and had to be sprinkled toward the veil and on the golden altar. [The omission of] one of these sprinklings invalidated [the ceremony]. The leftover blood was to be poured onto the western base of the outer altar. If this was not done, however, the omission did not invalidate [the ceremony]. All these offerings were burnt where the altar ashes were deposited.

The communal and individual sin-offerings – these are the communal sin-offerings: the he-goats offered on Rosh Ḥodesh and Festivals were slaughtered on the north side, their blood was received in a sacred vessel on the north side, and required four sprinklings, one on each of the four corners of the altar. How was this done? The priest ascended the ramp and turned [right] onto the surrounding ledge. He came to the southeast corner, then went to the northeast, then to the northwest, then to the southwest. The leftover blood he poured onto the southern base. [The meat of

בשבת:

במדבר כח

וּבְיוֹם הַשַּׁבָּת שְׁנֵי־כְבָשִׂים בְּנֵי־שָׁנָה תְּמִימִם, וּשְׁנֵי עֶשְׂרֹנִים סֹלֶת מִנְחָה בְּלוּלָה בַשֶּׁמֶן, וְנִסְכּוֹ: עֹלַת שַׁבַּת בְּשַׁבַּתּוֹ, עַל־עֹלַת הַתָּמִיד וְנִסְכָּהּ:

בראש חודש:

במדבר כח

וּבְרָאשֵׁי חָדְשֵׁיכֶם תַּקְרִיבוּ עֹלָה לַיהוה, פָּרִים בְּנֵי־בָקָר שְׁנַיִם, וְאַיִל אֶחָד, כְּבָשִׂים בְּנֵי־שָׁנָה שִׁבְעָה, תְּמִימִם: וּשְׁלֹשָׁה עֶשְׂרֹנִים סֹלֶת מִנְחָה בְּלוּלָה בַשֶּׁמֶן לַפָּר הָאֶחָד, וּשְׁנֵי עֶשְׂרֹנִים סֹלֶת מִנְחָה בְּלוּלָה בַשֶּׁמֶן לָאַיִל הָאֶחָד: וְעִשָּׂרֹן עִשָּׂרוֹן סֹלֶת מִנְחָה בְּלוּלָה בַשֶּׁמֶן לַכֶּבֶשׂ הָאֶחָד, עֹלָה רֵיחַ נִיחֹחַ, אִשֶּׁה לַיהוה: וְנִסְכֵּיהֶם, חֲצִי הַהִין יִהְיֶה לַפָּר, וּשְׁלִישִׁת הַהִין לָאַיִל, וּרְבִיעִת הַהִין לַכֶּבֶשׂ, יָיִן, זֹאת עֹלַת חֹדֶשׁ בְּחָדְשׁוֹ לְחָדְשֵׁי הַשָּׁנָה: וּשְׂעִיר עִזִּים אֶחָד לְחַטָּאת לַיהוה, עַל־עֹלַת הַתָּמִיד יֵעָשֶׂה, וְנִסְכּוֹ:

דיני זבחים

זבחים פרק ה

אֵיזֶהוּ מְקוֹמָן שֶׁל זְבָחִים. קָדְשֵׁי קָדָשִׁים שְׁחִיטָתָן בַּצָּפוֹן. פַּר וְשָׂעִיר שֶׁל יוֹם הַכִּפּוּרִים, שְׁחִיטָתָן בַּצָּפוֹן, וְקִבּוּל דָּמָן בִּכְלֵי שָׁרֵת בַּצָּפוֹן, וְדָמָן טָעוּן הַזָּיָה עַל בֵּין הַבַּדִּים, וְעַל הַפָּרֹכֶת, וְעַל מִזְבַּח הַזָּהָב. מַתָּנָה אַחַת מֵהֶן מְעַכָּבֶת. שְׁיָרֵי הַדָּם הָיָה שׁוֹפֵךְ עַל יְסוֹד מַעֲרָבִי שֶׁל מִזְבֵּחַ הַחִיצוֹן, אִם לֹא נָתַן לֹא עִכֵּב.

פָּרִים הַנִּשְׂרָפִים וּשְׂעִירִים הַנִּשְׂרָפִים, שְׁחִיטָתָן בַּצָּפוֹן, וְקִבּוּל דָּמָן בִּכְלֵי שָׁרֵת בַּצָּפוֹן, וְדָמָן טָעוּן הַזָּיָה עַל הַפָּרֹכֶת וְעַל מִזְבַּח הַזָּהָב. מַתָּנָה אַחַת מֵהֶן מְעַכָּבֶת. שְׁיָרֵי הַדָּם הָיָה שׁוֹפֵךְ עַל יְסוֹד מַעֲרָבִי שֶׁל מִזְבֵּחַ הַחִיצוֹן, אִם לֹא נָתַן לֹא עִכֵּב. אֵלּוּ וָאֵלּוּ נִשְׂרָפִין בְּבֵית הַדָּשֶׁן.

חַטֹּאת הַצִּבּוּר וְהַיָּחִיד. אֵלּוּ הֵן חַטֹּאת הַצִּבּוּר: שְׂעִירֵי רָאשֵׁי חֳדָשִׁים וְשֶׁל מוֹעֲדוֹת. שְׁחִיטָתָן בַּצָּפוֹן, וְקִבּוּל דָּמָן בִּכְלֵי שָׁרֵת בַּצָּפוֹן, וְדָמָן טָעוּן אַרְבַּע מַתָּנוֹת עַל אַרְבַּע קְרָנוֹת. כֵּיצַד, עָלָה בַכֶּבֶשׁ, וּפָנָה לַסּוֹבֵב, וּבָא לוֹ לְקֶרֶן דְּרוֹמִית מִזְרָחִית, מִזְרָחִית צְפוֹנִית, צְפוֹנִית מַעֲרָבִית, מַעֲרָבִית

these offerings], prepared in any manner, was eaten within the [courtyard] curtains, by males of the priest-hood, on that day and the following night, until midnight.

The burnt-offering was among the holiest of sacrifices. It was slaughtered on the north side, its blood was received in a sacred vessel on the north side, and required two sprinklings [at opposite corners of the altar], making four in all. The offering had to be flayed, dismembered and wholly consumed by fire.

The communal peace-offerings and the guilt-offerings – these are the guilt-offerings: the guilt-offering for robbery; the guilt-offering for profane use of a sacred object; the guilt-offering [for violating] a betrothed maidservant; the guilt-offering of a Nazirite [who had become defiled by a corpse]; the guilt-offering of a leper [at his cleansing]; and the guilt-offering in case of doubt. All these were slaughtered on the north side, their blood was received in a sacred vessel on the north side, and required two sprinklings [at opposite corners of the altar], making four in all. [The meat of these offerings], prepared in any manner, was eaten within the [courtyard] curtains, by males of the priesthood, on that day and the following night, until midnight.

The thanksgiving-offering and the ram of a Nazirite were offerings of lesser holiness. They could be slaughtered anywhere in the Temple court, and their blood required two sprinklings [at opposite corners of the altar], making four in all. The meat of these offerings, prepared in any manner, was eaten anywhere within the city [Jerusalem], by anyone during that day and the following night until midnight. This also applied to the portion of these sacrifices [given to the priests], except that the priests' portion was only to be eaten by the priests, their wives, children and servants.

Peace-offerings were [also] of lesser holiness. They could be slaughtered anywhere in the Temple court, and their blood required two sprinklings [at opposite corners of the altar], making four in all. The meat of these offerings, prepared in any manner, was eaten anywhere within the city [Jerusalem], by anyone, for two days and one night. This also applied to the portion of these sacrifices [given to the priests], except that the priests' portion was only to be eaten by the priests, their wives, children and servants.

The firstborn and tithe of cattle and the Pesaḥ lamb were sacrifices of lesser holiness. They could be slaughtered anywhere in the Temple court, and their blood required only one sprinkling, which had to be done at the base of the altar. They differed in their consumption: the firstborn was eaten only by priests, while the tithe could be eaten by anyone. Both could be eaten anywhere within the city, prepared in any manner, during two days and one night. The Pesaḥ lamb had to be eaten that night until midnight. It could only be eaten by those who had been numbered for it, and eaten only roasted.

דְּרוֹמִית. שְׁיָרֵי הַדָּם הָיָה שׁוֹפֵךְ עַל יְסוֹד דְּרוֹמִי. וְנֶאֱכָלִין לִפְנִים מִן הַקְּלָעִים, לְזִכְרֵי כְהֻנָּה, בְּכָל מַאֲכָל, לְיוֹם וָלַיְלָה עַד חֲצוֹת.

הָעוֹלָה קֹדֶשׁ קָדָשִׁים. שְׁחִיטָתָהּ בַּצָּפוֹן, וְקִבּוּל דָּמָהּ בִּכְלִי שָׁרֵת בַּצָּפוֹן, וְדָמָהּ טָעוּן שְׁתֵּי מַתָּנוֹת שֶׁהֵן אַרְבַּע, וּטְעוּנָה הֶפְשֵׁט וְנִתּוּחַ, וְכָלִיל לָאִשִּׁים.

זִבְחֵי שַׁלְמֵי צִבּוּר וַאֲשָׁמוֹת. אֵלּוּ הֵן אֲשָׁמוֹת: אֲשַׁם גְּזֵלוֹת, אֲשַׁם מְעִילוֹת, אֲשַׁם שִׁפְחָה חֲרוּפָה, אֲשַׁם נָזִיר, אֲשַׁם מְצֹרָע, אָשָׁם תָּלוּי. שְׁחִיטָתָן בַּצָּפוֹן, וְקִבּוּל דָּמָן בִּכְלִי שָׁרֵת בַּצָּפוֹן, וְדָמָן טָעוּן שְׁתֵּי מַתָּנוֹת שֶׁהֵן אַרְבַּע. וְנֶאֱכָלִין לִפְנִים מִן הַקְּלָעִים, לְזִכְרֵי כְהֻנָּה, בְּכָל מַאֲכָל, לְיוֹם וָלַיְלָה עַד חֲצוֹת.

הַתּוֹדָה וְאֵיל נָזִיר קָדָשִׁים קַלִּים. שְׁחִיטָתָן בְּכָל מָקוֹם בָּעֲזָרָה, וְדָמָן טָעוּן שְׁתֵּי מַתָּנוֹת שֶׁהֵן אַרְבַּע, וְנֶאֱכָלִין בְּכָל הָעִיר, לְכָל אָדָם, בְּכָל מַאֲכָל, לְיוֹם וָלַיְלָה עַד חֲצוֹת. הַמּוּרָם מֵהֶם כַּיּוֹצֵא בָהֶם, אֶלָּא שֶׁהַמּוּרָם נֶאֱכָל לַכֹּהֲנִים, לִנְשֵׁיהֶם, וְלִבְנֵיהֶם וּלְעַבְדֵיהֶם.

שְׁלָמִים קָדָשִׁים קַלִּים. שְׁחִיטָתָן בְּכָל מָקוֹם בָּעֲזָרָה, וְדָמָן טָעוּן שְׁתֵּי מַתָּנוֹת שֶׁהֵן אַרְבַּע, וְנֶאֱכָלִין בְּכָל הָעִיר, לְכָל אָדָם, בְּכָל מַאֲכָל, לִשְׁנֵי יָמִים וְלַיְלָה אֶחָד. הַמּוּרָם מֵהֶם כַּיּוֹצֵא בָהֶם, אֶלָּא שֶׁהַמּוּרָם נֶאֱכָל לַכֹּהֲנִים, לִנְשֵׁיהֶם, וְלִבְנֵיהֶם וּלְעַבְדֵיהֶם.

הַבְּכוֹר וְהַמַּעֲשֵׂר וְהַפֶּסַח קָדָשִׁים קַלִּים. שְׁחִיטָתָן בְּכָל מָקוֹם בָּעֲזָרָה, וְדָמָן טָעוּן מַתָּנָה אֶחָת, וּבִלְבַד שֶׁיִּתֵּן כְּנֶגֶד הַיְסוֹד. שִׁנָּה בַאֲכִילָתָן, הַבְּכוֹר נֶאֱכָל לַכֹּהֲנִים וְהַמַּעֲשֵׂר לְכָל אָדָם, וְנֶאֱכָלִין בְּכָל הָעִיר, בְּכָל מַאֲכָל, לִשְׁנֵי יָמִים וְלַיְלָה אֶחָד. הַפֶּסַח אֵינוֹ נֶאֱכָל אֶלָּא בַלַּיְלָה, וְאֵינוֹ נֶאֱכָל אֶלָּא עַד חֲצוֹת, וְאֵינוֹ נֶאֱכָל אֶלָּא לִמְנוּיָיו, וְאֵינוֹ נֶאֱכָל אֶלָּא צָלִי.

THE INTERPRETIVE PRINCIPLES OF RABBI YISHMAEL

רַבִּי יִשְׁמָעֵאל Rabbi Yishmael says:
The Torah is expounded by thirteen principles:

1. An inference from a lenient law to a strict one, and vice versa.
2. An inference drawn from identical words in two passages.
3. A general principle derived from one text or two related texts.
4. A general law followed by specific examples [where the law applies exclusively to those examples].
5. A specific example followed by a general law [where the law applies to everything implied in the general statement].
6. A general law followed by specific examples and concluding with a general law: here you may infer only cases similar to the examples.
7. When a general statement requires clarification by a specific example, or a specific example requires clarification by a general statement [then rules 4 and 5 do not apply].
8. When a particular case, already included in the general statement, is expressly mentioned to teach something new, that special provision applies to all other cases included in the general statement.
9. When a particular case, though included in the general statement, is expressly mentioned with a provision similar to the general law, such a case is singled out to lessen the severity of the law, not to increase it.
10. When a particular case, though included in the general statement, is explicitly mentioned with a provision differing from the general law, it is singled out to lessen in some respects, and in others to increase, the severity of the law.
11. When a particular case, though included in the general statement, is explicitly mentioned with a new provision, the terms of the general statement no longer apply to it, unless Scripture indicates explicitly that they do apply.
12. A matter elucidated from its context, or from the following passage.
13. ▸ Also, when two passages [seem to] contradict each other, [they are to be elucidated by] a third passage that reconciles them.

May it be Your will, Lord our God and God of our ancestors, that the Temple be speedily rebuilt in our days, and grant us our share in Your Torah. And may we serve You there in reverence, as in the days of old and as in former years.

Torah is interpreted" (Maimonides, Laws of Torah Study 1:11). It was chosen because it appears at the beginning of the *Sifra*, the halakhic commentary to Leviticus, which is the source of most of the laws of offerings. It also reminds us of the indissoluble connection between the Written Law (the Mosaic books) and the Oral Law (Mishna, Midrash and Talmud). Rabbi Yishmael's principles show how the latter can be derived from the former.

ברייתא דרבי ישמעאל

רַבִּי יִשְׁמָעֵאל אוֹמֵר: בִּשְׁלֹשׁ עֶשְׂרֵה מִדּוֹת הַתּוֹרָה נִדְרֶשֶׁת

א מִקַּל וָחֹמֶר

ב וּמִגְּזֵרָה שָׁוָה

ג מִבִּנְיַן אָב מִכָּתוּב אֶחָד, וּמִבִּנְיַן אָב מִשְּׁנֵי כְתוּבִים

ד מִכְּלָל וּפְרָט

ה מִפְּרָט וּכְלָל

ו כְּלָל וּפְרָט וּכְלָל, אִי אַתָּה דָן אֶלָּא כְּעֵין הַפְּרָט

ז מִכְּלָל שֶׁהוּא צָרִיךְ לִפְרָט, וּמִפְּרָט שֶׁהוּא צָרִיךְ לִכְלָל

ח כָּל דָּבָר שֶׁהָיָה בִּכְלָל, וְיָצָא מִן הַכְּלָל לְלַמֵּד
לֹא לְלַמֵּד עַל עַצְמוֹ יָצָא, אֶלָּא לְלַמֵּד עַל הַכְּלָל כֻּלּוֹ יָצָא

ט כָּל דָּבָר שֶׁהָיָה בִּכְלָל, וְיָצָא לִטְעֹן טֹעַן אֶחָד שֶׁהוּא כְעִנְיָנוֹ
יָצָא לְהָקֵל וְלֹא לְהַחֲמִיר

י כָּל דָּבָר שֶׁהָיָה בִּכְלָל, וְיָצָא לִטְעֹן טֹעַן אַחֵר שֶׁלֹּא כְעִנְיָנוֹ
יָצָא לְהָקֵל וּלְהַחֲמִיר

יא כָּל דָּבָר שֶׁהָיָה בִּכְלָל, וְיָצָא לִדּוֹן בַּדָּבָר הֶחָדָשׁ
אִי אַתָּה יָכוֹל לְהַחֲזִירוֹ לִכְלָלוֹ
עַד שֶׁיַּחֲזִירֶנּוּ הַכָּתוּב לִכְלָלוֹ בְּפֵרוּשׁ

יב דָּבָר הַלָּמֵד מֵעִנְיָנוֹ, וְדָבָר הַלָּמֵד מִסּוֹפוֹ

◂ יג וְכֵן שְׁנֵי כְתוּבִים הַמַּכְחִישִׁים זֶה אֶת זֶה
עַד שֶׁיָּבוֹא הַכָּתוּב הַשְּׁלִישִׁי וְיַכְרִיעַ בֵּינֵיהֶם.

יְהִי רָצוֹן מִלְּפָנֶיךָ, יהוה אֱלֹהֵינוּ וֵאלֹהֵי אֲבוֹתֵינוּ, שֶׁיִּבָּנֶה בֵּית הַמִּקְדָּשׁ בִּמְהֵרָה בְיָמֵינוּ, וְתֵן חֶלְקֵנוּ בְּתוֹרָתֶךָ, וְשָׁם נַעֲבָדְךָ בְּיִרְאָה כִּימֵי עוֹלָם וּכְשָׁנִים קַדְמוֹנִיּוֹת.

THE INTERPRETIVE PRINCIPLES OF RABBI YISHMAEL

This passage is included as an item of Talmud, defined in its broadest sense as "deducing conclusions from premises, developing implications of statements, comparing dicta, and studying the hermeneutical principles by which the

THE RABBIS' KADDISH

The following prayer, said by mourners, requires the presence of a minyan. A transliteration can be found on page 1333.

Mourner: יִתְגַּדַּל Magnified and sanctified
may His great name be,
in the world He created by His will.
May He establish His kingdom in your lifetime
and in your days,
and in the lifetime of all the house of Israel,
swiftly and soon –
and say: Amen.

All: May His great name be blessed for ever and all time.

Mourner: Blessed and praised,
glorified and exalted,
raised and honored,
uplifted and lauded
be the name of the Holy One,
blessed be He,
beyond any blessing,
song, praise and consolation uttered in the world –
and say: Amen.

---

mark the end of the Amida and its associated meditations; (3) the Mourner's Kaddish; (4) The Rabbis' Kaddish, said after a passage from the Oral Law; (5) the Kaddish of Renewal, said only at the conclusion of a tractate of the Talmud, or by a child at the funeral of a parent.

The Rabbis' Kaddish is a prayer not only for the establishment of God's kingdom but also for the teachers of Torah and their disciples. It is characteristic of Judaism's value system that this is the first Kaddish we say each morning. Judaism is a faith whose passion is education, whose heroes are teachers, and whose citadels are schools and houses of study. To learn, to teach, to internalize God's will, to join our minds with the great sages and scholars of the past – this is a supreme expression of Judaism, and the one from which all else flows.

קדיש דרבנן

The following prayer, said by mourners, requires the presence of a מנין.
A transliteration can be found on page 1333.

אבל: יִתְגַּדַּל וְיִתְקַדַּשׁ שְׁמֵהּ רַבָּא (קהל: אָמֵן)
בְּעָלְמָא דִּי בְרָא כִרְעוּתֵהּ
וְיַמְלִיךְ מַלְכוּתֵהּ
בְּחַיֵּיכוֹן וּבְיוֹמֵיכוֹן וּבְחַיֵּי דְכָל בֵּית יִשְׂרָאֵל
בַּעֲגָלָא וּבִזְמַן קָרִיב
וְאִמְרוּ אָמֵן. (קהל: אָמֵן)

קהל ואבל: יְהֵא שְׁמֵהּ רַבָּא מְבָרַךְ לְעָלַם וּלְעָלְמֵי עָלְמַיָּא.

אבל: יִתְבָּרַךְ וְיִשְׁתַּבַּח וְיִתְפָּאַר וְיִתְרוֹמַם וְיִתְנַשֵּׂא
וְיִתְהַדָּר וְיִתְעַלֶּה וְיִתְהַלָּל
שְׁמֵהּ דְּקֻדְשָׁא בְּרִיךְ הוּא (קהל: בְּרִיךְ הוּא)
לְעֵלָּא מִן כָּל בִּרְכָתָא
/בעשרת ימי תשובה: לְעֵלָּא לְעֵלָּא מִכָּל בִּרְכָתָא/
וְשִׁירָתָא, תֻּשְׁבְּחָתָא וְנֶחֱמָתָא, דַּאֲמִירָן בְּעָלְמָא
וְאִמְרוּ אָמֵן. (קהל: אָמֵן)

THE RABBIS' KADDISH

The Kaddish, one of the most important of all prayers, had its origins not in the synagogue but in the house of study. It grew out of a custom, still widely practiced, of ending every discourse or sermon with the hope that we may speedily see the coming of the messianic age, when the sovereignty of God will be recognized by all the dwellers on earth. It is written mainly in Aramaic, the language most widely spoken by Jews in the first centuries of the Common Era.

It has come to have five forms: (1) Half Kaddish, recited to mark the beginning or end of a section of the prayers; (2) Full Kaddish (*Titkabal*), to

To Israel, to the teachers,
their disciples and their disciples' disciples,
and to all who engage in the study of Torah,
in this (*in Israel add:* holy) place or elsewhere,
may there come to them and you great peace,
grace, kindness and compassion,
long life, ample sustenance and deliverance,
from their Father in Heaven –
and say: Amen.

May there be great peace from heaven,
and (good) life for us and all Israel –
and say: Amen.

Bow, take three steps back, as if taking leave of the Divine Presence, then bow, first left, then right, then center, while saying:

May He who makes peace in His high places,
in His compassion make peace for us and all Israel –
and say: Amen.

On Shabbat, Yom Tov, Hoshana Raba, and (in Israel and many communities outside Israel) on Yom HaAtzma'ut and Yom Yerushalayim, continue Shaḥarit on page 398.

A PSALM BEFORE VERSES OF PRAISE

מִזְמוֹר שִׁיר A psalm of David. A song for the dedication of the House. *Ps. 30*
I will exalt You, Lord, for You have lifted me up, and not let my enemies rejoice over me. Lord, my God, I cried to You for help and You healed me. Lord, You lifted my soul from the grave; You spared me from going down to the pit. Sing to the Lord, you His devoted ones, and give thanks to His holy name. For His anger is for a moment, but His favor for a lifetime. At night there may be weeping, but in the morning there is joy. When I felt secure, I said, "I shall never be shaken." Lord, when You favored me, You made me stand firm as a mountain, but when You hid Your face, I was terrified. To You, Lord, I called; I pleaded with my Lord: "What

עַל יִשְׂרָאֵל וְעַל רַבָּנָן
וְעַל תַּלְמִידֵיהוֹן וְעַל כָּל תַּלְמִידֵי תַלְמִידֵיהוֹן
וְעַל כָּל מָאן דְּעָסְקִין בְּאוֹרַיְתָא
דִּי בְּאַתְרָא (בארץ ישראל: קַדִּישָׁא) הָדֵין, וְדִי בְּכָל אֲתַר וַאֲתַר
יְהֵא לְהוֹן וּלְכוֹן שְׁלָמָא רַבָּא
חִנָּא וְחִסְדָּא, וְרַחֲמֵי, וְחַיֵּי אֲרִיכֵי, וּמְזוֹנֵי רְוִיחֵי
וּפֻרְקָנָא מִן קֳדָם אֲבוּהוֹן דִּי בִשְׁמַיָּא, וְאִמְרוּ אָמֵן. (קהל: אָמֵן)
יְהֵא שְׁלָמָא רַבָּא מִן שְׁמַיָּא
וְחַיִּים (טוֹבִים) עָלֵינוּ וְעַל כָּל יִשְׂרָאֵל, וְאִמְרוּ אָמֵן. (קהל: אָמֵן)

Bow, take three steps back, as if taking leave of the Divine Presence, then bow, first left, then right, then center, while saying:

עֹשֶׂה שָׁלוֹם/ בעשרת ימי תשובה: הַשָּׁלוֹם/ בִּמְרוֹמָיו
הוּא יַעֲשֶׂה בְרַחֲמָיו שָׁלוֹם
עָלֵינוּ וְעַל כָּל יִשְׂרָאֵל, וְאִמְרוּ אָמֵן. (קהל: אָמֵן)

On שבת, יום טוב, הושענא רבה, *and (in* ארץ ישראל *and many communities in* חוץ לארץ) יום ירושלים *and* יום העצמאות *on* שחרית *continue* *on page 399.*

מזמור לפני פסוקי דזמרה

תהלים ל מִזְמוֹר שִׁיר־חֲנֻכַּת הַבַּיִת לְדָוִד: אֲרוֹמִמְךָ יהוה כִּי דִלִּיתָנִי, וְלֹא־
שִׂמַּחְתָּ אֹיְבַי לִי: יהוה אֱלֹהָי, שִׁוַּעְתִּי אֵלֶיךָ וַתִּרְפָּאֵנִי: יהוה,
הֶעֱלִיתָ מִן־שְׁאוֹל נַפְשִׁי, חִיִּיתַנִי מִיָּרְדִי־בוֹר: זַמְּרוּ לַיהוה חֲסִידָיו,
וְהוֹדוּ לְזֵכֶר קָדְשׁוֹ: כִּי רֶגַע בְּאַפּוֹ, חַיִּים בִּרְצוֹנוֹ, בָּעֶרֶב יָלִין בֶּכִי
וְלַבֹּקֶר רִנָּה: וַאֲנִי אָמַרְתִּי בְשַׁלְוִי, בַּל־אֶמּוֹט לְעוֹלָם: יהוה, בִּרְצוֹנְךָ
הֶעֱמַדְתָּה לְהַרְרִי עֹז, הִסְתַּרְתָּ פָנֶיךָ הָיִיתִי נִבְהָל: אֵלֶיךָ יהוה
אֶקְרָא, וְאֶל־אֲדֹנָי אֶתְחַנָּן: מַה־בֶּצַע בְּדָמִי, בְּרִדְתִּי אֶל שָׁחַת,

gain would there be if I died and went down to the grave? Can dust thank You? Can it declare Your truth? Hear, LORD, and be gracious to me; LORD, be my help." ▸ You have turned my sorrow into dancing. You have removed my sackcloth and clothed me with joy, so that my soul may sing to You and not be silent. LORD my God, for ever will I thank You.

MOURNER'S KADDISH

The following prayer, said by mourners, requires the presence of a minyan.
A transliteration can be found on page 1334.

Mourner: יִתְגַּדַּל Magnified and sanctified
may His great name be,
in the world He created by His will.
May He establish His kingdom
in your lifetime and in your days,
and in the lifetime of all the house of Israel,
swiftly and soon – and say: Amen.

All: May His great name be blessed for ever and all time.

Mourner: Blessed and praised, glorified and exalted,
raised and honored, uplifted and lauded
be the name of the Holy One,
blessed be He,
beyond any blessing,
song, praise and consolation
uttered in the world – and say: Amen.

May there be great peace from heaven,
and life for us and all Israel – and say: Amen.

Bow, take three steps back, as if taking leave of the Divine Presence,
then bow, first left, then right, then center, while saying:

May He who makes peace in His high places,
make peace for us and all Israel –
and say: Amen.

הֲיוֹדְךָ עָפָר, הֲיַגִּיד אֲמִתֶּךָ: שְׁמַע־יהוה וְחָנֵּנִי, יהוה הֱיֵה־עֹזֵר לִי:
› הָפַכְתָּ מִסְפְּדִי לְמָחוֹל לִי, פִּתַּחְתָּ שַׂקִּי, וַתְּאַזְּרֵנִי שִׂמְחָה: לְמַעַן יְזַמֶּרְךָ כָבוֹד וְלֹא יִדֹּם, יהוה אֱלֹהַי, לְעוֹלָם אוֹדֶךָּ:

קדיש יתום

The following prayer, said by mourners, requires the presence of a מנין.
A transliteration can be found on page 1334.

אבל: יִתְגַּדַּל וְיִתְקַדַּשׁ שְׁמֵהּ רַבָּא (קהל: אָמֵן)
בְּעָלְמָא דִּי בְרָא כִרְעוּתֵהּ
וְיַמְלִיךְ מַלְכוּתֵהּ
בְּחַיֵּיכוֹן וּבְיוֹמֵיכוֹן וּבְחַיֵּי דְכָל בֵּית יִשְׂרָאֵל
בַּעֲגָלָא וּבִזְמַן קָרִיב, וְאִמְרוּ אָמֵן. (קהל: אָמֵן)

קהל ואבל: יְהֵא שְׁמֵהּ רַבָּא מְבָרַךְ לְעָלַם וּלְעָלְמֵי עָלְמַיָּא.

אבל: יִתְבָּרַךְ וְיִשְׁתַּבַּח וְיִתְפָּאַר
וְיִתְרוֹמַם וְיִתְנַשֵּׂא וְיִתְהַדָּר וְיִתְעַלֶּה וְיִתְהַלָּל
שְׁמֵהּ דְּקֻדְשָׁא בְּרִיךְ הוּא (קהל: בְּרִיךְ הוּא)
לְעֵלָּא מִן כָּל בִּרְכָתָא / בעשרת ימי תשובה: לְעֵלָּא לְעֵלָּא מִכָּל בִּרְכָתָא/
וְשִׁירָתָא, תֻּשְׁבְּחָתָא וְנֶחֱמָתָא
דַּאֲמִירָן בְּעָלְמָא, וְאִמְרוּ אָמֵן. (קהל: אָמֵן)

יְהֵא שְׁלָמָא רַבָּא מִן שְׁמַיָּא
וְחַיִּים, עָלֵינוּ וְעַל כָּל יִשְׂרָאֵל, וְאִמְרוּ אָמֵן. (קהל: אָמֵן)

Bow, take three steps back, as if taking leave of the Divine Presence, then bow, first left, then right, then center, while saying:

עֹשֶׂה שָׁלוֹם/ בעשרת ימי תשובה: הַשָּׁלוֹם/ בִּמְרוֹמָיו
הוּא יַעֲשֶׂה שָׁלוֹם
עָלֵינוּ וְעַל כָּל יִשְׂרָאֵל, וְאִמְרוּ אָמֵן. (קהל: אָמֵן)

PESUKEI DEZIMRA

The introductory blessing to the Pesukei DeZimra (Verses of Praise) is said standing, while holding the two front tzitziot of the tallit. They are kissed and released at the end of the blessing at "songs of praise" (on next page). From the beginning of this prayer to the end of the Amida, conversation is forbidden. See table on pages 1329–1331 for which congregational responses are permitted.

Some say:

I hereby prepare my mouth to thank, praise and laud my Creator, for the sake of the unification of the Holy One, blessed be He, and His Divine Presence, through that which is hidden and concealed, in the name of all Israel.

BLESSED IS HE WHO SPOKE

and the world came into being, blessed is He.
Blessed is He who creates the universe.
Blessed is He who speaks and acts.
Blessed is He who decrees and fulfills.
Blessed is He who shows compassion to the earth.
Blessed is He who shows compassion to all creatures.
Blessed is He who gives a good reward
to those who fear Him.
Blessed is He who lives for ever and exists to eternity.
Blessed is He who redeems and saves.
Blessed is His name.

---

structed in three movements, whose themes are: (1) *Creation:* God as He is in nature; (2) *Revelation:* God as He is in Torah and prayer; and (3) *Redemption:* God as He is in history and our lives. The theme of the Verses of Praise is Creation – God as Architect and Maker of a universe of splendor and diversity, whose orderliness testifies to the single creative will that underlies all that exists. The psalms tell this story not in scientific prose but majestic poetry, not *proving* but *proclaiming* the One at the heart of all.

The core elements of *Pesukei DeZimra* are: (1) Psalm 145 (*Ashrei*), a prayer to which the sages attached particular significance, specifying that it should be said three times daily; and (2) Psalms 146–150, which form the culmination and crescendo of the book of Psalms as a whole. These six psalms

פסוקי דזמרה

The introductory blessing to the פסוקי דזמרה *is said standing, while holding the two front* ציציות *of the* טלית*. They are kissed and released at the end of the blessing at* בַּתִּשְׁבָּחוֹת *(on next page). From the beginning of this prayer to the end of the* עמידה*, conversation is forbidden. See table on pages 1329–1331 for which congregational responses are permitted.*

Some say:

הֲרֵינִי מְזַמֵּן אֶת פִּי לְהוֹדוֹת וּלְהַלֵּל וּלְשַׁבֵּחַ אֶת בּוֹרְאִי, לְשֵׁם יִחוּד קֻדְשָׁא בְּרִיךְ הוּא וּשְׁכִינְתֵּהּ עַל יְדֵי הַהוּא טָמִיר וְנֶעְלָם בְּשֵׁם כָּל יִשְׂרָאֵל.

בָּרוּךְ שֶׁאָמַר וְהָיָה הָעוֹלָם, בָּרוּךְ הוּא.

בָּרוּךְ עוֹשֶׂה בְרֵאשִׁית

בָּרוּךְ אוֹמֵר וְעוֹשֶׂה

בָּרוּךְ גּוֹזֵר וּמְקַיֵּם

בָּרוּךְ מְרַחֵם עַל הָאָרֶץ

בָּרוּךְ מְרַחֵם עַל הַבְּרִיּוֹת

בָּרוּךְ מְשַׁלֵּם שָׂכָר טוֹב לִירֵאָיו

בָּרוּךְ חַי לָעַד וְקַיָּם לָנֶצַח

בָּרוּךְ פּוֹדֶה וּמַצִּיל

בָּרוּךְ שְׁמוֹ

PESUKEI DEZIMRA / VERSES OF PRAISE

"A person should first recount the praise of the Holy One, blessed be He, and then pray" (*Berakhot* 32b), hence the passages that follow, known as the "Verses of Praise." The morning service from this point until the end is con-

Blessed are You, LORD our God,
King of the Universe,
God, compassionate Father,
extolled by the mouth of His people,
praised and glorified by the tongue of His devoted ones and those who serve Him.
With the songs of Your servant David
we will praise You, O LORD our God.
With praises and psalms
we will magnify and praise You, glorify You,
speak Your name and proclaim Your kingship,
our King, our God, ▸ the only One, Giver of life to the worlds,
the King whose great name is praised
and glorified to all eternity.
Blessed are You, LORD,
the King extolled with songs of praise.

הוֹדוּ לַיהוה Thank the LORD, call on His name, make His acts known among the peoples. Sing to Him, make music to Him, tell of all His wonders. Glory in His holy name; let the hearts of those who seek the LORD rejoice. Search out the LORD and His strength; seek His presence at all times. Remember the wonders He has done, *1 Chr. 16*

Blessed are You: The second half of the blessing is a prelude to the biblical verses that follow, mainly from the book of Psalms ("With the songs of Your servant David we will exalt You") but also from the books of Chronicles and Nehemiah ("extolled by the mouth of His people"). To emphasize the significance of this declaration, we recite it standing and, at the end, kiss the two front fringes of the tallit.

הוֹדוּ לַיהוה *Thank the LORD:* A psalm of thanksgiving composed by King David to celebrate the moment when the Ark of the Covenant was brought to Jerusalem. In many communities, the Leader says the verse, "For all the gods," aloud to emphasize the need to make a pause between the word "idols" and the name of God.

בָּרוּךְ אַתָּה יהוה אֱלֹהֵינוּ מֶלֶךְ הָעוֹלָם
הָאֵל הָאָב הָרַחֲמָן הַמְהֻלָּל בְּפִי עַמּוֹ
מְשֻׁבָּח וּמְפֹאָר בִּלְשׁוֹן חֲסִידָיו וַעֲבָדָיו
וּבְשִׁירֵי דָוִד עַבְדֶּךָ
נְהַלֶּלְךָ יהוה אֱלֹהֵינוּ.
בִּשְׁבָחוֹת וּבִזְמִירוֹת
נְגַדֶּלְךָ וּנְשַׁבֵּחֲךָ וּנְפָאֶרְךָ
וְנַזְכִּיר שִׁמְךָ וְנַמְלִיכְךָ
מַלְכֵּנוּ אֱלֹהֵינוּ, ◂ יָחִיד חֵי הָעוֹלָמִים
מֶלֶךְ, מְשֻׁבָּח וּמְפֹאָר עֲדֵי עַד שְׁמוֹ הַגָּדוֹל
בָּרוּךְ אַתָּה יהוה, מֶלֶךְ מְהֻלָּל בַּתִּשְׁבָּחוֹת.

דברי הימים א, טז
הוֹדוּ לַיהוה קִרְאוּ בִשְׁמוֹ, הוֹדִיעוּ בָעַמִּים עֲלִילֹתָיו: שִׁירוּ לוֹ, זַמְּרוּ־לוֹ, שִׂיחוּ בְּכָל־נִפְלְאוֹתָיו: הִתְהַלְלוּ בְּשֵׁם קָדְשׁוֹ, יִשְׂמַח

---

correspond to the six days of creation; others are added on Shabbat and festivals. Around this inner core other passages have been woven: some from other biblical books and others from selected verses in the book of Psalms. The section begins and ends with a paragraph of blessings: "Blessed is He who spoke" (*Barukh SheAmar*) at the beginning, and "May Your name be praised for ever" (*Yishtabah*) at the end.

בָּרוּךְ שֶׁאָמַר *Blessed is He who spoke (previous page)*: An introductory blessing to the Verses of Praise, in two parts. The first is a ten-part litany of praise to God as Creator, each phrase introduced with the word "Blessed" (the second phrase, *barukh hu*, "blessed is He," is not a separate verse but was originally a congregational response). The number ten corresponds to the ten times the word *Vayomer*, "And He said," appears in the story of creation in Genesis 1, hence the rabbinic saying that "With ten utterances the world was created."

His miracles, and the judgments He pronounced. Descendants of Yisrael His servant, sons of Jacob His chosen ones: He is the LORD our God. His judgments are throughout the earth. Remember His covenant for ever, the word He commanded for a thousand generations. He made it with Abraham, vowed it to Isaac, and confirmed it to Jacob as a statute and to Israel as an everlasting covenant, saying, "To you I will give the land of Canaan as your allotted heritage." You were then small in number, few, strangers there, wandering from nation to nation, from one kingdom to another, but He let no man oppress them, and for their sake He rebuked kings: "Do not touch My anointed ones, and do My prophets no harm." Sing to the LORD, all the earth; proclaim His salvation daily. Declare His glory among the nations, His marvels among all the peoples. For great is the LORD and greatly to be praised; He is awesome beyond all heavenly powers. ▸ For all the gods of the peoples are mere idols; it was the LORD who made the heavens.

Before Him are majesty and splendor; there is strength and beauty in His holy place. Render to the LORD, families of the peoples, render to the LORD honor and might. Render to the LORD the glory due to His name; bring an offering and come before Him; bow down to the LORD in the splendor of holiness. Tremble before Him, all the earth; the world stands firm, it will not be shaken. Let the heavens rejoice and the earth be glad; let them declare among the nations, "The LORD is King." Let the sea roar, and all that is in it; let the fields be jubilant, and all they contain. Then the trees of the forest will sing for joy before the LORD, for He is coming to judge the earth. Thank the LORD for He is good; His loving-kindness is for ever. Say: "Save us, God of our salvation; gather us and rescue us from the nations, to acknowledge Your holy name and glory in Your praise. Blessed is the LORD, God of Israel, from this world to eternity." And let all the people say "Amen" and "Praise the LORD."

לֵב מְבַקְשֵׁי יהוה: דִּרְשׁוּ יהוה וְעֻזּוֹ, בַּקְּשׁוּ פָנָיו תָּמִיד: זִכְרוּ
נִפְלְאֹתָיו אֲשֶׁר עָשָׂה, מֹפְתָיו וּמִשְׁפְּטֵי־פִיהוּ: זֶרַע יִשְׂרָאֵל עַבְדּוֹ,
בְּנֵי יַעֲקֹב בְּחִירָיו: הוּא יהוה אֱלֹהֵינוּ בְּכָל־הָאָרֶץ מִשְׁפָּטָיו:
זִכְרוּ לְעוֹלָם בְּרִיתוֹ, דָּבָר צִוָּה לְאֶלֶף דּוֹר: אֲשֶׁר כָּרַת אֶת־
אַבְרָהָם, וּשְׁבוּעָתוֹ לְיִצְחָק: וַיַּעֲמִידֶהָ לְיַעֲקֹב לְחֹק, לְיִשְׂרָאֵל
בְּרִית עוֹלָם: לֵאמֹר, לְךָ אֶתֵּן אֶרֶץ־כְּנָעַן, חֶבֶל נַחֲלַתְכֶם:
בִּהְיוֹתְכֶם מְתֵי מִסְפָּר, כִּמְעַט וְגָרִים בָּהּ: וַיִּתְהַלְּכוּ מִגּוֹי אֶל־
גּוֹי, וּמִמַּמְלָכָה אֶל־עַם אַחֵר: לֹא־הִנִּיחַ לְאִישׁ לְעָשְׁקָם, וַיּוֹכַח
עֲלֵיהֶם מְלָכִים: אַל־תִּגְּעוּ בִּמְשִׁיחָי, וּבִנְבִיאַי אַל־תָּרֵעוּ: שִׁירוּ
לַיהוה כָּל־הָאָרֶץ, בַּשְּׂרוּ מִיּוֹם־אֶל־יוֹם יְשׁוּעָתוֹ: סַפְּרוּ בַגּוֹיִם
אֶת־כְּבוֹדוֹ, בְּכָל־הָעַמִּים נִפְלְאֹתָיו: כִּי גָדוֹל יהוה וּמְהֻלָּל מְאֹד,
וְנוֹרָא הוּא עַל־כָּל־אֱלֹהִים: ‹ כִּי כָּל־אֱלֹהֵי הָעַמִּים אֱלִילִים,
וַיהוה שָׁמַיִם עָשָׂה:

הוֹד וְהָדָר לְפָנָיו, עֹז וְחֶדְוָה בִּמְקֹמוֹ: הָבוּ לַיהוה מִשְׁפְּחוֹת
עַמִּים, הָבוּ לַיהוה כָּבוֹד וָעֹז: הָבוּ לַיהוה כְּבוֹד שְׁמוֹ, שְׂאוּ מִנְחָה
וּבֹאוּ לְפָנָיו, הִשְׁתַּחֲווּ לַיהוה בְּהַדְרַת־קֹדֶשׁ: חִילוּ מִלְּפָנָיו כָּל־
הָאָרֶץ, אַף־תִּכּוֹן תֵּבֵל בַּל־תִּמּוֹט: יִשְׂמְחוּ הַשָּׁמַיִם וְתָגֵל הָאָרֶץ,
וְיֹאמְרוּ בַגּוֹיִם יהוה מָלָךְ: יִרְעַם הַיָּם וּמְלוֹאוֹ, יַעֲלֹץ הַשָּׂדֶה
וְכָל־אֲשֶׁר־בּוֹ: אָז יְרַנְּנוּ עֲצֵי הַיָּעַר, מִלִּפְנֵי יהוה, כִּי־בָא לִשְׁפּוֹט
אֶת־הָאָרֶץ: הוֹדוּ לַיהוה כִּי טוֹב, כִּי לְעוֹלָם חַסְדּוֹ: וְאִמְרוּ,
הוֹשִׁיעֵנוּ אֱלֹהֵי יִשְׁעֵנוּ, וְקַבְּצֵנוּ וְהַצִּילֵנוּ מִן־הַגּוֹיִם, לְהֹדוֹת
לְשֵׁם קָדְשֶׁךָ, לְהִשְׁתַּבֵּחַ בִּתְהִלָּתֶךָ: בָּרוּךְ יהוה אֱלֹהֵי יִשְׂרָאֵל
מִן־הָעוֹלָם וְעַד־הָעֹלָם, וַיֹּאמְרוּ כָל־הָעָם אָמֵן, וְהַלֵּל לַיהוה:

▸ Exalt the LORD our God and bow before His footstool: He is Ps. 99
holy. Exalt the LORD our God and bow at His holy mountain; for
holy is the LORD our God.

He is compassionate. He forgives iniquity and does not destroy. Ps. 78
Repeatedly He suppresses His anger, not rousing His full wrath.
You, LORD: do not withhold Your compassion from me. May Your Ps. 40
loving-kindness and truth always guard me. Remember, LORD, Ps. 25
Your acts of compassion and love, for they have existed for ever.
Ascribe power to God, whose majesty is over Israel and whose Ps. 68
might is in the skies. You are awesome, God, in Your holy places.
It is the God of Israel who gives might and strength to the people,
may God be blessed. God of retribution, LORD, God of retribu- Ps. 94
tion, appear. Arise, Judge of the earth, to repay the arrogant their
just deserts. Salvation belongs to the LORD; may Your blessing rest Ps. 3
upon Your people, Selah! ▸ The LORD of hosts is with us, the God Ps. 46
of Jacob is our stronghold, Selah! LORD of hosts, happy is the one Ps. 84
who trusts in You. LORD, save! May the King answer us on the day Ps. 20
we call.

Save Your people and bless Your heritage; tend them and carry Ps. 28
them for ever. Our soul longs for the LORD; He is our Help and Ps. 33
Shield. For in Him our hearts rejoice, for in His holy name we have
trusted. May Your loving-kindness, LORD, be upon us, as we have
put our hope in You. Show us, LORD, Your loving-kindness and Ps. 85
grant us Your salvation. Arise, help us and redeem us for the sake Ps. 44
of Your love. I am the LORD your God who brought you up from Ps. 81
the land of Egypt: open your mouth wide and I will fill it. Happy Ps. 144
is the people for whom this is so; happy is the people whose God
is the LORD. ▸ As for me, I trust in Your loving-kindness; my heart Ps. 13
rejoices in Your salvation. I will sing to the LORD for He has been
good to me.

---

of King David to today. We may no longer have the Ark, but we still have the covenant.

› רוֹמְמוּ יהוה אֱלֹהֵינוּ וְהִשְׁתַּחֲווּ לַהֲדֹם רַגְלָיו, קָדוֹשׁ הוּא: תהלים צט
רוֹמְמוּ יהוה אֱלֹהֵינוּ וְהִשְׁתַּחֲווּ לְהַר קָדְשׁוֹ, כִּי־קָדוֹשׁ יהוה
אֱלֹהֵינוּ:

וְהוּא רַחוּם, יְכַפֵּר עָוֹן וְלֹא־יַשְׁחִית, וְהִרְבָּה לְהָשִׁיב אַפּוֹ, תהלים עח
וְלֹא־יָעִיר כָּל־חֲמָתוֹ: אַתָּה יהוה לֹא־תִכְלָא רַחֲמֶיךָ מִמֶּנִּי, חַסְדְּךָ תהלים מ
וַאֲמִתְּךָ תָּמִיד יִצְּרוּנִי: זְכֹר־רַחֲמֶיךָ יהוה וַחֲסָדֶיךָ, כִּי מֵעוֹלָם תהלים כה
הֵמָּה: תְּנוּ עֹז לֵאלֹהִים, עַל־יִשְׂרָאֵל גַּאֲוָתוֹ, וְעֻזּוֹ בַּשְּׁחָקִים: תהלים סח
נוֹרָא אֱלֹהִים מִמִּקְדָּשֶׁיךָ, אֵל יִשְׂרָאֵל הוּא נֹתֵן עֹז וְתַעֲצֻמוֹת
לָעָם, בָּרוּךְ אֱלֹהִים: אֵל־נְקָמוֹת יהוה, אֵל נְקָמוֹת הוֹפִיעַ: תהלים צד
הִנָּשֵׂא שֹׁפֵט הָאָרֶץ, הָשֵׁב גְּמוּל עַל־גֵּאִים: לַיהוה הַיְשׁוּעָה, תהלים ג
עַל־עַמְּךָ בִרְכָתֶךָ סֶּלָה: › יהוה צְבָאוֹת עִמָּנוּ, מִשְׂגָּב לָנוּ אֱלֹהֵי תהלים מו
יַעֲקֹב סֶלָה: יהוה צְבָאוֹת, אַשְׁרֵי אָדָם בֹּטֵחַ בָּךְ: יהוה הוֹשִׁיעָה, תהלים פד תהלים כ
הַמֶּלֶךְ יַעֲנֵנוּ בְיוֹם־קָרְאֵנוּ:

הוֹשִׁיעָה אֶת־עַמֶּךָ, וּבָרֵךְ אֶת־נַחֲלָתֶךָ, וּרְעֵם וְנַשְּׂאֵם עַד־ תהלים כח
הָעוֹלָם: נַפְשֵׁנוּ חִכְּתָה לַיהוה, עֶזְרֵנוּ וּמָגִנֵּנוּ הוּא: כִּי־בוֹ יִשְׂמַח תהלים לג
לִבֵּנוּ, כִּי בְשֵׁם קָדְשׁוֹ בָטָחְנוּ: יְהִי־חַסְדְּךָ יהוה עָלֵינוּ, כַּאֲשֶׁר
יִחַלְנוּ לָךְ: הַרְאֵנוּ יהוה חַסְדֶּךָ, וְיֶשְׁעֲךָ תִּתֶּן־לָנוּ: קוּמָה עֶזְרָתָה תהלים פה תהלים מד
לָּנוּ, וּפְדֵנוּ לְמַעַן חַסְדֶּךָ: אָנֹכִי יהוה אֱלֹהֶיךָ הַמַּעַלְךָ מֵאֶרֶץ תהלים פא
מִצְרָיִם, הַרְחֶב־פִּיךָ וַאֲמַלְאֵהוּ: אַשְׁרֵי הָעָם שֶׁכָּכָה לּוֹ, אַשְׁרֵי תהלים קמד
הָעָם שֶׁיהוה אֱלֹהָיו: › וַאֲנִי בְּחַסְדְּךָ בָטַחְתִּי, יָגֵל לִבִּי בִּישׁוּעָתֶךָ, תהלים יג
אָשִׁירָה לַיהוה, כִּי גָמַל עָלָי:

רוֹמְמוּ *Exalt:* These paragraphs (until כִּי גָמַל עָלָי, "for He has been good to me") are a selection of verses from the book of Psalms on the theme of hope and trust in God. It forms a moving transition from then to now, from the days

The following psalm recalls the thanksgiving-offering in Temple times.
It is not said on Erev Pesah, on Hol HaMo'ed Pesah, or Erev Yom Kippur
since no thanksgiving-offerings were brought on these days.
To emphasize its sacrificial nature, the custom is to say it standing.

מִזְמוֹר A psalm of thanksgiving. Shout joyously to the LORD, all the earth. Serve the LORD with joy. Come before Him with jubilation. Know that the LORD is God. He made us and we are His. We are His people and the flock He tends. Enter His gates with thanksgiving, His courts with praise. Thank Him and bless His name. ▸ For the LORD is good, His loving-kindness is everlasting, and His faithfulness is for every generation. *Ps. 100*

יְהִי כְבוֹד May the LORD's glory be for ever; may the LORD rejoice in His *Ps. 104*
works. May the LORD's name be blessed, now and for ever. From the *Ps. 113*
rising of the sun to its setting, may the LORD's name be praised. The
LORD is high above all nations; His glory is above the heavens. LORD, *Ps. 135*
Your name is for ever. Your renown, LORD, is for all generations. The *Ps. 103*
LORD has established His throne in heaven; His kingdom rules all. Let *1 Chr. 16*
the heavens rejoice and the earth be glad. Let them say among the
nations, "The LORD is King." The LORD is King, the LORD was King,
the LORD will be King for ever and all time. The LORD is King for ever *Ps. 10*
and all time; nations will perish from His land. The LORD foils the plans *Ps. 33*
of nations; He frustrates the intentions of peoples. Many are the inten- *Prov. 19*
tions in a person's mind, but the LORD's plan prevails. The LORD's plan *Ps. 33*
shall stand for ever, His mind's intent for all generations. For He spoke
and it was; He commanded and it stood firm. For the LORD has chosen *Ps. 132*
Zion; He desired it for His dwelling. For the LORD has chosen Jacob as *Ps. 135*
His own, Israel as His special treasure. For the LORD will not abandon *Ps. 94*
His people; nor will He forsake His heritage. ▸ He is compassionate. He *Ps. 78*
forgives iniquity and does not destroy. Repeatedly He suppresses His
anger, not rousing His full wrath. LORD, save! May the King answer us *Ps. 20*
on the day we call.

---

childbirth or danger) in place of the sacrifice. The psalm first appeared as part of the daily service in Yemenite and French prayer books of the Middle Ages. Its presence here is to emphasize the mood of thankfulness that dominates this section of the prayers.

The following psalm recalls the קרבן תודה *in Temple times. It is not said on* ערב פסח, חול המועד פסח *or* ערב יום כיפור*, since no* קורבנות תודה *were brought on these days. To emphasize its sacrificial nature, the custom is to say it standing.*

מִזְמוֹר לְתוֹדָה, הָרִיעוּ לַיהוה כָּל־הָאָרֶץ: עִבְדוּ אֶת־יהוה תהלים ק
בְּשִׂמְחָה, בֹּאוּ לְפָנָיו בִּרְנָנָה: דְּעוּ כִּי־יהוה הוּא אֱלֹהִים,
הוּא עָשָׂנוּ וְלוֹ אֲנַחְנוּ, עַמּוֹ וְצֹאן מַרְעִיתוֹ: בֹּאוּ שְׁעָרָיו
בְּתוֹדָה, חֲצֵרֹתָיו בִּתְהִלָּה, הוֹדוּ לוֹ, בָּרְכוּ שְׁמוֹ: ‹ כִּי־טוֹב
יהוה, לְעוֹלָם חַסְדּוֹ, וְעַד־דֹּר וָדֹר אֱמוּנָתוֹ:

יְהִי כְבוֹד יהוה לְעוֹלָם, יִשְׂמַח יהוה בְּמַעֲשָׂיו: יְהִי שֵׁם יהוה מְבֹרָךְ, תהלים קד / תהלים קיג
מֵעַתָּה וְעַד־עוֹלָם: מִמִּזְרַח־שֶׁמֶשׁ עַד־מְבוֹאוֹ, מְהֻלָּל שֵׁם יהוה:
רָם עַל־כָּל־גּוֹיִם יהוה, עַל הַשָּׁמַיִם כְּבוֹדוֹ: יהוה שִׁמְךָ לְעוֹלָם, תהלים קלה
יהוה זִכְרְךָ לְדֹר־וָדֹר: יהוה בַּשָּׁמַיִם הֵכִין כִּסְאוֹ, וּמַלְכוּתוֹ בַּכֹּל תהלים קג
מָשָׁלָה: יִשְׂמְחוּ הַשָּׁמַיִם וְתָגֵל הָאָרֶץ, וְיֹאמְרוּ בַגּוֹיִם יהוה מָלָךְ: דברי הימים א׳ טז
יהוה מֶלֶךְ, יהוה מָלָךְ, יהוה יִמְלֹךְ לְעוֹלָם וָעֶד. יהוה מֶלֶךְ עוֹלָם תהלים י
וָעֶד, אָבְדוּ גוֹיִם מֵאַרְצוֹ: יהוה הֵפִיר עֲצַת־גּוֹיִם, הֵנִיא מַחְשְׁבוֹת תהלים לג
עַמִּים: רַבּוֹת מַחֲשָׁבוֹת בְּלֶב־אִישׁ, וַעֲצַת יהוה הִיא תָקוּם: עֲצַת משלי יט / תהלים לג
יהוה לְעוֹלָם תַּעֲמֹד, מַחְשְׁבוֹת לִבּוֹ לְדֹר וָדֹר: כִּי הוּא אָמַר וַיֶּהִי,
הוּא־צִוָּה וַיַּעֲמֹד: כִּי־בָחַר יהוה בְּצִיּוֹן, אִוָּהּ לְמוֹשָׁב לוֹ: כִּי־יַעֲקֹב תהלים קלב / תהלים קלה
בָּחַר לוֹ יָהּ, יִשְׂרָאֵל לִסְגֻלָּתוֹ: כִּי לֹא־יִטֹּשׁ יהוה עַמּוֹ, וְנַחֲלָתוֹ לֹא תהלים צד
יַעֲזֹב: ‹ וְהוּא רַחוּם, יְכַפֵּר עָוֹן וְלֹא־יַשְׁחִית, וְהִרְבָּה לְהָשִׁיב אַפּוֹ, תהלים עח
וְלֹא־יָעִיר כָּל־חֲמָתוֹ: יהוה הוֹשִׁיעָה, הַמֶּלֶךְ יַעֲנֵנוּ בְיוֹם־קָרְאֵנוּ: תהלים כ

מִזְמוֹר לְתוֹדָה *A psalm of thanksgiving:* This psalm accompanied the *korban toda*, a thanksgiving-offering (Lev. 7:12), brought to express gratitude for coming safely through a hazardous situation (recovering from illness, completing a potentially dangerous journey or being released from captivity). Nowadays, we make the *HaGomel* blessing (which is said after surviving illness,

The line beginning with "You open Your hand" should be said with special concentration, representing as it does the key idea of this Psalm, and of Pesukei DeZimra as a whole, that God is the creator and sustainer of all. Some have the custom to touch the hand-tefillin at °, and the head-tefillin at °°.

אַשְׁרֵי Happy are those who dwell in Your House; they shall continue to praise You, Selah! *Ps. 84*
Happy are the people for whom this is so; happy are the people whose God is the Lord. *Ps. 144*
A song of praise by David. *Ps. 145*

א I will exalt You, my God, the King, and bless Your name for ever and all time. ב Every day I will bless You, and praise Your name for ever and all time. ג Great is the Lord and greatly to be praised; His greatness is unfathomable. ד One generation will praise Your works to the next, and tell of Your mighty deeds. ה On the glorious splendor of Your majesty I will meditate, and on the acts of Your wonders. ו They shall talk of the power of Your awesome deeds, and I will tell of Your greatness. ז They shall recite the record of Your great goodness, and sing with joy of Your righteousness. ח The Lord is gracious and compassionate, slow to anger and great in loving-kindness. ט The Lord is good to all, and His compassion extends to all His works. י All Your works shall thank You, Lord, and Your devoted ones shall bless You. כ They shall talk of the glory of Your kingship, and speak of Your might. ל To make known to mankind His mighty deeds and the glorious majesty of His kingship. מ Your kingdom is an everlasting kingdom, and Your reign is for all generations. ס The Lord supports all who fall, and raises all who are bowed down. ע All raise their eyes to You in hope, and You give them their food in due season. פ °You open Your hand, °°and satisfy every living thing with favor. צ The Lord is righteous in all His ways, and kind in all He does. ק The Lord is close to all who call on Him, to all who call on Him in truth. ר He fulfills the will of those who revere Him; He hears their cry and saves them. ש The Lord guards all who love Him, but all the wicked He will destroy. ► ת My mouth shall speak the praise of the Lord, and all creatures shall bless His holy name for ever and all time.

We will bless the Lord now and for ever. Halleluya! *Ps. 115*

The line beginning with פּוֹתֵחַ אֶת יָדֶךָ *should be said with special concentration, representing as it does the key idea of this psalm, and of* פסוקי דזמרה *as a whole, that God is the creator and sustainer of all. Some have the custom to touch the* תפילין של יד *at °, and the* תפילין של ראש *at °°.*

אַשְׁרֵי יוֹשְׁבֵי בֵיתֶךָ, עוֹד יְהַלְלוּךָ סֶּלָה: תהלים פד
אַשְׁרֵי הָעָם שֶׁכָּכָה לּוֹ, אַשְׁרֵי הָעָם שֶׁיהוה אֱלֹהָיו: תהלים קמד
תְּהִלָּה לְדָוִד תהלים קמה
א אֲרוֹמִמְךָ אֱלוֹהַי הַמֶּלֶךְ, וַאֲבָרְכָה שִׁמְךָ לְעוֹלָם וָעֶד:
ב בְּכָל־יוֹם אֲבָרְכֶךָּ, וַאֲהַלְלָה שִׁמְךָ לְעוֹלָם וָעֶד:
ג גָּדוֹל יהוה וּמְהֻלָּל מְאֹד, וְלִגְדֻלָּתוֹ אֵין חֵקֶר:
ד דּוֹר לְדוֹר יְשַׁבַּח מַעֲשֶׂיךָ, וּגְבוּרֹתֶיךָ יַגִּידוּ:
ה הֲדַר כְּבוֹד הוֹדֶךָ, וְדִבְרֵי נִפְלְאֹתֶיךָ אָשִׂיחָה:
ו וֶעֱזוּז נוֹרְאֹתֶיךָ יֹאמֵרוּ, וּגְדוּלָּתְךָ אֲסַפְּרֶנָּה:
ז זֵכֶר רַב־טוּבְךָ יַבִּיעוּ, וְצִדְקָתְךָ יְרַנֵּנוּ:
ח חַנּוּן וְרַחוּם יהוה, אֶרֶךְ אַפַּיִם וּגְדָל־חָסֶד:
ט טוֹב־יהוה לַכֹּל, וְרַחֲמָיו עַל־כָּל־מַעֲשָׂיו:
י יוֹדוּךָ יהוה כָּל־מַעֲשֶׂיךָ, וַחֲסִידֶיךָ יְבָרְכוּכָה:
כ כְּבוֹד מַלְכוּתְךָ יֹאמֵרוּ, וּגְבוּרָתְךָ יְדַבֵּרוּ:
ל לְהוֹדִיעַ לִבְנֵי הָאָדָם גְּבוּרֹתָיו, וּכְבוֹד הֲדַר מַלְכוּתוֹ:
מ מַלְכוּתְךָ מַלְכוּת כָּל־עֹלָמִים, וּמֶמְשַׁלְתְּךָ בְּכָל־דּוֹר וָדֹר:
ס סוֹמֵךְ יהוה לְכָל־הַנֹּפְלִים, וְזוֹקֵף לְכָל־הַכְּפוּפִים:
ע עֵינֵי־כֹל אֵלֶיךָ יְשַׂבֵּרוּ, וְאַתָּה נוֹתֵן־לָהֶם אֶת־אָכְלָם בְּעִתּוֹ:
פ °פּוֹתֵחַ אֶת־יָדֶךָ, °°וּמַשְׂבִּיעַ לְכָל־חַי רָצוֹן:
צ צַדִּיק יהוה בְּכָל־דְּרָכָיו, וְחָסִיד בְּכָל־מַעֲשָׂיו:
ק קָרוֹב יהוה לְכָל־קֹרְאָיו, לְכֹל אֲשֶׁר יִקְרָאֻהוּ בֶאֱמֶת:
ר רְצוֹן־יְרֵאָיו יַעֲשֶׂה, וְאֶת־שַׁוְעָתָם יִשְׁמַע, וְיוֹשִׁיעֵם:
ש שׁוֹמֵר יהוה אֶת־כָּל־אֹהֲבָיו, וְאֵת כָּל־הָרְשָׁעִים יַשְׁמִיד:
ת ◄ תְּהִלַּת יהוה יְדַבֶּר פִּי, וִיבָרֵךְ כָּל־בָּשָׂר שֵׁם קָדְשׁוֹ לְעוֹלָם וָעֶד:
וַאֲנַחְנוּ נְבָרֵךְ יָהּ מֵעַתָּה וְעַד־עוֹלָם, הַלְלוּיָהּ: תהלים קטו

הַלְלוּיָהּ Halleluya! Praise the LORD, my soul. I will praise the LORD *Ps. 146* all my life; I will sing to my God as long as I live. Put not your trust in princes, or in mortal man who cannot save. His breath expires, he returns to the earth; on that day his plans come to an end. Happy is he whose help is the God of Jacob, whose hope is in the LORD his God who made heaven and earth, the sea and all they contain; He who keeps faith for ever. He secures justice for the oppressed. He gives food to the hungry. The LORD sets captives free. The LORD gives sight to the blind. The LORD raises those bowed down. The LORD loves the righteous. The LORD protects the stranger. He gives courage to the orphan and widow. He thwarts the way of the wicked. ▸ The LORD shall reign for ever. He is your God, Zion, for all generations. Halleluya!

הַלְלוּיָהּ Halleluya! How good it is to sing songs to our God; how *Ps. 147* pleasant and fitting to praise Him. The LORD rebuilds Jerusalem. He gathers the scattered exiles of Israel. He heals the brokenhearted and binds up their wounds. He counts the number of the stars, calling each by name. Great is our LORD and mighty in power; His understanding has no limit. The LORD gives courage to the humble, but casts the wicked to the ground. Sing to the LORD in thanks; make music to our God on the harp. He covers the sky with clouds. He provides the earth with rain and makes grass grow on the hills. He gives food to the cattle and to the ravens when they cry. He does not take delight in the strength of horses nor pleasure in the fleetness of man. The LORD takes pleasure in those who fear Him, who put their hope in His loving care. Praise the LORD, Jerusalem; sing to your God, Zion, for He has strengthened the bars of your gates and blessed your children in your midst. He has brought peace to your borders, and satisfied you with the finest wheat. He sends His commandment to earth; swiftly runs His word. He spreads snow like fleece, sprinkles frost like ashes, scatters hail like crumbs. Who can stand His cold? He sends His word and melts them; He makes the wind blow and the waters flow. ▸ He has declared His words to Jacob, His statutes and laws to Israel. He has done this for no other nation; such laws they do not know. Halleluya!

תהלים קמו

הַלְלוּיָהּ, הַלְלִי נַפְשִׁי אֶת־יהוה: אֲהַלְלָה יהוה בְּחַיָּי, אֲזַמְּרָה
לֵאלֹהַי בְּעוֹדִי: אַל־תִּבְטְחוּ בִנְדִיבִים, בְּבֶן־אָדָם שֶׁאֵין לוֹ תְשׁוּעָה:
תֵּצֵא רוּחוֹ, יָשֻׁב לְאַדְמָתוֹ, בַּיּוֹם הַהוּא אָבְדוּ עֶשְׁתֹּנֹתָיו: אַשְׁרֵי
שֶׁאֵל יַעֲקֹב בְּעֶזְרוֹ, שִׂבְרוֹ עַל־יהוה אֱלֹהָיו: עֹשֶׂה שָׁמַיִם וָאָרֶץ,
אֶת־הַיָּם וְאֶת־כָּל־אֲשֶׁר־בָּם, הַשֹּׁמֵר אֱמֶת לְעוֹלָם: עֹשֶׂה מִשְׁפָּט
לַעֲשׁוּקִים, נֹתֵן לֶחֶם לָרְעֵבִים, יהוה מַתִּיר אֲסוּרִים: יהוה פֹּקֵחַ
עִוְרִים, יהוה זֹקֵף כְּפוּפִים, יהוה אֹהֵב צַדִּיקִים: יהוה שֹׁמֵר אֶת־
גֵּרִים, יָתוֹם וְאַלְמָנָה יְעוֹדֵד, וְדֶרֶךְ רְשָׁעִים יְעַוֵּת: ◂ יִמְלֹךְ יהוה
לְעוֹלָם, אֱלֹהַיִךְ צִיּוֹן לְדֹר וָדֹר, הַלְלוּיָהּ:

תהלים קמז

הַלְלוּיָהּ, כִּי־טוֹב זַמְּרָה אֱלֹהֵינוּ, כִּי־נָעִים נָאוָה תְהִלָּה: בּוֹנֵה
יְרוּשָׁלִַם יהוה, נִדְחֵי יִשְׂרָאֵל יְכַנֵּס: הָרֹפֵא לִשְׁבוּרֵי לֵב, וּמְחַבֵּשׁ
לְעַצְּבוֹתָם: מוֹנֶה מִסְפָּר לַכּוֹכָבִים, לְכֻלָּם שֵׁמוֹת יִקְרָא: גָּדוֹל
אֲדוֹנֵינוּ וְרַב־כֹּחַ, לִתְבוּנָתוֹ אֵין מִסְפָּר: מְעוֹדֵד עֲנָוִים יהוה, מַשְׁפִּיל
רְשָׁעִים עֲדֵי־אָרֶץ: עֱנוּ לַיהוה בְּתוֹדָה, זַמְּרוּ לֵאלֹהֵינוּ בְכִנּוֹר:
הַמְכַסֶּה שָׁמַיִם בְּעָבִים, הַמֵּכִין לָאָרֶץ מָטָר, הַמַּצְמִיחַ הָרִים חָצִיר:
נוֹתֵן לִבְהֵמָה לַחְמָהּ, לִבְנֵי עֹרֵב אֲשֶׁר יִקְרָאוּ: לֹא בִגְבוּרַת הַסּוּס
יֶחְפָּץ, לֹא־בְשׁוֹקֵי הָאִישׁ יִרְצֶה: רוֹצֶה יהוה אֶת־יְרֵאָיו, אֶת־
הַמְיַחֲלִים לְחַסְדּוֹ: שַׁבְּחִי יְרוּשָׁלִַם אֶת־יהוה, הַלְלִי אֱלֹהַיִךְ צִיּוֹן:
כִּי־חִזַּק בְּרִיחֵי שְׁעָרָיִךְ, בֵּרַךְ בָּנַיִךְ בְּקִרְבֵּךְ: הַשָּׂם־גְּבוּלֵךְ שָׁלוֹם,
חֵלֶב חִטִּים יַשְׂבִּיעֵךְ: הַשֹּׁלֵחַ אִמְרָתוֹ אָרֶץ, עַד־מְהֵרָה יָרוּץ דְּבָרוֹ:
הַנֹּתֵן שֶׁלֶג כַּצָּמֶר, כְּפוֹר כָּאֵפֶר יְפַזֵּר: מַשְׁלִיךְ קַרְחוֹ כְפִתִּים, לִפְנֵי
קָרָתוֹ מִי יַעֲמֹד: יִשְׁלַח דְּבָרוֹ וְיַמְסֵם, יַשֵּׁב רוּחוֹ יִזְּלוּ־מָיִם: ◂ מַגִּיד
דְּבָרָו לְיַעֲקֹב, חֻקָּיו וּמִשְׁפָּטָיו לְיִשְׂרָאֵל: לֹא עָשָׂה כֵן לְכָל־גּוֹי,
וּמִשְׁפָּטִים בַּל־יְדָעוּם, הַלְלוּיָהּ:

הַלְלוּיָהּ Halleluya! Praise the LORD from the heavens, praise Him in the heights. Praise Him, all His angels; praise Him, all His hosts. Praise Him, sun and moon; praise Him, all shining stars. Praise Him, highest heavens and the waters above the heavens. Let them praise the name of the LORD, for He commanded and they were created. He established them for ever and all time, issuing a decree that will never change. Praise the LORD from the earth: sea monsters and all the deep seas; fire and hail, snow and mist, storm winds that obey His word; mountains and all hills, fruit trees and all cedars; wild animals and all cattle, creeping things and winged birds; kings of the earth and all nations, princes and all judges on earth; youths and maidens, old and young. ▸ Let them praise the name of the LORD, for His name alone is sublime; His majesty is above earth and heaven. He has raised the pride of His people, for the glory of all His devoted ones, the children of Israel, the people close to Him. Halleluya! *Ps. 148*

הַלְלוּיָהּ Halleluya! Sing to the LORD a new song, His praise in the assembly of the devoted. Let Israel rejoice in its Maker; let the children of Zion exult in their King. Let them praise His name with dancing; sing praises to Him with timbrel and harp. For the LORD delights in His people; He adorns the humble with salvation. Let the devoted revel in glory; let them sing for joy on their beds. Let high praises of God be in their throats, and a two-edged sword in their hand: to impose retribution on the nations, punishment on the peoples, ▸ binding their kings with chains, their nobles with iron fetters, carrying out the judgment written against them. This is the glory of all His devoted ones. Halleluya! *Ps. 149*

הַלְלוּיָהּ Halleluya! Praise God in His holy place; praise Him in the heavens of His power. Praise Him for His mighty deeds; praise Him for His surpassing greatness. Praise Him with blasts of the shofar; praise Him with the harp and lyre. Praise Him with timbrel and dance; praise Him with strings and flute. Praise Him with clashing cymbals; praise Him with resounding cymbals. ▸ Let all that breathes praise the LORD. Halleluya! Let all that breathes praise the LORD. Halleluya! *Ps. 150*

הַלְלוּיָהּ, הַלְלוּ אֶת־יהוה מִן־הַשָּׁמַיִם, הַלְלוּהוּ בַּמְּרוֹמִים: הַלְלוּהוּ תהלים קמח
כָל־מַלְאָכָיו, הַלְלוּהוּ כָּל־צְבָאָו: הַלְלוּהוּ שֶׁמֶשׁ וְיָרֵחַ, הַלְלוּהוּ
כָּל־כּוֹכְבֵי אוֹר: הַלְלוּהוּ שְׁמֵי הַשָּׁמָיִם, וְהַמַּיִם אֲשֶׁר מֵעַל הַשָּׁמָיִם:
יְהַלְלוּ אֶת־שֵׁם יהוה, כִּי הוּא צִוָּה וְנִבְרָאוּ: וַיַּעֲמִידֵם לָעַד לְעוֹלָם,
חָק־נָתַן וְלֹא יַעֲבוֹר: הַלְלוּ אֶת־יהוה מִן־הָאָרֶץ, תַּנִּינִים וְכָל־
תְּהֹמוֹת: אֵשׁ וּבָרָד שֶׁלֶג וְקִיטוֹר, רוּחַ סְעָרָה עֹשָׂה דְבָרוֹ:
הֶהָרִים וְכָל־גְּבָעוֹת, עֵץ פְּרִי וְכָל־אֲרָזִים: הַחַיָּה וְכָל־בְּהֵמָה, רֶמֶשׂ
וְצִפּוֹר כָּנָף: מַלְכֵי־אֶרֶץ וְכָל־לְאֻמִּים, שָׂרִים וְכָל־שֹׁפְטֵי אָרֶץ:
בַּחוּרִים וְגַם־בְּתוּלוֹת, זְקֵנִים עִם־נְעָרִים: ‹ יְהַלְלוּ אֶת־שֵׁם יהוה,
כִּי־נִשְׂגָּב שְׁמוֹ לְבַדּוֹ, הוֹדוֹ עַל־אֶרֶץ וְשָׁמָיִם: וַיָּרֶם קֶרֶן לְעַמּוֹ,
תְּהִלָּה לְכָל־חֲסִידָיו, לִבְנֵי יִשְׂרָאֵל עַם קְרֹבוֹ, הַלְלוּיָהּ:

הַלְלוּיָהּ, שִׁירוּ לַיהוה שִׁיר חָדָשׁ, תְּהִלָּתוֹ בִּקְהַל חֲסִידִים: יִשְׂמַח תהלים קמט
יִשְׂרָאֵל בְּעֹשָׂיו, בְּנֵי־צִיּוֹן יָגִילוּ בְמַלְכָּם: יְהַלְלוּ שְׁמוֹ בְמָחוֹל, בְּתֹף
וְכִנּוֹר יְזַמְּרוּ־לוֹ: כִּי־רוֹצֶה יהוה בְּעַמּוֹ, יְפָאֵר עֲנָוִים בִּישׁוּעָה:
יַעְלְזוּ חֲסִידִים בְּכָבוֹד, יְרַנְּנוּ עַל־מִשְׁכְּבוֹתָם: רוֹמְמוֹת אֵל
בִּגְרוֹנָם, וְחֶרֶב פִּיפִיּוֹת בְּיָדָם: לַעֲשׂוֹת נְקָמָה בַּגּוֹיִם, תּוֹכֵחוֹת
בַּלְאֻמִּים: ‹ לֶאְסֹר מַלְכֵיהֶם בְּזִקִּים, וְנִכְבְּדֵיהֶם בְּכַבְלֵי בַרְזֶל:
לַעֲשׂוֹת בָּהֶם מִשְׁפָּט כָּתוּב, הָדָר הוּא לְכָל־חֲסִידָיו, הַלְלוּיָהּ:

הַלְלוּיָהּ, הַלְלוּ־אֵל בְּקָדְשׁוֹ, הַלְלוּהוּ בִּרְקִיעַ עֻזּוֹ: הַלְלוּהוּ תהלים קנ
בִגְבוּרֹתָיו, הַלְלוּהוּ כְּרֹב גֻּדְלוֹ: הַלְלוּהוּ בְּתֵקַע שׁוֹפָר, הַלְלוּהוּ
בְּנֵבֶל וְכִנּוֹר: הַלְלוּהוּ בְּתֹף וּמָחוֹל, הַלְלוּהוּ בְּמִנִּים וְעוּגָב: הַלְלוּהוּ
בְצִלְצְלֵי־שָׁמַע, הַלְלוּהוּ בְּצִלְצְלֵי תְרוּעָה: ‹ כֹּל הַנְּשָׁמָה תְּהַלֵּל
יָהּ, הַלְלוּיָהּ: כֹּל הַנְּשָׁמָה תְּהַלֵּל יָהּ, הַלְלוּיָהּ:

בָּרוּךְ Blessed be the LORD for ever. Amen and Amen. Ps. 89
Blessed from Zion be the LORD Ps. 135
who dwells in Jerusalem. Halleluya!
Blessed be the LORD, God of Israel, Ps. 72
who alone does wonders.
▸ Blessed be His glorious name for ever,
and may all the earth be filled with His glory.
Amen and Amen.

Stand (see commentary) until after "Bless the LORD" on page 88.

וַיְבָרֶךְ David blessed the LORD in front of the entire assembly. David *1 Chr. 29*
said, "Blessed are You, LORD, God of our father Yisrael, for ever and ever. Yours, LORD, are the greatness and the power, the glory, majesty and splendor, for everything in heaven and earth is Yours. Yours, LORD, is the kingdom; You are exalted as Head over all. Both riches and honor are in Your gift and You reign over all things. In Your hand are strength and might. It is in Your power to make great and give strength to all. Therefore, our God, we thank You and praise Your glorious name." You alone are the LORD. You *Neh. 9*
made the heavens, even the highest heavens, and all their hosts, the earth and all that is on it, the seas and all they contain. You give life to them all, and the hosts of heaven worship You. ▸ You are the LORD God who chose Abram and brought him out of Ur of the Chaldees, changing his name to Abraham. You found his heart faithful toward You, ◂ and You made a covenant with him to give to his descendants the land of the Canaanites, Hittites, Amorites,

---

money to charity at this point in the service. Some give this as the reason we stand at this point of the service, since we stand to fulfill a mitzva, in this case, giving to charity.

Others relate the act of standing to the next passage, "You alone," taken from the gathering in the days of Ezra and Nehemiah after the Babylonian exile and return, when the people renewed their covenant with God.

תהלים פט
בָּרוּךְ יהוה לְעוֹלָם, אָמֵן וְאָמֵן:

תהלים קלה
בָּרוּךְ יהוה מִצִּיּוֹן, שֹׁכֵן יְרוּשָׁלָֽםִ, הַלְלוּיָהּ:

תהלים עב
בָּרוּךְ יהוה אֱלֹהִים אֱלֹהֵי יִשְׂרָאֵל, עֹשֵׂה נִפְלָאוֹת לְבַדּוֹ:

‹ וּבָרוּךְ שֵׁם כְּבוֹדוֹ לְעוֹלָם
וְיִמָּלֵא כְבוֹדוֹ אֶת־כָּל־הָאָֽרֶץ
אָמֵן וְאָמֵן:

Stand (see commentary) until after בָּרְכוּ *on page 89.*

דברי הימים א, כט
וַיְבָֽרֶךְ דָּוִיד אֶת־יהוה לְעֵינֵי כָּל־הַקָּהָל, וַיֹּֽאמֶר דָּוִיד, בָּרוּךְ אַתָּה יהוה, אֱלֹהֵי יִשְׂרָאֵל אָבִֽינוּ, מֵעוֹלָם וְעַד־עוֹלָם: לְךָ יהוה הַגְּדֻלָּה וְהַגְּבוּרָה וְהַתִּפְאֶֽרֶת וְהַנֵּֽצַח וְהַהוֹד, כִּי־כֹל בַּשָּׁמַֽיִם וּבָאָֽרֶץ, לְךָ יהוה הַמַּמְלָכָה וְהַמִּתְנַשֵּׂא לְכֹל לְרֹאשׁ: וְהָעֹֽשֶׁר וְהַכָּבוֹד מִלְּפָנֶֽיךָ, וְאַתָּה מוֹשֵׁל בַּכֹּל, וּבְיָדְךָ כֹּֽחַ וּגְבוּרָה, וּבְיָדְךָ לְגַדֵּל וּלְחַזֵּק לַכֹּל: וְעַתָּה אֱלֹהֵֽינוּ מוֹדִים אֲנַֽחְנוּ לָךְ, וּמְהַלְלִים לְשֵׁם תִּפְאַרְתֶּֽךָ:

נחמיה ט
אַתָּה־הוּא יהוה לְבַדֶּֽךָ, אַתָּ עָשִֽׂיתָ אֶת־הַשָּׁמַֽיִם, שְׁמֵי הַשָּׁמַֽיִם וְכָל־צְבָאָם, הָאָֽרֶץ וְכָל־אֲשֶׁר עָלֶֽיהָ, הַיַּמִּים וְכָל־אֲשֶׁר בָּהֶם, וְאַתָּה מְחַיֶּה אֶת־כֻּלָּם, וּצְבָא הַשָּׁמַֽיִם לְךָ מִשְׁתַּחֲוִים: ‹ אַתָּה הוּא יהוה הָאֱלֹהִים אֲשֶׁר בָּחַֽרְתָּ בְּאַבְרָם, וְהוֹצֵאתוֹ מֵאוּר כַּשְׂדִּים, וְשַֽׂמְתָּ שְּׁמוֹ אַבְרָהָם: וּמָצָֽאתָ אֶת־לְבָבוֹ נֶאֱמָן לְפָנֶֽיךָ, ‹ וְכָרוֹת עִמּוֹ הַבְּרִית לָתֵת אֶת־אֶֽרֶץ הַכְּנַעֲנִי

וַיְבָֽרֶךְ דָּוִיד *David blessed:* This passage is part of the prayer of thanksgiving said by King David at the end of his life after he had gathered the resources to build the Temple in Jerusalem, to be undertaken by Solomon his son. As with the Tabernacle, the Temple was made out of the voluntary contributions of the people as a whole. For that reason, many have the custom to give

Perizzites, Jebusites and Girgashites. You fulfilled Your promise for You are righteous. You saw the suffering of our ancestors in Egypt. You heard their cry at the Sea of Reeds. You sent signs and wonders against Pharaoh, all his servants and all the people of his land, because You knew how arrogantly the Egyptians treated them. You created for Yourself renown that remains to this day. ▸ You divided the sea before them, so that they passed through the sea on dry land, but You cast their pursuers into the depths, like a stone into mighty waters.

וַיּוֹשַׁע That day the LORD saved Israel from the hands of the Egyptians, and Israel saw the Egyptians lying dead on the seashore. ▸ When Israel saw the great power the LORD had displayed against the Egyptians, the people feared the LORD, and believed in the LORD and in His servant, Moses. *Ex. 14*

אָז יָשִׁיר־מֹשֶׁה Then Moses and the Israelites sang this song to the LORD, saying: *Ex. 15*

I will sing to the LORD, for He has triumphed gloriously;
horse and rider He has hurled into the sea.
The LORD is my strength and song; He has become my salvation.
This is my God, and I will beautify Him,
my father's God, and I will exalt Him.
The LORD is a Master of war; LORD is His name.
Pharaoh's chariots and army He cast into the sea;
the best of his officers drowned in the Sea of Reeds.
The deep waters covered them;
they went down to the depths like a stone.
Your right hand, LORD, is majestic in power.
Your right hand, LORD, shatters the enemy.
In the greatness of Your majesty, You overthrew those who rose against You.
You sent out Your fury; it consumed them like stubble.

הַחִתִּי הָאֱמֹרִי וְהַפְּרִזִּי וְהַיְבוּסִי וְהַגִּרְגָּשִׁי, לָתֵת לְזַרְעוֹ, וַתָּקֶם
אֶת־דְּבָרֶיךָ, כִּי צַדִּיק אָתָּה: וַתֵּרֶא אֶת־עֳנִי אֲבֹתֵינוּ בְּמִצְרָיִם,
וְאֶת־זַעֲקָתָם שָׁמַעְתָּ עַל־יַם־סוּף: וַתִּתֵּן אֹתֹת וּמֹפְתִים בְּפַרְעֹה
וּבְכָל־עֲבָדָיו וּבְכָל־עַם אַרְצוֹ, כִּי יָדַעְתָּ כִּי הֵזִידוּ עֲלֵיהֶם, וַתַּעַשׂ־
לְךָ שֵׁם כְּהַיּוֹם הַזֶּה: › וְהַיָּם בָּקַעְתָּ לִפְנֵיהֶם, וַיַּעַבְרוּ בְתוֹךְ־הַיָּם
בַּיַּבָּשָׁה, וְאֶת־רֹדְפֵיהֶם הִשְׁלַכְתָּ בִמְצוֹלֹת כְּמוֹ־אֶבֶן, בְּמַיִם עַזִּים:

שמות יד וַיּוֹשַׁע יהוה בַּיּוֹם הַהוּא אֶת־יִשְׂרָאֵל מִיַּד מִצְרָיִם, וַיַּרְא יִשְׂרָאֵל
אֶת־מִצְרַיִם מֵת עַל־שְׂפַת הַיָּם: › וַיַּרְא יִשְׂרָאֵל אֶת־הַיָּד הַגְּדֹלָה
אֲשֶׁר עָשָׂה יהוה בְּמִצְרַיִם, וַיִּירְאוּ הָעָם אֶת־יהוה, וַיַּאֲמִינוּ
בַּיהוה וּבְמֹשֶׁה עַבְדּוֹ:

שמות טו אָז יָשִׁיר־מֹשֶׁה וּבְנֵי יִשְׂרָאֵל אֶת־הַשִּׁירָה הַזֹּאת לַיהוה, וַיֹּאמְרוּ
לֵאמֹר, אָשִׁירָה לַיהוה כִּי־גָאֹה גָּאָה, סוּס
וְרֹכְבוֹ רָמָה בַיָּם: עָזִּי וְזִמְרָת יָהּ וַיְהִי־לִי
לִישׁוּעָה, זֶה אֵלִי וְאַנְוֵהוּ, אֱלֹהֵי
אָבִי וַאֲרֹמְמֶנְהוּ: יהוה אִישׁ מִלְחָמָה, יהוה
שְׁמוֹ: מַרְכְּבֹת פַּרְעֹה וְחֵילוֹ יָרָה בַיָּם, וּמִבְחַר
שָׁלִשָׁיו טֻבְּעוּ בְיַם־סוּף: תְּהֹמֹת יְכַסְיֻמוּ, יָרְדוּ בִמְצוֹלֹת כְּמוֹ־
אָבֶן: יְמִינְךָ יהוה נֶאְדָּרִי בַּכֹּחַ, יְמִינְךָ
יהוה תִּרְעַץ אוֹיֵב: וּבְרֹב גְּאוֹנְךָ תַּהֲרֹס

Immediately prior to this passage, we read that the Levites called on the people to "Rise, bless the Lord your God" (Neh. 9:5). Hence we too stand in remembrance of that gathering (Rabbi Eli Munk).

By the blast of Your nostrils the waters piled up.
  The surging waters stood straight like a wall;
  the deeps congealed in the heart of the sea.
The enemy said, "I will pursue. I will overtake. I will divide the spoil.
  My desire shall have its fill of them.
  I will draw my sword. My hand will destroy them."
You blew with Your wind; the sea covered them.
  They sank in the mighty waters like lead.
Who is like You, LORD, among the mighty?
  Who is like You – majestic in holiness, awesome in glory,
  working wonders?
You stretched out Your right hand,
  the earth swallowed them.
In Your loving-kindness, You led the people You redeemed.
  In Your strength, You guided them to Your holy abode.
Nations heard and trembled;
  terror gripped Philistia's inhabitants.
The chiefs of Edom were dismayed,
  Moab's leaders were seized with trembling,
  the people of Canaan melted away.
Fear and dread fell upon them.
  By the power of Your arm, they were still as stone –
  until Your people crossed, LORD,
  until the people You acquired crossed over.
You will bring them and plant them
  on the mountain of Your heritage –
  the place, LORD, You made for Your dwelling,
  the Sanctuary, LORD, Your hands established.
  The LORD will reign for ever and all time.

The LORD will reign for ever and all time.
The LORD's kingship is established for ever and to all eternity.

When Pharaoh's horses, chariots and riders went into the sea,
  the LORD brought the waters of the sea back over them, but
  the Israelites walked on dry land through the sea.

קָמֶיךָ, תְּשַׁלַּח חֲרֹנְךָ יֹאכְלֵמוֹ כַּקַּשׁ: וּבְרוּחַ
אַפֶּיךָ נֶעֶרְמוּ מַיִם, נִצְּבוּ כְמוֹ־נֵד
נֹזְלִים, קָפְאוּ תְהֹמֹת בְּלֶב־יָם: אָמַר
אוֹיֵב אֶרְדֹּף, אַשִּׂיג, אֲחַלֵּק שָׁלָל, תִּמְלָאֵמוֹ
נַפְשִׁי, אָרִיק חַרְבִּי תּוֹרִישֵׁמוֹ יָדִי: נָשַׁפְתָּ
בְרוּחֲךָ כִּסָּמוֹ יָם, צָלְלוּ כַּעוֹפֶרֶת בְּמַיִם
אַדִּירִים: מִי־כָמֹכָה בָּאֵלִם יהוה, מִי
כָּמֹכָה נֶאְדָּר בַּקֹּדֶשׁ, נוֹרָא תְהִלֹּת עֹשֵׂה
פֶלֶא: נָטִיתָ יְמִינְךָ תִּבְלָעֵמוֹ אָרֶץ: נָחִיתָ
בְחַסְדְּךָ עַם־זוּ גָּאָלְתָּ, נֵהַלְתָּ בְעָזְּךָ אֶל־נְוֵה
קָדְשֶׁךָ: שָׁמְעוּ עַמִּים יִרְגָּזוּן, חִיל
אָחַז יֹשְׁבֵי פְּלָשֶׁת: אָז נִבְהֲלוּ אַלּוּפֵי
אֱדוֹם, אֵילֵי מוֹאָב יֹאחֲזֵמוֹ רָעַד, נָמֹגוּ
כֹּל יֹשְׁבֵי כְנָעַן: תִּפֹּל עֲלֵיהֶם אֵימָתָה
וָפַחַד, בִּגְדֹל זְרוֹעֲךָ יִדְּמוּ כָּאָבֶן, עַד־
יַעֲבֹר עַמְּךָ יהוה, עַד־יַעֲבֹר עַם־זוּ
קָנִיתָ: תְּבִאֵמוֹ וְתִטָּעֵמוֹ בְּהַר נַחֲלָתְךָ, מָכוֹן
לְשִׁבְתְּךָ פָּעַלְתָּ יהוה, מִקְּדָשׁ אֲדֹנָי כּוֹנְנוּ
יָדֶיךָ: יהוה ׀ יִמְלֹךְ לְעֹלָם וָעֶד:

יהוה יִמְלֹךְ לְעֹלָם וָעֶד.
יהוה מַלְכוּתֵהּ קָאֵם לְעָלַם וּלְעָלְמֵי עָלְמַיָּא.

כִּי
בָא סוּס פַּרְעֹה בְּרִכְבּוֹ וּבְפָרָשָׁיו בַּיָּם, וַיָּשֶׁב יהוה עֲלֵהֶם אֶת־מֵי
הַיָּם, וּבְנֵי יִשְׂרָאֵל הָלְכוּ בַיַּבָּשָׁה בְּתוֹךְ הַיָּם:

▸ For kingship is the LORD's *Ps. 22*
and He rules over the nations.
Saviors shall go up to Mount Zion *Ob. 1*
to judge Mount Esau,
and the LORD's shall be the kingdom.

Then the LORD shall be King over all the earth; *Zech. 14*
on that day the LORD shall be One and His name One,
(as it is written in Your Torah, saying:
Listen, Israel: the LORD is our God, the LORD is One.) *Deut. 6*

יִשְׁתַּבַּח May Your name be praised for ever, our King,
the great and holy God, King in heaven and on earth.
For to You,
LORD our God and God of our ancestors,
it is right to offer song and praise,
hymn and psalm,
strength and dominion,
eternity, greatness and power,
song of praise and glory,
holiness and kingship,
▸ blessings and thanks,
from now and for ever.
Blessed are You, LORD,
God and King,
exalted in praises,
God of thanksgivings,
Master of wonders,
who delights in hymns of song,
King, God, Giver of life to the worlds.

תהלים כב ‹ כִּי לַיהוה הַמְּלוּכָה וּמשֵׁל בַּגּוֹיִם:
עובדיה א וְעָלוּ מוֹשִׁעִים בְּהַר צִיּוֹן לִשְׁפֹּט אֶת־הַר עֵשָׂו
וְהָיְתָה לַיהוה הַמְּלוּכָה:
זכריה יד וְהָיָה יהוה לְמֶלֶךְ עַל־כָּל־הָאָרֶץ
בַּיּוֹם הַהוּא יִהְיֶה יהוה אֶחָד וּשְׁמוֹ אֶחָד:
דברים ו (וּבְתוֹרָתְךָ כָּתוּב לֵאמֹר, שְׁמַע יִשְׂרָאֵל, יהוה אֱלֹהֵינוּ יהוה אֶחָד:)

יִשְׁתַּבַּח

שִׁמְךָ לָעַד, מַלְכֵּנוּ
הָאֵל הַמֶּלֶךְ הַגָּדוֹל וְהַקָּדוֹשׁ בַּשָּׁמַיִם וּבָאָרֶץ
כִּי לְךָ נָאֶה, יהוה אֱלֹהֵינוּ וֵאלֹהֵי אֲבוֹתֵינוּ
שִׁיר וּשְׁבָחָה, הַלֵּל וְזִמְרָה
עֹז וּמֶמְשָׁלָה, נֶצַח, גְּדֻלָּה וּגְבוּרָה
תְּהִלָּה וְתִפְאֶרֶת, קְדֻשָּׁה וּמַלְכוּת
‹ בְּרָכוֹת וְהוֹדָאוֹת, מֵעַתָּה וְעַד עוֹלָם.
בָּרוּךְ אַתָּה יהוה
אֵל מֶלֶךְ גָּדוֹל בַּתִּשְׁבָּחוֹת
אֵל הַהוֹדָאוֹת
אֲדוֹן הַנִּפְלָאוֹת
הַבּוֹחֵר בְּשִׁירֵי זִמְרָה
מֶלֶךְ, אֵל, חֵי הָעוֹלָמִים.

Between Rosh HaShana and Yom Kippur, and on Hoshana Raba, many congregations open the Ark and say this psalm responsively, verse by verse.

שִׁיר הַמַּעֲלוֹת A song of ascents. From the depths I have called to You, LORD. *Ps. 130*
LORD, hear my voice; let Your ears be attentive to my plea. If You, LORD, should keep account of sins, O LORD, who could stand? But with You there is forgiveness, that You may be held in awe. I wait for the LORD, my soul waits, and in His word I put my hope. My soul waits for the LORD more than watchmen wait for the morning, more than watchmen wait for the morning. Israel, put your hope in the LORD, for with the LORD there is loving-kindness, and great is His power to redeem. It is He who will redeem Israel from all their sins.

HALF KADDISH

Leader: יִתְגַּדַּל Magnified and sanctified
may His great name be,
in the world He created by His will.
May He establish His kingdom
in your lifetime and in your days,
and in the lifetime of all the house of Israel,
swiftly and soon –
and say: Amen.

All: May His great name be blessed for ever and all time.

Leader: Blessed and praised,
glorified and exalted,
raised and honored,
uplifted and lauded
be the name of the Holy One,
blessed be He,
beyond any blessing,
song, praise and consolation
uttered in the world –
and say: Amen.

During the עשרת ימי תשובה*, and on* הושענא רבה*,*
many congregations open the ארון קודש *and say this psalm responsively, verse by verse.*

תהלים קל שִׁיר הַמַּעֲלוֹת, מִמַּעֲמַקִּים קְרָאתִיךָ יהוה: אֲדֹנָי שִׁמְעָה בְקוֹלִי, תִּהְיֶינָה אָזְנֶיךָ קַשֻּׁבוֹת לְקוֹל תַּחֲנוּנָי: אִם־עֲוֹנוֹת תִּשְׁמָר־יָהּ, אֲדֹנָי מִי יַעֲמֹד: כִּי־עִמְּךָ הַסְּלִיחָה, לְמַעַן תִּוָּרֵא: קִוִּיתִי יהוה קִוְּתָה נַפְשִׁי, וְלִדְבָרוֹ הוֹחָלְתִּי: נַפְשִׁי לַאדֹנָי, מִשֹּׁמְרִים לַבֹּקֶר, שֹׁמְרִים לַבֹּקֶר: יַחֵל יִשְׂרָאֵל אֶל יהוה, כִּי־עִם־יהוה הַחֶסֶד, וְהַרְבֵּה עִמּוֹ פְדוּת: וְהוּא יִפְדֶּה אֶת־יִשְׂרָאֵל, מִכֹּל עֲוֹנוֹתָיו:

חצי קדיש

ש״ץ: יִתְגַּדַּל וְיִתְקַדַּשׁ שְׁמֵהּ רַבָּא (קהל: אָמֵן)
בְּעָלְמָא דִּי בְרָא כִרְעוּתֵהּ
וְיַמְלִיךְ מַלְכוּתֵהּ
בְּחַיֵּיכוֹן וּבְיוֹמֵיכוֹן וּבְחַיֵּי דְכָל בֵּית יִשְׂרָאֵל
בַּעֲגָלָא וּבִזְמַן קָרִיב
וְאִמְרוּ אָמֵן. (קהל: אָמֵן)

קהל וש״ץ: יְהֵא שְׁמֵהּ רַבָּא מְבָרַךְ לְעָלַם וּלְעָלְמֵי עָלְמַיָּא.

ש״ץ: יִתְבָּרַךְ וְיִשְׁתַּבַּח וְיִתְפָּאַר וְיִתְרוֹמַם וְיִתְנַשֵּׂא
וְיִתְהַדַּר וְיִתְעַלֶּה וְיִתְהַלָּל
שְׁמֵהּ דְּקֻדְשָׁא בְּרִיךְ הוּא (קהל: בְּרִיךְ הוּא)
לְעֵלָּא מִן כָּל בִּרְכָתָא
/בעשרת ימי תשובה: לְעֵלָּא לְעֵלָּא מִכָּל בִּרְכָתָא/
וְשִׁירָתָא, תֻּשְׁבְּחָתָא וְנֶחֱמָתָא, דַּאֲמִירָן בְּעָלְמָא
וְאִמְרוּ אָמֵן. (קהל: אָמֵן)

BLESSINGS OF THE SHEMA

The following blessing and response are said only in the presence of a minyan. They represent a formal summons to the congregation to engage in an act of collective prayer. The custom of bowing at this point is based on 1 Chronicles 29:20, "David said to the whole assembly, 'Now bless the Lord your God.' All the assembly blessed the Lord God of their fathers and bowed their heads low to the Lord and the King." The Leader says the following, bowing at "Bless," standing straight at "the Lord." The congregation, followed by the Leader, responds, bowing at "Bless," standing straight at "the Lord."

Leader: **BLESS**
the Lord, the blessed One.

Congregation: Bless the Lord, the blessed One,
for ever and all time.

Leader: Bless the Lord, the blessed One,
for ever and all time.

The custom is to sit from this point until the Amida, since the predominant emotion of this section of the prayers is love rather than awe. Conversation is forbidden until after the Amida. See table on pages 1329–1331.

בָּרוּךְ Blessed are You, Lord our God,
King of the Universe,
who forms light and creates darkness, *Is. 45*
makes peace and creates all.

---

prayer). Saying the Shema twice daily (morning and evening, "when you lie down and when you rise up") is a biblical institution, and was part of the order of service in Temple times. The transition to congregational prayer is marked by a call – "Bless the Lord" – to those present to join in prayer as a community.

קריאת שמע וברכותיה

The following blessing and response are said only in the presence of a מנין.
They represent a formal summons to the קהל to engage in an act of collective prayer.
The custom of bowing at this point is based on דברי הימים א׳ כט, כ, "David said to the whole assembly, 'Now bless the LORD your God.' All the assembly blessed the LORD God of their fathers and bowed their heads low to the LORD and the King."
The שליח ציבור says the following, bowing at בָּרְכוּ, standing straight at ה׳. The קהל, followed by the שליח ציבור, responds, bowing at בָּרוּךְ, standing straight at ה׳.

ש״ץ: **בָּרְכוּ**

אֶת יהוה הַמְבֹרָךְ.

קהל: בָּרוּךְ יהוה הַמְבֹרָךְ לְעוֹלָם וָעֶד.

ש״ץ: בָּרוּךְ יהוה הַמְבֹרָךְ לְעוֹלָם וָעֶד.

The custom is to sit from this point until the עמידה, since the predominant emotion of this section of the prayers is love rather than awe.
Conversation is forbidden until after the עמידה. *See table on pages 1329–1331.*

בָּרוּךְ אַתָּה יהוה אֱלֹהֵינוּ מֶלֶךְ הָעוֹלָם
ישעיה מה יוֹצֵר אוֹר וּבוֹרֵא חֹשֶׁךְ
עֹשֶׂה שָׁלוֹם וּבוֹרֵא אֶת הַכֹּל.

THE SHEMA AND ITS BLESSINGS

The *Pesukei DeZimra* are a prelude to prayer. We now move to congregational prayer, the heart of which is the Shema and the Amida (the "standing"

הַמֵּאִיר In compassion He gives light to the earth
and its inhabitants,
and in His goodness continually renews the work of creation,
day after day.
How numerous are Your works, LORD; *Ps. 104*
You made them all in wisdom;
the earth is full of Your creations.
He is the King exalted alone since the beginning of time –
praised, glorified and elevated since the world began.
Eternal God,
in Your great compassion, have compassion on us,
LORD of our strength, Rock of our refuge,
Shield of our salvation, You are our stronghold.

The blessed God,
great in knowledge,
prepared and made the rays of the sun.
He who is good formed glory for His name,
surrounding His power with radiant stars.
The leaders of His hosts,
the holy ones,
exalt the Almighty,
constantly proclaiming God's glory and holiness.
Be blessed, LORD our God,
for the magnificence of Your handiwork
and for the radiant lights You have made.
May they glorify You, Selah!

---

day: the creation of light. Of this, there are two forms: the physical light of the sun, moon and stars, made on the fourth day of creation, and the spiritual light created on the first day ("Let there be light"). The prayer modulates from the first to the second: from the universe as we see it, to the mystical vision of God enthroned in glory, surrounded by angels.

הַמֵּאִיר לָאָֽרֶץ וְלַדָּרִים עָלֶֽיהָ בְּרַחֲמִים
וּבְטוּבוֹ מְחַדֵּשׁ בְּכָל יוֹם תָּמִיד מַעֲשֵׂה בְרֵאשִׁית.
מָה־רַבּוּ מַעֲשֶֽׂיךָ יהוה תהלים קד
כֻּלָּם בְּחָכְמָה עָשִֽׂיתָ
מָלְאָה הָאָֽרֶץ קִנְיָנֶֽךָ:
הַמֶּֽלֶךְ הַמְרוֹמָם לְבַדּוֹ מֵאָז
הַמְשֻׁבָּח וְהַמְפֹאָר וְהַמִּתְנַשֵּׂא מִימוֹת עוֹלָם.
אֱלֹהֵי עוֹלָם
בְּרַחֲמֶֽיךָ הָרַבִּים רַחֵם עָלֵֽינוּ
אֲדוֹן עֻזֵּֽנוּ, צוּר מִשְׂגַּבֵּֽנוּ
מָגֵן יִשְׁעֵֽנוּ, מִשְׂגָּב בַּעֲדֵֽנוּ.
אֵל בָּרוּךְ גְּדוֹל דֵּעָה
הֵכִין וּפָעַל זָהֳרֵי חַמָּה
טוֹב יָצַר כָּבוֹד לִשְׁמוֹ
מְאוֹרוֹת נָתַן סְבִיבוֹת עֻזּוֹ
פִּנּוֹת צְבָאָיו קְדוֹשִׁים, רוֹמְמֵי שַׁדַּי
תָּמִיד מְסַפְּרִים כְּבוֹד אֵל וּקְדֻשָּׁתוֹ.
תִּתְבָּרַךְ יהוה אֱלֹהֵֽינוּ
עַל שֶֽׁבַח מַעֲשֵׂה יָדֶֽיךָ.
וְעַל מְאֽוֹרֵי אוֹר שֶׁעָשִֽׂיתָ
יְפָאֲרֽוּךָ סֶּֽלָה.

אֵל בָּרוּךְ *The blessed God:* An alphabetical acrostic of twenty-two words. Although the first blessing is about creation as a whole, the morning prayer emphasizes the element of which we are most conscious at the start of the

תִּתְבָּרַךְ May You be blessed,
our Rock, King and Redeemer,
Creator of holy beings.
May Your name be praised for ever,
our King, Creator of the ministering angels,
all of whom stand in the universe's heights,
proclaiming together,
in awe, aloud,
the words of the living God, the eternal King.
They are all beloved, all pure, all mighty,
and all perform in awe and reverence the will of their Maker.
▸ All open their mouths in holiness and purity,
with song and psalm,
and bless, praise, glorify,
revere, sanctify and declare the sovereignty of – ◂
The name of the great, mighty
and awesome God and King,
holy is He.
▸ All accept on themselves,
one from another,
the yoke of the kingdom of heaven,
granting permission to one another
to sanctify the One who formed them,
in serene spirit,
pure speech and sweet melody.
All, as one,
proclaim His holiness,
saying in awe:

---

of the holy. For the main commentary on this section of the prayers, see page 455.

The theme of this section of the service is *revelation*: God as He has disclosed Himself in the words of the Torah. So at its heart are three passages

תִּתְבָּרַךְ
צוּרֵנוּ מַלְכֵּנוּ וְגוֹאֲלֵנוּ, בּוֹרֵא קְדוֹשִׁים
יִשְׁתַּבַּח שִׁמְךָ לָעַד
מַלְכֵּנוּ, יוֹצֵר מְשָׁרְתִים
וַאֲשֶׁר מְשָׁרְתָיו כֻּלָּם עוֹמְדִים בְּרוּם עוֹלָם
וּמַשְׁמִיעִים בְּיִרְאָה יַחַד בְּקוֹל
דִּבְרֵי אֱלֹהִים חַיִּים וּמֶלֶךְ עוֹלָם.
כֻּלָּם אֲהוּבִים, כֻּלָּם בְּרוּרִים, כֻּלָּם גִּבּוֹרִים
וְכֻלָּם עוֹשִׂים בְּאֵימָה וּבְיִרְאָה רְצוֹן קוֹנָם
◂ וְכֻלָּם פּוֹתְחִים אֶת פִּיהֶם בִּקְדֻשָּׁה וּבְטָהֳרָה
בְּשִׁירָה וּבְזִמְרָה
וּמְבָרְכִים וּמְשַׁבְּחִים וּמְפָאֲרִים
וּמַעֲרִיצִים וּמַקְדִּישִׁים וּמַמְלִיכִים ◂
אֶת שֵׁם הָאֵל הַמֶּלֶךְ הַגָּדוֹל, הַגִּבּוֹר וְהַנּוֹרָא
קָדוֹשׁ הוּא.
◂ וְכֻלָּם מְקַבְּלִים עֲלֵיהֶם עֹל מַלְכוּת שָׁמַיִם זֶה מִזֶּה
וְנוֹתְנִים רְשׁוּת זֶה לָזֶה
לְהַקְדִּישׁ לְיוֹצְרָם בְּנַחַת רוּחַ
בְּשָׂפָה בְרוּרָה וּבִנְעִימָה
קְדֻשָּׁה כֻּלָּם כְּאֶחָד
עוֹנִים וְאוֹמְרִים בְּיִרְאָה

The three blessings and the three paragraphs of the Shema form six passages, leading up to the seventh, the Amida. In Judaism, seven is the number

All say aloud: Holy, holy, holy is the LORD of hosts; *Is. 6*
the whole world is filled with His glory.

▸ Then the Ophanim and the Holy Ḥayyot,
with a roar of noise,
raise themselves toward the Seraphim and,
facing them, give praise, saying:

All say aloud: Blessed is the LORD's glory from His place. *Ezek. 3*

לָאֵל To the blessed God they offer melodies.
To the King, living and eternal God,
they say psalms and proclaim praises.
For it is He alone
who does mighty deeds
and creates new things,
who is Master of battles,
and sows righteousness,
who makes salvation grow
and creates cures,
who is revered in praises,
LORD of wonders,
who in His goodness,
continually renews the work of creation, day after day,
as it is said:
"[Praise] Him who made the great lights, *Ps. 136*
for His love endures for ever."
▸ May You make a new light shine over Zion,
and may we all soon be worthy of its light.
Blessed are You, LORD, who forms the radiant lights.

---

tion: the Torah, given in love. The third אֱמֶת וְיַצִּיב ("True and firm") is about redemption.

All say aloud קָדוֹשׁ, קָדוֹשׁ, קָדוֹשׁ יהוה צְבָאוֹת ישעיה ו
מְלֹא כָל־הָאָרֶץ כְּבוֹדוֹ:

▸ וְהָאוֹפַנִּים וְחַיּוֹת הַקֹּדֶשׁ
בְּרַעַשׁ גָּדוֹל מִתְנַשְּׂאִים לְעֻמַּת שְׂרָפִים
לְעֻמָּתָם מְשַׁבְּחִים וְאוֹמְרִים

All say aloud בָּרוּךְ כְּבוֹד־יהוה מִמְּקוֹמוֹ: יחזקאל ג

לָאֵל בָּרוּךְ נְעִימוֹת יִתֵּנוּ, לַמֶּלֶךְ אֵל חַי וְקַיָּם
זְמִירוֹת יֹאמֵרוּ וְתִשְׁבָּחוֹת יַשְׁמִיעוּ
כִּי הוּא לְבַדּוֹ
פּוֹעֵל גְּבוּרוֹת, עוֹשֶׂה חֲדָשׁוֹת
בַּעַל מִלְחָמוֹת, זוֹרֵעַ צְדָקוֹת
מַצְמִיחַ יְשׁוּעוֹת, בּוֹרֵא רְפוּאוֹת
נוֹרָא תְהִלּוֹת, אֲדוֹן הַנִּפְלָאוֹת
הַמְחַדֵּשׁ בְּטוּבוֹ בְּכָל יוֹם תָּמִיד מַעֲשֵׂה בְרֵאשִׁית
כָּאָמוּר
לְעֹשֵׂה אוֹרִים גְּדֹלִים, כִּי לְעוֹלָם חַסְדּוֹ: תהלים קלו
▸ אוֹר חָדָשׁ עַל צִיּוֹן תָּאִיר וְנִזְכֶּה כֻלָּנוּ מְהֵרָה לְאוֹרוֹ.
בָּרוּךְ אַתָּה יהוה, יוֹצֵר הַמְּאוֹרוֹת.

---

from the Torah, known collectively by their first word, *Shema*. Around it are three blessings, two before and one after the Shema. Like the morning service as a whole, their themes are creation, revelation and redemption. The first (continuing the theme of the *Pesukei DeZimra*) is about creation, renewed daily. The second אַהֲבָה רַבָּה ("You have loved us") is about revela-

אַהֲבָה You have loved us with great love, LORD our God,
and with surpassing compassion
have You had compassion on us.
Our Father, our King,
for the sake of our ancestors who trusted in You,
and to whom You taught the laws of life,
be gracious also to us and teach us.
Our Father, compassionate Father,
ever compassionate,
have compassion on us.
Instill in our hearts
the desire to understand and discern,
to listen, learn and teach,
to observe, perform and fulfill
all the teachings of Your Torah in love.
Enlighten our eyes in Your Torah
and let our hearts cling to Your commandments.
Unite our hearts to love and revere Your name,
so that we may never be ashamed.
And because we have trusted
in Your holy, great and revered name,
may we be glad and rejoice in Your salvation.

At this point, gather the four tzitziot of the tallit, holding them in the left hand.

Bring us back in peace from the four quarters of the earth
and lead us upright to our land.
▸ For You are a God who performs acts of salvation,
and You chose us from all peoples and tongues,
bringing us close to Your great name for ever in truth,
that we may thank You
and proclaim Your oneness in love.
Blessed are You, LORD,
who chooses His people Israel in love.

אַהֲבָה רַבָּה אֲהַבְתָּנוּ, יהוה אֱלֹהֵינוּ
חֶמְלָה גְדוֹלָה וִיתֵרָה חָמַלְתָּ עָלֵינוּ.
אָבִינוּ מַלְכֵּנוּ
בַּעֲבוּר אֲבוֹתֵינוּ שֶׁבָּטְחוּ בְךָ
וַתְּלַמְּדֵם חֻקֵּי חַיִּים
כֵּן תְּחָנֵּנוּ וּתְלַמְּדֵנוּ.
אָבִינוּ, הָאָב הָרַחֲמָן, הַמְרַחֵם
רַחֵם עָלֵינוּ
וְתֵן בְּלִבֵּנוּ לְהָבִין וּלְהַשְׂכִּיל
לִשְׁמֹעַ, לִלְמֹד וּלְלַמֵּד, לִשְׁמֹר וְלַעֲשׂוֹת, וּלְקַיֵּם
אֶת כָּל דִּבְרֵי תַלְמוּד תּוֹרָתֶךָ בְּאַהֲבָה.
וְהָאֵר עֵינֵינוּ בְּתוֹרָתֶךָ, וְדַבֵּק לִבֵּנוּ בְּמִצְוֹתֶיךָ
וְיַחֵד לְבָבֵנוּ לְאַהֲבָה וּלְיִרְאָה אֶת שְׁמֶךָ
וְלֹא נֵבוֹשׁ לְעוֹלָם וָעֶד.
כִּי בְשֵׁם קָדְשְׁךָ הַגָּדוֹל וְהַנּוֹרָא בָּטָחְנוּ
נָגִילָה וְנִשְׂמְחָה בִּישׁוּעָתֶךָ.

At this point, gather the four ציציות *of the* טלית*, holding them in the left hand.*

וַהֲבִיאֵנוּ לְשָׁלוֹם מֵאַרְבַּע כַּנְפוֹת הָאָרֶץ
וְתוֹלִיכֵנוּ קוֹמְמִיּוּת לְאַרְצֵנוּ.
◂ כִּי אֵל פּוֹעֵל יְשׁוּעוֹת אָתָּה
וּבָנוּ בָחַרְתָּ מִכָּל עַם וְלָשׁוֹן
וְקֵרַבְתָּנוּ לְשִׁמְךָ הַגָּדוֹל סֶלָה, בֶּאֱמֶת
לְהוֹדוֹת לְךָ וּלְיַחֶדְךָ בְּאַהֲבָה.
בָּרוּךְ אַתָּה יהוה, הַבּוֹחֵר בְּעַמּוֹ יִשְׂרָאֵל בְּאַהֲבָה.

The Shema must be said with intense concentration. In the first paragraph one should accept, with love, the sovereignty of God; in the second, the mitzvot as the will of God. The end of the third paragraph constitutes fulfillment of the mitzva to remember, morning and evening, the exodus from Egypt. See laws 346–355.

When not praying with a minyan, say:

God, faithful King!

The following verse should be said aloud, while covering the eyes with the right hand:

Listen, Israel: the LORD is our God, the LORD is One.

Deut. 6

Quietly: Blessed be the name of His glorious kingdom for ever and all time.

Touch the hand-tefillin at ° and the head-tefillin at °°.

וְאָהַבְתָּ Love the LORD your God with all your heart, with all your soul, and with all your might. These words which I command you today shall be on your heart. Teach them repeatedly to your children, speaking of them when you sit at home and when you travel on the way, when you lie down and when you rise. °Bind them as a sign on your hand, and °°they shall be an emblem between your eyes. Write them on the doorposts of your house and gates. *Deut. 6*

Touch the hand-tefillin at ° and the head-tefillin at °°.

וְהָיָה If you indeed heed My commandments with which I charge you today, to love the LORD your God and worship Him with all your heart and with all your soul, I will give rain in your land in its season, the early and late rain; and you shall gather in your grain, wine and oil. I will give grass in your field for your cattle, and you shall eat and be satisfied. Be careful lest your heart be tempted and *Deut. 11*

---

biblical readings. It is less a prayer than a prelude to prayer. In prayer, we speak to God. In the Shema, God, through the Torah, speaks to us. The word Shema itself means "listen," and the recital of the Shema is a supreme act of faith-as-listening: to the voice that brought the universe into being, created us in love and guides us through our lives.

The first paragraph represents *kabbalat ol malkhut shamayim*, "acceptance of the yoke of the kingship of heaven." We pledge allegiance to the One God, Sovereign of the universe, to whose authority all earthly powers are answer-

The שמע must be said with intense concentration. In the first paragraph one should accept, with love, the sovereignty of God; in the second, the מצוות as the will of God. The end of the third paragraph constitutes fulfillment of the מצווה to remember, morning and evening, the exodus from Egypt. See laws 346–355.

When not praying with a מנין, say:

אֵל מֶלֶךְ נֶאֱמָן

The following verse should be said aloud, while covering the eyes with the right hand:

דברים ו שְׁמַע יִשְׂרָאֵל, יְהוָה אֱלֹהֵינוּ, יְהוָה ׀ אֶחָד:

Quietly בָּרוּךְ שֵׁם כְּבוֹד מַלְכוּתוֹ לְעוֹלָם וָעֶד.

Touch the תפילין של יד at ° and the תפילין של ראש at °°.

דברים ו וְאָהַבְתָּ אֵת יְהוָה אֱלֹהֶיךָ, בְּכָל־לְבָבְךָ וּבְכָל־נַפְשְׁךָ וּבְכָל־
מְאֹדֶךָ: וְהָיוּ הַדְּבָרִים הָאֵלֶּה, אֲשֶׁר אָנֹכִי מְצַוְּךָ הַיּוֹם, עַל־לְבָבֶךָ:
וְשִׁנַּנְתָּם לְבָנֶיךָ וְדִבַּרְתָּ בָּם, בְּשִׁבְתְּךָ בְּבֵיתֶךָ וּבְלֶכְתְּךָ בַדֶּרֶךְ,
וּבְשָׁכְבְּךָ וּבְקוּמֶךָ: °וּקְשַׁרְתָּם לְאוֹת עַל־יָדֶךָ °°וְהָיוּ לְטֹטָפֹת
בֵּין עֵינֶיךָ: וּכְתַבְתָּם עַל־מְזֻזוֹת בֵּיתֶךָ וּבִשְׁעָרֶיךָ:

Touch the תפילין של יד at ° and the תפילין של ראש at °°.

דברים יא וְהָיָה אִם־שָׁמֹעַ תִּשְׁמְעוּ אֶל־מִצְוֺתַי אֲשֶׁר אָנֹכִי מְצַוֶּה אֶתְכֶם
הַיּוֹם, לְאַהֲבָה אֶת־יְהוָה אֱלֹהֵיכֶם וּלְעָבְדוֹ, בְּכָל־לְבַבְכֶם וּבְכָל־
נַפְשְׁכֶם: וְנָתַתִּי מְטַר־אַרְצְכֶם בְּעִתּוֹ, יוֹרֶה וּמַלְקוֹשׁ, וְאָסַפְתָּ
דְגָנֶךָ וְתִירֹשְׁךָ וְיִצְהָרֶךָ: וְנָתַתִּי עֵשֶׂב בְּשָׂדְךָ לִבְהֶמְתֶּךָ, וְאָכַלְתָּ
וְשָׂבָעְתָּ: הִשָּׁמְרוּ לָכֶם פֶּן־יִפְתֶּה לְבַבְכֶם, וְסַרְתֶּם וַעֲבַדְתֶּם

THE SHEMA

The Shema is the oldest and greatest of our prayers, part of the liturgy since Temple times, recited evening and morning, "when you lie down and when you rise." Its opening line is among the first words taught to a Jewish child, and among the last words spoken by those who went to their deaths because they were Jews. It is the supreme declaration of faith.

The Shema contains no human requests, no praise, no plea. It is a set of

you go astray and worship other gods, bowing down to them. Then the LORD's anger will flare against you and He will close the heavens so that there will be no rain. The land will not yield its crops, and you will perish swiftly from the good land that the LORD is giving you. Therefore, set these, My words, on your heart and soul. °Bind them as a sign on your hand, °°and they shall be an emblem between your eyes. Teach them to your children, speaking of them when you sit at home and when you travel on the way, when you lie down and when you rise. Write them on the doorposts of your house and gates, so that you and your children may live long in the land that the LORD swore to your ancestors to give them, for as long as the heavens are above the earth.

Hold the tzitziot in the right hand also (some transfer to the right hand), kissing them at °.

וַיֹּאמֶר The LORD spoke to Moses, saying: Speak to the Israelites and tell them to make °tassels on the corners of their garments for all generations. They shall attach to the °tassel at each corner a thread of blue. This shall be your °tassel, and you shall see it and remember all of the LORD's commandments and keep them, not straying after your heart and after your eyes, following your own sinful desires. Thus you will be reminded to keep all My commandments, and be holy to your God. I am the LORD your God, who brought you out of the land of Egypt to be your God. I am the LORD your God. *Num. 15*

°True –

The Leader repeats:

▸ The LORD your God is true –

---

commandments." Whereas the first paragraph speaks to us as individuals, the second speaks to us as a people, defined by our covenant with God and its 613 commandments. "Our nation is only a nation in virtue of its Torah," said Rabbi Sa'adia Gaon, and our collective fate depends on our collective faith. The third paragraph speaks of tzitzit, a perennial reminder of God's commandments. It then leads into the theme of the exodus from Egypt, which we are commanded to remember "all the days of our lives."

אֱלֹהִים אֲחֵרִים וְהִשְׁתַּחֲוִיתֶם לָהֶם: וְחָרָה אַף־יהוה בָּכֶם, וְעָצַר אֶת־הַשָּׁמַיִם וְלֹא־יִהְיֶה מָטָר, וְהָאֲדָמָה לֹא תִתֵּן אֶת־יְבוּלָהּ, וַאֲבַדְתֶּם מְהֵרָה מֵעַל הָאָרֶץ הַטֹּבָה אֲשֶׁר יהוה נֹתֵן לָכֶם: וְשַׂמְתֶּם אֶת־דְּבָרַי אֵלֶּה עַל־לְבַבְכֶם וְעַל־נַפְשְׁכֶם, °וּקְשַׁרְתֶּם אֹתָם לְאוֹת עַל־יֶדְכֶם, °°וְהָיוּ לְטוֹטָפֹת בֵּין עֵינֵיכֶם: וְלִמַּדְתֶּם אֹתָם אֶת־בְּנֵיכֶם לְדַבֵּר בָּם, בְּשִׁבְתְּךָ בְּבֵיתֶךָ וּבְלֶכְתְּךָ בַדֶּרֶךְ, וּבְשָׁכְבְּךָ וּבְקוּמֶךָ: וּכְתַבְתָּם עַל־מְזוּזוֹת בֵּיתֶךָ וּבִשְׁעָרֶיךָ: לְמַעַן יִרְבּוּ יְמֵיכֶם וִימֵי בְנֵיכֶם עַל הָאֲדָמָה אֲשֶׁר נִשְׁבַּע יהוה לַאֲבֹתֵיכֶם לָתֵת לָהֶם, כִּימֵי הַשָּׁמַיִם עַל־הָאָרֶץ:

Hold the ציציות *in the right hand also (some transfer to the right hand), kissing them at °.*

במדבר טו וַיֹּאמֶר יהוה אֶל־מֹשֶׁה לֵּאמֹר: דַּבֵּר אֶל־בְּנֵי יִשְׂרָאֵל וְאָמַרְתָּ אֲלֵהֶם, וְעָשׂוּ לָהֶם °צִיצִת עַל־כַּנְפֵי בִגְדֵיהֶם לְדֹרֹתָם, וְנָתְנוּ °עַל־צִיצִת הַכָּנָף פְּתִיל תְּכֵלֶת: וְהָיָה לָכֶם °לְצִיצִת, וּרְאִיתֶם אֹתוֹ וּזְכַרְתֶּם אֶת־כָּל־מִצְוֹת יהוה וַעֲשִׂיתֶם אֹתָם, וְלֹא תָתֻרוּ אַחֲרֵי לְבַבְכֶם וְאַחֲרֵי עֵינֵיכֶם, אֲשֶׁר־אַתֶּם זֹנִים אַחֲרֵיהֶם: לְמַעַן תִּזְכְּרוּ וַעֲשִׂיתֶם אֶת־כָּל־מִצְוֹתָי, וִהְיִיתֶם קְדֹשִׁים לֵאלֹהֵיכֶם: אֲנִי יהוה אֱלֹהֵיכֶם, אֲשֶׁר הוֹצֵאתִי אֶתְכֶם מֵאֶרֶץ מִצְרַיִם, לִהְיוֹת לָכֶם לֵאלֹהִים, אֲנִי יהוה אֱלֹהֵיכֶם:

°אֱמֶת

The שליח ציבור *repeats:*

◂ יהוה אֱלֹהֵיכֶם אֱמֶת

---

able. We do so not in fear but in love and with the totality of our being: all our heart, our soul, our might. That love suffuses all we do, from our relationships with our children to the homes we make.

The second paragraph represents *kabbalat ol mitzvot*, "acceptance of the

וְיַצִּיב And firm, established and enduring,
right, faithful,
beloved, cherished, delightful, pleasant,
awesome, mighty, perfect, accepted,
good and beautiful
is this faith for us for ever.
True is the eternal God, our King,
Rock of Jacob,
Shield of our salvation.
He exists and His name exists
through all generations.
His throne is established,
His kingship and faithfulness endure for ever.

At °, kiss the tzitziot and release them.

His words live and persist,
faithful and desirable
°for ever and all time.
▸ So they were for our ancestors,
so they are for us,
and so they will be for our children
and all our generations
and for all future generations
of the seed of Israel, Your servants. ◂
For the early and the later generations
this faith has proved good and enduring for ever –
True and faithful, an irrevocable law.

Israel," and the beginning of the Amida (*Berakhot* 14b, 9b). The connection between the two is *redemption*, the theme of this section. The Shema ends by speaking about redemption in the past. In the Amida we pray for redemption in the future. Connecting past and future is "truth" – our faith in God and in His covenant with us.

וְיַצִּיב, וְנָכוֹן וְקַיָּם, וְיָשָׁר וְנֶאֱמָן
וְאָהוּב וְחָבִיב, וְנֶחְמָד וְנָעִים
וְנוֹרָא וְאַדִּיר, וּמְתֻקָּן וּמְקֻבָּל
וְטוֹב וְיָפֶה
הַדָּבָר הַזֶּה עָלֵינוּ לְעוֹלָם וָעֶד.
אֱמֶת אֱלֹהֵי עוֹלָם מַלְכֵּנוּ
צוּר יַעֲקֹב מָגֵן יִשְׁעֵנוּ
לְדוֹר וָדוֹר הוּא קַיָּם וּשְׁמוֹ קַיָּם
וְכִסְאוֹ נָכוֹן
וּמַלְכוּתוֹ וֶאֱמוּנָתוֹ לָעַד קַיָּמֶת.

At °, kiss the ציצית *and release them.*

וּדְבָרָיו חָיִים וְקַיָּמִים
נֶאֱמָנִים וְנֶחֱמָדִים
°לָעַד וּלְעוֹלְמֵי עוֹלָמִים
◂ עַל אֲבוֹתֵינוּ וְעָלֵינוּ
עַל בָּנֵינוּ וְעַל דּוֹרוֹתֵינוּ
וְעַל כָּל דּוֹרוֹת זֶרַע יִשְׂרָאֵל עֲבָדֶיךָ. ◂
עַל הָרִאשׁוֹנִים וְעַל הָאַחֲרוֹנִים
דָּבָר טוֹב וְקַיָּם לְעוֹלָם וָעֶד
אֱמֶת וֶאֱמוּנָה, חֹק וְלֹא יַעֲבֹר.

וְיַצִּיב *And firm:* This section of prayer, joining the Shema to the Amida, goes back to Temple times. The sages emphasized that there must be no separation between the last words of the Shema, "I am the LORD your God," and the first word of the prayer, "*True* and firm," or between its last words, "who redeemed

True You are the LORD: our God and God of our ancestors,
▸ our King and King of our ancestors,
our Redeemer and Redeemer of our ancestors,
our Maker,
Rock of our salvation,
our Deliverer and Rescuer:
this has ever been Your name.
There is no God but You.

עֶזְרַת You have always been the help of our ancestors,
Shield and Savior of their children after them
in every generation.
Your dwelling is in the heights of the universe,
and Your judgments and righteousness
reach to the ends of the earth.
Happy is the one who obeys Your commandments
and takes to heart Your teaching and Your word.
True You are the Master of Your people
and a mighty King who pleads their cause.
True You are the first and You are the last.
Besides You, we have no king,
redeemer or savior.
From Egypt You redeemed us,
LORD our God,
and from the slave-house You delivered us.
All their firstborn You killed,
but Your firstborn You redeemed.
You split the Sea of Reeds
and drowned the arrogant.
You brought Your beloved ones across.
The water covered their foes; *Ps. 106*
not one of them was left.

אֱמֶת שָׁאַתָּה הוּא יהוה אֱלֹהֵינוּ וֵאלֹהֵי אֲבוֹתֵינוּ
‣ מַלְכֵּנוּ מֶלֶךְ אֲבוֹתֵינוּ
גּוֹאֲלֵנוּ גּוֹאֵל אֲבוֹתֵינוּ
יוֹצְרֵנוּ צוּר יְשׁוּעָתֵנוּ
פּוֹדֵנוּ וּמַצִּילֵנוּ מֵעוֹלָם שְׁמֶךָ
אֵין אֱלֹהִים זוּלָתֶךָ.

עֶזְרַת אֲבוֹתֵינוּ אַתָּה הוּא מֵעוֹלָם
מָגֵן וּמוֹשִׁיעַ לִבְנֵיהֶם אַחֲרֵיהֶם בְּכָל דּוֹר וָדוֹר.
בְּרוּם עוֹלָם מוֹשָׁבֶךָ
וּמִשְׁפָּטֶיךָ וְצִדְקָתְךָ עַד אַפְסֵי אָרֶץ.
אַשְׁרֵי אִישׁ שֶׁיִּשְׁמַע לְמִצְוֹתֶיךָ
וְתוֹרָתְךָ וּדְבָרְךָ יָשִׂים עַל לִבּוֹ.
אֱמֶת אַתָּה הוּא אָדוֹן לְעַמֶּךָ
וּמֶלֶךְ גִּבּוֹר לָרִיב רִיבָם.
אֱמֶת אַתָּה הוּא רִאשׁוֹן וְאַתָּה הוּא אַחֲרוֹן
וּמִבַּלְעָדֶיךָ אֵין לָנוּ מֶלֶךְ גּוֹאֵל וּמוֹשִׁיעַ.
מִמִּצְרַיִם גְּאַלְתָּנוּ, יהוה אֱלֹהֵינוּ
וּמִבֵּית עֲבָדִים פְּדִיתָנוּ
כָּל בְּכוֹרֵיהֶם הָרָגְתָּ, וּבְכוֹרְךָ גָּאָלְתָּ
וְיַם סוּף בָּקַעְתָּ
וְזֵדִים טִבַּעְתָּ
וִידִידִים הֶעֱבַרְתָּ
וַיְכַסּוּ־מַיִם צָרֵיהֶם, אֶחָד מֵהֶם לֹא נוֹתָר: תהלים קו

For this, the beloved ones praised and exalted God,
the cherished ones sang psalms, songs and praises,
blessings and thanksgivings to the King,
the living and enduring God.
High and exalted, great and awesome,
He humbles the haughty and raises the lowly,
freeing captives and redeeming those in need,
helping the poor
and answering His people when they cry out to Him.

Stand in preparation for the Amida. Take three steps back before beginning the Amida.

▸ Praises to God Most High,
the Blessed One who is blessed.
Moses and the children of Israel
recited to You a song with great joy,
and they all exclaimed:
"Who is like You, LORD, among the mighty? *Ex. 15*
Who is like You, majestic in holiness,
awesome in praises, doing wonders?"
▸ With a new song, the redeemed people praised
Your name at the seashore.
Together they all gave thanks,
proclaimed Your kingship,
and declared:
"The LORD shall reign for ever and ever." *Ex. 15*

Congregants should end the following blessing together with the Leader so as to be able to move directly from the words "redeemed Israel" to the Amida, without the interruption of saying Amen.

▸ צוּר יִשְׂרָאֵל Rock of Israel! Arise to the help of Israel.
Deliver, as You promised, Judah and Israel.
Our Redeemer, the LORD of hosts is His name, *Is. 47*
the Holy One of Israel.
Blessed are You, LORD, who redeemed Israel.

עַל זֹאת שִׁבְּחוּ אֲהוּבִים, וְרוֹמְמוּ אֵל
וְנָתְנוּ יְדִידִים זְמִירוֹת, שִׁירוֹת וְתִשְׁבָּחוֹת
בְּרָכוֹת וְהוֹדָאוֹת לְמֶלֶךְ אֵל חַי וְקַיָּם
רָם וְנִשָּׂא, גָּדוֹל וְנוֹרָא
מַשְׁפִּיל גֵּאִים וּמַגְבִּיהַּ שְׁפָלִים
מוֹצִיא אֲסִירִים, וּפוֹדֶה עֲנָוִים וְעוֹזֵר דַּלִּים
וְעוֹנֶה לְעַמּוֹ בְּעֵת שַׁוְּעָם אֵלָיו.

Stand in preparation for the עמידה*. Take three steps back before beginning the* עמידה*.*

▸ תְּהִלּוֹת לְאֵל עֶלְיוֹן, בָּרוּךְ הוּא וּמְבֹרָךְ
מֹשֶׁה וּבְנֵי יִשְׂרָאֵל
לְךָ עָנוּ שִׁירָה בְּשִׂמְחָה רַבָּה
וְאָמְרוּ כֻלָּם

מִי־כָמֹכָה בָּאֵלִם, יהוה שמות טו
מִי כָּמֹכָה נֶאְדָּר בַּקֹּדֶשׁ, נוֹרָא תְהִלֹּת, עֹשֵׂה פֶלֶא:

▸ שִׁירָה חֲדָשָׁה שִׁבְּחוּ גְאוּלִים
לְשִׁמְךָ עַל שְׂפַת הַיָּם
יַחַד כֻּלָּם הוֹדוּ וְהִמְלִיכוּ
וְאָמְרוּ

יהוה יִמְלֹךְ לְעֹלָם וָעֶד: שמות טו

The קהל *should end the following blessing together with the* שליח ציבור *so as to be able to move directly from the words* גאל ישראל *to the* עמידה*, without the interruption of saying* אמן*.*

▸ צוּר יִשְׂרָאֵל, קוּמָה בְּעֶזְרַת יִשְׂרָאֵל
וּפְדֵה כִנְאֻמֶךָ יְהוּדָה וְיִשְׂרָאֵל.
גֹּאֲלֵנוּ יהוה צְבָאוֹת שְׁמוֹ, קְדוֹשׁ יִשְׂרָאֵל: ישעיה מז
בָּרוּךְ אַתָּה יהוה, גָּאַל יִשְׂרָאֵל.

THE AMIDA

The following prayer, until "in former years" on page 134, is said standing with feet together in imitation of the angels in Ezekiel's vision (Ezek. 1:7). The Amida is said silently, following the precedent of Hannah when she prayed for a child (1 Sam. 1:13). If there is a minyan, it is repeated aloud by the Leader. Take three steps forward, as if formally entering the place of the Divine Presence. At the points indicated by ▾, bend the knees at the first word, bow at the second, and stand straight before saying God's name.

O Lord, open my lips, *Ps. 51*
so that my mouth may declare Your praise.

PATRIARCHS

▾בָּרוּךְ Blessed are You, Lord our God and God of our fathers,
God of Abraham, God of Isaac and God of Jacob;
the great, mighty and awesome God, God Most High,
who bestows acts of loving-kindness and creates all,
who remembers the loving-kindness of the fathers and will bring a Redeemer to their children's children
for the sake of His name, in love.

Between Rosh HaShana & Yom Kippur: Remember us for life, O King who desires life,
and write us in the book of life –
for Your sake, O God of life.

King, Helper, Savior, Shield:
▾Blessed are You, Lord, Shield of Abraham.

Several centuries later, it was canonized in a fuller form by Shimon HaPakuli in the days of Rabban Gamliel II (*Berakhot* 28b).

It is often called the *Shemoneh Esreh*, "Eighteen," because it originally consisted of eighteen blessings (now, nineteen). It has a three-part structure: (1) *praise* (blessings 1–3), (2) *requests* (blessings 4–16), and (3) *thanks* (17–19). Each of these has a tripartite form. The first and last sections each contain three blessings. The middle section is composed of twelve blessings (4–15), six personal requests and six collective ones. The first three personal requests are for spiritual goods (wisdom, repentance and forgiveness). The second are for physical goods (deliverance, healing and livelihood). The first three national requests are for physical events (ingathering of exiles, justice, and an end to internal conflicts). The second three are for the nation's spiritual needs

עמידה

The following prayer, until קַדְמֹנִיּוֹת *on page 135, is said standing with feet together in imitation of the angels in Ezekiel's vision* (יחזקאל א, ז). *The* עמידה *is said silently, following the precedent of Hannah when she prayed for a child* (שמואל א׳ א, יג). *If there is a* מנין, *it is repeated aloud by the* שליח ציבור. *Take three steps forward, as if formally entering the place of the Divine Presence. At the points indicated by* ׳, *bend the knees at the first word, bow at the second, and stand straight before saying God's name.*

אֲדֹנָי, שְׂפָתַי תִּפְתָּח, וּפִי יַגִּיד תְּהִלָּתֶךָ: תהלים נא

אבות

׳בָּרוּךְ אַתָּה יהוה, אֱלֹהֵינוּ וֵאלֹהֵי אֲבוֹתֵינוּ
אֱלֹהֵי אַבְרָהָם, אֱלֹהֵי יִצְחָק, וֵאלֹהֵי יַעֲקֹב
הָאֵל הַגָּדוֹל הַגִּבּוֹר וְהַנּוֹרָא, אֵל עֶלְיוֹן
גּוֹמֵל חֲסָדִים טוֹבִים, וְקוֹנֵה הַכֹּל
וְזוֹכֵר חַסְדֵי אָבוֹת
וּמֵבִיא גוֹאֵל לִבְנֵי בְנֵיהֶם לְמַעַן שְׁמוֹ בְּאַהֲבָה.

בעשרת ימי תשובה: זָכְרֵנוּ לְחַיִּים, מֶלֶךְ חָפֵץ בַּחַיִּים
וְכָתְבֵנוּ בְּסֵפֶר הַחַיִּים, לְמַעַנְךָ אֱלֹהִים חַיִּים.

מֶלֶךְ עוֹזֵר וּמוֹשִׁיעַ וּמָגֵן.
׳בָּרוּךְ אַתָּה יהוה, מָגֵן אַבְרָהָם.

THE AMIDA: THE STANDING PRAYER

The Amida is the summit of prayer: in it, we enter the holy of holies of religious experience. We say it standing because we are conscious of being in the unmediated presence of God. The name Amida is also related to its earliest setting: prayers said by the people of the *Ma'amad*, groups of laymen who, in Second Temple times, accompanied their local "watch" (*mishmar*) of priests who officiated in the Temple on a one-in-24-week schedule. The *Ma'amad* was one of the prototypes of congregational prayer.

According to tradition, the Amida in embryonic form dates back to the Great Assembly in the time of Ezra following the Jews' return from Babylon.

DIVINE MIGHT

אַתָּה גִּבּוֹר You are eternally mighty, Lord.
You give life to the dead and have great power to save.

The phrase "He makes the wind blow and the rain fall" is said from Simhat Torah until Pesah. In Israel the phrase "He causes the dew to fall" is said from Pesah until Shemini Atzeret. See laws 129–131.

In fall & winter: He makes the wind blow and the rain fall.
In Israel, in spring & summer: He causes the dew to fall.

He sustains the living with loving-kindness,
and with great compassion revives the dead.
He supports the fallen, heals the sick,
sets captives free,
and keeps His faith with those who sleep in the dust.
Who is like You, Master of might,
and who can compare to You,
O King who brings death and gives life,
and makes salvation grow?

Between Rosh HaShana & Yom Kippur: Who is like You, compassionate Father,
who remembers His creatures in compassion, for life?

Faithful are You to revive the dead.
Blessed are You, Lord, who revives the dead.

---

who was the first person to heed God's call. לְמַעַנְךָ אֱלֹהִים חַיִּים *For Your sake, O* God *of life:* the phrase literally means "Living God." The translation, however, conveys the poetic structure of this short but powerful prayer: four phrases, each ending with the word *hayim*, "life."

גבורות *Blessing 2: Divine might.* The fivefold reference to the resurrection of the dead reflects the controversy between the Sadducees and Pharisees in the late Second Temple era. The Sadducees rejected belief in resurrection; the Pharisees, whose heirs we are, affirmed it. Belief that those who died will one day live again is one of Judaism's great principles of hope, set out in the vision of Ezekiel of the valley of dry bones that came to life once more. Jews kept hope alive; hope kept the Jewish people alive.

גבורות

אַתָּה גִּבּוֹר לְעוֹלָם, אֲדֹנָי
מְחַיֵּה מֵתִים אַתָּה, רַב לְהוֹשִׁיעַ

The phrase מַשִּׁיב הָרְוּחַ *is said from* שמחת תורה *until* פסח.
In ארץ ישראל *the phrase* מוֹרִיד הַטָּל *is said from* פסח *until* שמיני עצרת. *See laws 129–131.*

בחורף: מַשִּׁיב הָרְוּחַ וּמוֹרִיד הַגֶּשֶׁם / בארץ ישראל בקיץ: מוֹרִיד הַטָּל

מְכַלְכֵּל חַיִּים בְּחֶסֶד, מְחַיֵּה מֵתִים בְּרַחֲמִים רַבִּים
סוֹמֵךְ נוֹפְלִים, וְרוֹפֵא חוֹלִים, וּמַתִּיר אֲסוּרִים
וּמְקַיֵּם אֱמוּנָתוֹ לִישֵׁנֵי עָפָר.
מִי כָמְוֹךָ, בַּעַל גְּבוּרוֹת
וּמִי דּוֹמֶה לָּךְ
מֶלֶךְ, מֵמִית וּמְחַיֶּה וּמַצְמִיחַ יְשׁוּעָה.

בעשרת ימי תשובה: מִי כָמְוֹךָ אַב הָרַחֲמִים
זוֹכֵר יְצוּרָיו לְחַיִּים בְּרַחֲמִים.

וְנֶאֱמָן אַתָּה לְהַחֲיוֹת מֵתִים.
בָּרוּךְ אַתָּה יהוה, מְחַיֵּה הַמֵּתִים.

(the righteous and pious, the rebuilding of Jerusalem, and the restoration of the Davidic monarchy). One blessing, "Listen to our voice" (the sixteenth, last of the "request" blessings), stands outside this structure because it is a prayer about prayer itself. It is also the point at which individuals can add their personal requests.

אבות *Blessing 1: Patriarchs.* In these opening chords we refer back to the dawn of our people's history – the days of the patriarchs, Abraham, Isaac and Jacob. In so doing, we echo Moses, who constantly referred to the patriarchs when praying for forgiveness for the people. God's love for, and covenant with, those who first heard His call is the supreme ground on which we stand when we turn to Him in prayer. The paragraph ends with a reference to Abraham,

When saying the Amida silently, continue with "You are holy" on the next page.

KEDUSHA

During the Leader's Repetition, the following is said standing with feet together, rising on the toes at the words indicated by ▴.

Cong. then Leader: נְקַדֵּשׁ We will sanctify Your name on earth,
as they sanctify it in the highest heavens,
as is written by Your prophet,
"And they [the angels] call to one another saying: *Is. 6*

Cong. then Leader: ▴Holy, ▴holy, ▴holy is the LORD of hosts
the whole world is filled with His glory."
Those facing them say "Blessed – "

Cong. then Leader: ▴"Blessed is the LORD's glory from His place." *Ezek. 3*
And in Your holy Writings it is written thus:

Cong. then Leader: ▴"The LORD shall reign for ever. He is your God, Zion, *Ps. 146*
from generation to generation, Halleluya!"

Leader: From generation to generation we will declare Your greatness,
and we will proclaim Your holiness for evermore.
Your praise, our God, shall not leave our mouth forever,
for You, God, are a great and holy King. Blessed are You, LORD,
the holy God. / *Between Rosh HaShana & Yom Kippur:* the holy King./

The Leader continues with "You grace humanity" on the next page.

---

do not require a *minyan* and are said sitting. The second requires a *minyan* and is said standing. The reason is that the first and third are descriptions of the song of the angels; the second is a reenactment. We stand, feet together, rising on our toes, as if we too were angels.

In the *Kedusha* we move beyond the priestly prayer-as-sacrifice and the prophetic prayer-as-dialogue, to prayer as a mystic experience. So holy is it that in Israel in ancient times it was said only on Shabbat and festivals. The *Zohar* interprets Jacob's vision of a ladder stretching from earth to heaven, with angels ascending and descending (Gen. 28:12), as a metaphor for prayer, and this, too, is part of the meaning of *Kedusha*. We have climbed the ladder from earth to heaven. As the Leader repeats the prayer on behalf of the entire community, we reach the summit of religious experience.

When saying the עמידה *silently, continue with* אַתָּה קָדוֹשׁ *on the next page.*

קדושה

During חזרת הש״ץ*, the following is said standing with feet together, rising on the toes at the words indicated by* ˄.

קהל *then* ש״ץ: נְקַדֵּשׁ אֶת שִׁמְךָ בָּעוֹלָם, כְּשֵׁם שֶׁמַּקְדִּישִׁים אוֹתוֹ בִּשְׁמֵי מָרוֹם
כַּכָּתוּב עַל יַד נְבִיאֶךָ, וְקָרָא זֶה אֶל־זֶה וְאָמַר ישעיה ו

קהל *then* ש״ץ: ˄קָדוֹשׁ, ˄קָדוֹשׁ, ˄קָדוֹשׁ, יהוה צְבָאוֹת, מְלֹא כָל־הָאָרֶץ כְּבוֹדוֹ:
לְעֻמָּתָם בָּרוּךְ יֹאמֵרוּ

קהל *then* ש״ץ: ˄בָּרוּךְ כְּבוֹד־יהוה מִמְּקוֹמוֹ: יחזקאל ג
וּבְדִבְרֵי קָדְשְׁךָ כָּתוּב לֵאמֹר

קהל *then* ש״ץ: ˄יִמְלֹךְ יהוה לְעוֹלָם, אֱלֹהַיִךְ צִיּוֹן לְדֹר וָדֹר, הַלְלוּיָהּ: תהלים קמו

ש״ץ: לְדוֹר וָדוֹר נַגִּיד גָּדְלֶךָ, וּלְנֵצַח נְצָחִים קְדֻשָּׁתְךָ נַקְדִּישׁ
וְשִׁבְחֲךָ אֱלֹהֵינוּ מִפִּינוּ לֹא יָמוּשׁ לְעוֹלָם וָעֶד
כִּי אֵל מֶלֶךְ גָּדוֹל וְקָדוֹשׁ אָתָּה.
בָּרוּךְ אַתָּה יהוה, הָאֵל הַקָּדוֹשׁ./בעשרת ימי תשובה: הַמֶּלֶךְ הַקָּדוֹשׁ./

The שליח ציבור *continues with* אַתָּה חוֹנֵן *on the next page.*

קדושה *Kedusha.* The *Kedusha* is the supreme moment of holiness in prayer. It takes several different forms. Common to them all is that they are built around the two supreme mystical visions in the Hebrew Bible, of Isaiah (chapter 6) and Ezekiel (chapters 1–3). The prophet sees God enthroned in glory, surrounded by angels singing His praises. Isaiah hears them singing, "Holy, holy, holy is the LORD of hosts; the whole world is filled with His glory." Ezekiel (3:12) hears them singing, "Blessed is the LORD's glory from His place." Together they constitute the most sublime expression of prayer as praise in the presence of God.

In the morning, *Kedusha* is said three times at different points in the service. There is *Kedushat Yotzer,* which appears in the first of the three Shema blessings (page 95), *Kedusha DeAmida,* said here during the Leader's Repetition; and *Kedusha DeSidra,* toward the end of the service. The first and third

HOLINESS

אַתָּה קָדוֹשׁ You are holy and Your name is holy,
and holy ones praise You daily, Selah!
Blessed are You, LORD,
the holy God. / *Between Rosh HaShana & Yom Kippur:* the holy King./
(If forgotten, repeat the Amida.)

KNOWLEDGE

אַתָּה חוֹנֵן You grace humanity with knowledge
and teach mortals understanding.
Grace us with the knowledge, understanding
and discernment that come from You.
Blessed are You, LORD, who graciously grants knowledge.

REPENTANCE

הֲשִׁיבֵנוּ Bring us back, our Father,
to Your Torah.
Draw us near, our King,
to Your service.
Lead us back to You in perfect repentance.
Blessed are You, LORD, who desires repentance.

דעת *Blessing 4: Knowledge.* This is the first of the "request" blessings. King Solomon, when asked by God to name the thing he most desired (1 Kings 3:5–15), asked for wisdom; so do we. Knowledge is prior to emotion, because "the heart is deceitful above all things" (Jer. 17:9). Untutored emotion can be misdirected, even destructive.

This paragraph replicates the structure of the Amida as a whole. It begins with praise ("You grace humanity with knowledge"), proceeds to request ("Grace us with the knowledge"), and ends in acknowledgment ("Who graciously grants knowledge").

תשובה *Blessing 5: Repentance.* Knowledge and understanding allow us to see where we have drifted from the right path of life. So we ask God to help us find the way back to repentance.

קדושת השם

אַתָּה קָדוֹשׁ וְשִׁמְךָ קָדוֹשׁ
וּקְדוֹשִׁים בְּכָל יוֹם יְהַלְלוּךָ סֶּלָה.
בָּרוּךְ אַתָּה יהוה, הָאֵל הַקָּדוֹשׁ./ בעשרת ימי תשובה: הַמֶּלֶךְ הַקָּדוֹשׁ./
(*If forgotten, repeat the* עמידה.)

דעת

אַתָּה חוֹנֵן לְאָדָם דַּעַת
וּמְלַמֵּד לֶאֱנוֹשׁ בִּינָה.
חָנֵּנוּ מֵאִתְּךָ דֵּעָה בִּינָה וְהַשְׂכֵּל.
בָּרוּךְ אַתָּה יהוה, חוֹנֵן הַדָּעַת.

תשובה

הֲשִׁיבֵנוּ אָבִינוּ לְתוֹרָתֶךָ
וְקָרְבֵנוּ מַלְכֵּנוּ לַעֲבוֹדָתֶךָ
וְהַחֲזִירֵנוּ בִּתְשׁוּבָה שְׁלֵמָה לְפָנֶיךָ.
בָּרוּךְ אַתָּה יהוה, הָרוֹצֶה בִּתְשׁוּבָה.

קדושת השם *Blessing 3: Holiness.* The threefold reference to holiness ("You are holy and Your name is holy, and holy ones praise You daily") mirrors the threefold declaration of the angels in Isaiah's vision: "Holy, holy, holy is the LORD of hosts." *Kadosh*, "holy," means "set apart, distinct." When used of God, it refers to His transcendence, the fact that He stands outside nature, creating and sustaining it. When used of Israel, it means that we too are summoned to stand apart from the idols of the age, living instead in close and continuous proximity to God.

The first three paragraphs of the Amida (excluding the *Kedusha*), form a composite unit. The first speaks of the beginning of covenantal time in the days of the patriarchs. The second is about the end of time: resurrection. The third is about holiness, beyond space and time.

FORGIVENESS

Strike the left side of the chest at °.

סְלַח לָנוּ Forgive us, our Father, for we have °sinned.
Pardon us, our King, for we have °transgressed;
for You pardon and forgive.
Blessed are You, LORD,
the gracious One who repeatedly forgives.

REDEMPTION

רְאֵה Look on our affliction, plead our cause,
and redeem us soon for Your name's sake,
for You are a powerful Redeemer.
Blessed are You, LORD, the Redeemer of Israel.

On Fast Days the Leader adds:

עֲנֵנוּ Answer us, LORD, answer us on our Fast Day, for we are in great distress. Look not at our wickedness. Do not hide Your face from us and do not ignore our plea. Be near to our cry; please let Your loving-kindness comfort us. Even before we call to You, answer us, as is said, "Before they call, I will answer. *Is. 65*
While they are still speaking, I will hear." For You, LORD, are the One who answers in time of distress, redeems and rescues in all times of trouble and anguish. Blessed are You, LORD, who answers in time of distress.

---

or affliction. Rabbi Samson Raphael Hirsch distinguishes between the first two phrases thus: "Look on our affliction" refers to suffering not caused by others, while "Plead our cause" refers to those who seek our harm. Rational argument is often insufficient to cure hatred; therefore we place our fate in the hands of God, asking Him to heal hostility (Rabbi J.H. Hertz). לְמַעַן שְׁמֶךָ *For Your name's sake:* may we be spared suffering not for our own sake but so that we may be free to worship You without distraction (Rabbi Yaakov Tzvi Mecklenburg). גּוֹאֵל יִשְׂרָאֵל *Redeemer of Israel:* in the present, as opposed to the blessing immediately prior to the Amida, which refers to acts of divine redemption in the past.

עֲנֵנוּ *Answer us:* A special prayer to be said on public fasts (*Ta'anit* 11a). The Leader recites it at this point in the Repetition of the Amida.

סליחה

Strike the left side of the chest at °.

סְלַח לָנוּ אָבִינוּ כִּי °חָטָאנוּ
מְחַל לָנוּ מַלְכֵּנוּ כִּי °פָשָׁעְנוּ
כִּי מוֹחֵל וְסוֹלֵחַ אָתָּה.
בָּרוּךְ אַתָּה יהוה, חַנּוּן הַמַּרְבֶּה לִסְלֹחַ.

גאולה

רְאֵה בְעָנְיֵנוּ, וְרִיבָה רִיבֵנוּ
וּגְאָלֵנוּ מְהֵרָה לְמַעַן שְׁמֶךָ
כִּי גּוֹאֵל חָזָק אָתָּה.
בָּרוּךְ אַתָּה יהוה, גּוֹאֵל יִשְׂרָאֵל.

On Fast Days the שליח ציבור *adds:*

עֲנֵנוּ יהוה עֲנֵנוּ בְּיוֹם צוֹם תַּעֲנִיתֵנוּ, כִּי בְצָרָה גְדוֹלָה אֲנָחְנוּ. אַל תֵּפֶן אֶל רִשְׁעֵנוּ, וְאַל תַּסְתֵּר פָּנֶיךָ מִמֶּנּוּ, וְאַל תִּתְעַלַּם מִתְּחִנָּתֵנוּ. הֱיֵה נָא קָרוֹב לְשַׁוְעָתֵנוּ, יְהִי נָא חַסְדְּךָ לְנַחֲמֵנוּ, טֶרֶם נִקְרָא אֵלֶיךָ עֲנֵנוּ, כַּדָּבָר שֶׁנֶּאֱמַר:
ישעיה סה וְהָיָה טֶרֶם יִקְרָאוּ וַאֲנִי אֶעֱנֶה, עוֹד הֵם מְדַבְּרִים וַאֲנִי אֶשְׁמָע: כִּי אַתָּה יהוה הָעוֹנֶה בְּעֵת צָרָה, פּוֹדֶה וּמַצִּיל בְּכָל עֵת צָרָה וְצוּקָה. בָּרוּךְ אַתָּה יהוה, הָעוֹנֶה בְּעֵת צָרָה.

סליחה *Blessing 6: Forgiveness.* Repentance involves asking God to forgive us. This applies to sins between us and God. Sins between us and our fellow human beings are only forgiven when we have apologized to, and tried to obtain the forgiveness of, those we have wronged. Knowledge, repentance and forgiveness are the three primary needs of the mind and soul.

גאולה *Blessing 7: Redemption.* The commentators explain that this request is not for national redemption, the subject of later blessings. Here the reference is to release from personal crises: captivity, persecution, misfortune

HEALING

רְפָאֵנוּ Heal us, LORD, and we shall be healed.
Save us and we shall be saved,
for You are our praise.
Bring complete recovery for all our ailments,

The following prayer for a sick person may be said here:
May it be Your will, O LORD my God and God of my ancestors, that You speedily send a complete recovery from heaven, a healing of both soul and body, to the patient (*name*), son/daughter of (*mother's name*) among the other afflicted of Israel.

---

for You, God, King, are a faithful and compassionate Healer.
Blessed are You, LORD, Healer of the sick of His people Israel.

PROSPERITY

The phrase "Grant dew and rain as a blessing" is said from December 5th (in the year before a civil leap year, December 6th) until Pesaḥ. In Israel, it is said from the 7th of Marḥeshvan. The phrase "Grant blessing" is said from Ḥol HaMo'ed Pesaḥ until December 4th (in the year before a civil leap year, December 5th). In Israel it is said through the 6th of Marḥeshvan. See laws 147–149.

בָּרֵךְ Bless this year for us, LORD our God,
and all its types of produce for good.

In winter: Grant dew and rain as a blessing
In other seasons: Grant blessing

on the face of the earth,
and from its goodness satisfy us,
blessing our year as the best of years.
Blessed are You, LORD, who blesses the years.

---

teaches its inhabitants the need for prayer. וְתֵן טַל וּמָטָר *Grant dew and rain:* unlike the praise "He makes the wind blow and the rain fall" (page 111), which we begin saying on Shemini Atzeret, the actual prayer for rain is said later to coincide with the rainy season itself. Outside Israel, it is said from the sixtieth day after "*Tekufat Tishrei*," the Jewish equivalent of the fall equinox (in the Northern Hemisphere).

רפואה

רְפָאֵנוּ יהוה וְנֵרָפֵא
הוֹשִׁיעֵנוּ וְנִוָּשֵׁעָה, כִּי תְהִלָּתֵנוּ אָתָּה
וְהַעֲלֵה רְפוּאָה שְׁלֵמָה לְכָל מַכּוֹתֵינוּ

The following prayer for a sick person may be said here:

יְהִי רָצוֹן מִלְּפָנֶיךָ יהוה אֱלֹהַי וֵאלֹהֵי אֲבוֹתַי, שֶׁתִּשְׁלַח מְהֵרָה רְפוּאָה שְׁלֵמָה
מִן הַשָּׁמַיִם רְפוּאַת הַנֶּפֶשׁ וּרְפוּאַת הַגּוּף לַחוֹלֶה/לַחוֹלָה *name of patient*
בֶּן/בַּת *mother's name* בְּתוֹךְ שְׁאָר חוֹלֵי יִשְׂרָאֵל.

כִּי אֵל מֶלֶךְ רוֹפֵא נֶאֱמָן וְרַחֲמָן אָתָּה.
בָּרוּךְ אַתָּה יהוה, רוֹפֵא חוֹלֵי עַמּוֹ יִשְׂרָאֵל.

ברכת השנים

The phrase וְתֵן טַל וּמָטָר לִבְרָכָה *is said from December 5th (in the year before a civil leap year, December 6th) until* פסח*. In* ארץ ישראל*, it is said from* ז׳ מרחשון*. The phrase* וְתֵן בְּרָכָה *is said from* חול המועד פסח *until December 4th (in the year before a civil leap year, December 5th). In* ארץ ישראל *it is said through* ו׳ מרחשון*. See laws 147–149.*

בָּרֵךְ עָלֵינוּ יהוה אֱלֹהֵינוּ אֶת הַשָּׁנָה הַזֹּאת
וְאֶת כָּל מִינֵי תְבוּאָתָהּ, לְטוֹבָה
בחורף: וְתֵן טַל וּמָטָר לִבְרָכָה / בקיץ: וְתֵן בְּרָכָה
עַל פְּנֵי הָאֲדָמָה, וְשַׂבְּעֵנוּ מִטּוּבָהּ
וּבָרֵךְ שְׁנָתֵנוּ כַּשָּׁנִים הַטּוֹבוֹת.
בָּרוּךְ אַתָּה יהוה, מְבָרֵךְ הַשָּׁנִים.

רפואה *Blessing 8: Healing.* We pray that medical treatment be successful, and that God Himself be part of the healing process. We are both body and soul: the health of one affects that of the other.

ברכת השנים *Blessing 9: Prosperity.* We pray for God's blessing on our efforts to earn a livelihood. Israel's agriculture depends on rain, so this blessing includes – during the winter months – a prayer for rain. Israel is a land that

INGATHERING OF EXILES

תְּקַע Sound the great shofar for our freedom,
raise high the banner to gather our exiles,
and gather us together from the four quarters of the earth.
Blessed are You, LORD,
who gathers the dispersed of His people Israel.

JUSTICE

הָשִׁיבָה Restore our judges as at first,
and our counselors as at the beginning,
and remove from us sorrow and sighing.
May You alone, LORD,
reign over us with loving-kindness and compassion,
and vindicate us in justice.
Blessed are You, LORD,
the King who loves righteousness and justice.
/ *Between Rosh HaShana & Yom Kippur, end the blessing:* the King of justice./

AGAINST INFORMERS

וְלַמַּלְשִׁינִים For the slanderers let there be no hope,
and may all wickedness perish in an instant.
May all Your people's enemies swiftly be cut down.
May You swiftly uproot, crush, cast down
and humble the arrogant swiftly in our days.
Blessed are You, LORD,
who destroys enemies and humbles the arrogant.

---

leaders of the people (Rabbi Abraham ben HaRambam). The prayer for the restoration of judges, following the ingathering of exiles, is thus a plea for the return of national sovereignty. וְהָסֵר מִמֶּנּוּ יָגוֹן וַאֲנָחָה *Remove from us sorrow and sighing:* the plaint of a people who have known the full precariousness of being dependent on the goodwill of others.

ברכת המינים *Blessing 12: Against Informers.* The text of this paragraph underwent several changes during the centuries. Its original object was the sectarianism that split the Jewish world during the late Second Temple period.

קבוץ גלויות

תְּקַע בְּשׁוֹפָר גָּדוֹל לְחֵרוּתֵנוּ, וְשָׂא נֵס לְקַבֵּץ גָּלֻיּוֹתֵינוּ
וְקַבְּצֵנוּ יַֽחַד מֵאַרְבַּע כַּנְפוֹת הָאָֽרֶץ.
בָּרוּךְ אַתָּה יהוה, מְקַבֵּץ נִדְחֵי עַמּוֹ יִשְׂרָאֵל.

השבת המשפט

הָשִֽׁיבָה שׁוֹפְטֵֽינוּ כְּבָרִאשׁוֹנָה וְיוֹעֲצֵֽינוּ כְּבַתְּחִלָּה
וְהָסֵר מִמֶּֽנּוּ יָגוֹן וַאֲנָחָה
וּמְלֹךְ עָלֵֽינוּ אַתָּה יהוה לְבַדְּךָ בְּחֶֽסֶד וּבְרַחֲמִים
וְצַדְּקֵֽנוּ בַּמִּשְׁפָּט.
בָּרוּךְ אַתָּה יהוה
מֶֽלֶךְ אוֹהֵב צְדָקָה וּמִשְׁפָּט. / בעשרת ימי תשובה: הַמֶּֽלֶךְ הַמִּשְׁפָּט./

ברכת המינים

וְלַמַּלְשִׁינִים אַל תְּהִי תִקְוָה, וְכָל הָרִשְׁעָה כְּרֶֽגַע תֹּאבֵד
וְכָל אוֹיְבֵי עַמְּךָ מְהֵרָה יִכָּרֵֽתוּ
וְהַזֵּדִים מְהֵרָה תְעַקֵּר וּתְשַׁבֵּר וּתְמַגֵּר וְתַכְנִֽיעַ בִּמְהֵרָה בְיָמֵֽינוּ.
בָּרוּךְ אַתָּה יהוה, שׁוֹבֵר אוֹיְבִים וּמַכְנִֽיעַ זֵדִים.

קבוץ גלויות *Blessing 10: Ingathering of exiles.* With this paragraph, the requests change from individual to collective hopes. They begin with three prayers for political-historical renewal: the return of exiles, the restoration of independence, and an end to the factionalism that caused great damage to the Israelites from the biblical era to the end of the Second Temple period. **תְּקַע בְּשׁוֹפָר גָּדוֹל** *Sound the great shofar:* A reference to Isaiah 27:13, "On that day a great shofar will sound." **וְשָׂא נֵס** *Raise high the banner:* Isaiah 11:12, "He will raise a banner for the nations and gather the exiles of Israel; He will assemble the scattered people of Judah from the four quarters of the earth."

משפט *Blessing 11: Justice.* A prayer for self-government. The "Judges" in the biblical book of that name were not merely judges in a legal sense; they were

THE RIGHTEOUS

עַל הַצַּדִּיקִים To the righteous, the pious,
the elders of Your people the house of Israel,
the remnant of their scholars,
the righteous converts, and to us,
may Your compassion be aroused,
LORD our God.
Grant a good reward to all who sincerely trust in Your name.
Set our lot with them,
so that we may never be ashamed, for in You we trust.
Blessed are You, LORD,
who is the support and trust of the righteous.

REBUILDING JERUSALEM

וְלִירוּשָׁלַיִם To Jerusalem, Your city,
may You return in compassion,
and may You dwell in it as You promised.
May You rebuild it rapidly in our days
as an everlasting structure,
and install within it soon the throne of David.
Blessed are You, LORD, who builds Jerusalem.

פְּלֵיטַת סוֹפְרֵיהֶם *The remnant of their scholars* is a reference to those Jews who endured religious persecution under the Greeks and Romans, and later, those who survived the Crusades and those who lived through the Holocaust. Judaism lost many of its greatest scholars as martyrs.

בניין ירושלים *Blessing 14: Rebuilding Jerusalem.* Jerusalem is the home of the Jewish soul, the place to which we turn in prayer and for whose restoration Jews prayed in every generation. The book of Psalms has left us an indelible description of how Jews felt when the city fell to the Babylonians in the sixth century BCE: "By the rivers of Babylon we sat and wept when we remembered Zion… May my tongue cling to the roof of my mouth if I do not remember you, if I do not consider Jerusalem my highest joy" (Psalm 137). Jerusalem is mentioned more than 600 times in the Hebrew Bible.

על הצדיקים

עַל הַצַּדִּיקִים וְעַל הַחֲסִידִים
וְעַל זִקְנֵי עַמְּךָ בֵּית יִשְׂרָאֵל
וְעַל פְּלֵיטַת סוֹפְרֵיהֶם
וְעַל גֵּרֵי הַצֶּדֶק, וְעָלֵינוּ
יֶהֱמוּ רַחֲמֶיךָ יהוה אֱלֹהֵינוּ
וְתֵן שָׂכָר טוֹב לְכָל הַבּוֹטְחִים בְּשִׁמְךָ בֶּאֱמֶת
וְשִׂים חֶלְקֵנוּ עִמָּהֶם, וּלְעוֹלָם לֹא נֵבוֹשׁ כִּי בְךָ בָּטָחְנוּ.
בָּרוּךְ אַתָּה יהוה, מִשְׁעָן וּמִבְטָח לַצַּדִּיקִים.

בניין ירושלים

וְלִירוּשָׁלַיִם עִירְךָ בְּרַחֲמִים תָּשׁוּב
וְתִשְׁכֹּן בְּתוֹכָהּ כַּאֲשֶׁר דִּבַּרְתָּ
וּבְנֵה אוֹתָהּ בְּקָרוֹב בְּיָמֵינוּ בִּנְיַן עוֹלָם
וְכִסֵּא דָוִד מְהֵרָה לְתוֹכָהּ תָּכִין.
בָּרוּךְ אַתָּה יהוה, בּוֹנֵה יְרוּשָׁלָיִם.

There were Jews in the Hellenistic age who turned against their own people. Faith (*emuna*) in Judaism involves the idea of loyalty – to a people and its heritage. This prayer is a protest against disloyalty.

The Talmud (*Berakhot* 28b) says that, to formulate this prayer, Rabban Gamliel turned to Shmuel HaKatan. Rabbi Kook pointed out that Shmuel HaKatan was known for his attachment to the principle, "Do not rejoice when your enemy falls" (*Avot* 4:24). Only a person who deeply loved his fellow human beings could be entrusted with the task of constructing this prayer, which must be free of animosity and *schadenfreude*.

על הצדיקים *Blessing 13:* **הַצַּדִּיקִים** *The righteous.* After mentioning those who harm the Jewish people, we go on to describe those who endow it with greatness: the righteous, the pious, the elders, scholars and converts.

KINGDOM OF DAVID

אֶת צֶמַח May the offshoot of Your servant David soon flower,
and may his pride be raised high by Your salvation,
for we wait for Your salvation all day.
Blessed are You, LORD, who makes the glory of salvation flourish.

RESPONSE TO PRAYER

שְׁמַע קוֹלֵנוּ Listen to our voice, LORD our God.
Spare us and have compassion on us,
and in compassion and favor accept our prayer,
for You, God, listen to prayers and pleas.
Do not turn us away, O our King,
empty-handed from Your presence,*
for You listen with compassion
to the prayer of Your people Israel.
Blessed are You, LORD, who listens to prayer.

**In times of drought in Israel, add:*

וַעֲנֵנוּ And answer us through the attribute of compassion, Creator of the universe who chooses His people Israel to make known His greatness and majestic glory. You who listen to prayer, grant dew and rain on the face of the earth, satisfying the whole universe from Your goodness. Fill our hands from Your blessings and Your hand's rich gift. Guard and deliver this year from all evil, all kinds of destruction and punishment, and give it hope and a peaceful end. Spare us and have compassion on us and on all our produce and fruit, blessing us with bounteous rain. May we merit life, plenty and peace as in the good years. Remove from us plague, sword and famine, wild animals, captivity and plunder, the evil instinct and serious and dangerous illnesses and events. Decree for us goodly decrees, and may Your compassion prevail over Your other attributes, that You may act toward Your children through the attribute of compassion, and in compassion and favor accept our prayer.

Continue with "for You listen" above.

---

in the messianic age. The word "Messiah" in Hebrew means "anointed"; that is, a duly appointed king of Davidic descent.

שומע תפלה *Blessing 16: Response to Prayer.* An all-inclusive prayer, that our

מלכות בית דוד

אֶת צֶמַח דָּוִד עַבְדְּךָ מְהֵרָה תַצְמִיחַ,
וְקַרְנוֹ תָּרוּם בִּישׁוּעָתֶךָ
כִּי לִישׁוּעָתְךָ קִוִּינוּ כָּל הַיּוֹם.
בָּרוּךְ אַתָּה יהוה, מַצְמִיחַ קֶרֶן יְשׁוּעָה.

שומע תפילה

שְׁמַע קוֹלֵנוּ יהוה אֱלֹהֵינוּ
חוּס וְרַחֵם עָלֵינוּ, וְקַבֵּל בְּרַחֲמִים וּבְרָצוֹן אֶת תְּפִלָּתֵנוּ
כִּי אֵל שׁוֹמֵעַ תְּפִלּוֹת וְתַחֲנוּנִים אָתָּה
וּמִלְּפָנֶיךָ מַלְכֵּנוּ רֵיקָם אַל תְּשִׁיבֵנוּ*
כִּי אַתָּה שׁוֹמֵעַ תְּפִלַּת עַמְּךָ יִשְׂרָאֵל בְּרַחֲמִים.
בָּרוּךְ אַתָּה יהוה, שׁוֹמֵעַ תְּפִלָּה.

**In times of drought in* ארץ ישראל*, add:*

וַעֲנֵנוּ בּוֹרֵא עוֹלָם בְּמִדַּת הָרַחֲמִים, בּוֹחֵר בְּעַמּוֹ יִשְׂרָאֵל לְהוֹדִיעַ גָּדְלוֹ וְהַדְרַת כְּבוֹדוֹ. שׁוֹמֵעַ תְּפִלָּה, תֵּן טַל וּמָטָר עַל פְּנֵי הָאֲדָמָה, וְתַשְׂבִּיעַ אֶת הָעוֹלָם כֻּלּוֹ מִטּוּבֶךָ, וּמַלֵּא יָדֵינוּ מִבִּרְכוֹתֶיךָ וּמֵעֹשֶׁר מַתְּנַת יָדֶךָ. שְׁמֹר וְהַצֵּל שָׁנָה זוֹ מִכָּל דָּבָר רָע, וּמִכָּל מִינֵי מַשְׁחִית וּמִכָּל מִינֵי פֻרְעָנִיּוֹת, וַעֲשֵׂה לָהּ תִּקְוָה וְאַחֲרִית שָׁלוֹם. חוּס וְרַחֵם עָלֵינוּ וְעַל כָּל תְּבוּאָתֵנוּ וּפֵרוֹתֵינוּ, וּבָרְכֵנוּ בְּגִשְׁמֵי בְרָכָה, וְנִזְכֶּה לְחַיִּים וְשֹׂבַע וְשָׁלוֹם כַּשָּׁנִים הַטּוֹבוֹת. וְהָסֵר מִמֶּנּוּ דֶּבֶר וְחֶרֶב וְרָעָב, וְחַיָּה רָעָה וּשְׁבִי וּבִזָּה, וְיֵצֶר הָרָע וָחֳלָיִים רָעִים וְקָשִׁים וּמְאֹרָעוֹת רָעִים וְקָשִׁים. וּגְזֹר עָלֵינוּ גְּזֵרוֹת טוֹבוֹת מִלְּפָנֶיךָ, וְיִגֹּלּוּ רַחֲמֶיךָ עַל מִדּוֹתֶיךָ, וְתִתְנַהֵג עִם בָּנֶיךָ בְּמִדַּת הָרַחֲמִים, וְקַבֵּל בְּרַחֲמִים וּבְרָצוֹן אֶת תְּפִלָּתֵנוּ.

Continue with כִּי אַתָּה שׁוֹמֵעַ *above.*

מלכות בית דוד *Blessing 15: Kingdom of David.* David was promised by God that the monarchy would always be the heritage of his children. The Davidic monarchy came to an end with the Babylonian conquest. It will be restored

TEMPLE SERVICE

רְצֵה Find favor, LORD our God,
in Your people Israel and their prayer.
Restore the service to Your most holy House,
and accept in love and favor
the fire-offerings of Israel and their prayer.
May the service of Your people Israel always find favor with You.

On Rosh Ḥodesh and Ḥol HaMo'ed, say:

אֱלֹהֵינוּ Our God and God of our ancestors, may there rise, come, reach, appear, be favored, heard, regarded and remembered before You, our recollection and remembrance, as well as the remembrance of our ancestors, and of the Messiah son of David Your servant, and of Jerusalem Your holy city, and of all Your people the house of Israel – for deliverance and well-being, grace, loving-kindness and compassion, life and peace, on this day of:

On Rosh Ḥodesh: Rosh Ḥodesh.
On Pesaḥ: the Festival of Matzot.
On Sukkot: the Festival of Sukkot.

On it remember us, LORD our God, for good; recollect us for blessing, and deliver us for life. In accord with Your promise of salvation and compassion, spare us and be gracious to us; have compassion on us and deliver us, for our eyes are turned to You because You, God, are a gracious and compassionate King.

וְתֶחֱזֶינָה And may our eyes witness
Your return to Zion in compassion.
Blessed are You, LORD,
who restores His Presence to Zion.

---

accepted. The priests then said *Modim,* "We give thanks to You" and blessed the people. According to *Tosafot,* this means that they said the threefold Priestly Blessing, but according to Maimonides it means that they said the prayer beginning שִׂים שָׁלוֹם, "Grant peace."

עבודה

רְצֵה יהוה אֱלֹהֵינוּ בְּעַמְּךָ יִשְׂרָאֵל, וּבִתְפִלָּתָם
וְהָשֵׁב אֶת הָעֲבוֹדָה לִדְבִיר בֵּיתֶךָ
וְאִשֵּׁי יִשְׂרָאֵל וּתְפִלָּתָם בְּאַהֲבָה תְקַבֵּל בְּרָצוֹן
וּתְהִי לְרָצוֹן תָּמִיד עֲבוֹדַת יִשְׂרָאֵל עַמֶּךָ.

On ראש חודש *and* חול המועד*, say:*

אֱלֹהֵינוּ וֵאלֹהֵי אֲבוֹתֵינוּ, יַעֲלֶה וְיָבוֹא וְיַגִּיעַ, וְיֵרָאֶה וְיֵרָצֶה וְיִשָּׁמַע, וְיִפָּקֵד וְיִזָּכֵר זִכְרוֹנֵנוּ וּפִקְדוֹנֵנוּ וְזִכְרוֹן אֲבוֹתֵינוּ, וְזִכְרוֹן מָשִׁיחַ בֶּן דָּוִד עַבְדֶּךָ, וְזִכְרוֹן יְרוּשָׁלַיִם עִיר קָדְשֶׁךָ, וְזִכְרוֹן כָּל עַמְּךָ בֵּית יִשְׂרָאֵל, לְפָנֶיךָ, לִפְלֵיטָה לְטוֹבָה, לְחֵן וּלְחֶסֶד וּלְרַחֲמִים, לְחַיִּים וּלְשָׁלוֹם בְּיוֹם

בראש חודש: רֹאשׁ הַחֹדֶשׁ / בפסח: חַג הַמַּצּוֹת / בסוכות: חַג הַסֻּכּוֹת הַזֶּה. זָכְרֵנוּ יהוה אֱלֹהֵינוּ בּוֹ לְטוֹבָה, וּפָקְדֵנוּ בוֹ לִבְרָכָה, וְהוֹשִׁיעֵנוּ בוֹ לְחַיִּים. וּבִדְבַר יְשׁוּעָה וְרַחֲמִים, חוּס וְחָנֵּנוּ וְרַחֵם עָלֵינוּ וְהוֹשִׁיעֵנוּ, כִּי אֵלֶיךָ עֵינֵינוּ, כִּי אֵל מֶלֶךְ חַנּוּן וְרַחוּם אָתָּה.

וְתֶחֱזֶינָה עֵינֵינוּ בְּשׁוּבְךָ לְצִיּוֹן בְּרַחֲמִים.
בָּרוּךְ אַתָּה יהוה
הַמַּחֲזִיר שְׁכִינָתוֹ לְצִיּוֹן.

---

prayers be heard. At this point in the silent Amida, the individual can include any of his or her personal requests.

עבודה *Blessing 17: Temple Service.* The last three blessings, called by the sages "Thanksgiving," are linked because they were said by the priests in the Temple (*Tamid* 5:1). This paragraph was originally a prayer that the day's sacrifices be

THANKSGIVING

Bow at the first nine words.

מוֹדִים We give thanks to You,
for You are the Lord our God
and God of our ancestors
for ever and all time.
You are the Rock of our lives,
Shield of our salvation
from generation to generation.
We will thank You and
declare Your praise for our lives,
which are entrusted
into Your hand;
for our souls,
which are placed in Your charge;
for Your miracles
which are with us every day;
and for Your wonders and favors
at all times, evening,
morning and midday.
You are good –
for Your compassion never fails.
You are compassionate –
for Your loving-
kindnesses never cease.
We have always
placed our hope in You.

During the Leader's Repetition, the congregation says quietly:

מוֹדִים We give thanks to You,
for You are the Lord
our God
and God of our ancestors,
God of all flesh,
who formed us
and formed the universe.
Blessings and thanks are due
to Your great
and holy name
for giving us life
and sustaining us.
May You continue
to give us life and sustain us;
and may You gather
our exiles
to Your holy courts,
to keep Your decrees,
do Your will and serve You
with a perfect heart,
for it is for us
to give You thanks.
Blessed be God
to whom
thanksgiving is due.

---

hidden miracles take place within them. God is present not only in signs and wonders, but also in the very laws that govern the universe. To see the miraculous in the everyday is part of the Judaic vision, beautifully expressed in these lines.

הודאה

Bow at the first five words.

מוֹדִים אֲנַחְנוּ לָךְ
שָׁאַתָּה הוּא יהוה אֱלֹהֵינוּ
וֵאלֹהֵי אֲבוֹתֵינוּ לְעוֹלָם וָעֶד.
צוּר חַיֵּינוּ, מָגֵן יִשְׁעֵנוּ
אַתָּה הוּא לְדוֹר וָדוֹר.
נוֹדֶה לְּךָ וּנְסַפֵּר תְּהִלָּתֶךָ
עַל חַיֵּינוּ הַמְּסוּרִים בְּיָדֶךָ
וְעַל נִשְׁמוֹתֵינוּ הַפְּקוּדוֹת לָךְ
וְעַל נִסֶּיךָ שֶׁבְּכָל יוֹם עִמָּנוּ
וְעַל נִפְלְאוֹתֶיךָ וְטוֹבוֹתֶיךָ
שֶׁבְּכָל עֵת
עֶרֶב וָבֹקֶר וְצָהֳרָיִם.
הַטּוֹב, כִּי לֹא כָלוּ רַחֲמֶיךָ
וְהַמְרַחֵם, כִּי לֹא תַמּוּ חֲסָדֶיךָ
מֵעוֹלָם קִוִּינוּ לָךְ.

During חזרת הש״ץ, *the* קהל *says quietly:*

מוֹדִים אֲנַחְנוּ לָךְ
שָׁאַתָּה הוּא יהוה אֱלֹהֵינוּ
וֵאלֹהֵי אֲבוֹתֵינוּ
אֱלֹהֵי כָל בָּשָׂר
יוֹצְרֵנוּ, יוֹצֵר בְּרֵאשִׁית.
בְּרָכוֹת וְהוֹדָאוֹת
לְשִׁמְךָ הַגָּדוֹל וְהַקָּדוֹשׁ
עַל שֶׁהֶחֱיִיתָנוּ וְקִיַּמְתָּנוּ.
כֵּן תְּחַיֵּנוּ וּתְקַיְּמֵנוּ
וְתֶאֱסֹף גָּלֻיּוֹתֵינוּ
לְחַצְרוֹת קָדְשֶׁךָ
לִשְׁמֹר חֻקֶּיךָ
וְלַעֲשׂוֹת רְצוֹנֶךָ וּלְעָבְדְּךָ
בְּלֵבָב שָׁלֵם
עַל שֶׁאֲנַחְנוּ מוֹדִים לָךְ.
בָּרוּךְ אֵל הַהוֹדָאוֹת.

הודאה *Blessing 18: Thanksgiving.* The root *y-d-h* has three meanings: (1) to bow (see *Targum* to II Samuel 16:4), hence we bow at the beginning and end of this blessing; (2) to confess or profess; and (3) to thank. The blessing begins as a confession of faith, and moves to thanks for God's blessings which surround us continually. וְעַל נִסֶּיךָ שֶׁבְּכָל יוֹם עִמָּנוּ *For Your miracles which are with us every day:* Nahmanides explained the difference between a "revealed" and a "hidden" miracle. Revealed miracles stand outside the laws of nature;

On Ḥanukka:

עַל הַנִּסִּים [We thank You also] for the miracles, the redemption, the mighty deeds, the salvations, and the victories in battle which You performed for our ancestors in those days, at this time.

בִּימֵי מַתִּתְיָהוּ In the days of Mattityahu, son of Yoḥanan, the High Priest, the Hasmonean, and his sons, the wicked Greek kingdom rose up against Your people Israel to make them forget Your Torah and to force them to transgress the statutes of Your will. It was then that You in Your great compassion stood by them in the time of their distress. You championed their cause, judged their claim, and avenged their wrong. You delivered the strong into the hands of the weak, the many into the hands of the few, the impure into the hands of the pure, the wicked into the hands of the righteous, and the arrogant into the hands of those who were engaged in the study of Your Torah. You made for Yourself great and holy renown in Your world, and for Your people Israel You performed a great salvation and redemption as of this very day. Your children then entered the holiest part of Your House, cleansed Your Temple, purified Your Sanctuary, kindled lights in Your holy courts, and designated these eight days of Ḥanukka for giving thanks and praise to Your great name.

Continue with "For all these things."

On Purim:

עַל הַנִּסִּים [We thank You also] for the miracles, the redemption, the mighty deeds, the salvations, and the victories in battle which You performed for our ancestors in those days, at this time.

בִּימֵי מָרְדְּכַי In the days of Mordekhai and Esther, in Shushan the capital, the wicked Haman rose up against them and sought to destroy, slay and exterminate *Esther 3*
all the Jews, young and old, children and women, on one day, the thirteenth day of the twelfth month, which is the month of Adar, and to plunder their possessions. Then You in Your great compassion thwarted his counsel, frustrated his plans, and caused his scheme to recoil on his own head, so that they hanged him and his sons on the gallows.

Continue with "For all these things."

וְעַל כֻּלָּם For all these things may Your name be blessed and exalted, our King, continually, for ever and all time.

Between Rosh HaShana & Yom Kippur: And write, for a good life, all the children of Your covenant.

Let all that lives thank You, Selah! and praise Your name in truth, God, our Savior and Help, Selah!

▾Blessed are You, Lord, whose name is "the Good" and to whom thanks are due.

בחנוכה:

עַל הַנִּסִּים וְעַל הַפֻּרְקָן וְעַל הַגְּבוּרוֹת וְעַל הַתְּשׁוּעוֹת וְעַל הַמִּלְחָמוֹת שֶׁעָשִׂיתָ לַאֲבוֹתֵינוּ בַּיָּמִים הָהֵם בִּזְּמַן הַזֶּה.

בִּימֵי מַתִּתְיָהוּ בֶּן יוֹחָנָן כֹּהֵן גָּדוֹל חַשְׁמוֹנַאי וּבָנָיו, כְּשֶׁעָמְדָה מַלְכוּת יָוָן הָרְשָׁעָה עַל עַמְּךָ יִשְׂרָאֵל לְהַשְׁכִּיחָם תּוֹרָתֶךָ וּלְהַעֲבִירָם מֵחֻקֵּי רְצוֹנֶךָ, וְאַתָּה בְּרַחֲמֶיךָ הָרַבִּים עָמַדְתָּ לָהֶם בְּעֵת צָרָתָם, רַבְתָּ אֶת רִיבָם, דַּנְתָּ אֶת דִּינָם, נָקַמְתָּ אֶת נִקְמָתָם, מָסַרְתָּ גִבּוֹרִים בְּיַד חַלָּשִׁים, וְרַבִּים בְּיַד מְעַטִּים, וּטְמֵאִים בְּיַד טְהוֹרִים, וּרְשָׁעִים בְּיַד צַדִּיקִים, וְזֵדִים בְּיַד עוֹסְקֵי תוֹרָתֶךָ, וּלְךָ עָשִׂיתָ שֵׁם גָּדוֹל וְקָדוֹשׁ בְּעוֹלָמֶךָ, וּלְעַמְּךָ יִשְׂרָאֵל עָשִׂיתָ תְּשׁוּעָה גְדוֹלָה וּפֻרְקָן כְּהַיּוֹם הַזֶּה. וְאַחַר כֵּן בָּאוּ בָנֶיךָ לִדְבִיר בֵּיתֶךָ, וּפִנּוּ אֶת הֵיכָלֶךָ, וְטִהֲרוּ אֶת מִקְדָּשֶׁךָ, וְהִדְלִיקוּ נֵרוֹת בְּחַצְרוֹת קָדְשֶׁךָ, וְקָבְעוּ שְׁמוֹנַת יְמֵי חֲנֻכָּה אֵלּוּ, לְהוֹדוֹת וּלְהַלֵּל לְשִׁמְךָ הַגָּדוֹל.

Continue with וְעַל כֻּלָּם.

בפורים:

עַל הַנִּסִּים וְעַל הַפֻּרְקָן וְעַל הַגְּבוּרוֹת וְעַל הַתְּשׁוּעוֹת וְעַל הַמִּלְחָמוֹת שֶׁעָשִׂיתָ לַאֲבוֹתֵינוּ בַּיָּמִים הָהֵם בִּזְּמַן הַזֶּה.

בִּימֵי מָרְדְּכַי וְאֶסְתֵּר בְּשׁוּשַׁן הַבִּירָה, כְּשֶׁעָמַד עֲלֵיהֶם הָמָן הָרָשָׁע, בִּקֵּשׁ לְהַשְׁמִיד לַהֲרֹג וּלְאַבֵּד אֶת־כָּל־הַיְּהוּדִים מִנַּעַר וְעַד־זָקֵן טַף וְנָשִׁים בְּיוֹם אֶחָד, בִּשְׁלוֹשָׁה עָשָׂר לְחֹדֶשׁ שְׁנֵים־עָשָׂר, הוּא־חֹדֶשׁ אֲדָר, וּשְׁלָלָם לָבוֹז: וְאַתָּה בְּרַחֲמֶיךָ הָרַבִּים הֵפַרְתָּ אֶת עֲצָתוֹ, וְקִלְקַלְתָּ אֶת מַחֲשַׁבְתּוֹ, וַהֲשֵׁבוֹתָ לּוֹ גְּמוּלוֹ בְּרֹאשׁוֹ, וְתָלוּ אוֹתוֹ וְאֶת בָּנָיו עַל הָעֵץ.

אסתר ג

Continue with וְעַל כֻּלָּם.

וְעַל כֻּלָּם יִתְבָּרַךְ וְיִתְרוֹמַם שִׁמְךָ מַלְכֵּנוּ תָּמִיד לְעוֹלָם וָעֶד.

בעשרת ימי תשובה: וּכְתֹב לְחַיִּים טוֹבִים כָּל בְּנֵי בְרִיתֶךָ.

וְכֹל הַחַיִּים יוֹדוּךָ סֶּלָה, וִיהַלְלוּ אֶת שִׁמְךָ בֶּאֱמֶת הָאֵל יְשׁוּעָתֵנוּ וְעֶזְרָתֵנוּ סֶלָה.

בָּרוּךְ אַתָּה יהוה, הַטּוֹב שִׁמְךָ וּלְךָ נָאֶה לְהוֹדוֹת.

The following is said by the Leader during the Repetition of the Amida, except in a house of mourning and on Tisha B'Av. In Israel, if Kohanim bless the congregation, *turn to page 838.* *See laws 370–377.*

Our God and God of our fathers, bless us with the threefold blessing in the Torah, written by the hand of Moses Your servant and pronounced by Aaron and his sons the priests, Your holy people, as it is said:

May the Lord bless you and protect you. *Num. 6*
Cong: May it be Your will.
May the Lord make His face shine on you and be gracious to you.
Cong: May it be Your will.
May the Lord turn His face toward you, and grant you peace.
Cong: May it be Your will.

PEACE

שִׂים שָׁלוֹם Grant peace, goodness and blessing,
grace, loving-kindness and compassion to us and all Israel Your people.
Bless us, our Father, all as one, with the light of Your face,
for by the light of Your face You have given us, Lord our God,
the Torah of life and love of kindness,
righteousness, blessing, compassion, life and peace.
May it be good in Your eyes to bless Your people Israel
at every time, in every hour, with Your peace.

Between Rosh HaShana & Yom Kippur: In the book of life, blessing, peace and prosperity,
may we and all Your people the house of Israel
be remembered and written before You
for a good life, and for peace.*

Blessed are You, Lord, who blesses His people Israel with peace.

**Between Rosh HaShana and Yom Kippur outside Israel, many end the blessing:*
Blessed are You, Lord, who makes peace.

The following verse concludes the Leader's Repetition of the Amida. Some also say it here as part of the silent Amida. See law 368.

May the words of my mouth and the meditation of my heart *Ps. 19*
find favor before You, Lord, my Rock and Redeemer.

---

famously in the words of Isaiah: "Nation shall not lift up sword against nation; neither shall they learn war anymore" (Is. 2:4). Peace is the ultimate hope of monotheism, with its belief that the world is the product of a single will, not the blind clash of conflicting elements.

The following is said by the שליח ציבור *during* חורת הש״ץ *except in a house of mourning and on* תשעה באב. *In* ארץ ישראל *if* כהנים *say* ברכת כהנים *turn to page 839. See laws 370–377.*

אֱלֹהֵינוּ וֵאלֹהֵי אֲבוֹתֵינוּ, בָּרְכֵנוּ בַּבְּרָכָה הַמְשֻׁלֶּשֶׁת בַּתּוֹרָה, הַכְּתוּבָה עַל יְדֵי מֹשֶׁה עַבְדֶּךָ, הָאֲמוּרָה מִפִּי אַהֲרֹן וּבָנָיו כֹּהֲנִים עַם קְדוֹשֶׁיךָ, כָּאָמוּר

יְבָרֶכְךָ יהוה וְיִשְׁמְרֶךָ: קהל: כֵּן יְהִי רָצוֹן במדבר ו
יָאֵר יהוה פָּנָיו אֵלֶיךָ וִיחֻנֶּךָּ: קהל: כֵּן יְהִי רָצוֹן
יִשָּׂא יהוה פָּנָיו אֵלֶיךָ וְיָשֵׂם לְךָ שָׁלוֹם: קהל: כֵּן יְהִי רָצוֹן

שלום
שִׂים שָׁלוֹם טוֹבָה וּבְרָכָה
חֵן וָחֶסֶד וְרַחֲמִים עָלֵינוּ וְעַל כָּל יִשְׂרָאֵל עַמֶּךָ.
בָּרְכֵנוּ אָבִינוּ כֻּלָּנוּ כְּאֶחָד בְּאוֹר פָּנֶיךָ
כִּי בְאוֹר פָּנֶיךָ נָתַתָּ לָּנוּ יהוה אֱלֹהֵינוּ
תּוֹרַת חַיִּים וְאַהֲבַת חֶסֶד
וּצְדָקָה וּבְרָכָה וְרַחֲמִים וְחַיִּים וְשָׁלוֹם.
וְטוֹב בְּעֵינֶיךָ לְבָרֵךְ אֶת עַמְּךָ יִשְׂרָאֵל
בְּכָל עֵת וּבְכָל שָׁעָה בִּשְׁלוֹמֶךָ.

בעשרת ימי תשובה: בְּסֵפֶר חַיִּים, בְּרָכָה וְשָׁלוֹם, וּפַרְנָסָה טוֹבָה
נִזָּכֵר וְנִכָּתֵב לְפָנֶיךָ, אֲנַחְנוּ וְכָל עַמְּךָ בֵּית יִשְׂרָאֵל
לְחַיִּים טוֹבִים וּלְשָׁלוֹם.*

בָּרוּךְ אַתָּה יהוה, הַמְבָרֵךְ אֶת עַמּוֹ יִשְׂרָאֵל בַּשָּׁלוֹם.

**During the* עשרת ימי תשובה *in* חוץ לארץ, *many end the blessing:*

בָּרוּךְ אַתָּה יהוה, עוֹשֶׂה הַשָּׁלוֹם.

The following verse concludes the חורת הש״ץ.
Some also say it here as part of the silent עמידה. *See law 368.*

יִהְיוּ לְרָצוֹן אִמְרֵי־פִי וְהֶגְיוֹן לִבִּי לְפָנֶיךָ, יהוה צוּרִי וְגֹאֲלִי: תהלים יט

שלום *Blessing 19: Peace. Shalom* means more than the English word "peace": it also means "completeness, perfection, harmonious interaction." The prophets of Israel were the first in history to conceive of peace as an ideal, most

אֱלֹהַי My God, Berakhot 17a
guard my tongue from evil and my lips from deceitful speech.
To those who curse me, let my soul be silent;
may my soul be to all like the dust.
Open my heart to Your Torah and let my soul
pursue Your commandments.
As for all who plan evil against me,
swiftly thwart their counsel and frustrate their plans.
Act for the sake of Your name; act for the sake of Your right hand;
act for the sake of Your holiness; act for the sake of Your Torah.
That Your beloved ones may be delivered, Ps. 60
save with Your right hand and answer me.
May the words of my mouth and the meditation of my heart Ps. 19
find favor before You, LORD, my Rock and Redeemer.

Bow, take three steps back, then bow, first left, then right, then center, while saying:

May He who makes peace in His high places,
make peace for us and all Israel – and say: Amen.

יְהִי רָצוֹן May it be Your will, LORD our God and God of our ancestors,
that the Temple be rebuilt speedily in our days,
and grant us a share in Your Torah. And there we will serve You
with reverence, as in the days of old and as in former years.
Then the offering of Judah and Jerusalem will be pleasing to the LORD Mal. 3
as in the days of old and as in former years.

When praying with a minyan, the Amida is repeated aloud by the Leader.

On days when Tahanun is said (see page 144), start Taḥanun on page 152.
On Mondays and Thursdays start Taḥanun on page 144.
In Israel, on days on which Taḥanun is said, some say Viduy and the
Thirteen Attributes of Divine Compassion on page 109. See law 478a.

On fast days (except Tisha B'Av) most congregations say Seliḥot
on page 924 before Avinu Malkenu on page 138.

Between Rosh HaShana and Yom Kippur (but not on Erev Yom Kippur,
unless it falls on Friday), say Avinu Malkenu on page 138.

On Rosh Ḥodesh, Ḥanukka, Ḥol HaMo'ed, Yom HaAtzma'ut and
Yom Yerushalayim, say Hallel on page 732.

On other days when Taḥanun is not said (see page 144),
the Leader says Half Kaddish on page 156.

ברכות יז. אֱלֹהַי

נְצֹר לְשׁוֹנִי מֵרָע וּשְׂפָתַי מִדַּבֵּר מִרְמָה
וְלִמְקַלְלַי נַפְשִׁי תִדֹּם, וְנַפְשִׁי כֶּעָפָר לַכֹּל תִּהְיֶה.
פְּתַח לִבִּי בְּתוֹרָתֶךָ, וּבְמִצְוֹתֶיךָ תִּרְדֹּף נַפְשִׁי.
וְכָל הַחוֹשְׁבִים עָלַי רָעָה
מְהֵרָה הָפֵר עֲצָתָם וְקַלְקֵל מַחֲשַׁבְתָּם.
עֲשֵׂה לְמַעַן שְׁמֶךָ, עֲשֵׂה לְמַעַן יְמִינֶךָ
עֲשֵׂה לְמַעַן קְדֻשָּׁתֶךָ, עֲשֵׂה לְמַעַן תּוֹרָתֶךָ.
תהלים ס לְמַעַן יֵחָלְצוּן יְדִידֶיךָ, הוֹשִׁיעָה יְמִינְךָ וַעֲנֵנִי:
תהלים יט יִהְיוּ לְרָצוֹן אִמְרֵי־פִי וְהֶגְיוֹן לִבִּי לְפָנֶיךָ, יהוה צוּרִי וְגֹאֲלִי:

Bow, take three steps back, then bow, first left, then right, then center, while saying:

עֹשֶׂה שָׁלוֹם/ בעשרת ימי תשובה: הַשָּׁלוֹם/ בִּמְרוֹמָיו
הוּא יַעֲשֶׂה שָׁלוֹם עָלֵינוּ וְעַל כָּל יִשְׂרָאֵל, וְאִמְרוּ אָמֵן.

יְהִי רָצוֹן מִלְּפָנֶיךָ יהוה אֱלֹהֵינוּ וֵאלֹהֵי אֲבוֹתֵינוּ
שֶׁיִּבָּנֶה בֵּית הַמִּקְדָּשׁ בִּמְהֵרָה בְיָמֵינוּ, וְתֵן חֶלְקֵנוּ בְּתוֹרָתֶךָ
וְשָׁם נַעֲבָדְךָ בְּיִרְאָה כִּימֵי עוֹלָם וּכְשָׁנִים קַדְמוֹנִיּוֹת.
מלאכי ג וְעָרְבָה לַיהוה מִנְחַת יְהוּדָה וִירוּשָׁלָםִ כִּימֵי עוֹלָם וּכְשָׁנִים קַדְמֹנִיּוֹת:

When praying with a מנין, the עמידה is repeated aloud by the שליח ציבור.

On days when תחנון is said (see page 145), start תחנון on page 153.
On Mondays and Thursdays start תחנון on page 145.
In ארץ ישראל, on days on which תחנון is said,
some say וידוי and the י״ג מדות on page 157. See law 478a.

On fast days (except תשעה באב) most congregations say
סליחות on page 925 before אבינו מלכנו on page 139.

During the עשרת ימי תשובה (but not on ערב יום כיפור,
unless it falls on Friday), say אבינו מלכנו on page 139.

On ראש חודש, חנוכה, חול המועד, יום העצמאות and יום ירושלים, say הלל on page 733.

On other days when תחנון is not said (see page 145),
the שליח ציבור says חצי קדיש on page 157.

VIDUY

In Israel on days on which Taḥanun is said (see page 144), some say Viduy and the Thirteen Attributes of Divine Compassion. See law 478a. The congregation stands and says:

אֱלֹהֵינוּ Our God and God of our fathers, let our prayer come before You, and do not hide Yourself from our plea, for we are not so arrogant or obstinate as to say before You, Lord, our God and God of our fathers, we are righteous and have not sinned, for in truth, we and our fathers have sinned.

At each expression, strike the chest on the left side:

אָשַׁמְנוּ We have been guilty, we have acted treacherously, we have robbed, we have spoken slander. We have acted perversely, we have acted wickedly, we have acted presumptuously, we have been violent, we have framed lies. We have given bad advice, we have deceived, we have scorned, we have rebelled, we have provoked, we have turned away, we have committed iniquity, we have transgressed, we have persecuted, we have been obstinate. We have acted wickedly, we have corrupted, we have acted abominably, we have strayed, we have led others astray.

We have turned away from Your commandments and good laws, to no avail, for You are just in all that has befallen us, for You have acted faithfully while we have done wickedly. *Neh. 9*

When praying without a minyan continue with "He is compassionate" on page 144.

THIRTEEN ATTRIBUTES OF DIVINE COMPASSION

אֵל אֶרֶךְ You are a God slow to anger, You are called Master of Compassion, and You have taught the way of repentance. May You remember today and every day the greatness of Your compassion and loving-kindness for the sake of the descendants of Your beloved ones. Turn toward us in compassion, for You are the Master of Compassion. We come before You in plea and prayer, as You in ancient times showed the humble one [Moses]. Turn from Your fierce anger, as is written in Your Torah. In the shadow of Your wings may we shelter and abide, as on the day when the Lord descended in the cloud. ▸ Disregard transgression and erase guilt as on the day You stood with him [Moses] there. Hear our cry and heed our word, as on the day You proclaimed in the name of the Lord, and there it is written:

All say aloud:

וַיַּעֲבֹר And the Lord passed by before him and proclaimed: *Ex. 34*

The Lord, the Lord, compassionate and gracious God, slow to anger,
abounding in loving-kindness and truth, extending loving-kindness to a
thousand generations, forgiving iniquity, rebellion and sin,
and absolving [the guilty who repent]. Forgive us our iniquity and our sin,
and take us as Your inheritance. Forgive us, our Father, for we have sinned.
Pardon us, our King, for we have transgressed. For You, Lord, are good *Ps. 86*
and forgiving, abounding in loving-kindness to all who call on You.

On Mondays and Thursdays continue with "He is compassionate" on page 144; on other days with "David said" on page 152.

וידוי

In ארץ ישראל on days on which תחנון is said (see page 145), some say וידוי and the י״ג מדות. See law 478a. The קהל stands and says:

אֱלֹהֵינוּ וֵאלֹהֵי אֲבוֹתֵינוּ, תָּבוֹא לְפָנֶיךָ תְּפִלָּתֵנוּ, וְאַל תִּתְעַלַּם מִתְּחִנָּתֵנוּ, שֶׁאֵין אֲנַחְנוּ עַזֵּי פָנִים וּקְשֵׁי עֹרֶף לוֹמַר לְפָנֶיךָ, יהוה אֱלֹהֵינוּ וֵאלֹהֵי אֲבוֹתֵינוּ, צַדִּיקִים אֲנַחְנוּ וְלֹא חָטָאנוּ, אֲבָל אֲנַחְנוּ וַאֲבוֹתֵינוּ חָטָאנוּ.

At each expression, strike the chest on the left side:

אָשַׁמְנוּ, בָּגַדְנוּ, גָּזַלְנוּ, דִּבַּרְנוּ דֹפִי, הֶעֱוִינוּ, וְהִרְשַׁעְנוּ, זַדְנוּ, חָמַסְנוּ, טָפַלְנוּ שֶׁקֶר, יָעַצְנוּ רָע, כִּזַּבְנוּ, לַצְנוּ, מָרַדְנוּ, נִאַצְנוּ, סָרַרְנוּ, עָוִינוּ, פָּשַׁעְנוּ, צָרַרְנוּ, קִשִּׁינוּ עֹרֶף, רָשַׁעְנוּ, שִׁחַתְנוּ, תִּעַבְנוּ, תָּעִינוּ, תִּעְתָּעְנוּ.

סַרְנוּ מִמִּצְוֹתֶיךָ וּמִמִּשְׁפָּטֶיךָ הַטּוֹבִים, וְלֹא שָׁוָה לָנוּ. וְאַתָּה צַדִּיק עַל כָּל־הַבָּא עָלֵינוּ, נחמיה ט
כִּי־אֱמֶת עָשִׂיתָ, וַאֲנַחְנוּ הִרְשָׁעְנוּ:

When praying without a מנין continue with וְהוּא רַחוּם on page 145.

י״ג מדות

אֵל אֶרֶךְ אַפַּיִם אַתָּה, וּבַעַל הָרַחֲמִים נִקְרֵאתָ, וְדֶרֶךְ תְּשׁוּבָה הוֹרֵיתָ. גְּדֻלַּת רַחֲמֶיךָ וַחֲסָדֶיךָ, תִּזְכֹּר הַיּוֹם וּבְכָל יוֹם לְזֶרַע יְדִידֶיךָ. תֵּפֶן אֵלֵינוּ בְּרַחֲמִים, כִּי אַתָּה הוּא בַּעַל הָרַחֲמִים. בְּתַחֲנוּן וּבִתְפִלָּה פָּנֶיךָ נְקַדֵּם, כְּהוֹדַעְתָּ לֶעָנָו מִקֶּדֶם. מֵחֲרוֹן אַפְּךָ שׁוּב, כְּמוֹ בְּתוֹרָתְךָ כָּתוּב. וּבְצֵל כְּנָפֶיךָ נֶחֱסֶה וְנִתְלוֹנָן, כְּיוֹם וַיֵּרֶד יהוה בֶּעָנָן. ◦ תַּעֲבֹר עַל פֶּשַׁע וְתִמְחֶה אָשָׁם, כְּיוֹם וַיִּתְיַצֵּב עִמּוֹ שָׁם. תַּאֲזִין שַׁוְעָתֵנוּ וְתַקְשִׁיב מֶנּוּ מַאֲמָר, כְּיוֹם וַיִּקְרָא בְשֵׁם יהוה, וְשָׁם נֶאֱמַר:

All say aloud:

וַיַּעֲבֹר יהוה עַל־פָּנָיו וַיִּקְרָא שמות לד

יהוה, יהוה, אֵל רַחוּם וְחַנּוּן, אֶרֶךְ אַפַּיִם וְרַב־חֶסֶד וֶאֱמֶת:
נֹצֵר חֶסֶד לָאֲלָפִים, נֹשֵׂא עָוֹן וָפֶשַׁע וְחַטָּאָה, וְנַקֵּה:
וְסָלַחְתָּ לַעֲוֹנֵנוּ וּלְחַטָּאתֵנוּ, וּנְחַלְתָּנוּ:

סְלַח לָנוּ אָבִינוּ כִּי חָטָאנוּ, מְחַל לָנוּ מַלְכֵּנוּ כִּי פָשָׁעְנוּ
כִּי־אַתָּה אֲדֹנָי טוֹב וְסַלָּח וְרַב־חֶסֶד לְכָל־קֹרְאֶיךָ: תהלים פו

On Mondays and Thursdays continue with וְהוּא רַחוּם on page 145; on other days with וַיֹּאמֶר דָּוִד on page 153.

AVINU MALKENU

On fast days (except Tisha B'Av) most congregations say Seliḥot on page 924 before Avinu Malkenu.

Between Rosh HaShana and Yom Kippur (but not on Erev Yom Kippur, unless it falls on Friday), say Avinu Malkenu below.

The Ark is opened.

אָבִינוּ מַלְכֵּנוּ Our Father, our King, we have sinned before You.
Our Father, our King, we have no king but You.
Our Father, our King, deal kindly with us for the sake of Your name.
Our Father our King, /*bless us with / a good year.
/ *Between Rosh HaShana & Yom Kippur: renew for us/
Our Father, our King, nullify all harsh decrees against us.
Our Father, our King, nullify the plans of those who hate us.
Our Father, our King, thwart the counsel of our enemies.
Our Father, our King, rid us of every oppressor and adversary.
Our Father, our King, close the mouths of our adversaries and accusers.
Our Father, our King, eradicate pestilence, sword, famine, captivity and destruction, iniquity and eradication from the people of Your covenant.
Our Father, our King, withhold the plague from Your heritage.
Our Father, our King, forgive and pardon all our iniquities.
Our Father, our King, wipe away and remove our transgressions and sins from Your sight.
Our Father, our King, erase in Your abundant mercy all records of our sins.

The following nine sentences are said responsively, first by the Leader, then by the congregation:

Our Father, our King, bring us back to You in perfect repentance.
Our Father, our King, send a complete healing to the sick of Your people.
Our Father, our King, tear up the evil decree against us.
Our Father, our King, remember us with a memory of favorable deeds before You.

---

the second by love, compassion and forgiveness. By placing the words in the reverse order, we mirror both history and faith: history because God called us His children ("My child, My firstborn, Israel") at Mount Sinai before He became Israel's King; faith because we ask God to let His parental love temper the severity of justice.

אבינו מלכנו

On fast days (except תשעה באב*) most congregations say* סליחות *on page 925 before* אבינו מלכנו.

During the עשרת ימי תשובה *(but not on* ערב יום כיפור*, unless it falls on Friday), say* אבינו מלכנו *below.*

The ארון קודש *is opened.*

אָבִינוּ מַלְכֵּנוּ, חָטָאנוּ לְפָנֶיךָ.

אָבִינוּ מַלְכֵּנוּ, אֵין לָנוּ מֶלֶךְ אֶלָּא אָתָּה.

אָבִינוּ מַלְכֵּנוּ, עֲשֵׂה עִמָּנוּ לְמַעַן שְׁמֶךָ.

אָבִינוּ מַלְכֵּנוּ, בָּרֵךְ/ בעשרת ימי תשובה: חַדֵּשׁ/ עָלֵינוּ שָׁנָה טוֹבָה.

אָבִינוּ מַלְכֵּנוּ, בַּטֵּל מֵעָלֵינוּ כָּל גְּזֵרוֹת קָשׁוֹת.

אָבִינוּ מַלְכֵּנוּ, בַּטֵּל מַחְשְׁבוֹת שׂוֹנְאֵינוּ.

אָבִינוּ מַלְכֵּנוּ, הָפֵר עֲצַת אוֹיְבֵינוּ.

אָבִינוּ מַלְכֵּנוּ, כַּלֵּה כָּל צַר וּמַשְׂטִין מֵעָלֵינוּ.

אָבִינוּ מַלְכֵּנוּ, סְתֹם פִּיּוֹת מַשְׂטִינֵנוּ וּמְקַטְרְגֵנוּ.

אָבִינוּ מַלְכֵּנוּ, כַּלֵּה דֶּבֶר וְחֶרֶב וְרָעָב וּשְׁבִי וּמַשְׁחִית וְעָוֹן וּשְׁמַד מִבְּנֵי בְרִיתֶךָ.

אָבִינוּ מַלְכֵּנוּ, מְנַע מַגֵּפָה מִנַּחֲלָתֶךָ.

אָבִינוּ מַלְכֵּנוּ, סְלַח וּמְחַל לְכָל עֲוֹנוֹתֵינוּ.

אָבִינוּ מַלְכֵּנוּ, מְחֵה וְהַעֲבֵר פְּשָׁעֵינוּ וְחַטֹּאתֵינוּ מִנֶּגֶד עֵינֶיךָ.

אָבִינוּ מַלְכֵּנוּ, מְחֹק בְּרַחֲמֶיךָ הָרַבִּים כָּל שִׁטְרֵי חוֹבוֹתֵינוּ.

The following nine sentences are said responsively, first by the שליח ציבור*, then by the* קהל:

אָבִינוּ מַלְכֵּנוּ, הַחֲזִירֵנוּ בִּתְשׁוּבָה שְׁלֵמָה לְפָנֶיךָ.

אָבִינוּ מַלְכֵּנוּ, שְׁלַח רְפוּאָה שְׁלֵמָה לְחוֹלֵי עַמֶּךָ.

אָבִינוּ מַלְכֵּנוּ, קְרַע רֹעַ גְּזַר דִּינֵנוּ.

אָבִינוּ מַלְכֵּנוּ, זָכְרֵנוּ בְּזִכָּרוֹן טוֹב לְפָנֶיךָ.

אָבִינוּ מַלְכֵּנוּ *Our Father, our King:* A prayer attributed, in its earliest form, to Rabbi Akiva. The opening two words juxtapose the two aspects of our relationship with God. He is our King and we are His subjects; He is our Parent and we are His children. The first relationship is governed by justice,

Between Rosh HaShana and Yom Kippur:

Our Father, our King, write us in the book of good life.

Our Father, our King, write us in the book of redemption and salvation.

Our Father, our King, write us in the book of livelihood and sustenance.

Our Father, our King, write us in the book of merit.

Our Father, our King, write us in the book of pardon and forgiveness.

On Fast Days:

Our Father, our King, remember us for a good life.

Our Father, our King, remember us for redemption and salvation.

Our Father, our King, remember us for livelihood and sustenance.

Our Father, our King, remember us for merit.

Our Father, our King, remember us for pardon and forgiveness.

End of responsive reading.

Our Father, our King, let salvation soon flourish for us.

Our Father, our King, raise the honor of Your people Israel.

Our Father, our King, raise the honor of Your anointed.

Our Father, our King, fill our hands with Your blessings.

Our Father, our King, fill our storehouses with abundance.

Our Father, our King, hear our voice, pity and be compassionate to us.

Our Father, our King, accept, with compassion and favor, our prayer.

Our Father, our King, open the gates of heaven to our prayer.

Our Father, our King, remember that we are dust.

Our Father, our King, please do not turn us away from You empty-handed.

Our Father, our King, may this moment be a moment of compassion and a time of favor before You.

Our Father, our King, have pity on us, our children and our infants.

Our Father, our King, act for the sake of those who were killed for Your holy name.

Our Father, our King, act for the sake of those who were slaughtered for proclaiming Your Unity.

Our Father, our King, act for the sake of those who went through fire and water to sanctify Your name.

During the עשרת ימי תשובה:

אָבִינוּ מַלְכֵּנוּ, כָּתְבֵנוּ בְּסֵפֶר חַיִּים טוֹבִים.

אָבִינוּ מַלְכֵּנוּ, כָּתְבֵנוּ בְּסֵפֶר גְּאֻלָּה וִישׁוּעָה.

אָבִינוּ מַלְכֵּנוּ, כָּתְבֵנוּ בְּסֵפֶר פַּרְנָסָה וְכַלְכָּלָה.

אָבִינוּ מַלְכֵּנוּ, כָּתְבֵנוּ בְּסֵפֶר זְכֻיּוֹת.

אָבִינוּ מַלְכֵּנוּ, כָּתְבֵנוּ בְּסֵפֶר סְלִיחָה וּמְחִילָה.

On Fast Days:

אָבִינוּ מַלְכֵּנוּ, זָכְרֵנוּ לְחַיִּים טוֹבִים.

אָבִינוּ מַלְכֵּנוּ, זָכְרֵנוּ לִגְאֻלָּה וִישׁוּעָה.

אָבִינוּ מַלְכֵּנוּ, זָכְרֵנוּ לְפַרְנָסָה וְכַלְכָּלָה.

אָבִינוּ מַלְכֵּנוּ, זָכְרֵנוּ לִזְכֻיּוֹת.

אָבִינוּ מַלְכֵּנוּ, זָכְרֵנוּ לִסְלִיחָה וּמְחִילָה.

End of responsive reading.

אָבִינוּ מַלְכֵּנוּ, הַצְמַח לָנוּ יְשׁוּעָה בְּקָרוֹב.
אָבִינוּ מַלְכֵּנוּ, הָרֵם קֶרֶן יִשְׂרָאֵל עַמֶּךָ.
אָבִינוּ מַלְכֵּנוּ, הָרֵם קֶרֶן מְשִׁיחֶךָ.
אָבִינוּ מַלְכֵּנוּ, מַלֵּא יָדֵינוּ מִבִּרְכוֹתֶיךָ.
אָבִינוּ מַלְכֵּנוּ, מַלֵּא אֲסָמֵינוּ שָׂבָע.
אָבִינוּ מַלְכֵּנוּ, שְׁמַע קוֹלֵנוּ, חוּס וְרַחֵם עָלֵינוּ.
אָבִינוּ מַלְכֵּנוּ, קַבֵּל בְּרַחֲמִים וּבְרָצוֹן אֶת תְּפִלָּתֵנוּ.
אָבִינוּ מַלְכֵּנוּ, פְּתַח שַׁעֲרֵי שָׁמַיִם לִתְפִלָּתֵנוּ.
אָבִינוּ מַלְכֵּנוּ, זְכֹר כִּי עָפָר אֲנָחְנוּ.
אָבִינוּ מַלְכֵּנוּ, נָא אַל תְּשִׁיבֵנוּ רֵיקָם מִלְּפָנֶיךָ.
אָבִינוּ מַלְכֵּנוּ, תְּהֵא הַשָּׁעָה הַזֹּאת שְׁעַת רַחֲמִים וְעֵת רָצוֹן מִלְּפָנֶיךָ.
אָבִינוּ מַלְכֵּנוּ, חֲמֹל עָלֵינוּ וְעַל עוֹלָלֵינוּ וְטַפֵּנוּ.
אָבִינוּ מַלְכֵּנוּ, עֲשֵׂה לְמַעַן הֲרוּגִים עַל שֵׁם קָדְשֶׁךָ.
אָבִינוּ מַלְכֵּנוּ, עֲשֵׂה לְמַעַן טְבוּחִים עַל יִחוּדֶךָ.
אָבִינוּ מַלְכֵּנוּ, עֲשֵׂה לְמַעַן בָּאֵי בָאֵשׁ וּבַמַּיִם עַל קִדּוּשׁ שְׁמֶךָ.

Our Father, our King, avenge before our eyes
the spilt blood of Your servants.
Our Father, our King, act for Your sake, if not for ours.
Our Father, our King, act for Your sake, and save us.
Our Father, our King, act for the sake of Your abundant compassion.
Our Father, our King, act for the sake of Your great, mighty and awesome
name by which we are called.
▸ Our Father, our King, be gracious to us and answer us, though we have
no worthy deeds; act with us in charity and
loving-kindness and save us.

The Ark is closed.

During Minḥa continue with Taḥanun on page 232.

---

faces to the ground, even after the destruction of the Temple. We preserve a trace of that gesture by resting our heads on our arms and covering our faces as we say Psalm 6. The Leader's Repetition of the Amida stands in place of the daily sacrifice, which is why we subsequently "fall on our faces."

The custom of attaching special significance to Mondays and Thursdays is also ancient. Already in the Second Temple period, Mondays and Thursdays were days on which the pious would fast. According to tradition, Moses began his ascent of Mount Sinai to receive the second tablets on a Thursday and descended forty days later on a Monday (the 10th of Tishrei, Yom Kippur). The second tablets were a sign of God's forgiveness. Hence, these days were seen as "days of favor." They were also market days when people would come from villages to towns. Congregations were larger; the Torah was read; law courts were in session. The heightened atmosphere was the setting for more extended penitential prayer; therefore, on Mondays and Thursdays, *Taḥanun* is longer.

One of the classic biblical instances of supplication was Daniel's prayer on behalf of the exiles in Babylon (Daniel, chapter 9). Sections of that prayer, together with other verses from the prophetic books and Psalms, form the core of these paragraphs. There are three sections, each containing eighteen mentions of God's name; thus we say them quietly, standing, as if they were forms of the Amida.

A tradition, found in the Geonic literature, dates these prayers to the period of persecution under the Romans, when three exiles crossed the

אָבִינוּ מַלְכֵּנוּ, נְקֹם לְעֵינֵינוּ נִקְמַת דַּם עֲבָדֶיךָ הַשָּׁפוּךְ.
אָבִינוּ מַלְכֵּנוּ, עֲשֵׂה לְמַעַנְךָ אִם לֹא לְמַעֲנֵנוּ.
אָבִינוּ מַלְכֵּנוּ, עֲשֵׂה לְמַעַנְךָ וְהוֹשִׁיעֵנוּ.
אָבִינוּ מַלְכֵּנוּ, עֲשֵׂה לְמַעַן רַחֲמֶיךָ הָרַבִּים.
אָבִינוּ מַלְכֵּנוּ, עֲשֵׂה לְמַעַן שִׁמְךָ הַגָּדוֹל הַגִּבּוֹר וְהַנּוֹרָא, שֶׁנִּקְרָא עָלֵינוּ.
◂ אָבִינוּ מַלְכֵּנוּ, חָנֵּנוּ וַעֲנֵנוּ, כִּי אֵין בָּנוּ מַעֲשִׂים
עֲשֵׂה עִמָּנוּ צְדָקָה וָחֶסֶד וְהוֹשִׁיעֵנוּ.

The ארון קודש *is closed.*

During מנחה *continue with* סדר תחנון *on page 233.*

TAHANUN: PLEADING WITH GOD

This section of the prayers, known as *Taḥanun*, "plea," is a return to private prayer, which began with the silent Amida. The siddur preserves a careful balance between the two ways in which we address God: as individuals with our personal hopes and fears, and as members of a community whose fate and aspirations we share. First we pray individually (the silent Amida), then communally (the Leader's Repetition), then individually in *Taḥanun* again.

Knowing that our time in the direct presence of the Supreme King of kings is drawing to an end, we approach Him directly, seeking, as it were, a private audience. Our voices drop; we whisper our deepest thoughts; we express our feelings of inadequacy and vulnerability. We know we are unworthy: we say nothing in our defense except that we have absolute faith in God.

The word *Taḥanun* derives from the root *ḥ-n-n* meaning, "to show favor, to be gracious, to forgive." What differentiates *Taḥanun* from other modes of prayer is the extent to which we emphasize our failings and our lack of good deeds. We express our dependence on God's unconditional grace and mercy. *Taḥanun* is the chamber music rather than the symphony of the soul, and it has a unique intensity of tone.

The practice of following public prayer with private intercession goes back to Temple times. After the daily sacrifice, "The Levites sang the Psalm [of the day]. When they reached the end of each section [the psalm was divided into three parts] they blew the shofar and the people prostrated themselves" (*Tamid* 7:3). Some communities continued the custom of prostration, with

TAḤANUN

On Mondays and Thursdays, when Taḥanun is said, begin with "He is compassionate" below. On other days when Taḥanun is said, begin with "David said" on page 152.

Taḥanun is not said on: Rosh Ḥodesh, Ḥanukka, Tu BiShvat, the 14th and 15th of Adar I, Purim and Shushan Purim, in the month of Nisan, Yom HaAtzma'ut, the 14th of Iyar (Pesaḥ Sheni), Lag BaOmer, Yom Yerushalayim, from Rosh Ḥodesh Sivan through the day after Shavuot (in Israel through 12th of Sivan), Tisha B'Av, Tu B'Av, Erev Rosh HaShana, and from Erev Yom Kippur through the day after Simḥat Torah (in Israel through Rosh Ḥodesh Marḥeshvan).

Taḥanun is also not said: on the morning of a Brit Mila, either where the brit will take place or where the father, Sandek or Mohel are present; if a groom is present (and some say a bride) on the day of his wedding or during the week of Sheva Berakhot; in a house of mourning.

In Israel on days on which Taḥanun is said, say Viduy and the Thirteen Attributes of Divine Compassion on page 136. See law 478a.

The following until "David said" on page 152 is said standing.

וְהוּא רַחוּם He is compassionate. He forgives iniquity and does not destroy. *Ps. 78*
Repeatedly He suppresses His anger, not rousing His full wrath. Lord, do not withhold Your compassion from us. May Your loving-kindness and truth always protect us. Save us, Lord our God, and gather us from among *Ps. 106*
the nations, that we may give thanks to Your holy name and glory in Your praise. If You, Lord, should keep account of sins, O Lord, who could stand? *Ps. 130*
But with You is forgiveness, that You may be revered. Do not deal with us according to our sins; do not repay us according to our iniquities. Though *Jer. 14*
our iniquities testify against us, Lord, act for Your name's sake. Remember, *Ps. 25*
Lord, Your compassion and loving-kindness, for they are everlasting. May *Ps. 20*
the Lord answer us when we are in distress; may the name of Jacob's God protect us. Lord, save! May the King answer us when we call. Our Father, our King, be gracious to us and answer us, though we have no worthy deeds;

---

of the divine promise, unbroken and unbreakable. Prayer sustains hope, and hope defeats tragedy. In these profound and moving words, Jews found the strength to survive.

With its intense penitential mood, *Taḥanun* is not said on days of festive joy; nor is it said on the Ninth of Av or in the house of a mourner.

וְהוּא רַחוּם *He is compassionate:* Penitential prayers woven from a variety of biblical texts, from Genesis and Exodus, Isaiah, Jeremiah and Joel, Lamentations, Daniel and Psalms. Lacking a Temple and sacrifices, we offer God our tears in their place: "The sacrifices of God are a broken spirit; a broken and humbled heart, God, You will not despise" (Psalm 51:19).

סדר תחנון

On Mondays and Thursdays, when תחנון *is said, begin with* וְהוּא רַחוּם *below.*
On other days when תחנון *is said, begin with* וַיֹּאמֶר דָּוִד *on page 153.*

תחנון *is not said on:* ראש חודש, חנוכה, ט״ו בשבט*, the 14th and 15th of* אדר א׳, פורים *and* שושן פורים*, in the month of* ניסן, יום העצמאות*, the 14th of* אייר (פסח שני), ל״ג בעומר*,* יום ירושלים*, from* ראש חודש סיון *through the day after* שבועות (*in* ארץ ישראל *through* י״ב סיון)*,* תשעה באב, ט״ו באב, ערב ראש השנה*, and from* ערב יום כיפור *through the day after* שמחת תורה (*in* ארץ ישראל *through* ראש חודש מרחשון).

תחנון *is also not said: on the morning of a* ברית מילה*, either where the* ברית *will take place or where the father,* סנדק *or* מוהל *are present; if a* חתן *is present (and some say a* כלה) *on the day of his wedding or during the week of* שבע ברכות*; in a house of mourning.*
In ארץ ישראל *on days on which* תחנון *is said, say* וידוי *and the* י״ג מדות *on page 137. See law 478a.*

The following until וַיֹּאמֶר דָּוִד *on page 153 is said standing.*

וְהוּא רַחוּם, יְכַפֵּר עָוֹן וְלֹא־יַשְׁחִית, וְהִרְבָּה לְהָשִׁיב אַפּוֹ וְלֹא־יָעִיר כָּל־ תהלים עח
חֲמָתוֹ: אַתָּה יהוה לֹא־תִכְלָא רַחֲמֶיךָ מִמֶּנּוּ, חַסְדְּךָ וַאֲמִתְּךָ תָּמִיד יִצְּרוּנוּ.
הוֹשִׁיעֵנוּ יהוה אֱלֹהֵינוּ וְקַבְּצֵנוּ מִן־הַגּוֹיִם, לְהוֹדוֹת לְשֵׁם קָדְשֶׁךָ, לְהִשְׁתַּבֵּחַ תהלים קו
בִּתְהִלָּתֶךָ: אִם־עֲוֹנוֹת תִּשְׁמָר־יָהּ, אֲדֹנָי מִי יַעֲמֹד: כִּי־עִמְּךָ הַסְּלִיחָה לְמַעַן תהלים קל
תִּוָּרֵא: לֹא כַחֲטָאֵינוּ תַּעֲשֶׂה לָנוּ, וְלֹא כַעֲוֹנוֹתֵינוּ תִּגְמֹל עָלֵינוּ. אִם־עֲוֹנֵינוּ ירמיה יד
עָנוּ בָנוּ, יהוה עֲשֵׂה לְמַעַן שְׁמֶךָ: זְכֹר־רַחֲמֶיךָ יהוה וַחֲסָדֶיךָ, כִּי מֵעוֹלָם תהלים כה
הֵמָּה: יַעֲנֵנוּ יהוה בְּיוֹם צָרָה, יְשַׂגְּבֵנוּ שֵׁם אֱלֹהֵי יַעֲקֹב. יהוה הוֹשִׁיעָה, תהלים כ

Mediterranean, found temporary refuge and then suffered renewed oppression. Some passages may have been added in the wake of the Gothic and Frankish persecutions in the seventh century. Their mood bespeaks the tears of Jews throughout the centuries of exile who experienced persecution, expulsion, humiliation, and often bloodshed at the hands of those amongst whom they lived. Even in times of freedom, we continue to say these prayers, keeping faith with our ancestors and remembering their tears.

What is remarkable about the prayers is the absence of anger or despair. If we ever doubt the power of prayer to transform the human situation, here we find an answer. Despite being treated as a pariah people, Jews never allowed themselves to be defined by their enemies. They wept and gave voice to pain: "God, see how low our glory has sunk among the nations. They abhor us as if we were impure." Yet they remained the people of the covenant, children

act charitably with us for Your name's sake. LORD our God, hear the sound of our pleas. Remember for us the covenant of our ancestors, and save us for Your name's sake.

וְעַתָּה And now, my LORD, our God, who took Your people out of the land of Egypt with a mighty hand, creating for Yourself renown to this day: we have sinned and acted wrongly. LORD, in keeping with all Your righteousness, please turn Your wrath and anger away from Jerusalem, Your holy mountain. Because of our sins and the iniquities of our ancestors, Jerusalem and Your people have become the scorn of all those around us. And now, our God, heed Your servant's prayer and pleas, and let Your face shine on Your desolate Sanctuary, for Your sake, O LORD. Incline Your ear, my God, and hear. Open Your eyes and see our desolation and that of the city called by Your name. Not because of our righteousness do we lay our pleas before You, but because of Your great compassion. LORD, hear! LORD, forgive! LORD, listen and act! Do not delay – for Your sake, my God, because Your city and Your people are called by Your name. *Dan. 9*

אָבִינוּ Our Father, compassionate Father, show us a sign for good, and gather our scattered ones from the four quarters of the earth. Let all the nations recognize and know that You are the LORD our God. And now, LORD, You *Is. 64* are our Father. We are the clay and You are our Potter; we are all the work of Your hand. Save us for the sake of Your name, our Rock, our King and our Redeemer. Pity Your people, LORD. Let not Your heritage become an object *Joel 2* of scorn, a byword among nations. Why should they say among the peoples, "Where is their God?" We know we have sinned and that there is no one to stand up for us. Let Your great name stand up for us in time of trouble. We know we have no merits of our own: therefore deal with us charitably for Your name's sake. As a father has compassion on his children, so, LORD, have compassion on us, and save us for the sake of Your name. Have mercy on Your people; have compassion for Your heritage; take pity in Your great

---

The passage weaves together three appeals to God's compassion: (1) we are Your children and You our Parent: have mercy on us as a parent forgives a child; (2) we are Your creation and You are our Creator: save us as an artist saves his most precious works of art; (3) we are Your witnesses, bearers of Your name: therefore save us for the sake of Your name. Let not the nations say, seeing our suffering, "Where is God?"

הַמֶּלֶךְ יַעֲנֵנוּ בְיוֹם־קָרְאֵנוּ: אָבִינוּ מַלְכֵּנוּ, חָנֵּנוּ וַעֲנֵנוּ, כִּי אֵין בָּנוּ מַעֲשִׂים,
צְדָקָה עֲשֵׂה עִמָּנוּ לְמַעַן שְׁמֶךָ. אֲדוֹנֵינוּ אֱלֹהֵינוּ, שְׁמַע קוֹל תַּחֲנוּנֵינוּ,
וּזְכָר לָנוּ אֶת בְּרִית אֲבוֹתֵינוּ וְהוֹשִׁיעֵנוּ לְמַעַן שְׁמֶךָ.

דניאל ט וְעַתָּה אֲדֹנָי אֱלֹהֵינוּ, אֲשֶׁר הוֹצֵאתָ אֶת־עַמְּךָ מֵאֶרֶץ מִצְרַיִם בְּיָד חֲזָקָה
וַתַּעַשׂ־לְךָ שֵׁם כַּיּוֹם הַזֶּה, חָטָאנוּ רָשָׁעְנוּ: אֲדֹנָי, כְּכָל־צִדְקֹתֶךָ יָשָׁב־נָא
אַפְּךָ וַחֲמָתְךָ, מֵעִירְךָ יְרוּשָׁלַיִם הַר־קָדְשֶׁךָ, כִּי בַחֲטָאֵינוּ וּבַעֲוֹנוֹת אֲבֹתֵינוּ,
יְרוּשָׁלַיִם וְעַמְּךָ לְחֶרְפָּה לְכָל־סְבִיבֹתֵינוּ: וְעַתָּה שְׁמַע אֱלֹהֵינוּ אֶל־תְּפִלַּת
עַבְדְּךָ וְאֶל־תַּחֲנוּנָיו, וְהָאֵר פָּנֶיךָ עַל־מִקְדָּשְׁךָ הַשָּׁמֵם, לְמַעַן אֲדֹנָי: הַטֵּה
אֱלֹהַי אָזְנְךָ וּשֲׁמָע, פְּקַח עֵינֶיךָ וּרְאֵה שֹׁמְמֹתֵינוּ וְהָעִיר אֲשֶׁר־נִקְרָא שִׁמְךָ
עָלֶיהָ, כִּי לֹא עַל־צִדְקֹתֵינוּ אֲנַחְנוּ מַפִּילִים תַּחֲנוּנֵינוּ לְפָנֶיךָ, כִּי עַל־רַחֲמֶיךָ
הָרַבִּים: אֲדֹנָי שְׁמָעָה, אֲדֹנָי סְלָחָה, אֲדֹנָי הַקְשִׁיבָה וַעֲשֵׂה אַל־תְּאַחַר,
לְמַעַנְךָ אֱלֹהַי, כִּי־שִׁמְךָ נִקְרָא עַל־עִירְךָ וְעַל־עַמֶּךָ:

אָבִינוּ הָאָב הָרַחֲמָן, הַרְאֵנוּ אוֹת לְטוֹבָה וְקַבֵּץ נְפוּצוֹתֵינוּ מֵאַרְבַּע כַּנְפוֹת
ישעיה סד הָאָרֶץ. יַכִּירוּ וְיֵדְעוּ כָּל הַגּוֹיִם כִּי אַתָּה יהוה אֱלֹהֵינוּ. וְעַתָּה יהוה אָבִינוּ
אָתָּה, אֲנַחְנוּ הַחֹמֶר וְאַתָּה יֹצְרֵנוּ וּמַעֲשֵׂה יָדְךָ כֻּלָּנוּ: הוֹשִׁיעֵנוּ לְמַעַן
יואל ב שְׁמֶךָ, צוּרֵנוּ מַלְכֵּנוּ וְגוֹאֲלֵנוּ. חוּסָה יהוה עַל־עַמֶּךָ, וְאַל־תִּתֵּן נַחֲלָתְךָ
לְחֶרְפָּה לִמְשָׁל־בָּם גּוֹיִם, לָמָּה יֹאמְרוּ בָעַמִּים אַיֵּה אֱלֹהֵיהֶם: יָדַעְנוּ כִּי
חָטָאנוּ וְאֵין מִי יַעֲמֹד בַּעֲדֵנוּ, שִׁמְךָ הַגָּדוֹל יַעֲמָד לָנוּ בְּעֵת צָרָה. יָדַעְנוּ
כִּי אֵין בָּנוּ מַעֲשִׂים, צְדָקָה עֲשֵׂה עִמָּנוּ לְמַעַן שְׁמֶךָ. כְּרַחֵם אָב עַל בָּנִים
כֵּן תְּרַחֵם יהוה עָלֵינוּ, וְהוֹשִׁיעֵנוּ לְמַעַן שְׁמֶךָ. חֲמֹל עַל עַמֶּךָ, רַחֵם עַל

וְעַתָּה *And now:* A prayer uttered by Daniel (9:15–19) in the first year of the reign of Xerxes, when he foresaw that the desolation of Jerusalem would last for seventy years. Fasting, dressed in sackcloth and ashes, he pleaded to God to forgive the people and bring an end to their suffering. These words play a key part in the Seliḥot (penitential prayers) on Fast Days.

אֲנַחְנוּ הַחֹמֶר *We are the clay and You are our Potter:* A verse from Isaiah (64:7) which became the basis of one of the liturgical poems on *Kol Nidrei* night.

compassion. Be gracious to us and answer us, for righteousness is Yours, Lord. Always You do wondrous things.

הַבֵּט נָא Please look, please swiftly have compassion for Your people for Your name's sake. In Your great compassion, Lord our God, have pity and compassion, and rescue the flock You tend. Let us not be ruled by wrath, for our eyes are turned toward You. Save us for Your name's sake. Have compassion on us for the sake of Your covenant. Look and answer us in time of trouble, for Yours, Lord, is the power to save. Our hope is in You, God of forgiveness. Please forgive, good and forgiving God, for You are a gracious, compassionate God and King.

אָנָּא מֶלֶךְ Please, gracious and compassionate King, remember and call to mind the Covenant between the Pieces [with Abraham] and let the binding of his only son [Isaac] appear before You for Israel's sake. Our Father, our King, be gracious to us and answer us, for we are called by Your great name. You who work miracles at all times, deal with us according to Your loving-kindness. Gracious and compassionate One, look and answer us in time of trouble, for salvation is Yours, Lord. Our Father, our King, our Refuge, do not act with us according to our evil deeds. Remember, Lord, Your tender mercies and Your love. Save us in Your great goodness, and have mercy on us, for we have no other god but You, our Rock. Do not abandon us, Lord our God, do not be distant from us, for we are worn out by the sword and captivity, pestilence and plague, and by every trouble and sorrow. Rescue us, for in You lies our hope. Put us not to shame, Lord our God. Let Your face shine upon us. Remember for us the covenant of our ancestors and save us for Your name's sake. See our troubles and heed the voice of our prayer, for You heed the prayer of every mouth.

אֵל רַחוּם וְחַנּוּן O Compassionate and gracious God, have compassion on us and on all Your works, for there is none like You, Lord our God. Please, we beg You, forgive our sins, our Father, our King, our Rock, our Redeemer, living and eternal God, mighty in strength, loving and good to all Your works, for You are the Lord our God. O God, slow to anger and full of compassion, act with us according to Your great compassion and save us for Your name's sake. Hear our prayer, our King, and save us from our enemies' hands. Heed our prayer, our King, and save us from all distress and sorrow. You are our Father, our King. We are called by Your name. Do not desert us. Do not abandon us, our Father. Do not cast us away, our Creator. Do not forget us, our Maker – for You are a gracious and compassionate God and King.

נַחֲלָתֶךָ, חוּסָה נָּא כְּרֹב רַחֲמֶיךָ, חָנֵּנוּ וַעֲנֵנוּ. כִּי לְךָ יהוה הַצְּדָקָה, עֹשֵׂה נִפְלָאוֹת בְּכָל עֵת.

הַבֶּט נָא, רַחֶם נָא עַל עַמְּךָ מְהֵרָה לְמַעַן שְׁמֶךָ. בְּרַחֲמֶיךָ הָרַבִּים יהוה אֱלֹהֵינוּ. חוּס וְרַחֵם וְהוֹשִׁיעָה צֹאן מַרְעִיתֶךָ, וְאַל יִמְשָׁל בָּנוּ קֶצֶף, כִּי לְךָ עֵינֵינוּ תְלוּיוֹת. הוֹשִׁיעֵנוּ לְמַעַן שְׁמֶךָ. רַחֵם עָלֵינוּ לְמַעַן בְּרִיתֶךָ. הַבִּיטָה וַעֲנֵנוּ בְּעֵת צָרָה, כִּי לְךָ יהוה הַיְשׁוּעָה. בְּךָ תוֹחַלְתֵּנוּ אֱלוֹהַּ סְלִיחוֹת, אָנָּא סְלַח נָא אֵל טוֹב וְסַלָּח, כִּי אֵל מֶלֶךְ חַנּוּן וְרַחוּם אָתָּה.

אָנָּא מֶלֶךְ חַנּוּן וְרַחוּם, זְכֹר וְהַבֵּט לִבְרִית בֵּין הַבְּתָרִים, וְתֵרָאֶה לְפָנֶיךָ עֲקֵדַת יָחִיד לְמַעַן יִשְׂרָאֵל. אָבִינוּ מַלְכֵּנוּ, חָנֵּנוּ וַעֲנֵנוּ, כִּי שִׁמְךָ הַגָּדוֹל נִקְרָא עָלֵינוּ. עֹשֵׂה נִפְלָאוֹת בְּכָל עֵת, עֲשֵׂה עִמָּנוּ כְּחַסְדֶּךָ. חַנּוּן וְרַחוּם, הַבִּיטָה וַעֲנֵנוּ בְּעֵת צָרָה, כִּי לְךָ יהוה הַיְשׁוּעָה. אָבִינוּ מַלְכֵּנוּ מַחְסֵנוּ, אַל תַּעַשׂ עִמָּנוּ כְּרֹעַ מַעֲלָלֵינוּ. זְכֹר רַחֲמֶיךָ יהוה וַחֲסָדֶיךָ, וּכְרֹב טוּבְךָ הוֹשִׁיעֵנוּ, וַחֲמָל נָא עָלֵינוּ, כִּי אֵין לָנוּ אֱלוֹהַּ אַחֵר מִבַּלְעָדֶיךָ צוּרֵנוּ. אַל תַּעַזְבֵנוּ יהוה אֱלֹהֵינוּ אַל תִּרְחַק מִמֶּנּוּ. כִּי נַפְשֵׁנוּ קְצָרָה, מֵחֶרֶב וּמִשְּׁבִי וּמִדֶּבֶר וּמִמַּגֵּפָה. וּמִכָּל צָרָה וְיָגוֹן הַצִּילֵנוּ, כִּי לְךָ קִוִּינוּ. וְאַל תַּכְלִימֵנוּ יהוה אֱלֹהֵינוּ, וְהָאֵר פָּנֶיךָ בָּנוּ, וּזְכָר לָנוּ אֶת בְּרִית אֲבוֹתֵינוּ וְהוֹשִׁיעֵנוּ לְמַעַן שְׁמֶךָ. רְאֵה בְצָרוֹתֵינוּ, וּשְׁמַע קוֹל תְּפִלָּתֵנוּ, כִּי אַתָּה שׁוֹמֵעַ תְּפִלַּת כָּל פֶּה.

אֵל רַחוּם וְחַנּוּן, רַחֵם עָלֵינוּ וְעַל כָּל מַעֲשֶׂיךָ, כִּי אֵין כָּמְוֹךָ יהוה אֱלֹהֵינוּ. אָנָּא שָׂא נָא פְשָׁעֵינוּ, אָבִינוּ מַלְכֵּנוּ צוּרֵנוּ וְגוֹאֲלֵנוּ, אֵל חַי וְקַיָּם הַחֲסִין בַּכֹּחַ, חָסִיד וָטוֹב עַל כָּל מַעֲשֶׂיךָ, כִּי אַתָּה הוּא יהוה אֱלֹהֵינוּ. אֵל אֶרֶךְ אַפַּיִם וּמָלֵא רַחֲמִים, עֲשֵׂה עִמָּנוּ כְּרֹב רַחֲמֶיךָ, וְהוֹשִׁיעֵנוּ לְמַעַן שְׁמֶךָ. שְׁמַע מַלְכֵּנוּ תְּפִלָּתֵנוּ, וּמִיַּד אוֹיְבֵינוּ הַצִּילֵנוּ. שְׁמַע מַלְכֵּנוּ תְּפִלָּתֵנוּ, וּמִכָּל צָרָה וְיָגוֹן הַצִּילֵנוּ. אָבִינוּ מַלְכֵּנוּ אָתָּה, וְשִׁמְךָ עָלֵינוּ נִקְרָא. אַל תַּנִּיחֵנוּ, אַל תַּעַזְבֵנוּ אָבִינוּ וְאַל תִּטְּשֵׁנוּ בּוֹרְאֵנוּ וְאַל תִּשְׁכָּחֵנוּ יוֹצְרֵנוּ, כִּי אֵל מֶלֶךְ חַנּוּן וְרַחוּם אָתָּה.

אֵין כָּמוֹךָ There is none like You in grace and compassion, LORD our God. There is none like You, God, slow to anger and abounding in loving-kindness and truth. Save us in Your great compassion; rescue us from storm and turmoil. Remember Your servants Abraham, Isaac and Jacob; do not attend to our stubbornness, wickedness and sinfulness. Turn from Your *Ex. 32* fierce anger, and relent from the evil meant for Your people. Remove from us the scourge of death, for You are compassionate. This is Your way, to show unearned loving-kindness to every generation. Have pity on Your people, LORD, and save us from Your wrath. Remove from us the scourge of plague and the harsh decree, for You are the Guardian of Israel. You are *Dan. 9* right, my LORD, and we are shamefaced. How can we complain? What can we say? What can we plead? How can we justify ourselves? Let us search our ways and examine them and return to You, for Your right hand is outstretched to receive those who return. Please, LORD, please save. Please, *Ps. 118* LORD, please send success. Please, LORD, answer us when we call. For You, LORD, we wait. For You, LORD, we hope. For You, LORD, we long. Do not be silent while we suffer, for the nations are saying, "Their hope is lost." To You alone every knee must bend, and those who hold themselves high bow down.

הַפּוֹתֵחַ יָד You who hold out an open hand of repentance to receive transgressors and sinners – our soul is overwhelmed by our great sorrow. Do not forget us for ever. Arise and save us, for we seek refuge in You. Our Father, our King, though we lack righteousness and good deeds, remember for us the covenant of our fathers, and our testimonies daily that "The LORD is One." Look on our affliction, for many are our sufferings and heartaches. Have pity on us, LORD, in the land of our captivity. Do not pour out Your wrath on us, for we are Your people, the children of Your covenant. God, see how low our glory has sunk among the nations. They abhor us as if we were impure. How long will Your strength be captive, and Your glory in the hand of the foe? Arouse Your strength and zeal against Your enemies. Let them be shamed and deprived of power. Let not our hardships seem small to You. Swiftly may Your compassion reach us in the day of our distress. If not for our sake, act for Yours, so that the memory of our survivors be not destroyed. Be gracious to the nation who, in constant love, proclaim twice daily the unity of Your name, saying, "Listen, Israel: the LORD is our God, *Deut. 6* the LORD is One."

אֵין כָּמְוֹךָ חַנּוּן וְרַחוּם יהוה אֱלֹהֵינוּ, אֵין כָּמְוֹךָ אֵל אֶרֶךְ אַפַּיִם וְרַב חֶסֶד וֶאֱמֶת. הוֹשִׁיעֵנוּ בְּרַחֲמֶיךָ הָרַבִּים, מֵרַעַשׁ וּמֵרְגֶז הַצִּילֵנוּ. זְכֹר לַעֲבָדֶיךָ לְאַבְרָהָם לְיִצְחָק וּלְיַעֲקֹב, אַל תֵּפֶן אֶל קָשְׁיֵנוּ וְאֶל רִשְׁעֵנוּ וְאֶל חַטָּאתֵנוּ.

שמות לב שׁוּב מֵחֲרוֹן אַפֶּךָ, וְהִנָּחֵם עַל־הָרָעָה לְעַמֶּךָ: וְהָסֵר מִמֶּנּוּ מַכַּת הַמָּוֶת כִּי רַחוּם אָתָּה, כִּי כֵן דַּרְכֶּךָ, עֹשֶׂה חֶסֶד חִנָּם בְּכָל דּוֹר וָדוֹר. חוּסָה יהוה עַל עַמֶּךָ וְהַצִּילֵנוּ מִזַּעְמֶךָ, וְהָסֵר מִמֶּנּוּ מַכַּת הַמַּגֵּפָה וּגְזֵרָה קָשָׁה, כִּי אַתָּה
דניאל ט שׁוֹמֵר יִשְׂרָאֵל. לְךָ אֲדֹנָי הַצְּדָקָה וְלָנוּ בֹּשֶׁת הַפָּנִים: מַה נִּתְאוֹנֵן, מַה נֹּאמַר, מַה נְּדַבֵּר וּמַה נִּצְטַדָּק. נַחְפְּשָׂה דְרָכֵינוּ וְנַחְקֹרָה וְנָשׁוּבָה אֵלֶיךָ, כִּי יְמִינְךָ
תהלים קיח פְּשׁוּטָה לְקַבֵּל שָׁבִים. אָנָּא יהוה הוֹשִׁיעָה נָּא, אָנָּא יהוה הַצְלִיחָה נָא: אָנָּא יהוה עֲנֵנוּ בְיוֹם קָרְאֵנוּ. לְךָ יהוה חִכִּינוּ, לְךָ יהוה קִוִּינוּ, לְךָ יהוה נְיַחֵל. אַל תֶּחֱשֶׁה וּתְעַנֵּנוּ, כִּי נָאֲמוּ גוֹיִם, אָבְדָה תִקְוָתָם. כָּל בֶּרֶךְ וְכָל קוֹמָה, לְךָ לְבַד תִּשְׁתַּחֲוֶה.

הַפּוֹתֵחַ יָד בִּתְשׁוּבָה לְקַבֵּל פּוֹשְׁעִים וְחַטָּאִים, נִבְהֲלָה נַפְשֵׁנוּ מֵרֹב עִצְּבוֹנֵנוּ. אַל תִּשְׁכָּחֵנוּ נֶצַח, קוּמָה וְהוֹשִׁיעֵנוּ כִּי חָסִינוּ בָךְ. אָבִינוּ מַלְכֵּנוּ, אִם אֵין בָּנוּ צְדָקָה וּמַעֲשִׂים טוֹבִים, זְכָר לָנוּ אֶת בְּרִית אֲבוֹתֵינוּ וְעֵדוֹתֵינוּ בְּכָל יוֹם יהוה אֶחָד. הַבִּיטָה בְעָנְיֵנוּ, כִּי רַבּוּ מַכְאוֹבֵינוּ וְצָרוֹת לְבָבֵנוּ. חוּסָה יהוה עָלֵינוּ בְּאֶרֶץ שִׁבְיֵנוּ, וְאַל תִּשְׁפֹּךְ חֲרוֹנְךָ עָלֵינוּ, כִּי אֲנַחְנוּ עַמְּךָ בְּנֵי בְרִיתֶךָ. אֵל, הַבִּיטָה, דַּל כְּבוֹדֵנוּ בַּגּוֹיִם וְשִׁקְּצוּנוּ כְּטֻמְאַת הַנִּדָּה. עַד מָתַי עֻזְּךָ בַּשְּׁבִי, וְתִפְאַרְתְּךָ בְּיַד צָר. עוֹרְרָה גְבוּרָתְךָ וְקִנְאָתְךָ עַל אוֹיְבֶיךָ. הֵם יֵבוֹשׁוּ וְיֵחַתּוּ מִגְּבוּרָתָם. וְאַל יִמְעֲטוּ לְפָנֶיךָ תְּלָאוֹתֵינוּ. מַהֵר יְקַדְּמוּנוּ רַחֲמֶיךָ בְּיוֹם צָרָתֵנוּ. וְאִם לֹא לְמַעֲנֵנוּ, לְמַעַנְךָ פְעַל, וְאַל תַּשְׁחִית זֵכֶר שְׁאֵרִיתֵנוּ, וְחֹן אֹם הַמְיַחֲדִים שִׁמְךָ פַּעֲמַיִם בְּכָל יוֹם תָּמִיד בְּאַהֲבָה,
דברים ו וְאוֹמְרִים, שְׁמַע יִשְׂרָאֵל, יהוה אֱלֹהֵינוּ, יהוה אֶחָד:

הַפּוֹתֵחַ יָד *You who hold out an open hand:* God's forgiveness stretches beyond strict retribution: "I do not desire the death of the wicked, but rather that they turn from their ways and live" (Ezek. 33:11).

LOWERING THE HEAD

On Sundays, Tuesdays, Wednesdays and Fridays, begin Taḥanun here. The following, until "We do not know" on page 156, is said sitting. When praying in a place where there is a Torah scroll, one should lean forward, resting one's head on the left arm (unless you are wearing tefillin on the left arm, in which case rest on the right arm out of respect for the tefillin), until in "sudden shame."

וַיֹּאמֶר דָּוִד David said to Gad, "I am in great distress. *II Sam. 24*
Let us fall into God's hand, for His mercy is great;
but do not let me fall into the hand of man."

Compassionate and gracious One, I have sinned before You.
Lord, full of compassion, have compassion on me and accept my pleas.

Lord, do not rebuke me in Your anger or chastise me in Your wrath. Be gracious to me, Lord, for I am weak. Heal me, Lord, for my bones are in agony. My soul is in anguish, and You, O Lord – how long? Turn, Lord, set my soul free; save me for the sake of Your love. For no one remembers You when he is dead. Who can praise You from the grave? I am weary with my sighing. Every night I drench my bed, I soak my couch with my tears. My eye grows dim from grief, worn out because of all my foes. Leave me, all you evildoers, for the Lord has heard the sound of my weeping. The Lord has heard my pleas. The Lord will accept my prayer. All my enemies will be shamed and utterly dismayed. They will turn back in sudden shame. *Ps. 6*

Sit upright. On Mondays and Thursdays, say the following. On other days, continue with "Guardian of Israel" on the next page.

Lord, God of Israel, turn away from Your fierce anger,
and relent from the evil against Your people.

Look down from heaven and see how we have become an object of scorn and derision among the nations. We are regarded as sheep led to the slaughter, to be killed, destroyed, beaten and humiliated. Yet, despite all this, we have not forgotten Your name. Please do not forget us.

Lord, God of Israel, turn away from Your fierce anger,
and relent from the evil against Your people.

Strangers say, "You have no hope or expectation." Be gracious to the nation whose hope is in Your name. O Pure One, bring our deliverance close. We are exhausted. We are given no rest. May Your compassion suppress Your anger against us. Please turn away from Your fierce anger, and have compassion on the people You chose as Your own.

---

when prayer becomes the ladder on which we climb from the pit of despair to the free air of hope.

הַבֵּט מִשָּׁמַיִם *Look down from heaven:* These heart-rending words were already known in Europe in the eleventh century, and recall the terrible persecutions Jews suffered during the early Middle Ages.

נפילת אפיים

On Sundays, Tuesdays, Wednesdays and Fridays, begin תחנון *here.*
The following, until וַאֲנַחְנוּ לֹא נֵדַע *on page 157, is said sitting. When praying in a place where there is a* ספר תורה*, one should lean forward, resting one's head on the left arm (unless you are wearing* תפילין *on the left arm, in which case rest on the right arm out of respect for the* תפילין*), until* יֵבֹשׁוּ רָגַע*.*

וַיֹּאמֶר דָּוִד אֶל־גָּד, צַר־לִי מְאֹד שמואל ב, כד
נִפְּלָה־נָּא בְיַד־יהוה, כִּי רַבִּים רַחֲמָו, וּבְיַד־אָדָם אַל־אֶפֹּלָה:

רַחוּם וְחַנּוּן, חָטָאתִי לְפָנֶיךָ. יהוה מָלֵא רַחֲמִים, רַחֵם עָלַי וְקַבֵּל תַּחֲנוּנָי.

יהוה, אַל־בְּאַפְּךָ תוֹכִיחֵנִי, וְאַל־בַּחֲמָתְךָ תְיַסְּרֵנִי: חָנֵּנִי יהוה, כִּי אֻמְלַל אָנִי, תהלים ו
רְפָאֵנִי יהוה, כִּי נִבְהֲלוּ עֲצָמָי: וְנַפְשִׁי נִבְהֲלָה מְאֹד, וְאַתְּ יהוה, עַד־מָתָי: שׁוּבָה
יהוה, חַלְּצָה נַפְשִׁי, הוֹשִׁיעֵנִי לְמַעַן חַסְדֶּךָ: כִּי אֵין בַּמָּוֶת זִכְרֶךָ, בִּשְׁאוֹל מִי
יוֹדֶה־לָּךְ: יָגַעְתִּי בְּאַנְחָתִי, אַשְׂחֶה בְכָל־לַיְלָה מִטָּתִי, בְּדִמְעָתִי עַרְשִׂי אַמְסֶה:
עָשְׁשָׁה מִכַּעַס עֵינִי, עָתְקָה בְּכָל־צוֹרְרָי: סוּרוּ מִמֶּנִּי כָּל־פֹּעֲלֵי אָוֶן, כִּי שָׁמַע
יהוה קוֹל בִּכְיִי: שָׁמַע יהוה תְּחִנָּתִי, יהוה תְּפִלָּתִי יִקָּח: יֵבֹשׁוּ וְיִבָּהֲלוּ מְאֹד
כָּל־אֹיְבָי, יָשֻׁבוּ יֵבֹשׁוּ רָגַע:

Sit upright. On Mondays and Thursdays, say the following.
On other days, continue with שׁוֹמֵר יִשְׂרָאֵל *on the next page.*

יהוה אֱלֹהֵי יִשְׂרָאֵל, שׁוּב מֵחֲרוֹן אַפֶּךָ וְהִנָּחֵם עַל הָרָעָה לְעַמֶּךָ.
הַבֵּט מִשָּׁמַיִם וּרְאֵה כִּי הָיִינוּ לַעַג וָקֶלֶס בַּגּוֹיִם, נֶחְשַׁבְנוּ כַּצֹּאן לַטֶּבַח יוּבָל, לַהֲרֹג וּלְאַבֵּד וּלְמַכָּה וּלְחֶרְפָּה. וּבְכָל זֹאת שִׁמְךָ לֹא שָׁכָחְנוּ, נָא אַל תִּשְׁכָּחֵנוּ.
יהוה אֱלֹהֵי יִשְׂרָאֵל, שׁוּב מֵחֲרוֹן אַפֶּךָ וְהִנָּחֵם עַל הָרָעָה לְעַמֶּךָ.
זָרִים אוֹמְרִים אֵין תּוֹחֶלֶת וְתִקְוָה, חֹן אֹם לְשִׁמְךָ מְקַוֶּה, טָהוֹר יְשׁוּעָתֵנוּ קָרְבָה, יָגַעְנוּ וְלֹא הוּנַח לָנוּ, רַחֲמֶיךָ יִכְבְּשׁוּ אֶת כַּעַסְךָ מֵעָלֵינוּ. אָנָּא שׁוּב מֵחֲרוֹנְךָ וְרַחֵם סְגֻלָּה אֲשֶׁר בָּחָרְתָּ.

וַיֹּאמֶר דָּוִד *David said to Gad:* Words spoken by David during a moment of crisis (II Sam. 24:14). The king had sinned by taking a census of the people. God, through the prophet Gad, offered him a choice: famine, war, or punishment directly from heaven. David replied: it is better to be punished by God than suffer the cruelty of man.

יהוה, אַל־בְּאַפְּךָ תוֹכִיחֵנִי *Lord, do not rebuke me in Your anger:* A psalm of intense emotional power, spoken out of fear's heart of darkness. **שָׁמַע יהוה תְּחִנָּתִי** *The Lord has heard my pleas:* from the deepest pain, strength is born,

Lord, God of Israel, turn away from Your fierce anger,
and relent from the evil against Your people.

Have pity on us, Lord, in Your compassion, and do not hand us over to cruel oppressors. Why should the nations say, "Where is their God now?" For Your own sake, deal kindly with us, and do not delay. Please turn away from Your fierce anger, and have compassion on the people You chose as Your own.

Lord, God of Israel, turn away from Your fierce anger,
and relent from the evil against Your people.

Heed our voice and be gracious. Do not abandon us into the hand of our enemies to blot out our name. Remember what You promised our fathers: "I will make your descendants as many as the stars of heaven" – yet now we are only a few left from many. Yet, despite all this, we have not forgotten Your name. Please do not forget us.

Lord, God of Israel, turn away from Your fierce anger,
and relent from the evil against Your people.

Help us, God of our salvation, for the sake of the glory of Your name. Save us and pardon our sins for Your name's sake. *Ps. 79*

Lord, God of Israel, turn away from Your fierce anger,
and relent from the evil against Your people.

On all days continue here:

שׁוֹמֵר יִשְׂרָאֵל Guardian of Israel, guard the remnant of Israel,
and let not Israel perish, who declare, "Listen, Israel."
Guardian of a unique nation, guard the remnant of a unique people,
and let not that unique nation perish, who proclaim the unity
of Your name [saying], "The Lord is our God, the Lord is One."
Guardian of a holy nation, guard the remnant of that holy people,
and let not the holy nation perish, who three times repeat
the threefold declaration of holiness to the Holy One.
You who are conciliated by calls for compassion and placated by pleas,
be conciliated and placated toward an afflicted generation,
for there is no other help.
Our Father, our King, be gracious to us and answer us, though we have no
worthy deeds; act with us in charity and loving-kindness and save us.

שׁוֹמֵר יִשְׂרָאֵל *Guardian of Israel:* A three-verse prayer set in motion by a phrase from Psalm 121: "See: the Guardian of Israel neither slumbers nor sleeps." An example of early liturgical poetry, it has the same structure as the poem preceding the morning Amida, "Rock of Israel! Arise to the help of Israel…" and

יהוה אֱלֹהֵי יִשְׂרָאֵל, שׁוּב מֵחֲרוֹן אַפֶּךָ וְהִנָּחֵם עַל הָרָעָה לְעַמֶּךָ.

חוּסָה יהוה עָלֵינוּ בְּרַחֲמֶיךָ, וְאַל תִּתְּנֵנוּ בִּידֵי אַכְזָרִים. לָמָּה יֹאמְרוּ הַגּוֹיִם אַיֵּה נָא אֱלֹהֵיהֶם, לְמַעַנְךָ עֲשֵׂה עִמָּנוּ חֶסֶד וְאַל תְּאַחַר. אָנָּא שׁוּב מֵחֲרוֹנְךָ וְרַחֵם סְגֻלָּה אֲשֶׁר בָּחָרְתָּ.

יהוה אֱלֹהֵי יִשְׂרָאֵל, שׁוּב מֵחֲרוֹן אַפֶּךָ וְהִנָּחֵם עַל הָרָעָה לְעַמֶּךָ.

קוֹלֵנוּ תִשְׁמַע וְתָחֹן, וְאַל תִּטְּשֵׁנוּ בְּיַד אֹיְבֵינוּ לִמְחוֹת אֶת שְׁמֵנוּ. זְכֹר אֲשֶׁר נִשְׁבַּעְתָּ לַאֲבוֹתֵינוּ כְּכוֹכְבֵי הַשָּׁמַיִם אַרְבֶּה אֶת זַרְעֲכֶם, וְעַתָּה נִשְׁאַרְנוּ מְעַט מֵהַרְבֵּה. וּבְכָל זֹאת שִׁמְךָ לֹא שָׁכָחְנוּ, נָא אַל תִּשְׁכָּחֵנוּ.

יהוה אֱלֹהֵי יִשְׂרָאֵל, שׁוּב מֵחֲרוֹן אַפֶּךָ וְהִנָּחֵם עַל הָרָעָה לְעַמֶּךָ.

עָזְרֵנוּ אֱלֹהֵי יִשְׁעֵנוּ עַל־דְּבַר כְּבוֹד־שְׁמֶךָ, וְהַצִּילֵנוּ וְכַפֵּר עַל־חַטֹּאתֵינוּ לְמַעַן שְׁמֶךָ: תהלים עט

יהוה אֱלֹהֵי יִשְׂרָאֵל, שׁוּב מֵחֲרוֹן אַפֶּךָ וְהִנָּחֵם עַל הָרָעָה לְעַמֶּךָ.

On all days continue here:

שׁוֹמֵר יִשְׂרָאֵל, שְׁמֹר שְׁאֵרִית יִשְׂרָאֵל, וְאַל יֹאבַד יִשְׂרָאֵל
הָאוֹמְרִים שְׁמַע יִשְׂרָאֵל.

שׁוֹמֵר גּוֹי אֶחָד, שְׁמֹר שְׁאֵרִית עַם אֶחָד, וְאַל יֹאבַד גּוֹי אֶחָד
הַמְיַחֲדִים שִׁמְךָ, יהוה אֱלֹהֵינוּ יהוה אֶחָד.

שׁוֹמֵר גּוֹי קָדוֹשׁ, שְׁמֹר שְׁאֵרִית עַם קָדוֹשׁ, וְאַל יֹאבַד גּוֹי קָדוֹשׁ
הַמְשַׁלְּשִׁים בְּשָׁלֹשׁ קְדֻשּׁוֹת לְקָדוֹשׁ.

מִתְרַצֶּה בְּרַחֲמִים וּמִתְפַּיֵּס בְּתַחֲנוּנִים, הִתְרַצֵּה וְהִתְפַּיֵּס לְדוֹר עָנִי
כִּי אֵין עוֹזֵר.

אָבִינוּ מַלְכֵּנוּ, חָנֵּנוּ וַעֲנֵנוּ, כִּי אֵין בָּנוּ מַעֲשִׂים
עֲשֵׂה עִמָּנוּ צְדָקָה וָחֶסֶד וְהוֹשִׁיעֵנוּ.

וּבְכָל זֹאת *Yet, despite all this:* After the Holocaust, the concentration camp at Theresienstadt was excavated. A hidden room was discovered, which had served as a secret place in which the prisoners would pray. On one of its walls were written the words: "Yet, despite all this, we have not forgotten Your name. Please do not forget us."

Stand at ▴.

וַאֲנַחְנוּ We do not know ▴what to do, but our eyes are turned to You. Remember, Lord, Your compassion and loving-kindness, for they are everlasting. May Your loving-kindness, Lord, be with us, for we have put our hope in You. Do not hold against us the sins of those who came before us. May Your mercies meet us swiftly, for we have been brought very low. Be gracious to us, Lord, be gracious to us, for we are sated with contempt. In wrath, remember mercy. He knows our nature; He remembers that we are dust. ▸ Help us, God of our salvation, for the sake of the glory of Your name. Save us and grant atonement for our sins for Your name's sake.

II Chr. 12 *Ps. 25* *Ps. 33* *Ps. 79* *Ps. 123* *Hab. 3* *Ps. 103* *Ps. 79*

HALF KADDISH

Leader: יִתְגַּדַּל Magnified and sanctified
may His great name be,
in the world He created by His will.
May He establish His kingdom
in your lifetime and in your days,
and in the lifetime of all the house of Israel,
swiftly and soon – and say: Amen.

All: May His great name be blessed for ever and all time.

Leader: Blessed and praised, glorified and exalted,
raised and honored, uplifted and lauded
be the name of the Holy One,
blessed be He,
beyond any blessing,
song, praise and consolation
uttered in the world –
and say: Amen.

---

intent on war (II Chr. 20:12). Our custom is to stand after these words. Abudarham explains that this is because – like Moses pleading on behalf of the people – we have prayed in every posture, sitting (before the Amida), standing (during the Amida), and "falling on our faces" (during *Tahanun*). We have exhausted the repertoire of prayer and do not know what else to do. We stand at this point to signal that our private supplications have come to an end.

Stand at *.

וַאֲנַחְנוּ לֹא נֵדַע מַה־נַּעֲשֶׂה, כִּי עָלֶיךָ עֵינֵינוּ: זְכֹר־רַחֲמֶיךָ יהוה וַחֲסָדֶיךָ, דברי הימים ב׳ כ תהלים כה
כִּי מֵעוֹלָם הֵמָּה: יְהִי־חַסְדְּךָ יהוה עָלֵינוּ, כַּאֲשֶׁר יִחַלְנוּ לָךְ: אַל־תִּזְכָּר־לָנוּ תהלים לג תהלים עט
עֲוֹנֹת רִאשֹׁנִים, מַהֵר יְקַדְּמוּנוּ רַחֲמֶיךָ, כִּי דַלּוֹנוּ מְאֹד: חָנֵּנוּ יהוה חָנֵּנוּ, תהלים קכג
כִּי־רַב שָׂבַעְנוּ בוּז: בְּרֹגֶז רַחֵם תִּזְכּוֹר: כִּי־הוּא יָדַע יִצְרֵנוּ, זָכוּר כִּי־עָפָר חבקוק ג תהלים קג
אֲנָחְנוּ: • עָזְרֵנוּ אֱלֹהֵי יִשְׁעֵנוּ עַל־דְּבַר כְּבוֹד־שְׁמֶךָ, וְהַצִּילֵנוּ וְכַפֵּר עַל־ תהלים עט
חַטֹּאתֵינוּ לְמַעַן שְׁמֶךָ:

חצי קדיש

ש״ץ: יִתְגַּדַּל וְיִתְקַדַּשׁ שְׁמֵהּ רַבָּא (קהל: אָמֵן)
בְּעָלְמָא דִּי בְרָא כִרְעוּתֵהּ
וְיַמְלִיךְ מַלְכוּתֵהּ
בְּחַיֵּיכוֹן וּבְיוֹמֵיכוֹן וּבְחַיֵּי דְכָל בֵּית יִשְׂרָאֵל
בַּעֲגָלָא וּבִזְמַן קָרִיב, וְאִמְרוּ אָמֵן. (קהל: אָמֵן)

קהל וש״ץ: יְהֵא שְׁמֵהּ רַבָּא מְבָרַךְ לְעָלַם וּלְעָלְמֵי עָלְמַיָּא.

ש״ץ: יִתְבָּרַךְ וְיִשְׁתַּבַּח וְיִתְפָּאַר וְיִתְרוֹמַם וְיִתְנַשֵּׂא
וְיִתְהַדָּר וְיִתְעַלֶּה וְיִתְהַלָּל
שְׁמֵהּ דְּקֻדְשָׁא בְּרִיךְ הוּא (קהל: בְּרִיךְ הוּא)
לְעֵלָּא מִן כָּל בִּרְכָתָא
/בעשרת ימי תשובה: לְעֵלָּא לְעֵלָּא מִכָּל בִּרְכָתָא/
וְשִׁירָתָא, תֻּשְׁבְּחָתָא וְנֶחֱמָתָא
דַּאֲמִירָן בְּעָלְמָא, וְאִמְרוּ אָמֵן. (קהל: אָמֵן)

---

the prayer said on the Ten Days of Penitence, "Remember us for life, O King who desires life…" In each case every verse contains four phrases, all ending with the same word (Rabbi Jeffrey Cohen). The prayer was transferred from the penitential prayers known as Selihot to the Daily Service.

וַאֲנַחְנוּ לֹא נֵדַע *We do not know:* A line taken from the prayer of King Jehoshaphat when the nation was confronted by a coalition of hostile powers

REMOVING THE TORAH FROM THE ARK

On Mondays and Thursdays, Rosh Ḥodesh, Ḥol HaMo'ed, Ḥanukka, Purim and Fast Days, the Torah is read when a minyan is present.
On all other days, continue with "Happy are those" on page 170.
Before taking the Torah out of the Ark, on Mondays and Thursdays, stand while reciting "God, slow to anger." It is not said on Rosh Ḥodesh, Ḥol HaMo'ed, Erev Pesaḥ, Ḥanukka, the 14th and 15th of Adar I, Purim and Shushan Purim, Yom HaAtzma'ut, Yom Yerushalayim, Tisha B'Av or in a house of mourning, and in Israel on Isru Ḥag. Most people say both paragraphs; some say only the first.

God, slow to anger, abounding
in loving-kindness and truth,
do not rebuke us in Your anger.
Have pity on Your people, LORD,
and save us from all evil.
We have sinned against You, LORD.
Please forgive in accordance with
Your great compassion, God.

God, slow to anger, full of compassion,
do not hide Your face from us.
Have pity on the remnant of Israel
Your people, LORD,
and deliver us from all evil.
We have sinned against You, LORD.
Please forgive in accordance with
Your great compassion, God.

The Ark is opened and the congregation stands. All say:

וַיְהִי בִּנְסֹעַ Whenever the Ark set out, Moses would say, "Arise, LORD, *Num. 10*
and may Your enemies be scattered. May those who hate You flee
before You." For the Torah shall come forth from Zion, and the *Is. 2*
word of the LORD from Jerusalem. Blessed is He who in His holiness gave the Torah to His people Israel.

---

them the entire Book of the Covenant which had been found in the LORD's Temple" (II Chr. 34:30).

The book of Nehemiah (8:1–12) contains a graphic description of the return of the Babylonian exiles to Israel. Ezra gathered the people at the Temple and read the Torah to them "from dawn until midday," assisted by Levites who "interpreted it and explained its meaning, so that they understood the verses."

These were national occasions. At a more local level, tradition holds that Moses instituted the practice that the Torah be read on Shabbat, Yom Tov, Ḥol HaMo'ed, and Rosh Ḥodesh. Ezra ordained that it also be read on Mondays and Thursdays (market days in ancient times) and on Shabbat afternoons (Yerushalmi, *Megilla* 4:1). The public reading of the Torah is as ancient an institution as prayer itself.

The synagogue thus became not only a house of prayer but also a house of study. The result is a dynamic tension between speaking and listening. In

הוצאת ספר תורה

On Mondays and Thursdays, ראש חודש, חול המועד, חנוכה, פורים *and Fast Days,*
the תורה *is read when a* מנין *is present. On all other days, continue with* אשרי *on page 171.*

Before taking the תורה *out of the* ארון קודש*, on Mondays and Thursdays, stand while reciting* אֵל אֶֽרֶךְ אַפַּֽיִם*. It is not said on:* ראש חודש, חול המועד, ערב פסח, חנוכה*, the 14th and 15th of* אדר א׳, פורים *and* שושן פורים, יום העצמאות, יום ירושלים, תשעה באב *or in a house of mourning, and in* ארץ ישראל *on* אסרו חג*. Most people say both paragraphs, some say only the first.*

אֵל אֶֽרֶךְ אַפַּֽיִם וְרַב חֶֽסֶד וֶאֱמֶת
אַל בְּאַפְּךָ תוֹכִיחֵֽנוּ.
חֽוּסָה יהוה עַל עַמֶּֽךָ
וְהוֹשִׁיעֵֽנוּ מִכָּל רָע.
חָטָֽאנוּ לְךָ אָדוֹן
סְלַח נָא כְּרֹב רַחֲמֶֽיךָ אֵל.

אֵל אֶֽרֶךְ אַפַּֽיִם וּמָלֵא רַחֲמִים
אַל תַּסְתֵּר פָּנֶֽיךָ מִמֶּֽנּוּ.
חֽוּסָה יהוה עַל שְׁאֵרִית יִשְׂרָאֵל עַמֶּֽךָ
וְהַצִּילֵֽנוּ מִכָּל רָע.
חָטָֽאנוּ לְךָ אָדוֹן
סְלַח נָא כְּרֹב רַחֲמֶֽיךָ אֵל.

The ארון קודש *is opened and the* קהל *stands. All say:*

במדבר י וַיְהִי בִּנְסֹֽעַ הָאָרֹן וַיֹּֽאמֶר מֹשֶׁה, קוּמָה יהוה וְיָפֻֽצוּ אֹיְבֶֽיךָ וְיָנֻֽסוּ
ישעיה ב מְשַׂנְאֶֽיךָ מִפָּנֶֽיךָ: כִּי מִצִּיּוֹן תֵּצֵא תוֹרָה וּדְבַר־יהוה מִירוּשָׁלָֽםִ:
בָּרוּךְ שֶׁנָּתַן תּוֹרָה לְעַמּוֹ יִשְׂרָאֵל בִּקְדֻשָּׁתוֹ.

READING OF THE TORAH

From earliest times, the public reading of the Torah has been a constitutive element of the spiritual life of Israel. At Mount Sinai, to confirm the covenant between the people and God, Moses "took the Book of the Covenant and read it aloud to the people" (Ex. 24:7). The penultimate commandment of the Torah specifies that every seven years (on Sukkot following the sabbatical year) there should be a national assembly at which "the people, men, women, children and the strangers in your communities" are to hear the Torah proclaimed "so that they may listen and learn to fear the LORD your God and observe faithfully all the words of this Torah" (Deut. 31:12).

At critical moments during the biblical era, when the people had drifted from their faith, national renewal was marked by a public Torah reading. King Jehoshaphat sent out officers who "taught throughout Judah, having with them a scroll of the LORD's Torah. They circulated throughout the towns of Judah and taught the people" (II Chr. 17:9).

King Josiah assembled "all the men of Judah, the inhabitants of Jerusalem, the priests, the Levites, and all the people, young and old alike, and read to

Blessed is the name of the Master of the Universe. Blessed is Your crown and Your place. May Your favor always be with Your people Israel. Show Your people the salvation of Your right hand in Your Temple. Grant us the gift of Your good light, and accept our prayers in mercy. May it be Your will to prolong our life in goodness. May I be counted among the righteous, so that You will have compassion on me and protect me and all that is mine and all that is Your people Israel's. You feed all; You sustain all; You rule over all; You rule over kings, for sovereignty is Yours. I am a servant of the Holy One, blessed be He, before whom and before whose glorious Torah I bow at all times. Not in man do I trust, nor on any angel do I rely, but on the God of heaven who is the God of truth, whose Torah is truth, whose prophets speak truth, and who abounds in acts of love and truth. ▸ In Him I trust, and to His holy and glorious name I offer praises. May it be Your will to open my heart to the Torah, and to fulfill the wishes of my heart and of the hearts of all Your people Israel for good, for life, and for peace. *Zohar, Vayak-hel*

The Leader takes the Torah scroll in his right arm, bows toward the Ark and says:

Magnify the LORD with me, and let us exalt His name together. *Ps. 34*

The Ark is closed. The Leader carries the Torah scroll to the bima and the congregation says:

לְךָ Yours, LORD, are the greatness and the power, the glory and the majesty and splendor, for everything in heaven and earth is Yours. Yours, LORD, is the kingdom; You are exalted as Head over all. *1 Chr. 29*

רוֹמְמוּ Exalt the LORD our God and bow to His footstool; He is holy. Exalt the LORD our God, and bow at His holy mountain, for holy is the LORD our God. *Ps. 99*

אַב הָרַחֲמִים May the Father of compassion have compassion on the people borne by Him. May He remember the covenant with the mighty [patriarchs], and deliver us from evil times. May He reproach the evil instinct in the people carried by Him, and graciously grant that we be an everlasting remnant. May He fulfill in good measure our requests for salvation and compassion.

---

literacy and lifelong learning. The Torah is not just written on parchment; it is meant to be engraved on the Jewish soul.

Keriat HaTorah, translated as "the reading of the Torah," also means "the proclamation of the Torah." The public reading symbolically affirms the Torah as the written constitution of the Jewish people as a nation under the sovereignty of God. It is a reenactment of the revelation at Mount Sinai when the Israelites first became a nation, bound by the Torah's laws, summoned to translate its ideals into life.

זוהר ויקהל בְּרִיךְ שְׁמֵהּ דְּמָרֵא עָלְמָא, בְּרִיךְ כִּתְרָךְ וְאַתְרָךְ. יְהֵא רְעוּתָךְ עִם עַמָּךְ יִשְׂרָאֵל לְעָלַם, וּפֻרְקַן יְמִינָךְ אַחֲזֵי לְעַמָּךְ בְּבֵית מַקְדְּשָׁךְ, וּלְאַמְטוּיֵי לָנָא מִטּוּב נְהוֹרָךְ, וּלְקַבֵּל צְלוֹתָנָא בְּרַחֲמִין. יְהֵא רַעֲוָא קֳדָמָךְ דְּתוֹרִיךְ לָן חַיִּין בְּטִיבוּ, וְלֶהֱוֵי אֲנָא פְקִידָא בְּגוֹ צַדִּיקַיָּא, לְמִרְחַם עָלַי וּלְמִנְטַר יָתִי וְיָת כָּל דִּי לִי וְדִי לְעַמָּךְ יִשְׂרָאֵל. אַנְתְּ הוּא זָן לְכֹלָּא וּמְפַרְנֵס לְכֹלָּא, אַנְתְּ הוּא שַׁלִּיט עַל כֹּלָּא, אַנְתְּ הוּא דְּשַׁלִּיט עַל מַלְכַיָּא, וּמַלְכוּתָא דִּילָךְ הִיא. אֲנָא עַבְדָּא דְקֻדְשָׁא בְּרִיךְ הוּא, דְּסָגִדְנָא קַמֵּהּ וּמִקַּמֵּי דִּיקַר אוֹרַיְתֵהּ בְּכָל עִדָּן וְעִדָּן. לָא עַל אֱנָשׁ רָחִיצְנָא וְלָא עַל בַּר אֱלָהִין סָמִיכְנָא, אֶלָּא בֶּאֱלָהָא דִשְׁמַיָּא, דְּהוּא אֱלָהָא קְשׁוֹט, וְאוֹרַיְתֵהּ קְשׁוֹט, וּנְבִיאוֹהִי קְשׁוֹט, וּמַסְגֵּא לְמֶעְבַּד טַבְוָן וּקְשׁוֹט. ◂ בֵּהּ אֲנָא רָחִיץ, וְלִשְׁמֵהּ קַדִּישָׁא יַקִּירָא אֲנָא אֵמַר תֻּשְׁבְּחָן. יְהֵא רַעֲוָא קֳדָמָךְ דְּתִפְתַּח לִבַּאי בְּאוֹרַיְתָא, וְתַשְׁלִים מִשְׁאֲלִין דְּלִבַּאי וְלִבָּא דְכָל עַמָּךְ יִשְׂרָאֵל לְטָב וּלְחַיִּין וְלִשְׁלָם.

The שליח ציבור *takes the* ספר תורה *in his right arm, bows toward the* ארון קודש *and says:*

תהלים לד גַּדְּלוּ לַיהוה אִתִּי וּנְרוֹמְמָה שְׁמוֹ יַחְדָּו:

The ארון קודש *is closed. The* שליח ציבור *carries the* ספר תורה *to the* בימה *and the* קהל *says:*

דברי הימים א, כט לְךָ יהוה הַגְּדֻלָּה וְהַגְּבוּרָה וְהַתִּפְאֶרֶת וְהַנֵּצַח וְהַהוֹד, כִּי־כֹל בַּשָּׁמַיִם וּבָאָרֶץ, לְךָ יהוה הַמַּמְלָכָה וְהַמִּתְנַשֵּׂא לְכֹל לְרֹאשׁ:

תהלים צט רוֹמְמוּ יהוה אֱלֹהֵינוּ וְהִשְׁתַּחֲווּ לַהֲדֹם רַגְלָיו, קָדוֹשׁ הוּא: רוֹמְמוּ יהוה אֱלֹהֵינוּ וְהִשְׁתַּחֲווּ לְהַר קָדְשׁוֹ, כִּי־קָדוֹשׁ יהוה אֱלֹהֵינוּ:

אַב הָרַחֲמִים הוּא יְרַחֵם עַם עֲמוּסִים, וְיִזְכֹּר בְּרִית אֵיתָנִים, וְיַצִּיל נַפְשׁוֹתֵינוּ מִן הַשָּׁעוֹת הָרָעוֹת, וְיִגְעַר בְּיֵצֶר הָרָע מִן הַנְּשׂוּאִים, וְיָחֹן אוֹתָנוּ לִפְלֵיטַת עוֹלָמִים, וִימַלֵּא מִשְׁאֲלוֹתֵינוּ בְּמִדָּה טוֹבָה יְשׁוּעָה וְרַחֲמִים.

---

prayer, we speak to God. In study we listen to God speaking to us, His word unchanged and undiminished across the centuries.

The assembly convened by Ezra, when the Torah was not only read but also explained, became the model for educational activities within the synagogue, of which the *derasha* ("sermon," or more precisely, "exposition") is only one of many forms. To an unparalleled degree, Judaism is predicated on universal

The Torah scroll is placed on the bima and the Gabbai calls a Kohen to the Torah. See laws 383–397.
May His kingship over us be soon revealed and made manifest. May He be gracious to our surviving remnant, the remnant of His people the house of Israel in grace, loving-kindness, compassion and favor, and let us say: Amen. Let us all render greatness to our God and give honor to the Torah. *Let the Kohen come forward. Arise (*name* son of *father's name*), the Kohen.

**If no Kohen is present, a Levi or Yisrael is called up as follows:*
/As there is no Kohen, arise (*name* son of *father's name*) in place of a Kohen./

Blessed is He who, in His holiness, gave the Torah to His people Israel.

Congregation followed by the Gabbai:
You who cling to the LORD your God are all alive today. Deut. 4

The appropriate Torah portions are to be found from page 1072; on Ḥol HaMo'ed, from page 1123.

The Reader shows the oleh the section to be read. The oleh touches the scroll at that place with the tzitzit of his tallit, which he then kisses. Holding the handles of the scroll, he says:

Oleh: Bless the LORD, the blessed One.

Cong: Bless the LORD, the blessed One, for ever and all time.

Oleh: Bless the LORD, the blessed One, for ever and all time.
Blessed are You, LORD our God, King of the Universe,
who has chosen us from all peoples and has given us His Torah.
Blessed are You, LORD, Giver of the Torah.

After the reading, the oleh says:

Oleh: Blessed are You, LORD our God, King of the Universe, who has given us the Torah of truth, planting everlasting life in our midst.
Blessed are You, LORD, Giver of the Torah.

One who has survived a situation of danger (see laws 398–399) says:

Blessed are You, LORD our God, King of the Universe,
who bestows good on the unworthy,
who has bestowed on me much good.

The congregation responds:

Amen. May He who bestowed much good on you continue to bestow on you much good, Selah.

Special blessings and memorial prayers may be said at this point. See pages 508–510 and 800.

After a Bar Mitzva boy has finished the Torah blessing, his father says aloud:

Blessed is He who has released me from the responsibility for this child.

The ספר תורה *is placed on the* שולחן *and the* גבאי *calls a* כהן *to the* תורה. *See laws 383–397.*

וְתִגָּלֶה וְתֵרָאֶה מַלְכוּתוֹ עָלֵינוּ בִּזְמַן קָרוֹב, וְיָחֹן פְּלֵיטָתֵנוּ וּפְלֵיטַת עַמּוֹ בֵּית יִשְׂרָאֵל לְחֵן וּלְחֶסֶד וּלְרַחֲמִים וּלְרָצוֹן וְנֹאמַר אָמֵן. הַכֹּל הָבוּ גֹדֶל לֵאלֹהֵינוּ וּתְנוּ כָבוֹד לַתּוֹרָה.

*כֹּהֵן קְרַב, יַעֲמֹד (פלוני בֶּן פלוני) הַכֹּהֵן.

**If no* כהן *is present, a* לוי *or* ישראל *is called up as follows:*

/אֵין כָּאן כֹּהֵן, יַעֲמֹד (פלוני בֶּן פלוני) בִּמְקוֹם כֹּהֵן./

בָּרוּךְ שֶׁנָּתַן תּוֹרָה לְעַמּוֹ יִשְׂרָאֵל בִּקְדֻשָּׁתוֹ.

קהל *followed by the* גבאי:

וְאַתֶּם הַדְּבֵקִים בַּיהוה אֱלֹהֵיכֶם חַיִּים כֻּלְּכֶם הַיּוֹם: דברים ד

The appropriate תורה *portions are to be found from page 1072; on* חול המועד, *from page 1123.*

The קורא *shows the* עולה *the section to be read. The* עולה *touches the* ספר תורה *at that place with the* ציצית *of his* טלית, *which he then kisses. Holding the handles of the* ספר תורה, *he says:*

עולה: בָּרְכוּ אֶת יהוה הַמְבֹרָךְ.

קהל: בָּרוּךְ יהוה הַמְבֹרָךְ לְעוֹלָם וָעֶד.

עולה: בָּרוּךְ יהוה הַמְבֹרָךְ לְעוֹלָם וָעֶד.
בָּרוּךְ אַתָּה יהוה, אֱלֹהֵינוּ מֶלֶךְ הָעוֹלָם
אֲשֶׁר בָּחַר בָּנוּ מִכָּל הָעַמִּים וְנָתַן לָנוּ אֶת תּוֹרָתוֹ.
בָּרוּךְ אַתָּה יהוה, נוֹתֵן הַתּוֹרָה.

After the קריאת התורה, *the* עולה *says:*

עולה: בָּרוּךְ אַתָּה יהוה אֱלֹהֵינוּ מֶלֶךְ הָעוֹלָם
אֲשֶׁר נָתַן לָנוּ תּוֹרַת אֱמֶת וְחַיֵּי עוֹלָם נָטַע בְּתוֹכֵנוּ.
בָּרוּךְ אַתָּה יהוה, נוֹתֵן הַתּוֹרָה.

One who has survived a situation of danger (see laws 398–399) says:

בָּרוּךְ אַתָּה יהוה אֱלֹהֵינוּ מֶלֶךְ הָעוֹלָם הַגּוֹמֵל לְחַיָּבִים טוֹבוֹת שֶׁגְּמָלַנִי כָּל טוֹב.

The קהל *responds:*

אָמֵן. מִי שֶׁגְּמָלְךָ כָּל טוֹב הוּא יִגְמָלְךָ כָּל טוֹב, סֶלָה.

Special מי שברך *and memorial prayers may be said at this point. See pages 509–511 and 801.*

After a בר מצווה *has finished the* תורה *blessing, his father says aloud:*

בָּרוּךְ שֶׁפְּטָרַנִי מֵעָנְשׁוֹ שֶׁלָּזֶה.

HALF KADDISH

After the Reading of the Torah, the Reader says Half Kaddish:

Reader: יִתְגַּדַּל Magnified and sanctified
may His great name be,
in the world He created by His will.
May He establish His kingdom
in your lifetime and in your days,
and in the lifetime of all the house of Israel,
swiftly and soon – and say: Amen.

All: May His great name be blessed for ever and all time.

Reader: Blessed and praised, glorified and exalted,
raised and honored, uplifted and lauded
be the name of the Holy One,
blessed be He,
beyond any blessing,
song, praise and consolation
uttered in the world –
and say: Amen.

The Torah scroll is lifted and the congregation says:

וְזֹאת הַתּוֹרָה This is the Torah *Deut. 4*
that Moses placed before the children of Israel,
at the LORD's commandment, by the hand of Moses. *Num. 9*

Some add:

It is a tree of life to those who grasp it, and those who uphold it are happy. *Prov. 3*
Its ways are ways of pleasantness, and all its paths are peace.
Long life is at its right hand; at its left, riches and honor.
It pleased the LORD for the sake of [Israel's] righteousness, *Is. 42*
to make the Torah great and glorious.

On those Mondays and Thursdays when Taḥanun is said,
the Leader says the following while the Torah scroll is being bound:

יְהִי רָצוֹן May it be the will of our Father in heaven to establish
(the Temple), home of our life,
and to restore His Presence to our midst,
swiftly in our days – and let us say: Amen.

חצי קדיש

After the קריאת התורה*, the* קורא *says* חצי קדיש:

קורא: יִתְגַּדַּל וְיִתְקַדַּשׁ שְׁמֵהּ רַבָּא (קהל: אָמֵן)
בְּעָלְמָא דִּי בְרָא כִרְעוּתֵהּ
וְיַמְלִיךְ מַלְכוּתֵהּ
בְּחַיֵּיכוֹן וּבְיוֹמֵיכוֹן וּבְחַיֵּי דְכָל בֵּית יִשְׂרָאֵל
בַּעֲגָלָא וּבִזְמַן קָרִיב, וְאִמְרוּ אָמֵן. (קהל: אָמֵן)

קורא וקהל: יְהֵא שְׁמֵהּ רַבָּא מְבָרַךְ לְעָלַם וּלְעָלְמֵי עָלְמַיָּא.

קורא: יִתְבָּרַךְ וְיִשְׁתַּבַּח וְיִתְפָּאַר וְיִתְרוֹמַם וְיִתְנַשֵּׂא
וְיִתְהַדָּר וְיִתְעַלֶּה וְיִתְהַלָּל
שְׁמֵהּ דְּקֻדְשָׁא בְּרִיךְ הוּא (קהל: בְּרִיךְ הוּא)
לְעֵלָּא מִן כָּל בִּרְכָתָא / בעשרת ימי תשובה: לְעֵלָּא לְעֵלָּא מִכָּל בִּרְכָתָא/
וְשִׁירָתָא, תֻּשְׁבְּחָתָא וְנֶחֱמָתָא
דַּאֲמִירָן בְּעָלְמָא, וְאִמְרוּ אָמֵן. (קהל: אָמֵן)

The ספר תורה *is lifted and the* קהל *says:*

וְזֹאת הַתּוֹרָה אֲשֶׁר־שָׂם מֹשֶׁה לִפְנֵי בְּנֵי יִשְׂרָאֵל: — דברים ד
עַל־פִּי יהוה בְּיַד־מֹשֶׁה: — במדבר ט

Some add:

עֵץ־חַיִּים הִיא לַמַּחֲזִיקִים בָּהּ וְתֹמְכֶיהָ מְאֻשָּׁר: — משלי ג
דְּרָכֶיהָ דַרְכֵי־נֹעַם וְכָל־נְתִיבֹתֶיהָ שָׁלוֹם:
אֹרֶךְ יָמִים בִּימִינָהּ, בִּשְׂמֹאולָהּ עֹשֶׁר וְכָבוֹד:
יהוה חָפֵץ לְמַעַן צִדְקוֹ יַגְדִּיל תּוֹרָה וְיַאְדִּיר: — ישעיה מב

On those Mondays and Thursdays when תחנון *is said,*
the שליח ציבור *says the following while the* ספר תורה *is being bound:*

יְהִי רָצוֹן מִלִּפְנֵי אָבִינוּ שֶׁבַּשָּׁמַיִם, לְכוֹנֵן אֶת בֵּית חַיֵּינוּ
וּלְהָשִׁיב אֶת שְׁכִינָתוֹ בְּתוֹכֵנוּ
בִּמְהֵרָה בְיָמֵינוּ, וְנֹאמַר אָמֵן.

יְהִי רָצוֹן May it be the will of our Father in heaven
to have compassion on us and our remnant,
and to keep destruction and plague away from us
and from all His people the house of Israel –
and let us say: Amen.

יְהִי רָצוֹן May it be the will of our Father in heaven
to preserve among us the sages of Israel:
them, their wives, their sons and daughters,
their disciples and their disciples' disciples,
in all their dwelling places – and let us say: Amen.

יְהִי רָצוֹן May it be the will of our Father in heaven
that we may hear and be given good tidings
of salvation and consolation,
and that our dispersed be gathered
from the four quarters of the earth – and let us say: Amen.

All:

אַחֵינוּ As for our brothers of the whole house of Israel who are in distress or captivity, on sea or land, may the All-Present have compassion on them and lead them from distress to relief, from darkness to light, and from oppression to freedom, now, swiftly and soon – and let us say: Amen.

In some congregations, during the week before a yahrzeit, "God, full of mercy" for a relative is said (page 800).

RETURNING THE TORAH TO THE ARK

The Ark is opened. The Leader takes the Torah scroll and says:

יְהַלְלוּ Let them praise the name of the LORD, Ps. 148
for His name alone is sublime.

The congregation responds:

הוֹדוֹ His majesty is above earth and heaven.
He has raised the horn of His people,
for the glory of all His devoted ones,
the children of Israel, the people close to Him.
Halleluya!

יְהִי רָצוֹן מִלִּפְנֵי אָבִינוּ שֶׁבַּשָּׁמַיִם, לְרַחֵם עָלֵינוּ וְעַל פְּלֵיטָתֵנוּ
וְלִמְנֹעַ מַשְׁחִית וּמַגֵּפָה מֵעָלֵינוּ
וּמֵעַל כָּל עַמּוֹ בֵּית יִשְׂרָאֵל, וְנֹאמַר אָמֵן.

יְהִי רָצוֹן מִלִּפְנֵי אָבִינוּ שֶׁבַּשָּׁמַיִם, לְקַיֵּם בָּנוּ חַכְמֵי יִשְׂרָאֵל
הֵם וּנְשֵׁיהֶם וּבְנֵיהֶם וּבְנוֹתֵיהֶם
וְתַלְמִידֵיהֶם וְתַלְמִידֵי תַלְמִידֵיהֶם
בְּכָל מְקוֹמוֹת מוֹשְׁבוֹתֵיהֶם, וְנֹאמַר אָמֵן.

יְהִי רָצוֹן מִלִּפְנֵי אָבִינוּ שֶׁבַּשָּׁמַיִם
שֶׁנִּשְׁמַע וְנִתְבַּשֵּׂר בְּשׂוֹרוֹת טוֹבוֹת, יְשׁוּעוֹת וְנֶחָמוֹת
וִיקַבֵּץ נִדָּחֵינוּ מֵאַרְבַּע כַּנְפוֹת הָאָרֶץ, וְנֹאמַר אָמֵן.

All:

אַחֵינוּ כָּל בֵּית יִשְׂרָאֵל, הַנְּתוּנִים בְּצָרָה וּבַשִּׁבְיָה, הָעוֹמְדִים בֵּין בַּיָּם וּבֵין בַּיַּבָּשָׁה, הַמָּקוֹם יְרַחֵם עֲלֵיהֶם וְיוֹצִיאֵם מִצָּרָה לִרְוָחָה, וּמֵאֲפֵלָה לְאוֹרָה, וּמִשִּׁעְבּוּד לִגְאֻלָּה, הַשְׁתָּא בַּעֲגָלָא וּבִזְמַן קָרִיב, וְנֹאמַר אָמֵן.

In some congregations, during the week before a yahrzeit,
אֵל מָלֵא רַחֲמִים for a relative is said (page 801).

הכנסת ספר תורה

The ארון קודש is opened. The שליח ציבור takes the ספר תורה and says:

יְהַלְלוּ אֶת־שֵׁם יהוה, כִּי נִשְׂגָּב־שְׁמוֹ, לְבַדּוֹ תהלים קמח

The קהל responds:

הוֹדוֹ עַל־אֶרֶץ וְשָׁמָיִם:
וַיָּרֶם קֶרֶן לְעַמּוֹ
תְּהִלָּה לְכָל־חֲסִידָיו
לִבְנֵי יִשְׂרָאֵל עַם קְרֹבוֹ, הַלְלוּיָהּ:

As the Torah scroll is returned to the Ark, say:

לְדָוִד מִזְמוֹר A psalm of David. The earth is the LORD's and all it contains, the world and all who live in it. For He founded it on the seas and established it on the streams. Who may climb the mountain of the LORD? Who may stand in His holy place? He who has clean hands and a pure heart, who has not taken My name in vain, or sworn deceitfully. He shall receive blessing from the LORD, and just reward from God, his salvation. This is a generation of those who seek Him, the descendants of Jacob who seek Your presence, Selah! Lift up your heads, O gates; be uplifted, eternal doors, so that the King of glory may enter. Who is the King of glory? It is the LORD, strong and mighty, the LORD mighty in battle. Lift up your heads, O gates; lift them up, eternal doors, so that the King of glory may enter. Who is He, the King of glory? The LORD of hosts, He is the King of glory, Selah! *Ps. 24*

As the Torah scroll is placed into the Ark, say:

וּבְנֻחֹה יֹאמַר When the Ark came to rest, Moses would say: "Return, *Num. 10*
O LORD, to the myriad thousands of Israel." Advance, LORD, to Your *Ps. 132*
resting place, You and Your mighty Ark. Your priests are clothed in righteousness, and Your devoted ones sing in joy. For the sake of Your servant David, do not reject Your anointed one. For I give you *Prov. 4*
good instruction; do not forsake My Torah. It is a tree of life to those *Prov. 3*
who grasp it, and those who uphold it are happy. Its ways are ways of pleasantness, and all its paths are peace. ▸ Turn us back, O LORD, to *Lam. 5*
You, and we will return. Renew our days as of old.

The Ark is closed.

וּבְנֻחֹה יֹאמַר *When the Ark came to rest:* These words, taken from Numbers 10:36, recall the journeys of the Israelites through the wilderness in the days of Moses. They parallel the words we say when the scroll is taken out, "Whenever the Ark set out" (page 159), said by the Israelites when they began a new journey. Throughout the centuries, wherever Jews went, they took the Torah with them: it became their "portable homeland." עֵץ־חַיִּים הִיא לַמַּחֲזִיקִים בָּהּ *It is a tree of life to those who grasp it:* though Adam and Eve were forbidden to eat the fruit of the tree of life (Gen. 3:22), the Torah is our intimation of eternity in the midst of time. Immortality is a matter, not of *how long* we live, but of *how* we live.

As the ספר תורה *is returned to the* ארון קודש*, say:*

לְדָוִד מִזְמוֹר, לַיהוה הָאָרֶץ וּמְלוֹאָהּ, תֵּבֵל וְיֹשְׁבֵי בָהּ: כִּי־הוּא תהלים כד
עַל־יַמִּים יְסָדָהּ, וְעַל־נְהָרוֹת יְכוֹנְנֶהָ: מִי־יַעֲלֶה בְהַר־יהוה,
וּמִי־יָקוּם בִּמְקוֹם קָדְשׁוֹ: נְקִי כַפַּיִם וּבַר־לֵבָב, אֲשֶׁר לֹא־נָשָׂא
לַשָּׁוְא נַפְשִׁי וְלֹא נִשְׁבַּע לְמִרְמָה: יִשָּׂא בְרָכָה מֵאֵת יהוה, וּצְדָקָה
מֵאֱלֹהֵי יִשְׁעוֹ: זֶה דּוֹר דֹּרְשָׁו, מְבַקְשֵׁי פָנֶיךָ, יַעֲקֹב, סֶלָה: שְׂאוּ
שְׁעָרִים רָאשֵׁיכֶם, וְהִנָּשְׂאוּ פִּתְחֵי עוֹלָם, וְיָבוֹא מֶלֶךְ הַכָּבוֹד:
מִי זֶה מֶלֶךְ הַכָּבוֹד, יהוה עִזּוּז וְגִבּוֹר, יהוה גִּבּוֹר מִלְחָמָה: שְׂאוּ
שְׁעָרִים רָאשֵׁיכֶם, וּשְׂאוּ פִּתְחֵי עוֹלָם, וְיָבֹא מֶלֶךְ הַכָּבוֹד: מִי הוּא
זֶה מֶלֶךְ הַכָּבוֹד, יהוה צְבָאוֹת הוּא מֶלֶךְ הַכָּבוֹד, סֶלָה:

As the ספר תורה *is placed into the* ארון קודש*, say:*

וּבְנֻחֹה יֹאמַר, שׁוּבָה יהוה רִבְבוֹת אַלְפֵי יִשְׂרָאֵל: קוּמָה יהוה במדבר י תהלים קלב
לִמְנוּחָתֶךָ, אַתָּה וַאֲרוֹן עֻזֶּךָ: כֹּהֲנֶיךָ יִלְבְּשׁוּ־צֶדֶק, וַחֲסִידֶיךָ יְרַנֵּנוּ:
בַּעֲבוּר דָּוִד עַבְדֶּךָ אַל־תָּשֵׁב פְּנֵי מְשִׁיחֶךָ: כִּי לֶקַח טוֹב נָתַתִּי משלי ד
לָכֶם, תּוֹרָתִי אַל־תַּעֲזֹבוּ: עֵץ־חַיִּים הִיא לַמַּחֲזִיקִים בָּהּ, וְתֹמְכֶיהָ משלי ג
מְאֻשָּׁר: דְּרָכֶיהָ דַרְכֵי־נֹעַם וְכָל־נְתִיבוֹתֶיהָ שָׁלוֹם: ‹ הֲשִׁיבֵנוּ יהוה איכה ה
אֵלֶיךָ וְנָשׁוּבָה, חַדֵּשׁ יָמֵינוּ כְּקֶדֶם:

The ארון קודש *is closed.*

לְדָוִד מִזְמוֹר *A psalm of David:* A psalm of joyous procession to the Temple. It begins with creation, "The earth is the Lord's," and moves directly to the moral requirements of the religious life: "Who may climb the mountain of the Lord?" Just as God created an orderly universe, so we are commanded to create an orderly society. Worshiping God at the Temple may not be divorced from honesty and integrity in everyday life. The latter part of the psalm, "Lift up your heads, O gates," was said by King Solomon when the Ark, containing the tablets of the covenant, was first brought into the Temple (*Shabbat* 30a). As the Torah scroll is returned to the Ark, we recall that historic scene.

CONCLUSION OF THE SERVICE

Some have the custom to touch the hand-tefillin at °, and the head-tefillin at °°.

אַשְׁרֵי Happy are those who dwell in Your House; Ps. 84
they shall continue to praise You, Selah!
Happy are the people for whom this is so; Ps. 144
happy are the people whose God is the Lord.
A song of praise by David. Ps. 145

א I will exalt You, my God, the King, and bless Your name for ever and all time. ב Every day I will bless You, and praise Your name for ever and all time. ג Great is the Lord and greatly to be praised; His greatness is unfathomable. ד One generation will praise Your works to the next, and tell of Your mighty deeds. ה On the glorious splendor of Your majesty I will meditate, and on the acts of Your wonders. ו They shall talk of the power of Your awesome deeds, and I will tell of Your greatness. ז They shall recite the record of Your great goodness, and sing with joy of Your righteousness. ח The Lord is gracious and compassionate, slow to anger and great in loving-kindness. ט The Lord is good to all, and His compassion extends to all His works. י All Your works shall thank You, Lord, and Your devoted ones shall bless You. כ They shall talk of the glory of Your kingship, and

---

the first of which speaks of redemption ("A redeemer will come to Zion"), and the second of which talks of Torah study ("My words I have placed in your mouth will not depart from your mouth, or from the mouth of your children"). Thus are joined study, the *internalization* of God's word, and redemption, the *externalization* of God's word as we prepare to enter the world of work, striving to live by the Torah's commandments.

אַשְׁרֵי *Happy are those:* Just as we say *Ashrei before* the Shema and the Amida, so do we say it *after*, following the custom of "the pious of old" who devoted time before prayer in preparation, and afterward in meditation. According to the Talmud, the practice was based on the first line of *Ashrei* itself: "Happy are those who dwell in Your House."

סיום התפילה

Some have the custom to touch the תפילין של יד *at* °, *and the* תפילין של ראש *at* °°.

אַשְׁרֵי יוֹשְׁבֵי בֵיתֶךָ, עוֹד יְהַלְלוּךָ סֶּלָה: תהלים פד
אַשְׁרֵי הָעָם שֶׁכָּכָה לּוֹ, אַשְׁרֵי הָעָם שֶׁיהוה אֱלֹהָיו: תהלים קמד
תְּהִלָּה לְדָוִד תהלים קמה
א אֲרוֹמִמְךָ אֱלוֹהַי הַמֶּלֶךְ, וַאֲבָרְכָה שִׁמְךָ לְעוֹלָם וָעֶד:
ב בְּכָל־יוֹם אֲבָרְכֶךָּ, וַאֲהַלְלָה שִׁמְךָ לְעוֹלָם וָעֶד:
ג גָּדוֹל יהוה וּמְהֻלָּל מְאֹד, וְלִגְדֻלָּתוֹ אֵין חֵקֶר:
ד דּוֹר לְדוֹר יְשַׁבַּח מַעֲשֶׂיךָ, וּגְבוּרֹתֶיךָ יַגִּידוּ:
ה הֲדַר כְּבוֹד הוֹדֶךָ, וְדִבְרֵי נִפְלְאֹתֶיךָ אָשִׂיחָה:
ו וֶעֱזוּז נוֹרְאֹתֶיךָ יֹאמֵרוּ, וּגְדוּלָּתְךָ אֲסַפְּרֶנָּה:
ז זֵכֶר רַב־טוּבְךָ יַבִּיעוּ, וְצִדְקָתְךָ יְרַנֵּנוּ:
ח חַנּוּן וְרַחוּם יהוה, אֶרֶךְ אַפַּיִם וּגְדָל־חָסֶד:
ט טוֹב־יהוה לַכֹּל, וְרַחֲמָיו עַל־כָּל־מַעֲשָׂיו:
י יוֹדוּךָ יהוה כָּל־מַעֲשֶׂיךָ, וַחֲסִידֶיךָ יְבָרְכוּכָה:
כ כְּבוֹד מַלְכוּתְךָ יֹאמֵרוּ, וּגְבוּרָתְךָ יְדַבֵּרוּ:

CONCLUSION OF THE SERVICE

The final section of the prayers now begins. It interweaves two distinct elements: one is a formal conclusion to the morning service, including *Aleinu* and the Daily Psalm, with an emphasis on the theme of Redemption; and the other is study. It was the custom in ancient times, and in many places today, to devote time after prayer to Torah learning. This originally included texts from the prophetic books. The close of a study session was marked by a series of prayers beginning "You are the Holy One." The Kaddish had its origin in such sessions.

The link between these two ideas – redemption and Torah study – is created in an inspired fashion, by reading two consecutive verses from Isaiah,

speak of Your might. ל To make known to mankind His mighty deeds and the glorious majesty of His kingship. מ Your kingdom is an everlasting kingdom, and Your reign is for all generations. ס The LORD supports all who fall, and raises all who are bowed down. ע All raise their eyes to You in hope, and You give them their food in due season. פ °You open Your hand, °°and satisfy every living thing with favor. צ The LORD is righteous in all His ways, and kind in all He does. ק The LORD is close to all who call on Him, to all who call on Him in truth. ר He fulfills the will of those who revere Him; He hears their cry and saves them. ש The LORD guards all who love Him, but all the wicked He will destroy. ▸ ת My mouth shall speak the praise of the LORD, and all creatures shall bless His holy name for ever and all time.

We will bless the LORD now and for ever. Halleluya! *Ps. 115*

Omit on Rosh Ḥodesh, Ḥol HaMo'ed, Erev Pesaḥ, Erev Yom Kippur, Ḥanukka, the 14th and 15th of Adar I, Purim and Shushan Purim, Yom HaAtzma'ut, Yom Yerushalayim, Tisha B'Av, or in a house of mourning, and in Israel on Isru Ḥag.

לַמְנַצֵּחַ For the conductor of music. A psalm of David. May the LORD answer you when you are in distress; may the name of Jacob's God protect you. May He send you help from the Sanctuary and support from Zion. May He remember all your meal-offerings and accept your burnt-offerings, Selah! May He give you your heart's desire and make all your plans succeed. We will shout for joy at Your salvation and lift a banner in the name of our God. May the LORD grant all your requests. Now I know that the LORD saves His anointed; He answers him from His holy heaven with the saving power of His right hand. Some trust in chariots, others in horses, but we call on the name of the LORD our God. They were brought to their knees and fell, but we rose up and stood firm. ▸ LORD, save! May the King answer us on the day we call. *Ps. 20*

---

mood, this psalm is omitted on festivals or in a house of mourning, so as not to subtract from the joy of the former, or add to the grief of the latter.

ל לְהוֹדִיעַ לִבְנֵי הָאָדָם גְּבוּרֹתָיו, וּכְבוֹד הֲדַר מַלְכוּתוֹ:
מ מַלְכוּתְךָ מַלְכוּת כָּל־עֹלָמִים, וּמֶמְשַׁלְתְּךָ בְּכָל־דּוֹר וָדֹר:
ס סוֹמֵךְ יהוה לְכָל־הַנֹּפְלִים, וְזוֹקֵף לְכָל־הַכְּפוּפִים:
ע עֵינֵי־כֹל אֵלֶיךָ יְשַׂבֵּרוּ, וְאַתָּה נוֹתֵן־לָהֶם אֶת־אָכְלָם בְּעִתּוֹ:
פ °פּוֹתֵחַ אֶת־יָדֶךָ, °°וּמַשְׂבִּיעַ לְכָל־חַי רָצוֹן:
צ צַדִּיק יהוה בְּכָל־דְּרָכָיו, וְחָסִיד בְּכָל־מַעֲשָׂיו:
ק קָרוֹב יהוה לְכָל־קֹרְאָיו, לְכֹל אֲשֶׁר יִקְרָאֻהוּ בֶאֱמֶת:
ר רְצוֹן־יְרֵאָיו יַעֲשֶׂה, וְאֶת־שַׁוְעָתָם יִשְׁמַע, וְיוֹשִׁיעֵם:
ש שׁוֹמֵר יהוה אֶת־כָּל־אֹהֲבָיו, וְאֵת כָּל־הָרְשָׁעִים יַשְׁמִיד:
ת ‹ תְּהִלַּת יהוה יְדַבֶּר פִּי, וִיבָרֵךְ כָּל־בָּשָׂר שֵׁם קָדְשׁוֹ לְעוֹלָם וָעֶד:
וַאֲנַחְנוּ נְבָרֵךְ יָהּ מֵעַתָּה וְעַד־עוֹלָם, הַלְלוּיָהּ: תהלים קטו

Omit on ראש חודש, חול המועד, ערב פסח, ערב יום כיפור, חנוכה,
the 14th and 15th of אדר א׳, פורים *and* שושן פורים, יום העצמאות,
אסרו חג *on* ארץ ישראל, תשעה באב, יום ירושלים*, or in a house of mourning, and in*.

לַמְנַצֵּחַ מִזְמוֹר לְדָוִד: יַעַנְךָ יהוה בְּיוֹם צָרָה, יְשַׂגֶּבְךָ שֵׁם אֱלֹהֵי תהלים כ
יַעֲקֹב: יִשְׁלַח־עֶזְרְךָ מִקֹּדֶשׁ, וּמִצִּיּוֹן יִסְעָדֶךָּ: יִזְכֹּר כָּל־מִנְחֹתֶךָ,
וְעוֹלָתְךָ יְדַשְּׁנֶה סֶלָה: יִתֶּן־לְךָ כִלְבָבֶךָ, וְכָל־עֲצָתְךָ יְמַלֵּא: נְרַנְּנָה
בִּישׁוּעָתֶךָ, וּבְשֵׁם־אֱלֹהֵינוּ נִדְגֹּל, יְמַלֵּא יהוה כָּל־מִשְׁאֲלוֹתֶיךָ: עַתָּה
יָדַעְתִּי כִּי הוֹשִׁיעַ יהוה מְשִׁיחוֹ, יַעֲנֵהוּ מִשְּׁמֵי קָדְשׁוֹ, בִּגְבֻרוֹת יֵשַׁע
יְמִינוֹ: אֵלֶּה בָרֶכֶב וְאֵלֶּה בַסּוּסִים, וַאֲנַחְנוּ בְּשֵׁם־יהוה אֱלֹהֵינוּ
נַזְכִּיר: הֵמָּה כָּרְעוּ וְנָפָלוּ, וַאֲנַחְנוּ קַמְנוּ וַנִּתְעוֹדָד: ‹ יהוה הוֹשִׁיעָה,
הַמֶּלֶךְ יַעֲנֵנוּ בְיוֹם־קָרְאֵנוּ:

לַמְנַצֵּחַ *Psalm 20:* A prayer for protection from harm. As prayer reaches its close, and we prepare to reenter the outside world with its hazards and dangers, we ask God to keep us from harm. Because of the solemnity of its

In a house of mourning and on Tisha B'Av omit the verse beginning "As for Me" and continue with "You are the Holy One."

וּבָא לְצִיּוֹן גּוֹאֵל "A redeemer will come to Zion, *Is. 59*
to those in Jacob who repent of their sins," declares the Lord.
"As for Me, this is My covenant with them," says the Lord.
"My spirit, that is on you, and My words I have placed in your mouth will not depart from your mouth, or from the mouth of your children, or from the mouth of their descendants from this time on and for ever," says the Lord.

▸ You are the Holy One, enthroned on the praises of Israel. *Ps. 22*
And (the angels) call to one another, saying, "Holy, holy, holy *Is. 6*
is the Lord of hosts; the whole world is filled with His glory."
And they receive permission from one another, saying: *Targum Yonatan Is. 6*
"Holy in the highest heavens, home of His Presence; holy on earth, the work of His strength; holy for ever and all time is the Lord of hosts; the whole earth is full of His radiant glory."

▸ Then a wind lifted me up and I heard behind me the sound of a *Ezek. 3*
great noise, saying, "Blessed is the Lord's glory from His place."
Then a wind lifted me up and I heard behind me *Targum Yonatan Ezek. 3*
the sound of a great tempest of those who uttered praise, saying,
"Blessed is the Lord's glory from the place of the home of His Presence."

The Lord shall reign for ever and all time. *Ex. 15*
The Lord's kingdom is established for ever and all time. *Targum Onkelos Ex. 15*

יהוה Lord, God of Abraham, Isaac and Yisrael, our ancestors, may *1 Chr. 29*
You keep this for ever so that it forms the thoughts in Your people's heart, and directs their heart toward You. He is compassionate. *Ps. 78*
He forgives iniquity and does not destroy. Repeatedly He suppresses His anger, not rousing His full wrath. For You, my Lord, are *Ps. 86*
good and forgiving, abundantly kind to all who call on You. Your *Ps. 119*

---

service, known as *Kedusha deSidra.* Here, it is incorporated into an act of study. Hence the verses of the *Kedusha* are followed by their Aramaic translations and expansions (Aramaic was for a long time the language of study).

In a house of mourning and on תשעה באב *omit the verse beginning* וַאֲנִי זֹאת בְּרִיתִי *and continue with* וְאַתָּה קָדוֹשׁ.

וּבָא לְצִיּוֹן גּוֹאֵל, וּלְשָׁבֵי פֶשַׁע בְּיַעֲקֹב, נְאֻם יהוה: ישעיה נט
וַאֲנִי זֹאת בְּרִיתִי אוֹתָם, אָמַר יהוה
רוּחִי אֲשֶׁר עָלֶיךָ וּדְבָרַי אֲשֶׁר־שַׂמְתִּי בְּפִיךָ
לֹא־יָמוּשׁוּ מִפִּיךָ וּמִפִּי זַרְעֲךָ וּמִפִּי זֶרַע זַרְעֲךָ
אָמַר יהוה, מֵעַתָּה וְעַד־עוֹלָם:

◂ וְאַתָּה קָדוֹשׁ יוֹשֵׁב תְּהִלּוֹת יִשְׂרָאֵל: וְקָרָא זֶה אֶל־זֶה וְאָמַר תהלים כב ישעיה ו
קָדוֹשׁ, קָדוֹשׁ, קָדוֹשׁ, יהוה צְבָאוֹת, מְלֹא כָל־הָאָרֶץ כְּבוֹדוֹ:
וּמְקַבְּלִין דֵּין מִן דֵּין וְאָמְרִין, קַדִּישׁ בִּשְׁמֵי מְרוֹמָא עִלָּאָה בֵּית שְׁכִינְתֵּהּ תרגום יונתן ישעיה ו
קַדִּישׁ עַל אַרְעָא עוֹבַד גְּבוּרְתֵּהּ, קַדִּישׁ לְעָלַם וּלְעָלְמֵי עָלְמַיָּא
יהוה צְבָאוֹת, מַלְיָא כָל אַרְעָא זִיו יְקָרֵהּ.

◂ וַתִּשָּׂאֵנִי רוּחַ, וָאֶשְׁמַע אַחֲרַי קוֹל רַעַשׁ גָּדוֹל יחזקאל ג
בָּרוּךְ כְּבוֹד־יהוה מִמְּקוֹמוֹ:
וּנְטָלַתְנִי רוּחָא, וְשִׁמְעִית בַּתְרַי קָל זִיעַ סַגִּיא, דִּמְשַׁבְּחִין וְאָמְרִין תרגום יונתן יחזקאל ג
בְּרִיךְ יְקָרָא דַיהוה מֵאֲתַר בֵּית שְׁכִינְתֵּהּ.

יהוה יִמְלֹךְ לְעֹלָם וָעֶד: שמות טו
יהוה מַלְכוּתֵהּ קָאֵם לְעָלַם וּלְעָלְמֵי עָלְמַיָּא. תרגום אונקלוס שמות טו

יהוה אֱלֹהֵי אַבְרָהָם יִצְחָק וְיִשְׂרָאֵל אֲבֹתֵינוּ, שָׁמְרָה־זֹּאת לְעוֹלָם דברי הימים א׳ כט
לְיֵצֶר מַחְשְׁבוֹת לְבַב עַמֶּךָ, וְהָכֵן לְבָבָם אֵלֶיךָ: וְהוּא רַחוּם יְכַפֵּר תהלים עח
עָוֹן וְלֹא־יַשְׁחִית, וְהִרְבָּה לְהָשִׁיב אַפּוֹ, וְלֹא־יָעִיר כָּל־חֲמָתוֹ:
כִּי־אַתָּה אֲדֹנָי טוֹב וְסַלָּח, וְרַב־חֶסֶד לְכָל־קֹרְאֶיךָ: צִדְקָתְךָ תהלים פו תהלים קיט

וּבָא לְצִיּוֹן גּוֹאֵל *A redeemer will come to Zion:* These two verses (from Isaiah), are all that remain of the ancient custom of studying prophetic texts after prayer.
וְאַתָּה קָדוֹשׁ *You are the Holy One:* the third and final *Kedusha* of the morning

righteousness is eternally righteous, and Your Torah is truth. Grant truth to Jacob, loving-kindness to Abraham, as You promised our ancestors in ancient times. Blessed is my LORD for day after day He burdens us [with His blessings]; God is our salvation, Selah! The LORD of hosts is with us; the God of Jacob is our refuge, Selah! LORD of hosts, happy is the one who trusts in You. LORD, save! May the King answer us on the day we call.

Mic. 7 *Ps. 68* *Ps. 46* *Ps. 84* *Ps. 20*

בָּרוּךְ Blessed is He, our God, who created us for His glory, separating us from those who go astray; who gave us the Torah of truth, planting within us eternal life. May He open our heart to His Torah, imbuing our heart with the love and awe of Him, that we may do His will and serve Him with a perfect heart, so that we neither toil in vain nor give birth to confusion.

יְהִי רָצוֹן May it be Your will, O LORD our God and God of our ancestors, that we keep Your laws in this world, and thus be worthy to live, see and inherit goodness and blessing in the Messianic Age and in the life of the World to Come. So that my soul may sing to You and not be silent. LORD, my God, for ever I will thank You. Blessed is the man who trusts in the LORD, whose trust is in the LORD alone. Trust in the LORD for evermore, for God, the LORD, is an everlasting Rock. ▸ Those who know Your name trust in You, for You, LORD, do not forsake those who seek You. The LORD desired, for the sake of Israel's merit, to make the Torah great and glorious.

Ps. 30 *Jer. 17* *Is. 26* *Ps. 9* *Is. 42*

On Rosh Hodesh and Hol HaMo'ed, the Leader says Half Kaddish, page 164. The service then continues with Musaf for Rosh Hodesh on page 744, for Hol HaMo'ed on page 806.

On other days, the Leader continues with Full Kaddish on the next page.

The prayer, by contrast, looks forward to the future, personal and collective: personal – may God help us to keep His commandments, and collective – may we see the coming of the Messianic Age.

צֶדֶק לְעוֹלָם וְתוֹרָתְךָ אֱמֶת: תִּתֵּן אֱמֶת לְיַעֲקֹב, חֶסֶד לְאַבְרָהָם, מיכה ז
אֲשֶׁר־נִשְׁבַּעְתָּ לַאֲבֹתֵינוּ מִימֵי קֶדֶם: בָּרוּךְ אֲדֹנָי יוֹם יוֹם יַעֲמָס־ תהלים סח
לָנוּ, הָאֵל יְשׁוּעָתֵנוּ סֶלָה: יהוה צְבָאוֹת עִמָּנוּ, מִשְׂגָּב לָנוּ אֱלֹהֵי תהלים מו
יַעֲקֹב סֶלָה: יהוה צְבָאוֹת, אַשְׁרֵי אָדָם בֹּטֵחַ בָּךְ: יהוה הוֹשִׁיעָה, תהלים פד תהלים כ
הַמֶּלֶךְ יַעֲנֵנוּ בְיוֹם־קָרְאֵנוּ:

בָּרוּךְ הוּא אֱלֹהֵינוּ שֶׁבְּרָאָנוּ לִכְבוֹדוֹ, וְהִבְדִּילָנוּ מִן הַתּוֹעִים, וְנָתַן לָנוּ תּוֹרַת אֱמֶת, וְחַיֵּי עוֹלָם נָטַע בְּתוֹכֵנוּ. הוּא יִפְתַּח לִבֵּנוּ בְּתוֹרָתוֹ, וְיָשֵׂם בְּלִבֵּנוּ אַהֲבָתוֹ וְיִרְאָתוֹ וְלַעֲשׂוֹת רְצוֹנוֹ וּלְעָבְדוֹ בְּלֵבָב שָׁלֵם, לְמַעַן לֹא נִיגַע לָרִיק וְלֹא נֵלֵד לַבֶּהָלָה.

יְהִי רָצוֹן מִלְּפָנֶיךָ יהוה אֱלֹהֵינוּ וֵאלֹהֵי אֲבוֹתֵינוּ, שֶׁנִּשְׁמֹר חֻקֶּיךָ
בָּעוֹלָם הַזֶּה, וְנִזְכֶּה וְנִחְיֶה וְנִרְאֶה וְנִירַשׁ טוֹבָה וּבְרָכָה, לִשְׁנֵי
יְמוֹת הַמָּשִׁיחַ וּלְחַיֵּי הָעוֹלָם הַבָּא. לְמַעַן יְזַמֶּרְךָ כָבוֹד וְלֹא יִדֹּם, תהלים ל
יהוה אֱלֹהַי, לְעוֹלָם אוֹדֶךָּ: בָּרוּךְ הַגֶּבֶר אֲשֶׁר יִבְטַח בַּיהוה, ירמיה יז
וְהָיָה יהוה מִבְטַחוֹ: בִּטְחוּ בַיהוה עֲדֵי־עַד, כִּי בְּיָהּ יהוה צוּר ישעיה כו
עוֹלָמִים: ▸ וְיִבְטְחוּ בְךָ יוֹדְעֵי שְׁמֶךָ, כִּי לֹא־עָזַבְתָּ דֹרְשֶׁיךָ, יהוה: תהלים ט
יהוה חָפֵץ לְמַעַן צִדְקוֹ, יַגְדִּיל תּוֹרָה וְיַאְדִּיר: ישעיה מב

On ראש חודש *and* חול המועד*, the* שליח ציבור *says* חצי קדיש*, page 165. The service then continues with* מוסף *for* ראש חודש *on page 745, for* חול המועד *on page 807.*

On other days the שליח ציבור *continues with* קדיש שלם *on the next page.*

בָּרוּךְ הוּא אֱלֹהֵינוּ *Blessed is He, our God:* There now follow a concluding blessing and a prayer. The blessing marks the end of a Torah study session (the counterpart of the two opening benedictions in the Blessings over the Torah).

FULL KADDISH

Leader: יִתְגַּדַּל Magnified and sanctified may His great name be,
in the world He created by His will.
May He establish His kingdom in your lifetime
and in your days,
and in the lifetime of all the house of Israel,
swiftly and soon –
and say: Amen.

All: May His great name be blessed for ever and all time.

Leader: Blessed and praised,
glorified and exalted,
raised and honored,
uplifted and lauded be
the name of the Holy One,
blessed be He,
beyond any blessing,
song, praise and consolation uttered in the world –
and say: Amen.

On Tisha B'Av, omit the next verse and continue with "May there be great peace."

May the prayers and pleas of all Israel
be accepted by their Father in heaven –
and say: Amen.

May there be great peace from heaven,
and life for us and all Israel –
and say: Amen.

Bow, take three steps back, as if taking leave of the Divine Presence, then bow, first left, then right, then center, while saying:

May He who makes peace in His high places,
make peace for us and all Israel –
and say: Amen.

קדיש שלם

ש״ץ: יִתְגַּדַּל וְיִתְקַדַּשׁ שְׁמֵהּ רַבָּא (קהל: אָמֵן)
בְּעָלְמָא דִּי בְרָא כִרְעוּתֵהּ
וְיַמְלִיךְ מַלְכוּתֵהּ
בְּחַיֵּיכוֹן וּבְיוֹמֵיכוֹן וּבְחַיֵּי דְכָל בֵּית יִשְׂרָאֵל
בַּעֲגָלָא וּבִזְמַן קָרִיב, וְאִמְרוּ אָמֵן. (קהל: אָמֵן)

קהל וש״ץ: יְהֵא שְׁמֵהּ רַבָּא מְבָרַךְ לְעָלַם וּלְעָלְמֵי עָלְמַיָּא.

ש״ץ: יִתְבָּרַךְ וְיִשְׁתַּבַּח וְיִתְפָּאַר
וְיִתְרוֹמַם וְיִתְנַשֵּׂא וְיִתְהַדָּר וְיִתְעַלֶּה וְיִתְהַלָּל
שְׁמֵהּ דְּקֻדְשָׁא בְּרִיךְ הוּא (קהל: בְּרִיךְ הוּא)
לְעֵלָּא מִן כָּל בִּרְכָתָא
/בעשרת ימי תשובה: לְעֵלָּא לְעֵלָּא מִכָּל בִּרְכָתָא/
וְשִׁירָתָא, תֻּשְׁבְּחָתָא וְנֶחֱמָתָא
דַּאֲמִירָן בְּעָלְמָא, וְאִמְרוּ אָמֵן. (קהל: אָמֵן)

On תשעה באב*, omit the next verse and continue with* יְהֵא שְׁלָמָא.

תִּתְקַבַּל צְלוֹתְהוֹן וּבָעוּתְהוֹן דְּכָל יִשְׂרָאֵל
קֳדָם אֲבוּהוֹן דִּי בִשְׁמַיָּא, וְאִמְרוּ אָמֵן. (קהל: אָמֵן)

יְהֵא שְׁלָמָא רַבָּא מִן שְׁמַיָּא
וְחַיִּים, עָלֵינוּ וְעַל כָּל יִשְׂרָאֵל, וְאִמְרוּ אָמֵן. (קהל: אָמֵן)

Bow, take three steps back, as if taking leave of the Divine Presence, then bow, first left, then right, then center, while saying:

עֹשֶׂה שָׁלוֹם/ בעשרת ימי תשובה: הַשָּׁלוֹם/ בִּמְרוֹמָיו
הוּא יַעֲשֶׂה שָׁלוֹם
עָלֵינוּ וְעַל כָּל יִשְׂרָאֵל, וְאִמְרוּ אָמֵן. (קהל: אָמֵן)

Stand while saying Aleinu. Bow at ▾.

עָלֵינוּ It is our duty to praise the Master of all,
and ascribe greatness to the Author of creation,
who has not made us like the nations of the lands
nor placed us like the families of the earth;
who has not made our portion like theirs,
nor our destiny like all their multitudes.
(For they worship vanity and emptiness,
and pray to a god who cannot save.)
▾But we bow in worship and thank the Supreme King of kings,
the Holy One, blessed be He,
who extends the heavens and establishes the earth,
whose throne of glory is in the heavens above,
and whose power's Presence is in the highest of heights.
He is our God; there is no other.
Truly He is our King, there is none else,
as it is written in His Torah:
"You shall know and take to heart this day that the Lord is God, *Deut. 4*
in heaven above and on earth below. There is no other."

Therefore, we place our hope in You, Lord our God,
that we may soon see the glory of Your power,
when You will remove abominations from the earth,
and idols will be utterly destroyed,
when the world will be perfected under the sovereignty of the Almighty,
when all humanity will call on Your name,
to turn all the earth's wicked toward You.
All the world's inhabitants will realize and know
that to You every knee must bow and every tongue swear loyalty.
Before You, Lord our God, they will kneel and bow down
and give honor to Your glorious name.

---

statement of the particularity of Jewish faith and its universal aspiration for humanity.

The first paragraph, was originally used (and still is) as an introduction to the Blessing of Kingship in the *Musaf* of Rosh HaShana. Less a prayer than a declaration of faith, it speaks of the singular vocation of the Jewish

Stand while saying עָלֵינוּ. *Bow at* ׳.

עָלֵינוּ לְשַׁבֵּחַ לַאֲדוֹן הַכֹּל, לָתֵת גְּדֻלָּה לְיוֹצֵר בְּרֵאשִׁית
שֶׁלֹּא עָשָׂנוּ כְּגוֹיֵי הָאֲרָצוֹת, וְלֹא שָׂמָנוּ כְּמִשְׁפְּחוֹת הָאֲדָמָה
שֶׁלֹּא שָׂם חֶלְקֵנוּ כָּהֶם וְגוֹרָלֵנוּ כְּכָל הֲמוֹנָם.
(שֶׁהֵם מִשְׁתַּחֲוִים לְהֶבֶל וָרִיק וּמִתְפַּלְלִים אֶל אֵל לֹא יוֹשִׁיעַ.)
׳וַאֲנַחְנוּ כּוֹרְעִים וּמִשְׁתַּחֲוִים וּמוֹדִים
לִפְנֵי מֶלֶךְ מַלְכֵי הַמְּלָכִים, הַקָּדוֹשׁ בָּרוּךְ הוּא
שֶׁהוּא נוֹטֶה שָׁמַיִם וְיוֹסֵד אָרֶץ, וּמוֹשַׁב יְקָרוֹ בַּשָּׁמַיִם מִמַּעַל
וּשְׁכִינַת עֻזּוֹ בְּגָבְהֵי מְרוֹמִים.
הוּא אֱלֹהֵינוּ, אֵין עוֹד.
אֱמֶת מַלְכֵּנוּ, אֶפֶס זוּלָתוֹ
כַּכָּתוּב בְּתוֹרָתוֹ
דברים ד וְיָדַעְתָּ הַיּוֹם וַהֲשֵׁבֹתָ אֶל־לְבָבֶךָ
כִּי יהוה הוּא הָאֱלֹהִים בַּשָּׁמַיִם מִמַּעַל וְעַל־הָאָרֶץ מִתָּחַת, אֵין עוֹד:

עַל כֵּן נְקַוֶּה לְּךָ יהוה אֱלֹהֵינוּ, לִרְאוֹת מְהֵרָה בְּתִפְאֶרֶת עֻזֶּךָ
לְהַעֲבִיר גִּלּוּלִים מִן הָאָרֶץ, וְהָאֱלִילִים כָּרוֹת יִכָּרֵתוּן
לְתַקֵּן עוֹלָם בְּמַלְכוּת שַׁדַּי.
וְכָל בְּנֵי בָשָׂר יִקְרְאוּ בִשְׁמֶךָ לְהַפְנוֹת אֵלֶיךָ כָּל רִשְׁעֵי אָרֶץ.
יַכִּירוּ וְיֵדְעוּ כָּל יוֹשְׁבֵי תֵבֵל
כִּי לְךָ תִּכְרַע כָּל בֶּרֶךְ, תִּשָּׁבַע כָּל לָשׁוֹן.
לְפָנֶיךָ יהוה אֱלֹהֵינוּ יִכְרְעוּ וְיִפֹּלוּ, וְלִכְבוֹד שִׁמְךָ יְקָר יִתֵּנוּ
וִיקַבְּלוּ כֻלָּם אֶת עֹל מַלְכוּתֶךָ
וְתִמְלֹךְ עֲלֵיהֶם מְהֵרָה לְעוֹלָם וָעֶד.

עָלֵינוּ *It is our duty:* Since the twelfth or thirteenth century, it has become the custom to bring all services to a close with the magnificent prayer known as *Aleinu*, a construct of two paragraphs, which together make a striking

They will all accept the yoke of Your kingdom,
and You will reign over them soon and for ever.
For the kingdom is Yours, and to all eternity You will reign in glory,
as it is written in Your Torah: "The LORD will reign for ever and ever." *Ex. 15*
▸ And it is said: "Then the LORD shall be King over all the earth; *Zech. 14*
on that day the LORD shall be One and His name One."

Some add:

Have no fear of sudden terror or of the ruin when it overtakes the wicked. *Prov. 3*
Devise your strategy, but it will be thwarted; propose your plan, *Is. 8*
but it will not stand, for God is with us.
When you grow old, I will still be the same. *Is. 46*
When your hair turns gray, I will still carry you.
I made you, I will bear you, I will carry you, and I will rescue you.

MOURNER'S KADDISH

The following prayer, said by mourners, requires the presence of a minyan.
A transliteration can be found on page 1334.

Mourner: יִתְגַּדַּל Magnified and sanctified
may His great name be,
in the world He created by His will.
May He establish His kingdom
in your lifetime and in your days,
and in the lifetime of all the house of Israel,
swiftly and soon – and say: Amen.

All: May His great name be blessed for ever and all time.

Mourner: Blessed and praised, glorified and exalted,
raised and honored, uplifted and lauded
be the name of the Holy One,
blessed be He,

No prayer more eloquently expresses the dual nature of the Jewish people: its singular history as the nation chosen to be God's witnesses on earth, and its universal aspiration for the time when all the inhabitants of earth will recognize the God in whose image we are formed.

כִּי הַמַּלְכוּת שֶׁלְּךָ הִיא וּלְעוֹלְמֵי עַד תִּמְלֹךְ בְּכָבוֹד
כַּכָּתוּב בְּתוֹרָתֶךָ, יהוה יִמְלֹךְ לְעֹלָם וָעֶד: שמות טו
◂ וְנֶאֱמַר, וְהָיָה יהוה לְמֶלֶךְ עַל־כָּל־הָאָרֶץ זכריה יד
בַּיּוֹם הַהוּא יִהְיֶה יהוה אֶחָד וּשְׁמוֹ אֶחָד:

Some add:

אַל־תִּירָא מִפַּחַד פִּתְאֹם וּמִשֹּׁאַת רְשָׁעִים כִּי תָבֹא: משלי ג
עֻצוּ עֵצָה וְתֻפָר, דַּבְּרוּ דָבָר וְלֹא יָקוּם, כִּי עִמָּנוּ אֵל: ישעיה ח
וְעַד־זִקְנָה אֲנִי הוּא, וְעַד־שֵׂיבָה אֲנִי אֶסְבֹּל, אֲנִי עָשִׂיתִי וַאֲנִי אֶשָּׂא וַאֲנִי אֶסְבֹּל וַאֲמַלֵּט: ישעיה מו

קדיש יתום

The following prayer, said by mourners, requires the presence of a מנין.
A transliteration can be found on page 1334.

אבל: יִתְגַּדַּל וְיִתְקַדַּשׁ שְׁמֵהּ רַבָּא (קהל: אָמֵן)
בְּעָלְמָא דִּי בְרָא כִרְעוּתֵהּ
וְיַמְלִיךְ מַלְכוּתֵהּ
בְּחַיֵּיכוֹן וּבְיוֹמֵיכוֹן וּבְחַיֵּי דְכָל בֵּית יִשְׂרָאֵל
בַּעֲגָלָא וּבִזְמַן קָרִיב, וְאִמְרוּ אָמֵן. (קהל: אָמֵן)

קהל ואבל: יְהֵא שְׁמֵהּ רַבָּא מְבָרַךְ לְעָלַם וּלְעָלְמֵי עָלְמַיָּא.

אבל: יִתְבָּרַךְ וְיִשְׁתַּבַּח וְיִתְפָּאַר
וְיִתְרוֹמַם וְיִתְנַשֵּׂא וְיִתְהַדָּר וְיִתְעַלֶּה וְיִתְהַלָּל
שְׁמֵהּ דְּקֻדְשָׁא בְּרִיךְ הוּא (קהל: בְּרִיךְ הוּא)

---

people as bearers of the message of monotheism. Twice, the prayer uses the expression, "There is no other," forcefully expressed in Hebrew by two monosyllabic words, *ein od.*

The second paragraph turns to God and to the future, to a time when all humanity will acknowledge the One God, a vision eloquently spoken of by the prophet Zechariah, from whose book the final verse is taken. It contains a phrase – "to perfect the world under the sovereignty of God" – which became a leading theme of Lurianic mysticism in the sixteenth century (*tikkun olam*).

beyond any blessing, song, praise and consolation
uttered in the world – and say: Amen.

May there be great peace from heaven,
and life for us and all Israel – and say: Amen.

Bow, take three steps back, as if taking leave of the Divine Presence, then bow, first left, then right, then center, while saying:

May He who makes peace in His high places,
make peace for us and all Israel – and say: Amen.

THE DAILY PSALM

One of the following psalms is said on the appropriate day of the week as indicated. After the psalm, the Mourner's Kaddish on page 182 is said.

After the Daily Psalm, on Rosh Hodesh, add Barekhi Nafshi, page 190 (in Israel, some only say Barekhi Nafshi). On Hanukka, add Psalm 30, page 58 followed by Mourner's Kaddish. From the second day of Rosh Hodesh Elul through Shemini Atzeret (in Israel, through Hoshana Raba), add Psalm 27 on page 192. In a house of mourning the service concludes on page 1060.

Sunday: Today is the first day of the week,
on which the Levites used to say this psalm in the Temple:

לְדָוִד מִזְמוֹר A psalm of David. The earth is the LORD's and all it contains, the world and all who live in it. For He founded it on the seas and established it on the streams. Who may climb the mountain of the LORD? Who may stand in His holy place? He who has clean hands and a pure heart, who has not taken My name in vain or sworn deceitfully. He shall receive a blessing from the LORD, and just reward from the God of his salvation. This is a generation of those who seek Him, the descendants of Jacob who seek Your presence, Selah! Lift up your heads, O gates; be uplifted, eternal doors, so that the King of glory may enter. Who is the King of glory? It is the LORD, strong and mighty, the LORD mighty in battle. Lift up your heads, O gates; lift them up, eternal doors, that the King of glory may enter. ▸ Who is He, the King of glory? The LORD of hosts, He is the King of glory, Selah! *Ps. 24*

Mourner's Kaddish (page 182)

לְדָוִד מִזְמוֹר *Sunday: Psalm 24.* The opening verses mirror the act of creation, reminding us that each week mirrors the seven days of creation itself. The psalm also alludes to the Temple, built on "the mountain of the LORD." The connection between the two is based on the idea that the Temple was a microcosm of the universe, and its construction a human counterpart to the divine creation of the cosmos.

לְעֵלָּא מִן כָּל בִּרְכָתָא
/ בעשרת ימי תשובה: לְעֵלָּא לְעֵלָּא מִכָּל בִּרְכָתָא/
וְשִׁירָתָא, תֻּשְׁבְּחָתָא וְנֶחֱמָתָא
דַּאֲמִירָן בְּעָלְמָא, וְאִמְרוּ אָמֵן. (קהל: אָמֵן)
יְהֵא שְׁלָמָא רַבָּא מִן שְׁמַיָּא
וְחַיִּים, עָלֵינוּ וְעַל כָּל יִשְׂרָאֵל, וְאִמְרוּ אָמֵן. (קהל: אָמֵן)

Bow, take three steps back, as if taking leave of the Divine Presence, then bow, first left, then right, then center, while saying:

עֹשֶׂה שָׁלוֹם/ בעשרת ימי תשובה: הַשָּׁלוֹם/ בִּמְרוֹמָיו
הוּא יַעֲשֶׂה שָׁלוֹם עָלֵינוּ וְעַל כָּל יִשְׂרָאֵל, וְאִמְרוּ אָמֵן. (קהל: אָמֵן)

שיר של יום

One of the following psalms is said on the appropriate day of the week as indicated. After the psalm, קדיש יתום *on page 183 is said.*

After שיר של יום*, on* ראש חודש*, add* בָּרְכִי נַפְשִׁי*, page 191 (in* ארץ ישראל*, some only say* בָּרְכִי נַפְשִׁי*). On* חנוכה*, add* מִזְמוֹר שִׁיר־חֲנֻכַּת הַבַּיִת*, page 59 followed by* קדיש יתום*. From the second day of* ראש חודש אלול *through* שמיני עצרת *(in* ארץ ישראל*, through* הושענא רבה*), add* לְדָוִד, יהוה אוֹרִי *on page 193. In a house of mourning the service concludes on page 1061.*

Sunday הַיּוֹם יוֹם רִאשׁוֹן בְּשַׁבָּת, שֶׁבּוֹ הָיוּ הַלְוִיִּם אוֹמְרִים בְּבֵית הַמִּקְדָּשׁ:

לְדָוִד מִזְמוֹר, לַיהוה הָאָרֶץ וּמְלוֹאָהּ, תֵּבֵל וְיֹשְׁבֵי בָהּ: כִּי־הוּא עַל־יַמִּים תהלים כד
יְסָדָהּ, וְעַל־נְהָרוֹת יְכוֹנְנֶהָ: מִי־יַעֲלֶה בְהַר־יהוה, וּמִי־יָקוּם בִּמְקוֹם קָדְשׁוֹ:
נְקִי כַפַּיִם וּבַר־לֵבָב, אֲשֶׁר לֹא־נָשָׂא לַשָּׁוְא נַפְשִׁי, וְלֹא נִשְׁבַּע לְמִרְמָה:
יִשָּׂא בְרָכָה מֵאֵת יהוה, וּצְדָקָה מֵאֱלֹהֵי יִשְׁעוֹ: זֶה דּוֹר דֹּרְשָׁו, מְבַקְשֵׁי
פָנֶיךָ יַעֲקֹב סֶלָה: שְׂאוּ שְׁעָרִים רָאשֵׁיכֶם, וְהִנָּשְׂאוּ פִּתְחֵי עוֹלָם, וְיָבוֹא
מֶלֶךְ הַכָּבוֹד: מִי זֶה מֶלֶךְ הַכָּבוֹד, יהוה עִזּוּז וְגִבּוֹר, יהוה גִּבּוֹר מִלְחָמָה:
שְׂאוּ שְׁעָרִים רָאשֵׁיכֶם, וּשְׂאוּ פִּתְחֵי עוֹלָם, וְיָבֹא מֶלֶךְ הַכָּבוֹד: ◂ מִי הוּא
זֶה מֶלֶךְ הַכָּבוֹד, יהוה צְבָאוֹת הוּא מֶלֶךְ הַכָּבוֹד סֶלָה:

קדיש יתום *(page 183)*

THE DAILY PSALM

A special psalm was said in the Temple on each of the seven days of the week. We say them still, in memory of those days and in hope of future restoration.

Monday: Today is the second day of the week,
on which the Levites used to say this psalm in the Temple:

שִׁיר מִזְמוֹר A song. A psalm of the sons of Koraḥ. Great is the LORD and greatly to be praised in the city of God, on His holy mountain – beautiful in its heights, joy of all the earth, Mount Zion on its northern side, city of the great King. In its citadels God is known as a stronghold. See how the kings joined forces, advancing together. They saw, they were astounded, they panicked, they fled. There fear seized them, like the pains of a woman giving birth, like ships of Tarshish wrecked by an eastern wind. What we had heard, now we have seen, in the city of the LORD of hosts, in the city of our God. May God preserve it for ever, Selah! In the midst of Your Temple, God, we meditate on Your love. As is Your name, God, so is Your praise: it reaches to the ends of the earth. Your right hand is filled with righteousness. Let Mount Zion rejoice, let the towns of Judah be glad, because of Your judgments. Walk around Zion and encircle it. Count its towers, note its strong walls, view its citadels, so that you may tell a future generation ▸ that this is God, our God, for ever and ever. He will guide us for evermore. *Ps. 48*

Mourner's Kaddish (page 182)

Tuesday: Today is the third day of the week,
on which the Levites used to say this psalm in the Temple:

מִזְמוֹר לְאָסָף A psalm of Asaph. God stands in the divine assembly. Among the judges He delivers judgment. How long will you judge unjustly, showing favor to the wicked? Selah. Do justice to the weak and the orphaned. Vindicate the poor and destitute. Rescue the weak and needy. Save them from the hand of the wicked. They do not know nor do they understand. They walk about in darkness while all the earth's foundations shake. I once said, "You are like gods, all of you are sons of the Most High." But you shall die like mere men, you will fall like any prince. ▸ Arise, O LORD, judge the earth, for all the nations are Your possession. *Ps. 82*

Mourner's Kaddish (page 182)

מִזְמוֹר לְאָסָף *Tuesday: Psalm 82.* The psalm for Tuesday is about judges and justice. Justice, the application of law, brings order to society as scientific law brings order to the cosmos. Justice ultimately belongs to God. A judge must therefore act with humility and integrity, bringing divine order to human chaos. "A judge who delivers a true judgment becomes a partner of the Holy One, blessed be He, in the work of creation" (*Shabbat* 10a).

Monday הַיּוֹם יוֹם שֵׁנִי בְּשַׁבָּת, שֶׁבּוֹ הָיוּ הַלְוִיִּם אוֹמְרִים בְּבֵית הַמִּקְדָּשׁ:

תהלים מח
שִׁיר מִזְמוֹר לִבְנֵי־קֹרַח: גָּדוֹל יהוה וּמְהֻלָּל מְאֹד, בְּעִיר אֱלֹהֵינוּ, הַר־קָדְשׁוֹ: יְפֵה נוֹף מְשׂוֹשׂ כָּל־הָאָרֶץ, הַר־צִיּוֹן יַרְכְּתֵי צָפוֹן, קִרְיַת מֶלֶךְ רָב: אֱלֹהִים בְּאַרְמְנוֹתֶיהָ נוֹדַע לְמִשְׂגָּב: כִּי־הִנֵּה הַמְּלָכִים נוֹעֲדוּ, עָבְרוּ יַחְדָּו: הֵמָּה רָאוּ כֵּן תָּמָהוּ, נִבְהֲלוּ נֶחְפָּזוּ: רְעָדָה אֲחָזָתַם שָׁם, חִיל כַּיּוֹלֵדָה: בְּרוּחַ קָדִים תְּשַׁבֵּר אֳנִיּוֹת תַּרְשִׁישׁ: כַּאֲשֶׁר שָׁמַעְנוּ כֵּן רָאִינוּ, בְּעִיר־יהוה צְבָאוֹת, בְּעִיר אֱלֹהֵינוּ, אֱלֹהִים יְכוֹנְנֶהָ עַד־עוֹלָם סֶלָה: דִּמִּינוּ אֱלֹהִים חַסְדֶּךָ, בְּקֶרֶב הֵיכָלֶךָ: כְּשִׁמְךָ אֱלֹהִים כֵּן תְּהִלָּתְךָ עַל־קַצְוֵי־אֶרֶץ, צֶדֶק מָלְאָה יְמִינֶךָ: יִשְׂמַח הַר־צִיּוֹן, תָּגֵלְנָה בְּנוֹת יְהוּדָה, לְמַעַן מִשְׁפָּטֶיךָ: סֹבּוּ צִיּוֹן וְהַקִּיפוּהָ, סִפְרוּ מִגְדָּלֶיהָ: שִׁיתוּ לִבְּכֶם לְחֵילָה, פַּסְּגוּ אַרְמְנוֹתֶיהָ, לְמַעַן תְּסַפְּרוּ לְדוֹר אַחֲרוֹן: ‹ כִּי זֶה אֱלֹהִים אֱלֹהֵינוּ עוֹלָם וָעֶד, הוּא יְנַהֲגֵנוּ עַל־מוּת:

קדיש יתום (*page 183*)

Tuesday הַיּוֹם יוֹם שְׁלִישִׁי בְּשַׁבָּת, שֶׁבּוֹ הָיוּ הַלְוִיִּם אוֹמְרִים בְּבֵית הַמִּקְדָּשׁ:

תהלים פב
מִזְמוֹר לְאָסָף, אֱלֹהִים נִצָּב בַּעֲדַת־אֵל, בְּקֶרֶב אֱלֹהִים יִשְׁפֹּט: עַד־מָתַי תִּשְׁפְּטוּ־עָוֶל, וּפְנֵי רְשָׁעִים תִּשְׂאוּ־סֶלָה: שִׁפְטוּ־דַל וְיָתוֹם, עָנִי וָרָשׁ הַצְדִּיקוּ: פַּלְּטוּ־דַל וְאֶבְיוֹן, מִיַּד רְשָׁעִים הַצִּילוּ: לֹא יָדְעוּ וְלֹא יָבִינוּ, בַּחֲשֵׁכָה יִתְהַלָּכוּ, יִמּוֹטוּ כָּל־מוֹסְדֵי אָרֶץ: אֲנִי־אָמַרְתִּי אֱלֹהִים אַתֶּם, וּבְנֵי עֶלְיוֹן כֻּלְּכֶם: אָכֵן כְּאָדָם תְּמוּתוּן, וּכְאַחַד הַשָּׂרִים תִּפֹּלוּ: ‹ קוּמָה אֱלֹהִים שָׁפְטָה הָאָרֶץ, כִּי־אַתָּה תִנְחַל בְּכָל־הַגּוֹיִם:

קדיש יתום (*page 183*)

שִׁיר מִזְמוֹר לִבְנֵי־קֹרַח *Monday: Psalm 48.* A hymn of praise to the beauty and endurance of Jerusalem, the city that outlived all those who sought to conquer it.

> A score of conquerors have held it as their choicest prize; and more than a dozen times has it been utterly destroyed. The Babylonians burnt it, and deported its population; the Romans slew a million of its inhabitants, razed it to the ground, passed the ploughshare over it, and strewed its furrows with salt; Hadrian banished its very name from the lips of men, changed it to *Aelia Capitolina*, and prohibited any Jew from entering its precincts on pain of death. Persians and Arabs, Barbarians and Crusaders and Turks took it and retook it, ravaged it and burnt it; and yet, marvelous to relate, it ever rises from its ashes to renewed life and glory. It is the Eternal City of the Eternal People. (Rabbi J.H. Hertz)

Wednesday: Today is the fourth day of the week,
on which the Levites used to say this psalm in the Temple:

אֵל־נְקָמוֹת God of retribution, LORD, God of retribution, appear! Rise up, Judge of the earth. Repay to the arrogant what they deserve. How long shall the wicked, LORD, how long shall the wicked triumph? They pour out insolent words. All the evildoers are full of boasting. They crush Your people, LORD, and oppress Your inheritance. They kill the widow and the stranger. They murder the orphaned. They say, "The LORD does not see. The God of Jacob pays no heed." Take heed, you most brutish people. You fools, when will you grow wise? Will He who implants the ear not hear? Will He who formed the eye not see? Will He who disciplines nations – He who teaches man knowledge – not punish? The LORD knows that the thoughts of man are a mere fleeting breath. Happy is the man whom You discipline, LORD, the one You instruct in Your Torah, giving him tranquility in days of trouble, until a pit is dug for the wicked. For the LORD will not forsake His people, nor abandon His heritage. Judgment shall again accord with justice, and all the upright in heart will follow it. Who will rise up for me against the wicked? Who will stand up for me against wrongdoers? Had the LORD not been my help, I would soon have dwelt in death's silence. When I thought my foot was slipping, Your loving-kindness, LORD, gave me support. When I was filled with anxiety, Your consolations soothed my soul. Can a corrupt throne be allied with You? Can injustice be framed into law? They join forces against the life of the righteous, and condemn the innocent to death. But the LORD is my stronghold, my God is the Rock of my refuge. He will bring back on them their wickedness, and destroy them for their evil deeds. The LORD our God will destroy them. *Ps. 94*

▸ Come, let us sing for joy to the LORD; let us shout aloud to the Rock of our salvation. Let us greet Him with thanksgiving, shout aloud to Him with songs of praise. For the LORD is the great God, the King great above all powers. *Ps. 95*

Mourner's Kaddish (page 182)

Thursday: Today is the fifth day of the week,
on which the Levites used to say this psalm in the Temple:

לַמְנַצֵּחַ For the conductor of music. On the Gittit. By Asaph. Sing for joy to God, our strength. Shout aloud to the God of Jacob. Raise a song, beat the drum, play the sweet harp and lyre. Sound the shofar on the new moon, on our feast *Ps. 81*

לַמְנַצֵּחַ *Thursday: Psalm 81.* God pleads with His people: a classic expression of one of the great themes of the prophetic literature, the divine pathos – God's love for, but exasperation with, His children. "If only My people would listen to Me."

Wednesday הַיּוֹם יוֹם רְבִיעִי בְּשַׁבָּת, שֶׁבּוֹ הָיוּ הַלְוִיִּם אוֹמְרִים בְּבֵית הַמִּקְדָּשׁ:

תהלים צד אֵל־נְקָמוֹת יהוה, אֵל נְקָמוֹת הוֹפִיעַ: הִנָּשֵׂא שֹׁפֵט הָאָרֶץ, הָשֵׁב גְּמוּל
עַל־גֵּאִים: עַד־מָתַי רְשָׁעִים, יהוה, עַד־מָתַי רְשָׁעִים יַעֲלֹזוּ: יַבִּיעוּ יְדַבְּרוּ
עָתָק, יִתְאַמְּרוּ כָּל־פֹּעֲלֵי אָוֶן: עַמְּךָ יהוה יְדַכְּאוּ, וְנַחֲלָתְךָ יְעַנּוּ: אַלְמָנָה
וְגֵר יַהֲרֹגוּ, וִיתוֹמִים יְרַצֵּחוּ: וַיֹּאמְרוּ לֹא יִרְאֶה־יָּהּ, וְלֹא־יָבִין אֱלֹהֵי יַעֲקֹב:
בִּינוּ בֹּעֲרִים בָּעָם, וּכְסִילִים מָתַי תַּשְׂכִּילוּ: הֲנֹטַע אֹזֶן הֲלֹא יִשְׁמָע, אִם־יֹצֵר
עַיִן הֲלֹא יַבִּיט: הֲיֹסֵר גּוֹיִם הֲלֹא יוֹכִיחַ, הַמְלַמֵּד אָדָם דָּעַת: יהוה יֹדֵעַ
מַחְשְׁבוֹת אָדָם, כִּי־הֵמָּה הָבֶל: אַשְׁרֵי הַגֶּבֶר אֲשֶׁר־תְּיַסְּרֶנּוּ יָּהּ, וּמִתּוֹרָתְךָ
תְלַמְּדֶנּוּ: לְהַשְׁקִיט לוֹ מִימֵי רָע, עַד יִכָּרֶה לָרָשָׁע שָׁחַת: כִּי לֹא־יִטֹּשׁ יהוה
עַמּוֹ, וְנַחֲלָתוֹ לֹא יַעֲזֹב: כִּי־עַד־צֶדֶק יָשׁוּב מִשְׁפָּט, וְאַחֲרָיו כָּל־יִשְׁרֵי־לֵב:
מִי־יָקוּם לִי עִם־מְרֵעִים, מִי־יִתְיַצֵּב לִי עִם־פֹּעֲלֵי אָוֶן: לוּלֵי יהוה עֶזְרָתָה לִּי,
כִּמְעַט שָׁכְנָה דוּמָה נַפְשִׁי: אִם־אָמַרְתִּי מָטָה רַגְלִי, חַסְדְּךָ יהוה יִסְעָדֵנִי:
בְּרֹב שַׂרְעַפַּי בְּקִרְבִּי, תַּנְחוּמֶיךָ יְשַׁעַשְׁעוּ נַפְשִׁי: הַיְחָבְרְךָ כִּסֵּא הַוּוֹת,
יֹצֵר עָמָל עֲלֵי־חֹק: יָגוֹדּוּ עַל־נֶפֶשׁ צַדִּיק, וְדָם נָקִי יַרְשִׁיעוּ: וַיְהִי יהוה לִי
לְמִשְׂגָּב, וֵאלֹהַי לְצוּר מַחְסִי: וַיָּשֶׁב עֲלֵיהֶם אֶת־אוֹנָם, וּבְרָעָתָם יַצְמִיתֵם,
יַצְמִיתֵם יהוה אֱלֹהֵינוּ:

תהלים צה ▸ לְכוּ נְרַנְּנָה לַיהוה, נָרִיעָה לְצוּר יִשְׁעֵנוּ: נְקַדְּמָה פָנָיו בְּתוֹדָה, בִּזְמִרוֹת
נָרִיעַ לוֹ: כִּי אֵל גָּדוֹל יהוה, וּמֶלֶךְ גָּדוֹל עַל־כָּל־אֱלֹהִים:

קדיש יתום (*page 183*)

Thursday הַיּוֹם יוֹם חֲמִישִׁי בְּשַׁבָּת, שֶׁבּוֹ הָיוּ הַלְוִיִּם אוֹמְרִים בְּבֵית הַמִּקְדָּשׁ:

תהלים פא לַמְנַצֵּחַ עַל־הַגִּתִּית לְאָסָף: הַרְנִינוּ לֵאלֹהִים עוּזֵּנוּ, הָרִיעוּ לֵאלֹהֵי יַעֲקֹב:
שְׂאוּ־זִמְרָה וּתְנוּ־תֹף, כִּנּוֹר נָעִים עִם־נָבֶל: תִּקְעוּ בַחֹדֶשׁ שׁוֹפָר, בַּכֶּסֶה
לְיוֹם חַגֵּנוּ: כִּי חֹק לְיִשְׂרָאֵל הוּא, מִשְׁפָּט לֵאלֹהֵי יַעֲקֹב: עֵדוּת בִּיהוֹסֵף

אֵל־נְקָמוֹת יהוה *Wednesday: Psalm 94.* Marking the midweek, this is a psalm of intense power about the connection between religious faith and ethical conduct and their opposite: lack of faith and a failure of humanity. When man begins to worship himself, he dreams of becoming a god but ends by becoming lower than the beasts. Appropriately, some communities recite this psalm on Yom HaSho'a, Holocaust Memorial Day (27 Nisan).

day when the moon is hidden. For it is a statute for Israel, an ordinance of the God of Jacob. He established it as a testimony for Joseph when He went forth against the land of Egypt, where I heard a language that I did not know. I relieved his shoulder of the burden. His hands were freed from the builder's basket. In distress you called and I rescued you. I answered you from the secret place of thunder; I tested you at the waters of Meribah, Selah! Hear, My people, and I will warn you. Israel, if you would only listen to Me! Let there be no strange god among you. Do not bow down to an alien god. I am the LORD your God who brought you out of the land of Egypt. Open your mouth wide and I will fill it. But My people would not listen to Me. Israel would have none of Me. So I left them to their stubborn hearts, letting them follow their own devices. If only My people would listen to Me, if Israel would walk in My ways, I would soon subdue their enemies, and turn My hand against their foes. Those who hate the LORD would cower before Him and their doom would last for ever. ▸ He would feed Israel with the finest wheat – with honey from the rock I would satisfy you.

Mourner's Kaddish (page 182)

Friday: Today is the sixth day of the week,
on which the Levites used to say this psalm in the Temple:

יהוה מָלָךְ The LORD reigns. He is robed in majesty. The LORD is robed, girded with strength. The world is firmly established; it cannot be moved. Your throne stands firm as of old; You are eternal. Rivers lift up, LORD, rivers lift up their voice, rivers lift up their crashing waves. Mightier than the noise of many waters, than the mighty waves of the sea is the LORD on high. ▸ Your testimonies are very sure; holiness adorns Your House, LORD, for evermore. *Ps. 93*

Mourner's Kaddish (page 182)

On Rosh Hodesh, the following psalm is said:

בָּרְכִי נַפְשִׁי Bless the LORD, my soul. LORD, my God, You are very great, clothed in majesty and splendor, wrapped in a robe of light. You have spread out the heavens like a tent. He has laid the beams of His lofts in the waters. He makes the clouds His chariot, riding on the wings of the wind. He makes the winds His messengers, flames of fire His ministers. He has fixed the earth on its foundations so that it will never be shaken. You covered it with the deep like a cloak; the waters stood above the mountains. At Your rebuke they fled; at the sound of Your thunder they rushed away, flowing over the hills, pouring down into the valleys to the place You appointed for them. You fixed a boundary they were not to pass, so that they would never cover the earth again. He makes springs flow in the valleys; they make their way between the hills, giving drink to all *Ps. 104*

שְׁמוֹ, בְּצֵאתוֹ עַל־אֶרֶץ מִצְרָיִם, שְׂפַת לֹא־יָדַעְתִּי אֶשְׁמָע: הֲסִירוֹתִי מִסֵּבֶל שִׁכְמוֹ, כַּפָּיו מִדּוּד תַּעֲבֹרְנָה: בַּצָּרָה קָרָאתָ וָאֲחַלְּצֶךָּ, אֶעֶנְךָ בְּסֵתֶר רַעַם, אֶבְחָנְךָ עַל־מֵי מְרִיבָה סֶלָה: שְׁמַע עַמִּי וְאָעִידָה בָּךְ, יִשְׂרָאֵל אִם־תִּשְׁמַע־לִי: לֹא־יִהְיֶה בְךָ אֵל זָר, וְלֹא תִשְׁתַּחֲוֶה לְאֵל נֵכָר: אָנֹכִי יהוה אֱלֹהֶיךָ, הַמַּעַלְךָ מֵאֶרֶץ מִצְרָיִם, הַרְחֶב־פִּיךָ וַאֲמַלְאֵהוּ: וְלֹא־שָׁמַע עַמִּי לְקוֹלִי, וְיִשְׂרָאֵל לֹא־אָבָה לִי: וָאֲשַׁלְּחֵהוּ בִּשְׁרִירוּת לִבָּם, יֵלְכוּ בְּמוֹעֲצוֹתֵיהֶם: לוּ עַמִּי שֹׁמֵעַ לִי, יִשְׂרָאֵל בִּדְרָכַי יְהַלֵּכוּ: כִּמְעַט אוֹיְבֵיהֶם אַכְנִיעַ, וְעַל־צָרֵיהֶם אָשִׁיב יָדִי: מְשַׂנְאֵי יהוה יְכַחֲשׁוּ־לוֹ, וִיהִי עִתָּם לְעוֹלָם: › וַיַּאֲכִילֵהוּ מֵחֵלֶב חִטָּה, וּמִצּוּר, דְּבַשׁ אַשְׂבִּיעֶךָ:

קדיש יתום (*page 183*)

Friday **הַיּוֹם יוֹם שִׁשִּׁי בְּשַׁבָּת, שֶׁבּוֹ הָיוּ הַלְוִיִּם אוֹמְרִים בְּבֵית הַמִּקְדָּשׁ**

יהוה מָלָךְ, גֵּאוּת לָבֵשׁ, לָבֵשׁ יהוה עֹז הִתְאַזָּר, אַף־תִּכּוֹן תֵּבֵל בַּל־תִּמּוֹט: תהלים צג
נָכוֹן כִּסְאֲךָ מֵאָז, מֵעוֹלָם אָתָּה: נָשְׂאוּ נְהָרוֹת יהוה, נָשְׂאוּ נְהָרוֹת קוֹלָם, יִשְׂאוּ נְהָרוֹת דָּכְיָם: מִקֹּלוֹת מַיִם רַבִּים, אַדִּירִים מִשְׁבְּרֵי־יָם, אַדִּיר בַּמָּרוֹם יהוה: › עֵדֹתֶיךָ נֶאֶמְנוּ מְאֹד, לְבֵיתְךָ נַאֲוָה־קֹדֶשׁ, יהוה לְאֹרֶךְ יָמִים:

קדיש יתום (*page 183*)

On ראש חודש*, the following psalm is said:*

בָּרְכִי נַפְשִׁי אֶת־יהוה, יהוה אֱלֹהַי גָּדַלְתָּ מְּאֹד, הוֹד וְהָדָר לָבָשְׁתָּ: עֹטֶה־אוֹר תהלים קד
כַּשַּׂלְמָה, נוֹטֶה שָׁמַיִם כַּיְרִיעָה: הַמְקָרֶה בַמַּיִם עֲלִיּוֹתָיו, הַשָּׂם־עָבִים רְכוּבוֹ, הַמְהַלֵּךְ עַל־כַּנְפֵי־רוּחַ: עֹשֶׂה מַלְאָכָיו רוּחוֹת, מְשָׁרְתָיו אֵשׁ לֹהֵט: יָסַד־אֶרֶץ עַל־מְכוֹנֶיהָ, בַּל־תִּמּוֹט עוֹלָם וָעֶד: תְּהוֹם כַּלְּבוּשׁ כִּסִּיתוֹ, עַל־הָרִים יַעַמְדוּ־מָיִם: מִן־גַּעֲרָתְךָ יְנוּסוּן, מִן־קוֹל רַעַמְךָ יֵחָפֵזוּן: יַעֲלוּ הָרִים, יֵרְדוּ בְקָעוֹת, אֶל־מְקוֹם זֶה יָסַדְתָּ לָהֶם: גְּבוּל־שַׂמְתָּ בַּל־יַעֲבֹרוּן, בַּל־יְשׁוּבוּן לְכַסּוֹת הָאָרֶץ: הַמְשַׁלֵּחַ מַעְיָנִים בַּנְּחָלִים, בֵּין הָרִים יְהַלֵּכוּן: יַשְׁקוּ כָּל־חַיְתוֹ שָׂדָי, יִשְׁבְּרוּ פְרָאִים צְמָאָם: עֲלֵיהֶם עוֹף־הַשָּׁמַיִם יִשְׁכּוֹן, מִבֵּין עֳפָאיִם יִתְּנוּ־קוֹל: מַשְׁקֶה

יהוה מלך *Friday: Psalm 93.* Speaking as it does of the completion of creation ("the world is firmly established"), this psalm is appropriate for the sixth day, when "the heavens and the earth were completed, and all their array."

the beasts of the field; the wild donkeys quench their thirst. The birds of the sky dwell beside them, singing among the foliage. He waters the mountains from His lofts: the earth is sated with the fruit of Your work. He makes grass grow for the cattle, and plants for the use of man, that he may produce bread from the earth, wine to cheer the heart of man, oil to make the face shine, and bread to sustain man's heart. The trees of the LORD drink their fill, the cedars of Lebanon which He planted. There, birds build their nests; the stork makes its home in the cypresses. High hills are for the wild goats; crags are shelter for the badgers. He made the moon to mark the seasons, and makes the sun know when to set. You bring darkness and it is night; then all the beasts of the forests stir. The young lions roar for prey, seeking their food from God. When the sun rises, they slink away and seek rest in their lairs. Man goes out to his work and his labor until evening. How numerous are Your works, LORD; You made them all in wisdom; the earth is full of Your creations. There is the vast, immeasurable sea with its countless swarming creatures, living things great and small. There ships sail. There is Leviathan You formed to sport there. All of them look to You in hope, to give them their food when it is due. What You give them, they gather up. When You open Your hand, they are sated with good. When You hide Your face, they are dismayed. When You take away their breath, they die and return to dust. When You send back Your breath, they are created, giving new life to the earth. May the glory of the LORD be for ever; may the LORD rejoice in His works. When He looks at the earth, it trembles. When He touches the mountains, they pour forth smoke. I will sing to the LORD as long as I live; I will sing psalms to my God all my life. ▸ May my meditation be pleasing to Him; I shall rejoice in the LORD. May sinners vanish from the earth, and the wicked be no more. Bless the LORD, my soul. Halleluya!

Mourner's Kaddish (page 182)

During the month of Elul (except Erev Rosh HaShana), the shofar is sounded (some sound the shofar after the psalm below). From the second day of Rosh Ḥodesh Elul through Shemini Atzeret (in Israel through Hoshana Raba), the following psalm is said:

לְדָוִד By David. The LORD is my light and my salvation – whom then shall I fear? *Ps. 27*
The LORD is the stronghold of my life – of whom shall I be afraid? When evil men close in on me to devour my flesh, it is they, my enemies and foes, who stumble and fall. Should an army besiege me, my heart would not fear. Should war break out against me, still I would be confident. One thing I ask of the LORD, only this do I seek: to live in the House of the LORD all the days of my life, to gaze on the beauty of the LORD and worship in His Temple. For He will keep me safe in His pavilion on the day of trouble. He will hide me under the cover of His tent. He will set me high upon a rock. Now my head is high above my enemies who surround me. I will sacrifice in His tent with shouts of joy. I will sing and chant praises to the LORD. LORD, hear my voice when I call. Be

הָרִים מֵעֲלִיּוֹתָיו, מִפְּרִי מַעֲשֶׂיךָ תִּשְׂבַּע הָאָרֶץ: מַצְמִיחַ חָצִיר לַבְּהֵמָה, וְעֵשֶׂב לַעֲבֹדַת הָאָדָם, לְהוֹצִיא לֶחֶם מִן־הָאָרֶץ: וְיַיִן יְשַׂמַּח לְבַב־אֱנוֹשׁ, לְהַצְהִיל פָּנִים מִשָּׁמֶן, וְלֶחֶם לְבַב־אֱנוֹשׁ יִסְעָד: יִשְׂבְּעוּ עֲצֵי יהוה, אַרְזֵי לְבָנוֹן אֲשֶׁר נָטָע: אֲשֶׁר־שָׁם צִפֳּרִים יְקַנֵּנוּ, חֲסִידָה בְּרוֹשִׁים בֵּיתָהּ: הָרִים הַגְּבֹהִים לַיְּעֵלִים, סְלָעִים מַחְסֶה לַשְׁפַנִּים: עָשָׂה יָרֵחַ לְמוֹעֲדִים, שֶׁמֶשׁ יָדַע מְבוֹאוֹ: תָּשֶׁת־חֹשֶׁךְ וִיהִי לָיְלָה, בּוֹ־תִרְמֹשׂ כָּל־חַיְתוֹ־יָעַר: הַכְּפִירִים שֹׁאֲגִים לַטָּרֶף, וּלְבַקֵּשׁ מֵאֵל אָכְלָם: תִּזְרַח הַשֶּׁמֶשׁ יֵאָסֵפוּן, וְאֶל־מְעוֹנֹתָם יִרְבָּצוּן: יֵצֵא אָדָם לְפָעֳלוֹ, וְלַעֲבֹדָתוֹ עֲדֵי־עָרֶב: מָה־רַבּוּ מַעֲשֶׂיךָ יהוה, כֻּלָּם בְּחָכְמָה עָשִׂיתָ, מָלְאָה הָאָרֶץ קִנְיָנֶךָ: זֶה הַיָּם גָּדוֹל וּרְחַב יָדָיִם, שָׁם־רֶמֶשׂ וְאֵין מִסְפָּר, חַיּוֹת קְטַנּוֹת עִם־גְּדֹלוֹת: שָׁם אֳנִיּוֹת יְהַלֵּכוּן, לִוְיָתָן זֶה־יָצַרְתָּ לְשַׂחֶק־בּוֹ: כֻּלָּם אֵלֶיךָ יְשַׂבֵּרוּן, לָתֵת אָכְלָם בְּעִתּוֹ: תִּתֵּן לָהֶם יִלְקֹטוּן, תִּפְתַּח יָדְךָ יִשְׂבְּעוּן טוֹב: תַּסְתִּיר פָּנֶיךָ יִבָּהֵלוּן, תֹּסֵף רוּחָם יִגְוָעוּן, וְאֶל־עֲפָרָם יְשׁוּבוּן: תְּשַׁלַּח רוּחֲךָ יִבָּרֵאוּן, וּתְחַדֵּשׁ פְּנֵי אֲדָמָה: יְהִי כְבוֹד יהוה לְעוֹלָם, יִשְׂמַח יהוה בְּמַעֲשָׂיו: הַמַּבִּיט לָאָרֶץ וַתִּרְעָד, יִגַּע בֶּהָרִים וְיֶעֱשָׁנוּ: אָשִׁירָה לַיהוה בְּחַיָּי, אֲזַמְּרָה לֵאלֹהַי בְּעוֹדִי: · יֶעֱרַב עָלָיו שִׂיחִי, אָנֹכִי אֶשְׂמַח בַּיהוה: יִתַּמּוּ חַטָּאִים מִן־הָאָרֶץ, וּרְשָׁעִים עוֹד אֵינָם, בָּרְכִי נַפְשִׁי אֶת־יהוה, הַלְלוּיָהּ:

קדיש יתום (*page 183*)

During the month of אלול (*except* ערב ראש השנה), *the* שופר *is sounded* (*some sound the* שופר *after the psalm below*). *From the second day of* ראש חודש אלול *through* שמיני עצרת (*in* ארץ ישראל *through* הושענא רבה), *the following psalm is said:*

תהלים כז

לְדָוִד, יהוה אוֹרִי וְיִשְׁעִי, מִמִּי אִירָא, יהוה מָעוֹז־חַיַּי, מִמִּי אֶפְחָד: בִּקְרֹב עָלַי מְרֵעִים לֶאֱכֹל אֶת־בְּשָׂרִי, צָרַי וְאֹיְבַי לִי, הֵמָּה כָשְׁלוּ וְנָפָלוּ: אִם־תַּחֲנֶה עָלַי מַחֲנֶה, לֹא־יִירָא לִבִּי, אִם־תָּקוּם עָלַי מִלְחָמָה, בְּזֹאת אֲנִי בוֹטֵחַ: אַחַת שָׁאַלְתִּי מֵאֵת־יהוה, אוֹתָהּ אֲבַקֵּשׁ, שִׁבְתִּי בְּבֵית־יהוה כָּל־יְמֵי חַיַּי, לַחֲזוֹת בְּנֹעַם־יהוה, וּלְבַקֵּר בְּהֵיכָלוֹ: כִּי יִצְפְּנֵנִי בְּסֻכֹּה בְּיוֹם רָעָה, יַסְתִּרֵנִי בְּסֵתֶר

לְדָוִד *Psalm 27*: A magnificent expression of trust in God's protection and unfailing love. An early Midrash (*Vayikra Raba* 21:4) relates it to the festivals of Tishrei: "*The Lord is my light* – on Rosh HaShana, *and my salvation* – on Yom Kippur." The phrase, "He will keep me safe in His pavilion [*beSukko*]" suggested Sukkot. It was accordingly adopted as a prayer for the penitential period up to and including these holy days, beginning on Rosh Ḥodesh Elul.

gracious to me and answer me. On Your behalf my heart says, "Seek My face." Your face, LORD, will I seek. Do not hide Your face from me. Do not turn Your servant away in anger. You have been my help. Do not reject or forsake me, God, my Savior. Were my father and my mother to forsake me, the LORD would take me in. Teach me Your way, LORD, and lead me on a level path, because of my oppressors. Do not abandon me to the will of my foes, for false witnesses have risen against me, breathing violence. ▸ Were it not for my faith that I shall see the LORD's goodness in the land of the living. Hope in the LORD. Be strong and of good courage, and hope in the LORD!

Mourner's Kaddish (page 182)

In Israel the following through "Bless the LORD," on page 196, is said:

אֵין כֵּאלֹהֵינוּ There is none like our God, none like our LORD, none like our King, none like our Savior. Who is like our God? Like our LORD? Like our King? Like our Savior? We will thank our God, thank our LORD, thank our King, thank our Savior. Blessed is our God, blessed our LORD, blessed our King, blessed our Savior. You are our God, You are our LORD, You are our King, You are our Savior. You are He to whom our ancestors offered the fragrant incense.

פִּטּוּם הַקְּטֹרֶת The incense mixture consisted of balsam, onycha, galbanum and frankincense, each weighing seventy manehs; myrrh, cassia, spikenard and saffron, each weighing sixteen manehs; twelve manehs of costus, three of aromatic bark; nine of cinnamon; nine kabs of Carsina lye; three seahs and three kabs of Cyprus wine. If Cyprus wine was not available, old white wine might be used. A quarter of a kab of Sodom salt, and a minute amount of a smoke-raising herb. Rabbi Nathan says: Also a minute amount of Jordan amber. If one added honey to the mixture, he rendered it unfit for sacred use. If he omitted any one of its ingredients, he is guilty of a capital offense. *Keritot 6a*

Rabban Shimon ben Gamliel says: "Balsam" refers to the sap that drips from the balsam tree. The Carsina lye was used for bleaching the onycha to improve it. The Cyprus wine was used to soak the onycha in it to make it pungent. Though urine is suitable for this purpose, it is not brought into the Temple out of respect.

It was taught in the Academy of Elijah: Whoever studies [Torah] laws every day is assured that he will be destined for the World to Come, as it is said, "The ways of the world are His" – read not, "ways" [*halikhot*] but "laws" [*halakhot*]. *Megilla 28b* *Hab. 3*

Rabbi Elazar said in the name of Rabbi Ḥanina: The disciples of the sages increase peace in the world, as it is said, "And all your children shall be taught of the LORD, and great shall be the peace of your children [*banayikh*]." Read not *banayikh*, "your children," but *bonayikh*, "your builders." Those who love Your Torah have great peace; there is no stumbling block for them. May there be peace within your ramparts, prosperity in your palaces. For the sake of my brothers and friends, I shall say, "Peace be within you." For the sake of the House of the LORD our God, I will seek your good. ▸ May the LORD grant strength to His people; may the LORD bless His people with peace. *Berakhot 64a* *Is. 54* *Ps. 119* *Ps. 122* *Ps. 29*

אָהֳלוֹ, בְּצוּר יְרוֹמְמֵנִי: וְעַתָּה יָרוּם רֹאשִׁי עַל אֹיְבַי סְבִיבוֹתַי, וְאֶזְבְּחָה בְאָהֳלוֹ זִבְחֵי תְרוּעָה, אָשִׁירָה וַאֲזַמְּרָה לַיהוה: שְׁמַע־יהוה קוֹלִי אֶקְרָא, וְחָנֵּנִי וַעֲנֵנִי: לְךָ אָמַר לִבִּי בַּקְּשׁוּ פָנָי, אֶת־פָּנֶיךָ יהוה אֲבַקֵּשׁ: אַל־תַּסְתֵּר פָּנֶיךָ מִמֶּנִּי, אַל תַּט־בְּאַף עַבְדֶּךָ, עֶזְרָתִי הָיִיתָ, אַל־תִּטְּשֵׁנִי וְאַל־תַּעַזְבֵנִי, אֱלֹהֵי יִשְׁעִי: כִּי־אָבִי וְאִמִּי עֲזָבוּנִי, וַיהוה יַאַסְפֵנִי: הוֹרֵנִי יהוה דַּרְכֶּךָ, וּנְחֵנִי בְּאֹרַח מִישׁוֹר, לְמַעַן שׁוֹרְרָי: אַל־תִּתְּנֵנִי בְּנֶפֶשׁ צָרָי, כִּי קָמוּ־בִי עֵדֵי־שֶׁקֶר, וִיפֵחַ חָמָס: ◦ לוּלֵא הֶאֱמַנְתִּי לִרְאוֹת בְּטוּב־יהוה בְּאֶרֶץ חַיִּים: קַוֵּה אֶל־יהוה, חֲזַק וְיַאֲמֵץ לִבֶּךָ, וְקַוֵּה אֶל־יהוה:

קדיש יתום (page 183)

In ארץ ישראל *the following through* בָּרְכוּ*, on page 197, is said:*

אֵין כֵּאלֹהֵינוּ, אֵין כַּאדוֹנֵינוּ, אֵין כְּמַלְכֵּנוּ, אֵין כְּמוֹשִׁיעֵנוּ. מִי כֵאלֹהֵינוּ, מִי כַאדוֹנֵינוּ, מִי כְמַלְכֵּנוּ, מִי כְמוֹשִׁיעֵנוּ. נוֹדֶה לֵאלֹהֵינוּ, נוֹדֶה לַאדוֹנֵינוּ, נוֹדֶה לְמַלְכֵּנוּ, נוֹדֶה לְמוֹשִׁיעֵנוּ. בָּרוּךְ אֱלֹהֵינוּ, בָּרוּךְ אֲדוֹנֵינוּ, בָּרוּךְ מַלְכֵּנוּ, בָּרוּךְ מוֹשִׁיעֵנוּ. אַתָּה הוּא אֱלֹהֵינוּ, אַתָּה הוּא אֲדוֹנֵינוּ, אַתָּה הוּא מַלְכֵּנוּ, אַתָּה הוּא מוֹשִׁיעֵנוּ. אַתָּה הוּא שֶׁהִקְטִירוּ אֲבוֹתֵינוּ לְפָנֶיךָ אֶת קְטֹרֶת הַסַּמִּים.

כריתות ו. פִּטּוּם הַקְּטֹרֶת: הַצְּרִי, וְהַצִּפֹּרֶן, וְהַחֶלְבְּנָה, וְהַלְּבוֹנָה מִשְׁקַל שִׁבְעִים שִׁבְעִים מָנֶה, מֹר, וּקְצִיעָה, שִׁבֹּלֶת נֵרְדְּ, וְכַרְכֹּם מִשְׁקַל שִׁשָּׁה עָשָׂר שִׁשָּׁה עָשָׂר מָנֶה, הַקֹּשְׁטְ שְׁנֵים עָשָׂר, קִלּוּפָה שְׁלֹשָׁה, וְקִנָּמוֹן תִּשְׁעָה, בֹּרִית כַּרְשִׁינָה תִּשְׁעָה קַבִּין, יֵין קַפְרִיסִין סְאִין תְּלָת וְקַבִּין תְּלָתָא, וְאִם אֵין לוֹ יֵין קַפְרִיסִין, מֵבִיא חֲמַר חִוַּרְיָן עַתִּיק. מֶלַח סְדוֹמִית רֹבַע, מַעֲלֶה עָשָׁן כָּל שֶׁהוּא. רַבִּי נָתָן הַבַּבְלִי אוֹמֵר: אַף כִּפַּת הַיַּרְדֵּן כָּל שֶׁהוּא, וְאִם נָתַן בָּהּ דְּבַשׁ פְּסָלָהּ, וְאִם חִסַּר אֶחָד מִכָּל סַמָּנֶיהָ, חַיָּב מִיתָה.

רַבָּן שִׁמְעוֹן בֶּן גַּמְלִיאֵל אוֹמֵר: הַצְּרִי אֵינוֹ אֶלָּא שְׂרָף הַנּוֹטֵף מֵעֲצֵי הַקְּטָף. בֹּרִית כַּרְשִׁינָה שֶׁשָּׁפִין בָּהּ אֶת הַצִּפֹּרֶן כְּדֵי שֶׁתְּהֵא נָאָה, יֵין קַפְרִיסִין שֶׁשּׁוֹרִין בּוֹ אֶת הַצִּפֹּרֶן כְּדֵי שֶׁתְּהֵא עַזָּה, וַהֲלֹא מֵי רַגְלַיִם יָפִין לָהּ, אֶלָּא שֶׁאֵין מַכְנִיסִין מֵי רַגְלַיִם בַּמִּקְדָּשׁ מִפְּנֵי הַכָּבוֹד.

מגילה כח: תָּנָא דְבֵי אֵלִיָּהוּ: כָּל הַשּׁוֹנֶה הֲלָכוֹת בְּכָל יוֹם, מֻבְטָח לוֹ שֶׁהוּא בֶּן עוֹלָם הַבָּא, שֶׁנֶּאֱמַר

חבקוק ג הֲלִיכוֹת עוֹלָם לוֹ: אַל תִּקְרֵי הֲלִיכוֹת אֶלָּא הֲלָכוֹת.

ברכות סד. אָמַר רַבִּי אֶלְעָזָר, אָמַר רַבִּי חֲנִינָא: תַּלְמִידֵי חֲכָמִים מַרְבִּים שָׁלוֹם בָּעוֹלָם, שֶׁנֶּאֱמַר

ישעיה נד וְכָל־בָּנַיִךְ לִמּוּדֵי יהוה, וְרַב שְׁלוֹם בָּנָיִךְ: אַל תִּקְרֵי בָּנָיִךְ, אֶלָּא בּוֹנָיִךְ. שָׁלוֹם רָב לְאֹהֲבֵי

תהלים קיט תוֹרָתֶךָ, וְאֵין־לָמוֹ מִכְשׁוֹל: יְהִי־שָׁלוֹם בְּחֵילֵךְ, שַׁלְוָה בְּאַרְמְנוֹתָיִךְ: לְמַעַן אַחַי וְרֵעָי

תהלים קכב אֲדַבְּרָה־נָּא שָׁלוֹם בָּךְ: לְמַעַן בֵּית־יהוה אֱלֹהֵינוּ אֲבַקְשָׁה טוֹב לָךְ: ◦ יהוה עֹז לְעַמּוֹ

תהלים כט יִתֵּן, יהוה יְבָרֵךְ אֶת־עַמּוֹ בַשָּׁלוֹם:

THE RABBIS' KADDISH

The following prayer, said by mourners, requires the presence of a minyan.
A transliteration can be found on page 1333.

Mourner: יִתְגַּדַּל Magnified and sanctified
may His great name be, in the world He created by His will.
May He establish His kingdom in your lifetime
and in your days, and in the lifetime of all the house of Israel,
swiftly and soon – and say: Amen.

All: May His great name be blessed for ever and all time.

Mourner: Blessed and praised, glorified and exalted,
raised and honored, uplifted and lauded be
the name of the Holy One, blessed be He,
beyond any blessing,
song, praise and consolation
uttered in the world – and say: Amen.

To Israel, to the teachers,
their disciples and their disciples' disciples,
and to all who engage in the study of Torah,
in this (*in Israel add:* holy) place or elsewhere,
may there come to them and you great peace,
grace, kindness and compassion, long life, ample sustenance
and deliverance, from their Father in Heaven – and say: Amen.

May there be great peace from heaven,
and (good) life for us and all Israel – and say: Amen.

Bow, take three steps back, as if taking leave of the Divine Presence,
then bow, first left, then right, then center, while saying:

May He who makes peace in His high places,
in His compassion make peace for us and all Israel –
and say: Amen.

In Israel, on days when the Torah is not read, the person saying Kaddish adds:

Bless the Lord, the blessed One.

and the congregation responds:

Bless the Lord, the blessed One, for ever and all time.

In Israel during Elul, some congregations blow shofar and say Psalm 27 *(page 192)* *at this point. In a house of mourning the service continues on page 1060.*

קדיש דרבנן

The following prayer, said by mourners, requires the presence of a מנין*.*
A transliteration can be found on page 1333.

אבל: יִתְגַּדַּל וְיִתְקַדַּשׁ שְׁמֵהּ רַבָּא (קהל: אָמֵן)
בְּעָלְמָא דִּי בְרָא כִרְעוּתֵהּ
וְיַמְלִיךְ מַלְכוּתֵהּ
בְּחַיֵּיכוֹן וּבְיוֹמֵיכוֹן וּבְחַיֵּי דְכָל בֵּית יִשְׂרָאֵל
בַּעֲגָלָא וּבִזְמַן קָרִיב, וְאִמְרוּ אָמֵן. (קהל: אָמֵן)

קהל ואבל: יְהֵא שְׁמֵהּ רַבָּא מְבָרַךְ לְעָלַם וּלְעָלְמֵי עָלְמַיָּא.

אבל: יִתְבָּרַךְ וְיִשְׁתַּבַּח וְיִתְפָּאַר וְיִתְרוֹמַם וְיִתְנַשֵּׂא
וְיִתְהַדַּר וְיִתְעַלֶּה וְיִתְהַלָּל, שְׁמֵהּ דְּקֻדְשָׁא בְּרִיךְ הוּא (קהל: בְּרִיךְ הוּא)
לְעֵלָּא מִן כָּל בִּרְכָתָא / בעשרת ימי תשובה: לְעֵלָּא לְעֵלָּא מִכָּל בִּרְכָתָא /
וְשִׁירָתָא, תֻּשְׁבְּחָתָא וְנֶחֱמָתָא, דַּאֲמִירָן בְּעָלְמָא, וְאִמְרוּ אָמֵן. (קהל: אָמֵן)
עַל יִשְׂרָאֵל וְעַל רַבָּנָן, וְעַל תַּלְמִידֵיהוֹן וְעַל כָּל תַּלְמִידֵי תַלְמִידֵיהוֹן
וְעַל כָּל מָאן דְּעָסְקִין בְּאוֹרַיְתָא
דִּי בְאַתְרָא (בארץ ישראל: קַדִּישָׁא) הָדֵין וְדִי בְכָל אֲתַר וַאֲתַר
יְהֵא לְהוֹן וּלְכוֹן שְׁלָמָא רַבָּא, חִנָּא וְחִסְדָּא, וְרַחֲמֵי, וְחַיֵּי אֲרִיכֵי, וּמְזוֹנֵי רְוִיחֵי
וּפֻרְקָנָא מִן קֳדָם אֲבוּהוֹן דִּי בִשְׁמַיָּא, וְאִמְרוּ אָמֵן. (קהל: אָמֵן)

יְהֵא שְׁלָמָא רַבָּא מִן שְׁמַיָּא
וְחַיִּים (טוֹבִים) עָלֵינוּ וְעַל כָּל יִשְׂרָאֵל, וְאִמְרוּ אָמֵן. (קהל: אָמֵן)

Bow, take three steps back, as if taking leave of the Divine Presence, then bow, first left, then right, then center, while saying:

עֹשֶׂה שָׁלוֹם/ בעשרת ימי תשובה: הַשָּׁלוֹם/ בִּמְרוֹמָיו
הוּא יַעֲשֶׂה בְרַחֲמָיו שָׁלוֹם, עָלֵינוּ וְעַל כָּל יִשְׂרָאֵל, וְאִמְרוּ אָמֵן. (קהל: אָמֵן)

In ארץ ישראל*, on days when the* תורה *is not read, the person saying* קדיש *adds:*

בָּרְכוּ אֶת יהוה הַמְבֹרָךְ.

and the קהל *responds:*

בָּרוּךְ יהוה הַמְבֹרָךְ לְעוֹלָם וָעֶד.

In ארץ ישראל *during* אלול*, some congregations blow* שופר *and say* לְדָוִד, יהוה אוֹרִי *(page 193) at this point. In a house of mourning the service continues on page 1061.*

READINGS AFTER THE SERVICE

Some say the following daily after morning prayers:

THE SIX REMEMBRANCES

The Exodus from Egypt

That you may remember the day you left the land of Egypt all the days of your life. *Deut. 16*

The Revelation at Mount Sinai

Only be careful and watch yourself very closely lest you forget the things your eyes have seen or let them slip from your heart all the days of your life. You shall make them known to your children and your children's children – the day you stood before the Lord your God at Horeb when the Lord said to me, "Assemble the people before Me and I will let them hear My words, so that they may learn to be in awe of Me as long as they live on earth, and they will teach them to their children." *Deut. 4*

Amalek

Remember what Amalek did to you on your way out of Egypt, how he met you on the way, cutting off those who were lagging behind, when you were tired and exhausted, and he did not fear God. So, when the Lord your God grants you rest from all your enemies around you in the land the Lord your God is about to give you to possess as an inheritance, you shall wipe out the memory of Amalek from under the heavens: you shall not forget. *Deut. 25*

The Golden Calf

Remember, and do not forget, how you provoked the Lord your God in the wilderness. *Deut. 9*

Miriam

Remember what the Lord your God did to Miriam on the way when you came out of Egypt. *Deut. 24*

The Shabbat

Remember the Shabbat day to hallow it. *Ex. 20*

---

golden calf reminds us of sins against God; Miriam's fate reminds us of sins against our fellows, especially through evil speech. Amalek's attack on the Israelites showed how a failure to fear God leads to cruelty against human beings.

אמירות לאחר התפילה

Some say the following daily after morning prayers:

שש זכירות

יציאת מצרים

לְמַעַן תִּזְכֹּר אֶת־יוֹם צֵאתְךָ מֵאֶרֶץ מִצְרַיִם כֹּל יְמֵי חַיֶּיךָ׃ דברים טז

מעמד הר סיני

רַק הִשָּׁמֶר לְךָ וּשְׁמֹר נַפְשְׁךָ מְאֹד פֶּן־תִּשְׁכַּח אֶת־הַדְּבָרִים אֲשֶׁר־רָאוּ עֵינֶיךָ וּפֶן־יָסוּרוּ מִלְּבָבְךָ כֹּל יְמֵי חַיֶּיךָ וְהוֹדַעְתָּם לְבָנֶיךָ וְלִבְנֵי בָנֶיךָ׃ יוֹם אֲשֶׁר עָמַדְתָּ לִפְנֵי יהוה אֱלֹהֶיךָ בְּחֹרֵב בֶּאֱמֹר יהוה אֵלַי הַקְהֶל־לִי אֶת־הָעָם וְאַשְׁמִעֵם אֶת־דְּבָרָי אֲשֶׁר יִלְמְדוּן לְיִרְאָה אֹתִי כָּל־הַיָּמִים אֲשֶׁר הֵם חַיִּים עַל־הָאֲדָמָה וְאֶת־בְּנֵיהֶם יְלַמֵּדוּן׃ דברים ד

מעשה עמלק ומחייתו

זָכוֹר אֵת אֲשֶׁר־עָשָׂה לְךָ עֲמָלֵק בַּדֶּרֶךְ בְּצֵאתְכֶם מִמִּצְרָיִם׃ אֲשֶׁר קָרְךָ בַּדֶּרֶךְ וַיְזַנֵּב בְּךָ כָּל־הַנֶּחֱשָׁלִים אַחֲרֶיךָ וְאַתָּה עָיֵף וְיָגֵעַ וְלֹא יָרֵא אֱלֹהִים׃ וְהָיָה בְּהָנִיחַ יהוה אֱלֹהֶיךָ ׀ לְךָ מִכָּל־אֹיְבֶיךָ מִסָּבִיב בָּאָרֶץ אֲשֶׁר־יהוה אֱלֹהֶיךָ נֹתֵן לְךָ נַחֲלָה לְרִשְׁתָּהּ תִּמְחֶה אֶת־זֵכֶר עֲמָלֵק מִתַּחַת הַשָּׁמָיִם לֹא תִּשְׁכָּח׃ דברים כה

מעשי אבותינו במדבר

זְכֹר אַל־תִּשְׁכַּח אֵת אֲשֶׁר־הִקְצַפְתָּ אֶת־יהוה אֱלֹהֶיךָ בַּמִּדְבָּר דברים ט

מעשה מרים

זָכוֹר אֵת אֲשֶׁר־עָשָׂה יהוה אֱלֹהֶיךָ לְמִרְיָם בַּדֶּרֶךְ בְּצֵאתְכֶם מִמִּצְרָיִם׃ דברים כד

שבת

זָכוֹר אֶת־יוֹם הַשַּׁבָּת לְקַדְּשׁוֹ׃ שמות כ

THE SIX REMEMBRANCES

These acts of remembrance define three positive and three negative parameters of Jewish faith and life. Positively, the exodus reminds us of divine redemption, Sinai of revelation, and the Sabbath of creation. Negatively, the

THE TEN COMMANDMENTS

God spoke all these words, saying: *Ex. 20*

1. אָנֹכִי I am the LORD your God who brought you out of the land of Egypt, from the slave-house.
2. לֹא־יִהְיֶה Have no other gods besides Me. Do not make a sculptured image for yourself, or any likeness of what is in the heavens above, or on the earth below, or in the waters under the earth. Do not bow down to them or worship them, for I am the LORD your God, a zealous God, visiting the guilt of the parents on the children to the third and fourth generation, if they also reject Me; but showing kindness to thousands of generations of those who love Me and keep My commandments.
3. לֹא תִשָּׂא Do not take the name of the LORD your God in vain. The LORD will not leave unpunished one who utters His name in vain.
4. זָכוֹר Remember the Sabbath and keep it holy. Six days you shall labor and do all your work, but the seventh day is a Sabbath of the LORD your God; on it you shall not do any work – you, your son or daughter, your male or female slaves, your cattle, or the stranger within your gates. For in six days the LORD made heaven and earth and sea, and all that is in them, and rested on the seventh day; therefore the LORD blessed the Sabbath day and made it holy.
5. כַּבֵּד Honor your father and your mother, so that you may live long in the land that the LORD your God is giving you.
6. לֹא תִרְצַח Do not murder.
7. לֹא תִנְאָף Do not commit adultery.
8. לֹא תִגְנֹב Do not steal.
9. לֹא־תַעֲנֶה Do not testify as a false witness against your neighbor.
10. לֹא תַחְמֹד Do not be envious of your neighbor's house. Do not be envious of your neighbor's wife, his male or female slave, his ox, his ass, or anything else that is your neighbor's.

---

when sectarians maintained that only these, and not the other commandments, were from God (*Berakhot* 12a). So deep was the attachment of Jews to this "sublime summary of human duties" (Rabbi J.H. Hertz), however, that the custom developed to say it privately after the end of the morning service.

עשרת הדברות

שמות כ

וַיְדַבֵּר אֱלֹהִים אֵת כׇּל־הַדְּבָרִים הָאֵלֶּה לֵאמֹר׃

א אָנֹכִי יהוה אֱלֹהֶיךָ אֲשֶׁר הוֹצֵאתִיךָ מֵאֶרֶץ מִצְרַיִם מִבֵּית עֲבָדִים׃

ב לֹא־יִהְיֶה לְךָ אֱלֹהִים אֲחֵרִים עַל־פָּנָי׃ לֹא־תַעֲשֶׂה לְךָ פֶסֶל וְכׇל־תְּמוּנָה
אֲשֶׁר בַּשָּׁמַיִם מִמַּעַל וַאֲשֶׁר בָּאָרֶץ מִתַּחַת וַאֲשֶׁר בַּמַּיִם מִתַּחַת לָאָרֶץ׃
לֹא־תִשְׁתַּחֲוֶה לָהֶם וְלֹא תׇעׇבְדֵם כִּי אָנֹכִי יהוה אֱלֹהֶיךָ אֵל קַנָּא פֹּקֵד עֲוֺן
אָבֹת עַל־בָּנִים עַל־שִׁלֵּשִׁים וְעַל־רִבֵּעִים לְשֹׂנְאָי׃ וְעֹשֶׂה חֶסֶד לַאֲלָפִים
לְאֹהֲבַי וּלְשֹׁמְרֵי מִצְוֺתָי׃

ג לֹא תִשָּׂא אֶת־שֵׁם־יהוה אֱלֹהֶיךָ לַשָּׁוְא כִּי לֹא יְנַקֶּה יהוה אֵת אֲשֶׁר־יִשָּׂא
אֶת־שְׁמוֹ לַשָּׁוְא׃

ד זָכוֹר אֶת־יוֹם הַשַּׁבָּת לְקַדְּשׁוֹ׃ שֵׁשֶׁת יָמִים תַּעֲבֹד וְעָשִׂיתָ כׇּל־מְלַאכְתֶּךָ׃
וְיוֹם הַשְּׁבִיעִי שַׁבָּת לַיהוה אֱלֹהֶיךָ לֹא־תַעֲשֶׂה כׇל־מְלָאכָה אַתָּה ׀ וּבִנְךָ
וּבִתֶּךָ עַבְדְּךָ וַאֲמָתְךָ וּבְהֶמְתֶּךָ וְגֵרְךָ אֲשֶׁר בִּשְׁעָרֶיךָ׃ כִּי שֵׁשֶׁת־יָמִים עָשָׂה
יהוה אֶת־הַשָּׁמַיִם וְאֶת־הָאָרֶץ אֶת־הַיָּם וְאֶת־כׇּל־אֲשֶׁר־בָּם וַיָּנַח בַּיּוֹם
הַשְּׁבִיעִי עַל־כֵּן בֵּרַךְ יהוה אֶת־יוֹם הַשַּׁבָּת וַיְקַדְּשֵׁהוּ׃

ה כַּבֵּד אֶת־אָבִיךָ וְאֶת־אִמֶּךָ לְמַעַן יַאֲרִכוּן יָמֶיךָ עַל הָאֲדָמָה אֲשֶׁר־יהוה
אֱלֹהֶיךָ נֹתֵן לָךְ׃

ו לֹא תִרְצָח

ז לֹא תִנְאָף

ח לֹא תִגְנֹב

ט לֹא־תַעֲנֶה בְרֵעֲךָ עֵד שָׁקֶר׃

י לֹא תַחְמֹד בֵּית רֵעֶךָ לֹא־תַחְמֹד אֵשֶׁת רֵעֶךָ וְעַבְדּוֹ וַאֲמָתוֹ וְשׁוֹרוֹ וַחֲמֹרוֹ
וְכֹל אֲשֶׁר לְרֵעֶךָ׃

THE TEN COMMANDMENTS

In Temple times, the Ten Commandments were recited as part of the daily prayers, immediately prior to the Shema. The practice was discontinued

THE THIRTEEN PRINCIPLES OF JEWISH FAITH

1. I believe with perfect faith
that the Creator,
blessed be His name,
creates and rules all creatures,
and that He alone made, makes, and will make, all things.

2. I believe with perfect faith
that the Creator,
blessed be His name, is One;
that there is no oneness like His in any way;
and that He alone is our God who was, is, and ever will be.

3. I believe with perfect faith
that the Creator,
blessed be His name, is not physical,
that no physical attributes can apply to Him,
and that there is nothing whatsoever to compare to Him.

4. I believe with perfect faith
that the Creator,
blessed be His name, is first and last.

5. I believe with perfect faith
that the Creator,
blessed be His name,
is the only one to whom it is proper to pray,
and that it is improper to pray to anyone else.

6. I believe with perfect faith
that all the words of the prophets are true.

7. I believe with perfect faith
that the prophecy of Moses our teacher,
peace be to him, was true,
and that he was the father of the prophets –
those who preceded him and those who followed him.

---

nity; and (5) the belief that He alone is to be worshiped. The next four are about revelation: (6) belief in prophecy; (7) the unique status of Moses as

שלושה עשר עיקרים

א אֲנִי מַאֲמִין בֶּאֱמוּנָה שְׁלֵמָה
שֶׁהַבּוֹרֵא יִתְבָּרַךְ שְׁמוֹ הוּא בּוֹרֵא וּמַנְהִיג לְכָל הַבְּרוּאִים
וְהוּא לְבַדּוֹ עָשָׂה וְעוֹשֶׂה וְיַעֲשֶׂה לְכָל הַמַּעֲשִׂים.

ב אֲנִי מַאֲמִין בֶּאֱמוּנָה שְׁלֵמָה
שֶׁהַבּוֹרֵא יִתְבָּרַךְ שְׁמוֹ הוּא יָחִיד
וְאֵין יְחִידוּת כָּמוֹהוּ בְּשׁוּם פָּנִים
וְהוּא לְבַדּוֹ אֱלֹהֵינוּ, הָיָה הֹוֶה וְיִהְיֶה.

ג אֲנִי מַאֲמִין בֶּאֱמוּנָה שְׁלֵמָה
שֶׁהַבּוֹרֵא יִתְבָּרַךְ שְׁמוֹ אֵינוֹ גוּף
וְלֹא יַשִּׂיגוּהוּ מַשִּׂיגֵי הַגּוּף
וְאֵין לוֹ שׁוּם דִּמְיוֹן כְּלָל.

ד אֲנִי מַאֲמִין בֶּאֱמוּנָה שְׁלֵמָה
שֶׁהַבּוֹרֵא יִתְבָּרַךְ שְׁמוֹ הוּא רִאשׁוֹן וְהוּא אַחֲרוֹן.

ה אֲנִי מַאֲמִין בֶּאֱמוּנָה שְׁלֵמָה
שֶׁהַבּוֹרֵא יִתְבָּרַךְ שְׁמוֹ לוֹ לְבַדּוֹ רָאוּי לְהִתְפַּלֵּל
וְאֵין רָאוּי לְהִתְפַּלֵּל לְזוּלָתוֹ.

ו אֲנִי מַאֲמִין בֶּאֱמוּנָה שְׁלֵמָה
שֶׁכָּל דִּבְרֵי נְבִיאִים אֱמֶת.

ז אֲנִי מַאֲמִין בֶּאֱמוּנָה שְׁלֵמָה
שֶׁנְּבוּאַת מֹשֶׁה רַבֵּנוּ עָלָיו הַשָּׁלוֹם הָיְתָה אֲמִתִּית
וְשֶׁהוּא הָיָה אָב לַנְּבִיאִים, לַקּוֹדְמִים לְפָנָיו וְלַבָּאִים אַחֲרָיו.

THE THIRTEEN PRINCIPLES OF JEWISH FAITH

A prose counterpart to the poetic Yigdal, both of which summarize the principles set out by Moses Maimonides (1135–1204). The first five are about God: (1) His existence; (2) His unity; (3) His incorporeality; (4) His eter-

8. I believe with perfect faith
that the entire Torah now in our hands
is the same one that was given to Moses our teacher,
peace be upon him.

9. I believe with perfect faith
that this Torah will not be changed,
nor will there be any other Torah from the Creator,
blessed be His name.

10. I believe with perfect faith
that the Creator, blessed be His name,
knows all the deeds and thoughts of humanity,
as it is said, "He fashions the hearts of them all, *Ps. 33*
comprehending all their deeds."

11. I believe with perfect faith
that the Creator, blessed be His name,
rewards those who keep His commandments,
and punishes those who transgress them.

12. I believe with perfect faith
in the coming of the Messiah,
and though he may delay,
I wait daily for his coming.

13. I believe with perfect faith
that the dead will live again
at a time of the Creator's choosing:
blessed be His name and exalted be His mention
for ever and all time.

---

punishes; (12) He will send the Messiah; and (13) in time to come, He will bring the dead back to life again. The presence of this passage is a reminder that the siddur is not just a book of prayer but also of faith.

ח אֲנִי מַאֲמִין בֶּאֱמוּנָה שְׁלֵמָה
שֶׁכָּל הַתּוֹרָה הַמְּצוּיָה עַתָּה בְיָדֵינוּ
הִיא הַנְּתוּנָה לְמשֶׁה רַבֵּנוּ עָלָיו הַשָּׁלוֹם.

ט אֲנִי מַאֲמִין בֶּאֱמוּנָה שְׁלֵמָה
שֶׁזֹּאת הַתּוֹרָה לֹא תְהֵא מֻחְלֶפֶת
וְלֹא תְהֵא תּוֹרָה אַחֶרֶת מֵאֵת הַבּוֹרֵא יִתְבָּרַךְ שְׁמוֹ.

י אֲנִי מַאֲמִין בֶּאֱמוּנָה שְׁלֵמָה
שֶׁהַבּוֹרֵא יִתְבָּרַךְ שְׁמוֹ
יוֹדֵעַ כָּל מַעֲשֵׂה בְנֵי אָדָם וְכָל מַחְשְׁבוֹתָם.
שֶׁנֶּאֱמַר: הַיֹּצֵר יַחַד לִבָּם, הַמֵּבִין אֶל־כָּל־מַעֲשֵׂיהֶם: תהלים לג

יא אֲנִי מַאֲמִין בֶּאֱמוּנָה שְׁלֵמָה
שֶׁהַבּוֹרֵא יִתְבָּרַךְ שְׁמוֹ גּוֹמֵל טוֹב לְשׁוֹמְרֵי מִצְוֹתָיו
וּמַעֲנִישׁ לְעוֹבְרֵי מִצְוֹתָיו.

יב אֲנִי מַאֲמִין בֶּאֱמוּנָה שְׁלֵמָה
בְּבִיאַת הַמָּשִׁיחַ
וְאַף עַל פִּי שֶׁיִּתְמַהְמֵהַּ עִם כָּל זֶה אֲחַכֶּה לּוֹ
בְּכָל יוֹם שֶׁיָּבוֹא.

יג אֲנִי מַאֲמִין בֶּאֱמוּנָה שְׁלֵמָה
שֶׁתִּהְיֶה תְּחִיַּת הַמֵּתִים
בְּעֵת שֶׁיַּעֲלֶה רָצוֹן מֵאֵת הַבּוֹרֵא
יִתְבָּרַךְ שְׁמוֹ וְיִתְעַלֶּה זִכְרוֹ לָעַד וּלְנֵצַח נְצָחִים.

---

the greatest of the prophets; (8) the divine authorship of the Torah; and (9) the immutability of the Torah. The last four are about reward, punishment and justice: (10) God knows our thoughts and deeds; (11) He rewards and

The following is said after morning and evening prayers:

יְהִי יהוה May the Lord our God be with us, as He was with our ancestors. *I Kings 8* May He never abandon us or forsake us, ever; as He turns our hearts toward Him, to follow all His paths and to keep His commands and His statutes and laws, as He charged our ancestors. And may these words with which I have pleaded before the Lord be close to the Lord our God, day and night, that He do justice for Your servant, and for Your people Israel, day by day. That all the peoples of the earth shall know that the Lord is God; there is no other.

יהוה נְחֵנִי Lead me, Lord, in Your righteousness, because of my foes; make *Ps. 5* Your way straight before me. As for me, I lead a blameless life; redeem me and *Ps. 26* show me favor. Turn to me and show me favor, for I am lonely and afflicted. *Ps. 25* My foot stands on level ground: in the assemblies I will bless the Lord. The *Ps. 26* Lord is my Guardian; the Lord is my Shade at my right hand. My help comes *Ps. 121* from the Lord, Maker of heaven and earth. The Lord will guard my coming and going, for life and for peace, now and for evermore. Gaze down from Your *Deut. 26* holy dwelling place, from the heavens, and bless Your people Israel, and the land that You have given us, as You promised our ancestors: a land flowing with milk and honey.

אֵל הַכָּבוֹד Glorious God, I bring before You song and praise; I shall worship You day and night. Blessed be the One and Only One – who was, who is and who will always be. Lord God, God of Israel, King, King of kings, Holy One, blessed be He. He is the living God, the living and ever, forever enduring King. Blessed be the name of His glorious kingdom for ever and ever. I long for Your *Gen. 49* salvation, Lord. All the nations will walk, each in the name of its god; and I will walk in the name of the Lord, the living God and eternal King. My help *Ps. 121* comes from the Lord, Maker of heaven and earth. The Lord will reign for *Ex. 15* ever and all time.

לַמְנַצֵּחַ For the Chief Musician; with stringed instruments. A psalm. A song. *Ps. 67* May God be gracious to us and bless us; may He cause His face to shine upon us, Selah, that Your way may be known on earth, Your salvation, among all nations. May the peoples praise You, God; may all the peoples praise You! The nations will rejoice and break into song; for You judge the peoples with equity and guide the nations of the earth, Selah. May the peoples praise You, God; may all the peoples praise You! The earth has yielded its produce; may God, our God, bless us. May God bless us, and may all the ends of the earth fear Him!

Some say Adon Olam (page 22) at this point.

The following is said after morning and evening prayers:

יְהִי יהוה אֱלֹהֵינוּ עִמָּנוּ כַּאֲשֶׁר הָיָה עִם־אֲבֹתֵינוּ, אַל־יַעַזְבֵנוּ וְאַל־יִטְּשֵׁנוּ: מלכים א׳ ח
לְהַטּוֹת לְבָבֵנוּ אֵלָיו, לָלֶכֶת בְּכָל־דְּרָכָיו וְלִשְׁמֹר מִצְוֹתָיו וְחֻקָּיו וּמִשְׁפָּטָיו
אֲשֶׁר צִוָּה אֶת־אֲבֹתֵינוּ: וְיִהְיוּ דְבָרַי אֵלֶּה אֲשֶׁר הִתְחַנַּנְתִּי לִפְנֵי יהוה,
קְרֹבִים אֶל־יהוה אֱלֹהֵינוּ יוֹמָם וָלָיְלָה, לַעֲשׂוֹת מִשְׁפַּט עַבְדּוֹ וּמִשְׁפַּט
עַמּוֹ יִשְׂרָאֵל דְּבַר־יוֹם בְּיוֹמוֹ: לְמַעַן דַּעַת כָּל־עַמֵּי הָאָרֶץ כִּי יהוה הוּא
הָאֱלֹהִים, אֵין עוֹד:

יהוה נְחֵנִי בְצִדְקָתֶךָ לְמַעַן שׁוֹרְרָי, הַיְשַׁר לְפָנַי דַּרְכֶּךָ: וַאֲנִי בְּתֻמִּי אֵלֵךְ, פְּדֵנִי תהלים ה תהלים כו
וְחָנֵּנִי: פְּנֵה־אֵלַי וְחָנֵּנִי כִּי־יָחִיד וְעָנִי אָנִי: רַגְלִי עָמְדָה בְמִישׁוֹר, בְּמַקְהֵלִים תהלים כה תהלים כו
אֲבָרֵךְ יהוה: יהוה שֹׁמְרִי, יהוה צִלִּי עַל־יַד יְמִינִי. עֶזְרִי מֵעִם יהוה, עֹשֵׂה תהלים קכא
שָׁמַיִם וָאָרֶץ: יהוה יִשְׁמֹר צֵאתִי וּבוֹאִי לְחַיִּים וּלְשָׁלוֹם, מֵעַתָּה וְעַד עוֹלָם.
הַשְׁקִיפָה מִמְּעוֹן קָדְשְׁךָ מִן־הַשָּׁמַיִם, וּבָרֵךְ אֶת־עַמְּךָ, אֶת־יִשְׂרָאֵל, וְאֵת דברים כו
הָאֲדָמָה אֲשֶׁר נָתַתָּה לָנוּ כַּאֲשֶׁר נִשְׁבַּעְתָּ לַאֲבֹתֵינוּ, אֶרֶץ זָבַת חָלָב
וּדְבָשׁ:

אֵל הַכָּבוֹד, אֶתֵּן לְךָ שִׁיר וְהַלֵּל וְאֶעֱבֹד לְךָ יוֹם וָלֵיל. בָּרוּךְ יָחִיד וּמְיֻחָד,
הָיָה הֹוֶה וְיִהְיֶה, יהוה אֱלֹהִים אֱלֹהֵי יִשְׂרָאֵל, מֶלֶךְ מַלְכֵי הַמְּלָכִים, הַקָּדוֹשׁ
בָּרוּךְ הוּא. הוּא אֱלֹהִים חַיִּים, מֶלֶךְ חַי וְקַיָּם לָעַד וּלְעוֹלְמֵי עַד. בָּרוּךְ שֵׁם
כְּבוֹד מַלְכוּתוֹ לְעוֹלָם וָעֶד. לִישׁוּעָתְךָ קִוִּיתִי יהוה: כִּי כָּל הָעַמִּים יֵלְכוּ בראשית מט
אִישׁ בְּשֵׁם אֱלֹהָיו, וַאֲנִי אֵלֵךְ בְּשֵׁם יהוה אֱלֹהִים חַיִּים וּמֶלֶךְ עוֹלָם. עֶזְרִי תהלים קכא
מֵעִם יהוה, עֹשֵׂה שָׁמַיִם וָאָרֶץ: יהוה יִמְלֹךְ לְעֹלָם וָעֶד: שמות טו

לַמְנַצֵּחַ בִּנְגִינֹת, מִזְמוֹר שִׁיר: אֱלֹהִים יְחָנֵּנוּ וִיבָרְכֵנוּ, יָאֵר פָּנָיו אִתָּנוּ סֶלָה: תהלים סז
לָדַעַת בָּאָרֶץ דַּרְכֶּךָ, בְּכָל־גּוֹיִם יְשׁוּעָתֶךָ: יוֹדוּךָ עַמִּים אֱלֹהִים, יוֹדוּךָ עַמִּים
כֻּלָּם: יִשְׂמְחוּ וִירַנְּנוּ לְאֻמִּים, כִּי־תִשְׁפֹּט עַמִּים מִישֹׁר, וּלְאֻמִּים בָּאָרֶץ
תַּנְחֵם סֶלָה: יוֹדוּךָ עַמִּים אֱלֹהִים, יוֹדוּךָ עַמִּים כֻּלָּם: אֶרֶץ נָתְנָה יְבוּלָהּ,
יְבָרְכֵנוּ אֱלֹהִים אֱלֹהֵינוּ: יְבָרְכֵנוּ אֱלֹהִים, וְיִירְאוּ אוֹתוֹ כָּל־אַפְסֵי־אָרֶץ:

Some say אדון עולם *(page 23) at this point.*

PRAYER UPON LEAVING THE SYNAGOGUE

Say while seated:

אַךְ Surely the righteous will praise Your name; Ps. 104
the upright shall live in Your presence.

Stand and say:

כִּי All the nations will walk, each in the name of its god;
and I will walk in the name of the LORD, the living God and eternal King.
My help comes from the LORD, Maker of heaven and earth. Ps. 121
The LORD will reign for ever and all time. Ex. 15

Walk toward the door of the synagogue, respectfully, without turning one's back, as one taking leave of the Divine Presence.
At the door, bow toward the Ark and say:

יהוה נְחֵנִי Lead me, LORD, in Your righteousness, Ps. 5
because of my foes; make Your way straight before me.

While leaving, say the following three verses:

גָּד Invaders may invade Gad, but he will invade at their heels. Gen. 49
David was wise in all that he did, and the LORD was with him. 1 Sam. 18
And Noah found favor in the eyes of the LORD. Gen. 6

One who will conduct business says:

עֶזְרִי My help comes from the LORD, Maker of heaven and earth. Cast your cares upon the LORD and He will sustain you. Watch the blameless, observe the upright, for there is a future for the peace-loving man. Trust in the LORD and do good, settle the land and cherish faithfulness. Behold, God is my salvation. I will trust and not be afraid. The LORD, the LORD, is my strength and my song. He has become my salvation. Master of the Universe, it is written in Your holy scriptures: "Love surrounds him who trusts in the LORD"; and it is written: "You give life to them all." LORD, God of truth, grant blessing and success to all the works of my hands. For I place my trust in You, that through my trade, through my profession, You will send me blessing, allowing me to sustain myself and the people of my household with ease, without suffering, by legal and not by forbidden means, for life and for peace. And may what is written be fulfilled in me: "Cast your cares upon the LORD and He will sustain you." Amen.

Ps. 121; Ps. 55; Ps. 37; Ibid.; Is. 12; Ps. 32; Neh. 9; Ps. 55

תפילה כשיוצא מבית הכנסת

Say while seated:

תהלים קמ אַךְ צַדִּיקִים יוֹדוּ לִשְׁמֶךָ, יֵשְׁבוּ יְשָׁרִים אֶת־פָּנֶיךָ:

Stand and say:

כִּי כָּל הָעַמִּים יֵלְכוּ אִישׁ בְּשֵׁם אֱלֹהָיו,
וַאֲנִי אֵלֵךְ בְּשֵׁם יהוה אֱלֹהִים חַיִּים וּמֶלֶךְ עוֹלָם.
תהלים קכא עֶזְרִי מֵעִם יהוה, עֹשֵׂה שָׁמַיִם וָאָרֶץ:
שמות טו יהוה יִמְלֹךְ לְעֹלָם וָעֶד:

Walk toward the door of the בית כנסת*, respectfully, without turning one's back, as one taking leave of the Divine Presence.*
At the door, bow toward the ארון קדש *and say:*

תהלים ה יהוה נְחֵנִי בְצִדְקָתֶךָ לְמַעַן שׁוֹרְרָי, הַיְשַׁר לְפָנַי דַּרְכֶּךָ:

While leaving, say the following three verses:

בראשית מט גָּד גְּדוּד יְגוּדֶנּוּ, וְהוּא יָגֻד עָקֵב:
שמואל א׳ יח וַיְהִי דָוִד לְכָל־דְּרָכָו מַשְׂכִּיל, וַיהוה עִמּוֹ:
בראשית ו וְנֹחַ מָצָא חֵן בְּעֵינֵי יהוה:

One who will conduct business says:

תהלים קכא תהלים נה עֶזְרִי מֵעִם יהוה, עֹשֵׂה שָׁמַיִם וָאָרֶץ: הַשְׁלֵךְ עַל־יהוה יְהָבְךָ וְהוּא יְכַלְכְּלֶךָ:
תהלים לז שם שְׁמָר־תָּם וּרְאֵה יָשָׁר, כִּי־אַחֲרִית לְאִישׁ שָׁלוֹם: בְּטַח בַּיהוה וַעֲשֵׂה־
ישעיה יב טוֹב, שְׁכָן־אֶרֶץ וּרְעֵה אֱמוּנָה: הִנֵּה אֵל יְשׁוּעָתִי אֶבְטַח וְלֹא אֶפְחָד, כִּי־עָזִּי
וְזִמְרָת יָהּ יהוה וַיְהִי־לִי לִישׁוּעָה: רִבּוֹנוֹ שֶׁל עוֹלָם, בְּדִבְרֵי קָדְשְׁךָ כָּתוּב
תהלים לב נחמיה ט לֵאמֹר, הַבּוֹטֵחַ בַּיהוה חֶסֶד יְסוֹבְבֶנּוּ: וּכְתִיב, וְאַתָּה מְחַיֶּה אֶת־כֻּלָּם:
יהוה אֱלֹהִים אֱמֶת, תֵּן בְּרָכָה וְהַצְלָחָה בְּכָל מַעֲשֵׂה יָדַי, כִּי בְטַחְתִּי
בְךָ שֶׁעַל יְדֵי מַשָּׂא וּמַתָּן וַעֲסָקִים שֶׁלִּי תִּשְׁלַח לִי בְּרָכָה, כְּדֵי שֶׁאוּכַל
לְפַרְנֵס אֶת עַצְמִי וּבְנֵי בֵיתִי בְּנַחַת וְלֹא בְצַעַר, בְּהֶתֵּר וְלֹא בְאִסּוּר,
תהלים נה לְחַיִּים וּלְשָׁלוֹם. וִיקֻיַּם בִּי מִקְרָא שֶׁכָּתוּב: הַשְׁלֵךְ עַל־יהוה יְהָבְךָ וְהוּא
יְכַלְכְּלֶךָ, אָמֵן.

PERSONAL SUPPLICATIONS

Some have the custom to read on a daily basis certain passages from the Torah, either in supplication to God that He may grant us our daily needs (both material and spiritual), or as a reminder that all our blessings come ultimately from Him.

THE CHAPTER OF THE MANNA

After the exodus from Egypt, the Israelites depended each day on the manna for their survival. Nowadays, we risk living under the illusion of self-reliance, and forgetting the true source of our sustenance. As early as the thirteenth century, the pupils of the Maharam of Rothenburg recommended reciting the verses which describe the miracle of the manna, as a declaration of faith and an expression of trust and gratitude.

יְהִי רָצוֹן May it be Your will, Lord our God, God of our ancestors, that you call forth sustenance for all Your people Israel, and among them, for me and for the people of my household. May it come with ease, without suffering, honorably, without shame, by legal and not by forbidden means, that we may perform Your service and learn Your Torah; just as You nourished our ancestors in the wilderness, in an arid, desert land.

וַיֹּאמֶר The Lord said to Moses: I shall rain bread down upon you from the sky. And the people shall go out and gather, each day their daily needs, so that I may test whether they will follow My Law or not. And on the sixth day, as they prepare what they bring home, it shall be twice what they gather every day. And so Moses and Aaron told all the people of Israel, "By evening you shall know that it was the Lord who brought you out of the land of Egypt, and in the morning you shall see the glory of God, who has heard all your protest against Him – as for us, who are we that you should stir up protest against us?" Moses said, "The Lord shall give you meat to eat in the evening, and bread in the morning to satisfy your hunger, when the Lord heeds the protest you have stirred up against Him – as for us, who are we? Your protest is not for us but for the Lord." Then Moses said to Aaron, "Tell all the congregation of Israel: Draw near to the Lord, for He has heard your protest." And when Aaron spoke to all the congregation of Israel, they turned toward the desert and there was the glory of God, revealed in a cloud. *Ex. 16*

The Lord said to Moses, "I have heard the protest of the people of Israel. Speak to them, tell them, by evening you shall eat meat, and in the morning, bread will satisfy you, and you shall know that I am the Lord your God." When evening came, quail rose up and covered the camp, and in the morning, a layer of dew surrounded the camp. And as the layer of dew lifted – there on the surface of the desert was a fine, round substance, fine as frost upon the land. And the

בקשות אישיות

Some have the custom to read on a daily basis certain passages from the תורה*, either in supplication to God that He may grant us our daily needs (both material and spiritual), or as a reminder that all our blessings come ultimately from Him.*

פרשת המן

After the exodus from Egypt, the Israelites depended each day on the manna for their survival. Nowadays, we risk living under the illusion of self-reliance, and forgetting the true source of our sustenance. As early as the thirteenth century, the pupils of the Maharam of Rothenburg recommended reciting the verses which describe the miracle of the manna, as a declaration of faith and an expression of trust and gratitude.

יְהִי רָצוֹן מִלְּפָנֶיךָ, יהוה אֱלֹהֵינוּ וֵאלֹהֵי אֲבוֹתֵינוּ, שֶׁתַּזְמִין פַּרְנָסָה לְכָל עַמְּךָ בֵּית יִשְׂרָאֵל, וּפַרְנָסָתִי וּפַרְנָסַת אַנְשֵׁי בֵיתִי בִּכְלָלָם, בְּנַחַת וְלֹא בְצַעַר, בְּכָבוֹד וְלֹא בְבִזּוּי, בְּהֶתֵּר וְלֹא בְאִסּוּר, כְּדֵי שֶׁנּוּכַל לַעֲבֹד עֲבוֹדָתֶךָ וְלִלְמֹד תּוֹרָתֶךָ, כְּמוֹ שֶׁזַּנְתָּ לַאֲבוֹתֵינוּ מָן בַּמִּדְבָּר, בְּאֶרֶץ צִיָּה וַעֲרָבָה.

וַיֹּאמֶר יהוה אֶל־מֹשֶׁה, הִנְנִי מַמְטִיר לָכֶם לֶחֶם מִן־הַשָּׁמָיִם, וְיָצָא הָעָם שמות טז
וְלָקְטוּ דְּבַר־יוֹם בְּיוֹמוֹ, לְמַעַן אֲנַסֶּנּוּ הֲיֵלֵךְ בְּתוֹרָתִי אִם־לֹא: וְהָיָה בַּיּוֹם הַשִּׁשִּׁי, וְהֵכִינוּ אֵת אֲשֶׁר־יָבִיאוּ, וְהָיָה מִשְׁנֶה עַל אֲשֶׁר־יִלְקְטוּ יוֹם יוֹם: וַיֹּאמֶר מֹשֶׁה וְאַהֲרֹן אֶל־כָּל־בְּנֵי יִשְׂרָאֵל, עֶרֶב וִידַעְתֶּם כִּי יהוה הוֹצִיא אֶתְכֶם מֵאֶרֶץ מִצְרָיִם: וּבֹקֶר וּרְאִיתֶם אֶת־כְּבוֹד יהוה, בְּשָׁמְעוֹ אֶת־תְּלֻנֹּתֵיכֶם עַל־יהוה, וְנַחְנוּ מָה כִּי תַלִּינוּ עָלֵינוּ: וַיֹּאמֶר מֹשֶׁה, בְּתֵת יהוה לָכֶם בָּעֶרֶב בָּשָׂר לֶאֱכֹל וְלֶחֶם בַּבֹּקֶר לִשְׂבֹּעַ, בִּשְׁמֹעַ יהוה אֶת־תְּלֻנֹּתֵיכֶם אֲשֶׁר־אַתֶּם מַלִּינִם עָלָיו, וְנַחְנוּ מָה, לֹא־עָלֵינוּ תְלֻנֹּתֵיכֶם כִּי עַל־יהוה: וַיֹּאמֶר מֹשֶׁה אֶל־אַהֲרֹן, אֱמֹר אֶל־כָּל־עֲדַת בְּנֵי יִשְׂרָאֵל, קִרְבוּ לִפְנֵי יהוה כִּי שָׁמַע אֵת תְּלֻנֹּתֵיכֶם: וַיְהִי כְּדַבֵּר אַהֲרֹן אֶל־כָּל־עֲדַת בְּנֵי־יִשְׂרָאֵל, וַיִּפְנוּ אֶל־הַמִּדְבָּר, וְהִנֵּה כְּבוֹד יהוה נִרְאָה בֶּעָנָן:

וַיְדַבֵּר יהוה אֶל־מֹשֶׁה לֵּאמֹר: שָׁמַעְתִּי אֶת־תְּלוּנֹּת בְּנֵי יִשְׂרָאֵל, דַּבֵּר אֲלֵהֶם לֵאמֹר בֵּין הָעַרְבַּיִם תֹּאכְלוּ בָשָׂר וּבַבֹּקֶר תִּשְׂבְּעוּ־לָחֶם, וִידַעְתֶּם כִּי אֲנִי יהוה אֱלֹהֵיכֶם: וַיְהִי בָעֶרֶב, וַתַּעַל הַשְּׂלָו וַתְּכַס אֶת־הַמַּחֲנֶה, וּבַבֹּקֶר הָיְתָה שִׁכְבַת הַטַּל סָבִיב לַמַּחֲנֶה: וַתַּעַל שִׁכְבַת הַטָּל, וְהִנֵּה עַל־פְּנֵי הַמִּדְבָּר דַּק מְחֻסְפָּס, דַּק כַּכְּפֹר עַל־הָאָרֶץ: וַיִּרְאוּ בְנֵי־יִשְׂרָאֵל וַיֹּאמְרוּ

children of Israel saw it and said one to another, "What is this?" not knowing what it could be. And Moses said, "This is the bread that the LORD has given you to eat. This is what the LORD has commanded: gather it, each person as much as he eats, an omer a head, as many as you are; let each man bring enough for the people in his tent." And so the people of Israel did; they each gathered; some much and some but little. And they measured what they had taken by the omer, and the ones who took much had no more, and the ones who took little had no less; each man had gathered as much as he would eat. Moses told them, "Let no man leave any of this behind until the morning." But they did not heed Moses, and some left some until the morning, and it became infested with worms and rotted, and Moses was furious with them. They gathered it early in the morning, each man as much as he would eat; and as the sun grew hot, it melted away. On the sixth day they gathered double bread, two omarim for each person, and all the princes of the congregation came and told Moses of it. And he said, "This is what the LORD has said: Tomorrow is a holy Sabbath of utter rest to the LORD – whatever you will bake, bake now, and whatever you will cook, cook; and all that is left over, save until the morning." So they left it for the morning as Moses had charged them; and it did not rot, and no worm was found in it. And Moses said, "Eat it today, for today is the Sabbath of the LORD; today you shall not find it outside. Six days shall you gather it, and on the seventh, the Sabbath, it will not be there." There were those of the people who went out on the seventh day to gather; but no manna did they find.

And the LORD said to Moses, "How long will you refuse to keep My commands and My Law? Look – the LORD has given you the Sabbath; and so He gave you two days' bread on the sixth day; each of you, sit in your places, and let no man leave his home on the seventh day." And so the people rested on the seventh day. The people of Israel named that substance, "Manna." And it looked like coriander seeds, but white, and its taste was that of flatbread made with honey. And Moses said, "This is what the LORD has commanded: An omer measure of this shall be kept down your generations, that you may see the bread that I fed you with in the desert when I brought you out of the land of Egypt." And Moses said to Aaron, "Take a jar and fill it with an omer of manna, and place it in the LORD's presence to be kept through the generations." So, as the LORD commanded Moses, Aaron placed it before the Testimony to be kept there. And the children of Israel ate the manna for forty years, until they arrived in settled land; they ate manna until they came to the borders of the Land of Canaan. An omer is the tenth of an ephah measure.

אִישׁ אֶל־אָחִיו מָן הוּא, כִּי לֹא יָדְעוּ מַה־הוּא, וַיֹּאמֶר מֹשֶׁה אֲלֵהֶם, הוּא הַלֶּחֶם אֲשֶׁר נָתַן יהוה לָכֶם לְאָכְלָה: זֶה הַדָּבָר אֲשֶׁר צִוָּה יהוה, לִקְטוּ מִמֶּנּוּ אִישׁ לְפִי אָכְלוֹ, עֹמֶר לַגֻּלְגֹּלֶת מִסְפַּר נַפְשֹׁתֵיכֶם, אִישׁ לַאֲשֶׁר בְּאָהֳלוֹ תִּקָּחוּ: וַיַּעֲשׂוּ־כֵן בְּנֵי יִשְׂרָאֵל, וַיִּלְקְטוּ הַמַּרְבֶּה וְהַמַּמְעִיט: וַיָּמֹדּוּ בָעֹמֶר, וְלֹא הֶעְדִּיף הַמַּרְבֶּה וְהַמַּמְעִיט לֹא הֶחְסִיר, אִישׁ לְפִי־אָכְלוֹ לָקָטוּ: וַיֹּאמֶר מֹשֶׁה אֲלֵהֶם, אִישׁ אַל־יוֹתֵר מִמֶּנּוּ עַד־בֹּקֶר: וְלֹא־שָׁמְעוּ אֶל־מֹשֶׁה, וַיּוֹתִרוּ אֲנָשִׁים מִמֶּנּוּ עַד־בֹּקֶר, וַיָּרֻם תּוֹלָעִים וַיִּבְאַשׁ, וַיִּקְצֹף עֲלֵהֶם מֹשֶׁה: וַיִּלְקְטוּ אֹתוֹ בַּבֹּקֶר בַּבֹּקֶר אִישׁ כְּפִי אָכְלוֹ, וְחַם הַשֶּׁמֶשׁ וְנָמָס: וַיְהִי בַּיּוֹם הַשִּׁשִּׁי לָקְטוּ לֶחֶם מִשְׁנֶה, שְׁנֵי הָעֹמֶר לָאֶחָד, וַיָּבֹאוּ כָּל־נְשִׂיאֵי הָעֵדָה וַיַּגִּידוּ לְמֹשֶׁה: וַיֹּאמֶר אֲלֵהֶם, הוּא אֲשֶׁר דִּבֶּר יהוה, שַׁבָּתוֹן שַׁבַּת־קֹדֶשׁ לַיהוה מָחָר, אֵת אֲשֶׁר־תֹּאפוּ אֵפוּ וְאֵת אֲשֶׁר־תְּבַשְּׁלוּ בַּשֵּׁלוּ, וְאֵת כָּל־הָעֹדֵף הַנִּיחוּ לָכֶם לְמִשְׁמֶרֶת עַד־הַבֹּקֶר: וַיַּנִּיחוּ אֹתוֹ עַד־הַבֹּקֶר כַּאֲשֶׁר צִוָּה מֹשֶׁה, וְלֹא הִבְאִישׁ וְרִמָּה לֹא־הָיְתָה בּוֹ: וַיֹּאמֶר מֹשֶׁה אִכְלֻהוּ הַיּוֹם כִּי־שַׁבָּת הַיּוֹם לַיהוה, הַיּוֹם לֹא תִמְצָאֻהוּ בַּשָּׂדֶה: שֵׁשֶׁת יָמִים תִּלְקְטֻהוּ, וּבַיּוֹם הַשְּׁבִיעִי שַׁבָּת לֹא יִהְיֶה־בּוֹ: וַיְהִי בַּיּוֹם הַשְּׁבִיעִי יָצְאוּ מִן־הָעָם לִלְקֹט, וְלֹא מָצָאוּ: וַיֹּאמֶר יהוה אֶל־מֹשֶׁה, עַד־אָנָה מֵאַנְתֶּם לִשְׁמֹר מִצְוֺתַי וְתוֹרֹתָי: רְאוּ כִּי־יהוה נָתַן לָכֶם הַשַּׁבָּת, עַל־כֵּן הוּא נֹתֵן לָכֶם בַּיּוֹם הַשִּׁשִּׁי לֶחֶם יוֹמָיִם, שְׁבוּ אִישׁ תַּחְתָּיו, אַל־יֵצֵא אִישׁ מִמְּקֹמוֹ בַּיּוֹם הַשְּׁבִיעִי: וַיִּשְׁבְּתוּ הָעָם בַּיּוֹם הַשְּׁבִעִי: וַיִּקְרְאוּ בֵית־יִשְׂרָאֵל אֶת־שְׁמוֹ מָן, וְהוּא כְּזֶרַע גַּד לָבָן, וְטַעְמוֹ כְּצַפִּיחִת בִּדְבָשׁ: וַיֹּאמֶר מֹשֶׁה זֶה הַדָּבָר אֲשֶׁר צִוָּה יהוה, מְלֹא הָעֹמֶר מִמֶּנּוּ לְמִשְׁמֶרֶת לְדֹרֹתֵיכֶם, לְמַעַן יִרְאוּ אֶת־הַלֶּחֶם אֲשֶׁר הֶאֱכַלְתִּי אֶתְכֶם בַּמִּדְבָּר, בְּהוֹצִיאִי אֶתְכֶם מֵאֶרֶץ מִצְרָיִם: וַיֹּאמֶר מֹשֶׁה אֶל־אַהֲרֹן, קַח צִנְצֶנֶת אַחַת וְתֶן־שָׁמָּה מְלֹא־הָעֹמֶר מָן, וְהַנַּח אֹתוֹ לִפְנֵי יהוה לְמִשְׁמֶרֶת לְדֹרֹתֵיכֶם: כַּאֲשֶׁר צִוָּה יהוה אֶל־מֹשֶׁה, וַיַּנִּיחֵהוּ אַהֲרֹן לִפְנֵי הָעֵדֻת לְמִשְׁמָרֶת: וּבְנֵי יִשְׂרָאֵל אָכְלוּ אֶת־הַמָּן אַרְבָּעִים שָׁנָה, עַד־בֹּאָם אֶל־אֶרֶץ נוֹשָׁבֶת, אֶת־הַמָּן אָכְלוּ עַד־בֹּאָם אֶל־קְצֵה אֶרֶץ כְּנָעַן: וְהָעֹמֶר עֲשִׂרִית הָאֵיפָה הוּא:

PRAYER FOR SUSTENANCE

אָנָּא Please, LORD who prepares sustenance for every creation, and calls forth clothing for all who have been made, and sends them their nourishment – grant me nourishment in plenty, provide for me and sustain me, and grant me and all the members of my household, and all of Israel, sustenance in plenty, honorable and obtained in serenity, without suffering, in legal ways and not forbidden ones, with honor and without disgrace, a sustenance with no shame or humiliation. A sustenance by which You will never make me needy of the gifts of other people, but only of Your full, broad hand; a sustenance that will allow me to engage in study of Your holy, pure and perfect Torah, pure meat, easily prepared; my bread and the bread of the people of my household – all our needs before we come to need them – so that my mind may be free of all worry to engage in study of the words of the Torah and to fulfill the commands, and to dwell in peace at my table, honorable, with all my household, without waiting to be invited to the tables of others. So that I will not be subject to any man, and that I will have the yoke of no man upon my shoulders, but only the yoke of Your kingship, making me serve You wholeheartedly, wearing clothes of honor; let our clothing be costly and not shameful. And save us from poverty, from vulnerability and shame, and allow me the merit of welcoming guests and dealing generously with every person. Send opportunities for me to give charity to those who deserve it, and let me not fall at the hands of dishonest people. Amen.

THE CHAPTER OF REVERENCE

In his final address before his death, Moses charges the people of Israel with loving God and holding Him in reverence, reminding them of God's combined majesty and humility (see "May God give you," page 702), and recounting the miracles He has done for them.

וְעַתָּה And now, Israel, what does the LORD your God ask of you, but that you hold the LORD your God in awe, walk in His ways and love Him, serving the LORD your God with all your heart and all your soul; keeping the commands of the LORD and His laws, as I charge you on this day, as a blessing. The sky, the highest heavens, the earth and all that fills it, belong to the LORD. Yet the LORD delighted in your ancestors, and loved them, and He chose their children after them – chose you – from all the other nations, as you see this day. Now, open your hearts, and stiffen your necks no longer. For the LORD your God is the God of gods, the LORD of lords, the great, mighty and awesome God, who does not favor the powerful, or accept any bribe. He does justice for the orphan and the widow, and loves the stranger, giving him bread and clothing. And you shall love the stranger, for you were strangers in the land of Egypt. Hold the LORD your God in awe and serve Him, cling to Him and swear by His name. For He *Deut. 10*

תפילה על הפרנסה

אָנָּא הָאֵל הַמֵּכִין פַּרְנָסָה לְכָל בְּרִיָּה, וּמַזְמִין מַלְבּוּשׁ לְכָל נִבְרָא, וְשׁוֹלֵחַ לָהֶם מִחְיָה, שֶׁתִּתֵּן לִי מִחְיָתִי בְּשֶׁפִי, שֶׁתְּכַלְכְּלֵנִי וּתְפַרְנְסֵנִי לִי וּלְכָל אַנְשֵׁי בֵיתִי וּלְכָל יִשְׂרָאֵל פַּרְנָסָה טוֹבָה שֶׁל כָּבוֹד, בְּנַחַת וְלֹא בְצַעַר, בְּהֶתֵּר וְלֹא בְאִסּוּר, בְּכָבוֹד וְלֹא בְבִזּוּי. פַּרְנָסָה שֶׁלֹּא תִהְיֶה בָהּ שׁוּם בּוּשָׁה וּכְלִמָּה, פַּרְנָסָה שֶׁלֹּא תַצְרִיכֵנִי בָהּ לִידֵי מַתְּנַת בָּשָׂר וָדָם, כִּי אִם לְיָדְךָ הַמְּלֵאָה וְהָרְחָבָה, פַּרְנָסָה שֶׁאוּכַל לַעֲסֹק בְּתוֹרָתְךָ הַקְּדוֹשָׁה וְהַטְּהוֹרָה וְהַתְּמִימָה, וְטֶרֶף נָקִי וּמְזֻמָּן וּמְזוֹנוֹתַי וּמְזוֹנוֹת אַנְשֵׁי בֵיתִי וְכָל צְרָכֵנוּ קֹדֶם שֶׁנִּצְטָרֵךְ לָהֶם, כְּדֵי שֶׁיִּהְיֶה לִבִּי פָּנוּי בְּלִי טִרְדָּה לַעֲסֹק בְּדִבְרֵי תוֹרָה וּלְקַיֵּם הַמִּצְוֹת, וְלֵישֵׁב בְּשָׁלוֹם עַל שֻׁלְחָנִי בְּכָבוֹד עִם כָּל בְּנֵי בֵיתִי. וְשֶׁלֹּא אֲצַפֶּה לְשֻׁלְחָן שֶׁל אֲחֵרִים, וְשֶׁלֹּא אֶצְטָרֵךְ לְהִשְׁתַּעְבֵּד לְשׁוּם אָדָם, וְשֶׁלֹּא יְהֵא עָלַי שׁוּם עֹל בָּשָׂר וָדָם, כִּי אִם עֹל מַלְכוּתְךָ לְעָבְדְּךָ בְּלֵבָב שָׁלֵם. וּבִגְדֵי כָבוֹד יִהְיוּ לְבוּשֵׁינוּ, בְּיֹקֶר וְלֹא בְבֹשֶׁת פָּנִים. וְהַצִּילֵנוּ מִן עֲנִיּוּת וּמִדַּלּוּת וְשִׁפְלוּת, וְאֶזְכֶּה לְהַכְנִיס אוֹרְחִים וְלִגְמֹל חֶסֶד לְכָל אָדָם. וְהַזְמֵן לִי לַעֲשׂוֹת צְדָקָה לָהֲרָאוּיִים לָהּ, וְלֹא אֶכָּשֵׁל בִּבְנֵי אָדָם שֶׁאֵינָם הֲגוּנִים, אָמֵן.

פרשת היראה

In his final address before his death, Moses charges the people of Israel with loving God and holding Him in reverence, reminding them of God's combined majesty and humility (see וַיִּתֶּן־לְךָ*, page 703), and recounting the miracles He has done for them.*

דברים י וְעַתָּה יִשְׂרָאֵל, מָה יהוה אֱלֹהֶיךָ שֹׁאֵל מֵעִמָּךְ, כִּי אִם־לְיִרְאָה אֶת־יהוה אֱלֹהֶיךָ לָלֶכֶת בְּכָל־דְּרָכָיו וּלְאַהֲבָה אֹתוֹ, וְלַעֲבֹד אֶת־יהוה אֱלֹהֶיךָ בְּכָל־לְבָבְךָ וּבְכָל־נַפְשֶׁךָ: לִשְׁמֹר אֶת־מִצְוֹת יהוה וְאֶת־חֻקֹּתָיו, אֲשֶׁר אָנֹכִי מְצַוְּךָ הַיּוֹם, לְטוֹב לָךְ: הֵן לַיהוה אֱלֹהֶיךָ הַשָּׁמַיִם וּשְׁמֵי הַשָּׁמָיִם, הָאָרֶץ וְכָל־אֲשֶׁר־בָּהּ: רַק בַּאֲבֹתֶיךָ חָשַׁק יהוה לְאַהֲבָה אוֹתָם, וַיִּבְחַר בְּזַרְעָם אַחֲרֵיהֶם, בָּכֶם מִכָּל־הָעַמִּים, כַּיּוֹם הַזֶּה: וּמַלְתֶּם אֵת עָרְלַת לְבַבְכֶם, וְעָרְפְּכֶם לֹא תַקְשׁוּ עוֹד: כִּי יהוה אֱלֹהֵיכֶם הוּא אֱלֹהֵי הָאֱלֹהִים וַאֲדֹנֵי הָאֲדֹנִים, הָאֵל הַגָּדֹל הַגִּבֹּר וְהַנּוֹרָא, אֲשֶׁר לֹא־יִשָּׂא פָנִים וְלֹא יִקַּח שֹׁחַד: עֹשֶׂה מִשְׁפַּט יָתוֹם וְאַלְמָנָה, וְאֹהֵב גֵּר לָתֶת לוֹ לֶחֶם וְשִׂמְלָה: וַאֲהַבְתֶּם אֶת־הַגֵּר, כִּי־גֵרִים הֱיִיתֶם בְּאֶרֶץ מִצְרָיִם: אֶת־יהוה אֱלֹהֶיךָ תִּירָא, אֹתוֹ תַעֲבֹד, וּבוֹ תִדְבָּק

is your glory and He is the God who performed with you these great and awesome things that your eyes have witnessed. Your ancestors were but seventy souls when they went down to Egypt, and now the LORD your God has made you as many as the stars of the sky.

You shall love the LORD your God, and keep what He gives you to guard, His statutes, His laws and His commands, every day of your lives. And know this day – for your children do not know and did not see what the LORD your God has taught you – His greatness, His mighty hand and His outstretched arm; His signs and the acts He has performed in Egypt, against Pharaoh, king of Egypt and all his land; and what He did to all the army of Egypt, its horses and its chariots, which He drowned in the waters of the Sea of Reeds before their eyes, as they chased after you – and the LORD destroyed them, gone to this very day; and what He did for you in the desert, until you came to this place; and what He did to Datan and to Aviram, the sons of Eliav, son of Reuben, when the earth opened her mouth and swallowed them, their families and their tents and everything that was theirs, in the very midst of all Israel – it is your eyes that have seen all the great work of the LORD that He has done. And you shall keep all the command that I charge you with on this day, that you may be strong and come and inherit the land that you are soon to cross over to and inherit; and so that you may live long upon the land that the LORD promised to give your ancestors and their descendants; a land flowing with milk and honey.

יְהִי רָצוֹן May it be Your will, LORD my God and God of my ancestors, that You plant the love and the awe of You in my heart, and in the hearts of all Israel, Your people, that we may revere Your great, mighty and awesome name, with all our heart and soul – in awe of the sublimity of the Infinite One; may Your name be blessed and raised high, for You are great and Your name is awesome, Amen, Selah.

THE CHAPTER OF REPENTANCE

This passage comes from the end of Moses' final address. After describing the blessings which might be conferred by keeping the covenant and the repercussions of breaking it, Moses promises the people that the punishment incurred will not be irrevocable; the gates of repentance are always open, and by returning to God the people might yet be redeemed. These verses were later interwoven into the prayer for the State of Israel (page 522) to express the hope that this first stage of redemption will lead to its full flowering, with the ingathering of all exiles and the opening of our hearts to truly loving and revering God.

וְהָיָה And when all these things come upon you, the blessing and the curse that I have laid before you now – you shall take this to heart, as you dwell with all the nations among whom the LORD your God has scattered you. And you will *Deut. 30*

וּבִשְׁמוֹ תִּשָּׁבֵעַ: הוּא תְהִלָּתְךָ וְהוּא אֱלֹהֶיךָ, אֲשֶׁר־עָשָׂה אִתְּךָ אֶת־הַגְּדֹלֹת וְאֶת־הַנּוֹרָאֹת הָאֵלֶּה אֲשֶׁר רָאוּ עֵינֶיךָ: בְּשִׁבְעִים נֶפֶשׁ יָרְדוּ אֲבֹתֶיךָ מִצְרָיְמָה, וְעַתָּה שָׂמְךָ יהוה אֱלֹהֶיךָ כְּכוֹכְבֵי הַשָּׁמַיִם לָרֹב: וְאָהַבְתָּ אֵת יהוה אֱלֹהֶיךָ, וְשָׁמַרְתָּ מִשְׁמַרְתּוֹ וְחֻקֹּתָיו וּמִשְׁפָּטָיו וּמִצְוֺתָיו כָּל־הַיָּמִים: וִידַעְתֶּם הַיּוֹם, כִּי לֹא אֶת־בְּנֵיכֶם אֲשֶׁר לֹא־יָדְעוּ וַאֲשֶׁר לֹא־רָאוּ אֶת־מוּסַר יהוה אֱלֹהֵיכֶם, אֶת־גָּדְלוֹ אֶת־יָדוֹ הַחֲזָקָה וּזְרֹעוֹ הַנְּטוּיָה: וְאֶת־אֹתֹתָיו וְאֶת־מַעֲשָׂיו אֲשֶׁר עָשָׂה בְּתוֹךְ מִצְרָיִם, לְפַרְעֹה מֶלֶךְ־מִצְרַיִם וּלְכָל־אַרְצוֹ: וַאֲשֶׁר עָשָׂה לְחֵיל מִצְרַיִם לְסוּסָיו וּלְרִכְבּוֹ, אֲשֶׁר הֵצִיף אֶת־מֵי יַם־סוּף עַל־פְּנֵיהֶם בְּרָדְפָם אַחֲרֵיכֶם, וַיְאַבְּדֵם יהוה עַד הַיּוֹם הַזֶּה: וַאֲשֶׁר עָשָׂה לָכֶם בַּמִּדְבָּר, עַד־בֹּאֲכֶם עַד־הַמָּקוֹם הַזֶּה: וַאֲשֶׁר עָשָׂה לְדָתָן וְלַאֲבִירָם בְּנֵי אֱלִיאָב בֶּן־רְאוּבֵן, אֲשֶׁר פָּצְתָה הָאָרֶץ אֶת־פִּיהָ וַתִּבְלָעֵם וְאֶת־בָּתֵּיהֶם וְאֶת־אָהֳלֵיהֶם, וְאֵת כָּל־הַיְקוּם אֲשֶׁר בְּרַגְלֵיהֶם בְּקֶרֶב כָּל־יִשְׂרָאֵל: כִּי עֵינֵיכֶם הָרֹאֹת אֵת כָּל־מַעֲשֵׂה יהוה הַגָּדֹל, אֲשֶׁר עָשָׂה: וּשְׁמַרְתֶּם אֶת־כָּל־הַמִּצְוָה אֲשֶׁר אָנֹכִי מְצַוְּךָ הַיּוֹם, לְמַעַן תֶּחֶזְקוּ וּבָאתֶם וִירִשְׁתֶּם אֶת־הָאָרֶץ אֲשֶׁר אַתֶּם עֹבְרִים שָׁמָּה לְרִשְׁתָּהּ: וּלְמַעַן תַּאֲרִיכוּ יָמִים עַל־הָאֲדָמָה אֲשֶׁר נִשְׁבַּע יהוה לַאֲבֹתֵיכֶם לָתֵת לָהֶם וּלְזַרְעָם, אֶרֶץ זָבַת חָלָב וּדְבָשׁ:

יְהִי רָצוֹן מִלְּפָנֶיךָ, יהוה אֱלֹהַי וֵאלֹהֵי אֲבוֹתַי, שֶׁתִּטַּע אַהֲבָתְךָ וְיִרְאָתְךָ בְּלִבִּי וּבְלֵב כָּל יִשְׂרָאֵל עַמֶּךָ, לְיִרְאָה אֶת שִׁמְךָ הַגָּדוֹל הַגִּבּוֹר וְהַנּוֹרָא בְּכָל לְבָבֵנוּ וּבְכָל נַפְשֵׁנוּ, יִרְאַת הָרוֹמְמוּת שֶׁל אֵין סוֹף בָּרוּךְ הוּא, וְיִתְעַלֶּה שִׁמְךָ. כִּי גָדוֹל אַתָּה וְנוֹרָא שְׁמֶךָ, אָמֵן סֶלָה.

פרשת התשובה

This passage comes from the end of Moses' final address. After describing the blessings which might be conferred by keeping the covenant and the repercussions of breaking it, Moses promises the people that the punishment incurred will not be irrevocable; the gates of repentance are always open, and by returning to God the people might yet be redeemed. These verses were later interwoven into the תפילה לשלום מדינת ישראל *(page 523) to express the hope that this first stage of redemption will lead to its full flowering, with the ingathering of all exiles and the opening of our hearts to truly loving and revering God.*

וְהָיָה כִי־יָבֹאוּ עָלֶיךָ כָּל־הַדְּבָרִים הָאֵלֶּה, הַבְּרָכָה וְהַקְּלָלָה אֲשֶׁר נָתַתִּי דברים ל
לְפָנֶיךָ, וַהֲשֵׁבֹתָ אֶל־לְבָבֶךָ בְּכָל־הַגּוֹיִם אֲשֶׁר הִדִּיחֲךָ יהוה אֱלֹהֶיךָ שָׁמָּה:

return to the LORD your God, and you will listen to His voice, just as I charge you on this day, you and your children, with all your heart and all your soul. And the LORD shall restore your fortunes, and have compassion for you, and will return and gather you in from all the nations among whom the LORD has dispersed you. Even if you are scattered to the furthermost lands under the heavens, from there the LORD your God will gather you and take you back. The LORD your God will bring you to the land your ancestors possessed and you will possess it; and He will make you more prosperous and numerous than your ancestors. Then the LORD your God will open up your heart and the heart of your descendants, to love the LORD your God with all your heart and with all your soul, that you may live. And as for all these curses the LORD your God will place them upon your enemies, upon those who hate you and who persecute you. And you will return and listen again to the voice of the LORD, and will fulfill all the commands that I charge you with this day. And the LORD your God will give you plenty in all the works of your hand, your young, the young of your cattle, the fruits of the land, for the good, for the LORD will come back to rejoice in you for the good, just as He rejoiced in your ancestors. For you shall listen to the voice of the LORD your God, keeping His commands and His statutes, as they are written in this scroll of the Torah, for you shall return to the LORD your God with all your heart and with all your soul.

יְהִי רָצוֹן May it be Your will, LORD my God and God of my ancestors, that You dig a passage for us beneath the walls to tunnel through to the throne of Your glory, returning all the sinners of Your people in full repentance – for Your right hand is outstretched to receive those who return, and You desire our repentance, Amen, Selah.

וְשַׁבְתָּ עַד־יהוה אֱלֹהֶיךָ וְשָׁמַעְתָּ בְקֹלוֹ, כְּכֹל אֲשֶׁר־אָנֹכִי מְצַוְּךָ הַיּוֹם, אַתָּה וּבָנֶיךָ בְּכָל־לְבָבְךָ וּבְכָל־נַפְשֶׁךָ: וְשָׁב יהוה אֱלֹהֶיךָ אֶת־שְׁבוּתְךָ וְרִחֲמֶךָ, וְשָׁב וְקִבֶּצְךָ מִכָּל־הָעַמִּים אֲשֶׁר הֱפִיצְךָ יהוה אֱלֹהֶיךָ שָׁמָּה: אִם־יִהְיֶה נִדַּחֲךָ בִּקְצֵה הַשָּׁמָיִם, מִשָּׁם יְקַבֶּצְךָ יהוה אֱלֹהֶיךָ וּמִשָּׁם יִקָּחֶךָ: וֶהֱבִיאֲךָ יהוה אֱלֹהֶיךָ אֶל־הָאָרֶץ אֲשֶׁר־יָרְשׁוּ אֲבֹתֶיךָ וִירִשְׁתָּהּ, וְהֵיטִבְךָ וְהִרְבְּךָ מֵאֲבֹתֶיךָ: וּמָל יהוה אֱלֹהֶיךָ אֶת־לְבָבְךָ וְאֶת־לְבַב זַרְעֶךָ, לְאַהֲבָה אֶת־יהוה אֱלֹהֶיךָ בְּכָל־לְבָבְךָ וּבְכָל־נַפְשְׁךָ, לְמַעַן חַיֶּיךָ: וְנָתַן יהוה אֱלֹהֶיךָ אֵת כָּל־הָאָלוֹת הָאֵלֶּה עַל־אֹיְבֶיךָ וְעַל־שֹׂנְאֶיךָ אֲשֶׁר רְדָפוּךָ: וְאַתָּה תָשׁוּב וְשָׁמַעְתָּ בְּקוֹל יהוה, וְעָשִׂיתָ אֶת־כָּל־מִצְוֹתָיו אֲשֶׁר אָנֹכִי מְצַוְּךָ הַיּוֹם: וְהוֹתִירְךָ יהוה אֱלֹהֶיךָ בְּכֹל מַעֲשֵׂה יָדֶךָ, בִּפְרִי בִטְנְךָ וּבִפְרִי בְהֶמְתְּךָ וּבִפְרִי אַדְמָתְךָ, לְטֹבָה, כִּי יָשׁוּב יהוה לָשׂוּשׂ עָלֶיךָ לְטוֹב כַּאֲשֶׁר־שָׂשׂ עַל־אֲבֹתֶיךָ: כִּי תִשְׁמַע בְּקוֹל יהוה אֱלֹהֶיךָ, לִשְׁמֹר מִצְוֹתָיו וְחֻקֹּתָיו הַכְּתוּבָה בְּסֵפֶר הַתּוֹרָה הַזֶּה, כִּי תָשׁוּב אֶל־יהוה אֱלֹהֶיךָ בְּכָל־לְבָבְךָ וּבְכָל־נַפְשֶׁךָ:

יְהִי רָצוֹן מִלְּפָנֶיךָ, יהוה אֱלֹהַי וֵאלֹהֵי אֲבוֹתַי, שֶׁתַּחְתֹּר חֲתִירָה מִתַּחַת כִּסֵּא כְבוֹדֶךָ לְהַחֲזִיר בִּתְשׁוּבָה שְׁלֵמָה לְכָל פּוֹשְׁעֵי עַמְּךָ בֵּית יִשְׂרָאֵל, וּבִכְלָלָם תַּחֲזִירֵנִי בִּתְשׁוּבָה שְׁלֵמָה לְפָנֶיךָ, כִּי יְמִינְךָ פְּשׁוּטָה לְקַבֵּל שָׁבִים וְרוֹצֶה אַתָּה בִּתְשׁוּבָה, אָמֵן סֶלָה.

FOR PROTECTION FROM THE EVIL EYE

The following prayer, based on Rabbi Tzvi Hirsch Kaidanover's Kav HaYashar (Frankfurt, 1705), incorporates biblical verses as a segula (charm) for God's protection.

נֶגַע When the plague of tzara'at is found in a man, *Lev. 13*
he shall be brought before the priest.
We will pass over armed before the LORD into the land of Canaan, *Num. 32*
and possess our inheritance here on this side of the Jordan.
The LORD your God will raise up a prophet from your midst for you, *Deut. 18*
one of your brethren, like me; and it is him that you shall heed.
There is a river whose streams bring joy to the city of God, *Ps. 46*
the holy dwelling-place of the Most High.
You led Your people like a flock by the hand of Moses and Aaron. *Ps. 77*
He performed wonders in the sight of their fathers, in the land of Egypt, *Ps. 78*
in the fields of Tzo'an.
I have perfumed my bed with myrrh, aloes, and cinnamon. *Prov. 7*
The spirit of man is the candle of the LORD, *Prov. 20*
searching out all his inner chambers.
Your lips drip nectar, my bride; honey and milk lie under your tongue, *Song. 4*
and on your dress lingers Lebanon's scent.
Flee out of the midst of Babylonia; depart from the land of the Kasdim; *Jer. 50*
and be as the he-goats running before the flocks.
They were armed with bows, and could use both the right hand *1 Chr. 12*
and the left, slinging stones and shooting arrows from their bows;
they were Saul's brethren, from Benjamin.

רִבּוֹנוֹ Master of the Universe, shelter Your people Israel from every kind of sorcery, from every evil eye. And just as You spread Your wings over our ancestors in the desert, and did not allow the evil eye of Balaam son of Beor to have hold over them, so may You spread Your wings over us, in Your great compassion, that we may be protected (protected and guided,) by Your holy names, from every evil eye.

You are my shelter, You will shield me from distress; *Ps. 32*
You will surround me with songs of deliverance. Selah.

שמירה נגד עין הרע

The following prayer, based on Rabbi Tzvi Hirsch Kaidanover's קב הישר *(Frankfurt, 1705), incorporates biblical verses as a* סגולה *(charm) for God's protection.*

נֶגַע צָרַעַת כִּי תִהְיֶה בְּאָדָם וְהוּבָא אֶל־הַכֹּהֵן: ויקרא יג
נַחְנוּ נַעֲבֹר חֲלוּצִים לִפְנֵי יהוה אֶרֶץ כְּנָעַן במדבר לב
וְאִתָּנוּ אֲחֻזַּת נַחֲלָתֵנוּ מֵעֵבֶר לַיַּרְדֵּן:
נָבִיא מִקִּרְבְּךָ מֵאַחֶיךָ כָּמֹנִי יָקִים לְךָ יהוה אֱלֹהֶיךָ, אֵלָיו תִּשְׁמָעוּן: דברים יח
נָהָר פְּלָגָיו יְשַׂמְּחוּ עִיר־אֱלֹהִים, קְדֹשׁ מִשְׁכְּנֵי עֶלְיוֹן: תהלים מו
נָחִיתָ כַצֹּאן עַמֶּךָ בְּיַד־מֹשֶׁה וְאַהֲרֹן: תהלים עז
נֶגֶד אֲבוֹתָם עָשָׂה פֶלֶא בְּאֶרֶץ מִצְרַיִם שְׂדֵה־צֹעַן: תהלים עח
נַפְתִּי מִשְׁכָּבִי מֹר אֲהָלִים וְקִנָּמוֹן: משלי ז
נֵר יהוה נִשְׁמַת אָדָם חֹפֵשׂ כָּל־חַדְרֵי־בָטֶן: משלי כ
נֹפֶת תִּטֹּפְנָה שִׂפְתוֹתַיִךְ כַּלָּה שיר השירים ד
דְּבַשׁ וְחָלָב תַּחַת לְשׁוֹנֵךְ וְרֵיחַ שַׂלְמֹתַיִךְ כְּרֵיחַ לְבָנוֹן:
נֻדוּ מִתּוֹךְ בָּבֶל וּמֵאֶרֶץ כַּשְׂדִּים צֵאוּ, וִהְיוּ כְּעַתּוּדִים לִפְנֵי־צֹאן: ירמיה נ
נֹשְׁקֵי קֶשֶׁת מַיְמִינִים וּמַשְׂמִאלִים בָּאֲבָנִים וּבַחִצִּים בַּקָּשֶׁת דברי הימים א יב
מֵאֲחֵי שָׁאוּל מִבִּנְיָמִן:

רִבּוֹנוֹ שֶׁל עוֹלָם, הַצֵּל עַמְּךָ בֵּית יִשְׂרָאֵל מִכָּל מִינֵי כְשׁוּפִים וּמִכָּל מִינֵי עַיִן הָרָע, וּכְשֵׁם שֶׁפָּרַשְׂתָּ כְּנָפֶיךָ עַל אֲבוֹתֵינוּ שֶׁבַּמִּדְבָּר, שֶׁלֹּא שָׁלַט עֲלֵיהֶם עֵינָא בִישָׁא דְּבִלְעָם בֶּן בְּעוֹר, כֵּן תִּפְרֹס כְּנָפֶיךָ עָלֵינוּ בְּרַחֲמֶיךָ הָרַבִּים לִהְיוֹתֵנוּ מְכֻסִּים (בְּמִכְסֶה וּבְהַגָּנָה) בִּשְׁמוֹתֶיךָ הַקְּדוֹשִׁים מִכָּל עֵינָא בִישָׁא.

אַתָּה סֵתֶר לִי מִצַּר תִּצְּרֵנִי רָנֵּי פַלֵּט תְּסוֹבְבֵנִי סֶלָה: תהלים כב

Minḥa for Weekdays

אַשְׁרֵי Happy are those who dwell in Your House; Ps. 84
they shall continue to praise You, Selah!
Happy are the people for whom this is so; Ps. 144
happy are the people whose God is the LORD.
A song of praise by David. Ps. 145

א I will exalt You, my God, the King, and bless Your name for ever and all time. ב Every day I will bless You, and praise Your name for ever and all time. ג Great is the LORD and greatly to be praised; His greatness is unfathomable. ד One generation will praise Your works to the next, and tell of Your mighty deeds. ה On the glorious splendor of Your majesty I will meditate, and on the acts of Your wonders. ו They shall talk of the power of Your awesome deeds, and I will tell of Your greatness. ז They shall recite the record of Your great goodness, and sing with joy of Your righteousness. ח The LORD is gracious and compassionate, slow to anger and great in loving-kindness. ט The LORD is good to all, and His compassion extends to all His works. י All Your works shall thank You, LORD, and Your devoted ones shall bless You. כ They shall talk of the glory of Your kingship, and speak of Your might. ל To make known to mankind His mighty

---

Its form is simple. It begins with *Ashrei* as a prelude to prayer, the third of three daily recitals. The Amida is the same as in the morning with two changes. In the Leader's Repetition, the passage referring to the priestly blessing is not said, since in the Temple the priests did not bless the congregation in the afternoon. Likewise, a shorter form of the final blessing (associated with the priestly blessing in the Temple) is said. *Taḥanun* is also said at Minḥa, on days when it is said in the morning, except on the afternoon before Shabbat and Yom Tov and certain other occasions (see page 233). The service ends with *Aleinu*.

מנחה לחול

אַשְׁרֵי יוֹשְׁבֵי בֵיתֶךָ, עוֹד יְהַלְלְוּךָ סֶּלָה: תהלים פד
אַשְׁרֵי הָעָם שֶׁכָּכָה לּוֹ, אַשְׁרֵי הָעָם שֶׁיהוה אֱלֹהָיו: תהלים קמד
תְּהִלָּה לְדָוִד תהלים קמה
א אֲרוֹמִמְךָ אֱלוֹהַי הַמֶּלֶךְ, וַאֲבָרְכָה שִׁמְךָ לְעוֹלָם וָעֶד:
ב בְּכָל־יוֹם אֲבָרְכֶךָּ, וַאֲהַלְלָה שִׁמְךָ לְעוֹלָם וָעֶד:
ג גָּדוֹל יהוה וּמְהֻלָּל מְאֹד, וְלִגְדֻלָּתוֹ אֵין חֵקֶר:
ד דּוֹר לְדוֹר יְשַׁבַּח מַעֲשֶׂיךָ, וּגְבוּרֹתֶיךָ יַגִּידוּ:
ה הֲדַר כְּבוֹד הוֹדֶךָ, וְדִבְרֵי נִפְלְאֹתֶיךָ אָשִׂיחָה:
ו וֶעֱזוּז נוֹרְאֹתֶיךָ יֹאמֵרוּ, וּגְדוּלָּתְךָ אֲסַפְּרֶנָּה:
ז זֵכֶר רַב־טוּבְךָ יַבִּיעוּ, וְצִדְקָתְךָ יְרַנֵּנוּ:
ח חַנּוּן וְרַחוּם יהוה, אֶרֶךְ אַפַּיִם וּגְדָל־חָסֶד:
ט טוֹב־יהוה לַכֹּל, וְרַחֲמָיו עַל־כָּל־מַעֲשָׂיו:
י יוֹדְוּךָ יהוה כָּל־מַעֲשֶׂיךָ, וַחֲסִידֶיךָ יְבָרְכוּכָה:
כ כְּבוֹד מַלְכוּתְךָ יֹאמֵרוּ, וּגְבוּרָתְךָ יְדַבֵּרוּ:
ל לְהוֹדִיעַ לִבְנֵי הָאָדָם גְּבוּרֹתָיו, וּכְבוֹד הֲדַר מַלְכוּתוֹ:

AFTERNOON SERVICE

The afternoon service corresponds to the daily afternoon sacrifice (Num. 28:4). *Minḥa*, the "meal-offering," was not unique to the afternoon. The prayer may have acquired this name because of the verse in Psalms (141:2): "May my prayer be like incense before You, the lifting up of my hands like the afternoon offering (*minḥat arev*)." The sages attached special significance to this prayer, noting that Elijah's prayer was answered at this time (1 Kings 18:36).

deeds and the glorious majesty of His kingship. מ Your kingdom is an everlasting kingdom, and Your reign is for all generations. ס The LORD supports all who fall, and raises all who are bowed down. ע All raise their eyes to You in hope, and You give them their food in due season. פ You open Your hand, and satisfy every living thing with favor. צ The LORD is righteous in all His ways, and kind in all He does. ק The LORD is close to all who call on Him, to all who call on Him in truth. ר He fulfills the will of those who revere Him; He hears their cry and saves them. ש The LORD guards all who love Him, but all the wicked He will destroy. ▸ ת My mouth shall speak the praise of the LORD, and all creatures shall bless His holy name for ever and all time.

We will bless the LORD now and for ever. Halleluya! *Ps. 115*

HALF KADDISH

Leader: יִתְגַּדַּל Magnified and sanctified
may His great name be,
in the world He created by His will.
May He establish His kingdom
in your lifetime and in your days,
and in the lifetime of all the house of Israel,
swiftly and soon –
and say: Amen.

All: May His great name be blessed for ever and all time.

Leader: Blessed and praised, glorified and exalted,
raised and honored, uplifted and lauded
be the name of the Holy One, blessed be He,
beyond any blessing,
song, praise and consolation
uttered in the world –
and say: Amen.

On fast days, turn to Removing the Torah on page 158. The Torah reading and Haftara for fast days are on page 1112. After the Torah is returned to the Ark, the Leader says Half Kaddish.

מ מַלְכוּתְךָ מַלְכוּת כָּל־עֹלָמִים, וּמֶמְשַׁלְתְּךָ בְּכָל־דּוֹר וָדֹר:
ס סוֹמֵךְ יהוה לְכָל־הַנֹּפְלִים, וְזוֹקֵף לְכָל־הַכְּפוּפִים:
ע עֵינֵי־כֹל אֵלֶיךָ יְשַׂבֵּרוּ, וְאַתָּה נוֹתֵן־לָהֶם אֶת־אָכְלָם בְּעִתּוֹ:
פ פּוֹתֵחַ אֶת־יָדֶךָ, וּמַשְׂבִּיעַ לְכָל־חַי רָצוֹן:
צ צַדִּיק יהוה בְּכָל־דְּרָכָיו, וְחָסִיד בְּכָל־מַעֲשָׂיו:
ק קָרוֹב יהוה לְכָל־קֹרְאָיו, לְכֹל אֲשֶׁר יִקְרָאֻהוּ בֶאֱמֶת:
ר רְצוֹן־יְרֵאָיו יַעֲשֶׂה, וְאֶת־שַׁוְעָתָם יִשְׁמַע, וְיוֹשִׁיעֵם:
ש שׁוֹמֵר יהוה אֶת־כָּל־אֹהֲבָיו, וְאֵת כָּל־הָרְשָׁעִים יַשְׁמִיד:
◄ ת תְּהִלַּת יהוה יְדַבֶּר פִּי, וִיבָרֵךְ כָּל־בָּשָׂר שֵׁם קָדְשׁוֹ לְעוֹלָם וָעֶד:
וַאֲנַחְנוּ נְבָרֵךְ יָהּ מֵעַתָּה וְעַד־עוֹלָם, הַלְלוּיָהּ: תהלים קטו

חצי קדיש

ש״ץ: יִתְגַּדַּל וְיִתְקַדַּשׁ שְׁמֵהּ רַבָּא (קהל: אָמֵן)
בְּעָלְמָא דִּי בְרָא כִרְעוּתֵהּ
וְיַמְלִיךְ מַלְכוּתֵהּ
בְּחַיֵּיכוֹן וּבְיוֹמֵיכוֹן וּבְחַיֵּי דְכָל בֵּית יִשְׂרָאֵל
בַּעֲגָלָא וּבִזְמַן קָרִיב, וְאִמְרוּ אָמֵן. (קהל: אָמֵן)

קהל וש״ץ: יְהֵא שְׁמֵהּ רַבָּא מְבָרַךְ לְעָלַם וּלְעָלְמֵי עָלְמַיָּא.

ש״ץ: יִתְבָּרַךְ וְיִשְׁתַּבַּח וְיִתְפָּאַר וְיִתְרוֹמַם וְיִתְנַשֵּׂא
וְיִתְהַדָּר וְיִתְעַלֶּה וְיִתְהַלָּל
שְׁמֵהּ דְּקֻדְשָׁא בְּרִיךְ הוּא (קהל: בְּרִיךְ הוּא)
לְעֵלָּא מִן כָּל בִּרְכָתָא / בעשרת ימי תשובה: לְעֵלָּא לְעֵלָּא מִכָּל בִּרְכָתָא/
וְשִׁירָתָא, תֻּשְׁבְּחָתָא וְנֶחֱמָתָא
דַּאֲמִירָן בְּעָלְמָא, וְאִמְרוּ אָמֵן. (קהל: אָמֵן)

On fast days, turn to הוצאת ספר תורה *on page 159. The* תורה *reading and* הפטרה *for fast days are on page 1112. After the* תורה *is returned to the* ארון קודש*, the* שליח ציבור *says* חצי קדיש.

THE AMIDA

The following prayer, until "in former years" on page 230, is said silently, standing with feet together. If there is a minyan, the Amida is repeated aloud by the Leader. Take three steps forward and at the points indicated by ▾, bend the knees at the first word, bow at the second, and stand straight before saying God's name.

When I proclaim the LORD's name, give glory to our God. *Deut. 32*
O LORD, open my lips, so that my mouth may declare Your praise. *Ps. 51*

PATRIARCHS

▾בָּרוּךְ Blessed are You, LORD our God and God of our fathers,
God of Abraham, God of Isaac and God of Jacob;
the great, mighty and awesome God, God Most High,
who bestows acts of loving-kindness and creates all,
who remembers the loving-kindness of the fathers
and will bring a Redeemer to their children's children
for the sake of His name, in love.

Between Rosh HaShana & Yom Kippur: Remember us for life, O King who desires life,
and write us in the book of life –
for Your sake, O God of life.

King, Helper, Savior, Shield:
▾Blessed are You, LORD, Shield of Abraham.

DIVINE MIGHT

אַתָּה גִּבּוֹר You are eternally mighty, LORD.
You give life to the dead and have great power to save.

The phrase "He makes the wind blow and the rain fall" is added from Simḥat Torah until Pesaḥ. In Israel the phrase "He causes the dew to fall" is added from Pesaḥ until Shemini Atzeret. See laws 129–131.

In fall & winter: He makes the wind blow and the rain fall.

In Israel, in spring & summer: He causes the dew to fall.

"I am not a man of words… I am heavy of speech and tongue." Isaiah said, "I am a man of unclean lips." Jeremiah said, "I cannot speak for I am a child." So our first prayer is for divine help in the act of prayer itself.

עמידה

The following prayer, until קַדְמֹנִיּוֹת *on page 231, is said silently, standing with feet together. If there is a* מנין, *the* עמידה *is repeated aloud by the* שליח ציבור. *Take three steps forward and at the points indicated by* ', *bend the knees at the first word, bow at the second, and stand straight before saying God's name.*

כִּי שֵׁם יהוה אֶקְרָא, הָבוּ גֹדֶל לֵאלֹהֵינוּ: דברים לב

אֲדֹנָי, שְׂפָתַי תִּפְתָּח, וּפִי יַגִּיד תְּהִלָּתֶךָ: תהלים נא

אבות

'בָּרוּךְ אַתָּה יהוה, אֱלֹהֵינוּ וֵאלֹהֵי אֲבוֹתֵינוּ
אֱלֹהֵי אַבְרָהָם, אֱלֹהֵי יִצְחָק, וֵאלֹהֵי יַעֲקֹב
הָאֵל הַגָּדוֹל הַגִּבּוֹר וְהַנּוֹרָא, אֵל עֶלְיוֹן
גּוֹמֵל חֲסָדִים טוֹבִים, וְקוֹנֵה הַכֹּל
וְזוֹכֵר חַסְדֵי אָבוֹת
וּמֵבִיא גוֹאֵל לִבְנֵי בְנֵיהֶם לְמַעַן שְׁמוֹ בְּאַהֲבָה.

בעשרת ימי תשובה: זָכְרֵנוּ לְחַיִּים, מֶלֶךְ חָפֵץ בַּחַיִּים
וְכָתְבֵנוּ בְּסֵפֶר הַחַיִּים, לְמַעַנְךָ אֱלֹהִים חַיִּים.

מֶלֶךְ עוֹזֵר וּמוֹשִׁיעַ וּמָגֵן.
'בָּרוּךְ אַתָּה יהוה, מָגֵן אַבְרָהָם.

גבורות

אַתָּה גִּבּוֹר לְעוֹלָם, אֲדֹנָי
מְחַיֵּה מֵתִים אַתָּה, רַב לְהוֹשִׁיעַ

The phrase מַשִּׁיב הָרְוּחַ *is added from* שמחת תורה *until* פסח.
In ארץ ישראל *the phrase* מוֹרִיד הַטָּל *is added from* פסח *until* שמיני עצרת. *See laws 129–131.*

בחורף: מַשִּׁיב הָרְוּחַ וּמוֹרִיד הַגֶּשֶׁם / בארץ ישראל בקיץ: מוֹרִיד הַטָּל

אֲדֹנָי, שְׂפָתַי תִּפְתָּח *O Lord, open my lips:* Standing in the presence of God, we feel our inadequacy. The greatest of the prophets felt tongue-tied. Moses said,

He sustains the living with loving-kindness,
and with great compassion revives the dead.
He supports the fallen, heals the sick,
sets captives free,
and keeps His faith with those who sleep in the dust.
Who is like You, Master of might,
and who can compare to You,
O King who brings death and gives life,
and makes salvation grow?

Between Rosh HaShana & Yom Kippur: Who is like You, compassionate Father,
who remembers His creatures in compassion, for life?

Faithful are You to revive the dead.
Blessed are You, Lord, who revives the dead.

When saying the Amida silently, continue with "You are holy" on the next page.

KEDUSHA

During the Leader's Repetition, the following is said standing with feet together, rising on the toes at the words indicated by ▲.

Cong. then Leader: נְקַדֵּשׁ We will sanctify Your name on earth,
as they sanctify it in the highest heavens,
as is written by Your prophet,
"And they [the angels] call to one another saying: *Is. 6*

Cong. then Leader: ▲Holy, ▲holy, ▲holy is the Lord of hosts
the whole world is filled with His glory."
Those facing them say "Blessed – "

Cong. then Leader: ▲"Blessed is the Lord's glory from His place." *Ezek. 3*
And in Your holy Writings it is written thus:

Cong. then Leader: ▲"The Lord shall reign for ever. He is your God, Zion, *Ps. 146*
from generation to generation, Halleluya!"

Leader: From generation to generation we will declare Your greatness,
and we will proclaim Your holiness for evermore.
Your praise, our God, shall not leave our mouth forever,
for You, God, are a great and holy King. Blessed are You, Lord,
the holy God. / *Between Rosh HaShana & Yom Kippur:* the holy King./

The Leader continues with "You grace humanity" on the next page.

מְכַלְכֵּל חַיִּים בְּחֶסֶד, מְחַיֵּה מֵתִים בְּרַחֲמִים רַבִּים
סוֹמֵךְ נוֹפְלִים, וְרוֹפֵא חוֹלִים, וּמַתִּיר אֲסוּרִים
וּמְקַיֵּם אֱמוּנָתוֹ לִישֵׁנֵי עָפָר.
מִי כָמְוֹךָ, בַּעַל גְּבוּרוֹת
וּמִי דּוֹמֶה לָּךְ
מֶלֶךְ, מֵמִית וּמְחַיֶּה וּמַצְמִיחַ יְשׁוּעָה.

בעשרת ימי תשובה: מִי כָמְוֹךָ אַב הָרַחֲמִים
זוֹכֵר יְצוּרָיו לְחַיִּים בְּרַחֲמִים.

וְנֶאֱמָן אַתָּה לְהַחֲיוֹת מֵתִים.
בָּרוּךְ אַתָּה יהוה, מְחַיֵּה הַמֵּתִים.

When saying the עמידה *silently, continue with* אַתָּה קָדוֹשׁ *on the next page.*

קדושה

During the חזרת הש״ץ*, the following is said standing with feet together, rising on the toes at the words indicated by* ˚.

קהל *then* ש״ץ: נְקַדֵּשׁ אֶת שִׁמְךָ בָּעוֹלָם, כְּשֵׁם שֶׁמַּקְדִּישִׁים אוֹתוֹ בִּשְׁמֵי מָרוֹם
כַּכָּתוּב עַל יַד נְבִיאֶךָ: וְקָרָא זֶה אֶל־זֶה וְאָמַר ישעיה ו

קהל *then* ש״ץ: ˚קָדוֹשׁ, ˚קָדוֹשׁ, ˚קָדוֹשׁ, יהוה צְבָאוֹת, מְלֹא כָל־הָאָרֶץ כְּבוֹדוֹ:
לְעֻמָּתָם בָּרוּךְ יֹאמֵרוּ

קהל *then* ש״ץ: ˚בָּרוּךְ כְּבוֹד־יהוה מִמְּקוֹמוֹ: יחזקאל ג
וּבְדִבְרֵי קָדְשְׁךָ כָּתוּב לֵאמֹר

קהל *then* ש״ץ: ˚יִמְלֹךְ יהוה לְעוֹלָם, אֱלֹהַיִךְ צִיּוֹן לְדֹר וָדֹר, הַלְלוּיָהּ: תהלים קמו

ש״ץ: לְדוֹר וָדוֹר נַגִּיד גָּדְלֶךָ, וּלְנֵצַח נְצָחִים קְדֻשָּׁתְךָ נַקְדִּישׁ
וְשִׁבְחֲךָ אֱלֹהֵינוּ מִפִּינוּ לֹא יָמוּשׁ לְעוֹלָם וָעֶד
כִּי אֵל מֶלֶךְ גָּדוֹל וְקָדוֹשׁ אָתָּה.
בָּרוּךְ אַתָּה יהוה, הָאֵל הַקָּדוֹשׁ./ בעשרת ימי תשובה: הַמֶּלֶךְ הַקָּדוֹשׁ./

The שליח ציבור *continues with* אַתָּה חוֹנֵן *on the next page.*

HOLINESS

אַתָּה קָדוֹשׁ You are holy and Your name is holy,
and holy ones praise You daily, Selah!
Blessed are You, LORD,
the holy God. / *Between Rosh HaShana & Yom Kippur:* the holy King./

(If forgotten, repeat the Amida.)

KNOWLEDGE

אַתָּה חוֹנֵן You grace humanity with knowledge
and teach mortals understanding.
Grace us with the knowledge, understanding
and discernment that come from You.
Blessed are You, LORD,
who graciously grants knowledge.

REPENTANCE

הֲשִׁיבֵנוּ Bring us back, our Father, to Your Torah.
Draw us near, our King, to Your service.
Lead us back to You in perfect repentance.
Blessed are You, LORD,
who desires repentance.

FORGIVENESS

Strike the left side of the chest at °.

סְלַח לָנוּ Forgive us, our Father, for we have °sinned.
Pardon us, our King, for we have °transgressed;
for You pardon and forgive.
Blessed are You, LORD,
the gracious One who repeatedly forgives.

REDEMPTION

רְאֵה Look on our affliction, plead our cause,
and redeem us soon for Your name's sake,
for You are a powerful Redeemer.
Blessed are You, LORD,
the Redeemer of Israel.

קדושת השם

אַתָּה קָדוֹשׁ וְשִׁמְךָ קָדוֹשׁ
וּקְדוֹשִׁים בְּכָל יוֹם יְהַלְלְוּךָ סֶּלָה.
בָּרוּךְ אַתָּה יהוה, הָאֵל הַקָּדוֹשׁ./ בעשרת ימי תשובה: הַמֶּלֶךְ הַקָּדוֹשׁ./

(*If forgotten, repeat the* עמידה.)

דעת

אַתָּה חוֹנֵן לְאָדָם דַּעַת, וּמְלַמֵּד לֶאֱנוֹשׁ בִּינָה.
חָנֵּנוּ מֵאִתְּךָ דֵּעָה בִּינָה וְהַשְׂכֵּל.
בָּרוּךְ אַתָּה יהוה, חוֹנֵן הַדָּעַת.

תשובה

הֲשִׁיבֵנוּ אָבִינוּ לְתוֹרָתֶךָ, וְקָרְבֵנוּ מַלְכֵּנוּ לַעֲבוֹדָתֶךָ
וְהַחֲזִירֵנוּ בִּתְשׁוּבָה שְׁלֵמָה לְפָנֶיךָ.
בָּרוּךְ אַתָּה יהוה, הָרוֹצֶה בִּתְשׁוּבָה.

סליחה

Strike the left side of the chest at °.

סְלַח לָנוּ אָבִינוּ כִּי °חָטָאנוּ
מְחַל לָנוּ מַלְכֵּנוּ כִּי °פָשָׁעְנוּ
כִּי מוֹחֵל וְסוֹלֵחַ אָתָּה.
בָּרוּךְ אַתָּה יהוה, חַנּוּן הַמַּרְבֶּה לִסְלֹחַ.

גאולה

רְאֵה בְעָנְיֵנוּ, וְרִיבָה רִיבֵנוּ
וּגְאָלֵנוּ מְהֵרָה לְמַעַן שְׁמֶךָ
כִּי גּוֹאֵל חָזָק אָתָּה.
בָּרוּךְ אַתָּה יהוה, גּוֹאֵל יִשְׂרָאֵל.

On fast days the Leader adds:

עֲנֵנוּ Answer us, Lord, answer us on our Fast Day, for we are in great distress. Look not at our wickedness. Do not hide Your face from us and do not ignore our plea. Be near to our cry; please let Your loving-kindness comfort us. Even before we call to You, answer us, as it is said, "Before they call, I will answer. While they are still speaking, I will hear." For You, Lord, are the One who answers in time of distress, redeems and rescues in all times of trouble and anguish. Blessed are You, Lord, who answers in time of distress. *Is. 65*

HEALING

רְפָאֵנוּ Heal us, Lord, and we shall be healed.
Save us and we shall be saved,
for You are our praise.
Bring complete recovery for all our ailments,

The following prayer for a sick person may be said here:

May it be Your will, O Lord my God and God of my ancestors, that You speedily send a complete recovery from heaven, a healing of both soul and body, to the patient (*name*), son/daughter of (*mother's name*) among the other afflicted of Israel.

for You, God, King, are a faithful and compassionate Healer.
Blessed are You, Lord, Healer of the sick of His people Israel.

PROSPERITY

The phrase "Grant dew and rain as a blessing" is said from December 5th (in the year before a civil leap year, December 6th) until Pesaḥ. In Israel, it is said from the 7th of Marḥeshvan. The phrase "Grant blessing" is said from Ḥol HaMo'ed Pesaḥ until December 4th (in the year before a civil leap year, December 5th). In Israel it is said through the 6th of Marḥeshvan. See laws 147–149.

בָּרֵךְ Bless this year for us, Lord our God,
and all its types of produce for good.

In winter: Grant dew and rain as a blessing
In other seasons: Grant blessing

on the face of the earth,
and from its goodness satisfy us,
blessing our year as the best of years.
Blessed are You, Lord, who blesses the years.

On fast days the שליח ציבור *adds:*

עֲנֵנוּ יהוה עֲנֵנוּ בְּיוֹם צוֹם תַּעֲנִיתֵנוּ, כִּי בְצָרָה גְדוֹלָה אֲנָחְנוּ. אַל תֵּפֶן אֶל רִשְׁעֵנוּ, וְאַל תַּסְתֵּר פָּנֶיךָ מִמֶּנּוּ, וְאַל תִּתְעַלַּם מִתְּחִנָּתֵנוּ. הֱיֵה נָא קָרוֹב לְשַׁוְעָתֵנוּ, יְהִי נָא חַסְדְּךָ לְנַחֲמֵנוּ, טֶרֶם נִקְרָא אֵלֶיךָ עֲנֵנוּ, כַּדָּבָר שֶׁנֶּאֱמַר: וְהָיָה טֶרֶם יִקְרָאוּ וַאֲנִי אֶעֱנֶה, עוֹד הֵם מְדַבְּרִים וַאֲנִי אֶשְׁמָע: כִּי אַתָּה יהוה ישעיה סה הָעוֹנֶה בְּעֵת צָרָה, פּוֹדֶה וּמַצִּיל בְּכָל עֵת צָרָה וְצוּקָה. בָּרוּךְ אַתָּה יהוה, הָעוֹנֶה בְּעֵת צָרָה.

רפואה

רְפָאֵנוּ יהוה וְנֵרָפֵא, הוֹשִׁיעֵנוּ וְנִוָּשֵׁעָה, כִּי תְהִלָּתֵנוּ אָתָּה
וְהַעֲלֵה רְפוּאָה שְׁלֵמָה לְכָל מַכּוֹתֵינוּ

The following prayer for a sick person may be said here:

יְהִי רָצוֹן מִלְּפָנֶיךָ יהוה אֱלֹהַי וֵאלֹהֵי אֲבוֹתַי, שֶׁתִּשְׁלַח מְהֵרָה רְפוּאָה שְׁלֵמָה מִן הַשָּׁמַיִם רְפוּאַת הַנֶּפֶשׁ וּרְפוּאַת הַגּוּף לְחוֹלֶה/לַחוֹלָה *name of patient* בֶּן/בַּת *mother's name* בְּתוֹךְ שְׁאָר חוֹלֵי יִשְׂרָאֵל.

כִּי אֵל מֶלֶךְ רוֹפֵא נֶאֱמָן וְרַחֲמָן אָתָּה.
בָּרוּךְ אַתָּה יהוה, רוֹפֵא חוֹלֵי עַמּוֹ יִשְׂרָאֵל.

ברכת השנים

The phrase וְתֵן טַל וּמָטָר לִבְרָכָה *is said from December 5th (in the year before a civil leap year, December 6th) until* פסח. *In* ארץ ישראל, *it is said from* ז׳ מרחשון.
The phrase וְתֵן בְּרָכָה *is said from* חול המועד פסח *until December 4th (in the year before a civil leap year, December 5th). In* ארץ ישראל *it is said through* ו׳ מרחשון. *See laws 147–149.*

בָּרֵךְ עָלֵינוּ יהוה אֱלֹהֵינוּ אֶת הַשָּׁנָה הַזֹּאת
וְאֶת כָּל מִינֵי תְבוּאָתָהּ, לְטוֹבָה
בחורף: וְתֵן טַל וּמָטָר לִבְרָכָה / בקיץ: וְתֵן בְּרָכָה
עַל פְּנֵי הָאֲדָמָה, וְשַׂבְּעֵנוּ מִטּוּבָהּ
וּבָרֵךְ שְׁנָתֵנוּ כַּשָּׁנִים הַטּוֹבוֹת.
בָּרוּךְ אַתָּה יהוה, מְבָרֵךְ הַשָּׁנִים.

INGATHERING OF EXILES

תְּקַע Sound the great shofar for our freedom,
raise high the banner to gather our exiles,
and gather us together from the four quarters of the earth.
Blessed are You, LORD,
who gathers the dispersed of His people Israel.

JUSTICE

הָשִׁיבָה Restore our judges as at first,
and our counselors as at the beginning,
and remove from us sorrow and sighing.
May You alone, LORD,
reign over us with loving-kindness and compassion,
and vindicate us in justice.
Blessed are You, LORD,
the King who loves righteousness and justice.
/*Between Rosh HaShana & Yom Kippur, end the blessing:* the King of justice./

AGAINST INFORMERS

וְלַמַּלְשִׁינִים For the slanderers let there be no hope,
and may all wickedness perish in an instant.
May all Your people's enemies swiftly be cut down.
May You swiftly uproot, crush, cast down
and humble the arrogant swiftly in our days.
Blessed are You, LORD,
who destroys enemies and humbles the arrogant.

THE RIGHTEOUS

עַל הַצַּדִּיקִים To the righteous, the pious,
the elders of Your people the house of Israel,
the remnant of their scholars,
the righteous converts, and to us,
may Your compassion be aroused, LORD our God.

קבוץ גלויות

תְּקַע בְּשׁוֹפָר גָּדוֹל לְחֵרוּתֵנוּ
וְשָׂא נֵס לְקַבֵּץ גָּלֻיּוֹתֵינוּ
וְקַבְּצֵנוּ יַחַד מֵאַרְבַּע כַּנְפוֹת הָאָרֶץ.
בָּרוּךְ אַתָּה יהוה, מְקַבֵּץ נִדְחֵי עַמּוֹ יִשְׂרָאֵל.

השבת המשפט

הָשִׁיבָה שׁוֹפְטֵינוּ כְּבָרִאשׁוֹנָה וְיוֹעֲצֵינוּ כְּבַתְּחִלָּה
וְהָסֵר מִמֶּנּוּ יָגוֹן וַאֲנָחָה
וּמְלֹךְ עָלֵינוּ אַתָּה יהוה לְבַדְּךָ בְּחֶסֶד וּבְרַחֲמִים
וְצַדְּקֵנוּ בַּמִּשְׁפָּט.
בָּרוּךְ אַתָּה יהוה
מֶלֶךְ אוֹהֵב צְדָקָה וּמִשְׁפָּט. / בעשרת ימי תשובה: הַמֶּלֶךְ הַמִּשְׁפָּט./

ברכת המינים

וְלַמַּלְשִׁינִים אַל תְּהִי תִקְוָה
וְכָל הָרִשְׁעָה כְּרֶגַע תֹּאבֵד
וְכָל אוֹיְבֵי עַמְּךָ מְהֵרָה יִכָּרֵתוּ
וְהַזֵּדִים מְהֵרָה תְעַקֵּר וּתְשַׁבֵּר וּתְמַגֵּר וְתַכְנִיעַ בִּמְהֵרָה בְיָמֵינוּ.
בָּרוּךְ אַתָּה יהוה, שׁוֹבֵר אוֹיְבִים וּמַכְנִיעַ זֵדִים.

על הצדיקים

עַל הַצַּדִּיקִים וְעַל הַחֲסִידִים
וְעַל זִקְנֵי עַמְּךָ בֵּית יִשְׂרָאֵל
וְעַל פְּלֵיטַת סוֹפְרֵיהֶם
וְעַל גֵּרֵי הַצֶּדֶק, וְעָלֵינוּ
יֶהֱמוּ רַחֲמֶיךָ יהוה אֱלֹהֵינוּ

Grant a good reward to all who sincerely trust in Your name.
Set our lot with them,
so that we may never be ashamed, for in You we trust.
Blessed are You, LORD,
who is the support and trust of the righteous.

REBUILDING JERUSALEM

וְלִירוּשָׁלַיִם To Jerusalem, Your city,
may You return in compassion,
and may You dwell in it as You promised.
May You rebuild it rapidly in our days
as an everlasting structure,
and install within it soon the throne of David.
*Blessed are You, LORD, who builds Jerusalem.

**On Tisha B'Av all conclude as follows:*

נַחֵם Console, O LORD our God, the mourners of Zion and the mourners of Jerusalem, and the city that is in sorrow, laid waste, scorned and desolate; that grieves for the loss of its children, that is laid waste of its dwellings, robbed of its glory, desolate without inhabitants. She sits with her head covered like a barren childless woman. Legions have devoured her; idolaters have taken possession of her; they have put Your people Israel to the sword and deliberately killed the devoted followers of the Most High. Therefore Zion weeps bitterly, and Jerusalem raises her voice. My heart, my heart grieves for those they killed; I am in anguish, I am in anguish for those they killed. For You, O LORD, consumed it with fire, and with fire You will rebuild it in the future, as is said, "And I Myself will be a wall of fire around it, says the LORD, *Zech. 2*
and I will be its glory within." Blessed are You, LORD, who consoles Zion and rebuilds Jerusalem.

Continue with "May the offshoot" below.

KINGDOM OF DAVID

אֶת צֶמַח May the offshoot of Your servant David soon flower,
and may his pride be raised high by Your salvation,
for we wait for Your salvation all day.
Blessed are You, LORD, who makes the glory of salvation flourish.

וְתֵן שָׂכָר טוֹב לְכָל הַבּוֹטְחִים בְּשִׁמְךָ בֶּאֱמֶת
וְשִׂים חֶלְקֵנוּ עִמָּהֶם
וּלְעוֹלָם לֹא נֵבוֹשׁ כִּי בְךָ בָּטָחְנוּ.
בָּרוּךְ אַתָּה יהוה, מִשְׁעָן וּמִבְטָח לַצַּדִּיקִים.

בניין ירושלים
וְלִירוּשָׁלַיִם עִירְךָ בְּרַחֲמִים תָּשׁוּב
וְתִשְׁכֹּן בְּתוֹכָהּ כַּאֲשֶׁר דִּבַּרְתָּ
וּבְנֵה אוֹתָהּ בְּקָרוֹב בְּיָמֵינוּ בִּנְיַן עוֹלָם
וְכִסֵּא דָוִד מְהֵרָה לְתוֹכָהּ תָּכִין.
*בָּרוּךְ אַתָּה יהוה, בּוֹנֵה יְרוּשָׁלָיִם.

**On תשעה באב, all conclude as follows:*

נַחֵם יהוה אֱלֹהֵינוּ אֶת אֲבֵלֵי צִיּוֹן וְאֶת אֲבֵלֵי יְרוּשָׁלָיִם, וְאֶת הָעִיר הָאֲבֵלָה
וְהַחֲרֵבָה וְהַבְּזוּיָה וְהַשּׁוֹמֵמָה. הָאֲבֵלָה מִבְּלִי בָנֶיהָ, וְהַחֲרֵבָה מִמְּעוֹנוֹתֶיהָ,
וְהַבְּזוּיָה מִכְּבוֹדָהּ, וְהַשּׁוֹמֵמָה מֵאֵין יוֹשֵׁב. וְהִיא יוֹשֶׁבֶת וְרֹאשָׁהּ חָפוּי, כְּאִשָּׁה
עֲקָרָה שֶׁלֹּא יָלָדָה. וַיְבַלְּעוּהָ לִגְיוֹנוֹת, וַיִּירָשׁוּהָ עוֹבְדֵי פְסִילִים, וַיָּטִילוּ אֶת
עַמְּךָ יִשְׂרָאֵל לֶחָרֶב, וַיַּהַרְגוּ בְזָדוֹן חֲסִידֵי עֶלְיוֹן. עַל כֵּן צִיּוֹן בְּמַר תִּבְכֶּה,
וִירוּשָׁלַיִם תִּתֵּן קוֹלָהּ. לִבִּי לִבִּי עַל חַלְלֵיהֶם, מֵעַי מֵעַי עַל חַלְלֵיהֶם, כִּי אַתָּה
יהוה בָּאֵשׁ הִצַּתָּהּ, וּבָאֵשׁ אַתָּה עָתִיד לִבְנוֹתָהּ. כָּאָמוּר: וַאֲנִי אֶהְיֶה־לָּהּ, זכריה ב
נְאֻם־יהוה, חוֹמַת אֵשׁ סָבִיב, וּלְכָבוֹד אֶהְיֶה בְתוֹכָהּ: בָּרוּךְ אַתָּה יהוה,
מְנַחֵם צִיּוֹן וּבוֹנֵה יְרוּשָׁלָיִם.

Continue with אֶת צֶמַח *below.*

משיח בן דוד
אֶת צֶמַח דָּוִד עַבְדְּךָ מְהֵרָה תַצְמִיחַ
וְקַרְנוֹ תָּרוּם בִּישׁוּעָתֶךָ, כִּי לִישׁוּעָתְךָ קִוִּינוּ כָּל הַיּוֹם.
בָּרוּךְ אַתָּה יהוה, מַצְמִיחַ קֶרֶן יְשׁוּעָה.

RESPONSE TO PRAYER

שְׁמַע קוֹלֵנוּ Listen to our voice, LORD our God.
Spare us and have compassion on us,
and in compassion and favor accept our prayer,
for You, God, listen to prayers and pleas.
Do not turn us away, O our King,
empty-handed from Your presence,*
for You listen with compassion
to the prayer of Your people Israel.
Blessed are You, LORD, who listens to prayer.

**At this point on fast days, the congregation adds "Answer us" below.*
In times of drought in Israel, say "And answer us" on page 124.

עֲנֵנוּ Answer us, LORD, answer us on our Fast Day, for we are in great distress. Look not at our wickedness. Do not hide Your face from us and do not ignore our plea. Be near to our cry; please let Your loving-kindness comfort us. Even before we call to You, answer us, as is said, "Before they call, I will answer. While they are still speaking, I will hear." For You, LORD, are the One who answers in time of distress, redeems and rescues in all times of trouble and anguish. *Is. 65*

Continue with "for You listen" above.

TEMPLE SERVICE

רְצֵה Find favor, LORD our God,
in Your people Israel and their prayer.
Restore the service to Your most holy House,
and accept in love and favor
the fire-offerings of Israel and their prayer.
May the service of Your people Israel always find favor with You.

On Rosh Ḥodesh and Ḥol HaMo'ed, say:

אֱלֹהֵינוּ Our God and God of our ancestors, may there rise, come, reach, appear, be favored, heard, regarded and remembered before You, our recollection and remembrance, as well as the remembrance of our ancestors, and of the Messiah son of David Your servant, and of Jerusalem Your holy city, and of all Your people the house of Israel – for deliverance and

שומע תפילה

שְׁמַע קוֹלֵנוּ יהוה אֱלֹהֵינוּ
חוּס וְרַחֵם עָלֵינוּ
וְקַבֵּל בְּרַחֲמִים וּבְרָצוֹן אֶת תְּפִלָּתֵנוּ
כִּי אֵל שׁוֹמֵעַ תְּפִלּוֹת וְתַחֲנוּנִים אָתָּה
וּמִלְּפָנֶיךָ מַלְכֵּנוּ רֵיקָם אַל תְּשִׁיבֵנוּ*
כִּי אַתָּה שׁוֹמֵעַ תְּפִלַּת עַמְּךָ יִשְׂרָאֵל בְּרַחֲמִים.
בָּרוּךְ אַתָּה יהוה, שׁוֹמֵעַ תְּפִלָּה.

**At this point on fast days, the* קהל *adds* עֲנֵנוּ *below.*
In times of drought in ארץ ישראל*, say* וַעֲנֵנוּ *on page 125.*

עֲנֵנוּ יהוה עֲנֵנוּ בְּיוֹם צוֹם תַּעֲנִיתֵנוּ, כִּי בְצָרָה גְדוֹלָה אֲנָחְנוּ. אַל תֵּפֶן אֶל
רִשְׁעֵנוּ, וְאַל תַּסְתֵּר פָּנֶיךָ מִמֶּנּוּ, וְאַל תִּתְעַלַּם מִתְּחִנָּתֵנוּ. הֱיֵה נָא קָרוֹב
לְשַׁוְעָתֵנוּ, יְהִי נָא חַסְדְּךָ לְנַחֲמֵנוּ, טֶרֶם נִקְרָא אֵלֶיךָ עֲנֵנוּ, כַּדָּבָר שֶׁנֶּאֱמַר: ישעיה סה
וְהָיָה טֶרֶם יִקְרָאוּ וַאֲנִי אֶעֱנֶה, עוֹד הֵם מְדַבְּרִים וַאֲנִי אֶשְׁמָע: כִּי אַתָּה
יהוה הָעוֹנֶה בְּעֵת צָרָה, פּוֹדֶה וּמַצִּיל בְּכָל עֵת צָרָה וְצוּקָה.

Continue with כִּי אַתָּה שׁוֹמֵעַ *above.*

עבודה

רְצֵה יהוה אֱלֹהֵינוּ בְּעַמְּךָ יִשְׂרָאֵל, וּבִתְפִלָּתָם
וְהָשֵׁב אֶת הָעֲבוֹדָה לִדְבִיר בֵּיתֶךָ
וְאִשֵּׁי יִשְׂרָאֵל וּתְפִלָּתָם בְּאַהֲבָה תְקַבֵּל בְּרָצוֹן
וּתְהִי לְרָצוֹן תָּמִיד עֲבוֹדַת יִשְׂרָאֵל עַמֶּךָ.

On ראש חודש *and* חול המועד*, say:*

אֱלֹהֵינוּ וֵאלֹהֵי אֲבוֹתֵינוּ, יַעֲלֶה וְיָבוֹא וְיַגִּיעַ, וְיֵרָאֶה וְיֵרָצֶה
וְיִשָּׁמַע, וְיִפָּקֵד וְיִזָּכֵר זִכְרוֹנֵנוּ וּפִקְדוֹנֵנוּ וְזִכְרוֹן אֲבוֹתֵינוּ, וְזִכְרוֹן
מָשִׁיחַ בֶּן דָּוִד עַבְדֶּךָ, וְזִכְרוֹן יְרוּשָׁלַיִם עִיר קָדְשֶׁךָ, וְזִכְרוֹן כָּל עַמְּךָ

well-being, grace, loving-kindness and compassion, life and peace, on this day of:

On Rosh Hodesh: Rosh Ḥodesh.
On Pesaḥ: the Festival of Matzot.
On Sukkot: the Festival of Sukkot.

On it remember us, LORD our God, for good; recollect us for blessing, and deliver us for life. In accord with Your promise of salvation and compassion, spare us and be gracious to us; have compassion on us and deliver us, for our eyes are turned to You because You, God, are a gracious and compassionate King.

וְתֶחֱזֶינָה And may our eyes witness Your return to Zion in compassion. Blessed are You, LORD, who restores His Presence to Zion.

THANKSGIVING

Bow at the first nine words.

מוֹדִים We give thanks to You,
for You are the LORD our God
and God of our ancestors
for ever and all time.
You are the Rock of our lives,
Shield of our salvation
from generation to generation.
We will thank You and
declare Your praise for our lives,
which are entrusted into Your hand;
for our souls,
which are placed in Your charge;
for Your miracles
which are with us every day;
and for Your wonders and favors
at all times, evening, morning and midday.
You are good –
for Your compassion never fails.
You are compassionate –
for Your loving-kindnesses never cease.
We have always placed our hope in You.

During the Leader's Repetition, the congregation says quietly:
מוֹדִים We give thanks to You,
for You are the LORD our God
and God of our ancestors,
God of all flesh,
who formed us
and formed the universe.
Blessings and thanks
are due to Your great
and holy name for giving us
life and sustaining us.
May You continue
to give us life and sustain us;
and may You gather our
exiles to Your holy courts,
to keep Your decrees,
do Your will and serve You
with a perfect heart,
for it is for us
to give You thanks.
Blessed be God to whom
thanksgiving is due.

בֵּית יִשְׂרָאֵל, לְפָנֶיךָ, לִפְלֵיטָה לְטוֹבָה, לְחֵן וּלְחֶסֶד וּלְרַחֲמִים, לְחַיִּים וּלְשָׁלוֹם בְּיוֹם

בראש חודש: רֹאשׁ הַחֹדֶשׁ / בפסח: חַג הַמַּצּוֹת / בסוכות: חַג הַסֻּכּוֹת הַזֶּה. זָכְרֵנוּ יהוה אֱלֹהֵינוּ בּוֹ לְטוֹבָה, וּפָקְדֵנוּ בוֹ לִבְרָכָה, וְהוֹשִׁיעֵנוּ בוֹ לְחַיִּים. וּבִדְבַר יְשׁוּעָה וְרַחֲמִים, חוּס וְחָנֵּנוּ וְרַחֵם עָלֵינוּ וְהוֹשִׁיעֵנוּ, כִּי אֵלֶיךָ עֵינֵינוּ, כִּי אֵל מֶלֶךְ חַנּוּן וְרַחוּם אָתָּה.

וְתֶחֱזֶינָה עֵינֵינוּ בְּשׁוּבְךָ לְצִיּוֹן בְּרַחֲמִים.
בָּרוּךְ אַתָּה יהוה, הַמַּחֲזִיר שְׁכִינָתוֹ לְצִיּוֹן.

הודאה

Bow at the first five words.

מוֹדִים אֲנַחְנוּ לָךְ
שָׁאַתָּה הוּא יהוה אֱלֹהֵינוּ
וֵאלֹהֵי אֲבוֹתֵינוּ לְעוֹלָם וָעֶד.
צוּר חַיֵּינוּ, מָגֵן יִשְׁעֵנוּ
אַתָּה הוּא לְדוֹר וָדוֹר.
נוֹדֶה לְּךָ וּנְסַפֵּר תְּהִלָּתֶךָ
עַל חַיֵּינוּ הַמְּסוּרִים בְּיָדֶךָ
וְעַל נִשְׁמוֹתֵינוּ הַפְּקוּדוֹת לָךְ
וְעַל נִסֶּיךָ שֶׁבְּכָל יוֹם עִמָּנוּ
וְעַל נִפְלְאוֹתֶיךָ וְטוֹבוֹתֶיךָ
שֶׁבְּכָל עֵת, עֶרֶב וָבֹקֶר וְצָהֳרָיִם.
הַטּוֹב, כִּי לֹא כָלוּ רַחֲמֶיךָ
וְהַמְרַחֵם, כִּי לֹא תַמּוּ חֲסָדֶיךָ
מֵעוֹלָם קִוִּינוּ לָךְ.

During the חזרת הש״ץ, *the* קהל *says quietly:*

מוֹדִים אֲנַחְנוּ לָךְ
שָׁאַתָּה הוּא יהוה אֱלֹהֵינוּ
וֵאלֹהֵי אֲבוֹתֵינוּ
אֱלֹהֵי כָל בָּשָׂר
יוֹצְרֵנוּ, יוֹצֵר בְּרֵאשִׁית.
בְּרָכוֹת וְהוֹדָאוֹת
לְשִׁמְךָ הַגָּדוֹל וְהַקָּדוֹשׁ
עַל שֶׁהֶחֱיִיתָנוּ וְקִיַּמְתָּנוּ.
כֵּן תְּחַיֵּנוּ וּתְקַיְּמֵנוּ
וְתֶאֱסֹף גָּלֻיּוֹתֵינוּ
לְחַצְרוֹת קָדְשֶׁךָ
לִשְׁמֹר חֻקֶּיךָ וְלַעֲשׂוֹת רְצוֹנֶךָ
וּלְעָבְדְּךָ בְּלֵבָב שָׁלֵם
עַל שֶׁאֲנַחְנוּ מוֹדִים לָךְ.
בָּרוּךְ אֵל הַהוֹדָאוֹת.

On Ḥanukka:

עַל הַנִּסִּים [We thank You also] for the miracles, the redemption, the mighty deeds, the salvations, and the victories in battle which You performed for our ancestors in those days, at this time.

בִּימֵי מַתִּתְיָהוּ In the days of Mattityahu, son of Yoḥanan, the High Priest, the Hasmonean, and his sons, the wicked Greek kingdom rose up against Your people Israel to make them forget Your Torah and to force them to transgress the statutes of Your will. It was then that You in Your great compassion stood by them in the time of their distress. You championed their cause, judged their claim, and avenged their wrong. You delivered the strong into the hands of the weak, the many into the hands of the few, the impure into the hands of the pure, the wicked into the hands of the righteous, and the arrogant into the hands of those who were engaged in the study of Your Torah. You made for Yourself great and holy renown in Your world, and for Your people Israel You performed a great salvation and redemption as of this very day. Your children then entered the holiest part of Your House, cleansed Your Temple, purified Your Sanctuary, kindled lights in Your holy courts, and designated these eight days of Ḥanukka for giving thanks and praise to Your great name.

Continue with "For all these things."

On Purim:

עַל הַנִּסִּים [We thank You also] for the miracles, the redemption, the mighty deeds, the salvations, and the victories in battle which You performed for our ancestors in those days, at this time.

בִּימֵי מָרְדְּכַי In the days of Mordekhai and Esther, in Shushan the capital, the wicked Haman rose up against them and sought to destroy, slay and exterminate *Esther 3* all the Jews, young and old, children and women, on one day, the thirteenth day of the twelfth month, which is the month of Adar, and to plunder their possessions. Then You in Your great compassion thwarted his counsel, frustrated his plans, and caused his scheme to recoil on his own head, so that they hanged him and his sons on the gallows.

Continue with "For all these things."

וְעַל כֻּלָּם For all these things may Your name be blessed and exalted, our King, continually, for ever and all time.

Between Rosh HaShana & Yom Kippur: And write, for a good life, all the children of Your covenant.

Let all that lives thank You, Selah! and praise Your name in truth, God, our Savior and Help, Selah!

▼Blessed are You, Lord, whose name is "the Good" and to whom thanks are due.

בחנוכה:

עַל הַנִּסִּים וְעַל הַפֻּרְקָן וְעַל הַגְּבוּרוֹת וְעַל הַתְּשׁוּעוֹת וְעַל הַמִּלְחָמוֹת שֶׁעָשִׂיתָ לַאֲבוֹתֵינוּ בַּיָּמִים הָהֵם בִּזְּמַן הַזֶּה.

בִּימֵי מַתִּתְיָהוּ בֶּן יוֹחָנָן כֹּהֵן גָּדוֹל חַשְׁמוֹנַאי וּבָנָיו, כְּשֶׁעָמְדָה מַלְכוּת יָוָן הָרְשָׁעָה עַל עַמְּךָ יִשְׂרָאֵל לְהַשְׁכִּיחָם תּוֹרָתֶךָ וּלְהַעֲבִירָם מֵחֻקֵּי רְצוֹנֶךָ, וְאַתָּה בְּרַחֲמֶיךָ הָרַבִּים עָמַדְתָּ לָהֶם בְּעֵת צָרָתָם, רַבְתָּ אֶת רִיבָם, דַּנְתָּ אֶת דִּינָם, נָקַמְתָּ אֶת נִקְמָתָם, מָסַרְתָּ גִבּוֹרִים בְּיַד חַלָּשִׁים, וְרַבִּים בְּיַד מְעַטִּים, וּטְמֵאִים בְּיַד טְהוֹרִים, וּרְשָׁעִים בְּיַד צַדִּיקִים, וְזֵדִים בְּיַד עוֹסְקֵי תוֹרָתֶךָ, וּלְךָ עָשִׂיתָ שֵׁם גָּדוֹל וְקָדוֹשׁ בְּעוֹלָמֶךָ, וּלְעַמְּךָ יִשְׂרָאֵל עָשִׂיתָ תְּשׁוּעָה גְדוֹלָה וּפֻרְקָן כְּהַיּוֹם הַזֶּה. וְאַחַר כֵּן בָּאוּ בָנֶיךָ לִדְבִיר בֵּיתֶךָ, וּפִנּוּ אֶת הֵיכָלֶךָ, וְטִהֲרוּ אֶת מִקְדָּשֶׁךָ, וְהִדְלִיקוּ נֵרוֹת בְּחַצְרוֹת קָדְשֶׁךָ, וְקָבְעוּ שְׁמוֹנַת יְמֵי חֲנֻכָּה אֵלּוּ, לְהוֹדוֹת וּלְהַלֵּל לְשִׁמְךָ הַגָּדוֹל.

Continue with וְעַל כֻּלָּם.

בפורים:

עַל הַנִּסִּים וְעַל הַפֻּרְקָן וְעַל הַגְּבוּרוֹת וְעַל הַתְּשׁוּעוֹת וְעַל הַמִּלְחָמוֹת שֶׁעָשִׂיתָ לַאֲבוֹתֵינוּ בַּיָּמִים הָהֵם בִּזְּמַן הַזֶּה.

בִּימֵי מָרְדְּכַי וְאֶסְתֵּר בְּשׁוּשַׁן הַבִּירָה, כְּשֶׁעָמַד עֲלֵיהֶם הָמָן הָרָשָׁע, בִּקֵּשׁ
אסתר ג לְהַשְׁמִיד לַהֲרֹג וּלְאַבֵּד אֶת־כָּל־הַיְּהוּדִים מִנַּעַר וְעַד־זָקֵן טַף וְנָשִׁים בְּיוֹם אֶחָד, בִּשְׁלוֹשָׁה עָשָׂר לְחֹדֶשׁ שְׁנֵים־עָשָׂר, הוּא־חֹדֶשׁ אֲדָר, וּשְׁלָלָם לָבוֹז: וְאַתָּה בְּרַחֲמֶיךָ הָרַבִּים הֵפַרְתָּ אֶת עֲצָתוֹ, וְקִלְקַלְתָּ אֶת מַחֲשַׁבְתּוֹ, וַהֲשֵׁבוֹתָ לּוֹ גְּמוּלוֹ בְּרֹאשׁוֹ, וְתָלוּ אוֹתוֹ וְאֶת בָּנָיו עַל הָעֵץ.

Continue with וְעַל כֻּלָּם.

וְעַל כֻּלָּם יִתְבָּרַךְ וְיִתְרוֹמַם שִׁמְךָ מַלְכֵּנוּ תָּמִיד לְעוֹלָם וָעֶד.

בעשרת ימי תשובה: וּכְתֹב לְחַיִּים טוֹבִים כָּל בְּנֵי בְרִיתֶךָ.

וְכֹל הַחַיִּים יוֹדוּךָ סֶּלָה, וִיהַלְלוּ אֶת שִׁמְךָ בֶּאֱמֶת הָאֵל יְשׁוּעָתֵנוּ וְעֶזְרָתֵנוּ סֶלָה.

ּבָּרוּךְ אַתָּה יהוה, הַטּוֹב שִׁמְךָ וּלְךָ נָאֶה לְהוֹדוֹת.

On public fast days only, the following is said by the Leader during the Repetition of the Amida, except in a house of mourning. In Israel, on Fast Days, if Kohanim bless the congregation, *turn to page 838. See laws 370–377.*

Our God and God of our fathers, bless us with the threefold blessing in the Torah, written by the hand of Moses Your servant and pronounced by Aaron and his sons the priests, Your holy people, as it is said:

May the LORD bless you and protect you. *Num. 6*
Cong: May it be Your will.
May the LORD make His face shine on you and be gracious to you.
Cong: May it be Your will.
May the LORD turn His face toward you, and grant you peace.
Cong: May it be Your will.

שָׁלוֹם רָב Grant great peace
to Your people Israel
for ever,
for You are
the sovereign LORD
of all peace;
and may it be good
in Your eyes
to bless Your people Israel
at every time,
at every hour,
with Your peace.

On fast days:
שִׂים שָׁלוֹם Grant peace,
goodness and blessing,
grace, loving-kindness and compassion
to us and all Israel Your people.
Bless us, our Father, all as one,
with the light of Your face,
for by the light of Your face
You have given us, LORD our God,
the Torah of life and love of kindness,
righteousness, blessing, compassion,
life and peace.
May it be good in Your eyes
to bless Your people Israel
at every time, in every hour,
with Your peace.

Between Rosh HaShana & Yom Kippur: In the book of life, blessing, peace and prosperity, may we and all Your people the house of Israel be remembered and written before You for a good life, and for peace.*

Blessed are You, LORD, who blesses His people Israel with peace.

**Between Rosh HaShana and Yom Kippur outside Israel, many end the blessing:*

Blessed are You, LORD, who makes peace.

The following verse concludes the Leader's Repetition of the Amida. Some also say it here as part of the silent Amida. See law 368.

May the words of my mouth and the meditation of my heart *Ps. 19*
find favor before You, LORD, my Rock and Redeemer.

On public fast days only, the following is said by the שליח ציבור *during the* חזרת הש״ץ *except in a house of mourning. In* ארץ ישראל*, on Fast Days, if* כהנים *say* ברכת כהנים *turn to page 839. See laws 370–377.*

אֱלֹהֵינוּ וֵאלֹהֵי אֲבוֹתֵינוּ, בָּרְכֵנוּ בַּבְּרָכָה הַמְשֻׁלֶּשֶׁת בַּתּוֹרָה, הַכְּתוּבָה עַל יְדֵי מֹשֶׁה עַבְדֶּךָ, הָאֲמוּרָה מִפִּי אַהֲרֹן וּבָנָיו כֹּהֲנִים עַם קְדוֹשֶׁיךָ, כָּאָמוּר

במדבר ו
יְבָרֶכְךָ יהוה וְיִשְׁמְרֶךָ: קהל: כֵּן יְהִי רָצוֹן
יָאֵר יהוה פָּנָיו אֵלֶיךָ וִיחֻנֶּךָּ: קהל: כֵּן יְהִי רָצוֹן
יִשָּׂא יהוה פָּנָיו אֵלֶיךָ וְיָשֵׂם לְךָ שָׁלוֹם: קהל: כֵּן יְהִי רָצוֹן

ברכת שלום

שָׁלוֹם רָב עַל יִשְׂרָאֵל
עַמְּךָ תָּשִׂים לְעוֹלָם
כִּי אַתָּה הוּא
מֶלֶךְ אָדוֹן לְכָל הַשָּׁלוֹם.
וְטוֹב בְּעֵינֶיךָ
לְבָרֵךְ אֶת עַמְּךָ יִשְׂרָאֵל
בְּכָל עֵת וּבְכָל שָׁעָה
בִּשְׁלוֹמֶךָ.

On fast days:
שִׂים שָׁלוֹם טוֹבָה וּבְרָכָה
חֵן וָחֶסֶד וְרַחֲמִים
עָלֵינוּ וְעַל כָּל יִשְׂרָאֵל עַמֶּךָ.
בָּרְכֵנוּ אָבִינוּ כֻּלָּנוּ כְּאֶחָד בְּאוֹר פָּנֶיךָ
כִּי בְאוֹר פָּנֶיךָ נָתַתָּ לָנוּ יהוה אֱלֹהֵינוּ
תּוֹרַת חַיִּים וְאַהֲבַת חֶסֶד
וּצְדָקָה וּבְרָכָה וְרַחֲמִים וְחַיִּים וְשָׁלוֹם.
וְטוֹב בְּעֵינֶיךָ לְבָרֵךְ אֶת עַמְּךָ יִשְׂרָאֵל
בְּכָל עֵת וּבְכָל שָׁעָה בִּשְׁלוֹמֶךָ.

בעשרת ימי תשובה: בְּסֵפֶר חַיִּים, בְּרָכָה וְשָׁלוֹם, וּפַרְנָסָה טוֹבָה
נִזָּכֵר וְנִכָּתֵב לְפָנֶיךָ, אֲנַחְנוּ וְכָל עַמְּךָ בֵּית יִשְׂרָאֵל
לְחַיִּים טוֹבִים וּלְשָׁלוֹם.*

בָּרוּךְ אַתָּה יהוה, הַמְבָרֵךְ אֶת עַמּוֹ יִשְׂרָאֵל בַּשָּׁלוֹם.

*During the עשרת ימי תשובה in חוץ לארץ, many end the blessing:
בָּרוּךְ אַתָּה יהוה, עוֹשֶׂה הַשָּׁלוֹם.

The following verse concludes the חזרת הש״ץ.
Some also say it here as part of the silent עמידה*. See law 368.*

תהלים יט
יִהְיוּ לְרָצוֹן אִמְרֵי־פִי וְהֶגְיוֹן לִבִּי לְפָנֶיךָ, יהוה צוּרִי וְגֹאֲלִי:

אֱלֹהַי My God, — Berakhot 17a
guard my tongue from evil and my lips from deceitful speech.
To those who curse me, let my soul be silent;
may my soul be to all like the dust.
Open my heart to Your Torah and let my soul
pursue Your commandments. As for all who plan evil against me,
swiftly thwart their counsel and frustrate their plans.
Act for the sake of Your name; act for the sake of Your right hand;
act for the sake of Your holiness; act for the sake of Your Torah.
That Your beloved ones may be delivered, — Ps. 60
save with Your right hand and answer me.
*May the words of my mouth and the meditation of my heart — Ps. 19
find favor before You, LORD, my Rock and Redeemer.

Bow, take three steps back, then bow, first left, then right, then center, while saying:
May He who makes peace in His high places,
make peace for us and all Israel – and say: Amen.

יְהִי רָצוֹן May it be Your will, LORD our God and God of our ancestors,
that the Temple be rebuilt speedily in our days,
and grant us a share in Your Torah.
And there we will serve You with reverence,
as in the days of old and as in former years.
Then the offering of Judah and Jerusalem will be pleasing to the LORD — Mal. 3
as in the days of old and as in former years.

On days when Taḥanun is not said, the Leader says Full Kaddish on page 234.

**A person undertaking a personal fast says the following at Minḥa before the fast:*

Master of all worlds, I hereby take upon myself before You a voluntary fast tomorrow. May it be Your will, LORD my God and God of my ancestors, that You accept me in love and favor, that my prayer may come before You, and that You may answer my entreaty in Your great compassion, for You hear the prayer of every mouth.

On the afternoon of the fast, the following is said:

Master of all worlds, it is revealed and known to You that when the Temple stood, a person who sinned would offer a sacrifice, of which were offered only the fat and blood, yet You in Your great compassion granted atonement. Now I have fasted, and my fat and blood have been diminished. May it be Your will that this diminution today of my fat and blood be as if I had offered them before You on the altar, and may You show me favor.

ברכות יז.

אֱלֹהַי

נְצֹר לְשׁוֹנִי מֵרָע וּשְׂפָתַי מִדַּבֵּר מִרְמָה

וְלִמְקַלְלַי נַפְשִׁי תִדֹּם, וְנַפְשִׁי כֶּעָפָר לַכֹּל תִּהְיֶה.

פְּתַח לִבִּי בְּתוֹרָתֶךָ, וּבְמִצְוֹתֶיךָ תִּרְדֹּף נַפְשִׁי.

וְכָל הַחוֹשְׁבִים עָלַי רָעָה

מְהֵרָה הָפֵר עֲצָתָם וְקַלְקֵל מַחֲשַׁבְתָּם.

עֲשֵׂה לְמַעַן שְׁמֶךָ, עֲשֵׂה לְמַעַן יְמִינֶךָ

עֲשֵׂה לְמַעַן קְדֻשָּׁתֶךָ, עֲשֵׂה לְמַעַן תּוֹרָתֶךָ.

תהלים ס

לְמַעַן יֵחָלְצוּן יְדִידֶיךָ, הוֹשִׁיעָה יְמִינְךָ וַעֲנֵנִי:

תהלים יט

*יִהְיוּ לְרָצוֹן אִמְרֵי־פִי וְהֶגְיוֹן לִבִּי לְפָנֶיךָ, יהוה צוּרִי וְגֹאֲלִי:

Bow, take three steps back, then bow, first left, then right, then center, while saying:

עֹשֶׂה שָׁלוֹם/ בעשרת ימי תשובה: הַשָּׁלוֹם/ בִּמְרוֹמָיו

הוּא יַעֲשֶׂה שָׁלוֹם עָלֵינוּ וְעַל כָּל יִשְׂרָאֵל, וְאִמְרוּ אָמֵן.

יְהִי רָצוֹן מִלְּפָנֶיךָ יהוה אֱלֹהֵינוּ וֵאלֹהֵי אֲבוֹתֵינוּ

שֶׁיִּבָּנֶה בֵּית הַמִּקְדָּשׁ בִּמְהֵרָה בְיָמֵינוּ, וְתֵן חֶלְקֵנוּ בְּתוֹרָתֶךָ

וְשָׁם נַעֲבָדְךָ בְּיִרְאָה כִּימֵי עוֹלָם וּכְשָׁנִים קַדְמוֹנִיּוֹת.

מלאכי ג

וְעָרְבָה לַיהוה מִנְחַת יְהוּדָה וִירוּשָׁלָםִ כִּימֵי עוֹלָם וּכְשָׁנִים קַדְמֹנִיּוֹת:

On days when תחנון *is not said, the* שליח ציבור *says* קדיש שלם *on page 235.*

**A person undertaking a personal fast says the following at* מנחה *before the fast:*

רִבּוֹן כָּל הָעוֹלָמִים, הֲרֵי אֲנִי לְפָנֶיךָ בְּתַעֲנִית נְדָבָה לְמָחָר. יְהִי רָצוֹן מִלְּפָנֶיךָ יהוה אֱלֹהַי וֵאלֹהֵי אֲבוֹתַי, שֶׁתְּקַבְּלֵנִי בְּאַהֲבָה וּבְרָצוֹן, וְתָבֹא לְפָנֶיךָ תְּפִלָּתִי, וְתַעֲנֶה עֲתִירָתִי בְּרַחֲמֶיךָ הָרַבִּים, כִּי אַתָּה שׁוֹמֵעַ תְּפִלַּת כָּל־פֶּה.

On the afternoon of the fast, the following is said:

רִבּוֹן כָּל הָעוֹלָמִים, גָּלוּי וְיָדוּעַ לְפָנֶיךָ, בִּזְמַן שֶׁבֵּית הַמִּקְדָּשׁ קַיָּם, אָדָם חוֹטֵא וּמַקְרִיב קָרְבָּן, וְאֵין מַקְרִיבִין מִמֶּנּוּ אֶלָּא חֶלְבּוֹ וְדָמוֹ, וְאַתָּה בְּרַחֲמֶיךָ הָרַבִּים מְכַפֵּר. וְעַכְשָׁו יָשַׁבְתִּי בְתַעֲנִית, וְנִתְמַעֵט חֶלְבִּי וְדָמִי. יְהִי רָצוֹן מִלְּפָנֶיךָ, שֶׁיְּהֵא מִעוּט חֶלְבִּי וְדָמִי שֶׁנִּתְמַעֵט הַיּוֹם, כְּאִלּוּ הִקְרַבְתִּיו עַל־גַּבֵּי הַמִּזְבֵּחַ, וְתִרְצֵנִי.

Between Rosh HaShana and Yom Kippur and on fast days, except days when Taḥanun is not said (see list below), Avinu Malkenu (on page 138) is said here.

TAḤANUN

Taḥanun is not said on Erev Shabbat and Erev Yom Tov. It is also not said on the following days: Rosh Ḥodesh, Ḥanukka, Tu BiShvat, the 14th and 15th of Adar I, Purim and Shushan Purim, Yom HaAtzma'ut, Lag BaOmer, Yom Yerushalayim, Tisha B'Av, Tu B'Av, and the preceding afternoons, the month of Nisan, the 14th of Iyar (Pesaḥ Sheni), from Rosh Ḥodesh Sivan through the day after Shavuot (in Israel through 12th of Sivan), and from Erev Yom Kippur through the day after Simḥat Torah (in Israel through Rosh Ḥodesh Marḥeshvan). Taḥanun is also not said: on the occasion of a Brit Mila, either where the brit will take place or where the father, Sandek or Mohel are present; if a groom is present (and some say, a bride) on the day of his wedding or during the week of Sheva Berakhot; in a house of mourning.

LOWERING THE HEAD

Say while sitting; in the presence of a Torah scroll say until "in sudden shame," leaning forward and resting one's head on the left arm.

וַיֹּאמֶר דָּוִד David said to Gad, "I am in great distress. *II Sam. 24*
Let us fall into God's hand, for His mercy is great;
but do not let me fall into the hand of man."

Compassionate and gracious One, I have sinned before You.
LORD, full of compassion, have compassion on me and accept my pleas.

LORD, do not rebuke me in Your anger or chastise me in Your wrath. *Ps. 6*
Be gracious to me, LORD, for I am weak.
Heal me, LORD, for my bones are in agony.
My soul is in anguish, and You, O LORD – how long?
Turn, LORD, set my soul free; save me for the sake of Your love.
For no one remembers You when he is dead.
Who can praise You from the grave? I am weary with my sighing.
Every night I drench my bed, I soak my couch with my tears.
My eye grows dim from grief, worn out because of all my foes.
Leave me, all you evildoers,
for the LORD has heard the sound of my weeping.
The LORD has heard my pleas. The LORD will accept my prayer.
All my enemies will be shamed and utterly dismayed.
They will turn back in sudden shame.

During the עשרת ימי תשובה *and on fast days, except days when* תחנון *is not said (see list below),* אבינו מלכנו *(on page 139) is said here.*

סדר תחנון

תחנון *is not said on* ערב שבת *and* ערב יום טוב*. It is also not said on the following days:* ראש חודש*,* חנוכה*,* ט״ו בשבט*, the 14th and 15th of* אדר א׳*,* פורים *and* שושן פורים*,* ט״ו באב*,* תשעה באב*,* יום ירושלים*,* ל״ג בעומר*,* יום העצמאות*, and the preceding afternoons, the month of* ניסן*, the 14th of* אייר *(*פסח שני*), from* ראש חודש סיון *through the day after* שבועות *(in* ארץ ישראל *through* י״ב סיון*), and from* ערב יום כיפור *through the day after* שמחת תורה *(in* ארץ ישראל *through* ראש חודש מרחשון*).* תחנון *is also not said: on the occasion of a* ברית מילה*, either where the* ברית *will take place or where the father,* סנדק *or* מוהל *are present; if a* חתן *is present (and some say, a* כלה*) on the day of his wedding or during the week of* שבע ברכות*; in a house of mourning.*

נפילת אפיים

Say while sitting; in the presence of a ספר תורה *say until* יֵבֹשׁוּ רָגַע*, leaning forward and resting one's head on the left arm.*

וַיֹּאמֶר דָּוִד אֶל־גָּד, צַר־לִי מְאֹד שמואל ב׳ כד
נִפְּלָה־נָּא בְיַד־יהוה, כִּי רַבִּים רַחֲמָו, וּבְיַד־אָדָם אַל־אֶפֹּלָה:

רַחוּם וְחַנּוּן, חָטָאתִי לְפָנֶיךָ.
יהוה מָלֵא רַחֲמִים, רַחֵם עָלַי וְקַבֵּל תַּחֲנוּנָי.

יהוה, אַל־בְּאַפְּךָ תוֹכִיחֵנִי, וְאַל־בַּחֲמָתְךָ תְיַסְּרֵנִי: תהלים ו
חָנֵּנִי יהוה, כִּי אֻמְלַל אָנִי, רְפָאֵנִי יהוה, כִּי נִבְהֲלוּ עֲצָמָי:
וְנַפְשִׁי נִבְהֲלָה מְאֹד, וְאַתָּ יהוה, עַד־מָתָי:
שׁוּבָה יהוה, חַלְּצָה נַפְשִׁי, הוֹשִׁיעֵנִי לְמַעַן חַסְדֶּךָ:
כִּי אֵין בַּמָּוֶת זִכְרֶךָ, בִּשְׁאוֹל מִי יוֹדֶה־לָּךְ:
יָגַעְתִּי בְּאַנְחָתִי, אַשְׂחֶה בְכָל־לַיְלָה מִטָּתִי, בְּדִמְעָתִי עַרְשִׂי אַמְסֶה:
עָשְׁשָׁה מִכַּעַס עֵינִי, עָתְקָה בְּכָל־צוֹרְרָי:
סוּרוּ מִמֶּנִּי כָּל־פֹּעֲלֵי אָוֶן, כִּי־שָׁמַע יהוה קוֹל בִּכְיִי:
שָׁמַע יהוה תְּחִנָּתִי, יהוה תְּפִלָּתִי יִקָּח:
יֵבֹשׁוּ וְיִבָּהֲלוּ מְאֹד כָּל־אֹיְבָי, יָשֻׁבוּ יֵבֹשׁוּ רָגַע:

Sit upright.

שׁוֹמֵר יִשְׂרָאֵל Guardian of Israel,
guard the remnant of Israel,
and let not Israel perish, who declare, "Listen, Israel."
Guardian of a unique nation, guard the remnant of a unique people,
and let not that unique nation perish, who proclaim the unity of Your name [saying], "The LORD is our God, the LORD is One."
Guardian of a holy nation, guard the remnant of that holy people,
and let not the holy nation perish, who three times repeat the threefold declaration of holiness to the Holy One.
You who are conciliated by calls for compassion and placated by pleas,
be conciliated and placated toward an afflicted generation,
for there is no other help.
Our Father, our King, be gracious to us and answer us,
though we have no worthy deeds;
act with us in charity and loving-kindness and save us.

Stand at ▲.

וַאֲנַחְנוּ We do not know ▲what to do, but our eyes are turned to You. *II Chr. 12*
Remember, LORD, Your compassion and loving-kindness, for they are *Ps. 25*
everlasting. May Your loving-kindness, LORD, be with us, for we have put *Ps. 33*
our hope in You. Do not hold against us the sins of those who came before *Ps. 79*
us. May Your mercies meet us swiftly, for we have been brought very low.
Be gracious to us, LORD, be gracious to us, for we are sated with contempt. *Ps. 123*
In wrath, remember mercy. He knows our nature; He remembers that *Hab. 3* *Ps. 103*
we are dust. ▸ Help us, God of our salvation, for the sake of the glory of *Ps. 79*
Your name. Save us and grant atonement for our sins for Your name's sake.

FULL KADDISH

Leader: יִתְגַּדַּל Magnified and sanctified may His great name be,
in the world He created by His will.
May He establish His kingdom
in your lifetime and in your days,
and in the lifetime of all the house of Israel,
swiftly and soon – and say: Amen.

All: May His great name be blessed for ever and all time.

Sit upright.

שׁוֹמֵר יִשְׂרָאֵל, שְׁמֹר שְׁאֵרִית יִשְׂרָאֵל, וְאַל יֹאבַד יִשְׂרָאֵל
הָאוֹמְרִים שְׁמַע יִשְׂרָאֵל.

שׁוֹמֵר גּוֹי אֶחָד, שְׁמֹר שְׁאֵרִית עַם אֶחָד, וְאַל יֹאבַד גּוֹי אֶחָד
הַמְיַחֲדִים שִׁמְךָ, יהוה אֱלֹהֵינוּ יהוה אֶחָד.

שׁוֹמֵר גּוֹי קָדוֹשׁ, שְׁמֹר שְׁאֵרִית עַם קָדוֹשׁ, וְאַל יֹאבַד גּוֹי קָדוֹשׁ
הַמְשַׁלְּשִׁים בְּשָׁלֹשׁ קְדֻשּׁוֹת לְקָדוֹשׁ.

מִתְרַצֶּה בְּרַחֲמִים וּמִתְפַּיֵּס בְּתַחֲנוּנִים, הִתְרַצֵּה וְהִתְפַּיֵּס לְדוֹר עָנִי
כִּי אֵין עוֹזֵר.

אָבִינוּ מַלְכֵּנוּ, חָנֵּנוּ וַעֲנֵנוּ, כִּי אֵין בָּנוּ מַעֲשִׂים
עֲשֵׂה עִמָּנוּ צְדָקָה וָחֶסֶד וְהוֹשִׁיעֵנוּ.

Stand at ▴.

וַאֲנַחְנוּ לֹא נֵדַע ▴מַה־נַּעֲשֶׂה, כִּי עָלֶיךָ עֵינֵינוּ: זְכֹר־רַחֲמֶיךָ יהוה דברי הימים ב׳ כ
וַחֲסָדֶיךָ, כִּי מֵעוֹלָם הֵמָּה: יְהִי־חַסְדְּךָ יהוה עָלֵינוּ, כַּאֲשֶׁר יִחַלְנוּ לָךְ: תהלים כה / תהלים לג
אַל־תִּזְכָּר־לָנוּ עֲוֹנֹת רִאשֹׁנִים, מַהֵר יְקַדְּמוּנוּ רַחֲמֶיךָ, כִּי דַלּוֹנוּ מְאֹד: תהלים עט
חָנֵּנוּ יהוה חָנֵּנוּ, כִּי־רַב שָׂבַעְנוּ בוּז: בְּרֹגֶז רַחֵם תִּזְכּוֹר: כִּי־הוּא יָדַע תהלים קכג / חבקוק ג / תהלים קג
יִצְרֵנוּ, זָכוּר כִּי־עָפָר אֲנָחְנוּ: ▸ עָזְרֵנוּ אֱלֹהֵי יִשְׁעֵנוּ עַל־דְּבַר כְּבוֹד־ תהלים עט
שְׁמֶךָ, וְהַצִּילֵנוּ וְכַפֵּר עַל־חַטֹּאתֵינוּ לְמַעַן שְׁמֶךָ:

קדיש שלם

ש״ץ: יִתְגַּדַּל וְיִתְקַדַּשׁ שְׁמֵהּ רַבָּא (קהל: אָמֵן)
בְּעָלְמָא דִּי בְרָא כִרְעוּתֵהּ
וְיַמְלִיךְ מַלְכוּתֵהּ
בְּחַיֵּיכוֹן וּבְיוֹמֵיכוֹן וּבְחַיֵּי דְכָל בֵּית יִשְׂרָאֵל
בַּעֲגָלָא וּבִזְמַן קָרִיב, וְאִמְרוּ אָמֵן. (קהל: אָמֵן)

קהל ושי״ץ: יְהֵא שְׁמֵהּ רַבָּא מְבָרַךְ לְעָלַם וּלְעָלְמֵי עָלְמַיָּא.

Leader: Blessed and praised,
glorified and exalted, raised and honored,
uplifted and lauded be
the name of the Holy One, blessed be He,
beyond any blessing,
song, praise and consolation uttered in the world –
and say: Amen.

May the prayers and pleas of all Israel
be accepted by their Father in heaven –
and say: Amen.

May there be great peace from heaven,
and life for us and all Israel –
and say: Amen.

Bow, take three steps back, as if taking leave of the Divine Presence, then bow, first left, then right, then center, while saying:

May He who makes peace in His high places,
make peace for us and all Israel –
and say: Amen.

Stand while saying Aleinu. Bow at ▾.

עָלֵינוּ It is our duty to praise the Master of all,
and ascribe greatness to the Author of creation,
who has not made us like the nations of the lands
nor placed us like the families of the earth;
who has not made our portion like theirs,
nor our destiny like all their multitudes.
(For they worship vanity and emptiness,
and pray to a god who cannot save.)
▾But we bow in worship
and thank the Supreme King of kings,
the Holy One, blessed be He,
who extends the heavens and establishes the earth,

ש״ץ: יִתְבָּרַךְ וְיִשְׁתַּבַּח וְיִתְפָּאַר
וְיִתְרוֹמַם וְיִתְנַשֵּׂא וְיִתְהַדָּר וְיִתְעַלֶּה וְיִתְהַלָּל
שְׁמֵהּ דְּקֻדְשָׁא בְּרִיךְ הוּא (קהל: בְּרִיךְ הוּא)
לְעֵלָּא מִן כָּל בִּרְכָתָא
/ בעשרת ימי תשובה: לְעֵלָּא לְעֵלָּא מִכָּל בִּרְכָתָא/
וְשִׁירָתָא, תֻּשְׁבְּחָתָא וְנֶחֱמָתָא
דַּאֲמִירָן בְּעָלְמָא, וְאִמְרוּ אָמֵן. (קהל: אָמֵן)
תִּתְקַבַּל צְלוֹתְהוֹן וּבָעוּתְהוֹן דְּכָל יִשְׂרָאֵל
קֳדָם אֲבוּהוֹן דִּי בִשְׁמַיָּא, וְאִמְרוּ אָמֵן. (קהל: אָמֵן)
יְהֵא שְׁלָמָא רַבָּא מִן שְׁמַיָּא
וְחַיִּים, עָלֵינוּ וְעַל כָּל יִשְׂרָאֵל
וְאִמְרוּ אָמֵן. (קהל: אָמֵן)

Bow, take three steps back, as if taking leave of the Divine Presence, then bow, first left, then right, then center, while saying:

עֹשֶׂה שָׁלוֹם/ בעשרת ימי תשובה: הַשָּׁלוֹם/ בִּמְרוֹמָיו
הוּא יַעֲשֶׂה שָׁלוֹם עָלֵינוּ וְעַל כָּל יִשְׂרָאֵל
וְאִמְרוּ אָמֵן. (קהל: אָמֵן)

Stand while saying עָלֵינוּ. *Bow at* ˚.

עָלֵינוּ לְשַׁבֵּחַ לַאֲדוֹן הַכֹּל, לָתֵת גְּדֻלָּה לְיוֹצֵר בְּרֵאשִׁית
שֶׁלֹּא עָשָׂנוּ כְּגוֹיֵי הָאֲרָצוֹת, וְלֹא שָׂמָנוּ כְּמִשְׁפְּחוֹת הָאֲדָמָה
שֶׁלֹּא שָׂם חֶלְקֵנוּ כָּהֶם וְגוֹרָלֵנוּ כְּכָל הֲמוֹנָם.
(שֶׁהֵם מִשְׁתַּחֲוִים לְהֶבֶל וָרִיק וּמִתְפַּלְלִים אֶל אֵל לֹא יוֹשִׁיעַ.)
˚וַאֲנַחְנוּ כּוֹרְעִים וּמִשְׁתַּחֲוִים וּמוֹדִים
לִפְנֵי מֶלֶךְ מַלְכֵי הַמְּלָכִים, הַקָּדוֹשׁ בָּרוּךְ הוּא
שֶׁהוּא נוֹטֶה שָׁמַיִם וְיוֹסֵד אָרֶץ

whose throne of glory is in the heavens above,
and whose power's Presence is in the highest of heights.
He is our God; there is no other.
Truly He is our King, there is none else,
as it is written in His Torah:
"You shall know and take to heart this day — *Deut. 4*
that the LORD is God,
in heaven above and on earth below. There is no other."

Therefore, we place our hope in You, LORD our God,
that we may soon see the glory of Your power,
when You will remove abominations from the earth,
and idols will be utterly destroyed,
when the world will be perfected
under the sovereignty of the Almighty,
when all humanity will call on Your name,
to turn all the earth's wicked toward You.
All the world's inhabitants will realize and know
that to You every knee must bow
and every tongue swear loyalty.
Before You, LORD our God, they will kneel and bow down
and give honor to Your glorious name.
They will all accept the yoke of Your kingdom,
and You will reign over them soon and for ever.
For the kingdom is Yours,
and to all eternity You will reign in glory,
as it is written in Your Torah:
"The LORD will reign for ever and ever." — *Ex. 15*
▸ And it is said: "Then the LORD shall be King over all the earth; — *Zech. 14*
on that day the LORD shall be One and His name One."

Some add:

Have no fear of sudden terror or of the ruin when it overtakes the wicked. — *Prov. 3*
Devise your strategy, but it will be thwarted; propose your plan, — *Is. 8*
but it will not stand, for God is with us. When you grow old, I will still be the same. — *Is. 46*
When your hair turns gray, I will still carry you. I made you, I will bear you,
I will carry you, and I will rescue you.

וּמוֹשַׁב יְקָרוֹ בַּשָּׁמַיִם מִמַּעַל
וּשְׁכִינַת עֻזּוֹ בְּגָבְהֵי מְרוֹמִים.
הוּא אֱלֹהֵינוּ, אֵין עוֹד.
אֱמֶת מַלְכֵּנוּ, אֶפֶס זוּלָתוֹ
כַּכָּתוּב בְּתוֹרָתוֹ
וְיָדַעְתָּ הַיּוֹם וַהֲשֵׁבֹתָ אֶל־לְבָבֶךָ דברים ד
כִּי יהוה הוּא הָאֱלֹהִים בַּשָּׁמַיִם מִמַּעַל וְעַל־הָאָרֶץ מִתָּחַת, **אֵין עוֹד:**

עַל כֵּן נְקַוֶּה לְּךָ יהוה אֱלֹהֵינוּ, לִרְאוֹת מְהֵרָה בְּתִפְאֶרֶת עֻזֶּךָ
לְהַעֲבִיר גִּלּוּלִים מִן הָאָרֶץ, וְהָאֱלִילִים כָּרוֹת יִכָּרֵתוּן
לְתַקֵּן עוֹלָם בְּמַלְכוּת שַׁדַּי.
וְכָל בְּנֵי בָשָׂר יִקְרְאוּ בִשְׁמֶךָ לְהַפְנוֹת אֵלֶיךָ כָּל רִשְׁעֵי אָרֶץ.
יַכִּירוּ וְיֵדְעוּ כָּל יוֹשְׁבֵי תֵבֵל
כִּי לְךָ תִּכְרַע כָּל בֶּרֶךְ, תִּשָּׁבַע כָּל לָשׁוֹן.
לְפָנֶיךָ יהוה אֱלֹהֵינוּ יִכְרְעוּ וְיִפֹּלוּ, וְלִכְבוֹד שִׁמְךָ יְקָר יִתֵּנוּ
וִיקַבְּלוּ כֻלָּם אֶת עֹל מַלְכוּתֶךָ
וְתִמְלֹךְ עֲלֵיהֶם מְהֵרָה לְעוֹלָם וָעֶד.
כִּי הַמַּלְכוּת שֶׁלְּךָ הִיא וּלְעוֹלְמֵי עַד תִּמְלֹךְ בְּכָבוֹד
כַּכָּתוּב בְּתוֹרָתֶךָ, יהוה יִמְלֹךְ לְעֹלָם וָעֶד: שמות טו
◂ וְנֶאֱמַר, וְהָיָה יהוה לְמֶלֶךְ עַל־כָּל־הָאָרֶץ זכריה יד
בַּיּוֹם הַהוּא יִהְיֶה יהוה אֶחָד וּשְׁמוֹ אֶחָד:

Some add:

אַל־תִּירָא מִפַּחַד פִּתְאֹם וּמִשֹּׁאַת רְשָׁעִים כִּי תָבֹא: משלי ג
עֻצוּ עֵצָה וְתֻפָר, דַּבְּרוּ דָבָר וְלֹא יָקוּם, כִּי עִמָּנוּ אֵל: ישעיה ח
וְעַד־זִקְנָה אֲנִי הוּא, וְעַד־שֵׂיבָה אֲנִי אֶסְבֹּל ישעיה מו
אֲנִי עָשִׂיתִי וַאֲנִי אֶשָּׂא וַאֲנִי אֶסְבֹּל וַאֲמַלֵּט:

MOURNER'S KADDISH

The following prayer, said by mourners, requires the presence of a minyan. A transliteration can be found on page 1334.

Mourner: יִתְגַּדַּל Magnified and sanctified
may His great name be,
in the world He created by His will.
May He establish His kingdom
in your lifetime
and in your days,
and in the lifetime
of all the house of Israel,
swiftly and soon –
and say: Amen.

All: May His great name be blessed for ever and all time.

Mourner: Blessed and praised,
glorified and exalted,
raised and honored,
uplifted and lauded
be the name of the Holy One,
blessed be He,
beyond any blessing,
song, praise and consolation
uttered in the world –
and say: Amen.

May there be great peace from heaven,
and life for us and all Israel –
and say: Amen.

Bow, take three steps back, as if taking leave of the Divine Presence, then bow, first left, then right, then center, while saying:

May He who makes peace in His high places,
make peace for us and all Israel –
and say: Amen.

קדיש יתום

The following prayer, said by mourners, requires the presence of a מנין*.*
A transliteration can be found on page 1334.

אבל: יִתְגַּדַּל וְיִתְקַדַּשׁ שְׁמֵהּ רַבָּא (קהל: אָמֵן)
בְּעָלְמָא דִּי בְרָא כִרְעוּתֵהּ
וְיַמְלִיךְ מַלְכוּתֵהּ
בְּחַיֵּיכוֹן וּבְיוֹמֵיכוֹן
וּבְחַיֵּי דְכָל בֵּית יִשְׂרָאֵל
בַּעֲגָלָא וּבִזְמַן קָרִיב
וְאִמְרוּ אָמֵן. (קהל: אָמֵן)

קהל ואבל: יְהֵא שְׁמֵהּ רַבָּא מְבָרַךְ לְעָלַם וּלְעָלְמֵי עָלְמַיָּא.

אבל: יִתְבָּרַךְ וְיִשְׁתַּבַּח וְיִתְפָּאַר
וְיִתְרוֹמַם וְיִתְנַשֵּׂא וְיִתְהַדָּר וְיִתְעַלֶּה וְיִתְהַלָּל
שְׁמֵהּ דְּקֻדְשָׁא בְּרִיךְ הוּא (קהל: בְּרִיךְ הוּא)
לְעֵלָּא מִן כָּל בִּרְכָתָא
/ בעשרת ימי תשובה: לְעֵלָּא לְעֵלָּא מִכָּל בִּרְכָתָא/
וְשִׁירָתָא, תֻּשְׁבְּחָתָא וְנֶחֱמָתָא
דַּאֲמִירָן בְּעָלְמָא
וְאִמְרוּ אָמֵן. (קהל: אָמֵן)
יְהֵא שְׁלָמָא רַבָּא מִן שְׁמַיָּא
וְחַיִּים, עָלֵינוּ וְעַל כָּל יִשְׂרָאֵל, וְאִמְרוּ אָמֵן. (קהל: אָמֵן)

Bow, take three steps back, as if taking leave of the Divine Presence,
then bow, first left, then right, then center, while saying:

עֹשֶׂה שָׁלוֹם/ בעשרת ימי תשובה: הַשָּׁלוֹם/ בִּמְרוֹמָיו
הוּא יַעֲשֶׂה שָׁלוֹם עָלֵינוּ וְעַל כָּל יִשְׂרָאֵל
וְאִמְרוּ אָמֵן. (קהל: אָמֵן)

Ma'ariv for Weekdays

On Motza'ei Shabbat some have the custom to sing Psalm 67 and Psalm 144 before the Ma'ariv Service (page 692).

וְהוּא רַחוּם He is compassionate. Ps. 78
He forgives iniquity and does not destroy.
Repeatedly He suppresses His anger, not rousing His full wrath.
LORD, save! May the King, answer us on the day we call. Ps. 20

BLESSINGS OF THE SHEMA

The Leader says the following, bowing at "Bless," standing straight at "the LORD"; the congregation, followed by the Leader, responds, bowing at "Bless," standing straight at "the LORD":

Leader: BLESS
the LORD, the blessed One.

Congregation: Bless the LORD, the blessed One,
for ever and all time.

Leader: Bless the LORD, the blessed One,
for ever and all time.

---

prayer: the ladder stretching from earth to heaven on which angels ascended and descended. During that vision, God promised Jacob that "I will protect you wherever you go" (Gen. 28:15). The evening service represents our trust in God during the dark and dangers of night.

וְהוּא רַחוּם *He is compassionate:* A prelude to prayer, from the book of Psalms, that serves as a brief equivalent to the Verses of Praise in the morning service. The verse (Psalm 78:38) contains thirteen words that are reminiscent of the thirteen attributes of divine mercy.

בָּרְכוּ אֶת יהוה *Bless the LORD:* As in the morning service, a call to the congregation to join in communal prayer, derived from the verse: "Magnify the LORD with me; let us exalt His name together" (Psalm 34:4).

מעריב לחול

On מוצאי שבת *some have the custom to sing* לְדָוִד, בָּרוּךְ יהוה צוּרִי *and* תפילת ערבית *before* מִזְמוֹר שִׁיר לַמְנַצֵּחַ בִּנְגִינֹת (*page 693*).

וְהוּא רַחוּם, יְכַפֵּר עָוֹן וְלֹא־יַשְׁחִית תהלים עח
וְהִרְבָּה לְהָשִׁיב אַפּוֹ, וְלֹא־יָעִיר כָּל־חֲמָתוֹ:
יהוה הוֹשִׁיעָה, הַמֶּלֶךְ יַעֲנֵנוּ בְיוֹם־קָרְאֵנוּ: תהלים כ

קריאת שמע וברכותיה

The שליח ציבור *says the following, bowing at* בָּרְכוּ*, standing straight at* ה'*; the* קהל*, followed by the* שליח ציבור*, responds, bowing at* בָּרוּךְ*, standing straight at* ה'*:*

שׁץ: בָּרְכוּ

אֶת יהוה הַמְבֹרָךְ.

קהל: בָּרוּךְ יהוה הַמְבֹרָךְ לְעוֹלָם וָעֶד.

שׁץ: בָּרוּךְ יהוה הַמְבֹרָךְ לְעוֹלָם וָעֶד.

EVENING SERVICE

The saying of Shema at night ("when you lie down") is a biblical imperative. In early post-Temple times there were some who held that the evening Amida was non-obligatory since – unlike the morning and afternoon services – there was no daily sacrifice to which it corresponded (*Berakhot* 27b–28a). So widespread was its observance, however, that it was eventually deemed obligatory. Notwithstanding, since the Amida at night does not correspond to a sacrifice, it is not repeated by the Leader.

Tradition identifies the evening prayer with Jacob, who had his most intense religious experiences at night, especially the vision most associated with

בָּרוּךְ Blessed are You, LORD our God, King of the Universe,
who by His word brings on evenings,
by His wisdom opens the gates of heaven,
with understanding makes time change and the seasons rotate,
and by His will
orders the stars in their constellations in the sky.
He creates day and night,
rolling away the light before the darkness,
and darkness before the light.
▸ He makes the day pass and brings on night,
distinguishing day from night:
the LORD of hosts is His name.
May the living and forever enduring God rule over us for all time.
Blessed are You, LORD, who brings on evenings.

אַהֲבַת עוֹלָם With everlasting love
have You loved Your people, the house of Israel.
You have taught us Torah and commandments,
decrees and laws of justice.
Therefore, LORD our God, when we lie down and when we rise up
we will speak of Your decrees, rejoicing in the words of Your Torah
and Your commandments for ever.
▸ For they are our life and the length of our days;
on them will we meditate day and night.
May You never take away Your love from us.
Blessed are You, LORD, who loves His people Israel.

"You have loved us with great love." Both speak of divine love in terms of revelation: God's gift to Israel of the Torah and its commandments. In the same way that God binds Himself to His people through word and deed, so do we bind ourselves to Him by the words of Torah and the deeds of the commandments. No simpler or more profound statement exists of the love of Jews for the life of the commandments than the phrase, "For they are our life and the length of our days."

בָּרוּךְ אַתָּה יהוה אֱלֹהֵינוּ מֶלֶךְ הָעוֹלָם
אֲשֶׁר בִּדְבָרוֹ מַעֲרִיב עֲרָבִים
בְּחָכְמָה פּוֹתֵחַ שְׁעָרִים
וּבִתְבוּנָה מְשַׁנֶּה עִתִּים וּמַחֲלִיף אֶת הַזְּמַנִּים
וּמְסַדֵּר אֶת הַכּוֹכָבִים בְּמִשְׁמְרוֹתֵיהֶם בָּרָקִיעַ כִּרְצוֹנוֹ.
בּוֹרֵא יוֹם וָלָיְלָה
גּוֹלֵל אוֹר מִפְּנֵי חֹשֶׁךְ וְחֹשֶׁךְ מִפְּנֵי אוֹר
‹ וּמַעֲבִיר יוֹם וּמֵבִיא לָיְלָה
וּמַבְדִּיל בֵּין יוֹם וּבֵין לָיְלָה
יהוה צְבָאוֹת שְׁמוֹ.
אֵל חַי וְקַיָּם תָּמִיד, יִמְלֹךְ עָלֵינוּ לְעוֹלָם וָעֶד.
בָּרוּךְ אַתָּה יהוה, הַמַּעֲרִיב עֲרָבִים.

אַהֲבַת עוֹלָם בֵּית יִשְׂרָאֵל עַמְּךָ אָהָבְתָּ
תּוֹרָה וּמִצְוֹת, חֻקִּים וּמִשְׁפָּטִים, אוֹתָנוּ לִמַּדְתָּ
עַל כֵּן יהוה אֱלֹהֵינוּ בְּשָׁכְבֵנוּ וּבְקוּמֵנוּ נָשִׂיחַ בְּחֻקֶּיךָ
וְנִשְׂמַח בְּדִבְרֵי תוֹרָתֶךָ וּבְמִצְוֹתֶיךָ לְעוֹלָם וָעֶד
‹ כִּי הֵם חַיֵּינוּ וְאֹרֶךְ יָמֵינוּ, וּבָהֶם נֶהְגֶּה יוֹמָם וָלָיְלָה.
וְאַהֲבָתְךָ אַל תָּסִיר מִמֶּנּוּ לְעוֹלָמִים.
בָּרוּךְ אַתָּה יהוה, אוֹהֵב עַמּוֹ יִשְׂרָאֵל.

הַמַּעֲרִיב עֲרָבִים *Who brings on evenings:* Praise of God as Creator of the universe, and hence of time itself. As with the morning service, the two blessings before the Shema, and the one immediately following, speak in turn of the three key elements of Jewish faith: creation, revelation and redemption.

אַהֲבַת עוֹלָם *With everlasting love:* A counterpart to the morning blessing,

The Shema must be said with intense concentration. See laws 349–353.

When not with a minyan, say:

God, faithful King!

The following verse should be said aloud, while covering the eyes with the right hand:

Listen, Israel: the LORD is our God, the LORD is One.

Deut. 6

Quietly: Blessed be the name of His glorious kingdom for ever and all time.

וְאָהַבְתָּ Love the LORD your God with all your heart, with all your soul, and with all your might. These words which I command you today shall be on your heart. Teach them repeatedly to your children, speaking of them when you sit at home and when you travel on the way, when you lie down and when you rise. Bind them as a sign on your hand, and they shall be an emblem between your eyes. Write them on the doorposts of your house and gates. *Deut. 6*

וְהָיָה If you indeed heed My commandments with which I charge you today, to love the LORD your God and worship Him with all your heart and with all your soul, I will give rain in your land in its season, the early and late rain; and you shall gather in your grain, wine and oil. I will give grass in your field for your cattle, and you shall eat and be satisfied. Be careful lest your heart be tempted and you go astray and worship other gods, bowing down to them. Then the LORD's anger will flare against you and He will close the heavens so that there will be no rain. The land will not yield its crops, and you will perish swiftly from the good land that the LORD is giving you. Therefore, set these, My words, on your heart and soul. Bind them as a sign on your hand, and they shall be an emblem between your eyes. Teach them to your children, speaking of them when you sit at home and when you travel on the way, when you lie down and when you rise. Write them on the doorposts of your house and gates, so that you and your children may live long in the land that the LORD swore to your ancestors to give them, for as long as the heavens are above the earth. *Deut. 11*

The שמע *must be said with intense concentration. See laws 349–353.*

When not with a מנין, *say:*

אֵל מֶלֶךְ נֶאֱמָן

The following verse should be said aloud, while covering the eyes with the right hand:

דברים ו

שְׁמַע יִשְׂרָאֵל, יְהוָה אֱלֹהֵינוּ, יְהוָה ׀ אֶחָד:

Quietly בָּרוּךְ שֵׁם כְּבוֹד מַלְכוּתוֹ לְעוֹלָם וָעֶד.

דברים ו

וְאָהַבְתָּ אֵת יְהוָה אֱלֹהֶיךָ, בְּכָל־לְבָבְךָ וּבְכָל־נַפְשְׁךָ וּבְכָל־מְאֹדֶךָ:
וְהָיוּ הַדְּבָרִים הָאֵלֶּה, אֲשֶׁר אָנֹכִי מְצַוְּךָ הַיּוֹם, עַל־לְבָבֶךָ: וְשִׁנַּנְתָּם
לְבָנֶיךָ וְדִבַּרְתָּ בָּם, בְּשִׁבְתְּךָ בְּבֵיתֶךָ וּבְלֶכְתְּךָ בַדֶּרֶךְ, וּבְשָׁכְבְּךָ
וּבְקוּמֶךָ: וּקְשַׁרְתָּם לְאוֹת עַל־יָדֶךָ וְהָיוּ לְטֹטָפֹת בֵּין עֵינֶיךָ:
וּכְתַבְתָּם עַל־מְזֻזוֹת בֵּיתֶךָ וּבִשְׁעָרֶיךָ:

דברים יא

וְהָיָה אִם־שָׁמֹעַ תִּשְׁמְעוּ אֶל־מִצְוֹתַי אֲשֶׁר אָנֹכִי מְצַוֶּה אֶתְכֶם
הַיּוֹם, לְאַהֲבָה אֶת־יְהוָה אֱלֹהֵיכֶם וּלְעָבְדוֹ, בְּכָל־לְבַבְכֶם וּבְכָל־
נַפְשְׁכֶם: וְנָתַתִּי מְטַר־אַרְצְכֶם בְּעִתּוֹ, יוֹרֶה וּמַלְקוֹשׁ, וְאָסַפְתָּ דְגָנֶךָ
וְתִירֹשְׁךָ וְיִצְהָרֶךָ: וְנָתַתִּי עֵשֶׂב בְּשָׂדְךָ לִבְהֶמְתֶּךָ, וְאָכַלְתָּ וְשָׂבָעְתָּ:
הִשָּׁמְרוּ לָכֶם פֶּן יִפְתֶּה לְבַבְכֶם, וְסַרְתֶּם וַעֲבַדְתֶּם אֱלֹהִים אֲחֵרִים
וְהִשְׁתַּחֲוִיתֶם לָהֶם: וְחָרָה אַף־יְהוָה בָּכֶם, וְעָצַר אֶת־הַשָּׁמַיִם
וְלֹא־יִהְיֶה מָטָר, וְהָאֲדָמָה לֹא תִתֵּן אֶת־יְבוּלָהּ, וַאֲבַדְתֶּם מְהֵרָה
מֵעַל הָאָרֶץ הַטֹּבָה אֲשֶׁר יְהוָה נֹתֵן לָכֶם: וְשַׂמְתֶּם אֶת־דְּבָרַי
אֵלֶּה עַל־לְבַבְכֶם וְעַל־נַפְשְׁכֶם, וּקְשַׁרְתֶּם אֹתָם לְאוֹת עַל־יֶדְכֶם,
וְהָיוּ לְטוֹטָפֹת בֵּין עֵינֵיכֶם: וְלִמַּדְתֶּם אֹתָם אֶת־בְּנֵיכֶם לְדַבֵּר בָּם,
בְּשִׁבְתְּךָ בְּבֵיתֶךָ וּבְלֶכְתְּךָ בַדֶּרֶךְ, וּבְשָׁכְבְּךָ וּבְקוּמֶךָ: וּכְתַבְתָּם
עַל־מְזוּזוֹת בֵּיתֶךָ וּבִשְׁעָרֶיךָ: לְמַעַן יִרְבּוּ יְמֵיכֶם וִימֵי בְנֵיכֶם עַל
הָאֲדָמָה אֲשֶׁר נִשְׁבַּע יְהוָה לַאֲבֹתֵיכֶם לָתֵת לָהֶם, כִּימֵי הַשָּׁמַיִם
עַל־הָאָרֶץ:

וַיֹּאמֶר The LORD spoke to Moses, saying: Speak to the Israelites and tell them to make tassels on the corners of their garments for all generations. They shall attach to the tassel at each corner a thread of blue. This shall be your tassel, and you shall see it and remember all of the LORD's commandments and keep them, not straying after your heart and after your eyes, following your own sinful desires. Thus you will be reminded to keep all My commandments, and be holy to your God. I am the LORD your God, who brought you out of the land of Egypt to be your God. I am the LORD your God. *Num. 15*

True –

The Leader repeats:

▸ The LORD your God is true –

וֶאֱמוּנָה – and faithful is all this,
and firmly established for us
that He is the LORD our God,
and there is none besides Him,
and that we, Israel, are His people.
He is our King, who redeems us from the hand of kings
and delivers us from the grasp of all tyrants.
He is our God,
who on our behalf repays our foes
and brings just retribution on our mortal enemies;
who performs great deeds beyond understanding
and wonders beyond number;
who kept us alive, not letting our foot slip; *Ps. 66*
who led us on the high places of our enemies,
raising our pride above all our foes;

---

faithfulness at night echoes the phrase from Psalm 92: "to tell of Your love in the morning, and Your faithfulness at night."

במדבר טו וַיֹּאמֶר יהוה אֶל־מֹשֶׁה לֵּאמֹר: דַּבֵּר אֶל־בְּנֵי יִשְׂרָאֵל וְאָמַרְתָּ אֲלֵהֶם, וְעָשׂוּ לָהֶם צִיצִת עַל־כַּנְפֵי בִגְדֵיהֶם לְדֹרֹתָם, וְנָתְנוּ עַל־צִיצִת הַכָּנָף פְּתִיל תְּכֵלֶת: וְהָיָה לָכֶם לְצִיצִת, וּרְאִיתֶם אֹתוֹ וּזְכַרְתֶּם אֶת־כָּל־מִצְוֹת יהוה וַעֲשִׂיתֶם אֹתָם, וְלֹא תָתֻרוּ אַחֲרֵי לְבַבְכֶם וְאַחֲרֵי עֵינֵיכֶם, אֲשֶׁר־אַתֶּם זֹנִים אַחֲרֵיהֶם: לְמַעַן תִּזְכְּרוּ וַעֲשִׂיתֶם אֶת־כָּל־מִצְוֹתָי, וִהְיִיתֶם קְדֹשִׁים לֵאלֹהֵיכֶם: אֲנִי יהוה אֱלֹהֵיכֶם, אֲשֶׁר הוֹצֵאתִי אֶתְכֶם מֵאֶרֶץ מִצְרַיִם, לִהְיוֹת לָכֶם לֵאלֹהִים, אֲנִי יהוה אֱלֹהֵיכֶם:

אֱמֶת

The שליח ציבור *repeats:*

◂ יהוה אֱלֹהֵיכֶם אֱמֶת

וֶאֱמוּנָה כָּל זֹאת וְקַיָּם עָלֵינוּ
כִּי הוּא יהוה אֱלֹהֵינוּ וְאֵין זוּלָתוֹ
וַאֲנַחְנוּ יִשְׂרָאֵל עַמּוֹ.
הַפּוֹדֵנוּ מִיַּד מְלָכִים
מַלְכֵּנוּ הַגּוֹאֲלֵנוּ מִכַּף כָּל הֶעָרִיצִים.
הָאֵל הַנִּפְרָע לָנוּ מִצָּרֵינוּ
וְהַמְשַׁלֵּם גְּמוּל לְכָל אוֹיְבֵי נַפְשֵׁנוּ.
הָעוֹשֶׂה גְדוֹלוֹת עַד אֵין חֵקֶר, וְנִפְלָאוֹת עַד אֵין מִסְפָּר
תהלים סו הַשָּׂם נַפְשֵׁנוּ בַּחַיִּים, וְלֹא־נָתַן לַמּוֹט רַגְלֵנוּ:
הַמַּדְרִיכֵנוּ עַל בָּמוֹת אוֹיְבֵינוּ
וַיָּרֶם קַרְנֵנוּ עַל כָּל שׂוֹנְאֵינוּ.

אֱמֶת וֶאֱמוּנָה *True and faithful:* A blessing about redemption, parallel to the blessing **אֱמֶת וְיַצִּיב**, "True and firm," in the morning. The special emphasis on

who did miracles for us
and brought vengeance against Pharaoh;
who performed signs and wonders
in the land of Ham's children;
who smote in His wrath all the firstborn of Egypt,
and brought out His people Israel from their midst
into everlasting freedom;
who led His children through the divided Reed Sea,
plunging their pursuers and enemies into the depths.
When His children saw His might,
they gave praise and thanks to His name,
▸ and willingly accepted His Sovereignty.
Moses and the children of Israel
then sang a song to You with great joy,
and they all exclaimed:

מִי־כָמֹכָה "Who is like You, LORD, among the mighty? *Ex. 15*
Who is like You, majestic in holiness,
awesome in praises, doing wonders?"

▸ Your children beheld Your majesty
as You parted the sea before Moses.
"This is my God!" they responded, and then said:

"The LORD shall reign for ever and ever." *Ex. 15*

▸ And it is said, "For the LORD has redeemed Jacob *Jer. 31*
and rescued him from a power stronger than his own."
Blessed are You, LORD, who redeemed Israel.

הַשְׁכִּיבֵנוּ Help us lie down, O LORD our God, in peace,
and rise up, O our King, to life.
Spread over us Your canopy of peace.
Direct us with Your good counsel,
and save us for the sake of Your name.

הַשְׁכִּיבֵנוּ *Help us lie down:* This blessing, which has no parallel in the morning service, is a prayer for protection against the hazards of the night.

הָעוֹשֶׂה לָּֽנוּ נִסִּים וּנְקָמָה בְּפַרְעֹה
אוֹתוֹת וּמוֹפְתִים בְּאַדְמַת בְּנֵי חָם.
הַמַּכֶּה בְעֶבְרָתוֹ כָּל בְּכוֹרֵי מִצְרָֽיִם
וַיּוֹצֵא אֶת עַמּוֹ יִשְׂרָאֵל מִתּוֹכָם לְחֵרוּת עוֹלָם.
הַמַּעֲבִיר בָּנָיו בֵּין גִּזְרֵי יַם סוּף
אֶת רוֹדְפֵיהֶם וְאֶת שׂוֹנְאֵיהֶם בִּתְהוֹמוֹת טִבַּע
וְרָאוּ בָנָיו גְּבוּרָתוֹ, שִׁבְּחוּ וְהוֹדוּ לִשְׁמוֹ
‹ וּמַלְכוּתוֹ בְּרָצוֹן קִבְּלוּ עֲלֵיהֶם.
מֹשֶׁה וּבְנֵי יִשְׂרָאֵל, לְךָ עָנוּ שִׁירָה בְּשִׂמְחָה רַבָּה
וְאָמְרוּ כֻלָּם

שמות טו מִי־כָמֹֽכָה בָּאֵלִם יהוה
מִי כָּמֹֽכָה נֶאְדָּר בַּקֹּֽדֶשׁ
נוֹרָא תְהִלֹּת עֹֽשֵׂה פֶֽלֶא:

‹ מַלְכוּתְךָ רָאוּ בָנֶֽיךָ, בּוֹקֵֽעַ יָם לִפְנֵי מֹשֶׁה
זֶה אֵלִי עָנוּ, וְאָמְרוּ
שמות טו יהוה יִמְלֹךְ לְעֹלָם וָעֶד:

‹ וְנֶאֱמַר
ירמיהו לא כִּי־פָדָה יהוה אֶת־יַעֲקֹב
וּגְאָלוֹ מִיַּד חָזָק מִמֶּֽנּוּ:
בָּרוּךְ אַתָּה יהוה, גָּאַל יִשְׂרָאֵל.

הַשְׁכִּיבֵֽנוּ יהוה אֱלֹהֵֽינוּ לְשָׁלוֹם
וְהַעֲמִידֵֽנוּ מַלְכֵּֽנוּ לְחַיִּים
וּפְרֹשׂ עָלֵֽינוּ סֻכַּת שְׁלוֹמֶֽךָ, וְתַקְּנֵֽנוּ בְּעֵצָה טוֹבָה מִלְּפָנֶֽיךָ
וְהוֹשִׁיעֵֽנוּ לְמַֽעַן שְׁמֶֽךָ.

Shield us and remove from us every enemy,
plague, sword, famine and sorrow.
Remove the adversary from before and behind us.
Shelter us in the shadow of Your wings,
for You, God, are our Guardian and Deliverer;
You, God, are a gracious and compassionate King.
▸ Guard our going out and our coming in,
for life and peace, from now and for ever.
Blessed are You, LORD, who guards His people Israel for ever.

In Israel the service continues with Half Kaddish on page 256.

בָּרוּךְ Blessed be the LORD for ever. Amen and Amen. *Ps. 89*
Blessed from Zion be the LORD *Ps. 135*
who dwells in Jerusalem. Halleluya!
Blessed be the LORD, God of Israel, *Ps. 72*
who alone does wondrous things.
Blessed be His glorious name for ever,
and may the whole earth be filled with His glory. Amen and Amen.
May the glory of the LORD endure for ever; *Ps. 104*
may the LORD rejoice in His works.
May the name of the LORD be blessed now and for all time. *Ps. 113*
For the sake of His great name *1 Sam. 12*
the LORD will not abandon His people,
for the LORD vowed to make you a people of His own.
When all the people saw [God's wonders] they fell on their faces *1 Kings 18*
and said: "The LORD, He is God; the LORD, He is God."
Then the LORD shall be King over all the earth; *Zech. 14*
on that day the LORD shall be One and His name One.
May Your loving-kindness, LORD, be upon us, *Ps. 33*
as we have put our hope in You.

God, was originally recited as a substitute for the evening Amida – possibly to shorten the evening service in synagogue so that participants could return home before dark. When conditions changed, the prayer was retained. Since it was a substitute for the weekday Amida, it is not said on Shabbat or Yom Tov.

וְהָגֵן בַּעֲדֵנוּ, וְהָסֵר מֵעָלֵינוּ אוֹיֵב, דֶּבֶר וְחֶרֶב וְרָעָב וְיָגוֹן
וְהָסֵר שָׂטָן מִלְּפָנֵינוּ וּמֵאַחֲרֵינוּ, וּבְצֵל כְּנָפֶיךָ תַּסְתִּירֵנוּ
כִּי אֵל שׁוֹמְרֵנוּ וּמַצִּילֵנוּ אָתָּה
כִּי אֵל מֶלֶךְ חַנּוּן וְרַחוּם אָתָּה.
◂ וּשְׁמֹר צֵאתֵנוּ וּבוֹאֵנוּ לְחַיִּים וּלְשָׁלוֹם מֵעַתָּה וְעַד עוֹלָם.
בָּרוּךְ אַתָּה יהוה, שׁוֹמֵר עַמּוֹ יִשְׂרָאֵל לָעַד.

In ארץ ישראל *the service continues with* חצי קדיש *on page 257.*

תהלים פט — בָּרוּךְ יהוה לְעוֹלָם, אָמֵן וְאָמֵן:
תהלים קלה — בָּרוּךְ יהוה מִצִּיּוֹן, שֹׁכֵן יְרוּשָׁלָםִ, הַלְלוּיָהּ:
תהלים עב — בָּרוּךְ יהוה אֱלֹהִים אֱלֹהֵי יִשְׂרָאֵל, עֹשֵׂה נִפְלָאוֹת לְבַדּוֹ:
וּבָרוּךְ שֵׁם כְּבוֹדוֹ לְעוֹלָם
וְיִמָּלֵא כְבוֹדוֹ אֶת־כָּל־הָאָרֶץ, אָמֵן וְאָמֵן:
תהלים קד — יְהִי כְבוֹד יהוה לְעוֹלָם, יִשְׂמַח יהוה בְּמַעֲשָׂיו:
תהלים קיג — יְהִי שֵׁם יהוה מְבֹרָךְ מֵעַתָּה וְעַד־עוֹלָם:
שמואל א, יב — כִּי לֹא־יִטֹּשׁ יהוה אֶת־עַמּוֹ בַּעֲבוּר שְׁמוֹ הַגָּדוֹל
כִּי הוֹאִיל יהוה לַעֲשׂוֹת אֶתְכֶם לוֹ לְעָם:
מלכים א, יח — וַיַּרְא כָּל־הָעָם וַיִּפְּלוּ עַל־פְּנֵיהֶם
וַיֹּאמְרוּ, יהוה הוּא הָאֱלֹהִים, יהוה הוּא הָאֱלֹהִים:
זכריה יד — וְהָיָה יהוה לְמֶלֶךְ עַל־כָּל־הָאָרֶץ
בַּיּוֹם הַהוּא יִהְיֶה יהוה אֶחָד וּשְׁמוֹ אֶחָד:
תהלים לג — יְהִי־חַסְדְּךָ יהוה עָלֵינוּ, כַּאֲשֶׁר יִחַלְנוּ לָךְ:

בָּרוּךְ יהוה לְעוֹלָם *Blessed be the LORD for ever:* This passage originated among Babylonian Jewry at a time when synagogues were not permitted within the town and were built in the fields outside. This made attendance at synagogue potentially hazardous at night. This prayer, with its eighteen references to

הוֹשִׁיעֵנוּ Save us, LORD our God, gather us *Ps. 106*
and deliver us from the nations,
to thank Your holy name, and glory in Your praise.
All the nations You made shall come and bow before You, LORD, *Ps. 86*
and pay honor to Your name,
for You are great and You perform wonders:
You alone are God.
We, Your people, the flock of Your pasture, will praise You for ever. *Ps. 79*
For all generations we will relate Your praise.

בָּרוּךְ Blessed is the LORD by day, blessed is the LORD by night.
Blessed is the LORD when we lie down;
blessed is the LORD when we rise.
For in Your hand are the souls of the living and the dead,
[as it is written:] "In His hand is every living soul, *Job 12*
and the breath of all mankind."
Into Your hand I entrust my spirit: *Ps. 31*
You redeemed me, LORD, God of truth.
Our God in heaven, bring unity to Your name,
establish Your kingdom constantly
and reign over us for ever and all time.

יִרְאוּ May our eyes see, our hearts rejoice,
and our souls be glad in Your true salvation,
when Zion is told, "Your God reigns."
The LORD is King, the LORD was King,
the LORD will be King for ever and all time.
▸ For sovereignty is Yours,
and to all eternity You will reign in glory,
for we have no king but You.
Blessed are You, LORD,
the King who in His constant glory will reign over us
and all His creation for ever and all time.

הוֹשִׁיעֵנוּ יהוה אֱלֹהֵינוּ, וְקַבְּצֵנוּ מִן־הַגּוֹיִם תהלים קו
לְהוֹדוֹת לְשֵׁם קָדְשֶׁךָ, לְהִשְׁתַּבֵּחַ בִּתְהִלָּתֶךָ:
כָּל־גּוֹיִם אֲשֶׁר עָשִׂיתָ, יָבוֹאוּ וְיִשְׁתַּחֲווּ לְפָנֶיךָ, אֲדֹנָי תהלים פו
וִיכַבְּדוּ לִשְׁמֶךָ:
כִּי־גָדוֹל אַתָּה וְעֹשֵׂה נִפְלָאוֹת, אַתָּה אֱלֹהִים לְבַדֶּךָ:
וַאֲנַחְנוּ עַמְּךָ וְצֹאן מַרְעִיתֶךָ, נוֹדֶה לְּךָ לְעוֹלָם תהלים עט
לְדוֹר וָדֹר נְסַפֵּר תְּהִלָּתֶךָ:

בָּרוּךְ יהוה בַּיּוֹם, בָּרוּךְ יהוה בַּלָּיְלָה
בָּרוּךְ יהוה בְּשָׁכְבֵנוּ, בָּרוּךְ יהוה בְּקוּמֵנוּ.
כִּי בְיָדְךָ נַפְשׁוֹת הַחַיִּים וְהַמֵּתִים.
אֲשֶׁר בְּיָדוֹ נֶפֶשׁ כָּל־חָי, וְרוּחַ כָּל־בְּשַׂר־אִישׁ: איוב יב
בְּיָדְךָ אַפְקִיד רוּחִי, פָּדִיתָה אוֹתִי יהוה אֵל אֱמֶת: תהלים לא
אֱלֹהֵינוּ שֶׁבַּשָּׁמַיִם, יַחֵד שִׁמְךָ וְקַיֵּם מַלְכוּתְךָ תָּמִיד
וּמְלֹךְ עָלֵינוּ לְעוֹלָם וָעֶד.

יִרְאוּ עֵינֵינוּ וְיִשְׂמַח לִבֵּנוּ
וְתָגֵל נַפְשֵׁנוּ בִּישׁוּעָתְךָ בֶּאֱמֶת
בֶּאֱמֹר לְצִיּוֹן מָלַךְ אֱלֹהָיִךְ.
יהוה מֶלֶךְ, יהוה מָלָךְ, יהוה יִמְלֹךְ לְעֹלָם וָעֶד.
◂ כִּי הַמַּלְכוּת שֶׁלְּךָ הִיא, וּלְעוֹלְמֵי עַד תִּמְלֹךְ בְּכָבוֹד
כִּי אֵין לָנוּ מֶלֶךְ אֶלָּא אָתָּה.
בָּרוּךְ אַתָּה יהוה
הַמֶּלֶךְ בִּכְבוֹדוֹ תָּמִיד, יִמְלֹךְ עָלֵינוּ לְעוֹלָם וָעֶד
וְעַל כָּל מַעֲשָׂיו.

HALF KADDISH

Leader: יִתְגַּדַּל Magnified and sanctified
may His great name be,
in the world He created by His will.
May He establish His kingdom
in your lifetime and in your days,
and in the lifetime of all the house of Israel,
swiftly and soon – and say: Amen.

All: May His great name be blessed
for ever and all time.

Leader: Blessed and praised, glorified and exalted,
raised and honored,
uplifted and lauded
be the name of the Holy One,
blessed be He,
beyond any blessing,
song, praise and consolation
uttered in the world –
and say: Amen.

THE AMIDA

The following prayer, until "in former years" on page 276, is said silently, standing with feet together. Take three steps forward and at the points indicated by ▾*, bend the knees at the first word, bow at the second, and stand straight before saying God's name.*

O Lord, open my lips, *Ps. 51*
so that my mouth may declare Your praise.

PATRIARCHS

▾בָּרוּךְ Blessed are You, Lord our God and God of our fathers,
God of Abraham, God of Isaac and God of Jacob;
the great, mighty and awesome God, God Most High,

חצי קדיש

ש״ץ: יִתְגַּדַּל וְיִתְקַדַּשׁ שְׁמֵהּ רַבָּא (קהל: אָמֵן)
בְּעָלְמָא דִּי בְרָא כִרְעוּתֵהּ
וְיַמְלִיךְ מַלְכוּתֵהּ
בְּחַיֵּיכוֹן וּבְיוֹמֵיכוֹן וּבְחַיֵּי דְכָל בֵּית יִשְׂרָאֵל
בַּעֲגָלָא וּבִזְמַן קָרִיב, וְאִמְרוּ אָמֵן. (קהל: אָמֵן)

קהל וש״ץ: יְהֵא שְׁמֵהּ רַבָּא מְבָרַךְ לְעָלַם וּלְעָלְמֵי עָלְמַיָּא.

ש״ץ: יִתְבָּרַךְ וְיִשְׁתַּבַּח וְיִתְפָּאַר וְיִתְרוֹמַם וְיִתְנַשֵּׂא
וְיִתְהַדָּר וְיִתְעַלֶּה וְיִתְהַלָּל
שְׁמֵהּ דְּקֻדְשָׁא בְּרִיךְ הוּא (קהל: בְּרִיךְ הוּא)
לְעֵלָּא מִן כָּל בִּרְכָתָא
/בעשרת ימי תשובה: לְעֵלָּא לְעֵלָּא מִכָּל בִּרְכָתָא/
וְשִׁירָתָא, תֻּשְׁבְּחָתָא וְנֶחֱמָתָא
דַּאֲמִירָן בְּעָלְמָא, וְאִמְרוּ אָמֵן. (קהל: אָמֵן)

עמידה

The following prayer, until קַדְמֹנִיּוֹת *on page 277, is said silently, standing with feet together. Take three steps forward and at the points indicated by* ׳*, bend the knees at the first word, bow at the second, and stand straight before saying God's name.*

אֲדֹנָי, שְׂפָתַי תִּפְתָּח, וּפִי יַגִּיד תְּהִלָּתֶךָ: תהלים נא

אבות

׳בָּרוּךְ אַתָּה יהוה, אֱלֹהֵינוּ וֵאלֹהֵי אֲבוֹתֵינוּ
אֱלֹהֵי אַבְרָהָם, אֱלֹהֵי יִצְחָק, וֵאלֹהֵי יַעֲקֹב
הָאֵל הַגָּדוֹל הַגִּבּוֹר וְהַנּוֹרָא, אֵל עֶלְיוֹן

who bestows acts of loving-kindness and creates all,
who remembers the loving-kindness of the fathers
and will bring a Redeemer to their children's children
for the sake of His name, in love.

Between Rosh HaShana & Yom Kippur: Remember us for life, O King who desires life,
and write us in the book of life –
for Your sake, O God of life.

King, Helper, Savior, Shield:
▾Blessed are You, LORD, Shield of Abraham.

DIVINE MIGHT

אַתָּה גִּבּוֹר You are eternally mighty, LORD.
You give life to the dead
and have great power to save.

The phrase "He makes the wind blow and the rain fall" is added from Simḥat Torah until Pesaḥ. In Israel the phrase "He causes the dew to fall" is added from Pesaḥ until Shemini Atzeret. See laws 129–131.

In fall & winter: He makes the wind blow and the rain fall.
In Israel, in spring & summer: He causes the dew to fall.

He sustains the living with loving-kindness,
and with great compassion revives the dead.
He supports the fallen, heals the sick, sets captives free,
and keeps His faith with those who sleep in the dust.
Who is like You, Master of might,
and who can compare to You,
O King who brings death and gives life,
and makes salvation grow?

Between Rosh HaShana & Yom Kippur: Who is like You, compassionate Father,
who remembers His creatures in compassion, for life?

Faithful are You to revive the dead.
Blessed are You, LORD, who revives the dead.

גּוֹמֵל חֲסָדִים טוֹבִים, וְקוֹנֵה הַכֹּל
וְזוֹכֵר חַסְדֵי אָבוֹת
וּמֵבִיא גוֹאֵל לִבְנֵי בְנֵיהֶם לְמַעַן שְׁמוֹ בְּאַהֲבָה.

בעשרת ימי תשובה: זָכְרֵנוּ לְחַיִּים, מֶלֶךְ חָפֵץ בַּחַיִּים
וְכָתְבֵנוּ בְּסֵפֶר הַחַיִּים, לְמַעַנְךָ אֱלֹהִים חַיִּים.

מֶלֶךְ עוֹזֵר וּמוֹשִׁיעַ וּמָגֵן.
ˆבָּרוּךְ אַתָּה יהוה, מָגֵן אַבְרָהָם.

גבורות

אַתָּה גִּבּוֹר לְעוֹלָם, אֲדֹנָי
מְחַיֵּה מֵתִים אַתָּה, רַב לְהוֹשִׁיעַ

The phrase מַשִּׁיב הָרְוּחַ *is added from* שמחת תורה *until* פסח. *In* ארץ ישראל *the phrase* מוֹרִיד הַטָּל *is added from* פסח *until* שמיני עצרת. *See laws 129–131.*

בחורף: מַשִּׁיב הָרְוּחַ וּמוֹרִיד הַגֶּשֶׁם / בארץ ישראל בקיץ: מוֹרִיד הַטָּל

מְכַלְכֵּל חַיִּים בְּחֶסֶד
מְחַיֵּה מֵתִים בְּרַחֲמִים רַבִּים
סוֹמֵךְ נוֹפְלִים, וְרוֹפֵא חוֹלִים, וּמַתִּיר אֲסוּרִים
וּמְקַיֵּם אֱמוּנָתוֹ לִישֵׁנֵי עָפָר.
מִי כָמְוֹךָ, בַּעַל גְּבוּרוֹת
וּמִי דּוֹמֶה לָּךְ
מֶלֶךְ, מֵמִית וּמְחַיֶּה וּמַצְמִיחַ יְשׁוּעָה.

בעשרת ימי תשובה: מִי כָמְוֹךָ אַב הָרַחֲמִים
זוֹכֵר יְצוּרָיו לְחַיִּים בְּרַחֲמִים.

וְנֶאֱמָן אַתָּה לְהַחֲיוֹת מֵתִים.
בָּרוּךְ אַתָּה יהוה, מְחַיֵּה הַמֵּתִים.

HOLINESS

אַתָּה קָדוֹשׁ You are holy and Your name is holy,
and holy ones praise You daily, Selah!
Blessed are You, LORD,
the holy God. / *Between Rosh HaShana & Yom Kippur:* the holy King./

(If forgotten, repeat the Amida.)

KNOWLEDGE

אַתָּה חוֹנֵן You grace humanity with knowledge
and teach mortals understanding.

On Motza'ei Shabbat and Motza'ei Yom Tov add:

אַתָּה חוֹנַנְתָּנוּ You have graced us with the knowledge of Your Torah, and taught us to perform the statutes of Your will. You have distinguished, LORD our God, between sacred and profane, light and darkness, Israel and the nations, and between the seventh day and the six days of work. Our Father, our King, may the days approaching us bring peace; may we be free from all sin, cleansed from all iniquity, holding fast to our reverence of You. And

---

Grace us with the knowledge, understanding
and discernment that come from You.
Blessed are You, LORD,
who graciously grants knowledge.

REPENTANCE

הֲשִׁיבֵנוּ Bring us back, our Father, to Your Torah.
Draw us near, our King, to Your service.
Lead us back to You in perfect repentance.
Blessed are You, LORD,
who desires repentance.

In nature there are no sharp boundaries. Day shades gradually into night; winter into spring; life into sentience. According to the Torah, what links man to God is our ability to separate, classify and name, and thus to see order amidst seeming chaos. As we begin the working week, we acknowledge the divine order of creation as the necessary prelude to human acts of creation.

קדושת השם

אַתָּה קָדוֹשׁ וְשִׁמְךָ קָדוֹשׁ
וּקְדוֹשִׁים בְּכָל יוֹם יְהַלְלוּךָ סֶּלָה.
בָּרוּךְ אַתָּה יהוה
הָאֵל הַקָּדוֹשׁ./ בעשרת ימי תשובה: הַמֶּלֶךְ הַקָּדוֹשׁ./

(*If forgotten, repeat the* עמידה.)

דעת

אַתָּה חוֹנֵן לְאָדָם דַּעַת, וּמְלַמֵּד לֶאֱנוֹשׁ בִּינָה.

On מוצאי שבת *and* מוצאי יום טוב *add:*

אַתָּה חוֹנַנְתָּנוּ לְמַדַּע תּוֹרָתֶךָ, וַתְּלַמְּדֵנוּ לַעֲשׂוֹת חֻקֵּי רְצוֹנֶךָ, וַתַּבְדֵּל יהוה אֱלֹהֵינוּ בֵּין קֹדֶשׁ לְחֹל, בֵּין אוֹר לְחֹשֶׁךְ, בֵּין יִשְׂרָאֵל לָעַמִּים, בֵּין יוֹם הַשְּׁבִיעִי לְשֵׁשֶׁת יְמֵי הַמַּעֲשֶׂה. אָבִינוּ מַלְכֵּנוּ, הָחֵל עָלֵינוּ הַיָּמִים הַבָּאִים לִקְרָאתֵנוּ לְשָׁלוֹם, חֲשׂוּכִים מִכָּל חֵטְא וּמְנֻקִּים מִכָּל עָוֹן וּמְדֻבָּקִים בְּיִרְאָתֶךָ. וְ

חָנֵּנוּ מֵאִתְּךָ דֵּעָה בִּינָה וְהַשְׂכֵּל.
בָּרוּךְ אַתָּה יהוה, חוֹנֵן הַדָּעַת.

תשובה

הֲשִׁיבֵנוּ אָבִינוּ לְתוֹרָתֶךָ, וְקָרְבֵנוּ מַלְכֵּנוּ לַעֲבוֹדָתֶךָ
וְהַחֲזִירֵנוּ בִּתְשׁוּבָה שְׁלֵמָה לְפָנֶיךָ.
בָּרוּךְ אַתָּה יהוה, הָרוֹצֶה בִּתְשׁוּבָה.

אַתָּה חוֹנַנְתָּנוּ *You have graced us:* From Talmudic times, this paragraph has been the way of marking Havdala – the transition between holy and secular time – within the Amida prayer. Havdala is repeated as a separate ceremony in the synagogue after prayer, and then again at home. Its positioning here, in the prayer for knowledge, indicates the essential connection between the human mind and the ability to make distinctions ("If there is no knowledge," says the Talmud Yerushalmi [*Berakhot* 5:2], "how can there be distinction?").

FORGIVENESS

Strike the left side of the chest at °.

סְלַח לָנוּ Forgive us, our Father,
for we have °sinned.
Pardon us, our King,
for we have °transgressed;
for You pardon and forgive.
Blessed are You, LORD, the gracious One who repeatedly forgives.

REDEMPTION

רְאֵה Look on our affliction,
plead our cause,
and redeem us soon for Your name's sake,
for You are a powerful Redeemer.
Blessed are You, LORD, the Redeemer of Israel.

HEALING

רְפָאֵנוּ Heal us, LORD, and we shall be healed.
Save us and we shall be saved,
for You are our praise.
Bring complete recovery for all our ailments,

The following prayer for a sick person may be said here:
May it be Your will, O LORD my God and God of my ancestors, that You speedily send a complete recovery from heaven, a healing of both soul and body, to the patient (*name*), son/daughter of (*mother's name*) among the other afflicted of Israel.

---

for You, God, King, are a faithful and compassionate Healer.
Blessed are You, LORD,
Healer of the sick of His people Israel.

סליחה

Strike the left side of the chest at °.

סְלַח לָנוּ אָבִינוּ כִּי °חָטָאנוּ
מְחַל לָנוּ מַלְכֵּנוּ כִּי °פָשָׁעְנוּ
כִּי מוֹחֵל וְסוֹלֵחַ אָתָּה.
בָּרוּךְ אַתָּה יהוה, חַנּוּן הַמַּרְבֶּה לִסְלֹחַ.

גאולה

רְאֵה בְעָנְיֵנוּ, וְרִיבָה רִיבֵנוּ
וּגְאָלֵנוּ מְהֵרָה לְמַעַן שְׁמֶךָ
כִּי גּוֹאֵל חָזָק אָתָּה.
בָּרוּךְ אַתָּה יהוה, גּוֹאֵל יִשְׂרָאֵל.

רפואה

רְפָאֵנוּ יהוה וְנֵרָפֵא
הוֹשִׁיעֵנוּ וְנִוָּשֵׁעָה, כִּי תְהִלָּתֵנוּ אָתָּה
וְהַעֲלֵה רְפוּאָה שְׁלֵמָה לְכָל מַכּוֹתֵינוּ

The following prayer for a sick person may be said here:

יְהִי רָצוֹן מִלְּפָנֶיךָ יהוה אֱלֹהַי וֵאלֹהֵי אֲבוֹתַי, שֶׁתִּשְׁלַח מְהֵרָה רְפוּאָה שְׁלֵמָה
מִן הַשָּׁמַיִם רְפוּאַת הַנֶּפֶשׁ וּרְפוּאַת הַגּוּף לַחוֹלֶה/לַחוֹלָה *name of patient*
בֶּן/בַּת *mother's name* בְּתוֹךְ שְׁאָר חוֹלֵי יִשְׂרָאֵל.

כִּי אֵל מֶלֶךְ רוֹפֵא נֶאֱמָן וְרַחֲמָן אָתָּה.
בָּרוּךְ אַתָּה יהוה, רוֹפֵא חוֹלֵי עַמּוֹ יִשְׂרָאֵל.

PROSPERITY

The phrase "Grant dew and rain as a blessing" is said from December 4th (in the year before a civil leap year, December 5th) until Pesaḥ. In Israel, it is said from the 7th of Marḥeshvan. The phrase "Grant blessing" is said from Ḥol HaMo'ed Pesaḥ until December 3rd (in the year before a civil leap year, December 4th). In Israel it is said through the 6th of Marḥeshvan. See laws 147–149.

בָּרֵךְ Bless this year for us, Lord our God,
and all its types of produce for good.

In winter: Grant dew and rain as a blessing
In other seasons: Grant blessing

on the face of the earth, and from its goodness satisfy us,
blessing our year as the best of years.
Blessed are You, Lord,
who blesses the years.

INGATHERING OF EXILES

תְּקַע Sound the great shofar for our freedom,
raise high the banner to gather our exiles,
and gather us together
from the four quarters of the earth.
Blessed are You, Lord,
who gathers the dispersed of His people Israel.

JUSTICE

הָשִׁיבָה Restore our judges as at first,
and our counselors as at the beginning,
and remove from us sorrow and sighing.
May You alone, Lord,
reign over us
with loving-kindness and compassion,
and vindicate us in justice.
Blessed are You, Lord,
the King who loves righteousness and justice.

/*Between Rosh HaShana & Yom Kippur, end the blessing:* the King of justice./

ברכת השנים

The phrase וְתֵן טַל וּמָטָר לִבְרָכָה *is said from December 4th (in the year before a civil leap year, December 5th) until* פסח. *In* ארץ ישראל*, it is said from* ז׳ מרחשון. *The phrase* וְתֵן בְּרָכָה *is said from* חול המועד פסח *until December 3rd (in the year before a civil leap year, December 4th). In* ארץ ישראל *it is said through* ו׳ מרחשון. *See laws 147–149.*

בָּרֵךְ עָלֵינוּ יהוה אֱלֹהֵינוּ אֶת הַשָּׁנָה הַזֹּאת
וְאֶת כָּל מִינֵי תְבוּאָתָהּ, לְטוֹבָה
בחורף: וְתֵן טַל וּמָטָר לִבְרָכָה / בקיץ: וְתֵן בְּרָכָה
עַל פְּנֵי הָאֲדָמָה, וְשַׂבְּעֵנוּ מִטּוּבָהּ
וּבָרֵךְ שְׁנָתֵנוּ כַּשָּׁנִים הַטּוֹבוֹת.
בָּרוּךְ אַתָּה יהוה, מְבָרֵךְ הַשָּׁנִים.

קבוץ גלויות

תְּקַע בְּשׁוֹפָר גָּדוֹל לְחֵרוּתֵנוּ
וְשָׂא נֵס לְקַבֵּץ גָּלֻיּוֹתֵינוּ
וְקַבְּצֵנוּ יַחַד מֵאַרְבַּע כַּנְפוֹת הָאָרֶץ.
בָּרוּךְ אַתָּה יהוה, מְקַבֵּץ נִדְחֵי עַמּוֹ יִשְׂרָאֵל.

השבת המשפט

הָשִׁיבָה שׁוֹפְטֵינוּ כְּבָרִאשׁוֹנָה
וְיוֹעֲצֵינוּ כְּבַתְּחִלָּה
וְהָסֵר מִמֶּנּוּ יָגוֹן וַאֲנָחָה
וּמְלֹךְ עָלֵינוּ אַתָּה יהוה לְבַדְּךָ בְּחֶסֶד וּבְרַחֲמִים
וְצַדְּקֵנוּ בַּמִּשְׁפָּט.
בָּרוּךְ אַתָּה יהוה
מֶלֶךְ אוֹהֵב צְדָקָה וּמִשְׁפָּט. / בעשרת ימי תשובה: הַמֶּלֶךְ הַמִּשְׁפָּט./

AGAINST INFORMERS

וְלַמַּלְשִׁינִים For the slanderers let there be no hope,
and may all wickedness perish in an instant.
May all Your people's enemies swiftly be cut down.
May You swiftly uproot, crush, cast down
and humble the arrogant swiftly in our days.
Blessed are You, LORD,
who destroys enemies and humbles the arrogant.

THE RIGHTEOUS

עַל הַצַּדִּיקִים To the righteous, the pious,
the elders of Your people the house of Israel,
the remnant of their scholars,
the righteous converts, and to us,
may Your compassion be aroused,
LORD our God.
Grant a good reward to all
who sincerely trust in Your name.
Set our lot with them,
so that we may never be ashamed,
for in You we trust.
Blessed are You, LORD,
who is the support and trust of the righteous.

REBUILDING JERUSALEM

וְלִירוּשָׁלַיִם To Jerusalem, Your city, may You return in compassion,
and may You dwell in it as You promised.
May You rebuild it rapidly in our days
as an everlasting structure,
and install within it soon the throne of David.
Blessed are You, LORD,
who builds Jerusalem.

ברכת המינים

וְלַמַּלְשִׁינִים אַל תְּהִי תִקְוָה
וְכָל הָרִשְׁעָה כְּרֶגַע תֹּאבֵד
וְכָל אוֹיְבֵי עַמְּךָ מְהֵרָה יִכָּרֵתוּ
וְהַזֵּדִים מְהֵרָה תְעַקֵּר וּתְשַׁבֵּר וּתְמַגֵּר וְתַכְנִיעַ בִּמְהֵרָה בְיָמֵינוּ.
בָּרוּךְ אַתָּה יהוה, שׁוֹבֵר אוֹיְבִים וּמַכְנִיעַ זֵדִים.

על הצדיקים

עַל הַצַּדִּיקִים וְעַל הַחֲסִידִים
וְעַל זִקְנֵי עַמְּךָ בֵּית יִשְׂרָאֵל
וְעַל פְּלֵיטַת סוֹפְרֵיהֶם
וְעַל גֵּרֵי הַצֶּדֶק, וְעָלֵינוּ
יֶהֱמוּ רַחֲמֶיךָ יהוה אֱלֹהֵינוּ
וְתֵן שָׂכָר טוֹב לְכָל הַבּוֹטְחִים בְּשִׁמְךָ בֶּאֱמֶת
וְשִׂים חֶלְקֵנוּ עִמָּהֶם
וּלְעוֹלָם לֹא נֵבוֹשׁ כִּי בְךָ בָטָחְנוּ.
בָּרוּךְ אַתָּה יהוה, מִשְׁעָן וּמִבְטָח לַצַּדִּיקִים.

בניין ירושלים

וְלִירוּשָׁלַיִם עִירְךָ בְּרַחֲמִים תָּשׁוּב
וְתִשְׁכֹּן בְּתוֹכָהּ כַּאֲשֶׁר דִּבַּרְתָּ
וּבְנֵה אוֹתָהּ בְּקָרוֹב בְּיָמֵינוּ בִּנְיַן עוֹלָם
וְכִסֵּא דָוִד מְהֵרָה לְתוֹכָהּ תָּכִין.
בָּרוּךְ אַתָּה יהוה, בּוֹנֵה יְרוּשָׁלָיִם.

KINGDOM OF DAVID

אֶת צֶמַח May the offshoot of Your servant David soon flower,
and may his pride be raised high by Your salvation,
for we wait for Your salvation all day.
Blessed are You, LORD,
who makes the glory of salvation flourish.

RESPONSE TO PRAYER

שְׁמַע קוֹלֵנוּ Listen to our voice, LORD our God.
Spare us and have compassion on us,
and in compassion and favor accept our prayer,
for You, God, listen to prayers and pleas.
Do not turn us away, O our King,
empty-handed from Your presence,*
for You listen with compassion
to the prayer of Your people Israel.
Blessed are You, LORD,
who listens to prayer.

At this point, in times of drought in Israel, say "And answer us" on page 124.

TEMPLE SERVICE

רְצֵה Find favor, LORD our God,
in Your people Israel and their prayer.
Restore the service to Your most holy House,
and accept in love and favor
the fire-offerings of Israel and their prayer.
May the service of Your people Israel always find favor with You.

On Rosh Ḥodesh and Ḥol HaMo'ed, say:

אֱלֹהֵינוּ Our God and God of our ancestors, may there rise, come, reach, appear, be favored, heard, regarded and remembered before You, our recollection and remembrance, as well as the remembrance of our ancestors, and of the Messiah son of David Your servant, and of Jerusalem Your holy city, and of all Your people the house of Israel – for deliverance and

משיח בן דוד

אֶת צֶמַח דָּוִד עַבְדְּךָ מְהֵרָה תַצְמִיחַ
וְקַרְנוֹ תָּרוּם בִּישׁוּעָתֶךָ
כִּי לִישׁוּעָתְךָ קִוִּינוּ כָּל הַיּוֹם.
בָּרוּךְ אַתָּה יהוה, מַצְמִיחַ קֶרֶן יְשׁוּעָה.

שומע תפילה

שְׁמַע קוֹלֵנוּ יהוה אֱלֹהֵינוּ
חוּס וְרַחֵם עָלֵינוּ
וְקַבֵּל בְּרַחֲמִים וּבְרָצוֹן אֶת תְּפִלָּתֵנוּ
כִּי אֵל שׁוֹמֵעַ תְּפִלּוֹת וְתַחֲנוּנִים אָתָּה
וּמִלְּפָנֶיךָ מַלְכֵּנוּ רֵיקָם אַל תְּשִׁיבֵנוּ*
כִּי אַתָּה שׁוֹמֵעַ תְּפִלַּת עַמְּךָ יִשְׂרָאֵל בְּרַחֲמִים.
בָּרוּךְ אַתָּה יהוה, שׁוֹמֵעַ תְּפִלָּה.

**At this point, in times of drought in* ארץ ישראל, *say* וַעֲנֵנוּ *on page 125.*

עבודה

רְצֵה יהוה אֱלֹהֵינוּ בְּעַמְּךָ יִשְׂרָאֵל, וּבִתְפִלָּתָם
וְהָשֵׁב אֶת הָעֲבוֹדָה לִדְבִיר בֵּיתֶךָ
וְאִשֵּׁי יִשְׂרָאֵל וּתְפִלָּתָם בְּאַהֲבָה תְקַבֵּל בְּרָצוֹן
וּתְהִי לְרָצוֹן תָּמִיד עֲבוֹדַת יִשְׂרָאֵל עַמֶּךָ.

On ראש חודש *and* חול המועד, *say:*

אֱלֹהֵינוּ וֵאלֹהֵי אֲבוֹתֵינוּ, יַעֲלֶה וְיָבוֹא וְיַגִּיעַ, וְיֵרָאֶה וְיֵרָצֶה וְיִשָּׁמַע, וְיִפָּקֵד וְיִזָּכֵר זִכְרוֹנֵנוּ וּפִקְדוֹנֵנוּ וְזִכְרוֹן אֲבוֹתֵינוּ, וְזִכְרוֹן מָשִׁיחַ בֶּן דָּוִד עַבְדֶּךָ, וְזִכְרוֹן יְרוּשָׁלַיִם עִיר קָדְשֶׁךָ, וְזִכְרוֹן כָּל עַמְּךָ

well-being, grace, loving-kindness and compassion, life and peace, on this day of:

On Rosh Ḥodesh: Rosh Hodesh.
On Pesaḥ: the Festival of Matzot.
On Sukkot: the Festival of Sukkot.

On it remember us, Lord our God, for good; recollect us for blessing, and deliver us for life. In accord with Your promise of salvation and compassion, spare us and be gracious to us; have compassion on us and deliver us, for our eyes are turned to You because You, God, are a gracious and compassionate King.

וְתֶחֱזֶינָה And may our eyes witness
Your return to Zion in compassion.
Blessed are You, Lord,
who restores His Presence to Zion.

THANKSGIVING

Bow at the first nine words.

מוֹדִים We give thanks to You,
for You are the Lord our God and God of our ancestors
for ever and all time.
You are the Rock of our lives,
Shield of our salvation from generation to generation.
We will thank You and declare Your praise for our lives,
which are entrusted into Your hand;
for our souls, which are placed in Your charge;
for Your miracles which are with us every day;
and for Your wonders and favors at all times,
evening, morning and midday.
You are good –
for Your compassion never fails.
You are compassionate –
for Your loving-kindnesses never cease.
We have always placed our hope in You.

בֵּית יִשְׂרָאֵל, לְפָנֶיךָ, לִפְלֵיטָה לְטוֹבָה, לְחֵן וּלְחֶסֶד וּלְרַחֲמִים,
לְחַיִּים וּלְשָׁלוֹם בְּיוֹם

בראש חודש: רֹאשׁ הַחֹדֶשׁ / בפסח: חַג הַמַּצּוֹת / בסוכות: חַג הַסֻּכּוֹת

הַזֶּה. זָכְרֵנוּ יהוה אֱלֹהֵינוּ בּוֹ לְטוֹבָה, וּפָקְדֵנוּ בוֹ לִבְרָכָה, וְהוֹשִׁיעֵנוּ בוֹ לְחַיִּים. וּבִדְבַר יְשׁוּעָה וְרַחֲמִים, חוּס וְחָנֵּנוּ וְרַחֵם עָלֵינוּ וְהוֹשִׁיעֵנוּ, כִּי אֵלֶיךָ עֵינֵינוּ, כִּי אֵל מֶלֶךְ חַנּוּן וְרַחוּם אָתָּה.

וְתֶחֱזֶינָה עֵינֵינוּ בְּשׁוּבְךָ לְצִיּוֹן בְּרַחֲמִים.
בָּרוּךְ אַתָּה יהוה, הַמַּחֲזִיר שְׁכִינָתוֹ לְצִיּוֹן.

הודאה

Bow at the first five words.

מוֹדִים אֲנַחְנוּ לָךְ
שָׁאַתָּה הוּא יהוה אֱלֹהֵינוּ וֵאלֹהֵי אֲבוֹתֵינוּ לְעוֹלָם וָעֶד.
צוּר חַיֵּינוּ, מָגֵן יִשְׁעֵנוּ
אַתָּה הוּא לְדוֹר וָדוֹר.
נוֹדֶה לְּךָ וּנְסַפֵּר תְּהִלָּתֶךָ
עַל חַיֵּינוּ הַמְּסוּרִים בְּיָדֶךָ
וְעַל נִשְׁמוֹתֵינוּ הַפְּקוּדוֹת לָךְ
וְעַל נִסֶּיךָ שֶׁבְּכָל יוֹם עִמָּנוּ
וְעַל נִפְלְאוֹתֶיךָ וְטוֹבוֹתֶיךָ שֶׁבְּכָל עֵת
עֶרֶב וָבֹקֶר וְצָהֳרָיִם.
הַטּוֹב, כִּי לֹא כָלוּ רַחֲמֶיךָ
וְהַמְרַחֵם, כִּי לֹא תַמּוּ חֲסָדֶיךָ
מֵעוֹלָם קִוִּינוּ לָךְ.

On Ḥanukka:

עַל הַנִּסִּים [We thank You also] for the miracles, the redemption, the mighty deeds, the salvations, and the victories in battle which You performed for our ancestors in those days, at this time.

בִּימֵי מַתִּתְיָהוּ In the days of Mattityahu, son of Yoḥanan, the High Priest, the Hasmonean, and his sons, the wicked Greek kingdom rose up against Your people Israel to make them forget Your Torah and to force them to transgress the statutes of Your will. It was then that You in Your great compassion stood by them in the time of their distress. You championed their cause, judged their claim, and avenged their wrong. You delivered the strong into the hands of the weak, the many into the hands of the few, the impure into the hands of the pure, the wicked into the hands of the righteous, and the arrogant into the hands of those who were engaged in the study of Your Torah. You made for Yourself great and holy renown in Your world, and for Your people Israel You performed a great salvation and redemption as of this very day. Your children then entered the holiest part of Your House, cleansed Your Temple, purified Your Sanctuary, kindled lights in Your holy courts, and designated these eight days of Ḥanukka for giving thanks and praise to Your great name.

Continue with "For all these things."

On Purim:

עַל הַנִּסִּים [We thank You also] for the miracles, the redemption, the mighty deeds, the salvations, and the victories in battle which You performed for our ancestors in those days at this time.

בִּימֵי מָרְדְּכַי In the days of Mordekhai and Esther, in Shushan the capital, the wicked Haman rose up against them and sought to destroy, slay and exterminate all the Jews, young and old, children and women, on one day, the thirteenth day of the twelfth month, which is the month of Adar, and to plunder their possessions. Then You in Your great compassion thwarted his counsel, frustrated his plans, and caused his scheme to recoil on his own head, so that they hanged him and his sons on the gallows. *Esther 3*

Continue with "For all these things."

וְעַל כֻּלָּם For all these things may Your name be blessed and exalted, our King, continually, for ever and all time.

Between Rosh HaShana & Yom Kippur: And write, for a good life, all the children of Your covenant.

Let all that lives thank You, Selah! and praise Your name in truth, God, our Savior and Help, Selah!

▼Blessed are You, Lord, whose name is "the Good" and to whom thanks are due.

בחנוכה:

עַל הַנִּסִּים וְעַל הַפֻּרְקָן וְעַל הַגְּבוּרוֹת וְעַל הַתְּשׁוּעוֹת וְעַל הַמִּלְחָמוֹת שֶׁעָשִׂיתָ לַאֲבוֹתֵינוּ בַּיָּמִים הָהֵם בַּזְּמַן הַזֶּה.

בִּימֵי מַתִּתְיָהוּ בֶּן יוֹחָנָן כֹּהֵן גָּדוֹל חַשְׁמוֹנַאי וּבָנָיו, כְּשֶׁעָמְדָה מַלְכוּת יָוָן הָרְשָׁעָה עַל עַמְּךָ יִשְׂרָאֵל לְהַשְׁכִּיחָם תּוֹרָתֶךָ וּלְהַעֲבִירָם מֵחֻקֵּי רְצוֹנֶךָ, וְאַתָּה בְּרַחֲמֶיךָ הָרַבִּים עָמַדְתָּ לָהֶם בְּעֵת צָרָתָם, רַבְתָּ אֶת רִיבָם, דַּנְתָּ אֶת דִּינָם, נָקַמְתָּ אֶת נִקְמָתָם, מָסַרְתָּ גִבּוֹרִים בְּיַד חַלָּשִׁים, וְרַבִּים בְּיַד מְעַטִּים, וּטְמֵאִים בְּיַד טְהוֹרִים, וּרְשָׁעִים בְּיַד צַדִּיקִים, וְזֵדִים בְּיַד עוֹסְקֵי תוֹרָתֶךָ, וּלְךָ עָשִׂיתָ שֵׁם גָּדוֹל וְקָדוֹשׁ בְּעוֹלָמֶךָ, וּלְעַמְּךָ יִשְׂרָאֵל עָשִׂיתָ תְּשׁוּעָה גְדוֹלָה וּפֻרְקָן כְּהַיּוֹם הַזֶּה. וְאַחַר כֵּן בָּאוּ בָנֶיךָ לִדְבִיר בֵּיתֶךָ, וּפִנּוּ אֶת הֵיכָלֶךָ, וְטִהֲרוּ אֶת מִקְדָּשֶׁךָ, וְהִדְלִיקוּ נֵרוֹת בְּחַצְרוֹת קָדְשֶׁךָ, וְקָבְעוּ שְׁמוֹנַת יְמֵי חֲנֻכָּה אֵלּוּ, לְהוֹדוֹת וּלְהַלֵּל לְשִׁמְךָ הַגָּדוֹל.

Continue with .וְעַל כֻּלָּם

בפורים:

עַל הַנִּסִּים וְעַל הַפֻּרְקָן וְעַל הַגְּבוּרוֹת וְעַל הַתְּשׁוּעוֹת וְעַל הַמִּלְחָמוֹת שֶׁעָשִׂיתָ לַאֲבוֹתֵינוּ בַּיָּמִים הָהֵם בַּזְּמַן הַזֶּה.

בִּימֵי מָרְדְּכַי וְאֶסְתֵּר בְּשׁוּשַׁן הַבִּירָה, כְּשֶׁעָמַד עֲלֵיהֶם הָמָן הָרָשָׁע, בִּקֵּשׁ לְהַשְׁמִיד לַהֲרֹג וּלְאַבֵּד אֶת־כָּל־הַיְּהוּדִים מִנַּעַר וְעַד־זָקֵן טַף וְנָשִׁים בְּיוֹם אֶחָד, בִּשְׁלוֹשָׁה עָשָׂר לְחֹדֶשׁ שְׁנֵים־עָשָׂר, הוּא־חֹדֶשׁ אֲדָר, וּשְׁלָלָם לָבוֹז: וְאַתָּה בְּרַחֲמֶיךָ הָרַבִּים הֵפַרְתָּ אֶת עֲצָתוֹ, וְקִלְקַלְתָּ אֶת מַחֲשַׁבְתּוֹ, וַהֲשֵׁבוֹתָ לּוֹ גְּמוּלוֹ בְּרֹאשׁוֹ, וְתָלוּ אוֹתוֹ וְאֶת בָּנָיו עַל הָעֵץ. אסתר ג

Continue with .וְעַל כֻּלָּם

וְעַל כֻּלָּם יִתְבָּרַךְ וְיִתְרוֹמַם שִׁמְךָ מַלְכֵּנוּ תָּמִיד לְעוֹלָם וָעֶד.

בעשרת ימי תשובה: וּכְתֹב לְחַיִּים טוֹבִים כָּל בְּנֵי בְרִיתֶךָ.

וְכֹל הַחַיִּים יוֹדְוּךָ סֶּלָה, וִיהַלְלוּ אֶת שִׁמְךָ בֶּאֱמֶת הָאֵל יְשׁוּעָתֵנוּ וְעֶזְרָתֵנוּ סֶלָה.

בָּרוּךְ אַתָּה יהוה, הַטּוֹב שִׁמְךָ וּלְךָ נָאֶה לְהוֹדוֹת.

PEACE

שָׁלוֹם רָב Grant great peace to Your people Israel for ever,
for You are the sovereign LORD of all peace;
and may it be good in Your eyes
to bless Your people Israel
at every time, at every hour, with Your peace.

Between Rosh HaShana & Yom Kippur: In the book of life, blessing, peace and prosperity,
may we and all Your people the house of Israel be remembered
and written before You for a good life, and for peace.*

Blessed are You, LORD, who blesses His people Israel with peace.

**Between Rosh HaShana and Yom Kippur outside Israel, many end the blessing:*
Blessed are You, LORD, who makes peace.

Some say the following verse (see law 368):
May the words of my mouth and the meditation of my heart *Ps. 19*
find favor before You, LORD, my Rock and Redeemer.

אֱלֹהַי My God, *Berakhot 17a*
guard my tongue from evil and my lips from deceitful speech.
To those who curse me, let my soul be silent;
may my soul be to all like the dust.
Open my heart to Your Torah
and let my soul pursue Your commandments.
As for all who plan evil against me,
swiftly thwart their counsel and frustrate their plans.
Act for the sake of Your name; act for the sake of Your right hand;
act for the sake of Your holiness; act for the sake of Your Torah.
That Your beloved ones may be delivered, *Ps. 60*
save with Your right hand and answer me.
May the words of my mouth *Ps. 19*
and the meditation of my heart find favor before You,
LORD, my Rock and Redeemer.

Bow, take three steps back, then bow, first left, then right, then center, while saying:
May He who makes peace in His high places,
make peace for us and all Israel – and say: Amen.

ברכת שלום

שָׁלוֹם רָב עַל יִשְׂרָאֵל עַמְּךָ תָּשִׂים לְעוֹלָם
כִּי אַתָּה הוּא מֶלֶךְ אָדוֹן לְכָל הַשָּׁלוֹם.
וְטוֹב בְּעֵינֶיךָ לְבָרֵךְ אֶת עַמְּךָ יִשְׂרָאֵל
בְּכָל עֵת וּבְכָל שָׁעָה בִּשְׁלוֹמֶךָ.

בעשרת ימי תשובה: בְּסֵפֶר חַיִּים, בְּרָכָה וְשָׁלוֹם, וּפַרְנָסָה טוֹבָה
נִזָּכֵר וְנִכָּתֵב לְפָנֶיךָ, אֲנַחְנוּ וְכָל עַמְּךָ בֵּית יִשְׂרָאֵל
לְחַיִּים טוֹבִים וּלְשָׁלוֹם.*

בָּרוּךְ אַתָּה יהוה, הַמְבָרֵךְ אֶת עַמּוֹ יִשְׂרָאֵל בַּשָּׁלוֹם.

**During the* עשרת ימי תשובה *in* חוץ לארץ*, many end the blessing:*

בָּרוּךְ אַתָּה יהוה, עוֹשֶׂה הַשָּׁלוֹם.

Some say the following verse (see law 368):

יִהְיוּ לְרָצוֹן אִמְרֵי־פִי וְהֶגְיוֹן לִבִּי לְפָנֶיךָ, יהוה צוּרִי וְגֹאֲלִי: תהלים יט

אֱלֹהַי ברכות יז.

נְצֹר לְשׁוֹנִי מֵרָע וּשְׂפָתַי מִדַּבֵּר מִרְמָה
וְלִמְקַלְלַי נַפְשִׁי תִדֹּם, וְנַפְשִׁי כֶּעָפָר לַכֹּל תִּהְיֶה.
פְּתַח לִבִּי בְּתוֹרָתֶךָ, וּבְמִצְוֹתֶיךָ תִּרְדֹּף נַפְשִׁי.
וְכָל הַחוֹשְׁבִים עָלַי רָעָה
מְהֵרָה הָפֵר עֲצָתָם וְקַלְקֵל מַחֲשַׁבְתָּם.
עֲשֵׂה לְמַעַן שְׁמֶךָ, עֲשֵׂה לְמַעַן יְמִינֶךָ
עֲשֵׂה לְמַעַן קְדֻשָּׁתֶךָ, עֲשֵׂה לְמַעַן תּוֹרָתֶךָ.
לְמַעַן יֵחָלְצוּן יְדִידֶיךָ, הוֹשִׁיעָה יְמִינְךָ וַעֲנֵנִי: תהלים ס
יִהְיוּ לְרָצוֹן אִמְרֵי־פִי וְהֶגְיוֹן לִבִּי לְפָנֶיךָ, יהוה צוּרִי וְגֹאֲלִי: תהלים יט

Bow, take three steps back, then bow, first left, then right, then center, while saying:

עֹשֶׂה שָׁלוֹם/ בעשרת ימי תשובה: הַשָּׁלוֹם/ בִּמְרוֹמָיו
הוּא יַעֲשֶׂה שָׁלוֹם עָלֵינוּ וְעַל כָּל יִשְׂרָאֵל, וְאִמְרוּ אָמֵן.

יְהִי רָצוֹן May it be Your will, Lord our God and God of our ancestors,
that the Temple be rebuilt speedily in our days, and grant us a share in Your Torah.
And there we will serve You with reverence,
as in the days of old and as in former years.
Then the offering of Judah and Jerusalem *Mal. 3*
will be pleasing to the Lord as in the days of old and as in former years.

On Motza'ei Shabbat (except when Yom Tov or Erev Pesah falls in the following week), the Leader continues with Half Kaddish on page 256, then "May the pleasantness" on page 694.
On Motza'ei Shabbat when Yom Tov falls in the following week, the service continues on page 700.
On other evenings the Leader says Full Kaddish:

FULL KADDISH

Leader: יִתְגַּדַּל Magnified and sanctified may His great name be,
in the world He created by His will.
May He establish His kingdom
in your lifetime and in your days,
and in the lifetime of all the house of Israel,
swiftly and soon –
and say: Amen.

All: May His great name be blessed for ever and all time.

Leader: Blessed and praised,
glorified and exalted,
raised and honored,
uplifted and lauded be
the name of the Holy One,
blessed be He, beyond any blessing,
song, praise and consolation
uttered in the world –
and say: Amen.

May the prayers and pleas of all Israel
be accepted by their Father in heaven –
and say: Amen.

יְהִי רָצוֹן מִלְּפָנֶיךָ יהוה אֱלֹהֵינוּ וֵאלֹהֵי אֲבוֹתֵינוּ
שֶׁיִּבָּנֶה בֵּית הַמִּקְדָּשׁ בִּמְהֵרָה בְיָמֵינוּ, וְתֵן חֶלְקֵנוּ בְּתוֹרָתֶךָ
וְשָׁם נַעֲבָדְךָ בְּיִרְאָה כִּימֵי עוֹלָם וּכְשָׁנִים קַדְמֹנִיּוֹת.
וְעָרְבָה לַיהוה מִנְחַת יְהוּדָה וִירוּשָׁלָםִ כִּימֵי עוֹלָם וּכְשָׁנִים קַדְמֹנִיּוֹת: מלאכי ג

On מוצאי שבת *(except when* יום טוב *or* ערב פסח *falls in the following week), the* שליח ציבור *continues with* חצי קדיש *on page 257, then* וִיהִי נֹעַם *on page 695.*

On מוצאי שבת *when* יום טוב *falls in the following week, the service continues on page 701.*

On other evenings the שליח ציבור *says* קדיש שלם*:*

קדיש שלם

ש״ץ: יִתְגַּדַּל וְיִתְקַדַּשׁ שְׁמֵהּ רַבָּא (קהל: אָמֵן)
בְּעָלְמָא דִּי בְרָא כִרְעוּתֵהּ
וְיַמְלִיךְ מַלְכוּתֵהּ
בְּחַיֵּיכוֹן וּבְיוֹמֵיכוֹן וּבְחַיֵּי דְכָל בֵּית יִשְׂרָאֵל
בַּעֲגָלָא וּבִזְמַן קָרִיב, וְאִמְרוּ אָמֵן. (קהל: אָמֵן)

קהל וש״ץ: יְהֵא שְׁמֵהּ רַבָּא מְבָרַךְ לְעָלַם וּלְעָלְמֵי עָלְמַיָּא.

ש״ץ: יִתְבָּרַךְ וְיִשְׁתַּבַּח וְיִתְפָּאַר וְיִתְרוֹמַם וְיִתְנַשֵּׂא
וְיִתְהַדָּר וְיִתְעַלֶּה וְיִתְהַלָּל
שְׁמֵהּ דְּקֻדְשָׁא בְּרִיךְ הוּא (קהל: בְּרִיךְ הוּא)
לְעֵלָּא מִן כָּל בִּרְכָתָא
/בעשרת ימי תשובה: לְעֵלָּא לְעֵלָּא מִכָּל בִּרְכָתָא/
וְשִׁירָתָא, תֻּשְׁבְּחָתָא וְנֶחֱמָתָא
דַּאֲמִירָן בְּעָלְמָא, וְאִמְרוּ אָמֵן. (קהל: אָמֵן)

תִּתְקַבַּל צְלוֹתְהוֹן וּבָעוּתְהוֹן דְּכָל יִשְׂרָאֵל
קֳדָם אֲבוּהוֹן דִּי בִשְׁמַיָּא, וְאִמְרוּ אָמֵן. (קהל: אָמֵן)

May there be great peace from heaven,
and life for us and all Israel –
and say: Amen.

Bow, take three steps back, as if taking leave of the Divine Presence, then bow, first left, then right, then center, while saying:

May He who makes peace in His high places,
make peace for us and all Israel –
and say: Amen.

On Yom HaAtzma'ut (in Israel and many communities outside Israel) the service continues with "Listen, Israel" *on* *page 916.*

From the second night of Pesaḥ until the night before Shavuot, the Omer is counted here *(page 284).*

On Purim, Megillat Esther is read (page 1224);
on Tisha B'Av, Megillat Eikha is read (page 1190).

Stand while saying Aleinu. Bow at ▾.

עָלֵינוּ It is our duty to praise the Master of all,
and ascribe greatness to the Author of creation,
who has not made us like the nations of the lands
nor placed us like the families of the earth;
who has not made our portion like theirs,
nor our destiny like all their multitudes.
(For they worship vanity and emptiness,
and pray to a god who cannot save.)
▾But we bow in worship
and thank the Supreme King of kings,
the Holy One, blessed be He,
who extends the heavens and establishes the earth,
whose throne of glory is in the heavens above,
and whose power's Presence is in the highest of heights.
He is our God; there is no other.
Truly He is our King, there is none else,
as it is written in His Torah:
"You shall know and take to heart this day *Deut. 4*
that the LORD is God,
in heaven above and on earth below. There is no other."

יְהֵא שְׁלָמָא רַבָּא מִן שְׁמַיָּא
וְחַיִּים, עָלֵינוּ וְעַל כָּל יִשְׂרָאֵל, וְאִמְרוּ אָמֵן. (קהל: אָמֵן)

Bow, take three steps back, as if taking leave of the Divine Presence, then bow, first left, then right, then center, while saying:

עֹשֶׂה שָׁלוֹם/ בעשרת ימי תשובה: הַשָּׁלוֹם/ בִּמְרוֹמָיו
הוּא יַעֲשֶׂה שָׁלוֹם
עָלֵינוּ וְעַל כָּל יִשְׂרָאֵל, וְאִמְרוּ אָמֵן. (קהל: אָמֵן)

On יום העצמאות *(in* ארץ ישראל *and many communities in* חוץ לארץ*)*
the service continues with שְׁמַע יִשְׂרָאֵל *on page 917.*
From the second night of פסח *until the night before* שבועות*, the* עומר *is counted here* (*page 285*).
On פורים*,* מגילת אסתר *is read* (page 1225); *on* תשעה באב*,* מגילת איכה *is read* (page 1191).

Stand while saying עָלֵינוּ*. Bow at* ".

עָלֵינוּ לְשַׁבֵּחַ לַאֲדוֹן הַכֹּל, לָתֵת גְּדֻלָּה לְיוֹצֵר בְּרֵאשִׁית
שֶׁלֹּא עָשָׂנוּ כְּגוֹיֵי הָאֲרָצוֹת, וְלֹא שָׂמָנוּ כְּמִשְׁפְּחוֹת הָאֲדָמָה
שֶׁלֹּא שָׂם חֶלְקֵנוּ כָּהֶם וְגוֹרָלֵנוּ כְּכָל הֲמוֹנָם.
(שֶׁהֵם מִשְׁתַּחֲוִים לְהֶבֶל וָרִיק וּמִתְפַּלְלִים אֶל אֵל לֹא יוֹשִׁיעַ.)
"וַאֲנַחְנוּ כּוֹרְעִים וּמִשְׁתַּחֲוִים וּמוֹדִים
לִפְנֵי מֶלֶךְ מַלְכֵי הַמְּלָכִים, הַקָּדוֹשׁ בָּרוּךְ הוּא
שֶׁהוּא נוֹטֶה שָׁמַיִם וְיוֹסֵד אָרֶץ
וּמוֹשַׁב יְקָרוֹ בַּשָּׁמַיִם מִמַּעַל
וּשְׁכִינַת עֻזּוֹ בְּגָבְהֵי מְרוֹמִים.
הוּא אֱלֹהֵינוּ, אֵין עוֹד.
אֱמֶת מַלְכֵּנוּ, אֶפֶס זוּלָתוֹ
כַּכָּתוּב בְּתוֹרָתוֹ
וְיָדַעְתָּ הַיּוֹם וַהֲשֵׁבֹתָ אֶל־לְבָבֶךָ דברים ד
כִּי יהוה הוּא הָאֱלֹהִים בַּשָּׁמַיִם מִמַּעַל וְעַל־הָאָרֶץ מִתָּחַת, אֵין עוֹד:

Therefore, we place our hope in You, LORD our God,
that we may soon see the glory of Your power,
when You will remove abominations from the earth,
and idols will be utterly destroyed,
when the world will be perfected
under the sovereignty of the Almighty,
when all humanity will call on Your name,
to turn all the earth's wicked toward You.
All the world's inhabitants will realize and know
that to You every knee must bow and every tongue swear loyalty.
Before You, LORD our God, they will kneel and bow down
and give honor to Your glorious name.
They will all accept the yoke of Your kingdom,
and You will reign over them soon and for ever.
For the kingdom is Yours, and to all eternity You will reign in glory,
as it is written in Your Torah: "The LORD will reign for ever and ever." *Ex. 15*
▸ And it is said: "Then the LORD shall be King over all the earth; *Zech. 14*
on that day the LORD shall be One and His name One."

Some add:

Have no fear of sudden terror or of the ruin when it overtakes the wicked. *Prov. 3*
Devise your strategy, but it will be thwarted; propose your plan, *Is. 8*
but it will not stand, for God is with us. When you grow old, I will still be the same. *Is. 46*
When your hair turns gray, I will still carry you. I made you, I will bear you,
I will carry you, and I will rescue you.

MOURNER'S KADDISH

The following prayer, said by mourners, requires the presence of a minyan.
A transliteration can be found on page 1334.

Mourner: יִתְגַּדַּל Magnified and sanctified may His great name be,
in the world He created by His will.
May He establish His kingdom
in your lifetime and in your days,
and in the lifetime of all the house of Israel,
swiftly and soon – and say: Amen.

All: May His great name be blessed for ever and all time.

עַל כֵּן נְקַוֶּה לְּךָ יהוה אֱלֹהֵינוּ, לִרְאוֹת מְהֵרָה בְּתִפְאֶרֶת עֻזֶּךָ
לְהַעֲבִיר גִּלּוּלִים מִן הָאָרֶץ, וְהָאֱלִילִים כָּרוֹת יִכָּרֵתוּן
לְתַקֵּן עוֹלָם בְּמַלְכוּת שַׁדַּי.
וְכָל בְּנֵי בָשָׂר יִקְרְאוּ בִשְׁמֶךָ לְהַפְנוֹת אֵלֶיךָ כָּל רִשְׁעֵי אָרֶץ.
יַכִּירוּ וְיֵדְעוּ כָּל יוֹשְׁבֵי תֵבֵל
כִּי לְךָ תִּכְרַע כָּל בֶּרֶךְ, תִּשָּׁבַע כָּל לָשׁוֹן.
לְפָנֶיךָ יהוה אֱלֹהֵינוּ יִכְרְעוּ וְיִפֹּלוּ, וְלִכְבוֹד שִׁמְךָ יְקָר יִתֵּנוּ
וִיקַבְּלוּ כֻלָּם אֶת עֹל מַלְכוּתֶךָ
וְתִמְלֹךְ עֲלֵיהֶם מְהֵרָה לְעוֹלָם וָעֶד.
כִּי הַמַּלְכוּת שֶׁלְּךָ הִיא וּלְעוֹלְמֵי עַד תִּמְלֹךְ בְּכָבוֹד
כַּכָּתוּב בְּתוֹרָתֶךָ, יהוה יִמְלֹךְ לְעֹלָם וָעֶד: שמות טו
► וְנֶאֱמַר, וְהָיָה יהוה לְמֶלֶךְ עַל־כָּל־הָאָרֶץ זכריה יד
בַּיּוֹם הַהוּא יִהְיֶה יהוה אֶחָד וּשְׁמוֹ אֶחָד:

Some add:

אַל־תִּירָא מִפַּחַד פִּתְאֹם וּמִשֹּׁאַת רְשָׁעִים כִּי תָבֹא: משלי ג
עֻצוּ עֵצָה וְתֻפָר, דַּבְּרוּ דָבָר וְלֹא יָקוּם, כִּי עִמָּנוּ אֵל: ישעיה ח
וְעַד־זִקְנָה אֲנִי הוּא, וְעַד־שֵׂיבָה אֲנִי אֶסְבֹּל אֲנִי עָשִׂיתִי וַאֲנִי אֶשָּׂא וַאֲנִי אֶסְבֹּל וַאֲמַלֵּט: ישעיה מו

קדיש יתום

The following prayer, said by mourners, requires the presence of a מנין.
A transliteration can be found on page 1334.

אבל: יִתְגַּדַּל וְיִתְקַדַּשׁ שְׁמֵהּ רַבָּא (קהל: אָמֵן)
בְּעָלְמָא דִּי בְרָא כִרְעוּתֵהּ
וְיַמְלִיךְ מַלְכוּתֵהּ
בְּחַיֵּיכוֹן וּבְיוֹמֵיכוֹן וּבְחַיֵּי דְכָל בֵּית יִשְׂרָאֵל
בַּעֲגָלָא וּבִזְמַן קָרִיב, וְאִמְרוּ אָמֵן. (קהל: אָמֵן)

קהל ואבל: יְהֵא שְׁמֵהּ רַבָּא מְבָרַךְ לְעָלַם וּלְעָלְמֵי עָלְמַיָּא.

Mourner: Blessed and praised, glorified and exalted,
raised and honored, uplifted and lauded
be the name of the Holy One,
blessed be He, beyond any blessing,
song, praise and consolation
uttered in the world – and say: Amen.

May there be great peace from heaven,
and life for us and all Israel – and say: Amen.

Bow, take three steps back, as if taking leave of the Divine Presence, then bow, first left, then right, then center, while saying:

May He who makes peace in His high places,
make peace for us and all Israel – and say: Amen.

From the second day of Rosh Ḥodesh Elul through Shemini Atzeret (in Israel through Hoshana Raba), the following psalm is said:

לְדָוִד By David. The LORD is my light and my salvation – whom then shall I fear? The LORD is the stronghold of my life – of whom shall I be afraid? When evil men close in on me to devour my flesh, it is they, my enemies and foes, who stumble and fall. Should an army besiege me, my heart would not fear. Should war break out against me, still I would be confident. One thing I ask of the LORD, only this do I seek: to live in the House of the LORD all the days of my life, to gaze on the beauty of the LORD and worship in His Temple. For He will keep me safe in His pavilion on the day of trouble. He will hide me under the cover of His tent. He will set me high upon a rock. Now my head is high above my enemies who surround me. I will sacrifice in His tent with shouts of joy. I will sing and chant praises to the LORD. LORD, hear my voice when I call. Be gracious to me and answer me. On Your behalf my heart says, "Seek My face." Your face, LORD, will I seek. Do not hide Your face from me. Do not turn Your servant away in anger. You have been my help. Do not reject or forsake me, God, my Savior. Were my father and my mother to forsake me, the LORD would take me in. Teach me Your way, LORD, and lead me on a level path, because of my oppressors. Do not abandon me to the will of my foes, for false witnesses have risen against me, breathing violence. ▸ Were it not for my faith that I shall see the LORD's goodness in the land of the living. Hope in the LORD. Be strong and of good courage, and hope in the LORD! *Ps. 27*

Mourner's Kaddish (on previous page)

In a house of mourning the service continues on page 1060.

אבל: יִתְבָּרַךְ וְיִשְׁתַּבַּח וְיִתְפָּאַר
וְיִתְרוֹמַם וְיִתְנַשֵּׂא וְיִתְהַדָּר וְיִתְעַלֶּה וְיִתְהַלָּל
שְׁמֵהּ דְּקֻדְשָׁא בְּרִיךְ הוּא (קהל: בְּרִיךְ הוּא)
לְעֵֽלָּא מִן כָּל בִּרְכָתָא
/בעשרת ימי תשובה: לְעֵֽלָּא לְעֵֽלָּא מִכָּל בִּרְכָתָא/
וְשִׁירָתָא, תֻּשְׁבְּחָתָא וְנֶחֱמָתָא
דַּאֲמִירָן בְּעָלְמָא, וְאִמְרוּ אָמֵן. (קהל: אָמֵן)

יְהֵא שְׁלָמָא רַבָּא מִן שְׁמַיָּא
וְחַיִּים, עָלֵֽינוּ וְעַל כָּל יִשְׂרָאֵל, וְאִמְרוּ אָמֵן. (קהל: אָמֵן)

Bow, take three steps back, as if taking leave of the Divine Presence, then bow, first left, then right, then center, while saying:

עֹשֶׂה שָׁלוֹם/בעשרת ימי תשובה: הַשָּׁלוֹם/ בִּמְרוֹמָיו
הוּא יַעֲשֶׂה שָׁלוֹם עָלֵֽינוּ וְעַל כָּל יִשְׂרָאֵל, וְאִמְרוּ אָמֵן. (קהל: אָמֵן)

From the second day of ראש חודש אלול *through* שמיני עצרת *(in* ארץ ישראל *through* הושענא רבה*), the following psalm is said:*

תהלים כז
לְדָוִד, יהוה אוֹרִי וְיִשְׁעִי, מִמִּי אִירָא, יהוה מָעוֹז־חַיַּי, מִמִּי אֶפְחָד: בִּקְרֹב עָלַי מְרֵעִים לֶאֱכֹל אֶת־בְּשָׂרִי, צָרַי וְאֹיְבַי לִי, הֵמָּה כָשְׁלוּ וְנָפָֽלוּ: אִם־תַּחֲנֶה עָלַי מַחֲנֶה, לֹא־יִירָא לִבִּי, אִם־תָּקוּם עָלַי מִלְחָמָה, בְּזֹאת אֲנִי בוֹטֵֽחַ: אַחַת שָׁאַֽלְתִּי מֵאֵת־יהוה, אוֹתָהּ אֲבַקֵּשׁ, שִׁבְתִּי בְּבֵית־יהוה כָּל־יְמֵי חַיַּי, לַחֲזוֹת בְּנֹֽעַם־יהוה, וּלְבַקֵּר בְּהֵיכָלוֹ: כִּי יִצְפְּנֵֽנִי בְּסֻכֹּה בְּיוֹם רָעָה, יַסְתִּרֵֽנִי בְּסֵֽתֶר אָהֳלוֹ, בְּצוּר יְרוֹמְמֵֽנִי: וְעַתָּה יָרוּם רֹאשִׁי עַל אֹיְבַי סְבִיבוֹתַי, וְאֶזְבְּחָה בְאָהֳלוֹ זִבְחֵי תְרוּעָה, אָשִֽׁירָה וַאֲזַמְּרָה לַיהוה: שְׁמַע־יהוה קוֹלִי אֶקְרָא, וְחָנֵּֽנִי וַעֲנֵֽנִי: לְךָ אָמַר לִבִּי בַּקְּשׁוּ פָנָי, אֶת־פָּנֶֽיךָ יהוה אֲבַקֵּשׁ: אַל־תַּסְתֵּר פָּנֶֽיךָ מִמֶּֽנִּי, אַל תַּט־בְּאַף עַבְדֶּֽךָ, עֶזְרָתִי הָיִֽיתָ, אַל־תִּטְּשֵֽׁנִי וְאַל־תַּעַזְבֵֽנִי, אֱלֹהֵי יִשְׁעִי: כִּי־אָבִי וְאִמִּי עֲזָבֽוּנִי, וַיהוה יַאַסְפֵֽנִי: הוֹרֵֽנִי יהוה דַּרְכֶּֽךָ, וּנְחֵֽנִי בְּאֹֽרַח מִישׁוֹר, לְמַֽעַן שׁוֹרְרָי: אַל־תִּתְּנֵֽנִי בְּנֶֽפֶשׁ צָרָי, כִּי קָֽמוּ־בִי עֵדֵי־שֶֽׁקֶר, וִיפֵֽחַ חָמָס: › לוּלֵא הֶאֱמַֽנְתִּי לִרְאוֹת בְּטוּב־יהוה בְּאֶֽרֶץ חַיִּים: קַוֵּה אֶל־יהוה, חֲזַק וְיַאֲמֵץ לִבֶּֽךָ, וְקַוֵּה אֶל־יהוה:

קדיש יתום *(on previous page)*

In a house of mourning the service continues on page 1061.

COUNTING OF THE OMER

The Omer is counted each night from the second night of Pesaḥ until the night before Shavuot. See laws 221–224.

Some say the following meditation before the blessing:

For the sake of the unification of the Holy One, blessed be He, and His Divine Presence, in reverence and love, to unify the name *Yod-Heh* with *Vav-Heh* in perfect unity in the name of all Israel.

הִנְנִי I am prepared and ready to fulfill the positive commandment of Counting the Omer, as is written in the Torah, "You shall count seven complete weeks from the day following the [Pesaḥ] rest day, when you brought the Omer as a wave-offering. To the day after the seventh week you shall count fifty days. Then you shall present a meal-offering of new grain to the LORD." *Lev. 23*
May the pleasantness of the LORD our God be upon us. Establish for us the work of our hands, O establish the work of our hands. *Ps. 90*

בָּרוּךְ Blessed are You, LORD our God, King of the Universe, who has made us holy through His commandments, and has commanded us about counting the Omer.

16 Nisan

1. Today is the first day of the Omer.

17 Nisan

2. Today is the second day of the Omer.

18 Nisan

3. Today is the third day of the Omer.

19 Nisan

4. Today is the fourth day of the Omer.

20 Nisan

5. Today is the fifth day of the Omer.

21 Nisan

6. Today is the sixth day of the Omer.

Egypt with the giving of the Torah at Mount Sinai, are a time of preparation and growth – of leaving a world of slavery and getting ready to enter a world of personal, social and spiritual responsibility. The Jewish mystics attached special significance to this period of the year as one in which the various facets of the soul were cleansed, one by one.

סדר ספירת העומר

The עומר is counted each night from the second night of פסח until the night before שבועות. See laws 221–224.

Some say the following meditation before the blessing:

לְשֵׁם יִחוּד קֻדְשָׁא בְּרִיךְ הוּא וּשְׁכִינְתֵּהּ בִּדְחִילוּ וּרְחִימוּ
לְיַחֵד שֵׁם י״ה בו״ה בְּיִחוּדָא שְׁלִים בְּשֵׁם כָּל יִשְׂרָאֵל.

הִנְנִי מוּכָן וּמְזֻמָּן לְקַיֵּם מִצְוַת עֲשֵׂה שֶׁל סְפִירַת הָעְמֶר. כְּמוֹ שֶׁכָּתוּב בַּתּוֹרָה,
ויקרא כג וּסְפַרְתֶּם לָכֶם מִמָּחֳרַת הַשַּׁבָּת, מִיּוֹם הֲבִיאֲכֶם אֶת־עְמֶר הַתְּנוּפָה, שֶׁבַע
שַׁבָּתוֹת תְּמִימֹת תִּהְיֶינָה: עַד מִמָּחֳרַת הַשַּׁבָּת הַשְּׁבִיעִת תִּסְפְּרוּ חֲמִשִּׁים
תהלים צ יוֹם, וְהִקְרַבְתֶּם מִנְחָה חֲדָשָׁה לַיהוה: וִיהִי נֹעַם אֲדֹנָי אֱלֹהֵינוּ עָלֵינוּ, וּמַעֲשֵׂה
יָדֵינוּ כּוֹנְנָה עָלֵינוּ, וּמַעֲשֵׂה יָדֵינוּ כּוֹנְנֵהוּ:

בָּרוּךְ אַתָּה יהוה אֱלֹהֵינוּ מֶלֶךְ הָעוֹלָם
אֲשֶׁר קִדְּשָׁנוּ בְּמִצְוֹתָיו וְצִוָּנוּ עַל סְפִירַת הָעְמֶר.

טו בניסן

1. הַיּוֹם יוֹם אֶחָד בָּעְמֶר.

חסד שבחסד

יז בניסן

2. הַיּוֹם שְׁנֵי יָמִים בָּעְמֶר.

גבורה שבחסד

יח בניסן

3. הַיּוֹם שְׁלֹשָׁה יָמִים בָּעְמֶר.

תפארת שבחסד

יט בניסן

4. הַיּוֹם אַרְבָּעָה יָמִים בָּעְמֶר.

נצח שבחסד

כ בניסן

5. הַיּוֹם חֲמִשָּׁה יָמִים בָּעְמֶר.

הוד שבחסד

כא בניסן

6. הַיּוֹם שִׁשָּׁה יָמִים בָּעְמֶר.

יסוד שבחסד

COUNTING THE OMER

When the Temple stood, on the day after the first day of Pesaḥ an offering was made of an Omer (approximately nine pounds) of new barley grain. There then began a count of forty-nine days – seven complete weeks – and on the fiftieth day, the festival of Shavuot was celebrated. When the Temple was destroyed, the sages ordained that we should continue to count the days as a memory of this practice. The forty-nine days, connecting the exodus from

22 Nisan

7. Today is the seventh day,
making one week
of the Omer.

23 Nisan

8. Today is the eighth day,
making one week and one day
of the Omer.

24 Nisan

9. Today is the ninth day,
making one week and two days
of the Omer.

25 Nisan

10. Today is the tenth day,
making one week and three
days of the Omer.

26 Nisan

11. Today is the eleventh day,
making one week and four
days of the Omer.

27 Nisan

12. Today is the twelfth day,
making one week and five days
of the Omer.

28 Nisan

13. Today is the thirteenth day,
making one week and six days
of the Omer.

29 Nisan

14. Today is the fourteenth day,
making two weeks
of the Omer.

30 Nisan, 1st day Rosh Ḥodesh

15. Today is the fifteenth day,
making two weeks and one day
of the Omer.

1 Iyar, 2nd day Rosh Ḥodesh

16. Today is the sixteenth day,
making two weeks and two
days of the Omer.

2 Iyar

17. Today is the seventeenth day,
making two weeks and three
days of the Omer.

3 Iyar

18. Today is the eighteenth day,
making two weeks and four
days of the Omer.

4 Iyar

19. Today is the nineteenth day,
making two weeks and five
days of the Omer.

5 Iyar, Yom HaAtzma'ut

20. Today is the twentieth day,
making two weeks and six days
of the Omer.

כב בניסן

7. הַיּוֹם שִׁבְעָה יָמִים שֶׁהֵם שָׁבְוּעַ אֶחָד בָּעְוֹמֶר. מלכות שבחסד

כג בניסן

8. הַיּוֹם שְׁמוֹנָה יָמִים שֶׁהֵם שָׁבְוּעַ אֶחָד וְיוֹם אֶחָד בָּעְוֹמֶר. חסד שבגבורה

כד בניסן

9. הַיּוֹם תִּשְׁעָה יָמִים שֶׁהֵם שָׁבְוּעַ אֶחָד וּשְׁנֵי יָמִים בָּעְוֹמֶר. גבורה שבגבורה

כה בניסן

10. הַיּוֹם עֲשָׂרָה יָמִים שֶׁהֵם שָׁבְוּעַ אֶחָד וּשְׁלֹשָׁה יָמִים בָּעְוֹמֶר. תפארת שבגבורה

כו בניסן

11. הַיּוֹם אַחַד עָשָׂר יוֹם שֶׁהֵם שָׁבְוּעַ אֶחָד וְאַרְבָּעָה יָמִים בָּעְוֹמֶר. נצח שבגבורה

כז בניסן

12. הַיּוֹם שְׁנֵים עָשָׂר יוֹם שֶׁהֵם שָׁבְוּעַ אֶחָד וַחֲמִשָּׁה יָמִים בָּעְוֹמֶר. הוד שבגבורה

כח בניסן

13. הַיּוֹם שְׁלֹשָׁה עָשָׂר יוֹם שֶׁהֵם שָׁבְוּעַ אֶחָד וְשִׁשָּׁה יָמִים בָּעְוֹמֶר. יסוד שבגבורה

כט בניסן

14. הַיּוֹם אַרְבָּעָה עָשָׂר יוֹם שֶׁהֵם שְׁנֵי שָׁבוּעוֹת בָּעְוֹמֶר. מלכות שבגבורה

ל בניסן, א׳ דראש חודש

15. הַיּוֹם חֲמִשָּׁה עָשָׂר יוֹם שֶׁהֵם שְׁנֵי שָׁבוּעוֹת וְיוֹם אֶחָד בָּעְוֹמֶר. חסד שבתפארת

א באייר, ב׳ דראש חודש

16. הַיּוֹם שִׁשָּׁה עָשָׂר יוֹם שֶׁהֵם שְׁנֵי שָׁבוּעוֹת וּשְׁנֵי יָמִים בָּעְוֹמֶר. גבורה שבתפארת

ב באייר

17. הַיּוֹם שִׁבְעָה עָשָׂר יוֹם שֶׁהֵם שְׁנֵי שָׁבוּעוֹת וּשְׁלֹשָׁה יָמִים בָּעְוֹמֶר. תפארת שבתפארת

ג באייר

18. הַיּוֹם שְׁמוֹנָה עָשָׂר יוֹם שֶׁהֵם שְׁנֵי שָׁבוּעוֹת וְאַרְבָּעָה יָמִים בָּעְוֹמֶר. נצח שבתפארת

ד באייר

19. הַיּוֹם תִּשְׁעָה עָשָׂר יוֹם שֶׁהֵם שְׁנֵי שָׁבוּעוֹת וַחֲמִשָּׁה יָמִים בָּעְוֹמֶר. הוד שבתפארת

ה באייר, יום העצמאות

20. הַיּוֹם עֶשְׂרִים יוֹם שֶׁהֵם שְׁנֵי שָׁבוּעוֹת וְשִׁשָּׁה יָמִים בָּעְוֹמֶר. יסוד שבתפארת

6 Iyar

21. Today is the twenty-first day, making three weeks of the Omer.

7 Iyar

22. Today is the twenty-second day, making three weeks and one day of the Omer.

8 Iyar

23. Today is the twenty-third day, making three weeks and two days of the Omer.

9 Iyar

24. Today is the twenty-fourth day, making three weeks and three days of the Omer.

10 Iyar

25. Today is the twenty-fifth day, making three weeks and four days of the Omer.

11 Iyar

26. Today is the twenty-sixth day, making three weeks and five days of the Omer.

12 Iyar

27. Today is the twenty-seventh day, making three weeks and six days of the Omer.

13 Iyar

28. Today is the twenty-eighth day, making four weeks of the Omer.

14 Iyar, Pesaḥ Sheni

29. Today is the twenty-ninth day, making four weeks and one day of the Omer.

15 Iyar

30. Today is the thirtieth day, making four weeks and two days of the Omer.

16 Iyar

31. Today is the thirty-first day, making four weeks and three days of the Omer.

17 Iyar

32. Today is the thirty-second day, making four weeks and four days of the Omer.

18 Iyar, Lag BaOmer

33. Today is the thirty-third day, making four weeks and five days of the Omer.

19 Iyar

34. Today is the thirty-fourth day, making four weeks and six days of the Omer.

ו באייר

21. הַיּוֹם אֶחָד וְעֶשְׂרִים יוֹם
שֶׁהֵם שְׁלֹשָׁה שָׁבוּעוֹת בָּעֹמֶר.
מלכות שבתפארת

ז באייר

22. הַיּוֹם שְׁנַיִם וְעֶשְׂרִים יוֹם
שֶׁהֵם שְׁלֹשָׁה שָׁבוּעוֹת
וְיוֹם אֶחָד בָּעֹמֶר. חסד שבנצח

ח באייר

23. הַיּוֹם שְׁלֹשָׁה וְעֶשְׂרִים יוֹם
שֶׁהֵם שְׁלֹשָׁה שָׁבוּעוֹת
וּשְׁנֵי יָמִים בָּעֹמֶר. גבורה שבנצח

ט באייר

24. הַיּוֹם אַרְבָּעָה וְעֶשְׂרִים יוֹם
שֶׁהֵם שְׁלֹשָׁה שָׁבוּעוֹת
וּשְׁלֹשָׁה יָמִים בָּעֹמֶר.
תפארת שבנצח

י באייר

25. הַיּוֹם חֲמִשָּׁה וְעֶשְׂרִים יוֹם
שֶׁהֵם שְׁלֹשָׁה שָׁבוּעוֹת
וְאַרְבָּעָה יָמִים בָּעֹמֶר. נצח שבנצח

יא באייר

26. הַיּוֹם שִׁשָּׁה וְעֶשְׂרִים יוֹם
שֶׁהֵם שְׁלֹשָׁה שָׁבוּעוֹת
וַחֲמִשָּׁה יָמִים בָּעֹמֶר. הוד שבנצח

יב באייר

27. הַיּוֹם שִׁבְעָה וְעֶשְׂרִים יוֹם
שֶׁהֵם שְׁלֹשָׁה שָׁבוּעוֹת
וְשִׁשָּׁה יָמִים בָּעֹמֶר. יסוד שבנצח

יג באייר

28. הַיּוֹם שְׁמוֹנָה וְעֶשְׂרִים יוֹם
שֶׁהֵם אַרְבָּעָה שָׁבוּעוֹת
בָּעֹמֶר. מלכות שבנצח

יד באייר, פסח שני

29. הַיּוֹם תִּשְׁעָה וְעֶשְׂרִים יוֹם
שֶׁהֵם אַרְבָּעָה שָׁבוּעוֹת
וְיוֹם אֶחָד בָּעֹמֶר. חסד שבהוד

טו באייר

30. הַיּוֹם שְׁלֹשִׁים יוֹם
שֶׁהֵם אַרְבָּעָה שָׁבוּעוֹת
וּשְׁנֵי יָמִים בָּעֹמֶר. גבורה שבהוד

טז באייר

31. הַיּוֹם אֶחָד וּשְׁלֹשִׁים יוֹם
שֶׁהֵם אַרְבָּעָה שָׁבוּעוֹת
וּשְׁלֹשָׁה יָמִים בָּעֹמֶר.
תפארת שבהוד

יז באייר

32. הַיּוֹם שְׁנַיִם וּשְׁלֹשִׁים יוֹם
שֶׁהֵם אַרְבָּעָה שָׁבוּעוֹת
וְאַרְבָּעָה יָמִים בָּעֹמֶר. נצח שבהוד

יח באייר, לג בעומר

33. הַיּוֹם שְׁלֹשָׁה וּשְׁלֹשִׁים יוֹם
שֶׁהֵם אַרְבָּעָה שָׁבוּעוֹת
וַחֲמִשָּׁה יָמִים בָּעֹמֶר. הוד שבהוד

יט באייר

34. הַיּוֹם אַרְבָּעָה וּשְׁלֹשִׁים יוֹם
שֶׁהֵם אַרְבָּעָה שָׁבוּעוֹת
וְשִׁשָּׁה יָמִים בָּעֹמֶר. יסוד שבהוד

20 Iyar

35. Today is the thirty-fifth day,
making five weeks
of the Omer.

21 Iyar

36. Today is the thirty-sixth day,
making five weeks and one day
of the Omer.

22 Iyar

37. Today is the thirty-seventh day,
making five weeks and two
days of the Omer.

23 Iyar

38. Today is the thirty-eighth day,
making five weeks and three
days of the Omer.

24 Iyar

39. Today is the thirty-ninth day,
making five weeks and four
days of the Omer.

25 Iyar

40. Today is the fortieth day,
making five weeks and five
days of the Omer.

26 Iyar

41. Today is the forty-first day,
making five weeks and six days
of the Omer.

27 Iyar

42. Today is the forty-second day,
making six weeks
of the Omer.

28 Iyar, Yom Yerushalayim

43. Today is the forty-third day,
making six weeks and one day
of the Omer.

29 Iyar

44. Today is the forty-fourth day,
making six weeks and two days
of the Omer.

1 Sivan, Rosh Ḥodesh

45. Today is the forty-fifth day,
making six weeks and three
days of the Omer.

2 Sivan

46. Today is the forty-sixth day,
making six weeks and four
days of the Omer.

3 Sivan

47. Today is the forty-seventh day,
making six weeks and five days
of the Omer.

4 Sivan

48. Today is the forty-eighth day,
making six weeks and six days
of the Omer.

כ באייר

35. הַיּוֹם חֲמִשָּׁה וּשְׁלֹשִׁים יוֹם
שֶׁהֵם חֲמִשָּׁה שָׁבוּעוֹת
בָּעֹֽמֶר. מלכות שבהוד

כא באייר

36. הַיּוֹם שִׁשָּׁה וּשְׁלֹשִׁים יוֹם
שֶׁהֵם חֲמִשָּׁה שָׁבוּעוֹת
וְיוֹם אֶחָד בָּעֹֽמֶר. חסד שביסוד

כב באייר

37. הַיּוֹם שִׁבְעָה וּשְׁלֹשִׁים יוֹם
שֶׁהֵם חֲמִשָּׁה שָׁבוּעוֹת
וּשְׁנֵי יָמִים בָּעֹֽמֶר. גבורה שביסוד

כג באייר

38. הַיּוֹם שְׁמוֹנָה וּשְׁלֹשִׁים יוֹם
שֶׁהֵם חֲמִשָּׁה שָׁבוּעוֹת
וּשְׁלֹשָׁה יָמִים בָּעֹֽמֶר.
תפארת שביסוד

כד באייר

39. הַיּוֹם תִּשְׁעָה וּשְׁלֹשִׁים יוֹם
שֶׁהֵם חֲמִשָּׁה שָׁבוּעוֹת
וְאַרְבָּעָה יָמִים בָּעֹֽמֶר. נצח שביסוד

כה באייר

40. הַיּוֹם אַרְבָּעִים יוֹם
שֶׁהֵם חֲמִשָּׁה שָׁבוּעוֹת
וַחֲמִשָּׁה יָמִים בָּעֹֽמֶר. הוד שביסוד

כו באייר

41. הַיּוֹם אֶחָד וְאַרְבָּעִים יוֹם
שֶׁהֵם חֲמִשָּׁה שָׁבוּעוֹת
וְשִׁשָּׁה יָמִים בָּעֹֽמֶר. יסוד שביסוד

כז באייר

42. הַיּוֹם שְׁנַיִם וְאַרְבָּעִים יוֹם
שֶׁהֵם שִׁשָּׁה שָׁבוּעוֹת
בָּעֹֽמֶר. מלכות שביסוד

כח באייר, יום ירושלים

43. הַיּוֹם שְׁלֹשָׁה וְאַרְבָּעִים יוֹם
שֶׁהֵם שִׁשָּׁה שָׁבוּעוֹת
וְיוֹם אֶחָד בָּעֹֽמֶר. חסד שבמלכות

כט באייר

44. הַיּוֹם אַרְבָּעָה וְאַרְבָּעִים יוֹם
שֶׁהֵם שִׁשָּׁה שָׁבוּעוֹת
וּשְׁנֵי יָמִים בָּעֹֽמֶר. גבורה שבמלכות

א בסיון, ראש חודש

45. הַיּוֹם חֲמִשָּׁה וְאַרְבָּעִים יוֹם
שֶׁהֵם שִׁשָּׁה שָׁבוּעוֹת וּשְׁלֹשָׁה
יָמִים בָּעֹֽמֶר. תפארת שבמלכות

ב בסיון

46. הַיּוֹם שִׁשָּׁה וְאַרְבָּעִים יוֹם
שֶׁהֵם שִׁשָּׁה שָׁבוּעוֹת וְאַרְבָּעָה
יָמִים בָּעֹֽמֶר. נצח שבמלכות

ג בסיון

47. הַיּוֹם שִׁבְעָה וְאַרְבָּעִים יוֹם
שֶׁהֵם שִׁשָּׁה שָׁבוּעוֹת וַחֲמִשָּׁה
יָמִים בָּעֹֽמֶר. הוד שבמלכות

ד בסיון

48. הַיּוֹם שְׁמוֹנָה וְאַרְבָּעִים יוֹם
שֶׁהֵם שִׁשָּׁה שָׁבוּעוֹת וְשִׁשָּׁה
יָמִים בָּעֹֽמֶר. יסוד שבמלכות

5 Sivan, Erev Shavuot

49. Today is the forty-ninth day,
making seven weeks of the Omer.

הָרַחֲמָן May the Compassionate One
restore the Temple service to its place
speedily in our days. Amen, Selah.

Some add:

לַמְנַצֵּחַ For the conductor of music. With stringed instruments. A psalm, a song. *Ps. 67* May God be gracious to us and bless us. May He make His face shine on us, Selah. Then will Your way be known on earth, Your salvation among all the nations. Let the peoples praise You, God; let all peoples praise You. Let nations rejoice and sing for joy, for You judge the peoples with equity, and guide the nations of the earth, Selah. Let the peoples praise You, God; let all peoples praise You. The earth has yielded its harvest. May God, our God, bless us. God will bless us, and all the ends of the earth will fear Him.

אָנָּא Please, by the power of Your great right hand, set the captive nation free. Accept Your people's prayer. Strengthen us, purify us, You who are revered. Please, Mighty One, guard like the pupil of the eye those who seek Your unity. Bless them, cleanse them, have compassion on them, grant them Your righteousness always. Mighty One, Holy One, in Your great goodness guide Your congregation. Only One, Exalted One, turn to Your people, who proclaim Your holiness. Accept our plea and heed our cry, You who know all secret thoughts. Blessed be the name of His glorious kingdom for ever and all time.

רִבּוֹנוֹ שֶׁל עוֹלָם Master of the Universe, You commanded us through Your servant Moses to count the Omer, to cleanse our carapaces and impurities, as You have written in Your Torah: "You shall count seven complete weeks from the day *Lev. 23* following the [Pesaḥ] rest day, when you brought the Omer as a wave-offering. To the day after the seventh week, you shall count fifty days." This is so that the souls of Your people Israel may be purified from their uncleanliness. May it also be Your will, Lord our God and God of our ancestors, that in the merit of the Omer count that I have counted today, there may be rectified any defect on my part in the counting of (*insert the appropriate sefira for each day*). May I be cleansed and sanctified with Your holiness on high, and through this may there flow a rich stream through all worlds, to rectify our lives, spirits and souls from any dross and defect, purifying and sanctifying us with Your sublime holiness. Amen, Selah.

The service continues with Aleinu on page 278.

ה בסיון, ערב שבועות

49. הַיּוֹם תִּשְׁעָה וְאַרְבָּעִים יוֹם
שֶׁהֵם שִׁבְעָה שָׁבוּעוֹת בָּעֹמֶר. מלכות שבמלכות

הָרַחֲמָן הוּא יַחֲזִיר לָנוּ עֲבוֹדַת בֵּית הַמִּקְדָּשׁ לִמְקוֹמָהּ בִּמְהֵרָה בְיָמֵינוּ, אָמֵן סֶלָה.

Some add:

לַמְנַצֵּחַ בִּנְגִינֹת, מִזְמוֹר שִׁיר: אֱלֹהִים יְחָנֵּנוּ וִיבָרְכֵנוּ, יָאֵר פָּנָיו אִתָּנוּ סֶלָה: לָדַעַת תהלים סז
בָּאָרֶץ דַּרְכֶּךָ, בְּכָל־גּוֹיִם יְשׁוּעָתֶךָ: יוֹדוּךָ עַמִּים אֱלֹהִים, יוֹדוּךָ עַמִּים כֻּלָּם: יִשְׂמְחוּ וִירַנְּנוּ
לְאֻמִּים, כִּי־תִשְׁפֹּט עַמִּים מִישֹׁר, וּלְאֻמִּים בָּאָרֶץ תַּנְחֵם סֶלָה: יוֹדוּךָ עַמִּים אֱלֹהִים,
יוֹדוּךָ עַמִּים כֻּלָּם: אֶרֶץ נָתְנָה יְבוּלָהּ, יְבָרְכֵנוּ אֱלֹהִים אֱלֹהֵינוּ: יְבָרְכֵנוּ אֱלֹהִים, וְיִירְאוּ
אוֹתוֹ כָּל־אַפְסֵי־אָרֶץ:

אָנָּא, בְּכֹחַ גְּדֻלַּת יְמִינְךָ, תַּתִּיר צְרוּרָה. קַבֵּל רִנַּת עַמְּךָ, שַׂגְּבֵנוּ, טַהֲרֵנוּ, נוֹרָא. נָא גִבּוֹר, דּוֹרְשֵׁי יִחוּדְךָ כְּבָבַת שָׁמְרֵם. בָּרְכֵם, טַהֲרֵם, רַחֲמֵם, צִדְקָתְךָ תָּמִיד גָּמְלֵם. חֲסִין קָדוֹשׁ, בְּרֹב טוּבְךָ נַהֵל עֲדָתֶךָ. יָחִיד גֵּאֶה, לְעַמְּךָ פְּנֵה, זוֹכְרֵי קְדֻשָּׁתֶךָ. שַׁוְעָתֵנוּ קַבֵּל וּשְׁמַע צַעֲקָתֵנוּ, יוֹדֵעַ תַּעֲלוּמוֹת. בָּרוּךְ שֵׁם כְּבוֹד מַלְכוּתוֹ לְעוֹלָם וָעֶד.

רִבּוֹנוֹ שֶׁל עוֹלָם, אַתָּה צִוִּיתָנוּ עַל יְדֵי מֹשֶׁה עַבְדְּךָ לִסְפֹּר סְפִירַת הָעֹמֶר, כְּדֵי לְטַהֲרֵנוּ
מִקְּלִפּוֹתֵינוּ וּמִטֻּמְאוֹתֵינוּ. כְּמוֹ שֶׁכָּתַבְתָּ בְּתוֹרָתֶךָ: וּסְפַרְתֶּם לָכֶם מִמָּחֳרַת הַשַּׁבָּת, ויקרא כג
מִיּוֹם הֲבִיאֲכֶם אֶת־עֹמֶר הַתְּנוּפָה, שֶׁבַע שַׁבָּתוֹת תְּמִימֹת תִּהְיֶינָה: עַד מִמָּחֳרַת הַשַּׁבָּת
הַשְּׁבִיעִת תִּסְפְּרוּ חֲמִשִּׁים יוֹם: כְּדֵי שֶׁיִּטָּהֲרוּ נַפְשׁוֹת עַמְּךָ יִשְׂרָאֵל מִזֻּהֲמָתָם. וּבְכֵן יְהִי
רָצוֹן מִלְּפָנֶיךָ יהוה אֱלֹהֵינוּ וֵאלֹהֵי אֲבוֹתֵינוּ, שֶׁבִּזְכוּת סְפִירַת הָעֹמֶר שֶׁסָּפַרְתִּי הַיּוֹם,
יְתֻקַּן מַה שֶּׁפָּגַמְתִּי בִּסְפִירָה (*insert appropriate* ספירה *for each day*) וְאֶטָּהֵר וְאֶתְקַדֵּשׁ
בִּקְדֻשָּׁה שֶׁל מַעְלָה, וְעַל יְדֵי זֶה יֻשְׁפַּע שֶׁפַע רַב בְּכָל הָעוֹלָמוֹת, לְתַקֵּן אֶת נַפְשׁוֹתֵינוּ
וְרוּחוֹתֵינוּ וְנִשְׁמוֹתֵינוּ מִכָּל סִיג וּפְגָם, וּלְטַהֲרֵנוּ וּלְקַדְּשֵׁנוּ בִּקְדֻשָּׁתְךָ הָעֶלְיוֹנָה, אָמֵן סֶלָה.

The service continues with עָלֵינוּ *on page 279.*

לַמְנַצֵּחַ *Psalm 67:* Selected to be said at this time because the psalm (excluding the first verse, which is a superscription and not part of the psalm itself) contains forty-nine words, corresponding to the days of the counting of the Omer.

רִבּוֹנוֹ שֶׁל עוֹלָם *Master of the Universe:* a prayer emphasizing the idea that the counting of the Omer is a time of spiritual purification.

SHEMA BEFORE SLEEP AT NIGHT

הֲרֵינִי I hereby forgive anyone who has angered or provoked me or sinned against me, physically or financially or by failing to give me due respect, or in any other matter relating to me, involuntarily or willingly, inadvertently or deliberately, whether in word or deed: let no one incur punishment because of me.

בָּרוּךְ Blessed are You, Lord our God, King of the Universe, who makes the bonds of sleep fall on my eyes, and slumber on my eyelids. May it be Your will, Lord my God and God of my fathers, that You make me lie down in peace and arise in peace. Let not my imagination, bad dreams or troubling thoughts disturb me. May my bed be flawless before You. Enlighten my eyes lest I sleep the sleep of death, for it is You who illuminates the pupil of the eye. Blessed are You, Lord, who gives light to the whole world in His glory.

When saying all three paragraphs of Shema, say:

God, faithful King!

The following verse should be said aloud, while covering the eyes with the right hand:

Listen, Israel: the Lord is our God, the Lord is One. *Deut. 6*

Quietly: Blessed be the name of His glorious kingdom for ever and all time.

וְאָהַבְתָּ Love the Lord your God with all your heart, with all your soul, and with all your might. These words which I command you today shall be on your heart. Teach them repeatedly to your children, speaking of them when you sit at home and when you travel on the way, when you lie down and when you rise. Bind them as a sign on your hand, and they shall be an emblem between your eyes. Write them on the doorposts of your house and gates. *Deut. 6*

---

from the evening service; (6) הַמַּלְאָךְ הַגֹּאֵל אֹתִי "May the angel who rescued me from all harm," a series of biblical verses about safety and security; (7) A verse about angels, based on "The Lord's angel encamps around those who fear Him, and He rescues them" (Psalm 34:8) and "He will command His angels about you, to guard you in all your ways" (Psalm 91:11); (8) Psalm 128, about work, recalling the phrase from Ecclesiastes (5:11), "Sweet is the sleep of one who labors"; (9) רִגְזוּ וְאַל־תֶּחֱטָאוּ "Tremble, and do not sin," from Psalm 4:5, mentioned in the Talmud (*Berakhot* 4b) as an appropriate verse before

קריאת שמע על המיטה

הֲרֵינִי מוֹחֵל לְכָל מִי שֶׁהִכְעִיס וְהִקְנִיט אוֹתִי אוֹ שֶׁחָטָא כְּנֶגְדִּי, בֵּין בְּגוּפִי בֵּין בְּמָמוֹנִי בֵּין בִּכְבוֹדִי בֵּין בְּכָל אֲשֶׁר לִי, בֵּין בְּאֹנֶס בֵּין בְּרָצוֹן, בֵּין בְּשׁוֹגֵג בֵּין בְּמֵזִיד, בֵּין בְּדִבּוּר בֵּין בְּמַעֲשֶׂה, וְלֹא יֵעָנֵשׁ שׁוּם אָדָם בְּסִבָּתִי.

בָּרוּךְ אַתָּה יהוה אֱלֹהֵינוּ מֶלֶךְ הָעוֹלָם, הַמַּפִּיל חֶבְלֵי שֵׁנָה עַל עֵינַי וּתְנוּמָה עַל עַפְעַפָּי. וִיהִי רָצוֹן מִלְּפָנֶיךָ, יהוה אֱלֹהַי וֵאלֹהֵי אֲבוֹתַי, שֶׁתַּשְׁכִּיבֵנִי לְשָׁלוֹם וְתַעֲמִידֵנִי לְשָׁלוֹם, וְאַל יְבַהֲלוּנִי רַעְיוֹנַי וַחֲלוֹמוֹת רָעִים וְהַרְהוּרִים רָעִים, וּתְהֵא מִטָּתִי שְׁלֵמָה לְפָנֶיךָ, וְהָאֵר עֵינַי פֶּן אִישַׁן הַמָּוֶת, כִּי אַתָּה הַמֵּאִיר לְאִישׁוֹן בַּת עָיִן. בָּרוּךְ אַתָּה יהוה, הַמֵּאִיר לָעוֹלָם כֻּלּוֹ בִּכְבוֹדוֹ.

When saying all three paragraphs of שמע*, say:*

אֵל מֶלֶךְ נֶאֱמָן

The following verse should be said aloud, while covering the eyes with the right hand:

דברים ו שְׁמַע יִשְׂרָאֵל, יהוה אֱלֹהֵינוּ, יהוה ׀ אֶחָד:

Quietly בָּרוּךְ שֵׁם כְּבוֹד מַלְכוּתוֹ לְעוֹלָם וָעֶד.

דברים ו וְאָהַבְתָּ אֵת יהוה אֱלֹהֶיךָ, בְּכָל־לְבָבְךָ וּבְכָל־נַפְשְׁךָ וּבְכָל־מְאֹדֶךָ: וְהָיוּ הַדְּבָרִים הָאֵלֶּה, אֲשֶׁר אָנֹכִי מְצַוְּךָ הַיּוֹם, עַל־לְבָבֶךָ: וְשִׁנַּנְתָּם לְבָנֶיךָ וְדִבַּרְתָּ בָּם, בְּשִׁבְתְּךָ בְּבֵיתֶךָ וּבְלֶכְתְּךָ בַדֶּרֶךְ, וּבְשָׁכְבְּךָ וּבְקוּמֶךָ: וּקְשַׁרְתָּם לְאוֹת עַל־יָדֶךָ וְהָיוּ לְטֹטָפֹת בֵּין עֵינֶיךָ: וּכְתַבְתָּם עַל־מְזֻזוֹת בֵּיתֶךָ וּבִשְׁעָרֶיךָ:

SHEMA BEFORE SLEEP AT NIGHT

Just as our first words in the morning should be words of prayer, so should our last at night. The night prayers consist of: (1) a prayer for peaceful sleep and a safe awakening, mentioned in the Talmud (*Berakhot* 60b); (2) the first paragraph of the Shema, ensuring these words are with us וּבְשָׁכְבְּךָ "when we lie down"; (3) Psalm 91, a prayer for protection from danger; (4) Psalm 3, chosen because of its reference to night: "I lie down to sleep and I wake again, for the LORD supports me"; (5) הַשְׁכִּיבֵנוּ "Help us lie down" – three paragraphs

וִיהִי May the pleasantness of the LORD our God be upon us. Establish for us the work of our hands, O establish the work of our hands. *Ps. 90*

יֹשֵׁב He who lives in the shelter of the Most High dwells in the shadow of the Almighty. I say of God, my Refuge and Stronghold, my LORD in whom I trust, that He will save you from the fowler's snare and the deadly pestilence. With His pinions He will cover you, and beneath His wings you will find shelter; His faithfulness is an encircling shield. You need not fear terror by night, nor the arrow that flies by day; not the pestilence that stalks in darkness, nor the plague that ravages at noon. A thousand may fall at your side, ten thousand at your right hand, but it will not come near you. You will only look with your eyes and see the punishment of the wicked. Because you [have said:] "The LORD is my Refuge," taking the Most High as your shelter, no harm will befall you, no plague come near your tent, for He will command His angels about you, to guard you in all your ways. They will lift you in their hands, lest your foot stumble on a stone. You will tread on lions and vipers; you will trample on young lions and snakes. [God says:] "Because he loves Me, I will rescue him; I will protect him, because he acknowledges My name. When he calls on Me, I will answer him; I will be with him in distress, I will deliver him and bring him honor. With long life I will satisfy him and show him My salvation. *Ps. 91*

With long life I will satisfy him and show him My salvation.

יהוה LORD, how numerous are my enemies, how many rise against me. Many say of me: "There is no help for him in God," Selah. But You, LORD, are a shield around me. You are my glory; You raise my head high. I cry aloud to the LORD, and He answers me from His holy mountain, Selah. I lie down to sleep and I wake again, for the LORD supports me. I will not fear the myriad forces ranged against me on all sides. Arise, LORD, save me, O my God; strike all my enemies across the cheek; break the teeth of the wicked. From the LORD comes deliverance; may Your blessing rest upon Your people, Selah. *Ps. 3*

הַשְׁכִּיבֵנוּ Help us lie down, O LORD our God, in peace, and rise up, O our King, to life. Spread over us Your canopy of peace. Direct us with Your good counsel, and save us for the sake of Your name. Shield us and remove from us every enemy, plague, sword, famine and sorrow. Remove the adversary from before and behind us. Shelter us in the shadow of Your wings, for You, God, are our Guardian and Deliverer; You, God, are a gracious and compassionate King. Guard our going out and our coming in, for life and peace, from now and for ever.

תהלים צ וִיהִי נֹעַם אֲדֹנָי אֱלֹהֵינוּ עָלֵינוּ וּמַעֲשֵׂה יָדֵינוּ כּוֹנְנָה עָלֵינוּ וּמַעֲשֵׂה יָדֵינוּ כּוֹנְנֵהוּ:

תהלים צא יֹשֵׁב בְּסֵתֶר עֶלְיוֹן, בְּצֵל שַׁדַּי יִתְלוֹנָן: אֹמַר לַיהוה מַחְסִי וּמְצוּדָתִי, אֱלֹהַי אֶבְטַח־בּוֹ: כִּי הוּא יַצִּילְךָ מִפַּח יָקוּשׁ, מִדֶּבֶר הַוּוֹת: בְּאֶבְרָתוֹ יָסֶךְ לָךְ, וְתַחַת־כְּנָפָיו תֶּחְסֶה, צִנָּה וְסֹחֵרָה אֲמִתּוֹ: לֹא־תִירָא מִפַּחַד לָיְלָה, מֵחֵץ יָעוּף יוֹמָם: מִדֶּבֶר בָּאֹפֶל יַהֲלֹךְ, מִקֶּטֶב יָשׁוּד צָהֳרָיִם: יִפֹּל מִצִּדְּךָ אֶלֶף, וּרְבָבָה מִימִינֶךָ, אֵלֶיךָ לֹא יִגָּשׁ: רַק בְּעֵינֶיךָ תַבִּיט, וְשִׁלֻּמַת רְשָׁעִים תִּרְאֶה: כִּי־אַתָּה יהוה מַחְסִי, עֶלְיוֹן שַׂמְתָּ מְעוֹנֶךָ: לֹא־תְאֻנֶּה אֵלֶיךָ רָעָה, וְנֶגַע לֹא־יִקְרַב בְּאָהֳלֶךָ: כִּי מַלְאָכָיו יְצַוֶּה־לָּךְ, לִשְׁמָרְךָ בְּכָל־דְּרָכֶיךָ: עַל־כַּפַּיִם יִשָּׂאוּנְךָ, פֶּן־תִּגֹּף בָּאֶבֶן רַגְלֶךָ: עַל־שַׁחַל וָפֶתֶן תִּדְרֹךְ, תִּרְמֹס כְּפִיר וְתַנִּין: כִּי בִי חָשַׁק וַאֲפַלְּטֵהוּ, אֲשַׂגְּבֵהוּ כִּי־יָדַע שְׁמִי: יִקְרָאֵנִי וְאֶעֱנֵהוּ, עִמּוֹ־אָנֹכִי בְצָרָה, אֲחַלְּצֵהוּ וַאֲכַבְּדֵהוּ: אֹרֶךְ יָמִים אַשְׂבִּיעֵהוּ, וְאַרְאֵהוּ בִּישׁוּעָתִי: אֹרֶךְ יָמִים אַשְׂבִּיעֵהוּ, וְאַרְאֵהוּ בִּישׁוּעָתִי:

תהלים ג יהוה מָה־רַבּוּ צָרָי, רַבִּים קָמִים עָלָי: רַבִּים אֹמְרִים לְנַפְשִׁי, אֵין יְשׁוּעָתָה לּוֹ בֵאלֹהִים, סֶלָה: וְאַתָּה יהוה מָגֵן בַּעֲדִי, כְּבוֹדִי וּמֵרִים רֹאשִׁי: קוֹלִי אֶל־יהוה אֶקְרָא, וַיַּעֲנֵנִי מֵהַר קָדְשׁוֹ, סֶלָה: אֲנִי שָׁכַבְתִּי וָאִישָׁנָה, הֱקִיצוֹתִי כִּי יהוה יִסְמְכֵנִי: לֹא־אִירָא מֵרִבְבוֹת עָם, אֲשֶׁר סָבִיב שָׁתוּ עָלָי: קוּמָה יהוה, הוֹשִׁיעֵנִי אֱלֹהַי, כִּי־הִכִּיתָ אֶת־כָּל־אֹיְבַי לֶחִי, שִׁנֵּי רְשָׁעִים שִׁבַּרְתָּ: לַיהוה הַיְשׁוּעָה, עַל־עַמְּךָ בִרְכָתֶךָ סֶּלָה:

הַשְׁכִּיבֵנוּ, יהוה אֱלֹהֵינוּ, לְשָׁלוֹם. וְהַעֲמִידֵנוּ, מַלְכֵּנוּ, לְחַיִּים. וּפְרֹשׂ עָלֵינוּ סֻכַּת שְׁלוֹמֶךָ, וְתַקְּנֵנוּ בְּעֵצָה טוֹבָה מִלְּפָנֶיךָ, וְהוֹשִׁיעֵנוּ לְמַעַן שְׁמֶךָ. וְהָגֵן בַּעֲדֵנוּ, וְהָסֵר מֵעָלֵינוּ אוֹיֵב, דֶּבֶר וְחֶרֶב וְרָעָב וְיָגוֹן. וְהָסֵר שָׂטָן מִלְּפָנֵינוּ וּמֵאַחֲרֵינוּ, וּבְצֵל כְּנָפֶיךָ תַּסְתִּירֵנוּ, כִּי אֵל שׁוֹמְרֵנוּ וּמַצִּילֵנוּ אָתָּה, כִּי אֵל מֶלֶךְ חַנּוּן וְרַחוּם אָתָּה. וּשְׁמֹר צֵאתֵנוּ וּבוֹאֵנוּ לְחַיִּים וּלְשָׁלוֹם מֵעַתָּה וְעַד עוֹלָם.

---

sleep; and (10) Adon Olam / "Lord of the Universe," said here because of its closing lines with their reference to entrusting our souls and bodies to God's safekeeping at night.

בָּרוּךְ Blessed is the Lord by day, blessed is the Lord by night. Blessed is the Lord when we lie down; blessed is the Lord when we rise. For in Your hand are the souls of the living and the dead, [as it is written:] "In His hand is every living soul, and the breath of all mankind." Into Your hand I entrust my spirit: You redeemed me, Lord, God of truth. Our God in heaven, bring unity to Your name, establish Your kingdom constantly and reign over us for ever and all time. *Job 12* *Ps. 31*

יִרְאוּ May our eyes see, our hearts rejoice, and our souls be glad in Your true salvation, when Zion is told, "Your God reigns." The Lord is King, the Lord was King, and the Lord will be King for ever and all time. For sovereignty is Yours, and to all eternity You will reign in glory, for we have no king but You.

הַמַּלְאָךְ May the angel who rescued me from all harm, bless these boys. May they be called by my name and the names of my fathers Abraham and Isaac, and may they increase greatly on the earth. *Gen. 48*

וַיֹּאמֶר He said, "If you listen carefully to the voice of the Lord your God and do what is right in His eyes, if you pay attention to His commandments and keep all His statutes, I will not bring on you any of the diseases I brought on the Egyptians, for I am the Lord who heals you." The Lord said to the accuser, "The Lord shall rebuke you, accuser. The Lord who has chosen Jerusalem shall rebuke you! Is not this man a burning stick snatched from the fire?" Look! It is Solomon's bed, escorted by sixty warriors, the noblest of Israel, all of them wearing the sword, experienced in battle, each with his sword at his side, prepared for the terror of the nights. *Ex. 15* *Zech. 3* *Song. 3*

Say three times:

יְבָרֶכְךָ May the Lord bless you and protect you. *Num. 6*
May the Lord make His face shine on you and be gracious to you.
May the Lord turn His face toward you and grant you peace.

Say three times:

הִנֵּה See – the Guardian of Israel neither slumbers nor sleeps. *Ps. 121*

Say three times:

לִישׁוּעָתְךָ For Your salvation I hope, Lord. *Gen. 49*
I hope, Lord, for Your salvation.
Lord, for Your salvation I hope.

בָּרוּךְ יהוה בַּיּוֹם, בָּרוּךְ יהוה בַּלָּיְלָה, בָּרוּךְ יהוה בְּשָׁכְבֵנוּ, בָּרוּךְ יהוה
איוב יב בְּקוּמֵנוּ. כִּי בְיָדְךָ נַפְשׁוֹת הַחַיִּים וְהַמֵּתִים. אֲשֶׁר בְּיָדוֹ נֶפֶשׁ כָּל־חָי, וְרוּחַ
תהלים לא כָּל־בְּשַׂר־אִישׁ: בְּיָדְךָ אַפְקִיד רוּחִי, פָּדִיתָה אוֹתִי יהוה אֵל אֱמֶת: אֱלֹהֵינוּ
שֶׁבַּשָּׁמַיִם, יַחֵד שִׁמְךָ וְקַיֵּם מַלְכוּתְךָ תָּמִיד, וּמְלֹךְ עָלֵינוּ לְעוֹלָם וָעֶד.

יִרְאוּ עֵינֵינוּ וְיִשְׂמַח לִבֵּנוּ, וְתָגֵל נַפְשֵׁנוּ בִּישׁוּעָתְךָ בֶּאֱמֶת, בֶּאֱמֹר לְצִיּוֹן
מָלַךְ אֱלֹהָיִךְ. יהוה מֶלֶךְ, יהוה מָלָךְ, יהוה יִמְלֹךְ לְעוֹלָם וָעֶד. כִּי הַמַּלְכוּת
שֶׁלְּךָ הִיא, וּלְעוֹלְמֵי עַד תִּמְלֹךְ בְּכָבוֹד, כִּי אֵין לָנוּ מֶלֶךְ אֶלָּא אָתָּה.

בראשית מח הַמַּלְאָךְ הַגֹּאֵל אֹתִי מִכָּל־רָע יְבָרֵךְ אֶת־הַנְּעָרִים, וְיִקָּרֵא בָהֶם שְׁמִי וְשֵׁם
אֲבֹתַי אַבְרָהָם וְיִצְחָק, וְיִדְגּוּ לָרֹב בְּקֶרֶב הָאָרֶץ:

שמות טו וַיֹּאמֶר אִם־שָׁמוֹעַ תִּשְׁמַע לְקוֹל יהוה אֱלֹהֶיךָ, וְהַיָּשָׁר בְּעֵינָיו תַּעֲשֶׂה,
וְהַאֲזַנְתָּ לְמִצְוֹתָיו וְשָׁמַרְתָּ כָּל־חֻקָּיו, כָּל־הַמַּחֲלָה אֲשֶׁר־שַׂמְתִּי בְמִצְרַיִם
זכריה ג לֹא־אָשִׂים עָלֶיךָ, כִּי אֲנִי יהוה רֹפְאֶךָ: וַיֹּאמֶר יהוה אֶל־הַשָּׂטָן, יִגְעַר יהוה
בְּךָ הַשָּׂטָן, וְיִגְעַר יהוה בְּךָ הַבֹּחֵר בִּירוּשָׁלָםִ, הֲלוֹא זֶה אוּד מֻצָּל מֵאֵשׁ:
שיר השירים ג הִנֵּה מִטָּתוֹ שֶׁלִּשְׁלֹמֹה, שִׁשִּׁים גִּבֹּרִים סָבִיב לָהּ, מִגִּבֹּרֵי יִשְׂרָאֵל: כֻּלָּם
אֲחֻזֵי חֶרֶב, מְלֻמְּדֵי מִלְחָמָה, אִישׁ חַרְבּוֹ עַל־יְרֵכוֹ מִפַּחַד בַּלֵּילוֹת:

Say three times:

במדבר ו יְבָרֶכְךָ יהוה וְיִשְׁמְרֶךָ:
יָאֵר יהוה פָּנָיו אֵלֶיךָ וִיחֻנֶּךָּ:
יִשָּׂא יהוה פָּנָיו אֵלֶיךָ וְיָשֵׂם לְךָ שָׁלוֹם:

Say three times:

תהלים קכא הִנֵּה לֹא־יָנוּם וְלֹא יִישָׁן שׁוֹמֵר יִשְׂרָאֵל:

Say three times:

בראשית מט לִישׁוּעָתְךָ קִוִּיתִי יהוה:
קִוִּיתִי יהוה לִישׁוּעָתְךָ
יהוה לִישׁוּעָתְךָ קִוִּיתִי

Say three times:

בְּשֵׁם In the name of the Lord, God of Israel:
may Michael be at my right hand,
Gabriel, at my left;
in front of me, Uriel,
behind me, Raphael;
and above my head the Presence of God.

שִׁיר הַמַּעֲלוֹת A song of ascents. Ps. 128
Happy are all who fear the Lord, who walk in His ways.
When you eat the fruit of your labor, happy and fortunate are you.
Your wife shall be like a fruitful vine within your house;
your sons like olive saplings around your table.
So shall the man who fears the Lord be blessed.
May the Lord bless you from Zion;
may you see the good of Jerusalem all the days of your life;
and may you live to see your children's children. Peace be on Israel!

Say three times:

רִגְזוּ Tremble, and do not sin. Ps. 4
Search your heart as you lie on your bed, and be silent. Selah.

אֲדוֹן עוֹלָם Lord of the Universe,
who reigned before the birth of any thing;
when by His will all things were made,
then was His name proclaimed King.
And when all things shall cease to be,
He alone will reign in awe.
He was, He is, and He shall be glorious for evermore.
He is One, there is none else, alone, unique, beyond compare;
Without beginning, without end, His might, His rule are everywhere.
He is my God; my Redeemer lives.
He is the Rock on whom I rely –
my banner and my safe retreat, my cup, my portion when I cry.
Into His hand my soul I place, when I awake and when I sleep.
The Lord is with me, I shall not fear;
body and soul from harm will He keep.

Say three times:

בְּשֵׁם יהוה אֱלֹהֵי יִשְׂרָאֵל
מִימִינִי מִיכָאֵל, וּמִשְּׂמֹאלִי גַּבְרִיאֵל
וּמִלְּפָנַי אוּרִיאֵל, וּמֵאֲחוֹרַי רְפָאֵל
וְעַל רֹאשִׁי שְׁכִינַת אֵל.

שִׁיר הַמַּעֲלוֹת, אַשְׁרֵי כָּל־יְרֵא יהוה, הַהֹלֵךְ בִּדְרָכָיו: תהלים קכח
יְגִיעַ כַּפֶּיךָ כִּי תֹאכֵל, אַשְׁרֶיךָ וְטוֹב לָךְ:
אֶשְׁתְּךָ כְּגֶפֶן פֹּרִיָּה בְּיַרְכְּתֵי בֵיתֶךָ
בָּנֶיךָ כִּשְׁתִלֵי זֵיתִים, סָבִיב לְשֻׁלְחָנֶךָ:
הִנֵּה כִי־כֵן יְבֹרַךְ גָּבֶר יְרֵא יהוה:
יְבָרֶכְךָ יהוה מִצִּיּוֹן, וּרְאֵה בְּטוּב יְרוּשָׁלָםִ, כֹּל יְמֵי חַיֶּיךָ:
וּרְאֵה־בָנִים לְבָנֶיךָ, שָׁלוֹם עַל־יִשְׂרָאֵל:

Say three times:

רִגְזוּ וְאַל־תֶּחֱטָאוּ תהלים ד
אִמְרוּ בִלְבַבְכֶם עַל־מִשְׁכַּבְכֶם, וְדֹמּוּ סֶלָה:

אֲדוֹן עוֹלָם אֲשֶׁר מָלַךְ בְּטֶרֶם כָּל־יְצִיר נִבְרָא.
לְעֵת נַעֲשָׂה בְחֶפְצוֹ כֹּל אֲזַי מֶלֶךְ שְׁמוֹ נִקְרָא.
וְאַחֲרֵי כִּכְלוֹת הַכֹּל לְבַדּוֹ יִמְלֹךְ נוֹרָא.
וְהוּא הָיָה וְהוּא הֹוֶה וְהוּא יִהְיֶה בְּתִפְאָרָה.
וְהוּא אֶחָד וְאֵין שֵׁנִי לְהַמְשִׁיל לוֹ לְהַחְבִּירָה.
בְּלִי רֵאשִׁית בְּלִי תַכְלִית וְלוֹ הָעֹז וְהַמִּשְׂרָה.
וְהוּא אֵלִי וְחַי גּוֹאֲלִי וְצוּר חֶבְלִי בְּעֵת צָרָה.
וְהוּא נִסִּי וּמָנוֹס לִי מְנָת כּוֹסִי בְּיוֹם אֶקְרָא.
בְּיָדוֹ אַפְקִיד רוּחִי בְּעֵת אִישַׁן וְאָעִירָה.
וְעִם רוּחִי גְּוִיָּתִי יהוה לִי וְלֹא אִירָא.

שבת

SHABBAT

Erev Shabbat and Yom Tov

EIRUV TEḤUMIN

On Shabbat and Yom Tov it is forbidden to walk more than 2000 cubits (about 3000 feet) beyond the boundary (teḥum) of the town where you live or are staying when the day begins. By placing food sufficient for two meals, before nightfall, at a point within 2000 cubits from the town limits, you confer on that place the status of a dwelling for the next day, and are then permitted to walk 2000 cubits from there.

בָּרוּךְ Blessed are You, Lord our God, King of the Universe,
who has made us holy through His commandments,
and has commanded us about the mitzva of Eiruv.

By this Eiruv may we be permitted to walk from this place, 2000 cubits in any direction.

EIRUV ḤATZEROT

On Shabbat it is forbidden to carry objects from one private domain to another, or from a private domain into space shared by others, such as a communal staircase, corridor or courtyard. An Eiruv Ḥatzerot is created when each of the Jewish households in a court or apartment block, before Shabbat, places a loaf of bread or matza in one of the homes. The entire court or block then becomes a single private domain within which it is permitted to carry.

בָּרוּךְ Blessed are You, Lord our God, King of the Universe,
who has made us holy through His commandments,
and has commanded us about the mitzva of Eiruv.

By this Eiruv may we be permitted to move, carry out and carry in from the houses to the courtyard, or from the courtyard to the houses, or from house to house, for all the houses within the courtyard.

For Eiruv Tavshilin see page 758.

CANDLE LIGHTING

On Erev Shabbat that is not a Yom Tov, cover the eyes with the hands after lighting the candles, and say:

בָּרוּךְ Blessed are You, Lord our God, King of the Universe,
who has made us holy through His commandments,
and has commanded us to light the Sabbath light.

On Erev Yom Tov, say the following blessing and then light the candles from an existing flame. If also Shabbat, cover the eyes with the hands after lighting the candles and say the following blessing, adding the words in parentheses.

בָּרוּךְ Blessed are You, Lord our God, King of the Universe,
who has made us holy through His commandments,
and has commanded us to light (the Sabbath light and) the festival light.

ערב שבת ויום טוב

עירוב תחומין

On שבת *and* יום טוב *it is forbidden to walk more than 2000 cubits (about 3000 feet) beyond the boundary (*תחום*) of the town where you live or are staying when the day begins. By placing food sufficient for two meals, before nightfall, at a point within 2000 cubits from the town limits, you confer on that place the status of a dwelling for the next day, and are then permitted to walk 2000 cubits from there.*

בָּרוּךְ אַתָּה יהוה אֱלֹהֵינוּ מֶלֶךְ הָעוֹלָם
אֲשֶׁר קִדְּשָׁנוּ בְּמִצְוֹתָיו וְצִוָּנוּ עַל מִצְוַת עֵרוּב.

בְּדֵין עֵרוּבָא יְהֵא שְׁרֵא לִי לְמֵיזַל מֵאַתְרָא הָדֵין תְּרֵין אַלְפִין אַמִּין לְכָל רוּחָא.

עירוב חצרות

On שבת *it is forbidden to carry objects from one private domain to another, or from a private domain into space shared by others, such as a communal staircase, corridor or courtyard. An* עירוב חצרות *is created when each of the Jewish households in a court or apartment block, before* שבת*, places a loaf of bread or matza in one of the homes. The entire court or block then becomes a single private domain within which it is permitted to carry.*

בָּרוּךְ אַתָּה יהוה אֱלֹהֵינוּ מֶלֶךְ הָעוֹלָם
אֲשֶׁר קִדְּשָׁנוּ בְּמִצְוֹתָיו וְצִוָּנוּ עַל מִצְוַת עֵרוּב.

בְּדֵין עֵרוּבָא יְהֵא שְׁרֵא לַנָא לְטַלְטוּלֵי וּלְאַפּוֹקֵי וּלְעַיּוֹלֵי מִן הַבָּתִּים לֶחָצֵר וּמִן הֶחָצֵר לַבָּתִּים וּמִבַּיִת לְבַיִת לְכָל הַבָּתִּים שֶׁבֶּחָצֵר.

For עירוב תבשילין *see page 759.*

הדלקת נרות

On ערב שבת *that is not a* יום טוב*, cover the eyes with the hands after lighting the candles, and say:*

בָּרוּךְ אַתָּה יהוה אֱלֹהֵינוּ מֶלֶךְ הָעוֹלָם
אֲשֶׁר קִדְּשָׁנוּ בְּמִצְוֹתָיו וְצִוָּנוּ לְהַדְלִיק נֵר שֶׁל שַׁבָּת.

On ערב יום טוב*, say the following blessing and then light the candles from an existing flame. If also* שבת*, cover the eyes with the hands after lighting the candles and say the following blessing, adding the words in parentheses.*

בָּרוּךְ אַתָּה יהוה אֱלֹהֵינוּ מֶלֶךְ הָעוֹלָם
אֲשֶׁר קִדְּשָׁנוּ בְּמִצְוֹתָיו וְצִוָּנוּ לְהַדְלִיק נֵר שֶׁל (שַׁבָּת וְשֶׁל) יוֹם טוֹב.

The blessing "Sheheḥeyanu" ("Who has given life") is said on Yom Tov evenings, except on the last evenings of Pesaḥ. (In Israel, it is not said on the last evening of Pesaḥ.)

בָּרוּךְ Blessed are You, Lord our God, King of the Universe, who has given us life, sustained us, and brought us to this time.

On Erev Yom Kippur, cover the eyes with the hands after lighting the candles, and say (on Shabbat add the words in parentheses):

בָּרוּךְ Blessed are You, Lord our God, King of the Universe, who has made us holy through His commandments, and has commanded us to light (the Sabbath light and) the light of the Day of Atonement.

בָּרוּךְ Blessed are You, Lord our God, King of the Universe, who has given us life, sustained us, and brought us to this time.

Prayer after candlelighting (add the words in parentheses as appropriate):

יְהִי May it be Your will, Lord my God and God of my forebears, that You give me grace – me (and my husband/and my father/and my mother/and my sons and my daughters) and all those close to me, and give us and all Israel good and long lives. And remember us with a memory that brings goodness and blessing; come to us with compassion and bless us with great blessings. Build our homes until they are complete, and allow Your Presence to live among us. And may I merit to raise children and grandchildren, each one wise and understanding, loving the Lord and in awe of God, people of truth, holy children, who will cling on to the Lord and light up the world with Torah and with good actions, and with all the kinds of work that serve the Creator. Please, hear my pleading at this time, by the merit of Sarah and Rebecca, Rachel and Leah our mothers, and light our candle that it should never go out, and light up Your face, so that we shall be saved, Amen.

The ancient custom is for women to perform this commandment since they are the primary guardians of the home. Our custom is to light two candles, representing the two dimensions of Shabbat: *shamor,* "guarding," observing the prohibitions of Shabbat; and *zakhor,* "remembering," keeping its positive commandments.

Normally we make a blessing over a commandment *before* performing it. In the case of Shabbat lights, however, the blessing is made afterward, so that the lighting precedes mental acceptance of the day and its prohibitions. The blessing is made while covering one's eyes, so that the blessing follows the act but precedes its benefit.

The blessing שֶׁהֶחֱיָנוּ *is said on* יום טוב *evenings, except on the last evenings of* פסח.
(*In* ארץ ישראל*, it is not said on the last evening of* פסח.)

בָּרוּךְ אַתָּה יהוה אֱלֹהֵינוּ מֶלֶךְ הָעוֹלָם
שֶׁהֶחֱיָנוּ וְקִיְּמָנוּ, וְהִגִּיעָנוּ לַזְּמַן הַזֶּה.

On ערב יום כיפור*, cover the eyes with the hands after lighting the candles, and say (on* שבת *add the words in parentheses):*

בָּרוּךְ אַתָּה יהוה אֱלֹהֵינוּ מֶלֶךְ הָעוֹלָם
אֲשֶׁר קִדְּשָׁנוּ בְּמִצְוֹתָיו וְצִוָּנוּ לְהַדְלִיק נֵר שֶׁל (שַׁבָּת וְשֶׁל) יוֹם הַכִּפּוּרִים.
בָּרוּךְ אַתָּה יהוה אֱלֹהֵינוּ מֶלֶךְ הָעוֹלָם
שֶׁהֶחֱיָנוּ וְקִיְּמָנוּ, וְהִגִּיעָנוּ לַזְּמַן הַזֶּה.

Prayer after candlelighting (add the words in parentheses as appropriate):

יְהִי רָצוֹן מִלְּפָנֶיךָ יהוה אֱלֹהַי וֵאלֹהֵי אֲבוֹתַי, שֶׁתְּחוֹנֵן אוֹתִי (וְאֶת אִישִׁי/ וְאֶת אָבִי/ וְאֶת אִמִּי/ וְאֶת בָּנַי וְאֶת בְּנוֹתַי) וְאֶת כָּל קְרוֹבַי, וְתִתֶּן לָנוּ וּלְכָל יִשְׂרָאֵל חַיִּים טוֹבִים וַאֲרֻכִּים, וְתִזְכְּרֵנוּ בְּזִכְרוֹן טוֹבָה וּבְרָכָה, וְתִפְקְדֵנוּ בִּפְקֻדַּת יְשׁוּעָה וְרַחֲמִים, וּתְבָרְכֵנוּ בְּרָכוֹת גְּדוֹלוֹת, וְתַשְׁלִים בָּתֵּינוּ וְתַשְׁכֵּן שְׁכִינָתְךָ בֵּינֵינוּ. וְזַכֵּנִי לְגַדֵּל בָּנִים וּבְנֵי בָנִים חֲכָמִים וּנְבוֹנִים, אוֹהֲבֵי יהוה יִרְאֵי אֱלֹהִים, אַנְשֵׁי אֱמֶת זֶרַע קֹדֶשׁ, בַּיהוה דְּבֵקִים וּמְאִירִים אֶת הָעוֹלָם בַּתּוֹרָה וּבְמַעֲשִׂים טוֹבִים וּבְכָל מְלֶאכֶת עֲבוֹדַת הַבּוֹרֵא. אָנָּא שְׁמַע אֶת תְּחִנָּתִי בָּעֵת הַזֹּאת בִּזְכוּת שָׂרָה וְרִבְקָה וְרָחֵל וְלֵאָה אִמּוֹתֵינוּ, וְהָאֵר נֵרֵנוּ שֶׁלֹּא יִכְבֶּה לְעוֹלָם וָעֶד, וְהָאֵר פָּנֶיךָ וְנִוָּשֵׁעָה. אָמֵן.

CANDLE LIGHTING

Lighting candles is a positive rabbinic commandment, symbolizing *shalom bayit*, domestic peace. By creating peace in the home, we are helping to make peace in the world.

The Shabbat candles also symbolize the light of the Divine Presence, which illuminates relationships within the home. Rabbi Akiva noted that the Hebrew words for man (*ish*) and woman (*isha*) both contain the letters of *esh*, "fire." Each contains one extra letter – *yod* in the case of man, *heh* in the case of woman, and these two letters together spell one of the names of God. He concluded: "When husband and wife are worthy, the Divine Presence dwells between them" (*Sota* 17a).

The service starts with Minḥa for Weekdays on page 206.
Most congregations sing "Beloved of the soul" before the Kabbalat Shabbat service.
On Yom Tov or Motza'ei Yom Tov falling on Shabbat, or on Shabbat Ḥol HaMo'ed, the service begins with Psalm 92 on page 324.
On Yom Tov falling on a weekday, the service begins with "Bless" on page 334.

יְדִיד Beloved of the soul, Father of compassion,
draw Your servant close to Your will.
Like a deer will Your servant run
and fall prostrate before Your beauty.
To him Your love is sweeter
than honey from the comb, than any taste.

הָדוּר Glorious, beautiful, radiance of the world,
my soul is sick with love for You.
Please, God, heal her now
by showing her Your tender radiance.
Then she will recover her strength and be healed,
Be Your servant for eternity.

וָתִיק Ancient of Days, let Your mercy be aroused;
please have pity on Your beloved child.
How long have I yearned
to see the glory of Your strength.
Please, my God, my heart's desire –
hasten; do not hide Yourself.

הִגָּלֵה Reveal Yourself, beloved, and spread over me
the tabernacle of Your peace.
Let the earth shine with Your glory,
let us be overjoyed and rejoice in You.
Hurry, beloved, for the appointed time has come,
and be gracious to me as in the times of old.

The service starts with מנחה לחול *on page 207.*
Most congregations sing יְדִיד נֶפֶשׁ *at this point before* קבלת שבת*.*
On יום טוב *or* מוצאי יום טוב *falling on* שבת*, or on* שבת חול המועד*,*
the service begins with מִזְמוֹר שִׁיר *on page 325.*
On יום טוב *falling on a weekday, the service begins with* בָּרְכוּ *on page 335.*

יְדִיד נֶפֶשׁ, אָב הָרַחֲמָן, מְשֹׁךְ עַבְדְּךָ אֶל רְצוֹנָךְ.
יָרוּץ עַבְדְּךָ כְּמוֹ אַיָּל, יִשְׁתַּחֲוֶה מוּל הֲדָרָךְ.
כִּי יֶעֱרַב לוֹ יְדִידוּתָךְ, מִנֹּפֶת צוּף וְכָל טָֽעַם.

הָדוּר, נָאֶה, זִיו הָעוֹלָם, נַפְשִׁי חוֹלַת אַהֲבָתָךְ.
אָנָּא, אֵל נָא, רְפָא נָא לָהּ, בְּהַרְאוֹת לָהּ נֹעַם זִיוָךְ.
אָז תִּתְחַזֵּק וְתִתְרַפֵּא, וְהָיְתָה לָךְ שִׁפְחַת עוֹלָם.

וָתִיק, יֶהֱמוּ רַחֲמֶיךָ, וְחוּסָה נָא עַל בֵּן אוֹהֲבָךְ.
כִּי זֶה כַּמֶּה נִכְסֹף נִכְסַף לִרְאוֹת בְּתִפְאֶרֶת עֻזָּךְ.
אָנָּא, אֵלִי, מַחְמַד לִבִּי, חוּשָׁה נָּא, וְאַל תִּתְעַלָּם.

הִגָּלֵה נָא וּפְרֹשׂ, חָבִיב, עָלַי אֶת סֻכַּת שְׁלוֹמָךְ.
תָּאִיר אֶֽרֶץ מִכְּבוֹדָךְ, נָגִֽילָה וְנִשְׂמְחָה בָךְ.
מַהֵר, אָהוּב, כִּי בָא מוֹעֵד, וְחָנֵּנִי כִּימֵי עוֹלָם.

יְדִיד נֶפֶשׁ *Beloved of the soul:* A song of passionate intensity, composed by the Safed kabbalist Rabbi Elazar Azikri (1533–1600). In language reminiscent of the Song of Songs, it speaks of Israel's yearning for God: Azikri himself called it "a prayer for union and the desire of love." The text here, differing in a number of details from that found in some other siddurim, is based on the original manuscript in the author's own hand. The initial letters of the four verses spell God's holiest name. **וְאַל תִּתְעַלָּם** *Do not hide Yourself:* refers to Israel's exile. The poet calls for God to reveal Himself at *the appointed time* of redemption, **כִּי בָא מוֹעֵד**.

Kabbalat Shabbat

Mourners during the week of Shiva leave the synagogue at this point, returning after "Come, my Beloved" on page 322.

לְכוּ נְרַנְּנָה Come, let us sing for joy to the LORD, let us shout aloud to the Rock of our salvation. Let us greet Him with thanksgiving, shout aloud to Him with songs of praise. For the LORD is the great God, the King great above all powers. In His hand are the depths of the earth, and the mountain peaks are His. The sea is His, for He made it; the dry land too, for His hands formed it. Come, let us bow in worship and bend the knee before the LORD our Maker. For He is our God, and we are the people of His pasture, the flock He tends – today, if you would heed His voice. Do not harden your hearts as you did at Meribah, as you did that day at Massah in the desert, *Ps. 95*

---

character of *Kabbalat Shabbat*, the custom in some synagogues is for the Leader to recite it from the *bima* rather than the *amud* (lectern) at the front of the synagogue.

The six psalms said before *Lekha Dodi* represent the six days of the week. The first five appear sequentially in the book of Psalms (95–99). They speak of the song creation sings to its Creator. These are followed by Psalm 29, understood by some as a description of the Giving of the Torah at Mount Sinai. *Lekha Dodi* looks forward to future redemption, and Psalms 92 and 93 envision the end of days. Thus the entire sequence is structured around the movement from creation to revelation to redemption.

לְכוּ נְרַנְּנָה *Psalm 95. Come, let us sing for joy*: The Psalmist calls on the people to serve God with joy, redeeming the sin of their ancestors who, though they had been rescued by God from slavery, were ungrateful and argumentative. *Massah and Meribah* (literally, "testing and quarreling"), were the names given to the place where, after crossing the Reed Sea, the Israelites complained of their lack of water (Ex. 17:1–7). אַרְבָּעִים שָׁנָה *For forty years* (*next page*): A reference to the episode of the spies (Num. chapters 13–14), when the people, demoralized by their report, rebelled. Their fate was to spend forty years in the desert. The Psalmist urges the people to do the opposite: to sing to God with joy.

קבלת שבת

Mourners during the week of שבעה *leave the* בית כנסת *at this point,*
returning after לְכָה דוֹדִי *on page 323.*

תהלים צה לְכוּ נְרַנְּנָה לַיהוה, נָרִיעָה לְצוּר יִשְׁעֵנוּ: נְקַדְּמָה פָנָיו בְּתוֹדָה, בִּזְמִרוֹת נָרִיעַ לוֹ: כִּי אֵל גָּדוֹל יהוה, וּמֶלֶךְ גָּדוֹל עַל־כָּל־אֱלֹהִים: אֲשֶׁר בְּיָדוֹ מֶחְקְרֵי־אָרֶץ, וְתוֹעֲפוֹת הָרִים לוֹ: אֲשֶׁר־לוֹ הַיָּם וְהוּא עָשָׂהוּ, וְיַבֶּשֶׁת יָדָיו יָצָרוּ: בֹּאוּ נִשְׁתַּחֲוֶה וְנִכְרָעָה, נִבְרְכָה לִפְנֵי־יהוה עֹשֵׂנוּ: כִּי הוּא אֱלֹהֵינוּ, וַאֲנַחְנוּ עַם מַרְעִיתוֹ וְצֹאן יָדוֹ, הַיּוֹם אִם־בְּקֹלוֹ תִשְׁמָעוּ: אַל־תַּקְשׁוּ לְבַבְכֶם כִּמְרִיבָה, כְּיוֹם

KABBALAT SHABBAT / WELCOMING SHABBAT

Already in Talmudic times Shabbat was seen as a bride, and the day itself as a wedding. "Rabbi Ḥanina robed himself and stood on the eve of Shabbat at sunset and said, 'Come, let us go and welcome Shabbat the queen.' Rabbi Yannai donned his robes and said, 'Come O bride, come O bride'" (*Shabbat* 119a).

In the late sixteenth century, this idea was developed with fresh intensity by a remarkable group of Jewish mystics in Safed. They included Rabbi Moses Cordovero who developed the custom of saying special psalms to greet the incoming Shabbat; his brother-in-law Rabbi Shlomo Alkabetz, composer of the song *Lekha Dodi* ("Come, my Beloved"); Rabbi Elazar Azikri, author of *Yedid Nefesh* ("Beloved of the Soul"); and Rabbi Isaac Luria (known as the "Ari" or "Arizal"), greatest of the Safed mystics, whose thought brought new depth to our understanding of prayer and observance of Shabbat as acts that help heal the spiritual fractures of the world.

By the twelfth century, the custom existed to say Psalm 92 as a song of welcome to Shabbat. The Safed kabbalists did more. Dressed in white, they would go out into the fields as the sun set, singing psalms and songs to the Shabbat bride. That is the origin of the custom (first mentioned by Rabbi Moshe ben Yehuda Makhir, *Seder HaYom*) to recite the six extra psalms (95–99, 29) prior to *Lekha Dodi*. A further reminder of the original custom is our practice of turning round to face west at the last verse of the song, facing, as they did, the setting sun, to welcome the incoming bride. To emphasize the non-statutory

when your ancestors tested and tried Me though they had seen My deeds. ▸ For forty years I strove with that generation. I said, "They are a people whose hearts go astray, who have not understood My ways." So I swore in My anger, "They shall not enter My place of rest."

שִׁירוּ Sing to the LORD a new song; sing to the LORD all the earth. *Ps. 96*
Sing to the LORD, bless His name; proclaim his deliverance day after day. Declare His glory among the nations, His marvels among all peoples. For great is the LORD and greatly to be praised; He is awesome beyond all heavenly powers. For all the gods of the peoples are mere idols: it was the LORD who made the heavens. Before Him are majesty and splendor; there are strength and beauty in His holy place. Render to the LORD, O families of the peoples; render to the LORD glory and might. Render to the LORD the glory due to His name; bring an offering and come into His courts. Bow down to the LORD in the splendor of holiness. Tremble before Him, all the earth. Say among the nations, "The LORD is King." The world stands firm, it will not be shaken. He will judge the peoples with equity. ▸ Let the heavens rejoice and the earth be glad. Let the sea roar, and all that is in it; let the fields be jubilant, and all they contain. Then the trees of the forest will sing for joy before the LORD, for He is coming to judge the earth. He will judge the world with justice, and the peoples with His faithfulness.

יהוה מָלָךְ The LORD reigns, let the earth be glad. Let the many *Ps. 97*
islands rejoice. Clouds and thick darkness surround Him; righteousness and justice are the foundation of His throne. Fire goes ahead of Him, consuming His enemies on every side. His lightning

---

יהוה מָלָךְ *Psalm 97. The LORD reigns, let the earth be glad:* God, Maker of the Universe, is the ultimate Sovereign. Therefore, all earthly rule and exercise of power is subject to His overarching authority: "The LORD reigns." History is not destined to be an endless story of the victory of might over right, the powerful over the powerless. At the heart of reality is a force that makes for justice, giving strength to the weak, and courage to the oppressed. "Light is sown for the righteous, and joy for the upright in heart."

מַסָּה בַּמִּדְבָּר: אֲשֶׁר נִסּוּנִי אֲבוֹתֵיכֶם, בְּחָנוּנִי גַּם רָאוּ פָעֳלִי:
› אַרְבָּעִים שָׁנָה אָקוּט בְּדוֹר, וָאֹמַר עַם תֹּעֵי לֵבָב הֵם, וְהֵם לֹא־
יָדְעוּ דְרָכָי: אֲשֶׁר־נִשְׁבַּעְתִּי בְאַפִּי, אִם־יְבֹאוּן אֶל מְנוּחָתִי:

תהלים צו שִׁירוּ לַיהוה שִׁיר חָדָשׁ, שִׁירוּ לַיהוה כָּל־הָאָרֶץ: שִׁירוּ לַיהוה,
בָּרְכוּ שְׁמוֹ, בַּשְּׂרוּ מִיּוֹם־לְיוֹם יְשׁוּעָתוֹ: סַפְּרוּ בַגּוֹיִם כְּבוֹדוֹ,
בְּכָל־הָעַמִּים נִפְלְאוֹתָיו: כִּי גָדוֹל יהוה וּמְהֻלָּל מְאֹד, נוֹרָא הוּא
עַל־כָּל־אֱלֹהִים: כִּי כָּל־אֱלֹהֵי הָעַמִּים אֱלִילִים, וַיהוה שָׁמַיִם
עָשָׂה: הוֹד־וְהָדָר לְפָנָיו, עֹז וְתִפְאֶרֶת בְּמִקְדָּשׁוֹ: הָבוּ לַיהוה
מִשְׁפְּחוֹת עַמִּים, הָבוּ לַיהוה כָּבוֹד וָעֹז: הָבוּ לַיהוה כְּבוֹד שְׁמוֹ,
שְׂאוּ־מִנְחָה וּבֹאוּ לְחַצְרוֹתָיו: הִשְׁתַּחֲווּ לַיהוה בְּהַדְרַת־קֹדֶשׁ,
חִילוּ מִפָּנָיו כָּל־הָאָרֶץ: אִמְרוּ בַגּוֹיִם יהוה מָלָךְ, אַף־תִּכּוֹן תֵּבֵל
בַּל־תִּמּוֹט, יָדִין עַמִּים בְּמֵישָׁרִים: › יִשְׂמְחוּ הַשָּׁמַיִם וְתָגֵל הָאָרֶץ,
יִרְעַם הַיָּם וּמְלֹאוֹ: יַעֲלֹז שָׂדַי וְכָל־אֲשֶׁר־בּוֹ, אָז יְרַנְּנוּ כָּל־עֲצֵי־
יָעַר: לִפְנֵי יהוה כִּי בָא, כִּי בָא לִשְׁפֹּט הָאָרֶץ, יִשְׁפֹּט־תֵּבֵל בְּצֶדֶק,
וְעַמִּים בֶּאֱמוּנָתוֹ:

תהלים צו יהוה מָלָךְ תָּגֵל הָאָרֶץ, יִשְׂמְחוּ אִיִּים רַבִּים: עָנָן וַעֲרָפֶל סְבִיבָיו,
צֶדֶק וּמִשְׁפָּט מְכוֹן כִּסְאוֹ: אֵשׁ לְפָנָיו תֵּלֵךְ, וּתְלַהֵט סָבִיב צָרָיו:

שִׁירוּ לַיהוה *Psalm 96. Sing to the Lord a new song*: One of the most difficult ideas for modern minds to grasp is that the universe might sing for joy at the coming of judgment and justice. Yet we believe not only in one God, Creator of heaven and earth, but also in the inseparable connection between *cosmos* and *ethos*, the world-that-is and the world-that-ought-to-be. God not only created the universe but also "saw that it was good." From the outset, the universe had an objective moral structure. As the natural world is governed by scientific law, so the human world is governed by moral law. Hence creation rejoices that *He is coming to judge the earth* כִּי בָא לִשְׁפֹּט הָאָרֶץ, that the world is governed by the rule of right rather than the rule of force.

lights up the world; the earth sees and trembles. Mountains melt like wax before the LORD, before the LORD of all the earth. The heavens proclaim His righteousness, and all the peoples see His glory. All who worship images and boast in idols are put to shame. Bow down to Him, all you heavenly powers. Zion hears and rejoices, and the towns of Judah are glad because of your judgments, LORD. For You, LORD, are supreme over all the earth; You are exalted far above all heavenly powers. ▸ Let those who love the LORD hate evil, for He protects the lives of his devoted ones, delivering them from the hand of the wicked. Light is sown for the righteous, and joy for the upright in heart. Rejoice in the LORD, you who are righteous, and give thanks to His holy name.

מִזְמוֹר A Psalm. Sing a new song to the LORD, for He has done wondrous things; He has saved by His right hand and His holy arm. The LORD has made His salvation known; He has displayed His righteousness in the sight of the nations. He remembered His loving-kindness and faithfulness to the house of Israel; all the ends of the earth have seen the victory of our LORD. Shout for joy to the LORD, all the earth; burst into song, sing with joy, play music. Play music to the LORD on the harp – on the harp with the sound of singing. With trumpets and the sound of the shofar, shout for joy before the LORD, the King. ▸ Let the sea and all that is in it thunder, the world and all who live in it. Let the rivers clap their hands, the mountains sing together for joy – before the LORD, for He is coming to judge the earth. He will judge the world with justice, and the peoples with equity. *Ps. 98*

יהוה מָלָךְ The LORD reigns, let the peoples tremble. He sits enthroned on the Cherubim, let the earth quake. Great is the LORD in *Ps. 99*

יהוה מָלָךְ *Psalm 99. The LORD reigns, let the peoples tremble:* Having declared God's sovereignty, the Psalmist now speaks of His holiness. The three sections of the psalm each end on this theme. The first two – about God's enthronement and His justice, end with the declaration, "He is holy." The

הֵאִירוּ בְרָקָיו תֵּבֵל, רָאֲתָה וַתָּחֵל הָאָרֶץ: הָרִים כַּדּוֹנַג נָמַסּוּ
מִלִּפְנֵי יהוה, מִלִּפְנֵי אֲדוֹן כָּל־הָאָרֶץ: הִגִּידוּ הַשָּׁמַיִם צִדְקוֹ, וְרָאוּ
כָל־הָעַמִּים כְּבוֹדוֹ: יֵבֹשׁוּ כָּל־עֹבְדֵי פֶסֶל הַמִּתְהַלְלִים בָּאֱלִילִים,
הִשְׁתַּחֲווּ־לוֹ כָּל־אֱלֹהִים: שָׁמְעָה וַתִּשְׂמַח צִיּוֹן, וַתָּגֵלְנָה בְּנוֹת
יְהוּדָה, לְמַעַן מִשְׁפָּטֶיךָ יהוה: כִּי־אַתָּה יהוה עֶלְיוֹן עַל־כָּל־
הָאָרֶץ, מְאֹד נַעֲלֵיתָ עַל־כָּל־אֱלֹהִים: › אֹהֲבֵי יהוה שִׂנְאוּ רָע,
שֹׁמֵר נַפְשׁוֹת חֲסִידָיו, מִיַּד רְשָׁעִים יַצִּילֵם: אוֹר זָרֻעַ לַצַּדִּיק,
וּלְיִשְׁרֵי־לֵב שִׂמְחָה: שִׂמְחוּ צַדִּיקִים בַּיהוה, וְהוֹדוּ לְזֵכֶר קָדְשׁוֹ:

מִזְמוֹר, שִׁירוּ לַיהוה שִׁיר חָדָשׁ כִּי־נִפְלָאוֹת עָשָׂה, הוֹשִׁיעָה־לּוֹ תהלים צח
יְמִינוֹ וּזְרוֹעַ קָדְשׁוֹ: הוֹדִיעַ יהוה יְשׁוּעָתוֹ, לְעֵינֵי הַגּוֹיִם גִּלָּה
צִדְקָתוֹ: זָכַר חַסְדּוֹ וֶאֱמוּנָתוֹ לְבֵית יִשְׂרָאֵל, רָאוּ כָל־אַפְסֵי־אָרֶץ
אֵת יְשׁוּעַת אֱלֹהֵינוּ: הָרִיעוּ לַיהוה כָּל־הָאָרֶץ, פִּצְחוּ וְרַנְּנוּ וְזַמֵּרוּ:
זַמְּרוּ לַיהוה בְּכִנּוֹר, בְּכִנּוֹר וְקוֹל זִמְרָה: בַּחֲצֹצְרוֹת וְקוֹל שׁוֹפָר,
הָרִיעוּ לִפְנֵי הַמֶּלֶךְ יהוה: › יִרְעַם הַיָּם וּמְלֹאוֹ, תֵּבֵל וְיֹשְׁבֵי בָהּ:
נְהָרוֹת יִמְחֲאוּ־כָף, יַחַד הָרִים יְרַנֵּנוּ: לִפְנֵי יהוה כִּי בָא לִשְׁפֹּט
הָאָרֶץ, יִשְׁפֹּט־תֵּבֵל בְּצֶדֶק, וְעַמִּים בְּמֵישָׁרִים:

יהוה מָלָךְ יִרְגְּזוּ עַמִּים, יֹשֵׁב כְּרוּבִים תָּנוּט הָאָרֶץ: יהוה בְּצִיּוֹן תהלים צט
גָּדוֹל, וְרָם הוּא עַל־כָּל־הָעַמִּים: יוֹדוּ שִׁמְךָ גָּדוֹל וְנוֹרָא קָדוֹשׁ

מִזְמוֹר *Psalm 98. A Psalm. Sing a new song to the Lord:* In this celebratory song, the Psalmist describes redemption in the vivid image of a royal arrival. The King who is also Judge and Deliverer is about to come. The trumpets sound a clarion to announce His entrance. A roar is heard, not just from the assembled people but from the universe itself: the sea, the earth, rivers and mountains. All herald His coming with joy, for they know that when He sits in judgment He will resolve all disputes with equity.

Zion, He is exalted over all the peoples. Let them praise Your name, O great and awesome One: He is holy! The King in His might loves justice. You have established equity. The justice and righteousness in Jacob is Your doing. Exalt the LORD our God, and bow at His footstool: He is holy! Moses and Aaron were among His priests; Samuel was among those who called on His name. They called on the LORD and He answered them. ▸ He spoke to them in a pillar of cloud; they observed His testimonies and the statute He gave them. LORD our God, You answered them. You were for them a forgiving God, though You punished their misdeeds. Exalt the LORD our God and bow at His holy mountain, for the LORD our God is holy.

The following psalm is said standing:

מִזְמוֹר לְדָוִד A psalm of David. Render to the LORD, you angelic powers, render to the LORD glory and might. Render to the LORD the glory due to His name. Bow to the LORD in the beauty of holiness. The LORD's voice echoes over the waters; the God of glory thunders; the LORD is over the mighty waters. The LORD's voice in power, the LORD's voice in beauty, the LORD's voice breaks cedars, the LORD shatters the cedars of Lebanon. He makes Lebanon skip like a calf, Sirion like a young wild ox. The LORD's voice cleaves flames of fire. The LORD's voice makes the desert quake, the LORD shakes the desert of Kadesh. ▸ The LORD's voice makes hinds calve and strips the forests bare, and in His temple all say: "Glory!" The LORD sat enthroned at the Flood, the LORD sits enthroned as King for ever. The LORD will give strength to His people; the LORD will bless His people with peace. *Ps. 29*

Torah. The Talmud Yerushalmi (*Berakhot* 4:3) relates its seven mentions of the word *kol*, "voice," to the seven blessings of the Shabbat Amida. Its mood is significant. It describes an earth-shattering storm which subsides, so that the last word of the psalm is "peace." So will the storm of human history one day be transfigured into peace. Redemption stands to history as does Shabbat to the six days of creation.

הוּא: וְעֹז מֶלֶךְ מִשְׁפָּט אָהֵב, אַתָּה כּוֹנַנְתָּ מֵישָׁרִים, מִשְׁפָּט
וּצְדָקָה בְּיַעֲקֹב אַתָּה עָשִׂיתָ: רוֹמְמוּ יהוה אֱלֹהֵינוּ, וְהִשְׁתַּחֲווּ
לַהֲדֹם רַגְלָיו, קָדוֹשׁ הוּא: מֹשֶׁה וְאַהֲרֹן בְּכֹהֲנָיו, וּשְׁמוּאֵל בְּקֹרְאֵי
שְׁמוֹ, קֹרְאִים אֶל־יהוה וְהוּא יַעֲנֵם: ‹ בְּעַמּוּד עָנָן יְדַבֵּר אֲלֵיהֶם,
שָׁמְרוּ עֵדֹתָיו וְחֹק נָתַן־לָמוֹ: יהוה אֱלֹהֵינוּ אַתָּה עֲנִיתָם, אֵל
נֹשֵׂא הָיִיתָ לָהֶם, וְנֹקֵם עַל־עֲלִילוֹתָם: רוֹמְמוּ יהוה אֱלֹהֵינוּ,
וְהִשְׁתַּחֲווּ לְהַר קָדְשׁוֹ, כִּי־קָדוֹשׁ יהוה אֱלֹהֵינוּ:

The following psalm is said standing:

תהלים כט מִזְמוֹר לְדָוִד, הָבוּ לַיהוה בְּנֵי אֵלִים, הָבוּ לַיהוה כָּבוֹד וָעֹז: הָבוּ
לַיהוה כְּבוֹד שְׁמוֹ, הִשְׁתַּחֲווּ לַיהוה בְּהַדְרַת־קֹדֶשׁ: קוֹל יהוה
עַל הַמָּיִם, אֵל־הַכָּבוֹד הִרְעִים, יהוה עַל־מַיִם רַבִּים: קוֹל־יהוה
בַּכֹּחַ, קוֹל יהוה בֶּהָדָר: קוֹל יהוה שֹׁבֵר אֲרָזִים, וַיְשַׁבֵּר יהוה אֶת־
אַרְזֵי הַלְּבָנוֹן: וַיַּרְקִידֵם כְּמוֹ־עֵגֶל, לְבָנוֹן וְשִׂרְיֹן כְּמוֹ בֶן־רְאֵמִים:
קוֹל־יהוה חֹצֵב לַהֲבוֹת אֵשׁ: קוֹל יהוה יָחִיל מִדְבָּר, יָחִיל יהוה
מִדְבַּר קָדֵשׁ: ‹ קוֹל יהוה יְחוֹלֵל אַיָּלוֹת וַיֶּחֱשֹׂף יְעָרוֹת, וּבְהֵיכָלוֹ,
כֻּלּוֹ אֹמֵר כָּבוֹד: יהוה לַמַּבּוּל יָשָׁב, וַיֵּשֶׁב יהוה מֶלֶךְ לְעוֹלָם:
יהוה עֹז לְעַמּוֹ יִתֵּן, יהוה יְבָרֵךְ אֶת־עַמּוֹ בַשָּׁלוֹם:

---

third ends with a double use of the word: "Bow at His *holy* mountain, for the Lord our God is *holy*." *Moses, Aaron, Samuel.* Respectively they represent the three "crowns" of leadership: prophecy, priesthood and kingship. Moses was the greatest of the prophets, Aaron the first High Priest, and Samuel the man who anointed Israel's first kings, Saul and David.

מזמור לדוד *Psalm 29. A psalm of David. Render to the Lord:* This psalm, powerful in both imagery and language, breaks the sequence of the previous psalms (95–99). Many interpret it as a poetic description of the giving of the

The following is said in some congregations:

Please, by the power of Your great right hand,
set the captive nation free.
Accept Your people's prayer. Strengthen us, purify us,
You who are revered.
Please, Mighty One, guard like the pupil of the eye
those who seek Your unity.
Bless them, cleanse them, have compassion on them,
grant them Your righteousness always.
Mighty One, Holy One, in Your great goodness
guide Your congregation.
Only One, Exalted One, turn to Your people,
who proclaim Your holiness.
Accept our plea and heed our cry,
You who know all secret thoughts.
Blessed be the name of His glorious kingdom for
ever and all time.

לְכָה דוֹדִי Come, my Beloved, to greet the bride;
let us welcome the Sabbath.

Come, my Beloved, to greet the bride;
let us welcome the Sabbath.

שָׁמוֹר "Observe" and "Remember" in one act of speech,
the One and Only God made us hear.
The Lord is One and His name is One,
for renown, for splendor, and for praise.

Come, my Beloved, to greet the bride;
let us welcome the Sabbath.

שָׁמוֹר וְזָכוֹר בְּדִבּוּר אֶחָד *"Observe" and "Remember" in one act of speech:* This refers to two versions of the Ten Commandments. In the first (Ex. 20:8), Israel was commanded to "Remember" the Sabbath; in the second (Deut. 5:12), to "observe" it. According to the sages, both were uttered at the same time. "Observe" refers to the negative commandment of Shabbat, the prohibition against work, while "Remember" refers to the positive commandment, to sanctify it in word and deed. The idea that both were spoken simultaneously teaches that the negative and positive aspects of holy time are inseparable. The prohibition against work creates space for rest and joy.

The following is said in some congregations:

אָנָּא, בְּכֹחַ גְּדֻלַּת יְמִינְךָ, תַּתִּיר צְרוּרָה.
קַבֵּל רִנַּת עַמְּךָ, שַׂגְּבֵנוּ, טַהֲרֵנוּ, נוֹרָא.
נָא גִבּוֹר, דּוֹרְשֵׁי יִחוּדְךָ כְּבָבַת שָׁמְרֵם.
בָּרְכֵם, טַהֲרֵם, רַחֲמֵם, צִדְקָתְךָ תָּמִיד גָּמְלֵם.
חֲסִין קָדוֹשׁ, בְּרֹב טוּבְךָ נַהֵל עֲדָתֶךָ.
יָחִיד גֵּאֶה, לְעַמְּךָ פְּנֵה, זוֹכְרֵי קְדֻשָּׁתֶךָ.
שַׁוְעָתֵנוּ קַבֵּל וּשְׁמַע צַעֲקָתֵנוּ, יוֹדֵעַ תַּעֲלוּמוֹת.
בָּרוּךְ שֵׁם כְּבוֹד מַלְכוּתוֹ לְעוֹלָם וָעֶד.

לְכָה דוֹדִי לִקְרַאת כַּלָּה, פְּנֵי שַׁבָּת נְקַבְּלָה.
לְכָה דוֹדִי לִקְרַאת כַּלָּה, פְּנֵי שַׁבָּת נְקַבְּלָה.

שָׁמוֹר וְזָכוֹר בְּדִבּוּר אֶחָד
הִשְׁמִיעָנוּ אֵל הַמְיֻחָד
יהוה אֶחָד וּשְׁמוֹ אֶחָד
לְשֵׁם וּלְתִפְאֶרֶת וְלִתְהִלָּה.

לְכָה דוֹדִי לִקְרַאת כַּלָּה, פְּנֵי שַׁבָּת נְקַבְּלָה.

אָנָּא, בְּכֹחַ *Please, by the power:* A hymn in seven lines, each of six words, whose initial letters spell out a mystical 42-letter name of God. It is attributed to Rabbi Neḥunya ben haKanah (second half of the first century CE).

לְכָה דוֹדִי *Come, my Beloved:* This song – the one original composition introduced into this service by the Safed kabbalists – was written by Rabbi Shlomo Alkabetz. It is a work of surpassing beauty, speaking in turn of Shabbat, Jerusalem, the Jewish people, and the Messiah, before returning in its last verse to the Shabbat again. Artfully woven from biblical quotations, many of them drawn from Isaiah's prophecies of consolation, together with Talmudic and midrashic ideas, its first eight verses form an acrostic, spelling out the name of its author, Shlomo HaLevi.

לִקְרַאת To greet the Sabbath, come let us go,
for of blessing, she is the source.
From the outset, as of old, ordained:
last in deed, first in thought.

Come, my Beloved, to greet the bride;
let us welcome the Sabbath.

מִקְדַּשׁ Sanctuary of the King, royal city,
arise, go forth from your ruined state.
Too long have you dwelt in the valley of tears.
He will shower compassion on you.

Come, my Beloved, to greet the bride;
let us welcome the Sabbath.

הִתְנַעֲרִי Shake yourself off, arise from the dust!
Put on your clothes of glory, My people.
Through the son of Jesse the Bethlehemite,
draw near to my soul and redeem it.

Come, my Beloved, to greet the bride;
let us welcome the Sabbath.

הִתְעוֹרְרִי Wake up, wake up,
for your light has come: rise, shine!
Awake, awake, break out in song,
for the Lord's glory is revealed on you.

Come, my Beloved, to greet the bride;
let us welcome the Sabbath.

---

people in his day. Using language drawn from Isaiah, he turns first to Jerusalem, then to the Jewish people, then to the land of Israel itself, summoning them to shake off their grief and rouse themselves to new glory. These verses radiate the hope born of faith, the victory of joy over despair.

לִקְרַאת שַׁבָּת לְכוּ וְנֵלְכָה
כִּי הִיא מְקוֹר הַבְּרָכָה
מֵרֹאשׁ מִקֶּדֶם נְסוּכָה
סוֹף מַעֲשֶׂה בְּמַחֲשָׁבָה תְּחִלָּה.
לְכָה דוֹדִי לִקְרַאת כַּלָּה, פְּנֵי שַׁבָּת נְקַבְּלָה.

מִקְדַּשׁ מֶלֶךְ עִיר מְלוּכָה
קוּמִי צְאִי מִתּוֹךְ הַהֲפֵכָה
רַב לָךְ שֶׁבֶת בְּעֵמֶק הַבָּכָא
וְהוּא יַחֲמֹל עָלַיִךְ חֶמְלָה.
לְכָה דוֹדִי לִקְרַאת כַּלָּה, פְּנֵי שַׁבָּת נְקַבְּלָה.

הִתְנַעֲרִי, מֵעָפָר קוּמִי
לִבְשִׁי בִּגְדֵי תִפְאַרְתֵּךְ עַמִּי
עַל יַד בֶּן יִשַׁי בֵּית הַלַּחְמִי
קָרְבָה אֶל נַפְשִׁי, גְּאָלָהּ.
לְכָה דוֹדִי לִקְרַאת כַּלָּה, פְּנֵי שַׁבָּת נְקַבְּלָה.

הִתְעוֹרְרִי הִתְעוֹרְרִי
כִּי בָא אוֹרֵךְ קוּמִי אוֹרִי
עוּרִי עוּרִי, שִׁיר דַּבֵּרִי
כְּבוֹד יהוה עָלַיִךְ נִגְלָה.
לְכָה דוֹדִי לִקְרַאת כַּלָּה, פְּנֵי שַׁבָּת נְקַבְּלָה.

מִקְדַּשׁ מֶלֶךְ עִיר מְלוּכָה *Sanctuary of the King, royal city:* In this and the next four verses, the poet speaks of the desolate condition of Jerusalem and the Jewish

לֹא תֵבֹשִׁי Do not be ashamed, do not be confounded.
Why be downcast? Why do you mourn?
In you the needy of My people find shelter,
and the city shall be rebuilt on its hill.

Come, my Beloved, to greet the bride;
let us welcome the Sabbath.

וְהָיוּ Those who despoiled you shall be despoiled,
and all who devoured you shall be far away.
Your God will rejoice over you
as a bridegroom rejoices over his bride.

Come, my Beloved, to greet the bride;
let us welcome the Sabbath.

יָמִין Right and left you shall spread out,
and the LORD you will revere.
Through the descendant of Peretz,
we shall rejoice and we shall be glad.

Come, my Beloved, to greet the bride;
let us welcome the Sabbath.

Stand and turn to face the door or the rear (usually western side) of the synagogue, as if to greet the incoming bride, bowing at the words "Enter, O bride!," then turn back.

בּוֹאִי Come in peace, O crown of her husband;
come with joy and jubilation,
among the faithful of the treasured people.
Enter, O bride! Enter, O bride!

Come, my Beloved, to greet the bride;
let us welcome the Sabbath.

Mourners during the week of Shiva return to the synagogue at this point. They are greeted with the following words of consolation:

הַמָּקוֹם May the Almighty comfort you
among the other mourners of Zion and Jerusalem.

בּוֹאִי בְשָׁלוֹם *Come in peace*: At this point our custom is to turn around to greet the Shabbat bride, as did the mystics in the fields of Safed.

לֹא תֵבֹשִׁי וְלֹא תִכָּלְמִי
מַה תִּשְׁתּוֹחֲחִי וּמַה תֶּהֱמִי
בָּךְ יֶחֱסוּ עֲנִיֵּי עַמִּי
וְנִבְנְתָה עִיר עַל תִּלָּהּ.
לְכָה דוֹדִי לִקְרַאת כַּלָּה, פְּנֵי שַׁבָּת נְקַבְּלָה.

וְהָיוּ לִמְשִׁסָּה שֹׁאסָיִךְ
וְרָחֲקוּ כָּל מְבַלְּעָיִךְ
יָשִׂישׂ עָלַיִךְ אֱלֹהָיִךְ
כִּמְשׂוֹשׂ חָתָן עַל כַּלָּה.
לְכָה דוֹדִי לִקְרַאת כַּלָּה, פְּנֵי שַׁבָּת נְקַבְּלָה.

יָמִין וּשְׂמֹאל תִּפְרֹצִי
וְאֶת יהוה תַּעֲרִיצִי
עַל יַד אִישׁ בֶּן פַּרְצִי
וְנִשְׂמְחָה וְנָגִילָה.
לְכָה דוֹדִי לִקְרַאת כַּלָּה, פְּנֵי שַׁבָּת נְקַבְּלָה.

Stand and turn to face the door or the rear (usually western side) of the בית כנסת*,*
as if to greet the incoming bride, bowing at the words בּוֹאִי כַלָּה*, then turn back.*

בּוֹאִי בְשָׁלוֹם עֲטֶרֶת בַּעְלָהּ
גַּם בְּשִׂמְחָה וּבְצָהֳלָה
תּוֹךְ אֱמוּנֵי עַם סְגֻלָּה
בּוֹאִי כַלָּה, בּוֹאִי כַלָּה.
לְכָה דוֹדִי לִקְרַאת כַּלָּה, פְּנֵי שַׁבָּת נְקַבְּלָה.

Mourners during the week of שבעה *return to the* בית כנסת *at this point.*
They are greeted with the following words of consolation:

הַמָּקוֹם יְנַחֵם אֶתְכֶם בְּתוֹךְ שְׁאָר אֲבֵלֵי צִיּוֹן וִירוּשָׁלָיִם.

On Yom Tov, Motza'ei Yom Tov or Shabbat Ḥol HaMo'ed, Kabbalat Shabbat begins here.

מִזְמוֹר A psalm. A song for the Sabbath day. It is good to thank the LORD and sing psalms to Your name, Most High – to tell of Your loving-kindness in the morning and Your faithfulness at night, to the music of the ten-stringed lyre and the melody of the harp. For You have made me rejoice by Your work, O LORD; I sing for joy at the deeds of Your hands. How great are Your deeds, LORD, and how very deep Your thoughts. A boor cannot know, nor can a fool understand, that though the wicked spring up like grass and all evildoers flourish, it is only that they may be destroyed for ever. But You, LORD, are eternally exalted. For behold Your enemies, LORD, behold Your enemies will perish; all evildoers will be scattered. You have raised my pride like that of a wild ox; I am anointed with fresh oil. My eyes shall look in triumph on my adversaries, my ears shall hear the downfall of the wicked who rise against me. ▸ The righteous will flourish like a palm tree and grow tall like a cedar in Lebanon. Planted in the LORD's House, blossoming in our God's courtyards, they will still bear fruit in old age, and stay vigorous and fresh, proclaiming that the LORD is upright: He is my Rock, in whom there is no wrong. *Ps. 92*

יהוה מָלָךְ The LORD reigns. He is robed in majesty. The LORD is robed, girded with strength. The world is firmly established; it cannot be moved. Your throne stands firm as of old; You are eternal. Rivers lift up, LORD, rivers lift up their voice, rivers lift up their crashing waves. ▸ Mightier than the noise of many waters, than the mighty waves of the sea is the LORD on high. Your testimonies are very sure; holiness adorns Your House, LORD, for evermore. *Ps. 93*

---

ished "like grass," it was short-lived, while the righteous grow slowly but stand tall "like the cedar of Lebanon." Because our time perspective is short, we seem to inhabit a world in which evil prevails. Were we able to see history as a whole, we would know that good wins the final victory; in the long run justice prevails.

On יום טוב, מוצאי יום טוב *or* שבת חול המועד, קבלת שבת *begins here.*

תהלים צב
מִזְמוֹר שִׁיר לְיוֹם הַשַּׁבָּת: טוֹב לְהֹדוֹת לַיהוה, וּלְזַמֵּר לְשִׁמְךָ
עֶלְיוֹן: לְהַגִּיד בַּבֹּקֶר חַסְדֶּךָ, וֶאֱמוּנָתְךָ בַּלֵּילוֹת: עֲלֵי־עָשׂוֹר
וַעֲלֵי־נָבֶל, עֲלֵי הִגָּיוֹן בְּכִנּוֹר: כִּי שִׂמַּחְתַּנִי יהוה בְּפָעֳלֶךָ, בְּמַעֲשֵׂי
יָדֶיךָ אֲרַנֵּן: מַה־גָּדְלוּ מַעֲשֶׂיךָ יהוה, מְאֹד עָמְקוּ מַחְשְׁבֹתֶיךָ:
אִישׁ־בַּעַר לֹא יֵדָע, וּכְסִיל לֹא־יָבִין אֶת־זֹאת: בִּפְרֹחַ רְשָׁעִים
כְּמוֹ עֵשֶׂב, וַיָּצִיצוּ כָּל־פֹּעֲלֵי אָוֶן, לְהִשָּׁמְדָם עֲדֵי־עַד: וְאַתָּה
מָרוֹם לְעֹלָם יהוה: כִּי הִנֵּה אֹיְבֶיךָ יהוה, כִּי־הִנֵּה אֹיְבֶיךָ יֹאבֵדוּ,
יִתְפָּרְדוּ כָּל־פֹּעֲלֵי אָוֶן: וַתָּרֶם כִּרְאֵים קַרְנִי, בַּלֹּתִי בְּשֶׁמֶן רַעֲנָן:
וַתַּבֵּט עֵינִי בְּשׁוּרָי, בַּקָּמִים עָלַי מְרֵעִים תִּשְׁמַעְנָה אָזְנָי: ‹ צַדִּיק
כַּתָּמָר יִפְרָח, כְּאֶרֶז בַּלְּבָנוֹן יִשְׂגֶּה: שְׁתוּלִים בְּבֵית יהוה, בְּחַצְרוֹת
אֱלֹהֵינוּ יַפְרִיחוּ: עוֹד יְנוּבוּן בְּשֵׂיבָה, דְּשֵׁנִים וְרַעֲנַנִּים יִהְיוּ: לְהַגִּיד
כִּי־יָשָׁר יהוה, צוּרִי, וְלֹא־עַוְלָתָה בּוֹ:

תהלים צג
יהוה מָלָךְ, גֵּאוּת לָבֵשׁ, לָבֵשׁ יהוה עֹז הִתְאַזָּר, אַף־תִּכּוֹן תֵּבֵל
בַּל־תִּמּוֹט: נָכוֹן כִּסְאֲךָ מֵאָז, מֵעוֹלָם אָתָּה: נָשְׂאוּ נְהָרוֹת יהוה,
נָשְׂאוּ נְהָרוֹת קוֹלָם, יִשְׂאוּ נְהָרוֹת דָּכְיָם: ‹ מִקֹּלוֹת מַיִם רַבִּים,
אַדִּירִים מִשְׁבְּרֵי־יָם, אַדִּיר בַּמָּרוֹם יהוה: עֵדֹתֶיךָ נֶאֶמְנוּ מְאֹד,
לְבֵיתְךָ נַאֲוָה־קֹדֶשׁ, יהוה לְאֹרֶךְ יָמִים:

מִזְמוֹר שִׁיר לְיוֹם הַשַּׁבָּת *A Psalm. A song for the Sabbath day:* This psalm, sung by the Levites on Shabbat, was already understood by the sages as "a song for the time to come, for the day that will be all Shabbat and rest in life everlasting." Shabbat is not merely a day of rest, it is a rehearsal, within time, for the age beyond time when humanity, guided by the call of God, moves beyond strife, evil and oppression, to create a world of harmony, respecting the integrity of creation as God's work, and the human person as God's image.

At that time, people looking back at history will see that though evil flour-

MOURNER'S KADDISH

The following prayer, said by mourners, requires the presence of a minyan. A transliteration can be found on page 1334.

Mourner: יִתְגַּדַּל Magnified and sanctified
may His great name be,
in the world He created by His will.
May He establish His kingdom
in your lifetime and in your days,
and in the lifetime of all the house of Israel,
swiftly and soon –
and say: Amen.

All: May His great name
be blessed for ever and all time.

Mourner: Blessed and praised,
glorified and exalted,
raised and honored,
uplifted and lauded
be the name of the Holy One,
blessed be He,
beyond any blessing,
song, praise and consolation
uttered in the world –
and say: Amen.

May there be great peace from heaven,
and life for us and all Israel –
and say: Amen.

Bow, take three steps back, as if taking leave of the Divine Presence, then bow, first left, then right, then center, while saying:

May He who makes peace in His high places,
make peace for us and all Israel –
and say: Amen.

קדיש יתום

The following prayer, said by mourners, requires the presence of a מנין*.*
A transliteration can be found on page 1334.

אבל: יִתְגַּדַּל וְיִתְקַדַּשׁ שְׁמֵהּ רַבָּא (קהל: אָמֵן)
בְּעָלְמָא דִּי בְרָא כִרְעוּתֵהּ
וְיַמְלִיךְ מַלְכוּתֵהּ
בְּחַיֵּיכוֹן וּבְיוֹמֵיכוֹן וּבְחַיֵּי דְכָל בֵּית יִשְׂרָאֵל
בַּעֲגָלָא וּבִזְמַן קָרִיב, וְאִמְרוּ אָמֵן. (קהל: אָמֵן)

קהל ואבל: יְהֵא שְׁמֵהּ רַבָּא מְבָרַךְ לְעָלַם וּלְעָלְמֵי עָלְמַיָּא.

אבל: יִתְבָּרַךְ וְיִשְׁתַּבַּח וְיִתְפָּאַר
וְיִתְרוֹמַם וְיִתְנַשֵּׂא וְיִתְהַדָּר וְיִתְעַלֶּה וְיִתְהַלָּל
שְׁמֵהּ דְּקֻדְשָׁא בְּרִיךְ הוּא (קהל: בְּרִיךְ הוּא)
לְעֵלָּא מִן כָּל בִּרְכָתָא
/בשבת שובה: לְעֵלָּא לְעֵלָּא מִכָּל בִּרְכָתָא/
וְשִׁירָתָא, תֻּשְׁבְּחָתָא וְנֶחֱמָתָא
דַּאֲמִירָן בְּעָלְמָא, וְאִמְרוּ אָמֵן. (קהל: אָמֵן)

יְהֵא שְׁלָמָא רַבָּא מִן שְׁמַיָּא
וְחַיִּים, עָלֵינוּ וְעַל כָּל יִשְׂרָאֵל
וְאִמְרוּ אָמֵן. (קהל: אָמֵן)

Bow, take three steps back, as if taking leave of the Divine Presence,
then bow, first left, then right, then center, while saying:

עֹשֶׂה שָׁלוֹם/בשבת שובה: הַשָּׁלוֹם/ בִּמְרוֹמָיו
הוּא יַעֲשֶׂה שָׁלוֹם עָלֵינוּ וְעַל כָּל יִשְׂרָאֵל
וְאִמְרוּ אָמֵן. (קהל: אָמֵן)

The following is not said on Yom Tov, Shabbat Ḥol HaMo'ed or Motza'ei Yom Tov.

1. בַּמֶּה מַדְלִיקִין With what wicks may we light the Sabbath lamp and with what may we not light? We may not use a wick of cedar bast, or uncombed flax, or raw silk, or a wick made of willow bast or desert weed, or seaweed. [For oil] we may not use pitch, or wax, or cottonseed oil or [contaminated consecrated] oil that must be destroyed by burning, or fat from sheeps' tails, or tallow. Naḥum the Mede says: We may use boiled tallow. But the sages say: Whether boiled or not boiled, we may not use it. *Mishna Shabbat, chapter 2*
2. [Contaminated consecrated] oil that must be destroyed by burning may not be used for a festival lamp. Rabbi Yishmael says: We may not use tar out of respect for the honor due to the Sabbath. But the sages permit all these oils: sesame oil, nut oil, radish oil, fish oil, gourd oil, tar or naphtha. Rabbi Tarfon, however, says: We may use only olive oil.
3. No product from a tree may be used as a wick for the Sabbath lamp, except flax. Also no product of a tree can contract "tent" uncleanness, except flax. If a wick was made from a cloth that has been twisted but not singed, Rabbi Eliezer declares, it is susceptible to contamination and may not be used for a Sabbath lamp; but Rabbi Akiva says, it is not susceptible to contamination, and may be used for the Sabbath lamp.
4. One may not pierce an eggshell, fill it with oil, and put it over the mouth of a lamp so that the oil may drip from it into the lamp, even if the vessel is of earthenware, but Rabbi Judah permits it. If, however, the potter had originally attached it to the lamp, it is permitted because it constitutes a single vessel. One may not fill a bowl with oil, put it beside a lamp, and put the end of the wick in it so that it draws oil from the bowl; but Rabbi Judah permits this.
5. One who extinguishes a lamp because he is afraid of heathens, robbers, or depression, or to enable a sick person to sleep, is not liable [for violating the Sabbath]. If he did it to spare the lamp, or the oil, or the wick, he is liable. Rabbi Yose absolves him in all these cases except that of sparing the wick, because he thereby turns it into charcoal.

Karaites) who denied it. The latter held that the commandment, "Do not light a fire in any of your dwellings on the Sabbath day" (Ex. 35:3), precluded the use of any light; the former held that it excluded only the act of kindling itself, and not the use of a light that had been lit before Shabbat. Hence the study of the section of the Mishna, part of the Oral Law, that deals with Shabbat lights (*Sefer HaIttim*).

The following is not said on יום טוב, שבת חול המועד *or* מוצאי יום טוב.

משנה שבת פרק שני

א בַּמֶּה מַדְלִיקִין וּבַמָּה אֵין מַדְלִיקִין. אֵין מַדְלִיקִין לֹא בְלֶכֶשׁ, וְלֹא בְחֹסֶן, וְלֹא בְכַלָּךְ, וְלֹא בִּפְתִילַת הָאִידָן, וְלֹא בִּפְתִילַת הַמִּדְבָּר, וְלֹא בִירוֹקָה שֶׁעַל פְּנֵי הַמָּיִם. וְלֹא בְזֶפֶת וְלֹא בְשַׁעֲוָה וְלֹא בְשֶׁמֶן קִיק וְלֹא בְשֶׁמֶן שְׂרֵפָה וְלֹא בְאַלְיָה וְלֹא בְחֵלֶב. נַחוּם הַמָּדִי אוֹמֵר: מַדְלִיקִין בְּחֵלֶב מְבֻשָּׁל, וַחֲכָמִים אוֹמְרִים: אֶחָד מְבֻשָּׁל וְאֶחָד שֶׁאֵינוֹ מְבֻשָּׁל, אֵין מַדְלִיקִין בּוֹ.

ב אֵין מַדְלִיקִין בְּשֶׁמֶן שְׂרֵפָה בְּיוֹם טוֹב. רַבִּי יִשְׁמָעֵאל אוֹמֵר: אֵין מַדְלִיקִין בְּעִטְרָן מִפְּנֵי כְּבוֹד הַשַּׁבָּת. וַחֲכָמִים מַתִּירִין בְּכָל הַשְּׁמָנִים, בְּשֶׁמֶן שֻׁמְשְׁמִין, בְּשֶׁמֶן אֱגוֹזִים, בְּשֶׁמֶן צְנוֹנוֹת, בְּשֶׁמֶן דָּגִים, בְּשֶׁמֶן פַּקֻּעוֹת, בְּעִטְרָן וּבְנֵפְט. רַבִּי טַרְפוֹן אוֹמֵר: אֵין מַדְלִיקִין אֶלָּא בְּשֶׁמֶן זַיִת בִּלְבָד.

ג כָּל הַיּוֹצֵא מִן הָעֵץ אֵין מַדְלִיקִין בּוֹ, אֶלָּא פִשְׁתָּן. וְכָל הַיּוֹצֵא מִן הָעֵץ אֵינוֹ מִטַּמֵּא טֻמְאַת אֹהָלִים, אֶלָּא פִשְׁתָּן. פְּתִילַת הַבֶּגֶד שֶׁקִּפְּלָהּ וְלֹא הִבְהֲבָהּ, רַבִּי אֱלִיעֶזֶר אוֹמֵר: טְמֵאָה הִיא, וְאֵין מַדְלִיקִין בָּהּ. רַבִּי עֲקִיבָא אוֹמֵר: טְהוֹרָה הִיא, וּמַדְלִיקִין בָּהּ.

ד לֹא יִקֹּב אָדָם שְׁפוֹפֶרֶת שֶׁל בֵּיצָה וִימַלְּאֶנָּה שֶׁמֶן וְיִתְּנֶנָּה עַל פִּי הַנֵּר, בִּשְׁבִיל שֶׁתְּהֵא מְנַטֶּפֶת, וַאֲפִלּוּ הִיא שֶׁל חֶרֶס. וְרַבִּי יְהוּדָה מַתִּיר. אֲבָל אִם חִבְּרָהּ הַיּוֹצֵר מִתְּחִלָּה מֻתָּר, מִפְּנֵי שֶׁהוּא כְּלִי אֶחָד. לֹא יְמַלֵּא אָדָם אֶת הַקְּעָרָה שֶׁמֶן וְיִתְּנֶנָּה בְּצַד הַנֵּר וְיִתֵּן רֹאשׁ הַפְּתִילָה בְּתוֹכָהּ, בִּשְׁבִיל שֶׁתְּהֵא שׁוֹאֶבֶת. וְרַבִּי יְהוּדָה מַתִּיר.

ה הַמְכַבֶּה אֶת הַנֵּר מִפְּנֵי שֶׁהוּא מִתְיָרֵא מִפְּנֵי גוֹיִם, מִפְּנֵי לִסְטִים, מִפְּנֵי רוּחַ רָעָה, אוֹ בִשְׁבִיל הַחוֹלֶה שֶׁיִּישַׁן, פָּטוּר. כְּחָס עַל הַנֵּר, כְּחָס עַל הַשֶּׁמֶן, כְּחָס עַל הַפְּתִילָה, חַיָּב. רַבִּי יוֹסֵי פּוֹטֵר בְּכֻלָּן חוּץ מִן הַפְּתִילָה, מִפְּנֵי שֶׁהוּא עוֹשָׂה פֶּחָם.

בַּמֶּה מַדְלִיקִין *With what wicks may we light?* This, the second chapter of the Mishna tractate *Shabbat*, was also added to prolong the service for the benefit of latecomers. Its recitation, however, is also related to an ancient controversy between those who accepted the Oral Law and those (Sadducees, and later,

6. For three transgressions women may die in childbirth: for being careless in observing the laws of menstruation, separating challah [dough-offering], and lighting the Sabbath light.
7. One should say three things at home on the eve of the Sabbath just before dark: Have you tithed? Have you prepared the Eiruv? Light the Sabbath lamp. If there is doubt whether or not darkness has fallen, we may not tithe definitely untithed produce, nor immerse [unclean] vessels, nor light the Sabbath lamp. We may tithe produce about which there is a doubt whether it has been tithed or not, we may prepare an Eiruv, and insulate hot food.

It was taught, Rabbi Ḥanina said: One should examine his clothing on the eve of the Sabbath before nightfall [to ensure that one is not carrying anything], for one may forget and go out. Rabbi Yosef said: This is an important law about the Sabbath [for it is easy to forget, and thus inadvertently violate the holiness of the day]. *Shabbat 12a*

Rabbi Elazar said in the name of Rabbi Ḥanina: The disciples of the sages *Berakhot 64a*
increase peace in the world, as it is said, "And all your children shall be taught *Is. 54*
of the LORD, and great shall be the peace of your children [*banayikh*]." Read
not *banayikh*, "your children," but *bonayikh*, "your builders." Those who love *Ps. 119*
Your Torah have great peace; there is no stumbling block for them. May there *Ps. 122*
be peace within your ramparts, prosperity in your palaces. For the sake of my
brothers and friends, I shall say, "Peace be within you." For the sake of the
House of the LORD our God, I will seek your good. ▸ May the LORD grant *Ps. 29*
strength to His people; may the LORD bless His people with peace.

THE RABBIS' KADDISH

The following prayer, said by mourners, requires the presence of a minyan.
A transliteration can be found on page 1333.

Mourner: יִתְגַּדַּל Magnified and sanctified may His great name be,
in the world He created by His will.
May He establish His kingdom in your lifetime
and in your days,
and in the lifetime of all the house of Israel,
swiftly and soon –
and say: Amen.

All: May His great name be blessed for ever and all time.

ו עַל שָׁלֹשׁ עֲבֵרוֹת נָשִׁים מֵתוֹת בִּשְׁעַת לֵדָתָן, עַל שֶׁאֵינָן זְהִירוֹת בְּנִדָּה, בְּחַלָּה וּבְהַדְלָקַת הַנֵּר.

ז שְׁלֹשָׁה דְבָרִים צָרִיךְ אָדָם לוֹמַר בְּתוֹךְ בֵּיתוֹ עֶרֶב שַׁבָּת עִם חֲשֵׁכָה: עִשַּׂרְתֶּם, עֵרַבְתֶּם, הַדְלִיקוּ אֶת הַנֵּר. סָפֵק חֲשֵׁכָה סָפֵק אֵינָהּ חֲשֵׁכָה, אֵין מְעַשְּׂרִין אֶת הַוַּדַּאי, וְאֵין מַטְבִּילִין אֶת הַכֵּלִים, וְאֵין מַדְלִיקִין אֶת הַנֵּרוֹת. אֲבָל מְעַשְּׂרִין אֶת הַדְּמַאי, וּמְעָרְבִין וְטוֹמְנִין אֶת הַחַמִּין.

שבת יב. תַּנְיָא, אָמַר רַבִּי חֲנִינָא: חַיָּב אָדָם לְמַשְׁמֵשׁ בְּגָדָיו בְּעֶרֶב שַׁבָּת עִם חֲשֵׁכָה, שֶׁמָּא יִשְׁכַּח וְיֵצֵא. אָמַר רַב יוֹסֵף: הִלְכְתָא רַבְּתָא לְשַׁבְּתָא.

ברכות סד. אָמַר רַבִּי אֶלְעָזָר, אָמַר רַבִּי חֲנִינָא: תַּלְמִידֵי חֲכָמִים מַרְבִּים שָׁלוֹם בָּעוֹלָם,
ישעיה נד שֶׁנֶּאֱמַר: וְכָל־בָּנַיִךְ לִמּוּדֵי יהוה, וְרַב שְׁלוֹם בָּנָיִךְ: אַל תִּקְרֵי בָּנָיִךְ, אֶלָּא
תהלים קיט תהלים קכב בּוֹנָיִךְ. שָׁלוֹם רָב לְאֹהֲבֵי תוֹרָתֶךָ, וְאֵין־לָמוֹ מִכְשׁוֹל: יְהִי־שָׁלוֹם בְּחֵילֵךְ,
שַׁלְוָה בְּאַרְמְנוֹתָיִךְ: לְמַעַן אַחַי וְרֵעָי אֲדַבְּרָה־נָּא שָׁלוֹם בָּךְ: לְמַעַן בֵּית־
תהלים כט יהוה אֱלֹהֵינוּ אֲבַקְשָׁה טוֹב לָךְ: ◂ יהוה עֹז לְעַמּוֹ יִתֵּן, יהוה יְבָרֵךְ אֶת־עַמּוֹ
בַשָּׁלוֹם:

קדיש דרבנן

The following prayer, said by mourners, requires the presence of a מנין*.*
A transliteration can be found on page 1333.

אבל: יִתְגַּדַּל וְיִתְקַדַּשׁ שְׁמֵהּ רַבָּא (קהל: אָמֵן)
בְּעָלְמָא דִּי בְרָא כִרְעוּתֵהּ
וְיַמְלִיךְ מַלְכוּתֵהּ
בְּחַיֵּיכוֹן וּבְיוֹמֵיכוֹן וּבְחַיֵּי דְכָל בֵּית יִשְׂרָאֵל
בַּעֲגָלָא וּבִזְמַן קָרִיב
וְאִמְרוּ אָמֵן. (קהל: אָמֵן)

קהל ואבל: יְהֵא שְׁמֵהּ רַבָּא מְבָרַךְ לְעָלַם וּלְעָלְמֵי עָלְמַיָּא.

Mourner: Blessed and praised,
glorified and exalted,
raised and honored,
uplifted and lauded
be the name of the Holy One,
blessed be He,
beyond any blessing,
song, praise and consolation
uttered in the world –
and say: Amen.

To Israel,
to the teachers,
their disciples and their disciples' disciples,
and to all who engage in the study of Torah,
in this (*In Israel add:* holy) place or elsewhere,
may there come to them
and you great peace,
grace, kindness and compassion,
long life, ample sustenance and deliverance,
from their Father in Heaven –
and say: Amen.

May there be great peace from heaven,
and (good) life for us and all Israel –
and say: Amen.

Bow, take three steps back, as if taking leave of the Divine Presence, then bow, first left, then right, then center, while saying:

May He who makes peace
in His high places,
in His compassion make peace for us and all Israel –
and say: Amen.

אבל: יִתְבָּרַךְ וְיִשְׁתַּבַּח וְיִתְפָּאַר וְיִתְרוֹמַם וְיִתְנַשֵּׂא
וְיִתְהַדָּר וְיִתְעַלֶּה וְיִתְהַלָּל
שְׁמֵהּ דְּקֻדְשָׁא בְּרִיךְ הוּא (קהל: בְּרִיךְ הוּא)
לְעֵלָּא מִן כָּל בִּרְכָתָא
/בשבת שובה: לְעֵלָּא לְעֵלָּא מִכָּל בִּרְכָתָא/
וְשִׁירָתָא, תֻּשְׁבְּחָתָא וְנֶחֱמָתָא, דַּאֲמִירָן בְּעָלְמָא
וְאִמְרוּ אָמֵן. (קהל: אָמֵן)

עַל יִשְׂרָאֵל וְעַל רַבָּנָן
וְעַל תַּלְמִידֵיהוֹן וְעַל כָּל תַּלְמִידֵי תַלְמִידֵיהוֹן
וְעַל כָּל מָאן דְּעָסְקִין בְּאוֹרַיְתָא
דִּי בְּאַתְרָא (בארץ ישראל: קַדִּישָׁא) הָדֵין, וְדִי בְּכָל אֲתַר וַאֲתַר
יְהֵא לְהוֹן וּלְכוֹן שְׁלָמָא רַבָּא
חִנָּא וְחִסְדָּא, וְרַחֲמֵי, וְחַיֵּי אֲרִיכֵי, וּמְזוֹנֵי רְוִיחֵי
וּפֻרְקָנָא מִן קֳדָם אֲבוּהוֹן דִּי בִשְׁמַיָּא
וְאִמְרוּ אָמֵן. (קהל: אָמֵן)

יְהֵא שְׁלָמָא רַבָּא מִן שְׁמַיָּא
וְחַיִּים (טוֹבִים) עָלֵינוּ וְעַל כָּל יִשְׂרָאֵל
וְאִמְרוּ אָמֵן. (קהל: אָמֵן)

Bow, take three steps back, as if taking leave of the Divine Presence, then bow, first left, then right, then center, while saying:

עֹשֶׂה שָׁלוֹם/ בשבת שובה: הַשָּׁלוֹם/ בִּמְרוֹמָיו
הוּא יַעֲשֶׂה בְרַחֲמָיו שָׁלוֹם, עָלֵינוּ וְעַל כָּל יִשְׂרָאֵל
וְאִמְרוּ אָמֵן. (קהל: אָמֵן)

Ma'ariv for Shabbat and Yom Tov

BLESSINGS OF THE SHEMA

The Leader says the following, bowing at "Bless," standing straight at "the LORD." The congregation, followed by the Leader, responds, bowing at "Bless," standing straight at "the LORD."

Leader: **BLESS**
the LORD, the blessed One.

Congregation: Bless the LORD, the blessed One,
for ever and all time.

Leader: Bless the LORD, the blessed One,
for ever and all time.

בָּרוּךְ Blessed are You, LORD our God, King of the Universe,
who by His word brings on evenings,
by His wisdom opens the gates of heaven,
with understanding makes time change and the seasons rotate,
and by His will
orders the stars in their constellations in the sky.
He creates day and night,
rolling away the light before the darkness,
and darkness before the light.
▸ He makes the day pass and brings on night,
distinguishing day from night:
the LORD of hosts is His name.
May the living and forever enduring God rule over us for all time.
Blessed are You, LORD, who brings on evenings.

אֲשֶׁר בִּדְבָרוֹ מַעֲרִיב עֲרָבִים *Who by His word brings on evenings:* The three key Jewish beliefs are creation (that God made the universe), revelation (that God speaks to mankind), and redemption (that God rescues humanity,

מעריב לשבת וליום טוב

קריאת שמע וברכותיה

The שליח ציבור *says the following, bowing at* בָּרְכוּ*, standing straight at* ה׳.
The קהל*, followed by the* שליח ציבור*, responds, bowing at* בָּרוּךְ*, standing straight at* ה׳.

ש״ץ: **בָּרְכוּ**

אֶת יהוה הַמְבֹרָךְ.

קהל: בָּרוּךְ יהוה הַמְבֹרָךְ לְעוֹלָם וָעֶד.

ש״ץ: בָּרוּךְ יהוה הַמְבֹרָךְ לְעוֹלָם וָעֶד.

בָּרוּךְ אַתָּה יהוה אֱלֹהֵינוּ מֶלֶךְ הָעוֹלָם
אֲשֶׁר בִּדְבָרוֹ מַעֲרִיב עֲרָבִים
בְּחָכְמָה פּוֹתֵחַ שְׁעָרִים
וּבִתְבוּנָה מְשַׁנֶּה עִתִּים וּמַחֲלִיף אֶת הַזְּמַנִּים
וּמְסַדֵּר אֶת הַכּוֹכָבִים בְּמִשְׁמְרוֹתֵיהֶם בָּרָקִיעַ כִּרְצוֹנוֹ.
בּוֹרֵא יוֹם וָלָיְלָה, גּוֹלֵל אוֹר מִפְּנֵי חֹשֶׁךְ וְחֹשֶׁךְ מִפְּנֵי אוֹר
◂ וּמַעֲבִיר יוֹם וּמֵבִיא לָיְלָה
וּמַבְדִּיל בֵּין יוֹם וּבֵין לָיְלָה
יהוה צְבָאוֹת שְׁמוֹ.
אֵל חַי וְקַיָּם תָּמִיד, יִמְלֹךְ עָלֵינוּ לְעוֹלָם וָעֶד.
בָּרוּךְ אַתָּה יהוה, הַמַּעֲרִיב עֲרָבִים.

אַהֲבַת עוֹלָם With everlasting love
have You loved Your people, the house of Israel.
You have taught us Torah and commandments,
decrees and laws of justice.
Therefore, LORD our God, when we lie down and when we rise up
we will speak of Your decrees, rejoicing in the words of Your Torah
and Your commandments for ever.
▸ For they are our life and the length of our days;
on them will we meditate day and night.
May You never take away Your love from us.
Blessed are You, LORD, who loves His people Israel.

The Shema must be said with intense concentration. See laws 349–353.
When not with a minyan, say:
God, faithful King!

The following verse should be said aloud, while covering the eyes with the right hand:

Listen, Israel: the LORD is our God, the LORD is One.

Deut. 6

Quietly: Blessed be the name of His glorious kingdom for ever and all time.

וְאָהַבְתָּ Love the LORD your God with all your heart, with all your soul, and with all your might. These words which I command you today shall be on your heart. Teach them repeatedly to your children, speaking of them when you sit at home and when you travel on the way, when you lie down and when you rise. Bind them as a sign on your hand, and they shall be an emblem between your eyes. Write them on the doorposts of your house and gates. Deut. 6

---

the people of Israel pour out their thanks for the gift of Torah and its "commandments, decrees and laws of justice." Here, law becomes love and love becomes law. God unites us to Him by teaching us how to act in accordance with His will – which becomes in turn "our life and the length of our days."

שְׁמַע יִשְׂרָאֵל *Listen, Israel: Shema* means not only "to hear" but also "to listen, understand, internalize, respond and obey." It is translated here as "Listen"

אַהֲבַת עוֹלָם בֵּית יִשְׂרָאֵל עַמְּךָ אָהָבְתָּ
תּוֹרָה וּמִצְוֹת, חֻקִּים וּמִשְׁפָּטִים, אוֹתָנוּ לִמַּדְתָּ
עַל כֵּן יהוה אֱלֹהֵינוּ בְּשָׁכְבֵנוּ וּבְקוּמֵנוּ נָשִׂיחַ בְּחֻקֶּיךָ
וְנִשְׂמַח בְּדִבְרֵי תוֹרָתֶךָ וּבְמִצְוֹתֶיךָ לְעוֹלָם וָעֶד
◂ כִּי הֵם חַיֵּינוּ וְאֹרֶךְ יָמֵינוּ, וּבָהֶם נֶהְגֶּה יוֹמָם וָלָיְלָה.
וְאַהֲבָתְךָ אַל תָּסִיר מִמֶּנּוּ לְעוֹלָמִים.
בָּרוּךְ אַתָּה יהוה, אוֹהֵב עַמּוֹ יִשְׂרָאֵל.

The שמע must be said with intense concentration. See laws 349–353.
When not with a מנין, say:

אֵל מֶלֶךְ נֶאֱמָן

The following verse should be said aloud, while covering the eyes with the right hand:

דברים ו שְׁמַע יִשְׂרָאֵל, יהוה אֱלֹהֵינוּ, יהוה ׀ אֶחָד:

Quietly בָּרוּךְ שֵׁם כְּבוֹד מַלְכוּתוֹ לְעוֹלָם וָעֶד.

דברים ו וְאָהַבְתָּ אֵת יהוה אֱלֹהֶיךָ, בְּכָל־לְבָבְךָ וּבְכָל־נַפְשְׁךָ וּבְכָל־
מְאֹדֶךָ: וְהָיוּ הַדְּבָרִים הָאֵלֶּה, אֲשֶׁר אָנֹכִי מְצַוְּךָ הַיּוֹם, עַל־לְבָבֶךָ:
וְשִׁנַּנְתָּם לְבָנֶיךָ וְדִבַּרְתָּ בָּם, בְּשִׁבְתְּךָ בְּבֵיתֶךָ וּבְלֶכְתְּךָ בַדֶּרֶךְ,
וּבְשָׁכְבְּךָ וּבְקוּמֶךָ: וּקְשַׁרְתָּם לְאוֹת עַל־יָדֶךָ וְהָיוּ לְטֹטָפֹת בֵּין
עֵינֶיךָ: וּכְתַבְתָּם עַל־מְזֻזוֹת בֵּיתֶךָ וּבִשְׁעָרֶיךָ:

---

teaching us how to act with justice and compassion). The blessings surrounding the Shema are constructed on this pattern. This, the first, speaks of creation – heaven and earth, light and darkness, day and night. The next speaks of revelation, God's gift of the Torah to the children of Israel. The third, immediately after the Shema, speaks of redemption ("who redeemed Israel"). The siddur is our tutorial in belief, teaching us to see the world through the eyes of faith.

אַהֲבַת עוֹלָם *With everlasting love:* Nothing more eloquently refutes the idea that Judaism is a dry, legalistic religion than this magnificent poem in which

וְהָיָה If you indeed heed My commandments with which I charge you today, to love the LORD your God and worship Him with all your heart and with all your soul, I will give rain in your land in its season, the early and late rain; and you shall gather in your grain, wine and oil. I will give grass in your field for your cattle, and you shall eat and be satisfied. Be careful lest your heart be tempted and you go astray and worship other gods, bowing down to them. Then the LORD's anger will flare against you and He will close the heavens so that there will be no rain. The land will not yield its crops, and you will perish swiftly from the good land that the LORD is giving you. Therefore, set these, My words, on your heart and soul. Bind them as a sign on your hand, and they shall be an emblem between your eyes. Teach them to your children, speaking of them when you sit at home and when you travel on the way, when you lie down and when you rise. Write them on the doorposts of your house and gates, so that you and your children may live long in the land that the LORD swore to your ancestors to give them, for as long as the heavens are above the earth. *Deut. 11*

וַיֹּאמֶר The LORD spoke to Moses, saying: Speak to the Israelites and tell them to make tassels on the corners of their garments for all generations. They shall attach to the tassel at each corner a thread of blue. This shall be your tassel, and you shall see it and remember all of the LORD's commandments and keep them, not straying after your heart and after your eyes, following your own sinful desires. Thus you will be reminded to keep all My *Num. 15*

Secular terms for understanding are permeated with visual images. We speak of insight, foresight, vision, observation, perspective; when we understand, we say "I see." Judaism, with its belief in an invisible, transcendent God, is a culture of the ear, not the eye. The patriarchs and prophets did not see God; they heard Him. To emphasize the non-visual nature of Jewish belief, it is our custom to cover our eyes as we say these words.

דברים יא וְהָיָה אִם־שָׁמֹעַ תִּשְׁמְעוּ אֶל־מִצְוֺתַי אֲשֶׁר אָנֹכִי מְצַוֶּה אֶתְכֶם
הַיּוֹם, לְאַהֲבָה אֶת־יהוה אֱלֹהֵיכֶם וּלְעָבְדוֹ, בְּכָל־לְבַבְכֶם וּבְכָל־
נַפְשְׁכֶם: וְנָתַתִּי מְטַר־אַרְצְכֶם בְּעִתּוֹ, יוֹרֶה וּמַלְקוֹשׁ, וְאָסַפְתָּ
דְגָנֶךָ וְתִירֹשְׁךָ וְיִצְהָרֶךָ: וְנָתַתִּי עֵשֶׂב בְּשָׂדְךָ לִבְהֶמְתֶּךָ, וְאָכַלְתָּ
וְשָׂבָעְתָּ: הִשָּׁמְרוּ לָכֶם פֶּן־יִפְתֶּה לְבַבְכֶם, וְסַרְתֶּם וַעֲבַדְתֶּם
אֱלֹהִים אֲחֵרִים וְהִשְׁתַּחֲוִיתֶם לָהֶם: וְחָרָה אַף־יהוה בָּכֶם, וְעָצַר
אֶת־הַשָּׁמַיִם וְלֹא־יִהְיֶה מָטָר, וְהָאֲדָמָה לֹא תִתֵּן אֶת־יְבוּלָהּ,
וַאֲבַדְתֶּם מְהֵרָה מֵעַל הָאָרֶץ הַטֹּבָה אֲשֶׁר יהוה נֹתֵן לָכֶם:
וְשַׂמְתֶּם אֶת־דְּבָרַי אֵלֶּה עַל־לְבַבְכֶם וְעַל־נַפְשְׁכֶם, וּקְשַׁרְתֶּם
אֹתָם לְאוֹת עַל־יֶדְכֶם, וְהָיוּ לְטוֹטָפֹת בֵּין עֵינֵיכֶם: וְלִמַּדְתֶּם
אֹתָם אֶת־בְּנֵיכֶם לְדַבֵּר בָּם, בְּשִׁבְתְּךָ בְּבֵיתֶךָ וּבְלֶכְתְּךָ בַדֶּרֶךְ,
וּבְשָׁכְבְּךָ וּבְקוּמֶךָ: וּכְתַבְתָּם עַל־מְזוּזוֹת בֵּיתֶךָ וּבִשְׁעָרֶיךָ: לְמַעַן
יִרְבּוּ יְמֵיכֶם וִימֵי בְנֵיכֶם עַל הָאֲדָמָה אֲשֶׁר נִשְׁבַּע יהוה לַאֲבֹתֵיכֶם
לָתֵת לָהֶם, כִּימֵי הַשָּׁמַיִם עַל־הָאָרֶץ:

במדבר טו וַיֹּאמֶר יהוה אֶל־מֹשֶׁה לֵּאמֹר: דַּבֵּר אֶל־בְּנֵי יִשְׂרָאֵל וְאָמַרְתָּ
אֲלֵהֶם, וְעָשׂוּ לָהֶם צִיצִת עַל־כַּנְפֵי בִגְדֵיהֶם לְדֹרֹתָם, וְנָתְנוּ
עַל־צִיצִת הַכָּנָף פְּתִיל תְּכֵלֶת: וְהָיָה לָכֶם לְצִיצִת, וּרְאִיתֶם אֹתוֹ
וּזְכַרְתֶּם אֶת־כָּל־מִצְוֺת יהוה וַעֲשִׂיתֶם אֹתָם, וְלֹא תָתוּרוּ אַחֲרֵי
לְבַבְכֶם וְאַחֲרֵי עֵינֵיכֶם, אֲשֶׁר־אַתֶּם זֹנִים אַחֲרֵיהֶם: לְמַעַן תִּזְכְּרוּ

---

because listening is active, while hearing is passive. This, the most famous line of Jewish prayer, is a call to action on the part of the mind, emotion and will. It asks us to reflect on, strive to understand, and to affirm the unity of God. God speaks in a "still, small voice" (I Kings 19:12), and to serve Him is to listen with the totality of our being.

commandments, and be holy to your God. I am the LORD your God, who brought you out of the land of Egypt to be your God. I am the LORD your God.

True –

The Leader repeats:

▸ The LORD your God is true –

וֶאֱמוּנָה – and faithful is all this,
and firmly established for us
that He is the LORD our God,
and there is none besides Him,
and that we, Israel, are His people.
He is our King, who redeems us from the hand of kings
and delivers us from the grasp of all tyrants.
He is our God,
who on our behalf repays our foes
and brings just retribution on our mortal enemies;
who performs great deeds beyond understanding
and wonders beyond number;
who kept us alive, not letting our foot slip; *Ps. 66*
who led us on the high places of our enemies,
raising our pride above all our foes;
who did miracles for us
and brought vengeance against Pharaoh;
who performed signs and wonders
in the land of Ham's children;
who smote in His wrath all the firstborn of Egypt,
and brought out His people Israel from their midst
into everlasting freedom;
who led His children through the divided Reed Sea,
plunging their pursuers and enemies into the depths.

וַעֲשִׂיתֶם אֶת־כָּל־מִצְוֺתָי, וִהְיִיתֶם קְדֹשִׁים לֵאלֹהֵיכֶם: אֲנִי יְהוָה אֱלֹהֵיכֶם, אֲשֶׁר הוֹצֵאתִי אֶתְכֶם מֵאֶרֶץ מִצְרַיִם, לִהְיוֹת לָכֶם לֵאלֹהִים, אֲנִי יְהוָה אֱלֹהֵיכֶם:

אֱמֶת

The שליח ציבור *repeats:*

◂ יהוה אֱלֹהֵיכֶם אֱמֶת

וֶאֱמוּנָה כָּל זֹאת וְקַיָּם עָלֵינוּ
כִּי הוּא יהוה אֱלֹהֵינוּ וְאֵין זוּלָתוֹ
וַאֲנַחְנוּ יִשְׂרָאֵל עַמּוֹ.
הַפּוֹדֵנוּ מִיַּד מְלָכִים
מַלְכֵּנוּ הַגּוֹאֲלֵנוּ מִכַּף כָּל הֶעָרִיצִים.
הָאֵל הַנִּפְרָע לָנוּ מִצָּרֵינוּ
וְהַמְשַׁלֵּם גְּמוּל לְכָל אוֹיְבֵי נַפְשֵׁנוּ.
הָעוֹשֶׂה גְדוֹלוֹת עַד אֵין חֵקֶר, וְנִפְלָאוֹת עַד אֵין מִסְפָּר
הַשָּׂם נַפְשֵׁנוּ בַּחַיִּים, וְלֹא־נָתַן לַמּוֹט רַגְלֵנוּ: תהלים סו
הַמַּדְרִיכֵנוּ עַל בָּמוֹת אוֹיְבֵינוּ
וַיָּרֶם קַרְנֵנוּ עַל כָּל שׂוֹנְאֵינוּ.
הָעוֹשֶׂה לָּנוּ נִסִּים וּנְקָמָה בְּפַרְעֹה
אוֹתוֹת וּמוֹפְתִים בְּאַדְמַת בְּנֵי חָם.
הַמַּכֶּה בְעֶבְרָתוֹ כָּל בְּכוֹרֵי מִצְרָיִם
וַיּוֹצֵא אֶת עַמּוֹ יִשְׂרָאֵל מִתּוֹכָם לְחֵרוּת עוֹלָם.
הַמַּעֲבִיר בָּנָיו בֵּין גִּזְרֵי יַם סוּף
אֶת רוֹדְפֵיהֶם וְאֶת שׂוֹנְאֵיהֶם בִּתְהוֹמוֹת טִבַּע

When His children saw His might,
they gave praise and thanks to His name,
▸ and willingly accepted His Sovereignty.
Moses and the children of Israel
then sang a song to You with great joy, and they all exclaimed:

"Who is like You, LORD, among the mighty? *Ex. 15*
Who is like You, majestic in holiness,
awesome in praises, doing wonders?"

▸ Your children beheld Your majesty
as You parted the sea before Moses.
"This is my God!" they responded, and then said:

"The LORD shall reign for ever and ever." *Ex. 15*

▸ And it is said,
"For the LORD has redeemed Jacob *Jer. 31*
and rescued him from a power stronger than his own."
Blessed are You, LORD, who redeemed Israel.

הַשְׁכִּיבֵנוּ Help us lie down, O LORD our God, in peace,
and rise up, O our King, to life.
Spread over us Your canopy of peace.
Direct us with Your good counsel,
and save us for the sake of Your name.
Shield us and remove from us every enemy,
plague, sword, famine and sorrow.
Remove the adversary from before and behind us.
Shelter us in the shadow of Your wings,
for You, God, are our Guardian and Deliverer;
You, God, are a gracious and compassionate King.
▸ Guard our going out and our coming in,
for life and peace, from now and for ever.
Spread over us Your canopy of peace.
Blessed are You, LORD, who spreads a canopy of peace over us,
over all His people Israel, and over Jerusalem.

וְרָאוּ בָנָיו גְּבוּרָתוֹ, שִׁבְּחוּ וְהוֹדוּ לִשְׁמוֹ
· וּמַלְכוּתוֹ בְּרָצוֹן קִבְּלוּ עֲלֵיהֶם.
מֹשֶׁה וּבְנֵי יִשְׂרָאֵל, לְךָ עָנוּ שִׁירָה בְּשִׂמְחָה רַבָּה
וְאָמְרוּ כֻלָּם

מִי־כָמֹכָה בָּאֵלִם יהוה (שמות טו)
מִי כָּמֹכָה נֶאְדָּר בַּקֹּדֶשׁ
נוֹרָא תְהִלֹּת עֹשֵׂה פֶלֶא:

· מַלְכוּתְךָ רָאוּ בָנֶיךָ, בּוֹקֵעַ יָם לִפְנֵי מֹשֶׁה
זֶה אֵלִי עָנוּ, וְאָמְרוּ
יהוה יִמְלֹךְ לְעֹלָם וָעֶד: (שמות טו)

· וְנֶאֱמַר
כִּי־פָדָה יהוה אֶת־יַעֲקֹב, וּגְאָלוֹ מִיַּד חָזָק מִמֶּנּוּ: (ירמיהו לא)
בָּרוּךְ אַתָּה יהוה, גָּאַל יִשְׂרָאֵל.

הַשְׁכִּיבֵנוּ יהוה אֱלֹהֵינוּ לְשָׁלוֹם, וְהַעֲמִידֵנוּ מַלְכֵּנוּ לְחַיִּים
וּפְרֹשׂ עָלֵינוּ סֻכַּת שְׁלוֹמֶךָ, וְתַקְּנֵנוּ בְּעֵצָה טוֹבָה מִלְּפָנֶיךָ
וְהוֹשִׁיעֵנוּ לְמַעַן שְׁמֶךָ.
וְהָגֵן בַּעֲדֵנוּ, וְהָסֵר מֵעָלֵינוּ אוֹיֵב, דֶּבֶר וְחֶרֶב וְרָעָב וְיָגוֹן
וְהָסֵר שָׂטָן מִלְּפָנֵינוּ וּמֵאַחֲרֵינוּ, וּבְצֵל כְּנָפֶיךָ תַּסְתִּירֵנוּ
כִּי אֵל שׁוֹמְרֵנוּ וּמַצִּילֵנוּ אָתָּה
כִּי אֵל מֶלֶךְ חַנּוּן וְרַחוּם אָתָּה.
· וּשְׁמֹר צֵאתֵנוּ וּבוֹאֵנוּ לְחַיִּים וּלְשָׁלוֹם מֵעַתָּה וְעַד עוֹלָם.
וּפְרֹשׂ עָלֵינוּ סֻכַּת שְׁלוֹמֶךָ.
בָּרוּךְ אַתָּה יהוה
הַפּוֹרֵשׂ סֻכַּת שָׁלוֹם עָלֵינוּ וְעַל כָּל עַמּוֹ יִשְׂרָאֵל וְעַל יְרוּשָׁלָיִם.

On Shabbat, the congregation stands and, together with the Leader, says:

וְשָׁמְרוּ The children of Israel must keep the Sabbath, *Ex. 31*
observing the Sabbath in every generation
as an everlasting covenant.
It is a sign between Me and the children of Israel for ever,
for in six days God made the heavens and the earth,
but on the seventh day He ceased work
and refreshed Himself.

On Yom Tov of the Three Festivals, say:

וַיְדַבֵּר Thus Moses announced the LORD's appointed seasons *Lev. 23*
to the children of Israel.

HALF KADDISH

Leader: יִתְגַּדַּל Magnified and sanctified may His great name be,
in the world He created by His will.
May He establish His kingdom
in your lifetime and in your days,
and in the lifetime of all the house of Israel,
swiftly and soon –
and say: Amen.

All: May His great name be blessed
for ever and all time.

Leader: Blessed and praised,
glorified and exalted,
raised and honored,
uplifted and lauded
be the name of the Holy One,
blessed be He,
beyond any blessing,
song, praise and consolation
uttered in the world –
and say: Amen.

On שבת*, the* קהל *stands and, together with the* שליח ציבור*, says:*

וְשָׁמְרוּ בְנֵי־יִשְׂרָאֵל אֶת־הַשַּׁבָּת שמות לא
לַעֲשׂוֹת אֶת־הַשַּׁבָּת לְדֹרֹתָם בְּרִית עוֹלָם:
בֵּינִי וּבֵין בְּנֵי יִשְׂרָאֵל, אוֹת הִוא לְעֹלָם
כִּי־שֵׁשֶׁת יָמִים עָשָׂה יהוה אֶת־הַשָּׁמַיִם וְאֶת־הָאָרֶץ
וּבַיּוֹם הַשְּׁבִיעִי שָׁבַת וַיִּנָּפַשׁ:

On יום טוב *of the* שלוש רגלים*, say:*

וַיְדַבֵּר מֹשֶׁה אֶת־מֹעֲדֵי יהוה אֶל־בְּנֵי יִשְׂרָאֵל: ויקרא כג

חצי קדיש

ש״ץ: יִתְגַּדַּל וְיִתְקַדַּשׁ שְׁמֵהּ רַבָּא (קהל: אָמֵן)
בְּעָלְמָא דִּי בְרָא כִרְעוּתֵהּ
וְיַמְלִיךְ מַלְכוּתֵהּ
בְּחַיֵּיכוֹן וּבְיוֹמֵיכוֹן וּבְחַיֵּי דְכָל בֵּית יִשְׂרָאֵל
בַּעֲגָלָא וּבִזְמַן קָרִיב
וְאִמְרוּ אָמֵן. (קהל: אָמֵן)

קהל וש״ץ: יְהֵא שְׁמֵהּ רַבָּא מְבָרַךְ לְעָלַם וּלְעָלְמֵי עָלְמַיָּא.

ש״ץ: יִתְבָּרַךְ וְיִשְׁתַּבַּח וְיִתְפָּאַר וְיִתְרוֹמַם וְיִתְנַשֵּׂא
וְיִתְהַדָּר וְיִתְעַלֶּה וְיִתְהַלָּל
שְׁמֵהּ דְּקֻדְשָׁא בְּרִיךְ הוּא (קהל: בְּרִיךְ הוּא)
לְעֵלָּא מִן כָּל בִּרְכָתָא
/בשבת שובה: לְעֵלָּא לְעֵלָּא מִכָּל בִּרְכָתָא/
וְשִׁירָתָא, תֻּשְׁבְּחָתָא וְנֶחֱמָתָא, דַּאֲמִירָן בְּעָלְמָא
וְאִמְרוּ אָמֵן. (קהל: אָמֵן)

On Yom Tov (including one that falls on Shabbat) say the appropriate Amida on page 770.

THE AMIDA

The following prayer, until "in former years" on page 358, is said silently, standing with feet together. Take three steps forward and at the points indicated by ▾, bend the knees at the first word, bow at the second, and stand straight before saying God's name.

O LORD, open my lips, Ps. 51
so that my mouth may declare Your praise.

PATRIARCHS

▾בָּרוּךְ Blessed are You, LORD our God and God of our fathers,
God of Abraham, God of Isaac and God of Jacob;
the great, mighty and awesome God, God Most High,
who bestows acts of loving-kindness and creates all,
who remembers the loving-kindness of the fathers
and will bring a Redeemer to their children's children
for the sake of His name, in love.

On Shabbat Shuva: Remember us for life, O King who desires life,
and write us in the book of life –
for Your sake, O God of life.

King, Helper, Savior, Shield:
▾Blessed are You, LORD, Shield of Abraham.

---

evening, we think of the birth of time; in the morning, of historical time, the remembered past and the living present; and in the afternoon, of the culmination of time, and the World to Come of which Shabbat is the foretaste. Shabbat becomes a journey through the three phases of faith: God's creation of the universe, His self-revelation to humanity, and His redemptive acts – collectively summoning us to build a world at peace with itself because it is at peace with God.

Another interpretation sees in the three stages of Shabbat the three parts of a wedding: first betrothal, *kiddushin*; then the marriage itself, symbolized by joy; then *yiḥud*, the coming together of the bride and groom (Abudarham). This idea, reflected in the language of the Amida, accords with the mystical understanding of Shabbat as a bride, and the day itself as a marriage of heaven and earth.

On יום טוב *(including one that falls on* שבת*) say the appropriate* עמידה *on page 771.*

עמידה

The following prayer, until קַדְמֹנִיּוֹת *on page 359, is said silently, standing with feet together. Take three steps forward and at the points indicated by* ', *bend the knees at the first word, bow at the second, and stand straight before saying God's name.*

אֲדֹנָי, שְׂפָתַי תִּפְתָּח, וּפִי יַגִּיד תְּהִלָּתֶךָ: תהלים נא

אבות

'בָּרוּךְ אַתָּה יהוה, אֱלֹהֵינוּ וֵאלֹהֵי אֲבוֹתֵינוּ
אֱלֹהֵי אַבְרָהָם, אֱלֹהֵי יִצְחָק, וֵאלֹהֵי יַעֲקֹב
הָאֵל הַגָּדוֹל הַגִּבּוֹר וְהַנּוֹרָא, אֵל עֶלְיוֹן
גּוֹמֵל חֲסָדִים טוֹבִים, וְקוֹנֵה הַכֹּל
וְזוֹכֵר חַסְדֵי אָבוֹת
וּמֵבִיא גּוֹאֵל לִבְנֵי בְנֵיהֶם לְמַעַן שְׁמוֹ בְּאַהֲבָה.

בשבת שובה: זָכְרֵנוּ לְחַיִּים, מֶלֶךְ חָפֵץ בַּחַיִּים
וְכָתְבֵנוּ בְּסֵפֶר הַחַיִּים, לְמַעַנְךָ אֱלֹהִים חַיִּים.

מֶלֶךְ עוֹזֵר וּמוֹשִׁיעַ וּמָגֵן.
'בָּרוּךְ אַתָּה יהוה, מָגֵן אַבְרָהָם.

THE FRIDAY NIGHT AMIDA

On Shabbat and Yom Tov, the Amida, the "standing prayer," consists not of nineteen but seven blessings (in Musaf of Rosh HaShana, nine). The first and last three are, with minor variations, the same throughout the year. The seventh (middle) blessing is dedicated to the special "sanctity of the day." Uniquely on Shabbat, this blessing is different for each of the three services; evening, morning and afternoon (the Musaf prayer is in a category of its own). The quality of time on Shabbat is different from other days: like a symphony, it has several movements.

On Friday evening, we speak of the Shabbat of creation; in the morning, of the Shabbat of revelation, as it was commanded on Mount Sinai; and in the afternoon, we look forward to the Shabbat of redemption. Thus in the

DIVINE MIGHT

אַתָּה גִּבּוֹר You are eternally mighty, Lord.
You give life to the dead and have great power to save.

The phrase "He makes the wind blow and the rain fall" is added from Simḥat Torah until Pesaḥ. In Israel, the phrase "He causes the dew to fall" is added from Pesaḥ until Shemini Atzeret. See laws 129–131.

In fall & winter: He makes the wind blow and the rain fall.
In Israel, in spring & summer: He causes the dew to fall.

He sustains the living with loving-kindness,
and with great compassion revives the dead.
He supports the fallen, heals the sick, sets captives free,
and keeps His faith with those who sleep in the dust.
Who is like You, Master of might, and and who can compare to You,
O King who brings death and gives life, and makes salvation grow?

On Shabbat Shuva: Who is like You, compassionate Father,
who remembers His creatures in compassion, for life?

Faithful are You to revive the dead.
Blessed are You, Lord, who revives the dead.

HOLINESS

אַתָּה קָדוֹשׁ You are holy and Your name is holy,
and holy ones praise You daily, Selah!
Blessed are You, Lord,
the holy God. / *On Shabbat Shuva:* the holy King./
(If forgotten, repeat the Amida.)

HOLINESS OF THE DAY

אַתָּה קִדַּשְׁתָּ You sanctified the seventh day
for Your name's sake,
as the culmination of the creation of heaven and earth.
Of all days, You blessed it; of all seasons You sanctified it –
and so it is written in Your Torah:

---

ning of time: the seventh day of creation when God rested and the universe was young. It also uses the word "sanctified," the key word of the betrothal declaration under the bridal canopy.

גבורות

אַתָּה גִּבּוֹר לְעוֹלָם, אֲדֹנָי
מְחַיֵּה מֵתִים אַתָּה, רַב לְהוֹשִׁיעַ

The phrase מַשִּׁיב הָרְוּחַ *is added from* שמחת תורה *until* פסח.
In ארץ ישראל *the phrase* מוֹרִיד הַטָּל *is added from* פסח *until* שמיני עצרת. *See laws 129–131.*

בחורף: מַשִּׁיב הָרְוּחַ וּמוֹרִיד הַגֶּשֶׁם / בארץ ישראל בקיץ: מוֹרִיד הַטָּל

מְכַלְכֵּל חַיִּים בְּחֶסֶד, מְחַיֵּה מֵתִים בְּרַחֲמִים רַבִּים
סוֹמֵךְ נוֹפְלִים, וְרוֹפֵא חוֹלִים, וּמַתִּיר אֲסוּרִים
וּמְקַיֵּם אֱמוּנָתוֹ לִישֵׁנֵי עָפָר.
מִי כָמְוֹךָ, בַּעַל גְּבוּרוֹת, וּמִי דּוֹמֶה לָּךְ
מֶלֶךְ, מֵמִית וּמְחַיֶּה וּמַצְמִיחַ יְשׁוּעָה.

בשבת שובה: מִי כָמְוֹךָ אַב הָרַחֲמִים, זוֹכֵר יְצוּרָיו לְחַיִּים בְּרַחֲמִים.

וְנֶאֱמָן אַתָּה לְהַחֲיוֹת מֵתִים.
בָּרוּךְ אַתָּה יהוה, מְחַיֵּה הַמֵּתִים.

קדושת השם

אַתָּה קָדוֹשׁ וְשִׁמְךָ קָדוֹשׁ, וּקְדוֹשִׁים בְּכָל יוֹם יְהַלְלְוּךָ סֶּלָה.
בָּרוּךְ אַתָּה יהוה, הָאֵל הַקָּדוֹשׁ. / בשבת שובה: הַמֶּלֶךְ הַקָּדוֹשׁ./

(*If forgotten, repeat the* עמידה.)

קדושת היום

אַתָּה קִדַּשְׁתָּ אֶת יוֹם הַשְּׁבִיעִי לִשְׁמֶךָ
תַּכְלִית מַעֲשֵׂה שָׁמַיִם וָאָרֶץ
וּבֵרַכְתּוֹ מִכָּל הַיָּמִים, וְקִדַּשְׁתּוֹ מִכָּל הַזְּמַנִּים
וְכֵן כָּתוּב בְּתוֹרָתֶךָ

אַתָּה קִדַּשְׁתָּ *You sanctified:* As signaled above, the Friday evening blessing speaks of creation: "You sanctified the seventh day for Your name's sake, as the culmination of the creation of heaven and earth." It refers to the begin-

וַיְכֻלּוּ Then the heavens and the earth were completed, Gen. 2
and all their array.
With the seventh day, God completed the work He had done.
He ceased on the seventh day from all the work He had done.
God blessed the seventh day and declared it holy,
because on it He ceased from all His work
He had created to do.

אֱלֹהֵינוּ Our God and God of our ancestors,
may You find favor in our rest.
Make us holy through Your commandments
and grant us our share in Your Torah.
Satisfy us with Your goodness, grant us joy in Your salvation,
and purify our hearts to serve You in truth.
In love and favor, O Lord our God,
grant us as our heritage Your holy Shabbat,
so that Israel, who sanctify Your name, may find rest on it.
Blessed are You, Lord,
who sanctifies the Sabbath.

TEMPLE SERVICE

רְצֵה Find favor, Lord our God,
in Your people Israel and their prayer.
Restore the service to Your most holy House,
and accept in love and favor
the fire-offerings of Israel and their prayer.
May the service of Your people Israel
always find favor with You.

וַיְקַדֵּשׁ אֹתוֹ *And declared it holy:* This is the first time the word "holy" appears in the Torah, indicating that time, not just space, is holy. The sages noted the similarities between Shabbat and the Sanctuary (*mishkan*) constructed by the Israelites in the wilderness. The thirty-nine categories of work performed in the building of the Sanctuary are the same as those forbidden on Shabbat. Shabbat is thus a "sanctuary in time," and Israel, the "eternal people," is the nation called on to sanctify time.

וַיְכֻלּוּ הַשָּׁמַיִם וְהָאָרֶץ וְכָל־צְבָאָם: בראשית ב
וַיְכַל אֱלֹהִים בַּיּוֹם הַשְּׁבִיעִי מְלַאכְתּוֹ אֲשֶׁר עָשָׂה
וַיִּשְׁבֹּת בַּיּוֹם הַשְּׁבִיעִי מִכָּל־מְלַאכְתּוֹ אֲשֶׁר עָשָׂה:
וַיְבָרֶךְ אֱלֹהִים אֶת־יוֹם הַשְּׁבִיעִי, וַיְקַדֵּשׁ אֹתוֹ
כִּי בוֹ שָׁבַת מִכָּל־מְלַאכְתּוֹ, אֲשֶׁר־בָּרָא אֱלֹהִים לַעֲשׂוֹת:

אֱלֹהֵינוּ וֵאלֹהֵי אֲבוֹתֵינוּ, רְצֵה בִמְנוּחָתֵנוּ.
קַדְּשֵׁנוּ בְּמִצְוֹתֶיךָ, וְתֵן חֶלְקֵנוּ בְּתוֹרָתֶךָ
שַׂבְּעֵנוּ מִטּוּבֶךָ, וְשַׂמְּחֵנוּ בִּישׁוּעָתֶךָ
וְטַהֵר לִבֵּנוּ לְעָבְדְּךָ בֶּאֱמֶת.
וְהַנְחִילֵנוּ, יהוה אֱלֹהֵינוּ, בְּאַהֲבָה וּבְרָצוֹן שַׁבַּת קָדְשֶׁךָ
וְיָנוּחוּ בָהּ יִשְׂרָאֵל מְקַדְּשֵׁי שְׁמֶךָ.
בָּרוּךְ אַתָּה יהוה, מְקַדֵּשׁ הַשַּׁבָּת.

עבודה

רְצֵה יהוה אֱלֹהֵינוּ בְּעַמְּךָ יִשְׂרָאֵל, וּבִתְפִלָּתָם
וְהָשֵׁב אֶת הָעֲבוֹדָה לִדְבִיר בֵּיתֶךָ
וְאִשֵּׁי יִשְׂרָאֵל וּתְפִלָּתָם בְּאַהֲבָה תְקַבֵּל בְּרָצוֹן
וּתְהִי לְרָצוֹן תָּמִיד עֲבוֹדַת יִשְׂרָאֵל עַמֶּךָ.

וַיְכֻלּוּ הַשָּׁמַיִם וְהָאָרֶץ *Then the heavens and the earth were completed:* These three verses conclude the biblical account of creation. They contain thirty-five (5×7) words. The entire creation narrative (Gen. 1:1–2:3) is constructed in multiples of seven. The word "good" appears seven times, the word "God" thirty-five times, and the word "earth" twenty-one times. The opening verse contains seven words, the second fourteen, and the complete text 469 (7×67) words. From the very outset, seven dominates, as if to signal from the beginning that the seventh day was the culmination and purpose of creation: "last in deed, first in thought."

On Rosh Ḥodesh and Ḥol HaMo'ed:
אֱלֹהֵינוּ Our God and God of our ancestors, may there rise, come, reach, appear, be favored, heard, regarded and remembered before You, our recollection and remembrance, as well as the remembrance of our ancestors, and of the Messiah son of David Your servant, and of Jerusalem Your holy city, and of all Your people the house of Israel – for deliverance and well-being, grace, loving-kindness and compassion, life and peace, on this day of:

On Rosh Ḥodesh: Rosh Ḥodesh.
On Pesaḥ: the Festival of Matzot.
On Sukkot: the Festival of Sukkot.

On it remember us, Lord our God, for good; recollect us for blessing, and deliver us for life. In accord with Your promise of salvation and compassion, spare us and be gracious to us; have compassion on us and deliver us, for our eyes are turned to You because You, God, are a gracious and compassionate King.

וְתֶחֱזֶינָה And may our eyes witness Your return to Zion in compassion. Blessed are You, Lord, who restores His Presence to Zion.

THANKSGIVING

Bow at the first nine words.

מוֹדִים We give thanks to You,
for You are the Lord our God and God of our ancestors
for ever and all time.
You are the Rock of our lives,
Shield of our salvation from generation to generation.
We will thank You and declare Your praise for our lives,
which are entrusted into Your hand;
for our souls, which are placed in Your charge;
for Your miracles which are with us every day;
and for Your wonders and favors
at all times, evening, morning and midday.
You are good – for Your compassion never fails.
You are compassionate – for Your loving-kindnesses never cease.
We have always placed our hope in You.

On ראש חודש *and* חול המועד:

אֱלֹהֵינוּ וֵאלֹהֵי אֲבוֹתֵינוּ, יַעֲלֶה וְיָבוֹא וְיַגִּיעַ, וְיֵרָאֶה וְיֵרָצֶה וְיִשָּׁמַע, וְיִפָּקֵד וְיִזָּכֵר זִכְרוֹנֵנוּ וּפִקְדּוֹנֵנוּ וְזִכְרוֹן אֲבוֹתֵינוּ, וְזִכְרוֹן מָשִׁיחַ בֶּן דָּוִד עַבְדֶּךָ, וְזִכְרוֹן יְרוּשָׁלַיִם עִיר קָדְשֶׁךָ, וְזִכְרוֹן כָּל עַמְּךָ בֵּית יִשְׂרָאֵל, לְפָנֶיךָ, לִפְלֵיטָה לְטוֹבָה, לְחֵן וּלְחֶסֶד וּלְרַחֲמִים, לְחַיִּים וּלְשָׁלוֹם בְּיוֹם

בראש חודש: רֹאשׁ הַחֹדֶשׁ / בפסח: חַג הַמַּצּוֹת / בסוכות: חַג הַסֻּכּוֹת

הַזֶּה. זָכְרֵנוּ יהוה אֱלֹהֵינוּ בּוֹ לְטוֹבָה, וּפָקְדֵנוּ בוֹ לִבְרָכָה, וְהוֹשִׁיעֵנוּ בוֹ לְחַיִּים. וּבִדְבַר יְשׁוּעָה וְרַחֲמִים, חוּס וְחָנֵּנוּ וְרַחֵם עָלֵינוּ וְהוֹשִׁיעֵנוּ, כִּי אֵלֶיךָ עֵינֵינוּ, כִּי אֵל מֶלֶךְ חַנּוּן וְרַחוּם אָתָּה.

וְתֶחֱזֶינָה עֵינֵינוּ בְּשׁוּבְךָ לְצִיּוֹן בְּרַחֲמִים.
בָּרוּךְ אַתָּה יהוה, הַמַּחֲזִיר שְׁכִינָתוֹ לְצִיּוֹן.

הודאה

Bow at the first five words.

מוֹדִים אֲנַחְנוּ לָךְ
שָׁאַתָּה הוּא יהוה אֱלֹהֵינוּ וֵאלֹהֵי אֲבוֹתֵינוּ לְעוֹלָם וָעֶד.
צוּר חַיֵּינוּ, מָגֵן יִשְׁעֵנוּ, אַתָּה הוּא לְדוֹר וָדוֹר.
נוֹדֶה לְּךָ וּנְסַפֵּר תְּהִלָּתֶךָ
עַל חַיֵּינוּ הַמְּסוּרִים בְּיָדֶךָ
וְעַל נִשְׁמוֹתֵינוּ הַפְּקוּדוֹת לָךְ
וְעַל נִסֶּיךָ שֶׁבְּכָל יוֹם עִמָּנוּ
וְעַל נִפְלְאוֹתֶיךָ וְטוֹבוֹתֶיךָ שֶׁבְּכָל עֵת, עֶרֶב וָבֹקֶר וְצָהֳרָיִם.
הַטּוֹב, כִּי לֹא כָלוּ רַחֲמֶיךָ
וְהַמְרַחֵם, כִּי לֹא תַמּוּ חֲסָדֶיךָ
מֵעוֹלָם קִוִּינוּ לָךְ.

On Ḥanukka:

עַל הַנִּסִּים [We thank You also] for the miracles, the redemption, the mighty deeds, the salvations, and the victories in battle which You performed for our ancestors in those days, at this time.

בִּימֵי מַתִּתְיָהוּ In the days of Mattityahu, son of Yoḥanan, the High Priest, the Hasmonean, and his sons, the wicked Greek kingdom rose up against Your people Israel to make them forget Your Torah and to force them to transgress the statutes of Your will. It was then that You in Your great compassion stood by them in the time of their distress. You championed their cause, judged their claim, and avenged their wrong. You delivered the strong into the hands of the weak, the many into the hands of the few, the impure into the hands of the pure, the wicked into the hands of the righteous, and the arrogant into the hands of those who were engaged in the study of Your Torah. You made for Yourself great and holy renown in Your world, and for Your people Israel You performed a great salvation and redemption as of this very day. Your children then entered the holiest part of Your House, cleansed Your Temple, purified Your Sanctuary, kindled lights in Your holy courts, and designated these eight days of Ḥanukka for giving thanks and praise to Your great name. *Continue with "For all these things."*

On Shushan Purim in Jerusalem:

עַל הַנִּסִּים [We thank You also] for the miracles, the redemption, the mighty deeds, the salvations, and the victories in battle which You performed for our ancestors in those days, at this time.

בִּימֵי מָרְדְּכַי In the days of Mordekhai and Esther, in Shushan the capital, the wicked Haman rose up against them and sought to destroy, slay and exterminate *Esther 3* all the Jews, young and old, children and women, on one day, the thirteenth day of the twelfth month, which is the month of Adar, and to plunder their possessions. Then You in Your great compassion thwarted his counsel, frustrated his plans, and caused his scheme to recoil on his own head, so that they hanged him and his sons on the gallows. *Continue with "For all these things."*

וְעַל כֻּלָּם For all these things may Your name be blessed and exalted, our King, continually, for ever and all time.

On Shabbat Shuva: And write, for a good life,
all the children of Your covenant.

Let all that lives thank You, Selah! and praise Your name in truth,
God, our Savior and Help, Selah!
▾Blessed are You, Lord, whose name is "the Good"
and to whom thanks are due.

בחנוכה:

עַל הַנִּסִּים וְעַל הַפֻּרְקָן וְעַל הַגְּבוּרוֹת וְעַל הַתְּשׁוּעוֹת וְעַל הַמִּלְחָמוֹת שֶׁעָשִׂיתָ לַאֲבוֹתֵינוּ בַּיָּמִים הָהֵם בַּזְּמַן הַזֶּה.

בִּימֵי מַתִּתְיָהוּ בֶּן יוֹחָנָן כֹּהֵן גָּדוֹל חַשְׁמוֹנַאי וּבָנָיו, כְּשֶׁעָמְדָה מַלְכוּת יָוָן הָרְשָׁעָה עַל עַמְּךָ יִשְׂרָאֵל לְהַשְׁכִּיחָם תּוֹרָתֶךָ וּלְהַעֲבִירָם מֵחֻקֵּי רְצוֹנֶךָ, וְאַתָּה בְּרַחֲמֶיךָ הָרַבִּים עָמַדְתָּ לָהֶם בְּעֵת צָרָתָם, רַבְתָּ אֶת רִיבָם, דַּנְתָּ אֶת דִּינָם, נָקַמְתָּ אֶת נִקְמָתָם, מָסַרְתָּ גִבּוֹרִים בְּיַד חַלָּשִׁים, וְרַבִּים בְּיַד מְעַטִּים, וּטְמֵאִים בְּיַד טְהוֹרִים, וּרְשָׁעִים בְּיַד צַדִּיקִים, וְזֵדִים בְּיַד עוֹסְקֵי תוֹרָתֶךָ, וּלְךָ עָשִׂיתָ שֵׁם גָּדוֹל וְקָדוֹשׁ בְּעוֹלָמֶךָ, וּלְעַמְּךָ יִשְׂרָאֵל עָשִׂיתָ תְּשׁוּעָה גְדוֹלָה וּפֻרְקָן כְּהַיּוֹם הַזֶּה. וְאַחַר כֵּן בָּאוּ בָנֶיךָ לִדְבִיר בֵּיתֶךָ, וּפִנּוּ אֶת הֵיכָלֶךָ, וְטִהֲרוּ אֶת מִקְדָּשֶׁךָ, וְהִדְלִיקוּ נֵרוֹת בְּחַצְרוֹת קָדְשֶׁךָ, וְקָבְעוּ שְׁמוֹנַת יְמֵי חֲנֻכָּה אֵלּוּ, לְהוֹדוֹת וּלְהַלֵּל לְשִׁמְךָ הַגָּדוֹל.

Continue with וְעַל כֻּלָּם.

בשושן פורים בירושלים:

עַל הַנִּסִּים וְעַל הַפֻּרְקָן וְעַל הַגְּבוּרוֹת וְעַל הַתְּשׁוּעוֹת וְעַל הַמִּלְחָמוֹת שֶׁעָשִׂיתָ לַאֲבוֹתֵינוּ בַּיָּמִים הָהֵם בַּזְּמַן הַזֶּה.

בִּימֵי מָרְדְּכַי וְאֶסְתֵּר בְּשׁוּשַׁן הַבִּירָה, כְּשֶׁעָמַד עֲלֵיהֶם הָמָן הָרָשָׁע, בִּקֵּשׁ לְהַשְׁמִיד לַהֲרֹג וּלְאַבֵּד אֶת־כָּל־הַיְּהוּדִים מִנַּעַר וְעַד־זָקֵן טַף וְנָשִׁים בְּיוֹם אֶחָד, בִּשְׁלוֹשָׁה עָשָׂר לְחֹדֶשׁ שְׁנֵים־עָשָׂר, הוּא־חֹדֶשׁ אֲדָר, וּשְׁלָלָם לָבוֹז: וְאַתָּה בְּרַחֲמֶיךָ הָרַבִּים הֵפַרְתָּ אֶת עֲצָתוֹ, וְקִלְקַלְתָּ אֶת מַחֲשַׁבְתּוֹ, וַהֲשֵׁבוֹתָ לּוֹ גְּמוּלוֹ בְּרֹאשׁוֹ, וְתָלוּ אוֹתוֹ וְאֶת בָּנָיו עַל הָעֵץ. אסתר ג

Continue with וְעַל כֻּלָּם.

וְעַל כֻּלָּם יִתְבָּרַךְ וְיִתְרוֹמַם שִׁמְךָ מַלְכֵּנוּ תָּמִיד לְעוֹלָם וָעֶד.

בשבת שובה: וּכְתֹב לְחַיִּים טוֹבִים כָּל בְּנֵי בְרִיתֶךָ.

וְכֹל הַחַיִּים יוֹדוּךָ סֶּלָה, וִיהַלְלוּ אֶת שִׁמְךָ בֶּאֱמֶת הָאֵל יְשׁוּעָתֵנוּ וְעֶזְרָתֵנוּ סֶלָה.

בָּרוּךְ אַתָּה יְהוָה, הַטּוֹב שִׁמְךָ וּלְךָ נָאֶה לְהוֹדוֹת.

PEACE

שָׁלוֹם רָב Grant great peace to Your people Israel for ever,
for You are the sovereign LORD of all peace;
and may it be good in Your eyes
to bless Your people Israel
at every time, at every hour, with Your peace.

On Shabbat Shuva: In the book of life, blessing, peace and prosperity,
may we and all Your people the house of Israel
be remembered and written before You
for a good life, and for peace.*

Blessed are You, LORD, who blesses His people Israel with peace.

**On Shabbat Shuva outside Israel, many end the blessing:*
Blessed are You, LORD, who makes peace.

Some say the following verse (see law 368):
May the words of my mouth and the meditation of my heart Ps. 19
find favor before You, LORD, my Rock and Redeemer.

אֱלֹהַי My God, Berakhot 17a
guard my tongue from evil and my lips from deceitful speech.
To those who curse me, let my soul be silent;
may my soul be to all like the dust.
Open my heart to Your Torah
and let my soul pursue Your commandments.
As for all who plan evil against me,
swiftly thwart their counsel and frustrate their plans.
Act for the sake of Your name; act for the sake of Your right hand;
act for the sake of Your holiness; act for the sake of Your Torah.
That Your beloved ones may be delivered, Ps. 60
save with Your right hand and answer me.
May the words of my mouth Ps. 19
and the meditation of my heart find favor before You,
LORD, my Rock and Redeemer.

Bow, take three steps back, then bow, first left, then right, then center, while saying:
May He who makes peace in His high places,
make peace for us and all Israel – and say: Amen.

ברכת שלום

שָׁלוֹם רָב עַל יִשְׂרָאֵל עַמְּךָ תָּשִׂים לְעוֹלָם
כִּי אַתָּה הוּא מֶלֶךְ אָדוֹן לְכָל הַשָּׁלוֹם.
וְטוֹב בְּעֵינֶיךָ לְבָרֵךְ אֶת עַמְּךָ יִשְׂרָאֵל
בְּכָל עֵת וּבְכָל שָׁעָה בִּשְׁלוֹמֶךָ.

בשבת שובה: בְּסֵפֶר חַיִּים, בְּרָכָה וְשָׁלוֹם, וּפַרְנָסָה טוֹבָה
נִזָּכֵר וְנִכָּתֵב לְפָנֶיךָ, אֲנַחְנוּ וְכָל עַמְּךָ בֵּית יִשְׂרָאֵל
לְחַיִּים טוֹבִים וּלְשָׁלוֹם.*

בָּרוּךְ אַתָּה יהוה, הַמְבָרֵךְ אֶת עַמּוֹ יִשְׂרָאֵל בַּשָּׁלוֹם.

On שבת שובה in חוץ לארץ, many end the blessing:

בָּרוּךְ אַתָּה יהוה, עוֹשֵׂה הַשָּׁלוֹם.

Some say the following verse (see law 368):

יִהְיוּ לְרָצוֹן אִמְרֵי־פִי וְהֶגְיוֹן לִבִּי לְפָנֶיךָ, יהוה צוּרִי וְגֹאֲלִי: תהלים יט

אֱלֹהַי ברכות יז.
נְצֹר לְשׁוֹנִי מֵרָע וּשְׂפָתַי מִדַּבֵּר מִרְמָה
וְלִמְקַלְלַי נַפְשִׁי תִדֹּם, וְנַפְשִׁי כֶּעָפָר לַכֹּל תִּהְיֶה.
פְּתַח לִבִּי בְּתוֹרָתֶךָ, וּבְמִצְוֹתֶיךָ תִּרְדֹּף נַפְשִׁי.
וְכָל הַחוֹשְׁבִים עָלַי רָעָה
מְהֵרָה הָפֵר עֲצָתָם וְקַלְקֵל מַחֲשַׁבְתָּם.
עֲשֵׂה לְמַעַן שְׁמֶךָ, עֲשֵׂה לְמַעַן יְמִינֶךָ
עֲשֵׂה לְמַעַן קְדֻשָּׁתֶךָ, עֲשֵׂה לְמַעַן תּוֹרָתֶךָ.
לְמַעַן יֵחָלְצוּן יְדִידֶיךָ, הוֹשִׁיעָה יְמִינְךָ וַעֲנֵנִי: תהלים ס
יִהְיוּ לְרָצוֹן אִמְרֵי־פִי וְהֶגְיוֹן לִבִּי לְפָנֶיךָ, יהוה צוּרִי וְגֹאֲלִי: תהלים יט

Bow, take three steps back, then bow, first left, then right, then center, while saying:

עֹשֶׂה שָׁלוֹם/ בשבת שובה: הַשָּׁלוֹם/ בִּמְרוֹמָיו
הוּא יַעֲשֶׂה שָׁלוֹם עָלֵינוּ וְעַל כָּל יִשְׂרָאֵל, וְאִמְרוּ אָמֵן.

יְהִי רָצוֹן May it be Your will, Lord our God and God of our ancestors,
that the Temple be rebuilt speedily in our days, and grant us a share in Your Torah.
And there we will serve You with reverence,
as in the days of old and as in former years.
Then the offering of Judah and Jerusalem *Mal. 3*
will be pleasing to the Lord as in the days of old and as in former years.

All stand and say:

וַיְכֻלּוּ Then the heavens and the earth were completed, *Gen. 2*
and all their array.
With the seventh day, God completed the work He had done.
He ceased on the seventh day from all the work He had done.
God blessed the seventh day and declared it holy,
because on it He ceased from all His work He had created to do.

On the first two nights of Pesaḥ (first night in Israel), some congregations recite Hallel (page 732) at this point. The following until "who sanctifies the Sabbath" on page 360, is omitted when praying with an occasional minyan or alone. See law 453. It is also omitted when the first day of Pesaḥ falls on Shabbat.

The Leader continues:

בָּרוּךְ Blessed are You, Lord our God and God of our fathers,
God of Abraham, God of Isaac and God of Jacob,
the great, mighty and awesome God,
God Most High, Creator of heaven and earth.

The congregation then the Leader:

מָגֵן אָבוֹת By His word, He was the Shield of our ancestors.
By His promise, He will revive the dead.
There is none like the holy God/*On Shabbat Shuva:* the holy King/
who gives rest to His people on His holy Sabbath day,
for He found them worthy of His favor to give them rest.
Before Him we will come in worship with reverence and awe,
giving thanks to His name daily, continually, with due blessings.

---

tion ascribes it to the fact that in Babylon – where synagogues were, for the most part, outside town – going home at night was fraught with danger. This prayer was added for the benefit of latecomers, so that the congregation could leave together.

יְהִי רָצוֹן מִלְּפָנֶיךָ יהוה אֱלֹהֵינוּ וֵאלֹהֵי אֲבוֹתֵינוּ
שֶׁיִּבָּנֶה בֵּית הַמִּקְדָּשׁ בִּמְהֵרָה בְיָמֵינוּ, וְתֵן חֶלְקֵנוּ בְּתוֹרָתֶךָ
וְשָׁם נַעֲבָדְךָ בְּיִרְאָה כִּימֵי עוֹלָם וּכְשָׁנִים קַדְמֹנִיּוֹת.
וְעָרְבָה לַיהוה מִנְחַת יְהוּדָה וִירוּשָׁלָםִ כִּימֵי עוֹלָם וּכְשָׁנִים קַדְמֹנִיּוֹת: מלאכי ג

All stand and say:

בראשית ב
וַיְכֻלּוּ הַשָּׁמַיִם וְהָאָרֶץ וְכָל־צְבָאָם:
וַיְכַל אֱלֹהִים בַּיּוֹם הַשְּׁבִיעִי מְלַאכְתּוֹ אֲשֶׁר עָשָׂה
וַיִּשְׁבֹּת בַּיּוֹם הַשְּׁבִיעִי מִכָּל־מְלַאכְתּוֹ אֲשֶׁר עָשָׂה:
וַיְבָרֶךְ אֱלֹהִים אֶת־יוֹם הַשְּׁבִיעִי, וַיְקַדֵּשׁ אֹתוֹ
כִּי בוֹ שָׁבַת מִכָּל־מְלַאכְתּוֹ, אֲשֶׁר־בָּרָא אֱלֹהִים, לַעֲשׂוֹת:

On the first two nights of פסח *(first night in* ארץ ישראל*), some congregations recite* הלל *(page 733) at this point. The following until* מְקַדֵּשׁ הַשַּׁבָּת *on page 361, is omitted when praying with an occasional* מנין *or alone. See law 453. It is also omitted when the first day of* פסח *falls on* שבת*.*

The שליח ציבור *continues:*

בָּרוּךְ אַתָּה יהוה, אֱלֹהֵינוּ וֵאלֹהֵי אֲבוֹתֵינוּ
אֱלֹהֵי אַבְרָהָם, אֱלֹהֵי יִצְחָק, וֵאלֹהֵי יַעֲקֹב
הָאֵל הַגָּדוֹל הַגִּבּוֹר וְהַנּוֹרָא, אֵל עֶלְיוֹן, קֹנֵה שָׁמַיִם וָאָרֶץ.

The קהל *then the* שליח ציבור*:*

מָגֵן אָבוֹת בִּדְבָרוֹ, מְחַיֵּה מֵתִים בְּמַאֲמָרוֹ
הָאֵל / בשבת שובה: הַמֶּלֶךְ / הַקָּדוֹשׁ שֶׁאֵין כָּמוֹהוּ
הַמֵּנִיחַ לְעַמּוֹ בְּיוֹם שַׁבַּת קָדְשׁוֹ
כִּי בָם רָצָה לְהָנִיחַ לָהֶם
לְפָנָיו נַעֲבֹד בְּיִרְאָה וָפַחַד
וְנוֹדֶה לִשְׁמוֹ בְּכָל יוֹם תָּמִיד, מֵעֵין הַבְּרָכוֹת

מָגֵן אָבוֹת בִּדְבָרוֹ *By His word, He was the Shield of our ancestors:* A summary of the seven blessings of the Amida, which is unique to Friday evening. Tradi-

He is God to whom thanks are due, the LORD of peace
who sanctifies the Sabbath and blesses the seventh day,
and in holiness gives rest to a people filled with delight,
in remembrance of the work of creation.

The Leader continues:

אֱלֹהֵינוּ Our God and God of our ancestors,
may You find favor in our rest.
Make us holy through Your commandments
and grant us our share in Your Torah.
Satisfy us with Your goodness, grant us joy in Your salvation,
and purify our hearts to serve You in truth.
In love and favor, LORD our God,
grant us as our heritage Your holy Sabbath,
so that Israel who sanctify Your name may find rest on it.
Blessed are You, LORD, who sanctifies the Sabbath.

FULL KADDISH

Leader: יִתְגַּדַּל Magnified and sanctified
may His great name be,
in the world He created by His will.
May He establish His kingdom
in your lifetime and in your days,
and in the lifetime of all the house of Israel,
swiftly and soon –
and say: Amen.

All: May His great name be blessed for ever and all time.

Leader: Blessed and praised,
glorified and exalted,
raised and honored,
uplifted and lauded be
the name of the Holy One,
blessed be He, beyond any blessing,

אֵל הַהוֹדָאוֹת, אֲדוֹן הַשָּׁלוֹם
מְקַדֵּשׁ הַשַּׁבָּת וּמְבָרֵךְ שְׁבִיעִי
וּמֵנִיחַ בִּקְדֻשָּׁה לְעַם מְדֻשְּׁנֵי עֹנֶג
זֵכֶר לְמַעֲשֵׂה בְרֵאשִׁית.

The שליח ציבור *continues:*

אֱלֹהֵינוּ וֵאלֹהֵי אֲבוֹתֵינוּ, רְצֵה בִמְנוּחָתֵנוּ.
קַדְּשֵׁנוּ בְּמִצְוֹתֶיךָ וְתֵן חֶלְקֵנוּ בְּתוֹרָתֶךָ
שַׂבְּעֵנוּ מִטּוּבֶךָ וְשַׂמְּחֵנוּ בִּישׁוּעָתֶךָ
וְטַהֵר לִבֵּנוּ לְעָבְדְּךָ בֶּאֱמֶת.
וְהַנְחִילֵנוּ יהוה אֱלֹהֵינוּ בְּאַהֲבָה וּבְרָצוֹן שַׁבַּת קָדְשֶׁךָ
וְיָנוּחוּ בָהּ יִשְׂרָאֵל מְקַדְּשֵׁי שְׁמֶךָ.
בָּרוּךְ אַתָּה יהוה, מְקַדֵּשׁ הַשַּׁבָּת.

קדיש שלם

ש״ץ: יִתְגַּדַּל וְיִתְקַדַּשׁ שְׁמֵהּ רַבָּא (קהל: אָמֵן)
בְּעָלְמָא דִּי בְרָא כִרְעוּתֵהּ
וְיַמְלִיךְ מַלְכוּתֵהּ
בְּחַיֵּיכוֹן וּבְיוֹמֵיכוֹן וּבְחַיֵּי דְכָל בֵּית יִשְׂרָאֵל
בַּעֲגָלָא וּבִזְמַן קָרִיב, וְאִמְרוּ אָמֵן. (קהל: אָמֵן)

קהל וש״ץ: יְהֵא שְׁמֵהּ רַבָּא מְבָרַךְ לְעָלַם וּלְעָלְמֵי עָלְמַיָּא.

ש״ץ: יִתְבָּרַךְ וְיִשְׁתַּבַּח וְיִתְפָּאַר
וְיִתְרוֹמַם וְיִתְנַשֵּׂא וְיִתְהַדָּר וְיִתְעַלֶּה וְיִתְהַלָּל
שְׁמֵהּ דְּקֻדְשָׁא בְּרִיךְ הוּא (קהל: בְּרִיךְ הוּא)
לְעֵלָּא מִן כָּל בִּרְכָתָא
/ בשבת שובה: לְעֵלָּא לְעֵלָּא מִכָּל בִּרְכָתָא/

song, praise and consolation uttered in the world –
and say: Amen.

May the prayers and pleas of all Israel
be accepted by their Father in heaven –
and say: Amen.

May there be great peace from heaven,
and life for us and all Israel – and say: Amen.

Bow, take three steps back, as if taking leave of the Divine Presence, then bow, first left, then right, then center, while saying:

May He who makes peace in His high places,
make peace for us and all Israel – and say: Amen.

On Yom Tov, say the Kiddush on page 760.

KIDDUSH IN THE SYNAGOGUE

The Leader raises a cup of wine and says:

Please pay attention, my masters.

בָּרוּךְ Blessed are You, LORD our God, King of the Universe,
who creates the fruit of the vine.

בָּרוּךְ Blessed are You, LORD our God, King of the Universe,
who has made us holy with His commandments, has favored us,
and in love and favor given us His holy Sabbath as a heritage,
a remembrance of the work of creation.
It is the first among the holy days of assembly,
a remembrance of the exodus from Egypt.
For You chose us and sanctified us from all the peoples,
and in love and favor gave us Your holy Sabbath as a heritage.
Blessed are You, LORD, who sanctifies the Sabbath.

The wine should be drunk by children under the age of Bar/Bat Mitzva or, if there are none, by the Leader.

קידוש *Kiddush.* As Kiddush is usually said "where we eat the meal," in order to avoid a blessing "said in vain," the wine is not drunk by an adult but by a child. The custom of saying Kiddush in the synagogue goes back to an age when the synagogue was also a hostel for visitors, who ate their meals nearby.

וְשִׁירָתָא, תֻּשְׁבְּחָתָא וְנֶחָמָתָא
דַּאֲמִירָן בְּעָלְמָא, וְאִמְרוּ אָמֵן. (קהל: אָמֵן)

תִּתְקַבַּל צְלוֹתְהוֹן וּבָעוּתְהוֹן דְּכָל יִשְׂרָאֵל
קֳדָם אֲבוּהוֹן דִּי בִשְׁמַיָּא, וְאִמְרוּ אָמֵן. (קהל: אָמֵן)

יְהֵא שְׁלָמָא רַבָּא מִן שְׁמַיָּא
וְחַיִּים, עָלֵינוּ וְעַל כָּל יִשְׂרָאֵל, וְאִמְרוּ אָמֵן. (קהל: אָמֵן)

Bow, take three steps back, as if taking leave of the Divine Presence, then bow, first left, then right, then center, while saying:

עֹשֶׂה שָׁלוֹם/ בשבת שובה: הַשָּׁלוֹם/ בִּמְרוֹמָיו
הוּא יַעֲשֶׂה שָׁלוֹם עָלֵינוּ וְעַל כָּל יִשְׂרָאֵל
וְאִמְרוּ אָמֵן. (קהל: אָמֵן)

On יום טוב*, say the* קידוש *on page 761.*

קידוש בבית הכנסת

The שליח ציבור *raises a cup of wine and says:*

סַבְרִי מָרָנָן
בָּרוּךְ אַתָּה יהוה אֱלֹהֵינוּ מֶלֶךְ הָעוֹלָם, בּוֹרֵא פְּרִי הַגָּפֶן.

בָּרוּךְ אַתָּה יהוה אֱלֹהֵינוּ מֶלֶךְ הָעוֹלָם
אֲשֶׁר קִדְּשָׁנוּ בְּמִצְוֹתָיו, וְרָצָה בָנוּ
וְשַׁבַּת קָדְשׁוֹ בְּאַהֲבָה וּבְרָצוֹן הִנְחִילָנוּ
זִכָּרוֹן לְמַעֲשֵׂה בְרֵאשִׁית
כִּי הוּא יוֹם תְּחִלָּה לְמִקְרָאֵי קֹדֶשׁ, זֵכֶר לִיצִיאַת מִצְרָיִם
כִּי בָנוּ בָחַרְתָּ וְאוֹתָנוּ קִדַּשְׁתָּ מִכָּל הָעַמִּים
וְשַׁבַּת קָדְשְׁךָ בְּאַהֲבָה וּבְרָצוֹן הִנְחַלְתָּנוּ.
בָּרוּךְ אַתָּה יהוה, מְקַדֵּשׁ הַשַּׁבָּת.

The wine should be drunk by children under the age of בר מצווה *or* בת מצווה *or, if there are none, by the* שליח ציבור*.*

From the second night of Pesaḥ until the night before Shavuot, the Omer is counted here (page 284).

Stand while saying Aleinu. Bow at ▾.

עָלֵינוּ It is our duty to praise the Master of all,
and ascribe greatness to the Author of creation,
who has not made us like the nations of the lands
nor placed us like the families of the earth;
who has not made our portion like theirs,
nor our destiny like all their multitudes.
(For they worship vanity and emptiness,
and pray to a god who cannot save.)
▾But we bow in worship
and thank the Supreme King of kings, the Holy One, blessed be He,
who extends the heavens and establishes the earth,
whose throne of glory is in the heavens above,
and whose power's Presence is in the highest of heights.
He is our God; there is no other.
Truly He is our King, there is none else,
as it is written in His Torah:
"You shall know and take to heart this day *Deut. 4*
that the LORD is God, in heaven above and on earth below.
There is no other."

Therefore, we place our hope in You, LORD our God,
that we may soon see the glory of Your power,
when You will remove abominations from the earth,
and idols will be utterly destroyed,
when the world will be perfected
under the sovereignty of the Almighty,
when all humanity will call on Your name,
to turn all the earth's wicked toward You.
All the world's inhabitants will realize and know
that to You every knee must bow and every tongue swear loyalty.
Before You, LORD our God, they will kneel and bow down
and give honor to Your glorious name.

From the second night of פסח *until the night before* שבועות*,*
the עומר *is counted here (page 285).*

Stand while saying עָלֵינוּ*. Bow at* ׳*.*

עָלֵינוּ לְשַׁבֵּחַ לַאֲדוֹן הַכֹּל, לָתֵת גְּדֻלָּה לְיוֹצֵר בְּרֵאשִׁית
שֶׁלֹּא עָשָׂנוּ כְּגוֹיֵי הָאֲרָצוֹת, וְלֹא שָׂמָנוּ כְּמִשְׁפְּחוֹת הָאֲדָמָה
שֶׁלֹּא שָׂם חֶלְקֵנוּ כָּהֶם וְגוֹרָלֵנוּ כְּכָל הֲמוֹנָם.
(שֶׁהֵם מִשְׁתַּחֲוִים לְהֶבֶל וָרִיק וּמִתְפַּלְלִים אֶל אֵל לֹא יוֹשִׁיעַ.)
׳וַאֲנַחְנוּ כּוֹרְעִים וּמִשְׁתַּחֲוִים וּמוֹדִים
לִפְנֵי מֶלֶךְ מַלְכֵי הַמְּלָכִים, הַקָּדוֹשׁ בָּרוּךְ הוּא
שֶׁהוּא נוֹטֶה שָׁמַיִם וְיוֹסֵד אָרֶץ
וּמוֹשַׁב יְקָרוֹ בַּשָּׁמַיִם מִמַּעַל
וּשְׁכִינַת עֻזּוֹ בְּגָבְהֵי מְרוֹמִים.
הוּא אֱלֹהֵינוּ, אֵין עוֹד.
אֱמֶת מַלְכֵּנוּ, אֶפֶס זוּלָתוֹ
כַּכָּתוּב בְּתוֹרָתוֹ
וְיָדַעְתָּ הַיּוֹם וַהֲשֵׁבֹתָ אֶל־לְבָבֶךָ דברים ד
כִּי יהוה הוּא הָאֱלֹהִים בַּשָּׁמַיִם מִמַּעַל וְעַל־הָאָרֶץ מִתָּחַת
אֵין עוֹד:

עַל כֵּן נְקַוֶּה לְךָ יהוה אֱלֹהֵינוּ, לִרְאוֹת מְהֵרָה בְּתִפְאֶרֶת עֻזֶּךָ
לְהַעֲבִיר גִּלּוּלִים מִן הָאָרֶץ, וְהָאֱלִילִים כָּרוֹת יִכָּרֵתוּן
לְתַקֵּן עוֹלָם בְּמַלְכוּת שַׁדַּי.
וְכָל בְּנֵי בָשָׂר יִקְרְאוּ בִשְׁמֶךָ לְהַפְנוֹת אֵלֶיךָ כָּל רִשְׁעֵי אָרֶץ.
יַכִּירוּ וְיֵדְעוּ כָּל יוֹשְׁבֵי תֵבֵל
כִּי לְךָ תִּכְרַע כָּל בֶּרֶךְ, תִּשָּׁבַע כָּל לָשׁוֹן.
לְפָנֶיךָ יהוה אֱלֹהֵינוּ יִכְרְעוּ וְיִפֹּלוּ, וְלִכְבוֹד שִׁמְךָ יְקָר יִתֵּנוּ

They will all accept the yoke of Your kingdom,
and You will reign over them soon and for ever.
For the kingdom is Yours,
and to all eternity You will reign in glory,
as it is written in Your Torah: "The LORD will reign for ever and ever." *Ex. 15*
▸ And it is said: "Then the LORD shall be King over all the earth; *Zech. 14*
on that day the LORD shall be One and His name One."

Some add:

Have no fear of sudden terror or of the ruin when it overtakes the wicked. *Prov. 3*
Devise your strategy, but it will be thwarted; *Is. 8*
propose your plan, but it will not stand, for God is with us.
When you grow old, I will still be the same. *Is. 46*
When your hair turns gray, I will still carry you.
I made you, I will bear you, I will carry you, and I will rescue you.

MOURNER'S KADDISH

The following prayer, said by mourners, requires the presence of a minyan. A transliteration can be found on page 1334.

Mourner: יִתְגַּדַּל Magnified and sanctified
may His great name be,
in the world He created by His will.
May He establish His kingdom
in your lifetime and in your days,
and in the lifetime of all the house of Israel,
swiftly and soon –
and say: Amen.

All: May His great name be blessed for ever and all time.

Mourner: Blessed and praised,
glorified and exalted,
raised and honored,
uplifted and lauded
be the name of the Holy One,
blessed be He, beyond any blessing,

וִיקַבְּלוּ כֻלָּם אֶת עֹל מַלְכוּתֶךָ
וְתִמְלֹךְ עֲלֵיהֶם מְהֵרָה לְעוֹלָם וָעֶד.
כִּי הַמַּלְכוּת שֶׁלְּךָ הִיא וּלְעוֹלְמֵי עַד תִּמְלֹךְ בְּכָבוֹד
כַּכָּתוּב בְּתוֹרָתֶךָ, יהוה יִמְלֹךְ לְעֹלָם וָעֶד: שמות טו
◂ וְנֶאֱמַר, וְהָיָה יהוה לְמֶלֶךְ עַל־כָּל־הָאָרֶץ זכריה יד
בַּיּוֹם הַהוּא יִהְיֶה יהוה אֶחָד וּשְׁמוֹ אֶחָד:

Some add:

אַל־תִּירָא מִפַּחַד פִּתְאֹם וּמִשֹּׁאַת רְשָׁעִים כִּי תָבֹא: משלי ג
עֻצוּ עֵצָה וְתֻפָר, דַּבְּרוּ דָבָר וְלֹא יָקוּם, כִּי עִמָּנוּ אֵל: ישעיה ח
וְעַד־זִקְנָה אֲנִי הוּא, וְעַד־שֵׂיבָה אֲנִי אֶסְבֹּל ישעיה מו
אֲנִי עָשִׂיתִי וַאֲנִי אֶשָּׂא וַאֲנִי אֶסְבֹּל וַאֲמַלֵּט:

קדיש יתום

The following prayer, said by mourners, requires the presence of a מנין.
A transliteration can be found on page 1334.

אבל: יִתְגַּדַּל וְיִתְקַדַּשׁ שְׁמֵהּ רַבָּא (קהל: אָמֵן)
בְּעָלְמָא דִּי בְרָא כִרְעוּתֵהּ
וְיַמְלִיךְ מַלְכוּתֵהּ
בְּחַיֵּיכוֹן וּבְיוֹמֵיכוֹן וּבְחַיֵּי דְכָל בֵּית יִשְׂרָאֵל
בַּעֲגָלָא וּבִזְמַן קָרִיב
וְאִמְרוּ אָמֵן. (קהל: אָמֵן)

קהל ואבל: יְהֵא שְׁמֵהּ רַבָּא מְבָרַךְ לְעָלַם וּלְעָלְמֵי עָלְמַיָּא.

אבל: יִתְבָּרַךְ וְיִשְׁתַּבַּח וְיִתְפָּאַר
וְיִתְרוֹמַם וְיִתְנַשֵּׂא וְיִתְהַדָּר וְיִתְעַלֶּה וְיִתְהַלָּל
שְׁמֵהּ דְּקֻדְשָׁא בְּרִיךְ הוּא (קהל: בְּרִיךְ הוּא)
לְעֵלָּא מִן כָּל בִּרְכָתָא
/בשבת שובה: לְעֵלָּא לְעֵלָּא מִכָּל בִּרְכָתָא/

song, praise and consolation
uttered in the world –
and say: Amen.

May there be great peace from heaven,
and life for us and all Israel –
and say: Amen.

Bow, take three steps back, as if taking leave of the Divine Presence, then bow, first left, then right, then center, while saying:

May He who makes peace in His high places,
make peace for us and all Israel –
and say: Amen.

From the second day of Rosh Ḥodesh Elul until and including Shemini Atzeret (in Israel until and including Hoshana Raba), the following psalm is said:

לְדָוִד A psalm of David. The LORD is my light and my salvation – whom then shall I fear? The LORD is the stronghold of my life – of whom shall I be afraid? When evil men close in on me to devour my flesh, it is they, my enemies and foes, who stumble and fall. Should an army besiege me, my heart would not fear. Should war break out against me, still I would be confident. One thing I ask of the LORD, only this do I seek: to live in the House of the LORD all the days of my life, to gaze on the beauty of the LORD and worship in His Temple. For He will keep me safe in His pavilion on the day of trouble. He will hide me under the cover of His tent. He will set me high upon a rock. Now my head is high above my enemies who surround me. I will sacrifice in His tent with shouts of joy. I will sing and chant praises to the LORD. LORD, hear my voice when I call. Be gracious to me and answer me. On Your behalf my heart says, "Seek My face." Your face, LORD, will I seek. Do not hide Your face from me. Do not turn Your servant away in anger. You have been my help. Do not reject or forsake me, God, my Savior. Were my father and my mother to forsake me, the LORD would take me in. Teach me Your way, LORD, and lead me on a level path, because of my oppressors. Do not abandon me to the will of my foes, for false witnesses have risen against me, breathing violence. ▸ Were it not for my faith that I shall see the LORD's goodness in the land of the living. Hope in the LORD. Be strong and of good courage, and hope in the LORD! Ps. 27

Mourner's Kaddish (on previous page)

וְשִׁירָתָא, תֻּשְׁבְּחָתָא וְנֶחֱמָתָא
דַּאֲמִירָן בְּעָלְמָא, וְאִמְרוּ אָמֵן. (קהל: אָמֵן)

יְהֵא שְׁלָמָא רַבָּא מִן שְׁמַיָּא
וְחַיִּים, עָלֵינוּ וְעַל כָּל יִשְׂרָאֵל
וְאִמְרוּ אָמֵן. (קהל: אָמֵן)

Bow, take three steps back, as if taking leave of the Divine Presence, then bow, first left, then right, then center, while saying:

עֹשֶׂה שָׁלוֹם/ בשבת שובה: הַשָּׁלוֹם/ בִּמְרוֹמָיו
הוּא יַעֲשֶׂה שָׁלוֹם עָלֵינוּ וְעַל כָּל יִשְׂרָאֵל
וְאִמְרוּ אָמֵן. (קהל: אָמֵן)

From the second day of ראש חודש אלול *until and including* שמיני עצרת *(in* ארץ ישראל *until and including* הושענא רבה*), the following psalm is said:*

לְדָוִד, יהוה אוֹרִי וְיִשְׁעִי, מִמִּי אִירָא, יהוה מָעוֹז־חַיַּי, מִמִּי אֶפְחָד: בִּקְרֹב תהלים כז
עָלַי מְרֵעִים לֶאֱכֹל אֶת־בְּשָׂרִי, צָרַי וְאֹיְבַי לִי, הֵמָּה כָשְׁלוּ וְנָפָלוּ: אִם־
תַּחֲנֶה עָלַי מַחֲנֶה, לֹא־יִירָא לִבִּי, אִם־תָּקוּם עָלַי מִלְחָמָה, בְּזֹאת אֲנִי
בוֹטֵחַ: אַחַת שָׁאַלְתִּי מֵאֵת־יהוה, אוֹתָהּ אֲבַקֵּשׁ, שִׁבְתִּי בְּבֵית־יהוה
כָּל־יְמֵי חַיַּי, לַחֲזוֹת בְּנֹעַם־יהוה, וּלְבַקֵּר בְּהֵיכָלוֹ: כִּי יִצְפְּנֵנִי בְּסֻכֹּה
בְּיוֹם רָעָה, יַסְתִּרֵנִי בְּסֵתֶר אָהֳלוֹ, בְּצוּר יְרוֹמְמֵנִי: וְעַתָּה יָרוּם רֹאשִׁי
עַל אֹיְבַי סְבִיבוֹתַי, וְאֶזְבְּחָה בְאָהֳלוֹ זִבְחֵי תְרוּעָה, אָשִׁירָה וַאֲזַמְּרָה
לַיהוה: שְׁמַע־יהוה קוֹלִי אֶקְרָא, וְחָנֵּנִי וַעֲנֵנִי: לְךָ אָמַר לִבִּי בַּקְּשׁוּ פָנָי,
אֶת־פָּנֶיךָ יהוה אֲבַקֵּשׁ: אַל־תַּסְתֵּר פָּנֶיךָ מִמֶּנִּי, אַל תַּט־בְּאַף עַבְדֶּךָ,
עֶזְרָתִי הָיִיתָ, אַל־תִּטְּשֵׁנִי וְאַל־תַּעַזְבֵנִי, אֱלֹהֵי יִשְׁעִי: כִּי־אָבִי וְאִמִּי
עֲזָבוּנִי, וַיהוה יַאַסְפֵנִי: הוֹרֵנִי יהוה דַּרְכֶּךָ, וּנְחֵנִי בְּאֹרַח מִישׁוֹר, לְמַעַן
שׁוֹרְרָי: אַל־תִּתְּנֵנִי בְּנֶפֶשׁ צָרָי, כִּי קָמוּ־בִי עֵדֵי־שֶׁקֶר, וִיפֵחַ חָמָס: ‹ לוּלֵא
הֶאֱמַנְתִּי לִרְאוֹת בְּטוּב־יהוה בְּאֶרֶץ חַיִּים: קַוֵּה אֶל־יהוה, חֲזַק וְיַאֲמֵץ
לִבֶּךָ, וְקַוֵּה אֶל־יהוה:

קדיש יתום (*on previous page*)

Most congregations sing Yigdal at this point.
In Israel, most congregations sing Adon Olam (*page* 22).

GREAT
is the living God and praised.
He exists, and His existence is beyond time.

He is One, and there is no unity like His.
Unfathomable, His oneness is infinite.

He has neither bodily form nor substance;
His holiness is beyond compare.

He preceded all that was created.
He was first: there was no beginning to His beginning.

Behold He is Master of the Universe; every creature
shows His greatness and majesty.

The rich flow of His prophecy He gave
to His treasured people in whom He gloried.

Never in Israel has there arisen another like Moses,
a prophet who beheld God's image.

God gave His people a Torah of truth
by the hand of His prophet, most faithful of His House.

God will not alter or change His law
for any other, for eternity.

He sees and knows our secret thoughts;
as soon as something is begun, He foresees its end.

He rewards people with loving-kindness according to their deeds;
He punishes the wicked according to his wickedness.

At the end of days He will send our Messiah,
to redeem those who await His final salvation.

God will revive the dead in His great loving-kindness.
Blessed for evermore is His glorious name!

Most congregations sing יגדל *at this point.*
In ארץ ישראל, *most congregations sing* אדון עולם (*page* 23).

יִגְדַּל

אֱלֹהִים חַי וְיִשְׁתַּבַּח, נִמְצָא וְאֵין עֵת אֶל מְצִיאוּתוֹ.
אֶחָד וְאֵין יָחִיד כְּיִחוּדוֹ, נֶעְלָם וְגַם אֵין סוֹף לְאַחְדוּתוֹ.
אֵין לוֹ דְּמוּת הַגּוּף וְאֵינוֹ גוּף, לֹא נַעֲרֹךְ אֵלָיו קְדֻשָּׁתוֹ.
קַדְמוֹן לְכָל דָּבָר אֲשֶׁר נִבְרָא, רִאשׁוֹן וְאֵין רֵאשִׁית לְרֵאשִׁיתוֹ.
הִנּוֹ אֲדוֹן עוֹלָם, וְכָל נוֹצָר יוֹרֶה גְדֻלָּתוֹ וּמַלְכוּתוֹ.
שֶׁפַע נְבוּאָתוֹ נְתָנוֹ אֶל־אַנְשֵׁי סְגֻלָּתוֹ וְתִפְאַרְתּוֹ.
לֹא קָם בְּיִשְׂרָאֵל כְּמֹשֶׁה עוֹד נָבִיא וּמַבִּיט אֶת תְּמוּנָתוֹ.
תּוֹרַת אֱמֶת נָתַן לְעַמּוֹ אֵל עַל יַד נְבִיאוֹ נֶאֱמַן בֵּיתוֹ.
לֹא יַחֲלִיף הָאֵל וְלֹא יָמִיר דָּתוֹ לְעוֹלָמִים לְזוּלָתוֹ.
צוֹפֶה וְיוֹדֵעַ סְתָרֵינוּ, מַבִּיט לְסוֹף דָּבָר בְּקַדְמָתוֹ.
גּוֹמֵל לְאִישׁ חֶסֶד כְּמִפְעָלוֹ, נוֹתֵן לְרָשָׁע רָע כְּרִשְׁעָתוֹ.
יִשְׁלַח לְקֵץ יָמִין מְשִׁיחֵנוּ לִפְדּוֹת מְחַכֵּי קֵץ יְשׁוּעָתוֹ.
מֵתִים יְחַיֶּה אֵל בְּרֹב חַסְדּוֹ, בָּרוּךְ עֲדֵי עַד שֵׁם תְּהִלָּתוֹ.

יִגְדַּל אֱלֹהִים חַי *Great is the living God:* A poetic setting of Maimonides' Thirteen Principles of Jewish Faith, written by Rabbi Daniel bar Judah (Rome, fourteenth century), each line representing one of the principles. Like Adon Olam, the presence of Yigdal in the siddur reminds us that it is not only a book of prayer but also the supreme book of Jewish faith. Judaism contains little systematic theology. We speak *to* God more than we speak *about* God. Yet Judaism *is* a faith whose distinctive beliefs find their home in the prayer book. We do not analyze faith in academic detachment. We sing it, affirming faith with joy.

Kiddush and Zemirot for Shabbat Evening

BLESSING THE CHILDREN

On the evenings of Shabbat and Yom Tov, many have the custom to bless their children.

To sons, say:

יְשִׂמְךָ May God
make you like Ephraim
and Manasseh.

To daughters, say:

יְשִׂימֵךְ May God
make you like Sarah, Rebecca,
Rachel and Leah.

יְבָרֶכְךָ May the LORD bless you and protect you. *Num. 6*
May the LORD make His face shine on you
and be gracious to you.
May the LORD turn His face toward you
and grant you peace.

---

invisible signs of God's protection; (4) praising the "woman of strength," guardian of the home; (5) Kiddush, the dimension of holiness; (6) the blessing over bread, a symbol of sustenance as God's gift; and (7) song and words of Torah, expressing our faith joyously.

BLESSING THE CHILDREN
The custom of parents blessing their children has its origin in the blessing Jacob gave to his grandsons: "By you shall Israel invoke blessings, saying, May God make you like Ephraim and Manasseh" (Gen. 48:20). The blessing for boys repeats this phrase. That for girls invokes the four biblical matriarchs: Sarah, Rebecca, Rachel and Leah. This is followed, in both cases, by the priestly blessing. It is a beautiful custom, symbolizing the continuity of the generations in a way that is both tender and deeply spiritual. In the only verse to describe why Abraham was chosen, God says: "I have chosen him so that he will teach his children and his household after him to keep the way of the LORD, doing righteousness and justice" (Gen. 18:19). The bond between parents and children represents the continuity of the covenant across the generations.

קידוש וזמירות לליל שבת

ברכת הבנים

On ליל שבת *and* ערב יום טוב*, many have the custom to bless their children.*

To daughters, say:	*To sons, say:*
יְשִׂימֵךְ אֱלֹהִים	יְשִׂמְךָ אֱלֹהִים
כְּשָׂרָה רִבְקָה רָחֵל וְלֵאָה.	כְּאֶפְרַיִם וְכִמְנַשֶּׁה:

בראשית מח

במדבר ו

יְבָרֶכְךָ יהוה וְיִשְׁמְרֶךָ:
יָאֵר יהוה פָּנָיו אֵלֶיךָ וִיחֻנֶּךָּ:
יִשָּׂא יהוה פָּנָיו אֵלֶיךָ וְיָשֵׂם לְךָ שָׁלוֹם:

SHABBAT AT HOME

Shabbat is a celebration of the Jewish home, and the home is the matrix of Judaism. The prophets compared the relationship between God and Israel with that between husband and wife, and between parent and child. The Hebrew word *emuna*, usually translated as "faith," in fact means "faithfulness, fidelity," the virtue born and sustained within the home. The love between husband and wife is the human redemption of solitude. The love between parent and child is the closest we come to immortality in this world, for it is through our children that we, and what we live for, live on.

Friday night is when, freed from the pressures of work, we can give time and loving attention to one another. It is also the time when we feel most profoundly the *Shekhina*, the Divine Presence, in the home. Our relationship to God and to those closest to us are both covenantal; that is to say, a mutual pledge of loyalty and love. Through the family and the quality of its relationships, divine blessings flow into the world.

Before the Friday evening meal, we enact sequentially the values on which the home is built: (1) lighting candles, symbolizing domestic peace; (2) blessing children, our responsibility and continuity; (3) welcoming angels,

Many people sing each of the four verses of the following song three times:

שָׁלוֹם עֲלֵיכֶם Welcome,
ministering angels, angels of the Most High,
from the Supreme King of kings,
the Holy One, blessed be He.

Enter in peace,
angels of peace, angels of the Most High,
from the Supreme King of kings,
the Holy One, blessed be He.

Bless me with peace,
angels of peace, angels of the Most High,
from the Supreme King of kings,
the Holy One, blessed be He.

Go in peace,
angels of peace, angels of the Most High,
from the Supreme King of kings,
the Holy One, blessed be He.

כִּי מַלְאָכָיו He will command His angels about you, *Ps. 91*
to guard you in all your ways.
May the LORD guard your going out and your return, *Ps. 121*
from now and for all time.

Shabbat, they bless the family. The author of the poem is unknown, but it is first mentioned in mystical circles in the seventeenth century.

Many people sing each of the four verses of the following song three times:

שָׁלוֹם עֲלֵיכֶם
מַלְאֲכֵי הַשָּׁרֵת, מַלְאֲכֵי עֶלְיוֹן
מִמֶּֽלֶךְ מַלְכֵי הַמְּלָכִים, הַקָּדוֹשׁ בָּרוּךְ הוּא.

בּוֹאֲכֶם לְשָׁלוֹם
מַלְאֲכֵי הַשָּׁלוֹם, מַלְאֲכֵי עֶלְיוֹן
מִמֶּֽלֶךְ מַלְכֵי הַמְּלָכִים, הַקָּדוֹשׁ בָּרוּךְ הוּא.

בָּרְכוּנִי לְשָׁלוֹם
מַלְאֲכֵי הַשָּׁלוֹם, מַלְאֲכֵי עֶלְיוֹן
מִמֶּֽלֶךְ מַלְכֵי הַמְּלָכִים, הַקָּדוֹשׁ בָּרוּךְ הוּא.

צֵאתְכֶם לְשָׁלוֹם
מַלְאֲכֵי הַשָּׁלוֹם, מַלְאֲכֵי עֶלְיוֹן
מִמֶּֽלֶךְ מַלְכֵי הַמְּלָכִים, הַקָּדוֹשׁ בָּרוּךְ הוּא.

כִּי מַלְאָכָיו יְצַוֶּה־לָּךְ, לִשְׁמָרְךָ בְּכָל־דְּרָכֶֽיךָ׃ תהלים צא
יהוה יִשְׁמָר־צֵאתְךָ וּבוֹאֶךָ, מֵעַתָּה וְעַד־עוֹלָם׃ תהלים קכא

שָׁלוֹם עֲלֵיכֶם *Welcome:* A poem based on the Talmudic passage (*Shabbat* 119b) that states that two ministering angels accompany a person on Friday night on his way from synagogue to home. When they see the home prepared for

Some say:

רִבּוֹן כָּל הָעוֹלָמִים Master of all worlds, LORD of all souls, LORD of peace, mighty, blessed and great King, King who speaks peace, King who is glorious, enduring and pure, King who gives life to worlds, King who is good and does good, King alone and unique, great King who robes Himself in compassion, King who reigns over all kings, who is exalted and supports those who fall, King who is Author of creation, who redeems and rescues, who is radiant and ruddy, King who is holy, high and exalted, King who hears prayer, King whose way is just: I thank You, LORD my God and God of my ancestors, for all the loving-kindness You have done and will do for me, and all the members of my household and all my fellow creatures. Blessed are Your angels, holy and pure, who do Your will. LORD of peace, King to whom peace belongs, bless me with peace, and grant me and the members of my household, and all Your people the house of Israel, a good and peaceful life. King exalted over all the heavenly array, who formed me and who formed creation, I entreat Your radiant presence, that You find me and all the members of my household worthy of grace and good favor in Your eyes and the eyes of all people and all who see us, that we may serve You. May we be worthy to receive Sabbaths amidst great joy, wealth and honor, and few sins. May You remove from me and all the members of my household and all Your people the house of Israel all sickness and disease, all poverty, hardship and destitution. Grant us a virtuous desire to serve You in truth, awe and love. May we find honor in Your eyes and the eyes of all who see us, for You are the King of honor: to You it belongs, to You it accords. Please, King who reigns over all kings, command Your angels, ministering angels who minister to the Most High, to act compassionately toward me when they enter my house on our holy day, for I have lit my lights, spread my couch and changed my clothes in honor of the Sabbath; I have come to Your House to lay my pleas before You that You remove my sighs; I have testified that in six days You created all things, and said it a second time, and will testify to it a third time over my cup, in joy, as You commanded me to remember it, delighting in the extra soul You have given me. On it [the Sabbath] I shall rest as You have commanded me, thereby to serve You. So too I will declare Your greatness in joyful song, for I have set the LORD before me, that You may have compassion upon me in my exile, redeeming me and awakening my heart to Your love. Then I will keep Your commands and statutes without sadness, praying correctly as is right and fitting. Angels of peace, come in peace and bless me with peace; declare blessed the table I have prepared, and go in peace, now and forever. Amen, Selah.

Some say:

רִבּוֹן כָּל הָעוֹלָמִים, אֲדוֹן כָּל הַנְּשָׁמוֹת, אֲדוֹן הַשָּׁלוֹם. מֶלֶךְ אַבִּיר, מֶלֶךְ בָּרוּךְ, מֶלֶךְ גָּדוֹל, מֶלֶךְ דּוֹבֵר שָׁלוֹם, מֶלֶךְ הָדוּר, מֶלֶךְ וָתִיק, מֶלֶךְ זַךְ, מֶלֶךְ חֵי הָעוֹלָמִים, מֶלֶךְ טוֹב וּמֵטִיב, מֶלֶךְ יָחִיד וּמְיֻחָד, מֶלֶךְ כַּבִּיר, מֶלֶךְ לוֹבֵשׁ רַחֲמִים, מֶלֶךְ מַלְכֵי הַמְּלָכִים, מֶלֶךְ נִשְׂגָּב, מֶלֶךְ סוֹמֵךְ נוֹפְלִים, מֶלֶךְ עֹשֶׂה מַעֲשֵׂה בְרֵאשִׁית, מֶלֶךְ פּוֹדֶה וּמַצִּיל, מֶלֶךְ צַח וְאָדֹם, מֶלֶךְ קָדוֹשׁ, מֶלֶךְ רָם וְנִשָּׂא, מֶלֶךְ שׁוֹמֵעַ תְּפִלָּה, מֶלֶךְ תָּמִים דַּרְכּוֹ. מוֹדֶה אֲנִי לְפָנֶיךָ, יהוה אֱלֹהַי וֵאלֹהֵי אֲבוֹתַי, עַל כָּל הַחֶסֶד אֲשֶׁר עָשִׂיתָ עִמָּדִי וַאֲשֶׁר אַתָּה עָתִיד לַעֲשׂוֹת עִמִּי וְעִם כָּל בְּנֵי בֵיתִי וְעִם כָּל בְּרִיּוֹתֶיךָ, בְּנֵי בְרִיתִי. וּבְרוּכִים הֵם מַלְאָכֶיךָ הַקְּדוֹשִׁים וְהַטְּהוֹרִים שֶׁעוֹשִׂים רְצוֹנֶךָ. אֲדוֹן הַשָּׁלוֹם, מֶלֶךְ שֶׁהַשָּׁלוֹם שֶׁלּוֹ, בָּרְכֵנִי בַשָּׁלוֹם, וְתִפְקֹד אוֹתִי וְאֶת כָּל בְּנֵי בֵיתִי וְכָל עַמְּךָ בֵּית יִשְׂרָאֵל לְחַיִּים טוֹבִים וּלְשָׁלוֹם. מֶלֶךְ עֶלְיוֹן עַל כָּל צְבָא מָרוֹם, יוֹצְרֵנוּ, יוֹצֵר בְּרֵאשִׁית, אֲחַלֶּה פָנֶיךָ הַמְּאִירִים, שֶׁתְּזַכֶּה אוֹתִי וְאֶת כָּל בְּנֵי בֵיתִי לִמְצֹא חֵן וְשֵׂכֶל טוֹב בְּעֵינֶיךָ וּבְעֵינֵי כָּל בְּנֵי אָדָם וּבְעֵינֵי כָל רוֹאֵינוּ לַעֲבוֹדָתֶךָ. וְזַכֵּנוּ לְקַבֵּל שַׁבָּתוֹת מִתּוֹךְ רֹב שִׂמְחָה וּמִתּוֹךְ עֹשֶׁר וְכָבוֹד וּמִתּוֹךְ מִעוּט עֲוֹנוֹת. וְהָסֵר מִמֶּנִּי וּמִכָּל בְּנֵי בֵיתִי וּמִכָּל עַמְּךָ בֵּית יִשְׂרָאֵל כָּל מִינֵי חֹלִי וְכָל מִינֵי מַדְוֶה וְכָל מִינֵי דַלּוּת וַעֲנִיּוּת וְאֶבְיוֹנוּת. וְתֵן בָּנוּ יֵצֶר טוֹב לְעָבְדְּךָ בֶּאֱמֶת וּבְיִרְאָה וּבְאַהֲבָה. וְנִהְיֶה מְכֻבָּדִים בְּעֵינֶיךָ וּבְעֵינֵי כָל רוֹאֵינוּ, כִּי אַתָּה הוּא מֶלֶךְ הַכָּבוֹד, כִּי לְךָ נָאֶה, כִּי לְךָ יָאֶה. אָנָּא, מֶלֶךְ מַלְכֵי הַמְּלָכִים, צַוֵּה לְמַלְאָכֶיךָ, מַלְאֲכֵי הַשָּׁרֵת, מְשָׁרְתֵי עֶלְיוֹן, שֶׁיִּפְקְדוּנִי בְּרַחֲמִים וִיבָרְכוּנִי בְּבוֹאָם לְבֵיתִי בְּיוֹם קָדְשֵׁנוּ, כִּי הִדְלַקְתִּי נֵרוֹתַי וְהִצַּעְתִּי מִטָּתִי וְהֶחֱלַפְתִּי שִׂמְלוֹתַי לִכְבוֹד יוֹם הַשַּׁבָּת וּבָאתִי לְבֵיתְךָ לְהַפִּיל תְּחִנָּתִי לְפָנֶיךָ, שֶׁתַּעֲבִיר אַנְחָתִי, וָאָעִיד אֲשֶׁר בָּרָאתָ בְשִׁשָּׁה יָמִים כָּל הַיְצוּר, וָאֶשְׁנֶה וַאֲשַׁלֵּשׁ עוֹד לְהָעִיד עַל כּוֹסִי בְּתוֹךְ שִׂמְחָתִי, כַּאֲשֶׁר צִוִּיתַנִי לְזָכְרוֹ וּלְהִתְעַנֵּג בְּיֶתֶר נִשְׁמָתִי אֲשֶׁר נָתַתָּ בִּי. בּוֹ אֶשְׁבֹּת כַּאֲשֶׁר צִוִּיתַנִי לְשָׁרְתֶךָ, וְכֵן אַגִּיד גְּדֻלָּתְךָ בְּרִנָּה, וְשִׁוִּיתִי יהוה לִקְרָאתִי שֶׁתְּרַחֲמֵנִי עוֹד בְּגָלוּתִי לְגָאֳלֵנִי לְעוֹרֵר לִבִּי לְאַהֲבָתֶךָ. וְאָז אֶשְׁמֹר פִּקּוּדֶיךָ וְחֻקֶּיךָ בְּלִי עֶצֶב, וְאֶתְפַּלֵּל כַּדָּת כָּרָאוּי וְכַנָּכוֹן. מַלְאֲכֵי הַשָּׁלוֹם, בּוֹאֲכֶם לְשָׁלוֹם, בָּרְכוּנִי לְשָׁלוֹם, וְאִמְרוּ בָּרוּךְ לְשֻׁלְחָנִי הֶעָרוּךְ, וְצֵאתְכֶם לְשָׁלוֹם מֵעַתָּה וְעַד עוֹלָם, אָמֵן סֶלָה.

א אֵשֶׁת־חַיִל A woman of strength, who can find? Her worth is far beyond pearls. *Prov. 31*
ב Her husband's heart trusts in her, and he has no lack of gain.
ג She brings him good, not harm, all the days of her life.
ד She seeks wool and linen, and works with willing hands.
ה She is like a ship laden with merchandise, bringing her food from afar.
ו She rises while it is still night, providing food for her household, portions for her maids.
ז She considers a field and buys it; from her earnings she plants a vineyard.
ח She girds herself with strength, and braces her arms for her tasks.
ט She sees that her business goes well; her lamp does not go out at night.
י She holds the distaff in her hand, and grasps the spindle with her palms.
כ She reaches out her palm to the poor, and extends her hand to the needy.
ל She has no fear for her family when it snows, for all her household is clothed in crimson wool.
מ She makes elegant coverings; her clothing is fine linen and purple wool.
נ Her husband is well known in the gates,
where he sits with the elders of the land.
ס She makes linen garments and sells them, and supplies merchants with sashes.
ע She is clothed with strength and dignity; she can laugh at the days to come.
פ She opens her mouth with wisdom,
and the law of kindness is on her tongue.
צ She watches over the ways of her household,
and never eats the bread of idleness.
ק Her children rise and call her happy; her husband also praises her:
ר "Many women have excelled, but you surpass them all."
ש Charm is deceptive and beauty vain:
it is the God-fearing woman who deserves praise.
ת Give her the reward she has earned;
let her deeds bring her praise in the gates.

---

word *ḥayil* in the opening phrase signifies strength, both moral and physical. Many of the commentators see the woman in this passage as a symbol of the Divine Presence (or Shabbat itself, personified as a bride). Without negating this allegorical meaning, the poem is also a hymn of thanks to the female head of the household for the blessings she brings to the family and the home.

משלי לא

א אֵֽשֶׁת־חַיִל מִי יִמְצָא, וְרָחֹק מִפְּנִינִים מִכְרָהּ:

ב בָּֽטַח בָּהּ לֵב בַּעְלָהּ, וְשָׁלָל לֹא יֶחְסָר:

ג גְּמָלַתְהוּ טוֹב וְלֹא־רָע, כֹּל יְמֵי חַיֶּיהָ:

ד דָּרְשָׁה צֶמֶר וּפִשְׁתִּים, וַתַּֽעַשׂ בְּחֵפֶץ כַּפֶּיהָ:

ה הָיְתָה כָּאֳנִיּוֹת סוֹחֵר, מִמֶּרְחָק תָּבִיא לַחְמָהּ:

ו וַתָּקָם בְּעוֹד לַיְלָה, וַתִּתֵּן טֶֽרֶף לְבֵיתָהּ, וְחֹק לְנַעֲרֹתֶֽיהָ:

ז זָמְמָה שָׂדֶה וַתִּקָּחֵֽהוּ, מִפְּרִי כַפֶּיהָ נָֽטְעָה כָּֽרֶם:

ח חָגְרָה בְעוֹז מָתְנֶיהָ, וַתְּאַמֵּץ זְרוֹעֹתֶֽיהָ:

ט טָעֲמָה כִּי־טוֹב סַחְרָהּ, לֹא־יִכְבֶּה בַלַּיְל נֵרָהּ:

י יָדֶיהָ שִׁלְּחָה בַכִּישׁוֹר, וְכַפֶּיהָ תָּמְכוּ פָֽלֶךְ:

כ כַּפָּהּ פָּרְשָׂה לֶעָנִי, וְיָדֶיהָ שִׁלְּחָה לָאֶבְיוֹן:

ל לֹא־תִירָא לְבֵיתָהּ מִשָּׁלֶג, כִּי כָל־בֵּיתָהּ לָבֻשׁ שָׁנִים:

מ מַרְבַדִּים עָשְׂתָה־לָּהּ, שֵׁשׁ וְאַרְגָּמָן לְבוּשָׁהּ:

נ נוֹדָע בַּשְּׁעָרִים בַּעְלָהּ, בְּשִׁבְתּוֹ עִם־זִקְנֵי־אָֽרֶץ:

ס סָדִין עָשְׂתָה וַתִּמְכֹּר, וַחֲגוֹר נָתְנָה לַכְּנַעֲנִי:

ע עוֹז־וְהָדָר לְבוּשָׁהּ, וַתִּשְׂחַק לְיוֹם אַחֲרוֹן:

פ פִּֽיהָ פָּתְחָה בְחָכְמָה, וְתוֹרַת־חֶֽסֶד עַל־לְשׁוֹנָהּ:

צ צוֹפִיָּה הֲלִיכוֹת בֵּיתָהּ, וְלֶֽחֶם עַצְלוּת לֹא תֹאכֵל:

ק קָֽמוּ בָנֶיהָ וַיְאַשְּׁרֽוּהָ, בַּעְלָהּ וַיְהַלְלָהּ:

ר רַבּוֹת בָּנוֹת עָֽשׂוּ חָֽיִל, וְאַתְּ עָלִית עַל־כֻּלָּֽנָה:

ש שֶֽׁקֶר הַחֵן וְהֶֽבֶל הַיֹּֽפִי, אִשָּׁה יִרְאַת־יהוה הִיא תִתְהַלָּל:

ת תְּנוּ־לָהּ מִפְּרִי יָדֶיהָ, וִיהַלְלֽוּהָ בַשְּׁעָרִים מַעֲשֶֽׂיהָ:

אֵֽשֶׁת־חַיִל *A woman of strength:* This text, an alphabetical acrostic, is taken from the closing chapter of the book of Proverbs. In a series of scenes it describes an ideal woman: active, practical, a businesswoman as well as director of the household, involved in the welfare of strangers as well as her family, a woman of wisdom and kindness, "clothed with strength and dignity." The

Some say:

Prepare the feast of perfect faith, joy of the holy King.
Prepare the royal feast.

This is the feast [mystically known as] 'the Field of Holy Apples' –
and 'the Small Face' and 'the Holy Ancient One'
[mystical terms for aspects of the Divine] come to partake in the feast with it.

With songs of praise I will cut away [evil forces],
to enter the holy gates of 'the Field of Apples.'
We now invite Her [the Divine Presence] with a newly prepared table
and a fine candelabrum spreading light upon our heads.
Between right and left is the bride, decked with jewelry, adorned and robed.
Her husband embraces her, and in the joy of their togetherness
[evil forces] are crushed.
Cries and suffering stop and cease; a new face comes upon spirits and souls.
She will have great and doubled joy; light will come, and bounteous blessing.
Come near, dear friends, and prepare delicacies of many kinds, and fish and fowl.
Renewing souls and spirits through the thirty-two [paths of wisdom]
and the three branches [of Scripture].
She [the Divine Presence] has seventy crowns, and above,
the King is crowned with all in the Holy of Holies.
Engraved and hidden with her are all worlds,
but the pestle of the Ancient of Days releases all that is hidden.
May it be His will that the Divine Presence rest on His people who,
for His name's sake, delight in sweet foods and honey.
To the south, I will arrange the candelabrum of hidden [wisdom],
to the north I will set the table with bread.
With wine in the cup, and myrtle clusters for bridegroom and bride,
the weak will be given strength.
Let us make them crowns of precious words, seventy crowns beyond the fifty.
May the Divine Presence be crowned with six loaves on each side, like
the two sets of six loaves [of showbread] and other articles [in the Temple].
[On the Sabbath] impure powers and afflicting angels cease and desist; and
those who are confined have respite.
To break bread the size of an olive or an egg, for there are two ways of
interpreting the *Yod* [of the divine name], restrictively or expansively.
It is like pure olive oil, pressed in a mill, flowing like rivers, whispering secrets.
Let us speak of mysteries, secrets unrevealed, hidden and concealed.
To crown the bride with mysteries above, at this,
the holy angels' wedding celebration.

Some say:

אַתְקִֽינוּ סְעוּדְתָא דִּמְהֵימְנוּתָא שְׁלִֽימְתָא
חֶדְוָתָא דְּמַלְכָּא קַדִּישָׁא.
אַתְקִֽינוּ סְעוּדְתָא דְּמַלְכָּא.

דָּא הִיא סְעוּדְתָא דַּחֲקַל תַּפּוּחִין קַדִּישִׁין
וּזְעֵיר אַנְפִּין וְעַתִּיקָא קַדִּישָׁא אָתְיָן לְסַעֲדָה בַּהֲדַהּ.

אֲזַמֵּר בִּשְׁבָחִין / לְמֵעַל גּוֹ פִתְחִין / דְּבַחֲקַל תַּפּוּחִין / דְּאִנּוּן קַדִּישִׁין.
נְזַמֵּן לַהּ הַשְׁתָּא / בְּפָתוֹרָא חַדְתָּא / וּבִמְנָרְתָא טָבְתָא / דְּנָהֲרָה עַל רֵישִׁין.
יְמִינָא וּשְׂמָאלָא / וּבֵינַיְהוּ כַלָּה / בְּקִשּׁוּטִין אָזְלָא / וּמָנִין וּלְבוּשִׁין.
יְחַבֵּק לַהּ בַּעְלָהּ / וּבִיסוֹדָא דִי לַהּ / דְּעָבֵד נַיְחָא לַהּ / יְהֵא כָתֵשׁ כְּתִישִׁין.
צְוָחִין אוּף עָקְתִין / בְּטֵילִין וּשְׁבִיתִין / בְּרַם אַנְפִּין חַדְתִּין / וְרוּחִין עִם נַפְשִׁין.
חֲדוּ סַגִּי יֵיתֵי / וְעַל חֲדָה תַּרְתֵּי / נְהוֹרָא לַהּ יַמְטֵי / וּבִרְכָן דִּנְפִישִׁין.
קְרִיבוּ שׁוֹשְׁבִינִין / עֲבִידוּ תִקּוּנִין / לְאַפָּשָׁה זֵינִין / וְנוּנִין עִם רַחְשִׁין.
לְמֶעְבַּד נִשְׁמָתִין / וְרוּחִין חַדְתִּין / בְּתַרְתֵּי וּתְלָתִין / וּבִתְלָתָא שִׁבְשִׁין.
וְעִטְרִין שַׁבְעִין לַהּ / וּמַלְכָּא דִּלְעֵלָּא / דְּיִתְעַטַּר כֹּלָּא / בְּקַדִּישׁ קַדִּישִׁין.
רְשִׁימִין וּסְתִימִין / בְּגַוַּהּ כָּל עָלְמִין / בְּרַם עַתִּיק יוֹמִין / הֲלָא בָטֵשׁ בְּטִישִׁין.
יְהֵא רַעֲוָה קַמֵּהּ / דְּתִשְׁרֵי עַל עַמֵּהּ / דְּיִתְעַנַּג לִשְׁמֵהּ / בִּמְתִיקִין וְדֻבְשִׁין.
אֲסַדֵּר לִדְרוֹמָא / מְנָרְתָא דִסְתִימָא / וְשֻׁלְחָן עִם נַהֲמָא / בִּצְפּוֹנָא אַדְשִׁין.
בְּחַמְרָא גוֹ כָסָא / וּמַדָּנֵי אָסָא / לְאָרוּס וַאֲרוּסָה / לְאַתְקָפָא חַלָּשִׁין.
נְעַבֵּד לוֹן כִּתְרִין / בְּמִלִּין יַקִּירִין / בְּשִׁבְעִין עִטּוּרִין / דְּעַל גַּבֵּי חַמְשִׁין.
שְׁכִינְתָא תִתְעַטַּר / בְּשִׁית נַהֲמֵי לִסְטַר / בְּוָוִין תִּתְקַטַּר / וְזֵינִין דִּכְנִישִׁין.
(שְׁבִיתִין וּשְׁבִיקִין / מְסָאֲבִין דְּדָחֲקִין / חֲבִילִין דִּמְעִיקִין / וְכָל זֵינֵי חַרְשִׁין.)
לְמִבְצַע עַל רִיפְתָא / כְּזֵיתָא וּכְבֵיעֲתָא / תְּרֵין יוּדִין נָקְטָא / סְתִימִין וּפְרִישִׁין.
מְשַׁח זֵיתָא דָכְיָא / דְּטָחֲנִין רֵיחַיָּא / וְנָגְדִין נַחֲלַיָּא / בְּגַוַּהּ בִּלְחִישִׁין.
הֲלָא נֵימָא רָזִין / וּמִלִּין דִּגְנִיזִין / דְּלֵיתֵיהוֹן מִתְחֲזִין / טְמִירִין וּכְבִישִׁין.
לְאַעְטָרָה כַלָּה / בְּרָזִין דִּלְעֵלָּא / בְּגוֹ הַאי הִלּוּלָה / דְּעִירִין קַדִּישִׁין.

KIDDUSH FOR SHABBAT EVENING

For Kiddush on Yom Tov see page 700, and on Rosh HaShana, see page 878.

Quietly: And it was evening, and it was morning – *Gen. 1*
יוֹם הַשִּׁשִּׁי the sixth day.

Then the heavens and the earth were completed, and all their array. *Gen. 2*
With the seventh day, God completed the work He had done.
He ceased on the seventh day from all the work He had done.
God blessed the seventh day and declared it holy,
because on it He ceased from all His work He had created to do.

When saying Kiddush for others, add:

Please pay attention, my masters.
Blessed are You, Lord our God, King of the Universe,
who creates the fruit of the vine.

Blessed are You, Lord our God, King of the Universe,
who has made us holy through His commandments,
who has favored us,
and in love and favor gave us His holy Sabbath as a heritage,
a remembrance of the work of creation.
It is the first among the holy days of assembly,
a remembrance of the exodus from Egypt.
For You chose us and sanctified us from all the peoples,
and in love and favor gave us Your holy Sabbath as a heritage.
Blessed are You, Lord, who sanctifies the Sabbath.

On Shabbat Ḥol HaMo'ed Sukkot, if Kiddush is made in the sukka, add:

Blessed are You, Lord our God, King of the Universe,
who has made us holy through his commandments and has
commanded us to dwell in the sukka.

It is customary for all present to drink of the wine.

---

completed creation and rested on the seventh day; (2) a blessing over wine; and (3) a blessing over the day itself.

It is our custom to begin the first paragraph with the last two words of the previous verse so that the first four Hebrew words of Kiddush – *Yom Hashishi Vayekhulu Hashamayim* – spell out the four-letter name of God. The previous words are said quietly. The blessing over the day recalls the two fundamental beliefs of which Shabbat is a reminder: creation and the exodus from Egypt.

קידוש לליל שבת

For קידוש *on* יום טוב *see page 761, and on* ראש השנה*, see page 879.*

Quietly וַיְהִי־עֶרֶב וַיְהִי־בֹקֶר בראשית א
יוֹם הַשִּׁשִּׁי:
וַיְכֻלּוּ הַשָּׁמַיִם וְהָאָרֶץ וְכָל־צְבָאָם: בראשית ב
וַיְכַל אֱלֹהִים בַּיּוֹם הַשְּׁבִיעִי מְלַאכְתּוֹ אֲשֶׁר עָשָׂה
וַיִּשְׁבֹּת בַּיּוֹם הַשְּׁבִיעִי מִכָּל־מְלַאכְתּוֹ אֲשֶׁר עָשָׂה:
וַיְבָרֶךְ אֱלֹהִים אֶת־יוֹם הַשְּׁבִיעִי, וַיְקַדֵּשׁ אֹתוֹ
כִּי בוֹ שָׁבַת מִכָּל־מְלַאכְתּוֹ, אֲשֶׁר־בָּרָא אֱלֹהִים, לַעֲשׂוֹת:

When saying קידוש *for others, add:*

סַבְרִי מָרָנָן

בָּרוּךְ אַתָּה יהוה אֱלֹהֵינוּ מֶלֶךְ הָעוֹלָם, בּוֹרֵא פְּרִי הַגָּפֶן.

בָּרוּךְ אַתָּה יהוה אֱלֹהֵינוּ מֶלֶךְ הָעוֹלָם
אֲשֶׁר קִדְּשָׁנוּ בְּמִצְוֹתָיו, וְרָצָה בָנוּ
וְשַׁבַּת קָדְשׁוֹ בְּאַהֲבָה וּבְרָצוֹן הִנְחִילָנוּ
זִכָּרוֹן לְמַעֲשֵׂה בְרֵאשִׁית
כִּי הוּא יוֹם תְּחִלָּה לְמִקְרָאֵי קֹדֶשׁ, זֵכֶר לִיצִיאַת מִצְרָיִם
כִּי בָנוּ בָחַרְתָּ וְאוֹתָנוּ קִדַּשְׁתָּ מִכָּל הָעַמִּים
וְשַׁבַּת קָדְשְׁךָ בְּאַהֲבָה וּבְרָצוֹן הִנְחַלְתָּנוּ.
בָּרוּךְ אַתָּה יהוה, מְקַדֵּשׁ הַשַּׁבָּת.

On שבת חול המועד סוכות*, if* קידוש *is made in the* סוכה*, add:*

בָּרוּךְ אַתָּה יהוה אֱלֹהֵינוּ מֶלֶךְ הָעוֹלָם
אֲשֶׁר קִדְּשָׁנוּ בְּמִצְוֹתָיו וְצִוָּנוּ לֵישֵׁב בַּסֻּכָּה.

It is customary for all present to drink of the wine.

קידוש *Kiddush:* In the Ten Commandments, we are commanded to "remember" the Shabbat day. This was understood to mean a verbal declaration, said over a cup of wine: hence Kiddush. The Friday night Kiddush contains three elements: (1) a biblical reading, referring to the first Shabbat when God

ZEMIROT FOR SHABBAT EVENING

כָּל מְקַדֵּשׁ All who fittingly sanctify the seventh day,
All who protect the Sabbath properly from desecration,
Will have great reward in accord with their deed.
"Each in his own camp, each under his own banner." *Num. 1*

Lovers of the LORD, who await the building of the Temple,
Be glad and joyful on the Sabbath as if receiving the gift of God's inheritance,
Raise your hands in holiness and say to God:
"Blessed is the LORD who has given rest to His people Israel." *1 Kings 8*

Seekers of the LORD, offspring of His beloved Abraham,
Who are slow to leave the Sabbath but hasten to enter it,
Who rejoice to keep it and make its *eiruv* –
"This is the day the LORD has made; let us rejoice and be glad in it." *Ps. 118*

Remember Moses' Torah, from which the laws of Sabbath are learned,
Engraved is the seventh day like a bedecked bride between her companions,
The pure inherit it and sanctify it with the words: "All that He had made…
With the seventh day God completed the work He had done." *Gen. 2*

It is a sacred day from beginning to end,
All Jacob's offspring will honor it as the King's word and decree,
Resting on it and rejoicing with delights of food and drink.
"All the congregation of Israel will observe it." *Ex. 12*

Extend Your loving-kindness to those who know You, zealous and retributive God,
Those who keep the seventh day, fulfilling "Remember" and "Observe,"
Grant them the joy of Jerusalem rebuilt, make them shine with the light of Your face.
"Fill them with the rich plenty of Your House, give them drink from Your river of delights." *Ps. 36*

Help those who, on the seventh day, rest from plow and harvest,
Who walk slowly, and eat three meals to bless You.
May their righteousness shine like the light of the seven days,
LORD God of Israel, grant completion. *1 Sam. 14*

מְנוּחָה וְשִׂמְחָה אוֹר לַיְּהוּדִים
יוֹם שַׁבָּתוֹן, יוֹם מַחֲמַדִּים
שׁוֹמְרָיו וְזוֹכְרָיו הֵמָּה מְעִידִים
כִּי לְשִׁשָּׁה כֹּל בְּרוּאִים וְעוֹמְדִים.

שְׁמֵי שָׁמַיִם, אֶרֶץ וְיַמִּים
כָּל צְבָא מָרוֹם גְּבוֹהִים וְרָמִים
תַּנִּין וְאָדָם וְחַיַּת רְאֵמִים
כִּי בְּיָהּ יהוה צוּר עוֹלָמִים.

הוּא אֲשֶׁר דִּבֶּר לְעַם סְגֻלָּתוֹ
שָׁמוֹר לְקַדְּשׁוֹ מִבּוֹאוֹ עַד צֵאתוֹ
שַׁבַּת קֹדֶשׁ יוֹם חֶמְדָּתוֹ
כִּי בוֹ שָׁבַת אֵל מִכָּל מְלַאכְתּוֹ.

בְּמִצְוַת שַׁבָּת אֵל יַחֲלִיצָךְ
קוּם קְרָא אֵלָיו, יָחִישׁ לְאַמְּצָךְ
נִשְׁמַת כָּל חַי וְגַם נַעֲרִיצָךְ
אֱכֹל בְּשִׂמְחָה כִּי כְבָר רָצָךְ.

בְּמִשְׁנֶה לֶחֶם וְקִדּוּשׁ רַבָּה
בְּרֹב מַטְעַמִּים וְרוּחַ נְדִיבָה
יִזְכּוּ לְרַב טוּב הַמִּתְעַנְּגִים בָּהּ
בְּבִיאַת גּוֹאֵל לְחַיֵּי הָעוֹלָם הַבָּא.

מַה־יְּדִידוּת How beloved is your rest, Sabbath Queen,
We run to greet you: Come, royal bride,
Dressed in fine robes. We light the light with blessing.
All labors end [as is said:] "You shall do no work."
To savor the delights of fowl, quail and fish.

In advance all kinds of tasty food have been prepared,
Fattened chickens made ready while it was still day.
Varied dishes set out, and fragrant wines to drink,
And special delicacies all three times.
To savor the delights of fowl, quail and fish.

They shall inherit Jacob's heritage, a heritage unbounded,
Rich and poor will honor [the Sabbath] and be worthy of redemption,
If you keep the Sabbath day you will be My special treasure,
Six days shall you labor – and on the seventh let us rejoice.
To savor the delights of fowl, quail and fish.

Your secular concerns are forbidden; so too are calculations.
Reflections are permitted, and arranging matches for girls,
And teaching a child a book, and singing songs of praise,
And meditating on fine words at every place and gathering.
To savor the delights of fowl, quail and fish.

Your walk shall be unhurried; you shall call the Sabbath a delight.
Sleep too is praiseworthy, for it refreshes the spirit.
Therefore my soul yearns for you, to rest in you in love,
As if within a fence of roses: on it son and daughter rest.
To savor the delights of fowl, quail and fish.

A foretaste of the World to Come is the day of Sabbath rest.
All who take delight in it will be worthy of great joy.
They will be delivered with relief from the birthpangs of the Messiah,
May our redemption spring forth, and sadness and sighing flee away.
To savor the delights of fowl, quail and fish.

מַה־יְּדִידוּת מְנוּחָתֵךְ, אַתְּ שַׁבָּת הַמַּלְכָּה
בְּכֵן נָרוּץ לִקְרָאתֵךְ, בּוֹאִי כַלָּה נְסוּכָה
לְבוּשׁ בִּגְדֵי חֲמוּדוֹת, לְהַדְלִיק נֵר בִּבְרָכָה
וַתֵּכֶל כָּל הָעֲבוֹדוֹת, לֹא תַעֲשׂוּ מְלָאכָה.
לְהִתְעַנֵּג בְּתַעֲנוּגִים בַּרְבּוּרִים וּשְׂלָו וְדָגִים.

מֵעֶרֶב מַזְמִינִים כָּל מִינֵי מַטְעַמִּים
מִבְּעוֹד יוֹם מוּכָנִים תַּרְנְגוֹלִים מְפֻטָּמִים
וְלַעֲרֹךְ כַּמָּה מִינִים, שְׁתוֹת יֵינוֹת מְבֻשָּׂמִים
וְתַפְנוּקֵי מַעֲדַנִּים בְּכָל שָׁלֹשׁ פְּעָמִים.
לְהִתְעַנֵּג בְּתַעֲנוּגִים בַּרְבּוּרִים וּשְׂלָו וְדָגִים.

נַחֲלַת יַעֲקֹב יִירָשׁ, בְּלִי מְצָרִים נַחֲלָה
וִיכַבְּדוּהוּ עָשִׁיר וָרָשׁ, וְתִזְכּוּ לִגְאֻלָּה
יוֹם שַׁבָּת אִם תְּכַבֵּדוּ וִהְיִיתֶם לִי סְגֻלָּה
שֵׁשֶׁת יָמִים תַּעֲבֹדוּ וּבַשְּׁבִיעִי נָגִילָה.
לְהִתְעַנֵּג בְּתַעֲנוּגִים בַּרְבּוּרִים וּשְׂלָו וְדָגִים.

חֲפָצֶיךָ אֲסוּרִים וְגַם לַחְשֹׁב חֶשְׁבּוֹנוֹת
הִרְהוּרִים מֻתָּרִים וּלְשַׁדֵּךְ הַבָּנוֹת
וְתִינוֹק לְלַמְּדוֹ סֵפֶר, לַמְנַצֵּחַ בִּנְגִינוֹת
וְלַהֲגוֹת בְּאִמְרֵי שֶׁפֶר בְּכָל פִּנּוֹת וּמַחֲנוֹת.
לְהִתְעַנֵּג בְּתַעֲנוּגִים בַּרְבּוּרִים וּשְׂלָו וְדָגִים.

הִלּוּכָךְ יְהֵא בְנַחַת, עֹנֶג קְרָא לַשַּׁבָּת
וְהַשֵּׁנָה מְשֻׁבַּחַת כְּדָת נֶפֶשׁ מְשִׁיבַת
בְּכֵן נַפְשִׁי לְךָ עָרְגָה וְלָנוּחַ בְּחִבַּת
כַּשּׁוֹשַׁנִּים סוּגָה, בּוֹ יָנוּחוּ בֵּן וּבַת.
לְהִתְעַנֵּג בְּתַעֲנוּגִים בַּרְבּוּרִים וּשְׂלָו וְדָגִים.

מֵעֵין עוֹלָם הַבָּא יוֹם שַׁבָּת מְנוּחָה
כָּל הַמִּתְעַנְּגִים בָּהּ יִזְכּוּ לְרֹב שִׂמְחָה
מֵחֶבְלֵי מָשִׁיחַ יֻצָּלוּ לִרְוָחָה
פְּדוּתֵנוּ תַצְמִיחַ, וְנָס יָגוֹן וַאֲנָחָה.
לְהִתְעַנֵּג בְּתַעֲנוּגִים בַּרְבּוּרִים וּשְׂלָו וְדָגִים.

יוֹם זֶה לְיִשְׂרָאֵל This day for Israel is light and joy,
a Sabbath of serenity.
At the assembly at Sinai You decreed the laws,
Sabbath and the festivals – to keep them all my years;
Setting a table before me with courses of fine food –
A Sabbath of serenity.
This day, for Israel, is light and joy, a Sabbath of serenity.

Heart's delight to a shattered people,
To suffering spirits, an extra soul.
From troubled hearts may it banish sighs –
A Sabbath of serenity.
This day, for Israel, is light and joy, a Sabbath of serenity.

You sanctified and blessed it above all other days.
In six days You finished the making of all worlds.
On it sad souls find quiet and safety –
A Sabbath of serenity.
This day, for Israel, is light and joy, a Sabbath of serenity.

All work is forbidden by the revered One's commandment,
I will merit royal glory if I keep the Sabbath day,
Bringing the awesome One a sweetly scented gift –
A Sabbath of serenity.
This day, for Israel, is light and joy, a Sabbath of serenity.

Renew our Sanctuary, remember the ruined city.
Bestow Your goodness, Savior, on one who is sad,
Yet still she spends the Sabbath in song and praise –
A Sabbath of serenity.
This day, for Israel, is light and joy, a Sabbath of serenity.

יוֹם זֶה לְיִשְׂרָאֵל אוֹרָה וְשִׂמְחָה, שַׁבַּת מְנוּחָה.

צִוִּיתָ פִּקּוּדִים בְּמַעֲמַד סִינַי
שַׁבָּת וּמוֹעֲדִים לִשְׁמֹר בְּכָל שָׁנַי
לַעֲרֹךְ לְפָנַי מַשְׂאֵת וַאֲרוּחָה שַׁבַּת מְנוּחָה.

יוֹם זֶה לְיִשְׂרָאֵל אוֹרָה וְשִׂמְחָה, שַׁבַּת מְנוּחָה.

חֶמְדַּת הַלְּבָבוֹת לְאֻמָּה שְׁבוּרָה
לִנְפָשׁוֹת נִכְאָבוֹת נְשָׁמָה יְתֵרָה
לְנֶפֶשׁ מְצֵרָה יָסִיר אֲנָחָה שַׁבַּת מְנוּחָה.

יוֹם זֶה לְיִשְׂרָאֵל אוֹרָה וְשִׂמְחָה, שַׁבַּת מְנוּחָה.

קִדַּשְׁתָּ בֵּרַכְתָּ אוֹתוֹ מִכָּל יָמִים
בְּשֵׁשֶׁת כִּלִּיתָ מְלֶאכֶת עוֹלָמִים
בּוֹ מָצְאוּ עֲגוּמִים הַשְׁקֵט וּבִטְחָה שַׁבַּת מְנוּחָה.

יוֹם זֶה לְיִשְׂרָאֵל אוֹרָה וְשִׂמְחָה, שַׁבַּת מְנוּחָה.

לְאִסּוּר מְלָאכָה צִוִּיתָנוּ נוֹרָא
אֶזְכֶּה הוֹד מְלוּכָה אִם שַׁבָּת אֶשְׁמְרָה
אַקְרִיב שַׁי לַמּוֹרָא, מִנְחָה מֶרְקָחָה שַׁבַּת מְנוּחָה.

יוֹם זֶה לְיִשְׂרָאֵל אוֹרָה וְשִׂמְחָה, שַׁבַּת מְנוּחָה.

חַדֵּשׁ מִקְדָּשֵׁנוּ, זָכְרָה נֶחֱרֶבֶת
טוּבְךָ, מוֹשִׁיעֵנוּ, תְּנָה לַנֶּעֱצֶבֶת
בְּשַׁבָּת יוֹשֶׁבֶת בְּזֶמֶר וּשְׁבָחָה שַׁבַּת מְנוּחָה.

יוֹם זֶה לְיִשְׂרָאֵל אוֹרָה וְשִׂמְחָה, שַׁבַּת מְנוּחָה.

יָהּ רִבּוֹן Master of all worlds, our God, adored,
King of kings, over all the Lord:
Your wondrous deeds to applaud
We sing to You with one accord.

God of all worlds, our God, adored;
King of kings, over all, the Lord.

Early and late my praise shall ring,
To You, holy Author of every thing:
Beasts of the field, birds that take wing.
Angels and mortals to You shall sing.

God of all worlds, our God, adored;
King of kings, over all, the Lord.

Your great good deeds are vast in scale,
You humble the proud, You lift the frail.
A thousand years would not avail
Of Your works to tell the tale.

God of all worlds, our God, adored;
King of kings, over all, the Lord.

Yours is the glory, the greatness too,
From the lion's jaw, Your flock rescue.
Bring Your exiles home to You:
The people You chose, deliver anew.

God of all worlds, our God, adored;
King of kings, over all, the Lord.

Come back to Your Temple, Your sacred shrine,
That there in joy our souls may entwine.
In song our voices to combine,
When Jerusalem's beauty again will shine.

God of all worlds, our God, adored;
King of kings, over all, the Lord.

יָהּ רִבּוֹן עָלַם וְעָלְמַיָּא
אַנְתְּ הוּא מַלְכָּא מֶלֶךְ מַלְכַיָּא
עוֹבַד גְּבוּרְתָּךְ וְתִמְהַיָּא
שְׁפַר קֳדָמָךְ לְהַחֲוָיָא.
יָהּ רִבּוֹן עָלַם וְעָלְמַיָּא, אַנְתְּ הוּא מַלְכָּא מֶלֶךְ מַלְכַיָּא.

שְׁבָחִין אֲסַדֵּר צַפְרָא וְרַמְשָׁא
לָךְ אֱלָהָא קַדִּישָׁא דִּי בְרָא כָּל נַפְשָׁא
עִירִין קַדִּישִׁין וּבְנֵי אֱנָשָׁא
חֵיוַת בָּרָא וְעוֹפֵי שְׁמַיָּא.
יָהּ רִבּוֹן עָלַם וְעָלְמַיָּא, אַנְתְּ הוּא מַלְכָּא מֶלֶךְ מַלְכַיָּא.

רַבְרְבִין עוֹבְדָיךְ וְתַקִּיפִין
מָכֵךְ רָמַיָּא וְזָקֵף כְּפִיפִין
לוּ יִחְיֶה גְבַר שְׁנִין אַלְפִין
לָא יֵעוֹל גְּבוּרְתָּךְ בְּחֻשְׁבְּנַיָּא.
יָהּ רִבּוֹן עָלַם וְעָלְמַיָּא, אַנְתְּ הוּא מַלְכָּא מֶלֶךְ מַלְכַיָּא.

אֱלָהָא דִּי לֵהּ יְקָר וּרְבוּתָא
פְּרוֹק יַת עָנָךְ מִפֻּם אַרְיְוָתָא
וְאַפֵּק יַת עַמָּךְ מִגּוֹ גָלוּתָא
עַמָּא דִּי בְחַרְתְּ מִכָּל אֻמַּיָּא.
יָהּ רִבּוֹן עָלַם וְעָלְמַיָּא, אַנְתְּ הוּא מַלְכָּא מֶלֶךְ מַלְכַיָּא.

לְמִקְדְּשָׁךְ תּוּב וּלְקֹדֶשׁ קֻדְשִׁין
אֲתַר דִּי בֵהּ יֶחֱדוּן רוּחִין וְנַפְשִׁין
וִיזַמְּרוּן לָךְ שִׁירִין וְרַחֲשִׁין
בִּירוּשְׁלֵם קַרְתָּא דְשֻׁפְרַיָּא.
יָהּ רִבּוֹן עָלַם וְעָלְמַיָּא, אַנְתְּ הוּא מַלְכָּא מֶלֶךְ מַלְכַיָּא.

צָמְאָה נַפְשִׁי My soul thirsts for God, the living God *Ps. 42*
My heart and flesh will sing joyfully to the living God. *Ps. 84*
The One God created me, and said "As I live,
No one shall see Me and live."

My soul thirsts for God, the living God
My heart and flesh will sing joyfully to the living God.

He created all with wisdom, design and deliberation,
Deeply hidden though it is from the eyes of all that live.
His glory is high above all, every mouth makes known His splendor,
Blessed is He in whose hands is the life-force of all that lives.

My soul thirsts for God, the living God
My heart and flesh will sing joyfully to the living God.

He set apart the quiet one's offspring, to teach them decrees,
Which if one performs them, thereby he shall live.
Who can vindicate himself? We are like specks of dust,
Truly none can vindicate itself before You, nothing that lives.

My soul thirsts for God, the living God
My heart and flesh will sing joyfully to the living God.

In the heart, the inclination is like a viper's poison,
How then can we return, and be like flesh that lives?
Those who have gone astray, if they wished, could turn from their way,
Before they go to their rest in the place destined for all that lives.

My soul thirsts for God, the living God
My heart and flesh will sing joyfully to the living God.

For everything, I shall thank You, every mouth shall declare Your oneness,
You who open Your hand and satisfy all that lives.
Recall the love of ancient times, and revive those who slumber,
Bring near the days when the Messiah shall live.

My soul thirsts for God, the living God
My heart and flesh will sing joyfully to the living God.

See who is the true mistress, when the handmaid says,
"No, your son is dead while my son lives."
I will bow face down and spread my hands toward you,
When I open my mouth to say: "The soul of all that lives."

My soul thirsts for God, the living God
My heart and flesh will sing joyfully to the living God.

צָמְאָה נַפְשִׁי לֵאלֹהִים לְאֵל חָי: לִבִּי וּבְשָׂרִי יְרַנְּנוּ אֶל אֵל־חָי: תהלים מב / תהלים פד
אֵל אֶחָד בְּרָאַנִי, וְאָמַר חַי אָנִי כִּי לֹא יִרְאַנִי הָאָדָם וָחָי.
צָמְאָה נַפְשִׁי לֵאלֹהִים לְאֵל חָי, לִבִּי וּבְשָׂרִי יְרַנְּנוּ אֶל אֵל־חָי.

בָּרָא כֹל בְּחָכְמָה, בְּעֵצָה וּבִמְזִמָּה מְאֹד נֶעְלָמָה מֵעֵינֵי כָּל חָי.
רָם עַל כֹּל כְּבוֹדוֹ, כָּל פֶּה יְחַוֶּה הוֹדוֹ בָּרוּךְ אֲשֶׁר בְּיָדוֹ נֶפֶשׁ כָּל חָי.
צָמְאָה נַפְשִׁי לֵאלֹהִים לְאֵל חָי, לִבִּי וּבְשָׂרִי יְרַנְּנוּ אֶל אֵל־חָי.

הִבְדִּיל נִינֵי תָם, חֻקִּים לְהוֹרוֹתָם אֲשֶׁר יַעֲשֶׂה אוֹתָם הָאָדָם וָחָי.
מִי זֶה יִצְטַדָּק, נִמְשַׁל לְאָבָק דָּק אֱמֶת, כִּי לֹא יִצְדַּק לְפָנֶיךָ כָּל חָי.
צָמְאָה נַפְשִׁי לֵאלֹהִים לְאֵל חָי, לִבִּי וּבְשָׂרִי יְרַנְּנוּ אֶל אֵל־חָי.

בְּלֵב יֵצֶר חָשׁוּב כִּדְמוּת חֲמַת עַכְשׁוּב וְאֵיכָכָה יָשׁוּב הַבָּשָׂר הֶחָי.
נְסוֹגִים אִם אָבוּ, וּמִדַּרְכָּם שָׁבוּ טֶרֶם יִשְׁכָּבוּ בֵּית מוֹעֵד לְכָל חָי.
צָמְאָה נַפְשִׁי לֵאלֹהִים לְאֵל חָי, לִבִּי וּבְשָׂרִי יְרַנְּנוּ אֶל אֵל־חָי.

עַל כֹּל אֲהוֹדֶךָ, כָּל פֶּה תְּיַחֲדֶךָ פּוֹתֵחַ אֶת יָדֶךָ וּמַשְׂבִּיעַ לְכָל חָי.
זְכֹר אַהֲבַת קְדוּמִים, וְהַחֲיֵה נִרְדָּמִים וְקָרֵב הַיָּמִים אֲשֶׁר בֶּן יִשַׁי חָי.
צָמְאָה נַפְשִׁי לֵאלֹהִים לְאֵל חָי, לִבִּי וּבְשָׂרִי יְרַנְּנוּ אֶל אֵל־חָי.

רְאֵה לִגְבֶרֶת אֱמֶת, שִׁפְחָה נוֹאֱמֶת לֹא כִי, בְּנֵךְ הַמֵּת וּבְנִי הֶחָי.
אֶקֹּד עַל אַפִּי, וְאֶפְרֹשׂ לְךָ כַּפִּי עֵת אֶפְתַּח פִּי בְּנִשְׁמַת כָּל חָי.
צָמְאָה נַפְשִׁי לֵאלֹהִים לְאֵל חָי, לִבִּי וּבְשָׂרִי יְרַנְּנוּ אֶל אֵל־חָי.

צוּר מִשֶּׁלּוֹ The Rock from whom we have eaten:
Bless Him, my faithful friends;
we have sufficed, we have left over,
just as the LORD said.

He feeds His world – our Shepherd, our Father,
we have eaten of His bread, His wine we have drunk.
So let us thank His name, let us praise Him with our mouths,
saying, singing: None is holy like the LORD.

> The Rock from whom we have eaten: Bless Him, my faithful friends;
> we have sufficed, we have left over, just as the LORD said.

With song and sound of thanks, we shall bless our God,
for the gift He gave our fathers: A lovely land.
With food and sustenance He has satisfied our souls.
His kindness overwhelms us: True is the LORD.

> The Rock from whom we have eaten: Bless Him, my faithful friends;
> we have sufficed, we have left over, just as the LORD said.

Have compassion in Your love for Your people, our Rock,
for Zion, Your home of glory, Temple of our splendor.
The son of David Your servant: may he come and redeem us,
breath of our life, anointed of the LORD.

> The Rock from whom we have eaten: Bless Him, my faithful friends;
> we have sufficed, we have left over, just as the LORD said.

May the Temple be rebuilt, Zion's city full again;
there we will sing a new song as we go up in joy,
to the Compassionate, the Holy One –
may He be blessed and raised on high –
with a full cup of wine, sign of the blessing of the LORD.

> The Rock from whom we have eaten: Bless Him, my faithful friends;
> we have sufficed, we have left over, just as the LORD said.

צוּר מִשֶּׁלּוֹ אָכַלְנוּ   בָּרְכוּ אֱמוּנַי
שָׂבַעְנוּ וְהוֹתַרְנוּ   כִּדְבַר יהוה.

הַזָּן אֶת עוֹלָמוֹ   רוֹעֵנוּ אָבִינוּ
אָכַלְנוּ אֶת לַחְמוֹ   וְיֵינוֹ שָׁתִינוּ
עַל כֵּן נוֹדֶה לִשְׁמוֹ   וּנְהַלְּלוֹ בְּפִינוּ
אָמַרְנוּ וְעָנִינוּ   אֵין קָדוֹשׁ כַּיהוה.

צוּר מִשֶּׁלּוֹ אָכַלְנוּ, בָּרְכוּ אֱמוּנַי, שָׂבַעְנוּ וְהוֹתַרְנוּ כִּדְבַר יהוה.

בְּשִׁיר וְקוֹל תּוֹדָה   נְבָרֵךְ אֱלֹהֵינוּ
עַל אֶרֶץ חֶמְדָּה   שֶׁהִנְחִיל לַאֲבוֹתֵינוּ
מָזוֹן וְצֵידָה   הִשְׂבִּיעַ לְנַפְשֵׁנוּ
חַסְדּוֹ גָּבַר עָלֵינוּ   וֶאֱמֶת יהוה.

צוּר מִשֶּׁלּוֹ אָכַלְנוּ, בָּרְכוּ אֱמוּנַי, שָׂבַעְנוּ וְהוֹתַרְנוּ כִּדְבַר יהוה.

רַחֵם בְּחַסְדֶּךָ   עַל עַמְּךָ צוּרֵנוּ
עַל צִיּוֹן מִשְׁכַּן כְּבוֹדֶךָ   זְבוּל בֵּית תִּפְאַרְתֵּנוּ
בֶּן דָּוִד עַבְדֶּךָ   יָבוֹא וְיִגְאָלֵנוּ
רוּחַ אַפֵּינוּ   מְשִׁיחַ יהוה.

צוּר מִשֶּׁלּוֹ אָכַלְנוּ, בָּרְכוּ אֱמוּנַי, שָׂבַעְנוּ וְהוֹתַרְנוּ כִּדְבַר יהוה.

יִבָּנֶה הַמִּקְדָּשׁ   עִיר צִיּוֹן תְּמַלֵּא
וְשָׁם נָשִׁיר שִׁיר חָדָשׁ   וּבִרְנָנָה נַעֲלֶה
הָרַחֲמָן הַנִּקְדָּשׁ   יִתְבָּרַךְ וְיִתְעַלֶּה
עַל כּוֹס יַיִן מָלֵא   כְּבִרְכַּת יהוה.

צוּר מִשֶּׁלּוֹ אָכַלְנוּ, בָּרְכוּ אֱמוּנַי, שָׂבַעְנוּ וְהוֹתַרְנוּ כִּדְבַר יהוה.

Shaḥarit for Shabbat and Yom Tov

Begin as on weekdays, from pages 4–58.

A PSALM BEFORE VERSES OF PRAISE

מִזְמוֹר שִׁיר A psalm of David. A song for the dedication of the House. *Ps. 30*
I will exalt You, LORD, for You have lifted me up, and not let my enemies rejoice over me. LORD, my God, I cried to You for help and You healed me. LORD, You lifted my soul from the grave; You spared me from going down to the pit. Sing to the LORD, you His devoted ones, and give thanks to His holy name. For His anger is for a moment, but His favor for a lifetime. At night there may be weeping, but in the morning there is joy. When I felt secure, I said, "I shall never be shaken." LORD, when You favored me, You made me stand firm as a mountain, but when You hid Your face, I was terrified. To You, LORD, I called; I pleaded with my LORD: "What gain would there be if I died and went down to the grave? Can dust thank You? Can it declare Your truth? Hear, LORD, and be gracious to me; LORD, be my help." You have turned my sorrow into dancing. ▸ You have removed my sackcloth and clothed me with joy, so that my soul may sing to You and not be silent. LORD my God, for ever will I thank You.

---

hitherto secure, was suddenly in danger. It was then that he prayed to God, "What gain would there be if I died and went down to the grave? … Can dust thank You?" So we, waking to the life of a new day, express our sense of joy, "so that my soul may sing to You and not be silent."

שחרית לשבת וליום טוב

Begin as on weekdays, from pages 5–59.

מזמור לפני פסוקי דזמרה

מִזְמוֹר שִׁיר־חֲנֻכַּת הַבַּיִת לְדָוִד: אֲרוֹמִמְךָ יהוה כִּי דִלִּיתָנִי, וְלֹא־ תהלים ל
שִׂמַּחְתָּ אֹיְבַי לִי: יהוה אֱלֹהָי, שִׁוַּעְתִּי אֵלֶיךָ וַתִּרְפָּאֵנִי: יהוה,
הֶעֱלִיתָ מִן־שְׁאוֹל נַפְשִׁי, חִיִּיתַנִי מִיָּרְדִי־בוֹר: זַמְּרוּ לַיהוה חֲסִידָיו,
וְהוֹדוּ לְזֵכֶר קׇדְשׁוֹ: כִּי רֶגַע בְּאַפּוֹ, חַיִּים בִּרְצוֹנוֹ, בָּעֶרֶב יָלִין בֶּכִי
וְלַבֹּקֶר רִנָּה: וַאֲנִי אָמַרְתִּי בְשַׁלְוִי, בַּל־אֶמּוֹט לְעוֹלָם: יהוה,
בִּרְצוֹנְךָ הֶעֱמַדְתָּה לְהַרְרִי עֹז, הִסְתַּרְתָּ פָנֶיךָ הָיִיתִי נִבְהָל: אֵלֶיךָ
יהוה אֶקְרָא, וְאֶל־אֲדֹנָי אֶתְחַנָּן: מַה־בֶּצַע בְּדָמִי, בְּרִדְתִּי אֶל שָׁחַת,
הֲיוֹדְךָ עָפָר, הֲיַגִּיד אֲמִתֶּךָ: שְׁמַע־יהוה וְחׇנֵּנִי, יהוה הֱיֵה־עֹזֵר לִי:
· הָפַכְתָּ מִסְפְּדִי לְמָחוֹל לִי, פִּתַּחְתָּ שַׂקִּי, וַתְּאַזְּרֵנִי שִׂמְחָה: לְמַעַן
יְזַמֶּרְךָ כָבוֹד וְלֹא יִדֹּם, יהוה אֱלֹהַי, לְעוֹלָם אוֹדֶךָּ:

מִזְמוֹר שִׁיר־חֲנֻכַּת הַבַּיִת *A song for the dedication of the House:* According to Rashi, David wrote this psalm to be sung at the inauguration of the Temple, though he knew it would only take place in the lifetime of his son, Solomon. The psalm first entered the siddur as a prayer to be said on Ḥanukka, and was later adopted as part of the daily prayers.

Its content is beautifully suited to be a bridge between the Morning Blessings and the *Pesukei DeZimra*. The connecting theme is the restoration of life as a reason for giving praise. The Psalmist recounts a crisis when his life,

MOURNER'S KADDISH

The following prayer, said by mourners, requires the presence of a minyan. A transliteration can be found on page 1334.

Mourner: יִתְגַּדַּל Magnified and sanctified
may His great name be,
in the world He created by His will.
May He establish His kingdom
in your lifetime and in your days,
and in the lifetime of all the house of Israel,
swiftly and soon – and say: Amen.

All: May His great name be blessed for ever and all time.

Mourner: Blessed and praised, glorified and exalted,
raised and honored,
uplifted and lauded
be the name of the Holy One,
blessed be He,
beyond any blessing,
song, praise and consolation
uttered in the world – and say: Amen.

May there be great peace from heaven,
and life for us and all Israel – and say: Amen.

Bow, take three steps back, as if taking leave of the Divine Presence, then bow, first left, then right, then center, while saying:

May He who makes peace in His high places,
make peace for us and all Israel – and say: Amen.

The most profound gift we can bring to the memory of one we have lost is to be a source of blessing to the deceased by the good deeds we do in his or her name. When we say Kaddish, we are the cause of the congregation saying, in response, "May His great name be blessed for ever and all time." This, according to the Talmud, brings great pleasure to God. By causing the congregation to praise God, we show that the recollection of the person we have lost moves us to good deeds – and thus that their memory continues to be a blessing.

קדיש יתום

The following prayer, said by mourners, requires the presence of a מנין.
A transliteration can be found on page 1334.

אבל: יִתְגַּדַּל וְיִתְקַדַּשׁ שְׁמֵהּ רַבָּא (קהל: אָמֵן)
בְּעָלְמָא דִּי בְרָא כִרְעוּתֵהּ
וְיַמְלִיךְ מַלְכוּתֵהּ
בְּחַיֵּיכוֹן וּבְיוֹמֵיכוֹן וּבְחַיֵּי דְכָל בֵּית יִשְׂרָאֵל
בַּעֲגָלָא וּבִזְמַן קָרִיב, וְאִמְרוּ אָמֵן. (קהל: אָמֵן)

קהל ואבל: יְהֵא שְׁמֵהּ רַבָּא מְבָרַךְ לְעָלַם וּלְעָלְמֵי עָלְמַיָּא.

אבל: יִתְבָּרַךְ וְיִשְׁתַּבַּח וְיִתְפָּאַר
וְיִתְרוֹמַם וְיִתְנַשֵּׂא וְיִתְהַדָּר וְיִתְעַלֶּה וְיִתְהַלָּל
שְׁמֵהּ דְּקֻדְשָׁא בְּרִיךְ הוּא (קהל: בְּרִיךְ הוּא)
לְעֵלָּא מִן כָּל בִּרְכָתָא / בשבת שובה: לְעֵלָּא לְעֵלָּא מִכָּל בִּרְכָתָא/
וְשִׁירָתָא, תֻּשְׁבְּחָתָא וְנֶחֱמָתָא
דַּאֲמִירָן בְּעָלְמָא, וְאִמְרוּ אָמֵן. (קהל: אָמֵן)

יְהֵא שְׁלָמָא רַבָּא מִן שְׁמַיָּא
וְחַיִּים, עָלֵינוּ וְעַל כָּל יִשְׂרָאֵל, וְאִמְרוּ אָמֵן. (קהל: אָמֵן)

Bow, take three steps back, as if taking leave of the Divine Presence, then bow, first left, then right, then center, while saying:

עֹשֶׂה שָׁלוֹם/ בשבת שובה: הַשָּׁלוֹם/ בִּמְרוֹמָיו
הוּא יַעֲשֶׂה שָׁלוֹם
עָלֵינוּ וְעַל כָּל יִשְׂרָאֵל, וְאִמְרוּ אָמֵן. (קהל: אָמֵן)

MOURNER'S KADDISH

The paradox has long been noted that the mourner's Kaddish contains no mention of death, bereavement or grief. In Judaism, we emerge from the pain of loss by re-immersing ourselves in life – and thus in God, the source of all life.

PESUKEI DEZIMRA

The following introductory blessing to the Pesukei DeZimra (Verses of Praise) is said standing, while holding the two front tzitziot of the tallit. They are kissed and released at the end of the blessing at "songs of praise" (on the next page). From the beginning of this prayer to the end of the Amida, conversation is forbidden. See table on pages 1329–1331 for which congregational responses are permitted.

Some say:
I hereby prepare my mouth to thank, praise and laud my Creator, for the sake of the unification of the Holy One, blessed be He, and His Divine Presence, through that which is hidden and concealed, in the name of all Israel.

BLESSED IS HE WHO SPOKE

and the world came into being, blessed is He.
Blessed is He who creates the universe.
Blessed is He who speaks and acts.
Blessed is He who decrees and fulfills.
Blessed is He who shows compassion to the earth.
Blessed is He who shows compassion to all creatures.
Blessed is He who gives a good reward
to those who fear Him.
Blessed is He who lives for ever and exists to eternity.
Blessed is He who redeems and saves.
Blessed is His name.

---

is impossible to move directly from worldly concerns to the intense concentration required for genuine prayer, and vice versa. The verse cited in support of this practice is "Happy are they that dwell in Your House" (Psalm 84:5), and this verse occupies a prominent place at the heart of the Verses of Praise. In addition to the six psalms said on weekdays, nine extra psalms are added on Shabbat and Yom Tov.

בָּרוּךְ שֶׁאָמַר *Blessed is He:* An introductory blessing to the *Pesukei DeZimra,* in two parts. The first is a ten-part litany of praise to God as creator, each phrase introduced with the word "Blessed" (the second phrase, "Blessed is He," is not a separate verse but originally a congregational response). The number

פסוקי דזמרה

The following introductory blessing to the פסוקי דזמרה *is said standing, while holding the two front* ציציות *of the* טלית. *They are kissed and released at the end of the blessing at* בַּתִּשְׁבָּחוֹת *(on the next page). From the beginning of this prayer to the end of the* עמידה, *conversation is forbidden. See table on pages 1329–1331 for which congregational responses are permitted.*

Some say:

הֲרֵינִי מְזַמֵּן אֶת פִּי לְהוֹדוֹת וּלְהַלֵּל וּלְשַׁבֵּחַ אֶת בּוֹרְאִי, לְשֵׁם יִחוּד קֻדְשָׁא בְּרִיךְ הוּא וּשְׁכִינְתֵּהּ עַל יְדֵי הַהוּא טָמִיר וְנֶעְלָם בְּשֵׁם כָּל יִשְׂרָאֵל.

בָּרוּךְ שֶׁאָמַר וְהָיָה הָעוֹלָם, בָּרוּךְ הוּא.

בָּרוּךְ עוֹשֶׂה בְרֵאשִׁית

בָּרוּךְ אוֹמֵר וְעוֹשֶׂה

בָּרוּךְ גּוֹזֵר וּמְקַיֵּם

בָּרוּךְ מְרַחֵם עַל הָאָרֶץ

בָּרוּךְ מְרַחֵם עַל הַבְּרִיּוֹת

בָּרוּךְ מְשַׁלֵּם שָׂכָר טוֹב לִירֵאָיו

בָּרוּךְ חַי לָעַד וְקַיָּם לָנֶצַח

בָּרוּךְ פּוֹדֶה וּמַצִּיל

בָּרוּךְ שְׁמוֹ

PESUKEI DEZIMRA / VERSES OF PRAISE

This section of the prayers is based on the Talmudic teaching (*Berakhot* 32a) that "The pious men of old used to wait for an hour [before praying], they prayed for an hour, and then waited again for an hour." Prayer requires mental preparation beforehand, as well as a gradual leave-taking afterward. It

Blessed are You, LORD our God,
King of the Universe,
God, compassionate Father,
extolled by the mouth of His people,
praised and glorified by the tongue of His devoted ones
and those who serve Him.
With the songs of Your servant David
we will praise You, O LORD our God.
With praises and psalms
we will magnify and praise You, glorify You,
speak Your name and proclaim Your kingship,
our King, our God, ▸ the only One, Giver of life to the worlds
the King whose great name is praised
and glorified to all eternity.
Blessed are You, LORD,
the King extolled with songs of praise.

הודו Thank the LORD, call on His name, make His acts known *1 Chr. 16*
among the peoples. Sing to Him, make music to Him, tell of all His wonders. Glory in His holy name; let the hearts of those who seek the LORD rejoice. Search out the LORD and His strength; seek His presence at all times. Remember the wonders He has done, His miracles, and the judgments He pronounced. Descendants of Yisrael His servant, sons of Jacob His chosen ones: He is the LORD our God. His judgments are throughout the earth. Remember

---

הודו *Thank the LORD:* The Bible gives us a vivid account (1 Chr. 15–16) of the moment when this passage was first recited: when King David brought the Ark of the Covenant to Jerusalem, newly established as the capital of the Jewish state. The Ark, which had been captured by the Philistines, was brought back by David to a temporary resting place. Later it was carried into Jerusalem to scenes of great jubilation. As on other momentous occasions in the life of biblical Israel, the leader (here David) reminds the people of the

בָּרוּךְ אַתָּה יהוה אֱלֹהֵינוּ מֶלֶךְ הָעוֹלָם
הָאֵל הָאָב הָרַחֲמָן הַמְהֻלָּל בְּפִי עַמּוֹ
מְשֻׁבָּח וּמְפֹאָר בִּלְשׁוֹן חֲסִידָיו וַעֲבָדָיו
וּבְשִׁירֵי דָוִד עַבְדֶּךָ
נְהַלֶּלְךָ יהוה אֱלֹהֵינוּ.
בִּשְׁבָחוֹת וּבִזְמִירוֹת
נְגַדֶּלְךָ וּנְשַׁבֵּחֲךָ וּנְפָאֶרְךָ
וְנַזְכִּיר שִׁמְךָ וְנַמְלִיכְךָ
מַלְכֵּנוּ אֱלֹהֵינוּ, ◂ יָחִיד חֵי הָעוֹלָמִים
מֶלֶךְ, מְשֻׁבָּח וּמְפֹאָר עֲדֵי עַד שְׁמוֹ הַגָּדוֹל
בָּרוּךְ אַתָּה יהוה, מֶלֶךְ מְהֻלָּל בַּתִּשְׁבָּחוֹת.

הוֹדוּ לַיהוה קִרְאוּ בִשְׁמוֹ, הוֹדִיעוּ בָעַמִּים עֲלִילֹתָיו: שִׁירוּ לוֹ, דברי הימים א׳ טז
זַמְּרוּ־לוֹ, שִׂיחוּ בְּכָל־נִפְלְאוֹתָיו: הִתְהַלְלוּ בְּשֵׁם קָדְשׁוֹ, יִשְׂמַח לֵב
מְבַקְשֵׁי יהוה: דִּרְשׁוּ יהוה וְעֻזּוֹ, בַּקְּשׁוּ פָנָיו תָּמִיד: זִכְרוּ נִפְלְאֹתָיו
אֲשֶׁר עָשָׂה, מֹפְתָיו וּמִשְׁפְּטֵי־פִיהוּ: זֶרַע יִשְׂרָאֵל עַבְדּוֹ, בְּנֵי יַעֲקֹב
בְּחִירָיו: הוּא יהוה אֱלֹהֵינוּ בְּכָל־הָאָרֶץ מִשְׁפָּטָיו: זִכְרוּ לְעוֹלָם

---

ten corresponds to the ten times the word *VaYomer,* "And He said," appears in the story of creation in Genesis 1. Hence the rabbinic saying that "With ten utterances the world was created" (*Avot* 5:1).

Blessed are You: The second half of the blessing is a prelude to the biblical verses that follow, mainly from the Psalms ("With the Psalms of your servant David we will exalt you") but also from the books of Chronicles and Nehemiah ("extolled by the mouth of His people"). To emphasize the significance of this declaration, we recite it standing and, at the end, kiss the two front fringes of the tallit.

His covenant for ever, the word He commanded for a thousand generations. He made it with Abraham, vowed it to Isaac, and confirmed it to Jacob as a statute and to Israel as an everlasting covenant, saying, "To you I will give the land of Canaan as your allotted heritage." You were then small in number, few, strangers there, wandering from nation to nation, from one kingdom to another, but He let no man oppress them, and for their sake He rebuked kings: "Do not touch My anointed ones, and do My prophets no harm." Sing to the LORD, all the earth; proclaim His salvation daily. Declare His glory among the nations, His marvels among all the peoples. For great is the LORD and greatly to be praised; He is awesome beyond all heavenly powers. ▸ For all the gods of the peoples are mere idols; it was the LORD who made the heavens.

Before Him are majesty and splendor; there is strength and beauty in His holy place. Render to the LORD, families of the peoples, render to the LORD honor and might. Render to the LORD the glory due to His name; bring an offering and come before Him; bow down to the LORD in the splendor of holiness. Tremble before Him, all the earth; the world stands firm, it will not be shaken. Let the heavens rejoice and the earth be glad; let them declare among the nations, "The LORD is King." Let the sea roar, and all that is in it; let the fields be jubilant, and all they contain. Then the trees of the forest will sing for joy before the LORD, for He is coming to judge the earth. Thank the LORD for He is good; His loving-kindness is for ever. Say: "Save us, God of our salvation; gather us and rescue us from the nations, to acknowledge Your holy name and glory in Your praise. Blessed is the LORD, God of Israel, from this world to eternity." And let all the people say "Amen" and "Praise the LORD."

---

as an accompaniment to the sacrifices, from that day until the inauguration of the Temple in the time of Solomon.

בְּרִיתוֹ, דָּבָר צִוָּה לְאֶלֶף דּוֹר: אֲשֶׁר כָּרַת אֶת־אַבְרָהָם, וּשְׁבוּעָתוֹ לְיִצְחָק: וַיַּעֲמִידֶהָ לְיַעֲקֹב לְחֹק, לְיִשְׂרָאֵל בְּרִית עוֹלָם: לֵאמֹר, לְךָ אֶתֵּן אֶרֶץ־כְּנָעַן, חֶבֶל נַחֲלַתְכֶם: בִּהְיוֹתְכֶם מְתֵי מִסְפָּר, כִּמְעַט וְגָרִים בָּהּ: וַיִּתְהַלְּכוּ מִגּוֹי אֶל־גּוֹי, וּמִמַּמְלָכָה אֶל־עַם אַחֵר: לֹא־הִנִּיחַ לְאִישׁ לְעָשְׁקָם, וַיּוֹכַח עֲלֵיהֶם מְלָכִים: אַל־תִּגְּעוּ בִּמְשִׁיחָי, וּבִנְבִיאַי אַל־תָּרֵעוּ: שִׁירוּ לַיהוה כָּל־הָאָרֶץ, בַּשְּׂרוּ מִיּוֹם־אֶל־יוֹם יְשׁוּעָתוֹ: סַפְּרוּ בַגּוֹיִם אֶת־כְּבוֹדוֹ, בְּכָל־הָעַמִּים נִפְלְאֹתָיו: כִּי גָדוֹל יהוה וּמְהֻלָּל מְאֹד, וְנוֹרָא הוּא עַל־כָּל־אֱלֹהִים: › כִּי כָּל־אֱלֹהֵי הָעַמִּים אֱלִילִים, וַיהוה שָׁמַיִם עָשָׂה:

הוֹד וְהָדָר לְפָנָיו, עֹז וְחֶדְוָה בִּמְקֹמוֹ: הָבוּ לַיהוה מִשְׁפְּחוֹת עַמִּים, הָבוּ לַיהוה כָּבוֹד וָעֹז: הָבוּ לַיהוה כְּבוֹד שְׁמוֹ, שְׂאוּ מִנְחָה וּבֹאוּ לְפָנָיו, הִשְׁתַּחֲווּ לַיהוה בְּהַדְרַת־קֹדֶשׁ: חִילוּ מִלְּפָנָיו כָּל־הָאָרֶץ, אַף־תִּכּוֹן תֵּבֵל בַּל־תִּמּוֹט: יִשְׂמְחוּ הַשָּׁמַיִם וְתָגֵל הָאָרֶץ, וְיֹאמְרוּ בַגּוֹיִם יהוה מָלָךְ: יִרְעַם הַיָּם וּמְלוֹאוֹ, יַעֲלֹץ הַשָּׂדֶה וְכָל־אֲשֶׁר־בּוֹ: אָז יְרַנְּנוּ עֲצֵי הַיָּעַר, מִלִּפְנֵי יהוה, כִּי־בָא לִשְׁפּוֹט אֶת־הָאָרֶץ: הוֹדוּ לַיהוה כִּי טוֹב, כִּי לְעוֹלָם חַסְדּוֹ: וְאִמְרוּ, הוֹשִׁיעֵנוּ אֱלֹהֵי יִשְׁעֵנוּ, וְקַבְּצֵנוּ וְהַצִּילֵנוּ מִן־הַגּוֹיִם, לְהֹדוֹת לְשֵׁם קָדְשֶׁךָ, לְהִשְׁתַּבֵּחַ בִּתְהִלָּתֶךָ: בָּרוּךְ יהוה אֱלֹהֵי יִשְׂרָאֵל מִן־הָעוֹלָם וְעַד־הָעֹלָם, וַיֹּאמְרוּ כָל־הָעָם אָמֵן, וְהַלֵּל לַיהוה:

---

history of the nation, and its dependence on divine providence. The passage ends with the response of the people: "And all the people said 'Amen' and 'Praise the Lord.'" According to *Seder Olam* (chapter 14), this passage was recited daily (in two halves: one in the morning, the other in the afternoon)

▸ Exalt the LORD our God and bow before His footstool: He is holy. Exalt the LORD our God and bow at His holy mountain; for holy is the LORD our God. *Ps. 99*

He is compassionate. He forgives iniquity and does not destroy. *Ps. 78*
Repeatedly He suppresses His anger, not rousing His full wrath.
You, LORD: do not withhold Your compassion from me. May Your *Ps. 40*
loving-kindness and truth always guard me. Remember, LORD, *Ps. 25*
Your acts of compassion and love, for they have existed for ever.
Ascribe power to God, whose majesty is over Israel and whose *Ps. 68*
might is in the skies. You are awesome, God, in Your holy places.
It is the God of Israel who gives might and strength to the people,
may God be blessed. God of retribution, LORD, God of retribu- *Ps. 94*
tion, appear. Arise, Judge of the earth, to repay the arrogant their
just deserts. Salvation belongs to the LORD; may Your blessing rest *Ps. 3*
upon Your people, Selah! ▸ The LORD of hosts is with us, the God *Ps. 46*
of Jacob is our stronghold, Selah! LORD of hosts, happy is the one *Ps. 84*
who trusts in You. LORD, save! May the King answer us on the day *Ps. 20*
we call.

Save Your people and bless Your heritage; tend them and carry *Ps. 28*
them for ever. Our soul longs for the LORD; He is our Help and *Ps. 33*
Shield. For in Him our hearts rejoice, for in His holy name we have
trusted. May Your loving-kindness, LORD, be upon us, as we have

---

we have more time to pray, and also because on Shabbat we reflect on God's creation, a theme of many of the psalms. The Ashkenazi custom is to say nine. Together with the six weekday psalms, they make fifteen, the number associated with the fifteen Songs of Ascents (Psalms 120–134), and the fifteen steps in the Temple on which the Levites stood and sang their songs.

There is a striking feature to this sequence of additional psalms. According to one interpretation (Meiri) the phrase "a song of ascents" means one begun softly and continued with ever-increasing volume. The extra psalms begin in Psalm 19 with the universe singing a silent song ("their voice is not heard") and end in Psalm 93 with a magnificent crescendo ("Mightier than the noise of many waters").

תהלים צט ▸ רוֹמְמוּ יהוה אֱלֹהֵינוּ וְהִשְׁתַּחֲווּ לַהֲדֹם רַגְלָיו, קָדוֹשׁ הוּא:
רוֹמְמוּ יהוה אֱלֹהֵינוּ וְהִשְׁתַּחֲווּ לְהַר קָדְשׁוֹ, כִּי־קָדוֹשׁ יהוה
אֱלֹהֵינוּ:

תהלים עח וְהוּא רַחוּם, יְכַפֵּר עָוֹן וְלֹא־יַשְׁחִית, וְהִרְבָּה לְהָשִׁיב אַפּוֹ,
תהלים מ וְלֹא־יָעִיר כָּל־חֲמָתוֹ: אַתָּה יהוה לֹא־תִכְלָא רַחֲמֶיךָ מִמֶּנִּי, חַסְדְּךָ
תהלים כה וַאֲמִתְּךָ תָּמִיד יִצְּרוּנִי: זְכֹר־רַחֲמֶיךָ יהוה וַחֲסָדֶיךָ, כִּי מֵעוֹלָם
תהלים סח הֵמָּה: תְּנוּ עֹז לֵאלֹהִים, עַל־יִשְׂרָאֵל גַּאֲוָתוֹ, וְעֻזּוֹ בַּשְּׁחָקִים:
נוֹרָא אֱלֹהִים מִמִּקְדָּשֶׁיךָ, אֵל יִשְׂרָאֵל הוּא נֹתֵן עֹז וְתַעֲצֻמוֹת
תהלים צד לָעָם, בָּרוּךְ אֱלֹהִים: אֵל־נְקָמוֹת יהוה, אֵל נְקָמוֹת הוֹפִיעַ: הִנָּשֵׂא
תהלים ג שֹׁפֵט הָאָרֶץ, הָשֵׁב גְּמוּל עַל־גֵּאִים: לַיהוה הַיְשׁוּעָה, עַל־עַמְּךָ
תהלים מו בִרְכָתֶךָ סֶּלָה: ▸ יהוה צְבָאוֹת עִמָּנוּ, מִשְׂגָּב לָנוּ אֱלֹהֵי יַעֲקֹב
תהלים פד תהלים כ סֶלָה: יהוה צְבָאוֹת, אַשְׁרֵי אָדָם בֹּטֵחַ בָּךְ: יהוה הוֹשִׁיעָה,
הַמֶּלֶךְ יַעֲנֵנוּ בְיוֹם־קָרְאֵנוּ:

תהלים כח הוֹשִׁיעָה אֶת־עַמֶּךָ, וּבָרֵךְ אֶת־נַחֲלָתֶךָ, וּרְעֵם וְנַשְּׂאֵם עַד־
תהלים לג הָעוֹלָם: נַפְשֵׁנוּ חִכְּתָה לַיהוה, עֶזְרֵנוּ וּמָגִנֵּנוּ הוּא: כִּי־בוֹ יִשְׂמַח
לִבֵּנוּ, כִּי בְשֵׁם קָדְשׁוֹ בָטָחְנוּ: יְהִי־חַסְדְּךָ יהוה עָלֵינוּ, כַּאֲשֶׁר

רוֹמְמוּ *Exalt the Lord our God:* A selection of verses from the book of Psalms, expressing hope and trust in God. The voice in these verses modulates from singular to plural, individual to nation. This frequent shift from public to private and back again is a distinctive feature of Jewish sensibility. We speak to God as individuals, from the depths of our being, yet we are also members of an extended family, a people, a nation, whose fate and destiny we share and on whose behalf we pray.

EXTRA PSALMS FOR SHABBAT AND YOM TOV

In the earliest siddurim, we already find the well-established custom of saying extra psalms on Shabbat and Yom Tov. This is because, work being forbidden,

put our hope in You. Show us, LORD, Your loving-kindness and grant Ps. 85
us Your salvation. Arise, help us and redeem us for the sake of Your Ps. 44
love. I am the LORD your God who brought you up from the land of Ps. 81
Egypt: open your mouth wide and I will fill it. Happy is the people Ps. 144
for whom this is so; happy is the people whose God is the LORD.
▸ As for me, I trust in Your loving-kindness; my heart rejoices in Your Ps. 13
salvation. I will sing to the LORD for He has been good to me.

On Hoshana Raba, Yom HaAtzma'ut and Yom Yerushalayim, the following psalm is said. The custom is to say it standing.

מִזְמוֹר A psalm of thanksgiving. Shout joyously to the LORD, all Ps. 100
the earth. Serve the LORD with joy. Come before Him with jubilation. Know that the LORD is God. He made us and we are His. We are His people and the flock He tends. Enter His gates with thanksgiving, His courts with praise. Thank Him and bless His name. ▸ For the LORD is good, His loving-kindness is everlasting, and His faithfulness is for every generation.

לַמְנַצֵּחַ For the conductor of music. A psalm of David. Ps. 19
The heavens declare the glory of God;
the skies proclaim the work of His hands.
Day to day they pour forth speech;
night to night they communicate knowledge.
There is no speech, there are no words,
their voice is not heard.
Yet their music carries throughout the earth,
their words to the end of the world.
In them He has set a tent for the sun.
It emerges like a groom from his marriage chamber,
rejoicing like a champion about to run a race.

---

and His revelation of the world-that-ought-to-be. קַוָּם *Yet their music:* literally "their line," perhaps the reverberating string of a musical instrument. Alternatively, it may mean the line marking a boundary – a reference to the order and "fearful symmetry" of the universe.

יְחַלְנוּ לָךְ: הַרְאֵנוּ יהוה חַסְדֶּךָ, וְיֶשְׁעֲךָ תִּתֶּן־לָנוּ: קוּמָה עֶזְרָתָה תהלים פה / תהלים מד
לָּנוּ, וּפְדֵנוּ לְמַעַן חַסְדֶּךָ: אָנֹכִי יהוה אֱלֹהֶיךָ הַמַּעַלְךָ מֵאֶרֶץ תהלים פא
מִצְרָיִם, הַרְחֶב־פִּיךָ וַאֲמַלְאֵהוּ: אַשְׁרֵי הָעָם שֶׁכָּכָה לּוֹ, אַשְׁרֵי תהלים קמד
הָעָם שֶׁיהוה אֱלֹהָיו: › וַאֲנִי בְּחַסְדְּךָ בָטַחְתִּי, יָגֵל לִבִּי בִּישׁוּעָתֶךָ, תהלים יג
אָשִׁירָה לַיהוה, כִּי גָמַל עָלָי:

On יום ירושלים *and* יום העצמאות, הושענא רבה,
the following psalm is said. The custom is to say it standing.

מִזְמוֹר לְתוֹדָה, הָרִיעוּ לַיהוה כׇּל־הָאָרֶץ: עִבְדוּ אֶת־יהוה בְּשִׂמְחָה, תהלים ק
בֹּאוּ לְפָנָיו בִּרְנָנָה: דְּעוּ כִּי־יהוה הוּא אֱלֹהִים, הוּא עָשָׂנוּ וְלוֹ אֲנַחְנוּ,
עַמּוֹ וְצֹאן מַרְעִיתוֹ: בֹּאוּ שְׁעָרָיו בְּתוֹדָה, חֲצֵרֹתָיו בִּתְהִלָּה, הוֹדוּ לוֹ,
בָּרְכוּ שְׁמוֹ: › כִּי־טוֹב יהוה, לְעוֹלָם חַסְדּוֹ, וְעַד־דֹּר וָדֹר אֱמוּנָתוֹ:

לַמְנַצֵּחַ מִזְמוֹר לְדָוִד: תהלים יט
הַשָּׁמַיִם מְסַפְּרִים כְּבוֹד־אֵל, וּמַעֲשֵׂה יָדָיו מַגִּיד הָרָקִיעַ:
יוֹם לְיוֹם יַבִּיעַ אֹמֶר, וְלַיְלָה לְּלַיְלָה יְחַוֶּה־דָּעַת:
אֵין־אֹמֶר וְאֵין דְּבָרִים, בְּלִי נִשְׁמָע קוֹלָם:
בְּכׇל־הָאָרֶץ יָצָא קַוָּם, וּבִקְצֵה תֵבֵל מִלֵּיהֶם
לַשֶּׁמֶשׁ שָׂם־אֹהֶל בָּהֶם:
וְהוּא כְּחָתָן יֹצֵא מֵחֻפָּתוֹ, יָשִׂישׂ כְּגִבּוֹר לָרוּץ אֹרַח:

לַמְנַצֵּחַ *Psalm 19. The heavens declare the glory of God:* A hymn of glory to the universe as God's work and the Torah as God's word. In the first half of the poem, the Psalmist speaks metaphorically of creation singing a song of praise to its Creator, a silent song yet one that can be heard by those whose ears are attuned to wonder. But God's word not only gives life to the natural universe: it instructs the human universe, the world we make by our actions and reactions. The Psalmist pours out his praise of God's creation of the world-that-is,

It rises at one end of the heaven
and makes its circuit to the other:
nothing is hidden from its heat.
The LORD's Torah is perfect, refreshing the soul.
The LORD's testimony is faithful, making the simple wise.
The LORD's precepts are just, gladdening the heart.
The LORD's commandment is radiant, giving light to the eyes.
The fear of the LORD is pure, enduring for ever.
The LORD's judgments are true, altogether righteous.
More precious than gold, than much fine gold.
They are sweeter than honey, than honey from the comb.
Your servant, too, is careful of them,
for in observing them there is great reward.
Yet who can discern his errors?
Cleanse me of hidden faults.
Keep Your servant also from willful sins;
let them not have dominion over me.
Then shall I be blameless,
and innocent of grave sin.
▸ May the words of my mouth and the meditation of my heart
find favor before You, LORD, my Rock and my Redeemer.

לְדָוִד Of David. When he pretended to be insane before Abimelech, *Ps. 34*
who drove him away, and he left.
I will bless the LORD at all times;
His praise will be always on my lips.
My soul will glory in the LORD;
let the lowly hear this and rejoice.
Magnify the LORD with me;
let us exalt His name together.
I sought the LORD, and He answered me;
He saved me from all my fears.
Those who look to Him are radiant;
Their faces are never downcast.

מִקְצֵה הַשָּׁמַיִם מוֹצָאוֹ, וּתְקוּפָתוֹ עַל־קְצוֹתָם
וְאֵין נִסְתָּר מֵחַמָּתוֹ:
תּוֹרַת יהוה תְּמִימָה, מְשִׁיבַת נָפֶשׁ
עֵדוּת יהוה נֶאֱמָנָה, מַחְכִּימַת פֶּתִי:
פִּקּוּדֵי יהוה יְשָׁרִים, מְשַׂמְּחֵי־לֵב
מִצְוַת יהוה בָּרָה, מְאִירַת עֵינָיִם:
יִרְאַת יהוה טְהוֹרָה, עוֹמֶדֶת לָעַד
מִשְׁפְּטֵי־יהוה אֱמֶת, צָדְקוּ יַחְדָּו:
הַנֶּחֱמָדִים מִזָּהָב וּמִפַּז רָב, וּמְתוּקִים מִדְּבַשׁ וְנֹפֶת צוּפִים:
גַּם־עַבְדְּךָ נִזְהָר בָּהֶם, בְּשָׁמְרָם עֵקֶב רָב:
שְׁגִיאוֹת מִי־יָבִין, מִנִּסְתָּרוֹת נַקֵּנִי:
גַּם מִזֵּדִים חֲשֹׂךְ עַבְדֶּךָ, אַל־יִמְשְׁלוּ־בִי אָז אֵיתָם,
וְנִקֵּיתִי מִפֶּשַׁע רָב:
◂ יִהְיוּ לְרָצוֹן אִמְרֵי־פִי וְהֶגְיוֹן לִבִּי לְפָנֶיךָ, יהוה, צוּרִי וְגֹאֲלִי:

לְדָוִד, בְּשַׁנּוֹתוֹ אֶת־טַעְמוֹ לִפְנֵי אֲבִימֶלֶךְ, וַיְגָרְשֵׁהוּ וַיֵּלַךְ: תהלים לד
אֲבָרְכָה אֶת־יהוה בְּכָל־עֵת, תָּמִיד תְּהִלָּתוֹ בְּפִי:
בַּיהוה תִּתְהַלֵּל נַפְשִׁי, יִשְׁמְעוּ עֲנָוִים וְיִשְׂמָחוּ:
גַּדְּלוּ לַיהוה אִתִּי, וּנְרוֹמְמָה שְׁמוֹ יַחְדָּו:
דָּרַשְׁתִּי אֶת־יהוה וְעָנָנִי, וּמִכָּל־מְגוּרוֹתַי הִצִּילָנִי:
הִבִּיטוּ אֵלָיו וְנָהָרוּ, וּפְנֵיהֶם אַל־יֶחְפָּרוּ:

לְדָוִד *Psalm 34:* During the period that David was fleeing from King Saul, he took refuge in the Philistine city of Gath. There, however, he was recognized and his life was again in danger. Feigning insanity in order to appear harmless,

This poor man called, and the LORD heard;
He saved him from all his troubles.
The LORD's angel encamps around those who fear Him,
and He rescues them.
Taste and see that the LORD is good;
happy is the man who takes refuge in Him.
Fear the LORD, you His holy ones,
for those who fear Him lack nothing.
Young lions may grow weak and hungry,
but those who seek the LORD lack no good thing.
Come, my children, listen to me;
I will teach you the fear of the LORD.
Who desires life,
loving each day to see good?
Then guard your tongue from evil
and your lips from speaking deceit.
Turn from evil and do good;
seek peace and pursue it.
The eyes of the LORD are on the righteous
and His ears attentive to their cry;
The LORD's face is set against those who do evil,
to erase their memory from the earth.
The righteous cry out, and the LORD hears them;
delivering them from all their troubles.
The LORD is close to the brokenhearted,
and saves those who are crushed in spirit.
Many troubles may befall the righteous,
but the LORD delivers him from them all;
He protects all his bones,
so that none of them will be broken.
Evil will slay the wicked;
the enemies of the righteous will be condemned.
▸ The LORD redeems His servants;
none who take refuge in Him shall be condemned.

זֶה עָנִי קָרָא, וַיהוה שָׁמֵעַ, וּמִכָּל־צָרוֹתָיו הוֹשִׁיעוֹ:
חֹנֶה מַלְאַךְ־יהוה סָבִיב לִירֵאָיו, וַיְחַלְּצֵם:
טַעֲמוּ וּרְאוּ כִּי־טוֹב יהוה, אַשְׁרֵי הַגֶּבֶר יֶחֱסֶה־בּוֹ:
יְראוּ אֶת־יהוה קְדֹשָׁיו, כִּי־אֵין מַחְסוֹר לִירֵאָיו:
כְּפִירִים רָשׁוּ וְרָעֵבוּ, וְדֹרְשֵׁי יהוה לֹא־יַחְסְרוּ כָל־טוֹב:
לְכוּ־בָנִים שִׁמְעוּ־לִי, יִרְאַת יהוה אֲלַמֶּדְכֶם:
מִי־הָאִישׁ הֶחָפֵץ חַיִּים, אֹהֵב יָמִים לִרְאוֹת טוֹב:
נְצֹר לְשׁוֹנְךָ מֵרָע, וּשְׂפָתֶיךָ מִדַּבֵּר מִרְמָה:
סוּר מֵרָע וַעֲשֵׂה־טוֹב, בַּקֵּשׁ שָׁלוֹם וְרָדְפֵהוּ:
עֵינֵי יהוה אֶל־צַדִּיקִים, וְאָזְנָיו אֶל־שַׁוְעָתָם:
פְּנֵי יהוה בְּעֹשֵׂי רָע, לְהַכְרִית מֵאֶרֶץ זִכְרָם:
צָעֲקוּ וַיהוה שָׁמֵעַ, וּמִכָּל־צָרוֹתָם הִצִּילָם:
קָרוֹב יהוה לְנִשְׁבְּרֵי־לֵב, וְאֶת־דַּכְּאֵי־רוּחַ יוֹשִׁיעַ:
רַבּוֹת רָעוֹת צַדִּיק, וּמִכֻּלָּם יַצִּילֶנּוּ יהוה:
שֹׁמֵר כָּל־עַצְמוֹתָיו, אַחַת מֵהֵנָּה לֹא נִשְׁבָּרָה:
תְּמוֹתֵת רָשָׁע רָעָה, וְשֹׂנְאֵי צַדִּיק יֶאְשָׁמוּ:
◂ פּוֹדֶה יהוה נֶפֶשׁ עֲבָדָיו, וְלֹא יֶאְשְׁמוּ כָּל־הַחֹסִים בּוֹ:

he was dismissed by the king and was able to escape (1 Sam. 21:11–16). The psalm of thanksgiving that follows is constructed as an alphabetical acrostic. An extra verse has been added at the end to avoid closing on a negative note. גַּדְּלוּ לַיהוה אִתִּי *Magnify the LORD with me*: this verse is taken by the sages as the source of the institution of summoning to prayer, as in the Grace after Meals. It is also said on taking the Torah scroll out of the Ark. טַעֲמוּ וּרְאוּ *Taste and see*: religious experience precedes religious understanding. God's goodness has to be felt before it can be thought. נְצֹר לְשׁוֹנְךָ מֵרָע *Then guard your tongue from evil*: the sages said about *lashon hara*, evil speech, that it harms the one who says it, the one it is said about, and the one who gives credence

תְּפִלָּה לְמֹשֶׁה A prayer of Moses, the man of God. LORD, You have been our shelter in every generation. Before the mountains were born, before You brought forth the earth and the world, from everlasting to everlasting You are God. You turn men back to dust, saying, "Return, you children of men." For a thousand years in Your sight are like yesterday when it has passed, like a watch in the night. You sweep men away; they sleep. In the morning they are like grass newly grown: in the morning it flourishes and is new, but by evening it withers and dries up. For we are consumed by Your anger, terrified by Your fury. You have set our iniquities before You, our secret sins in the light of Your presence. All our days pass away in Your wrath, we spend our years like a sigh. The span of our life is seventy years, or if we are strong, eighty years; but the best of them is trouble and sorrow, for they quickly pass, and we fly away. Who can know the force of Your anger? Your wrath matches the fear due to You. Teach us rightly to number our days, that we may gain a heart of wisdom. Relent, O LORD! How much longer? Be sorry for Your servants. Satisfy us in the morning with Your loving-kindness, that we may sing and rejoice all our days. Grant us joy for as many days as You have afflicted us, for as many years as we saw trouble. Let Your deeds be seen by Your servants, and Your glory by their children. ▸ May the pleasantness of the LORD our God be upon us. Establish for us the work of our hands, O establish the work of our hands. *Ps. 90*

Teach us to remember how short life is, that we may spend our time on the things that endure. וִיהִי נֹעַם אֲדֹנָי אֱלֹהֵינוּ עָלֵינוּ *May the pleasantness of the LORD our God be upon us:* according to the sages, this is the blessing Moses gave the Israelites when they finished constructing the Tabernacle, adding, "May the Divine Presence rest in the work of your hands" (*Bemidbar Raba* 12:9; quoted by Rashi on Exodus 39:43).

תהלים צ

תְּפִלָּה לְמֹשֶׁה אִישׁ־הָאֱלֹהִים, אֲדֹנָי, מָעוֹן אַתָּה הָיִיתָ לָּנוּ בְּדֹר וָדֹר: בְּטֶרֶם הָרִים יֻלָּדוּ, וַתְּחוֹלֵל אֶרֶץ וְתֵבֵל, וּמֵעוֹלָם עַד־עוֹלָם אַתָּה אֵל: תָּשֵׁב אֱנוֹשׁ עַד־דַּכָּא, וַתֹּאמֶר שׁוּבוּ בְנֵי־אָדָם: כִּי אֶלֶף שָׁנִים בְּעֵינֶיךָ, כְּיוֹם אֶתְמוֹל כִּי יַעֲבֹר, וְאַשְׁמוּרָה בַלָּיְלָה: זְרַמְתָּם, שֵׁנָה יִהְיוּ, בַּבֹּקֶר כֶּחָצִיר יַחֲלֹף: בַּבֹּקֶר יָצִיץ וְחָלָף, לָעֶרֶב יְמוֹלֵל וְיָבֵשׁ: כִּי־כָלִינוּ בְאַפֶּךָ, וּבַחֲמָתְךָ נִבְהָלְנוּ: שַׁתָּ עֲוֺנֹתֵינוּ לְנֶגְדֶּךָ, עֲלֻמֵנוּ לִמְאוֹר פָּנֶיךָ: כִּי כָל־יָמֵינוּ פָּנוּ בְעֶבְרָתֶךָ, כִּלִּינוּ שָׁנֵינוּ כְמוֹ־הֶגֶה: יְמֵי־שְׁנוֹתֵינוּ בָהֶם שִׁבְעִים שָׁנָה, וְאִם בִּגְבוּרֹת שְׁמוֹנִים שָׁנָה, וְרָהְבָּם עָמָל וָאָוֶן, כִּי־גָז חִישׁ וַנָּעֻפָה: מִי־יוֹדֵעַ עֹז אַפֶּךָ, וּכְיִרְאָתְךָ עֶבְרָתֶךָ: לִמְנוֹת יָמֵינוּ כֵּן הוֹדַע, וְנָבִא לְבַב חָכְמָה: שׁוּבָה יהוה עַד־מָתָי, וְהִנָּחֵם עַל־עֲבָדֶיךָ: שַׂבְּעֵנוּ בַבֹּקֶר חַסְדֶּךָ, וּנְרַנְּנָה וְנִשְׂמְחָה בְּכָל־יָמֵינוּ: שַׂמְּחֵנוּ כִּימוֹת עִנִּיתָנוּ, שְׁנוֹת רָאִינוּ רָעָה: יֵרָאֶה אֶל־עֲבָדֶיךָ פָעֳלֶךָ, וַהֲדָרְךָ עַל־בְּנֵיהֶם: · וִיהִי נֹעַם אֲדֹנָי אֱלֹהֵינוּ עָלֵינוּ, וּמַעֲשֵׂה יָדֵינוּ כּוֹנְנָה עָלֵינוּ, וּמַעֲשֵׂה יָדֵינוּ כּוֹנְנֵהוּ:

---

to it. בַּקֵּשׁ שָׁלוֹם וְרָדְפֵהוּ *Seek peace and pursue it*: "Seek peace where you are, and pursue it elsewhere" (Yerushalmi, *Pe'ah* 1:1).

תְּפִלָּה לְמֹשֶׁה *Psalm 90:* A moving meditation on the eternity of God and the shortness of our lives. זְרַמְתָּם *You sweep men away*: a succession of poetic images conveying the brevity of human life: it flows as fast as a swollen river; as quickly as a sleep or a dream; it is like grass in a parched land that withers by the end of the day; it is like a sigh, a mere breath, like a bird that briefly lands then flies away. The speed with which these metaphors succeed one another mirrors the rapidity with which the days and years pass. לִמְנוֹת יָמֵינוּ כֵּן הוֹדַע *Teach us rightly to number our days*: the moral at the heart of the psalm:

יֹשֵׁב בְּסֵתֶר He who lives in the shelter of the Most High dwells in the shadow of the Almighty. I say of the LORD, my Refuge and Stronghold, my God in whom I trust, that He will save you from the fowler's snare and the deadly pestilence. With His pinions He will cover you, and beneath His wings you will find shelter; His faithfulness is an encircling shield. You need not fear terror by night, nor the arrow that flies by day; not the pestilence that stalks in darkness, nor the plague that ravages at noon. A thousand may fall at your side, ten thousand at your right hand, but it will not come near you. You will only look with your eyes and see the punishment of the wicked. Because you [have said:] "The LORD is my Refuge," taking the Most High as your shelter, no harm will befall you, no plague will come near your tent, for He will command His angels about you, to guard you in all your ways. They will lift you in their hands, lest your foot stumble on a stone. You will tread on lions and vipers, you will trample on young lions and snakes. [God says] "Because he loves Me, I will rescue him; I will protect him, because he acknowledges My name. When he calls on Me, I will answer him, I will be with him in distress, I will deliver him and bring him honor. ▸ With long life I will satisfy him, and show him My salvation. With long life I will satisfy him, and show him My salvation." *Ps. 91*

הַלְלוּיָהּ Halleluya! Praise the name of the LORD. Praise Him, you servants of the LORD who stand in the LORD's House, in the courtyards of the House of our God. Praise the LORD, for the *Ps. 135*

"The Egyptian Hallel" since it contains a reference to the exodus from Egypt (others confined the description to Psalm 136 alone). It is likely that both were written for public worship in the Temple, and both are litanies: a series of invocations said by a leader of prayer, together with congregational responses. Psalm 136, with its refrain "His loving-kindness is for ever," is the only psalm in which the congregational responses are set out in full, line by line. In Psalm 135 the responses are likely to have been, for the first section, "Halleluya" (Praise God), and for the last, "Bless the LORD" (*Pesaḥim* 118a).

תהלים צא ישֵׁב בְּסֵתֶר עֶלְיוֹן, בְּצֵל שַׁדַּי יִתְלוֹנָן: אֹמַר לַיהוה מַחְסִי
וּמְצוּדָתִי, אֱלֹהַי אֶבְטַח־בּוֹ: כִּי הוּא יַצִּילְךָ מִפַּח יָקוּשׁ, מִדֶּבֶר
הַוּוֹת: בְּאֶבְרָתוֹ יָסֶךְ לָךְ, וְתַחַת־כְּנָפָיו תֶּחְסֶה, צִנָּה וְסֹחֵרָה
אֲמִתּוֹ: לֹא־תִירָא מִפַּחַד לָיְלָה, מֵחֵץ יָעוּף יוֹמָם: מִדֶּבֶר
בָּאֹפֶל יַהֲלֹךְ, מִקֶּטֶב יָשׁוּד צָהֳרָיִם: יִפֹּל מִצִּדְּךָ אֶלֶף, וּרְבָבָה
מִימִינֶךָ, אֵלֶיךָ לֹא יִגָּשׁ: רַק בְּעֵינֶיךָ תַבִּיט, וְשִׁלֻּמַת רְשָׁעִים
תִּרְאֶה: כִּי־אַתָּה יהוה מַחְסִי, עֶלְיוֹן שַׂמְתָּ מְעוֹנֶךָ: לֹא־תְאֻנֶּה
אֵלֶיךָ רָעָה, וְנֶגַע לֹא־יִקְרַב בְּאָהֳלֶךָ: כִּי מַלְאָכָיו יְצַוֶּה־לָּךְ,
לִשְׁמָרְךָ בְּכָל־דְּרָכֶיךָ: עַל־כַּפַּיִם יִשָּׂאוּנְךָ, פֶּן־תִּגֹּף בָּאֶבֶן
רַגְלֶךָ: עַל־שַׁחַל וָפֶתֶן תִּדְרֹךְ, תִּרְמֹס כְּפִיר וְתַנִּין: כִּי בִי חָשַׁק
וַאֲפַלְּטֵהוּ, אֲשַׂגְּבֵהוּ כִּי־יָדַע שְׁמִי: יִקְרָאֵנִי וְאֶעֱנֵהוּ, עִמּוֹ אָנֹכִי
בְצָרָה, אֲחַלְּצֵהוּ וַאֲכַבְּדֵהוּ: › אֹרֶךְ יָמִים אַשְׂבִּיעֵהוּ, וְאַרְאֵהוּ
בִּישׁוּעָתִי: אֹרֶךְ יָמִים אַשְׂבִּיעֵהוּ, וְאַרְאֵהוּ בִּישׁוּעָתִי:

תהלים קלה הַלְלוּיָהּ, הַלְלוּ אֶת־שֵׁם יהוה, הַלְלוּ עַבְדֵי יהוה: שֶׁעֹמְדִים
בְּבֵית יהוה, בְּחַצְרוֹת בֵּית אֱלֹהֵינוּ: הַלְלוּיָהּ כִּי־טוֹב יהוה,
זַמְּרוּ לִשְׁמוֹ כִּי נָעִים: כִּי־יַעֲקֹב בָּחַר לוֹ יָהּ, יִשְׂרָאֵל לִסְגֻלָּתוֹ:

ישֵׁב בְּסֵתֶר *Psalm 91:* A prayer for protection from danger and harm. The psalm uses many images for God's protection. To those who trust in Him, He is shelter, shadow, refuge, stronghold. He protects us beneath His wings, and encircles us like a shield. When we are in distress, He is with us. When we are in danger, we are not alone. Trust defeats terror, and faith conquers fear. The first speaker in the psalm is human; the second, God Himself (*Sanhedrin* 103a).

הַלְלוּיָהּ *Psalms 135–136*: Two psalms forming a single composite unit, similar in tone, vocabulary and literary structure to the group of Psalms 113–118 known as Hallel. Some sages (*Pesaḥim* 118a) called these two psalms "The Great Hallel" to distinguish them from Psalms 113–118 which they called

Lord is good; sing praises to His name, for it is lovely. For the Lord has chosen Jacob as His own, Israel as his treasure. For I know that the Lord is great, that our Lord is above all heavenly powers. Whatever pleases the Lord, He does, in heaven and on earth, in the seas and all the depths. He raises clouds from the ends of the earth; He sends lightning with the rain; He brings out the wind from His storehouses. He struck down the firstborn of Egypt, of both man and animals. He sent signs and wonders into your midst, Egypt – against Pharaoh and all his servants. He struck down many nations and slew mighty kings: Siḥon, King of the Amorites, Og, King of Bashan, and all the kingdoms of Canaan, giving their land as a heritage, a heritage for His people Israel. Your name, Lord, endures for ever; Your renown, Lord, for all generations. For the Lord will bring justice to His people, and have compassion on His servants. The idols of the nations are silver and gold, the work of human hands. They have mouths, but cannot speak; eyes, but cannot see; ears, but cannot hear; there is no breath in their mouths. Those who make them will become like them: so will all who trust in them. ▸ House of Israel, bless the Lord. House of Aaron, bless the Lord. House of Levi, bless the Lord. You who fear the Lord, bless the Lord. Blessed is the Lord from Zion, He who dwells in Jerusalem. Halleluya!

The custom is to stand for the following psalm.

הודו Thank the Lord for He is good; His loving-kindness is for ever. *Ps. 136*
Thank the God of gods, His loving-kindness is for ever.
Thank the Lord of lords, His loving-kindness is for ever.

הודו *Psalm 136:* Originally in the Temple, the leader of prayer said the first half of each verse, to which the congregation responded with the second half. As in several other psalms, the poem opens with cosmology and ends with history; it begins with God as Creator, and continues with God as Redeemer. The sages related the twenty-six verses of the psalm to the twenty-six genera-

כִּי אֲנִי יָדַעְתִּי כִּי־גָדוֹל יהוה, וַאֲדֹנֵינוּ מִכָּל־אֱלֹהִים: כָּל אֲשֶׁר־
חָפֵץ יהוה עָשָׂה, בַּשָּׁמַיִם וּבָאָרֶץ, בַּיַּמִּים וְכָל־תְּהֹמוֹת:
מַעֲלֶה נְשִׂאִים מִקְצֵה הָאָרֶץ, בְּרָקִים לַמָּטָר עָשָׂה, מוֹצֵא־רוּחַ
מֵאוֹצְרוֹתָיו: שֶׁהִכָּה בְּכוֹרֵי מִצְרָיִם, מֵאָדָם עַד־בְּהֵמָה: שָׁלַח
אוֹתֹת וּמֹפְתִים בְּתוֹכֵכִי מִצְרָיִם, בְּפַרְעֹה וּבְכָל־עֲבָדָיו: שֶׁהִכָּה
גּוֹיִם רַבִּים, וְהָרַג מְלָכִים עֲצוּמִים: לְסִיחוֹן מֶלֶךְ הָאֱמֹרִי, וּלְעוֹג
מֶלֶךְ הַבָּשָׁן, וּלְכֹל מַמְלְכוֹת כְּנָעַן: וְנָתַן אַרְצָם נַחֲלָה, נַחֲלָה
לְיִשְׂרָאֵל עַמּוֹ: יהוה שִׁמְךָ לְעוֹלָם, יהוה זִכְרְךָ לְדֹר־וָדֹר:
כִּי־יָדִין יהוה עַמּוֹ, וְעַל־עֲבָדָיו יִתְנֶחָם: עֲצַבֵּי הַגּוֹיִם כֶּסֶף
וְזָהָב, מַעֲשֵׂה יְדֵי אָדָם: פֶּה־לָהֶם וְלֹא יְדַבֵּרוּ, עֵינַיִם לָהֶם
וְלֹא יִרְאוּ: אָזְנַיִם לָהֶם וְלֹא יַאֲזִינוּ, אַף אֵין־יֶשׁ־רוּחַ בְּפִיהֶם:
כְּמוֹהֶם יִהְיוּ עֹשֵׂיהֶם, כֹּל אֲשֶׁר־בֹּטֵחַ בָּהֶם: ‹ בֵּית יִשְׂרָאֵל
בָּרְכוּ אֶת־יהוה, בֵּית אַהֲרֹן בָּרְכוּ אֶת־יהוה: בֵּית הַלֵּוִי בָּרְכוּ
אֶת־יהוה, יִרְאֵי יהוה בָּרְכוּ אֶת־יהוה: בָּרוּךְ יהוה מִצִּיּוֹן,
שֹׁכֵן יְרוּשָׁלָםִ, הַלְלוּיָהּ:

The custom is to stand for the following psalm.

תהלים קלו
הוֹדוּ לַיהוה כִּי־טוֹב   כִּי לְעוֹלָם חַסְדּוֹ:
הוֹדוּ לֵאלֹהֵי הָאֱלֹהִים   כִּי לְעוֹלָם חַסְדּוֹ:
הוֹדוּ לַאֲדֹנֵי הָאֲדֹנִים   כִּי לְעוֹלָם חַסְדּוֹ:

Psalm 135 is structured in three parts: the first and last speak about the truth of God and the falsity of idols, and the second about God's power over nature and history. The first part is five verses long; the second, seven; the third, nine. שֶׁהִכָּה בְּכוֹרֵי מִצְרָיִם *He struck down the firstborn of Egypt*: these lines are paralleled in the next psalm. עֲצַבֵּי הַגּוֹיִם כֶּסֶף וְזָהָב *The idols of the nations are silver and gold… You who fear the Lord, bless the Lord*: almost exactly paralleled in Hallel (Psalm 115:4–11).

To the One who alone
works great wonders, His loving-kindness is for ever.
Who made the heavens with wisdom, His loving-kindness is for ever.
Who spread the earth upon the waters, His loving-kindness is for ever.
Who made the great lights, His loving-kindness is for ever.
The sun to rule by day, His loving-kindness is for ever.
The moon and the stars to rule by night; His loving-kindness is for ever.
Who struck Egypt
through their firstborn, His loving-kindness is for ever.
And brought out Israel from their midst, His loving-kindness is for ever.
With a strong hand
and outstretched arm, His loving-kindness is for ever.
Who split the Reed Sea into parts, His loving-kindness is for ever.
And made Israel pass through it, His loving-kindness is for ever.
Casting Pharaoh and his army
into the Reed Sea; His loving-kindness is for ever.
Who led His people
through the wilderness; His loving-kindness is for ever.
Who struck down great kings, His loving-kindness is for ever.
And slew mighty kings, His loving-kindness is for ever.
Siḥon, King of the Amorites, His loving-kindness is for ever.
And Og, King of Bashan, His loving-kindness is for ever.
And gave their land as a heritage, His loving-kindness is for ever.
A heritage for His servant Israel; His loving-kindness is for ever.
Who remembered us in our lowly state, His loving-kindness is for ever.
And rescued us from our tormentors, His loving-kindness is for ever.
▸ Who gives food to all flesh, His loving-kindness is for ever.
Give thanks to the God of heaven. His loving-kindness is for ever.

---

tions between Adam and the Giving of the Torah – from creation to revelation. Because of its summary of the events of the exodus, it forms part of the Haggada on Pesaḥ.

לְעֹשֵׂה נִפְלָאוֹת גְּדֹלוֹת לְבַדּוֹ כִּי לְעוֹלָם חַסְדּוֹ:
לְעֹשֵׂה הַשָּׁמַיִם בִּתְבוּנָה כִּי לְעוֹלָם חַסְדּוֹ:
לְרֹקַע הָאָרֶץ עַל־הַמָּיִם כִּי לְעוֹלָם חַסְדּוֹ:
לְעֹשֵׂה אוֹרִים גְּדֹלִים כִּי לְעוֹלָם חַסְדּוֹ:
אֶת־הַשֶּׁמֶשׁ לְמֶמְשֶׁלֶת בַּיּוֹם כִּי לְעוֹלָם חַסְדּוֹ:
אֶת־הַיָּרֵחַ וְכוֹכָבִים לְמֶמְשְׁלוֹת בַּלָּיְלָה כִּי לְעוֹלָם חַסְדּוֹ:
לְמַכֵּה מִצְרַיִם בִּבְכוֹרֵיהֶם כִּי לְעוֹלָם חַסְדּוֹ:
וַיּוֹצֵא יִשְׂרָאֵל מִתּוֹכָם כִּי לְעוֹלָם חַסְדּוֹ:
בְּיָד חֲזָקָה וּבִזְרוֹעַ נְטוּיָה כִּי לְעוֹלָם חַסְדּוֹ:
לְגֹזֵר יַם־סוּף לִגְזָרִים כִּי לְעוֹלָם חַסְדּוֹ:
וְהֶעֱבִיר יִשְׂרָאֵל בְּתוֹכוֹ כִּי לְעוֹלָם חַסְדּוֹ:
וְנִעֵר פַּרְעֹה וְחֵילוֹ בְיַם־סוּף כִּי לְעוֹלָם חַסְדּוֹ:
לְמוֹלִיךְ עַמּוֹ בַּמִּדְבָּר כִּי לְעוֹלָם חַסְדּוֹ:
לְמַכֵּה מְלָכִים גְּדֹלִים כִּי לְעוֹלָם חַסְדּוֹ:
וַיַּהֲרֹג מְלָכִים אַדִּירִים כִּי לְעוֹלָם חַסְדּוֹ:
לְסִיחוֹן מֶלֶךְ הָאֱמֹרִי כִּי לְעוֹלָם חַסְדּוֹ:
וּלְעוֹג מֶלֶךְ הַבָּשָׁן כִּי לְעוֹלָם חַסְדּוֹ:
וְנָתַן אַרְצָם לְנַחֲלָה כִּי לְעוֹלָם חַסְדּוֹ:
נַחֲלָה לְיִשְׂרָאֵל עַבְדּוֹ כִּי לְעוֹלָם חַסְדּוֹ:
שֶׁבְּשִׁפְלֵנוּ זָכַר לָנוּ כִּי לְעוֹלָם חַסְדּוֹ:
וַיִּפְרְקֵנוּ מִצָּרֵינוּ כִּי לְעוֹלָם חַסְדּוֹ:
◂ נֹתֵן לֶחֶם לְכָל־בָּשָׂר כִּי לְעוֹלָם חַסְדּוֹ:
הוֹדוּ לְאֵל הַשָּׁמָיִם כִּי לְעוֹלָם חַסְדּוֹ:

רַנְּנוּ Sing joyfully to the LORD, you righteous, for praise from the upright is seemly. Give thanks to the LORD with the harp; make music to Him on the ten-stringed lute. Sing Him a new song, play skillfully with shouts of joy. For the LORD's word is right, and all His deeds are done in faith. He loves righteousness and justice; the earth is full of the LORD's loving-kindness. By the LORD's word the heavens were made, and all their starry host by the breath of His mouth. He gathers the sea waters as a heap, and places the deep in storehouses. Let all the earth fear the LORD, and all the world's inhabitants stand in awe of Him. For He spoke, and it was; He commanded, and it stood firm. The LORD foils the plans of nations; He thwarts the intentions of peoples. The LORD's plans stand for ever, His heart's intents for all generations. Happy is the nation whose God is the LORD, the people He has chosen as His own. From heaven the LORD looks down and sees all mankind; from His dwelling place He oversees all who live on earth. He forms the hearts of all, and discerns all their deeds. No king is saved by the size of his army; no warrior is delivered by great strength. A horse is a vain hope for deliverance; despite its great strength, it cannot save. The eye of the LORD is on those who fear Him, on those who place their hope in His unfailing love, to rescue their soul from death, and keep them alive in famine. Our soul waits for the LORD; He is our Help and Shield. ▸ In Him our hearts rejoice, for we trust in His holy name. May Your loving-kindness be upon us, LORD, as we have put our hope in You. *Ps. 33*

מִזְמוֹר שִׁיר A psalm. A song for the Sabbath day. It is good to thank the LORD and sing psalms to Your name, Most High – to tell of Your loving-kindness in the morning and Your faithfulness at night, to the music of the ten-stringed lyre and the melody of the harp. For You have made me rejoice by Your work, O LORD; I sing for joy at the deeds of Your hands. How great are Your deeds, LORD, and how very deep Your thoughts. A boor cannot know, nor can a fool understand, that though the wicked spring up like grass and all *Ps. 92*

תהלים לג רַנְּנוּ צַדִּיקִים בַּיהוה, לַיְשָׁרִים נָאוָה תְהִלָּה: הוֹדוּ לַיהוה בְּכִנּוֹר,
בְּנֵבֶל עָשׂוֹר זַמְּרוּ־לוֹ: שִׁירוּ־לוֹ שִׁיר חָדָשׁ, הֵיטִיבוּ נַגֵּן בִּתְרוּעָה:
כִּי־יָשָׁר דְּבַר־יהוה, וְכָל־מַעֲשֵׂהוּ בֶּאֱמוּנָה: אֹהֵב צְדָקָה וּמִשְׁפָּט,
חֶסֶד יהוה מָלְאָה הָאָרֶץ: בִּדְבַר יהוה שָׁמַיִם נַעֲשׂוּ, וּבְרוּחַ פִּיו
כָּל־צְבָאָם: כֹּנֵס כַּנֵּד מֵי הַיָּם, נֹתֵן בְּאוֹצָרוֹת תְּהוֹמוֹת: יִירְאוּ
מֵיהוה כָּל־הָאָרֶץ, מִמֶּנּוּ יָגוּרוּ כָּל־יֹשְׁבֵי תֵבֵל: כִּי הוּא אָמַר
וַיֶּהִי, הוּא־צִוָּה וַיַּעֲמֹד: יהוה הֵפִיר עֲצַת־גּוֹיִם, הֵנִיא מַחְשְׁבוֹת
עַמִּים: עֲצַת יהוה לְעוֹלָם תַּעֲמֹד, מַחְשְׁבוֹת לִבּוֹ לְדֹר וָדֹר:
אַשְׁרֵי הַגּוֹי אֲשֶׁר־יהוה אֱלֹהָיו, הָעָם בָּחַר לְנַחֲלָה לוֹ: מִשָּׁמַיִם
הִבִּיט יהוה, רָאָה אֶת־כָּל־בְּנֵי הָאָדָם: מִמְּכוֹן־שִׁבְתּוֹ הִשְׁגִּיחַ,
אֶל כָּל־יֹשְׁבֵי הָאָרֶץ: הַיֹּצֵר יַחַד לִבָּם, הַמֵּבִין אֶל־כָּל־מַעֲשֵׂיהֶם:
אֵין־הַמֶּלֶךְ נוֹשָׁע בְּרָב־חָיִל, גִּבּוֹר לֹא־יִנָּצֵל בְּרָב־כֹּחַ: שֶׁקֶר
הַסּוּס לִתְשׁוּעָה, וּבְרֹב חֵילוֹ לֹא יְמַלֵּט: הִנֵּה עֵין יהוה אֶל־יְרֵאָיו,
לַמְיַחֲלִים לְחַסְדּוֹ: לְהַצִּיל מִמָּוֶת נַפְשָׁם, וּלְחַיּוֹתָם בָּרָעָב: נַפְשֵׁנוּ
חִכְּתָה לַיהוה, עֶזְרֵנוּ וּמָגִנֵּנוּ הוּא: › כִּי־בוֹ יִשְׂמַח לִבֵּנוּ, כִּי בְשֵׁם
קָדְשׁוֹ בָטָחְנוּ: יְהִי־חַסְדְּךָ יהוה עָלֵינוּ, כַּאֲשֶׁר יִחַלְנוּ לָךְ:

תהלים צב מִזְמוֹר שִׁיר לְיוֹם הַשַּׁבָּת: טוֹב לְהֹדוֹת לַיהוה, וּלְזַמֵּר לְשִׁמְךָ
עֶלְיוֹן: לְהַגִּיד בַּבֹּקֶר חַסְדֶּךָ, וֶאֱמוּנָתְךָ בַּלֵּילוֹת: עֲלֵי־עָשׂוֹר
וַעֲלֵי־נָבֶל, עֲלֵי הִגָּיוֹן בְּכִנּוֹר: כִּי שִׂמַּחְתַּנִי יהוה בְּפָעֳלֶךָ, בְּמַעֲשֵׂי
יָדֶיךָ אֲרַנֵּן: מַה־גָּדְלוּ מַעֲשֶׂיךָ יהוה, מְאֹד עָמְקוּ מַחְשְׁבֹתֶיךָ:
אִישׁ־בַּעַר לֹא יֵדָע, וּכְסִיל לֹא־יָבִין אֶת־זֹאת: בִּפְרֹחַ רְשָׁעִים
כְּמוֹ עֵשֶׂב, וַיָּצִיצוּ כָּל־פֹּעֲלֵי אָוֶן, לְהִשָּׁמְדָם עֲדֵי־עַד: וְאַתָּה
מָרוֹם לְעֹלָם יהוה: כִּי הִנֵּה אֹיְבֶיךָ יהוה, כִּי־הִנֵּה אֹיְבֶיךָ יֹאבֵדוּ,
יִתְפָּרְדוּ כָּל־פֹּעֲלֵי אָוֶן: וַתָּרֶם כִּרְאֵים קַרְנִי, בַּלֹּתִי בְּשֶׁמֶן רַעֲנָן:

evildoers flourish, it is only that they may be destroyed for ever. But You, LORD, are eternally exalted. For behold Your enemies, LORD, behold Your enemies will perish; all evildoers will be scattered. You have raised my pride like that of a wild ox; I am anointed with fresh oil. My eyes shall look in triumph on my adversaries, my ears shall hear the downfall of the wicked who rise against me. ▸ The righteous will flourish like a palm tree and grow tall like a cedar in Lebanon. Planted in the LORD's House, blossoming in our God's courtyards, they will still bear fruit in old age, and stay vigorous and fresh, proclaiming that the LORD is upright: He is my Rock, in whom there is no wrong.

יהוה מָלָךְ The LORD reigns. He is robed in majesty. The LORD is robed, girded with strength. The world is firmly established; it cannot be moved. Your throne stands firm as of old; You are eternal. Rivers lift up, LORD, rivers lift up their voice, rivers lift up their Crashing waves. ▸ Mightier than the noise of many waters, than the mighty waves of the sea is the LORD on high. Your testimonies are very sure; holiness adorns Your House, LORD, for evermore. *Ps. 93*

יְהִי כְבוֹד May the LORD's glory be for ever; may the LORD rejoice *Ps. 104*
in His works. May the LORD's name be blessed, now and for ever. *Ps. 113*
From the rising of the sun to its setting, may the LORD's name be
praised. The LORD is high above all nations; His glory is above the
heavens. LORD, Your name is for ever. Your renown, LORD, is for all *Ps. 135*
generations. The LORD has established His throne in heaven; His *Ps. 103*
kingdom rules all. Let the heavens rejoice and the earth be glad. Let *1 Chr. 16*
them say among the nations, "The LORD is King." The LORD is King,
the LORD was King, the LORD will be King for ever and all time.
The LORD is King for ever and all time; nations will perish from *Ps. 10*
His land. The LORD foils the plans of nations; He frustrates the *Ps. 33*

---

nation whose very existence is dependent on its covenant with God. Because Israel recognizes no ultimate king other than God, it turns to Him in prayer.

וַתַּבֵּט עֵינִי בְּשׁוּרָי, בַּקָּמִים עָלַי מְרֵעִים תִּשְׁמַעְנָה אָזְנָי: ‹ צַדִּיק
כַּתָּמָר יִפְרָח, כְּאֶרֶז בַּלְּבָנוֹן יִשְׂגֶּה: שְׁתוּלִים בְּבֵית יהוה, בְּחַצְרוֹת
אֱלֹהֵינוּ יַפְרִיחוּ: עוֹד יְנוּבוּן בְּשֵׂיבָה, דְּשֵׁנִים וְרַעֲנַנִּים יִהְיוּ: לְהַגִּיד
כִּי־יָשָׁר יהוה, צוּרִי, וְלֹא־עַוְלָתָה בּוֹ:

יהוה מָלָךְ, גֵּאוּת לָבֵשׁ, לָבֵשׁ יהוה עֹז הִתְאַזָּר, אַף־תִּכּוֹן תֵּבֵל תהלים צג
בַּל־תִּמּוֹט: נָכוֹן כִּסְאֲךָ מֵאָז, מֵעוֹלָם אָתָּה: נָשְׂאוּ נְהָרוֹת יהוה,
נָשְׂאוּ נְהָרוֹת קוֹלָם, יִשְׂאוּ נְהָרוֹת דָּכְיָם: ‹ מִקֹּלוֹת מַיִם רַבִּים,
אַדִּירִים מִשְׁבְּרֵי־יָם, אַדִּיר בַּמָּרוֹם יהוה: עֵדֹתֶיךָ נֶאֶמְנוּ מְאֹד
לְבֵיתְךָ נַאֲוָה־קֹדֶשׁ, יהוה לְאֹרֶךְ יָמִים:

יְהִי כְבוֹד יהוה לְעוֹלָם, יִשְׂמַח יהוה בְּמַעֲשָׂיו: יְהִי שֵׁם יהוה מְבֹרָךְ, תהלים קד / תהלים קיג
מֵעַתָּה וְעַד־עוֹלָם: מִמִּזְרַח־שֶׁמֶשׁ עַד־מְבוֹאוֹ, מְהֻלָּל שֵׁם יהוה:
רָם עַל־כָּל־גּוֹיִם יהוה, עַל הַשָּׁמַיִם כְּבוֹדוֹ: יהוה שִׁמְךָ לְעוֹלָם, תהלים קלה
יהוה זִכְרְךָ לְדֹר־וָדֹר: יהוה בַּשָּׁמַיִם הֵכִין כִּסְאוֹ, וּמַלְכוּתוֹ בַּכֹּל תהלים קג
מָשָׁלָה: יִשְׂמְחוּ הַשָּׁמַיִם וְתָגֵל הָאָרֶץ, וְיֹאמְרוּ בַגּוֹיִם יהוה מָלָךְ: דברי הימים א׳ טז
יהוה מֶלֶךְ, יהוה מָלָךְ, יהוה יִמְלֹךְ לְעוֹלָם וָעֶד. יהוה מֶלֶךְ עוֹלָם תהלים י
וָעֶד, אָבְדוּ גוֹיִם מֵאַרְצוֹ: יהוה הֵפִיר עֲצַת־גּוֹיִם, הֵנִיא מַחְשְׁבוֹת תהלים לג

יְהִי כְבוֹד *May the Lord's glory:* An anthology of verses, mainly from Psalms, but also from Chronicles and Proverbs. One verse, "The Lord is King, the Lord was King, the Lord will be King for ever and all time," does not appear in this form in the Bible: it is a combination of three biblical phrases, two from Psalms, one from Exodus (at the end of the Song at the Sea). The verses take us through the following sequence of thought: God created the universe, therefore God is Sovereign over the universe. In the short term it may seem that human beings determine their own fate even against the will of heaven. However, it is not so: "The Lord's plan prevails." God has chosen a particular people (Zion, Jacob) to exemplify this truth, for Israel is the only

intentions of peoples. Many are the intentions in a person's mind, Prov. 19
but the LORD's plan prevails. The LORD's plan shall stand for ever, Ps. 33
His mind's intent for all generations. For He spoke and it was; He
commanded and it stood firm. For the LORD has chosen Zion; He Ps. 132
desired it for His dwelling. For the LORD has chosen Jacob, Israel Ps. 135
as His special treasure. For the LORD will not abandon His people; Ps. 94
nor will He forsake His heritage. ▸ He is compassionate. He forgives Ps. 78
iniquity and does not destroy. Repeatedly He suppresses His anger,
not rousing His full wrath. LORD, save! May the King answer us on Ps. 20
the day we call.

The line beginning with "You open Your hand" should be said with special concentration, representing as it does the key idea of this psalm, and of Pesukei DeZimra as a whole, that God is the creator and sustainer of all.

אַשְׁרֵי Happy are those who dwell in Your House; Ps. 84
they shall continue to praise You, Selah!
Happy are the people for whom this is so; Ps. 144
happy are the people whose God is the LORD.
A song of praise by David. Ps. 145

א I will exalt You, my God, the King, and bless Your name for ever and all time. ב Every day I will bless You, and praise Your name for ever and all time. ג Great is the LORD and greatly to be praised; His greatness is unfathomable. ד One generation will praise Your works to the next, and tell of Your mighty deeds. ה On the glorious splendor of Your majesty I will meditate, and on the acts of Your wonders. ו They shall talk of the power of Your awesome deeds, and I will tell of Your greatness. ז They shall recite the record of Your great goodness, and sing with joy of Your righteousness. ח The LORD is gracious and compassionate,

---

ruled (*Berakhot* 4b) that it be said three times each day (twice in the morning service, once in the afternoon).

There are other reasons for its prominence. It is the only one of the 150 Psalms to be called *Tehilla leDavid*, "A Song of Praise by David." It contains the phrase, "Every day I will bless You," suggesting that it be said daily. Its 21 lines are constructed in three groups of seven verses: 1–7 are about God's

עַמִּים: רַבּוֹת מַחֲשָׁבוֹת בְּלֶב־אִישׁ, וַעֲצַת יהוה הִיא תָקוּם: עֲצַת משלי יט / תהלים לג
יהוה לְעוֹלָם תַּעֲמֹד, מַחְשְׁבוֹת לִבּוֹ לְדֹר וָדֹר: כִּי הוּא אָמַר וַיֶּהִי,
הוּא־צִוָּה וַיַּעֲמֹד: כִּי־בָחַר יהוה בְּצִיּוֹן, אִוָּהּ לְמוֹשָׁב לוֹ: כִּי־יַעֲקֹב תהלים קלב / תהלים קלה
בָּחַר לוֹ יָהּ, יִשְׂרָאֵל לִסְגֻלָּתוֹ: כִּי לֹא־יִטֹּשׁ יהוה עַמּוֹ, וְנַחֲלָתוֹ לֹא תהלים צד
יַעֲזֹב: ◂ וְהוּא רַחוּם, יְכַפֵּר עָוֹן וְלֹא־יַשְׁחִית, וְהִרְבָּה לְהָשִׁיב אַפּוֹ, תהלים עח
וְלֹא־יָעִיר כָּל־חֲמָתוֹ: יהוה הוֹשִׁיעָה, הַמֶּלֶךְ יַעֲנֵנוּ בְיוֹם־קָרְאֵנוּ: תהלים כ

The line beginning with פּוֹתֵחַ אֶת יָדֶךָ *should be said with special concentration, representing as it does the key idea of this psalm, and of* פסוקי דזמרה *as a whole, that God is the creator and sustainer of all.*

אַשְׁרֵי יוֹשְׁבֵי בֵיתֶךָ, עוֹד יְהַלְלוּךָ סֶּלָה: תהלים פד
אַשְׁרֵי הָעָם שֶׁכָּכָה לּוֹ, אַשְׁרֵי הָעָם שֶׁיהוה אֱלֹהָיו: תהלים קמד
תְּהִלָּה לְדָוִד תהלים קמה
א אֲרוֹמִמְךָ אֱלוֹהַי הַמֶּלֶךְ, וַאֲבָרְכָה שִׁמְךָ לְעוֹלָם וָעֶד:
ב בְּכָל־יוֹם אֲבָרְכֶךָּ, וַאֲהַלְלָה שִׁמְךָ לְעוֹלָם וָעֶד:
ג גָּדוֹל יהוה וּמְהֻלָּל מְאֹד, וְלִגְדֻלָּתוֹ אֵין חֵקֶר:
ד דּוֹר לְדוֹר יְשַׁבַּח מַעֲשֶׂיךָ, וּגְבוּרֹתֶיךָ יַגִּידוּ:
ה הֲדַר כְּבוֹד הוֹדֶךָ, וְדִבְרֵי נִפְלְאֹתֶיךָ אָשִׂיחָה:
ו וֶעֱזוּז נוֹרְאֹתֶיךָ יֹאמֵרוּ, וּגְדוּלָּתְךָ אֲסַפְּרֶנָּה:
ז זֵכֶר רַב־טוּבְךָ יַבִּיעוּ, וְצִדְקָתְךָ יְרַנֵּנוּ:
ח חַנּוּן וְרַחוּם יהוה, אֶרֶךְ אַפַּיִם וּגְדָל־חָסֶד:

אַשְׁרֵי *Happy are those:* Psalm 145 is the single most important passage in the Verses of Praise. The sages saw it as the paradigm of praise, firstly because it is constructed as an alphabetic acrostic (with the exception of the letter *nun*), thus praising God with all the letters of the alphabet; second, because it contains the verse "You open Your hand, and satisfy every living thing with favor," encapsulating the idea that God did not merely create the universe in the beginning, but also sustains it and the life it contains daily. The sages

slow to anger and great in loving-kindness. ט The LORD is good to all, and His compassion extends to all His works. י All Your works shall thank You, LORD, and Your devoted ones shall bless You. כ They shall talk of the glory of Your kingship, and speak of Your might. ל To make known to mankind His mighty deeds and the glorious majesty of His kingship. מ Your kingdom is an everlasting kingdom, and Your reign is for all generations. ס The LORD supports all who fall, and raises all who are bowed down. ע All raise their eyes to You in hope, and You give them their food in due season. פ You open Your hand, and satisfy every living thing with favor. צ The LORD is righteous in all His ways, and kind in all He does. ק The LORD is close to all who call on Him, to all who call on Him in truth. ר He fulfills the will of those who revere Him; He hears their cry and saves them. ש The LORD guards all who love Him, but all the wicked He will destroy. ▸ ת My mouth shall speak the praise of the LORD, and all creatures shall bless His holy name for ever and all time.

We will bless the LORD now and for ever. Halleluya! Ps. 115

הַלְלוּיָהּ Halleluya! Praise the LORD, my soul. I will praise the LORD Ps. 146
all my life; I will sing to my God as long as I live. Put not your trust in princes, or in mortal man who cannot save. His breath expires, he returns to the earth; on that day his plans come to an end. Happy is he whose help is the God of Jacob, whose hope is in the LORD his

---

as a whole, which begins with the word *Ashrei* and ends with the word *Halleluya*.

הַלְלוּיָהּ *Psalm 146:* The contrast between human and divine rule. Human beings are mortal. They come from dust and return to dust. God is eternal, as are the values by which He governs the affairs of humankind. He brings justice to the oppressed, food to the hungry, freedom to captives, and hope to those at the margins of society. These principles of justice and compassion run through Jewish history as the governing ideals of a society under the sovereignty of God.

ט טוֹב־יהוה לַכֹּל, וְרַחֲמָיו עַל־כָּל־מַעֲשָׂיו:
י יוֹדוּךָ יהוה כָּל־מַעֲשֶׂיךָ, וַחֲסִידֶיךָ יְבָרְכוּכָה:
כ כְּבוֹד מַלְכוּתְךָ יֹאמֵרוּ, וּגְבוּרָתְךָ יְדַבֵּרוּ:
ל לְהוֹדִיעַ לִבְנֵי הָאָדָם גְּבוּרֹתָיו, וּכְבוֹד הֲדַר מַלְכוּתוֹ:
מ מַלְכוּתְךָ מַלְכוּת כָּל־עֹלָמִים, וּמֶמְשַׁלְתְּךָ בְּכָל־דּוֹר וָדֹר:
ס סוֹמֵךְ יהוה לְכָל־הַנֹּפְלִים, וְזוֹקֵף לְכָל־הַכְּפוּפִים:
ע עֵינֵי־כֹל אֵלֶיךָ יְשַׂבֵּרוּ, וְאַתָּה נוֹתֵן־לָהֶם אֶת־אָכְלָם בְּעִתּוֹ:
פ פּוֹתֵחַ אֶת־יָדֶךָ, וּמַשְׂבִּיעַ לְכָל־חַי רָצוֹן:
צ צַדִּיק יהוה בְּכָל־דְּרָכָיו, וְחָסִיד בְּכָל־מַעֲשָׂיו:
ק קָרוֹב יהוה לְכָל־קֹרְאָיו, לְכֹל אֲשֶׁר יִקְרָאֻהוּ בֶאֱמֶת:
ר רְצוֹן־יְרֵאָיו יַעֲשֶׂה, וְאֶת־שַׁוְעָתָם יִשְׁמַע, וְיוֹשִׁיעֵם:
ש שׁוֹמֵר יהוה אֶת־כָּל־אֹהֲבָיו, וְאֵת כָּל־הָרְשָׁעִים יַשְׁמִיד:
◂ ת תְּהִלַּת יהוה יְדַבֶּר פִּי, וִיבָרֵךְ כָּל־בָּשָׂר שֵׁם קָדְשׁוֹ לְעוֹלָם וָעֶד:
וַאֲנַחְנוּ נְבָרֵךְ יָהּ מֵעַתָּה וְעַד־עוֹלָם, הַלְלוּיָהּ: תהלים קטו

הַלְלוּיָהּ, הַלְלִי נַפְשִׁי אֶת־יהוה: אֲהַלְלָה יהוה בְּחַיָּי, אֲזַמְּרָה תהלים קמו
לֵאלֹהַי בְּעוֹדִי: אַל־תִּבְטְחוּ בִנְדִיבִים, בְּבֶן־אָדָם שֶׁאֵין לוֹ
תְשׁוּעָה: תֵּצֵא רוּחוֹ, יָשֻׁב לְאַדְמָתוֹ, בַּיּוֹם הַהוּא אָבְדוּ עֶשְׁתֹּנֹתָיו:
אַשְׁרֵי שֶׁאֵל יַעֲקֹב בְּעֶזְרוֹ, שִׂבְרוֹ עַל־יהוה אֱלֹהָיו: עֹשֶׂה שָׁמַיִם

---

praise throughout the generations; 8–14 depict God's kingship and compassion; and 15–21 are about how God heeds prayer. The psalm is built on numerical structures (3, 7, 10) that closely resemble the creation narrative in Genesis 1:1–2:3.

Added to Psalm 145 are verses from other psalms: two at the beginning, which include the word *Ashrei* (happy) three times; and one at the end, which ends with *Halleluya*. It thus epitomizes the book of Psalms

God who made heaven and earth, the sea and all they contain; He who keeps faith for ever. He secures justice for the oppressed. He gives food to the hungry. The LORD sets captives free. The LORD gives sight to the blind. The LORD raises those bowed down. The LORD loves the righteous. The LORD protects the stranger. He gives courage to the orphan and widow. He thwarts the way of the wicked. ▸ The LORD shall reign for ever. He is your God, Zion, for all generations. Halleluya!

הַלְלוּיָהּ Halleluya! How good it is to sing songs to our God; how pleasant and fitting to praise Him. The LORD rebuilds Jerusalem. He gathers the scattered exiles of Israel. He heals the brokenhearted and binds up their wounds. He counts the number of the stars, calling each by name. Great is our LORD and mighty in power; His understanding has no limit. The LORD gives courage to the humble, but casts the wicked to the ground. Sing to the LORD in thanks; make music to our God on the harp. He covers the sky with clouds. He provides the earth with rain and makes grass grow on the hills. He gives food to the cattle and to the ravens when they cry. He does not take delight in the strength of horses nor pleasure in the fleetness of man. The LORD takes pleasure in those who fear Him, who put their hope in His loving care. Praise the LORD, Jerusalem; sing to your God, Zion, for He has strengthened the bars of your gates and blessed your children in your midst. He has brought peace to your borders, and satisfied you with the finest wheat. He sends His commandment to earth; swiftly runs His word. He spreads snow like fleece, sprinkles frost like ashes, scatters hail like crumbs. Who can stand His cold? He sends His word and melts them; He makes the wind blow and the waters flow. ▸ He has declared His words to Jacob, His statutes and laws to Israel. He has done this for no other nation; such laws they do not know. Halleluya! *Ps. 147*

What matters ultimately is not power but humility in the face of God. He has chosen Israel uniquely to embody this truth in their constitution as a nation. Therefore He, not a human legislature, is the source of their laws.

וָאָרֶץ, אֶת־הַיָּם וְאֶת־כָּל־אֲשֶׁר־בָּם, הַשֹּׁמֵר אֱמֶת לְעוֹלָם: עֹשֶׂה
מִשְׁפָּט לָעֲשׁוּקִים, נֹתֵן לֶחֶם לָרְעֵבִים, יהוה מַתִּיר אֲסוּרִים:
יהוה פֹּקֵחַ עִוְרִים, יהוה זֹקֵף כְּפוּפִים, יהוה אֹהֵב צַדִּיקִים: יהוה
שֹׁמֵר אֶת־גֵּרִים, יָתוֹם וְאַלְמָנָה יְעוֹדֵד, וְדֶרֶךְ רְשָׁעִים יְעַוֵּת:
› יִמְלֹךְ יהוה לְעוֹלָם, אֱלֹהַיִךְ צִיּוֹן לְדֹר וָדֹר, הַלְלוּיָהּ:

הַלְלוּיָהּ, כִּי־טוֹב זַמְּרָה אֱלֹהֵינוּ, כִּי־נָעִים נָאוָה תְהִלָּה: בּוֹנֵה תהלים קמז
יְרוּשָׁלַםִ יהוה, נִדְחֵי יִשְׂרָאֵל יְכַנֵּס: הָרוֹפֵא לִשְׁבוּרֵי לֵב, וּמְחַבֵּשׁ
לְעַצְּבוֹתָם: מוֹנֶה מִסְפָּר לַכּוֹכָבִים, לְכֻלָּם שֵׁמוֹת יִקְרָא: גָּדוֹל
אֲדוֹנֵינוּ וְרַב־כֹּחַ, לִתְבוּנָתוֹ אֵין מִסְפָּר: מְעוֹדֵד עֲנָוִים יהוה,
מַשְׁפִּיל רְשָׁעִים עֲדֵי־אָרֶץ: עֱנוּ לַיהוה בְּתוֹדָה, זַמְּרוּ לֵאלֹהֵינוּ
בְכִנּוֹר: הַמְכַסֶּה שָׁמַיִם בְּעָבִים, הַמֵּכִין לָאָרֶץ מָטָר, הַמַּצְמִיחַ
הָרִים חָצִיר: נוֹתֵן לִבְהֵמָה לַחְמָהּ, לִבְנֵי עֹרֵב אֲשֶׁר יִקְרָאוּ: לֹא
בִגְבוּרַת הַסּוּס יֶחְפָּץ, לֹא־בְשׁוֹקֵי הָאִישׁ יִרְצֶה: רוֹצֶה יהוה אֶת־
יְרֵאָיו, אֶת־הַמְיַחֲלִים לְחַסְדּוֹ: שַׁבְּחִי יְרוּשָׁלַםִ אֶת־יהוה, הַלְלִי
אֱלֹהַיִךְ צִיּוֹן: כִּי־חִזַּק בְּרִיחֵי שְׁעָרָיִךְ, בֵּרַךְ בָּנַיִךְ בְּקִרְבֵּךְ: הַשָּׂם־
גְּבוּלֵךְ שָׁלוֹם, חֵלֶב חִטִּים יַשְׂבִּיעֵךְ: הַשֹּׁלֵחַ אִמְרָתוֹ אָרֶץ, עַד־
מְהֵרָה יָרוּץ דְּבָרוֹ: הַנֹּתֵן שֶׁלֶג כַּצָּמֶר, כְּפוֹר כָּאֵפֶר יְפַזֵּר: מַשְׁלִיךְ
קַרְחוֹ כְפִתִּים, לִפְנֵי קָרָתוֹ מִי יַעֲמֹד: יִשְׁלַח דְּבָרוֹ וְיַמְסֵם, יַשֵּׁב
רוּחוֹ יִזְּלוּ־מָיִם: › מַגִּיד דְּבָרָו לְיַעֲקֹב, חֻקָּיו וּמִשְׁפָּטָיו לְיִשְׂרָאֵל:
לֹא עָשָׂה כֵן לְכָל־גּוֹי, וּמִשְׁפָּטִים בַּל־יְדָעוּם, הַלְלוּיָהּ:

הַלְלוּיָהּ *Psalm 147:* A magnificent weaving together of the themes of nature, God's role in Israel's history, and the paradox of divine distance and closeness. God counts the stars: He rules the cosmos. At the same time, He also "heals the brokenhearted and binds up their wounds": He cares for each of us.

הַלְלוּיָהּ Halleluya! Praise the LORD from the heavens, praise Him in the heights. Praise Him, all His angels; praise Him, all His hosts. Praise Him, sun and moon; praise Him, all shining stars. Praise Him, highest heavens and the waters above the heavens. Let them praise the name of the LORD, for He commanded and they were created. He established them for ever and all time, issuing a decree that will never change. Praise the LORD from the earth: sea monsters and all the deep seas; fire and hail, snow and mist, storm winds that obey His word; mountains and all hills, fruit trees and all cedars; wild animals and all cattle, creeping things and winged birds; kings of the earth and all nations, princes and all judges on earth; youths and maidens, old and young. ▸ Let them praise the name of the LORD, for His name alone is sublime; His majesty is above earth and heaven. He has raised the pride of His people, for the glory of all His devoted ones, the children of Israel, the people close to Him. Halleluya! *Ps. 148*

הַלְלוּיָהּ Halleluya! Sing to the LORD a new song, His praise in the assembly of the devoted. Let Israel rejoice in its Maker; let the children of Zion exult in their King. Let them praise His name with dancing; sing praises to Him with timbrel and harp. For the LORD delights in His people; He adorns the humble with salvation. Let the devoted revel in glory; let them sing for joy on their beds. Let high praises of God be in their throats, and a two-edged sword in their hand: to impose retribution on the nations, punishment on the peoples, ▸ binding their kings with chains, their nobles with iron fetters, carrying out the judgment written against them. This is the glory of all His devoted ones. Halleluya! *Ps. 149*

---

granting them victory in war and ensuring the ultimate victory of justice over cruelty and aggression. The "two-edged sword" may be a reference to the dual nature of history: on the one hand the house of Israel must fight its own battles, on the other it must always be conscious of the providential pattern of history, the role of God in its survival and success.

תהלים קמח
הַלְלוּיָהּ, הַלְלוּ אֶת־יהוה מִן־הַשָּׁמַיִם, הַלְלוּהוּ בַּמְּרוֹמִים:
הַלְלוּהוּ כָל־מַלְאָכָיו, הַלְלוּהוּ כָּל־צְבָאוֹ: הַלְלוּהוּ שֶׁמֶשׁ וְיָרֵחַ,
הַלְלוּהוּ כָּל־כּוֹכְבֵי אוֹר: הַלְלוּהוּ שְׁמֵי הַשָּׁמָיִם, וְהַמַּיִם אֲשֶׁר
מֵעַל הַשָּׁמָיִם: יְהַלְלוּ אֶת־שֵׁם יהוה, כִּי הוּא צִוָּה וְנִבְרָאוּ:
וַיַּעֲמִידֵם לָעַד לְעוֹלָם, חָק־נָתַן וְלֹא יַעֲבוֹר: הַלְלוּ אֶת־יהוה
מִן־הָאָרֶץ, תַּנִּינִים וְכָל־תְּהֹמוֹת: אֵשׁ וּבָרָד שֶׁלֶג וְקִיטוֹר, רוּחַ
סְעָרָה עֹשָׂה דְבָרוֹ: הֶהָרִים וְכָל־גְּבָעוֹת, עֵץ פְּרִי וְכָל־אֲרָזִים:
הַחַיָּה וְכָל־בְּהֵמָה, רֶמֶשׂ וְצִפּוֹר כָּנָף: מַלְכֵי־אֶרֶץ וְכָל־לְאֻמִּים,
שָׂרִים וְכָל־שֹׁפְטֵי אָרֶץ: בַּחוּרִים וְגַם־בְּתוּלוֹת, זְקֵנִים עִם־נְעָרִים:
◂ יְהַלְלוּ אֶת־שֵׁם יהוה, כִּי־נִשְׂגָּב שְׁמוֹ לְבַדּוֹ, הוֹדוֹ עַל־אֶרֶץ
וְשָׁמָיִם: וַיָּרֶם קֶרֶן לְעַמּוֹ, תְּהִלָּה לְכָל־חֲסִידָיו, לִבְנֵי יִשְׂרָאֵל
עַם קְרֹבוֹ, הַלְלוּיָהּ:

תהלים קמט
הַלְלוּיָהּ, שִׁירוּ לַיהוה שִׁיר חָדָשׁ, תְּהִלָּתוֹ בִּקְהַל חֲסִידִים: יִשְׂמַח
יִשְׂרָאֵל בְּעֹשָׂיו, בְּנֵי־צִיּוֹן יָגִילוּ בְמַלְכָּם: יְהַלְלוּ שְׁמוֹ בְמָחוֹל, בְּתֹף
וְכִנּוֹר יְזַמְּרוּ־לוֹ: כִּי־רוֹצֶה יהוה בְּעַמּוֹ, יְפָאֵר עֲנָוִים בִּישׁוּעָה:
יַעְלְזוּ חֲסִידִים בְּכָבוֹד, יְרַנְּנוּ עַל־מִשְׁכְּבוֹתָם: רוֹמְמוֹת אֵל
בִּגְרוֹנָם, וְחֶרֶב פִּיפִיּוֹת בְּיָדָם: לַעֲשׂוֹת נְקָמָה בַּגּוֹיִם, תּוֹכֵחוֹת
בַּלְאֻמִּים: ◂ לֶאְסֹר מַלְכֵיהֶם בְּזִקִּים, וְנִכְבְּדֵיהֶם בְּכַבְלֵי בַרְזֶל:
לַעֲשׂוֹת בָּהֶם מִשְׁפָּט כָּתוּב, הָדָר הוּא לְכָל־חֲסִידָיו, הַלְלוּיָהּ:

הַלְלוּיָהּ *Psalm 148:* A creation psalm. The entire universe sings a song of praise to God. The first half of the psalm is about the heavens, the second about the earth. Each is a voice in the choral symphony of creation, in which all that exists testifies to its Maker.

הַלְלוּיָהּ *Psalm 149:* A psalm of thanksgiving for God's role in Israel's history,

הַלְלוּיָהּ Halleluya! *Ps. 150*
Praise God in His holy place;
praise Him in the heavens of His power.
Praise Him for His mighty deeds;
praise Him for His surpassing greatness.
Praise Him with blasts of the shofar;
praise Him with the harp and lyre.
Praise Him with timbrel and dance;
praise Him with strings and flute.
▸ Praise Him with clashing cymbals;
praise Him with resounding cymbals.
Let all that breathes praise the LORD. Halleluya!
Let all that breathes praise the LORD. Halleluya!

בָּרוּךְ Blessed be the LORD for ever. Amen and Amen. *Ps. 89*
Blessed from Zion be the LORD *Ps. 135*
who dwells in Jerusalem. Halleluya!
Blessed be the LORD, God of Israel, who alone does wonders. *Ps. 72*
▸ Blessed be His glorious name for ever,
and may all the earth be filled with His glory.
Amen and Amen.

Stand until "The soul" on page 444.

וַיְבָרֶךְ David blessed the LORD in front of the entire assembly. David *1 Chr. 29*
said, "Blessed are You, LORD, God of our father Yisrael, for ever and ever. Yours, LORD, are the greatness and the power, the glory, majesty and splendor, for everything in heaven and earth is Yours. Yours, LORD, is the kingdom; You are exalted as Head over all. Both

---

Temple Mount (Maimonides, *Bikkurim* 4:17). The repetition of the last verse is a convention signaling the end of a book or passage.

בָּרוּךְ ה׳ *Blessed be the LORD:* A passage marking the closure of the Verses of Praise. It is constructed out of three verses from the book of Psalms, chosen because they open with the word "Blessed."

תהלים קנ

הַלְלוּיָהּ
הַלְלוּ־אֵל בְּקָדְשׁוֹ, הַלְלוּהוּ בִּרְקִיעַ עֻזּוֹ:
הַלְלוּהוּ בִגְבוּרֹתָיו, הַלְלוּהוּ כְּרֹב גֻּדְלוֹ:
הַלְלוּהוּ בְּתֵקַע שׁוֹפָר, הַלְלוּהוּ בְּנֵבֶל וְכִנּוֹר:
הַלְלוּהוּ בְתֹף וּמָחוֹל, הַלְלוּהוּ בְּמִנִּים וְעֻגָב:
◂ הַלְלוּהוּ בְצִלְצְלֵי־שָׁמַע, הַלְלוּהוּ בְּצִלְצְלֵי תְרוּעָה:
כֹּל הַנְּשָׁמָה תְּהַלֵּל יָהּ, הַלְלוּיָהּ:
כֹּל הַנְּשָׁמָה תְּהַלֵּל יָהּ, הַלְלוּיָהּ:

תהלים פט — בָּרוּךְ יהוה לְעוֹלָם, אָמֵן וְאָמֵן:
תהלים קלה — בָּרוּךְ יהוה מִצִּיּוֹן, שֹׁכֵן יְרוּשָׁלָםִ, הַלְלוּיָהּ:
תהלים עב — בָּרוּךְ יהוה אֱלֹהִים אֱלֹהֵי יִשְׂרָאֵל, עֹשֵׂה נִפְלָאוֹת לְבַדּוֹ:
◂ וּבָרוּךְ שֵׁם כְּבוֹדוֹ לְעוֹלָם
וְיִמָּלֵא כְבוֹדוֹ אֶת־כָּל־הָאָרֶץ
אָמֵן וְאָמֵן:

Stand until נִשְׁמַת *on page 445.*

דברי הימים א׳ כט — וַיְבָרֶךְ דָּוִיד אֶת־יהוה לְעֵינֵי כָּל־הַקָּהָל, וַיֹּאמֶר דָּוִיד, בָּרוּךְ
אַתָּה יהוה, אֱלֹהֵי יִשְׂרָאֵל אָבִינוּ, מֵעוֹלָם וְעַד־עוֹלָם: לְךָ יהוה
הַגְּדֻלָּה וְהַגְּבוּרָה וְהַתִּפְאֶרֶת וְהַנֵּצַח וְהַהוֹד, כִּי־כֹל בַּשָּׁמַיִם
וּבָאָרֶץ, לְךָ יהוה הַמַּמְלָכָה וְהַמִּתְנַשֵּׂא לְכֹל לְרֹאשׁ: וְהָעֹשֶׁר

הַלְלוּיָהּ *Psalm 150:* The book of Psalms here reaches its crescendo in a magnificent song whose key word is praise (*hallel*), which appears in one or another form thirteen times in a single short paragraph. In ancient times it was recited by pilgrims bringing first fruits to Jerusalem, when they reached the

riches and honor are in Your gift and You reign over all things. In Your hand are strength and might. It is in Your power to make great and give strength to all. Therefore, our God, we thank You and praise Your glorious name." You alone are the LORD. You made the heavens, even the highest heavens, and all their hosts, the earth and all that is on it, the seas and all they contain. You give life to them all, and the hosts of heaven worship You. ▸ You are the LORD God who chose Abram and brought him out of Ur of the Chaldees, changing his name to Abraham. You found his heart faithful toward You, ◂ and You made a covenant with him to give to his descendants the land of the Canaanites, Hittites, Amorites, Perizzites, Jebusites and Girgashites. You fulfilled Your promise for You are righteous. You saw the suffering of our ancestors in Egypt. You heard their cry at the Sea of Reeds. You sent signs and wonders against Pharaoh, all his servants and all the people of his land, because You knew how arrogantly the Egyptians treated them. You created for Yourself renown that remains to this day. ▸ You divided the sea before them, so that they passed through the sea on dry land, but You cast their pursuers into the depths, like a stone into mighty waters. *Neh. 9*

וַיּוֹשַׁע That day the LORD saved Israel from the hands of the Egyptians, and Israel saw the Egyptians lying dead on the seashore. ▸ When Israel saw the great power the LORD had displayed against the Egyptians, the people feared the LORD, and believed in the LORD and in His servant, Moses. *Ex. 14*

One reason for their presence here is that thus far we have prayed as individuals. Communal prayer is about to begin. The three historic passages are about the constitution of a community of prayer.

In the first, David had made Jerusalem the capital of the nation and brought the Ark to it. Now at the end of his life he assembled the people and charged them with the sacred task of building the Temple. In the second, after the Babylonian exile, Ezra and Nehemiah summoned the people to reaffirm their historic covenant with God. The third, after the Israelites had crossed the

וְהַכָּבוֹד מִלְּפָנֶיךָ, וְאַתָּה מוֹשֵׁל בַּכֹּל, וּבְיָדְךָ כֹּחַ וּגְבוּרָה, וּבְיָדְךָ
לְגַדֵּל וּלְחַזֵּק לַכֹּל: וְעַתָּה אֱלֹהֵינוּ מוֹדִים אֲנַחְנוּ לָךְ, וּמְהַלְלִים
לְשֵׁם תִּפְאַרְתֶּךָ: אַתָּה־הוּא יהוה לְבַדֶּךָ, אַתָּה עָשִׂיתָ נחמיה ט
אֶת־הַשָּׁמַיִם, שְׁמֵי הַשָּׁמַיִם וְכָל־צְבָאָם, הָאָרֶץ וְכָל־אֲשֶׁר עָלֶיהָ,
הַיַּמִּים וְכָל־אֲשֶׁר בָּהֶם, וְאַתָּה מְחַיֶּה אֶת־כֻּלָּם, וּצְבָא הַשָּׁמַיִם לְךָ
מִשְׁתַּחֲוִים: · אַתָּה הוּא יהוה הָאֱלֹהִים אֲשֶׁר בָּחַרְתָּ בְּאַבְרָם,
וְהוֹצֵאתוֹ מֵאוּר כַּשְׂדִּים, וְשַׂמְתָּ שְּׁמוֹ אַבְרָהָם: וּמָצָאתָ אֶת־
לְבָבוֹ נֶאֱמָן לְפָנֶיךָ, · וְכָרוֹת עִמּוֹ הַבְּרִית לָתֵת אֶת־אֶרֶץ הַכְּנַעֲנִי
הַחִתִּי הָאֱמֹרִי וְהַפְּרִזִּי וְהַיְבוּסִי וְהַגִּרְגָּשִׁי, לָתֵת לְזַרְעוֹ, וַתָּקֶם
אֶת־דְּבָרֶיךָ, כִּי צַדִּיק אָתָּה: וַתֵּרֶא אֶת־עֳנִי אֲבֹתֵינוּ בְּמִצְרָיִם,
וְאֶת־זַעֲקָתָם שָׁמַעְתָּ עַל־יַם־סוּף: וַתִּתֵּן אֹתֹת וּמֹפְתִים בְּפַרְעֹה
וּבְכָל־עֲבָדָיו וּבְכָל־עַם אַרְצוֹ, כִּי יָדַעְתָּ כִּי הֵזִידוּ עֲלֵיהֶם, וַתַּעַשׂ־
לְךָ שֵׁם כְּהַיּוֹם הַזֶּה: · וְהַיָּם בָּקַעְתָּ לִפְנֵיהֶם, וַיַּעַבְרוּ בְתוֹךְ־
הַיָּם בַּיַּבָּשָׁה, וְאֶת־רֹדְפֵיהֶם הִשְׁלַכְתָּ בִמְצוֹלֹת כְּמוֹ־אֶבֶן, בְּמַיִם
עַזִּים:

וַיּוֹשַׁע יהוה בַּיּוֹם הַהוּא אֶת־יִשְׂרָאֵל מִיַּד מִצְרָיִם, וַיַּרְא יִשְׂרָאֵל שמות יד
אֶת־מִצְרַיִם מֵת עַל־שְׂפַת הַיָּם: · וַיַּרְא יִשְׂרָאֵל אֶת־הַיָּד הַגְּדֹלָה
אֲשֶׁר עָשָׂה יהוה בְּמִצְרַיִם, וַיִּירְאוּ הָעָם אֶת־יהוה, וַיַּאֲמִינוּ
בַּיהוה וּבְמֹשֶׁה עַבְדּוֹ:

וַיְבָרֶךְ דָּוִיד *David blessed:* The first of three passages marking historic transitions in the history of Israel: (1) King David's prayer for the building of the Temple; (2) the prayer said at the gathering convened by Ezra after the return from the Babylonian exile; and (3) the song Moses and the Israelites sang at the Sea of Reeds, after the waters had miraculously divided, allowing them to cross to safety.

אָז יָשִׁיר־מֹשֶׁה Then Moses and the Israelites sang this song to the LORD, saying: *Ex. 15*
I will sing to the LORD, for He has triumphed gloriously;
horse and rider He has hurled into the sea.
The LORD is my strength and song; He has become my salvation.
This is my God, and I will beautify Him,
my father's God, and I will exalt Him.
The LORD is a Master of war; LORD is His name.
Pharaoh's chariots and army He cast into the sea;
the best of his officers drowned in the Sea of Reeds.
The deep waters covered them;
they went down to the depths like a stone.
Your right hand, LORD, is majestic in power.
Your right hand, LORD, shatters the enemy.
In the greatness of Your majesty, You overthrew those who rose against You.
You sent out Your fury; it consumed them like stubble.
By the blast of Your nostrils the waters piled up.
The surging waters stood straight like a wall;
the deeps congealed in the heart of the sea.
The enemy said, "I will pursue. I will overtake. I will divide the spoil.
My desire shall have its fill of them.
I will draw my sword. My hand will destroy them."
You blew with Your wind; the sea covered them.
They sank in the mighty waters like lead.
Who is like You, LORD, among the mighty?
Who is like You – majestic in holiness, awesome in glory, working wonders?
You stretched out Your right hand,
the earth swallowed them.

---

of God. They were no longer mere individuals (returning exiles, escaping slaves) but a group, a nation, a community of faith.

אָז יָשִׁיר־מֹשֶׁה וּבְנֵי יִשְׂרָאֵל אֶת־הַשִּׁירָה הַזֹּאת לַיהוה, וַיֹּאמְרוּ שמות טו
לֵאמֹר, אָשִׁירָה לַיהוה כִּי־גָאֹה גָּאָה, סוּס
וְרֹכְבוֹ רָמָה בַיָּם: עָזִּי וְזִמְרָת יָהּ וַיְהִי־לִי
לִישׁוּעָה, זֶה אֵלִי וְאַנְוֵהוּ, אֱלֹהֵי
אָבִי וַאֲרֹמְמֶנְהוּ: יהוה אִישׁ מִלְחָמָה, יהוה
שְׁמוֹ: מַרְכְּבֹת פַּרְעֹה וְחֵילוֹ יָרָה בַיָּם, וּמִבְחַר
שָׁלִשָׁיו טֻבְּעוּ בְיַם־סוּף: תְּהֹמֹת יְכַסְיֻמוּ, יָרְדוּ בִמְצוֹלֹת כְּמוֹ־
אָבֶן: יְמִינְךָ יהוה נֶאְדָּרִי בַּכֹּחַ, יְמִינְךָ
יהוה תִּרְעַץ אוֹיֵב: וּבְרֹב גְּאוֹנְךָ תַּהֲרֹס
קָמֶיךָ, תְּשַׁלַּח חֲרֹנְךָ יֹאכְלֵמוֹ כַּקַּשׁ: וּבְרוּחַ
אַפֶּיךָ נֶעֶרְמוּ מַיִם, נִצְּבוּ כְמוֹ־נֵד
נֹזְלִים, קָפְאוּ תְהֹמֹת בְּלֶב־יָם: אָמַר
אוֹיֵב אֶרְדֹּף, אַשִּׂיג, אֲחַלֵּק שָׁלָל, תִּמְלָאֵמוֹ
נַפְשִׁי, אָרִיק חַרְבִּי, תּוֹרִישֵׁמוֹ יָדִי: נָשַׁפְתָּ
בְרוּחֲךָ כִּסָּמוֹ יָם, צָלְלוּ כַּעוֹפֶרֶת בְּמַיִם
אַדִּירִים: מִי־כָמֹכָה בָּאֵלִם יהוה, מִי
כָּמֹכָה נֶאְדָּר בַּקֹּדֶשׁ, נוֹרָא תְהִלֹּת עֹשֵׂה
פֶלֶא: נָטִיתָ יְמִינְךָ תִּבְלָעֵמוֹ אָרֶץ: נָחִיתָ

Sea of Reeds, was the moment when they left the land over which Pharaoh ruled. They were now God's people, under His sole domain. Common to all three passages is that they were said at historic moments when the people pledged themselves to be defined as a nation bound together by a sacred task.

Instead of simply moving from individual to communal worship, the siddur takes us through three transformative moments in Jewish history when the people constituted themselves as a nation dedicated to the service

In Your loving-kindness, You led the people You redeemed.
In Your strength, You guided them to Your holy abode.
Nations heard and trembled;
terror gripped Philistia's inhabitants.
The chiefs of Edom were dismayed,
Moab's leaders were seized with trembling,
the people of Canaan melted away.
Fear and dread fell upon them.
By the power of Your arm, they were still as stone –
until Your people crossed, LORD,
until the people You acquired crossed over.
You will bring them and plant them on the mountain of Your heritage –
the place, LORD, You made for Your dwelling,
the Sanctuary, LORD, Your hands established.
The LORD will reign for ever and all time.

The LORD will reign for ever and all time.
The LORD's kingship is established for ever and to all eternity.

When Pharaoh's horses, chariots and riders went into the sea,
the LORD brought the waters of the sea back over them,
but the Israelites walked on dry land through the sea.

▸ For kingship is the LORD's *Ps. 22*
and He rules over the nations.
Saviors shall go up to Mount Zion *Ob. 1*
to judge Mount Esau,
and the LORD's shall be the kingdom.
Then the LORD shall be King over all the earth; *Zech. 14*
on that day the LORD shall be One and His name One,
(as it is written in Your Torah, saying:
Listen, Israel: the LORD is our God, the LORD is One.) *Deut. 6*

On Hoshana Raba, Yom HaAtzma'ut and Yom Yerushalayim, continue with the weekday service, from "May Your name be praised" on page 84.

בְחַסְדְּךָ עַם־זוּ גָּאָֽלְתָּ, נֵהַֽלְתָּ בְעָזְּךָ אֶל־נְוֵה
קָדְשֶֽׁךָ: שָֽׁמְעוּ עַמִּים יִרְגָּזֽוּן, חִיל
אָחַז יֹשְׁבֵי פְּלָֽשֶׁת: אָז נִבְהֲלוּ אַלּוּפֵי
אֱדוֹם, אֵילֵי מוֹאָב יֹאחֲזֵמוֹ רָֽעַד, נָמֹגוּ
כֹּל יֹשְׁבֵי כְנָֽעַן: תִּפֹּל עֲלֵיהֶם אֵימָֽתָה
וָפַחַד, בִּגְדֹל זְרוֹעֲךָ יִדְּמוּ כָּאָֽבֶן, עַד־
יַעֲבֹר עַמְּךָ יהוה, עַד־יַעֲבֹר עַם־זוּ
קָנִֽיתָ: תְּבִאֵמוֹ וְתִטָּעֵמוֹ בְּהַר נַחֲלָֽתְךָ, מָכוֹן
לְשִׁבְתְּךָ פָּעַֽלְתָּ יהוה, מִקְּדָשׁ אֲדֹנָי כּוֹנְנוּ
יָדֶֽיךָ: יהוה ׀ יִמְלֹךְ לְעֹלָם וָעֶד:

יהוה יִמְלֹךְ לְעֹלָם וָעֶד.

יהוה מַלְכוּתֵהּ קָאֵם לְעָלַם וּלְעָלְמֵי עָלְמַיָּא.

כִּי
בָא סוּס פַּרְעֹה בְּרִכְבּוֹ וּבְפָרָשָׁיו בַּיָּם, וַיָּֽשֶׁב יהוה עֲלֵהֶם אֶת־מֵי
הַיָּם, וּבְנֵי יִשְׂרָאֵל הָלְכוּ בַיַּבָּשָׁה בְּתוֹךְ הַיָּם:

תהלים כב › כִּי לַיהוה הַמְּלוּכָה וּמֹשֵׁל בַּגּוֹיִם:
עובדיה א וְעָלוּ מוֹשִׁעִים בְּהַר צִיּוֹן לִשְׁפֹּט אֶת־הַר עֵשָׂו
וְהָיְתָה לַיהוה הַמְּלוּכָה:
זכריה יד וְהָיָה יהוה לְמֶֽלֶךְ עַל־כָּל־הָאָֽרֶץ
בַּיּוֹם הַהוּא יִהְיֶה יהוה אֶחָד וּשְׁמוֹ אֶחָד:
דברים ו (וּבְתוֹרָתְךָ כָּתוּב לֵאמֹר, שְׁמַע יִשְׂרָאֵל, יהוה אֱלֹהֵינוּ יהוה אֶחָד:)

On הושענא רבה, יום העצמאות *and* יום ירושלים *continue with* יִשְׁתַּבַּח *on page 85.*

THE SOUL

of all that lives shall bless Your name, Lord our God,
and the spirit of all flesh shall always glorify
and exalt Your remembrance, our King.
From eternity to eternity You are God.
Without You, we have no king, redeemer or savior,
who liberates, rescues, sustains
and shows compassion in every time of trouble and distress.
We have no king but You, God of the first and last,
God of all creatures, Master of all ages,
extolled by a multitude of praises,
who guides His world with loving-kindness
and His creatures with compassion.
The Lord neither slumbers nor sleeps.
He rouses the sleepers and wakens the slumberers.
He makes the dumb speak, sets the bound free,
supports the fallen, and raises those bowed down.
To You alone we give thanks:
If our mouths were as full of song as the sea,
and our tongue with jubilation as its myriad waves,
if our lips were full of praise like the spacious heavens,
and our eyes shone like the sun and moon,
if our hands were outstretched like eagles of the sky,
and our feet as swift as hinds –

---

mentioned in the Mishna as a conclusion to saying Hallel in the *seder* service on Pesaḥ (*Pesaḥim* 118a). Just as there, so here, it stands as a conclusion to the recitation of Psalms. The second part, beginning "To You alone we give thanks," is mentioned in the Talmud (*Berakhot* 59b) as a thanksgiving prayer for rain.

The first section is an extended meditation on the final words of the book of Psalms: "Let all that breathes praise the Lord." Hebrew has many words for soul, all deriving from verbs related to breathing. *Neshama* – the word linking this passage to the end of Psalms – means to breathe deeply, as we

נִשְׁמַת

כָּל חַי תְּבָרֵךְ אֶת שִׁמְךָ, יהוה אֱלֹהֵינוּ
וְרְוּחַ כָּל בָּשָׂר תְּפָאֵר וּתְרוֹמֵם זִכְרְךָ מַלְכֵּנוּ תָּמִיד.
מִן הָעוֹלָם וְעַד הָעוֹלָם אַתָּה אֵל
וּמִבַּלְעָדֶיךָ אֵין לָנוּ מֶלֶךְ גּוֹאֵל וּמוֹשִׁיעַ
פּוֹדֶה וּמַצִּיל וּמְפַרְנֵס וּמְרַחֵם
בְּכָל עֵת צָרָה וְצוּקָה אֵין לָנוּ מֶלֶךְ אֶלָּא אָתָּה.
אֱלֹהֵי הָרִאשׁוֹנִים וְהָאַחֲרוֹנִים, אֱלְוֹהַּ כָּל בְּרִיּוֹת
אֲדוֹן כָּל תּוֹלָדוֹת, הַמְהֻלָּל בְּרֹב הַתִּשְׁבָּחוֹת
הַמְנַהֵג עוֹלָמוֹ בְּחֶסֶד וּבְרִיּוֹתָיו בְּרַחֲמִים.
וַיהוה לֹא יָנוּם וְלֹא יִישָׁן
הַמְעוֹרֵר יְשֵׁנִים וְהַמֵּקִיץ נִרְדָּמִים
וְהַמֵּשִׂיחַ אִלְּמִים וְהַמַּתִּיר אֲסוּרִים
וְהַסּוֹמֵךְ נוֹפְלִים וְהַזּוֹקֵף כְּפוּפִים.
לְךָ לְבַדְּךָ אֲנַחְנוּ מוֹדִים.
אִלּוּ פִינוּ מָלֵא שִׁירָה כַּיָּם
וּלְשׁוֹנֵנוּ רִנָּה כַּהֲמוֹן גַּלָּיו
וְשִׂפְתוֹתֵינוּ שֶֽׁבַח כְּמֶרְחֲבֵי רָקִיעַ
וְעֵינֵינוּ מְאִירוֹת כַּשֶּׁמֶשׁ וְכַיָּרֵחַ
וְיָדֵינוּ פְרוּשׂוֹת כְּנִשְׁרֵי שָׁמָיִם
וְרַגְלֵינוּ קַלּוֹת כָּאַיָּלוֹת

נִשְׁמַת כָּל חַי *The soul of all that lives:* This magnificent poem is composed of two parts. The first, according to Rabbi Yoḥanan is the "blessing of the song"

still we could not thank You enough,
Lord our God and God of our ancestors,
or bless Your name
for even one of the thousand thousands
and myriad myriads of favors
You did for our ancestors and for us.
You redeemed us from Egypt, Lord our God,
and freed us from the house of bondage.
In famine You nourished us; in times of plenty You sustained us.
You delivered us from the sword, saved us from the plague,
and spared us from serious and lasting illness.
Until now Your mercies have helped us.
Your love has not forsaken us.
May You, Lord our God, never abandon us.
Therefore the limbs You formed within us,
the spirit and soul You breathed into our nostrils,
and the tongue You placed in our mouth –
they will thank and bless, praise and glorify, exalt and esteem,
hallow and do homage to Your name, O our King.
For every mouth shall give thanks to You,
every tongue vow allegiance to You,
every knee shall bend to You,
every upright body shall bow to You,
all hearts shall fear You,
and our innermost being sing praises to Your name,
as is written:

"All my bones shall say: Lord, who is like You? *Ps. 35*
You save the poor from one stronger than him,
the poor and needy from one who would rob him."

---

that lives sing a song of praise to God who brought the universe into being, sustains it, and guides the destinies of all things.

The second section is composed around a phrase from Psalms: "All my

אֵין אֲנַחְנוּ מַסְפִּיקִים לְהוֹדוֹת לְךָ
יהוה אֱלֹהֵינוּ וֵאלֹהֵי אֲבוֹתֵינוּ
וּלְבָרֵךְ אֶת שְׁמֶךָ
עַל אַחַת מֵאֶלֶף אֶלֶף אַלְפֵי אֲלָפִים
וְרִבֵּי רְבָבוֹת פְּעָמִים הַטּוֹבוֹת
שֶׁעָשִׂיתָ עִם אֲבוֹתֵינוּ וְעִמָּנוּ.
מִמִּצְרַיִם גְּאַלְתָּנוּ, יהוה אֱלֹהֵינוּ, וּמִבֵּית עֲבָדִים פְּדִיתָנוּ
בְּרָעָב זַנְתָּנוּ וּבְשָׂבָע כִּלְכַּלְתָּנוּ
מֵחֶרֶב הִצַּלְתָּנוּ וּמִדֶּבֶר מִלַּטְתָּנוּ
וּמֵחֳלָיִם רָעִים וְנֶאֱמָנִים דִּלִּיתָנוּ.
עַד הֵנָּה עֲזָרוּנוּ רַחֲמֶיךָ, וְלֹא עֲזָבוּנוּ חֲסָדֶיךָ
וְאַל תִּטְּשֵׁנוּ, יהוה אֱלֹהֵינוּ, לָנֶצַח.
עַל כֵּן אֵבָרִים שֶׁפִּלַּגְתָּ בָּנוּ
וְרוּחַ וּנְשָׁמָה שֶׁנָּפַחְתָּ בְּאַפֵּינוּ, וְלָשׁוֹן אֲשֶׁר שַׂמְתָּ בְּפִינוּ
הֵן הֵם יוֹדוּ וִיבָרְכוּ וִישַׁבְּחוּ וִיפָאֲרוּ
וִירוֹמְמוּ וְיַעֲרִיצוּ וְיַקְדִּישׁוּ וְיַמְלִיכוּ אֶת שִׁמְךָ מַלְכֵּנוּ
כִּי כָל פֶּה לְךָ יוֹדֶה וְכָל לָשׁוֹן לְךָ תִשָּׁבַע
וְכָל בֶּרֶךְ לְךָ תִכְרַע וְכָל קוֹמָה לְפָנֶיךָ תִשְׁתַּחֲוֶה
וְכָל לְבָבוֹת יִירָאוּךָ וְכָל קֶרֶב וּכְלָיוֹת יְזַמְּרוּ לִשְׁמֶךָ
כַּדָּבָר שֶׁכָּתוּב
כָּל עַצְמֹתַי תֹּאמַרְנָה יהוה מִי כָמוֹךָ תהלים לה
מַצִּיל עָנִי מֵחָזָק מִמֶּנּוּ, וְעָנִי וְאֶבְיוֹן מִגֹּזְלוֹ:

---

are able to do in a state of rest. Hence the sages said that on Shabbat we have "an extra soul." In the still silence of the turning world it is as if we hear all

Who is like You? Who is equal to You?
Who can be compared to You?
O great, mighty and awesome God, God Most High,
Maker of heaven and earth.
▸ We will laud, praise and glorify You and bless Your holy name,
as it is said:
"Of David. Bless the LORD, O my soul, *Ps. 103*
and all that is within me bless His holy name."

On Yom Tov the Leader begins here:

הָאֵל God – in Your absolute power,
Great – in the glory of Your name,
Mighty – for ever,
Awesome – in Your awe-inspiring deeds,
The King – who sits on a throne.
High and lofty

On Shabbat the Leader begins here:

HE INHABITS ETERNITY;
exalted and holy is His name.
And it is written:
Sing joyfully to the LORD, you righteous, *Ps. 33*
for praise from the upright is seemly.
▸ By the mouth of the upright You shall be praised.
By the words of the righteous You shall be blessed.
By the tongue of the devout You shall be extolled,
And in the midst of the holy You shall be sanctified.

---

the human inability to adequately thank God, itemizing how the various limbs ("All my bones") may praise Him.

שׁוֹכֵן עַד *He inhabits eternity:* The Leader begins at different points on different holy days of the year. On Shabbat he begins with "He inhabits eternity," emphasizing creation; on Yom Tov, with "God – in Your abolute power," laying stress on God as He acts in history; on Rosh HaShana and Yom Kippur, with "The King – enthroned," evoking ideas of justice and judgment.

מִי יִדְמֶה לָּךְ וּמִי יִשְׁוֶה לָּךְ וּמִי יַעֲרָךְ לָךְ
הָאֵל הַגָּדוֹל, הַגִּבּוֹר וְהַנּוֹרָא, אֵל עֶלְיוֹן, קוֹנֵה שָׁמַיִם וָאָרֶץ.
◂ נְהַלֶּלְךָ וּנְשַׁבֵּחֲךָ וּנְפָאֶרְךָ וּנְבָרֵךְ אֶת שֵׁם קָדְשֶׁךָ
כָּאָמוּר
לְדָוִד, בָּרְכִי נַפְשִׁי אֶת־יהוה, וְכׇל־קְרָבַי אֶת־שֵׁם קָדְשׁוֹ: תהלים קג

On יום טוב *the* שליח ציבור *begins here:*

הָאֵל בְּתַעֲצוּמוֹת עֻזֶּךָ
הַגָּדוֹל בִּכְבוֹד שְׁמֶךָ
הַגִּבּוֹר לָנֶצַח וְהַנּוֹרָא בְּנוֹרְאוֹתֶיךָ
הַמֶּלֶךְ הַיּוֹשֵׁב עַל כִּסֵּא
רָם וְנִשָּׂא

On שבת *the* שליח ציבור *begins here:*

שׁוֹכֵן עַד

מָרוֹם וְקָדוֹשׁ שְׁמוֹ
וְכָתוּב
רַנְּנוּ צַדִּיקִים בַּיהוה, לַיְשָׁרִים נָאוָה תְהִלָּה: תהלים לג
◂ בְּפִי יְשָׁרִים תִּתְהַלָּל
וּבְדִבְרֵי צַדִּיקִים תִּתְבָּרַךְ
וּבִלְשׁוֹן חֲסִידִים תִּתְרוֹמָם
וּבְקֶרֶב קְדוֹשִׁים תִּתְקַדָּשׁ

---

bones shall say, God, who is like You?" – thus ingeniously linking the psalms of praise with the שירת הים ("Song at the Sea"), which contains the same phrase, "Who is like You?" Through a fine series of images, the poet expresses

וּבְמַקְהֲלוֹת And in the assemblies
of tens of thousands of Your people, the house of Israel,
with joyous song shall Your name, our King,
be glorified in every generation.
▸ For this is the duty of all creatures before You,
LORD our God and God of our ancestors:
to thank, praise, laud, glorify, exalt,
honor, bless, raise high and acclaim –
even beyond all the words of song and praise
of David, son of Jesse, Your servant, Your anointed.

Stand until after "Barekhu" on page 454.

יִשְׁתַּבַּח May Your name be praised for ever, our King,
the great and holy God, King in heaven and on earth.
For to You, LORD our God and God of our ancestors,
it is right to offer song and praise,
hymn and psalm,
strength and dominion,
eternity, greatness and power,
song of praise and glory,
holiness and kingship,
▸ blessings and thanks, from now and for ever.
Blessed are You, LORD,
God and King, exalted in praises,
God of thanksgivings,
Master of wonders,
who delights in hymns of song,
King, God, Giver of life to the worlds.

"assemblies" refers to the large congregations present in synagogues on holy days, reminding us of the Temple, full at such times.

יִשְׁתַּבַּח שִׁמְךָ *May Your name be praised for ever:* The concluding blessing over the *Pesukei DeZimra* which, like the introductory blessing, is said standing. The fifteen terms of glorification equal the number of psalms in the *Pesukei DeZimra* on Shabbat and Yom Tov, as well as the number of "Songs of Ascents."

וּבְמַקְהֲלוֹת רִבְבוֹת עַמְּךָ בֵּית יִשְׂרָאֵל
בְּרִנָּה יִתְפָּאַר שִׁמְךָ מַלְכֵּנוּ בְּכָל דּוֹר וָדוֹר
◂ שֶׁכֵּן חוֹבַת כָּל הַיְצוּרִים
לְפָנֶיךָ יהוה אֱלֹהֵינוּ וֵאלֹהֵי אֲבוֹתֵינוּ
לְהוֹדוֹת, לְהַלֵּל, לְשַׁבֵּחַ, לְפָאֵר, לְרוֹמֵם
לְהַדֵּר, לְבָרֵךְ, לְעַלֵּה וּלְקַלֵּס
עַל כָּל דִּבְרֵי שִׁירוֹת וְתִשְׁבְּחוֹת
דָּוִד בֶּן יִשַׁי, עַבְדְּךָ מְשִׁיחֶךָ.

Stand until after בָּרְכוּ *on page 455.*

יִשְׁתַּבַּח שִׁמְךָ לָעַד, מַלְכֵּנוּ
הָאֵל הַמֶּלֶךְ הַגָּדוֹל וְהַקָּדוֹשׁ בַּשָּׁמַיִם וּבָאָרֶץ
כִּי לְךָ נָאֶה, יהוה אֱלֹהֵינוּ וֵאלֹהֵי אֲבוֹתֵינוּ
שִׁיר וּשְׁבָחָה, הַלֵּל וְזִמְרָה
עֹז וּמֶמְשָׁלָה, נֶצַח, גְּדֻלָּה וּגְבוּרָה
תְּהִלָּה וְתִפְאֶרֶת, קְדֻשָּׁה וּמַלְכוּת
◂ בְּרָכוֹת וְהוֹדָאוֹת, מֵעַתָּה וְעַד עוֹלָם.
בָּרוּךְ אַתָּה יהוה
אֵל מֶלֶךְ גָּדוֹל בַּתִּשְׁבָּחוֹת
אֵל הַהוֹדָאוֹת
אֲדוֹן הַנִּפְלָאוֹת
הַבּוֹחֵר בְּשִׁירֵי זִמְרָה
מֶלֶךְ, אֵל, חֵי הָעוֹלָמִים.

וּבְמַקְהֲלוֹת *And in the assemblies:* The list of nine words for praise corresponds to the nine additional psalms we say on Shabbat and Yom Tov. The word

On Shabbat Shuva, many congregations open the Ark and say this psalm responsively, verse by verse.

שִׁיר הַמַּעֲלוֹת A song of ascents. From the depths I have called to You, Lord. *Ps. 130*
Lord, hear my voice; let Your ears be attentive to my plea. If You, Lord, should keep account of sins, O Lord, who could stand? But with You there is forgiveness, that You may be held in awe. I wait for the Lord, my soul waits, and in His word I put my hope. My soul waits for the Lord more than watchmen wait for the morning, more than watchmen wait for the morning. Israel, put your hope in the Lord, for with the Lord there is loving-kindness, and great is His power to redeem. It is He who will redeem Israel from all their sins.

HALF KADDISH

Leader: יִתְגַּדַּל Magnified and sanctified
may His great name be,
in the world He created by His will.
May He establish His kingdom
in your lifetime and in your days,
and in the lifetime of all the house of Israel,
swiftly and soon –
and say: Amen.

All: May His great name be blessed
for ever and all time.

Leader: Blessed and praised, glorified and exalted,
raised and honored,
uplifted and lauded
be the name of the Holy One,
blessed be He,
beyond any blessing,
song, praise and consolation
uttered in the world –
and say: Amen.

On שבת שובה*, many congregations open the* ארון קודש *and say this psalm responsively, verse by verse.*

תהלים קל שִׁיר הַמַּעֲלוֹת, מִמַּעֲמַקִּים קְרָאתִיךָ יהוה: אֲדֹנָי שִׁמְעָה בְקוֹלִי, תִּהְיֶינָה אָזְנֶיךָ קַשֻּׁבוֹת לְקוֹל תַּחֲנוּנָי: אִם־עֲוֺנוֹת תִּשְׁמָר־יָהּ, אֲדֹנָי מִי יַעֲמֹד: כִּי־עִמְּךָ הַסְּלִיחָה, לְמַעַן תִּוָּרֵא: קִוִּיתִי יהוה קִוְּתָה נַפְשִׁי, וְלִדְבָרוֹ הוֹחָלְתִּי: נַפְשִׁי לַאדֹנָי, מִשֹּׁמְרִים לַבֹּקֶר, שֹׁמְרִים לַבֹּקֶר: יַחֵל יִשְׂרָאֵל אֶל יהוה, כִּי־עִם־יהוה הַחֶסֶד, וְהַרְבֵּה עִמּוֹ פְדוּת: וְהוּא יִפְדֶּה אֶת־יִשְׂרָאֵל, מִכֹּל עֲוֺנוֹתָיו:

חצי קדיש

ש״ץ: יִתְגַּדַּל וְיִתְקַדַּשׁ שְׁמֵהּ רַבָּא (קהל: אָמֵן)
בְּעָלְמָא דִּי בְרָא כִרְעוּתֵהּ
וְיַמְלִיךְ מַלְכוּתֵהּ
בְּחַיֵּיכוֹן וּבְיוֹמֵיכוֹן וּבְחַיֵּי דְכָל בֵּית יִשְׂרָאֵל
בַּעֲגָלָא וּבִזְמַן קָרִיב
וְאִמְרוּ אָמֵן. (קהל: אָמֵן)

קהל וש״ץ: יְהֵא שְׁמֵהּ רַבָּא מְבָרַךְ לְעָלַם וּלְעָלְמֵי עָלְמַיָּא.

ש״ץ: יִתְבָּרַךְ וְיִשְׁתַּבַּח וְיִתְפָּאַר וְיִתְרוֹמַם וְיִתְנַשֵּׂא
וְיִתְהַדָּר וְיִתְעַלֶּה וְיִתְהַלָּל
שְׁמֵהּ דְּקֻדְשָׁא בְּרִיךְ הוּא (קהל: בְּרִיךְ הוּא)
לְעֵלָּא מִן כָּל בִּרְכָתָא
/בשבת שובה: לְעֵלָּא לְעֵלָּא מִכָּל בִּרְכָתָא/
וְשִׁירָתָא, תֻּשְׁבְּחָתָא וְנֶחֱמָתָא, דַּאֲמִירָן בְּעָלְמָא
וְאִמְרוּ אָמֵן. (קהל: אָמֵן)

BLESSINGS OF THE SHEMA

The following blessing and response are said only in the presence of a minyan. They represent a formal summons to the congregation to engage in an act of collective prayer. The custom of bowing at this point is based on 1 Chronicles 29:20, "David said to the whole assembly, 'Now bless the Lord your God.' All the assembly blessed the Lord God of their fathers and bowed their heads low to the Lord and the King."

The Leader says the following, bowing at "Bless," standing straight at "the Lord." The congregation, followed by the Leader, responds, bowing at "Bless," standing straight at "the Lord."

Leader: **BLESS**
the Lord, the blessed One.

Congregation: Bless the Lord, the blessed One,
for ever and all time.

Leader: Bless the Lord, the blessed One,
for ever and all time.

The custom is to sit from this point until the Amida, since the predominant emotion of this section of the prayers is love rather than awe. Conversation is forbidden until after the Amida. See table on pages 1329–1331.

בָּרוּךְ Blessed are You, Lord our God,
King of the Universe,
who forms light and creates darkness, *Is. 45*
makes peace and creates all.

---

of the entire Jewish people. Since then, though Jews have been scattered and dispersed, wherever ten gather in prayer it is as if the whole Jewish people were present. The community is a microcosm of the nation.

BLESSINGS OF THE SHEMA

יוֹצֵר אוֹר *Who forms light:* A statement of faith that all things – good and apparently bad – come from the One God. The prayer is based on a verse in Isaiah (45:7). The original has the phrase "makes peace and creates evil"; this last

קריאת שמע וברכותיה

The following blessing and response are said only in the presence of a מנין.
They represent a formal summons to the קהל *to engage in an act of collective prayer.*
The custom of bowing at this point is based on דברי הימים א׳ כט, כ, *"David said to the whole assembly, 'Now bless the Lord your God.' All the assembly blessed the Lord God of their fathers and bowed their heads low to the Lord and the King."*

The שליח ציבור *says the following, bowing at* בָּרְכוּ, *standing straight at* ה׳.
The קהל, *followed by the* שליח ציבור, *responds, bowing at* בָּרוּךְ, *standing straight at* ה׳.

שׂ״ץ: **בָּרְכוּ**
אֶת יהוה הַמְבֹרָךְ.

קהל: בָּרוּךְ יהוה הַמְבֹרָךְ לְעוֹלָם וָעֶד.

שׂ״ץ: בָּרוּךְ יהוה הַמְבֹרָךְ לְעוֹלָם וָעֶד.

The custom is to sit from this point until the עמידה, *since the predominant emotion of this section of the prayers is love rather than awe.*
Conversation is forbidden until after the עמידה. *See table on pages 1329–1331.*

בָּרוּךְ אַתָּה יהוה אֱלֹהֵינוּ מֶלֶךְ הָעוֹלָם
יוֹצֵר אוֹר וּבוֹרֵא חֹשֶׁךְ ישעיה מה
עֹשֶׂה שָׁלוֹם וּבוֹרֵא אֶת הַכֹּל.

SUMMONS TO PRAYER

בָּרְכוּ *Bless the Lord:* An ancient formula (see Nehemiah 9:5) for summoning the congregation to prayer. From this point onward, communal prayer begins. Prayers of special sanctity require a *minyan*, a quorum of ten adult males. The ten spies who brought back a negative report about the land were called a "congregation." In response to Abraham's prayer about Sodom (Genesis, chapter 18), God assured him that if it contained ten righteous individuals, their merits would save the city. Ten is thus the minimum number to constitute a community. When the Temple stood, sacrifices were offered daily on behalf

If Yom Tov falls on a weekday continue with "In compassion" below the line.

All will thank You.
All will praise You.
All will declare:
Nothing is as holy as the LORD.
All will exalt You, Selah, You who form all –
the God who daily opens the doors of the gates of the East
and cleaves the windows of the sky,
who brings out the sun from its place
and the moon from its abode,
giving light to the whole world and its inhabitants
whom He created by the attribute of compassion.

If Yom Tov falls on a weekday continue here:

הַמֵּאִיר In compassion He gives light to the earth and its inhabitants, and in His goodness continually renews the work of creation, day after day. How numerous are Your works, LORD; You made them all in wisdom; *Ps. 104* the earth is full of Your creations. He is the King exalted alone since the beginning of time – praised, glorified and elevated since the world began. Eternal God, in Your great compassion, have compassion on us, LORD of our strength, Rock of our refuge, Shield of our salvation, You are our stronghold. The blessed God, great in knowledge, prepared and made the rays of the sun. He who is good formed glory for His name, surrounding His power with radiant stars. The leaders of His hosts, the holy ones, exalt the Almighty, constantly proclaiming God's glory and holiness. ▸ Be blessed, LORD our God, for the magnificence of Your handiwork and for the radiant lights You have made. May they glorify You, Selah!

Continue with "May You be blessed, our Rock" on page 462.

הַכֹּל יוֹדְוּךָ *All will thank You:* A short poem built around the last word of the previous line, "All," which is repeated here five times, four times at the beginning of a phrase, and once at the end. In monotheism, to worship anything less than the All is idolatry – be it worship of the self, the race, the nation, the ruler or the political system.

The paragraphs that follow are an expansion of the usual first blessing

If יום טוב *falls on a weekday continue with* הַמֵּאִיר לָאָרֶץ *below the line.*

הַכֹּל יוֹדְוּךָ וְהַכֹּל יְשַׁבְּחְוּךָ
וְהַכֹּל יֹאמְרוּ אֵין קָדוֹשׁ כַּיהוה
הַכֹּל יְרוֹמְמְוּךָ סֶּלָה, יוֹצֵר הַכֹּל.
הָאֵל הַפּוֹתֵחַ בְּכָל יוֹם דַּלְתוֹת שַׁעֲרֵי מִזְרָח
וּבוֹקֵעַ חַלּוֹנֵי רָקִיעַ
מוֹצִיא חַמָּה מִמְּקוֹמָהּ וּלְבָנָה מִמְּכוֹן שִׁבְתָּהּ
וּמֵאִיר לָעוֹלָם כֻּלּוֹ וּלְיוֹשְׁבָיו
שֶׁבָּרָא בְּמִדַּת הָרַחֲמִים.

If יום טוב *falls on a weekday continue here:*

הַמֵּאִיר לָאָרֶץ וְלַדָּרִים עָלֶיהָ בְּרַחֲמִים, וּבְטוּבוֹ מְחַדֵּשׁ בְּכָל יוֹם תָּמִיד מַעֲשֵׂה בְרֵאשִׁית. מָה רַבּוּ מַעֲשֶׂיךָ יהוה, כֻּלָּם בְּחָכְמָה עָשִׂיתָ, מָלְאָה הָאָרֶץ קִנְיָנֶךָ: תהלים קד הַמֶּלֶךְ הַמְרוֹמָם לְבַדּוֹ מֵאָז, הַמְשֻׁבָּח וְהַמְפֹאָר וְהַמִּתְנַשֵּׂא מִימוֹת עוֹלָם. אֱלֹהֵי עוֹלָם, בְּרַחֲמֶיךָ הָרַבִּים רַחֵם עָלֵינוּ, אֲדוֹן עֻזֵּנוּ, צוּר מִשְׂגַּבֵּנוּ, מָגֵן יִשְׁעֵנוּ, מִשְׂגָּב בַּעֲדֵנוּ. אֵל בָּרוּךְ גְּדוֹל דֵּעָה, הֵכִין וּפָעַל זָהֳרֵי חַמָּה, טוֹב יָצַר כָּבוֹד לִשְׁמוֹ, מְאוֹרוֹת נָתַן סְבִיבוֹת עֻזּוֹ, פִּנּוֹת צְבָאָיו קְדוֹשִׁים, רוֹמְמֵי שַׁדַּי, תָּמִיד מְסַפְּרִים כְּבוֹד אֵל וּקְדֻשָּׁתוֹ.
· תִּתְבָּרַךְ יהוה אֱלֹהֵינוּ עַל שֶׁבַח מַעֲשֵׂה יָדֶיךָ, וְעַל מְאוֹרֵי אוֹר שֶׁעָשִׂיתָ יְפָאֲרוּךָ סֶּלָה.

Continue with תִּתְבָּרַךְ, צוּרֵנוּ *on page 463.*

---

word has been changed to "all" to avoid speaking of evil in the context of prayer. The verse is directed against *dualism*: the perennial temptation to see in the suffering of the world, a force (evil, darkness, the devil) independent of, and opposed to, God. Dualism sees strife and war, contest and conquest, as part of the structure of reality itself. So profoundly did Judaism reject this idea, that it placed this counter-affirmation at the beginning of our collective prayers.

In compassion He gives light to the earth and its inhabitants,
and in His goodness daily, continually,
renews the work of creation.
He is the King who alone was exalted since time began,
praised, glorified and raised high from days of old.
Eternal God, in Your great compassion, have compassion on us,
LORD of our strength, Rock of our refuge,
Shield of our salvation, Stronghold of our safety.

אֵין כְּעֶרְכֶּךָ None can be compared to You,
there is none besides You;
None without You.
Who is like You?

▸ None can be compared to You,
LORD our God – in this world.
There is none besides You, our King –
in the life of the World to Come.
There is none but You, our Redeemer –
in the days of the Messiah.
There is none like You, our Savior –
at the resurrection of the dead.

אֵין כְּעֶרְכֶּךָ *None can be compared to You:* a fourfold statement of the uniqueness of God, each phrase of which is then expanded in the following lines. The fourfold structure of many early rabbinic prayers reflects the influence of Jewish mysticism, which saw reality in terms of four dimensions of increasing spirituality: the world of action, *Asiya*; the world of formation, *Yetzira*; the world of creation, *Beria*; and the world of Emanation, *Atzilut*.

This world… the World to Come: the prayer itemizes four time-zones: (1) this world that we inhabit now; (2) the World to Come, according to Maimonides, the realm of the soul after death; (3) the days of the Messiah, when the Temple will be rebuilt, the rule of David will be restored and peace and justice will prevail in the affairs of mankind; and (4) the resurrection of the dead, the final denouement of history, when those who have died will live again.

הַמֵּאִיר לָאָרֶץ וְלַדָּרִים עָלֶיהָ בְּרַחֲמִים
וּבְטוּבוֹ מְחַדֵּשׁ בְּכָל יוֹם תָּמִיד מַעֲשֵׂה בְרֵאשִׁית.
הַמֶּלֶךְ הַמְרוֹמָם לְבַדּוֹ מֵאָז
הַמְשֻׁבָּח וְהַמְפֹאָר וְהַמִּתְנַשֵּׂא מִימוֹת עוֹלָם.
אֱלֹהֵי עוֹלָם, בְּרַחֲמֶיךָ הָרַבִּים רַחֵם עָלֵינוּ
אֲדוֹן עֻזֵּנוּ, צוּר מִשְׂגַּבֵּנוּ, מָגֵן יִשְׁעֵנוּ, מִשְׂגָּב בַּעֲדֵנוּ.

אֵין כְּעֶרְכֶּךָ
וְאֵין זוּלָתֶךָ
אֶפֶס בִּלְתֶּךָ
וּמִי דּוֹמֶה לָּךְ.

◂ אֵין כְּעֶרְכְּךָ, יהוה אֱלֹהֵינוּ, בָּעוֹלָם הַזֶּה
וְאֵין זוּלָתְךָ, מַלְכֵּנוּ, לְחַיֵּי הָעוֹלָם הַבָּא
אֶפֶס בִּלְתְּךָ, גּוֹאֲלֵנוּ, לִימוֹת הַמָּשִׁיחַ
וְאֵין דּוֹמֶה לְּךָ, מוֹשִׁיעֵנוּ, לִתְחִיַּת הַמֵּתִים.

---

before the Shema. The first, but not the other blessings, is enlarged in honor of the Shabbat, because its theme is creation, and Shabbat is "a remembrance of the work of creation."

בְּכָל יוֹם תָּמִיד *Daily, continually, renews the work of creation:* Rabbi Yehuda HaLevi explained the difference between creation-from-something (*Yetzira*) and creation-from-nothing (*Beria*). When a carpenter makes a table from wood, the table continues to exist after the creative act is finished. When one makes something from nothing, however, the creative act must be continually renewed, otherwise the creation would cease to be. Divine creation is creation-from-nothing, and is thus perpetually renewed. This prayer invites us to a sense of wonder at the fact of existence: "It is not *how* the world is, but *that* it is, which is the mystical" (Wittgenstein).

א אֵל אָדוֹן God, LORD of all creation,
ב the Blessed, is blessed by every soul.
ג His greatness and goodness fill the world;
ד knowledge and wisdom surround Him.

ה Exalted above the holy Ḥayyot,
ו adorned in glory on the Chariot;
ז Merit and right are before His throne,
ח kindness and compassion before His glory.

ט Good are the radiant stars our God created;
י He formed them with knowledge,
understanding and deliberation.
כ He gave them strength and might
ל to rule throughout the world.

מ Full of splendor, radiating light,
נ beautiful is their splendor throughout the world.
ס Glad as they go forth, joyous as they return,
ע they fulfill with awe their Creator's will.

פ Glory and honor they give to His name,
צ jubilation and song at the mention of His majesty.
ק He called the sun into being and it shone with light.
ר He looked and fashioned the form of the moon.

ש All the hosts on high give Him praise;
ת the Seraphim, Ophanim and holy Ḥayyot
ascribe glory and greatness –

אֵל אָדוֹן *God, LORD of all creation:* A hymn of praise to God as Creator of the heavens, stars and celestial forces. The poem, structured as an alphabetical acrostic, is longer than its weekday counterpart (see אֵל בָּרוּךְ, "The blessed God" on pages 90–91) in honor of Shabbat. On weekdays each letter corresponds to a word; on Shabbat to a complete phrase. The poem contains traces of *Merkava* ("Chariot") mysticism, based on Ezekiel's vision of the divine chariot (Ezekiel, chapter 1).

א אֵל אָדוֹן עַל כָּל הַמַּעֲשִׂים

ב בָּרוּךְ וּמְבֹרָךְ בְּפִי כָּל נְשָׁמָה

ג גָּדְלוֹ וְטוּבוֹ מָלֵא עוֹלָם

ד דַּעַת וּתְבוּנָה סוֹבְבִים אוֹתוֹ.

ה הַמִּתְגָּאֶה עַל חַיּוֹת הַקֹּדֶשׁ

ו וְנֶהְדָּר בְּכָבוֹד עַל הַמֶּרְכָּבָה

ז זְכוּת וּמִישׁוֹר לִפְנֵי כִסְאוֹ

ח חֶסֶד וְרַחֲמִים לִפְנֵי כְבוֹדוֹ.

ט טוֹבִים מְאוֹרוֹת שֶׁבָּרָא אֱלֹהֵינוּ

י יְצָרָם בְּדַעַת בְּבִינָה וּבְהַשְׂכֵּל

כ כֹּחַ וּגְבוּרָה נָתַן בָּהֶם

ל לִהְיוֹת מוֹשְׁלִים בְּקֶרֶב תֵּבֵל.

מ מְלֵאִים זִיו וּמְפִיקִים נֹגַהּ

נ נָאֶה זִיוָם בְּכָל הָעוֹלָם

ס שְׂמֵחִים בְּצֵאתָם וְשָׂשִׂים בְּבוֹאָם

ע עוֹשִׂים בְּאֵימָה רְצוֹן קוֹנָם.

פ פְּאֵר וְכָבוֹד נוֹתְנִים לִשְׁמוֹ

צ צָהֳלָה וְרִנָּה לְזֵכֶר מַלְכוּתוֹ

ק קָרָא לַשֶּׁמֶשׁ וַיִּזְרַח אוֹר

ר רָאָה וְהִתְקִין צוּרַת הַלְּבָנָה.

ש שֶׁבַח נוֹתְנִים לוֹ כָּל צְבָא מָרוֹם

ת תִּפְאֶרֶת וּגְדֻלָּה, שְׂרָפִים וְאוֹפַנִּים וְחַיּוֹת הַקֹּדֶשׁ.

לָאֵל To God who rested from all works, and on the seventh day
ascended and sat on His throne of glory.
He robed the day of rest in glory
and called the Sabbath day a delight.
This is the praise of the seventh day,
that on it God rested from all His work.
The seventh day itself gives praise, saying,
"A psalm, a song for the Sabbath day. *Ps. 92*
It is good to give thanks to the LORD."
Therefore let all He has formed glorify and bless God.
Let them give praise, honor and grandeur to God,
the King, who formed all things
and in His holiness gave a heritage of rest
to His people Israel on the holy Sabbath day.
May Your name, O LORD our God, be sanctified,
and Your renown, O our King, be glorified
in the heavens above and on earth below.
May You be blessed, our Deliverer,
by the praises of Your handiwork,
and by the radiant lights You have made:
may they glorify You. Selah!

תִּתְבָּרַךְ May You be blessed,
our Rock, King and Redeemer, Creator of holy beings.
May Your name be praised for ever,
our King, Creator of the ministering angels,

Shabbat is a unique institution. The year is determined by the sun, the month by the phases of the moon, but there is no Shabbat in nature: nothing that corresponds to the seven-day cycle of work and rest, creation and cessation, doing and being.

The sages say that the creation of the first man and woman, their sin and their sentence to exile from the Garden of Eden all took place on the sixth day. Out of compassion, God allowed them to stay one full day in the Garden: the seventh day. Thus, the Shabbat is as close as we come to Paradise regained.

לָאֵל אֲשֶׁר שָׁבַת מִכָּל הַמַּעֲשִׂים
בַּיּוֹם הַשְּׁבִיעִי נִתְעַלָּה וְיָשַׁב עַל כִּסֵּא כְבוֹדוֹ.
תִּפְאֶרֶת עָטָה לְיוֹם הַמְּנוּחָה
עֹנֶג קָרָא לְיוֹם הַשַּׁבָּת.
זֶה שֶׁבַח שֶׁלְּיוֹם הַשְּׁבִיעִי
שֶׁבּוֹ שָׁבַת אֵל מִכָּל מְלַאכְתּוֹ
וְיוֹם הַשְּׁבִיעִי מְשַׁבֵּחַ וְאוֹמֵר
מִזְמוֹר שִׁיר לְיוֹם הַשַּׁבָּת, טוֹב לְהֹדוֹת לַיהוה: תהלים צב
לְפִיכָךְ יְפָאֲרוּ וִיבָרְכוּ לָאֵל כָּל יְצוּרָיו
שֶׁבַח יְקָר וּגְדֻלָּה יִתְּנוּ לָאֵל מֶלֶךְ יוֹצֵר כֹּל
הַמַּנְחִיל מְנוּחָה לְעַמּוֹ יִשְׂרָאֵל בִּקְדֻשָּׁתוֹ בְּיוֹם שַׁבַּת קֹדֶשׁ.
שִׁמְךָ יהוה אֱלֹהֵינוּ יִתְקַדַּשׁ, וְזִכְרְךָ מַלְכֵּנוּ יִתְפָּאַר
בַּשָּׁמַיִם מִמַּעַל וְעַל הָאָרֶץ מִתָּחַת.
תִּתְבָּרַךְ מוֹשִׁיעֵנוּ עַל שֶׁבַח מַעֲשֵׂה יָדֶיךָ
וְעַל מְאוֹרֵי אוֹר שֶׁעָשִׂיתָ, יְפָאֲרוּךָ סֶּלָה.

תִּתְבָּרַךְ
צוּרֵנוּ מַלְכֵּנוּ וְגוֹאֲלֵנוּ, בּוֹרֵא קְדוֹשִׁים
יִשְׁתַּבַּח שִׁמְךָ לָעַד
מַלְכֵּנוּ, יוֹצֵר מְשָׁרְתִים

לָאֵל *To God who rested:* A prayer on the theme of "the Sabbath of creation" at the dawn of time. Here, time itself is personified. Shabbat becomes a living presence, "robed in glory." The passage reflects a midrashic tradition that, at creation, each day sang its own song to God. The Sabbath sang Psalm 92 – the Midrash taking its opening phrase to mean not "a song for the Sabbath day" but "a song sung by the Sabbath day."

all of whom stand in the universe's heights,
proclaiming together,
in awe, aloud,
the words of the living God, the eternal King.
They are all beloved, all pure, all mighty,
and all perform in awe and reverence the will of their Maker.
▸ All open their mouths in holiness and purity,
with song and psalm,
and bless, praise, glorify,
revere, sanctify and declare the sovereignty of –
The name of the great, mighty
and awesome God and King,
holy is He.
▸ All accept on themselves,
one from another,
the yoke of the kingdom of heaven,
granting permission to one another
to sanctify the One who formed them, in serene spirit,
pure speech and sweet melody.
All, as one, proclaim His holiness,
saying in awe:

All say aloud:
Holy, holy, holy is the LORD of hosts; *Is. 6*
the whole world is filled with His glory.

---

and toward the end of prayer, except on Shabbat when the third is transferred to the afternoon.

This section of the prayers – the vision of the heavenly throne and the angels – is part of the mystical tradition in Judaism. Prayer is Jacob's ladder, stretching from earth to heaven, with "angels of the LORD" ascending and descending. The three *Kedushot* represent, respectively, the ascent, the summit, and the descent: the journey of the soul from earth to heaven and back again, transformed by our experience of the Divine.

נַחַת רוּחַ *Serene spirit:* The angels' praise has three elements, and by implication

וַאֲשֶׁר מְשָׁרְתָיו כֻּלָּם עוֹמְדִים בְּרוּם עוֹלָם
וּמַשְׁמִיעִים בְּיִרְאָה יַחַד בְּקוֹל
דִּבְרֵי אֱלֹהִים חַיִּים וּמֶלֶךְ עוֹלָם.
כֻּלָּם אֲהוּבִים, כֻּלָּם בְּרוּרִים, כֻּלָּם גִּבּוֹרִים
וְכֻלָּם עוֹשִׂים בְּאֵימָה וּבְיִרְאָה רְצוֹן קוֹנָם
◂ וְכֻלָּם פּוֹתְחִים אֶת פִּיהֶם בִּקְדֻשָּׁה וּבְטָהֳרָה
בְּשִׁירָה וּבְזִמְרָה
וּמְבָרְכִים וּמְשַׁבְּחִים וּמְפָאֲרִים
וּמַעֲרִיצִים וּמַקְדִּישִׁים וּמַמְלִיכִים ◂
אֶת שֵׁם הָאֵל הַמֶּלֶךְ הַגָּדוֹל, הַגִּבּוֹר וְהַנּוֹרָא
קָדוֹשׁ הוּא.
◂ וְכֻלָּם מְקַבְּלִים עֲלֵיהֶם עֹל מַלְכוּת שָׁמַיִם זֶה מִזֶּה
וְנוֹתְנִים רְשׁוּת זֶה לָזֶה
לְהַקְדִּישׁ לְיוֹצְרָם בְּנַחַת רוּחַ
בְּשָׂפָה בְרוּרָה וּבִנְעִימָה
קְדֻשָּׁה כֻּלָּם כְּאֶחָד
עוֹנִים וְאוֹמְרִים בְּיִרְאָה

All say aloud:

ישעיה ו קָדוֹשׁ, קָדוֹשׁ, קָדוֹשׁ יהוה צְבָאוֹת
מְלֹא כָל־הָאָרֶץ כְּבוֹדוֹ:

THE HOLINESS PRAYER

Two prophets, Isaiah and Ezekiel, saw mystical visions of God among His heavenly host, the choir of angels. These visions, together with the words the prophets heard the angels sing ("Holy, holy, holy" in Isaiah's vision, "Blessed is the LORD's glory from His place" in Ezekiel's), form the heart of *Kedusha*, the "Holiness" prayer. This is recited three times in the morning prayers – before the Shema, during the Leader's Repetition of the Amida;

▸ Then the Ophanim and the Holy Ḥayyot,
with a roar of noise,
raise themselves toward the Seraphim and,
facing them, give praise, saying:

All say aloud:

Blessed is the LORD's glory from His place. *Ezek. 3*

לָאֵל To the blessed God they offer melodies.
To the King,
living and eternal God,
they say psalms and proclaim praises.
For it is He alone
who does mighty deeds
and creates new things,
who is Master of battles
and sows righteousness,
who makes salvation grow
and creates cures,
who is is revered in praises,
the LORD of wonders,
who in His goodness,
continually renews the work of creation,
day after day,
as it is said:
"[Praise] Him who made the great lights, *Ps. 136*
for His love endures for ever."
▸ May You make a new light shine over Zion,
and may we all soon be worthy of its light.
Blessed are You, LORD,
who forms the radiant lights.

They form a heavenly retinue surrounding the divine throne, an angelic choir singing God's praises.

‹ וְהָאוֹפַנִּים וְחַיּוֹת הַקֹּדֶשׁ
בְּרַעַשׁ גָּדוֹל מִתְנַשְּׂאִים לְעֻמַּת שְׂרָפִים
לְעֻמָּתָם מְשַׁבְּחִים וְאוֹמְרִים

All say aloud:

בָּרוּךְ כְּבוֹד־יהוה מִמְּקוֹמוֹ: יחזקאל ג

לָאֵל בָּרוּךְ נְעִימוֹת יִתֵּנוּ
לַמֶּלֶךְ אֵל חַי וְקַיָּם
זְמִירוֹת יֹאמֵרוּ וְתִשְׁבָּחוֹת יַשְׁמִיעוּ
כִּי הוּא לְבַדּוֹ
פּוֹעֵל גְּבוּרוֹת, עוֹשֶׂה חֲדָשׁוֹת
בַּעַל מִלְחָמוֹת, זוֹרֵעַ צְדָקוֹת
מַצְמִיחַ יְשׁוּעוֹת, בּוֹרֵא רְפוּאוֹת
נוֹרָא תְהִלּוֹת, אֲדוֹן הַנִּפְלָאוֹת
הַמְחַדֵּשׁ בְּטוּבוֹ בְּכָל יוֹם תָּמִיד מַעֲשֵׂה בְרֵאשִׁית
כָּאָמוּר
לְעֹשֵׂה אוֹרִים גְּדֹלִים תהלים קלו
כִּי לְעוֹלָם חַסְדּוֹ:
‹ אוֹר חָדָשׁ עַל צִיּוֹן תָּאִיר וְנִזְכֶּה כֻלָּנוּ מְהֵרָה לְאוֹרוֹ.
בָּרוּךְ אַתָּה יהוה, יוֹצֵר הַמְּאוֹרוֹת.

---

so should ours: serene spirit (*naḥat ruaḥ*), pure speech (*safa berura*), and sweet melody (*ne'ima*). These are the three dimensions of prayer: spiritual *tranquillity*, cognitive *clarity*, and emotional-aesthetic *beauty*.

וְהָאוֹפַנִּים וְחַיּוֹת...שְׂרָפִים *Ophanim, Ḥayyot, Seraphim:* Three kinds of angels seen by Isaiah and Ezekiel in their visions. Seraphim are angels of fire. Ḥayyot are "living beings" surrounded by fire. Ophanim are "wheels within wheels."

אַהֲבָה You have loved us with great love, Lord our God,
and with surpassing compassion
have You had compassion on us.
Our Father, our King,
for the sake of our ancestors who trusted in You,
and to whom You taught the laws of life,
be gracious also to us and teach us.
Our Father, compassionate Father, ever compassionate,
have compassion on us.
Instill in our hearts the desire to understand and discern,
to listen, learn and teach, to observe, perform and fulfill
all the teachings of Your Torah in love.
Enlighten our eyes in Your Torah
and let our hearts cling to Your commandments.
Unite our hearts to love and revere Your name,
so that we may never be ashamed.
And because we have trusted in Your holy, great and revered name,
may we be glad and rejoice in Your salvation.

At this point, gather the four tzitziot of the tallit, holding them in the left hand.

Bring us back in peace from the four quarters of the earth
and lead us upright to our land.
▸ For You are a God who performs acts of salvation,
and You chose us from all peoples and tongues,
bringing us close to Your great name for ever in truth,
that we may thank You
and proclaim Your oneness in love.
Blessed are You, Lord, who chooses His people Israel in love.

The phrase *Our Father, compassionate Father, ever compassionate, have compassion on us,* with its twofold repetition of "Father" and threefold mention of compassion in the space of six Hebrew words, is one of the most concentrated expressions of the love and trust we feel in and for God – the God who said, "My child, My firstborn, Israel" (Ex. 4:22). The channel through which this love flows is the Torah, God's covenant with His people. This contains "the laws of life" in a double sense: laws that *guide* us in life, and laws that *give* us life.

אַהֲבָה רַבָּה אֲהַבְתָּנוּ, יהוה אֱלֹהֵינוּ
חֶמְלָה גְדוֹלָה וִיתֵרָה חָמַלְתָּ עָלֵינוּ.
אָבִינוּ מַלְכֵּנוּ
בַּעֲבוּר אֲבוֹתֵינוּ שֶׁבָּטְחוּ בְךָ
וַתְּלַמְּדֵם חֻקֵּי חַיִּים
כֵּן תְּחָנֵּנוּ וּתְלַמְּדֵנוּ.
אָבִינוּ, הָאָב הָרַחֲמָן, הַמְרַחֵם
רַחֵם עָלֵינוּ
וְתֵן בְּלִבֵּנוּ לְהָבִין וּלְהַשְׂכִּיל
לִשְׁמֹעַ, לִלְמֹד וּלְלַמֵּד, לִשְׁמֹר וְלַעֲשׂוֹת, וּלְקַיֵּם
אֶת כָּל דִּבְרֵי תַלְמוּד תּוֹרָתֶךָ בְּאַהֲבָה.
וְהָאֵר עֵינֵינוּ בְּתוֹרָתֶךָ, וְדַבֵּק לִבֵּנוּ בְּמִצְוֹתֶיךָ
וְיַחֵד לְבָבֵנוּ לְאַהֲבָה וּלְיִרְאָה אֶת שְׁמֶךָ
וְלֹא נֵבוֹשׁ לְעוֹלָם וָעֶד.
כִּי בְשֵׁם קָדְשְׁךָ הַגָּדוֹל וְהַנּוֹרָא בָּטָחְנוּ
נָגִילָה וְנִשְׂמְחָה בִּישׁוּעָתֶךָ.

At this point, gather the four ציצית *of the* טלית*, holding them in the left hand.*

וַהֲבִיאֵנוּ לְשָׁלוֹם מֵאַרְבַּע כַּנְפוֹת הָאָרֶץ
וְתוֹלִיכֵנוּ קוֹמְמִיּוּת לְאַרְצֵנוּ.
◂ כִּי אֵל פּוֹעֵל יְשׁוּעוֹת אָתָּה, וּבָנוּ בָחַרְתָּ מִכָּל עַם וְלָשׁוֹן
וְקֵרַבְתָּנוּ לְשִׁמְךָ הַגָּדוֹל סֶלָה, בֶּאֱמֶת
לְהוֹדוֹת לְךָ וּלְיַחֶדְךָ בְּאַהֲבָה.
בָּרוּךְ אַתָּה יהוה, הַבּוֹחֵר בְּעַמּוֹ יִשְׂרָאֵל בְּאַהֲבָה.

אַהֲבָה רַבָּה *You have loved us:* One of the supreme expressions of love in the liturgy. Having spoken of God's relationship to the universe, we now speak of His relationship to us, moving from cosmic grandeur to spiritual intimacy.

The Shema must be said with intense concentration. In the first paragraph one should accept, with love, the sovereignty of God; in the second, the mitzvot as the will of God. The end of the third paragraph constitutes fulfillment of the mitzva to remember, morning and evening, the exodus from Egypt. See laws 349–353.

When not praying with a minyan, say:

God, faithful King!

The following verse should be said aloud, while covering the eyes with the right hand:

Listen, Israel: the LORD is our God, the LORD is One. *Deut. 6*

Quietly: Blessed be the name of His glorious kingdom for ever and all time.

וְאָהַבְתָּ Love the LORD your God with all your heart, with all your soul, and with all your might. These words which I command you today shall be on your heart. Teach them repeatedly to your children, speaking of them when you sit at home and when you travel on the way, when you lie down and when you rise. Bind them as a sign on your hand, and they shall be an emblem between your eyes. Write them on the doorposts of your house and gates. *Deut. 6*

---

as a people. *The LORD is One:* among the many meanings of this phrase are: (1) there is only one God; (2) God is a unity, indivisible; (3) God is the only ultimate reality; (4) God is One despite the many appearances He has had throughout history; and (5) God alone is our King. This great sentence is the supreme declaration of Jewish faith: among the first Hebrew words learned by a child, often the last words of martyrs.

בָּרוּךְ שֵׁם *Blessed be the name:* This was the congregational response to the utterance in the Temple of the Tetragrammaton, God's holiest name. It is said here as a memory of the Temple service, but silently (except on Yom Kippur) because it is not part of the biblical text.

וְשִׁנַּנְתָּם *Teach them repeatedly:* Education is the responsibility, not only of schools, but also of parents. In Judaism, parents are educators, the home a matrix of learning, and education a conversation across the generations. Alshich connects this verse with the earlier one ("Love the LORD"): How do we teach our children? By showing them what we love.

The שמע *must be said with intense concentration. In the first paragraph one should accept, with love, the sovereignty of God; in the second, the* מצוות *as the will of God. The end of the third paragraph constitutes fulfillment of the* מצוה *to remember, morning and evening, the exodus from Egypt. See laws 349–353.*

When not praying with a מנין*, say:*

אֵל מֶלֶךְ נֶאֱמָן

The following verse should be said aloud, while covering the eyes with the right hand:

דברים ו **שְׁמַע יִשְׂרָאֵל, יהוה אֱלֹהֵינוּ, יהוה ׀ אֶחָד׃**

Quietly בָּרוּךְ שֵׁם כְּבוֹד מַלְכוּתוֹ לְעוֹלָם וָעֶד.

דברים ו וְאָהַבְתָּ אֵת יהוה אֱלֹהֶיךָ, בְּכָל־לְבָבְךָ וּבְכָל־נַפְשְׁךָ וּבְכָל־
מְאֹדֶךָ׃ וְהָיוּ הַדְּבָרִים הָאֵלֶּה, אֲשֶׁר אָנֹכִי מְצַוְּךָ הַיּוֹם, עַל־לְבָבֶךָ׃
וְשִׁנַּנְתָּם לְבָנֶיךָ וְדִבַּרְתָּ בָּם, בְּשִׁבְתְּךָ בְּבֵיתֶךָ וּבְלֶכְתְּךָ בַדֶּרֶךְ,
וּבְשָׁכְבְּךָ וּבְקוּמֶךָ׃ וּקְשַׁרְתָּם לְאוֹת עַל־יָדֶךָ וְהָיוּ לְטֹטָפֹת בֵּין
עֵינֶיךָ׃ וּכְתַבְתָּם עַל־מְזֻזוֹת בֵּיתֶךָ וּבִשְׁעָרֶיךָ׃

THE SHEMA

שְׁמַע *Listen, Israel:* The word *Shema* is untranslatable in English. It means (1) listen, (2) hear, (3) reflect on, (4) understand, (5) internalize, (6) respond in action, and hence (7) obey. In rabbinic Hebrew it developed yet other senses, such as "transmit, know about, infer, learn." I have translated it here as "Listen" rather than the traditional "Hear" because listening is active, hearing passive. The Shema is a call to an act of mind and soul, to meditate on, internalize and affirm the oneness of God.

Most civilizations have been cultures of the eye. Judaism, with its belief in the invisible God who transcends the universe, and its prohibition against visual representations of God, is supremely a civilization of the ear. The patriarchs and prophets did not see God; they heard Him. Hence, the key verb in Judaism is *Shema*, "listen." To give dramatic force to the idea that God is heard, not seen, we cover our eyes with our hand as we say these words.

יהוה אֱלֹהֵינוּ *The Lord is our God:* The sages called this declaration "acceptance of the yoke of the kingship of Heaven," meaning that we take God as our Sovereign, and our covenant with Him as the essence of our existence

וְהָיָה If you indeed heed My commandments with which I charge you today, to love the Lord your God and worship Him with all your heart and with all your soul, I will give rain in your land in its season, the early and late rain; and you shall gather in your grain, wine and oil. I will give grass in your field for your cattle, and you shall eat and be satisfied. Be careful lest your heart be tempted and you go astray and worship other gods, bowing down to them. Then the Lord's anger will flare against you and He will close the heavens so that there will be no rain. The land will not yield its crops, and you will perish swiftly from the good land that the Lord is giving you. Therefore, set these, My words, on your heart and soul. Bind them as a sign on your hand, and they shall be an emblem between your eyes. Teach them to your children, speaking of them when you sit at home and when you travel on the way, when you lie down and when you rise. Write them on the doorposts of your house and gates, so that you and your children may live long in the land that the Lord swore to your ancestors to give them, for as long as the heavens are above the earth. *Deut. 11*

Hold the tzitziot in the right hand also (some transfer to the right hand), kissing them at °.

וַיֹּאמֶר The Lord spoke to Moses, saying: Speak to the Israelites and tell them to make °tassels on the corners of their garments for all generations. They shall attach to the °tassel at each corner a thread of blue. This shall be your °tassel, and you shall see it and remember all of the Lord's commandments and keep them, not straying after your heart and after your eyes, following your own sinful desires. Thus you will be reminded to keep all My commandments, and be holy to your God. I am the Lord your *Num. 15*

---

(1) it deals with the third outward sign, tzitzit, which belongs together with the two mentioned in the previous paragraphs, tefillin and mezuza; and (2) it mentions the exodus, which we are commanded to remember "all the days of your life." *After your heart and after your eyes:* a principle of Judaism, as of cognitive psychology, is that our perceptions are filtered through our beliefs and emotions. What we feel affects what we see. The heart controls the eye.

דברים יא וְהָיָה אִם־שָׁמֹעַ תִּשְׁמְעוּ אֶל־מִצְוֹתַי אֲשֶׁר אָנֹכִי מְצַוֶּה אֶתְכֶם
הַיּוֹם, לְאַהֲבָה אֶת־יהוה אֱלֹהֵיכֶם וּלְעָבְדוֹ, בְּכָל־לְבַבְכֶם וּבְכָל־
נַפְשְׁכֶם: וְנָתַתִּי מְטַר־אַרְצְכֶם בְּעִתּוֹ, יוֹרֶה וּמַלְקוֹשׁ, וְאָסַפְתָּ
דְגָנֶךָ וְתִירֹשְׁךָ וְיִצְהָרֶךָ: וְנָתַתִּי עֵשֶׂב בְּשָׂדְךָ לִבְהֶמְתֶּךָ, וְאָכַלְתָּ
וְשָׂבָעְתָּ: הִשָּׁמְרוּ לָכֶם פֶּן־יִפְתֶּה לְבַבְכֶם, וְסַרְתֶּם וַעֲבַדְתֶּם
אֱלֹהִים אֲחֵרִים וְהִשְׁתַּחֲוִיתֶם לָהֶם: וְחָרָה אַף־יהוה בָּכֶם, וְעָצַר
אֶת־הַשָּׁמַיִם וְלֹא־יִהְיֶה מָטָר, וְהָאֲדָמָה לֹא תִתֵּן אֶת־יְבוּלָהּ,
וַאֲבַדְתֶּם מְהֵרָה מֵעַל הָאָרֶץ הַטֹּבָה אֲשֶׁר יהוה נֹתֵן לָכֶם:
וְשַׂמְתֶּם אֶת־דְּבָרַי אֵלֶּה עַל־לְבַבְכֶם וְעַל־נַפְשְׁכֶם, וּקְשַׁרְתֶּם
אֹתָם לְאוֹת עַל־יֶדְכֶם, וְהָיוּ לְטוֹטָפֹת בֵּין עֵינֵיכֶם: וְלִמַּדְתֶּם
אֹתָם אֶת־בְּנֵיכֶם לְדַבֵּר בָּם, בְּשִׁבְתְּךָ בְּבֵיתֶךָ וּבְלֶכְתְּךָ בַדֶּרֶךְ,
וּבְשָׁכְבְּךָ וּבְקוּמֶךָ: וּכְתַבְתָּם עַל־מְזוּזוֹת בֵּיתֶךָ וּבִשְׁעָרֶיךָ: לְמַעַן
יִרְבּוּ יְמֵיכֶם וִימֵי בְנֵיכֶם עַל הָאֲדָמָה אֲשֶׁר נִשְׁבַּע יהוה לַאֲבֹתֵיכֶם
לָתֵת לָהֶם, כִּימֵי הַשָּׁמַיִם עַל־הָאָרֶץ:

Hold the ציציות *in the right hand also (some transfer to the right hand), kissing them at °.*

במדבר טו וַיֹּאמֶר יהוה אֶל־מֹשֶׁה לֵּאמֹר: דַּבֵּר אֶל־בְּנֵי יִשְׂרָאֵל וְאָמַרְתָּ
אֲלֵהֶם, וְעָשׂוּ לָהֶם °צִיצִת עַל־כַּנְפֵי בִגְדֵיהֶם לְדֹרֹתָם, וְנָתְנוּ
°עַל־צִיצִת הַכָּנָף פְּתִיל תְּכֵלֶת: וְהָיָה לָכֶם °לְצִיצִת, וּרְאִיתֶם
אֹתוֹ וּזְכַרְתֶּם אֶת־כָּל־מִצְוֹת יהוה וַעֲשִׂיתֶם אֹתָם, וְלֹא תָתוּרוּ
אַחֲרֵי לְבַבְכֶם וְאַחֲרֵי עֵינֵיכֶם, אֲשֶׁר־אַתֶּם זֹנִים אַחֲרֵיהֶם: לְמַעַן

וְהָיָה אִם־שָׁמֹעַ תִּשְׁמְעוּ *If you indeed heed My commandments:* The sages called this "acceptance of the yoke of the commands." Having declared God our Sovereign, we go on to accept the laws He has given us, understanding that Israel's fate as a nation depends on its fidelity to them.

וַיֹּאמֶר יהוה *The LORD spoke:* This paragraph was included in the Shema because:

God, who brought you out of the land of Egypt to be your God. I am the Lord your God.

°True –

The Leader repeats:

▸ The Lord your God is true –

וְיַצִּיב And firm, established and enduring, right, faithful,
beloved, cherished, delightful, pleasant,
awesome, mighty, perfect, accepted,
good and beautiful
is this faith for us for ever.

True is the eternal God, our King, Rock of Jacob,
Shield of our salvation.
He exists and His name exists
through all generations.
His throne is established,
His kingship and faithfulness endure for ever.

At °, kiss the tzitziot and release them.

His words live and persist,
faithful and desirable
°for ever and all time.
▸ So they were for our ancestors, so they are for us,
and so they will be for our children
and all our generations and for all future generations
of the seed of Israel, Your servants.

---

blessings – which leads up to the Amida, the holiest of prayers, as the six days of the week lead to Shabbat, holiest of days.

The meaning of the word "true" here is similar to the word "Amen" said after a blessing. It is an act of affirmation and ratification, reminding us that the Shema is less a prayer than a declaration of faith. The passage recapitulates the main ideas of the Shema. Its primary emphasis, though, is on redemption. It contains the word "redeem" eight times, and is filled with redemption-related terms – deliverance, rescue, help, shield, Savior, as well as redemptive

תִּזְכְּרוּ וַעֲשִׂיתֶם אֶת־כָּל־מִצְוֺתָי, וִהְיִיתֶם קְדֹשִׁים לֵאלֹהֵיכֶם: אֲנִי יהוה אֱלֹהֵיכֶם, אֲשֶׁר הוֹצֵאתִי אֶתְכֶם מֵאֶרֶץ מִצְרַיִם, לִהְיוֹת לָכֶם לֵאלֹהִים, אֲנִי יהוה אֱלֹהֵיכֶם:

°אֱמֶת

The שליח ציבור *repeats:*

‹ יהוה אֱלֹהֵיכֶם אֱמֶת

וְיַצִּיב, וְנָכוֹן וְקַיָּם, וְיָשָׁר וְנֶאֱמָן
וְאָהוּב וְחָבִיב, וְנֶחְמָד וְנָעִים
וְנוֹרָא וְאַדִּיר, וּמְתֻקָּן וּמְקֻבָּל, וְטוֹב וְיָפֶה
הַדָּבָר הַזֶּה עָלֵינוּ לְעוֹלָם וָעֶד.

אֱמֶת אֱלֹהֵי עוֹלָם מַלְכֵּנוּ
צוּר יַעֲקֹב מָגֵן יִשְׁעֵנוּ
לְדוֹר וָדוֹר הוּא קַיָּם וּשְׁמוֹ קַיָּם
וְכִסְאוֹ נָכוֹן
וּמַלְכוּתוֹ וֶאֱמוּנָתוֹ לָעַד קַיֶּמֶת.

At °, kiss the ציציות *and release them.*

וּדְבָרָיו חָיִים וְקַיָּמִים
נֶאֱמָנִים וְנֶחֱמָדִים
°לָעַד וּלְעוֹלְמֵי עוֹלָמִים
‹ עַל אֲבוֹתֵינוּ וְעָלֵינוּ
עַל בָּנֵינוּ וְעַל דּוֹרוֹתֵינוּ
וְעַל כָּל דּוֹרוֹת זֶרַע יִשְׂרָאֵל עֲבָדֶיךָ.

אֱמֶת וְיַצִּיב *True and firm:* Fifteen adjectives mirroring the fifteen "Songs of Ascents" and the fifteen steps to the Temple courtyard. The prayer is structured around a six-part repetition of the word *Emet*: "true," mirroring the six-part sequence – the three paragraphs of the Shema and its three surrounding

For the early and the later generations
this faith has proved good and enduring for ever –
True and faithful, an irrevocable law.
True You are the LORD: our God and God of our ancestors,
▸ our King and King of our ancestors,
our Redeemer and Redeemer of our ancestors,
our Maker,
Rock of our salvation,
our Deliverer and Rescuer:
this has ever been Your name.
There is no God but You.

עֶזְרַת You have always been the help of our ancestors,
Shield and Savior of their children
after them in every generation.
Your dwelling is in the heights of the universe,
and Your judgments and righteousness
reach to the ends of the earth.
Happy is the one who obeys Your commandments
and takes to heart Your teaching and Your word.
True You are the Master of Your people
and a mighty King who pleads their cause.
True You are the first and You are the last.
Besides You, we have no king, redeemer or savior.
From Egypt You redeemed us, LORD our God,
and from the slave-house You delivered us.
All their firstborn You killed,
but Your firstborn You redeemed.
You split the Sea of Reeds and drowned the arrogant.
You brought Your beloved ones across.
The water covered their foes; not one of them was left. *Ps. 106*

---

activity – pleading a cause, raising the lowly, redeeming the meek, and helping the needy. Redemption refers to God's activity in history, liberating slaves, rewarding the faithful and ensuring justice.

עַל הָרִאשׁוֹנִים וְעַל הָאַחֲרוֹנִים
דָּבָר טוֹב וְקַיָּם לְעוֹלָם וָעֶד
אֱמֶת וֶאֱמוּנָה, חֹק וְלֹא יַעֲבֹר.
אֱמֶת שָׁאַתָּה הוּא יהוה אֱלֹהֵינוּ וֵאלֹהֵי אֲבוֹתֵינוּ
• מַלְכֵּנוּ מֶלֶךְ אֲבוֹתֵינוּ
גּוֹאֲלֵנוּ גּוֹאֵל אֲבוֹתֵינוּ
יוֹצְרֵנוּ צוּר יְשׁוּעָתֵנוּ
פּוֹדֵנוּ וּמַצִּילֵנוּ מֵעוֹלָם שְׁמֶךָ
אֵין אֱלֹהִים זוּלָתֶךָ.
עֶזְרַת אֲבוֹתֵינוּ אַתָּה הוּא מֵעוֹלָם
מָגֵן וּמוֹשִׁיעַ לִבְנֵיהֶם אַחֲרֵיהֶם בְּכָל דּוֹר וָדוֹר.
בְּרוּם עוֹלָם מוֹשָׁבֶךָ
וּמִשְׁפָּטֶיךָ וְצִדְקָתְךָ עַד אַפְסֵי אָרֶץ.
אַשְׁרֵי אִישׁ שֶׁיִּשְׁמַע לְמִצְוֹתֶיךָ
וְתוֹרָתְךָ וּדְבָרְךָ יָשִׂים עַל לִבּוֹ.
אֱמֶת אַתָּה הוּא אָדוֹן לְעַמֶּךָ
וּמֶלֶךְ גִּבּוֹר לָרִיב רִיבָם.
אֱמֶת אַתָּה הוּא רִאשׁוֹן וְאַתָּה הוּא אַחֲרוֹן
וּמִבַּלְעָדֶיךָ אֵין לָנוּ מֶלֶךְ גּוֹאֵל וּמוֹשִׁיעַ.
מִמִּצְרַיִם גְּאַלְתָּנוּ, יהוה אֱלֹהֵינוּ
וּמִבֵּית עֲבָדִים פְּדִיתָנוּ
כָּל בְּכוֹרֵיהֶם הָרַגְתָּ, וּבְכוֹרְךָ גָּאָלְתָּ
וְיַם סוּף בָּקַעְתָּ, וְזֵדִים טִבַּעְתָּ
וִידִידִים הֶעֱבַרְתָּ
וַיְכַסּוּ־מַיִם צָרֵיהֶם, אֶחָד מֵהֶם לֹא נוֹתָר: תהלים קו

For this, the beloved ones praised and exalted God,
the cherished ones sang psalms, songs and praises,
blessings and thanksgivings to the King,
the living and enduring God.
High and exalted, great and awesome,
He humbles the haughty and raises the lowly,
freeing captives and redeeming those in need, helping the poor
and answering His people when they cry out to Him.

Stand in preparation for the Amida. Take three steps back before beginning the Amida.

▸ Praises to God Most High, the Blessed One who is blessed.
Moses and the children of Israel
recited to You a song with great joy, and they all exclaimed:
"Who is like You, LORD, among the mighty? *Ex. 15*
Who is like You, majestic in holiness,
awesome in praises, doing wonders?"

▸ With a new song, the redeemed people praised
Your name at the seashore.
Together they all gave thanks,
proclaimed Your kingship, and declared:
"The LORD shall reign for ever and ever." *Ex. 15*

Congregants should end the following blessing together with the Leader so as to be able to move directly from the words "redeemed Israel" to the Amida, without the interruption of saying Amen.

▸ צוּר יִשְׂרָאֵל Rock of Israel! Arise to the help of Israel.
Deliver, as You promised, Judah and Israel.
Our Redeemer, the LORD of hosts is His name, *Is. 47*
the Holy One of Israel.

On Pesaḥ, in many congregations, a short piyut is said here before the Amida (page 1250).
No such piyut is said on the eighth day of Pesaḥ, unless it falls on a Shabbat.

Blessed are You, LORD, who redeemed Israel.

The God of the philosophers is a dimension of reality but not a personal presence, a shaper of history. One may meditate on such a being, but we cannot speak to Him, lay our innermost thoughts before Him, and place our fate in His hands. The God of the prophets – the God of redemption – is encountered in events, in history, in life (Judah HaLevi, *Kuzari*).

עַל זֹאת שִׁבְּחוּ אֲהוּבִים, וְרוֹמְמוּ אֵל
וְנָתְנוּ יְדִידִים זְמִירוֹת, שִׁירוֹת וְתִשְׁבָּחוֹת
בְּרָכוֹת וְהוֹדָאוֹת לְמֶלֶךְ אֵל חַי וְקַיָּם
רָם וְנִשָּׂא, גָּדוֹל וְנוֹרָא
מַשְׁפִּיל גֵּאִים וּמַגְבִּיהַּ שְׁפָלִים
מוֹצִיא אֲסִירִים, וּפוֹדֶה עֲנָוִים וְעוֹזֵר דַּלִּים
וְעוֹנֶה לְעַמּוֹ בְּעֵת שַׁוְּעָם אֵלָיו.

Stand in preparation for the עמידה*. Take three steps back before beginning the* עמידה.

▸ תְּהִלּוֹת לְאֵל עֶלְיוֹן, בָּרוּךְ הוּא וּמְבֹרָךְ
מֹשֶׁה וּבְנֵי יִשְׂרָאֵל, לְךָ עָנוּ שִׁירָה בְּשִׂמְחָה רַבָּה, וְאָמְרוּ כֻלָּם

שמות טו
מִי־כָמֹכָה בָּאֵלִם, יהוה
מִי כָּמֹכָה נֶאְדָּר בַּקֹּדֶשׁ, נוֹרָא תְהִלֹּת, עֹשֵׂה פֶלֶא:

▸ שִׁירָה חֲדָשָׁה שִׁבְּחוּ גְאוּלִים לְשִׁמְךָ עַל שְׂפַת הַיָּם
יַחַד כֻּלָּם הוֹדוּ וְהִמְלִיכוּ, וְאָמְרוּ

שמות טו
יהוה יִמְלֹךְ לְעֹלָם וָעֶד:

The קהל *should end the following blessing together with the* שליח ציבור *so as to be able to move directly from the words* גָּאַל יִשְׂרָאֵל *to the* עמידה*, without the interruption of saying* אמן.

▸ צוּר יִשְׂרָאֵל, קוּמָה בְּעֶזְרַת יִשְׂרָאֵל
וּפְדֵה כִנְאֻמֶךָ יְהוּדָה וְיִשְׂרָאֵל.

ישעיה מז
גֹּאֲלֵנוּ יהוה צְבָאוֹת שְׁמוֹ, קְדוֹשׁ יִשְׂרָאֵל:

On פסח*, in many congregations, a short piyut is said here before the* עמידה *(page 1251).*
No such piyut is said on the eighth day of פסח*, unless it falls on a* שבת.

(page 1251)

בָּרוּךְ אַתָּה יהוה, גָּאַל יִשְׂרָאֵל.

גָּאַל יִשְׂרָאֵל *Who redeemed Israel:* The sages attached great significance to the principle of "juxtaposing redemption and prayer," insisting that nothing should interrupt the transition from the words "who redeemed Israel" to the Amida itself (*Berakhot* 9b). The act of prayer *is* ultimately a request for redemption, a plea for God to intervene in our lives and the life of our people.

On Yom Tov (including one that falls on Shabbat) say the appropriate Amida on page 770.

THE AMIDA

The following prayer, until "in former years" on page 494, is said silently, standing with feet together. If there is a minyan, the Amida is repeated aloud by the Leader. Take three steps forward and at the points indicated by ▾, bend the knees at the first word, bow at the second, and stand straight before saying God's name.

O Lord, open my lips, so that my mouth may declare Your praise. *Ps. 51*

PATRIARCHS

▾בָּרוּךְ Blessed are You, Lord our God and God of our fathers,
God of Abraham, God of Isaac and God of Jacob;
the great, mighty and awesome God, God Most High,
who bestows acts of loving-kindness and creates all,
who remembers the loving-kindness of the fathers
and will bring a Redeemer to their children's children
for the sake of His name, in love.

On Shabbat Shuva: Remember us for life, O King who desires life,
and write us in the book of life – for Your sake, O God of life.

King, Helper, Savior, Shield:
▾Blessed are You, Lord, Shield of Abraham.

DIVINE MIGHT

אַתָּה גִּבּוֹר You are eternally mighty, Lord.
You give life to the dead and have great power to save.

The phrase "He makes the wind blow and the rain fall" is added from Simḥat Torah until Pesaḥ. In Israel the phrase "He causes the dew to fall" is added from Pesaḥ until Shemini Atzeret. See laws 129–131.

In fall & winter: He makes the wind blow and the rain fall.
In Israel, in spring & summer: He causes the dew to fall.

He sustains the living with loving-kindness,
and with great compassion revives the dead.
He supports the fallen, heals the sick, sets captives free,
and keeps His faith with those who sleep in the dust.
Who is like You, Master of might, and who can compare to You,
O King who brings death and gives life, and makes salvation grow?

On יום טוב *(including one that falls on* שבת*) say the appropriate* עמידה *on page 771.*

עמידה

The following prayer, until קַדְמֹנִיּוֹת *on page 495, is said silently, standing with feet together. If there is a* מנין*, the* עמידה *is repeated aloud by the* שליח ציבור*. Take three steps forward and at the points indicated by* ˚*, bend the knees at the first word, bow at the second, and stand straight before saying God's name.*

אֲדֹנָי, שְׂפָתַי תִּפְתָּח, וּפִי יַגִּיד תְּהִלָּתֶךָ: תהלים נא

אבות

˚בָּרוּךְ אַתָּה יהוה, אֱלֹהֵינוּ וֵאלֹהֵי אֲבוֹתֵינוּ
אֱלֹהֵי אַבְרָהָם, אֱלֹהֵי יִצְחָק, וֵאלֹהֵי יַעֲקֹב
הָאֵל הַגָּדוֹל הַגִּבּוֹר וְהַנּוֹרָא, אֵל עֶלְיוֹן
גּוֹמֵל חֲסָדִים טוֹבִים, וְקוֹנֵה הַכֹּל
וְזוֹכֵר חַסְדֵי אָבוֹת
וּמֵבִיא גוֹאֵל לִבְנֵי בְנֵיהֶם לְמַעַן שְׁמוֹ בְּאַהֲבָה.

בשבת שובה: זָכְרֵנוּ לְחַיִּים, מֶלֶךְ חָפֵץ בַּחַיִּים
וְכָתְבֵנוּ בְּסֵפֶר הַחַיִּים, לְמַעַנְךָ אֱלֹהִים חַיִּים.

מֶלֶךְ עוֹזֵר וּמוֹשִׁיעַ וּמָגֵן. ˚בָּרוּךְ אַתָּה יהוה, מָגֵן אַבְרָהָם.

גבורות

אַתָּה גִּבּוֹר לְעוֹלָם, אֲדֹנָי, מְחַיֵּה מֵתִים אַתָּה, רַב לְהוֹשִׁיעַ

The phrase מַשִּׁיב הָרוּחַ *is added from* שמחת תורה *until* פסח*.*
In ארץ ישראל *the phrase* מוֹרִיד הַטָּל *is added from* פסח *until* שמיני עצרת*. See laws 129–131.*

בחורף: מַשִּׁיב הָרוּחַ וּמוֹרִיד הַגֶּשֶׁם / בארץ ישראל בקיץ: מוֹרִיד הַטָּל

מְכַלְכֵּל חַיִּים בְּחֶסֶד, מְחַיֵּה מֵתִים בְּרַחֲמִים רַבִּים
סוֹמֵךְ נוֹפְלִים, וְרוֹפֵא חוֹלִים, וּמַתִּיר אֲסוּרִים
וּמְקַיֵּם אֱמוּנָתוֹ לִישֵׁנֵי עָפָר.
מִי כָמוֹךָ, בַּעַל גְּבוּרוֹת, וּמִי דּוֹמֶה לָּךְ
מֶלֶךְ, מֵמִית וּמְחַיֶּה וּמַצְמִיחַ יְשׁוּעָה.

On Shabbat Shuva: Who is like You, compassionate Father,
who remembers His creatures in compassion, for life?

Faithful are You to revive the dead.
Blessed are You, LORD, who revives the dead.

When saying the Amida silently, continue with "You are holy" on the next page.

KEDUSHA

During the Leader's Repetition, the following is said standing with feet together, rising on the toes at the words indicated by ▴.

Cong. then Leader: נְקַדֵּשׁ We will sanctify Your name on earth,
as they sanctify it in the highest heavens,
as is written by Your prophet,
"And they [the angels] call to one another saying: *Is. 6*

Cong. then Leader: ▴Holy, ▴holy, ▴holy is the LORD of hosts
the whole world is filled with His glory."
Then with a sound of mighty noise, majestic and strong,
they make their voice heard, raising themselves
toward the Seraphim, and facing them say: "Blessed…

Cong. then Leader: ▴"Blessed is the LORD's glory from His place." *Ezek. 3*
Reveal Yourself from Your place, O our King, and reign over us,
for we are waiting for You. When will You reign in Zion?
May it be soon in our days, and may You dwell there for ever
and all time. May You be exalted and sanctified in the midst of
Jerusalem, Your city, from generation to generation for evermore.
May our eyes see Your kingdom, as is said in the songs of Your
splendor, written by David your righteous anointed one:

Cong. then Leader: ▴"The LORD shall reign for ever. He is your God, Zion, *Ps. 146*
from generation to generation, Halleluya!"

Leader: From generation to generation we will declare Your greatness,
and we will proclaim Your holiness for evermore.
Your praise, our God, shall not leave our mouth forever,
for You, God, are a great and holy King. Blessed are You, LORD,
the holy God. / *On Shabbat Shuva:* the holy King./

The Leader continues with "Moses rejoiced" on the next page.

בשבת שובה: מִי כָמוֹךָ אַב הָרַחֲמִים, זוֹכֵר יְצוּרָיו לְחַיִּים בְּרַחֲמִים.

וְנֶאֱמָן אַתָּה לְהַחֲיוֹת מֵתִים. בָּרוּךְ אַתָּה יהוה, מְחַיֵּה הַמֵּתִים.

When saying the עמידה *silently, continue with* אַתָּה קָדוֹשׁ *on the next page.*

קדושה

During the חזרת הש״ץ*, the following is said standing with feet together, rising on the toes at the words indicated by* ˄.

then קהל ש״ץ: נְקַדֵּשׁ אֶת שִׁמְךָ בָּעוֹלָם, כְּשֵׁם שֶׁמַּקְדִּישִׁים אוֹתוֹ בִּשְׁמֵי מָרוֹם
כַּכָּתוּב עַל יַד נְבִיאֶךָ: וְקָרָא זֶה אֶל־זֶה וְאָמַר — ישעיה ו

then קהל ש״ץ: ˄קָדוֹשׁ, ˄קָדוֹשׁ, ˄קָדוֹשׁ, יהוה צְבָאוֹת, מְלֹא כָל־הָאָרֶץ כְּבוֹדוֹ:
אָז בְּקוֹל רַעַשׁ גָּדוֹל אַדִּיר וְחָזָק, מַשְׁמִיעִים קוֹל
מִתְנַשְּׂאִים לְעֻמַּת שְׂרָפִים, לְעֻמָּתָם בָּרוּךְ יֹאמֵרוּ

then קהל ש״ץ: ˄בָּרוּךְ כְּבוֹד־יהוה מִמְּקוֹמוֹ: — יחזקאל ג
מִמְּקוֹמְךָ מַלְכֵּנוּ תוֹפִיעַ וְתִמְלֹךְ עָלֵינוּ, כִּי מְחַכִּים אֲנַחְנוּ לָךְ
מָתַי תִּמְלֹךְ בְּצִיּוֹן, בְּקָרוֹב בְּיָמֵינוּ לְעוֹלָם וָעֶד תִּשְׁכֹּן
תִּתְגַּדַּל וְתִתְקַדַּשׁ בְּתוֹךְ יְרוּשָׁלַיִם עִירְךָ, לְדוֹר וָדוֹר וּלְנֵצַח נְצָחִים.
וְעֵינֵינוּ תִרְאֶינָה מַלְכוּתֶךָ
כַּדָּבָר הָאָמוּר בְּשִׁירֵי עֻזֶּךָ, עַל יְדֵי דָוִד מְשִׁיחַ צִדְקֶךָ

then קהל ש״ץ: ˄יִמְלֹךְ יהוה לְעוֹלָם, אֱלֹהַיִךְ צִיּוֹן לְדֹר וָדֹר, הַלְלוּיָהּ: — תהלים קמו

ש״ץ: לְדוֹר וָדוֹר נַגִּיד גָּדְלֶךָ, וּלְנֵצַח נְצָחִים קְדֻשָּׁתְךָ נַקְדִּישׁ
וְשִׁבְחֲךָ אֱלֹהֵינוּ מִפִּינוּ לֹא יָמוּשׁ לְעוֹלָם וָעֶד
כִּי אֵל מֶלֶךְ גָּדוֹל וְקָדוֹשׁ אָתָּה.
בָּרוּךְ אַתָּה יהוה, הָאֵל הַקָּדוֹשׁ./בשבת שובה: הַמֶּלֶךְ הַקָּדוֹשׁ./

The שליח ציבור *continues with* יִשְׂמַח מֹשֶׁה *on the next page.*

קדושה *Kedusha:* As on weekdays, the core of the *Kedusha* is comprised of the two lines said by the angels in the mystic visions of Isaiah ("Holy, holy, holy") and Ezekiel ("Blessed is the LORD's glory from His place"), together

/ *continued on page 485*

HOLINESS

אַתָּה קָדוֹשׁ You are holy and Your name is holy,
and holy ones praise You daily, Selah!
Blessed are You, LORD,
the holy God. / *On Shabbat Shuva:* the holy King./
(If forgotten, repeat the Amida.)

HOLINESS OF THE DAY

יִשְׂמַח Moses rejoiced at the gift of his portion
when You called him "faithful servant."
A crown of glory
You placed on his head
when he stood before You on Mount Sinai.
He brought down in his hands two tablets of stone
on which was engraved the observance of the Sabbath.
So it is written in Your Torah:

וְשָׁמְרוּ The children of Israel must keep the Sabbath, *Ex. 31*
observing the Sabbath in every generation
as an everlasting covenant.
It is a sign between Me and the children of Israel for ever,
for in six days God made the heavens and the earth,
but on the seventh day
He ceased work and refreshed Himself.

יִשְׂמַח מֹשֶׁה *Moses rejoiced:* As explained in the commentary for Friday night, the central blessings of the Shabbat evening, morning and afternoon services are different, forming a three-movement structure. This can be understood in three ways: (1) in terms of Jewish faith in creation, revelation and redemption; (2) in terms of eras: Shabbat past, present and future; and (3) as the three parts of a wedding: betrothal, marriage (marked by *simḥa,* rejoicing), and *yiḥud,* the coming together of bride and groom. The morning blessing fits all three patterns. It speaks about revelation – Moses bringing down the tablets of stone from Mount Sinai; about time present – the Israelites "observing the Sabbath throughout their generations"; and it speaks of joy – "Moses rejoiced."

קדושת השם
אַתָּה קָדוֹשׁ וְשִׁמְךָ קָדוֹשׁ
וּקְדוֹשִׁים בְּכָל יוֹם יְהַלְלוּךָ סֶּלָה.
בָּרוּךְ אַתָּה יהוה, הָאֵל הַקָּדוֹשׁ. / בשבת שובה: הַמֶּלֶךְ הַקָּדוֹשׁ./
(*If forgotten, repeat the* עמידה*.*)

קדושת היום
יִשְׂמַח מֹשֶׁה בְּמַתְּנַת חֶלְקוֹ
כִּי עֶבֶד נֶאֱמָן קָרָאתָ לּוֹ
כְּלִיל תִּפְאֶרֶת בְּרֹאשׁוֹ נָתַתָּ לּוֹ
בְּעָמְדוֹ לְפָנֶיךָ עַל הַר סִינַי
וּשְׁנֵי לוּחוֹת אֲבָנִים הוֹרִיד בְּיָדוֹ
וְכָתוּב בָּהֶם שְׁמִירַת שַׁבָּת
וְכֵן כָּתוּב בְּתוֹרָתֶךָ
וְשָׁמְרוּ בְנֵי־יִשְׂרָאֵל אֶת־הַשַּׁבָּת שמות לא
לַעֲשׂוֹת אֶת־הַשַּׁבָּת לְדֹרֹתָם בְּרִית עוֹלָם:
בֵּינִי וּבֵין בְּנֵי יִשְׂרָאֵל אוֹת הִוא לְעֹלָם
כִּי־שֵׁשֶׁת יָמִים עָשָׂה יהוה אֶת־הַשָּׁמַיִם וְאֶת־הָאָרֶץ
וּבַיּוֹם הַשְּׁבִיעִי שָׁבַת וַיִּנָּפַשׁ:

with a line from Psalms ("The Lord shall reign for ever"). The connecting passages, however, are longer than on weekdays.

The *Kedusha* is the supremely mystical moment in the prayers, and it may have had its origin in mystical circles in ancient times. So holy is it that in Israel until the era of the Geonim it was said only once a week, on Shabbat morning. In Babylon, however, it was said at every Leader's Repetition of the Amida. During its recital we stand with our feet together, rising on our toes at key words, as if we were angels, striving upward.

וְלֹא You, O Lord our God, did not give it
to the other nations of the world,
nor did You, our King, give it as a heritage to those who worship idols.
In its rest the uncircumcised do not dwell,
for You gave it in love to Israel Your people,
to the descendants of Jacob whom You chose.
May the people who sanctify the seventh day
all find satisfaction and delight in Your goodness,
for You favored the seventh day and made it holy,
calling it the most cherished of days,
a remembrance of the act of creation.

אֱלֹהֵינוּ Our God and God of our ancestors, find favor in our rest.
Make us holy through Your commandments
and grant us our share in Your Torah.
Satisfy us with Your goodness, grant us joy in Your salvation,
and purify our hearts to serve You in truth.
In love and favor, Lord our God,
grant us as our heritage Your holy Sabbath,
so that Israel who sanctify Your name may find rest on it.
Blessed are You, Lord, who sanctifies the Sabbath.

TEMPLE SERVICE

רְצֵה Find favor, Lord our God, in Your people Israel and their prayer.
Restore the service to Your most holy House,
and accept in love and favor the fire-offerings of Israel and their prayer.
May the service of Your people Israel always find favor with You.

On Rosh Hodesh and Hol HaMo'ed, say:

אֱלֹהֵינוּ Our God and God of our ancestors, may there rise, come, reach, appear, be favored, heard, regarded and remembered before You, our recollection and remembrance, as well as the remembrance of our ancestors, and of the Messiah son of David Your servant, and of Jerusalem Your holy city, and of all Your people the house of Israel – for deliverance and

---

the earth." Revelation, however, is particular – the unique covenant of love between God and His people – hence the emphasis on the special nature of the bond between Shabbat and the Jewish people.

וְלֹא נְתַתּוֹ, יהוה אֱלֹהֵינוּ, לְגוֹיֵי הָאֲרָצוֹת
וְלֹא הִנְחַלְתּוֹ, מַלְכֵּנוּ, לְעוֹבְדֵי פְסִילִים
וְגַם בִּמְנוּחָתוֹ לֹא יִשְׁכְּנוּ עֲרֵלִים
כִּי לְיִשְׂרָאֵל עַמְּךָ נְתַתּוֹ בְּאַהֲבָה, לְזֶרַע יַעֲקֹב אֲשֶׁר בָּם בָּחָרְתָּ.
עַם מְקַדְּשֵׁי שְׁבִיעִי
כֻּלָּם יִשְׂבְּעוּ וְיִתְעַנְּגוּ מִטּוּבֶךָ, וּבַשְּׁבִיעִי רָצִיתָ בּוֹ וְקִדַּשְׁתּוֹ
חֶמְדַּת יָמִים אוֹתוֹ קָרָאתָ, זֵכֶר לְמַעֲשֵׂה בְרֵאשִׁית.

אֱלֹהֵינוּ וֵאלֹהֵי אֲבוֹתֵינוּ, רְצֵה בִמְנוּחָתֵנוּ
קַדְּשֵׁנוּ בְּמִצְוֹתֶיךָ וְתֵן חֶלְקֵנוּ בְּתוֹרָתֶךָ
שַׂבְּעֵנוּ מִטּוּבֶךָ וְשַׂמְּחֵנוּ בִּישׁוּעָתֶךָ
וְטַהֵר לִבֵּנוּ לְעָבְדְּךָ בֶּאֱמֶת
וְהַנְחִילֵנוּ, יהוה אֱלֹהֵינוּ, בְּאַהֲבָה וּבְרָצוֹן שַׁבַּת קָדְשֶׁךָ
וְיָנוּחוּ בוֹ יִשְׂרָאֵל מְקַדְּשֵׁי שְׁמֶךָ.
בָּרוּךְ אַתָּה יהוה, מְקַדֵּשׁ הַשַּׁבָּת.

עבודה

רְצֵה יהוה אֱלֹהֵינוּ בְּעַמְּךָ יִשְׂרָאֵל, וּבִתְפִלָּתָם
וְהָשֵׁב אֶת הָעֲבוֹדָה לִדְבִיר בֵּיתֶךָ
וְאִשֵּׁי יִשְׂרָאֵל וּתְפִלָּתָם בְּאַהֲבָה תְקַבֵּל בְּרָצוֹן
וּתְהִי לְרָצוֹן תָּמִיד עֲבוֹדַת יִשְׂרָאֵל עַמֶּךָ.

On ראש חודש *and* חול המועד*, say:*

אֱלֹהֵינוּ וֵאלֹהֵי אֲבוֹתֵינוּ, יַעֲלֶה וְיָבוֹא וְיַגִּיעַ, וְיֵרָאֶה וְיֵרָצֶה
וְיִשָּׁמַע, וְיִפָּקֵד וְיִזָּכֵר זִכְרוֹנֵנוּ וּפִקְדוֹנֵנוּ וְזִכְרוֹן אֲבוֹתֵינוּ, וְזִכְרוֹן
מָשִׁיחַ בֶּן דָּוִד עַבְדֶּךָ, וְזִכְרוֹן יְרוּשָׁלַיִם עִיר קָדְשֶׁךָ, וְזִכְרוֹן כָּל עַמְּךָ

וְלֹא נְתַתּוֹ *You… did not give it to the other nations of the world:* Creation is universal; so is redemption, the time when "God will be Sovereign over all

well-being, grace, loving-kindness and compassion, life and peace, on this day of:

On Rosh Ḥodesh: Rosh Ḥodesh.
On Pesaḥ: the Festival of Matzot.
On Sukkot: the Festival of Sukkot.

On it remember us, LORD our God, for good; recollect us for blessing, and deliver us for life. In accord with Your promise of salvation and compassion, spare us and be gracious to us; have compassion on us and deliver us, for our eyes are turned to You because You, God, are a gracious and compassionate King.

וְתֶחֱזֶינָה And may our eyes witness Your return to Zion in compassion. Blessed are You, LORD, who restores His Presence to Zion.

THANKSGIVING

Bow at the first nine words.

מוֹדִים We give thanks to You,
for You are the LORD our God
and God of our ancestors
for ever and all time.
You are the Rock of our lives,
Shield of our salvation
from generation to generation.
We will thank You and
declare Your praise for our lives,
which are entrusted into Your hand;
for our souls,
which are placed in Your charge;
for Your miracles
which are with us every day;
and for Your wonders and favors
at all times, evening, morning and midday.
You are good –
for Your compassion never fails.
You are compassionate –
for Your loving-kindnesses never cease.
We have always placed our hope in You.

During the Leader's Repetition, the congregation says quietly:
מוֹדִים We give thanks to You,
for You are the LORD our God
and God of our ancestors,
God of all flesh,
who formed us
and formed the universe.
Blessings and thanks
are due to Your great
and holy name for giving us
life and sustaining us.
May You continue
to give us life and sustain us;
and may You gather our
exiles to Your holy courts,
to keep Your decrees,
do Your will and serve You
with a perfect heart,
for it is for us
to give You thanks.
Blessed be God to whom
thanksgiving is due.

בֵּית יִשְׂרָאֵל, לְפָנֶיךָ, לִפְלֵיטָה לְטוֹבָה, לְחֵן וּלְחֶסֶד וּלְרַחֲמִים,
לְחַיִּים וּלְשָׁלוֹם בְּיוֹם
בראש חודש: רֹאשׁ הַחֹדֶשׁ / בפסח: חַג הַמַּצּוֹת / בסוכות: חַג הַסֻּכּוֹת
הַזֶּה. זָכְרֵנוּ יהוה אֱלֹהֵינוּ בּוֹ לְטוֹבָה, וּפָקְדֵנוּ בוֹ לִבְרָכָה,
וְהוֹשִׁיעֵנוּ בוֹ לְחַיִּים. וּבִדְבַר יְשׁוּעָה וְרַחֲמִים, חוּס וְחָנֵּנוּ וְרַחֵם
עָלֵינוּ וְהוֹשִׁיעֵנוּ, כִּי אֵלֶיךָ עֵינֵינוּ, כִּי אֵל מֶלֶךְ חַנּוּן וְרַחוּם אָתָּה.

וְתֶחֱזֶינָה עֵינֵינוּ בְּשׁוּבְךָ לְצִיּוֹן בְּרַחֲמִים.
בָּרוּךְ אַתָּה יהוה, הַמַּחֲזִיר שְׁכִינָתוֹ לְצִיּוֹן.

הודאה

Bow at the first five words.

״מוֹדִים אֲנַחְנוּ לָךְ	*During the* חזרת הש״ץ, *the* קהל *says quietly:*
שָׁאַתָּה הוּא יהוה אֱלֹהֵינוּ	״מוֹדִים אֲנַחְנוּ לָךְ
וֵאלֹהֵי אֲבוֹתֵינוּ לְעוֹלָם וָעֶד.	שָׁאַתָּה הוּא יהוה אֱלֹהֵינוּ
צוּר חַיֵּינוּ, מָגֵן יִשְׁעֵנוּ	וֵאלֹהֵי אֲבוֹתֵינוּ אֱלֹהֵי כָל בָּשָׂר
אַתָּה הוּא לְדוֹר וָדוֹר.	יוֹצְרֵנוּ, יוֹצֵר בְּרֵאשִׁית.
נוֹדֶה לְּךָ וּנְסַפֵּר תְּהִלָּתֶךָ	בְּרָכוֹת וְהוֹדָאוֹת
עַל חַיֵּינוּ הַמְּסוּרִים בְּיָדֶךָ	לְשִׁמְךָ הַגָּדוֹל וְהַקָּדוֹשׁ
וְעַל נִשְׁמוֹתֵינוּ הַפְּקוּדוֹת לָךְ	עַל שֶׁהֶחֱיִיתָנוּ וְקִיַּמְתָּנוּ.
וְעַל נִסֶּיךָ שֶׁבְּכָל יוֹם עִמָּנוּ	כֵּן תְּחַיֵּנוּ וּתְקַיְּמֵנוּ
וְעַל נִפְלְאוֹתֶיךָ וְטוֹבוֹתֶיךָ	וְתֶאֱסֹף גָּלֻיּוֹתֵינוּ לְחַצְרוֹת קָדְשֶׁךָ
שֶׁבְּכָל עֵת, עֶרֶב וָבֹקֶר וְצָהֳרָיִם.	לִשְׁמֹר חֻקֶּיךָ וְלַעֲשׂוֹת רְצוֹנֶךָ
הַטּוֹב, כִּי לֹא כָלוּ רַחֲמֶיךָ	וּלְעָבְדְּךָ בְּלֵבָב שָׁלֵם
וְהַמְרַחֵם, כִּי לֹא תַמּוּ חֲסָדֶיךָ	עַל שֶׁאֲנַחְנוּ מוֹדִים לָךְ.
מֵעוֹלָם קִוִּינוּ לָךְ.	בָּרוּךְ אֵל הַהוֹדָאוֹת.

On Ḥanukka:

עַל הַנִּסִּים [We thank You also] for the miracles, the redemption, the mighty deeds, the salvations, and the victories in battle which You performed for our ancestors in those days, at this time.

בִּימֵי מַתִּתְיָהוּ In the days of Mattityahu, son of Yoḥanan, the High Priest, the Hasmonean, and his sons, the wicked Greek kingdom rose up against Your people Israel to make them forget Your Torah and to force them to transgress the statutes of Your will. It was then that You in Your great compassion stood by them in the time of their distress. You championed their cause, judged their claim, and avenged their wrong. You delivered the strong into the hands of the weak, the many into the hands of the few, the impure into the hands of the pure, the wicked into the hands of the righteous, and the arrogant into the hands of those who were engaged in the study of Your Torah. You made for Yourself great and holy renown in Your world, and for Your people Israel You performed a great salvation and redemption as of this very day. Your children then entered the holiest part of Your House, cleansed Your Temple, purified Your Sanctuary, kindled lights in Your holy courts, and designated these eight days of Ḥanukka for giving thanks and praise to Your great name.

Continue with "For all these things."

On Shushan Purim in Jerusalem:

עַל הַנִּסִּים [We thank You also] for the miracles, the redemption, the mighty deeds, the salvations, and the victories in battle which You performed for our ancestors in those days, at this time.

בִּימֵי מָרְדְּכַי In the days of Mordekhai and Esther, in Shushan the capital, the wicked Haman rose up against them and sought to destroy, slay and exterminate *Esther 3* all the Jews, young and old, children and women, on one day, the thirteenth day of the twelfth month, which is the month of Adar, and to plunder their possessions. Then You in Your great compassion thwarted his counsel, frustrated his plans, and caused his scheme to recoil on his own head, so that they hanged him and his sons on the gallows.

Continue with "For all these things."

וְעַל כֻּלָּם For all these things may Your name be blessed and exalted, our King, continually, for ever and all time.

On Shabbat Shuva: And write, for a good life, all the children of Your covenant.

Let all that lives thank You, Selah! and praise Your name in truth,
God, our Savior and Help, Selah!
▼Blessed are You, Lord, whose name is "the Good"
and to whom thanks are due.

בחנוכה:

עַל הַנִּסִּים וְעַל הַפֻּרְקָן וְעַל הַגְּבוּרוֹת וְעַל הַתְּשׁוּעוֹת וְעַל הַמִּלְחָמוֹת שֶׁעָשִׂיתָ לַאֲבוֹתֵינוּ בַּיָּמִים הָהֵם בַּזְּמַן הַזֶּה.

בִּימֵי מַתִּתְיָהוּ בֶּן יוֹחָנָן כֹּהֵן גָּדוֹל חַשְׁמוֹנַאי וּבָנָיו, כְּשֶׁעָמְדָה מַלְכוּת יָוָן הָרְשָׁעָה עַל עַמְּךָ יִשְׂרָאֵל לְהַשְׁכִּיחָם תּוֹרָתֶךָ וּלְהַעֲבִירָם מֵחֻקֵּי רְצוֹנֶךָ, וְאַתָּה בְּרַחֲמֶיךָ הָרַבִּים עָמַדְתָּ לָהֶם בְּעֵת צָרָתָם, רַבְתָּ אֶת רִיבָם, דַּנְתָּ אֶת דִּינָם, נָקַמְתָּ אֶת נִקְמָתָם, מָסַרְתָּ גִבּוֹרִים בְּיַד חַלָּשִׁים, וְרַבִּים בְּיַד מְעַטִּים, וּטְמֵאִים בְּיַד טְהוֹרִים, וּרְשָׁעִים בְּיַד צַדִּיקִים, וְזֵדִים בְּיַד עוֹסְקֵי תוֹרָתֶךָ, וּלְךָ עָשִׂיתָ שֵׁם גָּדוֹל וְקָדוֹשׁ בְּעוֹלָמֶךָ, וּלְעַמְּךָ יִשְׂרָאֵל עָשִׂיתָ תְּשׁוּעָה גְדוֹלָה וּפֻרְקָן כְּהַיּוֹם הַזֶּה. וְאַחַר כֵּן בָּאוּ בָנֶיךָ לִדְבִיר בֵּיתֶךָ, וּפִנּוּ אֶת הֵיכָלֶךָ, וְטִהֲרוּ אֶת מִקְדָּשֶׁךָ, וְהִדְלִיקוּ נֵרוֹת בְּחַצְרוֹת קָדְשֶׁךָ, וְקָבְעוּ שְׁמוֹנַת יְמֵי חֲנֻכָּה אֵלּוּ, לְהוֹדוֹת וּלְהַלֵּל לְשִׁמְךָ הַגָּדוֹל.

Continue with וְעַל כֻּלָּם.

בשושן פורים בירושלים:

עַל הַנִּסִּים וְעַל הַפֻּרְקָן וְעַל הַגְּבוּרוֹת וְעַל הַתְּשׁוּעוֹת וְעַל הַמִּלְחָמוֹת שֶׁעָשִׂיתָ לַאֲבוֹתֵינוּ בַּיָּמִים הָהֵם בַּזְּמַן הַזֶּה.

בִּימֵי מָרְדְּכַי וְאֶסְתֵּר בְּשׁוּשַׁן הַבִּירָה, כְּשֶׁעָמַד עֲלֵיהֶם הָמָן הָרָשָׁע, בִּקֵּשׁ
לְהַשְׁמִיד לַהֲרֹג וּלְאַבֵּד אֶת־כָּל־הַיְּהוּדִים מִנַּעַר וְעַד־זָקֵן טַף וְנָשִׁים בְּיוֹם אסתר ג
אֶחָד, בִּשְׁלוֹשָׁה עָשָׂר לְחֹדֶשׁ שְׁנֵים־עָשָׂר, הוּא־חֹדֶשׁ אֲדָר, וּשְׁלָלָם לָבוֹז: וְאַתָּה בְּרַחֲמֶיךָ הָרַבִּים הֵפַרְתָּ אֶת עֲצָתוֹ, וְקִלְקַלְתָּ אֶת מַחֲשַׁבְתּוֹ, וַהֲשֵׁבוֹתָ לּוֹ גְּמוּלוֹ בְּרֹאשׁוֹ, וְתָלוּ אוֹתוֹ וְאֶת בָּנָיו עַל הָעֵץ.

Continue with וְעַל כֻּלָּם.

וְעַל כֻּלָּם יִתְבָּרַךְ וְיִתְרוֹמַם שִׁמְךָ מַלְכֵּנוּ תָּמִיד לְעוֹלָם וָעֶד.

בשבת שובה: וּכְתֹב לְחַיִּים טוֹבִים כָּל בְּנֵי בְרִיתֶךָ.

וְכֹל הַחַיִּים יוֹדוּךָ סֶּלָה, וִיהַלְלוּ אֶת שִׁמְךָ בֶּאֱמֶת
הָאֵל יְשׁוּעָתֵנוּ וְעֶזְרָתֵנוּ סֶלָה.
בָּרוּךְ אַתָּה יהוה, הַטּוֹב שִׁמְךָ וּלְךָ נָאֶה לְהוֹדוֹת.

The following is said by the Leader during the Repetition of the Amida.
In Israel, if Kohanim bless the congregation, turn to page 838. See laws 370–377.

Our God and God of our fathers, bless us with the threefold blessing in the Torah, written by the hand of Moses Your servant and pronounced by Aaron and his sons the priests, Your holy people, as it is said:

May the Lord bless you and protect you. *Num. 6*
Cong: May it be Your will.
May the Lord make His face shine on you and be gracious to you.
Cong: May it be Your will.
May the Lord turn His face toward you, and grant you peace.
Cong: May it be Your will.

PEACE

שִׂים שָׁלוֹם Grant peace, goodness and blessing,
grace, loving-kindness and compassion to us
and all Israel Your people.
Bless us, our Father, all as one, with the light of Your face,
for by the light of Your face You have given us, Lord our God,
the Torah of life and love of kindness,
righteousness, blessing, compassion, life and peace.
May it be good in Your eyes to bless Your people Israel
at every time, in every hour, with Your peace.

On Shabbat Shuva: In the book of life, blessing,
peace and prosperity,
may we and all Your people
the house of Israel be remembered and written
before You for a good life, and for peace.*

Blessed are You, Lord,
who blesses His people Israel with peace.

**On Shabbat Shuva outside Israel, many end the blessing:*
Blessed are You, Lord, who makes peace.

The following verse concludes the Leader's Repetition of the Amida.
Some also say it here as part of the silent Amida. See law 368.

May the words of my mouth and the meditation of my heart *Ps. 19*
find favor before You, Lord, my Rock and Redeemer.

The following is said by the שליח ציבור *during* חורת הש״ץ.
In ארץ ישראל*, if* כהנים *say* ברכת כהנים*,* *turn to page 839. See laws 370–377.*

אֱלֹהֵינוּ וֵאלֹהֵי אֲבוֹתֵינוּ, בָּרְכֵנוּ בַבְּרָכָה הַמְשֻׁלֶּשֶׁת בַּתּוֹרָה, הַכְּתוּבָה עַל יְדֵי מֹשֶׁה עַבְדֶּךָ, הָאֲמוּרָה מִפִּי אַהֲרֹן וּבָנָיו כֹּהֲנִים עַם קְדוֹשֶׁיךָ, כָּאָמוּר

במדבר ו
יְבָרֶכְךָ יהוה וְיִשְׁמְרֶךָ: קהל: כֵּן יְהִי רָצוֹן
יָאֵר יהוה פָּנָיו אֵלֶיךָ וִיחֻנֶּךָּ: קהל: כֵּן יְהִי רָצוֹן
יִשָּׂא יהוה פָּנָיו אֵלֶיךָ וְיָשֵׂם לְךָ שָׁלוֹם: קהל: כֵּן יְהִי רָצוֹן

ברכת שלום

שִׂים שָׁלוֹם טוֹבָה וּבְרָכָה
חֵן וָחֶסֶד וְרַחֲמִים
עָלֵינוּ וְעַל כָּל יִשְׂרָאֵל עַמֶּךָ.
בָּרְכֵנוּ אָבִינוּ כֻּלָּנוּ כְּאֶחָד בְּאוֹר פָּנֶיךָ
כִּי בְאוֹר פָּנֶיךָ נָתַתָּ לָּנוּ, יהוה אֱלֹהֵינוּ
תּוֹרַת חַיִּים וְאַהֲבַת חֶסֶד
וּצְדָקָה וּבְרָכָה וְרַחֲמִים וְחַיִּים וְשָׁלוֹם.
וְטוֹב בְּעֵינֶיךָ לְבָרֵךְ אֶת עַמְּךָ יִשְׂרָאֵל
בְּכָל עֵת וּבְכָל שָׁעָה בִּשְׁלוֹמֶךָ.

בשבת שובה: בְּסֵפֶר חַיִּים, בְּרָכָה וְשָׁלוֹם, וּפַרְנָסָה טוֹבָה
נִזָּכֵר וְנִכָּתֵב לְפָנֶיךָ, אֲנַחְנוּ וְכָל עַמְּךָ בֵּית יִשְׂרָאֵל
לְחַיִּים טוֹבִים וּלְשָׁלוֹם.*

בָּרוּךְ אַתָּה יהוה, הַמְבָרֵךְ אֶת עַמּוֹ יִשְׂרָאֵל בַּשָּׁלוֹם.

**On* שבת שובה *in* חוץ לארץ*, many end the blessing:*

בָּרוּךְ אַתָּה יהוה, עוֹשֵׂה הַשָּׁלוֹם.

The following verse concludes the חורת הש״ץ.
Some also say it here as part of the silent עמידה*. See law 368.*

תהלים יט
יִהְיוּ לְרָצוֹן אִמְרֵי־פִי וְהֶגְיוֹן לִבִּי לְפָנֶיךָ, יהוה צוּרִי וְגֹאֲלִי:

אֱלֹהַי My God, *Berakhot 17a*
guard my tongue from evil
and my lips from deceitful speech.
To those who curse me, let my soul be silent;
may my soul be to all like the dust.
Open my heart to Your Torah
and let my soul pursue Your commandments.
As for all who plan evil against me,
swiftly thwart their counsel and frustrate their plans.

Act for the sake of Your name;
act for the sake of Your right hand;
act for the sake of Your holiness;
act for the sake of Your Torah.

That Your beloved ones may be delivered, *Ps. 60*
save with Your right hand and answer me.
May the words of my mouth *Ps. 19*
and the meditation of my heart
find favor before You, Lord, my Rock and Redeemer.

Bow, take three steps back, then bow, first left, then right, then center, while saying:

May He who makes peace in His high places,
make peace for us and all Israel – and say: Amen.

יְהִי רָצוֹן May it be Your will, Lord our God and God of our ancestors,
that the Temple be rebuilt speedily in our days, and grant us a share in Your Torah.
And there we will serve You with reverence,
as in the days of old and as in former years.
Then the offering of Judah and Jerusalem *Mal. 3*
will be pleasing to the Lord as in the days of old and as in former years.

On Rosh Hodesh, Hol HaMo'ed and Hanukka, the service continues with Hallel on page 732.

---

ence, we now ask Him to teach us what *not* to say in the presence of other human beings. We ask for help not to respond in kind to those who seek our harm. "The way of the righteous is to suffer humiliation but not to inflict it; to hear themselves insulted but not to reply" (*Yoma* 23a).

ברכות יז.

אֱלֹהַי
נְצֹר לְשׁוֹנִי מֵרָע, וּשְׂפָתַי מִדַּבֵּר מִרְמָה
וְלִמְקַלְלַי נַפְשִׁי תִדֹּם, וְנַפְשִׁי כֶּעָפָר לַכֹּל תִּהְיֶה.
פְּתַח לִבִּי בְּתוֹרָתֶךָ, וּבְמִצְוֹתֶיךָ תִּרְדֹּף נַפְשִׁי.
וְכָל הַחוֹשְׁבִים עָלַי רָעָה
מְהֵרָה הָפֵר עֲצָתָם וְקַלְקֵל מַחֲשַׁבְתָּם.
עֲשֵׂה לְמַעַן שְׁמֶךָ
עֲשֵׂה לְמַעַן יְמִינֶךָ
עֲשֵׂה לְמַעַן קְדֻשָּׁתֶךָ
עֲשֵׂה לְמַעַן תּוֹרָתֶךָ.

תהלים ס
לְמַעַן יֵחָלְצוּן יְדִידֶיךָ, הוֹשִׁיעָה יְמִינְךָ וַעֲנֵנִי:

תהלים יט
יִהְיוּ לְרָצוֹן אִמְרֵי־פִי וְהֶגְיוֹן לִבִּי לְפָנֶיךָ, יהוה צוּרִי וְגוֹאֲלִי:

Bow, take three steps back, then bow, first left, then right, then center, while saying:

עֹשֶׂה שָׁלוֹם/ בשבת שובה: הַשָּׁלוֹם/ בִּמְרוֹמָיו
הוּא יַעֲשֶׂה שָׁלוֹם עָלֵינוּ וְעַל כָּל יִשְׂרָאֵל, וְאִמְרוּ אָמֵן.

יְהִי רָצוֹן מִלְּפָנֶיךָ יהוה אֱלֹהֵינוּ וֵאלֹהֵי אֲבוֹתֵינוּ
שֶׁיִּבָּנֶה בֵּית הַמִּקְדָּשׁ בִּמְהֵרָה בְיָמֵינוּ, וְתֵן חֶלְקֵנוּ בְּתוֹרָתֶךָ
וְשָׁם נַעֲבָדְךָ בְּיִרְאָה כִּימֵי עוֹלָם וּכְשָׁנִים קַדְמֹנִיּוֹת.

מלאכי ג
וְעָרְבָה לַיהוה מִנְחַת יְהוּדָה וִירוּשָׁלָםִ כִּימֵי עוֹלָם וּכְשָׁנִים קַדְמֹנִיּוֹת:

On ראש חודש, חול המועד *and* חנוכה*, the service continues with* הלל *on page 733.*

אֱלֹהַי *My God:* A private meditation composed by the fourth-century scholar, Mar son of Ravina. It beautifully mirrors the opening meditation, "O Lord, open my lips." Having asked God to teach us what to say in His pres-

FULL KADDISH

Leader: יִתְגַּדַּל Magnified and sanctified
may His great name be,
in the world He created by His will.
May He establish His kingdom
in your lifetime and in your days,
and in the lifetime of all the house of Israel,
swiftly and soon –
and say: Amen.

All: May His great name
be blessed for ever and all time.

Leader: Blessed and praised,
glorified and exalted,
raised and honored,
uplifted and lauded be the name of the Holy One,
blessed be He, beyond any blessing,
song, praise and consolation
uttered in the world –
and say: Amen.

May the prayers and pleas of all Israel
be accepted by their Father in heaven –
and say: Amen.

May there be great peace from heaven,
and life for us and all Israel –
and say: Amen.

Bow, take three steps back, as if taking leave of the Divine Presence, then bow, first left, then right, then center, while saying:

May He who makes peace in His high places,
make peace for us and all Israel –
and say: Amen.

קדיש שלם

ש״ץ: יִתְגַּדַּל וְיִתְקַדַּשׁ שְׁמֵהּ רַבָּא (קהל: אָמֵן)
בְּעָלְמָא דִּי בְרָא כִרְעוּתֵהּ
וְיַמְלִיךְ מַלְכוּתֵהּ
בְּחַיֵּיכוֹן וּבְיוֹמֵיכוֹן וּבְחַיֵּי דְכָל בֵּית יִשְׂרָאֵל
בַּעֲגָלָא וּבִזְמַן קָרִיב, וְאִמְרוּ אָמֵן. (קהל: אָמֵן)

קהל וש״ץ: יְהֵא שְׁמֵהּ רַבָּא מְבָרַךְ לְעָלַם וּלְעָלְמֵי עָלְמַיָּא.

ש״ץ: יִתְבָּרַךְ וְיִשְׁתַּבַּח וְיִתְפָּאַר
וְיִתְרוֹמַם וְיִתְנַשֵּׂא וְיִתְהַדָּר וְיִתְעַלֶּה וְיִתְהַלָּל
שְׁמֵהּ דְּקֻדְשָׁא בְּרִיךְ הוּא (קהל: בְּרִיךְ הוּא)
לְעֵלָּא מִן כָּל בִּרְכָתָא
/בשבת שובה: לְעֵלָּא לְעֵלָּא מִכָּל בִּרְכָתָא/
וְשִׁירָתָא, תֻּשְׁבְּחָתָא וְנֶחֱמָתָא
דַּאֲמִירָן בְּעָלְמָא, וְאִמְרוּ אָמֵן. (קהל: אָמֵן)

תִּתְקַבַּל צְלוֹתְהוֹן וּבָעוּתְהוֹן דְּכָל יִשְׂרָאֵל
קֳדָם אֲבוּהוֹן דִּי בִשְׁמַיָּא, וְאִמְרוּ אָמֵן. (קהל: אָמֵן)

יְהֵא שְׁלָמָא רַבָּא מִן שְׁמַיָּא
וְחַיִּים, עָלֵינוּ וְעַל כָּל יִשְׂרָאֵל, וְאִמְרוּ אָמֵן. (קהל: אָמֵן)

Bow, take three steps back, as if taking leave of the Divine Presence, then bow, first left, then right, then center, while saying:

עֹשֶׂה שָׁלוֹם/ בשבת שובה: הַשָּׁלוֹם/ בִּמְרוֹמָיו
הוּא יַעֲשֶׂה שָׁלוֹם עָלֵינוּ וְעַל כָּל יִשְׂרָאֵל
וְאִמְרוּ אָמֵן. (קהל: אָמֵן)

REMOVING THE TORAH FROM THE ARK

אֵין־כָּמְוֹךָ There is none like You among the heavenly powers, *Ps. 86*
LORD, and there are no works like Yours.
Your kingdom is an eternal kingdom, *Ps. 145*
and Your dominion is for all generations.

The LORD is King, the LORD was King,
the LORD shall be King for ever and all time.
The LORD will give strength to His people; *Ps. 29*
the LORD will bless His people with peace.

Father of compassion,
favor Zion with Your goodness; rebuild the walls of Jerusalem. *Ps. 51*
For we trust in You alone, King, God,
high and exalted, Master of worlds.

The Ark is opened and the congregation stands. All say:

וַיְהִי בִּנְסֹעַ Whenever the Ark set out, Moses would say, *Num. 10*
"Arise, LORD, and may Your enemies be scattered.
May those who hate You flee before You."
For the Torah shall come forth from Zion, *Is. 2*
and the word of the LORD from Jerusalem.
Blessed is He who in His Holiness gave the Torah to His people Israel.

On Shabbat, continue with "Blessed is the name" on page 502.

---

study as well as prayer. During the Second Temple period and later eras, the reading was accompanied by verse-by-verse translation into the vernacular, mainly Aramaic. Over the course of time, the act of taking the Torah from, and returning it to, the Ark became ceremonial moments in their own right.

אֵין־כָּמְוֹךָ *There is none like You among the heavenly powers:* A collection of verses and phrases from the book of Psalms. וַיְהִי בִּנְסֹעַ הָאָרֹן *Whenever the Ark set out*: A description of the Ark during the journeys of the Israelites in the wilderness. The parallel verse, "When it came to rest," is recited when the Torah is returned to the Ark. Thus, the taking of the *Sefer Torah* from the Ark and its return recall the Ark of the covenant which accompanied the Israelites in the days of Moses.

כִּי מִצִּיּוֹן תֵּצֵא תוֹרָה *For the Torah shall come forth from Zion:* part of Isaiah's famous vision (2:2–4) of the end of days.

הוצאת ספר תורה

תהלים פו אֵין־כָּמְוֹךָ בָאֱלֹהִים, אֲדֹנָי, וְאֵין כְּמַעֲשֶׂיךָ:
תהלים קמה מַלְכוּתְךָ מַלְכוּת כָּל־עֹלָמִים, וּמֶמְשַׁלְתְּךָ בְּכָל־דּוֹר וָדֹר:
יהוה מֶלֶךְ, יהוה מָלָךְ, יהוה יִמְלֹךְ לְעֹלָם וָעֶד.
תהלים כט יהוה עֹז לְעַמּוֹ יִתֵּן, יהוה יְבָרֵךְ אֶת־עַמּוֹ בַשָּׁלוֹם:
תהלים נא אַב הָרַחֲמִים, הֵיטִיבָה בִרְצוֹנְךָ אֶת־צִיּוֹן תִּבְנֶה חוֹמוֹת יְרוּשָׁלָםִ:
כִּי בְךָ לְבַד בָּטָחְנוּ, מֶלֶךְ אֵל רָם וְנִשָּׂא, אֲדוֹן עוֹלָמִים.

The ארון קודש *is opened and the* קהל *stands. All say:*

במדבר י וַיְהִי בִּנְסֹעַ הָאָרֹן וַיֹּאמֶר מֹשֶׁה
קוּמָה יהוה וְיָפֻצוּ אֹיְבֶיךָ וְיָנֻסוּ מְשַׂנְאֶיךָ מִפָּנֶיךָ:
ישעיה ב כִּי מִצִּיּוֹן תֵּצֵא תוֹרָה וּדְבַר־יהוה מִירוּשָׁלָםִ:
בָּרוּךְ שֶׁנָּתַן תּוֹרָה לְעַמּוֹ יִשְׂרָאֵל בִּקְדֻשָּׁתוֹ.

On שבת*, continue with* בְּרִיךְ שְׁמֵהּ *on page 503.*

READING OF THE TORAH

Since the revelation at Mount Sinai, the Jewish people has been a nation defined by a book: the Torah. The Mosaic books are more than sacred literature, they are the written constitution of the house of Israel as a nation under the sovereignty of God, the basis of its collective memory, the record of its covenant with God, the template of its existence as "a kingdom of priests and a holy nation," and the detailed specification of the task it is called on to perform: to construct a society on the basis of justice and compassion and the inalienable dignity of the human person as the image of God. Just as the Torah is central to Jewish life, so the reading of the Torah is central to the synagogue service.

The Tanakh records several key moments in Jewish history when national rededication was accompanied by a public reading of the Torah, most famously in the days of King Josiah (II Kings, chapter 23) and Ezra (Nehemiah, chapter 8). According to tradition, Moses ordained that the Torah be read regularly and publicly, a long reading on Shabbat morning and shorter readings on Mondays and Thursdays. Ezra, reinstituting this practice, added the reading on Shabbat afternoon. Thus from its earliest days the synagogue was a place of

On Yom Tov (except when it falls on Shabbat) and on Hoshana Raba, say the following verses three times:

יהוה The LORD, the LORD, compassionate and gracious God, Ex. 34
slow to anger, abounding in loving-kindness and truth,
extending loving-kindness to a thousand generations, forgiving iniquity,
rebellion and sin, and absolving [the guilty who repent].

On Hoshana Raba continue:

Master of the Universe, fulfill my requests for good. Satisfy my desire, grant my request, and pardon me for all my iniquities and all iniquities of the members of my household, with the pardon of loving-kindness and compassion. Purify us from our sins, our iniquities and our transgressions; remember us with a memory of favorable deeds before You and be mindful of us in salvation and compassion. Remember us for a good life, for peace, for livelihood and sustenance, for bread to eat and clothes to wear, for wealth, honor and length of days dedicated to Your Torah and its commandments. Grant us discernment and understanding that we may understand and discern its deep secrets. Send healing for all our pain, and bless all the work of our hands. Ordain for us decrees of good, salvation and consolation, and nullify all hard and harsh decrees against us. And may the hearts of the government, its advisers and ministers / *in Israel:* And may the hearts of our ministers and their advisers, / be favorable toward us. Amen. May this be Your will.

On Yom Tov (except on Shabbat) continue, inserting appropriate phrase/s in parentheses:

Master of the Universe, fulfill my heart's requests for good. Satisfy my desire, grant my request, and enable me (*name*, son/daughter of *father's name*), (and my wife/ husband, and my sons/daughters) and all the members of my household to do Your will with a perfect heart. Deliver us from the evil impulse, grant us our share in Your Torah, and make us worthy that Your Presence may rest upon us. Confer on us a spirit of wisdom and understanding, and may there be fulfilled in us the verse: "The spirit of the LORD will rest upon him – a spirit of wisdom and understanding, a spirit of counsel and strength, a spirit of knowledge and reverence for the LORD." (Is. 11) So too may it be Your will, LORD our God and God of our ancestors, that we be worthy to do deeds that are good in Your sight, and to walk before You in the ways of the upright. Make us holy through Your holiness, so that we may be worthy of a good and long life, and of the World to Come. Guard us from evil deeds and bad times that threaten to bring turmoil to the world. May loving-kindness surround one who trusts in the LORD. Amen. (Ps. 32)

יִהְיוּ May the words of my mouth and the meditation of my Ps. 19
heart find favor before You, LORD, my Rock and Redeemer.

Say the following verse three times:

וַאֲנִי As for me, may my prayer come to You, LORD, Ps. 69
at a time of favor. O God, in Your great love,
answer me with Your faithful salvation.

---

lives and the lives of our family, that we may have a material and spiritual environment that will allow us to serve God without distraction or hindrance. The version of the prayer for Hoshana Raba (also said on Rosh HaShana and Yom Kippur) is more specifically tied to the details of our fate in the coming

On יום טוב (except when it falls on שבת) and on הושענא רבה,
say the following verses three times:

שמות לד

יְהוָה, יְהוָה, אֵל רַחוּם וְחַנּוּן, אֶרֶךְ אַפַּיִם וְרַב־חֶסֶד וֶאֱמֶת:
נֹצֵר חֶסֶד לָאֲלָפִים, נֹשֵׂא עָוֹן וָפֶשַׁע וְחַטָּאָה, וְנַקֵּה:

On הושענא רבה continue:

רִבּוֹנוֹ שֶׁל עוֹלָם, מַלֵּא מִשְׁאֲלוֹתַי לְטוֹבָה,
וְהָפֵק רְצוֹנִי וְתֵן שְׁאֵלָתִי, וּמְחַל לִי עַל כָּל
עֲוֹנוֹתַי וְעַל כָּל עֲוֹנוֹת אַנְשֵׁי בֵיתִי, מְחִילָה
בְּחֶסֶד מְחִילָה בְּרַחֲמִים, וְטַהֲרֵנוּ
מֵחֲטָאֵינוּ וּמֵעֲוֹנוֹתֵינוּ וּמִפְּשָׁעֵינוּ, וְזָכְרֵנוּ
בְּזִכָּרוֹן טוֹב לְפָנֶיךָ, וּפָקְדֵנוּ בִּפְקֻדַּת
יְשׁוּעָה וְרַחֲמִים. וְזָכְרֵנוּ לְחַיִּים טוֹבִים
וּלְשָׁלוֹם, וּפַרְנָסָה וְכַלְכָּלָה, וְלֶחֶם לֶאֱכֹל
וּבֶגֶד לִלְבֹּשׁ, וְעֹשֶׁר וְכָבוֹד, וְאֹרֶךְ יָמִים
לַהֲגוֹת בְּתוֹרָתֶךָ וּלְקַיֵּם מִצְוֹתֶיךָ, וְשֵׂכֶל
וּבִינָה לְהָבִין וּלְהַשְׂכִּיל עִמְקֵי סוֹדוֹתֶיךָ.
וְהָפֵק רְפוּאָה לְכָל מַכְאוֹבֵינוּ, וּבָרֵךְ כָּל
מַעֲשֵׂה יָדֵינוּ, וּגְזֹר עָלֵינוּ גְּזֵרוֹת טוֹבוֹת
יְשׁוּעוֹת וְנֶחָמוֹת, וּבַטֵּל מֵעָלֵינוּ כָּל גְּזֵרוֹת
קָשׁוֹת וְרָעוֹת, וְתֵן בְּלֵב הַמַּלְכוּת וְיוֹעֲצֶיהָ
וְשָׂרֶיהָ / בְּאֶרֶץ יִשְׂרָאֵל/ וְתֵן בְּלֵב שָׂרֵינוּ
וְיוֹעֲצֵינוּ/ עָלֵינוּ לְטוֹבָה. אָמֵן וְכֵן יְהִי רָצוֹן.

On יום טוב (except on שבת) continue,
inserting appropriate phrase/s in parentheses:

רִבּוֹנוֹ שֶׁל עוֹלָם, מַלֵּא מִשְׁאֲלוֹת לִבִּי
לְטוֹבָה, וְהָפֵק רְצוֹנִי וְתֵן שְׁאֵלָתִי, וְזַכֵּה
לִי (פלוני/ת) בֶּן/בַּת פלוני) (וְאִשְׁתִּי/בַּעֲלִי
וּבָנַי וּבְנוֹתַי) וְכָל בְּנֵי בֵיתִי, לַעֲשׂוֹת רְצוֹנְךָ
בְּלֵבָב שָׁלֵם, וּמַלְּטֵנוּ מִיֵּצֶר הָרָע, וְתֵן חֶלְקֵנוּ
בְּתוֹרָתֶךָ, וְזַכֵּנוּ שֶׁתִּשְׁרֶה שְׁכִינָתְךָ עָלֵינוּ,
וְהוֹפַע עָלֵינוּ רוּחַ חָכְמָה וּבִינָה. וִיְתְקַיֵּם
בָּנוּ מִקְרָא שֶׁכָּתוּב: וְנָחָה עָלָיו רוּחַ יְהוָה,

ישעיה יא

רוּחַ חָכְמָה וּבִינָה, רוּחַ עֵצָה וּגְבוּרָה, רוּחַ
דַּעַת וְיִרְאַת יְהוָה: וּבְכֵן יְהִי רָצוֹן מִלְּפָנֶיךָ
יְהוָה אֱלֹהֵינוּ וֵאלֹהֵי אֲבוֹתֵינוּ, שֶׁתְּזַכֵּנוּ
לַעֲשׂוֹת מַעֲשִׂים טוֹבִים בְּעֵינֶיךָ וְלָלֶכֶת
בְּדַרְכֵי יְשָׁרִים לְפָנֶיךָ, וְקַדְּשֵׁנוּ בִּקְדֻשָּׁתֶךָ
כְּדֵי שֶׁנִּזְכֶּה לְחַיִּים טוֹבִים וַאֲרוּכִים וּלְחַיֵּי
הָעוֹלָם הַבָּא, וְתִשְׁמְרֵנוּ מִמַּעֲשִׂים רָעִים
וּמִשָּׁעוֹת רָעוֹת הַמִּתְרַגְּשׁוֹת לָבוֹא לָעוֹלָם.

תהלים לב

וְהַבּוֹטֵחַ בַּיהוָה חֶסֶד יְסוֹבְבֶנּוּ: אָמֵן.

תהלים יט

יִהְיוּ לְרָצוֹן אִמְרֵי־פִי וְהֶגְיוֹן לִבִּי לְפָנֶיךָ, יְהוָה צוּרִי וְגֹאֲלִי:

Say the following verse three times:

תהלים סט

וַאֲנִי תְפִלָּתִי־לְךָ יְהוָה, עֵת רָצוֹן, אֱלֹהִים בְּרָב־חַסְדֶּךָ
עֲנֵנִי בֶּאֱמֶת יִשְׁעֶךָ:

רִבּוֹנוֹ שֶׁל עוֹלָם **Master of the Universe:** The festivals are heightened times of
holiness, and the opening of the Ark a moment when we most intensely
feel the transformative energy of the Divine Presence. Thus when these two
sacred moments coincide, we say a personal prayer for God's blessing in our

On Shabbat, Yom Tov and Hoshana Raba:

Blessed is the name of the Master of the Universe. Blessed is Your crown and Your place. May Your favor always be with Your people Israel. Show Your people the salvation of Your right hand in Your Temple. Grant us the gift of Your good light, and accept our prayers in mercy. May it be Your will to prolong our life in goodness. May I be counted among the righteous, so that You will have compassion on me and protect me and all that is mine and all that is Your people Israel's. You feed all; You sustain all; You rule over all; You rule over kings, for sovereignty is Yours. I am a servant of the Holy One, blessed be He, before whom and before whose glorious Torah I bow at all times. Not in man do I trust, nor on any angel do I rely, but on the God of heaven who is the God of truth, whose Torah is truth, whose prophets speak truth, and who abounds in acts of love and truth. ▸ In Him I trust, and to His holy and glorious name I offer praises. May it be Your will to open my heart to the Torah, and to fulfill the wishes of my heart and of the hearts of all Your people Israel for good, for life, and for peace. *Zohar, Vayak-hel*

The Leader takes the Torah scroll in his right arm. Leader then congregation:

Listen, Israel: the LORD is our God, the LORD is One. *Deut. 6*

Leader then congregation:

One is our God; great is our Master;
holy (*On Hoshana Raba:* and awesome) is His name.

The Leader turns to face the Ark, bows and says:

Magnify the LORD with me, and let us exalt His name together. *Ps. 34*

The Ark is closed. The Leader carries the Torah scroll to the bima and the congregation says:

לְךָ Yours, LORD, are the greatness and the power, the glory and the majesty and splendor, for everything in heaven and earth is Yours. Yours, LORD, is the kingdom; You are exalted as Head over all. *I Chr. 29*

רוֹמְמוּ Exalt the LORD our God and bow to His footstool; He is holy. Exalt the LORD our God, and bow at His holy mountain, for holy is the LORD our God. *Ps. 99*

בְּרִיךְ שְׁמֵהּ *Blessed is the name:* This passage, from the mystical text, the *Zohar* (*Vayak-hel* 206a), is prefaced in its original context with the words: "Rabbi Shimon said: When the scroll of the Torah is taken out to be read in public,

On שבת, יום טוב *and on* הושענא רבה:

זוהר ויקהל בְּרִיךְ שְׁמֵהּ דְּמָרֵא עָלְמָא, בְּרִיךְ כִּתְרָךְ וְאַתְרָךְ. יְהֵא רְעוּתָךְ עִם עַמָּךְ יִשְׂרָאֵל לְעָלַם, וּפֻרְקַן יְמִינָךְ אַחֲזֵי לְעַמָּךְ בְּבֵית מַקְדְּשָׁךְ, וּלְאַמְטוֹיֵי לַנָא מִטּוּב נְהוֹרָךְ, וּלְקַבֵּל צְלוֹתַנָא בְּרַחֲמִין. יְהֵא רַעֲוָא קֳדָמָךְ דְּתוֹרִיךְ לַן חַיִּין בְּטִיבוּ, וְלֶהֱוֵי אֲנָא פְקִידָא בְּגוֹ צַדִּיקַיָּא, לְמִרְחַם עָלַי וּלְמִנְטַר יָתִי וְיַת כָּל דִּי לִי וְדִי לְעַמָּךְ יִשְׂרָאֵל. אַנְתְּ הוּא זָן לְכֹלָּא וּמְפַרְנֵס לְכֹלָּא, אַנְתְּ הוּא שַׁלִּיט עַל כֹּלָּא, אַנְתְּ הוּא דְּשַׁלִּיט עַל מַלְכַיָּא, וּמַלְכוּתָא דִּילָךְ הִיא. אֲנָא עַבְדָּא דְקֻדְשָׁא בְּרִיךְ הוּא, דְּסָגֵדְנָא קַמֵּהּ וּמִקַּמֵּי דִּיקַר אוֹרַיְתֵהּ בְּכָל עִדָּן וְעִדָּן. לָא עַל אֱנָשׁ רָחִיצְנָא וְלָא עַל בַּר אֱלָהִין סָמִיכְנָא, אֶלָּא בֶּאֱלָהָא דִשְׁמַיָּא, דְּהוּא אֱלָהָא קְשׁוֹט, וְאוֹרַיְתֵהּ קְשׁוֹט, וּנְבִיאוֹהִי קְשׁוֹט, וּמַסְגֵּא לְמֶעְבַּד טַבְוָן וּקְשׁוֹט. ‹ בֵּהּ אֲנָא רָחִיץ, וְלִשְׁמֵהּ קַדִּישָׁא יַקִּירָא אֲנָא אֵמַר תֻּשְׁבְּחָן. יְהֵא רַעֲוָא קֳדָמָךְ דְּתִפְתַּח לִבַּאי בְּאוֹרַיְתָא, וְתַשְׁלִים מִשְׁאֲלִין דְּלִבַּאי וְלִבָּא דְכָל עַמָּךְ יִשְׂרָאֵל לְטָב וּלְחַיִּין וְלִשְׁלָם.

The שליח ציבור *takes the* ספר תורה *in his right arm.* שליח ציבור *then* קהל:

דברים ו שְׁמַע יִשְׂרָאֵל, יהוה אֱלֹהֵינוּ, יהוה אֶחָד:

קהל *then* שליח ציבור:

אֶחָד אֱלֹהֵינוּ, גָּדוֹל אֲדוֹנֵינוּ, קָדוֹשׁ (בהושענא רבה: וְנוֹרָא) שְׁמוֹ.

The שליח ציבור *turns to face the* ארון קודש*, bows and says:*

תהלים לד גַּדְּלוּ לַיהוה אִתִּי וּנְרוֹמְמָה שְׁמוֹ יַחְדָּו:

The ארון קודש *is closed. The* שליח ציבור *carries the* ספר תורה *to the* בימה *and the* קהל *says:*

דברי הימים א׳ כט לְךָ יהוה הַגְּדֻלָּה וְהַגְּבוּרָה וְהַתִּפְאֶרֶת וְהַנֵּצַח וְהַהוֹד, כִּי־כֹל בַּשָּׁמַיִם וּבָאָרֶץ, לְךָ יהוה הַמַּמְלָכָה וְהַמִּתְנַשֵּׂא לְכֹל לְרֹאשׁ:

תהלים צט רוֹמְמוּ יהוה אֱלֹהֵינוּ וְהִשְׁתַּחֲווּ לַהֲדֹם רַגְלָיו, קָדוֹשׁ הוּא: רוֹמְמוּ יהוה אֱלֹהֵינוּ וְהִשְׁתַּחֲווּ לְהַר קָדְשׁוֹ, כִּי־קָדוֹשׁ יהוה אֱלֹהֵינוּ:

---

year, inscribed on Rosh HaShana, sealed on Yom Kippur but not finalized until Hoshana Raba. Both prayers are preceded by the Thirteen Attributes of Compassion, used by Moses when praying for mercy and forgiveness, and taught to him, according to the Talmud, by God Himself.

Over all may the name of the Supreme King of kings, the Holy One blessed be He, be magnified and sanctified, praised and glorified, exalted and extolled, in the worlds that He has created – this world and the World to Come – in accordance with His will, and the will of those who fear Him, and the will of the whole house of Israel. He is the Rock of worlds, LORD of all creatures, God of all souls, who dwells in the spacious heights and inhabits the high heavens of old. His holiness is over the Ḥayyot and over the throne of glory. Therefore may Your name, LORD our God, be sanctified among us in the sight of all that lives. Let us sing before Him a new song, as it is written: "Sing to God, make music for His name, extol Him who rides the clouds – the LORD is His name – and exult before Him." And may we see Him eye to eye when He returns to His abode as it is written: "For they shall see eye to eye when the LORD returns to Zion." And it is said: "Then will the glory of the LORD be revealed, and all mankind together shall see that the mouth of the LORD has spoken." *Ps. 68* *Is. 52* *Is. 40*

Father of mercy, have compassion on the people borne by Him. May He remember the covenant with the mighty (patriarchs), and deliver us from evil times. May He reproach the evil instinct in the people carried by Him, and graciously grant that we be an eternal remnant. May He fulfill in good measure our requests for salvation and compassion.

The Torah scroll is placed on the bima and the Gabbai calls a Kohen to the Torah. See laws 383–397.

וְיַעֲזֹר May He help, shield and save all who seek refuge in Him,
and let us say: Amen. Let us all render greatness to our God
and give honor to the Torah. *Let the Kohen come forward.
Arise (*name* son of *father's name*), the Kohen.

**If no Kohen is present, a Levi or Yisrael is called up as follows:*

/As there is no Kohen, arise (*name* son of *father's name*) in place of a Kohen./

Blessed is He who, in His holiness, gave the Torah to His people Israel.

The congregation followed by the Gabbai:

You who cling to the LORD your God are all alive today. *Deut. 4*

The appropriate Torah portion is read.
The Torah portions for Yom Tov are to be found from page א1123; *see chart on page 1123.*

---

portion. Not everyone was able to do this, so the practice developed of entrusting the reading to one with expertise (commonly, though ungrammatically, known as the *ba'al koreh*), "so as not to shame those who do not know how to read" their own portions. Instead, they say the blessings before and after the portion, and recite the text silently along with the Reader.

עַל הַכֹּל יִתְגַּדַּל וְיִתְקַדַּשׁ וְיִשְׁתַּבַּח וְיִתְפָּאַר וְיִתְרוֹמַם וְיִתְנַשֵּׂא שְׁמוֹ שֶׁל מֶלֶךְ מַלְכֵי הַמְּלָכִים הַקָּדוֹשׁ בָּרוּךְ הוּא בָּעוֹלָמוֹת שֶׁבָּרָא, הָעוֹלָם הַזֶּה וְהָעוֹלָם הַבָּא, כִּרְצוֹנוֹ וְכִרְצוֹן יְרֵאָיו וְכִרְצוֹן כָּל בֵּית יִשְׂרָאֵל. צוּר הָעוֹלָמִים, אֲדוֹן כָּל הַבְּרִיּוֹת, אֱלוֹהַּ כָּל הַנְּפָשׁוֹת, הַיּוֹשֵׁב בְּמֶרְחֲבֵי מָרוֹם, הַשּׁוֹכֵן בִּשְׁמֵי שְׁמֵי קֶדֶם, קְדֻשָּׁתוֹ עַל הַחַיּוֹת, וּקְדֻשָּׁתוֹ עַל כִּסֵּא הַכָּבוֹד. וּבְכֵן יִתְקַדַּשׁ שִׁמְךָ בָּנוּ יהוה אֱלֹהֵינוּ לְעֵינֵי
תהלים סח כָּל חָי, וְנֹאמַר לְפָנָיו שִׁיר חָדָשׁ, כַּכָּתוּב: שִׁירוּ לֵאלֹהִים זַמְּרוּ שְׁמוֹ, סֹלּוּ לָרֹכֵב
ישעיה נב בָּעֲרָבוֹת, בְּיָהּ שְׁמוֹ, וְעִלְזוּ לְפָנָיו: וְנִרְאֵהוּ עַיִן בְּעַיִן בְּשׁוּבוֹ אֶל נָוֵהוּ, כַּכָּתוּב: כִּי
ישעיה מ עַיִן בְּעַיִן יִרְאוּ בְּשׁוּב יהוה צִיּוֹן: וְנֶאֱמַר: וְנִגְלָה כְּבוֹד יהוה, וְרָאוּ כָל־בָּשָׂר יַחְדָּו
כִּי פִּי יהוה דִּבֵּר:

אַב הָרַחֲמִים הוּא יְרַחֵם עַם עֲמוּסִים, וְיִזְכֹּר בְּרִית אֵיתָנִים, וְיַצִּיל נַפְשׁוֹתֵינוּ מִן הַשָּׁעוֹת הָרָעוֹת, וְיִגְעַר בְּיֵצֶר הָרָע מִן הַנְּשׂוּאִים, וְיָחֹן אוֹתָנוּ לִפְלֵיטַת עוֹלָמִים, וִימַלֵּא מִשְׁאֲלוֹתֵינוּ בְּמִדָּה טוֹבָה יְשׁוּעָה וְרַחֲמִים.

The ספר תורה *is placed on the* שולחן *and the* גבאי *calls a* כהן *to the* תורה*. See laws 383–397.*

וְיַעֲזֹר וְיָגֵן וְיוֹשִׁיעַ לְכָל הַחוֹסִים בּוֹ, וְנֹאמַר אָמֵן. הַכֹּל הָבוּ גֹדֶל לֵאלֹהֵינוּ וּתְנוּ כָבוֹד לַתּוֹרָה. *כֹּהֵן קְרַב, יַעֲמֹד (פלוני בֶּן פלוני) הַכֹּהֵן.

**If no* כהן *is present, a* לוי *or* ישראל *is called up as follows:*

/אֵין כָּאן כֹּהֵן, יַעֲמֹד (פלוני בֶּן פלוני) בִּמְקוֹם כֹּהֵן./

בָּרוּךְ שֶׁנָּתַן תּוֹרָה לְעַמּוֹ יִשְׂרָאֵל בִּקְדֻשָּׁתוֹ.

The קהל *followed by the* גבאי*:*

דברים ד וְאַתֶּם הַדְּבֵקִים בַּיהוה אֱלֹהֵיכֶם חַיִּים כֻּלְּכֶם הַיּוֹם:

The appropriate תורה *portion is read.*
The תורה *portions for* יום טוב *are to be found from page* 1123א*; see chart on page 1123.*

---

the Gates of Compassion are opened, and love is aroused on high. Therefore one should say (at this time): ….” The prayer “Blessed is the name” then follows. The custom of reciting it has its origins in the circle of mystics in Safed associated with Rabbi Isaac Luria.

ASCENT TO THE TORAH

The original custom was that each of those called to the Torah read his own

The Reader shows the oleh the section to be read. The oleh touches the scroll at that place with the tzitzit of his tallit, which he then kisses. Holding the handles of the scroll, he says:

Oleh: Bless the LORD, the blessed One.

Cong: Bless the LORD, the blessed One, for ever and all time.

Oleh: Bless the LORD, the blessed One, for ever and all time.
Blessed are You, LORD our God, King of the Universe,
who has chosen us from all peoples
and has given us His Torah.
Blessed are You, LORD, Giver of the Torah.

After the reading, the oleh says:

Oleh: Blessed are You, LORD our God, King of the Universe,
who has given us the Torah of truth,
planting everlasting life in our midst.
Blessed are You, LORD, Giver of the Torah.

One who has survived a situation of danger (see the commentary) says:

Blessed are You, LORD our God, King of the Universe, who bestows good on the unworthy, who has bestowed on me much good.

The congregation responds:

Amen. May He who bestowed much good on you
continue to bestow on you much good, Selah.

הַגּוֹמֵל *Who bestows good on the unworthy:* This blessing, known as *HaGomel* ("who bestows"), is mentioned in the Talmud (*Berakhot* 54b). It is to be said after the following four circumstances: (1) release from captivity, (2) recovery from a potentially life-threatening illness, (3) a dangerous journey, and (4) a sea-crossing (nowadays, many also say it after an air flight). It is said in the presence of a *minyan* (at least ten adult males), usually, though not necessarily, at the time of the reading of the Torah, and within three days of the event. הַגּוֹמֵל לְחַיָּבִים טוֹבוֹת *Who bestows good on the unworthy:* reminiscent of Jacob's prayer (Gen. 32:11), "I am unworthy of all the kindness and faithfulness You have shown Your servant."

The קורא *shows the* עולה *the section to be read. The* עולה *touches the scroll at that place with the* ציצית *of his* טלית*, which he then kisses. Holding the handles of the scroll, he says:*

עולה: בָּרְכוּ אֶת יהוה הַמְבֹרָךְ.

קהל: בָּרוּךְ יהוה הַמְבֹרָךְ לְעוֹלָם וָעֶד.

עולה: בָּרוּךְ יהוה הַמְבֹרָךְ לְעוֹלָם וָעֶד.
בָּרוּךְ אַתָּה יהוה אֱלֹהֵינוּ מֶלֶךְ הָעוֹלָם
אֲשֶׁר בָּחַר בָּנוּ מִכָּל הָעַמִּים וְנָתַן לָנוּ אֶת תּוֹרָתוֹ.
בָּרוּךְ אַתָּה יהוה, נוֹתֵן הַתּוֹרָה.

After the קריאת התורה*, the* עולה *says:*

עולה: בָּרוּךְ אַתָּה יהוה אֱלֹהֵינוּ מֶלֶךְ הָעוֹלָם
אֲשֶׁר נָתַן לָנוּ תּוֹרַת אֱמֶת וְחַיֵּי עוֹלָם נָטַע בְּתוֹכֵנוּ.
בָּרוּךְ אַתָּה יהוה, נוֹתֵן הַתּוֹרָה.

One who has survived a situation of danger (see the commentary) says:

בָּרוּךְ אַתָּה יהוה אֱלֹהֵינוּ מֶלֶךְ הָעוֹלָם, הַגּוֹמֵל לְחַיָּבִים טוֹבוֹת
שֶׁגְּמָלַנִי כָּל טוֹב.

The קהל *responds:*

אָמֵן. מִי שֶׁגְּמָלְךָ כָּל טוֹב הוּא יִגְמָלְךָ כָּל טוֹב, סֶלָה.

בָּרְכוּ *Bless the Lord:* An invitation to the congregation to join in blessing God, similar to the one that precedes communal prayer in the morning and evening services. אֲשֶׁר בָּחַר בָּנוּ מִכָּל הָעַמִּים *Who has chosen us from all peoples:* this ancient blessing, to be said before Torah study as well as before the public reading of the Torah, makes it clear that chosenness is not a right but a responsibility. אֲשֶׁר נָתַן לָנוּ תּוֹרַת אֱמֶת *Who has given us the Torah of truth:* an act of affirmation following the reading. The blessing, simply but beautifully, expresses the thought that in reading, studying and observing the word of the Eternal, we touch eternity.

After a Bar Mitzva boy has finished the Torah blessing, his father says aloud:

Blessed is He who has released me from the responsibility for this child.

In some congregations, during the week before a yahrzeit, "God, full of mercy" for a relative is said (*page 800*).

FOR AN OLEH

May He who blessed our fathers, Abraham, Isaac and Jacob, bless (*name*, son of *father's name*) who has been called up in honor of the All-Present, in honor of the Torah, and in honor of the Sabbath (*On Yom Tov:* and in honor of the festival). As a reward for this, may the Holy One, blessed be He, protect and deliver him from all trouble and distress, all infection and illness, and send blessing and success to all the work of his hands (*On Yom Tov:* and may he merit to go up to Jerusalem for the festivals), together with all Israel, his brethren, and let us say: Amen.

FOR A SICK MAN

May He who blessed our fathers, Abraham, Isaac and Jacob, Moses and Aaron, David and Solomon, bless and heal one who is ill, (*sick person's name*, son of *mother's name*), on whose behalf (*name of the one making the offering*) is making a contribution to charity. As a reward for this, may the Holy One, blessed be He, be filled with compassion for him, to restore his health, cure him, strengthen and revive him, sending him a swift and full recovery from heaven to all his 248 organs and 365 sinews, amongst the other sick ones in Israel, a healing of the spirit and a healing of the body – though on the Sabbath (*On Yom Tov:* on festivals) it is forbidden to cry out, may healing be quick to come – now, swiftly and soon, and let us say: Amen.

FOR A SICK WOMAN

May He who blessed our fathers, Abraham, Isaac and Jacob, Moses and Aaron, David and Solomon, bless and heal one who is ill, (*sick person's name*, daughter of *mother's name*), on whose behalf (*name of the one making the offering*) is making a contribution to charity. As a reward for this, may the Holy One, blessed be He, be filled with compassion for her, to restore her health, cure her, strengthen and revive her, sending her a swift and full recovery from heaven to all her organs and sinews, amongst the other sick ones in Israel, a healing of the spirit and a healing of the body – though on the Sabbath (*On Yom Tov:* on festivals) it is forbidden to cry out, may healing be quick to come – now, swiftly and soon, and let us say: Amen.

---

for his or her deeds. This blessing expresses the parents' gratitude for having lived to see their child reach the age of responsibility.

After a בר מצוה *has finished the* תורה *blessing, his father says aloud:*

בָּרוּךְ שֶׁפְּטָרַנִי מֵעָנְשׁוֹ שֶׁלָּזֶה.

In some congregations, during the week before a yahrzeit, אֵל מָלֵא רַחֲמִים *for a relative is said* *(page 801)**.*

מי שברך לעולה לתורה

מִי שֶׁבֵּרַךְ אֲבוֹתֵינוּ אַבְרָהָם יִצְחָק וְיַעֲקֹב, הוּא יְבָרֵךְ אֶת (פלוני בֶּן פלוני), בַּעֲבוּר שֶׁעָלָה לִכְבוֹד הַמָּקוֹם וְלִכְבוֹד הַתּוֹרָה וְלִכְבוֹד הַשַּׁבָּת (ביום טוב: וְלִכְבוֹד הָרֶגֶל). בִּשְׂכַר זֶה הַקָּדוֹשׁ בָּרוּךְ הוּא יִשְׁמְרֵהוּ וְיַצִּילֵהוּ מִכָּל צָרָה וְצוּקָה וּמִכָּל נֶגַע וּמַחֲלָה, וְיִשְׁלַח בְּרָכָה וְהַצְלָחָה בְּכָל מַעֲשֵׂה יָדָיו (ביום טוב: וְיִזְכֶּה לַעֲלוֹת לָרֶגֶל) עִם כָּל יִשְׂרָאֵל אֶחָיו, וְנֹאמַר אָמֵן.

מי שברך לחולה

מִי שֶׁבֵּרַךְ אֲבוֹתֵינוּ אַבְרָהָם יִצְחָק וְיַעֲקֹב, מֹשֶׁה וְאַהֲרֹן דָּוִד וּשְׁלֹמֹה הוּא יְבָרֵךְ וִירַפֵּא אֶת הַחוֹלֶה (פלוני בֶּן פלונית) בַּעֲבוּר שֶׁ(פלוני בֶּן פלוני) נוֹדֵר צְדָקָה בַּעֲבוּרוֹ. בִּשְׂכַר זֶה הַקָּדוֹשׁ בָּרוּךְ הוּא יִמָּלֵא רַחֲמִים עָלָיו לְהַחֲלִימוֹ וּלְרַפְּאֹתוֹ וּלְהַחֲזִיקוֹ וּלְהַחֲיוֹתוֹ וְיִשְׁלַח לוֹ מְהֵרָה רְפוּאָה שְׁלֵמָה מִן הַשָּׁמַיִם לִרְמַ״ח אֵבָרָיו וּשְׁסָ״ה גִּידָיו בְּתוֹךְ שְׁאָר חוֹלֵי יִשְׂרָאֵל, רְפוּאַת הַנֶּפֶשׁ וּרְפוּאַת הַגּוּף. שַׁבָּת הִיא מִלִּזְעֹק / ביום טוב: יוֹם טוֹב הוּא מִלִּזְעֹק/ וּרְפוּאָה קְרוֹבָה לָבוֹא, הַשְׁתָּא בַּעֲגָלָא וּבִזְמַן קָרִיב, וְנֹאמַר אָמֵן.

מי שברך לחולה

מִי שֶׁבֵּרַךְ אֲבוֹתֵינוּ אַבְרָהָם יִצְחָק וְיַעֲקֹב, מֹשֶׁה וְאַהֲרֹן דָּוִד וּשְׁלֹמֹה הוּא יְבָרֵךְ וִירַפֵּא אֶת הַחוֹלָה (פלונית בַּת פלונית) בַּעֲבוּר שֶׁ(פלוני בֶּן פלוני) נוֹדֵר צְדָקָה בַּעֲבוּרָהּ. בִּשְׂכַר זֶה הַקָּדוֹשׁ בָּרוּךְ הוּא יִמָּלֵא רַחֲמִים עָלֶיהָ לְהַחֲלִימָהּ וּלְרַפְּאֹתָהּ וּלְהַחֲזִיקָהּ וּלְהַחֲיוֹתָהּ וְיִשְׁלַח לָהּ מְהֵרָה רְפוּאָה שְׁלֵמָה מִן הַשָּׁמַיִם לְכָל אֵבָרֶיהָ וּלְכָל גִּידֶיהָ בְּתוֹךְ שְׁאָר חוֹלֵי יִשְׂרָאֵל, רְפוּאַת הַנֶּפֶשׁ וּרְפוּאַת הַגּוּף. שַׁבָּת הִיא מִלִּזְעֹק /ביום טוב: יוֹם טוֹב הוּא מִלִּזְעֹק/ וּרְפוּאָה קְרוֹבָה לָבוֹא, הַשְׁתָּא בַּעֲגָלָא וּבִזְמַן קָרִיב, וְנֹאמַר אָמֵן.

בָּרוּךְ שֶׁפְּטָרַנִי *Who has released me from the responsibility for this child:* Until a boy reaches the age of thirteen (twelve for girls), the parents are responsible

ON THE BIRTH OF A SON

May He who blessed our fathers, Abraham, Isaac and Jacob, Moses and Aaron, David and Solomon, Sarah, Rebecca, Rachel and Leah, bless the woman who has given birth (*name*, daughter of *father's name*), and her son who has been born to her as an auspicious sign. Her husband, the child's father, is making a contribution to charity. As a reward for this, may father and mother merit to bring the child into the covenant of Abraham and to a life of Torah, to the marriage canopy and to good deeds, and let us say: Amen.

ON THE BIRTH OF A DAUGHTER

May He who blessed our fathers, Abraham, Isaac and Jacob, Moses and Aaron, David and Solomon, Sarah, Rebecca, Rachel and Leah, bless the woman who has given birth (*name*, daughter of *father's name*), and her daughter who has been born to her as an auspicious sign; and may her name be called in Israel (*baby's name*, daughter of *father's name*). Her husband, the child's father, is making a contribution to charity. As a reward for this, may father and mother merit to raise her to a life of Torah, to the marriage canopy, and to good deeds, and let us say: Amen.

FOR A BAR MITZVA

May He who blessed our fathers, Abraham, Isaac and Jacob, bless (*name*, son of *father's name*) who has completed thirteen years and attained the age of the commandments, who has been called to the Torah to give praise and thanks to God, may His name be blessed, for all the good He has bestowed on him. May the Holy One, blessed be He, protect and sustain him and direct his heart to be perfect with God, to walk in His ways and keep the commandments all the days of his life, and let us say: Amen.

FOR A BAT MITZVA

May He who blessed our fathers, Abraham, Isaac and Jacob, Sarah, Rebecca, Rachel and Leah, bless (*name*, daughter of *father's name*) who has completed twelve years and attained the age of the commandments, and gives praise and thanks to God, may His name be blessed, for all the good He has bestowed on her. May the Holy One, blessed be He, protect and sustain her and direct her heart to be perfect with God, to walk in His ways and keep the commandments all the days of her life, and let us say: Amen.

מי שברך ליולדת בן

מִי שֶׁבֵּרַךְ אֲבוֹתֵינוּ אַבְרָהָם יִצְחָק וְיַעֲקֹב, מֹשֶׁה וְאַהֲרֹן דָּוִד וּשְׁלֹמֹה, שָׂרָה רִבְקָה רָחֵל וְלֵאָה הוּא יְבָרֵךְ אֶת הָאִשָּׁה הַיּוֹלֶדֶת (פלונית בַּת פלוני) וְאֶת בְּנָהּ שֶׁנּוֹלַד לָהּ לְמַזָּל טוֹב בַּעֲבוּר שֶׁבַּעְלָהּ וְאָבִיו נוֹדֵר צְדָקָה בַּעֲדָם. בִּשְׂכַר זֶה יִזְכּוּ אָבִיו וְאִמּוֹ לְהַכְנִיסוֹ בִּבְרִיתוֹ שֶׁל אַבְרָהָם אָבִינוּ וּלְגַדְּלוֹ לְתוֹרָה וּלְחֻפָּה וּלְמַעֲשִׂים טוֹבִים, וְנֹאמַר אָמֵן.

מי שברך ליולדת בת

מִי שֶׁבֵּרַךְ אֲבוֹתֵינוּ אַבְרָהָם יִצְחָק וְיַעֲקֹב, מֹשֶׁה וְאַהֲרֹן דָּוִד וּשְׁלֹמֹה, שָׂרָה רִבְקָה רָחֵל וְלֵאָה הוּא יְבָרֵךְ אֶת הָאִשָּׁה הַיּוֹלֶדֶת (פלונית בַּת פלוני) וְאֶת בִּתָּהּ שֶׁנּוֹלְדָה לָהּ לְמַזָּל טוֹב וְיִקָּרֵא שְׁמָהּ בְּיִשְׂרָאֵל (פלונית בַּת פלוני), בַּעֲבוּר שֶׁבַּעְלָהּ וְאָבִיהָ נוֹדֵר צְדָקָה בַּעֲדָן. בִּשְׂכַר זֶה יִזְכּוּ אָבִיהָ וְאִמָּהּ לְגַדְּלָהּ לְתוֹרָה וּלְחֻפָּה וּלְמַעֲשִׂים טוֹבִים, וְנֹאמַר אָמֵן.

מי שברך לבר מצווה

מִי שֶׁבֵּרַךְ אֲבוֹתֵינוּ אַבְרָהָם יִצְחָק וְיַעֲקֹב הוּא יְבָרֵךְ אֶת (פלוני בֶּן פלוני) שֶׁמָּלְאוּ לוֹ שְׁלֹשׁ עֶשְׂרֵה שָׁנָה וְהִגִּיעַ לְמִצְוֹת, וְעָלָה לַתּוֹרָה, לָתֵת שֶׁבַח וְהוֹדָיָה לְהַשֵּׁם יִתְבָּרַךְ עַל כָּל הַטּוֹבָה שֶׁגָּמַל אִתּוֹ. יִשְׁמְרֵהוּ הַקָּדוֹשׁ בָּרוּךְ הוּא וִיחַיֵּהוּ, וִיכוֹנֵן אֶת לִבּוֹ לִהְיוֹת שָׁלֵם עִם יהוה וְלָלֶכֶת בִּדְרָכָיו וְלִשְׁמֹר מִצְוֹתָיו כָּל הַיָּמִים, וְנֹאמַר אָמֵן.

מי שברך לבת מצווה

מִי שֶׁבֵּרַךְ אֲבוֹתֵינוּ אַבְרָהָם יִצְחָק וְיַעֲקֹב, שָׂרָה רִבְקָה רָחֵל וְלֵאָה, הוּא יְבָרֵךְ אֶת (פלונית בַּת פלוני) שֶׁמָּלְאוּ לָהּ שְׁתֵּים עֶשְׂרֵה שָׁנָה וְהִגִּיעָה לְמִצְוֹת, וְנוֹתֶנֶת שֶׁבַח וְהוֹדָיָה לְהַשֵּׁם יִתְבָּרַךְ עַל כָּל הַטּוֹבָה שֶׁגָּמַל אִתָּהּ. יִשְׁמְרֶהָ הַקָּדוֹשׁ בָּרוּךְ הוּא וִיחַיֶּהָ, וִיכוֹנֵן אֶת לִבָּהּ לִהְיוֹת שָׁלֵם עִם יהוה וְלָלֶכֶת בִּדְרָכָיו וְלִשְׁמֹר מִצְוֹתָיו כָּל הַיָּמִים, וְנֹאמַר אָמֵן.

HALF KADDISH

Before Maftir is read, the Reader says Half Kaddish:

Reader: יִתְגַּדַּל Magnified and sanctified
may His great name be,
in the world He created by His will.
May He establish His kingdom
in your lifetime and in your days,
and in the lifetime of all the house of Israel,
swiftly and soon –
and say: Amen.

All: May His great name be blessed for ever and all time.

Reader: Blessed and praised, glorified and exalted,
raised and honored, uplifted and lauded
be the name of the Holy One, blessed be He,
beyond any blessing,
song, praise and consolation
uttered in the world –
and say: Amen.

HAGBAHA AND GELILA

The Torah scroll is lifted and the congregation says:

וְזֹאת הַתּוֹרָה This is the Torah *Deut. 4*
that Moses placed before the children of Israel, *Num. 9*
at the Lord's commandment, by the hand of Moses.

Some add: It is a tree of life to those who grasp it, and those who uphold it are happy. *Prov. 3*
Its ways are ways of pleasantness, and all its paths are peace.
Long life is in its right hand; in its left, riches and honor.
It pleased the Lord for the sake of [Israel's] righteousness, *Is. 42*
to make the Torah great and glorious.

The Torah scroll is bound and covered.

---

commandment, by the hand of Moses" (the declaration is an amalgam of Deuteronomy 4:44 and Numbers 9:23).

חצי קדיש

Before מפטיר *is read, the* קורא *says* חצי קדיש:

קורא: יִתְגַּדַּל וְיִתְקַדַּשׁ שְׁמֵהּ רַבָּא (קהל: אָמֵן)
בְּעָלְמָא דִּי בְרָא כִרְעוּתֵהּ
וְיַמְלִיךְ מַלְכוּתֵהּ
בְּחַיֵּיכוֹן וּבְיוֹמֵיכוֹן וּבְחַיֵּי דְכָל בֵּית יִשְׂרָאֵל
בַּעֲגָלָא וּבִזְמַן קָרִיב, וְאִמְרוּ אָמֵן. (קהל: אָמֵן)

קהל וקורא: יְהֵא שְׁמֵהּ רַבָּא מְבָרַךְ לְעָלַם וּלְעָלְמֵי עָלְמַיָּא.

קורא: יִתְבָּרַךְ וְיִשְׁתַּבַּח וְיִתְפָּאַר וְיִתְרוֹמַם וְיִתְנַשֵּׂא
וְיִתְהַדָּר וְיִתְעַלֶּה וְיִתְהַלָּל
שְׁמֵהּ דְּקֻדְשָׁא בְּרִיךְ הוּא (קהל: בְּרִיךְ הוּא)
לְעֵלָּא מִן כָּל בִּרְכָתָא / בשבת שובה: לְעֵלָּא לְעֵלָּא מִכָּל בִּרְכָתָא/
וְשִׁירָתָא, תֻּשְׁבְּחָתָא וְנֶחֱמָתָא, דַּאֲמִירָן בְּעָלְמָא
וְאִמְרוּ אָמֵן. (קהל: אָמֵן)

הגבהה וגלילה

The ספר תורה *is lifted and the* קהל *says:*

וְזֹאת הַתּוֹרָה אֲשֶׁר־שָׂם מֹשֶׁה לִפְנֵי בְּנֵי יִשְׂרָאֵל: דברים ד
עַל־פִּי יהוה בְּיַד מֹשֶׁה: במדבר ט
Some add עֵץ־חַיִּים הִיא לַמַּחֲזִיקִים בָּהּ וְתֹמְכֶיהָ מְאֻשָּׁר: משלי ג
דְּרָכֶיהָ דַרְכֵי־נֹעַם וְכָל־נְתִיבוֹתֶיהָ שָׁלוֹם:
אֹרֶךְ יָמִים בִּימִינָהּ, בִּשְׂמֹאולָהּ עֹשֶׁר וְכָבוֹד:
יהוה חָפֵץ לְמַעַן צִדְקוֹ יַגְדִּיל תּוֹרָה וְיַאְדִּיר: ישעיה מב

The ספר תורה *is bound and covered.*

וְזֹאת הַתּוֹרָה *This is the Torah.* The raising (*hagbaha*) and rolling (*gelila*) of the Torah – ancient customs regarded as high honors, are accompanied by a reaffirmation of the holiness of the Torah as God's word, "at the LORD's

BLESSINGS BEFORE AND AFTER READING THE HAFTARA

Before reading the Haftara, the person called up for Maftir says:

בָּרוּךְ Blessed are You, LORD our God, King of the Universe, who chose good prophets and was pleased with their words, spoken in truth. Blessed are You, LORD, who chose the Torah, His servant Moses, His people Israel, and the prophets of truth and righteousness.

After the Haftara, the person called up for Maftir says the following blessings:

בָּרוּךְ Blessed are You, LORD our God, King of the Universe, Rock of all worlds, righteous for all generations, the faithful God who says and does, speaks and fulfills, all of whose words are truth and righteousness. You are faithful, LORD our God, and faithful are Your words, not one of which returns unfulfilled, for You, God, are a faithful (and compassionate) King. Blessed are You, LORD, faithful in all His words.

רַחֵם Have compassion on Zion for it is the source of our life, and save the one grieved in spirit swiftly in our days. Blessed are You, LORD, who makes Zion rejoice in her children.

שַׂמְּחֵנוּ Grant us joy, LORD our God, through Elijah the prophet Your servant, and through the kingdom of the house of David Your anointed – may he soon come and make our hearts glad. May no stranger sit on his throne, and may others not continue to inherit his glory, for You promised him by Your holy name that his light would never be extinguished. Blessed are You, LORD, Shield of David.

---

cally, with the Torah reading. Some *haftarot,* however, are related to the time of the year, such as the readings for Rosh Ḥodesh when it falls on a Shabbat, or before and after Tisha B'Av. The blessing before the reading emphasizes our faith in the truth of the words of the prophets. The four blessings afterwards speak of: (1) our faith in God's promises, through the prophets; (2) our hope for the restoration of Zion; (3) a prayer for the return of the Davidic monarchy (there are traces here of a polemic against rival claims to sovereignty, such as

ברכות ההפטרה

Before reading the הפטרה*, the person called up for* מפטיר *says:*

בָּרוּךְ אַתָּה יהוה אֱלֹהֵינוּ מֶלֶךְ הָעוֹלָם אֲשֶׁר בָּחַר בִּנְבִיאִים טוֹבִים, וְרָצָה בְדִבְרֵיהֶם הַנֶּאֱמָרִים בֶּאֱמֶת. בָּרוּךְ אַתָּה יהוה, הַבּוֹחֵר בַּתּוֹרָה וּבְמֹשֶׁה עַבְדּוֹ וּבְיִשְׂרָאֵל עַמּוֹ וּבִנְבִיאֵי הָאֱמֶת וָצֶדֶק.

After the הפטרה*, the person called up for* מפטיר *says the following blessings:*

בָּרוּךְ אַתָּה יהוה אֱלֹהֵינוּ מֶלֶךְ הָעוֹלָם, צוּר כָּל הָעוֹלָמִים, צַדִּיק בְּכָל הַדּוֹרוֹת, הָאֵל הַנֶּאֱמָן, הָאוֹמֵר וְעוֹשֶׂה, הַמְדַבֵּר וּמְקַיֵּם, שֶׁכָּל דְּבָרָיו אֱמֶת וָצֶדֶק. נֶאֱמָן אַתָּה הוּא יהוה אֱלֹהֵינוּ וְנֶאֱמָנִים דְּבָרֶיךָ, וְדָבָר אֶחָד מִדְּבָרֶיךָ אָחוֹר לֹא יָשׁוּב רֵיקָם, כִּי אֵל מֶלֶךְ נֶאֱמָן (וְרַחֲמָן) אָתָּה. בָּרוּךְ אַתָּה יהוה, הָאֵל הַנֶּאֱמָן בְּכָל דְּבָרָיו.

רַחֵם עַל צִיּוֹן כִּי הִיא בֵּית חַיֵּינוּ, וְלַעֲלוּבַת נֶפֶשׁ תּוֹשִׁיעַ בִּמְהֵרָה בְיָמֵינוּ. בָּרוּךְ אַתָּה יהוה, מְשַׂמֵּחַ צִיּוֹן בְּבָנֶיהָ.

שַׂמְּחֵנוּ יהוה אֱלֹהֵינוּ בְּאֵלִיָּהוּ הַנָּבִיא עַבְדֶּךָ, וּבְמַלְכוּת בֵּית דָּוִד מְשִׁיחֶךָ, בִּמְהֵרָה יָבוֹא וְיָגֵל לִבֵּנוּ. עַל כִּסְאוֹ לֹא יֵשֵׁב זָר, וְלֹא יִנְחֲלוּ עוֹד אֲחֵרִים אֶת כְּבוֹדוֹ, כִּי בְשֵׁם קָדְשְׁךָ נִשְׁבַּעְתָּ לּוֹ שֶׁלֹּא יִכְבֶּה נֵרוֹ לְעוֹלָם וָעֶד. בָּרוּךְ אַתָּה יהוה, מָגֵן דָּוִד.

THE HAFTARA

The reading of a passage from the prophetic works (the second of the three parts of Tanakh) dates back, in origin, to the period of the Second Temple. The word *haftara* means "conclusion" of the Torah reading. The person who reads the *haftara* is first called to the Torah (*maftir* – a rereading of the last verses of the weekly Torah portion) to emphasize the connection between the Mosaic and prophetic books. The *haftara* is usually connected, verbally or themati-

On Shabbat, including Shabbat Ḥol HaMo'ed Pesaḥ, say:

עַל הַתּוֹרָה For the Torah, for divine worship, for the prophets, and for this Sabbath day which You, Lord our God, have given us for holiness and rest, honor and glory – for all these we thank and bless You, Lord our God, and may Your name be blessed by the mouth of all that lives, continually, for ever and all time. Blessed are You, Lord, who sanctifies the Sabbath.

On Yom Tov and on Shabbat Ḥol HaMo'ed Sukkot, say (adding on Shabbat the words in parentheses):

For the Torah, for divine worship, for the prophets, (for this Sabbath day) and for this day of

On Pesaḥ:	the Festival of Matzot
On Shavuot:	the Festival of Shavuot
On Sukkot:	the Festival of Sukkot
On Shemini Atzeret and Simḥat Torah:	the Festival of Shemini Atzeret

which You, Lord our God, have given us (for holiness and rest), for joy and gladness, honor and glory – for all these we thank and bless You, Lord our God, and may Your name be blessed by the mouth of all that lives, continually, for ever and all time. Blessed are You, Lord, who sanctifies (the Sabbath,) Israel and the festivals.

The following three paragraphs are not said on a Yom Tov occurring on a weekday. They are only said when praying with a minyan (some say the first paragraph without a minyan).

יְקוּם פֻּרְקָן May deliverance arise from heaven, bringing grace, love and compassion, long life, ample sustenance and heavenly help, physical health and enlightenment of mind, living and thriving children who will neither interrupt nor cease from the words of the Torah – to our masters and teachers of the holy communities in the land of Israel and Babylon; to the leaders of assemblies and the

---

the world, the societies in which, and the governments under which, they live. Dating from different times and places, they reflect the diversity of Jewish life from ancient times to today.

יְקוּם פֻּרְקָן *May deliverance arise:* A prayer for the religious and lay leadership of Babylonian Jewry, dating from the Talmudic and Geonic eras, when Babylon was a major center of Jewish life.

On שבת*, including* שבת חול המועד פסח*, say:*

עַל הַתּוֹרָה וְעַל הָעֲבוֹדָה וְעַל הַנְּבִיאִים וְעַל יוֹם הַשַּׁבָּת הַזֶּה, שֶׁנָּתַתָּ לָּנוּ יהוה אֱלֹהֵינוּ לִקְדֻשָּׁה וְלִמְנוּחָה, לְכָבוֹד וּלְתִפְאָֽרֶת. עַל הַכֹּל יהוה אֱלֹהֵינוּ אֲנַחְנוּ מוֹדִים לָךְ וּמְבָרְכִים אוֹתָךְ, יִתְבָּרַךְ שִׁמְךָ בְּפִי כָּל חַי תָּמִיד לְעוֹלָם וָעֶד. בָּרוּךְ אַתָּה יהוה, מְקַדֵּשׁ הַשַּׁבָּת.

On יום טוב *and on* שבת חול המועד סוכות*, say (adding on* שבת *the words in parentheses):*

עַל הַתּוֹרָה וְעַל הָעֲבוֹדָה וְעַל הַנְּבִיאִים (בשבת: וְעַל יוֹם הַשַּׁבָּת הַזֶּה), וְעַל יוֹם

בפסח: חַג הַמַּצּוֹת הַזֶּה

בשבועות: חַג הַשָּׁבוּעוֹת הַזֶּה

בסוכות: חַג הַסֻּכּוֹת הַזֶּה

בשמיני עצרת ובש״ת: הַשְּׁמִינִי חַג הָעֲצֶרֶת הַזֶּה

שֶׁנָּתַתָּ לָּנוּ, יהוה אֱלֹהֵינוּ (בשבת: לִקְדֻשָּׁה וְלִמְנוּחָה) לְשָׂשׂוֹן וּלְשִׂמְחָה, לְכָבוֹד וּלְתִפְאָֽרֶת. עַל הַכֹּל יהוה אֱלֹהֵינוּ אֲנַחְנוּ מוֹדִים לָךְ וּמְבָרְכִים אוֹתָךְ. יִתְבָּרַךְ שִׁמְךָ בְּפִי כָּל חַי תָּמִיד לְעוֹלָם וָעֶד. בָּרוּךְ אַתָּה יהוה, מְקַדֵּשׁ (בשבת: הַשַּׁבָּת וְ)יִשְׂרָאֵל וְהַזְּמַנִּים.

The following three paragraphs are not said on a יום טוב *occurring on a weekday. They are only said when praying with a* מנין *(some say the first paragraph without a* מנין*).*

יְקוּם פֻּרְקָן מִן שְׁמַיָּא, חִנָּא וְחִסְדָּא וְרַחֲמֵי וְחַיֵּי אֲרִיכֵי וּמְזוֹנֵי רְוִיחֵי, וְסִיַּעְתָּא דִשְׁמַיָּא, וּבַרְיוּת גּוּפָא וּנְהוֹרָא מַעַלְיָא, זַרְעָא חַיָּא וְקַיָּמָא, זַרְעָא דִּי לָא יִפְסֻק וְדִי לָא יִבְטֻל מִפִּתְגָּמֵי אוֹרַיְתָא, לְמָרָנָן וְרַבָּנָן חֲבוּרָתָא קַדִּישָׁתָא דִּי בְאַרְעָא דְיִשְׂרָאֵל וְדִי בְבָבֶל, לְרֵישֵׁי כַלָּה, וּלְרֵישֵׁי גַלְוָתָא, וּלְרֵישֵׁי מְתִיבָתָא, וּלְדַיָּנֵי דְבָבָא, לְכָל תַּלְמִידֵיהוֹן,

---

that of the Hasmonean kings of the Second Temple period, who were not from the house of David); and (4) a hymn of praise to the day: Shabbat or Festival.

Special Prayers: A series of seven prayers for Jewish communities throughout

leaders of communities in exile; to the heads of academies and to the judges in the gates; to all their disciples and their disciples' disciples, and to all who occupy themselves in study of the Torah. May the King of the Universe bless them, prolonging their lives, increasing their days, and adding to their years. May they be redeemed and delivered from all distress and illness. May our Master in heaven be their help at all times and seasons; and let us say: Amen.

יְקוּם פֻּרְקָן May deliverance arise from heaven, bringing grace, love and compassion, long life, ample sustenance and heavenly help, physical health and enlightenment of mind, living and thriving children who will neither interrupt nor cease from the words of the Torah – to all this holy congregation, great and small, women and children. May the King of the Universe bless you, prolonging your lives, increasing your days, and adding to your years. May you be redeemed and delivered from all distress and illness. May our Master in heaven be your help at all times and seasons; and let us say: Amen.

מִי שֶׁבֵּרַךְ May He who blessed our fathers, Abraham, Isaac and Jacob, bless all this holy congregation, together with all other holy congregations: them, their wives, their sons and daughters, and all that is theirs. May He bless those who unite to form synagogues for prayer and those who come there to pray; those who provide lamps for light and wine for Kiddush and Havdala, food for visitors and charity for the poor, and all who faithfully occupy themselves with the needs of the community. May the Holy One, blessed be He, give them their reward; may He remove from them all illness, grant them complete healing, and forgive all their sins. May He send blessing and success to all the work of their hands, together with all Israel their brethren; and let us say: Amen.

Jewish worship, was made out of the voluntary contributions of the Israelites, so Jewish communities today are sustained by the voluntary contributions of their members, whether in the form of money or time.

וּלְכָל תַּלְמִידֵי תַלְמִידֵיהוֹן, וּלְכָל מָאן דְּעָסְקִין בְּאוֹרַיְתָא. מַלְכָּא דְעָלְמָא יְבָרֵךְ יָתְהוֹן, יַפֵּשׁ חַיֵּיהוֹן וְיַסְגֵּא יוֹמֵיהוֹן, וְיִתֵּן אַרְכָא לִשְׁנֵיהוֹן, וְיִתְפָּרְקוּן וְיִשְׁתֵּיזְבוּן מִן כָּל עָקָא וּמִן כָּל מַרְעִין בִּישִׁין. מָרַן דִּי בִשְׁמַיָּא יְהֵא בְסַעְדְּהוֹן כָּל זְמַן וְעִדָּן, וְנֹאמַר אָמֵן.

יְקוּם פֻּרְקָן מִן שְׁמַיָּא, חִנָּא וְחִסְדָּא וְרַחֲמֵי וְחַיֵּי אֲרִיכֵי וּמְזוֹנֵי רְוִיחֵי, וְסִיַּעְתָּא דִשְׁמַיָּא, וּבַרְיוּת גּוּפָא וּנְהוֹרָא מְעַלְּיָא, זַרְעָא חַיָּא וְקַיָּמָא, זַרְעָא דִּי לָא יִפְסֻק וְדִי לָא יִבְטֻל מִפִּתְגָּמֵי אוֹרַיְתָא, לְכָל קְהָלָא קַדִּישָׁא הָדֵין, רַבְרְבַיָּא עִם זְעֵרַיָּא, טַפְלָא וּנְשַׁיָּא. מַלְכָּא דְעָלְמָא יְבָרֵךְ יָתְכוֹן, יַפֵּשׁ חַיֵּיכוֹן וְיַסְגֵּא יוֹמֵיכוֹן, וְיִתֵּן אַרְכָא לִשְׁנֵיכוֹן, וְתִתְפָּרְקוּן וְתִשְׁתֵּיזְבוּן מִן כָּל עָקָא וּמִן כָּל מַרְעִין בִּישִׁין. מָרַן דִּי בִשְׁמַיָּא יְהֵא בְסַעְדְּכוֹן כָּל זְמַן וְעִדָּן, וְנֹאמַר אָמֵן.

מִי שֶׁבֵּרַךְ אֲבוֹתֵינוּ אַבְרָהָם יִצְחָק וְיַעֲקֹב, הוּא יְבָרֵךְ אֶת כָּל הַקָּהָל הַקָּדוֹשׁ הַזֶּה עִם כָּל קְהִלּוֹת הַקֹּדֶשׁ, הֵם וּנְשֵׁיהֶם וּבְנֵיהֶם וּבְנוֹתֵיהֶם וְכָל אֲשֶׁר לָהֶם, וּמִי שֶׁמְּיַחֲדִים בָּתֵּי כְנֵסִיּוֹת לִתְפִלָּה, וּמִי שֶׁבָּאִים בְּתוֹכָם לְהִתְפַּלֵּל, וּמִי שֶׁנּוֹתְנִים נֵר לַמָּאוֹר וְיַיִן לְקִדּוּשׁ וּלְהַבְדָּלָה וּפַת לָאוֹרְחִים וּצְדָקָה לָעֲנִיִּים, וְכָל מִי שֶׁעוֹסְקִים בְּצָרְכֵי צִבּוּר בֶּאֱמוּנָה. הַקָּדוֹשׁ בָּרוּךְ הוּא יְשַׁלֵּם שְׂכָרָם, וְיָסִיר מֵהֶם כָּל מַחֲלָה, וְיִרְפָּא לְכָל גּוּפָם, וְיִסְלַח לְכָל עֲוֹנָם, וְיִשְׁלַח בְּרָכָה וְהַצְלָחָה בְּכָל מַעֲשֵׂי יְדֵיהֶם עִם כָּל יִשְׂרָאֵל אֲחֵיהֶם, וְנֹאמַר אָמֵן.

יְקוּם פֻּרְקָן *May deliverance arise:* The second and third prayers, one in Aramaic and based on the previous prayer, the other in Hebrew, are for all those who work for the congregation. Just as the Tabernacle, the first collective house of

PRAYER FOR THE WELFARE OF THE AMERICAN GOVERNMENT

The Leader says the following:

הַנּוֹתֵן תְּשׁוּעָה May He who gives salvation to kings and dominion to princes, whose kingdom is an everlasting kingdom, who delivers His servant David from the evil sword, who makes a way in the sea and a path through the mighty waters, bless and protect, guard and help, exalt, magnify and uplift the President, Vice President and all officials of this land. May the Supreme King of kings in His mercy put into their hearts and the hearts of all their counselors and officials, to deal kindly with us and all Israel. In their days and in ours, may Judah be saved and Israel dwell in safety, and may the Redeemer come to Zion. May this be His will, and let us say: Amen.

PRAYER FOR THE SAFETY OF THE AMERICAN MILITARY

The Leader says the following:

אַדִּיר בַּמָּרוֹם God on high who dwells in might, the King to whom peace belongs, look down from Your holy habitation and bless the soldiers of the American military forces who risk their lives for the sake of peace on earth. Be their shelter and stronghold, and let them not falter. Give them the strength and courage to thwart the plans of the enemy and end the rule of evil. May their enemies be scattered and their foes flee before them, and may they rejoice in Your salvation. Bring them back safely to their homes, as is written: "The LORD will guard you from *Ps. 121*
all harm, He will guard your life. The LORD will guard your going and coming, now and for evermore." And may there be fulfilled for us the verse: "Nation shall not lift up sword against nation, nor shall they learn *Is. 2*
war any more." Let all the inhabitants on earth know that sovereignty is Yours and Your name inspires awe over all You have created – and let us say: Amen.

---

find peace." Similar guidance was given at a later period (first century CE) after the Roman conquest of Jerusalem: "Rabbi Ḥanina, the deputy High Priest, said: Pray for the welfare of the government, for were it not for fear of it, people would swallow one another alive" (*Avot* 3:2).

תפילה לשלום המלכות

The שליח ציבור *says the following:*

הַנּוֹתֵן תְּשׁוּעָה לַמְּלָכִים וּמֶמְשָׁלָה לַנְּסִיכִים, מַלְכוּתוֹ מַלְכוּת כָּל עוֹלָמִים, הַפּוֹצֶה אֶת דָּוִד עַבְדּוֹ מֵחֶרֶב רָעָה, הַנּוֹתֵן בַּיָּם דֶּרֶךְ וּבְמַיִם עַזִּים נְתִיבָה, הוּא יְבָרֵךְ וְיִשְׁמֹר וְיִנְצֹר וְיַעֲזֹר וִירוֹמֵם וִיגַדֵּל וִינַשֵּׂא לְמַעְלָה אֶת הַנָּשִׂיא וְאֶת מִשְׁנֵהוּ וְאֶת כָּל שָׂרֵי הָאָרֶץ הַזֹּאת. מֶלֶךְ מַלְכֵי הַמְּלָכִים, בְּרַחֲמָיו יִתֵּן בְּלִבָּם וּבְלֵב כָּל יוֹעֲצֵיהֶם וְשָׂרֵיהֶם לַעֲשׂוֹת טוֹבָה עִמָּנוּ וְעִם כָּל יִשְׂרָאֵל. בִּימֵיהֶם וּבְיָמֵינוּ תִּוָּשַׁע יְהוּדָה, וְיִשְׂרָאֵל יִשְׁכֹּן לָבֶטַח, וּבָא לְצִיּוֹן גּוֹאֵל. וְכֵן יְהִי רָצוֹן, וְנֹאמַר אָמֵן.

תפילה לשלום חיילי צבא ארצות הברית

The שליח ציבור *says the following:*

אַדִּיר בַּמָּרוֹם שׁוֹכֵן בִּגְבוּרָה, מֶלֶךְ שֶׁהַשָּׁלוֹם שֶׁלּוֹ, הַשְׁקִיפָה מִמְּעוֹן קָדְשְׁךָ, וּבָרֵךְ אֶת חַיָּלֵי צְבָא אַרְצוֹת הַבְּרִית, הַמְחָרְפִים נַפְשָׁם בְּלֶכְתָּם לָשִׂים שָׁלוֹם בָּאָרֶץ. הֱיֵה נָא לָהֶם מַחֲסֶה וּמָעוֹז, וְאַל תִּתֵּן לַמּוֹט רַגְלָם, חַזֵּק יְדֵיהֶם וְאַמֵּץ רוּחָם לְהָפֵר עֲצַת אוֹיֵב וּלְהַעֲבִיר מֶמְשֶׁלֶת זָדוֹן, יָפוּצוּ אוֹיְבֵיהֶם וְיָנוּסוּ מְשַׂנְאֵיהֶם מִפְּנֵיהֶם, וְיִשְׂמְחוּ

בִּישׁוּעָתֶךָ. הֲשִׁיבֵם בְּשָׁלוֹם אֶל בֵּיתָם, כַּכָּתוּב בְּדִבְרֵי קָדְשֶׁךָ: יהוה תהלים קכא

יִשְׁמָרְךָ מִכָּל־רָע, יִשְׁמֹר אֶת־נַפְשֶׁךָ: יהוה יִשְׁמָר־צֵאתְךָ וּבוֹאֶךָ,

מֵעַתָּה וְעַד־עוֹלָם: וְקַיֵּם בָּנוּ מִקְרָא שֶׁכָּתוּב: לֹא־יִשָּׂא גוֹי אֶל־גּוֹי ישעיה ב

חֶרֶב, וְלֹא־יִלְמְדוּ עוֹד מִלְחָמָה: וְיֵדְעוּ כָּל יוֹשְׁבֵי תֵבֵל כִּי לְךָ מְלוּכָה יָאֲתָה, וְשִׁמְךָ נוֹרָא עַל כָּל מַה שֶּׁבָּרָאתָ. וְנֹאמַר אָמֵן.

הַנּוֹתֵן תְּשׁוּעָה *Prayer for the Welfare of the Government.* This prayer echoes the instruction of Jeremiah (29:7) to those dispersed at the time of the Babylonian exile (sixth century BCE): "Seek the peace of the city to which I have carried you in exile. Pray to the LORD for it, because in its peace, you shall

PRAYER FOR THE STATE OF ISRAEL

The Leader says the following prayer:

אָבִינוּ שֶׁבַּשָּׁמַיִם Heavenly Father, Israel's Rock and Redeemer, bless the State of Israel, the first flowering of our redemption. Shield it under the wings of Your loving-kindness and spread over it the Tabernacle of Your peace. Send Your light and truth to its leaders, ministers and counselors, and direct them with good counsel before You.

Strengthen the hands of the defenders of our Holy Land; grant them deliverance, our God, and crown them with the crown of victory. Grant peace in the land and everlasting joy to its inhabitants.

As for our brothers, the whole house of Israel, remember them in all the lands of our (*In Israel say:* their) dispersion, and swiftly lead us (*In Israel say:* them) upright to Zion Your city, and Jerusalem Your dwelling place, as is written in the Torah of Moses Your servant: "Even if you *Deut. 30* are scattered to the furthermost lands under the heavens, from there the Lord your God will gather you and take you back. The Lord your God will bring you to the land your ancestors possessed and you will possess it; and He will make you more prosperous and numerous than your ancestors. Then the Lord your God will open up your heart and the heart of your descendants, to love the Lord your God with all your heart and with all your soul, that you may live."

Unite our hearts to love and revere Your name and observe all the words of Your Torah, and swiftly send us Your righteous anointed one of the house of David, to redeem those who long for Your salvation.

Appear in Your glorious majesty over all the dwellers on earth, and let all who breathe declare: The Lord God of Israel is King and His kingship has dominion over all. Amen, Selah.

---

verse from Deuteronomy – that Israel would one day be gathered from "the furthermost lands under the heavens," an astonishingly precise prediction of what actually happened. According to the third-century Babylonian teacher Shmuel, "The only difference between this world and the messianic age is subjection to foreign powers" (*Berakhot* 34b). In this view, Israel's independence was in itself a redemptive moment, a return to Jewish self-determination, self-government and self-defense under the sovereignty of God alone.

תפילה לשלום מדינת ישראל

The שליח ציבור *says the following prayer:*

אָבִינוּ שֶׁבַּשָּׁמַיִם, צוּר יִשְׂרָאֵל וְגוֹאֲלוֹ, בָּרֵךְ אֶת מְדִינַת יִשְׂרָאֵל, רֵאשִׁית צְמִיחַת גְּאֻלָּתֵנוּ. הָגֵן עָלֶיהָ בְּאֶבְרַת חַסְדֶּךָ וּפְרֹשׂ עָלֶיהָ סֻכַּת שְׁלוֹמֶךָ, וּשְׁלַח אוֹרְךָ וַאֲמִתְּךָ לְרָאשֶׁיהָ, שָׂרֶיהָ וְיוֹעֲצֶיהָ, וְתַקְּנֵם בְּעֵצָה טוֹבָה מִלְּפָנֶיךָ.

חַזֵּק אֶת יְדֵי מְגִנֵּי אֶרֶץ קָדְשֵׁנוּ, וְהַנְחִילֵם אֱלֹהֵינוּ יְשׁוּעָה וַעֲטֶרֶת נִצָּחוֹן תְּעַטְּרֵם, וְנָתַתָּ שָׁלוֹם בָּאָרֶץ וְשִׂמְחַת עוֹלָם לְיוֹשְׁבֶיהָ.

וְאֶת אַחֵינוּ כָּל בֵּית יִשְׂרָאֵל, פְּקָד נָא בְּכָל אַרְצוֹת פְּזוּרֵינוּ, וְתוֹלִיכֵנוּ
/בארץ ישראל: פְּזוּרֵיהֶם, וְתוֹלִיכֵם/ מְהֵרָה קוֹמְמִיּוּת לְצִיּוֹן עִירֶךָ וְלִירוּשָׁלַיִם
דברים ל מִשְׁכַּן שְׁמֶךָ, כַּכָּתוּב בְּתוֹרַת מֹשֶׁה עַבְדֶּךָ: אִם־יִהְיֶה נִדַּחֲךָ בִּקְצֵה הַשָּׁמָיִם, מִשָּׁם יְקַבֶּצְךָ יהוה אֱלֹהֶיךָ וּמִשָּׁם יִקָּחֶךָ: וֶהֱבִיאֲךָ יהוה אֱלֹהֶיךָ אֶל־הָאָרֶץ אֲשֶׁר־יָרְשׁוּ אֲבֹתֶיךָ וִירִשְׁתָּהּ, וְהֵיטִבְךָ וְהִרְבְּךָ מֵאֲבֹתֶיךָ: וּמָל יהוה אֱלֹהֶיךָ אֶת־לְבָבְךָ וְאֶת־לְבַב זַרְעֶךָ, לְאַהֲבָה אֶת־יהוה אֱלֹהֶיךָ בְּכָל־לְבָבְךָ וּבְכָל־נַפְשְׁךָ, לְמַעַן חַיֶּיךָ:

וְיַחֵד לְבָבֵנוּ לְאַהֲבָה וּלְיִרְאָה אֶת שְׁמֶךָ, וְלִשְׁמֹר אֶת כָּל דִּבְרֵי תּוֹרָתֶךָ, וּשְׁלַח לָנוּ מְהֵרָה בֶּן דָּוִד מְשִׁיחַ צִדְקֶךָ, לִפְדּוֹת מְחַכֵּי קֵץ יְשׁוּעָתֶךָ.

וְהוֹפַע בַּהֲדַר גְּאוֹן עֻזֶּךָ עַל כָּל יוֹשְׁבֵי תֵּבֵל אַרְצֶךָ וְיֹאמַר כֹּל אֲשֶׁר נְשָׁמָה בְאַפּוֹ, יהוה אֱלֹהֵי יִשְׂרָאֵל מֶלֶךְ וּמַלְכוּתוֹ בַּכֹּל מָשָׁלָה, אָמֵן סֶלָה.

אָבִינוּ שֶׁבַּשָּׁמַיִם *Prayer for the State of Israel:* Introduced after the birth of the modern State of Israel in 1948. A key element of the prayer is the phrase "the first flowering of our redemption." It means that the restoration of Israel as a sovereign nation in its own land was not merely an event in secular history. It was the fulfillment of the prophetic vision – first stated by Moses in the quoted

PRAYER FOR ISRAEL'S DEFENSE FORCES

The Leader says the following prayer:

מִי שֶׁבֵּרַךְ May He who blessed our ancestors, Abraham, Isaac and Jacob, bless the members of Israel's Defense Forces and its security services who stand guard over our land and the cities of our God from the Lebanese border to the Egyptian desert, from the Mediterranean sea to the approach of the Aravah, and wherever else they are, on land, in air and at sea. May the LORD make the enemies who rise against us be struck down before them. May the Holy One, blessed be He, protect and deliver them from all trouble and distress, affliction and illness, and send blessing and success to all the work of their hands. May He subdue our enemies under them and crown them with deliverance and victory. And may there be fulfilled in them the verse, "It is the LORD your God *Deut. 20* who goes with you to fight for you against your enemies, to deliver you." And let us say: Amen.

PRAYER FOR THOSE BEING HELD IN CAPTIVITY

If Israeli soldiers or civilians are being held in captivity, the Leader says the following:

מִי שֶׁבֵּרַךְ May He who blessed our ancestors, Abraham, Isaac and Jacob, Joseph, Moses and Aaron, David and Solomon, bless, protect and guard the members of Israel's Defense Forces missing in action or held captive, and other captives among our brethren, the whole house of Israel, who are in distress or captivity, as we, the members of this holy congregation, pray on their behalf. May the Holy One, blessed be He, have compassion on them and bring them out from darkness and the shadow of death; may He break their bonds, deliver them from their distress, and bring them swiftly back to their families' embrace. Give thanks to the LORD *Ps. 107* for His loving-kindness and for the wonders He does for the children of men; and may there be fulfilled in them the verse: "Those redeemed by *Is. 35* the LORD will return; they will enter Zion with singing, and everlasting joy will crown their heads. Gladness and joy will overtake them, and sorrow and sighing will flee away." And let us say: Amen.

---

before they went out to battle in biblical times (Deut. 20:4). Israel, always small, always outnumbered by its neighbors, places its faith in God and the justice of its cause, not on military might alone.

מי שברך לחיילי צה״ל

The שליח ציבור *says the following prayer:*

מִי שֶׁבֵּרַךְ אֲבוֹתֵינוּ אַבְרָהָם יִצְחָק וְיַעֲקֹב הוּא יְבָרֵךְ אֶת חַיָּלֵי צְבָא הַהֲגָנָה לְיִשְׂרָאֵל וְאַנְשֵׁי כֹּחוֹת הַבִּטָּחוֹן, הָעוֹמְדִים עַל מִשְׁמַר אַרְצֵנוּ וְעָרֵי אֱלֹהֵינוּ, מִגְּבוּל הַלְּבָנוֹן וְעַד מִדְבַּר מִצְרַיִם וּמִן הַיָּם הַגָּדוֹל עַד לְבוֹא הָעֲרָבָה וּבְכָל מָקוֹם שֶׁהֵם, בַּיַּבָּשָׁה, בָּאֲוִיר וּבַיָּם. יִתֵּן יהוה אֶת אוֹיְבֵינוּ הַקָּמִים עָלֵינוּ נִגָּפִים לִפְנֵיהֶם. הַקָּדוֹשׁ בָּרוּךְ הוּא יִשְׁמֹר וְיַצִּיל אֶת חַיָּלֵינוּ מִכָּל צָרָה וְצוּקָה וּמִכָּל נֶגַע וּמַחֲלָה, וְיִשְׁלַח בְּרָכָה וְהַצְלָחָה בְּכָל מַעֲשֵׂי יְדֵיהֶם. יַדְבֵּר שׂוֹנְאֵינוּ תַּחְתֵּיהֶם
דברים כ וִיעַטְּרֵם בְּכֶתֶר יְשׁוּעָה וּבַעֲטֶרֶת נִצָּחוֹן. וִיקֻיַּם בָּהֶם הַכָּתוּב: כִּי יהוה אֱלֹהֵיכֶם הַהֹלֵךְ עִמָּכֶם לְהִלָּחֵם לָכֶם עִם־אֹיְבֵיכֶם לְהוֹשִׁיעַ אֶתְכֶם: וְנֹאמַר אָמֵן.

מי שברך לשבויים

If Israeli soldiers or civilians are being held in captivity, the שליח ציבור *says the following:*

מִי שֶׁבֵּרַךְ אֲבוֹתֵינוּ אַבְרָהָם יִצְחָק וְיַעֲקֹב, יוֹסֵף מֹשֶׁה וְאַהֲרֹן, דָּוִד וּשְׁלֹמֹה, הוּא יְבָרֵךְ וְיִשְׁמֹר וְיִנְצֹר אֶת נֶעְדְּרֵי צְבָא הַהֲגָנָה לְיִשְׂרָאֵל וּשְׁבוּיָו, וְאֶת כָּל אַחֵינוּ הַנְּתוּנִים בְּצָרָה וּבְשִׁבְיָה, בַּעֲבוּר שֶׁכָּל הַקָּהָל הַקָּדוֹשׁ הַזֶּה מִתְפַּלֵּל בַּעֲבוּרָם. הַקָּדוֹשׁ בָּרוּךְ הוּא יִמָּלֵא רַחֲמִים עֲלֵיהֶם, וְיוֹצִיאֵם מֵחֹשֶׁךְ וְצַלְמָוֶת, וּמוֹסְרוֹתֵיהֶם יְנַתֵּק, וּמִמְּצוּקוֹתֵיהֶם יוֹשִׁיעֵם, וִישִׁיבֵם מְהֵרָה לְחֵיק מִשְׁפְּחוֹתֵיהֶם.
תהלים קז יוֹדוּ לַיהוה חַסְדּוֹ וְנִפְלְאוֹתָיו לִבְנֵי אָדָם: וִיקֻיַּם בָּהֶם מִקְרָא
ישעיה לה שֶׁכָּתוּב: וּפְדוּיֵי יהוה יְשֻׁבוּן, וּבָאוּ צִיּוֹן בְּרִנָּה, וְשִׂמְחַת עוֹלָם עַל־רֹאשָׁם, שָׂשׂוֹן וְשִׂמְחָה יַשִּׂיגוּ, וְנָסוּ יָגוֹן וַאֲנָחָה: וְנֹאמַר אָמֵן.

מִי שֶׁבֵּרַךְ *Prayer for Israel's Defense Forces:* The verse with which the prayer ends is taken from the speech that the "Kohen anointed for war" spoke to Israel

BLESSING THE NEW MONTH

On the Shabbat before Rosh Ḥodesh, the following is said by the congregation, and repeated by the Leader:

יְהִי רָצוֹן May it be Your will, LORD our God and God of our fathers, to renew for us this coming month for good and blessing. Grant us long life, a life of peace, a life of goodness, a life of blessing, a life of sustenance, a life of physical health, a life marked by reverence for heaven and dread of sin, a life without shame or disgrace, a life of wealth and honor, a life in which we have love for the Torah and reverence for heaven, a life in which our hearts' desires are fulfilled for good. Amen, Selah. ***Berakhot 16b***

The new moon is announced, then the Leader takes the Torah scroll in his right arm and says:

מִי שֶׁעָשָׂה May He who performed miracles for our ancestors
and redeemed them from slavery to freedom, redeem us soon,
and gather in our dispersed people from the four quarters of the earth,
so that all Israel may be united in friendship, and let us say: Amen.

The Leader, then the congregation:

The new month of (*Hebrew month*) will occur on (*day of week*).
May it come to us and all Israel for good.

The congregation and Leader continue:

Outside Israel:	*In Israel:*
May the Holy One, blessed be He, renew this new month for us and for all His people, the house of Israel, for life and peace, gladness and joy, salvation and consolation; and let us say: Amen.	May the Holy One, blessed be He, renew this month for us and for all His people the house of Israel, wherever they are, for good and blessing, gladness and joy, for salvation and consolation, livelihood and sustenance, for life and peace, good tidings and good news, (*In winter:* for rain in its due season,) for complete healing and imminent redemption, and let us say: Amen.

BLESSING OF THE NEW MOON
Originally the New Moon was determined by the Sanhedrin on the basis of eye-witness testimony. Since this could not be precisely predicted in advance, the decision of the court had to be communicated to the Jewish communities in Israel and elsewhere. At first this was done by lighting fire signals on

ברכת החודש

On the שבת *before* ראש חודש*, the following is said by the* קהל*, and repeated by the* שליח ציבור*:*

יְהִי רָצוֹן מִלְּפָנֶיךָ, יהוה אֱלֹהֵינוּ וֵאלֹהֵי אֲבוֹתֵינוּ, שֶׁתְּחַדֵּשׁ עָלֵינוּ אֶת הַחֹדֶשׁ הַזֶּה לְטוֹבָה וְלִבְרָכָה. וְתִתֶּן לָנוּ חַיִּים אֲרוּכִים, חַיִּים שֶׁל שָׁלוֹם, חַיִּים שֶׁל טוֹבָה, חַיִּים שֶׁל בְּרָכָה, חַיִּים שֶׁל פַּרְנָסָה, חַיִּים שֶׁל חִלּוּץ עֲצָמוֹת, חַיִּים שֶׁיֵּשׁ בָּהֶם יִרְאַת שָׁמַיִם וְיִרְאַת חֵטְא, חַיִּים שֶׁאֵין בָּהֶם בּוּשָׁה וּכְלִמָּה, חַיִּים שֶׁל עֹשֶׁר וְכָבוֹד, חַיִּים שֶׁתְּהֵא בָנוּ אַהֲבַת תּוֹרָה וְיִרְאַת שָׁמַיִם, חַיִּים שֶׁיְּמַלְּאוּ מִשְׁאֲלוֹת לִבֵּנוּ לְטוֹבָה, אָמֵן סֶלָה. ברכות טז:

The מולד *is announced, then the* שליח ציבור *takes the* ספר תורה *in his right arm and says:*

מִי שֶׁעָשָׂה נִסִּים לַאֲבוֹתֵינוּ וְגָאַל אוֹתָם מֵעַבְדוּת לְחֵרוּת
הוּא יִגְאַל אוֹתָנוּ בְּקָרוֹב וִיקַבֵּץ נִדָּחֵינוּ מֵאַרְבַּע כַּנְפוֹת הָאָרֶץ
חֲבֵרִים כָּל יִשְׂרָאֵל וְנֹאמַר אָמֵן.

The שליח ציבור*, then the* קהל*:*

רֹאשׁ חֹדֶשׁ *month* יִהְיֶה בְּיוֹם *day* (*וּבְיוֹם *day*)
הַבָּא עָלֵינוּ וְעַל כָּל יִשְׂרָאֵל לְטוֹבָה.

**if the second day falls on Sunday, then substitute:* וּלְמָחֳרָתוֹ בְּיוֹם

The שליח ציבור *and* קהל *continue:*

In חוץ לארץ *say:*	*In* ארץ ישראל *say:*
יְחַדְּשֵׁהוּ הַקָּדוֹשׁ בָּרוּךְ הוּא עָלֵינוּ וְעַל כָּל עַמּוֹ בֵּית יִשְׂרָאֵל לְחַיִּים וּלְשָׁלוֹם לְשָׂשׂוֹן וּלְשִׂמְחָה לִישׁוּעָה וּלְנֶחָמָה וְנֹאמַר אָמֵן.	יְחַדְּשֵׁהוּ הַקָּדוֹשׁ בָּרוּךְ הוּא עָלֵינוּ וְעַל כָּל עַמּוֹ בֵּית יִשְׂרָאֵל בְּכָל מָקוֹם שֶׁהֵם לְטוֹבָה וְלִבְרָכָה, לְשָׂשׂוֹן וּלְשִׂמְחָה לִישׁוּעָה וּלְנֶחָמָה לְפַרְנָסָה וּלְכַלְכָּלָה לְחַיִּים וּלְשָׁלוֹם לִשְׁמוּעוֹת טוֹבוֹת וְלִבְשׂוֹרוֹת טוֹבוֹת (בחורף: וְלִגְשָׁמִים בְּעִתָּם) וְלִרְפוּאָה שְׁלֵמָה, וְלִגְאֻלָּה קְרוֹבָה, וְנֹאמַר אָמֵן.

The following is omitted on days when Tahanun is not said (see page 144). It is also omitted on a Shabbat before Rosh Hodesh (except for the Shabbat before Rosh Hodesh Iyar and Rosh Hodesh Sivan) and on Shabbat Shekalim, Zakhor, Para and HaHodesh.

On the last day of Pesah, the second day of Shavuot (first day in Israel) and Shemini Atzeret, Yizkor is said, page 796.

On other Festivals continue with "Lord my God," page 804.

אַב הָרַחֲמִים Father of compassion, who dwells on high: may He remember in His compassion the pious, the upright and the blameless – holy communities who sacrificed their lives for the sanctification of God's name. Lovely and pleasant in their lives, in death they were not parted. They were swifter than eagles and stronger than lions to do the will of their Maker and the desire of their Creator. O our God, remember them for good with the other righteous of the world, and may He exact retribution for the shed blood of His servants,
as it is written in the Torah of Moses, the man of God: "O nations, acclaim *Deut. 32*
His people, for He will avenge the blood of His servants, wreak vengeance on His foes, and make clean His people's land." And by Your servants, the
prophets, it is written: "I shall cleanse their blood which I have not yet *Joel 4*
cleansed, says the Lord who dwells in Zion." And in the holy Writings it says:
"Why should the nations say: Where is their God? Before our eyes, may those *Ps. 79*
nations know that You avenge the shed blood of Your servants." And it also
says: "For the Avenger of blood remembers them and does not forget the cry *Ps. 9*
of the afflicted." And it further says: "He will execute judgment among the *Ps. 110*
nations, filled with the dead, crushing rulers far and wide. From the brook by the wayside he will drink, then he will hold his head high."

אַשְׁרֵי Happy are those who dwell in Your House; *Ps. 84*
they shall continue to praise You, Selah!
Happy are the people for whom this is so; *Ps. 144*
happy are the people whose God is the Lord.
A song of praise by David. *Ps. 145*

א I will exalt You, my God, the King, and bless Your name for ever and all time. ב Every day I will bless You, and praise Your name for ever and all time. ג Great is the Lord and greatly to be praised; His greatness is unfathomable. ד One generation will praise Your works to the next, and tell of Your mighty deeds. ה On the glorious splendor of Your majesty I will meditate, and

---

ordained that the new moon be determined by astronomical calculation. Our ceremony, though of a later date, recalls the earlier custom.

The following is omitted on days when תחנון *is not said (see page 145).*
It is also omitted on שבת מברכים *(except for the* שבת *before* ראש חודש אייר
and ראש חודש סיון*) and on the "*ארבע פרשיות*",* שקלים*,* זכור*,* פרה *and* החודש*.*
On the last day of פסח*, the second day of* שבועות *(first day in* ארץ ישראל*)*
and שמיני עצרת*,* יזכור *is said, page 797.*
On other חגים *continue with* יָהּ אֵלִי*, page 805.*

אַב הָרַחֲמִים שׁוֹכֵן מְרוֹמִים, בְּרַחֲמָיו הָעֲצוּמִים הוּא יִפְקֹד בְּרַחֲמִים
הַחֲסִידִים וְהַיְשָׁרִים וְהַתְּמִימִים, קְהִלּוֹת הַקֹּדֶשׁ שֶׁמָּסְרוּ נַפְשָׁם עַל קְדֻשַּׁת
הַשֵּׁם, הַנֶּאֱהָבִים וְהַנְּעִימִים בְּחַיֵּיהֶם, וּבְמוֹתָם לֹא נִפְרָדוּ, מִנְּשָׁרִים קַלּוּ
וּמֵאֲרָיוֹת גָּבֵרוּ לַעֲשׂוֹת רְצוֹן קוֹנָם וְחֵפֶץ צוּרָם. יִזְכְּרֵם אֱלֹהֵינוּ לְטוֹבָה
עִם שְׁאָר צַדִּיקֵי עוֹלָם, וְיִנְקֹם לְעֵינֵינוּ נִקְמַת דַּם עֲבָדָיו הַשָּׁפוּךְ, כַּכָּתוּב
דברים לב בְּתוֹרַת מֹשֶׁה אִישׁ הָאֱלֹהִים: הַרְנִינוּ גוֹיִם עַמּוֹ, כִּי דַם־עֲבָדָיו יִקּוֹם, וְנָקָם
יָשִׁיב לְצָרָיו, וְכִפֶּר אַדְמָתוֹ עַמּוֹ: וְעַל יְדֵי עֲבָדֶיךָ הַנְּבִיאִים כָּתוּב לֵאמֹר:
יואל ד וְנִקֵּיתִי, דָּמָם לֹא־נִקֵּיתִי, וַיהוה שֹׁכֵן בְּצִיּוֹן: וּבְכִתְבֵי הַקֹּדֶשׁ נֶאֱמַר: לָמָּה
תהלים עט יֹאמְרוּ הַגּוֹיִם אַיֵּה אֱלֹהֵיהֶם, יִוָּדַע בַּגּוֹיִם לְעֵינֵינוּ נִקְמַת דַּם־עֲבָדֶיךָ
תהלים ט הַשָּׁפוּךְ: וְאוֹמֵר: כִּי־דֹרֵשׁ דָּמִים אוֹתָם זָכָר, לֹא־שָׁכַח צַעֲקַת עֲנָוִים:
תהלים קי וְאוֹמֵר: יָדִין בַּגּוֹיִם מָלֵא גְוִיּוֹת, מָחַץ רֹאשׁ עַל־אֶרֶץ רַבָּה: מִנַּחַל בַּדֶּרֶךְ
יִשְׁתֶּה, עַל־כֵּן יָרִים רֹאשׁ:

תהלים פד אַשְׁרֵי יוֹשְׁבֵי בֵיתֶךָ, עוֹד יְהַלְלוּךָ סֶּלָה:
תהלים קמד אַשְׁרֵי הָעָם שֶׁכָּכָה לּוֹ, אַשְׁרֵי הָעָם שֶׁיהוה אֱלֹהָיו:
תהלים קמה תְּהִלָּה לְדָוִד

א אֲרוֹמִמְךָ אֱלוֹהַי הַמֶּלֶךְ, וַאֲבָרְכָה שִׁמְךָ לְעוֹלָם וָעֶד:
ב בְּכָל־יוֹם אֲבָרְכֶךָּ, וַאֲהַלְלָה שִׁמְךָ לְעוֹלָם וָעֶד:
ג גָּדוֹל יהוה וּמְהֻלָּל מְאֹד, וְלִגְדֻלָּתוֹ אֵין חֵקֶר:
ד דּוֹר לְדוֹר יְשַׁבַּח מַעֲשֶׂיךָ, וּגְבוּרֹתֶיךָ יַגִּידוּ:
ה הֲדַר כְּבוֹד הוֹדֶךָ, וְדִבְרֵי נִפְלְאֹתֶיךָ אָשִׂיחָה:

---

hill-tops. Later it was done by messengers, and in the fourth century, when much of the Jewish population had been forced to leave Israel, Hillel II

on the acts of Your wonders. ו They shall talk of the power of Your awesome deeds, and I will tell of Your greatness. ז They shall recite the record of Your great goodness, and sing with joy of Your righteousness. ח The LORD is gracious and compassionate, slow to anger and great in loving-kindness. ט The LORD is good to all, and His compassion extends to all His works. י All Your works shall thank You, LORD, and Your devoted ones shall bless You. כ They shall talk of the glory of Your kingship, and speak of Your might. ל To make known to mankind His mighty deeds and the glorious majesty of His kingship. מ Your kingdom is an everlasting kingdom, and Your reign is for all generations. ס The LORD supports all who fall, and raises all who are bowed down. ע All raise their eyes to You in hope, and You give them their food in due season. פ You open Your hand, and satisfy every living thing with favor. צ The LORD is righteous in all His ways, and kind in all He does. ק The LORD is close to all who call on Him, to all who call on Him in truth. ר He fulfills the will of those who revere Him; He hears their cry and saves them. ש The LORD guards all who love Him, but all the wicked He will destroy. ▸ ת My mouth shall speak the praise of the LORD, and all creatures shall bless His holy name for ever and all time.

We will bless the LORD now and for ever. Halleluya! *Ps. 115*

RETURNING THE TORAH TO THE ARK

The Ark is opened. All stand. The Leader takes the Torah scroll and says:

יְהַלְלוּ Let them praise the name of the LORD, *Ps. 148*
for His name alone is sublime.

The congregation responds:

הוֹדוֹ His majesty is above earth and heaven.
He has raised the horn of His people,
for the glory of all His devoted ones,
the children of Israel, the people close to Him.
Halleluya!

ו וֶעֱזוּז נוֹרְאֹתֶיךָ יֹאמֵרוּ, וּגְדוּלָּתְךָ אֲסַפְּרֶנָּה:
ז זֵכֶר רַב־טוּבְךָ יַבִּיעוּ, וְצִדְקָתְךָ יְרַנֵּנוּ:
ח חַנּוּן וְרַחוּם יהוה, אֶרֶךְ אַפַּיִם וּגְדָל־חָסֶד:
ט טוֹב־יהוה לַכֹּל, וְרַחֲמָיו עַל־כָּל־מַעֲשָׂיו:
י יוֹדוּךָ יהוה כָּל־מַעֲשֶׂיךָ, וַחֲסִידֶיךָ יְבָרְכוּכָה:
כ כְּבוֹד מַלְכוּתְךָ יֹאמֵרוּ, וּגְבוּרָתְךָ יְדַבֵּרוּ:
ל לְהוֹדִיעַ לִבְנֵי הָאָדָם גְּבוּרֹתָיו, וּכְבוֹד הֲדַר מַלְכוּתוֹ:
מ מַלְכוּתְךָ מַלְכוּת כָּל־עֹלָמִים, וּמֶמְשַׁלְתְּךָ בְּכָל־דּוֹר וָדֹר:
ס סוֹמֵךְ יהוה לְכָל־הַנֹּפְלִים, וְזוֹקֵף לְכָל־הַכְּפוּפִים:
ע עֵינֵי־כֹל אֵלֶיךָ יְשַׂבֵּרוּ, וְאַתָּה נוֹתֵן־לָהֶם אֶת־אָכְלָם בְּעִתּוֹ:
פ פּוֹתֵחַ אֶת־יָדֶךָ, וּמַשְׂבִּיעַ לְכָל־חַי רָצוֹן:
צ צַדִּיק יהוה בְּכָל־דְּרָכָיו, וְחָסִיד בְּכָל־מַעֲשָׂיו:
ק קָרוֹב יהוה לְכָל־קֹרְאָיו, לְכֹל אֲשֶׁר יִקְרָאֻהוּ בֶאֱמֶת:
ר רְצוֹן־יְרֵאָיו יַעֲשֶׂה, וְאֶת־שַׁוְעָתָם יִשְׁמַע, וְיוֹשִׁיעֵם:
ש שׁוֹמֵר יהוה אֶת־כָּל־אֹהֲבָיו, וְאֵת כָּל־הָרְשָׁעִים יַשְׁמִיד:
ת ◂ תְּהִלַּת יהוה יְדַבֶּר פִּי, וִיבָרֵךְ כָּל־בָּשָׂר שֵׁם קָדְשׁוֹ לְעוֹלָם וָעֶד:
וַאֲנַחְנוּ נְבָרֵךְ יָהּ מֵעַתָּה וְעַד־עוֹלָם, הַלְלוּיָהּ: תהלים קטו

הכנסת ספר תורה

The ארון קודש *is opened. All stand. The* שליח ציבור *takes the* ספר תורה *and says:*

יְהַלְלוּ אֶת־שֵׁם יהוה, כִּי־נִשְׂגָּב שְׁמוֹ, לְבַדּוֹ תהלים קמח

The קהל *responds:*

הוֹדוֹ עַל־אֶרֶץ וְשָׁמָיִם:
וַיָּרֶם קֶרֶן לְעַמּוֹ, תְּהִלָּה לְכָל־חֲסִידָיו
לִבְנֵי יִשְׂרָאֵל עַם קְרֹבוֹ, הַלְלוּיָהּ:

While the Torah scroll is being returned to the Ark, on Shabbat say:

מִזְמוֹר לְדָוִד A psalm of David. Render to the LORD, you angelic powers, render to the LORD glory and might. Render to the LORD the glory due to His name. Bow to the LORD in the beauty of holiness. The LORD's voice echoes over the waters; the God of glory thunders; the LORD is over the mighty waters. The LORD's voice in power, the LORD's voice in beauty, the LORD's voice breaks cedars, the LORD shatters the cedars of Lebanon. He makes Lebanon skip like a calf, Sirion like a young wild ox. The LORD's voice cleaves flames of fire. The LORD's voice makes the desert quake, the LORD shakes the desert of Kadesh. The LORD's voice makes hinds calve and strips the forests bare, and in His temple all say: "Glory!" The LORD sat enthroned at the Flood, the LORD sits enthroned as King for ever. The LORD will give strength to His people; the LORD will bless His people with peace. *Ps. 29*

On a Yom Tov occurring on a weekday say:

לְדָוִד מִזְמוֹר A psalm of David. The earth is the LORD's and all it contains, the world and all who live in it. For He founded it on the seas and established it on the streams. Who may climb the mountain of the LORD? Who may stand in His holy place? He who has clean hands and a pure heart, who has not taken My name in vain, or sworn deceitfully. He shall receive blessing from the LORD, and just reward from God, his salvation. This is a generation of those who seek Him, the descendants of Jacob who seek Your presence, Selah! Lift up your heads, O gates; be uplifted, eternal doors, so that the King of glory may enter. Who is the King of glory? It is the LORD, strong and mighty, the LORD mighty in battle. Lift up your heads, O gates; lift them up, eternal doors, so that the King of glory may enter. Who is He, the King of glory? The LORD of hosts, He is the King of glory, Selah! *Ps. 24*

---

with the giving of the Torah at Mount Sinai, accompanied by thunder and lightning, when the mountain "trembled violently" (Ex. 19:18).

While the ספר תורה *is being returned to the* ארון קודש*, on* שבת *say:*

תהלים כט
מִזְמוֹר לְדָוִד, הָבוּ לַיהוה בְּנֵי אֵלִים, הָבוּ לַיהוה כָּבוֹד וָעֹז: הָבוּ
לַיהוה כְּבוֹד שְׁמוֹ, הִשְׁתַּחֲווּ לַיהוה בְּהַדְרַת־קֹדֶשׁ: קוֹל יהוה
עַל־הַמָּיִם, אֵל־הַכָּבוֹד הִרְעִים, יהוה עַל־מַיִם רַבִּים: קוֹל־יהוה
בַּכֹּחַ, קוֹל יהוה בֶּהָדָר: קוֹל יהוה שֹׁבֵר אֲרָזִים, וַיְשַׁבֵּר יהוה אֶת־
אַרְזֵי הַלְּבָנוֹן: וַיַּרְקִידֵם כְּמוֹ־עֵגֶל, לְבָנוֹן וְשִׂרְיוֹן כְּמוֹ בֶן־רְאֵמִים:
קוֹל־יהוה חֹצֵב לַהֲבוֹת אֵשׁ: קוֹל יהוה יָחִיל מִדְבָּר, יָחִיל יהוה
מִדְבַּר קָדֵשׁ: קוֹל יהוה יְחוֹלֵל אַיָּלוֹת וַיֶּחֱשֹׂף יְעָרוֹת, וּבְהֵיכָלוֹ,
כֻּלּוֹ אֹמֵר כָּבוֹד: יהוה לַמַּבּוּל יָשָׁב, וַיֵּשֶׁב יהוה מֶלֶךְ לְעוֹלָם:
יהוה עֹז לְעַמּוֹ יִתֵּן, יהוה יְבָרֵךְ אֶת־עַמּוֹ בַשָּׁלוֹם:

On a יום טוב *occurring on a weekday say:*

תהלים כד
לְדָוִד מִזְמוֹר, לַיהוה הָאָרֶץ וּמְלוֹאָהּ, תֵּבֵל וְיֹשְׁבֵי בָהּ: כִּי־הוּא
עַל־יַמִּים יְסָדָהּ, וְעַל־נְהָרוֹת יְכוֹנְנֶהָ: מִי־יַעֲלֶה בְהַר־יהוה,
וּמִי־יָקוּם בִּמְקוֹם קָדְשׁוֹ: נְקִי כַפַּיִם וּבַר־לֵבָב, אֲשֶׁר לֹא־נָשָׂא
לַשָּׁוְא נַפְשִׁי וְלֹא נִשְׁבַּע לְמִרְמָה: יִשָּׂא בְרָכָה מֵאֵת יהוה, וּצְדָקָה
מֵאֱלֹהֵי יִשְׁעוֹ: זֶה דּוֹר דֹּרְשָׁו, מְבַקְשֵׁי פָנֶיךָ, יַעֲקֹב, סֶלָה: שְׂאוּ
שְׁעָרִים רָאשֵׁיכֶם, וְהִנָּשְׂאוּ פִּתְחֵי עוֹלָם, וְיָבוֹא מֶלֶךְ הַכָּבוֹד:
מִי זֶה מֶלֶךְ הַכָּבוֹד, יהוה עִזּוּז וְגִבּוֹר, יהוה גִּבּוֹר מִלְחָמָה: שְׂאוּ
שְׁעָרִים רָאשֵׁיכֶם, וּשְׂאוּ פִּתְחֵי עוֹלָם, וְיָבֹא מֶלֶךְ הַכָּבוֹד: מִי הוּא
זֶה מֶלֶךְ הַכָּבוֹד, יהוה צְבָאוֹת הוּא מֶלֶךְ הַכָּבוֹד, סֶלָה:

RETURN OF THE TORAH TO THE ARK

A ceremony parallel to that accompanying the taking out of the scroll(s).

מִזְמוֹר לְדָוִד *A psalm of David:* Psalm 29, with its sevenfold reference to "the LORD's voice" that makes the world tremble, was traditionally associated

As the Torah scroll is placed into the Ark, all say:

וּבְנֻחֹה יֹאמַר When the Ark came to rest, Moses would say: "Return, O Lord, to the myriad thousands of Israel." Advance, Lord, to Your resting place, You and Your mighty Ark. Your priests are clothed in righteousness, and Your devoted ones sing in joy. For the sake of Your servant David, do not reject Your anointed one. For I give you good instruction; do not forsake My Torah. It is a tree of life to those who grasp it, and those who uphold it are happy. Its ways are ways of pleasantness, and all its paths are peace. ▸ Turn us back, O Lord, to You, and we will return. Renew our days as of old.

Num. 10 *Ps. 132* *Prov. 4* *Prov. 3* *Lam. 5*

The Ark is closed.

HALF KADDISH

Leader: יִתְגַּדַּל Magnified and sanctified
may His great name be,
in the world He created by His will.
May He establish His kingdom
in your lifetime and in your days,
and in the lifetime of all the house of Israel,
swiftly and soon – and say: Amen.

All: May His great name be blessed for ever and all time.

Leader: Blessed and praised, glorified and exalted,
raised and honored, uplifted and lauded
be the name of the Holy One, blessed be He,
beyond any blessing,
song, praise and consolation uttered in the world –
and say: Amen.

---

when the Israelites carried the Ark, containing the Tablets, with them on all their journeys. Hence the poignancy of the last line, taken from the book of Lamentations, "Renew our days as of old." In Judaism – the world's oldest monotheistic faith – the new is old, and the old is new. The symbol of this constant renewal is the Torah, the word of the One who is beyond time.

As the ספר תורה *is placed into the* ארון קודש, *all say:*

וּבְנֻחֹה יֹאמַר, שׁוּבָה יהוה רִבְבוֹת אַלְפֵי יִשְׂרָאֵל: קוּמָה יהוה לִמְנוּחָתֶךָ, אַתָּה וַאֲרוֹן עֻזֶּךָ: כֹּהֲנֶיךָ יִלְבְּשׁוּ־צֶדֶק, וַחֲסִידֶיךָ יְרַנֵּנוּ: בַּעֲבוּר דָּוִד עַבְדֶּךָ אַל־תָּשֵׁב פְּנֵי מְשִׁיחֶךָ: כִּי לֶקַח טוֹב נָתַתִּי לָכֶם, תּוֹרָתִי אַל־תַּעֲזֹבוּ: עֵץ־חַיִּים הִיא לַמַּחֲזִיקִים בָּהּ, וְתֹמְכֶיהָ מְאֻשָּׁר: דְּרָכֶיהָ דַרְכֵי־נֹעַם וְכָל־נְתִיבוֹתֶיהָ שָׁלוֹם: › הֲשִׁיבֵנוּ יהוה אֵלֶיךָ וְנָשׁוּבָה, חַדֵּשׁ יָמֵינוּ כְּקֶדֶם:

במדבר י
תהלים קלב
משלי ד
משלי ג
איכה ה

The ארון קודש *is closed.*

חצי קדיש

ש״ץ: יִתְגַּדַּל וְיִתְקַדַּשׁ שְׁמֵהּ רַבָּא (קהל: אָמֵן)
בְּעָלְמָא דִּי בְרָא כִרְעוּתֵהּ
וְיַמְלִיךְ מַלְכוּתֵהּ
בְּחַיֵּיכוֹן וּבְיוֹמֵיכוֹן וּבְחַיֵּי דְכָל בֵּית יִשְׂרָאֵל
בַּעֲגָלָא וּבִזְמַן קָרִיב, וְאִמְרוּ אָמֵן. (קהל: אָמֵן)

קהל וש״ץ: יְהֵא שְׁמֵהּ רַבָּא מְבָרַךְ לְעָלַם וּלְעָלְמֵי עָלְמַיָּא.

ש״ץ: יִתְבָּרַךְ וְיִשְׁתַּבַּח וְיִתְפָּאַר וְיִתְרוֹמַם וְיִתְנַשֵּׂא
וְיִתְהַדָּר וְיִתְעַלֶּה וְיִתְהַלָּל
שְׁמֵהּ דְּקֻדְשָׁא בְּרִיךְ הוּא (קהל: בְּרִיךְ הוּא)
לְעֵלָּא מִן כָּל בִּרְכָתָא / בשבת שובה: לְעֵלָּא לְעֵלָּא מִכָּל בִּרְכָתָא/
וְשִׁירָתָא, תֻּשְׁבְּחָתָא וְנֶחֱמָתָא
דַּאֲמִירָן בְּעָלְמָא, וְאִמְרוּ אָמֵן. (קהל: אָמֵן)

וּבְנֻחֹה יֹאמַר *When the Ark came to rest:* The verse (Num. 10:36) describing the moments in the wilderness years when the Israelites encamped. As at the opening of the Ark, a ceremony in the present recalls the ancient past,

Musaf for Shabbat

On Yom Tov (including Shabbat Ḥol HaMo'ed) say the Musaf for Festivals on page 806.

THE AMIDA

The following prayer, until "in former years" on page 554, is said silently, standing with feet together. If there is a minyan, the Amida is repeated aloud by the Leader. Take three steps forward and at the points indicated by ▾, bend the knees at the first word, bow at the second, and stand straight before saying God's name.

When I proclaim the LORD's name, give glory to our God. *Deut. 32*
O LORD, open my lips, so that my mouth may declare Your praise. *Ps. 51*

PATRIARCHS

▾בָּרוּךְ Blessed are You, LORD our God and God of our fathers,
God of Abraham, God of Isaac and God of Jacob;
the great, mighty and awesome God, God Most High,
who bestows acts of loving-kindness and creates all,
who remembers the loving-kindness of the fathers
and will bring a Redeemer to their children's children
for the sake of His name, in love.

On Shabbat Shuva: Remember us for life, O King who desires life,
and write us in the book of life –
for Your sake, O God of life.

King, Helper, Savior, Shield:
▾Blessed are You, LORD, Shield of Abraham.

---

we may offer (the words of) our lips as the sacrifices of bulls." The Hebrew word for sacrifice, *korban*, derives from the root *k-r-b* meaning "to come, or bring close." The act of coming close to God involves sacrifice in the deepest sense of the word: surrendering something of ourselves to One greater than ourselves, the Author and ultimate Owner of all. Prayer-as-sacrifice means not asking God to do our will, but pledging ourselves to do His will. It is the supreme act of acknowledging our dependency on God.

מוסף לשבת

On יום טוב *(including* שבת חול המועד*) say the* מוסף לשלוש רגלים *on page 807.*

עמידה

The following prayer, until קַדְמֹנִיּוֹת *on page 555, is said standing with feet together. If there is a* מנין*, the* עמידה *is repeated aloud by the* שליח ציבור*. Take three steps forward and at the points indicated by* ', *bend the knees at the first word, bow at the second, and stand straight before saying God's name.*

דברים לב כִּי שֵׁם יהוה אֶקְרָא, הָבוּ גֹדֶל לֵאלֹהֵינוּ:

תהלים נא אֲדֹנָי, שְׂפָתַי תִּפְתָּח, וּפִי יַגִּיד תְּהִלָּתֶךָ:

אבות

'בָּרוּךְ אַתָּה יהוה, אֱלֹהֵינוּ וֵאלֹהֵי אֲבוֹתֵינוּ
אֱלֹהֵי אַבְרָהָם, אֱלֹהֵי יִצְחָק, וֵאלֹהֵי יַעֲקֹב
הָאֵל הַגָּדוֹל הַגִּבּוֹר וְהַנּוֹרָא, אֵל עֶלְיוֹן
גּוֹמֵל חֲסָדִים טוֹבִים, וְקוֹנֵה הַכֹּל, וְזוֹכֵר חַסְדֵי אָבוֹת
וּמֵבִיא גוֹאֵל לִבְנֵי בְנֵיהֶם לְמַעַן שְׁמוֹ בְּאַהֲבָה.

בשבת שובה: זָכְרֵנוּ לְחַיִּים, מֶלֶךְ חָפֵץ בַּחַיִּים
וְכָתְבֵנוּ בְּסֵפֶר הַחַיִּים, לְמַעַנְךָ אֱלֹהִים חַיִּים.

מֶלֶךְ עוֹזֵר וּמוֹשִׁיעַ וּמָגֵן.
'בָּרוּךְ אַתָּה יהוה, מָגֵן אַבְרָהָם.

THE ADDITIONAL SERVICE

On Shabbat, festivals and Rosh Ḥodesh, an extra sacrifice, Musaf, was brought in addition to the regular daily morning and afternoon offerings. The Musaf Amida corresponds to that sacrifice. Through it we ask God, in the absence of the Temple and its rites, to accept our prayer in place of sacrifice in the spirit of the words of Hosea (14:3), "Receive us graciously that

DIVINE MIGHT

אַתָּה גִּבּוֹר You are eternally mighty, LORD.
You give life to the dead
and have great power to save.

The phrase "He makes the wind blow and the rain fall" is added from Simḥat Torah until Pesaḥ. In Israel the phrase "He causes the dew to fall" is added from Pesaḥ until Shemini Atzeret. See laws 129–131.

In fall & winter: He makes the wind blow and the rain fall.
In Israel, in spring & summer: He causes the dew to fall.

He sustains the living with loving-kindness,
and with great compassion revives the dead.
He supports the fallen,
heals the sick,
sets captives free,
and keeps His faith with those who sleep in the dust.
Who is like You, Master of might,
and who can compare to You,
O King who brings death and gives life,
and makes salvation grow?

On Shabbat Shuva: Who is like You,
compassionate Father,
who remembers His creatures
in compassion, for life?

Faithful are You to revive the dead.
Blessed are You, LORD,
who revives the dead.

---

most notably by the inclusion of the first verse of the Shema. According to Rabbi Amram Gaon (ninth century) this originated at a time of persecution when Jews were forbidden to publicly declare their faith. They then incorporated the first verse into the Musaf Amida, where it remains to this day.

גבורות

אַתָּה גִּבּוֹר לְעוֹלָם, אֲדֹנָי
מְחַיֵּה מֵתִים אַתָּה, רַב לְהוֹשִׁיעַ

The phrase מַשִּׁיב הָרְוּחַ *is added from* שמחת תורה *until* פסח.
In ארץ ישראל *the phrase* מוֹרִיד הַטָּל *is added from* פסח *until* שמיני עצרת. *See laws 129–131.*

בחורף: מַשִּׁיב הָרְוּחַ וּמוֹרִיד הַגֶּשֶׁם / בארץ ישראל בקיץ: מוֹרִיד הַטָּל

מְכַלְכֵּל חַיִּים בְּחֶסֶד
מְחַיֵּה מֵתִים בְּרַחֲמִים רַבִּים
סוֹמֵךְ נוֹפְלִים
וְרוֹפֵא חוֹלִים
וּמַתִּיר אֲסוּרִים
וּמְקַיֵּם אֱמוּנָתוֹ לִישֵׁנֵי עָפָר.
מִי כָמְוֹךָ, בַּעַל גְּבוּרוֹת
וּמִי דְּוֹמֶה לָּךְ
מֶלֶךְ, מֵמִית וּמְחַיֶּה
וּמַצְמִיחַ יְשׁוּעָה.

בשבת שובה: מִי כָמְוֹךָ אַב הָרַחֲמִים
זוֹכֵר יְצוּרָיו לְחַיִּים בְּרַחֲמִים.

וְנֶאֱמָן אַתָּה לְהַחֲיוֹת מֵתִים.
בָּרוּךְ אַתָּה יהוה, מְחַיֵּה הַמֵּתִים.

קדושה *Kedusha:* As with all forms of the *Kedusha*, the central verses are the praises of the angels as described in the mystical visions of Isaiah and Ezekiel. The surrounding verses are different in Musaf from those of the other Amidot,

When saying the Amida silently, continue with "You are holy" on the next page.

KEDUSHA

During the Leader's Repetition, the following is said standing with feet together, rising on the toes at the words indicated by ▴.

Cong. then Leader: נְעֲרִיצְךָ We will revere and sanctify You with the words uttered by the holy Seraphim who sanctify Your name in the Sanctuary; as is written by Your prophet:
"They call out to one another, saying: *Is. 6*

Cong. then Leader: ▴Holy, ▴holy, ▴holy is the LORD of hosts;
the whole world is filled with His glory."
His glory fills the universe. His ministering angels ask each other, "Where is the place of His glory?"
Those facing them reply "Blessed –

Cong. then Leader: ▴"Blessed is the LORD's glory from His place." *Ezek. 3*
From His place may He turn with compassion
and be gracious to the people who proclaim the unity of His name, morning and evening, every day, continually,
twice each day reciting in love the Shema:

Cong. then Leader: "Listen, Israel: the LORD is our God, the LORD is One." *Deut. 6*
He is our God, He is our Father, He is our King,
He is our Savior – and He, in His compassion,
will let us hear a second time in the presence of all that lives,
His promise to be "Your God." *Num. 15*
"I am the LORD your God."

Leader: And in Your holy Writings it is written:

Cong. then Leader: ▴"The LORD shall reign for ever. He is your God, Zion, *Ps. 146*
from generation to generation, Halleluya!"

Leader: From generation to generation we will declare Your greatness, and we will proclaim Your holiness for evermore.
Your praise, our God, shall not leave our mouth forever,
for You, God, are a great and holy King.
Blessed are You, LORD,
the holy God. / *On Shabbat Shuva:* the holy King./

The Leader continues on the next page with "You instituted the Sabbath" on Shabbat and "Long ago You formed" on Rosh Ḥodesh.

When saying the עמידה silently, continue with אַתָּה קָדוֹשׁ on the next page.

קדושה

During the חזרת הש״ץ, the following is said standing with feet together, rising on the toes at the words indicated by ˄.

then קהל ש״ץ: נַעֲרִיצְךָ וְנַקְדִּישְׁךָ כְּסוֹד שִׂיחַ שַׂרְפֵי קֹדֶשׁ
הַמַּקְדִּישִׁים שִׁמְךָ בַּקֹּדֶשׁ, כַּכָּתוּב עַל יַד נְבִיאֶךָ:
ישעיה ו וְקָרָא זֶה אֶל־זֶה וְאָמַר

then קהל ש״ץ: ˄קָדוֹשׁ, ˄קָדוֹשׁ, ˄קָדוֹשׁ, יהוה צְבָאוֹת, מְלֹא כָל הָאָרֶץ כְּבוֹדוֹ:
כְּבוֹדוֹ מָלֵא עוֹלָם, מְשָׁרְתָיו שׁוֹאֲלִים זֶה לָזֶה, אַיֵּה מְקוֹם כְּבוֹדוֹ
לְעֻמָּתָם בָּרוּךְ יֹאמֵרוּ

יחזקאל ג then קהל ש״ץ: ˄בָּרוּךְ כְּבוֹד־יהוה מִמְּקוֹמוֹ:
מִמְּקוֹמוֹ הוּא יִפֶן בְּרַחֲמִים
וְיָחֹן עַם הַמְיַחֲדִים שְׁמוֹ, עֶרֶב וָבֹקֶר בְּכָל יוֹם תָּמִיד
פַּעֲמַיִם בְּאַהֲבָה שְׁמַע אוֹמְרִים

דברים ו then קהל ש״ץ: שְׁמַע יִשְׂרָאֵל, יהוה אֱלֹהֵינוּ, יהוה אֶחָד:
הוּא אֱלֹהֵינוּ, הוּא אָבִינוּ, הוּא מַלְכֵּנוּ, הוּא מוֹשִׁיעֵנוּ
וְהוּא יַשְׁמִיעֵנוּ בְּרַחֲמָיו שֵׁנִית לְעֵינֵי כָּל חָי
במדבר טו לִהְיוֹת לָכֶם לֵאלֹהִים
אֲנִי יהוה אֱלֹהֵיכֶם:

ש״ץ: וּבְדִבְרֵי קָדְשְׁךָ כָּתוּב לֵאמֹר

תהלים קמו then קהל ש״ץ: ˄יִמְלֹךְ יהוה לְעוֹלָם, אֱלֹהַיִךְ צִיּוֹן לְדֹר וָדֹר, הַלְלוּיָהּ:

ש״ץ: לְדוֹר וָדוֹר נַגִּיד גָּדְלֶךָ, וּלְנֵצַח נְצָחִים קְדֻשָּׁתְךָ נַקְדִּישׁ
וְשִׁבְחֲךָ אֱלֹהֵינוּ מִפִּינוּ לֹא יָמוּשׁ לְעוֹלָם וָעֶד
כִּי אֵל מֶלֶךְ גָּדוֹל וְקָדוֹשׁ אָתָּה.
בָּרוּךְ אַתָּה יהוה, הָאֵל הַקָּדוֹשׁ. /בשבת שובה: הַמֶּלֶךְ הַקָּדוֹשׁ./

The שליח ציבור continues on the next page with תִּכַּנְתָּ שַׁבָּת on שבת and אַתָּה יָצַרְתָּ on ראש חודש.

HOLINESS

אַתָּה קָדוֹשׁ You are holy and Your name is holy,
and holy ones praise You daily, Selah!
Blessed are You, LORD,
the holy God. / *On Shabbat Shuva:* the holy King./
(*If forgotten, repeat the Amida.*)

On Shabbat Rosh Ḥodesh say "Long ago You formed" below the line.

HOLINESS OF THE DAY

תִּכַּנְתָּ שַׁבָּת You instituted the Sabbath, You favored its offerings.
You commanded its specific laws
along with the order of its libations.
Those who delight in it inherit eternal glory,
those who relish it merit life,
and those who love its teachings have chosen greatness.
Even before Sinai they were commanded about it.
Then You, LORD our God, commanded us to offer on it
the additional offering of the Sabbath in the proper way.

On Shabbat Rosh Ḥodesh:

אַתָּה יָצַרְתָּ Long ago You formed Your world, completing Your work on the seventh day.
You loved us. You favored us, raising us above all languages.
You made us holy through Your commandments,
brought us near, O our King, to Your service,
and called us by Your great and holy name.
You also gave us in love, LORD our God,
Sabbaths for rest and New Moons for atonement.
But because we and our ancestors sinned against You,
our city was laid waste, our Sanctuary made desolate,
our splendor exiled, and the glory gone from our House of life.
We can no longer fulfill our obligations in Your chosen House,
the great and holy Temple called by Your name,
because of the hand that was stretched out against Your Sanctuary.

Continue below the line on the next page.

---

for the return of Jews to Israel and the restoration of the Temple service. The second, "Those who keep the Sabbath and call it a delight," speaks of the joyous nature of the day of rest.

קדושת השם

אַתָּה קָדוֹשׁ וְשִׁמְךָ קָדוֹשׁ, וּקְדוֹשִׁים בְּכָל יוֹם יְהַלְלְוּךָ סֶּלָה.
בָּרוּךְ אַתָּה יהוה, הָאֵל הַקָּדוֹשׁ. / בשבת שובה: **הַמֶּלֶךְ הַקָּדוֹשׁ./**

(*If forgotten, repeat the* עמידה.)

On שבת ראש חודש *say* אַתָּה יָצַרְתָּ *below the line.*

קדושת היום

תִּכַּנְתָּ שַׁבָּת, רָצִיתָ קָרְבְּנוֹתֶיהָ
צִוִּיתָ פֵּרוּשֶׁיהָ עִם סִדּוּרֵי נְסָכֶיהָ
מְעַנְּגֶיהָ לְעוֹלָם כָּבוֹד יִנְחָלוּ, טוֹעֲמֶיהָ חַיִּים זָכוּ
וְגַם הָאוֹהֲבִים דְּבָרֶיהָ גְּדֻלָּה בָּחָרוּ.
אָז מִסִּינַי נִצְטַוּוּ עָלֶיהָ
וַתְּצַוֵּנוּ יהוה אֱלֹהֵינוּ לְהַקְרִיב בָּהּ קָרְבַּן מוּסַף שַׁבָּת כָּרָאוּי.

בשבת ראש חודש:

אַתָּה יָצַרְתָּ עוֹלָמְךָ מִקֶּדֶם, כִּלִּיתָ מְלַאכְתְּךָ בַּיּוֹם הַשְּׁבִיעִי
אָהַבְתָּ אוֹתָנוּ וְרָצִיתָ בָּנוּ, וְרוֹמַמְתָּנוּ מִכָּל הַלְּשׁוֹנוֹת
וְקִדַּשְׁתָּנוּ בְּמִצְוֹתֶיךָ, וְקֵרַבְתָּנוּ מַלְכֵּנוּ לַעֲבוֹדָתֶךָ
וְשִׁמְךָ הַגָּדוֹל וְהַקָּדוֹשׁ עָלֵינוּ קָרָאתָ.
וַתִּתֶּן לָנוּ יהוה אֱלֹהֵינוּ בְּאַהֲבָה, שַׁבָּתוֹת לִמְנוּחָה וְרָאשֵׁי חֳדָשִׁים לְכַפָּרָה.
וּלְפִי שֶׁחָטָאנוּ לְפָנֶיךָ אֲנַחְנוּ וַאֲבוֹתֵינוּ
חָרְבָה עִירֵנוּ, וְשָׁמֵם בֵּית מִקְדָּשֵׁנוּ, וְגָלָה יְקָרֵנוּ, וְנִטַּל כָּבוֹד מִבֵּית חַיֵּינוּ
וְאֵין אֲנַחְנוּ יְכוֹלִים לַעֲשׂוֹת חוֹבוֹתֵינוּ בְּבֵית בְּחִירָתֶךָ
בַּבַּיִת הַגָּדוֹל וְהַקָּדוֹשׁ שֶׁנִּקְרָא שִׁמְךָ עָלָיו, מִפְּנֵי הַיָּד שֶׁנִּשְׁתַּלְּחָה בְּמִקְדָּשֶׁךָ.

Continue below the line on the next page.

תִּכַּנְתָּ שַׁבָּת *You instituted the Sabbath:* The central blessing of the Amida focuses on the biblical passage describing the additional Sabbath sacrifice (Num. 28:9–10). Surrounding it are two prayers. The first, "You instituted the Sabbath," opens with an acrostic: the initial letters of the first twenty-two words spell out the Hebrew alphabet in reverse. It continues with a prayer

On Shabbat continue here:

יְהִי רָצוֹן May it be Your will,
Lord our God and God of our ancestors, to lead us back in joy
to our land and to plant us within our borders.
There we will prepare for You our obligatory offerings:
the regular daily offerings in their order,
and the additional offerings according to their laws.

וְאֶת מוּסַף And the additional offering of this Sabbath day
we will prepare and offer before You in love,
in accord with Your will's commandment,
as You wrote for us in Your Torah
through Your servant Moses, by Your own word,
as it is said:

"On the Sabbath day, *Num. 28*
make an offering of two lambs a year old, without blemish,
together with two-tenths of an ephah of fine flour
mixed with oil as a meal-offering, and its appropriate libation.
This is the burnt-offering for every Sabbath,
in addition to the regular daily burnt-offering and its libation."

On Shabbat Rosh Ḥodesh continue here:

May it be Your will, Lord our God and God of our ancestors,
to lead us back in joy to our land, and to plant us within our borders.
There we will prepare for You our obligatory offerings:
the regular daily offerings in their order,
and the additional offerings according to their laws.
And the additional offerings of this Sabbath day, and of this New Moon day,
we will prepare and offer before You in love, in accord with Your will's commandment,
as You wrote for us in Your Torah through Your servant Moses,
by Your own word, as it is said:

"On the Sabbath day, make an offering of two lambs a year old, without blemish, together with two-tenths of an ephah of fine flour mixed with oil as a meal-offering, and its appropriate libation. This is the burnt-offering for every Sabbath, in addition to the regular daily burnt-offering and its libation." *Num. 28*

"And on your new moons, present as a burnt-offering to the Lord two young bulls, one ram, and seven yearling lambs without blemish." *Num. 28*

Continue below the line on the next page.

בשבת:

יְהִי רָצוֹן מִלְּפָנֶיךָ, יהוה אֱלֹהֵינוּ וֵאלֹהֵי אֲבוֹתֵינוּ
שֶׁתַּעֲלֵנוּ בְשִׂמְחָה לְאַרְצֵנוּ וְתִטָּעֵנוּ בִּגְבוּלֵנוּ
וְשָׁם נַעֲשֶׂה לְפָנֶיךָ אֶת קָרְבְּנוֹת חוֹבוֹתֵינוּ
תְּמִידִים כְּסִדְרָם וּמוּסָפִים כְּהִלְכָתָם.
וְאֶת מוּסַף יוֹם הַשַּׁבָּת הַזֶּה
נַעֲשֶׂה וְנַקְרִיב לְפָנֶיךָ בְּאַהֲבָה כְּמִצְוַת רְצוֹנֶךָ
כְּמוֹ שֶׁכָּתַבְתָּ עָלֵינוּ בְּתוֹרָתֶךָ
עַל יְדֵי מֹשֶׁה עַבְדֶּךָ מִפִּי כְבוֹדֶךָ
כָּאָמוּר
וּבְיוֹם הַשַּׁבָּת שְׁנֵי־כְבָשִׂים בְּנֵי־שָׁנָה תְּמִימִם במדבר כח
וּשְׁנֵי עֶשְׂרֹנִים סֹלֶת מִנְחָה בְּלוּלָה בַשֶּׁמֶן וְנִסְכּוֹ:
עֹלַת שַׁבַּת בְּשַׁבַּתּוֹ, עַל־עֹלַת הַתָּמִיד וְנִסְכָּהּ:

בשבת ראש חודש:

יְהִי רָצוֹן מִלְּפָנֶיךָ, יהוה אֱלֹהֵינוּ וֵאלֹהֵי אֲבוֹתֵינוּ
שֶׁתַּעֲלֵנוּ בְשִׂמְחָה לְאַרְצֵנוּ וְתִטָּעֵנוּ בִּגְבוּלֵנוּ
וְשָׁם נַעֲשֶׂה לְפָנֶיךָ אֶת קָרְבְּנוֹת חוֹבוֹתֵינוּ
תְּמִידִים כְּסִדְרָם וּמוּסָפִים כְּהִלְכָתָם.
וְאֶת מוּסְפֵי יוֹם הַשַּׁבָּת הַזֶּה וְיוֹם רֹאשׁ הַחֹדֶשׁ הַזֶּה
נַעֲשֶׂה וְנַקְרִיב לְפָנֶיךָ בְּאַהֲבָה כְּמִצְוַת רְצוֹנֶךָ
כְּמוֹ שֶׁכָּתַבְתָּ עָלֵינוּ בְּתוֹרָתֶךָ עַל יְדֵי מֹשֶׁה עַבְדֶּךָ מִפִּי כְבוֹדֶךָ, כָּאָמוּר
וּבְיוֹם הַשַּׁבָּת שְׁנֵי־כְבָשִׂים בְּנֵי־שָׁנָה תְּמִימִם, וּשְׁנֵי עֶשְׂרֹנִים סֹלֶת מִנְחָה בְּלוּלָה במדבר כח
בַשֶּׁמֶן וְנִסְכּוֹ: עֹלַת שַׁבַּת בְּשַׁבַּתּוֹ, עַל־עֹלַת הַתָּמִיד וְנִסְכָּהּ:
וּבְרָאשֵׁי חָדְשֵׁיכֶם תַּקְרִיבוּ עֹלָה לַיהוה, פָּרִים בְּנֵי־בָקָר שְׁנַיִם, וְאַיִל אֶחָד, במדבר כח
כְּבָשִׂים בְּנֵי־שָׁנָה שִׁבְעָה, תְּמִימִם:

Continue below the line on the next page.

On Shabbat continue here:

יִשְׂמְחוּ Those who keep the Sabbath and call it a delight
shall rejoice in Your kingship.
The people who sanctify the seventh day shall all be satisfied
and take delight in Your goodness,
for You favored the seventh day and declared it holy.
You called it "most desirable of days"
in remembrance of Creation.

אֱלֹהֵינוּ Our God and God of our ancestors, find favor in our rest.
Make us holy through Your commandments
and grant us our share in Your Torah.
Satisfy us with Your goodness,
grant us joy in Your salvation,
and purify our hearts to serve You in truth.
In love and favor, Lord our God,
grant us as our heritage Your holy Sabbath,
so that Israel who sanctify Your name may find rest on it.
Blessed are You, Lord, who sanctifies the Sabbath.

On Shabbat Rosh Ḥodesh continue here:

And their meal-offerings and wine-libations as ordained: three-tenths of an ephah for each bull, two-tenths of an ephah for the ram, one-tenth of an ephah for each lamb, wine for the libations, a male goat for atonement, and two regular daily offerings according to their law.

Those who keep the Sabbath and call it a delight
shall rejoice in Your kingship.
The people who sanctify the seventh day shall all be satisfied
and take delight in Your goodness,
for You favored the seventh day and declared it holy.
You called it "most desirable of days"
in remembrance of Creation.

Our God and God of our ancestors, find favor in our rest, and on this Sabbath day renew for us the coming month for good and blessing, joy and gladness, deliverance and consolation, sustenance and support, life and peace, pardon of sin and forgiveness of iniquity (*From Marḥeshvan to Adar II in a Jewish leap year (see page 1332):* and atonement of transgression). For You have chosen Your people Israel from all nations; You have made known to them Your holy Sabbath, and instituted for them rules for the New Moon. Blessed are You, Lord, who sanctifies the Sabbath, Israel and the New Moons.

Continue with "Find favor" on the next page.

בשבת:

יִשְׂמְחוּ בְמַלְכוּתְךָ שׁוֹמְרֵי שַׁבָּת וְקוֹרְאֵי עֹנֶג
עַם מְקַדְּשֵׁי שְׁבִיעִי
כֻּלָּם יִשְׂבְּעוּ וְיִתְעַנְּגוּ מִטּוּבֶךָ
וּבַשְּׁבִיעִי רָצִיתָ בּוֹ וְקִדַּשְׁתּוֹ
חֶמְדַּת יָמִים אוֹתוֹ קָרָאתָ, זֵכֶר לְמַעֲשֵׂה בְרֵאשִׁית.
אֱלֹהֵינוּ וֵאלֹהֵי אֲבוֹתֵינוּ, רְצֵה בִמְנוּחָתֵנוּ
קַדְּשֵׁנוּ בְּמִצְוֹתֶיךָ וְתֵן חֶלְקֵנוּ בְּתוֹרָתֶךָ
שַׂבְּעֵנוּ מִטּוּבֶךָ, וְשַׂמְּחֵנוּ בִּישׁוּעָתֶךָ
וְטַהֵר לִבֵּנוּ לְעָבְדְּךָ בֶּאֱמֶת
וְהַנְחִילֵנוּ יהוה אֱלֹהֵינוּ בְּאַהֲבָה וּבְרָצוֹן שַׁבַּת קָדְשֶׁךָ
וְיָנוּחוּ בוֹ יִשְׂרָאֵל מְקַדְּשֵׁי שְׁמֶךָ.
בָּרוּךְ אַתָּה יהוה, מְקַדֵּשׁ הַשַּׁבָּת.

בשבת ראש חודש:

וּמִנְחָתָם וְנִסְכֵּיהֶם כִּמְדֻבָּר, שְׁלֹשָׁה עֶשְׂרֹנִים לַפָּר, וּשְׁנֵי עֶשְׂרֹנִים לָאָיִל, וְעִשָּׂרוֹן לַכֶּבֶשׂ, וְיַיִן כְּנִסְכּוֹ, וְשָׂעִיר לְכַפֵּר, וּשְׁנֵי תְמִידִים כְּהִלְכָתָם.
יִשְׂמְחוּ בְמַלְכוּתְךָ שׁוֹמְרֵי שַׁבָּת וְקוֹרְאֵי עֹנֶג
עַם מְקַדְּשֵׁי שְׁבִיעִי, כֻּלָּם יִשְׂבְּעוּ וְיִתְעַנְּגוּ מִטּוּבֶךָ
וּבַשְּׁבִיעִי רָצִיתָ בּוֹ וְקִדַּשְׁתּוֹ
חֶמְדַּת יָמִים אוֹתוֹ קָרָאתָ, זֵכֶר לְמַעֲשֵׂה בְרֵאשִׁית.
אֱלֹהֵינוּ וֵאלֹהֵי אֲבוֹתֵינוּ, רְצֵה בִמְנוּחָתֵנוּ, וְחַדֵּשׁ עָלֵינוּ בְּיוֹם הַשַּׁבָּת הַזֶּה אֶת הַחֹדֶשׁ הַזֶּה, לְטוֹבָה וְלִבְרָכָה, לְשָׂשׂוֹן וּלְשִׂמְחָה, לִישׁוּעָה וּלְנֶחָמָה, לְפַרְנָסָה וּלְכַלְכָּלָה, לְחַיִּים וּלְשָׁלוֹם, לִמְחִילַת חֵטְא וְלִסְלִיחַת עָוֹן (*From* מרחשון *to* אדר שני *in a Jewish leap year* (*see page 1332*) וּלְכַפָּרַת פָּשַׁע), כִּי בְעַמְּךָ יִשְׂרָאֵל בָּחַרְתָּ מִכָּל הָאֻמּוֹת, וְשַׁבַּת קָדְשְׁךָ לָהֶם הוֹדַעְתָּ וְחֻקֵּי רָאשֵׁי חֳדָשִׁים לָהֶם קָבָעְתָּ. בָּרוּךְ אַתָּה יהוה, מְקַדֵּשׁ הַשַּׁבָּת וְיִשְׂרָאֵל וְרָאשֵׁי חֳדָשִׁים.

Continue with רְצֵה *on the next page.*

On all days continue here:

TEMPLE SERVICE

רְצֵה Find favor, LORD our God,
in Your people Israel and their prayer.
Restore the service to Your most holy House,
and accept in love and favor
the fire-offerings of Israel and their prayer.
May the service of Your people Israel
always find favor with You.
And may our eyes witness Your return to Zion in compassion.
Blessed are You, LORD, who restores His Presence to Zion.

THANKSGIVING

Bow at the first nine words.

מוֹדִים We give thanks to You,
for You are the LORD our God
and God of our ancestors
for ever and all time.
You are the Rock of our lives,
Shield of our salvation
from generation to generation.
We will thank You and
declare Your praise for our lives,
which are entrusted into Your hand;
for our souls,
which are placed in Your charge;
for Your miracles
which are with us every day;
and for Your wonders and favors
at all times,
evening, morning and midday.
You are good –
for Your compassion never fails.
You are compassionate –
for Your loving-kindnesses never cease.
We have always placed our hope in You.

During the Leader's Repetition, the congregation says quietly:
מוֹדִים We give thanks to You,
for You are the LORD our God
and God of our ancestors,
God of all flesh,
who formed us
and formed the universe.
Blessings and thanks
are due to Your great
and holy name for giving us
life and sustaining us.
May You continue
to give us life and sustain us;
and may You gather our
exiles to Your holy courts,
to keep Your decrees,
do Your will and serve You
with a perfect heart,
for it is for us
to give You thanks.
Blessed be God to whom
thanksgiving is due.

On all days continue here:

עבודה

רְצֵה יהוה אֱלֹהֵינוּ בְּעַמְּךָ יִשְׂרָאֵל, וּבִתְפִלָּתָם
וְהָשֵׁב אֶת הָעֲבוֹדָה לִדְבִיר בֵּיתֶךָ
וְאִשֵּׁי יִשְׂרָאֵל וּתְפִלָּתָם בְּאַהֲבָה תְקַבֵּל בְּרָצוֹן
וּתְהִי לְרָצוֹן תָּמִיד עֲבוֹדַת יִשְׂרָאֵל עַמֶּךָ.
וְתֶחֱזֶינָה עֵינֵינוּ בְּשׁוּבְךָ לְצִיּוֹן בְּרַחֲמִים.
בָּרוּךְ אַתָּה יהוה, הַמַּחֲזִיר שְׁכִינָתוֹ לְצִיּוֹן.

הודאה

Bow at the first five words.

מוֹדִים אֲנַחְנוּ לָךְ
שָׁאַתָּה הוּא יהוה אֱלֹהֵינוּ
וֵאלֹהֵי אֲבוֹתֵינוּ לְעוֹלָם וָעֶד.
צוּר חַיֵּינוּ, מָגֵן יִשְׁעֵנוּ
אַתָּה הוּא לְדוֹר וָדוֹר.
נוֹדֶה לְּךָ וּנְסַפֵּר תְּהִלָּתֶךָ
עַל חַיֵּינוּ הַמְּסוּרִים בְּיָדֶךָ
וְעַל נִשְׁמוֹתֵינוּ הַפְּקוּדוֹת לָךְ
וְעַל נִסֶּיךָ שֶׁבְּכָל יוֹם עִמָּנוּ
וְעַל נִפְלְאוֹתֶיךָ וְטוֹבוֹתֶיךָ
שֶׁבְּכָל עֵת, עֶרֶב וָבֹקֶר וְצָהֳרָיִם.
הַטּוֹב, כִּי לֹא כָלוּ רַחֲמֶיךָ
וְהַמְרַחֵם, כִּי לֹא תַמּוּ חֲסָדֶיךָ
מֵעוֹלָם קִוִּינוּ לָךְ.

During the חזרת הש״ץ, *the* קהל *says quietly:*

מוֹדִים אֲנַחְנוּ לָךְ
שָׁאַתָּה הוּא יהוה אֱלֹהֵינוּ
וֵאלֹהֵי אֲבוֹתֵינוּ
אֱלֹהֵי כָל בָּשָׂר
יוֹצְרֵנוּ, יוֹצֵר בְּרֵאשִׁית.
בְּרָכוֹת וְהוֹדָאוֹת
לְשִׁמְךָ הַגָּדוֹל וְהַקָּדוֹשׁ
עַל שֶׁהֶחֱיִיתָנוּ וְקִיַּמְתָּנוּ.
כֵּן תְּחַיֵּנוּ וּתְקַיְּמֵנוּ
וְתֶאֱסֹף גָּלֻיּוֹתֵינוּ
לְחַצְרוֹת קָדְשֶׁךָ
לִשְׁמֹר חֻקֶּיךָ וְלַעֲשׂוֹת רְצוֹנֶךָ
וּלְעָבְדְּךָ בְּלֵבָב שָׁלֵם
עַל שֶׁאֲנַחְנוּ מוֹדִים לָךְ.
בָּרוּךְ אֵל הַהוֹדָאוֹת.

On Ḥanukka:

עַל הַנִּסִּים [We thank You also] for the miracles, the redemption, the mighty deeds, the salvations, and the victories in battle which You performed for our ancestors in those days, at this time.

בִּימֵי מַתִּתְיָהוּ In the days of Mattityahu, son of Yoḥanan, the High Priest, the Hasmonean, and his sons, the wicked Greek kingdom rose up against Your people Israel to make them forget Your Torah and to force them to transgress the statutes of Your will. It was then that You in Your great compassion stood by them in the time of their distress. You championed their cause, judged their claim, and avenged their wrong. You delivered the strong into the hands of the weak, the many into the hands of the few, the impure into the hands of the pure, the wicked into the hands of the righteous, and the arrogant into the hands of those who were engaged in the study of Your Torah. You made for Yourself great and holy renown in Your world, and for Your people Israel You performed a great salvation and redemption as of this very day. Your children then entered the holiest part of Your House, cleansed Your Temple, purified Your Sanctuary, kindled lights in Your holy courts, and designated these eight days of Ḥanukka for giving thanks and praise to Your great name.

Continue with "For all these things."

On Shushan Purim in Jerusalem:

עַל הַנִּסִּים [We thank You also] for the miracles, the redemption, the mighty deeds, the salvations, and the victories in battle which You performed for our ancestors in those days at this time.

בִּימֵי מָרְדְּכַי In the days of Mordekhai and Esther, in Shushan the capital, the wicked Haman rose up against them and sought to destroy, slay and exterminate *Esther 3* all the Jews, young and old, children and women, on one day, the thirteenth day of the twelfth month, which is the month of Adar, and to plunder their possessions. Then You in Your great compassion thwarted his counsel, frustrated his plans, and caused his scheme to recoil on his own head, so that they hanged him and his sons on the gallows.

Continue with "For all these things."

וְעַל כֻּלָּם For all these things may Your name be blessed and exalted, our King, continually, for ever and all time.

On Shabbat Shuva: And write, for a good life, all the children of Your covenant.

Let all that lives thank You, Selah! and praise Your name in truth, God, our Savior and Help, Selah!

▾Blessed are You, Lord, whose name is "the Good" and to whom thanks are due.

בחנוכה:

עַל הַנִּסִּים וְעַל הַפֻּרְקָן וְעַל הַגְּבוּרוֹת וְעַל הַתְּשׁוּעוֹת וְעַל הַמִּלְחָמוֹת שֶׁעָשִׂיתָ לַאֲבוֹתֵינוּ בַּיָּמִים הָהֵם בִּזְּמַן הַזֶּה.

בִּימֵי מַתִּתְיָהוּ בֶּן יוֹחָנָן כֹּהֵן גָּדוֹל חַשְׁמוֹנַאי וּבָנָיו, כְּשֶׁעָמְדָה מַלְכוּת יָוָן הָרְשָׁעָה עַל עַמְּךָ יִשְׂרָאֵל לְהַשְׁכִּיחָם תּוֹרָתֶךָ וּלְהַעֲבִירָם מֵחֻקֵּי רְצוֹנֶךָ, וְאַתָּה בְּרַחֲמֶיךָ הָרַבִּים עָמַדְתָּ לָהֶם בְּעֵת צָרָתָם, רַבְתָּ אֶת רִיבָם, דַּנְתָּ אֶת דִּינָם, נָקַמְתָּ אֶת נִקְמָתָם, מָסַרְתָּ גִבּוֹרִים בְּיַד חַלָּשִׁים, וְרַבִּים בְּיַד מְעַטִּים, וּטְמֵאִים בְּיַד טְהוֹרִים, וּרְשָׁעִים בְּיַד צַדִּיקִים, וְזֵדִים בְּיַד עוֹסְקֵי תוֹרָתֶךָ, וּלְךָ עָשִׂיתָ שֵׁם גָּדוֹל וְקָדוֹשׁ בְּעוֹלָמֶךָ, וּלְעַמְּךָ יִשְׂרָאֵל עָשִׂיתָ תְּשׁוּעָה גְדוֹלָה וּפֻרְקָן כְּהַיּוֹם הַזֶּה. וְאַחַר כֵּן בָּאוּ בָנֶיךָ לִדְבִיר בֵּיתֶךָ, וּפִנּוּ אֶת הֵיכָלֶךָ, וְטִהֲרוּ אֶת מִקְדָּשֶׁךָ, וְהִדְלִיקוּ נֵרוֹת בְּחַצְרוֹת קָדְשֶׁךָ, וְקָבְעוּ שְׁמוֹנַת יְמֵי חֲנֻכָּה אֵלּוּ, לְהוֹדוֹת וּלְהַלֵּל לְשִׁמְךָ הַגָּדוֹל.

Continue with וְעַל כֻּלָּם.

בשושן פורים בירושלים:

עַל הַנִּסִּים וְעַל הַפֻּרְקָן וְעַל הַגְּבוּרוֹת וְעַל הַתְּשׁוּעוֹת וְעַל הַמִּלְחָמוֹת שֶׁעָשִׂיתָ לַאֲבוֹתֵינוּ בַּיָּמִים הָהֵם בִּזְּמַן הַזֶּה.

בִּימֵי מָרְדְּכַי וְאֶסְתֵּר בְּשׁוּשַׁן הַבִּירָה, כְּשֶׁעָמַד עֲלֵיהֶם הָמָן הָרָשָׁע, בִּקֵּשׁ לְהַשְׁמִיד לַהֲרֹג וּלְאַבֵּד אֶת־כָּל־הַיְּהוּדִים מִנַּעַר וְעַד־זָקֵן טַף וְנָשִׁים בְּיוֹם אֶחָד, בִּשְׁלוֹשָׁה עָשָׂר לְחֹדֶשׁ שְׁנֵים־עָשָׂר, הוּא־חֹדֶשׁ אֲדָר, וּשְׁלָלָם לָבוֹז: אסתר ג
וְאַתָּה בְּרַחֲמֶיךָ הָרַבִּים הֵפַרְתָּ אֶת עֲצָתוֹ, וְקִלְקַלְתָּ אֶת מַחֲשַׁבְתּוֹ, וַהֲשֵׁבוֹתָ לּוֹ גְּמוּלוֹ בְּרֹאשׁוֹ, וְתָלוּ אוֹתוֹ וְאֶת בָּנָיו עַל הָעֵץ.

Continue with וְעַל כֻּלָּם.

וְעַל כֻּלָּם יִתְבָּרַךְ וְיִתְרוֹמַם שִׁמְךָ מַלְכֵּנוּ תָּמִיד לְעוֹלָם וָעֶד.

בשבת שובה: וּכְתֹב לְחַיִּים טוֹבִים כָּל בְּנֵי בְרִיתֶךָ.

וְכֹל הַחַיִּים יוֹדְוּךָ סֶּלָה, וִיהַלְלוּ אֶת שִׁמְךָ בֶּאֱמֶת הָאֵל יְשׁוּעָתֵנוּ וְעֶזְרָתֵנוּ סֶלָה.
°בָּרוּךְ אַתָּה יהוה, הַטּוֹב שִׁמְךָ וּלְךָ נָאֶה לְהוֹדוֹת.

The following is said by the Leader during the Repetition of the Amida.
In Israel, if Kohanim bless the congregation, turn to page 838. See laws 370–377.

Our God and God of our fathers, bless us with the threefold blessing in the Torah, written by the hand of Moses Your servant and pronounced by Aaron and his sons the priests, Your holy people, as it is said:

May the Lord bless you and protect you. *Num. 6*
Cong: May it be Your will.
May the Lord make His face shine on you and be gracious to you.
Cong: May it be Your will.
May the Lord turn His face toward you, and grant you peace.
Cong: May it be Your will.

PEACE

שִׂים שָׁלוֹם Grant peace, goodness and blessing, grace,
loving-kindness and compassion to us
and all Israel Your people.
Bless us, our Father, all as one,
with the light of Your face,
for by the light of Your face You have given us,
Lord our God, the Torah of life and love of kindness,
righteousness, blessing, compassion, life and peace.
May it be good in Your eyes to bless Your people Israel
at every time, in every hour, with Your peace.

On Shabbat Shuva: In the book of life, blessing, peace and prosperity,
may we and all Your people the house of Israel
be remembered and written before You for a good life,
and for peace.*

Blessed are You, Lord, who blesses His people Israel with peace.

**On Shabbat Shuva outside Israel, many end the blessing:*
Blessed are You, Lord, who makes peace.

The following verse concludes the Leader's Repetition of the Amida.
Some also say it here as part of the silent Amida. See law 368.

May the words of my mouth and the meditation of my heart *Ps. 19*
find favor before You, Lord, my Rock and Redeemer.

The following is said by the שליח ציבור *during* חזרת הש״ץ.
In ארץ ישראל *if* כהנים *say* ברכת כהנים *turn to page 839. See laws 370–377.*

אֱלֹהֵינוּ וֵאלֹהֵי אֲבוֹתֵינוּ, בָּרְכֵנוּ בַבְּרָכָה הַמְשֻׁלֶּשֶׁת בַּתּוֹרָה, הַכְּתוּבָה עַל יְדֵי מֹשֶׁה עַבְדֶּךָ, הָאֲמוּרָה מִפִּי אַהֲרֹן וּבָנָיו כֹּהֲנִים עַם קְדוֹשֶׁיךָ, כָּאָמוּר

במדבר ו יְבָרֶכְךָ יהוה וְיִשְׁמְרֶךָ: קהל: כֵּן יְהִי רָצוֹן

יָאֵר יהוה פָּנָיו אֵלֶיךָ וִיחֻנֶּךָּ: קהל: כֵּן יְהִי רָצוֹן

יִשָּׂא יהוה פָּנָיו אֵלֶיךָ וְיָשֵׂם לְךָ שָׁלוֹם: קהל: כֵּן יְהִי רָצוֹן

ברכת שלום

שִׂים שָׁלוֹם טוֹבָה וּבְרָכָה
חֵן וָחֶסֶד וְרַחֲמִים עָלֵינוּ וְעַל כָּל יִשְׂרָאֵל עַמֶּךָ.
בָּרְכֵנוּ אָבִינוּ כֻּלָּנוּ כְּאֶחָד בְּאוֹר פָּנֶיךָ
כִּי בְאוֹר פָּנֶיךָ נָתַתָּ לָּנוּ, יהוה אֱלֹהֵינוּ
תּוֹרַת חַיִּים וְאַהֲבַת חֶסֶד
וּצְדָקָה וּבְרָכָה וְרַחֲמִים וְחַיִּים וְשָׁלוֹם.
וְטוֹב בְּעֵינֶיךָ לְבָרֵךְ אֶת עַמְּךָ יִשְׂרָאֵל
בְּכָל עֵת וּבְכָל שָׁעָה בִּשְׁלוֹמֶךָ.

בשבת שובה: בְּסֵפֶר חַיִּים, בְּרָכָה וְשָׁלוֹם, וּפַרְנָסָה טוֹבָה
נִזָּכֵר וְנִכָּתֵב לְפָנֶיךָ, אֲנַחְנוּ וְכָל עַמְּךָ בֵּית יִשְׂרָאֵל
לְחַיִּים טוֹבִים וּלְשָׁלוֹם.*

בָּרוּךְ אַתָּה יהוה, הַמְבָרֵךְ אֶת עַמּוֹ יִשְׂרָאֵל בַּשָּׁלוֹם.

*On שבת שובה *in* חוץ לארץ*, many end the blessing:*

בָּרוּךְ אַתָּה יהוה, עוֹשֵׂה הַשָּׁלוֹם.

The following verse concludes the חזרת הש״ץ.
Some also say it here as part of the silent עמידה*. See law 368.*

תהלים יט יִהְיוּ לְרָצוֹן אִמְרֵי־פִי וְהֶגְיוֹן לִבִּי לְפָנֶיךָ, יהוה צוּרִי וְגֹאֲלִי:

אֱלֹהַי My God, *Berakhot 17a*
guard my tongue from evil and my lips from deceitful speech.
To those who curse me, let my soul be silent;
may my soul be to all like the dust.
Open my heart to Your Torah
and let my soul pursue Your commandments.
As for all who plan evil against me,
swiftly thwart their counsel and frustrate their plans.
Act for the sake of Your name; act for the sake of Your right hand;
act for the sake of Your holiness; act for the sake of Your Torah.
That Your beloved ones may be delivered, *Ps. 60*
save with Your right hand and answer me.
May the words of my mouth and the meditation of my heart *Ps. 19*
find favor before You, Lord, my Rock and Redeemer.

Bow, take three steps back, then bow, first left, then right, then center, while saying:

May He who makes peace in His high places,
make peace for us and all Israel – and say: Amen.

יְהִי רָצוֹן May it be Your will, Lord our God and God of our ancestors,
that the Temple be rebuilt speedily in our days, and grant us a share in Your Torah.
And there we will serve You with reverence,
as in the days of old and as in former years.
Then the offering of Judah and Jerusalem *Mal. 3*
will be pleasing to the Lord as in the days of old and as in former years.

FULL KADDISH

Leader: יִתְגַּדַּל Magnified and sanctified
may His great name be,
in the world He created by His will.
May He establish His kingdom
in your lifetime and in your days,
and in the lifetime of all the house of Israel,
swiftly and soon – and say: Amen.

All: May His great name be blessed for ever and all time.

ברכות יז.
אֱלֹהַי
נְצֹר לְשׁוֹנִי מֵרָע וּשְׂפָתַי מִדַּבֵּר מִרְמָה
וְלִמְקַלְלַי נַפְשִׁי תִדֹּם, וְנַפְשִׁי כֶּעָפָר לַכֹּל תִּהְיֶה.
פְּתַח לִבִּי בְּתוֹרָתֶךָ, וּבְמִצְוֹתֶיךָ תִּרְדֹּף נַפְשִׁי.
וְכָל הַחוֹשְׁבִים עָלַי רָעָה
מְהֵרָה הָפֵר עֲצָתָם וְקַלְקֵל מַחֲשַׁבְתָּם.
עֲשֵׂה לְמַעַן שְׁמֶךָ, עֲשֵׂה לְמַעַן יְמִינֶךָ
עֲשֵׂה לְמַעַן קְדֻשָּׁתֶךָ, עֲשֵׂה לְמַעַן תּוֹרָתֶךָ.
תהלים ס
לְמַעַן יֵחָלְצוּן יְדִידֶיךָ, הוֹשִׁיעָה יְמִינְךָ וַעֲנֵנִי:
תהלים יט
יִהְיוּ לְרָצוֹן אִמְרֵי־פִי וְהֶגְיוֹן לִבִּי לְפָנֶיךָ, יהוה צוּרִי וְגֹאֲלִי:

Bow, take three steps back, then bow, first left, then right, then center, while saying:

עֹשֶׂה שָׁלוֹם/ בשבת שובה: הַשָּׁלוֹם/ בִּמְרוֹמָיו
הוּא יַעֲשֶׂה שָׁלוֹם עָלֵינוּ וְעַל כָּל יִשְׂרָאֵל, וְאִמְרוּ אָמֵן.

יְהִי רָצוֹן מִלְּפָנֶיךָ יהוה אֱלֹהֵינוּ וֵאלֹהֵי אֲבוֹתֵינוּ
שֶׁיִּבָּנֶה בֵּית הַמִּקְדָּשׁ בִּמְהֵרָה בְיָמֵינוּ, וְתֵן חֶלְקֵנוּ בְּתוֹרָתֶךָ
וְשָׁם נַעֲבָדְךָ בְּיִרְאָה כִּימֵי עוֹלָם וּכְשָׁנִים קַדְמֹנִיּוֹת.
מלאכי ג
וְעָרְבָה לַיהוה מִנְחַת יְהוּדָה וִירוּשָׁלָםִ כִּימֵי עוֹלָם וּכְשָׁנִים קַדְמֹנִיּוֹת:

קדיש שלם

ש״ץ: יִתְגַּדַּל וְיִתְקַדַּשׁ שְׁמֵהּ רַבָּא (קהל: אָמֵן)
בְּעָלְמָא דִּי בְרָא כִרְעוּתֵהּ
וְיַמְלִיךְ מַלְכוּתֵהּ
בְּחַיֵּיכוֹן וּבְיוֹמֵיכוֹן וּבְחַיֵּי דְכָל בֵּית יִשְׂרָאֵל
בַּעֲגָלָא וּבִזְמַן קָרִיב, וְאִמְרוּ אָמֵן. (קהל: אָמֵן)

קהל וש״ץ: יְהֵא שְׁמֵהּ רַבָּא מְבָרַךְ לְעָלַם וּלְעָלְמֵי עָלְמַיָּא.

Leader: Blessed and praised, glorified and exalted,
raised and honored,
uplifted and lauded be the name of the Holy One,
blessed be He, beyond any blessing,
song, praise and consolation uttered in the world –
and say: Amen.

May the prayers and pleas of all Israel
be accepted by their Father in heaven –
and say: Amen.

May there be great peace from heaven,
and life for us and all Israel – and say: Amen.

Bow, take three steps back, as if taking leave of the Divine Presence, then bow, first left, then right, then center, while saying:

May He who makes peace in His high places,
make peace for us and all Israel – and say: Amen.

אֵין כֵּאלֹהֵינוּ There is none like our God, none like our Lord,
none like our King, none like our Savior.
Who is like our God? Who is like our Lord?
Who is like our King? Who is like our Savior?
We will thank our God, we will thank our Lord,
we will thank our King, we will thank our Savior.
Blessed is our God, blessed is our Lord,
blessed is our King, blessed is our Savior.
You are our God, You are our Lord,
You are our King, You are our Savior.
You are He to whom our ancestors offered the fragrant incense.

Amen; the first words of the next two are "Blessed are You." Thus the poem is a way of reaffirming the preceding prayers, a coded coda to the service as a whole. Some suggest that the passage was intended to complete the "hundred blessings" to be said every day, since the Shabbat Amidot have fewer blessings than their weekday counterparts (Kol Bo).

ש״ץ: יִתְבָּרַךְ וְיִשְׁתַּבַּח וְיִתְפָּאַר
וְיִתְרוֹמַם וְיִתְנַשֵּׂא וְיִתְהַדָּר וְיִתְעַלֶּה וְיִתְהַלָּל
שְׁמֵהּ דְּקֻדְשָׁא בְּרִיךְ הוּא (קהל: בְּרִיךְ הוּא)
לְעֵלָּא מִן כָּל בִּרְכָתָא / בשבת שובה: לְעֵלָּא לְעֵלָּא מִכָּל בִּרְכָתָא/
וְשִׁירָתָא, תֻּשְׁבְּחָתָא וְנֶחֱמָתָא
דַּאֲמִירָן בְּעָלְמָא, וְאִמְרוּ אָמֵן. (קהל: אָמֵן)

תִּתְקַבַּל צְלוֹתְהוֹן וּבָעוּתְהוֹן דְּכָל יִשְׂרָאֵל
קֳדָם אֲבוּהוֹן דִּי בִשְׁמַיָּא, וְאִמְרוּ אָמֵן. (קהל: אָמֵן)

יְהֵא שְׁלָמָא רַבָּא מִן שְׁמַיָּא
וְחַיִּים, עָלֵינוּ וְעַל כָּל יִשְׂרָאֵל, וְאִמְרוּ אָמֵן. (קהל: אָמֵן)

Bow, take three steps back, as if taking leave of the Divine Presence, then bow, first left, then right, then center, while saying:

עֹשֶׂה שָׁלוֹם/ בשבת שובה: הַשָּׁלוֹם/ בִּמְרוֹמָיו
הוּא יַעֲשֶׂה שָׁלוֹם עָלֵינוּ וְעַל כָּל יִשְׂרָאֵל
וְאִמְרוּ אָמֵן. (קהל: אָמֵן)

אֵין כֵּאלֹהֵינוּ, אֵין כַּאדוֹנֵינוּ, אֵין כְּמַלְכֵּנוּ, אֵין כְּמוֹשִׁיעֵנוּ.
מִי כֵאלֹהֵינוּ, מִי כַאדוֹנֵינוּ, מִי כְמַלְכֵּנוּ, מִי כְמוֹשִׁיעֵנוּ.
נוֹדֶה לֵאלֹהֵינוּ, נוֹדֶה לַאדוֹנֵינוּ, נוֹדֶה לְמַלְכֵּנוּ, נוֹדֶה לְמוֹשִׁיעֵנוּ.
בָּרוּךְ אֱלֹהֵינוּ, בָּרוּךְ אֲדוֹנֵינוּ, בָּרוּךְ מַלְכֵּנוּ, בָּרוּךְ מוֹשִׁיעֵנוּ.
אַתָּה הוּא אֱלֹהֵינוּ, אַתָּה הוּא אֲדוֹנֵינוּ,
אַתָּה הוּא מַלְכֵּנוּ, אַתָּה הוּא מוֹשִׁיעֵנוּ.
אַתָּה הוּא שֶׁהִקְטִירוּ אֲבוֹתֵינוּ לְפָנֶיךָ אֶת קְטֹרֶת הַסַּמִּים.

אֵין כֵּאלֹהֵינוּ *There is none like our God:* This paragraph, usually sung in the synagogue, is a poetic introduction to the reading of the passage about the incense offering in the Temple. The initial letters of the first three lines spell

פִּטּוּם הַקְּטֹרֶת The incense mixture consisted of balsam, onycha, galbanum and frankincense, each weighing seventy manehs; myrrh, cassia, spikenard and saffron, each weighing sixteen manehs; twelve manehs of costus, three of aromatic bark; nine of cinnamon; nine kabs of Carsina lye; three seahs and three kabs of Cyprus wine. If Cyprus wine was not available, old white wine might be used. A quarter of a kab of Sodom salt, and a minute amount of a smoke-raising herb. Rabbi Nathan says: Also a minute amount of Jordan amber. If one added honey to the mixture, he rendered it unfit for sacred use. If he omitted any one of its ingredients, he is guilty of a capital offense. *Keritot 6a*

Rabban Shimon ben Gamliel says: "Balsam" refers to the sap that drips from the balsam tree. The Carsina lye was used for bleaching the onycha to improve it. The Cyprus wine was used to soak the onycha in it to make it pungent. Though urine is suitable for this purpose, it is not brought into the Temple out of respect.

These were the psalms which the Levites used to recite in the Temple: *Mishna, Tamid 7*
On the first day of the week they used to say: "The earth is the LORD's *Ps. 24*
and all it contains, the world and all who live in it."
On the second day they used to say: "Great is the LORD and *Ps. 48*
greatly to be praised in the city of God, on His holy mountain."
On the third day they used to say: "God stands in the divine assembly. *Ps. 82*
Among the judges He delivers judgment."
On the fourth day they used to say: "God of retribution, LORD, *Ps. 94*
God of retribution, appear."
On the fifth day they used to say: "Sing for joy to God, our strength. *Ps. 81*
Shout aloud to the God of Jacob."
On the sixth day they used to say: "The LORD reigns: He is robed in majesty; *Ps. 93*
the LORD is robed, girded with strength;
the world is firmly established; it cannot be moved."
On the Sabbath they used to say: "A psalm, a song for the Sabbath day" – *Ps. 92*
[meaning] a psalm and song for the time to come,
for the day which will be entirely Sabbath and rest for life everlasting.

It was taught in the Academy of Elijah: Whoever studies [Torah] laws every day is assured that he will be destined for the World to Come, as it is said, *Megilla 28b*
"The ways of the world are His" – read not, "ways" [*halikhot*] but "laws" [*halakhot*]. *Hab. 3*

---

used to recite in the Temple: Each day of the week, after the regular offerings in the Temple, the Levites would sing a particular psalm, signaling that each day has its own character, its own tasks, its own tonality in the symphony of time. We still say these psalms, usually at the end of the service. In this way, a further connection is made between our prayers and the Temple service.

פִּטּוּם הַקְּטֹרֶת. הַצֳּרִי, וְהַצִּפֹּרֶן, וְהַחֶלְבְּנָה, וְהַלְּבוֹנָה מִשְׁקַל שִׁבְעִים שִׁבְעִים כריתות ו.
מָנֶה, מֹר, וּקְצִיעָה, שִׁבֹּלֶת נֵרְדְּ, וְכַרְכֹּם מִשְׁקַל שִׁשָּׁה עָשָׂר שִׁשָּׁה עָשָׂר מָנֶה, הַקֹּשְׁטְ שְׁנֵים עָשָׂר, קִלּוּפָה שְׁלֹשָׁה, וְקִנָּמוֹן תִּשְׁעָה, בֹּרִית כַּרְשִׁינָה תִּשְׁעָה קַבִּין, יֵין קַפְרִיסִין סְאִין תְּלָת וְקַבִּין תְּלָתָא, וְאִם אֵין לוֹ יֵין קַפְרִיסִין, מֵבִיא חֲמַר חִוַּרְיָן עַתִּיק. מֶלַח סְדוֹמִית רֹבַע, מַעֲלֶה עָשָׁן כָּל שֶׁהוּא. רַבִּי נָתָן הַבַּבְלִי אוֹמֵר: אַף כִּפַּת הַיַּרְדֵּן כָּל שֶׁהוּא, וְאִם נָתַן בָּהּ דְּבַשׁ פְּסָלָהּ, וְאִם חִסַּר אֶחָד מִכָּל סַמָּנֶיהָ, חַיָּב מִיתָה.

רַבָּן שִׁמְעוֹן בֶּן גַּמְלִיאֵל אוֹמֵר: הַצֳּרִי אֵינוֹ אֶלָּא שְׂרָף הַנּוֹטֵף מֵעֲצֵי הַקְּטָף. בֹּרִית כַּרְשִׁינָה שֶׁשָּׁפִין בָּהּ אֶת הַצִּפֹּרֶן כְּדֵי שֶׁתְּהֵא נָאָה, יֵין קַפְרִיסִין שֶׁשּׁוֹרִין בּוֹ אֶת הַצִּפֹּרֶן כְּדֵי שֶׁתְּהֵא עַזָּה, וַהֲלֹא מֵי רַגְלַיִם יָפִין לָהּ, אֶלָּא שֶׁאֵין מַכְנִיסִין מֵי רַגְלַיִם בַּמִּקְדָּשׁ מִפְּנֵי הַכָּבוֹד.

משנה תמיד ז — הַשִּׁיר שֶׁהַלְוִיִּם הָיוּ אוֹמְרִים בְּבֵית הַמִּקְדָּשׁ:
תהלים כד — בַּיּוֹם הָרִאשׁוֹן הָיוּ אוֹמְרִים, לַיהוה הָאָרֶץ וּמְלוֹאָהּ, תֵּבֵל וְיֹשְׁבֵי בָהּ:
תהלים מח — בַּשֵּׁנִי הָיוּ אוֹמְרִים, גָּדוֹל יהוה וּמְהֻלָּל מְאֹד, בְּעִיר אֱלֹהֵינוּ הַר־קָדְשׁוֹ:
תהלים פב — בַּשְּׁלִישִׁי הָיוּ אוֹמְרִים, אֱלֹהִים נִצָּב בַּעֲדַת־אֵל, בְּקֶרֶב אֱלֹהִים יִשְׁפֹּט:
תהלים צד — בָּרְבִיעִי הָיוּ אוֹמְרִים, אֵל־נְקָמוֹת יהוה, אֵל נְקָמוֹת הוֹפִיעַ:
תהלים פא — בַּחֲמִישִׁי הָיוּ אוֹמְרִים, הַרְנִינוּ לֵאלֹהִים עוּזֵּנוּ, הָרִיעוּ לֵאלֹהֵי יַעֲקֹב:
תהלים צג — בַּשִּׁשִּׁי הָיוּ אוֹמְרִים, יהוה מָלָךְ גֵּאוּת לָבֵשׁ
לָבֵשׁ יהוה עֹז הִתְאַזָּר, אַף־תִּכּוֹן תֵּבֵל בַּל־תִּמּוֹט:
תהלים צב — בַּשַּׁבָּת הָיוּ אוֹמְרִים, מִזְמוֹר שִׁיר לְיוֹם הַשַּׁבָּת:
מִזְמוֹר שִׁיר לֶעָתִיד לָבוֹא, לְיוֹם שֶׁכֻּלּוֹ שַׁבָּת וּמְנוּחָה לְחַיֵּי הָעוֹלָמִים.

מגילה כח: — תָּנָא דְבֵי אֵלִיָּהוּ: כָּל הַשּׁוֹנֶה הֲלָכוֹת בְּכָל יוֹם
מֻבְטָח לוֹ שֶׁהוּא בֶּן עוֹלָם הַבָּא, שֶׁנֶּאֱמַר
חבקוק ג — הֲלִיכוֹת עוֹלָם לוֹ: אַל תִּקְרֵי הֲלִיכוֹת אֶלָּא הֲלָכוֹת.

פִּטּוּם הַקְּטֹרֶת *The incense mixture:* This paragraph is a Talmudic passage (*Keritot* 6a) describing the composition of the incense, burned in the Temple every morning and evening (Ex. 30:7–9).

הַשִּׁיר שֶׁהַלְוִיִּם הָיוּ אוֹמְרִים בְּבֵית הַמִּקְדָּשׁ *These were the psalms which the Levites*

Rabbi Elazar said in the name of Rabbi Ḥanina: The disciples of the sages increase peace in the world, as it is said, "And all your children shall be taught of the LORD, and great shall be the peace of your children [*banayikh*]." Read not *banayikh*, "your children," but *bonayikh*, "your builders." Those who love Your Torah have great peace; there is no stumbling block for them. May there be peace within your ramparts, prosperity in your palaces. For the sake of my brothers and friends, I shall say, "Peace be within you." For the sake of the House of the LORD our God, I will seek your good. ▸ May the LORD grant strength to His people; may the LORD bless His people with peace.

Berakhot 64a
Is. 54
Ps. 119
Ps. 122
Ps. 29

THE RABBIS' KADDISH

The following prayer, said by mourners, requires the presence of a minyan.
A transliteration can be found on page 1333.

Mourner: יִתְגַּדַּל Magnified and sanctified
may His great name be,
in the world He created by His will.
May He establish His kingdom in your lifetime
and in your days,
and in the lifetime of all the house of Israel,
swiftly and soon – and say: Amen.

All: May His great name be blessed for ever and all time.

Mourner: Blessed and praised,
glorified and exalted,
raised and honored,
uplifted and lauded
be the name of the Holy One, blessed be He,
beyond any blessing,
song, praise and consolation uttered in the world –
and say: Amen.

To Israel, to the teachers,
their disciples and their disciples' disciples,
and to all who engage
in the study of Torah,
in this (*in Israel add:* holy) place or elsewhere,
may there come to them and you great peace,

אָמַר רַבִּי אֶלְעָזָר, אָמַר רַבִּי חֲנִינָא: תַּלְמִידֵי חֲכָמִים מַרְבִּים שָׁלוֹם בָּעוֹלָם, ברכות סד.
שֶׁנֶּאֱמַר, וְכָל־בָּנַיִךְ לִמּוּדֵי יהוה, וְרַב שְׁלוֹם בָּנָיִךְ: אַל תִּקְרֵי בָּנָיִךְ, אֶלָּא ישעיה נד
בּוֹנָיִךְ. שָׁלוֹם רָב לְאֹהֲבֵי תוֹרָתֶךָ, וְאֵין־לָמוֹ מִכְשׁוֹל: יְהִי־שָׁלוֹם בְּחֵילֵךְ, תהלים קיט
שַׁלְוָה בְּאַרְמְנוֹתָיִךְ: לְמַעַן אַחַי וְרֵעָי אֲדַבְּרָה־נָּא שָׁלוֹם בָּךְ: לְמַעַן בֵּית־יהוה תהלים קכב
אֱלֹהֵינוּ אֲבַקְשָׁה טוֹב לָךְ: ◂ יהוה עֹז לְעַמּוֹ יִתֵּן, יהוה יְבָרֵךְ אֶת־עַמּוֹ בַשָּׁלוֹם: תהלים כט

קדיש דרבנן

The following prayer, said by mourners, requires the presence of a מנין.
A transliteration can be found on page 1333.

אבל: יִתְגַּדַּל וְיִתְקַדַּשׁ שְׁמֵהּ רַבָּא (קהל: אָמֵן)
בְּעָלְמָא דִּי בְרָא כִרְעוּתֵהּ
וְיַמְלִיךְ מַלְכוּתֵהּ
בְּחַיֵּיכוֹן וּבְיוֹמֵיכוֹן וּבְחַיֵּי דְכָל בֵּית יִשְׂרָאֵל
בַּעֲגָלָא וּבִזְמַן קָרִיב, וְאִמְרוּ אָמֵן. (קהל: אָמֵן)

קהל ואבל: יְהֵא שְׁמֵהּ רַבָּא מְבָרַךְ לְעָלַם וּלְעָלְמֵי עָלְמַיָּא.

אבל: יִתְבָּרַךְ וְיִשְׁתַּבַּח וְיִתְפָּאַר וְיִתְרוֹמַם וְיִתְנַשֵּׂא
וְיִתְהַדָּר וְיִתְעַלֶּה וְיִתְהַלָּל
שְׁמֵהּ דְּקֻדְשָׁא בְּרִיךְ הוּא (קהל: בְּרִיךְ הוּא)
לְעֵלָּא מִן כָּל בִּרְכָתָא / בשבת שובה: לְעֵלָּא לְעֵלָּא מִכָּל בִּרְכָתָא/
וְשִׁירָתָא, תֻּשְׁבְּחָתָא וְנֶחֱמָתָא, דַּאֲמִירָן בְּעָלְמָא
וְאִמְרוּ אָמֵן. (קהל: אָמֵן)

עַל יִשְׂרָאֵל וְעַל רַבָּנָן
וְעַל תַּלְמִידֵיהוֹן וְעַל כָּל תַּלְמִידֵי תַלְמִידֵיהוֹן
וְעַל כָּל מָאן דְּעָסְקִין בְּאוֹרַיְתָא
דִּי בְאַתְרָא (בארץ ישראל: קַדִּישָׁא) הָדֵין, וְדִי בְכָל אֲתַר וַאֲתַר
יְהֵא לְהוֹן וּלְכוֹן שְׁלָמָא רַבָּא

grace, kindness and compassion, long life, ample sustenance
and deliverance, from their Father in Heaven –
and say: Amen.

May there be great peace from heaven,
and (good) life for us and all Israel –
and say: Amen.

Bow, take three steps back, as if taking leave of the Divine Presence, then bow, first left, then right, then center, while saying:

May He who makes peace in His high places,
in His compassion make peace for us and all Israel –
and say: Amen.

Stand while saying Aleinu. Bow at ▾.

עָלֵינוּ It is our duty to praise the Master of all,
and ascribe greatness to the Author of creation,
who has not made us like the nations of the lands
nor placed us like the families of the earth;
who has not made our portion like theirs,
nor our destiny like all their multitudes.
(For they worship vanity and emptiness,
and pray to a god who cannot save.)
▾But we bow in worship
and thank the Supreme King of kings, the Holy One, blessed be He,
who extends the heavens and establishes the earth,
whose throne of glory is in the heavens above,
and whose power's Presence is in the highest of heights.
He is our God; there is no other.
Truly He is our King, there is none else,
as it is written in His Torah:
"You shall know and take to heart this day that the Lord is God, *Deut. 4*
in heaven above and on earth below. There is no other."

Therefore, we place our hope in You, Lord our God,
that we may soon see the glory of Your power,
when You will remove abominations from the earth,
and idols will be utterly destroyed,
when the world will be perfected under the sovereignty of the Almighty,

חִנָּא וְחִסְדָּא, וְרַחֲמֵי, וְחַיֵּי אֲרִיכֵי, וּמְזוֹנֵי רְוִיחֵי
וּפֻרְקָנָא מִן קֳדָם אֲבוּהוֹן דִּי בִשְׁמַיָּא, וְאִמְרוּ אָמֵן. (קהל: אָמֵן)

יְהֵא שְׁלָמָא רַבָּא מִן שְׁמַיָּא
וְחַיִּים (טוֹבִים) עָלֵינוּ וְעַל כָּל יִשְׂרָאֵל, וְאִמְרוּ אָמֵן. (קהל: אָמֵן)

Bow, take three steps back, as if taking leave of the Divine Presence, then bow, first left, then right, then center, while saying:

עֹשֶׂה שָׁלוֹם/ בשבת שובה: הַשָּׁלוֹם/ בִּמְרוֹמָיו
הוּא יַעֲשֶׂה בְרַחֲמָיו שָׁלוֹם, עָלֵינוּ וְעַל כָּל יִשְׂרָאֵל
וְאִמְרוּ אָמֵן. (קהל: אָמֵן)

Stand while saying עָלֵינוּ. *Bow at* ▼.

עָלֵינוּ לְשַׁבֵּחַ לַאֲדוֹן הַכֹּל, לָתֵת גְּדֻלָּה לְיוֹצֵר בְּרֵאשִׁית
שֶׁלֹּא עָשָׂנוּ כְּגוֹיֵי הָאֲרָצוֹת, וְלֹא שָׂמָנוּ כְּמִשְׁפְּחוֹת הָאֲדָמָה
שֶׁלֹּא שָׂם חֶלְקֵנוּ כָּהֶם וְגוֹרָלֵנוּ כְּכָל הֲמוֹנָם.
(שֶׁהֵם מִשְׁתַּחֲוִים לְהֶבֶל וָרִיק וּמִתְפַּלְלִים אֶל אֵל לֹא יוֹשִׁיעַ.)
▼וַאֲנַחְנוּ כּוֹרְעִים וּמִשְׁתַּחֲוִים וּמוֹדִים
לִפְנֵי מֶלֶךְ מַלְכֵי הַמְּלָכִים, הַקָּדוֹשׁ בָּרוּךְ הוּא
שֶׁהוּא נוֹטֶה שָׁמַיִם וְיוֹסֵד אָרֶץ
וּמוֹשַׁב יְקָרוֹ בַּשָּׁמַיִם מִמַּעַל
וּשְׁכִינַת עֻזּוֹ בְּגָבְהֵי מְרוֹמִים.
הוּא אֱלֹהֵינוּ, אֵין עוֹד.
אֱמֶת מַלְכֵּנוּ, אֶפֶס זוּלָתוֹ, כַּכָּתוּב בְּתוֹרָתוֹ
דברים ד וְיָדַעְתָּ הַיּוֹם וַהֲשֵׁבֹתָ אֶל־לְבָבֶךָ
כִּי יהוה הוּא הָאֱלֹהִים בַּשָּׁמַיִם מִמַּעַל וְעַל־הָאָרֶץ מִתָּחַת, אֵין עוֹד:

עַל כֵּן נְקַוֶּה לְּךָ יהוה אֱלֹהֵינוּ, לִרְאוֹת מְהֵרָה בְּתִפְאֶרֶת עֻזֶּךָ
לְהַעֲבִיר גִּלּוּלִים מִן הָאָרֶץ, וְהָאֱלִילִים כָּרוֹת יִכָּרֵתוּן
לְתַקֵּן עוֹלָם בְּמַלְכוּת שַׁדַּי.

when all humanity will call on Your name,
to turn all the earth's wicked toward You.
All the world's inhabitants will realize and know
that to You every knee must bow and every tongue swear loyalty.
Before You, LORD our God, they will kneel and bow down
and give honor to Your glorious name.
They will all accept the yoke of Your kingdom,
and You will reign over them soon and for ever.
For the kingdom is Yours,
and to all eternity You will reign in glory,
as it is written in Your Torah: "The LORD will reign for ever and ever." *Ex. 15*
▸ And it is said: "Then the LORD shall be King over all the earth; *Zech. 14*
on that day the LORD shall be One and His name One."

Some add:

Have no fear of sudden terror or of the ruin when it overtakes the wicked. *Prov. 3*
Devise your strategy, but it will be thwarted; propose your plan, *Is. 8*
but it will not stand, for God is with us.
When you grow old, I will still be the same. *Is. 46*
When your hair turns gray, I will still carry you.
I made you, I will bear you, I will carry you, and I will rescue you.

MOURNER'S KADDISH

The following prayer, said by mourners, requires the presence of a minyan.
A transliteration can be found on page 1334.

Mourner: יִתְגַּדַּל Magnified and sanctified
may His great name be,
in the world He created by His will.
May He establish His kingdom
in your lifetime and in your days,
and in the lifetime of all the house of Israel,
swiftly and soon – and say: Amen.

All: May His great name
be blessed for ever and all time.

Mourner: Blessed and praised, glorified and exalted,
raised and honored, uplifted and lauded
be the name of the Holy One, blessed be He,

וְכָל בְּנֵי בָשָׂר יִקְרְאוּ בִשְׁמֶךָ לְהַפְנוֹת אֵלֶיךָ כָּל רִשְׁעֵי אָרֶץ.
יַכִּירוּ וְיֵדְעוּ כָּל יוֹשְׁבֵי תֵבֵל
כִּי לְךָ תִּכְרַע כָּל בֶּרֶךְ, תִּשָּׁבַע כָּל לָשׁוֹן.
לְפָנֶיךָ יהוה אֱלֹהֵינוּ יִכְרְעוּ וְיִפֹּלוּ, וְלִכְבוֹד שִׁמְךָ יְקָר יִתֵּנוּ
וִיקַבְּלוּ כֻלָּם אֶת עֹל מַלְכוּתֶךָ
וְתִמְלֹךְ עֲלֵיהֶם מְהֵרָה לְעוֹלָם וָעֶד.
כִּי הַמַּלְכוּת שֶׁלְּךָ הִיא וּלְעוֹלְמֵי עַד תִּמְלֹךְ בְּכָבוֹד
כַּכָּתוּב בְּתוֹרָתֶךָ, יהוה יִמְלֹךְ לְעֹלָם וָעֶד: שמות טו
◂ וְנֶאֱמַר, וְהָיָה יהוה לְמֶלֶךְ עַל־כָּל־הָאָרֶץ זכריה יד
בַּיּוֹם הַהוּא יִהְיֶה יהוה אֶחָד וּשְׁמוֹ אֶחָד:

Some add:

אַל־תִּירָא מִפַּחַד פִּתְאֹם וּמִשֹּׁאַת רְשָׁעִים כִּי תָבֹא: משלי ג
עֻצוּ עֵצָה וְתֻפָר, דַּבְּרוּ דָבָר וְלֹא יָקוּם, כִּי עִמָּנוּ אֵל: ישעיה ח
וְעַד־זִקְנָה אֲנִי הוּא, וְעַד־שֵׂיבָה אֲנִי אֶסְבֹּל אֲנִי עָשִׂיתִי וַאֲנִי אֶשָּׂא וַאֲנִי אֶסְבֹּל וַאֲמַלֵּט: ישעיה מו

קדיש יתום

The following prayer, said by mourners, requires the presence of a מנין*.*
A transliteration can be found on page 1334.

אבל: יִתְגַּדַּל וְיִתְקַדַּשׁ שְׁמֵהּ רַבָּא (קהל: אָמֵן)
בְּעָלְמָא דִּי בְרָא כִרְעוּתֵהּ
וְיַמְלִיךְ מַלְכוּתֵהּ
בְּחַיֵּיכוֹן וּבְיוֹמֵיכוֹן וּבְחַיֵּי דְכָל בֵּית יִשְׂרָאֵל
בַּעֲגָלָא וּבִזְמַן קָרִיב, וְאִמְרוּ אָמֵן. (קהל: אָמֵן)

קהל ואבל: יְהֵא שְׁמֵהּ רַבָּא מְבָרַךְ לְעָלַם וּלְעָלְמֵי עָלְמַיָּא.

אבל: יִתְבָּרַךְ וְיִשְׁתַּבַּח וְיִתְפָּאַר
וְיִתְרוֹמַם וְיִתְנַשֵּׂא וְיִתְהַדָּר וְיִתְעַלֶּה וְיִתְהַלָּל
שְׁמֵהּ דְּקֻדְשָׁא בְּרִיךְ הוּא (קהל: בְּרִיךְ הוּא)

beyond any blessing,
song, praise and consolation
uttered in the world –
and say: Amen.

May there be great peace from heaven,
and life for us and all Israel –
and say: Amen.

Bow, take three steps back, as if taking leave of the Divine Presence, then bow, first left, then right, then center, while saying:

May He who makes peace in His high places,
make peace for us and all Israel –
and say: Amen.

On Yom Tov that falls on a weekday, say the appropriate Daily Psalm (page 184).
On Shabbat continue with the Daily Psalm below.
Many congregations say the Daily Psalm after the Song of Glory, page 570.
(In Israel on Shabbat Rosh Ḥodesh, some say Barekhi Nafshi, page 190, as the Daily Psalm.)

Today is the holy Sabbath,
on which the Levites used to say this psalm in the Temple:

מִזְמוֹר A psalm. A song for the Sabbath day. It is good to thank the LORD and sing psalms to Your name, Most High – to tell of Your loving-kindness in the morning and Your faithfulness at night, to the music of the ten-stringed lyre and the melody of the harp. For You have made me rejoice by Your work, O LORD; I sing for joy at the deeds of Your hands. How great are Your deeds, LORD, and how very deep Your thoughts. A boor cannot know, nor can a fool understand, that though the wicked spring up like grass and all evildoers flourish, it is only that they may be destroyed for ever. But You, LORD, are eternally exalted. For behold Your enemies, LORD, behold Your enemies will perish; all evildoers will be scattered. You have raised my pride like that of a wild ox; I am anointed with fresh oil. My eyes shall look in triumph on my adversaries; my ears shall hear the downfall of the wicked who rise against me. The righteous will flourish like a palm *Ps. 92*

לְעֵֽלָּא מִן כָּל בִּרְכָתָא
/בשבת שובה: לְעֵֽלָּא לְעֵֽלָּא מִכָּל בִּרְכָתָא/
וְשִׁירָתָא, תֻּשְׁבְּחָתָא וְנֶחֱמָתָא
דַּאֲמִירָן בְּעָלְמָא, וְאִמְרוּ אָמֵן. (קהל: אָמֵן)

יְהֵא שְׁלָמָא רַבָּא מִן שְׁמַיָּא
וְחַיִּים, עָלֵֽינוּ וְעַל כָּל יִשְׂרָאֵל
וְאִמְרוּ אָמֵן. (קהל: אָמֵן)

Bow, take three steps back, as if taking leave of the Divine Presence, then bow, first left, then right, then center, while saying:

עֹשֶׂה שָׁלוֹם/ בשבת שובה: הַשָּׁלוֹם/ בִּמְרוֹמָיו
הוּא יַעֲשֶׂה שָׁלוֹם עָלֵֽינוּ וְעַל כָּל יִשְׂרָאֵל
וְאִמְרוּ אָמֵן. (קהל: אָמֵן)

On יום טוב *that falls on a weekday, say the appropriate* שיר של יום *(page 185).*
On שבת *continue with the* שיר של יום *below. Many congregations say the* שיר של יום *after the* שיר הכבוד*, page 571.*
(In ארץ ישראל *on* שבת ראש חודש*, some say* בָּרְכִי נַפְשִׁי*, page 191, as the* שיר של יום*.)*

הַיּוֹם יוֹם שַׁבַּת קֹֽדֶשׁ, שֶׁבּוֹ הָיוּ הַלְוִיִּם אוֹמְרִים בְּבֵית הַמִּקְדָּשׁ:

מִזְמוֹר שִׁיר לְיוֹם הַשַּׁבָּת: טוֹב לְהֹדוֹת לַיהוה, וּלְזַמֵּר לְשִׁמְךָ תהלים צב
עֶלְיוֹן: לְהַגִּיד בַּבֹּֽקֶר חַסְדֶּֽךָ, וֶאֱמוּנָתְךָ בַּלֵּילוֹת: עֲלֵי־עָשׂוֹר
וַעֲלֵי־נָֽבֶל, עֲלֵי הִגָּיוֹן בְּכִנּוֹר: כִּי שִׂמַּחְתַּֽנִי יהוה בְּפָעֳלֶֽךָ, בְּמַעֲשֵׂי
יָדֶֽיךָ אֲרַנֵּן: מַה־גָּדְלוּ מַעֲשֶֽׂיךָ יהוה, מְאֹד עָמְקוּ מַחְשְׁבֹתֶֽיךָ:
אִישׁ־בַּֽעַר לֹא יֵדָע, וּכְסִיל לֹא־יָבִין אֶת־זֹאת: בִּפְרֹֽחַ רְשָׁעִים
כְּמוֹ־עֵֽשֶׂב, וַיָּצִֽיצוּ כָּל־פֹּֽעֲלֵי אָֽוֶן, לְהִשָּׁמְדָם עֲדֵי־עַד: וְאַתָּה
מָרוֹם לְעֹלָם יהוה: כִּי הִנֵּה אֹיְבֶֽיךָ יהוה, כִּי־הִנֵּה אֹיְבֶֽיךָ יֹאבֵֽדוּ,
יִתְפָּרְדוּ כָּל־פֹּֽעֲלֵי אָֽוֶן: וַתָּֽרֶם כִּרְאֵים קַרְנִי, בַּלֹּתִי בְּשֶֽׁמֶן רַעֲנָן:

tree and grow tall like a cedar in Lebanon. Planted in the LORD's House, blossoming in our God's courtyards, ▸ they will still bear fruit in old age, and stay vigorous and fresh, proclaiming that the LORD is upright: He is my Rock, in whom there is no wrong.

Mourner's Kaddish (page 564)

On Rosh Ḥodesh, say Barekhi Nafshi on page 190 followed by Mourner's Kaddish.
On Ḥanukka, many congregations add Psalm 30 on page 58 followed by Mourner's Kaddish.

From the second day of Rosh Ḥodesh Elul through Shemini Atzeret (in Israel through Hoshana Raba), the following psalm is said:

לְדָוִד A psalm of David. The LORD is my light and my salvation – Ps. 27
whom then shall I fear? The LORD is the stronghold of my life – of whom shall I be afraid? When evil men close in on me to devour my flesh, it is they, my enemies and foes, who stumble and fall. Should an army besiege me, my heart would not fear. Should war break out against me, still I would be confident. One thing I ask of the LORD, only this do I seek: to live in the House of the LORD all the days of my life, to gaze on the beauty of the LORD and worship in His Temple. For He will keep me safe in His pavilion on the day of trouble. He will hide me under the cover of His tent. He will set me high upon a rock. Now my head is high above my enemies who surround me. I will sacrifice in His tent with shouts of joy. I will sing and chant praises to the LORD. LORD, hear my voice when I call. Be gracious to me and answer me. On Your behalf my heart says, "Seek My face." Your face, LORD, will I seek. Do not hide Your face from me. Do not turn Your servant away in anger. You have been my help. Do not reject or forsake me, God, my Savior. Were my father and my mother to forsake me, the LORD would take me in. Teach me Your way, LORD, and lead me on a level path, because of my oppressors. Do not abandon me to the will of my foes, for false witnesses have risen against me, breathing violence. ▸ Were it not for my faith that I shall see the LORD's goodness in the land of the living. Hope in the LORD. Be strong and of good courage, and hope in the LORD!

Mourner's Kaddish (page 564)

וַתַּבֵּט עֵינִי בְּשׁוּרָי, בַּקָּמִים עָלַי מְרֵעִים תִּשְׁמַעְנָה אָזְנָי: צַדִּיק
כַּתָּמָר יִפְרָח, כְּאֶרֶז בַּלְּבָנוֹן יִשְׂגֶּה: שְׁתוּלִים בְּבֵית יהוה, בְּחַצְרוֹת
אֱלֹהֵינוּ יַפְרִיחוּ: ◂ עוֹד יְנוּבוּן בְּשֵׂיבָה, דְּשֵׁנִים וְרַעֲנַנִּים יִהְיוּ:
לְהַגִּיד כִּי־יָשָׁר יהוה, צוּרִי, וְלֹא־עַוְלָתָה בּוֹ:

קדיש יתום (*page 565*)

On ראש חודש*, say* בָּרְכִי נַפְשִׁי *on page 191 followed by* קדיש יתום.
On חנוכה*, many congregations add* מִזְמוֹר שִׁיר־חֲנֻכַּת הַבַּיִת *page 59 followed by* קדיש יתום.

From the second day of ראש חודש אלול *through* שמיני עצרת
(*in* ארץ ישראל *through* הושענא רבה), *the following psalm is said:*

לְדָוִד, יהוה אוֹרִי וְיִשְׁעִי, מִמִּי אִירָא, יהוה מָעוֹז־חַיַּי, מִמִּי תהלים כז
אֶפְחָד: בִּקְרֹב עָלַי מְרֵעִים לֶאֱכֹל אֶת־בְּשָׂרִי, צָרַי וְאֹיְבַי לִי,
הֵמָּה כָשְׁלוּ וְנָפָלוּ: אִם־תַּחֲנֶה עָלַי מַחֲנֶה, לֹא־יִירָא לִבִּי, אִם־
תָּקוּם עָלַי מִלְחָמָה, בְּזֹאת אֲנִי בוֹטֵחַ: אַחַת שָׁאַלְתִּי מֵאֵת־
יהוה, אוֹתָהּ אֲבַקֵּשׁ, שִׁבְתִּי בְּבֵית־יהוה כָּל־יְמֵי חַיַּי, לַחֲזוֹת
בְּנֹעַם־יהוה, וּלְבַקֵּר בְּהֵיכָלוֹ: כִּי יִצְפְּנֵנִי בְּסֻכֹּה בְּיוֹם רָעָה,
יַסְתִּרֵנִי בְּסֵתֶר אָהֳלוֹ, בְּצוּר יְרוֹמְמֵנִי: וְעַתָּה יָרוּם רֹאשִׁי עַל
אֹיְבַי סְבִיבוֹתַי, וְאֶזְבְּחָה בְאָהֳלוֹ זִבְחֵי תְרוּעָה, אָשִׁירָה וַאֲזַמְּרָה
לַיהוה: שְׁמַע־יהוה קוֹלִי אֶקְרָא, וְחָנֵּנִי וַעֲנֵנִי: לְךָ אָמַר לִבִּי
בַּקְּשׁוּ פָנָי, אֶת־פָּנֶיךָ יהוה אֲבַקֵּשׁ: אַל־תַּסְתֵּר פָּנֶיךָ מִמֶּנִּי, אַל
תַּט־בְּאַף עַבְדֶּךָ, עֶזְרָתִי הָיִיתָ, אַל־תִּטְּשֵׁנִי וְאַל־תַּעַזְבֵנִי, אֱלֹהֵי
יִשְׁעִי: כִּי־אָבִי וְאִמִּי עֲזָבוּנִי, וַיהוה יַאַסְפֵנִי: הוֹרֵנִי יהוה דַּרְכֶּךָ,
וּנְחֵנִי בְּאֹרַח מִישׁוֹר, לְמַעַן שׁוֹרְרָי: אַל־תִּתְּנֵנִי בְּנֶפֶשׁ צָרָי,
כִּי קָמוּ־בִי עֵדֵי־שֶׁקֶר, וִיפֵחַ חָמָס: ◂ לוּלֵא הֶאֱמַנְתִּי לִרְאוֹת
בְּטוּב־יהוה בְּאֶרֶץ חַיִּים: קַוֵּה אֶל־יהוה, חֲזַק וְיַאֲמֵץ לִבֶּךָ,
וְקַוֵּה אֶל־יהוה:

קדיש יתום (*page 565*)

SONG OF GLORY

The Ark is opened and all stand.

Leader: I will sing sweet psalms and I will weave songs,
to You for whom my soul longs.

Cong: My soul yearns for the shelter of Your hand,
that all Your mystic secrets I might understand.

Leader: Whenever I speak of Your glory above,
my heart is yearning for Your love.

Cong: So Your glories I will proclaim,
and in songs of love give honor to Your name.

Leader: I will tell of Your glory though I have not seen You,
imagine and describe You, though I have not known You.

Cong: By the hand of Your prophets, through Your servants' mystery,
You gave a glimpse of Your wondrous majesty.

Leader: Recounting Your grandeur and Your glory,
of Your great deeds they told the story.

Cong: They depicted You, though not as You are,
but as You do: Your acts, Your power.

Leader: They represented You in many visions;
through them all You are One without divisions.

Cong: They saw You, now old, then young,
Your head with gray, with black hair hung.

Leader: Aged on the day of judgment, yet on the day of war,
a young warrior with mighty hands they saw.

Cong: Triumph like a helmet He wore on his head;
His right hand and holy arm to victory have led.

Leader: His curls are filled with dew drops of light,
His locks with fragments of the night.

Cong: He will glory in me, for He delights in me;
My diadem of beauty He shall be.

Leader: His head is like pure beaten gold;
Engraved on His brow, His sacred name behold.

Cong: For grace and glory, beauty and renown,
His people have adorned Him with a crown.

שיר הכבוד

The ארון קודש *is opened and all stand.*

ש״ץ: אַנְעִים זְמִירוֹת וְשִׁירִים אֶאֱרֹג, כִּי אֵלֶיךָ נַפְשִׁי תַעֲרֹג.

קהל: נַפְשִׁי חָמְדָה בְּצֵל יָדֶךָ, לָדַעַת כָּל רָז סוֹדֶךָ.

ש״ץ: מִדֵּי דַבְּרִי בִּכְבוֹדֶךָ, הוֹמֶה לִבִּי אֶל דּוֹדֶיךָ.

קהל: עַל כֵּן אֲדַבֵּר בְּךָ נִכְבָּדוֹת, וְשִׁמְךָ אֲכַבֵּד בְּשִׁירֵי יְדִידוֹת.

ש״ץ: אֲסַפְּרָה כְבוֹדְךָ וְלֹא רְאִיתִיךָ, אֲדַמְּךָ אֲכַנְּךָ וְלֹא יְדַעְתִּיךָ.

קהל: בְּיַד נְבִיאֶיךָ בְּסוֹד עֲבָדֶיךָ, דִּמִּיתָ הֲדַר כְּבוֹד הוֹדֶךָ.

ש״ץ: גְּדֻלָּתְךָ וּגְבוּרָתֶךָ, כִּנּוּ לְתֹקֶף פְּעֻלָּתֶךָ.

קהל: דִּמּוּ אוֹתְךָ וְלֹא כְּפִי יֶשְׁךָ, וַיְשַׁוּוּךָ לְפִי מַעֲשֶׂיךָ.

ש״ץ: הִמְשִׁילְוּךָ בְּרֹב חֶזְיוֹנוֹת, הִנְּךָ אֶחָד בְּכָל דִּמְיוֹנוֹת.

קהל: וַיֶּחֱזוּ בְךָ זִקְנָה וּבַחֲרוּת, וּשְׂעַר רֹאשְׁךָ בְּשֵׂיבָה וְשַׁחֲרוּת.

ש״ץ: זִקְנָה בְּיוֹם דִּין וּבַחֲרוּת בְּיוֹם קְרָב, כְּאִישׁ מִלְחָמוֹת יָדָיו לוֹ רָב.

קהל: חָבַשׁ כּוֹבַע יְשׁוּעָה בְּרֹאשׁוֹ, הוֹשִׁיעָה לּוֹ יְמִינוֹ וּזְרוֹעַ קָדְשׁוֹ.

ש״ץ: טַלְלֵי אוֹרוֹת רֹאשׁוֹ נִמְלָא, קְוֻצּוֹתָיו רְסִיסֵי לָיְלָה.

קהל: יִתְפָּאֵר בִּי כִּי חָפֵץ בִּי, וְהוּא יִהְיֶה לִּי לַעֲטֶרֶת צְבִי.

ש״ץ: כֶּתֶם טָהוֹר פָּז דְּמוּת רֹאשׁוֹ, וְחַק עַל מֵצַח כְּבוֹד שֵׁם קָדְשׁוֹ.

קהל: לְחֵן וּלְכָבוֹד צְבִי תִפְאָרָה, אֻמָּתוֹ לוֹ עִטְּרָה עֲטָרָה.

אַנְעִים זְמִירוֹת *Song of Glory:* Attributed to either Rabbi Yehuda HeḤasid (d. 1217) or his father Rabbi Shmuel, this hymn is structured as an alphabetical acrostic, with a (non-acrostic) four-line introduction and a three-line conclusion, followed by biblical verses. The poem, with great grace and depth, speaks about the limits of language in describing the experience of God. On the one hand, God – infinite, eternal, invisible – is beyond the reach of language. On the other, we can only address Him in and through language.

Leader: Like a youth's, His hair in locks unfurls;
Its black tresses flowing in curls.

Cong: Jerusalem, His splendor, is the dwelling place of right;
may He prize it as His highest delight.

Leader: Like a crown in His hand may His treasured people be,
a turban of beauty and of majesty.

Cong: He bore them, carried them, with a crown He adorned them.
They were precious in His sight, and He honored them.

Leader: His glory is on me; my glory is on Him.
He is near to me when I call to Him.

Cong: He is bright and rosy; red will be His dress,
when He comes from Edom, treading the winepress.

Leader: He showed the tefillin-knot to Moses, humble, wise,
when the LORD's likeness was before his eyes.

Cong: He delights in His people; the humble He does raise –
He glories in them; He sits enthroned upon their praise.

Leader: Your first word, Your call to every age, is true:
O seek the people who seek You.

Cong: My many songs please take and hear
and may my hymn of joy to You come near.

Leader: May my praise be a crown for Your head,
and like incense before You, the prayers I have said.

Cong: May a poor man's song be precious in Your eyes,
like a song sung over sacrifice.

Leader: To the One who sustains all, may my blessing take flight:
Creator, Life-Giver, God of right and might.

Cong: And when I offer blessing, to me Your head incline:
accepting it as spice, fragrant and fine.

Leader: May my prayer be to You sweet song.
For You my soul will always long.

The Ark is closed.

Yours, LORD, are the greatness and the power, the glory, the majesty and *1 Chr. 29*
splendor, for everything in heaven and earth is Yours. Yours, LORD, is the
kingdom; You are exalted as Head over all. ▸ Who can tell of the mighty *Ps. 106*
acts of the LORD and make all His praise be heard?

שׁ״ץ: מַחְלְפוֹת רֹאשׁוֹ כְּבִימֵי בְחוּרוֹת, קְוֻצּוֹתָיו תַּלְתַּלִּים שְׁחוֹרוֹת.
קהל: נְוֵה הַצֶּדֶק צְבִי תִפְאַרְתּוֹ, יַעֲלֶה נָּא עַל רֹאשׁ שִׂמְחָתוֹ.

שׁ״ץ: סְגֻלָּתוֹ תְּהִי בְיָדוֹ עֲטֶרֶת, וּצְנִיף מְלוּכָה צְבִי תִפְאֶרֶת.
קהל: עֲמוּסִים נְשָׂאָם, עֲטֶרֶת עִנְּדָם, מֵאֲשֶׁר יָקְרוּ בְעֵינָיו כִּבְּדָם.

שׁ״ץ: פְּאֵרוֹ עָלַי וּפְאֵרִי עָלָיו, וְקָרוֹב אֵלַי בְּקָרְאִי אֵלָיו.
קהל: צַח וְאָדֹם לִלְבוּשׁוֹ אָדֹם, פּוּרָה בְדָרְכוֹ בְּבוֹאוֹ מֵאֱדוֹם.

שׁ״ץ: קֶשֶׁר תְּפִלִּין הֶרְאָה לֶעָנָו, תְּמוּנַת יהוה לְנֶגֶד עֵינָיו.
קהל: רוֹצֶה בְעַמּוֹ עֲנָוִים יְפָאֵר, יוֹשֵׁב תְּהִלּוֹת בָּם לְהִתְפָּאֵר.

שׁ״ץ: רֹאשׁ דְּבָרְךָ אֱמֶת קוֹרֵא מֵרֹאשׁ דּוֹר וָדוֹר, עַם דּוֹרֶשְׁךָ דְּרֹשׁ.
קהל: שִׁית הֲמוֹן שִׁירַי נָא עָלֶיךָ, וְרִנָּתִי תִּקְרַב אֵלֶיךָ.

שׁ״ץ: תְּהִלָּתִי תְּהִי לְרֹאשְׁךָ עֲטֶרֶת, וּתְפִלָּתִי תִּכּוֹן קְטֹרֶת.
קהל: תִּיקַר שִׁירַת רָשׁ בְּעֵינֶיךָ, כַּשִּׁיר יוּשַׁר עַל קָרְבָּנֶיךָ.

שׁ״ץ: בִּרְכָתִי תַעֲלֶה לְרֹאשׁ מַשְׁבִּיר, מְחוֹלֵל וּמוֹלִיד, צַדִּיק כַּבִּיר.
קהל: וּבְבִרְכָתִי תְנַעֲנַע לִי רֹאשׁ, וְאוֹתָהּ קַח לְךָ כִּבְשָׂמִים רֹאשׁ.

שׁ״ץ: יֶעֱרַב נָא שִׂיחִי עָלֶיךָ, כִּי נַפְשִׁי תַעֲרֹג אֵלֶיךָ.

The ארון קודש *is closed.*

לְךָ יהוה הַגְּדֻלָּה וְהַגְּבוּרָה וְהַתִּפְאֶרֶת וְהַנֵּצַח וְהַהוֹד, כִּי־כֹל בַּשָּׁמַיִם דברי הימים א׳ כט
וּבָאָרֶץ, לְךָ יהוה הַמַּמְלָכָה וְהַמִּתְנַשֵּׂא לְכֹל לְרֹאשׁ: › מִי יְמַלֵּל גְּבוּרוֹת תהלים קו
יהוה, יַשְׁמִיעַ כָּל־תְּהִלָּתוֹ:

Hence the various literary forms – metaphor, image, mystic vision – used by the prophets and poets and their successors to indicate, through words, that which lies beyond words. The images are many, but God is One.

In some communities the hymn is said each day. Many authorities, however, held that it was too sublime to be said daily, and limited its recital to Shabbat and Yom Tov.

MOURNER'S KADDISH

The following prayer, said by mourners, requires the presence of a minyan.
A transliteration can be found on page 1334.

Mourner: יִתְגַּדַּל Magnified and sanctified
may His great name be,
in the world He created by His will.
May He establish His kingdom
in your lifetime and in your days,
and in the lifetime of all the house of Israel,
swiftly and soon –
and say: Amen.

All: May His great name
be blessed for ever and all time.

Mourner: Blessed and praised,
glorified and exalted,
raised and honored,
uplifted and lauded
be the name of the Holy One,
blessed be He,
beyond any blessing,
song, praise and consolation
uttered in the world –
and say: Amen.

May there be great peace from heaven,
and life for us and all Israel –
and say: Amen.

Bow, take three steps back, as if taking leave of the Divine Presence, then bow, first left, then right, then center, while saying:

May He who makes peace in His high places,
make peace for us and all Israel –
and say: Amen.

קדיש יתום

The following prayer, said by mourners, requires the presence of a מנין*.*
A transliteration can be found on page 1334.

אבל: יִתְגַּדַּל וְיִתְקַדַּשׁ שְׁמֵהּ רַבָּא (קהל: אָמֵן)
בְּעָלְמָא דִּי בְרָא כִרְעוּתֵהּ
וְיַמְלִיךְ מַלְכוּתֵהּ
בְּחַיֵּיכוֹן וּבְיוֹמֵיכוֹן וּבְחַיֵּי דְכָל בֵּית יִשְׂרָאֵל
בַּעֲגָלָא וּבִזְמַן קָרִיב, וְאִמְרוּ אָמֵן. (קהל: אָמֵן)

קהל ואבל: יְהֵא שְׁמֵהּ רַבָּא מְבָרַךְ לְעָלַם וּלְעָלְמֵי עָלְמַיָּא.

אבל: יִתְבָּרַךְ וְיִשְׁתַּבַּח וְיִתְפָּאַר
וְיִתְרוֹמַם וְיִתְנַשֵּׂא וְיִתְהַדָּר וְיִתְעַלֶּה וְיִתְהַלָּל
שְׁמֵהּ דְּקֻדְשָׁא בְּרִיךְ הוּא (קהל: בְּרִיךְ הוּא)
לְעֵלָּא מִן כָּל בִּרְכָתָא
/ בשבת שובה: לְעֵלָּא לְעֵלָּא מִכָּל בִּרְכָתָא/
וְשִׁירָתָא, תֻּשְׁבְּחָתָא וְנֶחֱמָתָא
דַּאֲמִירָן בְּעָלְמָא
וְאִמְרוּ אָמֵן. (קהל: אָמֵן)

יְהֵא שְׁלָמָא רַבָּא מִן שְׁמַיָּא
וְחַיִּים, עָלֵינוּ וְעַל כָּל יִשְׂרָאֵל
וְאִמְרוּ אָמֵן. (קהל: אָמֵן)

Bow, take three steps back, as if taking leave of the Divine Presence,
then bow, first left, then right, then center, while saying:

עֹשֶׂה שָׁלוֹם/ בשבת שובה: הַשָּׁלוֹם/ בִּמְרוֹמָיו
הוּא יַעֲשֶׂה שָׁלוֹם עָלֵינוּ וְעַל כָּל יִשְׂרָאֵל
וְאִמְרוּ אָמֵן. (קהל: אָמֵן)

LORD OF THE UNIVERSE,
who reigned before the birth of any thing –

When by His will all things were made
then was His name proclaimed King.

And when all things shall cease to be
He alone will reign in awe.

He was, He is, and He shall be
glorious for evermore.

He is One, there is none else,
alone, unique, beyond compare;

Without beginning, without end,
His might, His rule are everywhere.

He is my God; my Redeemer lives.
He is the Rock on whom I rely –

My banner and my safe retreat,
my cup, my portion when I cry.

Into His hand my soul I place,
when I awake and when I sleep.

The LORD is with me, I shall not fear;
body and soul from harm will He keep.

---

a personal presence. Though He is unfathomably vast, He is also intensely close. I face the world without fear because I rest in His everlasting arms.

אֲדוֹן עוֹלָם

אֲשֶׁר מָלַךְ בְּטֶרֶם כׇּל־יְצִיר נִבְרָא.
לְעֵת נַעֲשָׂה בְחֶפְצוֹ כֹּל אֲזַי מֶלֶךְ שְׁמוֹ נִקְרָא.
וְאַחֲרֵי כִּכְלוֹת הַכֹּל לְבַדּוֹ יִמְלֹךְ נוֹרָא.
וְהוּא הָיָה וְהוּא הֹוֶה וְהוּא יִהְיֶה בְּתִפְאָרָה.
וְהוּא אֶחָד וְאֵין שֵׁנִי לְהַמְשִׁיל לוֹ לְהַחְבִּירָה.
בְּלִי רֵאשִׁית בְּלִי תַכְלִית וְלוֹ הָעֹז וְהַמִּשְׂרָה.
וְהוּא אֵלִי וְחַי גֹּאֲלִי וְצוּר חֶבְלִי בְּעֵת צָרָה.
וְהוּא נִסִּי וּמָנוֹס לִי מְנָת כּוֹסִי בְּיוֹם אֶקְרָא.
בְּיָדוֹ אַפְקִיד רוּחִי בְּעֵת אִישַׁן וְאָעִירָה.
וְעִם רוּחִי גְּוִיָּתִי יהוה לִי וְלֹא אִירָא.

אֲדוֹן עוֹלָם *Lord of the Universe:* A magnificent poem, attributed by some to the Spanish Jewish poet Solomon ibn Gabirol (1021–1070). Its power lies in its effortless transition from abstract theology to personal experience. The first six lines speak of God in cosmic terms; the last four lines turn to God as

Kiddush and Zemirot for Shabbat Morning

Some say:

אַתְקִינוּ Prepare the feast of perfect faith, joy of the holy King. Prepare the royal feast, this is the feast [mystically known as] "the Holy Ancient One" – and "the Small Face" and "the Field of Holy Apples" [mystical terms for aspects of the Divine] come to partake in the feast with it.

אֲסַדֵּר I will prepare the Sabbath morning feast, and invite to it "the Holy Ancient One." May His radiance shine on it, on the great Kiddush and goodly wine that gladdens the soul. May He send us His splendor; may we see His glory; may He reveal to us His whispered secrets. May He disclose to us the reason for the twelve loaves of bread, which are [the twelve combinations of the letters of] His name, and [the twelve sons of Jacob] the youngest patriarch. May we be united with the One above, who gives life to all; may our strength increase and [our prayers] reach [God's] head. Laborers in the field [of Torah] rejoice with speech and voice, speaking words sweet as honey. Before the Master of the Universe, reveal the meaning of, and give new interpretations to, matters veiled in mystery. To adorn the table with precious secrets, deep, esoteric, not widely to be shared. These words become sky; new heavens, and the sun then is the same. He will be lifted to a higher level, and [God] will take [Israel], from whom He had been separated, as His bride.

חַי יהוה The Lord lives; my Rock is blessed. My soul glories in the Lord. For the Lord gives light to my lamp; His radiance shines on my head. The Lord is my Shepherd, I shall not want. He leads me beside the still waters. He gives food to all flesh; He feeds me my daily bread. May it be Your will, You, my holy God, To prepare a table before me, to anoint my head with oil. Who will lay my rest before the Lord of peace, and grant that my children stay faithful, [blessed with] life and peace? May He send His angel before me, to accompany me on the way. I lift my face with a cup of salvation; my cup is filled to overflowing. My soul thirsts for the Lord; may He fill my store with plenty. I lift my eyes to the sages, [celebrating Shabbat] like Hillel, not Shammai. Most delightful of days and eternity's years; awake, my soul, awake. Above my head let there shine as one, the lamp of the commandments and the Torah's light. Advance, Lord, to where I rest; You and Your mighty Ark. Please, God, take my blessing and strengthen the shield of Your seer.

מִזְמוֹר לְדָוִד A psalm of David. The Lord is my Shepherd, I shall not want. He makes *Ps. 23*
me lie down in green pastures. He leads me beside the still waters. He refreshes my soul. He guides me in the paths of righteousness for His name's sake. Though I walk through the valley of the shadow of death, I will fear no evil, for You are with me; Your rod and Your staff, they comfort me. You set a table before me in the presence of my enemies; You anoint my head with oil; my cup is filled to overflowing. May goodness and kindness follow me all the days of my life, and may I live in the House of the Lord for evermore.

קידוש וזמירות ליום שבת

Some say:

אַתְקִֽינוּ סְעוּדְתָא דִמְהֵימְנוּתָא שְׁלִימְתָא, חֶדְוְתָא דְמַלְכָּא קַדִּישָׁא. אַתְקִֽינוּ סְעוּדְתָא דְמַלְכָּא. דָּא הִיא סְעוּדְתָא דְעַתִּיקָא קַדִּישָׁא, וּזְעֵיר אַנְפִּין וַחֲקַל תַּפּוּחִין קַדִּישִׁין אָתַיִן לְסַעֲדָה בַּהֲדֵהּ.

אֲסַדֵּר לִסְעוּדְתָא בְּצַפְרָא דְשַׁבַּתָּא   וְאַזְמִין בַּהּ הַשְׁתָּא עַתִּיקָא קַדִּישָׁא.
נְהוֹרֵהּ יִשְׁרֵי בַהּ בְּקִדּוּשָׁא רַבָּה   וּמֵחַמְרָא טָבָא דְּבֵהּ תֶּחְדֵּי נַפְשָׁא.
יְשַׁדַּר לַן שְׁפְרֵהּ וְנֶחֱזֵי בִיקָרֵהּ   וְיַחֲזֵי לַן סִתְרֵהּ דְּמִתְאֲמַר בִּלְחִישָׁא.
יְגַלֵּה לַן טַעֲמֵי דְּבִתְרֵיסַר נַהֲמֵי   דְּאִנּוּן אָת בִּשְׁמֵהּ כְּפִילָה וּקְלִישָׁא.
צְרוֹרָא דִלְעֵלָּא דְבֵהּ חַיֵּי כֹלָּא   וְיִתְרַבֵּי חֵילָא וְתִסַּק עַד רֵישָׁא.
חֲדוּ חַצְדֵי חַקְלָא בְּדִבּוּר וּבְקָלָא   וּמַלְּלוּ מִלָּה מְתִיקָא כְּדֻבְשָׁא.
קֳדָם רִבּוֹן עָלְמִין בְּמִלִּין סְתִימִין   תְּגַלּוּן פִּתְגָּמִין וְתֵימְרוּן חִדּוּשָׁא.
לְעַטֵּר פָּתוֹרָא בְּרָזָא יַקִּירָא   עֲמִיקָא וּטְמִירָא וְלָאו מִלְּתָא אֲוֹשָׁא.
וְאִלֵּין מִלַּיָּא יְהוֹן לִרְקִיעַיָּא   חֲדְתִין וּשְׁמַיָּא בְּכֵן הַהוּא שִׁמְשָׁא.
רְבוּ יַתִּיר יִסְגֵּי לְעֵילָּא מִן דַּרְגֵּהּ   וְיִסַּב בַּת זוּגֵהּ דַּהֲוָת פְּרִישָׁא.

חַי יהוה וּבָרוּךְ צוּרִי, בַּיהוה תִּתְהַלֵּל נַפְשִׁי, כִּי יהוה יָאִיר נֵרִי, בְּהִלּוֹ נֵרוֹ עֲלֵי רֹאשִׁי.
יהוה רוֹעִי לֹא אֶחְסָר, עַל מֵי מְנוּחוֹת יְנַהֲלֵנִי, נוֹתֵן לֶחֶם לְכָל בָּשָׂר, לֶחֶם חֻקִּי הַטְרִיפֵנִי.
יְהִי רָצוֹן מִלְּפָנֶיךָ, אַתָּה אֱלֹהַי קְדוֹשִׁי, תַּעֲרֹךְ לְפָנַי שֻׁלְחָנֶךָ, תְּדַשֵּׁן בַּשֶּׁמֶן רֹאשִׁי.
מִי יִתֵּן מְנוּחָתִי, לִפְנֵי אֲדוֹן הַשָּׁלוֹם, וְהָיְתָה שְׁלֵמָה מִטָּתִי, הַחַיִּים וְהַשָּׁלוֹם.
יִשְׁלַח מַלְאָכוֹ לְפָנַי, לְלַוּוֹתִי לְוָיָה, בְּכוֹס יְשׁוּעוֹת אֶשָּׂא פָנַי, מְנָת כּוֹסִי רְוָיָה.
צָמְאָה נַפְשִׁי אֶל יהוה, יְמַלֵּא שֹׂבַע אֲסָמַי, אֶל הֶהָרִים אֶשָּׂא עֵינַי, כְּהִלֵּל וְלֹא כְשַׁמַּאי.
חֶדְוַת יָמִים וּשְׁנוֹת עוֹלָמִים, עוּרָה כְבוֹדִי עוּרָה, וְעַל רֹאשִׁי יִהְיוּ תַמִּים,
נֵר מִצְוָה וְאוֹר תּוֹרָה.
קוּמָה יהוה לִמְנוּחָתִי, אַתָּה וַאֲרוֹן עֻזֶּךָ, קַח נָא אֵל אֶת בִּרְכָתִי, וְהַחֲזֵק מָגֵן חוֹזֶךָ.

תהלים כג מִזְמוֹר לְדָוִד, יהוה רֹעִי לֹא אֶחְסָר: בִּנְאוֹת דֶּשֶׁא יַרְבִּיצֵנִי, עַל־מֵי מְנֻחוֹת יְנַהֲלֵנִי: נַפְשִׁי יְשׁוֹבֵב, יַנְחֵנִי בְמַעְגְּלֵי־צֶדֶק לְמַעַן שְׁמוֹ: גַּם כִּי־אֵלֵךְ בְּגֵיא צַלְמָוֶת לֹא־אִירָא רָע, כִּי־אַתָּה עִמָּדִי, שִׁבְטְךָ וּמִשְׁעַנְתֶּךָ הֵמָּה יְנַחֲמֻנִי: תַּעֲרֹךְ לְפָנַי שֻׁלְחָן נֶגֶד צֹרְרָי, דִּשַּׁנְתָּ בַשֶּׁמֶן רֹאשִׁי, כּוֹסִי רְוָיָה: אַךְ טוֹב וָחֶסֶד יִרְדְּפוּנִי כָּל־יְמֵי חַיָּי, וְשַׁבְתִּי בְּבֵית־יהוה לְאֹרֶךְ יָמִים:

SHABBAT MORNING KIDDUSH

Some say:

אִם־תָּשִׁיב If you keep your feet from breaking the Sabbath, and from pursuing your affairs on My holy day, if you call the Sabbath a delight, and the LORD's holy day honorable, and if you honor it by not going your own way or attending to your own affairs, or speaking idle words, then you will find joy in the LORD, and I will cause you to ride on the heights of the earth and to feast on the inheritance of your father Jacob, for the mouth of the LORD has spoken. *Is. 58*

Most begin Kiddush here. On Yom Tov that falls on Shabbat, say the Kiddush on page 768.

וְשָׁמְרוּ The children of Israel must keep the Sabbath, observing the Sabbath in every generation as an everlasting covenant. It is a sign between Me and the children of Israel for ever, for in six days the LORD made the heavens and the earth, but on the seventh day He ceased work and refreshed Himself. *Ex. 31*

זָכוֹר Remember the Sabbath day to keep it holy. Six days you shall labor and do all your work, but the seventh day is a Sabbath of the LORD your God; on it you shall not do any work – you, your son or daughter, your male or female slave, or your cattle, or the stranger within your gates. For in six days the LORD made heaven and earth and sea and all that is in them, and rested on the seventh day; therefore the LORD blessed the Sabbath day and declared it holy. *Ex. 20*

When saying Kiddush for others, add:

Please pay attention, my masters.

בָּרוּךְ Blessed are You, LORD our God, King of the Universe,
who creates the fruit of the vine.

On Shabbat Ḥol HaMo'ed Sukkot, if Kiddush is made in the sukka, add:

Blessed are You, LORD our God, King of the Universe,
who has made us holy through His commandments,
and has commanded us to dwell in the sukka.

---

the author's name. חַי יהוה *The LORD lives*: A seventeenth-century poem whose verses spell out the name *Ḥayyim Yitzḥak*. אִם־תָּשִׁיב מִשַּׁבָּת רַגְלֶךָ *If you keep your feet*: the passage from Isaiah that is the source of the idea of *oneg Shabbat*, making the day a delight. וְשָׁמְרוּ בְנֵי־יִשְׂרָאֵל *The children of Israel:* Shabbat as a memorial of creation. זָכוֹר אֶת־יוֹם הַשַּׁבָּת *Remember the Sabbath day:* Shabbat as a memory of the exodus from Egypt. The freedom of Shabbat is the antithesis of slavery in Egypt.

קידושא רבה

Some say:

אִם־תָּשִׁיב מִשַּׁבָּת רַגְלֶךָ עֲשׂוֹת חֲפָצֶךָ בְּיוֹם קָדְשִׁי, וְקָרָאתָ לַשַּׁבָּת עֹנֶג לִקְדוֹשׁ ישעיה נח
יהוה מְכֻבָּד, וְכִבַּדְתּוֹ מֵעֲשׂוֹת דְּרָכֶיךָ מִמְּצוֹא חֶפְצְךָ וְדַבֵּר דָּבָר: אָז תִּתְעַנַּג עַל־
יהוה, וְהִרְכַּבְתִּיךָ עַל־בָּמֳתֵי אָרֶץ, וְהַאֲכַלְתִּיךָ נַחֲלַת יַעֲקֹב אָבִיךָ, כִּי פִּי יהוה דִּבֵּר:

Most begin קידוש *here. On* יום טוב *that falls on* שבת *say the* קידוש *on page 769.*

וְשָׁמְרוּ בְנֵי־יִשְׂרָאֵל אֶת־הַשַּׁבָּת, לַעֲשׂוֹת אֶת־הַשַּׁבָּת לְדֹרֹתָם שמות לא
בְּרִית עוֹלָם: בֵּינִי וּבֵין בְּנֵי יִשְׂרָאֵל אוֹת הִוא לְעֹלָם, כִּי־שֵׁשֶׁת יָמִים
עָשָׂה יהוה אֶת־הַשָּׁמַיִם וְאֶת־הָאָרֶץ וּבַיּוֹם הַשְּׁבִיעִי שָׁבַת וַיִּנָּפַשׁ:

זָכוֹר אֶת־יוֹם הַשַּׁבָּת לְקַדְּשׁוֹ: שֵׁשֶׁת יָמִים תַּעֲבֹד, וְעָשִׂיתָ כָּל־ שמות כ
מְלַאכְתֶּךָ: וְיוֹם הַשְּׁבִיעִי שַׁבָּת לַיהוה אֱלֹהֶיךָ, לֹא־תַעֲשֶׂה כָל־
מְלָאכָה אַתָּה וּבִנְךָ וּבִתֶּךָ, עַבְדְּךָ וַאֲמָתְךָ וּבְהֶמְתֶּךָ, וְגֵרְךָ אֲשֶׁר
בִּשְׁעָרֶיךָ: כִּי שֵׁשֶׁת־יָמִים עָשָׂה יהוה אֶת־הַשָּׁמַיִם וְאֶת־הָאָרֶץ
אֶת־הַיָּם וְאֶת־כָּל־אֲשֶׁר־בָּם, וַיָּנַח בַּיּוֹם הַשְּׁבִיעִי, עַל־כֵּן בֵּרַךְ יהוה
אֶת־יוֹם הַשַּׁבָּת וַיְקַדְּשֵׁהוּ:

When saying קידוש *for others, add:*

סַבְרִי מָרָנָן

בָּרוּךְ אַתָּה יהוה אֱלֹהֵינוּ מֶלֶךְ הָעוֹלָם, בּוֹרֵא פְּרִי הַגָּפֶן.

On שבת חול המועד סוכות *if* קידוש *is made in the* סוכה *add:*

בָּרוּךְ אַתָּה יהוה אֱלֹהֵינוּ מֶלֶךְ הָעוֹלָם
אֲשֶׁר קִדְּשָׁנוּ בְּמִצְוֹתָיו וְצִוָּנוּ לֵישֵׁב בַּסֻּכָּה.

SHABBAT MORNING KIDDUSH

The Kiddush of Shabbat morning is known as *Kiddusha Raba*, "the great Kiddush," despite or possibly because of its brevity: essentially it involves only the blessing over wine. Over the course of time additional texts were added, reflecting the varied customs of Jewish communities. אַתְקִינוּ סְעוּדָתָא *Prepare the feast* (on previous page): a mystical passage based in the *Zohar*. אֲסַדֵּר *I will prepare:* A poem written by R. Isaac Luria. The verses form an acrostic based on

ZEMIROT FOR SHABBAT DAY

בָּרוּךְ Blessed be the Lord who, day by day, carries our burden with salvation and redemption. We will rejoice in His name all day long, and raise our head high in His salvation. For He is a stronghold for the poor and a refuge for the needy.

The Lord's tribes are Israel's testimony: He was distressed in their distress, in their suffering and slavery. Through a pavement of sapphire He showed them the strength of His love, He revealed Himself, lifting them from the depths of the pit. For with the Lord is loving- *Ps. 130*
kindness; He abounds in redemption.

How precious is His loving-kindness; He shelters them under His shade. For their sake He went with them into exile in Babylon. When they went down in ships, He was counted among them. He ensured that they were treated mercifully by those who took them captive. For the Lord will not forsake His people, for the sake of His great name.

In Eilam He placed His throne, to rescue His beloved, to remove from them the stronghold of His rebels. He redeemed His servants from passing under the sword. He raised the pride of His people, for the glory of all His devoted ones. For though He afflicts, He also shows *Lam. 3*
compassion and loving-kindness.

When the he-goat [Greece] extended its power, and the vision of the four ascended to the heights, And in their hearts they intended to destroy those He loved, through His priests He laid low those who rose against Him: The Lord's kindness has not ended nor His *Lam. 3*
compassion ceased.

I was handed over to Edom [Rome] by my quarrelsome friends, who daily sated their appetite with my treasures. His help was with me, supporting my foundations, He will not forsake me all the days of my age. For the Lord does not reject forever. *Lam. 3*

When He comes from Edom with garments stained crimson, there will be slaughter in Botzra, and an execution of traitors, their blood will turn His garments red, in His great strength He will bring the leaders low. With His mighty blast like a day of the east wind. *Is. 27*

When the oppressor from Edom sees how it will be, He will think Botzra to be a refuge like Betzer, giving protection to angels and men, willful and accidental sinners alike. Love the *Ps. 31*
Lord, all His devoted ones: all His faithful ones He will guard.

The Rock in His kindness will command His communities to gather, coming together from the four winds, He will settle them upon the high mountains, He will return with us, gathering the dispersed, for it does not say, "He will bring back" but "He will return" and gather.

Blessed is our God who has bestowed good upon us. In His compassion and abundant kindness, He has done great things for us. Like these and those, may He do yet more for us, to magnify His great, mighty and awesome name, by which we are called.

Blessed is our God who created us for His glory, To praise and laud Him and tell of His majesty, His loving-kindness is greater to us than to any other nation. Therefore with all our heart and soul and might, let us proclaim His kingship and His unity.

May He to whom peace belongs, send us blessing and peace. From left and right, may Israel have peace. May the Compassionate One bless His people with peace, and may they merit to see children and children's children, occupied with Torah and the commandments, bringing Israel peace. Wondrous Counselor, mighty God, everlasting Father, Prince of peace. *Is. 9*

זמירות ליום שבת

בָּרוּךְ אֲדֹנָי יוֹם יוֹם, יַעֲמָס לָנוּ יֶשַׁע וּפִדְיוֹם, וּבִשְׁמוֹ נָגִיל כָּל הַיּוֹם, וּבִישׁוּעָתוֹ נָרִים רֹאשׁ עֶלְיוֹן. כִּי הוּא מָעוֹז לַדָּל וּמַחְסֶה לָאֶבְיוֹן.

שִׁבְטֵי יָהּ לְיִשְׂרָאֵל עֵדוּת, בְּצָרָתָם לוֹ צָר בְּסִבְלוּת וּבְעַבְדוּת, בְּלִבְנַת הַסַּפִּיר הֶרְאָם עֹז יְדִידוּת, וְנִגְלָה לְהַעֲלוֹתָם מֵעֹמֶק בּוֹר וָדוּת. כִּי־עִם־יהוה הַחֶסֶד, וְהַרְבֵּה עִמּוֹ פְדוּת: תהלים קל

מַה יָּקָר חַסְדּוֹ בְּצִלּוֹ לְגוֹנְנֵמוֹ, בְּגָלוּת בָּבֶלָה שֻׁלַּח לְמַעֲנֵמוֹ, לְהוֹרִיד בָּרִיחִים נִמְנָה בֵינֵימוֹ, וַיִּתְּנֵם לְרַחֲמִים לִפְנֵי שׁוֹבֵימוֹ. כִּי לֹא יִטֹּשׁ יהוה אֶת עַמּוֹ, בַּעֲבוּר הַגָּדוֹל שְׁמוֹ.

עֵילָם שָׁת כִּסְאוֹ לְהַצִּיל יְדִידָיו, לְהַאֲבִיד מִשָּׁם מָעֻזְנֵי מוֹרְדָיו, מֵעֲבֹר בַּשֶּׁלַח פָּדָה אֶת עֲבָדָיו, קֶרֶן לְעַמּוֹ יָרִים, תְּהִלָּה לְכָל חֲסִידָיו. כִּי אִם־הוֹגָה, וְרִחַם כְּרֹב חֲסָדָו: איכה ג

וּצְפִיר הָעִזִּים הִגְדִּיל עֲצוּמָיו, וְגַם חָזוֹת אַרְבַּע עָלוּ לִמְרוֹמָיו, וּבְלִבָּם דִּמּוּ לְהַשְׁחִית אֶת רְחוּמָיו, עַל יְדֵי כֹהֲנָיו מִגֵּר מִתְקוֹמְמָיו. חַסְדֵי יהוה כִּי לֹא־תָמְנוּ, כִּי לֹא כָלוּ רַחֲמָיו: איכה ג

נִסְגַּרְתִּי לֶאֱדוֹם בְּיַד רֵעַי מְדָנַי, שֶׁבְּכָל יוֹם מְמַלְּאִים כְּרֵסָם מֵעֲדָנַי, עֶזְרָתוֹ עִמִּי לִסְמֹךְ אֶת אֲדָנַי, וְלֹא נְטַשְׁתַּנִי כָּל יְמֵי עִדָּנַי. כִּי לֹא יִזְנַח לְעוֹלָם אֲדֹנָי: איכה ג

בְּבוֹאוֹ מֵאֱדוֹם חֲמוּץ בְּגָדִים, זֶבַח לוֹ בְּבָצְרָה וְטֶבַח לוֹ בְּבוֹגְדִים, וְיֵז נִצְחָם מַלְבּוּשָׁיו לְהַאְדִּים, בְּכֹחוֹ הַגָּדוֹל יִבְצֹר רוּחַ נְגִידִים. הָגָה בְּרוּחוֹ הַקָּשָׁה בְּיוֹם קָדִים: ישעיה כז

רְאוֹתוֹ כִּי כֵן אֲדוֹמִי הָעוֹצֵר, יַחְשֹׁב לוֹ בָּצְרָה תִּקְלֹט כְּבֶצֶר, וּמַלְאָךְ כְּאָדָם בְּתוֹכָהּ יִנָּצֵר, וּמֵזִיד כַּשּׁוֹגֵג בְּמִקְלָט יֵעָצֵר. אֶהֱבוּ אֶת־יהוה כָּל־חֲסִידָיו, אֱמוּנִים נֹצֵר: תהלים לא

יְצַוֶּה צוּר חַסְדּוֹ קְהִלּוֹתָיו לְקַבֵּץ, מֵאַרְבַּע רוּחוֹת עָדָיו לְהִקָּבֵץ, וּבְהַר מְרוֹם הָרִים אוֹתָנוּ לְהַרְבֵּץ, וְאִתָּנוּ יָשׁוּב נִדָּחִים קוֹבֵץ. יָשִׁיב לֹא נֶאֱמַר, כִּי אִם וְשָׁב וְקִבֵּץ.

בָּרוּךְ הוּא אֱלֹהֵינוּ אֲשֶׁר טוֹב גְּמָלָנוּ, כְּרַחֲמָיו וּכְרֹב חֲסָדָיו הִגְדִּיל לָנוּ, אֵלֶּה וְכָאֵלֶּה יוֹסֵף עִמָּנוּ, לְהַגְדִּיל שְׁמוֹ הַגָּדוֹל הַגִּבּוֹר וְהַנּוֹרָא, שֶׁנִּקְרָא עָלֵינוּ.

בָּרוּךְ הוּא אֱלֹהֵינוּ שֶׁבְּרָאָנוּ לִכְבוֹדוֹ, לְהַלְּלוֹ וּלְשַׁבְּחוֹ וּלְסַפֵּר הוֹדוֹ, מִכָּל אֹם גָּבַר עָלֵינוּ חַסְדּוֹ, לָכֵן בְּכָל לֵב וּבְכָל נֶפֶשׁ וּבְכָל מְאוֹדוֹ, נַמְלִיכוֹ וּנְיַחֲדוֹ.

שֶׁהַשָּׁלוֹם שֶׁלּוֹ יָשִׂים עָלֵינוּ בְּרָכָה וְשָׁלוֹם, מִשְּׂמֹאל וּמִיָּמִין עַל יִשְׂרָאֵל שָׁלוֹם, הָרַחֲמָן הוּא יְבָרֵךְ אֶת עַמּוֹ בַשָּׁלוֹם, וְיִזְכּוּ לִרְאוֹת בָּנִים וּבְנֵי בָנִים, עוֹסְקִים, בַּתּוֹרָה וּבְמִצְוֹת, עַל יִשְׂרָאֵל שָׁלוֹם. פֶּלֶא יוֹעֵץ אֵל גִּבּוֹר אֲבִי־עַד שַׂר־שָׁלוֹם: ישעיה ט

בָּרוּךְ אֵל עֶלְיוֹן Blessed is God Most High who has given us rest,
To relieve our souls from distress and pain.
May He seek the good of Zion, the outcast city.
How long must she grieve, her spirits downcast?
All who keep the Sabbath, man and woman alike, find favor like an offering made to God.

He who rides the heavens, King of worlds,
Gently told His people to rest,
With tasty food and delicacies of all kinds,
With elegant dress, as at a family feast.
All who keep the Sabbath, man and woman alike, find favor like an offering made to God.

Happy are all who await a double reward
From the One who sees all, though He dwells in dense dark.
He will grant him a heritage in hill and valley,
A heritage and resting place like [Jacob] on whom the sun shone.
All who keep the Sabbath, man and woman alike, find favor like an offering made to God.

Whoever keeps the Sabbath fully, not profaning it,
Shows that he is worthy; holy is his lot.
Happy is he who fulfills the day's duty;
It is like a gift presented to God who fashioned him.
All who keep the Sabbath, man and woman alike, find favor like an offering made to God.

The Rock, my God, called it "Beloved of days."
Happy are the faithful if it is kept intact.
He will set on their head a close-fitting crown.
On them the Rock of Eternity will make His spirit rest.
All who keep the Sabbath, man and woman alike, find favor like an offering made to God.

He who remembers the Sabbath day to keep it holy
Will gain high honor like a diadem on his head.
Therefore let each give to his soul
Delight and joy with which to be exalted.
All who keep the Sabbath, man and woman alike, find favor like an offering made to God.

Let her be holy to you – Sabbath the queen –
Placing a blessing in your home.
In all your dwellings, do no work,
Nor your sons and daughters, your servant or maid.
All who keep the Sabbath, man and woman alike, find favor like an offering made to God.

בָּרוּךְ אֵל עֶלְיוֹן
אֲשֶׁר נָתַן מְנוּחָה, לְנַפְשֵׁנוּ פִדְיוֹן מִשֵּׁאת וַאֲנָחָה
וְהוּא יִדְרֹשׁ לְצִיּוֹן, עִיר הַנִּדָּחָה, עַד אָנָה תּוּגְיוֹן נֶפֶשׁ נֶאֱנָחָה.
הַשּׁוֹמֵר שַׁבָּת הַבֵּן עִם הַבַּת, לָאֵל יֵרָצוּ כְּמִנְחָה עַל מַחֲבַת.

רוֹכֵב בָּעֲרָבוֹת, מֶלֶךְ עוֹלָמִים, אֶת עַמּוֹ לִשְׁבֹּת אִזֵּן בַּנְּעִימִים
בְּמַאֲכָלוֹת עֲרֵבוֹת בְּמִינֵי מַטְעַמִּים, בְּמַלְבּוּשֵׁי כָבוֹד זֶבַח מִשְׁפָּחָה.
הַשּׁוֹמֵר שַׁבָּת הַבֵּן עִם הַבַּת, לָאֵל יֵרָצוּ כְּמִנְחָה עַל מַחֲבַת.

וְאַשְׁרֵי כָּל חוֹכֶה לְתַשְׁלוּמֵי כֵפֶל, מֵאֵת כֹּל סוֹכֶה, שׁוֹכֵן בָּעֲרָפֶל
נַחֲלָה לוֹ יִזְכֶּה בָּהָר וּבַשָּׁפֶל, נַחֲלָה וּמְנוּחָה כַּשֶּׁמֶשׁ לוֹ זָרְחָה.
הַשּׁוֹמֵר שַׁבָּת הַבֵּן עִם הַבַּת, לָאֵל יֵרָצוּ כְּמִנְחָה עַל מַחֲבַת.

כָּל שׁוֹמֵר שַׁבָּת כַּדָּת מֵחַלְּלוֹ, הֵן הֶכְשֵׁר חִבַּת קֹדֶשׁ גּוֹרָלוֹ
וְאִם יֵצֵא חוֹבַת הַיּוֹם, אַשְׁרֵי לוֹ, אֶל אֵל אָדוֹן מְחוֹלְלוֹ מִנְחָה הִיא שְׁלוּחָה.
הַשּׁוֹמֵר שַׁבָּת הַבֵּן עִם הַבַּת, לָאֵל יֵרָצוּ כְּמִנְחָה עַל מַחֲבַת.

חֶמְדַּת הַיָּמִים קְרָאוֹ אֵלִי צוּר, וְאַשְׁרֵי לִתְמִימִים אִם יִהְיֶה נָצוּר
כֶּתֶר הִלּוּמִים עַל רֹאשָׁם יָצוּר, צוּר הָעוֹלָמִים, רוּחוֹ בָּם נָחָה.
הַשּׁוֹמֵר שַׁבָּת הַבֵּן עִם הַבַּת, לָאֵל יֵרָצוּ כְּמִנְחָה עַל מַחֲבַת.

זָכוֹר אֶת יוֹם הַשַּׁבָּת לְקַדְּשׁוֹ, קַרְנוֹ כִּי גָבְהָה נֵזֶר עַל רֹאשׁוֹ
עַל כֵּן יִתֵּן הָאָדָם לְנַפְשׁוֹ, עֹנֶג וְגַם שִׂמְחָה בָּהֶם לְמָשְׁחָה.
הַשּׁוֹמֵר שַׁבָּת הַבֵּן עִם הַבַּת, לָאֵל יֵרָצוּ כְּמִנְחָה עַל מַחֲבַת.

קֹדֶשׁ הִיא לָכֶם שַׁבָּת הַמַּלְכָּה, אֶל תּוֹךְ בָּתֵּיכֶם לְהָנִיחַ בְּרָכָה
בְּכָל מוֹשְׁבוֹתֵיכֶם לֹא תַעֲשׂוּ מְלָאכָה, בְּנֵיכֶם וּבְנוֹתֵיכֶם עֶבֶד וְגַם שִׁפְחָה.
הַשּׁוֹמֵר שַׁבָּת הַבֵּן עִם הַבַּת, לָאֵל יֵרָצוּ כְּמִנְחָה עַל מַחֲבַת.

יוֹם זֶה מְכֻבָּד This day is honored above all others,
For on it He who formed worlds found rest.

For six days, do your work
But the seventh day is God's:
On the Sabbath you shall do no work,
For in six days He made all.

This day is honored above all others,
for on it He who formed worlds found rest.

Foremost among sacred days
Is this day of rest, this holy Sabbath.
So let each say Kiddush over wine,
And break bread over two complete loaves.

This day is honored above all others,
for on it He who formed worlds found rest.

Eat choice food, drink sweet wine,
For God will give to those who cleave to Him
Clothes to wear, due portions of bread,
Meat and fish, and all tasty foods.

This day is honored above all others,
for on it He who formed worlds found rest.

On it you shall lack nothing – so eat,
Be satisfied and bless
The Lord your God, whom you love,
For He has blessed you from all peoples.

This day is honored above all others,
for on it He who formed worlds found rest.

The heavens declare His glory
And the earth is full of His loving-kindness.
See all these things His hand has made
For He is the Rock, His work is perfect.

This day is honored above all others,
for on it He who formed worlds found rest.

יוֹם זֶה מְכֻבָּד מִכָּל יָמִים, כִּי בוֹ שָׁבַת צוּר עוֹלָמִים.

שֵׁשֶׁת יָמִים תַּעֲשֶׂה מְלַאכְתֶּךָ
וְיוֹם הַשְּׁבִיעִי לֵאלֹהֶיךָ
שַׁבָּת לֹא תַעֲשֶׂה בוֹ מְלָאכָה
כִּי כֹל עָשָׂה שֵׁשֶׁת יָמִים.
יוֹם זֶה מְכֻבָּד מִכָּל יָמִים, כִּי בוֹ שָׁבַת צוּר עוֹלָמִים.

רִאשׁוֹן הוּא לְמִקְרָאֵי קֹדֶשׁ
יוֹם שַׁבָּתוֹן יוֹם שַׁבַּת קֹדֶשׁ
עַל כֵּן כָּל אִישׁ בְּיֵינוֹ יְקַדֵּשׁ
עַל שְׁתֵּי לֶחֶם יִבְצְעוּ תְמִימִים.
יוֹם זֶה מְכֻבָּד מִכָּל יָמִים, כִּי בוֹ שָׁבַת צוּר עוֹלָמִים.

אֱכֹל מַשְׁמַנִּים, שְׁתֵה מַמְתַקִּים
כִּי אֵל יִתֵּן לְכֹל בּוֹ דְבֵקִים
בֶּגֶד לִלְבֹּשׁ, לֶחֶם חֻקִּים
בָּשָׂר וְדָגִים וְכָל מַטְעַמִּים.
יוֹם זֶה מְכֻבָּד מִכָּל יָמִים, כִּי בוֹ שָׁבַת צוּר עוֹלָמִים.

לֹא תֶחְסַר כֹּל בּוֹ, וְאָכַלְתָּ
וְשָׂבָעְתָּ וּבֵרַכְתָּ
אֶת יהוה אֱלֹהֶיךָ אֲשֶׁר אָהַבְתָּ
כִּי בֵרַכְךָ מִכָּל הָעַמִּים.
יוֹם זֶה מְכֻבָּד מִכָּל יָמִים, כִּי בוֹ שָׁבַת צוּר עוֹלָמִים.

הַשָּׁמַיִם מְסַפְּרִים כְּבוֹדוֹ
וְגַם הָאָרֶץ מָלְאָה חַסְדּוֹ
רְאוּ כָּל אֵלֶּה עָשְׂתָה יָדוֹ
כִּי הוּא הַצּוּר פָּעֳלוֹ תָמִים.
יוֹם זֶה מְכֻבָּד מִכָּל יָמִים, כִּי בוֹ שָׁבַת צוּר עוֹלָמִים.

יוֹם שַׁבָּתוֹן The day of rest should not be forgotten, Its memory is like sweet fragrance,
On it the dove found rest, And in it the exhausted rest.

This day is honored by the people of faith. Parents and children guard it with care.
It was engraved on two tablets of stone,
By the greatness of His power and His unfailing strength.

On it the dove found rest, And in it the exhausted rest.

All came together in a covenant: "We will do and we will obey," they said as one.
Then they responded, saying, "The Lord is One" –
Blessed is He who gives the weary strength.

On it the dove found rest, And in it the exhausted rest.

He spoke in His holiness on the Mount of Myrrh [Sinai]:
"Remember and observe the seventh day."
And learn together all His commands: Gird your loins and muster strength.

On it the dove found rest, And in it the exhausted rest.

The people who have wandered like a straying flock –
May He remember the covenant and the oath,
So that no harm should happen to them, As You swore at the end of Noah's flood.

On it the dove found rest, And in it the exhausted rest.

שַׁבָּת הַיּוֹם Today is the Sabbath of the Lord. Celebrate greatly with my songs,
Multiply my delicacies, Keep it like the Lord's command.

Today is the Sabbath of the Lord.

Do not travel beyond boundaries, Do not labor on this day:
Eat, drink, make merry. This is the day the Lord has made.

Today is the Sabbath of the Lord.

If you keep it God will guard you like the pupil of His eye,
You, your son and daughter too. If you call the Sabbath a delight
Then you will find delight before the Lord.

Today is the Sabbath of the Lord.

Eat rich foods and delicacies, Tasty dishes of many kinds,
Soft-shelled nuts and pomegranates: Eat, be satisfied and bless the Lord.

Today is the Sabbath of the Lord.

Make ready on the table delicious bread, And make, this day, three meals.
Bless and thank His glorious name. Take care, observe and do, my sons.

Today is the Sabbath of the Lord.

יוֹם שַׁבָּתוֹן אֵין לִשְׁכֹּחַ, זִכְרוֹ כְּרֵיחַ הַנִּיחֹחַ
יוֹנָה מָצְאָה בוֹ מָנוֹחַ וְשָׁם יָנוּחוּ יְגִיעֵי כֹחַ.

הַיּוֹם נִכְבָּד לִבְנֵי אֱמוּנִים, זְהִירִים לְשָׁמְרוֹ אָבוֹת וּבָנִים
חָקוּק בִּשְׁנֵי לוּחוֹת אֲבָנִים, מֵרֹב אוֹנִים וְאַמִּיץ כֹּחַ.

יוֹנָה מָצְאָה בוֹ מָנוֹחַ וְשָׁם יָנוּחוּ יְגִיעֵי כֹחַ.

וּבָאוּ כֻלָּם בִּבְרִית יַחַד, נַעֲשֶׂה וְנִשְׁמַע אָמְרוּ כְּאֶחָד
וּפָתְחוּ וְעָנוּ יהוה אֶחָד, בָּרוּךְ נֹתֵן לַיָּעֵף כֹּחַ.

יוֹנָה מָצְאָה בוֹ מָנוֹחַ וְשָׁם יָנוּחוּ יְגִיעֵי כֹחַ.

דִּבֶּר בְּקָדְשׁוֹ בְּהַר הַמֹּר, יוֹם הַשְּׁבִיעִי זָכוֹר וְשָׁמוֹר
וְכָל פִּקּוּדָיו יַחַד לִגְמֹר, חַזֵּק מָתְנַיִם וְאַמֵּץ כֹּחַ.

יוֹנָה מָצְאָה בוֹ מָנוֹחַ וְשָׁם יָנוּחוּ יְגִיעֵי כֹחַ.

הָעָם אֲשֶׁר נָע, כַּצֹּאן תָּעָה, יִזְכֹּר לְפָקְדוֹ בְּרִית וּשְׁבוּעָה
לְבַל יַעֲבָר בָּם מִקְרֵה רָעָה, כַּאֲשֶׁר נִשְׁבַּעְתָּ עַל מֵי נֹחַ.

יוֹנָה מָצְאָה בוֹ מָנוֹחַ וְשָׁם יָנוּחוּ יְגִיעֵי כֹחַ.

שַׁבָּת הַיּוֹם לַיהוה, מְאֹד צַהֲלוּ בְּרִנּוּנַי
וְגַם הַרְבּוּ מַעֲדַנַּי, אוֹתוֹ לִשְׁמֹר כְּמִצְוַת יהוה. שַׁבָּת הַיּוֹם לַיהוה.

מֵעֲבֹר דֶּרֶךְ וּגְבוּלִים, מֵעֲשׂוֹת הַיּוֹם פְּעָלִים
לֶאֱכֹל וְלִשְׁתּוֹת בְּהִלּוּלִים, זֶה הַיּוֹם עָשָׂה יהוה. שַׁבָּת הַיּוֹם לַיהוה.

וְאִם תִּשְׁמְרֶנּוּ, יָהּ יִנְצָרְךָ כְּבָבַת, אַתָּה וּבִנְךָ וְגַם הַבַּת
וְקָרָאתָ עֹנֶג לַשַּׁבָּת, אָז תִּתְעַנַּג עַל יהוה. שַׁבָּת הַיּוֹם לַיהוה.

אֱכֹל מַשְׁמַנִּים וּמַעֲדַנִּים, וּמַטְעַמִּים הַרְבֵּה מִינִים
אֱגוֹזֵי פֶרֶךְ וְרִמּוֹנִים, וְאָכַלְתָּ וְשָׂבָעְתָּ וּבֵרַכְתָּ אֶת יהוה. שַׁבָּת הַיּוֹם לַיהוה.

לַעֲרֹךְ בְּשֻׁלְחָן לֶחֶם חֲמוּדוֹת, לַעֲשׂוֹת הַיּוֹם שָׁלֹשׁ סְעוּדוֹת
אֶת הַשֵּׁם הַנִּכְבָּד לְבָרֵךְ וּלְהוֹדוֹת, שִׁקְדוּ וְשִׁמְרוּ וַעֲשׂוּ בָנַי. שַׁבָּת הַיּוֹם לַיהוה.

שִׁמְרוּ שַׁבְּתוֹתַי Observe My Sabbaths, so that you are nourished and sated,
From the radiance of My blessings,
when you come to rest. Borrow on My account, My children,
Delight in My pleasures: Today is the Sabbath of the LORD.

Borrow on My account, My children,
Delight in My pleasures: Today is the Sabbath of the LORD.

Proclaim freedom from toil, then I will grant My blessing,
joining one to the next,
bringing gladness on My day of joy. Wear clothes of fine linen and wool.
And learn from My elders: Today is the Sabbath of the LORD.

Borrow on My account, My children,
Delight in My pleasures: Today is the Sabbath of the LORD.

Quickly bring the portion, obey Esther's command.
Make a reckoning with the Creator,
He will repay you for the food, and more. Trust in Me, My faithful ones,
And drink wine from My plentiful supply. Today is the Sabbath of the LORD.

Borrow on My account, My children,
Delight in My pleasures: Today is the Sabbath of the LORD.

Today is a day of redemption, if you observe the Sabbath;
Then you will be My special treasure.
Stay [for the night of exile], then pass on. Then you will live before Me.
And be filled from My hidden store. Today is the Sabbath of the LORD.

Borrow on My account, My children,
Delight in My pleasures: Today is the Sabbath of the LORD.

Make my city strong, God, the God most high.
Bring back my Temple,
With joy and words of song. There may my singers chant,
My Levites and my priests.
Then you will delight in the LORD. Today is the Sabbath of the LORD.

Borrow on My account, My children,
Delight in My pleasures: Today is the Sabbath of the LORD.

שָׁמְרוּ שַׁבְּתוֹתַי, לְמַעַן תִּינְקוּ וּשְׂבַעְתֶּם, מִזִּיו בִּרְכוֹתַי
אֶל הַמְּנוּחָה כִּי בָאתֶם, וְלִוּוּ עָלַי בָּנַי, וְעִדְנוּ מַעֲדַנַּי
שַׁבָּת הַיּוֹם לַיהוה.
וְלִוּוּ עָלַי בָּנַי, וְעִדְנוּ מַעֲדַנַּי, שַׁבָּת הַיּוֹם לַיהוה.

לְעָמֵל קִרְאוּ דְרוֹר, וְנָתַתִּי אֶת בִּרְכָתִי, אִשָּׁה אֶל אֲחוֹתָהּ לִצְרֹר
לִגְלוֹת עַל יוֹם שִׂמְחָתִי, בִּגְדֵי שֵׁשׁ עִם שָׁנִי, וְהִתְבּוֹנְנוּ מִזִּקְנֵי
שַׁבָּת הַיּוֹם לַיהוה.
וְלִוּוּ עָלַי בָּנַי, וְעִדְנוּ מַעֲדַנַּי, שַׁבָּת הַיּוֹם לַיהוה.

מַהֲרוּ אֶת הַמָּנֶה, לַעֲשׂוֹת אֶת דְּבַר אֶסְתֵּר, וְחִשְּׁבוּ עִם הַקּוֹנֶה
לְשַׁלֵּם אָכוֹל וְהוֹתֵר, בִּטְחוּ בִי אֱמוּנַי, וּשְׁתוּ יֵין מִשְׁמַנַּי
שַׁבָּת הַיּוֹם לַיהוה.
וְלִוּוּ עָלַי בָּנַי, וְעִדְנוּ מַעֲדַנַּי, שַׁבָּת הַיּוֹם לַיהוה.

הִנֵּה יוֹם גְּאֻלָּה, יוֹם שַׁבָּת אִם תִּשְׁמֹרוּ, וִהְיִיתֶם לִי סְגֻלָּה
לִינוּ וְאַחַר תַּעֲבֹרוּ, וְאָז תִּחְיוּ לְפָנַי, וְתִמָּלְאוּ צְפוּנַי
שַׁבָּת הַיּוֹם לַיהוה.
וְלִוּוּ עָלַי בָּנַי, וְעִדְנוּ מַעֲדַנַּי, שַׁבָּת הַיּוֹם לַיהוה.

חֲזַק קְרִיתִי, אֵל אֱלֹהִים עֶלְיוֹן, וְהָשֵׁב אֶת נְוָתִי
בְּשִׂמְחָה וּבְהִגָּיוֹן, יְשׁוֹרְרוּ שָׁם רְנָנַי, לְוִיַּי וְכֹהֲנַי, אָז תִּתְעַנַּג עַל יהוה
שַׁבָּת הַיּוֹם לַיהוה.
וְלִוּוּ עָלַי בָּנַי, וְעִדְנוּ מַעֲדַנַּי, שַׁבָּת הַיּוֹם לַיהוה.

כִּי אֶשְׁמְרָה If I keep the Sabbath, God will keep me,
It is an eternal sign between God and me.
It is an eternal sign between God and me.

It is forbidden to engage in business or to travel,
Even to speak about the things we need, or about matters of trade or state.
Instead I will study God's Torah and it will make me wise.
It is an eternal sign between God and me.

On it I always find refreshment for my soul.
See: My Holy One gave the first generation,
A sign, by giving them a double portion on the sixth day.
So may my food be doubled every sixth day!
It is an eternal sign between God and me.

Engraved in God's law is His priests' decree,
To prepare the Show-Bread in His presence.
So, His sages ruled, on it fasting is forbidden, except on sins' Atonement Day.
It is an eternal sign between God and me.

It is a day of honor, a day of delight, with bread and fine wine, meat and fish.
On it those who mourn are turned around,
For it is a joyous day and it will bring me joy.
It is an eternal sign between God and me.

Those who desecrate it by working will, in the end, be cut off.
Therefore I cleanse my heart with it as if with soap.
Evening and morning I will pray to God,
Additional and afternoon prayer also, and He will answer me.
It is an eternal sign between God and me.

דְּרוֹר יִקְרָא God proclaims freedom to boy and girl,
And guards you like the pupil of His eye.
Your name is pleasant, never will it cease. Rest and be at ease on the Sabbath day.

Seek my Temple and my hall, And show me a sign of salvation.
Plant a shoot in my vineyard. Hear the cry of my people.

Tread the winepress in Botzra, And in Babylon which overpowered.
Crush my foes in anger and wrath, Hear my voice on the day I cry.

God, let there be on the desert mountain, Myrtle, acacia, cypress and box tree.
To one who warns and one who is warned, Let peace flow like river waters.

Crush those who rise against me, zealous God, Melting their heart with grief.
Then we will open and fill our mouths, And tongues with songs of joy to You.

Know what is wisdom for your soul, And it will be a crown for your head.
Keep your Holy One's command, Observe your holy Sabbath day.

כִּי אֶשְׁמְרָה שַׁבָּת אֵל יִשְׁמְרֵנִי. אוֹת הִיא לְעוֹלְמֵי עַד בֵּינוֹ וּבֵינִי.

אוֹת הִיא לְעוֹלְמֵי עַד בֵּינוֹ וּבֵינִי.

אָסוּר מְצֹא חֵפֶץ, עֲשׂוֹת דְּרָכִים, גַּם מִלְּדַבֵּר בּוֹ דִּבְרֵי צְרָכִים
דִּבְרֵי סְחוֹרָה אַף דִּבְרֵי מְלָכִים, אֶהְגֶּה בְּתוֹרַת אֵל וּתְחַכְּמֵנִי.

אוֹת הִיא לְעוֹלְמֵי עַד בֵּינוֹ וּבֵינִי.

בּוֹ אֶמְצְאָה תָמִיד נֹפֶשׁ לְנַפְשִׁי, הִנֵּה לְדוֹר רִאשׁוֹן נָתַן קְדוֹשִׁי
מוֹפֵת, בְּתֵת לֶחֶם מִשְׁנֶה בַּשִּׁשִּׁי, כָּכָה בְּכָל שִׁשִּׁי יַכְפִּיל מְזוֹנִי.

אוֹת הִיא לְעוֹלְמֵי עַד בֵּינוֹ וּבֵינִי.

רָשַׁם בְּדַת הָאֵל חֹק אֶל סְגָנָיו, בּוֹ לַעֲרֹךְ לֶחֶם פָּנִים בְּפָנָיו
עַל כֵּן לְהִתְעַנּוֹת בּוֹ עַל פִּי נְבוֹנָיו, אָסוּר, לְבַד מִיּוֹם כִּפּוּר עֲוֹנִי.

אוֹת הִיא לְעוֹלְמֵי עַד בֵּינוֹ וּבֵינִי.

הוּא יוֹם מְכֻבָּד, הוּא יוֹם תַּעֲנוּגִים, לֶחֶם וְיַיִן טוֹב, בָּשָׂר וְדָגִים
הַמִּתְאַבְּלִים בּוֹ אָחוֹר נְסוֹגִים, כִּי יוֹם שְׂמָחוֹת הוּא וּתְשַׂמְּחֵנִי.

אוֹת הִיא לְעוֹלְמֵי עַד בֵּינוֹ וּבֵינִי.

מֵחֵל מְלָאכָה בּוֹ סוֹפוֹ לְהַכְרִית, עַל כֵּן אֲכַבֵּס בּוֹ לִבִּי כְּבוֹרִית
וְאֶתְפַּלְּלָה אֶל אֵל עַרְבִית וְשַׁחֲרִית, מוּסָף וְגַם מִנְחָה הוּא יַעֲנֵנִי.

אוֹת הִיא לְעוֹלְמֵי עַד בֵּינוֹ וּבֵינִי.

דְּרוֹר יִקְרָא לְבֵן עִם בַּת, וְיִנְצָרְכֶם כְּמוֹ בָבַת
נְעִים שִׁמְכֶם וְלֹא יֻשְׁבַּת, שְׁבוּ נוּחוּ בְּיוֹם שַׁבָּת

דְּרֹשׁ נָוִי וְאוּלָמִי, וְאוֹת יֶשַׁע עֲשֵׂה עִמִּי
נְטַע שׂוֹרֵק בְּתוֹךְ כַּרְמִי, שְׁעֵה שַׁוְעַת בְּנֵי עַמִּי.

דְּרֹךְ פּוּרָה בְּתוֹךְ בָּצְרָה, וְגַם בָּבֶל אֲשֶׁר גָּבְרָה
נְתֹץ צָרַי בְּאַף עֶבְרָה, שְׁמַע קוֹלִי בְּיוֹם אֶקְרָא.

אֱלֹהִים תֵּן בַּמִּדְבָּר הַר, הֲדַס שִׁטָּה בְּרוֹשׁ תִּדְהָר
וְלַמַּזְהִיר וְלַנִּזְהָר, שְׁלוֹמִים תֵּן כְּמֵי נָהָר.

הֲדֹךְ קָמַי, אֵל קַנָּא, בְּמוֹג לֵבָב וּבִמְגִנָּה
וְנַרְחִיב פֶּה וּנְמַלְּאֶנָּה, לְשׁוֹנֵנוּ לְךָ רִנָּה.

דְּעֵה חָכְמָה לְנַפְשֶׁךָ, וְהִיא כֶתֶר לְרֹאשֶׁךָ
נְצֹר מִצְוַת קְדוֹשֶׁךָ, שְׁמֹר שַׁבַּת קָדְשֶׁךָ.

Minḥa for Shabbat and Yom Tov

אַשְׁרֵי Happy are those who dwell in Your House; *Ps. 84*
they shall continue to praise You, Selah!
Happy are the people for whom this is so; *Ps. 144*
happy are the people whose God is the LORD.
A song of praise by David. *Ps. 145*

א I will exalt You, my God, the King, and bless Your name for ever and all time. ב Every day I will bless You, and praise Your name for ever and all time. ג Great is the LORD and greatly to be praised; His greatness is unfathomable. ד One generation will praise Your works to the next, and tell of Your mighty deeds. ה On the glorious splendor of Your majesty I will meditate, and on the acts of Your wonders. ו They shall talk of the power of Your awesome deeds, and I will tell of Your greatness. ז They shall recite the record of Your great goodness, and sing with joy of Your righteousness. ח The LORD is gracious and compassionate, slow to anger and great in loving-kindness. ט The LORD is good to all, and His compassion extends to all His works. י All Your works shall thank You, LORD, and Your devoted ones shall bless You. כ They shall talk of the glory of Your kingship, and speak of Your might. ל To make known to mankind His mighty deeds and the glorious majesty of His kingship. מ Your kingdom is an everlasting kingdom, and Your reign is for all generations. ס The LORD supports all who fall, and raises all who are bowed down. ע All raise their eyes to You in hope, and You give them their food in due season. פ You open Your hand, and satisfy every living thing

---

with the word *Ashrei*, the first word of the first psalm, and ends with *Halleluya*, the last word of the last psalm. It thus stands, in miniature, for the book of Psalms as a whole.

מנחה לשבת וליום טוב

תהלים פד אַשְׁרֵי יוֹשְׁבֵי בֵיתֶךָ, עוֹד יְהַלְלוּךָ סֶּלָה:

תהלים קמד אַשְׁרֵי הָעָם שֶׁכָּכָה לּוֹ, אַשְׁרֵי הָעָם שֶׁיהוה אֱלֹהָיו:

תהלים קמה תְּהִלָּה לְדָוִד

א אֲרוֹמִמְךָ אֱלוֹהַי הַמֶּלֶךְ, וַאֲבָרְכָה שִׁמְךָ לְעוֹלָם וָעֶד:

ב בְּכָל־יוֹם אֲבָרְכֶךָּ, וַאֲהַלְלָה שִׁמְךָ לְעוֹלָם וָעֶד:

ג גָּדוֹל יהוה וּמְהֻלָּל מְאֹד, וְלִגְדֻלָּתוֹ אֵין חֵקֶר:

ד דּוֹר לְדוֹר יְשַׁבַּח מַעֲשֶׂיךָ, וּגְבוּרֹתֶיךָ יַגִּידוּ:

ה הֲדַר כְּבוֹד הוֹדֶךָ, וְדִבְרֵי נִפְלְאֹתֶיךָ אָשִׂיחָה:

ו וֶעֱזוּז נוֹרְאֹתֶיךָ יֹאמֵרוּ, וּגְדוּלָּתְךָ אֲסַפְּרֶנָּה:

ז זֵכֶר רַב־טוּבְךָ יַבִּיעוּ, וְצִדְקָתְךָ יְרַנֵּנוּ:

ח חַנּוּן וְרַחוּם יהוה, אֶרֶךְ אַפַּיִם וּגְדָל־חָסֶד:

ט טוֹב־יהוה לַכֹּל, וְרַחֲמָיו עַל־כָּל־מַעֲשָׂיו:

י יוֹדוּךָ יהוה כָּל־מַעֲשֶׂיךָ, וַחֲסִידֶיךָ יְבָרְכוּכָה:

כ כְּבוֹד מַלְכוּתְךָ יֹאמֵרוּ, וּגְבוּרָתְךָ יְדַבֵּרוּ:

ל לְהוֹדִיעַ לִבְנֵי הָאָדָם גְּבוּרֹתָיו, וּכְבוֹד הֲדַר מַלְכוּתוֹ:

מ מַלְכוּתְךָ מַלְכוּת כָּל־עֹלָמִים, וּמֶמְשַׁלְתְּךָ בְּכָל־דּוֹר וָדֹר:

ס סוֹמֵךְ יהוה לְכָל־הַנֹּפְלִים, וְזוֹקֵף לְכָל־הַכְּפוּפִים:

ע עֵינֵי־כֹל אֵלֶיךָ יְשַׂבֵּרוּ, וְאַתָּה נוֹתֵן־לָהֶם אֶת־אָכְלָם בְּעִתּוֹ:

פ פּוֹתֵחַ אֶת־יָדֶךָ, וּמַשְׂבִּיעַ לְכָל־חַי רָצוֹן:

אַשְׁרֵי *Happy are those:* As on weekdays, the Minḥa Service begins with *Ashrei* as a prelude to prayer. The addition of two verses from other psalms at the beginning, and one verse at the end mean that the prayer, as we say it, begins

with favor. צ The LORD is righteous in all His ways, and kind in all He does. ק The LORD is close to all who call on Him, to all who call on Him in truth. ר He fulfills the will of those who revere Him; He hears their cry and saves them. ש The LORD guards all who love Him, but all the wicked He will destroy. ▸ ת My mouth shall speak the praise of the LORD, and all creatures shall bless His holy name for ever and all time.

We will bless the LORD now and for ever. Halleluya! Ps. 115

וּבָא לְצִיּוֹן גּוֹאֵל "A redeemer will come to Zion, Is. 59
to those of Jacob who repent of their sins," declares the LORD.
"As for Me, this is My covenant with them," says the LORD.
"My spirit, that is on you, and My words I have placed in your mouth will not depart from your mouth, or from the mouth of your children, or from the mouth of their descendants from this time on and for ever," says the LORD.

▸ You are the Holy One, enthroned on the praises of Israel. Ps. 22
And [the angels] call to one another, saying, ◂ "Holy, holy, holy is the LORD of hosts; the whole world is filled with His glory."
And they receive permission from one another, saying: Targum Yonatan Is. 6
"Holy in the highest heavens, home of His Presence; holy on earth,
the work of His strength; holy for ever and all time is the LORD of hosts;
the whole earth is full of His radiant glory."

▸ Then a wind lifted me up and I heard behind me the sound of a great noise, saying, ◂ "Blessed is the LORD's glory from His place." Ezek. 3
Then a wind lifted me up and I heard behind me Targum Yonatan Ezek. 3
the sound of a great tempest of those who uttered praise, saying,
"Blessed is the LORD's glory from the place of the home of His Presence."

---

composed of the following elements: (1) two consecutive verses from Isaiah about redemption; (2) the *Kedusha*, together with an Aramaic translation; (3) a collection of verses about faithfulness to God; (4) a blessing thanking God for the Torah and praying for the ability to fulfill the commandments; (5) a further collection of verses, about trust in God.

צ צַדִּיק יהוה בְּכָל־דְּרָכָיו, וְחָסִיד בְּכָל־מַעֲשָׂיו:
ק קָרוֹב יהוה לְכָל־קֹרְאָיו, לְכֹל אֲשֶׁר יִקְרָאֻהוּ בֶאֱמֶת:
ר רְצוֹן־יְרֵאָיו יַעֲשֶׂה, וְאֶת־שַׁוְעָתָם יִשְׁמַע, וְיוֹשִׁיעֵם:
ש שׁוֹמֵר יהוה אֶת־כָּל־אֹהֲבָיו, וְאֵת כָּל־הָרְשָׁעִים יַשְׁמִיד:
◂ ת תְּהִלַּת יהוה יְדַבֶּר פִּי, וִיבָרֵךְ כָּל־בָּשָׂר שֵׁם קָדְשׁוֹ לְעוֹלָם וָעֶד:
וַאֲנַחְנוּ נְבָרֵךְ יָהּ מֵעַתָּה וְעַד־עוֹלָם, הַלְלוּיָהּ: תהלים קטו

וּבָא לְצִיּוֹן גּוֹאֵל, וּלְשָׁבֵי פֶשַׁע בְּיַעֲקֹב, נְאֻם יהוה: ישעיה נט
וַאֲנִי זֹאת בְּרִיתִי אוֹתָם, אָמַר יהוה
רוּחִי אֲשֶׁר עָלֶיךָ וּדְבָרַי אֲשֶׁר־שַׂמְתִּי בְּפִיךָ
לֹא־יָמוּשׁוּ מִפִּיךָ וּמִפִּי זַרְעֲךָ וּמִפִּי זֶרַע זַרְעֲךָ
אָמַר יהוה, מֵעַתָּה וְעַד־עוֹלָם:

◂ וְאַתָּה קָדוֹשׁ יוֹשֵׁב תְּהִלּוֹת יִשְׂרָאֵל: וְקָרָא זֶה אֶל־זֶה וְאָמַר ◂ תהלים כב ישעיה ו
קָדוֹשׁ, קָדוֹשׁ, קָדוֹשׁ, יהוה צְבָאוֹת, מְלֹא כָל־הָאָרֶץ כְּבוֹדוֹ:
וּמְקַבְּלִין דֵּין מִן דֵּין וְאָמְרִין, קַדִּישׁ בִּשְׁמֵי מְרוֹמָא עִלָּאָה בֵּית שְׁכִינְתֵּהּ תרגום יונתן ישעיה ו
קַדִּישׁ עַל אַרְעָא עוֹבַד גְּבוּרְתֵּהּ, קַדִּישׁ לְעָלַם וּלְעָלְמֵי עָלְמַיָּא
יהוה צְבָאוֹת, מַלְיָא כָל אַרְעָא זִיו יְקָרֵהּ.

◂ וַתִּשָּׂאֵנִי רוּחַ, וָאֶשְׁמַע אַחֲרַי קוֹל רַעַשׁ גָּדוֹל ◂ יחזקאל ג
בָּרוּךְ כְּבוֹד־יהוה מִמְּקוֹמוֹ:
וּנְטָלַתְנִי רוּחָא, וּשְׁמָעִית בַּתְרַי קָל זִיעַ סַגִּיא, דִּמְשַׁבְּחִין וְאָמְרִין תרגום יונתן יחזקאל ג
בְּרִיךְ יְקָרָא דַיהוה מֵאֲתַר בֵּית שְׁכִינְתֵּהּ.

וּבָא לְצִיּוֹן גּוֹאֵל *A redeemer will come to Zion:* The proper place for this prayer, as on weekdays, is in the morning service. However, since the Shabbat morning prayers are already long, it was moved to the afternoon. Another possibility is that, since it was usually said after a period of study, it may testify to the custom of communal study before the afternoon prayer. The passage is

The LORD shall reign for ever and all time. *Ex. 15*

The LORD's kingdom is established for ever and all time. *Targum Onkelos Ex. 15*

יהוה LORD, God of Abraham, Isaac and Yisrael, our ancestors, may *1 Chr. 29*
You keep this for ever so that it forms the thoughts in Your people's
heart, and directs their heart toward You. He is compassionate. He *Ps. 78*
forgives iniquity and does not destroy. Repeatedly He suppresses
His anger, not rousing His full wrath. For You, my LORD, are good *Ps. 86*
and forgiving, abundantly kind to all who call on You. Your righ- *Ps. 119*
teousness is eternally righteous, and Your Torah is truth. Grant *Micah 7*
truth to Jacob, loving-kindness to Abraham, as You promised our
ancestors in ancient times. Blessed is my LORD for day after day He *Ps. 68*
burdens us [with His blessings]; is our salvation, Selah! The LORD *Ps. 46*
of hosts is with us; the God of Jacob is our refuge, Selah! LORD of *Ps. 84*
hosts, happy is the one who trusts in You. LORD, save. May the King *Ps. 20*
answer us on the day we call.

בָּרוּךְ Blessed is He, our God, who created us for His glory, separating us from those who go astray; who gave us the Torah of truth, planting within us eternal life. May He open our heart to His Torah, imbuing our heart with the love and awe of Him, that we may do His will and serve Him with a perfect heart, so that we neither toil in vain nor give birth to confusion.

יְהִי רָצוֹן May it be Your will, O LORD our God and God of our ancestors, that we keep Your laws in this world, and thus be worthy to live,
see and inherit goodness and blessing in the Messianic Age and in
the life of the World to Come. So that my soul may sing to You and *Ps. 30*
not be silent. LORD, my God, for ever I will thank You. Blessed is *Jer. 17*
the man who trusts in the LORD, whose trust is in the LORD alone.
Trust in the LORD for evermore, for God, the LORD, is an everlast- *Is. 26*
ing Rock. ▸ Those who know Your name trust in You, for You, LORD, *Ps. 9*
do not forsake those who seek You. The LORD desired, for the sake *Is. 42*
of Israel's merit, to make the Torah great and glorious.

יהוה יִמְלֹךְ לְעֹלָם וָעֶד: שמות טו
יהוה מַלְכוּתֵהּ קָאֵם לְעָלַם וּלְעָלְמֵי עָלְמַיָּא. תרגום אונקלוס שמות טו

יהוה אֱלֹהֵי אַבְרָהָם יִצְחָק וְיִשְׂרָאֵל אֲבֹתֵינוּ, שָׁמְרָה־זֹּאת לְעוֹלָם לְיֵצֶר מַחְשְׁבוֹת לְבַב עַמֶּךָ, וְהָכֵן לְבָבָם אֵלֶיךָ: וְהוּא רַחוּם יְכַפֵּר עָוֹן וְלֹא־יַשְׁחִית, וְהִרְבָּה לְהָשִׁיב אַפּוֹ, וְלֹא־יָעִיר כָּל־חֲמָתוֹ: כִּי־אַתָּה אֲדֹנָי טוֹב וְסַלָּח, וְרַב־חֶסֶד לְכָל־קֹרְאֶיךָ: צִדְקָתְךָ צֶדֶק לְעוֹלָם וְתוֹרָתְךָ אֱמֶת: תִּתֵּן אֱמֶת לְיַעֲקֹב, חֶסֶד לְאַבְרָהָם, אֲשֶׁר־נִשְׁבַּעְתָּ לַאֲבֹתֵינוּ מִימֵי קֶדֶם: בָּרוּךְ אֲדֹנָי יוֹם יוֹם יַעֲמָס־לָנוּ, הָאֵל יְשׁוּעָתֵנוּ סֶלָה: יהוה צְבָאוֹת עִמָּנוּ, מִשְׂגָּב לָנוּ אֱלֹהֵי יַעֲקֹב סֶלָה: יהוה צְבָאוֹת, אַשְׁרֵי אָדָם בֹּטֵחַ בָּךְ: יהוה הוֹשִׁיעָה, הַמֶּלֶךְ יַעֲנֵנוּ בְיוֹם־קָרְאֵנוּ:

דברי הימים א, כט · תהלים עח · תהלים פו · תהלים קיט · מיכה ז · תהלים סח · תהלים מו · תהלים פד · תהלים כ

בָּרוּךְ הוּא אֱלֹהֵינוּ שֶׁבְּרָאָנוּ לִכְבוֹדוֹ, וְהִבְדִּילָנוּ מִן הַתּוֹעִים, וְנָתַן לָנוּ תּוֹרַת אֱמֶת, וְחַיֵּי עוֹלָם נָטַע בְּתוֹכֵנוּ. הוּא יִפְתַּח לִבֵּנוּ בְּתוֹרָתוֹ, וְיָשֵׂם בְּלִבֵּנוּ אַהֲבָתוֹ וְיִרְאָתוֹ וְלַעֲשׂוֹת רְצוֹנוֹ וּלְעָבְדוֹ בְּלֵבָב שָׁלֵם, לְמַעַן לֹא נִיגַע לָרִיק וְלֹא נֵלֵד לַבֶּהָלָה.

יְהִי רָצוֹן מִלְּפָנֶיךָ יהוה אֱלֹהֵינוּ וֵאלֹהֵי אֲבוֹתֵינוּ, שֶׁנִּשְׁמֹר חֻקֶּיךָ בָּעוֹלָם הַזֶּה, וְנִזְכֶּה וְנִחְיֶה וְנִרְאֶה וְנִירַשׁ טוֹבָה וּבְרָכָה, לִשְׁנֵי יְמוֹת הַמָּשִׁיחַ וּלְחַיֵּי הָעוֹלָם הַבָּא. לְמַעַן יְזַמֶּרְךָ כָבוֹד וְלֹא יִדֹּם, יהוה אֱלֹהַי, לְעוֹלָם אוֹדֶךָּ: בָּרוּךְ הַגֶּבֶר אֲשֶׁר יִבְטַח בַּיהוה, וְהָיָה יהוה מִבְטַחוֹ: בִּטְחוּ בַיהוה עֲדֵי־עַד, כִּי בְּיָהּ יהוה צוּר עוֹלָמִים: ◂ וְיִבְטְחוּ בְךָ יוֹדְעֵי שְׁמֶךָ, כִּי לֹא־עָזַבְתָּ דֹרְשֶׁיךָ, יהוה: יהוה חָפֵץ לְמַעַן צִדְקוֹ, יַגְדִּיל תּוֹרָה וְיַאְדִּיר:

תהלים ל · ירמיה יז · ישעיה כו · תהלים ט · ישעיה מב

HALF KADDISH

Leader: יִתְגַּדַּל Magnified and sanctified
may His great name be,
in the world He created by His will.
May He establish His kingdom
in your lifetime and in your days,
and in the lifetime of all the house of Israel,
swiftly and soon – and say: Amen.

All: May His great name be blessed for ever and all time.

Leader: Blessed and praised, glorified and exalted,
raised and honored, uplifted and lauded
be the name of the Holy One, blessed be He,
beyond any blessing,
song, praise and consolation uttered in the world –
and say: Amen.

On Shabbat continue below. On Yom Tov falling on a weekday, say the Amida on page 770.

וַאֲנִי As for me, may my prayer come to You, Lord, *Ps. 69*
at a time of favor. O God, in Your great love,
answer me with Your faithful salvation.

The Ark is opened and the congregation stands. All say:

וַיְהִי בִּנְסֹעַ Whenever the Ark set out, Moses would say, *Num. 10*
"Arise, Lord, and may Your enemies be scattered.
May those who hate You flee before You."
For the Torah shall come forth from Zion, *Is. 2*
and the word of the Lord from Jerusalem.
Blessed is He who in His Holiness
gave the Torah to His people Israel.

READING OF THE TORAH

The custom of reading the opening section of the coming week's Torah portion on Shabbat afternoon is undoubtedly of ancient origin. It is attributed in the Talmud (*Bava Kama* 82a) to Ezra after the return of Jews from Babylon.

חצי קדיש

ש״ץ: יִתְגַּדַּל וְיִתְקַדַּשׁ שְׁמֵהּ רַבָּא (קהל: אָמֵן)
בְּעָלְמָא דִּי בְרָא כִרְעוּתֵהּ
וְיַמְלִיךְ מַלְכוּתֵהּ
בְּחַיֵּיכוֹן וּבְיוֹמֵיכוֹן וּבְחַיֵּי דְכָל בֵּית יִשְׂרָאֵל
בַּעֲגָלָא וּבִזְמַן קָרִיב, וְאִמְרוּ אָמֵן. (קהל: אָמֵן)

קהל וש״ץ: יְהֵא שְׁמֵהּ רַבָּא מְבָרַךְ לְעָלַם וּלְעָלְמֵי עָלְמַיָּא.

ש״ץ: יִתְבָּרַךְ וְיִשְׁתַּבַּח וְיִתְפָּאַר וְיִתְרוֹמַם וְיִתְנַשֵּׂא
וְיִתְהַדָּר וְיִתְעַלֶּה וְיִתְהַלָּל
שְׁמֵהּ דְּקֻדְשָׁא בְּרִיךְ הוּא (קהל: בְּרִיךְ הוּא)
לְעֵלָּא מִן כָּל בִּרְכָתָא / בשבת שובה: לְעֵלָּא לְעֵלָּא מִכָּל בִּרְכָתָא/
וְשִׁירָתָא, תֻּשְׁבְּחָתָא וְנֶחֱמָתָא
דַּאֲמִירָן בְּעָלְמָא, וְאִמְרוּ אָמֵן. (קהל: אָמֵן)

On שבת *continue below. On* יום טוב *falling on a weekday, say the* עמידה *on page 771.*

וַאֲנִי תְפִלָּתִי־לְךָ יהוה, עֵת רָצוֹן, אֱלֹהִים בְּרָב־חַסְדֶּךָ תהלים סט
עֲנֵנִי בֶּאֱמֶת יִשְׁעֶךָ:

The ארון קודש *is opened and the* קהל *stands. All say:*

וַיְהִי בִּנְסֹעַ הָאָרֹן וַיֹּאמֶר מֹשֶׁה במדבר י
קוּמָה יהוה וְיָפֻצוּ אֹיְבֶיךָ וְיָנֻסוּ מְשַׂנְאֶיךָ מִפָּנֶיךָ:
כִּי מִצִּיּוֹן תֵּצֵא תוֹרָה וּדְבַר־יהוה מִירוּשָׁלָםִ: ישעיה ב
בָּרוּךְ שֶׁנָּתַן תּוֹרָה לְעַמּוֹ יִשְׂרָאֵל בִּקְדֻשָּׁתוֹ.

וַאֲנִי תְפִלָּתִי־לְךָ *As for me, may my prayer come to You:* In the previous verse of Psalm 69, King David says, "I am the taunt of drunkards." The Midrash interprets this as a contrast between those who drink and carouse, and those who, in the midst of their celebrations, remember God. Thus we say this line on Shabbat afternoon, turning from our celebratory meal to pray (Abudarham).

Blessed is the name of the Master of the Universe. Blessed is Your crown and Your place. May Your favor always be with Your people Israel. Show Your people the salvation of Your right hand in Your Temple. Grant us the gift of Your good light, and accept our prayers in mercy. May it be Your will to prolong our life in goodness. May I be counted among the righteous, so that You will have compassion on me and protect me and all that is mine and all that is Your people Israel's. You feed all; You sustain all; You rule over all; You rule over kings, for sovereignty is Yours. I am a servant of the Holy One, blessed be He, before whom and before whose glorious Torah I bow at all times. Not in man do I trust, nor on any angel do I rely, but on the God of heaven who is the God of truth, whose Torah is truth, whose prophets speak truth, and who abounds in acts of love and truth. ▸ In Him I trust, and to His holy and glorious name I offer praises. May it be Your will to open my heart to the Torah, and to fulfill the wishes of my heart and of the hearts of all Your people Israel for good, for life, and for peace. *Zohar, Vayak-hel*

The Leader takes the Torah scroll in his right arm, bows toward the Ark and says:

Magnify the LORD with me, and let us exalt His name together. *Ps. 34*

The Ark is closed. The Leader carries the Torah scroll to the bima and the congregation says:

לְךָ Yours, LORD, are the greatness and the power, the glory and the majesty and splendor, for everything in heaven and earth is Yours. Yours, LORD, is the kingdom; You are exalted as Head over all. *1 Chr. 29*

רוֹמְמוּ Exalt the LORD our God and bow to His footstool; He is holy. Exalt the LORD our God, and bow at His holy mountain, for holy is the LORD our God. *Ps. 99*

אַב הָרַחֲמִים May the Father of compassion have compassion on the people borne by Him. May He remember the covenant with the mighty [patriarchs], and deliver us from evil times. May He reproach the evil instinct in the people carried by Him, and graciously grant that we be an everlasting remnant. May He fulfill in good measure our requests for salvation and compassion.

The Torah scroll is placed on the bima and the Gabbai calls a Kohen to the Torah. See laws 383–397.

וְתִגָּלֶה May His kingship over us be soon revealed and made manifest. May He be gracious to our surviving remnant, the remnant of His people the house of Israel in grace, loving-kindness, compassion and favor, and let us say: Amen. Let us all render greatness to our God and give honor to the Torah. *Let the Kohen come forward. Arise (*name* son of *father's name*), the Kohen.

**If no Kohen is present, a Levi or Yisrael is called up as follows:*

/As there is no Kohen, arise (*name* son of *father's name*) in place of a Kohen./

Blessed is He who, in His holiness, gave the Torah to His people Israel.

The congregation followed by the Gabbai:

You who cling to the LORD your God are all alive today. *Deut. 4*

זוהר ויקהל בְּרִיךְ שְׁמֵהּ דְּמָרֵא עָלְמָא, בְּרִיךְ כִּתְרָךְ וְאַתְרָךְ. יְהֵא רְעוּתָךְ עִם עַמָּךְ יִשְׂרָאֵל לְעָלַם, וּפֻרְקַן יְמִינָךְ אַחֲזֵי לְעַמָּךְ בְּבֵית מַקְדְּשָׁךְ, וּלְאַמְטוּיֵי לָנָא מִטּוּב נְהוֹרָךְ, וּלְקַבֵּל צְלוֹתָנָא בְּרַחֲמִין. יְהֵא רַעֲוָא קֳדָמָךְ דְּתוֹרִיךְ לַן חַיִּין בְּטִיבוּ, וְלֶהֱוֵי אֲנָא פְקִידָא בְּגוֹ צַדִּיקַיָּא, לְמִרְחַם עָלַי וּלְמִנְטַר יָתִי וְיַת כָּל דִּי לִי וְדִי לְעַמָּךְ יִשְׂרָאֵל. אַנְתְּ הוּא זָן לְכֹלָּא וּמְפַרְנֵס לְכֹלָּא, אַנְתְּ הוּא שַׁלִּיט עַל כֹּלָּא, אַנְתְּ הוּא דְּשַׁלִּיט עַל מַלְכַיָּא, וּמַלְכוּתָא דִּילָךְ הִיא. אֲנָא עַבְדָּא דְקֻדְשָׁא בְּרִיךְ הוּא, דְּסָגֵדְנָא קַמֵּהּ וּמִקַּמֵּי דִּיקַר אוֹרַיְתֵהּ בְּכָל עִדָּן וְעִדָּן. לָא עַל אֱנָשׁ רָחִיצְנָא וְלָא עַל בַּר אֱלָהִין סָמִיכְנָא, אֶלָּא בֶּאֱלָהָא דִשְׁמַיָּא, דְּהוּא אֱלָהָא קְשׁוֹט, וְאוֹרַיְתֵהּ קְשׁוֹט, וּנְבִיאוֹהִי קְשׁוֹט, וּמַסְגֵּא לְמֶעְבַּד טַבְוָן וּקְשׁוֹט. • בֵּהּ אֲנָא רָחִיץ, וְלִשְׁמֵהּ קַדִּישָׁא יַקִּירָא אֲנָא אֵמַר תֻּשְׁבְּחָן. יְהֵא רַעֲוָא קֳדָמָךְ דְּתִפְתַּח לִבָּאִי בְּאוֹרַיְתָא, וְתַשְׁלִים מִשְׁאֲלִין דְּלִבָּאִי וְלִבָּא דְכָל עַמָּךְ יִשְׂרָאֵל לְטָב וּלְחַיִּין וְלִשְׁלָם.

The שליח ציבור *takes the* ספר תורה *in his right arm, bows toward the* ארון קודש *and says:*

תהלים לד גַּדְּלוּ לַיהוה אִתִּי וּנְרוֹמְמָה שְׁמוֹ יַחְדָּו:

The ארון קודש *is closed. The* שליח ציבור *carries the* ספר תורה *to the* בימה *and the* קהל *says:*

דברי הימים א׳ כט לְךָ יהוה הַגְּדֻלָּה וְהַגְּבוּרָה וְהַתִּפְאֶרֶת וְהַנֵּצַח וְהַהוֹד, כִּי־כֹל בַּשָּׁמַיִם וּבָאָרֶץ: לְךָ יהוה הַמַּמְלָכָה וְהַמִּתְנַשֵּׂא לְכֹל לְרֹאשׁ:

תהלים צט רוֹמְמוּ יהוה אֱלֹהֵינוּ וְהִשְׁתַּחֲווּ לַהֲדֹם רַגְלָיו, קָדוֹשׁ הוּא: רוֹמְמוּ יהוה אֱלֹהֵינוּ וְהִשְׁתַּחֲווּ לְהַר קָדְשׁוֹ, כִּי־קָדוֹשׁ יהוה אֱלֹהֵינוּ:

אַב הָרַחֲמִים הוּא יְרַחֵם עַם עֲמוּסִים, וְיִזְכֹּר בְּרִית אֵיתָנִים, וְיַצִּיל נַפְשׁוֹתֵינוּ מִן הַשָּׁעוֹת הָרָעוֹת, וְיִגְעַר בְּיֵצֶר הָרָע מִן הַנְּשׂוּאִים, וְיָחֹן אוֹתָנוּ לִפְלֵיטַת עוֹלָמִים, וִימַלֵּא מִשְׁאֲלוֹתֵינוּ בְּמִדָּה טוֹבָה יְשׁוּעָה וְרַחֲמִים.

The ספר תורה *is placed on the* שולחן *and the* גבאי *calls a* כהן *to the* תורה. *See laws 383–397.*

וְתִגָּלֶה וְתֵרָאֶה מַלְכוּתוֹ עָלֵינוּ בִּזְמַן קָרוֹב, וְיָחֹן פְּלֵיטָתֵנוּ וּפְלֵיטַת עַמּוֹ בֵּית יִשְׂרָאֵל לְחֵן וּלְחֶסֶד וּלְרַחֲמִים וּלְרָצוֹן וְנֹאמַר אָמֵן. הַכֹּל הָבוּ גֹדֶל לֵאלֹהֵינוּ וּתְנוּ כָבוֹד לַתּוֹרָה. *כֹּהֵן קְרַב, יַעֲמֹד (פלוני בֶּן פלוני) הַכֹּהֵן.

**If no* כהן *is present, a* לוי *or* ישראל *is called up as follows:*

/אֵין כָּאן כֹּהֵן, יַעֲמֹד (פלוני בֶּן פלוני) בִּמְקוֹם כֹּהֵן./

בָּרוּךְ שֶׁנָּתַן תּוֹרָה לְעַמּוֹ יִשְׂרָאֵל בִּקְדֻשָּׁתוֹ.

The קהל *followed by the* גבאי:

דברים ד וְאַתֶּם הַדְּבֵקִים בַּיהוה אֱלֹהֵיכֶם חַיִּים כֻּלְּכֶם הַיּוֹם:

The appropriate Torah portions are to be found from page 1072.
The Reader shows the oleh the section to be read. The oleh touches the scroll at that place with the tzitzit of his tallit or the fabric belt of the Torah scroll, which he then kisses. Holding the handles of the scroll, he says:

Oleh: Bless the LORD, the blessed One.

Cong: Bless the LORD, the blessed One, for ever and all time.

Oleh: Bless the LORD, the blessed One, for ever and all time.
Blessed are You, LORD our God, King of the Universe, who has chosen us from all peoples and has given us His Torah. Blessed are You, LORD, Giver of the Torah.

After the reading, the oleh says:

Oleh: Blessed are You, LORD our God, King of the Universe, who has given us the Torah of truth, planting everlasting life in our midst. Blessed are You, LORD, Giver of the Torah.

The Torah scroll is lifted and the congregation says:

וְזֹאת הַתּוֹרָה This is the Torah that *Deut. 4*
Moses placed before the children of Israel,
at the LORD's commandment, by the hand of Moses. *Num. 9*

Some add: It is a tree of life to those who grasp it, and those who uphold it are happy. Its ways are ways of pleasantness, and all its paths are peace. Long life is in its right hand; in its left, riches and honor. It pleased the LORD for the sake of [Israel's] righteousness, to make the Torah great and glorious. *Prov. 3* *Is. 42*

The Torah scroll is bound and covered. In some congregations, during the week before a yahrzeit, "God, full of mercy" on page 804 is said.
The Ark is opened. The Leader takes the Torah scroll and says:

יְהַלְלוּ Let them praise the name of the LORD, *Ps. 148*
for His name alone is sublime.

The congregation responds:

הוֹדוֹ His majesty is above earth and heaven. He has raised the horn of His people, for the glory of all His devoted ones, the children of Israel, the people close to Him. Halleluya!

As the Torah scroll is returned to the Ark say:

לְדָוִד מִזְמוֹר A psalm of David. The earth is the LORD's and all it contains, *Ps. 24* the world and all who live in it. For He founded it on the seas and established it on the streams. Who may climb the mountain of the LORD? Who may stand in His holy place? He who has clean hands and a pure heart, who has not taken My name in vain, or sworn deceitfully. He shall receive blessing from the LORD, and just reward from God, his salvation.

The appropriate תורה *portions are to be found from page 1072.*
The קורא *shows the* עולה *the section to be read. The* עולה *touches the scroll at that place with the* ציצית *of his* טלית *or the gartel of the* ספר תורה*, which he then kisses. Holding the handles of the scroll, he says:*

עולה: בָּרְכוּ אֶת יהוה הַמְבֹרָךְ.

קהל: בָּרוּךְ יהוה הַמְבֹרָךְ לְעוֹלָם וָעֶד.

עולה: בָּרוּךְ יהוה הַמְבֹרָךְ לְעוֹלָם וָעֶד.

בָּרוּךְ אַתָּה יהוה אֱלֹהֵינוּ מֶלֶךְ הָעוֹלָם, אֲשֶׁר בָּחַר בָּנוּ מִכָּל הָעַמִּים וְנָתַן לָנוּ אֶת תּוֹרָתוֹ. בָּרוּךְ אַתָּה יהוה, נוֹתֵן הַתּוֹרָה.

After the קריאת התורה*, the* עולה *says:*

עולה: בָּרוּךְ אַתָּה יהוה אֱלֹהֵינוּ מֶלֶךְ הָעוֹלָם, אֲשֶׁר נָתַן לָנוּ תּוֹרַת אֱמֶת וְחַיֵּי עוֹלָם נָטַע בְּתוֹכֵנוּ. בָּרוּךְ אַתָּה יהוה, נוֹתֵן הַתּוֹרָה.

The ספר תורה *is lifted and the* קהל *says:*

דברים ד וְזֹאת הַתּוֹרָה אֲשֶׁר־שָׂם מֹשֶׁה לִפְנֵי בְּנֵי יִשְׂרָאֵל:
במדבר ט עַל־פִּי יהוה בְּיַד מֹשֶׁה:

Some add
משלי ג עֵץ־חַיִּים הִיא לַמַּחֲזִיקִים בָּהּ וְתֹמְכֶיהָ מְאֻשָּׁר: דְּרָכֶיהָ דַרְכֵי־נֹעַם וְכָל־נְתִיבֹתֶיהָ שָׁלוֹם: אֹרֶךְ יָמִים בִּימִינָהּ, בִּשְׂמֹאולָהּ עֹשֶׁר וְכָבוֹד:
ישעיה מב יהוה חָפֵץ לְמַעַן צִדְקוֹ יַגְדִּיל תּוֹרָה וְיַאְדִּיר:

The ספר תורה *is bound and covered.*
In some congregations, during the week before a yahrzeit, אֵל מָלֵא רַחֲמִים *on page 801 is said.*
The ארון קודש *is opened. The* שליח ציבור *takes the* ספר תורה *and says:*

תהלים קמח יְהַלְלוּ אֶת־שֵׁם יהוה, כִּי־נִשְׂגָּב שְׁמוֹ, לְבַדּוֹ

The קהל *responds:*

הוֹדוֹ עַל־אֶרֶץ וְשָׁמָיִם: וַיָּרֶם קֶרֶן לְעַמּוֹ, תְּהִלָּה לְכָל־חֲסִידָיו, לִבְנֵי יִשְׂרָאֵל עַם קְרֹבוֹ, הַלְלוּיָהּ:

As the ספר תורה *is returned to the* ארון קודש*, say:*

תהלים כד לְדָוִד מִזְמוֹר, לַיהוה הָאָרֶץ וּמְלוֹאָהּ, תֵּבֵל וְיֹשְׁבֵי בָהּ: כִּי־הוּא עַל־יַמִּים יְסָדָהּ, וְעַל־נְהָרוֹת יְכוֹנְנֶהָ: מִי־יַעֲלֶה בְהַר־יהוה, וּמִי־יָקוּם בִּמְקוֹם קָדְשׁוֹ: נְקִי כַפַּיִם וּבַר־לֵבָב, אֲשֶׁר לֹא־נָשָׂא לַשָּׁוְא נַפְשִׁי וְלֹא נִשְׁבַּע לְמִרְמָה: יִשָּׂא בְרָכָה מֵאֵת יהוה, וּצְדָקָה מֵאֱלֹהֵי יִשְׁעוֹ:

This is a generation of those who seek Him, the descendants of Jacob who seek Your presence, Selah! Lift up your heads, O gates; be uplifted, eternal doors, so that the King of glory may enter. Who is the King of glory? It is the LORD, strong and mighty, the LORD mighty in battle. Lift up your heads, O gates; lift them up, eternal doors, so that the King of glory may enter. Who is He, the King of glory? The LORD of hosts, He is the King of glory, Selah!

As the Torah scroll is placed into the Ark, say:

וּבְנֻחֹה יֹאמַר When the Ark came to rest, Moses would say: "Return, *Num. 10*
O LORD, to the myriad thousands of Israel." Advance, LORD, to Your *Ps. 132*
resting place, You and Your mighty Ark. Your priests are clothed in righteousness, and Your devoted ones sing in joy. For the sake of Your servant David, do not reject Your anointed one. For I give you good *Prov. 4*
instruction; do not forsake My Torah. It is a tree of life to those who *Prov. 3*
grasp it, and those who uphold it are happy. Its ways are ways of pleasantness, and all its paths are peace. ▸ Turn us back, O LORD, to You, and *Lam. 5*
we will return. Renew our days as of old.

The Ark is closed.

HALF KADDISH

Leader: יִתְגַּדַּל Magnified and sanctified
may His great name be,
in the world He created by His will.
May He establish His kingdom
in your lifetime and in your days,
and in the lifetime of all the house of Israel,
swiftly and soon – and say: Amen.

All: May His great name be blessed for ever and all time.

Leader: Blessed and praised, glorified and exalted,
raised and honored, uplifted and lauded
be the name of the Holy One, blessed be He,
beyond any blessing,
song, praise and consolation
uttered in the world –
and say: Amen.

זֶה דּוֹר דֹּרְשָׁו, מְבַקְשֵׁי פָנֶיךָ, יַעֲקֹב, סֶלָה: שְׂאוּ שְׁעָרִים רָאשֵׁיכֶם, וְהִנָּשְׂאוּ פִּתְחֵי עוֹלָם, וְיָבוֹא מֶלֶךְ הַכָּבוֹד: מִי זֶה מֶלֶךְ הַכָּבוֹד, יהוה עִזּוּז וְגִבּוֹר, יהוה גִּבּוֹר מִלְחָמָה: שְׂאוּ שְׁעָרִים רָאשֵׁיכֶם, וּשְׂאוּ פִּתְחֵי עוֹלָם, וְיָבֹא מֶלֶךְ הַכָּבוֹד: מִי הוּא זֶה מֶלֶךְ הַכָּבוֹד, יהוה צְבָאוֹת הוּא מֶלֶךְ הַכָּבוֹד, סֶלָה:

As the ספר תורה *is placed into the* ארון קודש*, say:*

במדבר י וּבְנֻחֹה יֹאמַר, שׁוּבָה יהוה רִבְבוֹת אַלְפֵי יִשְׂרָאֵל: קוּמָה יהוה
תהלים קלב לִמְנוּחָתֶךָ, אַתָּה וַאֲרוֹן עֻזֶּךָ: כֹּהֲנֶיךָ יִלְבְּשׁוּ־צֶדֶק, וַחֲסִידֶיךָ יְרַנֵּנוּ:
בַּעֲבוּר דָּוִד עַבְדֶּךָ אַל־תָּשֵׁב פְּנֵי מְשִׁיחֶךָ: כִּי לֶקַח טוֹב נָתַתִּי לָכֶם, משלי ד
תּוֹרָתִי אַל־תַּעֲזֹבוּ: עֵץ־חַיִּים הִיא לַמַּחֲזִיקִים בָּהּ, וְתֹמְכֶיהָ מְאֻשָּׁר: משלי ג
דְּרָכֶיהָ דַרְכֵי־נֹעַם וְכָל־נְתִיבוֹתֶיהָ שָׁלוֹם: ‹ הֲשִׁיבֵנוּ יהוה אֵלֶיךָ וְנָשׁוּבָה, איכה ה
חַדֵּשׁ יָמֵינוּ כְּקֶדֶם:

The ארון קודש *is closed.*

חצי קדיש

ש״ץ: יִתְגַּדַּל וְיִתְקַדַּשׁ שְׁמֵהּ רַבָּא (קהל: אָמֵן)
בְּעָלְמָא דִּי בְרָא כִרְעוּתֵהּ
וְיַמְלִיךְ מַלְכוּתֵהּ
בְּחַיֵּיכוֹן וּבְיוֹמֵיכוֹן, וּבְחַיֵּי דְכָל בֵּית יִשְׂרָאֵל
בַּעֲגָלָא וּבִזְמַן קָרִיב, וְאִמְרוּ אָמֵן. (קהל: אָמֵן)

קהל וש״ץ: יְהֵא שְׁמֵהּ רַבָּא מְבָרַךְ לְעָלַם וּלְעָלְמֵי עָלְמַיָּא.

ש״ץ: יִתְבָּרַךְ וְיִשְׁתַּבַּח וְיִתְפָּאַר וְיִתְרוֹמַם וְיִתְנַשֵּׂא
וְיִתְהַדָּר וְיִתְעַלֶּה וְיִתְהַלָּל
שְׁמֵהּ דְּקֻדְשָׁא בְּרִיךְ הוּא (קהל: בְּרִיךְ הוּא)
לְעֵלָּא מִן כָּל בִּרְכָתָא / בשבת שובה: לְעֵלָּא לְעֵלָּא מִכָּל בִּרְכָתָא/
וְשִׁירָתָא, תֻּשְׁבְּחָתָא וְנֶחֱמָתָא, דַּאֲמִירָן בְּעָלְמָא
וְאִמְרוּ אָמֵן. (קהל: אָמֵן)

On Yom Tov (including one that falls on Shabbat) say the appropriate Amida on page 770.

THE AMIDA

The following prayer, until "in former years" on page 620, is said silently, standing with feet together. If there is a minyan, the Amida is repeated aloud by the Leader. Take three steps forward and at the points indicated by ▾, bend the knees at the first word, bow at the second, and stand straight before saying God's name.

When I proclaim the LORD's name, give glory to our God. *Deut. 32*
O LORD, open my lips, so that my mouth may declare Your praise. *Ps. 51*

PATRIARCHS

▾בָּרוּךְ Blessed are You, LORD our God and God of our fathers,
God of Abraham, God of Isaac and God of Jacob;
the great, mighty and awesome God, God Most High,
who bestows acts of loving-kindness and creates all,
who remembers the loving-kindness of the fathers
and will bring a Redeemer to their children's children
for the sake of His name, in love.

On Shabbat Shuva: Remember us for life,
O King who desires life,
and write us in the book of life –
for Your sake, O God of life.

King, Helper, Savior, Shield:
▾Blessed are You, LORD, Shield of Abraham.

DIVINE MIGHT

אַתָּה גִּבּוֹר You are eternally mighty, LORD.
You give life to the dead and have great power to save.

The phrase "He makes the wind blow and the rain fall" is added from Simḥat Torah until Pesaḥ. In Israel, the phrase "He causes the dew to fall" is added from Pesaḥ until Shemini Atzeret. See laws 129–131.

In fall & winter: He makes the wind blow and the rain fall.

In Israel, in spring & summer: He causes the dew to fall.

On יום טוב *(including one that falls on* שבת*) say the appropriate* עמידה *on page 771.*

עמידה

The following prayer, until קַדְמֹנִיּוֹת *on page 621, is said silently, standing with feet together. If there is a* מנין*, the* עמידה *is repeated aloud by the* שליח ציבור*. Take three steps forward and at the points indicated by* ˅*, bend the knees at the first word, bow at the second, and stand straight before saying God's name.*

כִּי שֵׁם יהוה אֶקְרָא, הָבוּ גֹדֶל לֵאלֹהֵינוּ: דברים לב
אֲדֹנָי, שְׂפָתַי תִּפְתָּח, וּפִי יַגִּיד תְּהִלָּתֶךָ: תהלים נא

אבות

˅בָּרוּךְ אַתָּה יהוה, אֱלֹהֵינוּ וֵאלֹהֵי אֲבוֹתֵינוּ
אֱלֹהֵי אַבְרָהָם, אֱלֹהֵי יִצְחָק, וֵאלֹהֵי יַעֲקֹב
הָאֵל הַגָּדוֹל הַגִּבּוֹר וְהַנּוֹרָא, אֵל עֶלְיוֹן
גּוֹמֵל חֲסָדִים טוֹבִים, וְקוֹנֵה הַכֹּל
וְזוֹכֵר חַסְדֵי אָבוֹת
וּמֵבִיא גוֹאֵל לִבְנֵי בְנֵיהֶם לְמַעַן שְׁמוֹ בְּאַהֲבָה.

בשבת שובה: זָכְרֵנוּ לְחַיִּים, מֶלֶךְ חָפֵץ בַּחַיִּים
וְכָתְבֵנוּ בְּסֵפֶר הַחַיִּים
לְמַעַנְךָ אֱלֹהִים חַיִּים.

מֶלֶךְ עוֹזֵר וּמוֹשִׁיעַ וּמָגֵן.
˅בָּרוּךְ אַתָּה יהוה, מָגֵן אַבְרָהָם.

גבורות

אַתָּה גִּבּוֹר לְעוֹלָם, אֲדֹנָי
מְחַיֵּה מֵתִים אַתָּה, רַב לְהוֹשִׁיעַ

The phrase מַשִּׁיב הָרְוּחַ *is added from* שמחת תורה *until* פסח*.*
In ארץ ישראל*, the phrase* מוֹרִיד הַטָּל *is added from* פסח *until* שמיני עצרת*. See laws 129–131.*

בחורף: מַשִּׁיב הָרְוּחַ וּמוֹרִיד הַגֶּשֶׁם / בארץ ישראל בקיץ: מוֹרִיד הַטָּל

He sustains the living with loving-kindness,
and with great compassion revives the dead.
He supports the fallen, heals the sick, sets captives free,
and keeps His faith with those who sleep in the dust.
Who is like You, Master of might,
and who can compare to You,
O King who brings death and gives life,
and makes salvation grow?

On Shabbat Shuva: Who is like You, compassionate Father,
who remembers His creatures in compassion, for life?

Faithful are You to revive the dead.
Blessed are You, LORD, who revives the dead.

When saying the Amida silently, continue with "You are holy" on the next page.

KEDUSHA

During the Leader's Repetition, the following is said standing with feet together, rising on the toes at the words indicated by ▴.

Cong. then Leader: נְקַדֵּשׁ We will sanctify Your name on earth,
as they sanctify it in the highest heavens,
as is written by Your prophet,
"And they [the angels] call to one another saying: *Is. 6*

Cong. then Leader: ▴Holy, ▴holy, ▴holy is the LORD of hosts
the whole world is filled with His glory."
Those facing them say "Blessed – "

Cong. then Leader: ▴"Blessed is the LORD's glory from His place." *Ezek. 3*
And in Your holy Writings it is written thus:

Cong. then Leader: ▴"The LORD shall reign for ever. He is your God, Zion, *Ps. 146*
from generation to generation, Halleluya!"

Leader: From generation to generation we will declare Your greatness,
and we will proclaim Your holiness for evermore.
Your praise, our God, shall not leave our mouth forever,
for You, God, are a great and holy King. Blessed are You, LORD,
the holy God. / *On Shabbat Shuva:* the holy King./

The Leader continues with "You are One" on the next page.

מְכַלְכֵּל חַיִּים בְּחֶסֶד, מְחַיֵּה מֵתִים בְּרַחֲמִים רַבִּים
סוֹמֵךְ נוֹפְלִים, וְרוֹפֵא חוֹלִים, וּמַתִּיר אֲסוּרִים
וּמְקַיֵּם אֱמוּנָתוֹ לִישֵׁנֵי עָפָר.
מִי כָמְוֹךָ, בַּעַל גְּבוּרוֹת, וּמִי דּוֹמֶה לָּךְ
מֶלֶךְ, מֵמִית וּמְחַיֶּה וּמַצְמִיחַ יְשׁוּעָה.

בשבת שובה: מִי כָמְוֹךָ אַב הָרַחֲמִים
זוֹכֵר יְצוּרָיו לְחַיִּים בְּרַחֲמִים.

וְנֶאֱמָן אַתָּה לְהַחֲיוֹת מֵתִים.
בָּרוּךְ אַתָּה יהוה, מְחַיֵּה הַמֵּתִים.

When saying the עמידה *silently, continue with* אַתָּה קָדוֹשׁ *on the next page.*

קדושה

During the חזרת הש״ץ*, the following is said standing with feet together, rising on the toes at the words indicated by* ˄.

then קהל ש״ץ: נְקַדֵּשׁ אֶת שִׁמְךָ בָּעוֹלָם, כְּשֵׁם שֶׁמַּקְדִּישִׁים אוֹתוֹ בִּשְׁמֵי מָרוֹם
כַּכָּתוּב עַל יַד נְבִיאֶךָ: וְקָרָא זֶה אֶל־זֶה וְאָמַר ישעיה ו

then קהל ש״ץ: ˄קָדוֹשׁ, ˄קָדוֹשׁ, ˄קָדוֹשׁ, יהוה צְבָאוֹת, מְלֹא כָל־הָאָרֶץ כְּבוֹדוֹ:
לְעֻמָּתָם בָּרוּךְ יֹאמֵרוּ

then קהל ש״ץ: ˄בָּרוּךְ כְּבוֹד־יהוה מִמְּקוֹמוֹ: יחזקאל ג
וּבְדִבְרֵי קָדְשְׁךָ כָּתוּב לֵאמֹר

then קהל ש״ץ: ˄יִמְלֹךְ יהוה לְעוֹלָם, אֱלֹהַיִךְ צִיּוֹן לְדֹר וָדֹר, הַלְלוּיָהּ: תהלים קמו

ש״ץ: לְדוֹר וָדוֹר נַגִּיד גָּדְלֶךָ, וּלְנֵצַח נְצָחִים קְדֻשָּׁתְךָ נַקְדִּישׁ
וְשִׁבְחֲךָ אֱלֹהֵינוּ מִפִּינוּ לֹא יָמוּשׁ לְעוֹלָם וָעֶד
כִּי אֵל מֶלֶךְ גָּדוֹל וְקָדוֹשׁ אָתָּה. בָּרוּךְ אַתָּה יהוה
הָאֵל הַקָּדוֹשׁ. / בשבת שובה: הַמֶּלֶךְ הַקָּדוֹשׁ./

The שליח ציבור *continues with* אַתָּה אֶחָד *on the next page.*

HOLINESS

אַתָּה קָדוֹשׁ You are holy and Your name is holy,
and holy ones praise You daily, Selah!
Blessed are You, Lord,
the holy God. / *On Shabbat Shuva:* the holy King./
(*If forgotten, repeat the Amida.*)

HOLINESS OF THE DAY

אַתָּה You are One, Your name is One;
and who is like Your people Israel,
a nation unique on earth?
Splendor of greatness and a crown of salvation
is the day of rest and holiness You have given Your people.
Abraham will rejoice, Isaac will sing for joy,
Jacob and his children will find rest in it –
a rest of love and generosity,
a rest of truth and faith,
a rest of peace and tranquility,
calm and trust;
a complete rest in which You find favor.
May Your children recognize and know
that their rest comes from You,
and that by their rest they sanctify Your name.

---

the Sabbath all testify to one another; God and Israel testify to the holiness of the Sabbath; Israel and the Sabbath testify to the creative and redemptive power of God; God and the Sabbath testify to the uniqueness of Israel."

תִּפְאֶרֶת גְּדֻלָּה *Splendor of greatness:* As the day reaches its greatest intensity, the emphasis shifts to the experiential quality of the day itself. The word *menuḥa*, "rest, serenity," appears seven times in this one paragraph, together with an idyllic description of a world at peace with itself: "a rest of love and generosity, a rest of truth and faith, a rest of peace and tranquility, calm and trust." אַבְרָהָם יָגֵל *Abraham will rejoice:* a reference to the future, when the patriarchs will rejoice that their descendants have found peace and "the day that is wholly Sabbath."

קדושת השם

אַתָּה קָדוֹשׁ וְשִׁמְךָ קָדוֹשׁ
וּקְדוֹשִׁים בְּכָל יוֹם יְהַלְלְוּךָ סֶּלָה.
בָּרוּךְ אַתָּה יהוה
הָאֵל הַקָּדוֹשׁ. / בשבת שובה: הַמֶּלֶךְ הַקָּדוֹשׁ./

(*If forgotten, repeat the* עמידה.)

קדושת היום

אַתָּה אֶחָד וְשִׁמְךָ אֶחָד
וּמִי כְּעַמְּךָ יִשְׂרָאֵל גּוֹי אֶחָד בָּאָרֶץ.
תִּפְאֶרֶת גְּדֻלָּה וַעֲטֶרֶת יְשׁוּעָה
יוֹם מְנוּחָה וּקְדֻשָּׁה לְעַמְּךָ נָתָתָּ.
אַבְרָהָם יָגֵל, יִצְחָק יְרַנֵּן, יַעֲקֹב וּבָנָיו יָנְוּחוּ בוֹ
מְנוּחַת אַהֲבָה וּנְדָבָה, מְנוּחַת אֱמֶת וֶאֱמוּנָה
מְנוּחַת שָׁלוֹם וְשַׁלְוָה וְהַשְׁקֵט וָבֶטַח
מְנוּחָה שְׁלֵמָה שֶׁאַתָּה רוֹצֶה בָּהּ.
יַכִּירוּ בָנֶיךָ וְיֵדְעוּ, כִּי מֵאִתְּךָ הִיא מְנוּחָתָם
וְעַל מְנוּחָתָם יַקְדִּישׁוּ אֶת שְׁמֶךָ.

אַתָּה אֶחָד וְשִׁמְךָ אֶחָד *You are One, Your name is One:* As mentioned before, Shabbat is unique in that the central section of the evening, morning and afternoon Amida prayers is different on each occasion. There are three related explanations: (1) the prayers chart the movement from creation to revelation to redemption; (2) they speak of past, present and future; and (3) they describe the three stages of a wedding: betrothal, rejoicing and *yihud*, the coming together of bride and groom. The afternoon prayer fits this pattern closely. It speaks of redemption and the future, when "God shall be One and His name One," and of *yihud*, when the oneness of God joins the uniqueness of the Jewish people in perfect union. A Midrash teaches: "God, Israel and

אֱלֹהֵינוּ Our God and God of our ancestors,
find favor in our rest.
Make us holy through Your commandments
and grant us our share in Your Torah.
Satisfy us with Your goodness, grant us joy in Your salvation,
and purify our hearts to serve You in truth.
In love and favor, LORD our God,
grant us as our heritage Your holy Sabbaths,
so that Israel who sanctify Your name may find rest on them.
Blessed are You, LORD, who sanctifies the Sabbath.

TEMPLE SERVICE

רְצֵה Find favor, LORD our God,
in Your people Israel and their prayer.
Restore the service to Your most holy House,
and accept in love and favor
the fire-offerings of Israel and their prayer.
May the service of Your people Israel always find favor with You.

On Rosh Ḥodesh and Ḥol HaMo'ed:

אֱלֹהֵינוּ Our God and God of our ancestors, may there rise, come, reach, appear, be favored, heard, regarded and remembered before You, our recollection and remembrance, as well as the remembrance of our ancestors, and of the Messiah son of David Your servant, and of Jerusalem Your holy city, and of all Your people the house of Israel – for deliverance and well-being, grace, loving-kindness and compassion, life and peace, on this day of:

On Rosh Ḥodesh: Rosh Ḥodesh.
On Pesaḥ: the Festival of Matzot.
On Sukkot: the Festival of Sukkot.

On it remember us, LORD our God, for good; recollect us for blessing, and deliver us for life. In accord with Your promise of salvation and compassion, spare us and be gracious to us; have compassion on us and deliver us, for our eyes are turned to You because You, God, are a gracious and compassionate King.

וְתֶחֱזֶינָה And may our eyes
witness Your return to Zion in compassion.
Blessed are You, LORD, who restores His Presence to Zion.

אֱלֹהֵינוּ וֵאלֹהֵי אֲבוֹתֵינוּ
רְצֵה בִמְנוּחָתֵנוּ
קַדְּשֵׁנוּ בְּמִצְוֹתֶיךָ וְתֵן חֶלְקֵנוּ בְּתוֹרָתֶךָ
שַׂבְּעֵנוּ מִטּוּבֶךָ וְשַׂמְּחֵנוּ בִּישׁוּעָתֶךָ
וְטַהֵר לִבֵּנוּ לְעָבְדְּךָ בֶּאֱמֶת.
וְהַנְחִילֵנוּ יהוה אֱלֹהֵינוּ בְּאַהֲבָה וּבְרָצוֹן שַׁבְּתוֹת קָדְשֶׁךָ
וְיָנוּחוּ בָם יִשְׂרָאֵל מְקַדְּשֵׁי שְׁמֶךָ.
בָּרוּךְ אַתָּה יהוה, מְקַדֵּשׁ הַשַּׁבָּת.

עבודה

רְצֵה יהוה אֱלֹהֵינוּ בְּעַמְּךָ יִשְׂרָאֵל, וּבִתְפִלָּתָם
וְהָשֵׁב אֶת הָעֲבוֹדָה לִדְבִיר בֵּיתֶךָ
וְאִשֵּׁי יִשְׂרָאֵל וּתְפִלָּתָם בְּאַהֲבָה תְקַבֵּל בְּרָצוֹן
וּתְהִי לְרָצוֹן תָּמִיד עֲבוֹדַת יִשְׂרָאֵל עַמֶּךָ.

On ראש חודש *and* חול המועד:

אֱלֹהֵינוּ וֵאלֹהֵי אֲבוֹתֵינוּ, יַעֲלֶה וְיָבוֹא וְיַגִּיעַ, וְיֵרָאֶה וְיֵרָצֶה וְיִשָּׁמַע, וְיִפָּקֵד וְיִזָּכֵר זִכְרוֹנֵנוּ וּפִקְדוֹנֵנוּ, וְזִכְרוֹן אֲבוֹתֵינוּ, וְזִכְרוֹן מָשִׁיחַ בֶּן דָּוִד עַבְדֶּךָ, וְזִכְרוֹן יְרוּשָׁלַיִם עִיר קָדְשֶׁךָ, וְזִכְרוֹן כָּל עַמְּךָ בֵּית יִשְׂרָאֵל, לְפָנֶיךָ, לִפְלֵיטָה לְטוֹבָה, לְחֵן וּלְחֶסֶד וּלְרַחֲמִים, לְחַיִּים וּלְשָׁלוֹם בְּיוֹם

בראש חודש: רֹאשׁ הַחֹדֶשׁ / בפסח: חַג הַמַּצּוֹת / בסוכות: חַג הַסֻּכּוֹת

הַזֶּה. זָכְרֵנוּ יהוה אֱלֹהֵינוּ בּוֹ לְטוֹבָה, וּפָקְדֵנוּ בוֹ לִבְרָכָה, וְהוֹשִׁיעֵנוּ בוֹ לְחַיִּים. וּבִדְבַר יְשׁוּעָה וְרַחֲמִים, חוּס וְחָנֵּנוּ וְרַחֵם עָלֵינוּ וְהוֹשִׁיעֵנוּ, כִּי אֵלֶיךָ עֵינֵינוּ, כִּי אֵל מֶלֶךְ חַנּוּן וְרַחוּם אָתָּה.

וְתֶחֱזֶינָה עֵינֵינוּ בְּשׁוּבְךָ לְצִיּוֹן בְּרַחֲמִים.
בָּרוּךְ אַתָּה יהוה, הַמַּחֲזִיר שְׁכִינָתוֹ לְצִיּוֹן.

THANKSGIVING

Bow at the first nine words.

מוֹדִים We give thanks to You,
for You are the LORD our God
and God of our ancestors
for ever and all time.
You are the Rock of our lives,
Shield of our salvation
from generation to generation.
We will thank You and
declare Your praise for our lives,
which are entrusted into Your hand;
for our souls,
which are placed in Your charge;
for Your miracles which are with us every day;
and for Your wonders and favors
at all times, evening, morning and midday.
You are good –
for Your compassion never fails.
You are compassionate –
for Your loving-kindnesses never cease.
We have always placed our hope in You.

During the Leader's Repetition, the congregation says quietly:

מוֹדִים We give thanks to You,
for You are the LORD our God
and God of our ancestors,
God of all flesh, who formed us
and formed the universe.
Blessings and thanks
are due to Your great
and holy name for giving us
life and sustaining us.
May You continue
to give us life and sustain us;
and may You gather our exiles
to Your holy courts,
to keep Your decrees,
do Your will and serve You
with a perfect heart,
for it is for us
to give You thanks.
Blessed be God to whom
thanksgiving is due.

On Ḥanukka:

עַל הַנִּסִּים [We thank You also] for the miracles, the redemption, the mighty deeds, the salvations, and the victories in battle which You performed for our ancestors in those days, at this time.

בִּימֵי מַתִּתְיָהוּ In the days of Mattityahu, son of Yoḥanan, the High Priest, the Hasmonean, and his sons, the wicked Greek kingdom rose up against Your people Israel to make them forget Your Torah and to force them to transgress the statutes of Your will. It was then that You in Your great compassion stood by them in the time of their distress. You championed their cause, judged their claim, and avenged their wrong. You delivered the strong into the hands of the weak, the many into the hands of the few, the impure into the hands of the pure, the wicked into the hands of the righteous, and the arrogant into the hands of those who were engaged in the study of Your Torah. You made for Yourself great and holy renown in Your world, and for Your people Israel You performed a great salvation and redemption as of this very day. Your children then entered the holiest part of Your House, cleansed Your Temple, purified Your Sanctuary, kindled lights in Your holy courts, and designated these eight days of Ḥanukka for giving thanks and praise to Your great name.

Continue with "For all these things" on the next page.

הודאה

Bow at the first five words.

מוֹדִים אֲנַחְנוּ לָךְ
שָׁאַתָּה הוּא יהוה אֱלֹהֵינוּ
וֵאלֹהֵי אֲבוֹתֵינוּ לְעוֹלָם וָעֶד.
צוּר חַיֵּינוּ, מָגֵן יִשְׁעֵנוּ
אַתָּה הוּא לְדוֹר וָדוֹר.
נוֹדֶה לְּךָ וּנְסַפֵּר תְּהִלָּתֶךָ
עַל חַיֵּינוּ הַמְּסוּרִים בְּיָדֶךָ
וְעַל נִשְׁמוֹתֵינוּ הַפְּקוּדוֹת לָךְ
וְעַל נִסֶּיךָ שֶׁבְּכָל יוֹם עִמָּנוּ
וְעַל נִפְלְאוֹתֶיךָ וְטוֹבוֹתֶיךָ
שֶׁבְּכָל עֵת, עֶרֶב וָבֹקֶר וְצָהֳרָיִם.
הַטּוֹב, כִּי לֹא כָלוּ רַחֲמֶיךָ
וְהַמְרַחֵם, כִּי לֹא תַמּוּ חֲסָדֶיךָ
מֵעוֹלָם קִוִּינוּ לָךְ.

During the חזרת הש״ץ, *the* קהל *says quietly:*

מוֹדִים אֲנַחְנוּ לָךְ
שָׁאַתָּה הוּא יהוה אֱלֹהֵינוּ
וֵאלֹהֵי אֲבוֹתֵינוּ
אֱלֹהֵי כָל בָּשָׂר
יוֹצְרֵנוּ, יוֹצֵר בְּרֵאשִׁית.
בְּרָכוֹת וְהוֹדָאוֹת
לְשִׁמְךָ הַגָּדוֹל וְהַקָּדוֹשׁ
עַל שֶׁהֶחֱיִיתָנוּ וְקִיַּמְתָּנוּ.
כֵּן תְּחַיֵּנוּ וּתְקַיְּמֵנוּ
וְתֶאֱסֹף גָּלֻיּוֹתֵינוּ
לְחַצְרוֹת קָדְשֶׁךָ
לִשְׁמֹר חֻקֶּיךָ וְלַעֲשׂוֹת רְצוֹנֶךָ
וּלְעָבְדְּךָ בְּלֵבָב שָׁלֵם
עַל שֶׁאֲנַחְנוּ מוֹדִים לָךְ.
בָּרוּךְ אֵל הַהוֹדָאוֹת.

בחנוכה:

עַל הַנִּסִּים וְעַל הַפֻּרְקָן וְעַל הַגְּבוּרוֹת וְעַל הַתְּשׁוּעוֹת וְעַל הַמִּלְחָמוֹת שֶׁעָשִׂיתָ לַאֲבוֹתֵינוּ בַּיָּמִים הָהֵם בַּזְּמַן הַזֶּה.

בִּימֵי מַתִּתְיָהוּ בֶּן יוֹחָנָן כֹּהֵן גָּדוֹל חַשְׁמוֹנַאי וּבָנָיו, כְּשֶׁעָמְדָה מַלְכוּת יָוָן הָרְשָׁעָה עַל עַמְּךָ יִשְׂרָאֵל לְהַשְׁכִּיחָם תּוֹרָתֶךָ וּלְהַעֲבִירָם מֵחֻקֵּי רְצוֹנֶךָ, וְאַתָּה בְּרַחֲמֶיךָ הָרַבִּים עָמַדְתָּ לָהֶם בְּעֵת צָרָתָם, רַבְתָּ אֶת רִיבָם, דַּנְתָּ אֶת דִּינָם, נָקַמְתָּ אֶת נִקְמָתָם, מָסַרְתָּ גִבּוֹרִים בְּיַד חַלָּשִׁים, וְרַבִּים בְּיַד מְעַטִּים, וּטְמֵאִים בְּיַד טְהוֹרִים, וּרְשָׁעִים בְּיַד צַדִּיקִים, וְזֵדִים בְּיַד עוֹסְקֵי תוֹרָתֶךָ, וּלְךָ עָשִׂיתָ שֵׁם גָּדוֹל וְקָדוֹשׁ בְּעוֹלָמֶךָ, וּלְעַמְּךָ יִשְׂרָאֵל עָשִׂיתָ תְּשׁוּעָה גְדוֹלָה וּפֻרְקָן כְּהַיּוֹם הַזֶּה. וְאַחַר כֵּן בָּאוּ בָנֶיךָ לִדְבִיר בֵּיתֶךָ, וּפִנּוּ אֶת הֵיכָלֶךָ, וְטִהֲרוּ אֶת מִקְדָּשֶׁךָ, וְהִדְלִיקוּ נֵרוֹת בְּחַצְרוֹת קָדְשֶׁךָ, וְקָבְעוּ שְׁמוֹנַת יְמֵי חֲנֻכָּה אֵלּוּ, לְהוֹדוֹת וּלְהַלֵּל לְשִׁמְךָ הַגָּדוֹל.

Continue with וְעַל כֻּלָּם *on the next page.*

On Shushan Purim in Jerusalem:

עַל הַנִּסִּים [We thank You also] for the miracles, the redemption, the mighty deeds, the salvations, and the victories in battle which You performed for our ancestors in those days, at this time.

בִּימֵי מָרְדְּכַי In the days of Mordekhai and Esther, in Shushan the capital, the wicked Haman rose up against them and sought to destroy, slay and exterminate all the Jews, young and old, children and women, on one day, the thirteenth day of the twelfth month, which is the month of Adar, and to plunder their possessions. Then You in Your great compassion thwarted his counsel, frustrated his plans, and caused his scheme to recoil on his own head, so that they hanged him and his sons on the gallows. *Esther 3*

Continue with "For all these things."

וְעַל כֻּלָּם For all these things may Your name be blessed and exalted, our King, continually, for ever and all time.

On Shabbat Shuva: And write, for a good life,
all the children of Your covenant.

Let all that lives thank You, Selah! and praise Your name in truth, God, our Savior and Help, Selah!
▾Blessed are You, LORD, whose name is "the Good"
and to whom thanks are due.

PEACE

שָׁלוֹם רָב Grant
great peace
to Your people Israel
for ever,
for You are
the sovereign LORD
of all peace;
and may it be good
in Your eyes
to bless Your people Israel
at every time,
at every hour,
with Your peace.

In Israel:

שִׂים שָׁלוֹם Grant peace,
goodness and blessing,
grace, loving-kindness and compassion
to us and all Israel Your people.
Bless us, our Father, all as one,
with the light of Your face,
for by the light of Your face
You have given us, LORD our God,
the Torah of life and love of kindness,
righteousness, blessing, compassion,
life and peace.
May it be good in Your eyes
to bless Your people Israel
at every time, in every hour,
with Your peace.

בשושן פורים בירושלים:
עַל הַנִּסִּים וְעַל הַפֻּרְקָן וְעַל הַגְּבוּרוֹת וְעַל הַתְּשׁוּעוֹת וְעַל הַמִּלְחָמוֹת שֶׁעָשִׂיתָ לַאֲבוֹתֵינוּ בַּיָּמִים הָהֵם בַּזְּמַן הַזֶּה.

בִּימֵי מָרְדֳּכַי וְאֶסְתֵּר בְּשׁוּשַׁן הַבִּירָה, כְּשֶׁעָמַד עֲלֵיהֶם הָמָן הָרָשָׁע, בִּקֵּשׁ לְהַשְׁמִיד אסתר ג
לַהֲרֹג וּלְאַבֵּד אֶת־כָּל־הַיְּהוּדִים מִנַּעַר וְעַד־זָקֵן טַף וְנָשִׁים בְּיוֹם אֶחָד, בִּשְׁלוֹשָׁה עָשָׂר לְחֹדֶשׁ שְׁנֵים־עָשָׂר, הוּא־חֹדֶשׁ אֲדָר, וּשְׁלָלָם לָבוֹז: וְאַתָּה בְּרַחֲמֶיךָ הָרַבִּים הֵפַרְתָּ אֶת עֲצָתוֹ, וְקִלְקַלְתָּ אֶת מַחֲשַׁבְתּוֹ, וַהֲשֵׁבוֹתָ לּוֹ גְּמוּלוֹ בְּרֹאשׁוֹ, וְתָלוּ אוֹתוֹ וְאֶת בָּנָיו עַל הָעֵץ.

Continue with .וְעַל כֻּלָּם

וְעַל כֻּלָּם יִתְבָּרַךְ וְיִתְרוֹמַם שִׁמְךָ מַלְכֵּנוּ תָּמִיד לְעוֹלָם וָעֶד.

בשבת שובה: וּכְתֹב לְחַיִּים טוֹבִים כָּל בְּנֵי בְרִיתֶךָ.

וְכֹל הַחַיִּים יוֹדוּךָ סֶּלָה, וִיהַלְלוּ אֶת שִׁמְךָ בֶּאֱמֶת
הָאֵל יְשׁוּעָתֵנוּ וְעֶזְרָתֵנוּ סֶלָה.
בָּרוּךְ אַתָּה יהוה, הַטּוֹב שִׁמְךָ וּלְךָ נָאֶה לְהוֹדוֹת.

ברכת שלום

שָׁלוֹם רָב עַל יִשְׂרָאֵל עַמְּךָ
תָּשִׂים לְעוֹלָם
כִּי אַתָּה הוּא
מֶלֶךְ אָדוֹן לְכָל הַשָּׁלוֹם.
וְטוֹב בְּעֵינֶיךָ
לְבָרֵךְ אֶת עַמְּךָ יִשְׂרָאֵל
בְּכָל עֵת וּבְכָל שָׁעָה
בִּשְׁלוֹמֶךָ.

In ארץ ישראל:
שִׂים שָׁלוֹם טוֹבָה וּבְרָכָה
חֵן וָחֶסֶד וְרַחֲמִים
עָלֵינוּ וְעַל כָּל יִשְׂרָאֵל עַמֶּךָ.
בָּרְכֵנוּ אָבִינוּ כֻּלָּנוּ כְּאֶחָד בְּאוֹר פָּנֶיךָ
כִּי בְאוֹר פָּנֶיךָ נָתַתָּ לָּנוּ יהוה אֱלֹהֵינוּ
תּוֹרַת חַיִּים וְאַהֲבַת חֶסֶד
וּצְדָקָה וּבְרָכָה וְרַחֲמִים וְחַיִּים וְשָׁלוֹם.
וְטוֹב בְּעֵינֶיךָ לְבָרֵךְ אֶת עַמְּךָ יִשְׂרָאֵל
בְּכָל עֵת וּבְכָל שָׁעָה בִּשְׁלוֹמֶךָ.

On Shabbat Shuva: In the book of life, blessing, peace and prosperity,
may we and all Your people the house of Israel be remembered
and written before You for a good life, and for peace.*

Blessed are You, Lord, who blesses His people Israel with peace.

**On Shabbat Shuva outside Israel, many end the blessing:*
Blessed are You, Lord, who makes peace.

The following verse concludes the Leader's Repetition of the Amida. Some also say it here as part of the silent Amida. See law 368.

May the words of my mouth and the meditation of my heart *Ps. 19*
find favor before You, Lord, my Rock and Redeemer.

אֱלֹהַי My God, *Berakhot 17a*
guard my tongue from evil
and my lips from deceitful speech.
To those who curse me, let my soul be silent;
may my soul be to all like the dust.
Open my heart to Your Torah
and let my soul pursue Your commandments.
As for all who plan evil against me,
swiftly thwart their counsel and frustrate their plans.
Act for the sake of Your name; act for the sake of Your right hand;
act for the sake of Your holiness; act for the sake of Your Torah.
That Your beloved ones may be delivered, *Ps. 60*
save with Your right hand and answer me.
May the words of my mouth *Ps. 19*
and the meditation of my heart find favor before You,
Lord, my Rock and Redeemer.

Bow, take three steps back, then bow, first left, then right, then center, while saying:

May He who makes peace in His high places,
make peace for us and all Israel – and say: Amen.

יְהִי רָצוֹן May it be Your will, Lord our God and God of our ancestors,
that the Temple be rebuilt speedily in our days, and grant us a share in Your Torah.
And there we will serve You with reverence,
as in the days of old and as in former years.
Then the offering of Judah and Jerusalem *Mal. 3*
will be pleasing to the Lord as in the days of old and as in former years.

בשבת שובה: בְּסֵפֶר חַיִּים, בְּרָכָה וְשָׁלוֹם, וּפַרְנָסָה טוֹבָה
נִזָּכֵר וְנִכָּתֵב לְפָנֶיךָ, אֲנַחְנוּ וְכָל עַמְּךָ בֵּית יִשְׂרָאֵל
לְחַיִּים טוֹבִים וּלְשָׁלוֹם.*

בָּרוּךְ אַתָּה יהוה, הַמְבָרֵךְ אֶת עַמּוֹ יִשְׂרָאֵל בַּשָּׁלוֹם.

**On* שבת שובה *in* חוץ לארץ *many end the blessing:*

בָּרוּךְ אַתָּה יהוה, עוֹשֵׂה הַשָּׁלוֹם.

The following verse concludes the חזרת הש״ץ.
Some also say it here as part of the silent עמידה*. See law 368.*

יִהְיוּ לְרָצוֹן אִמְרֵי־פִי וְהֶגְיוֹן לִבִּי לְפָנֶיךָ, יהוה צוּרִי וְגוֹאֲלִי: תהלים יט

אֱלֹהַי ברכות יז.

נְצֹר לְשׁוֹנִי מֵרָע וּשְׂפָתַי מִדַּבֵּר מִרְמָה
וְלִמְקַלְלַי נַפְשִׁי תִדֹּם, וְנַפְשִׁי כֶּעָפָר לַכֹּל תִּהְיֶה.
פְּתַח לִבִּי בְּתוֹרָתֶךָ, וּבְמִצְוֹתֶיךָ תִּרְדֹּף נַפְשִׁי.
וְכָל הַחוֹשְׁבִים עָלַי רָעָה
מְהֵרָה הָפֵר עֲצָתָם וְקַלְקֵל מַחֲשַׁבְתָּם.
עֲשֵׂה לְמַעַן שְׁמֶךָ, עֲשֵׂה לְמַעַן יְמִינֶךָ
עֲשֵׂה לְמַעַן קְדֻשָּׁתֶךָ, עֲשֵׂה לְמַעַן תּוֹרָתֶךָ.
לְמַעַן יֵחָלְצוּן יְדִידֶיךָ, הוֹשִׁיעָה יְמִינְךָ וַעֲנֵנִי: תהלים ס
יִהְיוּ לְרָצוֹן אִמְרֵי־פִי וְהֶגְיוֹן לִבִּי לְפָנֶיךָ, יהוה צוּרִי וְגוֹאֲלִי: תהלים יט

Bow, take three steps back, then bow, first left, then right, then center, while saying:

עֹשֶׂה שָׁלוֹם/ בשבת שובה: הַשָּׁלוֹם/ בִּמְרוֹמָיו
הוּא יַעֲשֶׂה שָׁלוֹם עָלֵינוּ וְעַל כָּל יִשְׂרָאֵל, וְאִמְרוּ אָמֵן.

יְהִי רָצוֹן מִלְּפָנֶיךָ יהוה אֱלֹהֵינוּ וֵאלֹהֵי אֲבוֹתֵינוּ
שֶׁיִּבָּנֶה בֵּית הַמִּקְדָּשׁ בִּמְהֵרָה בְיָמֵינוּ, וְתֵן חֶלְקֵנוּ בְּתוֹרָתֶךָ
וְשָׁם נַעֲבָדְךָ בְּיִרְאָה כִּימֵי עוֹלָם וּכְשָׁנִים קַדְמוֹנִיּוֹת.
וְעָרְבָה לַיהוה מִנְחַת יְהוּדָה וִירוּשָׁלָםִ כִּימֵי עוֹלָם וּכְשָׁנִים קַדְמוֹנִיּוֹת: מלאכי ג

The following is omitted on days when Taḥanun is not said (see page 232).

צִדְקָתְךָ Your righteousness is an everlasting righteousness, and Your Torah is truth. Ps. 119
Your righteousness, O God, reaches to the highest heights, for You have done great things. Ps. 71
O God, who is like You?
Your righteousness is like the mighty mountains; Ps. 36
Your judgments like the great depths.
O Lord, You save both man and beast.

FULL KADDISH

Leader: יִתְגַּדַּל Magnified and sanctified
may His great name be,
in the world He created by His will.
May He establish His kingdom
in your lifetime and in your days,
and in the lifetime of all the house of Israel,
swiftly and soon –
and say: Amen.

All: May His great name be blessed for ever and all time.

Leader: Blessed and praised, glorified and exalted,
raised and honored, uplifted and lauded be
the name of the Holy One,
blessed be He, beyond any blessing,
song, praise and consolation uttered in the world –
and say: Amen.

---

to Joseph, Moses and David who, according to tradition, died on Shabbat afternoon. Like words we say at a funeral, they are an acceptance of loss as God's just decree. Because of these sad associations, the verses are not said at celebratory times of the year when *Taḥanun* is not said.

The following is omitted on days when תחנון *is not said* (*see page 233*).

צִדְקָתְךָ צֶדֶק לְעוֹלָם וְתוֹרָתְךָ אֱמֶת: תהלים קיט

וְצִדְקָתְךָ אֱלֹהִים עַד־מָרוֹם, אֲשֶׁר־עָשִׂיתָ גְדֹלוֹת תהלים עא
אֱלֹהִים, מִי כָמוֹךָ:

צִדְקָתְךָ כְּהַרְרֵי־אֵל, מִשְׁפָּטֶיךָ תְּהוֹם רַבָּה תהלים לו
אָדָם וּבְהֵמָה תוֹשִׁיעַ יהוה:

קדיש שלם

ש״ץ: יִתְגַּדַּל וְיִתְקַדַּשׁ שְׁמֵהּ רַבָּא (קהל: אָמֵן)
בְּעָלְמָא דִּי בְרָא כִרְעוּתֵהּ
וְיַמְלִיךְ מַלְכוּתֵהּ
בְּחַיֵּיכוֹן וּבְיוֹמֵיכוֹן וּבְחַיֵּי דְכָל בֵּית יִשְׂרָאֵל
בַּעֲגָלָא וּבִזְמַן קָרִיב, וְאִמְרוּ אָמֵן. (קהל: אָמֵן)

קהל וש״ץ: יְהֵא שְׁמֵהּ רַבָּא מְבָרַךְ לְעָלַם וּלְעָלְמֵי עָלְמַיָּא.

ש״ץ: יִתְבָּרַךְ וְיִשְׁתַּבַּח וְיִתְפָּאַר
וְיִתְרוֹמַם וְיִתְנַשֵּׂא וְיִתְהַדָּר וְיִתְעַלֶּה וְיִתְהַלָּל
שְׁמֵהּ דְּקֻדְשָׁא בְּרִיךְ הוּא (קהל: בְּרִיךְ הוּא)
לְעֵלָּא מִן כָּל בִּרְכָתָא
/בשבת שובה: לְעֵלָּא לְעֵלָּא מִכָּל בִּרְכָתָא/
וְשִׁירָתָא, תֻּשְׁבְּחָתָא וְנֶחֱמָתָא
דַּאֲמִירָן בְּעָלְמָא, וְאִמְרוּ אָמֵן. (קהל: אָמֵן)

צִדְקָתְךָ צֶדֶק לְעוֹלָם *Your righteousness is an everlasting righteousness:* Three verses vindicating God's justice. Their recitation at this point in the prayers dates back to the period of the Geonim, who explained them by reference

May the prayers and pleas of all Israel
be accepted by their Father in heaven –
and say: Amen.

May there be great peace from heaven,
and life for us and all Israel –
and say: Amen.

Bow, take three steps back, as if taking leave of the Divine Presence, then bow, first left, then right, then center, while saying:

May He who makes peace in His high places,
make peace for us and all Israel –
and say: Amen.

Between Sukkot and Pesaḥ, some recite Barekhi Nafshi, page 628, at this point.
Between Pesaḥ and Rosh HaShana some recite Ethics of the Fathers, page 640, at this point.

Stand while saying Aleinu. Bow at ▾.

עָלֵינוּ It is our duty to praise the Master of all,
and ascribe greatness to the Author of creation,
who has not made us like the nations of the lands
nor placed us like the families of the earth;
who has not made our portion like theirs,
nor our destiny like all their multitudes.
(For they worship vanity and emptiness,
and pray to a god who cannot save.)
▾But we bow in worship
and thank the Supreme King of kings,
the Holy One, blessed be He,
who extends the heavens and establishes the earth,
whose throne of glory is in the heavens above,
and whose power's Presence is in the highest of heights.
He is our God; there is no other.
Truly He is our King, there is none else,
as it is written in His Torah:
"You shall know and take to heart this day *Deut. 4*
that the LORD is God,
in heaven above and on earth below. There is no other."

תִּתְקַבַּל צְלוֹתְהוֹן וּבָעוּתְהוֹן דְּכָל יִשְׂרָאֵל
קֳדָם אֲבוּהוֹן דִּי בִשְׁמַיָּא, וְאִמְרוּ אָמֵן. (קהל: אָמֵן)

יְהֵא שְׁלָמָא רַבָּא מִן שְׁמַיָּא
וְחַיִּים, עָלֵינוּ וְעַל כָּל יִשְׂרָאֵל, וְאִמְרוּ אָמֵן. (קהל: אָמֵן)

Bow, take three steps back, as if taking leave of the Divine Presence, then bow, first left, then right, then center, while saying:

עֹשֶׂה שָׁלוֹם/ בשבת שובה: הַשָּׁלוֹם/ בִּמְרוֹמָיו
הוּא יַעֲשֶׂה שָׁלוֹם עָלֵינוּ וְעַל כָּל יִשְׂרָאֵל
וְאִמְרוּ אָמֵן. (קהל: אָמֵן)

Between סוכות *and* פסח*, some recite* ברכי נפשי*, page 629, at this point.*
Between פסח *and* ראש השנה *some recite* פרקי אבות*, page 641, at this point.*

Stand while saying עָלֵינוּ*. Bow at* *.

עָלֵינוּ לְשַׁבֵּחַ לַאֲדוֹן הַכֹּל, לָתֵת גְּדֻלָּה לְיוֹצֵר בְּרֵאשִׁית
שֶׁלֹּא עָשָׂנוּ כְּגוֹיֵי הָאֲרָצוֹת, וְלֹא שָׂמָנוּ כְּמִשְׁפְּחוֹת הָאֲדָמָה
שֶׁלֹּא שָׂם חֶלְקֵנוּ כָּהֶם וְגוֹרָלֵנוּ כְּכָל הֲמוֹנָם.
(שֶׁהֵם מִשְׁתַּחֲוִים לְהֶבֶל וָרִיק וּמִתְפַּלְלִים אֶל אֵל לֹא יוֹשִׁיעַ.)
*וַאֲנַחְנוּ כּוֹרְעִים וּמִשְׁתַּחֲוִים וּמוֹדִים
לִפְנֵי מֶלֶךְ מַלְכֵי הַמְּלָכִים, הַקָּדוֹשׁ בָּרוּךְ הוּא
שֶׁהוּא נוֹטֶה שָׁמַיִם וְיוֹסֵד אָרֶץ
וּמוֹשַׁב יְקָרוֹ בַּשָּׁמַיִם מִמַּעַל
וּשְׁכִינַת עֻזּוֹ בְּגָבְהֵי מְרוֹמִים.
הוּא אֱלֹהֵינוּ, אֵין עוֹד.
אֱמֶת מַלְכֵּנוּ, אֶפֶס זוּלָתוֹ
כַּכָּתוּב בְּתוֹרָתוֹ
וְיָדַעְתָּ הַיּוֹם וַהֲשֵׁבֹתָ אֶל־לְבָבֶךָ דברים ד
כִּי יהוה הוּא הָאֱלֹהִים בַּשָּׁמַיִם מִמַּעַל וְעַל־הָאָרֶץ מִתָּחַת, אֵין עוֹד:

Therefore, we place our hope in You, Lord our God,
that we may soon see the glory of Your power,
when You will remove abominations from the earth,
and idols will be utterly destroyed,
when the world will be perfected
under the sovereignty of the Almighty,
when all humanity will call on Your name,
to turn all the earth's wicked toward You.
All the world's inhabitants will realize and know
that to You every knee must bow and every tongue swear loyalty.
Before You, Lord our God, they will kneel and bow down
and give honor to Your glorious name.
They will all accept the yoke of Your kingdom,
and You will reign over them soon and for ever.
For the kingdom is Yours, and to all eternity You will reign in glory,
as it is written in Your Torah: "The Lord will reign for ever and ever." *Ex. 15*
▸ And it is said: "Then the Lord shall be King over all the earth; *Zech. 14*
on that day the Lord shall be One and His name One."

Some add:

Have no fear of sudden terror or of the ruin when it overtakes the wicked. *Prov. 3*
Devise your strategy, but it will be thwarted; propose your plan, *Is. 8*
but it will not stand, for God is with us. When you grow old, I will still be the same. *Is. 46*
When your hair turns gray, I will still carry you. I made you, I will bear you,
I will carry you, and I will rescue you.

MOURNER'S KADDISH

The following prayer, said by mourners, requires the presence of a minyan.
A transliteration can be found on page 1334.

Mourner: יִתְגַּדַּל Magnified and sanctified may His great name be,
in the world He created by His will.
May He establish His kingdom in your lifetime
and in your days,
and in the lifetime of all the house of Israel,
swiftly and soon – and say: Amen.

All: May His great name be blessed for ever and all time.

עַל כֵּן נְקַוֶּה לְּךָ יהוה אֱלֹהֵינוּ, לִרְאוֹת מְהֵרָה בְּתִפְאֶרֶת עֻזֶּךָ
לְהַעֲבִיר גִּלּוּלִים מִן הָאָרֶץ, וְהָאֱלִילִים כָּרוֹת יִכָּרֵתוּן
לְתַקֵּן עוֹלָם בְּמַלְכוּת שַׁדַּי.
וְכָל בְּנֵי בָשָׂר יִקְרְאוּ בִשְׁמֶךָ לְהַפְנוֹת אֵלֶיךָ כָּל רִשְׁעֵי אָרֶץ.
יַכִּירוּ וְיֵדְעוּ כָּל יוֹשְׁבֵי תֵבֵל
כִּי לְךָ תִּכְרַע כָּל בֶּרֶךְ, תִּשָּׁבַע כָּל לָשׁוֹן.
לְפָנֶיךָ יהוה אֱלֹהֵינוּ יִכְרְעוּ וְיִפֹּלוּ, וְלִכְבוֹד שִׁמְךָ יְקָר יִתֵּנוּ
וִיקַבְּלוּ כֻלָּם אֶת עֹל מַלְכוּתֶךָ
וְתִמְלֹךְ עֲלֵיהֶם מְהֵרָה לְעוֹלָם וָעֶד.
כִּי הַמַּלְכוּת שֶׁלְּךָ הִיא וּלְעוֹלְמֵי עַד תִּמְלֹךְ בְּכָבוֹד
כַּכָּתוּב בְּתוֹרָתֶךָ, יהוה יִמְלֹךְ לְעֹלָם וָעֶד: שמות טו
◂ וְנֶאֱמַר, וְהָיָה יהוה לְמֶלֶךְ עַל־כָּל־הָאָרֶץ זכריה יד
בַּיּוֹם הַהוּא יִהְיֶה יהוה אֶחָד וּשְׁמוֹ אֶחָד:

Some add:

אַל־תִּירָא מִפַּחַד פִּתְאֹם וּמִשֹּׁאַת רְשָׁעִים כִּי תָבֹא: משלי ג
עֻצוּ עֵצָה וְתֻפָר, דַּבְּרוּ דָבָר וְלֹא יָקוּם, כִּי עִמָּנוּ אֵל: ישעיה ח
וְעַד־זִקְנָה אֲנִי הוּא, וְעַד־שֵׂיבָה אֲנִי אֶסְבֹּל אֲנִי עָשִׂיתִי וַאֲנִי אֶשָּׂא וַאֲנִי אֶסְבֹּל וַאֲמַלֵּט: ישעיה מו

קדיש יתום

The following prayer, said by mourners, requires the presence of a מנין*.*
A transliteration can be found on page 1334.

אבל: יִתְגַּדַּל וְיִתְקַדַּשׁ שְׁמֵהּ רַבָּא (קהל: אָמֵן)
בְּעָלְמָא דִּי בְרָא כִרְעוּתֵהּ
וְיַמְלִיךְ מַלְכוּתֵהּ
בְּחַיֵּיכוֹן וּבְיוֹמֵיכוֹן וּבְחַיֵּי דְכָל בֵּית יִשְׂרָאֵל
בַּעֲגָלָא וּבִזְמַן קָרִיב, וְאִמְרוּ אָמֵן. (קהל: אָמֵן)

קהל ואבל: יְהֵא שְׁמֵהּ רַבָּא מְבָרַךְ לְעָלַם וּלְעָלְמֵי עָלְמַיָּא.

Mourner: Blessed and praised, glorified and exalted,
raised and honored, uplifted and lauded
be the name of the Holy One,
blessed be He,
beyond any blessing,
song, praise and consolation
uttered in the world –
and say: Amen.
May there be great peace from heaven,
and life for us and all Israel –
and say: Amen.

Bow, take three steps back, as if taking leave of the Divine Presence, then bow, first left, then right, then center, while saying:

May He who makes peace in His high places,
make peace for us and all Israel –
and say: Amen.

BAREKHI NAFSHI

The following psalms are said from the Shabbat after Simḥat Torah until (but not including) the Shabbat before Pesaḥ.

בָּרְכִי נַפְשִׁי Bless the LORD, my soul. LORD, my God, You are very great, *Ps. 104*
clothed in majesty and splendor, wrapped in a robe of light. You have spread out the heavens like a tent. He has laid the beams of His lofts in the waters. He makes the clouds His chariot, riding on the wings of the wind. He makes

---

accords with the tradition that creation took place in the month of Tishrei, while the exodus took place in Nisan (*Rosh HaShana* 10b). The winter months therefore correspond to the period through which God was known through creation rather than redemption (the exodus) and revelation (the giving of the Torah at Mount Sinai).

Psalm 104: Together with the first chapter of Genesis and chapters 38–41 of the book of Job, this psalm is one of the supreme celebrations of creation

אבל: יִתְבָּרַךְ וְיִשְׁתַּבַּח וְיִתְפָּאַר
וְיִתְרוֹמַם וְיִתְנַשֵּׂא וְיִתְהַדָּר וְיִתְעַלֶּה וְיִתְהַלָּל
שְׁמֵהּ דְּקֻדְשָׁא בְּרִיךְ הוּא (קהל: בְּרִיךְ הוּא)
לְעֵלָּא מִן כָּל בִּרְכָתָא
/ בשבת שובה: לְעֵלָּא לְעֵלָּא מִכָּל בִּרְכָתָא/
וְשִׁירָתָא, תֻּשְׁבְּחָתָא וְנֶחֱמָתָא
דַּאֲמִירָן בְּעָלְמָא, וְאִמְרוּ אָמֵן. (קהל: אָמֵן)
יְהֵא שְׁלָמָא רַבָּא מִן שְׁמַיָּא
וְחַיִּים, עָלֵינוּ וְעַל כָּל יִשְׂרָאֵל, וְאִמְרוּ אָמֵן. (קהל: אָמֵן)

Bow, take three steps back, as if taking leave of the Divine Presence, then bow, first left, then right, then center, while saying:

עֹשֶׂה שָׁלוֹם/ בשבת שובה: הַשָּׁלוֹם/ בִּמְרוֹמָיו
הוּא יַעֲשֶׂה שָׁלוֹם עָלֵינוּ וְעַל כָּל יִשְׂרָאֵל, וְאִמְרוּ אָמֵן. (קהל: אָמֵן)

ברכי נפשי

The following psalms are said from שבת בראשית *until (but not including)* שבת הגדול.

תהלים קד בָּרְכִי נַפְשִׁי אֶת־יהוה, יהוה אֱלֹהַי גָּדַלְתָּ מְּאֹד, הוֹד וְהָדָר לָבָשְׁתָּ: עֹטֶה־
אוֹר כַּשַּׂלְמָה, נוֹטֶה שָׁמַיִם כַּיְרִיעָה: הַמְקָרֶה בַמַּיִם עֲלִיּוֹתָיו, הַשָּׂם־עָבִים
רְכוּבוֹ, הַמְהַלֵּךְ עַל־כַּנְפֵי־רוּחַ: עֹשֶׂה מַלְאָכָיו רוּחוֹת, מְשָׁרְתָיו אֵשׁ לֹהֵט:

BAREKHI NAFSHI / SHABBAT AFTERNOON PSALMS

Between afternoon and evening services, customs varied. Some communities recited Ethics of the Fathers throughout the year; others between Pesaḥ and Shavuot. Our custom is to do so between Pesaḥ and the Shabbat before Rosh HaShana. Between Shabbat Bereshit and the week before Pesaḥ we recite Psalm 104 and the fifteen psalms known as "Songs of Ascents." The connection between Shabbat Bereshit and Psalm 104 is that both are about creation. In general, the saying of these psalms during the winter months

the winds His messengers, flames of fire His ministers. He has fixed the earth on its foundations so that it will never be shaken. You covered it with the deep like a cloak; the waters stood above the mountains. At Your rebuke they fled; at the sound of Your thunder they rushed away, flowing over the hills, pouring down into the valleys to the place You appointed for them. You fixed a boundary they were not to pass, so that they would never cover the earth again. He makes springs flow in the valleys; they make their way between the hills, giving drink to all the beasts of the field; the wild donkeys quench their thirst. The birds of the sky dwell beside them, singing among the foliage. He waters the mountains from His lofts: the earth is sated with the fruit of Your work. He makes grass grow for the cattle, and plants for the use of man, that he may produce bread from the earth, wine to cheer the heart of man, oil to make the face shine, and bread to sustain man's heart. The trees of the Lord drink their fill, the cedars of Lebanon which He planted. There, birds build their nests; the stork makes its home in the cypresses. High hills are for the wild goats; crags are shelter for the badgers. He made the moon to mark the seasons, and makes the sun know when to set. You bring darkness and it is night; then all the beasts of the forests stir. The young lions roar for prey, seeking their food from God. When the sun rises, they slink away and seek rest in their lairs. Man goes out to his work and his labor until evening. How numerous are Your works, Lord; You made them all in wisdom; the earth is full of Your creations. There is the vast, immeasurable sea with its countless swarming creatures, living things great and small. There ships sail. There is Leviathan You formed to sport there. All of them look to You in hope, to give them their food when it is due. What You give them, they gather up. When You open Your hand, they are sated with good. When You hide Your face, they are dismayed. When You take away their breath, they die and return to dust. When You send back Your breath, they are created, giving new life to the earth. May the glory of the Lord be for ever; may the Lord rejoice in His works. When He looks at the earth, it trembles. When He touches the mountains, they pour forth smoke. I will sing to the Lord as long as I live; I will sing psalms to my God all my life. May my meditation be pleasing to Him; I shall rejoice in the Lord. May sinners vanish from the earth, and the wicked be no more. Bless the Lord, my soul. Halleluya!

Psalmist that despite the vastness of the universe and the infinity of its Creator, He is close. He hears prayer. He attends to the human voice. This is the song

יָסַד־אֶרֶץ עַל־מְכוֹנֶיהָ, בַּל־תִּמּוֹט עוֹלָם וָעֶד: תְּהוֹם כַּלְּבוּשׁ כִּסִּיתוֹ, עַל־
הָרִים יַעַמְדוּ־מָיִם: מִן־גַּעֲרָתְךָ יְנוּסוּן, מִן־קוֹל רַעַמְךָ יֵחָפֵזוּן: יַעֲלוּ הָרִים,
יֵרְדוּ בְקָעוֹת, אֶל־מְקוֹם זֶה יָסַדְתָּ לָהֶם: גְּבוּל־שַׂמְתָּ בַּל־יַעֲבֹרוּן, בַּל־יְשׁוּבוּן
לְכַסּוֹת הָאָרֶץ: הַמְשַׁלֵּחַ מַעְיָנִים בַּנְּחָלִים, בֵּין הָרִים יְהַלֵּכוּן: יַשְׁקוּ כָּל־חַיְתוֹ
שָׂדָי, יִשְׁבְּרוּ פְרָאִים צְמָאָם: עֲלֵיהֶם עוֹף־הַשָּׁמַיִם יִשְׁכּוֹן, מִבֵּין עֳפָאיִם יִתְּנוּ־
קוֹל: מַשְׁקֶה הָרִים מֵעֲלִיּוֹתָיו, מִפְּרִי מַעֲשֶׂיךָ תִּשְׂבַּע הָאָרֶץ: מַצְמִיחַ חָצִיר
לַבְּהֵמָה, וְעֵשֶׂב לַעֲבֹדַת הָאָדָם, לְהוֹצִיא לֶחֶם מִן־הָאָרֶץ: וְיַיִן יְשַׂמַּח לְבַב־
אֱנוֹשׁ, לְהַצְהִיל פָּנִים מִשָּׁמֶן, וְלֶחֶם לְבַב־אֱנוֹשׁ יִסְעָד: יִשְׂבְּעוּ עֲצֵי יהוה,
אַרְזֵי לְבָנוֹן אֲשֶׁר נָטָע: אֲשֶׁר־שָׁם צִפֳּרִים יְקַנֵּנוּ, חֲסִידָה בְּרוֹשִׁים בֵּיתָהּ:
הָרִים הַגְּבֹהִים לַיְּעֵלִים, סְלָעִים מַחְסֶה לַשְׁפַנִּים: עָשָׂה יָרֵחַ לְמוֹעֲדִים, שֶׁמֶשׁ
יָדַע מְבוֹאוֹ: תָּשֶׁת־חֹשֶׁךְ וִיהִי לָיְלָה, בּוֹ־תִרְמֹשׂ כָּל־חַיְתוֹ־יָעַר: הַכְּפִירִים
שֹׁאֲגִים לַטָּרֶף, וּלְבַקֵּשׁ מֵאֵל אָכְלָם: תִּזְרַח הַשֶּׁמֶשׁ יֵאָסֵפוּן, וְאֶל־מְעוֹנֹתָם
יִרְבָּצוּן: יֵצֵא אָדָם לְפָעֳלוֹ, וְלַעֲבֹדָתוֹ עֲדֵי־עָרֶב: מָה־רַבּוּ מַעֲשֶׂיךָ יהוה,
כֻּלָּם בְּחָכְמָה עָשִׂיתָ, מָלְאָה הָאָרֶץ קִנְיָנֶךָ: זֶה הַיָּם גָּדוֹל וּרְחַב יָדָיִם, שָׁם־
רֶמֶשׂ וְאֵין מִסְפָּר, חַיּוֹת קְטַנּוֹת עִם־גְּדֹלוֹת: שָׁם אֳנִיּוֹת יְהַלֵּכוּן, לִוְיָתָן
זֶה־יָצַרְתָּ לְשַׂחֶק־בּוֹ: כֻּלָּם אֵלֶיךָ יְשַׂבֵּרוּן, לָתֵת אָכְלָם בְּעִתּוֹ: תִּתֵּן לָהֶם
יִלְקֹטוּן, תִּפְתַּח יָדְךָ יִשְׂבְּעוּן טוֹב: תַּסְתִּיר פָּנֶיךָ יִבָּהֵלוּן, תֹּסֵף רוּחָם יִגְוָעוּן,
וְאֶל־עֲפָרָם יְשׁוּבוּן: תְּשַׁלַּח רוּחֲךָ יִבָּרֵאוּן, וּתְחַדֵּשׁ פְּנֵי אֲדָמָה: יְהִי כְבוֹד
יהוה לְעוֹלָם, יִשְׂמַח יהוה בְּמַעֲשָׂיו: הַמַּבִּיט לָאָרֶץ וַתִּרְעָד, יִגַּע בֶּהָרִים
וְיֶעֱשָׁנוּ: אָשִׁירָה לַיהוה בְּחַיָּי, אֲזַמְּרָה לֵאלֹהַי בְּעוֹדִי: יֶעֱרַב עָלָיו שִׂיחִי, אָנֹכִי
אֶשְׂמַח בַּיהוה: יִתַּמּוּ חַטָּאִים מִן־הָאָרֶץ, וּרְשָׁעִים עוֹד אֵינָם, בָּרְכִי נַפְשִׁי אֶת־
יהוה, הַלְלוּיָהּ:

---

in Tanakh. Note the profound difference between these religious texts and scientific cosmologies. They speak in poetry, not prose; they express wonder rather than causal explanation; and they testify to the goodness of the world and its Creator rather than to blind, indifferent forces. The account in Psalm 104 is consistent with that of Genesis 1, though it is structured differently because the Psalmist wishes to emphasize the beauty and grandeur of creation rather than the order in which it emerged. What emerges above all – signaled by both beginning and end, "Bless the Lord, my soul" – is the sense of the

A song of ascents. I called to the LORD in my distress and He answered me. *Ps. 120*
"LORD, save my soul from lying lips, from a deceitful tongue." What will a deceitful tongue profit you? What will you gain? Only a warrior's sharp arrows, and hot coals of broom-wood. Woe to me that I dwell in Meshekh, that I live among the tents of Kedar. I have lived too long among those who hate peace. I am for peace, but whenever I speak of it, they are for war.

A song of ascents. I lift my eyes up to the hills; from where will my help come? *Ps. 121*
My help comes from the LORD, Maker of heaven and earth. He will not let your foot stumble; He who guards you does not slumber. See: the Guardian of Israel neither slumbers nor sleeps. The LORD is your Guardian; the LORD is your Shade at your right hand. The sun will not strike you by day, nor the moon by night. The LORD will guard you from all harm; He will guard your life. The LORD will guard your going and coming, now and for evermore.

A song of ascents. Of David. I rejoiced when they said to me, "Let us go to the *Ps. 122*
House of the LORD." Our feet stood within your gates, Jerusalem: Jerusalem built as a city joined together. There the tribes went up, the tribes of the LORD – as a testimony to Israel – to give thanks to the name of the LORD. For there the thrones of justice are set, the thrones of the house of David. Pray for the peace of Jerusalem: "May those who love you prosper. May there be peace within your ramparts, tranquility in your citadels." For the sake of my brothers and my friends, I shall say, "Peace be within you." For the sake of the House of the LORD our God, I shall seek your good.

---

near the Caspian Sea. Kedar: descendants of Ishmael (Gen. 25:12–13; 1 Chr. 1:29), a generic term for Arab tribes in the north of the Arabian peninsula. Though both were remote from Israel, they figure in the psalm as examples of warlike peoples.

Psalm 121: One of the great expressions of trust in God's protection, often recited in times of trouble. The Hebrew root *sh-m-r*, "guard, protect," appears six times in this short psalm.

Psalm 122: A song sung by pilgrims on the way to Jerusalem. The Hebrew is awash with alliterations on the *sh* sound – as in *sha'alu shelom Yerushalayim yishlayu* – echoing the sound of the second half of the name "Jerusalem," *shalayim*, related to *shalom*, "peace." Here, literary style mirrors substance: the gentle, soothing sounds evoke Jerusalem at peace.

תהלים קכ
שִׁיר הַמַּעֲלוֹת, אֶל־יהוה בַּצָּרָתָה לִּי, קָרָאתִי וַיַּעֲנֵנִי: יהוה הַצִּילָה נַפְשִׁי מִשְּׂפַת־שֶׁקֶר, מִלָּשׁוֹן רְמִיָּה: מַה־יִּתֵּן לְךָ וּמַה־יֹּסִיף לָךְ, לָשׁוֹן רְמִיָּה: חִצֵּי גִבּוֹר שְׁנוּנִים, עִם גַּחֲלֵי רְתָמִים: אוֹיָה־לִי כִּי־גַרְתִּי מֶשֶׁךְ, שָׁכַנְתִּי עִם־אָהֳלֵי קֵדָר: רַבַּת שָׁכְנָה־לָּהּ נַפְשִׁי, עִם שׂוֹנֵא שָׁלוֹם: אֲנִי־שָׁלוֹם וְכִי אֲדַבֵּר, הֵמָּה לַמִּלְחָמָה:

תהלים קכא
שִׁיר לַמַּעֲלוֹת, אֶשָּׂא עֵינַי אֶל־הֶהָרִים, מֵאַיִן יָבֹא עֶזְרִי: עֶזְרִי מֵעִם יהוה, עֹשֵׂה שָׁמַיִם וָאָרֶץ: אַל־יִתֵּן לַמּוֹט רַגְלֶךָ, אַל־יָנוּם שֹׁמְרֶךָ: הִנֵּה לֹא־יָנוּם וְלֹא יִישָׁן, שׁוֹמֵר יִשְׂרָאֵל: יהוה שֹׁמְרֶךָ, יהוה צִלְּךָ עַל־יַד יְמִינֶךָ: יוֹמָם הַשֶּׁמֶשׁ לֹא־יַכֶּכָּה, וְיָרֵחַ בַּלָּיְלָה: יהוה יִשְׁמָרְךָ מִכָּל־רָע, יִשְׁמֹר אֶת־נַפְשֶׁךָ: יהוה יִשְׁמָר־צֵאתְךָ וּבוֹאֶךָ, מֵעַתָּה וְעַד־עוֹלָם:

תהלים קכב
שִׁיר הַמַּעֲלוֹת לְדָוִד, שָׂמַחְתִּי בְּאֹמְרִים לִי בֵּית יהוה נֵלֵךְ: עֹמְדוֹת הָיוּ רַגְלֵינוּ, בִּשְׁעָרַיִךְ יְרוּשָׁלָםִ: יְרוּשָׁלַםִ הַבְּנוּיָה, כְּעִיר שֶׁחֻבְּרָה־לָּהּ יַחְדָּו: שֶׁשָּׁם עָלוּ שְׁבָטִים שִׁבְטֵי־יָהּ, עֵדוּת לְיִשְׂרָאֵל, לְהֹדוֹת לְשֵׁם יהוה: כִּי שָׁמָּה יָשְׁבוּ כִסְאוֹת לְמִשְׁפָּט, כִּסְאוֹת לְבֵית דָּוִד: שַׁאֲלוּ שְׁלוֹם יְרוּשָׁלָםִ, יִשְׁלָיוּ אֹהֲבָיִךְ: יְהִי־שָׁלוֹם בְּחֵילֵךְ, שַׁלְוָה בְּאַרְמְנוֹתָיִךְ: לְמַעַן אַחַי וְרֵעָי, אֲדַבְּרָה־נָּא שָׁלוֹם בָּךְ: לְמַעַן בֵּית־יהוה אֱלֹהֵינוּ, אֲבַקְשָׁה טוֹב לָךְ:

---

of one at home in the world, awed by its beauty, trusting in the graciousness of existence as God's gift.

Psalms 120–134: A sequence of fifteen psalms, all bearing the heading "A song of ascents." The meaning of this phrase is debated. Some relate it to the fifteen steps in the Temple between the men's and women's courtyards, on which the Levites would stand and sing. Others suggest that they were songs sung by the exiles returning from Babylon to Israel (ascending to the holy land). Radak argues that they were said by pilgrims on the three Pilgrimage festivals on their ascent to Jerusalem. Meiri argues that it is a musical direction, meaning a song begun softly and continued with ever-increasing volume. Others speculate that it may be a reference to the particular poetical style in which these psalms are written, in which a repeated phrase serves as a rung on which the poem ascends toward its final theme.

Psalm 120: Meshekh: Descendants of Noah's son Japhet (Gen. 10:2) who lived

A song of ascents. To You, enthroned in heaven, I lift my eyes. As the eyes of slaves turn to their master's hand, or the eyes of a slave-girl to the hand of her mistress, so our eyes are turned to the LORD our God, awaiting His favor. Show us favor, LORD, show us favor, for we have suffered more than enough contempt. Too long have we suffered the scorn of the complacent, the contempt of arrogant men. *Ps. 123*

A song of ascents. Of David. Had the LORD not been on our side – let Israel say it – had the LORD not been on our side when men rose up against us, they would have swallowed us alive when their anger raged against us. The waters would have engulfed us; the torrent would have swept over us; over us would have swept the raging waters. Blessed be the LORD who did not leave us as a prey for their teeth. We escaped like a bird from the fowler's trap; the trap broke and we escaped. Our help is in the name of the LORD, Maker of heaven and earth. *Ps. 124*

A song of ascents. Those who trust in the LORD are like Mount Zion that cannot be moved, that stands firm for ever. As hills surround Jerusalem so the LORD surrounds His people, now and forever. The scepter of the wicked shall not rest on the land allotted to the righteous, so that the righteous shall not set their hand to wrongdoing. Do good, LORD, to those who are good, to those who are upright in heart. As for those who turn aside to crooked ways, may the LORD make them go the way of evildoers. Peace be on Israel! *Ps. 125*

A song of ascents. When the LORD brought back the exiles of Zion we were like people who dream. Then were our mouths filled with laughter, and our tongues with songs of joy. Then was it said among the nations, "The LORD has done great things for them." The LORD did do great things for us and we rejoiced. Bring back our exiles, LORD, like streams in a dry land. May those who sowed in tears, reap in joy. May one who goes out weeping, carrying a bag of seed, come back with songs of joy, carrying his sheaves. *Ps. 126*

Psalm 126: The psalm sung as the song preceding *Birkat HaMazon* on Shabbat and festivals. Its interpretation is difficult because of the change of tenses from past (verses 1–3) to future (4–6). It may be entirely future-oriented, anticipating the ingathering of exiles and the restoration of national sovereignty, or it may be that the Psalmist prays for the future return of Jews to Zion by recalling events in the past. The current state of the people is compared in the last two verses to grain before the spring: though now it seems buried in the earth, it will eventually grow and yield a rich harvest.

תהלים קכג
שִׁיר הַמַּעֲלוֹת, אֵלֶיךָ נָשָׂאתִי אֶת־עֵינַי, הַיֹּשְׁבִי בַּשָּׁמָיִם: הִנֵּה כְעֵינֵי עֲבָדִים אֶל־יַד אֲדוֹנֵיהֶם, כְּעֵינֵי שִׁפְחָה אֶל־יַד גְּבִרְתָּהּ, כֵּן עֵינֵינוּ אֶל־יהוה אֱלֹהֵינוּ, עַד שֶׁיְּחָנֵּנוּ: חָנֵּנוּ יהוה חָנֵּנוּ, כִּי־רַב שָׂבַעְנוּ בוּז: רַבַּת שָׂבְעָה־לָּהּ נַפְשֵׁנוּ, הַלַּעַג הַשַּׁאֲנַנִּים, הַבּוּז לִגְאֵי יוֹנִים:

תהלים קכד
שִׁיר הַמַּעֲלוֹת לְדָוִד, לוּלֵי יהוה שֶׁהָיָה לָנוּ, יֹאמַר־נָא יִשְׂרָאֵל: לוּלֵי יהוה שֶׁהָיָה לָנוּ, בְּקוּם עָלֵינוּ אָדָם: אֲזַי חַיִּים בְּלָעוּנוּ, בַּחֲרוֹת אַפָּם בָּנוּ: אֲזַי הַמַּיִם שְׁטָפוּנוּ, נַחְלָה עָבַר עַל־נַפְשֵׁנוּ: אֲזַי עָבַר עַל־נַפְשֵׁנוּ, הַמַּיִם הַזֵּידוֹנִים: בָּרוּךְ יהוה, שֶׁלֹּא נְתָנָנוּ טֶרֶף לְשִׁנֵּיהֶם: נַפְשֵׁנוּ כְּצִפּוֹר נִמְלְטָה מִפַּח יוֹקְשִׁים, הַפַּח נִשְׁבָּר וַאֲנַחְנוּ נִמְלָטְנוּ: עֶזְרֵנוּ בְּשֵׁם יהוה, עֹשֵׂה שָׁמַיִם וָאָרֶץ:

תהלים קכה
שִׁיר הַמַּעֲלוֹת, הַבֹּטְחִים בַּיהוה, כְּהַר־צִיּוֹן לֹא־יִמּוֹט, לְעוֹלָם יֵשֵׁב: יְרוּשָׁלַםִ, הָרִים סָבִיב לָהּ, וַיהוה סָבִיב לְעַמּוֹ, מֵעַתָּה וְעַד־עוֹלָם: כִּי לֹא יָנוּחַ שֵׁבֶט הָרֶשַׁע עַל גּוֹרַל הַצַּדִּיקִים, לְמַעַן לֹא־יִשְׁלְחוּ הַצַּדִּיקִים בְּעַוְלָתָה יְדֵיהֶם: הֵיטִיבָה יהוה לַטּוֹבִים, וְלִישָׁרִים בְּלִבּוֹתָם: וְהַמַּטִּים עֲקַלְקַלּוֹתָם יוֹלִיכֵם יהוה אֶת־פֹּעֲלֵי הָאָוֶן, שָׁלוֹם עַל־יִשְׂרָאֵל:

תהלים קכו
שִׁיר הַמַּעֲלוֹת, בְּשׁוּב יהוה אֶת־שִׁיבַת צִיּוֹן, הָיִינוּ כְּחֹלְמִים: אָז יִמָּלֵא שְׂחוֹק פִּינוּ וּלְשׁוֹנֵנוּ רִנָּה, אָז יֹאמְרוּ בַגּוֹיִם הִגְדִּיל יהוה לַעֲשׂוֹת עִם־אֵלֶּה: הִגְדִּיל יהוה לַעֲשׂוֹת עִמָּנוּ, הָיִינוּ שְׂמֵחִים: שׁוּבָה יהוה אֶת־שְׁבִיתֵנוּ, כַּאֲפִיקִים בַּנֶּגֶב: הַזֹּרְעִים בְּדִמְעָה בְּרִנָּה יִקְצֹרוּ: הָלוֹךְ יֵלֵךְ וּבָכֹה נֹשֵׂא מֶשֶׁךְ־הַזָּרַע, בֹּא־יָבֹא בְרִנָּה נֹשֵׂא אֲלֻמֹּתָיו:

Psalm 124: A psalm of thanksgiving for deliverance, using – as often in Psalms – a rapid succession of different images: the people have been in danger of being swallowed, swept away as if in a flood, a prey to the enemy's teeth, captured in a hunter's trap. The images do not coalesce into a single metaphor. Rather, they combine to express a mood; in this case, the sense of sudden release from danger.

Psalm 125: A prayer expressing trust in God, likening divine protection to the hills that surround Jerusalem. The final phrase, "Peace be on Israel," became popular in later times and is found as part of the mosaic in the Byzantine synagogue of Jericho (sixth century CE).

A song of ascents. Of Solomon. Unless the LORD builds the house, its builders labor in vain. Unless the LORD guards the city, in vain does the guard keep watch. In vain do you rise early and go late to rest, toiling for the bread you eat. He provides for His loved ones while they sleep. Children are a heritage from the LORD; the fruit of the womb, His reward. Like arrows in the hand of a warrior are the sons of one's youth. Happy is the man who fills his quiver with them; they shall not be put to shame when they contend with the enemy at the gate. *Ps. 127*

A song of ascents. Happy are all who fear the LORD, who walk in His ways. When you eat the fruit of your labor, happy and fortunate are you. Your wife shall be like a fruitful vine within your house; your sons like olive saplings around your table. So shall the man who fears the LORD be blessed. May the LORD bless you from Zion; may you see the good of Jerusalem all the days of your life; and may you live to see your children's children. Peace be on Israel! *Ps. 128*

A song of ascents. Often since I was young I have been attacked – let Israel now say – often since I was young I have been attacked, but never have my attackers prevailed. Ploughmen ploughed across my back, making long furrows. But the LORD is just; He has cut the bonds of the wicked. Let all who hate Zion be driven back in shame. Let them be like the grass on roofs that fades before it can be pulled up. It will never fill a reaper's hand nor yield an armful for the gatherer of sheaves. No passersby will say to them: "The LORD's blessing be upon you. We bless you in the name of the LORD." *Ps. 129*

A song of ascents. From the depths I have called to You, O LORD. LORD, hear my voice; let Your ears be attentive to my plea. If You, LORD, should keep account of sins, O LORD, who could stand? But with You there is forgiveness, that You may be held in awe. I wait for the LORD, my soul waits, and in His word I put my hope. My soul waits for the LORD more than watchmen wait for the morning, more than watchmen wait for the morning. Israel, put your hope in the LORD, for with the LORD there is loving-kindness, and great is His power to redeem. It is He who will redeem Israel from all their sins. *Ps. 130*

A song of ascents. By David. LORD, my heart is not proud, nor are my eyes haughty. I do not busy myself with great affairs or with things beyond me. But I have made my soul still and quiet, like a weaned child with its mother; like a weaned child is my soul within me. Israel, put your hope in the LORD, now and for evermore. *Ps. 131*

שִׁיר הַמַּעֲלוֹת לִשְׁלֹמֹה, אִם־יהוה לֹא־יִבְנֶה בַיִת, שָׁוְא עָמְלוּ בוֹנָיו בּוֹ, אִם־ תהלים קכז
יהוה לֹא־יִשְׁמָר־עִיר, שָׁוְא שָׁקַד שׁוֹמֵר: שָׁוְא לָכֶם מַשְׁכִּימֵי קוּם מְאַחֲרֵי־
שֶׁבֶת, אֹכְלֵי לֶחֶם הָעֲצָבִים, כֵּן יִתֵּן לִידִידוֹ שֵׁנָא: הִנֵּה נַחֲלַת יהוה בָּנִים,
שָׂכָר פְּרִי הַבָּטֶן: כְּחִצִּים בְּיַד־גִּבּוֹר כֵּן בְּנֵי הַנְּעוּרִים: אַשְׁרֵי הַגֶּבֶר אֲשֶׁר מִלֵּא
אֶת־אַשְׁפָּתוֹ מֵהֶם, לֹא־יֵבֹשׁוּ כִּי־יְדַבְּרוּ אֶת־אוֹיְבִים בַּשָּׁעַר:

שִׁיר הַמַּעֲלוֹת, אַשְׁרֵי כָּל־יְרֵא יהוה, הַהֹלֵךְ בִּדְרָכָיו: יְגִיעַ כַּפֶּיךָ כִּי תֹאכֵל, תהלים קכח
אַשְׁרֶיךָ וְטוֹב לָךְ: אֶשְׁתְּךָ כְּגֶפֶן פֹּרִיָּה בְּיַרְכְּתֵי בֵיתֶךָ, בָּנֶיךָ כִּשְׁתִלֵי זֵיתִים, סָבִיב
לְשֻׁלְחָנֶךָ: הִנֵּה כִי־כֵן יְבֹרַךְ גָּבֶר יְרֵא יהוה: יְבָרֶכְךָ יהוה מִצִּיּוֹן, וּרְאֵה בְּטוּב
יְרוּשָׁלָםִ, כֹּל יְמֵי חַיֶּיךָ: וּרְאֵה־בָנִים לְבָנֶיךָ, שָׁלוֹם עַל־יִשְׂרָאֵל:

שִׁיר הַמַּעֲלוֹת, רַבַּת צְרָרוּנִי מִנְּעוּרָי, יֹאמַר־נָא יִשְׂרָאֵל: רַבַּת צְרָרוּנִי מִנְּעוּרָי, תהלים קכט
גַּם לֹא־יָכְלוּ לִי: עַל־גַּבִּי חָרְשׁוּ חֹרְשִׁים, הֶאֱרִיכוּ לְמַעֲנִיתָם: יהוה צַדִּיק, קִצֵּץ
עֲבוֹת רְשָׁעִים: יֵבֹשׁוּ וְיִסֹּגוּ אָחוֹר כֹּל שֹׂנְאֵי צִיּוֹן: יִהְיוּ כַּחֲצִיר גַּגּוֹת שֶׁקַּדְמַת
שָׁלַף יָבֵשׁ: שֶׁלֹּא מִלֵּא כַפּוֹ קוֹצֵר, וְחִצְנוֹ מְעַמֵּר: וְלֹא אָמְרוּ הָעֹבְרִים, בִּרְכַּת־
יהוה אֲלֵיכֶם, בֵּרַכְנוּ אֶתְכֶם בְּשֵׁם יהוה:

שִׁיר הַמַּעֲלוֹת, מִמַּעֲמַקִּים קְרָאתִיךָ יהוה: אֲדֹנָי שִׁמְעָה בְקוֹלִי, תִּהְיֶינָה תהלים קל
אָזְנֶיךָ קַשֻּׁבוֹת לְקוֹל תַּחֲנוּנָי: אִם־עֲוֹנוֹת תִּשְׁמָר־יָהּ, אֲדֹנָי מִי יַעֲמֹד: כִּי־עִמְּךָ
הַסְּלִיחָה, לְמַעַן תִּוָּרֵא: קִוִּיתִי יהוה קִוְּתָה נַפְשִׁי, וְלִדְבָרוֹ הוֹחָלְתִּי: נַפְשִׁי
לַאדֹנָי, מִשֹּׁמְרִים לַבֹּקֶר, שֹׁמְרִים לַבֹּקֶר: יַחֵל יִשְׂרָאֵל אֶל־יהוה, כִּי־עִם־יהוה
הַחֶסֶד, וְהַרְבֵּה עִמּוֹ פְדוּת: וְהוּא יִפְדֶּה אֶת־יִשְׂרָאֵל, מִכֹּל עֲוֹנוֹתָיו:

שִׁיר הַמַּעֲלוֹת לְדָוִד, יהוה לֹא־גָבַהּ לִבִּי, וְלֹא־רָמוּ עֵינַי, וְלֹא־הִלַּכְתִּי בִּגְדֹלוֹת תהלים קלא
וּבְנִפְלָאוֹת מִמֶּנִּי: אִם־לֹא שִׁוִּיתִי וְדוֹמַמְתִּי נַפְשִׁי, כְּגָמֻל עֲלֵי אִמּוֹ, כַּגָּמֻל עָלַי
נַפְשִׁי: יַחֵל יִשְׂרָאֵל אֶל־יהוה, מֵעַתָּה וְעַד־עוֹלָם:

Psalm 130: A penitential psalm, recited during the Ten Days of Repentance. מִמַּעֲמַקִּים *From the depths:* a graphic phrase, signaling closeness to despair or death, used in only one other psalm (Ps. 69). כִּי־עִמְּךָ הַסְּלִיחָה *With You there is forgiveness:* the Psalmist makes the powerful, paradoxical point that God is to be held in awe not because He punishes but because He forgives.

A song of ascents. Lord, remember David and all the hardship he endured. *Ps. 132*
He swore an oath to the Lord and made a vow to the Mighty One of Jacob: "I will not enter my house, nor go to bed; I will not give sleep to my eyes or slumber to my eyelids, until I find a place for the Lord, a dwelling for the Mighty One of Jacob." We heard of it in Efrat, we found it in the fields of Yaar. Let us enter His dwelling, worship at His footstool. Advance, Lord, to Your resting place, You and Your mighty Ark. Your priests are robed in righteousness; Your devoted ones sing for joy. For the sake of Your servant David, do not reject Your anointed one. The Lord swore to David a firm oath that He will not revoke: "One of your own descendants I will set upon your throne. If your sons keep My covenant and My decrees that I teach them, then their sons shall sit upon your throne for all time." For the Lord has chosen Zion; He desired it for His home. This is My resting place for all time; here I will dwell, for that is My desire. I will amply bless its store of food; its poor I will satisfy with bread. I will clothe its priests with salvation; its loyal ones shall sing for joy. There I will make David's dynasty flourish; I will prepare a lamp for My anointed one. I will clothe his enemies with shame, but on him will be a shining crown.

A song of ascents. By David. How good and pleasant it is when brothers dwell *Ps. 133*
together. It is like fragrant oil on the head, running down onto the beard, Aaron's beard, that runs down over the collar of his robes. It is like the dew of Hermon that falls on the mountains of Zion. There the Lord bestows His blessing, life for evermore.

A song of ascents. Come, bless the Lord, all you servants of the Lord, who *Ps. 134*
nightly stand in the House of the Lord. Lift up your hands toward the Sanctuary and bless the Lord. May the Lord, Maker of heaven and earth, bless you from Zion!

Priest, anointing oil was poured over his head (Ex. 29:7). Mount Hermon, in the north, was the highest mountain in Israel. Both images, of oil on the priest's head and dew on the mountain, are metaphors of plenitude.

Psalm 134: The last of the Psalms of Ascents brings the sequence to a close by calling on the people to bless God, and God to bless the people. The juxtaposition in the last verse, of "heaven and earth" and Zion, encapsulates the two dimensions of Judaism – the universal and the particular. God is everywhere, but it is in Zion that His Presence is most apparent.

תהלים קלב שִׁיר הַמַּעֲלוֹת, זְכוֹר־יהוה לְדָוִד אֵת כָּל־עֻנּוֹתוֹ: אֲשֶׁר נִשְׁבַּע לַיהוה, נָדַר
לַאֲבִיר יַעֲקֹב: אִם־אָבֹא בְּאֹהֶל בֵּיתִי, אִם־אֶעֱלֶה עַל־עֶרֶשׂ יְצוּעָי: אִם־אֶתֵּן
שְׁנַת לְעֵינָי, לְעַפְעַפַּי תְּנוּמָה: עַד־אֶמְצָא מָקוֹם לַיהוה, מִשְׁכָּנוֹת לַאֲבִיר
יַעֲקֹב: הִנֵּה־שְׁמַעֲנוּהָ בְאֶפְרָתָה, מְצָאנוּהָ בִּשְׂדֵי־יָעַר: נָבוֹאָה לְמִשְׁכְּנוֹתָיו,
נִשְׁתַּחֲוֶה לַהֲדֹם רַגְלָיו: קוּמָה יהוה לִמְנוּחָתֶךָ, אַתָּה וַאֲרוֹן עֻזֶּךָ: כֹּהֲנֶיךָ
יִלְבְּשׁוּ־צֶדֶק, וַחֲסִידֶיךָ יְרַנֵּנוּ: בַּעֲבוּר דָּוִד עַבְדֶּךָ, אַל־תָּשֵׁב פְּנֵי מְשִׁיחֶךָ:
נִשְׁבַּע־יהוה לְדָוִד, אֱמֶת לֹא־יָשׁוּב מִמֶּנָּה, מִפְּרִי בִטְנְךָ אָשִׁית לְכִסֵּא־לָךְ:
אִם־יִשְׁמְרוּ בָנֶיךָ בְּרִיתִי, וְעֵדֹתִי זוֹ אֲלַמְּדֵם, גַּם־בְּנֵיהֶם עֲדֵי־עַד, יֵשְׁבוּ לְכִסֵּא־
לָךְ: כִּי־בָחַר יהוה בְּצִיּוֹן, אִוָּהּ לְמוֹשָׁב לוֹ: זֹאת־מְנוּחָתִי עֲדֵי־עַד, פֹּה אֵשֵׁב
כִּי אִוִּתִיהָ: צֵידָהּ בָּרֵךְ אֲבָרֵךְ, אֶבְיוֹנֶיהָ אַשְׂבִּיעַ לָחֶם: וְכֹהֲנֶיהָ אַלְבִּישׁ יֶשַׁע,
וַחֲסִידֶיהָ רַנֵּן יְרַנֵּנוּ: שָׁם אַצְמִיחַ קֶרֶן לְדָוִד, עָרַכְתִּי נֵר לִמְשִׁיחִי: אוֹיְבָיו
אַלְבִּישׁ בֹּשֶׁת, וְעָלָיו יָצִיץ נִזְרוֹ:

תהלים קלג שִׁיר הַמַּעֲלוֹת לְדָוִד, הִנֵּה מַה־טּוֹב וּמַה־נָּעִים, שֶׁבֶת אַחִים גַּם־יָחַד: כַּשֶּׁמֶן
הַטּוֹב עַל־הָרֹאשׁ, יֹרֵד עַל־הַזָּקָן, זְקַן־אַהֲרֹן שֶׁיֹּרֵד עַל־פִּי מִדּוֹתָיו: כְּטַל־
חֶרְמוֹן שֶׁיֹּרֵד עַל־הַרְרֵי צִיּוֹן, כִּי שָׁם צִוָּה יהוה אֶת־הַבְּרָכָה, חַיִּים עַד־הָעוֹלָם:

תהלים קלד שִׁיר הַמַּעֲלוֹת, הִנֵּה בָּרְכוּ אֶת־יהוה כָּל־עַבְדֵי יהוה, הָעֹמְדִים בְּבֵית־יהוה
בַּלֵּילוֹת: שְׂאוּ־יְדֵכֶם קֹדֶשׁ, וּבָרְכוּ אֶת־יהוה: יְבָרֶכְךָ יהוה מִצִּיּוֹן, עֹשֵׂה
שָׁמַיִם וָאָרֶץ:

Psalm 132: A psalm about the Temple and its priests. The first five verses describe David's determination to build a House for God: "Here I am living in a house of cedar, while the Ark of the LORD is housed in a tent" (II Sam. 7:2). Verses 10–12 describe God's promise to David that the monarchy would be an eternal gift to his descendants: "Your family and your kingdom will be established for ever in My sight; your throne will endure for all time" (II Sam. 7:16).

Psalm 133: A short poem on the blessing of harmony between brothers – possibly a reference to the divided kingdom, Israel in the north, Judah in the south, with a hope for their reunification. When Aaron was ordained as High

ETHICS OF THE FATHERS

One of the following chapters is read each Shabbat after Pesaḥ until the Shabbat before Rosh HaShana. On the last three Shabbatot before Rosh HaShana, two chapters are read.

All Israel have a share in the World to Come, as it is said: *Sanhedrin 90a*
"Your people are all righteous; they shall inherit the land for ever; *Is. 60*
they are a shoot of My own planting,
a work of My own hands, that I may be glorified."

CHAPTER I

1. Moses received the Torah at Sinai and handed it on to Joshua; Joshua to the elders; the elders to the prophets; and the prophets handed it on to the men of the Great Assembly. They (the men of the Great Assembly) said three things: Be careful in judgment; raise up many disciples; and make a fence for the Torah.
2. Shimon the Just was one of the last survivors of the Great Assembly. He used to say: On three things the world stands: on the Torah, on divine worship, and on acts of loving-kindness.

---

grammatic, and at times even cryptic. The first two chapters are organized chronologically; chapters three and four are collections of sayings; chapter five records teachings whose common feature is that they are associated with numerical lists; and the sixth is a hymn of praise to the life of Torah and the virtues it requires.

No finer account exists of the way of life epitomized by the sages, which was quiet, scholarly, profoundly driven by a sense of justice and integrity, skeptical of politics and politicians, and dedicated to the life of the mind and to the spiritual drama of study as the highest connection between the mind of man and the will of God.

CHAPTER 1

1:1. *The elders:* Leaders of the people in the days of the Judges (see Judges 2:7). *Men of the Great Assembly:* a council of the sages convened by Ezra or shortly thereafter, during the Second Temple period. *Make a fence:* Rabbinic enactments designed to safeguard Torah observance.

פרקי אבות

One of the following chapters is read each שבת *after* פסח *until the* שבת *before* ראש השנה*. On the last three* שבתות *before* ראש השנה*, two chapters are read.*

כָּל יִשְׂרָאֵל יֵשׁ לָהֶם חֵלֶק לָעוֹלָם הַבָּא. שֶׁנֶּאֱמַר: סנהדרין צ.
וְעַמֵּךְ כֻּלָּם צַדִּיקִים, לְעוֹלָם יִירְשׁוּ אָרֶץ ישעיה ס
נֵצֶר מַטָּעַי, מַעֲשֵׂה יָדַי לְהִתְפָּאֵר:

פרק ראשון

א מֹשֶׁה קִבֵּל תּוֹרָה מִסִּינַי וּמְסָרָהּ לִיהוֹשֻׁעַ, וִיהוֹשֻׁעַ לִזְקֵנִים, וּזְקֵנִים לִנְבִיאִים, וּנְבִיאִים מְסָרוּהָ לְאַנְשֵׁי כְנֶסֶת הַגְּדוֹלָה. הֵם אָמְרוּ שְׁלֹשָׁה דְבָרִים: הֱווּ מְתוּנִים בַּדִּין, וְהַעֲמִידוּ תַלְמִידִים הַרְבֵּה, וַעֲשׂוּ סְיָג לַתּוֹרָה.

ב שִׁמְעוֹן הַצַּדִּיק הָיָה מִשְּׁיָרֵי כְנֶסֶת הַגְּדוֹלָה. הוּא הָיָה אוֹמֵר: עַל שְׁלֹשָׁה דְבָרִים הָעוֹלָם עוֹמֵד, עַל הַתּוֹרָה, וְעַל הָעֲבוֹדָה, וְעַל גְּמִילוּת חֲסָדִים.

ETHICS OF THE FATHERS

Ethics of the Fathers (*Pirkei Avot*) is the name given to the tractate of the Mishna that gathers together many of the ethical teachings of the sages. The word *Avot* may mean "fundamental principles," however it is more likely to mean "the fathers" of the oral tradition, the teachers of the Mishna and their predecessors. To the five chapters of the Mishna was added a sixth, not itself part of the Mishna but a later addition, similar in style and content. The need for such an addition arose in circles where the custom was to study one chapter each week during the six Shabbatot between Pesaḥ and Shavuot. It is our custom, however, to study *Avot* from Pesaḥ until the Shabbat before Rosh HaShana.

The tractate begins by tracing the unbroken continuity of the Oral Law from Moses to the sages. Interestingly, the sages traced their provenance to the prophets rather than the priests, who go unmentioned in the chain of succession.

The tractate ranges widely over matters of belief and conduct, but its primary concern is to set out values and virtues of a life dedicated to the study and practice of Torah. Its style is aphoristic; its statements brief, epi-

3. Antigonos of Sokho received [the Torah tradition] from Shimon the Just. He used to say: Do not be like servants who serve their master on condition of receiving a reward, but be like servants who serve their master not on condition of receiving a reward; and let the fear of Heaven be upon you.

4. Yose ben Yo'ezer of Zereda and Yose ben Yoḥanan of Jerusalem received [the tradition] from them. Yose ben Yo'ezer of Zereda used to say: Let your house be a meeting place for sages; sit in the dust at their feet, and with thirst, drink in their words.

5. Yose ben Yoḥanan of Jerusalem used to say: Let your house be open wide; let the poor join the members of your household; and do not gossip inordinately with women. This was said about one's own wife; all the more so does it apply to another man's wife. Hence the sages say: a man who talks too much with a woman brings trouble on himself, neglects the study of Torah, and in the end will inherit Gehinnom.

6. Yehoshua ben Peraḥya and Nittai the Arbelite received [the tradition] from them. Yehoshua ben Peraḥya used to say: Get yourself a teacher, acquire a companion, and give everyone the benefit of the doubt.

7. Nittai the Arbelite used to say: Keep far from a bad neighbor, do not associate with a bad person, and do not despair of divine retribution.

8. Yehuda ben Tabbai and Shimon ben Shataḥ received [the tradition] from them. Yehuda ben Tabbai used to say: [When sitting as a judge] do not act as an advocate; when the parties to a lawsuit appear before you, regard them both as guilty; but when they leave you, having accepted the verdict, regard them both as innocent.

9. Shimon ben Shataḥ used to say: Examine the witnesses thoroughly, and be careful in your words, lest through them they learn how to lie.

10. Shemaya and Avtalyon received [the tradition] from them. Shemaya used to say: Love work, hate public office, and do not become too intimate with the ruling power.

11. Avtalyon used to say: sages, be careful in what you say, lest you incur the penalty of exile and find yourself banished to a place of evil waters, where your disciples who follow you may drink from them and die, with the result that the name of Heaven will be profaned.

---

verdict has been delivered and accepted, there must be no ill-will on either side.

ג אַנְטִיגְנוֹס אִישׁ סוֹכוֹ קִבֵּל מִשִּׁמְעוֹן הַצַּדִּיק. הוּא הָיָה אוֹמֵר: אַל תִּהְיוּ כַּעֲבָדִים הַמְשַׁמְּשִׁים אֶת הָרַב עַל מְנָת לְקַבֵּל פְּרָס, אֶלָּא הֱווּ כַּעֲבָדִים הַמְשַׁמְּשִׁים אֶת הָרַב שֶׁלֹּא עַל מְנָת לְקַבֵּל פְּרָס, וִיהִי מוֹרָא שָׁמַיִם עֲלֵיכֶם.

ד יוֹסֵי בֶּן יוֹעֶזֶר אִישׁ צְרֵדָה וְיוֹסֵי בֶּן יוֹחָנָן אִישׁ יְרוּשָׁלַיִם קִבְּלוּ מֵהֶם. יוֹסֵי בֶּן יוֹעֶזֶר אִישׁ צְרֵדָה אוֹמֵר: יְהִי בֵיתְךָ בֵּית וַעַד לַחֲכָמִים, וֶהֱוֵי מִתְאַבֵּק בַּעֲפַר רַגְלֵיהֶם, וֶהֱוֵי שׁוֹתֶה בַצָּמָא אֶת דִּבְרֵיהֶם.

ה יוֹסֵי בֶּן יוֹחָנָן אִישׁ יְרוּשָׁלַיִם אוֹמֵר: יְהִי בֵיתְךָ פָּתוּחַ לִרְוָחָה, וְיִהְיוּ עֲנִיִּים בְּנֵי בֵיתֶךָ, וְאַל תַּרְבֶּה שִׂיחָה עִם הָאִשָּׁה. בְּאִשְׁתּוֹ אָמְרוּ, קַל וָחֹמֶר בְּאֵשֶׁת חֲבֵרוֹ. מִכָּאן אָמְרוּ חֲכָמִים: כָּל הַמַּרְבֶּה שִׂיחָה עִם הָאִשָּׁה, גּוֹרֵם רָעָה לְעַצְמוֹ, וּבוֹטֵל מִדִּבְרֵי תוֹרָה, וְסוֹפוֹ יוֹרֵשׁ גֵּיהִנָּם.

ו יְהוֹשֻׁעַ בֶּן פְּרַחְיָה וְנִתַּאי הָאַרְבֵּלִי קִבְּלוּ מֵהֶם. יְהוֹשֻׁעַ בֶּן פְּרַחְיָה אוֹמֵר: עֲשֵׂה לְךָ רַב, וּקְנֵה לְךָ חָבֵר, וֶהֱוֵי דָן אֶת כָּל הָאָדָם לְכַף זְכוּת.

ז נִתַּאי הָאַרְבֵּלִי אוֹמֵר: הַרְחֵק מִשָּׁכֵן רָע, וְאַל תִּתְחַבֵּר לָרָשָׁע, וְאַל תִּתְיָאֵשׁ מִן הַפֻּרְעָנוּת.

ח יְהוּדָה בֶּן טַבַּאי וְשִׁמְעוֹן בֶּן שָׁטָח קִבְּלוּ מֵהֶם. יְהוּדָה בֶּן טַבַּאי אוֹמֵר: אַל תַּעַשׂ עַצְמְךָ כְּעוֹרְכֵי הַדַּיָּנִין, וּכְשֶׁיִּהְיוּ בַּעֲלֵי הַדִּין עוֹמְדִים לְפָנֶיךָ יִהְיוּ בְעֵינֶיךָ כִּרְשָׁעִים, וּכְשֶׁנִּפְטָרִים מִלְּפָנֶיךָ יִהְיוּ בְעֵינֶיךָ כְּזַכָּאִין, כְּשֶׁקִּבְּלוּ עֲלֵיהֶם אֶת הַדִּין.

ט שִׁמְעוֹן בֶּן שָׁטָח אוֹמֵר: הֱוֵי מַרְבֶּה לַחְקֹר אֶת הָעֵדִים, וֶהֱוֵי זָהִיר בִּדְבָרֶיךָ, שֶׁמָּא מִתּוֹכָם יִלְמְדוּ לְשַׁקֵּר.

י שְׁמַעְיָה וְאַבְטַלְיוֹן קִבְּלוּ מֵהֶם. שְׁמַעְיָה אוֹמֵר: אֱהֹב אֶת הַמְּלָאכָה, וּשְׂנָא אֶת הָרַבָּנוּת, וְאַל תִּתְוַדַּע לָרָשׁוּת.

יא אַבְטַלְיוֹן אוֹמֵר: חֲכָמִים הִזָּהֲרוּ בְדִבְרֵיכֶם, שֶׁמָּא תָחוּבוּ חוֹבַת גָּלוּת, וְתִגְלוּ לִמְקוֹם מַיִם הָרָעִים, וְיִשְׁתּוּ הַתַּלְמִידִים הַבָּאִים אַחֲרֵיכֶם וְיָמוּתוּ, וְנִמְצָא שֵׁם שָׁמַיִם מִתְחַלֵּל.

1:8. *Do not act as an advocate:* A judge must maintain strict neutrality. While the case is being heard, the judge must exercise proper skepticism. Once the

12. Hillel and Shammai received [the tradition] from them. Hillel said: Be among the disciples of Aaron, loving peace and pursuing peace, loving people and drawing them close to the Torah.
13. He used to say: A name made great is a name destroyed. He who does not increase [his knowledge] loses it. He who does not study deserves to die, and he who makes worldly use of the crown [of Torah] passes away.
14. He used to say: If I am not for myself, who will be for me? And if I am only for myself, what am I? And if not now, when?
15. Shammai used to say: Make your Torah study a fixed habit. Say little and do much; and greet everyone cheerfully.
16. Rabban Gamliel used to say: Get yourself a teacher, avoid doubt, and do not make a habit of giving tithes by guessing.
17. Shimon, his son, used to say: All my life I grew up among sages and I found that nothing is better for a person than silence. Not learning but doing is the main thing; and one who talks too much causes sin.
18. Rabban Shimon ben Gamliel used to say: On three things does the world stand – on truth, justice and peace, as it is said, "Administer truth and the judgment of peace in your gates." *Zech. 8*

Rabbi Ḥananya ben Akashya said: The Holy One, blessed be He, wanted to confer merit on Israel. That is why He gave them a copious Torah and many commandments, as it is said, "It pleased the LORD, for the sake of [Israel's] righteousness, to make the Torah great and glorious." *Makkot 23b* *Is. 42*

If there is a minyan, mourners say the Rabbis' Kaddish (page 560).

* * *

---

away from situations in which you are called on to make a decision when the facts are unclear.

Rabbi Ḥananya ben Akashya: This paragraph is not part of the *Pirkei Avot* but a liturgical addition. According to Maimonides, its implication is that "It is a fundamental principle of Jewish faith that if a person fulfills even one of the 613 mitzvot fully and properly, without ulterior motive but simply for its own sake and out of love, he merits a share in the World to Come. Therefore Rabbi Ḥananya teaches that there are so many mitzvot that it is impossible that a person should not have fulfilled at least one in the course of a lifetime, and thereby merits eternal life" (commentary on the Mishna *Makkot* 3:17). The statement of Rabbi Ḥananya thus complements the teaching recited at the beginning, that "All Israel have a share in the World to Come."

יב הִלֵּל וְשַׁמַּאי קִבְּלוּ מֵהֶם. הִלֵּל אוֹמֵר: הֱוֵי מִתַּלְמִידָיו שֶׁל אַהֲרֹן, אוֹהֵב שָׁלוֹם וְרוֹדֵף שָׁלוֹם, אוֹהֵב אֶת הַבְּרִיּוֹת וּמְקָרְבָן לַתּוֹרָה.

יג הוּא הָיָה אוֹמֵר: נְגַד שְׁמָא אֲבַד שְׁמֵהּ, וּדְלָא מוֹסִיף יְסוּף, וּדְלָא יָלֵף קְטָלָא חַיָּב, וּדְאִשְׁתַּמֵּשׁ בְּתָגָא חֲלָף.

יד הוּא הָיָה אוֹמֵר: אִם אֵין אֲנִי לִי מִי לִי, וּכְשֶׁאֲנִי לְעַצְמִי מָה אֲנִי, וְאִם לֹא עַכְשָׁו אֵימָתָי.

טו שַׁמַּאי אוֹמֵר: עֲשֵׂה תוֹרָתְךָ קֶבַע, אֱמֹר מְעַט וַעֲשֵׂה הַרְבֵּה, וֶהֱוֵי מְקַבֵּל אֶת כָּל הָאָדָם בְּסֵבֶר פָּנִים יָפוֹת.

טז רַבָּן גַּמְלִיאֵל אוֹמֵר: עֲשֵׂה לְךָ רַב, וְהִסְתַּלֵּק מִן הַסָּפֵק, וְאַל תַּרְבֶּה לְעַשֵּׂר אֻמָּדוֹת.

יז שִׁמְעוֹן בְּנוֹ אוֹמֵר: כָּל יָמַי גָּדַלְתִּי בֵּין הַחֲכָמִים, וְלֹא מָצָאתִי לַגּוּף טוֹב מִשְּׁתִיקָה, וְלֹא הַמִּדְרָשׁ עִקָּר אֶלָּא הַמַּעֲשֶׂה, וְכָל הַמַּרְבֶּה דְבָרִים מֵבִיא חֵטְא.

יח רַבָּן שִׁמְעוֹן בֶּן גַּמְלִיאֵל אוֹמֵר: עַל שְׁלֹשָׁה דְבָרִים הָעוֹלָם קַיָּם, עַל הַדִּין, וְעַל הָאֱמֶת, וְעַל הַשָּׁלוֹם. שֶׁנֶּאֱמַר: אֱמֶת וּמִשְׁפַּט שָׁלוֹם שִׁפְטוּ בְּשַׁעֲרֵיכֶם: זכריה ח

רַבִּי חֲנַנְיָא בֶּן עֲקַשְׁיָא אוֹמֵר: רָצָה הַקָּדוֹשׁ בָּרוּךְ הוּא לְזַכּוֹת אֶת יִשְׂרָאֵל, לְפִיכָךְ מכות כג:
הִרְבָּה לָהֶם תּוֹרָה וּמִצְוֹת. שֶׁנֶּאֱמַר: יהוה חָפֵץ לְמַעַן צִדְקוֹ, יַגְדִּיל תּוֹרָה וְיַאְדִּיר: ישעיה מב

If there is a מנין*, mourners say* קדיש דרבנן *(page 561).*

* * *

1:13. *A name made great:* Those who take pride in fame will eventually lose it. *He who does not study:* life is learning, and learning is life. *He who makes worldly use of the crown:* Torah scholarship must never be used for personal advantage. It is for us to honor the Torah, and not use the Torah to honor ourselves.

1:14. *If I am not for myself:* A succinct summary of Judaism's philosophy of personal responsibility combined with social responsibility. *If not now:* a moment of opportunity, unseized, may never come again.

1:16. *Get yourself a teacher:* As with Yehoshua ben Perahya's teaching (above, 1:6), the emphasis is on the choice of one particular teacher as primary mentor and role model. Scholarship depends on discipleship. *Avoid doubt:* keep

All Israel have a share in the World to Come, as it is said: *Sanhedrin 90a*
"Your people are all righteous; they shall inherit the land for ever; *Is. 60*
they are a shoot of My own planting,
a work of My own hands, that I may be glorified."

CHAPTER 2

1. Rabbi [Judah the Prince] said: What is the right path a person should choose for himself? Whatever is honorable to one who chooses it and honorable in the eyes of others. Be as meticulous in the observance of a minor mitzva as a major one, for you do not know the reward for each mitzva. Against the loss that fulfilling a mitzva may entail, reckon its reward, and against the benefit a transgression may bring, reckon the loss it involves. Reflect on three things and you will not fall into transgression: know what is above you – a seeing eye, a hearing ear, and a book in which all your deeds are written.

2. Rabban Gamliel, son of Rabbi Judah the Prince, said: It is good to combine Torah study with a worldly occupation, for the effort involved in both makes one forget sin. Torah study without an occupation will in the end fail and lead to sin. And all who work for the community should do so for the sake of Heaven, for their ancestral merit will support them and their righteousness endures for ever. And as for you [God will say], I count you worthy of great reward as though you yourselves had accomplished it all.

3. Be wary in your dealings with the ruling power, for they only befriend a man when it serves their needs. When it is to their advantage, they appear as friends, but they do not stand by a person in his hour of need.

4. He used to say: Do His will as if it were yours, so that He may do your will as if it were His. Set aside your will for the sake of His, that He may set aside the will of others before yours.

5. Hillel said: Do not separate yourself from the community. Do not be sure of yourself until the day you die. Do not judge your fellow until you have stood in his place. Do not say anything that cannot be understood [at once] in the hope that it will eventually be understood. And do not say, I will study when I have the time, for you may never have the time.

6. He used to say: An uncouth person cannot be sin-fearing, nor can an ignoramus be pious. A shy person cannot learn, nor can an impatient one teach. A person over-occupied in business does not always become wise. In a place where there are no worthy people, strive to be worthy.

---

not say of anything you have been unable to understand that it is unintelligible. Eventually – through repeated study and fellowship – you will find that you can understand it."

כָּל יִשְׂרָאֵל יֵשׁ לָהֶם חֵלֶק לָעוֹלָם הַבָּא. שֶׁנֶּאֱמַר: סנהדרין צ.
וְעַמֵּךְ כֻּלָּם צַדִּיקִים, לְעוֹלָם יִירְשׁוּ אָרֶץ ישעיה ס
נֵצֶר מַטָּעַי, מַעֲשֵׂה יָדַי לְהִתְפָּאֵר:

פרק שני

א רַבִּי אוֹמֵר: אֵיזוֹ הִיא דֶרֶךְ יְשָׁרָה שֶׁיָּבֹר לוֹ הָאָדָם, כָּל שֶׁהִיא תִּפְאֶרֶת לְעֹשֶׂיהָ וְתִפְאֶרֶת לוֹ מִן הָאָדָם. וֶהֱוֵי זָהִיר בְּמִצְוָה קַלָּה כְּבַחֲמוּרָה, שֶׁאֵין אַתָּה יוֹדֵעַ מַתַּן שְׂכָרָן שֶׁל מִצְוֹת. וֶהֱוֵי מְחַשֵּׁב הֶפְסֵד מִצְוָה כְּנֶגֶד שְׂכָרָהּ, וּשְׂכַר עֲבֵרָה כְּנֶגֶד הֶפְסֵדָהּ. הִסְתַּכֵּל בִּשְׁלֹשָׁה דְבָרִים, וְאֵין אַתָּה בָא לִידֵי עֲבֵרָה. דַּע מַה לְּמַעְלָה מִמְּךָ, עַיִן רוֹאָה, וְאֹזֶן שׁוֹמַעַת, וְכָל מַעֲשֶׂיךָ בַּסֵּפֶר נִכְתָּבִים.

ב רַבָּן גַּמְלִיאֵל בְּנוֹ שֶׁל רַבִּי יְהוּדָה הַנָּשִׂיא אוֹמֵר: יָפֶה תַלְמוּד תּוֹרָה עִם דֶּרֶךְ אֶרֶץ, שֶׁיְּגִיעַת שְׁנֵיהֶם מְשַׁכַּחַת עָוֹן. וְכָל תּוֹרָה שֶׁאֵין עִמָּהּ מְלָאכָה, סוֹפָהּ בְּטֵלָה וְגוֹרֶרֶת עָוֹן. וְכָל הָעוֹסְקִים עִם הַצִּבּוּר, יִהְיוּ עוֹסְקִים עִמָּהֶם לְשֵׁם שָׁמַיִם, שֶׁזְּכוּת אֲבוֹתָם מְסַיַּעְתָּם, וְצִדְקָתָם עוֹמֶדֶת לָעַד. וְאַתֶּם, מַעֲלֶה אֲנִי עֲלֵיכֶם שָׂכָר הַרְבֵּה כְּאִלּוּ עֲשִׂיתֶם.

ג הֱווּ זְהִירִין בָּרָשׁוּת, שֶׁאֵין מְקָרְבִין לוֹ לָאָדָם אֶלָּא לְצֹרֶךְ עַצְמָן. נִרְאִין כְּאוֹהֲבִין בִּשְׁעַת הֲנָאָתָן, וְאֵין עוֹמְדִין לוֹ לָאָדָם בִּשְׁעַת דָּחְקוֹ.

ד הוּא הָיָה אוֹמֵר: עֲשֵׂה רְצוֹנוֹ כִּרְצוֹנְךָ, כְּדֵי שֶׁיַּעֲשֶׂה רְצוֹנְךָ כִּרְצוֹנוֹ. בַּטֵּל רְצוֹנְךָ מִפְּנֵי רְצוֹנוֹ, כְּדֵי שֶׁיְּבַטֵּל רְצוֹן אֲחֵרִים מִפְּנֵי רְצוֹנֶךָ.

ה הִלֵּל אוֹמֵר: אַל תִּפְרֹשׁ מִן הַצִּבּוּר, וְאַל תַּאֲמִין בְּעַצְמְךָ עַד יוֹם מוֹתְךָ, וְאַל תָּדִין אֶת חֲבֵרְךָ עַד שֶׁתַּגִּיעַ לִמְקוֹמוֹ. וְאַל תֹּאמַר דָּבָר שֶׁאִי אֶפְשַׁר לִשְׁמֹעַ, שֶׁסּוֹפוֹ לְהִשָּׁמַע. וְאַל תֹּאמַר לִכְשֶׁאֶפָּנֶה אֶשְׁנֶה, שֶׁמָּא לֹא תִפָּנֶה.

ו הוּא הָיָה אוֹמֵר: אֵין בּוּר יְרֵא חֵטְא, וְלֹא עַם הָאָרֶץ חָסִיד, וְלֹא הַבַּיְשָׁן לָמֵד, וְלֹא הַקַּפְּדָן מְלַמֵּד, וְלֹא כָל הַמַּרְבֶּה בִסְחוֹרָה מַחְכִּים. וּבְמָקוֹם שֶׁאֵין אֲנָשִׁים, הִשְׁתַּדֵּל לִהְיוֹת אִישׁ.

CHAPTER 2

The chapter continues the chronological sequence of the previous chapter, beginning with Rabbi (Judah the Prince) and his son, Rabban Gamliel, before reverting to the teachings of earlier sages, beginning with Hillel.

2:5. *Do not say anything that cannot be understood:* Alternative translation: "Do

7. Seeing a skull floating on the water, he said: "Because you drowned others, they drowned you, and those who drowned you will themselves eventually be drowned."

8. He used to say: The more flesh, the more worms. The more possessions, the more worries. The more wives, the more witchcraft. The more maidservants, the more lewdness. The more menservants, the more robbery. The more Torah, the more life. The more study, the more wisdom. The more counsel, the more understanding. The more charity, the more peace. Whoever acquires a good name acquires something for himself. Whoever acquires for himself words of Torah acquires for himself life in the World to Come.

9. Rabban Yoḥanan ben Zakkai received [the tradition] from Hillel and Shammai. He used to say: If you have learnt much Torah, take no special credit for yourself, for it was for this that you were created.

10. Rabban Yoḥanan ben Zakkai had five [pre-eminent] disciples, namely: Rabbi Eliezer ben Hyrcanus, Rabbi Yehoshua ben Ḥananya, Rabbi Yose the Priest, Rabbi Shimon ben Netanel and Rabbi Elazar ben Arakh.

11. He used to recount their praise: Eliezer ben Hyrcanus: a plastered well that never loses a drop. Yehoshua ben Ḥananya: happy the one who gave him birth. Yose the Priest: a pious man. Shimon ben Netanel: a man who fears sin. Elazar ben Arakh: an ever-flowing spring.

12. He used to say: If all the sages of Israel were in one scale of a balance and Eliezer ben Hyrcanus in the other, he would outweigh them all. However, Abba Saul said in his name: If all the sages of Israel, including Eliezer ben Hyrcanus, were in one scale of a balance, and Elazar ben Arakh in the other, he would outweigh them all.

13. He said to them: Go and see which is the right way to which one should cling. Rabbi Eliezer said: a good eye [generosity of spirit]. Rabbi Yehoshua said: a good companion. Rabbi Yose said: a good neighbor. Rabbi Shimon said: one who considers the consequences. Rabbi Elazar said: a good heart. Then he said to them: I prefer the answer of Elazar ben Arakh, for his view includes all of yours.

14. He said to them: Go and see which is the wrong way one should avoid. Rabbi Eliezer said: an evil eye [envy]. Rabbi Yehoshua said: an evil companion. Rabbi Yose said: an evil neighbor. Rabbi Shimon said: one who borrows and

---

2:10–11. *Rabban Yoḥanan ben Zakkai:* Rabban Yoḥanan was able to raise distinguished disciples because "he used to recount their praise." A great teacher is one who recognizes the distinctive potential of each student, and by praise and encouragement brings it to fruition.

ז אַף הוּא רָאָה גֻּלְגֹּלֶת אַחַת שֶׁצָּפָה עַל פְּנֵי הַמָּיִם. אָמַר לָהּ: עַל דַּאֲטֵפְתְּ אַטְיפוּךְ, וְסוֹף מְטִיפַיִךְ יְטוּפוּן.

ח הוּא הָיָה אוֹמֵר: מַרְבֶּה בָשָׂר, מַרְבֶּה רִמָּה. מַרְבֶּה נְכָסִים, מַרְבֶּה דְאָגָה. מַרְבֶּה נָשִׁים, מַרְבֶּה כְשָׁפִים. מַרְבֶּה שְׁפָחוֹת, מַרְבֶּה זִמָּה. מַרְבֶּה עֲבָדִים, מַרְבֶּה גָזֵל. מַרְבֶּה תוֹרָה, מַרְבֶּה חַיִּים. מַרְבֶּה יְשִׁיבָה, מַרְבֶּה חָכְמָה. מַרְבֶּה עֵצָה, מַרְבֶּה תְבוּנָה. מַרְבֶּה צְדָקָה, מַרְבֶּה שָׁלוֹם. קָנָה שֵׁם טוֹב, קָנָה לְעַצְמוֹ. קָנָה לוֹ דִבְרֵי תוֹרָה, קָנָה לוֹ חַיֵּי הָעוֹלָם הַבָּא.

ט רַבָּן יוֹחָנָן בֶּן זַכַּאי קִבֵּל מֵהִלֵּל וּמִשַּׁמַּאי. הוּא הָיָה אוֹמֵר: אִם לָמַדְתָּ תּוֹרָה הַרְבֵּה, אַל תַּחֲזִיק טוֹבָה לְעַצְמְךָ, כִּי לְכָךְ נוֹצָרְתָּ.

י חֲמִשָּׁה תַלְמִידִים הָיוּ לְרַבָּן יוֹחָנָן בֶּן זַכַּאי. וְאֵלּוּ הֵן: רַבִּי אֱלִיעֶזֶר בֶּן הוֹרְקָנוֹס, רַבִּי יְהוֹשֻׁעַ בֶּן חֲנַנְיָה, רַבִּי יוֹסֵי הַכֹּהֵן, רַבִּי שִׁמְעוֹן בֶּן נְתַנְאֵל, רַבִּי אֶלְעָזָר בֶּן עֲרָךְ.

יא הוּא הָיָה מוֹנֶה שִׁבְחָם: אֱלִיעֶזֶר בֶּן הוֹרְקָנוֹס, בּוֹר סוּד שֶׁאֵינוֹ מְאַבֵּד טִפָּה. יְהוֹשֻׁעַ בֶּן חֲנַנְיָה, אַשְׁרֵי יוֹלַדְתּוֹ. יוֹסֵי הַכֹּהֵן, חָסִיד. שִׁמְעוֹן בֶּן נְתַנְאֵל, יְרֵא חֵטְא. אֶלְעָזָר בֶּן עֲרָךְ, כְּמַעְיָן הַמִּתְגַּבֵּר.

יב הוּא הָיָה אוֹמֵר: אִם יִהְיוּ כָּל חַכְמֵי יִשְׂרָאֵל בְּכַף מֹאזְנַיִם, וֶאֱלִיעֶזֶר בֶּן הוֹרְקָנוֹס בְּכַף שְׁנִיָּה, מַכְרִיעַ אֶת כֻּלָּם. אַבָּא שָׁאוּל אוֹמֵר מִשְּׁמוֹ: אִם יִהְיוּ כָּל חַכְמֵי יִשְׂרָאֵל בְּכַף מֹאזְנַיִם, וֶאֱלִיעֶזֶר בֶּן הוֹרְקָנוֹס אַף עִמָּהֶם, וְאֶלְעָזָר בֶּן עֲרָךְ בְּכַף שְׁנִיָּה, מַכְרִיעַ אֶת כֻּלָּם.

יג אָמַר לָהֶם: צְאוּ וּרְאוּ אֵיזוֹ הִיא דֶּרֶךְ טוֹבָה, שֶׁיִּדְבַּק בָּהּ הָאָדָם. רַבִּי אֱלִיעֶזֶר אוֹמֵר: עַיִן טוֹבָה. רַבִּי יְהוֹשֻׁעַ אוֹמֵר: חָבֵר טוֹב. רַבִּי יוֹסֵי אוֹמֵר: שָׁכֵן טוֹב. רַבִּי שִׁמְעוֹן אוֹמֵר: הָרוֹאֶה אֶת הַנּוֹלָד. רַבִּי אֶלְעָזָר אוֹמֵר: לֵב טוֹב. אָמַר לָהֶם, רוֹאֶה אֲנִי אֶת דִּבְרֵי אֶלְעָזָר בֶּן עֲרָךְ מִדִּבְרֵיכֶם, שֶׁבִּכְלַל דְּבָרָיו דִּבְרֵיכֶם.

יד אָמַר לָהֶם: צְאוּ וּרְאוּ, אֵיזוֹ הִיא דֶּרֶךְ רָעָה, שֶׁיִּתְרַחֵק מִמֶּנָּה הָאָדָם. רַבִּי אֱלִיעֶזֶר אוֹמֵר: עַיִן רָעָה. רַבִּי יְהוֹשֻׁעַ אוֹמֵר: חָבֵר רָע. רַבִּי יוֹסֵי אוֹמֵר: שָׁכֵן

2:7. *A skull floating on the water:* The principle of measure for measure. This is one half of the basic ethic of Judaism. The first is the principle of altruism: Do not do to others what you would not wish them to do to you. The second is the principle of retributive justice: As you do to others, so shall others do to you.

does not repay, for borrowing from a person is like borrowing from God, as it is said, "The wicked borrows and does not repay, but the Righteous One is gracious and repays." Rabbi Elazar said: an evil heart. Then he said to them: I prefer the answer of Elazar ben Arakh, for his view includes all of yours. *Ps. 37*

15. Each of the disciples said three things. Rabbi Eliezer said: Let the honor of your fellow be as precious to you as your own. Do not be easily provoked to anger. Repent one day before you die. [He also said:] Warm yourself by the fire of the sages, but be careful of their glowing coals lest you be burnt; for their bite is the bite of a fox, their sting is the sting of a scorpion, their hiss is the hiss of a serpent, and all their words are like fiery coals.
16. Rabbi Yehoshua said: The evil eye [envy], the evil impulse, and hatred of humankind drive a person out of the world.
17. Rabbi Yose said: Let the property of your fellow be as precious to you as your own. Prepare yourself to study Torah, for it does not come to you as an inheritance. And let all your deeds be for the sake of Heaven.
18. Rabbi Shimon said: Be meticulous in reciting the Shema and the [Amida] prayer. When you pray, do not do so as a fixed routine, but as a plea for mercy and grace before God, as it is said, "For He is gracious and compassionate, slow to anger, abounding in kindness, and renouncing punishment." Do not be evil in your own eyes. *Joel 2*
19. Rabbi Elazar said: Be diligent in the study of Torah. Know how to answer a heretic. Know for whom you labor and who is your Employer who will pay you the reward of your work.
20. Rabbi Tarfon said: The day is short, the task is great, the laborers are lazy, the reward is much, and the Master insistent.
21. He used to say: It is not for you to complete the task, but neither are you free to stand aside from it. If you have studied much Torah, you will be given great reward, for your Employer will faithfully reward your work. Know, though, that the reward of the righteous is granted in the time to come.

---

all your deeds be for the sake of heaven – even those that are not specifically religious acts.

2:21. *It is not for you to complete the task:* The task of creating a society built on justice and compassion, freedom and respect for human dignity, cannot be achieved by one generation alone. It is a continuous struggle, in which each of us has a part to play; hence the idea of the covenant as a challenge extending over time, in which we build on the achievements of our ancestors and hand on our ideals to those who will come after us.

רָע. רַבִּי שִׁמְעוֹן אוֹמֵר: הַלֹּוֶה וְאֵינוֹ מְשַׁלֵּם, אֶחָד הַלֹּוֶה מִן הָאָדָם כְּלֹוֶה מִן הַמָּקוֹם, שֶׁנֶּאֱמַר: לֹוֶה רָשָׁע וְלֹא יְשַׁלֵּם, וְצַדִּיק חוֹנֵן וְנוֹתֵן: רַבִּי אֶלְעָזָר אוֹמֵר: לֵב רָע. אָמַר לָהֶם: רוֹאֶה אֲנִי אֶת דִּבְרֵי אֶלְעָזָר בֶּן עֲרָךְ מִדִּבְרֵיכֶם, שֶׁבִּכְלַל דְּבָרָיו דִּבְרֵיכֶם. תהלים לז

טו הֵם אָמְרוּ שְׁלֹשָׁה דְבָרִים. רַבִּי אֱלִיעֶזֶר אוֹמֵר: יְהִי כְבוֹד חֲבֵרְךָ חָבִיב עָלֶיךָ כְּשֶׁלָּךְ, וְאַל תְּהִי נוֹחַ לִכְעֹס. וְשׁוּב יוֹם אֶחָד לִפְנֵי מִיתָתְךָ. וֶהֱוֵי מִתְחַמֵּם כְּנֶגֶד אוּרָן שֶׁל חֲכָמִים, וֶהֱוֵי זָהִיר בְּגַחַלְתָּן שֶׁלֹּא תִכָּוֶה, שֶׁנְּשִׁיכָתָן נְשִׁיכַת שׁוּעָל, וַעֲקִיצָתָן עֲקִיצַת עַקְרָב, וּלְחִישָׁתָן לְחִישַׁת שָׂרָף, וְכָל דִּבְרֵיהֶם כְּגַחֲלֵי אֵשׁ.

טז רַבִּי יְהוֹשֻׁעַ אוֹמֵר: עַיִן הָרָע וְיֵצֶר הָרָע וְשִׂנְאַת הַבְּרִיּוֹת, מוֹצִיאִין אֶת הָאָדָם מִן הָעוֹלָם.

יז רַבִּי יוֹסֵי אוֹמֵר: יְהִי מָמוֹן חֲבֵרְךָ חָבִיב עָלֶיךָ כְּשֶׁלָּךְ. וְהַתְקֵן עַצְמְךָ לִלְמֹד תּוֹרָה, שֶׁאֵינָהּ יְרֻשָּׁה לָךְ. וְכָל מַעֲשֶׂיךָ יִהְיוּ לְשֵׁם שָׁמָיִם.

יח רַבִּי שִׁמְעוֹן אוֹמֵר: הֱוֵי זָהִיר בִּקְרִיאַת שְׁמַע וּבִתְפִלָּה. וּכְשֶׁאַתָּה מִתְפַּלֵּל אַל תַּעַשׂ תְּפִלָּתְךָ קֶבַע, אֶלָּא רַחֲמִים וְתַחֲנוּנִים לִפְנֵי הַמָּקוֹם, שֶׁנֶּאֱמַר: כִּי חַנּוּן וְרַחוּם הוּא, אֶרֶךְ אַפַּיִם וְרַב־חֶסֶד וְנִחָם עַל־הָרָעָה: וְאַל תְּהִי רָשָׁע בִּפְנֵי עַצְמְךָ. יואל ב

יט רַבִּי אֶלְעָזָר אוֹמֵר: הֱוֵי שָׁקוּד לִלְמֹד תּוֹרָה. וְדַע מַה שֶּׁתָּשִׁיב לְאֶפִּיקוֹרוֹס. וְדַע לִפְנֵי מִי אַתָּה עָמֵל, וּמִי הוּא בַּעַל מְלַאכְתְּךָ, שֶׁיְּשַׁלֶּם לְךָ שְׂכַר פְּעֻלָּתֶךָ.

כ רַבִּי טַרְפוֹן אוֹמֵר: הַיּוֹם קָצֵר, וְהַמְּלָאכָה מְרֻבָּה, וְהַפּוֹעֲלִים עֲצֵלִים, וְהַשָּׂכָר הַרְבֵּה, וּבַעַל הַבַּיִת דּוֹחֵק.

כא הוּא הָיָה אוֹמֵר: לֹא עָלֶיךָ הַמְּלָאכָה לִגְמֹר, וְלֹא אַתָּה בֶן חוֹרִין לִבָּטֵל מִמֶּנָּה. אִם לָמַדְתָּ תּוֹרָה הַרְבֵּה, נוֹתְנִין לְךָ שָׂכָר הַרְבֵּה. וְנֶאֱמָן הוּא בַּעַל מְלַאכְתְּךָ, שֶׁיְּשַׁלֶּם לְךָ שְׂכַר פְּעֻלָּתֶךָ. וְדַע, שֶׁמַּתַּן שְׂכָרָן שֶׁל צַדִּיקִים לֶעָתִיד לָבוֹא.

2:16. *Rabbi Yehoshua said:* Life is shortened by negative emotions. This has been confirmed by many medical studies.

2:17. *Prepare yourself to study Torah:* Though Torah is described as "the heritage of the congregation of Jacob" (Deut. 33:4), it does not pass automatically from one generation to the next. Only those who labor for it, acquire it. *Let*

Rabbi Ḥananya ben Akashya said: The Holy One, blessed be He, wanted to confer merit on Israel. That is why He gave them a copious Torah and many commandments, as it is said, "It pleased the LORD, for the sake of [Israel's] righteousness, to make the Torah great and glorious." *Makkot 23b* *Is. 42*

If there is a minyan, mourners say the Rabbis' Kaddish (page 560).

* * *

All Israel have a share in the World to Come, as it is said, *Sanhedrin 90a*
"Your people are all righteous; they shall inherit the land for ever; *Is. 60*
they are a shoot of My own planting,
a work of My own hands, that I may be glorified."

CHAPTER 3

1. Akavya ben Mahalalel said: Reflect on three things and you will avoid transgression: Know where you came from, where you are going, and before whom you will have to give an account and reckoning. "Where you came from" – from a putrid drop. "Where you are going" – to a place of dust, worms and maggots. "And before whom you will have to give an account and reckoning" – before the Supreme King of kings, the Holy One, blessed be He.
2. Rabbi Ḥanina, the deputy High Priest, said: Pray for the welfare of the government, for were it not for fear of it, people would swallow one another alive.
3. Rabbi Ḥanina ben Teradyon said: When two people sit together and no words of Torah pass between them, they are regarded as a company of scoffers, as it is said, "He does not sit in the company of scoffers." But when two people sit together and words of Torah do pass between them, the Divine Presence rests with them, as it is said, "Then those who feared the LORD talked together, and the LORD listened and heard, and a scroll of remembrance was written before Him concerning those who feared the LORD and cherished His name." This verse tells me about two people; from where can I learn that even one person who sits alone and studies Torah, the Holy One, blessed be He, grants him a reward? From the verse, "Though he sits alone and meditates quietly, He will grant him a reward." *Ps. 1* *Mal. 3* *Lam. 3*

---

of law, society would degenerate into a "war of all against all" in which life would be "solitary, poor, nasty, brutish, and short."

3:3. *Rabbi Ḥanina ben Teradyon:* A restatement of the argument of Psalm 1:1–2, "Happy is the man who does not… sit in the company of scoffers. But his delight is in the law of the LORD, and on his Torah he meditates day and night." Sharing words of Torah at the table transforms a physical act into a spiritual one, and those present into a learning fellowship.

רַבִּי חֲנַנְיָא בֶּן עֲקַשְׁיָא אוֹמֵר: רָצָה הַקָּדוֹשׁ בָּרוּךְ הוּא לְזַכּוֹת אֶת יִשְׂרָאֵל, לְפִיכָךְ הִרְבָּה לָהֶם תּוֹרָה וּמִצְוֹת. שֶׁנֶּאֱמַר: יהוה חָפֵץ לְמַעַן צִדְקוֹ, יַגְדִּיל תּוֹרָה וְיַאְדִּיר: מכות כג: ישעיה מב

If there is a מנין, *mourners say* קדיש דרבנן *(page 561).*

* * *

כָּל יִשְׂרָאֵל יֵשׁ לָהֶם חֵלֶק לָעוֹלָם הַבָּא. שֶׁנֶּאֱמַר: סנהדרין צ.
וְעַמֵּךְ כֻּלָּם צַדִּיקִים, לְעוֹלָם יִירְשׁוּ אָרֶץ ישעיה ס
נֵצֶר מַטָּעַי, מַעֲשֵׂה יָדַי לְהִתְפָּאֵר:

פרק שלישי

א עֲקַבְיָא בֶּן מַהֲלַלְאֵל אוֹמֵר: הִסְתַּכֵּל בִּשְׁלֹשָׁה דְבָרִים, וְאֵין אַתָּה בָא לִידֵי עֲבֵרָה. דַּע מֵאַיִן בָּאתָ, וּלְאָן אַתָּה הוֹלֵךְ, וְלִפְנֵי מִי אַתָּה עָתִיד לִתֵּן דִּין וְחֶשְׁבּוֹן. מֵאַיִן בָּאתָ, מִטִּפָּה סְרוּחָה. וּלְאָן אַתָּה הוֹלֵךְ, לִמְקוֹם עָפָר, רִמָּה וְתוֹלֵעָה. וְלִפְנֵי מִי אַתָּה עָתִיד לִתֵּן דִּין וְחֶשְׁבּוֹן, לִפְנֵי מֶלֶךְ מַלְכֵי הַמְּלָכִים, הַקָּדוֹשׁ בָּרוּךְ הוּא.

ב רַבִּי חֲנִינָא סְגַן הַכֹּהֲנִים אוֹמֵר: הֱוֵי מִתְפַּלֵּל בִּשְׁלוֹמָהּ שֶׁל מַלְכוּת, שֶׁאִלְמָלֵא מוֹרָאָהּ, אִישׁ אֶת רֵעֵהוּ חַיִּים בְּלָעוֹ.

ג רַבִּי חֲנִינָא בֶּן תְּרַדְיוֹן אוֹמֵר: שְׁנַיִם שֶׁיּוֹשְׁבִין, וְאֵין בֵּינֵיהֶם דִּבְרֵי תוֹרָה, הֲרֵי זֶה מוֹשַׁב לֵצִים, שֶׁנֶּאֱמַר: וּבְמוֹשַׁב לֵצִים לֹא יָשָׁב: אֲבָל שְׁנַיִם שֶׁיּוֹשְׁבִין, וְיֵשׁ בֵּינֵיהֶם דִּבְרֵי תוֹרָה, שְׁכִינָה שְׁרוּיָה בֵינֵיהֶם, שֶׁנֶּאֱמַר: אָז נִדְבְּרוּ יִרְאֵי יהוה אִישׁ אֶל־רֵעֵהוּ, וַיַּקְשֵׁב יהוה וַיִּשְׁמָע, וַיִּכָּתֵב סֵפֶר זִכָּרוֹן לְפָנָיו לְיִרְאֵי יהוה וּלְחֹשְׁבֵי שְׁמוֹ: אֵין לִי אֶלָּא שְׁנַיִם, מִנַּיִן אֲפִלּוּ אֶחָד שֶׁיּוֹשֵׁב וְעוֹסֵק בַּתּוֹרָה שֶׁהַקָּדוֹשׁ בָּרוּךְ הוּא קוֹבֵעַ לוֹ שָׂכָר, שֶׁנֶּאֱמַר: יֵשֵׁב בָּדָד וְיִדֹּם כִּי נָטַל עָלָיו: תהלים א מלאכי ג איכה ג

CHAPTER 3

3:1. *Akavya ben Mahalalel:* Considered as physical beings, we come from dust and to the dust we return. Only in matters of the spirit do we touch the wings of eternity.

3:2. *Rabbi Hanina, the deputy High Priest:* An anticipation, by some sixteen centuries, of the argument of Thomas Hobbes' political classic, *The Leviathan.* Without a centralized power, charged with the authority of enforcing the rule

4. Rabbi Shimon said: Three who eat at one table, and do not speak words of Torah, are as if they had eaten of sacrifices of dead idols, as it is said, "For all the tables are full of vomit and filth, when God is absent." However, three who eat at one table and speak words of Torah, it is as if they had eaten at God's table, as it is said, "And He spoke to me: This is the table before the LORD." *Is. 28* *Ezek. 41*

5. Rabbi Ḥanina ben Ḥakhinai said: One who stays awake at night, travels alone, or turns his mind to idle thoughts, endangers his soul.

6. Rabbi Neḥunya ben HaKanna said: One who takes on himself the yoke of Torah will be spared the yoke of government and the yoke of worldly responsibilities, but one who throws off the yoke of the Torah will bear the yoke of government and the yoke of worldly responsibilities.

7. Rabbi Ḥalafta ben Dosa of Kfar Ḥananya said: When ten people sit together and study Torah, the Divine Presence rests among them, as it is said, "God stands in the divine assembly." How do we know that the same applies to five? From the verse, "He has founded His group on the earth." And how do we know that it applies even to three? From the verse, "He judges among the judges." How do we know that the same applies even to two? From the verse, "Then those who feared the LORD talked together, and the LORD listened and heard." And how do we know that it applies even to one? From the verse, "In every place where I cause My name to be mentioned, I will come to you and bless you." *Ps. 82* *Amos 9* *Ps. 82* *Mal. 3* *Ex. 20*

8. Rabbi Elazar of Bartota said: Give Him what is His, for you and yours are His. This was also said by David: "For all things come from You, and we have given You only what is Yours." *I Chr. 29*

9. Rabbi Jacob said: One who is reviewing his Torah study while walking on the way, and interrupts his study to say, "What a beautiful tree" or "What a beautiful field," is regarded by Scripture as if he had endangered his soul.

10. Rabbi Dostai of Rabbi Yannai said in the name of Rabbi Meir: One who forgets even one thing of his Torah learning, Scripture regards him as if he had endangered his soul, for it is said, "Only take heed and guard your soul very carefully so that you do not forget the things that your eyes saw." One might think that this applies even to one who finds his studies too hard to remember. Therefore the verse adds, "Lest they be removed from your heart all the *Deut. 4* *Deut. 4*

3:9. *One who is reviewing his Torah study:* Judaism is a religion of the ear rather than the eye. Pagans *saw* the gods in the phenomena of nature; in Judaism, God cannot be seen, but *heard*. Hence one of the key words of the Bible is *Shema*, "listen, hear." One who gives priority to sight over sound has started to stray from the path of Jewish values.

ד רַבִּי שִׁמְעוֹן אוֹמֵר: שְׁלֹשָׁה שֶׁאָכְלוּ עַל שֻׁלְחָן אֶחָד וְלֹא אָמְרוּ עָלָיו דִּבְרֵי
תוֹרָה, כְּאִלּוּ אָכְלוּ מִזִּבְחֵי מֵתִים, שֶׁנֶּאֱמַר: כִּי כָּל־שֻׁלְחָנוֹת מָלְאוּ קִיא ישעיה כח
צֹאָה בְּלִי מָקוֹם: אֲבָל שְׁלֹשָׁה שֶׁאָכְלוּ עַל שֻׁלְחָן אֶחָד, וְאָמְרוּ עָלָיו דִּבְרֵי
תוֹרָה, כְּאִלּוּ אָכְלוּ מִשֻּׁלְחָנוֹ שֶׁל מָקוֹם, שֶׁנֶּאֱמַר: וַיְדַבֵּר אֵלַי, זֶה הַשֻּׁלְחָן יחזקאל מא
אֲשֶׁר לִפְנֵי יהוה:

ה רַבִּי חֲנִינָא בֶּן חֲכִינַאי אוֹמֵר: הַנֵּעוֹר בַּלַּיְלָה, וְהַמְהַלֵּךְ בַּדֶּרֶךְ יְחִידִי, וְהַמְפַנֶּה
לִבּוֹ לְבַטָּלָה, הֲרֵי זֶה מִתְחַיֵּב בְּנַפְשׁוֹ.

ו רַבִּי נְחוּנְיָא בֶּן הַקָּנָה אוֹמֵר: כָּל הַמְקַבֵּל עָלָיו עֹל תּוֹרָה, מַעֲבִירִין מִמֶּנּוּ עֹל
מַלְכוּת וְעֹל דֶּרֶךְ אֶרֶץ. וְכָל הַפּוֹרֵק מִמֶּנּוּ עֹל תּוֹרָה, נוֹתְנִין עָלָיו עֹל מַלְכוּת
וְעֹל דֶּרֶךְ אֶרֶץ.

ז רַבִּי חֲלַפְתָּא בֶּן דּוֹסָא אִישׁ כְּפַר חֲנַנְיָה אוֹמֵר: עֲשָׂרָה שֶׁיּוֹשְׁבִין וְעוֹסְקִין
בַּתּוֹרָה שְׁכִינָה שְׁרוּיָה בֵינֵיהֶם, שֶׁנֶּאֱמַר: אֱלֹהִים נִצָּב בַּעֲדַת־אֵל: וּמִנַּיִן אֲפִלּוּ תהלים פב
חֲמִשָּׁה, שֶׁנֶּאֱמַר: וַאֲגֻדָּתוֹ עַל־אֶרֶץ יְסָדָהּ: וּמִנַּיִן אֲפִלּוּ שְׁלֹשָׁה, שֶׁנֶּאֱמַר: עמוס ט
בְּקֶרֶב אֱלֹהִים יִשְׁפֹּט: וּמִנַּיִן אֲפִלּוּ שְׁנַיִם, שֶׁנֶּאֱמַר: אָז נִדְבְּרוּ יִרְאֵי יהוה אִישׁ תהלים פב מלאכי ג
אֶל־רֵעֵהוּ, וַיַּקְשֵׁב יהוה וַיִּשְׁמָע: וּמִנַּיִן אֲפִלּוּ אֶחָד, שֶׁנֶּאֱמַר: בְּכָל־הַמָּקוֹם שמות כ
אֲשֶׁר אַזְכִּיר אֶת־שְׁמִי, אָבוֹא אֵלֶיךָ וּבֵרַכְתִּיךָ:

ח רַבִּי אֶלְעָזָר אִישׁ בַּרְתּוֹתָא אוֹמֵר: תֶּן לוֹ מִשֶּׁלּוֹ, שֶׁאַתָּה וְשֶׁלְּךָ שֶׁלּוֹ. וְכֵן בְּדָוִד
הוּא אוֹמֵר: כִּי־מִמְּךָ הַכֹּל, וּמִיָּדְךָ נָתַנּוּ לָךְ: דברי הימים א׳ כט

ט רַבִּי יַעֲקֹב אוֹמֵר: הַמְהַלֵּךְ בַּדֶּרֶךְ וְשׁוֹנֶה, וּמַפְסִיק מִמִּשְׁנָתוֹ וְאוֹמֵר, מַה
נָּאֶה אִילָן זֶה, מַה נָּאֶה נִיר זֶה, מַעֲלֶה עָלָיו הַכָּתוּב כְּאִלּוּ מִתְחַיֵּב בְּנַפְשׁוֹ.

י רַבִּי דוֹסְתַּאי בְּרַבִּי יַנַּאי מִשּׁוּם רַבִּי מֵאִיר אוֹמֵר: כָּל הַשּׁוֹכֵחַ דָּבָר אֶחָד
מִמִּשְׁנָתוֹ, מַעֲלֶה עָלָיו הַכָּתוּב כְּאִלּוּ מִתְחַיֵּב בְּנַפְשׁוֹ, שֶׁנֶּאֱמַר: רַק הִשָּׁמֶר דברים ד
לְךָ וּשְׁמֹר נַפְשְׁךָ מְאֹד, פֶּן־תִּשְׁכַּח אֶת־הַדְּבָרִים אֲשֶׁר־רָאוּ עֵינֶיךָ: יָכוֹל אֲפִלּוּ

3:5. *Endangers his soul:* Literally, "is mortally guilty." The sages used this phrase to emphasize serious spiritual danger, rather than to suggest that an individual has committed a capital crime.

3:7. *Ten, five:* "Assembly" (*edah*), signifies ten as in the case of the spies who brought back an evil report about the land (Num. 14:27). "Group" (*aguda*), refers to that which can be held together in the five fingers of one hand: hence it signifies five.

days of your life." Thus, one does not endanger his soul unless he deliberately removes teachings from his heart.

11. Rabbi Ḥanina ben Dosa said: For one who puts fear of sin before wisdom, wisdom endures. For one who puts wisdom before fear of sin, wisdom does not endure.
12. He also used to say: For one whose good deeds exceed his wisdom, wisdom endures. For one whose wisdom exceeds his good deeds, wisdom does not endure.
13. He also used to say: In one in whom people delight, God delights. In one in whom people do not delight, God does not delight.
14. Rabbi Dosa ben Harkinas said: Sleeping late in the morning, drinking wine at midday, chattering with children and sitting in gatherings of the ignorant – these drive a person from the world.
15. Rabbi Elazar of Modin said: One who desecrates sacred things, despises the festivals, shames his fellow in public, nullifies the covenant of our father Abraham, or attributes meanings to the Torah contrary to normative law, even though he has to his credit Torah and good deeds, has no share in the World to Come.
16. Rabbi Yishmael said: Be yielding to a superior, pleasing to the young, and receive everyone cheerfully.
17. Rabbi Akiva said: Mocking and frivolity lead to immorality. The oral tradition (*Mesora*) is a fence protecting the Torah; tithes are a fence protecting wealth; vows are a fence protecting abstinence. The fence protecting wisdom is silence.
18. He used to say: Beloved is man, for he was created in the image of God. As a gesture of special love, it was made known to him that he was created in the image of God, as it is said, "For in the image of God He made man." Beloved *Gen. 9* are Israel for they are called God's children. As a gesture of special love, it was made known to them that they are called God's children, as it is said, "You *Deut. 14* are the children of the Lord your God." Beloved are Israel, for they were given a precious vessel [the Torah]. As a gesture of special love, it was made known to them that they were given the precious vessel through which the world was created, as it is said, "I have given you good instruction; do not *Prov. 4* forsake My Torah."

---

law: for instance, giving an allegorical meaning to commandments, arguing that they are not laws to be practiced, but rather philosophical statements to be contemplated.

תְּקֵפָה עָלָיו מִשְׁנָתוֹ, תַּלְמוּד לוֹמַר: וּפֶן יָסוּרוּ מִלְּבָבְךָ כֹּל יְמֵי חַיֶּיךָ: הָא אֵינוֹ מִתְחַיֵּב בְּנַפְשׁוֹ, עַד שֶׁיֵּשֵׁב וִיסִירֵם מִלִּבּוֹ. דברים ד

יא רַבִּי חֲנִינָא בֶּן דּוֹסָא אוֹמֵר: כָּל שֶׁיִּרְאַת חֶטְאוֹ קוֹדֶמֶת לְחָכְמָתוֹ, חָכְמָתוֹ מִתְקַיֶּמֶת. וְכָל שֶׁחָכְמָתוֹ קוֹדֶמֶת לְיִרְאַת חֶטְאוֹ, אֵין חָכְמָתוֹ מִתְקַיֶּמֶת.

יב הוּא הָיָה אוֹמֵר: כָּל שֶׁמַּעֲשָׂיו מְרֻבִּין מֵחָכְמָתוֹ, חָכְמָתוֹ מִתְקַיֶּמֶת. וְכָל שֶׁחָכְמָתוֹ מְרֻבָּה מִמַּעֲשָׂיו, אֵין חָכְמָתוֹ מִתְקַיֶּמֶת.

יג הוּא הָיָה אוֹמֵר: כָּל שֶׁרְוּחַ הַבְּרִיּוֹת נוֹחָה הֵימֶנּוּ, רְוּחַ הַמָּקוֹם נוֹחָה הֵימֶנּוּ. וְכָל שֶׁאֵין רְוּחַ הַבְּרִיּוֹת נוֹחָה הֵימֶנּוּ, אֵין רְוּחַ הַמָּקוֹם נוֹחָה הֵימֶנּוּ.

יד רַבִּי דוֹסָא בֶּן הַרְכִּינַס אוֹמֵר: שֵׁנָה שֶׁל שַׁחֲרִית, וְיַיִן שֶׁל צָהֳרַיִם, וְשִׂיחַת הַיְלָדִים, וִישִׁיבַת בָּתֵּי כְנֵסִיּוֹת שֶׁל עַמֵּי הָאָרֶץ, מוֹצִיאִין אֶת הָאָדָם מִן הָעוֹלָם.

טו רַבִּי אֶלְעָזָר הַמּוֹדָעִי אוֹמֵר: הַמְחַלֵּל אֶת הַקֳּדָשִׁים, וְהַמְבַזֶּה אֶת הַמּוֹעֲדוֹת, וְהַמַּלְבִּין פְּנֵי חֲבֵרוֹ בָּרַבִּים, וְהַמֵּפֵר בְּרִיתוֹ שֶׁל אַבְרָהָם אָבִינוּ, וְהַמְגַלֶּה פָנִים בַּתּוֹרָה שֶׁלֹּא כַהֲלָכָה, אַף עַל פִּי שֶׁיֵּשׁ בְּיָדוֹ תּוֹרָה וּמַעֲשִׂים טוֹבִים, אֵין לוֹ חֵלֶק לָעוֹלָם הַבָּא.

טז רַבִּי יִשְׁמָעֵאל אוֹמֵר: הֱוֵי קַל לְרֹאשׁ וְנוֹחַ לְתִשְׁחֹרֶת, וֶהֱוֵי מְקַבֵּל אֶת כָּל הָאָדָם בְּשִׂמְחָה.

יז רַבִּי עֲקִיבָא אוֹמֵר: שְׂחוֹק וְקַלּוּת רֹאשׁ מַרְגִּילִין אֶת הָאָדָם לְעֶרְוָה. מַסֹּרֶת סְיָג לַתּוֹרָה, מַעַשְׂרוֹת סְיָג לָעֹשֶׁר, נְדָרִים סְיָג לַפְּרִישׁוּת, סְיָג לַחָכְמָה שְׁתִיקָה.

יח הוּא הָיָה אוֹמֵר, חָבִיב אָדָם שֶׁנִּבְרָא בְצֶלֶם, חִבָּה יְתֵרָה נוֹדַעַת לוֹ שֶׁנִּבְרָא בְּצֶלֶם, שֶׁנֶּאֱמַר: כִּי בְּצֶלֶם אֱלֹהִים עָשָׂה אֶת־הָאָדָם: חֲבִיבִין יִשְׂרָאֵל שֶׁנִּקְרְאוּ בָנִים לַמָּקוֹם, חִבָּה יְתֵרָה נוֹדַעַת לָהֶם שֶׁנִּקְרְאוּ בָנִים לַמָּקוֹם, שֶׁנֶּאֱמַר: בָּנִים אַתֶּם לַיהוה אֱלֹהֵיכֶם: חֲבִיבִין יִשְׂרָאֵל שֶׁנִּתַּן לָהֶם כְּלִי חֶמְדָּה, חִבָּה יְתֵרָה נוֹדַעַת לָהֶם שֶׁנִּתַּן לָהֶם כְּלִי חֶמְדָּה שֶׁבּוֹ נִבְרָא הָעוֹלָם, שֶׁנֶּאֱמַר: כִּי לֶקַח טוֹב נָתַתִּי לָכֶם, תּוֹרָתִי אַל־תַּעֲזֹבוּ: בראשית ט דברים יד משלי ד

3:15. *One who… nullifies the covenant of our father Abraham:* The reference is to those who, under the influence of Hellenism, tried to remove the mark of circumcision. *Who… attributes meanings to the Torah contrary to normative*

19. All is foreseen, yet freedom of choice is given. The world is judged with goodness, but all depends on the majority of one's deeds.

20. He used to say: All is given on collateral, and a net is spread over all the living. The shop is open, the shopkeeper extends credit, the ledger is open, and the hand records. Whoever wishes to borrow may come and borrow. The collectors regularly make their daily rounds and collect payment from a person, whether he realizes it or not. They have [a record] on which they can rely; the judgment is just; and all is prepared for the banquet.

21. Rabbi Elazar ben Azariah said: If there is no Torah, there is no respect; if there is no respect, there is no Torah. If there is no wisdom, there is no reverence; if there is no reverence, there is no wisdom. If there is no knowledge, there is no understanding; if there is no understanding, there is no knowledge. If there is no flour [sustenance], there is no Torah; if there is no Torah, there is no flour.

22. He used to say: To what may one whose wisdom exceeds his deeds be compared? To a tree with many branches but few roots. When a wind comes, it uproots and overturns it, as it is said, "He shall be like a juniper tree in the desert, which does not sense the coming of good: it is set in the scorched places of the wilderness in a barren, uninhabited land." To what may one whose deeds exceed his wisdom be compared? To a tree with few branches but many roots. Even if all the winds of the world come and blow against it, they cannot dislodge it from its place, as it is said, "He shall be like a tree planted by waters, sending forth its roots by a stream: it does not sense the coming of heat; its leaves are ever fresh; it has no care in a year of drought; it does not cease to bear fruit." *Jer. 17* *Jer. 17*

23. Rabbi Elazar ben Ḥisma said: The laws of bird offerings and the calculation of menstrual periods are essential laws; astronomy and mathematics are adjuncts to wisdom.

Rabbi Ḥananya ben Akashya said: The Holy One, blessed be He, wanted to confer merit on Israel. That is why He gave them a copious Torah and many commandments, as it is said, "It pleased the LORD, for the sake of [Israel's] righteousness, to make the Torah great and glorious." *Makkot 23b* *Is. 42*

If there is a minyan, mourners say the Rabbis' Kaddish (page 560).

* * *

3:20. *All is given on collateral:* An extended metaphor on life under divine justice. Because we are not punished immediately for our misdeeds, we may come to think that bad behavior has no consequences. The reality is, however, that God is merely extending credit. He keeps a record of our deeds, and ultimately we will have to pay the price. The banquet refers to the World to Come.

יט הַכֹּל צָפוּי, וְהָרְשׁוּת נְתוּנָה, וּבְטוּב הָעוֹלָם נִדּוֹן, וְהַכֹּל לְפִי רֹב הַמַּעֲשֶׂה.

כ הוּא הָיָה אוֹמֵר: הַכֹּל נָתוּן בָּעֵרָבוֹן, וּמְצוּדָה פְרוּסָה עַל כָּל הַחַיִּים. הֶחָנוּת פְּתוּחָה, וְהַחֶנְוָנִי מַקִּיף, וְהַפִּנְקָס פָּתְוּחַ, וְהַיָּד כּוֹתֶבֶת, וְכָל הָרוֹצֶה לִלְווֹת יָבֹא וְיִלְוֶה. וְהַגַּבָּאִין מַחֲזִירִין תָּדִיר בְּכָל יוֹם, וְנִפְרָעִין מִן הָאָדָם מִדַּעְתּוֹ וְשֶׁלֹּא מִדַּעְתּוֹ, וְיֵשׁ לָהֶם עַל מַה שֶּׁיִּסְמְכוּ. וְהַדִּין, דִּין אֱמֶת. וְהַכֹּל מְתֻקָּן לַסְּעוּדָה.

כא רַבִּי אֶלְעָזָר בֶּן עֲזַרְיָה אוֹמֵר: אִם אֵין תּוֹרָה אֵין דֶּרֶךְ אֶרֶץ, אִם אֵין דֶּרֶךְ אֶרֶץ אֵין תּוֹרָה. אִם אֵין חָכְמָה אֵין יִרְאָה, אִם אֵין יִרְאָה אֵין חָכְמָה. אִם אֵין דַּעַת אֵין בִּינָה, אִם אֵין בִּינָה אֵין דַּעַת. אִם אֵין קֶמַח אֵין תּוֹרָה, אִם אֵין תּוֹרָה אֵין קֶמַח.

כב הוּא הָיָה אוֹמֵר: כָּל שֶׁחָכְמָתוֹ מְרֻבָּה מִמַּעֲשָׂיו, לְמָה הוּא דוֹמֶה, לְאִילָן שֶׁעֲנָפָיו מְרֻבִּין וְשָׁרָשָׁיו מֻעָטִין, וְהָרְוּחַ בָּאָה וְעוֹקַרְתּוֹ וְהוֹפַכְתּוֹ עַל פָּנָיו.
שֶׁנֶּאֱמַר, וְהָיָה כְּעַרְעָר בָּעֲרָבָה, וְלֹא יִרְאֶה כִּי־יָבוֹא טוֹב, וְשָׁכַן חֲרֵרִים ירמיה יז
בַּמִּדְבָּר, אֶרֶץ מְלֵחָה וְלֹא תֵשֵׁב: אֲבָל כָּל שֶׁמַּעֲשָׂיו מְרֻבִּין מֵחָכְמָתוֹ, לְמָה הוּא דוֹמֶה, לְאִילָן שֶׁעֲנָפָיו מֻעָטִין וְשָׁרָשָׁיו מְרֻבִּין, שֶׁאֲפִלּוּ כָּל הָרוּחוֹת
שֶׁבָּעוֹלָם בָּאוֹת וְנוֹשְׁבוֹת בּוֹ, אֵין מְזִיזִין אוֹתוֹ מִמְּקוֹמוֹ. שֶׁנֶּאֱמַר: וְהָיָה כְּעֵץ ירמיה יז
שָׁתוּל עַל־מַיִם, וְעַל־יוּבַל יְשַׁלַּח שָׁרָשָׁיו, וְלֹא יִרְאֶ כִּי־יָבֹא חֹם, וְהָיָה עָלֵהוּ רַעֲנָן, וּבִשְׁנַת בַּצֹּרֶת לֹא יִדְאָג, וְלֹא יָמִישׁ מֵעֲשׂוֹת פֶּרִי:

כג רַבִּי אֱלִיעֶזֶר בֶּן חִסְמָא אוֹמֵר: קִנִּין וּפִתְחֵי נִדָּה הֵן הֵן גּוּפֵי הֲלָכוֹת, תְּקוּפוֹת וְגִימַטְרִיָּאוֹת פַּרְפְּרָאוֹת לַחָכְמָה.

רַבִּי חֲנַנְיָא בֶּן עֲקַשְׁיָא אוֹמֵר: רָצָה הַקָּדוֹשׁ בָּרוּךְ הוּא לְזַכּוֹת אֶת יִשְׂרָאֵל, לְפִיכָךְ מכות כג:
הִרְבָּה לָהֶם תּוֹרָה וּמִצְוֹת. שֶׁנֶּאֱמַר: יהוה חָפֵץ לְמַעַן צִדְקוֹ, יַגְדִּיל תּוֹרָה וְיַאְדִּיר: ישעיה מב

If there is a מנין*, mourners say* קדיש דרבנן *(page 561).*

* * *

3:19. *All is foreseen:* This is the standard translation, according to which Rabbi Akiva sets out the paradox between divine foreknowledge and human free will. God knows in advance what we will do, but this does not negate our freedom to choose. An alternative translation is: "All is seen, yet freedom of choice is given." According to this, Rabbi Akiva is not speaking about divine foreknowledge. He is teaching that, though we are free to choose, we cannot escape responsibility for the consequences of our choice, because God sees all.

All Israel have a share in the World to Come, as it is said: *Sanhedrin 90a*
"Your people are all righteous; they shall inherit the land for ever; *Is. 60*
they are a shoot of My own planting,
a work of My own hands, that I may be glorified."

CHAPTER 4

1. Ben Zoma said: Who is wise? One who learns from everyone, as it is said, "From all my teachers I have learned, for Your testimonies are my meditation." *Ps. 119* Who is strong? One who masters his evil impulse, as it is said, "He who is slow to anger is better than the mighty, and he who rules over his spirit is better than he who conquers a city." *Prov. 16* Who is rich? One who rejoices in what he has, as it is said, "When you eat from the labor of your hands, you will be happy and all will be well with you." *Ps. 128* "You will be happy" – in this world, "and all will be well with you" – in the World to Come. Who is honored? One who honors others, as it is said, "Those who honor Me, I will honor; but those who scorn Me will be despised." *I Sam. 2*
2. Ben Azzai said: Run to do even a minor mitzva, and flee from sin, for one mitzva leads to another, and one sin leads to another – for the reward of a mitzva is another mitzva, and the recompense of a sin is another sin.
3. He used to say: Despise no one and disdain nothing, for there is no one who does not have his hour and there is nothing that does not have its place.
4. Rabbi Levitas of Yavne said: Have extreme humility of spirit, for the end of mortal man is the worm [the grave].
5. Rabbi Yoḥanan ben Beroka said: Whoever profanes God's name in secret will be punished in public. Profaning the name is the same whether done inadvertently or deliberately.
6. Rabbi Yishmael his son said: One who learns in order to teach will be given the opportunity to learn and teach. One who learns in order to do will be given the opportunity to learn, teach, keep and do.
7. Rabbi Tzaddok said: Do not separate yourself from the community. [When sitting as a judge] do not act as a lawyer. Do not use [the Torah] as a crown for self-glorification, or as a spade with which to dig. Likewise Hillel used to say: One who makes worldly use of the crown [of the Torah] shall fade away. From this you learn that one who seeks personal benefit from the words of Torah risks destroying his life.

---

who has everything he wants, but one who enjoys what he has. The greatest honors are not those we receive but those we give.

4:6. *One who learns in order to teach:* The best way to learn is to teach. The best way to teach is to practice what we preach.

כָּל יִשְׂרָאֵל יֵשׁ לָהֶם חֵלֶק לָעוֹלָם הַבָּא. שֶׁנֶּאֱמַר: סנהדרין צ.
וְעַמֵּךְ כֻּלָּם צַדִּיקִים, לְעוֹלָם יִירְשׁוּ אָרֶץ ישעיה ס
נֵצֶר מַטָּעַי, מַעֲשֵׂה יָדַי לְהִתְפָּאֵר:

פרק רביעי

א בֶּן זוֹמָא אוֹמֵר: אֵיזֶהוּ חָכָם, הַלּוֹמֵד מִכָּל אָדָם, שֶׁנֶּאֱמַר: מִכָּל־מְלַמְּדַי תהלים קיט
הִשְׂכַּלְתִּי, כִּי עֵדְוֹתֶיךָ שִׂיחָה לִּי: אֵיזֶהוּ גִבּוֹר, הַכּוֹבֵשׁ אֶת יִצְרוֹ, שֶׁנֶּאֱמַר: טוֹב משלי טז
אֶרֶךְ אַפַּיִם מִגִּבּוֹר וּמֹשֵׁל בְּרוּחוֹ מִלֹּכֵד עִיר: אֵיזֶהוּ עָשִׁיר, הַשָּׂמֵחַ בְּחֶלְקוֹ,
שֶׁנֶּאֱמַר: יְגִיעַ כַּפֶּיךָ כִּי תֹאכֵל אַשְׁרֶיךָ וְטוֹב לָךְ: אַשְׁרֶיךָ בָּעוֹלָם הַזֶּה וְטוֹב תהלים קכח
לָךְ לָעוֹלָם הַבָּא. אֵיזֶהוּ מְכֻבָּד, הַמְכַבֵּד אֶת הַבְּרִיּוֹת, שֶׁנֶּאֱמַר: כִּי־מְכַבְּדַי שמואל א׳ ב
אֲכַבֵּד, וּבֹזַי יֵקָלּוּ:

ב בֶּן עַזַּאי אוֹמֵר: הֱוֵי רָץ לְמִצְוָה קַלָּה וּבוֹרֵחַ מִן הָעֲבֵרָה. שֶׁמִּצְוָה גּוֹרֶרֶת מִצְוָה, וַעֲבֵרָה גּוֹרֶרֶת עֲבֵרָה. שֶׁשְּׂכַר מִצְוָה מִצְוָה, וּשְׂכַר עֲבֵרָה עֲבֵרָה.

ג הוּא הָיָה אוֹמֵר: אַל תְּהִי בָז לְכָל אָדָם, וְאַל תְּהִי מַפְלִיג לְכָל דָּבָר. שֶׁאֵין לְךָ אָדָם שֶׁאֵין לוֹ שָׁעָה, וְאֵין לְךָ דָבָר שֶׁאֵין לוֹ מָקוֹם.

ד רַבִּי לְוִיטַס אִישׁ יַבְנֶה אוֹמֵר: מְאֹד מְאֹד הֱוֵי שְׁפַל רוּחַ, שֶׁתִּקְוַת אֱנוֹשׁ רִמָּה.

ה רַבִּי יוֹחָנָן בֶּן בְּרוֹקָא אוֹמֵר: כָּל הַמְחַלֵּל שֵׁם שָׁמַיִם בַּסֵּתֶר, נִפְרָעִין מִמֶּנּוּ בַּגָּלוּי. אֶחָד שׁוֹגֵג וְאֶחָד מֵזִיד בְּחִלּוּל הַשֵּׁם.

ו רַבִּי יִשְׁמָעֵאל בְּנוֹ אוֹמֵר: הַלּוֹמֵד עַל מְנָת לְלַמֵּד, מַסְפִּיקִין בְּיָדוֹ לִלְמֹד וּלְלַמֵּד. וְהַלּוֹמֵד עַל מְנָת לַעֲשׂוֹת, מַסְפִּיקִין בְּיָדוֹ לִלְמֹד וּלְלַמֵּד, לִשְׁמֹר וְלַעֲשׂוֹת.

ז רַבִּי צָדוֹק אוֹמֵר: אַל תִּפְרֹשׁ מִן הַצִּבּוּר, וְאַל תַּעַשׂ עַצְמְךָ כְּעוֹרְכֵי הַדַּיָּנִין, וְאַל תַּעֲשֶׂהָ עֲטָרָה לְהִתְגַּדֶּל בָּהּ, וְלֹא קַרְדֹּם לַחְפֹּר בָּהּ. וְכָךְ הָיָה הִלֵּל אוֹמֵר: וּדְאִשְׁתַּמֵּשׁ בְּתָגָא חֲלָף. הָא לָמַדְתָּ, כָּל הַנֶּהֱנֶה מִדִּבְרֵי תוֹרָה, נוֹטֵל חַיָּיו מִן הָעוֹלָם.

CHAPTER 4

4:1. *Ben Zoma said:* Truth, argues Ben Zoma, is often the reverse of conventional wisdom. Who is wise? Not one who teaches, but one who is always willing to learn. Who is strong? Not one who can defeat his enemies but one who can defeat his own worst impulses (*Avot deRabbi Nathan* adds: Who is strong? One who turns an enemy into a friend). Who is rich? Not one

8. Rabbi Yose said: One who honors the Torah will be honored by mankind. One who disgraces the Torah will be disgraced by mankind.
9. Rabbi Yishmael his son said: One who avoids serving as a judge spares himself enmity, robbery and false swearing. One who is over-confident in giving decisions is foolish, wicked and arrogant.
10. He used to say: Do not act as a judge alone, for none may judge alone except the One. Do not say "Accept my view"; for they are permitted, not you.
11. Rabbi Yonatan said: Whoever keeps the Torah when poor will eventually keep it in wealth. Whoever neglects the Torah when wealthy will eventually neglect it in poverty.
12. Rabbi Meir said: Limit your business activities and occupy yourself with Torah. Have humility before everyone. If you neglect the Torah, you will have many excuses to neglect it, but if you labor in the Torah, He has great reward to give you.
13. Rabbi Eliezer ben Jacob said: One who performs a single mitzva acquires for himself an advocate. One who commits a single transgression acquires for himself an accuser. Repentance and good deeds are a shield against punishment.
14. Rabbi Yoḥanan the sandal maker said: Every gathering that meets for the sake of heaven will have an enduring effect. One that is not for the sake of heaven will not have an enduring effect.
15. Rabbi Elazar ben Shammua said: Let your student's honor be as precious to you as your own; let your colleague's honor be like the reverence due to your teacher; and let the reverence you have for your teacher be like the reverence due to Heaven.
16. Rabbi Judah said: Be careful when you study, for an inadvertent error in study is tantamount to an intentional sin.
17. Rabbi Shimon said: There are three crowns: the crown of Torah, the crown of priesthood, and the crown of kingship – but the crown of a good name surpasses them all.

---

ments are compelling; you do not have the right to put pressure on them to do so.

4:12. *Have humility before everyone:* Not just those who are greater than you. Behave toward everyone as if they were your superior. Greatness is humility, and humility is greatness.

4:17. *There are three crowns:* The Judaic principle of the separation of powers. Kingship is the crown of government; priesthood, the crown of religious

ח רַבִּי יוֹסֵי אוֹמֵר: כָּל הַמְכַבֵּד אֶת הַתּוֹרָה, גּוּפוֹ מְכֻבָּד עַל הַבְּרִיּוֹת. וְכָל הַמְחַלֵּל אֶת הַתּוֹרָה, גּוּפוֹ מְחֻלָּל עַל הַבְּרִיּוֹת.

ט רַבִּי יִשְׁמָעֵאל בְּנוֹ אוֹמֵר: הַחוֹשֵׂךְ עַצְמוֹ מִן הַדִּין, פּוֹרֵק מִמֶּנּוּ אֵיבָה וְגָזֵל וּשְׁבוּעַת שָׁוְא. וְהַגַּס לִבּוֹ בְּהוֹרָאָה, שׁוֹטֶה, רָשָׁע וְגַס רוּחַ.

י הוּא הָיָה אוֹמֵר: אַל תְּהִי דָן יְחִידִי, שֶׁאֵין דָּן יְחִידִי אֶלָּא אֶחָד. וְאַל תֹּאמַר קַבְּלוּ דַעְתִּי, שֶׁהֵן רַשָּׁאִין וְלֹא אָתָּה.

יא רַבִּי יוֹנָתָן אוֹמֵר: כָּל הַמְקַיֵּם אֶת הַתּוֹרָה מֵעֹנִי, סוֹפוֹ לְקַיְּמָהּ מֵעֹשֶׁר. וְכָל הַמְבַטֵּל אֶת הַתּוֹרָה מֵעֹשֶׁר, סוֹפוֹ לְבַטְּלָהּ מֵעֹנִי.

יב רַבִּי מֵאִיר אוֹמֵר: הֱוֵי מְמַעֵט בְּעֵסֶק וַעֲסֹק בַּתּוֹרָה, וֶהֱוֵי שְׁפַל רוּחַ בִּפְנֵי כָל אָדָם. וְאִם בָּטַלְתָּ מִן הַתּוֹרָה, יֵשׁ לְךָ בְּטֵלִים הַרְבֵּה כְּנֶגְדָּךְ. וְאִם עָמַלְתָּ בַּתּוֹרָה, יֶשׁ לוֹ שָׂכָר הַרְבֵּה לִתֶּן לָךְ.

יג רַבִּי אֱלִיעֶזֶר בֶּן יַעֲקֹב אוֹמֵר: הָעוֹשֶׂה מִצְוָה אַחַת, קוֹנֶה לּוֹ פְּרַקְלִיט אֶחָד. וְהָעוֹבֵר עֲבֵרָה אַחַת, קוֹנֶה לּוֹ קַטֵּגוֹר אֶחָד. תְּשׁוּבָה וּמַעֲשִׂים טוֹבִים, כִּתְרִיס בִּפְנֵי הַפֻּרְעָנוּת.

יד רַבִּי יוֹחָנָן הַסַּנְדְּלָר אוֹמֵר: כָּל כְּנֵסִיָּה שֶׁהִיא לְשֵׁם שָׁמַיִם, סוֹפָהּ לְהִתְקַיֵּם. וְשֶׁאֵינָהּ לְשֵׁם שָׁמַיִם, אֵין סוֹפָהּ לְהִתְקַיֵּם.

טו רַבִּי אֶלְעָזָר בֶּן שַׁמּוּעַ אוֹמֵר: יְהִי כְבוֹד תַּלְמִידְךָ חָבִיב עָלֶיךָ כְּשֶׁלָּךְ, וּכְבוֹד חֲבֵרְךָ כְּמוֹרָא רַבָּךְ, וּמוֹרָא רַבָּךְ כְּמוֹרָא שָׁמָיִם.

טז רַבִּי יְהוּדָה אוֹמֵר: הֱוֵי זָהִיר בְּתַלְמוּד, שֶׁשִּׁגְגַת תַּלְמוּד עוֹלָה זָדוֹן.

יז רַבִּי שִׁמְעוֹן אוֹמֵר: שְׁלֹשָׁה כְתָרִים הֵן, כֶּתֶר תּוֹרָה וְכֶתֶר כְּהֻנָּה וְכֶתֶר מַלְכוּת, וְכֶתֶר שֵׁם טוֹב עוֹלֶה עַל גַּבֵּיהֶן.

4:8. *One who honors the Torah:* No one wins honor by betraying his or her faith.

4:9. *Spares himself enmity, robbery and false swearing: Enmity* of the litigants; *robbery*, if the judge gives an incorrect verdict in a civil case, with the result that money is wrongfully transferred from one party to the other; *false swearing,* if the judge requires one of the litigants to take an oath, and he then testifies falsely.

4:10. *Do not say "Accept my view":* If your colleagues disagree, do not compel them to agree with you. They have the right to accept your view if your argu-

18. Rabbi Nehorai said: Exile yourself to a place of Torah, and do not assume that it will come after you, for your fellow students will ensure that it will remain with you. "Do not rely on your own understanding." *Prov. 3*
19. Rabbi Yannai said: It is not in our power to explain either the peace of the wicked or the suffering of the righteous.
20. Rabbi Matya ben Ḥarash said: Be first in greeting everyone. Be a tail to lions rather than a head to foxes.
21. Rabbi Jacob said: This world is like an antechamber before the World to Come. Prepare yourself in the antechamber so that you may enter the banqueting hall.
22. He used to say: Better one hour of repentance and good deeds in this world than all the life in the World to Come. Better one hour of bliss in the World to Come than the whole life of this world.
23. Rabbi Shimon ben Elazar said: Do not try to placate your fellow in his hour of anger. Do not try to comfort him while his dead lies before him. Do not question him about his vow at the time he is making it. Do not try to see him in his hour of disgrace.
24. Samuel the Younger used to quote: "If your enemy falls, do not rejoice; if he stumbles, let not your heart be glad; lest the Lord see it and be displeased, and divert His wrath from him to you." *Prov. 24*
25. Elisha ben Abuya said: When you learn as a child, what is it like? Like ink written on clean paper. When you learn in old age, what is it like? Like ink written on blotted paper.
26. Rabbi Yose bar Judah of Kfar Bavli said: When you learn from the young, what is it like? Like eating unripe grapes or drinking wine straight from the

---

4:19. *It is not in our power to explain:* Seen from beneath, a Turkish carpet looks like a meaningless tangle of threads. Only when we view it from the other side do we see its intricately designed pattern. So it is with the justice of events. On earth, we seem to see the righteous suffer and the wicked prosper. Only from the other side – Heaven – is it possible to see the logic, the pattern; but that is a vantage point we cannot attain in this life.

4:20. *Be a tail to lions:* The great seek the company of those greater than themselves.

4:23. *Do not try to placate:* There is a time and a place for everything, especially speech. The right word at the wrong time makes matters worse.

יח רַבִּי נְהוֹרַאי אוֹמֵר: הֱוֵי גוֹלֶה לִמְקוֹם תּוֹרָה. וְאַל תֹּאמַר שֶׁהִיא תָבוֹא אַחֲרֶיךָ,
שֶׁחֲבֵרֶיךָ יְקַיְּמוּהָ בְיָדֶךָ. וְאֶל־בִּינָתְךָ אַל־תִּשָּׁעֵן: משלי ג

יט רַבִּי יַנַּאי אוֹמֵר: אֵין בְּיָדֵינוּ לֹא מִשַּׁלְוַת הָרְשָׁעִים וְאַף לֹא מִיִּסּוּרֵי הַצַּדִּיקִים.

כ רַבִּי מַתְיָא בֶּן חָרָשׁ אוֹמֵר: הֱוֵי מַקְדִּים בִּשְׁלוֹם כָּל אָדָם, וֶהֱוֵי זָנָב לָאֲרָיוֹת,
וְאַל תְּהִי רֹאשׁ לַשּׁוּעָלִים.

כא רַבִּי יַעֲקֹב אוֹמֵר: הָעוֹלָם הַזֶּה דּוֹמֶה לִפְרוֹזְדוֹר בִּפְנֵי הָעוֹלָם הַבָּא. הַתְקֵן
עַצְמְךָ בַפְּרוֹזְדוֹר, כְּדֵי שֶׁתִּכָּנֵס לַטְּרַקְלִין.

כב הוּא הָיָה אוֹמֵר: יָפָה שָׁעָה אַחַת בִּתְשׁוּבָה וּמַעֲשִׂים טוֹבִים בָּעוֹלָם הַזֶּה,
מִכָּל חַיֵּי הָעוֹלָם הַבָּא. וְיָפָה שָׁעָה אַחַת שֶׁל קוֹרַת רוּחַ בָּעוֹלָם הַבָּא, מִכָּל
חַיֵּי הָעוֹלָם הַזֶּה.

כג רַבִּי שִׁמְעוֹן בֶּן אֶלְעָזָר אוֹמֵר: אַל תְּרַצֶּה אֶת חֲבֵרְךָ בִּשְׁעַת כַּעֲסוֹ, וְאַל
תְּנַחֲמֶהוּ בְּשָׁעָה שֶׁמֵּתוֹ מֻטָּל לְפָנָיו, וְאַל תִּשְׁאַל לוֹ בִּשְׁעַת נִדְרוֹ, וְאַל
תִּשְׁתַּדֵּל לִרְאוֹתוֹ בִּשְׁעַת קַלְקָלָתוֹ.

כד שְׁמוּאֵל הַקָּטָן אוֹמֵר: בִּנְפֹל אוֹיִבְךָ אַל־תִּשְׂמָח, וּבִכָּשְׁלוֹ אַל־יָגֵל לִבֶּךָ: פֶּן־ משלי כד
יִרְאֶה יהוה וְרַע בְּעֵינָיו, וְהֵשִׁיב מֵעָלָיו אַפּוֹ:

כה אֱלִישָׁע בֶּן אֲבוּיָה אוֹמֵר: הַלּוֹמֵד יֶלֶד, לְמָה הוּא דוֹמֶה, לִדְיוֹ כְתוּבָה עַל נְיָר
חָדָשׁ. וְהַלּוֹמֵד זָקֵן, לְמָה הוּא דוֹמֶה, לִדְיוֹ כְתוּבָה עַל נְיָר מָחוּק.

כו רַבִּי יוֹסֵי בַּר יְהוּדָה אִישׁ כְּפַר הַבַּבְלִי אוֹמֵר: הַלּוֹמֵד מִן הַקְּטַנִּים, לְמָה הוּא

---

worship; and Torah is the crown of Jewish study and education. The sages were critical of the Hasmonean kings, some of whom appointed themselves as High Priests, thus breaching the separation of the crowns of kingship and priesthood. *The crown of a good name:* an alternative translation is, "But the crown of a good name must accompany them all." Unlike the other crowns, which exist in virtue of office or accomplishment, a good name is won by the individual him- or herself, regardless of office or accomplishment, by the integrity and grace with which he or she relates to others.

4:18. *Exile yourself to a place of Torah:* Be prepared to travel to a center of Torah study where there are outstanding teachers and scholars. Torah is learned not only from books but also, and essentially, from people, their conduct, and the fellowship of argument.

vat. When you learn from the old, what is it like? Like eating ripe grapes and drinking old wine.

27. Rabbi Meir said: Do not look at the container but at what it contains, for a new flask may contain old wine, and an old flask may not contain anything, even new wine.

28. Rabbi Elazar HaKappar said: Envy, lust, and the seeking of honor, drive a person out of the world.

29. He used to say: Those who are born will one day die, those who die will live again, and the living will be judged. It is for us to know, make known, and confirm that He is God, He is the Maker; He is the Creator; He is the Discerner; He is the Judge; He is the Witness; He is the Plaintiff; and He will deliver the judgment. Blessed is He before whom there is no unrighteousness, no forgetfulness, no favoritism and no taking of bribes; and know that all is according to a strict reckoning. Do not let your evil impulse persuade you that the grave is, for you, a place of refuge: for without your consent you were formed, without your consent you were born, without your consent you live, without your consent you will die, and without your consent you will in the future have to give an account and reckoning before the Supreme King of kings, the Holy One, blessed be He.

Rabbi Ḥananya ben Akashya said: The Holy One, blessed be He, wanted to confer merit on Israel. That is why He gave them a copious Torah and many commandments, as it is said, "It pleased the LORD, for the sake of [Israel's] righteousness, to make the Torah great and glorious." *Makkot 23b* *Is. 42*

If there is a minyan, mourners say the Rabbis' Kaddish (page 560).

* * *

All Israel have a share in the World to Come, as it is said, *Sanhedrin 90a*
"Your people are all righteous; they shall inherit the land for ever; *Is. 60*
they are a shoot of My own planting,
a work of My own hands, that I may be glorified."

CHAPTER 5

1. By ten acts of speech the world was created. What does this teach us? Could not the world have been created by a single act of speech? It is to exact punishment from the wicked who destroy a world created by ten acts of speech, and richly to reward the righteous who sustain the world created by ten acts of speech.

5:1. *By ten acts of speech:* The word *VaYomer,* "and He said," appears ten times in Genesis chapter 1.

דּוֹמֶה, לְאוֹכֵל עֲנָבִים קֵהוֹת וְשׁוֹתֶה יַיִן מִגִּתּוֹ. וְהַלּוֹמֵד מִן הַזְּקֵנִים, לְמָה הוּא
דּוֹמֶה, לְאוֹכֵל עֲנָבִים בְּשׁוּלוֹת וְשׁוֹתֶה יַיִן יָשָׁן.

כז רַבִּי מֵאִיר אוֹמֵר: אַל תִּסְתַּכֵּל בַּקַּנְקַן, אֶלָּא בְּמַה שֶּׁיֵּשׁ בּוֹ. יֵשׁ קַנְקַן חָדָשׁ
מָלֵא יָשָׁן, וְיָשָׁן שֶׁאֲפִלּוּ חָדָשׁ אֵין בּוֹ.

כח רַבִּי אֶלְעָזָר הַקַּפָּר אוֹמֵר: הַקִּנְאָה וְהַתַּאֲוָה וְהַכָּבוֹד, מוֹצִיאִין אֶת הָאָדָם
מִן הָעוֹלָם.

כט הוּא הָיָה אוֹמֵר: הַיִּלּוֹדִים לָמוּת, וְהַמֵּתִים לְחָיוֹת, וְהַחַיִּים לִדּוֹן, לֵידַע
וּלְהוֹדִיעַ וּלְהִוָּדַע, שֶׁהוּא אֵל, הוּא הַיּוֹצֵר, הוּא הַבּוֹרֵא, הוּא הַמֵּבִין, הוּא
הַדַּיָּן, הוּא הָעֵד, הוּא בַּעַל דִּין, הוּא עָתִיד לָדוּן. בָּרוּךְ הוּא, שֶׁאֵין לְפָנָיו
לֹא עַוְלָה וְלֹא שִׁכְחָה, וְלֹא מַשּׂוֹא פָנִים וְלֹא מִקַּח שֹׁחַד, שֶׁהַכֹּל שֶׁלּוֹ. וְדַע,
שֶׁהַכֹּל לְפִי הַחֶשְׁבּוֹן. וְאַל יַבְטִיחֲךָ יִצְרְךָ שֶׁהַשְּׁאוֹל בֵּית מָנוֹס לָךְ, שֶׁעַל
כָּרְחֲךָ אַתָּה נוֹצָר, וְעַל כָּרְחֲךָ אַתָּה נוֹלָד, וְעַל כָּרְחֲךָ אַתָּה חַי, וְעַל כָּרְחֲךָ
אַתָּה מֵת, וְעַל כָּרְחֲךָ אַתָּה עָתִיד לִתֵּן דִּין וְחֶשְׁבּוֹן לִפְנֵי מֶלֶךְ מַלְכֵי הַמְּלָכִים
הַקָּדוֹשׁ בָּרוּךְ הוּא.

רַבִּי חֲנַנְיָא בֶּן עֲקַשְׁיָא אוֹמֵר: רָצָה הַקָּדוֹשׁ בָּרוּךְ הוּא לְזַכּוֹת אֶת יִשְׂרָאֵל, לְפִיכָךְ מכות כג:
הִרְבָּה לָהֶם תּוֹרָה וּמִצְוֹת. שֶׁנֶּאֱמַר: יהוה חָפֵץ לְמַעַן צִדְקוֹ, יַגְדִּיל תּוֹרָה וְיַאְדִּיר: ישעיה מב

If there is a מנין*, mourners say* קדיש דרבנן *(page 561).*

* * *

כָּל יִשְׂרָאֵל יֵשׁ לָהֶם חֵלֶק לָעוֹלָם הַבָּא. שֶׁנֶּאֱמַר: סנהדרין צ.
וְעַמֵּךְ כֻּלָּם צַדִּיקִים, לְעוֹלָם יִירְשׁוּ אָרֶץ ישעיה ס
נֵצֶר מַטָּעַי, מַעֲשֵׂה יָדַי לְהִתְפָּאֵר:

פרק חמישי

א בַּעֲשָׂרָה מַאֲמָרוֹת נִבְרָא הָעוֹלָם. וּמַה תַּלְמוּד לוֹמַר, וַהֲלֹא בְּמַאֲמָר אֶחָד
יָכוֹל לְהִבָּרְאוֹת, אֶלָּא לְהִפָּרַע מִן הָרְשָׁעִים, שֶׁמְּאַבְּדִין אֶת הָעוֹלָם שֶׁנִּבְרָא
בַּעֲשָׂרָה מַאֲמָרוֹת, וְלִתֵּן שָׂכָר טוֹב לַצַּדִּיקִים, שֶׁמְּקַיְּמִין אֶת הָעוֹלָם שֶׁנִּבְרָא
בַּעֲשָׂרָה מַאֲמָרוֹת.

CHAPTER 5

Unlike the previous chapters, where the emphasis was placed on the authors as well as their teachings, most of the passages in this final chapter of *Avot*, are presented anonymously. They begin with a series of numerical lists.

2. There were ten generations from Adam to Noah, to make known how patient God is, for all those generations increasingly provoked Him until He brought on them the waters of the Flood.
3. There were ten generations from Noah to Abraham, to make known how patient God is, for all those generations increasingly provoked Him until Abraham our father came and received the reward which could have been theirs.
4. Abraham our father was tested with ten trials and he withstood all of them, to make known how deep was our father Abraham's love of God.
5. Ten miracles were performed for our ancestors in Egypt, and ten at the Sea. The Holy One, blessed be He, brought ten plagues against the Egyptians in Egypt, and ten at the Sea.
6. With ten trials our ancestors tried the patience of the Holy One, blessed be He, in the wilderness, as it is written, "They have tested Me these ten times, *Num. 14* and did not listen to My voice."
7. Ten miracles were performed for our ancestors in the Temple: (1) No woman miscarried from the aroma of the sacrificial meat; (2) the sacrificial meat never became putrid; (3) no fly was seen in the slaughterhouse; (4) the High Priest never suffered ritual pollution on Yom Kippur; (5) rain never extinguished the fire of the wood-pile on the altar; (6) the wind never blew away the column of smoke that rose from the altar; (7) no defect was ever found in the Omer, the Two Loaves, or the Showbread; (8) the people stood crowded together, yet there was ample space when they prostrated themselves; (9) no serpent or scorpion ever harmed anyone in Jerusalem; and (10) no one ever said to his fellow, "There is no room for me to stay overnight in Jerusalem."
8. Ten things were created on the eve of the Sabbath at twilight. They were: (1) the mouth of the earth; (2) the mouth of the well; (3) the mouth of [Balaam's] ass; (4) the rainbow; (5) the manna; (6) the staff; (7) the Shamir; (8) the writing [on the Tablets]; (9) the inscription; and (10) the Tablets. Some say: also the demons, Moses' burial place, and the ram of our father Abraham. And some say: also tongs made with tongs.
9. Seven traits characterize an uncultured person, and seven a sage. A sage: (1) does not speak before one who is wiser than he; (2) does not interrupt the words of his fellow; (3) does not answer impetuously; (4) asks relevant questions and gives appropriate answers; (5) deals with first things first, and last things last; (6) about something he has not heard he says, "I have not

---

5:8. *Ten things were created:* Miraculous events which involved temporary suspension of natural or scientific law. The Mishna teaches that these events were programmed into nature at the outset. In general, Judaism emphasizes

ב עֲשָׂרָה דוֹרוֹת מֵאָדָם וְעַד נֹחַ, לְהוֹדִיעַ כַּמָּה אֶרֶךְ אַפַּיִם לְפָנָיו, שֶׁכָּל הַדּוֹרוֹת הָיוּ מַכְעִיסִין וּבָאִין, עַד שֶׁהֵבִיא עֲלֵיהֶם אֶת מֵי הַמַּבּוּל.

ג עֲשָׂרָה דוֹרוֹת מִנֹּחַ וְעַד אַבְרָהָם, לְהוֹדִיעַ כַּמָּה אֶרֶךְ אַפַּיִם לְפָנָיו, שֶׁכָּל הַדּוֹרוֹת הָיוּ מַכְעִיסִין וּבָאִין, עַד שֶׁבָּא אַבְרָהָם אָבִינוּ וְקִבֵּל שְׂכַר כֻּלָּם.

ד עֲשָׂרָה נִסְיוֹנוֹת נִתְנַסָּה אַבְרָהָם אָבִינוּ וְעָמַד בְּכֻלָּם, לְהוֹדִיעַ כַּמָּה חִבָּתוֹ שֶׁל אַבְרָהָם אָבִינוּ.

ה עֲשָׂרָה נִסִּים נַעֲשׂוּ לַאֲבוֹתֵינוּ בְּמִצְרַיִם, וַעֲשָׂרָה עַל הַיָּם. עֶשֶׂר מַכּוֹת הֵבִיא הַקָּדוֹשׁ בָּרוּךְ הוּא עַל הַמִּצְרִיִּים בְּמִצְרַיִם, וְעֶשֶׂר עַל הַיָּם.

ו עֲשָׂרָה נִסְיוֹנוֹת נִסּוּ אֲבוֹתֵינוּ אֶת הַקָּדוֹשׁ בָּרוּךְ הוּא בַּמִּדְבָּר, שֶׁנֶּאֱמַר: וַיְנַסּוּ אֹתִי זֶה עֶשֶׂר פְּעָמִים, וְלֹא שָׁמְעוּ בְּקוֹלִי: במדבר יד

ז עֲשָׂרָה נִסִּים נַעֲשׂוּ לַאֲבוֹתֵינוּ בְּבֵית הַמִּקְדָּשׁ. לֹא הִפִּילָה אִשָּׁה מֵרֵיחַ בְּשַׂר הַקֹּדֶשׁ, וְלֹא הִסְרִיחַ בְּשַׂר הַקֹּדֶשׁ מֵעוֹלָם, וְלֹא נִרְאָה זְבוּב בְּבֵית הַמִּטְבְּחַיִם, וְלֹא אֵרַע קֶרִי לְכֹהֵן גָּדוֹל בְּיוֹם הַכִּפּוּרִים, וְלֹא כִבּוּ הַגְּשָׁמִים אֵשׁ שֶׁל עֲצֵי הַמַּעֲרָכָה, וְלֹא נָצְחָה הָרוּחַ אֶת עַמּוּד הֶעָשָׁן, וְלֹא נִמְצָא פְסוּל בָּעֹמֶר וּבִשְׁתֵּי הַלֶּחֶם וּבְלֶחֶם הַפָּנִים, עוֹמְדִים צְפוּפִים וּמִשְׁתַּחֲוִים רְוָחִים, וְלֹא הִזִּיק נָחָשׁ וְעַקְרָב בִּירוּשָׁלַיִם מֵעוֹלָם, וְלֹא אָמַר אָדָם לַחֲבֵרוֹ: צַר לִי הַמָּקוֹם שֶׁאָלִין בִּירוּשָׁלַיִם.

ח עֲשָׂרָה דְבָרִים נִבְרְאוּ בְּעֶרֶב שַׁבָּת בֵּין הַשְּׁמָשׁוֹת. וְאֵלּוּ הֵן, פִּי הָאָרֶץ, פִּי הַבְּאֵר, פִּי הָאָתוֹן, הַקֶּשֶׁת, וְהַמָּן, וְהַמַּטֶּה, וְהַשָּׁמִיר, הַכְּתָב, וְהַמִּכְתָּב, וְהַלּוּחוֹת. וְיֵשׁ אוֹמְרִים, אַף הַמַּזִּיקִין, וּקְבוּרָתוֹ שֶׁל מֹשֶׁה, וְאֵילוֹ שֶׁל אַבְרָהָם אָבִינוּ. וְיֵשׁ אוֹמְרִים, אַף צְבָת בִּצְבָת עֲשׂוּיָה.

ט שִׁבְעָה דְבָרִים בַּגֹּלֶם, וְשִׁבְעָה בֶּחָכָם. חָכָם אֵינוֹ מְדַבֵּר לִפְנֵי מִי שֶׁגָּדוֹל מִמֶּנּוּ בְּחָכְמָה, וְאֵינוֹ נִכְנָס לְתוֹךְ דִּבְרֵי חֲבֵרוֹ, וְאֵינוֹ נִבְהָל לְהָשִׁיב, שׁוֹאֵל כָּעִנְיָן

5:4. *Ten trials:* Such as the commandment to leave his father's house; being forced by famine to go to Egypt; and the binding of Isaac. There are different midrashic traditions as to the precise enumeration.

5:6. *With ten trials our ancestors tried the patience:* Such as their rebellion at the Reed Sea; their complaints about the food and water; the golden calf; the report of the spies; and other provocations.

heard"; and (7) he acknowledges the truth. The opposites of these characterize an uncultured person.

10. Seven types of punishment come into the world for seven kinds of transgression: (1) If some tithe and others do not, a famine caused by drought occurs, so that some go hungry while others have sufficient. (2) If all decide not to tithe, a famine comes through tumult [of war] as well as drought. (3) If they also decide not to set apart ḥalla, a fatal famine ensues.
11. (4) Pestilence comes to the world for crimes that, according to the Torah, carry the death penalty, but are not the preserve of a human tribunal, and also for violation of the laws relating to produce of the seventh year. (5) The sword comes to the world for delay of justice, the perversion of justice, and for those who give a legal decision in violation of normative Torah law.
12. (6) Wild beasts come to the world because of perjury and the desecration of God's name. (7) Exile comes to the world for idolatry, sexual immorality and bloodshed, and for violating the sabbatical year of the land.
13. At four periods [of the seven-year sabbatical cycle] pestilence increases: in the fourth year, the seventh year, the year following the sabbatical year, and annually at the conclusion of the Festival of Sukkot. In the fourth year, [pestilence increases] because of neglect of the tithe for the poor in the third year; in the seventh year, because of neglect of the tithe for the poor in the sixth year; in the year following the sabbatical year, because of the violation of the laws of the seventh-year produce; and at the conclusion of the Festival of Sukkot, for robbing the poor of their gifts.
14. There are four types of human character: (1) One who says, "What is mine is mine, and what is yours is yours," is an average person, though some say this is a Sodom type. (2) One who says, "What is mine is yours and what is yours is mine," is an ignoramus. (3) One who says, "What is mine is yours and what

---

sought to understand national calamities as divine punishment, measure for measure, for national failings, religious, ethical or social. Thus the appropriate response to tragedy was collective penitence and rededication of the nation to the principles on which it was founded.

5:13. *Robbing the poor of their gifts:* The gleanings of the harvest, the corners of the field, and forgotten sheaves. These were to be left for the poor at harvest time; hence the connection with Sukkot, the harvest festival.

5:14. *Some say this is a Sodom type:* The sin of Sodom, according to Ezekiel 16:49, was that "they did not help the poor and needy." Insisting on property

וּמֵשִׁיב כַּהֲלָכָה, וְאוֹמֵר עַל רִאשׁוֹן רִאשׁוֹן וְעַל אַחֲרוֹן אַחֲרוֹן, וְעַל מַה שֶּׁלֹּא שָׁמַע אוֹמֵר לֹא שָׁמַעְתִּי, וּמוֹדֶה עַל הָאֱמֶת. וְחִלּוּפֵיהֶן בְּגֹלֶם.

י שִׁבְעָה מִינֵי פֻרְעָנִיּוֹת בָּאִין לָעוֹלָם עַל שִׁבְעָה גוּפֵי עֲבֵרָה. מִקְצָתָן מְעַשְּׂרִין וּמִקְצָתָן אֵינָן מְעַשְּׂרִין, רָעָב שֶׁל בַּצֹּרֶת בָּא, מִקְצָתָן רְעֵבִים וּמִקְצָתָן שְׂבֵעִים. גָּמְרוּ שֶׁלֹּא לְעַשֵּׂר, רָעָב שֶׁל מְהוּמָה וְשֶׁל בַּצֹּרֶת בָּא. וְשֶׁלֹּא לִטּוֹל אֶת הַחַלָּה, רָעָב שֶׁל כְּלָיָה בָּא.

יא דֶּבֶר בָּא לָעוֹלָם עַל מִיתוֹת הָאֲמוּרוֹת בַּתּוֹרָה שֶׁלֹּא נִמְסְרוּ לְבֵית דִּין, וְעַל פֵּרוֹת שְׁבִיעִית. חֶרֶב בָּאָה לָעוֹלָם עַל עִנּוּי הַדִּין, וְעַל עִוּוּת הַדִּין, וְעַל הַמּוֹרִים בַּתּוֹרָה שֶׁלֹּא כַהֲלָכָה.

יב חַיָּה רָעָה בָּאָה לָעוֹלָם עַל שְׁבוּעַת שָׁוְא וְעַל חִלּוּל הַשֵּׁם. גָּלוּת בָּאָה לָעוֹלָם עַל עֲבוֹדָה זָרָה, וְעַל גִּלּוּי עֲרָיוֹת, וְעַל שְׁפִיכוּת דָּמִים, וְעַל שְׁמִטַּת הָאָרֶץ.

יג בְּאַרְבָּעָה פְרָקִים הַדֶּבֶר מִתְרַבֶּה, בָּרְבִיעִית, וּבַשְּׁבִיעִית, וּבְמוֹצָאֵי שְׁבִיעִית, וּבְמוֹצָאֵי הֶחָג שֶׁבְּכָל שָׁנָה וְשָׁנָה. בָּרְבִיעִית, מִפְּנֵי מַעְשַׂר עָנִי שֶׁבַּשְּׁלִישִׁית. בַּשְּׁבִיעִית, מִפְּנֵי מַעְשַׂר עָנִי שֶׁבַּשִּׁשִּׁית. בְּמוֹצָאֵי שְׁבִיעִית, מִפְּנֵי פֵּרוֹת שְׁבִיעִית. בְּמוֹצָאֵי הֶחָג שֶׁבְּכָל שָׁנָה וְשָׁנָה, מִפְּנֵי גֵּזֶל מַתְּנוֹת עֲנִיִּים.

יד אַרְבַּע מִדּוֹת בָּאָדָם. הָאוֹמֵר שֶׁלִּי שֶׁלִּי וְשֶׁלְּךָ שֶׁלָּךְ, זוֹ מִדָּה בֵינוֹנִית, וְיֵשׁ

---

the law-like structure of the physical universe, as it says in Ecclesiastes, "There is nothing new under the sun" (1:9). *On the eve of the Sabbath at twilight* – between the six days of nature, and the seventh, which belongs to the One who transcends nature. *The mouth of the earth,* which opened to swallow Koraḥ; *the mouth of the well,* which accompanied the Israelites on their journey through the wilderness; *the mouth of [Balaam's] ass,* which spoke (Num. 22:28); *the rainbow,* which appeared after the Flood; *the manna,* which descended as "bread from heaven"; *the staff,* with which Moses performed signs and wonders; *the Shamir,* the miraculous worm which, according to tradition, split the stones from which the Temple was made; *the writing [on the Tablets],* which could be seen from both sides; *the inscription* of the Tablets and *the Tablets* themselves, hewn and inscribed by God. *Some say, also tongs made with tongs:* the infinite regress – what held the first implement forged by fire, if not another implement forged by fire?

5:10. *Seven types of punishment:* As heirs to the prophetic tradition, the sages

is yours is yours," is pious. (4) One who says, "What is yours is mine and what is mine is mine," is wicked.

15. There are four types of temperament: (1) One who is easily angered and easily pacified – his loss is cancelled by his gain. (2) One who is hard to anger and hard to pacify – his gain is cancelled by his loss. (3) One who is hard to anger and easily pacified is pious. (4) One who is easily angered and hard to pacify is wicked.
16. There are four types of student: (1) One who learns quickly and forgets quickly – his gain is cancelled by his loss. (2) One who learns slowly and forgets slowly – his loss is cancelled by his gain. (3) One who learns quickly and forgets slowly – his is a happy lot. (4) One who learns slowly and forgets quickly – his is a sad lot.
17. There are four types of donor to charity: (1) One who wishes to give but does not want others to give, begrudges others. (2) One who wants others to give, but does not himself give, begrudges himself. (3) One who gives and wants others to give is pious. (4) One who does not himself give and does not want others to give is wicked.
18. There are four types among those who attend the House of Study: (1) One who goes but does not practice [what he learns] receives a reward for going. (2) One who practices but does not go receives a reward for practicing. (3) One who goes and also practices is pious. (4) One who neither goes nor practices is wicked.
19. There are four types among those who sit before the sages: the sponge, the funnel, the strainer and the sieve. The sponge absorbs everything. The funnel takes in at one end and lets out at the other. The strainer lets out the wine and retains the sediment. The sieve allows the flour dust to pass through and retains the fine flour.
20. If love depends on a specific cause, when the cause ends, so does the love. If love does not depend on a specific cause, then it never ends. What is an example of love depending on a specific cause? The love of Amnon for Tamar. What is an example of love not dependent on a specific cause? The love of David and Jonathan.
21. Any dispute for the sake of Heaven will have enduring value, but any dispute not for the sake of Heaven will not have enduring value. What is an example of a dispute for the sake of heaven? The dispute between Hillel and Shammai. What is an example of one not for the sake of heaven? The dispute of Koraḥ and all his company.

---

by the truth is the only defeat that is also a victory, for by it we grow. "Just as I received reward for the exposition," said Rabbi Shimon HaAmsoni, "so I

אוֹמְרִים, זוֹ מִדַּת סְדוֹם. שֶׁלִּי שֶׁלָּךְ וְשֶׁלָּךְ שֶׁלִּי, עַם הָאָרֶץ. שֶׁלִּי שֶׁלָּךְ וְשֶׁלָּךְ שֶׁלָּךְ, חָסִיד. שֶׁלָּךְ שֶׁלִּי וְשֶׁלִּי שֶׁלִּי, רָשָׁע.

טו אַרְבַּע מִדּוֹת בַּדֵּעוֹת. נוֹחַ לִכְעֹס וְנוֹחַ לִרְצוֹת, יָצָא הֶפְסֵדוֹ בִשְׂכָרוֹ. קָשֶׁה לִכְעֹס וְקָשֶׁה לִרְצוֹת, יָצָא שְׂכָרוֹ בְהֶפְסֵדוֹ. קָשֶׁה לִכְעֹס וְנוֹחַ לִרְצוֹת, חָסִיד. נוֹחַ לִכְעֹס וְקָשֶׁה לִרְצוֹת, רָשָׁע.

טז אַרְבַּע מִדּוֹת בַּתַּלְמִידִים. מָהִיר לִשְׁמֹעַ וּמָהִיר לְאַבֵּד, יָצָא שְׂכָרוֹ בְהֶפְסֵדוֹ. קָשֶׁה לִשְׁמֹעַ וְקָשֶׁה לְאַבֵּד, יָצָא הֶפְסֵדוֹ בִשְׂכָרוֹ. מָהִיר לִשְׁמֹעַ וְקָשֶׁה לְאַבֵּד, זֶה חֵלֶק טוֹב. קָשֶׁה לִשְׁמֹעַ וּמָהִיר לְאַבֵּד, זֶה חֵלֶק רָע.

יז אַרְבַּע מִדּוֹת בְּנוֹתְנֵי צְדָקָה. הָרוֹצֶה שֶׁיִּתֵּן וְלֹא יִתְּנוּ אֲחֵרִים, עֵינוֹ רָעָה בְּשֶׁל אֲחֵרִים. יִתְּנוּ אֲחֵרִים וְהוּא לֹא יִתֵּן, עֵינוֹ רָעָה בְּשֶׁלּוֹ. יִתֵּן וְיִתְּנוּ אֲחֵרִים, חָסִיד. לֹא יִתֵּן וְלֹא יִתְּנוּ אֲחֵרִים, רָשָׁע.

יח אַרְבַּע מִדּוֹת בְּהוֹלְכֵי בֵית הַמִּדְרָשׁ. הוֹלֵךְ וְאֵינוֹ עוֹשֶׂה, שְׂכַר הֲלִיכָה בְּיָדוֹ. עוֹשֶׂה וְאֵינוֹ הוֹלֵךְ, שְׂכַר מַעֲשֶׂה בְּיָדוֹ. הוֹלֵךְ וְעוֹשֶׂה, חָסִיד. לֹא הוֹלֵךְ וְלֹא עוֹשֶׂה, רָשָׁע.

יט אַרְבַּע מִדּוֹת בְּיוֹשְׁבִים לִפְנֵי חֲכָמִים, סְפוֹג, וּמַשְׁפֵּךְ, מְשַׁמֶּרֶת, וְנָפָה. סְפוֹג, שֶׁהוּא סוֹפֵג אֶת הַכֹּל. וּמַשְׁפֵּךְ, שֶׁמַּכְנִיס בְּזוֹ וּמוֹצִיא בְזוֹ. מְשַׁמֶּרֶת, שֶׁמּוֹצִיאָה אֶת הַיַּיִן וְקוֹלֶטֶת אֶת הַשְּׁמָרִים. וְנָפָה, שֶׁמּוֹצִיאָה אֶת הַקֶּמַח וְקוֹלֶטֶת אֶת הַסֹּלֶת.

כ כָּל אַהֲבָה שֶׁהִיא תְלוּיָה בְדָבָר, בָּטֵל דָּבָר, בְּטֵלָה אַהֲבָה. וְשֶׁאֵינָהּ תְּלוּיָה בְדָבָר, אֵינָהּ בְּטֵלָה לְעוֹלָם. אֵיזוֹ הִיא אַהֲבָה שֶׁהִיא תְלוּיָה בְדָבָר, זוֹ אַהֲבַת אַמְנוֹן וְתָמָר. וְשֶׁאֵינָהּ תְּלוּיָה בְדָבָר, זוֹ אַהֲבַת דָּוִד וִיהוֹנָתָן.

כא כָּל מַחֲלֹקֶת שֶׁהִיא לְשֵׁם שָׁמַיִם, סוֹפָהּ לְהִתְקַיֵּם. וְשֶׁאֵינָהּ לְשֵׁם שָׁמַיִם, אֵין סוֹפָהּ לְהִתְקַיֵּם. אֵיזוֹ הִיא מַחֲלֹקֶת שֶׁהִיא לְשֵׁם שָׁמַיִם, זוֹ מַחֲלֹקֶת הִלֵּל וְשַׁמַּאי. וְשֶׁאֵינָהּ לְשֵׁם שָׁמַיִם, זוֹ מַחֲלֹקֶת קֹרַח וְכָל עֲדָתוֹ.

---

rights, they frowned on charity. *An ignoramus:* this, according to some scholars, is a critique of the property-sharing communes associated with the Essenes.

5:21. *Any dispute for the sake of Heaven* is an argument for the sake of truth. *Any dispute not for the sake of Heaven* is an argument for the sake of victory. In an argument for the sake of heaven, both sides win; one because his views are accepted, the other because he has learned something new. To be defeated

22. One who brings merit to the many will not be the cause of sin. One who causes the many to sin will be denied the means to repent. Moses attained merit and brought merit to the many; therefore the merit of the many was attributed to him, as it is said, "He carried out the LORD's righteousness and His ordinances with Israel." *Deut. 33* Jeroboam, son of Nebat, sinned and caused the many to sin; therefore the sin of the many was attributed to him, as it is said, "For the sins of Jeroboam that he committed and that he caused Israel to commit." *1 Kings 15*

23. Whoever possesses these three traits is one of the disciples of our father Abraham; whoever possesses the three opposite traits is one of the disciples of the wicked Balaam. A generous eye, a modest demeanor and a humble soul are the traits of the disciples of our father Abraham. An evil eye, an arrogant demeanor and an insatiable soul are attributes of the disciples of the wicked Balaam. What is the difference between our father Abraham's disciples and those of the wicked Balaam? Our father Abraham's disciples enjoy this world and inherit the World to Come, as it is said, "That I may cause those who love me to inherit substance and so that I may fill their treasures." *Prov. 8* The wicked Balaam's disciples inherit Gehinnom and go down to the pit of destruction, as it is said, "But You, God, will bring them down to the pit of destruction; bloodthirsty and deceitful men shall not live out half their days; but I trust in You." *Ps. 55*

24. Judah ben Tema said: Be strong as a leopard, light as an eagle, swift as a gazelle, and brave as a lion, to do the will of your Father in heaven. He used to say: The shameless go to Gehinnom; those who have a sense of shame are destined for the Garden of Eden. May it be Your will, O LORD our God and God of our ancestors that the Temple be speedily rebuilt in our days; and grant us our portion in Your Torah.

25. He used to say: Five years old is the age to begin studying Scripture; ten for Mishna; thirteen for the obligation of the commandments; fifteen for the study of Talmud; eighteen for marriage; twenty for seeking a livelihood; thirty for full strength; forty for understanding; fifty for giving counsel; sixty for old age; seventy for ripe old age; eighty for exceptional strength; and ninety for a bent back; at a hundred, one is as if he were dead and had left and gone from the world.

26. Ben Bag-Bag said: Turn it [the Torah] over and over, for everything is in it. Reflect on it, grow old and gray in it and do not stir from it, for there is no better portion for you than this. Ben Heh-Heh said: According to the effort is the reward.

5:24. *May it be Your will:* This passage originally marked the end of the chapter, and of the tractate, hence its formulaic character.

כב כׇּל הַמְזַכֶּה אֶת הָרַבִּים, אֵין חֵטְא בָּא עַל יָדוֹ. וְכׇל הַמַּחֲטִיא אֶת הָרַבִּים, אֵין
מַסְפִּיקִין בְּיָדוֹ לַעֲשׂוֹת תְּשׁוּבָה. מֹשֶׁה זָכָה וְזִכָּה אֶת הָרַבִּים, זְכוּת הָרַבִּים
תָּלוּי בּוֹ, שֶׁנֶּאֱמַר: צִדְקַת יהוה עָשָׂה וּמִשְׁפָּטָיו עִם־יִשְׂרָאֵל: יָרׇבְעָם בֶּן נְבָט, דברים לג
חָטָא וְהֶחֱטִיא אֶת הָרַבִּים, חֵטְא הָרַבִּים תָּלוּי בּוֹ, שֶׁנֶּאֱמַר: עַל־חַטֹּאות מלכים א׳ טו
יָרׇבְעָם אֲשֶׁר חָטָא וַאֲשֶׁר הֶחֱטִיא אֶת־יִשְׂרָאֵל:

כג כׇּל מִי שֶׁיֵּשׁ בּוֹ שְׁלֹשָׁה דְבָרִים הַלָּלוּ, הוּא מִתַּלְמִידָיו שֶׁל אַבְרָהָם אָבִינוּ,
וּשְׁלֹשָׁה דְבָרִים אֲחֵרִים, הוּא מִתַּלְמִידָיו שֶׁל בִּלְעָם הָרָשָׁע. עַיִן טוֹבָה, וְרוּחַ
נְמוּכָה, וְנֶפֶשׁ שְׁפָלָה, תַּלְמִידָיו שֶׁל אַבְרָהָם אָבִינוּ. עַיִן רָעָה, וְרוּחַ גְּבוֹהָה
וְנֶפֶשׁ רְחָבָה, תַּלְמִידָיו שֶׁל בִּלְעָם הָרָשָׁע. מַה בֵּין תַּלְמִידָיו שֶׁל אַבְרָהָם
אָבִינוּ לְתַלְמִידָיו שֶׁל בִּלְעָם הָרָשָׁע. תַּלְמִידָיו שֶׁל אַבְרָהָם אָבִינוּ אוֹכְלִין
בָּעוֹלָם הַזֶּה וְנוֹחֲלִין הָעוֹלָם הַבָּא, שֶׁנֶּאֱמַר: לְהַנְחִיל אֹהֲבַי יֵשׁ וְאֹצְרֹתֵיהֶם משלי ח
אֲמַלֵּא: אֲבָל תַּלְמִידָיו שֶׁל בִּלְעָם הָרָשָׁע יוֹרְשִׁין גֵּיהִנֹּם וְיוֹרְדִין לִבְאֵר שַׁחַת,
שֶׁנֶּאֱמַר: וְאַתָּה אֱלֹהִים תּוֹרִדֵם לִבְאֵר שַׁחַת, אַנְשֵׁי דָמִים וּמִרְמָה לֹא־יֶחֱצוּ תהלים נה
יְמֵיהֶם, וַאֲנִי אֶבְטַח־בָּךְ:

כד יְהוּדָה בֶּן תֵּימָא אוֹמֵר: הֱוֵי עַז כַּנָּמֵר וְקַל כַּנֶּשֶׁר, רָץ כַּצְּבִי וְגִבּוֹר כָּאֲרִי,
לַעֲשׂוֹת רְצוֹן אָבִיךָ שֶׁבַּשָּׁמַיִם. הוּא הָיָה אוֹמֵר: עַז פָּנִים לְגֵיהִנֹּם, וּבֹשֶׁת
פָּנִים לְגַן עֵדֶן. יְהִי רָצוֹן מִלְּפָנֶיךָ, יהוה אֱלֹהֵינוּ וֵאלֹהֵי אֲבוֹתֵינוּ, שֶׁיִּבָּנֶה בֵּית
הַמִּקְדָּשׁ בִּמְהֵרָה בְיָמֵינוּ, וְתֵן חֶלְקֵנוּ בְּתוֹרָתֶךָ.

כה הוּא הָיָה אוֹמֵר: בֶּן חָמֵשׁ שָׁנִים לַמִּקְרָא, בֶּן עֶשֶׂר שָׁנִים לַמִּשְׁנָה, בֶּן שְׁלֹשׁ
עֶשְׂרֵה לַמִּצְוֹת, בֶּן חֲמֵשׁ עֶשְׂרֵה לַגְּמָרָא, בֶּן שְׁמוֹנֶה עֶשְׂרֵה לַחֻפָּה, בֶּן עֶשְׂרִים
לִרְדֹּף, בֶּן שְׁלֹשִׁים לַכֹּחַ, בֶּן אַרְבָּעִים לַבִּינָה, בֶּן חֲמִשִּׁים לָעֵצָה, בֶּן שִׁשִּׁים
לַזִּקְנָה, בֶּן שִׁבְעִים לַשֵּׂיבָה, בֶּן שְׁמוֹנִים לַגְּבוּרָה, בֶּן תִּשְׁעִים לָשׁוּחַ, בֶּן מֵאָה
כְּאִלּוּ מֵת וְעָבַר וּבָטֵל מִן הָעוֹלָם.

כו בֶּן בַּג בַּג אוֹמֵר: הֲפָךְ בָּהּ וַהֲפָךְ בָּהּ דְּכֹלָּא בָהּ, וּבָהּ תֶּחֱזֵי, וְסִיב וּבְלֵה בָהּ,
וּמִנַּהּ לָא תְזוּעַ, שֶׁאֵין לְךָ מִדָּה טוֹבָה הֵימֶנָּה. בֶּן הֵא הֵא אוֹמֵר: לְפוּם
צַעֲרָא אַגְרָא.

---

will receive reward for the retraction" (*Bekhorot* 6b). In an argument for the sake of victory, both sides lose, even the victor, for in diminishing the other, he has diminished himself.

Rabbi Ḥananya ben Akashya said: The Holy One, blessed be He, wanted to confer merit on Israel. That is why He gave them a copious Torah and many commandments, as it is said, "It pleased the Lord, for the sake of [Israel's] righteousness, to make the Torah great and glorious." *Makkot 23b* *Is. 42*

If there is a minyan, mourners say the Rabbis' Kaddish (*page 560*).

* * *

All Israel have a share in the World to Come, as it is said, *Sanhedrin 90a*
"Your people are all righteous; they shall inherit the land for ever; *Is. 60*
they are a shoot of My own planting,
a work of My own hands, that I may be glorified."

CHAPTER 6

The sages taught the following in the style of the Mishna – blessed be He who chose them and their teaching.

1. Rabbi Meir said: Whoever engages in Torah study for its own sake merits many things; moreover, the whole world is worthwhile for his sake alone. He is called friend, beloved, a lover of God and a lover of mankind. He brings joy to God; he brings joy to mankind. [The Torah] clothes him with humility and reverence. It prepares him to be righteous, pious, upright and faithful. It keeps him far from sin and near to virtue. People benefit from his advice and wisdom, understanding and courage, as it is said, "Mine are counsel and wisdom; I am understanding, courage is mine." It gives him sovereignty, dominion and discerning judgment. To him the secrets of the Torah are revealed. He becomes like a never-failing fountain, like a river that never runs dry. He becomes modest and patient; he forgives insults. It makes him great, exalting him above all things. *Prov. 8*
2. Rabbi Yehoshua ben Levi said: Every day a heavenly voice resounds from Mount Horeb, proclaiming and saying: "Woe to mankind for their contempt of the Torah!" For whoever does not occupy himself with the Torah is called reprehensible, as it is said, "Like a gold ring in the snout of a pig is a beautiful woman bereft of sense." It also says, "The tablets were the work of God, and the writing was the writing of God, engraved (*ḥarut*) on the tablets." Read not *ḥarut* ("engraved") but *ḥerut* ("freedom"), for the only person who is truly free is one who occupies himself with Torah study; and whoever occupies himself with Torah study will be exalted, as it is said, "And from Mattana to Naḥaliel, and from Naḥaliel to Bamot." *Prov. 11* *Ex. 32* *Num. 21*

6:2. *The only person who is truly free:* Hebrew distinguishes two kinds of freedom, *ḥofesh* and *ḥerut*. *Ḥofesh* is negative liberty, the absence of coercion, while *ḥerut* is positive liberty, the freedom that honors the freedom of others. Positive freedom requires habits of self-restraint; hence it belongs only

רַבִּי חֲנַנְיָא בֶּן עֲקַשְׁיָא אוֹמֵר: רָצָה הַקָּדוֹשׁ בָּרוּךְ הוּא לְזַכּוֹת אֶת יִשְׂרָאֵל, לְפִיכָךְ הִרְבָּה לָהֶם תּוֹרָה וּמִצְוֹת. שֶׁנֶּאֱמַר: יהוה חָפֵץ לְמַעַן צִדְקוֹ, יַגְדִּיל תּוֹרָה וְיַאְדִּיר: מכות כג · ישעיה מב

If there is a מנין*, mourners say* קדיש דרבנן *(page 561).*

* * *

כָּל יִשְׂרָאֵל יֵשׁ לָהֶם חֵלֶק לָעוֹלָם הַבָּא. שֶׁנֶּאֱמַר: סנהדרין צ.
וְעַמֵּךְ כֻּלָּם צַדִּיקִים, לְעוֹלָם יִירְשׁוּ אָרֶץ ישעיה ס
נֵצֶר מַטָּעַי, מַעֲשֵׂה יָדַי לְהִתְפָּאֵר:

פרק שישי

שָׁנוּ חֲכָמִים בִּלְשׁוֹן הַמִּשְׁנָה, בָּרוּךְ שֶׁבָּחַר בָּהֶם וּבְמִשְׁנָתָם.

א רַבִּי מֵאִיר אוֹמֵר: כָּל הָעוֹסֵק בַּתּוֹרָה לִשְׁמָהּ, זוֹכֶה לִדְבָרִים הַרְבֵּה. וְלֹא עוֹד, אֶלָּא שֶׁכָּל הָעוֹלָם כֻּלּוֹ כְּדַאי הוּא לוֹ. נִקְרָא רֵעַ, אָהוּב, אוֹהֵב אֶת הַמָּקוֹם, אוֹהֵב אֶת הַבְּרִיּוֹת, מְשַׂמֵּחַ אֶת הַמָּקוֹם, מְשַׂמֵּחַ אֶת הַבְּרִיּוֹת, וּמַלְבַּשְׁתּוֹ עֲנָוָה וְיִרְאָה, וּמַכְשַׁרְתּוֹ לִהְיוֹת צַדִּיק, חָסִיד, יָשָׁר, וְנֶאֱמָן, וּמְרַחַקְתּוֹ מִן הַחֵטְא, וּמְקָרַבְתּוֹ לִידֵי זְכוּת, וְנֶהֱנִין מִמֶּנּוּ עֵצָה וְתוּשִׁיָּה, בִּינָה וּגְבוּרָה, שֶׁנֶּאֱמַר: לִי־עֵצָה וְתוּשִׁיָּה, אֲנִי בִינָה, לִי גְבוּרָה: וְנוֹתֶנֶת לוֹ מַלְכוּת וּמֶמְשָׁלָה, וְחִקּוּר דִּין, וּמְגַלִּין לוֹ רָזֵי תוֹרָה, וְנַעֲשֶׂה כְּמַעְיָן הַמִּתְגַּבֵּר וּכְנָהָר שֶׁאֵינוֹ פּוֹסֵק, וְהֹוֶה צָנוּעַ, וְאֶרֶךְ רוּחַ, וּמוֹחֵל עַל עֶלְבּוֹנוֹ, וּמְגַדַּלְתּוֹ וּמְרוֹמַמְתּוֹ עַל כָּל הַמַּעֲשִׂים. משלי ח

ב אָמַר רַבִּי יְהוֹשֻׁעַ בֶּן לֵוִי: בְּכָל יוֹם וָיוֹם, בַּת קוֹל יוֹצֵאת מֵהַר חוֹרֵב וּמַכְרֶזֶת וְאוֹמֶרֶת, אוֹי לָהֶם לַבְּרִיּוֹת מֵעֶלְבּוֹנָהּ שֶׁל תּוֹרָה, שֶׁכָּל מִי שֶׁאֵינוֹ עוֹסֵק בַּתּוֹרָה נִקְרָא נָזוּף, שֶׁנֶּאֱמַר: נֶזֶם זָהָב בְּאַף חֲזִיר, אִשָּׁה יָפָה וְסָרַת טָעַם: משלי יא
וְאוֹמֵר: וְהַלֻּחֹת מַעֲשֵׂה אֱלֹהִים הֵמָּה, וְהַמִּכְתָּב מִכְתַּב אֱלֹהִים הוּא, חָרוּת עַל־הַלֻּחֹת: אַל תִּקְרָא חָרוּת אֶלָּא חֵרוּת, שֶׁאֵין לְךָ בֶּן חוֹרִין אֶלָּא מִי שֶׁעוֹסֵק בְּתַלְמוּד תּוֹרָה. וְכָל מִי שֶׁעוֹסֵק בְּתַלְמוּד תּוֹרָה, הֲרֵי זֶה מִתְעַלֶּה, שֶׁנֶּאֱמַר: שמות לב
וּמִמַּתָּנָה נַחֲלִיאֵל, וּמִנַּחֲלִיאֵל בָּמוֹת: במדבר כא

CHAPTER 6

This chapter, as the text explains, is not part of the Tractate *Avot,* but is a later compilation. It is known as *The Chapter of* R. Meir, because of its first speaker, or *The Chapter of the Acquisition of Torah,* because of its central theme. Like Chapter 119 of the book of Psalms, it is a poetic expression of the love of a people for a book, the Book of Books, and a quintessential declaration of rabbinic faith.

3. Whoever learns from someone else a single chapter, a single law, a single verse, a single word, even a single letter, must treat him with honor, for so we find in the case of David, King of Israel, who learned only two things from Aḥitophel, yet he called him his teacher, his guide, and his close friend, for so it says, "But it is you, my equal, my guide, my close friend." The following *Ps. 55* inference can be derived: If David, King of Israel, who learned only two things from Aḥitophel, called him his teacher, guide and close friend, how much more must one who learns from someone else a chapter, a law, a verse, a word or even a single letter, treat him with honor! And honor is due only to Torah, as it is written, "The wise shall inherit honor," and "The wholehearted *Prov. 3* *Prov. 28* shall attain good," and "good" signifies Torah, as it is said, "I have given you *Prov. 4* good instruction; do not forsake My Torah."

4. This is the way of Torah: Eat bread with salt, drink water by measure, sleep on the ground, live a life of hardship, but toil in the Torah! If you do so, "You will be happy and it will be well with you": "You will be happy" in this world, "and it shall be well with you" in the World to Come.

5. Do not seek greatness for yourself, and do not long for honor. Let your deeds exceed your learning. Do not crave the table of kings, for your table is greater than theirs, your crown is greater than their crown, and your Employer can be relied upon to pay you your labor's reward.

6. The Torah is greater than priesthood and kingship, for kingship is acquired with thirty attainments, and priesthood is endowed with twenty-four [gifts], but the Torah is acquired by forty-eight virtues. They are: study, attentive listening, well-ordered speech, intuitive understanding, awe, reverence, humility, joy, purity, serving the wise, association with colleagues, debate with students, serenity, knowledge of Scripture and Mishna; minimizing time spent on business, worldly matters, pleasure, sleep, small talk or laughter; patience, a kindly heart, faith in the sages, and acceptance of suffering; knowing one's place, being happy with one's lot, restraining one's words, and claiming no credit for

---

the sages had a tradition that Psalm 55 was composed by David during Absolom's rebellion, and understood the following verses as referring to Aḥitophel: "If an enemy were insulting me, I could endure it… But it is you, a man like myself, my companion, my close friend, with whom I once enjoyed sweet fellowship as we walked with the throng at the House of God."

6:6. *Kingship is acquired with thirty attainments,* set out in Mishna, *Sanhedrin* 2:2–5. *Priesthood is endowed with twenty-four gifts,* derived from Numbers 18:8–32.

ג הַלּוֹמֵד מֵחֲבֵרוֹ פֶּרֶק אֶחָד, אוֹ הֲלָכָה אַחַת, אוֹ פָּסוּק אֶחָד, אוֹ דִבּוּר אֶחָד,
אוֹ אֲפִלּוּ אוֹת אַחַת, צָרִיךְ לִנְהָג בּוֹ כָּבוֹד. שֶׁכֵּן מָצִינוּ בְּדָוִד מֶלֶךְ יִשְׂרָאֵל,
שֶׁלֹּא לָמַד מֵאֲחִיתֹפֶל אֶלָּא שְׁנֵי דְבָרִים בִּלְבָד, קְרָאוֹ רַבּוֹ אַלּוּפוֹ וּמְיֻדָּעוֹ,
תהלים נה שֶׁנֶּאֱמַר: וְאַתָּה אֱנוֹשׁ כְּעֶרְכִּי, אַלּוּפִי וּמְיֻדָּעִי: וַהֲלֹא דְבָרִים קַל וָחֹמֶר. וּמַה
דָּוִד מֶלֶךְ יִשְׂרָאֵל, שֶׁלֹּא לָמַד מֵאֲחִיתֹפֶל אֶלָּא שְׁנֵי דְבָרִים בִּלְבָד, קְרָאוֹ
רַבּוֹ אַלּוּפוֹ וּמְיֻדָּעוֹ, הַלּוֹמֵד מֵחֲבֵרוֹ פֶּרֶק אֶחָד, אוֹ הֲלָכָה אַחַת, אוֹ פָּסוּק
אֶחָד, אוֹ דִבּוּר אֶחָד, אוֹ אֲפִלּוּ אוֹת אַחַת, עַל אַחַת כַּמָּה וְכַמָּה שֶׁצָּרִיךְ
משלי ג לִנְהָג בּוֹ כָּבוֹד. וְאֵין כָּבוֹד אֶלָּא תוֹרָה, שֶׁנֶּאֱמַר: כָּבוֹד חֲכָמִים יִנְחָלוּ:
משלי כח משלי ד וּתְמִימִים יִנְחֲלוּ־טוֹב: וְאֵין טוֹב אֶלָּא תוֹרָה, שֶׁנֶּאֱמַר: כִּי לֶקַח טוֹב נָתַתִּי
לָכֶם, תּוֹרָתִי אַל־תַּעֲזֹבוּ:

ד כָּךְ הִיא דַּרְכָּהּ שֶׁל תּוֹרָה. פַּת בַּמֶּלַח תֹּאכַל, וּמַיִם בַּמְּשׂוּרָה תִּשְׁתֶּה, וְעַל
הָאָרֶץ תִּישַׁן, וְחַיֵּי צַעַר תִּחְיֶה, וּבַתּוֹרָה אַתָּה עָמֵל. אִם אַתָּה עוֹשֶׂה כֵּן,
אַשְׁרֶיךָ וְטוֹב לָךְ, אַשְׁרֶיךָ בָּעוֹלָם הַזֶּה, וְטוֹב לָךְ לָעוֹלָם הַבָּא.

ה אַל תְּבַקֵּשׁ גְּדֻלָּה לְעַצְמְךָ, וְאַל תַּחְמֹד כָּבוֹד. יוֹתֵר מִלִּמּוּדְךָ עֲשֵׂה. וְאַל
תִּתְאַוֶּה לְשֻׁלְחָנָם שֶׁל מְלָכִים, שֶׁשֻּׁלְחָנְךָ גָּדוֹל מִשֻּׁלְחָנָם, וְכִתְרְךָ גָּדוֹל
מִכִּתְרָם. וְנֶאֱמָן הוּא בַּעַל מְלַאכְתְּךָ, שֶׁיְּשַׁלֶּם לְךָ שְׂכַר פְּעֻלָּתֶךָ.

ו גְּדוֹלָה תוֹרָה יוֹתֵר מִן הַכְּהֻנָּה וּמִן הַמַּלְכוּת. שֶׁהַמַּלְכוּת נִקְנֵית בִּשְׁלֹשִׁים
מַעֲלוֹת, וְהַכְּהֻנָּה בְּעֶשְׂרִים וְאַרְבַּע, וְהַתּוֹרָה נִקְנֵית בְּאַרְבָּעִים וּשְׁמוֹנָה
דְבָרִים. וְאֵלּוּ הֵן, בְּתַלְמוּד, בִּשְׁמִיעַת הָאֹזֶן, בַּעֲרִיכַת שְׂפָתַיִם, בְּבִינַת הַלֵּב,
בְּאֵימָה, בְּיִרְאָה, בַּעֲנָוָה, בְּשִׂמְחָה, בְּטָהֳרָה, בְּשִׁמּוּשׁ חֲכָמִים, בְּדִקְדּוּק
חֲבֵרִים, בְּפִלְפּוּל הַתַּלְמִידִים, בְּיִשּׁוּב, בְּמִקְרָא, בְּמִשְׁנָה, בְּמִעוּט סְחוֹרָה,

---

to those who have internalized the teachings of Torah. *"From Mattana to Naḥaliel, and from Naḥaliel to Bamot,"* reading the phrase as, "From the gift of Torah (*Mattana*) one reaches the heritage of God (*Naḥaliel*), and from there to the heights (*Bamot*)."

6:3. *Even a single letter:* Such as the correct text of a verse, which may depend on a single letter. *David and Aḥitophel:* the poignancy of this passage is that it was Aḥitophel who urged King David's son Absolom to rebel against him (II Samuel, chapter 16). He was therefore a traitor against the king. However,

oneself; being loved, loving God, loving mankind and loving righteousness, justice and admonishment; shunning honors, avoiding arrogance in one's learning or delight in giving decisions; sharing someone else's burden, giving him the benefit of the doubt, guiding him to truth and peace; concentrating on one's study, asking and answering questions, listening and adding to one's knowledge; learning in order to teach, learning in order to do, making one's teacher wiser, being precise in one's studies, and reporting a saying in the name of the one who said it. For you have learned: Whoever reports a saying in the name of the one who said it brings deliverance to the world, as it is said, "And Esther told the king in the name of Mordekhai." *Esther 2*

7. Great is Torah for it gives life to its practitioners in both this world and the World to Come, as it is said, "For they are life to those that find them, and *Prov. 4* healing to all their flesh"; and it says, "It shall be healing for your body and *Prov. 3* marrow for your bones"; and it says, "It is a tree of life to those who grasp it, and those who support it shall be happy"; and it says, "They shall be a garland *Prov. 1* of grace on your head, and pendants for your neck"; and it says, "It will adorn *Prov. 4* your head with a garland of grace, and bestow on you a crown of glory"; and it says, "Through me shall your days increase, and years of life shall be added *Prov. 9* to you"; and it says, "At its right hand is length of days; in its left, riches and *Prov. 3* honor"; and it says, "For length of days and years of life and peace shall they *Prov. 3* add to you."

8. Rabbi Shimon ben Menasya said in the name of Rabbi Shimon ben Yoḥai: Beauty, strength, wealth, honor, wisdom, old age, gray hair, and children are fitting for the righteous and for the world, as it is said: "Gray hair is a crown *Prov. 16* of glory; it is attained by the way of righteousness"; and it says, "The crown *Prov. 14* of the wise is their wealth"; and it says, "Grandchildren are the crown of *Prov. 17* their elders; the glory of children is their parents"; and it says, "The glory of *Prov. 20* the young is their strength; the majesty of the old is their gray hair"; and it says, "Then the moon shall be ashamed and the sun shall be abashed, for the *Is. 24* Lord of hosts will reign on Mount Zion and in Jerusalem, and glory shall be before His elders." Rabbi Shimon ben Menasya said: These seven qualities which the sages attributed to the righteous were all present in Rabbi [Judah the Prince] and his sons.

9. Rabbi Yose ben Kisma said: Once I was walking along the road when a man met and greeted me, and I returned his greeting. He said to me, "Rabbi, where do you come from?" I replied, "I come from a great city of sages and scribes." He said to me, "Rabbi, if you are willing to live with us in our place I will give you a million gold dinars, as well as precious stones and pearls." I replied, "Were you to give me all the silver and gold and precious stones and pearls

בְּמִעוּט דֶּרֶךְ אֶרֶץ, בְּמִעוּט תַּעֲנוּג, בְּמִעוּט שֵׁנָה, בְּמִעוּט שִׂיחָה, בְּמִעוּט שְׂחוֹק, בְּאֶרֶךְ אַפַּיִם, בְּלֵב טוֹב, בֶּאֱמוּנַת חֲכָמִים, בְּקַבָּלַת הַיִּסּוּרִין, הַמַּכִּיר אֶת מְקוֹמוֹ, וְהַשָּׂמֵחַ בְּחֶלְקוֹ, וְהָעוֹשֶׂה סְיָג לִדְבָרָיו, וְאֵינוֹ מַחֲזִיק טוֹבָה לְעַצְמוֹ, אָהוּב, אוֹהֵב אֶת הַמָּקוֹם, אוֹהֵב אֶת הַבְּרִיּוֹת, אוֹהֵב אֶת הַצְּדָקוֹת, אוֹהֵב אֶת הַמֵּישָׁרִים, אוֹהֵב אֶת הַתּוֹכָחוֹת, וּמִתְרַחֵק מִן הַכָּבוֹד, וְלֹא מֵגִיס לִבּוֹ בְּתַלְמוּדוֹ, וְאֵינוֹ שָׂמֵחַ בְּהוֹרָאָה, נוֹשֵׂא בְעֹל עִם חֲבֵרוֹ, וּמַכְרִיעוֹ לְכַף זְכוּת, וּמַעֲמִידוֹ עַל הָאֱמֶת, וּמַעֲמִידוֹ עַל הַשָּׁלוֹם, וּמִתְיַשֵּׁב לִבּוֹ בְּתַלְמוּדוֹ, שׁוֹאֵל וּמֵשִׁיב, שׁוֹמֵעַ וּמוֹסִיף, הַלּוֹמֵד עַל מְנָת לְלַמֵּד, וְהַלּוֹמֵד עַל מְנָת לַעֲשׂוֹת, הַמַּחְכִּים אֶת רַבּוֹ, וְהַמְכַוֵּן אֶת שְׁמוּעָתוֹ, וְהָאוֹמֵר דָּבָר בְּשֵׁם אוֹמְרוֹ. הָא לָמַדְתָּ, כָּל הָאוֹמֵר דָּבָר בְּשֵׁם אוֹמְרוֹ, מֵבִיא גְאֻלָּה לָעוֹלָם, שֶׁנֶּאֱמַר: וַתֹּאמֶר אֶסְתֵּר לַמֶּלֶךְ בְּשֵׁם מָרְדֳּכָי: אסתר ב

ז גְּדוֹלָה תוֹרָה, שֶׁהִיא נוֹתֶנֶת חַיִּים לְעוֹשֶׂיהָ בָּעוֹלָם הַזֶּה וּבָעוֹלָם הַבָּא, שֶׁנֶּאֱמַר: כִּי־חַיִּים הֵם לְמֹצְאֵיהֶם, וּלְכָל־בְּשָׂרוֹ מַרְפֵּא: וְאוֹמֵר: רִפְאוּת תְּהִי לְשָׁרֶּךָ, וְשִׁקּוּי לְעַצְמוֹתֶיךָ: וְאוֹמֵר: עֵץ־חַיִּים הִיא לַמַּחֲזִיקִים בָּהּ, וְתֹמְכֶיהָ מְאֻשָּׁר: וְאוֹמֵר: כִּי לִוְיַת חֵן הֵם לְרֹאשֶׁךָ, וַעֲנָקִים לְגַרְגְּרֹתֶךָ: וְאוֹמֵר: תִּתֵּן לְרֹאשְׁךָ לִוְיַת־חֵן, עֲטֶרֶת תִּפְאֶרֶת תְּמַגְּנֶךָּ: וְאוֹמֵר: כִּי־בִי יִרְבּוּ יָמֶיךָ, וְיוֹסִיפוּ לְּךָ שְׁנוֹת חַיִּים: וְאוֹמֵר: אֹרֶךְ יָמִים בִּימִינָהּ, בִּשְׂמֹאולָהּ עֹשֶׁר וְכָבוֹד: וְאוֹמֵר: כִּי אֹרֶךְ יָמִים וּשְׁנוֹת חַיִּים וְשָׁלוֹם יוֹסִיפוּ לָךְ: משלי ד משלי ג משלי ג משלי א משלי ד משלי ט משלי ג משלי ג

ח רַבִּי שִׁמְעוֹן בֶּן מְנַסְיָא מִשּׁוּם רַבִּי שִׁמְעוֹן בֶּן יוֹחָאי אוֹמֵר: הַנּוֹי, וְהַכֹּחַ, וְהָעֹשֶׁר, וְהַכָּבוֹד, וְהַחָכְמָה, וְהַזִּקְנָה, וְהַשֵּׂיבָה, וְהַבָּנִים, נָאֶה לַצַּדִּיקִים וְנָאֶה לָעוֹלָם, שֶׁנֶּאֱמַר: עֲטֶרֶת תִּפְאֶרֶת שֵׂיבָה, בְּדֶרֶךְ צְדָקָה תִּמָּצֵא: וְאוֹמֵר: עֲטֶרֶת חֲכָמִים עָשְׁרָם: וְאוֹמֵר: עֲטֶרֶת זְקֵנִים בְּנֵי בָנִים, וְתִפְאֶרֶת בָּנִים אֲבוֹתָם: וְאוֹמֵר: תִּפְאֶרֶת בַּחוּרִים כֹּחָם, וַהֲדַר זְקֵנִים שֵׂיבָה: וְאוֹמֵר: וְחָפְרָה הַלְּבָנָה וּבוֹשָׁה הַחַמָּה, כִּי־מָלַךְ יהוה צְבָאוֹת בְּהַר צִיּוֹן וּבִירוּשָׁלַםִ, וְנֶגֶד זְקֵנָיו כָּבוֹד: רַבִּי שִׁמְעוֹן בֶּן מְנַסְיָא אוֹמֵר: אֵלּוּ שֶׁבַע מִדּוֹת שֶׁמָּנוּ חֲכָמִים לַצַּדִּיקִים, כֻּלָּם נִתְקַיְּמוּ בְּרַבִּי וּבְבָנָיו. משלי טז משלי יד משלי יז משלי כ ישעיה כד

ט אָמַר רַבִּי יוֹסֵי בֶּן קִסְמָא: פַּעַם אַחַת הָיִיתִי מְהַלֵּךְ בַּדֶּרֶךְ, וּפָגַע בִּי אָדָם אֶחָד, וְנָתַן לִי שָׁלוֹם וְהֶחֱזַרְתִּי לוֹ שָׁלוֹם. אָמַר לִי, רַבִּי, מֵאֵיזֶה מָקוֹם אָתָּה.

in the world, I would not live anywhere except in a place of Torah, for so it is written in the book of Psalms by David, King of Israel, 'I prefer the Torah of your mouth to thousands of gold and silver pieces.' Furthermore, when a person departs from this world, neither silver nor gold nor precious stones nor pearls accompany him, but only Torah and good deeds, as it is said, 'When you walk, it will lead you; when you lie down, it will watch over you; and when you awake, it will talk with you.' 'When you walk, it will lead you' – in this world; 'when you lie down, it will watch over you' – in the grave; 'and when you awake, it will speak for you' – in the World to Come. And it says, 'Mine is the silver, and Mine is the gold, says the LORD of hosts.'" *Ps. 119* *Prov. 6* *Hag. 2*

10. Five possessions did the Holy One, blessed be He, declare as His own in His world, and they are: the Torah, heaven and earth, Abraham, Israel and the Temple. How do we know this about the Torah? Because it is written, "The LORD created me at the beginning of His way, as the first of His works in days of old." How do we know it about heaven and earth? Because it is written, "So says the LORD: the heaven is My throne, and the earth is My footstool; what house can you build for Me, and where is the place for My rest?"; and it also says, "How numerous are Your works, LORD; You made them all in wisdom; the earth is full of Your creations." How do we know it about Abraham? Because it is written, "And He blessed him and said, Blessed be Abram of God the Most High, owner of heaven and earth." How do we know it about Israel? Because it is written, "Until Your people pass over, O LORD, until this people You acquired pass over"; and it also says, "As for the holy ones who are on earth and for the mighty, all My delight is in them." How do we know it about the Temple? Because it is written, "Your dwelling place which You, LORD, have made; the Temple, O LORD, which Your hands established"; and it also says, "He brought them to His holy realm, the mountain His right hand had acquired." *Prov. 8* *Is. 66* *Ps. 104* *Gen. 14* *Ex. 15* *Ps. 16* *Ex. 15* *Ps. 78*

11. All that the Holy One, blessed be He, created in His world, He created solely for His glory, as it is said, "All that is called by My name, it is for My glory that I created it, formed it and made it"; and it also says, "The LORD shall reign for ever and ever." *Is. 43* *Ex. 15*

Rabbi Ḥananya ben Akashya said: The Holy One, blessed be He, wanted to confer merit on Israel. That is why He gave them a copious Torah and many commandments, as it is said, "It pleased the LORD, for the sake of [Israel's] righteousness, to make the Torah great and glorious." *Makkot 23b* *Is. 42*

If there is a minyan, mourners say the Rabbis' Kaddish (page 560).

אָמַרְתִּי לוֹ, מֵעִיר גְּדוֹלָה שֶׁל חֲכָמִים וְשֶׁל סוֹפְרִים אָנִי. אָמַר לִי, רַבִּי, רְצוֹנְךָ שֶׁתָּדוּר עִמָּנוּ בִּמְקוֹמֵנוּ, וַאֲנִי אֶתֵּן לְךָ אֶלֶף אֲלָפִים דִּינְרֵי זָהָב וַאֲבָנִים טוֹבוֹת וּמַרְגָּלִיּוֹת. אָמַרְתִּי לוֹ, אִם אַתָּה נוֹתֵן לִי כָּל כֶּסֶף וְזָהָב וַאֲבָנִים טוֹבוֹת וּמַרְגָּלִיּוֹת שֶׁבָּעוֹלָם, אֵינִי דָר אֶלָּא בִּמְקוֹם תּוֹרָה, וְכֵן כָּתוּב בְּסֵפֶר תְּהִלִּים עַל יְדֵי דָוִד מֶלֶךְ יִשְׂרָאֵל: טוֹב־לִי תוֹרַת־פִּיךָ מֵאַלְפֵי זָהָב וָכָסֶף: תהלים קיט
וְלֹא עוֹד, אֶלָּא שֶׁבִּשְׁעַת פְּטִירָתוֹ שֶׁל אָדָם, אֵין מְלַוִּין לוֹ לְאָדָם לֹא כֶסֶף וְלֹא זָהָב וְלֹא אֲבָנִים טוֹבוֹת וּמַרְגָּלִיּוֹת, אֶלָּא תּוֹרָה וּמַעֲשִׂים טוֹבִים בִּלְבָד, שֶׁנֶּאֱמַר: בְּהִתְהַלֶּכְךָ תַּנְחֶה אֹתָךְ, בְּשָׁכְבְּךָ תִּשְׁמֹר עָלֶיךָ, וַהֲקִיצוֹתָ הִיא תְשִׂיחֶךָ: משלי ו
בְּהִתְהַלֶּכְךָ תַּנְחֶה אֹתָךְ, בָּעוֹלָם הַזֶּה. בְּשָׁכְבְּךָ תִּשְׁמֹר עָלֶיךָ, בַּקֶּבֶר. וַהֲקִיצוֹתָ הִיא תְשִׂיחֶךָ, לָעוֹלָם הַבָּא. וְאוֹמֵר: לִי הַכֶּסֶף וְלִי הַזָּהָב, נְאֻם יהוה צְבָאוֹת: חגי ב

י חֲמִשָּׁה קִנְיָנִים קָנָה הַקָּדוֹשׁ בָּרוּךְ הוּא בְּעוֹלָמוֹ. וְאֵלּוּ הֵן, תּוֹרָה קִנְיָן אֶחָד, שָׁמַיִם וָאָרֶץ קִנְיָן אֶחָד, אַבְרָהָם קִנְיָן אֶחָד, יִשְׂרָאֵל קִנְיָן אֶחָד, בֵּית הַמִּקְדָּשׁ קִנְיָן אֶחָד. תּוֹרָה מִנַּיִן, דִּכְתִיב: יהוה קָנָנִי רֵאשִׁית דַּרְכּוֹ, קֶדֶם מִפְעָלָיו מֵאָז: משלי ח
שָׁמַיִם וָאָרֶץ מִנַּיִן, דִּכְתִיב: כֹּה אָמַר יהוה הַשָּׁמַיִם כִּסְאִי וְהָאָרֶץ הֲדֹם רַגְלָי, אֵי־זֶה בַיִת אֲשֶׁר תִּבְנוּ־לִי, וְאֵי־זֶה מָקוֹם מְנוּחָתִי: וְאוֹמֵר: מָה־רַבּוּ מַעֲשֶׂיךָ יהוה, כֻּלָּם בְּחָכְמָה עָשִׂיתָ, מָלְאָה הָאָרֶץ קִנְיָנֶךָ: אַבְרָהָם מִנַּיִן, דִּכְתִיב: וַיְבָרְכֵהוּ וַיֹּאמַר, בָּרוּךְ אַבְרָם לְאֵל עֶלְיוֹן, קֹנֵה שָׁמַיִם וָאָרֶץ: יִשְׂרָאֵל מִנַּיִן, דִּכְתִיב: עַד־יַעֲבֹר עַמְּךָ יהוה, עַד־יַעֲבֹר עַם־זוּ קָנִיתָ: וְאוֹמֵר: לִקְדוֹשִׁים אֲשֶׁר־בָּאָרֶץ הֵמָּה, וְאַדִּירֵי כָּל־חֶפְצִי־בָם: בֵּית הַמִּקְדָּשׁ מִנַּיִן, דִּכְתִיב: מָכוֹן לְשִׁבְתְּךָ פָּעַלְתָּ יהוה, מִקְּדָשׁ אֲדֹנָי כּוֹנְנוּ יָדֶיךָ: וְאוֹמֵר: וַיְבִיאֵם אֶל־גְּבוּל קָדְשׁוֹ, הַר־זֶה קָנְתָה יְמִינוֹ:

(ישעיה סו · תהלים קד · בראשית יד · שמות טו · תהלים טז · שמות טו · תהלים עח)

יא כָּל מַה שֶּׁבָּרָא הַקָּדוֹשׁ בָּרוּךְ הוּא בְּעוֹלָמוֹ, לֹא בְרָאוֹ אֶלָּא לִכְבוֹדוֹ, שֶׁנֶּאֱמַר: כֹּל הַנִּקְרָא בִשְׁמִי וְלִכְבוֹדִי בְּרָאתִיו, יְצַרְתִּיו אַף־עֲשִׂיתִיו: וְאוֹמֵר: יהוה יִמְלֹךְ לְעֹלָם וָעֶד: ישעיה מג · שמות טו

רַבִּי חֲנַנְיָא בֶּן עֲקַשְׁיָא אוֹמֵר: רָצָה הַקָּדוֹשׁ בָּרוּךְ הוּא לְזַכּוֹת אֶת יִשְׂרָאֵל, לְפִיכָךְ הִרְבָּה לָהֶם תּוֹרָה וּמִצְוֹת. שֶׁנֶּאֱמַר: יהוה חָפֵץ לְמַעַן צִדְקוֹ, יַגְדִּיל תּוֹרָה וְיַאְדִּיר: מכות כג: · ישעיה מב

If there is a מנין, *mourners say* קדיש דרבנן *(page 561)*.

Se'uda Shelishit for Shabbat

אַתְקִינוּ Prepare the feast of perfect faith, joy of the holy King.
Prepare the Royal feast,
this is the feast [mystically known as] "the Small Face,"
and "the Holy Ancient One" and "the Field of Holy Apples"
[mystical terms for aspects of the Divine]
come to partake in the feast with it.

Children of the palace
who yearn to see the radiance of "the Small Face,"
be here at this table
in which the King is engraved.
Long to join this gathering
together with the winged angels.
Rejoice now at this time of favor
when there is no displeasure.
Come close to me, see my strength,
for there are no harsh judgments:
Those brazen dogs are outside,
unable to enter.
So I invite the holy Ancient of Days, His brow of desire
as the moment fades,
And His will is revealed,
to annul all forces of impurity.
Hurl them into the abyss,
hide them in the clefts of rocks,
For now, at Minḥa-time,
is a time of joy for "the Small Face."

---

the words of Torah at the table more inward and profound. Yet there is also the knowledge that this charmed moment is the end of something, and the workday week, with its tensions and hazards, is about to begin. The Ḥassidim in particular seek to draw out these closing moments as long as possible, as if one could make time itself slow to a standstill. This is a time of spiritual longing, as we reluctantly prepare to leave the world-that-ought-to-be for the testing reality of the world-that-is.

סעודה שלישית של שבת

אַתְקִינוּ סְעוּדָתָא דִמְהֵימְנוּתָא שְׁלִימְתָא, חֶדְוָתָא דְמַלְכָּא קַדִּישָׁא.
אַתְקִינוּ סְעוּדָתָא דְמַלְכָּא.
דָא הִיא סְעוּדָתָא דִזְעֵיר אַנְפִּין
וְעַתִּיקָא קַדִּישָׁא וַחֲקַל תַּפּוּחִין קַדִּישִׁין אָתַיִן לְסַעֲדָה בַּהֲדֵהּ.

בְּנֵי הֵיכְלָא, דְּכַסִּיפִין לְמֶחֱזֵי זִיו זְעֵיר אַנְפִּין
יְהוֹן הָכָא, בְּהַאי תַּכָּא, דְּבֵהּ מַלְכָּא בְּגִלּוּפִין.
צְבוּ לַחֲדָא, בְּהַאי וַעֲדָא, בְּגוֹ עִירִין וְכָל גַּדְפִין.
חֲדוּ הַשְׁתָּא, בְּהַאי שַׁעְתָּא, דְּבֵהּ רַעֲוָא וְלֵית זַעְפִין.
קְרִיבוּ לִי, חֲזוּ חֵילִי, דְּלֵית דִּינִין דִּתְקִיפִין.
לְבַר נָטְלִין, וְלָא עָלִין, הָנֵי כַלְבִּין דַּחֲצִיפִין.
וְהָא אַזְמִין עַתִּיק יוֹמִין, לְמִצְחֵהּ עַד יְהוֹן חָלְפִין.
רְעוּ דִי לֵהּ, דְּגַלֵּי לֵהּ, לְבַטָּלָה בְּכָל קְלִיפִין.
יְשַׁוֵּי לוֹן, בְּנִקְבְּהוֹן, וְיִטַּמְרוּן בְּגוֹ כֵפִין.
אֲרֵי הַשְׁתָּא, בְּמִנְחֲתָא, בְּחֶדְוָתָא דִזְעֵיר אַנְפִּין.

SE'UDA SHELISHIT / THE THIRD SHABBAT MEAL

One of the ways in which Shabbat is honored is by eating a third meal, *Se'uda Shelishit*: on weekdays, in Talmudic times, only two meals were eaten. The third meal – often, especially in summer, eaten communally – is a time of great spiritual intensity. The special atmosphere of Shabbat here reaches its climax. We have passed through the Shabbat of creation, the theme of Friday night, and the Shabbat of revelation, the mood of Shabbat morning. We now enter the Shabbat of redemption, the distantly glimpsed future of a world in which God's sovereignty will be recognized by all, and life on earth will recover the harmonies it once had at the dawn of time.

Something of that serenity suffuses the third meal as the sun sinks low on the horizon, sending its slanting rays through the leaves and etching the landscape with red gold. The melodies of the third meal are more meditative, and

מִזְמוֹר לְדָוִד A psalm of David. Ps. 23
The Lord is my Shepherd,
I shall not want.
He makes me lie down in green pastures.
He leads me beside the still waters.
He refreshes my soul.
He guides me in the paths of righteousness
for His name's sake.
Though I walk through
the valley of the shadow of death,
I will fear no evil,
for You are with me;
Your rod and Your staff,
they comfort me.
You set a table before me
in the presence of my enemies;
You anoint my head with oil;
my cup is filled to overflowing.
May goodness and kindness
follow me all the days of my life,
and may I live in the House of the Lord
for evermore.

---

cup of wine filled to overflowing, his head anointed with oil (oil was placed on the heads of honored guests at banquets: see Ecclesiastes 9:8; Psalm 92:11). Though his enemies are close, they can do him no harm for he is under his host's protection. The last line delivers the unexpected denouement: the place where the poet experiences these rich feelings of safety is the Temple, "the House of the Lord."

Said here, toward the end of Shabbat, the psalm has particular force. Often Jews were all too conscious of the dangers that lay ahead as they left the refuge of Shabbat and prepared to reengage with the world outside. With them, however, they took the courage born of faith that "I will fear no evil, for You are with me."

תהלים כג

מִזְמוֹר לְדָוִד

יהוה רֹעִי לֹא אֶחְסָר:
בִּנְאוֹת דֶּשֶׁא יַרְבִּיצֵנִי
עַל־מֵי מְנֻחוֹת יְנַהֲלֵנִי:
נַפְשִׁי יְשׁוֹבֵב
יַנְחֵנִי בְמַעְגְּלֵי־צֶדֶק לְמַעַן שְׁמוֹ:
גַּם כִּי־אֵלֵךְ בְּגֵיא צַלְמָוֶת לֹא־אִירָא רָע
כִּי־אַתָּה עִמָּדִי
שִׁבְטְךָ וּמִשְׁעַנְתֶּךָ הֵמָּה יְנַחֲמֻנִי:
תַּעֲרֹךְ לְפָנַי שֻׁלְחָן נֶגֶד צֹרְרָי
דִּשַּׁנְתָּ בַשֶּׁמֶן רֹאשִׁי
כּוֹסִי רְוָיָה:
אַךְ טוֹב וָחֶסֶד יִרְדְּפוּנִי כָּל־יְמֵי חַיָּי
וְשַׁבְתִּי בְּבֵית־יהוה לְאֹרֶךְ יָמִים:

Psalm 23: One of the most sublime passages in all religious literature: a poetic masterpiece – a mere 57 words long – of trust in God's gentle care. In the first half, the Psalmist sees himself as a sheep of God's flock, vulnerable yet safe under the shepherd's protective eye. The tone of serenity is conveyed by a series of pastoral images: "green pastures," "still waters," and *ma'agelei tzedek*, "right (i.e. safe) paths."

The mood then quickens. The Psalmist speaks of "the valley of the shadow of death" (or "a valley of deep darkness"), perhaps a crevice in the rocks where the sun cannot penetrate and where there may be danger from predators. At this point, the psalm shifts from third to second person as the author turns directly to God, uttering in six simple Hebrew words one of the great declarations of faith: "I will fear no evil, for You are with me."

The metaphor then changes. Now the Psalmist is a guest at God's table, his

יְדִיד Beloved of the soul, Father of compassion,
draw Your servant close to Your will.
Like a deer will Your servant run
and fall prostrate before Your beauty.
To him Your love is sweeter
than honey from the comb, than any taste.

הָדוּר Glorious, beautiful, radiance of the world,
my soul is sick with love for You.
Please, God, heal her now
by showing her Your tender radiance.
Then she will recover her strength and be healed,
Be Your servant for eternity.

וָתִיק Ancient of Days, let Your mercy be aroused;
please have pity on Your beloved child.
How long have I yearned
to see the glory of Your strength.
Please, my God, my heart's desire –
hasten; do not hide Yourself.

הִגָּלֵה Reveal Yourself, beloved, and spread over me
the tabernacle of Your peace.
Let the earth shine with Your glory,
let us be overjoyed and rejoice in You.
Hurry, beloved, for the appointed time has come,
and be gracious to me as in the times of old.

Psalm 102:14, "You will surely arise and take pity on Zion, for it is time to be gracious to her; the appointed time has come" – a reference, in this context, to the messianic age.

יְדִיד נֶֽפֶשׁ, אָב הָרַחֲמָן, מְשֹׁךְ עַבְדְּךָ אֶל רְצוֹנָךְ
יָרוּץ עַבְדְּךָ כְּמוֹ אַיָּל, יִשְׁתַּחֲוֶה מוּל הֲדָרָךְ
כִּי יֶעֱרַב לוֹ יְדִידוּתָךְ, מִנֹּֽפֶת צוּף וְכָל טָֽעַם.

הָדוּר, נָאֶה, זִיו הָעוֹלָם, נַפְשִׁי חוֹלַת אַהֲבָתָךְ
אָנָּא, אֵל נָא, רְפָא נָא לָהּ, בְּהַרְאוֹת לָהּ נֹֽעַם זִיוָךְ
אָז תִּתְחַזֵּק וְתִתְרַפֵּא, וְהָיְתָה לָךְ שִׁפְחַת עוֹלָם.

וָתִיק, יֶהֱמוּ רַחֲמֶיךָ, וְחוּס נָא עַל בֵּן אוֹהֲבָךְ
כִּי זֶה כַּמֶּה נִכְסֹף נִכְסַף לִרְאוֹת בְּתִפְאֶֽרֶת עֻזָּךְ
אָנָּא, אֵלִי, מַחְמַד לִבִּי, חוּשָׁה נָּא, וְאַל תִּתְעַלָּם.

הִגָּלֶה נָא וּפְרֹשׂ, חָבִיב, עָלַי אֶת סֻכַּת שְׁלוֹמָךְ
תָּאִיר אֶֽרֶץ מִכְּבוֹדָךְ, נָגִֽילָה וְנִשְׂמְחָה בָךְ.
מַהֵר, אָהוּב, כִּי בָא מוֹעֵד, וְחָנֵּנִי כִּימֵי עוֹלָם.

יְדִיד נֶֽפֶשׁ *Beloved of the soul:* A poem of passionate love for God, written by the Safed kabbalist Rabbi Elazar ben Moses Azikri (1533–1600). Azikri was part of a mystical fellowship whose members undertook to relinquish all worldly activity and devote their time exclusively to study, prayer and meditation. He wrote "Beloved of the soul," which he called "a prayer for union and the desire of love," around 1584. It is one of the boldest expressions of love in Jewish literature, reminiscent in mood of the Song of Songs. יְדִיד נפש *Beloved of the soul:* in Jeremiah 12:7, God calls Israel, "the beloved of My soul." מְשֹׁךְ עַבְדְּךָ *Draw Your servant close:* Song of Songs 1:4, "Draw me after You, let us run!" אֵל נָא, רְפָא נָא לָהּ *Please, God, heal her now:* Moses' prayer on behalf of Miriam (Num. 12:13). כִּי בָא מוֹעֵד *For the appointed time has come:*

אֵל מִסְתַּתֵּר God hides Himself in the beauty of concealment, His wisdom opaque to all human thought; / Cause of causes, adorned with the highest crown, they [the angels] give You, LORD, a crown.

In the beginning was Your primordial Torah, inscribed with Your hermetic wisdom. Where can it be found? It is hidden. Wisdom begins in awe of the LORD.

Wider than a river, like never-ending streams, deep waters, that only an understanding man can draw, / its outcomes are the fifty gates of understanding. The faithful are guarded by the LORD.

Great God, all eyes are turned toward You. Your great kindness is higher than the heavens. / God of Abraham, remember Your servant, I will tell of the LORD's kindness, sing praises to the LORD.

Sublime, majestic in strength and might, who brings forth unparalleled light, "Awe of Isaac," make our judgment light. Forever, LORD, is Your might.

Who is like You, God, doing great deeds, Mighty One of Jacob, awesome in praise, Splendor of Israel, who listens to prayers, LORD who listens to those in need.

God, may the merit of the fathers be our shield. Eternal One of Israel, redeem us from distress. / Draw us, raise us, from the pit of exile, that we may loudly sing in service at the House of the LORD.

From right and left the prophets were inspired, finding within them Eternity and Glory, / known by the names of Yakhin and Boaz, and all your children shall be learned of the LORD.

Foundation, the Righteous, is hidden in Seven, the sign of the covenant to the world. Source of blessing, Righteous, Foundation of the world, righteous are You, LORD.

Restore, please, David and Solomon's kingdom, with the crown with which his mother crowned it. / The congregation of Israel is sweetly called a bride, a crown of splendor in the hand of the LORD.

Mighty One, unite the ten Sefirot as one. Those who divide them from the LORD will see no light. / Together they shine like sapphire. Bring my song close to You, the LORD.

Birkat HaMazon can be found on 974.

אֵל מִסְתַּתֵּר בְּשַׁפְרִיר חֶבְיוֹן, הַשֵּׂכֶל הַנֶּעְלָם מִכָּל רַעְיוֹן
עִלַּת הָעִלּוֹת מֻכְתָּר בְּכֶתֶר עֶלְיוֹן, כֶּתֶר יִתְּנוּ לְךָ יהוה.

בְּרֵאשִׁית תּוֹרָתְךָ הַקְּדוּמָה, רְשׁוּמָה חָכְמָתְךָ הַסְּתוּמָה
מֵאַיִן תִּמָּצֵא וְהִיא נֶעְלָמָה, רֵאשִׁית חָכְמָה יִרְאַת יהוה.

רְחוֹבוֹת הַנָּהָר נַחֲלֵי אֱמוּנָה, מַיִם עֲמֻקִּים יִדְלֵם אִישׁ תְּבוּנָה
תּוֹצְאוֹתֶיהָ חֲמִשִּׁים שַׁעֲרֵי בִינָה, אֱמוּנִים נוֹצֵר יהוה.

הָאֵל הַגָּדוֹל עֵינֵי כֹל נֶגְדֶּךָ, רַב חֶסֶד גָּדוֹל עַל הַשָּׁמַיִם חַסְדֶּךָ
אֱלֹהֵי אַבְרָהָם זְכֹר לְעַבְדֶּךָ, חַסְדֵי יהוה אַזְכִּיר תְּהִלּוֹת יהוה.

מָרוֹם נֶאְדָּר בְּכֹחַ וּגְבוּרָה, מוֹצִיא אוֹרָה מֵאֵין תְּמוּרָה
פַּחַד יִצְחָק מִשְׁפָּטֵנוּ הָאִירָה, אַתָּה גִּבּוֹר לְעוֹלָם יהוה.

מִי אֵל כָּמוֹךָ עוֹשֶׂה גְדוֹלוֹת, אֲבִיר יַעֲקֹב נוֹרָא תְהִלּוֹת
תִּפְאֶרֶת יִשְׂרָאֵל שׁוֹמֵעַ תְּפִלּוֹת, כִּי שׁוֹמֵעַ אֶל אֶבְיוֹנִים יהוה.

יָהּ, זְכוּת אָבוֹת יָגֵן עָלֵינוּ, נֵצַח יִשְׂרָאֵל מִצָּרוֹתֵינוּ גְּאָלֵנוּ
וּמִבּוֹר גָּלוּת דְּלֵנוּ וְהַעֲלֵנוּ, לְנַצֵּחַ עַל מְלֶאכֶת בֵּית יהוה.

מִיָּמִין וּמִשְּׂמֹאל יְנִיקַת הַנְּבִיאִים, נֵצַח וָהוֹד מֵהֶם נִמְצָאִים
יָכִין וּבֹעַז בְּשֵׁם נִקְרָאִים, וְכָל בָּנַיִךְ לִמּוּדֵי יהוה.

יְסוֹד צַדִּיק בְּשִׁבְעָה נֶעְלָם, אוֹת בְּרִית הוּא לְעוֹלָם
מַעְיַן הַבְּרָכָה צַדִּיק יְסוֹד עוֹלָם, צַדִּיק אַתָּה יהוה.

נָא הָקֵם מַלְכוּת דָּוִד וּשְׁלֹמֹה, בָּעֲטָרָה שֶׁעִטְּרָה לוֹ אִמּוֹ
כְּנֶסֶת יִשְׂרָאֵל כַּלָּה קְרוּאָה בִּנְעִימָה, עֲטֶרֶת תִּפְאֶרֶת בְּיַד יהוה.

חָזָק מְיַחֵד כְּאֶחָד עֶשֶׂר סְפִירוֹת, וּמַפְרִיד אַלּוּף לֹא יִרְאֶה מְאוֹרוֹת
סַפִּיר גִּזְרָתָם יַחַד מְאִירוֹת, תִּקְרַב רִנָּתִי לְפָנֶיךָ יהוה.

ברכת המזון *can be found on 975.*

Ma'ariv for Motza'ei Shabbat

In many congregations, the following two psalms are sung before Ma'ariv at the end of Shabbat.

לְדָוִד Of David. Blessed is the LORD, my Rock, who trains my hands for war, my fingers for battle. He is my Benefactor, my Fortress, my Stronghold and my Refuge, my Shield in whom I trust, He who subdues nations under me. LORD, what is man that You care for him, what are mortals that You think of them? Man is no more than a breath, his days like a fleeting shadow. LORD, part Your heavens and come down; touch the mountains so that they pour forth smoke. Flash forth lightning and scatter them; shoot Your arrows and panic them. Reach out Your hand from on high; deliver me and rescue me from the mighty waters, from the hands of strangers, whose every word is worthless, whose right hands are raised in falsehood. To You, God, I will sing a new song; to You I will play music on a ten-stringed harp. He who gives salvation to kings, who saved His servant David from the cruel sword: may He deliver me and rescue me from the hands of strangers, whose every word is worthless, whose right hands are raised in falsehood. Then our sons will be like saplings, well nurtured in their youth. Our daughters will be like pillars carved for a palace. Our barns will be filled with every kind of provision. Our sheep will increase by thousands, even

Ps. 144

The story is a parable of Jewish spirituality. Shabbat is our weekly return to the harmony and serenity of the Garden of Eden. As the day ends we, like Adam and Eve, prepare to reengage with the world – a world often fraught with dangers. We pray to God to be with us in the days ahead, to protect us from harm, and to bless the work of our hands.

לְדָוִד *Psalm 144:* As the arrival of Shabbat is greeted with psalms, so is its departure. Psalm 144 speaks with confidence about facing the battles that may lie ahead, and the blessings, human and material, that come from hard work. This is the song of a people who, trusting in God, face the future without fear.

מעריב למוצאי שבת

In many congregations, the following two psalms are sung before מעריב *on* מוצאי שבת*.*

לְדָוִד, בָּרוּךְ יהוה צוּרִי, הַמְלַמֵּד יָדַי לַקְרָב, אֶצְבְּעוֹתַי לַמִּלְחָמָה: תהלים קמד
חַסְדִּי וּמְצוּדָתִי מִשְׂגַּבִּי וּמְפַלְטִי לִי, מָגִנִּי וּבוֹ חָסִיתִי, הָרוֹדֵד
עַמִּי תַחְתָּי: יהוה מָה־אָדָם וַתֵּדָעֵהוּ, בֶּן־אֱנוֹשׁ וַתְּחַשְּׁבֵהוּ:
אָדָם לַהֶבֶל דָּמָה, יָמָיו כְּצֵל עוֹבֵר: יהוה הַט־שָׁמֶיךָ וְתֵרֵד,
גַּע בֶּהָרִים וְיֶעֱשָׁנוּ: בְּרוֹק בָּרָק וּתְפִיצֵם, שְׁלַח חִצֶּיךָ וּתְהֻמֵּם:
שְׁלַח יָדֶיךָ מִמָּרוֹם, פְּצֵנִי וְהַצִּילֵנִי מִמַּיִם רַבִּים, מִיַּד בְּנֵי נֵכָר:
אֲשֶׁר פִּיהֶם דִּבֶּר־שָׁוְא, וִימִינָם יְמִין שָׁקֶר: אֱלֹהִים שִׁיר חָדָשׁ
אָשִׁירָה לָּךְ, בְּנֵבֶל עָשׂוֹר אֲזַמְּרָה־לָּךְ: הַנּוֹתֵן תְּשׁוּעָה לַמְּלָכִים,
הַפּוֹצֶה אֶת־דָּוִד עַבְדּוֹ מֵחֶרֶב רָעָה: פְּצֵנִי וְהַצִּילֵנִי מִיַּד בְּנֵי נֵכָר,
אֲשֶׁר פִּיהֶם דִּבֶּר־שָׁוְא, וִימִינָם יְמִין שָׁקֶר: אֲשֶׁר בָּנֵינוּ כִּנְטִעִים,
מְגֻדָּלִים בִּנְעוּרֵיהֶם, בְּנוֹתֵינוּ כְזָוִיֹּת, מְחֻטָּבוֹת תַּבְנִית הֵיכָל:
מְזָוֵינוּ מְלֵאִים, מְפִיקִים מִזַּן אֶל־זַן, צֹאונֵנוּ מַאֲלִיפוֹת מְרֻבָּבוֹת

CONCLUSION OF SHABBAT

The end of Shabbat is one of the most intense Jewish experiences of time. According to rabbinic tradition (*Pirkei deRabbi Eliezer,* chapter 20), Adam and Eve were created, sinned, and were sentenced to exile from the Garden of Eden, all on the sixth day. God granted them stay of sentence, allowing them to spend one day, Shabbat itself, in the garden. During that day, say the sages, the sun did not set. As Shabbat came to an end, and darkness began to fall, the first human beings prepared to leave paradise and enter the world outside with its conflicts and challenges, hazards and fears. Assuring them that He would be with them, God gave them a gift: the ability to make light. Hence our custom of making a blessing over light in the Havdala service.

tens of thousands in our fields. Our oxen will draw heavy loads. There will be no breach in the walls, no going into captivity, no cries of distress in our streets. Happy are the people for whom this is so; happy are the people whose God is the LORD.

לַמְנַצֵּחַ For the conductor of music. With stringed instruments. A psalm, a song. May God be gracious to us and bless us. May He make His face shine on us, Selah. Then will Your way be known on earth, Your salvation among all the nations. Let the peoples praise You, God; let all peoples praise You. Let nations rejoice and sing for joy, for You judge the peoples with equity, and guide the nations of the earth, Selah. Let the peoples praise You, God; let all peoples praise You. The earth has yielded its harvest. May God, our God, bless us. God will bless us, and all the ends of the earth will fear Him. *Ps. 67*

The service continues with Ma'ariv for Weekdays on page 242. After the Amida, the Leader says Half Kaddish and the congregation continues below:

וִיהִי נֹעַם May the pleasantness of the LORD our God be upon us. Establish for us the work of our hands, O establish the work of our hands. *Ps. 90*

יֹשֵׁב He who lives in the shelter of the Most High dwells in the shadow of the Almighty. I say of the LORD, my Refuge and Stronghold, my God in whom I trust, that He will save you from the *Ps. 91*

---

deliverance from harm. It is said at the end of Shabbat as a prayer for God's protection against the dangers that may lie ahead in the coming week. It is prefaced by the last verse of the previous psalm. According to tradition (Rashi, Ex. 39:43), this was the blessing Moses gave to those who had helped build the Sanctuary, adding: "May the Divine Presence rest in the work of your hands." Said here at the beginning of the workday week, it is a prayer that God may send His blessings for our labors.

This and the following section are not said in a week in which a Festival falls, because we do not then face a full working week, and because the merit of the coming Festival itself is an augury of divine protection.

בְּחוּצוֹתֵֽינוּ: אַלּוּפֵֽינוּ מְסֻבָּלִים, אֵין פֶּֽרֶץ וְאֵין יוֹצֵאת, וְאֵין צְוָחָה
בִּרְחֹבֹתֵֽינוּ: אַשְׁרֵי הָעָם שֶׁכָּֽכָה לּוֹ, אַשְׁרֵי הָעָם שֶׁיהוה אֱלֹהָיו:

תהלים סז לַמְנַצֵּֽחַ בִּנְגִינֹת, מִזְמוֹר שִׁיר: אֱלֹהִים יְחָנֵּֽנוּ וִיבָרְכֵֽנוּ, יָאֵר פָּנָיו
אִתָּֽנוּ סֶֽלָה: לָדַֽעַת בָּאָֽרֶץ דַּרְכֶּֽךָ, בְּכָל־גּוֹיִם יְשׁוּעָתֶֽךָ: יוֹדֽוּךָ עַמִּים
אֱלֹהִים, יוֹדֽוּךָ עַמִּים כֻּלָּם: יִשְׂמְחוּ וִירַנְּנוּ לְאֻמִּים, כִּי־תִשְׁפֹּט עַמִּים
מִישֹׁר, וּלְאֻמִּים בָּאָֽרֶץ תַּנְחֵם סֶֽלָה: יוֹדֽוּךָ עַמִּים אֱלֹהִים, יוֹדֽוּךָ
עַמִּים כֻּלָּם: אֶֽרֶץ נָתְנָה יְבוּלָהּ, יְבָרְכֵֽנוּ אֱלֹהִים אֱלֹהֵֽינוּ: יְבָרְכֵֽנוּ
אֱלֹהִים, וְיִירְאוּ אוֹתוֹ כָּל־אַפְסֵי־אָֽרֶץ:

The service continues with מעריב לחול *on page 243. After the* עמידה*,*
the שליח ציבור *says* חצי קדיש *and the* קהל *continues below:*

תהלים צ וִיהִי נֹֽעַם אֲדֹנָי אֱלֹהֵֽינוּ עָלֵֽינוּ וּמַעֲשֵׂה יָדֵֽינוּ כּוֹנְנָה עָלֵֽינוּ וּמַעֲשֵׂה
יָדֵֽינוּ כּוֹנְנֵֽהוּ:

תהלים צא יֹשֵׁב בְּסֵֽתֶר עֶלְיוֹן, בְּצֵל שַׁדַּי יִתְלוֹנָן: אֹמַר לַיהוה מַחְסִי וּמְצוּדָתִי,
אֱלֹהַי אֶבְטַח־בּוֹ: כִּי הוּא יַצִּילְךָ מִפַּח יָקוּשׁ, מִדֶּֽבֶר הַוּוֹת:
בְּאֶבְרָתוֹ יָֽסֶךְ לָךְ, וְתַֽחַת־כְּנָפָיו תֶּחְסֶה, צִנָּה וְסֹחֵרָה אֲמִתּוֹ:
לֹא־תִירָא מִפַּֽחַד לָֽיְלָה, מֵחֵץ יָעוּף יוֹמָם: מִדֶּֽבֶר בָּאֹֽפֶל יַהֲלֹךְ,

---

לַמְנַצֵּֽחַ *Psalm 67:* A psalm of thanksgiving whose key phrase is "the earth has yielded its harvest." The second verse uses language reminiscent of the Priestly blessings. The word "earth" appears four times in a variety of senses, suggesting that when we do God's will on earth, the earth yields its blessings with the result that God is recognized by all nations of the earth. As we prepare to meet the time that recalls Adam's exile from Eden, we do so in a spirit directly opposite to the mood that prevailed then. Then it was said: "Cursed be the ground because of you" (Gen. 3:17). Now we pray for it to be blessed.

וִיהִי נֹֽעַם *May the pleasantness of the Lord:* Psalm 91 which follows immediately is known as the Psalm of Blessing and is the most famous of prayers for

fowler's snare and the deadly pestilence. With His pinions He will cover you, and beneath His wings you will find shelter; His faithfulness is an encircling shield. You need not fear terror by night, nor the arrow that flies by day; not the pestilence that stalks in darkness, nor the plague that ravages at noon. A thousand may fall at your side, ten thousand at your right hand, but it will not come near you. You will only look with your eyes and see the punishment of the wicked. Because you [have said:] "The LORD is my Refuge," taking the Most High as your shelter, no harm will befall you, no plague come near your tent, for He will command His angels about you, to guard you in all your ways. They will lift you in their hands, lest your foot stumble on a stone. You will tread on lions and vipers; you will trample on young lions and snakes. [God says:] "Because he loves Me, I will rescue him; I will protect him, because he acknowledges My name. When he calls on Me, I will answer him; I will be with him in distress, I will deliver him and bring him honor.
▸ With long life I will satisfy him and show him My salvation.
With long life I will satisfy him and show him My salvation.

▸ You are the Holy One, enthroned on the praises of Israel. *Ps. 22*
And [the angels] call to one another, saying, "Holy, holy, holy *Is. 6*
is the LORD of hosts; the whole world is filled with His glory."

And they receive permission from one another, saying: *Targum Yonatan Is. 6*
"Holy in the highest heavens, home of His Presence; holy on earth,
the work of His strength; holy for ever and all time is the LORD of hosts;
the whole earth is full of His radiant glory."

▸ Then a wind lifted me up and I heard behind me the sound of a *Ezek. 3*
great noise, saying, "Blessed is the LORD's glory from His place."

Then a wind lifted me up and I heard behind me *Targum Yonatan Ezek. 3*
the sound of a great tempest of those who uttered praise, saying,
"Blessed is the LORD's glory from the place of the home of His Presence."

The LORD shall reign for ever and all time. *Ex. 15*
The LORD's kingdom is established for ever and all time. *Targum Onkelos Ex. 15*

מִקֶּטֶב יָשׁוּד צָהֳרָיִם: יִפֹּל מִצִּדְּךָ אֶלֶף, וּרְבָבָה מִימִינֶךָ, אֵלֶיךָ
לֹא יִגָּשׁ: רַק בְּעֵינֶיךָ תַבִּיט, וְשִׁלֻּמַת רְשָׁעִים תִּרְאֶה: כִּי־אַתָּה
יהוה מַחְסִי, עֶלְיוֹן שַׂמְתָּ מְעוֹנֶךָ: לֹא־תְאֻנֶּה אֵלֶיךָ רָעָה, וְנֶגַע
לֹא־יִקְרַב בְּאָהֳלֶךָ: כִּי מַלְאָכָיו יְצַוֶּה־לָּךְ, לִשְׁמָרְךָ בְּכָל־דְּרָכֶיךָ:
עַל־כַּפַּיִם יִשָּׂאוּנְךָ, פֶּן־תִּגֹּף בָּאֶבֶן רַגְלֶךָ: עַל־שַׁחַל וָפֶתֶן תִּדְרֹךְ,
תִּרְמֹס כְּפִיר וְתַנִּין: כִּי בִי חָשַׁק וַאֲפַלְּטֵהוּ, אֲשַׂגְּבֵהוּ כִּי־יָדַע
שְׁמִי: יִקְרָאֵנִי וְאֶעֱנֵהוּ, עִמּוֹ אָנֹכִי בְצָרָה, אֲחַלְּצֵהוּ וַאֲכַבְּדֵהוּ:
◂ אֹרֶךְ יָמִים אַשְׂבִּיעֵהוּ, וְאַרְאֵהוּ בִּישׁוּעָתִי:
אֹרֶךְ יָמִים אַשְׂבִּיעֵהוּ, וְאַרְאֵהוּ בִּישׁוּעָתִי:

◂ וְאַתָּה קָדוֹשׁ יוֹשֵׁב תְּהִלּוֹת יִשְׂרָאֵל: וְקָרָא זֶה אֶל־זֶה וְאָמַר תהלים כב
קָדוֹשׁ, קָדוֹשׁ, קָדוֹשׁ, יהוה צְבָאוֹת, מְלֹא כָל־הָאָרֶץ כְּבוֹדוֹ: ישעיה ו
וּמְקַבְּלִין דֵּין מִן דֵּין וְאָמְרִין, קַדִּישׁ בִּשְׁמֵי מְרוֹמָא עִלָּאָה בֵּית שְׁכִינְתֵּהּ תרגום יונתן ישעיה ו
קַדִּישׁ עַל אַרְעָא עוֹבַד גְּבוּרְתֵּהּ, קַדִּישׁ לְעָלַם וּלְעָלְמֵי עָלְמַיָּא
יהוה צְבָאוֹת, מַלְיָא כָל אַרְעָא זִיו יְקָרֵהּ.

◂ וַתִּשָּׂאֵנִי רוּחַ, וָאֶשְׁמַע אַחֲרַי קוֹל רַעַשׁ גָּדוֹל יחזקאל ג
בָּרוּךְ כְּבוֹד־יהוה מִמְּקוֹמוֹ:
וּנְטָלַתְנִי רוּחָא, וּשְׁמָעִית בַּתְרַי קָל זִיעַ סַגִּיא, דִּמְשַׁבְּחִין וְאָמְרִין תרגום יונתן יחזקאל ג
בְּרִיךְ יְקָרָא דַיהוה מֵאֲתַר בֵּית שְׁכִינְתֵּהּ.

יהוה יִמְלֹךְ לְעֹלָם וָעֶד: שמות טו
יהוה מַלְכוּתֵהּ קָאֵם לְעָלַם וּלְעָלְמֵי עָלְמַיָּא. תרגום אונקלוס שמות טו

וְאַתָּה קָדוֹשׁ *You are the Holy One:* This prayer, with its parallels in the weekday morning and Shabbat afternoon services, was usually associated with periods of communal study. Its presence here may hark back to a time when it was customary to dedicate time to a period of study at the end of Shabbat.

יהוה Lord, God of Abraham, Isaac and Yisrael, our ancestors, may You keep this for ever so that it forms the thoughts in Your people's heart, and directs their heart toward You. He is compassionate. He forgives iniquity and does not destroy. Repeatedly He suppresses His anger, not rousing His full wrath. For You, my Lord, are good and forgiving, abundantly kind to all who call on You. Your righteousness is eternally righteous, and Your Torah is truth. Grant truth to Jacob, loving-kindness to Abraham, as You promised our ancestors in ancient times. Blessed is my Lord for day after day He burdens us [with His blessings]; God is our salvation, Selah! The Lord of hosts is with us; the God of Jacob is our refuge, Selah! Lord of hosts, happy is the one who trusts in You. Lord, save! May the King answer us on the day we call.

1 Chr. 29 *Ps. 78* *Ps. 86* *Ps. 119* *Micah 7* *Ps. 68* *Ps. 46* *Ps. 84* *Ps. 20*

בָּרוּךְ Blessed is He, our God, who created us for His glory, separating us from those who go astray; who gave us the Torah of truth, planting within us eternal life. May He open our heart to His Torah, imbuing our heart with the love and awe of Him, that we may do His will and serve Him with a perfect heart, so that we neither toil in vain nor give birth to confusion.

יְהִי רָצוֹן May it be Your will, O Lord our God and God of our ancestors, that we keep Your laws in this world, and thus be worthy to live, see and inherit goodness and blessing in the Messianic Age and in the life of the World to Come. So that my soul may sing to You and not be silent. Lord, my God, for ever I will thank You. Blessed is the man who trusts in the Lord, whose trust is in the Lord alone. Trust in the Lord for evermore, for God, the Lord, is an everlasting Rock. ▸ Those who know Your name trust in You, for You, Lord, do not forsake those who seek You. The Lord desired, for the sake of Israel's merit, to make the Torah great and glorious.

Ps. 30 *Jer. 17* *Is. 26* *Ps. 9* *Is. 42*

יהוה אֱלֹהֵי אַבְרָהָם יִצְחָק וְיִשְׂרָאֵל אֲבֹתֵינוּ, שָׁמְרָה־זֹּאת דברי הימים א׳ כט
לְעוֹלָם לְיֵצֶר מַחְשְׁבוֹת לְבַב עַמֶּךָ, וְהָכֵן לְבָבָם אֵלֶיךָ: וְהוּא תהלים עח
רַחוּם יְכַפֵּר עָוֹן וְלֹא־יַשְׁחִית, וְהִרְבָּה לְהָשִׁיב אַפּוֹ, וְלֹא־יָעִיר
כָּל־חֲמָתוֹ: כִּי־אַתָּה אֲדֹנָי טוֹב וְסַלָּח, וְרַב־חֶסֶד לְכָל־קֹרְאֶיךָ: תהלים פו
צִדְקָתְךָ צֶדֶק לְעוֹלָם וְתוֹרָתְךָ אֱמֶת: תִּתֵּן אֱמֶת לְיַעֲקֹב, חֶסֶד תהלים קיט מיכה ז
לְאַבְרָהָם, אֲשֶׁר־נִשְׁבַּעְתָּ לַאֲבֹתֵינוּ מִימֵי קֶדֶם: בָּרוּךְ אֲדֹנָי תהלים סח
יוֹם יוֹם יַעֲמָס־לָנוּ, הָאֵל יְשׁוּעָתֵנוּ סֶלָה: יהוה צְבָאוֹת עִמָּנוּ, תהלים מו
מִשְׂגָּב לָנוּ אֱלֹהֵי יַעֲקֹב סֶלָה: יהוה צְבָאוֹת, אַשְׁרֵי אָדָם בֹּטֵחַ תהלים פד
בָּךְ: יהוה הוֹשִׁיעָה, הַמֶּלֶךְ יַעֲנֵנוּ בְיוֹם־קָרְאֵנוּ: תהלים כ

בָּרוּךְ הוּא אֱלֹהֵינוּ שֶׁבְּרָאָנוּ לִכְבוֹדוֹ, וְהִבְדִּילָנוּ מִן הַתּוֹעִים, וְנָתַן לָנוּ תּוֹרַת אֱמֶת, וְחַיֵּי עוֹלָם נָטַע בְּתוֹכֵנוּ. הוּא יִפְתַּח לִבֵּנוּ בְּתוֹרָתוֹ, וְיָשֵׂם בְּלִבֵּנוּ אַהֲבָתוֹ וְיִרְאָתוֹ וְלַעֲשׂוֹת רְצוֹנוֹ וּלְעָבְדוֹ בְּלֵבָב שָׁלֵם, לְמַעַן לֹא נִיגַע לָרִיק וְלֹא נֵלֵד לַבֶּהָלָה.

יְהִי רָצוֹן מִלְּפָנֶיךָ יהוה אֱלֹהֵינוּ וֵאלֹהֵי אֲבוֹתֵינוּ, שֶׁנִּשְׁמֹר חֻקֶּיךָ
בָּעוֹלָם הַזֶּה, וְנִזְכֶּה וְנִחְיֶה וְנִרְאֶה וְנִירַשׁ טוֹבָה וּבְרָכָה, לִשְׁנֵי
יְמוֹת הַמָּשִׁיחַ וּלְחַיֵּי הָעוֹלָם הַבָּא. לְמַעַן יְזַמֶּרְךָ כָבוֹד וְלֹא יִדֹּם, תהלים ל
יהוה אֱלֹהַי, לְעוֹלָם אוֹדֶךָּ: בָּרוּךְ הַגֶּבֶר אֲשֶׁר יִבְטַח בַּיהוה, ירמיה יז
וְהָיָה יהוה מִבְטַחוֹ: בִּטְחוּ בַיהוה עֲדֵי־עַד, כִּי בְּיָהּ יהוה צוּר ישעיה כו
עוֹלָמִים: ‹ וְיִבְטְחוּ בְךָ יוֹדְעֵי שְׁמֶךָ, כִּי לֹא־עָזַבְתָּ דֹרְשֶׁיךָ, יהוה: תהלים ט
יהוה חָפֵץ לְמַעַן צִדְקוֹ, יַגְדִּיל תּוֹרָה וְיַאְדִּיר: ישעיה מב

FULL KADDISH

Leader: יִתְגַּדַּל Magnified and sanctified may His great name be,
in the world He created by His will.
May He establish His kingdom
in your lifetime and in your days,
and in the lifetime of all the house of Israel,
swiftly and soon –
and say: Amen.

All: May His great name be blessed for ever and all time.

Leader: Blessed and praised,
glorified and exalted,
raised and honored,
uplifted and lauded be
the name of the Holy One,
blessed be He,
beyond any blessing,
song, praise and consolation
uttered in the world –
and say: Amen.

On Purim and Tisha B'Av, omit the next verse and continue with "May there be great peace."

May the prayers and pleas of all Israel
be accepted by their Father in heaven –
and say: Amen.

May there be great peace from heaven,
and life for us and all Israel –
and say: Amen.

Bow, take three steps back, as if taking leave of the Divine Presence, then bow, first left, then right, then center, while saying:

May He who makes peace in His high places,
make peace for us and all Israel –
and say: Amen.

קדיש שלם

ש״ץ: יִתְגַּדַּל וְיִתְקַדַּשׁ שְׁמֵהּ רַבָּא (קהל: אָמֵן)
בְּעָלְמָא דִּי בְרָא כִרְעוּתֵהּ
וְיַמְלִיךְ מַלְכוּתֵהּ
בְּחַיֵּיכוֹן וּבְיוֹמֵיכוֹן וּבְחַיֵּי דְכָל בֵּית יִשְׂרָאֵל
בַּעֲגָלָא וּבִזְמַן קָרִיב, וְאִמְרוּ אָמֵן. (קהל: אָמֵן)

קהל וש״ץ: יְהֵא שְׁמֵהּ רַבָּא מְבָרַךְ לְעָלַם וּלְעָלְמֵי עָלְמַיָּא.

ש״ץ: יִתְבָּרַךְ וְיִשְׁתַּבַּח וְיִתְפָּאַר
וְיִתְרוֹמַם וְיִתְנַשֵּׂא וְיִתְהַדָּר וְיִתְעַלֶּה וְיִתְהַלָּל
שְׁמֵהּ דְּקֻדְשָׁא בְּרִיךְ הוּא (קהל: בְּרִיךְ הוּא)
לְעֵלָּא מִן כָּל בִּרְכָתָא
/בעשרת ימי תשובה: לְעֵלָּא לְעֵלָּא מִכָּל בִּרְכָתָא/
וְשִׁירָתָא, תֻּשְׁבְּחָתָא וְנֶחֱמָתָא
דַּאֲמִירָן בְּעָלְמָא, וְאִמְרוּ אָמֵן. (קהל: אָמֵן)

On פורים *and* תשעה באב*, omit the next verse and continue with* יְהֵא שְׁלָמָא.

תִּתְקַבַּל צְלוֹתְהוֹן וּבָעוּתְהוֹן דְּכָל יִשְׂרָאֵל
קֳדָם אֲבוּהוֹן דִּי בִשְׁמַיָּא, וְאִמְרוּ אָמֵן. (קהל: אָמֵן)

יְהֵא שְׁלָמָא רַבָּא מִן שְׁמַיָּא
וְחַיִּים, עָלֵינוּ וְעַל כָּל יִשְׂרָאֵל, וְאִמְרוּ אָמֵן. (קהל: אָמֵן)

Bow, take three steps back, as if taking leave of the Divine Presence, then bow, first left, then right, then center, while saying:

עֹשֶׂה שָׁלוֹם/בעשרת ימי תשובה: הַשָּׁלוֹם/ בִּמְרוֹמָיו
הוּא יַעֲשֶׂה שָׁלוֹם
עָלֵינוּ וְעַל כָּל יִשְׂרָאֵל, וְאִמְרוּ אָמֵן. (קהל: אָמֵן)

Between Pesaḥ and Shavuot the Omer is counted at this point on page 284.

On Ḥanukka, the candles are lit at this point, page 896.

On Tisha B'Av, the following prayers are omitted and the service continues with Aleinu on page 710.

BIBLICAL VERSES OF BLESSING

וְיִתֶּן־לְךָ May God give you dew from heaven and the richness of the earth, and corn and wine in plenty. May peoples serve you and nations bow down to you. Be lord over your brothers, and may your mother's sons bow down to you. A curse on those who curse you, but a blessing on those who bless you. *Gen. 27*

וְאֵל שַׁדַּי May God Almighty bless you; may He make you fruitful and numerous until you become an assembly of peoples. May He give you and your descendants the blessing of Abraham, that you may possess the land where you are now staying, the land God gave to Abraham. This comes from the God of your father – may He help you – and from the Almighty – may He bless you with blessings of the heaven above and the blessings of the deep that lies below, the blessings of breast and womb. The blessings of your father surpass the blessings of my fathers to the bounds of the endless hills. May they rest on the head of Joseph, on the brow of the prince among his brothers. He will love you and bless you and increase your numbers. He will bless the fruit of your womb and the fruit of your land: your corn, your wine and oil, the calves of your herds and the lambs of your flocks, in the land He swore to your fathers to give you. You will be blessed more than any other people. None of your men or women will be childless, nor any of your livestock without young. The LORD will keep you free from any disease. He will not inflict on you the terrible diseases you knew in Egypt, but He will inflict them on those who hate you. *Gen. 28* *Gen. 49* *Deut. 7*

הַמַּלְאָךְ May the angel who rescued me from all harm, bless these boys. May they be called by my name and the names of my fathers Abraham and Isaac, and may they increase greatly on the earth. The LORD your God has increased your numbers so that today you are as many as the stars in the sky. May the LORD, God of your fathers, increase you a thousand times, and bless you as He promised you. *Gen. 48* *Deut. 1*

---

to begin the next stage, confident in the knowledge that God is with us. They begin with the blessings of Isaac to Jacob, Jacob to Joseph and his brothers, and Moses' closing addresses to the Israelites in the book of Deuteronomy.

Between פסח *and* שבועות *the* עומר *is counted at this point on page 285.*

On חנוכה*, the candles are lit at this point, page 897.*

On תשעה באב*, the following prayers are omitted and the service continues with* עָלֵינוּ *on page 711.*

פסוקי ברכה

וְיִתֶּן־לְךָ הָאֱלֹהִים מִטַּל הַשָּׁמַיִם וּמִשְׁמַנֵּי הָאָרֶץ, וְרֹב דָּגָן וְתִירֹשׁ: יַעַבְדוּךָ בראשית כז
עַמִּים וְיִשְׁתַּחֲוֻ לְךָ לְאֻמִּים, הֱוֵה גְבִיר לְאַחֶיךָ וְיִשְׁתַּחֲווּ לְךָ בְּנֵי אִמֶּךָ,
אֹרְרֶיךָ אָרוּר וּמְבָרְכֶיךָ בָּרוּךְ:

וְאֵל שַׁדַּי יְבָרֵךְ אֹתְךָ וְיַפְרְךָ וְיַרְבֶּךָ, וְהָיִיתָ לִקְהַל עַמִּים: וְיִתֶּן־לְךָ אֶת־ בראשית כח
בִּרְכַּת אַבְרָהָם, לְךָ וּלְזַרְעֲךָ אִתָּךְ, לְרִשְׁתְּךָ אֶת־אֶרֶץ מְגֻרֶיךָ אֲשֶׁר־נָתַן
אֱלֹהִים לְאַבְרָהָם: מֵאֵל אָבִיךָ וְיַעְזְרֶךָּ וְאֵת שַׁדַּי וִיבָרְכֶךָּ, בִּרְכֹת שָׁמַיִם בראשית מט
מֵעָל בִּרְכֹת תְּהוֹם רֹבֶצֶת תָּחַת, בִּרְכֹת שָׁדַיִם וָרָחַם: בִּרְכֹת אָבִיךָ גָּבְרוּ
עַל־בִּרְכֹת הוֹרַי עַד־תַּאֲוַת גִּבְעֹת עוֹלָם, תִּהְיֶיןָ לְרֹאשׁ יוֹסֵף וּלְקָדְקֹד
נְזִיר אֶחָיו: וַאֲהֵבְךָ וּבֵרַכְךָ וְהִרְבֶּךָ, וּבֵרַךְ פְּרִי־בִטְנְךָ וּפְרִי־אַדְמָתֶךָ, דְּגָנְךָ דברים ז
וְתִירֹשְׁךָ וְיִצְהָרֶךָ, שְׁגַר־אֲלָפֶיךָ וְעַשְׁתְּרֹת צֹאנֶךָ, עַל הָאֲדָמָה אֲשֶׁר־נִשְׁבַּע
לַאֲבֹתֶיךָ לָתֶת לָךְ: בָּרוּךְ תִּהְיֶה מִכָּל־הָעַמִּים, לֹא־יִהְיֶה בְךָ עָקָר וַעֲקָרָה
וּבִבְהֶמְתֶּךָ: וְהֵסִיר יהוה מִמְּךָ כָּל־חֹלִי, וְכָל־מַדְוֵי מִצְרַיִם הָרָעִים אֲשֶׁר
יָדַעְתָּ, לֹא יְשִׂימָם בָּךְ, וּנְתָנָם בְּכָל־שֹׂנְאֶיךָ:

הַמַּלְאָךְ הַגֹּאֵל אֹתִי מִכָּל־רָע יְבָרֵךְ אֶת־הַנְּעָרִים, וְיִקָּרֵא בָהֶם שְׁמִי וְשֵׁם בראשית מח
אֲבֹתַי אַבְרָהָם וְיִצְחָק, וְיִדְגּוּ לָרֹב בְּקֶרֶב הָאָרֶץ: יהוה אֱלֹהֵיכֶם הִרְבָּה דברים א
אֶתְכֶם, וְהִנְּכֶם הַיּוֹם כְּכוֹכְבֵי הַשָּׁמַיִם לָרֹב: יהוה אֱלֹהֵי אֲבוֹתֵכֶם יֹסֵף
עֲלֵיכֶם כָּכֶם אֶלֶף פְּעָמִים, וִיבָרֵךְ אֶתְכֶם כַּאֲשֶׁר דִּבֶּר לָכֶם:

פסוקי ברכה *Biblical Verses of Blessing.* Setting out on a journey is a time to seek blessing and divine protection through the challenges that lie ahead, hence this long series of verses from Tanakh, including many of the blessings recorded in the Mosaic books. They are clustered around the themes of blessing, redemption and salvation; rescue and transformation; peace and consolation. Together they emphasize that time is a journey and we are about

בָּרוּךְ You will be blessed in the city, and blessed in the field. You will be blessed *Deut. 28* when you come in, and blessed when you go out. Your basket and your kneading trough will be blessed. The fruit of your womb will be blessed, and the crops of your land, and the young of your livestock, the calves of your herds and the lambs of your flocks. The LORD will send a blessing on your barns, and on everything you put your hand to. The LORD your God will bless you in the land He is giving you. The LORD will open for you the heavens, the storehouse of His bounty, to send rain on your land in season, and to bless all the work of your hands. You will lend to many nations but will borrow from none. For the LORD your God will bless you as He has promised: you will lend *Deut. 15* to many nations but will borrow from none. You will rule over many nations, but none will rule over you. Happy are you, Israel! Who is like you, a people *Deut. 33* saved by the LORD? He is your Shield and Helper and your glorious Sword. Your enemies will cower before you, and you will tread on their high places.

מָחִיתִי I have wiped away your transgressions like a cloud, your sins like the *Is. 44* morning mist. Return to Me for I have redeemed you. Sing for joy, O heavens, for the LORD has done this; shout aloud, you depths of the earth; burst into song, you mountains, you forests and all your trees, for the LORD has redeemed Jacob, and will glory in Israel. Our Redeemer, the LORD of hosts is *Is. 47* His name, the Holy One of Israel.

יִשְׂרָאֵל Israel is saved by the LORD with everlasting salvation. You will never *Is. 45* be ashamed or disgraced to time everlasting. You will eat your fill and praise *Joel 2* the name of the LORD your God, who has worked wonders for you. Never again shall My people be shamed. Then you will know that I am in the midst of Israel, that I am the LORD your God, and there is no other. Never again will My people be shamed. You will go out in joy and be led out in peace. The *Is. 55* mountains and hills will burst into song before you, and all the trees of the field will clap their hands. Behold, God is my salvation, I will trust and not *Is. 12* be afraid. The LORD, the LORD, is my strength and my song. He has become my salvation. With joy you will draw water from the springs of salvation. On that day you will say, "Thank the LORD, proclaim His name, make His deeds known among the nations." Declare that His name is exalted. Sing to the LORD, for He has done glorious things; let this be known throughout the world. Shout aloud and sing for joy, you who dwell in Zion, for great in your midst is the Holy One of Israel. On that day they will say, "See, this is our God; we *Is. 25* set our hope in Him and He saved us. This is the LORD in whom we hoped; let us rejoice and be glad in His salvation."

דברים כח בָּרוּךְ אַתָּה בָּעִיר, וּבָרוּךְ אַתָּה בַּשָּׂדֶה: בָּרוּךְ אַתָּה בְּבֹאֶךָ, וּבָרוּךְ אַתָּה
בְּצֵאתֶךָ: בָּרוּךְ טַנְאֲךָ וּמִשְׁאַרְתֶּךָ: בָּרוּךְ פְּרִי־בִטְנְךָ וּפְרִי אַדְמָתְךָ וּפְרִי
בְהֶמְתֶּךָ, שְׁגַר אֲלָפֶיךָ וְעַשְׁתְּרוֹת צֹאנֶךָ: יְצַו יהוה אִתְּךָ אֶת־הַבְּרָכָה
בַּאֲסָמֶיךָ וּבְכֹל מִשְׁלַח יָדֶךָ, וּבֵרַכְךָ בָּאָרֶץ אֲשֶׁר־יהוה אֱלֹהֶיךָ נֹתֵן לָךְ:
יִפְתַּח יהוה לְךָ אֶת־אוֹצָרוֹ הַטּוֹב אֶת־הַשָּׁמַיִם, לָתֵת מְטַר־אַרְצְךָ בְּעִתּוֹ,
דברים טו וּלְבָרֵךְ אֵת כָּל־מַעֲשֵׂה יָדֶךָ, וְהִלְוִיתָ גּוֹיִם רַבִּים וְאַתָּה לֹא תִלְוֶה: כִּי־יהוה
אֱלֹהֶיךָ בֵּרַכְךָ כַּאֲשֶׁר דִּבֶּר־לָךְ, וְהַעֲבַטְתָּ גּוֹיִם רַבִּים וְאַתָּה לֹא תַעֲבֹט,
דברים לג וּמָשַׁלְתָּ בְּגוֹיִם רַבִּים וּבְךָ לֹא יִמְשֹׁלוּ: אַשְׁרֶיךָ יִשְׂרָאֵל, מִי כָמוֹךָ, עַם
נוֹשַׁע בַּיהוה, מָגֵן עֶזְרֶךָ וַאֲשֶׁר־חֶרֶב גַּאֲוָתֶךָ, וְיִכָּחֲשׁוּ אֹיְבֶיךָ לָךְ, וְאַתָּה
עַל־בָּמוֹתֵימוֹ תִדְרֹךְ:

ישעיה מד מָחִיתִי כָעָב פְּשָׁעֶיךָ וְכֶעָנָן חַטֹּאותֶיךָ, שׁוּבָה אֵלַי כִּי גְאַלְתִּיךָ: רָנּוּ שָׁמַיִם
כִּי־עָשָׂה יהוה, הָרִיעוּ תַּחְתִּיּוֹת אָרֶץ, פִּצְחוּ הָרִים רִנָּה, יַעַר וְכָל־עֵץ בּוֹ,
ישעיה מז כִּי־גָאַל יהוה יַעֲקֹב וּבְיִשְׂרָאֵל יִתְפָּאָר: גֹּאֲלֵנוּ, יהוה צְבָאוֹת שְׁמוֹ, קְדוֹשׁ
יִשְׂרָאֵל:

ישעיה מה יִשְׂרָאֵל נוֹשַׁע בַּיהוה תְּשׁוּעַת עוֹלָמִים, לֹא־תֵבֹשׁוּ וְלֹא־תִכָּלְמוּ עַד־עוֹלְמֵי
יואל ב עַד: וַאֲכַלְתֶּם אָכוֹל וְשָׂבוֹעַ, וְהִלַּלְתֶּם אֶת־שֵׁם יהוה אֱלֹהֵיכֶם אֲשֶׁר־עָשָׂה
עִמָּכֶם לְהַפְלִיא, וְלֹא־יֵבֹשׁוּ עַמִּי לְעוֹלָם: וִידַעְתֶּם כִּי בְקֶרֶב יִשְׂרָאֵל
ישעיה נה אָנִי, וַאֲנִי יהוה אֱלֹהֵיכֶם וְאֵין עוֹד, וְלֹא־יֵבֹשׁוּ עַמִּי לְעוֹלָם: כִּי־בְשִׂמְחָה
תֵצֵאוּ וּבְשָׁלוֹם תּוּבָלוּן, הֶהָרִים וְהַגְּבָעוֹת יִפְצְחוּ לִפְנֵיכֶם רִנָּה, וְכָל־עֲצֵי
ישעיה יב הַשָּׂדֶה יִמְחֲאוּ־כָף: הִנֵּה אֵל יְשׁוּעָתִי אֶבְטַח, וְלֹא אֶפְחָד, כִּי־עָזִּי וְזִמְרָת
יָהּ יהוה, וַיְהִי־לִי לִישׁוּעָה: וּשְׁאַבְתֶּם־מַיִם בְּשָׂשׂוֹן, מִמַּעַיְנֵי הַיְשׁוּעָה:
וַאֲמַרְתֶּם בַּיּוֹם הַהוּא, הוֹדוּ לַיהוה קִרְאוּ בִשְׁמוֹ, הוֹדִיעוּ בָעַמִּים עֲלִילֹתָיו,
הַזְכִּירוּ כִּי נִשְׂגָּב שְׁמוֹ: זַמְּרוּ יהוה כִּי גֵאוּת עָשָׂה, מוּדַעַת זֹאת בְּכָל־
ישעיה כה הָאָרֶץ: צַהֲלִי וָרֹנִּי יוֹשֶׁבֶת צִיּוֹן, כִּי־גָדוֹל בְּקִרְבֵּךְ קְדוֹשׁ יִשְׂרָאֵל: וְאָמַר
בַּיּוֹם הַהוּא, הִנֵּה אֱלֹהֵינוּ זֶה קִוִּינוּ לוֹ וְיוֹשִׁיעֵנוּ, זֶה יהוה קִוִּינוּ לוֹ, נָגִילָה
וְנִשְׂמְחָה בִּישׁוּעָתוֹ:

בֵּית Come, house of Jacob: let us walk in the light of the LORD. He will be the sure foundation of your times; a rich store of salvation, wisdom and knowledge – the fear of the LORD is a person's treasure. In everything he did, David was successful, for the LORD was with him. *Is. 2* *Is. 32* *I Sam. 18*

פָּדָה He redeemed my soul in peace from the battle waged against me, for the sake of the many who were with me. The people said to Saul, "Shall Jonathan die – he who has brought about this great deliverance in Israel? Heaven forbid! As surely as the LORD lives, not a hair of his head shall fall to the ground, for he did this today with God's help." So the people rescued Jonathan and he did not die. Those redeemed by the LORD shall return; they will enter Zion singing; everlasting joy will crown their heads. Gladness and joy will overtake them, and sorrow and sighing will flee away. *Ps. 55* *I Sam. 14* *Is. 35*

הָפַכְתָּ You have turned my sorrow into dancing. You have removed my sackcloth and clothed me with joy. The LORD your God refused to listen to Balaam; instead the LORD your God turned the curse into a blessing, for the LORD your God loves you. Then maidens will dance and be glad; so too will young men and old together; I will turn their mourning into gladness; I will give them comfort and joy instead of sorrow. *Ps. 30* *Deut. 23* *Jer. 31*

בּוֹרֵא I create the speech of lips: Peace, peace to those far and near, says the LORD, and I will heal them. Then the spirit came upon Amasai, chief of the captains, and he said: "We are yours, David! We are with you, son of Jesse! Peace, peace to you, and peace to those who help you; for your God will help you." Then David received them and made them leaders of his troop. And you shall say: "To life! Peace be to you, peace to your household, and peace to all that is yours!" The LORD will give strength to His people; the LORD will bless His people with peace. *Is. 57* *I Chr. 12* *I Sam. 25* *Ps. 29*

אָמַר Rabbi Yoḥanan said: Wherever you find the greatness of the Holy One, blessed be He, there you find His humility. This is written in the Torah, repeated in the Prophets, and stated a third time in the Writings. It is written in the Torah: "For the LORD your God is God of gods and LORD of lords, the great, mighty and awe-inspiring God, who shows no favoritism and accepts no bribe." Immediately afterwards it is written, "He upholds the cause of the orphan and widow, and loves the stranger, giving him food and clothing." It is repeated in the Prophets, as it says: "So says the High and Exalted One, who lives for ever and whose name is Holy: I live in a high and holy place, but also with the contrite and lowly in spirit, to revive the spirit of the lowly, and to revive the heart of the *Megilla 31a* *Deut. 10* *Is. 57*

(*Megilla* 31a) telling us to learn from God that greatness is humility, and humility greatness. The Creator of all cares for all; the Power of powers cares for the powerless. The deeper our compassion, the higher we stand.

ישעיה ב ישעיה לב
בֵּית יַעֲקֹב לְכוּ וְנֵלְכָה בְּאוֹר יהוה: וְהָיָה אֱמוּנַת עִתֶּיךָ, חֹסֶן יְשׁוּעֹת חָכְמַת
שמואל א׳ יח
וָדָעַת, יִרְאַת יהוה הִיא אוֹצָרוֹ: וַיְהִי דָוִד לְכָל־דְּרָכָו מַשְׂכִּיל, וַיהוה עִמּוֹ:

תהלים נה שמואל א׳ יד
פָּדָה בְשָׁלוֹם נַפְשִׁי מִקְּרָב־לִי, כִּי־בְרַבִּים הָיוּ עִמָּדִי: וַיֹּאמֶר הָעָם אֶל־
שָׁאוּל, הֲיוֹנָתָן יָמוּת אֲשֶׁר עָשָׂה הַיְשׁוּעָה הַגְּדוֹלָה הַזֹּאת בְּיִשְׂרָאֵל,
חָלִילָה, חַי־יהוה אִם־יִפֹּל מִשַּׂעֲרַת רֹאשׁוֹ אַרְצָה, כִּי־עִם־אֱלֹהִים עָשָׂה
ישעיה לה
הַיּוֹם הַזֶּה, וַיִּפְדּוּ הָעָם אֶת־יוֹנָתָן וְלֹא־מֵת: וּפְדוּיֵי יהוה יְשֻׁבוּן וּבָאוּ צִיּוֹן
בְּרִנָּה, וְשִׂמְחַת עוֹלָם עַל־רֹאשָׁם, שָׂשׂוֹן וְשִׂמְחָה יַשִּׂיגוּ, וְנָסוּ יָגוֹן וַאֲנָחָה:

תהלים ל דברים כג
הָפַכְתָּ מִסְפְּדִי לְמָחוֹל לִי, פִּתַּחְתָּ שַׂקִּי, וַתְּאַזְּרֵנִי שִׂמְחָה: וְלֹא־אָבָה יהוה
אֱלֹהֶיךָ לִשְׁמֹעַ אֶל־בִּלְעָם, וַיַּהֲפֹךְ יהוה אֱלֹהֶיךָ לְּךָ אֶת־הַקְּלָלָה לִבְרָכָה,
ירמיה לא
כִּי אֲהֵבְךָ יהוה אֱלֹהֶיךָ: אָז תִּשְׂמַח בְּתוּלָה בְּמָחוֹל, וּבַחֻרִים וּזְקֵנִים יַחְדָּו,
וְהָפַכְתִּי אֶבְלָם לְשָׂשׂוֹן, וְנִחַמְתִּים, וְשִׂמַּחְתִּים מִיגוֹנָם:

ישעיה נז דברי הימים א׳ יב
בּוֹרֵא נִיב שְׂפָתָיִם, שָׁלוֹם שָׁלוֹם לָרָחוֹק וְלַקָּרוֹב אָמַר יהוה, וּרְפָאתִיו: וְרוּחַ
לָבְשָׁה אֶת־עֲמָשַׂי רֹאשׁ הַשָּׁלִישִׁים, לְךָ דָוִיד וְעִמְּךָ בֶן־יִשַׁי, שָׁלוֹם שָׁלוֹם
לְךָ וְשָׁלוֹם לְעֹזְרֶךָ, כִּי עֲזָרְךָ אֱלֹהֶיךָ, וַיְקַבְּלֵם דָּוִיד וַיִּתְּנֵם בְּרָאשֵׁי הַגְּדוּד:
שמואל א׳ כה תהלים כט
וַאֲמַרְתֶּם כֹּה לֶחָי, וְאַתָּה שָׁלוֹם וּבֵיתְךָ שָׁלוֹם וְכֹל אֲשֶׁר־לְךָ שָׁלוֹם: יהוה
עֹז לְעַמּוֹ יִתֵּן, יהוה יְבָרֵךְ אֶת־עַמּוֹ בַשָּׁלוֹם:

מגילה לא.
אָמַר רַבִּי יוֹחָנָן: בְּכָל מָקוֹם שֶׁאַתָּה מוֹצֵא גְּדֻלָּתוֹ שֶׁל הַקָּדוֹשׁ בָּרוּךְ
הוּא, שָׁם אַתָּה מוֹצֵא עַנְוְתָנוּתוֹ. דָּבָר זֶה כָּתוּב בַּתּוֹרָה, וְשָׁנוּי בַּנְּבִיאִים,
דברים י
וּמְשֻׁלָּשׁ בַּכְּתוּבִים. כָּתוּב בַּתּוֹרָה: כִּי יהוה אֱלֹהֵיכֶם הוּא אֱלֹהֵי הָאֱלֹהִים
וַאֲדֹנֵי הָאֲדֹנִים, הָאֵל הַגָּדֹל הַגִּבֹּר וְהַנּוֹרָא, אֲשֶׁר לֹא־יִשָּׂא פָנִים וְלֹא יִקַּח
שֹׁחַד: וּכְתִיב בַּתְרֵהּ: עֹשֶׂה מִשְׁפַּט יָתוֹם וְאַלְמָנָה, וְאֹהֵב גֵּר לָתֶת לוֹ לֶחֶם
ישעיה נז
וְשִׂמְלָה: שָׁנוּי בַּנְּבִיאִים, דִּכְתִיב: כִּי כֹה אָמַר רָם וְנִשָּׂא שֹׁכֵן עַד וְקָדוֹשׁ

פָּדָה *He redeemed my soul in peace:* There now follow three verses on the theme of redemption, three on transformation of fortune from bad to good, and three on peace. These three verses, according to the Talmud (*Berakhot* 55b), should be said to banish fear of misfortune.

אָמַר רַבִּי יוֹחָנָן *Rabbi Yoḥanan said:* A magnificent passage from the Talmud

contrite." It is stated a third time in the Writings: "Sing to God, make music for His name, extol Him who rides the clouds – the LORD is His name – and exult before Him." Immediately afterwards it is written: "Father of the orphans and Justice of widows, is God in His holy habitation." *Ps. 68*

יְהִי May the LORD our God be with us, as He was with our ancestors. May He never abandon us or forsake us. You who cleave to the LORD your God are all alive this day. For the LORD will comfort Zion, He will comfort all her ruins; He will make her wilderness like Eden, and her desert like a garden of the LORD. Joy and gladness will be found there, thanksgiving and the sound of singing. It pleased the LORD for the sake of [Israel's] righteousness to make the Torah great and glorious. *I Kings 8* *Deut. 4* *Is. 51* *Is. 42*

שִׁיר הַמַּעֲלוֹת A song of ascents. Happy are all who fear the LORD, who walk in His ways. When you eat the fruit of your labor, happy and fortunate are you. Your wife shall be like a fruitful vine within your house; your sons like olive saplings around your table. So shall the man who fears the LORD be blessed. May the LORD bless you from Zion; may you see the good of Jerusalem all the days of your life; and may you live to see your children's children. Peace be on Israel! *Ps. 128*

HAVDALA IN THE SYNAGOGUE

Some say the full Havdala on page 724.

On Motza'ei Yom Tov that is not a Motza'ei Shabbat, the blessings for the spices and flame are omitted. At the end of Yom Kippur, only the blessing for the spices is omitted. See laws 468, 471.

The Leader takes the cup of wine in his right hand, and says:

Please pay attention, my masters.

Blessed are You, LORD our God, King of the Universe, who creates the fruit of the vine.

Holding the spice box, the Leader says:

Blessed are You, LORD our God, King of the Universe, who creates the various spices.

The Leader smells the spices and puts the spice box down.
He lifts his hands toward the flame of the Havdala candle, and says:

Blessed are You, LORD our God, King of the Universe, who creates the lights of fire.

He lifts the cup of wine in his right hand, and says:

Blessed are You, LORD our God, King of the Universe, who distinguishes between sacred and secular, between light and darkness, between Israel and the nations, between the seventh day and the six days of work. Blessed are You, LORD, who distinguishes between sacred and secular.

שְׁמוֹ, מָרוֹם וְקָדוֹשׁ אֶשְׁכּוֹן, וְאֶת־דַּכָּא וּשְׁפַל־רוּחַ, לְהַחֲיוֹת רוּחַ שְׁפָלִים
וּלְהַחֲיוֹת לֵב נִדְכָּאִים: מְשֻׁלָּשׁ בִּכְתוּבִים, דִּכְתִיב: שִׁירוּ לֵאלֹהִים, זַמְּרוּ תהלים סח
שְׁמוֹ, סֹלּוּ לָרֹכֵב בָּעֲרָבוֹת בְּיָהּ שְׁמוֹ, וְעִלְזוּ לְפָנָיו: וּכְתִיב בָּתְרֵהּ: אֲבִי
יְתוֹמִים וְדַיַּן אַלְמָנוֹת, אֱלֹהִים בִּמְעוֹן קָדְשׁוֹ:

יְהִי יהוה אֱלֹהֵינוּ עִמָּנוּ כַּאֲשֶׁר הָיָה עִם־אֲבֹתֵינוּ, אַל־יַעַזְבֵנוּ וְאַל־יִטְּשֵׁנוּ: מלכים א׳ ח
וְאַתֶּם הַדְּבֵקִים בַּיהוה אֱלֹהֵיכֶם, חַיִּים כֻּלְּכֶם הַיּוֹם: כִּי־נִחַם יהוה צִיּוֹן, נִחַם דברים ד ישעיה נא
כָּל־חָרְבֹתֶיהָ, וַיָּשֶׂם מִדְבָּרָהּ כְּעֵדֶן וְעַרְבָתָהּ כְּגַן־יהוה, שָׂשׂוֹן וְשִׂמְחָה יִמָּצֵא
בָהּ, תּוֹדָה וְקוֹל זִמְרָה: יהוה חָפֵץ לְמַעַן צִדְקוֹ, יַגְדִּיל תּוֹרָה וְיַאְדִּיר: ישעיה מב

שִׁיר הַמַּעֲלוֹת, אַשְׁרֵי כָּל־יְרֵא יהוה, הַהֹלֵךְ בִּדְרָכָיו: יְגִיעַ כַּפֶּיךָ כִּי תֹאכֵל, תהלים קכח
אַשְׁרֶיךָ וְטוֹב לָךְ: אֶשְׁתְּךָ כְּגֶפֶן פֹּרִיָּה בְּיַרְכְּתֵי בֵיתֶךָ, בָּנֶיךָ כִּשְׁתִלֵי זֵיתִים,
סָבִיב לְשֻׁלְחָנֶךָ: הִנֵּה כִי־כֵן יְבֹרַךְ גָּבֶר יְרֵא יהוה: יְבָרֶכְךָ יהוה מִצִּיּוֹן, וּרְאֵה
בְּטוּב יְרוּשָׁלָםִ, כֹּל יְמֵי חַיֶּיךָ: וּרְאֵה־בָנִים לְבָנֶיךָ, שָׁלוֹם עַל־יִשְׂרָאֵל:

הבדלה בבית הכנסת

Some say the full הבדלה *on page 725.*

On מוצאי יום טוב *that is not a* מוצאי שבת*, the blessings for the spices and flame are omitted. At the end of* יום כפור*, only the blessing for the spices is omitted. See laws 468, 471.*

The שליח ציבור *takes the cup of wine in his right hand, and says:*

סַבְרִי מָרָנָן

בָּרוּךְ אַתָּה יהוה אֱלֹהֵינוּ מֶלֶךְ הָעוֹלָם, בּוֹרֵא פְּרִי הַגָּפֶן.

Holding the spice box, the שליח ציבור *says:*

בָּרוּךְ אַתָּה יהוה אֱלֹהֵינוּ מֶלֶךְ הָעוֹלָם, בּוֹרֵא מִינֵי בְשָׂמִים.

The שליח ציבור *smells the spices and puts the spice box down.*
He lifts his hands toward the flame of the הבדלה *candle, and says:*

בָּרוּךְ אַתָּה יהוה אֱלֹהֵינוּ מֶלֶךְ הָעוֹלָם, בּוֹרֵא מְאוֹרֵי הָאֵשׁ.

He lifts the cup of wine in his right hand, and says:

בָּרוּךְ אַתָּה יהוה אֱלֹהֵינוּ מֶלֶךְ הָעוֹלָם, הַמַּבְדִּיל בֵּין קֹדֶשׁ לְחֹל,
בֵּין אוֹר לְחֹשֶׁךְ, בֵּין יִשְׂרָאֵל לָעַמִּים, בֵּין יוֹם הַשְּׁבִיעִי לְשֵׁשֶׁת יְמֵי
הַמַּעֲשֶׂה. בָּרוּךְ אַתָּה יהוה, הַמַּבְדִּיל בֵּין קֹדֶשׁ לְחֹל.

Stand while saying Aleinu. Bow at ▾.

עָלֵינוּ It is our duty to praise the Master of all,
and ascribe greatness to the Author of creation,
who has not made us like the nations of the lands
nor placed us like the families of the earth;
who has not made our portion like theirs,
nor our destiny like all their multitudes.
(For they worship vanity and emptiness,
and pray to a god who cannot save.)
▾But we bow in worship and thank the Supreme King of kings,
the Holy One, blessed be He,
who extends the heavens and establishes the earth,
whose throne of glory is in the heavens above,
and whose power's Presence is in the highest of heights.
He is our God; there is no other.
Truly He is our King, there is none else, as it is written in His Torah:
"You shall know and take to heart this day that the LORD is God, *Deut. 4*
in heaven above and on earth below. There is no other."

Therefore, we place our hope in You, LORD our God,
that we may soon see the glory of Your power,
when You will remove abominations from the earth,
and idols will be utterly destroyed,
when the world will be perfected under the sovereignty of the Almighty,
when all humanity will call on Your name,
to turn all the earth's wicked toward You.
All the world's inhabitants will realize and know
that to You every knee must bow and every tongue swear loyalty.
Before You, LORD our God, they will kneel and bow down
and give honor to Your glorious name.
They will all accept the yoke of Your kingdom,
and You will reign over them soon and for ever.
For the kingdom is Yours, and to all eternity You will reign in glory,
as it is written in Your Torah:
"The LORD will reign for ever and ever." *Ex. 15*
▸ And it is said: "Then the LORD shall be King over all the earth; *Zech. 14*
on that day the LORD shall be One and His name One."

Stand while saying עָלֵינוּ*. Bow at* ‘.

עָלֵינוּ לְשַׁבֵּחַ לַאֲדוֹן הַכֹּל, לָתֵת גְּדֻלָּה לְיוֹצֵר בְּרֵאשִׁית
שֶׁלֹּא עָשָׂנוּ כְּגוֹיֵי הָאֲרָצוֹת, וְלֹא שָׂמָנוּ כְּמִשְׁפְּחוֹת הָאֲדָמָה
שֶׁלֹּא שָׂם חֶלְקֵנוּ כָּהֶם וְגוֹרָלֵנוּ כְּכָל הֲמוֹנָם.
(שֶׁהֵם מִשְׁתַּחֲוִים לְהֶבֶל וָרִיק וּמִתְפַּלְלִים אֶל אֵל לֹא יוֹשִׁיעַ.)
‘וַאֲנַחְנוּ כּוֹרְעִים וּמִשְׁתַּחֲוִים וּמוֹדִים
לִפְנֵי מֶלֶךְ מַלְכֵי הַמְּלָכִים, הַקָּדוֹשׁ בָּרוּךְ הוּא
שֶׁהוּא נוֹטֶה שָׁמַיִם וְיוֹסֵד אָרֶץ
וּמוֹשַׁב יְקָרוֹ בַּשָּׁמַיִם מִמַּעַל
וּשְׁכִינַת עֻזּוֹ בְּגָבְהֵי מְרוֹמִים.
הוּא אֱלֹהֵינוּ, אֵין עוֹד.
אֱמֶת מַלְכֵּנוּ, אֶפֶס זוּלָתוֹ, כַּכָּתוּב בְּתוֹרָתוֹ
וְיָדַעְתָּ הַיּוֹם וַהֲשֵׁבֹתָ אֶל־לְבָבֶךָ דברים ד
כִּי יהוה הוּא הָאֱלֹהִים בַּשָּׁמַיִם מִמַּעַל וְעַל־הָאָרֶץ מִתָּחַת, אֵין עוֹד:

עַל כֵּן נְקַוֶּה לְּךָ יהוה אֱלֹהֵינוּ, לִרְאוֹת מְהֵרָה בְּתִפְאֶרֶת עֻזֶּךָ
לְהַעֲבִיר גִּלּוּלִים מִן הָאָרֶץ, וְהָאֱלִילִים כָּרוֹת יִכָּרֵתוּן
לְתַקֵּן עוֹלָם בְּמַלְכוּת שַׁדַּי.
וְכָל בְּנֵי בָשָׂר יִקְרְאוּ בִשְׁמֶךָ לְהַפְנוֹת אֵלֶיךָ כָּל רִשְׁעֵי אָרֶץ.
יַכִּירוּ וְיֵדְעוּ כָּל יוֹשְׁבֵי תֵבֵל, כִּי לְךָ תִּכְרַע כָּל בֶּרֶךְ, תִּשָּׁבַע כָּל לָשׁוֹן.
לְפָנֶיךָ יהוה אֱלֹהֵינוּ יִכְרְעוּ וְיִפֹּלוּ, וְלִכְבוֹד שִׁמְךָ יְקָר יִתֵּנוּ
וִיקַבְּלוּ כֻלָּם אֶת עֹל מַלְכוּתֶךָ וְתִמְלֹךְ עֲלֵיהֶם מְהֵרָה לְעוֹלָם וָעֶד.
כִּי הַמַּלְכוּת שֶׁלְּךָ הִיא וּלְעוֹלְמֵי עַד תִּמְלֹךְ בְּכָבוֹד
כַּכָּתוּב בְּתוֹרָתֶךָ
יהוה יִמְלֹךְ לְעֹלָם וָעֶד: שמות טו
◂ וְנֶאֱמַר, וְהָיָה יהוה לְמֶלֶךְ עַל־כָּל־הָאָרֶץ זכריה יד
בַּיּוֹם הַהוּא יִהְיֶה יהוה אֶחָד וּשְׁמוֹ אֶחָד:

Some add:

Have no fear of sudden terror or of the ruin when it overtakes the wicked. *Prov. 3*
Devise your strategy, but it will be thwarted; propose your plan, *Is. 8*
but it will not stand, for God is with us. When you grow old, I will still be the same. *Is. 46*
When your hair turns gray, I will still carry you. I made you, I will bear you,
I will carry you, and I will rescue you.

MOURNER'S KADDISH

The following prayer, said by mourners, requires the presence of a minyan.
A transliteration can be found on page 1334.

Mourner: יִתְגַּדַּל Magnified and sanctified
may His great name be,
in the world He created by His will.
May He establish His kingdom
in your lifetime and in your days,
and in the lifetime of all the house of Israel,
swiftly and soon –
and say: Amen.

All: May His great name be blessed for ever and all time.

Mourner: Blessed and praised, glorified and exalted,
raised and honored, uplifted and lauded
be the name of the Holy One,
blessed be He,
beyond any blessing,
song, praise and consolation
uttered in the world –
and say: Amen.

May there be great peace from heaven,
and life for us and all Israel – and say: Amen.

Bow, take three steps back, as if taking leave of the Divine Presence,
then bow, first left, then right, then center, while saying:

May He who makes peace in His high places,
make peace for us and all Israel –
and say: Amen.

Some add:

אַל־תִּירָא מִפַּחַד פִּתְאֹם וּמִשֹּׁאַת רְשָׁעִים כִּי תָבֹא: משלי ג
עֻצוּ עֵצָה וְתֻפָר, דַּבְּרוּ דָבָר וְלֹא יָקוּם, כִּי עִמָּנוּ אֵל: ישעיה ח
וְעַד־זִקְנָה אֲנִי הוּא, וְעַד־שֵׂיבָה אֲנִי אֶסְבֹּל ישעיה מו
אֲנִי עָשִׂיתִי וַאֲנִי אֶשָּׂא וַאֲנִי אֶסְבֹּל וַאֲמַלֵּט:

קדיש יתום

The following prayer, said by mourners, requires the presence of a מנין.
A transliteration can be found on page 1334.

אבל: יִתְגַּדַּל וְיִתְקַדַּשׁ שְׁמֵהּ רַבָּא (קהל: אָמֵן)
בְּעָלְמָא דִּי בְרָא כִרְעוּתֵהּ
וְיַמְלִיךְ מַלְכוּתֵהּ
בְּחַיֵּיכוֹן וּבְיוֹמֵיכוֹן וּבְחַיֵּי דְכָל בֵּית יִשְׂרָאֵל
בַּעֲגָלָא וּבִזְמַן קָרִיב, וְאִמְרוּ אָמֵן. (קהל: אָמֵן)

קהל ואבל: יְהֵא שְׁמֵהּ רַבָּא מְבָרַךְ לְעָלַם וּלְעָלְמֵי עָלְמַיָּא.

אבל: יִתְבָּרַךְ וְיִשְׁתַּבַּח וְיִתְפָּאַר
וְיִתְרוֹמַם וְיִתְנַשֵּׂא וְיִתְהַדָּר וְיִתְעַלֶּה וְיִתְהַלָּל
שְׁמֵהּ דְּקֻדְשָׁא בְּרִיךְ הוּא (קהל: בְּרִיךְ הוּא)
לְעֵלָּא מִן כָּל בִּרְכָתָא / בעשרת ימי תשובה: לְעֵלָּא לְעֵלָּא מִכָּל בִּרְכָתָא/
וְשִׁירָתָא, תֻּשְׁבְּחָתָא וְנֶחֱמָתָא
דַּאֲמִירָן בְּעָלְמָא, וְאִמְרוּ אָמֵן. (קהל: אָמֵן)

יְהֵא שְׁלָמָא רַבָּא מִן שְׁמַיָּא
וְחַיִּים, עָלֵינוּ וְעַל כָּל יִשְׂרָאֵל, וְאִמְרוּ אָמֵן. (קהל: אָמֵן)

Bow, take three steps back, as if taking leave of the Divine Presence,
then bow, first left, then right, then center, while saying:

עֹשֶׂה שָׁלוֹם/ בעשרת ימי תשובה: הַשָּׁלוֹם / בִּמְרוֹמָיו
הוּא יַעֲשֶׂה שָׁלוֹם עָלֵינוּ וְעַל כָּל יִשְׂרָאֵל
וְאִמְרוּ אָמֵן. (קהל: אָמֵן)

From the second day of Rosh Ḥodesh Elul through Shemini Atzeret (in Israel through Hoshana Raba), the following psalm is said:

לְדָוִד By David. The LORD is my light and my salvation – whom then shall I fear? *Ps. 27*
The LORD is the stronghold of my life – of whom shall I be afraid? When evil men close in on me to devour my flesh, it is they, my enemies and foes, who stumble and fall. Should an army besiege me, my heart would not fear. Should war break out against me, still I would be confident. One thing I ask of the LORD, only this do I seek: to live in the House of the LORD all the days of my life, to gaze on the beauty of the LORD and worship in His Temple. For He will keep me safe in His pavilion on the day of trouble. He will hide me under the cover of His tent. He will set me high upon a rock. Now my head is high above my enemies who surround me. I will sacrifice in His tent with shouts of joy. I will sing and chant praises to the LORD. LORD, hear my voice when I call. Be gracious to me and answer me. On Your behalf my heart says, "Seek My face." Your face, LORD, will I seek. Do not hide Your face from me. Do not turn Your servant away in anger. You have been my help. Do not reject or forsake me, God, my Savior. Were my father and my mother to forsake me, the LORD would take me in. Teach me Your way, LORD, and lead me on a level path, because of my oppressors. Do not abandon me to the will of my foes, for false witnesses have risen against me, breathing violence.▸ Were it not for my faith that I shall see the LORD's goodness in the land of the living. Hope in the LORD. Be strong and of good courage, and hope in the LORD!

Mourner's Kaddish (previous page)

In a house of mourning the service continues on page 1060.

BLESSING OF THE NEW MOON

Kiddush Levana, the Blessing of the New Moon, is said between the third day and the middle day of each month. If possible, it should be said at the end of Shabbat, under the open sky, and in the presence of a minyan. See law 470.

הַלְלוּיָהּ Halleluya! Praise the LORD from the heavens, praise Him in *Ps. 148*
the heights. Praise Him, all His angels; praise Him, all His hosts. Praise Him, sun and moon; praise Him, all shining stars. Praise Him, highest heavens and the waters above the heavens. Let them praise the name of the LORD, for He commanded and they were created. He established them for ever and all time, issuing a decree that will never change.

---

a symbol of Jewish people who have seemed at times to face eclipse, yet they too have recovered and given light at dark times. Both themes are present in the Psalms and accompanying blessing. The physical act of stretching out on tiptoe to the moon is a gesture of faith that as the moon is beyond human reach and indestructible, so is the people it symbolizes.

From the second day of ראש חודש אלול *through* שמיני עצרת
(in ארץ ישראל *through* הושענא רבה*), the following psalm is said:*

תהלים כז לְדָוִד, יהוה אוֹרִי וְיִשְׁעִי, מִמִּי אִירָא, יהוה מָעוֹז־חַיַּי, מִמִּי אֶפְחָד: בִּקְרֹב עָלַי מְרֵעִים לֶאֱכֹל אֶת־בְּשָׂרִי, צָרַי וְאֹיְבַי לִי, הֵמָּה כָשְׁלוּ וְנָפָלוּ: אִם־תַּחֲנֶה עָלַי מַחֲנֶה, לֹא־יִירָא לִבִּי, אִם־תָּקוּם עָלַי מִלְחָמָה, בְּזֹאת אֲנִי בוֹטֵחַ: אַחַת שָׁאַלְתִּי מֵאֵת־יהוה, אוֹתָהּ אֲבַקֵּשׁ, שִׁבְתִּי בְּבֵית־יהוה כָּל־יְמֵי חַיַּי, לַחֲזוֹת בְּנֹעַם־יהוה, וּלְבַקֵּר בְּהֵיכָלוֹ: כִּי יִצְפְּנֵנִי בְּסֻכֹּה בְּיוֹם רָעָה, יַסְתִּרֵנִי בְּסֵתֶר אָהֳלוֹ, בְּצוּר יְרוֹמְמֵנִי: וְעַתָּה יָרוּם רֹאשִׁי עַל אֹיְבַי סְבִיבוֹתַי, וְאֶזְבְּחָה בְאָהֳלוֹ זִבְחֵי תְרוּעָה, אָשִׁירָה וַאֲזַמְּרָה לַיהוה: שְׁמַע־יהוה קוֹלִי אֶקְרָא, וְחָנֵּנִי וַעֲנֵנִי: לְךָ אָמַר לִבִּי בַּקְּשׁוּ פָנָי, אֶת־פָּנֶיךָ יהוה אֲבַקֵּשׁ: אַל־תַּסְתֵּר פָּנֶיךָ מִמֶּנִּי, אַל תַּט־בְּאַף עַבְדֶּךָ, עֶזְרָתִי הָיִיתָ, אַל־תִּטְּשֵׁנִי וְאַל־תַּעַזְבֵנִי, אֱלֹהֵי יִשְׁעִי: כִּי־אָבִי וְאִמִּי עֲזָבוּנִי, וַיהוה יַאַסְפֵנִי: הוֹרֵנִי יהוה דַּרְכֶּךָ, וּנְחֵנִי בְּאֹרַח מִישׁוֹר, לְמַעַן שׁוֹרְרָי: אַל־תִּתְּנֵנִי בְּנֶפֶשׁ צָרָי, כִּי קָמוּ־בִי עֵדֵי־שֶׁקֶר, וִיפֵחַ חָמָס: ◂ לוּלֵא הֶאֱמַנְתִּי לִרְאוֹת בְּטוּב־יהוה בְּאֶרֶץ חַיִּים: קַוֵּה אֶל־יהוה, חֲזַק וְיַאֲמֵץ לִבֶּךָ, וְקַוֵּה אֶל־יהוה:

קדיש יתום *(previous page)*

In a house of mourning the service continues on page 1061.

קידוש לבנה

קידוש לבנה*, the Blessing of the New Moon, is said between the third day and the middle day of each month. If possible, it should be said at the end of* שבת*, under the open sky, and in the presence of a* מנין*. See law 470.*

תהלים קמח הַלְלוּיָהּ, הַלְלוּ אֶת־יהוה מִן־הַשָּׁמַיִם, הַלְלוּהוּ בַּמְּרוֹמִים: הַלְלוּהוּ כָל־מַלְאָכָיו, הַלְלוּהוּ כָּל־צְבָאָו: הַלְלוּהוּ שֶׁמֶשׁ וְיָרֵחַ, הַלְלוּהוּ כָּל־כּוֹכְבֵי אוֹר: הַלְלוּהוּ שְׁמֵי הַשָּׁמָיִם, וְהַמַּיִם אֲשֶׁר מֵעַל הַשָּׁמָיִם: יְהַלְלוּ אֶת־שֵׁם יהוה, כִּי הוּא צִוָּה וְנִבְרָאוּ: וַיַּעֲמִידֵם לָעַד לְעוֹלָם, חָק־נָתַן וְלֹא יַעֲבוֹר:

These prayers, said on seeing the New Moon, have a dual dimension. First, they testify to the presence of God in creation. The regularity of the moon's waxing and waning are a visible reminder of the law-governed nature of the universe and the presence of an underlying order that surrounds us (Rabbenu Yonah). Second, the moon, endlessly reborn after seeming to decline, is

כִּי־אֶרְאֶה When I see Your heavens, the work of Your fingers, the moon and the stars which You have set in place: What is man that You are mindful of him, the son of man that You care for him? Ps. 8

Look at the moon, then say:

בָּרוּךְ Blessed are You, LORD our God, King of the Universe who by His word created the heavens, and by His breath all their host. He set for them laws and times, so that they should not deviate from their appointed task. They are joyous and glad to perform the will of their Owner, the Worker of truth whose work is truth. To the moon He said that it should renew itself as a crown of beauty for those He carried from the womb [Israel], for they are destined to be renewed like it, and to praise their Creator for the sake of His glorious majesty. Blessed are You, LORD, who renews the months.

The following five verses are each said three times:

Blessed is He who formed you; blessed is He who made you;
blessed is He who owns you; blessed is He who created you.

The following verse is said rising on the toes.

Just as I leap toward you but cannot touch you,
so may none of my enemies be able to touch me to do me harm.

May fear and dread fall upon them; Ex. 15
by the power of Your arm may they be still as stone.
May they be still as stone through the power of Your arm,
when dread and fear fall upon them.

David, King of Israel, lives and endures.

Turn to three people and say to each:

Peace upon you.

They respond:

Upon you, peace.

Say three times:

May it be a good sign and a good omen for us and all Israel. Amen.

קוֹל Hark! My beloved! Here he comes, leaping over the mountains, Song. 2
bounding over the hills. My beloved is like a gazelle, like a young deer. There he stands outside our wall, peering in through the windows, gazing through the lattice.

תהלים ח כִּי־אֶרְאֶה שָׁמֶיךָ מַעֲשֵׂה אֶצְבְּעֹתֶיךָ, יָרֵחַ וְכוֹכָבִים אֲשֶׁר כּוֹנָנְתָּה:
מָה־אֱנוֹשׁ כִּי־תִזְכְּרֶנּוּ, וּבֶן־אָדָם כִּי תִפְקְדֶנּוּ:

Look at the moon, then say:

בָּרוּךְ אַתָּה יהוה אֱלֹהֵינוּ מֶלֶךְ הָעוֹלָם, אֲשֶׁר בְּמַאֲמָרוֹ בָּרָא שְׁחָקִים,
וּבְרוּחַ פִּיו כָּל צְבָאָם, חֹק וּזְמַן נָתַן לָהֶם שֶׁלֹּא יְשַׁנּוּ אֶת תַּפְקִידָם.
שָׂשִׂים וּשְׂמֵחִים לַעֲשׂוֹת רְצוֹן קוֹנָם, פּוֹעֵל אֱמֶת שֶׁפְּעֻלָּתוֹ אֱמֶת.
וְלַלְּבָנָה אָמַר שֶׁתִּתְחַדֵּשׁ, עֲטֶרֶת תִּפְאֶרֶת לַעֲמוּסֵי בָטֶן, שֶׁהֵם
עֲתִידִים לְהִתְחַדֵּשׁ כְּמוֹתָהּ וּלְפָאֵר לְיוֹצְרָם עַל שֵׁם כְּבוֹד מַלְכוּתוֹ.
בָּרוּךְ אַתָּה יהוה, מְחַדֵּשׁ חֳדָשִׁים.

The following five verses are each said three times:

בָּרוּךְ יוֹצְרֵךְ, בָּרוּךְ עוֹשֵׂךְ, בָּרוּךְ קוֹנֵךְ, בָּרוּךְ בּוֹרְאֵךְ.

The following verse is said rising on the toes.

כְּשֵׁם שֶׁאֲנִי רוֹקֵד כְּנֶגְדֵּךְ וְאֵינִי יָכוֹל לִנְגֹּעַ בָּךְ
כָּךְ לֹא יוּכְלוּ כָּל אוֹיְבַי לִנְגֹּעַ בִּי לְרָעָה.

שמות טו תִּפֹּל עֲלֵיהֶם אֵימָתָה וָפַחַד, בִּגְדֹל זְרוֹעֲךָ יִדְּמוּ כָּאָבֶן:
כָּאָבֶן יִדְּמוּ זְרוֹעֲךָ בִּגְדֹל, וָפַחַד אֵימָתָה עֲלֵיהֶם תִּפֹּל.

דָּוִד מֶלֶךְ יִשְׂרָאֵל חַי וְקַיָּם.

Turn to three people and say to each:

שָׁלוֹם עֲלֵיכֶם.

They respond:

עֲלֵיכֶם שָׁלוֹם.

Say three times:

סִימָן טוֹב וּמַזָּל טוֹב יְהֵא לָנוּ וּלְכָל יִשְׂרָאֵל, אָמֵן.

שיר השירים ב קוֹל דּוֹדִי הִנֵּה־זֶה בָּא, מְדַלֵּג עַל־הֶהָרִים, מְקַפֵּץ עַל־הַגְּבָעוֹת:
דּוֹמֶה דוֹדִי לִצְבִי אוֹ לְעֹפֶר הָאַיָּלִים, הִנֵּה־זֶה עוֹמֵד אַחַר כָּתְלֵנוּ,
מַשְׁגִּיחַ מִן־הַחַלֹּנוֹת, מֵצִיץ מִן־הַחֲרַכִּים:

שִׁיר לַמַּעֲלוֹת A song of ascents. I lift my eyes up to the hills; from where will my help come? My help comes from the LORD, Maker of heaven and earth. He will not let your foot stumble; He who guards you does not slumber. See: the Guardian of Israel neither slumbers nor sleeps. The LORD is your Guardian; the LORD is your Shade at your right hand. The sun will not strike you by day, nor the moon by night. The LORD will guard you from all harm; He will guard your life. The LORD will guard your going and coming, now and for evermore. *Ps. 121*

הַלְלוּיָהּ Halleluya! Praise God in His holy place; praise Him in the heavens of His power. Praise Him for His mighty deeds; praise Him for His surpassing greatness. Praise Him with blasts of the ram's horn; praise Him with the harp and lyre. Praise Him with timbrel and dance; praise Him with strings and flute. Praise Him with clashing cymbals; praise Him with resounding cymbals. Let all that breathes praise the LORD. Halleluya! *Ps. 150*

תָּנָא In the academy of Rabbi Yishmael it was taught: Were the people of Israel privileged to greet the presence of their heavenly Father only once a month, it would have been sufficient for them. Abaye said: Therefore it [the blessing of the moon] should be said standing. Who is this coming up from the desert, leaning on her beloved? *Sanhedrin 42a* *Song. 8*

וִיהִי May it be Your will, LORD my God and God of my ancestors, to make good the deficiency of the moon, so that it is no longer in its diminished state. May the light of the moon be like the light of the sun and like the light of the seven days of creation as it was before it was diminished, as it says, "The two great luminaries." And may there be fulfilled for us the verse: "They shall seek the LORD their God, and David their king." Amen. *Gen. 1* *Hos. 3*

לַמְנַצֵּחַ For the conductor of music. With stringed instruments, a psalm. A song. May God be gracious to us and bless us. May He make His face shine on us, Selah. Then will Your way be known on earth, Your salvation among all the nations. Let the peoples praise You, God; let all peoples praise You. Let nations rejoice and sing for joy, for You judge the peoples with equity, and guide the nations of the earth, Selah. Let the peoples praise You, God; let all peoples praise You. The earth has yielded its harvest. May God, our God, bless us. God will bless us, and all the ends of the earth will fear Him. *Ps. 67*

תהלים קכא
שִׁיר לַמַּעֲלוֹת, אֶשָּׂא עֵינַי אֶל־הֶהָרִים, מֵאַיִן יָבֹא עֶזְרִי: עֶזְרִי מֵעִם יהוה, עֹשֵׂה שָׁמַיִם וָאָרֶץ: אַל־יִתֵּן לַמּוֹט רַגְלֶךָ, אַל־יָנוּם שֹׁמְרֶךָ: הִנֵּה לֹא־יָנוּם וְלֹא יִישָׁן, שׁוֹמֵר יִשְׂרָאֵל: יהוה שֹׁמְרֶךָ, יהוה צִלְּךָ עַל־יַד יְמִינֶךָ: יוֹמָם הַשֶּׁמֶשׁ לֹא־יַכֶּכָּה, וְיָרֵחַ בַּלָּיְלָה: יהוה יִשְׁמָרְךָ מִכָּל־רָע, יִשְׁמֹר אֶת־נַפְשֶׁךָ: יהוה יִשְׁמָר־צֵאתְךָ וּבוֹאֶךָ, מֵעַתָּה וְעַד־עוֹלָם:

תהלים קנ
הַלְלוּיָהּ, הַלְלוּ־אֵל בְּקָדְשׁוֹ, הַלְלוּהוּ בִּרְקִיעַ עֻזּוֹ: הַלְלוּהוּ בִגְבוּרֹתָיו, הַלְלוּהוּ כְּרֹב גֻּדְלוֹ: הַלְלוּהוּ בְּתֵקַע שׁוֹפָר, הַלְלוּהוּ בְּנֵבֶל וְכִנּוֹר: הַלְלוּהוּ בְתֹף וּמָחוֹל, הַלְלוּהוּ בְּמִנִּים וְעוּגָב: הַלְלוּהוּ בְצִלְצְלֵי־שָׁמַע, הַלְלוּהוּ בְּצִלְצְלֵי תְרוּעָה: כֹּל הַנְּשָׁמָה תְּהַלֵּל יָהּ, הַלְלוּיָהּ:

סנהדרין מב.
תָּנָא דְבֵי רַבִּי יִשְׁמָעֵאל: אִלְמָלֵי לֹא זָכוּ יִשְׂרָאֵל אֶלָּא לְהַקְבִּיל פְּנֵי אֲבִיהֶם שֶׁבַּשָּׁמַיִם פַּעַם אַחַת בַּחֹדֶשׁ, דַּיָּם. אָמַר אַבַּיֵּי: הִלְכָּךְ צָרִיךְ לְמֵימְרָא מְעֻמָּד. מִי זֹאת עֹלָה מִן־הַמִּדְבָּר, מִתְרַפֶּקֶת עַל־דּוֹדָהּ: שיר השירים ח

וִיהִי רָצוֹן מִלְּפָנֶיךָ יהוה אֱלֹהַי וֵאלֹהֵי אֲבוֹתַי, לְמַלֹּאת פְּגִימַת הַלְּבָנָה וְלֹא יִהְיֶה בָּהּ שׁוּם מִעוּט. וִיהִי אוֹר הַלְּבָנָה כְּאוֹר הַחַמָּה וּכְאוֹר שִׁבְעַת יְמֵי בְרֵאשִׁית, כְּמוֹ שֶׁהָיְתָה קֹדֶם מִעוּטָהּ, שֶׁנֶּאֱמַר: אֶת־שְׁנֵי הַמְּאֹרֹת הַגְּדֹלִים: וְיִתְקַיֵּם בָּנוּ מִקְרָא שֶׁכָּתוּב: וּבִקְשׁוּ אֶת־יהוה אֱלֹהֵיהֶם וְאֵת דָּוִיד מַלְכָּם: אָמֵן. בראשית א הושע ג

תהלים סז
לַמְנַצֵּחַ בִּנְגִינֹת, מִזְמוֹר שִׁיר: אֱלֹהִים יְחָנֵּנוּ וִיבָרְכֵנוּ, יָאֵר פָּנָיו אִתָּנוּ סֶלָה: לָדַעַת בָּאָרֶץ דַּרְכֶּךָ, בְּכָל־גּוֹיִם יְשׁוּעָתֶךָ: יוֹדוּךָ עַמִּים אֱלֹהִים, יוֹדוּךָ עַמִּים כֻּלָּם: יִשְׂמְחוּ וִירַנְּנוּ לְאֻמִּים, כִּי־תִשְׁפֹּט עַמִּים מִישֹׁר, וּלְאֻמִּים בָּאָרֶץ תַּנְחֵם סֶלָה: יוֹדוּךָ עַמִּים אֱלֹהִים, יוֹדוּךָ עַמִּים כֻּלָּם: אֶרֶץ נָתְנָה יְבוּלָהּ, יְבָרְכֵנוּ אֱלֹהִים אֱלֹהֵינוּ: יְבָרְכֵנוּ אֱלֹהִים, וְיִירְאוּ אוֹתוֹ כָּל־אַפְסֵי־אָרֶץ:

Stand while saying Aleinu. Bow at ▾.

עָלֵינוּ It is our duty to praise the Master of all, and ascribe greatness to the Author of creation, who has not made us like the nations of the lands nor placed us like the families of the earth; who has not made our portion like theirs, nor our destiny like all their multitudes. (For they worship vanity and emptiness, and pray to a god who cannot save.) ▾But we bow in worship and thank the Supreme King of kings, the Holy One, blessed be He, who extends the heavens and establishes the earth, whose throne of glory is in the heavens above, and whose power's Presence is in the highest of heights. He is our God; there is no other. Truly He is our King, there is none else, as it is written in His Torah: "You shall know and take to heart this day that the LORD is God, in heaven above and on earth below. There is no other." *Deut. 4*

Therefore, we place our hope in You, LORD our God, that we may soon see the glory of Your power, when You will remove abominations from the earth, and idols will be utterly destroyed, when the world will be perfected under the sovereignty of the Almighty, when all humanity will call on Your name, to turn all the earth's wicked toward You. All the world's inhabitants will realize and know that to You every knee must bow and every tongue swear loyalty. Before You, LORD our God, they will kneel and bow down and give honor to Your glorious name. They will all accept the yoke of Your kingdom, and You will reign over them soon and for ever. For the kingdom is Yours, and to all eternity You will reign in glory, as it is written in Your Torah: "The LORD will reign for ever and ever." *Ex. 15* ▸ And it is said: "Then the LORD shall be King over all the earth; on that day the LORD shall be One and His name One." *Zech. 14*

Some add:

Have no fear of sudden terror or of the ruin when it overtakes the wicked. *Prov. 3* Devise your strategy, but it will be thwarted; propose your plan, but it will not stand, for God is with us. *Is. 8* When you grow old, I will still be the same. When your hair turns gray, I will still carry you. I made you, I will bear you, I will carry you, and I will rescue you. *Is. 46*

MOURNER'S KADDISH

The following prayer, said by mourners, requires the presence of a minyan.
A transliteration can be found on page 1334.

Mourner: יִתְגַּדַּל Magnified and sanctified may His great name be,
in the world He created by His will.
May He establish His kingdom
in your lifetime and in your days,
and in the lifetime of all the house of Israel,
swiftly and soon – and say: Amen.

Stand while saying עָלֵינוּ. *Bow at* ◆.

עָלֵינוּ לְשַׁבֵּחַ לַאֲדוֹן הַכֹּל, לָתֵת גְּדֻלָּה לְיוֹצֵר בְּרֵאשִׁית, שֶׁלֹּא עָשָׂנוּ כְּגוֹיֵי הָאֲרָצוֹת, וְלֹא שָׂמָנוּ כְּמִשְׁפְּחוֹת הָאֲדָמָה, שֶׁלֹּא שָׂם חֶלְקֵנוּ כָּהֶם וְגוֹרָלֵנוּ כְּכָל הֲמוֹנָם. (שֶׁהֵם מִשְׁתַּחֲוִים לְהֶבֶל וָרִיק וּמִתְפַּלְלִים אֶל אֵל לֹא יוֹשִׁיעַ.) ◆וַאֲנַחְנוּ כּוֹרְעִים וּמִשְׁתַּחֲוִים וּמוֹדִים, לִפְנֵי מֶלֶךְ מַלְכֵי הַמְּלָכִים, הַקָּדוֹשׁ בָּרוּךְ הוּא, שֶׁהוּא נוֹטֶה שָׁמַיִם וְיוֹסֵד אָרֶץ, וּמוֹשַׁב יְקָרוֹ בַּשָּׁמַיִם מִמַּעַל, וּשְׁכִינַת עֻזּוֹ בְּגָבְהֵי מְרוֹמִים. הוּא אֱלֹהֵינוּ, אֵין עוֹד. אֱמֶת מַלְכֵּנוּ, אֶפֶס זוּלָתוֹ, כַּכָּתוּב בְּתוֹרָתוֹ, וְיָדַעְתָּ הַיּוֹם וַהֲשֵׁבֹתָ אֶל־לְבָבֶךָ, כִּי יהוה הוּא הָאֱלֹהִים בַּשָּׁמַיִם מִמַּעַל וְעַל־הָאָרֶץ מִתָּחַת, אֵין עוֹד: דברים ד

עַל כֵּן נְקַוֶּה לְּךָ יהוה אֱלֹהֵינוּ, לִרְאוֹת מְהֵרָה בְּתִפְאֶרֶת עֻזֶּךָ, לְהַעֲבִיר גִּלּוּלִים מִן הָאָרֶץ, וְהָאֱלִילִים כָּרוֹת יִכָּרֵתוּן, לְתַקֵּן עוֹלָם בְּמַלְכוּת שַׁדַּי. וְכָל בְּנֵי בָשָׂר יִקְרְאוּ בִשְׁמֶךָ לְהַפְנוֹת אֵלֶיךָ כָּל רִשְׁעֵי אָרֶץ. יַכִּירוּ וְיֵדְעוּ כָּל יוֹשְׁבֵי תֵבֵל, כִּי לְךָ תִּכְרַע כָּל בֶּרֶךְ, תִּשָּׁבַע כָּל לָשׁוֹן. לְפָנֶיךָ יהוה אֱלֹהֵינוּ יִכְרְעוּ וְיִפֹּלוּ, וְלִכְבוֹד שִׁמְךָ יְקָר יִתֵּנוּ, וִיקַבְּלוּ כֻלָּם אֶת עֹל מַלְכוּתֶךָ וְתִמְלֹךְ עֲלֵיהֶם מְהֵרָה לְעוֹלָם וָעֶד. כִּי הַמַּלְכוּת שֶׁלְּךָ הִיא וּלְעוֹלְמֵי עַד תִּמְלֹךְ בְּכָבוֹד, כַּכָּתוּב בְּתוֹרָתֶךָ, יהוה יִמְלֹךְ לְעֹלָם וָעֶד: ◂ וְנֶאֱמַר, וְהָיָה יהוה לְמֶלֶךְ עַל־כָּל־הָאָרֶץ, בַּיּוֹם הַהוּא יִהְיֶה יהוה אֶחָד וּשְׁמוֹ אֶחָד: שמות טו / זכריה יד

Some add:

אַל־תִּירָא מִפַּחַד פִּתְאֹם וּמִשֹּׁאַת רְשָׁעִים כִּי תָבֹא: עֻצוּ עֵצָה וְתֻפָר, דַּבְּרוּ דָבָר וְלֹא יָקוּם, כִּי עִמָּנוּ אֵל: וְעַד־זִקְנָה אֲנִי הוּא, וְעַד־שֵׂיבָה אֲנִי אֶסְבֹּל, אֲנִי עָשִׂיתִי וַאֲנִי אֶשָּׂא וַאֲנִי אֶסְבֹּל וַאֲמַלֵּט: משלי ג / ישעיה ח / ישעיה מו

קדיש יתום

The following prayer, said by mourners, requires the presence of a מנין*.*
A transliteration can be found on page 1334.

אבל: יִתְגַּדַּל וְיִתְקַדַּשׁ שְׁמֵהּ רַבָּא (קהל: אָמֵן)
בְּעָלְמָא דִּי בְרָא כִרְעוּתֵהּ
וְיַמְלִיךְ מַלְכוּתֵהּ
בְּחַיֵּיכוֹן וּבְיוֹמֵיכוֹן וּבְחַיֵּי דְכָל בֵּית יִשְׂרָאֵל
בַּעֲגָלָא וּבִזְמַן קָרִיב, וְאִמְרוּ אָמֵן. (קהל: אָמֵן)

All: May His great name be blessed for ever and all time.

Mourner: Blessed and praised,
glorified and exalted,
raised and honored,
uplifted and lauded
be the name of the Holy One,
blessed be He,
beyond any blessing,
song, praise and consolation
uttered in the world –
and say: Amen.

May there be great peace from heaven,
and life for us and all Israel –
and say: Amen.

Bow, take three steps back, as if taking leave of the Divine Presence, then bow, first left, then right, then center, while saying:

May He who makes peace in His high places,
make peace for us and all Israel –
and say: Amen.

All sing:

טוֹבִים Good are the radiant stars our God created;
He formed them with knowledge,
understanding and deliberation.
He gave them strength and might
to rule throughout the world.

Full of splendor, radiating light,
beautiful is their splendor throughout the world.
Glad as they go forth, joyous as they return,
they fulfill with awe their Creator's will.

Glory and honor they give to His name,
jubilation and song at the mention of His majesty.
He called the sun into being and it shone with light.
He looked and fashioned the form of the moon.

קהל ואבל: יְהֵא שְׁמֵהּ רַבָּא מְבָרַךְ לְעָלַם וּלְעָלְמֵי עָלְמַיָּא.

אבל: יִתְבָּרַךְ וְיִשְׁתַּבַּח וְיִתְפָּאַר
וְיִתְרוֹמַם וְיִתְנַשֵּׂא וְיִתְהַדָּר וְיִתְעַלֶּה וְיִתְהַלָּל
שְׁמֵהּ דְּקֻדְשָׁא בְּרִיךְ הוּא (קהל: בְּרִיךְ הוּא)
לְעֵלָּא מִן כָּל בִּרְכָתָא
/בעשרת ימי תשובה: לְעֵלָּא לְעֵלָּא מִכָּל בִּרְכָתָא/
וְשִׁירָתָא, תֻּשְׁבְּחָתָא וְנֶחֱמָתָא
דַּאֲמִירָן בְּעָלְמָא
וְאִמְרוּ אָמֵן. (קהל: אָמֵן)
יְהֵא שְׁלָמָא רַבָּא מִן שְׁמַיָּא
וְחַיִּים, עָלֵינוּ וְעַל כָּל יִשְׂרָאֵל
וְאִמְרוּ אָמֵן. (קהל: אָמֵן)

Bow, take three steps back, as if taking leave of the Divine Presence, then bow, first left, then right, then center, while saying:

עֹשֶׂה שָׁלוֹם/בעשרת ימי תשובה: הַשָּׁלוֹם/ בִּמְרוֹמָיו
הוּא יַעֲשֶׂה שָׁלוֹם עָלֵינוּ וְעַל כָּל יִשְׂרָאֵל
וְאִמְרוּ אָמֵן. (קהל: אָמֵן)

All sing:

טוֹבִים מְאוֹרוֹת שֶׁבָּרָא אֱלֹהֵינוּ, יְצָרָם בְּדַעַת בְּבִינָה וּבְהַשְׂכֵּל
כֹּחַ וּגְבוּרָה נָתַן בָּהֶם, לִהְיוֹת מוֹשְׁלִים בְּקֶרֶב תֵּבֵל.

מְלֵאִים זִיו וּמְפִיקִים נֹגַהּ, נָאֶה זִיוָם בְּכָל הָעוֹלָם
שְׂמֵחִים בְּצֵאתָם וְשָׂשִׂים בְּבוֹאָם, עוֹשִׂים בְּאֵימָה רְצוֹן קוֹנָם.

פְּאֵר וְכָבוֹד נוֹתְנִים לִשְׁמוֹ, צָהֳלָה וְרִנָּה לְזֵכֶר מַלְכוּתוֹ
קָרָא לַשֶּׁמֶשׁ וַיִּזְרַח אוֹר, רָאָה וְהִתְקִין צוּרַת הַלְּבָנָה.

HAVDALA AT HOME

On Motza'ei Yom Tov that is not a Motza'ei Shabbat, the first paragraph and the blessings for the spices and flame are omitted. At the end of Yom Kippur, only the blessing for the spices is omitted. See law 471.

Taking a cup of wine in the right hand, say:

הִנֵּה Behold, God is my salvation. I will trust and not be afraid. *Is. 12*
The LORD, the LORD, is my strength and my song.
He has become my salvation.
With joy you will draw water from the springs of salvation.
Salvation is the LORD's; on Your people is Your blessing, Selah. *Ps. 3*
The LORD of hosts is with us, the God of Jacob is our stronghold, Selah. *Ps. 46*
LORD of hosts: happy is the one who trusts in You. *Ps. 84*
LORD, save! May the King answer us on the day we call. *Ps. 20*
For the Jews there was light and gladness, joy and honor – so may it be for us. *Esther 8*
I will lift the cup of salvation and call on the name of the LORD. *Ps. 116*

When making Havdala for others, add:
Please pay attention, my masters.
Blessed are You, LORD our God, King of the Universe,
who creates the fruit of the vine.

Hold the spice box and say:

Blessed are You, LORD our God, King of the Universe,
who creates the various spices.

Smell the spices and put the spice box down.
Lift the hands toward the flame of the Havdala candle and say:

Blessed are You, LORD our God, King of the Universe,
who creates the lights of fire.

Holding the cup of wine again in the right hand, say:

בָּרוּךְ Blessed are You, LORD our God, King of the Universe, who distinguishes between sacred and secular, between light and darkness, between Israel and the nations, between the seventh day and the six days of work. Blessed are You, LORD, who distinguishes between sacred and secular.

On Sukkot, if Havdala is made in the sukka, add:
Blessed are You, LORD our God, King of the Universe,
who has made us holy through his commandments
and has commanded us to dwell in the sukka.

HAVDALA
Havdala is to the end of Shabbat what Kiddush is to the beginning: the marking of a transition from secular to holy time and vice versa. It is our way of

סדר הבדלה בבית

On מוצאי יום טוב that is not a מוצאי שבת, the first paragraph and the blessings for the spices and flame are omitted. At the end of יום כפור, only the blessing for the spices is omitted. See law 471.

Taking a cup of wine in the right hand, say:

ישעיה יב הִנֵּה אֵל יְשׁוּעָתִי אֶבְטַח, וְלֹא אֶפְחָד
כִּי־עָזִּי וְזִמְרָת יָהּ יהוה, וַיְהִי־לִי לִישׁוּעָה:
וּשְׁאַבְתֶּם־מַיִם בְּשָׂשׂוֹן, מִמַּעַיְנֵי הַיְשׁוּעָה:
תהלים ג לַיהוה הַיְשׁוּעָה, עַל־עַמְּךָ בִרְכָתֶךָ סֶּלָה:
תהלים מו יהוה צְבָאוֹת עִמָּנוּ, מִשְׂגָּב לָנוּ אֱלֹהֵי יַעֲקֹב סֶלָה:
תהלים פד יהוה צְבָאוֹת, אַשְׁרֵי אָדָם בֹּטֵחַ בָּךְ:
תהלים כ יהוה הוֹשִׁיעָה, הַמֶּלֶךְ יַעֲנֵנוּ בְיוֹם־קָרְאֵנוּ:
אסתר ח לַיְּהוּדִים הָיְתָה אוֹרָה וְשִׂמְחָה וְשָׂשֹׂן וִיקָר: כֵּן תִּהְיֶה לָּנוּ.
תהלים קטז כּוֹס־יְשׁוּעוֹת אֶשָּׂא, וּבְשֵׁם יהוה אֶקְרָא:

When making הבדלה for others, add:

סַבְרִי מָרָנָן

בָּרוּךְ אַתָּה יהוה אֱלֹהֵינוּ מֶלֶךְ הָעוֹלָם, בּוֹרֵא פְּרִי הַגָּפֶן.

Hold the spice box and say:

בָּרוּךְ אַתָּה יהוה אֱלֹהֵינוּ מֶלֶךְ הָעוֹלָם, בּוֹרֵא מִינֵי בְשָׂמִים.

Smell the spices and put the spice box down.
Lift the hands toward the flame of the הבדלה candle and say:

בָּרוּךְ אַתָּה יהוה אֱלֹהֵינוּ מֶלֶךְ הָעוֹלָם, בּוֹרֵא מְאוֹרֵי הָאֵשׁ.

Holding the cup of wine again in the right hand, say:

בָּרוּךְ אַתָּה יהוה אֱלֹהֵינוּ מֶלֶךְ הָעוֹלָם, הַמַּבְדִּיל בֵּין קֹדֶשׁ לְחֹל, בֵּין אוֹר לְחֹשֶׁךְ, בֵּין יִשְׂרָאֵל לָעַמִּים, בֵּין יוֹם הַשְּׁבִיעִי לְשֵׁשֶׁת יְמֵי הַמַּעֲשֶׂה. בָּרוּךְ אַתָּה יהוה, הַמַּבְדִּיל בֵּין קֹדֶשׁ לְחֹל.

On סוכות, if הבדלה is made in the סוכה, add:

בָּרוּךְ אַתָּה יהוה אֱלֹהֵינוּ מֶלֶךְ הָעוֹלָם
אֲשֶׁר קִדְּשָׁנוּ בְּמִצְוֹתָיו וְצִוָּנוּ לֵישֵׁב בַּסֻּכָּה.

הַמַּבְדִּיל He who distinguishes between sacred and secular,
may He forgive our sins.
May He multiply our offspring and wealth like the sand,
and like the stars at night.

The day has passed like a palm tree's shadow; I call on God to fulfill what the watchman said: "Morning comes, though now it is night." *Is. 21*

Your righteousness is as high as Mount Tabor. May You pass high over my sins.
[Let them be] like yesterday when it has passed, like a watch in the night. *Ps. 90*

The time of offerings has passed. Would that I might rest.
I am weary with my sighing, every night I drench [with tears]. *Ps. 6*

Hear my voice; let it not be cast aside. Open for me the lofty gate.
My head is filled with the dew of dawn, my hair with raindrops of the night. *Song. 5*

Heed my prayer, revered and awesome God. When I cry, grant me deliverance *Prov. 7*
at twilight, as the day fades, or in the darkness of the night.

I call to You, Lord: Save me. Make known to me the path of life.
Rescue me from misery before day turns to night.

Cleanse the defilement of my deeds, lest those who torment me say,
"Where is the God who made me, who gives cause for songs in the night?" *Job 35*

We are in Your hands like clay: please forgive our sins, light and grave.
Day to day they pour forth speech,
and night to night [they communicate knowledge].

---

light, so He taught humans how to make light – inviting them to become "His partners in the work of creation."

One of the key verbs in Genesis 1 is *b-d-l*, "to separate, distinguish, divide" – the root of the word *Havdala*. It appears five times in the chapter. By inviting human beings to engage in Havdala at the end of Shabbat, God invites us to create worlds. Creation involves the ability to make distinctions, to rescue order from chaos, to respect the integrity of creation. Havdala is thus not only a human blessing over the end of the day of rest, but as it were a divine blessing over the days of work. The Creator invites us to be creative – but always and only in a way that respects differences and distinctions, the laws of nature and the moral law. The message of Havdala is: if we respect the integrity of boundaries, we can turn chaos into order, darkness into light.

הַמַּבְדִּיל *He who distinguishes:* As we welcomed the arrival of Shabbat in song, so we bid our farewell to it in song. This beautiful hymn, originally part of the *Ne'ila* service on Yom Kippur, was composed by Isaac ibn Ḥayat (1030–1089).

הַמַּבְדִּיל בֵּין קֹדֶשׁ לְחֹל, חַטֹּאתֵינוּ הוּא יִמְחֹל
זַרְעֵנוּ וְכַסְפֵּנוּ יַרְבֶּה כַחוֹל וְכַכּוֹכָבִים בַּלָּיְלָה.

יוֹם פָּנָה כְּצֵל תֹּמֶר, אֶקְרָא לָאֵל עָלַי גּוֹמֵר
אָמַר שֹׁמֵר, אָתָא בֹקֶר וְגַם־לָיְלָה: ישעיה כא

צִדְקָתְךָ כְּהַר תָּבוֹר, עַל חֲטָאַי עָבוֹר תַּעֲבֹר
כְּיוֹם אֶתְמוֹל כִּי יַעֲבֹר, וְאַשְׁמוּרָה בַלָּיְלָה: תהלים צ

חָלְפָה עוֹנַת מִנְחָתִי, מִי יִתֵּן מְנוּחָתִי
יָגַעְתִּי בְאַנְחָתִי, אַשְׂחֶה בְכָל־לַיְלָה: תהלים ו

קוֹלִי בַּל יֻנְטַל, פְּתַח לִי שַׁעַר הַמְנֻטָּל
שֶׁרֹּאשִׁי נִמְלָא טָל, קְוֻצּוֹתַי רְסִיסֵי לָיְלָה: שיר השירים ה

הֵעָתֵר נוֹרָא וְאָיֹם, אֲשַׁוֵּעַ, תְּנָה פִדְיוֹם
בְּנֶשֶׁף־בְּעֶרֶב יוֹם, בְּאִישׁוֹן לָיְלָה: משלי ז

קְרָאתִיךָ יָהּ, הוֹשִׁיעֵנִי, אֹרַח חַיִּים תּוֹדִיעֵנִי
מִדַּלָּה תְבַצְּעֵנִי, מִיּוֹם עַד לָיְלָה.

טַהֵר טִנּוּף מַעֲשַׂי, פֶּן יֹאמְרוּ מַכְעִיסַי
אַיֵּה אֱלוֹהַ עֹשָׂי, נֹתֵן זְמִרוֹת בַּלָּיְלָה: איוב לה

נַחְנוּ בְיָדְךָ כַּחֹמֶר, סְלַח נָא עַל קַל וָחֹמֶר
יוֹם לְיוֹם יַבִּיעַ אֹמֶר, וְלַיְלָה לְלָיְלָה: תהלים יט

fulfilling the commandment to "Remember the Sabbath day," understood by the sages to mean: "Remember it at the beginning and at the end" (*Pesaḥim* 106a) – in both cases over a cup of wine.

Its deeper meaning recalls the moment at which Adam and Eve, exiled from Eden because of their sin, prepared to enter, for the first time, the world outside, with its darkness and dangers. As a gift, God showed them how to make light. Hence the light of Havdala.

This profound parable is the reverse of the Greek myth of Prometheus – who stole fire from the gods and was sentenced to everlasting torment. Judaism taught that God wants and blesses human creativity. Day 8, for humans, was the counterpart to Day 1 for God. Just as God began creation by making

[illegible]

[illegible] the commandment [illegible] "remember the Sabbath day," understood by the sages to mean, "Remember it at the beginning and at the end" [illegible] in both cases [illegible] the cup of wine.

[illegible] deeper meaning [illegible] recalls the moment at which Adam and Eve called [illegible] because [illegible] for the first time the world [illegible] with [illegible] God showed them how to make [illegible] the light of Havdala.

This profound [illegible] the reverse of the Greek myth of Prometheus, who stole fire from the gods and was eternally [illegible] tormented. Judaism taught that God [illegible] human creativity. [illegible] was the counterpart to [illegible] God began creation by making

חגים ומועדים
FESTIVALS

Blessing on Taking the Lulav

On Sukkot, except on Shabbat, the lulav and etrog are taken before Hallel.

Some say the following:

יְהִי רָצוֹן May it be Your will, LORD my God and God of my fathers, that through the fruit of the citron tree, the palm frond, the myrtle branches and willows of the brook, the letters of Your unique name draw close to one another and become united in my hand. Make it known I am called by Your name, so that [evil] will fear to come close to me. When I wave them, may a rich flow of blessings flow from the supreme Source of wisdom to the place of the Tabernacle and the site of the House of our God. May the command of these four species be considered by You as if I had fulfilled it in all its details and roots, as well as the 613 commandments dependent on it, for it is my intention to unify the name of the Holy One, blessed be He, and His Divine Presence, in reverence and love, to unify the name *Yod-Heh* with *Vav-Heh*, in perfect unity in the name of all Israel, Amen. Blessed is the LORD forever, Amen and Amen. *Ps. 89*

The lulav is taken in the right hand, with the myrtle leaves on the right, willow leaves on the left. The etrog is taken in the left hand, with its pointed end toward the floor. Then say the following blessing:

בָּרוּךְ Blessed are You, LORD our God, King of the Universe,
who has made us holy through His commandments,
and has commanded us about taking the lulav.

On the first day the lulav is taken, add:

בָּרוּךְ Blessed are You, LORD our God, King of the Universe,
who has given us life, sustained us and brought us to this time.

Invert the etrog, so that its pointed end is facing up. Face the front of the synagogue and wave the lulav and etrog in the following sequence, three times in each direction: ahead, right, back, left, up, down. Continue to hold the lulav and etrog during Hallel.

1662. The lulav, etrog, myrtle and willow leaves bear witness to the power of rain to give life to the earth and its produce. We offer them to God in the hope that He will continue to send rain in the coming year. The meditation speaks of the commandment in spiritual terms: just as we, on earth, dedicate this act to heaven, so may heaven grant a downward flow of God's blessings to earth.

סדר נטילת לולב

On סוכות, except on שבת, the לולב and אתרוג are taken before הלל.

Some say the following:

יְהִי רָצוֹן מִלְּפָנֶיךָ יהוה אֱלֹהַי וֵאלֹהֵי אֲבוֹתַי, בִּפְרִי עֵץ הָדָר וְכַפֹּת תְּמָרִים וַעֲנַף עֵץ עָבֹת וְעַרְבֵי נַחַל, אוֹתִיּוֹת שִׁמְךָ הַמְיֻחָד תְּקָרֵב אֶחָד אֶל אֶחָד וְהָיוּ לַאֲחָדִים בְּיָדִי, וְלֵידַע אֵיךְ שִׁמְךָ נִקְרָא עָלַי וְיִירְאוּ מִגֶּשֶׁת אֵלָי. וּבְנַעֲנוּעִי אוֹתָם תַּשְׁפִּיעַ שֶׁפַע בִּרְכוֹת מִדַּעַת עֶלְיוֹן לִנְוֵה אַפִּרְיוֹן לִמְכוֹן בֵּית אֱלֹהֵינוּ, וּתְהֵא חֲשׁוּבָה לְפָנֶיךָ מִצְוַת אַרְבָּעָה מִינִים אֵלּוּ כְּאִלּוּ קִיַּמְתִּיהָ בְּכָל פְּרָטוֹתֶיהָ וְשָׁרָשֶׁיהָ וְתַרְיַ״ג מִצְוֹת הַתְּלוּיוֹת בָּהּ, כִּי כַוָּנָתִי לְיַחֲדָא שְׁמָא דְקֻדְשָׁא בְּרִיךְ הוּא וּשְׁכִינְתֵּהּ בִּדְחִילוּ וּרְחִימוּ, לְיַחֵד שֵׁם י״ה בּו״ה בְּיִחוּדָא שְׁלִים בְּשֵׁם כָּל יִשְׂרָאֵל, אָמֵן. בָּרוּךְ יהוה לְעוֹלָם, אָמֵן וְאָמֵן: תהלים פט

The לולב is taken in the right hand, with the הדסים on the right, ערבות on the left. The אתרוג is taken in the left hand, with its pointed end toward the floor. Then say the following blessing:

בָּרוּךְ אַתָּה יהוה אֱלֹהֵינוּ מֶלֶךְ הָעוֹלָם
אֲשֶׁר קִדְּשָׁנוּ בְּמִצְוֹתָיו וְצִוָּנוּ עַל נְטִילַת לוּלָב.

On the first day the לולב is taken, add:

בָּרוּךְ אַתָּה יהוה אֱלֹהֵינוּ מֶלֶךְ הָעוֹלָם
שֶׁהֶחֱיָנוּ וְקִיְּמָנוּ וְהִגִּיעָנוּ לַזְּמַן הַזֶּה.

Invert the אתרוג, so that its pointed end is facing up. Face the front of the בית כנסת and wave the לולב and אתרוג in the following sequence, three times in each direction: ahead, right, back, left, up, down. Continue to hold the לולב and אתרוג during הלל.

MEDITATION AND BLESSING ON TAKING THE LULAV

Meditations before fulfilling commandments are a way of focusing our attention on the specific religious character of the act we are about to perform. They are a conscious declaration of *kavana*, sacred intent. This meditation first appeared in Rabbi Nathan Hannover's *Sha'arei Zion*, published in Prague,

Hallel

On the first two days of Pesaḥ (in Israel on the first evening and day); Shavuot; the entire festival of Sukkot, Shemini Atzeret and Simḥat Torah, Ḥanukka, Yom HaAtzma'ut and Yom Yerushalayim, Full Hallel is said. On Rosh Ḥodesh and the last six days of Pesaḥ, Half Hallel is said. See laws 438–439.

בָּרוּךְ Blessed are You, LORD our God, King of the Universe,
who has made us holy through His commandments
and has commanded us to recite the Hallel.

הַלְלוּיָהּ Halleluya! Servants of the LORD, give praise; praise the name of the LORD. Blessed be the name of the LORD now and for evermore. From the rising of the sun to its setting, may the LORD's name be praised. High is the LORD above all nations; His glory is above the heavens. Who is like the LORD our God, who sits enthroned so high, yet turns so low to see the heavens and the earth? ▸ He raises the poor from the dust and the needy from the refuse heap, giving them a place alongside princes, the princes of His people. He makes the woman in a childless house a happy mother of children. Halleluya! *Ps. 113*

---

at every epoch and at every trouble – may it not come to them! – and when they are redeemed, they recite it in thanks for their delivery" (*Pesaḥim* 117a). That is why we say it on Yom HaAtzma'ut and Yom Yerushalayim, the two most transformative events of modern Jewish history, in the faith that it is not human beings alone who shape the destiny of our people, but God working in and through His children.

Because of its association with history, Hallel is not said on Rosh HaShana or Yom Kippur, days dedicated less to national remembrance than to judgment, repentance and forgiveness.

מְקִימִי מֵעָפָר דָּל *He raises the poor from the dust:* A verse reminiscent of Hannah's prayer after the birth of her child (1 Sam. 2:8). The religions of the ancient world were deeply conservative, designed to vindicate and perpetuate hierarchies of power. Judaism, believing that human dignity is the prerogative of everyone, was an ongoing protest against such inequalities. God's greatness is evident in the fact that He can lift the poor and the needy to a place of honor alongside princes.

סדר הלל

On the first two days of פסח *(in* ארץ ישראל *on the first evening and day);*
שבועות; *the entire festival of* סוכות, שמיני עצרת *and* שמחת תורה, חנוכה,
יום העצמאות *and* יום ירושלים, הלל שלם *is said. On* ראש חודש *and*
the last six days of פסח, הלל בדילוג *is said. See laws 438–439.*

בָּרוּךְ אַתָּה יהוה אֱלֹהֵינוּ מֶלֶךְ הָעוֹלָם
אֲשֶׁר קִדְּשָׁנוּ בְּמִצְוֹתָיו וְצִוָּנוּ לִקְרֹא אֶת הַהַלֵּל.

תהלים קיג הַלְלוּיָהּ, הַלְלוּ עַבְדֵי יהוה, הַלְלוּ אֶת־שֵׁם יהוה: יְהִי שֵׁם יהוה
מְבֹרָךְ, מֵעַתָּה וְעַד־עוֹלָם: מִמִּזְרַח־שֶׁמֶשׁ עַד־מְבוֹאוֹ, מְהֻלָּל שֵׁם
יהוה: רָם עַל־כָּל־גּוֹיִם יהוה, עַל הַשָּׁמַיִם כְּבוֹדוֹ: מִי כַּיהוה אֱלֹהֵינוּ,
הַמַּגְבִּיהִי לָשָׁבֶת: הַמַּשְׁפִּילִי לִרְאוֹת, בַּשָּׁמַיִם וּבָאָרֶץ: ‹ מְקִימִי
מֵעָפָר דָּל, מֵאַשְׁפֹּת יָרִים אֶבְיוֹן: לְהוֹשִׁיבִי עִם־נְדִיבִים, עִם נְדִיבֵי
עַמּוֹ: מוֹשִׁיבִי עֲקֶרֶת הַבַּיִת, אֵם־הַבָּנִים שְׂמֵחָה, הַלְלוּיָהּ:

HALLEL

Psalms 113–118 – known as the Egyptian Hallel because of the reference in the second paragraph to the exodus from Egypt – are among the earliest prayers written to be recited in the Temple on days of national celebration. They were sung as accompaniment to the Pesaḥ sacrifice, and early rabbinic sources suggest that they were said on the pilgrimage festivals: Pesaḥ, Shavuot and Sukkot.

By the Talmudic era, a shortened form (known as "Half Hallel") was in use for Rosh Ḥodesh and the last six days of Pesaḥ. The Full Hallel was not said on Rosh Ḥodesh, because it is not a full festival, and on the last days of Pesaḥ because (a) the main event of the exodus took place on the first day, and (b) the miracle of the seventh day, the division of the Reed Sea, involved suffering for the Egyptians. According to the Talmud (*Megilla* 10b; *Sanhedrin* 39b), when the angels wished to sing the Song at the Sea, God refused, saying: "Shall you sing a song while My creatures are drowning in the sea?"

Hallel is a choral symphony of faith in the presence of God in history. The sages said that the prophets "enacted that the Israelites should recite it

בְּצֵאת When Israel came out of Egypt, the house of Jacob from a people of foreign tongue, Judah became His sanctuary, Israel His dominion. The sea saw and fled; the Jordan turned back. The mountains skipped like rams, the hills like lambs. ▸ Why was it, sea, that you fled? Jordan, why did you turn back? Why, mountains, did you skip like rams, and you, hills, like lambs? It was at the presence of the LORD, Creator of the earth, at the presence of the God of Jacob, who turned the rock into a pool of water, flint into a flowing spring. Ps. 114

Omit on Rosh Ḥodesh (except on Ḥanukka) and the last six days of Pesaḥ:

לֹא לָנוּ Not to us, LORD, not to us, but to Your name give glory, for Your love, for Your faithfulness. Why should the nations say, "Where now is their God?" Our God is in heaven; whatever He wills He does. Their idols are silver and gold, made by human hands. They have mouths but cannot speak; eyes but cannot see. They have ears but cannot hear; noses but cannot smell. They have hands but cannot feel; feet but cannot walk. No sound comes from their throat. Those who make them become like them; so will all who trust in them. ▸ Israel, trust in the LORD – He is their Help and their Shield. House of Aaron, trust in the LORD – He is their Help and their Shield. You who fear the LORD, trust in the LORD – He is their Help and their Shield. Ps. 115

יהוה זְכָרָנוּ The LORD remembers us and will bless us. He will bless the house of Israel. He will bless the house of Aaron. He will bless those who fear the LORD, small and great alike. May the LORD give you increase: you and your children. May you be blessed by the LORD, Maker of heaven and earth. ▸ The heavens are the LORD's, but the earth He has given over to mankind. It is not the dead who praise the LORD, nor those who go down to the silent grave. But we will bless the LORD, now and for ever. Halleluya!

---

yet imperfect, ideals. Idolatry is the worship of the part instead of the whole, one aspect of the universe in place of the Creator of all who transcends all.

יִרְאֵי יהוה *You who fear the LORD:* This may refer to converts to Judaism (Rashi), or God-fearers among the nations (Ibn Ezra).

וְהָאָרֶץ נָתַן לִבְנֵי־אָדָם *But the earth He has given over to mankind:* "Given over" rather than "given": placed in the guardianship of mankind. We do not own

תהלים קיד

בְּצֵאת יִשְׂרָאֵל מִמִּצְרָיִם, בֵּית יַעֲקֹב מֵעַם לֹעֵז: הָיְתָה יְהוּדָה
לְקָדְשׁוֹ, יִשְׂרָאֵל מַמְשְׁלוֹתָיו: הַיָּם רָאָה וַיָּנֹס, הַיַּרְדֵּן יִסֹּב לְאָחוֹר:
הֶהָרִים רָקְדוּ כְאֵילִים, גְּבָעוֹת כִּבְנֵי־צֹאן: • מַה־לְּךָ הַיָּם כִּי תָנוּס,
הַיַּרְדֵּן תִּסֹּב לְאָחוֹר: הֶהָרִים תִּרְקְדוּ כְאֵילִים, גְּבָעוֹת כִּבְנֵי־צֹאן:
מִלִּפְנֵי אָדוֹן חוּלִי אָרֶץ, מִלִּפְנֵי אֱלוֹהַּ יַעֲקֹב: הַהֹפְכִי הַצּוּר אֲגַם־
מָיִם, חַלָּמִישׁ לְמַעְיְנוֹ־מָיִם:

Omit on ראש חודש (*except on* חנוכה) *and the last six days of* פסח:

תהלים קטו

לֹא לָנוּ יהוה לֹא לָנוּ, כִּי־לְשִׁמְךָ תֵּן כָּבוֹד, עַל־חַסְדְּךָ עַל־אֲמִתֶּךָ: לָמָּה
יֹאמְרוּ הַגּוֹיִם אַיֵּה־נָא אֱלֹהֵיהֶם: וֵאלֹהֵינוּ בַשָּׁמָיִם, כֹּל אֲשֶׁר־חָפֵץ
עָשָׂה: עֲצַבֵּיהֶם כֶּסֶף וְזָהָב, מַעֲשֵׂה יְדֵי אָדָם: פֶּה־לָהֶם וְלֹא יְדַבֵּרוּ,
עֵינַיִם לָהֶם וְלֹא יִרְאוּ: אָזְנַיִם לָהֶם וְלֹא יִשְׁמָעוּ, אַף לָהֶם וְלֹא יְרִיחוּן:
יְדֵיהֶם וְלֹא יְמִישׁוּן, רַגְלֵיהֶם וְלֹא יְהַלֵּכוּ, לֹא־יֶהְגּוּ בִּגְרוֹנָם: כְּמוֹהֶם יִהְיוּ
עֹשֵׂיהֶם, כֹּל אֲשֶׁר־בֹּטֵחַ בָּהֶם: • יִשְׂרָאֵל בְּטַח בַּיהוה, עֶזְרָם וּמָגִנָּם
הוּא: בֵּית אַהֲרֹן בִּטְחוּ בַיהוה, עֶזְרָם וּמָגִנָּם הוּא: יִרְאֵי יהוה בִּטְחוּ
בַיהוה, עֶזְרָם וּמָגִנָּם הוּא:

יהוה זְכָרָנוּ יְבָרֵךְ, יְבָרֵךְ אֶת־בֵּית יִשְׂרָאֵל, יְבָרֵךְ אֶת־בֵּית אַהֲרֹן:
יְבָרֵךְ יִרְאֵי יהוה, הַקְּטַנִּים עִם־הַגְּדֹלִים: יֹסֵף יהוה עֲלֵיכֶם, עֲלֵיכֶם
וְעַל־בְּנֵיכֶם: בְּרוּכִים אַתֶּם לַיהוה, עֹשֵׂה שָׁמַיִם וָאָרֶץ: • הַשָּׁמַיִם
שָׁמַיִם לַיהוה, וְהָאָרֶץ נָתַן לִבְנֵי־אָדָם: לֹא הַמֵּתִים יְהַלְלוּ־יָהּ, וְלֹא
כָּל־יֹרְדֵי דוּמָה: וַאֲנַחְנוּ נְבָרֵךְ יָהּ, מֵעַתָּה וְעַד־עוֹלָם, הַלְלוּיָהּ:

בְּצֵאת יִשְׂרָאֵל מִמִּצְרָיִם *When Israel came out of Egypt:* A lyrical account of how nature itself trembled and rejoiced at the exodus, when the supreme Power intervened to rescue the powerless.

כְּמוֹהֶם יִהְיוּ עֹשֵׂיהֶם *Those who make them become like them:* Worshiping impersonal objects or forces eventually dehumanizes a culture and those who are part of it. Whether what is worshiped is an icon, a ruler, a race or a political ideology, the final outcome is the sacrifice of human lives on the altar of high,

Omit on Rosh Ḥodesh (except on Ḥanukka) and the last six days of Pesaḥ:

אָהַבְתִּי I love the LORD, for He hears my voice, my pleas. He turns His ear to me whenever I call. The bonds of death encompassed me, the anguish of the grave came upon me, I was overcome by trouble and sorrow. Then I called on the name of the LORD: "LORD, I pray, save my life." Gracious is the LORD, and righteous; our God is full of compassion. The LORD protects the simple hearted. When I was brought low, He saved me. My soul, be at peace once more, for the LORD has been good to you. For You have rescued me from death, my eyes from weeping, my feet from stumbling. ▸ I shall walk in the presence of the LORD in the land of the living. I had faith, even when I said, "I am greatly afflicted," even when I said rashly, "All men are liars." *Ps. 116*

מָה־אָשִׁיב How can I repay the LORD for all His goodness to me? I will lift the cup of salvation and call on the name of the LORD. I will fulfill my vows to the LORD in the presence of all His people. Grievous in the LORD's sight is the death of His devoted ones. Truly, LORD, I am Your servant; I am Your servant, the son of Your maidservant. You set me free from my chains. ▸ To You I shall bring a thanksgiving-offering and call on the LORD by name. I will fulfill my vows to the LORD in the presence of all His people, in the courts of the House of the LORD, in your midst, Jerusalem. Halleluya!

מָה־אָשִׁיב *How can I repay?* A rhetorical question: we can never repay God's kindnesses to us. All that we have is His. The very fact that we exist is due to His creative love. All we can do is express our thanks.

כּוֹס־יְשׁוּעוֹת אֶשָּׂא *I will lift the cup of salvation:* A reference to the wine-libation accompanying a thanksgiving-offering (Rashi). Alternatively, I will hold a feast of thanksgiving at which I will raise a glass of wine in thanks to God.
יָקָר בְּעֵינֵי יהוה, הַמָּוְתָה לַחֲסִידָיו *Grievous in the LORD's sight is the death of His devoted ones:* this is Rashi's understanding of the text; others translate it as "Precious in the LORD's sight." God does not wish His devoted ones to die. As the previous two paragraphs have made clear, God is the God of life; only idolatrous cultures worship death.

בֶּן־אֲמָתֶךָ *The son of Your maidservant:* Serving You comes naturally because my mother did likewise (Radak). A father teaches us "the discipline of

Omit on ראש חודש (*except on* חנוכה) *and the last six days of* פסח:

תהלים קטז

אָהַבְתִּי, כִּי־יִשְׁמַע יהוה, אֶת־קוֹלִי תַּחֲנוּנָי: כִּי־הִטָּה אָזְנוֹ לִי, וּבְיָמַי
אֶקְרָא: אֲפָפוּנִי חֶבְלֵי־מָוֶת, וּמְצָרֵי שְׁאוֹל מְצָאוּנִי, צָרָה וְיָגוֹן אֶמְצָא:
וּבְשֵׁם־יהוה אֶקְרָא, אָנָּה יהוה מַלְּטָה נַפְשִׁי: חַנּוּן יהוה וְצַדִּיק, וֵאלֹהֵינוּ
מְרַחֵם: שֹׁמֵר פְּתָאיִם יהוה, דַּלּוֹתִי וְלִי יְהוֹשִׁיעַ: שׁוּבִי נַפְשִׁי לִמְנוּחָיְכִי,
כִּי־יהוה גָּמַל עָלָיְכִי: כִּי חִלַּצְתָּ נַפְשִׁי מִמָּוֶת, אֶת־עֵינִי מִן־דִּמְעָה,
אֶת־רַגְלִי מִדֶּחִי: • אֶתְהַלֵּךְ לִפְנֵי יהוה, בְּאַרְצוֹת הַחַיִּים: הֶאֱמַנְתִּי כִּי
אֲדַבֵּר, אֲנִי עָנִיתִי מְאֹד: אֲנִי אָמַרְתִּי בְחָפְזִי, כָּל־הָאָדָם כֹּזֵב:

מָה־אָשִׁיב לַיהוה, כָּל־תַּגְמוּלוֹהִי עָלָי: כּוֹס־יְשׁוּעוֹת אֶשָּׂא, וּבְשֵׁם
יהוה אֶקְרָא: נְדָרַי לַיהוה אֲשַׁלֵּם, נֶגְדָה־נָּא לְכָל־עַמּוֹ: יָקָר בְּעֵינֵי
יהוה, הַמָּוְתָה לַחֲסִידָיו: אָנָּה יהוה כִּי־אֲנִי עַבְדֶּךָ, אֲנִי־עַבְדְּךָ
בֶּן־אֲמָתֶךָ, פִּתַּחְתָּ לְמוֹסֵרָי: • לְךָ־אֶזְבַּח זֶבַח תּוֹדָה, וּבְשֵׁם יהוה
אֶקְרָא: נְדָרַי לַיהוה אֲשַׁלֵּם, נֶגְדָה־נָּא לְכָל־עַמּוֹ: בְּחַצְרוֹת בֵּית
יהוה, בְּתוֹכֵכִי יְרוּשָׁלָםִ, הַלְלוּיָהּ:

---

the earth; we hold it in trust from God and there are conditions to that trust, namely that we respect the earth's integrity and the dignity of the human person; in short, that we honor God's laws.

אָהַבְתִּי *I love the* L*ORD:* This and the next paragraph form a single psalm. The psalmist turns from the collective to the individual. God has saved him from crisis and he gives public voice to his thanks. This prayer was included in Hallel because it spoke to the many among the pilgrims to Jerusalem who had vowed to bring thanksgiving-offerings, as is clear from the next paragraph. The juxtaposition of the individual and the collective is a significant feature of biblical texts generally. The Hebrew prophets and poets never saw the nation as an abstraction and the people an amorphous mass. The individual never loses his or her significance even in the presence of vast gatherings. **אֲנִי אָמַרְתִּי בְחָפְזִי, כָּל־הָאָדָם כֹּזֵב** *Even when I said rashly, "All men are liars"*: the commentators relate this to King David who, when forced to flee from Saul, felt betrayed by everyone. Alternatively: "Even when I was fleeing for my life, I knew that those [who preached despair] were false" (Radak).

הַלְלוּ Praise the LORD, all nations; acclaim Him, all you peoples; *Ps. 117*
for His loving-kindness to us is strong,
and the LORD's faithfulness is everlasting.
Halleluya!

The following verses are chanted by the Leader.
At the end of each verse, the congregation responds, "Thank the LORD for He is good; His loving-kindness is for ever." See law 439.

On Sukkot, the lulav and etrog are waved, three waves for each word of the verse (except God's name). On the first word, wave forward, then, on subsequent words, wave right, back, left, up and down respectively. The Leader waves only for the first two verses. The congregation waves each time the first verse is said in response.

הוֹדוּ Thank the LORD for He is good; His loving-kindness is for ever. *Ps. 118*
Let Israel say — His loving-kindness is for ever.
Let the house of Aaron say — His loving-kindness is for ever.
Let those who fear the LORD say — His loving-kindness is for ever.

מִן־הַמֵּצַר In my distress I called on the LORD. The LORD answered me and set me free. The LORD is with me; I will not be afraid. What can man do to me? The LORD is with me. He is my Helper. I will see the downfall of my enemies. It is better to take refuge in the LORD than to trust in man. It is better to take refuge in the LORD than to trust in princes. The nations all surrounded me, but in the LORD's name I drove them off. They surrounded me on every side, but in the LORD's name I drove them off. They surrounded me like bees, they attacked me as fire attacks brushwood, but in the LORD's name I drove them off. They thrust so hard against me, I nearly fell, but the LORD came to my help. The LORD is my strength and my song; He has become

---

has been for so long the guardian of prophecy and transmitted it to the rest of the world – such a nation cannot be destroyed. The Jew is everlasting as eternity itself" (Tolstoy).

הוֹדוּ לַיהוה כִּי־טוֹב *Thank the LORD for He is good:* This verse was first recited by King David when he brought the Ark to Jerusalem (1 Chr. 16:34).

מִן־הַמֵּצַר *In my distress... set me free:* The terms mean, respectively, "straits, confined space" and "broad space, expanse." The psalmist writes that he felt hemmed in by enemies; his eventual victory brings a sense of spaciousness and freedom.

הַלְלוּ אֶת־יהוה כָּל־גּוֹיִם, שַׁבְּחוּהוּ כָּל־הָאֻמִּים: תהלים קיז
כִּי גָבַר עָלֵינוּ חַסְדּוֹ, וֶאֱמֶת־יהוה לְעוֹלָם
הַלְלוּיָהּ:

The following verses are chanted by the שליח ציבור*.*
At the end of each verse, the קהל *responds:* הוֹדוּ לַיהוה כִּי־טוֹב, כִּי לְעוֹלָם חַסְדּוֹ*. See law 439.*
On סוכות*, the* לולב *and* אתרוג *are waved, three waves for each word of the verse (except God's name). On the first word, wave forward, then, on subsequent words, wave right, back, left, up and down respectively. The* שליח ציבור *waves only for the first two verses. The* קהל *waves each time the first verse is said in response.*

הוֹדוּ לַיהוה כִּי־טוֹב כִּי לְעוֹלָם חַסְדּוֹ: תהלים קיח
יֹאמַר־נָא יִשְׂרָאֵל כִּי לְעוֹלָם חַסְדּוֹ:
יֹאמְרוּ־נָא בֵית־אַהֲרֹן כִּי לְעוֹלָם חַסְדּוֹ:
יֹאמְרוּ־נָא יִרְאֵי יהוה כִּי לְעוֹלָם חַסְדּוֹ:

מִן־הַמֵּצַר קָרָאתִי יָּהּ, עָנָנִי בַמֶּרְחָב יָהּ: יהוה לִי לֹא אִירָא, מַה־
יַּעֲשֶׂה לִי אָדָם: יהוה לִי בְּעֹזְרָי, וַאֲנִי אֶרְאֶה בְשֹׂנְאָי: טוֹב לַחֲסוֹת
בַּיהוה, מִבְּטֹחַ בָּאָדָם: טוֹב לַחֲסוֹת בַּיהוה, מִבְּטֹחַ בִּנְדִיבִים:
כָּל־גּוֹיִם סְבָבוּנִי, בְּשֵׁם יהוה כִּי אֲמִילַם: סַבּוּנִי גַם־סְבָבוּנִי, בְּשֵׁם
יהוה כִּי אֲמִילַם: סַבּוּנִי כִדְבֹרִים, דֹּעֲכוּ כְּאֵשׁ קוֹצִים, בְּשֵׁם יהוה

thought as well as the discipline of action"; a mother teaches us the "living experience" of the commandments, their "flavor, scent and warmth." From her we learn "to feel the presence of the Almighty." "The fathers knew much about the Shabbat; the mothers lived the Shabbat, experienced her presence, and perceived her beauty and splendor" (Rabbi Joseph Soloveitchik).

הַלְלוּ אֶת־יהוה כָּל־גּוֹיִם *Praise the Lord, all nations:* The shortest of all the psalms, a mere two verses. The psalmist speaks of the universal significance of Israel's history. It is not Israel alone, but all the nations, who will see in the story of this people, something beyond mere history. "The Jew is the emblem of eternity. He who neither slaughter nor torture of thousands of years could destroy, he who neither fire nor sword nor inquisition was able to wipe off the face of the earth, he who was the first to produce the oracles of God, who

my salvation. Sounds of song and salvation resound in the tents of the righteous: "The LORD's right hand has done mighty deeds. The LORD's right hand is lifted high. The LORD's right hand has done mighty deeds." I will not die but live, and tell what the LORD has done. The LORD has chastened me severely, but He has not given me over to death. ▸ Open for me the gates of righteousness that I may enter them and thank the LORD. This is the gateway to the LORD; through it, the righteous shall enter.

אוֹדְךָ I will thank You, for You answered me, and became my salvation.
I will thank You, for You answered me, and became my salvation.

The stone the builders rejected has become the main cornerstone.
The stone the builders rejected has become the main cornerstone.

This is the LORD's doing; it is wondrous in our eyes.
This is the LORD's doing; it is wondrous in our eyes.

This is the day the LORD has made; let us rejoice and be glad in it.
This is the day the LORD has made; let us rejoice and be glad in it.

On Sukkot, the lulav and etrog are waved while saying "LORD, please, save us," three waves for each word of the verse (except God's name). On the first word, wave forward and right; third word: back and left; fourth word: up and down.

Leader followed by congregation:

אָנָּא LORD, please, save us.
LORD, please, save us.
LORD, please, grant us success.
LORD, please, grant us success.

אוֹדְךָ *I will thank You:* This and the next eight verses, the last of Psalm 118, are repeated. Litany – a prayer in which the Leader says a verse or phrase and the congregation responds – was an aspect of worship in the Temple, and is developed most fully in the *hakafot*, processions around the synagogue, on Sukkot.

אֶבֶן מָאֲסוּ הַבּוֹנִים *The stone the builders rejected:* This is a reference to the people of Israel. Two of the first references to Israel in non-Jewish sources – the Merneptah stele (Egypt, thirteenth century BCE) and the Mesha stele (Moab, ninth century BCE) – both declare that Israel has been destroyed. Israel is the people that outlives its obituaries.

כִּי אֲמִילַם: דָּחֹה דְחִיתַנִי לִנְפֹּל, וַיהוה עֲזָרָנִי: עָזִּי וְזִמְרָת יָהּ, וַיְהִי־לִי לִישׁוּעָה: קוֹל רִנָּה וִישׁוּעָה בְּאָהֳלֵי צַדִּיקִים, יְמִין יהוה עֹשָׂה חָיִל: יְמִין יהוה רוֹמֵמָה, יְמִין יהוה עֹשָׂה חָיִל: לֹא־אָמוּת כִּי־אֶחְיֶה, וַאֲסַפֵּר מַעֲשֵׂי יָהּ: יַסֹּר יִסְּרַנִּי יָּהּ, וְלַמָּוֶת לֹא נְתָנָנִי:
· פִּתְחוּ־לִי שַׁעֲרֵי־צֶדֶק, אָבֹא־בָם אוֹדֶה יָהּ: זֶה־הַשַּׁעַר לַיהוה, צַדִּיקִים יָבֹאוּ בוֹ:

אוֹדְךָ כִּי עֲנִיתָנִי, וַתְּהִי־לִי לִישׁוּעָה:
אוֹדְךָ כִּי עֲנִיתָנִי, וַתְּהִי־לִי לִישׁוּעָה:

אֶבֶן מָאֲסוּ הַבּוֹנִים, הָיְתָה לְרֹאשׁ פִּנָּה:
אֶבֶן מָאֲסוּ הַבּוֹנִים, הָיְתָה לְרֹאשׁ פִּנָּה:

מֵאֵת יהוה הָיְתָה זֹּאת, הִיא נִפְלָאת בְּעֵינֵינוּ:
מֵאֵת יהוה הָיְתָה זֹּאת, הִיא נִפְלָאת בְּעֵינֵינוּ:

זֶה־הַיּוֹם עָשָׂה יהוה, נָגִילָה וְנִשְׂמְחָה בוֹ:
זֶה־הַיּוֹם עָשָׂה יהוה, נָגִילָה וְנִשְׂמְחָה בוֹ:

On סוכות*, the* לולב *and* אתרוג *are waved while saying* אָנָּא יהוה הוֹשִׁיעָה נָּא*, three waves for each word of the verse (except God's name). On the first word, wave forward and right; third word: back and left; fourth word: up and down.*

שליח ציבור *followed by* קהל*:*

אָנָּא יהוה הוֹשִׁיעָה נָּא:
אָנָּא יהוה הוֹשִׁיעָה נָּא:
אָנָּא יהוה הַצְלִיחָה נָא:
אָנָּא יהוה הַצְלִיחָה נָא:

עָזִּי וְזִמְרָת יָהּ *The Lord is my strength and my song:* a quotation from *Shirat HaYam* (Ex. 15:2); it also appears in Isaiah 12:2.

פִּתְחוּ־לִי שַׁעֲרֵי־צֶדֶק *Open for me the gates of righteousness:* A reference to the gates of the Temple.

On Sukkot, the lulav and etrog are waved while saying "Thank the Lord…," three waves for each word of the verse (except God's name). On the first word, wave forward, then, on subsequent words, wave right, back, left, up and down respectively.

בָּרוּךְ Blessed is one who comes in the name of the Lord;
we bless you from the House of the Lord.
Blessed is one who comes in the name of the Lord;
we bless you from the House of the Lord.

The Lord is God; He has given us light. Bind the festival offering with thick cords [and bring it] to the horns of the altar.
The Lord is God; He has given us light. Bind the festival offering with thick cords [and bring it] to the horns of the altar.

You are my God and I will thank You; You are my God, I will exalt You.
You are my God and I will thank You; You are my God, I will exalt You.

Thank the Lord for He is good; His loving-kindness is for ever.
Thank the Lord for He is good; His loving-kindness is for ever.

יְהַלְלְוּךָ All Your works will praise You, Lord our God, and Your devoted ones – the righteous who do Your will, together with all Your people the house of Israel – will joyously thank, bless, praise, glorify, exalt, revere, sanctify, and proclaim the sovereignty of Your name, our King. ▸ For it is good to thank You and fitting to sing psalms to Your name, for from eternity to eternity You are God. Blessed are You, Lord, King who is extolled with praises.

On Sukkot some say at this point Hoshanot on page 852

On weekday Ḥanukka (except Rosh Ḥodesh Tevet), Yom HaAtzma'ut and Yom Yerushalayim, the service continues with Half Kaddish on page 156.

אֵלִי אַתָּה *You are my God:* The words of one who is bringing the offering. וְאוֹדֶךָּ *And I will thank You:* alternatively, "I will acknowledge You." These are words of dedication, meaning: This offering I bring is an expression of thanks and acknowledgment to God for all His kindnesses to me.

יְהַלְלְוּךָ *All Your works will praise You:* A concluding benediction, as at the end of the Verses of Praise.

On סוכות*, the* לולב *and* אתרוג *are waved while saying* הודוּ לַיהוה כִּי־טוֹב, כִּי לְעוֹלָם חַסְדּוֹ*, three waves for each word of the verse (except God's name). On the first word, wave forward, then, on subsequent words, wave right, back, left, up and down respectively.*

בָּרוּךְ הַבָּא בְּשֵׁם יהוה, בֵּרַכְנוּכֶם מִבֵּית יהוה:
בָּרוּךְ הַבָּא בְּשֵׁם יהוה, בֵּרַכְנוּכֶם מִבֵּית יהוה:

אֵל יהוה וַיָּאֶר לָנוּ, אִסְרוּ־חַג בַּעֲבֹתִים עַד־קַרְנוֹת הַמִּזְבֵּחַ:
אֵל יהוה וַיָּאֶר לָנוּ, אִסְרוּ־חַג בַּעֲבֹתִים עַד־קַרְנוֹת הַמִּזְבֵּחַ:

אֵלִי אַתָּה וְאוֹדֶךָּ, אֱלֹהַי אֲרוֹמְמֶךָּ:
אֵלִי אַתָּה וְאוֹדֶךָּ, אֱלֹהַי אֲרוֹמְמֶךָּ:

הוֹדוּ לַיהוה כִּי־טוֹב, כִּי לְעוֹלָם חַסְדּוֹ:
הוֹדוּ לַיהוה כִּי־טוֹב, כִּי לְעוֹלָם חַסְדּוֹ:

יְהַלְלוּךָ יהוה אֱלֹהֵינוּ כָּל מַעֲשֶׂיךָ, וַחֲסִידֶיךָ צַדִּיקִים עוֹשֵׂי רְצוֹנֶךָ, וְכָל עַמְּךָ בֵּית יִשְׂרָאֵל בְּרִנָּה יוֹדוּ וִיבָרְכוּ וִישַׁבְּחוּ וִיפָאֲרוּ וִירוֹמְמוּ וְיַעֲרִיצוּ וְיַקְדִּישׁוּ וְיַמְלִיכוּ אֶת שִׁמְךָ מַלְכֵּנוּ, • כִּי לְךָ טוֹב לְהוֹדוֹת וּלְשִׁמְךָ נָאֶה לְזַמֵּר, כִּי מֵעוֹלָם וְעַד עוֹלָם אַתָּה אֵל. בָּרוּךְ אַתָּה יהוה, מֶלֶךְ מְהֻלָּל בַּתִּשְׁבָּחוֹת.

On סוכות *some say at this point* הושענות *on page 853.*

On weekday חנוכה *(except* ראש חודש טבת*),* יום העצמאות *and* יום ירושלים*, the service continues with* חצי קדיש *on page 157.*

בָּרוּךְ הַבָּא *Blessed is one who comes:* A blessing made by the priests to those who came to worship in the Temple (Rashi, Radak). One of the tasks of the priests was to bless the people who came in pilgrimage to the Temple to make their offerings.

אִסְרוּ־חַג בַּעֲבֹתִים *Bind the festival offering with thick cords:* Alternatively, "Order the festival procession with boughs, up to the horns of the altar," a reference to the procession around the altar, with a lulav, on Sukkot (*Sukka* 45a).

FULL KADDISH

Leader: יִתְגַּדַּל Magnified and sanctified may His great name be,
in the world He created by His will.
May He establish His kingdom
in your lifetime and in your days,
and in the lifetime of all the house of Israel,
swiftly and soon – and say: Amen.

All: May His great name
be blessed for ever and all time.

Leader: Blessed and praised, glorified and exalted,
raised and honored, uplifted and lauded
be the name of the Holy One, blessed be He,
beyond any blessing, song, praise and consolation
uttered in the world – and say: Amen.

May the prayers and pleas of all Israel
be accepted by their Father in heaven – and say: Amen.

May there be great peace from heaven,
and life for us and all Israel – and say: Amen.

Bow, take three steps back, as if taking leave of the Divine Presence, then bow, first left, then right, then center, while saying:

May He who makes peace in His high places,
make peace for us and all Israel –
and say: Amen.

On Rosh Ḥodesh and Ḥol HaMo'ed, the service continues with the Reading of the Torah on page 158.

Shabbat, Yom Tov, and Hoshana Raba, the service continues with the Reading of the Torah on page 498.

On Shabbat Ḥol HaMo'ed, the appropriate megilla is read before the Torah Reading (on Pesaḥ, Shir HaShirim, on page 1170; on Sukkot, Kohelet, on page 1202). In the event that the first day of Yom Tov falls on Shabbat, the megilla is instead read on the last day of Pesaḥ or on Shemini Atzeret (in Israel, on the first day of Yom Tov).

On the second day of Shavuot, Megillat Ruth (page 1180) is read before the Torah Reading (in Israel, on the first day).

On Simḥat Torah, continue with Hakafot on page 788.

קדיש שלם

ש״ץ: יִתְגַּדַּל וְיִתְקַדַּשׁ שְׁמֵהּ רַבָּא (קהל: אָמֵן)
בְּעָלְמָא דִּי בְרָא כִרְעוּתֵהּ, וְיַמְלִיךְ מַלְכוּתֵהּ
בְּחַיֵּיכוֹן וּבְיוֹמֵיכוֹן וּבְחַיֵּי דְכָל בֵּית יִשְׂרָאֵל
בַּעֲגָלָא וּבִזְמַן קָרִיב, וְאִמְרוּ אָמֵן. (קהל: אָמֵן)

קהל ושי״ץ: יְהֵא שְׁמֵהּ רַבָּא מְבָרַךְ לְעָלַם וּלְעָלְמֵי עָלְמַיָּא.

ש״ץ: יִתְבָּרַךְ וְיִשְׁתַּבַּח וְיִתְפָּאַר
וְיִתְרוֹמַם וְיִתְנַשֵּׂא וְיִתְהַדָּר וְיִתְעַלֶּה וְיִתְהַלָּל
שְׁמֵהּ דְּקֻדְשָׁא בְּרִיךְ הוּא (קהל: בְּרִיךְ הוּא)
לְעֵלָּא מִן כָּל בִּרְכָתָא וְשִׁירָתָא, תֻּשְׁבְּחָתָא וְנֶחֱמָתָא
דַּאֲמִירָן בְּעָלְמָא, וְאִמְרוּ אָמֵן. (קהל: אָמֵן)

תִּתְקַבַּל צְלוֹתְהוֹן וּבָעוּתְהוֹן דְּכָל יִשְׂרָאֵל
קֳדָם אֲבוּהוֹן דִּי בִשְׁמַיָּא, וְאִמְרוּ אָמֵן. (קהל: אָמֵן)

יְהֵא שְׁלָמָא רַבָּא מִן שְׁמַיָּא
וְחַיִּים, עָלֵינוּ וְעַל כָּל יִשְׂרָאֵל, וְאִמְרוּ אָמֵן. (קהל: אָמֵן)

Bow, take three steps back, as if taking leave of the Divine Presence, then bow, first left, then right, then center, while saying:

עֹשֶׂה שָׁלוֹם בִּמְרוֹמָיו, הוּא יַעֲשֶׂה שָׁלוֹם עָלֵינוּ וְעַל כָּל יִשְׂרָאֵל
וְאִמְרוּ אָמֵן. (קהל: אָמֵן)

On ראש חודש *and* חול המועד*, the service continues with* קריאת התורה *on page 159.*

On יום טוב*,* שבת*, and* הושענא רבה *the service continues with* קריאת התורה *on page 499.*

On שבת חול המועד*, the appropriate* מגילה *is read before* קריאת התורה
(on פסח*,* שיר השירים*, on page 1171; on* סוכות*,* קהלת*, on page 1203).*
In the event that the first day of יום טוב *falls on* שבת*, the* מגילה *is instead read on the last day of* פסח *or on* שמיני עצרת *(in* ארץ ישראל*, on the first day of* יום טוב*).*

On the second day of שבועות*,* מגילת רות *(page 1181) is read before* קריאת התורה *(in* ארץ ישראל*, on the first day).*

On שמחת תורה*, continue with* הקפות *on page 789.*

Musaf for Rosh Ḥodesh

THE AMIDA

The following prayer, until "in former years" on page 756, is said silently, standing with feet together. If there is a minyan, the Amida is repeated aloud by the Leader. Take three steps forward and at the points indicated by ▾, bend the knees at the first word, bow at the second, and stand straight before saying God's name.

When I proclaim the LORD's name, give glory to our God. *Deut. 32*
O LORD, open my lips, so that my mouth may declare Your praise. *Ps. 51*

PATRIARCHS

▾בָּרוּךְ▾ Blessed are You, LORD our God and God of our fathers,
God of Abraham, God of Isaac and God of Jacob;
the great, mighty and awesome God, God Most High,
who bestows acts of loving-kindness and creates all,
who remembers the loving-kindness of the fathers and will bring
a Redeemer to their children's children
for the sake of His name, in love.
King, Helper, Savior, Shield:
▾Blessed are You, LORD, Shield of Abraham.

DIVINE MIGHT

אַתָּה גִּבּוֹר You are eternally mighty, LORD.
You give life to the dead and have great power to save.

The phrase "He makes the wind blow and the rain fall" is added from Simḥat Torah until Pesaḥ. In Israel the phrase "He causes the dew to fall" is added from Pesaḥ until Shemini Atzeret. See laws 129–131.

In fall & winter: He makes the wind blow and the rain fall.
In Israel, in spring & summer: He causes the dew to fall.

---

and seek to begin again. In Temple times a special offering was brought, of which the Musaf prayer is a memory. The central blessing of the Amida begins with a brief statement of the nature of the day, followed by a prayer for the restoration of the Temple and its sacrifices, a biblical passage describing the Rosh Ḥodesh offering, and a prayer that the new month be blessed for good.

מוסף לראש חודש

עמידה

The following prayer, until קַדְמֹנִיּוֹת *on page 757, is said silently, standing with feet together. If there is a* מנין*, the* עמידה *is repeated aloud by the* שליח ציבור*. Take three steps forward and at the points indicated by* ', *bend the knees at the first word, bow at the second, and stand straight before saying God's name.*

דברים לב כִּי שֵׁם יהוה אֶקְרָא, הָבוּ גֹדֶל לֵאלֹהֵינוּ:
תהלים נא אֲדֹנָי, שְׂפָתַי תִּפְתָּח, וּפִי יַגִּיד תְּהִלָּתֶךָ:

אבות

'בָּרוּךְ אַתָּה יהוה, אֱלֹהֵינוּ וֵאלֹהֵי אֲבוֹתֵינוּ
אֱלֹהֵי אַבְרָהָם, אֱלֹהֵי יִצְחָק, וֵאלֹהֵי יַעֲקֹב
הָאֵל הַגָּדוֹל הַגִּבּוֹר וְהַנּוֹרָא, אֵל עֶלְיוֹן
גּוֹמֵל חֲסָדִים טוֹבִים, וְקוֹנֵה הַכֹּל
וְזוֹכֵר חַסְדֵי אָבוֹת
וּמֵבִיא גוֹאֵל לִבְנֵי בְנֵיהֶם לְמַעַן שְׁמוֹ בְּאַהֲבָה.
מֶלֶךְ עוֹזֵר וּמוֹשִׁיעַ וּמָגֵן.
'בָּרוּךְ אַתָּה יהוה, מָגֵן אַבְרָהָם.

גבורות

אַתָּה גִּבּוֹר לְעוֹלָם, אֲדֹנָי
מְחַיֵּה מֵתִים אַתָּה, רַב לְהוֹשִׁיעַ

The phrase מַשִּׁיב הָרוּחַ *is added from* שמחת תורה *until* פסח.
In ארץ ישראל *the phrase* מוֹרִיד הַטָּל *is added from* פסח *until* שמיני עצרת. *See laws 129–131.*

בחורף: מַשִּׁיב הָרוּחַ וּמוֹרִיד הַגֶּשֶׁם / בארץ ישראל בקיץ: מוֹרִיד הַטָּל

ADDITIONAL SERVICE FOR THE NEW MOON
The New Moon, like the New Year, is understood in Judaism as a time of renewal and rededication, in which we pray for forgiveness and atonement

He sustains the living with loving-kindness,
and with great compassion revives the dead.
He supports the fallen, heals the sick, sets captives free,
and keeps His faith with those who sleep in the dust.
Who is like You, Master of might,
and who can compare to You,
O King who brings death and gives life,
and makes salvation grow?
Faithful are You to revive the dead.
Blessed are You, LORD, who revives the dead.

When saying the Amida silently, continue with "You are holy" on the next page.

KEDUSHA

During the Leader's Repetition, the following is said standing with feet together, rising on the toes at the words indicated by ▲.

Cong. then Leader: נְקַדֵּשׁ We will sanctify Your name on earth,
as they sanctify it in the highest heavens,
as is written by Your prophet,
"And they [the angels] call to one another saying: *Is. 6*

Cong. then Leader: ▲Holy, ▲holy, ▲holy is the LORD of hosts
the whole world is filled with His glory."
Those facing them say "Blessed – "

Cong. then Leader: ▲"Blessed is the LORD's glory from His place." *Ezek. 3*
And in Your holy Writings it is written thus:

Cong. then Leader: ▲"The LORD shall reign for ever. He is your God, Zion, *Ps. 146*
from generation to generation, Halleluya!"

Leader: From generation to generation we will declare Your greatness,
and we will proclaim Your holiness for evermore.
Your praise, our God, shall not leave our mouth forever,
for You, God, are a great and holy King.
Blessed are You, LORD, the holy God.

The Leader continues with "You have given New Moons" on the next page.

---

construction of the Tabernacle. From the first month of the second year after the exodus, the day the Tabernacle was dedicated, it became a women's festival (Rashi, *Megilla* 22b; *Shulḥan Arukh* OḤ 417:1).

מְכַלְכֵּל חַיִּים בְּחֶסֶד
מְחַיֵּה מֵתִים בְּרַחֲמִים רַבִּים
סוֹמֵךְ נוֹפְלִים, וְרוֹפֵא חוֹלִים, וּמַתִּיר אֲסוּרִים
וּמְקַיֵּם אֱמוּנָתוֹ לִישֵׁנֵי עָפָר.
מִי כָמְוֹךָ, בַּעַל גְּבוּרוֹת, וּמִי דּוֹמֶה לָּךְ
מֶלֶךְ, מֵמִית וּמְחַיֶּה וּמַצְמִיחַ יְשׁוּעָה.
וְנֶאֱמָן אַתָּה לְהַחֲיוֹת מֵתִים.
בָּרוּךְ אַתָּה יהוה, מְחַיֵּה הַמֵּתִים.

When saying the עמידה *silently, continue with* אַתָּה קָדוֹשׁ *on the next page.*

קדושה

During the חזרת הש״ץ*, the following is said standing with feet together, rising on the toes at the words indicated by* ˄*.*

then קהל ש״ץ: נְקַדֵּשׁ אֶת שִׁמְךָ בָּעוֹלָם, כְּשֵׁם שֶׁמַּקְדִּישִׁים אוֹתוֹ בִּשְׁמֵי מָרוֹם
כַּכָּתוּב עַל יַד נְבִיאֶךָ: וְקָרָא זֶה אֶל־זֶה וְאָמַר — ישעיה ו

then קהל ש״ץ: ˄קָדוֹשׁ, ˄קָדוֹשׁ, ˄קָדוֹשׁ, יהוה צְבָאוֹת, מְלֹא כָל־הָאָרֶץ כְּבוֹדוֹ:
לְעֻמָּתָם בָּרוּךְ יֹאמֵרוּ

then קהל ש״ץ: ˄בָּרוּךְ כְּבוֹד־יהוה מִמְּקוֹמוֹ: — יחזקאל ג
וּבְדִבְרֵי קָדְשְׁךָ כָּתוּב לֵאמֹר

then קהל ש״ץ: ˄יִמְלֹךְ יהוה לְעוֹלָם, אֱלֹהַיִךְ צִיּוֹן לְדֹר וָדֹר, הַלְלוּיָהּ: — תהלים קמו

ש״ץ: לְדוֹר וָדוֹר נַגִּיד גָּדְלֶךָ, וּלְנֵצַח נְצָחִים קְדֻשָּׁתְךָ נַקְדִּישׁ
וְשִׁבְחֲךָ אֱלֹהֵינוּ מִפִּינוּ לֹא יָמוּשׁ לְעוֹלָם וָעֶד
כִּי אֵל מֶלֶךְ גָּדוֹל וְקָדוֹשׁ אָתָּה.
בָּרוּךְ אַתָּה יהוה, הָאֵל הַקָּדוֹשׁ.

The שליח ציבור *continues with* רָאשֵׁי חֳדָשִׁים *on the next page.*

A midrashic tradition associates Rosh Ḥodesh with Jewish women, as a tribute to their faithfulness and to their generosity in providing gifts for the

HOLINESS

אַתָּה קָדוֹשׁ You are holy and Your name is holy,
and holy ones praise You daily, Selah!
Blessed are You, Lord, the holy God.

HOLINESS OF THE DAY

רָאשֵׁי חֳדָשִׁים You have given New Moons to Your people
as a time of atonement for all their offspring.
They would bring You offerings of goodwill,
and goats as sin-offerings for atonement.
May it serve as a remembrance for them all,
and a deliverance of their lives
from the hand of the enemy.
May You establish a new altar in Zion,
and may we offer on it
the New Moon burnt-offering,
and prepare goats in favor.
May we all rejoice in the Temple service,
and may the songs of David Your servant,
be heard in Your city,
chanted before Your altar.
Bestow on them everlasting love,
and remember the covenant of the fathers for their children.

וַהֲבִיאֵנוּ Bring us back, with song,
to Zion Your city,
and to Jerusalem Your Sanctuary with everlasting joy.
There we will prepare for You our obligatory offerings:
the regular daily offerings in their order,
and the additional offerings according to their law.

---

the moon shines with reflected light. So too with Israel: the light with which we shine comes not from ourselves but from God, of whose glory we are but a reflection (Seforno, Num. 28:11).

קדושת השם

אַתָּה קָדוֹשׁ וְשִׁמְךָ קָדוֹשׁ
וּקְדוֹשִׁים בְּכָל יוֹם יְהַלְלוּךָ סֶּלָה.
בָּרוּךְ אַתָּה יהוה, הָאֵל הַקָּדוֹשׁ.

קדושת היום

רָאשֵׁי חֳדָשִׁים לְעַמְּךָ נָתַתָּ
זְמַן כַּפָּרָה לְכָל תּוֹלְדוֹתָם
בִּהְיוֹתָם מַקְרִיבִים לְפָנֶיךָ זִבְחֵי רָצוֹן
וּשְׂעִירֵי חַטָּאת לְכַפֵּר בַּעֲדָם.
זִכָּרוֹן לְכֻלָּם יִהְיוּ, וּתְשׁוּעַת נַפְשָׁם מִיַּד שׂוֹנֵא.
מִזְבֵּחַ חָדָשׁ בְּצִיּוֹן תָּכִין
וְעוֹלַת רֹאשׁ חֹדֶשׁ נַעֲלֶה עָלָיו
וּשְׂעִירֵי עִזִּים נַעֲשֶׂה בְרָצוֹן
וּבַעֲבוֹדַת בֵּית הַמִּקְדָּשׁ נִשְׂמַח כֻּלָּנוּ
וּבְשִׁירֵי דָוִד עַבְדְּךָ הַנִּשְׁמָעִים בְּעִירֶךָ
הָאֲמוּרִים לִפְנֵי מִזְבְּחֶךָ.
אַהֲבַת עוֹלָם תָּבִיא לָהֶם, וּבְרִית אָבוֹת לַבָּנִים תִּזְכֹּר.
וַהֲבִיאֵנוּ לְצִיּוֹן עִירְךָ בְּרִנָּה
וְלִירוּשָׁלַיִם בֵּית מִקְדָּשְׁךָ בְּשִׂמְחַת עוֹלָם
וְשָׁם נַעֲשֶׂה לְפָנֶיךָ אֶת קָרְבְּנוֹת חוֹבוֹתֵינוּ
תְּמִידִים כְּסִדְרָם וּמוּסָפִים כְּהִלְכָתָם.

רָאשֵׁי חֳדָשִׁים *You have given New Moons to Your people:* The Jewish people is compared to the moon because, whereas the sun shines with its own light,

וְאֶת מוּסַף The additional offering of this New Moon day
we will prepare and offer to You
with love according to Your will's commandment,
as You have written for us in Your Torah
by Your own word, through Your servant Moses,
as it is said:

"On your new moons, *Num. 28*
present as a burnt-offering to the LORD,
two young bulls, one ram,
and seven yearling lambs without blemish."

וּמִנְחָתָם And their meal-offerings
and wine-libations as ordained:
three-tenths of an ephah for each bull,
two-tenths of an ephah for the ram,
one-tenth of an ephah for each lamb,
wine for the libations, a male goat for atonement,
and two regular daily offerings according to their law.

אֱלֹהֵינוּ O God and God of our ancestors,
renew for us the coming month for good and blessing,
joy and gladness, deliverance and consolation,
sustenance and support,
life and peace,
pardon of sin and forgiveness of iniquity
(*From Marḥeshvan to Adar II in a Jewish leap year (see page 1332)* and atonement of transgression).
For You have chosen Your people Israel from all nations,
and have instituted for them rules for the New Moon.
Blessed are You, LORD, who sanctifies Israel and the New Moons.

Ex. 12:2), hence the six double expressions of blessing. In a leap year there are seven months before Nisan, hence a seventh expression is added from Marḥeshvan to Adar II.

וְאֶת מוּסַף יוֹם רֹאשׁ הַחֹדֶשׁ הַזֶּה
נַעֲשֶׂה וְנַקְרִיב לְפָנֶיךָ בְּאַהֲבָה כְּמִצְוַת רְצוֹנֶךָ
כְּמוֹ שֶׁכָּתַבְתָּ עָלֵינוּ בְּתוֹרָתֶךָ
עַל יְדֵי מֹשֶׁה עַבְדֶּךָ מִפִּי כְבוֹדֶךָ
כָּאָמוּר
וּבְרָאשֵׁי חָדְשֵׁיכֶם תַּקְרִיבוּ עֹלָה לַיהוה במדבר כח
פָּרִים בְּנֵי־בָקָר שְׁנַיִם וְאַיִל אֶחָד
כְּבָשִׂים בְּנֵי־שָׁנָה שִׁבְעָה, תְּמִימִם:

וּמִנְחָתָם וְנִסְכֵּיהֶם כִּמְדֻבָּר
שְׁלֹשָׁה עֶשְׂרֹנִים לַפָּר, וּשְׁנֵי עֶשְׂרֹנִים לָאָיִל
וְעִשָּׂרוֹן לַכֶּבֶשׂ, וְיַיִן כְּנִסְכּוֹ, וְשָׂעִיר לְכַפֵּר
וּשְׁנֵי תְמִידִים כְּהִלְכָתָם.

אֱלֹהֵינוּ וֵאלֹהֵי אֲבוֹתֵינוּ
חַדֵּשׁ עָלֵינוּ אֶת הַחֹדֶשׁ הַזֶּה לְטוֹבָה וְלִבְרָכָה
לְשָׂשׂוֹן וּלְשִׂמְחָה, לִישׁוּעָה וּלְנֶחָמָה
לְפַרְנָסָה וּלְכַלְכָּלָה, לְחַיִּים וּלְשָׁלוֹם
לִמְחִילַת חֵטְא וְלִסְלִיחַת עָוֹן
(*From* מרחשון *to* אדר שני *in a Jewish leap year* (*see page 1332*) וּלְכַפָּרַת פָּשַׁע)
כִּי בְעַמְּךָ יִשְׂרָאֵל בָּחַרְתָּ מִכָּל הָאֻמּוֹת
וְחֻקֵּי רָאשֵׁי חֳדָשִׁים לָהֶם קָבָעְתָּ.
בָּרוּךְ אַתָּה יהוה, מְקַדֵּשׁ יִשְׂרָאֵל וְרָאשֵׁי חֳדָשִׁים.

וּלְכַפָּרַת פָּשַׁע *And atonement for transgression:* There are six months from Tishrei (Rosh HaShana, the beginning of the year) to Nisan (the first of months:

TEMPLE SERVICE

רְצֵה Find favor, LORD our God,
in Your people Israel and their prayer.
Restore the service to Your most holy House,
and accept in love and favor
the fire-offerings of Israel and their prayer.
May the service of Your people Israel always find favor with You
And may our eyes
witness Your return to Zion in compassion.
Blessed are You, LORD, who restores His Presence to Zion.

THANKSGIVING

Bow at the first nine words.

מוֹדִים We give thanks to You,
for You are the LORD our God
and God of our ancestors
for ever and all time.
You are the Rock of our lives,
Shield of our salvation
from generation to generation.
We will thank You and
declare Your praise for our lives,
which are entrusted into Your hand;
for our souls,
which are placed in Your charge;
for Your miracles
which are with us every day;
and for Your wonders and favors
at all times, evening, morning and midday.
You are good –
for Your compassion never fails.
You are compassionate –
for Your loving-kindnesses never cease.
We have always placed our hope in You.

During the Leader's Repetition, the congregation says quietly:

מוֹדִים We give thanks to You,
for You are the
LORD our God
and God of our ancestors,
God of all flesh,
who formed us
and formed the universe.
Blessings and thanks
are due to Your great
and holy name for giving us
life and sustaining us.
May You continue
to give us life and sustain us;
and may You gather our
exiles to Your holy courts,
to keep Your decrees,
do Your will and serve You
with a perfect heart,
for it is for us
to give You thanks.
Blessed be God to whom
thanksgiving is due.

עבודה

רְצֵה יהוה אֱלֹהֵינוּ בְּעַמְּךָ יִשְׂרָאֵל, וּבִתְפִלָּתָם
וְהָשֵׁב אֶת הָעֲבוֹדָה לִדְבִיר בֵּיתֶךָ
וְאִשֵּׁי יִשְׂרָאֵל וּתְפִלָּתָם בְּאַהֲבָה תְקַבֵּל בְּרָצוֹן
וּתְהִי לְרָצוֹן תָּמִיד עֲבוֹדַת יִשְׂרָאֵל עַמֶּךָ.
וְתֶחֱזֶינָה עֵינֵינוּ בְּשׁוּבְךָ לְצִיּוֹן בְּרַחֲמִים.
בָּרוּךְ אַתָּה יהוה, הַמַּחֲזִיר שְׁכִינָתוֹ לְצִיּוֹן.

הודאה

Bow at the first five words.

מוֹדִים אֲנַחְנוּ לָךְ
שָׁאַתָּה הוּא יהוה אֱלֹהֵינוּ
וֵאלֹהֵי אֲבוֹתֵינוּ לְעוֹלָם וָעֶד.
צוּר חַיֵּינוּ, מָגֵן יִשְׁעֵנוּ
אַתָּה הוּא לְדוֹר וָדוֹר.
נוֹדֶה לְּךָ וּנְסַפֵּר תְּהִלָּתֶךָ
עַל חַיֵּינוּ הַמְּסוּרִים בְּיָדֶךָ
וְעַל נִשְׁמוֹתֵינוּ הַפְּקוּדוֹת לָךְ
וְעַל נִסֶּיךָ שֶׁבְּכָל יוֹם עִמָּנוּ
וְעַל נִפְלְאוֹתֶיךָ וְטוֹבוֹתֶיךָ
שֶׁבְּכָל עֵת
עֶרֶב וָבֹקֶר וְצָהֳרָיִם.
הַטּוֹב, כִּי לֹא כָלוּ רַחֲמֶיךָ
וְהַמְרַחֵם, כִּי לֹא תַמּוּ חֲסָדֶיךָ
מֵעוֹלָם קִוִּינוּ לָךְ.

During the חזרת הש״ץ, *the* קהל *says quietly:*

מוֹדִים אֲנַחְנוּ לָךְ
שָׁאַתָּה הוּא יהוה אֱלֹהֵינוּ
וֵאלֹהֵי אֲבוֹתֵינוּ
אֱלֹהֵי כָל בָּשָׂר
יוֹצְרֵנוּ, יוֹצֵר בְּרֵאשִׁית.
בְּרָכוֹת וְהוֹדָאוֹת
לְשִׁמְךָ הַגָּדוֹל וְהַקָּדוֹשׁ
עַל שֶׁהֶחֱיִיתָנוּ וְקִיַּמְתָּנוּ.
כֵּן תְּחַיֵּנוּ וּתְקַיְּמֵנוּ
וְתֶאֱסֹף גָּלֻיּוֹתֵינוּ
לְחַצְרוֹת קָדְשֶׁךָ
לִשְׁמֹר חֻקֶּיךָ
וְלַעֲשׂוֹת רְצוֹנֶךָ וּלְעָבְדְּךָ
בְּלֵבָב שָׁלֵם
עַל שֶׁאֲנַחְנוּ מוֹדִים לָךְ.
בָּרוּךְ אֵל הַהוֹדָאוֹת.

On Ḥanukka:

עַל הַנִּסִּים [We thank You also] for the miracles, the redemption, the mighty deeds, the salvations, and the victories in battle which You performed for our ancestors in those days, at this time.

בִּימֵי מַתִּתְיָהוּ In the days of Mattityahu, son of Yoḥanan, the High Priest, the Hasmonean, and his sons, the wicked Greek kingdom rose up against Your people Israel to make them forget Your Torah and to force them to transgress the statutes of Your will. It was then that You in Your great compassion stood by them in the time of their distress. You championed their cause, judged their claim, and avenged their wrong. You delivered the strong into the hands of the weak, the many into the hands of the few, the impure into the hands of the pure, the wicked into the hands of the righteous, and the arrogant into the hands of those who were engaged in the study of Your Torah. You made for Yourself great and holy renown in Your world, and for Your people Israel You performed a great salvation and redemption as of this very day. Your children then entered the holiest part of Your House, cleansed Your Temple, purified Your Sanctuary, kindled lights in Your holy courts, and designated these eight days of Ḥanukka for giving thanks and praise to Your great name.

Continue with "For all these things."

וְעַל כֻּלָּם For all these things may Your name be blessed and exalted,
our King, continually, for ever and all time.
Let all that lives thank You, Selah! and praise Your name in truth,
God, our Savior and Help, Selah!
▾Blessed are You, Lord, whose name is "the Good"
and to whom thanks are due.

When saying the Amida silently, continue with "Grant peace" on the next page.

The following is said by the Leader during the Repetition of the Amida.
In Israel, if Kohanim bless the congregation, turn to page 838. See laws 370–377.

Our God and God of our fathers, bless us with the threefold blessing in the Torah, written by the hand of Moses Your servant and pronounced by Aaron and his sons the priests, Your holy people, as it is said:

May the Lord bless you and protect you. *Num. 6*
Cong: May it be Your will.
May the Lord make His face shine on you and be gracious to you.
Cong: May it be Your will.
May the Lord turn His face toward you, and grant you peace.
Cong: May it be Your will.

The Leader continues with "Grant peace" on the next page.

בחנוכה:

עַל הַנִּסִּים וְעַל הַפֻּרְקָן וְעַל הַגְּבוּרוֹת וְעַל הַתְּשׁוּעוֹת וְעַל הַמִּלְחָמוֹת שֶׁעָשִׂיתָ לַאֲבוֹתֵינוּ בַּיָּמִים הָהֵם בִּזְּמַן הַזֶּה.

בִּימֵי מַתִּתְיָהוּ בֶּן יוֹחָנָן כֹּהֵן גָּדוֹל חַשְׁמוֹנַאי וּבָנָיו, כְּשֶׁעָמְדָה מַלְכוּת יָוָן הָרְשָׁעָה עַל עַמְּךָ יִשְׂרָאֵל לְהַשְׁכִּיחָם תּוֹרָתֶךָ וּלְהַעֲבִירָם מֵחֻקֵּי רְצוֹנֶךָ, וְאַתָּה בְּרַחֲמֶיךָ הָרַבִּים עָמַדְתָּ לָהֶם בְּעֵת צָרָתָם, רַבְתָּ אֶת רִיבָם, דַּנְתָּ אֶת דִּינָם, נָקַמְתָּ אֶת נִקְמָתָם, מָסַרְתָּ גִבּוֹרִים בְּיַד חַלָּשִׁים, וְרַבִּים בְּיַד מְעַטִּים, וּטְמֵאִים בְּיַד טְהוֹרִים, וּרְשָׁעִים בְּיַד צַדִּיקִים, וְזֵדִים בְּיַד עוֹסְקֵי תוֹרָתֶךָ, וּלְךָ עָשִׂיתָ שֵׁם גָּדוֹל וְקָדוֹשׁ בְּעוֹלָמֶךָ, וּלְעַמְּךָ יִשְׂרָאֵל עָשִׂיתָ תְּשׁוּעָה גְדוֹלָה וּפֻרְקָן כְּהַיּוֹם הַזֶּה. וְאַחַר כֵּן בָּאוּ בָנֶיךָ לִדְבִיר בֵּיתֶךָ, וּפִנּוּ אֶת הֵיכָלֶךָ, וְטִהֲרוּ אֶת מִקְדָּשֶׁךָ, וְהִדְלִיקוּ נֵרוֹת בְּחַצְרוֹת קָדְשֶׁךָ, וְקָבְעוּ שְׁמוֹנַת יְמֵי חֲנֻכָּה אֵלּוּ, לְהוֹדוֹת וּלְהַלֵּל לְשִׁמְךָ הַגָּדוֹל.

Continue with וְעַל כֻּלָּם.

וְעַל כֻּלָּם יִתְבָּרַךְ וְיִתְרוֹמַם שִׁמְךָ מַלְכֵּנוּ תָּמִיד לְעוֹלָם וָעֶד.
וְכֹל הַחַיִּים יוֹדוּךָ סֶּלָה, וִיהַלְלוּ אֶת שִׁמְךָ בֶּאֱמֶת הָאֵל יְשׁוּעָתֵנוּ וְעֶזְרָתֵנוּ סֶלָה.
בָּרוּךְ אַתָּה יהוה, הַטּוֹב שִׁמְךָ וּלְךָ נָאֶה לְהוֹדוֹת.

When saying the עמידה *silently, continue with* שִׂים שָׁלוֹם *on the next page.*

The following is said by the שליח ציבור *during the* חזרת הש״ץ.
In ארץ ישראל, *if* כהנים *say* ברכת כהנים, *turn to page 839. See laws 370–377.*

אֱלֹהֵינוּ וֵאלֹהֵי אֲבוֹתֵינוּ, בָּרְכֵנוּ בַּבְּרָכָה הַמְשֻׁלֶּשֶׁת בַּתּוֹרָה, הַכְּתוּבָה עַל יְדֵי מֹשֶׁה עַבְדֶּךָ, הָאֲמוּרָה מִפִּי אַהֲרֹן וּבָנָיו כֹּהֲנִים עַם קְדוֹשֶׁיךָ, כָּאָמוּר

יְבָרֶכְךָ יהוה וְיִשְׁמְרֶךָ: קהל: כֵּן יְהִי רָצוֹן — במדבר ו
יָאֵר יהוה פָּנָיו אֵלֶיךָ וִיחֻנֶּךָּ: קהל: כֵּן יְהִי רָצוֹן
יִשָּׂא יהוה פָּנָיו אֵלֶיךָ וְיָשֵׂם לְךָ שָׁלוֹם: קהל: כֵּן יְהִי רָצוֹן

The שליח ציבור *continues with* שִׂים שָׁלוֹם *on the next page.*

PEACE

שִׂים שָׁלוֹם Grant peace, goodness and blessing,
grace, loving-kindness and compassion
to us and all Israel Your people.
Bless us, our Father, all as one, with the light of Your face,
for by the light of Your face You have given us, LORD our God,
the Torah of life and love of kindness,
righteousness, blessing, compassion, life and peace.
May it be good in Your eyes to bless Your people Israel
at every time, in every hour, with Your peace.
Blessed are You, LORD, who blesses His people Israel with peace.

The following verse concludes the Leader's Repetition of the Amida.
Some also say it here as part of the silent Amida. See law 368.

May the words of my mouth and the meditation of my heart *Ps. 19*
find favor before You, LORD, my Rock and Redeemer.

אֱלֹהַי My God, guard my tongue from evil *Berakhot 17a*
and my lips from deceitful speech.
To those who curse me, let my soul be silent;
may my soul be to all like the dust.
Open my heart to Your Torah and let my soul pursue Your commandments.
As for all who plan evil against me,
swiftly thwart their counsel and frustrate their plans.
Act for the sake of Your name; act for the sake of Your right hand;
act for the sake of Your holiness; act for the sake of Your Torah.
That Your beloved ones may be delivered, *Ps. 60*
save with Your right hand and answer me.
May the words of my mouth and the meditation of my heart *Ps. 19*
find favor before You, LORD, my Rock and Redeemer.

Bow, take three steps back, then bow, first left, then right, then center, while saying:

May He who makes peace in His high places,
make peace for us and all Israel – and say: Amen.

יְהִי רָצוֹן May it be Your will, LORD our God and God of our ancestors,
that the Temple be rebuilt speedily in our days, and grant us a share in Your Torah.
And there we will serve You with reverence, as in the days of old and as in former years.
Then the offering of Judah and Jerusalem *Mal. 3*
will be pleasing to the LORD as in the days of old and as in former years.

After the Leader's Repetition, the service continues with Full Kaddish (page 178),
followed by Aleinu (page 180), the Daily Psalm (page 184) and Barekhi Nafshi (page 190).

ברכת שלום

שִׂים שָׁלוֹם טוֹבָה וּבְרָכָה
חֵן וָחֶסֶד וְרַחֲמִים עָלֵינוּ וְעַל כָּל יִשְׂרָאֵל עַמֶּךָ.
בָּרְכֵנוּ אָבִינוּ כֻּלָּנוּ כְּאֶחָד בְּאוֹר פָּנֶיךָ
כִּי בְאוֹר פָּנֶיךָ נָתַתָּ לָּנוּ יהוה אֱלֹהֵינוּ
תּוֹרַת חַיִּים וְאַהֲבַת חֶסֶד וּצְדָקָה וּבְרָכָה וְרַחֲמִים וְחַיִּים וְשָׁלוֹם.
וְטוֹב בְּעֵינֶיךָ לְבָרֵךְ אֶת עַמְּךָ יִשְׂרָאֵל
בְּכָל עֵת וּבְכָל שָׁעָה בִּשְׁלוֹמֶךָ.
בָּרוּךְ אַתָּה יהוה, הַמְבָרֵךְ אֶת עַמּוֹ יִשְׂרָאֵל בַּשָּׁלוֹם.

The following verse concludes the חזרת הש״ץ*.*
Some also say it here as part of the silent עמידה*. See law 368.*

יִהְיוּ לְרָצוֹן אִמְרֵי־פִי וְהֶגְיוֹן לִבִּי לְפָנֶיךָ, יהוה צוּרִי וְגֹאֲלִי: תהלים יט

אֱלֹהַי, נְצֹר לְשׁוֹנִי מֵרָע וּשְׂפָתַי מִדַּבֵּר מִרְמָה ברכות יז.
וְלִמְקַלְלַי נַפְשִׁי תִדֹּם, וְנַפְשִׁי כֶּעָפָר לַכֹּל תִּהְיֶה.
פְּתַח לִבִּי בְּתוֹרָתֶךָ, וּבְמִצְוֹתֶיךָ תִּרְדֹּף נַפְשִׁי.
וְכָל הַחוֹשְׁבִים עָלַי רָעָה מְהֵרָה הָפֵר עֲצָתָם וְקַלְקֵל מַחֲשַׁבְתָּם.
עֲשֵׂה לְמַעַן שְׁמֶךָ, עֲשֵׂה לְמַעַן יְמִינֶךָ
עֲשֵׂה לְמַעַן קְדֻשָּׁתֶךָ, עֲשֵׂה לְמַעַן תּוֹרָתֶךָ.
לְמַעַן יֵחָלְצוּן יְדִידֶיךָ, הוֹשִׁיעָה יְמִינְךָ וַעֲנֵנִי: תהלים ס
יִהְיוּ לְרָצוֹן אִמְרֵי־פִי וְהֶגְיוֹן לִבִּי לְפָנֶיךָ, יהוה צוּרִי וְגֹאֲלִי: תהלים יט

Bow, take three steps back, then bow, first left, then right, then center, while saying:

עֹשֶׂה שָׁלוֹם בִּמְרוֹמָיו
הוּא יַעֲשֶׂה שָׁלוֹם עָלֵינוּ וְעַל כָּל יִשְׂרָאֵל, וְאִמְרוּ אָמֵן.

יְהִי רָצוֹן מִלְּפָנֶיךָ יהוה אֱלֹהֵינוּ וֵאלֹהֵי אֲבוֹתֵינוּ
שֶׁיִּבָּנֶה בֵּית הַמִּקְדָּשׁ בִּמְהֵרָה בְיָמֵינוּ, וְתֵן חֶלְקֵנוּ בְּתוֹרָתֶךָ
וְשָׁם נַעֲבָדְךָ בְּיִרְאָה כִּימֵי עוֹלָם וּכְשָׁנִים קַדְמוֹנִיּוֹת.
וְעָרְבָה לַיהוה מִנְחַת יְהוּדָה וִירוּשָׁלָםִ כִּימֵי עוֹלָם וּכְשָׁנִים קַדְמֹנִיּוֹת: מלאכי ג

After the חזרת הש״ץ*, the service continues with* קדיש שלם *(page 179),*
followed by עָלֵינוּ *(page 181),* שיר של יום *(page 185) and* בָּרְכִי נַפְשִׁי *(page 191).*

REMOVAL OF ḤAMETZ

On the night before Pesaḥ, a search for ḥametz, such as breadcrumbs, products containing leaven and grain alcohol, is made in the house. The custom is to do so at night by the light of a candle, but a flashlight may also be used. If Pesaḥ falls on Motza'ei Shabbat, the search is made on Thursday night. Those who plan to be away on Pesaḥ should conduct the search the night before their departure, but without making a blessing. Before the search, make the following blessing:

בָּרוּךְ Blessed are You, LORD our God, King of the Universe,
who has made us holy through His commandments,
and has commanded us about the removal of leaven.

After the search, say:

כָּל חֲמִירָא May all ḥametz or leaven that is in my possession
which I have not seen or removed
be annulled and deemed like the dust of the earth.

On the following morning after burning the ḥametz, say:

כָּל חֲמִירָא May all ḥametz or leaven that is in my possession,
whether I have seen it or not, whether I have removed it or not,
be annulled and deemed like the dust of the earth.

EIRUV TAVSHILIN

It is not permitted to cook for Shabbat when a Yom Tov falls on Thursday or Friday unless an Eiruv Tavshilin has been made prior to the Yom Tov. This is done by taking a loaf or piece of matza together with a boiled egg, or a piece of cooked fish or meat to be used on Shabbat. While holding them, say the following:

בָּרוּךְ Blessed are You, LORD our God, King of the Universe,
who has made us holy through His commandments,
and has commanded us about the mitzva of Eiruv.

By this Eiruv may we be permitted to bake, cook, insulate food, light a flame
and do everything necessary on the festival for the sake of Shabbat,
for us and for all Jews living in this city.

For Eiruv Teḥumin see page 304. For Candle Lighting see page 304.

---

to the search refers to the removal, since the search is a means to that end. The two declarations – one made at night after the search, the other in the morning after the removal – constitute a legal nullification and renunciation of ownership of any remaining *ḥametz*.

ביעור חמץ

On the night before פסח, a search for חמץ, such as breadcrumbs, products containing leaven and grain alcohol, is made in the house. The custom is to do so at night by the light of a candle, but a flashlight may also be used. If פסח falls on מוצאי שבת, the search is made on Thursday night. Those who plan to be away on פסח should conduct the search the night before their departure, but without making a blessing. Before the search, make the following blessing:

בָּרוּךְ אַתָּה יהוה אֱלֹהֵינוּ מֶלֶךְ הָעוֹלָם
אֲשֶׁר קִדְּשָׁנוּ בְּמִצְוֹתָיו וְצִוָּנוּ עַל בִּעוּר חָמֵץ.

After the search, say:

כָּל חֲמִירָא וַחֲמִיעָא דְּאִכָּא בִרְשׁוּתִי, דְּלָא חֲמִתֵּהּ וּדְלָא בִעַרְתֵּהּ
לִבְטִיל וְלֶהֱוֵי הֶפְקֵר כְּעַפְרָא דְאַרְעָא.

On the following morning after burning the חמץ, say:

כָּל חֲמִירָא וַחֲמִיעָא דְּאִכָּא בִרְשׁוּתִי, דַּחֲמִתֵּהּ וּדְלָא חֲמִתֵּהּ
דְּבִעַרְתֵּהּ וּדְלָא בִעַרְתֵּהּ, לִבְטִיל וְלֶהֱוֵי הֶפְקֵר כְּעַפְרָא דְאַרְעָא.

עירוב תבשילין

It is not permitted to cook for שבת when a יום טוב falls on Thursday or Friday unless an עירוב תבשילין has been made prior to the יום טוב. This is done by taking a loaf or piece of matza together with a boiled egg, or a piece of cooked fish or meat to be used on שבת. While holding them, say the following:

בָּרוּךְ אַתָּה יהוה אֱלֹהֵינוּ מֶלֶךְ הָעוֹלָם
אֲשֶׁר קִדְּשָׁנוּ בְּמִצְוֹתָיו וְצִוָּנוּ עַל מִצְוַת עֵרוּב.
בְּדֵין עֵרוּבָא יְהֵא שְׁרֵא לָנָא לְמֵיפָא וּלְבַשָּׁלָא וּלְאַטְמָנָא וּלְאַדְלָקָא שְׁרָגָא
וּלְמֶעְבַּד כָּל צָרְכָּנָא מִיּוֹמָא טָבָא לְשַׁבְּתָא, לָנוּ וּלְכָל יִשְׂרָאֵל הַדָּרִים בָּעִיר הַזֹּאת.

For עירוב תחומין see page 305. For הדלקת נרות see page 305.

SEARCH FOR ḤAMETZ

On Pesaḥ, not only is it forbidden to eat leavened products, it is also forbidden to have them in our possession (Ex. 12:19; 13:7). For that reason, a search was instituted on the night before the festival. All leaven is to be removed (usually destroyed by burning) the next morning. The blessing said prior

Kiddush for Festival Evening

On Shabbat add:

quietly: And it was evening, and it was morning – *Gen. 1*
יוֹם הַשִּׁשִּׁי the sixth day.

Then the heavens and the earth were completed, *Gen. 2*
and all their array.
With the seventh day, God completed the work He had done.
He ceased on the seventh day from all the work He had done.
God blessed the seventh day and declared it holy,
because on it He ceased from all His work He had created to do.

On other evenings Kiddush starts here:

When saying Kiddush for others, add:
Please pay attention, my masters.

Blessed are You, LORD our God, King of the Universe,
who creates the fruit of the vine.

On Shabbat, add the words in parentheses.

בָּרוּךְ Blessed are You, LORD our God,
King of the Universe,
who has chosen us from among all peoples,
raised us above all tongues,
and made us holy through His commandments.
You have given us, LORD our God, in love
(Sabbaths for rest), festivals for rejoicing,
holy days and seasons for joy, (this Sabbath day and) this day of:

---

the sukka" is said throughout the seven days of the festival whenever we eat in the sukka. The blessing "who has given us life" refers to two things: (1) the holiness of the day itself, and (2) the first act of sitting in the sukka. On the first night, "who has given us life" is said last so that it can refer to both. On the second night, it no longer refers to sitting in the sukka since this is not the first time we have done so. Thus, it is said immediately after Kiddush, since it only refers to the holiness of the day.

קידוש לליל שלוש רגלים

On שבת *add:*

בראשית א
quietly וַיְהִי־עֶרֶב וַיְהִי־בֹקֶר

יוֹם הַשִּׁשִּׁי:

בראשית ב
וַיְכֻלּוּ הַשָּׁמַיִם וְהָאָרֶץ וְכָל־צְבָאָם:
וַיְכַל אֱלֹהִים בַּיּוֹם הַשְּׁבִיעִי מְלַאכְתּוֹ אֲשֶׁר עָשָׂה
וַיִּשְׁבֹּת בַּיּוֹם הַשְּׁבִיעִי מִכָּל־מְלַאכְתּוֹ אֲשֶׁר עָשָׂה:
וַיְבָרֶךְ אֱלֹהִים אֶת־יוֹם הַשְּׁבִיעִי, וַיְקַדֵּשׁ אֹתוֹ
כִּי בוֹ שָׁבַת מִכָּל־מְלַאכְתּוֹ, אֲשֶׁר־בָּרָא אֱלֹהִים, לַעֲשׂוֹת:

On other evenings the קידוש *starts here:*

When saying קידוש *for others, add:*

סַבְרִי מָרָנָן

בָּרוּךְ אַתָּה יהוה אֱלֹהֵינוּ מֶלֶךְ הָעוֹלָם, בּוֹרֵא פְּרִי הַגָּפֶן.

On שבת*, add the words in parentheses.*

בָּרוּךְ אַתָּה יהוה אֱלֹהֵינוּ מֶלֶךְ הָעוֹלָם
אֲשֶׁר בָּחַר בָּנוּ מִכָּל עָם
וְרוֹמְמָנוּ מִכָּל לָשׁוֹן, וְקִדְּשָׁנוּ בְּמִצְוֹתָיו
וַתִּתֶּן לָנוּ יהוה אֱלֹהֵינוּ בְּאַהֲבָה
(שַׁבָּתוֹת לִמְנוּחָה וּ) מוֹעֲדִים לְשִׂמְחָה
חַגִּים וּזְמַנִּים לְשָׂשׂוֹן, אֶת יוֹם (הַשַּׁבָּת הַזֶּה וְאֶת יוֹם)

KIDDUSH FOR FESTIVALS

As in the Amida, the emphasis on the idea of the chosen people signifies that it was through the epic events of Israel's history recalled on the festivals – the exodus, the giving of the Torah, and the forty years of wandering in the wilderness – that God was made manifest in history.

Blessings in the sukka: The blessing "who has commanded us to dwell in

On Pesaḥ: the festival of Matzot,
the time of our freedom
On Shavuot: the festival of Shavuot,
the time of the giving of our Torah
On Sukkot: the festival of Sukkot,
our time of rejoicing
On Shemini Atzeret & Simḥat Torah: the festival of the eighth day, Shemini Atzeret,
our time of rejoicing

(with love), a holy assembly in memory of the exodus from Egypt.
For You have chosen us and sanctified us above all peoples,
and given us as our heritage (Your holy Sabbath in love and favor and)
Your holy festivals for joy and gladness.
Blessed are you, Lord,
who sanctifies (the Sabbath,) Israel and the festivals.

On Motza'ei Shabbat, the following Havdala is added:

בָּרוּךְ Blessed are You, Lord our God, King of the Universe,
who creates the lights of fire.

Blessed are You, Lord our God, King of the Universe, who distinguishes between sacred and secular, between light and darkness, between Israel and the nations, between the seventh day and the six days of work. You have made a distinction between the holiness of the Sabbath and the holiness of festivals, and have sanctified the seventh day above the six days of work. You have distinguished and sanctified Your people Israel with Your holiness. Blessed are You, Lord, who distinguishes between sacred and sacred.

On Sukkot, say the following blessing. On the first night it is said before the blessing "who has given us life"; on the second night, after it (some say it before on both nights).

בָּרוּךְ Blessed are You, Lord our God, King of the Universe,
who has made us holy though His commandments,
and has commanded us to dwell in the sukka.

The following blessing is omitted on the last two nights of Pesaḥ (in Israel, the last night).

בָּרוּךְ Blessed are You, Lord our God, King of the Universe,
who has given us life, sustained us, and brought us to this time.

It is customary for all present to drink of the wine.

בפסח: חַג הַמַּצּוֹת הַזֶּה, זְמַן חֵרוּתֵנוּ

בשבועות: חַג הַשָּׁבוּעוֹת הַזֶּה, זְמַן מַתַּן תּוֹרָתֵנוּ

בסוכות: חַג הַסֻּכּוֹת הַזֶּה, זְמַן שִׂמְחָתֵנוּ

בשמע״צ ובש״ת: הַשְּׁמִינִי חַג הָעֲצֶרֶת הַזֶּה, זְמַן שִׂמְחָתֵנוּ

(בְּאַהֲבָה) מִקְרָא קֹדֶשׁ, זֵכֶר לִיצִיאַת מִצְרָיִם
כִּי בָנוּ בָחַרְתָּ וְאוֹתָנוּ קִדַּשְׁתָּ מִכָּל הָעַמִּים (וְשַׁבָּת)
וּמוֹעֲדֵי קָדְשֶׁךָ (בְּאַהֲבָה וּבְרָצוֹן)
בְּשִׂמְחָה וּבְשָׂשׂוֹן הִנְחַלְתָּנוּ.

בָּרוּךְ אַתָּה יהוה, מְקַדֵּשׁ (הַשַּׁבָּת וְ) יִשְׂרָאֵל וְהַזְּמַנִּים.

On מוצאי שבת, the following הבדלה is added:

בָּרוּךְ אַתָּה יהוה אֱלֹהֵינוּ מֶלֶךְ הָעוֹלָם
בּוֹרֵא מְאוֹרֵי הָאֵשׁ.

בָּרוּךְ אַתָּה יהוה אֱלֹהֵינוּ מֶלֶךְ הָעוֹלָם, הַמַּבְדִּיל בֵּין קֹדֶשׁ לְחֹל, בֵּין אוֹר לְחֹשֶׁךְ, בֵּין יִשְׂרָאֵל לָעַמִּים, בֵּין יוֹם הַשְּׁבִיעִי לְשֵׁשֶׁת יְמֵי הַמַּעֲשֶׂה. בֵּין קְדֻשַּׁת שַׁבָּת לִקְדֻשַּׁת יוֹם טוֹב הִבְדַּלְתָּ, וְאֶת יוֹם הַשְּׁבִיעִי מִשֵּׁשֶׁת יְמֵי הַמַּעֲשֶׂה קִדַּשְׁתָּ, הִבְדַּלְתָּ וְקִדַּשְׁתָּ אֶת עַמְּךָ יִשְׂרָאֵל בִּקְדֻשָּׁתֶךָ. בָּרוּךְ אַתָּה יהוה, הַמַּבְדִּיל בֵּין קֹדֶשׁ לְקֹדֶשׁ.

On סוכות, say the following blessing. On the first night it is said before the blessing שֶׁהֶחֱיָנוּ; on the second night, after it (some say it before on both nights).

בָּרוּךְ אַתָּה יהוה אֱלֹהֵינוּ מֶלֶךְ הָעוֹלָם
אֲשֶׁר קִדְּשָׁנוּ בְּמִצְוֹתָיו וְצִוָּנוּ לֵישֵׁב בַּסֻּכָּה.

The following blessing is omitted on the last two nights of פסח (in ארץ ישראל, the last night).

בָּרוּךְ אַתָּה יהוה אֱלֹהֵינוּ מֶלֶךְ הָעוֹלָם
שֶׁהֶחֱיָנוּ וְקִיְּמָנוּ וְהִגִּיעָנוּ לַזְּמַן הַזֶּה.

It is customary for all present to drink of the wine.

Meditation in the Sukka

הֲרֵינִי I am hereby prepared and ready to fulfill the commandment of Sukka, as the Creator, blessed be His name has commanded me: "You shall live in booths for seven days; every citizen in Israel shall live in booths so that future generations will know that I made the Israelites live in booths when I brought them out of Egypt. I am the LORD your God." *Lev. 23*

Sit, sit, exalted guests. Sit, sit, holy guests. Sit, sit, guests in faith. Sit in the shade of the Holy One, blessed be He. Worthy is the portion of Israel, as is written, "For the LORD's portion is His people, Jacob His allotted inheritance." *Deut. 32*

May it be Your will, LORD my God and God of my fathers, that You cause Your Divine Presence to rest among us and that You spread over us the tabernacle of Your peace, in the merit of the commandment of Sukka which we are fulfilling to unify the name of the Holy One, blessed be He, and His Divine Presence, in reverence and love, to unify the name *Yod-Heh* with *Vav-Heh*, in perfect unity in the name of all Israel. May You surround it with the radiance of Your holy and pure glory, spread above their heads like an eagle that stirs up its nest, and from there may a rich flow of life stream down on your servant (*name* son of *mother's name*, Your servant). In the merit of leaving my house to go outside, running in the way of Your commandments, may I be considered as if I had wandered far. Cleanse me thoroughly from my iniquity and purify me from my sin. From the exalted guests, the guests in faith, may Your ears attend to much blessing. To the hungry and thirsty grant unfailing food and drink. Grant me the privilege of sitting and taking refuge under the shadow of Your wings when I take leave of this world, taking refuge from stream and rain when You rain fiery coals on the wicked. May this command of Sukka that I am fulfilling be considered by You as if I had fulfilled it in all its specifics, details and conditions, as well as all the commandments dependent on it. May the sealing of our fate be for good, and grant us the merit of living for many years on the soil of the Holy Land, serving You and revering You. Blessed is the LORD forever, Amen and Amen. *Ps. 89*

---

that I made the Israelites live in booths (*sukkot*) when I brought them out of Egypt; I am the LORD your God" (Lev. 23:43). The meditation, said on the first night of Sukkot, emphasizes the nature of the sukka as a symbol of God's protective presence.

תפילה כשנכנסין לסוכה

ויקרא כג הֲרֵינִי מוּכָן וּמְזֻמָּן לְקַיֵּם מִצְוַת סֻכָּה, כַּאֲשֶׁר צִוַּנִי הַבּוֹרֵא יִתְבָּרַךְ שְׁמוֹ: בַּסֻּכֹּת תֵּשְׁבוּ שִׁבְעַת יָמִים, כָּל־הָאֶזְרָח בְּיִשְׂרָאֵל יֵשְׁבוּ בַּסֻּכֹּת: לְמַעַן יֵדְעוּ דֹרֹתֵיכֶם, כִּי בַסֻּכּוֹת הוֹשַׁבְתִּי אֶת־בְּנֵי יִשְׂרָאֵל, בְּהוֹצִיאִי אוֹתָם מֵאֶרֶץ מִצְרָיִם:

תִּיבוּ תִּיבוּ אֻשְׁפִּיזִין עִלָּאִין, תִּיבוּ תִּיבוּ אֻשְׁפִּיזִין קַדִּישִׁין, תִּיבוּ תִּיבוּ אֻשְׁפִּיזִין דִּמְהֵימְנוּתָא. זַכָּאָה חֻלְקְהוֹן דְּיִשְׂרָאֵל, דִּכְתִיב: כִּי חֵלֶק יהוה עַמּוֹ, דברים לב יַעֲקֹב חֶבֶל נַחֲלָתוֹ:

יְהִי רָצוֹן מִלְּפָנֶיךָ יהוה אֱלֹהַי וֵאלֹהֵי אֲבוֹתַי, שֶׁתַּשְׁרֶה שְׁכִינָתְךָ בֵּינֵינוּ, וְתִפְרֹס עָלֵינוּ סֻכַּת שְׁלוֹמֶךָ, בִּזְכוּת מִצְוַת סֻכָּה שֶׁאֲנַחְנוּ מְקַיְּמִין לְיַחֲדָא שְׁמָא דְקֻדְשָׁא בְּרִיךְ הוּא וּשְׁכִינְתֵּהּ בִּדְחִילוּ וּרְחִימוּ, לְיַחֲדָא שֵׁם י״ה בו״ה בְּיִחוּדָא שְׁלִים בְּשֵׁם כָּל יִשְׂרָאֵל, וּלְהַקִּיף אוֹתָהּ מִזִּיו כְּבוֹדְךָ הַקָּדוֹשׁ וְהַטָּהוֹר, נָטוּי עַל רָאשֵׁיהֶם מִלְמַעְלָה כְּנֶשֶׁר יָעִיר קִנּוֹ, וּמִשָּׁם יַשְׁפִּיעַ שֶׁפַע הַחַיִּים לְעַבְדְּךָ (פלוני בֶּן פלונית אֲמָתֶךָ). וּבִזְכוּת צֵאתִי מִבֵּיתִי הַחוּצָה וְדֶרֶךְ מִצְוֹתֶיךָ אָרוּצָה, יֵחָשֵׁב לִי זֹאת כְּאִלּוּ הִרְחַקְתִּי נְדוֹד, וְהֶרֶב כַּבְּסֵנִי מֵעֲוֹנִי וּמֵחַטָּאתִי טַהֲרֵנִי, וּמֵאֻשְׁפִּיזִין עִלָּאִין אֻשְׁפִּיזִין דִּמְהֵימְנוּתָא תְּהֵיינָה אָזְנֶיךָ קַשֻּׁבוֹת רַב בְּרָכוֹת, וְלָרְעֵבִים גַּם צְמֵאִים תֶּן לַחְמָם וּמֵימָם הַנֶּאֱמָנִים, וְתִתֶּן לִי זְכוּת לָשֶׁבֶת וְלַחֲסוֹת בְּסֵתֶר צֵל כְּנָפֶיךָ בְּעֵת פְּטִירָתִי מִן הָעוֹלָם, וְלַחֲסוֹת מִזֶּרֶם וּמִמָּטָר, כִּי תַמְטִיר עַל רְשָׁעִים פַּחִים. וּתְהֵא חֲשׁוּבָה מִצְוַת סֻכָּה זוֹ שֶׁאֲנִי מְקַיֵּם, כְּאִלּוּ קִיַּמְתִּיהָ בְּכָל פְּרָטֶיהָ וְדִקְדּוּקֶיהָ וּתְנָאֶיהָ וְכָל מִצְוֹת הַתְּלוּיוֹת בָּהּ. וְתֵיטִיב לָנוּ הַחֲתִימָה, וּתְזַכֵּנוּ לֵישֵׁב יָמִים רַבִּים עַל הָאֲדָמָה אַדְמַת קֹדֶשׁ, בַּעֲבוֹדָתְךָ תהלים פט וּבְיִרְאָתֶךָ. בָּרוּךְ יהוה לְעוֹלָם אָמֵן וְאָמֵן:

MEDITATION IN THE SUKKA

Meditations before the fulfillment of mitzvot are especially important when an essential component of the mitzva is its symbolic content (for example, tzitzit serves as a reminder of the entire life of commandments, and tefillin reminds us of the bond of love between us and God). The Torah explicitly mentions the symbolism of the sukka: "So that your descendants will know

On entering the sukka and before saying Kiddush, many have the custom to welcome "guests" from the biblical past, who are said to join us as we sit in the sukka:

אֻזְמִין I invite to my meal the exalted guests,
Abraham, Isaac, Jacob, Joseph, Moses, Aaron, and David.

On the first day I pray you, Abraham, exalted guest,
that all the other exalted guests may sit here with me and you:
Isaac, Jacob, Joseph, Moses, Aaron, and David.

On the second day I pray you, Isaac, exalted guest,
that all the other exalted guests may sit here with me and you:
Abraham, Jacob, Joseph, Moses, Aaron, and David.

On the third day I pray you, Jacob, exalted guest,
that all the other exalted guests may sit here with me and you:
Abraham, Isaac, Joseph, Moses, Aaron, and David.

On the fourth day I pray you, Joseph, exalted guest,
that all the other exalted guests may sit here with me and you:
Abraham, Isaac, Jacob, Moses, Aaron, and David.

On the fifth day I pray you, Moses, exalted guest,
that all the other exalted guests may sit here with me and you:
Abraham, Isaac, Jacob, Joseph, Aaron, and David.

On the sixth day I pray you, Aaron, exalted guest,
that all the other exalted guests may sit here with me and you:
Abraham, Isaac, Jacob, Joseph, Moses, and David.

On Hoshana Raba I pray you, David, exalted guest,
that all the other exalted guests may sit here with me and you:
Abraham, Isaac, Jacob, Joseph, Moses and Aaron.

On the last day of Sukkot, on leaving the sukka:

May it be Your will, Lord our God and God of our fathers, that as I have fulfilled [Your commandment] and sat in this sukka, so next year may I have the privilege of sitting in the sukka made of the skin of Leviathan.

---

in the sukka, especially the poor and lonely, in keeping with the command to rejoice on the festivals together with "the stranger, the orphan, and the widow within your gates" (Deut. 16:14; see Maimonides, Laws of Festivals 6:18). *The skin of Leviathan:* A reference to the saying in the Talmud that at the End of Days, God will make a sukka for the righteous from the skin of Leviathan (*Bava Batra* 75a).

On entering the סוכה *and before saying* קידוש*, many have the custom to welcome "guests" from the biblical past, who are said to join us as we sit in the* סוכה*:*

אֲזַמִּין לִסְעוּדָתִי אֻשְׁפִּיזִין עִלָּאִין
אַבְרָהָם יִצְחָק יַעֲקֹב יוֹסֵף מֹשֶׁה אַהֲרֹן וְדָוִד.

On the first day
במטו מנך אברהם אשפיזי עלאי דתיתב עמי
וְעִמָּךְ כָּל אֻשְׁפִּיזֵי עִלָּאֵי: יִצְחָק יַעֲקֹב יוֹסֵף מֹשֶׁה אַהֲרֹן וְדָוִד.

On the second day
בְּמָטוּ מִנָּךְ יצחק אשפיזי עלאי דתיתב עמי
וְעִמָּךְ כָּל אֻשְׁפִּיזֵי עִלָּאֵי: אַבְרָהָם יַעֲקֹב יוֹסֵף מֹשֶׁה אַהֲרֹן וְדָוִד.

On the third day
בְּמָטוּ מִנָּךְ יַעֲקֹב אֻשְׁפִּיזִי עִלָּאִי דְּתֵיתֵב עִמִּי
וְעִמָּךְ כָּל אֻשְׁפִּיזֵי עִלָּאֵי: אַבְרָהָם יִצְחָק יוֹסֵף מֹשֶׁה אַהֲרֹן וְדָוִד.

On the fourth day
בְּמָטוּ מִנָּךְ יוֹסֵף אֻשְׁפִּיזִי עִלָּאִי דְּתֵיתֵב עִמִּי
וְעִמָּךְ כָּל אֻשְׁפִּיזֵי עִלָּאֵי: אַבְרָהָם יִצְחָק יַעֲקֹב מֹשֶׁה אַהֲרֹן וְדָוִד.

On the fifth day
בְּמָטוּ מִנָּךְ מֹשֶׁה אֻשְׁפִּיזִי עִלָּאִי דְּתֵיתֵב עִמִּי
וְעִמָּךְ כָּל אֻשְׁפִּיזֵי עִלָּאֵי: אַבְרָהָם יִצְחָק יַעֲקֹב יוֹסֵף אַהֲרֹן וְדָוִד.

On the sixth day
בְּמָטוּ מִנָּךְ אַהֲרֹן אֻשְׁפִּיזִי עִלָּאִי דְּתֵיתֵב עִמִּי
וְעִמָּךְ כָּל אֻשְׁפִּיזֵי עִלָּאֵי: אַבְרָהָם יִצְחָק יַעֲקֹב יוֹסֵף מֹשֶׁה וְדָוִד.

On הושענא רבה
בְּמָטוּ מִנָּךְ דָּוִד אֻשְׁפִּיזִי עִלָּאִי דְּתֵיתֵב עִמִּי
וְעִמָּךְ כָּל אֻשְׁפִּיזֵי עִלָּאֵי: אַבְרָהָם יִצְחָק יַעֲקֹב יוֹסֵף מֹשֶׁה וְאַהֲרֹן.

On the last day of סוכות *on leaving the* סוכה*:*

יְהִי רָצוֹן מִלְּפָנֶיךָ יהוה אֱלֹהֵינוּ וֵאלֹהֵי אֲבוֹתֵינוּ
כְּשֵׁם שֶׁקִּיַּמְתִּי וְיָשַׁבְתִּי בַּסֻּכָּה זוֹ
כֵּן אֶזְכֶּה לַשָּׁנָה הַבָּאָה לֵישֵׁב בְּסֻכַּת עוֹרוֹ שֶׁל לִוְיָתָן.

Ushpizin, the Aramaic for "guests," reflects a Jewish mystical tradition that on Sukkot, seven great figures from the biblical age, from Abraham to David, visit us as we sit in the sukka, a different guest entering first each day. Each of the seven figures suffered some form of exile from home to a temporary dwelling, and as we sit in the sukka we remember their fate, their faith and the continuity of the Jewish journey. We also remind ourselves of the importance of hospitality, said by the sages to be "greater even than receiving the Divine Presence" (*Shabbat* 127a). It is a mitzva to invite guests to join us

Kiddush for Yom Tov Morning

On Shabbat Ḥol HaMo'ed, turn to page 580.

On a Yom Tov that falls on Shabbat, start Kiddush here:

וְשָׁמְרוּ The children of Israel must keep the Sabbath, observing the Sabbath *Ex. 31*
in every generation as an everlasting covenant. It is a sign between Me and the children of Israel for ever, for in six days the LORD made the heavens and the earth, but on the seventh day He ceased work and refreshed Himself.

זָכוֹר Remember the Sabbath day to keep it holy. Six days you shall labor and *Ex. 20*
do all your work, but the seventh day is a Sabbath of the LORD your God; on it you shall not do any work – you, your son or daughter, your male or female slave, or your cattle, or the stranger within your gates. For in six days the LORD made heaven and earth and sea and all that is in them, and rested on the seventh day;

On a Yom Tov that falls on Shabbat, some start Kiddush here instead:

Therefore the LORD blessed the Sabbath day and declared it holy.

On a Yom Tov that falls on a weekday, start here:

אֵלֶּה These are the appointed times of the LORD, *Lev. 23*
sacred assemblies, which you shall announce in their due season.
Thus Moses announced the LORD's appointed seasons
to the children of Israel.

When saying Kiddush for others, add:

Please pay attention, my masters.

בָּרוּךְ Blessed are You, LORD our God, King of the Universe, who creates the fruit of the vine.

On Sukkot: בָּרוּךְ Blessed are You, LORD our God, King of the Universe,
who has made us holy through His commandments
and has commanded us to dwell in the sukka.

---

and celebration (Nahmanides); (3) holy days whose date is determined by the proclamation of the earthly court (Rashbam); (4) times whose date is made known throughout the nation by messengers or other signals by the court (Abrabanel); or (5) days in which, as it were, our souls summon us to holiness (Rabbi Yaakov Tzvi Mecklenburg).

קידושא רבה לשלוש רגלים

On שבת חול המועד turn to page 581.

On יום טוב that falls on שבת, start קידוש here:

שמות לא וְשָׁמְרוּ בְנֵי־יִשְׂרָאֵל אֶת־הַשַּׁבָּת, לַעֲשׂוֹת אֶת־הַשַּׁבָּת לְדֹרֹתָם בְּרִית עוֹלָם: בֵּינִי וּבֵין בְּנֵי יִשְׂרָאֵל אוֹת הִוא לְעֹלָם, כִּי־שֵׁשֶׁת יָמִים עָשָׂה יהוה אֶת־הַשָּׁמַיִם וְאֶת־הָאָרֶץ וּבַיּוֹם הַשְּׁבִיעִי שָׁבַת וַיִּנָּפַשׁ:

שמות כ זָכוֹר אֶת־יוֹם הַשַּׁבָּת לְקַדְּשׁוֹ: שֵׁשֶׁת יָמִים תַּעֲבֹד, וְעָשִׂיתָ כָּל־מְלַאכְתֶּךָ: וְיוֹם הַשְּׁבִיעִי שַׁבָּת לַיהוה אֱלֹהֶיךָ, לֹא־תַעֲשֶׂה כָל־מְלָאכָה אַתָּה וּבִנְךָ וּבִתֶּךָ, עַבְדְּךָ וַאֲמָתְךָ וּבְהֶמְתֶּךָ, וְגֵרְךָ אֲשֶׁר בִּשְׁעָרֶיךָ: כִּי שֵׁשֶׁת־יָמִים עָשָׂה יהוה אֶת־הַשָּׁמַיִם וְאֶת־הָאָרֶץ אֶת־הַיָּם וְאֶת־כָּל־אֲשֶׁר־בָּם, וַיָּנַח בַּיּוֹם הַשְּׁבִיעִי

On יום טוב that falls on שבת, some start קידוש here instead:

עַל־כֵּן בֵּרַךְ יהוה אֶת־יוֹם הַשַּׁבָּת וַיְקַדְּשֵׁהוּ:

On יום טוב that falls on a weekday, start here:

ויקרא כג אֵלֶּה מוֹעֲדֵי יהוה מִקְרָאֵי קֹדֶשׁ אֲשֶׁר־תִּקְרְאוּ אֹתָם בְּמוֹעֲדָם:
וַיְדַבֵּר מֹשֶׁה אֶת־מֹעֲדֵי יהוה אֶל־בְּנֵי יִשְׂרָאֵל:

When saying קידוש for others, add:

סַבְרִי מָרָנָן

בָּרוּךְ אַתָּה יהוה אֱלֹהֵינוּ מֶלֶךְ הָעוֹלָם
בּוֹרֵא פְּרִי הַגָּפֶן.

בסוכות: בָּרוּךְ אַתָּה יהוה אֱלֹהֵינוּ מֶלֶךְ הָעוֹלָם
אֲשֶׁר קִדְּשָׁנוּ בְּמִצְוֹתָיו וְצִוָּנוּ לֵישֵׁב בַּסֻּכָּה.

As on Shabbat, the morning Kiddush for Yom Tov is essentially only the blessing over the wine, since the blessing over the day has been made the previous night. We preface it with two verses taken from the beginning and end of the passage dealing with the festivals in Leviticus, chapter 23. The phrase *mikra'ei kodesh*, "sacred assemblies," may mean: (1) times whose holiness is proclaimed by the festive drink, food and dress of the day (Sifra); (2) times at which the community is summoned to come together in prayer

Service for Festivals

On Erev Yom Tov, Minḥa begins on page 206. On Shabbat Ḥol HaMo'ed, or when Yom Tov falls on Shabbat, Ma'ariv begins with Psalm 92 on page 324.

When Yom Tov falls on a weekday, Ma'ariv begins with Barekhu on page 334; when Ḥol HaMo'ed falls on a weekday, Ma'ariv begins with "He is compassionate" on page 242.

The following Amida is said at Shaḥarit, Minḥa and Ma'ariv on Yom Tov Pesaḥ, Shavuot, Sukkot, Shemini Atzeret and Simḥat Torah, but not on Ḥol HaMo'ed.

AMIDA FOR SHAḤARIT, MINḤA AND MA'ARIV

The following prayer, until "in former years" on page 786, is said silently, standing with feet together. If there is a minyan, the Amida is repeated aloud by the Leader, except during Ma'ariv. Take three steps forward and at the points indicated by ▾, bend the knees at the first word, bow at the second, and stand straight before saying God's name.

At Minḥa: When I proclaim the LORD's name, give glory to our God. *Deut. 32*
O LORD, open my lips, so that my mouth may declare Your praise. *Ps. 51*

PATRIARCHS

▾בָּרוּךְ Blessed are You, LORD our God and God of our fathers,
God of Abraham, God of Isaac and God of Jacob;
the great, mighty and awesome God, God Most High,
who bestows acts of loving-kindness and creates all,
who remembers the loving-kindness of the fathers
and will bring a Redeemer
to their children's children
for the sake of His name, in love.
King, Helper, Savior, Shield:
▾Blessed are You, LORD, Shield of Abraham.

DIVINE MIGHT

אַתָּה גִּבּוֹר You are eternally mighty, LORD.
You give life to the dead
and have great power to save.

From Minḥa of Shemini Atzeret,
through Shaḥarit on the first day of Pesaḥ (see laws 129–131):
He makes the wind blow and the rain fall.

In Israel, on other Festivals:
He causes the dew to fall.

שלוש רגלים

On ערב יום טוב *,*מנחה *begins on page 207. On* שבת חול המועד *or when* יום טוב *falls on* שבת*,* מעריב *begins with* מִזְמוֹר שִׁיר *on page 325.*
When יום טוב *falls on a weekday,* מעריב *begins with* בָּרְכוּ *on page 335;*
when חול המועד *falls on a weekday,* מעריב *begins with* וְהוּא רַחוּם *on page 243.*
The following עמידה *is said at* שחרית*,* מנחה *and* מעריב *of* פסח*,* שבועות*,* סוכות*,* שמיני עצרת *and* שמחת תורה*, but not on* חול המועד*.*

עמידה לשחרית, מנחה ומעריב

The following prayer, until קַדְמֹנִיּוֹת *on page 787, is said silently, standing with feet together. If there is a* מנין*, the* עמידה *is repeated aloud by the* שליח ציבור*, except during* מעריב*. Take three steps forward and at the points indicated by* °*, bend the knees at the first word, bow at the second, and stand straight before saying God's name.*

למנחה: כִּי שֵׁם יהוה אֶקְרָא, הָבוּ גֹדֶל לֵאלֹהֵינוּ: דברים לב
אֲדֹנָי, שְׂפָתַי תִּפְתָּח, וּפִי יַגִּיד תְּהִלָּתֶךָ: תהלים נא

אבות

°בָּרוּךְ אַתָּה יהוה, אֱלֹהֵינוּ וֵאלֹהֵי אֲבוֹתֵינוּ
אֱלֹהֵי אַבְרָהָם, אֱלֹהֵי יִצְחָק, וֵאלֹהֵי יַעֲקֹב
הָאֵל הַגָּדוֹל הַגִּבּוֹר וְהַנּוֹרָא, אֵל עֶלְיוֹן
גּוֹמֵל חֲסָדִים טוֹבִים, וְקוֹנֵה הַכֹּל
וְזוֹכֵר חַסְדֵי אָבוֹת
וּמֵבִיא גוֹאֵל לִבְנֵי בְנֵיהֶם לְמַעַן שְׁמוֹ בְּאַהֲבָה.
מֶלֶךְ עוֹזֵר וּמוֹשִׁיעַ וּמָגֵן.
°בָּרוּךְ אַתָּה יהוה, מָגֵן אַבְרָהָם.

גבורות

אַתָּה גִּבּוֹר לְעוֹלָם, אֲדֹנָי
מְחַיֵּה מֵתִים אַתָּה, רַב לְהוֹשִׁיעַ

From שמיני עצרת *of* מנחה
through שחרית *on the first day of* פסח *(see laws 129–131):*

מַשִּׁיב הָרְוּחַ וּמוֹרִיד הַגֶּשֶׁם

In ארץ ישראל *on other* חגים*:*

מוֹרִיד הַטָּל

He sustains the living with loving-kindness,
and with great compassion revives the dead.
He supports the fallen, heals the sick, sets captives free,
and keeps His faith with those who sleep in the dust.
Who is like You, Master of might,
and who can compare to You,
O King who brings death and gives life, and makes salvation grow?
Faithful are You to revive the dead.
Blessed are You, LORD, who revives the dead.

When saying the Amida silently, continue with "You are holy" on the next page.
During the Leader's Repetition of Minḥa, turn to the Kedusha on the next page.

KEDUSHA FOR SHAḤARIT

During the Leader's Repetition, the following is said standing with feet together, rising on the toes at the words indicated by ▲.

Cong. then Leader: נְקַדֵּשׁ We will sanctify Your name on earth, as they sanctify it in the highest heavens, as is written by Your prophet, "And they [the angels] call to one another saying: *Is. 6*

Cong. then Leader: ▲Holy, ▲holy, ▲holy is the LORD of hosts the whole world is filled with His glory."

Then with a sound of mighty noise, majestic and strong, they make their voice heard, raising themselves toward the Seraphim, and facing them say: "Blessed…

Cong. then Leader: ▲"Blessed is the LORD's glory from His place." *Ezek. 3*

Reveal Yourself from Your place, O our King, and reign over us, for we are waiting for You. When will You reign in Zion? May it be soon in our days, and may You dwell there for ever and all time. May You be exalted and sanctified in the midst of Jerusalem, Your city, from generation to generation for evermore. May our eyes see Your kingdom, as is said in the songs of Your splendor, written by David your righteous anointed one:

Cong. then Leader: ▲"The LORD shall reign for ever. He is your God, Zion, from generation to generation, Halleluya!" *Ps. 146*

Leader: From generation to generation we will declare Your greatness, and we will proclaim Your holiness for evermore. Your praise, our God, shall not leave our mouth forever, for You, God, are a great and holy King. Blessed are You, LORD, the holy God.

The Leader continues with "You have chosen us" on the next page.

מְכַלְכֵּל חַיִּים בְּחֶסֶד, מְחַיֵּה מֵתִים בְּרַחֲמִים רַבִּים
סוֹמֵךְ נוֹפְלִים, וְרוֹפֵא חוֹלִים, וּמַתִּיר אֲסוּרִים
וּמְקַיֵּם אֱמוּנָתוֹ לִישֵׁנֵי עָפָר.
מִי כָמְוֹךָ, בַּעַל גְּבוּרוֹת, וּמִי דְּוֹמֶה לָּךְ
מֶלֶךְ, מֵמִית וּמְחַיֶּה וּמַצְמִיחַ יְשׁוּעָה.
וְנֶאֱמָן אַתָּה לְהַחֲיוֹת מֵתִים.
בָּרוּךְ אַתָּה יהוה, מְחַיֵּה הַמֵּתִים.

When saying the עמידה *silently, continue with* אַתָּה קָדוֹשׁ *on the next page.*
During the חזרת הש״ץ *of* מנחה*, turn to the* קדושה *on the next page.*

קדושה לשחרית

During the חזרת הש״ץ*, the following is said standing with feet together, rising on the toes at the words indicated by* *.

קהל *then* ש״ץ: נְקַדֵּשׁ אֶת שִׁמְךָ בָּעוֹלָם, כְּשֵׁם שֶׁמַּקְדִּישִׁים אוֹתוֹ בִּשְׁמֵי מָרוֹם
כַּכָּתוּב עַל יַד נְבִיאֶךָ: וְקָרָא זֶה אֶל־זֶה וְאָמַר ישעיה ו

קהל *then* ש״ץ: *קָדוֹשׁ, *קָדוֹשׁ, *קָדוֹשׁ, יהוה צְבָאוֹת, מְלֹא כָל־הָאָרֶץ כְּבוֹדוֹ:
אָז בְּקוֹל רַעַשׁ גָּדוֹל אַדִּיר וְחָזָק, מַשְׁמִיעִים קוֹל
מִתְנַשְּׂאִים לְעֻמַּת שְׂרָפִים, לְעֻמָּתָם בָּרוּךְ יֹאמֵרוּ

קהל *then* ש״ץ: *בָּרוּךְ כְּבוֹד־יהוה מִמְּקוֹמוֹ: יחזקאל ג
מִמְּקוֹמְךָ מַלְכֵּנוּ תוֹפִיעַ וְתִמְלֹךְ עָלֵינוּ, כִּי מְחַכִּים אֲנַחְנוּ לָךְ
מָתַי תִּמְלֹךְ בְּצִיּוֹן, בְּקָרוֹב בְּיָמֵינוּ לְעוֹלָם וָעֶד תִּשְׁכֹּן
תִּתְגַּדַּל וְתִתְקַדַּשׁ בְּתוֹךְ יְרוּשָׁלַיִם עִירְךָ לְדוֹר וָדוֹר וּלְנֵצַח נְצָחִים.
וְעֵינֵינוּ תִרְאֶינָה מַלְכוּתֶךָ
כַּדָּבָר הָאָמוּר בְּשִׁירֵי עֻזֶּךָ עַל יְדֵי דָוִד מְשִׁיחַ צִדְקֶךָ

קהל *then* ש״ץ: *יִמְלֹךְ יהוה לְעוֹלָם, אֱלֹהַיִךְ צִיּוֹן לְדֹר וָדֹר, הַלְלוּיָהּ: תהלים קמו

ש״ץ: לְדוֹר וָדוֹר נַגִּיד גָּדְלֶךָ, וּלְנֵצַח נְצָחִים קְדֻשָּׁתְךָ נַקְדִּישׁ
וְשִׁבְחֲךָ אֱלֹהֵינוּ מִפִּינוּ לֹא יָמוּשׁ לְעוֹלָם וָעֶד
כִּי אֵל מֶלֶךְ גָּדוֹל וְקָדוֹשׁ אָתָּה. בָּרוּךְ אַתָּה יהוה, הָאֵל הַקָּדוֹשׁ.

The שליח ציבור *continues with* אַתָּה בְחַרְתָּנוּ *on the next page.*

KEDUSHA FOR MINḤA

During the Leader's Repetition, the following is said standing with feet together, rising on the toes at the words indicated by ▲.

Cong. then Leader: נְקַדֵּשׁ We will sanctify Your name on earth,
as they sanctify it in the highest heavens,
as is written by Your prophet,
"And they [the angels] call to one another saying: *Is. 6*

Cong. then Leader: ▲Holy, ▲holy, ▲holy is the LORD of hosts
the whole world is filled with His glory."
Those facing them say "Blessed – "

Cong. then Leader: ▲"Blessed is the LORD's glory from His place." *Ezek. 3*
And in Your holy Writings it is written thus:

Cong. then Leader: ▲"The LORD shall reign for ever. He is your God, Zion, *Ps. 146*
from generation to generation, Halleluya!"

Leader: From generation to generation we will declare Your greatness,
and we will proclaim Your holiness for evermore.
Your praise, our God, shall not leave our mouth forever,
for You, God, are a great and holy King.
Blessed are You, LORD, the holy God.

The Leader continues with "You have chosen us" below.

When saying the Amida silently, continue here:

HOLINESS

אַתָּה קָדוֹשׁ You are holy and Your name is holy,
and holy ones praise You daily, Selah!
Blessed are You, LORD, the holy God.

HOLINESS OF THE DAY

אַתָּה בְחַרְתָּנוּ You have chosen us from among all peoples.
You have loved and favored us.
You have raised us above all tongues.

אַתָּה בְחַרְתָּנוּ *You have chosen us:* Unlike Shabbat, which recalls pre-history (creation) and the end of history (ultimate redemption), the festivals recall specific moments within history: on Pesaḥ, the exodus from Egypt; on Shavuot, the giving of the Torah at Mount Sinai; and on Sukkot, the forty years of wandering in the wilderness. Hence the reference to the divine choice of

קדושה למנחה

*During the חזרת הש״ץ, the following is said standing with feet together, rising on the toes at the words indicated by *.*

then קהל ש״ץ: נְקַדֵּשׁ אֶת שִׁמְךָ בָּעוֹלָם, כְּשֵׁם שֶׁמַּקְדִּישִׁים אוֹתוֹ בִּשְׁמֵי מָרוֹם
כַּכָּתוּב עַל יַד נְבִיאֶךָ: וְקָרָא זֶה אֶל־זֶה וְאָמַר — ישעיה ו

then קהל ש״ץ: *קָדוֹשׁ, *קָדוֹשׁ, *קָדוֹשׁ, יהוה צְבָאוֹת, מְלֹא כָל־הָאָרֶץ כְּבוֹדוֹ:
לְעֻמָּתָם בָּרוּךְ יֹאמֵרוּ

then קהל ש״ץ: *בָּרוּךְ כְּבוֹד־יהוה מִמְּקוֹמוֹ: — יחזקאל ג
וּבְדִבְרֵי קָדְשְׁךָ כָּתוּב לֵאמֹר

then קהל ש״ץ: *יִמְלֹךְ יהוה לְעוֹלָם, אֱלֹהַיִךְ צִיּוֹן לְדֹר וָדֹר, הַלְלוּיָהּ: — תהלים קמו

ש״ץ: לְדוֹר וָדוֹר נַגִּיד גָּדְלֶךָ, וּלְנֵצַח נְצָחִים קְדֻשָּׁתְךָ נַקְדִּישׁ
וְשִׁבְחֲךָ אֱלֹהֵינוּ מִפִּינוּ לֹא יָמוּשׁ לְעוֹלָם וָעֶד
כִּי אֵל מֶלֶךְ גָּדוֹל וְקָדוֹשׁ אָתָּה.
בָּרוּךְ אַתָּה יהוה, הָאֵל הַקָּדוֹשׁ.

The שליח ציבור continues with אַתָּה בְחַרְתָּנוּ *below.*

When saying the עמידה silently, continue here:

קדושת השם

אַתָּה קָדוֹשׁ וְשִׁמְךָ קָדוֹשׁ
וּקְדוֹשִׁים בְּכָל יוֹם יְהַלְלוּךָ סֶּלָה.
בָּרוּךְ אַתָּה יהוה, הָאֵל הַקָּדוֹשׁ.

קדושת היום

אַתָּה בְחַרְתָּנוּ מִכָּל הָעַמִּים
אָהַבְתָּ אוֹתָנוּ וְרָצִיתָ בָּנוּ
וְרוֹמַמְתָּנוּ מִכָּל הַלְּשׁוֹנוֹת

THE FESTIVAL SERVICE

As on Shabbat, the Yom Tov Amida consists of seven blessings, of which the central one speaks of the holiness of the day.

You have made us holy through Your commandments.
You have brought us near, our King, to Your service,
and have called us by Your great and holy name.

On Motza'ei Shabbat:

וַתּוֹדִיעֵנוּ You have made known to us, LORD our God, Your righteous laws, and have taught us to perform Your will's decrees. You have given us, LORD our God, just laws and true teachings, good precepts and commandments. You have given us as our heritage seasons of joy, holy festivals, and occasions for presenting our freewill offerings. You have given us as our heritage the holiness of the Sabbath, the glory of the festival, and the festive offerings of the pilgrimage days. You have distinguished, LORD our God, between sacred and secular, between light and darkness, between Israel and the nations, between the seventh day and the six days of work. You have distinguished between the holiness of the Sabbath and the holiness of the festival, and have made the seventh day holy above the six days of work. You have distinguished and sanctified Your people Israel with Your holiness.

On Shabbat, add the words in parentheses:

וַתִּתֶּן לָנוּ And You, LORD our God, have given us in love
(Sabbaths for rest and) festivals for rejoicing,
holy days and seasons for joy,
(this Sabbath day and) this day of:

On Pesaḥ: the festival of Matzot,
the time of our freedom

On Shavuot: the festival of Shavuot,
the time of the giving of our Torah

On Sukkot: the festival of Sukkot,
our time of rejoicing

On Shemini Atzeret & Simḥat Torah: the festival of the eighth day, Shemini Atzeret,
our time of rejoicing

(with love), a holy assembly in memory of the exodus from Egypt.

---

and "the time of our freedom" is self-evident. It recalls liberation from Egypt and slavery. The connection between Shavuot and the giving of the To-

וְקִדַּשְׁתָּנוּ בְּמִצְוֹתֶיךָ
וְקֵרַבְתָּנוּ מַלְכֵּנוּ לַעֲבוֹדָתֶךָ
וְשִׁמְךָ הַגָּדוֹל וְהַקָּדוֹשׁ עָלֵינוּ קָרָאתָ.

On מוצאי שבת:

וַתּוֹדִיעֵנוּ יהוה אֱלֹהֵינוּ אֶת מִשְׁפְּטֵי צִדְקֶךָ, וַתְּלַמְּדֵנוּ לַעֲשׂוֹת חֻקֵּי רְצוֹנֶךָ, וַתִּתֶּן לָנוּ יהוה אֱלֹהֵינוּ מִשְׁפָּטִים יְשָׁרִים וְתוֹרוֹת אֱמֶת, חֻקִּים וּמִצְוֹת טוֹבִים, וַתַּנְחִילֵנוּ זְמַנֵּי שָׂשׂוֹן וּמוֹעֲדֵי קֹדֶשׁ וְחַגֵּי נְדָבָה, וַתּוֹרִישֵׁנוּ קְדֻשַּׁת שַׁבָּת וּכְבוֹד מוֹעֵד וַחֲגִיגַת הָרֶגֶל. וַתַּבְדֵּל יהוה אֱלֹהֵינוּ בֵּין קֹדֶשׁ לְחֹל, בֵּין אוֹר לְחֹשֶׁךְ, בֵּין יִשְׂרָאֵל לָעַמִּים, בֵּין יוֹם הַשְּׁבִיעִי לְשֵׁשֶׁת יְמֵי הַמַּעֲשֶׂה. בֵּין קְדֻשַּׁת שַׁבָּת לִקְדֻשַּׁת יוֹם טוֹב הִבְדַּלְתָּ, וְאֶת יוֹם הַשְּׁבִיעִי מִשֵּׁשֶׁת יְמֵי הַמַּעֲשֶׂה קִדַּשְׁתָּ, הִבְדַּלְתָּ וְקִדַּשְׁתָּ אֶת עַמְּךָ יִשְׂרָאֵל בִּקְדֻשָּׁתֶךָ.

On שבת*, add the words in parentheses:*

וַתִּתֶּן לָנוּ יהוה אֱלֹהֵינוּ בְּאַהֲבָה
(שַׁבָּתוֹת לִמְנוּחָה וּ) מוֹעֲדִים לְשִׂמְחָה, חַגִּים וּזְמַנִּים לְשָׂשׂוֹן
אֶת יוֹם (הַשַּׁבָּת הַזֶּה וְאֶת יוֹם)

בפסח: חַג הַמַּצּוֹת הַזֶּה, זְמַן חֵרוּתֵנוּ
בשבועות: חַג הַשָּׁבוּעוֹת הַזֶּה, זְמַן מַתַּן תּוֹרָתֵנוּ
בסוכות: חַג הַסֻּכּוֹת הַזֶּה, זְמַן שִׂמְחָתֵנוּ
בשמע״צ ובש״ת: הַשְּׁמִינִי חַג הָעֲצֶרֶת הַזֶּה, זְמַן שִׂמְחָתֵנוּ

(בְּאַהֲבָה) מִקְרָא קֹדֶשׁ, זֵכֶר לִיצִיאַת מִצְרָיִם.

Israel as the people who, through their singular history, bear witness to the role of God in history.

THE NAMES OF THE FESTIVALS.
The connection between Pesaḥ, "the festival of Matzot (unleavened bread)"

אֱלֹהֵינוּ Our God and God of our ancestors,
may there rise, come, reach,
appear, be favored, heard,
regarded and remembered before You,
our recollection and remembrance,
as well as the remembrance of our ancestors,
and of the Messiah son of David Your servant,
and of Jerusalem Your holy city,
and of all Your people the house of Israel –
for deliverance and well-being,
grace, loving-kindness and compassion,
life and peace, on this day of:

On Pesaḥ: the festival of Matzot.
On Shavuot: the festival of Shavuot.
On Sukkot: the festival of Sukkot.
On Shemini Atzeret & Simḥat Torah: the festival of Shemini Atzeret.

On it remember us, Lord our God, for good;
recollect us for blessing,
and deliver us for life.
In accord with Your promise
of salvation and compassion,
spare us and be gracious to us;
have compassion on us and deliver us,
for our eyes are turned to You
because You, God,
are a gracious and compassionate King.

---

time of rejoicing" because the word "rejoice" is mentioned three times in the Torah in connection with Sukkot (Lev. 23:40, Deut. 16:14, 15) – more than any other festival. Shemini Atzeret, while it shares in the joy of Sukkot, is, in some respects, a festival in its own right and is therefore referred to as such.

אֱלֹהֵינוּ וֵאלֹהֵי אֲבוֹתֵינוּ
יַעֲלֶה וְיָבוֹא וְיַגִּיעַ
וְיֵרָאֶה וְיֵרָצֶה וְיִשָּׁמַע
וְיִפָּקֵד וְיִזָּכֵר זִכְרוֹנֵנוּ וּפִקְדוֹנֵנוּ
וְזִכְרוֹן אֲבוֹתֵינוּ
וְזִכְרוֹן מָשִׁיחַ בֶּן דָּוִד עַבְדֶּךָ
וְזִכְרוֹן יְרוּשָׁלַיִם עִיר קָדְשֶׁךָ
וְזִכְרוֹן כָּל עַמְּךָ בֵּית יִשְׂרָאֵל, לְפָנֶיךָ
לִפְלֵיטָה, לְטוֹבָה, לְחֵן וּלְחֶסֶד וּלְרַחֲמִים
לְחַיִּים וּלְשָׁלוֹם בְּיוֹם

בפסח: חַג הַמַּצּוֹת הַזֶּה.
בשבועות: חַג הַשָּׁבוּעוֹת הַזֶּה.
בסוכות: חַג הַסֻּכּוֹת הַזֶּה.
בשמע״צ ובש״ת: הַשְּׁמִינִי חַג הָעֲצֶרֶת הַזֶּה.

זָכְרֵנוּ יהוה אֱלֹהֵינוּ בּוֹ לְטוֹבָה
וּפָקְדֵנוּ בוֹ לִבְרָכָה
וְהוֹשִׁיעֵנוּ בוֹ לְחַיִּים.
וּבִדְבַר יְשׁוּעָה וְרַחֲמִים
חוּס וְחָנֵּנוּ, וְרַחֵם עָלֵינוּ וְהוֹשִׁיעֵנוּ
כִּי אֵלֶיךָ עֵינֵינוּ, כִּי אֵל מֶלֶךְ חַנּוּן וְרַחוּם אָתָּה.

---

rah is not explicit in the Torah but is part of the Oral Tradition as well as calculation of dates by the sages (*Shabbat* 86b–88a). Because of this, the date of Shavuot became a subject of controversy in the Second Temple period and immediately thereafter among sects such as the Sadducees, who did not accept the authority of the Oral Tradition. Sukkot is called "our

On Shabbat, add the words in parentheses:

וְהַשִּׂיאֵנוּ Bestow on us, LORD our God,
the blessings of Your festivals
for good life and peace, joy and gladness,
as You desired and promised to bless us.
(Our God and God of our fathers, find favor in our rest.)
Make us holy through Your commandments
and grant us a share in Your Torah.
Satisfy us with Your goodness,
gladden us with Your salvation,
and purify our hearts to serve You in truth.
Grant us as our heritage,
LORD our God (with love and favor,)
with joy and gladness, Your holy (Sabbath and) festivals,
and may Israel, who sanctify Your name, rejoice in You.
Blessed are You, LORD,
who sanctifies (the Sabbath and) Israel and the festive seasons.

TEMPLE SERVICE

רְצֵה Find favor, LORD our God,
in Your people Israel and their prayer.
Restore the service to Your most holy House,
and accept in love and favor
the fire-offerings of Israel and their prayer.
May the service of Your people Israel
always find favor with You.
And may our eyes witness
Your return to Zion in compassion.
Blessed are You, LORD, who restores His Presence to Zion.

---

prior to that of the festivals. Shabbat, however, was determined by God on the seventh day of creation: hence its sanctity precedes the other two.

On שבת, add the words in parentheses:

וְהַשִּׂיאֵנוּ יהוה אֱלֹהֵינוּ אֶת בִּרְכַּת מוֹעֲדֶיךָ
לְחַיִּים וּלְשָׁלוֹם, לְשִׂמְחָה וּלְשָׂשׂוֹן
כַּאֲשֶׁר רָצִיתָ וְאָמַרְתָּ לְבָרְכֵנוּ.
(אֱלֹהֵינוּ וֵאלֹהֵי אֲבוֹתֵינוּ, רְצֵה בִמְנוּחָתֵנוּ)
קַדְּשֵׁנוּ בְּמִצְוֹתֶיךָ
וְתֵן חֶלְקֵנוּ בְּתוֹרָתֶךָ
שַׂבְּעֵנוּ מִטּוּבֶךָ, וְשַׂמְּחֵנוּ בִּישׁוּעָתֶךָ
וְטַהֵר לִבֵּנוּ לְעָבְדְּךָ בֶּאֱמֶת.
וְהַנְחִילֵנוּ יהוה אֱלֹהֵינוּ (בְּאַהֲבָה וּבְרָצוֹן)
בְּשִׂמְחָה וּבְשָׂשׂוֹן (שַׁבַּת וּ) מוֹעֲדֵי קָדְשֶׁךָ
וְיִשְׂמְחוּ בְךָ יִשְׂרָאֵל מְקַדְּשֵׁי שְׁמֶךָ.
בָּרוּךְ אַתָּה יהוה, מְקַדֵּשׁ (הַשַּׁבָּת וְ) יִשְׂרָאֵל וְהַזְּמַנִּים.

עבודה

רְצֵה יהוה אֱלֹהֵינוּ בְּעַמְּךָ יִשְׂרָאֵל, וּבִתְפִלָּתָם
וְהָשֵׁב אֶת הָעֲבוֹדָה לִדְבִיר בֵּיתֶךָ
וְאִשֵּׁי יִשְׂרָאֵל וּתְפִלָּתָם בְּאַהֲבָה תְקַבֵּל בְּרָצוֹן
וּתְהִי לְרָצוֹן תָּמִיד עֲבוֹדַת יִשְׂרָאֵל עַמֶּךָ.
וְתֶחֱזֶינָה עֵינֵינוּ בְּשׁוּבְךָ לְצִיּוֹן בְּרַחֲמִים.
בָּרוּךְ אַתָּה יהוה, הַמַּחֲזִיר שְׁכִינָתוֹ לְצִיּוֹן.

מְקַדֵּשׁ (הַשַּׁבָּת וְ)יִשְׂרָאֵל וְהַזְּמַנִּים *Who sanctifies* (*the Sabbath and*) *Israel and the festive seasons:* The precise order of the words is significant. It was the Israelites who were charged with determining the monthly and yearly calendar on which the festivals depend: hence the sanctity of the people of Israel is

THANKSGIVING

Bow at the first nine words.

מוֹדִים We give thanks to You,
for You are the LORD our God
and God of our ancestors
for ever and all time.
You are the Rock of our lives,
Shield of our salvation
from generation to generation.
We will thank You and
declare Your praise for our lives,
which are entrusted into Your hand;
for our souls,
which are placed in Your charge;
for Your miracles
which are with us every day;
and for Your wonders and favors
at all times, evening, morning and midday.
You are good –
for Your compassion never fails.
You are compassionate –
for Your loving-kindnesses never cease.
We have always placed our hope in You.

During the Leader's Repetition, the congregation says quietly:

מוֹדִים We give thanks to You,
for You are the LORD our God
and God of our ancestors,
God of all flesh,
who formed us
and formed the universe.
Blessings and thanks
are due to Your great
and holy name for giving us
life and sustaining us.
May You continue
to give us life and sustain us;
and may You gather our
exiles to Your holy courts,
to keep Your decrees,
do Your will and serve You
with a perfect heart,
for it is for us
to give You thanks.
Blessed be God to whom
thanksgiving is due.

וְעַל כֻּלָּם For all these things
may Your name be blessed and exalted, our King,
continually, for ever and all time.
Let all that lives thank You, Selah!
and praise Your name in truth,
God, our Savior and Help, Selah!
Blessed are You, LORD,
whose name is "the Good"
and to whom thanks are due.

הודאה

Bow at the first five words.

ˈמוֹדִים אֲנַחְנוּ לָךְ
שָׁאַתָּה הוּא יהוה אֱלֹהֵינוּ
וֵאלֹהֵי אֲבוֹתֵינוּ לְעוֹלָם וָעֶד.
צוּר חַיֵּינוּ, מָגֵן יִשְׁעֵנוּ
אַתָּה הוּא לְדוֹר וָדוֹר.
נוֹדֶה לְּךָ וּנְסַפֵּר תְּהִלָּתֶךָ
עַל חַיֵּינוּ הַמְּסוּרִים בְּיָדֶךָ
וְעַל נִשְׁמוֹתֵינוּ הַפְּקוּדוֹת לָךְ
וְעַל נִסֶּיךָ שֶׁבְּכָל יוֹם עִמָּנוּ
וְעַל נִפְלְאוֹתֶיךָ וְטוֹבוֹתֶיךָ
שֶׁבְּכָל עֵת
עֶרֶב וָבֹקֶר וְצָהֳרָיִם.
הַטּוֹב, כִּי לֹא כָלוּ רַחֲמֶיךָ
וְהַמְרַחֵם, כִּי לֹא תַמּוּ חֲסָדֶיךָ
מֵעוֹלָם קִוִּינוּ לָךְ.

During the חזרת הש״ץ, *the* קהל *says quietly:*

ˈמוֹדִים אֲנַחְנוּ לָךְ
שָׁאַתָּה הוּא יהוה אֱלֹהֵינוּ
וֵאלֹהֵי אֲבוֹתֵינוּ
אֱלֹהֵי כָל בָּשָׂר
יוֹצְרֵנוּ, יוֹצֵר בְּרֵאשִׁית.
בְּרָכוֹת וְהוֹדָאוֹת
לְשִׁמְךָ הַגָּדוֹל וְהַקָּדוֹשׁ
עַל שֶׁהֶחֱיִיתָנוּ וְקִיַּמְתָּנוּ.
כֵּן תְּחַיֵּנוּ וּתְקַיְּמֵנוּ
וְתֶאֱסֹף גָּלֻיּוֹתֵינוּ
לְחַצְרוֹת קָדְשֶׁךָ
לִשְׁמֹר חֻקֶּיךָ
וְלַעֲשׂוֹת רְצוֹנֶךָ וּלְעָבְדְּךָ
בְּלֵבָב שָׁלֵם
עַל שֶׁאֲנַחְנוּ מוֹדִים לָךְ.
בָּרוּךְ אֵל הַהוֹדָאוֹת.

וְעַל כֻּלָּם יִתְבָּרַךְ וְיִתְרוֹמַם שִׁמְךָ מַלְכֵּנוּ תָּמִיד לְעוֹלָם וָעֶד.
וְכֹל הַחַיִּים יוֹדוּךָ סֶּלָה, וִיהַלְלוּ אֶת שִׁמְךָ בֶּאֱמֶת
הָאֵל יְשׁוּעָתֵנוּ וְעֶזְרָתֵנוּ סֶלָה.
ˈבָּרוּךְ אַתָּה יהוה
הַטּוֹב שִׁמְךָ וּלְךָ נָאֶה לְהוֹדוֹת.

For the blessing of the Kohanim in Israel, see page 838.

The Leader says the following during the Repetition of the Shaharit Amida.
It is also said in Israel when no Kohanim bless the congregation. See laws 370–377.

Our God and God of our fathers, bless us with the threefold blessing in the Torah, written by the hand of Moses Your servant and pronounced by Aaron and his sons the priests, Your holy people, as it is said:

May the LORD bless you and protect you. *Num. 6*
Cong: May it be Your will.
May the LORD make His face shine on you and be gracious to you.
Cong: May it be Your will.
May the LORD turn His face toward you, and grant you peace.
Cong: May it be Your will.

PEACE

At Minha and Ma'ariv:

שָׁלוֹם רָב Grant
great peace
to Your people
Israel
for ever,
for You are
the sovereign LORD
of all peace;
and may it be good
in Your eyes
to bless
Your people Israel
at every time,
at every hour,
with Your peace.

At Shaharit and in Israel at Shabbat Minha:

שִׂים שָׁלוֹם Grant peace,
goodness and blessing,
grace, loving-kindness and compassion
to us and all Israel Your people.
Bless us, our Father, all as one,
with the light of Your face,
for by the light of Your face
You have given us, LORD our God,
the Torah of life and love of kindness,
righteousness, blessing, compassion,
life and peace.
May it be good in Your eyes
to bless Your people Israel
at every time, in every hour,
with Your peace.

Blessed are You, LORD, who blesses His people Israel with peace.

The following verse concludes the Leader's Repetition of the Amida.
Some also say it here as part of the silent Amida. See law 368.

May the words of my mouth and the meditation of my heart *Ps. 19*
find favor before You, LORD, my Rock and Redeemer.

For the blessing of the כהנים *in* ארץ ישראל *see page 839.*
The שליח ציבור *says the following during the* חורת הש״ץ *of* שחרית.
It is also said in ארץ ישראל *when no* כהנים *bless the congregation. See laws 370–377.*

אֱלֹהֵינוּ וֵאלֹהֵי אֲבוֹתֵינוּ, בָּרְכֵנוּ בַּבְּרָכָה הַמְשֻׁלֶּשֶׁת בַּתּוֹרָה, הַכְּתוּבָה עַל יְדֵי מֹשֶׁה עַבְדֶּךָ, הָאֲמוּרָה מִפִּי אַהֲרֹן וּבָנָיו כֹּהֲנִים עַם קְדוֹשֶׁיךָ, כָּאָמוּר

במדבר ו
יְבָרֶכְךָ יהוה וְיִשְׁמְרֶךָ: קהל: כֵּן יְהִי רָצוֹן
יָאֵר יהוה פָּנָיו אֵלֶיךָ וִיחֻנֶּךָּ: קהל: כֵּן יְהִי רָצוֹן
יִשָּׂא יהוה פָּנָיו אֵלֶיךָ וְיָשֵׂם לְךָ שָׁלוֹם: קהל: כֵּן יְהִי רָצוֹן

ברכת שלום

במנחה ובמעריב:	בשחרית ובארץ ישראל במנחה בשבת:
שָׁלוֹם רָב	שִׂים שָׁלוֹם טוֹבָה וּבְרָכָה
עַל יִשְׂרָאֵל עַמְּךָ	חֵן וָחֶסֶד וְרַחֲמִים
תָּשִׂים לְעוֹלָם	עָלֵינוּ וְעַל כָּל יִשְׂרָאֵל עַמֶּךָ.
כִּי אַתָּה הוּא	בָּרְכֵנוּ אָבִינוּ כֻּלָּנוּ כְּאֶחָד בְּאוֹר פָּנֶיךָ
מֶלֶךְ אָדוֹן	כִּי בְאוֹר פָּנֶיךָ
לְכָל הַשָּׁלוֹם.	נָתַתָּ לָּנוּ יהוה אֱלֹהֵינוּ
וְטוֹב בְּעֵינֶיךָ	תּוֹרַת חַיִּים וְאַהֲבַת חֶסֶד
לְבָרֵךְ	וּצְדָקָה וּבְרָכָה וְרַחֲמִים וְחַיִּים וְשָׁלוֹם.
אֶת עַמְּךָ יִשְׂרָאֵל	וְטוֹב בְּעֵינֶיךָ לְבָרֵךְ אֶת עַמְּךָ יִשְׂרָאֵל
בְּכָל עֵת וּבְכָל שָׁעָה	בְּכָל עֵת וּבְכָל שָׁעָה
בִּשְׁלוֹמֶךָ.	בִּשְׁלוֹמֶךָ.

בָּרוּךְ אַתָּה יהוה, הַמְבָרֵךְ אֶת עַמּוֹ יִשְׂרָאֵל בַּשָּׁלוֹם.

The following verse concludes the חורת הש״ץ
Some also say it here as part of the silent עמידה*. See law 368.*

תהלים יט
יִהְיוּ לְרָצוֹן אִמְרֵי־פִי וְהֶגְיוֹן לִבִּי לְפָנֶיךָ, יהוה צוּרִי וְגֹאֲלִי:

אֱלֹהַי My God, *Berakhot 17a*
guard my tongue from evil and my lips from deceitful speech.
To those who curse me, let my soul be silent;
may my soul be to all like the dust.
Open my heart to Your Torah
and let my soul pursue Your commandments.
As for all who plan evil against me,
swiftly thwart their counsel and frustrate their plans.
Act for the sake of Your name; act for the sake of Your right hand;
act for the sake of Your holiness; act for the sake of Your Torah.
That Your beloved ones may be delivered, *Ps. 60*
save with Your right hand and answer me.
May the words of my mouth and the meditation of my heart *Ps. 19*
find favor before You, LORD, my Rock and Redeemer.

Bow, take three steps back, then bow, first left, then right, then center, while saying:

May He who makes peace in His high places,
make peace for us and all Israel – and say: Amen.

יְהִי רָצוֹן May it be Your will, LORD our God and God of our ancestors,
that the Temple be rebuilt speedily in our days, and grant us a share in Your Torah.
And there we will serve You with reverence,
as in the days of old and as in former years.
Then the offering of Judah and Jerusalem *Mal. 3*
will be pleasing to the LORD as in the days of old and as in former years.

On Friday night, the service continues with "Then the heavens and the earth" on page 358.
If the first night of Pesaḥ falls on Shabbat, only the first paragraph is said.
On the Seder night many say Full Hallel (page 732) followed by Full Kaddish (page 360).
On the other Yamim Tovim, both at Minḥa and Ma'ariv, Full Kaddish (page 360) is said.
On the last nights of Pesaḥ, the Omer (page 284) is counted after Full Kaddish (page 360).
On Simḥat Torah, both at Ma'ariv and Shaḥarit say Full Kaddish (page 360), then continue with "You have been shown" and Hakafot on the next page.
At Shaḥarit, continue with Full Hallel (page 732), Full Kaddish (page 496), Torah Reading (page 498) and Musaf (page 806).
If the first day of Pesaḥ falls on Shabbat, then Shir HaShirim (page 1170) is read before the Torah reading at Shaḥarit on the last day (in Israel, on the first day). Otherwise it is read on Shabbat Ḥol HaMo'ed.
On the second day of Shavuot, Megillat Rut (page 1180) is read before the Torah reading at Shaḥarit (in Israel, on the first day).
If the first day of Sukkot falls on Shabbat, then Kohelet (page 1202) is read before the Torah reading at Shaḥarit on Shemini Atzeret (in Israel, on the first day of Sukkot). Otherwise it is read on Shabbat Ḥol HaMo'ed.

אֱלֹהַי   ברכות יז.
נְצֹר לְשׁוֹנִי מֵרָע וּשְׂפָתַי מִדַּבֵּר מִרְמָה
וְלִמְקַלְלַי נַפְשִׁי תִדֹּם, וְנַפְשִׁי כֶּעָפָר לַכֹּל תִּהְיֶה.
פְּתַח לִבִּי בְּתוֹרָתֶךָ, וּבְמִצְוֹתֶיךָ תִּרְדֹּף נַפְשִׁי.
וְכָל הַחוֹשְׁבִים עָלַי רָעָה
מְהֵרָה הָפֵר עֲצָתָם וְקַלְקֵל מַחֲשַׁבְתָּם.
עֲשֵׂה לְמַעַן שְׁמֶךָ, עֲשֵׂה לְמַעַן יְמִינֶךָ
עֲשֵׂה לְמַעַן קְדֻשָּׁתֶךָ, עֲשֵׂה לְמַעַן תּוֹרָתֶךָ.
לְמַעַן יֵחָלְצוּן יְדִידֶיךָ, הוֹשִׁיעָה יְמִינְךָ וַעֲנֵנִי: תהלים ס
יִהְיוּ לְרָצוֹן אִמְרֵי־פִי וְהֶגְיוֹן לִבִּי לְפָנֶיךָ, יהוה צוּרִי וְגֹאֲלִי: תהלים יט

Bow, take three steps back, then bow, first left, then right, then center, while saying:

עֹשֶׂה שָׁלוֹם בִּמְרוֹמָיו
הוּא יַעֲשֶׂה שָׁלוֹם עָלֵינוּ וְעַל כָּל יִשְׂרָאֵל, וְאִמְרוּ אָמֵן.
יְהִי רָצוֹן מִלְּפָנֶיךָ יהוה אֱלֹהֵינוּ וֵאלֹהֵי אֲבוֹתֵינוּ
שֶׁיִּבָּנֶה בֵּית הַמִּקְדָּשׁ בִּמְהֵרָה בְיָמֵינוּ, וְתֵן חֶלְקֵנוּ בְּתוֹרָתֶךָ
וְשָׁם נַעֲבָדְךָ בְּיִרְאָה כִּימֵי עוֹלָם וּכְשָׁנִים קַדְמוֹנִיּוֹת.
וְעָרְבָה לַיהוה מִנְחַת יְהוּדָה וִירוּשָׁלָםִ כִּימֵי עוֹלָם וּכְשָׁנִים קַדְמוֹנִיּוֹת: מלאכי ג

On Friday night, the service continues with וַיְכֻלּוּ *and* מעין שבע *on page 359.*
If the first night of פסח *falls on* שבת, מעין שבע *is omitted.*

On ליל הסדר *many say* הלל שלם *(page 733) followed by* קדיש שלם *(page 361).*
On the other ימים טובים*, both at* מנחה *and* מעריב, קדיש שלם *(page 361) is said.*

On the last nights of פסח*, the* עומר *(page 285) is counted after* קדיש שלם *(page 361).*

On שמחת תורה*, both at* מעריב *and* שחרית *say* קדיש שלם *(page 361),*
then continue with אַתָּה הׇרְאֵתָ *and* הקפות *on the next page.*

At שחרית*, continue with* הלל שלם *(page 733),* קדיש שלם *(page 497),*
קריאת התורה *(page 499) and* מוסף *(page 807).*

If the first day of פסח *falls on* שבת*, then* שיר השירים *(page 1171) is read before* קריאת התורה *at*
שחרית *on the last day (in* ארץ ישראל*, on the first day). Otherwise it is read on* שבת חול המועד.

On the second day of שבועות*,* רות *(page 1181) is read before* קריאת
התורה *at* שחרית *(in* ארץ ישראל*, on the first day).*

If the first day of סוכות *falls on* שבת*, then* קהלת *(page 1203) is read before* קריאת התורה
at שחרית *on* שמיני עצרת *(in* ארץ ישראל*, on the first day of* סוכות*).*
Otherwise it is read on שבת חול המועד.

HAKAFOT

At Ma'ariv and Shaḥarit of Simḥat Torah the following is said after Full Kaddish (page 496).

אַתָּה הָרְאֵתָ You have been shown [these things] so that you may know that the LORD is God; besides Him there is no other. *Deut. 4*
To the One who alone does great wonders, His loving-kindness is forever. *Ps. 136*
There is none like You among the heavenly powers, my LORD, *Ps. 86*
and there are no works like Yours.
May the LORD's glory be forever; may the LORD rejoice in His works. *Ps. 104*
May the LORD's name be blessed from now and forever. *Ps. 113*
May the LORD our God be with us as He was with our ancestors; *1 Kings 8*
may He never leave us or forsake us.
Say, "Save us, God our Savior; gather and deliver us from the nations, *1 Chr. 16*
that we may give thanks to Your holy name,
that we may glory in Your praise."
The LORD is King, the LORD was King,
the LORD will be King for ever and all time.
The LORD will give strength to His people; *Ps. 29*
the LORD will bless His people with peace.
May our words find favor before the LORD of all.

The Ark is opened.

Whenever the Ark set out, Moses would say, *Num. 10*
"Arise, LORD, and may Your enemies be scattered;
may those who hate You flee before You."
Advance, LORD, to Your resting place, You and Your mighty Ark. *Ps. 132*
Your priests are clothed in righteousness,
and Your devoted ones sing for joy.
For the sake of Your servant David, do not reject Your anointed one.
In that day they will say, *Is. 25*
"This is our God; we trusted in Him, and He saved us. This is the LORD,
we trusted in Him; let us rejoice and be glad in His salvation."
Your kingdom is an eternal kingdom, *Ps. 145*
and Your dominion is for all generations.
For the Torah shall come forth from Zion *Is. 2*
and the word of the LORD from Jerusalem.

Father of compassion, favor Zion with Your goodness; rebuild the walls of Jerusalem. *Ps. 51*
For we trust in You alone, King, God, high and exalted, Master of worlds.

סדר הקפות

At מעריב *and* שחרית *of* שמחת תורה*, the following is said after* קדיש שלם *(page 497).*

אַתָּה הָרְאֵתָ לָדַעַת, כִּי יהוה הוּא הָאֱלֹהִים, אֵין עוֹד מִלְּבַדּוֹ: דברים ד

לְעֹשֵׂה נִפְלָאוֹת גְּדֹלוֹת לְבַדּוֹ, כִּי לְעוֹלָם חַסְדּוֹ: תהלים קלו

אֵין־כָּמְוֹךָ בָאֱלֹהִים, אֲדֹנָי, וְאֵין כְּמַעֲשֶׂיךָ: תהלים פו

יְהִי כְבוֹד יהוה לְעוֹלָם, יִשְׂמַח יהוה בְּמַעֲשָׂיו: תהלים קד

יְהִי שֵׁם יהוה מְבֹרָךְ, מֵעַתָּה וְעַד־עוֹלָם: תהלים קיג

יְהִי יהוה אֱלֹהֵינוּ עִמָּנוּ, כַּאֲשֶׁר הָיָה עִם־אֲבֹתֵינוּ מלכים א׳ ח\
אַל־יַעַזְבֵנוּ וְאַל־יִטְּשֵׁנוּ:

וְאִמְרוּ, הוֹשִׁיעֵנוּ אֱלֹהֵי יִשְׁעֵנוּ, וְקַבְּצֵנוּ וְהַצִּילֵנוּ מִן־הַגּוֹיִם דברי הימים א׳ טז\
לְהֹדוֹת לְשֵׁם קָדְשֶׁךָ, לְהִשְׁתַּבֵּחַ בִּתְהִלָּתֶךָ:

יהוה מֶלֶךְ, יהוה מָלָךְ, יהוה יִמְלֹךְ לְעֹלָם וָעֶד.

יהוה עֹז לְעַמּוֹ יִתֵּן, יהוה יְבָרֵךְ אֶת־עַמּוֹ בַשָּׁלוֹם: תהלים כט

וְיִהְיוּ נָא אֲמָרֵינוּ לְרָצוֹן, לִפְנֵי אֲדוֹן כֹּל.

The ארון קודש *is opened.*

וַיְהִי בִּנְסֹעַ הָאָרֹן וַיֹּאמֶר מֹשֶׁה במדבר י\
קוּמָה יהוה וְיָפֻצוּ אֹיְבֶיךָ, וְיָנֻסוּ מְשַׂנְאֶיךָ מִפָּנֶיךָ:

קוּמָה יהוה לִמְנוּחָתֶךָ, אַתָּה וַאֲרוֹן עֻזֶּךָ: תהלים קלב\
כֹּהֲנֶיךָ יִלְבְּשׁוּ־צֶדֶק, וַחֲסִידֶיךָ יְרַנֵּנוּ:\
בַּעֲבוּר דָּוִד עַבְדֶּךָ, אַל־תָּשֵׁב פְּנֵי מְשִׁיחֶךָ:

וְאָמַר בַּיּוֹם הַהוּא ישעיה כה\
הִנֵּה אֱלֹהֵינוּ זֶה קִוִּינוּ לוֹ, וְיוֹשִׁיעֵנוּ\
זֶה יהוה קִוִּינוּ לוֹ, נָגִילָה וְנִשְׂמְחָה בִּישׁוּעָתוֹ:

מַלְכוּתְךָ מַלְכוּת כָּל־עֹלָמִים, וּמֶמְשַׁלְתְּךָ בְּכָל־דּוֹר וָדֹר: תהלים קמה

כִּי מִצִּיּוֹן תֵּצֵא תוֹרָה, וּדְבַר־יהוה מִירוּשָׁלָםִ: ישעיה ב

אַב הָרַחֲמִים, הֵיטִיבָה בִרְצוֹנְךָ אֶת־צִיּוֹן, תִּבְנֶה חוֹמוֹת יְרוּשָׁלָםִ: תהלים נא\
כִּי בְךָ לְבַד בָּטָחְנוּ, מֶלֶךְ אֵל רָם וְנִשָּׂא, אֲדוֹן עוֹלָמִים.

All the Torah scrolls are taken from the Ark.

First Hakafa

LORD, please save us. Ps. 118
LORD, please grant us success.
LORD, please answer us on the day we cry.

God of spirits, please save us.
Searcher of hearts, please grant us success.
Mighty Redeemer, answer us on the day we cry.

Second Hakafa

Speaker of righteousness, please save us.
Robed in majesty, please grant us success.
Ancient and loving One, answer us on the day we cry.

Third Hakafa

Pure and right, please save us.
Gracious and compassionate, please grant us success.
He who is good and does good, answer us on the day we cry.

Fourth Hakafa

He who knows thoughts, please save us.
Mighty and resplendent, please grant us success.
Robed in righteousness, answer us on the day we cry.

Fifth Hakafa

Eternal King, please save us.
Resplendent and mighty, please grant us success.
Supporter of the fallen, answer us on the day we cry.

Sixth Hakafa

Helper of the poor, please save us.
Redeemer and Rescuer, please grant us success.
Eternal Rock, answer us on the day we cry.

Seventh Hakafa

Holy and awesome, please save us.
Compassionate and gracious, please grant us success.
Dweller in the heavens, answer us on the day we cry.

Supporter of the innocent, please save us.
Eternally powerful, please grant us success.
Perfect in His deeds, answer us on the day we cry.

The Torah scrolls are returned to the Ark except for those used in the Torah Reading. At Ma'ariv, three (in some congregations, five) are called up and the "VeZot HaBerakha" Torah portion (pages 1161–1162) is read. See law 136. During Shaḥarit, the prevalent custom is to call up every adult male in the congregation. See law 139.

All the ספרי תורה *are taken from the* ארון קודש.

הקפה *First*

אָנָּא יהוה הוֹשִׁיעָה נָּא, אָנָּא יהוה הַצְלִיחָה נָא: תהלים קיח
אָנָּא יהוה עֲנֵנוּ בְיוֹם קָרְאֵנוּ.

אֱלֹהֵי הָרוּחוֹת הוֹשִׁיעָה נָּא, בּוֹחֵן לְבָבוֹת הַצְלִיחָה נָא
גּוֹאֵל חָזָק עֲנֵנוּ בְיוֹם קָרְאֵנוּ.

הקפה *Second*

דּוֹבֵר צְדָקוֹת הוֹשִׁיעָה נָּא, הָדוּר בִּלְבוּשׁוֹ הַצְלִיחָה נָא
וָתִיק וְחָסִיד עֲנֵנוּ בְיוֹם קָרְאֵנוּ.

הקפה *Third*

זַךְ וְיָשָׁר הוֹשִׁיעָה נָּא, חַנּוּן וְרַחוּם הַצְלִיחָה נָא
טוֹב וּמֵטִיב עֲנֵנוּ בְיוֹם קָרְאֵנוּ.

הקפה *Fourth*

יוֹדֵעַ מַחֲשָׁבוֹת הוֹשִׁיעָה נָּא, כַּבִּיר כֹּחַ הַצְלִיחָה נָא
לוֹבֵשׁ צְדָקוֹת עֲנֵנוּ בְיוֹם קָרְאֵנוּ.

הקפה *Fifth*

מֶלֶךְ עוֹלָמִים הוֹשִׁיעָה נָּא, נָאוֹר וְאַדִּיר הַצְלִיחָה נָא
סוֹמֵךְ וְסוֹעֵד עֲנֵנוּ בְיוֹם קָרְאֵנוּ.

הקפה *Sixth*

עוֹזֵר דַּלִּים הוֹשִׁיעָה נָּא, פּוֹדֶה וּמַצִּיל הַצְלִיחָה נָא
צוּר עוֹלָמִים עֲנֵנוּ בְיוֹם קָרְאֵנוּ.

הקפה *Seventh*

קָדוֹשׁ וְנוֹרָא הוֹשִׁיעָה נָּא, רַחוּם וְחַנּוּן הַצְלִיחָה נָא
שׁוֹכֵן שְׁחָקִים עֲנֵנוּ בְיוֹם קָרְאֵנוּ.

תּוֹמֵךְ תְּמִימִים הוֹשִׁיעָה נָּא, תַּקִּיף לָעַד הַצְלִיחָה נָא
תָּמִים בְּמַעֲשָׂיו עֲנֵנוּ בְיוֹם קָרְאֵנוּ.

The ספרי תורה *are returned to the* ארון קודש *except for those used in the* קריאת התורה.
At מעריב, *three (in some congregations, five) are called up and the* קריאה *of* וְזֹאת הַבְּרָכָה *(pages 1161–1162) is read. See law 136. During* שחרית, *the prevalent custom is to call up every adult male in the* קהל. *See law 139.*

AKDAMUT

On Shavuot, after the Kohen is called up to the Torah and before he makes the blessing, the following is said responsively by the Reader and the congregation.

Leader: The beginning of words – the opening of speech:
I shall ask permission and leave to begin.

Cong: Trembling I open my mouth with two matters and three,
by leave of the One who bears us through to old age.

Leader: His are eternal mighty acts,
which could not be laid out in words,
even were all the skies parchment, and all the forests reeds;

Cong: if all the seas were ink, and all the lakes,
and the all people, scribes and clerks.

Leader: The glorious Master of Heaven, Ruler of the land,
founded His world alone, and took control of it.

Cong: Without weariness He perfected it, without tiring at all;
by the lightest of letters, something without substance.

Leader: He summoned forth all creation in those six days;
and then His shining glory rose, to sit upon His throne of fire.

Cong: A heavenly host of a thousand thousands
and myriads serve Him –
created each morning anew, so great is His faithfulness.

Leader: Seraphim, covered with six wings, bow many times over,
and stand in utter silence until they have leave.

Cong: They receive leave from each other –
and at once, without pause,
His glory fills all the world, at their threefold sanctifying.

אקדמות

On שבועות, after the כהן is called up to the תורה and before he makes the ברכה, the following is said responsively by the שליח ציבור and the קהל.

ש״ץ: אַקְדָּמוּת מִלִּין וְשָׁרָיוּת שׁוּתָא
אַוְלָא שָׁקֵלְנָא הַרְמָן וּרְשׁוּתָא.

קהל: בְּבָבֵי תְּרֵי וּתְלָת דְּאֶפְתַּח בְּנַקְשׁוּתָא
בְּבָרֵי דְּבָרֵי וְטָרֵי עֲדֵי לְקַשִּׁישׁוּתָא.

ש״ץ: גְּבוּרָן עָלְמִין לֵהּ, וְלָא סָפֵק פְּרִישׁוּתָא
גְּוִיל אִלּוּ רְקִיעֵי, קְנֵי כָּל חֻרְשָׁתָא.

קהל: דְּיוֹ אִלּוּ יַמֵּי וְכָל מֵי כְנִישׁוּתָא
דָּיְרֵי אַרְעָא סָפְרֵי וְרָשְׁמֵי רַשְׁוָתָא.

ש״ץ: הֲדַר מָרֵי שְׁמַיָּא וְשַׁלִּיט בְּיַבֶּשְׁתָּא
הֲקֵים עָלְמָא יְחִידָאי, וְכַבְּשֵׁהּ בְּכַבְּשׁוּתָא.

קהל: וּבְלָא לֵאוּ שַׁכְלְלֵהּ, וּבְלָא תְשָׁשׁוּתָא
וּבְאָתָא קַלִּילָא דְּלֵית בַּהּ מְשָׁשׁוּתָא.

ש״ץ: זַמֵּן כָּל עֲבִידְתֵּהּ בְּהַךְ יוֹמֵי שִׁתָּא
זְהוֹר יְקָרֵהּ עַלִּי, עֲלֵי כֻרְסְיֵהּ דְּאֶשָּׁתָא.

קהל: חֵיל אֶלֶף אַלְפִין וְרִבּוֹא לְשַׁמָּשׁוּתָא
חַדְתִּין נְבוֹט לְצַפְרִין, סַגִּיאָה טְרָשׁוּתָא.

ש״ץ: טְפֵי יְקִידִין שְׂרָפִין, כְּלוּל גַּפֵּי שִׁתָּא
טְעֵם עַד יִתְיְהֵב לְהוֹן, שְׁתִיקִין בְּאַדִּשְׁתָּא.

קהל: יְקַבְּלוּן דֵּין מִן דֵּין שָׁוֵי דְּלָא בְשַׁשְׁתָּא
יְקָר מְלֵי כָל אַרְעָא לְתַלּוּתֵי קְדֻשְׁתָּא.

Leader: Like a voice from the Almighty, like the noise of many waters –
Cherubim raise themselves towards the Ophanim
in a roar of noise,

Cong: to see face to face what looks like sparks of the rainbow flying,
and wherever they are sent, they arrive in a flash of motion.

Leader: They bless His glory in every secret term,
from the place of the home of His Presence,
which cannot even be sought.

Cong: And all the hosts of heaven give praises in great fear,
of the sovereignty that will last through all ages, forever.

Leader: They each lay out His holiness in praise,
and when their moment has passed
it is gone forever; seven years will go by and it will not return.

Cong: His precious estate, Israel – they are more fortunate, for always
may they praise Him, dawn and dusk.

Leader: They are set apart, His portion, to perform His will,
and they will tell the wonders of His praise in speech.

Cong: He desires and values and yearns for them
to labor for Him to weariness,
and so He accepts their prayers; it is their pleas that are fulfilled.

Leader: And those pleas are joined, with a crown and an oath,
to the One who lives forever,
and worn with the phylacteries He binds to Himself always,

Cong: which are inscribed inside with wisdom and with insight,
with the greatness of Israel, who read the Shema.

Leader: And I, in the same way, praise the Master of the Universe,
and it befits me to speak of Him to those of other nations,

Cong: who come and form crowds, like waves all around,
doubting, asking about Him, about the signs He performs –

ש״ץ: כְּקָל מִן קֳדָם שַׁדַּי, כְּקָל מֵי נְפִישׁוּתָא
כְּרוּבִין קֳבֵל גַּלְגִּלִּין מְרוֹמְמִין בְּאַוְשָׁתָא.

קהל: לְמֶחֱזֵי בְּאַנְפָּא עֵין כְּוָת גִּירֵי קַשְׁתָּא
לְכָל אֲתַר דְּמִשְׁתַּלְּחִין, זְרִיזִין בְּאַשְׁוָתָא.

ש״ץ: מְבָרְכִין בְּרִיךְ יְקָרֵהּ בְּכָל לִשַּׁן לְחִישׁוּתָא
מֵאֲתַר בֵּית שְׁכִינְתֵּהּ, דְּלָא צְרִיךְ בְּחִישׁוּתָא.

קהל: נְהֵם כָּל חֵיל מְרוֹמָא, מְקַלְּסִין בַּחֲשַׁשְׁתָּא
נְהִירָא מַלְכוּתֵהּ לְדָר וְדָר לְאַפְרַשְׁתָּא.

ש״ץ: סְדִירָא בְהוֹן קְדֻשְׁתָּא, וְכַד חָלְפָא שַׁעְתָּא
סִיּוּמָא דִלְעָלַם, וְאוֹף לָא לְשִׁבְעֲתָא.

קהל: עֲדַב יְקַר אַחְסַנְתֵּהּ חֲבִיבִין, דְּבִקְבַעְתָּא
עֲבִידִין לֵהּ חֲטִיבָא בִּדְנַח וּשְׁקַעְתָּא.

ש״ץ: פְּרִישָׁן לְמָנָתֵהּ לְמֶעְבַּד לֵהּ רְעוּתָא
פְּרִישָׁתֵי שְׁבָחֵהּ יְחַוּוֹן בְּשָׁעוּתָא.

קהל: צְבִי וְחָמֵד וְרָגֵג דִּילְאוּן בִּלְעוּתָא
צְלוֹתְהוֹן בְּכֵן מְקַבֵּל, וְהָנְיָא בָעוּתָא.

ש״ץ: קְטִירָא לְחַי עָלְמָא בְּתָגָא בִּשְׁבוּעֲתָא
קֳבֵל יְקַר טוֹטַפְתָּא יְתִיבָא בִּקְבִיעֲתָא.

קהל: רְשִׁימָא הִיא גוּפָא בְּחָכְמְתָא וּבְדַעְתָּא
רְבוּתְהוֹן דְּיִשְׂרָאֵל, קָרָאֵי בִשְׁמַעְתָּא.

ש״ץ: שְׁבַח רִבּוֹן עָלְמָא, אֲמִירָא דְּכַוָּתָא
שַׁפַּר עֲלַי לְחַוּוֹיֵהּ בְּאַפֵּי מַלְכְּוָתָא.

קהל: תָּאִין וּמִתְכַּנְשִׁין כְּחֵזוּ אַדְוָתָא
תְּמֵהִין וְשַׁיְלִין לֵהּ בְּעֵסֶק אָתְוָתָא.

Leader: "Where is your Beloved from, yes who is He, who is so beautiful,
that you let yourselves be killed for Him in the lions' den?

Cong: "You would be more respected, lovelier,
if you bent yourselves to our rule:
your will would be done then wherever you would be."

Leader: With wisdom I reply to them, telling them of the end –
"If you only knew, if you only truly knew Him,

Cong: "and what your greatness is worth when compared to that glory,
or the greatness
I will be granted when my salvation comes...

Leader: "When light comes to me, and shame covers you over;
when His presence is revealed to me in might and in great pride."

Cong: He shall pay His enemies back in kind, the aggressors
of the distant isles,
and perform justice for the beloved people, rich in merit,

Leader: when He brings perfect happiness, and us as pure vessels;
when He brings the exiles back into the city of Jerusalem.

Cong: He shall cast His glory over them day and night,
as a canopy where they shall voice the splendor in
joyful songs,

Leader: for the shining of those clouds will make each canopy fine
as the actions of the one who sits in it; so will each shelter
be made.

Cong: On seats of finest gold, in seven tiers, sit the righteous
in their places before the One whose acts are manifold.

Leader: And they appear as seven tiers of joy,
like the dome of the sky in its brilliance, like stars of light.

Cong: This is a glory no mouth can express,
glory that the prophets never heard or saw in their visions.

ש״ץ: מְנָן וּמַאן הוּא רְחִימָךְ, שַׁפִּירָא בְרֵוָתָא
אֲרוּם בְּגִינֵהּ סְפֵית מְדוֹר אַרְיָוָתָא.

קהל: יְקָרָא וִיאָה אַתְּ, אִין תְּעָרְבִי לְמָרְוָתָא
רְעוּתֵךְ נַעֲבֵד לִיךְ בְּכָל אַתְרְוָתָא.

ש״ץ: בְּחָכְמְתָא מְתִיבְתָּא לְהוֹן, קְצָת לְהוֹדָעוּתָא
יְדַעְתּוּן חַכִּמִין לֵהּ בְּאִשְׁתְּמוֹדָעוּתָא.

קהל: רְבוּתְכוֹן מָה חֲשִׁיבָא קֳבֵל הַהִיא שִׁבְחָתָא
רְבוּתָא דְיַעֲבֵד לִי, כַּד מָטְיָא יְשׁוּעָתָא.

ש״ץ: בְּמֵיתֵי לִי נְהוֹרָא, וְתַחֲפֵי לְכוֹן בַּהֲתָא
יְקָרֵהּ כַּד אִתְגְּלֵי בְּתַקְפָא וּבְגֵיוְתָא.

קהל: יְשַׁלֵּם גְּמָלַיָּא לְסָנְאֵי וְנַגְוָתָא
צִדְקָתָא לְעַם חֲבִיב וְסַגִּי זַכְוָתָא.

ש״ץ: חֲדוּ שְׁלֵמָא בְּמֵיתֵי, וּמָנָא דְכִיָּתָא
קִרְיְתָא דִירוּשְׁלֵם כַּד יְכַנֵּשׁ גַּלְוָתָא.

קהל: יְקָרֵהּ מַטֵּל עֲלַהּ בְּיוֹמֵי וְלֵילְוָתָא
גְּנוּנֵהּ לְמֶעְבַּד בַּהּ בְּתֻשְׁבְּחָן כְּלִילָתָא.

ש״ץ: דְּזֵהוֹר עֲנָנַיָּא לְמִשְׁפַּר כִּילָתָא
לְפֻמֵּהּ דַּעֲבִידְתָּא עֲבִידָן מְטַלַּלְתָּא.

קהל: בְּתַכְתְּקֵי דְהַב פִּזָא, וְשִׁבְעָה מַעֲלָתָא
תְּחִימִין צַדִּיקֵי קֳדָם רַב פָּעֳלָתָא.

ש״ץ: וְרֵוֵיהוֹן דָּמֵי לְשָׁבְעָא חֶדְוָתָא
רְקִיעָא בְּזֵהוֹרֵהּ וְכוֹכְבֵי זִיוָתָא.

קהל: הַדְרָא דְּלָא אֶפְשַׁר לְמִפְרַט שִׂפְוָתָא
וְלָא אִשְׁתְּמַע וַחֲמֵי נְבִיאָן חֶזְוָתָא.

Leader: For no eye has ever overseen the Garden of Eden,
where the righteous circle the place of the dance, and the holy Presence among them.

Cong: And they point to Him, saying with awe, "It is He!
"The One for whom we longed when we were captives, in our powerful faith.

Leader: "And He will lead us in both worlds; and He will lead us dancing, as if we were young again;
lead us to our land, set aside from the beginning of the world for us."

Cong: He plays with the Leviathan, with the Behemoth of the high mountain,
and when they wrestle one another in their great duel,

Leader: the horns of the great Behemoth will gore,
and the mighty Leviathan will leap out at him with his fins,

Cong: and finally, his Creator will step forward with His great sword,
and prepare a meal, a feast, of that meat, for all the righteous.

Leader: And they shall sit at tables of rubies and gems,
with rivers of balsam flowing before them,

Cong: and quench their thirst in luxury with overflowing cups
of the wondrous wine stored up for them since the first days of creation.

Leader: My righteous listeners, as you have heard the praises in this song,
so may you be promised a place in those joyous circles.

Cong: And may you merit to sit in those heavenly rows,
for heeding God's words, which come forth in splendor.

Leader: Our God is in the highest heights, the first and the last,
desiring us and cherishing us, and giving us the Torah.

The service continues with the Torah Reading on page 1146.

ש״ץ: בְּלָא שָׁלְטָא בֵהּ עֵין, בְּגוֹ עֲדֶן גִּנְּתָא
מְטַיְּלֵי בֵהּ חִנְגָּא לְבַהֲדֵי דִשְׁכִינְתָּא.

קהל: עֲלֵהּ רָמְזֵי דֵּין הוּא, בְּרַם בְּאֵימְתָנוּתָא
שַׁבְרָנָא לֵהּ בְּשִׁבְיַן, תְּקוֹף הֵמָנוּתָא.

ש״ץ: יְדַבֵּר לַן עָלְמִין, עָלְמִין מְדַמּוּתָא
מְנָת דִּילַן דְּמִלְּקַדְמִין פָּרֵשׁ בַּאֲרָמוּתָא.

קהל: טְלוּלָא דְלִוְיָתָן וְתוֹר טוּר רָמוּתָא
וְחַד בְּחַד כִּי סָבֵךְ וְעָבֵד קְרָבוּתָא.

ש״ץ: בְּקַרְנוֹהִי מְנַגַּח בְּהֵמוֹת בְּרַבְרְבוּתָא
יְקַרְטַע נוּן לְקִבְלֵהּ בְּצִיצוֹי בִּגְבוּרְתָא.

קהל: מְקָרֵב לֵהּ בָּרְיֵהּ בְּחַרְבֵּהּ בְּרַבְרְבוּתָא
אֲרִסְטוֹן לְצַדִּיקֵי יְתַקַּן, וְשֵׁרוּתָא.

ש״ץ: מְסַחֲרִין עֲלֵי תַכֵּי דְּכַדְכֹּד וְגוּמַרְתָּא
נְגִידִין קָמֵיהוֹן אֲפַרְסְמוֹן נַהֲרָתָא.

קהל: וּמִתְפַּנְּקִין וְרָווּ בְּכַסֵּי רְוָיָתָא
חֲמַר מְרַת דְּמִבְּרֵאשִׁית נְטִיר בֵּי נַעֲוָתָא.

ש״ץ: זַכָּאִין, כַּד שְׁמַעְתּוּן שְׁבַח דָּא שִׁירָתָא
קְבִיעִין כֵּן תֶּהֱווֹן בְּהַנְהוּ חֲבוּרָתָא.

קהל: וְתִזְכּוּן דִּי תֵיתְּבוּן בְּעֵלָּא דָרָתָא
אֲרֵי תְצִיתוּן לְמִלּוֹי, דְּנָפְקִין בְּהַדְרָתָא.

ש״ץ: מְרוֹמַם הוּא אֱלָהִין בְּקַדְמָתָא וּבַתְרַיְתָא
צְבִי וְאִתְרְעִי בַן, וּמְסַר לַן אוֹרַיְתָא.

The service continues with קריאת התורה *on page 1147.*

YIZKOR

The Yizkor service is said on the last day of Pesaḥ, the second day of Shavuot (first day in Israel), Yom Kippur and Shemini Atzeret. In some communities, those who have not been bereaved of a parent or close relative do not participate in the service, but leave the synagogue and return at the end of Yizkor.

יהוה LORD, what is man that You care for him, a mortal that You notice him? *Ps. 144*
Man is like a fleeting breath, his days like a passing shadow.
In the morning he flourishes and grows; *Ps. 90*
in the evening he withers and dries up.
Teach us to number our days, that we may get a heart of wisdom.
Mark the blameless, note the upright, for the end of such a person is peace. *Ps. 37*
God will redeem my soul from the grave, for He will receive me, Selah. *Ps. 49*
My flesh and my heart may fail, *Ps. 73*
but God is the strength of my heart and my portion for ever.
The dust returns to the earth as it was, *Eccl. 12*
but the spirit returns to God who gave it.

ישב He who lives in the shelter of the Most High dwells in the shadow of the Almighty. I say of the LORD, my Refuge and Stronghold, my God in whom I trust, that He will save you from the fowler's snare and the deadly pestilence. With His pinions He will cover you, and beneath His wings you will find shelter; His faithfulness is an encircling shield. You need not fear terror by night, nor the arrow that flies by day; not the pestilence that stalks in darkness, nor the plague that ravages at noon. A thousand may fall at your side, ten thousand at your right hand, but it will not come near you. You will only look with your eyes and see the punishment of the wicked. Because you [have said:] "the LORD is my Refuge," taking the Most High as your shelter, no harm will befall you, no plague will come near your tent, for He will command His angels about you, to guard you in all your ways. They will lift you in their hands, lest your foot stumble on a stone. You will tread on lions and vipers; you will trample on young lions and snakes. [God says:] "Because he loves Me, I will rescue him; I will protect him, because he acknowledges My name. When he calls on Me, I will answer him; I will be with him in distress, I will deliver him and bring him honor. With long life I will satisfy him and show him My salvation. *Ps. 91*
With long life I will satisfy him and show him My salvation.

---

other festivals: the last day of Pesaḥ, the second day of Shavuot (first day in Israel), and the day of Shemini Atzeret.

Remembrance is fundamental to Judaism. The word *zakhor*, "remember," in one or other of its forms, appears no fewer than 169 times in the Hebrew

סדר הזכרת נשמות

The יזכור service is said on the last day of פסח, the second day of שבועות (first day in ארץ ישראל), שמיני עצרת and יום כיפור. In some communities, those who have not been bereaved of a parent or close relative do not participate in the service, but leave the בית כנסת and return at the end of סדר הזכרת נשמות.

יהוה מָה־אָדָם וַתֵּדָעֵהוּ, בֶּן־אֱנוֹשׁ וַתְּחַשְּׁבֵהוּ: תהלים קמד
אָדָם לַהֶבֶל דָּמָה, יָמָיו כְּצֵל עוֹבֵר:
בַּבֹּקֶר יָצִיץ וְחָלָף, לָעֶרֶב יְמוֹלֵל וְיָבֵשׁ: תהלים צ
לִמְנוֹת יָמֵינוּ כֵּן הוֹדַע, וְנָבִא לְבַב חָכְמָה:
שְׁמָר־תָּם וּרְאֵה יָשָׁר, כִּי־אַחֲרִית לְאִישׁ שָׁלוֹם: תהלים לז
אַךְ־אֱלֹהִים יִפְדֶּה נַפְשִׁי מִיַּד שְׁאוֹל, כִּי יִקָּחֵנִי סֶלָה: תהלים מט
כָּלָה שְׁאֵרִי וּלְבָבִי, צוּר־לְבָבִי וְחֶלְקִי אֱלֹהִים לְעוֹלָם: תהלים עג
וְיָשֹׁב הֶעָפָר עַל־הָאָרֶץ כְּשֶׁהָיָה, וְהָרְוּחַ תָּשׁוּב אֶל־הָאֱלֹהִים אֲשֶׁר נְתָנָהּ: קהלת יב

יֹשֵׁב בְּסֵתֶר עֶלְיוֹן, בְּצֵל שַׁדַּי יִתְלוֹנָן: אֹמַר לַיהוה מַחְסִי וּמְצוּדָתִי, תהלים צא
אֱלֹהַי אֶבְטַח־בּוֹ: כִּי הוּא יַצִּילְךָ מִפַּח יָקוּשׁ, מִדֶּבֶר הַוּוֹת: בְּאֶבְרָתוֹ
יָסֶךְ לָךְ, וְתַחַת־כְּנָפָיו תֶּחְסֶה, צִנָּה וְסֹחֵרָה אֲמִתּוֹ: לֹא־תִירָא מִפַּחַד
לָיְלָה, מֵחֵץ יָעוּף יוֹמָם: מִדֶּבֶר בָּאֹפֶל יַהֲלֹךְ, מִקֶּטֶב יָשׁוּד צָהֳרָיִם:
יִפֹּל מִצִּדְּךָ אֶלֶף, וּרְבָבָה מִימִינֶךָ, אֵלֶיךָ לֹא יִגָּשׁ: רַק בְּעֵינֶיךָ תַבִּיט,
וְשִׁלֻּמַת רְשָׁעִים תִּרְאֶה: כִּי־אַתָּה יהוה מַחְסִי, עֶלְיוֹן שַׂמְתָּ מְעוֹנֶךָ:
לֹא־תְאֻנֶּה אֵלֶיךָ רָעָה, וְנֶגַע לֹא־יִקְרַב בְּאָהֳלֶךָ: כִּי מַלְאָכָיו יְצַוֶּה־לָּךְ,
לִשְׁמָרְךָ בְּכָל־דְּרָכֶיךָ: עַל־כַּפַּיִם יִשָּׂאוּנְךָ, פֶּן־תִּגֹּף בָּאֶבֶן רַגְלֶךָ: עַל־
שַׁחַל וָפֶתֶן תִּדְרֹךְ, תִּרְמֹס כְּפִיר וְתַנִּין: כִּי בִי חָשַׁק וַאֲפַלְּטֵהוּ, אֲשַׂגְּבֵהוּ
כִּי־יָדַע שְׁמִי: יִקְרָאֵנִי וְאֶעֱנֵהוּ, עִמּוֹ־אָנֹכִי בְצָרָה, אֲחַלְּצֵהוּ וַאֲכַבְּדֵהוּ:
אֹרֶךְ יָמִים אַשְׂבִּיעֵהוּ, וְאַרְאֵהוּ בִּישׁוּעָתִי:
אֹרֶךְ יָמִים אַשְׂבִּיעֵהוּ, וְאַרְאֵהוּ בִּישׁוּעָתִי:

YIZKOR: MEMORIAL SERVICE FOR THE DEAD

From the eleventh century onward it has become customary to pray, at key moments in the year, for the souls of the departed. At first, this prayer was said only on Yom Kippur, but it was soon extended to the last days of the

For one's father:

יִזְכֹּר May God remember the soul of my father, my teacher (*name* son of *father's name*) who has gone to his eternal home, and to this I pledge (without formal vow) to give charity on his behalf, that his soul may be bound in the bond of everlasting life together with the souls of Abraham, Isaac and Jacob, Sarah, Rebecca, Rachel and Leah, and all the other righteous men and women in the Garden of Eden, and let us say: Amen.

For one's mother:

יִזְכֹּר May God remember the soul of my mother, my teacher (*name* daughter of *father's name*) who has gone to her eternal home, and to this I pledge (without formal vow) to give charity on her behalf, that her soul may be bound in the bond of everlasting life together with the souls of Abraham, Isaac and Jacob, Sarah, Rebecca, Rachel and Leah, and all the other righteous men and women in the Garden of Eden, and let us say: Amen.

For martyrs:

יִזְכֹּר May God remember the soul of (*name*, son/daughter of *father's name*), and the souls of all my relatives, on my father's or mother's side, who were killed, murdered, slaughtered, burned, drowned or strangled for the sanctification of God's name, and to this I pledge (without formal vow) to give charity in their memory. May their souls be bound in the bond of everlasting life together with the souls of Abraham, Isaac and Jacob, Sarah, Rebecca, Rachel and Leah, and all the other righteous men and women in the Garden of Eden, and let us say: Amen.

---

ence on us that we are in the synagogue; that we pray, and that we try to do good in this life. A connection is thus made between the dead and the living. We remember them; with God's help, their virtues live on in us. That is as much of immortality as we can know in the land of the living.

It is a custom at *Yizkor* also to remember the Jewish martyrs, including the victims of the Holocaust, for we are the guardians of their memory. The dead cannot be brought back to life, but we can act in such a way as to ensure that they did not die in vain, by showing that the faith for which they died still lives. To the *Yizkor* prayer itself have been added a series of biblical verses on life and death, together with a prayer that we may act in such a way as to honor the memory of those, especially our parents, who are no longer here.

For one's father:

יִזְכֹּר אֱלֹהִים נִשְׁמַת אָבִי מוֹרִי (פלוני בֶּן פלוני) שֶׁהָלַךְ לְעוֹלָמוֹ, בַּעֲבוּר שֶׁבְּלִי נֶדֶר אֶתֵּן צְדָקָה בַּעֲדוֹ. בִּשְׂכַר זֶה תְּהֵא נַפְשׁוֹ צְרוּרָה בִּצְרוֹר הַחַיִּים עִם נִשְׁמוֹת אַבְרָהָם יִצְחָק וְיַעֲקֹב, שָׂרָה רִבְקָה רָחֵל וְלֵאָה, וְעִם שְׁאָר צַדִּיקִים וְצִדְקָנִיּוֹת שֶׁבְּגַן עֵדֶן, וְנֹאמַר אָמֵן.

For one's mother:

יִזְכֹּר אֱלֹהִים נִשְׁמַת אִמִּי מוֹרָתִי (פלונית בַּת פלוני) שֶׁהָלְכָה לְעוֹלָמָהּ, בַּעֲבוּר שֶׁבְּלִי נֶדֶר אֶתֵּן צְדָקָה בַּעֲדָהּ. בִּשְׂכַר זֶה תְּהֵא נַפְשָׁהּ צְרוּרָה בִּצְרוֹר הַחַיִּים עִם נִשְׁמוֹת אַבְרָהָם יִצְחָק וְיַעֲקֹב, שָׂרָה רִבְקָה רָחֵל וְלֵאָה, וְעִם שְׁאָר צַדִּיקִים וְצִדְקָנִיּוֹת שֶׁבְּגַן עֵדֶן, וְנֹאמַר אָמֵן.

For martyrs:

יִזְכֹּר אֱלֹהִים נִשְׁמַת (*male* פלוני בֶּן פלוני / *female* פלונית בַּת פלוני) וְנִשְׁמוֹת כָּל קְרוֹבַי וּקְרוֹבוֹתַי, הֵן מִצַּד אָבִי הֵן מִצַּד אִמִּי, שֶׁהוּמְתוּ וְשֶׁנֶּהֶרְגוּ וְשֶׁנִּשְׁחֲטוּ וְשֶׁנִּשְׂרְפוּ וְשֶׁנִּטְבְּעוּ וְשֶׁנֶּחְנְקוּ עַל קִדּוּשׁ הַשֵּׁם, בַּעֲבוּר שֶׁבְּלִי נֶדֶר אֶתֵּן צְדָקָה בְּעַד הַזְכָּרַת נִשְׁמוֹתֵיהֶם. בִּשְׂכַר זֶה תִּהְיֶינָה נַפְשׁוֹתֵיהֶם צְרוּרוֹת בִּצְרוֹר הַחַיִּים עִם נִשְׁמוֹת אַבְרָהָם יִצְחָק וְיַעֲקֹב, שָׂרָה רִבְקָה רָחֵל וְלֵאָה, וְעִם שְׁאָר צַדִּיקִים וְצִדְקָנִיּוֹת שֶׁבְּגַן עֵדֶן, וְנֹאמַר אָמֵן.

Bible. The past is not lost: we remain connected to it to the extent that we remember it, honor it, and keep faith with it. We are its heirs – our lives are part of a story that began long before we were born and will continue long after we physically cease to be. Above all, God remembers – as we say in every Amida, He "remembers the loving-kindness of the fathers." For Him, there is no forgetting.

At *Yizkor*, our memory reaches out to that of God. We ask Him to remember those of our family who are no longer here. We ask Him to look on the good we do (it is a custom to donate a sum to charity at this time and attribute it to the souls of the departed ones), for it is because of their influ-

For a male close relative:

אֵל מָלֵא רַחֲמִים God, full of mercy, who dwells on high, grant fitting rest on the wings of the Divine Presence, in the heights of the holy and the pure who shine like the radiance of heaven, to the soul of (*name* son of *father's name*) who has gone to his eternal home, and to this I pledge (without formal vow) to give charity in his memory, may his resting place be in the Garden of Eden. Therefore, Master of compassion, shelter him in the shadow of Your wings forever and bind his soul in the bond of everlasting life. The LORD is his heritage; may he rest in peace, and let us say: Amen.

For a female close relative:

אֵל מָלֵא רַחֲמִים God, full of mercy, who dwells on high, grant fitting rest on the wings of the Divine Presence, in the heights of the holy and the pure who shine like the radiance of heaven, to the soul of (*name* daughter of *father's name*) who has gone to her eternal home, and to this I pledge (without formal vow) to give charity in her memory, may her resting place be in the Garden of Eden. Therefore, Master of compassion, shelter her in the shadow of Your wings forever and bind her soul in the bond of everlasting life. The LORD is her heritage; may she rest in peace, and let us say: Amen.

For the Israeli soldiers:

אֵל מָלֵא רַחֲמִים God, full of mercy, who dwells on high, grant fitting rest on the wings of the Divine Presence, in the heights of the holy, the pure and the brave, who shine like the radiance of heaven, to the souls of the holy ones who fought in any of Israel's battles, in clandestine operations and in Israel's Defense Forces, who fell in battle and sacrificed their lives for the consecration of God's name, for the people and the land, and for this we pray for the ascent of their souls. Therefore, Master of compassion, shelter them in the shadow of Your wings forever, and bind their souls in the bond of everlasting life. The LORD is their heritage; may the Garden of Eden be their resting place, may they rest in peace, may their merit stand for all Israel, and may they receive their reward at the End of Days, and let us say: Amen.

For a male close relative:

אֵל מָלֵא רַחֲמִים, שׁוֹכֵן בַּמְּרוֹמִים, הַמְצֵא מְנוּחָה נְכוֹנָה עַל כַּנְפֵי הַשְּׁכִינָה, בְּמַעֲלוֹת קְדוֹשִׁים וּטְהוֹרִים, כְּזְהַר הָרָקִיעַ מַזְהִירִים, לְנִשְׁמַת (פלוני בֶּן פלוני) שֶׁהָלַךְ לְעוֹלָמוֹ, בַּעֲבוּר שֶׁבְּלִי נֶדֶר אֶתֵּן צְדָקָה בְּעַד הַזְכָּרַת נִשְׁמָתוֹ, בְּגַן עֵדֶן תְּהֵא מְנוּחָתוֹ. לָכֵן, בַּעַל הָרַחֲמִים יַסְתִּירֵהוּ בְּסֵתֶר כְּנָפָיו לְעוֹלָמִים, וְיִצְרֹר בִּצְרוֹר הַחַיִּים אֶת נִשְׁמָתוֹ, יהוה הוּא נַחֲלָתוֹ, וְיָנְוּחַ בְּשָׁלוֹם עַל מִשְׁכָּבוֹ, וְנֹאמַר אָמֵן.

For a female close relative:

אֵל מָלֵא רַחֲמִים, שׁוֹכֵן בַּמְּרוֹמִים, הַמְצֵא מְנוּחָה נְכוֹנָה עַל כַּנְפֵי הַשְּׁכִינָה, בְּמַעֲלוֹת קְדוֹשִׁים וּטְהוֹרִים, כְּזְהַר הָרָקִיעַ מַזְהִירִים, לְנִשְׁמַת (פלונית בַּת פלוני) שֶׁהָלְכָה לְעוֹלָמָהּ, בַּעֲבוּר שֶׁבְּלִי נֶדֶר אֶתֵּן צְדָקָה בְּעַד הַזְכָּרַת נִשְׁמָתָהּ, בְּגַן עֵדֶן תְּהֵא מְנוּחָתָהּ. לָכֵן, בַּעַל הָרַחֲמִים יַסְתִּירֶהָ בְּסֵתֶר כְּנָפָיו לְעוֹלָמִים, וְיִצְרֹר בִּצְרוֹר הַחַיִּים אֶת נִשְׁמָתָהּ, יהוה הוּא נַחֲלָתָהּ, וְתָנְוּחַ בְּשָׁלוֹם עַל מִשְׁכָּבָהּ, וְנֹאמַר אָמֵן.

For the Israeli soldiers:

אֵל מָלֵא רַחֲמִים, שׁוֹכֵן בַּמְּרוֹמִים, הַמְצֵא מְנוּחָה נְכוֹנָה עַל כַּנְפֵי הַשְּׁכִינָה, בְּמַעֲלוֹת קְדוֹשִׁים טְהוֹרִים וְגִבּוֹרִים, כְּזְהַר הָרָקִיעַ מַזְהִירִים, לְנִשְׁמוֹת הַקְּדוֹשִׁים שֶׁנִּלְחֲמוּ בְּכָל מַעַרְכוֹת יִשְׂרָאֵל, בַּמַּחְתֶּרֶת וּבִצְבָא הַהֲגָנָה לְיִשְׂרָאֵל, וְשֶׁנָּפְלוּ בְּמִלְחַמְתָּם וּמָסְרוּ נַפְשָׁם עַל קְדֻשַּׁת הַשֵּׁם, הָעָם וְהָאָרֶץ, בַּעֲבוּר שֶׁאָנוּ מִתְפַּלְּלִים לְעִלּוּי נִשְׁמוֹתֵיהֶם. לָכֵן, בַּעַל הָרַחֲמִים יַסְתִּירֵם בְּסֵתֶר כְּנָפָיו לְעוֹלָמִים, וְיִצְרֹר בִּצְרוֹר הַחַיִּים אֶת נִשְׁמוֹתֵיהֶם, יהוה הוּא נַחֲלָתָם, בְּגַן עֵדֶן תְּהֵא מְנוּחָתָם, וְיָנְוּחוּ בְּשָׁלוֹם עַל מִשְׁכְּבוֹתֵיהֶם וְתַעֲמֹד לְכָל יִשְׂרָאֵל זְכוּתָם, וְיַעַמְדוּ לְגוֹרָלָם לְקֵץ הַיָּמִין, וְנֹאמַר אָמֵן.

For the Holocaust victims:

אֵל מָלֵא רַחֲמִים God, full of mercy, Justice of widows and Father of orphans, please do not be silent and hold Your peace for the blood of Israel that was shed like water. Grant fitting rest on the wings of the Divine Presence, in the heights of the holy and the pure who shine and radiate light like the radiance of heaven, to the souls of the millions of Jews, men, women and children, who were murdered, slaughtered, burned, strangled, and buried alive, in the lands touched by the German enemy and its followers. They were all holy and pure; among them were great scholars and righteous individuals, cedars of Lebanon and noble masters of Torah, may the Garden of Eden be their resting place. Therefore, Master of compassion, shelter them in the shadow of Your wings forever, and bind their souls in the bond of everlasting life. The Lord is their heritage; may they rest in peace, and let us say: Amen.

Congregation and Leader:

אַב הָרַחֲמִים Father of compassion, who dwells on high: may He remember in His compassion the pious, the upright and the blameless – holy communities who sacrificed their lives for the sanctification of God's name. Lovely and pleasant in their lives, in death they were not parted. They were swifter than eagles and stronger than lions to do the will of their Maker and the desire of their Creator. O our God, remember them for good with the other righteous of the world, and may He exact retribution for the shed blood of His servants, as it is written in the Torah of Moses, the man of God: "O nations, acclaim His people, for He will avenge the blood of His servants, wreak vengeance on His foes, and make clean His people's land." And by Your servants, the prophets, it is written: "I shall cleanse their blood which I have not yet cleansed, says the Lord who dwells in Zion." And in the holy Writings it says: "Why should the nations say: Where is their God? Before our eyes, may those nations know that You avenge the shed blood of Your servants." And it also says: "For the Avenger of blood remembers them and does not forget the cry of the afflicted." And it further says: "He will execute judgment among the nations, filled with the dead, crushing rulers far and wide. From the brook by the wayside he will drink, then he will hold his head high."

Deut. 32 · *Joel 4* · *Ps. 79* · *Ps. 9* · *Ps. 110*

For the Holocaust victims:

אֵל מָלֵא רַחֲמִים, דַּיַּן אַלְמָנוֹת וַאֲבִי יְתוֹמִים, אַל נָא תֶחֱשֶׁה
וְתִתְאַפַּק לְדַם יִשְׂרָאֵל שֶׁנִּשְׁפַּךְ כַּמַּיִם. הַמְצֵא מְנוּחָה נְכוֹנָה עַל
כַּנְפֵי הַשְּׁכִינָה, בְּמַעֲלוֹת קְדוֹשִׁים וּטְהוֹרִים, כְּזֹהַר הָרָקִיעַ מְאִירִים
וּמַזְהִירִים, לְנִשְׁמוֹתֵיהֶם שֶׁל רִבְבוֹת אַלְפֵי יִשְׂרָאֵל, אֲנָשִׁים וְנָשִׁים,
יְלָדִים וִילָדוֹת, שֶׁנֶּהֶרְגוּ וְנִשְׁחֲטוּ וְנִשְׂרְפוּ וְנֶחְנְקוּ וְנִקְבְּרוּ חַיִּים,
בָּאֲרָצוֹת אֲשֶׁר נָגְעָה בָהֶן יַד הַצּוֹרֵר הַגֶּרְמָנִי וּגְרוּרָיו. כֻּלָּם קְדוֹשִׁים
וּטְהוֹרִים, וּבָהֶם גְּאוֹנִים וְצַדִּיקִים, אַרְזֵי הַלְּבָנוֹן אַדִּירֵי הַתּוֹרָה.
בְּגַן עֵדֶן תְּהֵא מְנוּחָתָם. לָכֵן, בַּעַל הָרַחֲמִים יַסְתִּירֵם בְּסֵתֶר כְּנָפָיו
לְעוֹלָמִים, וְיִצְרֹר בִּצְרוֹר הַחַיִּים אֶת נִשְׁמָתָם, יהוה הוּא נַחֲלָתָם,
וְיָנוּחוּ בְשָׁלוֹם עַל מִשְׁכָּבָם, וְנֹאמַר אָמֵן.

קהל ושליח ציבור:

אַב הָרַחֲמִים שׁוֹכֵן מְרוֹמִים, בְּרַחֲמָיו הָעֲצוּמִים הוּא יִפְקֹד בְּרַחֲמִים
הַחֲסִידִים וְהַיְשָׁרִים וְהַתְּמִימִים, קְהִלּוֹת הַקֹּדֶשׁ שֶׁמָּסְרוּ נַפְשָׁם עַל
קְדֻשַּׁת הַשֵּׁם, הַנֶּאֱהָבִים וְהַנְּעִימִים בְּחַיֵּיהֶם, וּבְמוֹתָם לֹא נִפְרָדוּ,
מִנְּשָׁרִים קַלּוּ וּמֵאֲרָיוֹת גָּבֵרוּ לַעֲשׂוֹת רְצוֹן קוֹנָם וְחֵפֶץ צוּרָם. יִזְכְּרֵם
אֱלֹהֵינוּ לְטוֹבָה עִם שְׁאָר צַדִּיקֵי עוֹלָם, וְיִנְקֹם לְעֵינֵינוּ נִקְמַת דַּם
עֲבָדָיו הַשָּׁפוּךְ, כַּכָּתוּב בְּתוֹרַת מֹשֶׁה אִישׁ הָאֱלֹהִים, הַרְנִינוּ גוֹיִם דברים לב
עַמּוֹ, כִּי דַם־עֲבָדָיו יִקּוֹם, וְנָקָם יָשִׁיב לְצָרָיו, וְכִפֶּר אַדְמָתוֹ עַמּוֹ:
וְעַל יְדֵי עֲבָדֶיךָ הַנְּבִיאִים כָּתוּב לֵאמֹר, וְנִקֵּיתִי, דָּמָם לֹא־נִקֵּיתִי, יואל ד
וַיהוה שֹׁכֵן בְּצִיּוֹן: וּבְכִתְבֵי הַקֹּדֶשׁ נֶאֱמַר, לָמָּה יֹאמְרוּ הַגּוֹיִם אַיֵּה תהלים עט
אֱלֹהֵיהֶם, יִוָּדַע בַּגּוֹיִם לְעֵינֵינוּ נִקְמַת דַּם־עֲבָדֶיךָ הַשָּׁפוּךְ: וְאוֹמֵר,
כִּי־דֹרֵשׁ דָּמִים אוֹתָם זָכָר, לֹא־שָׁכַח צַעֲקַת עֲנָוִים: וְאוֹמֵר, יָדִין תהלים ט / תהלים קי
בַּגּוֹיִם מָלֵא גְוִיּוֹת, מָחַץ רֹאשׁ עַל־אֶרֶץ רַבָּה: מִנַּחַל בַּדֶּרֶךְ יִשְׁתֶּה,
עַל־כֵּן יָרִים רֹאשׁ:

Most congregations omit the following on days that Yizkor is said. Some also omit on Shabbat.

יָהּ אֵלִי LORD my God and Redeemer, I will stand to greet You;
[God] who was and will be, was and is,
the land of every nation is Yours.

The thanksgiving-offering, burnt-offering, meal-offering, sin-offering, guilt-offering, peace-offering and inauguration-offering are all offerings to You. Remember the weary nation that has borne much, and bring it back to Your land. I will always praise You with "Happy are those who dwell in Your House."

Fine beyond fine, undecipherable, His understanding is unfathomable, Awesome God who distinguishes between good and evil with a single glance.

The thanksgiving-offering, burnt-offering, meal-offering, sin-offering, guilt-offering, peace-offering and inauguration-offering are all offerings to You. Remember the weary nation that has borne much, and bring it back to Your land. I will always praise You with "Happy are those who dwell in Your House."

LORD of hosts, with many wonders, He joined all His tent,
making all blossom in the ways of the heart:
the Rock, perfect is His work.

The thanksgiving-offering, burnt-offering, meal-offering, sin-offering, guilt-offering, peace-offering and inauguration-offering are all offerings to You. Remember the weary nation that has borne much, and bring it back to Your land. I will always praise You with "Happy are those who dwell in Your House."

---

nation: a poignant reminder that the Jewish people, suffering and in exile, cannot yet be among those who "dwell in Your House," that is, the Temple.

דַּק עַל דַּק *Fine beyond fine:* beyond the reach of our human senses and understanding. בֵּין טוֹב לְרַע יְבַקֵּר *Who distinguishes between good and evil:* we cannot see God but He sees us; we cannot understand God but He understands us, instantly knowing our devices and desires.

חִבֵּר כָּל אָהֳלוֹ *He joined all His tent:* God constructed and connected all that exists under the canopy of the heavens. בִּנְתִיבוֹת לֵב לְבַלֵּב *The ways of the heart:* the Hebrew word for heart, *lev,* also stands for the number thirty-two, which according to the mystical *Sefer Yetzira,* represents the "thirty-two paths of wisdom" by which the universe was created (the word *Elohim* appears thirty-two times in the first chapter of the Torah).

Most congregations omit the following on days that יזכור *is said. Some also omit on* שבת.

יָהּ אֵלִי וְגוֹאֲלִי, אֶתְיַצְּבָה לִקְרָאתֶךָ
הָיָה וְיִהְיֶה, הָיָה וְהֹוֶה, כָּל גּוֹי אַדְמָתֶךָ.

וְתוֹדָה וְלָעוֹלָה וְלַמִּנְחָה וְלַחַטָּאת וְלָאָשָׁם
וְלַשְּׁלָמִים וְלַמִּלּוּאִים כָּל קָרְבָּנֶךָ.
זְכֹר נִלְאָה אֲשֶׁר נָשְׂאָה וְהָשִׁיבָה לְאַדְמָתֶךָ
סֶלָה אֲהַלֶּלְךָ בְּאַשְׁרֵי יוֹשְׁבֵי בֵיתֶךָ.

דַּק עַל דַּק, עַד אֵין נִבְדָּק, וְלִתְבוּנָתוֹ אֵין חֵקֶר
הָאֵל נוֹרָא, בְּאַחַת סְקִירָה, בֵּין טוֹב לָרַע יְבַקֵּר.

וְתוֹדָה וְלָעוֹלָה וְלַמִּנְחָה וְלַחַטָּאת וְלָאָשָׁם
וְלַשְּׁלָמִים וְלַמִּלּוּאִים כָּל קָרְבָּנֶךָ.
זְכֹר נִלְאָה אֲשֶׁר נָשְׂאָה וְהָשִׁיבָה לְאַדְמָתֶךָ
סֶלָה אֲהַלֶּלְךָ בְּאַשְׁרֵי יוֹשְׁבֵי בֵיתֶךָ.

אָדוֹן צְבָאוֹת, בְּרֹב פְּלָאוֹת, חִבֵּר כָּל אֲהָלוֹ
בִּנְתִיבוֹת לֵב לְבָבֵב, הַצּוּר תָּמִים פָּעֳלוֹ.

וְתוֹדָה וְלָעוֹלָה וְלַמִּנְחָה וְלַחַטָּאת וְלָאָשָׁם
וְלַשְּׁלָמִים וְלַמִּלּוּאִים כָּל קָרְבָּנֶךָ.
זְכֹר נִלְאָה אֲשֶׁר נָשְׂאָה וְהָשִׁיבָה לְאַדְמָתֶךָ
סֶלָה אֲהַלֶּלְךָ בְּאַשְׁרֵי יוֹשְׁבֵי בֵיתֶךָ.

יָהּ אֵלִי *LORD my God:* A poem written as a prelude to *Ashrei* ("Happy are those who dwell in Your House"), which first appeared in the siddur *Sha'ar Hashamayim* of R. Isaiah Horowitz (first published by his grandson in Amsterdam, 1717). Those who say it do so on festivals before the *Ashrei* that precedes Musaf; it is usually omitted on days on which *Yizkor* is said; some omit it on festivals that fall on Shabbat.

כָּל גּוֹי אַדְמָתֶךָ *The land of every nation,* that is, the whole world, *is Yours.* וְתוֹדָה *The thanksgiving-offering:* a list of sacrifices we are commanded to bring, but cannot, since the Temple no longer stands. זְכֹר נִלְאָה *Remember the weary*

Musaf for Festivals

The following Amida is said on Yom Tov and Ḥol HaMo'ed (including Shabbat Ḥol HaMo'ed).

On the first day of Pesaḥ, the Leader begins the Repetition with "Prayer for Dew" on page 840; on Shemini Atzeret, with "Prayer for Rain" on page 846. In Israel, these prayers are said before the silent recitation of the Amida.

The following prayer, until "in former years" on page 828, is said silently, standing with feet together. If there is a minyan, the Amida is repeated aloud by the Leader. Take three steps forward and at the points indicated by ▾, bend the knees at the first word, bow at the second, and stand straight before saying God's name.

When I proclaim the LORD's name, give glory to our God. *Deut. 32*

O LORD, open my lips, so that my mouth may declare Your praise. *Ps. 51*

PATRIARCHS

▾בָּרוּךְ Blessed are You, LORD our God and God of our fathers, God of Abraham, God of Isaac and God of Jacob; the great, mighty and awesome God, God Most High, who bestows acts of loving-kindness and creates all, who remembers the loving-kindness of the fathers and will bring a Redeemer to their children's children for the sake of His name, in love. King, Helper, Savior, Shield: ▾Blessed are You, LORD, Shield of Abraham.

DIVINE MIGHT

אַתָּה גִּבּוֹר You are eternally mighty, LORD.
You give life to the dead and have great power to save.

On Shemini Atzeret if announced (see law 128), Simḥat Torah and the first day of Pesaḥ (see laws 129–131):

He makes the wind blow and the rain fall.

In Israel, on other Festivals:

He causes the dew to fall.

He sustains the living with loving-kindness, and with great compassion revives the dead. He supports the fallen, heals the sick, sets captives free, and keeps His faith with those who sleep in the dust. Who is like You, Master of might, and who can compare to You, O King who brings death and gives life, and makes salvation grow? Faithful are You to revive the dead. Blessed are You, LORD, who revives the dead.

מוסף לשלוש רגלים

The following עמידה *is said on* יום טוב *and* חול המועד
(*including* שבת חול המועד).
On the first day of פסח*, the* שליח ציבור *begins the* חזרת הש״ץ *with* תפילת טל *on page 841;*
on שמיני עצרת*, with* תפילת גשם *on page 847.*
In ארץ ישראל*, these prayers are said before the silent recitation of the* עמידה.

The following prayer, until קַדְמֹנִיּוֹת *on page 829, is said silently, standing with feet together. If there is a* מנין*, the* עמידה *is repeated aloud by the* שליח ציבור.
Take three steps forward and at the points indicated by ׳*, bend the knees at the first word, bow at the second, and stand straight before saying God's name.*

כִּי שֵׁם יהוה אֶקְרָא, הָבוּ גֹדֶל לֵאלֹהֵינוּ: דברים לב
אֲדֹנָי, שְׂפָתַי תִּפְתָּח, וּפִי יַגִּיד תְּהִלָּתֶךָ: תהלים נא

אבות

׳בָּרוּךְ אַתָּה יהוה, אֱלֹהֵינוּ וֵאלֹהֵי אֲבוֹתֵינוּ, אֱלֹהֵי אַבְרָהָם, אֱלֹהֵי יִצְחָק, וֵאלֹהֵי יַעֲקֹב, הָאֵל הַגָּדוֹל הַגִּבּוֹר וְהַנּוֹרָא, אֵל עֶלְיוֹן, גּוֹמֵל חֲסָדִים טוֹבִים, וְקוֹנֵה הַכֹּל, וְזוֹכֵר חַסְדֵי אָבוֹת, וּמֵבִיא גוֹאֵל לִבְנֵי בְנֵיהֶם לְמַעַן שְׁמוֹ בְּאַהֲבָה. מֶלֶךְ עוֹזֵר וּמוֹשִׁיעַ וּמָגֵן. ׳בָּרוּךְ אַתָּה יהוה, מָגֵן אַבְרָהָם.

גבורות

אַתָּה גִּבּוֹר לְעוֹלָם, אֲדֹנָי, מְחַיֵּה מֵתִים אַתָּה, רַב לְהוֹשִׁיעַ

On שמיני עצרת *if announced (see law 128),* שמחת תורה
and the first day of פסח *(see laws 129–131):*

מַשִּׁיב הָרְוּחַ וּמוֹרִיד הַגֶּשֶׁם

In ארץ ישראל*, on other* חגים*:*

מוֹרִיד הַטָּל

מְכַלְכֵּל חַיִּים בְּחֶסֶד, מְחַיֵּה מֵתִים בְּרַחֲמִים רַבִּים, סוֹמֵךְ נוֹפְלִים, וְרוֹפֵא חוֹלִים, וּמַתִּיר אֲסוּרִים, וּמְקַיֵּם אֱמוּנָתוֹ לִישֵׁנֵי עָפָר. מִי כָמְוֹךָ, בַּעַל גְּבוּרוֹת, וּמִי דּוֹמֶה לָּךְ, מֶלֶךְ, מֵמִית וּמְחַיֶּה וּמַצְמִיחַ יְשׁוּעָה. וְנֶאֱמָן אַתָּה לְהַחֲיוֹת מֵתִים. בָּרוּךְ אַתָּה יהוה, מְחַיֵּה הַמֵּתִים.

When saying the Amida silently, continue with "You are holy" on page 810.

KEDUSHA

On Ḥol HaMo'ed, turn to the Kedusha on the next page. On Yom Tov, Shabbat Ḥol HaMo'ed and Hoshana Raba, during the Repetition, the following is said standing with feet together, rising on the toes at the words indicated by ˄.

Cong. then Leader: נַעֲרִיצְךָ We will revere and sanctify You with the words uttered by the holy Seraphim who sanctify Your name in the Sanctuary; as is written by Your prophet: "They call out to one another, saying: *Is. 6*

Cong. then Leader: ˄Holy, ˄holy, ˄holy is the LORD of hosts; the whole world is filled with His glory."

His glory fills the universe. His ministering angels ask each other, "Where is the place of His glory?" Those facing them reply "Blessed –

Cong. then Leader: ˄"Blessed is the LORD's glory from His place." *Ezek. 3*

From His place may He turn with compassion and be gracious to the people who proclaim the unity of His name, morning and evening, every day, continually, twice each day reciting in love the Shema:

Cong. then Leader: "Listen, Israel: the LORD is our God, the LORD is One." *Deut. 6*

He is our God, He is our Father, He is our King, He is our Savior – and He, in His compassion, will let us hear a second time in the presence of all that lives, His promise "to be Your God. *Num. 15* I am the LORD your God."

On Shabbat Ḥol HaMo'ed, the following paragraph is omitted:

Cong. then Leader: Glorious is our Glorious One, LORD our Master, and *Ps. 8* glorious is Your name throughout the earth. Then the *Zech. 14* LORD shall be King over all the earth; on that day the LORD shall be One and His name One.

Leader: And in Your holy Writings it is written:

Cong. then Leader: ˄"The LORD shall reign for ever. He is your God, Zion, from *Ps. 146* generation to generation, Halleluya!"

Leader: From generation to generation we will declare Your greatness, and we will proclaim Your holiness for evermore. Your praise, our God, shall not leave our mouth forever, for You, God, are a great and holy King. Blessed are You, LORD, the holy God.

The Leader continues with "You have chosen us" on the next page.

When saying the עמידה *silently, continue with* אַתָּה קָדוֹשׁ *on page 811.*

קדושה

On שבת חול המועד, *turn to the* קדושה *on the next page. On* יום טוב, חול המועד *and* הושענא רבה, *during the* חזרת הש״ץ, *the following is said standing with feet together, rising on the toes at the words indicated by* ˄.

then קהל ש״ץ: נַעֲרִיצְךָ וְנַקְדִּישְׁךָ כְּסוֹד שִׂיחַ שַׂרְפֵי קֹדֶשׁ, הַמַּקְדִּישִׁים שִׁמְךָ בַּקֹּדֶשׁ, כַּכָּתוּב עַל יַד נְבִיאֶךָ: וְקָרָא זֶה אֶל־זֶה וְאָמַר — ישעיה ו

then קהל ש״ץ: ˄קָדוֹשׁ, ˄קָדוֹשׁ, ˄קָדוֹשׁ, יהוה צְבָאוֹת, מְלֹא כָל הָאָרֶץ כְּבוֹדוֹ:
כְּבוֹדוֹ מָלֵא עוֹלָם, מְשָׁרְתָיו שׁוֹאֲלִים זֶה לָזֶה, אַיֵּה מְקוֹם כְּבוֹדוֹ, לְעֻמָּתָם בָּרוּךְ יֹאמֵרוּ

then קהל ש״ץ: ˄בָּרוּךְ כְּבוֹד־יהוה מִמְּקוֹמוֹ: — יחזקאל ג
מִמְּקוֹמוֹ הוּא יִפֶן בְּרַחֲמִים, וְיָחֹן עַם הַמְיַחֲדִים שְׁמוֹ, עֶרֶב וָבֹקֶר בְּכָל יוֹם תָּמִיד, פַּעֲמַיִם בְּאַהֲבָה שְׁמַע אוֹמְרִים

then קהל ש״ץ: שְׁמַע יִשְׂרָאֵל, יהוה אֱלֹהֵינוּ, יהוה אֶחָד: — דברים ו
הוּא אֱלֹהֵינוּ, הוּא אָבִינוּ, הוּא מַלְכֵּנוּ, הוּא מוֹשִׁיעֵנוּ, וְהוּא יַשְׁמִיעֵנוּ בְּרַחֲמָיו שֵׁנִית לְעֵינֵי כָּל חָי, לִהְיוֹת לָכֶם לֵאלֹהִים, — במדבר טו
אֲנִי יהוה אֱלֹהֵיכֶם:

On שבת חול המועד, *the following paragraph is omitted:*

then קהל ש״ץ: אַדִּיר אַדִּירֵנוּ, יהוה אֲדֹנֵינוּ, מָה־אַדִּיר שִׁמְךָ בְּכָל־הָאָרֶץ: — תהלים ח
וְהָיָה יהוה לְמֶלֶךְ עַל־כָּל־הָאָרֶץ, בַּיּוֹם הַהוּא יִהְיֶה יהוה אֶחָד וּשְׁמוֹ אֶחָד: — זכריה יד

ש״ץ: וּבְדִבְרֵי קָדְשְׁךָ כָּתוּב לֵאמֹר

then קהל ש״ץ: ˄יִמְלֹךְ יהוה לְעוֹלָם, אֱלֹהַיִךְ צִיּוֹן לְדֹר וָדֹר, הַלְלוּיָהּ: — תהלים קמו

ש״ץ: לְדוֹר וָדוֹר נַגִּיד גָּדְלֶךָ, וּלְנֵצַח נְצָחִים קְדֻשָּׁתְךָ נַקְדִּישׁ, וְשִׁבְחֲךָ אֱלֹהֵינוּ מִפִּינוּ לֹא יָמוּשׁ לְעוֹלָם וָעֶד, כִּי אֵל מֶלֶךְ גָּדוֹל וְקָדוֹשׁ אָתָּה. בָּרוּךְ אַתָּה יהוה, הָאֵל הַקָּדוֹשׁ.

The שליח ציבור *continues with* אַתָּה בְחַרְתָּנוּ *on the next page.*

KEDUSHA FOR ḤOL HAMO'ED

During the Leader's Repetition, the following is said standing with feet together, rising on the toes at the words indicated by ▲.

Cong. then Leader: נְקַדֵּשׁ We will sanctify Your name on earth, as they sanctify it in the highest heavens, as is written by Your prophet, "And they [the angels] call to one another saying: *Is. 6*

Cong. then Leader: ▲"Holy, ▲holy, ▲holy is the LORD of hosts the whole world is filled with His glory."

Those facing them say "Blessed – "

Cong. then Leader: ▲"Blessed is the LORD's glory from His place." *Ezek. 3*

And in Your holy Writings it is written thus:

Cong. then Leader: ▲"The LORD shall reign for ever. He is your God, Zion, from generation to generation, Halleluya!" *Ps. 146*

Leader: From generation to generation we will declare Your greatness, and we will proclaim Your holiness for evermore. Your praise, our God, shall not leave our mouth forever, for You, God, are a great and holy King. Blessed are You, LORD, the holy God.

The Leader continues with "You have chosen us" below.

When saying the Amida silently, continue here with "You are holy":

HOLINESS

אַתָּה קָדוֹשׁ You are holy and Your name is holy, and holy ones praise You daily, Selah! Blessed are You, LORD, the holy God.

HOLINESS OF THE DAY

אַתָּה בְחַרְתָּנוּ You have chosen us from among all peoples.
You have loved and favored us.
You have raised us above all tongues.
You have made us holy through Your commandments.
You have brought us near, our King, to Your service,
and have called us by Your great and holy name.

ADDITIONAL SERVICE FOR FESTIVALS

The Musaf on festivals, like that of Shabbat, corresponds to the additional sacrifice brought on these days. The Amida follows the normal form for prayers on holy days: the first and last three Amida blessings are the same as

קדושה לחול המועד

During the חזרת הש״ץ*, the following is said standing with feet together, rising on the toes at the words indicated by* *.

קהל then ש״ץ: נְקַדֵּשׁ אֶת שִׁמְךָ בָּעוֹלָם, כְּשֵׁם שֶׁמַּקְדִּישִׁים אוֹתוֹ בִּשְׁמֵי מָרוֹם
כַּכָּתוּב עַל יַד נְבִיאֶךָ: וְקָרָא זֶה אֶל־זֶה וְאָמַר — ישעיה ו

קהל then ש״ץ: *קָדוֹשׁ, *קָדוֹשׁ, *קָדוֹשׁ, יהוה צְבָאוֹת, מְלֹא כָל־הָאָרֶץ כְּבוֹדוֹ:
לְעֻמָּתָם בָּרוּךְ יֹאמֵרוּ

קהל then ש״ץ: *בָּרוּךְ כְּבוֹד־יהוה מִמְּקוֹמוֹ: — יחזקאל ג
וּבְדִבְרֵי קָדְשְׁךָ כָּתוּב לֵאמֹר

קהל then ש״ץ: *יִמְלֹךְ יהוה לְעוֹלָם, אֱלֹהַיִךְ צִיּוֹן לְדֹר וָדֹר, הַלְלוּיָהּ: — תהלים קמו

ש״ץ: לְדוֹר וָדוֹר נַגִּיד גָּדְלֶךָ, וּלְנֵצַח נְצָחִים קְדֻשָּׁתְךָ נַקְדִּישׁ, וְשִׁבְחֲךָ אֱלֹהֵינוּ מִפִּינוּ לֹא יָמוּשׁ לְעוֹלָם וָעֶד, כִּי אֵל מֶלֶךְ גָּדוֹל וְקָדוֹשׁ אָתָּה. בָּרוּךְ אַתָּה יהוה, הָאֵל הַקָּדוֹשׁ.

The שליח ציבור *continues with* אַתָּה בְחַרְתָּנוּ *below.*

When saying the עמידה *silently, continue here with* אַתָּה קָדוֹשׁ*:*

קדושת השם

אַתָּה קָדוֹשׁ וְשִׁמְךָ קָדוֹשׁ, וּקְדוֹשִׁים בְּכָל יוֹם יְהַלְלוּךָ סֶּלָה. בָּרוּךְ אַתָּה יהוה, הָאֵל הַקָּדוֹשׁ.

קדושת היום

אַתָּה בְחַרְתָּנוּ מִכָּל הָעַמִּים
אָהַבְתָּ אוֹתָנוּ וְרָצִיתָ בָּנוּ
וְרוֹמַמְתָּנוּ מִכָּל הַלְּשׁוֹנוֹת
וְקִדַּשְׁתָּנוּ בְּמִצְוֹתֶיךָ
וְקֵרַבְתָּנוּ מַלְכֵּנוּ לַעֲבוֹדָתֶךָ
וְשִׁמְךָ הַגָּדוֹל וְהַקָּדוֹשׁ עָלֵינוּ קָרָאתָ.

On Shabbat, add the words in parentheses:

וַתִּתֶּן לָנוּ And You, LORD our God, have given us in love
(Sabbaths for rest and) festivals for rejoicing,
holy days and seasons for joy,
(this Sabbath day and) this day of:

On Pesaḥ:	the festival of Matzot, the time of our freedom
On Shavuot:	the festival of Shavuot, the time of the giving of our Torah
On Sukkot:	the festival of Sukkot, our time of rejoicing
On Shemini Atzeret & Simḥat Torah:	the festival of the eighth day, Shemini Atzeret, our time of rejoicing

(with love), a holy assembly in memory of the exodus from Egypt.

וּמִפְּנֵי חֲטָאֵינוּ But because of our sins we were exiled from our land
and driven far from our country.
We cannot go up to appear and bow before You,
and to perform our duties in Your chosen House,
the great and holy Temple that was called by Your name,
because of the hand that was stretched out against Your Sanctuary.
May it be Your will, LORD our God and God of our ancestors,
merciful King,
that You in Your abounding compassion may once more
have mercy on us and on Your Sanctuary,
rebuilding it swiftly and adding to its glory.
Our Father, our King, reveal the glory of Your kingdom to us swiftly.
Appear and be exalted over us in the sight of all that lives.
Bring back our scattered ones from among the nations,
and gather our dispersed people from the ends of the earth.

---

festivals testify to the presence of God in history. Exile is the opposite. Not only is exile physical and geographical dispersion, it is also metaphysical: the "hiding of the face" of God (Deut. 31:18). The prayers for forgiveness, return to the land, the rebuilding of the Temple, and the reappearance of God in history, are thus intimately connected, and are most intensely felt on these days when we recall God's deliverances and saving acts in Israel's past.

On שבת*, add the words in parentheses:*

וַתִּתֶּן לָנוּ יהוה אֱלֹהֵינוּ בְּאַהֲבָה
(שַׁבָּתוֹת לִמְנוּחָה וּ) מוֹעֲדִים לְשִׂמְחָה, חַגִּים וּזְמַנִּים לְשָׂשׂוֹן
אֶת יוֹם (הַשַּׁבָּת הַזֶּה וְאֶת יוֹם)

בפסח: חַג הַמַּצּוֹת הַזֶּה, זְמַן חֵרוּתֵנוּ
בשבועות: חַג הַשָּׁבוּעוֹת הַזֶּה, זְמַן מַתַּן תּוֹרָתֵנוּ
בסוכות: חַג הַסֻּכּוֹת הַזֶּה, זְמַן שִׂמְחָתֵנוּ
בשמע״צ ובש״ת: הַשְּׁמִינִי חַג הָעֲצֶרֶת הַזֶּה, זְמַן שִׂמְחָתֵנוּ

(בְּאַהֲבָה) מִקְרָא קֹדֶשׁ, זֵכֶר לִיצִיאַת מִצְרָיִם.

וּמִפְּנֵי חֲטָאֵינוּ גָּלִינוּ מֵאַרְצֵנוּ, וְנִתְרַחַקְנוּ מֵעַל אַדְמָתֵנוּ
וְאֵין אֲנַחְנוּ יְכוֹלִים לַעֲלוֹת וְלֵרָאוֹת וּלְהִשְׁתַּחֲווֹת לְפָנֶיךָ
וְלַעֲשׂוֹת חוֹבוֹתֵינוּ בְּבֵית בְּחִירָתֶךָ
בַּבַּיִת הַגָּדוֹל וְהַקָּדוֹשׁ שֶׁנִּקְרָא שִׁמְךָ עָלָיו
מִפְּנֵי הַיָּד שֶׁנִּשְׁתַּלְּחָה בְּמִקְדָּשֶׁךָ.
יְהִי רָצוֹן מִלְּפָנֶיךָ יהוה אֱלֹהֵינוּ וֵאלֹהֵי אֲבוֹתֵינוּ, מֶלֶךְ רַחֲמָן
שֶׁתָּשׁוּב וּתְרַחֵם עָלֵינוּ וְעַל מִקְדָּשְׁךָ בְּרַחֲמֶיךָ הָרַבִּים
וְתִבְנֵהוּ מְהֵרָה וּתְגַדֵּל כְּבוֹדוֹ.
אָבִינוּ מַלְכֵּנוּ, גַּלֵּה כְּבוֹד מַלְכוּתְךָ עָלֵינוּ מְהֵרָה
וְהוֹפַע וְהִנָּשֵׂא עָלֵינוּ לְעֵינֵי כָּל חָי
וְקָרֵב פְּזוּרֵינוּ מִבֵּין הַגּוֹיִם, וּנְפוּצוֹתֵינוּ כַּנֵּס מִיַּרְכְּתֵי אָרֶץ.

---

on other days of the year; the middle blessing is specific to the "holiness of the day." On festivals, special emphasis is placed on rejoicing, mentioned in the Torah (Deut. 16:11–15) in connection with festivals.

וּמִפְּנֵי חֲטָאֵינוּ גָּלִינוּ מֵאַרְצֵנוּ *But because of our sins we were exiled from our land:* The concept of exile is emphasized on the festivals for two reasons. Firstly, the three pilgrimage festivals were occasions when people throughout the land went to Jerusalem to take part in the Temple celebrations. They are thus times in which we feel, most acutely, the absence of the Temple. Secondly, the

Lead us to Zion, Your city, in jubilation,
and to Jerusalem, home of Your Temple, with everlasting joy.
There we will prepare for You
our obligatory offerings:
the regular daily offerings in their order
and the additional offerings according to their law.
And the additional offering(s of this Sabbath day and) of this day of:

On Pesaḥ: the festival of Matzot.
On Shavuot: the festival of Shavuot.
On Sukkot: the festival of Sukkot.
On Shemini Atzeret & Simḥat Torah: the festival of Shemini Atzeret.

we will prepare and offer before You in love,
in accord with Your will's commandment,
as You wrote for us in Your Torah
through Your servant Moses, by Your own word, as it is said:

On Shabbat add:

וּבְיוֹם הַשַּׁבָּת On the Sabbath day, make an offering of two lambs a year old, without blemish, together with two-tenths of an ephah of fine flour mixed with oil as a meal-offering, and its appropriate libation. This is the burnt-offering for every Sabbath, in addition to the regular daily burnt-offering and its libation. *Num. 28*

On the first two days of Pesaḥ say (in Israel, on the first day only):

וּבַחֹדֶשׁ הָרִאשׁוֹן On the fourteenth day of the first month there shall be a Pesaḥ offering to the Lord. And on the fifteenth day of this month there shall be a festival: seven days unleavened bread shall be eaten. On the first day there shall be a sacred assembly: you shall do no laborious work. And you shall bring an offering consumed by fire, a burnt-offering to the Lord: two young bullocks, one ram, and seven yearling male lambs; they shall be to you unblemished. And their meal-offerings and wine-libations as ordained: three-tenths of an ephah for each bull, two-tenths of an ephah for the ram, one-tenth of an ephah for each lamb, wine for the libations, a male goat for atonement, and two regular daily offerings according to their law. *Num. 28*

On weekdays, continue with "Our God and God of our ancestors" on page 822.
On Shabbat, continue with "Those who keep the Sabbath" at the top of page 822.

וַהֲבִיאֵנוּ לְצִיּוֹן עִירְךָ בְּרִנָּה
וְלִירוּשָׁלַיִם בֵּית מִקְדָּשְׁךָ בְּשִׂמְחַת עוֹלָם
וְשָׁם נַעֲשֶׂה לְפָנֶיךָ אֶת קָרְבְּנוֹת חוֹבוֹתֵינוּ
תְּמִידִים כְּסִדְרָם וּמוּסָפִים כְּהִלְכָתָם
וְאֶת מוּסַף יוֹם / שבת: וְאֶת מוּסְפֵי יוֹם הַשַּׁבָּת הַזֶּה וְיוֹם/
בפסח: חַג הַמַּצּוֹת הַזֶּה
בשבועות: חַג הַשָּׁבוּעוֹת הַזֶּה
בסוכות: חַג הַסֻּכּוֹת הַזֶּה
בשמע״צ ובש״ת: הַשְּׁמִינִי חַג הָעֲצֶרֶת הַזֶּה
נַעֲשֶׂה וְנַקְרִיב לְפָנֶיךָ בְּאַהֲבָה כְּמִצְוַת רְצוֹנֶךָ
כְּמוֹ שֶׁכָּתַבְתָּ עָלֵינוּ בְּתוֹרָתֶךָ
עַל יְדֵי מֹשֶׁה עַבְדֶּךָ מִפִּי כְבוֹדֶךָ, כָּאָמוּר

On שבת *add:*

וּבְיוֹם הַשַּׁבָּת, שְׁנֵי־כְבָשִׂים בְּנֵי־שָׁנָה תְּמִימִם, וּשְׁנֵי עֶשְׂרֹנִים סֹלֶת מִנְחָה בְּלוּלָה בַשֶּׁמֶן וְנִסְכּוֹ: עֹלַת שַׁבַּת בְּשַׁבַּתּוֹ, עַל־עֹלַת הַתָּמִיד וְנִסְכָּהּ: במדבר כח

On the first two days of פסח *say (in* ארץ ישראל*, on the first day only):*

וּבַחֹדֶשׁ הָרִאשׁוֹן בְּאַרְבָּעָה עָשָׂר יוֹם לַחֹדֶשׁ, פֶּסַח לַיהוה: וּבַחֲמִשָּׁה עָשָׂר יוֹם לַחֹדֶשׁ הַזֶּה חָג, שִׁבְעַת יָמִים מַצּוֹת יֵאָכֵל: בַּיּוֹם הָרִאשׁוֹן מִקְרָא־קֹדֶשׁ, כָּל־מְלֶאכֶת עֲבֹדָה לֹא תַעֲשׂוּ: וְהִקְרַבְתֶּם אִשֶּׁה עֹלָה לַיהוה, פָּרִים בְּנֵי־בָקָר שְׁנַיִם וְאַיִל אֶחָד, וְשִׁבְעָה כְבָשִׂים בְּנֵי שָׁנָה תְּמִימִם יִהְיוּ לָכֶם: במדבר כח
וּמִנְחָתָם וְנִסְכֵּיהֶם כִּמְדֻבָּר, שְׁלֹשָׁה עֶשְׂרֹנִים לַפָּר וּשְׁנֵי עֶשְׂרֹנִים לָאָיִל, וְעִשָּׂרוֹן לַכֶּבֶשׂ, וְיַיִן כְּנִסְכּוֹ, וְשָׂעִיר לְכַפֵּר, וּשְׁנֵי תְמִידִים כְּהִלְכָתָם.

On weekdays, continue with אֱלֹהֵינוּ וֵאלֹהֵי אֲבוֹתֵינוּ *on page 823.*
On שבת*, continue with* יִשְׂמְחוּ בְמַלְכוּתְךָ *at the top of page 823.*

On the last six days of Pesaḥ say:

וְהִקְרַבְתֶּם And you shall bring an offering consumed by fire, a burnt-offering to the Lord: two young bullocks, one ram, and seven yearling male lambs; they shall be to you unblemished. And their meal-offerings and wine-libations as ordained: three-tenths of an ephah for each bull, two-tenths of an ephah for the ram, one-tenth of an ephah for each lamb, wine for the libations, a male goat for atonement, and two regular daily offerings according to their law. *Num. 28*

On weekdays, continue with "Our God and God of our ancestors" on page 822.
On Shabbat, continue with "Those who keep the Sabbath" at the top of page 822.

On Shavuot say:

וּבְיוֹם הַבִּכּוּרִים On the day of the first fruits, when you bring an offering of new grain to the Lord, on your Festival of Weeks, there shall be a sacred assembly: you shall do no laborious work. You shall offer a burnt-offering of pleasing aroma to the Lord: two young bullocks, one ram, and seven yearling male lambs. And their meal-offerings and wine-libations as ordained: three-tenths of an ephah for each bull, two-tenths of an ephah for the ram, one-tenth of an ephah for each lamb, wine for the libations, a male goat for atonement, and two regular daily offerings according to their law. *Num. 28*

On weekdays, continue with "Our God and God of our ancestors" on page 822.
On Shabbat, continue with "Those who keep the Sabbath" at the top of page 822.

On the first two days of Sukkot say (in Israel, the first day only):

וּבַחֲמִשָּׁה עָשָׂר On the fifteenth day of the seventh month you shall hold a sacred assembly. You shall do no laborious work, and you shall celebrate a festival to the Lord for seven days. You shall offer a burnt-offering, a fire-offering of pleasing aroma to the Lord: thirteen young bullocks, two rams, and fourteen yearling male lambs; they shall be without blemish. And their meal-offerings and wine-libations as ordained: three-tenths of an ephah for each bull, two-tenths of an ephah for each ram, one-tenth of an ephah for each lamb, wine for the libations, a male goat for atonement, and two regular daily offerings according to their law. *Num. 29*

On weekdays, continue with "Our God and God of our ancestors" on page 822.
On Shabbat, continue with "Those who keep the Sabbath" at the top of page 822.

On the first day of Ḥol HaMo'ed Sukkot,
say the following two paragraphs (in Israel say only the first):

וּבַיּוֹם הַשֵּׁנִי On the second day you shall offer twelve young bullocks, two rams, fourteen yearling male lambs without blemish. And their meal-offerings and wine-libations as ordained: three-tenths of an ephah for each bull, two-tenths of an ephah for each ram, one-tenth of an ephah for each lamb, wine for the libations, a male goat for atonement, and two regular daily offerings according to their law. *Num. 29*

Continue with "On the third day" at the top of the next page.

On the last six days of פסח *say:*

וְהִקְרַבְתֶּם אִשֶּׁה עֹלָה לַיהוה, פָּרִים בְּנֵי־בָקָר שְׁנַיִם וְאַיִל אֶחָד, וְשִׁבְעָה כְבָשִׂים בְּנֵי שָׁנָה, תְּמִימִם יִהְיוּ לָכֶם: וּמִנְחָתָם וְנִסְכֵּיהֶם כִּמְדֻבָּר, שְׁלֹשָׁה עֶשְׂרֹנִים לַפָּר וּשְׁנֵי עֶשְׂרֹנִים לָאָיִל, וְעִשָּׂרוֹן לַכֶּבֶשׂ, וְיַיִן כְּנִסְכּוֹ, וְשָׂעִיר לְכַפֵּר, וּשְׁנֵי תְמִידִים כְּהִלְכָתָם. במדבר כח

On weekdays, continue with אֱלֹהֵינוּ וֵאלֹהֵי אֲבוֹתֵינוּ *on page 823.*
On שבת*, continue with* יִשְׂמְחוּ בְמַלְכוּתְךָ *at the top of page 823.*

On שבועות *say:*

וּבְיוֹם הַבִּכּוּרִים, בְּהַקְרִיבְכֶם מִנְחָה חֲדָשָׁה לַיהוה בְּשָׁבֻעֹתֵיכֶם, מִקְרָא־קֹדֶשׁ יִהְיֶה לָכֶם, כָּל־מְלֶאכֶת עֲבֹדָה לֹא תַעֲשׂוּ: וְהִקְרַבְתֶּם עוֹלָה לְרֵיחַ נִיחֹחַ לַיהוה, פָּרִים בְּנֵי־בָקָר שְׁנַיִם, אַיִל אֶחָד, שִׁבְעָה כְבָשִׂים בְּנֵי שָׁנָה: וּמִנְחָתָם וְנִסְכֵּיהֶם כִּמְדֻבָּר, שְׁלֹשָׁה עֶשְׂרֹנִים לַפָּר וּשְׁנֵי עֶשְׂרֹנִים לָאָיִל, וְעִשָּׂרוֹן לַכֶּבֶשׂ, וְיַיִן כְּנִסְכּוֹ, וְשָׂעִיר לְכַפֵּר, וּשְׁנֵי תְמִידִים כְּהִלְכָתָם. במדבר כח

On weekdays, continue with אֱלֹהֵינוּ וֵאלֹהֵי אֲבוֹתֵינוּ *on page 823.*
On שבת*, continue with* יִשְׂמְחוּ בְמַלְכוּתְךָ *at the top of page 823.*

On the first two days of סוכות *say (in* ארץ ישראל*, the first day only):*

וּבַחֲמִשָּׁה עָשָׂר יוֹם לַחֹדֶשׁ הַשְּׁבִיעִי, מִקְרָא־קֹדֶשׁ יִהְיֶה לָכֶם, כָּל־מְלֶאכֶת עֲבֹדָה לֹא תַעֲשׂוּ, וְחַגֹּתֶם חַג לַיהוה שִׁבְעַת יָמִים: וְהִקְרַבְתֶּם עֹלָה אִשֵּׁה רֵיחַ נִיחֹחַ לַיהוה, פָּרִים בְּנֵי־בָקָר שְׁלֹשָׁה עָשָׂר, אֵילִם שְׁנָיִם, כְּבָשִׂים בְּנֵי־שָׁנָה אַרְבָּעָה עָשָׂר, תְּמִימִם יִהְיוּ: וּמִנְחָתָם וְנִסְכֵּיהֶם כִּמְדֻבָּר, שְׁלֹשָׁה עֶשְׂרֹנִים לַפָּר וּשְׁנֵי עֶשְׂרֹנִים לָאָיִל, וְעִשָּׂרוֹן לַכֶּבֶשׂ, וְיַיִן כְּנִסְכּוֹ, וְשָׂעִיר לְכַפֵּר, וּשְׁנֵי תְמִידִים כְּהִלְכָתָם. במדבר כט

On weekdays, continue with אֱלֹהֵינוּ וֵאלֹהֵי אֲבוֹתֵינוּ *on page 823.*
On שבת*, continue with* יִשְׂמְחוּ בְמַלְכוּתְךָ *at the top of page 823.*

On the first day of חול המועד סוכות*,*
say the following two paragraphs (in ארץ ישראל *say only the first):*

וּבַיּוֹם הַשֵּׁנִי, פָּרִים בְּנֵי־בָקָר שְׁנֵים עָשָׂר, אֵילִם שְׁנָיִם, כְּבָשִׂים בְּנֵי־שָׁנָה אַרְבָּעָה עָשָׂר, תְּמִימִם: וּמִנְחָתָם וְנִסְכֵּיהֶם כִּמְדֻבָּר, שְׁלֹשָׁה עֶשְׂרֹנִים לַפָּר, וּשְׁנֵי עֶשְׂרֹנִים לָאָיִל, וְעִשָּׂרוֹן לַכֶּבֶשׂ, וְיַיִן כְּנִסְכּוֹ, וְשָׂעִיר לְכַפֵּר, וּשְׁנֵי תְמִידִים כְּהִלְכָתָם. במדבר כט

Continue with וּבַיּוֹם הַשְּׁלִישִׁי *at the top of the next page.*

וּבַיּוֹם הַשְּׁלִישִׁי On the third day you shall offer eleven bullocks, two rams, fourteen yearling male lambs without blemish. And their meal-offerings and wine-libations as ordained: three-tenths of an ephah for each bull, two-tenths of an ephah for the ram, one-tenth of an ephah for each lamb, wine for the libations, a male goat for atonement, and two regular daily offerings according to their law. *Num. 29*

On weekdays, continue with "Our God and God of our ancestors" on page 822.
On Shabbat, continue with "Those who keep the Sabbath" at the top of page 822.

On the second day of Ḥol HaMo'ed Sukkot,
say the following two paragraphs (in Israel say only the first):

וּבַיּוֹם הַשְּׁלִישִׁי On the third day you shall offer eleven bullocks, two rams, fourteen yearling male lambs without blemish. And their meal-offerings and wine-libations as ordained: three-tenths of an ephah for each bull, two-tenths of an ephah for each ram, one-tenth of an ephah for each lamb, wine for the libations, a male goat for atonement, and two regular daily offerings according to their law. *Num. 29*

וּבַיּוֹם הָרְבִיעִי On the fourth day you shall offer ten bullocks, two rams, fourteen yearling male lambs without blemish. And their meal-offerings and wine-libations as ordained: three-tenths of an ephah for each bull, two-tenths of an ephah for each ram, one-tenth of an ephah for each lamb, wine for the libations, a male goat for atonement, and two regular daily offerings according to their law. *Num. 29*

On weekdays, continue with "Our God and God of our ancestors" on page 822.
On Shabbat, continue with "Those who keep the Sabbath" at the top of page 822.

On the third day of Ḥol HaMo'ed Sukkot,
say the following two paragraphs (in Israel say only the first):

וּבַיּוֹם הָרְבִיעִי On the fourth day you shall offer ten bullocks, two rams, fourteen yearling male lambs without blemish. And their meal-offerings and wine-libations as ordained: three-tenths of an ephah for each bull, two-tenths of an ephah for each ram, one-tenth of an ephah for each lamb, wine for the libations, a male goat for atonement, and two regular daily offerings according to their law. *Num. 29*

וּבַיּוֹם הַחֲמִישִׁי On the fifth day you shall offer nine bullocks, two rams, fourteen yearling male lambs without blemish. And their meal-offerings and wine-libations as ordained: three-tenths of an ephah for each bull, two-tenths of an ephah for each ram, one-tenth of an ephah for each lamb, wine for the libations, a male goat for atonement, and two regular daily offerings according to their law. *Num. 29*

On weekdays, continue with "Our God and God of our ancestors" on page 822.
On Shabbat, continue with "Those who keep the Sabbath" at the top of page 822.

וּבַיּוֹם הַשְּׁלִישִׁי, פָּרִים עַשְׁתֵּי־עָשָׂר, אֵילִם שְׁנָיִם, כְּבָשִׂים בְּנֵי־שָׁנָה אַרְבָּעָה עָשָׂר, תְּמִימִם: וּמִנְחָתָם וְנִסְכֵּיהֶם כִּמְדֻבָּר, שְׁלֹשָׁה עֶשְׂרֹנִים לַפָּר, וּשְׁנֵי עֶשְׂרֹנִים לָאָיִל, וְעִשָּׂרוֹן לַכֶּבֶשׂ, וְיַיִן כְּנִסְכּוֹ, וְשָׂעִיר לְכַפֵּר, וּשְׁנֵי תְמִידִים כְּהִלְכָתָם. במדבר כט

On weekdays, continue with אֱלֹהֵינוּ וֵאלֹהֵי אֲבוֹתֵינוּ *on page 823.*
On שבת*, continue with* יִשְׂמְחוּ בְמַלְכוּתְךָ *at the top of page 823.*

On the second day of חול המועד סוכות*,*
say the following two paragraphs (in ארץ ישראל *say only the first):*

וּבַיּוֹם הַשְּׁלִישִׁי, פָּרִים עַשְׁתֵּי־עָשָׂר, אֵילִם שְׁנָיִם, כְּבָשִׂים בְּנֵי־שָׁנָה אַרְבָּעָה עָשָׂר, תְּמִימִם: וּמִנְחָתָם וְנִסְכֵּיהֶם כִּמְדֻבָּר, שְׁלֹשָׁה עֶשְׂרֹנִים לַפָּר, וּשְׁנֵי עֶשְׂרֹנִים לָאָיִל, וְעִשָּׂרוֹן לַכֶּבֶשׂ, וְיַיִן כְּנִסְכּוֹ, וְשָׂעִיר לְכַפֵּר, וּשְׁנֵי תְמִידִים כְּהִלְכָתָם. במדבר כט

וּבַיּוֹם הָרְבִיעִי, פָּרִים עֲשָׂרָה, אֵילִם שְׁנָיִם, כְּבָשִׂים בְּנֵי־שָׁנָה אַרְבָּעָה עָשָׂר, תְּמִימִם: וּמִנְחָתָם וְנִסְכֵּיהֶם כִּמְדֻבָּר, שְׁלֹשָׁה עֶשְׂרֹנִים לַפָּר, וּשְׁנֵי עֶשְׂרֹנִים לָאָיִל, וְעִשָּׂרוֹן לַכֶּבֶשׂ, וְיַיִן כְּנִסְכּוֹ, וְשָׂעִיר לְכַפֵּר, וּשְׁנֵי תְמִידִים כְּהִלְכָתָם. במדבר כט

On weekdays, continue with אֱלֹהֵינוּ וֵאלֹהֵי אֲבוֹתֵינוּ *on page 823.*
On שבת*, continue with* יִשְׂמְחוּ בְמַלְכוּתְךָ *at the top of page 823.*

On the third day of חול המועד סוכות*,*
say the following two paragraphs (in ארץ ישראל *say only the first):*

וּבַיּוֹם הָרְבִיעִי, פָּרִים עֲשָׂרָה, אֵילִם שְׁנָיִם, כְּבָשִׂים בְּנֵי־שָׁנָה אַרְבָּעָה עָשָׂר, תְּמִימִם: וּמִנְחָתָם וְנִסְכֵּיהֶם כִּמְדֻבָּר, שְׁלֹשָׁה עֶשְׂרֹנִים לַפָּר, וּשְׁנֵי עֶשְׂרֹנִים לָאָיִל, וְעִשָּׂרוֹן לַכֶּבֶשׂ, וְיַיִן כְּנִסְכּוֹ, וְשָׂעִיר לְכַפֵּר, וּשְׁנֵי תְמִידִים כְּהִלְכָתָם. במדבר כט

וּבַיּוֹם הַחֲמִישִׁי, פָּרִים תִּשְׁעָה, אֵילִם שְׁנָיִם, כְּבָשִׂים בְּנֵי־שָׁנָה אַרְבָּעָה עָשָׂר, תְּמִימִם: וּמִנְחָתָם וְנִסְכֵּיהֶם כִּמְדֻבָּר, שְׁלֹשָׁה עֶשְׂרֹנִים לַפָּר, וּשְׁנֵי עֶשְׂרֹנִים לָאָיִל, וְעִשָּׂרוֹן לַכֶּבֶשׂ, וְיַיִן כְּנִסְכּוֹ, וְשָׂעִיר לְכַפֵּר, וּשְׁנֵי תְמִידִים כְּהִלְכָתָם. במדבר כט

On weekdays, continue with אֱלֹהֵינוּ וֵאלֹהֵי אֲבוֹתֵינוּ *on page 823.*
On שבת*, continue with* יִשְׂמְחוּ בְמַלְכוּתְךָ *at the top of page 823.*

On the fourth day of Ḥol HaMo'ed Sukkot,
say the following two paragraphs (in Israel say only the first):

וּבַיּוֹם הַחֲמִישִׁי On the fifth day you shall offer nine bullocks, two rams, fourteen yearling male lambs without blemish. And their meal-offerings and wine-libations as ordained: three-tenths of an ephah for each bull, two-tenths of an ephah for each ram, one-tenth of an ephah for each lamb, wine for the libations, a male goat for atonement, and two regular daily offerings according to their law. *Num. 29*

וּבַיּוֹם הַשִּׁשִּׁי On the sixth day you shall offer eight bullocks, two rams, fourteen yearling male lambs without blemish. And their meal-offerings and wine-libations as ordained: three-tenths of an ephah for each bull, two-tenths of an ephah for each ram, one-tenth of an ephah for each lamb, wine for the libations, a male goat for atonement, and two regular daily offerings according to their law. *Num. 29*

On weekdays, continue with "Our God and God of our ancestors" on the next page.
On Shabbat, continue with "Those who keep the Sabbath" at the top of the next page.

On Hoshana Raba, say the following two paragraphs.
In Israel, say the first paragraph on the fifth day of Ḥol HaMo'ed and the second on Hoshana Raba.

וּבַיּוֹם הַשִּׁשִּׁי On the sixth day you shall offer eight bullocks, two rams, fourteen yearling male lambs without blemish. And their meal-offerings and wine-libations as ordained: three-tenths of an ephah for each bull, two-tenths of an ephah for each ram, one-tenth of an ephah for each lamb, wine for the libations, a male goat for atonement, and two regular daily offerings according to their law. *Num. 29*

וּבַיּוֹם הַשְּׁבִיעִי On the seventh day you shall offer seven bullocks, two rams, fourteen yearling male lambs without blemish. And their meal-offerings and wine-libations as ordained: three-tenths of an ephah for each bull, two-tenths of an ephah for each ram, one-tenth of an ephah for each lamb, wine for the libations, a male goat for atonement, and two regular daily offerings according to their law. *Num. 29*

Continue with "Our God and God of our ancestors" on the next page.

On Shemini Atzeret and Simḥat Torah, say:

בַּיּוֹם הַשְּׁמִינִי On the eighth day you shall hold an assembly; you shall do no laborious work. And you shall offer a burnt-offering, a fire-offering of pleasing odor to the Lord: one bullock, one ram, seven yearling male lambs without blemish. And their meal-offerings and wine-libations as ordained: three-tenths of an ephah for each bull, two-tenths of an ephah for the ram, one-tenth of an ephah for each lamb, wine for the libations, a male goat for atonement, and two regular daily offerings according to their law. *Num. 29*

On weekdays, continue with "Our God and God of our ancestors" on the next page.
On Shabbat, continue with "Those who keep the Sabbath" at the top of the next page.

On the fourth day of חול המועד סוכות*, say the following two paragraphs (in* ארץ ישראל *say only the first):*

במדבר כט וּבַיּוֹם הַחֲמִישִׁי, פָּרִים תִּשְׁעָה, אֵילִם שְׁנָיִם, כְּבָשִׂים בְּנֵי־שָׁנָה אַרְבָּעָה עָשָׂר, תְּמִימִם: וּמִנְחָתָם וְנִסְכֵּיהֶם כִּמְדֻבָּר, שְׁלֹשָׁה עֶשְׂרֹנִים לַפָּר, וּשְׁנֵי עֶשְׂרֹנִים לָאָיִל, וְעִשָּׂרוֹן לַכֶּבֶשׂ, וְיַיִן כְּנִסְכּוֹ, וְשָׂעִיר לְכַפֵּר, וּשְׁנֵי תְמִידִים כְּהִלְכָתָם.

במדבר כט וּבַיּוֹם הַשִּׁשִּׁי, פָּרִים שְׁמֹנָה, אֵילִם שְׁנָיִם, כְּבָשִׂים בְּנֵי־שָׁנָה אַרְבָּעָה עָשָׂר, תְּמִימִם: וּמִנְחָתָם וְנִסְכֵּיהֶם כִּמְדֻבָּר, שְׁלֹשָׁה עֶשְׂרֹנִים לַפָּר, וּשְׁנֵי עֶשְׂרֹנִים לָאָיִל, וְעִשָּׂרוֹן לַכֶּבֶשׂ, וְיַיִן כְּנִסְכּוֹ, וְשָׂעִיר לְכַפֵּר, וּשְׁנֵי תְמִידִים כְּהִלְכָתָם.

On weekdays, continue with אֱלֹהֵינוּ וֵאלֹהֵי אֲבוֹתֵינוּ *on the next page.*
On שבת*, continue with* יִשְׂמְחוּ בְמַלְכוּתְךָ *at the top of the next page.*

On הושענא רבה*, say the following two paragraphs.*
In ארץ ישראל*, say the first paragraph on the fifth day of* חול המועד *and the second on* הושענא רבה*:*

במדבר כט וּבַיּוֹם הַשִּׁשִּׁי, פָּרִים שְׁמֹנָה, אֵילִם שְׁנָיִם, כְּבָשִׂים בְּנֵי־שָׁנָה אַרְבָּעָה עָשָׂר, תְּמִימִם: וּמִנְחָתָם וְנִסְכֵּיהֶם כִּמְדֻבָּר, שְׁלֹשָׁה עֶשְׂרֹנִים לַפָּר, וּשְׁנֵי עֶשְׂרֹנִים לָאָיִל, וְעִשָּׂרוֹן לַכֶּבֶשׂ, וְיַיִן כְּנִסְכּוֹ, וְשָׂעִיר לְכַפֵּר, וּשְׁנֵי תְמִידִים כְּהִלְכָתָם.

במדבר כט וּבַיּוֹם הַשְּׁבִיעִי, פָּרִים שִׁבְעָה, אֵילִם שְׁנָיִם, כְּבָשִׂים בְּנֵי־שָׁנָה אַרְבָּעָה עָשָׂר, תְּמִימִם: וּמִנְחָתָם וְנִסְכֵּיהֶם כִּמְדֻבָּר, שְׁלֹשָׁה עֶשְׂרֹנִים לַפָּר, וּשְׁנֵי עֶשְׂרֹנִים לָאָיִל, וְעִשָּׂרוֹן לַכֶּבֶשׂ, וְיַיִן כְּנִסְכּוֹ, וְשָׂעִיר לְכַפֵּר, וּשְׁנֵי תְמִידִים כְּהִלְכָתָם.

Continue with אֱלֹהֵינוּ וֵאלֹהֵי אֲבוֹתֵינוּ *on the next page.*

On שמיני עצרת *and* שמחת תורה*, say:*

במדבר כט בַּיּוֹם הַשְּׁמִינִי, עֲצֶרֶת תִּהְיֶה לָכֶם, כָּל־מְלֶאכֶת עֲבֹדָה לֹא תַעֲשׂוּ: וְהִקְרַבְתֶּם עֹלָה אִשֵּׁה רֵיחַ נִיחֹחַ לַיהוה, פַּר אֶחָד, אַיִל אֶחָד, כְּבָשִׂים בְּנֵי־שָׁנָה שִׁבְעָה, תְּמִימִם: וּמִנְחָתָם וְנִסְכֵּיהֶם כִּמְדֻבָּר, שְׁלֹשָׁה עֶשְׂרֹנִים לַפָּר וּשְׁנֵי עֶשְׂרֹנִים לָאָיִל, וְעִשָּׂרוֹן לַכֶּבֶשׂ, וְיַיִן כְּנִסְכּוֹ, וְשָׂעִיר לְכַפֵּר, וּשְׁנֵי תְמִידִים כְּהִלְכָתָם.

On weekdays, continue with אֱלֹהֵינוּ וֵאלֹהֵי אֲבוֹתֵינוּ *on the next page.*
On שבת*, continue with* יִשְׂמְחוּ בְמַלְכוּתְךָ *at the top of the next page.*

On Shabbat say:

יִשְׂמְחוּ Those who keep the Sabbath and call it a delight shall rejoice in Your kingship. The people who sanctify the seventh day shall all be satisfied and take delight in Your goodness, for You favored the seventh day and declared it holy. You called it "most desirable of days" in remembrance of Creation.

אֱלֹהֵינוּ Our God and God of our ancestors,
merciful King, have compassion upon us.
You who are good and do good, respond to our call.
Return to us in Your abounding mercy
for the sake of our fathers who did Your will.
Rebuild Your Temple as at the beginning,
and establish Your Sanctuary on its site.
Let us witness its rebuilding and gladden us by its restoration.
Bring the priests back to their service,
the Levites to their song and music,
and the Israelites to their homes.

וְשָׁם נַעֲלֶה There we will go up and appear and bow before You
on the three pilgrimage festivals, as is written in Your Torah:

"Three times in the year *Deut. 16*
all your males shall appear before the Lord your God
at the place He will choose:
on Pesaḥ, Shavuot and Sukkot.
They shall not appear before the Lord empty-handed.
Each shall bring such a gift as he can,
in proportion to the blessing
that the Lord your God grants you."

On Shabbat add the words in parentheses:

וְהַשִּׂיאֵנוּ Bestow on us, Lord our God,
the blessing of Your festivals
for life and peace, joy and gladness,
as You desired and promised to bless us.

On שבת *say:*

יִשְׂמְחוּ בְמַלְכוּתְךָ שׁוֹמְרֵי שַׁבָּת וְקוֹרְאֵי עֹנֶג. עַם מְקַדְּשֵׁי שְׁבִיעִי כֻּלָּם יִשְׂבְּעוּ וְיִתְעַנְּגוּ מִטּוּבֶךָ, וּבַשְּׁבִיעִי רָצִיתָ בּוֹ וְקִדַּשְׁתּוֹ, חֶמְדַּת יָמִים אוֹתוֹ קָרָאתָ, זֵכֶר לְמַעֲשֵׂה בְרֵאשִׁית.

אֱלֹהֵינוּ וֵאלֹהֵי אֲבוֹתֵינוּ
מֶלֶךְ רַחֲמָן רַחֵם עָלֵינוּ, טוֹב וּמֵטִיב הִדָּרֶשׁ לָנוּ
שׁוּבָה אֵלֵינוּ בַּהֲמוֹן רַחֲמֶיךָ, בִּגְלַל אָבוֹת שֶׁעָשׂוּ רְצוֹנֶךָ.
בְּנֵה בֵיתְךָ כְּבַתְּחִלָּה, וְכוֹנֵן מִקְדָּשְׁךָ עַל מְכוֹנוֹ
וְהַרְאֵנוּ בְּבִנְיָנוֹ, וְשַׂמְּחֵנוּ בְּתִקּוּנוֹ
וְהָשֵׁב כֹּהֲנִים לַעֲבוֹדָתָם, וּלְוִיִּם לְשִׁירָם וּלְזִמְרָם
וְהָשֵׁב יִשְׂרָאֵל לִנְוֵיהֶם.

וְשָׁם נַעֲלֶה וְנֵרָאֶה וְנִשְׁתַּחֲוֶה לְפָנֶיךָ בְּשָׁלֹשׁ פַּעֲמֵי רְגָלֵינוּ
כַּכָּתוּב בְּתוֹרָתֶךָ

שָׁלוֹשׁ פְּעָמִים בַּשָּׁנָה יֵרָאֶה כָל־זְכוּרְךָ אֶת־פְּנֵי יהוה אֱלֹהֶיךָ דברים טז
בַּמָּקוֹם אֲשֶׁר יִבְחָר
בְּחַג הַמַּצּוֹת, וּבְחַג הַשָּׁבֻעוֹת, וּבְחַג הַסֻּכּוֹת
וְלֹא יֵרָאֶה אֶת־פְּנֵי יהוה רֵיקָם:
אִישׁ כְּמַתְּנַת יָדוֹ
כְּבִרְכַּת יהוה אֱלֹהֶיךָ אֲשֶׁר נָתַן־לָךְ:

On שבת *add the words in parentheses:*

וְהַשִּׂיאֵנוּ יהוה אֱלֹהֵינוּ אֶת בִּרְכַּת מוֹעֲדֶיךָ
לְחַיִּים וּלְשָׁלוֹם, לְשִׂמְחָה וּלְשָׂשׂוֹן
כַּאֲשֶׁר רָצִיתָ וְאָמַרְתָּ לְבָרְכֵנוּ.

(Our God and God of our ancestors, be pleased with our rest.)
Make us holy through Your commandments
and grant us a share in Your Torah;
satisfy us with Your goodness, gladden us with Your salvation,
and purify our hearts to serve You in truth.
And grant us a heritage, LORD our God, (with love and favor,)
with joy and gladness Your holy (Sabbath and) festivals.
May Israel, who sanctify Your name, rejoice in You.
Blessed are You, LORD,
who sanctifies (the Sabbath and) Israel, and the festive seasons.

TEMPLE SERVICE

רְצֵה Find favor, LORD our God,
in Your people Israel and their prayer.
Restore the service to Your most holy House,
and accept in love and favor
the fire-offerings of Israel and their prayer.
May the service of Your people Israel always find favor with You.

If Kohanim bless the congregation during the Leader's Repetition, the following is said. It is not said on Ḥol HaMo'ed or Shabbat Ḥol HaMo'ed.

All: וְתֶעֱרַב May our entreaty be as pleasing to You as a burnt-offering and sacrifice. Please, Compassionate One, in Your abounding mercy restore Your Presence to Zion, Your city, and the order of the Temple service to Jerusalem. And may our eyes witness Your return to Zion in compassion, that there we may serve You with reverence as in the days of old and as in former years.

Leader: Blessed are You, LORD, for You alone do we serve with reverence.

Continue with "We give thanks" on the next page.

In Israel:

All: וְתֶעֱרַב May our entreaty be as pleasing to You as a burnt-offering and sacrifice. Please, Compassionate One, in Your abounding mercy restore Your Presence to Zion, Your city, and the order of the Temple service to Jerusalem. That there we may serve You with reverence as in the days of old and as in former years.

Continue with "And may our eyes" at the top of the next page.

(אֱלֹהֵינוּ וֵאלֹהֵי אֲבוֹתֵינוּ, רְצֵה בִמְנוּחָתֵנוּ)
קַדְּשֵׁנוּ בְּמִצְוֹתֶיךָ, וְתֵן חֶלְקֵנוּ בְּתוֹרָתֶךָ
שַׂבְּעֵנוּ מִטּוּבֶךָ, וְשַׂמְּחֵנוּ בִּישׁוּעָתֶךָ
וְטַהֵר לִבֵּנוּ לְעָבְדְּךָ בֶּאֱמֶת
וְהַנְחִילֵנוּ יהוה אֱלֹהֵינוּ (בְּאַהֲבָה וּבְרָצוֹן)
בְּשִׂמְחָה וּבְשָׂשׂוֹן (שַׁבָּת וּ) מוֹעֲדֵי קָדְשֶׁךָ
וְיִשְׂמְחוּ בְךָ יִשְׂרָאֵל מְקַדְּשֵׁי שְׁמֶךָ.
בָּרוּךְ אַתָּה יהוה, מְקַדֵּשׁ (הַשַּׁבָּת וְ) יִשְׂרָאֵל וְהַזְּמַנִּים.

עבודה
רְצֵה יהוה אֱלֹהֵינוּ בְּעַמְּךָ יִשְׂרָאֵל, וּבִתְפִלָּתָם
וְהָשֵׁב אֶת הָעֲבוֹדָה לִדְבִיר בֵּיתֶךָ
וְאִשֵּׁי יִשְׂרָאֵל וּתְפִלָּתָם בְּאַהֲבָה תְקַבֵּל בְּרָצוֹן
וּתְהִי לְרָצוֹן תָּמִיד עֲבוֹדַת יִשְׂרָאֵל עַמֶּךָ.

If כהנים *say* ברכת כהנים *during* חזרת הש״ץ*, the following is said. It is not said on* שבת חול המועד *or* חול המועד.

קהל וש״ץ: וְתֶעֱרַב עָלֶיךָ עֲתִירָתֵנוּ כְּעוֹלָה וּכְקָרְבָּן. אָנָּא רַחוּם, בְּרַחֲמֶיךָ הָרַבִּים הָשֵׁב שְׁכִינָתְךָ לְצִיּוֹן עִירְךָ, וְסֵדֶר הָעֲבוֹדָה לִירוּשָׁלָיִם. וְתֶחֱזֶינָה עֵינֵינוּ בְּשׁוּבְךָ לְצִיּוֹן בְּרַחֲמִים. וְשָׁם נַעֲבָדְךָ בְּיִרְאָה כִּימֵי עוֹלָם וּכְשָׁנִים קַדְמוֹנִיּוֹת.

ש״ץ: בָּרוּךְ אַתָּה יהוה, שֶׁאוֹתְךָ לְבַדְּךָ בְּיִרְאָה נַעֲבֹד.

Continue with מודים *on the next page.*

בארץ ישראל:
קהל וש״ץ: וְתֶעֱרַב עָלֶיךָ עֲתִירָתֵנוּ כְּעוֹלָה וּכְקָרְבָּן. אָנָּא רַחוּם, בְּרַחֲמֶיךָ הָרַבִּים הָשֵׁב שְׁכִינָתְךָ לְצִיּוֹן עִירְךָ, וְסֵדֶר הָעֲבוֹדָה לִירוּשָׁלָיִם. וְשָׁם נַעֲבָדְךָ בְּיִרְאָה כִּימֵי עוֹלָם וּכְשָׁנִים קַדְמוֹנִיּוֹת.

Continue with וְתֶחֱזֶינָה *at the top of the next page.*

וְתֶחֱזֶינָה And may our eyes witness Your return to Zion in compassion. Blessed are You, Lord, who restores His Presence to Zion.

THANKSGIVING

Bow at the first nine words.

▾מוֹדִים We give thanks to You,
for You are the Lord our God
and God of our ancestors
for ever and all time.
You are the Rock of our lives,
Shield of our salvation
from generation to generation.
We will thank You and
declare Your praise for our lives,
which are entrusted into Your hand;
for our souls,
which are placed in Your charge;
for Your miracles
which are with us every day;
and for Your wonders and favors
at all times, evening, morning and midday.
You are good –
for Your compassion never fails.
You are compassionate –
for Your loving-kindnesses never cease.
We have always placed our hope in You.

During the Leader's Repetition, the congregation says quietly:

▾מוֹדִים We give thanks to You,
for You are the Lord our God
and God of our ancestors,
God of all flesh,
who formed us
and formed the universe.
Blessings and thanks
are due to Your great
and holy name for giving us
life and sustaining us.
May You continue
to give us life and sustain us;
and may You gather our
exiles to Your holy courts,
to keep Your decrees,
do Your will and serve You
with a perfect heart,
for it is for us
to give You thanks.
Blessed be God to whom
thanksgiving is due.

וְעַל כֻּלָּם For all these things may Your name be blessed and exalted, our King, continually, for ever and all time. Let all that lives thank You, Selah! and praise Your name in truth, God, our Savior and Help, Selah! ▾Blessed are You, Lord, whose name is "the Good" and to whom thanks are due.

וְתֶחֱזֶינָה עֵינֵינוּ בְּשׁוּבְךָ לְצִיּוֹן בְּרַחֲמִים. בָּרוּךְ אַתָּה יהוה, הַמַּחֲזִיר שְׁכִינָתוֹ לְצִיּוֹן.

הודאה

Bow at the first five words.

מוֹדִים אֲנַחְנוּ לָךְ
שָׁאַתָּה הוּא יהוה אֱלֹהֵינוּ
וֵאלֹהֵי אֲבוֹתֵינוּ לְעוֹלָם וָעֶד.
צוּר חַיֵּינוּ, מָגֵן יִשְׁעֵנוּ
אַתָּה הוּא לְדוֹר וָדוֹר.
נוֹדֶה לְּךָ וּנְסַפֵּר תְּהִלָּתֶךָ
עַל חַיֵּינוּ הַמְּסוּרִים בְּיָדֶךָ
וְעַל נִשְׁמוֹתֵינוּ הַפְּקוּדוֹת לָךְ
וְעַל נִסֶּיךָ שֶׁבְּכָל יוֹם עִמָּנוּ
וְעַל נִפְלְאוֹתֶיךָ וְטוֹבוֹתֶיךָ
שֶׁבְּכָל עֵת, עֶרֶב וָבֹקֶר וְצָהֳרַיִם.
הַטּוֹב, כִּי לֹא כָלוּ רַחֲמֶיךָ
וְהַמְרַחֵם, כִּי לֹא תַמּוּ חֲסָדֶיךָ
מֵעוֹלָם קִוִּינוּ לָךְ.

During the חזרת הש״ץ, *the* קהל *says quietly:*

מוֹדִים אֲנַחְנוּ לָךְ
שָׁאַתָּה הוּא יהוה אֱלֹהֵינוּ
וֵאלֹהֵי אֲבוֹתֵינוּ
אֱלֹהֵי כָל בָּשָׂר
יוֹצְרֵנוּ, יוֹצֵר בְּרֵאשִׁית.
בְּרָכוֹת וְהוֹדָאוֹת
לְשִׁמְךָ הַגָּדוֹל וְהַקָּדוֹשׁ
עַל שֶׁהֶחֱיִיתָנוּ וְקִיַּמְתָּנוּ.
כֵּן תְּחַיֵּנוּ וּתְקַיְּמֵנוּ
וְתֶאֱסֹף גָּלֻיּוֹתֵינוּ
לְחַצְרוֹת קָדְשֶׁךָ
לִשְׁמֹר חֻקֶּיךָ וְלַעֲשׂוֹת רְצוֹנֶךָ
וּלְעָבְדְּךָ בְּלֵבָב שָׁלֵם
עַל שֶׁאֲנַחְנוּ מוֹדִים לָךְ.
בָּרוּךְ אֵל הַהוֹדָאוֹת.

וְעַל כֻּלָּם יִתְבָּרַךְ וְיִתְרוֹמַם שִׁמְךָ מַלְכֵּנוּ תָּמִיד לְעוֹלָם וָעֶד. וְכֹל הַחַיִּים יוֹדְוּךָ סֶּלָה, וִיהַלְלוּ אֶת שִׁמְךָ בֶּאֱמֶת, הָאֵל יְשׁוּעָתֵנוּ וְעֶזְרָתֵנוּ סֶלָה. בָּרוּךְ אַתָּה יהוה, הַטּוֹב שִׁמְךָ וּלְךָ נָאֶה לְהוֹדוֹת.

Outside Israel, if Kohanim bless the congregation during the Leader's Repetition, the service continues on page 830. In Israel, the regular Priestly Blessing on page 838 is said. If Kohanim do not ascend, the following is said. See laws 370–377.

Our God and God of our fathers, bless us with the threefold blessing in the Torah, written by the hand of Moses Your servant and pronounced by Aaron and his sons the priests, Your holy people, as it is said:

May the LORD bless you and protect you. (*Cong:* May it be Your will.) *Num. 6*
May the LORD make His face shine on you and be gracious to you.
(*Cong:* May it be Your will.)
May the LORD turn His face toward you, and grant you peace.
(*Cong:* May it be Your will.)

PEACE

שִׂים שָׁלוֹם Grant peace, goodness and blessing, grace, loving-kindness and compassion to us and all Israel Your people. Bless us, our Father, all as one, with the light of Your face, for by the light of Your face You have given us, LORD our God, the Torah of life and love of kindness, righteousness, blessing, compassion, life and peace. May it be good in Your eyes to bless Your people Israel at every time, in every hour, with Your peace. Blessed are You, LORD, who blesses His people Israel with peace.

The following verse concludes the Leader's Repetition of the Amida. Some also say it here as part of the silent Amida. See law 368.

May the words of my mouth and the meditation of my heart find favor before You, LORD, my Rock and Redeemer. *Ps. 19*

אֱלֹהַי My God, guard my tongue from evil and my lips from deceitful speech. To those who curse me, let my soul be silent; may my soul be to all like the dust. Open my heart to Your Torah and let my soul pursue Your commandments. As for all who plan evil against me, swiftly thwart their counsel and frustrate their plans. Act for the sake of Your name; act for the sake of Your right hand; act for the sake of Your holiness; act for the sake of Your Torah. That Your beloved ones may be delivered, save with Your right hand and answer me. May the words of my mouth and the meditation of my heart find favor before You, LORD, my Rock and Redeemer. *Berakhot 17a* *Ps. 60* *Ps. 19*

Bow, take three steps back, then bow, first left, then right, then center, while saying:

May He who makes peace in His high places, make peace for us and all Israel – and say: Amen.

יְהִי רָצוֹן May it be Your will, LORD our God and God of our ancestors, that the Temple be rebuilt speedily in our days, and grant us a share in Your Torah. And there we will serve You with reverence, as in the days of old and as in former years. Then the offering of Judah and Jerusalem will be pleasing to the LORD as in the days of old and as in former years. *Mal. 3*

On Sukkot, Hoshanot (page 853) are said at this point. On other days of Yom Tov and Shabbat Ḥol HaMo'ed, Full Kaddish (page 554) is said and the service continues with "There is none like our God" on page 556. On Ḥol HaMo'ed Pesaḥ, Full Kaddish (page 178) is said and the service continues with Aleinu (page 180).

In חוץ לארץ*, if* כהנים *say* ברכת כהנים*, during* חזרת הש״ץ *the service continues on page 831.*
In ארץ ישראל*, the regular* ברכת כהנים *on page 839 is said.*
If כהנים *do not ascend, the following is said. See laws 370–377.*

אֱלֹהֵינוּ וֵאלֹהֵי אֲבוֹתֵינוּ, בָּרְכֵנוּ בַּבְּרָכָה הַמְשֻׁלֶּשֶׁת בַּתּוֹרָה, הַכְּתוּבָה עַל יְדֵי מֹשֶׁה עַבְדֶּךָ, הָאֲמוּרָה מִפִּי אַהֲרֹן וּבָנָיו כֹּהֲנִים עַם קְדוֹשֶׁיךָ, כָּאָמוּר

במדבר ו יְבָרֶכְךָ יהוה וְיִשְׁמְרֶךָ: קהל: כֵּן יְהִי רָצוֹן
יָאֵר יהוה פָּנָיו אֵלֶיךָ וִיחֻנֶּךָּ: קהל: כֵּן יְהִי רָצוֹן
יִשָּׂא יהוה פָּנָיו אֵלֶיךָ וְיָשֵׂם לְךָ שָׁלוֹם: קהל: כֵּן יְהִי רָצוֹן

ברכת שלום

שִׂים שָׁלוֹם טוֹבָה וּבְרָכָה, חֵן וָחֶסֶד וְרַחֲמִים, עָלֵינוּ וְעַל כָּל יִשְׂרָאֵל עַמֶּךָ. בָּרְכֵנוּ אָבִינוּ כֻּלָּנוּ כְּאֶחָד בְּאוֹר פָּנֶיךָ, כִּי בְאוֹר פָּנֶיךָ נָתַתָּ לָּנוּ יהוה אֱלֹהֵינוּ, תּוֹרַת חַיִּים וְאַהֲבַת חֶסֶד, וּצְדָקָה וּבְרָכָה וְרַחֲמִים וְחַיִּים וְשָׁלוֹם. וְטוֹב בְּעֵינֶיךָ לְבָרֵךְ אֶת עַמְּךָ יִשְׂרָאֵל, בְּכָל עֵת וּבְכָל שָׁעָה בִּשְׁלוֹמֶךָ. בָּרוּךְ אַתָּה יהוה, הַמְבָרֵךְ אֶת עַמּוֹ יִשְׂרָאֵל בַּשָּׁלוֹם.

The following verse concludes the חזרת הש״ץ.
Some also say it here as part of the silent עמידה*. See law 368.*

תהלים יט יִהְיוּ לְרָצוֹן אִמְרֵי־פִי וְהֶגְיוֹן לִבִּי לְפָנֶיךָ, יהוה צוּרִי וְגֹאֲלִי:

ברכות יז. אֱלֹהַי, נְצֹר לְשׁוֹנִי מֵרָע וּשְׂפָתַי מִדַּבֵּר מִרְמָה, וְלִמְקַלְלַי נַפְשִׁי תִדֹּם, וְנַפְשִׁי כֶּעָפָר לַכֹּל תִּהְיֶה. פְּתַח לִבִּי בְּתוֹרָתֶךָ, וּבְמִצְוֹתֶיךָ תִּרְדֹּף נַפְשִׁי. וְכָל הַחוֹשְׁבִים עָלַי רָעָה, מְהֵרָה הָפֵר עֲצָתָם וְקַלְקֵל מַחֲשַׁבְתָּם. עֲשֵׂה לְמַעַן שְׁמֶךָ, עֲשֵׂה
תהלים ס לְמַעַן יְמִינֶךָ, עֲשֵׂה לְמַעַן קְדֻשָּׁתֶךָ, עֲשֵׂה לְמַעַן תּוֹרָתֶךָ. לְמַעַן יֵחָלְצוּן יְדִידֶיךָ,
תהלים יט הוֹשִׁיעָה יְמִינְךָ וַעֲנֵנִי: יִהְיוּ לְרָצוֹן אִמְרֵי־פִי וְהֶגְיוֹן לִבִּי לְפָנֶיךָ, יהוה צוּרִי וְגֹאֲלִי:

Bow, take three steps back, then bow, first left, then right, then center, while saying:

עֹשֶׂה שָׁלוֹם בִּמְרוֹמָיו, הוּא יַעֲשֶׂה שָׁלוֹם עָלֵינוּ וְעַל כָּל יִשְׂרָאֵל, וְאִמְרוּ אָמֵן.

יְהִי רָצוֹן מִלְּפָנֶיךָ יהוה אֱלֹהֵינוּ וֵאלֹהֵי אֲבוֹתֵינוּ, שֶׁיִּבָּנֶה בֵּית הַמִּקְדָּשׁ בִּמְהֵרָה בְיָמֵינוּ,
מלאכי ג וְתֵן חֶלְקֵנוּ בְּתוֹרָתֶךָ, וְשָׁם נַעֲבָדְךָ בְּיִרְאָה כִּימֵי עוֹלָם וּכְשָׁנִים קַדְמוֹנִיּוֹת. וְעָרְבָה לַיהוה מִנְחַת יְהוּדָה וִירוּשָׁלָםִ כִּימֵי עוֹלָם וּכְשָׁנִים קַדְמוֹנִיּוֹת:

On סוכות*,* הושענות *(page 853) are said at this point. On other days of* יום טוב *and* שבת חול המועד*,* קדיש שלם *(page 555) is said and the service continues with* אֵין כֵּאלֹהֵינוּ *on page 557. On* חול המועד פסח*,* קדיש שלם *(page 179) is said and the service continues with* עָלֵינוּ *(page 181).*

Birkat Kohanim

The following supplication is recited quietly while the Leader says "Let all that lives" (page 826):

In some communities, the congregation says:

יְהִי רָצוֹן May it be Your will, Lord our God and God of our ancestors, that this blessing with which You have commanded to bless Your people Israel should be a complete blessing, with neither hindrance nor sin, now and forever.

The Kohanim say:

יְהִי רָצוֹן May it be Your will, Lord our God and God of our ancestors, that this blessing with which You have commanded us to bless Your people Israel should be a complete blessing, with neither hindrance nor sin, now and forever.

The following is recited quietly by the Leader:

אֱלֹהֵינוּ Our God and God of our fathers,
bless us with the threefold blessing in the Torah,
written by the hand of Moses Your servant
and pronounced by Aaron and his sons:

The Leader says aloud:

Kohanim!

In most places, the congregation responds:

Your holy people, as it said:

The Kohanim say the following blessing in unison:

בָּרוּךְ Blessed are You, Lord our God, King of the Universe,
who has made us holy with the holiness of Aaron,
and has commanded us to bless His people Israel with love.

The first word in each sentence is said by the Leader, followed by the Kohanim. Some read silently the accompanying verses. One should remain silent and not look at the Kohanim while the blessings are being said.

May [He] bless you	May the Lord, Maker of heaven and earth, bless you from Zion.	*Ps. 134*
The Lord	Lord, our Master, how majestic is Your name throughout the earth.	*Ps. 8*
And protect you.	Protect me, God, for in You I take refuge.	*Ps. 16*

---

our most ancient prayer. The blessing is beautifully constructed. It grows in length: the first line has three words; the second, five; and the third, seven.

ברכת כהנים

The following supplication is recited quietly while the שליח ציבור *says* וְכֹל הַחַיִּים *(page 827):*

In some communities, the קהל *says:*

יְהִי רָצוֹן מִלְּפָנֶיךָ, יהוה אֱלֹהֵינוּ וֵאלֹהֵי אֲבוֹתֵינוּ, שֶׁתְּהֵא הַבְּרָכָה הַזֹּאת שֶׁצִּוִּיתָ לְבָרֵךְ אֶת עַמְּךָ יִשְׂרָאֵל בְּרָכָה שְׁלֵמָה, וְלֹא יִהְיֶה בָּהּ שׁוּם מִכְשׁוֹל וְעָוֹן מֵעַתָּה וְעַד עוֹלָם.

The כהנים *say:*

יְהִי רָצוֹן מִלְּפָנֶיךָ, יהוה אֱלֹהֵינוּ וֵאלֹהֵי אֲבוֹתֵינוּ, שֶׁתְּהֵא הַבְּרָכָה הַזֹּאת שֶׁצִּוִּיתָנוּ לְבָרֵךְ אֶת עַמְּךָ יִשְׂרָאֵל בְּרָכָה שְׁלֵמָה, וְלֹא יִהְיֶה בָּהּ שׁוּם מִכְשׁוֹל וְעָוֹן מֵעַתָּה וְעַד עוֹלָם.

The following is recited quietly by the שליח ציבור*:*

אֱלֹהֵינוּ וֵאלֹהֵי אֲבוֹתֵינוּ, בָּרְכֵנוּ בַּבְּרָכָה הַמְשֻׁלֶּשֶׁת בַּתּוֹרָה הַכְּתוּבָה עַל יְדֵי מֹשֶׁה עַבְדֶּךָ, הָאֲמוּרָה מִפִּי אַהֲרֹן וּבָנָיו

The שליח ציבור *says aloud:*

כֹּהֲנִים

In most places, the קהל *responds:*

עַם קְדוֹשֶׁךָ, כָּאָמוּר:

The כהנים *say the following blessing in unison:*

בָּרוּךְ אַתָּה יהוה אֱלֹהֵינוּ מֶלֶךְ הָעוֹלָם, אֲשֶׁר קִדְּשָׁנוּ בִּקְדֻשָּׁתוֹ שֶׁל אַהֲרֹן, וְצִוָּנוּ לְבָרֵךְ אֶת עַמּוֹ יִשְׂרָאֵל בְּאַהֲבָה.

The first word in each sentence is said by the שליח ציבור*, followed by the* כהנים*. Some read silently the accompanying verses. One should remain silent and not look at the* כהנים *while the blessings are being said.*

יְבָרֶכְךָ יְבָרֶכְךָ יהוה מִצִּיּוֹן, עֹשֵׂה שָׁמַיִם וָאָרֶץ: תהלים קלד

יהוה יהוה אֲדֹנֵינוּ, מָה־אַדִּיר שִׁמְךָ בְּכָל־הָאָרֶץ: תהלים ח

וְיִשְׁמְרֶךָ: שָׁמְרֵנִי אֵל, כִּי־חָסִיתִי בָךְ: תהלים טז

THE PRIESTLY BLESSING

The Priestly Blessing is unique among our prayers: not only is it ordained by the Torah itself, but so is its precise wording (Num. 6:24–26). It is therefore

Read the following silently while the Kohanim chant. Omit on Shabbat.

Master of the Universe, I am Yours and my dreams are Yours. I have dreamt a dream and I do not know what it means. May it be Your will, LORD my God and God of my fathers, that all my dreams be, for me and all Israel, for good, whether I have dreamt about myself, or about others, or others have dreamt about me. If they are good, strengthen and reinforce them, and may they be fulfilled in me and them like the dreams of the righteous Joseph. If, though, they need healing, heal them as You healed Hezekiah King of Judah from his illness, like Miriam the prophetess from her leprosy, like Na'aman from his leprosy, like the waters of Mara by Moses our teacher, and like the waters of Jericho by Elisha. And just as You turned the curses of Balaam the wicked from curse to blessing, so turn all my dreams about me and all Israel to good; protect me, be gracious to me and accept me. Amen.

May [He] make shine	May God be gracious to us and bless us; may He make His face shine upon us, Selah.	*Ps. 67*
The LORD	The LORD, the LORD, compassionate and gracious God, slow to anger, abounding in kindness and truth.	*Ex. 34*
His face	Turn to me and be gracious to me, for I am alone and afflicted.	*Ps. 25*
On you	To You, LORD, I lift up my soul.	*Ps. 25*
And be gracious to you.	As the eyes of slaves turn to their master's hand, or the eyes of a slave-girl to the hand of her mistress, so our eyes are turned to the LORD our God, awaiting His favor.	*Ps. 123*

Read the following silently while the Kohanim chant. Omit on Shabbat.

Master of the Universe, I am Yours and my dreams are Yours. I have dreamt a dream and I do not know what it means. May it be Your will, LORD my God and God of my fathers, that all my dreams be, for me and all Israel, for good, whether I have dreamt about myself, or about others, or others have dreamt about me. If they are good, strengthen and reinforce them, and may they be fulfilled in me and them like the dreams of the righteous Joseph. If, though, they need healing, heal them as You healed Hezekiah King of Judah from his illness, like Miriam the prophetess from her

---

name on the Israelites and I will bless them" (Num. 6:27). Thus it is not the Kohanim who bless the people, but God. The priests – whose entire life was dedicated to divine service – were holy vehicles through which divine

Read the following silently while the כהנים *chant. Omit on* שבת*.*

רִבּוֹנוֹ שֶׁל עוֹלָם, אֲנִי שֶׁלָּךְ וַחֲלוֹמוֹתַי שֶׁלָּךְ. חֲלוֹם חָלַמְתִּי וְאֵינִי יוֹדֵעַ מַה הוּא. יְהִי רָצוֹן מִלְּפָנֶיךָ, יהוה אֱלֹהַי וֵאלֹהֵי אֲבוֹתַי, שֶׁיִּהְיוּ כָּל חֲלוֹמוֹתַי עָלַי וְעַל כָּל יִשְׂרָאֵל לְטוֹבָה, בֵּין שֶׁחָלַמְתִּי עַל עַצְמִי, וּבֵין שֶׁחָלַמְתִּי עַל אֲחֵרִים, וּבֵין שֶׁחָלְמוּ אֲחֵרִים עָלָי. אִם טוֹבִים הֵם, חַזְּקֵם וְאַמְּצֵם, וְיִתְקַיְּמוּ בִי וּבָהֶם, כַּחֲלוֹמוֹתָיו שֶׁל יוֹסֵף הַצַּדִּיק. וְאִם צְרִיכִים רְפוּאָה, רְפָאֵם כְּחִזְקִיָּהוּ מֶלֶךְ יְהוּדָה מֵחָלְיוֹ, וּכְמִרְיָם הַנְּבִיאָה מִצָּרַעְתָּהּ, וּכְנַעֲמָן מִצָּרַעְתּוֹ, וּכְמֵי מָרָה עַל יְדֵי מֹשֶׁה רַבֵּנוּ, וּכְמֵי יְרִיחוֹ עַל יְדֵי אֱלִישָׁע. וּכְשֵׁם שֶׁהָפַכְתָּ אֶת קִלְלַת בִּלְעָם הָרָשָׁע מִקְּלָלָה לִבְרָכָה, כֵּן תַּהֲפֹךְ כָּל חֲלוֹמוֹתַי עָלַי וְעַל כָּל יִשְׂרָאֵל לְטוֹבָה, וְתִשְׁמְרֵנִי וּתְחָנֵּנִי וְתִרְצֵנִי. אָמֵן.

יָאֵר אֱלֹהִים יְחָנֵּנוּ וִיבָרְכֵנוּ, יָאֵר פָּנָיו אִתָּנוּ סֶלָה: תהלים סז

יהוה יהוה, יהוה, אֵל רַחוּם וְחַנּוּן, אֶרֶךְ אַפַּיִם וְרַב־חֶסֶד וֶאֱמֶת: שמות לד

פָּנָיו פְּנֵה־אֵלַי וְחָנֵּנִי, כִּי־יָחִיד וְעָנִי אָנִי: תהלים כה

אֵלֶיךָ אֵלֶיךָ יהוה נַפְשִׁי אֶשָּׂא: תהלים כה

וִיחֻנֶּךָּ: הִנֵּה כְעֵינֵי עֲבָדִים אֶל־יַד אֲדוֹנֵיהֶם תהלים קכג
כְּעֵינֵי שִׁפְחָה אֶל־יַד גְּבִרְתָּהּ, כֵּן עֵינֵינוּ אֶל־יהוה אֱלֹהֵינוּ
עַד שֶׁיְּחָנֵּנוּ:

Read the following silently while the כהנים *chant. Omit on* שבת*.*

רִבּוֹנוֹ שֶׁל עוֹלָם, אֲנִי שֶׁלָּךְ וַחֲלוֹמוֹתַי שֶׁלָּךְ. חֲלוֹם חָלַמְתִּי וְאֵינִי יוֹדֵעַ מַה הוּא. יְהִי רָצוֹן מִלְּפָנֶיךָ, יהוה אֱלֹהַי וֵאלֹהֵי אֲבוֹתַי, שֶׁיִּהְיוּ כָּל חֲלוֹמוֹתַי עָלַי וְעַל כָּל יִשְׂרָאֵל לְטוֹבָה, בֵּין שֶׁחָלַמְתִּי עַל עַצְמִי, וּבֵין שֶׁחָלַמְתִּי עַל אֲחֵרִים, וּבֵין שֶׁחָלְמוּ אֲחֵרִים עָלָי. אִם טוֹבִים הֵם, חַזְּקֵם וְאַמְּצֵם, וְיִתְקַיְּמוּ בִי וּבָהֶם, כַּחֲלוֹמוֹתָיו שֶׁל יוֹסֵף הַצַּדִּיק. וְאִם צְרִיכִים רְפוּאָה, רְפָאֵם כְּחִזְקִיָּהוּ מֶלֶךְ יְהוּדָה מֵחָלְיוֹ, וּכְמִרְיָם הַנְּבִיאָה מִצָּרַעְתָּהּ,

---

In each, God's holiest name is the second word of the blessing. The threefold blessing ascends thematically: the first is for material blessing, the second for spiritual blessing, the third for peace, without which no blessings can be enjoyed.

The Torah is careful to state: "So they [the Kohanim] shall place My

leprosy, like Na'aman from his leprosy, like the waters of Mara by Moses our teacher, and like the waters of Jericho by Elisha. And just as You turned the curses of Balaam the wicked from curse to blessing, so turn all my dreams about me and all Israel to good; protect me, be gracious to me and accept me. Amen.

May [He] turn	May he receive a blessing from the LORD and a just reward from the God of his salvation. And he will win grace and good favor in the eyes of God and man.	*Ps. 24* *Prov. 3*
The LORD	LORD, be gracious to us; we yearn for You. Be their strength every morning, our salvation in time of distress.	*Is. 33*
His face	Do not hide Your face from me in the day of my distress. Turn Your ear to me; on the day I call, swiftly answer me.	*Ps. 102*
Toward you	To You, enthroned in heaven, I lift my eyes.	*Ps. 123*
And give	They shall place My name on the children of Israel, and I will bless them.	*Num. 6*
You	Yours, LORD, are the greatness and the power, the glory, majesty and splendor, for everything in heaven and earth is Yours. Yours, LORD, is the kingdom; You are exalted as Head over all.	*1 Chr. 29*
Peace.	"Peace, peace, to those far and near," says the LORD, "and I will heal him."	*Is. 57*

Read the following silently while the Kohanim chant. Omit on Shabbat.

May it be Your will, LORD my God and God of my fathers, that You act for the sake of Your simple, sacred kindness and great compassion, and for the purity of Your great, mighty and awesome name of twenty-two letters derived from the verses of the priestly blessing spoken by Aaron and his sons, Your holy people. May You be close to me when I call to You. May You hear my prayer, plea and cry as You did the cry of Jacob Your perfect one who was called "a plain man." May You grant me and

---

During the Leader's Repetition of the Amida, and prior to the Priestly Blessings, the Kohanim wash their hands in water poured from a special vessel by the Levites. They remove their shoes. When the Leader reaches

וּכְנַעֲמָן מִצָּרַעְתּוֹ, וּכְמֵי מָרָה עַל יְדֵי מֹשֶׁה רַבֵּנוּ, וּכְמֵי יְרִיחוֹ עַל יְדֵי אֱלִישָׁע. וּכְשֵׁם שֶׁהָפַכְתָּ אֶת קִלְלַת בִּלְעָם הָרָשָׁע מִקְּלָלָה לִבְרָכָה, כֵּן תַּהֲפֹךְ כָּל חֲלוֹמוֹתַי עָלַי וְעַל כָּל יִשְׂרָאֵל לְטוֹבָה, וְתִשְׁמְרֵנִי וּתְחָנֵּנִי וְתִרְצֵנִי. אָמֵן.

יִשָּׂא יִשָּׂא בְרָכָה מֵאֵת יהוה, וּצְדָקָה מֵאֱלֹהֵי יִשְׁעוֹ: תהלים כד
וּמְצָא־חֵן וְשֵׂכֶל־טוֹב בְּעֵינֵי אֱלֹהִים וְאָדָם: משלי ג

יהוה יהוה חָנֵּנוּ, לְךָ קִוִּינוּ, הֱיֵה זְרֹעָם לַבְּקָרִים ישעיה לג
אַף־יְשׁוּעָתֵנוּ בְּעֵת צָרָה:

פָּנָיו אַל־תַּסְתֵּר פָּנֶיךָ מִמֶּנִּי בְּיוֹם צַר לִי, הַטֵּה־אֵלַי אָזְנֶךָ תהלים קב
בְּיוֹם אֶקְרָא מַהֵר עֲנֵנִי:

אֵלֶיךָ אֵלֶיךָ נָשָׂאתִי אֶת־עֵינַי, הַיֹּשְׁבִי בַּשָּׁמָיִם: תהלים קכג

וְיָשֵׂם וְשָׂמוּ אֶת־שְׁמִי עַל־בְּנֵי יִשְׂרָאֵל, וַאֲנִי אֲבָרְכֵם: במדבר ו

לְךָ לְךָ יהוה הַגְּדֻלָּה וְהַגְּבוּרָה וְהַתִּפְאֶרֶת וְהַנֵּצַח וְהַהוֹד דברי הימים א׳ כט
כִּי־כֹל בַּשָּׁמַיִם וּבָאָרֶץ, לְךָ יהוה הַמַּמְלָכָה
וְהַמִּתְנַשֵּׂא לְכֹל לְרֹאשׁ:

שָׁלוֹם: שָׁלוֹם שָׁלוֹם לָרָחוֹק וְלַקָּרוֹב, אָמַר יהוה, וּרְפָאתִיו: ישעיה נז

Read the following silently while the כהנים *chant. Omit on* שבת.

יְהִי רָצוֹן מִלְּפָנֶיךָ, יהוה אֱלֹהַי וֵאלֹהֵי אֲבוֹתַי, שֶׁתַּעֲשֶׂה לְמַעַן קְדֻשַּׁת חֲסָדֶיךָ וְגֹדֶל רַחֲמֶיךָ הַפְּשׁוּטִים, וּלְמַעַן טָהֳרַת שִׁמְךָ הַגָּדוֹל הַגִּבּוֹר וְהַנּוֹרָא, בֶּן עֶשְׂרִים וּשְׁתַּיִם אוֹתִיּוֹת הַיּוֹצֵא מִפְּסוּקִים שֶׁל בִּרְכַּת כֹּהֲנִים הָאֲמוּרָה מִפִּי אַהֲרֹן וּבָנָיו עַם קְדוֹשֶׁךָ, שֶׁתִּהְיֶה קָרוֹב לִי בְּקָרְאִי לָךְ, וְתִשְׁמַע תְּפִלָּתִי נַאֲקָתִי וְאֶנְקָתִי תָּמִיד, כְּשֵׁם שֶׁשָּׁמַעְתָּ אֶנְקַת יַעֲקֹב תְּמִימֶךָ הַנִּקְרָא אִישׁ תָּם. וְתִתֶּן לִי וּלְכָל נַפְשׁוֹת בֵּיתִי מְזוֹנוֹתֵינוּ וּפַרְנָסָתֵנוּ בְּרֶוַח וְלֹא בְצִמְצוּם, בְּהֶתֵּר וְלֹא בְאִסּוּר, בְּנַחַת וְלֹא בְצַעַר, מִתַּחַת יָדְךָ הָרְחָבָה, כְּשֵׁם שֶׁנָּתַתָּ פַּת לֶחֶם לֶאֱכֹל וּבֶגֶד לִלְבֹּשׁ לְיַעֲקֹב אָבִינוּ הַנִּקְרָא אִישׁ תָּם. וְתִתְּנֵנוּ

---

blessing flowed. In Temple times, the Kohanim blessed the people daily. That remains the custom in Israel. Outside Israel, the custom is that the Priestly Blessing is said only on Festivals, for only then do we experience some of the joy that those who live in God's land feel every day.

all the members of my household our food and sustenance, generously not meagerly, honestly not otherwise, with satisfaction not pain, from Your generous hand, just as You gave a portion of bread to eat and clothes to wear to Jacob our father who was called "a plain man." May we find love, grace, kindness and compassion in Your sight and in the eyes of all who see us. May my words in service to You be heard, as You granted Joseph Your righteous one, at the time when he was robed by his father in a cloak of fine wool, that he find grace, kindness and compassion in Your sight and in the eyes of all who saw him. May You do wonders and miracles with me, and a sign for good. Grant me success in my paths, and set in my heart understanding that I may understand, discern and fulfill all the words of Your Torah's teachings and mysteries. Save me from errors and purify my thoughts and my heart to serve You and be in awe of You. Prolong my days (*add, where appropriate:* and those of my father, mother, wife, husband, son/s, and daughter/s) in joy and happiness, with much strength and peace. Amen, Selah.

The Leader continues with "Grant peace" below.

The congregation says:
אַדִּיר Majestic One on high who dwells in power: You are peace and Your name is peace. May it be Your will to bestow on us and on Your people the house of Israel, life and blessing as a safeguard for peace.

The Kohanim say:
רִבּוֹנוֹ Master of the Universe: we have done what You have decreed for us. So too may You deal with us as You have promised us. Look down from Your holy dwelling place, from heaven, and bless Your people Israel and the land You have given us as You promised on oath to our ancestors, a land flowing with milk and honey. *Deut. 26*

The Leader continues:

שִׂים שָׁלוֹם Grant peace, goodness and blessing, grace, loving-kindness and compassion to us and all Israel Your people. Bless us, our Father, all as one, with the light of Your face, for by the light of Your face You have given us, Lord our God, the Torah of life and love of kindness, righteousness, blessing, compassion, life and peace. May it be good in Your eyes to bless Your people Israel at every time, in every hour, with Your peace. Blessed are You, Lord, who blesses His people Israel with peace.

The following verse concludes the Leader's Repetition of the Amida (see law 368).

May the words of my mouth and the meditation of my heart *Ps. 19*
find favor before You, Lord, my Rock and Redeemer.

---

at them while the blessings are being said. **אַדִּיר בַּמָּרוֹם** *Majestic One on high:* a prayer said by the congregation, echoing three times the last word of the Priestly Blessing: peace.

לְאַהֲבָה, לְחֵן וּלְחֶסֶד וּלְרַחֲמִים בְּעֵינֶיךָ וּבְעֵינֵי כָל רוֹאַי, וְיִהְיוּ דְבָרַי נִשְׁמָעִים לַעֲבוֹדָתֶךָ, כְּשֵׁם שֶׁנָּתַתָּ אֶת יוֹסֵף צַדִּיקֶךָ בְּשָׁעָה שֶׁהִלְבִּישׁוֹ אָבִיו כְּתֹנֶת פַּסִּים לְחֵן וּלְחֶסֶד וּלְרַחֲמִים בְּעֵינֶיךָ וּבְעֵינֵי כָל רוֹאָיו. וְתַעֲשֶׂה עִמִּי נִפְלָאוֹת וְנִסִּים, וּלְטוֹבָה אוֹת, וְתַצְלִיחֵנִי בִּדְרָכַי, וְתֵן בְּלִבִּי בִּינָה לְהָבִין וּלְהַשְׂכִּיל וּלְקַיֵּם אֶת כָּל דִּבְרֵי תַלְמוּד תּוֹרָתֶךָ וְסוֹדוֹתֶיהָ, וְתַצִּילֵנִי מִשְּׁגִיאוֹת, וּתְטַהֵר רַעְיוֹנַי וְלִבִּי לַעֲבוֹדָתֶךָ, וְתַאֲרִיךְ יָמַי (וִימֵי אָבִי וְאִמִּי / וְאִשְׁתִּי / וּבַעְלִי / וּבָנַי וּבְנוֹתַי) בְּטוֹב וּבִנְעִימוֹת, בְּרֹב עֹז וְשָׁלוֹם, אָמֵן סֶלָה.

The שליח ציבור *continues with* שִׂים שָׁלוֹם *below.*

The קהל *says:*

אַדִּיר בַּמָּרוֹם שׁוֹכֵן בִּגְבוּרָה, אַתָּה שָׁלוֹם וְשִׁמְךָ שָׁלוֹם. יְהִי רָצוֹן שֶׁתָּשִׂים עָלֵינוּ וְעַל כָּל עַמְּךָ בֵּית יִשְׂרָאֵל חַיִּים וּבְרָכָה לְמִשְׁמֶרֶת שָׁלוֹם.

The כהנים *say:*

רִבּוֹנוֹ שֶׁל עוֹלָם, עָשִׂינוּ מַה שֶּׁגָּזַרְתָּ עָלֵינוּ, אַף אַתָּה עֲשֵׂה עִמָּנוּ כְּמוֹ שֶׁהִבְטַחְתָּנוּ. הַשְׁקִיפָה מִמְּעוֹן קָדְשְׁךָ מִן־הַשָּׁמַיִם, וּבָרֵךְ אֶת־עַמְּךָ אֶת־יִשְׂרָאֵל, וְאֵת הָאֲדָמָה אֲשֶׁר נָתַתָּה לָנוּ, כַּאֲשֶׁר נִשְׁבַּעְתָּ לַאֲבֹתֵינוּ, אֶרֶץ זָבַת חָלָב וּדְבָשׁ: דברים כו

The שליח ציבור *continues:*

שִׂים שָׁלוֹם טוֹבָה וּבְרָכָה, חֵן וָחֶסֶד וְרַחֲמִים, עָלֵינוּ וְעַל כָּל יִשְׂרָאֵל עַמֶּךָ. בָּרְכֵנוּ אָבִינוּ כֻּלָּנוּ כְּאֶחָד בְּאוֹר פָּנֶיךָ, כִּי בְאוֹר פָּנֶיךָ נָתַתָּ לָּנוּ יהוה אֱלֹהֵינוּ, תּוֹרַת חַיִּים וְאַהֲבַת חֶסֶד, וּצְדָקָה וּבְרָכָה וְרַחֲמִים וְחַיִּים וְשָׁלוֹם. וְטוֹב בְּעֵינֶיךָ לְבָרֵךְ אֶת עַמְּךָ יִשְׂרָאֵל, בְּכָל עֵת וּבְכָל שָׁעָה בִּשְׁלוֹמֶךָ. בָּרוּךְ אַתָּה יהוה, הַמְבָרֵךְ אֶת עַמּוֹ יִשְׂרָאֵל בַּשָּׁלוֹם.

The following verse concludes the חזרת הש״ץ (*see law 368*).

תהלים יט יִהְיוּ לְרָצוֹן אִמְרֵי־פִי וְהֶגְיוֹן לִבִּי לְפָנֶיךָ, יהוה צוּרִי וְגֹאֲלִי:

"Find favor," they ascend to stand in front of the Ark. They cover the head and upper body with the tallit, and raise their arms and hands during the blessing in a special manner. During the blessings, which they repeat word for word after the Leader, all other members of the congregation should be in front of them: those sitting behind should move forward at this time. Their faces should be turned toward the Kohanim, but they should not look

BIRKAT KOHANIM IN ISRAEL

In Israel, the following is said by the Leader during the Repetition of the Amida when Kohanim bless the congregation. If there is more than one Kohen, a member of the congregation calls: (See laws 370–377.)

Kohanim!

The Kohanim respond:

Blessed are You, Lord our God, King of the Universe, who has made us holy with the holiness of Aaron, and has commanded us to bless His people Israel with love.

The Leader calls word by word, followed by the Kohanim:

יְבָרֶכְךָ May the LORD bless you and protect you. (*Cong:* Amen.) *Num. 6*
May the LORD make His face shine on you
and be gracious to you. (*Cong:* Amen.)
May the LORD turn His face toward you,
and grant you peace. (*Cong:* Amen.)

The Leader continues with "Grant peace" below.

The congregation says:

אַדִּיר Majestic One on high who dwells in power: You are peace and Your name is peace. May it be Your will to bestow on us and on Your people the house of Israel, life and blessing as a safeguard for peace.

The Kohanim say:

רִבּוֹנוֹ Master of the Universe: we have done what You have decreed for us. So too may You deal with us as You have promised us. Look down from Your holy dwelling place, from heaven, and bless Your people Israel and the land You have given us as You promised on oath to our ancestors, a land flowing with milk and honey. *Deut. 26*

The Leader continues:

שִׂים שָׁלוֹם Grant peace, goodness and blessing, grace, loving-kindness and compassion to us and all Israel Your people. Bless us, our Father, all as one, with the light of Your face, for by the light of Your face You have given us, LORD our God, the Torah of life and love of kindness, righteousness, blessing, compassion, life and peace. May it be good in Your eyes to bless Your people Israel at every time, in every hour, with Your peace.

Between Rosh HaShana & Yom Kippur: In the book of life, blessing, peace and prosperity, may we and all Your people the house of Israel be remembered and written before You for a good life, and for peace.

Blessed are You, LORD, who blesses His people Israel with peace.

The following verse concludes the Leader's Repetition of the Amida. See law 368.

May the words of my mouth and the meditation of my heart
find favor before You, LORD, my Rock and Redeemer. *Ps. 19*

ברכת כהנים בארץ ישראל

In ארץ ישראל*, the following is said by the* שליח ציבור *during the* חזרת הש״ץ *when* כהנים *say* ברכת כהנים*. If there is more than one* כהן*, a member of the* קהל *calls: (See laws 370–377.)*

כֹּהֲנִים

The כהנים *respond:*

בָּרוּךְ אַתָּה יהוה אֱלֹהֵינוּ מֶלֶךְ הָעוֹלָם, אֲשֶׁר קִדְּשָׁנוּ בִּקְדֻשָּׁתוֹ שֶׁל אַהֲרֹן
וְצִוָּנוּ לְבָרֵךְ אֶת עַמּוֹ יִשְׂרָאֵל בְּאַהֲבָה.

The שליח ציבור *calls word by word, followed by the* כהנים*:*

במדבר ו יְבָרֶכְךָ יהוה וְיִשְׁמְרֶךָ: קהל: אָמֵן
יָאֵר יהוה פָּנָיו אֵלֶיךָ וִיחֻנֶּךָּ: קהל: אָמֵן
יִשָּׂא יהוה פָּנָיו אֵלֶיךָ וְיָשֵׂם לְךָ שָׁלוֹם: קהל: אָמֵן

The שליח ציבור *continues with* שִׂים שָׁלוֹם *below.*

The קהל *says:*

אַדִּיר בַּמָּרוֹם שׁוֹכֵן בִּגְבוּרָה, אַתָּה שָׁלוֹם וְשִׁמְךָ שָׁלוֹם. יְהִי רָצוֹן שֶׁתָּשִׂים עָלֵינוּ וְעַל כָּל עַמְּךָ בֵּית יִשְׂרָאֵל חַיִּים וּבְרָכָה לְמִשְׁמֶרֶת שָׁלוֹם.

The כהנים *say:*

רִבּוֹנוֹ שֶׁל עוֹלָם, עָשִׂינוּ מַה שֶּׁגָּזַרְתָּ עָלֵינוּ, אַף אַתָּה עֲשֵׂה עִמָּנוּ כְּמוֹ שֶׁהִבְטַחְתָּנוּ. הַשְׁקִיפָה מִמְּעוֹן קָדְשְׁךָ מִן־הַשָּׁמַיִם, וּבָרֵךְ אֶת־עַמְּךָ אֶת־יִשְׂרָאֵל, וְאֵת הָאֲדָמָה אֲשֶׁר נָתַתָּה לָנוּ, כַּאֲשֶׁר נִשְׁבַּעְתָּ לַאֲבֹתֵינוּ, אֶרֶץ זָבַת חָלָב וּדְבָשׁ: דברים כו

The שליח ציבור *continues:*

שִׂים שָׁלוֹם טוֹבָה וּבְרָכָה, חֵן וָחֶסֶד וְרַחֲמִים עָלֵינוּ וְעַל כָּל יִשְׂרָאֵל עַמֶּךָ. בָּרְכֵנוּ אָבִינוּ כֻּלָּנוּ כְּאֶחָד בְּאוֹר פָּנֶיךָ, כִּי בְאוֹר פָּנֶיךָ נָתַתָּ לָּנוּ יהוה אֱלֹהֵינוּ, תּוֹרַת חַיִּים וְאַהֲבַת חֶסֶד, וּצְדָקָה וּבְרָכָה וְרַחֲמִים וְחַיִּים וְשָׁלוֹם. וְטוֹב בְּעֵינֶיךָ לְבָרֵךְ אֶת עַמְּךָ יִשְׂרָאֵל, בְּכָל עֵת וּבְכָל שָׁעָה בִּשְׁלוֹמֶךָ.

בעשרת ימי תשובה: בְּסֵפֶר חַיִּים, בְּרָכָה וְשָׁלוֹם, וּפַרְנָסָה טוֹבָה, נִזָּכֵר וְנִכָּתֵב לְפָנֶיךָ, אֲנַחְנוּ וְכָל עַמְּךָ בֵּית יִשְׂרָאֵל, לְחַיִּים טוֹבִים וּלְשָׁלוֹם.

בָּרוּךְ אַתָּה יהוה, הַמְבָרֵךְ אֶת עַמּוֹ יִשְׂרָאֵל בַּשָּׁלוֹם.

The following verse concludes the חזרת הש״ץ*. See law 368.*

תהלים יט יִהְיוּ לְרָצוֹן אִמְרֵי־פִי וְהֶגְיוֹן לִבִּי לְפָנֶיךָ, יהוה צוּרִי וְגֹאֲלִי:

Prayer for Dew

On the first day of Pesaḥ, the Ark is opened at the Repetition of the Musaf Amida. All stand.
In Israel, the Prayer for Dew is said before the silent Amida and starts on the next page.

When I proclaim the LORD's name, give glory to our God. *Deut. 32*
O LORD, open my lips, so that my mouth may declare Your praise. *Ps. 51*

PATRIARCHS

בָּרוּךְ Blessed are You, LORD our God and God of our fathers, God of Abraham, God of Isaac and God of Jacob; the great, mighty and awesome God, God Most High, who bestows acts of loving-kindness and creates all, who remembers the loving-kindness of the fathers and will bring a Redeemer to their children's children for the sake of His name, in love. King, Helper, Savior, Shield:

בְּדַעְתּוֹ With His consent I will speak of hidden things,
that for this people, by this prayer,
there may be joy in dew.
May the valley and its vegetation
be renewed through dew,
springing up under His shade anew.
Sign of regeneration,
shield of future generations – dew.

Blessed are You, LORD, Shield of Abraham.

---

to when and where he lived. Many believe him to have lived in the Mishnaic period; others that he lived in the sixth century. His compositions are full of allusions to rabbinic traditions; he coined many new words, and his style – intricate, erudite, full of wordplay and subtle acrostics – influenced many later liturgical poets.

בְּדַעְתּוֹ *With His consent:* The preamble to the prayer involves an untranslatable play on the similar-sounding words *ḥidot* ("hidden things"), *lehaḥadot* ("have joy"), and *laḥadot* ("be as new": an Aramaic form of the Hebrew *ḥadash*). The fourth line is a complex allusion to a wedding. It uses two

תפילת טל

On the first day of פסח*, the* ארון קודש *is opened at the* חזרת הש״ץ *of the* מוסף עמידה*. All stand. In* ארץ ישראל*,* תפילת טל *is said before the silent* עמידה *and starts on the next page.*

כִּי שֵׁם יהוה אֶקְרָא, הָבוּ גֹדֶל לֵאלֹהֵינוּ: דברים לב
אֲדֹנָי, שְׂפָתַי תִּפְתָּח, וּפִי יַגִּיד תְּהִלָּתֶךָ: תהלים נא

אבות

בָּרוּךְ אַתָּה יהוה, אֱלֹהֵינוּ וֵאלֹהֵי אֲבוֹתֵינוּ, אֱלֹהֵי אַבְרָהָם, אֱלֹהֵי יִצְחָק, וֵאלֹהֵי יַעֲקֹב, הָאֵל הַגָּדוֹל הַגִּבּוֹר וְהַנּוֹרָא, אֵל עֶלְיוֹן, גּוֹמֵל חֲסָדִים טוֹבִים, וְקוֹנֵה הַכֹּל, וְזוֹכֵר חַסְדֵי אָבוֹת, וּמֵבִיא גוֹאֵל לִבְנֵי בְנֵיהֶם לְמַעַן שְׁמוֹ בְּאַהֲבָה. מֶלֶךְ עוֹזֵר וּמוֹשִׁיעַ וּמָגֵן.

בְּדַעְתּוֹ אַבִּיעָה חִידוֹת
בְּעַם זוּ בְּזוֹ בְּטַל לְהַחֲדוֹת.
טַל גַּיְא וּדְשָׁאֶיהָ לַחֲדוֹת
דָּצִים בְּצִלּוֹ לְהַחֲדוֹת.
אוֹת יַלְדוּת טַל, לְהָגֵן לְתוֹלָדוֹת

בָּרוּךְ אַתָּה יהוה, מָגֵן אַבְרָהָם.

PRAYER FOR DEW

Pesaḥ, the "festival of spring," marks the end of the rainy season. Accordingly, on the first day at Musaf, we stop saying, "He makes the wind blow and the rain fall" in the second paragraph of the Amida. The Sephardi and Israeli custom is to say instead, "who causes the dew to fall"; we do not have this custom. Nonetheless, to mark the transition, we recite a special liturgical poem (*piyut*).

Its author is the greatest of Jewry's liturgical poets, Elazar Kalir. Despite his genius and the sheer number of his compositions (many previously unknown works of his were discovered in the Cairo Geniza), we remain uncertain as

אַתָּה גִּבּוֹר You are eternally mighty, Lord.
You give life to the dead and have great power to save.

תְּהוֹמוֹת The depths of the earth yearn for drops of dew;
all the green pastures long for them.
The mention of dew adds to His might,
inscribed as we approach in the Musaf prayer.
Dew – to revive those [buried] in the clefts of the rocks.

In Israel start here:

Our God and God of our fathers:

טַל Dew – Grant it to favor Your land;
in Your jubilation, set us as a blessing.
Increase for us our corn and wine.
Establish the city in which You delight – With dew.

טַל Dew – Decree it for a good and resplendent year;
may the fruit of the earth be fine and fair.
As for the city now deserted like a hut,
place it in Your hand like a crown – With dew.

טַל Dew – May it drop gently on the blessed land;
satisfy us with a blessing of the rich gifts of heaven.
Send light in the midst of darkness
to the stock [Israel] who are drawn to You – With dew.

---

phrase which also means, "Dew is mentioned in [the second paragraph of the Amida known as] 'His might.'"

טַל תֵּן לִרְצוֹת אַרְצָךְ *Dew – Grant it to favor Your land:* The six verses of the poem begin and end with the word "Dew," and the whole is constructed as a reverse alphabetical acrostic, the last two letters (*bet* and *aleph*) each being allocated two lines. (Note that in such *piyutim*, the letters *sin* and *samekh* are interchangeable.) The poem deftly intertwines the themes of nature (spring, renewal) and history (asking God to bring His people back from the winter of exile to a spring of national renewal). כַּנָּה *To the stock:* the root or stem

אַתָּה גִּבּוֹר לְעוֹלָם אֲדֹנָי
מְחַיֵּה מֵתִים אַתָּה, רַב לְהוֹשִׁיעַ

תְּהוֹמוֹת הֲדוֹם לִרְסִיסוֹ כְסוּפִים
וְכָל נְאוֹת דֶּשֶׁא לוֹ נִכְסָפִים.
טַל זִכְרוֹ גְּבוּרוֹת מוּסִיפִים
חָקוּק בְּגִישַׁת מוּסָפִים
טַל, לְהַחֲיוֹת בּוֹ נְקוּקֵי סְעִיפִים.

In ארץ ישראל *start here:*

אֱלֹהֵינוּ וֵאלֹהֵי אֲבוֹתֵינוּ

טַל תֵּן לִרְצוֹת אַרְצָךְ שִׁיתֵנוּ בְרָכָה בְּדִיצָךְ
רֹב דָּגָן וְתִירוֹשׁ בְּהַפְרִיצָךְ קוֹמֵם עִיר בָּהּ חֶפְצָךְ בְּטָל.

טַל צַוֵּה שָׁנָה טוֹבָה וּמְעֻטֶּרֶת פְּרִי הָאָרֶץ לְגָאוֹן וּלְתִפְאֶרֶת
עִיר כַּסֻּכָּה נוֹתֶרֶת שִׂימָהּ בְּיָדְךָ עֲטֶרֶת בְּטָל.

טַל נוֹפֵף עֲלֵי אֶרֶץ בְּרוּכָה מִמֶּגֶד שָׁמַיִם שַׂבְּעֵנוּ בְרָכָה
לְהָאִיר מִתּוֹךְ חֲשֵׁכָה כַּנָּה אַחֲרֶיךָ מְשׁוּכָה בְּטָל.

---

words that appear together in the last of the seven marriage blessings (*ditza* and *ḥedva*). The word "shade" (meaning both cloud and divine protection) may also be an allusion to the bridal canopy. Thus Kalir, through complex verbal resonances, strikes a mood of joy as if spring were the wedding of heaven and earth.

תְּהוֹמוֹת *The depths of the earth:* A meditation on the fact that dew (and rain) are mentioned in the second paragraph of the Amida, known as *Gevurot*, "Divine might," whose dominant theme is the resurrection of the dead. Just as at the end of time God will revive the dead ("those buried in the clefts of the rocks"), so does dew now revive the earth and make it green again. **טַל זִכְרוֹ גְּבוּרוֹת מוּסִיפִים** *The mention of dew adds to His might:* an ambiguous

טַל Dew – Let it sweeten the mountain streams;
let the chosen ones taste Your magnanimity.
Free Your beloved ones from captivity,
then sweetly we will raise our voices and sing –
With dew.

טַל Dew – May it fill our granaries to overflowing.
Would that now You might renew our days.
Beloved! Let our name endure as Yours.
Make us like a well-watered garden – With dew.

טַל Dew – With it bless our food;
in our fertile lands may there be no scarcity.
The nation You once led like a flock,
on her please, we pray, bestow Your favor – With dew.

Leader:

For You, LORD our God,
make the wind blow and the dew fall.

Congregation then Leader, responsively:

For blessing, and not for curse. *Cong:* Amen.
For life, and not for death. *Cong:* Amen.
For plenty, and not for scarcity. *Cong:* Amen.

The Ark is closed. Outside Israel, the Leader continues the Repetition with "He sustains the living" on page 806. In Israel, the Leader says Half Kaddish and the Musaf Amida is recited with the addition of "He makes the dew fall."

לִבְרָכָה וְלֹא לִקְלָלָה *For blessing, and not for curse:* In this rousing three-line climax (paralleled in the Prayer for Rain), Leader and congregation join in fervent prayer that the forces of nature, under the care of the Maker of nature, should bring blessing to the land and its people.

טַל יַעֲסִיס צוּף הָרִים טְעֵם בִּמְאוֹדֶיךָ מֻבְחָרִים
חֲנוּנֶיךָ חַלֵּץ מִמַּסְגֵּרִים זִמְרָה נַנְעִים וְקוֹל נָרִים בְּטָל.

טַל וְשֹׂבַע מַלֵּא אֲסָמֵינוּ הֲכָעֵת תְּחַדֵּשׁ יָמֵינוּ
דּוֹד, כְּעֶרְכְּךָ הַעֲמֵד שְׁמֵנוּ גַּן רָוֶה שִׂימֵנוּ בְּטָל.

טַל בּוֹ תְּבָרֵךְ מָזוֹן בְּמַשְׁמַנֵּינוּ אַל יְהִי רָזוֹן
אֲיֻמָּה אֲשֶׁר הִסַּעְתָּ כַּצֹּאן אָנָּא תָּפֵק לָהּ רָצוֹן בְּטָל.

שליח ציבור:

שָׁאַתָּה הוּא יהוה אֱלֹהֵינוּ
מַשִּׁיב הָרְוּחַ וּמוֹרִיד הַטָּל

קהל then שליח ציבור, responsively:

לִבְרָכָה וְלֹא לִקְלָלָה קהל: אָמֵן
לְחַיִּים וְלֹא לְמָוֶת קהל: אָמֵן
לְשֹׂבַע וְלֹא לְרָזוֹן קהל: אָמֵן

The ארון קודש *is closed. In* חוץ לארץ*, the* שליח ציבור *continues the* חזרת הש״ץ *with* מְכַלְכֵּל חַיִּים *on page 807. In* ארץ ישראל*, the* שליח ציבור *says* חצי קדיש *and the* מוסף עמידה *is recited with the addition of* מוֹרִיד הַטָּל*.*

---

of a vine, a metaphor for Israel (see Psalm 80:16 and commentaries thereto). By comparing Israel to a plant, the poet can extend the metaphor of dew to the fortunes of the nation. כְּעֶרְכְּךָ הַעֲמֵד שְׁמֵנוּ *Let our name endure as Yours:* just as God is eternal, so may be the people who carry His name ("Then all the peoples on earth will see that you are called by the name of the Lord," Deut. 28:10). בְּמַשְׁמַנֵּינוּ *In our fertile lands:* literally, "In our fat places may there be no leanness."

Prayer for Rain

On Shemini Atzeret, the Ark is opened at the Repetition of the Musaf Amida. All stand. In Israel, the Prayer for Rain is said before the silent Amida and starts on the next page.

When I proclaim the Lord's name, give glory to our God. Deut. 32
O Lord, open my lips, so that my mouth may declare Your praise. Ps. 51

PATRIARCHS

ˀבָּרוּךְ Blessed are You, Lord our God and God of our fathers, God of Abraham, God of Isaac and God of Jacob; the great, mighty and awesome God, God Most High, who bestows acts of loving-kindness and creates all, who remembers the loving-kindness of the fathers and will bring a Redeemer to their children's children for the sake of His name, in love. King, Helper, Savior, Shield:

אַף־בְּרִי Af-bri is the name of the angel of rain,
Who overcasts [the sky],
forms clouds and precipitates them, making them rain
Water to crown the valley with green.
May rain not be withheld from us because of our unpaid debts.
May the merit of the faithful Patriarchs
protect their offspring who pray for rain.

ˀBlessed are You, Lord, Shield of Abraham.

אַתָּה You are eternally mighty, Lord.
You give life to the dead and have great power to save.

---

and each line ends with the word "water." The six verses enumerate events related to water in six lives: those of the patriarchs, Abraham, Isaac and Jacob; the leaders of the Israelites in the wilderness, Moses and Aaron; and the people of Israel as a whole.

אַף־בְּרִי *Af-bri is the name of the angel of rain:* Job 37:11 reads: "Even when it is clear [*af-bri*], He gives the dense clouds their load, and the clouds spread His mist abroad." Rashi interprets the phrase *Af-bri* as "the angel of rain," a personification of the two aspects of rain. At times it is fierce, like anger (*af*); at others it is gentle, healing (*bri*) the earth's thirst.

תפילת גשם

On שמיני עצרת*, the* ארון קודש *is opened at the* חזרת הש״ץ *of the* מוסף עמידה*. All stand.*
In ארץ ישראל*,* תפילת גשם *is said before the silent* עמידה *and starts on the next page.*

כִּי שֵׁם יהוה אֶקְרָא, הָבוּ גֹדֶל לֵאלֹהֵינוּ: דברים לב
אֲדֹנָי, שְׂפָתַי תִּפְתָּח, וּפִי יַגִּיד תְּהִלָּתֶךָ: תהלים נא

אבות

בָּרוּךְ אַתָּה יהוה, אֱלֹהֵינוּ וֵאלֹהֵי אֲבוֹתֵינוּ, אֱלֹהֵי אַבְרָהָם, אֱלֹהֵי יִצְחָק, וֵאלֹהֵי יַעֲקֹב, הָאֵל הַגָּדוֹל הַגִּבּוֹר וְהַנּוֹרָא, אֵל עֶלְיוֹן, גּוֹמֵל חֲסָדִים טוֹבִים, וְקוֹנֵה הַכֹּל, וְזוֹכֵר חַסְדֵי אָבוֹת, וּמֵבִיא גוֹאֵל לִבְנֵי בְנֵיהֶם לְמַעַן שְׁמוֹ בְּאַהֲבָה. מֶלֶךְ עוֹזֵר וּמוֹשִׁיעַ וּמָגֵן.

אַף־בְּרִי אֻתַּת שֵׁם שַׂר מָטָר
לְהַעֲבִיב וּלְהַעֲנִין לְהָרִיק וּלְהַמְטַר
מַיִם אִבִּים בָּם גֵּיא לַעֲטַר
לְבַל יֵעָצְרוּ בְּנִשְׁיוֹן שְׁטָר
אֱמוּנִים גְּנוֹן בָּם, שׁוֹאֲלֵי מָטָר.

בָּרוּךְ אַתָּה יהוה, מָגֵן אַבְרָהָם.

אַתָּה גִּבּוֹר לְעוֹלָם אֲדֹנָי, מְחַיֵּה מֵתִים אַתָּה, רַב לְהוֹשִׁיעַ

PRAYER FOR RAIN

"On the festival [of Sukkot] the rainfall of the world is judged" (Mishna, *Rosh HaShana* 1:2). Israel is peculiarly dependent on rain, as Moses told the Israelites: "The land you are crossing the Jordan to take possession of is a land of mountains and valleys that drinks rain from heaven. It is a land the LORD your God cares for; the eyes of the LORD your God are continually on it from the beginning of the year to its end" (Deut. 11:11–12). Sukkot is the festival closest to the start of the rainy season. In theory, the prayer for rain should be said at the beginning of Sukkot, but since rainfall would interfere with the command to eat in the sukka, it was deferred to Shemini Atzeret. The liturgical poem that precedes the prayer was, like that for dew, composed by Elazar Kalir. The initial letter of each line spells out an alphabetical acrostic,

יַטְרִיחַ May He make him apportion due portions of rain,
Moistening the earth with drops pure as opal.
In the Torah You symbolized Your might by water.
Its drops refresh those in whom was breathed the breath of life,
Reviving those who make mention of the powers of rain.

In Israel start here:

Our God and God of our fathers.

זְכוֹר Remember the Patriarch [Abraham]
who followed You like water.
You blessed him like a tree planted beside streams of water.
You shielded him and rescued him from fire and water.
You sought him because he sowed [righteousness] by all waters.
Cong: For his sake do not withhold water.

זְכוֹר Remember [Isaac] whose birth was foretold
when [Abraham said] "Let there be brought some water." *Gen. 18*
You told his father to offer him, to shed his blood like water.
[Isaac], too, cared and poured out his soul like water.
When he dug, he discovered wells of water.
Cong: For his righteousness' sake grant abundant water.

זְכוֹר Remember [Jacob] who carried his staff
and crossed the Jordan's water.
With steadfast heart he rolled away the stone
from the well of water.
He wrestled with an angel composed of fire and water,
So You promised to be with him through fire and water.
Cong: For his sake do not withhold water.

זְכוֹר הַנּוֹלָד *Remember [Isaac] whose birth was foretold* when the three angels visited Abraham, and he urged them to stay, rest, eat and drink water. חָפַר *When he dug*: Isaac reopened the wells Abraham had dug, which had been stopped up by the Philistines (Gen. 26:18).

וְגָל אֶבֶן מִפִּי בְאֵר מַיִם *He rolled away the stone from the well of water:* When Jacob arrived at Haran and saw Rachel coming to water the sheep, Jacob removed the stone covering the well (Gen. 29:10). שַׂר בָּלוּל מֵאֵשׁ וּמִמַּיִם *An angel composed of fire and water:* the Talmud Yerushalmi (*Rosh HaShana* 2:4)

יַטְרִיחַ לְפַלֵּג מִפֶּלֶג גֶּשֶׁם
לְמוֹגֵג פְּנֵי נֶשִׁי בְּצַחוּת לְשֶׁם
מַיִם לְאַדְרָךְ כִּנִּיתָ בְּרֶשֶׁם
לְהַרְגִּיעַ בְּרַעְפָּם לְנִפּוּחֵי נֶשֶׁם
לְהַחֲיוֹת מַזְכִּירִים גְּבוּרוֹת הַגָּשֶׁם.

In ארץ ישראל *start here:*

אֱלֹהֵינוּ וֵאלֹהֵי אֲבוֹתֵינוּ

זְכוֹר אָב נִמְשַׁךְ אַחֲרֶיךָ כַּמַּיִם
בֵּרַכְתּוֹ כְּעֵץ שָׁתוּל עַל פַּלְגֵי מַיִם
גְּנַנְתּוֹ, הִצַּלְתּוֹ מֵאֵשׁ וּמִמַּיִם
דְּרַשְׁתּוֹ בְּזָרְעוֹ עַל כָּל מָיִם.
קהל: בַּעֲבוּרוֹ אַל תִּמְנַע מָיִם.

זְכוֹר הַנּוֹלָד בִּבְשׂוֹרַת יֻקַּח־נָא מְעַט־מַיִם בראשית יח
וְשַׂחְתָּ לְהוֹרוֹ לְשָׁחֲטוֹ לִשְׁפֹּךְ דָּמוֹ כַּמַּיִם
זִהֵר גַּם הוּא לִשְׁפֹּךְ לֵב כַּמַּיִם
חָפַר וּמָצָא בְּאֵרוֹת מָיִם.
קהל: בְּצִדְקוֹ חֹן חַשְׁרַת מָיִם.

זְכוֹר טָעַן מַקְלוֹ וְעָבַר יַרְדֵּן מַיִם
יִחֵד לֵב וְגָל אֶבֶן מִפִּי בְּאֵר מַיִם
כְּנֶאֱבַק לוֹ שַׂר בָּלוּל מֵאֵשׁ וּמִמַּיִם
לָכֵן הִבְטַחְתּוֹ הֱיוֹת עִמּוֹ בָּאֵשׁ וּבַמָּיִם.
קהל: בַּעֲבוּרוֹ אַל תִּמְנַע מָיִם.

גְּנַנְתּוֹ, הִצַּלְתּוֹ מֵאֵשׁ וּמִמַּיִם *You shielded him and rescued him from fire and water:* According to rabbinic tradition, Abraham was cast into a fiery furnace by Nimrod and was saved by God. Satan created a river to block Abraham's way on his journey to the binding of Isaac. Abraham walked undaunted into the water; when it came up to his neck, God rebuked Satan and the river vanished.

זְכוֹר Remember [Moses] who in a reed basket
was drawn out of the water.
They said: "He drew water for us, and gave the flock water."
When Your treasured people thirsted for water,
He struck the rock and out gushed water.

Cong: For his righteousness' sake grant abundant water.

זְכוֹר Remember [Aaron], chief officer of the Temple,
who immersed five times in water.
He went and washed his hands in the sanctifying water.
He called out and sprinkled blood,
purifying the people as if with water.
He kept apart from the people who were as unruly as water.

Cong: For his sake do not withhold water.

זְכוֹר Remember the twelve tribes
You brought through the divided water,
For whom You sweetened the bitterness of the water.
For Your sake their descendants' blood was spilled like water.
Turn to us, for troubles engulf our souls like water.

Cong: For their righteousness' sake grant abundant water.

Leader:

For You, Lord our God,
make the wind blow and the rain fall.

Congregation then Leader, responsively:

For blessing, and not for curse. *Cong:* Amen.
For life, and not for death. *Cong:* Amen.
For plenty, and not for scarcity. *Cong:* Amen.

The Ark is closed. The Leader continues the Repetition with "He sustains the living" on page 806. In Israel, the Leader says Half Kaddish, and the Musaf Amida is said with the addition of "He makes the wind blow and the rain fall."

---

about Moses (Ex. 2:19). עַל הַסֶּלַע הָךְ *He struck the rock:* the reference is to Exodus 17:6, shortly after the crossing of the Reed Sea (and not to the later episode, Numbers, chapter 20, when God instructed Moses to speak to the rock). טוֹבֵל חָמֵשׁ טְבִילוֹת בַּמַּיִם *Who immersed five times in water:* as part of the rites of Yom Kippur.

זְכוֹר מָשׁוּי בְּתֵבַת גֹּמֶא מִן הַמַּיִם

נָמוּ דָּלֹה דָלָה וְהִשְׁקָה צֹאן מַיִם

סְגוּלֶיךָ עֵת צָמְאוּ לַמַּיִם

עַל הַסֶּלַע הָךְ, וַיֵּצְאוּ מָיִם.

קהל: בְּצִדְקוֹ חֹן חַשְׁרַת מָיִם.

זְכוֹר פְּקִיד שָׁתוֹת, טוֹבֵל חָמֵשׁ טְבִילוֹת בַּמַּיִם

צוֹעֶה וּמַרְחִיץ כַּפָּיו בְּקִדּוּשׁ מַיִם

קוֹרֵא וּמַזֶּה טָהֳרַת מַיִם

רֻחַק מֵעַם פַּחַז כַּמָּיִם.

קהל: בַּעֲבוּרוֹ אַל תִּמְנַע מָיִם.

זְכוֹר שְׁנֵים עָשָׂר שְׁבָטִים, שֶׁהֶעֱבַרְתָּ בְּגִזְרַת מַיִם

שֶׁהִמְתַּקְתָּ לָמוֹ מְרִירוּת מַיִם

תּוֹלְדוֹתָם נִשְׁפַּךְ דָּמָם עָלֶיךָ כַּמַּיִם

תֵּפֶן, כִּי נַפְשֵׁנוּ אָפְפוּ מָיִם.

קהל: בְּצִדְקָם חֹן חַשְׁרַת מָיִם.

שליח ציבור:

שָׁאַתָּה הוּא יהוה אֱלֹהֵינוּ

מַשִּׁיב הָרוּחַ וּמוֹרִיד הַגָּשֶׁם

then קהל *,* שליח ציבור *responsively:*

לִבְרָכָה וְלֹא לִקְלָלָה   קהל: אָמֵן

לְחַיִּים וְלֹא לְמָוֶת   קהל: אָמֵן

לְשֹׂבַע וְלֹא לְרָזוֹן   קהל: אָמֵן

The ארון קודש *is closed. The* שליח ציבור *continues the* חזרת הש״ץ *with* מְכַלְכֵּל חַיִּים *on page 807. In* ארץ ישראל*, the* שליח ציבור *says* חצי קדיש*, and the* מוסף עמידה *is said with the addition of* מַשִּׁיב הָרוּחַ וּמוֹרִיד הַגֶּשֶׁם.

describes the angel with whom Jacob wrestled as "half water, half fire." נָמוּ דָּלֹה דָלָה *They said: "He drew water for us"*: the daughters of Jethro said this

Hoshanot

Hoshanot are said after the Leader's Repetition of the Amida of Musaf (and in some congregations after Hallel) on every day of Sukkot.
On weekdays, the Ark is opened, and a Torah scroll is taken to the Bima. Members of the congregation who have a Lulav and Etrog make a circuit around the Bima and say Hoshanot. Mourners do not participate in the circuit.
At the conclusion of the Hoshanot, the Torah scroll is returned to the Ark, which is then closed.
On Shabbat, turn to page 856. On Hoshana Raba, turn to page 858.

If first day of Sukkot falls on	*On first day*	*On second day*	*On third day*	*On fourth day*	*On fifth day*	*On sixth day*
Monday	For the sake of Your truth	The Foundation Stone	I shall lay out my prayer	"I am a wall," said the people	God of all salvation	A people guarded
Tuesday	For the sake of Your truth	The Foundation Stone	I shall lay out my prayer	God of all salvation	A people guarded	Lord and Savior
Thursday	For the sake of Your truth	The Foundation Stone	A people guarded	I shall lay out my prayer	God of all salvation	Lord and Savior
Shabbat	A people guarded	For the sake of Your truth	I shall lay out my prayer	The Foundation Stone	God of all salvation	Lord and Savior

Leader then Congregation:

הוֹשַׁע נָא Save us, please for Your sake, our God, save us, please.

Leader then Congregation:

Save us, please for Your sake, our Creator, save us, please.

Leader then Congregation:

Save us, please for Your sake, our Redeemer, save us, please.

Leader then Congregation:

Save us, please for Your sake, You who seek us, save us, please.

Save us, please –

לְמַעַן אֲמִתָּךְ For the sake of Your truth – for the sake of Your covenant – for the sake of Your greatness and glory – for the sake of Your Law – for the sake of Your majesty – for the sake of Your promise – for the sake of Your remembrance – for the sake of Your love – for the sake of Your goodness – for the sake of Your

הושענות

הושענות are said after the חזרת הש״ץ of the מוסף עמידה
(and in some congregations after הלל) on every day of סוכות.
On weekdays, the ארון קודש is opened, and a ספר תורה is taken to the בימה.
Members of the קהל who have a לולב and אתרוג make a circuit around the בימה and say הושענות. Mourners do not participate in the circuit.
At the conclusion of the הושענות, the ספר תורה is returned to the ארון קודש, which is then closed.
On שבת, turn to page 857. On הושענא רבה, turn to page 859.

On sixth day	*On fifth day*	*On fourth day*	*On third day*	*On second day*	*On first day*	*If first day of סוכות falls on*
אוֹם נְצוּרָה	אֵל לְמוֹשָׁעוֹת	אוֹם אֲנִי חוֹמָה	אֶעֱרֹךְ שׁוּעִי	אֶבֶן שְׁתִיָּה	לְמַעַן אֲמִתָּךְ	*Monday*
אָדוֹן הַמּוֹשִׁיעַ	אוֹם נְצוּרָה	אֵל לְמוֹשָׁעוֹת	אֶעֱרֹךְ שׁוּעִי	אֶבֶן שְׁתִיָּה	לְמַעַן אֲמִתָּךְ	*Tuesday*
אָדוֹן הַמּוֹשִׁיעַ	אֵל לְמוֹשָׁעוֹת	אֶעֱרֹךְ שׁוּעִי	אוֹם נְצוּרָה	אֶבֶן שְׁתִיָּה	לְמַעַן אֲמִתָּךְ	*Thursday*
אָדוֹן הַמּוֹשִׁיעַ	אֵל לְמוֹשָׁעוֹת	אֶבֶן שְׁתִיָּה	אֶעֱרֹךְ שׁוּעִי	לְמַעַן אֲמִתָּךְ	אוֹם נְצוּרָה	שבת

קהל then שליח ציבור:

הוֹשַׁע נָא לְמַעַנְךָ אֱלֹהֵינוּ הוֹשַׁע נָא.

קהל then שליח ציבור:

הוֹשַׁע נָא לְמַעַנְךָ בּוֹרְאֵנוּ הוֹשַׁע נָא.

קהל then שליח ציבור:

הוֹשַׁע נָא לְמַעַנְךָ גּוֹאֲלֵנוּ הוֹשַׁע נָא.

קהל then שליח ציבור:

הוֹשַׁע נָא לְמַעַנְךָ דּוֹרְשֵׁנוּ הוֹשַׁע נָא.

הוֹשַׁע נָא

לְמַעַן אֲמִתָּךְ. לְמַעַן בְּרִיתָךְ. לְמַעַן גָּדְלָךְ וְתִפְאַרְתָּךְ. לְמַעַן דָּתָךְ. לְמַעַן הוֹדָךְ. לְמַעַן וִעוּדָךְ. לְמַעַן זִכְרָךְ. לְמַעַן חַסְדָּךְ. לְמַעַן טוּבָךְ. לְמַעַן יִחוּדָךְ.

oneness – for the sake of Your honor – for the sake of Your wisdom – for the sake of Your kingship – for the sake of Your eternity – for the sake of Your mystery – for the sake of Your might – for the sake of Your splendor – for the sake of Your righteousness – for the sake of Your holiness – for the sake of Your great compassion – for the sake of Your Presence – for the sake of Your praise – Save us, please.

Continue with "I and HE: save us, please" on the next page.

Save us, please –

אֶבֶן שְׁתִיָּה The Foundation Stone – the House You chose – the threshing-floor of Ornan – the hidden Shrine – Mount Moriah – where the LORD shall be seen – Your glorious Sanctuary – where David camped – the best of Lebanon – the Beauty of Heights, Joy of all the earth – the Place of Perfect Beauty – the Lodge of goodness – the Place of Your dwelling – the Shelter of Shalem – the tribes' Pilgrimage – the precious Cornerstone – shining Zion – the Holy of Holies – [the walls] lined with love – Residence of Your glory – the Hill toward which all mouths pray – Save us, please.

Continue with "I and HE: save us, please" on the next page.

Save us, please –

אֶעֱרֹךְ שׁוּעִי I shall lay out my prayer – in the house of my prayer – I found my sin, fasting – I seek You from there, to save me – heed the sound of my prayer – and rise up to my aid – remember with compassion, my Savior – making life my delight – Beneficent One, hear my groaning – quickly, bring my savior – put an end to my accuser – that he condemn me no more – quickly, God of my salvation – make eternal my salvation – bear the iniquity of my wickedness – pass over my sin – turn to me and save me – righteous Rock, my Savior – receive, please, my prayer – raise the horn of my salvation – Almighty One, my Savior – come, show Yourself and save me – Save us, please.

Continue with "I and HE: save us, please" on the next page.

Save us, please –

אוֹם אֲנִי חוֹמָה "I am a wall," said the people – bright as the sun – exiled and reviled – fair like a date palm – killed on account of You – like sheep to the slaughter – dispersed among tormentors – wrapped in Your embrace, clinging to You – bearing Your yoke – the one to know Your Oneness – beaten down in exile – learning the awe of You – our faces scratched – given over to the violent – weighed down beneath Your burden – oppressed and in turmoil – redeemed by [Moses] Toviya – holy flock – the communities of Jacob – marked out with Your name – roaring, "Save us, please!" – leaning on You – Save us, please.

Continue with "I and HE: save us, please" on the next page.

לְמַעַן כְּבוֹדָךְ. לְמַעַן לִמּוּדָךְ. לְמַעַן מַלְכוּתָךְ. לְמַעַן נִצְחָךְ. לְמַעַן סוֹדָךְ. לְמַעַן עֻזָּךְ. לְמַעַן פְּאֵרָךְ. לְמַעַן צִדְקָתָךְ. לְמַעַן קְדֻשָּׁתָךְ. לְמַעַן רַחֲמֶיךָ הָרַבִּים. לְמַעַן שְׁכִינָתָךְ. לְמַעַן תְּהִלָּתָךְ. הוֹשַׁע נָא.

Continue with אֲנִי וָהוּ הוֹשִׁיעָה נָּא *on the next page.*

הוֹשַׁע נָא

אֶבֶן שְׁתִיָּה. בֵּית הַבְּחִירָה. גֹּרֶן אָרְנָן. דְּבִיר הַמֻּצְנָע. הַר הַמּוֹרִיָּה. וְהַר יֵרָאֶה. זְבוּל תִּפְאַרְתֶּךָ. חָנָה דָוִד. טוֹב הַלְּבָנוֹן. יְפֵה נוֹף מְשׂוֹשׂ כָּל הָאָרֶץ. כְּלִילַת יֹפִי. לִינַת הַצֶּדֶק. מָכוֹן לְשִׁבְתֶּךָ. נָוֶה שַׁאֲנָן. סֻכַּת שָׁלֵם. עֲלִיַּת שְׁבָטִים. פִּנַּת יִקְרַת. צִיּוֹן הַמְצֻיֶּנֶת. קֹדֶשׁ הַקֳּדָשִׁים. רָצוּף אַהֲבָה. שְׁכִינַת כְּבוֹדֶךָ. תֵּל תַּלְפִּיּוֹת. הוֹשַׁע נָא.

Continue with אֲנִי וָהוּ הוֹשִׁיעָה נָּא *on the next page.*

הוֹשַׁע נָא

אֶעֱרֹךְ שׁוּעִי. בְּבֵית שַׁוְעִי. גָּלִיתִי בַצּוֹם פִּשְׁעִי. דְּרַשְׁתִּיךָ בּוֹ לְהוֹשִׁיעִי. הַקְשִׁיבָה לְקוֹל שַׁוְעִי. וְקוּמָה וְהוֹשִׁיעִי. זְכֹר וְרַחֵם מוֹשִׁיעִי. חַי כֵּן תְּשַׁעַשְׁעִי. טוֹב בְּאֶנֶק שְׁעִי. יוֹחַשׁ מוֹשִׁיעִי. כַּלֵּה מַרְשִׁיעִי. לְבַל עוֹד יַרְשִׁיעִי. מַהֵר אֱלֹהֵי יִשְׁעִי. נֶצַח לְהוֹשִׁיעִי. שָׂא נָא עֲוֹן רִשְׁעִי. עֲבֹר עַל פִּשְׁעִי. פְּנֵה נָא לְהוֹשִׁיעִי. צוּר צַדִּיק מוֹשִׁיעִי. קַבֵּל נָא שַׁוְעִי. רוֹמֵם קֶרֶן יִשְׁעִי. שַׁדַּי מוֹשִׁיעִי. תּוֹפִיעַ וְתוֹשִׁיעִי. הוֹשַׁע נָא.

Continue with אֲנִי וָהוּ הוֹשִׁיעָה נָּא *on the next page.*

הוֹשַׁע נָא

אֹם אֲנִי חוֹמָה. בָּרָה כַּחַמָּה. גּוֹלָה וְסוּרָה. דָּמְתָה לְתָמָר. הַהֲרוּגָה עָלֶיךָ. וְנֶחְשֶׁבֶת כְּצֹאן טִבְחָה. זְרוּיָה בֵּין מַכְעִיסֶיהָ. חֲבוּקָה וּדְבוּקָה בָךְ. טוֹעֶנֶת עֻלָּךְ. יְחִידָה לְיַחֲדָךְ. כְּבוּשָׁה בַּגּוֹלָה. לוֹמֶדֶת יִרְאָתָךְ. מְרוּטַת לֶחִי. נְתוּנָה לְמַכִּים. סוֹבֶלֶת סִבְלָךְ. עֲנִיָּה סוֹעֲרָה. פְּדוּיַת טוֹבִיָּה. צֹאן קָדָשִׁים. קְהִלּוֹת יַעֲקֹב. רְשׁוּמִים בִּשְׁמֶךָ. שׁוֹאֲגִים הוֹשַׁע נָא. תְּמוּכִים עָלֶיךָ. הוֹשַׁע נָא.

Continue with אֲנִי וָהוּ הוֹשִׁיעָה נָּא *on the next page.*

Save us, please –

אֵל לְמוֹשָׁעוֹת God of all salvation – for keeping our four vows – we who draw close in prayer – who come knocking to lay out our prayer – who speak Your words of delight – who revel in their questions – crying out to be heard – we who watch for the Redemption – hear those who hold on to You – who understand Your calendar – who bow to You and pray – to comprehend Your message – as it comes from Your mouth – (You who give salvation) – telling their stories – making known Your testament – You who work salvation – bring a righteous [leader] for the saved – bring close our salvations – with noise, amid thundering – in three brief hours – speed us our salvation – Save us, please.

Continue with "I and HE: save us, please" below.

Save us, please –

אָדוֹן הַמּוֹשִׁיעַ LORD and Savior – there is no one else – mighty, with great power to save – when I was brought low, He saved me – God who saves – who delivers and saves – save those who cry out to You – those who yet watch for You – nourish Your young lambs – make the harvest lavish – sprout every growing thing and save us – do not condemn this valley – make the good fruits sweet and save us – carry the clouds to us – shake down the raindrops – do not hold back the clouds – You who open Your hand and satisfy – relieve those who thirst for You – save those who call to You – save those You have loved – rescue those who rise to seek You – save Your innocent ones – Save us, please.

Continue with "I and HE: save us, please" below.

I and HE: save us, please.

כְּהוֹשַׁעְתָּ As You saved the mighty ones in Lud with You
coming down for Your people's deliverance – save us, please.

As You saved nation and God together
[the people] called for God's salvation – save us, please.

As You saved the crowding hosts,
and angelic hosts along with them – save us, please.

As You saved pure ones from the grip of slavery,
Gracious One; enslaved in cruel hands – save us, please.

הוֹשַׁע נָא

אֵל לְמוֹשָׁעוֹת. בְּאַרְבַּע שְׁבוּעוֹת. גָּשִׁים בְּשַׁוְעוֹת. דּוֹפְקֵי עֶרֶךְ שׁוּעוֹת. הוֹגֵי שַׁעֲשׁוּעוֹת. וְחִידוֹת מִשְׁתַּעְשְׁעוֹת. זוֹעֲקִים לְהַשְׁעוֹת. חוֹכֵי יְשׁוּעוֹת. טְפוּלִים בְּךָ שְׁעוֹת. יוֹדְעֵי בִּין שָׁעוֹת. כּוֹרְעֶיךָ בְּשַׁוְעוֹת. לְהָבִין שְׁמוּעוֹת. מְפִּיךָ נִשְׁמָעוֹת. נוֹתֵן תְּשׁוּעוֹת. סְפוּרוֹת מַשְׁמָעוֹת. עֵדוֹת מַשְׁמִיעוֹת. פּוֹעֵל יְשׁוּעוֹת. צַדִּיק נוֹשָׁעוֹת. קִרְיַת תְּשׁוּעוֹת. רֶגֶשׁ תְּשׁוּאוֹת. שָׁלֹשׁ שָׁעוֹת. תָּחִישׁ לִתְשׁוּעוֹת. הוֹשַׁע נָא.

Continue with אֲנִי וָהוּ הוֹשִׁיעָה נָּא *below.*

הוֹשַׁע נָא

אָדוֹן הַמּוֹשִׁיעַ. בִּלְתְּךָ אֵין לְהוֹשִׁיעַ. גִּבּוֹר וְרַב לְהוֹשִׁיעַ. דַּלּוֹתִי וְלִי יְהוֹשִׁיעַ. הָאֵל הַמּוֹשִׁיעַ. וּמַצִּיל וּמוֹשִׁיעַ. זוֹעֲקֶיךָ תּוֹשִׁיעַ. חוֹכֶיךָ הוֹשִׁיעַ. טְלָאֶיךָ תַּשְׂבִּיעַ. יְבוּל לְהַשְׁפִּיעַ. כָּל שִׂיחַ תַּדְשֵׁא וְתוֹשִׁיעַ. לְגֵיא בַּל תַּרְשִׁיעַ. מְגָדִים תַּמְתִּיק וְתוֹשִׁיעַ. נְשִׂיאִים לְהַסִּיעַ. שְׂעִירִים לְהָנִיעַ. עֲנָנִים מִלְּהַמְנִיעַ. פּוֹתֵחַ יָד וּמַשְׂבִּיעַ. צְמֵאֶיךָ תַּשְׂבִּיעַ. קוֹרְאֶיךָ תּוֹשִׁיעַ. רְחוּמֶיךָ תּוֹשִׁיעַ. שׁוֹחֲרֶיךָ הוֹשִׁיעַ. תְּמִימֶיךָ תּוֹשִׁיעַ. הוֹשַׁע נָא.

Continue with אֲנִי וָהוּ הוֹשִׁיעָה נָּא *below.*

אֲנִי וָהוּ הוֹשִׁיעָה נָּא.

כְּהוֹשַׁעְתָּ אֵלִים בְּלוּד עִמָּךְ.
בְּצֵאתְךָ לְיֵשַׁע עַמָּךְ.   כֵּן הוֹשַׁע נָא.

כְּהוֹשַׁעְתָּ גּוֹי וֵאלֹהִים.
דְּרוּשִׁים לְיֵשַׁע אֱלֹהִים.   כֵּן הוֹשַׁע נָא.

כְּהוֹשַׁעְתָּ הֲמוֹן צְבָאוֹת.
וְעִמָּם מַלְאֲכֵי צְבָאוֹת.   כֵּן הוֹשַׁע נָא.

כְּהוֹשַׁעְתָּ זַכִּים מִבֵּית עֲבָדִים.
חַנּוּן בְּיָדָם מַעֲבִידִים.   כֵּן הוֹשַׁע נָא.

As You saved those submerged between slices of the deep,
and brought Your own glory through it with them – save us, please.

As You saved the stem as they sang "And God saved" –
but the Deliverer reads it "God was saved" – save us, please.

As You saved, and You said, "I took you out,"
but let it be pointed "I was taken out with You" – save us, please.

As You saved those who encompassed the Altar,
bearing their willows to encircle the Altar – save us, please.

As You saved the Ark of wonders that was wronged,
tormenting Philistia with fury, and saving it – save us, please.

As You saved the communities You sent away to Babylon,
being sent too, for them, Your compassionate Self – save us, please.

As You saved the returning exiles of the tribes of Jacob;
so come back and return the exiles of the tents of Jacob – and save us, please.

As You saved those who kept Your commandments and waited for
salvation, / God of all salvation – and save us, please.

I and HE: save us, please.

The Torah scroll is returned to the Ark.

הוֹשִׁיעָה Save Your people; bless Your legacy; tend them and carry them forever. Let these words with which I have pleaded with the LORD be close to the LORD our God day and night, that He may do justice for His servant, and justice for His people Israel, day after day; so that all the peoples of the earth will know that the LORD is God. There is no other. *Ps. 28* *1 Kings 8*

The Ark is closed. On Yom Tov the Leader continues the service with Full Kaddish on page 554; on Ḥol HaMo'ed, with Full Kaddish on page 178.

כְּהוֹשַׁעְתָּ טְבוּעִים בְּצוּל גְּזָרִים.
יְקָרְךָ עִמָּם מַעֲבִירִים. כֵּן הוֹשַׁע נָא.

כְּהוֹשַׁעְתָּ כַּנָּה מְשׁוֹרֶרֶת וַיּוֹשַׁע.
לְגוֹחָהּ מְצַיֶּנֶת וַיִּוָּשַׁע. כֵּן הוֹשַׁע נָא.

כְּהוֹשַׁעְתָּ מַאֲמָר וְהוֹצֵאתִי אֶתְכֶם.
נָקוּב וְהוּצֵאתִי אִתְּכֶם. כֵּן הוֹשַׁע נָא.

כְּהוֹשַׁעְתָּ סוֹבְבֵי מִזְבֵּחַ.
עוֹמְסֵי עֲרָבָה לְהַקִּיף מִזְבֵּחַ. כֵּן הוֹשַׁע נָא.

כְּהוֹשַׁעְתָּ פִלְאֵי אָרוֹן כְּהֻפְשַׁע.
צִעֵר פְּלֶשֶׁת בַּחֲרוֹן אַף, וְנוֹשַׁע. כֵּן הוֹשַׁע נָא.

כְּהוֹשַׁעְתָּ קְהִלּוֹת בָּבֶלָה שִׁלַּחְתָּ.
רַחוּם לְמַעֲנָם שֻׁלַּחְתָּ. כֵּן הוֹשַׁע נָא.

כְּהוֹשַׁעְתָּ שְׁבוּת שִׁבְטֵי יַעֲקֹב.
תָּשׁוּב וְתָשִׁיב שְׁבוּת אָהֳלֵי יַעֲקֹב. וְהוֹשִׁיעָה נָּא.

כְּהוֹשַׁעְתָּ שׁוֹמְרֵי מִצְוֹת וְחוֹכֵי יְשׁוּעוֹת.
אֵל לְמוֹשָׁעוֹת. וְהוֹשִׁיעָה נָּא.

אֲנִי וָהוֹ הוֹשִׁיעָה נָּא.

The ספר תורה *is returned to the* ארון קודש.

הוֹשִׁיעָה אֶת־עַמֶּךָ, וּבָרֵךְ אֶת־נַחֲלָתֶךָ, וּרְעֵם וְנַשְּׂאֵם עַד־הָעוֹלָם: תהלים כח
וְיִהְיוּ דְבָרַי אֵלֶּה, אֲשֶׁר הִתְחַנַּנְתִּי לִפְנֵי יהוה, קְרֹבִים אֶל־ מלכים א׳ ח
יהוה אֱלֹהֵינוּ יוֹמָם וָלָיְלָה, לַעֲשׂוֹת מִשְׁפַּט עַבְדּוֹ וּמִשְׁפַּט עַמּוֹ
יִשְׂרָאֵל, דְּבַר־יוֹם בְּיוֹמוֹ: לְמַעַן דַּעַת כָּל־עַמֵּי הָאָרֶץ כִּי יהוה
הוּא הָאֱלֹהִים, אֵין עוֹד:

The ארון קודש *is closed. On* יום טוב *the* שליח ציבור *continues the service with* קדיש שלם *on page 555; on* חול המועד*, with* קדיש שלם *on page 179.*

HOSHANOT FOR SHABBAT

The Ark is opened but no Torah scrolls are taken out.
The congregation does not walk around the Bima.

Leader then Congregation:

הוֹשַׁע נָא Save us, please for Your sake, our God, save us, please.

Leader then Congregation:

Save us, please for Your sake, our Creator, save us, please.

Leader then Congregation:

Save us, please for Your sake, our Redeemer, save us, please.

Leader then Congregation:

Save us, please for Your sake, You who seek us, save us, please.

Save us, please –

אֹם נְצוּרָה כְּבָבַת A people guarded like the pupil of Your eye – who understand the Law that refreshes the spirit – who learn through all the laws of the Sabbath – who unfold the rules of carrying on the Sabbath – who fix two thousand cubits as our boundary for the Sabbath – and keep our feet from breaking the Sabbath – who remember early and keep hold of the Sabbath – and speed to hasten in the Sabbath – who for six days work hard for the Sabbath – who sit patiently on before ending the Sabbath – who call her an honor, delight, our Sabbath – who change their clothes, and dress for the Sabbath – who prepare themselves feast and drink for the Sabbath – laying a spread of sweet things on the Sabbath – holding three festive meals for the Sabbath – who break bread over two loaves on the Sabbath – distinguishing four domains on the Sabbath – who light the candles for the command, for the Sabbath – who sanctify the day on the Sabbath – who speak seven blessings [in the Amida] of the Sabbath – who read seven portions of Torah on the Sabbath – bring us into what is ours, the day that will be entirely Sabbath – Save us, please.

I and HE: save us, please.

כְּהוֹשַׁעְתָּ As You saved Adam, formed in Your hands, and protected him, making the holy Sabbath his ransom, clemency – so, save us, please.

הושענות לשבת

The ארון קודש *is opened but no* ספרי תורה *are taken out. The* קהל *does not walk around the* בימה.

קהל *then* שליח ציבור:

הוֹשַׁע נָא לְמַעַנְךָ אֱלֹהֵינוּ הוֹשַׁע נָא.

קהל *then* שליח ציבור:

הוֹשַׁע נָא לְמַעַנְךָ בּוֹרְאֵנוּ הוֹשַׁע נָא.

קהל *then* שליח ציבור:

הוֹשַׁע נָא לְמַעַנְךָ גּוֹאֲלֵנוּ הוֹשַׁע נָא.

קהל *then* שליח ציבור:

הוֹשַׁע נָא לְמַעַנְךָ דּוֹרְשֵׁנוּ הוֹשַׁע נָא.

הוֹשַׁע נָא

אֹם נְצוּרָה כְּבָבַת. בּוֹנֶנֶת בְּדָת נֶפֶשׁ מְשִׁיבַת. גּוֹמֶרֶת הִלְכוֹת שַׁבָּת. דּוֹרֶשֶׁת מַשְׂאַת שַׁבָּת. הַקּוֹבַעַת אַלְפַּיִם תְּחוּם שַׁבָּת. וּמְשִׁיבַת רֶגֶל מִשַּׁבָּת. זָכוֹר וְשָׁמוֹר מְקַיֶּמֶת בַּשַּׁבָּת. חָשָׁה לְמַהֵר בִּיאַת שַׁבָּת. טוֹרַחַת כָּל מִשְׁשָׁה לַשַּׁבָּת. יוֹשֶׁבֶת וּמַמְתֶּנֶת עַד כְּלוֹת שַׁבָּת. כָּבוֹד וָעֹנֶג קוֹרְאָה לַשַּׁבָּת. לְבוּשׁ וּכְסוּת מַחֲלֶפֶת בַּשַּׁבָּת. מַאֲכָל וּמִשְׁתֶּה מְכִינָה לַשַּׁבָּת. נֹעַם מְגָדִים מְנַעֶמֶת לַשַּׁבָּת. סְעוּדוֹת שָׁלֹשׁ מְקַיֶּמֶת בַּשַּׁבָּת. עַל שְׁתֵּי כִכָּרוֹת בּוֹצַעַת בַּשַּׁבָּת. פּוֹרֶטֶת אַרְבַּע רְשֻׁיּוֹת שַׁבָּת. צִוּוּי הַדְלָקַת נֵר מַדְלֶקֶת בַּשַּׁבָּת. קִדּוּשׁ הַיּוֹם מְקַדֶּשֶׁת בַּשַּׁבָּת. רֶנֶן שֶׁבַע מְפַלֶּלֶת בַּשַּׁבָּת. שִׁבְעָה בְּדָת קוֹרְאָה בַּשַּׁבָּת. תַּנְחִילֵנָה לְיוֹם שֶׁכֻּלּוֹ שַׁבָּת. הוֹשַׁע נָא.

אֲנִי וָהוּ הוֹשִׁיעָה נָּא.

כְּהוֹשַׁעְתָּ אָדָם יְצִיר כַּפֶּיךָ לְגוֹנְנָה.

בְּשַׁבַּת קֹדֶשׁ הִמְצֵאתוֹ כֹּפֶר וַחֲנִינָה. כֵּן הוֹשַׁע נָא.

As You saved the people who remained distinct while longing for freedom –
in their thoughts already marking out the seventh day for rest –
so, save us, please.

As You saved the people You led and guided as Your flock
and gave a Law at Mara, by the still waters – so, save us, please.

As You saved those who received Your gift in the Wilderness of Sin, the camp,
who were taught and collected two-fold bread on a Friday –
so, save us, please.

As You saved those who clung to You, who learned of their own mind to
prepare for the Sabbath, / and [Moses] their shepherd blessed their
strength and concurred – so, save us, please.

As You saved those who ate [manna] stored up on [their day of] delight,
and it looked no different and its scent had not spoiled –
so, save us, please.

As You saved those who learned every law of a journey on the Sabbath,
who rested, stopped, and kept the boundaries of domain and
encampment – so, save us, please.

As You saved those who could hear the fourth commandment at Sinai:
both "Remember" and "Keep" to make the seventh day holy –
so, save us, please.

As You saved those commanded to march seven times round Jericho,
besieging her to strike until she fell on the Sabbath – so, save us, please.

As You saved Kohelet [Solomon] and his people in the eternal House,
when they came to please You for seven days and seven –
so, save us, please.

As You saved those who returned, rising up from Exile, redeemed,
as they read Your Torah on this Festival, each day – so, save us, please.

As You saved those who rejoiced for You in the second House, renewed,
in the Sanctuary where they took up the lulav all seven days –
so, save us, please.

As You saved those whose willow beating overrode the Sabbath,
who placed branches from Motza at the base of the Altar –
so, save us, please.

כְּהוֹשַׁעְתָּ גּוֹי מְצַיֵּן מְקַוִּים חֹפֶשׁ.
דֵּעָה כִּוְּנוּ לָבוּר שְׁבִיעִי לְנֹפֶשׁ. כֵּן הוֹשַׁע נָא.

כְּהוֹשַׁעְתָּ הָעָם נִהַגְתָּ כַּצֹּאן לְהַנְחוֹת.
וְחֹק שַׂמְתָּ בְּמָרָה עַל מֵי מְנוּחוֹת. כֵּן הוֹשַׁע נָא.

כְּהוֹשַׁעְתָּ זְבוּדֶיךָ בְּמִדְבַּר סִין בְּמַחֲנֶה.
חָכְמוּ וְלָקְטוּ בַּשִּׁשִּׁי לֶחֶם מִשְׁנֶה. כֵּן הוֹשַׁע נָא.

כְּהוֹשַׁעְתָּ טְפוּלֶיךָ הוֹרוּ הֲכָנָה בְּמַדָּעִם.
יִשַׁר כֹּחָם, וְהוֹדָה לָמוֹ רוֹעָם. כֵּן הוֹשַׁע נָא.

כְּהוֹשַׁעְתָּ כִּלְכַּלְתּוֹ בְּעֹנֶג מָן הַמְשֻׁמָּר.
לֹא הָפַךְ עֵינוֹ וְרֵיחוֹ לֹא נָמָר. כֵּן הוֹשַׁע נָא.

כְּהוֹשַׁעְתָּ מִשְׁפְּטֵי מַשְׂאוֹת שַׁבָּת גָּמָרוּ.
נָחוּ וְשָׁבְתוּ, רְשֻׁיּוֹת וּתְחוּמִים שָׁמָרוּ. כֵּן הוֹשַׁע נָא.

כְּהוֹשַׁעְתָּ סִינַי הָשְׁמְעוּ בְּדִבּוּר רְבִיעִי.
עִנְיַן זָכוֹר וְשָׁמוֹר לְקַדֵּשׁ שְׁבִיעִי. כֵּן הוֹשַׁע נָא.

כְּהוֹשַׁעְתָּ פְּקֻדּוּ יְרִיחוֹ שֶׁבַע לְהַקֵּף.
צָרוּ עַד רִדְתָּהּ בַּשַּׁבָּת לְתַקֵּף. כֵּן הוֹשַׁע נָא.

כְּהוֹשַׁעְתָּ קֹהֶלֶת וְעַמּוֹ בְּבֵית עוֹלָמִים.
רִצּוּךָ בְּחָגְגָם שִׁבְעָה וְשִׁבְעָה יָמִים. כֵּן הוֹשַׁע נָא.

כְּהוֹשַׁעְתָּ שָׁבִים עוֹלֵי גוֹלָה לְפִדְיוֹם.
תּוֹרָתְךָ בְּקָרְאָם בֶּחָג יוֹם יוֹם. כֵּן הוֹשַׁע נָא.

כְּהוֹשַׁעְתָּ מְשַׂמְּחֶיךָ בְּבִנְיַן שֵׁנִי הַמְחֻדָּשׁ.
נוֹטְלִין לוּלָב כָּל שִׁבְעָה בַּמִּקְדָּשׁ. כֵּן הוֹשַׁע נָא.

כְּהוֹשַׁעְתָּ חִבּוּט עֲרָבָה שַׁבָּת מַדְחִים.
מְרֻבִּיּוֹת מוֹצָא לִיסוֹד מִזְבֵּחַ מַנִּיחִים. כֵּן הוֹשַׁע נָא.

As You saved those who rejoiced with supple, long, high willows, as they parted from the place calling "Praise to you, Altar!" – so, save us, please.

As You saved those who gave thanks and who prayed and were true to their words, / all of them repeating "We are the LORD's and to Him our eyes are turned" – so, save us, please.

As You saved those circling [the Altar,] the wine-vat You carved out, with luscious willows, / as they sang out, "I and HE: save us, please" – so, save us, please.

As You saved the eager legion [of priests], hastening to serve on the day of rest, / bringing a double Sabbath offering, burnt-offering and meal-offering – so, save us, please.

As You saved Your Levites, making them many on their platform, singing "A psalm. A song for the Sabbath day" – so, save us, please.

As You saved those You comforted, always delighting in Your commands, and desired and delivered them, bringing them safe to respite and peace – so, save us, please.

As You saved the returning exiles of the tribes of Jacob, so come back and return the exiles of the tents of Jacob – and save us, please.

As You saved those who kept Your commandments and waited for salvation, God of all salvation – and save us, please.

I and HE: save us, please.

הוֹשִׁיעָה Save Your people; bless Your legacy; tend them and carry them forever. Let these words with which I have pleaded with the LORD be close to the LORD our God day and night, that He may do justice for His servant, and justice for His people Israel, day after day; so that all the peoples of the earth will know that the LORD is God. There is no other. *Ps. 28* *1 Kings 8*

The Ark is closed and the Leader continues the service with Full Kaddish on page 554.

כְּהוֹשַׁעְתָּ בְּרֻכּוֹת וַאֲרֻכּוֹת וּגְבוֹהוֹת מְעֻלָּסִים.
בְּפַטִּירָתָן יֹפִי לְךָ מִזְבֵּחַ מְקַלְּסִים. כֵּן הוֹשַׁע נָא.

כְּהוֹשַׁעְתָּ מוֹדִים וּמְיַחֲלִים וְלֹא מְשַׁנִּים.
כֻּלָּנוּ אָנוּ לְיָהּ וְעֵינֵינוּ לְיָהּ שׁוֹנִים. כֵּן הוֹשַׁע נָא.

כְּהוֹשַׁעְתָּ יֶקֶב מֵחֲצֵבֶיךָ סוֹבְבִים בִּרְנָנָה.
רוֹנְנִים אֲנִי וָהוֹ הוֹשִׁיעָה נָּא. כֵּן הוֹשַׁע נָא.

כְּהוֹשַׁעְתָּ חֵיל זְרִיזִים מְשָׁרְתִים בִּמְנוּחָה.
קָרְבַּן שַׁבָּת כָּפוּל, עוֹלָה וּמִנְחָה. כֵּן הוֹשַׁע נָא.

כְּהוֹשַׁעְתָּ לְוִיֶּיךָ עַל דּוּכָנָם לְהַרְבַּת.
אוֹמְרִים מִזְמוֹר שִׁיר לְיוֹם הַשַּׁבָּת. כֵּן הוֹשַׁע נָא.

כְּהוֹשַׁעְתָּ נְחוּמֶיךָ בְּמִצְוֹתֶיךָ תָּמִיד יִשְׁתַּעַשְׁעוּן.
וּרְצֵם וְהַחֲלִיצֵם בְּשׁוּבָה וָנַחַת יִוָּשֵׁעוּן. כֵּן הוֹשַׁע נָא.

כְּהוֹשַׁעְתָּ שְׁבוּת שִׁבְטֵי יַעֲקֹב.
תָּשׁוּב וְתָשִׁיב שְׁבוּת אָהֳלֵי יַעֲקֹב. וְהוֹשִׁיעָה נָּא.

כְּהוֹשַׁעְתָּ שׁוֹמְרֵי מִצְוֹת וְחוֹכֵי יְשׁוּעוֹת.
אֵל לְמוֹשָׁעוֹת. וְהוֹשִׁיעָה נָּא.

אֲנִי וָהוֹ הוֹשִׁיעָה נָּא.

תהלים כח הוֹשִׁיעָה אֶת־עַמֶּךָ, וּבָרֵךְ אֶת־נַחֲלָתֶךָ, וּרְעֵם וְנַשְּׂאֵם עַד־הָעוֹלָם:
מלכים א׳ ח וְיִהְיוּ דְבָרַי אֵלֶּה, אֲשֶׁר הִתְחַנַּנְתִּי לִפְנֵי יהוה, קְרֹבִים אֶל־
יהוה אֱלֹהֵינוּ יוֹמָם וָלָיְלָה, לַעֲשׂוֹת מִשְׁפַּט עַבְדּוֹ וּמִשְׁפַּט עַמּוֹ
יִשְׂרָאֵל, דְּבַר־יוֹם בְּיוֹמוֹ: לְמַעַן דַּעַת כָּל־עַמֵּי הָאָרֶץ כִּי יהוה
הוּא הָאֱלֹהִים, אֵין עוֹד:

The ארון קודש *is closed and the* שליח ציבור *continues the service with* קדיש שלם *on page 555.*

HOSHANOT FOR HOSHANA RABA

It is the custom to leave the Ark open until the end of the Hoshanot. All of the Torah scrolls are held on the Bima. Members of the congregation who have a Lulav and Etrog circle the Bima seven times while the Hoshanot are read. After finishing the first circuit, say "For I said" and immediately proceed to make another circuit, saying "The Foundation Stone," etc.

Leader then Congregation:

הוֹשַׁע נָא Save us, please   for Your sake, our God,   save us, please.

Leader then Congregation:

Save us, please   for Your sake, our Creator,   save us, please.

Leader then Congregation:

Save us, please   for Your sake, our Redeemer,   save us, please.

Leader then Congregation:

Save us, please   for Your sake, You who seek us,   save us, please.

Save us, please –

First Hakafa:

לְמַעַן אֲמִתָּךְ For the sake of Your truth – for the sake of Your covenant – for the sake of Your greatness and glory – for the sake of Your Law – for the sake of Your majesty – for the sake of Your promise – for the sake of Your remembrance – for the sake of Your love – for the sake of Your goodness – for the sake of Your oneness – for the sake of Your honor – for the sake of Your wisdom – for the sake of Your kingship – for the sake of Your eternity – for the sake of Your mystery – for the sake of Your might – for the sake of Your splendor – for the sake of Your righteousness – for the sake of Your holiness – for the sake of Your great compassion – for the sake of Your Presence – for the sake of Your praise – Save us, please.

After circling the Bima the first time, say:

For I said, the world is built by loving-kindness. *Ps. 89*

Save us, please –

Second Hakafa:

אֶבֶן שְׁתִיָּה The Foundation Stone – the House You chose – the threshing-floor of Ornan – the hidden Shrine – Mount Moriah – where the Lord shall be seen – Your glorious Sanctuary – where David camped – the best of

הושענות להושענא רבה

It is the custom to leave the ארון קודש open until the end of the הושענות.
All of the ספרי תורה are held on the בימה. Members of the קהל who have a לולב and אתרוג circle the בימה seven times while the הושענות are read. After finishing the first circuit, say כִּי־אָמַרְתִּי *and immediately proceed to make another circuit, saying* אֶבֶן שְׁתִיָּה*, etc.*

קהל then שליח ציבור:

הוֹשַׁע נָא   לְמַעַנְךָ אֱלֹהֵינוּ   הוֹשַׁע נָא.

קהל then שליח ציבור:

הוֹשַׁע נָא   לְמַעַנְךָ בּוֹרְאֵנוּ   הוֹשַׁע נָא.

קהל then שליח ציבור:

הוֹשַׁע נָא   לְמַעַנְךָ גּוֹאֲלֵנוּ   הוֹשַׁע נָא.

קהל then שליח ציבור:

הוֹשַׁע נָא   לְמַעַנְךָ דּוֹרְשֵׁנוּ   הוֹשַׁע נָא.

הוֹשַׁע נָא

First הקפה:

לְמַעַן אֲמִתָּךְ. לְמַעַן בְּרִיתָךְ. לְמַעַן גָּדְלָךְ וְתִפְאַרְתָּךְ. לְמַעַן דָּתָךְ. לְמַעַן הוֹדָךְ. לְמַעַן וִעוּדָךְ. לְמַעַן זִכְרָךְ. לְמַעַן חַסְדָּךְ. לְמַעַן טוּבָךְ. לְמַעַן יִחוּדָךְ. לְמַעַן כְּבוֹדָךְ. לְמַעַן לִמּוּדָךְ. לְמַעַן מַלְכוּתָךְ. לְמַעַן נִצְחָךְ. לְמַעַן סוֹדָךְ. לְמַעַן עֻזָּךְ. לְמַעַן פְּאֵרָךְ. לְמַעַן צִדְקָתָךְ. לְמַעַן קְדֻשָּׁתָךְ. לְמַעַן רַחֲמֶיךָ הָרַבִּים. לְמַעַן שְׁכִינָתָךְ. לְמַעַן תְּהִלָּתָךְ. הוֹשַׁע נָא.

After circling the בימה the first time, say:

כִּי־אָמַרְתִּי עוֹלָם חֶסֶד יִבָּנֶה: תהלים פט

הוֹשַׁע נָא

Second הקפה:

אֶבֶן שְׁתִיָּה. בֵּית הַבְּחִירָה. גֹּרֶן אָרְנָן. דְּבִיר הַמֻּצְנָע. הַר הַמּוֹרִיָּה. וְהַר יֵרָאֶה. זְבוּל תִּפְאַרְתֶּךָ. חָנָה דָוִד. טוֹב הַלְּבָנוֹן. יְפֵה נוֹף מְשׂוֹשׂ כָּל

Lebanon – the Beauty of Heights, Joy of all the earth – the Place of Perfect Beauty – the Lodge of goodness – the Place of Your dwelling – the Shelter of Shalem – the tribes' Pilgrimage – the precious Cornerstone – shining Zion – the Holy of Holies – [the walls] lined with love – Residence of Your glory – the Hill toward which all mouths pray – Save us, please.

After circling the Bima the second time, say:

A strong arm is Yours, might is Yours; Ps. 89
Your hand holds its power, Your right hand raised.

Save us, please –

Third Hakafa:

אֹם אֲנִי חוֹמָה "I am a wall," said the people – bright as the sun – exiled and reviled – fair like a date palm – killed on account of You – like sheep to the slaughter – dispersed among tormentors – wrapped in Your embrace, clinging to You – bearing Your yoke – the one to know Your Oneness – beaten down in exile – learning the awe of You – our faces scratched – given over to the violent – weighed down beneath Your burden – oppressed and in turmoil – redeemed by [Moses] Toviya – holy flock – the communities of Jacob – marked out with Your name – roaring, "Save us, please!" – leaning on You – Save us, please.

After circling the Bima the third time, say:

Grant truth to Jacob, Micah 7
loving-kindness to Abraham.

Save us, please –

Fourth Hakafa:

אָדוֹן הַמּוֹשִׁיעַ Lord and Savior – there is no one else – mighty, with great power to save – when I was brought low, He saved me – God who saves – who delivers and saves – save those who cry out to You – those who yet watch for You – nourish Your young lambs – make the harvest lavish – sprout every growing thing and save us – do not condemn this valley – make the good fruits sweet and save us – carry the clouds to us – shake down the raindrops – do not hold back the clouds – You who open Your hand and satisfy – relieve those who thirst for You – save those who call to You – save those You have loved – rescue those who rise to seek You – save Your innocent ones – Save us, please.

After circling the Bima the fourth time, say:

At Your hand, bliss for evermore. Ps. 16

הָאָרֶץ. כְּלִילַת יֹפִי. לִינַת הַצֶּדֶק. מָכוֹן לְשִׁבְתֶּךָ. נָוֶה שַׁאֲנָן. סֻכַּת שָׁלֵם. עֲלִיַּת שְׁבָטִים. פִּנַּת יִקְרַת. צִיּוֹן הַמְצֻיֶּנֶת. קֹדֶשׁ הַקֳּדָשִׁים. רָצוּף אַהֲבָה. שְׁכִינַת כְּבוֹדֶךָ. תֵּל תַּלְפִּיּוֹת. הוֹשַׁע נָא.

After circling the בימה *the second time, say:*

תהלים פט לְךָ זְרוֹעַ עִם־גְּבוּרָה, תָּעֹז יָדְךָ תָּרוּם יְמִינֶךָ:

הוֹשַׁע נָא

Third הקפה:

אֹם אֲנִי חוֹמָה. בָּרָה כַּחַמָּה. גּוֹלָה וְסוּרָה. דָּמְתָה לְתָמָר. הַהֲרוּגָה עָלֶיךָ. וְנֶחְשֶׁבֶת כְּצֹאן טִבְחָה. זְרוּיָה בֵּין מַכְעִיסֶיהָ. חֲבוּקָה וּדְבוּקָה בָּךְ. טוֹעֶנֶת עֻלָּךְ. יְחִידָה לְיַחֲדָךְ. כְּבוּשָׁה בַּגּוֹלָה. לוֹמֶדֶת יִרְאָתָךְ. מְרוּטַת לֶחִי. נְתוּנָה לְמַכִּים. סוֹבֶלֶת סִבְלָךְ. עֲנִיָּה סוֹעֲרָה. פְּדוּיַת טוֹבִיָּה. צֹאן קָדָשִׁים. קְהִלּוֹת יַעֲקֹב. רְשׁוּמִים בִּשְׁמֶךָ. שׁוֹאֲגִים הוֹשַׁע נָא. תְּמוּכִים עָלֶיךָ. הוֹשַׁע נָא.

After circling the בימה *the third time, say:*

מיכה ז תִּתֵּן אֱמֶת לְיַעֲקֹב, חֶסֶד לְאַבְרָהָם:

הוֹשַׁע נָא

Fourth הקפה:

אָדוֹן הַמּוֹשִׁיעַ. בִּלְתְּךָ אֵין לְהוֹשִׁיעַ. גִּבּוֹר וְרַב לְהוֹשִׁיעַ. דַּלּוֹתִי וְלִי יְהוֹשִׁיעַ. הָאֵל הַמּוֹשִׁיעַ. וּמַצִּיל וּמוֹשִׁיעַ. זוֹעֲקֶיךָ תּוֹשִׁיעַ. חוֹכֶיךָ הוֹשִׁיעַ. טְלָאֶיךָ תַּשְׂבִּיעַ. יְבוּל לְהַשְׁפִּיעַ. כָּל שִׂיחַ תַּדְשֵׁא וְתוֹשִׁיעַ. לְגִיא בַּל תַּרְשִׁיעַ. מְגָדִים תַּמְתִּיק וְתוֹשִׁיעַ. נְשִׂיאִים לְהַסִּיעַ. שְׂעִירִים לְהָנִיעַ. עֲנָנִים מִלְּהַמְנִיעַ. פּוֹתֵחַ יָד וּמַשְׂבִּיעַ. צְמֵאֶיךָ תַּשְׂבִּיעַ. קוֹרְאֶיךָ תּוֹשִׁיעַ. רְחוּמֶיךָ תּוֹשִׁיעַ. שׁוֹחֲרֶיךָ הוֹשִׁיעַ. תְּמִימֶיךָ תּוֹשִׁיעַ. הוֹשַׁע נָא.

After circling the בימה *the fourth time, say:*

תהלים טז נְעִמוֹת בִּימִינְךָ נֶצַח:

Save us, please –

Fifth Hakafa:

אָדָם וּבְהֵמָה Man and beast – body, spirit and soul – muscle, bone, skin – likeness and image woven – glory reduced to mere breath – likened to beasts that fall silent – light and beauty and stature – renew the face of the land – planting trees on desolate ground – winepress and bounty of meadows – vineyard and sycamore fig – bring to the land renowned – mighty rain to scent spices – to recover a devastated place – to raise up the shrub – to make the delightful fruits robust – to make the land glorious with flowers – to soak the plants with rain – to make cool waters flow – to fill out the raindrops – to raise up the earth – the earth that is hung over nothingness – Save us, please.

After circling the Bima the fifth time, say:

LORD our Master, how majestic is Your name throughout the earth, *Ps. 8*
Your glory over all the heavens.

Save us, please –

Sixth Hakafa:

אֲדָמָה מֵאֵרֶר Save earth from cursedness – save cattle from miscarriage – save threshing floor from pest – save grain from burning – save wealth from want – save sustenance from terror – save olive from windfall – save wheat from grasshopper – save food from vermin – save wine-vat from maggot – save vineyard from worm – save late harvest from locust – save bounty from crickets – save souls from horror – save abundance from insects – save herds from infirmity – save fruits from the gales – save flocks from destruction – save crops from the curse – save plenty from poverty – save the wheat-ears from leanness – save produce from pestilence – Save us, please.

After circling the Bima the sixth time, say:

The LORD is righteous in all His ways, *Ps. 145*
and kind in all He does.

Save us, please –

Seventh Hakafa:

לְמַעַן אֵיתָן For the sake of steadfast [Abraham], who was thrown into flames of fire –
for the sake of his son [Isaac] who was bound on the wood of the fire –
for the sake of the mighty [Jacob] who struggled with a prince of fire –
for the sake of the flags [of the tribes] You led in light and a cloud of fire –

הוֹשַׁע נָא

Fifth הקפה:

אָדָם וּבְהֵמָה. בָּשָׂר וְרוּחַ וּנְשָׁמָה. גִּיד וְעֶצֶם וְקָרְמָה. דְּמוּת וְצֶלֶם וְרִקְמָה. הוֹד לַהֶבֶל דָּמָה. וְנִמְשַׁל כַּבְּהֵמוֹת נִדְמָה. זִיו וְתֹאַר וְקוֹמָה. חִדּוּשׁ פְּנֵי אֲדָמָה. טִיעַת עֲצֵי נְשַׁמָּה. יְקָבִים וְקָמָה. כְּרָמִים וְשִׁקְמָה. לְתֵבֵל הַמְסֻיָּמָה. מְטָרוֹת עֹז לְסַמְּמָה. נְשִׁיָּה לְקַיְּמָה. שִׂיחִים לְקוֹמְמָה. עֲדָנִים לְעָצְמָה. פְּרָחִים לְהַעֲצִימָה. צְמָחִים לְגַשְּׁמָה. קָרִים לְזָרְמָה. רְבִיבִים לְשַׁלְּמָה. שְׁתִיָּה לְרוֹמְמָה. תְּלוּיָה עַל בְּלִימָה. הוֹשַׁע נָא.

After circling the בימה *the fifth time, say:*

יְהוָה אֲדֹנֵינוּ מָה־אַדִּיר שִׁמְךָ בְּכָל־הָאָרֶץ תהלים ח
אֲשֶׁר־תְּנָה הוֹדְךָ עַל־הַשָּׁמָיִם:

הוֹשַׁע נָא

Sixth הקפה:

אֲדָמָה מֵאֶרֶר. בְּהֵמָה מִמְּשַׁכֶּלֶת. גֹּרֶן מִגָּזָם. דָּגָן מִדַּלֶּקֶת. הוֹן מִמְּאֵרָה. וָאֹכֶל מִמְּהוּמָה. זַיִת מִנֶּשֶׁל. חִטָּה מֵחָגָב. טֶרֶף מִגּוֹבַי. יֶקֶב מִיֶּלֶק. כֶּרֶם מִתּוֹלַעַת. לֶקֶשׁ מֵאַרְבֶּה. מֶגֶד מִצְּלָצַל. נֶפֶשׁ מִבֶּהָלָה. שֹׂבַע מִסָּלְעָם. עֲדָרִים מִדַּלּוּת. פֵּרוֹת מִשִּׁדָּפוֹן. צֹאן מִצְּמִיתוּת. קָצִיר מִקְּלָלָה. רֹב מֵרָזוֹן. שִׁבֹּלֶת מִצִּנָּמוֹן. תְּבוּאָה מֵחָסִיל. הוֹשַׁע נָא.

After circling the בימה *the sixth time, say:*

צַדִּיק יְהוָה בְּכָל־דְּרָכָיו, וְחָסִיד בְּכָל־מַעֲשָׂיו: תהלים קמה

הוֹשַׁע נָא

Seventh הקפה:

לְמַעַן אֵיתָן הַנִּזְרָק בְּלַהַב אֵשׁ.
לְמַעַן בֵּן הַנֶּעֱקַד עַל עֵצִים וָאֵשׁ.
לְמַעַן גִּבּוֹר הַנֶּאֱבַק עִם שַׂר אֵשׁ.
לְמַעַן דְּגָלִים נָחִיתָ בְּאוֹר וַעֲנַן אֵשׁ.

for the sake of one who was raised up to the heights and rose, like an angel of fire –
for the sake of one who is to You like a deputy among erelim of fire –
for the sake of the gift of commandments made in fire –
for the sake of the curtained Tent [of Meeting] and its cloud of fire –
for the sake of that scene on the mountain, of Your coming down to it in fire –
for the sake of the loveliness of that House You preferred above heavens of fire –
for the sake of [Moses] who yearned until the dying of the fire –
for the sake of [Aaron] who took a fire pan to quell a rage of fire –
for the sake of [Pinehas] who burned with a great jealousy, Your fire –
for the sake of [Joshua] who raised his hand and brought down stones of fire –
for the sake of [Samuel] who burned a milk lamb wholly in the fire –
for the sake of [David] who stood in the threshing floor and found favor again through fire –
for the sake of [Solomon] who spoke in the Courtyard and down came fire –
for the sake of Your messenger [Elijah] who rose and was raised up in a chariot with horses of fire –
for the sake of [Hananiah, Mishael and Azariah,] the holy ones flung into fire –
for the sake of [Daniel] who saw the thousands of myriad [angels], the rivers of fire –
for the sake of the desolate remains of Your city burnt up by fire –
for the sake of the past of these clans of Judah whom You shall make as a basin of fire – Save us, please.

After circling the Bima the seventh time, say:

לְךָ Yours, LORD, are the greatness and the power, *1 Chr. 29*
the glory and the majesty and splendor,
for everything in heaven and earth is Yours.
Yours, LORD, is the kingdom; You are exalted as head over all.
Then the LORD shall be King over all the earth; *Zech. 14*
on that day the LORD shall be One and His name One.
And in Your Torah it is written:
Listen, Israel: the LORD is our God, the LORD is One. *Deut. 6*
Blessed be the name of His glorious kingdom for ever and all time.

לְמַעַן הָעֲלָה לַמָּרוֹם, וְנִתְעַלָּה כְּמַלְאֲכֵי אֵשׁ.
לְמַעַן וְהוּא לְךָ כְּסָגָן בְּאֶרְאֶלֵּי אֵשׁ.
לְמַעַן זֶבֶד הַדִּבְּרוֹת הַנְּתוּנוֹת מֵאֵשׁ.
לְמַעַן חִפּוּי יְרִיעוֹת וַעֲנַן אֵשׁ.
לְמַעַן טֶכֶס הַר יָרַדְתָּ עָלָיו בָּאֵשׁ.
לְמַעַן יְדִידוּת בַּיִת אֲשֶׁר אָהַבְתָּ מִשְּׁמֵי אֵשׁ.
לְמַעַן כָּמַהּ עַד שָׁקְעָה הָאֵשׁ.
לְמַעַן לָקַח מַחְתַּת אֵשׁ וְהֵסִיר חֲרוֹן אֵשׁ.
לְמַעַן מְקַנֵּא קִנְאָה גְדוֹלָה בָּאֵשׁ.
לְמַעַן נָף יָדוֹ וְיָרְדוּ אַבְנֵי אֵשׁ.
לְמַעַן שָׂם טְלֵה חָלָב כְּלִיל אֵשׁ.
לְמַעַן עָמַד בַּגֹּרֶן וְנִתְרַצָּה בָאֵשׁ.
לְמַעַן פִּלֵּל בָּעֲזָרָה וְיָרְדָה הָאֵשׁ.
לְמַעַן צִיר עָלָה וְנִתְעַלָּה בְּרֶכֶב וְסוּסֵי אֵשׁ.
לְמַעַן קְדוֹשִׁים מֻשְׁלָכִים בָּאֵשׁ.
לְמַעַן רִבּוֹ רִבְבָן חָזוּ וְנַהֲרֵי אֵשׁ.
לְמַעַן שְׁמָמוֹת עִירְךָ הַשְּׂרוּפָה בָאֵשׁ.
לְמַעַן תּוֹלְדוֹת אַלּוּפֵי יְהוּדָה, תָּשִׂים כְּכִיּוֹר אֵשׁ. הוֹשַׁע נָא.

After circling the בימה *the seventh time, say:*

לְךָ יהוה הַגְּדֻלָּה וְהַגְּבוּרָה וְהַתִּפְאֶרֶת וְהַנֵּצַח וְהַהוֹד — דברי הימים א׳ כט
כִּי־כֹל בַּשָּׁמַיִם וּבָאָרֶץ
לְךָ יהוה הַמַּמְלָכָה וְהַמִּתְנַשֵּׂא לְכֹל לְרֹאשׁ:
וְהָיָה יהוה לְמֶלֶךְ עַל־כָּל־הָאָרֶץ — זכריה יד
בַּיּוֹם הַהוּא יִהְיֶה יהוה אֶחָד וּשְׁמוֹ אֶחָד:
וּבְתוֹרָתְךָ כָּתוּב לֵאמֹר: שְׁמַע יִשְׂרָאֵל, יהוה אֱלֹהֵינוּ, יהוה אֶחָד: — דברים ו
בָּרוּךְ שֵׁם כְּבוֹד מַלְכוּתוֹ לְעוֹלָם וָעֶד.

I and HE: save us, please.

כְּהוֹשַׁעְתָּ As You saved the mighty ones in Lud with You
coming down for Your people's deliverance – save us, please.

As You saved nation and God together
[the people] called for God's salvation – save us, please.

As You saved the crowding hosts,
and angelic hosts along with them – save us, please.

As You saved pure ones from the grip of slavery,
Gracious One; enslaved in cruel hands – save us, please.

As You saved those submerged between slices of the deep,
and brought Your own glory through it with them – save us, please.

As You saved the stem as they sang "And God saved" –
but the Deliverer reads it "God was saved" – save us, please.

As You saved, and You said, "I took you out,"
but let it be pointed "I was taken out with You" – save us, please.

As You saved those who encompassed the Altar,
bearing their willows to encircle the Altar – save us, please.

As You saved the Ark of wonders that was wronged,
tormenting Philistia with fury, and saving it – save us, please.

As You saved the communities You sent away to Babylon,
being sent too, for them, Your compassionate Self – save us, please.

As You saved the returning exiles of the tribes of Jacob;
so come back and return the exiles of the tents of Jacob –
and save us, please.

As You saved those who kept Your commandments and waited for
salvation, / God of all salvation – and save us, please.

אֲנִי וָהוּ הוֹשִׁיעָה נָּא.

כְּהוֹשַׁעְתָּ אֵלִים בְּלוּד עִמָּךְ.
בְּצֵאתְךָ לְיֵשַׁע עַמָּךְ. כֵּן הוֹשַׁע נָא.
כְּהוֹשַׁעְתָּ גּוֹי וֵאלֹהִים.
דְּרוּשִׁים לְיֵשַׁע אֱלֹהִים. כֵּן הוֹשַׁע נָא.
כְּהוֹשַׁעְתָּ הֲמוֹן צְבָאוֹת.
וְעִמָּם מַלְאֲכֵי צְבָאוֹת. כֵּן הוֹשַׁע נָא.
כְּהוֹשַׁעְתָּ זַכִּים מִבֵּית עֲבָדִים.
חַנּוּן בְּיָדָם מַעֲבִידִים. כֵּן הוֹשַׁע נָא.
כְּהוֹשַׁעְתָּ טְבוּעִים בְּצוּל גְּזָרִים.
יְקָרְךָ עִמָּם מַעֲבִירִים. כֵּן הוֹשַׁע נָא.
כְּהוֹשַׁעְתָּ כַּנָּה מְשׁוֹרֶרֶת וַיּוֹשַׁע.
לְגוֹחָהּ מְצֻיֶּנֶת וַיִּוָּשַׁע. כֵּן הוֹשַׁע נָא.
כְּהוֹשַׁעְתָּ מַאֲמָר וְהוֹצֵאתִי אֶתְכֶם.
נָקוּב וְהוּצֵאתִי אִתְּכֶם. כֵּן הוֹשַׁע נָא.
כְּהוֹשַׁעְתָּ סוֹבְבֵי מִזְבֵּחַ.
עוֹמְסֵי עֲרָבָה לְהַקִּיף מִזְבֵּחַ. כֵּן הוֹשַׁע נָא.
כְּהוֹשַׁעְתָּ פִּלְאֵי אָרוֹן כְּהֻפְשַׁע.
צִעֵר פְּלֶשֶׁת בַּחֲרוֹן אַף, וְנוֹשַׁע. כֵּן הוֹשַׁע נָא.
כְּהוֹשַׁעְתָּ קְהִלּוֹת בָּבֶלָה שִׁלַּחְתָּ.
רַחוּם לְמַעֲנָם שֻׁלַּחְתָּ. כֵּן הוֹשַׁע נָא.
כְּהוֹשַׁעְתָּ שְׁבוּת שִׁבְטֵי יַעֲקֹב.
תָּשׁוּב וְתָשִׁיב שְׁבוּת אָהֳלֵי יַעֲקֹב. וְהוֹשִׁיעָה נָּא.
כְּהוֹשַׁעְתָּ שׁוֹמְרֵי מִצְוֹת וְחוֹכֵי יְשׁוּעוֹת.
אֵל לְמוֹשָׁעוֹת. וְהוֹשִׁיעָה נָּא.

I and HE: save us, please.

תְּתְּנֵנוּ לְשֵׁם Grant us name and honor / return us to our home, our land / raise us up, up above / gather us to the House of prayer / plant us as a tree on streams of water / redeem us from infection and illness / crown us with bridal love / have us rejoice in the House of prayer / lead us beside the still waters forever / fill us with wisdom and insight / clothe us with strength and dignity / crown us with the finest crown / guide us straight along a paved avenue / set us down upon a straight pathway / grace us with compassion and mercy / remember us, "Who is this rising?" / save us, to the end, to Redemption / have us glow with the splendor of the crowd / bind us about You like a loincloth girt / make us greater with Your great hand / bring us to Your House in song, in jubilation / make us majestic with salvation and joy / strengthen us in Your relief and rescue / sweep our hearts up in the building of Your city anew / awaken us to Zion in her completion / grant us the honor to see the city rebuilt on its hill / set us down to pasture in happiness and joy / strengthen us, God of Jacob, always –

Save us, please.

Leader then congregation:

Please: save us, please.

אָנָּא Please – listen to the plea of those who hunger for your rescue
as they bring willows of the stream to delight You –
and save us, please.

Please – redeem this stem You planted,
as You sweep away Duma – sun and save us, please.

Please – look to the covenant You have sealed in us,
as You destroy the dark places of this earth–
and save us, please.

אֲנִי וָהוֹ הוֹשִׁיעָה נָּא.

תְּתְנֵנוּ לְשֵׁם וְלִתְהִלָּה. תְּחָנֵנוּ בְּרַחֲמִים וּבְחֶמְלָה.
תְּשִׁיבֵנוּ אֶל הַחֶבֶל וְאֶל הַנַּחֲלָה. תְּזַכִּירֵנוּ בְּמִי זֹאת עוֹלָה.
תְּרוֹמְמֵנוּ לְמַעְלָה לְמַעְלָה. תּוֹשִׁיעֵנוּ לְקֵץ הַגְּאֻלָּה.
תְּקַבְּצֵנוּ לְבֵית הַתְּפִלָּה. תְּהַדְּרֵנוּ בְּזִיו הַמִּלָּה.
תְּצִיבֵנוּ כְּעֵץ עַל פַּלְגֵי מַיִם שְׁתוּלָה. תַּדְבִּיקֵנוּ כְּאֵזוֹר חֲתוּלָה.
תִּפְדֵּנוּ מִכָּל נֶגַע וּמַחֲלָה. תְּגַדְּלֵנוּ בְּיָד הַגְּדוֹלָה.
תְּעַטְּרֵנוּ בְּאַהֲבָה כְלוּלָה. תְּבִיאֵנוּ לְבֵיתְךָ בְּרִנָּה וְצָהֳלָה.
תְּשַׂמְּחֵנוּ בְּבֵית הַתְּפִלָּה. תְּאַדְּרֵנוּ בְּיֶשַׁע וְגִילָה.
תְּנַהֲלֵנוּ עַל מֵי מְנוּחוֹת סֶלָה. תְּאַמְּצֵנוּ בְּרֶוַח וְהַצָּלָה.
תְּמַלְּאֵנוּ חָכְמָה וְשִׂכְלָה. תְּלַבְּבֵנוּ בְּבִנְיַן עִירְךָ כְּבַתְּחִלָּה.
תַּלְבִּישֵׁנוּ עֹז וּגְדֻלָּה. תְּעוֹרְרֵנוּ לְצִיּוֹן בְּשִׁכְלוּלָהּ.
תַּכְתִּירֵנוּ בְּכֶתֶר כְּלוּלָה. תְּזַכֵּנוּ בְּנִבְנְתָה הָעִיר עַל תִּלָּהּ.
תְּיַשְּׁרֵנוּ בְּאֹרַח סְלוּלָה. תַּרְבִּיצֵנוּ בְּשָׂשׂוֹן וְגִילָה.
תִּטָּעֵנוּ בְּיֹשֶׁר מְסִלָּה. תְּחַזְּקֵנוּ אֱלֹהֵי יַעֲקֹב סֶלָה.

הוֹשַׁע נָא.

then שליח ציבור :קהל

אָנָּא, הוֹשִׁיעָה נָּא.

אָנָּא אֱזֹן חִין תְּאֵבֵי יִשְׁעָךְ.
בְּעַרְבֵי נַחַל לְשַׁעְשְׁעָךְ. וְהוֹשִׁיעָה נָּא.
אָנָּא גְּאַל כַּנַּת נִטְעָךְ.
דּוּמָה בְּטַאטְאָךְ. וְהוֹשִׁיעָה נָּא.
אָנָּא הַבֵּט לַבְּרִית טִבְעָךְ.
וּמַחְשַׁכֵּי אֶרֶץ בְּהַטְבִּיעָךְ. וְהוֹשִׁיעָה נָּא.

Please – remember for our sake our father] Abraham [who knew You,
as You make Your love known to] the others–
and save us, please.

Please – as You perform miracles for the pure of heart,
make it known that these are Your own wonders –
and save us, please.

Please – You whose strength is immense, grant us Your salvation
as You swore to our forefathers – and save us, please.

Please – answer the wishes of the people who entreat You
like the prayer of [Isaac] bound on the Mountain of
Myrrh – and save us, please.

Please – strengthen [Israel,] the tamarisks You planted
as You push aside oppressors – and save us, please.

Please – open for us Your treasuries of rain,
as from them You water arid land – and save us, please.

Please – when You shake the earth, lead those who call on You
to pasture in the best of Your meadows –
and save us, please.

Please – lift the gates of Your [House] from their destruction,
as You raise the ruins each mouth prays towards –
and save us, please.

Leader then congregation:

Please; God, please; save, please; save us, please

אֵל נָא God, please; we have gone astray like lost sheep;
do not erase our name from Your book save, please; save us, please.

God, please; tend the flock destined to slaughter,
raged against, killed in Your name save, please; save us, please.

God, please; Your flock, the flock You tend,
Your creation, Your beloved save, please; save us, please.

אָנָּא זְכָר לָנוּ אָב יְדָעֲךָ.
חַסְדְּךָ לָמוֹ בְּהוֹדִיעָךְ. וְהוֹשִׁיעָה נָּא.

אָנָּא טְהוֹרֵי לֵב בְּהַפְלִיאָךְ.
יוֹדֵעַ כִּי הוּא פִלְאָךְ. וְהוֹשִׁיעָה נָּא.

אָנָּא כַּבִּיר כֹּחַ תֶּן לָנוּ יִשְׁעָךְ.
לַאֲבוֹתֵינוּ כְּהִשָּׁבְעָךְ. וְהוֹשִׁיעָה נָּא.

אָנָּא מָלֵא מִשְׁאֲלוֹת עַם מְשַׁוְּעָךְ.
נֶעֱקַד בְּהַר מוֹר כְּמוֹ שׁוֹעֲךָ. וְהוֹשִׁיעָה נָּא.

אָנָּא סַגֵּב אֶשְׁלֵי נִטְעָךְ.
עָרִיצִים בְּהַנִיעָךְ. וְהוֹשִׁיעָה נָּא.

אָנָּא פְּתַח לָנוּ אוֹצְרוֹת רִבְעָךְ.
צִיָּה מֵהֶם בְּהַרְבִּיעָךְ. וְהוֹשִׁיעָה נָּא.

אָנָּא קוֹרְאֶיךָ אֶרֶץ בְּרוֹעֲעָךְ.
רְעֵם בְּטוּב מִרְעָךְ. וְהוֹשִׁיעָה נָּא.

אָנָּא שְׁעָרֶיךָ תַּעַל מִמְּשׁוֹאָךְ.
תֵּל תַּלְפִּיּוֹת בְּהַשִּׂיאָךְ. וְהוֹשִׁיעָה נָּא.

קהל *then* שליח ציבור:

אָנָּא, אֵל נָא, הוֹשַׁע נָא וְהוֹשִׁיעָה נָּא.

אֵל נָא תָּעִינוּ כְּשֶׂה אוֹבֵד
שְׁמֵנוּ מִסִּפְרְךָ אַל תְּאַבֵּד הוֹשַׁע נָא וְהוֹשִׁיעָה נָּא.

אֵל נָא רְעֵה אֶת צֹאן הַהֲרֵגָה
קְצוּפָה, וְעָלֶיךָ הֲרוּגָה הוֹשַׁע נָא וְהוֹשִׁיעָה נָּא.

אֵל נָא צֹאנְךָ וְצֹאן מַרְעִיתֶךָ
פְּעֻלָּתְךָ וְרַעְיָתֶךָ הוֹשַׁע נָא וְהוֹשִׁיעָה נָּא.

God, please; the poorest of the flock –
answer their prayer at a time of favor save, please; save us, please.

God, please; those who raise their eyes to You –
may those who rise against You be as nothing beside them
save, please; save us, please.

God, please; those who pour water out before You –
from the wellsprings of salvation, let them draw water
save, please; save us, please.

God, please; let the redeemers go up to Zion,
leaning upon You, saved in Your name save, please; save us, please.

God, please; Your clothes red with blood,
rage and shake away all those who betray
save, please; save us, please.

God, please; surely remember,
those sold away for a letekh of grain, for a kor
save, please; save us, please.

God, please; those who seek You with stems of willow,
hear their weeping from the highest heaven
save, please; save us, please.

God, please; crown this year with blessing,
and hear my words as I pray, on the day of Hoshana
save, please; save us, please.

Leader then congregation:

Please; God, please;
save, please; save us, please;
You are our Father.

לְמַעַן For the sake of one perfect in his generation,
who escaped in his righteousness,
saved from the flood, when there came down a deluge of water –
the people that says "I am a wall" –
save, please: save us, please: You are our Father.

אֵל נָא עֲנִיֵּי הַצֹּאן
שִׂיחָם עֲנֵה בְּעֵת רָצוֹן הוֹשַׁע נָא וְהוֹשִׁיעָה נָּא.
אֵל נָא נוֹשְׂאֵי לְךָ עַיִן
מִתְקוֹמְמֶיךָ יִהְיוּ כְאַיִן הוֹשַׁע נָא וְהוֹשִׁיעָה נָּא.
אֵל נָא לִמְנַסְּכֵי לְךָ מַיִם
כְּמִמַּעַיְנֵי הַיְשׁוּעָה
יִשְׁאֲבוּן מַיִם הוֹשַׁע נָא וְהוֹשִׁיעָה נָּא.
אֵל נָא יַעֲלוּ לְצִיּוֹן מוֹשִׁיעִים
טְפוּלִים בָּךְ וּבִשְׁמְךָ נוֹשָׁעִים הוֹשַׁע נָא וְהוֹשִׁיעָה נָּא.
אֵל נָא חֲמוּץ בְּגָדִים
זְעוֹם לִנְעֹר כָּל בּוֹגְדִים הוֹשַׁע נָא וְהוֹשִׁיעָה נָּא.
אֵל נָא וְזָכוֹר תִּזְכֹּר
הַנִּכּוֹרִים בְּלֶתֶךְ וָכֹר הוֹשַׁע נָא וְהוֹשִׁיעָה נָּא.
אֵל נָא דּוֹרְשֶׁיךָ בְּעַנְפֵי עֲרָבוֹת
גְּעִים שְׁעֵה מֵעֲרָבוֹת הוֹשַׁע נָא וְהוֹשִׁיעָה נָּא.
אֵל נָא בָּרֵךְ בְּעִטּוּר שָׁנָה
אֲמָרַי רְצֵה בְּפִלּוּלִי
בְּיוֹם הוֹשַׁעְנָא הוֹשַׁע נָא וְהוֹשִׁיעָה נָּא.

קהל *then* שליח ציבור:

אָנָּא, אֵל נָא, הוֹשַׁע נָא וְהוֹשִׁיעָה נָּא, אָבִינוּ אָתָּה.

לְמַעַן תָּמִים בְּדוֹרוֹתָיו, הַנִּמְלָט בְּרֹב צִדְקוֹתָיו
מֻצָּל מִשֶּׁטֶף בְּבוֹא מַבּוּל מָיִם.
לְאֹם אֲנִי חוֹמָה הוֹשַׁע נָא וְהוֹשִׁיעָה נָּא, אָבִינוּ אָתָּה.

For the sake of one whole in all his doings, tested with ten trials,
who saw angels and said, "Please, bring a little water" –
the people shining like the sun –
save, please: save us, please: You are our Father.

For the sake of a tender, only child, young fruit borne to a man of a hundred,
who cried out "Where is the lamb for the burnt offering?!"
Whose servants brought him news: "We have found water!" –
the people expelled and banished –
save, please: save us, please: You are our Father.

For the sake of one who came in first to bear blessing,
who gained a foe and waited for salvation by Your name;
who made goats fertile with branches, by troughs of water –
the people likened to a date palm –
save, please: save us, please: You are our Father.

For the sake of the one righteous enough to be chosen as Your priest,
serving You like a bridegroom adorned,
tested at Masa, by the Mei Meriva water –
the good mountain – save, please: save us, please: You are our Father.

For the sake of the one raised to be master of his brothers,
Judah who became the most powerful of brothers,
numerous as dust; his pail overflows with water –
not for us, but for Your sake –
save, please: save us, please: You are our Father.

For the sake of the humblest of men, the most faithful,
for whose righteous sake the manna fell,
pulled to be redeemer, drawn forth from the water –
this people, gazing out – save, please: save us, please: You are our Father.

For the sake of one You raised like angels of the heights, clad with the urim and tumim, commanded to come into the Temple with sanctified hands and feet, bathed in water –
this people sick with love –
save, please: save us, please: You are our Father.

For the sake of the prophetess who danced between the camps;
to whom the people on their yearning journey raised their eyes [to lead them]; for her sake it moved, it rose and it rested, the well of water –
the people of the goodly tents –
save, please: save us, please: You are our Father.

לְמַעַן שָׁלֵם בְּכָל מַעֲשִׂים, הַמְנֻסֶּה בַּעֲשָׂרָה נִסִּים
כְּשֶׂר מַלְאָכִים, נָם יֻקַּח נָא מְעַט מַיִם.
לְבָרָה כַּחַמָּה הוֹשַׁע נָא וְהוֹשִׁיעָה נָּא, אָבִינוּ אָתָּה.

לְמַעַן רַךְ וְיָחִיד נֶחֱנַט פְּרִי לְמֵאָה, זָעַק אַיֵּה הַשֶּׂה לְעֹלָה
בִּשְּׂרוּהוּ עֲבָדָיו מָצָאנוּ מַיִם.
לְגוֹלָה וְסוּרָה הוֹשַׁע נָא וְהוֹשִׁיעָה נָּא, אָבִינוּ אָתָּה.

לְמַעַן קָדַם שְׂאֵת בְּרָכָה, הַנִּשְׂטָם וּלְשִׁמְךָ חִכָּה
מְיֻחָם בְּמַקְלוֹת בְּשִׁקְתוֹת הַמָּיִם.
לְדָמְתָה לְתָמָר הוֹשַׁע נָא וְהוֹשִׁיעָה נָּא, אָבִינוּ אָתָּה.

לְמַעַן צֶדֶק הֱיוֹת לְךָ לְכַהֵן, כֶּחָתָן פְּאֵר יְכַהֵן
מְנֻסֶּה בְּמַסָּה בְּמֵי מְרִיבַת מַיִם.
לְהָהָר הַטּוֹב הוֹשַׁע נָא וְהוֹשִׁיעָה נָּא, אָבִינוּ אָתָּה.

לְמַעַן פְּאֵר הֱיוֹת גְּבִיר לְאֶחָיו, יְהוּדָה אֲשֶׁר גָּבַר בְּאֶחָיו
מִסְפַּר רֹבַע מִדָּלְיָו יִזַּל מַיִם.
לֹא לָנוּ כִּי אִם לְמַעַנְךָ הוֹשַׁע נָא וְהוֹשִׁיעָה נָּא, אָבִינוּ אָתָּה.

לְמַעַן עָנָו מִכֹּל וְנֶאֱמָן, אֲשֶׁר בְּצִדְקוֹ כִּלְכֵּל הַמָּן
מָשׁוּךְ לְגוֹאֵל וּמָשׁוּי מִמַּיִם.
לְזֹאת הַנִּשְׁקָפָה הוֹשַׁע נָא וְהוֹשִׁיעָה נָּא, אָבִינוּ אָתָּה.

לְמַעַן שַׂמְתּוֹ כְּמַלְאֲכֵי מְרוֹמִים, הַלּוֹבֵשׁ אוּרִים וְתֻמִּים
מְצֻוֶּה לָבוֹא בְּמִקְדָּשׁ בְּקִדּוּשׁ יָדַיִם וְרַגְלַיִם וּרְחִיצַת מַיִם.
לְחוֹלַת אַהֲבָה הוֹשַׁע נָא וְהוֹשִׁיעָה נָּא, אָבִינוּ אָתָּה.

לְמַעַן נְבִיאָה מְחוֹלַת מַחֲנַיִם, לִכְמֵהֵי לֵב הוּשְׂמָה עֵינַיִם
לְרַגְלָהּ רָצָה עָלוֹת וְרֶדֶת בְּאֵר מַיִם.
לְטוֹבוּ אֹהָלָיו הוֹשַׁע נָא וְהוֹשִׁיעָה נָּא, אָבִינוּ אָתָּה.

For the sake of the servant who never left the Tent, over whom the holy
spirit rested, for whose sake the Jordan parted its water –
the people beautiful and shining –
save, please: save us, please: You are our Father.

For the sake of the one taught to read a sign of good things,
who cried out, "Where are the wonders now?"
But later wrung rain from the wool – a whole bowl full of water –
the bride of Lebanon –
save, please: save us, please: You are our Father.

For the sake of one who ground his enemies alone, dedicated from the womb
a Nazirite, from the hollow of a jawbone You brought him forth water –
for Your holy name's sake –
save, please: save us, please: You are our Father.

For the sake of those included in the army of Your war,
at whose hands You gave Your salvation,
marked out from the people as from their hands they lapped up water –
those who never betrayed –
save, please: save us, please: You are our Father.

For the sake of the good child growing more and more,
who never allowed himself to take from the people;
when the people repented he said, "Draw forth water!" –
the people, lovely as Jerusalem –
save, please: save us, please: You are our Father.

For the sake of one who laughed and danced in song,
who taught the Torah through any instrument of music,
who libated before You, though he longed to drink water –
those who placed their hope in You –
save, please: save us, please: You are our Father.

For the sake of the pure one who went up in a storm cloud,
who was jealous for You and who turned back Your rage,
at whose word down came fire to lick the dust and water –
the people whose eyes are like pools –
save, please: save us, please: You are our Father.

For the sake of one who served his teacher truly,
and was assigned a double measure of his spirit.
When he called the musician to play, the pools were filled with water –
those who said "Who is like You?" –
save, please: save us, please: You are our Father.

לְמַעַן מְשָׁרֵת לֹא מָשׁ מֵאֹהֶל, וְרוּחַ הַקֹּדֶשׁ עָלָיו אִהֵל
בְּעָבְרוֹ בַּיַּרְדֵּן נִכְרְתוּ הַמַּיִם.
לְיָפָה וּבָרָה הוֹשַׁע נָא וְהוֹשִׁיעָה נָּא, אָבִינוּ אָתָּה.

לְמַעַן לָמַד רְאוֹת לְטוֹבָה אוֹת, זָעַק אַיֵּה נִפְלָאוֹת
מִצָּה טַל מִגִּזָּה מְלֹא הַסֵּפֶל מַיִם.
לְכַלַּת לְבָנוֹן הוֹשַׁע נָא וְהוֹשִׁיעָה נָּא, אָבִינוּ אָתָּה.

לְמַעַן כְּלוּלֵי עֲשׂוֹת מִלְחַמְתֶּךָ, אֲשֶׁר בְּיָדָם תַּתָּה יְשׁוּעָתֶךָ
צְרוּפֵי מִגּוּי בְּלָקְקָם בְּיָדָם מַיִם.
לְלֹא בָגְדוּ בָךְ הוֹשַׁע נָא וְהוֹשִׁיעָה נָּא, אָבִינוּ אָתָּה.

לְמַעַן יָחִיד צוֹרְרִים דָּשׁ, אֲשֶׁר מֵרֶחֶם לְנָזִיר הֻקְדָּשׁ
מִמַּכְתֵּשׁ לֶחִי הִבְקַעְתָּ לוֹ מַיִם.
לְמַעַן שֵׁם קָדְשָׁךְ הוֹשַׁע נָא וְהוֹשִׁיעָה נָּא, אָבִינוּ אָתָּה.

לְמַעַן טוֹב הוֹלֵךְ וְגָדֵל, אֲשֶׁר מֵעֹשֶׁק עֵדָה חִדֵּל
בְּשׁוּב עָם מֵחֵטְא צִוָּה שְׁאֹב מַיִם.
לְנָאוָה כִּירוּשָׁלָיִם הוֹשַׁע נָא וְהוֹשִׁיעָה נָּא, אָבִינוּ אָתָּה.

לְמַעַן חַיָּךְ מְכַרְכֵּר בְּשִׁיר, הַמְלַמֵּד תּוֹרָה בְּכָל כְּלֵי שִׁיר
מְנַסֵּךְ לְפָנֶיךָ כְּתָאֵב שְׁתוֹת מַיִם.
לְשָׁמוּ בְךָ סִבְרָם הוֹשַׁע נָא וְהוֹשִׁיעָה נָּא, אָבִינוּ אָתָּה.

לְמַעַן זָךְ עָלָה בַּסְּעָרָה, הַמְקַנֵּא וּמֵשִׁיב עֶבְרָה
לְפִלּוּלוֹ יָרְדָה אֵשׁ וְלִחֲכָה עָפָר וּמַיִם.
לְעֵינֶיהָ בְּרֵכוֹת הוֹשַׁע נָא וְהוֹשִׁיעָה נָּא, אָבִינוּ אָתָּה.

לְמַעַן וְשֵׁרֵת בֶּאֱמֶת לְרַבּוֹ, פִּי שְׁנַיִם בְּרוּחוֹ נֶאֱצַל בּוֹ
בְּקַחְתּוֹ מְנַגֵּן נִתְמַלְּאוּ גֵּבִים מַיִם.
לְפָצוּ מִי כָמֹכָה הוֹשַׁע נָא וְהוֹשִׁיעָה נָּא, אָבִינוּ אָתָּה.

For the sake of one who thought to do Your will,
who declared repentance to all Your flock;
then, when the blasphemer came, he stopped up all springs of water –
Zion, perfect beauty –
save, please: save us, please: You are our Father.

For the sake of those who sought You from the heart of Exile,
to whom Your secrets were revealed,
and not to be tainted [by meat and wine]
they asked for grains and water –
those who cry out to You from their distress –
save, please: save us, please: You are our Father.

For the sake of one who learned wisdom and insight,
the keen-minded scribe who set forth a pledge,
the one who made us wiser with words deep as oceans of water –
the [city that] flocked with people –
save, please: save us, please: You are our Father.

For the sake of those who come to You today with all their hearts,
who pour out their words without two minds,
who ask of You Your mighty torrents of water –
those who sang at the sea –
save, please: save us, please: You are our Father.

For the sake of those who say "May Your name be magnified" –
and they are Your inheritance, Your people;
who thirst for Your salvation as an arid land thirsts water –
those for whom You sought out a resting place –
save, please: save us, please: You are our Father.

Leader then congregation:

Save, please, God, please,
save us, please.
Save, please, please forgive
and grant us success, please.
Save us, God who is our Refuge.

Put down the Lulav and Etrog and pick up the Hoshanot.

לְמַעַן הִרְהֵר עֲשׂוֹת רְצוֹנֶךָ, הַמַּכְרִיז תְּשׁוּבָה לְצֹאנֶךָ
אָז בְּבוֹא מַחְרֵף סָתַם עֵינוֹת מָיִם.
לְצִיּוֹן מִכְלַל יֹפִי הוֹשַׁע נָא וְהוֹשִׁיעָה נָּא, אָבִינוּ אָתָּה.

לְמַעַן דָּרְשׁוּךָ בְּתוֹךְ הַגּוֹלָה, וְסוֹדְךָ לָמוֹ נִגְלָה
בְּלִי לְהִתְגָּאֵל דָּרְשׁוּ זֵרְעוֹנִים וּמָיִם.
לְקוֹרְאֶיךָ בַּצָּר הוֹשַׁע נָא וְהוֹשִׁיעָה נָּא, אָבִינוּ אָתָּה.

לְמַעַן גְּמַר חָכְמָה וּבִינָה, סוֹפֵר מָהִיר מְפַלֵּשׁ אֲמָנָה
מַחְכִּימֵנוּ אֲמָרִים הַמְשׁוּלִים בְּרַהֲבֵי מָיִם.
לְרַבָּתִי עָם הוֹשַׁע נָא וְהוֹשִׁיעָה נָּא, אָבִינוּ אָתָּה.

לְמַעַן בָּאֵי לְךָ הַיּוֹם בְּכָל לֵב, שׁוֹפְכִים לְךָ שִׂיחַ בְּלֹא לֵב וָלֵב
שׁוֹאֲלִים מִמְּךָ עֹז מְטְרוֹת מָיִם.
לְשׁוֹרְרוּ בַּיָּם הוֹשַׁע נָא וְהוֹשִׁיעָה נָּא, אָבִינוּ אָתָּה.

לְמַעַן אוֹמְרֵי יִגְדַּל שְׁמֶךָ, וְהֵם נַחֲלָתְךָ וְעַמֶּךָ
צְמֵאִים לְיֶשְׁעֲךָ כְּאֶרֶץ עֲיֵפָה לַמָּיִם.
לְתָרַתְּ לָמוֹ מְנוּחָה הוֹשַׁע נָא וְהוֹשִׁיעָה נָּא, אָבִינוּ אָתָּה.

קהל then שליח ציבור:

הוֹשַׁע נָא, אֵל נָא
אָנָּא הוֹשִׁיעָה נָּא.
הוֹשַׁע נָא, סְלַח נָא
וְהַצְלִיחָה נָא
וְהוֹשִׁיעֵנוּ אֵל מָעֻזֵּנוּ.

Put down the לולב and אתרוג and pick up the הושענות.

תַּעֲנֶה Answer the faithful ones who pour out their hearts
to You like water – and save us, please;
for the sake of [Abraham] who came through
fire and water – and grant us success, please;
He gave the order and said, "Please, bring
a little water" – save us, God our Refuge.

Answer the flagged tribes who went swift through the split sea – and save us, please;
for the sake of [Isaac who was] bound at the
gate of heaven – and grant us success, please;
he who yet lived to return and to dig out
wells of water – save us, God our Refuge.

Answer the pure ones encamped on the water – and save us, please;
for the sake of smooth-skinned [Jacob] who
peeled branches by troughs of water – and grant us success, please;
he who heaved and rolled a rock from the
well of water – save us, God our Refuge.

Answer the beloved ones, heirs to a Law likened to water – and save us, please;
for the sake of those [princes in the wilderness]
whose staffs drew forth water – and grant us success, please;
to prepare for them and for their children –
water – save us, God our Refuge.

Answer those who plead as in the wilderness for water – and save us, please;
for the sake of [Moses], trusted in Your household,
who provided the people with water – and grant us success, please;
he hit the rock and out flowed water – save us, God our Refuge.

Answer those who sang in the wilderness, "Spring up, well
of water!" – and save us, please;
for the sake of [Aaron,] commanded at the
Mei Meriva water – and grant us success, please;
commanded to give those who thirsted, water – save us, God our Refuge.

Answerthe holy ones who pour before You water – and save us, please;
for the sake of [David] father of song-makers
who longed to drink water – and grant us success, please;
but who held back and poured before You water – save us, God our Refuge.

Answer those who come to beseech You with four species
grown by water – and save us, please;
for the sake of the Hill of ruins all mouths pray
towards, the source of water – and grant us success, please;
open up the earth and let the heavens rain down water –
and save us, God our Refuge.

תַּעֲנֶה אֱמוּנִים שׁוֹפְכִים לְךָ לֵב כַּמַּיִם וְהוֹשִׁיעָה נָּא.
לְמַעַן בָּא בָאֵשׁ וּבַמַּיִם וְהַצְלִיחָה נָא.
גָּזַר וְנָם יֻקַּח נָא מְעַט מַיִם וְהוֹשִׁיעֵנוּ אֵל מָעֻזֵּנוּ.

תַּעֲנֶה דְגָלִים גִּזּוּ גִּזְרֵי מַיִם וְהוֹשִׁיעָה נָּא.
לְמַעַן הַנֶּעֱקַד בְּשַׁעַר הַשָּׁמַיִם וְהַצְלִיחָה נָא.
וְשָׁב וְחָפַר בְּאֵרוֹת מַיִם וְהוֹשִׁיעֵנוּ אֵל מָעֻזֵּנוּ.

תַּעֲנֶה זַכִּים חוֹנִים עֲלֵי מַיִם וְהוֹשִׁיעָה נָּא.
לְמַעַן חָלָק מְפַצֵּל מַקְלוֹת בְּשִׁקְתוֹת הַמַּיִם וְהַצְלִיחָה נָא.
טָעַן וְגָל אֶבֶן מִבְּאֵר מַיִם וְהוֹשִׁיעֵנוּ אֵל מָעֻזֵּנוּ.

תַּעֲנֶה יְדִידִים נוֹחֲלֵי דָת מְשׁוּלַת מַיִם וְהוֹשִׁיעָה נָּא.
לְמַעַן כָּרוּ בְּמִשְׁעֲנוֹתָם מַיִם וְהַצְלִיחָה נָא.
לְהָכִין לָמוֹ וּלְצֶאֱצָאֵימוֹ מַיִם וְהוֹשִׁיעֵנוּ אֵל מָעֻזֵּנוּ.

תַּעֲנֶה מִתְחַנְּנִים כְּבִישִׁימוֹן עֲלֵי מַיִם וְהוֹשִׁיעָה נָּא.
לְמַעַן נֶאֱמַן בַּיִת מַסְפִּיק לָעָם מַיִם וְהַצְלִיחָה נָא.
סֶלַע הָךְ וַיָּזוּבוּ מַיִם וְהוֹשִׁיעֵנוּ אֵל מָעֻזֵּנוּ.

תַּעֲנֶה עוֹנִים עֲלֵי בְּאֵר מַיִם וְהוֹשִׁיעָה נָּא.
לְמַעַן פָּקַד בְּמֵי מְרִיבַת מַיִם וְהַצְלִיחָה נָא.
צְמֵאִים לְהַשְׁקוֹת מַיִם וְהוֹשִׁיעֵנוּ אֵל מָעֻזֵּנוּ.

תַּעֲנֶה קְדוֹשִׁים מְנַסְּכִים לְךָ מַיִם וְהוֹשִׁיעָה נָּא.
לְמַעַן רֹאשׁ מְשׁוֹרְרִים כְּתָאֵב שְׁתוֹת מַיִם וְהַצְלִיחָה נָא.
שָׁב וְנָסַךְ לְךָ מַיִם וְהוֹשִׁיעֵנוּ אֵל מָעֻזֵּנוּ.

תַּעֲנֶה שׁוֹאֲלִים בְּרִבּוּעַ אֶשְׁלֵי מַיִם וְהוֹשִׁיעָה נָּא.
לְמַעַן תֵּל תַּלְפִּיּוֹת מוֹצָא מַיִם וְהַצְלִיחָה נָא.
תִּפְתַּח אֶרֶץ וְתַרְעִיף שָׁמַיִם וְהוֹשִׁיעֵנוּ אֵל מָעֻזֵּנוּ.

Leader then congregation:

Have compassion, please, for the community of the people of Yeshurun; forgive and pardon their iniquity, and save us, God of our salvation.

אז As the eyes of slaves are raised / to their masters' hands
we come before You, judged save us, God of our salvation.

Proud Lord of lords, / they have brought us to conflict;
they have trampled us; other lords have mastered us
so save us, God of our salvation.

We have come today, pleading – / before You, Compassionate and Gracious One,
telling and repeating Your wondrous acts now save us, God of our salvation.

Please do not dry up / what flowed with milk and honey;
heal the land's pain with clouds full of water and save us, God of our salvation.

Plant us in luscious land, / at the hand of the seven shepherds, the eight princes,
righteous, upright God of faithfulness yes, save us, God of our salvation.

You forged a covenant with the land / for as long as the earth will be,
never to break it apart again so save us, God of our salvation.

Those who plead with You for water / as willows thirst over streams of water –
remember for them the libation of water and save us, God of our salvation.

As they plead they carry with them / plants, held straight as they grow;
answer their prayer, their voice and save us, God of our salvation.

You who work salvations, / turn to hear their prayers,
and vindicate them, God of salvation to save us, God of our salvation.

Listen to the voice of their crowds who come, / and open the earth, to bear fruit of salvation,
You who are great in saving, who desire no evil save us, God of our salvation.

Open the gates of heaven, / and throw open Your treasury of good.
Save us, and do not press Your claims against us
but save us, God of our salvation.

Leader then congregation:

Open the gates of heaven,
and Your treasure-house of goodness – open for us.
Save us and do not extend judgment against us –
and save us, God of our salvation.

קהל *then* שליח ציבור:

רַחֶם נָא קְהַל עֲדַת יְשׁוּרוּן, סְלַח וּמְחַל עֲוֹנָם
וְהוֹשִׁיעֵנוּ אֱלֹהֵי יִשְׁעֵנוּ.

אָז כְּעֵינֵי עֲבָדִים אֶל יַד אֲדוֹנִים
בָּאנוּ לְפָנֶיךָ נְדוֹנִים. וְהוֹשִׁיעֵנוּ אֱלֹהֵי יִשְׁעֵנוּ.

גֵּאָה אֲדוֹנֵי הָאֲדוֹנִים, נִתְגָּרוּ בָנוּ מְדָנִים
דְּשׁוּנוּ וּבְעָלוּנוּ זוּלָתְךָ אֲדוֹנִים. וְהוֹשִׁיעֵנוּ אֱלֹהֵי יִשְׁעֵנוּ.

הֵן גַּשְׁנוּ הַיּוֹם בְּתַחֲנוּן, עָדֶיךָ רַחוּם וְחַנּוּן
וְסִפְּרָנוּ נִפְלְאוֹתֶיךָ בְּשִׁנּוּן. וְהוֹשִׁיעֵנוּ אֱלֹהֵי יִשְׁעֵנוּ.

זָבַת חָלָב וּדְבָשׁ, נָא אַל תִּיבַשׁ
חֲשׁוּרַת מַיִם כְּאָבָה תֶּחְבַּשׁ. וְהוֹשִׁיעֵנוּ אֱלֹהֵי יִשְׁעֵנוּ.

טְעוּנֵי בִּשְׁמֹנָה, בְּיַד שִׁבְעָה וּשְׁמוֹנָה
יָשָׁר צַדִּיק אֵל אֱמוּנָה. וְהוֹשִׁיעֵנוּ אֱלֹהֵי יִשְׁעֵנוּ.

כָּרַתָּ בְרִית לָאָרֶץ, עוֹד כָּל יְמֵי הָאָרֶץ
לְבִלְתִּי פְּרָץ בָּהּ פָּרֶץ. וְהוֹשִׁיעֵנוּ אֱלֹהֵי יִשְׁעֵנוּ.

מִתְחַנְּנִים עֲלֵי מַיִם, כַּעֲרָבִים עַל יִבְלֵי מַיִם
נָא זְכָר לָמוֹ נִסּוּךְ הַמַּיִם. וְהוֹשִׁיעֵנוּ אֱלֹהֵי יִשְׁעֵנוּ.

שִׂיחִים בְּדֶרֶךְ מַטָּעָתָם, עוֹמְסִים בְּשַׁוְעָתָם
עֲנֵם בְּקוֹל פְּגִיעָתָם. וְהוֹשִׁיעֵנוּ אֱלֹהֵי יִשְׁעֵנוּ.

פּוֹעֵל יְשׁוּעוֹת, פְּנֵה לְפִלּוּלָם שְׁעוֹת
צַדְּקֵם אֵל לְמוֹשָׁעוֹת. וְהוֹשִׁיעֵנוּ אֱלֹהֵי יִשְׁעֵנוּ.

קוֹל רִגְשָׁם תִּשַׁע, תִּפְתַּח אֶרֶץ וְיִפְרוּ יֶשַׁע
רַב לְהוֹשִׁיעַ וְלֹא חָפֵץ רֶשַׁע. וְהוֹשִׁיעֵנוּ אֱלֹהֵי יִשְׁעֵנוּ.

קהל *then* שליח ציבור:

שַׁעֲרֵי שָׁמַיִם פְּתַח, וְאוֹצָרְךָ הַטּוֹב לָנוּ תִפְתַּח.
תּוֹשִׁיעֵנוּ וְרִיב אַל תִּמְתַּח. וְהוֹשִׁיעֵנוּ אֱלֹהֵי יִשְׁעֵנוּ.

Leader then congregation:

The voice of the herald, he heralds and says –

אֹמֶן Your true salvation is coming; / the voice of my Beloved, here He is coming – heralding, saying / A voice: He is coming with myriad [heavenly] legions, / coming to stand on the Mount of Olives – heralding, saying / A voice: He is coming to sound the shofar, / as the mount is broken in half beneath Him – heralding, saying – / A voice: He knocks, He looks, He shines out, / and half the mount is moved from the east – heralding, saying / A voice: He is fulfilling the words He spoke / and coming, and all His holy ones with Him – heralding, saying / A voice: and for all who have come into this world, / the echo is heard in all the world – heralding, saying / A voice: the children borne of His womb, / were born in a day like a child of his mother – heralding, saying / A voice: she labored and bore – who is this? / Who has heard of anything like this? – heralding, saying / A voice: *Is. 66*
the Pure One who wrought all this – / and who has seen anything like this? – *Ibid.*
heralding, saying / A voice: salvation, its time already set; / can the land give *Ibid.*
birth all in a day? – heralding, saying / A voice: the One mighty above and below, / can a nation be born all in one birth? – heralding, saying / A voice: *Ibid.*
when the shining One redeems His people, / as evening falls, there shall be *Zech. 14*
light – heralding, saying / A voice: saviors shall go up to Mount Zion: / for Zion has labored and has given birth – heralding, saying / A voice is heard *Is. 66*
throughout your borders: / "Broaden the spread of your tents!" – heralding, *Is. 54*
saying / A voice: "Let your home extend as far as Damascus; / receive your sons and your daughters" – heralding, saying / A voice: "Be joyful, dune flower of the coast; / for the [forebears] who slept in Hebron are awoken" – heralding, saying / A voice: "Turn to Me and be saved; / today, if you heed *Is. 45*
My voice" – heralding, saying / A voice: a [savior] has grown up, Tzemaḥ his name, / and he is none other than David himself – heralding, saying / A voice: "Rise up, you who lie in the ashes; / awaken and sing, you who *Is. 26*
sleep in the dust" – heralding, saying / A voice: the city flocking with people for his crowning: / a tower of salvation, His own king – heralding, saying / *II Sam. 22*
A voice to silence the names of the wicked; / dealing kindly with his anointed, *Ibid.*
David – heralding, saying / A voice: grant salvation to an eternal people; / *Ibid.*
to David and his descendants forever – heralding, saying

The Leader says three times then congregations repeats three times:

The voice of the herald, he heralds and says –

קהל *then* שליח ציבור:

קוֹל מְבַשֵּׂר מְבַשֵּׂר וְאוֹמֵר.

אֹמֶן יֶשְׁעֲךָ בָּא, קוֹל דּוֹדִי הִנֵּה זֶה בָּא. מְבַשֵּׂר וְאוֹמֵר.
בָּא בְּרִבְבוֹת כִּתִּים, לַעֲמֹד עַל הַר הַזֵּיתִים. מְבַשֵּׂר וְאוֹמֵר.
גִּשְׁתּוֹ בַּשּׁוֹפָר לִתְקֹעַ, תַּחְתָּיו הַר יִבָּקֵעַ. מְבַשֵּׂר וְאוֹמֵר.
דָּפַק וְהֵצִיץ וְזָרַח, וּמָשׁ חֲצִי הָהָר מִמִּזְרָח. מְבַשֵּׂר וְאוֹמֵר.
הֵקִים מִלּוּל נְאֻמוֹ, וּבָא הוּא וְכָל קְדוֹשָׁיו עִמּוֹ. מְבַשֵּׂר וְאוֹמֵר.
וּלְכָל בָּאֵי הָעוֹלָם, בַּת קוֹל יִשָּׁמַע בָּעוֹלָם. מְבַשֵּׂר וְאוֹמֵר.
זֶרַע עֲמוּסֵי רַחְמוֹ, נוֹלְדוּ כְּיֶלֶד מִמְּעֵי אִמּוֹ. מְבַשֵּׂר וְאוֹמֵר.
חָלָה וְיָלְדָה מִי זֹאת, מִי־שָׁמַע כָּזֹאת. מְבַשֵּׂר וְאוֹמֵר. ישעיה סו
טָהוֹר פָּעַל כָּל אֵלֶּה, מִי רָאָה כָּאֵלֶּה. מְבַשֵּׂר וְאוֹמֵר. ישעיה סו
יֶשַׁע וּזְמַן הוּחַד, הֲיוּחַל אֶרֶץ בְּיוֹם אֶחָד. מְבַשֵּׂר וְאוֹמֵר. ישעיה סו
כַּבִּיר רוּם וָתַחַת, אִם־יִוָּלֵד גּוֹי פַּעַם אֶחָת. מְבַשֵּׂר וְאוֹמֵר. ישעיה סו
לְעֵת יִגְאַל עַמּוֹ נָאוֹר, וְהָיָה לְעֵת־עֶרֶב יִהְיֶה־אוֹר. מְבַשֵּׂר וְאוֹמֵר. זכריה יד
מוֹשִׁיעִים יַעֲלוּ לְהַר צִיּוֹן, כִּי־חָלָה גַּם־יָלְדָה צִיּוֹן. מְבַשֵּׂר וְאוֹמֵר. ישעיה סו
נִשְׁמַע בְּכָל גְּבוּלֵךְ, הַרְחִיבִי מְקוֹם אָהֳלֵךְ. מְבַשֵּׂר וְאוֹמֵר. ישעיה נד
שִׂימִי עַד דַּמֶּשֶׂק מִשְׁכְּנוֹתַיִךְ, קַבְּלִי בָנַיִךְ וּבְנוֹתַיִךְ. מְבַשֵּׂר וְאוֹמֵר.
עִלְזִי חֲבַצֶּלֶת הַשָּׁרוֹן, כִּי קָמוּ יְשֵׁנֵי חֶבְרוֹן. מְבַשֵּׂר וְאוֹמֵר.
פְּנוּ אֵלַי וְהִוָּשְׁעוּ, הַיּוֹם אִם בְּקוֹלִי תִשְׁמָעוּ. מְבַשֵּׂר וְאוֹמֵר.
צֶמַח אִישׁ צֶמַח שְׁמוֹ, הוּא דָוִד בְּעַצְמוֹ. מְבַשֵּׂר וְאוֹמֵר.
קוּמוּ כְּפוּשֵׁי עָפָר, הָקִיצוּ וְרַנְּנוּ שֹׁכְנֵי עָפָר. מְבַשֵּׂר וְאוֹמֵר. ישעיה כו
רַבָּתִי עָם בְּהַמְלִיכוֹ, מִגְדּוֹל יְשׁוּעוֹת מַלְכּוֹ. מְבַשֵּׂר וְאוֹמֵר. שמואל ב׳ כב
שֵׁם רְשָׁעִים לְהַאֲבִיד, עֹשֶׂה־חֶסֶד לִמְשִׁיחוֹ לְדָוִד. מְבַשֵּׂר וְאוֹמֵר. שמואל ב׳ כב
תְּנָה יְשׁוּעוֹת לְעַם עוֹלָם, לְדָוִד וּלְזַרְעוֹ עַד־עוֹלָם. מְבַשֵּׂר וְאוֹמֵר. שמואל ב׳ כב

שליח ציבור *says three times then* קהל *repeats three times:*

קוֹל מְבַשֵּׂר מְבַשֵּׂר וְאוֹמֵר.

Beat the Hoshanot against a chair or the floor five times, then say the following (see law 118):

הוֹשִׁיעָה Save Your people; bless Your legacy; Ps. 28
tend them and carry them forever.
Let these words with which I have pleaded with the LORD 1 Kings 8
be close to the LORD our God day and night,
that they may do justice for His servant,
and justice for His people Israel, day after day;
so that all the peoples of the earth will know
that the LORD is God. There is no other.

The Torah scrolls are returned to the Ark, which is then closed.

May it be Your will, LORD our God, God of our ancestors, who chooses good prophets, and their good customs – to receive our prayers and our circlings with compassion and favor. Remember for us the merit of Your seven perfect ones, and remove the wall of iron that separates us from You, and hear our pleas, and to seal us a good judgment – You who suspends the world over nothingness. And seal us in the book of good life.

On this day, invest Your mighty Presence with the five sweetened powers – by means of the beating of the willows, the custom of Your holy prophets – and let love be awakened among them. Kiss us with the kisses of Your mouth, which sweetens all might and all judgments. Shine light upon Your mighty Presence, by the name *Yod-Heh-Vav*, which is the dew that is a dew of light. And from that place, emanate plenty to Your servant, who prays here before You; lengthen his life and forgive him his sins and iniquities and rebellions. And extend Your hand, Your right hand, to receive him in full repentance before You. Open Your treasury of good, to satisfy the yearning soul with water, as it is written, "The LORD will open His good treasury for You, open the heavens, to grant your land its rain in its right time, and to bless all the work of your hands:" Amen. Deut. 28

The Leader continues with Full Kaddish on page 554.

Beat the הושענות against a chair or the floor five times, then say the following (see law 118):

תהלים כח
הוֹשִׁיעָה אֶת־עַמֶּךָ, וּבָרֵךְ אֶת־נַחֲלָתֶךָ
וּרְעֵם וְנַשְּׂאֵם עַד־הָעוֹלָם:
מלכים א׳ ח
וְיִהְיוּ דְבָרַי אֵלֶּה, אֲשֶׁר הִתְחַנַּנְתִּי לִפְנֵי יהוה
קְרֹבִים אֶל־יהוה אֱלֹהֵינוּ יוֹמָם וָלָיְלָה
לַעֲשׂוֹת מִשְׁפַּט עַבְדּוֹ וּמִשְׁפַּט עַמּוֹ יִשְׂרָאֵל
דְּבַר־יוֹם בְּיוֹמוֹ:
לְמַעַן דַּעַת כָּל־עַמֵּי הָאָרֶץ כִּי יהוה הוּא הָאֱלֹהִים
אֵין עוֹד:

The ספרי תורה are returned to the ארון קודש, which is then closed.

יְהִי רָצוֹן מִלְּפָנֶיךָ יהוה אֱלֹהֵינוּ וֵאלֹהֵי אֲבוֹתֵינוּ, הַבּוֹחֵר בִּנְבִיאִים טוֹבִים וּבְמִנְהֲגֵיהֶם הַטּוֹבִים, שֶׁתְּקַבֵּל בְּרַחֲמִים וּבְרָצוֹן אֶת תְּפִלָּתֵנוּ וְהַקָּפוֹתֵינוּ. וּזְכָר לָנוּ זְכוּת שִׁבְעַת תְּמִימֶיךָ, וְתָסִיר מְחִצַּת הַבַּרְזֶל הַמַּפְסֶקֶת בֵּינֵינוּ וּבֵינֶךָ, וְתַאֲזִין שַׁוְעָתֵנוּ, וְתֵיטִיב לָנוּ הַחֲתִימָה, תּוֹלֶה אֶרֶץ עַל בְּלִימָה, וְחָתְמֵנוּ בְּסֵפֶר חַיִּים טוֹבִים.

וְהַיּוֹם הַזֶּה תִּתֵּן בִּשְׁכִינַת עֻזֶּךָ חָמֵשׁ גְּבוּרוֹת מְמֻתָּקוֹת, עַל יְדֵי חֲבִיטַת עֲרָבָה מִנְהַג נְבִיאֶיךָ הַקְּדוֹשִׁים, וְתִתְעוֹרֵר הָאַהֲבָה בֵּינֵיהֶם. וּתְנַשְּׁקֵנוּ מִנְּשִׁיקוֹת פִּיךָ, מְמַתֶּקֶת כָּל הַגְּבוּרוֹת וְכָל הַדִּינִין. וְתָאִיר לִשְׁכִינַת עֻזְּךָ בְּשֵׁם יו״ד הֵ״א וָא״ו שֶׁהוּא טַל אוֹרוֹת טַלֶּךָ, וּמִשָּׁם תַּשְׁפִּיעַ שֶׁפַע לְעַבְדְּךָ הַמִּתְפַּלֵּל לְפָנֶיךָ, שֶׁתַּאֲרִיךְ יָמָיו וְתִמְחֹל לוֹ חֲטָאָיו וַעֲוֹנוֹתָיו וּפְשָׁעָיו. וְתִפְשֹׁט יְמִינְךָ וְיָדְךָ לְקַבְּלוֹ בִּתְשׁוּבָה שְׁלֵמָה לְפָנֶיךָ. וְאוֹצָרְךָ
דברים כח
הַטּוֹב תִּפְתַּח לְהַשְׂבִּיעַ מַיִם נֶפֶשׁ שׁוֹקֵקָה, כְּמוֹ שֶׁכָּתוּב: יִפְתַּח יהוה לְךָ אֶת־אוֹצָרוֹ הַטּוֹב אֶת־הַשָּׁמַיִם לָתֵת מְטַר־אַרְצְךָ בְּעִתּוֹ, וּלְבָרֵךְ אֵת כָּל־מַעֲשֵׂה יָדֶךָ: אָמֵן.

The שליח ציבור continues with קדיש שלם on page 555.

ANNULMENT OF VOWS

On the morning before Rosh HaShana, one should annul vows before three men, who sit as judges, saying:

שִׁמְעוּ נָא Listen, please, my masters (expert judges): every vow or oath or prohibition or restriction or ban that I have vowed or sworn, whether awake or in a dream, or that I swore with one of the holy names that may not be erased, or by the holy four-letter name of God, blessed be He, or any naziriteship that I accepted on myself, even a naziriteship like that of Samson, or any prohibition, even against enjoyment, whether I forbade it to myself or others, by any expression of prohibition, whether using the language of prohibition or restriction or ban, or any positive commitment, even to perform a [non-obligatory] commandment, that I undertook by way of a vow or voluntary undertaking or oath or naziriteship or any other such expression, whether it was done by handshake or vow or voluntary undertaking or commandment-mandated custom I have customarily practiced, or any utterance that I have verbalized, or any non-obligatory commandment or good practice or conduct I have vowed and resolved in my heart to do, and have done three times without specifying that it does not have the force of a vow, whether it relates to myself or others, both those known to me and those I have already forgotten – regarding all of them, I hereby express my retroactive regret, and ask and seek their annulment from you, my eminences. For I fear that I may stumble and be trapped, Heaven forbid, in the sin of vows, oaths, naziriteships, bans, prohibitions, restrictions and agreements. I do not regret, Heaven forbid, the performance of the good deeds I have done. I regret, rather, having accepted them on myself in the language of vow, oath, naziriteship, prohibition, ban, restriction, agreement or acceptance of the heart.

Therefore I request annulment for them all.

Judaism is a religion that stresses the sanctity of language, especially when used to accept or impose obligations on oneself. Deep significance attaches to vows and other verbal undertakings: "If a man makes a vow to God, or makes an oath to obligate himself, he must not break his word. He must do everything he said" (Num. 30:3). In general, it is preferable not to invest voluntary commitments with the sacred status of a vow. "If you refrain from making a vow, you will not be guilty" (Deut. 23:23). "It is better not to vow than to make a vow and not fulfill it" (Eccl. 5:4).

התרת נדרים

On the morning before ראש השנה*, one should annul vows before three men, who sit as judges, saying:*

שִׁמְעוּ נָא רַבּוֹתַי (דַּיָּנִים מֻמְחִים), כָּל נֶדֶר אוֹ שְׁבוּעָה אוֹ אִסָּר אוֹ קוֹנָם אוֹ חֵרֶם שֶׁנָּדַרְתִּי אוֹ נִשְׁבַּעְתִּי בְּהָקִיץ אוֹ בַחֲלוֹם, אוֹ נִשְׁבַּעְתִּי בְּשֵׁמוֹת הַקְּדוֹשִׁים שֶׁאֵינָם נִמְחָקִים וּבְשֵׁם הוי״ה בָּרוּךְ הוּא, וְכָל מִינֵי נְזִירוּת שֶׁקִּבַּלְתִּי עָלַי וַאֲפִלּוּ נְזִירוּת שִׁמְשׁוֹן, וְכָל שׁוּם אִסּוּר וַאֲפִלּוּ אִסּוּר הֲנָאָה שֶׁאָסַרְתִּי עָלַי אוֹ עַל אֲחֵרִים בְּכָל לָשׁוֹן שֶׁל אִסּוּר בֵּין בִּלְשׁוֹן אִסּוּר אוֹ חֵרֶם אוֹ קוֹנָם, וְכָל שׁוּם קַבָּלָה אֲפִלּוּ שֶׁל מִצְוָה שֶׁקִּבַּלְתִּי עָלַי בֵּין בִּלְשׁוֹן נֶדֶר בֵּין בִּלְשׁוֹן נְדָבָה בֵּין בִּלְשׁוֹן שְׁבוּעָה בֵּין בִּלְשׁוֹן נְזִירוּת בֵּין בְּכָל לָשׁוֹן, וְגַם הַנַּעֲשֶׂה בִּתְקִיעַת כָּף. בֵּין כָּל נֶדֶר וּבֵין כָּל נְדָבָה וּבֵין שׁוּם מִנְהָג שֶׁל מִצְוָה שֶׁנָּהַגְתִּי אֶת עַצְמִי, וְכָל מוֹצָא שְׂפָתַי שֶׁיָּצָא מִפִּי אוֹ שֶׁנָּדַרְתִּי וְגָמַרְתִּי בְּלִבִּי לַעֲשׂוֹת שׁוּם מִצְוָה מֵהַמִּצְוֹת אוֹ אֵיזוֹ הַנְהָגָה טוֹבָה אוֹ אֵיזֶה דָבָר טוֹב שֶׁנָּהַגְתִּי שָׁלֹשׁ פְּעָמִים, וְלֹא הִתְנֵיתִי שֶׁיְּהֵא בְּלִי נֶדֶר. הֵן דָּבָר שֶׁעָשִׂיתִי, הֵן עַל עַצְמִי הֵן עַל אֲחֵרִים, הֵן אוֹתָן הַיְדוּעִים לִי הֵן אוֹתָן שֶׁכְּבָר שָׁכַחְתִּי. בְּכֻלְּהוֹן אִתְחֲרַטְנָא בְהוֹן מֵעִקָּרָא, וְשׁוֹאֵל וּמְבַקֵּשׁ אֲנִי מִמַּעֲלַתְכֶם הַתָּרָה עֲלֵיהֶם, כִּי יָרֵאתִי פֶּן אֶכָּשֵׁל וְנִלְכַּדְתִּי, חַס וְשָׁלוֹם, בַּעֲוֹן נְדָרִים וּשְׁבוּעוֹת וּנְזִירוֹת וַחֲרָמוֹת וְאִסּוּרִין וְקוֹנָמוֹת וְהַסְכָּמוֹת. וְאֵין אֲנִי תוֹהֵא, חַס וְשָׁלוֹם, עַל קִיּוּם הַמַּעֲשִׂים הַטּוֹבִים הָהֵם שֶׁעָשִׂיתִי, רַק אֲנִי מִתְחָרֵט עַל קַבָּלַת הָעִנְיָנִים בִּלְשׁוֹן נֶדֶר אוֹ שְׁבוּעָה אוֹ נְזִירוּת אוֹ אִסּוּר אוֹ חֵרֶם אוֹ קוֹנָם אוֹ הַסְכָּמָה אוֹ קַבָּלָה בְלֵב, וּמִתְחָרֵט אֲנִי עַל זֶה שֶׁלֹּא אָמַרְתִּי הִנְנִי עוֹשֶׂה דָבָר זֶה בְּלִי נֶדֶר וּשְׁבוּעָה וּנְזִירוּת וְחֵרֶם וְאִסּוּר וְקוֹנָם וְקַבָּלָה בְלֵב.

לָכֵן אֲנִי שׁוֹאֵל הַתָּרָה בְּכֻלְּהוֹן.

ANNULMENT OF VOWS

To avoid entering the High Holy Days under the pressure of unfulfilled undertakings to God, our custom is to annul or "release" vows on the morning before Rosh HaShana. A similar, though more solemn, ceremony takes place immediately prior to Yom Kippur in the form of *Kol Nidrei*.

I regret all these things I have mentioned, whether they related to monetary matters, or to the body or to the soul.

In relation to them all, I regret the language of vow, oath, naziriteship, prohibition, ban, penalty, and acceptance of the heart.

To be sure, according to the law, one who regrets and seeks annulment must specify the vow [from which he seeks release]. But please know, my masters, that it is impossible to specify them, for they are many. I do not seek release from vows that cannot be annulled. Therefore, may it be in your eyes as if I had specified them.

The judges say the following three times:

May all be permitted to you. May all be forgiven you. May all be allowed to you. There is now no vow, oath, naziriteship, ban, prohibition, penalty, ostracism, excommunication, or curse. There is now pardon, forgiveness and atonement. And just as the earthly court has granted permission, so may the heavenly court grant permission.

The one seeking annulment of vows says:

Behold I make a formal declaration before you that I cancel from now onward all vows and all oaths, naziriteships, prohibitions, penalties, bans, agreements and acceptances of the heart that I may accept upon myself, whether awake or in a dream, except a vow to fast that I undertake at the time of the afternoon prayer. If I forget the conditions of this declaration and make a vow from this day onward, as of now I retroactively regret them and declare them to be null and void, without effect or validity, and they shall have no force whatsoever. Regarding them all, I regret them from now and for ever.

---

a sacrifice. *Nezirut*, the acceptance, usually for a period of thirty days, of the status of a nazirite (Num. 6:1–21), involves abstaining from wine or grapes, cutting one's hair, or contact with a corpse.

The basis of release is regret: had one known what one knows now, one would not have undertaken the vow. The release is performed by three adult men sitting as a court, and its effect is retroactive: it is as if the vow had never been made. The entire process emphasizes the solemnity of verbal commitments. We must be true to our word and never lightly promise to do what we may not be able to fulfill.

אֲנִי מִתְחָרֵט עַל כָּל הַנִּזְכָּר, בֵּין אִם הָיוּ הַמַּעֲשִׂים מִדְּבָרִים הַנּוֹגְעִים בְּמָמוֹן, בֵּין מֵהַדְּבָרִים הַנּוֹגְעִים בְּגוּף, בֵּין מֵהַדְּבָרִים הַנּוֹגְעִים אֶל הַנְּשָׁמָה.

בְּכֻלְּהוֹן אֲנִי מִתְחָרֵט עַל לְשׁוֹן נֶדֶר וּשְׁבוּעָה וּנְזִירוּת וְאִסּוּר וְחֵרֶם וְקוֹנָם וְקַבָּלָה בְלֵב.

וְהִנֵּה מִצַּד הַדִּין הַמִּתְחָרֵט וְהַמְבַקֵּשׁ הַתָּרָה צָרִיךְ לִפְרֹט הַנֶּדֶר, אַךְ דְּעוּ נָא רַבּוֹתַי, כִּי אִי אֶפְשָׁר לְפָרְטָם, כִּי רַבִּים הֵם. וְאֵין אֲנִי מְבַקֵּשׁ הַתָּרָה עַל אוֹתָם הַנְּדָרִים שֶׁאֵין לְהַתִּיר אוֹתָם, עַל כֵּן יִהְיוּ נָא בְעֵינֵיכֶם כְּאִלּוּ הָיִיתִי פוֹרְטָם.

The judges say the following three times:

הַכֹּל יִהְיוּ מֻתָּרִים לָךְ, הַכֹּל מְחוּלִים לָךְ, הַכֹּל שְׁרוּיִים לָךְ. אֵין כָּאן לֹא נֶדֶר וְלֹא שְׁבוּעָה וְלֹא נְזִירוּת וְלֹא חֵרֶם וְלֹא אִסּוּר וְלֹא קוֹנָם וְלֹא נִדּוּי וְלֹא שַׁמְתָּא וְלֹא אָרוּר. אֲבָל יֵשׁ כָּאן מְחִילָה וּסְלִיחָה וְכַפָּרָה. וּכְשֵׁם שֶׁמַּתִּירִים בְּבֵית דִּין שֶׁל מַטָּה, כָּךְ יִהְיוּ מֻתָּרִים מִבֵּית דִּין שֶׁל מַעְלָה.

The one seeking annulment of vows says:

הֲרֵי אֲנִי מוֹסֵר מוֹדָעָה לִפְנֵיכֶם, וַאֲנִי מְבַטֵּל מִכָּאן וּלְהַבָּא כָּל הַנְּדָרִים וְכָל שְׁבוּעוֹת וּנְזִירוּת וְאִסּוּרִין וְקוֹנָמוֹת וַחֲרָמוֹת וְהַסְכָּמוֹת וְקַבָּלָה בְלֵב שֶׁאֲקַבֵּל עָלַי בְּעַצְמִי, הֵן בְּהָקִיץ הֵן בַּחֲלוֹם, חוּץ מִנִּדְרֵי תַעֲנִית בִּשְׁעַת מִנְחָה. וּבְאִם אֶשְׁכַּח לִתְנַאי מוֹדָעָה הַזֹּאת וְאֶדֹּר מֵהַיּוֹם עוֹד, מֵעַתָּה אֲנִי מִתְחָרֵט עֲלֵיהֶם וּמַתְנֶה עֲלֵיהֶם שֶׁיִּהְיוּ כֻּלָּן בְּטֵלִין וּמְבֻטָּלִין, לָא שְׁרִירִין וְלָא קַיָּמִין, וְלָא יְהוֹן חָלִין כְּלָל וּכְלָל. בְּכֻלָּן אִתְחֲרַטְנָא בְּהוֹן מֵעַתָּה וְעַד עוֹלָם.

The undertakings involved here relate to vows made to God in respect of behavior not categorically demanded or forbidden by Jewish law. The declaration covers a range of such commitments. A *neder* is a vow forbidding something to oneself; an *isar* is a more general category of self-imposed prohibition. A *shevu'a* is an oath relating to action rather than an object: a promise to do or not to do a certain act. A *ḥerem* renders an object forbidden by designating it as sacred property; a *konam* designates it as if it were

KIDDUSH FOR ROSH HASHANA EVENING

On Shabbat add:

quietly: And it was evening, and it was morning – Gen. 1
יוֹם הַשִּׁשִּׁי the sixth day.

Then the heavens and the earth were completed, Gen. 2
and all their array.
With the seventh day, God completed the work He had done.
He ceased on the seventh day from all the work He had done.
God blessed the seventh day and declared it holy,
because on it He ceased from all His work He had created to do.

On other evenings start Kiddush here:

When saying Kiddush for others: Please pay attention, my masters.

Blessed are You, Lord our God, King of the Universe,
who creates the fruit of the vine.

On Shabbat, add the words in parentheses.

בָּרוּךְ Blessed are You, Lord our God,
King of the Universe,
who has chosen us from among all peoples,
raised us above all tongues,
and made us holy through His commandments.
You have given us, Lord our God, in love, this
(Sabbath and this) Day of Remembrance,
a day of (remembering) blowing the shofar (in love),
a holy assembly in memory of the exodus from Egypt,
for You have chosen us
and sanctified us above all peoples,
and Your word is true and endures for ever.
Blessed are You, Lord, King over all the earth,
who sanctifies (the Sabbath,)
Israel and the Day of Remembrance.

קידוש לליל ראש השנה

On שבת *add:*

quietly וַיְהִי־עֶרֶב וַיְהִי־בֹקֶר בראשית א

יוֹם הַשִּׁשִּׁי:

וַיְכֻלּוּ הַשָּׁמַיִם וְהָאָרֶץ וְכָל־צְבָאָם: בראשית ב

וַיְכַל אֱלֹהִים בַּיּוֹם הַשְּׁבִיעִי מְלַאכְתּוֹ אֲשֶׁר עָשָׂה

וַיִּשְׁבֹּת בַּיּוֹם הַשְּׁבִיעִי מִכָּל־מְלַאכְתּוֹ אֲשֶׁר עָשָׂה:

וַיְבָרֶךְ אֱלֹהִים אֶת־יוֹם הַשְּׁבִיעִי, וַיְקַדֵּשׁ אֹתוֹ

כִּי בוֹ שָׁבַת מִכָּל־מְלַאכְתּוֹ, אֲשֶׁר־בָּרָא אֱלֹהִים, לַעֲשׂוֹת:

On other evenings start קידוש *here:*

When saying קידוש *for others* סַבְרִי מָרָנָן

בָּרוּךְ אַתָּה יהוה אֱלֹהֵינוּ מֶלֶךְ הָעוֹלָם, בּוֹרֵא פְּרִי הַגָּפֶן.

On שבת*, add the words in parentheses.*

בָּרוּךְ אַתָּה יהוה אֱלֹהֵינוּ מֶלֶךְ הָעוֹלָם

אֲשֶׁר בָּחַר בָּנוּ מִכָּל עָם

וְרוֹמְמָנוּ מִכָּל לָשׁוֹן, וְקִדְּשָׁנוּ בְּמִצְוֹתָיו

וַתִּתֶּן לָנוּ יהוה אֱלֹהֵינוּ בְּאַהֲבָה

אֶת יוֹם (הַשַּׁבָּת הַזֶּה וְאֶת יוֹם)

הַזִּכָּרוֹן הַזֶּה, יוֹם (זִכְרוֹן) תְּרוּעָה

(בְּאַהֲבָה) מִקְרָא קֹדֶשׁ, זֵכֶר לִיצִיאַת מִצְרָיִם

כִּי בָנוּ בָחַרְתָּ וְאוֹתָנוּ קִדַּשְׁתָּ מִכָּל הָעַמִּים

וּדְבָרְךָ אֱמֶת וְקַיָּם לָעַד.

בָּרוּךְ אַתָּה יהוה, מֶלֶךְ עַל כָּל הָאָרֶץ

מְקַדֵּשׁ (הַשַּׁבָּת וְ) יִשְׂרָאֵל וְיוֹם הַזִּכָּרוֹן.

On Motza'ei Shabbat, the following Havdala is added:

בָּרוּךְ Blessed are You, Lord our God, King of the Universe, who creates the lights of fire.

Blessed are You, Lord our God, King of the Universe, who distinguishes between sacred and secular, between light and darkness, between Israel and the nations, between the seventh day and the six days of work. You have made a distinction between the holiness of the Sabbath and the holiness of festivals, and have sanctified the seventh day above the six days of work. You have distinguished and sanctified Your people Israel with Your holiness. Blessed are You, Lord, who distinguishes between sacred and sacred.

The following blessing is said on both nights of Rosh HaShana. On the second night, new fruit is placed on the table, and one should have in mind that the blessing is also on the new fruit.

בָּרוּךְ Blessed are You, Lord our God, King of the Universe, who has given us life, sustained us, and brought us to this time.

It is customary for all present to drink of the wine.

On the first night, following Kiddush and "HaMotzi," an apple is dipped in honey and the following is said:

בָּרוּךְ Blessed are You, Lord our God, King of the Universe, who creates the fruit of the tree.

After eating some of the apple and honey, say:

יְהִי רָצוֹן May it be Your will, Lord our God and God of our fathers, that You renew for us a good and sweet year.

KIDDUSH FOR ROSH HASHANA DAY

On Shabbat first say "The children of Israel must keep" and "Remember the Sabbath day" on page 580.

On a Yom Tov that falls on a weekday, some start here:

אֵלֶּה These are the appointed times of the Lord, sacred assemblies, which you shall announce in their due season. Thus Moses announced the Lord's appointed seasons to the children of Israel. *Lev. 23*

On a Yom Tov that falls on a weekday, start here:

תִּקְעוּ Sound the shofar on the new moon, *Ps. 81*
on our feast day when the moon is hidden.
For it is a statute for Israel, an ordinance of the God of Jacob.

When saying Kiddush for others: Please pay attention, my masters.

בָּרוּךְ Blessed are You, Lord our God, King of the Universe, who creates the fruit of the vine.

On מוצאי שבת*, the following* הבדלה *is added:*

בָּרוּךְ אַתָּה יהוה אֱלֹהֵינוּ מֶלֶךְ הָעוֹלָם, בּוֹרֵא מְאוֹרֵי הָאֵשׁ.

בָּרוּךְ אַתָּה יהוה אֱלֹהֵינוּ מֶלֶךְ הָעוֹלָם, הַמַּבְדִּיל בֵּין קֹדֶשׁ לְחֹל, בֵּין אוֹר לְחֹשֶׁךְ, בֵּין יִשְׂרָאֵל לָעַמִּים, בֵּין יוֹם הַשְּׁבִיעִי לְשֵׁשֶׁת יְמֵי הַמַּעֲשֶׂה. בֵּין קְדֻשַּׁת שַׁבָּת לִקְדֻשַּׁת יוֹם טוֹב הִבְדַּלְתָּ, וְאֶת יוֹם הַשְּׁבִיעִי מִשֵּׁשֶׁת יְמֵי הַמַּעֲשֶׂה קִדַּשְׁתָּ, הִבְדַּלְתָּ וְקִדַּשְׁתָּ אֶת עַמְּךָ יִשְׂרָאֵל בִּקְדֻשָּׁתֶךָ. בָּרוּךְ אַתָּה יהוה, הַמַּבְדִּיל בֵּין קֹדֶשׁ לְקֹדֶשׁ.

The following blessing is said on both nights of ראש השנה*. On the second night, new fruit is placed on the table, and one should have in mind that the blessing is also on the new fruit.*

בָּרוּךְ אַתָּה יהוה אֱלֹהֵינוּ מֶלֶךְ הָעוֹלָם
שֶׁהֶחֱיָנוּ וְקִיְּמָנוּ וְהִגִּיעָנוּ לַזְּמַן הַזֶּה.

It is customary for all present to drink of the wine.

On the first night, following קידוש *and* המוציא*,*
an apple is dipped in honey and the following is said:

בָּרוּךְ אַתָּה יהוה אֱלֹהֵינוּ מֶלֶךְ הָעוֹלָם, בּוֹרֵא פְּרִי הָעֵץ.

After eating some of the apple and honey, say:

יְהִי רָצוֹן מִלְּפָנֶיךָ יהוה אֱלֹהֵינוּ וֵאלֹהֵי אֲבוֹתֵינוּ
שֶׁתְּחַדֵּשׁ עָלֵינוּ שָׁנָה טוֹבָה וּמְתוּקָה.

קידושא רבה לראש השנה

On שבת *first say* וְשָׁמְרוּ *and* זָכוֹר *on page 581.*

On יום טוב *that falls on a weekday, some start here:*

אֵלֶּה מוֹעֲדֵי יהוה מִקְרָאֵי קֹדֶשׁ אֲשֶׁר־תִּקְרְאוּ אֹתָם בְּמוֹעֲדָם: ויקרא כג
וַיְדַבֵּר מֹשֶׁה אֶת־מֹעֲדֵי יהוה אֶל־בְּנֵי יִשְׂרָאֵל:

On יום טוב *that falls on a weekday, start here:*

תִּקְעוּ בַחֹדֶשׁ שׁוֹפָר, בַּכֶּסֶה לְיוֹם חַגֵּנוּ: תהלים פא
כִּי חֹק לְיִשְׂרָאֵל הוּא, מִשְׁפָּט לֵאלֹהֵי יַעֲקֹב:

When saying קידוש *for others* סַבְרִי מָרָנָן

בָּרוּךְ אַתָּה יהוה אֱלֹהֵינוּ מֶלֶךְ הָעוֹלָם, בּוֹרֵא פְּרִי הַגָּפֶן.

TASHLIKH

On the first day of Rosh HaShana (or, if that day is Shabbat, on the second day), it is customary, in the afternoon after Minḥa, to go to the banks of a river, or of any stretch of flowing water, and say the following (see law 36):

מִי־אֵל כָּמוֹךָ Who, God, is like You, *Mic. 7*
who pardons iniquity and forgives the transgression
of the remnant of His heritage?
He does not stay angry for ever,
but delights in loving-kindness.
He will again have compassion on us, suppress our iniquities,
and cast into the depths of the sea all their sins.
Grant truth to Jacob, kindness to Abraham,
as You promised our ancestors in ancient times.

מִן־הַמֵּצַר In my distress I called on the Lord. *Ps. 118*
The Lord answered me and set me free.
The Lord is with me; I will not be afraid.
What can man do to me? The Lord is with me.
He is my Helper. I will see the downfall of my enemies.
It is better to take refuge in the Lord than to trust in man.
It is better to take refuge in the Lord than to trust in princes.

Water, too, is a symbol of Torah – of the knowledge that leads to virtue and peace: "They will neither harm nor destroy on all My holy mountain, for the earth will be full of the knowledge of the Lord as the waters cover the sea" (Is. 11:9).

Rivers are a symbol of tears (*Avot deRabbi Nathan,* chapter 31) and thus a sign of repentance and remorse. "By the rivers of Babylon, there we sat and wept as we remembered Zion" (Psalm 137:1). Flowing water is also a symbol of time, mortality and the shortness of life: "One generation goes, another comes… All streams flow into the sea, yet the sea is never full." Consciousness of mortality is a fundamental theme of Rosh HaShana ("Write us in the book of life").

Some have the custom to shake the hems of their clothing, in accordance with Nehemiah 5:13, "Also I shook out my lap, and said: So may God shake out…" (*Maḥzor Oholei Yaakov*).

סדר תשליך

On the first day of ראש השנה *(or, if that day is* שבת*, on the second day),*
it is customary, in the afternoon after מנחה*, to go to the banks of a river,*
or of any stretch of flowing water, and say the following (see law 36):

מיכה ז
מִי־אֵל כָּמְוֹךָ
נֹשֵׂא עָוֹן וְעֹבֵר עַל־פֶּשַׁע לִשְׁאֵרִית נַחֲלָתוֹ
לֹא־הֶחֱזִיק לָעַד אַפּוֹ
כִּי־חָפֵץ חֶסֶד הוּא:
יָשׁוּב יְרַחֲמֵנוּ, יִכְבֹּשׁ עֲוֹנֹתֵינוּ
וְתַשְׁלִיךְ בִּמְצֻלוֹת יָם כָּל־חַטֹּאתָם:
תִּתֵּן אֱמֶת לְיַעֲקֹב, חֶסֶד לְאַבְרָהָם
אֲשֶׁר־נִשְׁבַּעְתָּ לַאֲבֹתֵינוּ מִימֵי קֶדֶם:

תהלים קיח
מִן־הַמֵּצַר קָרָאתִי יָּהּ, עָנָנִי בַמֶּרְחָב יָהּ:
יהוה לִי לֹא אִירָא, מַה־יַּעֲשֶׂה לִי אָדָם:
יהוה לִי בְּעֹזְרָי, וַאֲנִי אֶרְאֶה בְשֹׂנְאָי:
טוֹב לַחֲסוֹת בַּיהוה, מִבְּטֹחַ בָּאָדָם:
טוֹב לַחֲסוֹת בַּיהוה, מִבְּטֹחַ בִּנְדִיבִים:

TASHLIKH: THE CASTING

It is a custom, on the afternoon of the first day of Rosh HaShana (or second, if the first is Shabbat) to go to the shore of the sea, the bank of a river, or other running stream of water, as a symbolic enactment of the words of the prophet Micah: "You will cast (*tashlikh*) into the depths of the sea all their sins" (7:19).

The first mention of the custom is in *Sefer Maharil* of Rabbi Jacob Moellin (d. 1425). Various explanations have been given. Rabbi Moellin himself relates the custom to a midrashic tradition about the binding of Isaac (on Rosh HaShana, according to the Talmud, we blow the ram's horn in memory of the ram Abraham offered as a sacrifice in place of his son). On the journey, the Accuser placed a river in his way. Abraham was undeterred and walked straight through (*Tanhuma, VaYera* 22). Thus, as with the blowing of the shofar, we ask God to forgive us in the merit of Abraham.

KAPAROT

Taking a rooster (men), or a hen (women) in the right hand
(alternatively one may use money), say the following paragraph three times:

בְּנֵי אָדָם Children of men,
those who sat in darkness and the shadow of death, *Ps. 107*
cruelly bound in iron chains –
He brought them out from darkness
and the shadow of death and broke open their chains.
Some were fools with sinful ways,
and suffered affliction because of their iniquities.
They found all food repulsive, and came close to the gates of death.
Then they cried to the Lord in their trouble,
and He saved them from their distress.
He sent His word and healed them; He rescued them from their destruction.
Let them thank the Lord for his loving-kindness
and His wondrous deeds for humankind.
If there is one angel out of a thousand in his defense, *Job 33*
to declare his righteousness on his behalf, He will be gracious to him
and say, "Spare him from going down to the pit; I have found atonement."

A man revolves the rooster around his head and says:

זֶה חֲלִיפָתִי Let this be my exchange, let this be my substitute,
let this be my atonement,
let this rooster go to death
while I go and enter a good, long life and peace.

A woman revolves the hen around her head and says:

זֹאת חֲלִיפָתִי Let this be my exchange, let this be my substitute,
let this be my atonement,
let this hen go to death
while I go and enter a good, long life and peace.

If money is used, then revolve the money around the head and say:

אֵלּוּ חֲלִיפָתִי Let this be my exchange, let this be my substitute,
let this be my atonement,
let this money go to charity
while I go and enter a good, long life and peace.

High Priest confessed the sins of Israel on Yom Kippur (Leviticus, chapter 16). Maimonides explains that though sins cannot be transferred, the rite had a powerful psychological effect, signaling the act of distancing ourselves from past wrongs. Many have the custom of donating money to charity instead.

סדר כפרות

Taking a rooster (men), or a hen (women) in the right hand (alternatively one may use money), say the following paragraph three times:

בְּנֵי אָדָם

יֹשְׁבֵי חֹשֶׁךְ וְצַלְמָוֶת, אֲסִירֵי עֳנִי וּבַרְזֶל: תהלים קז

יוֹצִיאֵם מֵחֹשֶׁךְ וְצַלְמָוֶת, וּמוֹסְרוֹתֵיהֶם יְנַתֵּק:

אֱוִלִים מִדֶּרֶךְ פִּשְׁעָם, וּמֵעֲוֹנֹתֵיהֶם יִתְעַנּוּ:

כָּל־אֹכֶל תְּתַעֵב נַפְשָׁם, וַיַּגִּיעוּ עַד־שַׁעֲרֵי מָוֶת:

וַיִּזְעֲקוּ אֶל־יהוה בַּצַּר לָהֶם, מִמְּצֻקוֹתֵיהֶם יוֹשִׁיעֵם:

יִשְׁלַח דְּבָרוֹ וְיִרְפָּאֵם, וִימַלֵּט מִשְּׁחִיתוֹתָם:

יוֹדוּ לַיהוה חַסְדּוֹ, וְנִפְלְאוֹתָיו לִבְנֵי אָדָם:

אִם־יֵשׁ עָלָיו מַלְאָךְ מֵלִיץ אֶחָד מִנִּי־אָלֶף, לְהַגִּיד לְאָדָם יָשְׁרוֹ: איוב לג

וַיְחֻנֶּנּוּ, וַיֹּאמֶר פְּדָעֵהוּ מֵרֶדֶת שַׁחַת, מָצָאתִי כֹפֶר:

A man revolves the rooster around his head and says:

זֶה חֲלִיפָתִי, זֶה תְּמוּרָתִי, זֶה כַּפָּרָתִי.
זֶה הַתַּרְנְגוֹל יֵלֵךְ לְמִיתָה
וַאֲנִי אֵלֵךְ וְאֶכָּנֵס לְחַיִּים טוֹבִים אֲרֻכִּים וּלְשָׁלוֹם.

A woman revolves the hen around her head and says:

זֹאת חֲלִיפָתִי, זֹאת תְּמוּרָתִי, זֹאת כַּפָּרָתִי.
זֹאת הַתַּרְנְגֹלֶת תֵּלֵךְ לְמִיתָה
וַאֲנִי אֵלֵךְ וְאֶכָּנֵס לְחַיִּים טוֹבִים אֲרֻכִּים וּלְשָׁלוֹם.

If money is used, then revolve the money around the head and say:

אֵלּוּ חֲלִיפָתִי, אֵלּוּ תְּמוּרָתִי, אֵלּוּ כַּפָּרָתִי.
אֵלּוּ הַמָּעוֹת יֵלְכוּ לִצְדָקָה
וַאֲנִי אֵלֵךְ וְאֶכָּנֵס לְחַיִּים טוֹבִים אֲרֻכִּים וּלְשָׁלוֹם.

Kaparot: Literally "atonements," this ritual is first mentioned as a custom in the ninth century. Opposed by some authorities, it was endorsed by others, especially Jewish mystics. Traditionally a chicken was used, so that the rite could not be confused with a sacrificial act (chickens were not offered in the Temple). The symbolic transfer of sins recalls the rite of the goat on which the

VIDUY FOR MINḤA OF EREV YOM KIPPUR

The following is said on Erev Yom Kippur (and by a bride and groom on the eve of their wedding), in the Amida before "My God, guard":

אֱלֹהֵינוּ Our God and God of our fathers,
let our prayer come before You,
and do not hide Yourself from our plea,
for we are not so arrogant or obstinate as to say before You,
LORD, our God and God of our fathers,
we are righteous and have not sinned,
for in truth, we and our fathers have sinned.

Strike the left side of the chest with the right fist while saying each of the sins:

אָשַׁמְנוּ We have sinned, we have acted treacherously,
we have robbed, we have spoken slander.
We have acted perversely, we have acted wickedly,
we have acted presumptuously, we have been violent, we have framed lies.
We have given bad advice, we have deceived, we have scorned,
we have rebelled, we have provoked, we have turned away,
we have committed iniquity, we have transgressed,
we have persecuted, we have been obstinate.
We have acted wickedly, we have corrupted,
we have acted abominably, we have strayed, we have led others astray.

סַרְנוּ We have turned away from Your commandments and good laws,
to no avail, for You are just in all that has befallen us,
for You have acted faithfully while we have done wickedly.

מַה נֹּאמַר What can we say before You, You who dwell on high?
What can we declare before You, You who abide in heaven?
Do You not know all, the hidden and revealed alike?

אַתָּה יוֹדֵעַ You know every secret since the world began,
and what is hidden deep inside every living thing.
You search each person's inner chambers examining conscience and mind.
Nothing is shrouded from You, and nothing is hidden, before Your eyes.
And so, may it be Your will, LORD our God and God of our ancestors,
that You forgive us all our sins,
pardon all our iniquities
and grant us atonement for all of our transgressions.

וידוי למנחה בערב יום הכיפורים

The following is said on ערב יום הכיפורים *(and by a* חתן *and* כלה *on the eve of their wedding), in the Amida before* אֱלֹהַי, נְצֹר*:*

אֱלֹהֵינוּ וֵאלֹהֵי אֲבוֹתֵינוּ
תָּבוֹא לְפָנֶיךָ תְּפִלָּתֵנוּ, וְאַל תִּתְעַלַּם מִתְּחִנָּתֵנוּ.
שֶׁאֵין אֲנַחְנוּ עַזֵּי פָנִים וּקְשֵׁי עֹרֶף לוֹמַר לְפָנֶיךָ
יהוה אֱלֹהֵינוּ וֵאלֹהֵי אֲבוֹתֵינוּ
צַדִּיקִים אֲנַחְנוּ וְלֹא חָטָאנוּ. אֲבָל אֲנַחְנוּ וַאֲבוֹתֵינוּ חָטָאנוּ.

Strike the left side of the chest with the right fist while saying each of the sins:

אָשַׁמְנוּ, בָּגַדְנוּ, גָּזַלְנוּ, דִּבַּרְנוּ דֹפִי
הֶעֱוִינוּ, וְהִרְשַׁעְנוּ, זַדְנוּ, חָמַסְנוּ, טָפַלְנוּ שֶׁקֶר
יָעַצְנוּ רָע, כִּזַּבְנוּ, לַצְנוּ, מָרַדְנוּ, נִאַצְנוּ, סָרַרְנוּ
עָוִינוּ, פָּשַׁעְנוּ, צָרַרְנוּ, קִשִּׁינוּ עֹרֶף
רָשַׁעְנוּ, שִׁחַתְנוּ, תִּעַבְנוּ, תָּעִינוּ, תִּעְתָּעְנוּ.

סַרְנוּ מִמִּצְוֹתֶיךָ וּמִמִּשְׁפָּטֶיךָ הַטּוֹבִים, וְלֹא שָׁוָה לָנוּ.
וְאַתָּה צַדִּיק עַל כָּל הַבָּא עָלֵינוּ
כִּי אֱמֶת עָשִׂיתָ, וַאֲנַחְנוּ הִרְשָׁעְנוּ.

מַה נֹּאמַר לְפָנֶיךָ יוֹשֵׁב מָרוֹם, וּמַה נְּסַפֵּר לְפָנֶיךָ שׁוֹכֵן שְׁחָקִים
הֲלֹא כָּל הַנִּסְתָּרוֹת וְהַנִּגְלוֹת אַתָּה יוֹדֵעַ.

אַתָּה יוֹדֵעַ רָזֵי עוֹלָם וְתַעֲלוּמוֹת סִתְרֵי כָּל חָי.
אַתָּה חוֹפֵשׂ כָּל חַדְרֵי בָטֶן וּבוֹחֵן כְּלָיוֹת וָלֵב.
אֵין דָּבָר נֶעְלָם מִמֶּךָּ וְאֵין נִסְתָּר מִנֶּגֶד עֵינֶיךָ.
וּבְכֵן, יְהִי רָצוֹן מִלְּפָנֶיךָ, יהוה אֱלֹהֵינוּ וֵאלֹהֵי אֲבוֹתֵינוּ
שֶׁתִּסְלַח לָנוּ עַל כָּל חַטֹּאתֵינוּ
וְתִמְחַל לָנוּ עַל כָּל עֲוֹנוֹתֵינוּ
וּתְכַפֵּר לָנוּ עַל כָּל פְּשָׁעֵינוּ.

Strike the left side of the chest with the right fist while saying each of the sins.

עַל חֵטְא For the sin we have sinned before You under duress or freewill,
and for the sin we have sinned before You in hardness of heart.

For the sin we have sinned before You unwittingly,
and for the sin we have sinned before You by an utterance of our lips.

For the sin we have sinned before You by unchastity,
and for the sin we have sinned before You openly or secretly.

For the sin we have sinned before You knowingly and deceitfully,
and for the sin we have sinned before You in speech.

For the sin we have sinned before You by wronging a neighbor,
and for the sin we have sinned before You by thoughts of the heart.

For the sin we have sinned before You in a gathering for immorality,
and for the sin we have sinned before You by insincere confession.

For the sin we have sinned before You by contempt for parents and teachers,
and for the sin we have sinned before You willfully or in error.

For the sin we have sinned before You by force,
and for the sin we have sinned before You by desecrating Your name.

For the sin we have sinned before You by impure lips,
and for the sin we have sinned before You by foolish speech.

For the sin we have sinned before You by the evil inclination,
and for the sin we have sinned before You knowingly or unwittingly.

For all these, God of forgiveness,
forgive us, pardon us, grant us atonement.

עַל חֵטְא *For the sin:* It is a custom to confess sins as part of the Afternoon Service before Yom Kippur so as to enter the holy of holies of Jewish time in the appropriate mood of penitence. Confession is an essential element of *teshuva*, "repentance," and according to Maimonides, its biblical source. God forgives our wrongs, but only if we acknowledge them as wrongs. The

Strike the left side of the chest with the right fist while saying each of the sins.

עַל חֵטְא שֶׁחָטָאנוּ לְפָנֶיךָ בְּאֹנֶס וּבְרָצוֹן
וְעַל חֵטְא שֶׁחָטָאנוּ לְפָנֶיךָ בְּאִמּוּץ הַלֵּב

עַל חֵטְא שֶׁחָטָאנוּ לְפָנֶיךָ בִּבְלִי דָעַת
וְעַל חֵטְא שֶׁחָטָאנוּ לְפָנֶיךָ בְּבִטּוּי שְׂפָתָיִם

עַל חֵטְא שֶׁחָטָאנוּ לְפָנֶיךָ בְּגִלּוּי עֲרָיוֹת
וְעַל חֵטְא שֶׁחָטָאנוּ לְפָנֶיךָ בְּגָלוּי וּבַסָּתֶר

עַל חֵטְא שֶׁחָטָאנוּ לְפָנֶיךָ בְּדַעַת וּבְמִרְמָה
וְעַל חֵטְא שֶׁחָטָאנוּ לְפָנֶיךָ בְּדִבּוּר פֶּה

עַל חֵטְא שֶׁחָטָאנוּ לְפָנֶיךָ בְּהוֹנָאַת רֵעַ
וְעַל חֵטְא שֶׁחָטָאנוּ לְפָנֶיךָ בְּהַרְהוֹר הַלֵּב

עַל חֵטְא שֶׁחָטָאנוּ לְפָנֶיךָ בִּוְעִידַת זְנוּת
וְעַל חֵטְא שֶׁחָטָאנוּ לְפָנֶיךָ בְּוִדּוּי פֶּה

עַל חֵטְא שֶׁחָטָאנוּ לְפָנֶיךָ בְּזִלְזוּל הוֹרִים וּמוֹרִים
וְעַל חֵטְא שֶׁחָטָאנוּ לְפָנֶיךָ בְּזָדוֹן וּבִשְׁגָגָה

עַל חֵטְא שֶׁחָטָאנוּ לְפָנֶיךָ בְּחֹזֶק יָד
וְעַל חֵטְא שֶׁחָטָאנוּ לְפָנֶיךָ בְּחִלּוּל הַשֵּׁם

עַל חֵטְא שֶׁחָטָאנוּ לְפָנֶיךָ בְּטֻמְאַת שְׂפָתָיִם
וְעַל חֵטְא שֶׁחָטָאנוּ לְפָנֶיךָ בְּטִפְשׁוּת פֶּה

עַל חֵטְא שֶׁחָטָאנוּ לְפָנֶיךָ בְּיֵצֶר הָרָע
וְעַל חֵטְא שֶׁחָטָאנוּ לְפָנֶיךָ בְּיוֹדְעִים וּבְלֹא יוֹדְעִים

וְעַל כֻּלָּם אֱלוֹהַּ סְלִיחוֹת סְלַח לָנוּ, מְחַל לָנוּ, כַּפֶּר לָנוּ.

For the sin we have sinned before You by deceit and lies,
and for the sin we have sinned before You by bribery.

For the sin we have sinned before You by scorn,
and for the sin we have sinned before You by evil speech.

For the sin we have sinned before You in business,
and for the sin we have sinned before You with food and drink.

For the sin we have sinned before You by interest and extortion,
and for the sin we have sinned before You by being haughty.

For the sin we have sinned before You by the idle chatter of our lips,
and for the sin we have sinned before You by prying eyes.

For the sin we have sinned before You by arrogance,
and for the sin we have sinned before You by insolence.

For all these, God of forgiveness,
forgive us, pardon us, grant us atonement.

For the sin we have sinned before You by casting off the yoke,
and for the sin we have sinned before You by perverting judgment.

For the sin we have sinned before You by entrapping a neighbor,
and for the sin we have sinned before You by envy.

For the sin we have sinned before You by lack of seriousness,
and for the sin we have sinned before You by obstinacy.

For the sin we have sinned before You by running to do evil,
and for the sin we have sinned before You by gossip.

---

two forms of confession, *Ashamnu*, "We have been guilty" and *Al ḥet*, "For the sin," are both arranged as alphabetical acrostics, as if to say, we confess with every letter of the alphabet and for every possible transgression. Divine forgiveness makes it possible for us to admit our failings and engage in moral and spiritual growth, defeating the rationalizations and self-justifications that may otherwise imprison people in their past and their shortcomings.

עַל חֵטְא שֶׁחָטָאנוּ לְפָנֶיךָ בְּכַחַשׁ וּבְכָזָב
וְעַל חֵטְא שֶׁחָטָאנוּ לְפָנֶיךָ בְּכַפַּת שֹׁחַד

עַל חֵטְא שֶׁחָטָאנוּ לְפָנֶיךָ בְּלָצוֹן
וְעַל חֵטְא שֶׁחָטָאנוּ לְפָנֶיךָ בְּלָשׁוֹן הָרָע

עַל חֵטְא שֶׁחָטָאנוּ לְפָנֶיךָ בְּמַשָּׂא וּבְמַתָּן
וְעַל חֵטְא שֶׁחָטָאנוּ לְפָנֶיךָ בְּמַאֲכָל וּבְמִשְׁתֶּה

עַל חֵטְא שֶׁחָטָאנוּ לְפָנֶיךָ בְּנֶשֶׁךְ וּבְמַרְבִּית
וְעַל חֵטְא שֶׁחָטָאנוּ לְפָנֶיךָ בִּנְטִיַּת גָּרוֹן

עַל חֵטְא שֶׁחָטָאנוּ לְפָנֶיךָ בְּשִׂיחַ שִׂפְתוֹתֵינוּ
וְעַל חֵטְא שֶׁחָטָאנוּ לְפָנֶיךָ בְּשִׂקּוּר עָיִן

עַל חֵטְא שֶׁחָטָאנוּ לְפָנֶיךָ בְּעֵינַיִם רָמוֹת
וְעַל חֵטְא שֶׁחָטָאנוּ לְפָנֶיךָ בְּעַזּוּת מֵצַח

וְעַל כֻּלָּם אֱלוֹהַּ סְלִיחוֹת סְלַח לָנוּ, מְחַל לָנוּ, כַּפֶּר לָנוּ.

עַל חֵטְא שֶׁחָטָאנוּ לְפָנֶיךָ בִּפְרִיקַת עֹל
וְעַל חֵטְא שֶׁחָטָאנוּ לְפָנֶיךָ בִּפְלִילוּת

עַל חֵטְא שֶׁחָטָאנוּ לְפָנֶיךָ בִּצְדִיַּת רֵעַ
וְעַל חֵטְא שֶׁחָטָאנוּ לְפָנֶיךָ בְּצָרוּת עָיִן

עַל חֵטְא שֶׁחָטָאנוּ לְפָנֶיךָ בְּקַלּוּת רֹאשׁ
וְעַל חֵטְא שֶׁחָטָאנוּ לְפָנֶיךָ בְּקַשְׁיוּת עֹרֶף

עַל חֵטְא שֶׁחָטָאנוּ לְפָנֶיךָ בְּרִיצַת רַגְלַיִם לְהָרַע
וְעַל חֵטְא שֶׁחָטָאנוּ לְפָנֶיךָ בִּרְכִילוּת

For the sin we have sinned before You by vain oath,
and for the sin we have sinned before You by baseless hatred.

For the sin we have sinned before You by breach of trust,
and for the sin we have sinned before You by confusion of heart.

For all these, God of forgiveness,
forgive us, pardon us, grant us atonement.

וְעַל חֲטָאִים And for the sins for which we are liable to bring a burnt-offering,
and for the sins for which we are liable to bring a sin-offering,
and for the sins for which we are liable to bring an offering according to our means,
and for the sins for which we are liable to bring a guilt-offering for certain or possible sin,
and for the sins for which we are liable to lashes for rebellion,
and for the sins for which we are liable to forty lashes,
and for the sins for which we are liable to death by the hands of Heaven,
and for the sins for which we are liable to be cut off and childless,
and for the sins for which we are liable to the four death penalties inflicted by the court: stoning, burning, beheading and strangling.

For positive and negative commandments,
whether they can be remedied by an act or not,
for sins known to us and for those that are unknown –
for those that are known,
we have already declared them before You
and confessed them to You;
and for those that are unknown,
before You they are revealed and known,
as it is said,
"The secret things belong to the LORD our God, *Deut. 29*
but the things that are revealed are for us and our children for ever,
that we may fulfill all the words of this Torah."
For You are He who forgives Israel
and pardons the tribes of Yeshurun in every generation,
and besides You we have no king who pardons and forgives, only You.

עַל חֵטְא שֶׁחָטָאנוּ לְפָנֶיךָ בִּשְׁבוּעַת שָׁוְא
וְעַל חֵטְא שֶׁחָטָאנוּ לְפָנֶיךָ בְּשִׂנְאַת חִנָּם

עַל חֵטְא שֶׁחָטָאנוּ לְפָנֶיךָ בִּתְשׂוּמֶת יָד
וְעַל חֵטְא שֶׁחָטָאנוּ לְפָנֶיךָ בְּתִמְהוֹן לֵבָב

וְעַל כֻּלָּם אֱלוֹהַּ סְלִיחוֹת סְלַח לָנוּ, מְחַל לָנוּ, כַּפֶּר לָנוּ.

וְעַל חֲטָאִים שֶׁאָנוּ חַיָּבִים עֲלֵיהֶם עוֹלָה
וְעַל חֲטָאִים שֶׁאָנוּ חַיָּבִים עֲלֵיהֶם חַטָּאת
וְעַל חֲטָאִים שֶׁאָנוּ חַיָּבִים עֲלֵיהֶם קָרְבַּן עוֹלֶה וְיוֹרֵד
וְעַל חֲטָאִים שֶׁאָנוּ חַיָּבִים עֲלֵיהֶם אָשָׁם וַדַּאי וְתָלוּי
וְעַל חֲטָאִים שֶׁאָנוּ חַיָּבִים עֲלֵיהֶם מַכַּת מַרְדּוּת
וְעַל חֲטָאִים שֶׁאָנוּ חַיָּבִים עֲלֵיהֶם מַלְקוּת אַרְבָּעִים
וְעַל חֲטָאִים שֶׁאָנוּ חַיָּבִים עֲלֵיהֶם מִיתָה בִּידֵי שָׁמָיִם
וְעַל חֲטָאִים שֶׁאָנוּ חַיָּבִים עֲלֵיהֶם כָּרֵת וַעֲרִירִי
וְעַל חֲטָאִים שֶׁאָנוּ חַיָּבִים עֲלֵיהֶם אַרְבַּע מִיתוֹת בֵּית דִּין
סְקִילָה, שְׂרֵפָה, הֶרֶג, וְחֶנֶק.

עַל מִצְוַת עֲשֵׂה וְעַל מִצְוַת לֹא תַעֲשֶׂה.
בֵּין שֶׁיֵּשׁ בָּהּ קוּם עֲשֵׂה וּבֵין שֶׁאֵין בָּהּ קוּם עֲשֵׂה.
אֶת הַגְּלוּיִים לָנוּ וְאֶת שֶׁאֵינָם גְּלוּיִים לָנוּ
אֶת הַגְּלוּיִים לָנוּ, כְּבָר אֲמַרְנוּם לְפָנֶיךָ, וְהוֹדִינוּ לְךָ עֲלֵיהֶם
וְאֶת שֶׁאֵינָם גְּלוּיִים לָנוּ, לְפָנֶיךָ הֵם גְּלוּיִים וִידוּעִים
כַּדָּבָר שֶׁנֶּאֱמַר
הַנִּסְתָּרֹת לַיהוה אֱלֹהֵינוּ (דברים כט)
וְהַנִּגְלֹת לָנוּ וּלְבָנֵינוּ עַד־עוֹלָם
לַעֲשׂוֹת אֶת־כָּל־דִּבְרֵי הַתּוֹרָה הַזֹּאת:
כִּי אַתָּה סָלְחָן לְיִשְׂרָאֵל וּמָחֳלָן לְשִׁבְטֵי יְשֻׁרוּן בְּכָל דּוֹר וָדוֹר
וּמִבַּלְעָדֶיךָ אֵין לָנוּ מֶלֶךְ מוֹחֵל וְסוֹלֵחַ אֶלָּא אָתָּה.

אֱלֹהַי My God,
before I was formed I was unworthy,
and now that I have been formed it is as if I had not been formed.
I am dust while alive,
how much more so when I am dead.
See, I am before You like a vessel filled with shame and disgrace.
May it be Your will, LORD my God and God of my fathers,
that I may sin no more,
and as for the sins I have committed before You,
erase them in Your great compassion,
but not by suffering or severe illness.

אֱלֹהַי My God, *Berakhot 17a*
guard my tongue from evil
and my lips from deceitful speech.
To those who curse me, let my soul be silent;
may my soul be to all like the dust.
Open my heart to Your Torah
and let my soul pursue Your commandments.
As for all who plan evil against me,
swiftly thwart their counsel and frustrate their plans.
Act for the sake of Your name; act for the sake of Your right hand;
act for the sake of Your holiness; act for the sake of Your Torah.
That Your beloved ones may be delivered, *Ps. 60*
save with Your right hand and answer me.
May the words of my mouth and the meditation of my heart *Ps. 19*
find favor before You, LORD, my Rock and Redeemer.

Bow, take three steps back, then bow, first left, then right, then center, while saying:
May He who makes peace in His high places,
make peace for us and all Israel – and say: Amen.

יְהִי רָצוֹן May it be Your will, LORD our God and God of our ancestors,
that the Temple be rebuilt speedily in our days,
and grant us a share in Your Torah.
And there we will serve You with reverence,
as in the days of old and as in former years.
Then the offering of Judah and Jerusalem *Mal. 3*
will be pleasing to the LORD as in the days of old and as in former years.

אֱלֹהַי
עַד שֶׁלֹּא נוֹצַרְתִּי אֵינִי כְדַאי
וְעַכְשָׁיו שֶׁנּוֹצַרְתִּי, כְּאִלּוּ לֹא נוֹצַרְתִּי
עָפָר אֲנִי בְּחַיַּי, קַל וָחֹמֶר בְּמִיתָתִי.
הֲרֵי אֲנִי לְפָנֶיךָ כִּכְלִי מָלֵא בוּשָׁה וּכְלִמָּה.
יְהִי רָצוֹן מִלְּפָנֶיךָ, יהוה אֱלֹהַי וֵאלֹהֵי אֲבוֹתַי
שֶׁלֹּא אֶחֱטָא עוֹד.
וּמַה שֶּׁחָטָאתִי לְפָנֶיךָ, מְחֹק בְּרַחֲמֶיךָ הָרַבִּים
אֲבָל לֹא עַל יְדֵי יִסּוּרִים וָחֳלָיִם רָעִים.

ברכות יז. אֱלֹהַי
נְצֹר לְשׁוֹנִי מֵרָע וּשְׂפָתַי מִדַּבֵּר מִרְמָה
וְלִמְקַלְלַי נַפְשִׁי תִדֹּם, וְנַפְשִׁי כֶּעָפָר לַכֹּל תִּהְיֶה.
פְּתַח לִבִּי בְּתוֹרָתֶךָ, וּבְמִצְוֹתֶיךָ תִּרְדֹּף נַפְשִׁי.
וְכָל הַחוֹשְׁבִים עָלַי רָעָה
מְהֵרָה הָפֵר עֲצָתָם וְקַלְקֵל מַחֲשַׁבְתָּם.
עֲשֵׂה לְמַעַן שְׁמֶךָ, עֲשֵׂה לְמַעַן יְמִינֶךָ
עֲשֵׂה לְמַעַן קְדֻשָּׁתֶךָ, עֲשֵׂה לְמַעַן תּוֹרָתֶךָ.
תהלים ס לְמַעַן יֵחָלְצוּן יְדִידֶיךָ, הוֹשִׁיעָה יְמִינְךָ וַעֲנֵנִי:
תהלים יט יִהְיוּ לְרָצוֹן אִמְרֵי פִי וְהֶגְיוֹן לִבִּי לְפָנֶיךָ, יהוה צוּרִי וְגֹאֲלִי:

Bow, take three steps back, then bow, first left, then right, then center, while saying:

עֹשֶׂה שָׁלוֹם / בעשרת ימי תשובה: הַשָּׁלוֹם/ בִּמְרוֹמָיו
הוּא יַעֲשֶׂה שָׁלוֹם עָלֵינוּ וְעַל כָּל יִשְׂרָאֵל וְאִמְרוּ אָמֵן.

יְהִי רָצוֹן מִלְּפָנֶיךָ יהוה אֱלֹהֵינוּ וֵאלֹהֵי אֲבוֹתֵינוּ
שֶׁיִּבָּנֶה בֵּית הַמִּקְדָּשׁ בִּמְהֵרָה בְיָמֵינוּ, וְתֵן חֶלְקֵנוּ בְּתוֹרָתֶךָ
וְשָׁם נַעֲבָדְךָ בְּיִרְאָה כִּימֵי עוֹלָם וּכְשָׁנִים קַדְמֹנִיּוֹת.
מלאכי ג וְעָרְבָה לַיהוה מִנְחַת יְהוּדָה וִירוּשָׁלָםִ כִּימֵי עוֹלָם וּכְשָׁנִים קַדְמֹנִיּוֹת:

SERVICE FOR ḤANUKKA

On each of the eight nights of Ḥanukka, the lights of the menora are lit: one on the first night, two on the second, and so on. On the first night, the rightmost branch of the menora is used; on each subsequent night, an additional light is added to the left. Each night, the new light is lit first, then the others, moving rightwards. If possible, the menora should be displayed near a window so that it is visible from the street.

The lights are lit using a separate flame known as the shamash. The lighting should be carried out as soon as possible after nightfall. On Friday night, it must be done before the beginning of Shabbat. See laws 151–157. Before lighting the Ḥanukka lights, say:

בָּרוּךְ Blessed are You, LORD our God, King of the Universe,
who has made us holy through His commandments,
and has commanded us to light the Ḥanukka lights.

בָּרוּךְ Blessed are You, LORD our God, King of the Universe,
who performed miracles for our ancestors in those days,
at this time.

On the first night, add:

בָּרוּךְ Blessed are You, LORD our God, King of the Universe,
who has given us life, sustained us, and brought us to this time.

---

forces out of Jerusalem and rededicating the desecrated Temple. Ḥanukka is the anniversary of that ceremony of rededication, celebrating not only the military victory and the restoration of Jewish self-government, but also the spiritual victory of Jewish faith over enforced assimilation. Shortly afterward, it was decided to hold an annual eight-day celebration in memory of those events, including the recitation of Hallel.

One incident came to hold immense symbolic significance: the fact that among the debris of the Temple, a single cruse of oil was found, its seal intact, with which the menora – the Temple candelabrum – could be lit. The oil that would normally have lasted for one day burned for eight, the full period of the rededication ceremony. Even after the Temple was destroyed more than two centuries later by the Romans, the Ḥanukka lights bore witness to the fact that after the worst desecration, something pure remains, lighting a way to the future. The Ḥanukka lights became one of the great symbols of Jewish hope.

סדר הדלקת נרות חנוכה

On each of the eight nights of חנוכה, the lights of the חנוכיה are lit: one on the first night, two on the second, and so on. On the first night, the rightmost branch of the חנוכיה is used; on each subsequent night, an additional light is added to the left. Each night, the new light is lit first, then the others, moving rightwards. If possible, the חנוכיה should be displayed near a window so that it is visible from the street.

The lights are lit using a separate flame known as the שמש. The lighting should be carried out as soon as possible after nightfall. On Friday night, it must be done before the beginning of שבת. See laws 151–157. Before lighting the חנוכה lights, say:

בָּרוּךְ אַתָּה יהוה אֱלֹהֵינוּ מֶלֶךְ הָעוֹלָם
אֲשֶׁר קִדְּשָׁנוּ בְּמִצְוֹתָיו וְצִוָּנוּ לְהַדְלִיק נֵר שֶׁל חֲנֻכָּה.

בָּרוּךְ אַתָּה יהוה אֱלֹהֵינוּ מֶלֶךְ הָעוֹלָם
שֶׁעָשָׂה נִסִּים לַאֲבוֹתֵינוּ בַּיָּמִים הָהֵם בַּזְּמַן הַזֶּה.

On the first night, add:

בָּרוּךְ אַתָּה יהוה אֱלֹהֵינוּ מֶלֶךְ הָעוֹלָם
שֶׁהֶחֱיָנוּ וְקִיְּמָנוּ וְהִגִּיעָנוּ לַזְּמַן הַזֶּה.

ḤANUKKA

After the conquests of Alexander the Great, Israel came under the rule of Greece, in the third century BCE under the Ptolemies, based in Egypt; then in the second century BCE under the Seleucids, based in Syria. Beginning in 175 BCE, one of the Seleucid rulers, Antiochus Epiphanes, decided to embark on a campaign of enforced Hellenization of the Jews in Israel. A gymnasium was built at the foot of the Temple Mount. Temple funds were diverted to Greek athletic and cultural events. Eventually, in 167 BCE, the public practice of Judaism was forbidden and a statue of Zeus erected in the Temple. Many Jews went to their death as martyrs rather than abandon their faith.

A group of pious Jews, led by an elderly priest, Mattityahu, and his sons – including most famously Judah, known as the Maccabee – rose in revolt. Over the next three years they fought a successful campaign, driving the Greek

After lighting the first light, say:

הַנֵּרוֹת הַלָּלוּ We light these lights
because of the miracles and wonders,
deliverances and victories
You performed for our ancestors
n those days, at this time,
through Your holy priests.

Sofrim ch. 20

Throughout the eight days of Ḥanukka
these lights are holy
and we are not permitted
to make any other use of them,
except to look at them,

that we may give thanks and praise to Your great name
for Your miracles, Your wonders and Your deliverances.

After all the lights are lit:

מָעוֹז צוּר Refuge, Rock of my salvation:
to You it is a delight to give praise.
Restore my House of prayer,
so that there I may offer You thanksgiving.
When You silence the loud-mouthed foe,
then will I complete, with song and psalm, the altar's dedication.

Shabbat lights, those of Ḥanukka are not lit for the sake of the light they give, but rather are lit in order to "publicize the miracle." A separate light or candle, the *shamash*, is used to light the others, and is placed slightly higher, so that if we benefit from the light, it is from the *shamash*, and not those that form part of the mitzva itself.

מָעוֹז צוּר יְשׁוּעָתִי *Refuge, Rock of my salvation:* Composed in Germany in the thirteenth century. The first letters of the verses spell out the name Mordekhai; other than this we cannot identify the author. The first verse recalls the rededication of the Temple and looks forward to its future restoration. The

After lighting the first light, say:

מסכת סופרים פרק כ

הַנֵּרוֹת הַלָּלוּ אֲנוּ מַדְלִיקִים
עַל הַנִּסִּים וְעַל הַנִּפְלָאוֹת וְעַל הַתְּשׁוּעוֹת וְעַל הַמִּלְחָמוֹת
שֶׁעָשִׂיתָ לַאֲבוֹתֵינוּ בַּיָּמִים הָהֵם בַּזְּמַן הַזֶּה
עַל יְדֵי כֹּהֲנֶיךָ הַקְּדוֹשִׁים.

וְכָל שְׁמוֹנַת יְמֵי חֲנֻכָּה
הַנֵּרוֹת הַלָּלוּ קֹדֶשׁ הֵם
וְאֵין לָנוּ רְשׁוּת לְהִשְׁתַּמֵּשׁ בָּהֶם
אֶלָּא לִרְאוֹתָם בִּלְבָד

כְּדֵי לְהוֹדוֹת וּלְהַלֵּל לְשִׁמְךָ הַגָּדוֹל
עַל נִסֶּיךָ וְעַל נִפְלְאוֹתֶיךָ וְעַל יְשׁוּעָתֶךָ.

After all the lights are lit:

מָעוֹז צוּר יְשׁוּעָתִי לְךָ נָאֶה לְשַׁבֵּחַ
תִּכּוֹן בֵּית תְּפִלָּתִי וְשָׁם תּוֹדָה נְזַבֵּחַ
לְעֵת תָּכִין מַטְבֵּחַ מִצָּר הַמְנַבֵּחַ
אָז אֶגְמֹר בְּשִׁיר מִזְמוֹר חֲנֻכַּת הַמִּזְבֵּחַ.

They are lit at home, at nightfall or soon thereafter, preferably in a position where they can be seen by passersby. Our custom is to light one candle (or olive-oil lamp) on the first night, two on the second, and so on. The first candle is placed at the right of the menora; on each night, the first light to be lit is the leftmost.

הַנֵּרוֹת הַלָּלוּ *We light these lights:* A hymn about the holiness of the lights and why we light them. The text is known from the rabbinic tractate, *Sofrim*, though it has undergone some changes in the intervening centuries. **וְאֵין לָנוּ רְשׁוּת לְהִשְׁתַּמֵּשׁ בָּהֶם** *We are not permitted to make any other use of them:* Unlike

רָעוֹת Troubles sated my soul; my strength was spent with sorrow.
They embittered my life with hardship,
when I was enslaved under Egyptian rule.
But God with His great power
brought out His treasured people,
while Pharaoh's host and followers sank like a stone into the deep.

דְּבִיר He brought me to His holy abode,
but even there I found no rest.
The oppressor came and exiled me,
because I had served strange gods.
I had drunk poisoned wine. I almost perished.
Then Babylon fell, Zerubbabel came: within seventy years I was saved.

כְּרֹת The Agagite, son of Hammedatha,
sought to cut down the tall fir tree,
but it became a trap to him,
and his arrogance was brought to an end.
You raised the head of the Benjaminite,
and the enemy's name You blotted out.
His many sons and his household You hanged on the gallows.

יְוָנִים Then the Greeks gathered against me,
in the days of the Hasmoneans.
They broke down the walls of my towers,
and defiled all the oils.
But from the last remaining flask
a miracle was wrought for Your beloved.
Therefore the sages ordained these eight days for song and praise.

חֲשֹׂף Bare Your holy arm, and hasten the time of salvation.
Take retribution against the evil nation
on behalf of Your servants,
for the hour [of deliverance] has been too long delayed;
there seems no end to the evil days.
Thrust the enemy into the darkness of death,
and establish for us the seven Shepherds.

רָעוֹת שָׂבְעָה נַפְשִׁי   בְּיָגוֹן כֹּחִי כָּלָה
חַיַּי מֵרְרוּ בְקֹשִׁי   בְּשִׁעְבּוּד מַלְכוּת עֶגְלָה
וּבְיָדוֹ הַגְּדוֹלָה   הוֹצִיא אֶת הַסְּגֻלָּה
חֵיל פַּרְעֹה   וְכָל זַרְעוֹ   יָרְדוּ כְּאֶבֶן מְצוּלָה.

דְּבִיר קָדְשׁוֹ הֱבִיאַנִי   וְגַם שָׁם לֹא שָׁקַטְתִּי
וּבָא נוֹגֵשׂ וְהִגְלַנִי   כִּי זָרִים עָבַדְתִּי
וְיֵין רַעַל מָסַכְתִּי   כִּמְעַט שֶׁעָבַרְתִּי
קֵץ בָּבֶל   זְרֻבָּבֶל   לְקֵץ שִׁבְעִים נוֹשַׁעְתִּי.

כְּרֹת קוֹמַת בְּרוֹשׁ בִּקֵּשׁ   אֲגָגִי בֶּן הַמְּדָתָא
וְנִהְיְתָה לּוֹ לְפַח וּלְמוֹקֵשׁ   וְגַאֲוָתוֹ נִשְׁבָּתָה
רֹאשׁ יְמִינִי נִשֵּׂאתָ   וְאוֹיֵב שְׁמוֹ מָחִיתָ
רֹב בָּנָיו   וְקִנְיָנָיו   עַל הָעֵץ תָּלִיתָ.

יְוָנִים נִקְבְּצוּ עָלַי   אֲזַי בִּימֵי חַשְׁמַנִּים
וּפָרְצוּ חוֹמוֹת מִגְדָּלַי   וְטִמְּאוּ כָּל הַשְּׁמָנִים
וּמִנּוֹתַר קַנְקַנִּים   נַעֲשָׂה נֵס לַשּׁוֹשַׁנִּים
בְּנֵי בִינָה   יְמֵי שְׁמוֹנָה   קָבְעוּ שִׁיר וּרְנָנִים.

חֲשׂוֹף זְרוֹעַ קָדְשֶׁךָ   וְקָרֵב קֵץ הַיְשׁוּעָה
נְקֹם נִקְמַת עֲבָדֶיךָ   מֵאֻמָּה הָרְשָׁעָה
כִּי אָרְכָה לָנוּ הַשָּׁעָה   וְאֵין קֵץ לִימֵי הָרָעָה
דְּחֵה אַדְמוֹן   בְּצֵל צַלְמוֹן   הָקֵם לָנוּ רוֹעִים שִׁבְעָה.

---

next four describe, sequentially, four crises and deliverances of Jewish history – slavery in Egypt, the Babylonian exile, Purim, and Ḥanukka itself. The last verse, missing from some manuscripts, may have been a later addition; alternatively it may have been part of the original text, but was censored by the non-Jewish authorities.

SERVICE FOR PURIM

Before the reading of Megillat Esther, the congregation stands and the Reader says the following three blessings:

בָּרוּךְ Blessed are You, Lord our God, King of the Universe,
who has made us holy through His commandments,
and has commanded us about reading the Megilla.

בָּרוּךְ Blessed are You, Lord our God, King of the Universe,
who performed miracles for our ancestors
in those days at this time.

בָּרוּךְ Blessed are You, Lord our God, King of the Universe,
who has given us life, sustained us, and brought us to this time.

The Megilla is read (page 1224). When the reading is completed, the scroll is rolled up and, if a minyan is present, the Reader continues:

בָּרוּךְ Blessed are You, Lord our God, King of the Universe,
who pleads our cause, judges our claim, avenges our wrong,
brings retribution to our enemies, and punishes our foes.
Blessed are You, Lord,
who on behalf of His people Israel,
exacts punishment from all their foes,
the God who brings salvation.

The following is said after the night reading of the Megilla:

אֲשֶׁר הֵנִיא [God] frustrated the plan of the nations,
thwarted the intentions of the crafty.
An evil man rose up against us,
an arrogant branch of Amalek's tree,
haughty, rich, he dug his own pit.
His hubris became his own snare.
He was trapped in the trap he set for others.
Seeking to destroy, he was destroyed.
Haman shared his ancestors' hate,
and stirred against children the hostility of brothers.
He did not remember Saul's act of mercy,
his pity for Agag, through which a new enemy was born.
The wicked planned to cut off the righteous,
but the impure was defeated by the pure.

סדר קריאת המגילה בפורים

Before the reading of מגילת אסתר, the קהל stands and the קורא says the following three blessings:

בָּרוּךְ אַתָּה יהוה אֱלֹהֵינוּ מֶלֶךְ הָעוֹלָם
אֲשֶׁר קִדְּשָׁנוּ בְּמִצְוֹתָיו וְצִוָּנוּ עַל מִקְרָא מְגִלָּה.

בָּרוּךְ אַתָּה יהוה אֱלֹהֵינוּ מֶלֶךְ הָעוֹלָם
שֶׁעָשָׂה נִסִּים לַאֲבוֹתֵינוּ בַּיָּמִים הָהֵם בַּזְּמַן הַזֶּה.

בָּרוּךְ אַתָּה יהוה אֱלֹהֵינוּ מֶלֶךְ הָעוֹלָם
שֶׁהֶחֱיָנוּ וְקִיְּמָנוּ וְהִגִּיעָנוּ לַזְּמַן הַזֶּה.

The מגילה is read (page 1225). When the reading is completed, the scroll is rolled up and, if a מנין is present, the קורא continues:

בָּרוּךְ אַתָּה יהוה אֱלֹהֵינוּ מֶלֶךְ הָעוֹלָם
הָרָב אֶת רִיבֵנוּ, וְהַדָּן אֶת דִּינֵנוּ, וְהַנּוֹקֵם אֶת נִקְמָתֵנוּ
וְהַמְשַׁלֵּם גְּמוּל לְכָל אוֹיְבֵי נַפְשֵׁנוּ, וְהַנִּפְרָע לָנוּ מִצָּרֵינוּ.
בָּרוּךְ אַתָּה יהוה
הַנִּפְרָע לְעַמּוֹ יִשְׂרָאֵל מִכָּל צָרֵיהֶם, הָאֵל הַמּוֹשִׁיעַ.

The following is said after the night reading of the מגילה:

אֲשֶׁר הֵנִיא עֲצַת גּוֹיִם, וַיָּפֶר מַחְשְׁבוֹת עֲרוּמִים.
בְּקוּם עָלֵינוּ אָדָם רָשָׁע, נֵצֶר זָדוֹן מִזֶּרַע עֲמָלֵק.
גָּאָה בְעָשְׁרוֹ וְכָרָה לוֹ בּוֹר, וּגְדֻלָּתוֹ יָקְשָׁה לּוֹ לָכֶד.
דִּמָּה בְנַפְשׁוֹ לִלְכֹּד וְנִלְכַּד, בִּקֵּשׁ לְהַשְׁמִיד וְנִשְׁמַד מְהֵרָה.
הָמָן הוֹדִיעַ אֵיבַת אֲבוֹתָיו, וְעוֹרֵר שִׂנְאַת אַחִים לַבָּנִים.
וְלֹא זָכַר רַחֲמֵי שָׁאוּל, כִּי בְחֶמְלָתוֹ עַל אֲגָג נוֹלַד אוֹיֵב.
זָמַם רָשָׁע לְהַכְרִית צַדִּיק, וְנִלְכַּד טָמֵא בִּידֵי טָהוֹר.

PURIM

Purim is the annual remembrance and celebration of the events described in the book of Esther. During the reign of Aḥashverosh of Persia, one of his

[Mordekhai's] goodness overcame the father's [Saul's] error,
but the evil [Haman] piled sin upon sin.
He hid in his heart his cunning schemes,
intent on his evildoing.
He stretched out his hand against God's holy ones;
he spent his wealth to destroy every memory of them.
When Mordekhai saw the wrath go forth,
and Haman's decrees issued in Shushan,
he put on sackcloth, wrapped himself in mourning,
decreed a fast and sat on ashes.
"Who will arise to atone for error,
and find forgiveness for our ancestors' sins?"
A flower blossomed from the palm tree;
Hadassa arose to wake those who slept.
Her servants hastened Haman to come,
to serve him wine with the venom of serpents.
He had risen by his wealth, but fell by his evil.
He made the very gallows by which he was hanged.
All the inhabitants of the world were amazed
when Haman's ploy (*pur*) became our joy (*Purim*).
The righteous one was saved from evil hands,
the perpetrator suffered the fate of his intended victim.
They undertook to celebrate Purim,
and to rejoice on it year after year.
You heeded the prayer of Mordekhai and Esther;
and Haman and his sons were hanged on the gallows.

The following is said after both night and morning readings of the Megilla:

שׁוֹשַׁנַּת יַעֲקֹב The lily of Jacob rejoiced and was glad,
when, together, they saw Mordekhai robed in royal blue.
You have been their eternal salvation, their hope in every generation;
to make known that all who hope in You will not be put to shame,
all who trust in You will never be humiliated.
Cursed be Haman who sought to destroy me. Blessed be Mordekhai the Yehudi.
Cursed be Zeresh, wife of the one who terrified me.
Blessed be Esther [whose actions saved] me.
Cursed be all the wicked; blessed be all Israel.
And may Ḥarvona, too, be remembered for good.

After the night reading, Ma'ariv continues with "You are Holy" to "great and glorious" on pages 696–698 (on Motza'ei Shabbat, begin with "May the pleasantness" on page 694). The Leader then continues with Full Kaddish on page 700 (omitting the line "May the prayers and pleas"). (On Motza'ei Shabbat, continue with "May God give you" on page 702.) The service continues with Aleinu on page 710, and Mourner's Kaddish on page 712.

In the morning, continue with Ashrei on page 170 and "A redeemer will come" on page 174.

חֶסֶד גָּבַר עַל שִׁגְגַת אָב, וְרָשָׁע הוֹסִיף חֵטְא עַל חֲטָאָיו.
טָמַן בְּלִבּוֹ מַחְשְׁבוֹת עֲרוּמָיו, וַיִּתְמַכֵּר לַעֲשׂוֹת רָעָה.
יָדוֹ שָׁלַח בִּקְדוֹשֵׁי אֵל, כַּסְפּוֹ נָתַן לְהַכְרִית זִכְרָם.
כִּרְאוֹת מָרְדְּכַי כִּי יָצָא קֶצֶף, וְדָתֵי הָמָן נִתְּנוּ בְשׁוּשָׁן.
לָבַשׁ שַׂק וְקָשַׁר מִסְפֵּד וְגָזַר צוֹם וַיֵּשֶׁב עַל הָאֵפֶר.
מִי זֶה יַעֲמֹד לְכַפֵּר שְׁגָגָה, וְלִמְחֹל חַטַּאת עֲוֹן אֲבוֹתֵינוּ.
נֵץ פָּרַח מִלּוּלָב, הֵן הֲדַסָּה עָמְדָה לְעוֹרֵר יְשֵׁנִים.
סָרִיסֶיהָ הִבְהִילוּ לְהָמָן, לְהַשְׁקוֹתוֹ יֵין חֲמַת תַּנִּינִים.
עָמַד בְּעָשְׁרוֹ וְנָפַל בְּרִשְׁעוֹ, עָשָׂה לוֹ עֵץ וְנִתְלָה עָלָיו.
פִּיהֶם פָּתְחוּ כָּל יוֹשְׁבֵי תֵבֵל, כִּי פוּר הָמָן נֶהְפַּךְ לְפוּרֵנוּ.
צַדִּיק נֶחֱלַץ מִיַּד רָשָׁע, אוֹיֵב נִתַּן תַּחַת נַפְשׁוֹ.
קִיְּמוּ עֲלֵיהֶם לַעֲשׂוֹת פּוּרִים וְלִשְׂמֹחַ בְּכָל שָׁנָה וְשָׁנָה.
רָאִיתָ אֶת תְּפִלַּת מָרְדְּכַי וְאֶסְתֵּר, הָמָן וּבָנָיו עַל הָעֵץ תָּלִיתָ.

The following is said after both night and morning readings of the מגילה*:*

שׁוֹשַׁנַּת יַעֲקֹב צָהֲלָה וְשָׂמֵחָה בִּרְאוֹתָם יַחַד תְּכֵלֶת מָרְדְּכָי.
תְּשׁוּעָתָם הָיִיתָ לָנֶצַח, וְתִקְוָתָם בְּכָל דּוֹר וָדוֹר.
לְהוֹדִיעַ שֶׁכָּל קוֶֹיךָ לֹא יֵבֹשׁוּ, וְלֹא יִכָּלְמוּ לָנֶצַח כָּל הַחוֹסִים בָּךְ.
אָרוּר הָמָן אֲשֶׁר בִּקֵּשׁ לְאַבְּדִי, בָּרוּךְ מָרְדְּכַי הַיְּהוּדִי.
אֲרוּרָה זֶרֶשׁ אֵשֶׁת מַפְחִידִי, בְּרוּכָה אֶסְתֵּר בַּעֲדִי.
אֲרוּרִים כָּל הָרְשָׁעִים, בְּרוּכִים כָּל יִשְׂרָאֵל, וְגַם חַרְבוֹנָה זָכוּר לַטּוֹב.

After the night reading, מעריב *continues with* וְאַתָּה קָדוֹשׁ *to* וַיַּאְדִּיר *on pages 697–699 (on* מוצאי שבת*, begin with* וִיהִי נֹעַם *on page 695). The* שליח ציבור *then continues with* קדיש שלם *on page 701 (omitting the line* תִּתְקַבַּל*). (On* מוצאי שבת*, continue with* וְיִתֶּן־לְךָ *on page 703.) The service continues with* עָלֵינוּ *on page 711, and* קדיש יתום *on page 713.*

In the morning, continue with אַשְׁרֵי *on page 171 and* וּבָא לְצִיּוֹן *on page 175.*

---

senior officials, Haman, conspired to "destroy, kill and annihilate all the Jews, young and old, women and children, on a single day" (Esther 3:13) – the day chosen by the lottery (*pur*) that gives the festival its name. The Jews were saved by a combination of the defiance of Mordekhai and the plea of his cousin Esther, who had been taken into the royal harem and was a favorite of the king. Haman's plan was thwarted, and he and his sons were hanged on the gallows they had prepared for Mordekhai.

Memorial Day

At the end of Shaḥarit, after Full Kaddish, the Ark is opened and the following is said by some congregations:

לַמְנַצֵּחַ For the conductor of music. Upon the death of Labben. A psalm of David. *Ps. 9*
I will thank You, LORD, with all my heart; I will tell of all Your wonders.
I will rejoice and exult in You; I will sing praise to Your name, Most High.
My enemies retreat; they stumble and perish before You.
For You have upheld my case and my cause; You have sat enthroned as righteous Judge.
You have rebuked nations and destroyed the wicked, blotting out their name for ever and all time.
The enemy are finished, ruined forever; You have overthrown their cities; even the memory of them is lost.
But the LORD abides forever; He has established His throne for judgment.
He will judge the world with righteousness, and try the cause of peoples with justice.
The LORD is a refuge for the oppressed, a stronghold in times of trouble.
Those who know Your name trust in You, for You, LORD, do not forsake those who seek You.
Sing praise to the LORD who dwells in Zion; tell the peoples of His deeds.
For He who avenges blood remembers; He does not forget the cry of the afflicted.
Have mercy on me, LORD, see how my enemies afflict me. Lift me up from the gates of death,
That in the gates of the Daughter of Zion I may tell all Your praises and rejoice in Your deliverance.
The nations have fallen into the pit they dug; their feet are caught in the net they hid.
The LORD is known by His justice; the wicked is ensnared by the work of his own hands. Reflect on this, Selah.
The wicked return to the grave, all the nations that forget God.
The needy will not be forgotten forever, nor the hope of the afflicted ever be lost.
Arise, LORD, let not man have power; let the nations be judged in Your presence.
Strike them with fear, LORD; let the nations know they are only men. Selah.

The Ark is closed.

סדר תפילת שחרית ליום הזיכרון

At the end of שחרית*, after* קדיש שלם*, the* ארון קודש *is opened and the following is said by some congregations:*

לַמְנַצֵּחַ עַל־מוּת לַבֵּן מִזְמוֹר לְדָוִד: תהלים ט
אוֹדֶה יהוה בְּכָל־לִבִּי, אֲסַפְּרָה כָּל־נִפְלְאוֹתֶיךָ:
אֶשְׂמְחָה וְאֶעֶלְצָה בָךְ, אֲזַמְּרָה שִׁמְךָ עֶלְיוֹן:
בְּשׁוּב־אוֹיְבַי אָחוֹר, יִכָּשְׁלוּ וְיֹאבְדוּ מִפָּנֶיךָ:
כִּי־עָשִׂיתָ מִשְׁפָּטִי וְדִינִי, יָשַׁבְתָּ לְכִסֵּא שׁוֹפֵט צֶדֶק:
גָּעַרְתָּ גוֹיִם אִבַּדְתָּ רָשָׁע, שְׁמָם מָחִיתָ לְעוֹלָם וָעֶד:
הָאוֹיֵב תַּמּוּ חֳרָבוֹת לָנֶצַח, וְעָרִים נָתַשְׁתָּ, אָבַד זִכְרָם הֵמָּה:
וַיהוה לְעוֹלָם יֵשֵׁב, כּוֹנֵן לַמִּשְׁפָּט כִּסְאוֹ:
וְהוּא יִשְׁפֹּט־תֵּבֵל בְּצֶדֶק, יָדִין לְאֻמִּים בְּמֵישָׁרִים:
וִיהִי יהוה מִשְׂגָּב לַדָּךְ, מִשְׂגָּב לְעִתּוֹת בַּצָּרָה:
וְיִבְטְחוּ בְךָ יוֹדְעֵי שְׁמֶךָ, כִּי לֹא־עָזַבְתָּ דֹרְשֶׁיךָ, יהוה:
זַמְּרוּ לַיהוה יֹשֵׁב צִיּוֹן, הַגִּידוּ בָעַמִּים עֲלִילוֹתָיו:
כִּי־דֹרֵשׁ דָּמִים אוֹתָם זָכָר, לֹא־שָׁכַח צַעֲקַת עֲנָוִים:
חָנְנֵנִי יהוה רְאֵה עָנְיִי מִשֹּׂנְאָי, מְרוֹמְמִי מִשַּׁעֲרֵי־מָוֶת:
לְמַעַן אֲסַפְּרָה כָּל־תְּהִלָּתֶיךָ, בְּשַׁעֲרֵי בַת־צִיּוֹן אָגִילָה בִּישׁוּעָתֶךָ:
טָבְעוּ גוֹיִם בְּשַׁחַת עָשׂוּ, בְּרֶשֶׁת־זוּ טָמָנוּ נִלְכְּדָה רַגְלָם:
נוֹדַע יהוה מִשְׁפָּט עָשָׂה, בְּפֹעַל כַּפָּיו נוֹקֵשׁ רָשָׁע, הִגָּיוֹן סֶלָה:
יָשׁוּבוּ רְשָׁעִים לִשְׁאוֹלָה, כָּל־גּוֹיִם שְׁכֵחֵי אֱלֹהִים:
כִּי לֹא לָנֶצַח יִשָּׁכַח אֶבְיוֹן, תִּקְוַת עֲנִיִּים תֹּאבַד לָעַד:
קוּמָה יהוה אַל־יָעֹז אֱנוֹשׁ, יִשָּׁפְטוּ גוֹיִם עַל־פָּנֶיךָ:
שִׁיתָה יהוה מוֹרָה לָהֶם, יֵדְעוּ גוֹיִם, אֱנוֹשׁ הֵמָּה סֶּלָה:

The ארון קודש *is closed.*

Memorial Prayer for Fallen Israeli Soldiers

אָבִינוּ שֶׁבַּשָּׁמַיִם Heavenly Father, God, Source of the spirits of all flesh,
remember, we pray You, the pure souls of our sons and daughters
who heroically gave their lives
in defense of the people and the Land.
Swifter than eagles, stronger than lions,
they fought for the liberation of their people and homeland,
sacrificing their lives for Israel's rebirth in its holy land.
They breathed a spirit of strength and courage
into the whole house of Israel,
in the Land and the Diaspora,
inspiring it to go forward toward its redemption and liberation.
Remember them, our God, for good,
together with the myriad holy ones and heroes of Israel from ancient times.
May their souls be bound in the bonds of everlasting life,
may the Garden of Eden be their resting place,
may they rest in peace
and receive their reward at the End of Days.
Amen.

לְדָוִד Of David. Blessed is the LORD, my Rock, who trains my hands for war, my fingers for battle. He is my Benefactor, my Fortress, my Stronghold and my Refuge, my Shield in whom I trust, He who subdues nations under me. LORD, what is man that You care for him, what are mortals that You think of them? Man is no more than a breath, his days like a fleeting shadow. LORD, part Your heavens and come down; touch the mountains so that they pour forth smoke. Flash forth lightning and scatter them; shoot Your arrows and panic them. Reach out Your hand from on high; deliver me and rescue me from the mighty waters, from the hands of strangers, whose every word is worthless, whose right hands are raised in falsehood. To You, God, I will sing a new song; to You I will play music on a ten-stringed harp. He who gives salvation to kings, who saved His servant David from the cruel sword: may He deliver me and rescue me from the hands of strangers, whose every word is worthless, whose right hands are raised in falsehood. Then our sons will be like saplings, well nurtured in their youth. Our daughters will be like pillars carved for a palace. Our barns will be filled with every kind of provision. Our sheep will increase by thousands, even tens of thousands in our fields. Our oxen will draw heavy loads. There will be no breach in the walls, no going into captivity, no cries of distress in our streets. Happy are the people for whom this is so; happy are the people whose God is the LORD. *Ps. 144*

Memorial Prayer for Fallen Israeli Soldiers

אָבִינוּ שֶׁבַּשָּׁמַיִם, אֵל אֱלֹהֵי הָרוּחוֹת לְכָל בָּשָׂר
זְכֹר נָא אֶת הַנְּשָׁמוֹת הַזַּכּוֹת וְהַטְּהוֹרוֹת שֶׁל בָּנֵינוּ וּבְנוֹתֵינוּ
אֲשֶׁר הֶעֱרוּ אֶת נַפְשָׁם לַמָּוֶת מוֹת גִּבּוֹרִים
בְּהֵחָלְצָם לְעֶזְרַת הָעָם וְהָאָרֶץ.
מִנְּשָׁרִים קַלּוּ מֵאֲרָיוֹת גָּבֵרוּ
בְּמִלְחַמְתָּם לְמַעַן שִׁחְרוּר עַמָּם וּמוֹלַדְתָּם.
בַּעֲלוֹתָם עַל מִזְבַּח תְּקוּמַת יִשְׂרָאֵל בְּאֶרֶץ קָדְשׁוֹ
הֵפִיחוּ רוּחַ עֹז וּגְבוּרָה בְּכָל בֵּית יִשְׂרָאֵל בָּאָרֶץ וּבַתְּפוּצוֹת
וַיִּתְעוֹרֵר לִקְרַאת גְּאֻלָּתוֹ וּפְדוּת נַפְשׁוֹ.
יִזְכְּרֵם אֱלֹהֵינוּ לְטוֹבָה
עִם רִבְבוֹת אַלְפֵי קְדוֹשֵׁי יִשְׂרָאֵל וְגִבּוֹרָיו מִימֵי עוֹלָם
בִּצְרוֹר הַחַיִּים יִצְרֹר אֶת נִשְׁמָתָם
בְּגַן עֵדֶן תְּהֵא מְנוּחָתָם
וְיָנוּחוּ בְשָׁלוֹם עַל מִשְׁכָּבָם
וְיַעַמְדוּ לְגוֹרָלָם לְקֵץ הַיָּמִין
אָמֵן.

תהלים קמד

לְדָוִד בָּרוּךְ יהוה צוּרִי הַמְלַמֵּד יָדַי לַקְרָב, אֶצְבְּעוֹתַי לַמִּלְחָמָה: חַסְדִּי וּמְצוּדָתִי מִשְׂגַּבִּי וּמְפַלְטִי לִי מָגִנִּי וּבוֹ חָסִיתִי הָרוֹדֵד עַמִּי תַחְתָּי: יהוה מָה־אָדָם וַתֵּדָעֵהוּ, בֶּן־אֱנוֹשׁ וַתְּחַשְּׁבֵהוּ: אָדָם לַהֶבֶל דָּמָה יָמָיו כְּצֵל עוֹבֵר: יהוה הַט־שָׁמֶיךָ וְתֵרֵד גַּע בֶּהָרִים וְיֶעֱשָׁנוּ: בְּרוֹק בָּרָק וּתְפִיצֵם, שְׁלַח חִצֶּיךָ וּתְהֻמֵּם: שְׁלַח יָדֶיךָ מִמָּרוֹם פְּצֵנִי וְהַצִּילֵנִי מִמַּיִם רַבִּים מִיַּד בְּנֵי נֵכָר: אֲשֶׁר פִּיהֶם דִּבֶּר־שָׁוְא, וִימִינָם יְמִין שָׁקֶר: אֱלֹהִים שִׁיר חָדָשׁ אָשִׁירָה לָּךְ, בְּנֵבֶל עָשׂוֹר אֲזַמְּרָה־לָּךְ: הַנּוֹתֵן תְּשׁוּעָה לַמְּלָכִים הַפּוֹצֶה אֶת־דָּוִד עַבְדּוֹ מֵחֶרֶב רָעָה: פְּצֵנִי וְהַצִּילֵנִי מִיַּד בְּנֵי־נֵכָר אֲשֶׁר פִּיהֶם דִּבֶּר־שָׁוְא וִימִינָם יְמִין שָׁקֶר: אֲשֶׁר בָּנֵינוּ כִּנְטִעִים מְגֻדָּלִים בִּנְעוּרֵיהֶם בְּנוֹתֵינוּ כְזָוִיֹּת מְחֻטָּבוֹת תַּבְנִית הֵיכָל: מְזָוֵינוּ מְלֵאִים מְפִיקִים מִזַּן אֶל־זַן צֹאונֵנוּ מַאֲלִיפוֹת מְרֻבָּבוֹת בְּחוּצוֹתֵינוּ: אַלּוּפֵינוּ מְסֻבָּלִים אֵין פֶּרֶץ וְאֵין יוֹצֵאת וְאֵין צְוָחָה בִּרְחֹבֹתֵינוּ: אַשְׁרֵי הָעָם שֶׁכָּכָה לּוֹ אַשְׁרֵי הָעָם שֶׁיהוה אֱלֹהָיו:

Ma'ariv for Yom HaAtzma'ut

In Israel and many communities outside Israel the following is said before Ma'ariv:

הודו Thank the LORD for He is good; His loving-kindness is for ever. *Ps. 107*
Let those the LORD redeemed say this – those He redeemed from the enemy's hand, those He gathered from the lands, from east and west, from north and south. Some lost their way in desert wastelands, finding no way to a city where they could live. They were hungry and thirsty, and their spirit grew faint. Then they cried out to the LORD in their trouble, and He rescued them from their distress. He led them by a straight path to a city where they could live. Let them thank the LORD for His loving-kindness and His wondrous deeds for humankind, for He satisfies the thirsty and fills the hungry with good. Some sat in darkness and the shadow of death, cruelly bound in iron chains, for they had rebelled against God's words and despised the counsel of the Most High. He humbled their hearts with hard labor; they stumbled, and there was none to help. Then they cried to the LORD in their trouble, and He saved them from their distress. He brought them out from darkness and the shadow of death and broke open their chains. Let them thank the LORD for His loving-kindness and His wondrous deeds for humankind, for He shattered gates of bronze and broke their iron bars. Some were fools with sinful ways, and suffered affliction because of their iniquities. They found all food repulsive, and came close to the gates of death. Then they cried to the LORD in their trouble, and He saved them from their distress. He sent His word and healed them; He rescued them from their destruction. Let them thank the LORD for His loving-kindness and His wondrous

---

and his descendants were summoned to create a new kind of society, based on the sanctity of human life and the equal dignity of all, where they would be subject to the sovereignty of God alone, constantly conscious of the Divine Presence while striving to be true to the covenant that charged them with being "a kingdom of priests and a holy nation."

Nahmanides (commentary to Lev. 18:25) says that the primary fulfillment of all the commandments, not just those that relate to the land, occurs only

מעריב ליום העצמאות

In ארץ ישראל *and many communities in* חוץ לארץ *the following is said before* מעריב*:*

הֹדוּ לַיהוה כִּי־טוֹב, כִּי לְעוֹלָם חַסְדּוֹ: יֹאמְרוּ גְּאוּלֵי יהוה, אֲשֶׁר תהלים קז
גְּאָלָם מִיַּד־צָר: וּמֵאֲרָצוֹת קִבְּצָם, מִמִּזְרָח וּמִמַּעֲרָב, מִצָּפוֹן
וּמִיָּם: תָּעוּ בַמִּדְבָּר, בִּישִׁימוֹן דָּרֶךְ, עִיר מוֹשָׁב לֹא מָצָאוּ: רְעֵבִים
גַּם־צְמֵאִים, נַפְשָׁם בָּהֶם תִּתְעַטָּף: וַיִּצְעֲקוּ אֶל־יהוה בַּצַּר לָהֶם,
מִמְּצוּקוֹתֵיהֶם יַצִּילֵם: וַיַּדְרִיכֵם בְּדֶרֶךְ יְשָׁרָה, לָלֶכֶת אֶל־עִיר
מוֹשָׁב: יוֹדוּ לַיהוה חַסְדּוֹ, וְנִפְלְאוֹתָיו לִבְנֵי אָדָם: כִּי־הִשְׂבִּיעַ
נֶפֶשׁ שֹׁקֵקָה, וְנֶפֶשׁ רְעֵבָה מִלֵּא־טוֹב: יֹשְׁבֵי חֹשֶׁךְ וְצַלְמָוֶת,
אֲסִירֵי עֳנִי וּבַרְזֶל: כִּי־הִמְרוּ אִמְרֵי־אֵל, וַעֲצַת עֶלְיוֹן נָאָצוּ:
וַיַּכְנַע בֶּעָמָל לִבָּם, כָּשְׁלוּ וְאֵין עֹזֵר: וַיִּזְעֲקוּ אֶל־יהוה בַּצַּר לָהֶם,
מִמְּצֻקוֹתֵיהֶם יוֹשִׁיעֵם: יוֹצִיאֵם מֵחֹשֶׁךְ וְצַלְמָוֶת, וּמוֹסְרוֹתֵיהֶם
יְנַתֵּק: יוֹדוּ לַיהוה חַסְדּוֹ, וְנִפְלְאוֹתָיו לִבְנֵי אָדָם: כִּי־שִׁבַּר דַּלְתוֹת
נְחֹשֶׁת, וּבְרִיחֵי בַרְזֶל גִּדֵּעַ: אֱוִלִים מִדֶּרֶךְ פִּשְׁעָם, וּמֵעֲוֹנֹתֵיהֶם
יִתְעַנּוּ: כָּל־אֹכֶל תְּתַעֵב נַפְשָׁם, וַיַּגִּיעוּ עַד־שַׁעֲרֵי מָוֶת: וַיִּזְעֲקוּ
אֶל־יהוה בַּצַּר לָהֶם, מִמְּצֻקוֹתֵיהֶם יוֹשִׁיעֵם: יִשְׁלַח דְּבָרוֹ וְיִרְפָּאֵם,

---

YOM HAATZMA'UT

Yom HaAtzma'ut, Israel's Independence Day, 5th Iyar 5708, marks the moment when the Jewish people recovered their independence and sovereignty after a lapse of some two thousand years. The longest exile ever endured by a people was at an end. For the first time in two millennia Jews had a home in the sense given by the poet Robert Frost, a place that, "when you have to go there, they have to take you in." Jews had once again returned to the arena of history as a self-determining nation in the land to which Abraham journeyed in his day, and Moses and the Israelites in theirs.

The significance of Israel to Judaism is more than geographical, historical and political. It is spiritual. Israel was and is the Holy Land to which Abraham

deeds for humankind. Let them sacrifice thanksgiving-offerings and tell His deeds with songs of joy. Those who go to sea in ships, plying their trade in the mighty waters, have seen the works of the LORD, His wondrous deeds in the deep. He spoke and stirred up a tempest that lifted high the waves. They rose to the heavens and plunged down to the depths; their souls melted in misery. They reeled and staggered like drunkards; all their skill was to no avail. Then they cried to the LORD in their trouble, and He brought them out of their distress. He stilled the storm to a whisper, and the waves of the sea grew calm. They rejoiced when all was quiet, then He guided them to their destination. Let them thank the LORD for His loving-kindness and His wondrous deeds for humankind. Let them exalt Him in the assembly of the people and praise Him in the council of the elders. He turns rivers into a desert, springs of water into parched land, fruitful land into a salt marsh, because of the wickedness of its inhabitants. He turns the desert into pools of water, parched land into flowing springs; He brings the hungry to live there, they build themselves a town in which to live. They sow fields and plant vineyards that yield a fruitful harvest; He blesses them, and they increase greatly, their herds do not decrease, though they had been few and brought low by oppression, adversity and sorrow. He pours contempt on nobles and makes them wander in a pathless waste. ▸ He lifts the destitute from poverty and enlarges their families like flocks. The upright see and rejoice, but the mouth of all wrongdoers is stopped. Whoever is wise, let him lay these things to heart, and reflect on the loving-kindness of the LORD.

יהוה מָלָךְ The LORD reigns, let the earth be glad. Let the many islands Ps. 97
rejoice. Clouds and thick darkness surround Him; righteousness and justice are the foundation of His throne. Fire goes ahead of Him, consuming His enemies on every side. His lightning lights up the

---

the form of a just, gracious and compassionate social order. It is a code for "societal beatitude" (Rabbi Aharon Lichtenstein), and is predicated on a free, self-governing nation in its own land.

Though Jews, in the long centuries of their dispersion, were scattered over the face of the earth, only in Israel have they formed a majority and

וִימַלְּטֵם מִשְּׁחִיתוֹתָם: יוֹדוּ לַיהוה חַסְדּוֹ, וְנִפְלְאוֹתָיו לִבְנֵי אָדָם: וְיִזְבְּחוּ זִבְחֵי תוֹדָה וִיסַפְּרוּ מַעֲשָׂיו בְּרִנָּה: יוֹרְדֵי הַיָּם בָּאֳנִיּוֹת, עֹשֵׂי מְלָאכָה בְּמַיִם רַבִּים: הֵמָּה רָאוּ מַעֲשֵׂי יהוה, וְנִפְלְאוֹתָיו בִּמְצוּלָה: וַיֹּאמֶר, וַיַּעֲמֵד רוּחַ סְעָרָה, וַתְּרוֹמֵם גַּלָּיו: יַעֲלוּ שָׁמַיִם, יֵרְדוּ תְהוֹמוֹת, נַפְשָׁם בְּרָעָה תִתְמוֹגָג: יָחוֹגּוּ וְיָנוּעוּ כַּשִּׁכּוֹר, וְכָל־חָכְמָתָם תִּתְבַּלָּע: וַיִּצְעֲקוּ אֶל־יהוה בַּצַּר לָהֶם, וּמִמְּצוּקֹתֵיהֶם יוֹצִיאֵם: יָקֵם סְעָרָה לִדְמָמָה, וַיֶּחֱשׁוּ גַּלֵּיהֶם: וַיִּשְׂמְחוּ כִי־יִשְׁתֹּקוּ, וַיַּנְחֵם אֶל־מְחוֹז חֶפְצָם: יוֹדוּ לַיהוה חַסְדּוֹ, וְנִפְלְאוֹתָיו לִבְנֵי אָדָם: וִירוֹמְמוּהוּ בִּקְהַל־עָם, וּבְמוֹשַׁב זְקֵנִים יְהַלְלוּהוּ: יָשֵׂם נְהָרוֹת לְמִדְבָּר, וּמֹצָאֵי מַיִם לְצִמָּאוֹן: אֶרֶץ פְּרִי לִמְלֵחָה, מֵרָעַת יוֹשְׁבֵי בָהּ: יָשֵׂם מִדְבָּר לַאֲגַם־מַיִם, וְאֶרֶץ צִיָּה לְמֹצָאֵי מָיִם: וַיּוֹשֶׁב שָׁם רְעֵבִים, וַיְכוֹנְנוּ עִיר מוֹשָׁב: וַיִּזְרְעוּ שָׂדוֹת, וַיִּטְּעוּ כְרָמִים, וַיַּעֲשׂוּ פְּרִי תְבוּאָה: וַיְבָרְכֵם וַיִּרְבּוּ מְאֹד, וּבְהֶמְתָּם לֹא יַמְעִיט: וַיִּמְעֲטוּ וַיָּשֹׁחוּ, מֵעֹצֶר רָעָה וְיָגוֹן: שֹׁפֵךְ בּוּז עַל־נְדִיבִים, וַיַּתְעֵם בְּתֹהוּ לֹא־דָרֶךְ: ‹ וַיְשַׂגֵּב אֶבְיוֹן מֵעוֹנִי, וַיָּשֶׂם כַּצֹּאן מִשְׁפָּחוֹת: יִרְאוּ יְשָׁרִים וְיִשְׂמָחוּ, וְכָל־עַוְלָה קָפְצָה פִּיהָ: מִי־חָכָם וְיִשְׁמָר־אֵלֶּה, וְיִתְבּוֹנְנוּ חַסְדֵי יהוה:

תהלים צז יהוה מָלָךְ תָּגֵל הָאָרֶץ, יִשְׂמְחוּ אִיִּים רַבִּים: עָנָן וַעֲרָפֶל סְבִיבָיו, צֶדֶק וּמִשְׁפָּט מְכוֹן כִּסְאוֹ: אֵשׁ לְפָנָיו תֵּלֵךְ, וּתְלַהֵט סָבִיב צָרָיו:

"when living in the land of God." Interpreted non-mystically, this means that the Torah represents the architecture of a society; it is not just a code for the salvation of the soul. The Torah includes laws relating to welfare, the environment, the administration of justice, employer-employee relationships, and many other matters not normally thought of as religious. It is less about the ascent of the soul to heaven, than about bringing heaven down to earth in

world; the earth sees and trembles. Mountains melt like wax before the LORD, before the LORD of all the earth. The heavens proclaim His righteousness, and all the peoples see His glory. All who worship images and boast in idols are put to shame. Bow down to Him, all you heavenly powers. Zion hears and rejoices, and the towns of Judah are glad because of Your judgments, LORD. For You, LORD, are supreme over all the earth; You are exalted far above all heavenly powers. Let those who love the LORD hate evil, for He protects the lives of His devoted ones, delivering them from the hand of the wicked. ▸ Light is sown for the righteous, and joy for the upright in heart. Rejoice in the LORD, you who are righteous, and give thanks to His holy name.

מִזְמוֹר A Psalm. Sing a new song to the LORD, for He has done wondrous things; He has saved by His right hand and His holy arm. The LORD has made His salvation known; He has displayed His righteousness in the sight of the nations. He remembered His loving-kindness and faithfulness to the house of Israel; all the ends of the earth have seen the victory of our LORD. Shout for joy to the LORD, all the earth; burst into song, sing with joy, play music. Play music to the LORD on the harp – on the harp with the sound of singing. With trumpets and the sound of the shofar, shout for joy before the LORD, the King. ▸ Let the sea and all that is in it thunder, the world and all who live in it. Let the rivers clap their hands, the mountains sing together for joy – before the LORD, for He is coming to judge the earth. He will judge the world with justice, and the peoples with equity. *Ps. 98*

---

millennia recovered it again. Ravaged by the Holocaust a mere three years earlier, the declaration of Israel's independence was a remarkable act of faith, an everlasting symbol of the victory of life over death, hope over despair.

Some thirty-three centuries ago, Moses prophesied: "Even if you have been dispersed to the most distant land under the heavens, from there the LORD your God will gather you and bring you back" (Deut. 30:4), and so it happened. If, as we believe, there are events that bear the signature of Heaven, this surely was one. Therefore we give thanks to God for bringing the land back to the people, and the people back to the land – the land where our people was born in ancient times, and reborn in ours.

הֵאִירוּ בְרָקָיו תֵּבֵל, רָאֲתָה וַתָּחֵל הָאָרֶץ: הָרִים כַּדּוֹנַג נָמַסּוּ
מִלִּפְנֵי יהוה, מִלִּפְנֵי אֲדוֹן כָּל־הָאָרֶץ: הִגִּידוּ הַשָּׁמַיִם צִדְקוֹ,
וְרָאוּ כָל־הָעַמִּים כְּבוֹדוֹ: יֵבֹשׁוּ כָּל־עֹבְדֵי פֶסֶל הַמִּתְהַלְלִים
בָּאֱלִילִים, הִשְׁתַּחֲווּ־לוֹ כָּל־אֱלֹהִים: שָׁמְעָה וַתִּשְׂמַח צִיּוֹן,
וַתָּגֵלְנָה בְּנוֹת יְהוּדָה, לְמַעַן מִשְׁפָּטֶיךָ יהוה: כִּי־אַתָּה יהוה
עֶלְיוֹן עַל־כָּל־הָאָרֶץ, מְאֹד נַעֲלֵיתָ עַל־כָּל־אֱלֹהִים: אֹהֲבֵי יהוה
שִׂנְאוּ רָע, שֹׁמֵר נַפְשׁוֹת חֲסִידָיו, מִיַּד רְשָׁעִים יַצִּילֵם: ‹ אוֹר
זָרֻעַ לַצַּדִּיק, וּלְיִשְׁרֵי־לֵב שִׂמְחָה: שִׂמְחוּ צַדִּיקִים בַּיהוה, וְהוֹדוּ
לְזֵכֶר קָדְשׁוֹ:

מִזְמוֹר, שִׁירוּ לַיהוה שִׁיר חָדָשׁ כִּי־נִפְלָאוֹת עָשָׂה, הוֹשִׁיעָה־לּוֹ תהלים צח
יְמִינוֹ וּזְרוֹעַ קָדְשׁוֹ: הוֹדִיעַ יהוה יְשׁוּעָתוֹ, לְעֵינֵי הַגּוֹיִם גִּלָּה
צִדְקָתוֹ: זָכַר חַסְדּוֹ וֶאֱמוּנָתוֹ לְבֵית יִשְׂרָאֵל, רָאוּ כָל־אַפְסֵי־אָרֶץ
אֵת יְשׁוּעַת אֱלֹהֵינוּ: הָרִיעוּ לַיהוה כָּל־הָאָרֶץ, פִּצְחוּ וְרַנְּנוּ וְזַמֵּרוּ:
זַמְּרוּ לַיהוה בְּכִנּוֹר, בְּכִנּוֹר וְקוֹל זִמְרָה: בַּחֲצֹצְרוֹת וְקוֹל שׁוֹפָר,
הָרִיעוּ לִפְנֵי הַמֶּלֶךְ יהוה: ‹ יִרְעַם הַיָּם וּמְלֹאוֹ, תֵּבֵל וְיֹשְׁבֵי בָהּ:
נְהָרוֹת יִמְחֲאוּ־כָף, יַחַד הָרִים יְרַנֵּנוּ: לִפְנֵי־יהוה כִּי בָא לִשְׁפֹּט
הָאָרֶץ, יִשְׁפֹּט־תֵּבֵל בְּצֶדֶק, וְעַמִּים בְּמֵישָׁרִים:

---

been able to rule and defend themselves. Only in Israel can a Jew speak a Jewish language, see a Jewish landscape, walk where our ancestors walked and continue the story they began. Only in Israel have Jews been able to live as a nation shaping its own destiny, constructing a society according to its own principles and laws.

Jews were the first to see God in history, to see the unfolding of events as a meaningful narrative, the ongoing story of the covenant between God and His people. The celebration of Yom HaAtzma'ut as a religious festival is part of this faith. Never before had a people survived so long an exile, its identity intact. Never before had a nation that had not known sovereignty for two

It is customary to sing:

הִתְעוֹרְרִי Wake up, wake up,
For your light has come: rise, shine!
Awake, awake, break out in song,
For the LORD's glory is revealed on you.

This is the day the LORD has made; Ps. 118
let us rejoice and be glad in it.

לֹא תֵבֹשִׁי Do not be ashamed, do not be confounded.
Why be downcast? Why do you mourn?
In you the needy of My people find shelter,
And the city shall be rebuilt on its hill.

This is the day the LORD has made;
let us rejoice and be glad in it.

יָמִין Right and left you shall spread out,
And God you will revere.
Through the descendant of Peretz,
We shall rejoice and we shall be glad.

This is the day the LORD has made;
let us rejoice and be glad in it.

Ma'ariv for Weekdays (page 242) is said at this point, in the Yom Tov melody. After Full Kaddish, the Ark is opened and the following is said responsively by the Leader and congregation.

Listen, Israel: the LORD is our God, the LORD is One. Deut. 6

The following is said three times responsively:

The LORD, He is God.

The Leader says the following which is repeated by the congregation.

מִי שֶׁעָשָׂה May He who performed miracles for our ancestors and for us,
redeeming us from slavery to freedom,
grant us a complete redemption soon,
and gather in our dispersed people
from the four quarters of the earth,
so that all Israel may be united in friendship,
and let us say: Amen.

The Ark is closed.

It is customary to sing:

הִתְעוֹרְרִי הִתְעוֹרְרִי
כִּי בָא אוֹרֵךְ קוּמִי אוֹרִי
עוּרִי עוּרִי, שִׁיר דַּבֵּרִי
כְּבוֹד יהוה עָלַיִךְ נִגְלָה.

תהלים קיח
זֶה־הַיּוֹם עָשָׂה יהוה, נָגִילָה וְנִשְׂמְחָה בוֹ:

לֹא תֵבֹשִׁי וְלֹא תִכָּלְמִי
מַה תִּשְׁתּוֹחֲחִי וּמַה תֶּהֱמִי
בָּךְ יֶחֱסוּ עֲנִיֵּי עַמִּי
וְנִבְנְתָה עִיר עַל תִּלָּהּ.
זֶה־הַיּוֹם עָשָׂה יהוה, נָגִילָה וְנִשְׂמְחָה בוֹ:

יָמִין וּשְׂמֹאל תִּפְרֹצִי
וְאֶת יהוה תַּעֲרִיצִי
עַל יַד אִישׁ בֶּן פַּרְצִי
וְנִשְׂמְחָה וְנָגִילָה.
זֶה־הַיּוֹם עָשָׂה יהוה, נָגִילָה וְנִשְׂמְחָה בוֹ:

קדיש שלם, מעריב לחול (page 243) is said at this point, in the יום טוב melody. After קדיש שלם, the ארון קודש is opened and the following is said responsively by the שליח ציבור and the קהל.

דברים ו
שְׁמַע יִשְׂרָאֵל, יהוה אֱלֹהֵינוּ, יהוה אֶחָד:

The following is said three times responsively:

יהוה הוּא הָאֱלֹהִים.

The שליח ציבור says the following which is repeated by the קהל.

מִי שֶׁעָשָׂה נִסִּים לַאֲבוֹתֵינוּ וְלָנוּ
וּגְאָלָנוּ מֵעַבְדוּת לְחֵרוּת
הוּא יִגְאָלֵנוּ גְּאֻלָּה שְׁלֵמָה בְּקָרוֹב
וִיקַבֵּץ נִדָּחֵינוּ מֵאַרְבַּע כַּנְפוֹת הָאָרֶץ
חֲבֵרִים כָּל יִשְׂרָאֵל, וְנֹאמַר אָמֵן.

The ארון קודש is closed.

The Leader continues:

וְכִי־תָבֹאוּ When you go into battle in your land against an enemy who is attacking you, sound a staccato blast on the trumpets. Then you will be remembered by the LORD your God and you will be delivered from your enemies. On your days of rejoicing – your festivals and new moon celebrations – you shall sound a note on the trumpets over your burnt- and peace-offerings, and they will be a remembrance for you before your God. I am the LORD your God. *Num. 10*

The shofar is sounded with a Tekia Gedola and the following is said aloud:

Next year in Jerusalem rebuilt.

All:

May it be Your will, LORD our God and God of our fathers,
That as we have merited to witness the beginning of redemption,
So may we merit to hear the sound of the shofar
of our righteous anointed one, swiftly in our days.

All sing:

שִׁיר הַמַּעֲלוֹת A song of ascents. When the LORD brought back the exiles of Zion we were like people who dream. Then were our mouths filled with laughter, and our tongues with songs of joy. Then was it said among the nations, "The LORD has done great things for them." The LORD did do great things for us and we rejoiced. Bring back our exiles, LORD, like streams in a dry land. May those who sowed in tears, reap in joy. May one who goes out weeping, carrying a bag of seed, come back with songs of joy, carrying his sheaves. *Ps. 126*

The Omer is counted (page 284), followed by Aleinu (page 278).

All sing:

אֲנִי מַאֲמִין I believe with perfect faith
in the coming of the Messiah,
and though he may delay,
I wait daily for his coming.

It is customary to greet each other with the following phrase:

Happy festival; to a complete redemption!

The שליח ציבור *continues:*

במדבר י וְכִי־תָבֹאוּ מִלְחָמָה בְּאַרְצְכֶם עַל־הַצַּר הַצֹּרֵר אֶתְכֶם, וַהֲרֵעֹתֶם בַּחֲצֹצְרֹת, וְנִזְכַּרְתֶּם לִפְנֵי יהוה אֱלֹהֵיכֶם, וְנוֹשַׁעְתֶּם מֵאֹיְבֵיכֶם: וּבְיוֹם שִׂמְחַתְכֶם וּבְמוֹעֲדֵיכֶם וּבְרָאשֵׁי חָדְשֵׁכֶם, וּתְקַעְתֶּם בַּחֲצֹצְרֹת עַל עֹלֹתֵיכֶם וְעַל זִבְחֵי שַׁלְמֵיכֶם, וְהָיוּ לָכֶם לְזִכָּרוֹן לִפְנֵי אֱלֹהֵיכֶם, אֲנִי יהוה אֱלֹהֵיכֶם:

The שופר *is sounded with a* תקיעה גדולה *and the following is said aloud:*

לַשָּׁנָה הַבָּאָה בִּירוּשָׁלַיִם הַבְּנוּיָה.

All:

יְהִי רָצוֹן מִלְּפָנֶיךָ יהוה אֱלֹהֵינוּ וֵאלֹהֵי אֲבוֹתֵינוּ
שֶׁכְּשֵׁם שֶׁזָּכִינוּ לְאַתְחַלְתָּא דִגְאֻלָּה
כֵּן נִזְכֶּה לִשְׁמֹעַ קוֹל שׁוֹפָרוֹ שֶׁל מְשִׁיחַ צִדְקֵנוּ בִּמְהֵרָה בְיָמֵינוּ.

All sing:

תהלים קכו שִׁיר הַמַּעֲלוֹת, בְּשׁוּב יהוה אֶת־שִׁיבַת צִיּוֹן, הָיִינוּ כְּחֹלְמִים: אָז יִמָּלֵא שְׂחוֹק פִּינוּ וּלְשׁוֹנֵנוּ רִנָּה, אָז יֹאמְרוּ בַגּוֹיִם הִגְדִּיל יהוה לַעֲשׂוֹת עִם־אֵלֶּה: הִגְדִּיל יהוה לַעֲשׂוֹת עִמָּנוּ, הָיִינוּ שְׂמֵחִים: שׁוּבָה יהוה אֶת־שְׁבִיתֵנוּ, כַּאֲפִיקִים בַּנֶּגֶב: הַזֹּרְעִים בְּדִמְעָה בְּרִנָּה יִקְצֹרוּ: הָלוֹךְ יֵלֵךְ וּבָכֹה נֹשֵׂא מֶשֶׁךְ־הַזָּרַע, בֹּא־יָבֹא בְרִנָּה נֹשֵׂא אֲלֻמֹּתָיו:

The עומר *is counted (page 285), followed by* עָלֵינוּ *(page 279).*

All sing:

אֲנִי מַאֲמִין בֶּאֱמוּנָה שְׁלֵמָה בְּבִיאַת הַמָּשִׁיחַ
וְאַף עַל פִּי שֶׁיִּתְמַהְמֵהַּ
עִם כָּל זֶה אֲחַכֶּה לּוֹ בְּכָל יוֹם שֶׁיָּבוֹא.

It is customary to greet each other with the following phrase:

מוֹעֲדִים לְשִׂמְחָה לִגְאֻלָּה שְׁלֵמָה

Shaḥarit for Yom HaAtzma'ut

In Israel and many congregations outside Israel, Pesukei DeZimra of Yom Tov on page 398 are said. Shirat HaYam (page 440) is said verse by verse. After the Leader's Repetition, Full Hallel (page 732) is said followed by Half Kaddish (page 156). On Thursdays the Torah is read (page 158). On all days, the following Haftara is read. See law 261.

עוֹד הַיּוֹם This day he will halt at Nob; he will wave his hand, mountain of the daughter of Zion, hill of Jerusalem. See, the sovereign LORD of hosts will lop off the boughs with an axe. The tall trees will be felled, the lofty ones laid low. He will cut down the forest thickets with an axe. Lebanon will fall before the Mighty One. A shoot will grow from the stump of Jesse; from his roots a branch will bear fruit. The spirit of the LORD will rest on him – a spirit of wisdom and understanding, a spirit of counsel and power, a spirit of knowledge and the fear of the LORD, and he will delight in the fear of the LORD. He will not judge by what his eyes see, or decide by what his ears hear; with justice he will judge the poor, and with equity defend the humble in the land. He will strike the earth with the rod of his mouth; with the breath of his lips he will slay the wicked. Justice will be his belt and faithfulness the sash around his waist. The wolf will live with the lamb, the leopard will lie down with the kid, the calf and the lion and the yearling together; and a little child will lead them. The cow will graze with the bear, their young will lie down together, and the lion will eat straw like the ox. An infant will play near the cobra's hole, and a young child put his hand into the viper's nest. They will neither harm nor destroy on all My holy mountain, for the earth will be full of the knowledge of the LORD as the waters cover the sea. On that day the stock of Jesse will stand as a banner for the peoples; nations will rally to him, and his place of rest will be glorious. On that day the LORD will reach out His hand a second time to reclaim the remnant that is left of His people from Assyria, Lower Egypt, Pathros, Cush, Elam, Shinar, Hamath and the islands of the sea. He will raise a banner for the nations and gather the exiles of Israel; He will assemble the scattered people of Judah from the four quarters of the earth. Ephraim's jealousy will

Is. 10:32–12:6

שחרית ליום העצמאות

In ארץ ישראל *and many congregations in* חוץ לארץ, פסוקי דזמרה *of* יום טוב *on page 399 are said.* שירת הים *(page 441) is said verse by verse. After* חזרת הש״ץ, הלל שלם *(page 733) is said followed by* חצי קדיש *(page 157). On Thursdays the* תורה *is read (page 159).*
On all days, the following הפטרה *is read. See law 261.*

ישעיה י:לב–יב:

עוֹד הַיּוֹם בְּנֹב לַעֲמֹד יְנֹפֵף יָדוֹ הַר בַּת־צִיּוֹן גִּבְעַת
יְרוּשָׁלָםִ׃ הִנֵּה הָאָדוֹן יהוה צְבָאוֹת מְסָעֵף פֻּארָה
בְּמַעֲרָצָה וְרָמֵי הַקּוֹמָה גְּדֻעִים וְהַגְּבֹהִים יִשְׁפָּלוּ׃ וְנִקַּף סִבְכֵי
הַיַּעַר בַּבַּרְזֶל וְהַלְּבָנוֹן בְּאַדִּיר יִפּוֹל׃ וְיָצָא חֹטֶר מִגֵּזַע
יִשָׁי וְנֵצֶר מִשָּׁרָשָׁיו יִפְרֶה׃ וְנָחָה עָלָיו רוּחַ יהוה רוּחַ חׇכְמָה וּבִינָה
רוּחַ עֵצָה וּגְבוּרָה רוּחַ דַּעַת וְיִרְאַת יהוה׃ וַהֲרִיחוֹ בְּיִרְאַת יהוה
וְלֹא־לְמַרְאֵה עֵינָיו יִשְׁפּוֹט וְלֹא־לְמִשְׁמַע אׇזְנָיו יוֹכִיחַ׃ וְשָׁפַט
בְּצֶדֶק דַּלִּים וְהוֹכִיחַ בְּמִישׁוֹר לְעַנְוֵי־אָרֶץ וְהִכָּה־אֶרֶץ בְּשֵׁבֶט
פִּיו וּבְרוּחַ שְׂפָתָיו יָמִית רָשָׁע׃ וְהָיָה צֶדֶק אֵזוֹר מׇתְנָיו וְהָאֱמוּנָה
אֵזוֹר חֲלָצָיו׃ וְגָר זְאֵב עִם־כֶּבֶשׂ וְנָמֵר עִם־גְּדִי יִרְבָּץ וְעֵגֶל וּכְפִיר
וּמְרִיא יַחְדָּו וְנַעַר קָטֹן נֹהֵג בָּם׃ וּפָרָה וָדֹב תִּרְעֶינָה יַחְדָּו יִרְבְּצוּ
יַלְדֵיהֶן וְאַרְיֵה כַּבָּקָר יֹאכַל־תֶּבֶן׃ וְשִׁעֲשַׁע יוֹנֵק עַל־חֻר פָּתֶן
וְעַל מְאוּרַת צִפְעוֹנִי גָּמוּל יָדוֹ הָדָה׃ לֹא־יָרֵעוּ וְלֹא־יַשְׁחִיתוּ
בְּכׇל־הַר קׇדְשִׁי כִּי־מָלְאָה הָאָרֶץ דֵּעָה אֶת־יהוה כַּמַּיִם לַיָּם
מְכַסִּים׃ וְהָיָה בַּיּוֹם הַהוּא שֹׁרֶשׁ יִשַׁי אֲשֶׁר עֹמֵד לְנֵס
עַמִּים אֵלָיו גּוֹיִם יִדְרֹשׁוּ וְהָיְתָה מְנֻחָתוֹ כָּבוֹד׃ וְהָיָה ׀
בַּיּוֹם הַהוּא יוֹסִיף אֲדֹנָי ׀ שֵׁנִית יָדוֹ לִקְנוֹת אֶת־שְׁאָר עַמּוֹ אֲשֶׁר
יִשָּׁאֵר מֵאַשּׁוּר וּמִמִּצְרַיִם וּמִפַּתְרוֹס וּמִכּוּשׁ וּמֵעֵילָם וּמִשִּׁנְעָר
וּמֵחֲמָת וּמֵאִיֵּי הַיָּם׃ וְנָשָׂא נֵס לַגּוֹיִם וְאָסַף נִדְחֵי יִשְׂרָאֵל וּנְפֻצוֹת

vanish, and Judah's harassment will end. Ephraim will not be jealous of Judah, nor will Judah be hostile toward Ephraim. They will swoop down on the slopes of Philistia to the west; together they will plunder the people to the east. Edom and Moab will be subject to them, and the Ammonites shall obey them. The LORD will dry up the gulf of the Egyptian sea; with a scorching wind He will sweep His hand over the Euphrates River. He will break it up into seven streams so that people can cross over in sandals. There will be a highway for the remnant of His people that is left from Assyria, as there was for Israel when they came up from Egypt. In that day you will say: "I will praise You, O LORD. Although You were angry with me, Your anger has turned away and You have comforted me. Surely God is my salvation; I will trust and not be afraid. The LORD, the LORD, is my strength and my song; He has become my salvation." With joy you will draw water from the wells of salvation. In that day you will say: "Give thanks to the LORD, call on His name; make known among the nations what He has done, and proclaim that His name is exalted. Sing to the LORD, for He has done glorious things; let this be known to all the world. Shout aloud and sing for joy, people of Zion, for great is the Holy One of Israel among you."

After the Haftara, the Prayer for the State of Israel (page 522) followed by the Memorial for Fallen Israeli Soldiers (page 908) is said. The service then continues with Ashrei until the end of Shaḥarit. At the end of the service, sing:

אֲנִי מַאֲמִין I believe with perfect faith
in the coming of the Messiah,
and though he may delay,
I wait daily for his coming.

YOM YERUSHALAYIM

At Minḥa before Yom Yerushalayim, Taḥanun is omitted. (If Shabbat, Tzidkatekha on page 622 is omitted.) In the evening, Ma'ariv for weekdays is said in the Yom Tov melody. The Omer is counted. Many have the custom to add prayers of thanksgiving at the end of Ma'ariv.

In Shaḥarit, many communities outside Israel and in Israel say the Pesukei DeZimra of Yom Tov (page 398). After the Leader's Repetition, Full Hallel (page 732) is said and the regular service continues.

יְהוּדָה יְקַבֵּץ מֵאַרְבַּע כַּנְפוֹת הָאָרֶץ: וְסָרָה קִנְאַת אֶפְרַיִם וְצֹרְרֵי
יְהוּדָה יִכָּרֵתוּ אֶפְרַיִם לֹא־יְקַנֵּא אֶת־יְהוּדָה וִיהוּדָה לֹא־יָצֹר
אֶת־אֶפְרָיִם: וְעָפוּ בְכָתֵף פְּלִשְׁתִּים יָמָּה יַחְדָּו יָבֹזּוּ אֶת־בְּנֵי־
קֶדֶם אֱדוֹם וּמוֹאָב מִשְׁלוֹח יָדָם וּבְנֵי עַמּוֹן מִשְׁמַעְתָּם: וְהֶחֱרִים
יהוה אֵת לְשׁוֹן יָם־מִצְרַיִם וְהֵנִיף יָדוֹ עַל־הַנָּהָר בַּעְיָם רוּחוֹ
וְהִכָּהוּ לְשִׁבְעָה נְחָלִים וְהִדְרִיךְ בַּנְּעָלִים: וְהָיְתָה מְסִלָּה לִשְׁאָר
עַמּוֹ אֲשֶׁר יִשָּׁאֵר מֵאַשּׁוּר כַּאֲשֶׁר הָיְתָה לְיִשְׂרָאֵל בְּיוֹם עֲלֹתוֹ
מֵאֶרֶץ מִצְרָיִם: וְאָמַרְתָּ בַּיּוֹם הַהוּא אוֹדְךָ יהוה כִּי אָנַפְתָּ בִּי
יָשֹׁב אַפְּךָ וּתְנַחֲמֵנִי: הִנֵּה אֵל יְשׁוּעָתִי אֶבְטַח וְלֹא אֶפְחָד כִּי־
עָזִּי וְזִמְרָת יָהּ יהוה וַיְהִי־לִי לִישׁוּעָה: וּשְׁאַבְתֶּם־מַיִם בְּשָׂשׂוֹן
מִמַּעַיְנֵי הַיְשׁוּעָה: וַאֲמַרְתֶּם בַּיּוֹם הַהוּא הוֹדוּ לַיהוה קִרְאוּ בִשְׁמוֹ
הוֹדִיעוּ בָעַמִּים עֲלִילֹתָיו הַזְכִּירוּ כִּי נִשְׂגָּב שְׁמוֹ: זַמְּרוּ יהוה כִּי
גֵאוּת עָשָׂה מוּדַעַת זֹאת בְּכָל־הָאָרֶץ: צַהֲלִי וָרֹנִּי יוֹשֶׁבֶת צִיּוֹן
כִּי־גָדוֹל בְּקִרְבֵּךְ קְדוֹשׁ יִשְׂרָאֵל:

After the הפטרה, the Prayer for the State of Israel (page 523) followed by the אזכרה for Fallen Israeli Soldiers (page 909) is said. The service then continues with אַשְׁרֵי and וּבָא לְצִיּוֹן until the end of שחרית. At the end of the service, sing:

אֲנִי מַאֲמִין בֶּאֱמוּנָה שְׁלֵמָה, בְּבִיאַת הַמָּשִׁיחַ
וְאַף עַל פִּי שֶׁיִּתְמַהְמֵהַּ
עִם כָּל זֶה אֲחַכֶּה לּוֹ בְּכָל יוֹם שֶׁיָּבוֹא.

יום חירות ירושלים

At מנחה before יום ירושלים, תחנון is omitted. (If שבת, צִדְקָתְךָ on page 623 is omitted.)
In the evening, מעריב לחול is said in the יום טוב melody. The עומר is counted.
Many have the custom to add prayers of thanksgiving at the end of מעריב.

In many communities in חוץ לארץ and in ארץ ישראל say the פסוקי דזמרה of יום טוב שחרית (page 399). After חזרת הש״ץ, הלל שלם (page 733) is said and the regular service continues.

Seliḥot

Seliḥot are said on Fast Days. On Tisha B'Av, Kinot are said instead.
On the Fast of Gedalya, the Seliḥot for the Ten Days of Repentance are said.

SELIḤOT FOR THE TENTH OF TEVET

סְלַח לָנוּ Forgive us, our Father, for in our great foolishness we have blundered. Pardon us, our King, for our iniquities are many.

אֵל אֶרֶךְ You are a God slow to anger, You are called the Master of Compassion, and You have taught the way of repentance. May You remember today and every day the greatness of Your compassion and kindness, for the sake of the descendants of Your beloved ones. Turn toward us in compassion, for You are the Master of Compassion. We come before You in plea and prayer, as You in ancient times showed the humble one [Moses]. Turn from Your fierce anger, as is written in Your Torah. In the shadow of Your wings may we shelter and abide, as on the day when the LORD descended in the cloud. ▸ Overlook sin and wipe away guilt, as on the day when "He stood beside him there." Give ear to our pleading and listen to our speech, as on the day when "he called upon the name of the LORD," and in that place is said –

Congregation then Leader:

And the LORD passed by before him and proclaimed: *Ex. 34*

All say aloud:

יהוה The LORD, the LORD, compassionate and gracious God, slow to anger, abounding in loving-kindness and truth, extending loving-kindness to a thousand generations, forgiving iniquity, rebellion and sin, and absolving [the guilty who repent]. Forgive us our iniquity and our sin, and take us as Your inheritance.

Continue:

סְלַח לָנוּ Forgive us, our Father, for we have sinned. Pardon us, our King, for we have transgressed. For You, LORD, are good and forgiving, abounding in loving-kindness to all who call on You. *Ps. 86*

For with the LORD there is loving-kindness, and great is His power to redeem. *Ps. 130*
LORD, save Israel from all its troubles. It is He who will redeem Israel from *Ps. 25* *Ps. 130*
all its sins. The LORD redeems His servants; those who take refuge in Him *Ps. 34*
shall not be condemned.

סליחות

סליחות *are said on Fast Days. On* תשעה באב, קינות *are said instead.*
On צום גדליה, *the* סליחות *for the* עשרת ימי תשובה *are said.*

סליחות לעשרה בטבת

סְלַח לָנוּ, אָבִינוּ, כִּי בְּרֹב אִוַּלְתֵּנוּ שָׁגִינוּ.
מְחַל לָנוּ, מַלְכֵּנוּ, כִּי רַבּוּ עֲוֹנֵינוּ.

אֵל אֶרֶךְ אַפַּיִם אַתָּה, וּבַעַל הָרַחֲמִים נִקְרֵאתָ, וְדֶרֶךְ תְּשׁוּבָה הוֹרֵיתָ. גְּדֻלַּת רַחֲמֶיךָ וַחֲסָדֶיךָ, תִּזְכֹּר הַיּוֹם וּבְכָל יוֹם לְזֶרַע יְדִידֶיךָ. תֵּפֶן אֵלֵינוּ בְּרַחֲמִים, כִּי אַתָּה הוּא בַּעַל הָרַחֲמִים. בְּתַחֲנוּן וּבִתְפִלָּה פָּנֶיךָ נְקַדֵּם, כְּהוֹדַעְתָּ לֶעָנָו מִקֶּדֶם. מֵחֲרוֹן אַפְּךָ שׁוּב, כְּמוֹ בְּתוֹרָתְךָ כָּתוּב. וּבְצֵל כְּנָפֶיךָ נֶחֱסֶה וְנִתְלוֹנָן, כְּיוֹם וַיֵּרֶד יהוה בֶּעָנָן. ‹ תַּעֲבֹר עַל פֶּשַׁע וְתִמְחֶה אָשָׁם, כְּיוֹם וַיִּתְיַצֵּב עִמּוֹ שָׁם. תַּאֲזִין שַׁוְעָתֵנוּ וְתַקְשִׁיב מֶנּוּ מַאֲמָר, כְּיוֹם וַיִּקְרָא בְשֵׁם יהוה, וְשָׁם נֶאֱמַר

:שליח ציבור then קהל

וַיַּעֲבֹר יהוה עַל־פָּנָיו וַיִּקְרָא שמות לד

All say aloud:

יהוה, יהוה, אֵל רַחוּם וְחַנּוּן, אֶרֶךְ אַפַּיִם, וְרַב־חֶסֶד וֶאֱמֶת: נֹצֵר חֶסֶד לָאֲלָפִים, נֹשֵׂא עָוֹן וָפֶשַׁע וְחַטָּאָה, וְנַקֵּה: וְסָלַחְתָּ לַעֲוֹנֵנוּ וּלְחַטָּאתֵנוּ, וּנְחַלְתָּנוּ:

Continue:

סְלַח לָנוּ אָבִינוּ כִּי חָטָאנוּ, מְחַל לָנוּ מַלְכֵּנוּ כִּי פָשָׁעְנוּ. כִּי־אַתָּה אֲדֹנָי טוֹב תהלים פו
וְסַלָּח, וְרַב־חֶסֶד לְכָל־קֹרְאֶיךָ:

כִּי־עִם־יהוה הַחֶסֶד, וְהַרְבֵּה עִמּוֹ פְדוּת: פְּדֵה אֱלֹהִים אֶת־יִשְׂרָאֵל מִכֹּל תהלים קל / תהלים כה
צָרוֹתָיו: וְהוּא יִפְדֶּה אֶת־יִשְׂרָאֵל מִכֹּל עֲוֹנֹתָיו: פּוֹדֶה יהוה נֶפֶשׁ עֲבָדָיו, תהלים קל / תהלים לד
וְלֹא יֶאְשְׁמוּ כָּל־הַחֹסִים בּוֹ:

כְּרַחֵם As a father has compassion for his children,
so, LORD, have compassion for us.
Salvation is the LORD's; on Your people is Your blessing, Selah! *Ps. 3*
The LORD of hosts is with us, the God of Jacob is our stronghold, Selah! *Ps. 46*
LORD of hosts, happy is the one who trusts in You. *Ps. 84*
LORD, save! May the King answer us on the day we call. *Ps. 20*

▸ Forgive, please, this people's iniquity, *Num. 14*
in the abundance of Your kindness,
and as You have forgiven this people from the time of Egypt until now,
and there it is written:

Congregation then Leader:

And the LORD said, I have forgiven as you asked.

Continue:

הַטֵּה Give ear, my God and hear; open Your eyes and see our desolation, and the city that bears Your name, for it is not on the strength of our righteousness that we throw down our pleadings before You, but on the strength of Your great compassion. LORD, hear me; LORD, forgive; LORD, listen and act and do not delay – for Your sake, my God; for Your city and Your people bear Your name. *Dan. 9*

Our God and God of our fathers:

אֶזְכְּרָה I shall recall the anguish that came to me; He inflicted three blows upon me in this month. He cut me off, He veered me aside, He beat me – but now He has finally drained me out. *Job 16* On the eighth of the month He darkened my right and my left; I marked out all three days for fasting. The king of Greece forced me to write the Torah in his tongue. The ploughmen have ploughed across my back; they made the furrows long. I raged, on the ninth, in shame and disgrace, my mantle of glory and my wreath were taken from me. The man who gave us the words of Heaven was torn from us on that day – that was Ezra the Scribe. On the tenth, Ezekiel the Seer, son of Buzi was commanded, "Write this happening in the scroll, for the remembrance of a people melted away and disgraced; write this very day." *Ezek. 24* The tenth was listed last among the fasts to show the order of the months. My own mouth gapes open with weeping and wailing, and this chronicle of troubles burns within my heart – as the fugitive came to me and said, "The city is crushed." For these things I have scattered dust upon my face. I have spoken now of all four – would that I could shoot an arrow through my heart. For these great torments, I have dug my own grave. "The LORD is righteous; I have rebelled against His word." *Lam. 1* I have called out Your name as I grieve my troubles. Witness my oppression and hear my voice in its entreaty. Hear my pleading, please, hasten my salvation. Do not block Your ears to my sighing, to my cry. *Lam. 3* ▸ In the month of Tevet I was stricken sorely. The world changed its course, from where I stand. I was stubborn, I sinned – yet may He reveal His goodness to me; the One who told the ocean, "Only thus far, come."

כְּרַחֵם אָב עַל בָּנִים, כֵּן תְּרַחֵם יהוה עָלֵינוּ.
לַיהוה הַיְשׁוּעָה, עַל־עַמְּךָ בִרְכָתֶךָ סֶּלָה: תהלים ג
יהוה צְבָאוֹת עִמָּנוּ, מִשְׂגָּב לָנוּ אֱלֹהֵי יַעֲקֹב סֶלָה: תהלים מו
יהוה צְבָאוֹת, אַשְׁרֵי אָדָם בֹּטֵחַ בָּךְ: תהלים פד
יהוה הוֹשִׁיעָה, הַמֶּלֶךְ יַעֲנֵנוּ בְיוֹם־קָרְאֵנוּ: תהלים כ

› סְלַח־נָא לַעֲוֹן הָעָם הַזֶּה כְּגֹדֶל חַסְדֶּךָ במדבר יד
וְכַאֲשֶׁר נָשָׂאתָה לָעָם הַזֶּה מִמִּצְרַיִם וְעַד־הֵנָּה:
וְשָׁם נֶאֱמַר

קהל then שליח ציבור:

וַיֹּאמֶר יהוה, סָלַחְתִּי כִּדְבָרֶךָ:

Continue:

הַטֵּה אֱלֹהַי אָזְנְךָ וּשְׁמָע, פְּקַח עֵינֶיךָ וּרְאֵה שֹׁמְמֹתֵינוּ וְהָעִיר אֲשֶׁר־נִקְרָא שִׁמְךָ דניאל ט
עָלֶיהָ, כִּי לֹא עַל־צִדְקֹתֵינוּ אֲנַחְנוּ מַפִּילִים תַּחֲנוּנֵינוּ לְפָנֶיךָ, כִּי עַל־רַחֲמֶיךָ
הָרַבִּים: אֲדֹנָי שְׁמָעָה, אֲדֹנָי סְלָחָה, אֲדֹנָי הַקְשִׁיבָה וַעֲשֵׂה אַל־תְּאַחַר, לְמַעַנְךָ
אֱלֹהַי, כִּי־שִׁמְךָ נִקְרָא עַל־עִירְךָ וְעַל־עַמֶּךָ:

אֱלֹהֵינוּ וֵאלֹהֵי אֲבוֹתֵינוּ

אֶזְכְּרָה מָצוֹק אֲשֶׁר קְרָאַנִי. בְּשָׁלֹשׁ מַכּוֹת בְּחֹדֶשׁ הַזֶּה הִכַּנִי. גְּדָעַנִי הֱנִיאַנִי
הִכְאַנִי. אַף־עַתָּה הֶלְאָנִי: דִּעְכַנִי בִּשְׁמוֹנָה בוֹ שְׂמָאלִית וִימָנִית. הֲלֹא שְׁלָשְׁתָּן איוב טז
קָבַעְתִּי תַעֲנִית. וּמֶלֶךְ יָוָן אֲנָסַנִי לִכְתֹּב דָּת, יְוָנִית. עַל גַּבִּי חָרְשׁוּ חוֹרְשִׁים,
הֶאֱרִיכוּ מַעֲנִית. זָעַמְתִּי בְּתִשְׁעָה בוֹ בִּכְלִמָּה וָחֵפֶר. חָשַׁךְ מֵעָלַי מְעִיל הוֹד
וָצֶפֶר. טֹרַף טָרַף בּוֹ הַנּוֹתֵן אִמְרֵי שֶׁפֶר. הוּא עֶזְרָא הַסּוֹפֵר. יוֹם עֲשִׂירִי, צֻוָּה
בֶּן בּוּזִי הַחוֹזֶה. כְּתָב לְךָ בְּסֵפֶר הַמַּחֲזֶה. לְזִכָּרוֹן לְעַם נִמְאָס וְנִבְזֶה. אֶת־עֶצֶם יחזקאל כד
הַיּוֹם הַזֶּה: מִנְיַן סֵדֶר חֳדָשִׁים בַּעֲשָׂרָה בוֹ הָעִיר. נְהִי וִילֵל בְּמוֹ פִי אַפְעִיר.
סֵדֶר פִּרְעָנִיּוֹת בְּתוֹךְ לְבָבִי יַבְעִיר. בְּבֹא אֵלַי הַפָּלִיט לֵאמֹר הֻכְּתָה הָעִיר. עַל
אֵלֶּה, עַל פְּנֵי אָבָק זֵרִיתִי. פַּצְתִּי עַל אַרְבַּעְתָּן, לוֹ חֵץ בִּלְבָבִי יָרִיתִי. צָרוֹת עַל
אֵלֶּה, קֶבֶר לִי כָּרִיתִי. צַדִּיק הוּא יהוה, כִּי פִיהוּ מָרִיתִי: קָרָאתִי שִׁמְךָ, מִתְנַחֵם איכה א
עַל רָעָתִי. רְאֵה עָנְיִי וּשְׁמַע קוֹל פְּגִיעָתִי. שְׁמַע תְּחִנָּתִי, חִישׁ נָא יְשׁוּעָתִי.
אַל־תַּעְלֵם אָזְנְךָ לְרַוְחָתִי לְשַׁוְעָתִי: › יֶרַח טֵבֵת, מְאֹד לָקִיתִי בּוֹ. וְנִשְׁתַּנּוּ איכה ג
עָלַי סִדְרֵי נְתִיבוֹ. סָרַרְתִּי, פָּשַׁעְתִּי, יְגַלֶּה לִי טוּבוֹ. הָאוֹמֵר לַיָּם עַד פֹּה תָבוֹא.

אֵל מֶלֶךְ God, King who sits upon a throne of compassion, who acts with loving-kindness, who pardons the iniquities of His people, passing them before Him in order; who forgives sinners and pardons transgressors; who performs righteousness with all flesh and spirit, do not repay their bad actions in kind. ▸ God, You taught us to speak thirteen attributes: recall for us today the covenant of the thirteen attributes, as You in ancient times showed the humble one [Moses], as is written: The LORD descended in the cloud and stood with him there, and proclaimed in the name of the LORD: *Ex. 34*

Congregation then Leader:

And the LORD passed by before him and proclaimed: *Ex. 34*

All say aloud:

יהוה The LORD, the LORD, compassionate and gracious God, slow to anger, abounding in loving-kindness and truth, extending loving-kindness to a thousand generations, forgiving iniquity, rebellion and sin, and absolving [the guilty who repent]. Forgive us our iniquity and our sin, and take us as Your inheritance.

Continue:

סְלַח לָנוּ Forgive us, our Father, for we have sinned. Pardon us, our King, for we have transgressed. For You, LORD, are good and forgiving, abounding in loving-kindness to all who call on You. *Ps. 86*

God, nations came into Your inheritance, they made Your holy Sanctuary impure, they reduced Jerusalem to ruins. God, wanton people came up against us and a gang of oppressors sought out our lives, and did not place You before them. *Ps. 79*

כְּרַחֵם As a father has compassion for his children,
so, LORD, have compassion for us.
Salvation is the LORD's; on Your people is Your blessing, Selah! *Ps. 3*
The LORD of hosts is with us, the God of Jacob is our stronghold, Selah! *Ps. 46*
LORD of hosts, happy is the one who trusts in You. *Ps. 84*
LORD, save! May the King answer us on the day we call. *Ps. 20*

Our God and God of our fathers:

אֶבֶן הָרֹאשָׁה The Temple, Top Stone, is laid to ruin and ploughed over, and the Torah's heirs, Israel, a derision among nations. Within me an aching heart, sickened and pained – we are left as if fatherless, become like orphans. Israel, delicate and refined, fenced by lilies of the Law, has now become mournful, given over to assailants. The faithful city has become like a widow, the countless

אֵל מֶלֶךְ יוֹשֵׁב עַל כִּסֵּא רַחֲמִים, מִתְנַהֵג בַּחֲסִידוּת. מוֹחֵל עֲוֹנוֹת עַמּוֹ, מַעֲבִיר רִאשׁוֹן רִאשׁוֹן. מַרְבֶּה מְחִילָה לְחַטָּאִים, וּסְלִיחָה לְפוֹשְׁעִים. עֹשֶׂה צְדָקוֹת עִם כָּל בָּשָׂר וָרוּחַ, לֹא כְרָעָתָם תִּגְמֹל. ∙ אֵל, הוֹרֵיתָ לָּנוּ לוֹמַר שְׁלֹשׁ עֶשְׂרֵה, וּזְכָר לָנוּ הַיּוֹם בְּרִית שְׁלֹשׁ עֶשְׂרֵה, כְּמוֹ שֶׁהוֹדַעְתָּ לֶעָנָו מִקֶּדֶם, כְּמוֹ שֶׁכָּתוּב: וַיֵּרֶד יהוה בֶּעָנָן, וַיִּתְיַצֵּב עִמּוֹ שָׁם, וַיִּקְרָא בְשֵׁם, יהוה: שמות לד

then שליח ציבור קהל:

וַיַּעֲבֹר יהוה עַל־פָּנָיו וַיִּקְרָא שמות לד

All say aloud:

יהוה, יהוה, אֵל רַחוּם וְחַנּוּן, אֶרֶךְ אַפַּיִם, וְרַב־חֶסֶד וֶאֱמֶת: נֹצֵר חֶסֶד לָאֲלָפִים, נֹשֵׂא עָוֹן וָפֶשַׁע וְחַטָּאָה, וְנַקֵּה: וְסָלַחְתָּ לַעֲוֹנֵנוּ וּלְחַטָּאתֵנוּ, וּנְחַלְתָּנוּ:

Continue:

סְלַח לָנוּ אָבִינוּ כִּי חָטָאנוּ, מְחַל לָנוּ מַלְכֵּנוּ כִּי פָשָׁעְנוּ. כִּי־אַתָּה אֲדֹנָי טוֹב וְסַלָּח, וְרַב־חֶסֶד לְכָל־קֹרְאֶיךָ: תהלים פו

אֱלֹהִים בָּאוּ גוֹיִם בְּנַחֲלָתֶךָ, טִמְּאוּ אֶת־הֵיכַל קָדְשֶׁךָ, שָׂמוּ אֶת־יְרוּשָׁלַםִ לְעִיִּים: אֱלֹהִים, זֵדִים קָמוּ עָלֵינוּ, וַעֲדַת עָרִיצִים בִּקְשׁוּ נַפְשֵׁנוּ, וְלֹא שָׂמוּךָ לְנֶגְדָּם. תהלים עט

כְּרַחֵם אָב עַל בָּנִים, כֵּן תְּרַחֵם יהוה עָלֵינוּ.

לַיהוה הַיְשׁוּעָה, עַל־עַמְּךָ בִרְכָתֶךָ סֶּלָה: תהלים ג

יהוה צְבָאוֹת עִמָּנוּ, מִשְׂגָּב לָנוּ אֱלֹהֵי יַעֲקֹב סֶלָה: תהלים מו

יהוה צְבָאוֹת, אַשְׁרֵי אָדָם בֹּטֵחַ בָּךְ: תהלים פד

יהוה הוֹשִׁיעָה, הַמֶּלֶךְ יַעֲנֵנוּ בְיוֹם־קָרְאֵנוּ: תהלים כ

אֱלֹהֵינוּ וֵאלֹהֵי אֲבוֹתֵינוּ

אֶבֶן הָרֹאשָׁה, לְעִיִּים וְלַחֲרִישָׁה, וְנוֹחֲלֵי מוֹרָשָׁה, מְנוֹד רֹאשׁ בַּלְאֻמִּים. בְּקִרְבִּי לֵב נִכְאָב, נִדְוֶה וְנִדְאָב, נִשְׁאַרְנוּ כְּאֵין אָב, וְהָיִינוּ כִּיתוֹמִים. רַכָּה וַעֲנֻגָּה, בַּשּׁוֹשַׁנִּים סוּגָה, וְעַתָּה הִיא נוּגָה, מְסוּרָה בְּיַד קָמִים. הָיְתָה

descendants of Jacob have been sold for no price. Refined and delicate, worthy of royalty, they have been ploughed across in long furrows over many years and days. The house of Jacob is given over to plunder, to jeering and slander, and the joyous city to plantations of vines. Doused in poison by lawless ones, is the people once desired like offerings, like fragrant incense. They have despised and neglected the Torah of Moses Avi-Zanoaḥ, they can find no rest by night or by day. Awesome, highest God, may the desire arise in You to bring a year of recompense for Israel's strife. Renew our days as of old, Dwelling Place who is our God of old. And wash our red guilt white as wool; our stains as snow. ▸ Strengthen us in awe of You, and in the keeping of Your Law. And come to us, in Your salvation, God who is full of compassion.

אֵל מֶלֶךְ God, King who sits upon a throne of compassion, who acts with loving-kindness, who pardons the iniquities of His people, passing them before Him in order; who forgives sinners and pardons transgressors; who performs righteousness with all flesh and spirit, do not repay their bad actions in kind. ▸ God, You taught us to speak thirteen attributes: recall for us today the covenant of the thirteen attributes, as You in ancient times showed the humble one [Moses], as is written: The Lord descended in the cloud and stood with him there, and *Ex. 34*
proclaimed in the name of the Lord:

Congregation then Leader:

And the Lord passed by before him and proclaimed: *Ex. 34*

All say aloud:

יהוה The Lord, the Lord, compassionate and gracious God, slow to anger, abounding in loving-kindness and truth, extending loving-kindness to a thousand generations, forgiving iniquity, rebellion and sin, and absolving [the guilty who repent]. Forgive us our iniquity and our sin, and take us as Your inheritance.

Continue:

סְלַח לָנוּ Forgive us, our Father, for we have sinned. Pardon us, our King, for we have transgressed. For You, Lord, are good and forgiving, abounding in *Ps. 86*
loving-kindness to all who call on You.

The following is said responsively:

אֲבוֹתַי When my forebears trusted in the name of God, my Rock,
they grew and were successful and also gave forth fruit.
And from the time when they were drawn away to walk with Him in enmity,
they diminished and diminished until the tenth month. *Gen. 8*

כְּאַלְמָנָה, קִרְיָה נֶאֱמָנָה, וְזֶרַע מִי מָנָה, נִמְכְּרוּ בְּלֹא דָמִים. מְעֻנָּגָה וְרַכָּה, צָלְחָה לִמְלוּכָה, וּמְעֻנֵּיתָהּ אֲרֻכָּה, זֶה כַּמָּה שָׁנִים וְיָמִים. בֵּית יַעֲקֹב לְבִזָּה, לְלַעַג וּלְעַזָּה, וְהָעִיר הָעַלִּיזָה, לְמַטְּעֵי כְרָמִים. רְוּוּיָה תַּרְעֵלָה, בְּיַד בְּנֵי עַוְלָה, הָרְצוּיָה כְּעוֹלָה, וְכִקְטֹרֶת הַסַּמִּים. מָאֲסָה לִזְנֹחַ, תּוֹרַת אֲבִי זָנוֹחַ, וְלֹא מָצְאָה מָנוֹחַ, לֵילוֹת וְגַם יָמִים. נוֹרָא אֵל עֶלְיוֹן, מִמְּךָ יְהִי צִבְיוֹן, לְהָשִׁיב לְרִיב צִיּוֹן, שְׁנַת שִׁלּוּמִים. חַדֵּשׁ יָמֵינוּ כְּקֶדֶם, מְעוֹנָה אֱלֹהֵי קֶדֶם, וְלַבֵּן כְּצֶמֶר אָדֹם, וּכְשֶׁלֶג כְּתָמִים. ‹ חַזְּקֵנוּ בְּיִרְאָתֶךָ, וּבְקִיּוּם תּוֹרָתֶךָ, וּפָקְדֵנוּ בִּישׁוּעָתֶךָ, אֵל מָלֵא רַחֲמִים.

אֵל מֶלֶךְ יוֹשֵׁב עַל כִּסֵּא רַחֲמִים, מִתְנַהֵג בַּחֲסִידוּת. מוֹחֵל עֲוֹנוֹת עַמּוֹ, מַעֲבִיר רִאשׁוֹן רִאשׁוֹן. מַרְבֶּה מְחִילָה לְחַטָּאִים, וּסְלִיחָה לְפוֹשְׁעִים. עֹשֶׂה צְדָקוֹת עִם כָּל בָּשָׂר וָרוּחַ, לֹא כְרָעָתָם תִּגְמֹל. ‹ אֵל, הוֹרֵיתָ לָּנוּ לוֹמַר שְׁלֹשׁ עֶשְׂרֵה, וּזְכָר לָנוּ הַיּוֹם בְּרִית שְׁלֹשׁ עֶשְׂרֵה, כְּמוֹ שֶׁהוֹדַעְתָּ לֶעָנָו מִקֶּדֶם, כְּמוֹ שֶׁכָּתוּב: וַיֵּרֶד יהוה בֶּעָנָן, וַיִּתְיַצֵּב עִמּוֹ שָׁם, וַיִּקְרָא בְשֵׁם, יהוה: שמות לד

קהל then שליח ציבור:

וַיַּעֲבֹר יהוה עַל־פָּנָיו וַיִּקְרָא שמות לד

All say aloud:

יהוה, יהוה, אֵל רַחוּם וְחַנּוּן, אֶרֶךְ אַפַּיִם, וְרַב־חֶסֶד וֶאֱמֶת: נֹצֵר חֶסֶד לָאֲלָפִים, נֹשֵׂא עָוֹן וָפֶשַׁע וְחַטָּאָה, וְנַקֵּה: וְסָלַחְתָּ לַעֲוֹנֵנוּ וּלְחַטָּאתֵנוּ, וּנְחַלְתָּנוּ:

Continue:

סְלַח לָנוּ אָבִינוּ כִּי חָטָאנוּ, מְחַל לָנוּ מַלְכֵּנוּ כִּי פָשָׁעְנוּ. כִּי־אַתָּה אֲדֹנָי טוֹב וְסַלָּח, וְרַב־חֶסֶד לְכָל־קֹרְאֶיךָ: תהלים פו

The following is said responsively:

אֲבוֹתַי כִּי בָטְחוּ בְּשֵׁם אֱלֹהֵי צוּרִי\
גָּדְלוּ וְהִצְלִיחוּ וְגַם עָשׂוּ פְרִי\
וּמֵעֵת הֻדְּחוּ וְהָלְכוּ עִמּוֹ קֶרִי\
הָיוּ הָלוֹךְ וְחָסוֹר עַד הַחֹדֶשׁ הָעֲשִׂירִי. בראשית ח

On the tenth, the king of Babylon laid siege on the city,
and beleaguered it. The chief of the army arrived,
and I was yielded to be trampled,
was tormented in fetters,
and from month to month my harp turned to grief.

Once like the first figs of a new tree,
they were the very first to be destroyed.
They spoke the names of others,
and sin closed their destiny.
They did not recognize God's face and were swept off by the flood –
agony like that of a first childbirth, soars up as high as Heaven.

God brought us a day of evil and siege,
ordered enemies about me to harvest my last fruits.
The day my heart was quelled, no strength to resist,
and He said to the prophet,
"Preach this to the rebellious house."

He took the cloak of authority from the judges at the gate.
His rage burned like fire
and He raised the crown away,
and He cast down the splendor of the Temple, Forest of Lebanon,
and rushing wind and storm make my flesh bristle and shiver.

Once you were called most beautiful;
now you are darkened,
for you have stumbled over iniquity
and your heart has turned back.
You have been attacked from behind,
have been weakened, once, then twice,
and even the slightest dressing or balm not offered you.

The Righteous One, perfect Rock,
who forgives iniquity almost too great to bear,
flew from the cherubs to the threshold,
and from there to a corner of the roof,
because of the iniquity marked out; the scream of it rose up,
their evil as abundant as a fruit-tree's crop.

בַּעֲשִׂירִי לַחֹדֶשׁ סָמַךְ מֶלֶךְ בָּבֶל
וְצָר עַל עִיר הַקֹּדֶשׁ, וְנִקְרַב רַב הַחוֹבֵל
נָתַתִּי הֲדַשׁ וְעָנִיתִי בַּכֶּבֶל
וְהָיָה מִדֵּי חֹדֶשׁ לְאֵבֶל כִּנּוֹרִי.

רֵאשִׁית בִּכּוּרָה לְרֵאשִׁית הַחֵרֶם
שֵׁם אֲחֵרִים הִזְכִּירָה, וְהֶעָוֹן גּוֹרֵם
פְּנֵי אֵל לֹא הִכִּירָה, וְשֻׁטְּפָה בְזֶרֶם
צָרָה כְּמַבְכִּירָה כָּעֵת בַּמָּרוֹם תַּמְרִיא.

הָאֱלֹהִים הֵבִיא יוֹם רָעָה וּמָצוֹר
צִוָּה צָרַי סְבִיבַי עוֹלָלַי לִבְצוֹר
יוֹם הֻרַךְ לְבָבִי וְאֵין כֹּחַ לַעְצוֹר
וַדַּבֵּר אֶל נָבִיא, מְשֹׁל אֶל בֵּית הַמֶּרִי.

מִיּוֹשְׁבֵי שַׁעַר הֶעֱבִיר אַדֶּרֶת
חֲמָתוֹ כָּאֵשׁ בָּעַר, וְהֵרִים עֲטֶרֶת
וּמִלְּבָנוֹן יַעַר הִשְׁלִיךְ תִּפְאֶרֶת
וְרוּחַ סוֹעָה וָסַעַר תְּסַמֵּר שַׂעֲרַת בְּשָׂרִי.

יְפֵיפִית נִמְשַׁלְתְּ, וְעַתָּה קְדוֹרַנִּית
בְּעָוֹן כִּי כָשַׁלְתְּ, וְלִבֵּךְ אֲחוֹרַנִּית
זִנְבוּךְ וְנֶחֱשַׁלְתְּ רִאשׁוֹנָה וְשֵׁנִית
וְהָחֵל לֹא חִתַּלְתְּ מְעַט צֳרִי.

צַדִּיק הַצּוּר תָּם, נָשָׂא עָוֹן נִלְאָה
מִכְּרוּב לְמִפְתָּן, לְפִנַּת גַּג דָּאָה
מֵעֲוֹן הִכִּתָם, וְצַעֲקָתָם בָּאָה
רַבָּה רָעָתָם כְּעֵץ עֹשֶׂה פֶּרִי.

The One who weighs the actions of people,
strengthened all my attackers,
for my days had been filled with malignant deeds,
and in the shamefulness of my youth
I forgot the good granted me,
and the One who gives me my bread and water,
my flax and my wool.

My attackers opened wide their mouths and swallowed up my legacy.
They overcame me utterly, drank my blood and gulped it down.
Strangers became my enemies, they injured my brothers –
strangers who called out, "Destroy, destroy!"
Descendants of Seir the Horite.

They said, "Come, let us finish them off,
and put an end to their memory."
Jealous, vengeful God, grant retribution;
let them load the burden of their own ruin.
Pay them back for their actions
and have their hopes disgrace them,
like the baker who dreamt his dream
of three baskets of white bread.

My wound was not softened, my bruise enough to kill me,
and my eyes have grown dim with watching for my bright-faced Love.
Is His anger even now not forever forgotten?
Why has He done this; why this burning rage?

This God of mine is compassionate; He shall not forever reject.
The days of my grief have grown long and still my heart sighs.
Return, God, to my tent; do not abandon Your place.
Close the days of my grief. Bring my recompense.

Lord who is the portion allotted me,
come to me quickly, help me,
and loosen my sackcloth,
wrap me around in joy,
and dazzle my darkness with Your light – light up
the twilight I once longed for, for it is You who are my lamp.

חִזֵּק כָּל קָמַי, תּוֹכֵן הָעֲלִילוֹת
כִּי מָלְאוּ יָמַי בֶּרֶגַע מִפְעָלוֹת
וּמִבֹּשֶׁת עֲלוּמַי שָׁכַחְתִּי גְמוּלוֹת
נוֹתֵן לַחְמִי וּמֵימַי, פִּשְׁתִּי וְצַמְרִי.

קָמַי פִּיהֶם פָּעֲרוּ וְנַחֲלָתִי בִלֵּעוּ
מְאֹד עָלַי גָּבְרוּ וְדָמִי שָׁתוּ וְלָעוּ
נָכְרִים עָלַי צָרוּ וְאֶת אַחַי הֵרֵעוּ
הָאוֹמְרִים עָרוּ עָרוּ, בְּנֵי שֵׂעִיר הַחֹרִי.

אָמְרוּ לְכוּ נְכַלֵּם, וְנַשְׁבִּיתָה זִכְרָם
אֵל קַנּוֹא וְנוֹקֵם, גָּמְלֵם, יִשְׂאוּ אֶת שִׁבְרָם
כְּמַעֲשֵׂיהֶם שַׁלֵּם וְיֵבוֹשׁוּ מִשִּׁבְרָם
כְּאִישׁ חֲלוֹם חוֹלֵם שְׁלֹשָׁה סַלֵּי חֹרִי.

פְּצָעַי לֹא רֻכְּכָה וְחַבּוּרוֹתַי רֶצַח
וְעֵינַי הַכְּהָתָה, צוֹפָה לְדוֹדִי צַח
הַעוֹד לֹא שָׁכְכָה חֲמָתוֹ לָנֶצַח
עַל מֶה עָשָׂה כָּכָה וּמֶה חָרִי.

רַחוּם זֶה אֵלִי, אַל לָעַד תִּזְנַח
אָרְכוּ יְמֵי אֶבְלִי וְעוֹד לִבִּי נֶאֱנָח
שׁוּבָה אֶל לְאָהֳלִי, מְקוֹמְךָ אַל תַּנַּח
שַׁלֵּם יְמֵי אֶבְלִי כִּי תָבוֹא עַל שְׂכָרִי.

יהוה מְנָת חֶלְקִי, חוּשָׁה לִּי לְעֶזְרָה
וּפִתַּחְתָּ שַׂקִּי, שִׂמְחָה לִי לְאַזְּרָה
וְתַגִּיהַּ אֶת חָשְׁכִּי בְּאוֹרְךָ לְהָאִירָה
אֶת נֶשֶׁף חִשְׁקִי, כִּי אַתָּה נֵרִי.

Redeem my soul from anguish and sighing,
grant Your people remission, my King and my Holy One.
And turn into relief the fast of Av;
into gladness and joy, the fast of Tammuz and the fast of Tevet.

Continue with "God, King who sits" on page 958.

SELIḤOT FOR THE FAST OF ESTHER

סְלַח לָנוּ Forgive us, our Father, for in our great foolishness we have blundered. Pardon us, our King, for our iniquities are many.

אֵל אֶרֶךְ You are a God slow to anger, You are called the Master of Compassion, and You have taught the way of repentance. May You remember today and every day the greatness of Your compassion and kindness, for the sake of the descendants of Your beloved ones. Turn toward us in compassion, for You are the Master of Compassion. We come before You in plea and prayer, as You in ancient times showed the humble one [Moses]. Turn from Your fierce anger, as is written in Your Torah. In the shadow of Your wings may we shelter and abide, as on the day when the LORD descended in the cloud. ▸ Disregard transgression and erase guilt as on the day You stood with him [Moses] there. Hear our cry and heed our word, as on the day You proclaimed in the name of the LORD, and there it is written:

Congregation then Leader:

And the LORD passed by before him and proclaimed: *Ex. 34*

All say aloud:

יהוה The LORD, the LORD, compassionate and gracious God, slow to anger, abounding in loving-kindness and truth, extending loving-kindness to a thousand generations, forgiving iniquity, rebellion and sin, and absolving [the guilty who repent]. Forgive us our iniquity and our sin, and take us as Your inheritance.

Continue:

סְלַח לָנוּ Forgive us, our Father, for we have sinned. Pardon us, our King, for we have transgressed. For You, LORD, are good and forgiving, abounding in loving-kindness to all who call on You. *Ps. 86*

מִיָּגוֹן וַאֲנָחָה, פְּדֵה אֵל אֶת נַפְשִׁי
עֲשֵׂה לְעַמְּךָ הֲנָחָה, מַלְכִּי וּקְדוֹשִׁי
תַּהֲפוֹךְ לִרְוָחָה אֶת צוֹם הַחֲמִישִׁי
לְשָׂשׂוֹן וּלְשִׂמְחָה, צוֹם הָרְבִיעִי וְצוֹם הָעֲשִׂירִי.

Continue with אֵל מֶלֶךְ יוֹשֵׁב *on page 959.*

סליחות לתענית אסתר

סְלַח לָנוּ, אָבִינוּ, כִּי בְּרֹב אִוַּלְתֵּנוּ שָׁגִינוּ.
מְחַל לָנוּ, מַלְכֵּנוּ, כִּי רַבּוּ עֲוֹנֵינוּ.

אֵל אֶרֶךְ אַפַּיִם אַתָּה, וּבַעַל הָרַחֲמִים נִקְרֵאתָ, וְדֶרֶךְ תְּשׁוּבָה הוֹרֵיתָ. גְּדֻלַּת רַחֲמֶיךָ וַחֲסָדֶיךָ, תִּזְכֹּר הַיּוֹם וּבְכָל יוֹם לְזֶרַע יְדִידֶיךָ. תֵּפֶן אֵלֵינוּ בְּרַחֲמִים, כִּי אַתָּה הוּא בַּעַל הָרַחֲמִים. בְּתַחֲנוּן וּבִתְפִלָּה פָּנֶיךָ נְקַדֵּם, כְּהוֹדַעְתָּ לֶעָנָו מִקֶּדֶם. מֵחֲרוֹן אַפְּךָ שׁוּב, כְּמוֹ בְּתוֹרָתְךָ כָּתוּב. וּבְצֵל כְּנָפֶיךָ נֶחֱסֶה וְנִתְלוֹנָן, כְּיוֹם וַיֵּרֶד יהוה בֶּעָנָן. ‹ תַּעֲבֹר עַל פֶּשַׁע וְתִמְחֶה אָשָׁם, כְּיוֹם וַיִּתְיַצֵּב עִמּוֹ שָׁם. תַּאֲזִין שַׁוְעָתֵנוּ וְתַקְשִׁיב מֶנּוּ מַאֲמָר, כְּיוֹם וַיִּקְרָא בְשֵׁם יהוה, וְשָׁם נֶאֱמַר

שליח ציבור then *קהל:*

שמות לד וַיַּעֲבֹר יהוה עַל־פָּנָיו וַיִּקְרָא

All say aloud:

יהוה, יהוה, אֵל רַחוּם וְחַנּוּן, אֶרֶךְ אַפַּיִם, וְרַב־חֶסֶד וֶאֱמֶת: נֹצֵר חֶסֶד לָאֲלָפִים, נֹשֵׂא עָוֹן וָפֶשַׁע וְחַטָּאָה, וְנַקֵּה: וְסָלַחְתָּ לַעֲוֹנֵנוּ וּלְחַטָּאתֵנוּ, וּנְחַלְתָּנוּ:

Continue:

תהלים פו סְלַח לָנוּ אָבִינוּ כִּי חָטָאנוּ, מְחַל לָנוּ מַלְכֵּנוּ כִּי פָשָׁעְנוּ. כִּי־אַתָּה אֲדֹנָי טוֹב וְסַלָּח, וְרַב־חֶסֶד לְכָל־קֹרְאֶיךָ:

We have waited patiently for the LORD, and He has turned toward us and heard our cry. And on the path of Your laws, LORD, we have waited for You, for it is Your name and Your memory that are our souls' desire. *Is. 26*

כְּרַחֵם As a father has compassion for his children,
so, LORD, have compassion for us.
Salvation is the LORD's; on Your people is Your blessing, Selah! *Ps. 3*
The LORD of hosts is with us, the God of Jacob is our stronghold, Selah! *Ps. 46*
LORD of hosts, happy is the one who trusts in You. *Ps. 84*
LORD, save! May the King answer us on the day we call. *Ps. 20*

▸ Forgive, please, this people's iniquity, *Num. 14*
in the abundance of Your kindness,
and as You have forgiven this people from the time of Egypt until now,
and there it is written:

Congregation then Leader:

And the LORD said, I have forgiven as you asked.

Continue:

הַטֵּה Give ear, my God and hear; open Your eyes and see our desolation, and the city that bears Your name, for it is not on the strength of our righteousness that we throw down our pleadings before You, but on the strength of Your great compassion. LORD, hear me; LORD, forgive, LORD, listen and act and do not delay – for Your sake, my God; for Your city and Your people bear Your name. *Dan. 9*

Our God and God of our fathers:

אָדָם When a man rose up against us, convulsions of trembling seized us. When he attached himself to a government of flattery, we almost stumbled and fell. They cheerfully closed an agreement to sell us, as a person with an unwanted mound gives it away quite freely to one with an unwanted pit. There was no defense. They said, "Come, let us annihilate them from among nations: the name of Israel shall be recalled no more." *Ps. 83* My eyes turned heavenward and I called on You to curse my enemies: "Cut off name and remnant; expunge their name, let it rot. And be Enemy to my enemies; bring them down in the very deceptions with which they deceived the people of Jacob." And they said, "The LORD will not see; the God of Jacob will not comprehend." *Ps. 94* Yet God tormented the scattered ones and made them mournful – but did not mean to destroy them utterly. They were guilty on the face of things, and so He terrorized them. By the taking off of a ring, He made them tremble. But God fulfilled the good of His word, raising them up in the view of nations. "In their enemies' land He did not reject them, and did not detest them to the point of destruction." *Lev. 26* He revealed the premonition of events for a nation begrimed and scratched over. He wrote "I shall surely hide (*astir*) Myself" to hint at Esther, and fragrant "pure myrrh," translated "mar-dokh," to hint at Mordekhai; all to put an end to Haman on the

ישעיה כו קַוֵּה קִוִּינוּ יהוה, וַיֵּט אֵלֵינוּ וַיִּשְׁמַע שַׁוְעָתֵנוּ. אַף אֹרַח מִשְׁפָּטֶיךָ יהוה קִוִּינוּךָ, לְשִׁמְךָ וּלְזִכְרְךָ תַּאֲוַת נָפֶשׁ:

כְּרַחֵם אָב עַל בָּנִים, כֵּן תְּרַחֵם יהוה עָלֵינוּ.

תהלים ג לַיהוה הַיְשׁוּעָה, עַל עַמְּךָ בִרְכָתֶךָ סֶּלָה:

תהלים מו יהוה צְבָאוֹת עִמָּנוּ, מִשְׂגָּב לָנוּ אֱלֹהֵי יַעֲקֹב סֶלָה:

תהלים פד יהוה צְבָאוֹת, אַשְׁרֵי אָדָם בֹּטֵחַ בָּךְ:

תהלים כ יהוה הוֹשִׁיעָה, הַמֶּלֶךְ יַעֲנֵנוּ בְיוֹם קָרְאֵנוּ:

במדבר יד ◄ סְלַח נָא לַעֲוֹן הָעָם הַזֶּה כְּגֹדֶל חַסְדֶּךָ

וְכַאֲשֶׁר נָשָׂאתָה לָעָם הַזֶּה מִמִּצְרַיִם וְעַד הֵנָּה:

וְשָׁם נֶאֱמַר

then קהל *:*שליח ציבור

וַיֹּאמֶר יהוה, סָלַחְתִּי כִּדְבָרֶךָ:

Continue:

דניאל ט הַטֵּה אֱלֹהַי אָזְנְךָ וּשְׁמָע, פְּקַח עֵינֶיךָ וּרְאֵה שֹׁמְמֹתֵינוּ וְהָעִיר אֲשֶׁר נִקְרָא שִׁמְךָ עָלֶיהָ, כִּי לֹא עַל צִדְקֹתֵינוּ אֲנַחְנוּ מַפִּילִים תַּחֲנוּנֵינוּ לְפָנֶיךָ, כִּי עַל רַחֲמֶיךָ הָרַבִּים: אֲדֹנָי שְׁמָעָה, אֲדֹנָי סְלָחָה, אֲדֹנָי הַקְשִׁיבָה וַעֲשֵׂה אַל תְּאַחַר, לְמַעַנְךָ אֱלֹהַי, כִּי שִׁמְךָ נִקְרָא עַל עִירְךָ וְעַל עַמֶּךָ:

אֱלֹהֵינוּ וֵאלֹהֵי אֲבוֹתֵינוּ

אָדָם בְּקוּם עָלֵינוּ, חִיל אֲחָזָתְנוּ לִרְעֹד. בְּהִסְתַּפְּחוֹ לְמַלְכוּת חָנֵף, כִּמְעַט
תהלים פג כָּשַׁלְנוּ לִמְעֹד. גָּמְרוּ לְמַכְרֵנוּ כְּתַל וְחָרִיץ בְּלִי מִסְעוֹד. אָמְרוּ לְכוּ וְנַכְחִידֵם
מִגּוֹי, וְלֹא יִזָּכֵר שֵׁם יִשְׂרָאֵל עוֹד: דַּלּוּ עֵינַי לַמָּרוֹם, קְרָאתִיךָ אוֹיְבַי לָקֹב.
הַכְרֵת שֵׁם וּשְׁאָר, וּמְחֵה שֵׁם לִרְקֹב. וְצַר צוֹרְרֵי בְּנִכְלֵיהֶם אֲשֶׁר נִכְּלוּ
תהלים צד לְעָקֹב. וַיֹּאמְרוּ, לֹא יִרְאֶה יָּהּ, וְלֹא יָבִין אֱלֹהֵי יַעֲקֹב: זְרוּיִים עָנָה וַיָּגָה,
וְלֹא מִלֵּב לְכַלּוֹתָם. חָבוּ לְפָנִים, וְרוֹדִים בְּהֵסֶרַת טַבַּעַת לְהַחְלוֹתָם. טוֹב
ויקרא כו דְּבָרוֹ הֵקִים לְעֵינֵי הַגּוֹיִם לְהַעֲלוֹתָם. בְּאֶרֶץ אֹיְבֵיהֶם לֹא מְאַסְתִּים וְלֹא

morrow, "From (*hamin*) the tree" foreshadowing his gallows. "In place of the thorn bush, shall rise up a cypress, and in place of the nettle, shall rise up myrtle." The king who listened to lies, dictated accusation and sorrow. He wrapped himself in priestly clothes, Ahasuerus, having mistaken his reckoning of the End. He ordered "other vessels" to be used, from the Quarry from which the world was hewn; and the devil too, came and placed himself among them. When the people in Shushan ate of their destroyer's meat, the king opened his mouth wide to accuse them, to give them over into the hands of the one who was ready to pay their price. The Rock, meanwhile, agreed to write a letter to destroy their hope; "I said that I would yield them up, would put an end to their memory among mankind." The angels, messengers of peace, wept bitterly, crying out, "Compassionate One, look to the covenant and do not break it, pushing it away!" The Torah, too, heard of it and put on clothes of widowhood and sorrow; and she laid her hands upon her head and walked along, crying as she went. [Elijah] The Tishbite wrapped a covering of sackcloth around his waist. He hurried and told the three fathers who sleep in the Cave of Makhpelah, and then hastened to the Shepherd, [Moses] – "What do you mean by sleeping? Rouse yourself! Get up and call out to your God – perhaps He may change His mind!" He told [Mordekhai] Bilshan of the pronouncement that had been sealed in clay – but not in blood. They learnt from the example of Nineveh how to overturn anger after a decree; the son of Kish knocked at the door of the school, and covered himself in sackcloth and sat down on the earth. For three days he gathered the children before him – thirsty, hidden from by God – so that, in the voice of Jacob, they might weaken the hand of the bold-faced king. His hands raised steadily to God, Mordekhai prayed, "Save us now from insult; that he should not come and slaughter us, mothers and children together." Those and those, from all sides, the children of my mighty ones and teachers, all cried out, and their plea rose up to the Lord. And God, when those plaintive calls reached Him, asked, "And what is this bleating of sheep that meets My ears?" The shepherd Moses answered Him, "These are the little ones of the holy offspring. Lord, save ones condemned to die, from the evil enemy." The compassion of the Gracious One was stirred, and He was moved to weep for what had happened. And so it was that when the King of Israel read the letter, He tore it to pieces. The Jew suspended sons below and father above. Each man covered three *amot*; the fourth *amah* above was space exposed. Mordekhai saw a double revenge, was delighted, and spoke praises: "I was returned to my post and he was hanged!" Esther wrote with emphasis, that a Hallel of thanks should be read on that day; and what the beloved ones accepted down below was established above. A banner shall be raised by those who bear witness, to make the wonder known now, as it was then. And at this time – may relief and salvation rise up for the Jews.

Is. 55

Job 2

Deut. 32

II Sam. 13

Jonah 1

Jonah 3

Gen. 32

I Sam. 15

II Kings 5

Gen. 41

Esther 4

אֵל מֶלֶךְ God, King who sits upon a throne of compassion, who acts with loving-kindness, who pardons the iniquities of His people, passing them before Him in order; who forgives sinners and pardons transgressors; who performs righteousness with all

גַּעֲלְתִּים לְכַלּוֹתָם: יַדַע רֶמֶז הַקּוֹרוֹת לְעַם מְעֻפָּר וּמְהֻדָּס. כְּתָב הַסְתֵּר
אַסְתִּיר וּמָר דְּרוֹר מְפֹרָדָס. לְשַׁבֹּת הָמָן מִמָּחֳרָת, הֲמַן הָעֵץ קְנָדָס. תַּחַת הַנַּעֲצוּץ יַעֲלֶה בְרוֹשׁ וְתַחַת הַסִּרְפַּד יַעֲלֶה הֲדַס: מַקְשִׁיב דְּבַר שֶׁקֶר כָּתַב ישעיה נה
שִׂטְנָה וָעֶצֶב. נִתְעַטֵּף בְּבִגְדֵי שְׂרָד כְּטָעָה בְּמִנְיַן קֶצֶב. סָדַר לְהִשְׁתַּמֵּשׁ
בְּשׁוֹנִים כְּלֵי הַמַּחְצֵב. וַיָּבוֹא גַם־הַשָּׂטָן בְּתֹכָם לְהִתְיַצֵּב: עַם הַנִּמְצָאִים איוב ב
בְּשׁוּשָׁן, בְּאָכְלָם מִזֶּבַח עוֹכְרָם. פָּעַר פִּיו לְהַשְׂטִינָם, וּלְהַסְגִּירָם בְּיַד
נוֹתֵן מִכְרָם. צוּר הִסְכִּים לִכְתֹּב אִגֶּרֶת לְאַבֵּד שִׁבְרָם. אָמַרְתִּי אַפְאֵיהֶם, דברים לב
אַשְׁבִּיתָה מֵאֱנוֹשׁ זִכְרָם: קְדוֹשִׁים מַלְאֲכֵי שָׁלוֹם מַר יִבְכָּיוּן בִּצְעָקָה.
רַחוּם הַבֵּט לַבְּרִית וְאַל תָּפֵר לְהַרְחִיקָה. שָׁמְעָה מוֹרָשָׁה, וַתִּלְבַּשׁ בִּגְדֵי
אַלְמְנוּת וּמוּעָקָה. וַתָּשֶׂם יָדָהּ עַל־רֹאשָׁהּ, וַתֵּלֶךְ הָלוֹךְ וְזָעָקָה: תִּשְׁבִּי שָׁם שמואל ב׳ יג
אֵזוֹר שַׂק בְּמָתְנָיו תַּחְבֹּשֶׁת. מִהֵר וְהוֹדִיעַ יְשֵׁנֵי מַכְפֵּל, אָבוֹת שְׁלֹשֶׁת. נָחַץ
לְרוֹעֶה, מַה לְּךָ נִרְדָּם לְהִתְעַשֵּׁת. קוּם קְרָא אֶל־אֱלֹהֶיךָ, אוּלַי יִתְעַשֵּׁת: יונה א
חוֹתַם טִיט אֲשֶׁר נַעֲשָׂה, לְבִלְשָׁן סִפֵּר. מְנִינֵהוּ לָמְדוּ לְאַחַר גְּזֵרָה כְּעַס
לְהָפֵר. בֶּן קִישׁ הִקִּישׁ דַּלְתוֹת בֵּית הַסֵּפֶר. וַיְכַס שַׂק, וַיֵּשֶׁב עַל־הָאֵפֶר: יונה ג
רִבֵּץ תִּינוֹקוֹת לְפָנָיו יָמִים שְׁלֹשָׁה, צְמֵאִים וּמְכֻפָּנִים. בְּקוֹל יַעֲקֹב לַחֲלֹשׁ
יְדֵי עַז פָּנִים. יָדָיו אֱמוּנָה לָאֵל, הַצִּילֵנִי נָא מֵעֶלְבּוֹנִים. פֶּן־יָבוֹא וְהִכַּנִי בראשית לב
אֵם עַל־בָּנִים: מִזֶּה אֵלֶּה וּמִזֶּה אֵלֶּה, בְּנֵי אֵיתָנַי וְרַבָּנַי. כֻּלָּם צָעֲקוּ, וַתַּעַל
שַׁוְעָתָם אֶל יהוה. יָהּ, לְקוֹל רִנּוּן כְּבוֹא, שָׁאַל לְפָנַי. וּמֶה קוֹל־הַצֹּאן הַזֶּה שמואל א׳ טו
בְּאָזְנָי: רוֹעֶה הֱשִׁיבוֹ, הֵם קְטַנֵּי קֹדֶשׁ זֶרַע. יָהּ, הַצֵּל לְקוּחִים לַמָּוֶת מֵאוֹיֵב
הָרָע. חַנּוּן נִכְמְרוּ רַחֲמָיו וַיְבַקֵּשׁ לִבְכּוֹת הַמְאֹרָע. וַיְהִי כִּקְרֹא מֶלֶךְ־יִשְׂרָאֵל מלכים ב׳ ה
אֶת־הַסֵּפֶר, וַיִּקְרַע: יְהוּדִי הוֹקִיעַ, יְלָדָיו לְמַטָּה וַאֲבִיהֶם לְמַעְלָה. אִישׁ
אִישׁ בְּשָׁלֹשׁ אַמּוֹת, וְהָרְבִיעִית אֲוִיר מְגֻלָּה. מִשְׁנֶה נָקַם חָזָה, וְשָׂמַח וְשָׁח
תְּהִלָּה. אֹתִי הֵשִׁיב עַל־כַּנִּי וְאֹתוֹ תָלָה: ◂ וַתִּכְתֹּב אֶסְתֵּר תֹּקֶף, לִקְרֹא בראשית מא
כִּבְהַלֵּל מְהוֹדִים. מִלְמַעְלָה קִיְּמוּ מַה שֶּׁקִּבְּלוּ לְמַטָּה דוֹדִים. נֵס יְנוֹסֵס
לְפַרְסֵם כְּאָז פְּלָאוֹ מַסְהִידִים. בָּעֵת הַזֹּאת רֶוַח וְהַצָּלָה יַעֲמוֹד לַיְּהוּדִים: אסתר ד

אֵל מֶלֶךְ יוֹשֵׁב עַל כִּסֵּא רַחֲמִים, מִתְנַהֵג בַּחֲסִידוּת. מוֹחֵל עֲוֹנוֹת עַמּוֹ,
מַעֲבִיר רִאשׁוֹן רִאשׁוֹן. מַרְבֶּה מְחִילָה לְחַטָּאִים, וּסְלִיחָה לְפוֹשְׁעִים. עֹשֶׂה

flesh and spirit, do not repay their bad actions in kind. God, You taught us to speak thirteen attributes: recall for us today the covenant of the thirteen attributes, as You in ancient times showed the humble one [Moses], as is written: The LORD descended in the cloud and stood with him there, and proclaimed in the name of the LORD:

Congregation then Leader:

And the LORD passed by before him and proclaimed: *Ex. 34*

All say aloud:

יהוה The LORD, the LORD, compassionate and gracious God, slow to anger, abounding in loving-kindness and truth, extending loving-kindness to a thousand generations, forgiving iniquity, rebellion and sin, and absolving [the guilty who repent]. Forgive us our iniquity and our sin, and take us as Your inheritance.

Continue:

סְלַח לָנוּ Forgive us, our Father, for we have sinned. Pardon us, our King, for we have transgressed. For You, LORD, are good and forgiving, abounding in loving-kindness to all who call on You. *Ps. 86*

כִּי־עִמְּךָ For in You there is a wellspring of life; in Your light shall we see light. As we call You, God of our righteousness, answer us. In a narrow place You have opened out our horizon; be gracious to us and hear our prayer. And now let the strength of the LORD be great, as You have said. *Ps. 36* *Num. 14*

כְּרַחֵם As a father has compassion for his children,
so, LORD, have compassion for us.
Salvation is the LORD's; on Your people is Your blessing, Selah! *Ps. 3*
The LORD of hosts is with us, the God of Jacob is our stronghold, Selah! *Ps. 46*
LORD of hosts, happy is the one who trusts in You. *Ps. 84*
LORD, save! May the King answer us on the day we call. *Ps. 20*

Our God and God of our fathers:

אַתָּה הָאֵל It is You who are the God of wonders. You have made known among nations Your terrifying strength. You redeemed Your people by might from torments, suppressed their foes with ignominious death, when the enemy rose to awaken strife, and seemed about to cut down the exquisite flowers, Israel. He plotted to measure out into the masters' treasuries, a hundred times the silver talents of the sockets in the Tabernacle. You warned Your lambs to announce the shekel offering early; You knew what would be. You warned us to be punctual, and to find a way to douse the fire of ones who sought to burn us. And so, those once

צְדָקוֹת עִם כָּל בָּשָׂר וָרְוּחַ, לֹא כְרָעָתָם תִּגְמֹל. ❖ אֵל, הוֹרֵיתָ לָּנוּ לוֹמַר שְׁלֹשׁ עֶשְׂרֵה, וּזְכָר לָנוּ הַיּוֹם בְּרִית שְׁלֹשׁ עֶשְׂרֵה, כְּמוֹ שֶׁהוֹדַעְתָּ לֶעָנָו מִקֶּדֶם, כְּמוֹ שֶׁכָּתוּב: וַיֵּרֶד יהוה בֶּעָנָן, וַיִּתְיַצֵּב עִמּוֹ שָׁם, וַיִּקְרָא בְשֵׁם, יהוה:

then שליח ציבור קהל:

שמות לד וַיַּעֲבֹר יהוה עַל־פָּנָיו וַיִּקְרָא

All say aloud:

יהוה, יהוה, אֵל רַחוּם וְחַנּוּן, אֶרֶךְ אַפַּיִם, וְרַב־חֶסֶד וֶאֱמֶת: נֹצֵר חֶסֶד לָאֲלָפִים, נֹשֵׂא עָוֹן וָפֶשַׁע וְחַטָּאָה, וְנַקֵּה: וְסָלַחְתָּ לַעֲוֹנֵנוּ וּלְחַטָּאתֵנוּ, וּנְחַלְתָּנוּ:

Continue:

תהלים פו סְלַח לָנוּ אָבִינוּ כִּי חָטָאנוּ, מְחַל לָנוּ מַלְכֵּנוּ כִּי פָשָׁעְנוּ. כִּי־אַתָּה אֲדֹנָי טוֹב וְסַלָּח, וְרַב־חֶסֶד לְכָל־קֹרְאֶיךָ:

תהלים לו כִּי־עִמְּךָ מְקוֹר חַיִּים, בְּאוֹרְךָ נִרְאֶה־אוֹר: בְּקָרְאֵנוּ עֲנֵנוּ אֱלֹהֵי צִדְקֵנוּ,
במדבר יד בַּצָּר הִרְחַבְתָּ לָּנוּ, חָנֵּנוּ וּשְׁמַע תְּפִלָּתֵנוּ. וְעַתָּה יִגְדַּל־נָא כֹּחַ אֲדֹנָי, כַּאֲשֶׁר דִּבַּרְתָּ לֵאמֹר:

כְּרַחֵם אָב עַל בָּנִים, כֵּן תְּרַחֵם יהוה עָלֵינוּ.
תהלים ג לַיהוה הַיְשׁוּעָה, עַל־עַמְּךָ בִרְכָתֶךָ סֶּלָה:
תהלים מו יהוה צְבָאוֹת עִמָּנוּ, מִשְׂגָּב לָנוּ אֱלֹהֵי יַעֲקֹב סֶלָה:
תהלים פד יהוה צְבָאוֹת, אַשְׁרֵי אָדָם בֹּטֵחַ בָּךְ:
תהלים כ יהוה הוֹשִׁיעָה, הַמֶּלֶךְ יַעֲנֵנוּ בְיוֹם־קָרְאֵנוּ:

אֱלֹהֵינוּ וֵאלֹהֵי אֲבוֹתֵינוּ

אַתָּה הָאֵל עוֹשֵׂה פְלָאוֹת, בָּעַמִּים הוֹדַעְתָּ עֹז נוֹרָאוֹת, גָּאַלְתָּ בִּזְרוֹעַ עַמְּךָ מִתְּלָאוֹת, דִּכִּיתָ צָרֵיהֶם בְּמוֹתֵי תַחֲלוּאוֹת. הָאוֹיֵב בְּקוּמוֹ לְעוֹרֵר מְדָנִים, וְדִמָּה לְהַכְרִית פִּרְחֵי עֲדָנִים, זָמַם לִשְׁקֹל לְגִנְזֵי אֲדוֹנִים, חֲלִיפֵי מְאַת כִּכָּרֵי

condemned to death – are marked out for resurrection. When (for appearances,) they worshiped a narrow image, they were yielded up to be clipped off: all those offshoots and grapes. Traps surrounded them on all sides; they turned their eyes to You, they were concealed in Your hiddenness. The lots were overturned, they ruled over their enemies, and the gallows was prepared to receive Haman the Agagite. God struck and swallowed the façade of covering that covered, and He entombed His people's enemies in darkness. Peace and truth were written on all sides; power of salvation, steady rock and fortress. The plunderer was plundered, he was caught in his own trap. The one who spoke against me was swept away; destroyed; eyed disdainfully. The people made celebrations, and these were fixed for all generations. Amalek had entered the Scriptures three times – how could there be a fourth? Yet on High it was agreed and here below it was sealed, and the reason for all that had been fixed, was inscribed in the scroll. Your hand is lifted high to forgive sinners. You set Mordekhai the Jew and Hadassah Esther in their place as saviors, and now their righteousness remains forever to delight us, and the study of their honor to recall to You those who were saved. Be zealous for Your name, Awesome and Sanctified One. Witness Your vineyard, destroyed, trampled; gather our scattered ones and their song to You will be renewed. Sustain them and revive them with the building of the Temple. ▸ And as You did awe-inspiring things in those days, so perform with us the wonder of salvation for all time. Find in Your presence our ransom, our appeasement – God, King who sits upon a throne of compassion.

God, King who sits upon a throne of compassion, who acts with loving-kindness, who pardons the iniquities of His people, passing them before Him in order; who forgives sinners and pardons transgressors; who performs righteousness with all flesh and spirit, do not repay their bad actions in kind. ▸ God, You taught us to speak thirteen attributes: recall for us today the covenant of the thirteen attributes, as You in ancient times showed the humble one [Moses], as is written: The Lord descended in the cloud and stood with him there, and proclaimed in the name of the Lord:

Congregation then Leader:

And the Lord passed by before him and proclaimed: *Ex. 34*

All say aloud:

יהוה The Lord, the Lord, compassionate and gracious God, slow to anger, abounding in loving-kindness and truth, extending loving-kindness to a thousand generations, forgiving iniquity, rebellion and sin, and absolving [the guilty who repent]. Forgive us our iniquity and our sin, and take us as Your inheritance.

אֲדָנִים. טְלָאֶיךָ הַזְּהִרְתָּ שְׁקָלֵיהֶם לְהַקְדִּים, יָדַעְתָּ הָעֲתִידוֹת וְדָרַשְׁתָּ נִשְׁקָדִים, כִּבּוּי לְהַמְצִיא לְלַהַב יוֹקְדִים, לְקוֹחִים לַמָּוֶת לְתַחִי נִפְקָדִים. מַסֵּכָה צָרָה בְּעָבְדָם לְפָנִים, נִמְסְרוּ לְהָתֵז קְנוּקְנוֹת וּגְפָנִים, סְבָבוּם מוֹקְשִׁים בְּכָל דְּפָנִים, עֵינֵיהֶם לְךָ תוֹלִים וּבְסִתְרְךָ נִצְפָּנִים. פּוּר נֶהְפַּךְ בְּאוֹיְבִים לִשְׁלֹט, צְלִיבָה הוּכַן אֲגָגִי לִקְלֹט, קְלַע וּבְלַע פְּנֵי הַלּוֹט הַלּוֹט, רִיבֵי עָם בְּאַשְׁמַנִּים לְעַלֵּט. שָׁלוֹם וֶאֱמֶת נִכְתַּב מִכָּל צַד, תְּקַף יֵשַׁע סֶלַע וּמְצָד, שׁוֹדֵד הַשֹּׁדֵד וּבְרִשְׁתּוֹ נוֹצַד, מַלְשְׁנֵי נִסְחַף נִצְמַת וְנִרְצָד. עָשׂוּ שְׂמָחוֹת וְלַדּוֹרוֹת קְבָעוּם, וּמִקְרָאוֹת שְׁלֹשׁוּם וְלֹא רִבְעוּם, נִסְכְּמוּ מִמַּעַל וּלְמַטָּה טְבָעוּם, בְּסֵפֶר נֶחְקַק עַל מָה קְבָעוּם. רָמָה יָדְךָ לִסְלֹחַ לַפּוֹשְׁעִים, יְהוּדִי וַהֲדַסָּה הֲקָמַת מוֹשִׁיעִים, צִדְקָתָם עוֹמֶדֶת לָעַד לְשַׁעֲשׁוּעִים, חֲקֹר כְּבוֹדָם לְהִזָּכֵר לְנוֹשָׁעִים. קַנֵּא לְשִׁמְךָ נוֹרָא וְנִקְדָּשׁ, חַזֵּה כַּרְמְךָ נֶהֱרַס וְנִדָּשׁ, זֵרוּיֵינוּ קַבֵּץ וְשִׁיר לְךָ יְחֻדָּשׁ, קַיְּמֵם וְהַחֲיֵם בְּבִנְיַן בֵּית הַמִּקְדָּשׁ. ‹ וּכְעָשׂוֹתְךָ נוֹרָאוֹת בְּאוֹתָן הַיָּמִים, אִתָּנוּ הַפְלֵא תְּשׁוּעַת עוֹלָמִים, מָצוֹא לְפָנֶיךָ כֹּפֶר וְתַנְחוּמִים, אֵל מֶלֶךְ יוֹשֵׁב עַל כִּסֵּא רַחֲמִים.

אֵל מֶלֶךְ יוֹשֵׁב עַל כִּסֵּא רַחֲמִים, מִתְנַהֵג בַּחֲסִידוּת. מוֹחֵל עֲוֹנוֹת עַמּוֹ, מַעֲבִיר רִאשׁוֹן רִאשׁוֹן. מַרְבֶּה מְחִילָה לְחַטָּאִים, וּסְלִיחָה לְפוֹשְׁעִים. עֹשֶׂה צְדָקוֹת עִם כָּל בָּשָׂר וָרוּחַ, לֹא כְרָעָתָם תִּגְמֹל. ‹ אֵל, הוֹרֵיתָ לָּנוּ לוֹמַר שְׁלֹשׁ עֶשְׂרֵה, וּזְכֹר לָנוּ הַיּוֹם בְּרִית שְׁלֹשׁ עֶשְׂרֵה, כְּמוֹ שֶׁהוֹדַעְתָּ לֶעָנָו מִקֶּדֶם, כְּמוֹ שֶׁכָּתוּב: וַיֵּרֶד יהוה בֶּעָנָן, וַיִּתְיַצֵּב עִמּוֹ שָׁם, וַיִּקְרָא בְשֵׁם, יהוה:

שליח ציבור then קהל:

וַיַּעֲבֹר יהוה עַל־פָּנָיו וַיִּקְרָא שמות לד

All say aloud:

יהוה, יהוה, אֵל רַחוּם וְחַנּוּן, אֶרֶךְ אַפַּיִם, וְרַב־חֶסֶד וֶאֱמֶת: נֹצֵר חֶסֶד לָאֲלָפִים, נֹשֵׂא עָוֺן וָפֶשַׁע וְחַטָּאָה, וְנַקֵּה: וְסָלַחְתָּ לַעֲוֺנֵנוּ וּלְחַטָּאתֵנוּ, וּנְחַלְתָּנוּ:

Continue:

סְלַח לָנוּ Forgive us, our Father, for we have sinned. Pardon us, our King, for we have transgressed. For You, LORD, are good and forgiving, abounding in loving-kindness to all who call on You. *Ps. 86*

The following is said responsively:

Small of number we stand pleading before You: do not block Your ears to the cry of people crushed. Listen to their entreaty from the Heaven where You dwell, as You saved Your children in the days of Myrrh and Myrtle [Mordekhai and Esther].

On Israel's praises You sit enthroned, hearing their cry, listening to their prayer. Bringing healing even before the blow, counting it out to help the ones You have acquired; to settle their homes again.

A foe and enemy fixed his eyes like knives on Israel; he opened wide his mouth to swallow up the humble man. He deliberated within him to destroy Mordekhai's great community; in the letter, he etched his intent to destroy the treasured people.

You who take revenge upon foes and persist in Your claim against enemies; You measured them out with the very measure they used against Your loved ones. The fighter and his descendants were hanged, suspended; they were strung up together, like fish on a thread.

On the day on which the enemies hoped to lay carnage among the people You harbor, the rule was overturned and bodies fell; they bore the brunt and fury of Your rage – they were trodden underfoot and washed away.

And so may Your name be raised up, exalted. Your glory covers all the highest heavens. As You lift the downtrodden, those yielded up as plunder, Your praise fills up the valleys to their very ends.

Consider our thoughts, now, and witness our suffering. Rise up, in Your rage, against the bitter enemy. Master, we have called You from a narrow place. Please, take us out into the open, and release us from anguish.

Bring us much, abundant pardon. Hear our prayer, and what is crude in us – pass over. Bring down those who press us and fill them with horror. And as for us – do not forever withhold Your compassion.

Continue with "God, King who sits" on page 958.

Continue:

סְלַח לָנוּ אָבִינוּ כִּי חָטָאנוּ, מְחַל לָנוּ מַלְכֵּנוּ כִּי פָשָׁעְנוּ. כִּי־אַתָּה אֲדֹנָי טוֹב וְסַלָּח, וְרַב־חֶסֶד לְכָל־קֹרְאֶיךָ: תהלים פו

The following is said responsively:

בְּמְתֵי מִסְפָּר חִלִּינוּ פָנֶיךָ. לְשַׁוְעַת נִבְאִים אַל תַּעְלֵם אָזְנֶךָ.
הַקְשֵׁב תְּחִנָּתָם מִשְּׁמֵי מְעוֹנֶךָ. כְּבִימֵי מֹר וַהֲדַס הוֹשַׁעְתָּ בָנֶיךָ.

תְּהִלּוֹת יִשְׂרָאֵל אַתָּה יוֹשֵׁב. שַׁוְעָתָם מַאֲזִין וְרִנָּתָם קוֹשֵׁב.
רְפָאוֹת לְמַחַץ מַקְדִּים וּמְחַשֵּׁב. קְנוּיֶיךָ לְהֵיטִיב וּנְוֵיהֶם לְיַשֵּׁב.

צַר וְאוֹיֵב הִלְטִישׁ עֵינָיו. פִּיהוּ פָּעַר לִשְׁאֹף עָנָו.
עָשָׂת בְּשַׁלְוֹ לְהַשְׁמִיד קְהַל הֲמוֹנָיו. סְגַל לְאַבֵּד חָרַת בְּנִשְׁתְּוָנָיו.

נוֹקֵם לְצָרִים וְנוֹטֵר לְאוֹיְבִים. מְדַדְתָּ מִדָּתָם כְּזָדוּ לַאֲהוּבִים.
לוֹחֵם וְנִינָיו הָתְלוּ מִצְלָבִים. כִּבְחֵרוֹת דָּגִים חֹרְזוּ תְּחוּבִים.

יוֹם אֲשֶׁר שִׁבְּרוּ צוֹרְרִים. טִבְחָה לָשִׁית בְּעַם נְצוּרִים.
חֻלְּפָה הַדָּת וְנָפְלוּ פְגָרִים. זָלְעֲפוּ וְזָעֲמוּ מוּבָסִים מְגֻרִים.

וּבְכֵן יִתְעַלֶּה שִׁמְךָ וְיִתְנַשֵּׂא. הוֹדְךָ שְׁמֵי שָׁמַיִם כִּסָּה.
דַּכִּים בְּרוֹמְמְךָ נְתוּנִים לִמְשִׁסָּה. גֵּיא וְאַפְסֶיהָ תְּהִלָּתְךָ מְכַסָּה.

בִּינָה הֲגִיגֵנוּ עַתָּה, וּרְאֵה בַּצָּר. בְּאַפְּךָ קוּמָה עַל צוֹרֵר הַצָּר.
אָדוֹן, קְרָאנוּךָ מִן הַמֵּצַר. אָנָּא הוֹצִיאֵנוּ לַמֶּרְחָב וְחַלְּצֵנוּ מִצָּר.

מְאֹד תַּרְבֶּה לָנוּ מְחִילָה. שְׁמַע תְּפִלָּה, וְהַעֲבֵר תִּפְלָה.
לוֹחֲצֵינוּ הַמְעֵד וּמַלְאָם חַלְחָלָה. מִמְּנוּ רַחֲמֶיךָ לָעַד לֹא תִּכְלָא.

Continue with אֵל מֶלֶךְ יוֹשֵׁב *on page 959.*

SELIḤOT FOR THE SEVENTEENTH OF TAMMUZ

סְלַח לָנוּ Forgive us, our Father, for in our great foolishness we have blundered. Pardon us, our King, for our iniquities are many.

אֵל אֶרֶךְ You are a God slow to anger, You are called the Master of Compassion, and You have taught the way of repentance. May You remember today and every day the greatness of Your compassion and kindness, for the sake of the descendants of Your beloved ones. Turn toward us in compassion, for You are the Master of Compassion. We come before You in plea and prayer, as You in ancient times showed the humble one [Moses]. Turn from Your fierce anger, as is written in Your Torah. In the shadow of Your wings may we shelter and abide, as on the day when the LORD descended in the cloud. ▸ Disregard transgression and erase guilt as on the day You stood with him [Moses] there. Hear our cry and heed our word, as on the day You proclaimed in the name of the LORD, and there it is written:

Congregation then Leader:

And the LORD passed by before him and proclaimed: *Ex. 34*

All say aloud:

יהוה The LORD, the LORD, compassionate and gracious God, slow to anger, abounding in loving-kindness and truth, extending loving-kindness to a thousand generations, forgiving iniquity, rebellion and sin, and absolving [the guilty who repent]. Forgive us our iniquity and our sin, and take us as Your inheritance.

Continue:

סְלַח לָנוּ Forgive us, our Father, for we have sinned. Pardon us, our King, for we have transgressed. For You, LORD, are good and forgiving, abounding in *Ps. 86* loving-kindness to all who call on You.

And do not let Him rest, until He establishes, until He makes Jerusalem the *Is. 62* praise of all the earth. For in You there is a wellspring of life; in Your light shall *Ps. 36* we see light. Our God, we are ashamed of our actions, distraught at our sins.

כְּרַחֵם As a father has compassion for his children,
so, LORD, have compassion for us.
Salvation is the LORD's; on Your people is Your blessing, Selah! *Ps. 3*
The LORD of hosts is with us, the God of Jacob is our stronghold, Selah! *Ps. 46*

סליחות לשבעה עשר בתמוז

סְלַח לָנוּ, אָבִינוּ, כִּי בְּרֹב אִוַּלְתֵּנוּ שָׁגִינוּ.
מְחַל לָנוּ, מַלְכֵּנוּ, כִּי רַבּוּ עֲוֹנֵינוּ.

אֵל אֶרֶךְ אַפַּיִם אַתָּה, וּבַעַל הָרַחֲמִים נִקְרֵאתָ, וְדֶרֶךְ תְּשׁוּבָה הוֹרֵיתָ. גְּדֻלַּת רַחֲמֶיךָ וַחֲסָדֶיךָ, תִּזְכֹּר הַיּוֹם וּבְכָל יוֹם לְזֶרַע יְדִידֶיךָ. תֵּפֶן אֵלֵינוּ בְּרַחֲמִים, כִּי אַתָּה הוּא בַּעַל הָרַחֲמִים. בְּתַחֲנוּן וּבִתְפִלָּה פָּנֶיךָ נְקַדֵּם, כְּהוֹדַעְתָּ לֶעָנָו מִקֶּדֶם. מֵחֲרוֹן אַפְּךָ שׁוּב, כְּמוֹ בְּתוֹרָתְךָ כָּתוּב. וּבְצֵל כְּנָפֶיךָ נֶחֱסֶה וְנִתְלוֹנָן, כְּיוֹם וַיֵּרֶד יהוה בֶּעָנָן. ‹ תַּעֲבֹר עַל פֶּשַׁע וְתִמְחֶה אָשָׁם, כְּיוֹם וַיִּתְיַצֵּב עִמּוֹ שָׁם. תַּאֲזִין שַׁוְעָתֵנוּ וְתַקְשִׁיב מֶנּוּ מַאֲמָר, כְּיוֹם וַיִּקְרָא בְשֵׁם יהוה, וְשָׁם נֶאֱמַר

שליח ציבור then קהל:

וַיַּעֲבֹר יהוה עַל־פָּנָיו וַיִּקְרָא — שמות לד

All say aloud:

יהוה, יהוה, אֵל רַחוּם וְחַנּוּן, אֶרֶךְ אַפַּיִם, וְרַב־חֶסֶד וֶאֱמֶת: נֹצֵר חֶסֶד לָאֲלָפִים, נֹשֵׂא עָוֹן וָפֶשַׁע וְחַטָּאָה, וְנַקֵּה: וְסָלַחְתָּ לַעֲוֹנֵנוּ וּלְחַטָּאתֵנוּ, וּנְחַלְתָּנוּ:

Continue:

סְלַח לָנוּ אָבִינוּ כִּי חָטָאנוּ, מְחַל לָנוּ מַלְכֵּנוּ כִּי פָשָׁעְנוּ. כִּי־אַתָּה אֲדֹנָי טוֹב וְסַלָּח, וְרַב־חֶסֶד לְכָל־קֹרְאֶיךָ: — תהלים פו

וְאַל־תִּתְּנוּ דֳמִי לוֹ, עַד־יְכוֹנֵן וְעַד־יָשִׂים אֶת־יְרוּשָׁלַםִ תְּהִלָּה בָּאָרֶץ: כִּי־עִמְּךָ מְקוֹר חַיִּים, בְּאוֹרְךָ נִרְאֶה־אוֹר: אֱלֹהֵינוּ, בֹּשְׁנוּ בְּמַעֲשֵׂינוּ וְנִכְלַמְנוּ בַּעֲוֹנֵינוּ. — ישעיה סב / תהלים לו

כְּרַחֵם אָב עַל בָּנִים, כֵּן תְּרַחֵם יהוה עָלֵינוּ.
לַיהוה הַיְשׁוּעָה, עַל־עַמְּךָ בִרְכָתֶךָ סֶּלָה: — תהלים ג
יהוה צְבָאוֹת עִמָּנוּ, מִשְׂגָּב לָנוּ אֱלֹהֵי יַעֲקֹב סֶלָה: — תהלים מו

Lord of hosts, happy is the one who trusts in You. *Ps. 84*
Lord, save! May the King answer us on the day we call. *Ps. 20*

▸ Forgive, please, this people's iniquity, *Num. 14*
in the abundance of Your kindness,
and as You have forgiven this people from the time of Egypt until now,
and there it is written:

Congregation then Leader:

And the Lord said, I have forgiven as you asked.

Continue:

הַטֵּה Give ear, my God and hear; open Your eyes and see our desolation, and the city that bears Your name, for it is not on the strength of our righteousness that we throw down our pleadings before You, but on the strength of Your great compassion. Lord, hear me; Lord, forgive; Lord, listen and act and do not delay – for Your sake, my God; for Your city and Your people bear Your name. *Dan. 9*

Our God and God of our fathers:

אָתָנוּ We come before You, Former of the winds. In our many iniquities our sighs have grown heavy; the decrees against us powerful and our screams so many – for on the Seventeenth of Tammuz, the Tablets were smashed. We have been exiled from the House of Your choosing; our judgment was sealed, the decree laid down. And the light has darkened over us – for on the Seventeenth of Tammuz, the Torah scroll was burnt. Our enemies destroyed the Sanctuary, the Divine Presence fled from Its corner, and we were yielded up to the hands of the wanton, to be consumed – for on the Seventeenth of Tammuz, an idol was set up in the Temple. We were scattered from city to city, and old and young of us were seized. The place of our delight was destroyed, and fire raged through her – for on the Seventeenth of Tammuz the city was broken through. The lethal foe took hold of our Temple, and the cherubs, bride and bridegroom were deprived of all their ornament. Because we angered You we were given up to destruction – for on the Seventeenth of Tammuz, the daily offering ceased. All glory and praise there ended. The enemy drew his sword and brandished its point against us; small children and babies were prepared for the slaughter – for on the Seventeenth of Tammuz, the offerings and sacrifices ceased. We rebelled against the One who inhabits the Heavens, and so we were dispersed to all the corners of the world. All our dancing was turned to lament – for on the Seventeenth of Tammuz, the Temple service ended. We acted obstinately with You in the discord of tongues, and so our own tongue has learnt lamentation; we have been abandoned in countless numbers – for on the Seventeenth of Tammuz, sin decided our destiny. We have been dispersed and found no relief, and so our sighs have multiplied within us; Rock, see how

יהוה צְבָאוֹת, אַשְׁרֵי אָדָם בֹּטֵחַ בָּךְ: תהלים פד

יהוה הוֹשִׁיעָה, הַמֶּלֶךְ יַעֲנֵנוּ בְיוֹם־קָרְאֵנוּ: תהלים כ

‹ סְלַח־נָא לַעֲוֹן הָעָם הַזֶּה כְּגֹדֶל חַסְדֶּךָ במדבר יד

וְכַאֲשֶׁר נָשָׂאתָה לָעָם הַזֶּה מִמִּצְרַיִם וְעַד־הֵנָּה:

וְשָׁם נֶאֱמַר

שליח ציבור then קהל:

וַיֹּאמֶר יהוה, סָלַחְתִּי כִּדְבָרֶךָ:

Continue:

הַטֵּה אֱלֹהַי אָזְנְךָ וּשְׁמָע, פְּקַח עֵינֶיךָ וּרְאֵה שֹׁמְמֹתֵינוּ וְהָעִיר אֲשֶׁר־נִקְרָא שִׁמְךָ עָלֶיהָ, כִּי לֹא עַל־צִדְקֹתֵינוּ אֲנַחְנוּ מַפִּילִים תַּחֲנוּנֵינוּ לְפָנֶיךָ, כִּי עַל־רַחֲמֶיךָ הָרַבִּים: אֲדֹנָי שְׁמָעָה, אֲדֹנָי סְלָחָה, אֲדֹנָי הַקְשִׁיבָה וַעֲשֵׂה אַל־תְּאַחַר, לְמַעַנְךָ אֱלֹהַי, כִּי־שִׁמְךָ נִקְרָא עַל־עִירְךָ וְעַל־עַמֶּךָ: דניאל ט

אֱלֹהֵינוּ וֵאלֹהֵי אֲבוֹתֵינוּ

אָתָנוּ לְךָ יוֹצֵר רוּחוֹת, בְּרוֹב עֲוֹנֵינוּ כָּבְדוּ אֲנָחוֹת, גָּזְרוּ עַצְמוּ וְרַבּוּ צְרִיחוֹת, כִּי בְּשִׁבְעָה עָשָׂר בְּתַמּוּז נִשְׁתַּבְּרוּ הַלֻּחוֹת. גָּלִינוּ מִבֵּית הַבְּחִירָה, דִּינֵנוּ נֶחְתַּם וְנִגְזְרָה גְזֵרָה, וְחָשַׁךְ בַּעֲדֵנוּ אוֹרָה, כִּי בְּשִׁבְעָה עָשָׂר בְּתַמּוּז נִשְׂרְפָה הַתּוֹרָה. הָרְסוּ אוֹיְבֵינוּ הַהֵיכָל, וּבָרְחָה שְׁכִינָה מִזָּוִית הֵיכָל, וְנִמְסַרְנוּ בִּידֵי זֵדִים לְהִתְאַכָּל, כִּי בְּשִׁבְעָה עָשָׂר בְּתַמּוּז הָעֳמַד צֶלֶם בַּהֵיכָל. זֹרִינוּ מֵעִיר אֶל עִיר, וְנִלְכַּד מִמֶּנּוּ רַב וְצָעִיר, חָרְבָה מְשׂוֹשֵׂנוּ וְאֵשׁ בָּהּ הִבְעִיר, כִּי בְּשִׁבְעָה עָשָׂר בְּתַמּוּז הֻבְקְעָה הָעִיר. טָפַשׁ מִקְדָּשֵׁנוּ צַר הַמַּשְׁמִיד, וְנָטַל מַחְתָּן וְכִלָּה אֶצְעָדָה וְצָמִיד, יַעַן כְּעַסְנוּךָ נִתְּנוּ לְהַשְׁמִיד, כִּי בְּשִׁבְעָה עָשָׂר בְּתַמּוּז בָּטַל הַתָּמִיד. כָּלָה מִנּוּ כָּל הוֹד וָשֶׁבֶת, חַרְבּוֹ שָׁלַף אוֹיֵב עָלֵינוּ לְאַבֵּת, לִהְיוֹת עוֹלְלִים וְיוֹנְקִים מוּכָנִים לַטֶּבַח, כִּי בְּשִׁבְעָה עָשָׂר בְּתַמּוּז בָּטְלוּ עוֹלָה וָזֶבַח. מָרַדְנוּ לְשׁוֹכֵן מְעוֹנוֹת, לָכֵן נִתְפַּזַּרְנוּ בְּכָל פִּנּוֹת, נֶהְפַּךְ מְחוֹלֵנוּ לְקִינוֹת, כִּי בְּשִׁבְעָה עָשָׂר בְּתַמּוּז בָּטְלוּ קָרְבָּנוֹת. סָרַרְנוּ לְפָנֶיךָ מֵרִיב לְשׁוֹנוֹת, לָכֵן לָמְדָה לְשׁוֹנֵנוּ לוֹמַר קִינוֹת, עֻזַּבְנוּ בְּלִי לְהִמָּנוֹת, כִּי בְּשִׁבְעָה עָשָׂר בְּתַמּוּז גָּרְמוּ לָנוּ עֲוֹנוֹת. פֹּזַּרְנוּ בְּלִי מְצוֹא רְוָחָה, לָכֵן רַבָּתָה

our souls have been bowed low – and turn our Seventeenth of Tammuz into gladness and joy. We have been obstinate and many calamities have met us; and so we have been yielded up to the plunder, have been pushed into the mud. See, LORD, and release us from disaster – and turn our Seventeenth of Tammuz into joy and gladness. ▸ Turn to us, You who reside on High, and gather in our scattered ones from the very ends of the earth. Say to Zion, "Come, get up," – and turn our Seventeenth of Tammuz to a day of salvation and comfort.

אֵל מֶלֶךְ God, King who sits upon a throne of compassion, who acts with loving-kindness, who pardons the iniquities of His people, passing them before Him in order; who forgives sinners and pardons transgressors; who performs righteousness with all flesh and spirit, do not repay their bad actions in kind. ▸ God, You taught us to speak thirteen attributes: recall for us today the covenant of the thirteen attributes, as You in ancient times showed the humble one [Moses], as is written: The LORD descended in the cloud and stood with him there, and proclaimed in the name of the LORD.

Congregation then Leader:

And the LORD passed by before him and proclaimed: *Ex. 34*

All say aloud:

יהוה The LORD, the LORD, compassionate and gracious God, slow to anger, abounding in loving-kindness and truth, extending loving-kindness to a thousand generations, forgiving iniquity, rebellion and sin, and absolving [the guilty who repent]. Forgive us our iniquity and our sin, and take us as Your inheritance.

Continue:

סְלַח לָנוּ Forgive us, our Father, for we have sinned. Pardon us, our King, for we have transgressed. For You, LORD, are good and forgiving, abounding in loving- *Ps. 86*
kindness to all who call on You.

God, do not rest, do not be silent and do not be still, for Your enemies clamor *Ps. 83*
and those who hate You hold their heads high. God of retribution, *Ps. 94*
LORD; God of retribution, appear

כְּרַחֵם As a father has compassion for his children,
so, LORD, have compassion for us.
Salvation is the LORD's; on Your people is Your blessing, Selah! *Ps. 3*
The LORD of hosts is with us, the God of Jacob is our stronghold, Selah! *Ps. 46*
LORD of hosts: happy is the one who trusts in You. *Ps. 84*
LORD, save! May the King answer us on the day we call. *Ps. 20*

בָּנוּ אֲנָחָה, צוּר רְאֵה נַפְשֵׁנוּ כִּי שָׁחָה, וְשִׁבְעָה עָשָׂר בְּתַמּוּז הֲפָךְ לָנוּ לְשָׂשׂוֹן וּלְשִׂמְחָה. קָשִׁינוּ עֹרֶף וְרָבְתָה בָּנוּ אָסוֹן, לָכֵן נִתַּנּוּ לִמְשִׁסָּה וְרִפְשׂוֹן, רְאֵה יהוה וְחַלְּצֵנוּ מֵאָסוֹן, וְשִׁבְעָה עָשָׂר בְּתַמּוּז הֲפָךְ לָנוּ לְשִׂמְחָה וּלְשָׂשׂוֹן. • שְׁעֵנוּ שׁוֹכֵן רוּמָה, וְקַבֵּץ נְפוּצוֹתֵינוּ מִקְּצוֹת אֲדָמָה, תֹּאמַר לְצִיּוֹן קוּמָה, וְשִׁבְעָה עָשָׂר בְּתַמּוּז הֲפָךְ לָנוּ לְיוֹם יְשׁוּעָה וְנֶחָמָה.

אֵל מֶלֶךְ יוֹשֵׁב עַל כִּסֵּא רַחֲמִים, מִתְנַהֵג בַּחֲסִידוּת. מוֹחֵל עֲוֹנוֹת עַמּוֹ, מַעֲבִיר רִאשׁוֹן רִאשׁוֹן. מַרְבֶּה מְחִילָה לְחַטָּאִים, וּסְלִיחָה לְפוֹשְׁעִים. עֹשֶׂה צְדָקוֹת עִם כָּל בָּשָׂר וָרוּחַ, לֹא כְרָעָתָם תִּגְמֹל. • אֵל, הוֹרֵיתָ לָּנוּ לוֹמַר שְׁלֹשׁ עֶשְׂרֵה, וּזְכָר לָנוּ הַיּוֹם בְּרִית שְׁלֹשׁ עֶשְׂרֵה, כְּמוֹ שֶׁהוֹדַעְתָּ לֶעָנָו מִקֶּדֶם, כְּמוֹ שֶׁכָּתוּב: וַיֵּרֶד יהוה בֶּעָנָן, וַיִּתְיַצֵּב עִמּוֹ שָׁם, וַיִּקְרָא בְשֵׁם, יהוה:

קהל then שליח ציבור:

וַיַּעֲבֹר יהוה עַל־פָּנָיו וַיִּקְרָא — שמות לד

All say aloud:

יהוה, יהוה, אֵל רַחוּם וְחַנּוּן, אֶרֶךְ אַפַּיִם, וְרַב־חֶסֶד וֶאֱמֶת: נֹצֵר חֶסֶד לָאֲלָפִים, נֹשֵׂא עָוֹן וָפֶשַׁע וְחַטָּאָה, וְנַקֵּה: וְסָלַחְתָּ לַעֲוֹנֵנוּ וּלְחַטָּאתֵנוּ, וּנְחַלְתָּנוּ:

Continue:

תהלים פו — סְלַח לָנוּ אָבִינוּ כִּי חָטָאנוּ, מְחַל לָנוּ מַלְכֵּנוּ כִּי פָשָׁעְנוּ. כִּי־אַתָּה אֲדֹנָי טוֹב וְסַלָּח, וְרַב־חֶסֶד לְכָל־קֹרְאֶיךָ:

תהלים פג — אֱלֹהִים אַל־דֳּמִי־לָךְ, אַל־תֶּחֱרַשׁ וְאַל־תִּשְׁקֹט אֵל: כִּי־הִנֵּה אוֹיְבֶיךָ יֶהֱמָיוּן, וּמְשַׂנְאֶיךָ נָשְׂאוּ רֹאשׁ: אֵל־נְקָמוֹת יהוה, אֵל נְקָמוֹת הוֹפִיעַ: — תהלים צד

כְּרַחֵם אָב עַל בָּנִים, כֵּן תְּרַחֵם יהוה עָלֵינוּ.

תהלים ג — לַיהוה הַיְשׁוּעָה, עַל־עַמְּךָ בִרְכָתֶךָ סֶּלָה:

תהלים מו — יהוה צְבָאוֹת עִמָּנוּ, מִשְׂגָּב לָנוּ אֱלֹהֵי יַעֲקֹב סֶלָה:

תהלים פד — יהוה צְבָאוֹת, אַשְׁרֵי אָדָם בֹּטֵחַ בָּךְ:

תהלים כ — יהוה הוֹשִׁיעָה, הַמֶּלֶךְ יַעֲנֵנוּ בְיוֹם־קָרְאֵנוּ:

Our God and God of our fathers:

אֶמְרַר It is bitterly that I weep, over the Hand raised against our ruins. I blasphemed Him in His House, in my unfaithfulness and thieving. The Holy Presence broke out and fled, flew ten stretches and rose up to the seventh Heaven. God cut me off, tormented me, burnt me, in the fourth month. He closed the time set for Him to break those young boys, who were like boughs just sprouting. He shot us with His arrows twice, melted and weakened us, as heedless women wept for Tammuz in the Temple. He condemned me and became Enemy to me, then, in the month of Tammuz. Five traps were laid for me, deep in the Scripture of sufferings sent. Those people overcame me for my impurity on the seventeenth of the month. For I was ensnared like a wretched bride, unfaithful beneath a wedding canopy of peace and success. I did not wait for Moses, my shepherd, until the sixth hour, and the Tablets were smashed. From His hand was I ornamented with jewelry of fine gold, brooch and bracelet. They flowed away on the day of His rage, when I corrupted my way, and denounced my faith. I broke off the order of His service and the constant supplies of the altar – from the Chamber of the Lambs, the daily offering is ended. Israel is crumbled to pieces, scattered, storm battered, oppressed. Likened to a ship without a captain, tossed about like a boat. You have taken her by the head for her sins, exposed her twice over to mourning and moaning. Her enemies waged war on her on this day, and the city was broken through again. She fled out like a chased gazelle to hide, when none sought her. They sharpened their tongues, they made her like a lamb, and left her wool and milk for all takers. She cries out for the cherished thing with which she was crowned: the beloved of her eyes eluded her as Apostomus burnt the Torah. A fool cursed those oppressed and broken to vex them; he taunted abject people: "They shall be consumed;" "God shall hide His face from seeing." When idols were placed in the Temple, God avenged one's hand at the hand of the other, a disgusting item consumed. This, at the time when He gathered anguish over us; for an image was set up in the Sanctuary of God. Miserable and plagued are these children, who were once the very first. Their troubles have come close on one another's heels these many years; stricken as if by the stings of bees and scorpions. They think their hope is gone, that as they sit in this darkness they have no more chance. ▸ Zealous God, in Your restraint towards those who incite You they have flourished fat and succulent. Raise up those who still await You; let them stand firm always, like something planted, or carved out with love. It is on fast days that truth and peace are hewn out. May they become forever times of joy and celebration – festive days.

אֵל מֶלֶךְ God, King who sits upon a throne of compassion, who acts with loving-kindness, who pardons the iniquities of His people, passing them before Him in order; who forgives sinners and pardons transgressors; who performs righteousness with all flesh and spirit, do not repay their bad actions in kind. ▸ God, You taught us to speak thirteen attributes: recall for us today the covenant of the thirteen attributes, as You in ancient times showed the humble one [Moses], as is written: The Lord descended in the cloud and stood with him there, and proclaimed in the name of the Lord:

Congregation then Leader:

And the Lord passed by before him and proclaimed: *Ex. 34*

אֱלֹהֵינוּ וֵאלֹהֵי אֲבוֹתֵינוּ

אֶמְרַר בִּבְכִי מִפְּנֵי יַד שְׁלוּחָה בְּעִי. בְּנָאצִי בְּתוֹךְ בֵּיתוֹ בְּבִגְדֵי וְקָבְעִי. גָּח וּבָרַח וְנָסַע עָשָׂר וְעָלָה לְשְׁבִיעִי. דִּמְנִי הֵצִיקָנִי הֵשִׂיקָנִי בְּחֹדֶשׁ הָרְבִיעִי. הֵבִיא מוֹעֵד בִּמְלַאכְתּוֹ לִשְׁבֹּר בַּחוּרֵי גְמוּז. וְרַבָּה בּוֹ פְּעָמִים בְּמִסְמוּס וּמִזְמוּז. זְבוּלוֹ כְּשֶׁר שַׁאֲנָנוּת מְבַכּוֹת אֶת הַתַּמּוּז. חִיְּבַנִי וְאִיְּבַנִי אֲזַי בְּיֶרַח תַּמּוּז. טָמְנוּ פַּחִים חֲמִשָּׁה בְּמִקְרָא תְּלָאוֹת מְשֻׁלָּחוֹת. יָכְלוּ לִי בְּשִׁבְעָה עָשָׂר בּוֹ בַּאֲלִיחוֹת. כִּי נוֹקַשְׁתִּי כְּכַלָּה עֲלוּבָה בְּחֻפַּת שַׁלְוָה וְהַצְלָחוֹת. לְרוֹעִי לֹא הִמְתַּנְתִּי שֵׁשׁ, וְנִשְׁתַּבְּרוּ הַלֻּחוֹת. מִיָּדוֹ עֲדִיתִי חֲלִי כֶתֶם, אֶצְעָדָה וְצָמִיד. נִגְּרוֹת בְּיוֹם אַפּוֹ, כְּשִׁחַתִּי דְרָכַי לְהַשְׁמִיד. סֵדֶר עֲבוֹדָתוֹ וְקֵץ מִזְבְּחוֹ קִצְּתִי לְהַעֲמִיד. עַל כֵּן מִלִּשְׁכַּת הַטְּלָאִים בָּטַל הַתָּמִיד. פּוֹר הִתְפּוֹרְרָה וְנִתְפַּזְּרָה סֹעֲרָה עֲנִיָּה. צִי נִמְשְׁלָה מִבְּלִי חוֹבֵל, וְנִטְרְפָה כָּאֳנִיָּה. קָחְתָה בְּחַטָּאתָהּ בְּרֹאשָׁהּ, וּבְכֶפֶל תַּאֲנִיָּה וַאֲנִיָּה. רִיבוּהָ צָרֶיהָ כְּהַיּוֹם, וְהָבְקְעָה הָעִיר בַּשְּׁנִיָּה. שֻׁלְּחָה כִּצְבִי מֻדָּח מֵאֵין דּוֹרֵשׁ לְהַסְתִּירָה. שָׁנְנוּ לְשׁוֹנָם וּנְתָנוּהָ כְּשֶׂה, צַמְרָהּ וַחֲלָבָהּ לְהַתִּירָה. תִּצְעַק עַל כְּלֵי חֶמְדָּה שֶׁבּוֹ נִכְתָּרָה. תַּחְמוּד עֵינֶיהָ נְצַל כְּשָׂרָף אַפּוֹסְטֹמוּס הַתּוֹרָה. חֵרֵף עֲשׁוּקִים וּרְצוּצִים בַּעֲבוּר הַרְעִימָם סָכָל. יְרוּדִים בּוֹהֶיהָ לֶאֱכוֹל וּבְהַסְתֵּר פָּנִים מִלְּהִסְתַּכֵּל. יַד הִשְׁלִים מִכְּנַף שִׁקּוּצִים נֶאֱכָל. עֵת צָרָה כְּהִתְכַּנֵּס וְהָעֳמַד צֶלֶם בְּהֵיכָל. דְּוּוִים סְגוּפִים בָּנִים הָיוּ מִקֶּדֶם רִאשׁוֹנִים. סְמוּכוֹת צָרוֹתֵיהֶם זוֹ לְזוֹ כַּמָּה שָׁנִים. לוֹקִים כַּאֲשֶׁר תַּעֲשֶׂינָה הַדְּבוֹרִים, וְהָעַקְרַבִּים שׁוֹנִים. הוֹגִים אַבַּד שִׁבְרָם וּבָטֵל סִכּוּיִם בָּאִישׁוֹנִים. · אֵל קַנָּא, בְּהִתְאַפֵּק בִּמְקַנְאֶיךָ דְּשֵׁנִים וְרַטֻבִּים. מְחַכִּים תְּקִים עוֹמְדִים לְעוֹלָמִים, כִּנְטִיעִים מְחֻטָּבִים בַּאֲהָבִים. הָאֱמֶת וְהַשָּׁלוֹם בְּצוֹמוֹת חֲטוּבִים. נֶצַח הֱיוֹתָם לְשִׂמְחָה וּלְשָׂשׂוֹן וּלְמוֹעֲדִים טוֹבִים.

אֵל מֶלֶךְ יוֹשֵׁב עַל כִּסֵּא רַחֲמִים, מִתְנַהֵג בַּחֲסִידוּת. מוֹחֵל עֲוֹנוֹת עַמּוֹ, מַעֲבִיר רִאשׁוֹן רִאשׁוֹן. מַרְבֶּה מְחִילָה לְחַטָּאִים, וּסְלִיחָה לְפוֹשְׁעִים. עֹשֶׂה צְדָקוֹת עִם כָּל בָּשָׂר וָרוּחַ, לֹא כְרָעָתָם תִּגְמֹל. · אֵל, הוֹרֵיתָ לָּנוּ לוֹמַר שְׁלֹשׁ עֶשְׂרֵה, וּזְכָר לָנוּ הַיּוֹם בְּרִית שְׁלֹשׁ עֶשְׂרֵה, כְּמוֹ שֶׁהוֹדַעְתָּ לֶעָנָו מִקֶּדֶם, כְּמוֹ שֶׁכָּתוּב: וַיֵּרֶד יהוה בֶּעָנָן, וַיִּתְיַצֵּב עִמּוֹ שָׁם, וַיִּקְרָא בְשֵׁם, יהוה:

then קהל שליח ציבור:

שמות לד — וַיַּעֲבֹר יהוה עַל־פָּנָיו וַיִּקְרָא

All say aloud:

יהוה The Lord, the Lord, compassionate and gracious God, slow to anger, abounding in loving-kindness and truth, extending loving-kindness to a thousand generations, forgiving iniquity, rebellion and sin, and absolving [the guilty who repent]. Forgive us our iniquity and our sin, and take us as Your inheritance.

Continue:

סְלַח לָנוּ Forgive us, our Father, for we have sinned. Pardon us, our King, for we have transgressed. For You, Lord, are good and forgiving, abounding in loving-kindness to all who call on You. *Ps. 86*

The following is said responsively:

Turn to this prisoner who has been yielded up,
to the hand of Babylon and then of Seir;
to You he has been calling all these years, and he pleads like a small child,
on the day the enemy prevailed and the city was broken through.

And so I bow myself and strike my hands together,
on this day of five disasters that scattered me about,
for at the time of the golden calf, the Tablets left me.
And the daily offering was annulled, and they brought me away in a cage.
And an idol was placed in the Sanctuary that was my crowning glory,
and I was deprived of His counsel.
The meal-offering was ended, and Your Law – the foe sent it up in flames,
on the day the enemy prevailed and the city was broken through.

I tremble terribly, I stand horrified, on the day the Lord pushed me aside,
And Sennacherib, the Viper of the north, swept me away like a deluge.
My light grew dark, and Sheshakh [Babylon] too, tossed me about like a ball.
And the hunter stretched out his hand, and the goat of Greece,
the hairy one of Rome,
on the day the enemy prevailed and the city was broken through.

The glory of my heart, my Stronghold, will Your rage fume forever?
Will You not see this weary nation, blackened as if by the furnace?
Close, with the descendant of Peretz, the breach in my fence,
and, from among the thorns, pick out the lily.
Build the Temple, and return the borders of the Carmel and of Bashan.
And open Your eyes, exact vengeance from Etzer and Dishan.
Judge a people struck dumb, so that the damages be paid,
by the one who destroys, the one who burns –
on the day the enemy prevailed and the city was broken through.

All say aloud:

יהוה, יהוה, אֵל רַחוּם וְחַנּוּן, אֶרֶךְ אַפַּיִם, וְרַב־חֶסֶד וֶאֱמֶת: נֹצֵר חֶסֶד לָאֲלָפִים, נֹשֵׂא עָוֹן וָפֶשַׁע וְחַטָּאָה, וְנַקֵּה: וְסָלַחְתָּ לַעֲוֹנֵנוּ וּלְחַטָּאתֵנוּ, וּנְחַלְתָּנוּ:

Continue:

סְלַח לָנוּ אָבִינוּ כִּי חָטָאנוּ, מְחַל לָנוּ מַלְכֵּנוּ כִּי פָשָׁעְנוּ. כִּי־אַתָּה אֲדֹנָי טוֹב וְסַלָּח, וְרַב־חֶסֶד לְכָל־קֹרְאֶיךָ: תהלים פו

The following is said responsively:

שְׁעֵה נֶאֱסַר, אֲשֶׁר נִמְסַר, בְּיַד בָּבֶל וְגַם שֵׂעִיר.
לְךָ יֶהֱמֶה, זֶה כַּמֶּה, וְיִתְחַנֵּן כְּבֵן צָעִיר.
יוֹם גָּבַר הָאוֹיֵב וַתִּבָּקַע הָעִיר.

לְזֹאת אֶכַּף, וְאֶסְפֹּק כַּף, בְּיוֹם חֲמֵשׁ פְּזוּרוֹנִי.
וְעַל רֶגֶל הָעֵגֶל, הַלֻּחוֹת יְצָאוּנִי.
וְגַם הִשְׁמִיד הַתָּמִיד, וּבַסּוּגַר הֱבִיאַנִי.
וְהוּשַׂם אֱלִיל בְּהֵיכַל כְּלִיל, וּמֵעֲצָתוֹ כְּלָאַנִי.
וְהַמִּנְחָה הוּנְחָה, וְדָתְךָ, צָר בָּאֵשׁ הִבְעִיר.
יוֹם גָּבַר הָאוֹיֵב וַתִּבָּקַע הָעִיר.

מְאֹד אֶתְחַל, וְאֶתְחַלְחַל, בְּיוֹם שַׁדַּי דְּחָפַנִי.
וְהַשְּׁפִיפוֹן מִצָּפוֹן, כְּשִׁבֹּלֶת שְׁטָפַנִי.
מְאוֹר חָשַׁךְ, וְגַם שֵׁשַׁךְ, כְּמוֹ כַדּוּר צְנָפַנִי.
וְהַצַּיָּד שָׁלַח יָד, וְהַצָּפִיר וְהַשָּׂעִיר.
יוֹם גָּבַר הָאוֹיֵב וַתִּבָּקַע הָעִיר.

הוֹד לִבִּי וּמִשְׂגַּבִּי, הֲלָעַד אַפְּךָ יֶעְשַׁן.
הֲלֹא תִרְאֶה עַם נִלְאֶה, אֲשֶׁר הָשְׁחַר כְּמוֹ כִבְשָׁן.
גְּדֹר פִּרְצִי בְּבֶן פַּרְצִי, וּמֵחֶדֶק לְקֹט שׁוֹשָׁן.
בְּנֵה בֵּית זְבוּל, וְהָשֵׁב גְּבוּל הַכַּרְמֶל וְהַבָּשָׁן.
וְעַיִן פְּקַח, וְנָקָם קַח מֵאֶצֶר וּמִדִּישָׁן.
שְׁפֹט אִלֵּם, וְאָז יְשַׁלֵּם הַמַּבְעֶה וְהַמַּבְעִיר.
יוֹם גָּבַר הָאוֹיֵב וַתִּבָּקַע הָעִיר.

On all days continue:

אֵל מֶלֶךְ God, King who sits upon a throne of compassion, who acts with loving-kindness, who pardons the iniquities of His people, passing them before Him in order; who forgives sinners and pardons transgressors; who performs righteousness with all flesh and spirit, do not repay their bad actions in kind. God, You taught us to speak thirteen attributes: recall for us today the covenant of the thirteen attributes, as You in ancient times showed the humble one [Moses], as is written: The LORD descended in the cloud and stood with him there, and proclaimed in the name of the LORD:

Congregation then Leader:

And the LORD passed by before him and proclaimed: *Ex. 34*

All say aloud:

יהוה The LORD, the LORD, compassionate and gracious God, slow to anger, abounding in loving-kindness and truth, extending loving-kindness to a thousand generations, forgiving iniquity, rebellion and sin, and absolving [the guilty who repent]. Forgive us our iniquity and our sin, and take us as Your inheritance.

Continue:

סְלַח לָנוּ Forgive us, our Father, for we have sinned. Pardon us, our King, for we have transgressed. For You, LORD, are good and forgiving, abounding in loving-kindness to all who call on You. *Ps. 86*

זְכֹר Remember, LORD, Your compassion and loving-kindness, *Ps. 25*
for they are everlasting. Remember us, LORD, in favoring Your people;
redeem us with Your salvation.

זְכֹר Remember Your congregation, the one that You acquired long ago, *Ps. 74*
the tribe of Your inheritance that You redeemed,
this Mount Zion that You have dwelt in.

זְכֹר Remember, LORD, the fondness of Jerusalem; do not forever forget the
love of Zion. You shall rise up and have compassion for Zion, *Ps. 102*
for now it is right to be gracious, for the time has come.

זְכֹר Remember, LORD, what the Edomites did on the day Jerusalem fell. *Ps. 137*
They said, "Tear it down, tear it down to its very foundations!"

זְכֹר Remember Abraham, Isaac and Jacob, to whom You swore by Your *Ex. 32*
own self, when You said to them, "I shall make Your descendants
as numerous as the stars in the sky, and I shall give all this Land that
I spoke of to your descendants, and they shall inherit it forever."

זְכֹר Remember Your servants, Abraham, Isaac and Jacob; do not attend to *Deut. 9*
the stubbornness of this people, to their wickedness or sinfulness.

On all days continue:

אֵל מֶלֶךְ יוֹשֵׁב עַל כִּסֵּא רַחֲמִים, מִתְנַהֵג בַּחֲסִידוּת. מוֹחֵל עֲוֹנוֹת עַמּוֹ, מַעֲבִיר רִאשׁוֹן רִאשׁוֹן. מַרְבֶּה מְחִילָה לְחַטָּאִים, וּסְלִיחָה לְפוֹשְׁעִים. עֹשֶׂה צְדָקוֹת עִם כָּל בָּשָׂר וָרוּחַ, לֹא כְרָעָתָם תִּגְמֹל. ‹ אֵל, הוֹרֵיתָ לָּנוּ לוֹמַר שְׁלֹשׁ עֶשְׂרֵה, וּזְכָר לָנוּ הַיּוֹם בְּרִית שְׁלֹשׁ עֶשְׂרֵה, כְּמוֹ שֶׁהוֹדַעְתָּ לֶעָנָו מִקֶּדֶם, כְּמוֹ שֶׁכָּתוּב: וַיֵּרֶד יהוה בֶּעָנָן, וַיִּתְיַצֵּב עִמּוֹ שָׁם, וַיִּקְרָא בְשֵׁם, יהוה:

קהל *then* שליח ציבור*:*

שמות לד וַיַּעֲבֹר יהוה עַל־פָּנָיו וַיִּקְרָא

All say aloud:

יהוה, יהוה, אֵל רַחוּם וְחַנּוּן, אֶרֶךְ אַפַּיִם, וְרַב־חֶסֶד וֶאֱמֶת: נֹצֵר חֶסֶד לָאֲלָפִים, נֹשֵׂא עָוֹן וָפֶשַׁע וְחַטָּאָה, וְנַקֵּה: וְסָלַחְתָּ לַעֲוֹנֵנוּ וּלְחַטָּאתֵנוּ, וּנְחַלְתָּנוּ:

Continue:

תהלים פו סְלַח לָנוּ אָבִינוּ כִּי חָטָאנוּ, מְחַל לָנוּ מַלְכֵּנוּ כִּי פָשָׁעְנוּ. כִּי־אַתָּה אֲדֹנָי טוֹב וְסַלָּח, וְרַב־חֶסֶד לְכָל־קֹרְאֶיךָ:

תהלים כה זְכֹר־רַחֲמֶיךָ יהוה וַחֲסָדֶיךָ, כִּי מֵעוֹלָם הֵמָּה:

זָכְרֵנוּ יהוה בִּרְצוֹן עַמֶּךָ, פָּקְדֵנוּ בִּישׁוּעָתֶךָ.

תהלים עד זְכֹר עֲדָתְךָ קָנִיתָ קֶּדֶם, גָּאַלְתָּ שֵׁבֶט נַחֲלָתֶךָ

הַר־צִיּוֹן זֶה שָׁכַנְתָּ בּוֹ:

זְכֹר יהוה חִבַּת יְרוּשָׁלָיִם, אַהֲבַת צִיּוֹן אַל תִּשְׁכַּח לָנֶצַח.

תהלים קב אַתָּה תָקוּם תְּרַחֵם צִיּוֹן, כִּי־עֵת לְחֶנְנָהּ, כִּי־בָא מוֹעֵד:

תהלים קלז זְכֹר יהוה לִבְנֵי אֱדוֹם אֵת יוֹם יְרוּשָׁלָיִם

הָאֹמְרִים עָרוּ עָרוּ, עַד הַיְסוֹד בָּהּ:

שמות לב זְכֹר לְאַבְרָהָם לְיִצְחָק וּלְיִשְׂרָאֵל עֲבָדֶיךָ, אֲשֶׁר נִשְׁבַּעְתָּ לָהֶם בָּךְ

וַתְּדַבֵּר אֲלֵהֶם, אַרְבֶּה אֶת־זַרְעֲכֶם כְּכוֹכְבֵי הַשָּׁמָיִם

וְכָל־הָאָרֶץ הַזֹּאת אֲשֶׁר אָמַרְתִּי אֶתֵּן לְזַרְעֲכֶם, וְנָחֲלוּ לְעֹלָם:

דברים ט זְכֹר לַעֲבָדֶיךָ לְאַבְרָהָם לְיִצְחָק וּלְיַעֲקֹב

אַל־תֵּפֶן אֶל־קְשִׁי הָעָם הַזֶּה וְאֶל־רִשְׁעוֹ וְאֶל־חַטָּאתוֹ:

אַל־נָא Please, do not hold against us the sin
that we committed so foolishly, that we have sinned. *Num. 12*
We have sinned, our Rock; forgive us, our Creator.

Some say responsively (all continue with "Remember the covenant" on the next page):

אֵל נָא God, please, heal please, the diseases of this fruitful vine,
ashamed, disgraced and miserable are her fruits.
Redeem her from destruction and from the seeping wound;
answer us as You answered our father Abraham on Mount Moriah –
We have sinned, our Rock;
forgive us, our Creator.

Let the flags of the people redeemed by Your revealed arm,
be spared from plague; let them not be cut down,
and answer our call, and desire the creations of Your hands.
Answer us as You answered our fathers at the Reed Sea –
We have sinned, our Rock;
forgive us, our Creator.

Reveal now the merit of Abraham and Sarah,
the rock from which we were hewn.
Spare us from rage and lead us on a straight path.
Clear our impurity, and open our eyes to the light of Your Torah.
Answer us as You answered Joshua at Gilgal –
We have sinned, our Rock;
forgive us, our Creator.

LORD, witness the ashes of bound Isaac; make our cure spring up.
Put an end to plunder and brokenness, tempest and storm.
Teach us and make us wise with Your perfect word.
Answer us as You answered Samuel at Mitzpah –
We have sinned, our Rock;
forgive us, our Creator.

Jacob who emerged perfect from the womb – do not let his roots dry up.
Cleanse us of all stain and blemish, and do not have us wither.
Help us and we shall be saved,
and receive of Your ways of kindness.
Answer us as You answered Elijah on Mount Carmel –
We have sinned, our Rock;
forgive us, our Creator.

אַל־נָא תָשֵׁת עָלֵינוּ חַטָּאת אֲשֶׁר נוֹאַלְנוּ וַאֲשֶׁר חָטָאנוּ: במדבר יב
חָטָאנוּ צוּרֵנוּ, סְלַח לָנוּ יוֹצְרֵנוּ.

Some say responsively (all continue with זְכָר לָנוּ בְּרִית *on the next page):*

אֵל נָא, רְפָא נָא תַּחֲלוּאֵי גֶּפֶן פּוֹרִיָּה
בּוֹשָׁה וְחָפְרָה, וְאֻמְלַל פִּרְיָהּ
גְּאָלֶנָּה מִשַּׁחַת וּמִמַּכָּה טְרִיָּה.
עֲנֵנוּ כְּשֶׁעָנִיתָ לְאַבְרָהָם אָבִינוּ בְּהַר הַמּוֹרִיָּה.
חָטָאנוּ צוּרֵנוּ, סְלַח לָנוּ יוֹצְרֵנוּ.

דְּגָלֵי עָם, פְּדוּיֵי בִּזְרוֹעַ חָשׂוּף
הַצֵּל מִנֶּגֶף וְאַל יִהְיוּ לְשִׁסּוּף
וְתַעֲנֶה קְרִיאָתֵנוּ וּלְמַעֲשֵׂה יָדֶיךָ תִּכְסֹף
עֲנֵנוּ כְּשֶׁעָנִיתָ לַאֲבוֹתֵינוּ עַל יַם סוּף.
חָטָאנוּ צוּרֵנוּ, סְלַח לָנוּ יוֹצְרֵנוּ.

זְכוּת צוּר חֻצַּב הַיּוֹם לָנוּ תָגֵל
חָשְׁכֵנוּ מֵאֱנֹף וּנְחֵנוּ בְּיֹשֶׁר מַעְגָּל
טַהֵר טֻמְאָתֵנוּ וְלִמְאוֹר תּוֹרָתְךָ עֵינֵינוּ גַל
עֲנֵנוּ כְּשֶׁעָנִיתָ לִיהוֹשֻׁעַ בַּגִּלְגָּל.
חָטָאנוּ צוּרֵנוּ, סְלַח לָנוּ יוֹצְרֵנוּ.

יָהּ, רְאֵה דֶּשֶׁן עָקוּד, וְהַצְמַח לָנוּ תְרוּפָה
כַּלֵּה שֹׁד וָשֶׁבֶר, סַעַר וְסוּפָה
לַמְּדֵנוּ וְחַכְּמֵנוּ אִמְרָתְךָ הַצְּרוּפָה
עֲנֵנוּ כְּשֶׁעָנִיתָ לִשְׁמוּאֵל בַּמִּצְפָּה.
חָטָאנוּ צוּרֵנוּ, סְלַח לָנוּ יוֹצְרֵנוּ.

מְתֻמִּם מְרַחֵם, שָׁרָשָׁיו אַל תְּקַמֵּל
נְקֵנוּ מִכְּתָם וְשֶׁמֶץ, וְלֹא נֶאֱמַל
סְעָדֵנוּ וְנִוָּשֵׁעָה, וְאָרְחוֹת חֲסָדֶיךָ נִגְמַל
עֲנֵנוּ כְּשֶׁעָנִיתָ לְאֵלִיָּהוּ בְּהַר הַכַּרְמֶל.
חָטָאנוּ צוּרֵנוּ, סְלַח לָנוּ יוֹצְרֵנוּ.

Strengthen us by the righteousness of Moses, drawn from water,
and atone our crimes, wanton or foolish.
Free us from the terror of death that thrusts us back,
rule for our salvation; do not let us melt away in our sins.
Answer us as You answered Jonah in the belly of the fish –

We have sinned, our Rock;
forgive us, our Creator.

Remember Your devoted Aaron's sanctity,
for the sake of Israel of the pleasing steps.
Awaken Your compassion, for we are doubly stricken.
Return us resolutely to our awe of You, do not expose us.
Answer us as You answered David, and Solomon his son in Jerusalem –

We have sinned, our Rock;
forgive us, our Creator.

On the Fast of Esther add:

Answer those who call You; listen out from Your residence.
Hear the cry of those who call out to You, You who listen to the destitute.
Have compassion for Your children, as a father has for his.
Answer us as You answered Mordekhai and Esther:
and on a fifty-cubit gallows they hanged father and sons –

We have sinned, our Rock.
Forgive us, our Creator.

All continue:

זְכֹר Remember the covenant of our fathers, as You have said,
"I shall remember My covenant with Jacob, and My covenant *Lev. 26*
with Isaac, and I shall remember My covenant with Abraham,
and I shall remember the Land."

זְכֹר Remember the covenant of the early ones, as You have said,
"I shall remember for them the covenant of the early ones, *Lev. 26*
those I took out of the Land of Egypt before the eyes of the nations,
in order to be their God: I am the LORD."

עֲשֵׂה Deal kindly with us as You have promised, "Even so, when they are in the land of their enemies I shall not reject them and shall not detest them to the point of destruction, to the point of breaking My covenant with them, for I am the LORD their God." Restore our fortunes, and have compassion for us as is written, "And God shall restore your fortunes and have compassion for you, and shall return and gather you in from all the nations among whom the LORD *Lev. 26* *Deut. 30*

עוֹדְדֵנוּ בְּצֶדֶק מְשׁוּי מִמַּיִם, וְכַפֵּר זָדוֹן וּמְשׁוּגָה
פְּדֵנוּ מִמְּהוּמַת מָוֶת, וְאָחוֹר בַּל נִסּוֹגָה
צַוֵּה יְשׁוּעָתֵנוּ, וּבַעֲוֹנוֹתֵינוּ אַל נִתְמוֹגְגָה
עֲנֵנוּ כְּשֶׁעָנִיתָ לְיוֹנָה בִּמְעֵי הַדָּגָה.
חָטָאנוּ צוּרֵנוּ, סְלַח לָנוּ יוֹצְרֵנוּ.

קְדֻשַּׁת אִישׁ חֲסִידֶךָ זְכֹר לִיפַת פְּעָמִים
רַחֲמֶיךָ תְּעוֹרֵר כִּי לָקִינוּ בְּכִפְלַיִם
שׁוּבֵנוּ תֹּקֶף לְיִרְאָתֶךָ וְלֹא נֶחְשַׁף שׁוּלַיִם
עֲנֵנוּ כְּשֶׁעָנִיתָ לְדָוִד וְלִשְׁלֹמֹה בְנוֹ בִּירוּשָׁלָיִם.
חָטָאנוּ צוּרֵנוּ, סְלַח לָנוּ יוֹצְרֵנוּ.

On תענית אסתר *add:*

תַּעֲנֶה לְקוֹרְאֶיךָ, וְהַסְכֵּת מִמְּעוֹנִים
תִּשְׁמַע שַׁוְעַת צוֹעֲקֶיךָ, שׁוֹמֵעַ אֶל אֶבְיוֹנִים
תְּרַחֵם עַל בָּנֶיךָ כְּרַחֵם אָב עַל בָּנִים
עֲנֵנוּ כְּמוֹ שֶׁעָנִיתָ לְמָרְדְּכַי וְאֶסְתֵּר
וְתָלוּ עַל עֵץ־חֲמִשִּׁים הָאָב עִם בָּנִים.
חָטָאנוּ צוּרֵנוּ, סְלַח לָנוּ יוֹצְרֵנוּ.

All continue:

זְכֹר לָנוּ בְּרִית אָבוֹת כַּאֲשֶׁר אָמַרְתָּ: וְזָכַרְתִּי אֶת־בְּרִיתִי יַעֲקוֹב וְאַף אֶת־בְּרִיתִי יִצְחָק וְאַף אֶת־בְּרִיתִי אַבְרָהָם אֶזְכֹּר וְהָאָרֶץ אֶזְכֹּר: ויקרא כו

זְכֹר לָנוּ בְּרִית רִאשׁוֹנִים כַּאֲשֶׁר אָמַרְתָּ: וְזָכַרְתִּי לָהֶם בְּרִית רִאשֹׁנִים אֲשֶׁר הוֹצֵאתִי־אֹתָם מֵאֶרֶץ מִצְרַיִם לְעֵינֵי הַגּוֹיִם לִהְיוֹת לָהֶם לֵאלֹהִים, אֲנִי יהוה: ויקרא כו

עֲשֵׂה עִמָּנוּ כְּמָה שֶׁהִבְטַחְתָּנוּ: וְאַף גַּם־זֹאת בִּהְיוֹתָם בְּאֶרֶץ אֹיְבֵיהֶם, ויקרא כו
לֹא־מְאַסְתִּים וְלֹא־גְעַלְתִּים לְכַלֹּתָם, לְהָפֵר בְּרִיתִי אִתָּם, כִּי אֲנִי יהוה
אֱלֹהֵיהֶם: הָשֵׁב שְׁבוּתֵנוּ וְרַחֲמֵנוּ כְּמָה שֶׁכָּתוּב: וְשָׁב יהוה אֱלֹהֶיךָ אֶת־ דברים ל

has scattered you." Gather those of us who have been distanced, as is written, "If your distanced ones are at the very ends of the heavens, from there shall the LORD your God gather you; from there shall He bring You." Wipe out our crimes as if they were a cloud, as if they were a haze, as is written, "I have wiped out your crimes like a cloud, and as a haze your sins; come back to Me for I have redeemed you." Wipe out our crimes for Your sake, as You have said, "I, I am the one who shall wipe out your crimes for My sake, and I shall not recall your sins." Whiten our sins as snow and as wool, as is written, "Come now, let us reason together, says the LORD; If your sins are like scarlet, they shall be whitened like snow; should they be as red as crimson, they shall become like wool." Throw over us pure waters and purify us, as is written, "I shall throw pure waters over you and you shall be pure. I shall purify you of all your impurities and of all your idolatry." Have compassion for us and do not destroy us, as is written, "For the LORD your God is a compassionate God; He will not cease to hold you and He will not destroy you, and will not forget the covenant of your fathers that He pledged to them." Circumcise our hearts to love Your name, as is written, "And the LORD will circumcise your heart and the heart of your descendants to love the LORD your God with all your heart and with all your soul, so that you shall live." Let us find You when we seek You, as is written, "And if from there you seek the LORD your God, you shall find Him, when you seek Him out with all your heart and with all your soul." Bring us to Your holy mountain, and let us rejoice in Your house of prayer, as is written, "I shall bring them to My holy mountain, and I shall make them rejoice in My house of prayer; their offerings and their sacrifices will be accepted, desired on My altar, for My House will be called a house of prayer for all peoples."

Deut. 30 · Is. 44 · Is. 43 · Is. 1 · Ezek. 36 · Deut. 4 · Deut. 30 · Deut. 4 · Is. 56

The Ark is opened. The following until ◂ is said responsively, verse by verse:

שְׁמַע קוֹלֵנוּ Listen to our voice, LORD our God. Spare us and have compassion on us, and in compassion and favor accept our prayer. Turn us back, O LORD, to You, and we will return. Renew our days as of old. Do not cast us away from You, and do not take Your holy spirit from us. Do not cast us away in our old age; when our strength is gone do not desert us.◂ Do not desert us, LORD; our God, do not be distant from us. Give us a sign of good things, and those who hate us shall see it and be ashamed, for You, LORD, will help us and console us. Hear our speech, LORD, consider our thoughts. May the words of our mouths and the thoughts within our hearts be pleasing to You, LORD, our Rock and our Redeemer. For it is You, LORD, that we have longed for; You shall answer us, LORD our God.

Lam. 5

The Ark is closed.

שְׁבוּתְךָ וְרִחֲמֶךָ, וְשָׁב וְקִבֶּצְךָ מִכׇּל־הָעַמִּים אֲשֶׁר הֱפִיצְךָ יהוה אֱלֹהֶיךָ
שָׁמָּה: קַבֵּץ נִדָּחֵינוּ כְּמָה שֶׁכָּתוּב: אִם־יִהְיֶה נִדַּחֲךָ בִּקְצֵה הַשָּׁמָיִם, מִשָּׁם דברים ל
יְקַבֶּצְךָ יהוה אֱלֹהֶיךָ וּמִשָּׁם יִקָּחֶךָ: מְחֵה פְשָׁעֵינוּ כָּעָב וְכֶעָנָן כְּמָה שֶׁכָּתוּב:
מָחִיתִי כָעָב פְּשָׁעֶיךָ וְכֶעָנָן חַטֹּאותֶיךָ, שׁוּבָה אֵלַי כִּי גְאַלְתִּיךָ: מְחֵה פְשָׁעֵינוּ ישעיה מד
לְמַעַנְךָ כַּאֲשֶׁר אָמַרְתָּ: אָנֹכִי אָנֹכִי הוּא מֹחֶה פְשָׁעֶיךָ לְמַעֲנִי, וְחַטֹּאתֶיךָ ישעיה מג
לֹא אֶזְכֹּר: הַלְבֵּן חֲטָאֵינוּ כַּשֶּׁלֶג וְכַצֶּמֶר כְּמָה שֶׁכָּתוּב: לְכוּ־נָא וְנִוָּכְחָה ישעיה א
יֹאמַר יהוה, אִם־יִהְיוּ חֲטָאֵיכֶם כַּשָּׁנִים כַּשֶּׁלֶג יַלְבִּינוּ, אִם־יַאְדִּימוּ כַתּוֹלָע
כַּצֶּמֶר יִהְיוּ: זְרֹק עָלֵינוּ מַיִם טְהוֹרִים וְטַהֲרֵנוּ כְּמָה שֶׁכָּתוּב: וְזָרַקְתִּי עֲלֵיכֶם יחזקאל לו
מַיִם טְהוֹרִים וּטְהַרְתֶּם, מִכֹּל טֻמְאוֹתֵיכֶם וּמִכׇּל־גִּלּוּלֵיכֶם אֲטַהֵר אֶתְכֶם:
רַחֵם עָלֵינוּ וְאַל תַּשְׁחִיתֵנוּ כְּמָה שֶׁכָּתוּב: כִּי אֵל רַחוּם יהוה אֱלֹהֶיךָ, לֹא דברים ד
יַרְפְּךָ וְלֹא יַשְׁחִיתֶךָ, וְלֹא יִשְׁכַּח אֶת־בְּרִית אֲבֹתֶיךָ אֲשֶׁר נִשְׁבַּע לָהֶם: מוֹל
אֶת לְבָבֵנוּ לְאַהֲבָה אֶת שְׁמֶךָ כְּמָה שֶׁכָּתוּב: וּמָל יהוה אֱלֹהֶיךָ אֶת־לְבָבְךָ דברים ל
וְאֶת־לְבַב זַרְעֶךָ, לְאַהֲבָה אֶת־יהוה אֱלֹהֶיךָ בְּכׇל־לְבָבְךָ וּבְכׇל־נַפְשְׁךָ,
לְמַעַן חַיֶּיךָ: הִמָּצֵא לָנוּ בְּבַקָּשָׁתֵנוּ כְּמָה שֶׁכָּתוּב: וּבִקַּשְׁתֶּם מִשָּׁם אֶת־ דברים ד
יהוה אֱלֹהֶיךָ וּמָצָאתָ, כִּי תִדְרְשֶׁנּוּ בְּכׇל־לְבָבְךָ וּבְכׇל־נַפְשֶׁךָ: תְּבִיאֵנוּ אֶל
הַר קׇדְשֶׁךָ וְשַׂמְּחֵנוּ בְּבֵית תְּפִלָּתֶךָ כְּמָה שֶׁכָּתוּב: וַהֲבִיאוֹתִים אֶל־הַר ישעיה נו
קׇדְשִׁי וְשִׂמַּחְתִּים בְּבֵית תְּפִלָּתִי, עוֹלֹתֵיהֶם וְזִבְחֵיהֶם לְרָצוֹן עַל־מִזְבְּחִי,
כִּי בֵיתִי בֵּית־תְּפִלָּה יִקָּרֵא לְכׇל־הָעַמִּים:

The ארון קודש is opened. The following until ▸ is said responsively, verse by verse:

שְׁמַע קוֹלֵנוּ, יהוה אֱלֹהֵינוּ, חוּס וְרַחֵם עָלֵינוּ וְקַבֵּל בְּרַחֲמִים וּבְרָצוֹן אֶת
תְּפִלָּתֵנוּ. הֲשִׁיבֵנוּ יהוה אֵלֶיךָ וְנָשׁוּבָה, חַדֵּשׁ יָמֵינוּ כְּקֶדֶם: אַל תַּשְׁלִיכֵנוּ איכה ה
מִלְּפָנֶיךָ, וְרוּחַ קׇדְשְׁךָ אַל תִּקַּח מִמֶּנּוּ. אַל תַּשְׁלִיכֵנוּ לְעֵת זִקְנָה, כִּכְלוֹת
כֹּחֵנוּ אַל תַּעַזְבֵנוּ. ◂ אַל תַּעַזְבֵנוּ יהוה, אֱלֹהֵינוּ אַל תִּרְחַק מִמֶּנּוּ. עֲשֵׂה
עִמָּנוּ אוֹת לְטוֹבָה, וְיִרְאוּ שׂוֹנְאֵינוּ וְיֵבֹשׁוּ, כִּי אַתָּה יהוה עֲזַרְתָּנוּ וְנִחַמְתָּנוּ.
אֲמָרֵינוּ הַאֲזִינָה יהוה, בִּינָה הֲגִיגֵנוּ. יִהְיוּ לְרָצוֹן אִמְרֵי פִינוּ וְהֶגְיוֹן לִבֵּנוּ
לְפָנֶיךָ, יהוה צוּרֵנוּ וְגוֹאֲלֵנוּ. כִּי לְךָ יהוה הוֹחָלְנוּ, אַתָּה תַעֲנֶה אֲדֹנָי אֱלֹהֵינוּ.

The ארון קודש is closed.

CONFESSION

אֱלֹהֵינוּ Our God and God of our fathers,
let our prayer come before You, and do not hide Yourself from our plea,
for we are not so arrogant or obstinate as to say before You,
Lord, our God and God of our fathers,
we are righteous and have not sinned,
for in truth, we and our fathers have sinned.

Strike the left side of the chest with the right fist while saying each of the sins.

אָשַׁמְנוּ We have been guilty, we have acted treacherously, we have robbed, we have spoken slander. We have acted perversely, we have acted wickedly, we have acted presumptuously, we have been violent, we have framed lies. We have given bad advice, we have deceived, we have scorned, we have rebelled, we have provoked, we have turned away, we have committed iniquity, we have transgressed, we have persecuted, we have been obstinate. We have acted wickedly, we have corrupted, we have acted abominably, we have strayed, we have led others astray.

סַרְנוּ We have turned away from Your commandments, and good laws, to no avail, for You are just in all that has befallen us, for You have acted faithfully *Neh. 9*
while we have done wickedly.

הִרְשַׁעְנוּ We have been wicked and we have done wrong, and so we have not been saved. Place it in our hearts to abandon the way of wickedness, and hasten our salvation, as is written by Your prophet, "Let each wicked person *Is. 55*
abandon his ways, each man of iniquity his thoughts, and let him come back to the Lord and He will have compassion for him; back to our God for He will forgive abundantly."

מָשִׁיחַ Your righteous anointed one said to You, "Who can discern his own *Ps. 19*
mistakes? Cleanse me of my hidden faults." Cleanse us, Lord our God, of all our sins, and purify us of all our impurities and throw clear waters over us to purify us, as was written by Your prophet, "I shall throw clear waters over you *Ezek. 36*
and you shall be pure. I shall purify you of all your impurities and of all your idolatry." Your people, Your inheritance, famished of Your good, thirsting for Your loving-kindness, craving Your salvation – they shall recognize and know that compassion and forgiveness belong to the Lord our God.

On days when Taḥanun is not said (such as on the morning of a Brit Mila, or when a bridegroom is present), continue with Avinu Malkenu on page 138 followed by Half Kaddish (page 156).

וידוי

אֱלֹהֵינוּ וֵאלֹהֵי אֲבוֹתֵינוּ
תָּבֹא לְפָנֶיךָ תְּפִלָּתֵנוּ, וְאַל תִּתְעַלַּם מִתְּחִנָּתֵנוּ.
שֶׁאֵין אֲנוּ עַזֵּי פָנִים וּקְשֵׁי עֹרֶף לוֹמַר לְפָנֶיךָ
יהוה אֱלֹהֵינוּ וֵאלֹהֵי אֲבוֹתֵינוּ, צַדִּיקִים אֲנַחְנוּ וְלֹא חָטָאנוּ.
אֲבָל אֲנַחְנוּ וַאֲבוֹתֵינוּ חָטָאנוּ.

Strike the left side of the chest with the right fist while saying each of the sins.

אָשַׁמְנוּ, בָּגַדְנוּ, גָּזַלְנוּ, דִּבַּרְנוּ דֹפִי. הֶעֱוִינוּ, וְהִרְשַׁעְנוּ, זַדְנוּ, חָמַסְנוּ, טָפַלְנוּ שֶׁקֶר. יָעַצְנוּ רָע, כִּזַּבְנוּ, לַצְנוּ, מָרַדְנוּ, נִאַצְנוּ, סָרַרְנוּ, עָוִינוּ, פָּשַׁעְנוּ, צָרַרְנוּ, קִשִּׁינוּ עֹרֶף. רָשַׁעְנוּ, שִׁחַתְנוּ, תִּעַבְנוּ, תָּעִינוּ, תִּעְתָּעְנוּ.

סַרְנוּ מִמִּצְוֹתֶיךָ וּמִמִּשְׁפָּטֶיךָ הַטּוֹבִים, וְלֹא שָׁוָה לָנוּ. וְאַתָּה צַדִּיק עַל כָּל־הַבָּא עָלֵינוּ, כִּי־אֱמֶת עָשִׂיתָ וַאֲנַחְנוּ הִרְשָׁעְנוּ. נחמיה ט

הִרְשַׁעְנוּ וּפָשַׁעְנוּ לָכֵן לֹא נוֹשָׁעְנוּ. וְתֵן בְּלִבֵּנוּ לַעֲזֹב דֶּרֶךְ רֶשַׁע, וְחִישׁ לָנוּ יֶשַׁע, כַּכָּתוּב עַל יַד נְבִיאֶךָ: יַעֲזֹב רָשָׁע דַּרְכּוֹ וְאִישׁ אָוֶן מַחְשְׁבֹתָיו, וְיָשֹׁב אֶל־יהוה וִירַחֲמֵהוּ וְאֶל־אֱלֹהֵינוּ כִּי־יַרְבֶּה לִסְלוֹחַ: ישעיה נה

מְשִׁיחַ צִדְקֶךָ אָמַר לְפָנֶיךָ: שְׁגִיאוֹת מִי־יָבִין, מִנִּסְתָּרוֹת נַקֵּנִי: נַקֵּנוּ יהוה אֱלֹהֵינוּ מִכָּל פְּשָׁעֵינוּ וְטַהֲרֵנוּ מִכָּל טֻמְאוֹתֵינוּ וּזְרֹק עָלֵינוּ מַיִם טְהוֹרִים וְטַהֲרֵנוּ, כַּכָּתוּב עַל יַד נְבִיאֶךָ: וְזָרַקְתִּי עֲלֵיכֶם מַיִם טְהוֹרִים וּטְהַרְתֶּם, מִכֹּל טֻמְאוֹתֵיכֶם וּמִכָּל־גִּלּוּלֵיכֶם אֲטַהֵר אֶתְכֶם: עַמְּךָ וְנַחֲלָתְךָ רְעֵבֵי טוּבְךָ, צְמֵאֵי חַסְדְּךָ, תְּאֵבֵי יִשְׁעֶךָ. יַכִּירוּ וְיֵדְעוּ, כִּי לַיהוה אֱלֹהֵינוּ הָרַחֲמִים וְהַסְּלִיחוֹת.

תהלים יט · יחזקאל לו

On days when תחנון *is not said (such as on the morning of a* ברית מילה*, or when a* חתן *is present), continue with* אבינו מלכנו *on page 139 followed by* חצי קדיש *(page 157).*

אֵל רַחוּם Compassionate God is Your name; Gracious God is Your name. We are called by Your name; LORD, act for the sake of Your name. Act for the sake of Your truth. Act for the sake of Your covenant. Act for the sake of Your greatness and glory. Act for the sake of Your Law. Act for the sake of Your majesty. Act for the sake of Your promise. Act for the sake of Your remembrance. Act for the sake of Your loving-kindness. Act for the sake of Your goodness. Act for the sake of Your oneness. Act for the sake of Your honor. Act for the sake of Your wisdom. Act for the sake of Your kingship. Act for the sake of Your eternity. Act for the sake of Your mystery. Act for the sake of Your might. Act for the sake of Your splendor. Act for the sake of Your righteousness. Act for the sake of Your holiness. Act for the sake of Your great compassion. Act for the sake of Your Presence. Act for the sake of Your praise. Act for the sake of those who loved You, who now dwell in the dust. Act for the sake of Abraham, Isaac and Jacob. Act for the sake of Moses and Aaron. Act for the sake of David and Solomon. Act for the sake of Jerusalem, Your holy city. Act for the sake of Zion, the dwelling place of Your glory. Act for the sake of the desolate site of Your Temple. Act for the sake of the ruins of Your altar. Act for the sake of those killed in sanctification of Your name. Act for the sake of those slaughtered over Your unity. Act for the sake of those who have gone through fire and water in sanctification of Your name. Act for the sake of suckling infants who have not sinned. Act for the sake of little ones just weaned who have done no wrong. Act for the sake of schoolchildren. Act for Your own sake if not for ours. Act for Your own sake, and save us.

עֲנֵנוּ Answer us, LORD, answer us. Answer us, our God, answer us. Answer us, our Father, answer us. Answer us, our Creator, answer us. Answer us, our Redeemer, answer us. Answer us, You who seek us, answer us. Answer us, God who is faithful, answer us. Answer us, You who are ancient and kind, answer us. Answer us, You who are pure and upright, answer us. Answer us, You who are alive and remain, answer us. Answer us, You who are good and do good, answer us. Answer us, You who know our impulses, answer us. Answer us, You who conquer rage, answer us. Answer us, You who clothe Yourself in righteousness, answer us. Answer us, Supreme King of kings, answer us. Answer us, You who are awesome and elevated, answer us. Answer us, You who forgive and pardon, answer us. Answer us, You who answer in times of trouble, answer us. Answer us, You who redeem and save, answer us. Answer us, You who are righteous and straightforward, answer us. Answer us, You who are close to those who call, answer us. Answer us, You who are compassionate and gracious, answer us. Answer us, You who listen to the destitute, answer us. Answer us, You who support the innocent, answer us. Answer us, God of our fathers, answer us. Answer us, God of Abraham, answer us. Answer us, Terror of Isaac, answer us. Answer us, Champion of Jacob, answer us. Answer us, Help of the tribes, answer us. Answer us, Stronghold of the mothers, answer us. Answer us, You who are slow to anger, answer us. Answer us, You who are lightly appeased, answer us. Answer us, You who answer at times of favor, answer us. Answer us, Father of orphans, answer us. Answer us, Justice of widows, answer us.

אֵל רַחוּם שְׁמֶךָ. אֵל חַנּוּן שְׁמֶךָ. בָּנוּ נִקְרָא שְׁמֶךָ. יהוה עֲשֵׂה לְמַעַן שְׁמֶךָ. עֲשֵׂה לְמַעַן אֲמִתָּךְ. עֲשֵׂה לְמַעַן בְּרִיתָךְ. עֲשֵׂה לְמַעַן גָּדְלָךְ וְתִפְאַרְתָּךְ. עֲשֵׂה לְמַעַן דָּתָךְ. עֲשֵׂה לְמַעַן הוֹדָךְ. עֲשֵׂה לְמַעַן וַעוּדָךְ. עֲשֵׂה לְמַעַן זִכְרָךְ. עֲשֵׂה לְמַעַן חַסְדָּךְ. עֲשֵׂה לְמַעַן טוּבָךְ. עֲשֵׂה לְמַעַן יִחוּדָךְ. עֲשֵׂה לְמַעַן כְּבוֹדָךְ. עֲשֵׂה לְמַעַן לִמּוּדָךְ. עֲשֵׂה לְמַעַן מַלְכוּתָךְ. עֲשֵׂה לְמַעַן נִצְחָךְ. עֲשֵׂה לְמַעַן סוֹדָךְ. עֲשֵׂה לְמַעַן עֻזָּךְ. עֲשֵׂה לְמַעַן פְּאֵרָךְ. עֲשֵׂה לְמַעַן צִדְקָתָךְ. עֲשֵׂה לְמַעַן קְדֻשָּׁתָךְ. עֲשֵׂה לְמַעַן רַחֲמֶיךָ הָרַבִּים. עֲשֵׂה לְמַעַן שְׁכִינָתָךְ. עֲשֵׂה לְמַעַן תְּהִלָּתָךְ. עֲשֵׂה לְמַעַן אוֹהֲבֶיךָ שׁוֹכְנֵי עָפָר. עֲשֵׂה לְמַעַן אַבְרָהָם יִצְחָק וְיַעֲקֹב. עֲשֵׂה לְמַעַן מֹשֶׁה וְאַהֲרֹן. עֲשֵׂה לְמַעַן דָּוִד וּשְׁלֹמֹה. עֲשֵׂה לְמַעַן יְרוּשָׁלַיִם עִיר קָדְשֶׁךָ. עֲשֵׂה לְמַעַן צִיּוֹן מִשְׁכַּן כְּבוֹדֶךָ. עֲשֵׂה לְמַעַן שִׁמְמוֹת הֵיכָלֶךָ. עֲשֵׂה לְמַעַן הֲרִיסוּת מִזְבְּחֶךָ. עֲשֵׂה לְמַעַן הֲרוּגִים עַל שֵׁם קָדְשֶׁךָ. עֲשֵׂה לְמַעַן טְבוּחִים עַל יִחוּדֶךָ. עֲשֵׂה לְמַעַן בָּאֵי בָאֵשׁ וּבַמַּיִם עַל קִדּוּשׁ שְׁמֶךָ. עֲשֵׂה לְמַעַן יוֹנְקֵי שָׁדַיִם שֶׁלֹּא חָטְאוּ. עֲשֵׂה לְמַעַן גְּמוּלֵי חָלָב שֶׁלֹּא פָשְׁעוּ. עֲשֵׂה לְמַעַן תִּינוֹקוֹת שֶׁל בֵּית רַבָּן. עֲשֵׂה לְמַעַנְךָ אִם לֹא לְמַעֲנֵנוּ. עֲשֵׂה לְמַעַנְךָ וְהוֹשִׁיעֵנוּ.

עֲנֵנוּ יהוה עֲנֵנוּ. עֲנֵנוּ אֱלֹהֵינוּ עֲנֵנוּ. עֲנֵנוּ אָבִינוּ עֲנֵנוּ. עֲנֵנוּ בּוֹרְאֵנוּ עֲנֵנוּ. עֲנֵנוּ גּוֹאֲלֵנוּ עֲנֵנוּ. עֲנֵנוּ דּוֹרְשֵׁנוּ עֲנֵנוּ. עֲנֵנוּ הָאֵל הַנֶּאֱמָן עֲנֵנוּ. עֲנֵנוּ וָתִיק וְחָסִיד עֲנֵנוּ. עֲנֵנוּ זַךְ וְיָשָׁר עֲנֵנוּ. עֲנֵנוּ חַי וְקַיָּם עֲנֵנוּ. עֲנֵנוּ טוֹב וּמֵטִיב עֲנֵנוּ. עֲנֵנוּ יוֹדֵעַ יֵצֶר עֲנֵנוּ. עֲנֵנוּ כּוֹבֵשׁ כְּעָסִים עֲנֵנוּ. עֲנֵנוּ לוֹבֵשׁ צְדָקוֹת עֲנֵנוּ. עֲנֵנוּ מֶלֶךְ מַלְכֵי הַמְּלָכִים עֲנֵנוּ. עֲנֵנוּ נוֹרָא וְנִשְׂגָּב עֲנֵנוּ. עֲנֵנוּ סוֹלֵחַ וּמוֹחֵל עֲנֵנוּ. עֲנֵנוּ עוֹנֶה בְּעֵת צָרָה עֲנֵנוּ. עֲנֵנוּ פּוֹדֶה וּמַצִּיל עֲנֵנוּ. עֲנֵנוּ צַדִּיק וְיָשָׁר עֲנֵנוּ. עֲנֵנוּ קָרוֹב לְקוֹרְאָיו עֲנֵנוּ. עֲנֵנוּ רַחוּם וְחַנּוּן עֲנֵנוּ. עֲנֵנוּ שׁוֹמֵעַ אֶל אֶבְיוֹנִים עֲנֵנוּ. עֲנֵנוּ תּוֹמֵךְ תְּמִימִים עֲנֵנוּ. עֲנֵנוּ אֱלֹהֵי אֲבוֹתֵינוּ עֲנֵנוּ. עֲנֵנוּ אֱלֹהֵי אַבְרָהָם עֲנֵנוּ. עֲנֵנוּ פַּחַד יִצְחָק עֲנֵנוּ. עֲנֵנוּ אֲבִיר יַעֲקֹב עֲנֵנוּ. עֲנֵנוּ עֶזְרַת הַשְּׁבָטִים עֲנֵנוּ. עֲנֵנוּ מִשְׂגַּב אִמָּהוֹת עֲנֵנוּ. עֲנֵנוּ קָשֶׁה לִכְעֹס עֲנֵנוּ. עֲנֵנוּ רַךְ לִרְצוֹת עֲנֵנוּ. עֲנֵנוּ עוֹנֶה בְּעֵת רָצוֹן עֲנֵנוּ. עֲנֵנוּ אֲבִי יְתוֹמִים עֲנֵנוּ. עֲנֵנוּ דַּיַּן אַלְמָנוֹת עֲנֵנוּ.

מִי שֶׁעָנָה The One who answered Abraham our father on Mount Moriah – answer us.
The One who answered Isaac his son, when he was bound upon the altar – answer us.
The One who answered Jacob in Beth-El – answer us.
The One who answered Joseph in prison – answer us.
The One who answered our fathers at the Reed Sea – answer us.
The One who answered Moses at Horeb – answer us.
The One who answered Aaron over his firepan – answer us.
The One who answered Pinehas when he stood up from among the congregation – answer us.
The One who answered Joshua at Gilgal – answer us.
The One who answered Samuel at Mitzpah – answer us.
The One who answered David and Solomon his son in Jerusalem – answer us.
The One who answered Elijah on Mount Carmel – answer us.
The One who answered Elisha at Jericho – answer us.
The One who answered Jonah in the belly of the fish – answer us.
The One who answered Hezekiah the king of Judah in his illness – answer us.
The One who answered Hananiah, Mishael and Azariah in the furnace of fire – answer us.
The One who answered Daniel in the lions' den – answer us.
The One who answered Mordekhai and Esther in Shushan the capital city – answer us.
The One who answered Ezra in his exile – answer us.
The One who answered so many righteous, devoted, innocent and upright people – answer us.

רַחֲמָנָא Loving God, who answers the oppressed: answer us.
Loving God, who answers the broken hearted: answer us.
Loving God, who answers those of humbled spirit: answer us.
Loving God, answer us.
Loving God, spare; Loving God, release; Loving God, save us.
Loving God, have compassion for us now, swiftly, at a time soon coming.

Continue with "Avinu Malkenu" on page 138.

מִי שֶׁעָנָה לְאַבְרָהָם אָבִינוּ בְּהַר הַמּוֹרִיָּה, הוּא יַעֲנֵנוּ.
מִי שֶׁעָנָה לְיִצְחָק בְּנוֹ כְּשֶׁנֶּעֱקַד עַל גַּבֵּי הַמִּזְבֵּחַ, הוּא יַעֲנֵנוּ.
מִי שֶׁעָנָה לְיַעֲקֹב בְּבֵית אֵל, הוּא יַעֲנֵנוּ.
מִי שֶׁעָנָה לְיוֹסֵף בְּבֵית הָאֲסוּרִים, הוּא יַעֲנֵנוּ.
מִי שֶׁעָנָה לַאֲבוֹתֵינוּ עַל יַם סוּף, הוּא יַעֲנֵנוּ.
מִי שֶׁעָנָה לְמֹשֶׁה בְּחוֹרֵב, הוּא יַעֲנֵנוּ.
מִי שֶׁעָנָה לְאַהֲרֹן בַּמַּחְתָּה, הוּא יַעֲנֵנוּ.
מִי שֶׁעָנָה לְפִינְחָס בְּקוּמוֹ מִתּוֹךְ הָעֵדָה, הוּא יַעֲנֵנוּ.
מִי שֶׁעָנָה לִיהוֹשֻׁעַ בַּגִּלְגָּל, הוּא יַעֲנֵנוּ.
מִי שֶׁעָנָה לִשְׁמוּאֵל בַּמִּצְפָּה, הוּא יַעֲנֵנוּ.
מִי שֶׁעָנָה לְדָוִד וּשְׁלֹמֹה בְנוֹ בִּירוּשָׁלַיִם, הוּא יַעֲנֵנוּ.
מִי שֶׁעָנָה לְאֵלִיָּהוּ בְּהַר הַכַּרְמֶל, הוּא יַעֲנֵנוּ.
מִי שֶׁעָנָה לֶאֱלִישָׁע בִּירִיחוֹ, הוּא יַעֲנֵנוּ.
מִי שֶׁעָנָה לְיוֹנָה בִּמְעֵי הַדָּגָה, הוּא יַעֲנֵנוּ.
מִי שֶׁעָנָה לְחִזְקִיָּהוּ מֶלֶךְ יְהוּדָה בְּחָלְיוֹ, הוּא יַעֲנֵנוּ.
מִי שֶׁעָנָה לַחֲנַנְיָה מִישָׁאֵל וַעֲזַרְיָה בְּתוֹךְ כִּבְשַׁן הָאֵשׁ, הוּא יַעֲנֵנוּ.
מִי שֶׁעָנָה לְדָנִיֵּאל בְּגוֹב הָאֲרָיוֹת, הוּא יַעֲנֵנוּ.
מִי שֶׁעָנָה לְמָרְדְּכַי וְאֶסְתֵּר בְּשׁוּשַׁן הַבִּירָה, הוּא יַעֲנֵנוּ.
מִי שֶׁעָנָה לְעֶזְרָא בַּגּוֹלָה, הוּא יַעֲנֵנוּ.
מִי שֶׁעָנָה לְכָל הַצַּדִּיקִים וְהַחֲסִידִים וְהַתְּמִימִים וְהַיְשָׁרִים, הוּא יַעֲנֵנוּ.

רַחֲמָנָא דְּעָנֵי לַעֲנִיֵּי עֲנֵינָן.
רַחֲמָנָא דְּעָנֵי לִתְבִירֵי לִבָּא עֲנֵינָן.
רַחֲמָנָא דְּעָנֵי לְמַכִּיכֵי רוּחָא עֲנֵינָן.
רַחֲמָנָא עֲנֵינָן.
רַחֲמָנָא חוּס, רַחֲמָנָא פְּרֽק, רַחֲמָנָא שֵׁיזִב.
רַחֲמָנָא רְחֵם עֲלָן, הַשְׁתָּא בַּעֲגָלָא וּבִזְמַן קָרִיב.

Continue with אבינו מלכנו *on page 139.*

ברכות
GIVING THANKS

THE MEAL AND ITS BLESSINGS

On washing hands before eating bread (see laws 409–413):

Blessed are You, Lord our God, King of the Universe,
who has made us holy through His commandments,
and has commanded us about washing hands.

Before eating bread:

Blessed are You, Lord our God, King of the Universe,
who brings forth bread from the earth.

BIRKAT HAMAZON / GRACE AFTER MEALS

On days when Taḥanun is said:

עַל־נַהֲרוֹת By the rivers of Babylon we sat and wept as we remembered Zion. There on the willow trees we hung up our harps, for there our captors asked us for songs, our tormentors, for amusement, said: "Sing us one of the songs of Zion!" How can we sing the Lord's song on foreign soil? If I forget you, Jerusalem, may my right hand forget its skill. May my tongue cling to the roof of my mouth if I do not remember you, if I do not set Jerusalem above my highest joy. Remember, Lord, what the Edomites did on the day Jerusalem fell. They said, "Tear it down, tear it down to its very foundations!" Daughter of Babylon, doomed to destruction, happy is he who repays you for what you have done to us, who seizes your infants and dashes them against the rocks. *Ps. 137*

On days when Taḥanun is omitted (such as Shabbat and Yom Tov, see full list on page 144):

שִׁיר הַמַּעֲלוֹת A song of ascents. When the Lord brought back the exiles of Zion we were like people who dream. Then were our mouths filled with laughter, and our tongues with songs of joy. Then was it said among the nations, "The Lord has done great things for them." The Lord did do great things for us and we rejoiced. Bring back our exiles, Lord, like streams in a dry land. May those who sowed in tears, reap in joy. May one who goes out weeping, carrying a bag of seed, come back with songs of joy, carrying his sheaves. *Ps. 126*

The original form of Grace consisted of three blessings, which move sequentially from the universal to the particular. In the first, we thank God for sustaining the world and all that lives. The second is national: we thank God for the land of Israel as well as for the other blessings of Jewish life: the covenant and its sign, circumcision, and the Torah. The third turns to Jerusalem. The fourth paragraph is a later addition: according to the Talmud (*Berakhot* 48b), it was added after the Bar Kokhba rebellion, c. 135 CE. Over the course of time, it has expanded considerably.

סדר סעודה וברכותיה

On washing hands before eating bread (see laws 409–413):

בָּרוּךְ אַתָּה יהוה אֱלֹהֵינוּ מֶלֶךְ הָעוֹלָם
אֲשֶׁר קִדְּשָׁנוּ בְּמִצְוֹתָיו וְצִוָּנוּ עַל נְטִילַת יָדָיִם.

Before eating bread:

בָּרוּךְ אַתָּה יהוה אֱלֹהֵינוּ מֶלֶךְ הָעוֹלָם, הַמּוֹצִיא לֶחֶם מִן הָאָרֶץ.

ברכת המזון

On days when תחנון *is said:*

תהלים קלז עַל־נַהֲרוֹת בָּבֶל, שָׁם יָשַׁבְנוּ גַּם־בָּכִינוּ, בְּזָכְרֵנוּ אֶת־צִיּוֹן: עַל־עֲרָבִים בְּתוֹכָהּ תָּלִינוּ כִּנֹּרוֹתֵינוּ: כִּי שָׁם שְׁאֵלוּנוּ שׁוֹבֵינוּ דִּבְרֵי־שִׁיר וְתוֹלָלֵינוּ שִׂמְחָה, שִׁירוּ לָנוּ מִשִּׁיר צִיּוֹן: אֵיךְ נָשִׁיר אֶת־שִׁיר־יהוה עַל אַדְמַת נֵכָר: אִם־אֶשְׁכָּחֵךְ יְרוּשָׁלָםִ, תִּשְׁכַּח יְמִינִי: תִּדְבַּק לְשׁוֹנִי לְחִכִּי אִם־לֹא אֶזְכְּרֵכִי, אִם־לֹא אַעֲלֶה אֶת־יְרוּשָׁלַםִ עַל רֹאשׁ שִׂמְחָתִי: זְכֹר יהוה לִבְנֵי אֱדוֹם אֵת יוֹם יְרוּשָׁלָםִ, הָאֹמְרִים עָרוּ עָרוּ עַד הַיְסוֹד בָּהּ: בַּת־בָּבֶל הַשְּׁדוּדָה, אַשְׁרֵי שֶׁיְשַׁלֶּם־לָךְ אֶת־גְּמוּלֵךְ שֶׁגָּמַלְתְּ לָנוּ: אַשְׁרֵי שֶׁיֹּאחֵז, וְנִפֵּץ אֶת־עֹלָלַיִךְ אֶל־הַסָּלַע:

On days when תחנון *is omitted (such as* שבת *and* יום טוב*, see full list on page 145):*

תהלים קכו שִׁיר הַמַּעֲלוֹת, בְּשׁוּב יהוה אֶת־שִׁיבַת צִיּוֹן, הָיִינוּ כְּחֹלְמִים: אָז יִמָּלֵא שְׂחוֹק פִּינוּ וּלְשׁוֹנֵנוּ רִנָּה, אָז יֹאמְרוּ בַגּוֹיִם הִגְדִּיל יהוה לַעֲשׂוֹת עִם־אֵלֶּה: הִגְדִּיל יהוה לַעֲשׂוֹת עִמָּנוּ, הָיִינוּ שְׂמֵחִים: שׁוּבָה יהוה אֶת־שְׁבִיתֵנוּ, כַּאֲפִיקִים בַּנֶּגֶב: הַזֹּרְעִים בְּדִמְעָה בְּרִנָּה יִקְצֹרוּ: הָלוֹךְ יֵלֵךְ וּבָכֹה נֹשֵׂא מֶשֶׁךְ־הַזָּרַע, בֹּא־יָבֹא בְרִנָּה נֹשֵׂא אֲלֻמֹּתָיו:

BIRKAT HAMAZON / GRACE AFTER MEALS
Grace after Meals is specifically mandated by the Torah itself: "You shall eat and be satisfied and bless the Lord your God" (Deut. 8:10). Thanksgiving, Moses taught the Israelites, is central to Jewish life, "lest your heart grow haughty and you forget the Lord your God… and you say to yourselves, 'My own power and the might of my own hand have won this wealth for me'" (ibid, vv. 14–17). Bereft of a sense of gratitude and of a power higher than humans, nations, like individuals, eventually decay.

Some say:

תְּהִלַּת My mouth shall speak the praise of God, and all creatures shall bless His holy name for ever and all time. — Ps. 145
We will bless God now and for ever. — Ps. 115
Halleluya! Thank the LORD for He is good; His loving-kindness is for ever. — Ps. 136
Who can tell of the LORD's mighty acts and make all His praise be heard? — Ps. 106

ZIMMUN / INVITATION

For the zimmun said at a wedding or during the week of Sheva Berakhot, see page 1042. At a Brit, see page 1020. In the house of a mourner when there are three or more men, see page 1068.

When three or more men say Birkat HaMazon together, the following zimmun is said. When three or more women say Birkat HaMazon, substitute "Friends" for "Gentlemen." The leader should ask permission from those with precedence to lead the Birkat HaMazon.

Leader Gentlemen, let us say grace.

Others May the name of the LORD be blessed from now and for ever. — Ps. 113

Leader May the name of the LORD be blessed from now and for ever.
With your permission, (my father and teacher / my mother and teacher / the Kohanim present / our teacher the Rabbi / the master of this house / the mistress of this house)
my masters and teachers,
let us bless (*in a minyan:* our God,) the One
from whose food we have eaten.

Others Blessed be (*in a minyan:* our God,) the One
from whose food we have eaten, and by whose goodness we live.

**People present who have not taken part in the meal say:*
*Blessed be (*in a minyan:* our God,) the One
whose name is continually blessed for ever and all time.

Leader Blessed be (*in a minyan:* our God,) the One
from whose food we have eaten, and by whose goodness we live.
Blessed be He, and blessed be His name.

---

to join in the act of praise is similar to the recitation of *Barekhu*, "Bless the LORD," with which morning and evening services begin. It emphasizes the essentially communal nature of prayer in Judaism. In addition to the regular *zimmun* here, there are special forms of *zimmun* for (1) a wedding meal, (2) a meal after a circumcision, and (3) a meal in a house of mourning.

Some say:

תְּהִלַּת יהוה יְדַבֶּר פִּי, וִיבָרֵךְ כָּל־בָּשָׂר שֵׁם קָדְשׁוֹ לְעוֹלָם וָעֶד: וַאֲנַחְנוּ תהלים קמה / תהלים קטו
נְבָרֵךְ יָהּ מֵעַתָּה וְעַד־עוֹלָם, הַלְלוּיָהּ: הוֹדוּ לַיהוה כִּי־טוֹב, כִּי לְעוֹלָם תהלים קלו
חַסְדּוֹ: מִי יְמַלֵּל גְּבוּרוֹת יהוה, יַשְׁמִיעַ כָּל־תְּהִלָּתוֹ: תהלים קו

סדר הזימון

For the זימון *said at a wedding or during the week of* שבע ברכות*, see page 1043.*
At a ברית*, see page 1021. In a* בית אבל *when there are three or more men, see page 1069.*

When three or more men say ברכת המזון *together, the following* זימון *is said.*
When three or more women say ברכת המזון*, substitute* חֲבֵרוֹתַי *for* רַבּוֹתַי*.*
The leader should ask permission from those with precedence to lead the ברכת המזון*.*

Leader רַבּוֹתַי, נְבָרֵךְ.

Others יְהִי שֵׁם יהוה מְבֹרָךְ מֵעַתָּה וְעַד־עוֹלָם: תהלים קיג

Leader יְהִי שֵׁם יהוה מְבֹרָךְ מֵעַתָּה וְעַד־עוֹלָם:
בִּרְשׁוּת (אָבִי מוֹרִי / אִמִּי מוֹרָתִי / כֹּהֲנִים / מוֹרֵנוּ הָרַב /
בַּעַל הַבַּיִת הַזֶּה / בַּעֲלַת הַבַּיִת הַזֶּה)
מָרָנָן וְרַבָּנָן וְרַבּוֹתַי
נְבָרֵךְ (במנין: אֱלֹהֵינוּ) שֶׁאָכַלְנוּ מִשֶּׁלּוֹ.

Others בָּרוּךְ (במנין: אֱלֹהֵינוּ) שֶׁאָכַלְנוּ מִשֶּׁלּוֹ וּבְטוּבוֹ חָיִינוּ.

**People present who have not taken part in the meal say:*
*בָּרוּךְ (במנין: אֱלֹהֵינוּ) וּמְבֹרָךְ שְׁמוֹ תָּמִיד לְעוֹלָם וָעֶד.

Leader בָּרוּךְ (במנין: אֱלֹהֵינוּ) שֶׁאָכַלְנוּ מִשֶּׁלּוֹ וּבְטוּבוֹ חָיִינוּ.
בָּרוּךְ הוּא וּבָרוּךְ שְׁמוֹ.

ZIMMUN

A meal at which there are three adult males requires a formal invitation, *zimmun*, to say Grace. The Talmud derives this from the verse, "Magnify the Lord with me; let us exalt His name together" (Psalm 34:4). A slightly longer version is used when at least ten are present. The act of inviting those present

BLESSING OF NOURISHMENT

בָּרוּךְ Blessed are You, Lord our God, King of the Universe,
who in His goodness feeds the whole world
with grace, kindness and compassion.
He gives food to all living things,
for His kindness is for ever.
Because of His continual great goodness,
we have never lacked food,
nor may we ever lack it, for the sake of His great name.
For He is God who feeds and sustains all,
does good to all,
and prepares food for all creatures He has created.
Blessed are You, Lord, who feeds all.

BLESSING OF LAND

נוֹדֶה We thank You, Lord our God,
for having granted as a heritage to our ancestors
a desirable, good and spacious land;
for bringing us out, Lord our God, from the land of Egypt,
freeing us from the house of slavery;
for Your covenant which You sealed in our flesh;
for Your Torah which You taught us;
for Your laws which You made known to us;
for the life, grace and kindness You have bestowed on us;
and for the food by which You continually feed and sustain us,
every day, every season, every hour.

נוֹדֶה *We thank:* After thanking God for the land, the paragraph goes on to add thanks for God's other kindnesses to Israel: the exodus from Egypt, the covenant and its sign, circumcision, the giving of the Torah and the commandments. On Ḥanukka and Purim, *Al HaNissim* ("[We thank You also] for the miracles") is said here, as it is in the Amida in the parallel paragraph of "Thanks" (*Modim*).

ברכת הזן

בָּרוּךְ אַתָּה יהוה אֱלֹהֵינוּ מֶלֶךְ הָעוֹלָם
הַזָּן אֶת הָעוֹלָם כֻּלּוֹ בְּטוּבוֹ
בְּחֵן בְּחֶסֶד וּבְרַחֲמִים
הוּא נוֹתֵן לֶחֶם לְכָל בָּשָׂר
כִּי לְעוֹלָם חַסְדּוֹ.
וּבְטוּבוֹ הַגָּדוֹל, תָּמִיד לֹא חָסַר לָנוּ
וְאַל יֶחְסַר לָנוּ מָזוֹן לְעוֹלָם וָעֶד
בַּעֲבוּר שְׁמוֹ הַגָּדוֹל.
כִּי הוּא אֵל זָן וּמְפַרְנֵס לַכֹּל
וּמֵטִיב לַכֹּל
וּמֵכִין מָזוֹן לְכָל בְּרִיּוֹתָיו אֲשֶׁר בָּרָא.
בָּרוּךְ אַתָּה יהוה, הַזָּן אֶת הַכֹּל.

ברכת הארץ

נוֹדֶה לְּךָ, יהוה אֱלֹהֵינוּ
עַל שֶׁהִנְחַלְתָּ לַאֲבוֹתֵינוּ אֶרֶץ חֶמְדָּה טוֹבָה וּרְחָבָה
וְעַל שֶׁהוֹצֵאתָנוּ יהוה אֱלֹהֵינוּ מֵאֶרֶץ מִצְרַיִם
וּפְדִיתָנוּ מִבֵּית עֲבָדִים
וְעַל בְּרִיתְךָ שֶׁחָתַמְתָּ בִּבְשָׂרֵנוּ
וְעַל תּוֹרָתְךָ שֶׁלִּמַּדְתָּנוּ
וְעַל חֻקֶּיךָ שֶׁהוֹדַעְתָּנוּ
וְעַל חַיִּים חֵן וָחֶסֶד שֶׁחוֹנַנְתָּנוּ
וְעַל אֲכִילַת מָזוֹן שָׁאַתָּה זָן וּמְפַרְנֵס אוֹתָנוּ תָּמִיד
בְּכָל יוֹם וּבְכָל עֵת וּבְכָל שָׁעָה.

On Ḥanukka:

עַל הַנִּסִּים [We thank You also] for the miracles, the redemption, the mighty deeds, the salvations, and the victories in battle which You performed for our ancestors in those days, at this time.

בִּימֵי מַתִּתְיָהוּ In the days of Mattityahu, son of Yoḥanan, the High Priest, the Hasmonean, and his sons, the wicked Greek kingdom rose up against Your people Israel to make them forget Your Torah and to force them to transgress the statutes of Your will. It was then that You in Your great compassion stood by them in the time of their distress. You championed their cause, judged their claim, and avenged their wrong. You delivered the strong into the hands of the weak, the many into the hands of the few, the impure into the hands of the pure, the wicked into the hands of the righteous, and the arrogant into the hands of those who were engaged in the study of Your Torah. You made for Yourself great and holy renown in Your world, and for Your people Israel You performed a great salvation and redemption as of this very day. Your children then entered the holiest part of Your House, cleansed Your Temple, purified Your Sanctuary, kindled lights in Your holy courts, and designated these eight days of Ḥanukka for giving thanks and praise to Your great name.

Continue with "For all this."

On Purim:

עַל הַנִּסִּים [We thank You also] for the miracles, the redemption, the mighty deeds, the salvations, and the victories in battle which You performed for our ancestors in those days, at this time.

בִּימֵי מָרְדְּכַי In the days of Mordekhai and Esther, in Shushan the capital, the wicked Haman rose up against them and sought to destroy, slay and exterminate all the Jews, young and old, children and women, on one day, the thirteenth day of the twelfth month, which is the month of Adar, and to plunder their possessions. Then You in Your great compassion thwarted his counsel, frustrated his plans, and caused his scheme to recoil on his own head, so that they hanged him and his sons on the gallows. *Esther 3*

Continue with "For all this."

וְעַל הַכֹּל For all this, Lord our God, we thank and bless You.
May Your name be blessed continually
by the mouth of all that lives, for ever and all time –
for so it is written: "You will eat and be satisfied, then you shall bless the Lord your God for the good land He has given you." *Deut. 8*
Blessed are You, Lord, for the land and for the food.

בחנוכה:

עַל הַנִּסִּים וְעַל הַפֻּרְקָן וְעַל הַגְּבוּרוֹת וְעַל הַתְּשׁוּעוֹת וְעַל הַמִּלְחָמוֹת שֶׁעָשִׂיתָ לַאֲבוֹתֵינוּ בַּיָּמִים הָהֵם בַּזְּמַן הַזֶּה.

בִּימֵי מַתִּתְיָהוּ בֶּן יוֹחָנָן כֹּהֵן גָּדוֹל חַשְׁמוֹנַאי וּבָנָיו, כְּשֶׁעָמְדָה מַלְכוּת יָוָן הָרְשָׁעָה עַל עַמְּךָ יִשְׂרָאֵל לְהַשְׁכִּיחָם תּוֹרָתֶךָ וּלְהַעֲבִירָם מֵחֻקֵּי רְצוֹנֶךָ, וְאַתָּה בְּרַחֲמֶיךָ הָרַבִּים עָמַדְתָּ לָהֶם בְּעֵת צָרָתָם, רַבְתָּ אֶת רִיבָם, דַּנְתָּ אֶת דִּינָם, נָקַמְתָּ אֶת נִקְמָתָם, מָסַרְתָּ גִבּוֹרִים בְּיַד חַלָּשִׁים, וְרַבִּים בְּיַד מְעַטִּים, וּטְמֵאִים בְּיַד טְהוֹרִים, וּרְשָׁעִים בְּיַד צַדִּיקִים, וְזֵדִים בְּיַד עוֹסְקֵי תוֹרָתֶךָ, וּלְךָ עָשִׂיתָ שֵׁם גָּדוֹל וְקָדוֹשׁ בְּעוֹלָמֶךָ, וּלְעַמְּךָ יִשְׂרָאֵל עָשִׂיתָ תְּשׁוּעָה גְדוֹלָה וּפֻרְקָן כְּהַיּוֹם הַזֶּה. וְאַחַר כֵּן בָּאוּ בָנֶיךָ לִדְבִיר בֵּיתֶךָ, וּפִנּוּ אֶת הֵיכָלֶךָ, וְטִהֲרוּ אֶת מִקְדָּשֶׁךָ, וְהִדְלִיקוּ נֵרוֹת בְּחַצְרוֹת קָדְשֶׁךָ, וְקָבְעוּ שְׁמוֹנַת יְמֵי חֲנֻכָּה אֵלּוּ, לְהוֹדוֹת וּלְהַלֵּל לְשִׁמְךָ הַגָּדוֹל.

Continue with וְעַל הַכֹּל.

בפורים:

עַל הַנִּסִּים וְעַל הַפֻּרְקָן וְעַל הַגְּבוּרוֹת וְעַל הַתְּשׁוּעוֹת וְעַל הַמִּלְחָמוֹת שֶׁעָשִׂיתָ לַאֲבוֹתֵינוּ בַּיָּמִים הָהֵם בַּזְּמַן הַזֶּה.

בִּימֵי מָרְדְּכַי וְאֶסְתֵּר בְּשׁוּשַׁן הַבִּירָה, כְּשֶׁעָמַד עֲלֵיהֶם הָמָן הָרָשָׁע, בִּקֵּשׁ
לְהַשְׁמִיד לַהֲרֹג וּלְאַבֵּד אֶת־כָּל־הַיְּהוּדִים מִנַּעַר וְעַד־זָקֵן טַף וְנָשִׁים בְּיוֹם אסתר ג
אֶחָד, בִּשְׁלוֹשָׁה עָשָׂר לְחֹדֶשׁ שְׁנֵים־עָשָׂר, הוּא־חֹדֶשׁ אֲדָר, וּשְׁלָלָם לָבוֹז: וְאַתָּה בְּרַחֲמֶיךָ הָרַבִּים הֵפַרְתָּ אֶת עֲצָתוֹ, וְקִלְקַלְתָּ אֶת מַחֲשַׁבְתּוֹ, וַהֲשֵׁבוֹתָ לּוֹ גְּמוּלוֹ בְּרֹאשׁוֹ, וְתָלוּ אוֹתוֹ וְאֶת בָּנָיו עַל הָעֵץ.

Continue with וְעַל הַכֹּל.

וְעַל הַכֹּל, יהוה אֱלֹהֵינוּ
אֲנַחְנוּ מוֹדִים לָךְ וּמְבָרְכִים אוֹתָךְ
יִתְבָּרַךְ שִׁמְךָ בְּפִי כָּל חַי תָּמִיד לְעוֹלָם וָעֶד
כַּכָּתוּב: וְאָכַלְתָּ וְשָׂבָעְתָּ, וּבֵרַכְתָּ אֶת־יהוה אֱלֹהֶיךָ דברים ח
עַל־הָאָרֶץ הַטֹּבָה אֲשֶׁר נָתַן־לָךְ:
בָּרוּךְ אַתָּה יהוה, עַל הָאָרֶץ וְעַל הַמָּזוֹן.

BLESSING FOR JERUSALEM

רַחֵם נָא Have compassion, please,
Lord our God,
on Israel Your people,
on Jerusalem Your city,
on Zion the dwelling place of Your glory,
on the royal house of David Your anointed,
and on the great and holy House that bears Your name.
Our God, our Father,
tend us, feed us,
sustain us and support us,
relieve us and send us relief,
Lord our God,
swiftly from all our troubles.
Please, Lord our God,
do not make us dependent
on the gifts or loans of other people,
but only on Your full, open, holy and generous hand
so that we may suffer neither shame nor humiliation
for ever and all time.

On Shabbat, say:

רְצֵה Favor and strengthen us, Lord our God,
through Your commandments,
especially through the commandment of the seventh day,
this great and holy Sabbath.
For it is, for You, a great and holy day.
On it we cease work and rest in love
in accord with Your will's commandment.
May it be Your will, Lord our God,
to grant us rest without distress,
grief, or lament on our day of rest.
May You show us the consolation of Zion Your city,
and the rebuilding of Jerusalem Your holy city,
for You are the Master of salvation and consolation.

ברכת ירושלים

רַחֵם נָא, יהוה אֱלֹהֵינוּ
עַל יִשְׂרָאֵל עַמֶּךָ
וְעַל יְרוּשָׁלַיִם עִירֶךָ
וְעַל צִיּוֹן מִשְׁכַּן כְּבוֹדֶךָ
וְעַל מַלְכוּת בֵּית דָּוִד מְשִׁיחֶךָ
וְעַל הַבַּיִת הַגָּדוֹל וְהַקָּדוֹשׁ שֶׁנִּקְרָא שִׁמְךָ עָלָיו.
אֱלֹהֵינוּ, אָבִינוּ
רְעֵנוּ, זוּנֵנוּ, פַּרְנְסֵנוּ וְכַלְכְּלֵנוּ
וְהַרְוִיחֵנוּ, וְהַרְוַח לָנוּ יהוה אֱלֹהֵינוּ מְהֵרָה מִכָּל צָרוֹתֵינוּ.
וְנָא אַל תַּצְרִיכֵנוּ, יהוה אֱלֹהֵינוּ
לֹא לִידֵי מַתְּנַת בָּשָׂר וָדָם
וְלֹא לִידֵי הַלְוָאָתָם
כִּי אִם לְיָדְךָ הַמְּלֵאָה, הַפְּתוּחָה, הַקְּדוֹשָׁה וְהָרְחָבָה
שֶׁלֹּא נֵבוֹשׁ וְלֹא נִכָּלֵם לְעוֹלָם וָעֶד.

On שבת*, say:*

רְצֵה וְהַחֲלִיצֵנוּ, יהוה אֱלֹהֵינוּ, בְּמִצְוֹתֶיךָ
וּבְמִצְוַת יוֹם הַשְּׁבִיעִי הַשַּׁבָּת הַגָּדוֹל וְהַקָּדוֹשׁ הַזֶּה
כִּי יוֹם זֶה גָּדוֹל וְקָדוֹשׁ הוּא לְפָנֶיךָ
לִשְׁבָּת בּוֹ, וְלָנוּחַ בּוֹ בְּאַהֲבָה כְּמִצְוַת רְצוֹנֶךָ
וּבִרְצוֹנְךָ הָנִיחַ לָנוּ, יהוה אֱלֹהֵינוּ
שֶׁלֹּא תְהֵא צָרָה וְיָגוֹן וַאֲנָחָה בְּיוֹם מְנוּחָתֵנוּ
וְהַרְאֵנוּ, יהוה אֱלֹהֵינוּ, בְּנֶחָמַת צִיּוֹן עִירֶךָ
וּבְבִנְיַן יְרוּשָׁלַיִם עִיר קָדְשֶׁךָ
כִּי אַתָּה הוּא בַּעַל הַיְשׁוּעוֹת וּבַעַל הַנֶּחָמוֹת.

On Rosh Ḥodesh and Festivals, say:

אֱלֹהֵינוּ Our God and God of our ancestors,
may there rise, come, reach, appear, be favored, heard, regarded
and remembered before You, our recollection and remembrance,
as well as the remembrance of our ancestors,
and of the Messiah son of David Your servant,
and of Jerusalem Your holy city,
and of all Your people the house of Israel –
for deliverance and well-being, grace, loving-kindness and compassion,
life and peace, on this day of:

On Rosh Ḥodesh: Rosh Ḥodesh.
On Rosh HaShana: the Day of Memorial.
On Pesaḥ: the Festival of Matzot.
On Shavuot: the Festival of Shavuot.
On Sukkot: the Festival of Sukkot.
On Shemini Atzeret & Simḥat Torah: the Festival of Shemini Atzeret.

On it remember us, Lord our God, for good;
recollect us for blessing,
and deliver us for life.
In accord with Your promise of salvation and compassion,
spare us and be gracious to us;
have compassion on us and deliver us,
for our eyes are turned to You because You are God,
gracious and compassionate (*on Rosh HaShana:* King).

In the house of a mourner, "Comfort" on page 1068 is substituted for the next two paragraphs.

וּבְנֵה And may Jerusalem the holy city be rebuilt soon, in our time.
Blessed are You, Lord, who in His compassion
will rebuild Jerusalem. Amen.

---

with compassion, and there My House will be rebuilt" (1:16). According to tradition, the Divine Presence never left Jerusalem, even when the city lay in ruins. בּוֹנֶה בְרַחֲמָיו יְרוּשָׁלָיִם, אָמֵן *Who in His compassion will rebuild Jerusalem. Amen:* the unusual appearance of the word *Amen* in this passage (normally we do not say it after our own blessings) signals that this was originally the end of Grace.

On ראש חודש *and* חגים*, say:*

אֱלֹהֵינוּ וֵאלֹהֵי אֲבוֹתֵינוּ
יַעֲלֶה וְיָבוֹא וְיַגִּיעַ, וְיֵרָאֶה וְיֵרָצֶה וְיִשָּׁמַע
וְיִפָּקֵד וְיִזָּכֵר זִכְרוֹנֵנוּ וּפִקְדּוֹנֵנוּ, וְזִכְרוֹן אֲבוֹתֵינוּ
וְזִכְרוֹן מָשִׁיחַ בֶּן דָּוִד עַבְדֶּךָ
וְזִכְרוֹן יְרוּשָׁלַיִם עִיר קָדְשֶׁךָ
וְזִכְרוֹן כָּל עַמְּךָ בֵּית יִשְׂרָאֵל
לְפָנֶיךָ, לִפְלֵיטָה לְטוֹבָה, לְחֵן וּלְחֶסֶד וּלְרַחֲמִים
לְחַיִּים וּלְשָׁלוֹם בְּיוֹם

בראש חודש: רֹאשׁ הַחֹדֶשׁ הַזֶּה.
בראש השנה: הַזִּכָּרוֹן הַזֶּה.
בפסח: חַג הַמַּצּוֹת הַזֶּה.
בשבועות: חַג הַשָּׁבוּעוֹת הַזֶּה.
בסוכות: חַג הַסֻּכּוֹת הַזֶּה.
בשמיני עצרת ושמחת תורה: הַשְּׁמִינִי חַג הָעֲצֶרֶת הַזֶּה.

זָכְרֵנוּ יהוה אֱלֹהֵינוּ בּוֹ לְטוֹבָה
וּפָקְדֵנוּ בוֹ לִבְרָכָה
וְהוֹשִׁיעֵנוּ בוֹ לְחַיִּים.
וּבִדְבַר יְשׁוּעָה וְרַחֲמִים, חוּס וְחָנֵּנוּ וְרַחֵם עָלֵינוּ, וְהוֹשִׁיעֵנוּ
כִּי אֵלֶיךָ עֵינֵינוּ, כִּי אֵל (בראש השנה: מֶלֶךְ) חַנּוּן וְרַחוּם אָתָּה.

In the house of a mourner, **נַחֵם** ***on page 1069 is substituted for the next two paragraphs.***

וּבְנֵה יְרוּשָׁלַיִם עִיר הַקֹּדֶשׁ בִּמְהֵרָה בְיָמֵינוּ.
בָּרוּךְ אַתָּה יהוה, בּוֹנֵה בְרַחֲמָיו יְרוּשָׁלָיִם, אָמֵן.

וּבְנֵה יְרוּשָׁלַיִם *And may Jerusalem.* The third blessing speaks of Jerusalem, home of God's glory, as well as the Davidic monarchy and the Temple, for the restoration of which we pray. As is often the case in the siddur, Jerusalem is associated with the divine attribute of compassion, reflecting the words of Zechariah: "Therefore, this is what the Lord says: I will return to Jerusalem

BLESSING OF GOD'S GOODNESS

בָּרוּךְ Blessed are You, LORD our God, King of the Universe –
God our Father, our King, our Sovereign,
our Creator, our Redeemer, our Maker,
our Holy One, the Holy One of Jacob.
He is our Shepherd, Israel's Shepherd,
the good King who does good to all.
Every day He has done, is doing, and will do good to us.
He has acted, is acting, and will always act kindly toward us for ever,
granting us grace, kindness and compassion, relief and rescue,
prosperity, blessing, redemption and comfort,
sustenance and support, compassion, life, peace and all good things,
and of all good things may He never let us lack.

ADDITIONAL REQUESTS

הָרַחֲמָן May the Compassionate One reign over us
for ever and all time.
May the Compassionate One be blessed
in heaven and on earth.
May the Compassionate One be praised from generation to generation,
be glorified by us to all eternity,
and honored among us for ever and all time.
May the Compassionate One
grant us an honorable livelihood.
May the Compassionate One break the yoke from our neck
and lead us upright to our land.
May the Compassionate One send us many blessings to this house
and this table at which we have eaten.

---

by starvation. Nine hundred and eighty-five towns, villages and settlements were destroyed. Jerusalem was leveled to the ground and rebuilt as a Roman city, Aelia Capitolina. The fact that the sages were able to salvage a fragment of consolation from the fact that the dead were not denied the dignity of burial is testimony to an extraordinary ability to survive catastrophe and preserve the lineaments of hope. The passage is built around threefold references to God's kingship, goodness and bestowal of kindness.

ברכת הטוב והמטיב

בָּרוּךְ אַתָּה יהוה אֱלֹהֵינוּ מֶלֶךְ הָעוֹלָם
הָאֵל אָבִינוּ, מַלְכֵּנוּ, אַדִּירֵנוּ
בּוֹרְאֵנוּ, גּוֹאֲלֵנוּ, יוֹצְרֵנוּ, קְדוֹשֵׁנוּ, קְדוֹשׁ יַעֲקֹב
רוֹעֵנוּ, רוֹעֵה יִשְׂרָאֵל, הַמֶּלֶךְ הַטּוֹב וְהַמֵּיטִיב לַכֹּל, שֶׁבְּכָל יוֹם וָיוֹם
הוּא הֵיטִיב, הוּא מֵיטִיב, הוּא יֵיטִיב לָנוּ
הוּא גְמָלָנוּ, הוּא גוֹמְלֵנוּ, הוּא יִגְמְלֵנוּ לָעַד
לְחֵן וּלְחֶסֶד וּלְרַחֲמִים, וּלְרֶוַח, הַצָּלָה וְהַצְלָחָה
בְּרָכָה וִישׁוּעָה, נֶחָמָה, פַּרְנָסָה וְכַלְכָּלָה
וְרַחֲמִים וְחַיִּים וְשָׁלוֹם וְכָל טוֹב, וּמִכָּל טוּב לְעוֹלָם אַל יְחַסְּרֵנוּ.

בקשות נוספות

הָרַחֲמָן הוּא יִמְלֹךְ עָלֵינוּ לְעוֹלָם וָעֶד.
הָרַחֲמָן הוּא יִתְבָּרַךְ בַּשָּׁמַיִם וּבָאָרֶץ.
הָרַחֲמָן הוּא יִשְׁתַּבַּח לְדוֹר דּוֹרִים, וְיִתְפָּאַר בָּנוּ לָעַד וּלְנֵצַח נְצָחִים
וְיִתְהַדַּר בָּנוּ לָעַד וּלְעוֹלְמֵי עוֹלָמִים.
הָרַחֲמָן הוּא יְפַרְנְסֵנוּ בְּכָבוֹד.
הָרַחֲמָן הוּא יִשְׁבֹּר עֻלֵּנוּ מֵעַל צַוָּארֵנוּ
וְהוּא יוֹלִיכֵנוּ קוֹמְמִיּוּת לְאַרְצֵנוּ.
הָרַחֲמָן הוּא יִשְׁלַח לָנוּ בְּרָכָה מְרֻבָּה בַּבַּיִת הַזֶּה
וְעַל שֻׁלְחָן זֶה שֶׁאָכַלְנוּ עָלָיו.

בָּרוּךְ *Blessed:* A later addition, dated by the Talmud (*Berakhot* 48b) to the period following the Bar Kokhba rebellion when, after a long delay, the Romans gave permission to the Jews to bury their dead. The failure of the Bar Kokhba rebellion was one of the low points of Jewish history. According to the Roman historian Dio, 580,000 Jews died in the fighting and many others

May the Compassionate One send us Elijah the prophet –
may he be remembered for good –
to bring us good tidings of salvation and consolation.
May the Compassionate One bless the State of Israel,
first flowering of our redemption.
May the Compassionate One bless
the members of Israel's Defense Forces,
who stand guard over our land.

A guest says:

יְהִי רָצוֹן May it be Your will that the master of this house shall not suffer shame in this world, nor humiliation in the World to Come. May all he owns prosper greatly, and may his and our possessions be successful and close to hand. Let not the Accuser hold sway over his deeds or ours, and may no thought of sin, iniquity or transgression enter him or us from now and for evermore.

הָרַחֲמָן May the Compassionate One bless –

When eating at one's own table, say (include the words in parentheses that apply):
me, (my wife/husband, / my father, my teacher / my mother,
my teacher/ my children,) and all that is mine,

A guest at someone else's table says (include the words in parentheses that apply):
the master of this house, him (and his wife,
the mistress of this house / and his children,) and all that is his,

Children at their parents' table say (include the words in parentheses that apply):
my father, my teacher, (master of this house,) and my mother,
my teacher, (mistress of this house,) them, their household, their children, and all that is theirs.

For all other guests, add:
and all the diners here,

---

sages, is how Abraham and Sarah brought monotheism to the world. They would provide hospitality to strangers. When the meal was over, and the guests would begin to thank them, Abraham would reply, "Thank the One from whom all we have enjoyed has come."

הָרַחֲמָן הוּא יִשְׁלַח לָנוּ אֶת אֵלִיָּהוּ הַנָּבִיא זָכוּר לַטּוֹב
וִיבַשֶּׂר לָנוּ בְּשׂוֹרוֹת טוֹבוֹת יְשׁוּעוֹת וְנֶחָמוֹת.
הָרַחֲמָן הוּא יְבָרֵךְ אֶת מְדִינַת יִשְׂרָאֵל, רֵאשִׁית צְמִיחַת גְּאֻלָּתֵנוּ.
הָרַחֲמָן הוּא יְבָרֵךְ אֶת חַיָּלֵי צְבָא הַהֲגַנָּה לְיִשְׂרָאֵל
הָעוֹמְדִים עַל מִשְׁמַר אַרְצֵנוּ.

A guest says:

יְהִי רָצוֹן שֶׁלֹּא יֵבוֹשׁ בַּעַל הַבַּיִת בָּעוֹלָם הַזֶּה, וְלֹא יִכָּלֵם לָעוֹלָם הַבָּא, וְיַצְלִיחַ מְאֹד בְּכָל נְכָסָיו, וְיִהְיוּ נְכָסָיו וּנְכָסֵינוּ מֻצְלָחִים וּקְרוֹבִים לָעִיר, וְאַל יִשְׁלֹט שָׂטָן לֹא בְּמַעֲשֵׂה יָדָיו וְלֹא בְּמַעֲשֵׂה יָדֵינוּ. וְאַל יִזְדַּקֵּק לֹא לְפָנָיו וְלֹא לְפָנֵינוּ שׁוּם דְּבַר הִרְהוּר חֵטְא, עֲבֵרָה וְעָוֹן, מֵעַתָּה וְעַד עוֹלָם.

הָרַחֲמָן הוּא יְבָרֵךְ

When eating at one's own table, say (include the words in parentheses that apply):

אוֹתִי (וְאֶת אִשְׁתִּי / וְאֶת בַּעְלִי / וְאֶת אָבִי מוֹרִי /
וְאֶת אִמִּי מוֹרָתִי / וְאֶת זַרְעִי) וְאֶת כָּל אֲשֶׁר לִי.

A guest at someone else's table says (include the words in parentheses that apply):

אֶת בַּעַל הַבַּיִת הַזֶּה, אוֹתוֹ (וְאֶת אִשְׁתּוֹ בַּעֲלַת הַבַּיִת הַזֶּה /
וְאֶת זַרְעוֹ) וְאֶת כָּל אֲשֶׁר לוֹ.

Children at their parents' table say (include the words in parentheses that apply):

אֶת אָבִי מוֹרִי (בַּעַל הַבַּיִת הַזֶּה), וְאֶת אִמִּי מוֹרָתִי (בַּעֲלַת הַבַּיִת
הַזֶּה), אוֹתָם וְאֶת בֵּיתָם וְאֶת זַרְעָם וְאֶת כָּל אֲשֶׁר לָהֶם

For all other guests, add:

וְאֶת כָּל הַמְּסֻבִּין כָּאן

הָרַחֲמָן *May the Compassionate One:* A series of additional prayers, dating from the Geonic period. The oldest is the one in which a guest invokes blessings on the hosts and their family. This is immediately preceded by a prayer that Elijah may come and announce the coming of the Messiah. The juxtaposition is striking: we bring redemption by acts of hospitality. This, according to the

אוֹתָנוּ – together with us and all that is ours.
Just as our forefathers
Abraham, Isaac and Jacob were blessed in all, from all, with all,
so may He bless all of us together with a complete blessing,
and let us say: Amen.

בַּמָּרוֹם On high, may grace be invoked for them and for us,
as a safeguard of peace.
May we receive a blessing from the Lord
and a just reward from the God of our salvation,
and may we find grace and good favor in the eyes of God and man.

At a circumcision feast add here "May the Compassionate One bless the father" on page 1022.

On Shabbat: May the Compassionate One let us inherit
the time, that will be entirely Shabbat
and rest for life everlasting.

On Rosh Ḥodesh: May the Compassionate One renew this month for us,
for good and blessing.

On Rosh HaShana: May the Compassionate One renew for us this year,
for good and blessing.

On Yom Tov: May the Compassionate One let us inherit the day,
that is all good.

On Sukkot: May the Compassionate One restore for us,
the fallen Tabernacle of David.

הָרַחֲמָן May the Compassionate One make us worthy
of the Messianic Age and life in the World to Come.
He gives great / *On Shabbat, Festivals, and Rosh Ḥodesh:* He is a tower of / *II Sam. 22*
salvation to His king, showing kindness to His anointed,
to David and his descendants for ever.
He who makes peace in His high places,
may He make peace for us and all Israel,
and let us say: Amen.

אוֹתָנוּ וְאֶת כָּל אֲשֶׁר לָנוּ

כְּמוֹ שֶׁנִּתְבָּרְכוּ אֲבוֹתֵינוּ

אַבְרָהָם יִצְחָק וְיַעֲקֹב, בַּכֹּל, מִכֹּל, כֹּל

כֵּן יְבָרֵךְ אוֹתָנוּ כֻּלָּנוּ יַחַד בִּבְרָכָה שְׁלֵמָה, וְנֹאמַר אָמֵן.

בַּמָּרוֹם יְלַמְּדוּ עֲלֵיהֶם וְעָלֵינוּ זְכוּת שֶׁתְּהֵא לְמִשְׁמֶרֶת שָׁלוֹם

וְנִשָּׂא בְרָכָה מֵאֵת יהוה וּצְדָקָה מֵאֱלֹהֵי יִשְׁעֵנוּ

וְנִמְצָא חֵן וְשֵׂכֶל טוֹב בְּעֵינֵי אֱלֹהִים וְאָדָם.

At a meal after a ברית *add here* הָרַחֲמָן הוּא יְבָרֵךְ אֲבִי הַיֶּלֶד *on page 1023.*

בשבת: הָרַחֲמָן הוּא יַנְחִילֵנוּ

יוֹם שֶׁכֻּלּוֹ שַׁבָּת וּמְנוּחָה לְחַיֵּי הָעוֹלָמִים.

בראש חודש: הָרַחֲמָן הוּא יְחַדֵּשׁ עָלֵינוּ

אֶת הַחֹדֶשׁ הַזֶּה לְטוֹבָה וְלִבְרָכָה.

בראש השנה: הָרַחֲמָן הוּא יְחַדֵּשׁ עָלֵינוּ

אֶת הַשָּׁנָה הַזֹּאת לְטוֹבָה וְלִבְרָכָה.

ביום טוב: הָרַחֲמָן הוּא יַנְחִילֵנוּ יוֹם שֶׁכֻּלּוֹ טוֹב.

בסוכות: הָרַחֲמָן הוּא יָקִים לָנוּ אֶת סֻכַּת דָּוִד הַנּוֹפֶלֶת.

הָרַחֲמָן הוּא יְזַכֵּנוּ לִימוֹת הַמָּשִׁיחַ וּלְחַיֵּי הָעוֹלָם הַבָּא

מַגְדִּיל / *On* שבת, חגים, *and* ראש חודש מִגְדּוֹל / יְשׁוּעוֹת מַלְכּוֹ שמואל ב׳ כב

וְעֹשֶׂה־חֶסֶד לִמְשִׁיחוֹ, לְדָוִד וּלְזַרְעוֹ עַד־עוֹלָם:

עֹשֶׂה שָׁלוֹם בִּמְרוֹמָיו

הוּא יַעֲשֶׂה שָׁלוֹם עָלֵינוּ וְעַל כָּל יִשְׂרָאֵל

וְאִמְרוּ אָמֵן.

יְראוּ Fear the LORD, you His holy ones; Ps. 34
those who fear Him lack nothing.
Young lions may grow weak and hungry,
but those who seek the LORD
lack no good thing.
Thank the LORD for He is good; Ps. 118
His loving-kindness is for ever.
You open Your hand, Ps. 145
and satisfy every living thing with favor.
Blessed is the person Jer. 17
who trusts in the LORD,
whose trust is in the LORD alone.
Once I was young, and now I am old, Ps. 37
yet I have never watched
a righteous man forsaken
or his children begging for bread.
The LORD will give His people strength. Ps. 29
The LORD will bless His people with peace.

If Birkat HaMazon was made on a cup of wine, then the blessing over wine is made and the majority of the cup is drunk, after which Al HaMiḥya, page 994, is said.

At a wedding or Sheva Berakhot, turn to page 1040.

dred?" (8:6). The verb there means "stand as a passive witness to." Taken in this sense, Psalm 37:25 should be understood as, "When the righteous was forsaken or his children forced to search for bread, I never merely stood and watched." Understood thus, it is a warning against being a mere bystander while other people suffer. It thus brings the Grace to a symmetrical close: It began by speaking of God's goodness in feeding the hungry and ends with an injunction for us to do likewise. This too is part of "walking in God's ways."

יְראוּ אֶת־יהוה קְדֹשָׁיו תהלים לד
כִּי־אֵין מַחְסוֹר לִירֵאָיו:
כְּפִירִים רָשׁוּ וְרָעֵבוּ
וְדֹרְשֵׁי יהוה לֹא־יַחְסְרוּ כָל־טוֹב:
הוֹדוּ לַיהוה כִּי־טוֹב תהלים קיח
כִּי לְעוֹלָם חַסְדּוֹ:
פּוֹתֵחַ אֶת־יָדֶךָ תהלים קמה
וּמַשְׂבִּיעַ לְכָל־חַי רָצוֹן:
בָּרוּךְ הַגֶּבֶר אֲשֶׁר יִבְטַח בַּיהוה ירמיה יז
וְהָיָה יהוה מִבְטַחוֹ:
נַעַר הָיִיתִי גַּם־זָקַנְתִּי תהלים לז
וְלֹא־רָאִיתִי צַדִּיק נֶעֱזָב וְזַרְעוֹ מְבַקֶּשׁ־לָחֶם:
יהוה עֹז לְעַמּוֹ יִתֵּן תהלים כט
יהוה יְבָרֵךְ אֶת־עַמּוֹ בַשָּׁלוֹם:

If ברכת המזון *was made on a cup of wine, then* בּוֹרֵא פְּרִי הַגָּפֶן *is said and the majority of the cup is drunk, after which* ברכה מעין שלוש*, page 995, is said.*

At a wedding or שבע ברכות*, turn to page 1041.*

נער הייתי *Once I was young:* The standard translation of this verse (Psalm 37:25) is "I was young and now am old and I have not seen the righteous forsaken or his children searching for bread." I have translated it here according to a fine insight, author unknown, suggesting that the verb *ra'iti* should be understood in the sense in which it appears in the book of Esther, when Esther, pleading on behalf of Jewry, says: "For how can I watch the evil that shall come unto my people? Or how can I watch the destruction of my kin-

Before eating food, other than bread or matza, made from the five species of grain (wheat, barley, rye, oats and spelt), or rice:

Blessed are You, the LORD our God, King of the Universe,
who creates the various kinds of nourishment.

Before drinking wine or grape juice:

Blessed are You, LORD our God, King of the Universe,
who creates the fruit of the vine.

Before eating fruit that grows on trees:

Blessed are You, LORD our God, King of the Universe,
who creates the fruit of the tree.

Before eating vegetables, or fruit that does not grow on trees:

Blessed are You, LORD our God, King of the Universe,
who creates the fruit of the ground.

Before eating other food or drinking other liquids:

Blessed are You, LORD our God, King of the Universe,
by whose word all things came to be.

Before eating fruit for the first time in a season, the following is said. This blessing is also said when buying or wearing a new garment of significant value (e.g. a dress or suit); entering a new home for the first time; or hearing personal good news.

Blessed are You, LORD our God, King of the Universe,
who has given us life, sustained us, and brought us to this time.

BLESSING AFTER FOOD – AL HAMIḤYA

Grace after eating from the "seven species" of produce with which Israel is blessed: food made from the five grains (but not bread); wine or grape juice; grapes, figs, pomegranates, olives, or dates.

בָּרוּךְ Blessed are You, LORD our God, King of the Universe,

After grain products (but not bread or matza):	*After wine or grape juice:*	*After grapes, figs, olives, pomegranates or dates:*
for the nourishment and sustenance,	for the vine and the fruit of the vine,	for the tree and the fruit of the tree,

After grain products (but not bread or matza), and wine or grape juice:

for the nourishment and sustenance
and for the vine and the fruit of the vine,

(1) food made from wheat, barley, rye, oats or spelt; (2) grape wine or juice; or (3) grapes, figs, pomegranates, olives or dates.

Before eating food, other than bread or מצה*,*
made from the five species of grain (wheat, barley, rye, oats and spelt), or rice:

בָּרוּךְ אַתָּה יהוה אֱלֹהֵינוּ מֶלֶךְ הָעוֹלָם, בּוֹרֵא מִינֵי מְזוֹנוֹת.

Before drinking wine or grape juice:

בָּרוּךְ אַתָּה יהוה אֱלֹהֵינוּ מֶלֶךְ הָעוֹלָם, בּוֹרֵא פְּרִי הַגָּפֶן.

Before eating fruit that grows on trees:

בָּרוּךְ אַתָּה יהוה אֱלֹהֵינוּ מֶלֶךְ הָעוֹלָם, בּוֹרֵא פְּרִי הָעֵץ.

Before eating vegetables, or fruit that does not grow on trees:

בָּרוּךְ אַתָּה יהוה אֱלֹהֵינוּ מֶלֶךְ הָעוֹלָם, בּוֹרֵא פְּרִי הָאֲדָמָה.

Before eating other food or drinking other liquids:

בָּרוּךְ אַתָּה יהוה אֱלֹהֵינוּ מֶלֶךְ הָעוֹלָם, שֶׁהַכֹּל נִהְיָה בִּדְבָרוֹ.

Before eating fruit for the first time in a season, the following שֶׁהֶחֱיָנוּ *is said.*
This blessing is also said when buying or wearing a new garment of significant value (e.g. a dress or suit); entering a new home for the first time; or hearing personal good news.

בָּרוּךְ אַתָּה יהוה אֱלֹהֵינוּ מֶלֶךְ הָעוֹלָם
שֶׁהֶחֱיָנוּ וְקִיְּמָנוּ וְהִגִּיעָנוּ לַזְּמַן הַזֶּה.

ברכה מעין שלוש

Grace after eating from the "seven species" of produce with which ארץ ישראל *is blessed: food made from the five grains (but not bread); wine or grape juice; grapes, figs, pomegranates, olives, or dates.*

בָּרוּךְ אַתָּה יהוה אֱלֹהֵינוּ מֶלֶךְ הָעוֹלָם, עַל

After grain products (but not bread or מצה*):*
הַמִּחְיָה וְעַל הַכַּלְכָּלָה

After wine or grape juice:
הַגֶּפֶן וְעַל פְּרִי הַגֶּפֶן

After grapes, figs, olives, pomegranates or dates:
הָעֵץ וְעַל פְּרִי הָעֵץ

After grain products (but not bread or מצה*), and wine or grape juice:*

הַמִּחְיָה וְעַל הַכַּלְכָּלָה וְעַל הַגֶּפֶן וְעַל פְּרִי הַגֶּפֶן

עַל הַמִּחְיָה *A blessing after other food or drink:* Known as the "three-in-one" blessing, this prayer summarizes the first three paragraphs of the Grace after Meals. It is said after consuming any of the "seven kinds" of produce for which Israel is praised in the Torah (Deut. 8:8) other than bread or matza, namely:

and for the produce of the field; for the desirable, good and spacious land that You willingly gave as heritage to our ancestors, that they might eat of its fruit and be satisfied with its goodness. Have compassion, please, LORD our God, on Israel Your people, on Jerusalem, Your city, on Zion the home of Your glory, on Your altar and Your Temple. May You rebuild Jerusalem, the holy city swiftly in our time, and may You bring us back there, rejoicing in its rebuilding, eating from its fruit, satisfied by its goodness, and blessing You for it in holiness and purity.

On Shabbat: Be pleased to refresh us on this Sabbath Day.

On Rosh Ḥodesh: Remember us for good on this day of the New Moon.

On Rosh HaShana: Remember us for good on this Day of Remembrance.

On Pesaḥ: Grant us joy on this Festival of Matzot.

On Shavuot: Grant us joy on this Festival of Shavuot.

On Sukkot: Grant us joy on this Festival of Sukkot.

On Shemini Atzeret & Simḥat Torah: Grant us joy on this Festival of Shemini Atzeret.

For You, LORD, are good and do good to all and we thank You for the land

After grain products (but not bread or matza):	*After wine or grape juice:*	*After grapes, figs, olives, pomegranates or dates:*
and for the nourishment. Blessed are You, LORD, for the land and for the nourishment.	and for the fruit of the vine.* Blessed are You, LORD, for the land and for the fruit of the vine.*	and for the fruit.** Blessed are You, LORD, for the land and for the fruit.**

After grain products (but not bread or matza), and wine or grape juice:

and for the nourishment and for the fruit of the vine.* Blessed are You, LORD, for the land and for the nourishment and the fruit of the vine.*

* *If the wine is from Israel, then substitute "her vine" for "the vine."*
** *If the fruit is from Israel, then substitute "her fruit" for "the fruit."*

BLESSING AFTER FOOD – BOREH NEFASHOT

After food or drink that does not require Birkat HaMazon or Al HaMiḥya – such as meat, fish, dairy products, vegetables, beverages, or fruit other than grapes, figs, pomegranates, olives or dates – say:

בָּרוּךְ Blessed are You, LORD our God, King of the Universe, who creates the many forms of life and their needs. For all You have created to sustain the life of all that lives, blessed be He, Giver of life to the worlds.

וְעַל תְּנוּבַת הַשָּׂדֶה וְעַל אֶרֶץ חֶמְדָּה טוֹבָה וּרְחָבָה, שֶׁרָצִיתָ וְהִנְחַלְתָּ לַאֲבוֹתֵינוּ לֶאֱכֹל מִפִּרְיָהּ וְלִשְׂבֹּעַ מִטּוּבָהּ. רַחֵם נָא יהוה אֱלֹהֵינוּ עַל יִשְׂרָאֵל עַמֶּךָ וְעַל יְרוּשָׁלַיִם עִירֶךָ וְעַל צִיּוֹן מִשְׁכַּן כְּבוֹדֶךָ וְעַל מִזְבְּחֶךָ וְעַל הֵיכָלֶךָ. וּבְנֵה יְרוּשָׁלַיִם עִיר הַקֹּדֶשׁ בִּמְהֵרָה בְיָמֵינוּ, וְהַעֲלֵנוּ לְתוֹכָהּ וְשַׂמְּחֵנוּ בְּבִנְיָנָהּ וְנֹאכַל מִפִּרְיָהּ וְנִשְׂבַּע מִטּוּבָהּ, וּנְבָרֶכְךָ עָלֶיהָ בִּקְדֻשָּׁה וּבְטָהֳרָה.

בשבת: וּרְצֵה וְהַחֲלִיצֵנוּ בְּיוֹם הַשַּׁבָּת הַזֶּה

בראש חודש: וְזָכְרֵנוּ לְטוֹבָה בְּיוֹם רֹאשׁ הַחֹדֶשׁ הַזֶּה

בראש השנה: וְזָכְרֵנוּ לְטוֹבָה בְּיוֹם הַזִּכָּרוֹן הַזֶּה

בפסח: וְשַׂמְּחֵנוּ בְּיוֹם חַג הַמַּצּוֹת הַזֶּה

בשבועות: וְשַׂמְּחֵנוּ בְּיוֹם חַג הַשָּׁבוּעוֹת הַזֶּה

בסוכות: וְשַׂמְּחֵנוּ בְּיוֹם חַג הַסֻּכּוֹת הַזֶּה

בשמיני עצרת ושמחת תורה: וְשַׂמְּחֵנוּ בְּיוֹם הַשְּׁמִינִי חַג הָעֲצֶרֶת הַזֶּה

כִּי אַתָּה יהוה טוֹב וּמֵטִיב לַכֹּל, וְנוֹדֶה לְּךָ עַל הָאָרֶץ

After grain products (but not bread or מצה*):*	*After wine or grape juice:*	*After grapes, figs, olives, pomegranates or dates:*
וְעַל הַמִּחְיָה.	וְעַל פְּרִי הַגָּפֶן.*	וְעַל הַפֵּרוֹת.**
בָּרוּךְ אַתָּה יהוה, עַל הָאָרֶץ וְעַל הַמִּחְיָה.	בָּרוּךְ אַתָּה יהוה, עַל הָאָרֶץ וְעַל פְּרִי הַגָּפֶן.*	בָּרוּךְ אַתָּה יהוה, עַל הָאָרֶץ וְעַל הַפֵּרוֹת.**

After grain products (but not bread or מצה*), and wine or grape juice:*

וְעַל הַמִּחְיָה וְעַל פְּרִי הַגָּפֶן.*

בָּרוּךְ אַתָּה יהוה, עַל הָאָרֶץ וְעַל הַמִּחְיָה וְעַל פְּרִי הַגָּפֶן.*

*If the wine is from ארץ ישראל, then substitute הגפן for גפנה.

**If the fruit is from ארץ ישראל, then substitute הפרות for פרותיה.

בורא נפשות

After food or drink that does not require ברכת המזון *or* מעין שלוש *– such as meat, fish, dairy products, vegetables, beverages, or fruit other than grapes, figs, pomegranates, olives or dates – say:*

בָּרוּךְ אַתָּה יהוה אֱלֹהֵינוּ מֶלֶךְ הָעוֹלָם, בּוֹרֵא נְפָשׁוֹת רַבּוֹת וְחֶסְרוֹנָן עַל כָּל מַה שֶּׁבָּרָאתָ לְהַחֲיוֹת בָּהֶם נֶפֶשׁ כָּל חָי. בָּרוּךְ חֵי הָעוֹלָמִים.

BLESSINGS

BLESSINGS ON MITZVOT

In Israel on separating teruma and first tithe (if there is doubt as to whether the teruma and first tithe have been taken, the following blessing is not said, but the subsequent declaration is):

Blessed are You, LORD our God, King of the Universe,
who has made us holy through His commandments,
and has commanded us to separate *terumot* and tithes.

Whatever [of the allocated portion] is more than one in a hundred of everything here, is hereby declared to be *teruma gedola* [the priestly portion] and is the northern portion. The one in a hundred that remains here, together with nine equal portions on the upper side of this produce are declared to be the first [levitical] tithe. The one in a hundred I have made first tithe is hereby declared to be *terumat maaser* [the tithe-of-the-tithe set aside for the priests]. Nine other equal portions on the lower side of the produce are declared to be second tithe, but if this produce must have the tithe of the poor separated from it, let them be the tithe of the poor.

In Israel on separating and redeeming the second tithe (if there is doubt as to whether the second tithe has been taken, the following blessing is not said, but the subsequent declaration is):

Blessed are You, LORD our God, King of the Universe,
who has made us holy through His commandments,
and has commanded us about the redemption of the second tithe.

This second tithe, together with its additional fifth, is hereby redeemed by one *peruta* of the coins I have set aside for the redemption of the second tithe.

On taking ḥalla:

Blessed are You, LORD our God, King of the Universe,
who has made us holy through His commandments,
and has commanded us to set aside ḥalla from the dough.

On redeeming fourth-year fruit:

Blessed are You, LORD our God, King of the Universe,
who has made us holy through His commandments,
and has commanded us about the redemption of fruit of the fourth year.

On fixing a mezuza to the doorpost:

Blessed are You, LORD our God, King of the Universe,
who has made us holy through His commandments,
and has commanded us to affix the mezuza.

---

ed us about…" The most common explanation – though there are exceptions – is that the former is used when fulfilling a commandment which I personally am obligated to do, while the latter relates to fulfilling a commandment on behalf of others (as when a *mohel* circumcises a child on behalf of its parents).

ברכות

ברכות המצוות

In ארץ ישראל *on separating* תרומה *and* מעשר ראשון (*if there is doubt as to whether the* תרומה *and* מעשר ראשון *have been taken, the following blessing is not said, but the subsequent declaration is*):

בָּרוּךְ אַתָּה יהוה אֱלֹהֵינוּ מֶלֶךְ הָעוֹלָם, אֲשֶׁר קִדְּשָׁנוּ בְּמִצְוֹתָיו
וְצִוָּנוּ לְהַפְרִישׁ תְּרוּמוֹת וּמַעַשְׂרוֹת.

מַה שֶּׁהוּא יוֹתֵר מֵאֶחָד מִמֵּאָה מִן הַכֹּל שֶׁיֵּשׁ כָּאן, הֲרֵי הוּא תְּרוּמָה גְדוֹלָה בִּצְפוֹנוֹ, וְהָאֶחָד מִמֵּאָה שֶׁנִּשְׁאַר כָּאן עִם תִּשְׁעָה חֲלָקִים כָּמוֹהוּ בְּצַד הָעֶלְיוֹן שֶׁל הַפֵּרוֹת הַלָּלוּ, הֲרֵי הֵם מַעֲשֵׂר רִאשׁוֹן. אוֹתוֹ הָאֶחָד מִמֵּאָה שֶׁעֲשִׂיתִיו מַעֲשֵׂר רִאשׁוֹן הֲרֵי הוּא תְּרוּמַת מַעֲשֵׂר. עוֹד תִּשְׁעָה חֲלָקִים כָּאֵלֶּה בְּצַד הַתַּחְתּוֹן שֶׁל הַפֵּרוֹת הֲרֵי הֵם מַעֲשֵׂר שֵׁנִי, וְאִם הֵם חַיָּבִים בְּמַעֲשַׂר עָנִי, הֲרֵי הֵם מַעֲשַׂר עָנִי.

In ארץ ישראל *on separating and redeeming the* מעשר שני (*if there is doubt as to whether the* מעשר שני *has been taken, the following blessing is not said, but the subsequent declaration is*):

בָּרוּךְ אַתָּה יהוה אֱלֹהֵינוּ מֶלֶךְ הָעוֹלָם, אֲשֶׁר קִדְּשָׁנוּ בְּמִצְוֹתָיו
וְצִוָּנוּ עַל פִּדְיוֹן מַעֲשֵׂר שֵׁנִי.

מַעֲשֵׂר שֵׁנִי זֶה, הוּא וְחֻמְשׁוֹ, הֲרֵי הוּא מְחֻלָּל עַל פְּרוּטָה אַחַת מִן הַמַּטְבֵּעַ שֶׁיִּחַדְתִּי לְפִדְיוֹן מַעֲשֵׂר שֵׁנִי.

On taking חלה:

בָּרוּךְ אַתָּה יהוה אֱלֹהֵינוּ מֶלֶךְ הָעוֹלָם, אֲשֶׁר קִדְּשָׁנוּ בְּמִצְוֹתָיו
וְצִוָּנוּ לְהַפְרִישׁ חַלָּה מִן הָעִסָּה.

On redeeming נטע רבעי:

בָּרוּךְ אַתָּה יהוה אֱלֹהֵינוּ מֶלֶךְ הָעוֹלָם, אֲשֶׁר קִדְּשָׁנוּ בְּמִצְוֹתָיו
וְצִוָּנוּ עַל פִּדְיוֹן נֶטַע רְבָעִי.

On fixing a מזוזה *to the doorpost:*

בָּרוּךְ אַתָּה יהוה אֱלֹהֵינוּ מֶלֶךְ הָעוֹלָם, אֲשֶׁר קִדְּשָׁנוּ בְּמִצְוֹתָיו
וְצִוָּנוּ לִקְבֹּעַ מְזוּזָה.

BLESSINGS ON MITZVOT

Most mitzvot, except those "between man and man," require a blessing prior to their performance. The blessing is, in effect, the declaration of an intention to fulfill the commandment, an expression of *kavana*, sacred intent. There are two basic formulae, "Who has commanded us to…" and "Who has command-

On making a protective railing around one's roof, or a fence around a pit:
Blessed are You, Lord our God, King of the Universe,
who has made us holy through His commandments,
and has commanded us to to affix a guard-rail.

A woman on ritual immersion:
Blessed are You, Lord our God, King of the Universe,
who has made us holy through His commandments,
and has commanded us about ritual immersion.

On immersing utensils made by or bought from a gentile:
Blessed are You, Lord our God, King of the Universe,
who has made us holy through His commandments,
and has commanded us about immersing a vessel (vessels).

BLESSINGS ON PLEASURES, SIGHTS AND SOUNDS

On wearing new clothes:
Blessed are You, Lord our God, King of the Universe, who clothes the naked.

On smelling fragrant shrubs or trees:
Blessed are You, Lord our God, King of the Universe,
who creates fragrant trees.

On smelling fragrant herbs, grasses or flowers:
Blessed are You, Lord our God, King of the Universe,
who creates fragrant plants.

On smelling fragrant fruit:
Blessed are You, Lord our God, King of the Universe,
who gives pleasant fragrance to fruits.

On smelling persimmon oil:
Blessed are You, Lord our God, King of the Universe,
who creates pleasing perfume.

On all other scents:
Blessed are You, Lord our God, King of the Universe,
who creates the various spices.

On seeing the wonders of nature, such as lightning, and on the 28-year solar cycle:
Blessed are You, Lord our God, King of the Universe, Author of creation.

On hearing thunder or experiencing a hurricane:
Blessed are You, Lord our God, King of the Universe,
whose power and might fill the world.

On seeing a rainbow:
Blessed are You, Lord our God, King of the Universe,
who remembers the covenant, is faithful to the covenant, and fulfills His word.

On making a protective railing around one's roof, or a fence around a pit:

בָּרוּךְ אַתָּה יהוה אֱלֹהֵינוּ מֶלֶךְ הָעוֹלָם, אֲשֶׁר קִדְּשָׁנוּ בְּמִצְוֹתָיו
וְצִוָּנוּ לַעֲשׂוֹת מַעֲקֶה.

A woman on ritual immersion:

בָּרוּךְ אַתָּה יהוה אֱלֹהֵינוּ מֶלֶךְ הָעוֹלָם, אֲשֶׁר קִדְּשָׁנוּ בְּמִצְוֹתָיו
וְצִוָּנוּ עַל הַטְּבִילָה.

On immersing utensils made by or bought from a gentile:

בָּרוּךְ אַתָּה יהוה אֱלֹהֵינוּ מֶלֶךְ הָעוֹלָם, אֲשֶׁר קִדְּשָׁנוּ בְּמִצְוֹתָיו
וְצִוָּנוּ עַל טְבִילַת כְּלִי (כֵּלִים).

ברכות הנהנין, הראייה והשמיעה

On wearing new clothes:

בָּרוּךְ אַתָּה יהוה אֱלֹהֵינוּ מֶלֶךְ הָעוֹלָם, מַלְבִּישׁ עֲרֻמִּים.

On smelling fragrant shrubs or trees:

בָּרוּךְ אַתָּה יהוה אֱלֹהֵינוּ מֶלֶךְ הָעוֹלָם, בּוֹרֵא עֲצֵי בְשָׂמִים.

On smelling fragrant herbs, grasses or flowers:

בָּרוּךְ אַתָּה יהוה אֱלֹהֵינוּ מֶלֶךְ הָעוֹלָם, בּוֹרֵא עִשְׂבֵי בְשָׂמִים.

On smelling fragrant fruit:

בָּרוּךְ אַתָּה יהוה אֱלֹהֵינוּ מֶלֶךְ הָעוֹלָם, הַנּוֹתֵן רֵיחַ טוֹב בַּפֵּרוֹת.

On smelling persimmon oil:

בָּרוּךְ אַתָּה יהוה אֱלֹהֵינוּ מֶלֶךְ הָעוֹלָם, בּוֹרֵא שֶׁמֶן עָרֵב.

On all other scents:

בָּרוּךְ אַתָּה יהוה אֱלֹהֵינוּ מֶלֶךְ הָעוֹלָם, בּוֹרֵא מִינֵי בְשָׂמִים.

On seeing the wonders of nature, such as lightning, and ברכת החמה*:*

בָּרוּךְ אַתָּה יהוה אֱלֹהֵינוּ מֶלֶךְ הָעוֹלָם, עוֹשֶׂה מַעֲשֵׂה בְרֵאשִׁית.

On hearing thunder or experiencing a hurricane:

בָּרוּךְ אַתָּה יהוה אֱלֹהֵינוּ מֶלֶךְ הָעוֹלָם, שֶׁכֹּחוֹ וּגְבוּרָתוֹ מָלֵא עוֹלָם.

On seeing a rainbow:

בָּרוּךְ אַתָּה יהוה אֱלֹהֵינוּ מֶלֶךְ הָעוֹלָם
זוֹכֵר הַבְּרִית וְנֶאֱמָן בִּבְרִיתוֹ וְקַיָּם בְּמַאֲמָרוֹ.

On seeing the ocean or the Mediterranean Sea for the first time in thirty days:
Blessed are You, LORD our God, King of the Universe,
who has made the great sea.

On seeing trees blossoming for the first time in the year:
Blessed are You, LORD our God, King of the Universe,
who has withheld nothing from His world,
but has created in it beautiful creatures and trees for human beings to enjoy.

On seeing beautiful scenes of nature:
Blessed are You, LORD our God, King of the Universe,
who has [created] such things in His world.

On seeing unusual people or animals:
Blessed are You, LORD our God, King of the Universe,
who makes [all] creatures different.

On hearing good news from which others as well as oneself will benefit:
Blessed are You, LORD our God, King of the Universe,
who is good and does good.

On hearing bad news, and said by a mourner before the ritual tearing of the garment:
Blessed are You, LORD our God, King of the Universe, the true Judge.

On seeing an outstanding Torah scholar:
Blessed are You, LORD our God, King of the Universe,
who has shared of His wisdom with those who revere Him.

On seeing an outstanding secular scholar:
Blessed are You, LORD our God, King of the Universe,
who has given of His wisdom with human beings.

On seeing a Monarch or Head of State:
Blessed are You, LORD our God, King of the Universe,
who has given of His glory to human beings.

On seeing 600,000 Jews together in Israel:
Blessed are You, LORD our God, King of the Universe,
who knows all secrets.

On seeing Jewish settlements in Israel:
Blessed are You, LORD our God, King of the Universe,
who establishes the border of the widow.

On seeing the place where miracles occurred to the Jewish people:
Blessed are You, LORD our God, King of the Universe,
who performed miracles for our ancestors in this place.

On seeing the place where miracles occurred to oneself or one's family (insert the relevant words):
Blessed are You, LORD our God, King of the Universe, who performed a
miracle for me (my father / my mother / my ancestors) in this place.

On seeing the ocean or the Mediterranean Sea for the first time in thirty days:

בָּרוּךְ אַתָּה יהוה אֱלֹהֵינוּ מֶלֶךְ הָעוֹלָם, שֶׁעָשָׂה אֶת הַיָּם הַגָּדוֹל.

On seeing trees blossoming for the first time in the year:

בָּרוּךְ אַתָּה יהוה אֱלֹהֵינוּ מֶלֶךְ הָעוֹלָם, שֶׁלֹּא חִסַּר בְּעוֹלָמוֹ כְּלוּם
וּבָרָא בוֹ בְּרִיּוֹת טוֹבוֹת וְאִילָנוֹת טוֹבִים לְהַנּוֹת בָּהֶם בְּנֵי אָדָם.

On seeing beautiful scenes of nature:

בָּרוּךְ אַתָּה יהוה אֱלֹהֵינוּ מֶלֶךְ הָעוֹלָם, שֶׁכָּכָה לוֹ בְּעוֹלָמוֹ.

On seeing unusual people or animals:

בָּרוּךְ אַתָּה יהוה אֱלֹהֵינוּ מֶלֶךְ הָעוֹלָם, מְשַׁנֶּה הַבְּרִיּוֹת.

On hearing good news from which others as well as oneself will benefit:

בָּרוּךְ אַתָּה יהוה אֱלֹהֵינוּ מֶלֶךְ הָעוֹלָם, הַטּוֹב וְהַמֵּטִיב.

On hearing bad news, and said by a mourner before the ritual tearing of the garment:

בָּרוּךְ אַתָּה יהוה אֱלֹהֵינוּ מֶלֶךְ הָעוֹלָם, דַּיַּן הָאֱמֶת.

On seeing an outstanding Torah scholar:

בָּרוּךְ אַתָּה יהוה אֱלֹהֵינוּ מֶלֶךְ הָעוֹלָם, שֶׁחָלַק מֵחָכְמָתוֹ לִירֵאָיו.

On seeing an outstanding secular scholar:

בָּרוּךְ אַתָּה יהוה אֱלֹהֵינוּ מֶלֶךְ הָעוֹלָם, שֶׁנָּתַן מֵחָכְמָתוֹ לְבָשָׂר וָדָם.

On seeing a Monarch or Head of State:

בָּרוּךְ אַתָּה יהוה אֱלֹהֵינוּ מֶלֶךְ הָעוֹלָם, שֶׁנָּתַן מִכְּבוֹדוֹ לְבָשָׂר וָדָם.

On seeing 600,000 Jews together in ארץ ישראל*:*

בָּרוּךְ אַתָּה יהוה אֱלֹהֵינוּ מֶלֶךְ הָעוֹלָם, חֲכַם הָרָזִים.

On seeing Jewish settlements in ארץ ישראל*:*

בָּרוּךְ אַתָּה יהוה אֱלֹהֵינוּ מֶלֶךְ הָעוֹלָם
מַצִּיב גְּבוּל אַלְמָנָה.

On seeing the place where miracles occurred to the Jewish people:

בָּרוּךְ אַתָּה יהוה אֱלֹהֵינוּ מֶלֶךְ הָעוֹלָם
שֶׁעָשָׂה נִסִּים לַאֲבוֹתֵינוּ בַּמָּקוֹם הַזֶּה.

On seeing the place where miracles occurred to oneself or one's family (insert the relevant words):

בָּרוּךְ אַתָּה יהוה אֱלֹהֵינוּ מֶלֶךְ הָעוֹלָם
שֶׁעָשָׂה לִי (לְאָבִי/לְאִמִּי/לַאֲבוֹתַי) נֵס בַּמָּקוֹם הַזֶּה.

ADDITIONAL BLESSINGS

After relieving oneself and washing one's hands, say:

Blessed are You, Lord our God, King of the Universe, who formed man in wisdom and created in him many orifices and cavities. It is revealed and known before the throne of Your glory that were one of them to be ruptured or blocked, it would be impossible to survive and stand before You. Blessed are You, Lord, Healer of all flesh who does wondrous deeds.

On visiting a cemetery, or seeing a Jewish grave, for the first time in thirty days:

Blessed are You, Lord our God, King of the Universe, who formed you in judgment, who nourished and sustained you in judgment, who brought death on you in judgment, who knows the number of you all in judgment, and who in the future will restore you to life in judgment. Blessed are You, Lord, who revives the dead.

You are eternally mighty, Lord. You give life to the dead and have great power to save. He sustains the living with loving-kindness, and with great compassion revives the dead. He supports the fallen, heals the sick, sets captives free, and keeps His faith with those who sleep in the dust. Who is like You, Master of might, and who can compare to You, O King who brings death and gives life, and makes salvation grow? Faithful are You to revive the dead.

In special cases of urgency only (see law 363), the following short form of the Amida may be said. First say the first three blessings of the Amida from "O Lord" on page 108 until "the holy God" page 114, then say:

הֲבִינֵנוּ Grant us understanding, Lord our God, to know Your ways. Sensitize our hearts so that we may revere You, and forgive us so that we may be redeemed. Keep us far from suffering and satisfy us with the pastures of Your land. Gather our scattered people from the four quarters of the earth. May those who go astray be judged according to Your will: raise Your hand against the wicked. May the righteous rejoice in the rebuilding of Your city, the restoration of Your Temple, the flowering of Your servant David's glory, and the radiant light of the son of Jesse, Your anointed. May You answer us even before we call. Blessed are You, Lord, who hears prayer.

Continue with the final three blessings from "Find favor" on page 126 until the end.

In extreme cases where there is no time to say the abbreviated Amida above, one may say the following. However, if prayer is then possible at a later time, one should say the complete Amida.

צָרְכֵי The needs of Your people Israel are many, and their patience is thin. May it be Your will, Lord our God and God of our ancestors, to give each one of them enough to sustain him, and to every single body, all that it lacks – and perform what is right in Your eyes. Blessed are You, Lord, who listens to prayer.

ברכות נוספות

After relieving oneself and washing one's hands, say:

בָּרוּךְ אַתָּה יהוה אֱלֹהֵינוּ מֶלֶךְ הָעוֹלָם, אֲשֶׁר יָצַר אֶת הָאָדָם בְּחָכְמָה, וּבָרָא בוֹ נְקָבִים נְקָבִים, חֲלוּלִים חֲלוּלִים. גָּלוּי וְיָדוּעַ לִפְנֵי כִסֵּא כְבוֹדֶךָ, שֶׁאִם יִפָּתֵחַ אֶחָד מֵהֶם אוֹ יִסָּתֵם אֶחָד מֵהֶם, אִי אֶפְשַׁר לְהִתְקַיֵּם וְלַעֲמֹד לְפָנֶיךָ. בָּרוּךְ אַתָּה יהוה, רוֹפֵא כָל בָּשָׂר וּמַפְלִיא לַעֲשׂוֹת.

On visiting a cemetery, or seeing a Jewish grave, for the first time in thirty days:

בָּרוּךְ אַתָּה יהוה אֱלֹהֵינוּ מֶלֶךְ הָעוֹלָם, אֲשֶׁר יָצַר אֶתְכֶם בַּדִּין, וְזָן וְכִלְכֵּל אֶתְכֶם בַּדִּין, וְהֵמִית אֶתְכֶם בַּדִּין, וְיוֹדֵעַ מִסְפַּר כֻּלְּכֶם בַּדִּין, וְהוּא עָתִיד לְהַחֲיוֹתְכֶם וּלְקַיֵּם אֶתְכֶם בַּדִּין. בָּרוּךְ אַתָּה יהוה, מְחַיֵּה הַמֵּתִים.

אַתָּה גִּבּוֹר לְעוֹלָם אֲדֹנָי, מְחַיֵּה מֵתִים אַתָּה, רַב לְהוֹשִׁיעַ, מְכַלְכֵּל חַיִּים בְּחֶסֶד, מְחַיֵּה מֵתִים בְּרַחֲמִים רַבִּים, סוֹמֵךְ נוֹפְלִים, וְרוֹפֵא חוֹלִים, וּמַתִּיר אֲסוּרִים, וּמְקַיֵּם אֱמוּנָתוֹ לִישֵׁנֵי עָפָר. מִי כָמוֹךָ בַּעַל גְּבוּרוֹת וּמִי דּוֹמֶה לָּךְ, מֶלֶךְ מֵמִית וּמְחַיֶּה וּמַצְמִיחַ יְשׁוּעָה, וְנֶאֱמָן אַתָּה לְהַחֲיוֹת מֵתִים.

In special cases of urgency only (see law 363), the following short form of the עמידה *may be said. First say the first three* ברכות *of the* עמידה *from* אֲדֹנָי, שְׂפָתַי תִּפְתָּח *on page 109 until* הַקָּדוֹשׁ *on page 115, then say:*

הֲבִינֵנוּ יהוה אֱלֹהֵינוּ לָדַעַת דְּרָכֶיךָ, וּמוֹל אֶת לְבָבֵנוּ לְיִרְאָתֶךָ, וְתִסְלַח לָנוּ לִהְיוֹת גְּאוּלִים, וְרַחֲקֵנוּ מִמַּכְאוֹב, וְדַשְּׁנֵנוּ בִּנְאוֹת אַרְצֶךָ, וּנְפוּצוֹתֵינוּ מֵאַרְבַּע תְּקַבֵּץ, וְהַתּוֹעִים עַל דַּעְתְּךָ יִשָּׁפֵטוּ, וְעַל הָרְשָׁעִים תָּנִיף יָדֶךָ, וְיִשְׂמְחוּ צַדִּיקִים בְּבִנְיַן עִירֶךָ וּבְתִקּוּן הֵיכָלֶךָ, וּבִצְמִיחַת קֶרֶן לְדָוִד עַבְדֶּךָ וּבַעֲרִיכַת נֵר לְבֶן יִשַׁי מְשִׁיחֶךָ, טֶרֶם נִקְרָא אַתָּה תַעֲנֶה. בָּרוּךְ אַתָּה יהוה, שׁוֹמֵעַ תְּפִלָּה.

Continue with the final three ברכות*, from* רְצֵה *on page 127 until the end.*

In extreme cases where there is no time to say the abbreviated עמידה *above, one may say the following. However, if prayer is then possible at a later time, one should say the complete* עמידה*.*

צָרְכֵי עַמְּךָ יִשְׂרָאֵל מְרֻבִּים וְדַעְתָּם קְצָרָה. יְהִי רָצוֹן מִלְּפָנֶיךָ יהוה אֱלֹהֵינוּ וֵאלֹהֵי אֲבוֹתֵינוּ, שֶׁתִּתֵּן לְכָל אֶחָד וְאֶחָד כְּדֵי פַרְנָסָתוֹ, וּלְכָל גְּוִיָּה וּגְוִיָּה דֵּי מַחְסוֹרָהּ, וְהַטּוֹב בְּעֵינֶיךָ עֲשֵׂה. בָּרוּךְ אַתָּה יהוה, שׁוֹמֵעַ תְּפִלָּה.

SERVICE AT THE CONSECRATION OF A HOUSE

מִזְמוֹר A psalm of David. A song for the dedication of the House. I will exalt You, LORD, for You have lifted me up, and not let my enemies rejoice over me. LORD, my God, I cried to You for help and You healed me. LORD, You lifted my soul from the grave; You spared me from going down to the pit. Sing to the LORD, you His devoted ones, and give thanks to His holy name. For His anger is for a moment, but His favor for a lifetime. At night there may be weeping, but in the morning there is joy. When I felt secure, I said, "I shall never be shaken." LORD, when You favored me, You made me stand firm as a mountain, but when You hid Your face, I was terrified. To You, LORD, I called; I pleaded with my LORD: "What gain would there be if I died and went down to the grave? Can dust thank You? Can it declare Your truth? Hear, LORD, and be gracious to me; LORD, be my help." You have turned my sorrow into dancing. You have removed my sackcloth and clothed me with joy, so that my soul may sing to You and not be silent. LORD my God, for ever will I thank You. *Ps. 30*

מִזְמוֹר A Psalm of David. LORD, who may dwell in Your tent? Who may live on Your holy mountain? One who walks in integrity, does what is right, and speaks the truth from his heart; who has no malice on his tongue, does no wrong to his fellow, nor casts a slur on his neighbor; who scorns those who are vile, but honors those who fear the LORD; who keeps his oath even when it hurts; who does not demand interest on his loans and never takes a bribe against the innocent. One who does these things will never be shaken. *Ps. 15*

Solomon Hirschell; another was compiled by Chief Rabbi Dr. Hermann Adler, which is the basis of the present text.

Where appropriate, the ceremony should begin with the fixing of mezuzot with the appropriate blessing, together with *Sheheḥeyanu* (page 999 and 995).

Psalm 30 is then recited because of its superscription, "A song for the dedication of the House." Psalm 15 speaks of the qualities required for "dwelling in the tent" of God – "tent" being understood by the sages (as in "How beautiful are your tents, Jacob") as a metaphor for the Jewish home.

סדר חנוכת הבית

תהלים ל
מִזְמוֹר שִׁיר־חֲנֻכַּת הַבַּיִת לְדָוִד: אֲרוֹמִמְךָ יהוה כִּי דִלִּיתָנִי, וְלֹא־שִׂמַּחְתָּ אֹיְבַי לִי: יהוה אֱלֹהָי, שִׁוַּעְתִּי אֵלֶיךָ וַתִּרְפָּאֵנִי: יהוה, הֶעֱלִיתָ מִן־שְׁאוֹל נַפְשִׁי, חִיִּיתַנִי מִיָּרְדִי־בוֹר: זַמְּרוּ לַיהוה חֲסִידָיו, וְהוֹדוּ לְזֵכֶר קָדְשׁוֹ: כִּי רֶגַע בְּאַפּוֹ, חַיִּים בִּרְצוֹנוֹ, בָּעֶרֶב יָלִין בֶּכִי וְלַבֹּקֶר רִנָּה: וַאֲנִי אָמַרְתִּי בְשַׁלְוִי, בַּל־אֶמּוֹט לְעוֹלָם: יהוה, בִּרְצוֹנְךָ הֶעֱמַדְתָּה לְהַרְרִי עֹז, הִסְתַּרְתָּ פָנֶיךָ הָיִיתִי נִבְהָל: אֵלֶיךָ יהוה אֶקְרָא, וְאֶל־אֲדֹנָי אֶתְחַנָּן: מַה־בֶּצַע בְּדָמִי, בְּרִדְתִּי אֶל שָׁחַת, הֲיוֹדְךָ עָפָר, הֲיַגִּיד אֲמִתֶּךָ: שְׁמַע־יהוה וְחָנֵּנִי, יהוה הֱיֵה־עֹזֵר לִי: הָפַכְתָּ מִסְפְּדִי לְמָחוֹל לִי, פִּתַּחְתָּ שַׂקִּי, וַתְּאַזְּרֵנִי שִׂמְחָה: לְמַעַן יְזַמֶּרְךָ כָבוֹד וְלֹא יִדֹּם, יהוה אֱלֹהַי, לְעוֹלָם אוֹדֶךָּ:

תהלים טו
מִזְמוֹר לְדָוִד, יהוה מִי־יָגוּר בְּאָהֳלֶךָ, מִי־יִשְׁכֹּן בְּהַר קָדְשֶׁךָ: הוֹלֵךְ תָּמִים וּפֹעֵל צֶדֶק, וְדֹבֵר אֱמֶת בִּלְבָבוֹ: לֹא־רָגַל עַל־לְשֹׁנוֹ, לֹא־עָשָׂה לְרֵעֵהוּ רָעָה, וְחֶרְפָּה לֹא־נָשָׂא עַל־קְרֹבוֹ: נִבְזֶה בְּעֵינָיו נִמְאָס, וְאֶת־יִרְאֵי יהוה יְכַבֵּד, נִשְׁבַּע לְהָרַע וְלֹא יָמִר: כַּסְפּוֹ לֹא־נָתַן בְּנֶשֶׁךְ, וְשֹׁחַד עַל־נָקִי לֹא לָקָח, עֹשֵׂה אֵלֶּה, לֹא יִמּוֹט לְעוֹלָם:

SERVICE AT THE CONSECRATION OF A HOUSE

The Torah mentions the dedication of a house: "The officials shall say to the troops: Has anyone built a new house and not dedicated it? Let him go home, or he may die in battle and someone else may dedicate it" (Deut. 20:5). There are also descriptions of the consecration of the altar (Numbers, chapter 7) and of the Temple (1 Kings, chapter 8).

No formal ceremony for the consecration of a house is mentioned in the early rabbinic literature, other than saying *Sheheḥeyanu* ("Who has given us life, sustained us, and brought us to this day") and the blessing on fixing the mezuza. The current ceremony is a longstanding part of Anglo-Jewish custom. A service for the consecration of a house was compiled by Chief Rabbi

רִבּוֹן הָעוֹלָם Master of the Universe, look down from Your holy dwelling place, and in compassion and favor accept the prayer and plea of Your children, who are gathered here to consecrate this house, and to offer You their thanksgiving for all the kindness and truth You have shown them. Please do let not Your kindness depart, nor Your covenant of Your peace be removed from them. Shield this their home so that no evil befalls it. May illness and sadness never come near it, nor the sound of sorrow be heard within its walls. May the members of this household live together in this home in fellowship and friendship. May they love and revere You, hold fast to You, meditating in Your Torah, and living faithfully by its commandments.

Where appropriate, add the words in parentheses:

הָרֵךְ Bestow Your blessings on the owner of this house. LORD bless *Deut. 33*
his resources and find favor in the work of his hands. Keep him far from sin and transgression. May Your tender love be upon him, and establish the work of our hands. May Your kindness be with his wife, she who watches over the affairs of her household, know- *Prov. 31*
ing that it is the God-fearing woman who deserves praise. (Bestow on their sons and daughters a spirit of wisdom and understanding. Lead them in the path of Your commandments, so that all who *Is. 61*
see them recognise that they are children blessed by the LORD, knowing Your Torah and revering You.) Protect them from all evil; protect their lives. May this [Your promise] be fulfilled in them: "You will be blessed when you come in, and blessed when you go *Deut. 28*
out." And as we have been able to consecrate the house, so together may we witness the consecration of the great and holy Temple in Jerusalem Your city, city of our sacred assemblies, swiftly in our days. Amen.

---

greater than receiving the Divine Presence. And it is where we create *shelom bayit*, "peace in the home," from which, we believe, flows peace to the world (See Maimonides, Laws of Ḥanukka 4:14).

רִבּוֹן הָעוֹלָם, הַשְׁקִיפָה מִמְּעוֹן קָדְשְׁךָ, וְקַבֵּל בְּרַחֲמִים וּבְרָצוֹן אֶת תְּפִלַּת בָּנֶיךָ וְתַחֲנוּנָם, אֲשֶׁר הִתְאַסְּפוּ פֹּה לַחֲנֹךְ אֶת הַבַּיִת הַזֶּה וּלְהַקְרִיב לְפָנֶיךָ אֶת תּוֹדָתָם עַל כָּל הַחֶסֶד וְהָאֱמֶת אֲשֶׁר עָשִׂיתָ אִתָּם. אָנָּא חַסְדְּךָ מֵאִתָּם אַל יָמוּשׁ, וּבְרִית שְׁלוֹמְךָ אַל תָּמוּט. הָגֵן בְּעַד בֵּית מְגוּרֵיהֶם, לֹא תְאֻנֶּה אֵלָיו רָעָה, וְנֶגַע וְצַעַר לֹא יִקְרְבוּ אֵלָיו, וְלֹא יִשָּׁמַע קוֹל צְוָחָה בְּתוֹכוֹ. זַכֵּה אֶת בְּנֵי הַבַּיִת לָשֶׁבֶת בְּמִשְׁכְּנָם בְּאַחֲוָה וְרֵעוּת, לְאַהֲבָה וּלְיִרְאָה אוֹתְךָ וּלְדָבְקָה בָךְ, לַהֲגוֹת בְּתוֹרָתְךָ וּלְקַיֵּם מִצְוֹתֶיהָ.

Where appropriate, add the words in parentheses:

הָרֵק בִּרְכוֹתֶיךָ עַל בַּעַל הַבָּיִת. בָּרֵךְ יהוה חֵילוֹ, וּפֹעַל יָדָיו דברים לג
תִּרְצֶה: הַרְחִיקֵהוּ מִידֵי עֲבֵרָה וְעָוֹן, וִיהִי נֹעַמְךָ עָלָיו, וּמַעֲשֵׂה
יָדָיו כּוֹנְנֵהוּ. יְהִי נָא חַסְדְּךָ אֶת אִשְׁתּוֹ, צוֹפִיָּה הֲלִיכוֹת בֵּיתָהּ: משלי לא
וְתֵדַע כִּי, אִשָּׁה יִרְאַת־יהוה הִיא תִתְהַלָּל: (הוֹפַע עַל בְּנֵיהֶם
וּבְנוֹתֵיהֶם רוּחַ חָכְמָה וּבִינָה, הַדְרִיכֵם בִּנְתִיב מִצְוֹתֶיךָ, וְכָל־ ישעיה סא
רוֹאֵיהֶם יַכִּירוּם כִּי הֵם זֶרַע בֵּרַךְ יהוה, בְּרוּכִים בַּתּוֹרָה וּבְיִרְאַת
שָׁמַיִם.) שָׁמְרֵם מִכָּל רָע, שְׁמֹר אֶת נַפְשָׁם, וִיקֻיַּם בָּהֶם: בָּרוּךְ דברים כח
אַתָּה בְּבֹאֶךָ, וּבָרוּךְ אַתָּה בְּצֵאתֶךָ: וְכַאֲשֶׁר זָכִינוּ לַחֲנֹךְ אֶת
הַבַּיִת הַזֶּה עַתָּה, כֵּן נִזְכֶּה גַּם יַחַד לִרְאוֹת חֲנֻכַּת הַבַּיִת הַגָּדוֹל
וְהַקָּדוֹשׁ בִּירוּשָׁלַיִם עִירֶךָ, קִרְיַת מוֹעֲדֵינוּ, בִּמְהֵרָה בְיָמֵינוּ, אָמֵן.

רִבּוֹן הָעוֹלָם *Master of the Universe:* A prayer of thanksgiving, followed by prayers for the welfare of those who will live in the house. The sanctity of the home is fundamental to Judaism. It is where we celebrate the love between husband and wife – which is symbolic of the love between God and Israel. It is where, with God's blessing, parents pass on their faith and teachings to their children. It is where we practice hospitality, said by the sages to be even

THE TRAVELER'S PRAYER

If one intends to return home on the same day, add the words in parentheses:

יְהִי רָצוֹן May it be Your will,
Lord our God and God of our fathers,
to lead us to peace, direct our steps to peace,
guide us to peace, and bring us to our desired destination in life,
joy and peace
(and bring us back to our home in peace).
Rescue us from any enemy or ambush on the way,
and from all afflictions that trouble the world.
Send blessing to the work of our hands,
and let us find grace, kindness and compassion
from You and from all who see us.
Hear our pleas,
for You are a God who hears prayer and pleas.
Blessed are You, Lord, who listens to prayer.

May the Lord guard your going out and your return, *Ps. 121*
from now and for all time.

Repeat three times:

וְיַעֲקֹב And Jacob went on his way *Gen. 32*
and angels of God met him.
When he saw them, Jacob said, "This is God's camp"
and he named the place Maḥanaim [two camps].

Repeat three times:

יְבָרֶכְךָ May the Lord bless you and protect you. *Num. 6*
May the Lord make His face shine on you and be gracious to you.
May the Lord turn His face toward you and grant you peace.

שִׁיר לַמַּעֲלוֹת A song of ascents. I lift my eyes up to the hills; from where will my help come? My help comes from the Lord, Maker of heaven and earth. He will not let your foot stumble; He who guards you does not slumber. See: the Guardian of Israel neither slumbers nor sleeps. The Lord is your Guardian; the Lord is your Shade at your right hand. The sun will not strike you by day, nor the moon by night. The Lord will guard you from all harm; He will guard your life. The Lord will guard your going and coming, now and for evermore. *Ps. 121*

תפילת הדרך

If one intends to return home on the same day, add the words in parentheses:

יְהִי רָצוֹן מִלְּפָנֶיךָ, יהוה אֱלֹהֵינוּ וֵאלֹהֵי אֲבוֹתֵינוּ
שֶׁתּוֹלִיכֵנוּ לְשָׁלוֹם, וְתַצְעִידֵנוּ לְשָׁלוֹם, וְתַדְרִיכֵנוּ לְשָׁלוֹם
וְתַגִּיעֵנוּ לִמְחוֹז חֶפְצֵנוּ לְחַיִּים וּלְשִׂמְחָה וּלְשָׁלוֹם
(וְתַחֲזִירֵנוּ לְבֵיתֵנוּ לְשָׁלוֹם)
וְתַצִּילֵנוּ מִכַּף כָּל אוֹיֵב וְאוֹרֵב בַּדֶּרֶךְ
וּמִכָּל מִינֵי פֻּרְעָנִיּוֹת הַמִּתְרַגְּשׁוֹת לָבוֹא לָעוֹלָם
וְתִשְׁלַח בְּרָכָה בְּמַעֲשֵׂה יָדֵינוּ
וְתִתְּנֵנוּ לְחֵן וּלְחֶסֶד וּלְרַחֲמִים בְּעֵינֶיךָ וּבְעֵינֵי כָל רוֹאֵינוּ
וְתִשְׁמַע קוֹל תַּחֲנוּנֵינוּ
כִּי אֵל שׁוֹמֵעַ תְּפִלָּה וְתַחֲנוּן אָתָּה.
בָּרוּךְ אַתָּה יהוה, שׁוֹמֵעַ תְּפִלָּה.

תהלים קכא יהוה יִשְׁמָר־צֵאתְךָ וּבוֹאֶךָ, מֵעַתָּה וְעַד־עוֹלָם:

Repeat three times:

בראשית לב וְיַעֲקֹב הָלַךְ לְדַרְכּוֹ, וַיִּפְגְּעוּ־בוֹ מַלְאֲכֵי אֱלֹהִים:
וַיֹּאמֶר יַעֲקֹב כַּאֲשֶׁר רָאָם, מַחֲנֵה אֱלֹהִים זֶה
וַיִּקְרָא שֵׁם־הַמָּקוֹם הַהוּא מַחֲנָיִם:

Repeat three times:

במדבר ו יְבָרֶכְךָ יהוה וְיִשְׁמְרֶךָ:
יָאֵר יהוה פָּנָיו אֵלֶיךָ וִיחֻנֶּךָּ:
יִשָּׂא יהוה פָּנָיו אֵלֶיךָ וְיָשֵׂם לְךָ שָׁלוֹם:

תהלים קכא שִׁיר לַמַּעֲלוֹת, אֶשָּׂא עֵינַי אֶל־הֶהָרִים, מֵאַיִן יָבֹא עֶזְרִי: עֶזְרִי מֵעִם יהוה, עֹשֵׂה שָׁמַיִם וָאָרֶץ: אַל־יִתֵּן לַמּוֹט רַגְלֶךָ, אַל־יָנוּם שֹׁמְרֶךָ: הִנֵּה לֹא־יָנוּם וְלֹא יִישָׁן, שׁוֹמֵר יִשְׂרָאֵל: יהוה שֹׁמְרֶךָ, יהוה צִלְּךָ עַל־יַד יְמִינֶךָ: יוֹמָם הַשֶּׁמֶשׁ לֹא־יַכֶּכָּה, וְיָרֵחַ בַּלָּיְלָה: יהוה יִשְׁמָרְךָ מִכָּל־רָע, יִשְׁמֹר אֶת־נַפְשֶׁךָ: יהוה יִשְׁמָר־צֵאתְךָ וּבוֹאֶךָ, מֵעַתָּה וְעַד־עוֹלָם:

מעגל החיים

THE CYCLE OF LIFE

BRIT MILA

When the baby is brought in, all stand and say:

Blessed is he who comes.

The mohel (in some congregations, all) say (in Israel omit):

וַיְדַבֵּר The LORD spoke to Moses, saying: Pinehas the son of Elazar, the son of Aaron the priest, turned back My rage from the children of Israel, when he was zealous for Me among them, and I did not annihilate the children of Israel in My own zeal. And so tell him, that I now give him My covenant for peace. *Num. 25*

The following verses, through "LORD, please, grant us success," are only said in Israel.

Mohel: Happy are those You choose and bring near to dwell in Your courts. *Ps. 65*

All: May we be sated with the goodness of Your House,
Your holy Temple.

The father takes the baby in his hands and says quietly:

אִם אֶשְׁכָּחֵךְ If I forget you, O Jerusalem, may my right hand forget its skill. May my tongue cling to the roof of my mouth, if I do not remember you, if I do not set Jerusalem above my highest joy. *Ps. 137*

The father says aloud, followed by the congregation:

Listen, Israel: the LORD is our God, the LORD is One. *Deut. 6*

The Mohel, followed by the congregation,
recites each of the following three phrases:

The LORD is King, the LORD was King,
the LORD shall be King for ever and all time.
LORD, please, save us. *Ps. 118*
LORD, please, grant us success.

The baby is placed on Eliyahu's seat, and the Mohel says:

This is the throne of Elijah the prophet, may he be remembered for good.

The Mohel continues:

לִישׁוּעָתְךָ For Your salvation I wait, O LORD. I await Your deliverance, LORD, and I observe Your commandments. Elijah, angel of the covenant, behold: yours is before you. Stand at my right hand and be close to me. *Gen. 49* *Ps. 119*

סדר ברית מילה

When the baby is brought in, all stand and say:

בָּרוּךְ הַבָּא.

The מוהל *(in some congregations, all) say (in* ארץ ישראל *omit):*

במדבר כה וַיְדַבֵּר יהוה אֶל־מֹשֶׁה לֵּאמֹר: פִּינְחָס בֶּן־אֶלְעָזָר בֶּן־אַהֲרֹן הַכֹּהֵן הֵשִׁיב אֶת־חֲמָתִי מֵעַל בְּנֵי־יִשְׂרָאֵל, בְּקַנְאוֹ אֶת־קִנְאָתִי בְּתוֹכָם, וְלֹא־כִלִּיתִי אֶת־בְּנֵי־יִשְׂרָאֵל בְּקִנְאָתִי: לָכֵן אֱמֹר, הִנְנִי נֹתֵן לוֹ אֶת־בְּרִיתִי שָׁלוֹם:

The following verses, through אָנָּא יהוה הַצְלִיחָה נָא *are only said in Israel.*

תהלים סה המוהל: אַשְׁרֵי תִּבְחַר וּתְקָרֵב, יִשְׁכֹּן חֲצֵרֶיךָ

הקהל: נִשְׂבְּעָה בְּטוּב בֵּיתֶךָ, קְדֹשׁ הֵיכָלֶךָ:

The father takes the baby in his hands and says quietly:

תהלים קלז אִם־אֶשְׁכָּחֵךְ יְרוּשָׁלָםִ, תִּשְׁכַּח יְמִינִי: תִּדְבַּק לְשׁוֹנִי לְחִכִּי

אִם־לֹא אֶזְכְּרֵכִי, אִם־לֹא אַעֲלֶה אֶת־יְרוּשָׁלַםִ עַל רֹאשׁ שִׂמְחָתִי:

The father says aloud, followed by the קהל*:*

דברים ו שְׁמַע יִשְׂרָאֵל, יהוה אֱלֹהֵינוּ, יהוה אֶחָד:

The מוהל*, followed by the* קהל*, repeats each of the following three phrases:*

יהוה מֶלֶךְ, יהוה מָלָךְ, יהוה יִמְלֹךְ לְעוֹלָם וָעֶד.

תהלים קיח אָנָּא יהוה הוֹשִׁיעָה נָּא

אָנָּא יהוה הַצְלִיחָה נָא:

The baby is placed on the כסא של אליהו*, and the* מוהל *says:*

זֶה הַכִּסֵּא שֶׁל אֵלִיָּהוּ הַנָּבִיא זָכוּר לַטּוֹב.

The מוהל *continues:*

בראשית מט / תהלים קיט לִישׁוּעָתְךָ קִוִּיתִי יהוה: שִׂבַּרְתִּי לִישׁוּעָתְךָ יהוה, וּמִצְוֹתֶיךָ עָשִׂיתִי: אֵלִיָּהוּ מַלְאַךְ הַבְּרִית, הִנֵּה שֶׁלְּךָ לְפָנֶיךָ, עֲמֹד עַל יְמִינִי וְסָמְכֵנִי.

I await Your deliverance, LORD. I rejoice in Your word like one who finds much spoil. Those who love Your Torah have great peace, and there is no stumbling block before them. Happy are those You choose and bring near to dwell in Your courts. Ps. 119 Ps. 65

All respond:

May we be sated with the goodness of Your House, Your holy Temple.

The baby is placed on the knees of the Sandak, and the Mohel says:

בָּרוּךְ Blessed are You, LORD our God, King of the Universe,
who has made us holy through His commandments,
and has commanded us concerning circumcision.

Immediately after the circumcision, the father says:

בָּרוּךְ Blessed are You, LORD our God, King of the Universe,
who has made us holy through His commandments,
and has commanded us to bring him [our son]
into the covenant of Abraham, our father.

In Israel the father adds (some outside Israel add it as well):

בָּרוּךְ Blessed are You, LORD our God, King of the Universe,
who has given us life, sustained us, and brought us to this time.

All respond:

אָמֵן Amen. Just as he has entered into the covenant,
so may he enter into Torah, marriage and good deeds.

---

the covenant of Abraham, our father – a separate blessing, referring not to the circumcision itself, but what it is a sign of – namely entry into the life of the covenant, under the sheltering wings of the Divine Presence (*Arukh HaShulḥan, Yoreh De'ah* 365:2); (3) *Who made the beloved one* [*Isaac*] *holy from the womb* – a blessing of acknowledgment. Isaac was the first child to have a circumcision at the age of eight days. He was consecrated before birth, Abraham having been told that it would be Isaac who would continue the covenant (Gen. 17:19–21).

כְּשֵׁם שֶׁנִּכְנַס לַבְּרִית *Just as he has entered into the covenant:* Mentioned already in early rabbinic sources as the response of those present. The three phrases refer to the duties of a parent to a child: (1) to teach him Torah; (2) to ensure that he marries; and (3) to train him to do good deeds, as the Torah says in the case of Abraham: "For I have singled him out so that he may instruct his children and his posterity to keep the way of the LORD by doing what is just and right" (Gen. 18:19).

שִׂבַּרְתִּי לִישׁוּעָתְךָ יהוה: שָׂשׂ אָנֹכִי עַל־אִמְרָתֶךָ, כְּמוֹצֵא שָׁלָל רָב: תהלים קיט
שָׁלוֹם רָב לְאֹהֲבֵי תוֹרָתֶךָ, וְאֵין־לָמוֹ מִכְשׁוֹל: אַשְׁרֵי תִּבְחַר וּתְקָרֵב, תהלים סה
יִשְׁכֹּן חֲצֵרֶיךָ

All respond:

נִשְׂבְּעָה בְּטוּב בֵּיתֶךָ, קְדֹשׁ הֵיכָלֶךָ:

The baby is placed on the knees of the סנדק*, and the* מוהל *says:*

בָּרוּךְ אַתָּה יהוה אֱלֹהֵינוּ מֶלֶךְ הָעוֹלָם
אֲשֶׁר קִדְּשָׁנוּ בְּמִצְוֹתָיו וְצִוָּנוּ עַל הַמִּילָה.

Immediately after the circumcision, the father says:

בָּרוּךְ אַתָּה יהוה אֱלֹהֵינוּ מֶלֶךְ הָעוֹלָם, אֲשֶׁר קִדְּשָׁנוּ בְּמִצְוֹתָיו
וְצִוָּנוּ לְהַכְנִיסוֹ בִּבְרִיתוֹ שֶׁל אַבְרָהָם אָבִינוּ.

In ארץ ישראל *the father adds (some in* חוץ לארץ *add it as well):*

בָּרוּךְ אַתָּה יהוה אֱלֹהֵינוּ מֶלֶךְ הָעוֹלָם
שֶׁהֶחֱיָנוּ וְקִיְּמָנוּ וְהִגִּיעָנוּ לַזְּמַן הַזֶּה.

All respond:

אָמֵן. כְּשֵׁם שֶׁנִּכְנַס לַבְּרִית, כֵּן יִכָּנֵס לְתוֹרָה וּלְחֻפָּה וּלְמַעֲשִׂים טוֹבִים.

SERVICE AT A CIRCUMCISION
Since the days of Abraham (Gen. 17:4–14), circumcision has been the sign, for Jewish males, of the covenant between God and His people. Despite the fact that the law was restated by Moses (Lev. 12:3), it remains known as the "Covenant of Abraham." The ceremony – always performed on the eighth day, even on Shabbat, unless there are medical reasons for delay – marks the entry of the child into the covenant of Jewish fate and destiny. The duty of circumcision devolves, in principle, on the father of the child; in practice it is performed only by a qualified *mohel.*

בָּרוּךְ *Blessed are You:* There are three blessings to be said at a circumcision: (1) *And has commanded us concerning circumcision* – a blessing over the commandment itself, the "about" formula signaling that the *mohel* is performing the commandment on behalf of the father; (2) *To bring him [our son] into*

After the circumcision has been completed, the Mohel (or another honoree) takes a cup of wine and says:

בָּרוּךְ Blessed are You, Lord our God, King of the Universe, who creates the fruit of the vine.

בָּרוּךְ Blessed are You, Lord our God, King of the Universe, who made the beloved one [Isaac] holy from the womb, marked the decree of circumcision in his flesh, and gave his descendants the seal and sign of the holy covenant. As a reward for this, the Living God, our Portion, our Rock, did order deliverance from destruction for the beloved of our flesh, for the sake of His covenant that He set in our flesh. Blessed are You, Lord, who establishes the covenant.

אֱלֹהֵינוּ Our God and God of our fathers, preserve this child to his father and mother, and let his name be called in Israel (*baby's name* son of *father's name*). May the father rejoice in the issue of his body, and the mother be glad with the fruit of her womb, as is written, "May your father and mother rejoice, and she who bore you be glad." And it is said, *Prov. 23*
"Then I passed by you and saw you downtrodden in your blood, and I said to you: In your blood, live; and I said to you: In your blood, live." *Ezek. 16*

וְנֶאֱמַר And it is said, "He remembered His covenant for ever; the word He ordained for a thousand generations; the covenant He made with Abraham and gave on oath to Isaac, confirming it as a statute for Jacob, an everlasting covenant for Israel." And it is said, *Ps. 105*
"And Abraham circumcised his son Isaac at the age of eight days, as *Gen. 21*
God had commanded him." Thank the Lord for He is good; His loving-kindness is for ever. *Ps. 118*

All respond:

Thank the Lord for He is good; His loving-kindness is for ever.

The Mohel (or honoree) continues:

May this child (*baby's name* son of *father's name*) become great. Just as he has entered into the covenant, so may he enter into Torah, marriage and good deeds.

The Sandak also drinks some of the wine; some drops are given to the baby. The cup is then sent to the mother, who also drinks from it.

All say Aleinu on page 180, and Mourner's Kaddish on page 182.

After the circumcision has been completed, the מוהל *(or another honoree) takes a cup of wine and says:*

בָּרוּךְ אַתָּה יהוה אֱלֹהֵינוּ מֶלֶךְ הָעוֹלָם, בּוֹרֵא פְּרִי הַגָּפֶן.

בָּרוּךְ אַתָּה יהוה אֱלֹהֵינוּ מֶלֶךְ הָעוֹלָם, אֲשֶׁר קִדַּשׁ יְדִיד מִבֶּטֶן, וְחֹק בִּשְׁאֵרוֹ שָׂם, וְצֶאֱצָאָיו חָתַם בְּאוֹת בְּרִית קֹדֶשׁ. עַל כֵּן בִּשְׂכַר זֹאת, אֵל חַי חֶלְקֵנוּ צוּרֵנוּ צַוֵּה לְהַצִּיל יְדִידוּת שְׁאֵרֵנוּ מִשַּׁחַת, לְמַעַן בְּרִיתוֹ אֲשֶׁר שָׂם בִּבְשָׂרֵנוּ. בָּרוּךְ אַתָּה יהוה, כּוֹרֵת הַבְּרִית.

אֱלֹהֵינוּ וֵאלֹהֵי אֲבוֹתֵינוּ, קַיֵּם אֶת הַיֶּלֶד הַזֶּה לְאָבִיו וּלְאִמּוֹ, וְיִקָּרֵא שְׁמוֹ בְּיִשְׂרָאֵל (פלוני בֶּן פלוני). יִשְׂמַח הָאָב בְּיוֹצֵא חֲלָצָיו וְתָגֵל
אִמּוֹ בִּפְרִי בִטְנָהּ, כַּכָּתוּב: יִשְׂמַח־אָבִיךָ וְאִמֶּךָ, וְתָגֵל יוֹלַדְתֶּךָ: משלי כג
וְנֶאֱמַר: וָאֶעֱבֹר עָלַיִךְ וָאֶרְאֵךְ מִתְבּוֹסֶסֶת בְּדָמָיִךְ, וָאֹמַר לָךְ יחזקאל טז
בְּדָמַיִךְ חֲיִי, וָאֹמַר לָךְ בְּדָמַיִךְ חֲיִי:

וְנֶאֱמַר: זָכַר לְעוֹלָם בְּרִיתוֹ, דָּבָר צִוָּה לְאֶלֶף דּוֹר: אֲשֶׁר כָּרַת אֶת־ תהלים קה
אַבְרָהָם, וּשְׁבוּעָתוֹ לְיִשְׂחָק: וַיַּעֲמִידֶהָ לְיַעֲקֹב לְחֹק, לְיִשְׂרָאֵל
בְּרִית עוֹלָם: וְנֶאֱמַר: וַיָּמָל אַבְרָהָם אֶת־יִצְחָק בְּנוֹ בֶּן־שְׁמֹנַת בראשית כא
יָמִים, כַּאֲשֶׁר צִוָּה אֹתוֹ אֱלֹהִים: הוֹדוּ לַיהוה כִּי־טוֹב, כִּי לְעוֹלָם תהלים קיח
חַסְדּוֹ:

All respond:

הוֹדוּ לַיהוה כִּי־טוֹב, כִּי לְעוֹלָם חַסְדּוֹ:

The מוהל *(or honoree) continues:*

(פלוני בֶּן פלוני) זֶה הַקָּטָן גָּדוֹל יִהְיֶה, כְּשֵׁם שֶׁנִּכְנַס לַבְּרִית, כֵּן יִכָּנֵס לְתוֹרָה וּלְחֻפָּה וּלְמַעֲשִׂים טוֹבִים.

The סנדק *also drinks some of the wine; some drops are given to the baby.*
The cup is then sent to the mother, who also drinks from it.

All say עָלֵינוּ*, on page 181, and* קדיש יתום *on page 183.*

BIRKAT HAMAZON AT A BRIT MILA

Leader Gentlemen, let us say grace.
Others May the name of the LORD be blessed from now and for ever. *Ps. 113*
Leader May the name of the LORD be blessed from now and for ever.

Leader then others We give thanks to Your name among the faithful.
Blessed are you to the LORD.

Leader With permission of the Almighty, awesome and revered,
a refuge in times of trouble,
Almighty, girded with strength –
majestic on high, the LORD.

Others We give thanks to Your name among the faithful.
Blessed are you to the LORD.

Leader With permission of the holy Torah,
pure and clear,
given to us as a heritage
by Moses the servant of the LORD.

Others We give thanks to Your name among the faithful.
Blessed are you to the LORD.

Leader With permission of the priests, the Levites,
I call upon the God of the Hebrews,
declaring His glory to the furthest isles,
and offering blessings to the LORD.

Others We give thanks to Your name among the faithful.
Blessed are you to the LORD.

---

from God, the Torah, Kohanim and Levites, and the assembled company, dating from the Middle Ages. Originally said at other festive occasions, it has come, over the course of time, to be associated specifically with the celebration of a circumcision.

ברכת המזון לברית מילה

Leader רַבּוֹתַי, נְבָרֵךְ.

Others יְהִי שֵׁם יהוה מְבֹרָךְ מֵעַתָּה וְעַד־עוֹלָם: תהלים קיג

Leader יְהִי שֵׁם יהוה מְבֹרָךְ מֵעַתָּה וְעַד־עוֹלָם:

Leader then others נוֹדֶה לְשִׁמְךָ בְּתוֹךְ אֱמוּנַי, בְּרוּכִים אַתֶּם לַיהוה.

Leader בִּרְשׁוּת אֵל אָיֹם וְנוֹרָא
מִשְׂגָּב לְעִתּוֹת בַּצָּרָה
אֵל נֶאְזָר בִּגְבוּרָה
אַדִּיר בַּמָּרוֹם יהוה.

Others נוֹדֶה לְשִׁמְךָ בְּתוֹךְ אֱמוּנַי, בְּרוּכִים אַתֶּם לַיהוה.

Leader בִּרְשׁוּת הַתּוֹרָה הַקְּדוֹשָׁה
טְהוֹרָה הִיא וְגַם פְּרוּשָׁה
צִוָּה לָנוּ מוֹרָשָׁה
מֹשֶׁה עֶבֶד יהוה.

Others נוֹדֶה לְשִׁמְךָ בְּתוֹךְ אֱמוּנַי, בְּרוּכִים אַתֶּם לַיהוה.

Leader בִּרְשׁוּת הַכֹּהֲנִים וְהַלְוִיִּם
אֶקְרָא לֵאלֹהֵי הָעִבְרִיִּים
אֲהוֹדֶנּוּ בְּכָל אִיִּים
אֲבָרְכָה אֶת יהוה.

Others נוֹדֶה לְשִׁמְךָ בְּתוֹךְ אֱמוּנַי, בְּרוּכִים אַתֶּם לַיהוה.

BIRKAT HAMAZON AT A BRIT MILA

נוֹדֶה לְשִׁמְךָ בְּתוֹךְ אֱמוּנַי *We give thanks to Your name among the faithful:* A highly stylized form of the invitation to say Grace, asking permission respectively

Leader With the permission of the rabbis, teachers and friends,
I open my lips with song,
saying from my innermost being:
"Blessed is he that comes in the name of the LORD."

Others We give thanks to Your name among the faithful.
Blessed are you to the LORD.

Leader With your permission, my masters and teachers,
let us bless (*in a minyan:* our God,) the One
from whose food we have eaten.

Others Blessed be (*in a minyan:* our God,) the One
from whose food we have eaten,
and by whose goodness we live.

Leader Blessed be (*in a minyan:* our God,) the One
from whose food we have eaten,
and by whose goodness we live.
Blessed be He, and blessed be His name.

Continue with Birkat HaMazon on page 978 until
"in the eyes of God and man" on page 990. Then continue:

Someone other than the father says:

הָרַחֲמָן May the Compassionate One
bless the father and mother of this child.
May they be worthy to raise him,
educate him, and train him in wisdom.
From this eighth day onward may his blood be accepted,
and may the LORD his God be with him always.

Someone other than the Sandak says:

הָרַחֲמָן May the Compassionate One bless him [the Sandak]
who assisted in the covenant of circumcision
and rejoiced to do this pious deed.
May God doubly reward him for his deed,
exalting him ever higher.

Leader בִּרְשׁוּת מָרָנָן וְרַבָּנָן וְרַבּוֹתַי
אֶפְתְּחָה בְּשִׁיר פִּי וּשְׂפָתַי
וְתֹאמַרְנָה עַצְמוֹתַי
בָּרוּךְ הַבָּא בְּשֵׁם יהוה.

Others נוֹדֶה לְשִׁמְךָ בְּתוֹךְ אֱמוּנַי, בְּרוּכִים אַתֶּם לַיהוה.

Leader בִּרְשׁוּת מָרָנָן וְרַבָּנָן וְרַבּוֹתַי
נְבָרֵךְ (במנין: אֱלֹהֵינוּ) שֶׁאָכַלְנוּ מִשֶּׁלּוֹ.

Others בָּרוּךְ (במנין: אֱלֹהֵינוּ) שֶׁאָכַלְנוּ מִשֶּׁלּוֹ וּבְטוּבוֹ חָיִינוּ.

Leader בָּרוּךְ (במנין: אֱלֹהֵינוּ) שֶׁאָכַלְנוּ מִשֶּׁלּוֹ וּבְטוּבוֹ חָיִינוּ.
בָּרוּךְ הוּא וּבָרוּךְ שְׁמוֹ.

Continue with ברכת המזון *on page 979 until* בְּעֵינֵי אֱלֹהִים וְאָדָם *on page 991. Then continue:*

Someone other than the father says:

הָרַחֲמָן הוּא יְבָרֵךְ אֲבִי הַיֶּלֶד וְאִמּוֹ
וְיִזְכּוּ לְגַדְּלוֹ וּלְחַנְּכוֹ וּלְחַכְּמוֹ
מִיּוֹם הַשְּׁמִינִי וָהָלְאָה יֵרָצֶה דָמוֹ
וִיהִי יהוה אֱלֹהָיו עִמּוֹ.

Someone other than the סנדק *says:*

הָרַחֲמָן הוּא יְבָרֵךְ בַּעַל בְּרִית הַמִּילָה
אֲשֶׁר שָׂשׂ לַעֲשׂוֹת צֶדֶק בְּגִילָה
וִישַׁלֵּם פָּעֳלוֹ וּמַשְׂכֻּרְתּוֹ כְּפוּלָה
וְיִתְּנֵהוּ לְמַעְלָה לְמָעְלָה.

הָרַחֲמָן *May the Compassionate One:* A series of special blessings for the parents of the child, the *Sandak*, the child, and the *mohel*. The fifth and sixth are prayers for the coming of the Messiah, and for Elijah, who is believed to be

הָרַחֲמָן May the Compassionate One
bless the tender child, circumcised on his eighth day.
May his heart and hands be firm with God,
and may he be worthy to witness the Divine Presence
three times a year.

Someone other than the Mohel says:

הָרַחֲמָן May the Compassionate One
bless him who performed the circumcision,
and fulfilled every part of the precept.
The service of the faint-hearted would not be acceptable
if he failed to perform
the three essentials of the precept.

הָרַחֲמָן May the Compassionate One
send us His anointed, blameless in life,
through the merit of this child
groomed by the blood of circumcision,
to proclaim good news and consolations
to the unique people scattered
and dispersed among the nations.

הָרַחֲמָן May the Compassionate One
send us the righteous priest,
who was taken into hiding,
until a throne, bright as the sun, radiant as a diamond,
is prepared for him;
the prophet who covered his face with his mantle
and wrapped himself in it [when God declared]:
My covenant is with him for life and peace.

Continue with "May the Compassionate One make us worthy of the Messianic Age" on page 990.

On Shabbat, Rosh Ḥodesh or Yom Tov, continue with the appropriate "May the Compassionate One" on page 990.

הָרַחֲמָן הוּא יְבָרֵךְ רַךְ הַנִּמּוֹל לִשְׁמוֹנָה
וְיִהְיוּ יָדָיו וְלִבּוֹ לָאֵל אֱמוּנָה
וְיִזְכֶּה לִרְאוֹת פְּנֵי הַשְּׁכִינָה
שָׁלֹשׁ פְּעָמִים בַּשָּׁנָה.

Someone other than the מוהל *says:*

הָרַחֲמָן הוּא יְבָרֵךְ הַמָּל בְּשַׂר הָעָרְלָה
וּפָרַע וּמָצַץ דְּמֵי הַמִּילָה
אִישׁ הַיָּרֵא וְרַךְ הַלֵּבָב עֲבוֹדָתוֹ פְּסוּלָה
אִם שְׁלָשׁ אֵלֶּה לֹא יַעֲשֶׂה לָהּ.

הָרַחֲמָן הוּא יִשְׁלַח לָנוּ מְשִׁיחוֹ הוֹלֵךְ תָּמִים
בִּזְכוּת חֲתַן לַמּוּלוֹת דָּמִים
לְבַשֵּׂר בְּשׂוֹרוֹת טוֹבוֹת וְנִחוּמִים
לְעַם אֶחָד מְפֻזָּר וּמְפֹרָד בֵּין הָעַמִּים.

הָרַחֲמָן הוּא יִשְׁלַח לָנוּ כֹּהֵן צֶדֶק אֲשֶׁר לֻקַּח לְעֵילוֹם
עַד הוּכַן כִּסְאוֹ כַּשֶּׁמֶשׁ וְיַהֲלוֹם
וַיָּלֶט פָּנָיו בְּאַדַּרְתּוֹ וַיִּגְלֹם
בְּרִיתִי הָיְתָה אִתּוֹ הַחַיִּים וְהַשָּׁלוֹם.

Continue with הָרַחֲמָן הוּא יְזַכֵּנוּ לִימוֹת הַמָּשִׁיחַ *on page 991.*
On שבת*,* ראש חודש *or* יום טוב*, continue with the appropriate* הָרַחֲמָן *on page 991.*

present at the circumcision. The author has left his name, Abraham, in an acrostic formed by the initial letters of the third-to-last word in the first line of the first five blessings.

REDEMPTION OF THE FIRSTBORN

A firstborn male child, must be redeemed on the 31st day of his birth – unless the father is a Kohen or Levi, or the mother is a daughter of a Kohen or a Levi. If the 31st day falls on Shabbat or Yom Tov, the ceremony is postponed to the following weekday.

The father, presenting his child to the Kohen, declares:

זֶה This is my firstborn son, the first issue of his mother's womb. The Holy One, blessed be He, has commanded us to redeem him, as is said,

"Those who are to be redeemed, you must redeem from the age of one month, at the fixed price of five shekels of silver by the sacred standard, which is twenty gerahs to the shekel." *Num. 18*

And it is also stated,

"Consecrate to Me every firstborn; the first of every womb among the people of Israel, whether of man or beast, belongs to Me." *Ex. 13*

The Kohen checks with the mother that this is her firstborn, and then asks if she has miscarried before this child. If her answer is no, he asks the father:

מַאי Which do you prefer:
to give me your firstborn son,
the first birth of his mother,
or to redeem him for five selas
as you are bound to do according to the Torah?

---

prescribes a ceremony of redemption, in which the father of the child makes a monetary offering to a Kohen, symbolically exchanging it for his son. The substance of the ceremony has not changed since biblical times, though its wording is first mentioned in the Talmud.

מַאי בָּעֵית טְפֵי *Which do you prefer:* A notional question. In fact, the father has no choice but to redeem the child. The question is asked to ensure that the father understands the nature of the ceremony. The present text is in Aramaic, but it can be said in any language.

סדר פדיון הבן

A firstborn male child, must be redeemed on the 31st day of his birth – unless the father is a כהן or לוי, or the mother is a daughter of a כהן or a לוי. If the 31st day falls on שבת or יום טוב, the ceremony is postponed to the following weekday.

The father, presenting his child to the כהן, declares:

זֶה בְּנִי בְכוֹרִי הוּא פֶּטֶר רֶחֶם לְאִמּוֹ
וְהַקָּדוֹשׁ בָּרוּךְ הוּא צִוָּה לִפְדּוֹתוֹ
שֶׁנֶּאֱמַר
וּפְדוּיָו מִבֶּן־חֹדֶשׁ תִּפְדֶּה, בְּעֶרְכְּךָ כֶּסֶף חֲמֵשֶׁת שְׁקָלִים בְּשֶׁקֶל הַקֹּדֶשׁ, עֶשְׂרִים גֵּרָה הוּא: במדבר יח
וְנֶאֱמַר
קַדֶּשׁ־לִי כָל־בְּכוֹר פֶּטֶר כָּל־רֶחֶם בִּבְנֵי יִשְׂרָאֵל בָּאָדָם וּבַבְּהֵמָה, לִי הוּא: שמות יג

The כהן checks with the mother that this is her firstborn, and then asks if she has miscarried before this child. If her answer is no, he asks the father:

מַאי בָּעֵית טְפֵי
לִתֵּן לִי בִּנְךָ בְּכוֹרְךָ שֶׁהוּא פֶּטֶר רֶחֶם לְאִמּוֹ
אוֹ בָּעֵית לִפְדּוֹתוֹ בְּעַד חָמֵשׁ סְלָעִים
כְּדִמְחֻיַּבְתְּ מִדְּאוֹרַיְתָא.

REDEMPTION OF THE FIRSTBORN

According to the Torah, firstborn males originally carried a special sanctity. Their lives spared during the last of the ten plagues, the firstborns were to become God's special ministers, who would dedicate themselves to His service. (The supreme biblical example is Samuel, dedicated to God by his mother Hannah, I Sam. 1:11.) After the sin of the golden calf, that responsibility was transferred to the Levites, the only tribe that did not take part in the sin (Num. 3:11–13). In memory of the earlier sanctity, however, the Torah

The father replies:

חָפֵץ I wish to redeem my son.
I present you with the cost of his redemption
which I am bound to give according to the Torah.

Holding the redemption money, the father says:

בָּרוּךְ Blessed are You, Lord our God, King of the Universe,
who has made us holy through His commandments,
and has commanded us concerning the redemption of a son.

בָּרוּךְ Blessed are You, Lord our God, King of the Universe,
who has given us life, sustained us, and brought us to this time.

The redemption money is given to the Kohen, who then returns the child to his father.
The Kohen takes a cup of wine and says:

בָּרוּךְ Blessed are You, Lord our God, King of the Universe,
who creates the fruit of the vine.

Placing his right hand on the head of the child, the Kohen blesses him as follows:

יְשִׂמְךָ May God make you like *Gen. 48*
Ephraim and Manasseh.
May the Lord bless you and protect you. *Num. 6*
May the Lord make His face shine on you
and be gracious to you.
May the Lord turn His face toward you
and grant you peace.
The Lord is your Guardian; *Ps. 121*
the Lord is your protection at your right hand.
The Lord will guard you against all harm.
He will guard your life.
For length of days, years of life, and peace *Prov. 3*
He will increase for you.

The father replies:

חָפֵץ אֲנִי לִפְדּוֹת אֶת בְּנִי

וְהֵילָךְ דְּמֵי פִדְיוֹנוֹ כִּדְמִחַיַּבְנָא מִדְּאוֹרַיְתָא.

Holding the redemption money, the father says:

בָּרוּךְ אַתָּה יהוה אֱלֹהֵינוּ מֶלֶךְ הָעוֹלָם

אֲשֶׁר קִדְּשָׁנוּ בְּמִצְוֹתָיו וְצִוָּנוּ עַל פִּדְיוֹן הַבֵּן.

בָּרוּךְ אַתָּה יהוה אֱלֹהֵינוּ מֶלֶךְ הָעוֹלָם

שֶׁהֶחֱיָנוּ וְקִיְּמָנוּ וְהִגִּיעָנוּ לַזְּמַן הַזֶּה.

The redemption money is given to the כהן, who then returns the child to his father.
The כהן takes a cup of wine and says:

בָּרוּךְ אַתָּה יהוה אֱלֹהֵינוּ מֶלֶךְ הָעוֹלָם, בּוֹרֵא פְּרִי הַגָּפֶן.

Placing his right hand on the head of the child, the כהן blesses him as follows:

בראשית מח — יְשִׂמְךָ אֱלֹהִים כְּאֶפְרַיִם וְכִמְנַשֶּׁה:

במדבר ו — יְבָרֶכְךָ יהוה וְיִשְׁמְרֶךָ:

יָאֵר יהוה פָּנָיו אֵלֶיךָ וִיחֻנֶּךָּ:

יִשָּׂא יהוה פָּנָיו אֵלֶיךָ וְיָשֵׂם לְךָ שָׁלוֹם:

תהלים קכא — יהוה שֹׁמְרֶךָ, יהוה צִלְּךָ עַל־יַד יְמִינֶךָ:

יהוה יִשְׁמָרְךָ מִכָּל־רָע, יִשְׁמֹר אֶת־נַפְשֶׁךָ:

משלי ג — כִּי אֹרֶךְ יָמִים וּשְׁנוֹת חַיִּים וְשָׁלוֹם יוֹסִיפוּ לָךְ:

THANKSGIVING PRAYER AFTER CHILDBIRTH

On entering the synagogue, say:

וַאֲנִי As for me, by Your great love, *Ps. 5*
I will come into Your House.
I will bow down toward Your holy Temple in awe of You.

אָהַבְתִּי I love the Lord, for He hears my voice, my pleas. *Ps. 116*
He turns His ear to me whenever I call.
The bonds of death encompassed me,
the anguish of the grave came upon me,
I was overcome by trouble and sorrow.
Then I called on the name of the Lord: "Lord, I pray, save my life."
Gracious is the Lord, and righteous; our God is full of compassion.
The Lord protects the simple hearted.
When I was brought low, He saved me.
My soul, be at peace once more, for the Lord has been good to you.
For You have rescued me from death,
my eyes from weeping, my feet from stumbling.
I shall walk in the presence of the Lord in the land of the living.
I had faith, even when I said, "I am greatly afflicted,"
even when I said rashly, "All men are liars."

מָה־אָשִׁיב How can I repay the Lord for all His goodness to me? *Ps. 116*
To You I shall bring a thanksgiving-offering
and call on the Lord by name.
I will fulfill my vows to the Lord in the presence of all His people,
in the courts of the House of the Lord,
in your midst, Jerusalem. Halleluya!

---

above prayer is composed of the following elements: (1) a prayer on entry to the synagogue; (2) verses of thanksgiving from Hallel; (3) the blessing "Who bestows good things" (*HaGomel*) together with the congregational response; and (4) prayers for recovery from the pains of birth, and for success in raising the child.

סדר תפילה ליולדת

On entering the בית כנסת*, say:*

תהלים ה
וַאֲנִי בְּרֹב חַסְדְּךָ אָבוֹא בֵיתֶךָ
אֶשְׁתַּחֲוֶה אֶל־הֵיכַל־קָדְשְׁךָ בְּיִרְאָתֶךָ:

תהלים קטז
אָהַבְתִּי, כִּי־יִשְׁמַע יהוה, אֶת־קוֹלִי תַּחֲנוּנָי:
כִּי־הִטָּה אָזְנוֹ לִי, וּבְיָמַי אֶקְרָא:
אֲפָפוּנִי חֶבְלֵי־מָוֶת, וּמְצָרֵי שְׁאוֹל מְצָאוּנִי, צָרָה וְיָגוֹן אֶמְצָא:
וּבְשֵׁם־יהוה אֶקְרָא, אָנָּה יהוה מַלְּטָה נַפְשִׁי:
חַנּוּן יהוה וְצַדִּיק, וֵאלֹהֵינוּ מְרַחֵם:
שֹׁמֵר פְּתָאִים יהוה, דַּלּוֹתִי וְלִי יְהוֹשִׁיעַ:
שׁוּבִי נַפְשִׁי לִמְנוּחָיְכִי, כִּי־יהוה גָּמַל עָלָיְכִי:
כִּי חִלַּצְתָּ נַפְשִׁי מִמָּוֶת, אֶת־עֵינִי מִן־דִּמְעָה, אֶת־רַגְלִי מִדֶּחִי:
אֶתְהַלֵּךְ לִפְנֵי יהוה, בְּאַרְצוֹת הַחַיִּים:
הֶאֱמַנְתִּי כִּי אֲדַבֵּר, אֲנִי עָנִיתִי מְאֹד:
אֲנִי אָמַרְתִּי בְחָפְזִי, כָּל־הָאָדָם כֹּזֵב:

תהלים קטז
מָה־אָשִׁיב לַיהוה, כָּל־תַּגְמוּלוֹהִי עָלָי:
לְךָ־אֶזְבַּח זֶבַח תּוֹדָה, וּבְשֵׁם יהוה אֶקְרָא:
נְדָרַי לַיהוה אֲשַׁלֵּם, נֶגְדָה־נָּא לְכָל־עַמּוֹ:
בְּחַצְרוֹת בֵּית יהוה, בְּתוֹכֵכִי יְרוּשָׁלָםִ, הַלְלוּיָהּ:

THANKSGIVING PRAYER AFTER CHILDBIRTH

In Temple times, mothers would offer a sacrifice after the birth of a child (Lev. 12:6–8). No record exists of a formal prayer offered on such occasions: there may have been no fixed text. Hannah's prayer after the birth of Samuel (1 Sam. 2:1–10) is, however, a powerful example of such a song of thanksgiving. The

The mother says:

בָּרוּךְ Blessed are You, LORD our God, King of the Universe,
who bestows good things on the unworthy,
who has bestowed on me much good.

All respond:

אָמֵן Amen. May He who bestowed much good on you,
continue to bestow on you much good. Selah.

אָנָּא O great, mighty and revered God. By Your great love I now come into Your House, to offer You a thanksgiving-offering for all the good You have bestowed on me. Travail beset me, pains seized me. In my distress I cried to You, and from Your habitation You heard my voice and helped me. You healed all my sickness, and crowned me with kindness and compassion. Until now Your mercy has helped me. I pray to You, God, never forsake me. Bestow Your blessing upon Your handmaid. Strengthen and support me together with my husband, that we may raise

For a boy:

הַיֶּלֶד the boy that has been born to us, to revere You and serve You in truth, and to walk in the path of righteousness. Protect our tender child in all his ways. Favor him with knowledge, understanding and discernment, and let his portion be in Your Torah, so that he may sanctify Your great name, and become a comfort to us as we grow old. As for me, may my prayer come to You, LORD, at a time of favor. *Ps. 69*
O God, in Your great love, answer me with Your faithful salvation.

For a girl:

הַיַּלְדָּה the girl that has been born to us, to revere You and serve You in truth, and to walk in the path of righteousness. Protect our tender child in all her ways. Favor her with knowledge, understanding and discernment, and let her portion be in Your Torah, so that she may sanctify Your great name, and become a comfort to us as we grow old. As for me, may my prayer come to You, LORD, at a time of favor. *Ps. 69*
O God, in Your great love, answer me with Your faithful salvation.

If the baby is brought to the synagogue, the Rabbi says the following blessings over him/her:

יְבָרֶכְךָ May the LORD bless you and protect you. *Num. 6*
May the LORD make His face shine on you and be gracious to you.
May the LORD turn His face toward you and grant you peace.

The mother says:

בָּרוּךְ אַתָּה יהוה אֱלֹהֵינוּ מֶלֶךְ הָעוֹלָם
הַגּוֹמֵל לְחַיָּבִים טוֹבוֹת, שֶׁגְּמָלַנִי כָּל טוֹב.

All respond:

אָמֵן. מִי שֶׁגְּמָלֵךְ כָּל טוֹב, הוּא יִגְמְלֵךְ כָּל טוֹב, סֶלָה.

אָנָּא הָאֵל הַגָּדוֹל הַגִּבּוֹר וְהַנּוֹרָא, בְּרֹב חַסְדְּךָ אָבוֹא בֵיתֶךָ, לִזְבֹּחַ לְךָ זֶבַח תּוֹדָה עַל כָּל הַטּוֹבוֹת אֲשֶׁר גָּמַלְתָּ עָלָי. אֲפָפוּנִי חֲבָלִים וְצִירִים אֲחָזוּנִי, בַּצַּר לִי קָרָאתִי אֵלֶיךָ, וְשָׁמַעְתָּ מֵהֵיכָלְךָ קוֹלִי וְהָיִיתָ בְּעֶזְרִי, רוֹפֵא לְכָל תַּחֲלוּאַי, עִטַּרְתַּנִי חֶסֶד וְרַחֲמִים, עַד הֵנָּה עֲזָרוּנִי רַחֲמֶיךָ, אָנָּא אַל תִּטְּשֵׁנִי לָנֶצַח. הוֹאֵל אֱלוֹהַּ, וּבָרֵךְ אֶת אֲמָתֶךָ, חַזְּקֵנִי וְאַמְּצֵנִי, אוֹתִי וְאֶת בַּעְלִי, וּנְגַדֵּל אֶת

For a boy:

הַיֶּלֶד אֲשֶׁר יֻלַּד לָנוּ, לְיִרְאָתְךָ וּלְעָבְדְךָ בֶּאֱמֶת, וְלָלֶכֶת אֹרַח מֵישָׁרִים. שְׁמֹר אֶת הַיֶּלֶד הָרַךְ בְּכָל דְּרָכָיו, חָנֵּהוּ דֵּעָה בִּינָה וְהַשְׂכֵּל, וְתֵן חֶלְקוֹ בְּתוֹרָתֶךָ, וִיקַדֵּשׁ אֶת שִׁמְךָ הַגָּדוֹל, וְהָיָה לָנוּ לְמֵשִׁיב נֶפֶשׁ בִּימֵי שֵׂיבָתֵנוּ. וַאֲנִי תְפִלָּתִי־לְךָ יהוה עֵת רָצוֹן, תהלים סט
אֱלֹהִים בְּרָב־חַסְדֶּךָ, עֲנֵנִי בֶּאֱמֶת יִשְׁעֶךָ:

For a girl:

הַיַּלְדָּה אֲשֶׁר יֻלְּדָה לָנוּ, לְיִרְאָתְךָ וּלְעָבְדְךָ בֶּאֱמֶת, וְלָלֶכֶת אֹרַח מֵישָׁרִים. שְׁמֹר אֶת הַיַּלְדָּה הָרַכָּה בְּכָל דְּרָכֶיהָ, חָנֶּהָ דֵּעָה בִּינָה וְהַשְׂכֵּל, וְתֵן חֶלְקָהּ בְּתוֹרָתֶךָ, וּתְקַדֵּשׁ אֶת שִׁמְךָ הַגָּדוֹל, וְהָיְתָה לָנוּ לִמְשִׁיבַת נֶפֶשׁ בִּימֵי שֵׂיבָתֵנוּ. וַאֲנִי תְפִלָּתִי־לְךָ יהוה עֵת רָצוֹן, תהלים סט
אֱלֹהִים בְּרָב־חַסְדֶּךָ, עֲנֵנִי בֶּאֱמֶת יִשְׁעֶךָ:

If the baby is brought to the בית כנסת*, the Rabbi says the following blessings over him/her:*

יְבָרֶכְךָ יהוה וְיִשְׁמְרֶךָ: יָאֵר יהוה פָּנָיו אֵלֶיךָ וִיחֻנֶּךָּ: במדבר ו
יִשָּׂא יהוה פָּנָיו אֵלֶיךָ, וְיָשֵׂם לְךָ שָׁלוֹם:

ZEVED HABAT

The mother or father says:

יוֹנָתִי My dove in the clefts of the rock, *Song. 2*
in the hiding places of the mountain side,
show me your face, let me hear your voice;
for your voice is sweet, and your face is lovely.

If this is their first daughter, they add:

אַחַת There is one alone, my dove, my perfect one, *Song. 6*
her mother's only child,
the favorite of the one who bore her.
Maidens see her and called her blessed;
queens and concubines praise her.

The Rabbi says:

מִי שֶׁבֵּרַךְ He who blessed our ancestors,
Abraham, Isaac and Jacob, Moses and Aaron, David and Solomon,
Sarah, Rebecca, Rachel and Leah –
may He bless (*mother's name* daughter of *her mother's name*),
who has given birth.

If the baby has already been named in the synagogue:
and her newborn daughter, (*baby's name* daughter of *father's name*),
born in favor.

If the baby has not been named in the synagogue:
and her newborn daughter, born in favor, whose name in Israel
shall be called (*baby's name* daughter of *father's name*).

Bless, we pray to You, her parents
that they may have the merit to raise her to the Torah,
to the marriage canopy and to good deeds; and let us say: Amen.

---

her life. If food is served at the ceremony, the meal has religious significance (*seudat mitzva*), and should be accompanied by words of Torah.

יוֹנָתִי *My dove in the clefts of the rock:* Song of Songs 2:14. אַחַת הִיא *There is one alone:* Song of Songs 6:9.

סדר זבד הבת

The mother or father says:

שיר השירים ב

יוֹנָתִי בְּחַגְוֵי הַסֶּלַע, בְּסֵתֶר הַמַּדְרֵגָה
הַרְאִינִי אֶת־מַרְאַיִךְ, הַשְׁמִיעִנִי אֶת־קוֹלֵךְ
כִּי־קוֹלֵךְ עָרֵב וּמַרְאֵיךְ נָאוֶה:

If this is their first daughter, they add:

שיר השירים ו

אַחַת הִיא יוֹנָתִי תַמָּתִי
אַחַת הִיא לְאִמָּהּ, בָּרָה הִיא לְיוֹלַדְתָּהּ
רָאוּהָ בָנוֹת וַיְאַשְּׁרוּהָ, מְלָכוֹת וּפִילַגְשִׁים וַיְהַלְלוּהָ:

The Rabbi says:

מִי שֶׁבֵּרַךְ אֲבוֹתֵינוּ אַבְרָהָם יִצְחָק וְיַעֲקֹב
מֹשֶׁה וְאַהֲרֹן דָּוִד וּשְׁלֹמֹה, שָׂרָה רִבְקָה רָחֵל וְלֵאָה
הוּא יְבָרֵךְ אֶת הָאִשָּׁה הַיּוֹלֶדֶת (פלונית בַּת פלונית)

If the baby has already been named in the בית כנסת*:*

וְאֶת בִּתָּהּ (פלונית בַּת פלוני) שֶׁנּוֹלְדָה לָהּ בְּמַזָּל טוֹב.

If the baby has not been named in the בית כנסת*:*

וְאֶת בִּתָּהּ שֶׁנּוֹלְדָה לָהּ בְּמַזָּל טוֹב
וְיִקָּרֵא שְׁמָהּ בְּיִשְׂרָאֵל (פלונית בַּת פלוני).

אָנָּא בָּרֵךְ אֶת אָבִיהָ וְאֶת אִמָּהּ
וְיִזְכּוּ לְגַדְּלָהּ לְתוֹרָה וּלְחֻפָּה וּלְמַעֲשִׂים טוֹבִים, וְנֹאמַר אָמֵן.

ZEVED HABAT

There has long been a custom among Sephardim – increasingly adopted by Ashkenazim – to mark the birth of a daughter with a special ceremony known as *Zeved HaBat* ("the gift of a daughter"), during which the baby is named and blessed. We give expression to our thanks to God for the miracle of a new life, and pray that His blessings should accompany her through the course of

The parents bless the child:

יְשִׂמֵךְ May God make you like Sarah, Rebecca, Rachel and Leah.
May the Lord bless you and protect you. *Num. 6*
May the Lord make His face shine on you and be gracious to you.
May the Lord turn His face toward you and grant you peace.

וִיהִי רָצוֹן May it be the will of our Father in heaven,
that He set in your heart the love and awe of Him all your days,
so that you do not come to sin.
May your desire be for the Torah and the commandments.
May your eyes look straight before you;
may your mouth speak wisdom
and your heart meditate in awe;
may your hands be occupied with the commandments
and may your feet run to do the will of your Father in heaven.

If grandparents are present, they say the following blessing:

הָאֱלֹהִים May God before whom my fathers *Gen. 48*
Abraham and Isaac walked –
God who has been my Shepherd all my life to this day,
the angel who has rescued me from all harm –
may He bless the children.
May they be called by my name
and the names of my fathers Abraham and Isaac,
and may they increase greatly on earth.

All say:

Our sister, may you grow to become thousands of myriads. *Gen. 24*

הָאֱלֹהִים אֲשֶׁר הִתְהַלְּכוּ אֲבֹתַי לְפָנָיו *May God before whom my fathers:* the blessing given by Jacob to the children of Joseph (Gen. 48:15–16), the only instance in the Torah of a grandparent blessing grandchildren. אֲחֹתֵנוּ *Our sister:* the blessing given to Rebecca by her family (Gen. 24:60).

The parents bless the child:

יְשִׂמֵךְ אֱלֹהִים כְּשָׂרָה רִבְקָה רָחֵל וְלֵאָה.

במדבר ו יְבָרֶכְךָ יהוה וְיִשְׁמְרֶךָ:
יָאֵר יהוה פָּנָיו אֵלֶיךָ וִיחֻנֶּךָּ:
יִשָּׂא יהוה פָּנָיו אֵלֶיךָ, וְיָשֵׂם לְךָ שָׁלוֹם:

וִיהִי רָצוֹן מִלִּפְנֵי אָבִינוּ שֶׁבַּשָּׁמַיִם, שֶׁיִּתֵּן בְּלִבֵּךְ אַהֲבָתוֹ וְיִרְאָתוֹ
וְתִהְיֶה יִרְאַת יהוה עַל פָּנַיִךְ כָּל יָמַיִךְ שֶׁלֹּא תֶחֱטָאִי
וִיהִי חֶשְׁקֵךְ בַּתּוֹרָה וּבַמִּצְוֹת.
עֵינַיִךְ לְנֹכַח יַבִּיטוּ, פִּיךְ יְדַבֵּר חָכְמוֹת וְלִבֵּךְ יֶהְגֶּה אֵימוֹת
יָדַיִךְ יַעַסְקוּ בְּמִצְוֹת
וְרַגְלַיִךְ יָרוּצוּ לַעֲשׂוֹת רְצוֹן אָבִיךְ שֶׁבַּשָּׁמַיִם.

If grandparents are present, they say the following blessing:

בראשית מח הָאֱלֹהִים אֲשֶׁר הִתְהַלְּכוּ אֲבֹתַי לְפָנָיו, אַבְרָהָם וְיִצְחָק
הָאֱלֹהִים הָרֹעֶה אֹתִי, מֵעוֹדִי עַד־הַיּוֹם הַזֶּה:
הַמַּלְאָךְ הַגֹּאֵל אֹתִי מִכָּל־רָע, יְבָרֵךְ אֶת־הַנְּעָרִים
וְיִקָּרֵא בָהֶם שְׁמִי, וְשֵׁם אֲבֹתַי אַבְרָהָם וְיִצְחָק
וְיִדְגּוּ לָרֹב בְּקֶרֶב הָאָרֶץ:

All say:

בראשית כד אֲחֹתֵנוּ, אַתְּ הֲיִי לְאַלְפֵי רְבָבָה:

יְשִׂמֵךְ *May God make you like:* the traditional blessing given by parents to daughters. יְבָרֶכְךָ יהוה *May the Lord bless you:* the Priestly Blessing (Num. 6:24–26).

וִיהִי רָצוֹן *May it be the will:* Taken from a traditional blessing given by parents to children on the eve of Yom Kippur.

MARRIAGE SERVICE

BLESSINGS OF BETROTHAL

The Rabbi performing the ceremony takes a cup of wine and says:

בָּרוּךְ Blessed are You, LORD our God, King of the Universe, who creates the fruit of the vine.

בָּרוּךְ Blessed are You, LORD our God, King of the Universe, who has made us holy through His commandments, and has commanded us concerning forbidden unions, forbidding us those who are betrothed, permitting us those who are wedded to us through the rite of the canopy and sacred covenant of marriage. Blessed are You, LORD, who sanctifies His people Israel by the rite of the canopy and sacred covenant of marriage.

The bride and bridegroom both drink from the wine. The bridegroom takes the ring and, holding it ready to be placed on the forefinger of the bride's right hand, says:

הֲרֵי Behold you are consecrated to me by this ring
in accordance with the law of Moses and of Israel.

He then places the ring on the forefinger of the bride's right hand. The Ketuba is read and the bridegroom hands it to the bride. A second cup of wine is taken, and over it, the Sheva Berakhot on the next page are said; the same person should preferably say the first two.

---

blessings said over a cup of wine, and nowadays they are separated by the reading of the marriage contract (*Ketuba*). The betrothal blessing spells out the fact that both ceremonies must be observed for the marriage to be complete.

הֲרֵי אַתְּ מְקֻדֶּשֶׁת לִי *Behold you are consecrated to me:* The declaration accompanying the giving of the ring by the groom to the bride. The use of the word "consecration" in the context of marriage signals the sacred nature of the bond between the partners. כְּדַת מֹשֶׁה וְיִשְׂרָאֵל *The law of Moses and of Israel:* the bridegroom undertakes to honor his obligations according to both biblical (Moses) and rabbinic (Israel) law.

THE MARRIAGE CONTRACT

Read in its original Aramaic, it spells out the duty of a Jewish husband to his wife, to "work for, honor, support and maintain" her, and to meet all financial obligations arising out of the marriage. The *Ketuba* dates back more than two thousand years, and was intended to secure the bride's legal rights within the marriage. It is made binding by the bridegroom raising an object, usually a handkerchief, in the presence of two witnesses. These witnesses sign the document, which is also usually signed by the bridegroom.

סדר קידושין ונישואין

ברכות האירוסין

The מסדר קידושין *takes a cup of wine and says:*

בָּרוּךְ אַתָּה יהוה אֱלֹהֵינוּ מֶלֶךְ הָעוֹלָם, בּוֹרֵא פְּרִי הַגָּפֶן.

בָּרוּךְ אַתָּה יהוה אֱלֹהֵינוּ מֶלֶךְ הָעוֹלָם, אֲשֶׁר קִדְּשָׁנוּ בְּמִצְוֹתָיו וְצִוָּנוּ עַל הָעֲרָיוֹת, וְאָסַר לָנוּ אֶת הָאֲרוּסוֹת, וְהִתִּיר לָנוּ אֶת הַנְּשׂוּאוֹת לָנוּ עַל יְדֵי חֻפָּה וְקִדּוּשִׁין. בָּרוּךְ אַתָּה יהוה, מְקַדֵּשׁ עַמּוֹ יִשְׂרָאֵל עַל יְדֵי חֻפָּה וְקִדּוּשִׁין.

The חתן *and* כלה *both drink from the wine. The* חתן *takes the ring and, holding it ready to be placed on the forefinger of the* כלה*'s right hand, says:*

הֲרֵי אַתְּ מְקֻדֶּשֶׁת לִי בְּטַבַּעַת זוּ כְּדַת מֹשֶׁה וְיִשְׂרָאֵל.

He then places the ring on the forefinger of the כלה*'s right hand. The* כתובה *is read and the* חתן *hands it to the* כלה*. A second cup of wine is taken, and over it, the* שבע ברכות *on the next page are said; the same person should preferably say the first two.*

MARRIAGE SERVICE

"The Lord God said: It is not good for man to be alone, I will make a partner suited to him ... That is why a man leaves his father and mother and attaches himself to his wife, and they become one flesh" (Gen. 2:18, 2:24). Marriage is one of the supreme institutions of Judaism, the first mentioned in the Bible, and the one spoken of by the prophets in their deepest moments as the most compelling metaphor for God's relationship with His people. In marriage, the bridegroom and bride pledge themselves to one another in a bond of loyalty and love, each respecting the integrity of the other while joining their destinies to achieve together what neither could achieve alone. The very word *ḥayyim*, "life," in Hebrew is plural, as if to suggest that life, at its fullest, is to be shared. Marriage is the moralization of passion, love translated into a covenant of mutual responsibility through which, by sharing our vulnerabilities, we redeem our solitude and discover strength.

בָּרוּךְ *Blessed are You:* Marriage originally took the form of two distinct moments. The first, *Erusin* or *Kiddushin*, "betrothal," joined the couple in a mutual pledge. Bride and groom then returned to their respective families. A year or so later, the bride would be brought under the bridal canopy to the groom and they would begin their life together. This was called *Nissu'in*, and was accompanied by its own blessings. During the upheavals of Jewish life in the early Middle Ages, the two ceremonies were brought together. Each involves

THE SEVEN BLESSINGS OF MARRIAGE

בָּרוּךְ Blessed are You, Lord our God, King of the Universe,
who creates the fruit of the vine.

בָּרוּךְ Blessed are You, Lord our God, King of the Universe,
who has created all for His glory.

בָּרוּךְ Blessed are You, Lord our God, King of the Universe,
Creator of mankind.

בָּרוּךְ Blessed are You, Lord our God, King of the Universe,
who made humanity in His image, the image of His likeness,
and out of His very self formed a building for eternity.
Blessed are You, Lord, Creator of mankind.

שׂוֹשׂ Bring great happiness and joy to one who was barren [Zion],
as her children return to her in joy.
Blessed are You, Lord, who gladdens Zion through her children.

שַׂמֵּחַ Bring great joy to these loving friends,
as You gave joy to Your creations in the Garden of Eden.
Blessed are You, Lord, who gives joy to the bridegroom and bride.

בָּרוּךְ Blessed are You, Lord our God, King of the Universe,
who created joy and gladness, bridegroom and bride,
happiness and jubilation, cheer and delight,
love, fellowship, peace and friendship.
Soon, Lord our God, may there be heard in the cities of Judah,
and in the streets of Jerusalem, the sounds of joy and gladness,
the sounds of the bridegroom and bride,
the joyous sounds of bridegrooms from their wedding canopy and
of young people at their feasts of song.
Blessed are You, Lord,
who makes the bridegroom rejoice with the bride.

---

become "a building for eternity" through their descendants. The fifth movingly speaks about the Jewish people (Zion) as a whole, renewed through this marriage of her children. The sixth prays that the bride and groom should find joy together and bring joy to God. The seventh and longest brings all of these themes together, invoking the words of the prophet Jeremiah (33:10–11) that in the future there will be heard "the sounds of joy and gladness, the sounds of bridegroom and bride."

שבע ברכות הנשואין

בָּרוּךְ אַתָּה יהוה אֱלֹהֵינוּ מֶלֶךְ הָעוֹלָם, בּוֹרֵא פְּרִי הַגָּפֶן.

בָּרוּךְ אַתָּה יהוה אֱלֹהֵינוּ מֶלֶךְ הָעוֹלָם, שֶׁהַכֹּל בָּרָא לִכְבוֹדוֹ.

בָּרוּךְ אַתָּה יהוה אֱלֹהֵינוּ מֶלֶךְ הָעוֹלָם, יוֹצֵר הָאָדָם.

בָּרוּךְ אַתָּה יהוה אֱלֹהֵינוּ מֶלֶךְ הָעוֹלָם
אֲשֶׁר יָצַר אֶת הָאָדָם בְּצַלְמוֹ, בְּצֶלֶם דְּמוּת תַּבְנִיתוֹ
וְהִתְקִין לוֹ מִמֶּנּוּ בִּנְיַן עֲדֵי עַד.
בָּרוּךְ אַתָּה יהוה, יוֹצֵר הָאָדָם.

שׂוֹשׂ תָּשִׂישׂ וְתָגֵל הָעֲקָרָה בְּקִבּוּץ בָּנֶיהָ לְתוֹכָהּ בְּשִׂמְחָה.
בָּרוּךְ אַתָּה יהוה, מְשַׂמֵּחַ צִיּוֹן בְּבָנֶיהָ.

שַׂמֵּחַ תְּשַׂמַּח רֵעִים הָאֲהוּבִים כְּשַׂמֵּחֲךָ יְצִירְךָ בְּגַן עֵדֶן מִקֶּדֶם.
בָּרוּךְ אַתָּה יהוה, מְשַׂמֵּחַ חָתָן וְכַלָּה.

בָּרוּךְ אַתָּה יהוה אֱלֹהֵינוּ מֶלֶךְ הָעוֹלָם
אֲשֶׁר בָּרָא שָׂשׂוֹן וְשִׂמְחָה, חָתָן וְכַלָּה
גִּילָה, רִנָּה, דִּיצָה וְחֶדְוָה, אַהֲבָה וְאַחֲוָה וְשָׁלוֹם וְרֵעוּת.
מְהֵרָה יהוה אֱלֹהֵינוּ
יִשָּׁמַע בְּעָרֵי יְהוּדָה וּבְחוּצוֹת יְרוּשָׁלַיִם
קוֹל שָׂשׂוֹן וְקוֹל שִׂמְחָה, קוֹל חָתָן וְקוֹל כַּלָּה
קוֹל מִצְהֲלוֹת חֲתָנִים מֵחֻפָּתָם וּנְעָרִים מִמִּשְׁתֵּה נְגִינָתָם.
בָּרוּךְ אַתָּה יהוה, מְשַׂמֵּחַ הֶחָתָן עִם הַכַּלָּה.

SHEVA BERAKHOT / THE SEVEN BLESSINGS

These blessings, accompanying the second stage of the marriage, date back to early rabbinic times. After the blessing over wine, the remaining six benedictions move sequentially from the universal to the particular. The second praises God as Creator of all. The third speaks of His creation of man. The fourth alludes to the second chapter of Genesis in which God, seeing that the man was alone, formed "out of His very self" a partner so that they could

The bride and bridegroom both drink from the wine.
The bridegroom breaks a glass in memory of the destruction of the Temple. Some say the following beforehand:

אִם־אֶשְׁכָּחֵךְ If I forget you, O Jerusalem, may my right hand forget its skill. *Ps. 137*
May my tongue cling to the roof of my mouth if I do not remember you,
if I do not set Jerusalem above my highest joy.

ZIMMUN AFTER A WEDDING OR SHEVA BERAKHOT FEAST

The leader takes a cup of wine in his hand and says:

Leader Gentlemen, let us say grace.

Others May the name of the Lord be blessed from now and for ever. *Ps. 113*

Leader May the name of the Lord be blessed from now and for ever.

Banish grief and anger. Let even the mute celebrate in song.
Guide us in the paths of righteousness.
Hear the blessing of the children of Aaron.

Add the appropriate words in parentheses (see page 976):

With your permission, (my father and teacher / my mother and teacher / the Kohanim present / our teacher the Rabbi / the master of this house / the mistress of this house) my masters and teachers, let us bless our God, in whose dwelling place is joy, from whose food we have eaten.

Others Blessed be our God in whose dwelling place is joy,
from whose food we have eaten, and by whose goodness we live.

Leader Blessed be our God in whose dwelling place is joy,
from whose food we have eaten, and by whose goodness we live.
Blessed be He, and blessed be His name.

Continue with Birkat HaMazon on page 978, at the end of which say the Sheva Berakhot (on previous page) over a cup of wine, beginning with the second blessing, "who has created all," and ending with the first blessing, that over the wine.

GRACE AFTER THE WEDDING FEAST

The special invocation, with its phrase "in whose dwelling place is joy," is mentioned in the Talmud (*Ketubot* 8a). דְּוַי הָסֵר וְגַם חָרוֹן *Banish grief and anger:* a poem written by the tenth-century linguist and poet, Dunash ben Labrat. The initial letters of the four phrases spell out his name.

The חתן *and* כלה *both drink from the wine.*
The חתן *breaks a glass in memory of the destruction of the* בית המקדש*. Some say the following beforehand:*

אִם־אֶשְׁכָּחֵךְ יְרוּשָׁלָםִ, תִּשְׁכַּח יְמִינִי: תִּדְבַּק לְשׁוֹנִי לְחִכִּי אִם־לֹא אֶזְכְּרֵכִי, תהלים קלז
אִם־לֹא אַעֲלֶה אֶת־יְרוּשָׁלַםִ עַל רֹאשׁ שִׂמְחָתִי:

זימון לסעודת שבע ברכות

The leader takes a cup of wine in his hand and says:

Leader רַבּוֹתַי, נְבָרֵךְ.

Others יְהִי שֵׁם יהוה מְבֹרָךְ מֵעַתָּה וְעַד־עוֹלָם: תהלים קיג

Leader יְהִי שֵׁם יהוה מְבֹרָךְ מֵעַתָּה וְעַד־עוֹלָם:

דְּוַי הָסֵר וְגַם חָרוֹן　　וְאָז אִלֵּם בְּשִׁיר יָרֹן.
נְחֵנוּ בְּמַעְגְּלֵי צֶדֶק　　שְׁעֵה בִּרְכַּת בְּנֵי אַהֲרֹן.

Add the appropriate words in parentheses (see page 977):

בִּרְשׁוּת (אָבִי מוֹרִי / אִמִּי מוֹרָתִי / כֹּהֲנִים / מוֹרֵנוּ הָרַב /
בַּעַל הַבַּיִת הַזֶּה / בַּעֲלַת הַבַּיִת הַזֶּה) מָרָנָן וְרַבָּנָן וְרַבּוֹתַי
נְבָרֵךְ אֱלֹהֵינוּ שֶׁהַשִּׂמְחָה בִּמְעוֹנוֹ וְשֶׁאָכַלְנוּ מִשֶּׁלּוֹ.

Others בָּרוּךְ אֱלֹהֵינוּ שֶׁהַשִּׂמְחָה בִּמְעוֹנוֹ, שֶׁאָכַלְנוּ מִשֶּׁלּוֹ וּבְטוּבוֹ חָיִינוּ.

Leader בָּרוּךְ אֱלֹהֵינוּ שֶׁהַשִּׂמְחָה בִּמְעוֹנוֹ, שֶׁאָכַלְנוּ מִשֶּׁלּוֹ וּבְטוּבוֹ חָיִינוּ.
בָּרוּךְ הוּא וּבָרוּךְ שְׁמוֹ.

Continue with ברכת המזון *on page 979, at the end of which say the* שבע ברכות *(on previous page) over a cup of wine, beginning with the second blessing,* שֶׁהַכֹּל בָּרָא לִכְבוֹדוֹ*, and ending with the first blessing,* בּוֹרֵא פְּרִי הַגָּפֶן.

BREAKING THE GLASS

An ancient custom, reminding us that while the Temple remains unbuilt, our joy cannot be complete. It has become a custom to preface this by reciting the verse from Psalm 137, "If I forget you, O Jerusalem," said by the exiles in Babylon after the destruction of the First Temple.

PRAYER FOR RECOVERY FROM ILLNESS

מִזְמוֹר לְדָוִד A psalm of David. The LORD is my Shepherd, I shall not want. He makes me lie down in green pastures. He leads me beside the still waters. He refreshes my soul. He guides me in the paths of righteousness for His name's sake. Though I walk through the valley of the shadow of death, I will fear no evil, for You are with me; Your rod and Your staff, they comfort me. You set a table before me in the presence of my enemies; You anoint my head with oil; my cup is filled to overflowing. May goodness and kindness follow me all the days of my life, and may I live in the House of the LORD for evermore. *Ps. 23*

לְדָוִד By David. Bless the LORD, my soul; with all my being I bless His holy name. Bless the LORD, my soul, and forget none of His benefits. He forgives all your sins. He heals all your ills. He redeems your life from the pit. He crowns you with love and compassion. He satisfies your soul with good things, so that your youth is renewed like the eagle's. The LORD is righteous in all He does; He brings justice to all the oppressed. He made known His ways to Moses, His deeds to the people of Israel. The LORD is compassionate and gracious, slow to anger, abounding in love. He will not always accuse or nurse His anger for ever. He has not treated us as our sins deserve, or repaid us according to our misdeeds. For as high as the heavens are above the earth, so great is His love for those who fear Him. As far as the east is from the west, so far has He removed our transgressions from us. As a father has compassion on his children, so the LORD has compassion on those who fear Him. For He knows how we are formed; He remembers that we are dust. As for man, his days are like grass; like a flower of the field he flourishes. For a wind passes over it and it is gone, and its place knows it no more. But the kindness of the LORD is for all eternity to those who fear Him; His righteousness is with their children's children – with those who keep His covenant, and remember to obey His precepts. The LORD has established His throne in heaven, and His kingdom rules over all. Bless the LORD, you His angels, mighty in power, who do His bidding, who obey His word. Bless the LORD, all you His host, the ministers who do His will. Bless the LORD, all His works, everywhere in His dominion. Bless the LORD, my soul. *Ps. 103*

לַמְנַצֵּחַ For the conductor of music. A psalm of David. O LORD, You have examined me and You know me. You know when I sit and when I rise; You understand my thoughts from afar. You encompass my going out and lying down. You are familiar with all my ways. Before a word is on my tongue, You, LORD, know it all. You keep close guard behind and before me. You have laid Your hand upon me. Knowledge so wonderful is beyond me; so high, it is *Ps. 139*

תפילה לחולה

תהלים כג

מִזְמוֹר לְדָוִד, יהוה רֹעִי לֹא אֶחְסָר: בִּנְאוֹת דֶּשֶׁא יַרְבִּיצֵנִי, עַל־מֵי מְנֻחוֹת יְנַהֲלֵנִי: נַפְשִׁי יְשׁוֹבֵב, יַנְחֵנִי בְמַעְגְּלֵי־צֶדֶק לְמַעַן שְׁמוֹ: גַּם כִּי־אֵלֵךְ בְּגֵיא צַלְמָוֶת לֹא־אִירָא רָע, כִּי־אַתָּה עִמָּדִי, שִׁבְטְךָ וּמִשְׁעַנְתֶּךָ הֵמָּה יְנַחֲמֻנִי: תַּעֲרֹךְ לְפָנַי שֻׁלְחָן נֶגֶד צֹרְרָי, דִּשַּׁנְתָּ בַשֶּׁמֶן רֹאשִׁי, כּוֹסִי רְוָיָה: אַךְ טוֹב וָחֶסֶד יִרְדְּפוּנִי כָּל־יְמֵי חַיָּי, וְשַׁבְתִּי בְּבֵית־יהוה לְאֹרֶךְ יָמִים:

תהלים קג

לְדָוִד, בָּרְכִי נַפְשִׁי אֶת־יהוה, וְכָל־קְרָבַי אֶת־שֵׁם קָדְשׁוֹ: בָּרְכִי נַפְשִׁי אֶת־יהוה, וְאַל־תִּשְׁכְּחִי כָּל־גְּמוּלָיו: הַסֹּלֵחַ לְכָל־עֲוֺנֵכִי, הָרֹפֵא לְכָל־תַּחֲלוּאָיְכִי: הַגּוֹאֵל מִשַּׁחַת חַיָּיְכִי, הַמְעַטְּרֵכִי חֶסֶד וְרַחֲמִים: הַמַּשְׂבִּיעַ בַּטּוֹב עֶדְיֵךְ, תִּתְחַדֵּשׁ כַּנֶּשֶׁר נְעוּרָיְכִי: עֹשֵׂה צְדָקוֹת יהוה, וּמִשְׁפָּטִים לְכָל־עֲשׁוּקִים: יוֹדִיעַ דְּרָכָיו לְמֹשֶׁה, לִבְנֵי יִשְׂרָאֵל עֲלִילוֹתָיו: רַחוּם וְחַנּוּן יהוה, אֶרֶךְ אַפַּיִם וְרַב־חָסֶד: לֹא־לָנֶצַח יָרִיב, וְלֹא לְעוֹלָם יִטּוֹר: לֹא כַחֲטָאֵינוּ עָשָׂה לָנוּ, וְלֹא כַעֲוֺנֹתֵינוּ גָּמַל עָלֵינוּ: כִּי כִגְבֹהַּ שָׁמַיִם עַל־הָאָרֶץ, גָּבַר חַסְדּוֹ עַל־יְרֵאָיו: כִּרְחֹק מִזְרָח מִמַּעֲרָב, הִרְחִיק מִמֶּנּוּ אֶת־פְּשָׁעֵינוּ: כְּרַחֵם אָב עַל־בָּנִים, רִחַם יהוה עַל־יְרֵאָיו: כִּי־הוּא יָדַע יִצְרֵנוּ, זָכוּר כִּי־עָפָר אֲנָחְנוּ: אֱנוֹשׁ כֶּחָצִיר יָמָיו, כְּצִיץ הַשָּׂדֶה כֵּן יָצִיץ: כִּי רוּחַ עָבְרָה־בּוֹ וְאֵינֶנּוּ, וְלֹא־יַכִּירֶנּוּ עוֹד מְקוֹמוֹ: וְחֶסֶד יהוה מֵעוֹלָם וְעַד־עוֹלָם עַל־יְרֵאָיו, וְצִדְקָתוֹ לִבְנֵי בָנִים: לְשֹׁמְרֵי בְרִיתוֹ, וּלְזֹכְרֵי פִקֻּדָיו לַעֲשׂוֹתָם: יהוה בַּשָּׁמַיִם הֵכִין כִּסְאוֹ, וּמַלְכוּתוֹ בַּכֹּל מָשָׁלָה: בָּרְכוּ יהוה מַלְאָכָיו, גִּבֹּרֵי כֹחַ עֹשֵׂי דְבָרוֹ, לִשְׁמֹעַ בְּקוֹל דְּבָרוֹ: בָּרְכוּ יהוה כָּל־צְבָאָיו, מְשָׁרְתָיו עֹשֵׂי רְצוֹנוֹ: בָּרְכוּ יהוה כָּל־מַעֲשָׂיו, בְּכָל־מְקֹמוֹת מֶמְשַׁלְתּוֹ, בָּרְכִי נַפְשִׁי אֶת־יהוה:

תהלים קלט

לַמְנַצֵּחַ לְדָוִד מִזְמוֹר, יהוה חֲקַרְתַּנִי וַתֵּדָע: אַתָּה יָדַעְתָּ שִׁבְתִּי וְקוּמִי, בַּנְתָּה לְרֵעִי מֵרָחוֹק: אָרְחִי וְרִבְעִי זֵרִיתָ, וְכָל־דְּרָכַי הִסְכַּנְתָּה: כִּי אֵין מִלָּה בִּלְשׁוֹנִי, הֵן יהוה יָדַעְתָּ כֻלָּהּ: אָחוֹר וָקֶדֶם צַרְתָּנִי, וַתָּשֶׁת עָלַי כַּפֶּכָה: פְּלִיאָה דַעַת מִמֶּנִּי, נִשְׂגְּבָה לֹא־אוּכַל לָהּ: אָנָה אֵלֵךְ מֵרוּחֶךָ, וְאָנָה מִפָּנֶיךָ אֶבְרָח: אִם־אֶסַּק שָׁמַיִם שָׁם אָתָּה, וְאַצִּיעָה שְּׁאוֹל הִנֶּךָּ: אֶשָּׂא כַנְפֵי־שָׁחַר, אֶשְׁכְּנָה בְּאַחֲרִית יָם: גַּם־שָׁם יָדְךָ תַנְחֵנִי, וְתֹאחֲזֵנִי יְמִינֶךָ:

above my reach. Where can I escape from Your spirit? Where can I flee from Your presence? If I climb to heaven, You are there; if I make my bed in the underworld, You are there. If I rise on the wings of the dawn, if I settle on the far side of the sea, even there Your hand will guide me, Your right hand will hold me fast. Were I to say, "Surely the darkness will hide me, and light become night around me," to You the darkness would not be dark; night is light as day; to You dark and light are one. For You created my innermost being; You knitted me together in my mother's womb. I praise You because I am awesomely, wondrously made; wonderful are Your works; I know that full well. My frame was not hidden from You when I was formed in the secret place, woven in the depths of the earth. Your eyes saw my unformed body. All the days ordained for me were written in Your book before one of them came to be. How precious to me are Your thoughts, God, how vast in number they are. Were I to count them, they would outnumber the grains of the sand. I awake and I am still with You. God, if only You would slay the wicked – away from me, you bloodthirsty men. They speak of You with evil intent; Your adversaries misuse Your name. Do I not hate those who hate You, LORD, and loathe those who rise up against You? I have nothing but hatred for them; I count them my enemies. Search me, God, and know my heart; test me and know my innermost thoughts. See if there is grief in the way I follow, and lead me in the everlasting way.

תְּפִלָּה לְעָנִי A prayer of one who is afflicted, when he is faint, and pours out his anguish before the LORD. LORD, hear my prayer and let my cry come before You. Do not hide Your face from me in my day of distress. Turn Your ear toward me; answer me swiftly on the day I call. *Ps. 102*

אָנָּא Please, LORD, Healer of all flesh, have pity on me, and support me on my sick bed, in Your great love, for I am weak. Send relief and healing to me and to the others of Your children who are sick. Heal my pain and renew my youth as the eagle's. Grant wisdom to the physician that he may cure my illness, so that my healing may spring up swiftly. Hear my prayer, prolong my life, and let me complete my years in happiness, so that I may be able to serve You and keep Your precepts with a perfect heart. Grant me the understanding to know that this bitter trial has come upon me for my welfare. Let me not reject Your discipline or spurn Your rebuke.

---

sages consist of three psalms long associated with deliverance from harm, together with two prayers, one for healing, the other for forgiveness, since, our tradition tells us, illness is a time for self-examination and rededication.

וָאֹמַר אַךְ־חֹשֶׁךְ יְשׁוּפֵנִי, וְלַיְלָה אוֹר בַּעֲדֵנִי: גַּם־חֹשֶׁךְ לֹא־יַחְשִׁיךְ מִמֶּךָּ, וְלַיְלָה כַּיּוֹם יָאִיר, כַּחֲשֵׁיכָה כָּאוֹרָה: כִּי־אַתָּה קָנִיתָ כִלְיֹתָי, תְּסֻכֵּנִי בְּבֶטֶן אִמִּי: אוֹדְךָ עַל כִּי נוֹרָאוֹת נִפְלֵיתִי, נִפְלָאִים מַעֲשֶׂיךָ, וְנַפְשִׁי יֹדַעַת מְאֹד: לֹא־נִכְחַד עָצְמִי מִמֶּךָּ, אֲשֶׁר־עֻשֵּׂיתִי בַסֵּתֶר, רֻקַּמְתִּי בְּתַחְתִּיּוֹת אָרֶץ: גָּלְמִי רָאוּ עֵינֶיךָ, וְעַל־סִפְרְךָ כֻּלָּם יִכָּתֵבוּ, יָמִים יֻצָּרוּ, וְלוֹ אֶחָד בָּהֶם: וְלִי מַה־יָּקְרוּ רֵעֶיךָ אֵל, מֶה עָצְמוּ רָאשֵׁיהֶם: אֶסְפְּרֵם מֵחוֹל יִרְבּוּן, הֱקִיצֹתִי וְעוֹדִי עִמָּךְ: אִם־תִּקְטֹל אֱלוֹהַּ רָשָׁע, וְאַנְשֵׁי דָמִים סוּרוּ מֶנִּי: אֲשֶׁר יֹמְרֻךָ לִמְזִמָּה, נָשֻׂא לַשָּׁוְא עָרֶיךָ: הֲלוֹא־מְשַׂנְאֶיךָ יהוה אֶשְׂנָא, וּבִתְקוֹמְמֶיךָ אֶתְקוֹטָט: תַּכְלִית שִׂנְאָה שְׂנֵאתִים, לְאוֹיְבִים הָיוּ לִי: חָקְרֵנִי אֵל וְדַע לְבָבִי, בְּחָנֵנִי וְדַע שַׂרְעַפָּי: וּרְאֵה אִם־דֶּרֶךְ־עֹצֶב בִּי, וּנְחֵנִי בְּדֶרֶךְ עוֹלָם:

תהלים קב תְּפִלָּה לְעָנִי כִי־יַעֲטֹף, וְלִפְנֵי יהוה יִשְׁפֹּךְ שִׂיחוֹ: יהוה שִׁמְעָה תְפִלָּתִי, וְשַׁוְעָתִי אֵלֶיךָ תָבוֹא: אַל־תַּסְתֵּר פָּנֶיךָ מִמֶּנִּי בְּיוֹם צַר לִי, הַטֵּה־אֵלַי אָזְנֶךָ, בְּיוֹם אֶקְרָא מַהֵר עֲנֵנִי:

אָנָּא יהוה רוֹפֵא כָל בָּשָׂר, רַחֵם עָלַי, וְסַעֲדֵנִי בְּחַסְדְּךָ הַגָּדוֹל עַל עֶרֶשׂ דְּוַי, כִּי אֻמְלַל אָנִי. שְׁלַח לִי תְּרוּפָה וּתְעָלָה, בְּתוֹךְ שְׁאָר חוֹלֵי יִשְׂרָאֵל. רְפָא אֶת מַכְאוֹבִי, וְחַדֵּשׁ כַּנֶּשֶׁר נְעוּרָי. תֵּן בִּינָה לָרוֹפֵא, וְיִגְהֶה מִמֶּנִּי מְזוֹרִי, וַאֲרוּכָתִי מְהֵרָה תִצְמַח. שְׁמַע תְּפִלָּתִי, וְהוֹסֵף יָמִים עַל יָמַי, וַאֲכַלֶּה שְׁנוֹתַי בַּנְּעִימִים, לְמַעַן אוּכַל לַעֲבֹד אוֹתְךָ, וְלִשְׁמֹר פִּקּוּדֶיךָ בְּלֵב שָׁלֵם. הֲבִינֵנִי וְאֵדְעָה, כִּי לְשָׁלוֹמִי מַר לִי מָר. וְאַל אֶמְאַס אֶת מוּסָרְךָ, וּבְתוֹכַחְתְּךָ אַל אָקוּץ.

PRAYER FOR RECOVERY FROM ILLNESS

Since the birth of faith, people have turned to God "who heals the broken-hearted and binds up their wounds" for strength and recovery in times of sickness. Many of the psalms are supreme examples of such prayers. There is a deep connection, still not fully understood by medical science, between "healing of the spirit and healing of the body." Prayer, said the sages, is not a substitute for medicine, but neither is medicine a substitute for prayer: both have their part to play in the healing process. Prayer gives strength, as does the knowledge that God is close to all who call on Him in truth. The above pas-

אֱלוֹהַּ סְלִיחוֹת God of forgiveness, gracious and compassionate, slow to anger, abounding in love, I acknowledge before You with a broken and contrite heart that I have sinned and done evil in Your sight. I hereby repent of my evil and turn to You in complete repentance. Help me, God of my salvation, that I may not turn to folly again, but instead walk before You in truth and integrity. Gladden Your servant's heart, for to You, LORD, I lift up my soul. *Ps. 86*
Heal me, LORD, and I will be healed, save me and I will be saved, for You are *Jer. 17*
my glory. Amen and Amen!

THANKSGIVING PRAYER AFTER RECOVERY FROM ILLNESS

Say Psalms 23 and 103 on page 1044. Then continue with:

אָנָּא O great, mighty and awesome God: By Your great love I come before You to offer thanks for all the good You have bestowed on me. In my distress I called to You and You answered me; from my sick bed I cried to You, and You heard my voice and my pleas. You chastened me severely, LORD, but You did not hand me over to death. In Your love and compassion You lifted my soul from the grave. For Your anger is for a moment, Your favor for a lifetime.
At night there may be weeping, but in the morning there is joy. The living, *Is. 38*
only the living, praise You as I do this day. My soul which You have redeemed shall tell of Your wonders to the children of men. Blessed are You, the faithful Healer of all flesh.

אֵל רַחוּם O God, compassionate and gracious, who grants favors to the undeserving: I am not worthy of all the kindness You have shown to me until now. Purify, please, my heart that I may be worthy to walk before You in the way of the upright. Extend Your help to Your servant. Grant me the strength and resolution to overcome my weakness, and bless me with physical health. Keep sorrow and grief far from me; protect me from all harm, and guide me with Your counsel. May the sun of righteousness shine for me, bringing healing in
its wings. May the words of my mouth and the meditation of my heart find *Ps. 19*
favor before You, O LORD, my Rock and my Redeemer. Amen.

---

life-threatening, the *HaGomel* blessing (page 507) should be said on the first occasion one is able to attend the synagogue, either weekday, Shabbat or Festival.

אֱלוֹהַּ סְלִיחוֹת, חַנּוּן וְרַחוּם אֶרֶךְ אַפַּיִם וְרַב חֶסֶד, מוֹדֶה אֲנִי לְפָנֶיךָ בְּלֵב נִשְׁבָּר וְנִדְכֶּה כִּי חָטָאתִי, וְהָרַע בְּעֵינֶיךָ עָשִׂיתִי. הִנֵּה נִחַמְתִּי עַל רָעָתִי, וָאָשׁוּב בִּתְשׁוּבָה שְׁלֵמָה לְפָנֶיךָ. עָזְרֵנִי אֱלֹהֵי יִשְׁעִי, וְלֹא אָשׁוּב לְכִסְלָה,
וְאֶתְהַלֵּךְ לְפָנֶיךָ בֶּאֱמֶת וּבְתָמִים. שַׂמֵּחַ נֶפֶשׁ עַבְדֶּךָ, כִּי־אֵלֶיךָ אֲדֹנָי, תהלים פו
נַפְשִׁי אֶשָּׂא: רְפָאֵנִי יהוה וְאֵרָפֵא, הוֹשִׁיעֵנִי וְאִוָּשֵׁעָה, כִּי תְהִלָּתִי אָתָּה: ירמיה יז
אָמֵן וְאָמֵן.

תפילה לעומד מחליו

Say תהלים כג *and* קג *on page 1045. Then continue with:*

אָנָּא הָאֵל הַגָּדוֹל הַגִּבּוֹר וְהַנּוֹרָא, בְּרֹב חַסְדְּךָ אָבוֹא לְפָנֶיךָ לְהוֹדוֹת לְךָ עַל כָּל הַטּוֹבוֹת אֲשֶׁר גָּמַלְתָּ עָלַי. מִן הַמֵּצַר קְרָאתִיךָ וַתַּעֲנֵנִי, מֵעֶרֶשׂ דְּוַי שִׁוַּעְתִּי אֵלֶיךָ, וַתִּשְׁמַע אֶת קוֹלִי תַּחֲנוּנַי. יַסֹּר יִסְּרַנִּי יָּהּ, וְלַמָּוֶת לֹא נְתָנָנִי. בְּאַהֲבָתְךָ וּבְחֶמְלָתְךָ הֶעֱלִיתָ מִן שְׁאוֹל נַפְשִׁי. כִּי רֶגַע בְּאַפּוֹ,
חַיִּים בִּרְצוֹנוֹ, בָּעֶרֶב יָלִין בֶּכִי וְלַבֹּקֶר רִנָּה. חַי חַי הוּא יוֹדֶךָ, כָּמוֹנִי הַיּוֹם: ישעיה לח
וְנַפְשִׁי אֲשֶׁר פָּדִיתָ, תְּסַפֵּר נִפְלְאוֹתֶיךָ לִבְנֵי אָדָם. בָּרוּךְ אַתָּה, רוֹפֵא נֶאֱמָן לְכָל בָּשָׂר.

אֵל רַחוּם וְחַנּוּן, הַגּוֹמֵל לְחַיָּבִים טוֹבוֹת, קָטֹנְתִּי מִכֹּל הַחֲסָדִים אֲשֶׁר עָשִׂיתָ עִמָּדִי עַד הֵנָּה. אָנָּא טַהֵר לְבָבִי, וְזַכֵּנִי לָלֶכֶת בְּדֶרֶךְ יְשָׁרִים לְפָנֶיךָ, וּמְשֹׁךְ עֶזְרְךָ לְעַבְדֶּךָ. חַזְּקֵנִי וְאַמְּצֵנִי מֵרִפְיוֹן, וּבְחִלּוּץ עֲצָמוֹת תְּבָרְכֵנִי. הַרְחֵק מֵעָלַי כָּל צָרָה וְתוּגָה, שָׁמְרֵנִי מִכָּל רָע, וּבַעֲצָתְךָ תַּנְחֵנִי. וְזָרְחָה לִי
שֶׁמֶשׁ צְדָקָה, וּמַרְפֵּא בִּכְנָפֶיהָ. יִהְיוּ לְרָצוֹן אִמְרֵי־פִי וְהֶגְיוֹן לִבִּי לְפָנֶיךָ, תהלים יט
יהוה צוּרִי וְגֹאֲלִי: אָמֵן.

THANKSGIVING PRAYER AFTER RECOVERY FROM ILLNESS

No less important than prayer *for* recovery is thanksgiving *after* recovery. There are many psalms which share this theme; two are suggested here, together with a thanksgiving prayer. If the illness is felt to have been potentially

CONFESSION BEFORE DEATH

The following confession is said by one near death.
He or she should be told: "Do not fear. Many confessed their sins, and then recovered.
Everyone who does confess has reward in the World to Come" (Shabbat 32a).

מוֹדֶה אֲנִי I acknowledge before You, LORD my God and God of my ancestors, that my cure and my death are in Your hands. May it be Your will to send me a perfect healing. Yet if my death is fully determined by You, I accept it in love at Your hand. May my death be an atonement for all the sins, iniquities and transgressions I have committed before You. Grant me of the great happiness that is stored up for the righteous. Make known to me the path of life, in Your presence is fullness of joy; at Your right hand bliss for evermore. *Ps. 16*

אֲבִי יְתוֹמִים Father of orphans and Justice of widows, protect my cherished family, whose souls are bound with mine. Into Your hand I entrust my spirit. May You redeem me, LORD, God of truth. Amen and Amen. *Ps. 31*

When the end is approaching, the following should be said.

Repeat three times:

The LORD is King, the LORD was King,
and the LORD will be King for ever and ever.

Repeat three times:

Blessed be the name of His glorious
kingdom for ever and all time.

Repeat seven times:

The LORD, He is God.

Once:

Listen, Israel: the LORD is our God, the LORD is One. *Deut. 6*

(*Shabbat* 32a). These prayers are supreme testimonies of faith, as the human soul reaches upward to the world of souls.

וידוי שכיב מרע

The following confession is said by one near death.
He or she should be told: "Do not fear. Many confessed their sins, and then recovered.
Everyone who does confess has reward in the World to Come" (Shabbat 32a).

מוֹדֶה אֲנִי לְפָנֶיךָ, יהוה אֱלֹהַי וֵאלֹהֵי אֲבוֹתַי, שֶׁרְפוּאָתִי וּמִיתָתִי בְּיָדֶךָ. יְהִי רָצוֹן מִלְּפָנֶיךָ, שֶׁתִּרְפָּאֵנִי רְפוּאָה שְׁלֵמָה, וְאִם אָמוּת, תְּהִי מִיתָתִי כַּפָּרָה עַל כָּל חֲטָאִים וַעֲוֹנוֹת וּפְשָׁעִים שֶׁחָטָאתִי וְשֶׁעָוִיתִי וְשֶׁפָּשַׁעְתִּי לְפָנֶיךָ.

תהלים טז
וְזַכֵּנִי לָעוֹלָם הַבָּא הַצָּפוּן לַצַּדִּיקִים. תּוֹדִיעֵנִי אֹרַח חַיִּים, שֹׂבַע שְׂמָחוֹת אֶת־פָּנֶיךָ, נְעִמוֹת בִּימִינְךָ נֶצַח:

אֲבִי יְתוֹמִים וְדַיַּן אַלְמָנוֹת, הָגֵן בְּעַד קְרוֹבַי הַיְקָרִים, אֲשֶׁר נַפְשִׁי קְשׁוּרָה

תהלים לא
בְּנַפְשָׁם. בְּיָדְךָ אַפְקִיד רוּחִי, פָּדִיתָה אוֹתִי יהוה אֵל אֱמֶת: אָמֵן וְאָמֵן.

When the end is approaching, the following should be said.

Repeat three times:

יהוה מֶלֶךְ, יהוה מָלָךְ, יהוה יִמְלֹךְ לְעוֹלָם וָעֶד.

Repeat three times:

בָּרוּךְ שֵׁם כְּבוֹד מַלְכוּתוֹ לְעוֹלָם וָעֶד.

Repeat seven times:

יהוה הוּא הָאֱלֹהִים.

Once:

דברים ו
שְׁמַע יִשְׂרָאֵל, יהוה אֱלֹהֵינוּ, יהוה אֶחָד:

CONFESSION BEFORE DEATH

"One who confesses and renounces his sins finds mercy" (Prov. 28:13). "When a person is sick and close to death, he or she is told: make a confession"

FUNERAL SERVICE

עֲקַבְיָא Akavya ben Mahalalel said: Reflect on three things and you will avoid transgression: Know where you came from, where you are going, and before whom you will have to give an account and reckoning. "Where you came from" – from a putrid drop. "Where you are going" – to a place of dust, worms and maggots. "And before whom you will have to give an account and reckoning" – before the Supreme King of kings, the Holy One, blessed be He. *Mishna Avot 3:1*

While on the way to the grave, say:

יֹשֵׁב בְּסֵתֶר He who lives in the shelter of the Most High dwells in the shadow of the Almighty. I say of the LORD, my Refuge and Stronghold, my God in whom I trust, that He will save you from the fowler's snare and the deadly pestilence. With His pinions He will cover you, and beneath His wings you will find shelter; His faithfulness is an encircling shield. You need not fear terror by night, nor the arrow that flies by day; not the pestilence that stalks in darkness, nor the plague that ravages at noon. A thousand may fall at your side, ten thousand at your right hand, but it will not come near you. You will only look with your eyes and see the punishment of the wicked. Because you [have said:] "The LORD is my Refuge," taking the Most High as your shelter, no harm will befall you, no plague will come near your tent, for He will command His angels about you, to guard you in all your ways. They will lift you in their hands, lest your foot stumble on a stone. You will tread on lions and vipers, you will trample on young lions and snakes. [God says] "Because he loves Me, I will rescue him; I will protect him, because he acknowledges My name. When he calls on Me, I will answer him, I will be with him in distress, I will deliver him and bring him honor. With long life I will satisfy him, and show him My salvation. With long life I will satisfy him, and show him My salvation." *Ps. 91*

---

there is suffering and death, we reaffirm our faith, tried and tested though it may be, that there is an ultimate order and justice in the universe. הַצּוּר *The Rock:* a symbol, taken from the Song of Moses (Deut. 32) signifying the eternity of God in the face of the transience of life.

לוויית המת

עֲקַבְיָא בֶּן מַהֲלַלְאֵל אוֹמֵר: הִסְתַּכֵּל בִּשְׁלֹשָׁה דְבָרִים, וְאֵין אַתָּה בָא לִידֵי עֲבֵרָה. דַּע מֵאַיִן בָּאתָ, וּלְאָן אַתָּה הוֹלֵךְ, וְלִפְנֵי מִי אַתָּה עָתִיד לִתֵּן דִּין וְחֶשְׁבּוֹן. מֵאַיִן בָּאתָ, מִטִּפָּה סְרוּחָה. וּלְאָן אַתָּה הוֹלֵךְ, לִמְקוֹם עָפָר, רִמָּה וְתוֹלֵעָה. וְלִפְנֵי מִי אַתָּה עָתִיד לִתֵּן דִּין וְחֶשְׁבּוֹן, לִפְנֵי מֶלֶךְ מַלְכֵי הַמְּלָכִים, הַקָּדוֹשׁ בָּרוּךְ הוּא. משנה אבות ג:א

While on the way to the grave, say:

יֹשֵׁב בְּסֵתֶר עֶלְיוֹן, בְּצֵל שַׁדַּי יִתְלוֹנָן: אֹמַר לַיהוה מַחְסִי וּמְצוּדָתִי, אֱלֹהַי אֶבְטַח־בּוֹ: כִּי הוּא יַצִּילְךָ מִפַּח יָקוּשׁ, מִדֶּבֶר הַוּוֹת: בְּאֶבְרָתוֹ יָסֶךְ לָךְ, וְתַחַת־כְּנָפָיו תֶּחְסֶה, צִנָּה וְסֹחֵרָה אֲמִתּוֹ: לֹא־תִירָא מִפַּחַד לָיְלָה, מֵחֵץ יָעוּף יוֹמָם: מִדֶּבֶר בָּאֹפֶל יַהֲלֹךְ, מִקֶּטֶב יָשׁוּד צָהֳרָיִם: יִפֹּל מִצִּדְּךָ אֶלֶף, וּרְבָבָה מִימִינֶךָ, אֵלֶיךָ לֹא יִגָּשׁ: רַק בְּעֵינֶיךָ תַבִּיט, וְשִׁלֻּמַת רְשָׁעִים תִּרְאֶה: כִּי־אַתָּה יהוה מַחְסִי, עֶלְיוֹן שַׂמְתָּ מְעוֹנֶךָ: לֹא־תְאֻנֶּה אֵלֶיךָ רָעָה, וְנֶגַע לֹא־יִקְרַב בְּאָהֳלֶךָ: כִּי מַלְאָכָיו יְצַוֶּה־לָּךְ, לִשְׁמָרְךָ בְּכָל־דְּרָכֶיךָ: עַל־כַּפַּיִם יִשָּׂאוּנְךָ, פֶּן־תִּגֹּף בָּאֶבֶן רַגְלֶךָ: עַל־שַׁחַל וָפֶתֶן תִּדְרֹךְ, תִּרְמֹס כְּפִיר וְתַנִּין: כִּי בִי חָשַׁק וַאֲפַלְּטֵהוּ, אֲשַׂגְּבֵהוּ כִּי־יָדַע שְׁמִי: יִקְרָאֵנִי וְאֶעֱנֵהוּ, עִמּוֹ אָנֹכִי בְצָרָה, אֲחַלְּצֵהוּ וַאֲכַבְּדֵהוּ: אֹרֶךְ יָמִים אַשְׂבִּיעֵהוּ, וְאַרְאֵהוּ בִּישׁוּעָתִי: תהלים צא

אֹרֶךְ יָמִים אַשְׂבִּיעֵהוּ, וְאַרְאֵהוּ בִּישׁוּעָתִי:

Bereavement is doubly devastating. One who was part of our life is no longer there and our world threatens to fall apart. And we come face to face with mortality itself, the knowledge that all that lives, dies. At such times, prayer helps us make the transition from *aninut*, the inarticulate shock of grief, to *avelut*, the work of mourning and recovering faith in life (R. Joseph Soloveitchik). *Tzidduk HaDin*, "The Acceptance of Judgment" (on next page), is the ultimate act of humility in the face of loss. Though we cannot understand why

After the funeral, the following is said, except on days on which Taḥanun is omitted, or after nightfall. Some say the following before the funeral.

THE ACCEPTANCE OF JUDGMENT

הַצּוּר The Rock, His work is perfect, for all His ways are just; *Deut. 32*
A faithful God who does no wrong, righteous and fair is He.

The Rock, perfect in every deed:
Who can say to Him, "What have You done?"
He rules below and above. He brings death and gives life, *1 Sam. 2*
bringing down to the grave and raising up again.

The Rock, perfect in every act:
Who can say to Him, "Why do You so act?"
You who speak and act: show us kindness we do not deserve,
and in the merit of the one who was bound like a lamb, hear us and act.

Righteous in all His ways, the Rock who is perfect,
slow to anger and full of compassion,
please have pity and spare parents and children,
for Yours, LORD, are forgiveness and compassion.

You are righteous, LORD, in bringing death and giving life.
In Your hand is the safekeeping of all spirits.
Far be it from You to erase our remembrance.
May Your eyes be open to us in compassion,
for Yours, LORD, are compassion and forgiveness.

If one lives for a year or a thousand years,
what does it profit him? He shall be as if he had never been.
Blessed is the true Judge who brings death and gives life.

Blessed is He for His judgment is true, and in His sight He surveys all.
He repays man in accord with his account and just desert,
and all must render acknowledgment to His name.

We know, LORD, that Your judgment is just.
You are just when You speak and fair when You judge.
It is not for us to criticize Your manner of judgment.
You are righteous, LORD, and Your judgments are fair. *Ps. 119*

After the funeral, the following is said, except on days on which תחנון *is omitted, or after nightfall. Some say the following before the funeral.*

צדוק הדין

הַצּוּר תָּמִים פָּעֳלוֹ, כִּי כָל־דְּרָכָיו מִשְׁפָּט דברים לב
אֵל אֱמוּנָה וְאֵין עָוֶל, צַדִּיק וְיָשָׁר הוּא:

הַצּוּר תָּמִים בְּכָל פֹּעַל, מִי יֹאמַר לוֹ מַה תִּפְעַל
הַשַּׁלִּיט בְּמַטָּה וּבְמַעַל. מֵמִית וּמְחַיֶּה, מוֹרִיד שְׁאוֹל וַיָּעַל: שמואל א׳ ב
הַצּוּר תָּמִים בְּכָל מַעֲשֶׂה, מִי יֹאמַר לוֹ מַה תַּעֲשֶׂה
הָאוֹמֵר וְעוֹשֶׂה, חֶסֶד חִנָּם לָנוּ תַעֲשֶׂה
וּבִזְכוּת הַנֶּעֱקַד כְּשֶׂה, הַקְשִׁיבָה וַעֲשֵׂה.
צַדִּיק בְּכָל דְּרָכָיו הַצּוּר תָּמִים, אֶרֶךְ אַפַּיִם וּמָלֵא רַחֲמִים
חֲמָל נָא וְחוּס נָא עַל אָבוֹת וּבָנִים
כִּי לְךָ אָדוֹן הַסְּלִיחוֹת וְהָרַחֲמִים.
צַדִּיק אַתָּה יהוה לְהָמִית וּלְהַחֲיוֹת
אֲשֶׁר בְּיָדְךָ פִּקְדוֹן כָּל רוּחוֹת, חָלִילָה לְּךָ זִכְרוֹנֵנוּ לִמְחוֹת
וְיִהְיוּ נָא עֵינֶיךָ בְּרַחֲמִים עָלֵינוּ פְקוּחוֹת
כִּי לְךָ אָדוֹן הָרַחֲמִים וְהַסְּלִיחוֹת.
אָדָם אִם בֶּן שָׁנָה יִהְיֶה, אוֹ אֶלֶף שָׁנִים יִחְיֶה
מַה יִּתְרוֹן לוֹ, כְּלֹא הָיָה יִהְיֶה
בָּרוּךְ דַּיַּן הָאֱמֶת, מֵמִית וּמְחַיֶּה.
בָּרוּךְ הוּא כִּי אֱמֶת דִּינוֹ, וּמְשׁוֹטֵט הַכֹּל בְּעֵינוֹ
וּמְשַׁלֵּם לְאָדָם חֶשְׁבּוֹנוֹ וְדִינוֹ, וְהַכֹּל לִשְׁמוֹ הוֹדָיָה יִתֵּנוּ.
יָדַעְנוּ יהוה כִּי צֶדֶק מִשְׁפָּטֶךָ, תִּצְדַּק בְּדָבְרֶךָ וְתִזְכֶּה בְשָׁפְטֶךָ
וְאֵין לְהַרְהֵר אַחַר מִדַּת שָׁפְטֶךָ. צַדִּיק אַתָּה יהוה, וְיָשָׁר מִשְׁפָּטֶיךָ: תהלים קיט

True Judge, Judge of righteousness and truth:
Blessed is the true Judge for all His judgments are righteous and true.

In Your hand is the soul of every living thing. Your right hand and power are full of righteousness.
Have compassion on the remnant of the flock of those who serve You, and say to the angel [of death], "Stay your hand."

Great in counsel and mighty in deed, *Jer. 32*
Your eyes are open to all the ways of men,
giving each according to his ways and the fruit of his deeds:

to proclaim that the LORD is upright; *Ps. 92*
He is my Rock, in whom there is no wrong.

The LORD has given and the LORD has taken away: *Job 1*
blessed be the name of the LORD.

He is compassionate; He forgives iniquity and does not destroy. *Ps. 78*
Repeatedly He suppresses His anger, not rousing His full wrath.

The following Kaddish, said by the mourners, requires the presence of a minyan.

Mourner: Magnified and sanctified may His great name be,
in the world that will in future be renewed,
reviving the dead and raising them up to eternal life.
He will rebuild the city of Jerusalem
and in it reestablish His Temple.
He will remove alien worship from the earth
and restore to its place the worship of Heaven.
Then the Holy One, blessed be He,
will reign in His sovereignty and splendor.
May it be in your lifetime and in your days,
and in the lifetime of all the house of Israel,
swiftly and soon – and say: Amen.

All: May His great name be blessed for ever and all time.

---

resurrection of the dead. Death is not final: it is a prelude to eternal life and eventual rebirth.

דַּיַּן אֱמֶת, שׁוֹפֵט צֶדֶק וֶאֱמֶת
בָּרוּךְ דַּיַּן הָאֱמֶת, שֶׁכָּל מִשְׁפָּטָיו צֶדֶק וֶאֱמֶת.
נֶפֶשׁ כָּל חַי בְּיָדֶךָ, צֶדֶק מָלְאָה יְמִינְךָ וְיָדֶךָ
רַחֵם עַל פְּלֵטַת צֹאן עֲבָדֶיךָ, וְתֹאמַר לַמַּלְאָךְ הֶרֶף יָדֶךָ.

גְּדֹל הָעֵצָה וְרַב הָעֲלִילִיָּה — ירמיה לב
אֲשֶׁר־עֵינֶיךָ פְקֻחוֹת עַל־כָּל־דַּרְכֵי בְּנֵי אָדָם
לָתֵת לְאִישׁ כִּדְרָכָיו, וְכִפְרִי מַעֲלָלָיו:

לְהַגִּיד כִּי־יָשָׁר יהוה, צוּרִי וְלֹא־עַוְלָתָה בּוֹ: — תהלים צב

יהוה נָתַן וַיהוה לָקָח, יְהִי שֵׁם יהוה מְבֹרָךְ: — איוב א

וְהוּא רַחוּם, יְכַפֵּר עָוֹן וְלֹא־יַשְׁחִית — תהלים עח
וְהִרְבָּה לְהָשִׁיב אַפּוֹ, וְלֹא־יָעִיר כָּל־חֲמָתוֹ:

The following קדיש*, said by the mourners, requires the presence of a* מנין.

אבל: יִתְגַּדַּל וְיִתְקַדַּשׁ שְׁמֵהּ רַבָּא (קהל: אָמֵן)
בְּעָלְמָא דְּהוּא עָתִיד לְאִתְחַדָּתָא
וּלְאַחֲיָאָה מֵתַיָּא, וּלְאַסָּקָא יָתְהוֹן לְחַיֵּי עָלְמָא
וּלְמִבְנֵא קַרְתָּא דִירוּשְׁלֵם, וּלְשַׁכְלָלָא הֵיכְלֵהּ בְּגַוַּהּ
וּלְמֶעְקַר פֻּלְחָנָא נֻכְרָאָה מֵאַרְעָא
וְלַאֲתָבָא פֻּלְחָנָא דִשְׁמַיָּא לְאַתְרֵהּ
וְיַמְלִיךְ קֻדְשָׁא בְּרִיךְ הוּא בְּמַלְכוּתֵהּ וִיקָרֵהּ
בְּחַיֵּיכוֹן וּבְיוֹמֵיכוֹן וּבְחַיֵּי דְכָל בֵּית יִשְׂרָאֵל
בַּעֲגָלָא וּבִזְמַן קָרִיב, וְאִמְרוּ אָמֵן. (קהל: אָמֵן)

קהל ואבל: יְהֵא שְׁמֵהּ רַבָּא מְבָרַךְ לְעָלַם וּלְעָלְמֵי עָלְמַיָּא.

The long Kaddish, said only by a mourner after the funeral and by one who completes a tractate of the Oral Law, is unique in its reference to the

Mourner: Blessed and praised, glorified and exalted,
raised and honored, uplifted and lauded
be the name of the Holy One, blessed be He,
beyond any blessing,
song, praise and consolation
uttered in the world – and say: Amen.

May there be great peace from heaven,
and life for us and all Israel – and say: Amen.

Bow, take three steps back, as if taking leave of the Divine Presence, then bow, first left, then right, then center, while saying:

May He who makes peace in His high places,
make peace for us and all Israel – and say: Amen.

After the funeral, those present form two rows, the mourners pass between them, and the following is said to them:

May the Almighty comfort you among the
other mourners of Zion and Jerusalem.

Some conclude with:

May you have no further grief.

Some have the custom to pick blades of grass and throw them over their shoulders, saying:

May they of the city grow like the grass of the earth. *Ps. 72*

Or:

Remember that we are dust. *Ps. 103*

After leaving the cemetery, it is customary to wash one's hands and say:

He will destroy death for ever, and the Lord God will wipe away the tears from all faces and remove the reproach of His people from the whole earth, for the Lord has spoken. *Is. 25*

הַמָּקוֹם יְנַחֵם *May the Almighty comfort you:* By comforting the mourners, we help reintegrate them into the community of the living, and into the larger hope that just as Jerusalem will be rebuilt, so will our fractured lives.

אבל: יִתְבָּרַךְ וְיִשְׁתַּבַּח וְיִתְפָּאַר
וְיִתְרוֹמַם וְיִתְנַשֵּׂא וְיִתְהַדָּר וְיִתְעַלֶּה וְיִתְהַלָּל
שְׁמֵהּ דְּקֻדְשָׁא בְּרִיךְ הוּא (קהל: בְּרִיךְ הוּא)
לְעֵלָּא מִן כָּל בִּרְכָתָא
/בעשרת ימי תשובה: לְעֵלָּא לְעֵלָּא מִכָּל בִּרְכָתָא/
וְשִׁירָתָא, תֻּשְׁבְּחָתָא וְנֶחֱמָתָא
דַּאֲמִירָן בְּעָלְמָא, וְאִמְרוּ אָמֵן. (קהל: אָמֵן)
יְהֵא שְׁלָמָא רַבָּא מִן שְׁמַיָּא
וְחַיִּים, עָלֵינוּ וְעַל כָּל יִשְׂרָאֵל, וְאִמְרוּ אָמֵן. (קהל: אָמֵן)

Bow, take three steps back, as if taking leave of the Divine Presence, then bow, first left, then right, then center, while saying:

עֹשֶׂה שָׁלוֹם/ בעשרת ימי תשובה: הַשָּׁלוֹם/ בִּמְרוֹמָיו
הוּא יַעֲשֶׂה שָׁלוֹם, עָלֵינוּ וְעַל כָּל יִשְׂרָאֵל
וְאִמְרוּ אָמֵן. (קהל: אָמֵן)

After the funeral, those present form two rows, the mourners pass between them, and the following is said to them:

הַמָּקוֹם יְנַחֵם אוֹתְךָ/אוֹתָךְ/אֶתְכֶם
בְּתוֹךְ שְׁאָר אֲבֵלֵי צִיּוֹן וִירוּשָׁלָיִם.

Some conclude with:

וְלֹא תוֹסִיפוּ לְדַאֲבָה עוֹד.

Some have the custom to pick blades of grass and throw them over their shoulders, saying:

תהלים עב וְיָצִיצוּ מֵעִיר כְּעֵשֶׂב הָאָרֶץ:

Or:

תהלים קג זָכוּר כִּי־עָפָר אֲנָחְנוּ:

After leaving the cemetery, it is customary to wash one's hands and say:

ישעיה כה בִּלַּע הַמָּוֶת לָנֶצַח, וּמָחָה אֲדֹנָי יֱהֹוִה דִּמְעָה מֵעַל כָּל־פָּנִים, וְחֶרְפַּת
עַמּוֹ יָסִיר מֵעַל כָּל־הָאָרֶץ, כִּי יהוה דִּבֵּר:

PRAYER IN A HOUSE OF MOURNING

After the regular service, the following psalm is read in a house of mourning during the shiva week. On those days on which Taḥanun is not said, Psalm 16 (below) is substituted.

לַמְנַצֵּחַ For the conductor of music. Of the sons of Koraḥ. A sacred song. Hear this, all you peoples. Listen, all inhabitants of the world, low and high, rich and poor alike. My mouth will speak words of wisdom; the utterance of my heart will give understanding. I listen with care to a parable; I expound my mystery to the music of the harp. Why should I fear when evil days come, when the wickedness of my foes surrounds me, trusting in their wealth, boasting of their great riches? No man can redeem his brother or pay God the price of his release, for the ransom of a life is costly; no payment is ever enough that would let him live for ever, never seeing the grave. For all can see that wise men die, that the foolish and senseless all perish and leave their wealth to others. They think their houses will remain for ever, their dwellings for all generations; they give their names to their estates. But man, despite his splendor, does not endure; he is like the beasts that perish. Such is the fate of the foolish and their followers who approve their words, Selah. Like sheep they are destined for the grave: death will be their shepherd. The upright will rule over them in the morning. Their forms will decay in the grave, far from their mansions. But God will redeem my life from the grave; He will surely take me to Himself, Selah. Do not be overawed when a man grows rich, when the glory of his house increases, for he will take nothing with him when he dies; his wealth will not descend with him. Though while he lived he counted himself blessed – men always praise you when you prosper – he will join the generation of his ancestors who will never again see the light. A man who, despite his splendor, lacks understanding, is like the beasts that perish. *Ps. 49*

On those days on which Taḥanun is not said, substitute:

מִכְתָּם לְדָוִד A musical composition of David. Protect me, God, for in You I have found refuge. I have said to the LORD: You are my LORD: from You alone comes the good I enjoy. All my delight is in the holy ones, the mighty in the land. Those who run after other gods multiply their sorrows. I shall never offer them libations of blood, nor will their names pass my lips. The LORD *Ps. 16*

מִכְתָּם לְדָוִד *Psalm 16.* On days when *Taḥanun* is not said, we recite this psalm, quite different in mood from Psalm 49. The psalm reflects that, despite our loss, we are here, alive, and with much for which to thank God. This is a poem of reaffirmation.

תפילה בבית האבל

After the regular service, the following psalm is read in a house of mourning during the שבעה *week. On those days on which* תחנון *is not said,* תהלים טז *(below) is substituted.*

לַמְנַצֵּחַ לִבְנֵי־קֹרַח מִזְמוֹר: שִׁמְעוּ־זֹאת כָּל־הָעַמִּים, הַאֲזִינוּ כָּל־יֹשְׁבֵי חָלֶד: תהלים מט
גַּם־בְּנֵי אָדָם, גַּם־בְּנֵי־אִישׁ, יַחַד עָשִׁיר וְאֶבְיוֹן: פִּי יְדַבֵּר חָכְמוֹת, וְהָגוּת
לִבִּי תְבוּנוֹת: אַטֶּה לְמָשָׁל אָזְנִי, אֶפְתַּח בְּכִנּוֹר חִידָתִי: לָמָּה אִירָא בִּימֵי
רָע, עֲוֹן עֲקֵבַי יְסֻבֵּנִי: הַבֹּטְחִים עַל־חֵילָם, וּבְרֹב עָשְׁרָם יִתְהַלָּלוּ: אָח לֹא־
פָדֹה יִפְדֶּה אִישׁ, לֹא־יִתֵּן לֵאלֹהִים כָּפְרוֹ: וְיֵקַר פִּדְיוֹן נַפְשָׁם, וְחָדַל לְעוֹלָם:
וִיחִי־עוֹד לָנֶצַח, לֹא יִרְאֶה הַשָּׁחַת: כִּי יִרְאֶה חֲכָמִים יָמוּתוּ, יַחַד כְּסִיל
וָבַעַר יֹאבֵדוּ, וְעָזְבוּ לַאֲחֵרִים חֵילָם: קִרְבָּם בָּתֵּימוֹ לְעוֹלָם, מִשְׁכְּנֹתָם לְדוֹר
וָדֹר, קָרְאוּ בִשְׁמוֹתָם עֲלֵי אֲדָמוֹת: וְאָדָם בִּיקָר בַּל־יָלִין, נִמְשַׁל כַּבְּהֵמוֹת
נִדְמוּ: זֶה דַרְכָּם, כֵּסֶל לָמוֹ, וְאַחֲרֵיהֶם בְּפִיהֶם יִרְצוּ סֶלָה: כַּצֹּאן לִשְׁאוֹל
שַׁתּוּ, מָוֶת יִרְעֵם, וַיִּרְדּוּ בָם יְשָׁרִים לַבֹּקֶר, וְצוּרָם לְבַלּוֹת שְׁאוֹל מִזְּבֻל לוֹ:
אַךְ־אֱלֹהִים יִפְדֶּה נַפְשִׁי מִיַּד שְׁאוֹל, כִּי יִקָּחֵנִי סֶלָה: אַל־תִּירָא כִּי־יַעֲשִׁר
אִישׁ, כִּי־יִרְבֶּה כְּבוֹד בֵּיתוֹ: כִּי לֹא בְמוֹתוֹ יִקַּח הַכֹּל, לֹא־יֵרֵד אַחֲרָיו כְּבוֹדוֹ:
כִּי־נַפְשׁוֹ בְּחַיָּיו יְבָרֵךְ, וְיוֹדֻךָ כִּי־תֵיטִיב לָךְ: תָּבוֹא עַד־דּוֹר אֲבוֹתָיו, עַד־נֵצַח
לֹא יִרְאוּ־אוֹר: אָדָם בִּיקָר וְלֹא יָבִין, נִמְשַׁל כַּבְּהֵמוֹת נִדְמוּ:

On those days on which תחנון *is not said, substitute:*

מִכְתָּם לְדָוִד, שָׁמְרֵנִי אֵל כִּי־חָסִיתִי בָךְ: אָמַרְתְּ לַיהוה, אֲדֹנָי אָתָּה, טוֹבָתִי תהלים טז
בַּל־עָלֶיךָ: לִקְדוֹשִׁים אֲשֶׁר־בָּאָרֶץ הֵמָּה, וְאַדִּירֵי כָּל־חֶפְצִי־בָם: יִרְבּוּ
עַצְּבוֹתָם אַחֵר מָהָרוּ, בַּל־אַסִּיךְ נִסְכֵּיהֶם מִדָּם, וּבַל־אֶשָּׂא אֶת־שְׁמוֹתָם

PRAYER IN A HOUSE OF MOURNING

לַמְנַצֵּחַ *Psalm 49.* Repentance is part of the process of mourning (Maimonides). Confronted with an awareness of our mortality, we begin to rethink our priorities, knowing that what occupy our energies and thoughts much of the time, are often matters of relatively minor significance when weighed against the fullness of eternity and the brevity of our lives on earth. Psalm 49 is a most powerful expression of this idea. What lives on after us is not our wealth but the ideals for which we live and the good we do.

is my allotted portion and my cup: You direct my fate. The lines have fallen for me in pleasant places; I am well content with my inheritance. I will bless the LORD who has guided me; at night my innermost being admonishes me. I have set the LORD before me at all times. He is at my right hand: I shall not be shaken. Therefore my heart is glad, my spirit rejoices, and my body rests secure. For You will not abandon me to the grave, nor let Your faithful one see the pit. You will teach me the path of life. In Your presence is fullness of joy; at Your right hand, bliss for evermore.

MEMORIAL PRAYER

אֵל O LORD and King, full of compassion, God of the spirits of all flesh, in whose hand are the souls of the living and the dead, receive, we pray You, in Your great love the soul of

For a man, say:

(*name* son of *father's name*) who has been gathered to his people. Have mercy on him, pardon all his transgressions, for there is no one so righteous on earth as to have done only good and never sinned. Remember the righteousness that he did, and let his reward be with him, his recompense before him. O shelter his soul in the shadow of Your wings. Make known to him the path of life. In Your presence is fullness of joy, at Your right hand bliss for evermore. Bestow upon him the great goodness that is stored up for the righteous. *Eccl. 7*

For a woman, say:

(*name* daughter of *father's name*) who has been gathered to her people. Have mercy on her, pardon all her transgressions, for there is no one so righteous on earth as to have done only good and never sinned. Remember the righteousness that she did, and let her reward be with her, her recompense before her. O shelter her soul in the shadow of Your wings. Make known to her the path of life. In Your presence is fullness of joy, at Your right hand bliss for evermore. Bestow upon her the great goodness that is stored up for the righteous. *Eccl. 7*

For a boy, say:

(*name* son of *father's name*) who has been gathered to his people. Remember the righteousness that he did, and let his reward be with him, his recompense before him. O shelter his soul in the shadow of Your wings. Make known to him the path of life. In Your presence is fullness of joy, at Your right hand bliss for evermore. Bestow upon him the great goodness that is stored up for the righteous.

עַל־שְׂפָתָי: יהוה, מְנָת־חֶלְקִי וְכוֹסִי, אַתָּה תּוֹמִיךְ גּוֹרָלִי: חֲבָלִים נָפְלוּ־לִי בַּנְּעִמִים, אַף־נַחֲלַת שָׁפְרָה עָלָי: אֲבָרֵךְ אֶת־יהוה אֲשֶׁר יְעָצָנִי, אַף־לֵילוֹת יִסְּרוּנִי כִלְיוֹתָי: שִׁוִּיתִי יהוה לְנֶגְדִּי תָמִיד, כִּי מִימִינִי בַּל־אֶמּוֹט: לָכֵן שָׂמַח לִבִּי וַיָּגֶל כְּבוֹדִי, אַף־בְּשָׂרִי יִשְׁכֹּן לָבֶטַח: כִּי לֹא־תַעֲזֹב נַפְשִׁי לִשְׁאוֹל, לֹא־תִתֵּן חֲסִידְךָ לִרְאוֹת שָׁחַת: תּוֹדִיעֵנִי אֹרַח חַיִּים, שֹׂבַע שְׂמָחוֹת אֶת־פָּנֶיךָ, נְעִמוֹת בִּימִינְךָ נֶצַח:

אזכרה

אָנָּא יהוה מֶלֶךְ מָלֵא רַחֲמִים, אֱלֹהֵי הָרוּחוֹת לְכָל בָּשָׂר, אֲשֶׁר בְּיָדְךָ נַפְשׁוֹת הַחַיִּים וְהַמֵּתִים, אָנָּא קַבֵּל בְּחַסְדְּךָ הַגָּדוֹל אֶת נִשְׁמַת

For a man, say:

(פלוני בֶּן פלוני) אֲשֶׁר נֶאֱסַף אֶל עַמָּיו. חוּס וַחֲמֹל עָלָיו, סְלַח וּמְחַל לְכָל פְּשָׁעָיו. כִּי אָדָם אֵין צַדִּיק בָּאָרֶץ, אֲשֶׁר יַעֲשֶׂה־טּוֹב וְלֹא יֶחֱטָא: קהלת ז
זְכֹר לוֹ צִדְקָתוֹ אֲשֶׁר עָשָׂה, וִיהִי שְׂכָרוֹ אִתּוֹ, וּפְעֻלָּתוֹ לְפָנָיו. אָנָּא הַסְתֵּר אֶת נִשְׁמָתוֹ בְּצֵל כְּנָפֶיךָ, הוֹדִיעֵהוּ אֹרַח חַיִּים, שֹׂבַע שְׂמָחוֹת אֶת פָּנֶיךָ, נְעִימוֹת בִּימִינְךָ נֶצַח, וְתַשְׁפִּיעַ לוֹ מֵרַב טוּב הַצָּפוּן לַצַּדִּיקִים.

For a woman, say:

(פלונית בַּת פלוני) אֲשֶׁר נֶאֶסְפָה אֶל עַמֶּיהָ. חוּס וַחֲמֹל עָלֶיהָ, סְלַח וּמְחַל לְכָל פְּשָׁעֶיהָ. כִּי אָדָם אֵין צַדִּיק בָּאָרֶץ, אֲשֶׁר יַעֲשֶׂה־טּוֹב וְלֹא יֶחֱטָא: קהלת ז
זְכֹר לָהּ צִדְקָתָהּ אֲשֶׁר עָשְׂתָה, וִיהִי שְׂכָרָהּ אִתָּהּ, וּפְעֻלָּתָהּ לְפָנֶיהָ. אָנָּא הַסְתֵּר אֶת נִשְׁמָתָהּ בְּצֵל כְּנָפֶיךָ, הוֹדִיעֶהָ אֹרַח חַיִּים, שֹׂבַע שְׂמָחוֹת אֶת פָּנֶיךָ, נְעִימוֹת בִּימִינְךָ נֶצַח, וְתַשְׁפִּיעַ לָהּ מֵרַב טוּב הַצָּפוּן לַצַּדִּיקִים.

For a boy, say:

(פלוני בֶּן פלוני) אֲשֶׁר נֶאֱסַף אֶל עַמָּיו. זְכֹר לוֹ צִדְקָתוֹ אֲשֶׁר עָשָׂה, וִיהִי שְׂכָרוֹ אִתּוֹ, וּפְעֻלָּתוֹ לְפָנָיו. אָנָּא הַסְתֵּר אֶת נִשְׁמָתוֹ בְּצֵל כְּנָפֶיךָ, הוֹדִיעֵהוּ אֹרַח חַיִּים, שֹׂבַע שְׂמָחוֹת אֶת פָּנֶיךָ, נְעִימוֹת בִּימִינְךָ נֶצַח, וְתַשְׁפִּיעַ לוֹ מֵרַב טוּב הַצָּפוּן לַצַּדִּיקִים.

For a girl, say:

(*name* daughter of *father's name*) who has been gathered to her people. Remember the righteousness that she did, and let her reward be with her, her recompense before her. O shelter her soul in the shadow of Your wings. Make known to her the path of life. In Your presence is fullness of joy, at Your right hand bliss for evermore. Bestow upon her the great goodness that is stored up for the righteous.

As it is written, "How great is Your goodness which You have stored up for those who revere You, which You bestow on those that trust in You before the children of men." *Ps. 31*

אָנָּא May the LORD who heals the brokenhearted and binds up their wounds, grant consolation to the mourners.

For a young boy, add:

May the death of this boy
mark the end of all anguish and sorrow for his parents.

For a young girl, add:

May the death of this girl
mark the end of all anguish and sorrow for her parents.

If the mourners have children, add the words in parentheses:

חַזְּקֵם Strengthen and support them in the day of their sadness and grief; and remember them (and their children) for a long and good life. Put into their hearts love and reverence for You, so that they may serve You with a perfect heart; and let their end be peace. Amen.

כְּאִישׁ As a mother comforts her son, *Is. 66*
so will I comfort you;
and in Jerusalem you shall find comfort.
Your sun shall no more set, *Is. 60*
your moon shall no more withdraw itself,
for the LORD shall be your everlasting light,
and your days of mourning shall be ended.
He will destroy death for ever; *Is. 25*
and the LORD God will wipe away the tears from all faces,
and remove the reproach of His people from the whole earth;
for the LORD has spoken it.

For a girl, say:

(פלונית בַּת פלוני) אֲשֶׁר נֶאֶסְפָה אֶל עַמֶּיהָ. זְכוֹר לָהּ צִדְקָתָהּ אֲשֶׁר עָשְׂתָה, וִיהִי שְׂכָרָהּ אִתָּהּ, וּפְעֻלָּתָהּ לְפָנֶיהָ. אָנָּא הַסְתֵּר אֶת נִשְׁמָתָהּ בְּצֵל כְּנָפֶיךָ, הוֹדִיעֶהָ אֹרַח חַיִּים, שֹׂבַע שְׂמָחוֹת אֶת פָּנֶיךָ, נְעִימוֹת בִּימִינְךָ נֶצַח, וְתַשְׁפִּיעַ לָהּ מֵרֹב טוּב הַצָּפוּן לַצַּדִּיקִים.

תהלים לא כְּמוֹ שֶׁכָּתוּב: מָה רַב טוּבְךָ אֲשֶׁר־צָפַנְתָּ לִּירֵאֶיךָ, פָּעַלְתָּ לַחוֹסִים בָּךְ נֶגֶד בְּנֵי אָדָם:

אָנָּא יהוה, הָרוֹפֵא לִשְׁבוּרֵי לֵב וּמְחַבֵּשׁ לְעַצְּבוֹתָם, שַׁלֵּם נִחוּמִים לָאֲבֵלִים.

For a young boy, add:

וּתְהִי פְּטִירַת הַיֶּלֶד הַזֶּה קֵץ לְכָל צָרָה וְצוּקָה לְאָבִיו וּלְאִמּוֹ.

For a young girl, add:

וּתְהִי פְּטִירַת הַיַּלְדָּה הַזֹּאת קֵץ לְכָל צָרָה וְצוּקָה לְאָבִיהָ וּלְאִמָּהּ.

If the mourners have children, add the words in parentheses:

חַזְּקֵם וְאַמְּצֵם בְּיוֹם אֶבְלָם וִיגוֹנָם, וְזָכְרֵם (וּזְכֹר אֶת בְּנֵי בֵיתָם) לְחַיִּים טוֹבִים וַאֲרֻכִּים. תֵּן בְּלִבָּם יִרְאָתְךָ וְאַהֲבָתְךָ לְעָבְדְךָ בְּלֵבָב שָׁלֵם, וּתְהִי אַחֲרִיתָם שָׁלוֹם, אָמֵן.

ישעיה סו כְּאִישׁ אֲשֶׁר אִמּוֹ תְּנַחֲמֶנּוּ
כֵּן אָנֹכִי אֲנַחֶמְכֶם
וּבִירוּשָׁלַםִ תְּנֻחָמוּ:
ישעיה ס לֹא־יָבוֹא עוֹד שִׁמְשֵׁךְ, וִירֵחֵךְ לֹא יֵאָסֵף
כִּי יהוה יִהְיֶה־לָּךְ לְאוֹר עוֹלָם
וְשָׁלְמוּ יְמֵי אֶבְלֵךְ:
ישעיה כה בִּלַּע הַמָּוֶת לָנֶצַח
וּמָחָה אֲדֹנָי יֱהוִה דִּמְעָה מֵעַל כָּל־פָּנִים
וְחֶרְפַּת עַמּוֹ יָסִיר מֵעַל כָּל־הָאָרֶץ
כִּי יהוה דִּבֵּר:

MOURNER'S KADDISH

The following prayer, said by mourners, requires the presence of a minyan. A transliteration can be found on page 1334.

Mourner: יִתְגַּדַּל Magnified and sanctified
may His great name be,
in the world He created by His will.
May He establish His kingdom
in your lifetime and in your days,
and in the lifetime of all the house of Israel,
swiftly and soon –
and say: Amen.

All: May His great name be blessed
for ever and all time.

Mourner: Blessed and praised,
glorified and exalted,
raised and honored,
uplifted and lauded
be the name of the Holy One,
blessed be He,
beyond any blessing,
song, praise and consolation
uttered in the world –
and say: Amen.

May there be great peace from heaven,
and life for us and all Israel –
and say: Amen.

Bow, take three steps back, as if taking leave of the Divine Presence, then bow, first left, then right, then center, while saying:

May He who makes peace in His high places,
make peace for us and all Israel –
and say: Amen.

קדיש יתום

The following prayer, said by mourners, requires the presence of a מנין.
A transliteration can be found on page 1334.

אבל: יִתְגַּדַּל וְיִתְקַדַּשׁ שְׁמֵהּ רַבָּא (קהל: אָמֵן)
בְּעָלְמָא דִּי בְרָא כִרְעוּתֵהּ
וְיַמְלִיךְ מַלְכוּתֵהּ
בְּחַיֵּיכוֹן וּבְיוֹמֵיכוֹן וּבְחַיֵּי דְכָל בֵּית יִשְׂרָאֵל
בַּעֲגָלָא וּבִזְמַן קָרִיב
וְאִמְרוּ אָמֵן. (קהל: אָמֵן)

קהל ואבל: יְהֵא שְׁמֵהּ רַבָּא מְבָרַךְ לְעָלַם וּלְעָלְמֵי עָלְמַיָּא.

אבל: יִתְבָּרַךְ וְיִשְׁתַּבַּח וְיִתְפָּאַר
וְיִתְרוֹמַם וְיִתְנַשֵּׂא וְיִתְהַדָּר וְיִתְעַלֶּה וְיִתְהַלָּל
שְׁמֵהּ דְּקֻדְשָׁא בְּרִיךְ הוּא (קהל: בְּרִיךְ הוּא)
לְעֵלָּא מִן כָּל בִּרְכָתָא / בעשרת ימי תשובה: לְעֵלָּא לְעֵלָּא מִכָּל בִּרְכָתָא/
וְשִׁירָתָא, תֻּשְׁבְּחָתָא וְנֶחֱמָתָא
דַּאֲמִירָן בְּעָלְמָא
וְאִמְרוּ אָמֵן. (קהל: אָמֵן)

יְהֵא שְׁלָמָא רַבָּא מִן שְׁמַיָּא
וְחַיִּים, עָלֵינוּ וְעַל כָּל יִשְׂרָאֵל
וְאִמְרוּ אָמֵן. (קהל: אָמֵן)

Bow, take three steps back, as if taking leave of the Divine Presence,
then bow, first left, then right, then center, while saying:

עֹשֶׂה שָׁלוֹם/ בעשרת ימי תשובה: הַשָּׁלוֹם/ בִּמְרוֹמָיו
הוּא יַעֲשֶׂה שָׁלוֹם עָלֵינוּ וְעַל כָּל יִשְׂרָאֵל
וְאִמְרוּ אָמֵן. (קהל: אָמֵן)

BIRKAT HAMAZON IN A HOUSE OF MOURNING

Leader Gentlemen, let us say grace.

Others May the name of the Lord be blessed from now and for ever. *Ps. 113*

Leader May the name of the Lord be blessed from now and for ever.
With your permission,
let us bless the One who comforts mourners
from whose food we have eaten.

Others Blessed be the One who comforts mourners,
from whose food we have eaten, and by whose goodness we live.

**People present who have not taken part in the meal say:*
*Blessed be the One who comforts mourners,
whose name is continually blessed for ever and all time.

Leader Blessed be the One who comforts mourners,
from whose food we have eaten, and by whose goodness we live.
Blessed be He, and blessed be His name.

Continue with Birkat HaMazon on page 978 until "And may Jerusalem" on page 984. Then say:

נַחֵם Comfort, O Lord our God, the mourners of Jerusalem and those who mourn here. Grant them consolation in their mourning and gladness in their grief, as it is said, "As a mother comforts her son, so will I comfort *Is. 66* you, and in Jerusalem you shall find comfort." Blessed are You, Lord, who brings comfort to Zion through the rebuilding of Jerusalem. Amen.

בָּרוּךְ Blessed are You, Lord our God, King of the Universe – God our Father, our King, our Sovereign, our Creator, our Redeemer, our Maker, our Holy One, the Holy One of Jacob. He is our Shepherd, Israel's Sheperd, our living King who is good and does good, the true God, the true Judge, who judges righteously and takes back souls in judgment. He rules the world according to His will, for all His ways are just, and we are His people and His servants. For everything, we are duty bound to acknowledge and bless Him. May He who repairs the breaches in Israel, repair this breach in us and grant us life and peace. May He always bestow on us grace, kindness, compassion and all good things. Of all that is good, may He never let us lack.

Continue with "May the Compassionate One reign" on page 986.

ברכת המזון בבית האבל

Leader רַבּוֹתַי, נְבָרֵךְ.

Others יְהִי שֵׁם יהוה מְבֹרָךְ מֵעַתָּה וְעַד־עוֹלָם: תהלים קיג

Leader יְהִי שֵׁם יהוה מְבֹרָךְ מֵעַתָּה וְעַד־עוֹלָם:
בִּרְשׁוּת רַבּוֹתַי, נְבָרֵךְ מְנַחֵם אֲבֵלִים שֶׁאָכַֽלְנוּ מִשֶּׁלּוֹ.

Others בָּרוּךְ מְנַחֵם אֲבֵלִים, שֶׁאָכַֽלְנוּ מִשֶּׁלּוֹ וּבְטוּבוֹ חָיִֽינוּ.

**People present who have not taken part in the meal say:*

*בָּרוּךְ מְנַחֵם אֲבֵלִים, וּמְבֹרָךְ שְׁמוֹ תָּמִיד לְעוֹלָם וָעֶד.

Leader בָּרוּךְ מְנַחֵם אֲבֵלִים, שֶׁאָכַֽלְנוּ מִשֶּׁלּוֹ וּבְטוּבוֹ חָיִֽינוּ.
בָּרוּךְ הוּא וּבָרוּךְ שְׁמוֹ.

Continue with בִּרְכַּת הַמָּזוֹן *on page 979 until* וּבְנֵה יְרוּשָׁלַיִם *on page 985. Then say:*

נַחֵם יהוה אֱלֹהֵֽינוּ אֶת אֲבֵלֵי יְרוּשָׁלַֽיִם, וְאֶת הָאֲבֵלִים הַמִּתְאַבְּלִים בָּאֵֽבֶל הַזֶּה. נַחֲמֵם מֵאֶבְלָם וְשַׂמְּחֵם מִיגוֹנָם, כָּאָמוּר: כְּאִישׁ אֲשֶׁר ישעיה סו
אִמּוֹ תְּנַחֲמֶֽנּוּ, כֵּן אָנֹכִי אֲנַחֶמְכֶם וּבִירוּשָׁלַֽםִ תְּנֻחָֽמוּ: בָּרוּךְ אַתָּה יהוה, מְנַחֵם צִיּוֹן בְּבִנְיַן יְרוּשָׁלָֽיִם. אָמֵן.

בָּרוּךְ אַתָּה יהוה אֱלֹהֵֽינוּ מֶֽלֶךְ הָעוֹלָם, הָאֵל אָבִֽינוּ מַלְכֵּֽנוּ אַדִּירֵֽנוּ בּוֹרְאֵֽנוּ גּוֹאֲלֵֽנוּ יוֹצְרֵֽנוּ קְדוֹשֵֽׁנוּ קְדוֹשׁ יַעֲקֹב, רוֹעֵֽנוּ רוֹעֵה יִשְׂרָאֵל, הַמֶּֽלֶךְ הַחַי, הַטּוֹב וְהַמֵּטִיב. אֵל אֱמֶת, דַּיַּן אֱמֶת, שׁוֹפֵט צֶֽדֶק, לוֹקֵֽחַ נְפָשׁוֹת בְּמִשְׁפָּט, וְשַׁלִּיט בְּעוֹלָמוֹ לַעֲשׂוֹת בּוֹ כִּרְצוֹנוֹ, כִּי כָל דְּרָכָיו מִשְׁפָּט, וַאֲנַֽחְנוּ עַמּוֹ וַעֲבָדָיו, וְעַל הַכֹּל אֲנַֽחְנוּ חַיָּבִים לְהוֹדוֹת לוֹ וּלְבָרְכוֹ. גּוֹדֵר פִּרְצוֹת יִשְׂרָאֵל, הוּא יִגְדֹּר אֶת הַפִּרְצָה הַזֹּאת מֵעָלֵֽינוּ לְחַיִּים וּלְשָׁלוֹם. הוּא יִגְמְלֵֽנוּ לָעַד חֵן וָחֶֽסֶד וְרַחֲמִים וְכָל טוֹב, וּמִכָּל טוּב לְעוֹלָם אַל יְחַסְּרֵֽנוּ.

Continue with הָרַחֲמָן הוּא יִמְלוֹךְ *on page 987.*

קריאת התורה
TORAH READINGS

קריאת התורה לימי שני וחמישי
ובמנחה של שבת

THE READING OF THE TORAH
FOR MONDAYS, THURSDAYS, AND SHABBAT MINḤA

בראשית

BERESHIT

בראשית א:
א-כג

בְּרֵאשִׁ֖ית בָּרָ֣א אֱלֹהִ֑ים אֵ֥ת הַשָּׁמַ֖יִם וְאֵ֥ת הָאָֽרֶץ: וְהָאָ֗רֶץ הָיְתָ֥ה תֹ֨הוּ֙ וָבֹ֔הוּ
וְחֹ֖שֶׁךְ עַל־פְּנֵ֣י תְה֑וֹם וְר֣וּחַ אֱלֹהִ֔ים מְרַחֶ֖פֶת עַל־פְּנֵ֥י הַמָּֽיִם: וַיֹּ֥אמֶר אֱלֹהִ֖ים
יְהִ֣י א֑וֹר וַֽיְהִי־אֽוֹר: וַיַּ֧רְא אֱלֹהִ֛ים אֶת־הָא֖וֹר כִּי־ט֑וֹב וַיַּבְדֵּ֣ל אֱלֹהִ֔ים בֵּ֥ין הָא֖וֹר
וּבֵ֥ין הַחֹֽשֶׁךְ: וַיִּקְרָ֨א אֱלֹהִ֤ים ׀ לָאוֹר֙ י֔וֹם וְלַחֹ֖שֶׁךְ קָ֣רָא לָ֑יְלָה וַֽיְהִי־עֶ֥רֶב וַֽיְהִי־
בֹ֖קֶר י֥וֹם אֶחָֽד:

לוי
וַיֹּ֣אמֶר אֱלֹהִ֔ים יְהִ֥י רָקִ֖יעַ בְּת֣וֹךְ הַמָּ֑יִם וִיהִ֣י מַבְדִּ֔יל בֵּ֥ין מַ֖יִם לָמָֽיִם: וַיַּ֣עַשׂ
אֱלֹהִים֮ אֶת־הָֽרָקִיעַ֒ וַיַּבְדֵּ֗ל בֵּ֤ין הַמַּ֨יִם֙ אֲשֶׁר֙ מִתַּ֣חַת לָֽרָקִ֔יעַ וּבֵ֣ין הַמַּ֔יִם אֲשֶׁ֖ר
מֵעַ֣ל לָֽרָקִ֑יעַ וַֽיְהִי־כֵֽן: וַיִּקְרָ֧א אֱלֹהִ֛ים לָֽרָקִ֖יעַ שָׁמָ֑יִם וַֽיְהִי־עֶ֥רֶב וַֽיְהִי־בֹ֖קֶר
י֥וֹם שֵׁנִֽי:

ישראל
וַיֹּ֣אמֶר אֱלֹהִ֗ים יִקָּו֨וּ הַמַּ֜יִם מִתַּ֤חַת הַשָּׁמַ֨יִם֙ אֶל־מָק֣וֹם אֶחָ֔ד וְתֵרָאֶ֖ה הַיַּבָּשָׁ֑ה
וַֽיְהִי־כֵֽן: וַיִּקְרָ֨א אֱלֹהִ֤ים ׀ לַיַּבָּשָׁה֙ אֶ֔רֶץ וּלְמִקְוֵ֥ה הַמַּ֖יִם קָרָ֣א יַמִּ֑ים וַיַּ֥רְא
אֱלֹהִ֖ים כִּי־טֽוֹב: וַיֹּ֣אמֶר אֱלֹהִ֗ים תַּֽדְשֵׁ֤א הָאָ֨רֶץ֙ דֶּ֔שֶׁא עֵ֚שֶׂב מַזְרִ֣יעַ זֶ֔רַע עֵ֣ץ
פְּרִ֞י עֹ֤שֶׂה פְּרִי֙ לְמִינ֔וֹ אֲשֶׁ֥ר זַרְעוֹ־ב֖וֹ עַל־הָאָ֑רֶץ וַֽיְהִי־כֵֽן: וַתּוֹצֵ֨א הָאָ֜רֶץ דֶּ֠שֶׁא
עֵ֣שֶׂב מַזְרִ֤יעַ זֶ֨רַע֙ לְמִינֵ֔הוּ וְעֵ֧ץ עֹֽשֶׂה־פְּרִ֛י אֲשֶׁ֥ר זַרְעוֹ־ב֖וֹ לְמִינֵ֑הוּ וַיַּ֥רְא אֱלֹהִ֖ים
כִּי־טֽוֹב: וַֽיְהִי־עֶ֥רֶב וַֽיְהִי־בֹ֖קֶר י֥וֹם שְׁלִישִֽׁי:

Some extend the ישראל *portion on the Thursday reading:*

וַיֹּ֣אמֶר אֱלֹהִ֗ים יְהִ֤י מְאֹרֹת֙ בִּרְקִ֣יעַ הַשָּׁמַ֔יִם לְהַבְדִּ֕יל בֵּ֥ין הַיּ֖וֹם וּבֵ֣ין הַלָּ֑יְלָה
וְהָי֤וּ לְאֹתֹת֙ וּלְמ֣וֹעֲדִ֔ים וּלְיָמִ֖ים וְשָׁנִֽים: וְהָי֤וּ לִמְאוֹרֹת֙ בִּרְקִ֣יעַ הַשָּׁמַ֔יִם לְהָאִ֖יר
עַל־הָאָ֑רֶץ וַֽיְהִי־כֵֽן: וַיַּ֣עַשׂ אֱלֹהִ֔ים אֶת־שְׁנֵ֥י הַמְּאֹרֹ֖ת הַגְּדֹלִ֑ים אֶת־הַמָּא֤וֹר
הַגָּדֹל֙ לְמֶמְשֶׁ֣לֶת הַיּ֔וֹם וְאֶת־הַמָּא֤וֹר הַקָּטֹן֙ לְמֶמְשֶׁ֣לֶת הַלַּ֔יְלָה וְאֵ֖ת הַכּֽוֹכָבִֽים:
וַיִּתֵּ֥ן אֹתָ֛ם אֱלֹהִ֖ים בִּרְקִ֣יעַ הַשָּׁמָ֑יִם לְהָאִ֖יר עַל־הָאָֽרֶץ: וְלִמְשֹׁל֙ בַּיּ֣וֹם וּבַלַּ֔יְלָה

וּלְהַבְדִּיל בֵּין הָאוֹר וּבֵין הַחֹשֶׁךְ וַיַּרְא אֱלֹהִים כִּי־טוֹב׃ וַיְהִי־עֶרֶב וַיְהִי־בֹקֶר
יוֹם רְבִיעִי׃
וַיֹּאמֶר אֱלֹהִים יִשְׁרְצוּ הַמַּיִם שֶׁרֶץ נֶפֶשׁ חַיָּה וְעוֹף יְעוֹפֵף עַל־הָאָרֶץ עַל־פְּנֵי
רְקִיעַ הַשָּׁמָיִם׃ וַיִּבְרָא אֱלֹהִים אֶת־הַתַּנִּינִם הַגְּדֹלִים וְאֵת כָּל־נֶפֶשׁ הַחַיָּה ׀
הָרֹמֶשֶׂת אֲשֶׁר שָׁרְצוּ הַמַּיִם לְמִינֵהֶם וְאֵת כָּל־עוֹף כָּנָף לְמִינֵהוּ וַיַּרְא אֱלֹהִים
כִּי־טוֹב׃ וַיְבָרֶךְ אֹתָם אֱלֹהִים לֵאמֹר פְּרוּ וּרְבוּ וּמִלְאוּ אֶת־הַמַּיִם בַּיַּמִּים וְהָעוֹף
יִרֶב בָּאָרֶץ׃ וַיְהִי־עֶרֶב וַיְהִי־בֹקֶר יוֹם חֲמִישִׁי׃

NOAH נח

אֵלֶּה תּוֹלְדֹת נֹחַ נֹחַ אִישׁ צַדִּיק תָּמִים הָיָה בְּדֹרֹתָיו אֶת־הָאֱלֹהִים הִתְהַלֶּךְ־ בראשית ו: ט–כב
נֹחַ׃ וַיּוֹלֶד נֹחַ שְׁלֹשָׁה בָנִים אֶת־שֵׁם אֶת־חָם וְאֶת־יָפֶת׃ וַתִּשָּׁחֵת הָאָרֶץ
לִפְנֵי הָאֱלֹהִים וַתִּמָּלֵא הָאָרֶץ חָמָס׃ וַיַּרְא אֱלֹהִים אֶת־הָאָרֶץ וְהִנֵּה נִשְׁחָתָה
כִּי־הִשְׁחִית כָּל־בָּשָׂר אֶת־דַּרְכּוֹ עַל־הָאָרֶץ׃ וַיֹּאמֶר אֱלֹהִים
לְנֹחַ קֵץ כָּל־בָּשָׂר בָּא לְפָנַי כִּי־מָלְאָה הָאָרֶץ חָמָס מִפְּנֵיהֶם וְהִנְנִי מַשְׁחִיתָם
אֶת־הָאָרֶץ׃ עֲשֵׂה לְךָ תֵּבַת עֲצֵי־גֹפֶר קִנִּים תַּעֲשֶׂה אֶת־הַתֵּבָה וְכָפַרְתָּ אֹתָהּ
מִבַּיִת וּמִחוּץ בַּכֹּפֶר׃ וְזֶה אֲשֶׁר תַּעֲשֶׂה אֹתָהּ שְׁלֹשׁ מֵאוֹת אַמָּה אֹרֶךְ הַתֵּבָה
חֲמִשִּׁים אַמָּה רָחְבָּהּ וּשְׁלֹשִׁים אַמָּה קוֹמָתָהּ׃ צֹהַר ׀ תַּעֲשֶׂה לַתֵּבָה וְאֶל־אַמָּה
תְּכַלֶּנָּה מִלְמַעְלָה וּפֶתַח הַתֵּבָה בְּצִדָּהּ תָּשִׂים תַּחְתִּיִּם שְׁנִיִּם וּשְׁלִשִׁים תַּעֲשֶׂהָ׃
*וַאֲנִי הִנְנִי מֵבִיא אֶת־הַמַּבּוּל מַיִם עַל־הָאָרֶץ לְשַׁחֵת כָּל־בָּשָׂר אֲשֶׁר־בּוֹ לוי
רוּחַ חַיִּים מִתַּחַת הַשָּׁמָיִם כֹּל אֲשֶׁר־בָּאָרֶץ יִגְוָע׃ וַהֲקִמֹתִי אֶת־בְּרִיתִי אִתָּךְ
וּבָאתָ אֶל־הַתֵּבָה אַתָּה וּבָנֶיךָ וְאִשְׁתְּךָ וּנְשֵׁי־בָנֶיךָ אִתָּךְ׃ וּמִכָּל־הָחַי מִכָּל־
בָּשָׂר שְׁנַיִם מִכֹּל תָּבִיא אֶל־הַתֵּבָה לְהַחֲיֹת אִתָּךְ זָכָר וּנְקֵבָה יִהְיוּ׃ *מֵהָעוֹף ישראל
לְמִינֵהוּ וּמִן־הַבְּהֵמָה לְמִינָהּ מִכֹּל רֶמֶשׂ הָאֲדָמָה לְמִינֵהוּ שְׁנַיִם מִכֹּל יָבֹאוּ
אֵלֶיךָ לְהַחֲיוֹת׃ וְאַתָּה קַח־לְךָ מִכָּל־מַאֲכָל אֲשֶׁר יֵאָכֵל וְאָסַפְתָּ אֵלֶיךָ וְהָיָה
לְךָ וְלָהֶם לְאָכְלָה׃ וַיַּעַשׂ נֹחַ כְּכֹל אֲשֶׁר צִוָּה אֹתוֹ אֱלֹהִים כֵּן עָשָׂה׃

LEKH LEKHA לך לך

וַיֹּאמֶר יהוה אֶל־אַבְרָם לֶךְ־לְךָ מֵאַרְצְךָ וּמִמּוֹלַדְתְּךָ וּמִבֵּית אָבִיךָ אֶל־הָאָרֶץ בראשית יב: א–יג
אֲשֶׁר אַרְאֶךָּ׃ וְאֶעֶשְׂךָ לְגוֹי גָּדוֹל וַאֲבָרֶכְךָ וַאֲגַדְּלָה שְׁמֶךָ וֶהְיֵה בְּרָכָה׃ וַאֲבָרְכָה

לוי מְבָרְכֶיךָ וּמְקַלֶּלְךָ אָאֹר וְנִבְרְכוּ בְךָ כֹּל מִשְׁפְּחֹת הָאֲדָמָה: *וַיֵּלֶךְ אַבְרָם כַּאֲשֶׁר
דִּבֶּר אֵלָיו יהוה וַיֵּלֶךְ אִתּוֹ לוֹט וְאַבְרָם בֶּן־חָמֵשׁ שָׁנִים וְשִׁבְעִים שָׁנָה בְּצֵאתוֹ
מֵחָרָן: וַיִּקַּח אַבְרָם אֶת־שָׂרַי אִשְׁתּוֹ וְאֶת־לוֹט בֶּן־אָחִיו וְאֶת־כָּל־רְכוּשָׁם
אֲשֶׁר רָכָשׁוּ וְאֶת־הַנֶּפֶשׁ אֲשֶׁר־עָשׂוּ בְחָרָן וַיֵּצְאוּ לָלֶכֶת אַרְצָה כְּנַעַן וַיָּבֹאוּ
אַרְצָה כְּנָעַן: וַיַּעֲבֹר אַבְרָם בָּאָרֶץ עַד מְקוֹם שְׁכֶם עַד אֵלוֹן מוֹרֶה וְהַכְּנַעֲנִי
אָז בָּאָרֶץ: וַיֵּרָא יהוה אֶל־אַבְרָם וַיֹּאמֶר לְזַרְעֲךָ אֶתֵּן אֶת־הָאָרֶץ הַזֹּאת וַיִּבֶן
שָׁם מִזְבֵּחַ לַיהוה הַנִּרְאֶה אֵלָיו: וַיַּעְתֵּק מִשָּׁם הָהָרָה מִקֶּדֶם לְבֵית־אֵל וַיֵּט
אָהֳלֹה בֵּית־אֵל מִיָּם וְהָעַי מִקֶּדֶם וַיִּבֶן־שָׁם מִזְבֵּחַ לַיהוה וַיִּקְרָא בְּשֵׁם יהוה:
וַיִּסַּע אַבְרָם הָלוֹךְ וְנָסוֹעַ הַנֶּגְבָּה:

ישראל וַיְהִי רָעָב בָּאָרֶץ וַיֵּרֶד אַבְרָם מִצְרַיְמָה לָגוּר שָׁם כִּי־כָבֵד הָרָעָב בָּאָרֶץ:
וַיְהִי כַּאֲשֶׁר הִקְרִיב לָבוֹא מִצְרָיְמָה וַיֹּאמֶר אֶל־שָׂרַי אִשְׁתּוֹ הִנֵּה־נָא יָדַעְתִּי
כִּי אִשָּׁה יְפַת־מַרְאֶה אָתְּ: וְהָיָה כִּי־יִרְאוּ אֹתָךְ הַמִּצְרִים וְאָמְרוּ אִשְׁתּוֹ זֹאת
וְהָרְגוּ אֹתִי וְאֹתָךְ יְחַיּוּ: אִמְרִי־נָא אֲחֹתִי אָתְּ לְמַעַן יִיטַב־לִי בַעֲבוּרֵךְ וְחָיְתָה
נַפְשִׁי בִּגְלָלֵךְ:

VAYERA וירא

בראשית יח: א–יד וַיֵּרָא אֵלָיו יהוה בְּאֵלֹנֵי מַמְרֵא וְהוּא יֹשֵׁב פֶּתַח־הָאֹהֶל כְּחֹם הַיּוֹם: וַיִּשָּׂא
עֵינָיו וַיַּרְא וְהִנֵּה שְׁלֹשָׁה אֲנָשִׁים נִצָּבִים עָלָיו וַיַּרְא וַיָּרָץ לִקְרָאתָם מִפֶּתַח
הָאֹהֶל וַיִּשְׁתַּחוּ אָרְצָה: וַיֹּאמַר אֲדֹנָי אִם־נָא מָצָאתִי חֵן בְּעֵינֶיךָ אַל־נָא
תַעֲבֹר מֵעַל עַבְדֶּךָ: יֻקַּח־נָא מְעַט־מַיִם וְרַחֲצוּ רַגְלֵיכֶם וְהִשָּׁעֲנוּ תַּחַת הָעֵץ:
וְאֶקְחָה פַת־לֶחֶם וְסַעֲדוּ לִבְּכֶם אַחַר תַּעֲבֹרוּ כִּי־עַל־כֵּן עֲבַרְתֶּם עַל־עַבְדְּכֶם
לוי וַיֹּאמְרוּ כֵּן תַּעֲשֶׂה כַּאֲשֶׁר דִּבַּרְתָּ: *וַיְמַהֵר אַבְרָהָם הָאֹהֱלָה אֶל־שָׂרָה וַיֹּאמֶר
מַהֲרִי שְׁלֹשׁ סְאִים קֶמַח סֹלֶת לוּשִׁי וַעֲשִׂי עֻגוֹת: וְאֶל־הַבָּקָר רָץ אַבְרָהָם
וַיִּקַּח בֶּן־בָּקָר רַךְ וָטוֹב וַיִּתֵּן אֶל־הַנַּעַר וַיְמַהֵר לַעֲשׂוֹת אֹתוֹ: וַיִּקַּח חֶמְאָה
וְחָלָב וּבֶן־הַבָּקָר אֲשֶׁר עָשָׂה וַיִּתֵּן לִפְנֵיהֶם וְהוּא עֹמֵד עֲלֵיהֶם תַּחַת הָעֵץ
ישראל וַיֹּאכֵלוּ: *וַיֹּאמְרוּ אֵלָיו אַיֵּה שָׂרָה אִשְׁתֶּךָ וַיֹּאמֶר הִנֵּה בָאֹהֶל: וַיֹּאמֶר שׁוֹב
אָשׁוּב אֵלֶיךָ כָּעֵת חַיָּה וְהִנֵּה־בֵן לְשָׂרָה אִשְׁתֶּךָ וְשָׂרָה שֹׁמַעַת פֶּתַח הָאֹהֶל
וְהוּא אַחֲרָיו: וְאַבְרָהָם וְשָׂרָה זְקֵנִים בָּאִים בַּיָּמִים חָדַל לִהְיוֹת לְשָׂרָה אֹרַח
כַּנָּשִׁים: וַתִּצְחַק שָׂרָה בְּקִרְבָּהּ לֵאמֹר אַחֲרֵי בְלֹתִי הָיְתָה־לִּי עֶדְנָה וַאדֹנִי

זָקֵן: וַיֹּאמֶר יְהוָה אֶל־אַבְרָהָם לָמָּה זֶּה צָחֲקָה שָׂרָה לֵאמֹר הַאַף אֻמְנָם אֵלֵד
וַאֲנִי זָקַנְתִּי: הֲיִפָּלֵא מֵיְהוָה דָּבָר לַמּוֹעֵד אָשׁוּב אֵלֶיךָ כָּעֵת חַיָּה וּלְשָׂרָה בֵן:

ḤAYYEI SARA

חיי שרה

בראשית כג:
א-טז

וַיִּהְיוּ חַיֵּי שָׂרָה מֵאָה שָׁנָה וְעֶשְׂרִים שָׁנָה וְשֶׁבַע שָׁנִים שְׁנֵי חַיֵּי שָׂרָה: וַתָּמָת
שָׂרָה בְּקִרְיַת אַרְבַּע הִוא חֶבְרוֹן בְּאֶרֶץ כְּנָעַן וַיָּבֹא אַבְרָהָם לִסְפֹּד לְשָׂרָה
וְלִבְכֹּתָהּ: וַיָּקָם אַבְרָהָם מֵעַל פְּנֵי מֵתוֹ וַיְדַבֵּר אֶל־בְּנֵי־חֵת לֵאמֹר: גֵּר־וְתוֹשָׁב
אָנֹכִי עִמָּכֶם תְּנוּ לִי אֲחֻזַּת־קֶבֶר עִמָּכֶם וְאֶקְבְּרָה מֵתִי מִלְּפָנָי: וַיַּעֲנוּ בְנֵי־חֵת
אֶת־אַבְרָהָם לֵאמֹר לוֹ: שְׁמָעֵנוּ ׀ אֲדֹנִי נְשִׂיא אֱלֹהִים אַתָּה בְּתוֹכֵנוּ בְּמִבְחַר
קְבָרֵינוּ קְבֹר אֶת־מֵתֶךָ אִישׁ מִמֶּנּוּ אֶת־קִבְרוֹ לֹא־יִכְלֶה מִמְּךָ מִקְּבֹר מֵתֶךָ:
וַיָּקָם אַבְרָהָם וַיִּשְׁתַּחוּ לְעַם־הָאָרֶץ לִבְנֵי־חֵת: לוי וַיְדַבֵּר אִתָּם לֵאמֹר אִם־יֵשׁ
אֶת־נַפְשְׁכֶם לִקְבֹּר אֶת־מֵתִי מִלְּפָנַי שְׁמָעוּנִי וּפִגְעוּ־לִי בְּעֶפְרוֹן בֶּן־צֹחַר:
וְיִתֶּן־לִי אֶת־מְעָרַת הַמַּכְפֵּלָה אֲשֶׁר־לוֹ אֲשֶׁר בִּקְצֵה שָׂדֵהוּ בְּכֶסֶף מָלֵא יִתְּנֶנָּה
לִי בְּתוֹכְכֶם לַאֲחֻזַּת־קָבֶר: וְעֶפְרוֹן יֹשֵׁב בְּתוֹךְ בְּנֵי־חֵת וַיַּעַן עֶפְרוֹן הַחִתִּי
אֶת־אַבְרָהָם בְּאָזְנֵי בְנֵי־חֵת לְכֹל בָּאֵי שַׁעַר־עִירוֹ לֵאמֹר: לֹא־אֲדֹנִי שְׁמָעֵנִי
הַשָּׂדֶה נָתַתִּי לָךְ וְהַמְּעָרָה אֲשֶׁר־בּוֹ לְךָ נְתַתִּיהָ לְעֵינֵי בְנֵי־עַמִּי נְתַתִּיהָ לָּךְ
קְבֹר מֵתֶךָ: ישראל וַיִּשְׁתַּחוּ אַבְרָהָם לִפְנֵי עַם־הָאָרֶץ: *וַיְדַבֵּר אֶל־עֶפְרוֹן בְּאָזְנֵי עַם־
הָאָרֶץ לֵאמֹר אַךְ אִם־אַתָּה לוּ שְׁמָעֵנִי נָתַתִּי כֶּסֶף הַשָּׂדֶה קַח מִמֶּנִּי וְאֶקְבְּרָה
אֶת־מֵתִי שָׁמָּה: וַיַּעַן עֶפְרוֹן אֶת־אַבְרָהָם לֵאמֹר לוֹ: אֲדֹנִי שְׁמָעֵנִי אֶרֶץ אַרְבַּע
מֵאֹת שֶׁקֶל־כֶּסֶף בֵּינִי וּבֵינְךָ מַה־הִוא וְאֶת־מֵתְךָ קְבֹר: וַיִּשְׁמַע אַבְרָהָם אֶל־
עֶפְרוֹן וַיִּשְׁקֹל אַבְרָהָם לְעֶפְרֹן אֶת־הַכֶּסֶף אֲשֶׁר דִּבֶּר בְּאָזְנֵי בְנֵי־חֵת אַרְבַּע
מֵאוֹת שֶׁקֶל כֶּסֶף עֹבֵר לַסֹּחֵר:

TOLEDOT

תולדות

בראשית
כה:יט-כו:ה

וְאֵלֶּה תּוֹלְדֹת יִצְחָק בֶּן־אַבְרָהָם אַבְרָהָם הוֹלִיד אֶת־יִצְחָק: וַיְהִי יִצְחָק בֶּן־
אַרְבָּעִים שָׁנָה בְּקַחְתּוֹ אֶת־רִבְקָה בַּת־בְּתוּאֵל הָאֲרַמִּי מִפַּדַּן אֲרָם אֲחוֹת לָבָן
הָאֲרַמִּי לוֹ לְאִשָּׁה: וַיֶּעְתַּר יִצְחָק לַיהוָה לְנֹכַח אִשְׁתּוֹ כִּי עֲקָרָה הִוא וַיֵּעָתֶר
לוֹ יְהוָה וַתַּהַר רִבְקָה אִשְׁתּוֹ: וַיִּתְרֹצֲצוּ הַבָּנִים בְּקִרְבָּהּ וַתֹּאמֶר אִם־כֵּן לָמָּה
זֶּה אָנֹכִי וַתֵּלֶךְ לִדְרֹשׁ אֶת־יְהוָה: *וַיֹּאמֶר יְהוָה לָהּ שְׁנֵי גֹיִים בְּבִטְנֵךְ וּשְׁנֵי לוי
גוים

לְאֻמִּים מִמֵּעַיִךְ יִפָּרֵדוּ וּלְאֹם מִלְאֹם יֶאֱמָץ וְרַב יַעֲבֹד צָעִיר: וַיִּמְלְאוּ יָמֶיהָ
לָלֶדֶת וְהִנֵּה תוֹמִם בְּבִטְנָהּ: וַיֵּצֵא הָרִאשׁוֹן אַדְמוֹנִי כֻּלּוֹ כְּאַדֶּרֶת שֵׂעָר וַיִּקְרְאוּ
שְׁמוֹ עֵשָׂו: וְאַחֲרֵי־כֵן יָצָא אָחִיו וְיָדוֹ אֹחֶזֶת בַּעֲקֵב עֵשָׂו וַיִּקְרָא שְׁמוֹ יַעֲקֹב
ישראל וְיִצְחָק בֶּן־שִׁשִּׁים שָׁנָה בְּלֶדֶת אֹתָם: *וַיִּגְדְּלוּ הַנְּעָרִים וַיְהִי עֵשָׂו אִישׁ יֹדֵעַ צַיִד
אִישׁ שָׂדֶה וְיַעֲקֹב אִישׁ תָּם יֹשֵׁב אֹהָלִים: וַיֶּאֱהַב יִצְחָק אֶת־עֵשָׂו כִּי־צַיִד בְּפִיו
וְרִבְקָה אֹהֶבֶת אֶת־יַעֲקֹב: וַיָּזֶד יַעֲקֹב נָזִיד וַיָּבֹא עֵשָׂו מִן־הַשָּׂדֶה וְהוּא עָיֵף:
וַיֹּאמֶר עֵשָׂו אֶל־יַעֲקֹב הַלְעִיטֵנִי נָא מִן־הָאָדֹם הָאָדֹם הַזֶּה כִּי עָיֵף אָנֹכִי עַל־
כֵּן קָרָא־שְׁמוֹ אֱדוֹם: וַיֹּאמֶר יַעֲקֹב מִכְרָה כַיּוֹם אֶת־בְּכֹרָתְךָ לִי: וַיֹּאמֶר עֵשָׂו
הִנֵּה אָנֹכִי הוֹלֵךְ לָמוּת וְלָמָּה־זֶּה לִי בְּכֹרָה: וַיֹּאמֶר יַעֲקֹב הִשָּׁבְעָה לִּי כַּיּוֹם
וַיִּשָּׁבַע לוֹ וַיִּמְכֹּר אֶת־בְּכֹרָתוֹ לְיַעֲקֹב: וְיַעֲקֹב נָתַן לְעֵשָׂו לֶחֶם וּנְזִיד עֲדָשִׁים
וַיֹּאכַל וַיֵּשְׁתְּ וַיָּקָם וַיֵּלַךְ וַיִּבֶז עֵשָׂו אֶת־הַבְּכֹרָה:

וַיְהִי רָעָב בָּאָרֶץ מִלְּבַד הָרָעָב הָרִאשׁוֹן אֲשֶׁר הָיָה בִּימֵי אַבְרָהָם וַיֵּלֶךְ יִצְחָק
אֶל־אֲבִימֶלֶךְ מֶלֶךְ־פְּלִשְׁתִּים גְּרָרָה: וַיֵּרָא אֵלָיו יהוה וַיֹּאמֶר אַל־תֵּרֵד מִצְרָיְמָה
שְׁכֹן בָּאָרֶץ אֲשֶׁר אֹמַר אֵלֶיךָ: גּוּר בָּאָרֶץ הַזֹּאת וְאֶהְיֶה עִמְּךָ וַאֲבָרְכֶךָּ כִּי־לְךָ
וּלְזַרְעֲךָ אֶתֵּן אֶת־כָּל־הָאֲרָצֹת הָאֵל וַהֲקִמֹתִי אֶת־הַשְּׁבֻעָה אֲשֶׁר נִשְׁבַּעְתִּי
לְאַבְרָהָם אָבִיךָ: וְהִרְבֵּיתִי אֶת־זַרְעֲךָ כְּכוֹכְבֵי הַשָּׁמַיִם וְנָתַתִּי לְזַרְעֲךָ אֵת כָּל־
הָאֲרָצֹת הָאֵל וְהִתְבָּרְכוּ בְזַרְעֲךָ כֹּל גּוֹיֵי הָאָרֶץ: עֵקֶב אֲשֶׁר־שָׁמַע אַבְרָהָם
בְּקֹלִי וַיִּשְׁמֹר מִשְׁמַרְתִּי מִצְוֹתַי חֻקּוֹתַי וְתוֹרֹתָי:

ויצא VAYETZEH

בראשית כח:י–כב וַיֵּצֵא יַעֲקֹב מִבְּאֵר שָׁבַע וַיֵּלֶךְ חָרָנָה: וַיִּפְגַּע בַּמָּקוֹם וַיָּלֶן שָׁם כִּי־בָא הַשֶּׁמֶשׁ
וַיִּקַּח מֵאַבְנֵי הַמָּקוֹם וַיָּשֶׂם מְרַאֲשֹׁתָיו וַיִּשְׁכַּב בַּמָּקוֹם הַהוּא: וַיַּחֲלֹם וְהִנֵּה
סֻלָּם מֻצָּב אַרְצָה וְרֹאשׁוֹ מַגִּיעַ הַשָּׁמָיְמָה וְהִנֵּה מַלְאֲכֵי אֱלֹהִים עֹלִים וְיֹרְדִים
לוי בּוֹ: *וְהִנֵּה יהוה נִצָּב עָלָיו וַיֹּאמַר אֲנִי יהוה אֱלֹהֵי אַבְרָהָם אָבִיךָ וֵאלֹהֵי יִצְחָק
הָאָרֶץ אֲשֶׁר אַתָּה שֹׁכֵב עָלֶיהָ לְךָ אֶתְּנֶנָּה וּלְזַרְעֶךָ: וְהָיָה זַרְעֲךָ כַּעֲפַר הָאָרֶץ
וּפָרַצְתָּ יָמָּה וָקֵדְמָה וְצָפֹנָה וָנֶגְבָּה וְנִבְרְכוּ בְךָ כָּל־מִשְׁפְּחֹת הָאֲדָמָה וּבְזַרְעֶךָ:
וְהִנֵּה אָנֹכִי עִמָּךְ וּשְׁמַרְתִּיךָ בְּכֹל אֲשֶׁר־תֵּלֵךְ וַהֲשִׁבֹתִיךָ אֶל־הָאֲדָמָה הַזֹּאת כִּי
לֹא אֶעֱזָבְךָ עַד אֲשֶׁר אִם־עָשִׂיתִי אֵת אֲשֶׁר־דִּבַּרְתִּי לָךְ: וַיִּיקַץ יַעֲקֹב מִשְּׁנָתוֹ

וַיֹּאמֶר אָכֵן יֵשׁ יְהוָה בַּמָּקוֹם הַזֶּה וְאָנֹכִי לֹא יָדָעְתִּי: וַיִּירָא וַיֹּאמַר מַה־נּוֹרָא הַמָּקוֹם הַזֶּה אֵין זֶה כִּי אִם־בֵּית אֱלֹהִים וְזֶה שַׁעַר הַשָּׁמָיִם: וַיַּשְׁכֵּם יַעֲקֹב בַּבֹּקֶר וַיִּקַּח אֶת־הָאֶבֶן אֲשֶׁר־שָׂם מְרַאֲשֹׁתָיו וַיָּשֶׂם אֹתָהּ מַצֵּבָה וַיִּצֹק שֶׁמֶן עַל־רֹאשָׁהּ: וַיִּקְרָא אֶת־שֵׁם־הַמָּקוֹם הַהוּא בֵּית־אֵל וְאוּלָם לוּז שֵׁם־הָעִיר לָרִאשֹׁנָה: וַיִּדַּר יַעֲקֹב נֶדֶר לֵאמֹר אִם־יִהְיֶה אֱלֹהִים עִמָּדִי וּשְׁמָרַנִי בַּדֶּרֶךְ הַזֶּה אֲשֶׁר אָנֹכִי הוֹלֵךְ וְנָתַן־לִי לֶחֶם לֶאֱכֹל וּבֶגֶד לִלְבֹּשׁ: וְשַׁבְתִּי בְשָׁלוֹם אֶל־בֵּית אָבִי וְהָיָה יְהוָה לִי לֵאלֹהִים: וְהָאֶבֶן הַזֹּאת אֲשֶׁר־שַׂמְתִּי מַצֵּבָה יִהְיֶה בֵּית אֱלֹהִים וְכֹל אֲשֶׁר תִּתֶּן־לִי עַשֵּׂר אֲעַשְּׂרֶנּוּ לָךְ:

ויישלח
VAYISHLAH

וַיִּשְׁלַח יַעֲקֹב מַלְאָכִים לְפָנָיו אֶל־עֵשָׂו אָחִיו אַרְצָה שֵׂעִיר שְׂדֵה אֱדוֹם: וַיְצַו אֹתָם לֵאמֹר כֹּה תֹאמְרוּן לַאדֹנִי לְעֵשָׂו כֹּה אָמַר עַבְדְּךָ יַעֲקֹב עִם־לָבָן גַּרְתִּי וָאֵחַר עַד־עָתָּה: וַיְהִי־לִי שׁוֹר וַחֲמוֹר צֹאן וְעֶבֶד וְשִׁפְחָה וָאֶשְׁלְחָה לְהַגִּיד לַאדֹנִי לִמְצֹא־חֵן בְּעֵינֶיךָ: וַיָּשֻׁבוּ הַמַּלְאָכִים אֶל־יַעֲקֹב לֵאמֹר בָּאנוּ אֶל־אָחִיךָ אֶל־עֵשָׂו וְגַם הֹלֵךְ לִקְרָאתְךָ וְאַרְבַּע־מֵאוֹת אִישׁ עִמּוֹ: וַיִּירָא יַעֲקֹב מְאֹד וַיֵּצֶר לוֹ וַיַּחַץ אֶת־הָעָם אֲשֶׁר־אִתּוֹ וְאֶת־הַצֹּאן וְאֶת־הַבָּקָר וְהַגְּמַלִּים לִשְׁנֵי מַחֲנוֹת: וַיֹּאמֶר אִם־יָבוֹא עֵשָׂו אֶל־הַמַּחֲנֶה הָאַחַת וְהִכָּהוּ וְהָיָה הַמַּחֲנֶה הַנִּשְׁאָר לִפְלֵיטָה: וַיֹּאמֶר יַעֲקֹב אֱלֹהֵי אָבִי אַבְרָהָם וֵאלֹהֵי אָבִי יִצְחָק יְהוָה הָאֹמֵר אֵלַי שׁוּב לְאַרְצְךָ וּלְמוֹלַדְתְּךָ וְאֵיטִיבָה עִמָּךְ: קָטֹנְתִּי מִכֹּל הַחֲסָדִים וּמִכָּל־הָאֱמֶת אֲשֶׁר עָשִׂיתָ אֶת־עַבְדֶּךָ כִּי בְמַקְלִי עָבַרְתִּי אֶת־הַיַּרְדֵּן הַזֶּה וְעַתָּה הָיִיתִי לִשְׁנֵי מַחֲנוֹת: הַצִּילֵנִי נָא מִיַּד אָחִי מִיַּד עֵשָׂו כִּי־יָרֵא אָנֹכִי אֹתוֹ פֶּן־יָבוֹא וְהִכַּנִי אֵם עַל־בָּנִים: וְאַתָּה אָמַרְתָּ הֵיטֵב אֵיטִיב עִמָּךְ וְשַׂמְתִּי אֶת־זַרְעֲךָ כְּחוֹל הַיָּם אֲשֶׁר לֹא־יִסָּפֵר מֵרֹב:

ויישב
VAYESHEV

וַיֵּשֶׁב יַעֲקֹב בְּאֶרֶץ מְגוּרֵי אָבִיו בְּאֶרֶץ כְּנָעַן: אֵלֶּה ׀ תֹּלְדוֹת יַעֲקֹב יוֹסֵף בֶּן־שְׁבַע־עֶשְׂרֵה שָׁנָה הָיָה רֹעֶה אֶת־אֶחָיו בַּצֹּאן וְהוּא נַעַר אֶת־בְּנֵי בִלְהָה וְאֶת־בְּנֵי זִלְפָּה נְשֵׁי אָבִיו וַיָּבֵא יוֹסֵף אֶת־דִּבָּתָם רָעָה אֶל־אֲבִיהֶם: וְיִשְׂרָאֵל

לוי אָהַב אֶת־יוֹסֵף מִכָּל־בָּנָיו כִּי־בֶן־זְקֻנִים הוּא לוֹ וְעָשָׂה לוֹ כְּתֹנֶת פַּסִּים׃ *וַיִּרְאוּ
אֶחָיו כִּי־אֹתוֹ אָהַב אֲבִיהֶם מִכָּל־אֶחָיו וַיִּשְׂנְאוּ אֹתוֹ וְלֹא יָכְלוּ דַּבְּרוֹ לְשָׁלֹם׃
וַיַּחֲלֹם יוֹסֵף חֲלוֹם וַיַּגֵּד לְאֶחָיו וַיּוֹסִפוּ עוֹד שְׂנֹא אֹתוֹ׃ וַיֹּאמֶר אֲלֵיהֶם שִׁמְעוּ־
נָא הַחֲלוֹם הַזֶּה אֲשֶׁר חָלָמְתִּי׃ וְהִנֵּה אֲנַחְנוּ מְאַלְּמִים אֲלֻמִּים בְּתוֹךְ הַשָּׂדֶה
וְהִנֵּה קָמָה אֲלֻמָּתִי וְגַם־נִצָּבָה וְהִנֵּה תְסֻבֶּינָה אֲלֻמֹּתֵיכֶם וַתִּשְׁתַּחֲוֶיןָ לַאֲלֻמָּתִי׃
ישראל *וַיֹּאמְרוּ לוֹ אֶחָיו הֲמָלֹךְ תִּמְלֹךְ עָלֵינוּ אִם־מָשׁוֹל תִּמְשֹׁל בָּנוּ וַיּוֹסִפוּ עוֹד
שְׂנֹא אֹתוֹ עַל־חֲלֹמֹתָיו וְעַל־דְּבָרָיו׃ וַיַּחֲלֹם עוֹד חֲלוֹם אַחֵר וַיְסַפֵּר אֹתוֹ
לְאֶחָיו וַיֹּאמֶר הִנֵּה חָלַמְתִּי חֲלוֹם עוֹד וְהִנֵּה הַשֶּׁמֶשׁ וְהַיָּרֵחַ וְאַחַד עָשָׂר
כּוֹכָבִים מִשְׁתַּחֲוִים לִי׃ וַיְסַפֵּר אֶל־אָבִיו וְאֶל־אֶחָיו וַיִּגְעַר־בּוֹ אָבִיו וַיֹּאמֶר לוֹ
מָה הַחֲלוֹם הַזֶּה אֲשֶׁר חָלָמְתָּ הֲבוֹא נָבוֹא אֲנִי וְאִמְּךָ וְאַחֶיךָ לְהִשְׁתַּחֲוֺת לְךָ
אָרְצָה׃ וַיְקַנְאוּ־בוֹ אֶחָיו וְאָבִיו שָׁמַר אֶת־הַדָּבָר׃

מקץ MIKETZ

בראשית מא:א-יד וַיְהִי מִקֵּץ שְׁנָתַיִם יָמִים וּפַרְעֹה חֹלֵם וְהִנֵּה עֹמֵד עַל־הַיְאֹר׃ וְהִנֵּה מִן־הַיְאֹר
עֹלֹת שֶׁבַע פָּרוֹת יְפוֹת מַרְאֶה וּבְרִיאֹת בָּשָׂר וַתִּרְעֶינָה בָּאָחוּ׃ וְהִנֵּה שֶׁבַע
פָּרוֹת אֲחֵרוֹת עֹלוֹת אַחֲרֵיהֶן מִן־הַיְאֹר רָעוֹת מַרְאֶה וְדַקּוֹת בָּשָׂר וַתַּעֲמֹדְנָה
אֵצֶל הַפָּרוֹת עַל־שְׂפַת הַיְאֹר׃ וַתֹּאכַלְנָה הַפָּרוֹת רָעוֹת הַמַּרְאֶה וְדַקֹּת הַבָּשָׂר
לוי אֵת שֶׁבַע הַפָּרוֹת יְפֹת הַמַּרְאֶה וְהַבְּרִיאֹת וַיִּיקַץ פַּרְעֹה׃ *וַיִּישָׁן וַיַּחֲלֹם שֵׁנִית
וְהִנֵּה ׀ שֶׁבַע שִׁבֳּלִים עֹלוֹת בְּקָנֶה אֶחָד בְּרִיאוֹת וְטֹבוֹת׃ וְהִנֵּה שֶׁבַע שִׁבֳּלִים
דַּקּוֹת וּשְׁדוּפֹת קָדִים צֹמְחוֹת אַחֲרֵיהֶן׃ וַתִּבְלַעְנָה הַשִּׁבֳּלִים הַדַּקּוֹת אֵת
ישראל שֶׁבַע הַשִּׁבֳּלִים הַבְּרִיאוֹת וְהַמְּלֵאוֹת וַיִּיקַץ פַּרְעֹה וְהִנֵּה חֲלוֹם׃ *וַיְהִי בַבֹּקֶר
וַתִּפָּעֶם רוּחוֹ וַיִּשְׁלַח וַיִּקְרָא אֶת־כָּל־חַרְטֻמֵּי מִצְרַיִם וְאֶת־כָּל־חֲכָמֶיהָ וַיְסַפֵּר
פַּרְעֹה לָהֶם אֶת־חֲלֹמוֹ וְאֵין־פּוֹתֵר אוֹתָם לְפַרְעֹה׃ וַיְדַבֵּר שַׂר הַמַּשְׁקִים אֶת־
פַּרְעֹה לֵאמֹר אֶת־חֲטָאַי אֲנִי מַזְכִּיר הַיּוֹם׃ פַּרְעֹה קָצַף עַל־עֲבָדָיו וַיִּתֵּן אֹתִי
בְּמִשְׁמַר בֵּית שַׂר הַטַּבָּחִים אֹתִי וְאֵת שַׂר הָאֹפִים׃ וַנַּחַלְמָה חֲלוֹם בְּלַיְלָה
אֶחָד אֲנִי וָהוּא אִישׁ כְּפִתְרוֹן חֲלֹמוֹ חָלָמְנוּ׃ וְשָׁם אִתָּנוּ נַעַר עִבְרִי עֶבֶד לְשַׂר
הַטַּבָּחִים וַנְּסַפֶּר־לוֹ וַיִּפְתָּר־לָנוּ אֶת־חֲלֹמֹתֵינוּ אִישׁ כַּחֲלֹמוֹ פָּתָר׃ וַיְהִי כַּאֲשֶׁר
פָּתַר־לָנוּ כֵּן הָיָה אֹתִי הֵשִׁיב עַל־כַּנִּי וְאֹתוֹ תָלָה׃ וַיִּשְׁלַח פַּרְעֹה וַיִּקְרָא אֶת־
יוֹסֵף וַיְרִיצֻהוּ מִן־הַבּוֹר וַיְגַלַּח וַיְחַלֵּף שִׂמְלֹתָיו וַיָּבֹא אֶל־פַּרְעֹה׃

VAYIGASH ויגש

בראשית מד:יח-ל

וַיִּגַּשׁ אֵלָיו יְהוּדָה וַיֹּאמֶר בִּי אֲדֹנִי יְדַבֶּר־נָא עַבְדְּךָ דָבָר בְּאׇזְנֵי אֲדֹנִי וְאַל־יִחַר
אַפְּךָ בְּעַבְדֶּךָ כִּי כָמוֹךָ כְּפַרְעֹה׃ אֲדֹנִי שָׁאַל אֶת־עֲבָדָיו לֵאמֹר הֲיֵשׁ־לָכֶם אָב
אוֹ־אָח׃ וַנֹּאמֶר אֶל־אֲדֹנִי יֶשׁ־לָנוּ אָב זָקֵן וְיֶלֶד זְקֻנִים קָטָן וְאָחִיו מֵת וַיִּוָּתֵר הוּא
לוי לְבַדּוֹ לְאִמּוֹ וְאָבִיו אֲהֵבוֹ׃ *וַתֹּאמֶר אֶל־עֲבָדֶיךָ הוֹרִדֻהוּ אֵלָי וְאָשִׂימָה עֵינִי
עָלָיו׃ וַנֹּאמֶר אֶל־אֲדֹנִי לֹא־יוּכַל הַנַּעַר לַעֲזֹב אֶת־אָבִיו וְעָזַב אֶת־אָבִיו וָמֵת׃
וַתֹּאמֶר אֶל־עֲבָדֶיךָ אִם־לֹא יֵרֵד אֲחִיכֶם הַקָּטֹן אִתְּכֶם לֹא תֹסִפוּן לִרְאוֹת פָּנָי׃
ישראל וַיְהִי כִּי עָלִינוּ אֶל־עַבְדְּךָ אָבִי וַנַּגֶּד־לוֹ אֵת דִּבְרֵי אֲדֹנִי׃ *וַיֹּאמֶר אָבִינוּ שֻׁבוּ
שִׁבְרוּ־לָנוּ מְעַט־אֹכֶל׃ וַנֹּאמֶר לֹא נוּכַל לָרֶדֶת אִם־יֵשׁ אָחִינוּ הַקָּטֹן אִתָּנוּ
וְיָרַדְנוּ כִּי־לֹא נוּכַל לִרְאוֹת פְּנֵי הָאִישׁ וְאָחִינוּ הַקָּטֹן אֵינֶנּוּ אִתָּנוּ׃ וַיֹּאמֶר
עַבְדְּךָ אָבִי אֵלֵינוּ אַתֶּם יְדַעְתֶּם כִּי שְׁנַיִם יָלְדָה־לִּי אִשְׁתִּי׃ וַיֵּצֵא הָאֶחָד מֵאִתִּי
וָאֹמַר אַךְ טָרֹף טֹרָף וְלֹא רְאִיתִיו עַד־הֵנָּה׃ וּלְקַחְתֶּם גַּם־אֶת־זֶה מֵעִם פָּנַי
וְקָרָהוּ אָסוֹן וְהוֹרַדְתֶּם אֶת־שֵׂיבָתִי בְּרָעָה שְׁאֹלָה׃ וְעַתָּה כְּבֹאִי אֶל־עַבְדְּךָ
אָבִי וְהַנַּעַר אֵינֶנּוּ אִתָּנוּ וְנַפְשׁוֹ קְשׁוּרָה בְנַפְשׁוֹ׃

VAYHI ויחי

בראשית מז:כח-מח:ט

וַיְחִי יַעֲקֹב בְּאֶרֶץ מִצְרַיִם שְׁבַע עֶשְׂרֵה שָׁנָה וַיְהִי יְמֵי־יַעֲקֹב שְׁנֵי חַיָּיו שֶׁבַע
שָׁנִים וְאַרְבָּעִים וּמְאַת שָׁנָה׃ וַיִּקְרְבוּ יְמֵי־יִשְׂרָאֵל לָמוּת וַיִּקְרָא ׀ לִבְנוֹ לְיוֹסֵף
וַיֹּאמֶר לוֹ אִם־נָא מָצָאתִי חֵן בְּעֵינֶיךָ שִׂים־נָא יָדְךָ תַּחַת יְרֵכִי וְעָשִׂיתָ עִמָּדִי
חֶסֶד וֶאֱמֶת אַל־נָא תִקְבְּרֵנִי בְּמִצְרָיִם׃ וְשָׁכַבְתִּי עִם־אֲבֹתַי וּנְשָׂאתַנִי מִמִּצְרַיִם
וּקְבַרְתַּנִי בִּקְבֻרָתָם וַיֹּאמַר אָנֹכִי אֶעֱשֶׂה כִדְבָרֶךָ׃ וַיֹּאמֶר הִשָּׁבְעָה לִי וַיִּשָּׁבַע
לוֹ וַיִּשְׁתַּחוּ יִשְׂרָאֵל עַל־רֹאשׁ הַמִּטָּה׃
לוי וַיְהִי אַחֲרֵי הַדְּבָרִים הָאֵלֶּה וַיֹּאמֶר לְיוֹסֵף הִנֵּה אָבִיךָ חֹלֶה וַיִּקַּח אֶת־שְׁנֵי בָנָיו
עִמּוֹ אֶת־מְנַשֶּׁה וְאֶת־אֶפְרָיִם׃ וַיַּגֵּד לְיַעֲקֹב וַיֹּאמֶר הִנֵּה בִּנְךָ יוֹסֵף בָּא אֵלֶיךָ
וַיִּתְחַזֵּק יִשְׂרָאֵל וַיֵּשֶׁב עַל־הַמִּטָּה׃ וַיֹּאמֶר יַעֲקֹב אֶל־יוֹסֵף אֵל שַׁדַּי נִרְאָה־אֵלַי
ישראל בְּלוּז בְּאֶרֶץ כְּנָעַן וַיְבָרֶךְ אֹתִי׃ *וַיֹּאמֶר אֵלַי הִנְנִי מַפְרְךָ וְהִרְבִּיתִךָ וּנְתַתִּיךָ
לִקְהַל עַמִּים וְנָתַתִּי אֶת־הָאָרֶץ הַזֹּאת לְזַרְעֲךָ אַחֲרֶיךָ אֲחֻזַּת עוֹלָם׃ וְעַתָּה
שְׁנֵי־בָנֶיךָ הַנּוֹלָדִים לְךָ בְּאֶרֶץ מִצְרַיִם עַד־בֹּאִי אֵלֶיךָ מִצְרַיְמָה לִי־הֵם אֶפְרַיִם
וּמְנַשֶּׁה כִּרְאוּבֵן וְשִׁמְעוֹן יִהְיוּ־לִי׃ וּמוֹלַדְתְּךָ אֲשֶׁר־הוֹלַדְתָּ אַחֲרֵיהֶם לְךָ יִהְיוּ

עַל שֵׁם אֲחֵיהֶם יִקָּרְאוּ בְּנַחֲלָתָם: וַאֲנִי | בְּבֹאִי מִפַּדָּן מֵתָה עָלַי רָחֵל בְּאֶרֶץ
כְּנַעַן בַּדֶּרֶךְ בְּעוֹד כִּבְרַת־אֶרֶץ לָבֹא אֶפְרָתָה וָאֶקְבְּרֶהָ שָּׁם בְּדֶרֶךְ אֶפְרָת
הִוא בֵּית לָחֶם: וַיַּרְא יִשְׂרָאֵל אֶת־בְּנֵי יוֹסֵף וַיֹּאמֶר מִי־אֵלֶּה: וַיֹּאמֶר יוֹסֵף
אֶל־אָבִיו בָּנַי הֵם אֲשֶׁר־נָתַן־לִי אֱלֹהִים בָּזֶה וַיֹּאמַר קָחֶם־נָא אֵלַי וַאֲבָרְכֵם:

שמות SHEMOT

שמות א:א–יז וְאֵלֶּה שְׁמוֹת בְּנֵי יִשְׂרָאֵל הַבָּאִים מִצְרָיְמָה אֵת יַעֲקֹב אִישׁ וּבֵיתוֹ בָּאוּ:
רְאוּבֵן שִׁמְעוֹן לֵוִי וִיהוּדָה: יִשָּׂשכָר זְבוּלֻן וּבִנְיָמִן: דָּן וְנַפְתָּלִי גָּד וְאָשֵׁר:
וַיְהִי כָּל־נֶפֶשׁ יֹצְאֵי יֶרֶךְ־יַעֲקֹב שִׁבְעִים נָפֶשׁ וְיוֹסֵף הָיָה בְמִצְרָיִם: וַיָּמָת יוֹסֵף
וְכָל־אֶחָיו וְכֹל הַדּוֹר הַהוּא: וּבְנֵי יִשְׂרָאֵל פָּרוּ וַיִּשְׁרְצוּ וַיִּרְבּוּ וַיַּעַצְמוּ בִּמְאֹד
מְאֹד וַתִּמָּלֵא הָאָרֶץ אֹתָם:

לוי וַיָּקָם מֶלֶךְ־חָדָשׁ עַל־מִצְרָיִם אֲשֶׁר לֹא־יָדַע אֶת־יוֹסֵף: וַיֹּאמֶר אֶל־עַמּוֹ הִנֵּה עַם
בְּנֵי יִשְׂרָאֵל רַב וְעָצוּם מִמֶּנּוּ: הָבָה נִתְחַכְּמָה לוֹ פֶּן־יִרְבֶּה וְהָיָה כִּי־תִקְרֶאנָה
מִלְחָמָה וְנוֹסַף גַּם־הוּא עַל־שֹׂנְאֵינוּ וְנִלְחַם־בָּנוּ וְעָלָה מִן־הָאָרֶץ: וַיָּשִׂימוּ
עָלָיו שָׂרֵי מִסִּים לְמַעַן עַנֹּתוֹ בְּסִבְלֹתָם וַיִּבֶן עָרֵי מִסְכְּנוֹת לְפַרְעֹה אֶת־פִּתֹם
וְאֶת־רַעַמְסֵס: וְכַאֲשֶׁר יְעַנּוּ אֹתוֹ כֵּן יִרְבֶּה וְכֵן יִפְרֹץ וַיָּקֻצוּ מִפְּנֵי בְּנֵי יִשְׂרָאֵל:

ישראל *וַיַּעֲבִדוּ מִצְרַיִם אֶת־בְּנֵי יִשְׂרָאֵל בְּפָרֶךְ: וַיְמָרְרוּ אֶת־חַיֵּיהֶם בַּעֲבֹדָה קָשָׁה
בְּחֹמֶר וּבִלְבֵנִים וּבְכָל־עֲבֹדָה בַּשָּׂדֶה אֵת כָּל־עֲבֹדָתָם אֲשֶׁר־עָבְדוּ בָהֶם
בְּפָרֶךְ: וַיֹּאמֶר מֶלֶךְ מִצְרַיִם לַמְיַלְּדֹת הָעִבְרִיֹּת אֲשֶׁר שֵׁם הָאַחַת שִׁפְרָה וְשֵׁם
הַשֵּׁנִית פּוּעָה: וַיֹּאמֶר בְּיַלֶּדְכֶן אֶת־הָעִבְרִיּוֹת וּרְאִיתֶן עַל־הָאָבְנָיִם אִם־בֵּן
הוּא וַהֲמִתֶּן אֹתוֹ וְאִם־בַּת הִוא וָחָיָה: וַתִּירֶאןָ הַמְיַלְּדֹת אֶת־הָאֱלֹהִים וְלֹא
עָשׂוּ כַּאֲשֶׁר דִּבֶּר אֲלֵיהֶן מֶלֶךְ מִצְרָיִם וַתְּחַיֶּיןָ אֶת־הַיְלָדִים:

וארא VA'ERA

שמות ו:ב–יג וַיְדַבֵּר אֱלֹהִים אֶל־מֹשֶׁה וַיֹּאמֶר אֵלָיו אֲנִי יהוה: וָאֵרָא אֶל־אַבְרָהָם אֶל־יִצְחָק
וְאֶל־יַעֲקֹב בְּאֵל שַׁדָּי וּשְׁמִי יהוה לֹא נוֹדַעְתִּי לָהֶם: וְגַם הֲקִמֹתִי אֶת־בְּרִיתִי
אִתָּם לָתֵת לָהֶם אֶת־אֶרֶץ כְּנָעַן אֵת אֶרֶץ מְגֻרֵיהֶם אֲשֶׁר־גָּרוּ בָהּ: וְגַם | אֲנִי
שָׁמַעְתִּי אֶת־נַאֲקַת בְּנֵי יִשְׂרָאֵל אֲשֶׁר מִצְרַיִם מַעֲבִדִים אֹתָם וָאֶזְכֹּר אֶת־

בְּרִיתִי: *לָכֵן אֱמֹר לִבְנֵי־יִשְׂרָאֵל אֲנִי יהוה וְהוֹצֵאתִי אֶתְכֶם מִתַּחַת סִבְלֹת לוי
מִצְרַיִם וְהִצַּלְתִּי אֶתְכֶם מֵעֲבֹדָתָם וְגָאַלְתִּי אֶתְכֶם בִּזְרוֹעַ נְטוּיָה וּבִשְׁפָטִים
גְּדֹלִים: וְלָקַחְתִּי אֶתְכֶם לִי לְעָם וְהָיִיתִי לָכֶם לֵאלֹהִים וִידַעְתֶּם כִּי אֲנִי יהוה
אֱלֹהֵיכֶם הַמּוֹצִיא אֶתְכֶם מִתַּחַת סִבְלוֹת מִצְרָיִם: וְהֵבֵאתִי אֶתְכֶם אֶל־הָאָרֶץ
אֲשֶׁר נָשָׂאתִי אֶת־יָדִי לָתֵת אֹתָהּ לְאַבְרָהָם לְיִצְחָק וּלְיַעֲקֹב וְנָתַתִּי אֹתָהּ לָכֶם
מוֹרָשָׁה אֲנִי יהוה: וַיְדַבֵּר מֹשֶׁה כֵּן אֶל־בְּנֵי יִשְׂרָאֵל וְלֹא שָׁמְעוּ אֶל־מֹשֶׁה
מִקֹּצֶר רוּחַ וּמֵעֲבֹדָה קָשָׁה:

וַיְדַבֵּר יהוה אֶל־מֹשֶׁה לֵּאמֹר: בֹּא דַבֵּר אֶל־פַּרְעֹה מֶלֶךְ מִצְרָיִם וִישַׁלַּח אֶת־ ישראל
בְּנֵי־יִשְׂרָאֵל מֵאַרְצוֹ: וַיְדַבֵּר מֹשֶׁה לִפְנֵי יהוה לֵאמֹר הֵן בְּנֵי־יִשְׂרָאֵל לֹא־שָׁמְעוּ
אֵלַי וְאֵיךְ יִשְׁמָעֵנִי פַרְעֹה וַאֲנִי עֲרַל שְׂפָתָיִם:

וַיְדַבֵּר יהוה אֶל־מֹשֶׁה וְאֶל־אַהֲרֹן וַיְצַוֵּם אֶל־בְּנֵי יִשְׂרָאֵל וְאֶל־פַּרְעֹה מֶלֶךְ
מִצְרָיִם לְהוֹצִיא אֶת־בְּנֵי־יִשְׂרָאֵל מֵאֶרֶץ מִצְרָיִם:

BO בא

וַיֹּאמֶר יהוה אֶל־מֹשֶׁה בֹּא אֶל־פַּרְעֹה כִּי־אֲנִי הִכְבַּדְתִּי אֶת־לִבּוֹ וְאֶת־לֵב שמות י:א–יא
עֲבָדָיו לְמַעַן שִׁתִי אֹתֹתַי אֵלֶּה בְּקִרְבּוֹ: וּלְמַעַן תְּסַפֵּר בְּאָזְנֵי בִנְךָ וּבֶן־בִּנְךָ אֵת
אֲשֶׁר הִתְעַלַּלְתִּי בְּמִצְרַיִם וְאֶת־אֹתֹתַי אֲשֶׁר־שַׂמְתִּי בָם וִידַעְתֶּם כִּי־אֲנִי יהוה:
וַיָּבֹא מֹשֶׁה וְאַהֲרֹן אֶל־פַּרְעֹה וַיֹּאמְרוּ אֵלָיו כֹּה־אָמַר יהוה אֱלֹהֵי הָעִבְרִים
עַד־מָתַי מֵאַנְתָּ לֵעָנֹת מִפָּנָי שַׁלַּח עַמִּי וְיַעַבְדֻנִי: *כִּי אִם־מָאֵן אַתָּה לְשַׁלֵּחַ לוי
אֶת־עַמִּי הִנְנִי מֵבִיא מָחָר אַרְבֶּה בִּגְבֻלֶךָ: וְכִסָּה אֶת־עֵין הָאָרֶץ וְלֹא יוּכַל
לִרְאֹת אֶת־הָאָרֶץ וְאָכַל ׀ אֶת־יֶתֶר הַפְּלֵטָה הַנִּשְׁאֶרֶת לָכֶם מִן־הַבָּרָד וְאָכַל
אֶת־כָּל־הָעֵץ הַצֹּמֵחַ לָכֶם מִן־הַשָּׂדֶה: וּמָלְאוּ בָתֶּיךָ וּבָתֵּי כָל־עֲבָדֶיךָ וּבָתֵּי
כָל־מִצְרַיִם אֲשֶׁר לֹא־רָאוּ אֲבֹתֶיךָ וַאֲבוֹת אֲבֹתֶיךָ מִיּוֹם הֱיוֹתָם עַל־הָאֲדָמָה
עַד הַיּוֹם הַזֶּה וַיִּפֶן וַיֵּצֵא מֵעִם פַּרְעֹה: *וַיֹּאמְרוּ עַבְדֵי פַרְעֹה אֵלָיו עַד־מָתַי ישראל
יִהְיֶה זֶה לָנוּ לְמוֹקֵשׁ שַׁלַּח אֶת־הָאֲנָשִׁים וְיַעַבְדוּ אֶת־יהוה אֱלֹהֵיהֶם הֲטֶרֶם
תֵּדַע כִּי אָבְדָה מִצְרָיִם: וַיּוּשַׁב אֶת־מֹשֶׁה וְאֶת־אַהֲרֹן אֶל־פַּרְעֹה וַיֹּאמֶר
אֲלֵהֶם לְכוּ עִבְדוּ אֶת־יהוה אֱלֹהֵיכֶם מִי וָמִי הַהֹלְכִים: וַיֹּאמֶר מֹשֶׁה בִּנְעָרֵינוּ
וּבִזְקֵנֵינוּ נֵלֵךְ בְּבָנֵינוּ וּבִבְנוֹתֵנוּ בְּצֹאנֵנוּ וּבִבְקָרֵנוּ נֵלֵךְ כִּי חַג־יהוה לָנוּ: וַיֹּאמֶר

אֲלֵהֶם יְהִי כֵן יהוה עִמָּכֶם כַּאֲשֶׁר אֲשַׁלַּח אֶתְכֶם וְאֶת־טַפְּכֶם רְאוּ כִּי רָעָה
נֶגֶד פְּנֵיכֶם: לֹא כֵן לְכוּ־נָא הַגְּבָרִים וְעִבְדוּ אֶת־יהוה כִּי אֹתָהּ אַתֶּם מְבַקְשִׁים
וַיְגָרֶשׁ אֹתָם מֵאֵת פְּנֵי פַרְעֹה:

בשלח BESHALLAḤ

שמות יג:יז–יד:ח וַיְהִי בְּשַׁלַּח פַּרְעֹה אֶת־הָעָם וְלֹא־נָחָם אֱלֹהִים דֶּרֶךְ אֶרֶץ פְּלִשְׁתִּים כִּי קָרוֹב
הוּא כִּי ׀ אָמַר אֱלֹהִים פֶּן־יִנָּחֵם הָעָם בִּרְאֹתָם מִלְחָמָה וְשָׁבוּ מִצְרָיְמָה: וַיַּסֵּב
אֱלֹהִים ׀ אֶת־הָעָם דֶּרֶךְ הַמִּדְבָּר יַם־סוּף וַחֲמֻשִׁים עָלוּ בְנֵי־יִשְׂרָאֵל מֵאֶרֶץ
מִצְרָיִם: וַיִּקַּח מֹשֶׁה אֶת־עַצְמוֹת יוֹסֵף עִמּוֹ כִּי הַשְׁבֵּעַ הִשְׁבִּיעַ אֶת־בְּנֵי יִשְׂרָאֵל
לֵאמֹר פָּקֹד יִפְקֹד אֱלֹהִים אֶתְכֶם וְהַעֲלִיתֶם אֶת־עַצְמֹתַי מִזֶּה אִתְּכֶם: וַיִּסְעוּ
מִסֻּכֹּת וַיַּחֲנוּ בְאֵתָם בִּקְצֵה הַמִּדְבָּר: וַיהוה הֹלֵךְ לִפְנֵיהֶם יוֹמָם בְּעַמּוּד עָנָן
לַנְחֹתָם הַדֶּרֶךְ וְלַיְלָה בְּעַמּוּד אֵשׁ לְהָאִיר לָהֶם לָלֶכֶת יוֹמָם וָלָיְלָה: לֹא־יָמִישׁ
עַמּוּד הֶעָנָן יוֹמָם וְעַמּוּד הָאֵשׁ לָיְלָה לִפְנֵי הָעָם:
לוי וַיְדַבֵּר יהוה אֶל־מֹשֶׁה לֵּאמֹר: דַּבֵּר אֶל־בְּנֵי יִשְׂרָאֵל וְיָשֻׁבוּ וְיַחֲנוּ לִפְנֵי פִּי
הַחִירֹת בֵּין מִגְדֹּל וּבֵין הַיָּם לִפְנֵי בַּעַל צְפֹן נִכְחוֹ תַחֲנוּ עַל־הַיָּם: וְאָמַר פַּרְעֹה
לִבְנֵי יִשְׂרָאֵל נְבֻכִים הֵם בָּאָרֶץ סָגַר עֲלֵיהֶם הַמִּדְבָּר: וְחִזַּקְתִּי אֶת־לֵב־פַּרְעֹה
וְרָדַף אַחֲרֵיהֶם וְאִכָּבְדָה בְּפַרְעֹה וּבְכָל־חֵילוֹ וְיָדְעוּ מִצְרַיִם כִּי־אֲנִי יהוה וַיַּעֲשׂוּ־
ישראל כֵן: *וַיֻּגַּד לְמֶלֶךְ מִצְרַיִם כִּי בָרַח הָעָם וַיֵּהָפֵךְ לְבַב פַּרְעֹה וַעֲבָדָיו אֶל־הָעָם
וַיֹּאמְרוּ מַה־זֹּאת עָשִׂינוּ כִּי־שִׁלַּחְנוּ אֶת־יִשְׂרָאֵל מֵעָבְדֵנוּ: וַיֶּאְסֹר אֶת־רִכְבּוֹ
וְאֶת־עַמּוֹ לָקַח עִמּוֹ: וַיִּקַּח שֵׁשׁ־מֵאוֹת רֶכֶב בָּחוּר וְכֹל רֶכֶב מִצְרָיִם וְשָׁלִשִׁם
עַל־כֻּלּוֹ: וַיְחַזֵּק יהוה אֶת־לֵב פַּרְעֹה מֶלֶךְ מִצְרַיִם וַיִּרְדֹּף אַחֲרֵי בְּנֵי יִשְׂרָאֵל
וּבְנֵי יִשְׂרָאֵל יֹצְאִים בְּיָד רָמָה:

יתרו YITRO

שמות יח:א-יב וַיִּשְׁמַע יִתְרוֹ כֹהֵן מִדְיָן חֹתֵן מֹשֶׁה אֵת כָּל־אֲשֶׁר עָשָׂה אֱלֹהִים לְמֹשֶׁה
וּלְיִשְׂרָאֵל עַמּוֹ כִּי־הוֹצִיא יהוה אֶת־יִשְׂרָאֵל מִמִּצְרָיִם: וַיִּקַּח יִתְרוֹ חֹתֵן
מֹשֶׁה אֶת־צִפֹּרָה אֵשֶׁת מֹשֶׁה אַחַר שִׁלּוּחֶיהָ: וְאֵת שְׁנֵי בָנֶיהָ אֲשֶׁר שֵׁם הָאֶחָד
גֵּרְשֹׁם כִּי אָמַר גֵּר הָיִיתִי בְּאֶרֶץ נָכְרִיָּה: וְשֵׁם הָאֶחָד אֱלִיעֶזֶר כִּי־אֱלֹהֵי אָבִי

לוי בְּעֶזְרִי וַיַּצִּלֵנִי מֵחֶרֶב פַּרְעֹה: *וַיָּבֹא יִתְרוֹ חֹתֵן מֹשֶׁה וּבָנָיו וְאִשְׁתּוֹ אֶל־מֹשֶׁה
אֶל־הַמִּדְבָּר אֲשֶׁר־הוּא חֹנֶה שָׁם הַר הָאֱלֹהִים: וַיֹּאמֶר אֶל־מֹשֶׁה אֲנִי חֹתֶנְךָ
יִתְרוֹ בָּא אֵלֶיךָ וְאִשְׁתְּךָ וּשְׁנֵי בָנֶיהָ עִמָּהּ: וַיֵּצֵא מֹשֶׁה לִקְרַאת חֹתְנוֹ וַיִּשְׁתַּחוּ
וַיִּשַּׁק־לוֹ וַיִּשְׁאֲלוּ אִישׁ־לְרֵעֵהוּ לְשָׁלוֹם וַיָּבֹאוּ הָאֹהֱלָה: וַיְסַפֵּר מֹשֶׁה לְחֹתְנוֹ
אֵת כָּל־אֲשֶׁר עָשָׂה יהוה לְפַרְעֹה וּלְמִצְרַיִם עַל אוֹדֹת יִשְׂרָאֵל אֵת כָּל־הַתְּלָאָה
ישראל אֲשֶׁר מְצָאָתַם בַּדֶּרֶךְ וַיַּצִּלֵם יהוה: *וַיִּחַדְּ יִתְרוֹ עַל כָּל־הַטּוֹבָה אֲשֶׁר־עָשָׂה
יהוה לְיִשְׂרָאֵל אֲשֶׁר הִצִּילוֹ מִיַּד מִצְרָיִם: וַיֹּאמֶר יִתְרוֹ בָּרוּךְ יהוה אֲשֶׁר הִצִּיל
אֶתְכֶם מִיַּד מִצְרַיִם וּמִיַּד פַּרְעֹה אֲשֶׁר הִצִּיל אֶת־הָעָם מִתַּחַת יַד־מִצְרָיִם:
עַתָּה יָדַעְתִּי כִּי־גָדוֹל יהוה מִכָּל־הָאֱלֹהִים כִּי בַדָּבָר אֲשֶׁר זָדוּ עֲלֵיהֶם: וַיִּקַּח
יִתְרוֹ חֹתֵן מֹשֶׁה עֹלָה וּזְבָחִים לֵאלֹהִים וַיָּבֹא אַהֲרֹן וְכֹל ׀ זִקְנֵי יִשְׂרָאֵל לֶאֱכָל־
לֶחֶם עִם־חֹתֵן מֹשֶׁה לִפְנֵי הָאֱלֹהִים:

משפטים MISHPATIM

שמות כא:א-יט וְאֵלֶּה הַמִּשְׁפָּטִים אֲשֶׁר תָּשִׂים לִפְנֵיהֶם: כִּי תִקְנֶה עֶבֶד עִבְרִי שֵׁשׁ שָׁנִים
יַעֲבֹד וּבַשְּׁבִעִת יֵצֵא לַחָפְשִׁי חִנָּם: אִם־בְּגַפּוֹ יָבֹא בְּגַפּוֹ יֵצֵא אִם־בַּעַל אִשָּׁה
הוּא וְיָצְאָה אִשְׁתּוֹ עִמּוֹ: אִם־אֲדֹנָיו יִתֶּן־לוֹ אִשָּׁה וְיָלְדָה־לוֹ בָנִים אוֹ בָנוֹת
הָאִשָּׁה וִילָדֶיהָ תִּהְיֶה לַאדֹנֶיהָ וְהוּא יֵצֵא בְגַפּוֹ: וְאִם־אָמֹר יֹאמַר הָעֶבֶד
אָהַבְתִּי אֶת־אֲדֹנִי אֶת־אִשְׁתִּי וְאֶת־בָּנָי לֹא אֵצֵא חָפְשִׁי: וְהִגִּישׁוֹ אֲדֹנָיו
אֶל־הָאֱלֹהִים וְהִגִּישׁוֹ אֶל־הַדֶּלֶת אוֹ אֶל־הַמְּזוּזָה וְרָצַע אֲדֹנָיו אֶת־אָזְנוֹ
לוי בַּמַּרְצֵעַ וַעֲבָדוֹ לְעֹלָם: *וְכִי־יִמְכֹּר אִישׁ אֶת־בִּתּוֹ לְאָמָה לֹא
לוֹ תֵצֵא כְּצֵאת הָעֲבָדִים: אִם־רָעָה בְּעֵינֵי אֲדֹנֶיהָ אֲשֶׁר־לֹא יְעָדָהּ וְהֶפְדָּהּ לְעַם
נָכְרִי לֹא־יִמְשֹׁל לְמָכְרָהּ בְּבִגְדוֹ־בָהּ: וְאִם־לִבְנוֹ יִיעָדֶנָּה כְּמִשְׁפַּט הַבָּנוֹת
יַעֲשֶׂה־לָּהּ: אִם־אַחֶרֶת יִקַּח־לוֹ שְׁאֵרָהּ כְּסוּתָהּ וְעֹנָתָהּ לֹא יִגְרָע: וְאִם־שְׁלָשׁ־
ישראל אֵלֶּה לֹא יַעֲשֶׂה לָהּ וְיָצְאָה חִנָּם אֵין כָּסֶף: *מַכֵּה אִישׁ וָמֵת מוֹת
יוּמָת: וַאֲשֶׁר לֹא צָדָה וְהָאֱלֹהִים אִנָּה לְיָדוֹ וְשַׂמְתִּי לְךָ מָקוֹם אֲשֶׁר יָנוּס
שָׁמָּה: וְכִי־יָזִד אִישׁ עַל־רֵעֵהוּ לְהָרְגוֹ בְעָרְמָה מֵעִם מִזְבְּחִי
תִּקָּחֶנּוּ לָמוּת: וּמַכֵּה אָבִיו וְאִמּוֹ מוֹת יוּמָת: וְגֹנֵב
אִישׁ וּמְכָרוֹ וְנִמְצָא בְיָדוֹ מוֹת יוּמָת: וּמְקַלֵּל אָבִיו וְאִמּוֹ מוֹת

יוּמָת: וְכִי־יְרִיבֻן אֲנָשִׁים וְהִכָּה־אִישׁ אֶת־רֵעֵהוּ בְּאֶבֶן אוֹ בְאֶגְרֹף
וְלֹא יָמוּת וְנָפַל לְמִשְׁכָּב: אִם־יָקוּם וְהִתְהַלֵּךְ בַּחוּץ עַל־מִשְׁעַנְתּוֹ וְנִקָּה הַמַּכֶּה
רַק שִׁבְתּוֹ יִתֵּן וְרַפֹּא יְרַפֵּא:

תרומה TERUMA

שמות כה:א–טז וַיְדַבֵּר יְהֹוָה אֶל־מֹשֶׁה לֵּאמֹר: דַּבֵּר אֶל־בְּנֵי יִשְׂרָאֵל וְיִקְחוּ־לִי תְּרוּמָה מֵאֵת
כָּל־אִישׁ אֲשֶׁר יִדְּבֶנּוּ לִבּוֹ תִּקְחוּ אֶת־תְּרוּמָתִי: וְזֹאת הַתְּרוּמָה אֲשֶׁר תִּקְחוּ
מֵאִתָּם זָהָב וָכֶסֶף וּנְחֹשֶׁת: וּתְכֵלֶת וְאַרְגָּמָן וְתוֹלַעַת שָׁנִי וְשֵׁשׁ וְעִזִּים: וְעֹרֹת
לוי אֵילִם מְאָדָּמִים וְעֹרֹת תְּחָשִׁים וַעֲצֵי שִׁטִּים: *שֶׁמֶן לַמָּאֹר בְּשָׂמִים לְשֶׁמֶן
הַמִּשְׁחָה וְלִקְטֹרֶת הַסַּמִּים: אַבְנֵי־שֹׁהַם וְאַבְנֵי מִלֻּאִים לָאֵפֹד וְלַחֹשֶׁן: וְעָשׂוּ
לִי מִקְדָּשׁ וְשָׁכַנְתִּי בְּתוֹכָם: כְּכֹל אֲשֶׁר אֲנִי מַרְאֶה אוֹתְךָ אֵת תַּבְנִית הַמִּשְׁכָּן
ישראל וְאֵת תַּבְנִית כָּל־כֵּלָיו וְכֵן תַּעֲשׂוּ: *וְעָשׂוּ אֲרוֹן עֲצֵי שִׁטִּים אַמָּתַיִם
וָחֵצִי אָרְכּוֹ וְאַמָּה וָחֵצִי רָחְבּוֹ וְאַמָּה וָחֵצִי קֹמָתוֹ: וְצִפִּיתָ אֹתוֹ זָהָב טָהוֹר
מִבַּיִת וּמִחוּץ תְּצַפֶּנּוּ וְעָשִׂיתָ עָלָיו זֵר זָהָב סָבִיב: וְיָצַקְתָּ לּוֹ אַרְבַּע טַבְּעֹת
זָהָב וְנָתַתָּה עַל אַרְבַּע פַּעֲמֹתָיו וּשְׁתֵּי טַבָּעֹת עַל־צַלְעוֹ הָאֶחָת וּשְׁתֵּי טַבָּעֹת
עַל־צַלְעוֹ הַשֵּׁנִית: וְעָשִׂיתָ בַדֵּי עֲצֵי שִׁטִּים וְצִפִּיתָ אֹתָם זָהָב: וְהֵבֵאתָ אֶת־
הַבַּדִּים בַּטַּבָּעֹת עַל צַלְעֹת הָאָרֹן לָשֵׂאת אֶת־הָאָרֹן בָּהֶם: בְּטַבְּעֹת הָאָרֹן
יִהְיוּ הַבַּדִּים לֹא יָסֻרוּ מִמֶּנּוּ: וְנָתַתָּ אֶל־הָאָרֹן אֵת הָעֵדֻת אֲשֶׁר אֶתֵּן אֵלֶיךָ:

תצוה TETZAVEH

שמות כז:כ–כח:יב וְאַתָּה תְּצַוֶּה ׀ אֶת־בְּנֵי יִשְׂרָאֵל וְיִקְחוּ אֵלֶיךָ שֶׁמֶן זַיִת זָךְ כָּתִית לַמָּאוֹר
לְהַעֲלֹת נֵר תָּמִיד: בְּאֹהֶל מוֹעֵד מִחוּץ לַפָּרֹכֶת אֲשֶׁר עַל־הָעֵדֻת יַעֲרֹךְ
אֹתוֹ אַהֲרֹן וּבָנָיו מֵעֶרֶב עַד־בֹּקֶר לִפְנֵי יְהֹוָה חֻקַּת עוֹלָם לְדֹרֹתָם מֵאֵת בְּנֵי
יִשְׂרָאֵל: וְאַתָּה הַקְרֵב אֵלֶיךָ אֶת־אַהֲרֹן אָחִיךָ וְאֶת־בָּנָיו אִתּוֹ מִתּוֹךְ
בְּנֵי יִשְׂרָאֵל לְכַהֲנוֹ־לִי אַהֲרֹן נָדָב וַאֲבִיהוּא אֶלְעָזָר וְאִיתָמָר בְּנֵי אַהֲרֹן: וְעָשִׂיתָ
בִגְדֵי־קֹדֶשׁ לְאַהֲרֹן אָחִיךָ לְכָבוֹד וּלְתִפְאָרֶת: וְאַתָּה תְּדַבֵּר אֶל־כָּל־חַכְמֵי־לֵב
אֲשֶׁר מִלֵּאתִיו רוּחַ חָכְמָה וְעָשׂוּ אֶת־בִּגְדֵי אַהֲרֹן לְקַדְּשׁוֹ לְכַהֲנוֹ־לִי: וְאֵלֶּה
הַבְּגָדִים אֲשֶׁר יַעֲשׂוּ חֹשֶׁן וְאֵפוֹד וּמְעִיל וּכְתֹנֶת תַּשְׁבֵּץ מִצְנֶפֶת וְאַבְנֵט וְעָשׂוּ
בִגְדֵי־קֹדֶשׁ לְאַהֲרֹן אָחִיךָ וּלְבָנָיו לְכַהֲנוֹ־לִי: וְהֵם יִקְחוּ אֶת־הַזָּהָב וְאֶת־הַתְּכֵלֶת

וְאֶת־הָאַרְגָּמָן וְאֶת־תּוֹלַעַת הַשָּׁנִי וְאֶת־הַשֵּׁשׁ׃
לוי וְעָשׂוּ אֶת־הָאֵפֹד זָהָב תְּכֵלֶת וְאַרְגָּמָן תּוֹלַעַת שָׁנִי וְשֵׁשׁ מָשְׁזָר מַעֲשֵׂה חֹשֵׁב׃
שְׁתֵּי כְתֵפֹת חֹבְרֹת יִהְיֶה־לּוֹ אֶל־שְׁנֵי קְצוֹתָיו וְחֻבָּר׃ וְחֵשֶׁב אֲפֻדָּתוֹ אֲשֶׁר עָלָיו
כְּמַעֲשֵׂהוּ מִמֶּנּוּ יִהְיֶה זָהָב תְּכֵלֶת וְאַרְגָּמָן וְתוֹלַעַת שָׁנִי וְשֵׁשׁ מָשְׁזָר׃ וְלָקַחְתָּ
ישראל אֶת־שְׁתֵּי אַבְנֵי־שֹׁהַם וּפִתַּחְתָּ עֲלֵיהֶם שְׁמוֹת בְּנֵי יִשְׂרָאֵל׃ *שִׁשָּׁה מִשְּׁמֹתָם עַל
הָאֶבֶן הָאֶחָת וְאֶת־שְׁמוֹת הַשִּׁשָּׁה הַנּוֹתָרִים עַל־הָאֶבֶן הַשֵּׁנִית כְּתוֹלְדֹתָם׃
מַעֲשֵׂה חָרַשׁ אֶבֶן פִּתּוּחֵי חֹתָם תְּפַתַּח אֶת־שְׁתֵּי הָאֲבָנִים עַל־שְׁמֹת בְּנֵי
יִשְׂרָאֵל מֻסַבֹּת מִשְׁבְּצוֹת זָהָב תַּעֲשֶׂה אֹתָם׃ וְשַׂמְתָּ אֶת־שְׁתֵּי הָאֲבָנִים עַל
כִּתְפֹת הָאֵפֹד אַבְנֵי זִכָּרֹן לִבְנֵי יִשְׂרָאֵל וְנָשָׂא אַהֲרֹן אֶת־שְׁמוֹתָם לִפְנֵי יְהוָה
עַל־שְׁתֵּי כְתֵפָיו לְזִכָּרֹן׃

כי תשא KI TISSA

שמות ל:יא–כא וַיְדַבֵּר יְהוָה אֶל־מֹשֶׁה לֵּאמֹר׃ כִּי תִשָּׂא אֶת־רֹאשׁ בְּנֵי־יִשְׂרָאֵל לִפְקֻדֵיהֶם
וְנָתְנוּ אִישׁ כֹּפֶר נַפְשׁוֹ לַיהוָה בִּפְקֹד אֹתָם וְלֹא־יִהְיֶה בָהֶם נֶגֶף בִּפְקֹד אֹתָם׃
זֶה ׀ יִתְּנוּ כָּל־הָעֹבֵר עַל־הַפְּקֻדִים מַחֲצִית הַשֶּׁקֶל בְּשֶׁקֶל הַקֹּדֶשׁ עֶשְׂרִים
לוי גֵּרָה הַשֶּׁקֶל מַחֲצִית הַשֶּׁקֶל תְּרוּמָה לַיהוָה׃ *כֹּל הָעֹבֵר עַל־הַפְּקֻדִים מִבֶּן
עֶשְׂרִים שָׁנָה וָמָעְלָה יִתֵּן תְּרוּמַת יְהוָה׃ הֶעָשִׁיר לֹא־יַרְבֶּה וְהַדַּל לֹא יַמְעִיט
מִמַּחֲצִית הַשָּׁקֶל לָתֵת אֶת־תְּרוּמַת יְהוָה לְכַפֵּר עַל־נַפְשֹׁתֵיכֶם׃ וְלָקַחְתָּ
אֶת־כֶּסֶף הַכִּפֻּרִים מֵאֵת בְּנֵי יִשְׂרָאֵל וְנָתַתָּ אֹתוֹ עַל־עֲבֹדַת אֹהֶל מוֹעֵד וְהָיָה
לִבְנֵי יִשְׂרָאֵל לְזִכָּרוֹן לִפְנֵי יְהוָה לְכַפֵּר עַל־נַפְשֹׁתֵיכֶם׃
ישראל וַיְדַבֵּר יְהוָה אֶל־מֹשֶׁה לֵּאמֹר׃ וְעָשִׂיתָ כִּיּוֹר נְחֹשֶׁת וְכַנּוֹ נְחֹשֶׁת לְרָחְצָה וְנָתַתָּ
אֹתוֹ בֵּין־אֹהֶל מוֹעֵד וּבֵין הַמִּזְבֵּחַ וְנָתַתָּ שָׁמָּה מָיִם׃ וְרָחֲצוּ אַהֲרֹן וּבָנָיו מִמֶּנּוּ
אֶת־יְדֵיהֶם וְאֶת־רַגְלֵיהֶם׃ בְּבֹאָם אֶל־אֹהֶל מוֹעֵד יִרְחֲצוּ־מַיִם וְלֹא יָמֻתוּ אוֹ
בְגִשְׁתָּם אֶל־הַמִּזְבֵּחַ לְשָׁרֵת לְהַקְטִיר אִשֶּׁה לַיהוָה׃ וְרָחֲצוּ יְדֵיהֶם וְרַגְלֵיהֶם
וְלֹא יָמֻתוּ וְהָיְתָה לָהֶם חָק־עוֹלָם לוֹ וּלְזַרְעוֹ לְדֹרֹתָם׃

ויקהל VAYAK-HEL

שמות לה:א–כ וַיַּקְהֵל מֹשֶׁה אֶת־כָּל־עֲדַת בְּנֵי יִשְׂרָאֵל וַיֹּאמֶר אֲלֵהֶם אֵלֶּה הַדְּבָרִים אֲשֶׁר־
צִוָּה יְהוָה לַעֲשֹׂת אֹתָם׃ שֵׁשֶׁת יָמִים תֵּעָשֶׂה מְלָאכָה וּבַיּוֹם הַשְּׁבִיעִי יִהְיֶה

לָכֶם קֹדֶשׁ שַׁבַּת שַׁבָּתוֹן לַיהוָה כָּל־הָעֹשֶׂה בוֹ מְלָאכָה יוּמָת׃ לֹא־תְבַעֲרוּ
אֵשׁ בְּכֹל מֹשְׁבֹתֵיכֶם בְּיוֹם הַשַּׁבָּת׃
לוי וַיֹּאמֶר מֹשֶׁה אֶל־כָּל־עֲדַת בְּנֵי־יִשְׂרָאֵל לֵאמֹר זֶה הַדָּבָר אֲשֶׁר־צִוָּה יְהוָה
לֵאמֹר׃ קְחוּ מֵאִתְּכֶם תְּרוּמָה לַיהוָה כֹּל נְדִיב לִבּוֹ יְבִיאֶהָ אֵת תְּרוּמַת יְהוָה
זָהָב וָכֶסֶף וּנְחֹשֶׁת׃ וּתְכֵלֶת וְאַרְגָּמָן וְתוֹלַעַת שָׁנִי וְשֵׁשׁ וְעִזִּים׃ וְעֹרֹת אֵילִם
מְאָדָּמִים וְעֹרֹת תְּחָשִׁים וַעֲצֵי שִׁטִּים׃ וְשֶׁמֶן לַמָּאוֹר וּבְשָׂמִים לְשֶׁמֶן הַמִּשְׁחָה
וְלִקְטֹרֶת הַסַּמִּים׃ וְאַבְנֵי־שֹׁהַם וְאַבְנֵי מִלֻּאִים לָאֵפוֹד וְלַחֹשֶׁן׃ וְכָל־חֲכַם־לֵב
ישראל בָּכֶם יָבֹאוּ וְיַעֲשׂוּ אֵת כָּל־אֲשֶׁר צִוָּה יְהוָה׃ *אֶת־הַמִּשְׁכָּן אֶת־אָהֳלוֹ וְאֶת־
מִכְסֵהוּ אֶת־קְרָסָיו וְאֶת־קְרָשָׁיו אֶת־בְּרִיחָו אֶת־עַמֻּדָיו וְאֶת־אֲדָנָיו׃ אֶת־
הָאָרֹן וְאֶת־בַּדָּיו אֶת־הַכַּפֹּרֶת וְאֵת פָּרֹכֶת הַמָּסָךְ׃ אֶת־הַשֻּׁלְחָן וְאֶת־בַּדָּיו
וְאֶת־כָּל־כֵּלָיו וְאֵת לֶחֶם הַפָּנִים׃ וְאֶת־מְנֹרַת הַמָּאוֹר וְאֶת־כֵּלֶיהָ וְאֶת־נֵרֹתֶיהָ
וְאֵת שֶׁמֶן הַמָּאוֹר׃ וְאֶת־מִזְבַּח הַקְּטֹרֶת וְאֶת־בַּדָּיו וְאֵת שֶׁמֶן הַמִּשְׁחָה וְאֵת
קְטֹרֶת הַסַּמִּים וְאֶת־מָסַךְ הַפֶּתַח לְפֶתַח הַמִּשְׁכָּן׃ אֵת ׀ מִזְבַּח הָעֹלָה וְאֶת־
מִכְבַּר הַנְּחֹשֶׁת אֲשֶׁר־לוֹ אֶת־בַּדָּיו וְאֶת־כָּל־כֵּלָיו אֶת־הַכִּיֹּר וְאֶת־כַּנּוֹ׃ אֵת
קַלְעֵי הֶחָצֵר אֶת־עַמֻּדָיו וְאֶת־אֲדָנֶיהָ וְאֵת מָסַךְ שַׁעַר הֶחָצֵר׃ אֶת־יִתְדֹת
הַמִּשְׁכָּן וְאֶת־יִתְדֹת הֶחָצֵר וְאֶת־מֵיתְרֵיהֶם׃ אֶת־בִּגְדֵי הַשְּׂרָד לְשָׁרֵת בַּקֹּדֶשׁ
אֶת־בִּגְדֵי הַקֹּדֶשׁ לְאַהֲרֹן הַכֹּהֵן וְאֶת־בִּגְדֵי בָנָיו לְכַהֵן׃ וַיֵּצְאוּ כָּל־עֲדַת בְּנֵי־
יִשְׂרָאֵל מִלִּפְנֵי מֹשֶׁה׃

פקודי PEKUDEI

שמות לח:כא–לט:א אֵלֶּה פְקוּדֵי הַמִּשְׁכָּן מִשְׁכַּן הָעֵדֻת אֲשֶׁר פֻּקַּד עַל־פִּי מֹשֶׁה עֲבֹדַת הַלְוִיִּם בְּיַד
אִיתָמָר בֶּן־אַהֲרֹן הַכֹּהֵן׃ וּבְצַלְאֵל בֶּן־אוּרִי בֶן־חוּר לְמַטֵּה יְהוּדָה עָשָׂה אֵת
כָּל־אֲשֶׁר־צִוָּה יְהוָה אֶת־מֹשֶׁה׃ וְאִתּוֹ אָהֳלִיאָב בֶּן־אֲחִיסָמָךְ לְמַטֵּה־דָן חָרָשׁ
לוי וְחֹשֵׁב וְרֹקֵם בַּתְּכֵלֶת וּבָאַרְגָּמָן וּבְתוֹלַעַת הַשָּׁנִי וּבַשֵּׁשׁ׃ *כָּל־הַזָּהָב
הֶעָשׂוּי לַמְּלָאכָה בְּכֹל מְלֶאכֶת הַקֹּדֶשׁ וַיְהִי ׀ זְהַב הַתְּנוּפָה תֵּשַׁע וְעֶשְׂרִים
כִּכָּר וּשְׁבַע מֵאוֹת וּשְׁלֹשִׁים שֶׁקֶל בְּשֶׁקֶל הַקֹּדֶשׁ׃ וְכֶסֶף פְּקוּדֵי הָעֵדָה מְאַת
כִּכָּר וְאֶלֶף וּשְׁבַע מֵאוֹת וַחֲמִשָּׁה וְשִׁבְעִים שֶׁקֶל בְּשֶׁקֶל הַקֹּדֶשׁ׃ בֶּקַע לַגֻּלְגֹּלֶת
מַחֲצִית הַשֶּׁקֶל בְּשֶׁקֶל הַקֹּדֶשׁ לְכֹל הָעֹבֵר עַל־הַפְּקֻדִים מִבֶּן עֶשְׂרִים שָׁנָה

וּלְמַ֨עְלָה לְשֵׁשׁ־מֵא֥וֹת אֶ֙לֶף֙ וּשְׁלֹ֣שֶׁת אֲלָפִ֔ים וַחֲמֵ֥שׁ מֵא֖וֹת וַחֲמִשִּֽׁים׃ וַֽיְהִ֗י
מְאַת֙ כִּכַּ֣ר הַכֶּ֔סֶף לָצֶ֗קֶת אֵ֚ת אַדְנֵ֣י הַקֹּ֔דֶשׁ וְאֵ֖ת אַדְנֵ֣י הַפָּרֹ֑כֶת מְאַ֧ת אֲדָנִ֛ים
לִמְאַ֥ת הַכִּכָּ֖ר כִּכָּ֥ר לָאָֽדֶן׃ *וְֽאֶת־הָאֶ֜לֶף וּשְׁבַ֧ע הַמֵּא֗וֹת וַחֲמִשָּׁה֙ וְשִׁבְעִ֔ים ישראל
עָשָׂ֥ה וָוִ֖ים לָעַמּוּדִ֑ים וְצִפָּ֥ה רָאשֵׁיהֶ֖ם וְחִשַּׁ֥ק אֹתָֽם׃ וּנְח֥שֶׁת הַתְּנוּפָ֖ה שִׁבְעִ֣ים
כִּכָּ֑ר וְאַלְפַּ֥יִם וְאַרְבַּע־מֵא֖וֹת שָֽׁקֶל׃ וַיַּ֣עַשׂ בָּ֗הּ אֶת־אַדְנֵי֙ פֶּ֚תַח אֹ֣הֶל מוֹעֵ֔ד
וְאֵת֙ מִזְבַּ֣ח הַנְּחֹ֔שֶׁת וְאֶת־מִכְבַּ֥ר הַנְּח֖שֶׁת אֲשֶׁר־ל֑וֹ וְאֵ֖ת כָּל־כְּלֵ֥י הַמִּזְבֵּֽחַ׃
וְאֶת־אַדְנֵ֤י הֶֽחָצֵר֙ סָבִ֔יב וְאֶת־אַדְנֵ֖י שַׁ֣עַר הֶחָצֵ֑ר וְאֵ֨ת כָּל־יִתְדֹ֧ת הַמִּשְׁכָּ֛ן
וְאֶת־כָּל־יִתְדֹ֥ת הֶחָצֵ֖ר סָבִֽיב׃ וּמִן־הַתְּכֵ֤לֶת וְהָֽאַרְגָּמָן֙ וְתוֹלַ֣עַת הַשָּׁנִ֔י עָשׂ֥וּ
בִגְדֵי־שְׂרָ֖ד לְשָׁרֵ֣ת בַּקֹּ֑דֶשׁ וַֽיַּעֲשׂ֞וּ אֶת־בִּגְדֵ֤י הַקֹּ֙דֶשׁ֙ אֲשֶׁ֣ר לְאַהֲרֹ֔ן כַּאֲשֶׁ֛ר צִוָּ֥ה
יהוה֖ אֶת־מֹשֶֽׁה׃

VAYIKRA ויקרא

וַיִּקְרָ֖א אֶל־מֹשֶׁ֑ה וַיְדַבֵּ֤ר יהוה֙ אֵלָ֔יו מֵאֹ֥הֶל מוֹעֵ֖ד לֵאמֹֽר׃ דַּבֵּ֞ר אֶל־בְּנֵ֤י יִשְׂרָאֵל֙ ויקרא א:א–יג
וְאָמַרְתָּ֣ אֲלֵהֶ֔ם אָדָ֗ם כִּֽי־יַקְרִ֥יב מִכֶּ֛ם קָרְבָּ֖ן לַיהוה מִן־הַבְּהֵמָ֗ה מִן־הַבָּקָר֙
וּמִן־הַצֹּ֔אן תַּקְרִ֖יבוּ אֶת־קָרְבַּנְכֶֽם׃ אִם־עֹלָ֤ה קָרְבָּנוֹ֙ מִן־הַבָּקָ֔ר זָכָ֥ר תָּמִ֖ים
יַקְרִיבֶ֑נּוּ אֶל־פֶּ֜תַח אֹ֤הֶל מוֹעֵד֙ יַקְרִ֣יב אֹת֔וֹ לִרְצֹנ֖וֹ לִפְנֵ֥י יהוה׃ וְסָמַ֣ךְ יָד֔וֹ עַ֖ל
רֹ֣אשׁ הָעֹלָ֑ה וְנִרְצָ֥ה ל֖וֹ לְכַפֵּ֥ר עָלָֽיו׃ *וְשָׁחַ֛ט אֶת־בֶּ֥ן הַבָּקָ֖ר לִפְנֵ֣י יהוה וְהִקְרִ֡יבוּ לוי
בְּנֵ֨י אַהֲרֹ֤ן הַכֹּהֲנִים֙ אֶת־הַדָּ֔ם וְזָרְק֨וּ אֶת־הַדָּ֤ם עַל־הַמִּזְבֵּ֙חַ֙ סָבִ֔יב אֲשֶׁר־פֶּ֖תַח
אֹ֥הֶל מוֹעֵֽד׃ וְהִפְשִׁ֖יט אֶת־הָעֹלָ֑ה וְנִתַּ֥ח אֹתָ֖הּ לִנְתָחֶֽיהָ׃ וְנָ֨תְנ֜וּ בְּנֵ֨י אַהֲרֹ֧ן
הַכֹּהֵ֛ן אֵ֖שׁ עַל־הַמִּזְבֵּ֑חַ וְעָרְכ֥וּ עֵצִ֖ים עַל־הָאֵֽשׁ׃ וְעָרְכ֗וּ בְּנֵ֤י אַהֲרֹן֙ הַכֹּ֣הֲנִ֔ים
אֵ֚ת הַנְּתָחִ֔ים אֶת־הָרֹ֖אשׁ וְאֶת־הַפָּ֑דֶר עַל־הָֽעֵצִים֙ אֲשֶׁ֣ר עַל־הָאֵ֔שׁ אֲשֶׁ֖ר עַל־
הַמִּזְבֵּֽחַ׃ וְקִרְבּ֥וֹ וּכְרָעָ֖יו יִרְחַ֣ץ בַּמָּ֑יִם וְהִקְטִ֨יר הַכֹּהֵ֤ן אֶת־הַכֹּל֙ הַמִּזְבֵּ֔חָה עֹלָ֛ה
אִשֵּׁ֥ה רֵֽיחַ־נִיח֖וֹחַ לַיהוה׃ *וְאִם־מִן־הַצֹּ֨אן קָרְבָּנ֧וֹ מִן־הַכְּשָׂבִ֛ים ישראל
א֥וֹ מִן־הָעִזִּ֖ים לְעֹלָ֑ה זָכָ֥ר תָּמִ֖ים יַקְרִיבֶֽנּוּ׃ וְשָׁחַ֨ט אֹת֜וֹ עַ֣ל יֶ֧רֶךְ הַמִּזְבֵּ֛חַ צָפֹ֖נָה
לִפְנֵ֣י יהוה וְזָרְק֡וּ בְּנֵי֩ אַהֲרֹ֨ן הַכֹּהֲנִ֧ים אֶת־דָּמ֛וֹ עַל־הַמִּזְבֵּ֖חַ סָבִֽיב׃ וְנִתַּ֤ח אֹתוֹ֙
לִנְתָחָ֔יו וְאֶת־רֹאשׁ֖וֹ וְאֶת־פִּדְר֑וֹ וְעָרַ֤ךְ הַכֹּהֵן֙ אֹתָ֔ם עַל־הָעֵצִים֙ אֲשֶׁ֣ר עַל־הָאֵ֔שׁ
אֲשֶׁ֖ר עַל־הַמִּזְבֵּֽחַ׃ וְהַקֶּ֥רֶב וְהַכְּרָעַ֖יִם יִרְחַ֣ץ בַּמָּ֑יִם וְהִקְרִ֨יב הַכֹּהֵ֤ן אֶת־הַכֹּל֙
וְהִקְטִ֣יר הַמִּזְבֵּ֔חָה עֹלָ֣ה ה֗וּא אִשֵּׁ֛ה רֵ֥יחַ נִיחֹ֖חַ לַיהוה׃

צו TZAV

ויקרא ו:א–יא וַיְדַבֵּר יהוה אֶל־מֹשֶׁה לֵּאמֹר: צַו אֶת־אַהֲרֹן וְאֶת־בָּנָיו לֵאמֹר זֹאת תּוֹרַת
הָעֹלָה הִוא הָעֹלָה עַל מוֹקְדָה עַל־הַמִּזְבֵּחַ כָּל־הַלַּיְלָה עַד־הַבֹּקֶר וְאֵשׁ הַמִּזְבֵּחַ
תּוּקַד בּוֹ: וְלָבַשׁ הַכֹּהֵן מִדּוֹ בַד וּמִכְנְסֵי־בַד יִלְבַּשׁ עַל־בְּשָׂרוֹ וְהֵרִים אֶת־הַדֶּשֶׁן
לוי אֲשֶׁר תֹּאכַל הָאֵשׁ אֶת־הָעֹלָה עַל־הַמִּזְבֵּחַ וְשָׂמוֹ אֵצֶל הַמִּזְבֵּחַ: *וּפָשַׁט אֶת־
בְּגָדָיו וְלָבַשׁ בְּגָדִים אֲחֵרִים וְהוֹצִיא אֶת־הַדֶּשֶׁן אֶל־מִחוּץ לַמַּחֲנֶה אֶל־מָקוֹם
טָהוֹר: וְהָאֵשׁ עַל־הַמִּזְבֵּחַ תּוּקַד־בּוֹ לֹא תִכְבֶּה וּבִעֵר עָלֶיהָ הַכֹּהֵן עֵצִים בַּבֹּקֶר
בַּבֹּקֶר וְעָרַךְ עָלֶיהָ הָעֹלָה וְהִקְטִיר עָלֶיהָ חֶלְבֵי הַשְּׁלָמִים: אֵשׁ תָּמִיד תּוּקַד
ישראל עַל־הַמִּזְבֵּחַ לֹא תִכְבֶּה: *וְזֹאת תּוֹרַת הַמִּנְחָה הַקְרֵב אֹתָהּ
בְּנֵי־אַהֲרֹן לִפְנֵי יהוה אֶל־פְּנֵי הַמִּזְבֵּחַ: וְהֵרִים מִמֶּנּוּ בְּקֻמְצוֹ מִסֹּלֶת הַמִּנְחָה
וּמִשַּׁמְנָהּ וְאֵת כָּל־הַלְּבֹנָה אֲשֶׁר עַל־הַמִּנְחָה וְהִקְטִיר הַמִּזְבֵּחַ רֵיחַ נִיחֹחַ
אַזְכָּרָתָהּ לַיהוה: וְהַנּוֹתֶרֶת מִמֶּנָּה יֹאכְלוּ אַהֲרֹן וּבָנָיו מַצּוֹת תֵּאָכֵל בְּמָקוֹם
קָדֹשׁ בַּחֲצַר אֹהֶל־מוֹעֵד יֹאכְלוּהָ: לֹא תֵאָפֶה חָמֵץ חֶלְקָם נָתַתִּי אֹתָהּ מֵאִשָּׁי
קֹדֶשׁ קָדָשִׁים הִוא כַּחַטָּאת וְכָאָשָׁם: כָּל־זָכָר בִּבְנֵי אַהֲרֹן יֹאכֲלֶנָּה חָק־עוֹלָם
לְדֹרֹתֵיכֶם מֵאִשֵּׁי יהוה כֹּל אֲשֶׁר־יִגַּע בָּהֶם יִקְדָּשׁ:

שמיני SHEMINI

ויקרא ט:א–טז וַיְהִי בַּיּוֹם הַשְּׁמִינִי קָרָא מֹשֶׁה לְאַהֲרֹן וּלְבָנָיו וּלְזִקְנֵי יִשְׂרָאֵל: וַיֹּאמֶר אֶל־אַהֲרֹן
קַח־לְךָ עֵגֶל בֶּן־בָּקָר לְחַטָּאת וְאַיִל לְעֹלָה תְּמִימִם וְהַקְרֵב לִפְנֵי יהוה: וְאֶל־
בְּנֵי יִשְׂרָאֵל תְּדַבֵּר לֵאמֹר קְחוּ שְׂעִיר־עִזִּים לְחַטָּאת וְעֵגֶל וָכֶבֶשׂ בְּנֵי־שָׁנָה
תְּמִימִם לְעֹלָה: וְשׁוֹר וָאַיִל לִשְׁלָמִים לִזְבֹּחַ לִפְנֵי יהוה וּמִנְחָה בְּלוּלָה בַשָּׁמֶן
כִּי הַיּוֹם יהוה נִרְאָה אֲלֵיכֶם: וַיִּקְחוּ אֵת אֲשֶׁר צִוָּה מֹשֶׁה אֶל־פְּנֵי אֹהֶל מוֹעֵד
וַיִּקְרְבוּ כָּל־הָעֵדָה וַיַּעַמְדוּ לִפְנֵי יהוה: וַיֹּאמֶר מֹשֶׁה זֶה הַדָּבָר אֲשֶׁר־צִוָּה יהוה
לוי תַּעֲשׂוּ וְיֵרָא אֲלֵיכֶם כְּבוֹד יהוה: *וַיֹּאמֶר מֹשֶׁה אֶל־אַהֲרֹן קְרַב אֶל־הַמִּזְבֵּחַ
וַעֲשֵׂה אֶת־חַטָּאתְךָ וְאֶת־עֹלָתֶךָ וְכַפֵּר בַּעַדְךָ וּבְעַד הָעָם וַעֲשֵׂה אֶת־קָרְבַּן
הָעָם וְכַפֵּר בַּעֲדָם כַּאֲשֶׁר צִוָּה יהוה: וַיִּקְרַב אַהֲרֹן אֶל־הַמִּזְבֵּחַ וַיִּשְׁחַט אֶת־
עֵגֶל הַחַטָּאת אֲשֶׁר־לוֹ: וַיַּקְרִבוּ בְּנֵי אַהֲרֹן אֶת־הַדָּם אֵלָיו וַיִּטְבֹּל אֶצְבָּעוֹ
בַּדָּם וַיִּתֵּן עַל־קַרְנוֹת הַמִּזְבֵּחַ וְאֶת־הַדָּם יָצַק אֶל־יְסוֹד הַמִּזְבֵּחַ: וְאֶת־הַחֵלֶב
וְאֶת־הַכְּלָיֹת וְאֶת־הַיֹּתֶרֶת מִן־הַכָּבֵד מִן־הַחַטָּאת הִקְטִיר הַמִּזְבֵּחָה כַּאֲשֶׁר

ישראל

צִוָּה יְהוָה אֶת־מֹשֶׁה׃ *וְאֶת־הַבָּשָׂר וְאֶת־הָעוֹר שָׂרַף בָּאֵשׁ מִחוּץ לַמַּחֲנֶה׃ וַיִּשְׁחַט אֶת־הָעֹלָה וַיַּמְצִאוּ בְּנֵי אַהֲרֹן אֵלָיו אֶת־הַדָּם וַיִּזְרְקֵהוּ עַל־הַמִּזְבֵּחַ סָבִיב׃ וְאֶת־הָעֹלָה הִמְצִיאוּ אֵלָיו לִנְתָחֶיהָ וְאֶת־הָרֹאשׁ וַיַּקְטֵר עַל־הַמִּזְבֵּחַ׃ וַיִּרְחַץ אֶת־הַקֶּרֶב וְאֶת־הַכְּרָעָיִם וַיַּקְטֵר עַל־הָעֹלָה הַמִּזְבֵּחָה׃ וַיַּקְרֵב אֵת קָרְבַּן הָעָם וַיִּקַּח אֶת־שְׂעִיר הַחַטָּאת אֲשֶׁר לָעָם וַיִּשְׁחָטֵהוּ וַיְחַטְּאֵהוּ כָּרִאשׁוֹן׃ וַיַּקְרֵב אֶת־הָעֹלָה וַיַּעֲשֶׂהָ כַּמִּשְׁפָּט׃

תזריע TAZRIA

ויקרא יב:א–יג:ה

וַיְדַבֵּר יְהוָה אֶל־מֹשֶׁה לֵּאמֹר׃ דַּבֵּר אֶל־בְּנֵי יִשְׂרָאֵל לֵאמֹר אִשָּׁה כִּי תַזְרִיעַ וְיָלְדָה זָכָר וְטָמְאָה שִׁבְעַת יָמִים כִּימֵי נִדַּת דְּוֺתָהּ תִּטְמָא׃ וּבַיּוֹם הַשְּׁמִינִי יִמּוֹל בְּשַׂר עָרְלָתוֹ׃ וּשְׁלֹשִׁים יוֹם וּשְׁלֹשֶׁת יָמִים תֵּשֵׁב בִּדְמֵי טָהֳרָה בְּכָל־קֹדֶשׁ לֹא־תִגָּע וְאֶל־הַמִּקְדָּשׁ לֹא תָבֹא עַד־מְלֹאת יְמֵי טָהֳרָהּ׃

לוי

*וְאִם־נְקֵבָה תֵלֵד וְטָמְאָה שְׁבֻעַיִם כְּנִדָּתָהּ וְשִׁשִּׁים יוֹם וְשֵׁשֶׁת יָמִים תֵּשֵׁב עַל־דְּמֵי טָהֳרָה׃ וּבִמְלֹאת ׀ יְמֵי טָהֳרָהּ לְבֵן אוֹ לְבַת תָּבִיא כֶּבֶשׂ בֶּן־שְׁנָתוֹ לְעֹלָה וּבֶן־יוֹנָה אוֹ־תֹר לְחַטָּאת אֶל־פֶּתַח אֹהֶל־מוֹעֵד אֶל־הַכֹּהֵן׃ וְהִקְרִיבוֹ לִפְנֵי יְהוָה וְכִפֶּר עָלֶיהָ וְטָהֲרָה מִמְּקֹר דָּמֶיהָ זֹאת תּוֹרַת הַיֹּלֶדֶת לַזָּכָר אוֹ לַנְּקֵבָה׃ וְאִם־לֹא תִמְצָא יָדָהּ דֵּי שֶׂה וְלָקְחָה שְׁתֵּי־תֹרִים אוֹ שְׁנֵי בְּנֵי יוֹנָה אֶחָד לְעֹלָה וְאֶחָד לְחַטָּאת וְכִפֶּר עָלֶיהָ הַכֹּהֵן וְטָהֵרָה׃

ישראל

וַיְדַבֵּר יְהוָה אֶל־מֹשֶׁה וְאֶל־אַהֲרֹן לֵאמֹר׃ אָדָם כִּי־יִהְיֶה בְעוֹר־בְּשָׂרוֹ שְׂאֵת אוֹ־סַפַּחַת אוֹ בַהֶרֶת וְהָיָה בְעוֹר־בְּשָׂרוֹ לְנֶגַע צָרָעַת וְהוּבָא אֶל־אַהֲרֹן הַכֹּהֵן אוֹ אֶל־אַחַד מִבָּנָיו הַכֹּהֲנִים׃ וְרָאָה הַכֹּהֵן אֶת־הַנֶּגַע בְּעוֹר־הַבָּשָׂר וְשֵׂעָר בַּנֶּגַע הָפַךְ ׀ לָבָן וּמַרְאֵה הַנֶּגַע עָמֹק מֵעוֹר בְּשָׂרוֹ נֶגַע צָרַעַת הוּא וְרָאָהוּ הַכֹּהֵן וְטִמֵּא אֹתוֹ׃ וְאִם־בַּהֶרֶת לְבָנָה הִוא בְּעוֹר בְּשָׂרוֹ וְעָמֹק אֵין־מַרְאֶהָ מִן־הָעוֹר וּשְׂעָרָה לֹא־הָפַךְ לָבָן וְהִסְגִּיר הַכֹּהֵן אֶת־הַנֶּגַע שִׁבְעַת יָמִים׃ וְרָאָהוּ הַכֹּהֵן בַּיּוֹם הַשְּׁבִיעִי וְהִנֵּה הַנֶּגַע עָמַד בְּעֵינָיו לֹא־פָשָׂה הַנֶּגַע בָּעוֹר וְהִסְגִּירוֹ הַכֹּהֵן שִׁבְעַת יָמִים שֵׁנִית׃

מצורע METZORA

ויקרא יד:א–יב

וַיְדַבֵּר יְהוָה אֶל־מֹשֶׁה לֵּאמֹר׃ זֹאת תִּהְיֶה תּוֹרַת הַמְּצֹרָע בְּיוֹם טָהֳרָתוֹ

וְהוּבָא אֶל־הַכֹּהֵן׃ וְיָצָא הַכֹּהֵן אֶל־מִחוּץ לַמַּחֲנֶה וְרָאָה הַכֹּהֵן וְהִנֵּה נִרְפָּא
נֶגַע־הַצָּרַעַת מִן־הַצָּרוּעַ׃ וְצִוָּה הַכֹּהֵן וְלָקַח לַמִּטַּהֵר שְׁתֵּי־צִפֳּרִים חַיּוֹת
טְהֹרוֹת וְעֵץ אֶרֶז וּשְׁנִי תוֹלַעַת וְאֵזֹב׃ וְצִוָּה הַכֹּהֵן וְשָׁחַט אֶת־הַצִּפּוֹר הָאֶחָת
לוי אֶל־כְּלִי־חֶרֶשׂ עַל־מַיִם חַיִּים׃ *אֶת־הַצִּפֹּר הַחַיָּה יִקַּח אֹתָהּ וְאֶת־עֵץ הָאֶרֶז
וְאֶת־שְׁנִי הַתּוֹלַעַת וְאֶת־הָאֵזֹב וְטָבַל אוֹתָם וְאֵת ׀ הַצִּפֹּר הַחַיָּה בְּדַם הַצִּפֹּר
הַשְּׁחֻטָה עַל הַמַּיִם הַחַיִּים׃ וְהִזָּה עַל הַמִּטַּהֵר מִן־הַצָּרַעַת שֶׁבַע פְּעָמִים
וְטִהֲרוֹ וְשִׁלַּח אֶת־הַצִּפֹּר הַחַיָּה עַל־פְּנֵי הַשָּׂדֶה׃ וְכִבֶּס הַמִּטַּהֵר אֶת־בְּגָדָיו
וְגִלַּח אֶת־כָּל־שְׂעָרוֹ וְרָחַץ בַּמַּיִם וְטָהֵר וְאַחַר יָבוֹא אֶל־הַמַּחֲנֶה וְיָשַׁב מִחוּץ
לְאָהֳלוֹ שִׁבְעַת יָמִים׃ וְהָיָה בַיּוֹם הַשְּׁבִיעִי יְגַלַּח אֶת־כָּל־שְׂעָרוֹ אֶת־רֹאשׁוֹ
וְאֶת־זְקָנוֹ וְאֵת גַּבֹּת עֵינָיו וְאֶת־כָּל־שְׂעָרוֹ יְגַלֵּחַ וְכִבֶּס אֶת־בְּגָדָיו וְרָחַץ אֶת־
ישראל בְּשָׂרוֹ בַּמַּיִם וְטָהֵר׃ *וּבַיּוֹם הַשְּׁמִינִי יִקַּח שְׁנֵי־כְבָשִׂים תְּמִימִם וְכַבְשָׂה אַחַת
בַּת־שְׁנָתָהּ תְּמִימָה וּשְׁלֹשָׁה עֶשְׂרֹנִים סֹלֶת מִנְחָה בְּלוּלָה בַשֶּׁמֶן וְלֹג אֶחָד
שָׁמֶן׃ וְהֶעֱמִיד הַכֹּהֵן הַמְטַהֵר אֵת הָאִישׁ הַמִּטַּהֵר וְאֹתָם לִפְנֵי יהוה פֶּתַח
אֹהֶל מוֹעֵד׃ וְלָקַח הַכֹּהֵן אֶת־הַכֶּבֶשׂ הָאֶחָד וְהִקְרִיב אֹתוֹ לְאָשָׁם וְאֶת־לֹג
הַשֶּׁמֶן וְהֵנִיף אֹתָם תְּנוּפָה לִפְנֵי יהוה׃

אחרי מות AHAREI MOT

ויקרא טז:א–יז וַיְדַבֵּר יהוה אֶל־מֹשֶׁה אַחֲרֵי מוֹת שְׁנֵי בְּנֵי אַהֲרֹן בְּקָרְבָתָם לִפְנֵי־יהוה וַיָּמֻתוּ׃
וַיֹּאמֶר יהוה אֶל־מֹשֶׁה דַּבֵּר אֶל־אַהֲרֹן אָחִיךָ וְאַל־יָבֹא בְכָל־עֵת אֶל־הַקֹּדֶשׁ
מִבֵּית לַפָּרֹכֶת אֶל־פְּנֵי הַכַּפֹּרֶת אֲשֶׁר עַל־הָאָרֹן וְלֹא יָמוּת כִּי בֶּעָנָן אֵרָאֶה
עַל־הַכַּפֹּרֶת׃ בְּזֹאת יָבֹא אַהֲרֹן אֶל־הַקֹּדֶשׁ בְּפַר בֶּן־בָּקָר לְחַטָּאת וְאַיִל
לְעֹלָה׃ כְּתֹנֶת־בַּד קֹדֶשׁ יִלְבָּשׁ וּמִכְנְסֵי־בַד יִהְיוּ עַל־בְּשָׂרוֹ וּבְאַבְנֵט בַּד
יַחְגֹּר וּבְמִצְנֶפֶת בַּד יִצְנֹף בִּגְדֵי־קֹדֶשׁ הֵם וְרָחַץ בַּמַּיִם אֶת־בְּשָׂרוֹ וּלְבֵשָׁם׃
וּמֵאֵת עֲדַת בְּנֵי יִשְׂרָאֵל יִקַּח שְׁנֵי־שְׂעִירֵי עִזִּים לְחַטָּאת וְאַיִל אֶחָד לְעֹלָה׃
לוי וְהִקְרִיב אַהֲרֹן אֶת־פַּר הַחַטָּאת אֲשֶׁר־לוֹ וְכִפֶּר בַּעֲדוֹ וּבְעַד בֵּיתוֹ׃ *וְלָקַח
אֶת־שְׁנֵי הַשְּׂעִירִם וְהֶעֱמִיד אֹתָם לִפְנֵי יהוה פֶּתַח אֹהֶל מוֹעֵד׃ וְנָתַן אַהֲרֹן
עַל־שְׁנֵי הַשְּׂעִירִם גֹּרָלוֹת גּוֹרָל אֶחָד לַיהוה וְגוֹרָל אֶחָד לַעֲזָאזֵל׃ וְהִקְרִיב
אַהֲרֹן אֶת־הַשָּׂעִיר אֲשֶׁר עָלָה עָלָיו הַגּוֹרָל לַיהוה וְעָשָׂהוּ חַטָּאת׃ וְהַשָּׂעִיר
אֲשֶׁר עָלָה עָלָיו הַגּוֹרָל לַעֲזָאזֵל יָעֳמַד־חַי לִפְנֵי יהוה לְכַפֵּר עָלָיו לְשַׁלַּח

אֹתוֹ לַעֲזָאזֵל הַמִּדְבָּרָה: וְהִקְרִיב אַהֲרֹן אֶת־פַּר הַחַטָּאת אֲשֶׁר־לוֹ וְכִפֶּר
בַּעֲדוֹ וּבְעַד בֵּיתוֹ וְשָׁחַט אֶת־פַּר הַחַטָּאת אֲשֶׁר־לוֹ: *וְלָקַח מְלֹא־הַמַּחְתָּה ישראל
גַּחֲלֵי־אֵשׁ מֵעַל הַמִּזְבֵּחַ מִלִּפְנֵי יהוה וּמְלֹא חָפְנָיו קְטֹרֶת סַמִּים דַּקָּה וְהֵבִיא
מִבֵּית לַפָּרֹכֶת: וְנָתַן אֶת־הַקְּטֹרֶת עַל־הָאֵשׁ לִפְנֵי יהוה וְכִסָּה ׀ עֲנַן הַקְּטֹרֶת
אֶת־הַכַּפֹּרֶת אֲשֶׁר עַל־הָעֵדוּת וְלֹא יָמוּת: וְלָקַח מִדַּם הַפָּר וְהִזָּה בְאֶצְבָּעוֹ
עַל־פְּנֵי הַכַּפֹּרֶת קֵדְמָה וְלִפְנֵי הַכַּפֹּרֶת יַזֶּה שֶׁבַע־פְּעָמִים מִן־הַדָּם בְּאֶצְבָּעוֹ:
וְשָׁחַט אֶת־שְׂעִיר הַחַטָּאת אֲשֶׁר לָעָם וְהֵבִיא אֶת־דָּמוֹ אֶל־מִבֵּית לַפָּרֹכֶת
וְעָשָׂה אֶת־דָּמוֹ כַּאֲשֶׁר עָשָׂה לְדַם הַפָּר וְהִזָּה אֹתוֹ עַל־הַכַּפֹּרֶת וְלִפְנֵי הַכַּפֹּרֶת:
וְכִפֶּר עַל־הַקֹּדֶשׁ מִטֻּמְאֹת בְּנֵי יִשְׂרָאֵל וּמִפִּשְׁעֵיהֶם לְכָל־חַטֹּאתָם וְכֵן יַעֲשֶׂה
לְאֹהֶל מוֹעֵד הַשֹּׁכֵן אִתָּם בְּתוֹךְ טֻמְאֹתָם: וְכָל־אָדָם לֹא־יִהְיֶה ׀ בְּאֹהֶל מוֹעֵד
בְּבֹאוֹ לְכַפֵּר בַּקֹּדֶשׁ עַד־צֵאתוֹ וְכִפֶּר בַּעֲדוֹ וּבְעַד בֵּיתוֹ וּבְעַד כָּל־קְהַל יִשְׂרָאֵל:

קדושים KEDOSHIM

וַיְדַבֵּר יהוה אֶל־מֹשֶׁה לֵּאמֹר: דַּבֵּר אֶל־כָּל־עֲדַת בְּנֵי־יִשְׂרָאֵל וְאָמַרְתָּ אֲלֵהֶם ויקרא יט:א–יד
קְדֹשִׁים תִּהְיוּ כִּי קָדוֹשׁ אֲנִי יהוה אֱלֹהֵיכֶם: אִישׁ אִמּוֹ וְאָבִיו תִּירָאוּ וְאֶת־
שַׁבְּתֹתַי תִּשְׁמֹרוּ אֲנִי יהוה אֱלֹהֵיכֶם: אַל־תִּפְנוּ אֶל־הָאֱלִילִם וֵאלֹהֵי מַסֵּכָה
לֹא תַעֲשׂוּ לָכֶם אֲנִי יהוה אֱלֹהֵיכֶם: *וְכִי תִזְבְּחוּ זֶבַח שְׁלָמִים לַיהוה לִרְצֹנְכֶם לוי
תִּזְבָּחֻהוּ: בְּיוֹם זִבְחֲכֶם יֵאָכֵל וּמִמָּחֳרָת וְהַנּוֹתָר עַד־יוֹם הַשְּׁלִישִׁי בָּאֵשׁ יִשָּׂרֵף:
וְאִם הֵאָכֹל יֵאָכֵל בַּיּוֹם הַשְּׁלִישִׁי פִּגּוּל הוּא לֹא יֵרָצֶה: וְאֹכְלָיו עֲוֺנוֹ יִשָּׂא כִּי־
אֶת־קֹדֶשׁ יהוה חִלֵּל וְנִכְרְתָה הַנֶּפֶשׁ הַהִוא מֵעַמֶּיהָ: וּבְקֻצְרְכֶם אֶת־קְצִיר
אַרְצְכֶם לֹא תְכַלֶּה פְּאַת שָׂדְךָ לִקְצֹר וְלֶקֶט קְצִירְךָ לֹא תְלַקֵּט: וְכַרְמְךָ לֹא
תְעוֹלֵל וּפֶרֶט כַּרְמְךָ לֹא תְלַקֵּט לֶעָנִי וְלַגֵּר תַּעֲזֹב אֹתָם אֲנִי יהוה אֱלֹהֵיכֶם:
*לֹא תִּגְנֹבוּ וְלֹא־תְכַחֲשׁוּ וְלֹא־תְשַׁקְּרוּ אִישׁ בַּעֲמִיתוֹ: וְלֹא־תִשָּׁבְעוּ בִשְׁמִי ישראל
לַשָּׁקֶר וְחִלַּלְתָּ אֶת־שֵׁם אֱלֹהֶיךָ אֲנִי יהוה: לֹא־תַעֲשֹׁק אֶת־רֵעֲךָ וְלֹא תִגְזֹל
לֹא־תָלִין פְּעֻלַּת שָׂכִיר אִתְּךָ עַד־בֹּקֶר: לֹא־תְקַלֵּל חֵרֵשׁ וְלִפְנֵי עִוֵּר לֹא תִתֵּן
מִכְשֹׁל וְיָרֵאתָ מֵּאֱלֹהֶיךָ אֲנִי יהוה:

אמור EMOR

וַיֹּאמֶר יהוה אֶל־מֹשֶׁה אֱמֹר אֶל־הַכֹּהֲנִים בְּנֵי אַהֲרֹן וְאָמַרְתָּ אֲלֵהֶם לְנֶפֶשׁ ויקרא כא:א–טו

לֹא־יִטַּמָּא בְּעַמָּיו: כִּי אִם־לִשְׁאֵרוֹ הַקָּרֹב אֵלָיו לְאִמּוֹ וּלְאָבִיו וְלִבְנוֹ וּלְבִתּוֹ
וּלְאָחִיו: וְלַאֲחֹתוֹ הַבְּתוּלָה הַקְּרוֹבָה אֵלָיו אֲשֶׁר לֹא־הָיְתָה לְאִישׁ לָהּ יִטַּמָּא:
יִקְרְחוּ לֹא יִטַּמָּא בַּעַל בְּעַמָּיו לְהֵחַלּוֹ: לֹא־יקרחה קָרְחָה בְּרֹאשָׁם וּפְאַת זְקָנָם
לֹא יְגַלֵּחוּ וּבִבְשָׂרָם לֹא יִשְׂרְטוּ שָׂרָטֶת: קְדֹשִׁים יִהְיוּ לֵאלֹהֵיהֶם וְלֹא יְחַלְּלוּ
שֵׁם אֱלֹהֵיהֶם כִּי אֶת־אִשֵּׁי יהוה לֶחֶם אֱלֹהֵיהֶם הֵם מַקְרִיבִם וְהָיוּ קֹדֶשׁ:
לוי *אִשָּׁה זֹנָה וַחֲלָלָה לֹא יִקָּחוּ וְאִשָּׁה גְּרוּשָׁה מֵאִישָׁהּ לֹא יִקָּחוּ כִּי־קָדֹשׁ הוּא
לֵאלֹהָיו: וְקִדַּשְׁתּוֹ כִּי־אֶת־לֶחֶם אֱלֹהֶיךָ הוּא מַקְרִיב קָדֹשׁ יִהְיֶה־לָּךְ כִּי קָדוֹשׁ
אֲנִי יהוה מְקַדִּשְׁכֶם: וּבַת אִישׁ כֹּהֵן כִּי תֵחֵל לִזְנוֹת אֶת־אָבִיהָ הִיא מְחַלֶּלֶת
בָּאֵשׁ תִּשָּׂרֵף: וְהַכֹּהֵן הַגָּדוֹל מֵאֶחָיו אֲשֶׁר־יוּצַק עַל־רֹאשׁוֹ ׀ שֶׁמֶן
הַמִּשְׁחָה וּמִלֵּא אֶת־יָדוֹ לִלְבֹּשׁ אֶת־הַבְּגָדִים אֶת־רֹאשׁוֹ לֹא יִפְרָע וּבְגָדָיו לֹא
יִפְרֹם: וְעַל כָּל־נַפְשֹׁת מֵת לֹא יָבֹא לְאָבִיו וּלְאִמּוֹ לֹא יִטַּמָּא: וּמִן־הַמִּקְדָּשׁ
לֹא יֵצֵא וְלֹא יְחַלֵּל אֵת מִקְדַּשׁ אֱלֹהָיו כִּי נֵזֶר שֶׁמֶן מִשְׁחַת אֱלֹהָיו עָלָיו אֲנִי
ישראל יהוה: *וְהוּא אִשָּׁה בִבְתוּלֶיהָ יִקָּח: אַלְמָנָה וּגְרוּשָׁה וַחֲלָלָה זֹנָה אֶת־אֵלֶּה
לֹא יִקָּח כִּי אִם־בְּתוּלָה מֵעַמָּיו יִקַּח אִשָּׁה: וְלֹא־יְחַלֵּל זַרְעוֹ בְּעַמָּיו כִּי אֲנִי
יהוה מְקַדְּשׁוֹ:

BEHAR בהר

ויקרא כה:א–יג וַיְדַבֵּר יהוה אֶל־מֹשֶׁה בְּהַר סִינַי לֵאמֹר: דַּבֵּר אֶל־בְּנֵי יִשְׂרָאֵל וְאָמַרְתָּ
אֲלֵהֶם כִּי תָבֹאוּ אֶל־הָאָרֶץ אֲשֶׁר אֲנִי נֹתֵן לָכֶם וְשָׁבְתָה הָאָרֶץ שַׁבָּת לַיהוה:
שֵׁשׁ שָׁנִים תִּזְרַע שָׂדֶךָ וְשֵׁשׁ שָׁנִים תִּזְמֹר כַּרְמֶךָ וְאָסַפְתָּ אֶת־תְּבוּאָתָהּ:
לוי *וּבַשָּׁנָה הַשְּׁבִיעִת שַׁבַּת שַׁבָּתוֹן יִהְיֶה לָאָרֶץ שַׁבָּת לַיהוה שָׂדְךָ לֹא תִזְרָע
וְכַרְמְךָ לֹא תִזְמֹר: אֵת סְפִיחַ קְצִירְךָ לֹא תִקְצוֹר וְאֶת־עִנְּבֵי נְזִירֶךָ לֹא תִבְצֹר
שְׁנַת שַׁבָּתוֹן יִהְיֶה לָאָרֶץ: וְהָיְתָה שַׁבַּת הָאָרֶץ לָכֶם לְאָכְלָה לְךָ וּלְעַבְדְּךָ
וְלַאֲמָתֶךָ וְלִשְׂכִירְךָ וּלְתוֹשָׁבְךָ הַגָּרִים עִמָּךְ: וְלִבְהֶמְתְּךָ וְלַחַיָּה אֲשֶׁר בְּאַרְצֶךָ
ישראל תִּהְיֶה כָל־תְּבוּאָתָהּ לֶאֱכֹל: *וְסָפַרְתָּ לְךָ שֶׁבַע שַׁבְּתֹת שָׁנִים
שֶׁבַע שָׁנִים שֶׁבַע פְּעָמִים וְהָיוּ לְךָ יְמֵי שֶׁבַע שַׁבְּתֹת הַשָּׁנִים תֵּשַׁע וְאַרְבָּעִים
שָׁנָה: וְהַעֲבַרְתָּ שׁוֹפַר תְּרוּעָה בַּחֹדֶשׁ הַשְּׁבִעִי בֶּעָשׂוֹר לַחֹדֶשׁ בְּיוֹם הַכִּפֻּרִים
תַּעֲבִירוּ שׁוֹפָר בְּכָל־אַרְצְכֶם: וְקִדַּשְׁתֶּם אֵת שְׁנַת הַחֲמִשִּׁים שָׁנָה וּקְרָאתֶם
דְּרוֹר בָּאָרֶץ לְכָל־יֹשְׁבֶיהָ יוֹבֵל הִוא תִּהְיֶה לָכֶם וְשַׁבְתֶּם אִישׁ אֶל־אֲחֻזָּתוֹ

וְאִישׁ אֶל־מִשְׁפַּחְתּוֹ תָּשֻׁבוּ: יוֹבֵל הִוא שְׁנַת הַחֲמִשִּׁים שָׁנָה תִּהְיֶה לָכֶם לֹא
תִזְרָעוּ וְלֹא תִקְצְרוּ אֶת־סְפִיחֶיהָ וְלֹא תִבְצְרוּ אֶת־נְזִרֶיהָ: כִּי יוֹבֵל הִוא קֹדֶשׁ
תִּהְיֶה לָכֶם מִן־הַשָּׂדֶה תֹּאכְלוּ אֶת־תְּבוּאָתָהּ: בִּשְׁנַת הַיּוֹבֵל הַזֹּאת תָּשֻׁבוּ
אִישׁ אֶל־אֲחֻזָּתוֹ:

בחוקותי BEḤUKKOTAI

אִם־בְּחֻקֹּתַי תֵּלֵכוּ וְאֶת־מִצְוֹתַי תִּשְׁמְרוּ וַעֲשִׂיתֶם אֹתָם: וְנָתַתִּי גִשְׁמֵיכֶם בְּעִתָּם ויקרא כו:ג–יג
וְנָתְנָה הָאָרֶץ יְבוּלָהּ וְעֵץ הַשָּׂדֶה יִתֵּן פִּרְיוֹ: וְהִשִּׂיג לָכֶם דַּיִשׁ אֶת־בָּצִיר וּבָצִיר
יַשִּׂיג אֶת־זָרַע וַאֲכַלְתֶּם לַחְמְכֶם לָשֹׂבַע וִישַׁבְתֶּם לָבֶטַח בְּאַרְצְכֶם: *וְנָתַתִּי לוי
שָׁלוֹם בָּאָרֶץ וּשְׁכַבְתֶּם וְאֵין מַחֲרִיד וְהִשְׁבַּתִּי חַיָּה רָעָה מִן־הָאָרֶץ וְחֶרֶב
לֹא־תַעֲבֹר בְּאַרְצְכֶם: וּרְדַפְתֶּם אֶת־אֹיְבֵיכֶם וְנָפְלוּ לִפְנֵיכֶם לֶחָרֶב: וְרָדְפוּ
מִכֶּם חֲמִשָּׁה מֵאָה וּמֵאָה מִכֶּם רְבָבָה יִרְדֹּפוּ וְנָפְלוּ אֹיְבֵיכֶם לִפְנֵיכֶם לֶחָרֶב:
וּפָנִיתִי אֲלֵיכֶם וְהִפְרֵיתִי אֶתְכֶם וְהִרְבֵּיתִי אֶתְכֶם וַהֲקִימֹתִי אֶת־בְּרִיתִי אִתְּכֶם:
*וַאֲכַלְתֶּם יָשָׁן נוֹשָׁן וְיָשָׁן מִפְּנֵי חָדָשׁ תּוֹצִיאוּ: וְנָתַתִּי מִשְׁכָּנִי בְּתוֹכְכֶם וְלֹא־ ישראל
תִגְעַל נַפְשִׁי אֶתְכֶם: וְהִתְהַלַּכְתִּי בְּתוֹכְכֶם וְהָיִיתִי לָכֶם לֵאלֹהִים וְאַתֶּם תִּהְיוּ־לִי
לְעָם: אֲנִי יְהוָה אֱלֹהֵיכֶם אֲשֶׁר הוֹצֵאתִי אֶתְכֶם מֵאֶרֶץ מִצְרַיִם מִהְיֹת לָהֶם
עֲבָדִים וָאֶשְׁבֹּר מֹטֹת עֻלְּכֶם וָאוֹלֵךְ אֶתְכֶם קוֹמְמִיּוּת:

במדבר BEMIDBAR

וַיְדַבֵּר יְהוָה אֶל־מֹשֶׁה בְּמִדְבַּר סִינַי בְּאֹהֶל מוֹעֵד בְּאֶחָד לַחֹדֶשׁ הַשֵּׁנִי בַּשָּׁנָה במדבר א:א–יט
הַשֵּׁנִית לְצֵאתָם מֵאֶרֶץ מִצְרַיִם לֵאמֹר: שְׂאוּ אֶת־רֹאשׁ כָּל־עֲדַת בְּנֵי־יִשְׂרָאֵל
לְמִשְׁפְּחֹתָם לְבֵית אֲבֹתָם בְּמִסְפַּר שֵׁמוֹת כָּל־זָכָר לְגֻלְגְּלֹתָם: מִבֶּן עֶשְׂרִים
שָׁנָה וָמַעְלָה כָּל־יֹצֵא צָבָא בְּיִשְׂרָאֵל תִּפְקְדוּ אֹתָם לְצִבְאֹתָם אַתָּה וְאַהֲרֹן:
וְאִתְּכֶם יִהְיוּ אִישׁ אִישׁ לַמַּטֶּה אִישׁ רֹאשׁ לְבֵית־אֲבֹתָיו הוּא: *וְאֵלֶּה שְׁמוֹת לוי
הָאֲנָשִׁים אֲשֶׁר יַעַמְדוּ אִתְּכֶם לִרְאוּבֵן אֱלִיצוּר בֶּן־שְׁדֵיאוּר: לְשִׁמְעוֹן שְׁלֻמִיאֵל
בֶּן־צוּרִישַׁדָּי: לִיהוּדָה נַחְשׁוֹן בֶּן־עַמִּינָדָב: לְיִשָּׂשכָר נְתַנְאֵל בֶּן־צוּעָר:
לִזְבוּלֻן אֱלִיאָב בֶּן־חֵלֹן: לִבְנֵי יוֹסֵף לְאֶפְרַיִם אֱלִישָׁמָע בֶּן־עַמִּיהוּד לִמְנַשֶּׁה
גַּמְלִיאֵל בֶּן־פְּדָהצוּר: לְבִנְיָמִן אֲבִידָן בֶּן־גִּדְעֹנִי: לְדָן אֲחִיעֶזֶר בֶּן־עַמִּישַׁדָּי:
לְאָשֵׁר פַּגְעִיאֵל בֶּן־עָכְרָן: לְגָד אֶלְיָסָף בֶּן־דְּעוּאֵל: לְנַפְתָּלִי אֲחִירַע בֶּן־

קְרוּאֵי עֵינָן: אֵלֶּה קריאֵי הָעֵדָה נְשִׂיאֵי מַטּוֹת אֲבוֹתָם רָאשֵׁי אַלְפֵי יִשְׂרָאֵל הֵם:
ישראל *וַיִּקַּח מֹשֶׁה וְאַהֲרֹן אֵת הָאֲנָשִׁים הָאֵלֶּה אֲשֶׁר נִקְּבוּ בְּשֵׁמוֹת: וְאֵת כָּל־הָעֵדָה
הִקְהִילוּ בְּאֶחָד לַחֹדֶשׁ הַשֵּׁנִי וַיִּתְיַלְדוּ עַל־מִשְׁפְּחֹתָם לְבֵית אֲבֹתָם בְּמִסְפַּר
שֵׁמוֹת מִבֶּן עֶשְׂרִים שָׁנָה וָמַעְלָה לְגֻלְגְּלֹתָם: כַּאֲשֶׁר צִוָּה יהוה אֶת־מֹשֶׁה
וַיִּפְקְדֵם בְּמִדְבַּר סִינָי:

נשא NASO

במדבר ד:כא–לז
וַיְדַבֵּר יהוה אֶל־מֹשֶׁה לֵּאמֹר: נָשֹׂא אֶת־רֹאשׁ בְּנֵי גֵרְשׁוֹן גַּם־הֵם לְבֵית אֲבֹתָם
לְמִשְׁפְּחֹתָם: מִבֶּן שְׁלֹשִׁים שָׁנָה וָמַעְלָה עַד בֶּן־חֲמִשִּׁים שָׁנָה תִּפְקֹד אוֹתָם
כָּל־הַבָּא לִצְבֹא צָבָא לַעֲבֹד עֲבֹדָה בְּאֹהֶל מוֹעֵד: זֹאת עֲבֹדַת מִשְׁפְּחֹת
לוי הַגֵּרְשֻׁנִּי לַעֲבֹד וּלְמַשָּׂא: *וְנָשְׂאוּ אֶת־יְרִיעֹת הַמִּשְׁכָּן וְאֶת־אֹהֶל מוֹעֵד מִכְסֵהוּ
וּמִכְסֵה הַתַּחַשׁ אֲשֶׁר־עָלָיו מִלְמָעְלָה וְאֶת־מָסַךְ פֶּתַח אֹהֶל מוֹעֵד: וְאֵת קַלְעֵי
הֶחָצֵר וְאֶת־מָסַךְ ׀ פֶּתַח ׀ שַׁעַר הֶחָצֵר אֲשֶׁר עַל־הַמִּשְׁכָּן וְעַל־הַמִּזְבֵּחַ סָבִיב
וְאֵת מֵיתְרֵיהֶם וְאֶת־כָּל־כְּלֵי עֲבֹדָתָם וְאֵת כָּל־אֲשֶׁר יֵעָשֶׂה לָהֶם וְעָבָדוּ:
עַל־פִּי אַהֲרֹן וּבָנָיו תִּהְיֶה כָּל־עֲבֹדַת בְּנֵי הַגֵּרְשֻׁנִּי לְכָל־מַשָּׂאָם וּלְכֹל עֲבֹדָתָם
וּפְקַדְתֶּם עֲלֵהֶם בְּמִשְׁמֶרֶת אֵת כָּל־מַשָּׂאָם: זֹאת עֲבֹדַת מִשְׁפְּחֹת בְּנֵי הַגֵּרְשֻׁנִּי
ישראל בְּאֹהֶל מוֹעֵד וּמִשְׁמַרְתָּם בְּיַד אִיתָמָר בֶּן־אַהֲרֹן הַכֹּהֵן: *בְּנֵי מְרָרִי
לְמִשְׁפְּחֹתָם לְבֵית־אֲבֹתָם תִּפְקֹד אֹתָם: מִבֶּן שְׁלֹשִׁים שָׁנָה וָמַעְלָה וְעַד בֶּן־
חֲמִשִּׁים שָׁנָה תִּפְקְדֵם כָּל־הַבָּא לַצָּבָא לַעֲבֹד אֶת־עֲבֹדַת אֹהֶל מוֹעֵד: וְזֹאת
מִשְׁמֶרֶת מַשָּׂאָם לְכָל־עֲבֹדָתָם בְּאֹהֶל מוֹעֵד קַרְשֵׁי הַמִּשְׁכָּן וּבְרִיחָיו וְעַמּוּדָיו
וַאֲדָנָיו: וְעַמּוּדֵי הֶחָצֵר סָבִיב וְאַדְנֵיהֶם וִיתֵדֹתָם וּמֵיתְרֵיהֶם לְכָל־כְּלֵיהֶם וּלְכֹל
עֲבֹדָתָם וּבְשֵׁמֹת תִּפְקְדוּ אֶת־כְּלֵי מִשְׁמֶרֶת מַשָּׂאָם: זֹאת עֲבֹדַת מִשְׁפְּחֹת בְּנֵי
מְרָרִי לְכָל־עֲבֹדָתָם בְּאֹהֶל מוֹעֵד בְּיַד אִיתָמָר בֶּן־אַהֲרֹן הַכֹּהֵן:

Some extend the ישראל *portion:*

וַיִּפְקֹד מֹשֶׁה וְאַהֲרֹן וּנְשִׂיאֵי הָעֵדָה אֶת־בְּנֵי הַקְּהָתִי לְמִשְׁפְּחֹתָם וּלְבֵית אֲבֹתָם:
מִבֶּן שְׁלֹשִׁים שָׁנָה וָמַעְלָה וְעַד בֶּן־חֲמִשִּׁים שָׁנָה כָּל־הַבָּא לַצָּבָא לַעֲבֹדָה
בְּאֹהֶל מוֹעֵד: וַיִּהְיוּ פְקֻדֵיהֶם לְמִשְׁפְּחֹתָם אַלְפַּיִם שְׁבַע מֵאוֹת וַחֲמִשִּׁים: אֵלֶּה
פְקוּדֵי מִשְׁפְּחֹת הַקְּהָתִי כָּל־הָעֹבֵד בְּאֹהֶל מוֹעֵד אֲשֶׁר פָּקַד מֹשֶׁה וְאַהֲרֹן
עַל־פִּי יהוה בְּיַד־מֹשֶׁה:

בהעלותך BEHA'ALOTEKHA

במדבר ח:א-יד וַיְדַבֵּר יְהוָה אֶל־מֹשֶׁה לֵּאמֹר: דַּבֵּר אֶל־אַהֲרֹן וְאָמַרְתָּ אֵלָיו בְּהַעֲלֹתְךָ אֶת־
הַנֵּרֹת אֶל־מוּל פְּנֵי הַמְּנוֹרָה יָאִירוּ שִׁבְעַת הַנֵּרוֹת: וַיַּעַשׂ כֵּן אַהֲרֹן אֶל־מוּל
פְּנֵי הַמְּנוֹרָה הֶעֱלָה נֵרֹתֶיהָ כַּאֲשֶׁר צִוָּה יְהוָה אֶת־מֹשֶׁה: וְזֶה מַעֲשֵׂה הַמְּנֹרָה
מִקְשָׁה זָהָב עַד־יְרֵכָהּ עַד־פִּרְחָהּ מִקְשָׁה הִוא כַּמַּרְאֶה אֲשֶׁר הֶרְאָה יְהוָה
אֶת־מֹשֶׁה כֵּן עָשָׂה אֶת־הַמְּנֹרָה:
לוי וַיְדַבֵּר יְהוָה אֶל־מֹשֶׁה לֵּאמֹר: קַח אֶת־הַלְוִיִּם מִתּוֹךְ בְּנֵי יִשְׂרָאֵל וְטִהַרְתָּ
אֹתָם: וְכֹה־תַעֲשֶׂה לָהֶם לְטַהֲרָם הַזֵּה עֲלֵיהֶם מֵי חַטָּאת וְהֶעֱבִירוּ תַעַר עַל־
כָּל־בְּשָׂרָם וְכִבְּסוּ בִגְדֵיהֶם וְהִטֶּהָרוּ: וְלָקְחוּ פַּר בֶּן־בָּקָר וּמִנְחָתוֹ סֹלֶת בְּלוּלָה
בַשָּׁמֶן וּפַר־שֵׁנִי בֶן־בָּקָר תִּקַּח לְחַטָּאת: וְהִקְרַבְתָּ אֶת־הַלְוִיִּם לִפְנֵי אֹהֶל
ישראל מוֹעֵד וְהִקְהַלְתָּ אֶת־כָּל־עֲדַת בְּנֵי יִשְׂרָאֵל: *וְהִקְרַבְתָּ אֶת־הַלְוִיִּם לִפְנֵי יְהוָה
וְסָמְכוּ בְנֵי־יִשְׂרָאֵל אֶת־יְדֵיהֶם עַל־הַלְוִיִּם: וְהֵנִיף אַהֲרֹן אֶת־הַלְוִיִּם תְּנוּפָה
לִפְנֵי יְהוָה מֵאֵת בְּנֵי יִשְׂרָאֵל וְהָיוּ לַעֲבֹד אֶת־עֲבֹדַת יְהוָה: וְהַלְוִיִּם יִסְמְכוּ
אֶת־יְדֵיהֶם עַל רֹאשׁ הַפָּרִים וַעֲשֵׂה אֶת־הָאֶחָד חַטָּאת וְאֶת־הָאֶחָד עֹלָה
לַיהוָה לְכַפֵּר עַל־הַלְוִיִּם: וְהַעֲמַדְתָּ אֶת־הַלְוִיִּם לִפְנֵי אַהֲרֹן וְלִפְנֵי בָנָיו וְהֵנַפְתָּ
אֹתָם תְּנוּפָה לַיהוָה: וְהִבְדַּלְתָּ אֶת־הַלְוִיִּם מִתּוֹךְ בְּנֵי יִשְׂרָאֵל וְהָיוּ לִי הַלְוִיִּם:

שלח SHELAḤ

במדבר יג:א-כ וַיְדַבֵּר יְהוָה אֶל־מֹשֶׁה לֵּאמֹר: שְׁלַח־לְךָ אֲנָשִׁים וְיָתֻרוּ אֶת־אֶרֶץ כְּנַעַן אֲשֶׁר־
אֲנִי נֹתֵן לִבְנֵי יִשְׂרָאֵל אִישׁ אֶחָד אִישׁ אֶחָד לְמַטֵּה אֲבֹתָיו תִּשְׁלָחוּ כֹּל נָשִׂיא
בָהֶם: וַיִּשְׁלַח אֹתָם מֹשֶׁה מִמִּדְבַּר פָּארָן עַל־פִּי יְהוָה כֻּלָּם אֲנָשִׁים רָאשֵׁי
לוי בְנֵי־יִשְׂרָאֵל הֵמָּה: *וְאֵלֶּה שְׁמוֹתָם לְמַטֵּה רְאוּבֵן שַׁמּוּעַ בֶּן־זַכּוּר: לְמַטֵּה
שִׁמְעוֹן שָׁפָט בֶּן־חוֹרִי: לְמַטֵּה יְהוּדָה כָּלֵב בֶּן־יְפֻנֶּה: לְמַטֵּה יִשָּׂשכָר יִגְאָל
בֶּן־יוֹסֵף: לְמַטֵּה אֶפְרָיִם הוֹשֵׁעַ בִּן־נוּן: לְמַטֵּה בִנְיָמִן פַּלְטִי בֶּן־רָפוּא: לְמַטֵּה
זְבוּלֻן גַּדִּיאֵל בֶּן־סוֹדִי: לְמַטֵּה יוֹסֵף לְמַטֵּה מְנַשֶּׁה גַּדִּי בֶּן־סוּסִי: לְמַטֵּה דָן
עַמִּיאֵל בֶּן־גְּמַלִּי: לְמַטֵּה אָשֵׁר סְתוּר בֶּן־מִיכָאֵל: לְמַטֵּה נַפְתָּלִי נַחְבִּי בֶּן־
וָפְסִי: לְמַטֵּה גָד גְּאוּאֵל בֶּן־מָכִי: אֵלֶּה שְׁמוֹת הָאֲנָשִׁים אֲשֶׁר־שָׁלַח מֹשֶׁה
ישראל לָתוּר אֶת־הָאָרֶץ וַיִּקְרָא מֹשֶׁה לְהוֹשֵׁעַ בִּן־נוּן יְהוֹשֻׁעַ: *וַיִּשְׁלַח אֹתָם מֹשֶׁה
לָתוּר אֶת־אֶרֶץ כְּנָעַן וַיֹּאמֶר אֲלֵהֶם עֲלוּ זֶה בַּנֶּגֶב וַעֲלִיתֶם אֶת־הָהָר: וּרְאִיתֶם

אֶת־הָאָ֗רֶץ מַה־הִ֔וא וְאֶת־הָעָם֙ הַיֹּשֵׁ֣ב עָלֶ֔יהָ הֶחָזָ֥ק הוּא֙ הֲרָפֶ֔ה הַמְעַ֥ט ה֖וּא אִם־רָ֑ב: וּמָ֣ה הָאָ֗רֶץ אֲשֶׁר־הוּא֙ יֹשֵׁ֣ב בָּ֔הּ הֲטוֹבָ֥ה הִ֖וא אִם־רָעָ֑ה וּמָ֣ה הֶעָרִ֗ים אֲשֶׁר־הוּא֙ יוֹשֵׁ֣ב בָּהֵ֔נָּה הַבְּמַֽחֲנִ֖ים אִ֥ם בְּמִבְצָרִֽים: וּמָ֣ה הָ֠אָ֠רֶץ הַשְּׁמֵנָ֨ה הִ֜וא אִם־רָזָ֗ה הֲיֵשׁ־בָּ֥הּ עֵץ֙ אִם־אַ֔יִן וְהִ֨תְחַזַּקְתֶּ֔ם וּלְקַחְתֶּ֖ם מִפְּרִ֣י הָאָ֑רֶץ וְהַ֨יָּמִ֔ים יְמֵ֖י בִּכּוּרֵ֥י עֲנָבִֽים:

KORAH

קרח

במדבר
ט״ז:א-ג

וַיִּקַּ֣ח קֹ֔רַח בֶּן־יִצְהָ֥ר בֶּן־קְהָ֖ת בֶּן־לֵוִ֑י וְדָתָ֨ן וַאֲבִירָ֜ם בְּנֵ֧י אֱלִיאָ֛ב וְא֥וֹן בֶּן־ פֶּ֖לֶת בְּנֵ֥י רְאוּבֵֽן: וַיָּקֻ֨מוּ לִפְנֵ֣י מֹשֶׁ֗ה וַאֲנָשִׁ֥ים מִבְּנֵֽי־יִשְׂרָאֵ֖ל חֲמִשִּׁ֣ים וּמָאתָ֑יִם נְשִׂיאֵ֥י עֵדָ֛ה קְרִאֵ֥י מוֹעֵ֖ד אַנְשֵׁי־שֵֽׁם: וַיִּקָּהֲל֞וּ עַל־מֹשֶׁ֣ה וְעַֽל־אַהֲרֹ֗ן וַיֹּאמְר֣וּ אֲלֵהֶם֮ רַב־לָכֶם֒ כִּ֤י כָל־הָֽעֵדָה֙ כֻּלָּ֣ם קְדֹשִׁ֔ים וּבְתוֹכָ֖ם יהו֑ה וּמַדּ֥וּעַ תִּֽתְנַשְּׂא֖וּ

לוי

עַל־קְהַ֥ל יהוֽה: וַיִּשְׁמַ֣ע מֹשֶׁ֔ה וַיִּפֹּ֖ל עַל־פָּנָֽיו: וַיְדַבֵּ֨ר אֶל־קֹ֜רַח וְאֶֽל־כָּל־עֲדָתוֹ֮ לֵאמֹר֒ בֹּ֠קֶר וְיֹדַ֨ע יהו֧ה אֶת־אֲשֶׁר־ל֛וֹ וְאֶת־הַקָּד֖וֹשׁ וְהִקְרִ֣יב אֵלָ֑יו וְאֵ֛ת אֲשֶׁ֥ר יִבְחַר־בּ֖וֹ יַקְרִ֥יב אֵלָֽיו: זֹ֖את עֲשׂ֑וּ קְחוּ־לָכֶ֣ם מַחְתּ֔וֹת קֹ֖רַח וְכָל־עֲדָתֽוֹ: וּתְנ֣וּ בָהֵ֣ן ׀ אֵ֗שׁ וְשִׂימוּ֩ עֲלֵיהֶ֨ן קְטֹ֜רֶת לִפְנֵ֤י יהוה֙ מָחָ֔ר וְהָיָ֗ה הָאִ֛ישׁ אֲשֶׁר־יִבְחַ֥ר

ישראל

יהו֖ה ה֣וּא הַקָּד֑וֹשׁ רַב־לָכֶ֖ם בְּנֵ֥י לֵוִֽי: וַיֹּ֥אמֶר מֹשֶׁ֖ה אֶל־קֹ֑רַח שִׁמְעוּ־נָ֖א בְּנֵ֥י לֵוִֽי: הַמְעַ֣ט מִכֶּ֗ם כִּֽי־הִבְדִּיל֩ אֱלֹהֵ֨י יִשְׂרָאֵ֤ל אֶתְכֶם֙ מֵעֲדַ֣ת יִשְׂרָאֵ֔ל לְהַקְרִ֥יב אֶתְכֶ֖ם אֵלָ֑יו לַעֲבֹ֗ד אֶת־עֲבֹדַת֙ מִשְׁכַּ֣ן יהו֔ה וְלַעֲמֹ֛ד לִפְנֵ֥י הָעֵדָ֖ה לְשָׁרְתָֽם: וַיַּקְרֵב֙ אֹֽתְךָ֔ וְאֶת־כָּל־אַחֶ֥יךָ בְנֵֽי־לֵוִ֖י אִתָּ֑ךְ וּבִקַּשְׁתֶּ֖ם גַּם־כְּהֻנָּֽה: לָכֵ֗ן אַתָּה֙

תליש

וְכָל־עֲדָ֣תְךָ֔ הַנֹּעָדִ֖ים עַל־יהו֑ה וְאַהֲרֹ֣ן מַה־ה֔וּא כִּ֥י תַלִּ֖ונוּ עָלָֽיו: וַיִּשְׁלַ֣ח מֹשֶׁ֔ה לִקְרֹ֛א לְדָתָ֥ן וְלַאֲבִירָ֖ם בְּנֵ֣י אֱלִיאָ֑ב וַיֹּאמְר֖וּ לֹ֥א נַעֲלֶֽה: הַמְעַ֗ט כִּ֤י הֶֽעֱלִיתָ֙נוּ֙ מֵאֶ֨רֶץ זָבַ֤ת חָלָב֙ וּדְבַ֔שׁ לַהֲמִיתֵ֖נוּ בַּמִּדְבָּ֑ר כִּֽי־תִשְׂתָּרֵ֥ר עָלֵ֖ינוּ גַּם־הִשְׂתָּרֵֽר:

HUKAT

חקת

במדבר
י״ט:א-ה

וַיְדַבֵּ֣ר יהו֔ה אֶל־מֹשֶׁ֥ה וְאֶֽל־אַהֲרֹ֖ן לֵאמֹֽר: זֹ֚את חֻקַּ֣ת הַתּוֹרָ֔ה אֲשֶׁר־צִוָּ֥ה יהו֖ה לֵאמֹ֑ר דַּבֵּ֣ר ׀ אֶל־בְּנֵ֣י יִשְׂרָאֵ֗ל וְיִקְח֣וּ אֵלֶ֩יךָ֩ פָרָ֨ה אֲדֻמָּ֜ה תְּמִימָ֗ה אֲשֶׁ֤ר אֵֽין־בָּהּ֙ מ֔וּם אֲשֶׁ֛ר לֹא־עָלָ֥ה עָלֶ֖יהָ עֹֽל: וּנְתַתֶּ֣ם אֹתָ֔הּ אֶל־אֶלְעָזָ֖ר הַכֹּהֵ֑ן וְהוֹצִ֤יא אֹתָהּ֙ אֶל־מִח֣וּץ לַֽמַּחֲנֶ֔ה וְשָׁחַ֥ט אֹתָ֖הּ לְפָנָֽיו: וְלָקַ֞ח אֶלְעָזָ֤ר הַכֹּהֵן֙ מִדָּמָ֖הּ בְּאֶצְבָּע֑וֹ וְהִזָּ֞ה אֶל־נֹ֨כַח פְּנֵ֧י אֹֽהֶל־מוֹעֵ֛ד מִדָּמָ֖הּ שֶׁ֥בַע פְּעָמִֽים: וְשָׂרַ֥ף אֶת־הַפָּרָ֖ה לְעֵינָ֑יו

אֶת־עֹרָהּ וְאֶת־בְּשָׂרָהּ וְאֶת־דָּמָהּ עַל־פִּרְשָׁהּ יִשְׂרֹף: וְלָקַח הַכֹּהֵן עֵץ אֶרֶז
וְאֵזוֹב וּשְׁנִי תוֹלָעַת וְהִשְׁלִיךְ אֶל־תּוֹךְ שְׂרֵפַת הַפָּרָה: וְכִבֶּס בְּגָדָיו הַכֹּהֵן לוי
וְרָחַץ בְּשָׂרוֹ בַּמַּיִם וְאַחַר יָבֹא אֶל־הַמַּחֲנֶה וְטָמֵא הַכֹּהֵן עַד־הָעָרֶב: וְהַשֹּׂרֵף
אֹתָהּ יְכַבֵּס בְּגָדָיו בַּמַּיִם וְרָחַץ בְּשָׂרוֹ בַּמָּיִם וְטָמֵא עַד־הָעָרֶב: וְאָסַף ׀ אִישׁ
טָהוֹר אֵת אֵפֶר הַפָּרָה וְהִנִּיחַ מִחוּץ לַמַּחֲנֶה בְּמָקוֹם טָהוֹר וְהָיְתָה לַעֲדַת
בְּנֵי־יִשְׂרָאֵל לְמִשְׁמֶרֶת לְמֵי נִדָּה חַטָּאת הִוא: וְכִבֶּס הָאֹסֵף אֶת־אֵפֶר הַפָּרָה ישראל
אֶת־בְּגָדָיו וְטָמֵא עַד־הָעָרֶב וְהָיְתָה לִבְנֵי יִשְׂרָאֵל וְלַגֵּר הַגָּר בְּתוֹכָם לְחֻקַּת
עוֹלָם: הַנֹּגֵעַ בְּמֵת לְכָל־נֶפֶשׁ אָדָם וְטָמֵא שִׁבְעַת יָמִים: הוּא יִתְחַטָּא־בוֹ
בַּיּוֹם הַשְּׁלִישִׁי וּבַיּוֹם הַשְּׁבִיעִי יִטְהָר וְאִם־לֹא יִתְחַטָּא בַּיּוֹם הַשְּׁלִישִׁי וּבַיּוֹם
הַשְּׁבִיעִי לֹא יִטְהָר: כָּל־הַנֹּגֵעַ בְּמֵת בְּנֶפֶשׁ הָאָדָם אֲשֶׁר־יָמוּת וְלֹא יִתְחַטָּא
אֶת־מִשְׁכַּן יְהוָה טִמֵּא וְנִכְרְתָה הַנֶּפֶשׁ הַהִוא מִיִּשְׂרָאֵל כִּי מֵי נִדָּה לֹא־זֹרַק
עָלָיו טָמֵא יִהְיֶה עוֹד טֻמְאָתוֹ בוֹ: זֹאת הַתּוֹרָה אָדָם כִּי־יָמוּת בְּאֹהֶל כָּל־
הַבָּא אֶל־הָאֹהֶל וְכָל־אֲשֶׁר בָּאֹהֶל יִטְמָא שִׁבְעַת יָמִים: וְכֹל כְּלִי פָתוּחַ אֲשֶׁר
אֵין־צָמִיד פָּתִיל עָלָיו טָמֵא הוּא: וְכֹל אֲשֶׁר־יִגַּע עַל־פְּנֵי הַשָּׂדֶה בַּחֲלַל־חֶרֶב
אוֹ בְמֵת אוֹ־בְעֶצֶם אָדָם אוֹ בְקָבֶר יִטְמָא שִׁבְעַת יָמִים: וְלָקְחוּ לַטָּמֵא מֵעֲפַר
שְׂרֵפַת הַחַטָּאת וְנָתַן עָלָיו מַיִם חַיִּים אֶל־כֶּלִי:

בלק
BALAK

וַיַּרְא בָּלָק בֶּן־צִפּוֹר אֵת כָּל־אֲשֶׁר־עָשָׂה יִשְׂרָאֵל לָאֱמֹרִי: וַיָּגָר מוֹאָב מִפְּנֵי במדבר כב:ב-יב
הָעָם מְאֹד כִּי רַב־הוּא וַיָּקָץ מוֹאָב מִפְּנֵי בְּנֵי יִשְׂרָאֵל: וַיֹּאמֶר מוֹאָב אֶל־זִקְנֵי
מִדְיָן עַתָּה יְלַחֲכוּ הַקָּהָל אֶת־כָּל־סְבִיבֹתֵינוּ כִּלְחֹךְ הַשּׁוֹר אֵת יֶרֶק הַשָּׂדֶה
וּבָלָק בֶּן־צִפּוֹר מֶלֶךְ לְמוֹאָב בָּעֵת הַהִוא: וַיִּשְׁלַח מַלְאָכִים אֶל־בִּלְעָם לוי
בֶּן־בְּעֹר פְּתוֹרָה אֲשֶׁר עַל־הַנָּהָר אֶרֶץ בְּנֵי־עַמּוֹ לִקְרֹא־לוֹ לֵאמֹר הִנֵּה עַם
יָצָא מִמִּצְרַיִם הִנֵּה כִסָּה אֶת־עֵין הָאָרֶץ וְהוּא יֹשֵׁב מִמֻּלִי: וְעַתָּה לְכָה־נָּא
אָרָה־לִּי אֶת־הָעָם הַזֶּה כִּי־עָצוּם הוּא מִמֶּנִּי אוּלַי אוּכַל נַכֶּה־בּוֹ וַאֲגָרְשֶׁנּוּ
מִן־הָאָרֶץ כִּי יָדַעְתִּי אֵת אֲשֶׁר־תְּבָרֵךְ מְבֹרָךְ וַאֲשֶׁר תָּאֹר יוּאָר: וַיֵּלְכוּ זִקְנֵי
מוֹאָב וְזִקְנֵי מִדְיָן וּקְסָמִים בְּיָדָם וַיָּבֹאוּ אֶל־בִּלְעָם וַיְדַבְּרוּ אֵלָיו דִּבְרֵי בָלָק:
וַיֹּאמֶר אֲלֵיהֶם לִינוּ פֹה הַלַּיְלָה וַהֲשִׁבֹתִי אֶתְכֶם דָּבָר כַּאֲשֶׁר יְדַבֵּר יְהוָה אֵלָי ישראל
וַיֵּשְׁבוּ שָׂרֵי־מוֹאָב עִם־בִּלְעָם: וַיָּבֹא אֱלֹהִים אֶל־בִּלְעָם וַיֹּאמֶר מִי הָאֲנָשִׁים

הָאֵלֶּה עִמָּךְ: וַיֹּאמֶר בִּלְעָם אֶל־הָאֱלֹהִים בָּלָק בֶּן־צִפֹּר מֶלֶךְ מוֹאָב שָׁלַח
אֵלָי: הִנֵּה הָעָם הַיֹּצֵא מִמִּצְרַיִם וַיְכַס אֶת־עֵין הָאָרֶץ עַתָּה לְכָה קָבָה־לִּי אֹתוֹ
אוּלַי אוּכַל לְהִלָּחֶם בּוֹ וְגֵרַשְׁתִּיו: וַיֹּאמֶר אֱלֹהִים אֶל־בִּלְעָם לֹא תֵלֵךְ עִמָּהֶם
לֹא תָאֹר אֶת־הָעָם כִּי בָרוּךְ הוּא:

פינחס PINEHAS

במדבר כה:י–כו:ד

וַיְדַבֵּר יְהוָה אֶל־מֹשֶׁה לֵּאמֹר: פִּינְחָס בֶּן־אֶלְעָזָר בֶּן־אַהֲרֹן הַכֹּהֵן הֵשִׁיב
אֶת־חֲמָתִי מֵעַל בְּנֵי־יִשְׂרָאֵל בְּקַנְאוֹ אֶת־קִנְאָתִי בְּתוֹכָם וְלֹא־כִלִּיתִי אֶת־
לוי בְּנֵי־יִשְׂרָאֵל בְּקִנְאָתִי: לָכֵן אֱמֹר הִנְנִי נֹתֵן לוֹ אֶת־בְּרִיתִי שָׁלוֹם: *וְהָיְתָה לּוֹ
וּלְזַרְעוֹ אַחֲרָיו בְּרִית כְּהֻנַּת עוֹלָם תַּחַת אֲשֶׁר קִנֵּא לֵאלֹהָיו וַיְכַפֵּר עַל־בְּנֵי
יִשְׂרָאֵל: וְשֵׁם אִישׁ יִשְׂרָאֵל הַמֻּכֶּה אֲשֶׁר הֻכָּה אֶת־הַמִּדְיָנִית זִמְרִי בֶּן־סָלוּא
נְשִׂיא בֵית־אָב לַשִּׁמְעֹנִי: וְשֵׁם הָאִשָּׁה הַמֻּכָּה הַמִּדְיָנִית כָּזְבִּי בַת־צוּר רֹאשׁ
אֻמּוֹת בֵּית־אָב בְּמִדְיָן הוּא:
ישראל וַיְדַבֵּר יְהוָה אֶל־מֹשֶׁה לֵּאמֹר: צָרוֹר אֶת־הַמִּדְיָנִים וְהִכִּיתֶם אוֹתָם: כִּי
צֹרְרִים הֵם לָכֶם בְּנִכְלֵיהֶם אֲשֶׁר־נִכְּלוּ לָכֶם עַל־דְּבַר פְּעוֹר וְעַל־דְּבַר כָּזְבִּי
בַת־נְשִׂיא מִדְיָן אֲחֹתָם הַמֻּכָּה בְיוֹם־הַמַּגֵּפָה עַל־דְּבַר פְּעוֹר: וַיְהִי אַחֲרֵי
הַמַּגֵּפָה
וַיֹּאמֶר יְהוָה אֶל־מֹשֶׁה וְאֶל אֶלְעָזָר בֶּן־אַהֲרֹן הַכֹּהֵן לֵאמֹר: שְׂאוּ אֶת־רֹאשׁ
כָּל־עֲדַת בְּנֵי־יִשְׂרָאֵל מִבֶּן עֶשְׂרִים שָׁנָה וָמַעְלָה לְבֵית אֲבֹתָם כָּל־יֹצֵא צָבָא
בְּיִשְׂרָאֵל: וַיְדַבֵּר מֹשֶׁה וְאֶלְעָזָר הַכֹּהֵן אֹתָם בְּעַרְבֹת מוֹאָב עַל־יַרְדֵּן יְרֵחוֹ
לֵאמֹר: מִבֶּן עֶשְׂרִים שָׁנָה וָמָעְלָה כַּאֲשֶׁר צִוָּה יְהוָה אֶת־מֹשֶׁה וּבְנֵי יִשְׂרָאֵל
הַיֹּצְאִים מֵאֶרֶץ מִצְרָיִם:

מטות MATOT

במדבר ל:ב–ז

וַיְדַבֵּר מֹשֶׁה אֶל־רָאשֵׁי הַמַּטּוֹת לִבְנֵי יִשְׂרָאֵל לֵאמֹר זֶה הַדָּבָר אֲשֶׁר צִוָּה
יְהוָה: אִישׁ כִּי־יִדֹּר נֶדֶר לַיהוָה אוֹ־הִשָּׁבַע שְׁבֻעָה לֶאְסֹר אִסָּר עַל־נַפְשׁוֹ
לֹא יַחֵל דְּבָרוֹ כְּכָל־הַיֹּצֵא מִפִּיו יַעֲשֶׂה: וְאִשָּׁה כִּי־תִדֹּר נֶדֶר לַיהוָה וְאָסְרָה
אִסָּר בְּבֵית אָבִיהָ בִּנְעֻרֶיהָ: וְשָׁמַע אָבִיהָ אֶת־נִדְרָהּ וֶאֱסָרָהּ אֲשֶׁר אָסְרָה
עַל־נַפְשָׁהּ וְהֶחֱרִישׁ לָהּ אָבִיהָ וְקָמוּ כָּל־נְדָרֶיהָ וְכָל־אִסָּר אֲשֶׁר־אָסְרָה

עַל־נַפְשָׁהּ יָקוּם׃ וְאִם־הֵנִיא אָבִיהָ אֹתָהּ בְּיוֹם שָׁמְעוֹ כָּל־נְדָרֶיהָ וֶאֱסָרֶיהָ
אֲשֶׁר־אָסְרָה עַל־נַפְשָׁהּ לֹא יָקוּם וַיהוה יִסְלַח־לָהּ כִּי־הֵנִיא אָבִיהָ אֹתָהּ׃
וְאִם־הָיוֹ תִהְיֶה לְאִישׁ וּנְדָרֶיהָ עָלֶיהָ אוֹ מִבְטָא שְׂפָתֶיהָ אֲשֶׁר אָסְרָה עַל־
נַפְשָׁהּ׃ וְשָׁמַע אִישָׁהּ בְּיוֹם שָׁמְעוֹ וְהֶחֱרִישׁ לָהּ וְקָמוּ נְדָרֶיהָ וֶאֱסָרֶהָ אֲשֶׁר־
אָסְרָה עַל־נַפְשָׁהּ יָקֻמוּ׃ וְאִם בְּיוֹם שְׁמֹעַ אִישָׁהּ יָנִיא אוֹתָהּ וְהֵפֵר אֶת־נִדְרָהּ
אֲשֶׁר עָלֶיהָ וְאֵת מִבְטָא שְׂפָתֶיהָ אֲשֶׁר אָסְרָה עַל־נַפְשָׁהּ וַיהוה יִסְלַח־לָהּ׃
*וְנֵדֶר אַלְמָנָה וּגְרוּשָׁה כֹּל אֲשֶׁר־אָסְרָה עַל־נַפְשָׁהּ יָקוּם עָלֶיהָ׃ וְאִם־בֵּית לוי
אִישָׁהּ נָדָרָה אוֹ־אָסְרָה אִסָּר עַל־נַפְשָׁהּ בִּשְׁבֻעָה׃ וְשָׁמַע אִישָׁהּ וְהֶחֱרִשׁ לָהּ
לֹא הֵנִיא אֹתָהּ וְקָמוּ כָּל־נְדָרֶיהָ וְכָל־אִסָּר אֲשֶׁר־אָסְרָה עַל־נַפְשָׁהּ יָקוּם׃
וְאִם־הָפֵר יָפֵר אֹתָם ׀ אִישָׁהּ בְּיוֹם שָׁמְעוֹ כָּל־מוֹצָא שְׂפָתֶיהָ לִנְדָרֶיהָ וּלְאִסַּר
נַפְשָׁהּ לֹא יָקוּם אִישָׁהּ הֲפֵרָם וַיהוה יִסְלַח־לָהּ׃ *כָּל־נֵדֶר וְכָל־שְׁבֻעַת אִסָּר ישראל
לְעַנֹּת נָפֶשׁ אִישָׁהּ יְקִימֶנּוּ וְאִישָׁהּ יְפֵרֶנּוּ׃ וְאִם־הַחֲרֵשׁ יַחֲרִישׁ לָהּ אִישָׁהּ
מִיּוֹם אֶל־יוֹם וְהֵקִים אֶת־כָּל־נְדָרֶיהָ אוֹ אֶת־כָּל־אֱסָרֶיהָ אֲשֶׁר עָלֶיהָ הֵקִים
אֹתָם כִּי־הֶחֱרִשׁ לָהּ בְּיוֹם שָׁמְעוֹ׃ וְאִם־הָפֵר יָפֵר אֹתָם אַחֲרֵי שָׁמְעוֹ וְנָשָׂא
אֶת־עֲוֺנָהּ׃ אֵלֶּה הַחֻקִּים אֲשֶׁר צִוָּה יהוה אֶת־מֹשֶׁה בֵּין אִישׁ לְאִשְׁתּוֹ בֵּין־
אָב לְבִתּוֹ בִּנְעֻרֶיהָ בֵּית אָבִיהָ׃

MASEI מסעי

אֵלֶּה מַסְעֵי בְנֵי־יִשְׂרָאֵל אֲשֶׁר יָצְאוּ מֵאֶרֶץ מִצְרַיִם לְצִבְאֹתָם בְּיַד־מֹשֶׁה במדבר לג:א–נג
וְאַהֲרֹן׃ וַיִּכְתֹּב מֹשֶׁה אֶת־מוֹצָאֵיהֶם לְמַסְעֵיהֶם עַל־פִּי יהוה וְאֵלֶּה מַסְעֵיהֶם
לְמוֹצָאֵיהֶם׃ וַיִּסְעוּ מֵרַעְמְסֵס בַּחֹדֶשׁ הָרִאשׁוֹן בַּחֲמִשָּׁה עָשָׂר יוֹם לַחֹדֶשׁ
הָרִאשׁוֹן מִמָּחֳרַת הַפֶּסַח יָצְאוּ בְנֵי־יִשְׂרָאֵל בְּיָד רָמָה לְעֵינֵי כָּל־מִצְרָיִם׃
*וּמִצְרַיִם מְקַבְּרִים אֵת אֲשֶׁר הִכָּה יהוה בָּהֶם כָּל־בְּכוֹר וּבֵאלֹהֵיהֶם עָשָׂה לוי
יהוה שְׁפָטִים׃ וַיִּסְעוּ בְנֵי־יִשְׂרָאֵל מֵרַעְמְסֵס וַיַּחֲנוּ בְּסֻכֹּת׃ וַיִּסְעוּ מִסֻּכֹּת
וַיַּחֲנוּ בְאֵתָם אֲשֶׁר בִּקְצֵה הַמִּדְבָּר׃ *וַיִּסְעוּ מֵאֵתָם וַיָּשָׁב עַל־פִּי הַחִירֹת אֲשֶׁר ישראל
עַל־פְּנֵי בַּעַל צְפוֹן וַיַּחֲנוּ לִפְנֵי מִגְדֹּל׃ וַיִּסְעוּ מִפְּנֵי הַחִירֹת וַיַּעַבְרוּ בְתוֹךְ־הַיָּם
הַמִּדְבָּרָה וַיֵּלְכוּ דֶּרֶךְ שְׁלֹשֶׁת יָמִים בְּמִדְבַּר אֵתָם וַיַּחֲנוּ בְּמָרָה׃ וַיִּסְעוּ מִמָּרָה
וַיָּבֹאוּ אֵילִמָה וּבְאֵילִם שְׁתֵּים עֶשְׂרֵה עֵינֹת מַיִם וְשִׁבְעִים תְּמָרִים וַיַּחֲנוּ־שָׁם׃
וַיִּסְעוּ מֵאֵילִם וַיַּחֲנוּ עַל־יַם־סוּף׃

Some extend the לוי *portion:*

וַיִּסְעוּ מִיַּם־סוּף וַיַּחֲנוּ בְּמִדְבַּר־סִין: וַיִּסְעוּ מִמִּדְבַּר־סִין וַיַּחֲנוּ בְּדָפְקָה: וַיִּסְעוּ מִדָּפְקָה וַיַּחֲנוּ בְּאָלוּשׁ: וַיִּסְעוּ מֵאָלוּשׁ וַיַּחֲנוּ בִּרְפִידִם וְלֹא־הָיָה שָׁם מַיִם לָעָם לִשְׁתּוֹת: וַיִּסְעוּ מֵרְפִידִם וַיַּחֲנוּ בְּמִדְבַּר סִינָי: וַיִּסְעוּ מִמִּדְבַּר סִינָי וַיַּחֲנוּ בְּקִבְרֹת הַתַּאֲוָה: וַיִּסְעוּ מִקִּבְרֹת הַתַּאֲוָה וַיַּחֲנוּ בַּחֲצֵרֹת: וַיִּסְעוּ מֵחֲצֵרֹת וַיַּחֲנוּ בְּרִתְמָה: וַיִּסְעוּ מֵרִתְמָה וַיַּחֲנוּ בְּרִמֹּן פָּרֶץ: וַיִּסְעוּ מֵרִמֹּן פָּרֶץ וַיַּחֲנוּ בְּלִבְנָה: וַיִּסְעוּ מִלִּבְנָה וַיַּחֲנוּ בְּרִסָּה: וַיִּסְעוּ מֵרִסָּה וַיַּחֲנוּ בִּקְהֵלָתָה: וַיִּסְעוּ מִקְּהֵלָתָה וַיַּחֲנוּ בְּהַר־שָׁפֶר: וַיִּסְעוּ מֵהַר־שָׁפֶר וַיַּחֲנוּ בַּחֲרָדָה: וַיִּסְעוּ מֵחֲרָדָה וַיַּחֲנוּ בְּמַקְהֵלֹת: וַיִּסְעוּ מִמַּקְהֵלֹת וַיַּחֲנוּ בְּתָחַת: וַיִּסְעוּ מִתָּחַת וַיַּחֲנוּ בְּתָרַח: וַיִּסְעוּ מִתָּרַח וַיַּחֲנוּ בְּמִתְקָה: וַיִּסְעוּ מִמִּתְקָה וַיַּחֲנוּ בְּחַשְׁמֹנָה: וַיִּסְעוּ מֵחַשְׁמֹנָה וַיַּחֲנוּ בְּמֹסֵרוֹת: וַיִּסְעוּ מִמֹּסֵרוֹת וַיַּחֲנוּ בִּבְנֵי יַעֲקָן: וַיִּסְעוּ מִבְּנֵי יַעֲקָן וַיַּחֲנוּ בְּחֹר הַגִּדְגָּד: וַיִּסְעוּ מֵחֹר הַגִּדְגָּד וַיַּחֲנוּ בְּיָטְבָתָה: וַיִּסְעוּ מִיָּטְבָתָה וַיַּחֲנוּ בְּעַבְרֹנָה: וַיִּסְעוּ מֵעַבְרֹנָה וַיַּחֲנוּ בְּעֶצְיֹן גָּבֶר: וַיִּסְעוּ מֵעֶצְיֹן גָּבֶר וַיַּחֲנוּ בְמִדְבַּר־צִן הִוא קָדֵשׁ: וַיִּסְעוּ מִקָּדֵשׁ וַיַּחֲנוּ בְּהֹר הָהָר בִּקְצֵה אֶרֶץ אֱדוֹם: וַיַּעַל אַהֲרֹן הַכֹּהֵן אֶל־הֹר הָהָר עַל־פִּי יְהוָה וַיָּמָת שָׁם בִּשְׁנַת הָאַרְבָּעִים לְצֵאת בְּנֵי־יִשְׂרָאֵל מֵאֶרֶץ מִצְרַיִם בַּחֹדֶשׁ הַחֲמִישִׁי בְּאֶחָד לַחֹדֶשׁ: וְאַהֲרֹן בֶּן־שָׁלֹשׁ וְעֶשְׂרִים וּמְאַת שָׁנָה בְּמֹתוֹ בְּהֹר הָהָר:

וַיִּשְׁמַע הַכְּנַעֲנִי מֶלֶךְ עֲרָד וְהוּא־יֹשֵׁב בַּנֶּגֶב בְּאֶרֶץ כְּנָעַן בְּבֹא בְּנֵי יִשְׂרָאֵל: וַיִּסְעוּ מֵהֹר הָהָר וַיַּחֲנוּ בְּצַלְמֹנָה: וַיִּסְעוּ מִצַּלְמֹנָה וַיַּחֲנוּ בְּפוּנֹן: וַיִּסְעוּ מִפּוּנֹן וַיַּחֲנוּ בְּאֹבֹת: וַיִּסְעוּ מֵאֹבֹת וַיַּחֲנוּ בְּעִיֵּי הָעֲבָרִים בִּגְבוּל מוֹאָב: וַיִּסְעוּ מֵעִיִּים וַיַּחֲנוּ בְּדִיבֹן גָּד: וַיִּסְעוּ מִדִּיבֹן גָּד וַיַּחֲנוּ בְּעַלְמֹן דִּבְלָתָיְמָה: וַיִּסְעוּ מֵעַלְמֹן דִּבְלָתָיְמָה וַיַּחֲנוּ בְּהָרֵי הָעֲבָרִים לִפְנֵי נְבוֹ: וַיִּסְעוּ מֵהָרֵי הָעֲבָרִים וַיַּחֲנוּ בְּעַרְבֹת מוֹאָב עַל יַרְדֵּן יְרֵחוֹ: וַיַּחֲנוּ עַל־הַיַּרְדֵּן מִבֵּית הַיְשִׁמֹת עַד אָבֵל הַשִּׁטִּים בְּעַרְבֹת מוֹאָב:

ישראל *וַיְדַבֵּר יְהוָה אֶל־מֹשֶׁה בְּעַרְבֹת מוֹאָב עַל־יַרְדֵּן יְרֵחוֹ לֵאמֹר: דַּבֵּר אֶל־בְּנֵי יִשְׂרָאֵל וְאָמַרְתָּ אֲלֵהֶם כִּי אַתֶּם עֹבְרִים אֶת־הַיַּרְדֵּן אֶל־אֶרֶץ כְּנָעַן: וְהוֹרַשְׁתֶּם אֶת־כָּל־יֹשְׁבֵי הָאָרֶץ מִפְּנֵיכֶם וְאִבַּדְתֶּם אֵת כָּל־מַשְׂכִּיֹּתָם וְאֵת כָּל־צַלְמֵי מַסֵּכֹתָם תְּאַבֵּדוּ וְאֵת כָּל־בָּמוֹתָם תַּשְׁמִידוּ: וְהוֹרַשְׁתֶּם אֶת־הָאָרֶץ וִישַׁבְתֶּם־בָּהּ כִּי לָכֶם נָתַתִּי אֶת־הָאָרֶץ לָרֶשֶׁת אֹתָהּ:

דברים

DEVARIM

אֵ֣לֶּה הַדְּבָרִ֗ים אֲשֶׁ֨ר דִּבֶּ֤ר מֹשֶׁה֙ אֶל־כָּל־יִשְׂרָאֵ֔ל בְּעֵ֖בֶר הַיַּרְדֵּ֑ן בַּמִּדְבָּ֣ר בָּֽעֲרָבָ֡ה
מ֣וֹל סוּף֩ בֵּֽין־פָּארָ֨ן וּבֵֽין־תֹּ֜פֶל וְלָבָ֤ן וַחֲצֵרֹת֙ וְדִ֣י זָהָ֔ב: אַחַ֨ד עָשָׂ֥ר יוֹם֙ מֵֽחֹרֵ֔ב
דֶּ֖רֶךְ הַר־שֵׂעִ֑יר עַ֖ד קָדֵ֥שׁ בַּרְנֵֽעַ: וַיְהִי֙ בְּאַרְבָּעִ֣ים שָׁנָ֔ה בְּעַשְׁתֵּֽי־עָשָׂ֥ר חֹ֖דֶשׁ
בְּאֶחָ֣ד לַחֹ֑דֶשׁ דִּבֶּ֤ר מֹשֶׁה֙ אֶל־בְּנֵ֣י יִשְׂרָאֵ֔ל כְּכֹל֩ אֲשֶׁ֨ר צִוָּ֧ה יְהוָ֛ה אֹת֖וֹ אֲלֵהֶֽם:
אַֽחֲרֵ֣י הַכֹּת֗וֹ אֵ֚ת סִיחֹן֙ מֶ֣לֶךְ הָֽאֱמֹרִ֔י אֲשֶׁ֥ר יוֹשֵׁ֖ב בְּחֶשְׁבּ֑וֹן וְאֵ֗ת ע֚וֹג מֶ֣לֶךְ
הַבָּשָׁ֔ן אֲשֶׁר־יוֹשֵׁ֥ב בְּעַשְׁתָּרֹ֖ת בְּאֶדְרֶֽעִי: בְּעֵ֥בֶר הַיַּרְדֵּ֖ן בְּאֶ֣רֶץ מוֹאָ֑ב הוֹאִ֣יל
מֹשֶׁ֔ה בֵּאֵ֛ר אֶת־הַתּוֹרָ֥ה הַזֹּ֖את לֵאמֹֽר: יְהוָ֧ה אֱלֹהֵ֛ינוּ דִּבֶּ֥ר אֵלֵ֖ינוּ בְּחֹרֵ֣ב לֵאמֹ֑ר
רַב־לָכֶ֥ם שֶׁ֖בֶת בָּהָ֥ר הַזֶּֽה: פְּנ֣וּ | וּסְע֣וּ לָכֶ֗ם וּבֹ֨אוּ הַ֥ר הָֽאֱמֹרִי֮ וְאֶל־כָּל־שְׁכֵנָיו֒
בָּֽעֲרָבָ֥ה בָהָ֛ר וּבַשְּׁפֵלָ֥ה וּבַנֶּ֖גֶב וּבְח֣וֹף הַיָּ֑ם אֶ֤רֶץ הַֽכְּנַֽעֲנִי֙ וְהַלְּבָנ֔וֹן עַד־הַנָּהָ֥ר
הַגָּדֹ֖ל נְהַר־פְּרָֽת: רְאֵ֛ה נָתַ֥תִּי לִפְנֵיכֶ֖ם אֶת־הָאָ֑רֶץ בֹּ֚אוּ וּרְשׁ֣וּ אֶת־הָאָ֔רֶץ
אֲשֶׁ֣ר נִשְׁבַּ֣ע יְ֠הוָה לַֽאֲבֹֽתֵיכֶ֞ם לְאַבְרָהָ֨ם לְיִצְחָ֤ק וּֽלְיַֽעֲקֹב֙ לָתֵ֣ת לָהֶ֔ם וּלְזַרְעָ֖ם
אַֽחֲרֵיהֶֽם: וָֽאֹמַ֣ר אֲלֵכֶ֔ם בָּעֵ֥ת הַהִ֖וא לֵאמֹ֑ר לֹֽא־אוּכַ֥ל לְבַדִּ֖י שְׂאֵ֥ת אֶתְכֶֽם:
יְהוָ֥ה אֱלֹֽהֵיכֶ֖ם הִרְבָּ֣ה אֶתְכֶ֑ם וְהִנְּכֶ֣ם הַיּ֔וֹם כְּכֽוֹכְבֵ֥י הַשָּׁמַ֖יִם לָרֹֽב: יְהֹוָ֞ה אֱלֹהֵ֣י
אֲבֽוֹתֵכֶ֗ם יֹסֵ֧ף עֲלֵיכֶ֛ם כָּכֶ֖ם אֶ֣לֶף פְּעָמִ֑ים וִיבָרֵ֣ךְ אֶתְכֶ֔ם כַּֽאֲשֶׁ֖ר דִּבֶּ֥ר לָכֶֽם:

דברים
א:א–י"א

לוי

ישראל

ואתחנן

VA'ET-HANAN

וָֽאֶתְחַנַּ֖ן אֶל־יְהוָ֑ה בָּעֵ֥ת הַהִ֖וא לֵאמֹֽר: אֲדֹנָ֣י יְהֹוִ֗ה אַתָּ֤ה הַֽחִלּ֨וֹתָ֙ לְהַרְא֣וֹת
אֶֽת־עַבְדְּךָ֔ אֶ֨ת־גָּדְלְךָ֔ וְאֶת־יָֽדְךָ֖ הַחֲזָקָ֑ה אֲשֶׁ֤ר מִי־אֵל֙ בַּשָּׁמַ֣יִם וּבָאָ֔רֶץ אֲשֶׁר־
יַֽעֲשֶׂ֥ה כְמַֽעֲשֶׂ֖יךָ וְכִגְבֽוּרֹתֶֽךָ: אֶעְבְּרָה־נָּ֗א וְאֶרְאֶה֙ אֶת־הָאָ֣רֶץ הַטּוֹבָ֔ה אֲשֶׁ֖ר
בְּעֵ֣בֶר הַיַּרְדֵּ֑ן הָהָ֥ר הַטּ֛וֹב הַזֶּ֖ה וְהַלְּבָנֹֽן: וַיִּתְעַבֵּ֨ר יְהוָ֥ה בִּי֙ לְמַ֣עַנְכֶ֔ם וְלֹ֥א
שָׁמַ֖ע אֵלָ֑י וַיֹּ֨אמֶר יְהוָ֤ה אֵלַי֙ רַב־לָ֔ךְ אַל־תּ֗וֹסֶף דַּבֵּ֥ר אֵלַ֛י ע֖וֹד בַּדָּבָ֥ר הַזֶּֽה:
עֲלֵ֣ה | רֹ֣אשׁ הַפִּסְגָּ֗ה וְשָׂ֥א עֵינֶ֛יךָ יָ֧מָּה וְצָפֹ֛נָה וְתֵימָ֥נָה וּמִזְרָ֖חָה וּרְאֵ֣ה בְעֵינֶ֑יךָ
כִּֽי־לֹ֥א תַֽעֲבֹ֖ר אֶת־הַיַּרְדֵּ֥ן הַזֶּֽה: וְצַ֥ו אֶת־יְהוֹשֻׁ֖עַ וְחַזְּקֵ֣הוּ וְאַמְּצֵ֑הוּ כִּי־ה֣וּא
יַֽעֲבֹ֗ר לִפְנֵי֙ הָעָ֣ם הַזֶּ֔ה וְהוּא֙ יַנְחִ֣יל אוֹתָ֔ם אֶת־הָאָ֖רֶץ אֲשֶׁ֣ר תִּרְאֶ֑ה: וַנֵּ֣שֶׁב
בַּגָּ֔יְא מ֖וּל בֵּ֥ית פְּעֽוֹר:
וְעַתָּ֣ה יִשְׂרָאֵ֗ל שְׁמַ֤ע אֶל־הַֽחֻקִּים֙ וְאֶל־הַמִּשְׁפָּטִ֔ים אֲשֶׁ֧ר אָֽנֹכִ֛י מְלַמֵּ֥ד אֶתְכֶ֖ם
לַֽעֲשׂ֑וֹת לְמַ֣עַן תִּֽחְי֗וּ וּבָאתֶם֙ וִֽירִשְׁתֶּ֣ם אֶת־הָאָ֔רֶץ אֲשֶׁ֧ר יְהוָ֛ה אֱלֹהֵ֥י אֲבֹֽתֵיכֶ֖ם

דברים
ג:כג–ד:ח

לוי

נֹתֵן לָכֶם: לֹא תֹסִפוּ עַל־הַדָּבָר אֲשֶׁר אָנֹכִי מְצַוֶּה אֶתְכֶם וְלֹא תִגְרְעוּ מִמֶּנּוּ
לִשְׁמֹר אֶת־מִצְוֹת יהוה אֱלֹהֵיכֶם אֲשֶׁר אָנֹכִי מְצַוֶּה אֶתְכֶם: עֵינֵיכֶם הָרֹאוֹת
אֵת אֲשֶׁר־עָשָׂה יהוה בְּבַעַל פְּעוֹר כִּי כָל־הָאִישׁ אֲשֶׁר הָלַךְ אַחֲרֵי בַעַל־
פְּעוֹר הִשְׁמִידוֹ יהוה אֱלֹהֶיךָ מִקִּרְבֶּךָ: וְאַתֶּם הַדְּבֵקִים בַּיהוה אֱלֹהֵיכֶם חַיִּים
ישראל כֻּלְּכֶם הַיּוֹם: *רְאֵה | לִמַּדְתִּי אֶתְכֶם חֻקִּים וּמִשְׁפָּטִים כַּאֲשֶׁר צִוַּנִי יהוה
אֱלֹהָי לַעֲשׂוֹת כֵּן בְּקֶרֶב הָאָרֶץ אֲשֶׁר אַתֶּם בָּאִים שָׁמָּה לְרִשְׁתָּהּ: וּשְׁמַרְתֶּם
וַעֲשִׂיתֶם כִּי הִוא חָכְמַתְכֶם וּבִינַתְכֶם לְעֵינֵי הָעַמִּים אֲשֶׁר יִשְׁמְעוּן אֵת כָּל־
הַחֻקִּים הָאֵלֶּה וְאָמְרוּ רַק עַם־חָכָם וְנָבוֹן הַגּוֹי הַגָּדוֹל הַזֶּה: כִּי מִי־גוֹי גָּדוֹל
אֲשֶׁר־לוֹ אֱלֹהִים קְרֹבִים אֵלָיו כַּיהוה אֱלֹהֵינוּ בְּכָל־קָרְאֵנוּ אֵלָיו: וּמִי גּוֹי גָּדוֹל
אֲשֶׁר־לוֹ חֻקִּים וּמִשְׁפָּטִים צַדִּיקִם כְּכֹל הַתּוֹרָה הַזֹּאת אֲשֶׁר אָנֹכִי נֹתֵן לִפְנֵיכֶם
הַיּוֹם:

עקב EKEV

דברים ז:יב–ח:י
וְהָיָה | עֵקֶב תִּשְׁמְעוּן אֵת הַמִּשְׁפָּטִים הָאֵלֶּה וּשְׁמַרְתֶּם וַעֲשִׂיתֶם אֹתָם וְשָׁמַר
יהוה אֱלֹהֶיךָ לְךָ אֶת־הַבְּרִית וְאֶת־הַחֶסֶד אֲשֶׁר נִשְׁבַּע לַאֲבֹתֶיךָ: וַאֲהֵבְךָ
וּבֵרַכְךָ וְהִרְבֶּךָ וּבֵרַךְ פְּרִי־בִטְנְךָ וּפְרִי־אַדְמָתֶךָ דְּגָנְךָ וְתִירֹשְׁךָ וְיִצְהָרֶךָ שְׁגַר־
אֲלָפֶיךָ וְעַשְׁתְּרֹת צֹאנֶךָ עַל הָאֲדָמָה אֲשֶׁר־נִשְׁבַּע לַאֲבֹתֶיךָ לָתֶת לָךְ: בָּרוּךְ
תִּהְיֶה מִכָּל־הָעַמִּים לֹא־יִהְיֶה בְךָ עָקָר וַעֲקָרָה וּבִבְהֶמְתֶּךָ: וְהֵסִיר יהוה
מִמְּךָ כָּל־חֹלִי וְכָל־מַדְוֵי מִצְרַיִם הָרָעִים אֲשֶׁר יָדַעְתָּ לֹא יְשִׂימָם בָּךְ וּנְתָנָם
בְּכָל־שֹׂנְאֶיךָ: וְאָכַלְתָּ אֶת־כָּל־הָעַמִּים אֲשֶׁר יהוה אֱלֹהֶיךָ נֹתֵן לָךְ לֹא־תָחוֹס
עֵינְךָ עֲלֵיהֶם וְלֹא תַעֲבֹד אֶת־אֱלֹהֵיהֶם כִּי־מוֹקֵשׁ הוּא לָךְ: כִּי
תֹאמַר בִּלְבָבְךָ רַבִּים הַגּוֹיִם הָאֵלֶּה מִמֶּנִּי אֵיכָה אוּכַל לְהוֹרִישָׁם: לֹא תִירָא
מֵהֶם זָכֹר תִּזְכֹּר אֵת אֲשֶׁר־עָשָׂה יהוה אֱלֹהֶיךָ לְפַרְעֹה וּלְכָל־מִצְרָיִם: הַמַּסֹּת
הַגְּדֹלֹת אֲשֶׁר־רָאוּ עֵינֶיךָ וְהָאֹתֹת וְהַמֹּפְתִים וְהַיָּד הַחֲזָקָה וְהַזְּרֹעַ הַנְּטוּיָה
אֲשֶׁר הוֹצִאֲךָ יהוה אֱלֹהֶיךָ כֵּן־יַעֲשֶׂה יהוה אֱלֹהֶיךָ לְכָל־הָעַמִּים אֲשֶׁר־אַתָּה
יָרֵא מִפְּנֵיהֶם: וְגַם אֶת־הַצִּרְעָה יְשַׁלַּח יהוה אֱלֹהֶיךָ בָּם עַד־אֲבֹד הַנִּשְׁאָרִים
וְהַנִּסְתָּרִים מִפָּנֶיךָ: לֹא תַעֲרֹץ מִפְּנֵיהֶם כִּי־יהוה אֱלֹהֶיךָ בְּקִרְבֶּךָ אֵל גָּדוֹל
לוי וְנוֹרָא: *וְנָשַׁל יהוה אֱלֹהֶיךָ אֶת־הַגּוֹיִם הָאֵל מִפָּנֶיךָ מְעַט מְעָט לֹא תוּכַל
כַּלֹּתָם מַהֵר פֶּן־תִּרְבֶּה עָלֶיךָ חַיַּת הַשָּׂדֶה: וּנְתָנָם יהוה אֱלֹהֶיךָ לְפָנֶיךָ וְהָמָם

מֵהֻמָה גְדֹלָה עַד הִשָּׁמְדָם: וְנָתַן מַלְכֵיהֶם בְּיָדֶךָ וְהַאֲבַדְתָּ אֶת־שְׁמָם מִתַּחַת הַשָּׁמָיִם לֹא־יִתְיַצֵּב אִישׁ בְּפָנֶיךָ עַד הִשְׁמִדְךָ אֹתָם: פְּסִילֵי אֱלֹהֵיהֶם תִּשְׂרְפוּן בָּאֵשׁ לֹא־תַחְמֹד כֶּסֶף וְזָהָב עֲלֵיהֶם וְלָקַחְתָּ לָךְ פֶּן תִּוָּקֵשׁ בּוֹ כִּי תוֹעֲבַת יְהוָה אֱלֹהֶיךָ הוּא: וְלֹא־תָבִיא תוֹעֵבָה אֶל־בֵּיתֶךָ וְהָיִיתָ חֵרֶם כָּמֹהוּ שַׁקֵּץ ׀ תְּשַׁקְּצֶנּוּ וְתַעֵב ׀ תְּתַעֲבֶנּוּ כִּי־חֵרֶם הוּא:

כָּל־הַמִּצְוָה אֲשֶׁר אָנֹכִי מְצַוְּךָ הַיּוֹם תִּשְׁמְרוּן לַעֲשׂוֹת לְמַעַן תִּחְיוּן וּרְבִיתֶם וּבָאתֶם וִירִשְׁתֶּם אֶת־הָאָרֶץ אֲשֶׁר־נִשְׁבַּע יְהוָה לַאֲבֹתֵיכֶם: וְזָכַרְתָּ אֶת־כָּל־הַדֶּרֶךְ אֲשֶׁר הוֹלִיכֲךָ יְהוָה אֱלֹהֶיךָ זֶה אַרְבָּעִים שָׁנָה בַּמִּדְבָּר לְמַעַן עַנֹּתְךָ לְנַסֹּתְךָ לָדַעַת אֶת־אֲשֶׁר בִּלְבָבְךָ הֲתִשְׁמֹר מִצְוֹתָו אִם־לֹא: וַיְעַנְּךָ וַיַּרְעִבֶךָ וַיַּאֲכִלְךָ אֶת־הַמָּן אֲשֶׁר לֹא־יָדַעְתָּ וְלֹא יָדְעוּן אֲבֹתֶיךָ לְמַעַן הוֹדִיעֲךָ כִּי לֹא עַל־הַלֶּחֶם לְבַדּוֹ יִחְיֶה הָאָדָם כִּי עַל־כָּל־מוֹצָא פִי־יְהוָה יִחְיֶה הָאָדָם:
ישראל
*שִׂמְלָתְךָ לֹא בָלְתָה מֵעָלֶיךָ וְרַגְלְךָ לֹא בָצֵקָה זֶה אַרְבָּעִים שָׁנָה: וְיָדַעְתָּ עִם־לְבָבֶךָ כִּי כַּאֲשֶׁר יְיַסֵּר אִישׁ אֶת־בְּנוֹ יְהוָה אֱלֹהֶיךָ מְיַסְּרֶךָּ: וְשָׁמַרְתָּ אֶת־מִצְוֹת יְהוָה אֱלֹהֶיךָ לָלֶכֶת בִּדְרָכָיו וּלְיִרְאָה אֹתוֹ: כִּי יְהוָה אֱלֹהֶיךָ מְבִיאֲךָ אֶל־אֶרֶץ טוֹבָה אֶרֶץ נַחֲלֵי מָיִם עֲיָנֹת וּתְהֹמֹת יֹצְאִים בַּבִּקְעָה וּבָהָר: אֶרֶץ חִטָּה וּשְׂעֹרָה וְגֶפֶן וּתְאֵנָה וְרִמּוֹן אֶרֶץ־זֵית שֶׁמֶן וּדְבָשׁ: אֶרֶץ אֲשֶׁר לֹא בְמִסְכֵּנֻת תֹּאכַל־בָּהּ לֶחֶם לֹא־תֶחְסַר כֹּל בָּהּ אֶרֶץ אֲשֶׁר אֲבָנֶיהָ בַרְזֶל וּמֵהֲרָרֶיהָ תַּחְצֹב נְחֹשֶׁת: וְאָכַלְתָּ וְשָׂבָעְתָּ וּבֵרַכְתָּ אֶת־יְהוָה אֱלֹהֶיךָ עַל־הָאָרֶץ הַטֹּבָה אֲשֶׁר נָתַן־לָךְ:

RE'EH

ראה
דברים
יא:כו-יב:י
רְאֵה אָנֹכִי נֹתֵן לִפְנֵיכֶם הַיּוֹם בְּרָכָה וּקְלָלָה: אֶת־הַבְּרָכָה אֲשֶׁר תִּשְׁמְעוּ אֶל־מִצְוֹת יְהוָה אֱלֹהֵיכֶם אֲשֶׁר אָנֹכִי מְצַוֶּה אֶתְכֶם הַיּוֹם: וְהַקְּלָלָה אִם־לֹא תִשְׁמְעוּ אֶל־מִצְוֹת יְהוָה אֱלֹהֵיכֶם וְסַרְתֶּם מִן־הַדֶּרֶךְ אֲשֶׁר אָנֹכִי מְצַוֶּה אֶתְכֶם הַיּוֹם לָלֶכֶת אַחֲרֵי אֱלֹהִים אֲחֵרִים אֲשֶׁר לֹא־יְדַעְתֶּם: וְהָיָה כִּי יְבִיאֲךָ יְהוָה אֱלֹהֶיךָ אֶל־הָאָרֶץ אֲשֶׁר־אַתָּה בָא־שָׁמָּה לְרִשְׁתָּהּ וְנָתַתָּה אֶת־הַבְּרָכָה עַל־הַר גְּרִזִים וְאֶת־הַקְּלָלָה עַל־הַר עֵיבָל: הֲלֹא־הֵמָּה בְּעֵבֶר הַיַּרְדֵּן אַחֲרֵי דֶּרֶךְ מְבוֹא הַשֶּׁמֶשׁ בְּאֶרֶץ הַכְּנַעֲנִי הַיֹּשֵׁב בָּעֲרָבָה מוּל הַגִּלְגָּל אֵצֶל אֵלוֹנֵי מֹרֶה: כִּי אַתֶּם עֹבְרִים אֶת־הַיַּרְדֵּן לָבֹא לָרֶשֶׁת אֶת־הָאָרֶץ אֲשֶׁר־יְהוָה אֱלֹהֵיכֶם

לוי נתן לכם וירשתם אתה וישבתם־בה: *ושמרתם לעשות את כל־החקים
ואת־המשפטים אשר אנכי נתן לפניכם היום: אלה החקים והמשפטים
אשר תשמרון לעשות בארץ אשר נתן יהוה אלהי אבתיך לך לרשתה
כל־הימים אשר־אתם חיים על־האדמה: אבד תאבדון את־כל־המקמות
אשר עבדו־שם הגוים אשר אתם ירשים אתם את־אלהיהם על־ההרים
הרמים ועל־הגבעות ותחת כל־עץ רענן: ונתצתם את־מזבחתם ושברתם
את־מצבתם ואשריהם תשרפון באש ופסילי אלהיהם תגדעון ואבדתם
את־שמם מן־המקום ההוא: לא־תעשון כן ליהוה אלהיכם: כי אם־אל־
המקום אשר־יבחר יהוה אלהיכם מכל־שבטיכם לשום את־שמו שם
ישראל לשכנו תדרשו ובאת שמה: *והבאתם שמה עלתיכם וזבחיכם ואת
מעשרתיכם ואת תרומת ידכם ונדריכם ונדבתיכם ובכרת בקרכם וצאנכם:
ואכלתם־שם לפני יהוה אלהיכם ושמחתם בכל משלח ידכם אתם ובתיכם
אשר ברכך יהוה אלהיך: לא תעשון ככל אשר אנחנו עשים פה היום
איש כל־הישר בעיניו: כי לא־באתם עד־עתה אל־המנוחה ואל־הנחלה
אשר־יהוה אלהיך נתן לך: ועברתם את־הירדן וישבתם בארץ אשר־
יהוה אלהיכם מנחיל אתכם והניח לכם מכל־איביכם מסביב וישבתם־
בטח:

SHOFETIM שופטים

דברים טז:יח–יז:יג
שפטים ושטרים תתן־לך בכל־שעריך אשר יהוה אלהיך נתן לך לשבטיך
ושפטו את־העם משפט־צדק: לא־תטה משפט לא תכיר פנים ולא־תקח
שחד כי השחד יעור עיני חכמים ויסלף דברי צדיקים: צדק צדק תרדף למען
לוי תחיה וירשת את־הארץ אשר־יהוה אלהיך נתן לך: *לא־
תטע לך אשרה כל־עץ אצל מזבח יהוה אלהיך אשר תעשה־לך: ולא־
תקים לך מצבה אשר שנא יהוה אלהיך: לא־תזבח ליהוה
אלהיך שור ושה אשר יהיה בו מום כל דבר רע כי תועבת יהוה אלהיך
הוא: כי־ימצא בקרבך באחד שעריך אשר־יהוה אלהיך נתן
לך איש או־אשה אשר יעשה את־הרע בעיני יהוה־אלהיך לעבר בריתו:
וילך ויעבד אלהים אחרים וישתחו להם ולשמש | או לירח או לכל־צבא

הַשָּׁמַיִם אֲשֶׁר לֹא־צִוִּיתִי׃ וְהֻגַּד־לְךָ וְשָׁמָעְתָּ וְדָרַשְׁתָּ הֵיטֵב וְהִנֵּה אֱמֶת נָכוֹן
הַדָּבָר נֶעֶשְׂתָה הַתּוֹעֵבָה הַזֹּאת בְּיִשְׂרָאֵל׃ וְהוֹצֵאתָ אֶת־הָאִישׁ הַהוּא אוֹ
אֶת־הָאִשָּׁה הַהִוא אֲשֶׁר עָשׂוּ אֶת־הַדָּבָר הָרָע הַזֶּה אֶל־שְׁעָרֶיךָ אֶת־הָאִישׁ
אוֹ אֶת־הָאִשָּׁה וּסְקַלְתָּם בָּאֲבָנִים וָמֵתוּ׃ עַל־פִּי ׀ שְׁנַיִם עֵדִים אוֹ שְׁלֹשָׁה
עֵדִים יוּמַת הַמֵּת לֹא יוּמַת עַל־פִּי עֵד אֶחָד׃ יַד הָעֵדִים תִּהְיֶה־בּוֹ בָרִאשֹׁנָה
לַהֲמִיתוֹ וְיַד כָּל־הָעָם בָּאַחֲרֹנָה וּבִעַרְתָּ הָרָע מִקִּרְבֶּךָ׃
כִּי יִפָּלֵא מִמְּךָ דָבָר לַמִּשְׁפָּט בֵּין־דָּם ׀ לְדָם בֵּין־דִּין לְדִין וּבֵין נֶגַע לָנֶגַע דִּבְרֵי
רִיבֹת בִּשְׁעָרֶיךָ וְקַמְתָּ וְעָלִיתָ אֶל־הַמָּקוֹם אֲשֶׁר יִבְחַר יהוה אֱלֹהֶיךָ בּוֹ׃ וּבָאתָ
אֶל־הַכֹּהֲנִים הַלְוִיִּם וְאֶל־הַשֹּׁפֵט אֲשֶׁר יִהְיֶה בַּיָּמִים הָהֵם וְדָרַשְׁתָּ וְהִגִּידוּ לְךָ
אֵת דְּבַר הַמִּשְׁפָּט׃ וְעָשִׂיתָ עַל־פִּי הַדָּבָר אֲשֶׁר יַגִּידוּ לְךָ מִן־הַמָּקוֹם הַהוּא
אֲשֶׁר יִבְחַר יהוה וְשָׁמַרְתָּ לַעֲשׂוֹת כְּכֹל אֲשֶׁר יוֹרוּךָ׃ *עַל־פִּי הַתּוֹרָה אֲשֶׁר ישראל
יוֹרוּךָ וְעַל־הַמִּשְׁפָּט אֲשֶׁר־יֹאמְרוּ לְךָ תַּעֲשֶׂה לֹא תָסוּר מִן־הַדָּבָר אֲשֶׁר־יַגִּידוּ
לְךָ יָמִין וּשְׂמֹאל׃ וְהָאִישׁ אֲשֶׁר־יַעֲשֶׂה בְזָדוֹן לְבִלְתִּי שְׁמֹעַ אֶל־הַכֹּהֵן הָעֹמֵד
לְשָׁרֶת שָׁם אֶת־יהוה אֱלֹהֶיךָ אוֹ אֶל־הַשֹּׁפֵט וּמֵת הָאִישׁ הַהוּא וּבִעַרְתָּ הָרָע
מִיִּשְׂרָאֵל׃ וְכָל־הָעָם יִשְׁמְעוּ וְיִרָאוּ וְלֹא יְזִידוּן עוֹד׃

כי תצא KI TETZEH

כִּי־תֵצֵא לַמִּלְחָמָה עַל־אֹיְבֶיךָ וּנְתָנוֹ יהוה אֱלֹהֶיךָ בְּיָדֶךָ וְשָׁבִיתָ שִׁבְיוֹ׃ וְרָאִיתָ דברים כא:י–כא
בַּשִּׁבְיָה אֵשֶׁת יְפַת־תֹּאַר וְחָשַׁקְתָּ בָהּ וְלָקַחְתָּ לְךָ לְאִשָּׁה׃ וַהֲבֵאתָהּ אֶל־
תּוֹךְ בֵּיתֶךָ וְגִלְּחָה אֶת־רֹאשָׁהּ וְעָשְׂתָה אֶת־צִפָּרְנֶיהָ׃ וְהֵסִירָה אֶת־שִׂמְלַת
שִׁבְיָהּ מֵעָלֶיהָ וְיָשְׁבָה בְּבֵיתֶךָ וּבָכְתָה אֶת־אָבִיהָ וְאֶת־אִמָּהּ יֶרַח יָמִים
וְאַחַר כֵּן תָּבוֹא אֵלֶיהָ וּבְעַלְתָּהּ וְהָיְתָה לְךָ לְאִשָּׁה׃ וְהָיָה אִם־לֹא חָפַצְתָּ בָּהּ
וְשִׁלַּחְתָּהּ לְנַפְשָׁהּ וּמָכֹר לֹא־תִמְכְּרֶנָּה בַּכָּסֶף לֹא־תִתְעַמֵּר בָּהּ תַּחַת אֲשֶׁר
עִנִּיתָהּ׃ *כִּי־תִהְיֶיןָ לְאִישׁ שְׁתֵּי נָשִׁים הָאַחַת אֲהוּבָה וְהָאַחַת לוי
שְׂנוּאָה וְיָלְדוּ־לוֹ בָנִים הָאֲהוּבָה וְהַשְּׂנוּאָה וְהָיָה הַבֵּן הַבְּכֹר לַשְּׂנִיאָה׃ וְהָיָה
בְּיוֹם הַנְחִילוֹ אֶת־בָּנָיו אֵת אֲשֶׁר־יִהְיֶה לוֹ לֹא יוּכַל לְבַכֵּר אֶת־בֶּן־הָאֲהוּבָה
עַל־פְּנֵי בֶן־הַשְּׂנוּאָה הַבְּכֹר׃ כִּי אֶת־הַבְּכֹר בֶּן־הַשְּׂנוּאָה יַכִּיר לָתֶת לוֹ פִּי שְׁנַיִם
בְּכֹל אֲשֶׁר־יִמָּצֵא לוֹ כִּי־הוּא רֵאשִׁית אֹנוֹ לוֹ מִשְׁפַּט הַבְּכֹרָה׃ *כִּי־ ישראל
יִהְיֶה לְאִישׁ בֵּן סוֹרֵר וּמוֹרֶה אֵינֶנּוּ שֹׁמֵעַ בְּקוֹל אָבִיו וּבְקוֹל אִמּוֹ וְיִסְּרוּ אֹתוֹ

וְלֹא יִשְׁמַע אֲלֵיהֶם: וְתָפְשׂוּ בוֹ אָבִיו וְאִמּוֹ וְהוֹצִיאוּ אֹתוֹ אֶל־זִקְנֵי עִירוֹ וְאֶל־
שַׁעַר מְקֹמוֹ: וְאָמְרוּ אֶל־זִקְנֵי עִירוֹ בְּנֵנוּ זֶה סוֹרֵר וּמֹרֶה אֵינֶנּוּ שֹׁמֵעַ בְּקֹלֵנוּ
זוֹלֵל וְסֹבֵא: וּרְגָמֻהוּ כָּל־אַנְשֵׁי עִירוֹ בָאֲבָנִים וָמֵת וּבִעַרְתָּ הָרָע מִקִּרְבֶּךָ
וְכָל־יִשְׂרָאֵל יִשְׁמְעוּ וְיִרָאוּ:

כי תבוא — KI TAVO

דברים כו:א–טו וְהָיָה כִּי־תָבוֹא אֶל־הָאָרֶץ אֲשֶׁר יְהוָה אֱלֹהֶיךָ נֹתֵן לְךָ נַחֲלָה וִירִשְׁתָּהּ
וְיָשַׁבְתָּ בָּהּ: וְלָקַחְתָּ מֵרֵאשִׁית | כָּל־פְּרִי הָאֲדָמָה אֲשֶׁר תָּבִיא מֵאַרְצְךָ אֲשֶׁר
יְהוָה אֱלֹהֶיךָ נֹתֵן לָךְ וְשַׂמְתָּ בַטֶּנֶא וְהָלַכְתָּ אֶל־הַמָּקוֹם אֲשֶׁר יִבְחַר יְהוָה
אֱלֹהֶיךָ לְשַׁכֵּן שְׁמוֹ שָׁם: וּבָאתָ אֶל־הַכֹּהֵן אֲשֶׁר יִהְיֶה בַּיָּמִים הָהֵם וְאָמַרְתָּ
אֵלָיו הִגַּדְתִּי הַיּוֹם לַיהוָה אֱלֹהֶיךָ כִּי־בָאתִי אֶל־הָאָרֶץ אֲשֶׁר נִשְׁבַּע יְהוָה
לוי לַאֲבֹתֵינוּ לָתֶת לָנוּ: *וְלָקַח הַכֹּהֵן הַטֶּנֶא מִיָּדֶךָ וְהִנִּיחוֹ לִפְנֵי מִזְבַּח יְהוָה
אֱלֹהֶיךָ: וְעָנִיתָ וְאָמַרְתָּ לִפְנֵי | יְהוָה אֱלֹהֶיךָ אֲרַמִּי אֹבֵד אָבִי וַיֵּרֶד מִצְרַיְמָה
וַיָּגָר שָׁם בִּמְתֵי מְעָט וַיְהִי־שָׁם לְגוֹי גָּדוֹל עָצוּם וָרָב: וַיָּרֵעוּ אֹתָנוּ הַמִּצְרִים
וַיְעַנּוּנוּ וַיִּתְּנוּ עָלֵינוּ עֲבֹדָה קָשָׁה: וַנִּצְעַק אֶל־יְהוָה אֱלֹהֵי אֲבֹתֵינוּ וַיִּשְׁמַע
יְהוָה אֶת־קֹלֵנוּ וַיַּרְא אֶת־עָנְיֵנוּ וְאֶת־עֲמָלֵנוּ וְאֶת־לַחֲצֵנוּ: וַיּוֹצִאֵנוּ יְהוָה
מִמִּצְרַיִם בְּיָד חֲזָקָה וּבִזְרֹעַ נְטוּיָה וּבְמֹרָא גָּדֹל וּבְאֹתוֹת וּבְמֹפְתִים: וַיְבִאֵנוּ
אֶל־הַמָּקוֹם הַזֶּה וַיִּתֶּן־לָנוּ אֶת־הָאָרֶץ הַזֹּאת אֶרֶץ זָבַת חָלָב וּדְבָשׁ: וְעַתָּה
הִנֵּה הֵבֵאתִי אֶת־רֵאשִׁית פְּרִי הָאֲדָמָה אֲשֶׁר־נָתַתָּה לִּי יְהוָה וְהִנַּחְתּוֹ לִפְנֵי
יְהוָה אֱלֹהֶיךָ וְהִשְׁתַּחֲוִיתָ לִפְנֵי יְהוָה אֱלֹהֶיךָ: וְשָׂמַחְתָּ בְכָל־הַטּוֹב אֲשֶׁר נָתַן־
ישראל לְךָ יְהוָה אֱלֹהֶיךָ וּלְבֵיתֶךָ אַתָּה וְהַלֵּוִי וְהַגֵּר אֲשֶׁר בְּקִרְבֶּךָ: *כִּי
תְכַלֶּה לַעְשֵׂר אֶת־כָּל־מַעְשַׂר תְּבוּאָתְךָ בַּשָּׁנָה הַשְּׁלִישִׁת שְׁנַת הַמַּעֲשֵׂר
וְנָתַתָּה לַלֵּוִי לַגֵּר לַיָּתוֹם וְלָאַלְמָנָה וְאָכְלוּ בִשְׁעָרֶיךָ וְשָׂבֵעוּ: וְאָמַרְתָּ לִפְנֵי
יְהוָה אֱלֹהֶיךָ בִּעַרְתִּי הַקֹּדֶשׁ מִן־הַבַּיִת וְגַם נְתַתִּיו לַלֵּוִי וְלַגֵּר לַיָּתוֹם וְלָאַלְמָנָה
כְּכָל־מִצְוָתְךָ אֲשֶׁר צִוִּיתָנִי לֹא־עָבַרְתִּי מִמִּצְוֺתֶיךָ וְלֹא שָׁכָחְתִּי: לֹא־אָכַלְתִּי
בְאֹנִי מִמֶּנּוּ וְלֹא־בִעַרְתִּי מִמֶּנּוּ בְּטָמֵא וְלֹא־נָתַתִּי מִמֶּנּוּ לְמֵת שָׁמַעְתִּי בְּקוֹל
יְהוָה אֱלֹהָי עָשִׂיתִי כְּכֹל אֲשֶׁר צִוִּיתָנִי: הַשְׁקִיפָה מִמְּעוֹן קָדְשְׁךָ מִן־הַשָּׁמַיִם
וּבָרֵךְ אֶת־עַמְּךָ אֶת־יִשְׂרָאֵל וְאֵת הָאֲדָמָה אֲשֶׁר נָתַתָּה לָנוּ כַּאֲשֶׁר נִשְׁבַּעְתָּ
לַאֲבֹתֵינוּ אֶרֶץ זָבַת חָלָב וּדְבָשׁ:

NITZAVIM
נצבים

אַתֶּם נִצָּבִים הַיּוֹם כֻּלְּכֶם לִפְנֵי יהוה אֱלֹהֵיכֶם רָאשֵׁיכֶם שִׁבְטֵיכֶם זִקְנֵיכֶם דברים
וְשֹׁטְרֵיכֶם כֹּל אִישׁ יִשְׂרָאֵל: טַפְּכֶם נְשֵׁיכֶם וְגֵרְךָ אֲשֶׁר בְּקֶרֶב מַחֲנֶיךָ מֵחֹטֵב כט:ט-כח
עֵצֶיךָ עַד שֹׁאֵב מֵימֶיךָ: לְעָבְרְךָ בִּבְרִית יהוה אֱלֹהֶיךָ וּבְאָלָתוֹ אֲשֶׁר יהוה
אֱלֹהֶיךָ כֹּרֵת עִמְּךָ הַיּוֹם: *לְמַעַן הָקִים־אֹתְךָ הַיּוֹם ׀ לוֹ לְעָם וְהוּא יִהְיֶה־לְּךָ לוי
לֵאלֹהִים כַּאֲשֶׁר דִּבֶּר־לָךְ וְכַאֲשֶׁר נִשְׁבַּע לַאֲבֹתֶיךָ לְאַבְרָהָם לְיִצְחָק וּלְיַעֲקֹב:
וְלֹא אִתְּכֶם לְבַדְּכֶם אָנֹכִי כֹּרֵת אֶת־הַבְּרִית הַזֹּאת וְאֶת־הָאָלָה הַזֹּאת: כִּי
אֶת־אֲשֶׁר יֶשְׁנוֹ פֹּה עִמָּנוּ עֹמֵד הַיּוֹם לִפְנֵי יהוה אֱלֹהֵינוּ וְאֵת אֲשֶׁר אֵינֶנּוּ פֹּה
עִמָּנוּ הַיּוֹם: *כִּי־אַתֶּם יְדַעְתֶּם אֵת אֲשֶׁר־יָשַׁבְנוּ בְּאֶרֶץ מִצְרָיִם וְאֵת אֲשֶׁר־ ישראל
עָבַרְנוּ בְּקֶרֶב הַגּוֹיִם אֲשֶׁר עֲבַרְתֶּם: וַתִּרְאוּ אֶת־שִׁקּוּצֵיהֶם וְאֵת גִּלֻּלֵיהֶם
עֵץ וָאֶבֶן כֶּסֶף וְזָהָב אֲשֶׁר עִמָּהֶם: פֶּן־יֵשׁ בָּכֶם אִישׁ אוֹ־אִשָּׁה אוֹ מִשְׁפָּחָה
אוֹ־שֵׁבֶט אֲשֶׁר לְבָבוֹ פֹנֶה הַיּוֹם מֵעִם יהוה אֱלֹהֵינוּ לָלֶכֶת לַעֲבֹד אֶת־אֱלֹהֵי
הַגּוֹיִם הָהֵם פֶּן־יֵשׁ בָּכֶם שֹׁרֶשׁ פֹּרֶה רֹאשׁ וְלַעֲנָה: וְהָיָה בְּשָׁמְעוֹ אֶת־דִּבְרֵי
הָאָלָה הַזֹּאת וְהִתְבָּרֵךְ בִּלְבָבוֹ לֵאמֹר שָׁלוֹם יִהְיֶה־לִּי כִּי בִּשְׁרִרוּת לִבִּי אֵלֵךְ
לְמַעַן סְפוֹת הָרָוָה אֶת־הַצְּמֵאָה: לֹא־יֹאבֶה יהוה סְלֹחַ לוֹ כִּי אָז יֶעְשַׁן אַף־
יהוה וְקִנְאָתוֹ בָּאִישׁ הַהוּא וְרָבְצָה בּוֹ כָּל־הָאָלָה הַכְּתוּבָה בַּסֵּפֶר הַזֶּה וּמָחָה
יהוה אֶת־שְׁמוֹ מִתַּחַת הַשָּׁמָיִם: וְהִבְדִּילוֹ יהוה לְרָעָה מִכֹּל שִׁבְטֵי יִשְׂרָאֵל
כְּכֹל אָלוֹת הַבְּרִית הַכְּתוּבָה בְּסֵפֶר הַתּוֹרָה הַזֶּה: וְאָמַר הַדּוֹר הָאַחֲרוֹן בְּנֵיכֶם
אֲשֶׁר יָקוּמוּ מֵאַחֲרֵיכֶם וְהַנָּכְרִי אֲשֶׁר יָבֹא מֵאֶרֶץ רְחוֹקָה וְרָאוּ אֶת־מַכּוֹת
הָאָרֶץ הַהִוא וְאֶת־תַּחֲלֻאֶיהָ אֲשֶׁר־חִלָּה יהוה בָּהּ: גָּפְרִית וָמֶלַח שְׂרֵפָה כָל־
אַרְצָהּ לֹא תִזָּרַע וְלֹא תַצְמִחַ וְלֹא־יַעֲלֶה בָהּ כָּל־עֵשֶׂב כְּמַהְפֵּכַת סְדֹם וַעֲמֹרָה
אַדְמָה וצביים אֲשֶׁר הָפַךְ יהוה בְּאַפּוֹ וּבַחֲמָתוֹ: וְאָמְרוּ כָּל־הַגּוֹיִם עַל־מֶה וּצְבוֹיִם
עָשָׂה יהוה כָּכָה לָאָרֶץ הַזֹּאת מֶה חֳרִי הָאַף הַגָּדוֹל הַזֶּה: וְאָמְרוּ עַל אֲשֶׁר
עָזְבוּ אֶת־בְּרִית יהוה אֱלֹהֵי אֲבֹתָם אֲשֶׁר כָּרַת עִמָּם בְּהוֹצִיאוֹ אֹתָם מֵאֶרֶץ
מִצְרָיִם: וַיֵּלְכוּ וַיַּעַבְדוּ אֱלֹהִים אֲחֵרִים וַיִּשְׁתַּחֲווּ לָהֶם אֱלֹהִים אֲשֶׁר לֹא־יְדָעוּם
וְלֹא חָלַק לָהֶם: וַיִּחַר־אַף יהוה בָּאָרֶץ הַהִוא לְהָבִיא עָלֶיהָ אֶת־כָּל־הַקְּלָלָה
הַכְּתוּבָה בַּסֵּפֶר הַזֶּה: וַיִּתְּשֵׁם יהוה מֵעַל אַדְמָתָם בְּאַף וּבְחֵמָה וּבְקֶצֶף גָּדוֹל
וַיַּשְׁלִכֵם אֶל־אֶרֶץ אַחֶרֶת כַּיּוֹם הַזֶּה: הַנִּסְתָּרֹת לַיהוה אֱלֹהֵינוּ וְהַנִּגְלֹת לָנוּ
וּלְבָנֵינוּ עַד־עוֹלָם לַעֲשׂוֹת אֶת־כָּל־דִּבְרֵי הַתּוֹרָה הַזֹּאת:

VAYELEKH
וילך

דברים לא:א-יג

וַיֵּלֶךְ מֹשֶׁה וַיְדַבֵּר אֶת־הַדְּבָרִים הָאֵלֶּה אֶל־כָּל־יִשְׂרָאֵל׃ וַיֹּאמֶר אֲלֵהֶם בֶּן־
מֵאָה וְעֶשְׂרִים שָׁנָה אָנֹכִי הַיּוֹם לֹא־אוּכַל עוֹד לָצֵאת וְלָבוֹא וַיהוה אָמַר אֵלַי
לֹא תַעֲבֹר אֶת־הַיַּרְדֵּן הַזֶּה׃ יהוה אֱלֹהֶיךָ הוּא ׀ עֹבֵר לְפָנֶיךָ הוּא־יַשְׁמִיד
אֶת־הַגּוֹיִם הָאֵלֶּה מִלְּפָנֶיךָ וִירִשְׁתָּם יְהוֹשֻׁעַ הוּא עֹבֵר לְפָנֶיךָ כַּאֲשֶׁר דִּבֶּר
לוי יהוה׃ *וְעָשָׂה יהוה לָהֶם כַּאֲשֶׁר עָשָׂה לְסִיחוֹן וּלְעוֹג מַלְכֵי הָאֱמֹרִי וּלְאַרְצָם
אֲשֶׁר הִשְׁמִיד אֹתָם׃ וּנְתָנָם יהוה לִפְנֵיכֶם וַעֲשִׂיתֶם לָהֶם כְּכָל־הַמִּצְוָה אֲשֶׁר
צִוִּיתִי אֶתְכֶם׃ חִזְקוּ וְאִמְצוּ אַל־תִּירְאוּ וְאַל־תַּעַרְצוּ מִפְּנֵיהֶם כִּי ׀ יהוה אֱלֹהֶיךָ
ישראל הוּא הַהֹלֵךְ עִמָּךְ לֹא יַרְפְּךָ וְלֹא יַעַזְבֶךָּ׃ *וַיִּקְרָא מֹשֶׁה לִיהוֹשֻׁעַ
וַיֹּאמֶר אֵלָיו לְעֵינֵי כָל־יִשְׂרָאֵל חֲזַק וֶאֱמָץ כִּי אַתָּה תָּבוֹא אֶת־הָעָם הַזֶּה
אֶל־הָאָרֶץ אֲשֶׁר נִשְׁבַּע יהוה לַאֲבֹתָם לָתֵת לָהֶם וְאַתָּה תַּנְחִילֶנָּה אוֹתָם׃
וַיהוה הוּא ׀ הַהֹלֵךְ לְפָנֶיךָ הוּא יִהְיֶה עִמָּךְ לֹא יַרְפְּךָ וְלֹא יַעַזְבֶךָּ לֹא תִירָא וְלֹא
תֵחָת׃ וַיִּכְתֹּב מֹשֶׁה אֶת־הַתּוֹרָה הַזֹּאת וַיִּתְּנָהּ אֶל־הַכֹּהֲנִים בְּנֵי לֵוִי הַנֹּשְׂאִים
אֶת־אֲרוֹן בְּרִית יהוה וְאֶל־כָּל־זִקְנֵי יִשְׂרָאֵל׃ וַיְצַו מֹשֶׁה אוֹתָם לֵאמֹר מִקֵּץ ׀
שֶׁבַע שָׁנִים בְּמֹעֵד שְׁנַת הַשְּׁמִטָּה בְּחַג הַסֻּכּוֹת׃ בְּבוֹא כָל־יִשְׂרָאֵל לֵרָאוֹת
אֶת־פְּנֵי יהוה אֱלֹהֶיךָ בַּמָּקוֹם אֲשֶׁר יִבְחָר תִּקְרָא אֶת־הַתּוֹרָה הַזֹּאת נֶגֶד
כָּל־יִשְׂרָאֵל בְּאָזְנֵיהֶם׃ הַקְהֵל אֶת־הָעָם הָאֲנָשִׁים וְהַנָּשִׁים וְהַטַּף וְגֵרְךָ אֲשֶׁר
בִּשְׁעָרֶיךָ לְמַעַן יִשְׁמְעוּ וּלְמַעַן יִלְמְדוּ וְיָרְאוּ אֶת־יהוה אֱלֹהֵיכֶם וְשָׁמְרוּ
לַעֲשׂוֹת אֶת־כָּל־דִּבְרֵי הַתּוֹרָה הַזֹּאת׃ וּבְנֵיהֶם אֲשֶׁר לֹא־יָדְעוּ יִשְׁמְעוּ וְלָמְדוּ
לְיִרְאָה אֶת־יהוה אֱלֹהֵיכֶם כָּל־הַיָּמִים אֲשֶׁר אַתֶּם חַיִּים עַל־הָאֲדָמָה אֲשֶׁר
אַתֶּם עֹבְרִים אֶת־הַיַּרְדֵּן שָׁמָּה לְרִשְׁתָּהּ׃

HA'AZINU
האזינו

דברים לב:א-יח

הַאֲזִינוּ הַשָּׁמַיִם וַאֲדַבֵּרָה   וְתִשְׁמַע הָאָרֶץ אִמְרֵי־פִי׃
יַעֲרֹף כַּמָּטָר לִקְחִי   תִּזַּל כַּטַּל אִמְרָתִי
כִּשְׂעִירִם עֲלֵי־דֶשֶׁא   וְכִרְבִיבִים עֲלֵי־עֵשֶׂב׃
כִּי שֵׁם יהוה אֶקְרָא   הָבוּ גֹדֶל לֵאלֹהֵינוּ׃

*הַצּוּר תָּמִים פָּעֳלוֹ   כִּי כָל־דְּרָכָיו מִשְׁפָּט   לוי
אֵל אֱמוּנָה וְאֵין עָוֶל   צַדִּיק וְיָשָׁר הוּא׃
שִׁחֵת לוֹ לֹא בָּנָיו מוּמָם   דּוֹר עִקֵּשׁ וּפְתַלְתֹּל׃
הֲ לַיהוה תִּגְמְלוּ־זֹאת   עַם נָבָל וְלֹא חָכָם
הֲלוֹא־הוּא אָבִיךָ קָּנֶךָ   הוּא עָשְׂךָ וַיְכֹנְנֶךָ׃

Some start the לוי portion here:

*זְכֹר יְמוֹת עוֹלָם   בִּינוּ שְׁנוֹת דֹּר־וָדֹר   ישראל
שְׁאַל אָבִיךָ וְיַגֵּדְךָ   זְקֵנֶיךָ וְיֹאמְרוּ לָךְ׃
בְּהַנְחֵל עֶלְיוֹן גּוֹיִם   בְּהַפְרִידוֹ בְּנֵי אָדָם
יַצֵּב גְּבֻלֹת עַמִּים   לְמִסְפַּר בְּנֵי יִשְׂרָאֵל׃
כִּי חֵלֶק יהוה עַמּוֹ   יַעֲקֹב חֶבֶל נַחֲלָתוֹ׃
יִמְצָאֵהוּ בְּאֶרֶץ מִדְבָּר   וּבְתֹהוּ יְלֵל יְשִׁמֹן
יְסֹבְבֶנְהוּ יְבוֹנְנֵהוּ   יִצְּרֶנְהוּ כְּאִישׁוֹן עֵינוֹ׃
כְּנֶשֶׁר יָעִיר קִנּוֹ   עַל־גּוֹזָלָיו יְרַחֵף
יִפְרֹשׂ כְּנָפָיו יִקָּחֵהוּ   יִשָּׂאֵהוּ עַל־אֶבְרָתוֹ׃
יהוה בָּדָד יַנְחֶנּוּ   וְאֵין עִמּוֹ אֵל נֵכָר׃

Most finish here; some start the ישראל portion here:

*יַרְכִּבֵהוּ עַל־בָּמֳותֵי אָרֶץ   וַיֹּאכַל תְּנוּבֹת שָׂדָי   בָּמֳתֵי
וַיֵּנִקֵהוּ דְבַשׁ מִסֶּלַע   וְשֶׁמֶן מֵחַלְמִישׁ צוּר׃
חֶמְאַת בָּקָר וַחֲלֵב צֹאן   עִם־חֵלֶב כָּרִים
וְאֵילִים בְּנֵי־בָשָׁן וְעַתּוּדִים   עִם־חֵלֶב כִּלְיוֹת חִטָּה
וְדַם־עֵנָב תִּשְׁתֶּה־חָמֶר׃   וַיִּשְׁמַן יְשֻׁרוּן וַיִּבְעָט
שָׁמַנְתָּ עָבִיתָ כָּשִׂיתָ   וַיִּטֹּשׁ אֱלוֹהַּ עָשָׂהוּ
וַיְנַבֵּל צוּר יְשֻׁעָתוֹ׃   יַקְנִאֻהוּ בְּזָרִים
בְּתוֹעֵבֹת יַכְעִיסֻהוּ׃   יִזְבְּחוּ לַשֵּׁדִים לֹא אֱלֹהַּ
אֱלֹהִים לֹא יְדָעוּם   חֲדָשִׁים מִקָּרֹב בָּאוּ
לֹא שְׂעָרוּם אֲבֹתֵיכֶם׃   צוּר יְלָדְךָ תֶּשִׁי
וַתִּשְׁכַּח אֵל מְחֹלְלֶךָ׃

VEZOT HABERAKHA
וזאת הברכה

דברים לג:א–יז
וְזֹ֣את הַבְּרָכָ֗ה אֲשֶׁ֨ר בֵּרַ֥ךְ מֹשֶׁ֛ה אִ֥ישׁ הָאֱלֹהִ֖ים אֶת־בְּנֵ֣י יִשְׂרָאֵ֑ל לִפְנֵ֖י מוֹתֽוֹ׃
וַיֹּאמַ֗ר יְהֹוָ֞ה מִסִּינַ֥י בָּא֙ וְזָרַ֤ח מִשֵּׂעִיר֙ לָ֔מוֹ הוֹפִ֙יעַ֙ מֵהַ֣ר פָּארָ֔ן וְאָתָ֖ה מֵרִבְבֹ֣ת
אֵ֥שׁ דָּ֖ת קֹ֑דֶשׁ מִֽימִינ֕וֹ אשדת לָֽמוֹ׃ אַ֚ף חֹבֵ֣ב עַמִּ֔ים כׇּל־קְדֹשָׁ֖יו בְּיָדֶ֑ךָ וְהֵם֙ תֻּכּ֣וּ לְרַגְלֶ֔ךָ
יִשָּׂ֖א מִדַּבְּרֹתֶֽיךָ׃ תּוֹרָ֥ה צִוָּה־לָ֖נוּ מֹשֶׁ֑ה מוֹרָשָׁ֖ה קְהִלַּ֥ת יַעֲקֹֽב׃ וַיְהִ֥י בִישֻׁר֖וּן
מֶ֑לֶךְ בְּהִתְאַסֵּף֙ רָ֣אשֵׁי עָ֔ם יַ֖חַד שִׁבְטֵ֥י יִשְׂרָאֵֽל׃ יְחִ֥י רְאוּבֵ֖ן וְאַל־יָמֹ֑ת וִיהִ֥י מְתָ֖יו
מִסְפָּֽר׃ וְזֹ֣את לִֽיהוּדָה֮ וַיֹּאמַר֒ שְׁמַ֤ע יְהֹוָה֙ ק֣וֹל יְהוּדָ֔ה וְאֶל־עַמּ֖וֹ
תְּבִיאֶ֑נּוּ יָדָיו֙ רָ֣ב ל֔וֹ וְעֵ֥זֶר מִצָּרָ֖יו תִּהְיֶֽה׃
לוי וּלְלֵוִ֣י אָמַ֔ר תֻּמֶּ֥יךָ וְאוּרֶ֖יךָ לְאִ֣ישׁ חֲסִידֶ֑ךָ אֲשֶׁ֤ר נִסִּיתוֹ֙ בְּמַסָּ֔ה תְּרִיבֵ֖הוּ עַל־מֵ֥י
מְרִיבָֽה׃ הָאֹמֵ֞ר לְאָבִ֤יו וּלְאִמּוֹ֙ לֹ֣א רְאִיתִ֔יו וְאֶת־אֶחָיו֙ לֹ֣א הִכִּ֔יר וְאֶת־בָּנָ֖ו לֹ֣א
יָדָ֑ע כִּ֤י שָֽׁמְרוּ֙ אִמְרָתֶ֔ךָ וּבְרִֽיתְךָ֖ יִנְצֹֽרוּ׃ יוֹר֤וּ מִשְׁפָּטֶ֙יךָ֙ לְיַעֲקֹ֔ב וְתוֹרָתְךָ֖ לְיִשְׂרָאֵ֑ל
יָשִׂ֤ימוּ קְטוֹרָה֙ בְּאַפֶּ֔ךָ וְכָלִ֖יל עַֽל־מִזְבְּחֶֽךָ׃ בָּרֵ֤ךְ יְהֹוָה֙ חֵיל֔וֹ וּפֹ֥עַל יָדָ֖יו תִּרְצֶ֑ה
מְחַ֨ץ מׇתְנַ֧יִם קָמָ֛יו וּמְשַׂנְאָ֖יו מִן־יְקוּמֽוּן׃ לְבִנְיָמִ֣ן אָמַ֔ר יְדִ֣יד יְהֹוָ֔ה
ישראל יִשְׁכֹּ֥ן לָבֶ֖טַח עָלָ֑יו חֹפֵ֤ף עָלָיו֙ כׇּל־הַיּ֔וֹם וּבֵ֥ין כְּתֵפָ֖יו שָׁכֵֽן׃ *וּלְיוֹסֵ֣ף
אָמַ֔ר מְבֹרֶ֥כֶת יְהֹוָ֖ה אַרְצ֑וֹ מִמֶּ֤גֶד שָׁמַ֙יִם֙ מִטָּ֔ל וּמִתְּה֖וֹם רֹבֶ֥צֶת תָּֽחַת׃ וּמִמֶּ֖גֶד
תְּבוּאֹ֣ת שָׁ֑מֶשׁ וּמִמֶּ֖גֶד גֶּ֥רֶשׁ יְרָחִֽים׃ וּמֵרֹ֖אשׁ הַרְרֵי־קֶ֑דֶם וּמִמֶּ֖גֶד גִּבְע֥וֹת עוֹלָֽם׃
וּמִמֶּ֗גֶד אֶ֚רֶץ וּמְלֹאָ֔הּ וּרְצ֥וֹן שֹׁכְנִ֖י סְנֶ֑ה תָּב֙וֹאתָה֙ לְרֹ֣אשׁ יוֹסֵ֔ף וּלְקׇדְקֹ֖ד נְזִ֥יר
אֶחָֽיו׃ בְּכ֨וֹר שׁוֹר֜וֹ הָדָ֣ר ל֗וֹ וְקַרְנֵ֤י רְאֵם֙ קַרְנָ֔יו בָּהֶ֗ם עַמִּ֛ים יְנַגַּ֥ח יַחְדָּ֖ו אַפְסֵי־
אָ֑רֶץ וְהֵם֙ רִבְב֣וֹת אֶפְרַ֔יִם וְהֵ֖ם אַלְפֵ֥י מְנַשֶּֽׁה׃

קריאת התורה לראש חודש, לתעניות ציבור, לחנוכה ולפורים

THE READING OF THE TORAH FOR ROSH ḤODESH, FAST DAYS, ḤANUKKA AND PURIM

READING FOR ROSH ḤODESH — קריאה לראש חודש

For the כהן, the first three verses are read up to עֹלָה תָּמִיד. For the לוי, the third verse is repeated and starts with וְאָמַרְתָּ לָהֶם. For שלישי, continue from עֹלַת תָּמִיד up to וְנִסְכָּהּ. For רביעי, read from וּבְרָאשֵׁי חׇדְשֵׁיכֶם until the end. In ארץ ישראל, some read as follows: For the כהן read until רְבִיעִת הַהִין, for the לוי read from אֶת־הַכֶּבֶשׂ until רֵיחַ נִיחֹחַ לַה׳, for שלישי, the last verse is repeated and starts at עֹלַת תָּמִיד up to וְנִסְכָּהּ, and for רביעי, from וּבְרָאשֵׁי חׇדְשֵׁיכֶם until the end. On ראש חודש טבת, the כהן reads until רְבִיעִת הַהִין, the לוי reads the portion for שלישי and the שלישי the portion of רביעי; the fourth עולה reads the appropriate day of חנוכה on page 1119.

במדבר כח:א–טו וַיְדַבֵּר יְהוָה אֶל־מֹשֶׁה לֵּאמֹר: צַו אֶת־בְּנֵי יִשְׂרָאֵל וְאָמַרְתָּ אֲלֵהֶם אֶת־
לוי קׇרְבָּנִי לַחְמִי לְאִשַּׁי רֵיחַ נִיחֹחִי תִּשְׁמְרוּ לְהַקְרִיב לִי בְּמוֹעֲדוֹ: *וְאָמַרְתָּ
לָהֶם זֶה הָאִשֶּׁה אֲשֶׁר תַּקְרִיבוּ לַיהוָה כְּבָשִׂים בְּנֵי־שָׁנָה תְמִימִם שְׁנַיִם לַיּוֹם
עד כאן לכהן עֹלָה תָמִיד: *אֶת־הַכֶּבֶשׂ אֶחָד תַּעֲשֶׂה בַבֹּקֶר וְאֵת הַכֶּבֶשׂ הַשֵּׁנִי תַּעֲשֶׂה
בֵּין הָעַרְבָּיִם: וַעֲשִׂירִית הָאֵיפָה סֹלֶת לְמִנְחָה בְּלוּלָה בְּשֶׁמֶן כָּתִית רְבִיעִת
שלישי הַהִין: *עֹלַת תָּמִיד הָעֲשֻׂיָה בְּהַר סִינַי לְרֵיחַ נִיחֹחַ אִשֶּׁה לַיהוָה: וְנִסְכּוֹ
רְבִיעִת הַהִין לַכֶּבֶשׂ הָאֶחָד בַּקֹּדֶשׁ הַסֵּךְ נֶסֶךְ שֵׁכָר לַיהוָה: וְאֵת הַכֶּבֶשׂ
הַשֵּׁנִי תַּעֲשֶׂה בֵּין הָעַרְבָּיִם כְּמִנְחַת הַבֹּקֶר וּכְנִסְכּוֹ תַּעֲשֶׂה אִשֵּׁה רֵיחַ נִיחֹחַ
לַיהוָה:

וּבְיוֹם הַשַּׁבָּת שְׁנֵי־כְבָשִׂים בְּנֵי־שָׁנָה תְּמִימִם וּשְׁנֵי עֶשְׂרֹנִים סֹלֶת מִנְחָה בְּלוּלָה
בַשֶּׁמֶן וְנִסְכּוֹ: עֹלַת שַׁבַּת בְּשַׁבַּתּוֹ עַל־עֹלַת הַתָּמִיד וְנִסְכָּהּ:

רביעי וּבְרָאשֵׁי חׇדְשֵׁיכֶם תַּקְרִיבוּ עֹלָה לַיהוָה פָּרִים בְּנֵי־בָקָר שְׁנַיִם וְאַיִל אֶחָד
כְּבָשִׂים בְּנֵי־שָׁנָה שִׁבְעָה תְּמִימִם: וּשְׁלֹשָׁה עֶשְׂרֹנִים סֹלֶת מִנְחָה בְּלוּלָה
בַשֶּׁמֶן לַפָּר הָאֶחָד וּשְׁנֵי עֶשְׂרֹנִים סֹלֶת מִנְחָה בְּלוּלָה בַשֶּׁמֶן לָאַיִל הָאֶחָד:
וְעִשָּׂרֹן עִשָּׂרוֹן סֹלֶת מִנְחָה בְּלוּלָה בַשֶּׁמֶן לַכֶּבֶשׂ הָאֶחָד עֹלָה רֵיחַ נִיחֹחַ
אִשֶּׁה לַיהוָה: וְנִסְכֵּיהֶם חֲצִי הַהִין יִהְיֶה לַפָּר וּשְׁלִישִׁת הַהִין לָאַיִל וּרְבִיעִת
הַהִין לַכֶּבֶשׂ יָיִן זֹאת עֹלַת חֹדֶשׁ בְּחׇדְשׁוֹ לְחׇדְשֵׁי הַשָּׁנָה: וּשְׂעִיר עִזִּים אֶחָד
לְחַטָּאת לַיהוָה עַל־עֹלַת הַתָּמִיד יֵעָשֶׂה וְנִסְכּוֹ:

READING FOR FAST DAYS / קריאה לתענית ציבור

The following is read on a תענית ציבור *(except* תשעה באב*) in both* שחרית *and* מנחה.
At מנחה, *the person called up for* שלישי *also reads the* הפטרה.
It is customary for the קהל *to say aloud the passages marked by arrows, followed by the* קורא *(see law 51).*

שמות לב: יא–יד וַיְחַל מֹשֶׁה אֶת־פְּנֵי יהוה אֱלֹהָיו וַיֹּאמֶר לָמָה יהוה יֶחֱרֶה אַפְּךָ בְּעַמֶּךָ אֲשֶׁר
הוֹצֵאתָ מֵאֶרֶץ מִצְרַיִם בְּכֹחַ גָּדוֹל וּבְיָד חֲזָקָה: לָמָּה יֹאמְרוּ מִצְרַיִם לֵאמֹר
בְּרָעָה הוֹצִיאָם לַהֲרֹג אֹתָם בֶּהָרִים וּלְכַלֹּתָם מֵעַל פְּנֵי הָאֲדָמָה ◂ שׁוּב מֵחֲרוֹן
אַפֶּךָ וְהִנָּחֵם עַל־הָרָעָה לְעַמֶּךָ: ◂ זְכֹר לְאַבְרָהָם לְיִצְחָק וּלְיִשְׂרָאֵל עֲבָדֶיךָ
אֲשֶׁר נִשְׁבַּעְתָּ לָהֶם בָּךְ וַתְּדַבֵּר אֲלֵהֶם אַרְבֶּה אֶת־זַרְעֲכֶם כְּכוֹכְבֵי הַשָּׁמָיִם
וְכָל־הָאָרֶץ הַזֹּאת אֲשֶׁר אָמַרְתִּי אֶתֵּן לְזַרְעֲכֶם וְנָחֲלוּ לְעֹלָם: וַיִּנָּחֶם יהוה
עַל־הָרָעָה אֲשֶׁר דִּבֶּר לַעֲשׂוֹת לְעַמּוֹ:

שמות לד: א–י לוי וַיֹּאמֶר יהוה אֶל־מֹשֶׁה פְּסָל־לְךָ שְׁנֵי־לֻחֹת אֲבָנִים כָּרִאשֹׁנִים וְכָתַבְתִּי עַל־
הַלֻּחֹת אֶת־הַדְּבָרִים אֲשֶׁר הָיוּ עַל־הַלֻּחֹת הָרִאשֹׁנִים אֲשֶׁר שִׁבַּרְתָּ: וֶהְיֵה נָכוֹן
לַבֹּקֶר וְעָלִיתָ בַבֹּקֶר אֶל־הַר סִינַי וְנִצַּבְתָּ לִי שָׁם עַל־רֹאשׁ הָהָר: וְאִישׁ לֹא־
יַעֲלֶה עִמָּךְ וְגַם־אִישׁ אַל־יֵרָא בְּכָל־הָהָר גַּם־הַצֹּאן וְהַבָּקָר אַל־יִרְעוּ אֶל־מוּל
ישראל הָהָר הַהוּא: *וַיִּפְסֹל שְׁנֵי־לֻחֹת אֲבָנִים כָּרִאשֹׁנִים וַיַּשְׁכֵּם מֹשֶׁה בַבֹּקֶר וַיַּעַל
אֶל־הַר סִינַי כַּאֲשֶׁר צִוָּה יהוה אֹתוֹ וַיִּקַּח בְּיָדוֹ שְׁנֵי לֻחֹת אֲבָנִים: וַיֵּרֶד יהוה
בֶּעָנָן וַיִּתְיַצֵּב עִמּוֹ שָׁם וַיִּקְרָא בְשֵׁם יהוה: וַיַּעֲבֹר יהוה ׀ עַל־פָּנָיו וַיִּקְרָא ◂ יהוה ׀
יהוה אֵל רַחוּם וְחַנּוּן אֶרֶךְ אַפַּיִם וְרַב־חֶסֶד וֶאֱמֶת: נֹצֵר חֶסֶד לָאֲלָפִים נֹשֵׂא
עָוֺן וָפֶשַׁע וְחַטָּאָה וְנַקֵּה ◂ לֹא יְנַקֶּה פֹּקֵד ׀ עֲוֺן אָבוֹת עַל־בָּנִים וְעַל־בְּנֵי בָנִים
עַל־שִׁלֵּשִׁים וְעַל־רִבֵּעִים: וַיְמַהֵר מֹשֶׁה וַיִּקֹּד אַרְצָה וַיִּשְׁתָּחוּ: וַיֹּאמֶר אִם־נָא
מָצָאתִי חֵן בְּעֵינֶיךָ אֲדֹנָי יֵלֶךְ־נָא אֲדֹנָי בְּקִרְבֵּנוּ כִּי עַם־קְשֵׁה־עֹרֶף הוּא ◂ וְסָלַחְתָּ
לַעֲוֺנֵנוּ וּלְחַטָּאתֵנוּ וּנְחַלְתָּנוּ: ◂ וַיֹּאמֶר הִנֵּה אָנֹכִי כֹּרֵת בְּרִית נֶגֶד כָּל־עַמְּךָ
אֶעֱשֶׂה נִפְלָאֹת אֲשֶׁר לֹא־נִבְרְאוּ בְכָל־הָאָרֶץ וּבְכָל־הַגּוֹיִם וְרָאָה כָל־הָעָם
אֲשֶׁר־אַתָּה בְקִרְבּוֹ אֶת־מַעֲשֵׂה יהוה כִּי־נוֹרָא הוּא אֲשֶׁר אֲנִי עֹשֶׂה עִמָּךְ:

HAFTARA FOR FAST DAYS / הפטרה לתענית ציבור

The blessings for the הפטרה *can be found on page 515.*

ישעיה נה:ו–נו:ח דִּרְשׁוּ יהוה בְּהִמָּצְאוֹ קְרָאֻהוּ בִּהְיוֹתוֹ קָרוֹב: יַעֲזֹב רָשָׁע דַּרְכּוֹ וְאִישׁ אָוֶן
מַחְשְׁבֹתָיו וְיָשֹׁב אֶל־יהוה וִירַחֲמֵהוּ וְאֶל־אֱלֹהֵינוּ כִּי־יַרְבֶּה לִסְלוֹחַ: כִּי לֹא

מַחְשְׁבוֹתַי מַחְשְׁבוֹתֵיכֶם וְלֹא דַרְכֵיכֶם דְּרָכָי נְאֻם יְהֹוָה: כִּי־גָבְהוּ שָׁמַיִם
מֵאָרֶץ כֵּן גָּבְהוּ דְרָכַי מִדַּרְכֵיכֶם וּמַחְשְׁבֹתַי מִמַּחְשְׁבֹתֵיכֶם: כִּי כַּאֲשֶׁר יֵרֵד
הַגֶּשֶׁם וְהַשֶּׁלֶג מִן־הַשָּׁמַיִם וְשָׁמָּה לֹא יָשׁוּב כִּי אִם־הִרְוָה אֶת־הָאָרֶץ וְהוֹלִידָהּ
וְהִצְמִיחָהּ וְנָתַן זֶרַע לַזֹּרֵעַ וְלֶחֶם לָאֹכֵל: כֵּן יִהְיֶה דְבָרִי אֲשֶׁר יֵצֵא מִפִּי לֹא־
יָשׁוּב אֵלַי רֵיקָם כִּי אִם־עָשָׂה אֶת־אֲשֶׁר חָפַצְתִּי וְהִצְלִיחַ אֲשֶׁר שְׁלַחְתִּיו:
כִּי־בְשִׂמְחָה תֵצֵאוּ וּבְשָׁלוֹם תּוּבָלוּן הֶהָרִים וְהַגְּבָעוֹת יִפְצְחוּ לִפְנֵיכֶם רִנָּה
וְכָל־עֲצֵי הַשָּׂדֶה יִמְחֲאוּ־כָף: תַּחַת הַנַּעֲצוּץ יַעֲלֶה בְרוֹשׁ תַּחַת הַסִּרְפַּד וְתַחַת
יַעֲלֶה הֲדַס וְהָיָה לַיהֹוָה לְשֵׁם לְאוֹת עוֹלָם לֹא יִכָּרֵת: כֹּה אָמַר

יְהֹוָה שִׁמְרוּ מִשְׁפָּט וַעֲשׂוּ צְדָקָה כִּי־קְרוֹבָה יְשׁוּעָתִי לָבוֹא וְצִדְקָתִי לְהִגָּלוֹת:
אַשְׁרֵי אֱנוֹשׁ יַעֲשֶׂה־זֹּאת וּבֶן־אָדָם יַחֲזִיק בָּהּ שֹׁמֵר שַׁבָּת מֵחַלְּלוֹ וְשֹׁמֵר
יָדוֹ מֵעֲשׂוֹת כָּל־רָע: וְאַל־יֹאמַר בֶּן־הַנֵּכָר הַנִּלְוָה אֶל־יְהֹוָה לֵאמֹר הַבְדֵּל
יַבְדִּילַנִי יְהֹוָה מֵעַל עַמּוֹ וְאַל־יֹאמַר הַסָּרִיס הֵן אֲנִי עֵץ יָבֵשׁ: כִּי־

כֹה ׀ אָמַר יְהֹוָה לַסָּרִיסִים אֲשֶׁר יִשְׁמְרוּ אֶת־שַׁבְּתוֹתַי וּבָחֲרוּ בַּאֲשֶׁר חָפָצְתִּי
וּמַחֲזִיקִים בִּבְרִיתִי: וְנָתַתִּי לָהֶם בְּבֵיתִי וּבְחוֹמֹתַי יָד וָשֵׁם טוֹב מִבָּנִים
וּמִבָּנוֹת שֵׁם עוֹלָם אֶתֶּן־לוֹ אֲשֶׁר לֹא יִכָּרֵת: וּבְנֵי הַנֵּכָר הַנִּלְוִים
עַל־יְהֹוָה לְשָׁרְתוֹ וּלְאַהֲבָה אֶת־שֵׁם יְהֹוָה לִהְיוֹת לוֹ לַעֲבָדִים כָּל־שֹׁמֵר
שַׁבָּת מֵחַלְּלוֹ וּמַחֲזִיקִים בִּבְרִיתִי: וַהֲבִיאוֹתִים אֶל־הַר קָדְשִׁי וְשִׂמַּחְתִּים
בְּבֵית תְּפִלָּתִי עוֹלֹתֵיהֶם וְזִבְחֵיהֶם לְרָצוֹן עַל־מִזְבְּחִי כִּי בֵיתִי בֵּית־תְּפִלָּה
יִקָּרֵא לְכָל־הָעַמִּים: נְאֻם אֲדֹנָי יֱהֹוִה מְקַבֵּץ נִדְחֵי יִשְׂרָאֵל עוֹד אֲקַבֵּץ עָלָיו
לְנִקְבָּצָיו:

READING FOR TISHA B'AV · קריאה לתשעה באב

The following is read during שחרית *of* תשעה באב. *The person called up for* שלישי *also
reads the* הפטרה. *At* מנחה, *the* קריאת התורה *and* הפטרה *are those for regular Fast Days.*

דברים
ד:כה-מ

כִּי־תוֹלִיד בָּנִים וּבְנֵי בָנִים וְנוֹשַׁנְתֶּם בָּאָרֶץ וְהִשְׁחַתֶּם וַעֲשִׂיתֶם פֶּסֶל תְּמוּנַת
כֹּל וַעֲשִׂיתֶם הָרַע בְּעֵינֵי־יְהֹוָה אֱלֹהֶיךָ לְהַכְעִיסוֹ: הַעִידֹתִי בָכֶם הַיּוֹם אֶת־
הַשָּׁמַיִם וְאֶת־הָאָרֶץ כִּי־אָבֹד תֹּאבֵדוּן מַהֵר מֵעַל הָאָרֶץ אֲשֶׁר אַתֶּם עֹבְרִים
אֶת־הַיַּרְדֵּן שָׁמָּה לְרִשְׁתָּהּ לֹא־תַאֲרִיכֻן יָמִים עָלֶיהָ כִּי הִשָּׁמֵד תִּשָּׁמֵדוּן:
וְהֵפִיץ יְהֹוָה אֶתְכֶם בָּעַמִּים וְנִשְׁאַרְתֶּם מְתֵי מִסְפָּר בַּגּוֹיִם אֲשֶׁר יְנַהֵג יְהֹוָה
אֶתְכֶם שָׁמָּה: וַעֲבַדְתֶּם־שָׁם אֱלֹהִים מַעֲשֵׂה יְדֵי אָדָם עֵץ וָאֶבֶן אֲשֶׁר לֹא־

יִרְאוּן וְלֹא יִשְׁמְעוּן וְלֹא יֹאכְלוּן וְלֹא יְרִיחֻן: וּבִקַּשְׁתֶּם מִשָּׁם אֶת־יהוה אֱלֹהֶיךָ
לוי וּמָצָאתָ כִּי תִדְרְשֶׁנּוּ בְּכָל־לְבָבְךָ וּבְכָל־נַפְשֶׁךָ: *בַּצַּר לְךָ וּמְצָאוּךָ כֹּל הַדְּבָרִים
הָאֵלֶּה בְּאַחֲרִית הַיָּמִים וְשַׁבְתָּ עַד־יהוה אֱלֹהֶיךָ וְשָׁמַעְתָּ בְּקֹלוֹ: כִּי אֵל
רַחוּם יהוה אֱלֹהֶיךָ לֹא יַרְפְּךָ וְלֹא יַשְׁחִיתֶךָ וְלֹא יִשְׁכַּח אֶת־בְּרִית אֲבֹתֶיךָ
אֲשֶׁר נִשְׁבַּע לָהֶם: כִּי שְׁאַל־נָא לְיָמִים רִאשֹׁנִים אֲשֶׁר־הָיוּ לְפָנֶיךָ לְמִן־הַיּוֹם
אֲשֶׁר בָּרָא אֱלֹהִים ׀ אָדָם עַל־הָאָרֶץ וּלְמִקְצֵה הַשָּׁמַיִם וְעַד־קְצֵה הַשָּׁמָיִם
הֲנִהְיָה כַּדָּבָר הַגָּדוֹל הַזֶּה אוֹ הֲנִשְׁמַע כָּמֹהוּ: הֲשָׁמַע עָם קוֹל אֱלֹהִים מְדַבֵּר
מִתּוֹךְ־הָאֵשׁ כַּאֲשֶׁר־שָׁמַעְתָּ אַתָּה וַיֶּחִי: אוֹ ׀ הֲנִסָּה אֱלֹהִים לָבוֹא לָקַחַת לוֹ
גוֹי מִקֶּרֶב גּוֹי בְּמַסֹּת בְּאֹתֹת וּבְמוֹפְתִים וּבְמִלְחָמָה וּבְיָד חֲזָקָה וּבִזְרוֹעַ נְטוּיָה
וּבְמוֹרָאִים גְּדֹלִים כְּכֹל אֲשֶׁר־עָשָׂה לָכֶם יהוה אֱלֹהֵיכֶם בְּמִצְרַיִם לְעֵינֶיךָ:
ישראל אַתָּה הָרְאֵתָ לָדַעַת כִּי יהוה הוּא הָאֱלֹהִים אֵין עוֹד מִלְּבַדּוֹ: *מִן־הַשָּׁמַיִם
הִשְׁמִיעֲךָ אֶת־קֹלוֹ לְיַסְּרֶךָּ וְעַל־הָאָרֶץ הֶרְאֲךָ אֶת־אִשּׁוֹ הַגְּדוֹלָה וּדְבָרָיו
שָׁמַעְתָּ מִתּוֹךְ הָאֵשׁ: וְתַחַת כִּי אָהַב אֶת־אֲבֹתֶיךָ וַיִּבְחַר בְּזַרְעוֹ אַחֲרָיו
וַיּוֹצִאֲךָ בְּפָנָיו בְּכֹחוֹ הַגָּדֹל מִמִּצְרָיִם: לְהוֹרִישׁ גּוֹיִם גְּדֹלִים וַעֲצֻמִים מִמְּךָ
מִפָּנֶיךָ לַהֲבִיאֲךָ לָתֶת־לְךָ אֶת־אַרְצָם נַחֲלָה כַּיּוֹם הַזֶּה: וְיָדַעְתָּ הַיּוֹם וַהֲשֵׁבֹתָ
אֶל־לְבָבֶךָ כִּי יהוה הוּא הָאֱלֹהִים בַּשָּׁמַיִם מִמַּעַל וְעַל־הָאָרֶץ מִתָּחַת אֵין
עוֹד: וְשָׁמַרְתָּ אֶת־חֻקָּיו וְאֶת־מִצְוֺתָיו אֲשֶׁר אָנֹכִי מְצַוְּךָ הַיּוֹם אֲשֶׁר יִיטַב לְךָ
וּלְבָנֶיךָ אַחֲרֶיךָ וּלְמַעַן תַּאֲרִיךְ יָמִים עַל־הָאֲדָמָה אֲשֶׁר יהוה אֱלֹהֶיךָ נֹתֵן לְךָ
כָּל־הַיָּמִים:

הפטרה לתשעה באב — HAFTARA FOR TISHA B'AV

ירמיהו ח:יג–ט:כג
אָסֹף אֲסִיפֵם נְאֻם־יהוה אֵין עֲנָבִים בַּגֶּפֶן וְאֵין תְּאֵנִים בַּתְּאֵנָה וְהֶעָלֶה נָבֵל
וָאֶתֵּן לָהֶם יַעַבְרוּם: עַל־מָה אֲנַחְנוּ יֹשְׁבִים הֵאָסְפוּ וְנָבוֹא אֶל־עָרֵי הַמִּבְצָר
וְנִדְּמָה־שָּׁם כִּי יהוה אֱלֹהֵינוּ הֲדִמָּנוּ וַיַּשְׁקֵנוּ מֵי־רֹאשׁ כִּי חָטָאנוּ לַיהוה: קַוֵּה
לְשָׁלוֹם וְאֵין טוֹב לְעֵת מַרְפֵּה וְהִנֵּה בְעָתָה: מִדָּן נִשְׁמַע נַחְרַת סוּסָיו מִקּוֹל
מִצְהֲלוֹת אַבִּירָיו רָעֲשָׁה כָּל־הָאָרֶץ וַיָּבוֹאוּ וַיֹּאכְלוּ אֶרֶץ וּמְלוֹאָהּ עִיר וְיֹשְׁבֵי
בָהּ: כִּי הִנְנִי מְשַׁלֵּחַ בָּכֶם נְחָשִׁים צִפְעֹנִים אֲשֶׁר אֵין־לָהֶם לָחַשׁ וְנִשְּׁכוּ אֶתְכֶם
נְאֻם־יהוה: מַבְלִיגִיתִי עֲלֵי יָגוֹן עָלַי לִבִּי דַוָּי: הִנֵּה־קוֹל שַׁוְעַת

בַּת־עַמִּי מֵאֶרֶץ מַרְחַקִּים הַיהוָה אֵין בְּצִיּוֹן אִם־מַלְכָּהּ אֵין בָּהּ מַדּוּעַ הִכְעִסוּנִי
בִּפְסִלֵיהֶם בְּהַבְלֵי נֵכָר: עָבַר קָצִיר כָּלָה קָיִץ וַאֲנַחְנוּ לוֹא נוֹשָׁעְנוּ: עַל־שֶׁבֶר
בַּת־עַמִּי הָשְׁבָּרְתִּי קָדַרְתִּי שַׁמָּה הֶחֱזִקָתְנִי: הַצֳרִי אֵין בְּגִלְעָד אִם־רֹפֵא אֵין
שָׁם כִּי מַדּוּעַ לֹא עָלְתָה אֲרֻכַת בַּת־עַמִּי: מִי־יִתֵּן רֹאשִׁי מַיִם וְעֵינִי
מְקוֹר דִּמְעָה וְאֶבְכֶּה יוֹמָם וָלַיְלָה אֵת חַלְלֵי בַת־עַמִּי: מִי־יִתְּנֵנִי בַמִּדְבָּר מְלוֹן
אֹרְחִים וְאֶעֶזְבָה אֶת־עַמִּי וְאֵלְכָה מֵאִתָּם כִּי כֻלָּם מְנָאֲפִים עֲצֶרֶת בֹּגְדִים:
וַיַּדְרְכוּ אֶת־לְשׁוֹנָם קַשְׁתָּם שֶׁקֶר וְלֹא לֶאֱמוּנָה גָּבְרוּ בָאָרֶץ כִּי מֵרָעָה אֶל־
רָעָה ׀ יָצָאוּ וְאֹתִי לֹא־יָדָעוּ נְאֻם־יְהוָה: אִישׁ מֵרֵעֵהוּ הִשָּׁמֵרוּ וְעַל־כָּל־אָח
אַל־תִּבְטָחוּ כִּי כָל־אָח עָקוֹב יַעְקֹב וְכָל־רֵעַ רָכִיל יַהֲלֹךְ: וְאִישׁ בְּרֵעֵהוּ יְהָתֵלּוּ
וֶאֱמֶת לֹא יְדַבֵּרוּ לִמְּדוּ לְשׁוֹנָם דַּבֶּר־שֶׁקֶר הַעֲוֵה נִלְאוּ: שִׁבְתְּךָ בְּתוֹךְ מִרְמָה
בְּמִרְמָה מֵאֲנוּ דַעַת־אוֹתִי נְאֻם־יְהוָה: לָכֵן כֹּה אָמַר יְהוָה צְבָאוֹת
הִנְנִי צוֹרְפָם וּבְחַנְתִּים כִּי־אֵיךְ אֶעֱשֶׂה מִפְּנֵי בַּת־עַמִּי: חֵץ שׁוֹחֵט לְשׁוֹנָם מִרְמָה שָׁחֵט
דִבֵּר בְּפִיו שָׁלוֹם אֶת־רֵעֵהוּ יְדַבֵּר וּבְקִרְבּוֹ יָשִׂים אָרְבּוֹ: הַעַל־אֵלֶּה לֹא־אֶפְקָד־
בָּם נְאֻם־יְהוָה אִם בְּגוֹי אֲשֶׁר־כָּזֶה לֹא תִתְנַקֵּם נַפְשִׁי: עַל־הֶהָרִים
אֶשָּׂא בְכִי וָנֶהִי וְעַל־נְאוֹת מִדְבָּר קִינָה כִּי נִצְּתוּ מִבְּלִי־אִישׁ עֹבֵר וְלֹא שָׁמְעוּ
קוֹל מִקְנֶה מֵעוֹף הַשָּׁמַיִם וְעַד־בְּהֵמָה נָדְדוּ הָלָכוּ: וְנָתַתִּי אֶת־יְרוּשָׁלַ͏ִם
לְגַלִּים מְעוֹן תַּנִּים וְאֶת־עָרֵי יְהוּדָה אֶתֵּן שְׁמָמָה מִבְּלִי יוֹשֵׁב: מִי־
הָאִישׁ הֶחָכָם וְיָבֵן אֶת־זֹאת וַאֲשֶׁר דִּבֶּר פִּי־יְהוָה אֵלָיו וְיַגִּדָהּ עַל־מָה אָבְדָה
הָאָרֶץ נִצְּתָה כַמִּדְבָּר מִבְּלִי עֹבֵר: וַיֹּאמֶר יְהוָה עַל־עָזְבָם
אֶת־תּוֹרָתִי אֲשֶׁר נָתַתִּי לִפְנֵיהֶם וְלֹא־שָׁמְעוּ בְקוֹלִי וְלֹא־הָלְכוּ בָהּ: וַיֵּלְכוּ
אַחֲרֵי שְׁרִרוּת לִבָּם וְאַחֲרֵי הַבְּעָלִים אֲשֶׁר לִמְּדוּם אֲבוֹתָם: לָכֵן
כֹּה־אָמַר יְהוָה צְבָאוֹת אֱלֹהֵי יִשְׂרָאֵל הִנְנִי מַאֲכִילָם אֶת־הָעָם הַזֶּה לַעֲנָה
וְהִשְׁקִיתִים מֵי־רֹאשׁ: וַהֲפִצוֹתִים בַּגּוֹיִם אֲשֶׁר לֹא יָדְעוּ הֵמָּה וַאֲבוֹתָם וְשִׁלַּחְתִּי
אַחֲרֵיהֶם אֶת־הַחֶרֶב עַד כַּלּוֹתִי אוֹתָם: כֹּה אָמַר יְהוָה צְבָאוֹת
הִתְבּוֹנְנוּ וְקִרְאוּ לַמְקוֹנְנוֹת וּתְבוֹאֶינָה וְאֶל־הַחֲכָמוֹת שִׁלְחוּ וְתָבוֹאנָה:
וּתְמַהֵרְנָה וְתִשֶּׂנָה עָלֵינוּ נֶהִי וְתֵרַדְנָה עֵינֵינוּ דִּמְעָה וְעַפְעַפֵּינוּ יִזְּלוּ־מָיִם:
כִּי קוֹל נְהִי נִשְׁמַע מִצִּיּוֹן אֵיךְ שֻׁדָּדְנוּ בֹּשְׁנוּ מְאֹד כִּי־עָזַבְנוּ אָרֶץ כִּי הִשְׁלִיכוּ
מִשְׁכְּנוֹתֵינוּ: כִּי־שְׁמַעְנָה נָשִׁים דְּבַר־יְהוָה וְתִקַּח אָזְנְכֶם דְּבַר־

פִּיו וְלַמֵּדְנָה בְנוֹתֵיכֶם נֶהִי וְאִשָּׁה רְעוּתָהּ קִינָה: כִּי־עָלָה מָוֶת בְּחַלּוֹנֵינוּ בָּא
בְּאַרְמְנוֹתֵינוּ לְהַכְרִית עוֹלָל מִחוּץ בַּחוּרִים מֵרְחֹבוֹת: דַּבֵּר כֹּה נְאֻם־יהוה
וְנָפְלָה נִבְלַת הָאָדָם כְּדֹמֶן עַל־פְּנֵי הַשָּׂדֶה וּכְעָמִיר מֵאַחֲרֵי הַקֹּצֵר וְאֵין
מְאַסֵּף: כֹּה | אָמַר יהוה אַל־יִתְהַלֵּל חָכָם בְּחָכְמָתוֹ וְאַל־יִתְהַלֵּל
הַגִּבּוֹר בִּגְבוּרָתוֹ אַל־יִתְהַלֵּל עָשִׁיר בְּעָשְׁרוֹ: כִּי אִם־בְּזֹאת יִתְהַלֵּל הַמִּתְהַלֵּל
הַשְׂכֵּל וְיָדֹעַ אוֹתִי כִּי אֲנִי יהוה עֹשֶׂה חֶסֶד מִשְׁפָּט וּצְדָקָה בָּאָרֶץ כִּי־בְאֵלֶּה
חָפַצְתִּי נְאֻם־יהוה:

קריאה ליום הראשון של חנוכה FIRST DAY OF ḤANUKKA

במדבר ז:א–יז
וַיְהִי בְּיוֹם כַּלּוֹת מֹשֶׁה לְהָקִים אֶת־הַמִּשְׁכָּן וַיִּמְשַׁח אֹתוֹ וַיְקַדֵּשׁ אֹתוֹ וְאֶת־
כָּל־כֵּלָיו וְאֶת־הַמִּזְבֵּחַ וְאֶת־כָּל־כֵּלָיו וַיִּמְשָׁחֵם וַיְקַדֵּשׁ אֹתָם: וַיַּקְרִיבוּ נְשִׂיאֵי
יִשְׂרָאֵל רָאשֵׁי בֵּית אֲבֹתָם הֵם נְשִׂיאֵי הַמַּטֹּת הֵם הָעֹמְדִים עַל־הַפְּקֻדִים:
וַיָּבִיאוּ אֶת־קָרְבָּנָם לִפְנֵי יהוה שֵׁשׁ־עֶגְלֹת צָב וּשְׁנֵי־עָשָׂר בָּקָר עֲגָלָה עַל־שְׁנֵי
הַנְּשִׂאִים וְשׁוֹר לְאֶחָד וַיַּקְרִיבוּ אוֹתָם לִפְנֵי הַמִּשְׁכָּן: וַיֹּאמֶר יהוה אֶל־מֹשֶׁה
לֵּאמֹר: קַח מֵאִתָּם וְהָיוּ לַעֲבֹד אֶת־עֲבֹדַת אֹהֶל מוֹעֵד וְנָתַתָּה אוֹתָם אֶל־
הַלְוִיִּם אִישׁ כְּפִי עֲבֹדָתוֹ: וַיִּקַּח מֹשֶׁה אֶת־הָעֲגָלֹת וְאֶת־הַבָּקָר וַיִּתֵּן אוֹתָם
אֶל־הַלְוִיִּם: אֵת | שְׁתֵּי הָעֲגָלוֹת וְאֵת אַרְבַּעַת הַבָּקָר נָתַן לִבְנֵי גֵרְשׁוֹן כְּפִי
עֲבֹדָתָם: וְאֵת | אַרְבַּע הָעֲגָלֹת וְאֵת שְׁמֹנַת הַבָּקָר נָתַן לִבְנֵי מְרָרִי כְּפִי עֲבֹדָתָם
בְּיַד אִיתָמָר בֶּן־אַהֲרֹן הַכֹּהֵן: וְלִבְנֵי קְהָת לֹא נָתָן כִּי־עֲבֹדַת הַקֹּדֶשׁ עֲלֵהֶם
בַּכָּתֵף יִשָּׂאוּ: וַיַּקְרִיבוּ הַנְּשִׂאִים אֵת חֲנֻכַּת הַמִּזְבֵּחַ בְּיוֹם הִמָּשַׁח אֹתוֹ וַיַּקְרִיבוּ
הַנְּשִׂיאִם אֶת־קָרְבָּנָם לִפְנֵי הַמִּזְבֵּחַ: וַיֹּאמֶר יהוה אֶל־מֹשֶׁה נָשִׂיא אֶחָד לַיּוֹם
לוי נָשִׂיא אֶחָד לַיּוֹם יַקְרִיבוּ אֶת־קָרְבָּנָם לַחֲנֻכַּת הַמִּזְבֵּחַ: *וַיְהִי
הַמַּקְרִיב בַּיּוֹם הָרִאשׁוֹן אֶת־קָרְבָּנוֹ נַחְשׁוֹן בֶּן־עַמִּינָדָב לְמַטֵּה יְהוּדָה: וְקָרְבָּנוֹ
קַעֲרַת־כֶּסֶף אַחַת שְׁלֹשִׁים וּמֵאָה מִשְׁקָלָהּ מִזְרָק אֶחָד כֶּסֶף שִׁבְעִים שֶׁקֶל
בְּשֶׁקֶל הַקֹּדֶשׁ שְׁנֵיהֶם | מְלֵאִים סֹלֶת בְּלוּלָה בַשֶּׁמֶן לְמִנְחָה: כַּף אַחַת
ישראל עֲשָׂרָה זָהָב מְלֵאָה קְטֹרֶת: *פַּר אֶחָד בֶּן־בָּקָר אַיִל אֶחָד כֶּבֶשׂ־אֶחָד בֶּן־
שְׁנָתוֹ לְעֹלָה: שְׂעִיר־עִזִּים אֶחָד לְחַטָּאת: וּלְזֶבַח הַשְּׁלָמִים בָּקָר שְׁנַיִם
אֵילִם חֲמִשָּׁה עַתֻּדִים חֲמִשָּׁה כְּבָשִׂים בְּנֵי־שָׁנָה חֲמִשָּׁה זֶה קָרְבַּן נַחְשׁוֹן
בֶּן־עַמִּינָדָב:

SECOND DAY OF ḤANUKKA — קריאה ליום השני של חנוכה

In ארץ ישראל, *for* שלישי *repeat the first paragraph:* בַּיּוֹם הַשֵּׁנִי *until* נְתַנְאֵל בֶּן־צוּעָר.

במדבר ז:יח–כט
בַּיּוֹם הַשֵּׁנִי הִקְרִיב נְתַנְאֵל בֶּן־צוּעָר נְשִׂיא יִשָּׂשכָר: הִקְרִב אֶת־קָרְבָּנוֹ קַעֲרַת־
כֶּסֶף אַחַת שְׁלֹשִׁים וּמֵאָה מִשְׁקָלָהּ מִזְרָק אֶחָד כֶּסֶף שִׁבְעִים שֶׁקֶל בְּשֶׁקֶל
הַקֹּדֶשׁ שְׁנֵיהֶם ׀ מְלֵאִים סֹלֶת בְּלוּלָה בַשֶּׁמֶן לְמִנְחָה: כַּף אַחַת עֲשָׂרָה זָהָב
לוי מְלֵאָה קְטֹרֶת: *פַּר אֶחָד בֶּן־בָּקָר אַיִל אֶחָד כֶּבֶשׂ־אֶחָד בֶּן־שְׁנָתוֹ לְעֹלָה:
שְׂעִיר־עִזִּים אֶחָד לְחַטָּאת: וּלְזֶבַח הַשְּׁלָמִים בָּקָר שְׁנַיִם אֵילִם חֲמִשָּׁה עַתֻּדִים
חֲמִשָּׁה כְּבָשִׂים בְּנֵי־שָׁנָה חֲמִשָּׁה זֶה קָרְבַּן נְתַנְאֵל בֶּן־צוּעָר:

ישראל בַּיּוֹם הַשְּׁלִישִׁי נָשִׂיא לִבְנֵי זְבוּלֻן אֱלִיאָב בֶּן־חֵלֹן: קָרְבָּנוֹ קַעֲרַת־כֶּסֶף אַחַת
שְׁלֹשִׁים וּמֵאָה מִשְׁקָלָהּ מִזְרָק אֶחָד כֶּסֶף שִׁבְעִים שֶׁקֶל בְּשֶׁקֶל הַקֹּדֶשׁ שְׁנֵיהֶם ׀
מְלֵאִים סֹלֶת בְּלוּלָה בַשֶּׁמֶן לְמִנְחָה: כַּף אַחַת עֲשָׂרָה זָהָב מְלֵאָה קְטֹרֶת:
פַּר אֶחָד בֶּן־בָּקָר אַיִל אֶחָד כֶּבֶשׂ־אֶחָד בֶּן־שְׁנָתוֹ לְעֹלָה: שְׂעִיר־עִזִּים אֶחָד
לְחַטָּאת: וּלְזֶבַח הַשְּׁלָמִים בָּקָר שְׁנַיִם אֵילִם חֲמִשָּׁה עַתֻּדִים חֲמִשָּׁה כְּבָשִׂים
בְּנֵי־שָׁנָה חֲמִשָּׁה זֶה קָרְבַּן אֱלִיאָב בֶּן־חֵלֹן:

THIRD DAY OF ḤANUKKA — קריאה ליום השלישי של חנוכה

In ארץ ישראל, *for* שלישי *repeat the first paragraph:* בַּיּוֹם הַשְּׁלִישִׁי *until* אֱלִיאָב בֶּן־חֵלֹן.

במדבר ז:כד–לה
בַּיּוֹם הַשְּׁלִישִׁי נָשִׂיא לִבְנֵי זְבוּלֻן אֱלִיאָב בֶּן־חֵלֹן: קָרְבָּנוֹ קַעֲרַת־כֶּסֶף אַחַת
שְׁלֹשִׁים וּמֵאָה מִשְׁקָלָהּ מִזְרָק אֶחָד כֶּסֶף שִׁבְעִים שֶׁקֶל בְּשֶׁקֶל הַקֹּדֶשׁ שְׁנֵיהֶם ׀
מְלֵאִים סֹלֶת בְּלוּלָה בַשֶּׁמֶן לְמִנְחָה: כַּף אַחַת עֲשָׂרָה זָהָב מְלֵאָה קְטֹרֶת:
לוי *פַּר אֶחָד בֶּן־בָּקָר אַיִל אֶחָד כֶּבֶשׂ־אֶחָד בֶּן־שְׁנָתוֹ לְעֹלָה: שְׂעִיר־עִזִּים אֶחָד
לְחַטָּאת: וּלְזֶבַח הַשְּׁלָמִים בָּקָר שְׁנַיִם אֵילִם חֲמִשָּׁה עַתֻּדִים חֲמִשָּׁה כְּבָשִׂים
בְּנֵי־שָׁנָה חֲמִשָּׁה זֶה קָרְבַּן אֱלִיאָב בֶּן־חֵלֹן:

ישראל בַּיּוֹם הָרְבִיעִי נָשִׂיא לִבְנֵי רְאוּבֵן אֱלִיצוּר בֶּן־שְׁדֵיאוּר: קָרְבָּנוֹ קַעֲרַת־כֶּסֶף
אַחַת שְׁלֹשִׁים וּמֵאָה מִשְׁקָלָהּ מִזְרָק אֶחָד כֶּסֶף שִׁבְעִים שֶׁקֶל בְּשֶׁקֶל הַקֹּדֶשׁ
שְׁנֵיהֶם ׀ מְלֵאִים סֹלֶת בְּלוּלָה בַשֶּׁמֶן לְמִנְחָה: כַּף אַחַת עֲשָׂרָה זָהָב מְלֵאָה
קְטֹרֶת: פַּר אֶחָד בֶּן־בָּקָר אַיִל אֶחָד כֶּבֶשׂ־אֶחָד בֶּן־שְׁנָתוֹ לְעֹלָה: שְׂעִיר־עִזִּים
אֶחָד לְחַטָּאת: וּלְזֶבַח הַשְּׁלָמִים בָּקָר שְׁנַיִם אֵילִם חֲמִשָּׁה עַתֻּדִים חֲמִשָּׁה
כְּבָשִׂים בְּנֵי־שָׁנָה חֲמִשָּׁה זֶה קָרְבַּן אֱלִיצוּר בֶּן־שְׁדֵיאוּר:

FOURTH DAY OF ḤANUKKA — קריאה ליום הרביעי של חנוכה

In ארץ ישראל, *for* שלישי *repeat the first paragraph:* בַּיּוֹם הָרְבִיעִי *until* אֱלִיצוּר בֶּן־שְׁדֵיאוּר.

במדבר ז:ל–מא
בַּיּוֹם הָרְבִיעִי נָשִׂיא לִבְנֵי רְאוּבֵן אֱלִיצוּר בֶּן־שְׁדֵיאוּר: קָרְבָּנוֹ קַעֲרַת־כֶּסֶף
אַחַת שְׁלֹשִׁים וּמֵאָה מִשְׁקָלָהּ מִזְרָק אֶחָד כֶּסֶף שִׁבְעִים שֶׁקֶל בְּשֶׁקֶל הַקֹּדֶשׁ
שְׁנֵיהֶם ׀ מְלֵאִים סֹלֶת בְּלוּלָה בַשֶּׁמֶן לְמִנְחָה: כַּף אַחַת עֲשָׂרָה זָהָב מְלֵאָה
לוי קְטֹרֶת: *פַּר אֶחָד בֶּן־בָּקָר אַיִל אֶחָד כֶּבֶשׂ־אֶחָד בֶּן־שְׁנָתוֹ לְעֹלָה: שְׂעִיר־
עִזִּים אֶחָד לְחַטָּאת: וּלְזֶבַח הַשְּׁלָמִים בָּקָר שְׁנַיִם אֵילִם חֲמִשָּׁה עַתֻּדִים חֲמִשָּׁה
כְּבָשִׂים בְּנֵי־שָׁנָה חֲמִשָּׁה זֶה קָרְבַּן אֱלִיצוּר בֶּן־שְׁדֵיאוּר:
ישראל בַּיּוֹם הַחֲמִישִׁי נָשִׂיא לִבְנֵי שִׁמְעוֹן שְׁלֻמִיאֵל בֶּן־צוּרִישַׁדָּי: קָרְבָּנוֹ קַעֲרַת־כֶּסֶף
אַחַת שְׁלֹשִׁים וּמֵאָה מִשְׁקָלָהּ מִזְרָק אֶחָד כֶּסֶף שִׁבְעִים שֶׁקֶל בְּשֶׁקֶל הַקֹּדֶשׁ
שְׁנֵיהֶם ׀ מְלֵאִים סֹלֶת בְּלוּלָה בַשֶּׁמֶן לְמִנְחָה: כַּף אַחַת עֲשָׂרָה זָהָב מְלֵאָה
קְטֹרֶת: פַּר אֶחָד בֶּן־בָּקָר אַיִל אֶחָד כֶּבֶשׂ־אֶחָד בֶּן־שְׁנָתוֹ לְעֹלָה: שְׂעִיר־עִזִּים
אֶחָד לְחַטָּאת: וּלְזֶבַח הַשְּׁלָמִים בָּקָר שְׁנַיִם אֵילִם חֲמִשָּׁה עַתֻּדִים חֲמִשָּׁה
כְּבָשִׂים בְּנֵי־שָׁנָה חֲמִשָּׁה זֶה קָרְבַּן שְׁלֻמִיאֵל בֶּן־צוּרִישַׁדָּי:

FIFTH DAY OF ḤANUKKA — קריאה ליום החמישי של חנוכה

In ארץ ישראל, *for* שלישי *repeat the first paragraph:* בַּיּוֹם הַחֲמִישִׁי *until* שְׁלֻמִיאֵל בֶּן־צוּרִישַׁדָּי.

במדבר ז:לו–מז
בַּיּוֹם הַחֲמִישִׁי נָשִׂיא לִבְנֵי שִׁמְעוֹן שְׁלֻמִיאֵל בֶּן־צוּרִישַׁדָּי: קָרְבָּנוֹ קַעֲרַת־
כֶּסֶף אַחַת שְׁלֹשִׁים וּמֵאָה מִשְׁקָלָהּ מִזְרָק אֶחָד כֶּסֶף שִׁבְעִים שֶׁקֶל בְּשֶׁקֶל
הַקֹּדֶשׁ שְׁנֵיהֶם ׀ מְלֵאִים סֹלֶת בְּלוּלָה בַשֶּׁמֶן לְמִנְחָה: כַּף אַחַת עֲשָׂרָה זָהָב
לוי מְלֵאָה קְטֹרֶת: *פַּר אֶחָד בֶּן־בָּקָר אַיִל אֶחָד כֶּבֶשׂ־אֶחָד בֶּן־שְׁנָתוֹ לְעֹלָה:
שְׂעִיר־עִזִּים אֶחָד לְחַטָּאת: וּלְזֶבַח הַשְּׁלָמִים בָּקָר שְׁנַיִם אֵילִם חֲמִשָּׁה עַתֻּדִים
חֲמִשָּׁה כְּבָשִׂים בְּנֵי־שָׁנָה חֲמִשָּׁה זֶה קָרְבַּן שְׁלֻמִיאֵל בֶּן־צוּרִישַׁדָּי:
ישראל בַּיּוֹם הַשִּׁשִּׁי נָשִׂיא לִבְנֵי גָד אֶלְיָסָף בֶּן־דְּעוּאֵל: קָרְבָּנוֹ קַעֲרַת־כֶּסֶף אַחַת
שְׁלֹשִׁים וּמֵאָה מִשְׁקָלָהּ מִזְרָק אֶחָד כֶּסֶף שִׁבְעִים שֶׁקֶל בְּשֶׁקֶל הַקֹּדֶשׁ שְׁנֵיהֶם ׀
מְלֵאִים סֹלֶת בְּלוּלָה בַשֶּׁמֶן לְמִנְחָה: כַּף אַחַת עֲשָׂרָה זָהָב מְלֵאָה קְטֹרֶת:
פַּר אֶחָד בֶּן־בָּקָר אַיִל אֶחָד כֶּבֶשׂ־אֶחָד בֶּן־שְׁנָתוֹ לְעֹלָה: שְׂעִיר־עִזִּים אֶחָד
לְחַטָּאת: וּלְזֶבַח הַשְּׁלָמִים בָּקָר שְׁנַיִם אֵילִם חֲמִשָּׁה עַתֻּדִים חֲמִשָּׁה כְּבָשִׂים
בְּנֵי־שָׁנָה חֲמִשָּׁה זֶה קָרְבַּן אֶלְיָסָף בֶּן־דְּעוּאֵל:

קריאה ליום השישי של חנוכה וראש חודש
SIXTH DAY OF ḤANUKKA AND ROSH ḤODESH

The sixth day is ראש חודש טבת*. Two* ספרי תורה *are taken out of the* ארון קודש*. From the first, read the* קריאת התורה *for* ראש חודש *(page 1111), from the second, read* בַּיּוֹם הַשִּׁשִּׁי*:*

במדבר ז:מב–מז בַּיּוֹם הַשִּׁשִּׁי נָשִׂיא לִבְנֵי גָד אֶלְיָסָף בֶּן־דְּעוּאֵל: קָרְבָּנוֹ קַעֲרַת־כֶּסֶף אַחַת שְׁלֹשִׁים וּמֵאָה מִשְׁקָלָהּ מִזְרָק אֶחָד כֶּסֶף שִׁבְעִים שֶׁקֶל בְּשֶׁקֶל הַקֹּדֶשׁ שְׁנֵיהֶם ׀ מְלֵאִים סֹלֶת בְּלוּלָה בַשֶּׁמֶן לְמִנְחָה: כַּף אַחַת עֲשָׂרָה זָהָב מְלֵאָה קְטֹרֶת: פַּר אֶחָד בֶּן־בָּקָר אַיִל אֶחָד כֶּבֶשׂ־אֶחָד בֶּן־שְׁנָתוֹ לְעֹלָה: שְׂעִיר־עִזִּים אֶחָד לְחַטָּאת: וּלְזֶבַח הַשְּׁלָמִים בָּקָר שְׁנַיִם אֵילִם חֲמִשָּׁה עַתֻּדִים חֲמִשָּׁה כְּבָשִׂים בְּנֵי־שָׁנָה חֲמִשָּׁה זֶה קָרְבַּן אֶלְיָסָף בֶּן־דְּעוּאֵל:

קריאה ליום השביעי של חנוכה וראש חודש
SEVENTH DAY OF ḤANUKKA AND ROSH ḤODESH

If the seventh day is also ראש חודש*, then two* ספרי תורה *are taken out of the* ארון קודש*. From the first, read the* קריאת התורה *for* ראש חודש *(page 1111), from the second, read* בַּיּוֹם הַשְּׁבִיעִי*:*

במדבר ז:מח–נג בַּיּוֹם הַשְּׁבִיעִי נָשִׂיא לִבְנֵי אֶפְרָיִם אֱלִישָׁמָע בֶּן־עַמִּיהוּד: קָרְבָּנוֹ קַעֲרַת־כֶּסֶף אַחַת שְׁלֹשִׁים וּמֵאָה מִשְׁקָלָהּ מִזְרָק אֶחָד כֶּסֶף שִׁבְעִים שֶׁקֶל בְּשֶׁקֶל הַקֹּדֶשׁ שְׁנֵיהֶם ׀ מְלֵאִים סֹלֶת בְּלוּלָה בַשֶּׁמֶן לְמִנְחָה: כַּף אַחַת עֲשָׂרָה זָהָב מְלֵאָה קְטֹרֶת: פַּר אֶחָד בֶּן־בָּקָר אַיִל אֶחָד כֶּבֶשׂ־אֶחָד בֶּן־שְׁנָתוֹ לְעֹלָה: שְׂעִיר־עִזִּים אֶחָד לְחַטָּאת: וּלְזֶבַח הַשְּׁלָמִים בָּקָר שְׁנַיִם אֵילִם חֲמִשָּׁה עַתֻּדִים חֲמִשָּׁה כְּבָשִׂים בְּנֵי־שָׁנָה חֲמִשָּׁה זֶה קָרְבַּן אֱלִישָׁמָע בֶּן־עַמִּיהוּד:

קריאה ליום השביעי של חנוכה SEVENTH DAY OF ḤANUKKA

If the seventh day is not ראש חודש*, then read as below. In* ארץ ישראל*, for* שלישי *repeat the first paragraph:* בַּיּוֹם הַשְּׁבִיעִי *until* אֱלִישָׁמָע בֶּן־עַמִּיהוּד*.*

במדבר ז:מח–נט בַּיּוֹם הַשְּׁבִיעִי נָשִׂיא לִבְנֵי אֶפְרָיִם אֱלִישָׁמָע בֶּן־עַמִּיהוּד: קָרְבָּנוֹ קַעֲרַת־כֶּסֶף אַחַת שְׁלֹשִׁים וּמֵאָה מִשְׁקָלָהּ מִזְרָק אֶחָד כֶּסֶף שִׁבְעִים שֶׁקֶל בְּשֶׁקֶל הַקֹּדֶשׁ שְׁנֵיהֶם ׀ מְלֵאִים סֹלֶת בְּלוּלָה בַשֶּׁמֶן לְמִנְחָה: כַּף אַחַת עֲשָׂרָה זָהָב מְלֵאָה קְטֹרֶת: *פַּר אֶחָד בֶּן־בָּקָר אַיִל אֶחָד כֶּבֶשׂ־אֶחָד בֶּן־שְׁנָתוֹ לְעֹלָה: שְׂעִיר־ לוי

עִזִּים אֶחָד לְחַטָּאת: וּלְזֶבַח הַשְּׁלָמִים בָּקָר שְׁנַיִם אֵילִם חֲמִשָּׁה עַתֻּדִים
חֲמִשָּׁה כְּבָשִׂים בְּנֵי־שָׁנָה חֲמִשָּׁה זֶה קָרְבַּן אֱלִישָׁמָע בֶּן־עַמִּיהוּד:

ישראל בַּיּוֹם הַשְּׁמִינִי נָשִׂיא לִבְנֵי מְנַשֶּׁה גַּמְלִיאֵל בֶּן־פְּדָהצוּר: קָרְבָּנוֹ קַעֲרַת־כֶּסֶף
אַחַת שְׁלֹשִׁים וּמֵאָה מִשְׁקָלָהּ מִזְרָק אֶחָד כֶּסֶף שִׁבְעִים שֶׁקֶל בְּשֶׁקֶל הַקֹּדֶשׁ
שְׁנֵיהֶם ׀ מְלֵאִים סֹלֶת בְּלוּלָה בַשֶּׁמֶן לְמִנְחָה: כַּף אַחַת עֲשָׂרָה זָהָב מְלֵאָה
קְטֹרֶת: פַּר אֶחָד בֶּן־בָּקָר אַיִל אֶחָד כֶּבֶשׂ־אֶחָד בֶּן־שְׁנָתוֹ לְעֹלָה: שְׂעִיר־עִזִּים
אֶחָד לְחַטָּאת: וּלְזֶבַח הַשְּׁלָמִים בָּקָר שְׁנַיִם אֵילִם חֲמִשָּׁה עַתֻּדִים חֲמִשָּׁה
כְּבָשִׂים בְּנֵי־שָׁנָה חֲמִשָּׁה זֶה קָרְבַּן גַּמְלִיאֵל בֶּן־פְּדָהצוּר:

קריאה ליום השמיני של חנוכה
EIGHTH DAY OF HANUKKA

במדבר ז:נד–ח:ד

בַּיּוֹם הַשְּׁמִינִי נָשִׂיא לִבְנֵי מְנַשֶּׁה גַּמְלִיאֵל בֶּן־פְּדָהצוּר: קָרְבָּנוֹ קַעֲרַת־כֶּסֶף
אַחַת שְׁלֹשִׁים וּמֵאָה מִשְׁקָלָהּ מִזְרָק אֶחָד כֶּסֶף שִׁבְעִים שֶׁקֶל בְּשֶׁקֶל הַקֹּדֶשׁ
שְׁנֵיהֶם ׀ מְלֵאִים סֹלֶת בְּלוּלָה בַשֶּׁמֶן לְמִנְחָה: כַּף אַחַת עֲשָׂרָה זָהָב מְלֵאָה
לוי קְטֹרֶת: *פַּר אֶחָד בֶּן־בָּקָר אַיִל אֶחָד כֶּבֶשׂ־אֶחָד בֶּן־שְׁנָתוֹ לְעֹלָה: שְׂעִיר־עִזִּים
אֶחָד לְחַטָּאת: וּלְזֶבַח הַשְּׁלָמִים בָּקָר שְׁנַיִם אֵילִם חֲמִשָּׁה עַתֻּדִים חֲמִשָּׁה
כְּבָשִׂים בְּנֵי־שָׁנָה חֲמִשָּׁה זֶה קָרְבַּן גַּמְלִיאֵל בֶּן־פְּדָהצוּר:

ישראל בַּיּוֹם הַתְּשִׁיעִי נָשִׂיא לִבְנֵי בִנְיָמִן אֲבִידָן בֶּן־גִּדְעֹנִי: קָרְבָּנוֹ קַעֲרַת־כֶּסֶף אַחַת
שְׁלֹשִׁים וּמֵאָה מִשְׁקָלָהּ מִזְרָק אֶחָד כֶּסֶף שִׁבְעִים שֶׁקֶל בְּשֶׁקֶל הַקֹּדֶשׁ שְׁנֵיהֶם ׀
מְלֵאִים סֹלֶת בְּלוּלָה בַשֶּׁמֶן לְמִנְחָה: כַּף אַחַת עֲשָׂרָה זָהָב מְלֵאָה קְטֹרֶת:
פַּר אֶחָד בֶּן־בָּקָר אַיִל אֶחָד כֶּבֶשׂ־אֶחָד בֶּן־שְׁנָתוֹ לְעֹלָה: שְׂעִיר־עִזִּים אֶחָד
לְחַטָּאת: וּלְזֶבַח הַשְּׁלָמִים בָּקָר שְׁנַיִם אֵילִם חֲמִשָּׁה עַתֻּדִים חֲמִשָּׁה כְּבָשִׂים
בְּנֵי־שָׁנָה חֲמִשָּׁה זֶה קָרְבַּן אֲבִידָן בֶּן־גִּדְעֹנִי:

בַּיּוֹם הָעֲשִׂירִי נָשִׂיא לִבְנֵי דָן אֲחִיעֶזֶר בֶּן־עַמִּישַׁדָּי: קָרְבָּנוֹ קַעֲרַת־כֶּסֶף אַחַת
שְׁלֹשִׁים וּמֵאָה מִשְׁקָלָהּ מִזְרָק אֶחָד כֶּסֶף שִׁבְעִים שֶׁקֶל בְּשֶׁקֶל הַקֹּדֶשׁ שְׁנֵיהֶם ׀
מְלֵאִים סֹלֶת בְּלוּלָה בַשֶּׁמֶן לְמִנְחָה: כַּף אַחַת עֲשָׂרָה זָהָב מְלֵאָה קְטֹרֶת:
פַּר אֶחָד בֶּן־בָּקָר אַיִל אֶחָד כֶּבֶשׂ־אֶחָד בֶּן־שְׁנָתוֹ לְעֹלָה: שְׂעִיר־עִזִּים אֶחָד
לְחַטָּאת: וּלְזֶבַח הַשְּׁלָמִים בָּקָר שְׁנַיִם אֵילִם חֲמִשָּׁה עַתֻּדִים חֲמִשָּׁה כְּבָשִׂים
בְּנֵי־שָׁנָה חֲמִשָּׁה זֶה קָרְבַּן אֲחִיעֶזֶר בֶּן־עַמִּישַׁדָּי:

בְּיוֹם֙ עַשְׁתֵּ֣י עָשָׂ֣ר י֔וֹם נָשִׂ֖יא לִבְנֵ֣י אֲשֵׁ֑ר פַּגְעִיאֵ֖ל בֶּן־עָכְרָֽן׃ קָרְבָּנ֞וֹ קַעֲרַת־כֶּ֣סֶף
אַחַ֗ת שְׁלֹשִׁ֣ים וּמֵאָה֮ מִשְׁקָלָהּ֒ מִזְרָ֤ק אֶחָד֙ כֶּ֔סֶף שִׁבְעִ֥ים שֶׁ֖קֶל בְּשֶׁ֣קֶל הַקֹּ֑דֶשׁ
שְׁנֵיהֶ֣ם ׀ מְלֵאִ֗ים סֹ֛לֶת בְּלוּלָ֥ה בַשֶּׁ֖מֶן לְמִנְחָֽה׃ כַּ֚ף אַחַ֣ת עֲשָׂרָ֣ה זָהָ֔ב מְלֵאָ֖ה
קְטֹֽרֶת׃ פַּ֣ר אֶחָ֞ד בֶּן־בָּקָ֗ר אַ֧יִל אֶחָ֛ד כֶּֽבֶשׂ־אֶחָ֥ד בֶּן־שְׁנָת֖וֹ לְעֹלָֽה׃ שְׂעִיר־עִזִּ֥ים
אֶחָ֖ד לְחַטָּֽאת׃ וּלְזֶ֣בַח הַשְּׁלָמִים֮ בָּקָ֣ר שְׁנַ֒יִם֒ אֵילִ֤ם חֲמִשָּׁה֙ עַתֻּדִ֣ים חֲמִשָּׁ֔ה
כְּבָשִׂ֥ים בְּנֵֽי־שָׁנָ֖ה חֲמִשָּׁ֑ה זֶ֛ה קָרְבַּ֥ן פַּגְעִיאֵ֖ל בֶּן־עָכְרָֽן׃

בְּיוֹם֙ שְׁנֵ֣ים עָשָׂ֣ר י֔וֹם נָשִׂ֖יא לִבְנֵ֣י נַפְתָּלִ֑י אֲחִירַ֖ע בֶּן־עֵינָֽן׃ קָרְבָּנ֞וֹ קַעֲרַת־כֶּ֣סֶף
אַחַ֗ת שְׁלֹשִׁ֣ים וּמֵאָה֮ מִשְׁקָלָהּ֒ מִזְרָ֤ק אֶחָד֙ כֶּ֔סֶף שִׁבְעִ֥ים שֶׁ֖קֶל בְּשֶׁ֣קֶל הַקֹּ֑דֶשׁ
שְׁנֵיהֶ֣ם ׀ מְלֵאִ֗ים סֹ֛לֶת בְּלוּלָ֥ה בַשֶּׁ֖מֶן לְמִנְחָֽה׃ כַּ֚ף אַחַ֣ת עֲשָׂרָ֣ה זָהָ֔ב מְלֵאָ֖ה
קְטֹֽרֶת׃ פַּ֣ר אֶחָ֞ד בֶּן־בָּקָ֗ר אַ֧יִל אֶחָ֛ד כֶּֽבֶשׂ־אֶחָ֥ד בֶּן־שְׁנָת֖וֹ לְעֹלָֽה׃ שְׂעִיר־עִזִּ֥ים
אֶחָ֖ד לְחַטָּֽאת׃ וּלְזֶ֣בַח הַשְּׁלָמִים֮ בָּקָ֣ר שְׁנַ֒יִם֒ אֵילִ֤ם חֲמִשָּׁה֙ עַתֻּדִ֣ים חֲמִשָּׁ֔ה
כְּבָשִׂ֥ים בְּנֵֽי־שָׁנָ֖ה חֲמִשָּׁ֑ה זֶ֛ה קָרְבַּ֥ן אֲחִירַ֖ע בֶּן־עֵינָֽן׃

זֹ֣את ׀ חֲנֻכַּ֣ת הַמִּזְבֵּ֗חַ בְּי֚וֹם הִמָּשַׁ֣ח אֹת֔וֹ מֵאֵ֖ת נְשִׂיאֵ֣י יִשְׂרָאֵ֑ל קַעֲרֹ֨ת כֶּ֜סֶף
שְׁתֵּ֣ים עֶשְׂרֵ֗ה מִֽזְרְקֵי־כֶ֙סֶף֙ שְׁנֵ֣ים עָשָׂ֔ר כַּפּ֥וֹת זָהָ֖ב שְׁתֵּ֥ים עֶשְׂרֵֽה׃ שְׁלֹשִׁ֣ים
וּמֵאָ֗ה הַקְּעָרָ֤ה הָֽאַחַת֙ כֶּ֔סֶף וְשִׁבְעִ֖ים הַמִּזְרָ֣ק הָאֶחָ֑ד כֹּ֚ל כֶּ֣סֶף הַכֵּלִ֔ים אַלְפַּ֥יִם
וְאַרְבַּע־מֵא֖וֹת בְּשֶׁ֥קֶל הַקֹּֽדֶשׁ׃ כַּפּ֨וֹת זָהָ֤ב שְׁתֵּים־עֶשְׂרֵה֙ מְלֵאֹ֣ת קְטֹ֔רֶת
עֲשָׂרָ֧ה עֲשָׂרָ֛ה הַכַּ֖ף בְּשֶׁ֣קֶל הַקֹּ֑דֶשׁ כָּל־זְהַ֥ב הַכַּפּ֖וֹת עֶשְׂרִ֥ים וּמֵאָֽה׃ כָּל־
הַבָּקָ֨ר לָעֹלָ֜ה שְׁנֵ֧ים עָשָׂ֣ר פָּרִ֗ים אֵילִ֤ם שְׁנֵים־עָשָׂר֙ כְּבָשִׂ֧ים בְּנֵֽי־שָׁנָ֛ה שְׁנֵ֥ים
עָשָׂ֖ר וּמִנְחָתָ֑ם וּשְׂעִירֵ֥י עִזִּ֛ים שְׁנֵ֥ים עָשָׂ֖ר לְחַטָּֽאת׃ וְכֹ֞ל בְּקַ֣ר ׀ זֶ֣בַח הַשְּׁלָמִ֗ים
עֶשְׂרִ֣ים וְאַרְבָּעָה֮ פָּרִים֒ אֵילִ֤ם שִׁשִּׁים֙ עַתֻּדִ֣ים שִׁשִּׁ֔ים כְּבָשִׂ֥ים בְּנֵֽי־שָׁנָ֖ה שִׁשִּׁ֑ים
זֹ֚את חֲנֻכַּ֣ת הַמִּזְבֵּ֔חַ אַחֲרֵ֖י הִמָּשַׁ֥ח אֹתֽוֹ׃ וּבְבֹ֨א מֹשֶׁ֜ה אֶל־אֹ֣הֶל מוֹעֵד֮ לְדַבֵּ֣ר
אִתּוֹ֒ וַיִּשְׁמַ֞ע אֶת־הַקּ֗וֹל מִדַּבֵּ֣ר אֵלָ֔יו מֵעַ֤ל הַכַּפֹּ֙רֶת֙ אֲשֶׁר֙ עַל־אֲרֹ֣ן הָעֵדֻ֔ת מִבֵּ֖ין
שְׁנֵ֣י הַכְּרֻבִ֑ים וַיְדַבֵּ֖ר אֵלָֽיו׃

וַיְדַבֵּ֥ר יְהוָ֖ה אֶל־מֹשֶׁ֥ה לֵּאמֹֽר׃ דַּבֵּר֙ אֶֽל־אַהֲרֹ֔ן וְאָמַרְתָּ֖ אֵלָ֑יו בְּהַעֲלֹֽתְךָ֙ אֶת־
הַנֵּרֹ֔ת אֶל־מוּל֙ פְּנֵ֣י הַמְּנוֹרָ֔ה יָאִ֖ירוּ שִׁבְעַ֥ת הַנֵּרֽוֹת׃ וַיַּ֤עַשׂ כֵּן֙ אַהֲרֹ֔ן אֶל־מוּל֙
פְּנֵ֣י הַמְּנוֹרָ֔ה הֶעֱלָ֖ה נֵרֹתֶ֑יהָ כַּֽאֲשֶׁ֛ר צִוָּ֥ה יְהוָ֖ה אֶת־מֹשֶֽׁה׃ וְזֶ֨ה מַעֲשֵׂ֤ה הַמְּנֹרָה֙
מִקְשָׁ֣ה זָהָ֔ב עַד־יְרֵכָ֥הּ עַד־פִּרְחָ֖הּ מִקְשָׁ֣ה הִ֑וא כַּמַּרְאֶ֗ה אֲשֶׁ֨ר הֶרְאָ֤ה יְהוָה֙
אֶת־מֹשֶׁ֔ה כֵּ֥ן עָשָׂ֖ה אֶת־הַמְּנֹרָֽה׃

קריאה לפורים PURIM

שמות יז:ח–טז וַיָּבֹא עֲמָלֵק וַיִּלָּחֶם עִם־יִשְׂרָאֵל בִּרְפִידִם: וַיֹּאמֶר מֹשֶׁה אֶל־יְהוֹשֻׁעַ בְּחַר־
לָנוּ אֲנָשִׁים וְצֵא הִלָּחֵם בַּעֲמָלֵק מָחָר אָנֹכִי נִצָּב עַל־רֹאשׁ הַגִּבְעָה וּמַטֵּה
הָאֱלֹהִים בְּיָדִי: וַיַּעַשׂ יְהוֹשֻׁעַ כַּאֲשֶׁר אָמַר־לוֹ מֹשֶׁה לְהִלָּחֵם בַּעֲמָלֵק
לוי וּמֹשֶׁה אַהֲרֹן וְחוּר עָלוּ רֹאשׁ הַגִּבְעָה: *וְהָיָה כַּאֲשֶׁר יָרִים מֹשֶׁה יָדוֹ וְגָבַר
יִשְׂרָאֵל וְכַאֲשֶׁר יָנִיחַ יָדוֹ וְגָבַר עֲמָלֵק: וִידֵי מֹשֶׁה כְּבֵדִים וַיִּקְחוּ־אֶבֶן וַיָּשִׂימוּ
תַחְתָּיו וַיֵּשֶׁב עָלֶיהָ וְאַהֲרֹן וְחוּר תָּמְכוּ בְיָדָיו מִזֶּה אֶחָד וּמִזֶּה אֶחָד וַיְהִי
יָדָיו אֱמוּנָה עַד־בֹּא הַשָּׁמֶשׁ: וַיַּחֲלֹשׁ יְהוֹשֻׁעַ אֶת־עֲמָלֵק וְאֶת־עַמּוֹ לְפִי־
חָרֶב:

ישראל וַיֹּאמֶר יְהוָה אֶל־מֹשֶׁה כְּתֹב זֹאת זִכָּרוֹן בַּסֵּפֶר וְשִׂים בְּאָזְנֵי יְהוֹשֻׁעַ כִּי־מָחֹה
אֶמְחֶה אֶת־זֵכֶר עֲמָלֵק מִתַּחַת הַשָּׁמָיִם: וַיִּבֶן מֹשֶׁה מִזְבֵּחַ וַיִּקְרָא שְׁמוֹ יְהוָה ׀
נִסִּי: וַיֹּאמֶר כִּי־יָד עַל־כֵּס יָהּ מִלְחָמָה לַיהוָה בַּעֲמָלֵק מִדֹּר דֹּר:

קריאת התורה לשלוש רגלים

DIRECTORY OF TORAH PORTIONS FOR PESAḤ, SHAVUOT AND SUKKOT

Day	*Torah portion*	*Maftir*	*Haftara*
First day of Pesaḥ	א1123	1125	1125
Second day of Pesaḥ (outside Israel)	1127	1125	1129
First day of Ḥol HaMo'ed Pesaḥ	א1129		
Second day of Ḥol HaMo'ed Pesaḥ	א1131		
Third day of Ḥol HaMo'ed Pesaḥ	1133		
Fourth day of Ḥol HaMo'ed Pesaḥ	ב1133		
Shabbat Ḥol HaMo'ed Pesaḥ	1135	1135	1137
Seventh day of Pesaḥ	א1137	1141	1141
Last day of Pesaḥ (outside Israel)	1143	1141	א1145
First day of Shavuot	1147	1149	א1149
Second day of Shavuot (outside Israel)	1143	1149	1151
First day of Sukkot	1127	1153	1153
Second day of Sukkot (outside Israel)	1127	1153	1155
First day of Ḥol HaMo'ed Sukkot	א1155		
Second day of Ḥol HaMo'ed Sukkot	1157		
Third day of Ḥol HaMo'ed Sukkot	א1157		
Fourth day of Ḥol HaMo'ed Sukkot	א1157		
Fifth day of Ḥol HaMo'ed Sukkot (in Israel)	1159		
Shabbat Ḥol HaMo'ed Sukkot	1135	א1155–1159	א1159
Hoshana Raba	1159		
Shemini Atzeret (outside Israel)	1143	1161	1161
Simḥat Torah	א1161	1161	1167

TORAH READING FOR THE FIRST DAY OF PESAḤ

Moses called for all of the elders of Israel and told them, "Select and take lambs for yourselves, one for each family, and slaughter them as a Pesaḥ offering. Then take a bunch of hyssop, dip it in the blood that is on the threshold and apply of that blood to the lintel and the two side-posts; no man may exit the door of his house until morning. And the LORD shall come to strike Egypt; when He sees the blood upon the lintel and the two side-posts, He will pass over the opening and will not allow the Destroyer to come into your houses to strike you. You must observe this as a statute for you and for your children forever. *And when you enter the land which the LORD shall give you as He promised, you shall observe this rite. And if your children should say to you: 'What is this service to you?' You shall say: 'It is a Pesaḥ offering for the LORD, for He passed over the houses of the children of Israel in Egypt while He struck the Egyptians, but saved those in our homes'" – and the people bowed and prostrated themselves. So the children of Israel went and did just as the LORD had commanded Moses and Aaron; so it was done. *Ex. 12:21–51* LEVI

And when midnight came, the LORD slew every firstborn in the land of Egypt: from the firstborn of Pharaoh sitting on his throne to the firstborn of the captive in prison, and the firstborns of all their livestock. And Pharaoh arose at night, he and all of his servants and all of Egypt; and there was a great cry in Egypt, for no house was without one dead. So he called for Moses and Aaron at night, and said: "Rise up, leave the midst of my people, you and the children of Israel, and go worship the LORD as you said! Take both your sheep and your cattle, as you requested, and go – and you shall also bless me." *All of Egypt urged the people, making haste to expel them from their land – for they said, "We are all dying!" So the people carried their dough before it was leavened, their kneading-troughs SHELISHI (*Shabbat:* REVI'I)

Note the emphasis on children in this passage. Ancient Egypt and ancient Israel were two civilizations that asked the fundamental question: how do we

קריאה ליום הראשון של פסח

וַיִּקְרָא מֹשֶׁה לְכׇל־זִקְנֵי יִשְׂרָאֵל וַיֹּאמֶר אֲלֵהֶם מִשְׁכוּ וּקְחוּ לָכֶם צֹאן שמות יב:כא–נא
לְמִשְׁפְּחֹתֵיכֶם וְשַׁחֲטוּ הַפָּסַח: וּלְקַחְתֶּם אֲגֻדַּת אֵזוֹב וּטְבַלְתֶּם בַּדָּם אֲשֶׁר־
בַּסַּף וְהִגַּעְתֶּם אֶל־הַמַּשְׁקוֹף וְאֶל־שְׁתֵּי הַמְּזוּזֹת מִן־הַדָּם אֲשֶׁר בַּסָּף וְאַתֶּם
לֹא תֵצְאוּ אִישׁ מִפֶּתַח־בֵּיתוֹ עַד־בֹּקֶר: וְעָבַר יהוה לִנְגֹּף אֶת־מִצְרַיִם וְרָאָה
אֶת־הַדָּם עַל־הַמַּשְׁקוֹף וְעַל שְׁתֵּי הַמְּזוּזֹת וּפָסַח יהוה עַל־הַפֶּתַח וְלֹא
יִתֵּן הַמַּשְׁחִית לָבֹא אֶל־בָּתֵּיכֶם לִנְגֹּף: וּשְׁמַרְתֶּם אֶת־הַדָּבָר הַזֶּה לְחׇק־
לְךָ וּלְבָנֶיךָ עַד־עוֹלָם: *וְהָיָה כִּי־תָבֹאוּ אֶל־הָאָרֶץ אֲשֶׁר יִתֵּן יהוה לָכֶם לוי
כַּאֲשֶׁר דִּבֵּר וּשְׁמַרְתֶּם אֶת־הָעֲבֹדָה הַזֹּאת: וְהָיָה כִּי־יֹאמְרוּ אֲלֵיכֶם בְּנֵיכֶם
מָה הָעֲבֹדָה הַזֹּאת לָכֶם: וַאֲמַרְתֶּם זֶבַח־פֶּסַח הוּא לַיהוה אֲשֶׁר פָּסַח עַל־
בָּתֵּי בְנֵי־יִשְׂרָאֵל בְּמִצְרַיִם בְּנׇגְפּוֹ אֶת־מִצְרַיִם וְאֶת־בָּתֵּינוּ הִצִּיל וַיִּקֹּד הָעָם
וַיִּשְׁתַּחֲווּ: וַיֵּלְכוּ וַיַּעֲשׂוּ בְּנֵי יִשְׂרָאֵל כַּאֲשֶׁר צִוָּה יהוה אֶת־מֹשֶׁה וְאַהֲרֹן כֵּן
עָשׂוּ: *וַיְהִי ׀ בַּחֲצִי הַלַּיְלָה וַיהוה הִכָּה כׇל־בְּכוֹר בְּאֶרֶץ מִצְרַיִם שלישי
מִבְּכֹר פַּרְעֹה הַיֹּשֵׁב עַל־כִּסְאוֹ עַד בְּכוֹר הַשְּׁבִי אֲשֶׁר בְּבֵית הַבּוֹר וְכֹל בְּכוֹר
בְּהֵמָה: וַיָּקׇם פַּרְעֹה לַיְלָה הוּא וְכׇל־עֲבָדָיו וְכׇל־מִצְרַיִם וַתְּהִי צְעָקָה גְדֹלָה
בְּמִצְרָיִם כִּי־אֵין בַּיִת אֲשֶׁר אֵין־שָׁם מֵת: וַיִּקְרָא לְמֹשֶׁה וּלְאַהֲרֹן לַיְלָה
וַיֹּאמֶר קוּמוּ צְּאוּ מִתּוֹךְ עַמִּי גַּם־אַתֶּם גַּם־בְּנֵי יִשְׂרָאֵל וּלְכוּ עִבְדוּ אֶת־
יהוה כְּדַבֶּרְכֶם: גַּם־צֹאנְכֶם גַּם־בְּקַרְכֶם קְחוּ כַּאֲשֶׁר דִּבַּרְתֶּם וָלֵכוּ וּבֵרַכְתֶּם
גַּם־אֹתִי: *וַתֶּחֱזַק מִצְרַיִם עַל־הָעָם לְמַהֵר לְשַׁלְּחָם מִן־הָאָרֶץ כִּי אָמְרוּ (בשבת רביעי)
כֻּלָּנוּ מֵתִים: וַיִּשָּׂא הָעָם אֶת־בְּצֵקוֹ טֶרֶם יֶחְמָץ מִשְׁאֲרֹתָם צְרֻרֹת בְּשִׂמְלֹתָם

TORAH READING FOR THE FIRST DAY OF PESAH

This is Moses' address prior to the exodus, preparing the people for what they must do on their last night in captivity. They were to offer a sacrifice, sprinkling its blood on their doorposts. The Israelites had to perform an act of spiritual liberation as preparation for their physical/political liberation. By engaging in an act foreign to their Egyptian neighbors, and by being willing to signal the fact on the doorposts of their houses, they showed they were unafraid to be different: to take a risk for the sake of God.

bound up in their clothes, slung over their shoulders. And the children of Israel did as Moses commanded: they asked the Egyptians for silver vessels, golden vessels, and clothing. And the LORD caused the people to find favor in the eyes of the Egyptians – they let them have what they asked, and [thus the Israelites] depleted Egypt.

The children of Israel then traveled from Rameses to Sukkot – about six hundred thousand men on foot, as well as children. A mixed multitude went up with them as well, and sheep and cattle, herds of great number. They baked the dough they had taken out of Egypt, matza rounds, for they had not risen; for they were expelled from Egypt and could not delay, and they had not prepared any provisions for themselves. The children of Israel had dwelled in Egypt for four hundred and thirty years. And when four hundred and thirty years came to an end, on that very day, the LORD's hosts left Egypt. It was a night of guarding to the LORD, so as to bring them out of Egypt – this night is therefore safeguarded for the LORD, by all of the children of Israel for all generations. REVI'I (*Shabbat:* ḤAMISHI)

The LORD spoke to Moses and Aaron: These are the laws of the Pesaḥ offering: no stranger shall eat of it. Every man's slave that is bought for money must first be circumcised; after that he may eat of it. A sojourner or hired laborer may not eat of it. It must be eaten in one house – you may not take any of its meat outside the house, and you may not break any of its bones. All the community of Israel shall observe this. *If a proselyte lives among you and brings a Pesaḥ offering to the LORD, he must circumcise all of his males – then he may come and offer it, just as one home-born in your land – no one uncircumcised may partake of it. The same law shall apply to one born in your land and to the proselyte who dwells among you. All of the children of Israel did as the LORD commanded Moses and Aaron; that is what they did. ḤAMISHI (*Shabbat:* SHISHI) (*Shabbat:* SHEVI'I)

It was on that very day that the LORD brought the children of Israel out of the land of Egypt, in all their hosts.

עַל־שִׁכְמָם: וּבְנֵי־יִשְׂרָאֵל עָשׂוּ כִּדְבַר מֹשֶׁה וַיִּשְׁאֲלוּ מִמִּצְרַיִם כְּלֵי־כֶסֶף וּכְלֵי
זָהָב וּשְׂמָלֹת: וַיהֹוָה נָתַן אֶת־חֵן הָעָם בְּעֵינֵי מִצְרַיִם וַיַּשְׁאִלוּם וַיְנַצְּלוּ אֶת־
מִצְרָיִם:

רביעי
(בשבת
חמישי)

וַיִּסְעוּ בְנֵי־יִשְׂרָאֵל מֵרַעְמְסֵס סֻכֹּתָה כְּשֵׁשׁ־מֵאוֹת אֶלֶף רַגְלִי הַגְּבָרִים לְבַד
מִטָּף: וְגַם־עֵרֶב רַב עָלָה אִתָּם וְצֹאן וּבָקָר מִקְנֶה כָּבֵד מְאֹד: וַיֹּאפוּ אֶת־
הַבָּצֵק אֲשֶׁר הוֹצִיאוּ מִמִּצְרַיִם עֻגֹת מַצּוֹת כִּי לֹא חָמֵץ כִּי־גֹרְשׁוּ מִמִּצְרַיִם וְלֹא
יָכְלוּ לְהִתְמַהְמֵהַּ וְגַם־צֵדָה לֹא־עָשׂוּ לָהֶם: וּמוֹשַׁב בְּנֵי יִשְׂרָאֵל אֲשֶׁר יָשְׁבוּ
בְּמִצְרָיִם שְׁלֹשִׁים שָׁנָה וְאַרְבַּע מֵאוֹת שָׁנָה: וַיְהִי מִקֵּץ שְׁלֹשִׁים שָׁנָה וְאַרְבַּע
מֵאוֹת שָׁנָה וַיְהִי בְּעֶצֶם הַיּוֹם הַזֶּה יָצְאוּ כָּל־צִבְאוֹת יְהֹוָה מֵאֶרֶץ מִצְרָיִם:
לֵיל שִׁמֻּרִים הוּא לַיהֹוָה לְהוֹצִיאָם מֵאֶרֶץ מִצְרָיִם הוּא־הַלַּיְלָה הַזֶּה לַיהֹוָה
שִׁמֻּרִים לְכָל־בְּנֵי יִשְׂרָאֵל לְדֹרֹתָם:

חמישי
(בשבת
שישי)

וַיֹּאמֶר יְהֹוָה אֶל־מֹשֶׁה וְאַהֲרֹן זֹאת חֻקַּת הַפָּסַח כָּל־בֶּן־נֵכָר לֹא־יֹאכַל בּוֹ:
וְכָל־עֶבֶד אִישׁ מִקְנַת־כָּסֶף וּמַלְתָּה אֹתוֹ אָז יֹאכַל בּוֹ: תּוֹשָׁב וְשָׂכִיר לֹא־
יֹאכַל בּוֹ: בְּבַיִת אֶחָד יֵאָכֵל לֹא־תוֹצִיא מִן־הַבַּיִת מִן־הַבָּשָׂר חוּצָה וְעֶצֶם
לֹא תִשְׁבְּרוּ־בוֹ: כָּל־עֲדַת יִשְׂרָאֵל יַעֲשׂוּ אֹתוֹ: וְכִי־יָגוּר אִתְּךָ גֵּר וְעָשָׂה פֶסַח
לַיהֹוָה הִמּוֹל לוֹ כָל־זָכָר וְאָז יִקְרַב לַעֲשֹׂתוֹ וְהָיָה כְּאֶזְרַח הָאָרֶץ וְכָל־עָרֵל
לֹא־יֹאכַל בּוֹ: תּוֹרָה אַחַת יִהְיֶה לָאֶזְרָח וְלַגֵּר הַגָּר בְּתוֹכְכֶם: וַיַּעֲשׂוּ כָּל־בְּנֵי
יִשְׂרָאֵל כַּאֲשֶׁר צִוָּה יְהֹוָה אֶת־מֹשֶׁה וְאֶת־אַהֲרֹן כֵּן עָשׂוּ: וַיְהִי בְּעֶצֶם
הַיּוֹם הַזֶּה הוֹצִיא יְהֹוָה אֶת־בְּנֵי יִשְׂרָאֵל מֵאֶרֶץ מִצְרַיִם עַל־צִבְאֹתָם:

(בשבת
שביעי)

achieve immortality? How do we ensure that something of us lives on? They
gave opposite answers. The Egyptians built pyramids, monuments in stone
that would outlast the sands and winds of time. Moses took a quite different
path. We become immortal by engraving our values on the hearts of their
children, and they on theirs, and so on to the end of time. Israel became the
first people in history to predicate its survival on education – and it began
here, in Moses' words shortly before the exodus. Already he is asking the
Israelites to think not just about tomorrow but about the distant future and
the education of their children.

MAFTIR FOR THE FIRST AND SECOND DAY OF PESAḤ

After Half Kaddish (page 512), the Maftir is read from the second Torah scroll on both the first and second days of Pesaḥ.

On the fourteenth day of the first month there shall be a Pesaḥ offering to the LORD. And on the fifteenth day of this month there shall be a festival: seven days unleavened bread shall be eaten. On the first day there shall be a sacred assembly: you shall do no laborious work. And you shall bring an offering consumed by fire, a burnt-offering to the LORD: two young bullocks, one ram, and seven yearling male lambs; they shall be to you unblemished. And you shall perform their meal-offerings, fine flour mixed with oil, three-tenths of an ephah for each bull, two-tenths of an ephah for the ram; and one-tenth of an ephah for each of the seven lambs; and one goat for a sin-offering, to make atonement for you. All this aside from the morning burnt-offering, the daily offering; You shall offer all of these as food, on each of the seven days, a burnt-offering by fire of pleasing aroma to the LORD, along with the regular daily offering and its libation. On the seventh day there shall be a sacred assembly: you shall do no laborious work. *Num. 28:16–25*

HAFTARA FOR THE FIRST DAY OF PESAḤ

*In some congregations, the Haftara begins at "At that time" below (at the *).*

Joshua said to the people, "Sanctify yourselves, for tomorrow the LORD shall work wonders in your midst." And Joshua said to the priests, "Lift up the Ark of the Covenant and walk ahead of the people" – and so they walked out ahead of the people. *Josh. 3:5–7*

The LORD said to Joshua, "On this day I shall begin to exalt you in the eyes of all Israel, to have them know that just as I was with Moses, so will I be with you."

*At that time, the LORD said to Joshua: make knives of flint for yourself and circumcise the children of Israel again. So Joshua made for himself knives of flint and circumcised the children of Israel on the Hill of Aralot [foreskins]. This is why Joshua had to circumcise them. All of the males who had left Egypt, all the men of battle, had died in the desert on their way up from Egypt. For all of the nation who had left *Josh. 5:2–6:1*

מפטיר ליום הראשון והשני של פסח

After חצי קדיש *(page 513), the* מפטיר *is read from the second* ספר תורה *on both the first and second days of* פסח.

במדבר כח:טז–כה וּבַחֹדֶשׁ הָרִאשׁוֹן בְּאַרְבָּעָה עָשָׂר יוֹם לַחֹדֶשׁ פֶּסַח לַיהוָה: וּבַחֲמִשָּׁה עָשָׂר
יוֹם לַחֹדֶשׁ הַזֶּה חָג שִׁבְעַת יָמִים מַצּוֹת יֵאָכֵל: בַּיּוֹם הָרִאשׁוֹן מִקְרָא־קֹדֶשׁ
כָּל־מְלֶאכֶת עֲבֹדָה לֹא תַעֲשׂוּ: וְהִקְרַבְתֶּם אִשֶּׁה עֹלָה לַיהוָה פָּרִים בְּנֵי־בָקָר
שְׁנַיִם וְאַיִל אֶחָד וְשִׁבְעָה כְבָשִׂים בְּנֵי שָׁנָה תְּמִימִם יִהְיוּ לָכֶם: וּמִנְחָתָם סֹלֶת
בְּלוּלָה בַשָּׁמֶן שְׁלֹשָׁה עֶשְׂרֹנִים לַפָּר וּשְׁנֵי עֶשְׂרֹנִים לָאַיִל תַּעֲשׂוּ: עִשָּׂרוֹן
עִשָּׂרוֹן תַּעֲשֶׂה לַכֶּבֶשׂ הָאֶחָד לְשִׁבְעַת הַכְּבָשִׂים: וּשְׂעִיר חַטָּאת אֶחָד לְכַפֵּר
עֲלֵיכֶם: מִלְּבַד עֹלַת הַבֹּקֶר אֲשֶׁר לְעֹלַת הַתָּמִיד תַּעֲשׂוּ אֶת־אֵלֶּה: כָּאֵלֶּה
תַּעֲשׂוּ לַיּוֹם שִׁבְעַת יָמִים לֶחֶם אִשֵּׁה רֵיחַ־נִיחֹחַ לַיהוָה עַל־עוֹלַת הַתָּמִיד
יֵעָשֶׂה וְנִסְכּוֹ: וּבַיּוֹם הַשְּׁבִיעִי מִקְרָא־קֹדֶשׁ יִהְיֶה לָכֶם כָּל־מְלֶאכֶת עֲבֹדָה
לֹא תַעֲשׂוּ:

הפטרה ליום הראשון של פסח

In some congregations, the הפטרה *begins at* בָּעֵת הַהִיא *below (at the *).*

יהושע ג:ה–ז וַיֹּאמֶר יְהוֹשֻׁעַ אֶל־הָעָם הִתְקַדָּשׁוּ כִּי מָחָר יַעֲשֶׂה יְהוָה בְּקִרְבְּכֶם נִפְלָאוֹת:
וַיֹּאמֶר יְהוֹשֻׁעַ אֶל־הַכֹּהֲנִים לֵאמֹר שְׂאוּ אֶת־אֲרוֹן הַבְּרִית וְעִבְרוּ לִפְנֵי הָעָם
וַיִּשְׂאוּ אֶת־אֲרוֹן הַבְּרִית וַיֵּלְכוּ לִפְנֵי הָעָם: וַיֹּאמֶר יְהוָה אֶל־
יְהוֹשֻׁעַ הַיּוֹם הַזֶּה אָחֵל גַּדֶּלְךָ בְּעֵינֵי כָּל־יִשְׂרָאֵל אֲשֶׁר יֵדְעוּן כִּי כַּאֲשֶׁר הָיִיתִי
עִם־מֹשֶׁה אֶהְיֶה עִמָּךְ:

יהושע ה:ב–ו:א *בָּעֵת הַהִיא אָמַר יְהוָה אֶל־יְהוֹשֻׁעַ עֲשֵׂה לְךָ חַרְבוֹת צֻרִים וְשׁוּב מֹל אֶת־
בְּנֵי־יִשְׂרָאֵל שֵׁנִית: וַיַּעַשׂ־לוֹ יְהוֹשֻׁעַ חַרְבוֹת צֻרִים וַיָּמָל אֶת־בְּנֵי יִשְׂרָאֵל
אֶל־גִּבְעַת הָעֲרָלוֹת: וְזֶה הַדָּבָר אֲשֶׁר־מָל יְהוֹשֻׁעַ כָּל־הָעָם הַיֹּצֵא מִמִּצְרַיִם
הַזְּכָרִים כֹּל | אַנְשֵׁי הַמִּלְחָמָה מֵתוּ בַמִּדְבָּר בַּדֶּרֶךְ בְּצֵאתָם מִמִּצְרָיִם: כִּי־
מֻלִים הָיוּ כָּל־הָעָם הַיֹּצְאִים וְכָל־הָעָם הַיִּלֹּדִים בַּמִּדְבָּר בַּדֶּרֶךְ בְּצֵאתָם

HAFTARA FOR THE FIRST DAY OF PESAḤ

The Torah portion spoke of the first Pesaḥ in Egypt prior to the exodus. The Haftara speaks of the first Pesaḥ the Israelites celebrated in the Promised

[Egypt] had been circumcised, but all of those born in the desert on the way up from Egypt had not been circumcised. For the children of Israel had journeyed in the desert for forty years until all of the people, the men of battle who had left Egypt, had perished, for they had not heeded the voice of the Lord, the Lord had sworn to them that they were not to see the land which the Lord had promised to their forefathers to give to us, a land flowing with milk and honey. But their children who survived them – they were circumcised by Joshua, for they were still uncircumcised, as they had not been circumcised on the journey. When all of the people had been circumcised, they stayed in the camp until they healed.

The Lord said to Joshua, "Today I have rolled the shame of Egypt away from you," and he named that place Gilgal ["rolling"], and so it is known to this day. The children of Israel camped at Gilgal and they made the Pesaḥ offering on the fourteenth day of the month in the evening, on the plains of Jericho. They ate of the produce of the land on the day after the Pesaḥ, matzot and roasted grain, on that very day. And the manna ceased [to come down] the next day, when they ate of the produce of the land, and the children of Israel no longer had manna; they ate of the crops of the land of Canaan that year.

When Joshua was in Jericho, he raised his eyes and looked up – and a man was standing opposite him, with his sword drawn in his hand; Joshua approached him and said to him, "Are you for us or are you for our adversaries?" [The man] said, "No, for I am captain of the Lord's hosts; I have just arrived" – and Joshua fell upon his face to the ground and prostrated himself and said, "What words has my master to speak to his servant?" And the captain of the Lord's hosts said to Joshua, "Remove the shoes from your feet, for the place upon which you are standing is sanctified." And Joshua did as he had said. And Jericho was completely closed off for fear of the children of Israel: none went out and none came in.

Some add:

And the Lord was with Joshua, and his fame spread throughout the land. *Josh. 6:27*

Continue with the blessings after the Haftara on page 514.

מִמִּצְרָ֑יִם לֹא־מָֽלוּ׃ כִּ֣י ׀ אַרְבָּעִ֣ים שָׁנָ֗ה הָלְכ֣וּ בְנֵֽי־יִשְׂרָאֵל֮ בַּמִּדְבָּר֒ עַד־תֹּ֨ם
כָּל־הַגּ֜וֹי אַנְשֵׁ֤י הַמִּלְחָמָה֙ הַיֹּצְאִ֣ים מִמִּצְרַ֔יִם אֲשֶׁ֥ר לֹא־שָׁמְע֖וּ בְּק֣וֹל יהוה
אֲשֶׁ֨ר נִשְׁבַּ֤ע יהוה֙ לָהֶ֔ם לְבִלְתִּ֞י הַרְאוֹתָ֣ם אֶת־הָאָ֗רֶץ אֲשֶׁר֩ נִשְׁבַּ֨ע יהוה
לַאֲבוֹתָם֙ לָ֣תֶת לָ֔נוּ אֶ֛רֶץ זָבַ֥ת חָלָ֖ב וּדְבָֽשׁ׃ וְאֶת־בְּנֵיהֶם֙ הֵקִ֣ים תַּחְתָּ֔ם אֹתָ֖ם
מָ֣ל יְהוֹשֻׁ֑עַ כִּֽי־עֲרֵלִ֣ים הָי֔וּ כִּ֛י לֹא־מָ֥לוּ אוֹתָ֖ם בַּדָּֽרֶךְ׃ וַיְהִ֛י כַּאֲשֶׁר־תַּ֥מּוּ כָל־
הַגּ֖וֹי לְהִמּ֑וֹל וַיֵּשְׁב֥וּ תַחְתָּ֛ם בַּֽמַּחֲנֶ֖ה עַ֥ד חֲיוֹתָֽם׃ וַיֹּ֤אמֶר יהוה
אֶל־יְהוֹשֻׁ֔עַ הַיּ֗וֹם גַּלּ֛וֹתִי אֶת־חֶרְפַּ֥ת מִצְרַ֖יִם מֵעֲלֵיכֶ֑ם וַיִּקְרָ֞א שֵׁ֣ם הַמָּק֤וֹם
הַהוּא֙ גִּלְגָּ֔ל עַ֖ד הַיּ֥וֹם הַזֶּֽה׃ וַיַּחֲנ֥וּ בְנֵֽי־יִשְׂרָאֵ֖ל בַּגִּלְגָּ֑ל וַיַּעֲשׂ֣וּ אֶת־הַפֶּ֡סַח
בְּאַרְבָּעָה֩ עָשָׂ֨ר י֥וֹם לַחֹ֛דֶשׁ בָּעֶ֖רֶב בְּעַֽרְב֥וֹת יְרִיחֽוֹ׃ וַיֹּ֨אכְל֜וּ מֵעֲב֥וּר הָאָ֛רֶץ
מִמָּחֳרַ֥ת הַפֶּ֖סַח מַצּ֣וֹת וְקָל֑וּי בְּעֶ֖צֶם הַיּ֥וֹם הַזֶּֽה׃ וַיִּשְׁבֹּ֨ת הַמָּ֜ן מִֽמָּחֳרָ֗ת בְּאָכְלָם֙
מֵעֲב֣וּר הָאָ֔רֶץ וְלֹא־הָ֥יָה ע֛וֹד לִבְנֵ֥י יִשְׂרָאֵ֖ל מָ֑ן וַיֹּאכְל֗וּ מִתְּבוּאַת֙ אֶ֣רֶץ כְּנַ֔עַן
בַּשָּׁנָ֖ה הַהִֽיא׃ וַיְהִ֗י בִּֽהְי֣וֹת יְהוֹשֻׁעַ֮ בִּירִיחוֹ֒ וַיִּשָּׂ֤א עֵינָיו֙ וַיַּ֔רְא
וְהִנֵּה־אִישׁ֙ עֹמֵ֣ד לְנֶגְדּ֔וֹ וְחַרְבּ֥וֹ שְׁלוּפָ֖ה בְּיָד֑וֹ וַיֵּ֨לֶךְ יְהוֹשֻׁ֤עַ אֵלָיו֙ וַיֹּ֣אמֶר ל֔וֹ
הֲלָ֥נוּ אַתָּ֖ה אִם־לְצָרֵֽינוּ׃ וַיֹּ֣אמֶר ׀ לֹ֗א כִּ֛י אֲנִ֥י שַׂר־צְבָֽא־יהוה עַתָּ֣ה בָ֑אתִי
וַיִּפֹּל֩ יְהוֹשֻׁ֨עַ אֶל־פָּנָ֥יו אַ֙רְצָה֙ וַיִּשְׁתָּ֔חוּ וַיֹּ֣אמֶר ל֔וֹ מָ֥ה אֲדֹנִ֖י מְדַבֵּ֥ר אֶל־עַבְדּֽוֹ׃
וַיֹּאמֶר֩ שַׂר־צְבָ֨א יהוה אֶל־יְהוֹשֻׁ֜עַ שַׁל־נַֽעַלְךָ֙ מֵעַ֣ל רַגְלֶ֔ךָ כִּ֣י הַמָּק֔וֹם אֲשֶׁ֥ר
אַתָּ֛ה עֹמֵ֥ד עָלָ֖יו קֹ֣דֶשׁ ה֑וּא וַיַּ֥עַשׂ יְהוֹשֻׁ֖עַ כֵּֽן׃ וִירִיחוֹ֙ סֹגֶ֣רֶת וּמְסֻגֶּ֔רֶת מִפְּנֵ֖י בְּנֵ֣י
יִשְׂרָאֵ֑ל אֵ֥ין יוֹצֵ֖א וְאֵ֥ין בָּֽא׃

Some add:

יהושע ו:כז וַיְהִ֥י יהוה אֶת־יְהוֹשֻׁ֑עַ וַיְהִ֥י שָׁמְע֖וֹ בְּכָל־הָאָֽרֶץ׃

Continue with the blessings after the הפטרה *on page 515.*

Land, bringing the long story of the exodus to a close after forty years. The passage also describes the second circumcision, that is, the second mass ceremony: the first had taken place in Egypt. The Torah stipulates that an uncircumcised male may not eat the Paschal offering (Ex. 12:48). Those born in the wilderness had not been circumcised because of the dangers involved in performing the operation during a journey. The people never knew in advance when they might have to set off, and this would have endangered the newly circumcised children. So the new generation of males had to be circumcised in order to celebrate Pesaḥ.

TORAH READING FOR THE SECOND DAY OF PESAḤ, THE FIRST DAY OF SUKKOT AND THE SECOND DAY OUTSIDE ISRAEL

On the first day of Ḥol HaMo'ed in Israel, for Levi start where Revi'i on Shabbat would otherwise start, for Shelishi read to the end, and for Revi'i read from the second Torah scroll.

The Lord spoke to Moses, saying: When a bullock or lamb or goat is born, it shall remain with its mother for seven days; from the eighth day onwards it will be accepted as a sacrifice, a fire-offering to the Lord. Whether a bullock or a sheep, you may not slaughter the animal and its offspring on the same day. If you bring an offering of thanksgiving to God, offer it so that it will be accepted from you. It must be eaten on that very day; let none of it remain until morning; I am the Lord. Safeguard My commandments and perform them; I am the Lord. Do not profane My holy name; I shall be sanctified among the children of Israel; I am the Lord who sanctifies you, who has taken you out of the land of Egypt to be your God: I am the Lord. *Lev. 22:26–23:44*

The Lord spoke to Moses, saying: Speak to the children of Israel, saying to them: The appointed times of the Lord which you shall proclaim to be days of sacred assembly: these are My appointed times: For six days shall work be done, but the seventh day is a Sabbath of utter rest, a sacred assembly; you may not do any work. It is a Sabbath for the Lord in all of your dwellings. (*Shabbat:* LEVI)

These are the appointed times of the Lord, sacred assemblies, which you shall announce in their due seasons: In the first month, on the fourteenth of that month, in the afternoon, the Pesaḥ [offering shall be brought] to the Lord. And the fifteenth day of that month will be the festival of Matzot to the Lord; for seven days you shall eat matzot. On the first day there will be a sacred assembly; you shall do no laborious work. And you shall bring an offering consumed by fire to the Lord on each of the seven days; on the seventh day there shall be a sacred assembly: you shall do no laborious work. LEVI (*Shabbat:* SHELISHI)

The Lord spoke to Moses, saying: Speak to the children of Israel and tell them: When you enter the land which I am giving you, and you harvest its grains, you shall bring the first omer measure of your harvest to the priest. He shall wave the omer in the presence of the Lord so that it may be accepted from you; the priest shall wave it on (*Shabbat:* REVI'I LEVI *on Ḥol HaMo'ed Pesaḥ*)

קריאה ליום השני של פסח,
וכן ליום הראשון של סוכות ויום טוב שני בחוץ לארץ

On the first day of פסח המועד חול in ישראל ארץ, for לוי start
where שבת on שבת would otherwise start, for שלישי read to
the end, and for רביעי read from the second תורה ספר.

ויקרא כב:
כו-כג:מד
וַיְדַבֵּ֥ר יְהֹוָ֖ה אֶל־מֹשֶׁ֥ה לֵּאמֹֽר׃ שׁ֣וֹר אוֹ־כֶ֤שֶׂב אוֹ־עֵז֙ כִּ֣י יִוָּלֵ֔ד וְהָיָ֛ה שִׁבְעַ֥ת יָמִ֖ים תַּ֣חַת אִמּ֑וֹ וּמִיּ֤וֹם הַשְּׁמִינִי֙ וָהָ֔לְאָה יֵֽרָצֶ֕ה לְקׇרְבַּ֥ן אִשֶּׁ֖ה לַֽיהֹוָֽה׃ וְשׁ֖וֹר אוֹ־שֶׂ֑ה אֹת֣וֹ וְאֶת־בְּנ֔וֹ לֹ֥א תִשְׁחֲט֖וּ בְּי֥וֹם אֶחָֽד׃ וְכִֽי־תִזְבְּח֥וּ זֶֽבַח־תּוֹדָ֖ה לַֽיהֹוָ֑ה לִֽרְצֹנְכֶ֖ם תִּזְבָּֽחוּ׃ בַּיּ֤וֹם הַהוּא֙ יֵֽאָכֵ֔ל לֹֽא־תוֹתִ֥ירוּ מִמֶּ֖נּוּ עַד־בֹּ֑קֶר אֲנִ֖י יְהֹוָֽה׃ וּשְׁמַרְתֶּם֙ מִצְוֺתַ֔י וַֽעֲשִׂיתֶ֖ם אֹתָ֑ם אֲנִ֖י יְהֹוָֽה׃ וְלֹ֤א תְחַלְּלוּ֙ אֶת־שֵׁ֣ם קׇדְשִׁ֔י וְנִ֨קְדַּשְׁתִּ֔י בְּת֖וֹךְ בְּנֵ֣י יִשְׂרָאֵ֑ל אֲנִ֥י יְהֹוָ֖ה מְקַדִּשְׁכֶֽם׃ הַמּוֹצִ֤יא אֶתְכֶם֙ מֵאֶ֣רֶץ מִצְרַ֔יִם לִֽהְי֥וֹת לָכֶ֖ם לֵֽאלֹהִ֑ים אֲנִ֖י יְהֹוָֽה׃

(בשבת
לוי)
וַיְדַבֵּ֥ר יְהֹוָ֖ה אֶל־מֹשֶׁ֥ה לֵּאמֹֽר׃ דַּבֵּ֞ר אֶל־בְּנֵ֤י יִשְׂרָאֵל֙ וְאָֽמַרְתָּ֣ אֲלֵהֶ֔ם מֽוֹעֲדֵ֣י יְהֹוָ֔ה אֲשֶׁר־תִּקְרְא֥וּ אֹתָ֖ם מִקְרָאֵ֣י קֹ֑דֶשׁ אֵ֥לֶּה הֵ֖ם מֽוֹעֲדָֽי׃ שֵׁ֣שֶׁת יָמִים֮ תֵּֽעָשֶׂ֣ה מְלָאכָה֒ וּבַיּ֣וֹם הַשְּׁבִיעִ֗י שַׁבַּ֤ת שַׁבָּתוֹן֙ מִקְרָא־קֹ֔דֶשׁ כׇּל־מְלָאכָ֖ה לֹ֣א תַֽעֲשׂ֑וּ שַׁבָּ֥ת הִוא֙ לַֽיהֹוָ֔ה בְּכֹ֖ל מֽוֹשְׁבֹֽתֵיכֶֽם׃

לוי
(בשבת
שלישי)
אֵ֚לֶּה מֽוֹעֲדֵ֣י יְהֹוָ֔ה מִקְרָאֵ֖י קֹ֑דֶשׁ אֲשֶׁר־תִּקְרְא֥וּ אֹתָ֖ם בְּמֽוֹעֲדָֽם׃ בַּחֹ֣דֶשׁ הָֽרִאשׁ֗וֹן בְּאַרְבָּעָ֥ה עָשָׂ֛ר לַחֹ֖דֶשׁ בֵּ֣ין הָֽעַרְבָּ֑יִם פֶּ֖סַח לַֽיהֹוָֽה׃ וּבַֽחֲמִשָּׁ֨ה עָשָׂ֥ר יוֹם֙ לַחֹ֣דֶשׁ הַזֶּ֔ה חַ֥ג הַמַּצּ֖וֹת לַֽיהֹוָ֑ה שִׁבְעַ֥ת יָמִ֖ים מַצּ֥וֹת תֹּאכֵֽלוּ׃ בַּיּוֹם֙ הָֽרִאשׁ֔וֹן מִקְרָא־קֹ֖דֶשׁ יִֽהְיֶ֣ה לָכֶ֑ם כׇּל־מְלֶ֥אכֶת עֲבֹדָ֖ה לֹ֥א תַֽעֲשֽׂוּ׃ וְהִקְרַבְתֶּ֥ם אִשֶּׁ֛ה לַֽיהֹוָ֖ה שִׁבְעַ֣ת יָמִ֑ים בַּיּ֤וֹם הַשְּׁבִיעִי֙ מִקְרָא־קֹ֔דֶשׁ כׇּל־מְלֶ֥אכֶת עֲבֹדָ֖ה לֹ֥א תַֽעֲשֽׂוּ׃

(בשבת
רביעי
לוי בחוהמ
פסח)
וַיְדַבֵּ֥ר יְהֹוָ֖ה אֶל־מֹשֶׁ֥ה לֵּאמֹֽר׃ דַּבֵּ֞ר אֶל־בְּנֵ֤י יִשְׂרָאֵל֙ וְאָֽמַרְתָּ֣ אֲלֵהֶ֔ם כִּֽי־תָבֹ֣אוּ אֶל־הָאָ֗רֶץ אֲשֶׁ֤ר אֲנִי֙ נֹתֵ֣ן לָכֶ֔ם וּקְצַרְתֶּ֖ם אֶת־קְצִירָ֑הּ וַֽהֲבֵאתֶ֥ם אֶת־עֹ֛מֶר רֵאשִׁ֥ית קְצִֽירְכֶ֖ם אֶל־הַכֹּהֵֽן׃ וְהֵנִ֧יף אֶת־הָעֹ֛מֶר לִפְנֵ֥י יְהֹוָ֖ה לִֽרְצֹנְכֶ֑ם

TORAH READING FOR THE FIRST TWO DAYS

The core reading is Leviticus 22–23, the first of three extended accounts of
the festivals in the Torah. This sets out the basic structure of the Jewish
calendar as a rhythm of holiness in time. The second, in Numbers 28–29, is
a detailed account of the sacrifices to be offered on these days. The third, in

the day following the [Pesaḥ] rest day. And on the day of waving the omer, you shall offer an unblemished yearling lamb as a burnt-offering to the LORD. And its meal-offering shall be two tenths of an ephah of fine flour mixed with oil, an offering consumed by fire, a pleasing scent for the LORD; its libation shall be a fourth of a hin of wine. You may not eat any bread, roasted grains or fresh kernels (of the new harvest) until this day, until you bring the offering of your God – this is an eternal ordinance for all your generations in all of your dwellings.

SHELISHI (*Shabbat:* ḤAMISHI)

And you shall count seven complete weeks from the day following the [Pesaḥ] rest day, when you brought the omer as a wave-offering. To the day after the seventh week you shall count fifty days. Then you shall present a meal-offering of new grain to the LORD. You shall bring two loaves from your settlements as a wave-offering: they shall be made from two tenths of an ephah of fine flour; they shall be baked as leavened bread; first harvest for the LORD. And with this bread you shall offer seven unblemished yearling lambs, one young bullock and two rams: all as a burnt-offering to the LORD along with their meal-offerings and wine-libations, an offering consumed by fire, a pleasant scent for the LORD. And you shall bring one male goat for atonement and two yearling lambs as a peace-offering. And the priest shall wave them over the loaves made from the first harvest as a wave-offering in the presence of the LORD, and upon the two lambs – they shall be sanctified to the LORD, for the priest. And you shall proclaim on that day – it shall be a sacred assembly for you: you may not perform any laborious work – this is an eternal ordinance for all your generations in all of your dwellings. And when you reap the grain of your land, do not finish reaping the corner of your field, and do not collect the fallen remnants of your harvest: you must leave them for the poor and for the stranger – I am the LORD your God.

REVI'I (*Shabbat:* SHISHI)

The LORD spoke to Moses, saying: Speak to the children of Israel, saying: In the seventh month, on the first day of the month, you shall hold a rest day of remembrance by the shofar, a sacred assembly. You may not perform any laborious work, and you shall bring a fire-offering to the LORD.

The LORD spoke to Moses, saying: Speak to the children of Israel, saying: On the tenth day of that seventh month, there shall be a Day of Atonement; it is a sacred assembly for you; you shall afflict your souls,

מִמָּחֳרַת הַשַּׁבָּת יְנִיפֶנּוּ הַכֹּהֵן: וַעֲשִׂיתֶם בְּיוֹם הֲנִיפְכֶם אֶת־הָעֹמֶר כֶּבֶשׂ
תָּמִים בֶּן־שְׁנָתוֹ לְעֹלָה לַיהוה: וּמִנְחָתוֹ שְׁנֵי עֶשְׂרֹנִים סֹלֶת בְּלוּלָה בַשֶּׁמֶן
אִשֶּׁה לַיהוה רֵיחַ נִיחֹחַ וְנִסְכֹּה יַיִן רְבִיעִת הַהִין: וְלֶחֶם וְקָלִי וְכַרְמֶל לֹא
תֹאכְלוּ עַד־עֶצֶם הַיּוֹם הַזֶּה עַד הֲבִיאֲכֶם אֶת־קָרְבַּן אֱלֹהֵיכֶם חֻקַּת עוֹלָם
שלישי ביו״ט ובחוה״מ (בשבת חמישי) לְדֹרֹתֵיכֶם בְּכֹל מֹשְׁבֹתֵיכֶם: *וּסְפַרְתֶּם לָכֶם מִמָּחֳרַת הַשַּׁבָּת מִיּוֹם
הֲבִיאֲכֶם אֶת־עֹמֶר הַתְּנוּפָה שֶׁבַע שַׁבָּתוֹת תְּמִימֹת תִּהְיֶינָה: עַד מִמָּחֳרַת
הַשַּׁבָּת הַשְּׁבִיעִת תִּסְפְּרוּ חֲמִשִּׁים יוֹם וְהִקְרַבְתֶּם מִנְחָה חֲדָשָׁה לַיהוה:
מִמּוֹשְׁבֹתֵיכֶם תָּבִיאוּ | לֶחֶם תְּנוּפָה שְׁתַּיִם שְׁנֵי עֶשְׂרֹנִים סֹלֶת תִּהְיֶינָה חָמֵץ
תֵּאָפֶינָה בִּכּוּרִים לַיהוה: וְהִקְרַבְתֶּם עַל־הַלֶּחֶם שִׁבְעַת כְּבָשִׂים תְּמִימִם בְּנֵי
שָׁנָה וּפַר בֶּן־בָּקָר אֶחָד וְאֵילִם שְׁנָיִם יִהְיוּ עֹלָה לַיהוה וּמִנְחָתָם וְנִסְכֵּיהֶם
אִשֵּׁה רֵיחַ־נִיחֹחַ לַיהוה: וַעֲשִׂיתֶם שְׂעִיר־עִזִּים אֶחָד לְחַטָּאת וּשְׁנֵי כְבָשִׂים
בְּנֵי שָׁנָה לְזֶבַח שְׁלָמִים: וְהֵנִיף הַכֹּהֵן | אֹתָם עַל לֶחֶם הַבִּכֻּרִים תְּנוּפָה לִפְנֵי
יהוה עַל־שְׁנֵי כְּבָשִׂים קֹדֶשׁ יִהְיוּ לַיהוה לַכֹּהֵן: וּקְרָאתֶם בְּעֶצֶם | הַיּוֹם
הַזֶּה מִקְרָא־קֹדֶשׁ יִהְיֶה לָכֶם כָּל־מְלֶאכֶת עֲבֹדָה לֹא תַעֲשׂוּ חֻקַּת עוֹלָם
בְּכָל־מוֹשְׁבֹתֵיכֶם לְדֹרֹתֵיכֶם: וּבְקֻצְרְכֶם אֶת־קְצִיר אַרְצְכֶם לֹא־תְכַלֶּה פְּאַת
שָׂדְךָ בְּקֻצְרֶךָ וְלֶקֶט קְצִירְךָ לֹא תְלַקֵּט לֶעָנִי וְלַגֵּר תַּעֲזֹב אֹתָם אֲנִי יהוה
אֱלֹהֵיכֶם:
רביעי (בשבת שישי) וַיְדַבֵּר יהוה אֶל־מֹשֶׁה לֵּאמֹר: דַּבֵּר אֶל־בְּנֵי יִשְׂרָאֵל לֵאמֹר בַּחֹדֶשׁ הַשְּׁבִיעִי
בְּאֶחָד לַחֹדֶשׁ יִהְיֶה לָכֶם שַׁבָּתוֹן זִכְרוֹן תְּרוּעָה מִקְרָא־קֹדֶשׁ: כָּל־מְלֶאכֶת
עֲבֹדָה לֹא תַעֲשׂוּ וְהִקְרַבְתֶּם אִשֶּׁה לַיהוה: וַיְדַבֵּר יהוה אֶל־
מֹשֶׁה לֵּאמֹר: אַךְ בֶּעָשׂוֹר לַחֹדֶשׁ הַשְּׁבִיעִי הַזֶּה יוֹם הַכִּפֻּרִים הוּא מִקְרָא־קֹדֶשׁ
יִהְיֶה לָכֶם וְעִנִּיתֶם אֶת־נַפְשֹׁתֵיכֶם וְהִקְרַבְתֶּם אִשֶּׁה לַיהוה: וְכָל־מְלָאכָה לֹא

Deuteronomy 16, emphasizes the pilgrimage character of Pesaḥ, Shavuot and Sukkot, together with the principle of social inclusion – they were days on which the widow, orphan, Levite, and stranger were all to be included in the celebration. Note the significance of the number seven in the architectonics of holy time. The seventh day, Shabbat, is holy. There are seven other holy days: the first and last day of Pesaḥ, Shavuot, Rosh HaShana, Yom Kippur, Sukkot and Shemini Atzeret. The greatest concentration of festivals is in the seventh month.

and bring a fire-offering to the LORD. You may not perform any work on this day, for it is a Day of Atonements, to atone for you before the LORD your God. For any soul that is not afflicted on this very day will be cut off from its people. And any soul that performs any work on this very day – I shall cause that soul to be lost from among its people. You shall perform no work – this is an eternal ordinance for all your generations in all of your dwellings. It is a Sabbath of Sabbaths for you; you shall afflict your souls from the ninth of the month in the evening; you shall rest on your Sabbath until the following evening.

HAMISHI (*Shabbat:* SHEVI'I)

The LORD spoke to Moses, saying: Speak to the children of Israel, and tell them: On the fifteenth day of this seventh month, there shall be a Festival of Booths for the LORD, for seven days. On the first day there shall be a sacred assembly; you shall do no laborious work. For seven days, you shall bring fire-offerings to the LORD; on the eighth day there will be a sacred assembly, and you shall bring another fire-offering to the LORD – it is a day of gathering; you shall do no laborious work. These are the appointed times of the LORD which you shall proclaim to be days of sacred assembly, bringing fire-offerings to the LORD: burnt-offerings, meal-offerings, peace-offerings and wine-libations, as ordained for each day, in addition to the LORD's Sabbath offerings, and your donated offerings, and all the vows and voluntary offerings which you may offer to the LORD. But on the fifteenth day of the seventh month, when you gather the harvest of the land, you shall celebrate the LORD's holiday for seven days; the first day shall be a day of rest, and the eighth day shall be a day of rest. And on the first day, you shall take for yourselves a fruit of the citron tree, palm fronds, myrtle branches and willows of the brook, and be joyous in the presence of the LORD your God for seven days. You shall celebrate it, a holiday for the LORD, seven days a year – this is an eternal ordinance for all your generations – you shall celebrate it in the seventh month. You shall dwell in booths for seven days; all those born among Israel shall dwell in booths, so that your descendants will know that I settled the children of Israel in booths when I brought them out of the land of Egypt; I am the LORD your God. And Moses related all of the LORD's festivals to the children of Israel.

Half Kaddish (page 512) is said. The Maftir is read from the second Torah scroll: for the second day of Pesaḥ on page 1124 and for for the first two days of Sukkot on page 1152.

תַעֲשׂוּ בְּעֶצֶם הַיּוֹם הַזֶּה כִּי יוֹם כִּפֻּרִים הוּא לְכַפֵּר עֲלֵיכֶם לִפְנֵי יהוה אֱלֹהֵיכֶם:
כִּי כָל־הַנֶּפֶשׁ אֲשֶׁר לֹא־תְעֻנֶּה בְּעֶצֶם הַיּוֹם הַזֶּה וְנִכְרְתָה מֵעַמֶּיהָ: וְכָל־הַנֶּפֶשׁ
אֲשֶׁר תַּעֲשֶׂה כָּל־מְלָאכָה בְּעֶצֶם הַיּוֹם הַזֶּה וְהַאֲבַדְתִּי אֶת־הַנֶּפֶשׁ הַהִוא
מִקֶּרֶב עַמָּהּ: כָּל־מְלָאכָה לֹא תַעֲשׂוּ חֻקַּת עוֹלָם לְדֹרֹתֵיכֶם בְּכֹל מֹשְׁבֹתֵיכֶם:
שַׁבַּת שַׁבָּתוֹן הוּא לָכֶם וְעִנִּיתֶם אֶת־נַפְשֹׁתֵיכֶם בְּתִשְׁעָה לַחֹדֶשׁ בָּעֶרֶב מֵעֶרֶב
עַד־עֶרֶב תִּשְׁבְּתוּ שַׁבַּתְּכֶם:

חמישי (בשבת שביעי)

וַיְדַבֵּר יהוה אֶל־מֹשֶׁה לֵּאמֹר: דַּבֵּר אֶל־בְּנֵי יִשְׂרָאֵל לֵאמֹר בַּחֲמִשָּׁה עָשָׂר
יוֹם לַחֹדֶשׁ הַשְּׁבִיעִי הַזֶּה חַג הַסֻּכּוֹת שִׁבְעַת יָמִים לַיהוה: בַּיּוֹם הָרִאשׁוֹן
מִקְרָא־קֹדֶשׁ כָּל־מְלֶאכֶת עֲבֹדָה לֹא תַעֲשׂוּ: שִׁבְעַת יָמִים תַּקְרִיבוּ אִשֶּׁה
לַיהוה בַּיּוֹם הַשְּׁמִינִי מִקְרָא־קֹדֶשׁ יִהְיֶה לָכֶם וְהִקְרַבְתֶּם אִשֶּׁה לַיהוה עֲצֶרֶת
הִוא כָּל־מְלֶאכֶת עֲבֹדָה לֹא תַעֲשׂוּ: אֵלֶּה מוֹעֲדֵי יהוה אֲשֶׁר־תִּקְרְאוּ אֹתָם
מִקְרָאֵי קֹדֶשׁ לְהַקְרִיב אִשֶּׁה לַיהוה עֹלָה וּמִנְחָה זֶבַח וּנְסָכִים דְּבַר־יוֹם
בְּיוֹמוֹ: מִלְּבַד שַׁבְּתֹת יהוה וּמִלְּבַד מַתְּנוֹתֵיכֶם וּמִלְּבַד כָּל־נִדְרֵיכֶם וּמִלְּבַד
כָּל־נִדְבֹתֵיכֶם אֲשֶׁר תִּתְּנוּ לַיהוה: אַךְ בַּחֲמִשָּׁה עָשָׂר יוֹם לַחֹדֶשׁ הַשְּׁבִיעִי
בְּאָסְפְּכֶם אֶת־תְּבוּאַת הָאָרֶץ תָּחֹגּוּ אֶת־חַג־יהוה שִׁבְעַת יָמִים בַּיּוֹם הָרִאשׁוֹן
שַׁבָּתוֹן וּבַיּוֹם הַשְּׁמִינִי שַׁבָּתוֹן: וּלְקַחְתֶּם לָכֶם בַּיּוֹם הָרִאשׁוֹן פְּרִי עֵץ הָדָר כַּפֹּת
תְּמָרִים וַעֲנַף עֵץ־עָבֹת וְעַרְבֵי־נָחַל וּשְׂמַחְתֶּם לִפְנֵי יהוה אֱלֹהֵיכֶם שִׁבְעַת
יָמִים: וְחַגֹּתֶם אֹתוֹ חַג לַיהוה שִׁבְעַת יָמִים בַּשָּׁנָה חֻקַּת עוֹלָם לְדֹרֹתֵיכֶם
בַּחֹדֶשׁ הַשְּׁבִיעִי תָּחֹגּוּ אֹתוֹ: בַּסֻּכֹּת תֵּשְׁבוּ שִׁבְעַת יָמִים כָּל־הָאֶזְרָח בְּיִשְׂרָאֵל
יֵשְׁבוּ בַּסֻּכֹּת: לְמַעַן יֵדְעוּ דֹרֹתֵיכֶם כִּי בַסֻּכּוֹת הוֹשַׁבְתִּי אֶת־בְּנֵי יִשְׂרָאֵל
בְּהוֹצִיאִי אוֹתָם מֵאֶרֶץ מִצְרָיִם אֲנִי יהוה אֱלֹהֵיכֶם: וַיְדַבֵּר מֹשֶׁה אֶת־מֹעֲדֵי
יהוה אֶל־בְּנֵי יִשְׂרָאֵל:

חצי קדיש *(page 513) is said.*
The מפטיר *is read from the second* ספר תורה*:*
for the second day of פסח *on page 1125 and for the first two days of* סוכות *on page 1155.*

לְמַעַן יֵדְעוּ דֹרֹתֵיכֶם *So that your descendants will know.* As well as marking the cycle of seasons and the agricultural year, the festivals are also times of remembering and reenacting the history of the nation and handing on that memory across the generations. To be a Jew is to live history, celebrating the present in the context of past and future, memory and hope.

HAFTARA FOR THE SECOND DAY OF PESAḤ (OUTSIDE ISRAEL)

*In some congregations, the Haftara begins at "Then the king commanded" below (at the *).*

So the king sent for all the elders of Judah and Jerusalem, and they came to him. The king went up to the Temple along with all the men of Judah and the inhabitants of Jerusalem and the priests and the prophets, and all the people, young and old, and he read to them all that was written in the Book of the Covenant that had been found in the Temple. The king stood on his platform and made a covenant before the Lord, [pledging] to walk after Him and to observe His commandments and statutes and laws with all his heart and all his soul, to observe the words of that covenant written in the scroll of the Torah – and all the people committed themselves to the covenant. *Then the king commanded Ḥilkiyahu the high priest and the priests second in rank and the gatekeepers, to take all of the vessels that had been made for Ba'al and Ashera and for all the hosts of the heavens out of the Lord's sanctuary; he burned all of these outside Jerusalem, on the fields of Kidron, and carried their ashes to Beit El. He put an end to the practice of the idolatrous priests who had been appointed by the kings of Judah, those who had offered up incense on the high places of worship in the cities of Judah and in places all around Jerusalem, as well as those who had burned incense to Ba'al and to the sun and moon and constellations and to all of the hosts of heaven. He took the Ashera out of the Temple and brought it out of Jerusalem to the Kidron Valley and burned it there, grinding it to fine dust, and threw its ashes upon the graves of the people. He destroyed the rooms of the male temple-prostitutes in the House of the Lord, where the women would weave hangings in honor of the Ashera. He brought in all of the priests from the cities of Judah; he defiled the high places upon which the priests had worshiped, from Geva [in the north] all the way to Be'er Sheva [in the south]; he shattered the high places of the gate which were at the gate of Joshua, the city sentry, to the left of those who entered the city's gates. But the priests of the high

II Kings, 23:1–9

Some begin here

---

covenant. The mood of national religious revival led to a spectacular celebration of Pesaḥ, on a scale and with a fervor that had not been seen for many centuries.

הפטרה ליום טוב שני של פסח בחוץ לארץ

In some congregations, the הפטרה *begins at* וַיְצַו הַמֶּלֶךְ *below (at the* **).*

מלכים ב
כג:א-ט

וַיִּשְׁלַח הַמֶּלֶךְ וַיַּאַסְפוּ אֵלָיו כָּל־זִקְנֵי יְהוּדָה וִירוּשָׁלָ͏ִם: וַיַּעַל הַמֶּלֶךְ בֵּית־יהוֹה
וְכָל־אִישׁ יְהוּדָה וְכָל־יֹשְׁבֵי יְרוּשָׁלַ͏ִם אִתּוֹ וְהַכֹּהֲנִים וְהַנְּבִיאִים וְכָל־הָעָם
לְמִקָּטֹן וְעַד־גָּדוֹל וַיִּקְרָא בְאָזְנֵיהֶם אֶת־כָּל־דִּבְרֵי סֵפֶר הַבְּרִית הַנִּמְצָא בְּבֵית
יהוֹה: וַיַּעֲמֹד הַמֶּלֶךְ עַל־הָעַמּוּד וַיִּכְרֹת אֶת־הַבְּרִית לִפְנֵי יהוֹה לָלֶכֶת אַחַר
יהוֹה וְלִשְׁמֹר מִצְוֺתָיו וְאֶת־עֵדְוֺתָיו וְאֶת־חֻקֹּתָיו בְּכָל־לֵב וּבְכָל־נֶפֶשׁ לְהָקִים
אֶת־דִּבְרֵי הַבְּרִית הַזֹּאת הַכְּתֻבִים עַל־הַסֵּפֶר הַזֶּה וַיַּעֲמֹד כָּל־הָעָם בַּבְּרִית:
*וַיְצַו הַמֶּלֶךְ אֶת־חִלְקִיָּהוּ הַכֹּהֵן הַגָּדוֹל וְאֶת־כֹּהֲנֵי הַמִּשְׁנֶה וְאֶת־שֹׁמְרֵי הַסַּף
לְהוֹצִיא מֵהֵיכַל יהוֹה אֵת כָּל־הַכֵּלִים הָעֲשׂוּיִם לַבַּעַל וְלָאֲשֵׁרָה וּלְכֹל צְבָא
הַשָּׁמָיִם וַיִּשְׂרְפֵם מִחוּץ לִירוּשָׁלַ͏ִם בְּשַׁדְמוֹת קִדְרוֹן וְנָשָׂא אֶת־עֲפָרָם בֵּית־
אֵל: וְהִשְׁבִּית אֶת־הַכְּמָרִים אֲשֶׁר נָתְנוּ מַלְכֵי יְהוּדָה וַיְקַטֵּר בַּבָּמוֹת בְּעָרֵי
יְהוּדָה וּמְסִבֵּי יְרוּשָׁלָ͏ִם וְאֶת־הַמְקַטְּרִים לַבַּעַל לַשֶּׁמֶשׁ וְלַיָּרֵחַ וְלַמַּזָּלוֹת וּלְכֹל
צְבָא הַשָּׁמָיִם: וַיֹּצֵא אֶת־הָאֲשֵׁרָה מִבֵּית יהוֹה מִחוּץ לִירוּשָׁלַ͏ִם אֶל־נַחַל
קִדְרוֹן וַיִּשְׂרֹף אֹתָהּ בְּנַחַל קִדְרוֹן וַיָּדֶק לְעָפָר וַיַּשְׁלֵךְ אֶת־עֲפָרָהּ עַל־קֶבֶר
בְּנֵי הָעָם: וַיִּתֹּץ אֶת־בָּתֵּי הַקְּדֵשִׁים אֲשֶׁר בְּבֵית יהוֹה אֲשֶׁר הַנָּשִׁים אֹרְגוֹת
שָׁם בָּתִּים לָאֲשֵׁרָה: וַיָּבֵא אֶת־כָּל־הַכֹּהֲנִים מֵעָרֵי יְהוּדָה וַיְטַמֵּא אֶת־הַבָּמוֹת
אֲשֶׁר קִטְּרוּ־שָׁמָּה הַכֹּהֲנִים מִגֶּבַע עַד־בְּאֵר שָׁבַע וְנָתַץ אֶת־בָּמוֹת הַשְּׁעָרִים
אֲשֶׁר־פֶּתַח שַׁעַר יְהוֹשֻׁעַ שַׂר־הָעִיר אֲשֶׁר־עַל־שְׂמֹאול אִישׁ בְּשַׁעַר הָעִיר:

Some
begin here

HAFTARA FOR THE SECOND DAY OF PESAḤ

Having read about one historic Pesaḥ on the first day, on the second we
read about another, one of the great moments of religious renewal in the
life of the nation. During the long reign of King Manasseh, the kingdom
of Judah had lapsed into the worst forms of idolatry. Manasseh's grandson
Josiah, ascending to the throne at the age of eight, presided over a period of
national rededication.

In the course of repairs to the Temple, Hilkiah the priest made the
momentous discovery of a Torah scroll, probably hidden during Manasseh's
reign to avoid destruction. On hearing the curses of Deuteronomy fore-
telling national catastrophe as a result of faithlessness, the king was moved
to tears. Tearing his clothes as a sign of mourning and repentance, Josiah
read the Torah to the people, and together with them reaffirmed the

places were not allowed to go up the LORD's altar in Jerusalem, but only to eat matzot among their brethren.

The king commanded all the people, saying: "Observe the Pesaḥ in honor of the LORD your God, as prescribed in this Book of the Covenant. For the Pesaḥ had not been observed [with such ceremony] since the days of the judges who judged Israel, nor throughout the times of all of the kings of Israel or the kings of Judea. Only in the eighteenth year of King Josiah was the Pesaḥ observed so, in honor of the LORD in Jerusalem. Moreover, those who divined by a ghost or a familiar spirit, and the idols and the graven images and all the detestable things which had ever been seen in the land of Judea and Jerusalem were also destroyed by King Josiah, to uphold the covenant prescribed in the scroll which Ḥilkiyahu the priest had found in the Temple. And like him there was no king before him, who returned to the LORD with all his heart and all his soul and all his might, following all that was written in the Torah of Moses; and none like him came after. *II Kings 23:21–25*

Continue with the blessings after the Haftara on page 514.

TORAH READING FOR THE FIRST DAY OF ḤOL HAMO'ED PESAḤ

If the third day of Pesaḥ falls on Shabbat, the Reading for Shabbat Ḥol HaMo'ed is read (page 1134). In Israel, the Torah portion of the first day of Ḥol HaMo'ed is that of the second day of Yom Tov (page 1126).

And the LORD spoke to Moses, saying: Consecrate every firstborn to Me; that which first opens the wombs of the children of Israel, their people and their livestock, shall be Mine. And Moses said to the people: Remember this day, the day you came out of Egypt, out of the house of slavery, for it was with the strength of His hand that the LORD took you out of this place; no leaven may be eaten. You are going out today, in the month of Aviv. *When the LORD brings you to the land of the Canaanites, the Hittites, the Amorites, the Hivites and the Jebusites as He swore to your ancestors, giving you a land flowing with milk and honey, you must observe this rite in this month. For seven days you shall eat matzot, and the seventh day shall be a festival for the LORD. Matzot shall be eaten all these seven days; no leavened bread shall be seen by you, nor shall any leaven be seen by you within *Ex. 13:1–16* LEVI

אַ֣ךְ לֹ֣א יַעֲל֗וּ כֹּהֲנֵ֤י הַבָּמוֹת֙ אֶל־מִזְבַּ֣ח יהוה בִּירֽוּשָׁלָ֑͏ִם כִּ֛י אִם־אָכְל֥וּ מַצּ֖וֹת
בְּת֥וֹךְ אֲחֵיהֶֽם:

מלכים ב
כג:כא-כה

*וַיְצַ֤ו הַמֶּ֨לֶךְ֙ אֶת־כׇּל־הָעָ֣ם לֵאמֹ֔ר עֲשׂ֣וּ פֶ֔סַח לַֽיהוה אֱלֹֽהֵיכֶ֑ם כַּכָּת֕וּב עַ֖ל סֵ֥פֶר
הַבְּרִ֥ית הַזֶּֽה: כִּ֣י לֹ֤א נַֽעֲשָׂה֙ כַּפֶּ֣סַח הַזֶּ֔ה מִימֵי֙ הַשֹּׁ֣פְטִ֔ים אֲשֶׁ֥ר שָׁפְט֖וּ אֶת־
יִשְׂרָאֵ֑ל וְכֹ֗ל יְמֵ֛י מַלְכֵ֥י יִשְׂרָאֵ֖ל וּמַלְכֵ֥י יְהוּדָֽה: כִּ֗י אִם־בִּשְׁמֹנֶ֤ה עֶשְׂרֵה֙ שָׁנָ֔ה
לַמֶּ֖לֶךְ יֹֽאשִׁיָּ֑הוּ נַֽעֲשָׂ֞ה הַפֶּ֧סַח הַזֶּ֛ה לַֽיהוה בִּירֽוּשָׁלָֽ͏ִם: וְגַ֣ם אֶת־הָֽאֹב֣וֹת וְאֶת־
הַ֠יִּדְּעֹנִ֠ים וְאֶת־הַתְּרָפִ֨ים וְאֶת־הַגִּלֻּלִ֜ים וְאֵ֣ת כׇּל־הַשִּׁקֻּצִ֗ים אֲשֶׁ֤ר נִרְאוּ֙ בְּאֶ֤רֶץ
יְהוּדָה֙ וּבִיר֣וּשָׁלַ֔͏ִם בִּעֵ֖ר יֹֽאשִׁיָּ֑הוּ לְ֠מַ֠עַן הָקִ֞ים אֶת־דִּבְרֵ֤י הַתּוֹרָה֙ הַכְּתֻבִ֣ים
עַל־הַסֵּ֔פֶר אֲשֶׁ֥ר מָצָ֛א חִלְקִיָּ֥הוּ הַכֹּהֵ֖ן בֵּ֣ית יהוה: וְכָמֹ֩הוּ֩ לֹֽא־הָיָ֨ה לְפָנָ֜יו מֶ֗לֶךְ
אֲשֶׁר־שָׁ֣ב אֶל־יהוה בְּכׇל־לְבָב֤וֹ וּבְכׇל־נַפְשׁוֹ֙ וּבְכׇל־מְאֹד֔וֹ כְּכֹ֖ל תּוֹרַ֣ת מֹשֶׁ֑ה
וְאַֽחֲרָ֖יו לֹֽא־קָ֥ם כָּמֹֽהוּ:

Continue with the blessings after the הפטרה on page 515.

קריאה ליום א׳ דחול המועד פסח

*If the third day of פסח falls on שבת, the קריאת התורה for שבת חול המועד
is read (page 1135). In ארץ ישראל, the קריאת התורה of the first day of
Hol HaMo'ed is that of the second day of יום טוב (page 1127).*

שמות
יג:א-טז

וַיְדַבֵּ֥ר יהוה אֶל־מֹשֶׁ֥ה לֵּאמֹֽר: קַדֶּשׁ־לִ֨י כׇל־בְּכ֜וֹר פֶּ֤טֶר כׇּל־רֶ֨חֶם֙ בִּבְנֵ֣י יִשְׂרָאֵ֔ל
בָּֽאָדָ֖ם וּבַבְּהֵמָ֑ה לִ֖י הֽוּא: וַיֹּ֨אמֶר מֹשֶׁ֜ה אֶל־הָעָ֗ם זָכ֞וֹר אֶת־הַיּ֤וֹם הַזֶּה֙ אֲשֶׁ֨ר
יְצָאתֶ֤ם מִמִּצְרַ֨יִם֙ מִבֵּ֣ית עֲבָדִ֔ים כִּ֚י בְּחֹ֣זֶק יָ֔ד הוֹצִ֧יא יהוה אֶתְכֶ֖ם מִזֶּ֑ה וְלֹ֥א
יֵֽאָכֵ֖ל חָמֵֽץ: הַיּ֖וֹם אַתֶּ֣ם יֹֽצְאִ֑ים בְּחֹ֖דֶשׁ הָֽאָבִֽיב: לוי *וְהָיָ֣ה כִֽי־יְבִֽיאֲךָ֣ יהוה
אֶל־אֶ֣רֶץ הַֽ֠כְּנַֽעֲנִ֠י וְהַֽחִתִּ֨י וְהָֽאֱמֹרִ֜י וְהַֽחִוִּ֣י וְהַיְבוּסִ֗י אֲשֶׁ֨ר נִשְׁבַּ֤ע לַֽאֲבֹתֶ֨יךָ֙
לָ֣תֶת לָ֔ךְ אֶ֛רֶץ זָבַ֥ת חָלָ֖ב וּדְבָ֑שׁ וְעָֽבַדְתָּ֛ אֶת־הָֽעֲבֹדָ֥ה הַזֹּ֖את בַּחֹ֥דֶשׁ הַזֶּֽה:
שִׁבְעַ֥ת יָמִ֖ים תֹּאכַ֣ל מַצֹּ֑ת וּבַיּוֹם֙ הַשְּׁבִיעִ֔י חַ֖ג לַֽיהוה: מַצּוֹת֙ יֵֽאָכֵ֔ל אֵ֖ת שִׁבְעַ֣ת
הַיָּמִ֑ים וְלֹֽא־יֵֽרָאֶ֨ה לְךָ֜ חָמֵ֗ץ וְלֹֽא־יֵֽרָאֶ֥ה לְךָ֛ שְׂאֹ֖ר בְּכׇל־גְּבֻלֶֽךָ: וְהִגַּדְתָּ֣ לְבִנְךָ֞

TORAH READING FOR THE THIRD DAY OF PESAḤ

This passage is part of God's and Moses' instructions to the Israelites prior
to the exodus so that they would never forget the significance of that event
throughout all future generations.

זָכוֹר אֶת־הַיּוֹם הַזֶּה *Remember this day.* Remember it each year on the anni-

any of your borders. And you shall explain to your child on that day, "It is because of what the LORD did for me when I went out of Egypt." And this should be a sign on your arm, a remembrance between your eyes, that the LORD's Torah be on your tongue always; for it was with a strong hand that the LORD took you out of Egypt. And you shall observe these laws at their appointed time, each and every year.

When the LORD brings you to the land of the Canaanites, as He swore SHELISHI to you and to your forefathers, and gives it to you, you shall set aside for the LORD all that first opens the womb; all that opens the womb, the offspring of livestock belonging to you – the males shall be for the LORD. And every firstborn donkey shall be redeemed with a lamb; if you do not redeem it, you must behead it. And every human firstborn among your sons you must redeem. And if in time to come your child should ask you, "What is this?" You shall say to him: "With a strong hand the LORD brought us out of Egypt, from the house of slavery. And when Pharaoh harshly refused to release us, the LORD slew every firstborn in the land of Egypt, from the firstborn sons to the firstborn cattle; that is why I offer up to the LORD every male animal that first opens the womb; and any firstborn son born to me I must redeem." This shall be a sign upon your hand and an emblem between your eyes; for by the strength of His hand the LORD took us out of Egypt.

The first Torah scroll is lifted up (page 164) and Revi'i is read from the second Torah scroll:

And you shall bring an offering consumed by fire, a burnt-offering *Num. 28:19–25* to the LORD: two young bullocks, one ram, and seven yearling male lambs; they shall be to you unblemished. And you shall perform their meal-offerings, fine flour mixed with oil, three-tenths of an ephah for each bull, two-tenths of an ephah for the ram; and one-tenth of an ephah for each of the seven lambs; and one goat for a sin-offering, to make atonement for you. All this aside from the morning burnt-offering, the daily offering; You shall offer all of these as food, on each of the seven days, a burnt-offering by fire of pleasing aroma to the LORD, along with the regular daily offering and its libation. On the seventh day there shall be a sacred assembly: you shall do no laborious work.

Half Kaddish is said, and the second Torah scroll is lifted up (page 164). Both Torah scrolls are returned to the Ark (page 166).

בַּיּוֹם הַהוּא לֵאמֹר בַּעֲבוּר זֶה עָשָׂה יְהֹוָה לִי בְּצֵאתִי מִמִּצְרָיִם: וְהָיָה לְךָ
לְאוֹת עַל־יָדְךָ וּלְזִכָּרוֹן בֵּין עֵינֶיךָ לְמַעַן תִּהְיֶה תּוֹרַת יְהֹוָה בְּפִיךָ כִּי בְּיָד
חֲזָקָה הוֹצִאֲךָ יְהֹוָה מִמִּצְרָיִם: וְשָׁמַרְתָּ אֶת־הַחֻקָּה הַזֹּאת לְמוֹעֲדָהּ מִיָּמִים
יָמִימָה:

שלישי
וְהָיָה כִּי־יְבִאֲךָ יְהֹוָה אֶל־אֶרֶץ הַכְּנַעֲנִי כַּאֲשֶׁר נִשְׁבַּע לְךָ וְלַאֲבֹתֶיךָ וּנְתָנָהּ
לָךְ: וְהַעֲבַרְתָּ כָל־פֶּטֶר־רֶחֶם לַיהֹוָה וְכָל־פֶּטֶר ׀ שֶׁגֶר בְּהֵמָה אֲשֶׁר יִהְיֶה
לְךָ הַזְּכָרִים לַיהֹוָה: וְכָל־פֶּטֶר חֲמֹר תִּפְדֶּה בְשֶׂה וְאִם־לֹא תִפְדֶּה וַעֲרַפְתּוֹ
וְכֹל בְּכוֹר אָדָם בְּבָנֶיךָ תִּפְדֶּה: וְהָיָה כִּי־יִשְׁאָלְךָ בִנְךָ מָחָר לֵאמֹר מַה־זֹּאת
וְאָמַרְתָּ אֵלָיו בְּחֹזֶק יָד הוֹצִיאָנוּ יְהֹוָה מִמִּצְרַיִם מִבֵּית עֲבָדִים: וַיְהִי כִּי־
הִקְשָׁה פַרְעֹה לְשַׁלְּחֵנוּ וַיַּהֲרֹג יְהֹוָה כָּל־בְּכוֹר בְּאֶרֶץ מִצְרַיִם מִבְּכֹר אָדָם
וְעַד־בְּכוֹר בְּהֵמָה עַל־כֵּן אֲנִי זֹבֵחַ לַיהֹוָה כָּל־פֶּטֶר רֶחֶם הַזְּכָרִים וְכָל־בְּכוֹר בָּנַי
אֶפְדֶּה: וְהָיָה לְאוֹת עַל־יָדְכָה וּלְטוֹטָפֹת בֵּין עֵינֶיךָ כִּי בְּחֹזֶק יָד הוֹצִיאָנוּ יְהֹוָה
מִמִּצְרָיִם:

The first ספר תורה *is lifted up* (page 165) *and* רביעי *is read from the second* ספר תורה:

במדבר כח:
יט-כה
וְהִקְרַבְתֶּם אִשֶּׁה עֹלָה לַיהֹוָה פָּרִים בְּנֵי־בָקָר שְׁנַיִם וְאַיִל אֶחָד וְשִׁבְעָה כְבָשִׂים
בְּנֵי שָׁנָה תְּמִימִם יִהְיוּ לָכֶם: וּמִנְחָתָם סֹלֶת בְּלוּלָה בַשָּׁמֶן שְׁלֹשָׁה עֶשְׂרֹנִים
לַפָּר וּשְׁנֵי עֶשְׂרֹנִים לָאַיִל תַּעֲשׂוּ: עִשָּׂרוֹן עִשָּׂרוֹן תַּעֲשֶׂה לַכֶּבֶשׂ הָאֶחָד לְשִׁבְעַת
הַכְּבָשִׂים: וּשְׂעִיר חַטָּאת אֶחָד לְכַפֵּר עֲלֵיכֶם: מִלְּבַד עֹלַת הַבֹּקֶר אֲשֶׁר לְעֹלַת
הַתָּמִיד תַּעֲשׂוּ אֶת־אֵלֶּה: כָּאֵלֶּה תַּעֲשׂוּ לַיּוֹם שִׁבְעַת יָמִים לֶחֶם אִשֵּׁה רֵיחַ־
נִיחֹחַ לַיהֹוָה עַל־עוֹלַת הַתָּמִיד יֵעָשֶׂה וְנִסְכּוֹ: וּבַיּוֹם הַשְּׁבִיעִי מִקְרָא־קֹדֶשׁ
יִהְיֶה לָכֶם כָּל־מְלֶאכֶת עֲבֹדָה לֹא תַעֲשׂוּ:

חֲצִי קַדִּישׁ *is said, and the second* ספר תורה *is lifted up* (page 165).
Both ספרי תורה *are returned to the* ארון קודש (page 167).

versary of the exodus. Here, for the first time in history, remembering becomes a religious duty. There is a difference between history and memory.
History is a record of the past; memory is the living presence of the past. In
Judaism, history is transformed into memory so that it becomes part of who
we are and how we live.

TORAH READING FOR THE SECOND DAY OF ḤOL HAMO'ED PESAḤ (THIRD DAY OF ḤOL HAMO'ED IN ISRAEL)

If the fourth day of Pesaḥ falls on Sunday, the Reading for the third day is read (*page 1128*).

Should you lend money to one of My people, to a poor man among you, do not conduct yourself toward him as a usurer: do not burden him with interest. Should you take the robe of your kinsman as collateral, you must return it to him before the sun sets. For that is his only clothing – the robe he wears upon his skin – with what is he to lie down? If he cries out to Me I will listen; for I am compassionate. *Ex. 22:24–23:19*

LEVI You shall not blaspheme God, nor shall you curse a leader among your people. You may not delay your bringing of the fullness of your harvest or the outflow of your presses. You shall give Me the firstborn of your sons. You shall do the same with your oxen and your flock – the young shall stay with their mothers for seven days, but on the eighth day you shall offer them to Me. Be sanctified people unto Me: do not eat meat that has been torn up in the field, but cast it away to the dogs.

Do not utter a false report; do not join hands with a wicked man by acting as a false witness. Do not follow a majority to condemn; do not follow the majority to speak in a dispute in a way which will pervert judgment. And neither may you favor a poor man in his case at law.

If you encounter your enemy's ox or donkey gone astray, you must certainly return it to him. If you see the donkey of your enemy stooping under its load, and you hesitate to help – you must certainly help him.

SHELISHI Do not pervert the judgment of your poor in his case at law. Keep your distance from false speech, and do not cause the innocent and righteous to die; for I will not allow the wicked to be acquitted. And do not take bribes, for bribes blind those who see and pervert the words of the righteous. Do not press the stranger; you know the soul of the stranger, for you yourselves were strangers in the land of Egypt. For six years you may plant your land and gather its harvest. But in the seventh year

---

וְהַשְּׁבִיעִת *The seventh year.* The seventh year, like the seventh day, must be a time of rest – in this case for the land. The law, with its stipulation that the produce of the field should be available to all, appears here because of its association with other commands to have care for the poor.

קריאה ליום ב׳ דחול המועד פסח (יום ג׳ בארץ ישראל)

If the fourth day of פסח *falls on Sunday, the* קריאת התורה *for the third day is read* (*page 1129*).

אִם־כֶּסֶף ׀ תַּלְוֶה אֶת־עַמִּי אֶת־הֶעָנִי עִמָּךְ לֹא־תִהְיֶה לוֹ כְּנֹשֶׁה לֹא־תְשִׂימוּן שמות כב:כד–כג:יט
עָלָיו נֶשֶׁךְ: אִם־חָבֹל תַּחְבֹּל שַׂלְמַת רֵעֶךָ עַד־בֹּא הַשֶּׁמֶשׁ תְּשִׁיבֶנּוּ לוֹ: כִּי הִוא
כְסוּתֹה לְבַדָּהּ הִוא שִׂמְלָתוֹ לְעֹרוֹ בַּמֶּה יִשְׁכָּב וְהָיָה כִּי־יִצְעַק אֵלַי וְשָׁמַעְתִּי
כִּי־חַנּוּן אָנִי: *אֱלֹהִים לֹא תְקַלֵּל וְנָשִׂיא בְעַמְּךָ לֹא תָאֹר: מְלֵאָתְךָ לוי
וְדִמְעֲךָ לֹא תְאַחֵר בְּכוֹר בָּנֶיךָ תִּתֶּן־לִּי: כֵּן־תַּעֲשֶׂה לְשֹׁרְךָ לְצֹאנֶךָ שִׁבְעַת יָמִים
יִהְיֶה עִם־אִמּוֹ בַּיּוֹם הַשְּׁמִינִי תִּתְּנוֹ־לִי: וְאַנְשֵׁי־קֹדֶשׁ תִּהְיוּן לִי וּבָשָׂר בַּשָּׂדֶה
טְרֵפָה לֹא תֹאכֵלוּ לַכֶּלֶב תַּשְׁלִכוּן אֹתוֹ: לֹא תִשָּׂא שֵׁמַע שָׁוְא
אַל־תָּשֶׁת יָדְךָ עִם־רָשָׁע לִהְיֹת עֵד חָמָס: לֹא־תִהְיֶה אַחֲרֵי־רַבִּים לְרָעֹת וְלֹא־
תַעֲנֶה עַל־רִב לִנְטֹת אַחֲרֵי רַבִּים לְהַטֹּת: וְדָל לֹא תֶהְדַּר בְּרִיבוֹ: כִּי
תִפְגַּע שׁוֹר אֹיִבְךָ אוֹ חֲמֹרוֹ תֹּעֶה הָשֵׁב תְּשִׁיבֶנּוּ לוֹ: כִּי־תִרְאֶה חֲמוֹר
שֹׂנַאֲךָ רֹבֵץ תַּחַת מַשָּׂאוֹ וְחָדַלְתָּ מֵעֲזֹב לוֹ עָזֹב תַּעֲזֹב עִמּוֹ: *לֹא שלישי
תַטֶּה מִשְׁפַּט אֶבְיֹנְךָ בְּרִיבוֹ: מִדְּבַר־שֶׁקֶר תִּרְחָק וְנָקִי וְצַדִּיק אַל־תַּהֲרֹג
כִּי לֹא־אַצְדִּיק רָשָׁע: וְשֹׁחַד לֹא תִקָּח כִּי הַשֹּׁחַד יְעַוֵּר פִּקְחִים וִיסַלֵּף דִּבְרֵי
צַדִּיקִים: וְגֵר לֹא תִלְחָץ וְאַתֶּם יְדַעְתֶּם אֶת־נֶפֶשׁ הַגֵּר כִּי־גֵרִים הֱיִיתֶם בְּאֶרֶץ
מִצְרָיִם: וְשֵׁשׁ שָׁנִים תִּזְרַע אֶת־אַרְצֶךָ וְאָסַפְתָּ אֶת־תְּבוּאָתָהּ: וְהַשְּׁבִיעִת

TORAH READING FOR THE FOURTH DAY OF PESAH

אִם־כֶּסֶף תַּלְוֶה *Should you lend money.* The word "should" is to be understood as "when." Helping the poor is not an option but an obligation.

כְּנֹשֶׁה *As a usurer.* Do not humiliate those unable to repay. The Torah consistently stresses not just the material needs of the poor but also their psychological need for self-respect. Human dignity is to be honored, especially when it is most vulnerable.

אַחֲרֵי־רַבִּים לְרָעֹת *Do not follow a majority to condemn.* Do not assume that a majority is always right. The "herd instinct" is to be avoided. Popular sentiment often conflicts with truth and justice. We must never sacrifice individual judgment to conform to the crowd when we suspect they may be wrong.

וְדָל לֹא תֶהְדַּר *Neither may you favor a poor man.* Charity is one thing, justice another. We must never pervert the latter for the sake of the former. Each has its specific place in the moral life and they must not be confused.

you must leave it be and let it lie fallow, so that the poor among your people might eat of it, and the beasts of the field might eat what remains; this is what you shall do with your vineyards and olive orchards. Six days you may perform your work, but on the seventh day, you shall refrain from working, so that your ox and donkey might rest, and so that the child of your female slave, and the stranger, might find respite. Take care to adhere to all that I have commanded you, and do not pronounce the name of any foreign god; none of them should be heard from your mouth. You shall celebrate three festivals each year for Me. Keep the Festival of Matzot: eat matzot for seven days, as I have commanded you, in the season of the month of the Aviv, for that is when you came out of Egypt – do not come before Me empty-handed; and the Festival of Harvest, [when you shall offer] the first produce of the grain that you plant in the field, and the Festival of Gathering, at the end of the year, when you gather your harvest from the field. Three times a year all males shall present themselves before their Master, the LORD. Do not offer the blood of My sacrifice with leaven; the fats of My festive [Pesaḥ] offering may not remain until the morning. You shall bring the first fruits of your land to the House of the LORD your God. You may not cook a kid in its mother's milk.

The first Torah scroll is lifted up (page 164) and Revi'i is read from the second Torah scroll:

And you shall bring an offering consumed by fire, a burnt-offering to the LORD: two young bullocks, one ram, and seven yearling male lambs; they shall be to you unblemished. And you shall perform their meal-offerings, fine flour mixed with oil, three-tenths of an ephah for each bull, two-tenths of an ephah for the ram; and one-tenth of an ephah for each of the seven lambs; and one goat for a sin-offering, to make atonement for you. All this aside from the morning burnt-offering, the daily offering; You shall offer all of these as food, on each of the seven days, a burnt-offering by fire of pleasing aroma to the LORD, along with the regular daily offering and its libation. On the seventh day there shall be a sacred assembly: you shall do no laborious work. *Num. 28:19–25*

Half Kaddish is said, and the second Torah scroll is lifted up (page 164). Both Torah scrolls are returned to the Ark (page 166).

---

times in the Torah to forbid (1) the cooking itself, (2) eating, and (3) deriving benefit from the mixture.

תִּשְׁמְטֶנָּה וּנְטַשְׁתָּהּ וְאָכְלוּ אֶבְיֹנֵי עַמֶּךָ וְיִתְרָם תֹּאכַל חַיַּת הַשָּׂדֶה כֵּן־תַּעֲשֶׂה
לְכַרְמְךָ לְזֵיתֶךָ׃ שֵׁשֶׁת יָמִים תַּעֲשֶׂה מַעֲשֶׂיךָ וּבַיּוֹם הַשְּׁבִיעִי תִּשְׁבֹּת לְמַעַן
יָנוּחַ שׁוֹרְךָ וַחֲמֹרֶךָ וְיִנָּפֵשׁ בֶּן־אֲמָתְךָ וְהַגֵּר׃ וּבְכֹל אֲשֶׁר־אָמַרְתִּי אֲלֵיכֶם
תִּשָּׁמֵרוּ וְשֵׁם אֱלֹהִים אֲחֵרִים לֹא תַזְכִּירוּ לֹא יִשָּׁמַע עַל־פִּיךָ׃ שָׁלֹשׁ רְגָלִים
תָּחֹג לִי בַּשָּׁנָה׃ אֶת־חַג הַמַּצּוֹת תִּשְׁמֹר שִׁבְעַת יָמִים תֹּאכַל מַצּוֹת כַּאֲשֶׁר
צִוִּיתִךָ לְמוֹעֵד חֹדֶשׁ הָאָבִיב כִּי־בוֹ יָצָאתָ מִמִּצְרָיִם וְלֹא־יֵרָאוּ פָנַי רֵיקָם׃
וְחַג הַקָּצִיר בִּכּוּרֵי מַעֲשֶׂיךָ אֲשֶׁר תִּזְרַע בַּשָּׂדֶה וְחַג הָאָסִף בְּצֵאת הַשָּׁנָה
בְּאָסְפְּךָ אֶת־מַעֲשֶׂיךָ מִן־הַשָּׂדֶה׃ שָׁלֹשׁ פְּעָמִים בַּשָּׁנָה יֵרָאֶה כָּל־זְכוּרְךָ
אֶל־פְּנֵי הָאָדֹן ׀ יהוה׃ לֹא־תִזְבַּח עַל־חָמֵץ דַּם־זִבְחִי וְלֹא־יָלִין חֵלֶב־חַגִּי
עַד־בֹּקֶר׃ רֵאשִׁית בִּכּוּרֵי אַדְמָתְךָ תָּבִיא בֵּית יהוה אֱלֹהֶיךָ לֹא־תְבַשֵּׁל גְּדִי
בַּחֲלֵב אִמּוֹ׃

The first ספר תורה *is lifted up* (*page 165*) *and* רביעי *is read from the second* ספר תורה*:*

במדבר כח: יט–כה
וְהִקְרַבְתֶּם אִשֶּׁה עֹלָה לַיהוה פָּרִים בְּנֵי־בָקָר שְׁנַיִם וְאַיִל אֶחָד וְשִׁבְעָה כְבָשִׂים
בְּנֵי שָׁנָה תְּמִימִם יִהְיוּ לָכֶם׃ וּמִנְחָתָם סֹלֶת בְּלוּלָה בַשָּׁמֶן שְׁלֹשָׁה עֶשְׂרֹנִים
לַפָּר וּשְׁנֵי עֶשְׂרֹנִים לָאַיִל תַּעֲשׂוּ׃ עִשָּׂרוֹן עִשָּׂרוֹן תַּעֲשֶׂה לַכֶּבֶשׂ הָאֶחָד לְשִׁבְעַת
הַכְּבָשִׂים׃ וּשְׂעִיר חַטָּאת אֶחָד לְכַפֵּר עֲלֵיכֶם׃ מִלְּבַד עֹלַת הַבֹּקֶר אֲשֶׁר לְעֹלַת
הַתָּמִיד תַּעֲשׂוּ אֶת־אֵלֶּה׃ כָּאֵלֶּה תַּעֲשׂוּ לַיּוֹם שִׁבְעַת יָמִים לֶחֶם אִשֵּׁה רֵיחַ־
נִיחֹחַ לַיהוה עַל־עוֹלַת הַתָּמִיד יֵעָשֶׂה וְנִסְכּוֹ׃ וּבַיּוֹם הַשְּׁבִיעִי מִקְרָא־קֹדֶשׁ
יִהְיֶה לָכֶם כָּל־מְלֶאכֶת עֲבֹדָה לֹא תַעֲשׂוּ׃

חצי קדיש *is said, and the second* ספר תורה *is lifted up* (*page 165*).
Both ספרי תורה *are returned to the* ארון קודש (*page 167*).

תִּשְׁמְטֶנָּה *You shall refrain from working.* This verse emphasizes the social and moral dimension of Shabbat as a time when servants and domestic animals are, for a day each week, granted the experience of freedom.

שָׁלֹשׁ רְגָלִים *Three festivals each year.* There were to be three pilgrimage festivals, corresponding to key moments in the agricultural year: Pesaḥ in spring when the first grain ripens, Shavuot the time of first-fruits, and Sukkot, the festival of ingathering when the harvest is stored to protect it from the early autumn rain.

לֹא־תְבַשֵּׁל גְּדִי בַּחֲלֵב אִמּוֹ *You may not cook a kid in its mother's milk.* A specific instance of the general prohibition of mixing meat and milk, stated three

TORAH READING FOR THE THIRD DAY OF ḤOL HAMO'ED PESAḤ (FOURTH DAY OF ḤOL HAMO'ED IN ISRAEL)

If the fifth day of Pesaḥ falls on Shabbat, the Reading for Shabbat Ḥol HaMo'ed is read (page 1134); if it falls on Monday, the Reading for the fourth day is read (page 1130).

The LORD said to Moses: Carve out two stone tablets for yourself, like the first ones, and I will inscribe on them the same words that were on the first tablets, which you broke. Prepare yourself by morning, for in the morning you shall go up to Mount Sinai and stand before Me there, at the summit. No one shall go up with you, nor shall anyone be seen anywhere on the mountain; even the sheep and cattle may not graze in front of that mountain. *So he carved out two stone tablets like the first ones; Moses arose early in the morning and walked up Mount Sinai as the LORD had commanded him, taking in his hand the two stone tablets. The LORD descended in a cloud, and stood with him there; and proclaimed in the name of the LORD. And the LORD passed by before him and proclaimed: "The LORD, the LORD, compassionate and gracious God, slow to anger, abounding in loving-kindness and truth, extending loving-kindness to a thousand generations, forgiving iniquity, rebellion and sin, He shall not absolve [those who do not repent], but shall visit the punishment of fathers' sins upon their children and grandchildren to the third and fourth generation." And Moses hastened to bow to the ground, prostrating himself. He said: "O LORD, if I find favor in Your eyes, please, let the LORD go forth in our midst, for this is a stiff-necked people; forgive us our iniquity and our sin, and take us as Your inheritance." He said: "Behold, I will forge a covenant: in the presence of your entire people I will work wonders like none ever formed in all the world or for any nation; this people among whom you dwell shall witness the works of the LORD, for what I will do for you is awesome indeed. *Keep what I command you today; I shall expel the Amorites, the Canaanites, the Hittites, the Perizites, the Hivites and the Jebusites for you. Guard yourselves against forging any covenant with the inhabitants of the land that you are about to enter, so that they do not become a snare in your path. Instead, shatter their altars, break apart their sacred pillars, and cut down their worshiped trees. For you may not bow to any other god, for the LORD's name is Jealous; He is a jealous God. [And so do this,] lest you make a covenant with an inhabitant of the land and, when they stray

Ex. 34:1–26

LEVI

SHELISHI

קריאה ליום ג' דחול המועד פסח (יום ד' בארץ ישראל)

If the fifth day of פסח falls on שבת, the קריאת התורה for שבת חול המועד is read (page 1135),
if it falls on Monday, the קריאת התורה for the fourth day is read (page 1131).

שמות
לד: א-כו

וַיֹּאמֶר יְהוָה אֶל־מֹשֶׁה פְּסָל־לְךָ שְׁנֵי־לֻחֹת אֲבָנִים כָּרִאשֹׁנִים וְכָתַבְתִּי עַל־
הַלֻּחֹת אֶת־הַדְּבָרִים אֲשֶׁר הָיוּ עַל־הַלֻּחֹת הָרִאשֹׁנִים אֲשֶׁר שִׁבַּרְתָּ: וֶהְיֵה
נָכוֹן לַבֹּקֶר וְעָלִיתָ בַבֹּקֶר אֶל־הַר סִינַי וְנִצַּבְתָּ לִי שָׁם עַל־רֹאשׁ הָהָר: וְאִישׁ
לֹא־יַעֲלֶה עִמָּךְ וְגַם־אִישׁ אַל־יֵרָא בְּכָל־הָהָר גַּם־הַצֹּאן וְהַבָּקָר אַל־יִרְעוּ אֶל־
מוּל הָהָר הַהוּא: *וַיִּפְסֹל שְׁנֵי־לֻחֹת אֲבָנִים כָּרִאשֹׁנִים וַיַּשְׁכֵּם מֹשֶׁה בַבֹּקֶר

לוי

וַיַּעַל אֶל־הַר סִינַי כַּאֲשֶׁר צִוָּה יְהוָה אֹתוֹ וַיִּקַּח בְּיָדוֹ שְׁנֵי לֻחֹת אֲבָנִים: וַיֵּרֶד
יְהוָה בֶּעָנָן וַיִּתְיַצֵּב עִמּוֹ שָׁם וַיִּקְרָא בְשֵׁם יְהוָה: וַיַּעֲבֹר יְהוָה ׀ עַל־פָּנָיו וַיִּקְרָא
יְהוָה ׀ יְהוָה אֵל רַחוּם וְחַנּוּן אֶרֶךְ אַפַּיִם וְרַב־חֶסֶד וֶאֱמֶת: נֹצֵר חֶסֶד לָאֲלָפִים
נֹשֵׂא עָוֺן וָפֶשַׁע וְחַטָּאָה וְנַקֵּה לֹא יְנַקֶּה פֹּקֵד ׀ עֲוֺן אָבוֹת עַל־בָּנִים וְעַל־בְּנֵי
בָנִים עַל־שִׁלֵּשִׁים וְעַל־רִבֵּעִים: וַיְמַהֵר מֹשֶׁה וַיִּקֹּד אַרְצָה וַיִּשְׁתָּחוּ: וַיֹּאמֶר
אִם־נָא מָצָאתִי חֵן בְּעֵינֶיךָ אֲדֹנָי יֵלֶךְ־נָא אֲדֹנָי בְּקִרְבֵּנוּ כִּי עַם־קְשֵׁה־עֹרֶף
הוּא וְסָלַחְתָּ לַעֲוֺנֵנוּ וּלְחַטָּאתֵנוּ וּנְחַלְתָּנוּ: וַיֹּאמֶר הִנֵּה אָנֹכִי כֹּרֵת בְּרִית נֶגֶד
כָּל־עַמְּךָ אֶעֱשֶׂה נִפְלָאֹת אֲשֶׁר לֹא־נִבְרְאוּ בְכָל־הָאָרֶץ וּבְכָל־הַגּוֹיִם וְרָאָה
כָל־הָעָם אֲשֶׁר־אַתָּה בְקִרְבּוֹ אֶת־מַעֲשֵׂה יְהוָה כִּי־נוֹרָא הוּא אֲשֶׁר אֲנִי עֹשֶׂה

שלישי

עִמָּךְ: שְׁמָר־לְךָ אֵת אֲשֶׁר אָנֹכִי מְצַוְּךָ הַיּוֹם הִנְנִי גֹרֵשׁ מִפָּנֶיךָ אֶת־הָאֱמֹרִי
וְהַכְּנַעֲנִי וְהַחִתִּי וְהַפְּרִזִּי וְהַחִוִּי וְהַיְבוּסִי: הִשָּׁמֶר לְךָ פֶּן־תִּכְרֹת בְּרִית לְיוֹשֵׁב
הָאָרֶץ אֲשֶׁר אַתָּה בָּא עָלֶיהָ פֶּן־יִהְיֶה לְמוֹקֵשׁ בְּקִרְבֶּךָ: כִּי אֶת־מִזְבְּחֹתָם
תִּתֹּצוּן וְאֶת־מַצֵּבֹתָם תְּשַׁבֵּרוּן וְאֶת־אֲשֵׁרָיו תִּכְרֹתוּן: כִּי לֹא תִשְׁתַּחֲוֶה לְאֵל
אַחֵר כִּי יְהוָה קַנָּא שְׁמוֹ אֵל קַנָּא הוּא: פֶּן־תִּכְרֹת בְּרִית לְיוֹשֵׁב הָאָרֶץ וְזָנוּ ׀

TORAH READING FOR THE FIFTH DAY OF PESAḤ

Moses' plea for divine forgiveness after the sin of the golden calf has been
accepted. God now commands him to prepare two tablets of stone to replace
those that had been broken when Moses first descended and saw the people
in disarray. These were to be a visible sign that the covenant between the
people and God had been restored.

וַיַּעֲבֹר יהוה *And the LORD passed by.* According to the sages, God showed
Moses how to pray on future occasions when Israel sinned, by invoking
the qualities known as the "Thirteen Attributes of Mercy" (*Rosh HaShana*

after their gods and offer sacrifices to them, he invite you to partake of his sacrifice, and you do. And lest you take of his daughters to marry your sons; and these daughters stray after their gods and cause your sons to worship them too. Do not make molten gods for yourselves. Observe the Festival of Matzot: you shall eat matzot for seven days as I have commanded you, at the season of the month of Aviv, for in the month of Aviv you went out of Egypt. Every firstborn that opens the womb is Mine, as well as every firstborn male of your herd, whether bullock or lamb. A firstborn donkey must be redeemed with a lamb, and if you do not redeem it, you must behead it; each of your own firstborn sons must be redeemed: do not approach Me empty-handed. Six days you shall do your work but on the seventh day you shall rest: in plowing and in sowing seasons too, you must rest. You shall celebrate a Festival of Weeks [Shavuot] at the time of the first wheat harvest, and a festival of ingathering [Sukkot] at the completion of the year. Three times a year all males shall present themselves before their Master, the Lord God of Israel. When I conquer nations for you and extend your borders, no one will covet your land when you go up to be seen by the Lord your God, three times each year. Do not slaughter My [Pesaḥ] offering along with leaven; the offering of the Pesaḥ festival must not be allowed to remain until morning. You shall bring the first fruits of your land to the House of the Lord your God. Do not cook a kid in its mother's milk.

The first Torah scroll is lifted up (page 164) and Revi'i is read from the second Torah scroll:

And you shall bring an offering consumed by fire, a burnt-offering to the Lord: two young bullocks, one ram, and seven yearling male lambs; they shall be to you unblemished. And you shall perform their meal-offerings, fine flour mixed with oil, three-tenths of an ephah for each bull, two-tenths of an ephah for the ram; and one-tenth of an ephah for each of the seven lambs; and one goat for a sin-offering, to make atonement for you. All this aside from the morning burnt-offering, the daily offering; You shall offer all of these as food, on each of the seven days, a burnt-offering by fire of pleasing aroma to the Lord, along with the regular daily offering and its libation. On the seventh day there shall be a sacred assembly: you shall do no laborious work.

Half Kaddish is said, and the second Torah scroll is lifted up (page 164). Both Torah scrolls are returned to the Ark (page 166).

אַחֲרֵי אֱלֹהֵיהֶם וְזָבְחוּ לֵאלֹהֵיהֶם וְקָרָא לְךָ וְאָכַלְתָּ מִזִּבְחוֹ: וְלָקַחְתָּ מִבְּנֹתָיו
לְבָנֶיךָ וְזָנוּ בְנֹתָיו אַחֲרֵי אֱלֹהֵיהֶן וְהִזְנוּ אֶת־בָּנֶיךָ אַחֲרֵי אֱלֹהֵיהֶן: אֱלֹהֵי מַסֵּכָה
לֹא תַעֲשֶׂה־לָּךְ: אֶת־חַג הַמַּצּוֹת תִּשְׁמֹר שִׁבְעַת יָמִים תֹּאכַל מַצּוֹת אֲשֶׁר
צִוִּיתִךָ לְמוֹעֵד חֹדֶשׁ הָאָבִיב כִּי בְּחֹדֶשׁ הָאָבִיב יָצָאתָ מִמִּצְרָיִם: כָּל־פֶּטֶר
רֶחֶם לִי וְכָל־מִקְנְךָ תִּזָּכָר פֶּטֶר שׁוֹר וָשֶׂה: וּפֶטֶר חֲמוֹר תִּפְדֶּה בְשֶׂה וְאִם־
לֹא תִפְדֶּה וַעֲרַפְתּוֹ כֹּל בְּכוֹר בָּנֶיךָ תִּפְדֶּה וְלֹא־יֵרָאוּ פָנַי רֵיקָם: שֵׁשֶׁת יָמִים
תַּעֲבֹד וּבַיּוֹם הַשְּׁבִיעִי תִּשְׁבֹּת בֶּחָרִישׁ וּבַקָּצִיר תִּשְׁבֹּת: וְחַג שָׁבֻעֹת תַּעֲשֶׂה
לְךָ בִּכּוּרֵי קְצִיר חִטִּים וְחַג הָאָסִיף תְּקוּפַת הַשָּׁנָה: שָׁלֹשׁ פְּעָמִים בַּשָּׁנָה
יֵרָאֶה כָּל־זְכוּרְךָ אֶת־פְּנֵי הָאָדֹן ׀ יְהוָה אֱלֹהֵי יִשְׂרָאֵל: כִּי־אוֹרִישׁ גּוֹיִם מִפָּנֶיךָ
וְהִרְחַבְתִּי אֶת־גְּבֻלֶךָ וְלֹא־יַחְמֹד אִישׁ אֶת־אַרְצְךָ בַּעֲלֹתְךָ לֵרָאוֹת אֶת־פְּנֵי
יְהוָה אֱלֹהֶיךָ שָׁלֹשׁ פְּעָמִים בַּשָּׁנָה: לֹא־תִשְׁחַט עַל־חָמֵץ דַּם־זִבְחִי וְלֹא־יָלִין
לַבֹּקֶר זֶבַח חַג הַפָּסַח: רֵאשִׁית בִּכּוּרֵי אַדְמָתְךָ תָּבִיא בֵּית יְהוָה אֱלֹהֶיךָ
לֹא־תְבַשֵּׁל גְּדִי בַּחֲלֵב אִמּוֹ:

The first ספר תורה *is lifted up (page 165) and* רביעי *is read from the second* ספר תורה*:*

במדבר כח:יט–כה
וְהִקְרַבְתֶּם אִשֶּׁה עֹלָה לַיהוָה פָּרִים בְּנֵי־בָקָר שְׁנַיִם וְאַיִל אֶחָד וְשִׁבְעָה כְבָשִׂים
בְּנֵי שָׁנָה תְּמִימִם יִהְיוּ לָכֶם: וּמִנְחָתָם סֹלֶת בְּלוּלָה בַשָּׁמֶן שְׁלֹשָׁה עֶשְׂרֹנִים
לַפָּר וּשְׁנֵי עֶשְׂרֹנִים לָאַיִל תַּעֲשׂוּ: עִשָּׂרוֹן עִשָּׂרוֹן תַּעֲשֶׂה לַכֶּבֶשׂ הָאֶחָד לְשִׁבְעַת
הַכְּבָשִׂים: וּשְׂעִיר חַטָּאת אֶחָד לְכַפֵּר עֲלֵיכֶם: מִלְּבַד עֹלַת הַבֹּקֶר אֲשֶׁר לְעֹלַת
הַתָּמִיד תַּעֲשׂוּ אֶת־אֵלֶּה: כָּאֵלֶּה תַּעֲשׂוּ לַיּוֹם שִׁבְעַת יָמִים לֶחֶם אִשֵּׁה רֵיחַ־
נִיחֹחַ לַיהוָה עַל־עוֹלַת הַתָּמִיד יֵעָשֶׂה וְנִסְכּוֹ: וּבַיּוֹם הַשְּׁבִיעִי מִקְרָא־קֹדֶשׁ
יִהְיֶה לָכֶם כָּל־מְלֶאכֶת עֲבֹדָה לֹא תַעֲשׂוּ:

חצי קדיש *is said, and the second* ספר תורה *is lifted up (page 165).*
Both ספרי תורה *are returned to the* ארון קודש *(page 167).*

17b). These subsequently became the basis of *seliḥot*, penitential prayer, in Judaism.

בֶּחָרִישׁ וּבַקָּצִיר *In plowing and in sowing seasons too.* Even during the busiest times of the year, the command to rest on Shabbat must be kept.

וְלֹא־יַחְמֹד אִישׁ אֶת־אַרְצְךָ *No one will covet your land.* The people should not fail to keep the pilgrimage festivals for fear that while they are away from their homes and fields their enemies would attack and conquer their territory.

TORAH READING FOR THE FOURTH DAY OF ḤOL HAMO'ED PESAḤ (FIFTH DAY OF ḤOL HAMO'ED IN ISRAEL)

The LORD spoke to Moses in the Sinai Desert, in the first month of the second year after their exodus from Egypt, saying, "The children of Israel must bring the Pesaḥ offering at its appointed time. It shall be offered on the fourteenth day of this month, in the afternoon, at its appointed time; all its statutes and rules must be observed." And Moses spoke to the children of Israel, and told them to bring the Pesaḥ offering. And so they brought the Pesaḥ offering on the afternoon of the fourteenth day of the first month, in the Sinai Desert; just as the LORD commanded Moses, so did the children of Israel do. *There were some men who had been defiled by contact with death, so that they could not bring the Pesaḥ offering on that day; they approached Moses and Aaron on that very day. And the men said to Moses, "We are defiled by death; why should we be be excluded from bringing the LORD's sacrifice at its appointed time with the rest of the children of Israel?" Moses said to them, "Stand here, and I will hear what the LORD commands you to do." *Num. 9:1–14* LEVI

Then the LORD spoke to Moses, saying: "Any man who is defiled by death, or is on a long journey – now or in future generations – may still bring a Pesaḥ offering to the LORD. In the second month, on the afternoon of the fourteenth day shall they bring it; they must eat it with matzot and bitter herbs. They may not leave any of it until the morning, nor may they break any of its bones; they should bring it in accordance with all the rules of the Pesaḥ offering. But a man who is pure, and is not on a journey, and who neglects to bring the Pesaḥ offering – that soul will be cut off from among its people, for that man did not bring the LORD's offering at its appointed time, and he must bear his sin. If a proselyte lives among you and brings a Pesaḥ offering to the LORD, he must follow all the statutes and rules of the Pesaḥ offering; the same law shall apply to you, to the proselyte and to those born in your land. SHELISHI

---

community of Israel, participating in its covenant of fate: hence the severity of the punishment for one who deliberately does not do so.

קריאה ליום ד' דחול המועד פסח (יום ה' בארץ ישראל)

במדבר
ט:א-יד

וַיְדַבֵּ֨ר יְהֹוָ֧ה אֶל־מֹשֶׁ֛ה בְמִדְבַּר־סִינַ֛י בַּשָּׁנָ֥ה הַשֵּׁנִ֛ית לְצֵאתָ֥ם מֵאֶ֥רֶץ מִצְרַ֖יִם בַּחֹ֥דֶשׁ הָרִאשׁ֖וֹן לֵאמֹֽר: וְיַעֲשׂ֥וּ בְנֵֽי־יִשְׂרָאֵ֖ל אֶת־הַפֶּ֥סַח בְּמֽוֹעֲדֽוֹ: בְּאַרְבָּעָ֣ה עָשָׂר־י֠וֹם בַּחֹ֨דֶשׁ הַזֶּ֜ה בֵּ֣ין הָעַרְבַּ֗יִם תַּעֲשׂ֥וּ אֹת֖וֹ בְּמֹֽעֲד֑וֹ כְּכָל־חֻקֹּתָ֥יו וּכְכָל־מִשְׁפָּטָ֖יו תַּעֲשׂ֥וּ אֹתֽוֹ: וַיְדַבֵּ֥ר מֹשֶׁ֛ה אֶל־בְּנֵ֥י יִשְׂרָאֵ֖ל לַעֲשֹׂ֥ת הַפָּֽסַח: וַיַּעֲשׂ֣וּ אֶת־הַפֶּ֡סַח בָּרִאשׁ֡וֹן בְּאַרְבָּעָה֩ עָשָׂ֨ר י֥וֹם לַחֹ֛דֶשׁ בֵּ֥ין הָעַרְבַּ֖יִם בְּמִדְבַּ֣ר סִינָ֑י

לוי

כְּ֠כֹ֠ל אֲשֶׁ֨ר צִוָּ֤ה יְהֹוָה֙ אֶת־מֹשֶׁ֔ה כֵּ֥ן עָשׂ֖וּ בְּנֵ֥י יִשְׂרָאֵֽל: וַיְהִ֣י אֲנָשִׁ֗ים אֲשֶׁ֨ר הָי֤וּ טְמֵאִים֙ לְנֶ֣פֶשׁ אָדָ֔ם וְלֹא־יָכְל֥וּ לַעֲשֹׂת־הַפֶּ֖סַח בַּיּ֣וֹם הַה֑וּא וַיִּקְרְב֞וּ לִפְנֵ֥י מֹשֶׁ֛ה וְלִפְנֵ֥י אַהֲרֹ֖ן בַּיּ֥וֹם הַהֽוּא: וַיֹּאמְר֠וּ הָאֲנָשִׁ֤ים הָהֵ֙מָּה֙ אֵלָ֔יו אֲנַ֥חְנוּ טְמֵאִ֖ים לְנֶ֣פֶשׁ אָדָ֑ם לָ֣מָּה נִגָּרַ֗ע לְבִלְתִּ֨י הַקְרִ֜ב אֶת־קָרְבַּ֤ן יְהֹוָה֙ בְּמֹ֣עֲד֔וֹ בְּת֖וֹךְ בְּנֵ֥י יִשְׂרָאֵֽל: וַיֹּ֥אמֶר אֲלֵהֶ֖ם מֹשֶׁ֑ה עִמְד֣וּ וְאֶשְׁמְעָ֔ה מַה־יְצַוֶּ֥ה יְהֹוָ֖ה לָכֶֽם:

שלישי

וַיְדַבֵּ֥ר יְהֹוָ֖ה אֶל־מֹשֶׁ֥ה לֵּאמֹֽר: דַּבֵּ֛ר אֶל־בְּנֵ֥י יִשְׂרָאֵ֖ל לֵאמֹ֑ר אִ֣ישׁ אִ֣ישׁ כִּֽי־יִהְיֶֽה־טָמֵ֣א ׀ לָנֶ֡פֶשׁ אוֹ֩ בְדֶ֨רֶךְ רְחֹקָ֜הֿ לָכֶ֗ם א֚וֹ לְדֹרֹ֣תֵיכֶ֔ם וְעָ֥שָׂה פֶ֖סַח לַיהֹוָֽה: בַּחֹ֨דֶשׁ הַשֵּׁנִ֜י בְּאַרְבָּעָ֨ה עָשָׂ֥ר י֛וֹם בֵּ֥ין הָעַרְבַּ֖יִם יַעֲשׂ֣וּ אֹת֑וֹ עַל־מַצּ֥וֹת וּמְרֹרִ֖ים יֹאכְלֻֽהוּ: לֹֽא־יַשְׁאִ֤ירוּ מִמֶּ֙נּוּ֙ עַד־בֹּ֔קֶר וְעֶ֖צֶם לֹ֣א יִשְׁבְּרוּ־ב֑וֹ כְּכָל־חֻקַּ֥ת הַפֶּ֖סַח יַעֲשׂ֥וּ אֹתֽוֹ: וְהָאִישׁ֩ אֲשֶׁר־ה֨וּא טָה֜וֹר וּבְדֶ֣רֶךְ לֹא־הָיָ֗ה וְחָדַל֙ לַעֲשׂ֣וֹת הַפֶּ֔סַח וְנִכְרְתָ֛ה הַנֶּ֥פֶשׁ הַהִ֖וא מֵעַמֶּ֑יהָ כִּ֣י ׀ קָרְבַּ֣ן יְהֹוָ֗ה לֹ֤א הִקְרִיב֙ בְּמֹ֣עֲד֔וֹ חֶטְא֥וֹ יִשָּׂ֖א הָאִ֥ישׁ הַהֽוּא: וְכִֽי־יָג֨וּר אִתְּכֶ֜ם גֵּ֗ר וְעָ֤שָֽׂה פֶ֙סַח֙ לַֽיהֹוָ֔ה כְּחֻקַּ֥ת הַפֶּ֖סַח וּכְמִשְׁפָּט֑וֹ כֵּ֣ן יַעֲשֶׂ֑ה חֻקָּ֤ה אַחַת֙ יִהְיֶ֣ה לָכֶ֔ם וְלַגֵּ֖ר וּלְאֶזְרַ֥ח הָאָֽרֶץ:

TORAH READING FOR THE SIXTH DAY OF PESAḤ
The children of Israel must bring the Pesaḥ offering. In the book of Exodus, in addition to the Paschal sacrifice they offered in Egypt immediately prior to their departure, the Israelites were commanded to celebrate Pesaḥ only after arriving in the land of Israel (Ex. 12:25, 13:5). So this additional command was necessary to signal that it was to be celebrated also in their first year in the wilderness.

וְנִכְרְתָה הַנֶּפֶשׁ הַהִוא מֵעַמֶּיהָ That soul will be cut off from among its people. The act of observing Pesaḥ is a fundamental affirmation of membership in the

The first Torah scroll is lifted up (page 512) and Revi'i is read from the second Torah scroll:

And you shall bring an offering consumed by fire, a burnt-offering to the LORD: two young bullocks, one ram, and seven yearling male lambs; they shall be to you unblemished. And you shall perform their meal-offerings, fine flour mixed with oil, three-tenths of an ephah for each bull, two-tenths of an ephah for the ram; and one-tenth of an ephah for each of the seven lambs; and one goat for a sin-offering, to make atonement for you. All this aside from the morning burnt-offering, the daily offering; You shall offer all of these as food, on each of the seven days, a burnt-offering by fire of pleasing aroma to the LORD, along with the regular daily offering and its libation. On the seventh day there shall be a sacred assembly: you shall do no laborious work. *Num. 28:19–25*

Half Kaddish is said, and the second Torah scroll is lifted up (page 512). Both Torah scrolls are returned to the Ark (page 530).

TORAH READING FOR SHABBAT ḤOL HAMO'ED

Moses said to the LORD: Behold, You have told me to bring this people up [to the Land], but You have yet to inform me whom You shall send along with me; You have told me that You have singled me out and that I have found favor in Your eyes. Now, if I indeed find favor in Your eyes, let me know Your ways, so that I might become acquainted with You, so that I find favor in Your eyes: behold, this people is Your nation! He replied: My presence shall go forth and guide You. He said to Him: If Your countenance does not go with us, do not remove us from this place. How am I to know that I have found favor in Your eyes – I and Your people – if not through Your presence among us? Let me and Your people be chosen from all other nations in the land. *Ex. 33:12*

LEVI

The LORD said to Moses: I shall do this thing that you said, for you have found favor in My eyes, and I recognize you by name. He said: Please, show me Your glory! He said: I shall pass all My beneficence before you, calling out the name of the LORD in your presence, and

---

that God should reaffirm that Israel is indeed His people – that He has not distanced Himself from them.

The first ספר תורה *is lifted up (page 513) and* רביעי *is read from the second* ספר תורה*:*

במדבר כח: יט–כה

וְהִקְרַבְתֶּם אִשֶּׁה עֹלָה לַיהוה פָּרִים בְּנֵי־בָקָר שְׁנַיִם וְאַיִל אֶחָד וְשִׁבְעָה כְבָשִׂים
בְּנֵי שָׁנָה תְּמִימִם יִהְיוּ לָכֶם: וּמִנְחָתָם סֹלֶת בְּלוּלָה בַשָּׁמֶן שְׁלֹשָׁה עֶשְׂרֹנִים
לַפָּר וּשְׁנֵי עֶשְׂרֹנִים לָאַיִל תַּעֲשׂוּ: עִשָּׂרוֹן עִשָּׂרוֹן תַּעֲשֶׂה לַכֶּבֶשׂ הָאֶחָד לְשִׁבְעַת
הַכְּבָשִׂים: וּשְׂעִיר חַטָּאת אֶחָד לְכַפֵּר עֲלֵיכֶם: מִלְּבַד עֹלַת הַבֹּקֶר אֲשֶׁר לְעֹלַת
הַתָּמִיד תַּעֲשׂוּ אֶת־אֵלֶּה: כָּאֵלֶּה תַּעֲשׂוּ לַיּוֹם שִׁבְעַת יָמִים לֶחֶם אִשֵּׁה רֵיחַ־
נִיחֹחַ לַיהוה עַל־עוֹלַת הַתָּמִיד יֵעָשֶׂה וְנִסְכּוֹ: וּבַיּוֹם הַשְּׁבִיעִי מִקְרָא־קֹדֶשׁ
יִהְיֶה לָכֶם כָּל־מְלֶאכֶת עֲבֹדָה לֹא תַעֲשׂוּ:

חצי קדיש *is said, and the second* ספר תורה *is lifted up (page 513).*
Both ספרי תורה *are returned to the* ארון קודש *(page 531).*

קריאה לשבת חול המועד

שמות לג: יב–לד:כו

וַיֹּאמֶר מֹשֶׁה אֶל־יהוה רְאֵה אַתָּה אֹמֵר אֵלַי הַעַל אֶת־הָעָם הַזֶּה וְאַתָּה לֹא
הוֹדַעְתַּנִי אֵת אֲשֶׁר־תִּשְׁלַח עִמִּי וְאַתָּה אָמַרְתָּ יְדַעְתִּיךָ בְשֵׁם וְגַם־מָצָאתָ
חֵן בְּעֵינָי: וְעַתָּה אִם־נָא מָצָאתִי חֵן בְּעֵינֶיךָ הוֹדִעֵנִי נָא אֶת־דְּרָכֶךָ וְאֵדָעֲךָ
לְמַעַן אֶמְצָא־חֵן בְּעֵינֶיךָ וּרְאֵה כִּי עַמְּךָ הַגּוֹי הַזֶּה: וַיֹּאמַר פָּנַי יֵלֵכוּ וַהֲנִחֹתִי
לָךְ: וַיֹּאמֶר אֵלָיו אִם־אֵין פָּנֶיךָ הֹלְכִים אַל־תַּעֲלֵנוּ מִזֶּה: וּבַמֶּה | יִוָּדַע אֵפוֹא
כִּי־מָצָאתִי חֵן בְּעֵינֶיךָ אֲנִי וְעַמֶּךָ הֲלוֹא בְּלֶכְתְּךָ עִמָּנוּ וְנִפְלֵינוּ אֲנִי וְעַמְּךָ
מִכָּל־הָעָם אֲשֶׁר עַל־פְּנֵי הָאֲדָמָה:
לוי וַיֹּאמֶר יהוה אֶל־מֹשֶׁה גַּם אֶת־הַדָּבָר הַזֶּה אֲשֶׁר דִּבַּרְתָּ אֶעֱשֶׂה כִּי־מָצָאתָ
חֵן בְּעֵינַי וָאֵדָעֲךָ בְּשֵׁם: וַיֹּאמַר הַרְאֵנִי נָא אֶת־כְּבֹדֶךָ: וַיֹּאמֶר אֲנִי אַעֲבִיר

TORAH READING FOR SHABBAT OF ḤOL HAMO'ED

וַיֹּאמֶר מֹשֶׁה *Moses said.* The Israelites had made a golden calf, one of their most grievous sins in the wilderness. Moses had interceded with God on their behalf, descended, smashed the tablets, reprimanded the people, and punished the wrongdoers. Now Moses ascends the mountain to plead on their behalf again. He asks three things of God, first that His presence, not just an angel, should go with the people; second, that God "let him know His ways" so that he can understand the nature of divine justice; and third

I shall be gracious to whom I shall be gracious; I shall be merciful to whom I shall be merciful. *He said: You cannot see My face, for no man can see Me and live. The LORD said: Behold, there is a place near Me, where you can stand upon the rock. When My glory passes, I shall put you in the rock's cave, and cover you with My palm until I pass. Then I shall remove My palm and you shall see My back, but My face may not be seen. SHELISHI

The LORD said to Moses: Carve out two stone tablets for yourself, like the first ones, and I will inscribe on them the same words that were on the first tablets, which you broke. Prepare yourself by morning, for in the morning you shall go up to Mount Sinai and stand before Me there, at the summit. No one shall go up with you, nor shall anyone be seen anywhere on the mountain; even the sheep and cattle may not graze in front of that mountain. *So he carved out two stone tablets like the first ones; Moses arose early in the morning and walked up Mount Sinai as the LORD had commanded him, taking in his hand the two stone tablets. The LORD descended in a cloud, and stood with him there; and proclaimed in the name of the LORD. And the LORD passed by before him and proclaimed: "The LORD, the LORD, compassionate and gracious God, slow to anger, abounding in loving-kindness and truth, extending loving-kindness to a thousand generations, forgiving iniquity, rebellion and sin, and absolving [the guilty who repent]; He shall not absolve [those who do not repent], but shall visit the punishment of fathers' sins upon their children and grandchildren to the third and fourth generation." And Moses hastened to bow to the ground, prostrating himself. He said: "O LORD, if I find favor in Your eyes, please, let the LORD go forth in our midst, for this is a stiff-necked people; forgive us our iniquity and our sin, and take us as Your inheritance." He said: "Behold, I will forge a covenant: in the presence of your entire people I will work wonders like none ever formed in all the world or for any nation; this people among whom you dwell shall witness the works of the LORD, for what I will do for you is REVI'I HAMISHI

וַיֹּאמֶר הִנֵּה אָנֹכִי כֹּרֵת בְּרִית *He said: Behold, I will forge a covenant.* God renews the covenant in response to Moses' prayer.

כָּל־טוּבִי עַל־פָּנֶיךָ וְקָרָאתִי בְשֵׁם יהוה לְפָנֶיךָ וְחַנֹּתִי אֶת־אֲשֶׁר אָחֹן וְרִחַמְתִּי
שלישי אֶת־אֲשֶׁר אֲרַחֵם: *וַיֹּאמֶר לֹא תוּכַל לִרְאֹת אֶת־פָּנָי כִּי לֹא־יִרְאַנִי הָאָדָם וָחָי:
וַיֹּאמֶר יהוה הִנֵּה מָקוֹם אִתִּי וְנִצַּבְתָּ עַל־הַצּוּר: וְהָיָה בַּעֲבֹר כְּבֹדִי וְשַׂמְתִּיךָ
בְּנִקְרַת הַצּוּר וְשַׂכֹּתִי כַפִּי עָלֶיךָ עַד־עָבְרִי: וַהֲסִרֹתִי אֶת־כַּפִּי וְרָאִיתָ אֶת־
אֲחֹרָי וּפָנַי לֹא יֵרָאוּ:

רביעי וַיֹּאמֶר יהוה אֶל־מֹשֶׁה פְּסָל־לְךָ שְׁנֵי־לֻחֹת אֲבָנִים כָּרִאשֹׁנִים וְכָתַבְתִּי עַל־
הַלֻּחֹת אֶת־הַדְּבָרִים אֲשֶׁר הָיוּ עַל־הַלֻּחֹת הָרִאשֹׁנִים אֲשֶׁר שִׁבַּרְתָּ: וֶהְיֵה
נָכוֹן לַבֹּקֶר וְעָלִיתָ בַבֹּקֶר אֶל־הַר סִינַי וְנִצַּבְתָּ לִי שָׁם עַל־רֹאשׁ הָהָר: וְאִישׁ
לֹא־יַעֲלֶה עִמָּךְ וְגַם־אִישׁ אַל־יֵרָא בְּכָל־הָהָר גַּם־הַצֹּאן וְהַבָּקָר אַל־יִרְעוּ
חמישי אֶל־מוּל הָהָר הַהוּא: *וַיִּפְסֹל שְׁנֵי־לֻחֹת אֲבָנִים כָּרִאשֹׁנִים וַיַּשְׁכֵּם מֹשֶׁה
בַבֹּקֶר וַיַּעַל אֶל־הַר סִינַי כַּאֲשֶׁר צִוָּה יהוה אֹתוֹ וַיִּקַּח בְּיָדוֹ שְׁנֵי לֻחֹת אֲבָנִים:
וַיֵּרֶד יהוה בֶּעָנָן וַיִּתְיַצֵּב עִמּוֹ שָׁם וַיִּקְרָא בְשֵׁם יהוה: וַיַּעֲבֹר יהוה | עַל־פָּנָיו
וַיִּקְרָא יהוה | יהוה אֵל רַחוּם וְחַנּוּן אֶרֶךְ אַפַּיִם וְרַב־חֶסֶד וֶאֱמֶת: נֹצֵר חֶסֶד
לָאֲלָפִים נֹשֵׂא עָוֺן וָפֶשַׁע וְחַטָּאָה וְנַקֵּה לֹא יְנַקֶּה פֹּקֵד | עֲוֺן אָבוֹת עַל־בָּנִים
וְעַל־בְּנֵי בָנִים עַל־שִׁלֵּשִׁים וְעַל־רִבֵּעִים: וַיְמַהֵר מֹשֶׁה וַיִּקֹּד אַרְצָה וַיִּשְׁתָּחוּ:
וַיֹּאמֶר אִם־נָא מָצָאתִי חֵן בְּעֵינֶיךָ אֲדֹנָי יֵלֶךְ־נָא אֲדֹנָי בְּקִרְבֵּנוּ כִּי עַם־קְשֵׁה־
עֹרֶף הוּא וְסָלַחְתָּ לַעֲוֺנֵנוּ וּלְחַטָּאתֵנוּ וּנְחַלְתָּנוּ: וַיֹּאמֶר הִנֵּה אָנֹכִי כֹּרֵת בְּרִית
נֶגֶד כָּל־עַמְּךָ אֶעֱשֶׂה נִפְלָאֹת אֲשֶׁר לֹא־נִבְרְאוּ בְכָל־הָאָרֶץ וּבְכָל־הַגּוֹיִם
וְרָאָה כָל־הָעָם אֲשֶׁר־אַתָּה בְקִרְבּוֹ אֶת־מַעֲשֵׂה יהוה כִּי־נוֹרָא הוּא אֲשֶׁר

וְרָאִיתָ אֶת־אֲחֹרָי וּפָנַי לֹא יֵרָאוּ *You shall see My back, but My face may not be seen.* A metaphorical way of saying that only in retrospect do we see the presence of God in events. We live life forward but understand it only backward.

פְּסָל־לְךָ שְׁנֵי־לֻחֹת אֲבָנִים *Carve out two stone tablets.* The first tablets, entirely the work of God, were broken. The second, the work of God but with the participation of man, endured. So it is in the life of the spirit. The Divine Presence rests securely in this world only when we do something to create space for it.

עֲוֺן אָבוֹת עַל־בָּנִים *Visit the punishment of fathers' sins upon their children.* According to the Talmud (*Berakhot* 7a), only when the children repeat the sins of the fathers.

awesome indeed. *Keep what I command you today; I shall expel the Amorites, the Canaanites, the Hittites, the Perizites, the Hivites and the Jebusites for you. Guard yourselves against forging any covenant with the inhabitants of the land that you are about to enter, so that they do not become a snare in your path. Instead, shatter their altars, break apart their sacred pillars, and cut down their worshiped trees. For you may not bow to any other god, for the LORD's name is Jealous; He is a jealous God. [And so do this,] lest you make a covenant with an inhabitant of the land and, when they stray after their gods and offer sacrifices to them, he invite you to partake of his sacrifice, and you do. And lest you take of his daughters to marry your sons; and these daughters stray after their gods and cause your sons to worship them too. Do not make molten gods for yourselves. *Observe the Festival of Matzot: you shall eat matzot for seven days as I have commanded you, at the season of the month of Aviv, for in the month of Aviv you went out of Egypt. Every firstborn that opens the womb is Mine, as well as every firstborn male of your herd, whether bullock or lamb. A firstborn donkey must be redeemed with a lamb, and if you do not redeem it, you must behead it; each of your own firstborn sons must be redeemed: do not approach Me empty-handed. Six days you shall do your work but on the seventh day you shall rest: in plowing and in sowing seasons too, you must rest. You shall celebrate a Festival of Weeks [Shavuot] at the time of the first wheat harvest, and a festival of ingathering [Sukkot] at the completion of the year. Three times a year all males shall present themselves before their Master, the LORD God of Israel. When I conquer nations for you and extend your borders, no one will covet your land when you go up to be seen by the LORD your God, three times each year. Do not slaughter My [Pesaḥ] offering along with leaven; the offering of the Pesaḥ festival must not be allowed to remain until morning. You shall bring the first fruits of your land to the house of the LORD your God. Do not cook a kid in its mother's milk.

SHISHI

SHEVI'I

Continue with Half Kaddish on page 512. The Maftir is read from the the second Torah scroll. The Maftir for Shabbat Ḥol HaMo'ed Pesaḥ (page 1134) is the same as that for the other days of Ḥol HaMo'ed Pesaḥ. The Maftir for Shabbat Ḥol HaMo'ed Sukkot is the Torah reading of the day of Ḥol HaMo'ed Sukkot on which Shabbat falls (pages א1154–1158).

ששי אֲנִי עֹשֶׂה עִמָּךְ: *שְׁמׇר־לְךָ אֵת אֲשֶׁר אָנֹכִי מְצַוְּךָ הַיּוֹם הִנְנִי גֹרֵשׁ מִפָּנֶיךָ
אֶת־הָאֱמֹרִי וְהַכְּנַעֲנִי וְהַחִתִּי וְהַפְּרִזִּי וְהַחִוִּי וְהַיְבוּסִי: הִשָּׁמֶר לְךָ פֶּן־תִּכְרֹת
בְּרִית לְיוֹשֵׁב הָאָרֶץ אֲשֶׁר אַתָּה בָּא עָלֶיהָ פֶּן־יִהְיֶה לְמוֹקֵשׁ בְּקִרְבֶּךָ: כִּי
אֶת־מִזְבְּחֹתָם תִּתֹּצוּן וְאֶת־מַצֵּבֹתָם תְּשַׁבֵּרוּן וְאֶת־אֲשֵׁרָיו תִּכְרֹתוּן: כִּי לֹא
תִשְׁתַּחֲוֶה לְאֵל אַחֵר כִּי יהוה קַנָּא שְׁמוֹ אֵל קַנָּא הוּא: פֶּן־תִּכְרֹת בְּרִית
לְיוֹשֵׁב הָאָרֶץ וְזָנוּ ׀ אַחֲרֵי אֱלֹהֵיהֶם וְזָבְחוּ לֵאלֹהֵיהֶם וְקָרָא לְךָ וְאָכַלְתָּ
מִזִּבְחוֹ: וְלָקַחְתָּ מִבְּנֹתָיו לְבָנֶיךָ וְזָנוּ בְנֹתָיו אַחֲרֵי אֱלֹהֵיהֶן וְהִזְנוּ אֶת־בָּנֶיךָ
שביעי אַחֲרֵי אֱלֹהֵיהֶן: אֱלֹהֵי מַסֵּכָה לֹא תַעֲשֶׂה־לָּךְ: *אֶת־חַג הַמַּצּוֹת תִּשְׁמֹר
שִׁבְעַת יָמִים תֹּאכַל מַצּוֹת אֲשֶׁר צִוִּיתִךָ לְמוֹעֵד חֹדֶשׁ הָאָבִיב כִּי בְּחֹדֶשׁ
הָאָבִיב יָצָאתָ מִמִּצְרָיִם: כׇּל־פֶּטֶר רֶחֶם לִי וְכׇל־מִקְנְךָ תִּזָּכָר פֶּטֶר שׁוֹר וָשֶׂה:
וּפֶטֶר חֲמוֹר תִּפְדֶּה בְשֶׂה וְאִם־לֹא תִפְדֶּה וַעֲרַפְתּוֹ כֹּל בְּכוֹר בָּנֶיךָ תִּפְדֶּה
וְלֹא־יֵרָאוּ פָנַי רֵיקָם: שֵׁשֶׁת יָמִים תַּעֲבֹד וּבַיּוֹם הַשְּׁבִיעִי תִּשְׁבֹּת בֶּחָרִישׁ
וּבַקָּצִיר תִּשְׁבֹּת: וְחַג שָׁבֻעֹת תַּעֲשֶׂה לְךָ בִּכּוּרֵי קְצִיר חִטִּים וְחַג הָאָסִיף
תְּקוּפַת הַשָּׁנָה: שָׁלֹשׁ פְּעָמִים בַּשָּׁנָה יֵרָאֶה כׇּל־זְכוּרְךָ אֶת־פְּנֵי הָאָדֹן ׀ יהוה
אֱלֹהֵי יִשְׂרָאֵל: כִּי־אוֹרִישׁ גּוֹיִם מִפָּנֶיךָ וְהִרְחַבְתִּי אֶת־גְּבֻלֶךָ וְלֹא־יַחְמֹד אִישׁ
אֶת־אַרְצְךָ בַּעֲלֹתְךָ לֵרָאוֹת אֶת־פְּנֵי יהוה אֱלֹהֶיךָ שָׁלֹשׁ פְּעָמִים בַּשָּׁנָה: לֹא־
תִשְׁחַט עַל־חָמֵץ דַּם־זִבְחִי וְלֹא־יָלִין לַבֹּקֶר זֶבַח חַג הַפָּסַח: רֵאשִׁית בִּכּוּרֵי
אַדְמָתְךָ תָּבִיא בֵּית יהוה אֱלֹהֶיךָ לֹא־תְבַשֵּׁל גְּדִי בַּחֲלֵב אִמּוֹ:

Continue with חצי קדיש *on page 513. The* מפטיר *is read from the second* ספר תורה.
The מפטיר *for* שבת חול המועד פסח *is the same as that for the other days of* חול המועד פסח,
page 1135. The מפטיר *for* שבת חול המועד סוכות *is the* קריאת התורה *of the day*
of חול המועד סוכות *on which* שבת *falls* (*pages* א1155–1159).

שְׁמׇר־לְךָ... בַּחֲלֵב אִמּוֹ *Keep what I command you...in its mother's milk* (34:11–26). The prohibition of idolatry and anything that might lead to it, followed by an account of the three pilgrimage festivals. These are essential terms of the covenant. The prohibition of idolatry follows from Israel's exclusive covenant of loyalty with God. The festivals testify to God's presence in Israel's history.

לֹא־תְבַשֵּׁל גְּדִי בַּחֲלֵב אִמּוֹ *Do not cook a kid in its mother's milk.* The origin of the prohibition against mixing meat and milk. Maimonides infers from its

HAFTARA FOR SHABBAT ḤOL HAMO'ED PESAḤ

The LORD pressed His hand upon me; He brought me out with His wind and placed me in the valley; it was filled with bones. He made me traverse them all around; and there were very many of them all over the valley, and they were very dry. He said to me, "Son of man, can these bones be revived?" And I said, "LORD, O God, You alone know." He said to me, "Prophesy over these bones; say to them, 'O dry bones, listen to the word of the LORD! For so says the LORD God to these bones: Behold, I shall place My spirit within you and you shall live. I will place sinews upon you, pad you with flesh, and cover you with skin, and I shall place a spirit within you and you shall live; and you will know that I am the LORD.'" So I prophesied as I was commanded; and as I prophesied, there was a sound, a rattling noise – and the bones came together, each bone to its bone. And I watched as sinews were placed upon them, and flesh padded them, and skin covered them on the surface – but they were without breath. He said to me, "Prophesy, son of man, prophesy to the wind; say to the wind, 'Thus said the LORD God: Come, wind, from all four directions, and breathe into these slain ones, so that they might live.'" And I prophesied as He had commanded me, and the wind breathed into them and they were alive, and they stood upon their feet, an exceedingly vast army. He said to me, "Son of man, these bones are all the house of Israel: behold, they say, 'Our bones have dried, our hope is lost, our decree has been sealed.' Therefore, prophesy, saying to them, 'Thus spoke the LORD God: Behold, I shall open your graves and lift you out of your graves, My people; I shall bring you to the land of Israel. And you will know that I am the LORD when I open your graves and lift you out of your graves, My people. I shall breathe My spirit into you and you shall live, and I shall place you upon your land, and you will know that I am the LORD: I have spoken and performed,' says the LORD." *Ezek. 37:1–14*

Continue with the blessings after the Haftara on page 514.

הפטרה לשבת חול המועד פסח

יחזקאל לז:א–יד

הָיְתָה עָלַי יַד־יְהוָה וַיּוֹצִאֵנִי בְרוּחַ יְהוָה וַיְנִיחֵנִי בְּתוֹךְ הַבִּקְעָה וְהִיא
מְלֵאָה עֲצָמוֹת: וְהֶעֱבִירַנִי עֲלֵיהֶם סָבִיב ׀ סָבִיב וְהִנֵּה רַבּוֹת מְאֹד עַל־פְּנֵי
הַבִּקְעָה וְהִנֵּה יְבֵשׁוֹת מְאֹד: וַיֹּאמֶר אֵלַי בֶּן־אָדָם הֲתִחְיֶינָה הָעֲצָמוֹת
הָאֵלֶּה וָאֹמַר אֲדֹנָי יֱהוִה אַתָּה יָדָעְתָּ: וַיֹּאמֶר אֵלַי הִנָּבֵא עַל־הָעֲצָמוֹת
הָאֵלֶּה וְאָמַרְתָּ אֲלֵיהֶם הָעֲצָמוֹת הַיְבֵשׁוֹת שִׁמְעוּ דְּבַר־יְהוָה: כֹּה אָמַר
אֲדֹנָי יֱהוִה לָעֲצָמוֹת הָאֵלֶּה הִנֵּה אֲנִי מֵבִיא בָכֶם רוּחַ וִחְיִיתֶם: וְנָתַתִּי
עֲלֵיכֶם גִּידִים וְהַעֲלֵתִי עֲלֵיכֶם בָּשָׂר וְקָרַמְתִּי עֲלֵיכֶם עוֹר וְנָתַתִּי בָכֶם רוּחַ
וִחְיִיתֶם וִידַעְתֶּם כִּי־אֲנִי יְהוָה: וְנִבֵּאתִי כַּאֲשֶׁר צֻוֵּיתִי וַיְהִי־קוֹל כְּהִנָּבְאִי
וְהִנֵּה־רַעַשׁ וַתִּקְרְבוּ עֲצָמוֹת עֶצֶם אֶל־עַצְמוֹ: וְרָאִיתִי וְהִנֵּה־עֲלֵיהֶם גִּדִים
וּבָשָׂר עָלָה וַיִּקְרַם עֲלֵיהֶם עוֹר מִלְמָעְלָה וְרוּחַ אֵין בָּהֶם: וַיֹּאמֶר אֵלַי
הִנָּבֵא אֶל־הָרוּחַ הִנָּבֵא בֶן־אָדָם וְאָמַרְתָּ אֶל־הָרוּחַ כֹּה־אָמַר ׀ אֲדֹנָי
יֱהוִה מֵאַרְבַּע רוּחוֹת בֹּאִי הָרוּחַ וּפְחִי בַּהֲרוּגִים הָאֵלֶּה וְיִחְיוּ: וְהִנַּבֵּאתִי
כַּאֲשֶׁר צִוָּנִי וַתָּבוֹא בָהֶם הָרוּחַ וַיִּחְיוּ וַיַּעַמְדוּ עַל־רַגְלֵיהֶם חַיִל גָּדוֹל מְאֹד
מְאֹד: וַיֹּאמֶר אֵלַי בֶּן־אָדָם הָעֲצָמוֹת הָאֵלֶּה כָּל־בֵּית יִשְׂרָאֵל הֵמָּה הִנֵּה
אֹמְרִים יָבְשׁוּ עַצְמוֹתֵינוּ וְאָבְדָה תִקְוָתֵנוּ נִגְזַרְנוּ לָנוּ: לָכֵן הִנָּבֵא וְאָמַרְתָּ
אֲלֵיהֶם כֹּה־אָמַר אֲדֹנָי יֱהוִה הִנֵּה אֲנִי פֹתֵחַ אֶת־קִבְרוֹתֵיכֶם וְהַעֲלֵיתִי
אֶתְכֶם מִקִּבְרוֹתֵיכֶם עַמִּי וְהֵבֵאתִי אֶתְכֶם אֶל־אַדְמַת יִשְׂרָאֵל: וִידַעְתֶּם
כִּי־אֲנִי יְהוָה בְּפִתְחִי אֶת־קִבְרוֹתֵיכֶם וּבְהַעֲלוֹתִי אֶתְכֶם מִקִּבְרוֹתֵיכֶם עַמִּי:
וְנָתַתִּי רוּחִי בָכֶם וִחְיִיתֶם וְהִנַּחְתִּי אֶתְכֶם עַל־אַדְמַתְכֶם וִידַעְתֶּם כִּי אֲנִי
יְהוָה דִּבַּרְתִּי וְעָשִׂיתִי נְאֻם־יְהוָה:

Continue with the blessings after the הפטרה *on page 515.*

association with the festivals that this was an idolatrous practice associated with pagan festivities (*Guide for the Perplexed* 3:48). The biblical imagination is predicated on clear boundaries. The pagan imagination often celebrated the blurring of boundaries: man-god, man-beast, androgyny, and other hybrids.

TORAH READING FOR THE SEVENTH DAY OF PESAḤ

And so it was, when Pharaoh let the people go, God did not lead them by way of the land of the Philistines, which was near; for He said, "The people may change their minds when they see battle, and return to Egypt." So God led the people round about, by way of the wilderness of the Sea of Reeds; it was armed that the children of Israel ascended from the land of Egypt. And Moses carried the bones of Joseph with him, for [Joseph] had adjured the children of Israel, saying: "When God redeems you, you must take my bones up with you from this place." *They journeyed from Sukkot and encamped at Etam, at the edge of the wilderness. And the LORD went before them: by day in a pillar of cloud to show them the way; and by night in a pillar of fire to illuminate their path, so that they might walk by day and by night. Never did the pillar of cloud depart from before the people by day, nor the pillar of fire at night. *Ex. 13:17–15:26* (*Shabbat:* LEVI)

The LORD spoke to Moses, saying: "Speak to the children of Israel; they must turn back and encamp near Pi HaḤirot, between Migdol and the sea, before Ba'al Tzefon; it is opposite this place that you shall encamp, alongside the sea. Pharaoh will say of the children of Israel: 'They are lost in the land: the wilderness has shut them in.' And I shall strengthen Pharaoh's heart, and he will pursue them, and I will be glorified through Pharaoh and all of his hosts; all of Egypt shall know that I am the LORD." And they did as [God had commanded]. *Word reached the king of Egypt that the people had fled, and the hearts of Pharaoh and his servants changed with regard to the people. They said, "What is it that we have done, releasing the Israelites from servitude to us?" He harnessed his chariot and took his men along with him: six hundred choice chariots he took, and all the other chariots of Egypt, with officers over all of them. The LORD strengthened the heart of Pharaoh, King of Egypt, and he pursued the children of Israel as they went out with an uplifted hand. *The Egyptians pursued them and overtook them while they were encamped at the sea – all of Pharaoh's horses and chariots and his horsemen and army – at Pi HaḤirot, opposite Ba'al Tzefon. As Pharaoh drew near, the children of Israel raised their eyes and they saw: all of Egypt was marching LEVI (*Shabbat:* SHELISHI) (*Shabbat:* REVI'I) SHELISHI (*Shabbat:* ḤAMISHI)

קריאה לשביעי של פסח

שמות יג:יז–טו:כו וַיְהִי בְּשַׁלַּח פַּרְעֹה אֶת־הָעָם וְלֹא־נָחָם אֱלֹהִים דֶּרֶךְ אֶרֶץ פְּלִשְׁתִּים כִּי קָרוֹב
הוּא כִּי | אָמַר אֱלֹהִים פֶּן־יִנָּחֵם הָעָם בִּרְאֹתָם מִלְחָמָה וְשָׁבוּ מִצְרָיְמָה: וַיַּסֵּב
אֱלֹהִים | אֶת־הָעָם דֶּרֶךְ הַמִּדְבָּר יַם־סוּף וַחֲמֻשִׁים עָלוּ בְנֵי־יִשְׂרָאֵל מֵאֶרֶץ
מִצְרָיִם: וַיִּקַּח מֹשֶׁה אֶת־עַצְמוֹת יוֹסֵף עִמּוֹ כִּי הַשְׁבֵּעַ הִשְׁבִּיעַ אֶת־בְּנֵי יִשְׂרָאֵל
(בשבת לוי) לֵאמֹר פָּקֹד יִפְקֹד אֱלֹהִים אֶתְכֶם וְהַעֲלִיתֶם אֶת־עַצְמֹתַי מִזֶּה אִתְּכֶם: *וַיִּסְעוּ
מִסֻּכֹּת וַיַּחֲנוּ בְאֵתָם בִּקְצֵה הַמִּדְבָּר: וַיהוה הֹלֵךְ לִפְנֵיהֶם יוֹמָם בְּעַמּוּד עָנָן
לַנְחֹתָם הַדֶּרֶךְ וְלַיְלָה בְּעַמּוּד אֵשׁ לְהָאִיר לָהֶם לָלֶכֶת יוֹמָם וָלָיְלָה: לֹא־יָמִישׁ
עַמּוּד הֶעָנָן יוֹמָם וְעַמּוּד הָאֵשׁ לָיְלָה לִפְנֵי הָעָם:
לוי וַיְדַבֵּר יהוה אֶל־מֹשֶׁה לֵּאמֹר: דַּבֵּר אֶל־בְּנֵי יִשְׂרָאֵל וְיָשֻׁבוּ וְיַחֲנוּ לִפְנֵי פִּי
(בשבת שלישי) הַחִירֹת בֵּין מִגְדֹּל וּבֵין הַיָּם לִפְנֵי בַּעַל צְפֹן נִכְחוֹ תַחֲנוּ עַל־הַיָּם: וְאָמַר פַּרְעֹה
לִבְנֵי יִשְׂרָאֵל נְבֻכִים הֵם בָּאָרֶץ סָגַר עֲלֵיהֶם הַמִּדְבָּר: וְחִזַּקְתִּי אֶת־לֵב־פַּרְעֹה
וְרָדַף אַחֲרֵיהֶם וְאִכָּבְדָה בְּפַרְעֹה וּבְכָל־חֵילוֹ וְיָדְעוּ מִצְרַיִם כִּי־אֲנִי יהוה וַיַּעֲשׂוּ־
(בשבת רביעי) כֵן: *וַיֻּגַּד לְמֶלֶךְ מִצְרַיִם כִּי בָרַח הָעָם וַיֵּהָפֵךְ לְבַב פַּרְעֹה וַעֲבָדָיו אֶל־הָעָם
וַיֹּאמְרוּ מַה־זֹּאת עָשִׂינוּ כִּי־שִׁלַּחְנוּ אֶת־יִשְׂרָאֵל מֵעָבְדֵנוּ: וַיֶּאְסֹר אֶת־רִכְבּוֹ
וְאֶת־עַמּוֹ לָקַח עִמּוֹ: וַיִּקַּח שֵׁשׁ־מֵאוֹת רֶכֶב בָּחוּר וְכֹל רֶכֶב מִצְרָיִם וְשָׁלִשִׁם
עַל־כֻּלּוֹ: וַיְחַזֵּק יהוה אֶת־לֵב פַּרְעֹה מֶלֶךְ מִצְרַיִם וַיִּרְדֹּף אַחֲרֵי בְּנֵי יִשְׂרָאֵל
שלישי וּבְנֵי יִשְׂרָאֵל יֹצְאִים בְּיָד רָמָה: *וַיִּרְדְּפוּ מִצְרַיִם אַחֲרֵיהֶם וַיַּשִּׂיגוּ אוֹתָם חֹנִים
(בשבת חמישי) עַל־הַיָּם כָּל־סוּס רֶכֶב פַּרְעֹה וּפָרָשָׁיו וְחֵילוֹ עַל־פִּי הַחִירֹת לִפְנֵי בַּעַל צְפֹן:
וּפַרְעֹה הִקְרִיב וַיִּשְׂאוּ בְנֵי־יִשְׂרָאֵל אֶת־עֵינֵיהֶם וְהִנֵּה מִצְרַיִם | נֹסֵעַ אַחֲרֵיהֶם

TORAH READING FOR THE SEVENTH DAY OF PESAḤ

בְּשַׁלַּח פַּרְעֹה *When Pharaoh let the people go.* The verb *sh-l-ḥ* can also mean liberating a slave (see Deuteronomy 15:13). Thus it conveys a twofold sense of release: physical and legal.

וַחֲמֻשִׁים *Armed.* In preparation for later battles. It was not because they were unarmed that God led them on a more circuitous route, but rather that they were psychologically unprepared for war at this point.

עַצְמוֹת יוֹסֵף *Bones of Joseph.* A moving fulfillment of Joseph's last request, shortly before he died (Gen. 50:25). It was a mark of honor that they were carried by Moses himself. A metaphor, also, of the Jewish condition: we keep

behind them. They were very much afraid – and the children of Israel cried out to the LORD. They said to Moses, "Does Egypt lack graves, that you have brought us to die in the desert? What have you done to us, bringing us out of Egypt? Is this not exactly what we told you when we were still there – 'Leave us be, just let us serve Egypt, for it is better for us to serve Egypt than to die in the desert!'" But Moses said to the people, "Do not fear. Stand here and witness the salvation that the LORD will perform for you today; for as you see the Egyptians today, you will not see them again as long as you live. The LORD will wage war for you, and you need only remain silent."

REVI'I (*Shabbat:* SHISHI)

The LORD said to Moses, "Why do you cry out to Me? Tell the children of Israel that they must depart. And as for you – raise your staff and stretch your hand out over the sea and divide it, so that the children of Israel may come through the sea on dry land. And I – I shall make the hearts of Egypt bold and they will enter in after them, and I will be glorified through Pharaoh and all of his hosts, his chariots and horsemen; the Egyptians will know that I am the LORD when I am glorified through Pharaoh and all of his hosts, his chariots and horsemen. So the angel of God who walked before the Israelite camp departed and went behind them; and the pillar of cloud departed from in front of them and came to rest behind. And they came between the camp of Egypt and the camp of Israel; and when cloud and darkness came, the night was lit up – and one camp did not come near the other all that night. Moses raised his hand over the sea, and the LORD moved the sea with a strong easterly wind all that night; it turned the sea into dry land, and the waters were divided. So the children of Israel walked into the midst of the sea on dry land, and the water was like a wall for them on their right and on their left. The Egyptians pursued them, entering in after them, all the horses of Pharaoh, his chariots and horsemen, into the sea. And when the morning watch arrived, the LORD looked upon the Egyptian camp in a pillar of cloud and fire, and threw the Egyptian camp into confusion. The wheels of their chariots were unfastened and drove with difficulty. "Let us escape from Israel," said the Egyptians, "for the LORD is waging war for them against Egypt!"

ḤAMISHI (*Shabbat:* SHEVI'I)

The LORD said to Moses, "Raise your hand over the sea, and the waters

וַיִּירְאוּ מְאֹד וַיִּצְעֲקוּ בְנֵי־יִשְׂרָאֵל אֶל־יהוה: וַיֹּאמְרוּ אֶל־מֹשֶׁה הֲמִבְּלִי אֵין־
קְבָרִים בְּמִצְרַיִם לְקַחְתָּנוּ לָמוּת בַּמִּדְבָּר מַה־זֹּאת עָשִׂיתָ לָּנוּ לְהוֹצִיאָנוּ
מִמִּצְרָיִם: הֲלֹא־זֶה הַדָּבָר אֲשֶׁר דִּבַּרְנוּ אֵלֶיךָ בְמִצְרַיִם לֵאמֹר חֲדַל מִמֶּנּוּ
וְנַעַבְדָה אֶת־מִצְרָיִם כִּי טוֹב לָנוּ עֲבֹד אֶת־מִצְרַיִם מִמֻּתֵנוּ בַּמִּדְבָּר: וַיֹּאמֶר
מֹשֶׁה אֶל־הָעָם אַל־תִּירָאוּ הִתְיַצְּבוּ וּרְאוּ אֶת־יְשׁוּעַת יהוה אֲשֶׁר־יַעֲשֶׂה לָכֶם
הַיּוֹם כִּי אֲשֶׁר רְאִיתֶם אֶת־מִצְרַיִם הַיּוֹם לֹא תֹסִפוּ לִרְאֹתָם עוֹד עַד־עוֹלָם:
יהוה יִלָּחֵם לָכֶם וְאַתֶּם תַּחֲרִשׁוּן:

רביעי (בשבת ששי)
וַיֹּאמֶר יהוה אֶל־מֹשֶׁה מַה־תִּצְעַק אֵלָי דַּבֵּר אֶל־בְּנֵי־יִשְׂרָאֵל וְיִסָּעוּ: וְאַתָּה
הָרֵם אֶת־מַטְּךָ וּנְטֵה אֶת־יָדְךָ עַל־הַיָּם וּבְקָעֵהוּ וְיָבֹאוּ בְנֵי־יִשְׂרָאֵל בְּתוֹךְ הַיָּם
בַּיַּבָּשָׁה: וַאֲנִי הִנְנִי מְחַזֵּק אֶת־לֵב מִצְרַיִם וְיָבֹאוּ אַחֲרֵיהֶם וְאִכָּבְדָה בְּפַרְעֹה
וּבְכָל־חֵילוֹ בְּרִכְבּוֹ וּבְפָרָשָׁיו: וְיָדְעוּ מִצְרַיִם כִּי־אֲנִי יהוה בְּהִכָּבְדִי בְּפַרְעֹה
בְּרִכְבּוֹ וּבְפָרָשָׁיו: וַיִּסַּע מַלְאַךְ הָאֱלֹהִים הַהֹלֵךְ לִפְנֵי מַחֲנֵה יִשְׂרָאֵל וַיֵּלֶךְ
מֵאַחֲרֵיהֶם וַיִּסַּע עַמּוּד הֶעָנָן מִפְּנֵיהֶם וַיַּעֲמֹד מֵאַחֲרֵיהֶם: וַיָּבֹא בֵּין ׀ מַחֲנֵה
מִצְרַיִם וּבֵין מַחֲנֵה יִשְׂרָאֵל וַיְהִי הֶעָנָן וְהַחֹשֶׁךְ וַיָּאֶר אֶת־הַלָּיְלָה וְלֹא־קָרַב
זֶה אֶל־זֶה כָּל־הַלָּיְלָה: וַיֵּט מֹשֶׁה אֶת־יָדוֹ עַל־הַיָּם וַיּוֹלֶךְ יהוה ׀ אֶת־הַיָּם
בְּרוּחַ קָדִים עַזָּה כָּל־הַלַּיְלָה וַיָּשֶׂם אֶת־הַיָּם לֶחָרָבָה וַיִּבָּקְעוּ הַמָּיִם: וַיָּבֹאוּ
בְנֵי־יִשְׂרָאֵל בְּתוֹךְ הַיָּם בַּיַּבָּשָׁה וְהַמַּיִם לָהֶם חוֹמָה מִימִינָם וּמִשְּׂמֹאלָם:
וַיִּרְדְּפוּ מִצְרַיִם וַיָּבֹאוּ אַחֲרֵיהֶם כֹּל סוּס פַּרְעֹה רִכְבּוֹ וּפָרָשָׁיו אֶל־תּוֹךְ הַיָּם:
וַיְהִי בְּאַשְׁמֹרֶת הַבֹּקֶר וַיַּשְׁקֵף יהוה אֶל־מַחֲנֵה מִצְרַיִם בְּעַמּוּד אֵשׁ וְעָנָן וַיָּהָם
אֵת מַחֲנֵה מִצְרָיִם: וַיָּסַר אֵת אֹפַן מַרְכְּבֹתָיו וַיְנַהֲגֵהוּ בִּכְבֵדֻת וַיֹּאמֶר מִצְרַיִם
אָנוּסָה מִפְּנֵי יִשְׂרָאֵל כִּי יהוה נִלְחָם לָהֶם בְּמִצְרָיִם:

חמישי (בשבת שביעי)
וַיֹּאמֶר יהוה אֶל־מֹשֶׁה נְטֵה אֶת־יָדְךָ עַל־הַיָּם וְיָשֻׁבוּ הַמַּיִם עַל־מִצְרַיִם עַל־

---

our faith with those who came before us by carrying their memory with us. We do not live *in* the past, but *with* the past.

מַה־זֹּאת עָשִׂיתָ לָּנוּ *What have you done to us?* The people blame Moses, as if the decision were his, not God's – an ominous precursor of many complaints that were to follow during their time in the wilderness.

מַה־תִּצְעַק אֵלָי *Why do you cry out to Me?* An elision, since no prayer of Moses at the Reed Sea has been mentioned. God's reply does not mean that Moses was wrong to pray, but rather, now is the time for action not words.

will come down upon the Egyptians, their chariots and horsemen." Moses raised his hand over the sea, and as morning approached, the sea returned to its strength: all the Egyptians fled against it – and the LORD shook the Egyptians into the sea. The waters returned, covering the chariots and horsemen, along with all of Pharaoh's hosts who had entered the sea after them – not one survived. But the children of Israel walked on dry land in the midst of the sea, and the water was like a wall for them on their right and on their left. That day the LORD saved Israel from the hands of the Egyptians, and Israel saw the Egyptians lying dead on the seashore. When Israel saw the great power the LORD had displayed against the Egyptians, the people feared the LORD, and believed in the LORD and in His servant, Moses.

Then Moses and the Israelites sang this song to the LORD, saying:
I will sing to the LORD, for He has triumphed gloriously; horse and rider He has hurled into the sea.
The LORD is my strength and song; He has become my salvation. This is my God, and I will beautify Him, my father's God, and I will exalt Him.
The LORD is a Master of war; LORD is His name.
Pharaoh's chariots and army He cast into the sea; the best of his officers drowned in the Sea of Reeds.
The deep waters covered them; they went down to the depths like a stone.
Your right hand, LORD, is majestic in power. Your right hand, LORD, shatters the enemy.
In the greatness of Your majesty, You overthrew those who rose against You. You sent out Your fury; it consumed them like stubble.
By the blast of Your nostrils the waters piled up. The surging waters stood straight like a wall; the deeps congealed in the heart of the sea.
The enemy said, "I will pursue. I will overtake. I will divide the spoil. My desire shall have its fill of them. I will draw my sword. My hand will destroy them."
You blew with Your wind; the sea covered them. They sank in the mighty waters like lead.

רִכְבּוֹ וְעַל־פָּרָשָׁיו: וַיֵּט מֹשֶׁה אֶת־יָדוֹ עַל־הַיָּם וַיָּשָׁב הַיָּם לִפְנוֹת בֹּקֶר לְאֵיתָנוֹ
וּמִצְרַיִם נָסִים לִקְרָאתוֹ וַיְנַעֵר יהוה אֶת־מִצְרַיִם בְּתוֹךְ הַיָּם: וַיָּשֻׁבוּ הַמַּיִם וַיְכַסּוּ
אֶת־הָרֶכֶב וְאֶת־הַפָּרָשִׁים לְכֹל חֵיל פַּרְעֹה הַבָּאִים אַחֲרֵיהֶם בַּיָּם לֹא־נִשְׁאַר
בָּהֶם עַד־אֶחָד: וּבְנֵי יִשְׂרָאֵל הָלְכוּ בַיַּבָּשָׁה בְּתוֹךְ הַיָּם וְהַמַּיִם לָהֶם חֹמָה
מִימִינָם וּמִשְּׂמֹאלָם: וַיּוֹשַׁע יהוה בַּיּוֹם הַהוּא אֶת־יִשְׂרָאֵל מִיַּד מִצְרָיִם וַיַּרְא
יִשְׂרָאֵל אֶת־מִצְרַיִם מֵת עַל־שְׂפַת הַיָּם: וַיַּרְא יִשְׂרָאֵל אֶת־הַיָּד הַגְּדֹלָה אֲשֶׁר
עָשָׂה יהוה בְּמִצְרַיִם וַיִּירְאוּ הָעָם אֶת־יהוה וַיַּאֲמִינוּ בַּיהוה וּבְמֹשֶׁה עַבְדּוֹ:

אָז יָשִׁיר־מֹשֶׁה וּבְנֵי יִשְׂרָאֵל אֶת־הַשִּׁירָה הַזֹּאת לַיהוה וַיֹּאמְרוּ
לֵאמֹר   אָשִׁירָה לַיהוה כִּי־גָאֹה גָּאָה   סוּס
וְרֹכְבוֹ רָמָה בַיָּם: עָזִּי וְזִמְרָת יָהּ וַיְהִי־לִי
לִישׁוּעָה   זֶה אֵלִי וְאַנְוֵהוּ   אֱלֹהֵי
אָבִי וַאֲרֹמְמֶנְהוּ:   יהוה אִישׁ מִלְחָמָה יהוה
שְׁמוֹ:   מַרְכְּבֹת פַּרְעֹה וְחֵילוֹ יָרָה בַיָּם   וּמִבְחַר
שָׁלִשָׁיו טֻבְּעוּ בְיַם־סוּף: תְּהֹמֹת יְכַסְיֻמוּ יָרְדוּ בִמְצוֹלֹת כְּמוֹ־
אָבֶן: יְמִינְךָ יהוה נֶאְדָּרִי בַּכֹּחַ   יְמִינְךָ
יהוה תִּרְעַץ אוֹיֵב: וּבְרֹב גְּאוֹנְךָ תַּהֲרֹס
קָמֶיךָ   תְּשַׁלַּח חֲרֹנְךָ יֹאכְלֵמוֹ כַּקַּשׁ:   וּבְרוּחַ
אַפֶּיךָ נֶעֶרְמוּ מַיִם   נִצְּבוּ כְמוֹ־נֵד
נֹזְלִים   קָפְאוּ תְהֹמֹת בְּלֶב־יָם: אָמַר
אוֹיֵב אֶרְדֹּף אַשִּׂיג   אֲחַלֵּק שָׁלָל תִּמְלָאֵמוֹ
נַפְשִׁי   אָרִיק חַרְבִּי תּוֹרִישֵׁמוֹ יָדִי: נָשַׁפְתָּ
בְרוּחֲךָ כִּסָּמוֹ יָם   צָלְלוּ כַּעוֹפֶרֶת בְּמַיִם

ויאמינו *And believed.* Free of Egypt, on the far side of the sea, knowing that God had delivered them, the Israelites are suddenly liberated from fear and break out in song. This is one of the turning points of Jewish history – the first spontaneous, collective expression of faith. We recite it every day in our prayers.

ובמשה עבדו *And in His servant, Moses.* The phrase is pointed. The rulers of the ancient world saw themselves as demigods who commanded obedience. The Torah insists that the truth is the opposite: greatness is humility, and to be a leader is to be a servant.

Who is like You, LORD, among the mighty? Who is like You – majestic in holiness, awesome in glory, working wonders?
You stretched out Your right hand, the earth swallowed them.
In Your loving-kindness, You led the people You redeemed. In Your strength, You guided them to Your holy abode.
Nations heard and trembled; terror gripped Philistia's inhabitants.
The chiefs of Edom were dismayed, Moab's leaders were seized with trembling, the people of Canaan melted away.
Fear and dread fell upon them. By the power of Your arm, they were still as stone – until Your people crossed, LORD, until the people You acquired crossed over.
You will bring them and plant them on the mountain of Your heritage – the place, LORD, You made for Your dwelling, the Sanctuary, LORD, Your hands established. The LORD will reign for ever and all time.
When Pharaoh's horses, chariots and riders went into the sea, the LORD brought the waters of the sea back over them, but the Israelites walked on dry land through the sea.

Miriam the prophetess, the sister of Aaron, took a tambourine in her hand, and all the women followed after her, with tambourines and dances. And Miriam led them singing, "Sing to the LORD, for He has triumphed gloriously; horse and rider He has hurled into the sea."

Moses led the Israelites away from the Sea of Reeds, setting out towards the wilderness of Shur; they walked across the wilderness for three days and did not find any water. And when they came to Marah, they could not drink water there, for it was bitter; and so that place was named Marah [Bitter]. So the people complained to Moses, saying, "What shall we drink?" He cried out to the LORD, and the LORD showed him a tree; he cast it into the waters, and the waters were sweetened; at that place He gave them statutes and ordinances, and there He tested them. He said, "If you heed the voice of the LORD your God, and do what is right in His eyes, listening to all of His commandments and guarding all His statutes, I will not inflict upon you any of the diseases which I put upon the Egyptians, for I am the LORD, your Healer."

אַדִּירִים: מִי־כָמֹכָה בָּאֵלִם יהוה מִי
כָּמֹכָה נֶאְדָּר בַּקֹּדֶשׁ נוֹרָא תְהִלֹּת עֹשֵׂה
פֶלֶא: נָטִיתָ יְמִינְךָ תִּבְלָעֵמוֹ אָרֶץ: נָחִיתָ
בְחַסְדְּךָ עַם־זוּ גָּאָלְתָּ נֵהַלְתָּ בְעָזְּךָ אֶל־נְוֵה
קָדְשֶׁךָ: שָׁמְעוּ עַמִּים יִרְגָּזוּן חִיל
אָחַז יֹשְׁבֵי פְּלָשֶׁת: אָז נִבְהֲלוּ אַלּוּפֵי
אֱדוֹם אֵילֵי מוֹאָב יֹאחֲזֵמוֹ רָעַד נָמֹגוּ
כֹּל יֹשְׁבֵי כְנָעַן: תִּפֹּל עֲלֵיהֶם אֵימָתָה
וָפַחַד בִּגְדֹל זְרוֹעֲךָ יִדְּמוּ כָּאָבֶן עַד־
יַעֲבֹר עַמְּךָ יהוה עַד־יַעֲבֹר עַם־זוּ
קָנִיתָ: תְּבִאֵמוֹ וְתִטָּעֵמוֹ בְּהַר נַחֲלָתְךָ מָכוֹן
לְשִׁבְתְּךָ פָּעַלְתָּ יהוה מִקְּדָשׁ אֲדֹנָי כּוֹנְנוּ
יָדֶיךָ: יהוה ׀ יִמְלֹךְ לְעֹלָם וָעֶד: כִּי
בָא סוּס פַּרְעֹה בְּרִכְבּוֹ וּבְפָרָשָׁיו בַּיָּם וַיָּשֶׁב יהוה עֲלֵהֶם אֶת־מֵי
הַיָּם וּבְנֵי יִשְׂרָאֵל הָלְכוּ בַיַּבָּשָׁה בְּתוֹךְ הַיָּם:

וַתִּקַּח מִרְיָם הַנְּבִיאָה אֲחוֹת אַהֲרֹן אֶת־הַתֹּף בְּיָדָהּ וַתֵּצֶאןָ כָל־הַנָּשִׁים אַחֲרֶיהָ בְּתֻפִּים וּבִמְחֹלֹת: וַתַּעַן לָהֶם מִרְיָם שִׁירוּ לַיהוה כִּי־גָאֹה גָּאָה סוּס וְרֹכְבוֹ רָמָה בַיָּם: וַיַּסַּע מֹשֶׁה אֶת־יִשְׂרָאֵל מִיַּם־סוּף וַיֵּצְאוּ אֶל־מִדְבַּר־שׁוּר וַיֵּלְכוּ שְׁלֹשֶׁת־יָמִים בַּמִּדְבָּר וְלֹא־מָצְאוּ מָיִם: וַיָּבֹאוּ מָרָתָה וְלֹא יָכְלוּ לִשְׁתֹּת מַיִם מִמָּרָה כִּי מָרִים הֵם עַל־כֵּן קָרָא־שְׁמָהּ מָרָה: וַיִּלֹּנוּ הָעָם עַל־מֹשֶׁה לֵּאמֹר מַה־נִּשְׁתֶּה: וַיִּצְעַק אֶל־יהוה וַיּוֹרֵהוּ יהוה עֵץ וַיַּשְׁלֵךְ אֶל־הַמַּיִם וַיִּמְתְּקוּ הַמָּיִם שָׁם שָׂם לוֹ חֹק וּמִשְׁפָּט וְשָׁם נִסָּהוּ: וַיֹּאמֶר אִם־שָׁמוֹעַ תִּשְׁמַע לְקוֹל ׀ יהוה אֱלֹהֶיךָ וְהַיָּשָׁר בְּעֵינָיו תַּעֲשֶׂה וְהַאֲזַנְתָּ לְמִצְוֹתָיו וְשָׁמַרְתָּ כָּל־חֻקָּיו כָּל־הַמַּחֲלָה אֲשֶׁר־שַׂמְתִּי בְמִצְרַיִם לֹא־אָשִׂים עָלֶיךָ כִּי אֲנִי יהוה רֹפְאֶךָ:

יהוה יִמְלֹךְ *The Lord will reign.* A key verse, marking the first time in the Torah that God has been described as a King. Crossing the sea has been for the Israelites not just a miraculous experience, nor merely an escape from defeat and death, but also a fundamental "rite of passage": Israel has become the nation whose sovereign is God Himself.

MAFTIR FOR THE SEVENTH DAY OF PESAḤ

The first Torah scroll is lifted up (page 512) and Maftir is read from the second Torah scroll:

And you shall bring an offering consumed by fire, a burnt-offering to the LORD: two young bullocks, one ram, and seven yearling male lambs; they shall be to you unblemished. And you shall perform their meal-offerings, fine flour mixed with oil, three-tenths of an ephah for each bull, two-tenths of an ephah for the ram; and one-tenth of an ephah for each of the seven lambs; and one goat for a sin-offering, to make atonement for you. All this aside from the morning burnt-offering, the daily offering; You shall offer all of these as food, on each of the seven days, a burnt-offering by fire of pleasing aroma to the LORD, along with the regular daily offering and its libation. On the seventh day there shall be a sacred assembly: you shall do no laborious work. *Num. 28:19–25*

HAFTARA FOR THE SEVENTH DAY OF PESAḤ

And David spoke the words of this song to the LORD – on the day the LORD saved him from the hand of all his enemies, and from the hand of Saul. And he said: *II Sam. 22:1–51*

LORD, my Rock, my Fortress – and my Deliverer;
my God, my Rock – I shelter in Him; my Shield and the Strength for my salvation; my Keep and my Refuge, my Savior;
You save me from violence. Praised One! I call to the LORD, and from my enemies I am saved – for breaking-waves of death were all around me, torrents of evil assailed me;
the ropes of the grave encircled me, traps of death were in front of me.
In my anguish I called to the LORD – to my God, I called out – and He heard from His sanctuary, my voice and my pleas were in His ears.

The superscription describes this as a song David sang "on the day the LORD saved him from the hand of all his enemies, and from the hand of Saul," though it reads as if it was composed late in David's life. If so, then it would show that his deliverance from Saul stayed vivid in his memory until the end (Rashi, Radak). Abrabanel, however, believed that David wrote it in his youth, sang it at various points in his life on occasions of deliverance from danger, and eventually edited it for public use in the form we have as Psalm 18.

מפטיר לשביעי של פסח

The first תורה ספר *is lifted up (page 513) and* מפטיר *is read from the second* תורה ספר:

במדבר
כח:יט-כה

וְהִקְרַבְתֶּ֨ם אִשֶּׁ֤ה עֹלָה֙ לַֽיהוָ֔ה פָּרִ֨ים בְּנֵי־בָקָ֥ר שְׁנַ֛יִם וְאַ֥יִל אֶחָ֖ד וְשִׁבְעָ֣ה כְבָשִׂ֑ים
בְּנֵ֤י שָׁנָה֙ תְּמִימִ֣ם יִֽהְי֣וּ לָכֶ֔ם: וּמִ֨נְחָתָ֔ם סֹ֖לֶת בְּלוּלָ֣ה בַשָּׁ֑מֶן שְׁלֹשָׁ֣ה עֶשְׂרֹנִ֗ים
לַפָּ֜ר וּשְׁנֵ֤י עֶשְׂרֹנִים֙ לָאַ֣יִל תַּֽעֲשֽׂוּ: עִשָּׂר֗וֹן עִשָּׂרוֹן֙ תַּֽעֲשֶׂ֔ה לַכֶּ֖בֶשׂ הָֽאֶחָ֑ד לְשִׁבְעַ֖ת
הַכְּבָשִֽׂים: וּשְׂעִ֥יר חַטָּ֖את אֶחָ֑ד לְכַפֵּ֖ר עֲלֵיכֶֽם: מִלְּבַד֩ עֹלַ֨ת הַבֹּ֜קֶר אֲשֶׁ֣ר לְעֹלַ֣ת
הַתָּמִ֗יד תַּֽעֲשׂ֖וּ אֶת־אֵֽלֶּה: כָּאֵ֜לֶּה תַּֽעֲשׂ֤וּ לַיּוֹם֙ שִׁבְעַ֣ת יָמִ֔ים לֶ֛חֶם אִשֵּׁ֥ה רֵֽיחַ־
נִיחֹ֖חַ לַֽיהוָ֑ה עַל־עוֹלַ֧ת הַתָּמִ֛יד יֵֽעָשֶׂ֖ה וְנִסְכּֽוֹ: וּבַיּוֹם֙ הַשְּׁבִיעִ֔י מִקְרָא־קֹ֖דֶשׁ
יִֽהְיֶ֣ה לָכֶ֑ם כָּל־מְלֶ֥אכֶת עֲבֹדָ֖ה לֹ֥א תַֽעֲשֽׂוּ:

הפטרה לשביעי של פסח

שמואל ב
כב:א-נא

וַיְדַבֵּ֤ר דָּוִד֙ לַֽיהוָ֔ה אֶת־דִּבְרֵ֖י הַשִּׁירָ֣ה הַזֹּ֑את בְּי֨וֹם
הִצִּ֨יל יְהוָ֥ה אֹת֛וֹ מִכַּ֥ף כָּל־אֹֽיְבָ֖יו וּמִכַּ֥ף שָׁאֽוּל:
וַיֹּאמַ֑ר יְהוָ֛ה סַֽלְעִ֥י וּמְצֻֽדָתִ֖י וּמְפַלְטִי־לִֽי: אֱלֹהֵ֥י
צוּרִ֖י אֶֽחֱסֶה־בּ֑וֹ מָֽגִנִּ֞י וְקֶ֣רֶן יִשְׁעִ֗י מִשְׂגַּבִּי֙
וּמְנוּסִ֔י מֹֽשִׁעִ֕י מֵֽחָמָ֖ס תֹּֽשִׁעֵֽנִי: מְהֻלָּ֖ל
אֶקְרָ֣א יְהוָ֑ה וּמֵאֹֽיְבַ֖י אִוָּשֵֽׁעַ: כִּ֥י אֲפָפֻ֖נִי מִשְׁבְּרֵי־
מָ֔וֶת נַֽחֲלֵ֥י בְלִיַּ֖עַל יְבַֽעֲתֻֽנִי: חֶבְלֵ֥י
שְׁא֖וֹל סַבֻּ֑נִי קִדְּמֻ֖נִי מֹ֥קְשֵׁי־
מָֽוֶת: בַּצַּר־לִי֙ אֶקְרָ֣א יְהוָ֔ה וְאֶל־
אֱלֹהַ֖י אֶקְרָ֑א וַיִּשְׁמַ֤ע מֵהֵֽיכָלוֹ֙
קוֹלִ֔י וְשַׁוְעָתִ֖י בְּאָזְנָֽיו: וַתִּגְעַ֤שׁ וַתִּרְעַשׁ֙

HAFTARA FOR THE SEVENTH DAY OF PESAH

David's great song of deliverance, taken here from II Samuel 22, also appears
in the book of Psalms (with minor differences) as Psalm 18. Its kinship with
the Torah reading, the Song at the Sea, is obvious. Both are songs of thanksgiving after great danger. David uses imagery that echoes the Song at the Sea.
He speaks of being almost overwhelmed by "breakers" and "torrents." He
says, "Channel-beds of the sea appeared … from the force of breath from His
nostrils." He feels as if God had "reached from the heights, He took me, He
drew me out from a mass of waters." The intertextuality – the linguistic and
metaphorical parallels between the two songs – is unmistakable.

The land shook and quaked, the foundations of the heavens trembled
and shook from His anger;
smoke rose from His nostrils, consuming fire from His mouth; coals
flamed from Him.
And He bent the heavens and descended, heavy mist beneath His feet;
upon a cherub He rode, He flew and appeared on the wings of the wind.
He placed darkness as pavilions around Him, glooms of water, clouds
of the sky;
from the brilliance before Him, fire-coals flamed.
The LORD thundered from heaven, the High One sounded His voice.
He sent down arrows and scattered them, lightning and stunned them;
channel-beds of the sea appeared, the foundations of the world were
revealed – from the LORD's rebuke, from the force of breath
from His nostrils.
He reached from the heights, He took me, He drew me out from a
mass of waters;
He saved me from my strong enemy, from my haters who were mightier
than me:
they overtook me on my day of calamity, but the LORD was my stay:
He brought me out to an open place, He delivered me – for He delighted
in me.
The LORD has rewarded me, according to my merit, according to the
cleanness of my hands He has repaid me;
because I kept the ways of the LORD, and was not corrupted away from
my God;
all His laws are before me and His statutes; I will not turn from them.
I have been faultless before Him, and have kept myself from sin;
the LORD has repaid me according to my merit, my cleanness before
His eyes.
With the constant person, You are constant; with the faultless hero,
You are faultless;
with the pure, You act with purity; with the perverse, You act with
subtlety; an oppressed people,
You save, and Your eyes on the haughty, humble them.
You are my Lamp, LORD; the LORD illuminates my darkness.
With You, I can run against a battalion; with my God, I can jump
city walls.

וַתִּרְעַשׁ הָאָרֶץ מוֹסְדוֹת הַשָּׁמַיִם
יִרְגָּזוּ וַיִּתְגָּעֲשׁוּ כִּי־חָרָה לוֹ׃ עָלָה
עָשָׁן בְּאַפּוֹ וְאֵשׁ מִפִּיו
תֹּאכֵל גֶּחָלִים בָּעֲרוּ מִמֶּנּוּ׃ וַיֵּט
שָׁמַיִם וַיֵּרַד וַעֲרָפֶל תַּחַת
רַגְלָיו׃ וַיִּרְכַּב עַל־כְּרוּב וַיָּעֹף וַיֵּרָא
עַל־כַּנְפֵי־רוּחַ׃ וַיָּשֶׁת חֹשֶׁךְ סְבִיבֹתָיו
סֻכּוֹת חַשְׁרַת־מַיִם עָבֵי שְׁחָקִים׃ מִנֹּגַהּ
נֶגְדּוֹ בָּעֲרוּ גַּחֲלֵי־אֵשׁ׃ יַרְעֵם מִן־שָׁמַיִם
יְהוָה וְעֶלְיוֹן יִתֵּן קוֹלוֹ׃ וַיִּשְׁלַח
חִצִּים וַיְפִיצֵם בָּרָק ויהמם׃ וַיֵּרָאוּ אֲפִקֵי וַיָּהֹם
יָם יִגָּלוּ מֹסְדוֹת תֵּבֵל בְּגַעֲרַת
יְהוָה מִנִּשְׁמַת רוּחַ אַפּוֹ׃ יִשְׁלַח מִמָּרוֹם
יִקָּחֵנִי יַמְשֵׁנִי מִמַּיִם רַבִּים׃ יַצִּילֵנִי
מֵאֹיְבִי עָז מִשֹּׂנְאַי כִּי אָמְצוּ
מִמֶּנִּי׃ יְקַדְּמֻנִי בְּיוֹם אֵידִי וַיְהִי
יְהוָה מִשְׁעָן לִי׃ וַיֹּצֵא לַמֶּרְחָב
אֹתִי יְחַלְּצֵנִי כִּי־חָפֵץ בִּי׃ יִגְמְלֵנִי
יְהוָה כְּצִדְקָתִי כְּבֹר יָדַי יָשִׁיב
לִי׃ כִּי שָׁמַרְתִּי דַּרְכֵי יְהוָה וְלֹא
רָשַׁעְתִּי מֵאֱלֹהָי׃ כִּי כָל־מִשְׁפָּטָו
לְנֶגְדִּי וְחֻקֹּתָיו לֹא־אָסוּר מִמֶּנָּה׃ וָאֶהְיֶה
תָמִים לוֹ וָאֶשְׁתַּמְּרָה מֵעֲוֹנִי׃ וַיָּשֶׁב יְהוָה לִי
כְּצִדְקָתִי כְּבֹרִי לְנֶגֶד עֵינָיו׃ עִם־
חָסִיד תִּתְחַסָּד עִם־גִּבּוֹר תָּמִים
תִּתַּמָּם׃ עִם־נָבָר תִּתָּבָר וְעִם־
עִקֵּשׁ תִּתַּפָּל׃ וְאֶת־עַם עָנִי
תּוֹשִׁיעַ וְעֵינֶיךָ עַל־רָמִים תַּשְׁפִּיל׃ כִּי־
אַתָּה נֵירִי יְהוָה וַיהוָה יַגִּיהַּ
חָשְׁכִּי׃ כִּי בְכָה אָרוּץ גְּדוּד בֵּאלֹהַי

Awesome God, His way is perfect; the Lord's words are pure, He is the shield of all who take refuge in Him;
for who is God, if not the Lord? Who is a Rock, if not our God?
Awesome God, my Stronghold of strength, who perfects my way;
He makes my feet like a deer's, and stands me here in high places;
He trains my hands for war, and He sets a copper bow in my arms.
You have given me Your shield of protection; in descending to me, You have made me great.
You widened my steps beneath me and my feet did not stumble;
I pursued my enemies and destroyed them, I did not return until they were consumed;
I consumed and crushed them so they could not rise, and they fell beneath my feet.
You have girded me with the strength for war; those who rose against me, You have subdued beneath me;
You gave me the necks of my enemies, my haters, so I could cut them down.
They looked for help, but there was no rescuer; to the Lord, but they were not answered.
And I ground them like dust of the earth, like mud in the streets I stamped and crushed them.
You have saved me from disputes in my people; You have kept me to be a ruler of nations – a people I have not known will serve me, a foreign people will submit to me;
when they hear of me, they will heed me; a foreign people will become weak and come trembling out of their fortresses.
The Lord lives, blessed is my Rock, exalted; God, Rock of my salvation.
Awesome God who avenges me, and who sinks peoples beneath me,
who brings me out from before my enemies, and raises me above those who rise against me; from the man of violence, You save me.
Therefore, I will thank You, Lord, among the nations, and to Your name I will sing praise.
Tower of Salvation to His king, He shows kindness to His anointed, to David and his descendants for ever.

Continue with the blessings after the Haftara on page 514.

אֲדַלֶּג־שׁוּר: הָאֵל תָּמִים
דַּרְכּוֹ אִמְרַת יְהוָה צְרוּפָה מָגֵן
הוּא לְכֹל הַחֹסִים בּוֹ: כִּי מִי־אֵל מִבַּלְעֲדֵי
יְהוָה וּמִי צוּר מִבַּלְעֲדֵי אֱלֹהֵינוּ: הָאֵל
מָעוּזִּי חָיִל וַיַּתֵּר תָּמִים
דרכו: מְשַׁוֶּה רגליו כָּאַיָּלוֹת וְעַל־ רַגְלַי דַּרְכִּי
בָּמוֹתַי יַעֲמִידֵנִי: מְלַמֵּד יָדַי
לַמִּלְחָמָה וְנִחַת קֶשֶׁת־נְחוּשָׁה זְרֹעֹתָי: וַתִּתֶּן־
לִי מָגֵן יִשְׁעֶךָ וַעֲנֹתְךָ תַּרְבֵּנִי: תַּרְחִיב צַעֲדִי
תַּחְתֵּנִי וְלֹא מָעֲדוּ קַרְסֻלָּי: אֶרְדְּפָה
אֹיְבַי וָאַשְׁמִידֵם וְלֹא אָשׁוּב עַד־
כַּלּוֹתָם: וָאֲכַלֵּם וָאֶמְחָצֵם וְלֹא יְקוּמוּן וַיִּפְּלוּ
תַּחַת רַגְלָי: וַתַּזְרֵנִי חַיִל
לַמִּלְחָמָה תַּכְרִיעַ קָמַי תַּחְתֵּנִי: וְאֹיְבַי
תַּתָּה לִּי עֹרֶף מְשַׂנְאַי וָאַצְמִיתֵם: יִשְׁעוּ וְאֵין
מֹשִׁיעַ אֶל־יְהוָה וְלֹא עָנָם: וְאֶשְׁחָקֵם
כַּעֲפַר־אָרֶץ כְּטִיט־חוּצוֹת אֲדִקֵּם
אֶרְקָעֵם: וַתְּפַלְּטֵנִי מֵרִיבֵי עַמִּי תִּשְׁמְרֵנִי
לְרֹאשׁ גּוֹיִם עַם לֹא־יָדַעְתִּי
יַעַבְדֻנִי: בְּנֵי נֵכָר יִתְכַּחֲשׁוּ־לִי לִשְׁמוֹעַ
אֹזֶן יִשָּׁמְעוּ לִי: בְּנֵי נֵכָר יִבֹּלוּ וְיַחְגְּרוּ
מִמִּסְגְּרוֹתָם: חַי־יְהוָה וּבָרוּךְ צוּרִי וְיָרֻם
אֱלֹהֵי צוּר יִשְׁעִי: הָאֵל הַנֹּתֵן נְקָמֹת
לִי וּמוֹרִיד עַמִּים תַּחְתֵּנִי: וּמוֹצִיאִי
מֵאֹיְבָי וּמִקָּמַי תְּרוֹמְמֵנִי מֵאִישׁ חֲמָסִים
תַּצִּילֵנִי: עַל־כֵּן אוֹדְךָ יְהוָה בַּגּוֹיִם וּלְשִׁמְךָ
אֲזַמֵּר: מגדיל יְשׁוּעוֹת מִגְדּוֹל
מַלְכּוֹ וְעֹשֶׂה־חֶסֶד לִמְשִׁיחוֹ
לְדָוִד וּלְזַרְעוֹ עַד־עוֹלָם:

Continue with the blessings after the הפטרה *on page 515.*

TORAH READING FOR THE LAST DAY OF PESAḤ AND SHAVUOT, AND SHEMINI ATZERET OUTSIDE ISRAEL

If the last day of Pesaḥ or the second day of Shavuot falls on Shabbat, start here. If it falls on a weekday, start with "Every male firstborn" on page 1144. On Shemini Atzeret start here.

You must tithe all the produce of your grain, that which grows in the field, each year. You shall then eat it in the presence of the Lord your God, at the place He will choose as a dwelling place for His name; the tithes of your grain, wine and oil as well as the firstborn of your herd and flock, so that you might learn to hold the Lord your God in awe as long as you live. If the distance is very great for you, so that you cannot carry it all; if the place the Lord your God chooses as a dwelling place for His name is far away from you, and the Lord your God blesses you with plenty, then you may sell your produce for money and, holding that money in your hand, go to the place which the Lord your God will choose. You may purchase with that money anything you may wish for of the herd or flock, of wine or intoxicating drinks: anything your heart desires; and you shall eat there, in the presence of the Lord your God, and you and your household shall rejoice. As for the Levite who dwells within your gates – you shall not forsake him, for he does not have a portion or an inheritance among you. *Deut. 14:22–16:17*

At the end of every third year, you must take out all the tithes of your harvest from that year, and set them down within your gates. Then the Levite, who does not have a portion or an inheritance among you, along with the stranger and orphan and widow within your gates, shall come and eat and be satisfied; do this, so that the Lord your God might bless you in all that you do.

LEVI

At the end of every seven years, you shall institute a release. And this is the manner of the release: every creditor shall let go of what he is entitled to from his debtor; he may not demand payment from his fellow or his kinsman, for a release has been proclaimed for [the honor of] the Lord. You may ask payment of a gentile, but any claim you hold against your kinsmen must be released. Nevertheless, you will not have paupers among you, for the Lord shall surely bless you in the land that He is giving you as a portion, to inherit it – but only if you heed the voice of the Lord your God, safeguarding and keeping all of

קריאה ליום אחרון של פסח או שבועות, ולשמיני עצרת בחוץ לארץ

If the last day of פסח *or the second day of* שבועות *falls on* שבת*, start here.*
If it falls on a weekday, start with כׇּל־הַבְּכוֹר *on page page 1145. On* שמיני עצרת *start here.*

דברים יד:כב–טו:ו עַשֵּׂר תְּעַשֵּׂר אֵת כׇּל־תְּבוּאַת זַרְעֶךָ הַיֹּצֵא הַשָּׂדֶה שָׁנָה שָׁנָה: וְאָכַלְתָּ לִפְנֵי ׀
יהוה אֱלֹהֶיךָ בַּמָּקוֹם אֲשֶׁר־יִבְחַר לְשַׁכֵּן שְׁמוֹ שָׁם מַעְשַׂר דְּגָנְךָ תִּירֹשְׁךָ וְיִצְהָרֶךָ
וּבְכֹרֹת בְּקָרְךָ וְצֹאנֶךָ לְמַעַן תִּלְמַד לְיִרְאָה אֶת־יהוה אֱלֹהֶיךָ כׇּל־הַיָּמִים: וְכִי־
יִרְבֶּה מִמְּךָ הַדֶּרֶךְ כִּי לֹא תוּכַל שְׂאֵתוֹ כִּי־יִרְחַק מִמְּךָ הַמָּקוֹם אֲשֶׁר יִבְחַר יהוה
אֱלֹהֶיךָ לָשׂוּם שְׁמוֹ שָׁם כִּי יְבָרֶכְךָ יהוה אֱלֹהֶיךָ: וְנָתַתָּה בַּכָּסֶף וְצַרְתָּ הַכֶּסֶף
בְּיָדְךָ וְהָלַכְתָּ אֶל־הַמָּקוֹם אֲשֶׁר יִבְחַר יהוה אֱלֹהֶיךָ בּוֹ: וְנָתַתָּה הַכֶּסֶף בְּכֹל
אֲשֶׁר־תְּאַוֶּה נַפְשְׁךָ בַּבָּקָר וּבַצֹּאן וּבַיַּיִן וּבַשֵּׁכָר וּבְכֹל אֲשֶׁר תִּשְׁאָלְךָ נַפְשֶׁךָ
וְאָכַלְתָּ שָּׁם לִפְנֵי יהוה אֱלֹהֶיךָ וְשָׂמַחְתָּ אַתָּה וּבֵיתֶךָ: וְהַלֵּוִי אֲשֶׁר־בִּשְׁעָרֶיךָ לֹא
תַעַזְבֶנּוּ כִּי אֵין לוֹ חֵלֶק וְנַחֲלָה עִמָּךְ: מִקְצֵה ׀ שָׁלֹשׁ שָׁנִים תּוֹצִיא
אֶת־כׇּל־מַעְשַׂר תְּבוּאָתְךָ בַּשָּׁנָה הַהִוא וְהִנַּחְתָּ בִּשְׁעָרֶיךָ: וּבָא הַלֵּוִי כִּי אֵין־
לוֹ חֵלֶק וְנַחֲלָה עִמָּךְ וְהַגֵּר וְהַיָּתוֹם וְהָאַלְמָנָה אֲשֶׁר בִּשְׁעָרֶיךָ וְאָכְלוּ וְשָׂבֵעוּ
(בשבת לוי) לְמַעַן יְבָרֶכְךָ יהוה אֱלֹהֶיךָ בְּכׇל־מַעֲשֵׂה יָדְךָ אֲשֶׁר תַּעֲשֶׂה: *מִקֵּץ
שֶׁבַע־שָׁנִים תַּעֲשֶׂה שְׁמִטָּה: וְזֶה דְּבַר הַשְּׁמִטָּה שָׁמוֹט כׇּל־בַּעַל מַשֵּׁה יָדוֹ
אֲשֶׁר יַשֶּׁה בְּרֵעֵהוּ לֹא־יִגֹּשׂ אֶת־רֵעֵהוּ וְאֶת־אָחִיו כִּי־קָרָא שְׁמִטָּה לַיהוה:
אֶת־הַנׇּכְרִי תִּגֹּשׂ וַאֲשֶׁר יִהְיֶה לְךָ אֶת־אָחִיךָ תַּשְׁמֵט יָדֶךָ: אֶפֶס כִּי לֹא יִהְיֶה־
בְּךָ אֶבְיוֹן כִּי־בָרֵךְ יְבָרֶכְךָ יהוה בָּאָרֶץ אֲשֶׁר יהוה אֱלֹהֶיךָ נֹתֵן־לְךָ נַחֲלָה
לְרִשְׁתָּהּ: רַק אִם־שָׁמוֹעַ תִּשְׁמַע בְּקוֹל יהוה אֱלֹהֶיךָ לִשְׁמֹר לַעֲשׂוֹת אֶת־
כׇּל־הַמִּצְוָה הַזֹּאת אֲשֶׁר אָנֹכִי מְצַוְּךָ הַיּוֹם: כִּי־יהוה אֱלֹהֶיךָ בֵּרַכְךָ כַּאֲשֶׁר
דִּבֶּר־לָךְ וְהַעֲבַטְתָּ גּוֹיִם רַבִּים וְאַתָּה לֹא תַעֲבֹט וּמָשַׁלְתָּ בְּגוֹיִם רַבִּים וּבְךָ לֹא

READING OF THE TORAH: LAST DAY OF PESAḤ AND SHAVUOT, AND SHEMINI ATZERET OUTSIDE ISRAEL

The core of this reading is the passage dealing with the festivals in the book of Deuteronomy. The festivals are extensively described in three places in the Torah, in Leviticus (23), in Numbers (28–29), and here (Deut. 16). The sages explained that the first is to establish their order, the second to prescribe their sacrifices, and the third to explain them to the public (Sifrei).

the commandments I am commanding you today. For the Lord your God will bless you as He has promised you: you shall lend to many nations and you shall not borrow; you shall rule over many nations and shall not be ruled by others.

If there should be a poor person among you, one of your kinsmen in one of the cities in your land, which the Lord your God has given to you, you must not harden your heart and you must not close your hand to your impoverished kinsman. Rather, you must open your hand to him, making him a loan to tide him over his lack. Take care, lest evil thoughts enter your heart, saying: "The seventh year, the year of release draws near," causing you to treat your impoverished kinsman meanly, withholding loans from him; he might then call out to God because of you and it will be held against you as a sin. You must certainly give to him, and let your heart not be grudging when you give, for because of this deed, the Lord your God shall bless you in all that you do and in all of your endeavors. For there will never cease to be poor people in the land; and so I am commanding you: you must open your hand to your kinsman, to the poor and destitute in your land.

If your Hebrew kinsman or kinswoman is sold to you, he shall work for you for six years, and in the seventh year, you must release him from your service, free. When you set him free from your service you must not send him away empty-handed. You must give generously to him of your flock, your granary and your wine-vat with which the Lord your God has blessed you; so you shall give him. And you shall remember that you were once a slave in the land of Egypt and the Lord your God redeemed you; this is why, today, I command you thus. Should [the slave] say: "I would not leave your home;" because he is fond of you and of your household, and is happy living with you, then you shall take an awl and pierce his ear upon the door with it, and he shall then be your slave forever; the same should be done with your female slave. Do not feel it a hardship when you release him from your service, free; for he has served you for six years – twice a hired hand's work, and now the Lord your God will bless you in all that you do.

יִמְשֹׁלוּ׃ כִּי־יִהְיֶה בְךָ אֶבְיוֹן מֵאַחַד אַחֶיךָ בְּאַחַד שְׁעָרֶיךָ בְּאַרְצְךָ
אֲשֶׁר־יהוה אֱלֹהֶיךָ נֹתֵן לָךְ לֹא תְאַמֵּץ אֶת־לְבָבְךָ וְלֹא תִקְפֹּץ אֶת־יָדְךָ מֵאָחִיךָ
הָאֶבְיוֹן׃ כִּי־פָתֹחַ תִּפְתַּח אֶת־יָדְךָ לוֹ וְהַעֲבֵט תַּעֲבִיטֶנּוּ דֵּי מַחְסֹרוֹ אֲשֶׁר
יֶחְסַר לוֹ׃ הִשָּׁמֶר לְךָ פֶּן־יִהְיֶה דָבָר עִם־לְבָבְךָ בְלִיַּעַל לֵאמֹר קָרְבָה שְׁנַת־
הַשֶּׁבַע שְׁנַת הַשְּׁמִטָּה וְרָעָה עֵינְךָ בְּאָחִיךָ הָאֶבְיוֹן וְלֹא תִתֵּן לוֹ וְקָרָא עָלֶיךָ
אֶל־יהוה וְהָיָה בְךָ חֵטְא׃ נָתוֹן תִּתֵּן לוֹ וְלֹא־יֵרַע לְבָבְךָ בְּתִתְּךָ לוֹ כִּי בִּגְלַל ׀
הַדָּבָר הַזֶּה יְבָרֶכְךָ יהוה אֱלֹהֶיךָ בְּכָל־מַעֲשֶׂךָ וּבְכֹל מִשְׁלַח יָדֶךָ׃ כִּי לֹא־יֶחְדַּל
אֶבְיוֹן מִקֶּרֶב הָאָרֶץ עַל־כֵּן אָנֹכִי מְצַוְּךָ לֵאמֹר פָּתֹחַ תִּפְתַּח אֶת־יָדְךָ לְאָחִיךָ
לַעֲנִיֶּךָ וּלְאֶבְיֹנְךָ בְּאַרְצֶךָ׃ כִּי־יִמָּכֵר לְךָ אָחִיךָ הָעִבְרִי אוֹ הָעִבְרִיָּה
וַעֲבָדְךָ שֵׁשׁ שָׁנִים וּבַשָּׁנָה הַשְּׁבִיעִת תְּשַׁלְּחֶנּוּ חָפְשִׁי מֵעִמָּךְ׃ וְכִי־תְשַׁלְּחֶנּוּ
חָפְשִׁי מֵעִמָּךְ לֹא תְשַׁלְּחֶנּוּ רֵיקָם׃ הַעֲנֵיק תַּעֲנִיק לוֹ מִצֹּאנְךָ וּמִגָּרְנְךָ וּמִיִּקְבֶךָ
אֲשֶׁר בֵּרַכְךָ יהוה אֱלֹהֶיךָ תִּתֶּן־לוֹ׃ וְזָכַרְתָּ כִּי עֶבֶד הָיִיתָ בְּאֶרֶץ מִצְרַיִם וַיִּפְדְּךָ
יהוה אֱלֹהֶיךָ עַל־כֵּן אָנֹכִי מְצַוְּךָ אֶת־הַדָּבָר הַזֶּה הַיּוֹם׃ וְהָיָה כִּי־יֹאמַר אֵלֶיךָ
לֹא אֵצֵא מֵעִמָּךְ כִּי אֲהֵבְךָ וְאֶת־בֵּיתֶךָ כִּי־טוֹב לוֹ עִמָּךְ׃ וְלָקַחְתָּ אֶת־הַמַּרְצֵעַ
וְנָתַתָּה בְאָזְנוֹ וּבַדֶּלֶת וְהָיָה לְךָ עֶבֶד עוֹלָם וְאַף לַאֲמָתְךָ תַּעֲשֶׂה־כֵּן׃ לֹא־
יִקְשֶׁה בְעֵינֶךָ בְּשַׁלֵּחֲךָ אֹתוֹ חָפְשִׁי מֵעִמָּךְ כִּי מִשְׁנֶה שְׂכַר שָׂכִיר עֲבָדְךָ שֵׁשׁ
שָׁנִים וּבֵרַכְךָ יהוה אֱלֹהֶיךָ בְּכֹל אֲשֶׁר תַּעֲשֶׂה׃

Throughout Deuteronomy, Moses explains the laws to the people as a whole, reminding them of the historical background against which they are set, and the future of which they are the parameters. In the case of the festivals, Moses' presentation here has a strong emphasis on the seasons of the agricultural year: Pesaḥ is the festival of spring, the countdown to Shavuot begins from "when the sickle begins to cut the standing grain," and Sukkot is celebrated at the time when "when you gather into your granary and wine-vat." These are dimensions of the festivals the people have not yet experienced as desert nomads but which they will once they enter and make their home in the land which the Lord has blessed.

Moses also emphasizes the important dimension of social inclusion. They are times when people are to invite those at the margins of society: the widow, the orphan, the Levites who have no land of their own, the temporary residents, as well as slaves. No one is to be left out.

If the eighth day of Pesaḥ or the second day of Shavuot falls on a weekday, start here:

Every male firstborn that is delivered among your herd and your flock, you shall consecrate to the LORD your God: you may not perform work with the male firstborn of your oxen, nor shear the male firstborn of your sheep. You shall eat them in the presence of the LORD your God each year, you and your household, in the place which the LORD will choose. If it is blemished: lame or blind, or with any other serious blemish, you may not offer it to the LORD your God. Eat it within your gates; [it may be eaten by] pure and impure alike, as the gazelle and as the hart. But its blood you may not eat; you must spill it on the ground like water. (*Shabbat:* SHELISHI)

Remember the month of Spring: bring a Pesaḥ offering to the LORD your God, for in the month of Spring, the LORD your God took you out of Egypt at night. You shall bring a Pesaḥ offering to the LORD your God, sheep and cattle, at the place the LORD shall choose as a dwelling place for His name. You may not eat leaven with it; you must eat matzot, the bread of oppression, with it for seven days – for you left Egypt in great haste – so that you remember the day of your exodus from Egypt all the days of your life. *And no leaven shall be seen by you within all your borders for seven days, and none of the meat which you offer in the evening of the first day shall be allowed to remain until morning. You may not sacrifice the Pesaḥ offering in any one of your cities, which the LORD your God gives you. Only at the place which the LORD your God shall choose as a dwelling place for His name – that is where you should sacrifice the Pesaḥ offering in the evening, before sunset, in the season of your exodus from Egypt. You shall cook it and eat it in the place the LORD your God will choose, and in the morning you shall turn back and go to your abode. For six days, you shall eat matzot; the seventh day is a day of assembly for the LORD your God: on it, you may not perform work. LEVI (*Shabbat:* REVI'I) SHELISHI (*Shabbat:* ḤAMISHI)

Count for yourselves seven weeks; when the sickle begins to cut the standing grain, then shall you begin to count the seven weeks. And you shall celebrate a Festival of Weeks [Shavuot] for the LORD your God, bringing a free-will offering, as much as you can afford, according to the blessing the LORD your God has given you. And you shall rejoice in the presence of the LORD your God: you and your sons and daughters, REVI'I (*Shabbat:* SHISHI)

If the eighth day of פסח *or the second day of* שבועות *falls on a weekday, start here:*

(בשבת שלישי) כָּל־הַבְּכוֹר אֲשֶׁר יִוָּלֵד בִּבְקָרְךָ וּבְצֹאנְךָ הַזָּכָר תַּקְדִּישׁ לַיהוה אֱלֹהֶיךָ לֹא
תַעֲבֹד בִּבְכֹר שׁוֹרֶךָ וְלֹא תָגֹז בְּכוֹר צֹאנֶךָ: לִפְנֵי יהוה אֱלֹהֶיךָ תֹאכְלֶנּוּ שָׁנָה
בְשָׁנָה בַּמָּקוֹם אֲשֶׁר־יִבְחַר יהוה אַתָּה וּבֵיתֶךָ: וְכִי־יִהְיֶה בוֹ מוּם פִּסֵּחַ אוֹ
עִוֵּר כֹּל מוּם רָע לֹא תִזְבָּחֶנּוּ לַיהוה אֱלֹהֶיךָ: בִּשְׁעָרֶיךָ תֹּאכְלֶנּוּ הַטָּמֵא
וְהַטָּהוֹר יַחְדָּו כַּצְּבִי וְכָאַיָּל: רַק אֶת־דָּמוֹ לֹא תֹאכֵל עַל־הָאָרֶץ תִּשְׁפְּכֶנּוּ
כַּמָּיִם:

לוי (בשבת רביעי) שָׁמוֹר אֶת־חֹדֶשׁ הָאָבִיב וְעָשִׂיתָ פֶּסַח לַיהוה אֱלֹהֶיךָ כִּי בְּחֹדֶשׁ הָאָבִיב
הוֹצִיאֲךָ יהוה אֱלֹהֶיךָ מִמִּצְרַיִם לָיְלָה: וְזָבַחְתָּ פֶּסַח לַיהוה אֱלֹהֶיךָ צֹאן
וּבָקָר בַּמָּקוֹם אֲשֶׁר יִבְחַר יהוה לְשַׁכֵּן שְׁמוֹ שָׁם: לֹא־תֹאכַל עָלָיו חָמֵץ
שִׁבְעַת יָמִים תֹּאכַל־עָלָיו מַצּוֹת לֶחֶם עֹנִי כִּי בְחִפָּזוֹן יָצָאתָ מֵאֶרֶץ מִצְרַיִם
שלישי (בשבת חמישי) לְמַעַן תִּזְכֹּר אֶת־יוֹם צֵאתְךָ מֵאֶרֶץ מִצְרַיִם כֹּל יְמֵי חַיֶּיךָ: *וְלֹא־יֵרָאֶה לְךָ
שְׂאֹר בְּכָל־גְּבֻלְךָ שִׁבְעַת יָמִים וְלֹא־יָלִין מִן־הַבָּשָׂר אֲשֶׁר תִּזְבַּח בָּעֶרֶב בַּיּוֹם
הָרִאשׁוֹן לַבֹּקֶר: לֹא תוּכַל לִזְבֹּחַ אֶת־הַפָּסַח בְּאַחַד שְׁעָרֶיךָ אֲשֶׁר־יהוה
אֱלֹהֶיךָ נֹתֵן לָךְ: כִּי אִם־אֶל־הַמָּקוֹם אֲשֶׁר־יִבְחַר יהוה אֱלֹהֶיךָ לְשַׁכֵּן שְׁמוֹ
שָׁם תִּזְבַּח אֶת־הַפֶּסַח בָּעָרֶב כְּבוֹא הַשֶּׁמֶשׁ מוֹעֵד צֵאתְךָ מִמִּצְרָיִם: וּבִשַּׁלְתָּ
וְאָכַלְתָּ בַּמָּקוֹם אֲשֶׁר יִבְחַר יהוה אֱלֹהֶיךָ בּוֹ וּפָנִיתָ בַבֹּקֶר וְהָלַכְתָּ לְאֹהָלֶיךָ:
שֵׁשֶׁת יָמִים תֹּאכַל מַצּוֹת וּבַיּוֹם הַשְּׁבִיעִי עֲצֶרֶת לַיהוה אֱלֹהֶיךָ לֹא תַעֲשֶׂה
רביעי (בשבת שישי) מְלָאכָה: *שִׁבְעָה שָׁבֻעֹת תִּסְפָּר־לָךְ מֵהָחֵל חֶרְמֵשׁ בַּקָּמָה תָּחֵל
לִסְפֹּר שִׁבְעָה שָׁבֻעוֹת: וְעָשִׂיתָ חַג שָׁבֻעוֹת לַיהוה אֱלֹהֶיךָ מִסַּת נִדְבַת יָדְךָ
אֲשֶׁר תִּתֵּן כַּאֲשֶׁר יְבָרֶכְךָ יהוה אֱלֹהֶיךָ: וְשָׂמַחְתָּ לִפְנֵי ׀ יהוה אֱלֹהֶיךָ אַתָּה

וְשָׂמַחְתָּ *You shall rejoice.* There is greater emphasis on rejoicing in Deuteronomy than elsewhere in the Torah. The root *s-m-ḥ*, "to rejoice," appears only once in each of the books of Genesis, Exodus, Leviticus and Numbers, but twelve times in Deuteronomy as a whole. The previous books have been about the long journey, begun by Abraham, toward the fulfillment of the divine promises of children and a homeland. Deuteronomy is about the destination: a land where the people of the covenant can be free to pursue their vocation as a holy nation in a holy land, keeping God's law, sensing His presence and celebrating His blessings. Note, however, that the word "rejoice"

your male and female slaves, and the Levite who dwells within your gates, along with the stranger and orphan and widow that are among you, at the place that the LORD your God shall choose as a dwelling place for His name. And you shall remember that you were once a slave in Egypt; keep and fulfill all of these statutes.

You shall celebrate a Festival of Booths [Sukkot] for yourselves for seven days, when you gather [your produce] into your granary and wine-vat. And you shall rejoice on your festival: you and your sons and daughters, your male and female slaves, and the Levite, the stranger and orphan and widow that dwell within your gates. You shall celebrate for seven days for the LORD your God in the place which the LORD shall choose, for the LORD your God shall bless you in all of your produce and all that you do; and you will be truly joyful. Three times in the year, all your males shall appear before the LORD your God at the place He will choose: on Pesaḥ, Shavuot and Sukkot. They shall not appear before the LORD empty-handed. Each shall bring such a gift as he can, in proportion to the blessing the LORD your God grants you. ḤAMISHI (*Shabbat:* SHEVI'I)

The Maftir for the last day of Pesaḥ is the same as that for the other days of Ḥol HaMo'ed, page 1140. The Maftir for Shavuot appears on page 1148, and the Haftara for the second day of Shavuot appears on page 1150. Both the Maftir and the Haftara for Shemini Atzeret appear on page 1161.

HAFTARA FOR THE LAST DAY OF PESAḤ

This day he will halt at Nob; he will wave his hand, mountain of the daughter of Zion, hill of Jerusalem. *Is. 10:32–12:6*

See, the sovereign LORD of hosts will lop off the boughs with an axe. The tall trees will be felled, the lofty ones laid low. He will cut down the forest thickets with an axe. Lebanon will fall before the Mighty One.

A shoot will grow from the stump of Jesse; from his roots a branch will bear fruit. The spirit of the LORD will rest on him – a spirit of wisdom and understanding, a spirit of counsel and power, a spirit of knowledge and the fear of the LORD, and he will delight in the fear of the LORD. He will not judge by what his eyes see, or decide by what his ears hear; with justice he will judge the poor, and with equity defend the humble in the land. He will strike the earth with the rod of his mouth; with the breath of his lips he will slay the wicked. Justice will be his belt and faithfulness

ובנך ובתך ועבדך ואמתך והלוי אשר בשעריך והגר והיתום והאלמנה
אשר בקרבך במקום אשר יבחר יהוה אלהיך לשכן שמו שם: וזכרת כי־
עבד היית במצרים ושמרת ועשית את־החקים האלה:
חמישי (בשבת שביעי) חג הסכת תעשה לך שבעת ימים באספך מגרנך ומיקבך: ושמחת בחגך
אתה ובנך ובתך ועבדך ואמתך והלוי והגר והיתום והאלמנה אשר
בשעריך: שבעת ימים תחג ליהוה אלהיך במקום אשר־יבחר יהוה כי
יברכך יהוה אלהיך בכל־תבואתך ובכל מעשה ידיך והיית אך שמח:
שלוש פעמים | בשנה יראה כל־זכורך את־פני | יהוה אלהיך במקום אשר
יבחר בחג המצות ובחג השבעות ובחג הסכות ולא יראה את־פני יהוה
ריקם: איש כמתנת ידו כברכת יהוה אלהיך אשר נתן־לך:

The מפטיר *for* יום שמיני של פסח *is the same as that for the other days of* חול המועד פסח*, page 1141. The* מפטיר *for* יום שני של שבועות *appears on page 1149, and the* הפטרה *for* שבועות *appears on page 1151. Both the* מפטיר *and the* הפטרה *for* שמיני עצרת *appear on page 1161.*

הפטרה ליום האחרון של פסח

בת ישעיהו י:לב–יב:ו עוד היום בנב לעמד ינפף ידו הר בית־ציון גבעת ירושלם: הנה
האדון יהוה צבאות מסעף פארה במערצה ורמי הקומה גדעים והגבהים
ישפלו: ונקף סבכי היער בברזל והלבנון באדיר יפול: ויצא
חטר מגזע ישי ונצר משרשיו יפרה: ונחה עליו רוח יהוה רוח חכמה ובינה
רוח עצה וגבורה רוח דעת ויראת יהוה: והריחו ביראת יהוה ולא־למראה
עיניו ישפוט ולא־למשמע אזניו יוכיח: ושפט בצדק דלים והוכיח במישור
לענוי־ארץ והכה־ארץ בשבט פיו וברוח שפתיו ימית רשע: והיה צדק אזור

does not appear in the context of Pesah, for it recalls two periods of suffering, the suffering inflicted on the Israelites by the Egyptians, and the subsequent suffering of the Egyptians themselves. Halakhically there is a mitzva of *simha* on Pesah, but it comes on the first day(s) mixed with the taste of affliction *and bitterness* (matza and *maror*) and on the last with the memory of the Egyptians who died at the Sea of Reeds, and as Proverbs 24:17 states, "Do not rejoice when your enemy falls" (*Yalkut Shimoni, Emor*, 654).

HAFTARA FOR THE LAST DAY OF PESAH

The exodus was not only an event in the past; it is also a prefiguration and

the sash around his waist. The wolf will live with the lamb, the leopard will lie down with the kid, the calf and the lion and the yearling together; and a little child will lead them. The cow will graze with the bear, their young will lie down together, and the lion will eat straw like the ox. An infant will play near the cobra's hole, and a young child put his hand into the viper's nest. They will neither harm nor destroy on all My holy mountain, for the earth will be full of the knowledge of the LORD as the waters cover the sea.

On that day the stock of Jesse will stand as a banner for the peoples; nations will rally to him, and his place of rest will be glorious.

On that day the LORD will reach out His hand a second time to reclaim the remnant that is left of His people from Assyria, Lower Egypt, Pathros, Cush, Elam, Shinar, Hamath and the islands of the sea. He will raise a banner for the nations and gather the exiles of Israel; He will assemble the scattered people of Judah from the four quarters of the earth. Ephraim's jealousy will vanish, and Judah's harassment will end. Ephraim will not be jealous of Judah, nor will Judah be hostile toward Ephraim. They will swoop down on the slopes of Philistia to the west; together they will plunder the people to the east. Edom and Moab will be subject to them, and the Ammonites shall obey them. The LORD will dry up the gulf of the Egyptian sea; with a scorching wind He will sweep His hand over the Euphrates River. He will break it up into seven streams so that people can cross over in sandals. There will be a highway for the remnant of His people that is left from Assyria, as there was for Israel when they came up from Egypt. In that day you will say: "I will praise You, O LORD. Although You were angry with me, Your anger has turned away and You have comforted me. Behold, God is my salvation; I will trust and not be afraid. The LORD, the LORD, is my strength and my song. He has become my salvation." With joy you will draw water from the springs of salvation. In that day you will say: "Give thanks to the LORD, call on His name; make known among the nations what He has done, and proclaim that His name is exalted. Sing to the LORD, for He has done glorious things; let this be known throughout the world. Shout aloud and sing for joy, people of Zion, for great is the Holy One of Israel among you."

Continue with the blessings after the Haftara on page 514.

מָתְנָיו וְהָאֱמוּנָה אֵזוֹר חֲלָצָיו: וְגָר זְאֵב עִם־כֶּבֶשׂ וְנָמֵר עִם־גְּדִי יִרְבָּץ וְעֵגֶל
וּכְפִיר וּמְרִיא יַחְדָּו וְנַעַר קָטֹן נֹהֵג בָּם: וּפָרָה וָדֹב תִּרְעֶינָה יַחְדָּו יִרְבְּצוּ יַלְדֵיהֶן
וְאַרְיֵה כַּבָּקָר יֹאכַל־תֶּבֶן: וְשִׁעֲשַׁע יוֹנֵק עַל־חֻר פָּתֶן וְעַל מְאוּרַת צִפְעוֹנִי
גָּמוּל יָדוֹ הָדָה: לֹא־יָרֵעוּ וְלֹא־יַשְׁחִיתוּ בְּכָל־הַר קָדְשִׁי כִּי־מָלְאָה הָאָרֶץ דֵּעָה
אֶת־יהוה כַּמַּיִם לַיָּם מְכַסִּים: וְהָיָה בַּיּוֹם הַהוּא שֹׁרֶשׁ יִשַׁי אֲשֶׁר
עֹמֵד לְנֵס עַמִּים אֵלָיו גּוֹיִם יִדְרֹשׁוּ וְהָיְתָה מְנֻחָתוֹ כָּבוֹד: וְהָיָה ׀
בַּיּוֹם הַהוּא יוֹסִיף אֲדֹנָי ׀ שֵׁנִית יָדוֹ לִקְנוֹת אֶת־שְׁאָר עַמּוֹ אֲשֶׁר יִשָּׁאֵר מֵאַשּׁוּר
וּמִמִּצְרַיִם וּמִפַּתְרוֹס וּמִכּוּשׁ וּמֵעֵילָם וּמִשִּׁנְעָר וּמֵחֲמָת וּמֵאִיֵּי הַיָּם: וְנָשָׂא נֵס
לַגּוֹיִם וְאָסַף נִדְחֵי יִשְׂרָאֵל וּנְפֻצוֹת יְהוּדָה יְקַבֵּץ מֵאַרְבַּע כַּנְפוֹת הָאָרֶץ: וְסָרָה
קִנְאַת אֶפְרַיִם וְצֹרְרֵי יְהוּדָה יִכָּרֵתוּ אֶפְרַיִם לֹא־יְקַנֵּא אֶת־יְהוּדָה וִיהוּדָה לֹא־
יָצֹר אֶת־אֶפְרָיִם: וְעָפוּ בְכָתֵף פְּלִשְׁתִּים יָמָּה יַחְדָּו יָבֹזּוּ אֶת־בְּנֵי־קֶדֶם אֱדוֹם
וּמוֹאָב מִשְׁלוֹח יָדָם וּבְנֵי עַמּוֹן מִשְׁמַעְתָּם: וְהֶחֱרִים יהוה אֵת לְשׁוֹן יָם־מִצְרַיִם
וְהֵנִיף יָדוֹ עַל־הַנָּהָר בַּעְיָם רוּחוֹ וְהִכָּהוּ לְשִׁבְעָה נְחָלִים וְהִדְרִיךְ בַּנְּעָלִים:
וְהָיְתָה מְסִלָּה לִשְׁאָר עַמּוֹ אֲשֶׁר יִשָּׁאֵר מֵאַשּׁוּר כַּאֲשֶׁר הָיְתָה לְיִשְׂרָאֵל בְּיוֹם
עֲלֹתוֹ מֵאֶרֶץ מִצְרָיִם: וְאָמַרְתָּ בַּיּוֹם הַהוּא אוֹדְךָ יהוה כִּי אָנַפְתָּ בִּי יָשֹׁב אַפְּךָ
וּתְנַחֲמֵנִי: הִנֵּה אֵל יְשׁוּעָתִי אֶבְטַח וְלֹא אֶפְחָד כִּי־עָזִּי וְזִמְרָת יָהּ יהוה וַיְהִי־
לִי לִישׁוּעָה: וּשְׁאַבְתֶּם־מַיִם בְּשָׂשׂוֹן מִמַּעַיְנֵי הַיְשׁוּעָה: וַאֲמַרְתֶּם בַּיּוֹם הַהוּא
הוֹדוּ לַיהוה קִרְאוּ בִשְׁמוֹ הוֹדִיעוּ בָעַמִּים עֲלִילֹתָיו הַזְכִּירוּ כִּי נִשְׂגָּב שְׁמוֹ:
זַמְּרוּ יהוה כִּי גֵאוּת עָשָׂה מידעת זֹאת בְּכָל־הָאָרֶץ: צַהֲלִי וָרֹנִּי יוֹשֶׁבֶת צִיּוֹן מוּדַעַת
כִּי־גָדוֹל בְּקִרְבֵּךְ קְדוֹשׁ יִשְׂרָאֵל:

Continue with the blessings after the הפטרה *on page 515.*

---

promise of future redemption: "As in the days when I brought you out of Egypt, I will show them miracles" (Mic. 7:15). So on the last day of Pesaḥ, the Haftara speaks of future redemption in one of the most justly famous passages in the entire prophetic literature, in the words of Isaiah, the poet laureate of hope. Isaiah spells out the connection between past and future in the words, "On that day the Lord will reach out His hand a second time to reclaim the remnant that is left of His people" (11:11), this time bringing them back not from one place of exile but "from the four quarters of the earth."

TORAH READING FOR THE FIRST DAY OF SHAVUOT

Akdamut appears on page 792.

On the third new moon after the people of Israel had left the land of Egypt, on that first day, they arrived at the wilderness of Sinai. They had traveled from Refidim and they arrived in the wilderness of Sinai, and encamped there in the desert; there, in view of the mountain, Israel laid out its camp. And there Moses ascended to God; and the LORD called out to him from the mountain, telling him, "This you must say to the house of Jacob, must tell the house of Israel: You have seen what I did in Egypt; and how I lifted you high, on the wings of eagles, and brought you to Me. And now – if you will listen to My voice, if you will guard close My covenant, you shall be My treasure among all the peoples – for all the earth is Mine; but you shall be a kingdom of priests to Me, a holy nation. These are the words you must say to the children of Israel." *Ex. 19:1–20:23*

LEVI So Moses came back, and called together the elders of the people, and laid out before them all these words with which the LORD had charged him. And all the people responded as one: "All that the LORD has spoken, we shall perform." And Moses brought the words of the people back to the LORD.

The LORD said to Moses, "I shall come to you in the thick of the cloud, that the people may hear as I speak to you, that they should believe in you also, forever," and Moses told the LORD what the people had said. "Go to the people," said the LORD to Moses, "And have them consecrate themselves today and tomorrow, and wash their clothes. Be sure they are ready for the third day, for on the third day the LORD shall descend to Mount Sinai, in the sight of all the people. Mark a boundary for the people around, and tell them: Take care not to climb the mountain, or even to touch its edge, for anyone who touches the mountain shall die. Let no hand touch it, for that person will be stoned or shot down; man or beast, he shall not live. Only when the horn sounds a long blast, may you ascend the mountain again."

---

your God" (Ex. 6:7). This would mark the culmination of their seven-week journey from servitude to law-governed liberty.

קריאה ליום טוב ראשון של שבועות

אקדמות *appears on page 793.*

שמות
יט:א-כ:כג

בַּחֹ֙דֶשׁ֙ הַשְּׁלִישִׁ֔י לְצֵ֥את בְּנֵֽי־יִשְׂרָאֵ֖ל מֵאֶ֣רֶץ מִצְרָ֑יִם בַּיּ֣וֹם הַזֶּ֔ה בָּ֖אוּ מִדְבַּ֥ר
סִינָֽי: וַיִּסְע֣וּ מֵרְפִידִ֗ים וַיָּבֹ֙אוּ֙ מִדְבַּ֣ר סִינַ֔י וַֽיַּחֲנ֖וּ בַּמִּדְבָּ֑ר וַיִּֽחַן־שָׁ֥ם יִשְׂרָאֵ֖ל
נֶ֥גֶד הָהָֽר: וּמֹשֶׁ֥ה עָלָ֖ה אֶל־הָאֱלֹהִ֑ים וַיִּקְרָ֙א אֵלָ֤יו יהו֙ה מִן־הָהָ֣ר לֵאמֹ֔ר כֹּ֤ה
תֹאמַר֙ לְבֵ֣ית יַעֲקֹ֔ב וְתַגֵּ֖יד לִבְנֵ֥י יִשְׂרָאֵֽל: אַתֶּ֣ם רְאִיתֶ֔ם אֲשֶׁ֥ר עָשִׂ֖יתִי לְמִצְרָ֑יִם
וָאֶשָּׂ֤א אֶתְכֶם֙ עַל־כַּנְפֵ֣י נְשָׁרִ֔ים וָאָבִ֥א אֶתְכֶ֖ם אֵלָֽי: וְעַתָּ֗ה אִם־שָׁמ֤וֹעַ תִּשְׁמְעוּ֙
בְּקֹלִ֔י וּשְׁמַרְתֶּ֖ם אֶת־בְּרִיתִ֑י וִהְיִ֙יתֶם לִ֤י סְגֻלָּה֙ מִכָּל־הָ֣עַמִּ֔ים כִּי־לִ֖י כָּל־הָאָֽרֶץ:
וְאַתֶּ֧ם תִּֽהְיוּ־לִ֛י מַמְלֶ֥כֶת כֹּהֲנִ֖ים וְג֣וֹי קָד֑וֹשׁ אֵ֚לֶּה הַדְּבָרִ֔ים אֲשֶׁ֥ר תְּדַבֵּ֖ר אֶל־
בְּנֵ֥י יִשְׂרָאֵֽל: וַיָּבֹ֣א מֹשֶׁ֔ה וַיִּקְרָ֖א לְזִקְנֵ֣י הָעָ֑ם וַיָּ֣שֶׂם לִפְנֵיהֶ֗ם אֵ֚ת כָּל־הַדְּבָרִ֣ים לוי
הָאֵ֔לֶּה אֲשֶׁ֥ר צִוָּ֖הוּ יהוֽה: וַיַּעֲנ֙וּ כָל־הָעָ֤ם יַחְדָּו֙ וַיֹּ֣אמְר֔וּ כֹּ֛ל אֲשֶׁר־דִּבֶּ֥ר יהו֖ה
נַעֲשֶׂ֑ה וַיָּ֧שֶׁב מֹשֶׁ֛ה אֶת־דִּבְרֵ֥י הָעָ֖ם אֶל־יהוֽה: וַיֹּ֨אמֶר יהו֜ה אֶל־מֹשֶׁ֗ה הִנֵּ֙ה
אָנֹכִ֜י בָּ֣א אֵלֶ֘יךָ֘ בְּעַ֣ב הֶֽעָנָן֒ בַּעֲב֞וּר יִשְׁמַ֤ע הָעָם֙ בְּדַבְּרִ֣י עִמָּ֔ךְ וְגַם־בְּךָ֖ יַאֲמִ֣ינוּ
לְעוֹלָ֑ם וַיַּגֵּ֥ד מֹשֶׁ֛ה אֶת־דִּבְרֵ֥י הָעָ֖ם אֶל־יהוֽה: וַיֹּ֨אמֶר יהו֤ה אֶל־מֹשֶׁה֙ לֵ֣ךְ
אֶל־הָעָ֔ם וְקִדַּשְׁתָּ֥ם הַיּ֖וֹם וּמָחָ֑ר וְכִבְּס֖וּ שִׂמְלֹתָֽם: וְהָי֥וּ נְכֹנִ֖ים לַיּ֣וֹם הַשְּׁלִישִׁ֑י
כִּ֣י ׀ בַּיּ֣וֹם הַשְּׁלִשִׁ֗י יֵרֵ֧ד יהו֛ה לְעֵינֵ֥י כָל־הָעָ֖ם עַל־הַ֥ר סִינָֽי: וְהִגְבַּלְתָּ֤ אֶת־הָעָם֙
סָבִ֣יב לֵאמֹ֔ר הִשָּׁמְר֥וּ לָכֶ֛ם עֲל֥וֹת בָּהָ֖ר וּנְגֹ֣עַ בְּקָצֵ֑הוּ כָּל־הַנֹּגֵ֥עַ בָּהָ֖ר מ֥וֹת יוּמָֽת:
לֹֽא־תִגַּ֙ע בּ֜וֹ יָ֗ד כִּֽי־סָק֤וֹל יִסָּקֵל֙ אֽוֹ־יָרֹ֣ה יִיָּרֶ֔ה אִם־בְּהֵמָ֥ה אִם־אִ֖ישׁ לֹ֣א יִחְיֶ֑ה

READING OF THE TORAH FOR THE FIRST DAY OF SHAVUOT
The reading for the first day describes the revelation at Mount Sinai, the event
commemorated by Shavuot and the defining moment of Jewish history. It
was then that, uniquely, God revealed Himself to an entire people, making
a covenant with them that would charge them with the mission of becoming
a holy nation, dedicated to God and an inspiration to the world. It was also
the occasion on which God spoke the Ten Commandments or "Utterances"
that eventually became the world's most famous moral code.

אַתֶּם רְאִיתֶם *You have seen.* The emphasis is on the immediacy of the experience. The people had witnessed a divine intervention into history. They had
been redeemed from slavery under Pharaoh. God was now proposing that
they become a nation under His own direct sovereignty in fulfillment of
what He had earlier told Moses: "I will take you as My people, and I will be

Moses descended the mountain to the people, and he consecrated them, and they washed their clothes. "Be ready," he told the people, "for three days' time; let no man come close to a woman." SHELISHI

On the third day, in the early morning – thunder and lightning; heavy cloud covered the mountain, there was a very loud sound of the shofar, and all of the people in the camp quaked. And Moses went apart from the people, to meet God, leaving the camp behind, and the people came to stand at the foot of the mountain. And Mount Sinai was all enveloped in smoke, for the LORD had descended upon it in fire, and its smoke rose up like the smoke of a furnace, and all the mountain shook. And the sound of the shofar grew ever louder – Moses spoke, and God answered him with a voice.

The LORD descended to Mount Sinai, to the mountain top – and the LORD called Moses forth to the top of the mountain, and Moses ascended. "Now go down," said the LORD to Moses, "and warn the people, lest they break away to come to see the LORD, and fall in their great numbers. Even the priests who draw near the LORD – let them, too, set themselves apart, lest the LORD bursts in among them." But Moses told the LORD, "The people cannot ascend to Mount Sinai, for You have already warned us, 'Mark a boundary to the mountain around and consecrate it.'" So the LORD said to him, "Go down and ascend again, together with Aaron, but let the priests and the people not break away to ascend to the LORD, lest disaster burst out upon them." So Moses descended to the people and told them. REVI'I

And God spoke all these words, saying:

I am the LORD your God who brought you out of the land of Egypt, from the slave-house. Have no other gods besides Me. Do not make a

---

the God of all humankind, but He is also, especially in His relationship with Israel, the God of history. Having freed the people from enslavement, He is now giving them their constitution of liberty as a law-governed society under the sovereignty of God.

לֹא־יִהְיֶה לְךָ אֱלֹהִים אֲחֵרִים *Have no other gods.* Monotheism is more than belief in one God. It is also undivided loyalty to the one God, involving a moral bond, not just an intellectual one. It was this exclusivity of worship that was

שלישי בִּמְשֹׁךְ הַיֹּבֵל הֵמָּה יַעֲלוּ בָהָר׃ *וַיֵּרֶד מֹשֶׁה מִן־הָהָר אֶל־הָעָם וַיְקַדֵּשׁ אֶת־
הָעָם וַיְכַבְּסוּ שִׂמְלֹתָם׃ וַיֹּאמֶר אֶל־הָעָם הֱיוּ נְכֹנִים לִשְׁלֹשֶׁת יָמִים אַל־תִּגְּשׁוּ
אֶל־אִשָּׁה׃ וַיְהִי בַיּוֹם הַשְּׁלִישִׁי בִּהְיֹת הַבֹּקֶר וַיְהִי קֹלֹת וּבְרָקִים וְעָנָן כָּבֵד
עַל־הָהָר וְקֹל שֹׁפָר חָזָק מְאֹד וַיֶּחֱרַד כָּל־הָעָם אֲשֶׁר בַּמַּחֲנֶה׃ וַיּוֹצֵא מֹשֶׁה
אֶת־הָעָם לִקְרַאת הָאֱלֹהִים מִן־הַמַּחֲנֶה וַיִּתְיַצְּבוּ בְּתַחְתִּית הָהָר׃ וְהַר סִינַי
עָשַׁן כֻּלּוֹ מִפְּנֵי אֲשֶׁר יָרַד עָלָיו יהוה בָּאֵשׁ וַיַּעַל עֲשָׁנוֹ כְּעֶשֶׁן הַכִּבְשָׁן וַיֶּחֱרַד
כָּל־הָהָר מְאֹד׃ וַיְהִי קוֹל הַשֹּׁפָר הוֹלֵךְ וְחָזֵק מְאֹד מֹשֶׁה יְדַבֵּר וְהָאֱלֹהִים
רביעי יַעֲנֶנּוּ בְקוֹל׃ *וַיֵּרֶד יהוה עַל־הַר סִינַי אֶל־רֹאשׁ הָהָר וַיִּקְרָא יהוה לְמֹשֶׁה
אֶל־רֹאשׁ הָהָר וַיַּעַל מֹשֶׁה׃ וַיֹּאמֶר יהוה אֶל־מֹשֶׁה רֵד הָעֵד בָּעָם פֶּן־יֶהֶרְסוּ
אֶל־יהוה לִרְאוֹת וְנָפַל מִמֶּנּוּ רָב׃ וְגַם הַכֹּהֲנִים הַנִּגָּשִׁים אֶל־יהוה יִתְקַדָּשׁוּ
פֶּן־יִפְרֹץ בָּהֶם יהוה׃ וַיֹּאמֶר מֹשֶׁה אֶל־יהוה לֹא־יוּכַל הָעָם לַעֲלֹת אֶל־הַר
סִינָי כִּי־אַתָּה הַעֵדֹתָה בָּנוּ לֵאמֹר הַגְבֵּל אֶת־הָהָר וְקִדַּשְׁתּוֹ׃ וַיֹּאמֶר אֵלָיו
יהוה לֶךְ־רֵד וְעָלִיתָ אַתָּה וְאַהֲרֹן עִמָּךְ וְהַכֹּהֲנִים וְהָעָם אַל־יֶהֶרְסוּ לַעֲלֹת
אֶל־יהוה פֶּן־יִפְרָץ־בָּם׃ וַיֵּרֶד מֹשֶׁה אֶל־הָעָם וַיֹּאמֶר אֲלֵהֶם׃ וַיְדַבֵּר
אֱלֹהִים אֵת כָּל־הַדְּבָרִים הָאֵלֶּה לֵאמֹר׃ אָנֹכִי יהוה אֱלֹהֶיךָ אֲשֶׁר
הוֹצֵאתִיךָ מֵאֶרֶץ מִצְרַיִם מִבֵּית עֲבָדִים׃ לֹא־יִהְיֶה לְךָ אֱלֹהִים אֲחֵרִים עַל־

מֹשֶׁה יְדַבֵּר וְהָאֱלֹהִים יַעֲנֶנּוּ בְקוֹל *Moses spoke, and God answered him with a voice.* This refers not to the Ten Commandments but to the conversation about preparations for that event (Ramban). Moses' words were inaudible against the sound of the shofar but the voice of God could be heard by all (Rashbam). R. Elie Munk, citing the *Zohar* (*VaYikra* 7a), suggests a larger idea, that God would confirm what Moses said, even when he spoke on his own initiative. Likewise God ratifies the decisions of the sages in each generation when they apply the principles of the Oral Law.

רֵד *Now go down.* God wanted Moses to be at the foot of the mountain not at the top, so that he would be among the people, not apart from them, when the revelation took place.

אָנֹכִי יהוה אֱלֹהֶיךָ *I am the Lord your God.* According to Maimonides, this is the first command: to believe in God. According to Nahmanides, it is a prelude and prologue to the commands. Judah HaLevi in the *Kuzari* (1:11–25) notes that God does not identify himself as Creator of heaven and earth, but as He who brought the people out of slavery. God as Creator of the universe is

sculptured image for yourself, or any likeness of what is in the heavens above, or on the earth below, or in the waters under the earth. Do not bow down to them or worship them, for I am the LORD your God, a zealous God, visiting the guilt of the parents on the children to the third and fourth generation, if they also reject Me; but showing kindness to thousands of generations of those who love Me and keep My commandments.

Do not take the name of the LORD your God in vain. The LORD will not leave unpunished one who utters His name in vain.

Remember the Sabbath and keep it holy. Six days you shall labor and do all your work, but the seventh day is a Sabbath of the LORD your God; on it you shall not do any work – you, your son or daughter, your male or female slaves, your cattle, or the stranger within your gates. For in six days the LORD made heaven and earth and sea, and all that is in them, and rested on the seventh day; therefore the LORD blessed the Sabbath day and made it holy.

Honor your father and your mother, so that you may live long in the land that the LORD your God is giving you.

Do not murder.

Do not commit adultery.

Do not steal.

Do not testify as a false witness against your neighbor.

Do not be envious of your neighbor's house.

Do not be envious of your neighbor's wife, his male or female slave, his ox, his ass, or anything else that is your neighbor's.

---

choose. It is part of public time, the way a park is part of public space. It and the freedom it represents belong to everyone equally. Thus it is essential that on Shabbat no one – not slaves, servants, employees, even farm animals – can be made to work against their will.

לְמַעַן יַאֲרִכוּן יָמֶיךָ עַל הָאֲדָמָה *So that you may live long in the land.* "People will not look forward to posterity who never look backward to their ancestors" (Edmund Burke).

פָּנָֽי לֹֽא תַֽעֲשֶׂה־לְךָ֣ פֶּ֣סֶל ׀ וְכׇל־תְּמוּנָ֡ה אֲשֶׁ֣ר בַּשָּׁמַ֣יִם ׀ מִמַּ֡עַל וַאֲשֶׁ֣ר בָּאָ֣רֶץ
מִתַּ֡חַת וַאֲשֶׁ֣ר בַּמַּ֣יִם ׀ מִתַּ֣חַת לָאָ֗רֶץ לֹֽא־תִשְׁתַּחֲוֶ֥ה לָהֶ֛ם וְלֹ֥א תָֽעׇבְדֵ֖ם כִּ֣י
אָנֹכִ֞י יהו֤ה אֱלֹהֶ֙יךָ֙ אֵ֣ל קַנָּ֔א פֹּ֠קֵד עֲוֺ֨ן אָבֹ֧ת עַל־בָּנִ֛ים עַל־שִׁלֵּשִׁ֥ים וְעַל־רִבֵּעִ֖ים
לְשֹׂנְאָ֑י וְעֹ֤שֶׂה חֶ֙סֶד֙ לַאֲלָפִ֔ים לְאֹהֲבַ֖י וּלְשֹׁמְרֵ֥י מִצְוֺתָֽי׃ לֹ֥א תִשָּׂ֛א
אֶת־שֵׁם־יהו֥ה אֱלֹהֶ֖יךָ לַשָּׁ֑וְא כִּ֣י לֹ֤א יְנַקֶּה֙ יהו֔ה אֵ֛ת אֲשֶׁר־יִשָּׂ֥א אֶת־שְׁמ֖וֹ
לַשָּֽׁוְא׃

זָכ֛וֹר אֶת־י֥וֹם הַשַּׁבָּ֖ת לְקַדְּשׁ֑וֹ שֵׁ֤שֶׁת יָמִים֙ תַּֽעֲבֹ֔ד וְעָשִׂ֖יתָ כׇּל־מְלַאכְתֶּֽךָ
וְי֙וֹם֙ הַשְּׁבִיעִ֜י שַׁבָּ֣ת ׀ לַיהו֣ה אֱלֹהֶ֗יךָ לֹ֣א תַעֲשֶׂ֣ה כׇל־מְלָאכָ֡ה אַתָּ֣ה ׀ וּבִנְךָ֣
וּ֠בִתֶּ֠ךָ עַבְדְּךָ֨ וַאֲמָתְךָ֜ וּבְהֶמְתֶּ֗ךָ וְגֵרְךָ֙ אֲשֶׁ֣ר בִּשְׁעָרֶ֔יךָ כִּ֣י שֵֽׁשֶׁת־יָמִ֡ים עָשָׂ֣ה
יהו֩ה אֶת־הַשָּׁמַ֨יִם וְאֶת־הָאָ֜רֶץ אֶת־הַיָּ֗ם וְאֶת־כׇּל־אֲשֶׁר־בָּ֔ם וַיָּ֖נַח בַּיּ֣וֹם
הַשְּׁבִיעִ֑י עַל־כֵּ֗ן בֵּרַ֧ךְ יהו֛ה אֶת־י֥וֹם הַשַּׁבָּ֖ת וַֽיְקַדְּשֵֽׁהוּ׃ כַּבֵּ֥ד
אֶת־אָבִ֖יךָ וְאֶת־אִמֶּ֑ךָ לְמַ֙עַן֙ יַאֲרִכ֣וּן יָמֶ֔יךָ עַ֚ל הָאֲדָמָ֔ה אֲשֶׁר־יהו֥ה אֱלֹהֶ֖יךָ
נֹתֵ֥ן לָֽךְ׃ לֹ֖א תִּֿרְצָֽח׃ לֹ֖א
תִּֿנְאָֽף׃ לֹ֖א תִּֿגְנֹֽב׃ לֹֽא־
תַעֲנֶ֥ה בְרֵעֲךָ֖ עֵ֥ד שָֽׁקֶר׃ לֹ֥א
תַחְמֹ֖ד בֵּ֣ית רֵעֶ֑ךָ לֹֽא־
תַחְמֹ֞ד אֵ֣שֶׁת רֵעֶ֗ךָ וְעַבְדּ֤וֹ וַאֲמָתוֹ֙ וְשׁוֹר֣וֹ וַחֲמֹר֔וֹ וְכֹ֖ל אֲשֶׁ֥ר
לְרֵעֶֽךָ׃

---

unique in the ancient world, making faith in Judaism akin to faithfulness in marriage.

עַל־שִׁלֵּשִׁים וְעַל־רִבֵּעִים לְשֹׂנְאָי *To the third and fourth generation, if they also reject Me.* Deuteronomy 24:16, Jeremiah 31:28–29 and Ezekiel 18:2–4 all make clear that there is no intergenerational transfer of guilt. Children are only punished for the sins of their parents if they themselves commit those sins. The phrase is therefore a warning to parents not to have a negative influence on their children, not a statement of vicarious guilt or punishment.

אַתָּה וּבִנְךָ וּבִתֶּךָ עַבְדְּךָ ... וּבְהֶמְתֶּךָ וְגֵרְךָ *You, your son or daughter… slaves… cattle… stranger.* The difference between a holiday and a holy day is that a holiday is private; a holy day is public. We take a vacation as individuals choosing to do so for our own enjoyment. By contrast, a holy day is not something we

And all the people saw the thunder and the flames, and the sound of the shofar, and the mountain asmoke; the people saw and they staggered, and stood far back. They called out to Moses, "You speak to us and we shall listen, but let God not speak to us, lest we die." "Do not be afraid," said Moses, "For it is to test you that God comes so, and that His awe may be upon you, that you should not sin." The people stood at a distance, and Moses approached the mist, in which God was. HAMISHI

The LORD said to Moses, "Say this to the people of Israel: You have seen now that I have spoken to you from the heavens. Make yourself no silver gods or golden gods alongside Me. Make Me an earthen altar, and sacrifice your burnt offerings and your peace offerings on that, of your flock and of your herd. In those places where I shall recall My name, there I shall come to you and bless you. And if you should build Me an altar of stone, let it not be of stone that is hewn – for if you pass your sword-blade over it, it will be desecrated. And do not ascend My altar by steps, for over it you may not expose your naked flesh."

MAFTIR FOR SHAVUOT

The following Maftir is read from the second Torah scroll on both days of Shavuot.

On the day of the first fruits, when you bring an offering of new grain to the LORD, on your Festival of Weeks, there shall be a sacred assembly: you shall do no laborious work. You shall offer a burnt-offering of pleasing aroma to the LORD: two young bullocks, one ram, and seven yearling male lambs. And also their meal-offerings, fine flour mixed with oil, three-tenths of an ephah for each of the bulls, two-tenths of an ephah for the ram, and one tenth of an ephah each for every one of the seven lambs. And one male goat as a sin-offering, as well as the regular daily sacrifice with its meal-offering; and they shall all be perfect for you, they and their libations. *Num. 28: 26–31*

לֹא־תִבְנֶה אֶתְהֶן גָּזִית *Let it not be of stone that is hewn.* The sword shortens life; the altar prolongs it. The sword symbolizes strife; the altar is a symbol of peace. That is why the sword, and metal instruments generally, were not to be used to hew stones for the altar (Mishna, *Midot* 3:4).

חמישי וְכָל־הָעָם֩ רֹאִ֨ים אֶת־הַקּוֹלֹ֜ת וְאֶת־הַלַּפִּידִ֗ם וְאֵת֙ ק֣וֹל הַשֹּׁפָ֔ר וְאֶת־הָהָ֖ר
עָשֵׁ֑ן וַיַּ֤רְא הָעָם֙ וַיָּנֻ֔עוּ וַיַּֽעַמְד֖וּ מֵֽרָחֹֽק׃ וַיֹּֽאמְרוּ֙ אֶל־מֹשֶׁ֔ה דַּבֵּר־אַתָּ֥ה עִמָּ֖נוּ
וְנִשְׁמָ֑עָה וְאַל־יְדַבֵּ֥ר עִמָּ֛נוּ אֱלֹהִ֖ים פֶּן־נָמֽוּת׃ וַיֹּ֨אמֶר מֹשֶׁ֣ה אֶל־הָעָם֮ אַל־
תִּירָאוּ֒ כִּ֗י לְבַֽעֲבוּר֙ נַסּ֣וֹת אֶתְכֶ֔ם בָּ֖א הָֽאֱלֹהִ֑ים וּבַעֲב֗וּר תִּהְיֶ֧ה יִרְאָת֛וֹ עַל־פְּנֵיכֶ֖ם
לְבִלְתִּ֥י תֶחֱטָֽאוּ׃ וַיַּעֲמֹ֥ד הָעָ֖ם מֵרָחֹ֑ק וּמֹשֶׁה֙ נִגַּ֣שׁ אֶל־הָעֲרָפֶ֔ל אֲשֶׁר־שָׁ֖ם
הָאֱלֹהִֽים׃ וַיֹּ֤אמֶר יהוה֙ אֶל־מֹשֶׁ֔ה כֹּ֥ה תֹאמַ֖ר אֶל־בְּנֵ֣י יִשְׂרָאֵ֑ל
אַתֶּ֣ם רְאִיתֶ֔ם כִּ֚י מִן־הַשָּׁמַ֔יִם דִּבַּ֖רְתִּי עִמָּכֶֽם׃ לֹ֥א תַעֲשׂ֖וּן אִתִּ֑י אֱלֹ֤הֵי כֶ֙סֶף֙
וֵאלֹהֵ֣י זָהָ֔ב לֹ֥א תַעֲשׂ֖וּ לָכֶֽם׃ מִזְבַּ֣ח אֲדָמָה֮ תַּעֲשֶׂה־לִּי֒ וְזָבַחְתָּ֣ עָלָ֗יו אֶת־עֹלֹתֶ֙יךָ֙
וְאֶת־שְׁלָמֶ֔יךָ אֶת־צֹֽאנְךָ֖ וְאֶת־בְּקָרֶ֑ךָ בְּכָל־הַמָּקוֹם֙ אֲשֶׁ֣ר אַזְכִּ֣יר אֶת־שְׁמִ֔י
אָב֥וֹא אֵלֶ֖יךָ וּבֵרַכְתִּֽיךָ׃ וְאִם־מִזְבַּ֤ח אֲבָנִים֙ תַּעֲשֶׂה־לִּ֔י לֹֽא־תִבְנֶ֥ה אֶתְהֶ֖ן גָּזִ֑ית
כִּ֧י חַרְבְּךָ֛ הֵנַ֥פְתָּ עָלֶ֖יהָ וַתְּחַלְלֶֽהָ׃ וְלֹא־תַעֲלֶ֥ה בְמַעֲלֹ֖ת עַל־מִזְבְּחִ֑י אֲשֶׁ֛ר לֹא־
תִגָּלֶ֥ה עֶרְוָתְךָ֖ עָלָֽיו׃

מפטיר לשבועות

The following מפטיר *is read from the second* ספר תורה *on both days of* שבועות*:*

במדבר כח:כו–לא וּבְי֣וֹם הַבִּכּוּרִ֗ים בְּהַקְרִיבְכֶ֞ם מִנְחָ֤ה חֲדָשָׁה֙ לַֽיהוה בְּשָׁבֻעֹ֖תֵיכֶ֑ם מִֽקְרָא־
קֹ֙דֶשׁ֙ יִהְיֶ֣ה לָכֶ֔ם כָּל־מְלֶ֥אכֶת עֲבֹדָ֖ה לֹ֥א תַעֲשֽׂוּ׃ וְהִקְרַבְתֶּ֨ם עוֹלָ֜ה לְרֵ֤יחַ
נִיחֹ֙חַ֙ לַֽיהוה פָּרִ֧ים בְּנֵֽי־בָקָ֛ר שְׁנַ֖יִם אַ֣יִל אֶחָ֑ד שִׁבְעָ֥ה כְבָשִׂ֖ים בְּנֵ֥י שָׁנָֽה׃
וּמִ֨נְחָתָ֔ם סֹ֖לֶת בְּלוּלָ֣ה בַשָּׁ֑מֶן שְׁלֹשָׁ֤ה עֶשְׂרֹנִים֙ לַפָּ֣ר הָאֶחָ֔ד שְׁנֵי֙ עֶשְׂרֹנִ֔ים
לָאַ֖יִל הָאֶחָֽד׃ עִשָּׂרוֹן֙ עִשָּׂר֔וֹן לַכֶּ֖בֶשׂ הָאֶחָ֑ד לְשִׁבְעַ֖ת הַכְּבָשִֽׂים׃ שְׂעִ֥יר עִזִּ֖ים
אֶחָ֑ד לְכַפֵּ֖ר עֲלֵיכֶֽם׃ מִלְּבַ֛ד עֹלַ֥ת הַתָּמִ֖יד וּמִנְחָת֑וֹ תַּעֲשׂ֕וּ תְּמִימִ֥ם יִֽהְיוּ־לָכֶ֖ם
וְנִסְכֵּיהֶֽם׃

וְכָל־הָעָם רֹאִים אֶת־הַקּוֹלֹת *And all the people saw the thunder.* Literally, "they saw the sounds." According to some, this means they experienced synesthesia: they saw what is normally only heard. An auditory experience became a visual one (*Mekhilta*, Rashi). Moses emphasized later how it was the sound that was the essential element of revelation: "Then God spoke to you out of the fire. You heard the sound of words, but saw no image; there was only a voice" (Deut. 4:12).

HAFTARA FOR FIRST DAY OF SHAVUOT

And it was in the thirtieth year, in the fourth month on the fifth day of the month: I was out in the exile, by the river Kevar, and the heavens opened up and I saw visions of God; on the fifth day of the month – it was the fifth year of the exile of king Jehoiachin. *Ezek. 1:1–28*

And so it was: the word of the LORD came to Ezekiel, the son of Buzi, the priest, in the land of Kasdim, by the river Kevar; the hand of the LORD was upon him there.

And I saw: behold, a storm-wind came from the north, a great cloud and a flaring fire with a bright glow about it, and inside it, within the fire, a semblance of amber; and within that was the form of four living beings – this was their appearance: they had the form of a man, and each one had four faces, and each of these had four wings; and their legs were straight-standing, and their feet were like a calf's hoof, and they gleamed with a semblance of burnished copper; they had man's hands beneath their wings, on their four sides, and the four of them had wings and faces.

Their wings were joined to each other; they did not turn when they moved: each one moved in the direction of its face. And their faces were in the form of the face of a man, with the face of a lion on the right of the four, the face of an ox on the left of the four, and the face of an eagle. Their faces, and their wings were separate above: each one had two joining it to the other, and two covering its body; each one moved in the direction of its face – wherever the spirit wished to move, they moved – they did not turn when they moved; and the form of the living beings, their appearance, was like coals burning, like the appearance of torch-flames, it passed among the living beings; the fire had a bright glow, and lightning flashed out from the fire. And the living beings ran forward and back, like the appearance of darting-flames.

And I saw the living beings – and behold, a wheel was on the ground with the living beings with the four faces. And the appearance of the wheels and their action had a semblance of topaz, and there was one form to each of the four; their appearance and their actions were as though one wheel were inside the other. When they moved, they moved on each of their four sides; they did not turn as they moved. Their rims were high, fearful; and the rims of all four of them were covered with eyes, all around. And when the living beings moved, the wheels moved with them; and when the living beings rose up above the ground, the wheels also rose up; wherever the spirit wished to move, they moved, there where the spirit moved,

הפטרה ליום טוב ראשון של שבועות

וַיְהִי ׀ בִּשְׁלֹשִׁים שָׁנָה בָּרְבִיעִי בַּחֲמִשָּׁה לַחֹדֶשׁ וַאֲנִי בְתוֹךְ־הַגּוֹלָה עַל־נְהַר־ יחזקאל א:א–כח
כְּבָר נִפְתְּחוּ הַשָּׁמַיִם וָאֶרְאֶה מַרְאוֹת אֱלֹהִים: בַּחֲמִשָּׁה לַחֹדֶשׁ הִיא הַשָּׁנָה
הַחֲמִישִׁית לְגָלוּת הַמֶּלֶךְ יוֹיָכִין: הָיֹה הָיָה דְבַר־יהוה אֶל־יְחֶזְקֵאל בֶּן־בּוּזִי
הַכֹּהֵן בְּאֶרֶץ כַּשְׂדִּים עַל־נְהַר־כְּבָר וַתְּהִי עָלָיו שָׁם יַד־יהוה: וָאֵרֶא וְהִנֵּה
רוּחַ סְעָרָה בָּאָה מִן־הַצָּפוֹן עָנָן גָּדוֹל וְאֵשׁ מִתְלַקַּחַת וְנֹגַהּ לוֹ סָבִיב וּמִתּוֹכָהּ
כְּעֵין הַחַשְׁמַל מִתּוֹךְ הָאֵשׁ: וּמִתּוֹכָהּ דְּמוּת אַרְבַּע חַיּוֹת וְזֶה מַרְאֵיהֶן דְּמוּת
אָדָם לָהֵנָּה: וְאַרְבָּעָה פָנִים לְאֶחָת וְאַרְבַּע כְּנָפַיִם לְאַחַת לָהֶם: וְרַגְלֵיהֶם רֶגֶל
יְשָׁרָה וְכַף רַגְלֵיהֶם כְּכַף רֶגֶל עֵגֶל וְנֹצְצִים כְּעֵין נְחֹשֶׁת קָלָל: וידו אָדָם מִתַּחַת וִידֵי
כַּנְפֵיהֶם עַל אַרְבַּעַת רִבְעֵיהֶם וּפְנֵיהֶם וְכַנְפֵיהֶם לְאַרְבַּעְתָּם: חֹבְרֹת אִשָּׁה
אֶל־אֲחוֹתָהּ כַּנְפֵיהֶם לֹא־יִסַּבּוּ בְלֶכְתָּן אִישׁ אֶל־עֵבֶר פָּנָיו יֵלֵכוּ: וּדְמוּת פְּנֵיהֶם
פְּנֵי אָדָם וּפְנֵי אַרְיֵה אֶל־הַיָּמִין לְאַרְבַּעְתָּם וּפְנֵי־שׁוֹר מֵהַשְּׂמֹאול לְאַרְבַּעְתָּן
וּפְנֵי־נֶשֶׁר לְאַרְבַּעְתָּן: וּפְנֵיהֶם וְכַנְפֵיהֶם פְּרֻדוֹת מִלְמָעְלָה לְאִישׁ שְׁתַּיִם חֹבְרוֹת
אִישׁ וּשְׁתַּיִם מְכַסּוֹת אֵת גְּוִיֹתֵיהֶנָה: וְאִישׁ אֶל־עֵבֶר פָּנָיו יֵלֵכוּ אֶל אֲשֶׁר
יִהְיֶה־שָׁמָּה הָרוּחַ לָלֶכֶת יֵלֵכוּ לֹא יִסַּבּוּ בְּלֶכְתָּן: וּדְמוּת הַחַיּוֹת מַרְאֵיהֶם
כְּגַחֲלֵי־אֵשׁ בֹּעֲרוֹת כְּמַרְאֵה הַלַּפִּדִים הִיא מִתְהַלֶּכֶת בֵּין הַחַיּוֹת וְנֹגַהּ לָאֵשׁ
וּמִן־הָאֵשׁ יוֹצֵא בָרָק: וְהַחַיּוֹת רָצוֹא וָשׁוֹב כְּמַרְאֵה הַבָּזָק: וָאֵרֶא הַחַיּוֹת וְהִנֵּה
אוֹפַן אֶחָד בָּאָרֶץ אֵצֶל הַחַיּוֹת לְאַרְבַּעַת פָּנָיו: מַרְאֵה הָאוֹפַנִּים וּמַעֲשֵׂיהֶם
כְּעֵין תַּרְשִׁישׁ וּדְמוּת אֶחָד לְאַרְבַּעְתָּן וּמַרְאֵיהֶם וּמַעֲשֵׂיהֶם כַּאֲשֶׁר יִהְיֶה
הָאוֹפַן בְּתוֹךְ הָאוֹפָן: עַל־אַרְבַּעַת רִבְעֵיהֶן בְּלֶכְתָּם יֵלֵכוּ לֹא יִסַּבּוּ בְּלֶכְתָּן:
וְגַבֵּיהֶן וְגֹבַהּ לָהֶם וְיִרְאָה לָהֶם וְגַבֹּתָם מְלֵאֹת עֵינַיִם סָבִיב לְאַרְבַּעְתָּן: וּבְלֶכֶת
הַחַיּוֹת יֵלְכוּ הָאוֹפַנִּים אֶצְלָם וּבְהִנָּשֵׂא הַחַיּוֹת מֵעַל הָאָרֶץ יִנָּשְׂאוּ הָאוֹפַנִּים:
עַל אֲשֶׁר יִהְיֶה־שָּׁם הָרוּחַ לָלֶכֶת יֵלֵכוּ שָׁמָּה הָרוּחַ לָלֶכֶת וְהָאוֹפַנִּים יִנָּשְׂאוּ

HAFTARA FOR THE FIRST DAY OF SHAVUOT

The Haftara for the first day is taken from the opening of the book of Ezekiel. The connection between it and the Torah reading is Revelation: the direct unmediated encounter with the transcendental God, that, in the days of Moses, transformed the Israelites into "a kingdom of priests and a holy nation," and that turned Ezekiel, a priest, into the great prophet of exile, bringing hope to his contemporaries who, like him, had been carried captive to Babylon.

the wheels rose up with them, for the spirit of the living being was also in the wheels: when they moved, they too moved, and when they stood, they too stood, and when they rose up from the ground, the wheels too rose up with them, because the spirit of the living being was in the wheels. And above the heads of the living beings there was the form of a dome, with a semblance of the terrible ice, suspended over their heads from above; and beneath the dome, their wings were straightened out towards each other, a pair covering them here, and another pair covering them there, over their bodies. And I heard the sound of their wings and it was like the sound of a mass of waters, like the voice of the Almighty, when they moved; the sound of roaring, like the sound of an encampment. Standing still, they lowered their wings; a voice came from upon the dome which was over their heads – standing still, they lowered their wings.

And above the dome which was over their heads, with the appearance of a sapphire, was the form of a throne; and on the form of the throne there was a form with the appearance of a man, upon it, from above. And I saw: a semblance of amber, the appearance of fire encasing it, from what appeared to be his waist and above; and from what appeared to be his waist and below, I saw an appearance like fire with a brightness around it – it was like the appearance of the rainbow in the clouds on a rainy day, the brightness around it had that appearance. This was the appearance of the form of the glory of God – and I saw it, and I fell upon my face, and I heard a voice speak.

Then a wind lifted me up and I heard behind me the sound of a great noise, *Ezek. 3:12*
saying, "Blessed is the Lord's glory from His place."

Continue with the blessings after the Haftara on page 514.

---

falls on his face and hears a voice speak. The Haftara then moves to the close of the vision, in which Ezekiel, lifted by a wind, hears a great voice saying, "Blessed is the Lord's glory from His place."

Much of this is deeply obscure, and became the basis of an esoteric tradition known as *Merkava*, or "chariot," mysticism. This vision, mysteriously transmitted as it were from the Temple in Jerusalem to the prophet in exile, carried with it the assurance that God was still with His people, that their defeat and dispersion were not permanent, that the covenant was still in place, and that when the spirit lifts us, as the wind lifted Ezekiel, we can still sense the glory of God, however opaque, for though we may seem far from Him, He is never far from us.

לְעֻמָּתָם כִּי רוּחַ הַחַיָּה בָּאוֹפַנִּים׃ בְּלֶכְתָּם יֵלֵכוּ וּבְעָמְדָם יַעֲמֹדוּ וּבְהִנָּשְׂאָם
מֵעַל הָאָרֶץ יִנָּשְׂאוּ הָאוֹפַנִּים לְעֻמָּתָם כִּי רוּחַ הַחַיָּה בָּאוֹפַנִּים׃ וּדְמוּת עַל־
רָאשֵׁי הַחַיָּה רָקִיעַ כְּעֵין הַקֶּרַח הַנּוֹרָא נָטוּי עַל־רָאשֵׁיהֶם מִלְמָעְלָה׃ וְתַחַת
הָרָקִיעַ כַּנְפֵיהֶם יְשָׁרוֹת אִשָּׁה אֶל־אֲחוֹתָהּ לְאִישׁ שְׁתַּיִם מְכַסּוֹת לָהֵנָּה
וּלְאִישׁ שְׁתַּיִם מְכַסּוֹת לָהֵנָּה אֵת גְּוִיֹּתֵיהֶם׃ וָאֶשְׁמַע אֶת־קוֹל כַּנְפֵיהֶם כְּקוֹל
מַיִם רַבִּים כְּקוֹל־שַׁדַּי בְּלֶכְתָּם קוֹל הֲמֻלָּה כְּקוֹל מַחֲנֶה בְּעָמְדָם תְּרַפֶּינָה
כַנְפֵיהֶן׃ וַיְהִי־קוֹל מֵעַל לָרָקִיעַ אֲשֶׁר עַל־רֹאשָׁם בְּעָמְדָם תְּרַפֶּינָה כַנְפֵיהֶן׃
וּמִמַּעַל לָרָקִיעַ אֲשֶׁר עַל־רֹאשָׁם כְּמַרְאֵה אֶבֶן־סַפִּיר דְּמוּת כִּסֵּא וְעַל דְּמוּת
הַכִּסֵּא דְּמוּת כְּמַרְאֵה אָדָם עָלָיו מִלְמָעְלָה׃ וָאֵרֶא ׀ כְּעֵין חַשְׁמַל כְּמַרְאֵה־
אֵשׁ בֵּית־לָהּ סָבִיב מִמַּרְאֵה מָתְנָיו וּלְמָעְלָה וּמִמַּרְאֵה מָתְנָיו וּלְמַטָּה רָאִיתִי
כְּמַרְאֵה־אֵשׁ וְנֹגַהּ לוֹ סָבִיב׃ כְּמַרְאֵה הַקֶּשֶׁת אֲשֶׁר יִהְיֶה בֶעָנָן בְּיוֹם הַגֶּשֶׁם
כֵּן מַרְאֵה הַנֹּגַהּ סָבִיב הוּא מַרְאֵה דְּמוּת כְּבוֹד־יְהוָה וָאֶרְאֶה וָאֶפֹּל עַל־פָּנַי
וָאֶשְׁמַע קוֹל מְדַבֵּר׃

וַתִּשָּׂאֵנִי רוּחַ וָאֶשְׁמַע אַחֲרַי קוֹל רַעַשׁ גָּדוֹל בָּרוּךְ כְּבוֹד־יְהוָה מִמְּקוֹמוֹ׃ יחזקאל ג:יב

Continue with the blessings after the הפטרה *on page 515.*

Ezekiel lived through one of the great crises of Jewish history. After the death of Solomon, the kingdom had split in two. The northern kingdom, Israel, defeated by the Assyrians in 722 BCE, mostly disappeared, becoming known to history as the Lost Ten Tribes. The southern kingdom, Judah, was conquered by the Babylonians under Nebuchadnezzar in 597 BCE. The king, Jehoiakim, was taken captive to Babylon, together with the elite of the population, Ezekiel among them. Some years later, those who remained rose in rebellion and were defeated a second time. Jerusalem fell in 586 BCE, and the Temple was destroyed.

The Haftara opens by locating itself in time. The Temple was still standing in Jerusalem. The revolt that would lead to its destruction had not yet taken place. But Ezekiel, like his older contemporary Jeremiah, believed that disaster was imminent. Both prophets were charged by God to warn the people of the coming catastrophe, to urge them to repent, and to provide a compelling narrative of hope. If the people returned to God, God would return to them and bring them home.

Ezekiel's prophetic mission began with the dazzling vision set out in the Haftara, the most vivid of its kind anywhere in Tanakh. Terrified, the prophet

TORAH READING FOR THE SECOND DAY OF SHAVUOT

The Torah reading for the second day of Shavuot is the same as that of the eighth day of Pesaḥ on page 1142. The Maftir is the same as that of the first day of Shavuot (page 1148).

HAFTARA FOR THE SECOND DAY OF SHAVUOT

The LORD is in His holy Sanctuary: hush before Him, all the earth! A prayer of Habakkuk the prophet, upon Shigyonot: *Habakkuk 2:30–3:19*

Many say the following "May this praise" in the Haftara.

יַצִּיב פִּתְגָם May this praise be desired, for God, Sign and Witness, alone among myriad myriad angels.
Where is it that He dwells, among that company of angels who dismissed the four great mountains [and chose Sinai].
Out before Him springs and flows, into His wells, a river of fire.
In a mountain of snow bright light shines out, and sparks and brands of fire,
and He creates and sees all that lies in darkness, for present with Him is all light.
He oversees all distances, judging without hastiness, and to Him are revealed all the world's secrets.
From Him will I ask permission to read; and afterwards also from the people before me,
who know the Law the Mishna, Tosefta, Sifra and Sifrei.
The King who lives for evermore will destroy the people that subjugates them.
For they have been told that they will be like sand, too many to be counted, like dust of the earth.
Make their valleys white today, with produce, their vats flowing over with wine.
Bring what they wish for, make their faces shine – let them shine out like morning light.
Grant me strength, and lift Your eyes to see Your enemies, those who deny You,
and make them like straw within the bricks; like stones, silent and ashamed.

Middle Ages, and Aramaic ceased to be the language of everyday speech, but, as with *Akdamut*, the introductory poem remained.

קריאה ליום טוב שני של שבועות

The קריאת התורה *for the second day of* שבועות *is the same as that of the eighth day of* פסח *on page 1143. The* מפטיר *is the same as that of the first day of* שבועות *(page 1149).*

הפטרה ליום טוב שני של שבועות

וַיהוָה בְּהֵיכַל קׇדְשׁוֹ הַס מִפָּנָיו כׇּל־הָאָרֶץ׃ תְּפִלָּה לַחֲבַקּוּק חבקוק ב:כ–ג:יט
הַנָּבִיא עַל שִׁגְיֹנוֹת׃

Many say the following יַצִּיב פִּתְגָם *in the* הפטרה.

יַצִּיב פִּתְגָם, לְאָת וּדְגַם, בְּרִבּוֹ רִבְבָן עִירִין.
עֲנֵה אֲנָא, בְּמִנְיָנָא, דְּפַסְלִין אַרְבְּעָה טוּרִין.
קֳדָמוֹהִי, לְגוֹ מוֹהִי, נְגִיד וּנְפִיק נְהַר דִּי נוּרִין.
בְּטוּר תַּלְגָּא, נְהוֹר שְׁרָגָא, וְזִיקִין דִּי נוּר וּבָעוֹרִין.
בְּרָא וּסְכָא, מַה בַּחֲשׁוֹכָא, וְעִמֵּהּ שָׁרְיָין נְהוֹרִין.
רְחִיקִין צְפָא, בְּלָא שְׁטָפָא, וּגְלֵין לֵהּ דְּמִטַּמְּרִין.
בְּעֵית מִנֵּהּ, יָת הַרְמָנֵהּ, וּבָתְרוֹהִי עֲדֵי גֻבְרִין.
יָדְעֵי הִלְכְתָא, וּמַתְנִיתָא, וְתוֹסֶפְתָּא סִפְרָא וְסִפְרִין.
מֶלֶךְ חַיָּא, לְעָלְמַיָּא, יְמַגַּר עַם לְהוֹן מְשַׁחֲרִין.
אֲמִיר עֲלֵיהוֹן, כְּחָלָא יְהוֹן, וְלָא יִתְמְנוּן הֵיךְ עַפְרִין.
יַחֲוְרוּן כְּעַן, לְהוֹן בִּקְעָן, יְטוּפוּן נַעֲוֵי חַמְרִין.
רְעוּתְהוֹן הַב, וְאַפֵּיהוֹן צְהַב, יְנַהֲרוּן כִּנְהוֹר צַפְרִין.
לִי הַב תְּקוֹף, וְעֵינָךְ זְקוֹף, חֲזִי עָרָךְ דְּבָךְ כָּפְרִין.
יְהוֹן כְּתִבְנָא, בְּגוֹ לִבְנָא, כְּאַבְנָא יִשְׁתְּקוּן חָפְרִין.

YATZIV PITGAM: MAY THIS PRAISE BE DESIRED

This poem, like *Akdamut* said on the first day, is a *reshut,* a request for permission to recite the Aramaic translation of the text about to be read, in this case the Haftara from Habakkuk. The reason it is not said on the first day is that the passage read then – the vision of Ezekiel – was considered too mystical and open to misinterpretation to be translated into the vernacular. The custom of verse-by-verse translation of the biblical Hebrew into Aramaic lapsed as the center of Jewish life moved from Babylon to Europe in the

As I stand here, translating the words of the most superior of books,
the LORD has given [Torah] through the humble [Moses], and so to
Him – our gracious thanks.

LORD, I heard tell of You, and I feared; LORD, in these years, revive Your work, in these years, make it known; in wrath, remember mercy. God is coming, from Teiman, the Holy One, from Mount Paran, Selah. His glory covers the heavens, His praise fills the earth, its brilliance like light, beams, from His hand, from the hidden place of His might. Plague will go before Him, fire following His feet; He stands, and measures up the land, He looks, and the nations tremble; ancient mountains shatter, age-old hills collapse – the world's ways are His. I saw the tents of Kushan distressed, the curtains of the land of Midian quivering. Is the LORD angry at the rivers – is Your fury against the rivers, Your wrath, against the sea, that You ride upon Your horses, upon Your chariot of deliverance? Your bow is bared, uncovered, according to the promise said to the tribes, Selah. You slice the land into rivers; seeing You, the mountains quake, rushing waters flow past, the deep raises its voice, lifts its hands skyward. The sun, the moon, stand still, in their place – by the light of Your arrows the world goes on, in the brilliance from Your shining spear. In rage, You walk over the land, in fury, You trample nations: You come forth, to deliver Your people, to deliver Your anointed. You crush the head of the house of the wicked, baring the foundation up to its neck, Selah. You pierce with his own sticks the head of his leaders – who come like a storm to scatter me, exultant as though secretly devouring the poor. You drive Your horses through the sea, the mass of raging waters. I hear and my stomach churns, at the sound my lips stutter, a rot enters my bones, I quiver where I stand yet I calmly wait for the day of trouble, when he comes up against the people to attack them. The fig tree does not blossom, and there is no yield from the vines; the olive grows gaunt, and the grain fields grow no food; the sheep are gone from the pens, and there are

---

were to be taken from me, I would still have God, and it would be more than enough. To live in the presence of God, knowing that He is with us whatever fate brings, is to experience ultimate existential joy: joy in the simple fact that He is and we are, that we are *because* He is. Nothing can separate us from the Source of our being. We live in the light of His presence, and thus in hope and joy.

כְּקַדְמָנָא, וְתַרְגְּמָנָא, בְּמִלּוֹי דִּבְחִיר סַפְרִין.
יְהוֹנָתָן, גְּבַר עִנְוְתָן, בְּכֵן נַמְטִין אַפְרִין.

יהוה שָׁמַעְתִּי שִׁמְעֲךָ יָרֵאתִי יהוה פָּעָלְךָ בְּקֶרֶב שָׁנִים חַיֵּיהוּ בְּקֶרֶב שָׁנִים
תּוֹדִיעַ בְּרֹגֶז רַחֵם תִּזְכּוֹר: אֱלוֹהַּ מִתֵּימָן יָבוֹא וְקָדוֹשׁ מֵהַר־פָּארָן סֶלָה כִּסָּה
שָׁמַיִם הוֹדוֹ וּתְהִלָּתוֹ מָלְאָה הָאָרֶץ: וְנֹגַהּ כָּאוֹר תִּהְיֶה קַרְנַיִם מִיָּדוֹ לוֹ וְשָׁם
חֶבְיוֹן עֻזֹּה: לְפָנָיו יֵלֶךְ דָּבֶר וְיֵצֵא רֶשֶׁף לְרַגְלָיו: עָמַד ׀ וַיְמֹדֶד אֶרֶץ רָאָה וַיַּתֵּר
גּוֹיִם וַיִּתְפֹּצְצוּ הַרְרֵי־עַד שַׁחוּ גִּבְעוֹת עוֹלָם הֲלִיכוֹת עוֹלָם לוֹ: תַּחַת אָוֶן
רָאִיתִי אָהֳלֵי כוּשָׁן יִרְגְּזוּן יְרִיעוֹת אֶרֶץ מִדְיָן: הֲבִנְהָרִים חָרָה
יהוה אִם בַּנְּהָרִים אַפֶּךָ אִם־בַּיָּם עֶבְרָתֶךָ כִּי תִרְכַּב עַל־סוּסֶיךָ מַרְכְּבֹתֶיךָ
יְשׁוּעָה: עֶרְיָה תֵעוֹר קַשְׁתֶּךָ שְׁבֻעוֹת מַטּוֹת אֹמֶר סֶלָה נְהָרוֹת תְּבַקַּע־אָרֶץ:
רָאוּךָ יָחִילוּ הָרִים זֶרֶם מַיִם עָבָר נָתַן תְּהוֹם קוֹלוֹ רוֹם יָדֵיהוּ נָשָׂא: שֶׁמֶשׁ יָרֵחַ
עָמַד זְבֻלָה לְאוֹר חִצֶּיךָ יְהַלֵּכוּ לְנֹגַהּ בְּרַק חֲנִיתֶךָ: בְּזַעַם תִּצְעַד־אָרֶץ בְּאַף
תָּדוּשׁ גּוֹיִם: יָצָאתָ לְיֵשַׁע עַמֶּךָ לְיֵשַׁע אֶת־מְשִׁיחֶךָ מָחַצְתָּ רֹּאשׁ מִבֵּית רָשָׁע
עָרוֹת יְסוֹד עַד־צַוָּאר סֶלָה: נָקַבְתָּ בְמַטָּיו רֹאשׁ פְּרָזָו יִסְעֲרוּ
לַהֲפִיצֵנִי עֲלִיצֻתָם כְּמוֹ־לֶאֱכֹל עָנִי בַּמִּסְתָּר: דָּרַכְתָּ בַיָּם סוּסֶיךָ חֹמֶר מַיִם
רַבִּים: שָׁמַעְתִּי ׀ וַתִּרְגַּז בִּטְנִי לְקוֹל צָלְלוּ שְׂפָתַי יָבוֹא רָקָב בַּעֲצָמַי וְתַחְתַּי
אֶרְגָּז אֲשֶׁר אָנוּחַ לְיוֹם צָרָה לַעֲלוֹת לְעַם יְגוּדֶנּוּ: כִּי־תְאֵנָה לֹא־תִפְרָח וְאֵין
יְבוּל בַּגְּפָנִים כִּחֵשׁ מַעֲשֵׂה־זַיִת וּשְׁדֵמוֹת לֹא־עָשָׂה אֹכֶל גָּזַר מִמִּכְלָה צֹאן

HAFTARA FOR THE SECOND DAY OF SHAVUOT

The Haftara, taken from the conclusion of the short prophetic book of Habakkuk, was chosen because it describes a future revelation similar, at least in externals, to the one that took place on Mount Sinai on the first Shavuot. As then, so in the future, God will make an appearance in history, shaking the earth to its foundations. Ancient mountains will shatter, age-old hills will collapse – language reminiscent of the theophany at Sinai as described in Deuteronomy 33:2–5, Judges 5:4, and Psalms 68:8–9.

The passage culminates in one of the most beautiful sentiments in the entire prophetic literature. Though the fig tree does not blossom and there are no grapes on the vines, though there is no grain in the fields and the flocks and herds have gone, still "I will rejoice in the LORD, will exult in the God who delivers me." This is faith at its most sublime. Though everything else

no cattle in the sheds. But I – I will rejoice in the LORD, will exult in the God who delivers me: God, my LORD, my Strength, who makes my feet like the deer's, who leads me to my highest places.

To the conductor: to be sung with my instruments.

Continue with the blessings after the Haftara on page 514.

MAFTIR FOR FIRST DAY OF SUKKOT, AND SECOND DAY OUTSIDE ISRAEL

The Torah Reading for the first two days of Sukkot (in Israel, the first day only) is the same as that of the second day of Pesaḥ (page 1126). The following Maftir is then read from the second scroll:

On the fifteenth day of the seventh month you shall hold a sacred assembly. You shall do no laborious work, and you shall celebrate a festival to the LORD for seven days. You shall offer a burnt-offering, a fire-offering of pleasing aroma to the LORD: thirteen young bullocks, two rams, and fourteen yearling male lambs; they shall be without blemish. And also their meal-offerings, fine flour mixed with oil, three-tenths of an ephah for each of the thirteen bulls, two-tenths of an ephah for each of the two rams, and an ephah each for every one of the fourteen lambs. And one male goat as a sin-offering, as well as the regular daily sacrifice, its meal-offering and its libation. *Num. 29: 12–16*

HAFTARA FOR THE FIRST DAY OF SUKKOT

Behold, a day of the LORD is coming; your spoil will be divided up in your midst. I will gather all the nations to Jerusalem for war: the city will be taken, the houses will be plundered, and the women will be raped; half of the city will go out into exile, but the remainder of the people will not be cut off from the city. And the LORD will go out and He will fight against these nations, as He has fought on days of battle: on that day, His feet will stand upon the Mount of Olives which faces Jerusalem on the east, and the Mount of Olives will split through its middle – in to a very great valley – from east to west; and half the mountain will shift northward and half southward. And you will flee from this Valley of the Mountains – the Valley of the Mountains will reach as far as Atzal – you will flee as you fled from the earthquake in the days of Uziah the King of Judah; and the LORD will come, my God, all the holy ones with You. And it will be: on that day there will be neither bright light nor thick darkness. And it will be: this one day *Zech. 14:1–21*

וְאֵין בָּקָר בָּרְפָתִים: וַאֲנִי בַּיהוָה אֶעְלוֹזָה אָגִילָה בֵּאלֹהֵי יִשְׁעִי: יֱהֹוִה אֲדֹנָי
חֵילִי וַיָּשֶׂם רַגְלַי כָּאַיָּלוֹת וְעַל־בָּמוֹתַי יַדְרִכֵנִי לַמְנַצֵּחַ בִּנְגִינוֹתָי:

Continue with the blessings after the הפטרה *on page 515.*

מפטיר ליום הראשון של סוכות, ויום טוב שני בחוץ לארץ

The קריאת התורה *for the first two days of* סוכות *(in* ארץ ישראל*, the first day only) is the same as that of the second day of* פסח *(page 1127). The following* מפטיר *is then read from the second* ספר תורה*:*

במדבר כט:יב–טז
וּבַחֲמִשָּׁה עָשָׂר יוֹם לַחֹדֶשׁ הַשְּׁבִיעִי מִקְרָא־קֹדֶשׁ יִהְיֶה לָכֶם כָּל־מְלֶאכֶת
עֲבֹדָה לֹא תַעֲשׂוּ וְחַגֹּתֶם חַג לַיהוָה שִׁבְעַת יָמִים: וְהִקְרַבְתֶּם עֹלָה אִשֵּׁה
רֵיחַ נִיחֹחַ לַיהוָה פָּרִים בְּנֵי־בָקָר שְׁלֹשָׁה עָשָׂר אֵילִם שְׁנָיִם כְּבָשִׂים בְּנֵי־שָׁנָה
אַרְבָּעָה עָשָׂר תְּמִימִם יִהְיוּ: וּמִנְחָתָם סֹלֶת בְּלוּלָה בַשָּׁמֶן שְׁלֹשָׁה עֶשְׂרֹנִים
לַפָּר הָאֶחָד לִשְׁלֹשָׁה עָשָׂר פָּרִים שְׁנֵי עֶשְׂרֹנִים לָאַיִל הָאֶחָד לִשְׁנֵי הָאֵילִם:
וְעִשָּׂרוֹן עִשָּׂרוֹן לַכֶּבֶשׂ הָאֶחָד לְאַרְבָּעָה עָשָׂר כְּבָשִׂים: וּשְׂעִיר־עִזִּים אֶחָד
חַטָּאת מִלְּבַד עֹלַת הַתָּמִיד מִנְחָתָהּ וְנִסְכָּהּ:

הפטרה ליום הראשון של סוכות

זכריה יד:א–כא
הִנֵּה יוֹם־בָּא לַיהוָה וְחֻלַּק שְׁלָלֵךְ בְּקִרְבֵּךְ: וְאָסַפְתִּי אֶת־כָּל־הַגּוֹיִם ׀ אֶל־
יְרוּשָׁלַםִ לַמִּלְחָמָה וְנִלְכְּדָה הָעִיר וְנָשַׁסּוּ הַבָּתִּים וְהַנָּשִׁים תשגלנה וְיָצָא חֲצִי (תִּשָּׁכַבְנָה)
הָעִיר בַּגּוֹלָה וְיֶתֶר הָעָם לֹא יִכָּרֵת מִן־הָעִיר: וְיָצָא יְהוָה וְנִלְחַם בַּגּוֹיִם הָהֵם
כְּיוֹם הִלָּחֲמוֹ בְּיוֹם קְרָב: וְעָמְדוּ רַגְלָיו בַּיּוֹם־הַהוּא עַל־הַר הַזֵּיתִים אֲשֶׁר
עַל־פְּנֵי יְרוּשָׁלַםִ מִקֶּדֶם וְנִבְקַע הַר הַזֵּיתִים מֵחֶצְיוֹ מִזְרָחָה וָיָמָּה גֵּיא גְּדוֹלָה
מְאֹד וּמָשׁ חֲצִי הָהָר צָפוֹנָה וְחֶצְיוֹ נֶגְבָּה: וְנַסְתֶּם גֵּיא־הָרַי כִּי־יַגִּיעַ גֵּי־הָרִים
אֶל־אָצַל וְנַסְתֶּם כַּאֲשֶׁר נַסְתֶּם מִפְּנֵי הָרַעַשׁ בִּימֵי עֻזִּיָּה מֶלֶךְ־יְהוּדָה וּבָא יְהוָה
אֱלֹהַי כָּל־קְדֹשִׁים עִמָּךְ: וְהָיָה בַּיּוֹם הַהוּא לֹא־יִהְיֶה אוֹר יְקָרוֹת יקפאון: וְהָיָה (וְקִפָּאוֹן)

HAFTARA FOR THE FIRST DAY OF SUKKOT

Zechariah was one of the last of the prophets. He began his prophetic career around the year 520 BCE, as the first of the exiles were returning from Babylon. Along with the prophet Haggai he encouraged the rebuilding of the Temple and the revitalizing of Jewish life under Joshua the High Priest and the governor Zerubavel. The connection between the haftara, the last

will be known as the LORD's, it will be neither day nor night but at evening time there will be light. And it will be: on that day living waters will flow out from Jerusalem, half to the eastern sea and half to the western sea; in summer and winter it will be so. Then the LORD shall be King over all the earth; on that day the LORD shall be One and His name One. The whole country will be smoothed out like the Arava, from Geva to Rimon south of Jerusalem – and [Jerusalem] will be lifted up, in her place; and from the gate of Binyamin to the site of the first gate and to the corner gate, and from the tower of Ḥananel to the king's winery, they will inhabit her. There will be no more devastation – and Jerusalem will live in safety.

And this will be the plague that the LORD will bring upon all the peoples who fought against Jerusalem: their flesh will rot away as they stand on their feet, their eyes will rot in their sockets and their tongues will rot in their mouths. And it will be: on that day, the turmoil the LORD brings on them will be great and each man will seize his neighbor by the arm to raise his hand against his neighbor's hand. And Judah too will fight in Jerusalem and the wealth of all the surrounding nations, great quantities of gold, silver and clothing, will be gathered in. And there will be a plague just like this plague, on the horse, the mule, the camel and the donkey and on every animal in those camps.

And it will be: those remaining from all the nations who came up against Jerusalem will go up year upon year to bow down to the King, LORD of Hosts, and to celebrate the Festival of Sukkot. And it will be: those from the earth's families who do not go up to Jerusalem and bow down to the King, LORD of Hosts – rain shall not fall for them; and if the family of Egypt does not go up, does not come – they will have no [overflow]. This will be the plague that the LORD will bring upon the nations who do not go up to celebrate the Festival of Sukkot; such will be the punishment

---

the people of the covenant, at a low ebb economically, politically and spiritually, are caught in a vortex of alien forces.

The late prophets lost none of their faith in the eventual restoration of Israel and the rebuilding of the Temple. But there is a mounting sense that this will not happen within the normal terms of history. There will be a major confrontation in which the universe will be shaken to its foundations, after which Israel will emerge triumphant and at peace, and Jerusalem, especially on Sukkot, will be acknowledged as the spiritual center of the world.

יוֹם־אֶחָ֔ד ה֣וּא יִוָּדַ֣ע לַֽיהוָ֔ה לֹא־י֖וֹם וְלֹא־לָ֑יְלָה וְהָיָ֥ה לְעֵֽת־עֶ֖רֶב יִֽהְיֶה־אֽוֹר:
וְהָיָ֣ה ׀ בַּיּ֣וֹם הַה֗וּא יֵצְא֤וּ מַֽיִם־חַיִּים֙ מִיר֣וּשָׁלַ֔͏ִם חֶצְיָ֗ם אֶל־הַיָּם֙ הַקַּדְמוֹנִ֔י וְחֶצְיָ֖ם
אֶל־הַיָּ֣ם הָאַחֲר֑וֹן בַּקַּ֥יִץ וּבָחֹ֖רֶף יִהְיֶֽה: וְהָיָ֧ה יְהוָ֛ה לְמֶ֖לֶךְ עַל־כָּל־הָאָ֑רֶץ בַּיּ֣וֹם
הַה֗וּא יִהְיֶ֧ה יְהוָ֛ה אֶחָ֖ד וּשְׁמ֥וֹ אֶחָֽד: יִסּ֨וֹב כָּל־הָאָ֜רֶץ כָּעֲרָבָ֗ה מִגֶּ֛בַע לְרִמּ֖וֹן נֶ֣גֶב
יְרוּשָׁלָ֑͏ִם וְֽרָאֲמָ֡ה וְיָ֣שְׁבָה תַחְתֶּיהָ֩ לְמִשַּׁ֨עַר בִּנְיָמִ֜ן עַד־מְק֣וֹם שַׁ֣עַר הָֽרִאשׁ֗וֹן עַד־
שַׁ֣עַר הַפִּנִּ֔ים וּמִגְדַּ֣ל חֲנַנְאֵ֔ל עַ֖ד יִקְבֵ֥י הַמֶּֽלֶךְ: וְיָ֣שְׁבוּ בָ֔הּ וְחֵ֖רֶם לֹ֣א יִֽהְיֶה־ע֑וֹד
וְיָשְׁבָ֥ה יְרוּשָׁלַ֖͏ִם לָבֶֽטַח: וְזֹ֣את ׀ תִּֽהְיֶ֣ה הַמַּגֵּפָ֗ה אֲשֶׁ֨ר יִגֹּ֤ף יְהוָה֙
אֶת־כָּל־הָ֣עַמִּ֔ים אֲשֶׁ֥ר צָבְא֖וּ עַל־יְרֽוּשָׁלָ֑͏ִם הָמֵ֣ק ׀ בְּשָׂר֗וֹ וְהוּא֙ עֹמֵ֣ד עַל־רַגְלָ֔יו
וְעֵינָיו֙ תִּמַּ֣קְנָה בְחֹֽרֵיהֶ֔ן וּלְשׁוֹנ֖וֹ תִּמַּ֥ק בְּפִיהֶֽם: וְהָיָה֙ בַּיּ֣וֹם הַה֔וּא תִּֽהְיֶ֧ה מְהֽוּמַת־
יְהוָ֛ה רַבָּ֖ה בָּהֶ֑ם וְהֶחֱזִ֗יקוּ אִ֚ישׁ יַ֣ד רֵעֵ֔הוּ וְעָלְתָ֥ה יָד֖וֹ עַל־יַ֥ד רֵעֵֽהוּ: וְגַם־יְהוּדָ֕ה
תִּלָּחֵ֖ם בִּירֽוּשָׁלָ֑͏ִם וְאֻסַּף֩ חֵ֨יל כָּל־הַגּוֹיִ֜ם סָבִ֗יב זָהָ֥ב וָכֶ֛סֶף וּבְגָדִ֖ים לָרֹ֥ב מְאֹֽד: וְכֵ֨ן
תִּֽהְיֶ֜ה מַגֵּפַ֣ת הַסּ֗וּס הַפֶּ֙רֶד֙ הַגָּמָ֣ל וְהַֽחֲמ֔וֹר וְכָ֨ל־הַבְּהֵמָ֔ה אֲשֶׁ֥ר יִֽהְיֶ֖ה בַּמַּחֲנ֣וֹת
הָהֵ֑מָּה כַּמַּגֵּפָ֖ה הַזֹּֽאת: וְהָיָ֗ה כָּל־הַנּוֹתָר֙ מִכָּל־הַגּוֹיִ֔ם הַבָּאִ֖ים עַל־יְרֽוּשָׁלָ֑͏ִם
וְעָל֣וּ מִדֵּ֣י שָׁנָ֣ה בְשָׁנָ֗ה לְהִֽשְׁתַּחֲוֺת֙ לְמֶ֙לֶךְ֙ יְהוָ֣ה צְבָא֔וֹת וְלָחֹ֖ג אֶת־חַ֥ג הַסֻּכּֽוֹת:
וְ֠הָיָ֠ה אֲשֶׁ֨ר לֹֽא־יַעֲלֶ֜ה מֵאֵ֨ת מִשְׁפְּח֤וֹת הָאָ֙רֶץ֙ אֶל־יְר֣וּשָׁלַ֔͏ִם לְהִֽשְׁתַּחֲוֺ֔ת לְמֶ֖לֶךְ
יְהוָ֣ה צְבָא֑וֹת וְלֹ֥א עֲלֵיהֶ֖ם יִהְיֶ֥ה הַגָּֽשֶׁם: וְאִם־מִשְׁפַּ֨חַת מִצְרַ֧יִם לֹֽא־תַעֲלֶ֣ה וְלֹ֣א
בָאָ֗ה וְלֹ֤א עֲלֵיהֶם֙ תִּֽהְיֶ֣ה הַמַּגֵּפָ֔ה אֲשֶׁ֨ר יִגֹּ֤ף יְהוָה֙ אֶת־הַגּוֹיִ֔ם אֲשֶׁ֥ר לֹ֣א יַעֲל֔וּ
לָחֹ֖ג אֶת־חַ֣ג הַסֻּכּֽוֹת: זֹ֥את תִּהְיֶ֖ה חַטַּ֣את מִצְרָ֑יִם וְחַטַּאת֙ כָּל־הַגּוֹיִ֔ם אֲשֶׁ֖ר לֹ֣א

---

chapter of his book, and Sukkot, is direct. In a verse that became one of the
best known in the prayer book, Zechariah foresees a day when all the nations
of the world will acknowledge the sovereignty of God ("On that day the
Lᴏʀᴅ shall be One and His name One"). They will come to worship in Jerusalem to celebrate Sukkot, which will become the universal festival of rain.

Before that happens, however, there will be a major confrontation between
Israel and its enemies. Initially Jews will suffer setbacks, but God will then fight
for His people and defeat its enemies for all time. Jerusalem will re-emerge
as the diadem of the earth, the world center of faith in a new order of peace.

A new tone entered prophecy during and especially after the Babylonian
exile. Beginning in Babylon with Ezekiel, we gain a sense of the prophets
"wandering between two worlds," a past that has gone, and a future seemingly
powerless to be born. The times are out of joint, there is global disorder, new
empires are battling for supremacy, barbarians are invading the region, and

of Egypt and the punishment of all the nations who do not come up to celebrate the Festival of Sukkot.

On that day even the bells of the horses will be inscribed "sacred to the Lord"; and the pots in the House of the Lord will be like basins before the Altar. And it will be: every pot in Jerusalem and in Judah will be sacred to the Lord of Hosts, and all those who come to sacrifice will take them and will cook in them; and on that day, there will be no more need for traders in the House of the Lord of Hosts.

Continue with the blessings after the Haftara on page 514.

HAFTARA FOR THE SECOND DAY OF SUKKOT

It was in the month of Eitanim, at the Festival (in the seventh month, that is), that all the people of Israel gathered together to King Solomon. All the elders of Israel came; and the Priests were bearing the Ark with them. The Priests and the Levites brought the Ark of the Lord, and the Tent of Meeting and all the holy vessels that used to be in it, up [to the top of Mount Zion]. And King Solomon, and all the people of Israel who had come with him before the Ark, brought offerings from the flock and the herd; offerings that could not be counted or listed, so numerous were they. The priests brought the Ark of the Lord's Covenant to its place: to the Sanctuary of the House – to the Holy of Holies – to the shade of the Cherubim's wings. For the Cherubim stretched their wings out over the place of the Ark; and they covered the Ark and its poles above. The poles themselves extended outwards, and their ends were discernible from the Holy Place, the Sanctuary, but they could not be seen from outside; and this is where they remain to this day. The Ark held nothing else but the two stone tablets that Moses had placed there at Ḥorev, that the Lord had hewed out with the children of Israel as they left Egypt. *1 Kings 8:2–21*

And when the Priests left the Holy Place, the cloud filled the House of the Lord. And the Priests could not stand up to serve because of the cloud – for the glory of the Lord filled the Lord's House.

The construction took seven years. Eleven months later the formal consecration took place, the celebrations lasting for two weeks. The second week coincided with Sukkot, which thereafter became associated with the Temple and its consecration. The Second Temple was also inaugurated on Sukkot (Ezra 3:1–6), and even the re-consecration by the Maccabees after the

יַעֲלוּ לָחֹג אֶת־חַג הַסֻּכּוֹת׃ בַּיּוֹם הַהוּא יִהְיֶה עַל־מְצִלּוֹת הַסּוּס קֹדֶשׁ לַיהוָה
וְהָיָה הַסִּירוֹת בְּבֵית יהוה כַּמִּזְרָקִים לִפְנֵי הַמִּזְבֵּחַ׃ וְהָיָה כָּל־סִיר בִּירוּשָׁלִַם
וּבִיהוּדָה קֹדֶשׁ לַיהוָה צְבָאוֹת וּבָאוּ כָּל־הַזֹּבְחִים וְלָקְחוּ מֵהֶם וּבִשְּׁלוּ בָהֶם
וְלֹא־יִהְיֶה כְנַעֲנִי עוֹד בְּבֵית־יְהוָה צְבָאוֹת בַּיּוֹם הַהוּא׃

Continue with the blessings after the הפטרה *on page 515.*

הפטרה ליום טוב שני של סוכות

מלכים א׳ ח:ב–כא
וַיִּקָּהֲלוּ אֶל־הַמֶּלֶךְ שְׁלֹמֹה כָּל־אִישׁ יִשְׂרָאֵל בְּיֶרַח הָאֵתָנִים בֶּחָג הוּא הַחֹדֶשׁ
הַשְּׁבִיעִי׃ וַיָּבֹאוּ כֹּל זִקְנֵי יִשְׂרָאֵל וַיִּשְׂאוּ הַכֹּהֲנִים אֶת־הָאָרוֹן׃ וַיַּעֲלוּ אֶת־אֲרוֹן
יְהוָה וְאֶת־אֹהֶל מוֹעֵד וְאֶת־כָּל־כְּלֵי הַקֹּדֶשׁ אֲשֶׁר בָּאֹהֶל וַיַּעֲלוּ אֹתָם הַכֹּהֲנִים
וְהַלְוִיִּם׃ וְהַמֶּלֶךְ שְׁלֹמֹה וְכָל־עֲדַת יִשְׂרָאֵל הַנּוֹעָדִים עָלָיו אִתּוֹ לִפְנֵי הָאָרוֹן
מְזַבְּחִים צֹאן וּבָקָר אֲשֶׁר לֹא־יִסָּפְרוּ וְלֹא יִמָּנוּ מֵרֹב׃ וַיָּבִאוּ הַכֹּהֲנִים אֶת־אֲרוֹן
בְּרִית־יְהוָה אֶל־מְקוֹמוֹ אֶל־דְּבִיר הַבַּיִת אֶל־קֹדֶשׁ הַקֳּדָשִׁים אֶל־תַּחַת כַּנְפֵי
הַכְּרוּבִים׃ כִּי הַכְּרוּבִים פֹּרְשִׂים כְּנָפַיִם אֶל־מְקוֹם הָאָרוֹן וַיָּסֹכּוּ הַכְּרֻבִים עַל־
הָאָרוֹן וְעַל־בַּדָּיו מִלְמָעְלָה׃ וַיַּאֲרִכוּ הַבַּדִּים וַיֵּרָאוּ רָאשֵׁי הַבַּדִּים מִן־הַקֹּדֶשׁ
עַל־פְּנֵי הַדְּבִיר וְלֹא יֵרָאוּ הַחוּצָה וַיִּהְיוּ שָׁם עַד הַיּוֹם הַזֶּה׃ אֵין בָּאָרוֹן רַק שְׁנֵי
לֻחוֹת הָאֲבָנִים אֲשֶׁר הִנִּחַ שָׁם מֹשֶׁה בְּחֹרֵב אֲשֶׁר כָּרַת יהוה עִם־בְּנֵי יִשְׂרָאֵל
בְּצֵאתָם מֵאֶרֶץ מִצְרָיִם׃ וַיְהִי בְּצֵאת הַכֹּהֲנִים מִן־הַקֹּדֶשׁ וְהֶעָנָן מָלֵא אֶת־
בֵּית יהוה׃ וְלֹא־יָכְלוּ הַכֹּהֲנִים לַעֲמֹד לְשָׁרֵת מִפְּנֵי הֶעָנָן כִּי־מָלֵא כְבוֹד־יהוה

HAFTARA FOR THE SECOND DAY OF SUKKOT

Four hundred and eighty years after the exodus, King Solomon set in motion the building of the Temple, bringing the entire journey of slavery-to-freedom to its culmination. The nation now had a land, a king, and a capital city, Jerusalem. But there was as yet no permanent home for God at the spiritual center-point of the nation. The plan to build a Temple had been conceived by King David, but he was told by God, through the prophet Nathan, that it would be his son who would build it (II Sam. 7). The idea of such a sanctuary had been anticipated long before, in the Song at the Sea, at a critical moment in the exodus itself: "You will bring them in and plant them on the mountain of Your inheritance – the place, LORD, You made for Your dwelling, the sanctuary, LORD, Your hands established" (Ex. 15:17).

It was then that Solomon said: "The Lord said His Presence would rest in the darkness. I have built, I have built You a House of Worship; a place for Your dwelling forever."
Then the king turned his face and blessed all the congregation of Israel: "Blessed be the Lord God of Israel, whose mouth spoke to David my father, and whose hand fulfilled; for He said: 'From the day I brought My people Israel from Egypt I never chose a town in all the tribes of Israel to build My House, to rest My name there; but now I choose David to rule My people Israel.' And He was with the heart of my father, David, who longed to build a House for the name of the Lord God of Israel, and He said to my father, David: 'Because it was in your heart to build a House for My name, you pleased Me but by having this in your heart. You shall not build the House – but your son, your seed, will build a House for My name.' And the Lord has fulfilled the word He spoke, and I have followed my father David, to sit upon the throne of Israel, as the Lord promised. And I have built a House for the name of the Lord God of Israel. And there I made a place for the Ark with the Lord's Covenant in it; the one that He hewed out with our fathers, when He brought them out of the Land of Egypt."

Continue with the blessings after the Haftara on page 514.

TORAH READING FOR THE FIRST DAY OF ḤOL HAMO'ED SUKKOT

In Israel, the first three verses, "On the second day" through "its meal offering and their libations," are read for each of the four aliyot.

On the second day, twelve young bullocks, two rams, and fourteen unblemished yearling male lambs. And you shall perform their meal-offerings and their libations, for each of the bullocks, the rams and the lambs, in the proper quantities, according to the law. And likewise a male goat for atonement, as well as the regular daily offering and its meal offering and their libations. *Num. 29:17–25*

LEVI On the third day, eleven young bullocks, two rams, and fourteen unblemished yearling male lambs. And you shall perform their meal-offerings and their libations, for each of the bullocks, the rams and the lambs, in the proper quantities, according to the law. And likewise a male goat for atonement, as well as the regular daily offering and its meal offering and its libation.

SHELISHI On the fourth day, ten young bullocks, two rams, and fourteen unblemished yearling male lambs. And you shall perform their meal-offerings and their libations, for each of the bullocks, the rams and the lambs, in the proper quantities, according to the law. And likewise a male goat for atonement, as well as the regular daily offering and its meal offering and its libation.

אֶת־בֵּית יהוה: אָז אָמַר שְׁלֹמֹה יהוה אָמַר לִשְׁכֹּן בָּעֲרָפֶל: בָּנֹה
בָנִיתִי בֵּית זְבֻל לָךְ מָכוֹן לְשִׁבְתְּךָ עוֹלָמִים: וַיַּסֵּב הַמֶּלֶךְ אֶת־פָּנָיו וַיְבָרֶךְ אֵת
כָּל־קְהַל יִשְׂרָאֵל וְכָל־קְהַל יִשְׂרָאֵל עֹמֵד: וַיֹּאמֶר בָּרוּךְ יהוה אֱלֹהֵי יִשְׂרָאֵל
אֲשֶׁר דִּבֶּר בְּפִיו אֵת דָּוִד אָבִי וּבְיָדוֹ מִלֵּא לֵאמֹר: מִן־הַיּוֹם אֲשֶׁר הוֹצֵאתִי
אֶת־עַמִּי אֶת־יִשְׂרָאֵל מִמִּצְרַיִם לֹא־בָחַרְתִּי בְעִיר מִכֹּל שִׁבְטֵי יִשְׂרָאֵל לִבְנוֹת
בַּיִת לִהְיוֹת שְׁמִי שָׁם וָאֶבְחַר בְּדָוִד לִהְיוֹת עַל־עַמִּי יִשְׂרָאֵל: וַיְהִי עִם־לְבַב
דָּוִד אָבִי לִבְנוֹת בַּיִת לְשֵׁם יהוה אֱלֹהֵי יִשְׂרָאֵל: וַיֹּאמֶר יהוה אֶל־דָּוִד אָבִי
יַעַן אֲשֶׁר הָיָה עִם־לְבָבְךָ לִבְנוֹת בַּיִת לִשְׁמִי הֱטִיבֹתָ כִּי הָיָה עִם־לְבָבֶךָ: רַק
אַתָּה לֹא תִבְנֶה הַבָּיִת כִּי אִם־בִּנְךָ הַיֹּצֵא מֵחֲלָצֶיךָ הוּא־יִבְנֶה הַבַּיִת לִשְׁמִי:
וַיָּקֶם יהוה אֶת־דְּבָרוֹ אֲשֶׁר דִּבֵּר וָאָקֻם תַּחַת דָּוִד אָבִי וָאֵשֵׁב ׀ עַל־כִּסֵּא
יִשְׂרָאֵל כַּאֲשֶׁר דִּבֶּר יהוה וָאֶבְנֶה הַבַּיִת לְשֵׁם יהוה אֱלֹהֵי יִשְׂרָאֵל: וָאָשִׂם
שָׁם מָקוֹם לָאָרוֹן אֲשֶׁר־שָׁם בְּרִית יהוה אֲשֶׁר כָּרַת עִם־אֲבֹתֵינוּ בְּהוֹצִיאוֹ
אֹתָם מֵאֶרֶץ מִצְרָיִם:

Continue with the blessings after the הפטרה *on page 515.*

קריאה לא׳ דחול המועד סוכות

In ארץ ישראל*, the first three verses,* וּבַיּוֹם הַשֵּׁנִי *through* וּמִנְחָתָהּ וְנִסְכֵּיהֶם*,*
are read for each of the four עליות*.*

במדבר כט:יז–כה וּבַיּוֹם הַשֵּׁנִי פָּרִים בְּנֵי־בָקָר שְׁנֵים עָשָׂר אֵילִם שְׁנָיִם כְּבָשִׂים בְּנֵי־שָׁנָה
אַרְבָּעָה עָשָׂר תְּמִימִם: וּמִנְחָתָם וְנִסְכֵּיהֶם לַפָּרִים לָאֵילִם וְלַכְּבָשִׂים
בְּמִסְפָּרָם כַּמִּשְׁפָּט: וּשְׂעִיר־עִזִּים אֶחָד חַטָּאת מִלְּבַד עֹלַת הַתָּמִיד וּמִנְחָתָהּ
לוי וְנִסְכֵּיהֶם: *וּבַיּוֹם הַשְּׁלִישִׁי פָּרִים עַשְׁתֵּי־עָשָׂר אֵילִם שְׁנָיִם כְּבָשִׂים
בְּנֵי־שָׁנָה אַרְבָּעָה עָשָׂר תְּמִימִם: וּמִנְחָתָם וְנִסְכֵּיהֶם לַפָּרִים לָאֵילִם וְלַכְּבָשִׂים
בְּמִסְפָּרָם כַּמִּשְׁפָּט: וּשְׂעִיר חַטָּאת אֶחָד מִלְּבַד עֹלַת הַתָּמִיד וּמִנְחָתָהּ
שלישי וְנִסְכָּהּ: *וּבַיּוֹם הָרְבִיעִי פָּרִים עֲשָׂרָה אֵילִם שְׁנָיִם כְּבָשִׂים בְּנֵי־שָׁנָה
אַרְבָּעָה עָשָׂר תְּמִימִם: מִנְחָתָם וְנִסְכֵּיהֶם לַפָּרִים לָאֵילִם וְלַכְּבָשִׂים בְּמִסְפָּרָם
כַּמִּשְׁפָּט: וּשְׂעִיר־עִזִּים אֶחָד חַטָּאת מִלְּבַד עֹלַת הַתָּמִיד מִנְחָתָהּ וְנִסְכָּהּ:

defilement of the Greeks, though it took place later in the year, on Ḥanukka, was also modeled on Sukkot (see II Maccabees 10:6–8).

On the second day, twelve young bullocks, two rams, and fourteen unblemished yearling male lambs. And you shall perform their meal-offerings and their libations, for each of the bullocks, the rams and the lambs, in the proper quantities, according to the law. And likewise a male goat for atonement, as well as the regular daily offering and its meal offering and their libations. REVI'I

On the third day, eleven young bullocks, two rams, and fourteen unblemished yearling male lambs. And you shall perform their meal-offerings and their libations, for each of the bullocks, the rams and the lambs, in the proper quantities, according to the law. And likewise a male goat for atonement, as well as the regular daily offering and its meal offering and its libation.

TORAH READING FOR THE SECOND DAY OF ḤOL HAMO'ED SUKKOT

In Israel, the first three verses, "On the third day" through "its meal offering and its libation," are read for each of the four aliyot.

On the third day, eleven young bullocks, two rams, and fourteen unblemished yearling male lambs. And you shall perform their meal-offerings and their libations, for each of the bullocks, the rams and the lambs, in the proper quantities, according to the law. And likewise a male goat for atonement, as well as the regular daily offering and its meal offering and its libation. *Num.* 29:20–28

On the fourth day, ten young bullocks, two rams, and fourteen unblemished yearling male lambs. And you shall perform their meal-offerings and their libations, for each of the bullocks, the rams and the lambs, in the proper quantities, according to the law. And likewise a male goat for atonement, as well as the regular daily offering and its meal offering and its libation. LEVI

On the fifth day, nine young bullocks, two rams, and fourteen unblemished yearling male lambs. And you shall perform their meal-offerings and their libations, for each of the bullocks, the rams and the lambs, in the proper quantities, according to the law. And likewise a male goat for atonement, as well as the regular daily offering and its meal offering and its libation. SHELISHI

On the third day, eleven young bullocks, two rams, and fourteen unblemished yearling male lambs. And you shall perform their meal-offerings and their libations, for each of the bullocks, the rams and the lambs, in the proper quantities, according to the law. And likewise a male goat for atonement, as well as the regular daily offering and its meal offering and its libation. REVI'I

On the fourth day, ten young bullocks, two rams, and fourteen unblemished yearling male lambs. And you shall perform their meal-offerings and their libations, for each of the bullocks, the rams and the lambs, in the proper quantities, according to the law. And likewise a male goat for atonement, as well as the regular daily offering and its meal offering and its libation.

רביעי וּבַיּוֹם הַשֵּׁנִי פָּרִים בְּנֵי־בָקָר שְׁנֵים עָשָׂר אֵילִם שְׁנָיִם כְּבָשִׂים בְּנֵי־שָׁנָה
אַרְבָּעָה עָשָׂר תְּמִימִם: וּמִנְחָתָם וְנִסְכֵּיהֶם לַפָּרִים לָאֵילִם וְלַכְּבָשִׂים
בְּמִסְפָּרָם כַּמִּשְׁפָּט: וּשְׂעִיר־עִזִּים אֶחָד חַטָּאת מִלְּבַד עֹלַת הַתָּמִיד
וּמִנְחָתָהּ וְנִסְכֵּיהֶם: וּבַיּוֹם הַשְּׁלִישִׁי פָּרִים עַשְׁתֵּי־עָשָׂר אֵילִם
שְׁנָיִם כְּבָשִׂים בְּנֵי־שָׁנָה אַרְבָּעָה עָשָׂר תְּמִימִם: וּמִנְחָתָם וְנִסְכֵּיהֶם לַפָּרִים
לָאֵילִם וְלַכְּבָשִׂים בְּמִסְפָּרָם כַּמִּשְׁפָּט: וּשְׂעִיר חַטָּאת אֶחָד מִלְּבַד עֹלַת
הַתָּמִיד וּמִנְחָתָהּ וְנִסְכָּהּ:

קריאה ליום ב׳ דחול המועד סוכות

In ארץ ישראל*, the first three verses,* וּבַיּוֹם הַשְּׁלִישִׁי *through* וּמִנְחָתָהּ וְנִסְכָּהּ*,*
are read for each of the four עליות*.*

במדבר כט:כ–כח וּבַיּוֹם הַשְּׁלִישִׁי פָּרִים עַשְׁתֵּי־עָשָׂר אֵילִם שְׁנָיִם כְּבָשִׂים בְּנֵי־שָׁנָה
אַרְבָּעָה עָשָׂר תְּמִימִם: וּמִנְחָתָם וְנִסְכֵּיהֶם לַפָּרִים לָאֵילִם וְלַכְּבָשִׂים
בְּמִסְפָּרָם כַּמִּשְׁפָּט: וּשְׂעִיר חַטָּאת אֶחָד מִלְּבַד עֹלַת הַתָּמִיד וּמִנְחָתָהּ
לוי וְנִסְכָּהּ: *וּבַיּוֹם הָרְבִיעִי פָּרִים עֲשָׂרָה אֵילִם שְׁנָיִם כְּבָשִׂים בְּנֵי־
שָׁנָה אַרְבָּעָה עָשָׂר תְּמִימִם: מִנְחָתָם וְנִסְכֵּיהֶם לַפָּרִים לָאֵילִם וְלַכְּבָשִׂים
בְּמִסְפָּרָם כַּמִּשְׁפָּט: וּשְׂעִיר־עִזִּים אֶחָד חַטָּאת מִלְּבַד עֹלַת הַתָּמִיד מִנְחָתָהּ
שלישי וְנִסְכָּהּ: *וּבַיּוֹם הַחֲמִישִׁי פָּרִים תִּשְׁעָה אֵילִם שְׁנָיִם כְּבָשִׂים
בְּנֵי־שָׁנָה אַרְבָּעָה עָשָׂר תְּמִימִם: וּמִנְחָתָם וְנִסְכֵּיהֶם לַפָּרִים לָאֵילִם
וְלַכְּבָשִׂים בְּמִסְפָּרָם כַּמִּשְׁפָּט: וּשְׂעִיר חַטָּאת אֶחָד מִלְּבַד עֹלַת הַתָּמִיד
וּמִנְחָתָהּ וְנִסְכָּהּ:

רביעי וּבַיּוֹם הַשְּׁלִישִׁי פָּרִים עַשְׁתֵּי־עָשָׂר אֵילִם שְׁנָיִם כְּבָשִׂים בְּנֵי־שָׁנָה
אַרְבָּעָה עָשָׂר תְּמִימִם: וּמִנְחָתָם וְנִסְכֵּיהֶם לַפָּרִים לָאֵילִם וְלַכְּבָשִׂים
בְּמִסְפָּרָם כַּמִּשְׁפָּט: וּשְׂעִיר חַטָּאת אֶחָד מִלְּבַד עֹלַת הַתָּמִיד וּמִנְחָתָהּ
וְנִסְכָּהּ: וּבַיּוֹם הָרְבִיעִי פָּרִים עֲשָׂרָה אֵילִם שְׁנָיִם כְּבָשִׂים
בְּנֵי־שָׁנָה אַרְבָּעָה עָשָׂר תְּמִימִם: מִנְחָתָם וְנִסְכֵּיהֶם לַפָּרִים לָאֵילִם
וְלַכְּבָשִׂים בְּמִסְפָּרָם כַּמִּשְׁפָּט: וּשְׂעִיר־עִזִּים אֶחָד חַטָּאת מִלְּבַד עֹלַת
הַתָּמִיד מִנְחָתָהּ וְנִסְכָּהּ:

TORAH READING FOR THE THIRD DAY OF ḤOL HAMO'ED SUKKOT

In Israel, the first three verses, "On the fourth day" through "its meal offering and its libation," are read for each of the four aliyot.

On the fourth day, ten young bullocks, two rams, and fourteen unblemished yearling male lambs. And you shall perform their meal-offerings and their libations, for each of the bullocks, the rams and the lambs, in the proper quantities, according to the law. And likewise a male goat for atonement, as well as the regular daily offering and its meal offering and its libation. *Num. 29:23–31*

LEVI On the fifth day, nine young bullocks, two rams, and fourteen unblemished yearling male lambs. And you shall perform their meal-offerings and their libations, for each of the bullocks, the rams and the lambs, in the proper quantities, according to the law. And likewise a male goat for atonement, as well as the regular daily offering and its meal offering and its libation.

SHELISHI On the sixth day, eighth young bullocks, two rams, and fourteen unblemished yearling male lambs. And you shall perform their meal-offerings and their libations, for each of the bullocks, the rams and the lambs, in the proper quantities, according to the law. And likewise a male goat for atonement, as well as the regular daily offering and its meal offering and its libations.

REVI'I On the fourth day, ten young bullocks, two rams, and fourteen unblemished yearling male lambs. And you shall perform their meal-offerings and their libations, for each of the bullocks, the rams and the lambs, in the proper quantities, according to the law. And likewise a male goat for atonement, as well as the regular daily offering and its meal offering and its libation.

On the fifth day, nine young bullocks, two rams, and fourteen unblemished yearling male lambs. And you shall perform their meal-offerings and their libations, for each of the bullocks, the rams and the lambs, in the proper quantities, according to the law. And likewise a male goat for atonement, as well as the regular daily offering and its meal offering and its libation.

TORAH READING FOR THE FOURTH DAY OF ḤOL HAMO'ED SUKKOT

In Israel, the first three verses, "On the fifth day" through "its meal offering and its libations," are read for each of the four aliyot.

On the fifth day, nine young bullocks, two rams, and fourteen unblemished yearling male lambs. And you shall perform their meal-offerings and their libations, for each of the bullocks, the rams and the lambs, in the proper quantities, according to the law. And likewise a male goat for atonement, as well as the regular daily offering and its meal offering and its libations. *Num. 29:26–34*

LEVI On the sixth day, eight young bullocks, two rams, and fourteen unblemished yearling male lambs. And you shall perform their meal-offerings and their libations, for each of the bullocks, the rams and the lambs, in the proper quantities, according to the law. And likewise a male goat for atonement, as well as the regular daily offering and its meal offering and its libations.

קריאה ליום ג׳ דחול המועד סוכות

In ארץ ישראל*, the first three verses,* וּבַיּוֹם הָרְבִיעִי *through* מִנְחָתָהּ וְנִסְכָּהּ*,*
are read for each of the four עליות*.*

במדבר כט:כג–לא
וּבַיּוֹם הָרְבִיעִי פָּרִים עֲשָׂרָה אֵילִם שְׁנָיִם כְּבָשִׂים בְּנֵי־שָׁנָה אַרְבָּעָה
עָשָׂר תְּמִימִם: מִנְחָתָם וְנִסְכֵּיהֶם לַפָּרִים לָאֵילִם וְלַכְּבָשִׂים בְּמִסְפָּרָם
כַּמִּשְׁפָּט: וּשְׂעִיר־עִזִּים אֶחָד חַטָּאת מִלְּבַד עֹלַת הַתָּמִיד מִנְחָתָהּ
לוי וְנִסְכָּהּ: *וּבַיּוֹם הַחֲמִישִׁי פָּרִים תִּשְׁעָה אֵילִם שְׁנָיִם כְּבָשִׂים
בְּנֵי־שָׁנָה אַרְבָּעָה עָשָׂר תְּמִימִם: וּמִנְחָתָם וְנִסְכֵּיהֶם לַפָּרִים לָאֵילִם
וְלַכְּבָשִׂים בְּמִסְפָּרָם כַּמִּשְׁפָּט: וּשְׂעִיר חַטָּאת אֶחָד מִלְּבַד עֹלַת הַתָּמִיד
שלישי וּמִנְחָתָהּ וְנִסְכָּהּ: *וּבַיּוֹם הַשִּׁשִּׁי פָּרִים שְׁמֹנָה אֵילִם שְׁנָיִם
כְּבָשִׂים בְּנֵי־שָׁנָה אַרְבָּעָה עָשָׂר תְּמִימִם: וּמִנְחָתָם וְנִסְכֵּיהֶם לַפָּרִים לָאֵילִם
וְלַכְּבָשִׂים בְּמִסְפָּרָם כַּמִּשְׁפָּט: וּשְׂעִיר חַטָּאת אֶחָד מִלְּבַד עֹלַת הַתָּמִיד
מִנְחָתָהּ וּנְסָכֶיהָ:

רביעי וּבַיּוֹם הָרְבִיעִי פָּרִים עֲשָׂרָה אֵילִם שְׁנָיִם כְּבָשִׂים בְּנֵי־שָׁנָה אַרְבָּעָה
עָשָׂר תְּמִימִם: מִנְחָתָם וְנִסְכֵּיהֶם לַפָּרִים לָאֵילִם וְלַכְּבָשִׂים בְּמִסְפָּרָם
כַּמִּשְׁפָּט: וּשְׂעִיר־עִזִּים אֶחָד חַטָּאת מִלְּבַד עֹלַת הַתָּמִיד מִנְחָתָהּ
וְנִסְכָּהּ: וּבַיּוֹם הַחֲמִישִׁי פָּרִים תִּשְׁעָה אֵילִם שְׁנָיִם כְּבָשִׂים
בְּנֵי־שָׁנָה אַרְבָּעָה עָשָׂר תְּמִימִם: וּמִנְחָתָם וְנִסְכֵּיהֶם לַפָּרִים לָאֵילִם
וְלַכְּבָשִׂים בְּמִסְפָּרָם כַּמִּשְׁפָּט: וּשְׂעִיר חַטָּאת אֶחָד מִלְּבַד עֹלַת הַתָּמִיד
וּמִנְחָתָהּ וְנִסְכָּהּ:

קריאה ליום ד׳ דחול המועד סוכות

In ארץ ישראל*, the first three verses,* וּבַיּוֹם הַחֲמִישִׁי *through* וּמִנְחָתָהּ וְנִסְכָּהּ*,*
are read for each of the four עליות*.*

במדבר כט:כו–לד
וּבַיּוֹם הַחֲמִישִׁי פָּרִים תִּשְׁעָה אֵילִם שְׁנָיִם כְּבָשִׂים בְּנֵי־שָׁנָה אַרְבָּעָה עָשָׂר
תְּמִימִם: וּמִנְחָתָם וְנִסְכֵּיהֶם לַפָּרִים לָאֵילִם וְלַכְּבָשִׂים בְּמִסְפָּרָם כַּמִּשְׁפָּט:
לוי וּשְׂעִיר חַטָּאת אֶחָד מִלְּבַד עֹלַת הַתָּמִיד וּמִנְחָתָהּ וְנִסְכָּהּ: *וּבַיּוֹם
הַשִּׁשִּׁי פָּרִים שְׁמֹנָה אֵילִם שְׁנָיִם כְּבָשִׂים בְּנֵי־שָׁנָה אַרְבָּעָה עָשָׂר תְּמִימִם:
וּמִנְחָתָם וְנִסְכֵּיהֶם לַפָּרִים לָאֵילִם וְלַכְּבָשִׂים בְּמִסְפָּרָם כַּמִּשְׁפָּט: וּשְׂעִיר

On the seventh day, seven young bullocks, two rams, and fourteen unblemished yearling male lambs. And you shall perform their meal-offerings and their libations, for each of the bullocks, the rams and the lambs, in the proper quantities, according to the law. And likewise a male goat for atonement, as well as the regular daily offering and its meal offering and its libation. SHELISHI

On the fifth day, nine young bullocks, two rams, and fourteen unblemished yearling male lambs. And you shall perform their meal-offerings and their libations, for each of the bullocks, the rams and the lambs, in the proper quantities, according to the law. And likewise a male goat for atonement, as well as the regular daily offering and its meal offering and its libations. REVI'I

On the sixth day, eight young bullocks, two rams, and fourteen unblemished yearling male lambs. And you shall perform their meal-offerings and their libations, for each of the bullocks, the rams and the lambs, in the proper quantities, according to the law. And likewise a male goat for atonement, as well as the regular daily offering and its meal offering and its libations.

TORAH READING FOR THE FIFTH DAY OF ḤOL HAMO'ED SUKKOT IN ISRAEL

In Israel, the following is read for each of the four aliyot.

On the sixth day, eight young bullocks, two rams, and fourteen unblemished yearling male lambs. And you shall perform their meal-offerings and their libations, for each of the bullocks, the rams and the lambs, in the proper quantities, according to the law. And likewise a male goat for atonement, as well as the regular daily offering and its meal offering and its libations. *Num. 29:29–31*

TORAH READING FOR HOSHANA RABA

In Israel, the last three verses, "On the seventh day" through "its meal offering and its libation," are read for each of the four aliyot.

On the fifth day, nine young bullocks, two rams, and fourteen unblemished yearling male lambs. And you shall perform their meal-offerings and their libations, for each of the bullocks, the rams and the lambs, in the proper quantities, according to the law. And likewise a male goat for atonement, as well as the regular daily offering and its meal offering and its libations. *Num. 29:26–34*

On the sixth day, eight young bullocks, two rams, and fourteen unblemished yearling male lambs. And you shall perform their meal-offerings and their libations, for each of the bullocks, the rams and the lambs, in the proper quantities, according to the law. And likewise a male goat for atonement, as well as the regular daily offering and its meal offering and its libations. LEVI

On the seventh day, seven young bullocks, two rams, and fourteen unblemished yearling male lambs. And you shall perform their meal-offerings and their libations, for each of the bullocks, the rams and the lambs, in the proper quantities, according to the law. And likewise a male goat for atonement, as well as the regular daily offering and its meal offering and its libation. SHELISHI

שלישי חַטָּאת אֶחָד מִלְּבַד עֹלַת הַתָּמִיד מִנְחָתָהּ וּנְסָכֶיהָ: *וּבַיּוֹם
הַשְּׁבִיעִי פָּרִים שִׁבְעָה אֵילִם שְׁנָיִם כְּבָשִׂים בְּנֵי־שָׁנָה אַרְבָּעָה עָשָׂר תְּמִימִם:
וּמִנְחָתָם וְנִסְכֵּהֶם לַפָּרִים לָאֵילִם וְלַכְּבָשִׂים בְּמִסְפָּרָם כְּמִשְׁפָּטָם: וּשְׂעִיר
חַטָּאת אֶחָד מִלְּבַד עֹלַת הַתָּמִיד מִנְחָתָהּ וְנִסְכָּהּ:

רביעי וּבַיּוֹם הַחֲמִישִׁי פָּרִים תִּשְׁעָה אֵילִם שְׁנָיִם כְּבָשִׂים בְּנֵי־שָׁנָה אַרְבָּעָה עָשָׂר
תְּמִימִם: וּמִנְחָתָם וְנִסְכֵּיהֶם לַפָּרִים לָאֵילִם וְלַכְּבָשִׂים בְּמִסְפָּרָם כַּמִּשְׁפָּט:
וּשְׂעִיר חַטָּאת אֶחָד מִלְּבַד עֹלַת הַתָּמִיד וּמִנְחָתָהּ וְנִסְכָּהּ: וּבַיּוֹם
הַשִּׁשִּׁי פָּרִים שְׁמֹנָה אֵילִם שְׁנָיִם כְּבָשִׂים בְּנֵי־שָׁנָה אַרְבָּעָה עָשָׂר תְּמִימִם:
וּמִנְחָתָם וְנִסְכֵּיהֶם לַפָּרִים לָאֵילִם וְלַכְּבָשִׂים בְּמִסְפָּרָם כַּמִּשְׁפָּט: וּשְׂעִיר
חַטָּאת אֶחָד מִלְּבַד עֹלַת הַתָּמִיד מִנְחָתָהּ וּנְסָכֶיהָ:

קריאה ליום ה׳ דחול המועד סוכות בארץ ישראל

In ארץ ישראל*, the following is read for each of the four* עליות*.*

במדבר כט:כט–לא

וּבַיּוֹם הַשִּׁשִּׁי פָּרִים שְׁמֹנָה אֵילִם שְׁנָיִם כְּבָשִׂים בְּנֵי־שָׁנָה אַרְבָּעָה עָשָׂר
תְּמִימִם: וּמִנְחָתָם וְנִסְכֵּיהֶם לַפָּרִים לָאֵילִם וְלַכְּבָשִׂים בְּמִסְפָּרָם כַּמִּשְׁפָּט:
וּשְׂעִיר חַטָּאת אֶחָד מִלְּבַד עֹלַת הַתָּמִיד מִנְחָתָהּ וּנְסָכֶיהָ:

קריאה להושענא רבה

In ארץ ישראל*, the three verses from* וּבַיּוֹם הַשְּׁבִיעִי *through* מִנְחָתָהּ וְנִסְכָּהּ *are read for each of the four* עליות°.

במדבר כט:כו–לד

וּבַיּוֹם הַחֲמִישִׁי פָּרִים תִּשְׁעָה אֵילִם שְׁנָיִם כְּבָשִׂים בְּנֵי־שָׁנָה אַרְבָּעָה עָשָׂר
תְּמִימִם: וּמִנְחָתָם וְנִסְכֵּיהֶם לַפָּרִים לָאֵילִם וְלַכְּבָשִׂים בְּמִסְפָּרָם כַּמִּשְׁפָּט:
לוי וּשְׂעִיר חַטָּאת אֶחָד מִלְּבַד עֹלַת הַתָּמִיד וּמִנְחָתָהּ וְנִסְכָּהּ: *וּבַיּוֹם
הַשִּׁשִּׁי פָּרִים שְׁמֹנָה אֵילִם שְׁנָיִם כְּבָשִׂים בְּנֵי־שָׁנָה אַרְבָּעָה עָשָׂר תְּמִימִם:
וּמִנְחָתָם וְנִסְכֵּיהֶם לַפָּרִים לָאֵילִם וְלַכְּבָשִׂים בְּמִסְפָּרָם כַּמִּשְׁפָּט: וּשְׂעִיר
שלישי חַטָּאת אֶחָד מִלְּבַד עֹלַת הַתָּמִיד מִנְחָתָהּ וּנְסָכֶיהָ: *וּבַיּוֹם
הַשְּׁבִיעִי פָּרִים שִׁבְעָה אֵילִם שְׁנָיִם כְּבָשִׂים בְּנֵי־שָׁנָה אַרְבָּעָה עָשָׂר תְּמִימִם:
וּמִנְחָתָם וְנִסְכֵּהֶם לַפָּרִים לָאֵילִם וְלַכְּבָשִׂים בְּמִסְפָּרָם כְּמִשְׁפָּטָם: וּשְׂעִיר
חַטָּאת אֶחָד מִלְּבַד עֹלַת הַתָּמִיד מִנְחָתָהּ וְנִסְכָּהּ:

On the sixth day, eight young bullocks, two rams, and fourteen unblemished yearling male lambs. And you shall perform their meal-offerings and their libations, for each of the bullocks, the rams and the lambs, in the proper quantities, according to the law. And likewise a male goat for atonement, as well as the regular daily offering and its meal offering and its libations. REVI'I

On the seventh day, seven young bullocks, two rams, and fourteen unblemished yearling male lambs. And you shall perform their meal-offerings and their libations, for each of the bullocks, the rams and the lambs, in the proper quantities, according to the law. And likewise a male goat for atonement, as well as the regular daily offering and its meal offering and its libation.

TORAH READING FOR SHABBAT ḤOL HAMO'ED SUKKOT

The Torah reading for Shabbat Ḥol HaMo'ed Sukkot is the same as that of Shabbat Ḥol HaMo'ed Pesaḥ (page 1135). The Maftir is the Torah reading of the day of Ḥol HaMo'ed Sukkot on which Shabbat falls.

HAFTARA FOR SHABBAT ḤOL HAMO'ED SUKKOT

Ezek. 38:18–39:16

And it shall be, on the day that Gog comes onto the soil of Israel, says the LORD God: My anger will rise up in My nostrils; in My fury, in the fire of My rage, I have spoken: Surely, on that day there will be a great quaking upon the ground of Israel; the fish of the seas and the birds of the sky, the animals of the land, every creeping thing that crawls upon the earth and every man on the face of the earth will quake before Me; the mountains will be demolished, the terraces will collapse, and every wall shall fall to the ground. I will call the sword down on him from all My mountains, says the LORD God: each man's sword will be turned against his brother. I will call judgment on him with pestilence and blood; I will pour down torrential rain and crystal hailstone, fire and sulphur over him and his troops, and over the many peoples who are with him. And so I will be magnified and sanctified, I will make Myself known in the eyes of many nations – and they will know that I am the LORD.

And you, Man, prophesy against Gog and say: so says the LORD God: behold I am against you, Gog, prince, leader of Meshech and Tuval. I will turn you around, I will incite you on, and I will take you from the far-edge of the north and bring you to the mountains of Israel. I will strike

רביעי וביום הששי פרים שמנה אילם שנים כבשים בני־שנה ארבעה עשר
תמימם: ומנחתם ונסכיהם לפרים לאילם ולכבשים במספרם כמשפט:
ושעיר חטאת אחד מלבד עלת התמיד מנחתה ונסכיה: °וביום
השביעי פרים שבעה אילם שנים כבשים בני־שנה ארבעה עשר תמימם:
ומנחתם ונסכהם לפרים לאילם ולכבשים במספרם כמשפטם: ושעיר
חטאת אחד מלבד עלת התמיד מנחתה ונסכה:

קריאה לשבת חול המועד סוכות

The קריאת התורה *for* שבת חול המועד סוכות *is the same as that of* שבת חול המועד פסח *(page 1135). The* מפטיר *is the* קריאת התורה *of the day of* חול המועד סוכות *on which* שבת *falls.*

הפטרה לשבת חול המועד סוכות

יחזקאל לח:יח–לט:טז

והיה | ביום ההוא ביום בוא גוג על־אדמת ישראל נאם אדני יהוה תעלה
חמתי באפי: ובקנאתי באש־עברתי דברתי אם־לא | ביום ההוא יהיה
רעש גדול על אדמת ישראל: ורעשו מפני דגי הים ועוף השמים וחית
השדה וכל־הרמש הרמש על־האדמה וכל האדם אשר על־פני האדמה
ונהרסו ההרים ונפלו המדרגות וכל־חומה לארץ תפול: וקראתי עליו
לכל־הרי חרב נאם אדני יהוה חרב איש באחיו תהיה: ונשפטתי אתו
בדבר ובדם וגשם שוטף ואבני אלגביש אש וגפרית אמטיר עליו ועל־
אגפיו ועל־עמים רבים אשר אתו: והתגדלתי והתקדשתי ונודעתי לעיני
גוים רבים וידעו כי־אני יהוה: ואתה בן־אדם הנבא על־גוג
ואמרת כה אמר אדני יהוה הנני אליך גוג נשיא ראש משך ותבל:
ושבבתיך וששאתיך והעליתיך מירכתי צפון והבאותיך על־הרי ישראל:
והכיתי קשתך מיד שמאולך וחציך מיד ימינך אפיל: על־הרי ישראל

HAFTARA FOR SHABBAT HOL HAMO'ED SUKKOT

A graphic vision of a battle that will take place at the end of days, in which Israel's enemies will be defeated, and God's name will be made great among the nations.

The connection with Sukkot lies in the similarity between this vision and

your bow from your left hand, I will make the arrows fall from your right; upon the mountains of Israel, you will fall – you and your troops and all the peoples who are with you; I will give you up to the birds of prey, to every winged creature, to the animals of the land, to feed from; upon the open field, you will fall; so have I spoken, says the LORD God. And I will send fire on Magog and on those who live securely in their isles; they will know that I am the LORD.

I will make My holy name known among My people, Israel; I will no longer have My holy name profaned; and the nations will know that I am the LORD, holy among Israel. Behold: it is coming, it will be, says the LORD God: This is the day of which I have spoken.

And the inhabitants of the cities of Israel will come out, and they will kindle and burn the weapons, the shields and guards, the bows and arrows, the truncheons and spears; they will burn them for seven years, for fire: they will not take wood from the land, nor will they chop down any from the forests, for they will make their fires of weapons; they will despoil those who despoiled them, and plunder those who plundered them, says the LORD God.

And it will happen, on that day: I will grant Gog a burial-place there, in Israel, the Valley of the Travelers, east of the sea, and it will block the travelers; here they will bury Gog and his horde, they will call it the Valley of the Hordes of Gog. For seven months, the house of Israel will bury them, to purify the land; all the people in the land will bury them, and it will make their name; it will be the day of My glory, says the LORD God. And they will select men to cross the land perpetually, burying those remains that lie upon the ground – with the travelers – to purify it; they will search from the end of seven months, and travelers passing through the land, whenever they see a human bone, will place a sign next to it, until the buriers have buried it in the Valley of the Hordes of Gog. A city will be named Hamona, [for his Hordes]. And so will they purify the land.

Continue with the blessings after the Haftara on page 514.

---

were unable to protect His people. This, for Ezekiel, was a *ḥillul Hashem*, a "desecration of God's name."

תִּפּוֹל אַתָּה וְכׇל־אֲגַפֶּיךָ וְעַמִּים אֲשֶׁר אִתָּךְ לְעֵיט צִפּוֹר כׇּל־כָּנָף וְחַיַּת הַשָּׂדֶה
נְתַתִּיךָ לְאׇכְלָה׃ עַל־פְּנֵי הַשָּׂדֶה תִּפּוֹל כִּי אֲנִי דִּבַּרְתִּי נְאֻם אֲדֹנָי יֱהֹוִה׃
וְשִׁלַּחְתִּי־אֵשׁ בְּמָגוֹג וּבְיֹשְׁבֵי הָאִיִּים לָבֶטַח וְיָדְעוּ כִּי־אֲנִי יְהֹוָה׃ וְאֶת־שֵׁם
קׇדְשִׁי אוֹדִיעַ בְּתוֹךְ עַמִּי יִשְׂרָאֵל וְלֹא־אַחֵל אֶת־שֵׁם־קׇדְשִׁי עוֹד וְיָדְעוּ
הַגּוֹיִם כִּי־אֲנִי יְהֹוָה קָדוֹשׁ בְּיִשְׂרָאֵל׃ הִנֵּה בָאָה וְנִהְיָתָה נְאֻם אֲדֹנָי יֱהֹוִה
הוּא הַיּוֹם אֲשֶׁר דִּבַּרְתִּי׃ וְיָצְאוּ יֹשְׁבֵי ׀ עָרֵי יִשְׂרָאֵל וּבִעֲרוּ וְהִשִּׂיקוּ בְּנֶשֶׁק
וּמָגֵן וְצִנָּה בְּקֶשֶׁת וּבְחִצִּים וּבְמַקֵּל יָד וּבְרֹמַח וּבִעֲרוּ בָהֶם אֵשׁ שֶׁבַע שָׁנִים׃
וְלֹא־יִשְׂאוּ עֵצִים מִן־הַשָּׂדֶה וְלֹא יַחְטְבוּ מִן־הַיְּעָרִים כִּי בַנֶּשֶׁק יְבַעֲרוּ־אֵשׁ
וְשָׁלְלוּ אֶת־שֹׁלְלֵיהֶם וּבָזְזוּ אֶת־בֹּזְזֵיהֶם נְאֻם אֲדֹנָי יֱהֹוִה׃ וְהָיָה
בַיּוֹם הַהוּא אֶתֵּן לְגוֹג ׀ מְקוֹם־שָׁם קֶבֶר בְּיִשְׂרָאֵל גֵּי הָעֹבְרִים קִדְמַת הַיָּם
וְחֹסֶמֶת הִיא אֶת־הָעֹבְרִים וְקָבְרוּ שָׁם אֶת־גּוֹג וְאֶת־כׇּל־הֲמוֹנֹה וְקָרְאוּ גֵּיא
הֲמוֹן גּוֹג׃ וּקְבָרוּם בֵּית יִשְׂרָאֵל לְמַעַן טַהֵר אֶת־הָאָרֶץ שִׁבְעָה חֳדָשִׁים׃
וְקָבְרוּ כׇּל־עַם הָאָרֶץ וְהָיָה לָהֶם לְשֵׁם יוֹם הִכָּבְדִי נְאֻם אֲדֹנָי יֱהֹוִה׃ וְאַנְשֵׁי
תָמִיד יַבְדִּילוּ עֹבְרִים בָּאָרֶץ מְקַבְּרִים אֶת־הָעֹבְרִים אֶת־הַנּוֹתָרִים עַל־פְּנֵי
הָאָרֶץ לְטַהֲרָהּ מִקְצֵה שִׁבְעָה־חֳדָשִׁים יַחְקֹרוּ׃ וְעָבְרוּ הָעֹבְרִים בָּאָרֶץ וְרָאָה
עֶצֶם אָדָם וּבָנָה אֶצְלוֹ צִיּוּן עַד קָבְרוּ אֹתוֹ הַמְקַבְּרִים אֶל־גֵּיא הֲמוֹן גּוֹג׃ וְגַם
שֶׁם־עִיר הֲמוֹנָה וְטִהֲרוּ הָאָרֶץ׃

Continue with the blessings after the הפטרה *on page 515.*

---

that of Zechariah 14 (the *haftara* for the first day), with its explicit reference to Sukkot. Since this was the time when both the first and second Temples were dedicated, it was natural to associate it with the restoration of cosmic order, in which Israel will be at peace, Jerusalem the spiritual center of the world, and God's presence manifest to all.

וְהִתְגַּדִּלְתִּי וְהִתְקַדִּשְׁתִּי *I will be magnified and sanctified.* These words were adapted to become the opening words of the Kaddish, itself a prayer for the recognition of God's sovereignty throughout the world.

וְלֹא־אַחֵל אֶת־שֵׁם־קׇדְשִׁי עוֹד *I will no longer have My holy name profaned.* To a unique degree, Ezekiel saw Israel's exile as a tragedy not only for Israel, but, as it were, for God Himself, since it seemed to the nations as if He

MAFTIR FOR SHEMINI ATZERET AND SIMḤAT TORAH

Outside Israel, the Torah Reading for Shemini Atzeret is the same as that of the eighth day of Pesaḥ, page 1142. In Israel the Torah Reading for Shemini Atzeret is that of Simḥat Torah, page 1160. The following Maftir is then read:

On the eighth day, you shall hold an assembly: you shall do no laborious work. And you shall bring a burnt-offering, an offering consumed by fire, of pleasing aroma to the LORD: one bull, one ram, and seven yearling male lambs; they shall be without blemish. The meal-offerings and the libations for the bull, the ram and the lambs in their number shall be according to the ordinance, and one goat for a sin-offering; all of this aside from the regular daily burnt-offering with its meal-offering and its libation. You shall offer these to the LORD at your appointed festival-times, besides for your vows and your freewill-offerings, your burnt-offerings, your meal-offerings, your libations, and your peace-offerings. And Moses told the children of Israel, according to all that the LORD had commanded Moses. *Num. 29:35–30:1*

HAFTARA FOR SHEMINI ATZERET OUTSIDE ISRAEL

In Israel, the Haftara for Shemini Atzeret is that of Simḥat Torah, on page 1166.

When Solomon had finished uttering this prayer and this plea to the LORD, he rose up from before the altar of the LORD, and bowed down upon his knees, his palms outstretched towards the heavens. And he stood and blessed all the congregation of Israel, in a loud voice, saying: *I Kings. 8:54–9:1*

"Blessed be the LORD, who has granted rest to His people Israel just as He promised; no word of the good that the LORD promised through His servant has failed us. May the LORD our God be with us as He was with our ancestors; may He never leave us or forsake us. May He incline our hearts towards Him, that we follow in all His ways and keep His commands and all the statutes and laws with which He charged our ancestors. Let these words with which I have pleaded with the LORD be close to the LORD our God day and night, that He do justice for His servant, and justice for His people Israel, day after day; so that all the peoples of the earth will know that the LORD is God. There is no other. And may your hearts be wholly with the LORD our God, to follow His statutes and to keep His commands as you do on this day."

Then the king and all of his people, Israel, brought offerings before the LORD. The peace offering that Solomon brought to the LORD consisted of

---

the nation. They must have felt that the journey had been completed: they had arrived at their destination.

Solomon did what the great Jewish leaders of the biblical age always did at key moments in the life of the nation: he told the story of the people thus far,

מפטיר לשמיני עצרת ולשמחת תורה

In חוץ לארץ, the קריאת התורה for שמיני עצרת is the same as that of the
eighth day of פסח, page 1143. In ארץ ישראל the קריאת התורה for שמיני עצרת
is that of שמחת תורה, page 1161. The following מפטיר is then read:

במדבר
כט:לה-ל:א

בַּיּוֹם֙ הַשְּׁמִינִ֔י עֲצֶ֖רֶת תִּהְיֶ֣ה לָכֶ֑ם כָּל־מְלֶ֥אכֶת עֲבֹדָ֖ה לֹ֥א תַעֲשֽׂוּ׃ וְהִקְרַבְתֶּ֨ם
עֹלָ֜ה אִשֵּׁ֨ה רֵ֤יחַ נִיחֹ֨חַ֙ לַֽיהֹוָ֔ה פַּ֥ר אֶחָ֖ד אַ֣יִל אֶחָ֑ד כְּבָשִׂ֧ים בְּנֵֽי־שָׁנָ֛ה שִׁבְעָ֖ה
תְּמִימִֽם׃ מִנְחָתָ֣ם וְנִסְכֵּיהֶ֗ם לַפָּ֨ר לָאַ֧יִל וְלַכְּבָשִׂ֛ים בְּמִסְפָּרָ֖ם כַּמִּשְׁפָּֽט׃ וּשְׂעִ֥יר
חַטָּ֖את אֶחָ֑ד מִלְּבַד֙ עֹלַ֣ת הַתָּמִ֔יד וּמִנְחָתָ֖הּ וְנִסְכָּֽהּ׃ אֵ֛לֶּה תַּעֲשׂ֥וּ לַֽיהֹוָ֖ה
בְּמוֹעֲדֵיכֶ֑ם לְבַ֨ד מִנִּדְרֵיכֶ֜ם וְנִדְבֹֽתֵיכֶ֗ם לְעֹלֹֽתֵיכֶם֙ וּלְמִנְחֹ֣תֵיכֶ֔ם וּלְנִסְכֵּיכֶ֖ם
וּֽלְשַׁלְמֵיכֶֽם׃ וַיֹּ֣אמֶר מֹשֶׁ֔ה אֶל־בְּנֵ֖י יִשְׂרָאֵ֑ל כְּכֹ֛ל אֲשֶׁר־צִוָּ֥ה יְהֹוָ֖ה אֶת־
מֹשֶֽׁה׃

הפטרה לשמיני עצרת בחוץ לארץ

In ארץ ישראל, the הפטרה for שמיני עצרת is that of שמחת תורה, page 1167.

מלכים א
ח:נד-ט:א

וַיְהִ֣י ׀ כְּכַלּ֣וֹת שְׁלֹמֹ֗ה לְהִתְפַּלֵּל֙ אֶל־יְהֹוָ֔ה אֵ֛ת כָּל־הַתְּפִלָּ֥ה וְהַתְּחִנָּ֖ה הַזֹּ֑את
קָ֞ם מִלִּפְנֵ֨י מִזְבַּ֤ח יְהֹוָה֙ מִכְּרֹ֣עַ עַל־בִּרְכָּ֔יו וְכַפָּ֖יו פְּרֻשׂ֥וֹת הַשָּׁמָֽיִם׃ וַיַּעֲמֹ֕ד וַיְבָ֕רֶךְ
אֵ֖ת כָּל־קְהַ֣ל יִשְׂרָאֵ֑ל ק֥וֹל גָּד֖וֹל לֵאמֹֽר׃ בָּר֣וּךְ יְהֹוָ֗ה אֲשֶׁ֨ר נָתַ֤ן מְנוּחָה֙ לְעַמּ֣וֹ
יִשְׂרָאֵ֔ל כְּכֹ֖ל אֲשֶׁ֣ר דִּבֵּ֑ר לֹֽא־נָפַ֞ל דָּבָ֣ר אֶחָ֗ד מִכֹּל֙ דְּבָר֣וֹ הַטּ֔וֹב אֲשֶׁ֣ר דִּבֶּ֔ר בְּיַ֖ד
מֹשֶׁ֥ה עַבְדּֽוֹ׃ יְהִ֨י יְהֹוָ֤ה אֱלֹהֵ֨ינוּ֙ עִמָּ֔נוּ כַּאֲשֶׁ֥ר הָיָ֖ה עִם־אֲבֹתֵ֑ינוּ אַל־יַעַזְבֵ֖נוּ
וְאַֽל־יִטְּשֵֽׁנוּ׃ לְהַטּ֥וֹת לְבָבֵ֖נוּ אֵלָ֑יו לָלֶ֣כֶת בְּכָל־דְּרָכָ֗יו וְלִשְׁמֹ֨ר מִצְוֺתָ֤יו וְחֻקָּיו֙
וּמִשְׁפָּטָ֔יו אֲשֶׁ֥ר צִוָּ֖ה אֶת־אֲבֹתֵֽינוּ׃ וְיִֽהְי֨וּ דְבָרַ֜י אֵ֗לֶּה אֲשֶׁ֤ר הִתְחַנַּ֨נְתִּי֙ לִפְנֵ֣י יְהֹוָ֔ה
קְרֹבִ֛ים אֶל־יְהֹוָ֥ה אֱלֹהֵ֖ינוּ יוֹמָ֣ם וָלָ֑יְלָה לַעֲשׂ֣וֹת ׀ מִשְׁפַּ֣ט עַבְדּ֗וֹ וּמִשְׁפַּ֛ט עַמּ֥וֹ
יִשְׂרָאֵ֖ל דְּבַר־י֥וֹם בְּיוֹמֽוֹ׃ לְמַ֗עַן דַּ֚עַת כָּל־עַמֵּ֣י הָאָ֔רֶץ כִּ֥י יְהֹוָ֖ה ה֣וּא הָאֱלֹהִ֑ים
אֵ֖ין עֽוֹד׃ וְהָיָ֤ה לְבַבְכֶם֙ שָׁלֵ֔ם עִ֖ם יְהֹוָ֣ה אֱלֹהֵ֑ינוּ לָלֶ֧כֶת בְּחֻקָּ֛יו וְלִשְׁמֹ֥ר מִצְוֺתָ֖יו
כַּיּ֥וֹם הַזֶּֽה׃ וְהַמֶּ֨לֶךְ וְכָל־יִשְׂרָאֵ֤ל עִמּוֹ֙ זֹבְחִ֣ים זֶ֔בַח לִפְנֵ֖י יְהֹוָֽה׃ וַיִּזְבַּ֣ח שְׁלֹמֹ֗ה

HAFTARA: THE CONCLUSION OF THE DEDICATION OF THE TEMPLE

The *haftara* for Shemini Atzeret describes the end of the ceremony of the
dedication of the Temple, conceived by David, and built under the direction
of Solomon his son. The celebration lasted for two weeks, the first of which
was the dedication itself, while the second took place on Sukkot. The sense
of closure must have been immense. Sukkot reminded the people of the years
when their ancestors wandered the desert without house or home. Now, some
480 years later (1 Kings 6:1), they had a land, a king, a capital city, Jerusalem,
and finally a Temple, the visible home of the Divine Presence in the midst of

twenty-two thousand heads of cattle and one hundred and twenty thousand sheep; and thus did the king and all the people of Israel dedicate the House of the Lord.

On that day, the king consecrated the center of the Courtyard before the House of the Lord, for there he prepared the burnt-offering, the meal-offering and fats of the peace-offerings; for the Brass Altar that stood before the Lord was too small to contain all the burnt-offerings and the meal-offerings and the fat of the peace-offerings. It was then that Solomon celebrated the Festival, and all of Israel his people with him, a vast congregation from all the land, from the border of Ḥamat to the river of Egypt, before the Lord our God for seven days and for seven days more, fourteen days all told. And then, on the eighth day, Solomon sent the people on their way, and they blessed the king, going back to their tents happy and buoyant of heart over all the goodness that the Lord had performed for His servant, David, and for His people, Israel.

And so it was, when Solomon had finished building the House of the Lord and the palace of the king, all of Solomon's heart's desire, all that he had wished to do.

Continue with the blessings after the Haftara on page 514.

TORAH READING FOR SIMḤAT TORAH

In Israel, if Simḥat Torah falls on Shabbat, the first three verses of the reading for the Ḥatan Torah (page 1162b), from "Your sanctuary" through "their high places," are read for Shishi.

This is the blessing with which Moses, the man of God, blessed the children of Israel before he died. Moses said: "The Lord came to them from Sinai; He shone out from Seir. He appeared over the crest of Paran, and came, among myriad angels, at His right hand a law of fire, for them. And He embraces the tribes, their holy ones all in His hands; they are drawn after Your steps, and carry Your words. Moses gave us a Law, a heritage to the people of Jacob. There is a King in Yeshurun, as the heads of the people are gathered, the tribes of Israel together. *Deut. 33:1–26*

"May Reuben live; let him not die, nor be left slight in number."

And this to Judah: he said, "Heed, Lord, the voice of Judah, and bring him home to his people. His arms alone need fight for him; You are his Support against his foes."

---

benediction. Following the precedent of Jacob on his death-bed (Gen. 49), Moses takes leave of the living by conferring on them his blessings.

אֶת זֶבַח הַשְּׁלָמִים אֲשֶׁר זָבַח לַיהוה בָּקָר עֶשְׂרִים וּשְׁנַיִם אֶלֶף וְצֹאן מֵאָה
וְעֶשְׂרִים אָלֶף וַיַּחְנְכוּ אֶת־בֵּית יהוה הַמֶּלֶךְ וְכׇל־בְּנֵי יִשְׂרָאֵל: בַּיּוֹם הַהוּא קִדַּשׁ
הַמֶּלֶךְ אֶת־תּוֹךְ הֶחָצֵר אֲשֶׁר לִפְנֵי בֵית־יהוה כִּי־עָשָׂה שָׁם אֶת־הָעֹלָה וְאֶת־
הַמִּנְחָה וְאֵת חֶלְבֵי הַשְּׁלָמִים כִּי־מִזְבַּח הַנְּחֹשֶׁת אֲשֶׁר לִפְנֵי יהוה קָטֹן מֵהָכִיל
אֶת־הָעֹלָה וְאֶת־הַמִּנְחָה וְאֵת חֶלְבֵי הַשְּׁלָמִים: וַיַּעַשׂ שְׁלֹמֹה בָעֵת־הַהִיא ׀
אֶת־הֶחָג וְכׇל־יִשְׂרָאֵל עִמּוֹ קָהָל גָּדוֹל מִלְּבוֹא חֲמָת ׀ עַד־נַחַל מִצְרַיִם לִפְנֵי
יהוה אֱלֹהֵינוּ שִׁבְעַת יָמִים וְשִׁבְעַת יָמִים אַרְבָּעָה עָשָׂר יוֹם: בַּיּוֹם הַשְּׁמִינִי
שִׁלַּח אֶת־הָעָם וַיְבָרְכוּ אֶת־הַמֶּלֶךְ וַיֵּלְכוּ לְאׇהֳלֵיהֶם שְׂמֵחִים וְטוֹבֵי לֵב עַל
כׇּל־הַטּוֹבָה אֲשֶׁר עָשָׂה יהוה לְדָוִד עַבְדּוֹ וּלְיִשְׂרָאֵל עַמּוֹ: וַיְהִי
כְּכַלּוֹת שְׁלֹמֹה לִבְנוֹת אֶת־בֵּית־יהוה וְאֶת־בֵּית הַמֶּלֶךְ וְאֵת כׇּל־חֵשֶׁק שְׁלֹמֹה
אֲשֶׁר חָפֵץ לַעֲשׂוֹת:

Continue with the blessings after the הפטרה *on page 515.*

קריאה לשמחת תורה

In ארץ ישראל*, if* שמחת תורה *falls on* שבת*, the first three verses of the* קריאה לחתן תורה *(page 1163ב) from* מְעֹנָה אֱלֹהֵי קֶדֶם *through* עַל־בָּמוֹתֵימוֹ תִדְרֹךְ *are read for* שישי*.*

דברים לג:א–כו וְזֹאת הַבְּרָכָה אֲשֶׁר בֵּרַךְ מֹשֶׁה אִישׁ הָאֱלֹהִים אֶת־בְּנֵי יִשְׂרָאֵל לִפְנֵי מוֹתוֹ:
וַיֹּאמַר יהוה מִסִּינַי בָּא וְזָרַח מִשֵּׂעִיר לָמוֹ הוֹפִיעַ מֵהַר פָּארָן וְאָתָה מֵרִבְבֹת
קֹדֶשׁ מִימִינוֹ אשדת לָמוֹ: אַף חֹבֵב עַמִּים כׇּל־קְדֹשָׁיו בְּיָדֶךָ וְהֵם תֻּכּוּ לְרַגְלֶךָ אֵשׁ דָּת
יִשָּׂא מִדַּבְּרֹתֶיךָ: תּוֹרָה צִוָּה־לָנוּ מֹשֶׁה מוֹרָשָׁה קְהִלַּת יַעֲקֹב: וַיְהִי בִישֻׁרוּן
מֶלֶךְ בְּהִתְאַסֵּף רָאשֵׁי עָם יַחַד שִׁבְטֵי יִשְׂרָאֵל: יְחִי רְאוּבֵן וְאַל־יָמֹת וִיהִי מְתָיו
מִסְפָּר: וְזֹאת לִיהוּדָה וַיֹּאמַר שְׁמַע יהוה קוֹל יְהוּדָה וְאֶל־עַמּוֹ
תְּבִיאֶנּוּ יָדָיו רָב לוֹ וְעֵזֶר מִצָּרָיו תִּהְיֶה:

---

recalling its history, emphasizing the decisive role of God in the shape and outcome of events, His faithfulness to the covenant, and the way in which all His promises to the patriarchs and to Moses have come true. This is history through the eyes of faith, and it represents a profound moralization of politics.

וְזֹאת הַבְּרָכָה *This is the blessing.* In one of the most intense convergences in Jewish time, this Torah reading brings together the last day in the life of Israel's greatest leader, the completion of the Torah, the last day of the "season of our joy," and the culmination of the long sequence of the holy days of the seventh month that began on Rosh HaShana. Appropriately, it consists of words of

To Levi he said, "Your Tumim and Urim are with Your devoted, the one You tested at Masa, and wrestled at Meriva; who said, of his father and mother: I have seen them not; who did not recognize his brothers, nor know his own sons, for he kept Your words, and guarded close Your covenant. They will teach Your laws to Jacob, and Your Torah to Israel. They will place before You the scent of incense, and offerings burnt on Your Altar. LORD, bless his strength, and receive the work of his hands. Those who rise against him – crush their bearing; all his enemies, until they rise no more." LEVI

To Benjamin he said, "Beloved of the LORD, he shall rest on Him in safety; and all through the day He shelters him, and rests between his shoulders."

To Joseph he said, "His land is blessed of the LORD, with the fruit of the skies, of rain, and of the deeps that bide below, and of the fruit of the sun's harvest, all the fruits of the moon's yield, of the heights of primeval mountains, of the fruit of the ancient hills, and the fruit of the world and its fullness – and the favor of that Presence at the Bush. May this come to the head of Joseph, to the crown of one raised above his brothers. His glory is that of a firstborn bull, his horns the grand horns of the oryx. With these he can gore nations; the ends of the earth together – yes, these are the myriads of Ephraim, the thousands of Manasseh." SHELISHI

And to Zebulun he said, "Find happiness, Zebulun, in your journeys, and Issachar in your tents. Tribes shall be called to the mountain, to bring righteous offerings there. For they will draw of the plenty of oceans, and of the hidden, buried riches of the sands." To Gad he said, "Blessed be the One who broadens Gad's borders; for he crouches like a lioness, to tear arm and head from his prey. He chose the first place for his own, for the grave of a law-giver hides there. He came with the heads of the people; he performed the LORD's righteousness, and dealt uprightly with Israel." REVI'I

And to Dan he said, "Dan is a lion cub, leaping from Bashan." And to Naftali he said, "Naftali is sated with favor; filled with the LORD's blessing: go and form your inheritance seaward and south." To Asher he said, "Most blessed of sons is Asher – may he be beloved of his brothers; may his feet be steeped in oil. Your doors are locked with iron and bronze, and your strength is as long as your days. "There is none like God, Yeshurun, riding the skies to help you, the heavens in His grandeur." HAMISHI*

* THE CHILDREN'S ALIYA

In many congregations, the children participate in the last aliya before calling up the Hatan Torah. All the children gather on the Bima, a tallit is spread over them and they say the blessings aloud together with the Oleh. After the blessing which follows the Reading, the whole congregation sing together:

הַמַּלְאָךְ May the angel who rescued me from all harm, bless these boys. May they be called by my name and the names of my fathers Abraham and Isaac, and may they increase greatly on the earth. *Gen. 48*

Some add:

יְבָרֶכְךָ May the LORD bless you and protect you. May the LORD make His face shine on you and be gracious to you. May the LORD turn His face toward you and grant you peace. *Num. 6*

לוי

וּלְלֵוִ֣י אָמַ֗ר תֻּמֶּ֤יךָ וְאוּרֶ֨יךָ֙ לְאִ֣ישׁ חֲסִידֶ֔ךָ אֲשֶׁ֤ר נִסִּיתוֹ֙ בְּמַסָּ֔ה תְּרִיבֵ֖הוּ עַל־מֵ֥י מְרִיבָֽה: הָאֹמֵ֞ר לְאָבִ֤יו וּלְאִמּוֹ֙ לֹ֣א רְאִיתִ֔יו וְאֶת־אֶחָיו֙ לֹ֣א הִכִּ֔יר וְאֶת־בָּנָ֖ו לֹ֣א יָדָ֑ע כִּ֤י שָֽׁמְרוּ֙ אִמְרָתֶ֔ךָ וּבְרִֽיתְךָ֖ יִנְצֹֽרוּ: יוֹר֤וּ מִשְׁפָּטֶ֨יךָ֙ לְיַעֲקֹ֔ב וְתוֹרָֽתְךָ֖ לְיִשְׂרָאֵ֑ל יָשִׂ֤ימוּ קְטוֹרָה֙ בְּאַפֶּ֔ךָ וְכָלִ֖יל עַֽל־מִזְבְּחֶֽךָ: בָּרֵ֤ךְ יהו֙ה חֵיל֔וֹ וּפֹ֥עַל יָדָ֖יו תִּרְצֶ֑ה מְחַ֨ץ מָתְנַ֧יִם קָמָ֛יו וּמְשַׂנְאָ֖יו מִן־יְקוּמֽוּן:

לבנימן

לְבִנְיָמִ֣ן אָמַ֔ר יְדִ֣יד יהו֔ה יִשְׁכֹּ֥ן לָבֶ֖טַח עָלָ֑יו חֹפֵ֤ף עָלָיו֙ כָּל־הַיּ֔וֹם וּבֵ֥ין כְּתֵפָ֖יו שָׁכֵֽן:

שלישי

*וּלְיוֹסֵ֣ף אָמַ֔ר מְבֹרֶ֥כֶת יהו֖ה אַרְצ֑וֹ מִמֶּ֤גֶד שָׁמַ֨יִם֙ מִטָּ֔ל וּמִתְּה֖וֹם רֹבֶ֥צֶת תָּֽחַת: וּמִמֶּ֤גֶד תְּבוּאֹ֣ת שָׁ֔מֶשׁ וּמִמֶּ֖גֶד גֶּ֥רֶשׁ יְרָחִֽים: וּמֵרֹ֖אשׁ הַרְרֵי־קֶ֑דֶם וּמִמֶּ֖גֶד גִּבְע֥וֹת עוֹלָֽם: וּמִמֶּ֗גֶד אֶ֚רֶץ וּמְלֹאָ֔הּ וּרְצ֥וֹן שֹׁכְנִ֖י סְנֶ֑ה תָּב֨וֹאתָה֙ לְרֹ֣אשׁ יוֹסֵ֔ף וּלְקָדְקֹ֖ד נְזִ֥יר אֶחָֽיו: בְּכ֨וֹר שׁוֹר֜וֹ הָדָ֣ר ל֗וֹ וְקַרְנֵ֤י רְאֵם֙ קַרְנָ֔יו בָּהֶ֗ם עַמִּ֛ים יְנַגַּ֥ח יַחְדָּ֖ו אַפְסֵי־אָ֑רֶץ וְהֵם֙ רִבְב֣וֹת אֶפְרַ֔יִם וְהֵ֖ם אַלְפֵ֥י מְנַשֶּֽׁה:

רביעי

*וְלִזְבוּלֻ֣ן אָמַ֔ר שְׂמַ֥ח זְבוּלֻ֖ן בְּצֵאתֶ֑ךָ וְיִשָּׂשכָ֖ר בְּאֹהָלֶֽיךָ: עַמִּים֙ הַר־יִקְרָ֔אוּ שָׁ֖ם יִזְבְּח֣וּ זִבְחֵי־צֶ֑דֶק כִּ֣י שֶׁ֤פַע יַמִּים֙ יִינָ֔קוּ וּשְׂפוּנֵ֖י טְמ֥וּנֵי חֽוֹל:

וּלְגָ֣ד אָמַ֔ר בָּר֖וּךְ מַרְחִ֣יב גָּ֑ד כְּלָבִ֣יא שָׁכֵ֔ן וְטָרַ֥ף זְר֖וֹעַ אַף־קָדְקֹֽד: וַיַּ֤רְא רֵאשִׁית֙ ל֔וֹ כִּי־שָׁ֛ם חֶלְקַ֥ת מְחֹקֵ֖ק סָפ֑וּן וַיֵּתֵא֙ רָ֣אשֵׁי עָ֔ם צִדְקַ֤ת יהו֙ה עָשָׂ֔ה וּמִשְׁפָּטָ֖יו עִם־יִשְׂרָאֵֽל:

חמישי *

*וּלְדָ֣ן אָמַ֔ר דָּ֖ן גּ֣וּר אַרְיֵ֑ה יְזַנֵּ֖ק מִן־הַבָּשָֽׁן: וּלְנַפְתָּלִ֣י אָמַ֔ר נַפְתָּלִי֙ שְׂבַ֣ע רָצ֔וֹן וּמָלֵ֖א בִּרְכַּ֣ת יהו֑ה יָ֥ם וְדָר֖וֹם יְרָֽשָׁה: וּלְאָשֵׁ֣ר אָמַ֔ר בָּר֥וּךְ מִבָּנִ֖ים אָשֵׁ֑ר יְהִ֤י רְצוּי֙ אֶחָ֔יו וְטֹבֵ֥ל בַּשֶּׁ֖מֶן רַגְלֽוֹ: בַּרְזֶ֣ל וּנְחֹ֖שֶׁת מִנְעָלֶ֑ךָ וּכְיָמֶ֖יךָ דָּבְאֶֽךָ: אֵ֥ין כָּאֵ֖ל יְשֻׁר֑וּן רֹכֵ֤ב שָׁמַ֨יִם֙ בְּעֶזְרֶ֔ךָ וּבְגַאֲוָת֖וֹ שְׁחָקִֽים:

עֲלִיַּת כָּל הַנְּעָרִים *

*In many congregations, the children participate in the last עליה before calling up the חתן תורה. All the children gather on the בימה, a טלית is spread over them and they say the blessings aloud together with the עולה. After the blessing which follows the Reading, the whole congregation sing together:

בראשית מח

הַמַּלְאָ֞ךְ הַגֹּאֵ֣ל אֹתִי֮ מִכָּל־רָע֒ יְבָרֵךְ֮ אֶת־הַנְּעָרִים֒ וְיִקָּרֵ֤א בָהֶם֙ שְׁמִ֔י וְשֵׁ֖ם אֲבֹתַ֣י אַבְרָהָ֣ם וְיִצְחָ֑ק וְיִדְגּ֥וּ לָרֹ֖ב בְּקֶ֥רֶב הָאָֽרֶץ:

Some add:

במדברו

יְבָרֶכְךָ֥ יהו֖ה וְיִשְׁמְרֶֽךָ: יָאֵ֨ר יהו֧ה פָּנָ֛יו אֵלֶ֖יךָ וִֽיחֻנֶּֽךָּ: יִשָּׂ֨א יהו֤ה פָּנָיו֙ אֵלֶ֔יךָ וְיָשֵׂ֥ם לְךָ֖ שָׁלֽוֹם:

RESHUT FOR THE ḤATAN TORAH

The following is said by the Gabbai to call up the Ḥatan Torah to his aliya:

By leave of great, mighty and awesome God; by leave of [the Torah] who is more precious than fine gold and pearls; by leave of the holy and chosen Sanhedrin, the leaders in Torah and heads of the academies, and the elders and young men seated in their rows: I shall open my mouth in poetry and song, in thanks and praise to the One encircled in light, who gives us life, sustains us, in pure awe, who brings us to rejoice at this Simḥat Torah that delights the heart and lights up the eyes, gives life and richness, dignity and splendor, brings happiness to those who walk the straight path of goodness, lengthens life, heightens strength of those who love and keep her with care, attentively, those busy with her, who guard her in love and awe. And so, from the Mighty One, it should be His will that grace, kindness and life, crown and diadem, be given to (*name* son of *father's name*), the one chosen to complete the Torah. Strengthen him, bless him, nurture him in the learning of Torah, make him sought after, praised, included in the company of learners, make him worthy, vital, honor him in the splendor of light, make him strong, crown him, teach him Torah and its way of thinking, protect him, elevate him, support him with direct assistance, give him sustenance, make him refined and righteous among Your created people, bring him close, show him mercy, guard him from pain and precipice, give him fortitude, sustain him, make him whole in broken spirit. Stand, stand, stand (*name* son of *father's name*), groom to the Torah, give honor to great, awesome God; for this you shall merit from the awesome God to see your children and grandchildren busy themselves in Torah and fulfill the commandments amongst this beautiful, pure people; and you shall be worthy of rejoicing in the joy of the Temple, the Chosen House, and your face should light up in righteousness like [the Presence of God through] shining glass, as Isaiah, filled with the spirit of wisdom and strength, prophesied: Rejoice with Jerusalem, be happy with her, soon, rejoice with her in joyfulness, all you who grieved in pain and mourning. Stand, stand, stand (*name* son of *father's name*), groom to the Torah; by leave of this holy congregation, complete the Torah. Arise (*name* son of *father's name*), Ḥatan HaTorah.

---

legally constituted) authority under which the act is taking place. Permission would be asked, first of God, then of the Torah, then of the local religious authorities, then of the congregation. This gave the act, in this case, the blessing, its gravitas as an official honor, one of the highest the community could bestow.

רשות לחתן תורה

The following is said by the גבאי *to call up the* חתן תורה *to his* עליה:

מֵרְשׁוּת הָאֵל הַגָּדוֹל הַגִּבּוֹר וְהַנּוֹרָא, וּמֵרְשׁוּת מִפָּז וּמִפְּנִינִים יְקָרָה, וּמֵרְשׁוּת סַנְהֶדְרִין הַקְּדוֹשָׁה וְהַבְּחוּרָה, וּמֵרְשׁוּת רָאשֵׁי יְשִׁיבוֹת וְאַלּוּפֵי תוֹרָה, וּמֵרְשׁוּת זְקֵנִים וּנְעָרִים יוֹשְׁבֵי שׁוּרָה, אֶפְתַּח פִּי בְּשִׁיר וּבְזִמְרָה, לְהוֹדוֹת לְהַלֵּל לְדָר בִּנְהוֹרָא, שֶׁהֶחֱיָנוּ וְקִיְּמָנוּ בְּיִרְאָתוֹ הַטְּהוֹרָה, וְהִגִּיעָנוּ לִשְׂמֹחַ בְּשִׂמְחַת הַתּוֹרָה, הַמְשַׂמַּחַת לֵב וְעֵינַיִם מְאִירָה, הַנּוֹתֶנֶת חַיִּים וְעֹשֶׁר וְכָבוֹד וְתִפְאָרָה, הַמְאַשֶּׁרֶת הוֹלְכִים בְּדֶרֶךְ הַטּוֹבָה וְהַיְשָׁרָה, הַמַּאֲרֶכֶת יָמִים וּמוֹסֶפֶת גְּבוּרָה, לְאוֹהֲבֶיהָ וּלְשׁוֹמְרֶיהָ בְּצִוּוּי וְאַזְהָרָה, לְעוֹסְקֶיהָ וּלְנוֹצְרֶיהָ בְּאַהַב וּבְמוֹרָא. וּבְכֵן יְהִי רָצוֹן מִלִּפְנֵי הַגְּבוּרָה, לָתֵת חֵן וָחֶסֶד וְחַיִּים וָנֵזֶר וַעֲטָרָה, לְרַבִּי (פלוני ב״ר פלוני) הַנִּבְחָר לְהַשְׁלִים הַתּוֹרָה, לְאַמְּצוֹ לְבָרְכוֹ לְגַדְּלוֹ בְּתַלְמוּד תּוֹרָה, לְדָרְשׁוֹ לְהַדְּרוֹ לְוַעֲדוֹ בַּחֲבוּרָה, לְזַכּוֹתוֹ לְחַיּוֹתוֹ לְטַכְּסוֹ בְּטֶכֶס אוֹרָה, לְיַשְּׁרוֹ לְכַלְּלוֹ לְלַמְּדוֹ לֶקַח וּסְבָרָה, לְמַלְּטוֹ לְנַשְּׂאוֹ לְסַעֲדוֹ בְּסַעַד בְּרוּרָה, לְעַדְּנוֹ לְפַרְנְסוֹ לְצַדְּקוֹ בְּעַם נִבְרָא, לְקָרְבוֹ לְרַחֲמוֹ לְשָׁמְרוֹ מִכָּל צוּקָה וְצָרָה, לְתַקְּפוֹ לְתָמְכוֹ לְתוֹמְמוֹ בְּרוּחַ נִשְׁבָּרָה. עֲמֹד עֲמֹד רַבִּי (פלוני ב״ר פלוני) חֲתַן הַתּוֹרָה, וְתֵן כָּבוֹד לְאֵל גָּדוֹל וְנוֹרָא, וּבִשְׂכַר זֶה תִּזְכֶּה מֵאֵל נוֹרָא, לִרְאוֹת בָּנִים וּבְנֵי בָנִים עוֹסְקִים בַּתּוֹרָה, וּמְקַיְּמֵי מִצְוֹת בְּתוֹךְ עַם יָפָה וּבָרָה, וְתִזְכֶּה לִשְׂמֹחַ בְּשִׂמְחַת בֵּית הַבְּחִירָה, וּפָנֶיךָ לְהָאִיר בִּצְדָקָה כְּאַסְפַּקְלַרְיָא הַמְּאִירָה, כִּנְבָא יְשַׁעְיָהוּ מָלֵא רוּחַ עֵצָה וּגְבוּרָה, שִׂמְחוּ אֶת יְרוּשָׁלַיִם וְגִילוּ בָהּ מְהֵרָה, שִׂישׂוּ אִתָּהּ מָשׂוֹשׂ כָּל הַמִּתְאַבְּלִים בַּאֲבֵלָה וְצָרָה, עֲמֹד עֲמֹד רַבִּי (פלוני ב״ר פלוני) חֲתַן הַתּוֹרָה, מֵרְשׁוּת כָּל הַקָּהָל הַקָּדוֹשׁ הַזֶּה וְהַשְׁלֵם הַתּוֹרָה. יַעֲמֹד רַבִּי (פלוני ב״ר פלוני) חֲתַן הַתּוֹרָה.

RESHUT FOR THE ḤATAN TORAH

The custom of calling up the *Ḥatan Torah* with an elaborate invocation is first found in the *Maḥzor Vitry*, written by a student of Rashi in eleventh century France. In those days it was the custom to call bridegrooms to the Torah with a similar invocation, on the Shabbat after their wedding. Prefacing a religious act – as we do, for example, in the Grace after Meals if three men are present – with a request for *reshut*, permission, is a formal acknowledgment of the (often

READING FOR THE ḤATAN TORAH

Deut. 33:27–34:12 (On Shabbat: SHISHI)

Your sanctuary the God of time immemorial, you rest in eternal arms. And He dispels every foe before you, saying: "Destroy." And Israel will rest in safety, untouched, the fountain of Jacob; in a land of grain and wine, its skies dripping with dew. Happy are you, Israel; who is like you, a people surviving through the LORD? He is the shield of your strength; the sword of your grandeur – your enemies may deny you, but you shall traverse their high places."

(On Shabbat: Ḥatan Torah)

And Moses ascended from the Moab plains to Mount Nevo, to the very summit, looking out towards Jericho. And the LORD showed him all of the land, across Gilead to Dan; all of Naftali, and the lands of Ephraim and Manasseh, and all the domain of Judah to the far ocean, the Negev and the plain, the valley of Jericho, city of palms, and as far as Tzo'ar. And the LORD said to him, "This is the land I promised to Abraham, to Isaac and to Jacob, saying, 'I shall give this to your children.' Now I have let your eyes see it – but you shall not cross over there."

And there, in the land of Moab, Moses, the servant of the LORD, died at the word of the LORD. He buried him there in the valley, in the land of Moab, opposite Beit Peor, and no man knows his burial place to this day. Moses was a hundred and twenty years old when he died; his sight had never dimmed, nor his strength evaded him. And the children of Israel wept for Moses thirty days, there in the plains of Moab. Then the days of weeping ended, the days of mourning for Moses. And Joshua son of Nun was filled with a spirit of wisdom, Moses having pressed his hands upon him; and the children of Israel heeded him, and did as the LORD had commanded Moses.

No other prophet like Moses has ever risen up in Israel; one whom the LORD knew face to face. None was like him, with the signs and wonders the LORD sent him to perform in the land of Egypt; before Pharaoh and all his servants and all of his land. None like him with all the mighty power and all the great awe that he brought down, before the eyes of all Israel.

Be strong, be strong, and let us strengthen one another.

---

will not himself enter it: he will merely see it from afar. Thus he became the symbol both of the possibilities of a human life and of its limits. "It is not for you to complete the task," said Rabbi Tarfon, "but neither are you free to stand aside from it" (*Avot* 2:21). For each of us there is a Jordan we will not

קריאה לחתן תורה

דברים לג:כו–לד:יב

מְעֹנָה֙ אֱלֹ֣הֵי קֶ֔דֶם וּמִתַּ֖חַת זְרֹעֹ֣ת עוֹלָ֑ם וַיְגָ֧רֶשׁ מִפָּנֶ֛יךָ אוֹיֵ֖ב וַיֹּ֥אמֶר הַשְׁמֵֽד׃
וַיִּשְׁכֹּן֩ יִשְׂרָאֵ֨ל בֶּ֤טַח בָּדָד֙ עֵ֣ין יַעֲקֹ֔ב אֶל־אֶ֖רֶץ דָּגָ֣ן וְתִיר֑וֹשׁ אַף־שָׁמָ֖יו יַ֥עַרְפוּ־
טָֽל׃ אַשְׁרֶ֨יךָ יִשְׂרָאֵ֜ל מִ֣י כָמ֗וֹךָ עַ֚ם נוֹשַׁ֣ע בַּֽיהוָ֔ה מָגֵ֣ן עֶזְרֶ֔ךָ וַאֲשֶׁר־חֶ֖רֶב גַּאֲוָתֶ֑ךָ
וְיִכָּחֲשׁ֤וּ אֹיְבֶ֙יךָ֙ לָ֔ךְ וְאַתָּ֖ה עַל־בָּמוֹתֵ֥ימוֹ תִדְרֹֽךְ׃ (On Shabbat: חתן תורה) וַיַּ֨עַל מֹשֶׁ֜ה מֵעַרְבֹ֤ת
מוֹאָב֙ אֶל־הַ֣ר נְב֔וֹ רֹ֚אשׁ הַפִּסְגָּ֔ה אֲשֶׁ֖ר עַל־פְּנֵ֣י יְרֵח֑וֹ וַיַּרְאֵ֨הוּ יְהוָ֧ה אֶת־כָּל־
הָאָ֛רֶץ אֶת־הַגִּלְעָ֖ד עַד־דָּֽן׃ וְאֵת֙ כָּל־נַפְתָּלִ֔י וְאֶת־אֶ֥רֶץ אֶפְרַ֖יִם וּמְנַשֶּׁ֑ה וְאֵת֙
כָּל־אֶ֣רֶץ יְהוּדָ֔ה עַ֖ד הַיָּ֥ם הָאַחֲרֽוֹן׃ וְאֶת־הַנֶּ֗גֶב וְאֶת־הַכִּכָּ֞ר בִּקְעַ֧ת יְרֵח֛וֹ עִ֥יר
הַתְּמָרִ֖ים עַד־צֹֽעַר׃ וַיֹּ֨אמֶר יְהוָ֜ה אֵלָ֗יו זֹ֤את הָאָ֙רֶץ֙ אֲשֶׁ֨ר נִשְׁבַּ֜עְתִּי לְאַבְרָהָ֨ם
לְיִצְחָ֤ק וּֽלְיַעֲקֹב֙ לֵאמֹ֔ר לְזַרְעֲךָ֖ אֶתְּנֶ֑נָּה הֶרְאִיתִ֣יךָ בְעֵינֶ֔יךָ וְשָׁ֖מָּה לֹ֥א תַעֲבֹֽר׃
וַיָּ֨מָת שָׁ֜ם מֹשֶׁ֧ה עֶֽבֶד־יְהוָ֛ה בְּאֶ֥רֶץ מוֹאָ֖ב עַל־פִּ֥י יְהוָֽה׃ וַיִּקְבֹּ֨ר אֹת֤וֹ בַגַּיְ֙ בְּאֶ֣רֶץ
מוֹאָ֔ב מ֖וּל בֵּ֣ית פְּע֑וֹר וְלֹא־יָדַ֥ע אִישׁ֙ אֶת־קְבֻ֣רָת֔וֹ עַ֖ד הַיּ֥וֹם הַזֶּֽה׃ וּמֹשֶׁ֗ה בֶּן־
מֵאָ֧ה וְעֶשְׂרִ֛ים שָׁנָ֖ה בְּמֹת֑וֹ לֹא־כָהֲתָ֥ה עֵינ֖וֹ וְלֹא־נָ֥ס לֵחֹֽה׃ וַיִּבְכּוּ֩ בְנֵ֨י יִשְׂרָאֵ֧ל
אֶת־מֹשֶׁ֛ה בְּעַרְבֹ֥ת מוֹאָ֖ב שְׁלֹשִׁ֣ים י֑וֹם וַיִּתְּמ֕וּ יְמֵ֥י בְכִ֖י אֵ֥בֶל מֹשֶֽׁה׃ וִיהוֹשֻׁ֣עַ
בִּן־נ֗וּן מָלֵא֙ ר֣וּחַ חָכְמָ֔ה כִּֽי־סָמַ֥ךְ מֹשֶׁ֛ה אֶת־יָדָ֖יו עָלָ֑יו וַיִּשְׁמְע֨וּ אֵלָ֤יו בְּנֵֽי־
יִשְׂרָאֵל֙ וַֽיַּעֲשׂ֔וּ כַּאֲשֶׁ֛ר צִוָּ֥ה יְהוָ֖ה אֶת־מֹשֶֽׁה׃ וְלֹֽא־קָ֨ם נָבִ֥יא ע֛וֹד בְּיִשְׂרָאֵ֖ל
כְּמֹשֶׁ֑ה אֲשֶׁר֙ יְדָע֣וֹ יְהוָ֔ה פָּנִ֖ים אֶל־פָּנִֽים׃ לְכָל־הָ֨אֹתֹ֜ת וְהַמּוֹפְתִ֗ים אֲשֶׁ֤ר שְׁלָחוֹ֙
יְהוָ֔ה לַעֲשׂ֖וֹת בְּאֶ֣רֶץ מִצְרָ֑יִם לְפַרְעֹ֥ה וּלְכָל־עֲבָדָ֖יו וּלְכָל־אַרְצֽוֹ׃ וּלְכֹל֙ הַיָּ֣ד
הַחֲזָקָ֔ה וּלְכֹ֖ל הַמּוֹרָ֣א הַגָּד֑וֹל אֲשֶׁר֙ עָשָׂ֣ה מֹשֶׁ֔ה לְעֵינֵ֖י כָּל־יִשְׂרָאֵֽל׃

חֲזַק חֲזַק וְנִתְחַזֵּק

אַשְׁרֶיךָ יִשְׂרָאֵל *Happy are you, Israel.* Moses' last words to the people he had led from slavery to freedom, through the wilderness, to the brink of the Promised Land. His message is moving and clear: If the people stay faithful to God, they will be safe from their enemies, and need have no fear. The real challenge will not be military but spiritual. So it was, so it is, so it will always be: Israel is summoned to be a small nation, made great not by its own power, but by *its fidelity* to a Power greater than itself, larger than humankind, beyond the hazards of history and the winds of time.

THE DEATH OF MOSES

One of the most poignant moments in religious history. Moses, who had spent forty years leading the Israelites to the Promised Land, is told that he

RESHUT FOR THE ḤATAN BERESHIT

The following is said by the Gabbai to call up the Ḥatan Bereshit to his aliya:

By leave of the One higher than all poetry and blessing, awesome above all praise and song, wise-hearted, powerful, mighty, Ruler of the world, Master of every creation; and by leave of [the Torah], this King's daughter whose glory lies concealed, within her, created first and hidden away, for two thousand years, pure, perfect, who restores the soul, returns it; and with permission from Yeshurun – she is their legacy, given to be kept and nurtured, and the great leaders of Jacob – who learn to open her, to complete her, the crowning splendor of the prince of the Beit Din whose authority is great, the rabbinical judges, who turn back conflict from her gate, the academy heads, leaders of this dispersed exile. And by leave of this righteous company, this joyous congregation, elders and youths of each rank, together, gathered, today, here, for Simḥat Torah, collected to finish, and to begin again, with happiness and awe, the one as beloved as on the day she was given in all her glory: they delight in her, not as though old and past, but as new, thirsty to drink in and enjoy her precious brilliance for she makes the heart joyous, effaces sadness, her comfort delights the soul of those who take pride in her, who delve into the written and the spoken, the Mishna and the Gemara, who run to bring their little ones to the house of prayer, and go out, do everything to keep her with care – so, great is their reward from the Mighty One, everlasting joy is upon their heads, they long to see the Temple, the chosen house. And so I have been appointed by the choice of us all to elevate one man, from all the people among this company; I found in him a wise heart for elucidating the Torah, He seeks justice and kindness with integrity, his heart has inspired him, awakening his spirit to giving – he should be the first, foremost, to begin the Torah. And now, arise (*name* son of *father's name*), stand, take courage, come, present yourself, stand to my right and read out the Beginning – created by the Rock for His glory for which reason we immediately follow completion by beginning again so the accusing angel will not be able to tell lies of this people. Since you are the first to do this perfect commandment – how great will be the goodness, how abundant your reward: you who are so generous, may you have no constraint upon your giving; from the blessing of your Creator, give, do not curb your hand, for the one who honors the Torah with majesty should be honored with healthy contentment. So, quickly: stand, stand, stand (*name* son of *father's name*), groom to "In the beginning," with permission from this holy congregation, and bless awesome, mighty God – quickly, all will answer after you: Amen. Arise (*name* son of *father's name*), Ḥatan Bereshit.

רשות לחתן בראשית

The following is said by the גבאי *to call up the* חתן בראשית *to his* עליה*:*

מֵרְשׁוּת מְרוֹמָם עַל כָּל בְּרָכָה וְשִׁירָה, נוֹרָא עַל כָּל תְּהִלָּה וְזִמְרָה, חֲכַם לֵבָב וְאַמִּיץ כֹּחַ וּגְבוּרָה, מוֹשֵׁל עוֹלָם אֲדוֹן כָּל יְצִירָה, וּמֵרְשׁוּת כְּבוּדָּה בַּת מֶלֶךְ פְּנִימָה וַעֲצוּרָה, רֵאשִׁית קִנְיָנָהּ אַלְפַּיִם אֲצוּרָה, בָּרָה תְּמִימָה מְשִׁיבַת נֶפֶשׁ וּמַחֲזִירָה, יְשֻׁרוּן נִתְּנָה מוֹרָשָׁה לְעָבְדָהּ וּלְשָׁמְרָהּ, מְלַמְּדֶיהָ גְּאוֹנֵי יַעֲקֹב לְפָתְחָהּ וּלְסָגְרָהּ, כְּלִיל הוֹד נְשִׂיא מַרְבֵּה הַמִּשְׂרָה, יוֹשְׁבֵי מִדִּין מְשִׁיבֵי מִלְחָמָה שַׁעְרָה, רָאשֵׁי יְשִׁיבוֹת רָאשֵׁי גוֹלָה פְּזוּרָה, וּמֵרְשׁוּת חֲבוּרַת צֶדֶק עֵדָה זוּ הַמְאֻשָּׁרָה, זְקֵנִים וּנְעָרִים יַחַד בְּכָל שׁוּרָה, קְבוּצִים פֹּה הַיּוֹם לְשִׂמְחַת תּוֹרָה, וְנֶעֱצָרִים לְסַיֵּם וּלְהָחֵל בְּגִיל וּבְמוֹרָא, אוֹתָהּ מְחַבְּבִים כְּיוֹם נְתִינָתָהּ בַּהֲדָרָה, מְסַלְסְלִים בָּהּ כַּחֲדָשָׁה וְלֹא כִּישָׁנָה שֶׁעָבְרָה, צְמֵאִים לָמֹץ וּלְהִתְעַנֵּג מִזִּיו יְקָרָהּ, בְּיַעַן מְשַׂמַּחַת לֵב וְעֶצֶב מְסִירָה, תַּנְחוּמֶיהָ יְשַׁעַשְׁעוּ נַפְשָׁם בָּהּ לְהִתְפָּאֲרָה, וְהוֹגִים בְּמִקְרָא וְהַגָּדָה בְּמִשְׁנָה וּגְמָרָא, רָצִים וּמְבִיאִים טַף לְבֵית הָעֲתִירָה, הוֹלְכִים וְעוֹשִׂים לְהַזְהִירָה, לָכֵן גָּדוֹל שְׂכָרָם מֵאֵת הַגְּבוּרָה, עַל רֹאשָׁם שִׂמְחַת עוֹלָם קְשׁוּרָה, דָּאִים לִרְאוֹת בְּבֵית הַבְּחִירָה, וּבְכֵן נִסְמַכְתִּי דַּעַת כֻּלָּם לְבָרְרָה, בָּחוּר הֲרִימוֹתִי מֵעַם תּוֹךְ הַחֲבוּרָה, מְצָאתִיו לֵב נָבוֹן לְהַסְבִּירָה, צֶדֶק וָחֶסֶד רוֹדֵף בְּאֹרַח יְשָׁרָה, וּנְשָׂאוֹ לִבּוֹ וְנָדְבָה רוּחוֹ לְהִתְעוֹרְרָה, תְּחִלָּה וְרִאשׁוֹן הֱיוֹת לְהַתְחִיל הַתּוֹרָה. וְעַתָּה קוּם רַבִּי (פלוני ב״ר פלוני) עֲמֹד לְהִתְאַזְּרָה, בֹּא וְהִתְיַצֵּב וַעֲמֹד לִימִינִי וּקְרָא, מַעֲשֵׂה בְרֵאשִׁית לִכְבוֹדוֹ צוּר בָּרָא, עַל זֹאת מַתְכִּיפִין הַתְחָלָה לְהַשְׁלָמָה בִּתְדִירָה, שָׂטָן שֶׁלֹּא יְרַגֵּל בְּעַם זוּ לְשַׁקְּרָה, יַעַן נַעֲשֵׂית רִאשׁוֹן לְמִצְוָה גְּמוּרָה, מַה רַב טוּבְךָ וּמַשְׂכֻּרְתְּךָ יְתֵרָה, טוֹב עַיִן תְּבֹרַךְ בְּנִדְבָתְךָ מִלְּעָצְרָה, וּמְבָרְכַת בּוֹרַאֲךָ תְּדוּר יָדְךָ מִלְּקַצְּרָה, בַּעֲבוּר שֶׁכָּל הַמְכַבֵּד תּוֹרָה בִּצְפִירָה, יְהֵא גוּפוֹ מְכֻבָּד לְהִתְאַשְּׁרָה. מַהֵר עֲמֹד עֲמֹד עֲמֹד רַבִּי (פלוני ב״ר פלוני) חֲתַן בְּרֵאשִׁית בָּרָא, מֵרְשׁוּת הַקָּהָל הַקָּדוֹשׁ הַזֶּה וּבָרֵךְ אֵל גָּדוֹל וְנוֹרָא, אָמֵן יַעֲנוּ אַחֲרֶיךָ הַכֹּל מְהֵרָה. יַעֲמֹד רַבִּי (פלוני ב״ר פלוני) חֲתַן בְּרֵאשִׁית.

---

cross, a destination we will not reach, a fulfillment we will not see. Hence the importance, in Judaism, of handing the tradition on across the generations – through our children, as in the case of Aaron, or our disciples, as in the case of Moses.

READING FOR THE ḤATAN BERESHIT

It is customary for the congregation to say aloud the passages marked by arrows, followed by the Reader.

Bereshit 1:1–2:3

In the beginning, God created heaven and earth. And the earth was desolate emptiness, and darkness over the deep; but the spirit of God moved over the waters. And God said: "Let there be light." Light came to be. And He saw that the light was good, and divided light from darkness. God named the light, "Day;" and the darkness He named, "Night." ▸ There was evening; then there was morning: one day. ◂

God said: "Let there be a clear dome amid the waters, dividing water from water." And He shaped the dome, dividing the waters below the dome from the waters above it – and so it came to be. And God named that dome, "Sky." ▸ And there was evening; then there was morning: a second day. ◂

God said, "Let all the waters below the sky be gathered to one place; let dry ground be revealed." And so it came to be. And He named the dry ground, "Land"; and the gathering of waters He named "Seas." And God saw that it was good. And God said, "Let the land sprout green plants that seed, and fruit trees, each bearing fruit with its own seeds in them, overspreading the land." And so it came to be. The land brought forth green, seeding plants, each with its own seeds,

---

ing of the universe from mystery, magic and myth. All ancient religions had creation myths to explain why the world is as it is. Always they involved a multiplicity of gods, fighting and struggling among themselves for dominance. The opening chapter of the Torah represents a decisive break from that entire mindset. There is only one God, and it is His creative will alone that made the universe as it is. As sociologist Max Weber pointed out, the roots of Western rationality lie here.

However, the point of Genesis 1 is not to tell us *how* the world came into being. It is neither science nor proto-science. We see this in the sheer brevity of the account, a mere thirty-four verses, less than a tenth of the space the Torah dedicates to the other creative act it describes, namely the Israelites' construction of the Sanctuary (Ex. 25–40). The Torah is telling us not

קריאה לחתן בראשית

It is customary for the קהל *to say aloud the passages marked by arrows, followed by the* קורא*.*

בראשית א:א–ב:ג

בְּרֵאשִׁית בָּרָא אֱלֹהִים אֵת הַשָּׁמַיִם וְאֵת הָאָרֶץ׃ וְהָאָרֶץ הָיְתָה תֹהוּ וָבֹהוּ
וְחֹשֶׁךְ עַל־פְּנֵי תְהוֹם וְרוּחַ אֱלֹהִים מְרַחֶפֶת עַל־פְּנֵי הַמָּיִם׃ וַיֹּאמֶר אֱלֹהִים
יְהִי־אוֹר וַיְהִי־אוֹר׃ וַיַּרְא אֱלֹהִים אֶת־הָאוֹר כִּי־טוֹב וַיַּבְדֵּל אֱלֹהִים בֵּין הָאוֹר
וּבֵין הַחֹשֶׁךְ׃ וַיִּקְרָא אֱלֹהִים ׀ לָאוֹר יוֹם וְלַחֹשֶׁךְ קָרָא לָיְלָה ◂ וַיְהִי־עֶרֶב וַיְהִי־
בֹקֶר יוֹם אֶחָד׃ ◂

וַיֹּאמֶר אֱלֹהִים יְהִי רָקִיעַ בְּתוֹךְ הַמָּיִם וִיהִי מַבְדִּיל בֵּין מַיִם לָמָיִם׃ וַיַּעַשׂ
אֱלֹהִים אֶת־הָרָקִיעַ וַיַּבְדֵּל בֵּין הַמַּיִם אֲשֶׁר מִתַּחַת לָרָקִיעַ וּבֵין הַמַּיִם אֲשֶׁר
מֵעַל לָרָקִיעַ וַיְהִי־כֵן׃ וַיִּקְרָא אֱלֹהִים לָרָקִיעַ שָׁמָיִם ◂ וַיְהִי־עֶרֶב וַיְהִי־בֹקֶר
יוֹם שֵׁנִי׃ ◂

וַיֹּאמֶר אֱלֹהִים יִקָּווּ הַמַּיִם מִתַּחַת הַשָּׁמַיִם אֶל־מָקוֹם אֶחָד וְתֵרָאֶה הַיַּבָּשָׁה
וַיְהִי־כֵן׃ וַיִּקְרָא אֱלֹהִים ׀ לַיַּבָּשָׁה אֶרֶץ וּלְמִקְוֵה הַמַּיִם קָרָא יַמִּים וַיַּרְא
אֱלֹהִים כִּי־טוֹב׃ וַיֹּאמֶר אֱלֹהִים תַּדְשֵׁא הָאָרֶץ דֶּשֶׁא עֵשֶׂב מַזְרִיעַ זֶרַע עֵץ
פְּרִי עֹשֶׂה פְּרִי לְמִינוֹ אֲשֶׁר זַרְעוֹ־בוֹ עַל־הָאָרֶץ וַיְהִי־כֵן׃ וַתּוֹצֵא הָאָרֶץ דֶּשֶׁא

TORAH READING FOR ḤATAN BERESHIT

This act of beginning the Torah reading anew exemplifies one of the most remarkable principles of Judaism: the idea of perpetual study.

In this unique point of the Jewish year, we make the transition from the end of the Torah to a new beginning. The last letter of the Torah is the *lamed* of Yisrael, the first is the *beit* of Bereshit. When we join the end of the Torah to the beginning, the connection spells the word *Lev*, "heart." *So long as the Jewish people never stops studying, the Jewish heart will never stop beating.* "You gave us a Torah of truth, thereby planting everlasting life in our midst," says the blessing after the reading of the Torah. The word of the Eternal is, this side of Heaven, our one taste of eternity.

IN THE BEGINNING

This majestic opening sets out, for the first time, principles that were not only to shape Judaism, but eventually also to transform the imagination of the West. Genesis 1 represents the emancipation of the human understand-

and trees bearing fruit, each with its own seeds in it. And God saw that it was good. ▸ There was evening; then there was morning: a third day. ◂

God said, "Let there be lights in the dome of the sky, to divide day from night; let them mark out signs and seasons, days and years; and let them be lights in the dome of the sky to light up the land." Thus it came to be. God made the two great lights – the greater light to rule over the day, and the smaller light to rule over the night, and the stars. And He hung them in the dome of the sky, to light up the earth; to rule by day and by night, and to divide light from darkness; and God saw that it was good. ▸ There was evening; then there was morning: a fourth day. ◂

God said, "Let the water swarm with schools of living things; and let flying creatures fly across the land, against the dome of the sky. And God created the great sea beasts, and living things of all kinds that crawl and that swarm within the waters, and winged, flying creatures of all kinds; and He saw that it was good. God blessed them: "Be fruitful, grow numerous, fill the waters of the seas; and let the creatures that fly grow many on the land." ▸ There was evening; then there was morning: a fifth day. ◂

---

here that the universe has a precisely calibrated mathematical structure at every level, from the microscopic to the cosmological.

The text is also designed to show that creation has an underlying order. For the first three days, God establishes a series of distinct domains from the undifferentiated void: On the first day, He separates light from darkness and day from night, on the second, the upper and lower waters, on the third, sea from dry land. For the next three days God furnishes each of the domains with the appropriate objects and life-forms: On the fourth day, the sun, moon and stars, on the fifth, birds and fish, on the sixth, animals and humankind.

The key verb, appearing five times, is ב-ד-ל, meaning "to distinguish, demarcate, separate." This will eventually become a key word relating to the priests: they will be charged with distinguishing between pure and impure, holy and mundane. There is a sacred ontology, a God-given structure to the universe whose integrity we are commanded to respect and preserve.

עֵשֶׂב מַזְרִיעַ זֶרַע לְמִינֵהוּ וְעֵץ עֹשֶׂה־פְּרִי אֲשֶׁר זַרְעוֹ־בוֹ לְמִינֵהוּ וַיַּרְא אֱלֹהִים
כִּי־טוֹב: • וַיְהִי־עֶרֶב וַיְהִי־בֹקֶר יוֹם שְׁלִישִׁי: •
וַיֹּאמֶר אֱלֹהִים יְהִי מְאֹרֹת בִּרְקִיעַ הַשָּׁמַיִם לְהַבְדִּיל בֵּין הַיּוֹם וּבֵין הַלָּיְלָה
וְהָיוּ לְאֹתֹת וּלְמוֹעֲדִים וּלְיָמִים וְשָׁנִים: וְהָיוּ לִמְאוֹרֹת בִּרְקִיעַ הַשָּׁמַיִם לְהָאִיר
עַל־הָאָרֶץ וַיְהִי־כֵן: וַיַּעַשׂ אֱלֹהִים אֶת־שְׁנֵי הַמְּאֹרֹת הַגְּדֹלִים אֶת־הַמָּאוֹר
הַגָּדֹל לְמֶמְשֶׁלֶת הַיּוֹם וְאֶת־הַמָּאוֹר הַקָּטֹן לְמֶמְשֶׁלֶת הַלַּיְלָה וְאֵת הַכּוֹכָבִים:
וַיִּתֵּן אֹתָם אֱלֹהִים בִּרְקִיעַ הַשָּׁמָיִם לְהָאִיר עַל־הָאָרֶץ: וְלִמְשֹׁל בַּיּוֹם וּבַלַּיְלָה
וּלֲהַבְדִּיל בֵּין הָאוֹר וּבֵין הַחֹשֶׁךְ וַיַּרְא אֱלֹהִים כִּי־טוֹב: • וַיְהִי־עֶרֶב וַיְהִי־בֹקֶר
יוֹם רְבִיעִי: •
וַיֹּאמֶר אֱלֹהִים יִשְׁרְצוּ הַמַּיִם שֶׁרֶץ נֶפֶשׁ חַיָּה וְעוֹף יְעוֹפֵף עַל־הָאָרֶץ עַל־פְּנֵי
רְקִיעַ הַשָּׁמָיִם: וַיִּבְרָא אֱלֹהִים אֶת־הַתַּנִּינִם הַגְּדֹלִים וְאֵת כָּל־נֶפֶשׁ הַחַיָּה
הָרֹמֶשֶׂת אֲשֶׁר שָׁרְצוּ הַמַּיִם לְמִינֵהֶם וְאֵת כָּל־עוֹף כָּנָף לְמִינֵהוּ וַיַּרְא אֱלֹהִים
כִּי־טוֹב: וַיְבָרֶךְ אֹתָם אֱלֹהִים לֵאמֹר פְּרוּ וּרְבוּ וּמִלְאוּ אֶת־הַמַּיִם בַּיַּמִּים וְהָעוֹף
יִרֶב בָּאָרֶץ: • וַיְהִי־עֶרֶב וַיְהִי־בֹקֶר יוֹם חֲמִישִׁי: •

---

how God created the world, but *that* God created the world. It did not merely happen. Behind the emergent order of the universe is a God who loves creativity and order.

The creation narrative is not a substitute for science, but rather the articulation of fundamental moral principles that govern our understanding of the universe and our place within it. The first is that the world is *good* – the word chimes like a motif, no less than seven times. This in itself is a radical rejection of the view, widespread in the ancient world, and to some extent throughout history, that the physical world is bad, the arena of pain, suffering and injustice, from which we are liberated only by death and life-after-death.

Then there is the deep structure of the text itself. As modern commentators have noted, the pattern of seven – a universe created in seven days – lies not only on the surface, but is also replicated in less obvious ways throughout. So, for example, there are seven words in the first verse, fourteen in the second, thirty-five in the closing three verses describing the seventh day. The word *Elokim*, "God," appears thirty-five times, *eretz*, "earth," twenty-one times, and the passage as a whole contains 469 (7×67) words. There is an intimation

God said, "Let the land bring forth living beings, cattle and creeping things and land animals of all kinds;" and so it came to be. He made land animals of all kinds, cattle of all kinds, and all the kinds of creature that crawl upon the earth; and God saw that it was good. And He said, "Let Us make man, in Our image, Our likeness, to rule the fish of the sea and the flying creatures of the sky, cattle and all the animals of the land, and the crawling things that creep across the land." God created mankind in His image; in the image of God He created man; He created them male and female. And He blessed them: "Be fruitful, grow numerous; fill the earth and conquer it. Rule the fish of the sea and the flying creatures of the sky, and everything that creeps upon the earth." And God said, "I have given to you the green plants with their seeds that cover the land, and the trees that bear fruits with their seeds; these shall be yours to eat. And all the animals of the land, and all the flying creatures of the sky, and all that creeps upon the land that has a living spirit in it shall have all the green plants to eat." So it came to be. And God saw all that He had done – and it was very good. ▸ There was evening; then there was morning: the sixth day. ◂

▸ Then the heavens and the earth were completed, and all their array. With the seventh day, God completed the work He had done. He ceased on the seventh day from all the work He had done. God blessed the seventh day and declared it holy, because on it He ceased from all His work He had created to do. ◂

The Maftir for Simḥat Torah is the same as that of Shemini Atzeret on page 1161.

---

a universe, and that the first human was created alone so that no one would be able to say, my ancestor was greater than yours. The connection between this principle and the sanctity of human life is made explicit in the covenant with Noah: "Whoever sheds the blood of man, by man shall his blood be shed, for in the image of God He made man" (Gen. 9:6).

Finally, the Genesis creation narrative establishes the jurisprudential principle on which the entire Judaic structure of social ethics rests: that God, as Creator of the universe, owns the universe, and we, as its temporary residents, are bound by His sovereignty. Thus God rules, not by virtue of might, but of right.

וַיֹּאמֶר אֱלֹהִים תּוֹצֵא הָאָרֶץ נֶפֶשׁ חַיָּה לְמִינָהּ בְּהֵמָה וָרֶמֶשׂ וְחַיְתוֹ־אֶרֶץ
לְמִינָהּ וַיְהִי־כֵן: וַיַּעַשׂ אֱלֹהִים אֶת־חַיַּת הָאָרֶץ לְמִינָהּ וְאֶת־הַבְּהֵמָה לְמִינָהּ
וְאֵת כָּל־רֶמֶשׂ הָאֲדָמָה לְמִינֵהוּ וַיַּרְא אֱלֹהִים כִּי־טוֹב: וַיֹּאמֶר אֱלֹהִים נַעֲשֶׂה
אָדָם בְּצַלְמֵנוּ כִּדְמוּתֵנוּ וְיִרְדּוּ בִדְגַת הַיָּם וּבְעוֹף הַשָּׁמַיִם וּבַבְּהֵמָה וּבְכָל־הָאָרֶץ
וּבְכָל־הָרֶמֶשׂ הָרֹמֵשׂ עַל־הָאָרֶץ: וַיִּבְרָא אֱלֹהִים ׀ אֶת־הָאָדָם בְּצַלְמוֹ בְּצֶלֶם
אֱלֹהִים בָּרָא אֹתוֹ זָכָר וּנְקֵבָה בָּרָא אֹתָם: וַיְבָרֶךְ אֹתָם אֱלֹהִים וַיֹּאמֶר לָהֶם
אֱלֹהִים פְּרוּ וּרְבוּ וּמִלְאוּ אֶת־הָאָרֶץ וְכִבְשֻׁהָ וּרְדוּ בִּדְגַת הַיָּם וּבְעוֹף הַשָּׁמַיִם
וּבְכָל־חַיָּה הָרֹמֶשֶׂת עַל־הָאָרֶץ: וַיֹּאמֶר אֱלֹהִים הִנֵּה נָתַתִּי לָכֶם אֶת־כָּל־
עֵשֶׂב ׀ זֹרֵעַ זֶרַע אֲשֶׁר עַל־פְּנֵי כָל־הָאָרֶץ וְאֶת־כָּל־הָעֵץ אֲשֶׁר־בּוֹ פְרִי־עֵץ
זֹרֵעַ זָרַע לָכֶם יִהְיֶה לְאָכְלָה: וּלְכָל־חַיַּת הָאָרֶץ וּלְכָל־עוֹף הַשָּׁמַיִם וּלְכֹל ׀
רוֹמֵשׂ עַל־הָאָרֶץ אֲשֶׁר־בּוֹ נֶפֶשׁ חַיָּה אֶת־כָּל־יֶרֶק עֵשֶׂב לְאָכְלָה וַיְהִי־כֵן:
וַיַּרְא אֱלֹהִים אֶת־כָּל־אֲשֶׁר עָשָׂה וְהִנֵּה־טוֹב מְאֹד · וַיְהִי־עֶרֶב וַיְהִי־בֹקֶר
יוֹם הַשִּׁשִּׁי: ·

· וַיְכֻלּוּ הַשָּׁמַיִם וְהָאָרֶץ וְכָל־צְבָאָם: וַיְכַל אֱלֹהִים בַּיּוֹם הַשְּׁבִיעִי מְלַאכְתּוֹ
אֲשֶׁר עָשָׂה וַיִּשְׁבֹּת בַּיּוֹם הַשְּׁבִיעִי מִכָּל־מְלַאכְתּוֹ אֲשֶׁר עָשָׂה: וַיְבָרֶךְ אֱלֹהִים
אֶת־יוֹם הַשְּׁבִיעִי וַיְקַדֵּשׁ אֹתוֹ כִּי בוֹ שָׁבַת מִכָּל־מְלַאכְתּוֹ אֲשֶׁר־בָּרָא אֱלֹהִים
לַעֲשׂוֹת: ·

The מפטיר *for* שמחת תורה *is the same as that of* שמיני עצרת *on page 1161.*

Then there is the single most transformative sentence in the religious history of humankind: "Let Us make man, in Our image, Our likeness." What is revolutionary about this idea is not that a human being could be in the image of God. That belief was commonplace in the ancient world: it is what rulers, emperors, pharaohs, and kings were imagined to be, a child of the gods or their chief intermediary. What was unprecedented was the idea that *every* human being, regardless of color, culture, class or caste, is in the image and likeness of God. The whole of the Torah's ethics and politics are already foreshadowed in this one verse.

It was to this that Rabbi Akiva was alluding when he said: "Beloved is man, for he was created in the image of God" (*Avot* 3:18). It is what the sages meant when they taught (Mishna, *Sanhedrin* 37a) that whoever destroys a life is as if he destroyed a universe, and whoever saves a life is as if he saved

HAFTARA FOR SIMḤAT TORAH

Then, after the death of the LORD's servant, Moses, the LORD spoke to Moses' disciple, Joshua son of Nun. "Moses, My servant, has died. Now come, you and all this people; rise up and cross this Jordan River to the land that I am giving them, giving to the children of Israel. Every place your feet should tread – I have given to you. This I told Moses: from the desert and the Lebanon, to the great river, the river Perat, all the land of the Hittites, and as far as the great ocean that lies towards the sunset; these shall be your borders. No man shall stand in your way all the days of your life; as I was with Moses, so shall I be with you. I shall not let go of you, nor shall I leave you. Be strong, be determined – for you shall endow this people with the land that I swore to give their ancestors. Only be very strong, be very determined, to keep all the Torah with which Moses My servant charged you. Be sure not to stray from it rightward or left; and then you shall be successful in every course you take. Let the Torah in this scroll never leave your lips; meditate upon it day and night, that you may keep and perform all that is written there, for then shall all your ventures be fruitful; then shall you succeed. Know that I have *Josh. 1:1–18*

---

as the Israelites move from the desert to the land, from exile and exodus to homecoming, and from journey to destination.

רַק חֲזַק וֶאֱמַץ *Only be very strong, be very determined.* Dayan Yeḥezkel Abramsky noted that in the previous verse, speaking of the conquest of the land, God tells Joshua to be "strong and of good courage." Now, speaking of the religious challenge of remaining faithful to God's law, a far more emphatic form of words is used, signaling that the spiritual dimension of leadership demands greater strength and courage than the military or political dimension.

לֹא־יָמוּשׁ סֵפֶר הַתּוֹרָה הַזֶּה *Let the Torah in this scroll never leave your lips.* A command stated in the Torah in relation to a king (Deut. 17:18–20), thus conveying another fundamental rule of leadership: the heavier the responsibility, the greater the need for constant moral and spiritual guidance. A leader who guides people into the unmapped territory of the future needs, above

הפטרה לשמחת תורה

יהושע א:א–יח וַיְהִי אַחֲרֵי מוֹת מֹשֶׁה עֶבֶד יהוה וַיֹּאמֶר יהוה אֶל־יְהוֹשֻׁעַ בִּן־נוּן מְשָׁרֵת מֹשֶׁה
לֵאמֹר: מֹשֶׁה עַבְדִּי מֵת וְעַתָּה קוּם עֲבֹר אֶת־הַיַּרְדֵּן הַזֶּה אַתָּה וְכָל־הָעָם
הַזֶּה אֶל־הָאָרֶץ אֲשֶׁר אָנֹכִי נֹתֵן לָהֶם לִבְנֵי יִשְׂרָאֵל: כָּל־מָקוֹם אֲשֶׁר תִּדְרֹךְ
כַּף־רַגְלְכֶם בּוֹ לָכֶם נְתַתִּיו כַּאֲשֶׁר דִּבַּרְתִּי אֶל־מֹשֶׁה: מֵהַמִּדְבָּר וְהַלְּבָנוֹן הַזֶּה
וְעַד־הַנָּהָר הַגָּדוֹל נְהַר־פְּרָת כֹּל אֶרֶץ הַחִתִּים וְעַד־הַיָּם הַגָּדוֹל מְבוֹא הַשָּׁמֶשׁ
יִהְיֶה גְּבוּלְכֶם: לֹא־יִתְיַצֵּב אִישׁ לְפָנֶיךָ כֹּל יְמֵי חַיֶּיךָ כַּאֲשֶׁר הָיִיתִי עִם־מֹשֶׁה
אֶהְיֶה עִמָּךְ לֹא אַרְפְּךָ וְלֹא אֶעֶזְבֶךָּ: חֲזַק וֶאֱמָץ כִּי אַתָּה תַּנְחִיל אֶת־הָעָם
הַזֶּה אֶת־הָאָרֶץ אֲשֶׁר־נִשְׁבַּעְתִּי לַאֲבוֹתָם לָתֵת לָהֶם: רַק חֲזַק וֶאֱמַץ מְאֹד
לִשְׁמֹר לַעֲשׂוֹת כְּכָל־הַתּוֹרָה אֲשֶׁר צִוְּךָ מֹשֶׁה עַבְדִּי אַל־תָּסוּר מִמֶּנּוּ יָמִין
וּשְׂמֹאול לְמַעַן תַּשְׂכִּיל בְּכֹל אֲשֶׁר תֵּלֵךְ: לֹא־יָמוּשׁ סֵפֶר הַתּוֹרָה הַזֶּה מִפִּיךָ
וְהָגִיתָ בּוֹ יוֹמָם וָלַיְלָה לְמַעַן תִּשְׁמֹר לַעֲשׂוֹת כְּכָל־הַכָּתוּב בּוֹ כִּי־אָז תַּצְלִיחַ

HAFTARA FOR SIMḤAT TORAH

There are, in Judaism, (at least) two conceptions of time: cyclical and historical. Cyclical time is time as it is in nature: in the succession of nights and days, the seasons, and the lifecycle. Historical time – held by many scholars to have been first conceived in the Hebrew Bible – is time as a narrative, with a beginning, middle, and end, or as a journey, with a starting-point and a destination. History in Judaism is an arena of change, as we come closer to, or drift further from, what R. Aaron Lichtenstein called "societal beatitude" – a world of justice, compassion and peace.

The three festivals, Pesaḥ, Shavuot, and Sukkot, all have this dual character. They are cyclical, seasonal, representing respectively spring, first fruits, and harvest. And they are also historical, commemorating first the exodus, then the revelation at Sinai, then the forty years of wandering without a permanent home.

On Simḥat Torah, after concluding the last of the Mosaic books, we make a dramatic entry into both systems of time: cyclical as we move directly from the last word of the Torah to the first, ensuring that our cycle of Torah reading will be unbroken. Immediately thereafter, we take a decisive step into historical time, as Moses dies and his successor Joshua takes on the role of leadership. A new generation, and a new chapter in the Jewish story, begins,

charged you: be strong, be determined, do not be terrified and do not fear, for the LORD your God is with you wherever you go.

And Yehoshua charged the leaders of the people, saying, "Pass throughout the camp, commanding the people: 'Prepare yourselves provisions, for in three days' time you shall cross this Jordan river, to come into and to take possession of the land that the LORD your God is giving you as an inheritance.'"

And to the people of Reuben and Gad, and to half of the tribe of Manasseh, Joshua said, "Remember the words Moses the LORD's servant charged you with; the LORD your God will let you remain; He is giving you this land. The women and children among you, and your cattle, may settle now in this land that Moses gave you beyond the Jordan. But all your strong fighting men shall cross the river armed before your brothers, and help them, until the LORD has granted your brothers rest like yours, and they too shall inherit the land that the LORD has given them. And then shall you return to your own inheritance, which the LORD's servant Moses granted you, and take possession of it, here beyond the Jordan, towards the sunrise.

And they answered Joshua: "All that you charge us with, we shall fulfill, and wherever you send us we shall go. Just as we listened to Moses, so shall we listen to you. Only let the LORD your God be with you, as He used to be with Moses. If any man rebels against your word, and refuses to listen to your voice, to all that you charge us with – let that man die. Only be strong, be determined."

Continue with the blessings after the Haftara on page 514.

כְּכֹל אֲשֶׁר־שָׁמַעְנוּ אֶל־מֹשֶׁה *Just as we listened to Moses.* The people give their consent and pledge their allegiance to Joshua as Moses' successor, an instance of a fundamental principle of Judaism, as of the American Declaration of Independence, that leaders and governments derive their authority from the consent of the governed.

אֶת־דְּרָכֶךָ וְאָז תַּשְׂכִּיל׃ הֲלוֹא צִוִּיתִיךָ חֲזַק וֶאֱמָץ אַל־תַּעֲרֹץ וְאַל־תֵּחָת
כִּי עִמְּךָ יהוה אֱלֹהֶיךָ בְּכֹל אֲשֶׁר תֵּלֵךְ׃ וַיְצַו יְהוֹשֻׁעַ אֶת־שֹׁטְרֵי
הָעָם לֵאמֹר׃ עִבְרוּ ׀ בְּקֶרֶב הַמַּחֲנֶה וְצַוּוּ אֶת־הָעָם לֵאמֹר הָכִינוּ לָכֶם צֵידָה כִּי
בְּעוֹד ׀ שְׁלֹשֶׁת יָמִים אַתֶּם עֹבְרִים אֶת־הַיַּרְדֵּן הַזֶּה לָבוֹא לָרֶשֶׁת אֶת־הָאָרֶץ
אֲשֶׁר יהוה אֱלֹהֵיכֶם נֹתֵן לָכֶם לְרִשְׁתָּהּ׃ וְלָראוּבֵנִי וְלַגָּדִי וְלַחֲצִי
שֵׁבֶט הַמְנַשֶּׁה אָמַר יְהוֹשֻׁעַ לֵאמֹר׃ זָכוֹר אֶת־הַדָּבָר אֲשֶׁר צִוָּה אֶתְכֶם מֹשֶׁה
עֶבֶד־יהוה לֵאמֹר יהוה אֱלֹהֵיכֶם מֵנִיחַ לָכֶם וְנָתַן לָכֶם אֶת־הָאָרֶץ הַזֹּאת׃
נְשֵׁיכֶם טַפְּכֶם וּמִקְנֵיכֶם יֵשְׁבוּ בָּאָרֶץ אֲשֶׁר נָתַן לָכֶם מֹשֶׁה בְּעֵבֶר הַיַּרְדֵּן
וְאַתֶּם תַּעַבְרוּ חֲמֻשִׁים לִפְנֵי אֲחֵיכֶם כֹּל גִּבּוֹרֵי הַחַיִל וַעֲזַרְתֶּם אוֹתָם׃ עַד
אֲשֶׁר־יָנִיחַ יהוה ׀ לַאֲחֵיכֶם כָּכֶם וְיָרְשׁוּ גַם־הֵמָּה אֶת־הָאָרֶץ אֲשֶׁר־יהוה
אֱלֹהֵיכֶם נֹתֵן לָהֶם וְשַׁבְתֶּם לְאֶרֶץ יְרֻשַּׁתְכֶם וִירִשְׁתֶּם אוֹתָהּ אֲשֶׁר ׀ נָתַן לָכֶם
מֹשֶׁה עֶבֶד יהוה בְּעֵבֶר הַיַּרְדֵּן מִזְרַח הַשָּׁמֶשׁ׃ וַיַּעֲנוּ אֶת־יְהוֹשֻׁעַ לֵאמֹר כֹּל
אֲשֶׁר־צִוִּיתָנוּ נַעֲשֶׂה וְאֶל־כָּל־אֲשֶׁר תִּשְׁלָחֵנוּ נֵלֵךְ׃ כְּכֹל אֲשֶׁר־שָׁמַעְנוּ אֶל־
מֹשֶׁה כֵּן נִשְׁמַע אֵלֶיךָ רַק יִהְיֶה יהוה אֱלֹהֶיךָ עִמָּךְ כַּאֲשֶׁר הָיָה עִם־מֹשֶׁה׃
כָּל־אִישׁ אֲשֶׁר־יַמְרֶה אֶת־פִּיךָ וְלֹא־יִשְׁמַע אֶת־דְּבָרֶיךָ לְכֹל אֲשֶׁר־תְּצַוֶּנּוּ
יוּמָת רַק חֲזַק וֶאֱמָץ׃

Continue with the blessings after the הפטרה *on page 515.*

---

all, an inner compass, to avoid the moral drift that is otherwise the fate of those who allow themselves to be merely reactive to events.

וְאַל־תֵּחָת *Do not be terrified.* Faith is the antidote to fear. "The Lord is my light and my salvation - whom then shall I fear?" (Ps. 27:1).

וְלָראוּבֵנִי וְלַגָּדִי *And to the people of Reuben and Gad.* A reminder of the agreement they made with Moses (Num. 32), that though they would settle on the east bank of the Jordan, they would first honor their commitment to lead the Israelites into battle against the Canaanites. Only when the land was conquered and settled would they return to their families.

מגילות

MEGILLOT

SONG OF SONGS

1 1 Solomon's Song of Songs.

2 [*She*] Would that he kiss me with that mouth. Better than any wine is your love;
3 the fragrance of your oils, finer. Your very name flows forth like scented oil; what
4 wonder then that young girls love you? Come, draw me after you, let us run – the
king has brought me into his chambers.

[*Friends*] In you our joy, our happiness: your love possesses us more than any wine; flowing freely falls this love.

5 [*She*] I am dark yet fair, daughters of Jerusalem; black as the tents of Kedar, as
6 Solomon's curtains. Do not look at me, I am scorched black: the sun has stared
at me. My mother's sons were furious. They made me a keeper of the vineyards;
my own vineyard, I did not keep.

7 [*She*] Tell me, you that I have loved, where will you pasture, where will you rest your flock at noon? Do not make me swathe my face and wander, among all the herds of your friends.

8 [*Friends*] If you do not know, most beautiful of women, then go out in the tracks of the flock; bring your own young goats to pasture where the shepherds' huts stand.

9 [*He*] My mare among Pharaoh's chariots, that is what you are to me, my love,
10 11 your cheeks fair in their strings of beads, your neck, jewelled; I would make you
strings of solid gold – with silver grains.

12 13 [*She*] As long as my king reclined to eat, my musk-root gave its scent; my beloved
14 a bundle of myrrh to me resting between my breasts, my beloved a cluster of
henna to me, in the spice-beds of Ein Gedi.

15 [*He*] You are beautiful, my love, how beautiful, your eyes like doves.

16 [*She*] How beautiful you are, beloved, and how good. Our bed is green, luscious.
17 Our house is roofed with cedars; its rafters are juniper trees.

2 1 [*She*] I am a dune flower of the coast, I am a lily of the valleys.

2 [*He*] A lily among thorn weeds is my love among the girls.

3 [*She*] Amid the forest, an apple tree is my beloved among men. I treasure his shade, there I rest – and his fruit fills my mouth with sweetness.

4 [*She*] He has brought me to the wine house, and his flag flying over me is love.
5 Sustain me now with raisin cakes, spread a bed for me among apples – for I am
6 7 sick with love. My head rests in his left hand; his right arm is around me. Swear
to me, daughters of Jerusalem, by the she-gazelles, by the does of the field; swear
that you will not waken, will not rouse, this love before its time.

8 [*She*] The voice of my beloved – I hear him coming – springing over the hills, leap-
9 ing the slopes; he is like a gazelle, my beloved, he is like a young deer – here he
stands, behind our wall, gazing through the windows, glimpsing through every gap.

שיר השירים

א ב שִׁיר הַשִּׁירִים אֲשֶׁר לִשְׁלֹמֹה: יִשָּׁקֵנִי מִנְּשִׁיקוֹת פִּיהוּ כִּי־טוֹבִים דֹּדֶיךָ
ג מִיָּיִן: לְרֵיחַ שְׁמָנֶיךָ טוֹבִים שֶׁמֶן תּוּרַק שְׁמֶךָ עַל־כֵּן עֲלָמוֹת אֲהֵבוּךָ:
ד מָשְׁכֵנִי אַחֲרֶיךָ נָּרוּצָה הֱבִיאַנִי הַמֶּלֶךְ חֲדָרָיו נָגִילָה וְנִשְׂמְחָה בָּךְ
ה נַזְכִּירָה דֹדֶיךָ מִיַּיִן מֵישָׁרִים אֲהֵבוּךָ: שְׁחוֹרָה אֲנִי וְנָאוָה
ו בְּנוֹת יְרוּשָׁלָםִ כְּאָהֳלֵי קֵדָר כִּירִיעוֹת שְׁלֹמֹה: אַל־תִּרְאוּנִי שֶׁאֲנִי
שְׁחַרְחֹרֶת שֶׁשְּׁזָפַתְנִי הַשָּׁמֶשׁ בְּנֵי אִמִּי נִחֲרוּ־בִי שָׂמֻנִי נֹטֵרָה אֶת־
ז הַכְּרָמִים כַּרְמִי שֶׁלִּי לֹא נָטָרְתִּי: הַגִּידָה לִּי שֶׁאָהֲבָה נַפְשִׁי אֵיכָה
תִרְעֶה אֵיכָה תַּרְבִּיץ בַּצָּהֳרָיִם שַׁלָּמָה אֶהְיֶה כְּעֹטְיָה עַל עֶדְרֵי חֲבֵרֶיךָ:
ח אִם־לֹא תֵדְעִי לָךְ הַיָּפָה בַּנָּשִׁים צְאִי־לָךְ בְּעִקְבֵי הַצֹּאן וּרְעִי אֶת־
ט גְּדִיֹּתַיִךְ עַל מִשְׁכְּנוֹת הָרֹעִים: לְסֻסָתִי בְּרִכְבֵי פַרְעֹה
י יא דִּמִּיתִיךְ רַעְיָתִי: נָאווּ לְחָיַיִךְ בַּתֹּרִים צַוָּארֵךְ בַּחֲרוּזִים: תּוֹרֵי זָהָב
יב נַעֲשֶׂה־לָּךְ עִם נְקֻדּוֹת הַכָּסֶף: עַד־שֶׁהַמֶּלֶךְ בִּמְסִבּוֹ נִרְדִּי נָתַן רֵיחוֹ:
יג יד צְרוֹר הַמֹּר ׀ דּוֹדִי לִי בֵּין שָׁדַי יָלִין: אֶשְׁכֹּל הַכֹּפֶר ׀ דּוֹדִי לִי בְּכַרְמֵי
טו טז עֵין גֶּדִי: הִנָּךְ יָפָה רַעְיָתִי הִנָּךְ יָפָה עֵינַיִךְ יוֹנִים: הִנְּךָ יָפֶה
יז דוֹדִי אַף נָעִים אַף־עַרְשֵׂנוּ רַעֲנָנָה: קֹרוֹת בָּתֵּינוּ אֲרָזִים רחיטנו רָהִיטֵנוּ
ב ב בְּרוֹתִים: אֲנִי חֲבַצֶּלֶת הַשָּׁרוֹן שׁוֹשַׁנַּת הָעֲמָקִים: כְּשׁוֹשַׁנָּה בֵּין
ג הַחוֹחִים כֵּן רַעְיָתִי בֵּין הַבָּנוֹת: כְּתַפּוּחַ בַּעֲצֵי הַיַּעַר כֵּן דּוֹדִי בֵּין הַבָּנִים
ד בְּצִלּוֹ חִמַּדְתִּי וְיָשַׁבְתִּי וּפִרְיוֹ מָתוֹק לְחִכִּי: הֱבִיאַנִי אֶל־בֵּית הַיָּיִן וְדִגְלוֹ
ה עָלַי אַהֲבָה: סַמְּכוּנִי בָּאֲשִׁישׁוֹת רַפְּדוּנִי בַּתַּפּוּחִים כִּי־חוֹלַת אַהֲבָה
ו ז אָנִי: שְׂמֹאלוֹ תַּחַת לְרֹאשִׁי וִימִינוֹ תְּחַבְּקֵנִי: הִשְׁבַּעְתִּי אֶתְכֶם בְּנוֹת
יְרוּשָׁלַםִ בִּצְבָאוֹת אוֹ בְּאַיְלוֹת הַשָּׂדֶה אִם־תָּעִירוּ ׀ וְאִם־תְּעוֹרְרוּ
ח אֶת־הָאַהֲבָה עַד שֶׁתֶּחְפָּץ: קוֹל דּוֹדִי הִנֵּה־זֶה בָּא מְדַלֵּג
ט עַל־הֶהָרִים מְקַפֵּץ עַל־הַגְּבָעוֹת: דּוֹמֶה דוֹדִי לִצְבִי אוֹ לְעֹפֶר הָאַיָּלִים
הִנֵּה־זֶה עוֹמֵד אַחַר כָּתְלֵנוּ מַשְׁגִּיחַ מִן־הַחֲלֹּנוֹת מֵצִיץ מִן־הַחֲרַכִּים:

10 My beloved, he spoke, he said to me, "Come, rise, my love, my beautiful one,
11 12 let us leave. Winter is over. The rains have passed and left us. On the land,
buds have appeared. The songbirds' time has come, and the turtle-dove's
13 call sounds over our land. The fig has put out her young fruits, and the
flowering vines give scent – so come, rise, my love, my beautiful one, let us
leave."

14 [*He*] My dove, in the rock's cleft, in the cliff's shadow – show me your face,
let me hear your voice, for it is lovely, your voice; your face so fair.

15 [*She*] Catch the foxes, the little foxes, ravaging the vineyards, just as our vine-
16 yard is in flower. My beloved is my own and I am his, who pastures among
17 lilies. Until the day has breathed its light and the shadows have flown, turn
like a gazelle, my beloved, turn like a young deer, to the riven hills.

3 1 [*She*] Upon my bed at night I search for the one I love; I search for him, I do
2 not find him. I shall rise, I shall go all around the town, through the streets,
across the squares; I am searching for the one I love – I search for him, I do
3 not find him. The guards find me, those who go around the town: "The one
4 that I love – have you seen him?" I have scarcely moved away from them
when I find the one I love. I catch hold of him; I will not let him go, until I
have brought him to my mother's house, to the chamber where I was con-
5 ceived. Swear to me, daughters of Jerusalem, by the she-gazelles, by the does
of the field; swear that you will not waken, will not rouse, this love before its
time.

6 [*Friends*] Who is this, rising from the desert, like plumes of smoke, perfumed
with myrrh and frankincense, and all the merchants' powders?

7 8 Here stands Solomon's bed, sixty soldiers all around it, heroes of Israel. Each
carrying his sword, each learned in war, each with his sword at his thigh
9 10 for very fear at night. King Solomon built a palace of Lebanon wood; He
plated the pillars with silver, made the pillows of gold; his couch is purple
11 silk, and all the space is lined with love by the daughters of Jerusalem. Go
out and see, daughters of Zion, look at Solomon the king, in the crown
his mother gave to him, on this his wedding day; on the day his heart
rejoiced.

4 1 [*He*] How beautiful you are, my love, how beautiful, your eyes like doves
seen through your tresses; your hair like a flock of goats flowing down Mount
2 Gilead. Your teeth are like a flock of sheep, rising up from cleaning, each bear-
3 ing twins, two and two, not one among them lost. Your lips are like a scarlet
ribbon, and your speech is fair; your forehead, like a pomegranate glowing

י יא עָנָה דוֹדִי וְאָמַר לִי קוּמִי לָךְ רַעְיָתִי יָפָתִי וּלְכִי־לָךְ: כִּי־הִנֵּה הַסְּתָו
יב עָבַר הַגֶּשֶׁם חָלַף הָלַךְ לוֹ: הַנִּצָּנִים נִרְאוּ בָאָרֶץ עֵת הַזָּמִיר הִגִּיעַ
יג וְקוֹל הַתּוֹר נִשְׁמַע בְּאַרְצֵנוּ: הַתְּאֵנָה חָנְטָה פַגֶּיהָ וְהַגְּפָנִים ׀ סְמָדַר
יד נָתְנוּ רֵיחַ קוּמִי לכי רַעְיָתִי יָפָתִי וּלְכִי־לָךְ: יוֹנָתִי בְּחַגְוֵי לָךְ
הַסֶּלַע בְּסֵתֶר הַמַּדְרֵגָה הַרְאִינִי אֶת־מַרְאַיִךְ הַשְׁמִיעִנִי אֶת־קוֹלֵךְ
טו כִּי־קוֹלֵךְ עָרֵב וּמַרְאֵיךְ נָאוֶה: אֶחֱזוּ־לָנוּ שׁוּעָלִים שֻׁעָלִים
טז קְטַנִּים מְחַבְּלִים כְּרָמִים וּכְרָמֵינוּ סְמָדַר: דּוֹדִי לִי וַאֲנִי לוֹ הָרֹעֶה
יז בַּשּׁוֹשַׁנִּים: עַד שֶׁיָּפוּחַ הַיּוֹם וְנָסוּ הַצְּלָלִים סֹב דְּמֵה־לְךָ דוֹדִי לִצְבִי
ג א אוֹ לְעֹפֶר הָאַיָּלִים עַל־הָרֵי בָתֶר: עַל־מִשְׁכָּבִי בַּלֵּילוֹת
ב בִּקַּשְׁתִּי אֵת שֶׁאָהֲבָה נַפְשִׁי בִּקַּשְׁתִּיו וְלֹא מְצָאתִיו: אָקוּמָה נָּא
וַאֲסוֹבְבָה בָעִיר בַּשְּׁוָקִים וּבָרְחֹבוֹת אֲבַקְשָׁה אֵת שֶׁאָהֲבָה נַפְשִׁי
ג בִּקַּשְׁתִּיו וְלֹא מְצָאתִיו: מְצָאוּנִי הַשֹּׁמְרִים הַסֹּבְבִים בָּעִיר אֵת שֶׁאָהֲבָה
ד נַפְשִׁי רְאִיתֶם: כִּמְעַט שֶׁעָבַרְתִּי מֵהֶם עַד שֶׁמָּצָאתִי אֵת שֶׁאָהֲבָה
נַפְשִׁי אֲחַזְתִּיו וְלֹא אַרְפֶּנּוּ עַד־שֶׁהֲבֵיאתִיו אֶל־בֵּית אִמִּי וְאֶל־חֶדֶר
ה הוֹרָתִי: הִשְׁבַּעְתִּי אֶתְכֶם בְּנוֹת יְרוּשָׁלִַם בִּצְבָאוֹת אוֹ בְּאַיְלוֹת הַשָּׂדֶה
ו אִם־תָּעִירוּ ׀ וְאִם־תְּעוֹרְרוּ אֶת־הָאַהֲבָה עַד שֶׁתֶּחְפָּץ: מִי
זֹאת עֹלָה מִן־הַמִּדְבָּר כְּתִימְרוֹת עָשָׁן מְקֻטֶּרֶת מֹר וּלְבוֹנָה מִכֹּל
ז אַבְקַת רוֹכֵל: הִנֵּה מִטָּתוֹ שֶׁלִּשְׁלֹמֹה שִׁשִּׁים גִּבֹּרִים סָבִיב לָהּ מִגִּבֹּרֵי
ח יִשְׂרָאֵל: כֻּלָּם אֲחֻזֵי חֶרֶב מְלֻמְּדֵי מִלְחָמָה אִישׁ חַרְבּוֹ עַל־יְרֵכוֹ מִפַּחַד
ט בַּלֵּילוֹת: אַפִּרְיוֹן עָשָׂה לוֹ הַמֶּלֶךְ שְׁלֹמֹה מֵעֲצֵי הַלְּבָנוֹן:
י עַמּוּדָיו עָשָׂה כֶסֶף רְפִידָתוֹ זָהָב מֶרְכָּבוֹ אַרְגָּמָן תּוֹכוֹ רָצוּף אַהֲבָה
יא מִבְּנוֹת יְרוּשָׁלִָם: צְאֶינָה ׀ וּרְאֶינָה בְּנוֹת צִיּוֹן בַּמֶּלֶךְ שְׁלֹמֹה בָּעֲטָרָה
ד א שֶׁעִטְּרָה־לּוֹ אִמּוֹ בְּיוֹם חֲתֻנָּתוֹ וּבְיוֹם שִׂמְחַת לִבּוֹ: הִנָּךְ
יָפָה רַעְיָתִי הִנָּךְ יָפָה עֵינַיִךְ יוֹנִים מִבַּעַד לְצַמָּתֵךְ שַׂעְרֵךְ כְּעֵדֶר הָעִזִּים
ב שֶׁגָּלְשׁוּ מֵהַר גִּלְעָד: שִׁנַּיִךְ כְּעֵדֶר הַקְּצוּבוֹת שֶׁעָלוּ מִן־הָרַחְצָה שֶׁכֻּלָּם
ג מַתְאִימוֹת וְשַׁכֻּלָה אֵין בָּהֶם: כְּחוּט הַשָּׁנִי שִׂפְתֹתַיִךְ וּמִדְבָּרֵיךְ נָאוֶה

4 through your tresses. Your neck is like the Tower of David, built in splendor, a
5 thousand shields adorning it, the shields of all the heroes. Your two breasts are
6 like young twins of a she-gazelle, pasturing in lilies. Until the day has breathed
its light, and the shadows have flown, I am going to the hill of myrrh, to the
7 slopes of frankincense. And all of you is beauty, my love, is flawless; wholly.

8 Come with me from Lebanon, bride, come down with me from Lebanon; from
the peak of Amana descend, from the peaks of Senir and Hermon, from the
9 lions' haunts, the leopards' hills. You have taken my heart, my sister, my bride;
either one of your eyes would take my heart, any strand of the necklace you
10 wear. How beautiful your love is, my sister, my bride, how much better than
11 any wine your love, and finer than all perfumes the scent of your oils. Your lips
drip nectar, my bride; honey and milk lie under your tongue, and on your dress
lingers Lebanon's scent.

12 13 A locked garden is my sister, my bride, a locked well, a spring sealed up – yet your
dry ground is a grove of pomegranates, of the sweetest of fruits, henna plants,
14 musk-root; musk-root and saffron, calamus, cinnamon, every kind of fragrant
15 tree. With myrrh plants and aloe, with all the finest spices; and a spring to water
gardens, a well of living waters, waters flowing down from Lebanon.

16 [*She*] Wake now, north wind, south wind, come: breathe life into my garden, let
its perfumes flow. Let my beloved come to his garden, and eat his sweetest fruits.

5 1 [*He*] I have come into my garden, my sister, my bride; I have gathered my
myrrh and my balsam, I have eaten my honeycomb with honey, I have drunk
my wine with milk –

[*Friends*] Eat, loved ones, eat; drink, drink deep of love.

2 [*She*] I am asleep; my heart is awake – my beloved's voice, knocking – "Open
for me, my sister, my love, my dove, my perfection, for my head is covered with
3 dew, my locks with fragments of the night." "I have taken off my dress, how can
4 I put it on again? I have already washed my feet, how can I dirty them?" My
5 beloved stretches his hand through the door – and my being longs for him. I rise
to open the door for my beloved; my hands are dripping with myrrh, my fingers
6 are streaming with myrrh oil, all over the handles of the latch. I open for my
beloved – he has slipped away; gone. I had fainted for him as he spoke – I search
7 for him, I cannot find him; I call out, but he does not answer. The guards find
me, those who go around the town; they beat me, they wound me, they pull my
8 scarf from me, those guardians of the walls. Swear to me, daughters of Jerusalem;
if you find my beloved, swear that you will tell him – tell him I am sick with love.

9 [*Friends*] What makes your lover so much more than other lovers, you most
beautiful of women? What makes your lover so much more than other men,
that this is what you have us swear?

ד כְּפֶלַח הָרִמּוֹן רַקָּתֵךְ מִבַּעַד לְצַמָּתֵךְ׃ כְּמִגְדַּל דָּוִיד צַוָּארֵךְ בָּנוּי
ה לְתַלְפִּיּוֹת אֶלֶף הַמָּגֵן תָּלוּי עָלָיו כֹּל שִׁלְטֵי הַגִּבֹּרִים׃ שְׁנֵי שָׁדַיִךְ כִּשְׁנֵי
ו עֳפָרִים תְּאוֹמֵי צְבִיָּה הָרוֹעִים בַּשּׁוֹשַׁנִּים׃ עַד שֶׁיָּפוּחַ הַיּוֹם וְנָסוּ
ז הַצְּלָלִים אֵלֶךְ לִי אֶל־הַר הַמּוֹר וְאֶל־גִּבְעַת הַלְּבוֹנָה׃ כֻּלָּךְ יָפָה רַעְיָתִי
ח וּמוּם אֵין בָּךְ׃ אִתִּי מִלְּבָנוֹן כַּלָּה אִתִּי מִלְּבָנוֹן תָּבוֹאִי
תָּשׁוּרִי ׀ מֵרֹאשׁ אֲמָנָה מֵרֹאשׁ שְׂנִיר וְחֶרְמוֹן מִמְּעֹנוֹת אֲרָיוֹת מֵהַרְרֵי
ט נְמֵרִים׃ לִבַּבְתִּנִי אֲחֹתִי כַלָּה לִבַּבְתִּינִי באחד מֵעֵינַיִךְ בְּאַחַד עֲנָק בְּאַחַת
י מִצַּוְּרֹנָיִךְ׃ מַה־יָּפוּ דֹדַיִךְ אֲחֹתִי כַלָּה מַה־טֹּבוּ דֹדַיִךְ מִיַּיִן וְרֵיחַ שְׁמָנַיִךְ
יא מִכָּל־בְּשָׂמִים׃ נֹפֶת תִּטֹּפְנָה שִׂפְתוֹתַיִךְ כַּלָּה דְּבַשׁ וְחָלָב תַּחַת
יב לְשׁוֹנֵךְ וְרֵיחַ שַׂלְמֹתַיִךְ כְּרֵיחַ לְבָנוֹן׃ גַּן ׀ נָעוּל אֲחֹתִי כַלָּה
יג גַּל נָעוּל מַעְיָן חָתוּם׃ שְׁלָחַיִךְ פַּרְדֵּס רִמּוֹנִים עִם פְּרִי מְגָדִים כְּפָרִים
יד עִם־נְרָדִים׃ נֵרְדְּ ׀ וְכַרְכֹּם קָנֶה וְקִנָּמוֹן עִם כָּל־עֲצֵי לְבוֹנָה מֹר וַאֲהָלוֹת
טו עִם כָּל־רָאשֵׁי בְשָׂמִים׃ מַעְיַן גַּנִּים בְּאֵר מַיִם חַיִּים וְנֹזְלִים מִן־לְבָנוֹן׃
טז עוּרִי צָפוֹן וּבוֹאִי תֵימָן הָפִיחִי גַנִּי יִזְּלוּ בְשָׂמָיו יָבֹא דוֹדִי לְגַנּוֹ וְיֹאכַל
ה א פְּרִי מְגָדָיו׃ בָּאתִי לְגַנִּי אֲחֹתִי כַלָּה אָרִיתִי מוֹרִי עִם־בְּשָׂמִי אָכַלְתִּי
יַעְרִי עִם־דִּבְשִׁי שָׁתִיתִי יֵינִי עִם־חֲלָבִי אִכְלוּ רֵעִים שְׁתוּ וְשִׁכְרוּ
ב דּוֹדִים׃ אֲנִי יְשֵׁנָה וְלִבִּי עֵר קוֹל ׀ דּוֹדִי דוֹפֵק פִּתְחִי־לִי
אֲחֹתִי רַעְיָתִי יוֹנָתִי תַמָּתִי שֶׁרֹּאשִׁי נִמְלָא־טָל קְוֻצּוֹתַי רְסִיסֵי לָיְלָה׃
ג פָּשַׁטְתִּי אֶת־כֻּתָּנְתִּי אֵיכָכָה אֶלְבָּשֶׁנָּה רָחַצְתִּי אֶת־רַגְלַי אֵיכָכָה
ד ה אֲטַנְּפֵם׃ דּוֹדִי שָׁלַח יָדוֹ מִן־הַחֹר וּמֵעַי הָמוּ עָלָיו׃ קַמְתִּי אֲנִי לִפְתֹּחַ
ו לְדוֹדִי וְיָדַי נָטְפוּ־מוֹר וְאֶצְבְּעֹתַי מוֹר עֹבֵר עַל כַּפּוֹת הַמַּנְעוּל׃ פָּתַחְתִּי
אֲנִי לְדוֹדִי וְדוֹדִי חָמַק עָבָר נַפְשִׁי יָצְאָה בְדַבְּרוֹ בִּקַּשְׁתִּיהוּ וְלֹא
ז מְצָאתִיהוּ קְרָאתִיו וְלֹא עָנָנִי׃ מְצָאֻנִי הַשֹּׁמְרִים הַסֹּבְבִים בָּעִיר הִכּוּנִי
ח פְצָעוּנִי נָשְׂאוּ אֶת־רְדִידִי מֵעָלַי שֹׁמְרֵי הַחֹמוֹת׃ הִשְׁבַּעְתִּי אֶתְכֶם
בְּנוֹת יְרוּשָׁלִָם אִם־תִּמְצְאוּ אֶת־דּוֹדִי מַה־תַּגִּידוּ לוֹ שֶׁחוֹלַת אַהֲבָה
ט אָנִי׃ מַה־דּוֹדֵךְ מִדּוֹד הַיָּפָה בַּנָּשִׁים מַה־דּוֹדֵךְ מִדּוֹד שֶׁכָּכָה הִשְׁבַּעְתָּנוּ׃

10 [*She*] He is bright, my beloved, he is blooming; you would know him among ten
11 thousand. His face glows like gold, fine gold, his hair in locks like palm-flowers,
12 raven black. Yet his eyes are like doves, drinking at springs, washed in milk, at
13 rest by the well. His cheeks are like beds of balsam, where perfume herbs are
14 grown. His lips smell like lilies, flowing with myrrh oil. His arms are like golden
bars, set with beryl stones. His stomach is hewn like solid ivory, inlaid with lapis
15 lazuli. His legs stand firm as marble pillars, fixed on gold foundations. Seeing
16 him is like looking at Lebanon, and he is as choice as its cedars. His mouth is
filled with sweetness, for all of him, my longing. This is my beloved, this is my
love, daughters of Jerusalem.

6 1 [*Friends*] Where has your beloved gone, most beautiful of women? Where has
your beloved turned? We shall search for him with you.

2 [*She*] My beloved has gone to his garden, down to the beds of balsam; to pasture
3 in the gardens, to gather in lilies. I am my beloved's – my beloved is my own, who
pastures among the lilies.

4 [*He*] My love, you are as beautiful as Tirzah, as lovely as Jerusalem, terrifying
5 as the flagged armies. Turn your eyes from me, for they have overwhelmed me.
6 Your hair is like a flock of goats streaming down from Gilead. Your teeth are like
a flock of ewes rising up from cleaning; each bears twins, two and two, not one
7 among them lost. Your forehead, like a pomegranate, glows through your tresses.
8 Queens there are sixty; eighty concubines, and maids there are without number.
9 But my dove, my perfection, is one; one, unique to her mother – the shining one
she bore. Look at her, you girls, acknowledge she is blessed; look, queens and
concubines – and praise her."

10 [*Friends*] Who is this, gazing out like morning, beautiful as the moon, shining
like the sun, terrifying as the flagged armies?

11 [*He*] I went down to the nut-garden, to see the plants of the stream; to see
whether the vines were in flower, and if the pomegranate buds had burst.

12 [*She*] I did not know myself – I found myself – amid the chariots of my princely
people.

7 1 [*Friends*] Turn, turn back, Shulamite girl; turn back, turn, let us see you.
[*He*] Why do you gaze at the Shulamite girl as if she were a Maḥanaim dancer?
2 How lovely are your steps in sandals, prince's daughter, the turn of your thighs
3 like jewelry, work of the artist's hands; your navel a circular bowl – may it never
4 lack wine; your waist curved like baled wheat, bounded round with lilies. Your
5 two breasts are like young twins of a she-gazelle; your neck an ivory tower, your
eyes like pools in Ḥeshbon, like pools by the Bat Rabbim Gate; your nose like
6 the Tower of Lebanon gazing out to Damascus. Your head rises from you like the
7 Carmel, its curls shine like purple silk – a king is tangled up in its tresses. How
8 beautiful you are, how good; my love, in all its joys. Your bearing is like a date

יא דּוֹדִי צַח וְאָדוֹם דָּגוּל מֵרְבָבָה: רֹאשׁוֹ כֶּתֶם פָּז קְוֻצּוֹתָיו תַּלְתַּלִּים
יב שְׁחֹרוֹת כָּעוֹרֵב: עֵינָיו כְּיוֹנִים עַל־אֲפִיקֵי מָיִם רֹחֲצוֹת בֶּחָלָב יֹשְׁבוֹת
יג עַל־מִלֵּאת: לְחָיָו כַּעֲרוּגַת הַבֹּשֶׂם מִגְדְּלוֹת מֶרְקָחִים שִׂפְתוֹתָיו
יד שׁוֹשַׁנִּים נֹטְפוֹת מוֹר עֹבֵר: יָדָיו גְּלִילֵי זָהָב מְמֻלָּאִים בַּתַּרְשִׁישׁ מֵעָיו
טו עֶשֶׁת שֵׁן מְעֻלֶּפֶת סַפִּירִים: שׁוֹקָיו עַמּוּדֵי שֵׁשׁ מְיֻסָּדִים עַל־אַדְנֵי־פָז
טז מַרְאֵהוּ כַּלְּבָנוֹן בָּחוּר כָּאֲרָזִים: חִכּוֹ מַמְתַקִּים וְכֻלּוֹ מַחֲמַדִּים זֶה דוֹדִי
ו א וְזֶה רֵעִי בְּנוֹת יְרוּשָׁלִָם: אָנָה הָלַךְ דּוֹדֵךְ הַיָּפָה בַּנָּשִׁים אָנָה פָּנָה
ב דוֹדֵךְ וּנְבַקְשֶׁנּוּ עִמָּךְ: דּוֹדִי יָרַד לְגַנּוֹ לַעֲרוּגוֹת הַבֹּשֶׂם לִרְעוֹת בַּגַּנִּים
ג וְלִלְקֹט שׁוֹשַׁנִּים: אֲנִי לְדוֹדִי וְדוֹדִי לִי הָרֹעֶה בַּשּׁוֹשַׁנִּים:
ד יָפָה אַתְּ רַעְיָתִי כְּתִרְצָה נָאוָה כִּירוּשָׁלִָם אֲיֻמָּה כַּנִּדְגָּלוֹת: הָסֵבִּי
ה עֵינַיִךְ מִנֶּגְדִּי שֶׁהֵם הִרְהִיבֻנִי שַׂעְרֵךְ כְּעֵדֶר הָעִזִּים שֶׁגָּלְשׁוּ מִן־הַגִּלְעָד:
ו שִׁנַּיִךְ כְּעֵדֶר הָרְחֵלִים שֶׁעָלוּ מִן־הָרַחְצָה שֶׁכֻּלָּם מַתְאִימוֹת וְשַׁכֻּלָה
ז ח אֵין בָּהֶם: כְּפֶלַח הָרִמּוֹן רַקָּתֵךְ מִבַּעַד לְצַמָּתֵךְ: שִׁשִּׁים הֵמָּה מְלָכוֹת
ט וּשְׁמֹנִים פִּילַגְשִׁים וַעֲלָמוֹת אֵין מִסְפָּר: אַחַת הִיא יוֹנָתִי תַמָּתִי
אַחַת הִיא לְאִמָּהּ בָּרָה הִיא לְיוֹלַדְתָּהּ רָאוּהָ בָנוֹת וַיְאַשְּׁרוּהָ מְלָכוֹת
י וּפִילַגְשִׁים וַיְהַלְלוּהָ: מִי־זֹאת הַנִּשְׁקָפָה כְּמוֹ־שָׁחַר יָפָה
יא כַלְּבָנָה בָּרָה כַּחַמָּה אֲיֻמָּה כַּנִּדְגָּלוֹת: אֶל־גִּנַּת אֱגוֹז יָרַדְתִּי לִרְאוֹת
יב בְּאִבֵּי הַנָּחַל לִרְאוֹת הֲפָרְחָה הַגֶּפֶן הֵנֵצוּ הָרִמֹּנִים: לֹא יָדַעְתִּי נַפְשִׁי
ז א שָׂמַתְנִי מַרְכְּבוֹת עַמִּי נָדִיב: שׁוּבִי שׁוּבִי הַשּׁוּלַמִּית שׁוּבִי שׁוּבִי
ב וְנֶחֱזֶה־בָּךְ מַה־תֶּחֱזוּ בַּשּׁוּלַמִּית כִּמְחֹלַת הַמַּחֲנָיִם: מַה־יָּפוּ פְעָמַיִךְ
ג בַּנְּעָלִים בַּת־נָדִיב חַמּוּקֵי יְרֵכַיִךְ כְּמוֹ חֲלָאִים מַעֲשֵׂה יְדֵי אָמָּן: שָׁרְרֵךְ
אַגַּן הַסַּהַר אַל־יֶחְסַר הַמָּזֶג בִּטְנֵךְ עֲרֵמַת חִטִּים סוּגָה בַּשּׁוֹשַׁנִּים:
ד ה שְׁנֵי שָׁדַיִךְ כִּשְׁנֵי עֳפָרִים תָּאֳמֵי צְבִיָּה: צַוָּארֵךְ כְּמִגְדַּל הַשֵּׁן עֵינַיִךְ
בְּרֵכוֹת בְּחֶשְׁבּוֹן עַל־שַׁעַר בַּת־רַבִּים אַפֵּךְ כְּמִגְדַּל הַלְּבָנוֹן צוֹפֶה
ו פְּנֵי דַמָּשֶׂק: רֹאשֵׁךְ עָלַיִךְ כַּכַּרְמֶל וְדַלַּת רֹאשֵׁךְ כָּאַרְגָּמָן מֶלֶךְ אָסוּר
ז ח בָּרְהָטִים: מַה־יָּפִית וּמַה־נָּעַמְתְּ אַהֲבָה בַּתַּעֲנוּגִים: זֹאת קוֹמָתֵךְ

9 palm, your breasts its clustered fruits; but I said, "I shall climb the date palm, I
shall take hold of its stems," and your breasts will be like clustered grapes, your
10 breath, the scent of apples. And your mouth is like good wine, inside –

11 [*She*] It is for my beloved, flowing freely, bringing words to sleeping lips. I am my
beloved's; and his longing is for me.

12 13 Come, my beloved, let us go to the field, let us lodge in the villages; we will get up
early and go to the vineyards, to see if the vine has flowered, whether its blossoms
have opened out, if the pomegranate buds have burst; and there shall I give you
14 my love. The mandrakes give their scent, and on our own doorstep, the sweetest
of fruits, new and old; my beloved, I have hoarded them for you.

8 1 [*She*] If only you could have been my brother; could have suckled at my mother's
breast. I would find you outside, I would kiss you, yet no one would shame me.
2 I would lead you, I would bring you to my mother's house, you would teach me.
3 I would give you to drink, spiced wine, my pomegranate juice. My head rests in
4 his left hand, and his right arm is around me. Swear to me, daughters of Jerusalem,
tell me, why do you seek to waken, why to rouse, this love before its time?

5 [*Friends*] Who is this, rising from the desert, leaning on her beloved?

[*She*] Beneath the apple tree I woke you; where your mother bore you, where in
6 suffering she gave you birth. Set me like a seal upon your heart, like the seal upon
your arm – for love is as powerful as death itself, and jealousy as unyielding as
7 the grave; it burns with sparks of fire, with the Lord's own flame. Great waters
cannot quench love, nor torrents sweep it by. If a man offered all his inheritance
for love – they would laugh him to shame.

8 [*The Brothers*] We have a little sister, her breasts are not yet grown; what shall we
9 do for our sister when a man comes for her? If she were a wall we would build a
silver watchtower; if a door, then we would bar her up with cedar.

10 [*She*] But I am a wall. My breasts are like towers. It was when I was so that I
found peace in his eyes.

11 Once, Solomon had a vineyard at Ba'al Hamon. He gave the vineyard over to
12 the keepers; each keeper brought him in a silver thousand from the fruits. My
vineyard stands before me, my own: Solomon, keep your thousand; pay two
hundred to each keeper of the vines.

13 [*He*] "You who still sit in the gardens, friends listen for your voice. Have me hear."

14 [*She*] Away with you, my beloved, like a gazelle, or a young deer, over perfumed
hills.

Continue with Removing the Torah from the Ark on page 498.

ט דָּמְתָה לְתָמָר וְשָׁדַיִךְ לְאַשְׁכֹּלוֹת: אָמַרְתִּי אֶעֱלֶה בְתָמָר אֹחֲזָה
י בְּסַנְסִנָּיו וְיִהְיוּ־נָא שָׁדַיִךְ כְּאֶשְׁכְּלוֹת הַגֶּפֶן וְרֵיחַ אַפֵּךְ כַּתַּפּוּחִים: וְחִכֵּךְ
יא כְּיֵין הַטּוֹב הוֹלֵךְ לְדוֹדִי לְמֵישָׁרִים דּוֹבֵב שִׂפְתֵי יְשֵׁנִים: אֲנִי לְדוֹדִי
יב יג וְעָלַי תְּשׁוּקָתוֹ: לְכָה דוֹדִי נֵצֵא הַשָּׂדֶה נָלִינָה בַּכְּפָרִים: נַשְׁכִּימָה
לַכְּרָמִים נִרְאֶה אִם־פָּרְחָה הַגֶּפֶן פִּתַּח הַסְּמָדַר הֵנֵצוּ הָרִמּוֹנִים שָׁם
יד אֶתֵּן אֶת־דֹּדַי לָךְ: הַדּוּדָאִים נָתְנוּ־רֵיחַ וְעַל־פְּתָחֵינוּ כָּל־מְגָדִים
ח א חֲדָשִׁים גַּם־יְשָׁנִים דּוֹדִי צָפַנְתִּי לָךְ: מִי יִתֶּנְךָ כְּאָח לִי יוֹנֵק שְׁדֵי אִמִּי
ב אֶמְצָאֲךָ בַחוּץ אֶשָּׁקְךָ גַּם לֹא־יָבוּזוּ לִי: אֶנְהָגֲךָ אֲבִיאֲךָ אֶל־בֵּית
ג אִמִּי תְּלַמְּדֵנִי אַשְׁקְךָ מִיַּיִן הָרֶקַח מֵעֲסִיס רִמֹּנִי: שְׂמֹאלוֹ תַּחַת רֹאשִׁי
ד וִימִינוֹ תְּחַבְּקֵנִי: הִשְׁבַּעְתִּי אֶתְכֶם בְּנוֹת יְרוּשָׁלָםִ מַה־תָּעִירוּ ׀ וּמַה־
ה תְּעֹרְרוּ אֶת־הָאַהֲבָה עַד שֶׁתֶּחְפָּץ: מִי זֹאת עֹלָה מִן־
הַמִּדְבָּר מִתְרַפֶּקֶת עַל־דּוֹדָהּ תַּחַת הַתַּפּוּחַ עוֹרַרְתִּיךָ שָׁמָּה חִבְּלַתְךָ
ו אִמֶּךָ שָׁמָּה חִבְּלָה יְלָדַתְךָ: שִׂימֵנִי כַחוֹתָם עַל־לִבֶּךָ כַּחוֹתָם עַל־
זְרוֹעֶךָ כִּי־עַזָּה כַמָּוֶת אַהֲבָה קָשָׁה כִשְׁאוֹל קִנְאָה רְשָׁפֶיהָ רִשְׁפֵּי
ז אֵשׁ שַׁלְהֶבֶתְיָה: מַיִם רַבִּים לֹא יוּכְלוּ לְכַבּוֹת אֶת־הָאַהֲבָה וּנְהָרוֹת
לֹא יִשְׁטְפוּהָ אִם־יִתֵּן אִישׁ אֶת־כָּל־הוֹן בֵּיתוֹ בָּאַהֲבָה בּוֹז יָבוּזוּ
ח לוֹ: אָחוֹת לָנוּ קְטַנָּה וְשָׁדַיִם אֵין לָהּ מַה־נַּעֲשֶׂה לַאֲחֹתֵנוּ
ט בַּיּוֹם שֶׁיְּדֻבַּר־בָּהּ: אִם־חוֹמָה הִיא נִבְנֶה עָלֶיהָ טִירַת כָּסֶף וְאִם־דֶּלֶת
י הִיא נָצוּר עָלֶיהָ לוּחַ אָרֶז: אֲנִי חוֹמָה וְשָׁדַי כַּמִּגְדָּלוֹת אָז הָיִיתִי
יא בְעֵינָיו כְּמוֹצְאֵת שָׁלוֹם: כֶּרֶם הָיָה לִשְׁלֹמֹה בְּבַעַל הָמוֹן נָתַן אֶת־
יב הַכֶּרֶם לַנֹּטְרִים אִישׁ יָבִא בְּפִרְיוֹ אֶלֶף כָּסֶף: כַּרְמִי שֶׁלִּי לְפָנָי הָאֶלֶף
יג לְךָ שְׁלֹמֹה וּמָאתַיִם לְנֹטְרִים אֶת־פִּרְיוֹ: הַיּוֹשֶׁבֶת בַּגַּנִּים חֲבֵרִים
יד מַקְשִׁיבִים לְקוֹלֵךְ הַשְׁמִיעִנִי: בְּרַח ׀ דּוֹדִי וּדְמֵה־לְךָ לִצְבִי אוֹ לְעֹפֶר
הָאַיָּלִים עַל הָרֵי בְשָׂמִים:

Continue with הוצאת ספר תורה *on page 499.*

RUTH

1 1 Once, in the days when the Judges judged, there was a famine in the land. And
one man set out from Bethlehem of Judah and journeyed to live for a while in
2 the land of Moab, and his wife and two sons came with him. This man's name
was Elimelekh, his wife's was Naomi, and his two sons' names were Maḥlon and
Kilyon, all Efratites from Bethlehem of Judah. They duly arrived in the land of
Moab, and there they stayed.

3 But then Elimelekh, Naomi's husband, died, and she was left there with her
4 two sons. Both of them married Moabite women – the first was called Orpah,
and the second was called Ruth – and they lived on there for some ten years.
5 And after that, the two of them – Maḥlon and Kilyon – died as well, and the
6 woman was left bereaved of both her children and of her husband. And she got
up, her daughters-in-law with her, to return from the land of Moab; for word
had reached her in the land of Moab, that the Lord had brought His people to
mind, and granted them bread.

7 So she left the place where she had been, both of her daughters-in-law with her,
8 and set off back to the land of Judah. But to her two daughters-in-law she said, "Go
on now, please, turn back, each to your own mother's house, and may the Lord
9 show you that same kindness that you have shown the dead, and me. May the
Lord grant that you find your resting place, each in her husband's home –" and
10 as she kissed them, they wept aloud. And they said to her, "No. We are returning
with you to your people."

11 Said Naomi, "Turn back, daughters, why would you come with me? Have I still
12 sons in my womb who could be husbands to you? Turn back, my daughters, go;
I am too old to be with a man. Even were I to say, 'there is hope for me still';
13 were I even this night to be married, even if I could bear sons again – are you to
wait for them as they grow? Would you be chained to them, never to be another
man's? No, daughters, your presence is very bitter to me now, for the hand of
the Lord has beaten me."

14 Aloud they wept, still more, and then Orpah kissed her mother-in-law – but
Ruth clung to her.

15 And Naomi said, "Your sister-in-law has turned back, to her people, to her gods.
Turn back after your sister-in-law."

16 But Ruth replied, "Do not entreat me to leave you, to turn back and not to go
after you. Wherever you walk, I shall walk; wherever you lie down, there shall
17 I lie. Your people is my people; your God is my God. Wherever you die, there
I die, and there shall I be buried. All of this may the Lord show me, and more,
for death alone will part me from you."

רות

א א וַיְהִי בִּימֵי שְׁפֹט הַשֹּׁפְטִים וַיְהִי רָעָב בָּאָרֶץ וַיֵּלֶךְ אִישׁ מִבֵּית לֶחֶם
ב יְהוּדָה לָגוּר בִּשְׂדֵי מוֹאָב הוּא וְאִשְׁתּוֹ וּשְׁנֵי בָנָיו׃ וְשֵׁם הָאִישׁ אֱלִימֶלֶךְ
וְשֵׁם אִשְׁתּוֹ נָעֳמִי וְשֵׁם שְׁנֵי־בָנָיו ׀ מַחְלוֹן וְכִלְיוֹן אֶפְרָתִים מִבֵּית לֶחֶם
ג יְהוּדָה וַיָּבֹאוּ שְׂדֵי־מוֹאָב וַיִּהְיוּ־שָׁם׃ וַיָּמָת אֱלִימֶלֶךְ אִישׁ נָעֳמִי
ד וַתִּשָּׁאֵר הִיא וּשְׁנֵי בָנֶיהָ׃ וַיִּשְׂאוּ לָהֶם נָשִׁים מֹאֲבִיּוֹת שֵׁם הָאַחַת
ה עָרְפָּה וְשֵׁם הַשֵּׁנִית רוּת וַיֵּשְׁבוּ שָׁם כְּעֶשֶׂר שָׁנִים׃ וַיָּמוּתוּ גַם־שְׁנֵיהֶם
ו מַחְלוֹן וְכִלְיוֹן וַתִּשָּׁאֵר הָאִשָּׁה מִשְּׁנֵי יְלָדֶיהָ וּמֵאִישָׁהּ׃ וַתָּקָם הִיא
וְכַלֹּתֶיהָ וַתָּשָׁב מִשְּׂדֵי מוֹאָב כִּי שָׁמְעָה בִּשְׂדֵה מוֹאָב כִּי־פָקַד יהוה
ז אֶת־עַמּוֹ לָתֵת לָהֶם לָחֶם׃ וַתֵּצֵא מִן־הַמָּקוֹם אֲשֶׁר הָיְתָה־שָׁמָּה
ח וּשְׁתֵּי כַלֹּתֶיהָ עִמָּהּ וַתֵּלַכְנָה בַדֶּרֶךְ לָשׁוּב אֶל־אֶרֶץ יְהוּדָה׃ וַתֹּאמֶר
נָעֳמִי לִשְׁתֵּי כַלֹּתֶיהָ לֵכְנָה שֹּׁבְנָה אִשָּׁה לְבֵית אִמָּהּ יַעֲשֶׂה יהוה יַעַשׂ
ט עִמָּכֶם חֶסֶד כַּאֲשֶׁר עֲשִׂיתֶם עִם־הַמֵּתִים וְעִמָּדִי׃ יִתֵּן יהוה לָכֶם
וּמְצֶאןָ מְנוּחָה אִשָּׁה בֵּית אִישָׁהּ וַתִּשַּׁק לָהֶן וַתִּשֶּׂאנָה קוֹלָן וַתִּבְכֶּינָה׃
י יא וַתֹּאמַרְנָה־לָּהּ כִּי־אִתָּךְ נָשׁוּב לְעַמֵּךְ׃ וַתֹּאמֶר נָעֳמִי שֹׁבְנָה בְנֹתַי
יב לָמָּה תֵלַכְנָה עִמִּי הַעוֹד־לִי בָנִים בְּמֵעַי וְהָיוּ לָכֶם לַאֲנָשִׁים׃ שֹׁבְנָה
בְנֹתַי לֵכְןָ כִּי זָקַנְתִּי מִהְיוֹת לְאִישׁ כִּי אָמַרְתִּי יֶשׁ־לִי תִקְוָה גַּם הָיִיתִי
יג הַלַּיְלָה לְאִישׁ וְגַם יָלַדְתִּי בָנִים׃ הֲלָהֵן ׀ תְּשַׂבֵּרְנָה עַד אֲשֶׁר יִגְדָּלוּ
הֲלָהֵן תֵּעָגֵנָה לְבִלְתִּי הֱיוֹת לְאִישׁ אַל בְּנֹתַי כִּי־מַר־לִי מְאֹד מִכֶּם
יד כִּי־יָצְאָה בִי יַד־יהוה׃ וַתִּשֶּׂנָה קוֹלָן וַתִּבְכֶּינָה עוֹד וַתִּשַּׁק עָרְפָּה
טו לַחֲמוֹתָהּ וְרוּת דָּבְקָה בָּהּ׃ וַתֹּאמֶר הִנֵּה שָׁבָה יְבִמְתֵּךְ אֶל־עַמָּהּ
טז וְאֶל־אֱלֹהֶיהָ שׁוּבִי אַחֲרֵי יְבִמְתֵּךְ׃ וַתֹּאמֶר רוּת אַל־תִּפְגְּעִי־בִי לְעָזְבֵךְ
לָשׁוּב מֵאַחֲרָיִךְ כִּי אֶל־אֲשֶׁר תֵּלְכִי אֵלֵךְ וּבַאֲשֶׁר תָּלִינִי אָלִין עַמֵּךְ
יז עַמִּי וֵאלֹהַיִךְ אֱלֹהָי׃ בַּאֲשֶׁר תָּמוּתִי אָמוּת וְשָׁם אֶקָּבֵר כֹּה יַעֲשֶׂה
יח יהוה לִי וְכֹה יֹסִיף כִּי הַמָּוֶת יַפְרִיד בֵּינִי וּבֵינֵךְ׃ וַתֵּרֶא כִּי־מִתְאַמֶּצֶת

18 Naomi saw that Ruth was determined to come with her, and she spoke to her
19 no more. The two of them walked on until they came to Bethlehem; and when
they arrived at Bethlehem the whole town crowded round, the women saying,
"Can this be Naomi?"

20 She said, "Call me not Naomi. Call me Bitter, for the Almighty has made my
21 life bitter beyond words. I was full when I left this place, and empty has the
LORD returned me. Why call me, 'Naomi'? The LORD has spoken up against
me, the Almighty, and ruined me."

22 This is how Naomi, returning from the land of Moab, and, with her, her daughter-in-law, Ruth the Moabitess, returned. And they arrived at Bethlehem just as the barley harvest began.

2 1 Naomi had a relation from her husband Elimelekh's family: a man of substance
2 and great strength; his name was Boaz. Ruth the Moabitess said to Naomi, "I
shall go and gather the fallen grains among the barley-stalks – go after anyone
3 who should show me favor." Naomi said, "Go then, my daughter." And so she
went, to gather in the field after the harvestmen. And it was the field-plot of
Boaz she chanced to come to; that man of Elimelekh's family.

4 And there, indeed, came Boaz, arriving from Bethlehem, and saying to the harvestmen, "The LORD be with you." "Be blessed of the LORD," they replied.

5 "Whose is that young woman over there?" asked Boaz of his servant, who was
6 in charge of the harvestmen. "That is some Moabite girl," replied the servant in
charge of the harvestmen, "the one who came back with Naomi from the land of
7 Moab. She said, 'Let me come gleaning, gathering the fallen grains from among
the bundles, where the harvestmen have been'; and so she came, and has been
standing out here from early morning until now, and hardly sat at all in the shelter."

8 Boaz went to Ruth and said, "Daughter, take heed. Do not go gleaning in any
9 other field, and do not leave this one; cling close by my young women. Keep
your eyes on the field they are harvesting from and follow after them. I have
instructed the young men, of course, not to touch you. When you are thirsty,
go to the jugs and drink of the water the young men have drawn."

10 Ruth bowed down low, to the ground, and she asked him, "Why is it that I have found favor in your eyes, that you give me recognition such as this, when I am a stranger?"

11 Boaz said, "I have heard what you have done for your mother-in-law, since your
husband died; of how you left your father, your mother, the land of your birth,
12 and came to a people you knew not the day before. May the LORD repay your
labors; may your reward be full, at the hand of the LORD, the God of Israel,
under whose mantle you come to take shelter."

יט הִיא לָלֶכֶת אִתָּהּ וַתֶּחְדַּל לְדַבֵּר אֵלֶיהָ: וַתֵּלַכְנָה שְׁתֵּיהֶם עַד־בּוֹאָנָה
בֵּית לֶחֶם וַיְהִי כְּבוֹאָנָה בֵּית לֶחֶם וַתֵּהֹם כָּל־הָעִיר עֲלֵיהֶן וַתֹּאמַרְנָה
כ הֲזֹאת נָעֳמִי: וַתֹּאמֶר אֲלֵיהֶן אַל־תִּקְרֶאנָה לִי נָעֳמִי קְרֶאןָ לִי מָרָא
כא כִּי־הֵמַר שַׁדַּי לִי מְאֹד: אֲנִי מְלֵאָה הָלַכְתִּי וְרֵיקָם הֱשִׁיבַנִי יְהוָה
לָמָּה תִקְרֶאנָה לִי נָעֳמִי וַיהוָה עָנָה בִי וְשַׁדַּי הֵרַע לִי: וַתָּשָׁב נָעֳמִי
כב וְרוּת הַמּוֹאֲבִיָּה כַלָּתָהּ עִמָּהּ הַשָּׁבָה מִשְּׂדֵי מוֹאָב וְהֵמָּה בָּאוּ בֵּית
בא לֶחֶם בִּתְחִלַּת קְצִיר שְׂעֹרִים: וּלְנָעֳמִי מֵידָע לְאִישָׁהּ אִישׁ גִּבּוֹר חַיִל מוֹדַע
ב מִמִּשְׁפַּחַת אֱלִימֶלֶךְ וּשְׁמוֹ בֹּעַז: וַתֹּאמֶר רוּת הַמּוֹאֲבִיָּה אֶל־נָעֳמִי
אֵלְכָה־נָּא הַשָּׂדֶה וַאֲלַקֳטָה בַשִּׁבֳּלִים אַחַר אֲשֶׁר אֶמְצָא־חֵן בְּעֵינָיו
ג וַתֹּאמֶר לָהּ לְכִי בִתִּי: וַתֵּלֶךְ וַתָּבוֹא וַתְּלַקֵּט בַּשָּׂדֶה אַחֲרֵי הַקֹּצְרִים
ד וַיִּקֶר מִקְרֶהָ חֶלְקַת הַשָּׂדֶה לְבֹעַז אֲשֶׁר מִמִּשְׁפַּחַת אֱלִימֶלֶךְ: וְהִנֵּה־
בֹעַז בָּא מִבֵּית לֶחֶם וַיֹּאמֶר לַקּוֹצְרִים יְהוָה עִמָּכֶם וַיֹּאמְרוּ לוֹ יְבָרֶכְךָ
ה יְהוָה: וַיֹּאמֶר בֹּעַז לְנַעֲרוֹ הַנִּצָּב עַל־הַקּוֹצְרִים לְמִי הַנַּעֲרָה הַזֹּאת:
ו וַיַּעַן הַנַּעַר הַנִּצָּב עַל־הַקּוֹצְרִים וַיֹּאמַר נַעֲרָה מוֹאֲבִיָּה הִיא הַשָּׁבָה
ז עִם־נָעֳמִי מִשְּׂדֵה מוֹאָב: וַתֹּאמֶר אֲלַקֳטָה־נָּא וְאָסַפְתִּי בָעֳמָרִים אַחֲרֵי
הַקּוֹצְרִים וַתָּבוֹא וַתַּעֲמוֹד מֵאָז הַבֹּקֶר וְעַד־עַתָּה זֶה שִׁבְתָּהּ הַבַּיִת
ח מְעָט: וַיֹּאמֶר בֹּעַז אֶל־רוּת הֲלוֹא שָׁמַעַתְּ בִּתִּי אַל־תֵּלְכִי לִלְקֹט
ט בְּשָׂדֶה אַחֵר וְגַם לֹא תַעֲבוּרִי מִזֶּה וְכֹה תִדְבָּקִין עִם־נַעֲרֹתָי: עֵינַיִךְ
בַּשָּׂדֶה אֲשֶׁר־יִקְצֹרוּן וְהָלַכְתְּ אַחֲרֵיהֶן הֲלוֹא צִוִּיתִי אֶת־הַנְּעָרִים
לְבִלְתִּי נָגְעֵךְ וְצָמִת וְהָלַכְתְּ אֶל־הַכֵּלִים וְשָׁתִית מֵאֲשֶׁר יִשְׁאֲבוּן
י הַנְּעָרִים: וַתִּפֹּל עַל־פָּנֶיהָ וַתִּשְׁתַּחוּ אָרְצָה וַתֹּאמֶר אֵלָיו מַדּוּעַ מָצָאתִי
יא חֵן בְּעֵינֶיךָ לְהַכִּירֵנִי וְאָנֹכִי נָכְרִיָּה: וַיַּעַן בֹּעַז וַיֹּאמֶר לָהּ הֻגֵּד הֻגַּד לִי
כֹּל אֲשֶׁר־עָשִׂית אֶת־חֲמוֹתֵךְ אַחֲרֵי מוֹת אִישֵׁךְ וַתַּעַזְבִי אָבִיךְ וְאִמֵּךְ
וְאֶרֶץ מוֹלַדְתֵּךְ וַתֵּלְכִי אֶל־עַם אֲשֶׁר לֹא־יָדַעַתְּ תְּמוֹל שִׁלְשׁוֹם: יְשַׁלֵּם
יב יְהוָה פָּעֳלֵךְ וּתְהִי מַשְׂכֻּרְתֵּךְ שְׁלֵמָה מֵעִם יְהוָה אֱלֹהֵי יִשְׂרָאֵל אֲשֶׁר־
יג בָּאת לַחֲסוֹת תַּחַת־כְּנָפָיו: וַתֹּאמֶר אֶמְצָא־חֵן בְּעֵינֶיךָ אֲדֹנִי כִּי

13 "Sir," she said, "I hope to find favor in your eyes, for you give me solace. For
you have spoken to your servant's heart, though I am not like your servants."
14 When the time came for eating, Boaz said to her, "Come here, eat of this food,
and dip your bread in the vinegar." She sat down beside the harvestmen and he
15 served her roasted grains, and she ate, and had her fill, and more left over. And
when she stood up to begin gleaning again, Boaz instructed his workers, "Let her
16 glean among the sheaves as well, do not disgrace her. And drop some ears from
the bunches as well; leave them, let her glean them and do not reproach her."

17 Ruth carried on gleaning in the field until evening and then threshed what
18 she had gleaned; it was almost an ephah of barley. She picked it up and came
into the city; her mother-in-law saw what she had gleaned; and she produced
all that was left beyond her fill, and gave it to her.

19 "Where did you gather today," she asked, "where were you? Bless whoever gave
you this recognition." So Ruth told her mother-in-law under whose patronage
20 she had worked: "The man's name is Boaz, with whom I worked today." Said
Naomi to her daughter-in-law, "The Lord bless him; for he has not left behind
his kindness for the living or the dead –" and Naomi told her, "The man is our
relative; one of our redeemers."

21 "He said to me, as well," said Ruth the Moabitess: "'Cling by my young men,
22 until they finish all my harvest,'" and Naomi told her daughter-in-law Ruth,
"That is well, my daughter. Go out with his young women; do not go and come
to harm in other fields."

23 And so it was that she clung by Boaz's young women to glean, until the barley
harvest was over, and then the wheat; and after that she sat at home with her
mother-in-law.

3 1 One day her mother-in-law Naomi said to her, "Daughter, do I not wish I
2 could find you a resting place that would be good for you? Now there is Boaz,
our relative, whose young women you were with – and he will be doing his
3 winnowing in the barley shed tonight. And you are going to wash yourself
and anoint yourself and put on your dress, and go down to that shed. Do not
let the man know that you are there until he has finished eating and drinking.
4 And when he lies down, take note of the place where he lies, and afterwards go
there, uncover his feet and lie down also – and he will tell you what to do next."

5 "I shall do," said Ruth, "all that you tell me to do."

6 She went down to the shed and did exactly as her mother-in-law had instructed
7 her. Boaz ate, and drank, and was happy, and he went and lay down at the edge
of the heap of grain; and then she came to him silently, uncovered his feet and
lay herself down.

נִחַמְתָּ֔נִי וְכִ֥י דִבַּ֖רְתָּ עַל־לֵ֣ב שִׁפְחָתֶ֑ךָ וְאָֽנֹכִי֙ לֹ֣א אֶֽהְיֶ֔ה כְּאַחַ֖ת שִׁפְחֹתֶֽיךָ׃
יד וַיֹּאמֶר֩ לָ֨ה בֹ֜עַז לְעֵ֣ת הָאֹ֗כֶל גֹּ֤שִֽׁי הֲלֹם֙ וְאָכַ֣לְתְּ מִן־הַלֶּ֔חֶם וְטָבַ֥לְתְּ
פִּתֵּ֖ךְ בַּחֹ֑מֶץ וַתֵּ֙שֶׁב֙ מִצַּ֣ד הַקֹּֽצְרִ֔ים וַיִּצְבָּט־לָ֣הּ קָלִ֔י וַתֹּ֥אכַל וַתִּשְׂבַּ֖ע
טו וַתֹּתַֽר׃ וַתָּ֖קָם לְלַקֵּ֑ט וַיְצַו֩ בֹּ֨עַז אֶת־נְעָרָ֜יו לֵאמֹ֗ר גַּ֣ם בֵּ֧ין הָֽעֳמָרִ֛ים
טז תְּלַקֵּ֖ט וְלֹ֥א תַכְלִימֽוּהָ׃ וְגַ֛ם שֹׁל־תָּשֹׁ֥לּוּ לָ֖הּ מִן־הַצְּבָתִ֑ים וַעֲזַבְתֶּ֥ם
יז וְלִקְּטָ֖ה וְלֹ֥א תִגְעֲרוּ־בָֽהּ׃ וַתְּלַקֵּ֥ט בַּשָּׂדֶ֖ה עַד־הָעָ֑רֶב וַתַּחְבֹּט֙ אֵ֣ת
יח אֲשֶׁר־לִקֵּ֔טָה וַיְהִ֖י כְּאֵיפָ֥ה שְׂעֹרִֽים׃ וַתִּשָּׂא֙ וַתָּב֣וֹא הָעִ֔יר וַתֵּ֥רֶא חֲמוֹתָ֖הּ
אֵ֣ת אֲשֶׁר־לִקֵּ֑טָה וַתּוֹצֵא֙ וַתִּתֶּן־לָ֔הּ אֵ֥ת אֲשֶׁר־הוֹתִ֖רָה מִשָּׂבְעָֽהּ׃
יט וַתֹּאמֶר֩ לָ֨הּ חֲמוֹתָ֜הּ אֵיפֹ֨ה לִקַּ֤טְתְּ הַיּוֹם֙ וְאָ֣נָה עָשִׂ֔ית יְהִ֥י מַכִּירֵ֖ךְ בָּר֑וּךְ
וַתַּגֵּ֣ד לַחֲמוֹתָ֗הּ אֵ֤ת אֲשֶׁר־עָשְׂתָה֙ עִמּ֔וֹ וַתֹּ֗אמֶר שֵׁ֤ם הָאִישׁ֙ אֲשֶׁ֨ר
כ עָשִׂ֧יתִי עִמּ֛וֹ הַיּ֖וֹם בֹּֽעַז׃ וַתֹּ֨אמֶר נָעֳמִ֜י לְכַלָּתָ֗הּ בָּר֥וּךְ הוּא֙ לַֽיהֹוָ֔ה
אֲשֶׁר֙ לֹא־עָזַ֣ב חַסְדּ֔וֹ אֶת־הַחַיִּ֖ים וְאֶת־הַמֵּתִ֑ים וַתֹּ֧אמֶר לָ֣הּ נָעֳמִ֗י
כא קָר֥וֹב לָ֙נוּ֙ הָאִ֔ישׁ מִגֹּאֲלֵ֖נוּ הֽוּא׃ וַתֹּ֖אמֶר ר֣וּת הַמּוֹאֲבִיָּ֑ה גַּ֣ם ׀ כִּֽי־אָמַ֣ר
אֵלַ֗י עִם־הַנְּעָרִ֤ים אֲשֶׁר־לִי֙ תִּדְבָּקִ֔ין עַ֣ד אִם־כִּלּ֔וּ אֵ֥ת כָּל־הַקָּצִ֖יר
כב אֲשֶׁר־לִֽי׃ וַתֹּ֥אמֶר נָעֳמִ֖י אֶל־ר֣וּת כַּלָּתָ֑הּ ט֣וֹב בִּתִּ֗י כִּ֤י תֵֽצְאִי֙ עִם־
כג נַעֲרוֹתָ֔יו וְלֹ֥א יִפְגְּעוּ־בָ֖ךְ בְּשָׂדֶ֥ה אַחֵֽר׃ וַתִּדְבַּ֞ק בְּנַעֲר֥וֹת בֹּ֙עַז֙ לְלַקֵּ֔ט
עַד־כְּל֥וֹת קְצִיר־הַשְּׂעֹרִ֖ים וּקְצִ֣יר הַחִטִּ֑ים וַתֵּ֖שֶׁב אֶת־חֲמוֹתָֽהּ׃
ג א וַתֹּ֥אמֶר לָ֖הּ נָעֳמִ֣י חֲמוֹתָ֑הּ בִּתִּ֗י הֲלֹ֧א אֲבַקֶּשׁ־לָ֛ךְ מָנ֖וֹחַ אֲשֶׁ֥ר יִֽיטַב־
ב לָֽךְ׃ וְעַתָּ֗ה הֲלֹ֥א בֹ֙עַז֙ מֹֽדַעְתָּ֔נוּ אֲשֶׁ֥ר הָיִ֖ית אֶת־נַעֲרוֹתָ֑יו הִנֵּה־ה֗וּא
ג זֹרֶ֛ה אֶת־גֹּ֥רֶן הַשְּׂעֹרִ֖ים הַלָּֽיְלָה׃ וְרָחַ֣צְתְּ ׀ וָסַ֗כְתְּ וְשַׂ֥מְתְּ שמלתך שִׂמְלֹתַ֛יִךְ
עָלַ֖יִךְ וירדתי הַגֹּ֑רֶן אַל־תִּוָּ֣דְעִ֣י לָאִ֔ישׁ עַ֥ד כַּלֹּת֖וֹ לֶאֱכֹ֥ל וְלִשְׁתּֽוֹת׃ וְיָרַ֣דְתְּ
ד וִיהִ֣י בְשָׁכְב֗וֹ וְיָדַ֙עַתְּ֙ אֶת־הַמָּקוֹם֙ אֲשֶׁ֣ר יִשְׁכַּב־שָׁ֔ם וּבָ֛את וְגִלִּ֥ית
ה מַרְגְּלֹתָ֖יו ושכבתי וְה֗וּא יַגִּ֣יד לָ֔ךְ אֵ֖ת אֲשֶׁ֥ר תַּעֲשִֽׂין׃ וַתֹּ֖אמֶר אֵלֶ֑יהָ וְשָׁכָ֑בְתְּ
ו כֹּ֛ל אֲשֶׁר־תֹּאמְרִ֥י   אֶֽעֱשֶֽׂה׃ וַתֵּ֖רֶד הַגֹּ֑רֶן וַתַּ֕עַשׂ כְּכֹ֥ל אֲשֶׁר־צִוַּ֖תָּה אֵלַ֖י
ז חֲמוֹתָֽהּ׃ וַיֹּ֨אכַל בֹּ֤עַז וַיֵּשְׁתְּ֙ וַיִּיטַ֣ב לִבּ֔וֹ וַיָּבֹ֕א לִשְׁכַּ֖ב בִּקְצֵ֣ה הָעֲרֵמָ֑ה
ח וַתָּבֹ֣א בַלָּ֔ט וַתְּגַ֥ל מַרְגְּלֹתָ֖יו וַתִּשְׁכָּֽב׃ וַיְהִי֙ בַּחֲצִ֣י הַלַּ֔יְלָה וַיֶּחֱרַ֥ד הָאִ֖ישׁ

8 At midnight the man started and turned over – there was a woman lying
9 at his feet. "Who are you?" he said, and she answered, "I am your servant
Ruth – spread your mantle over your maidservant, for you are a redeemer."
10 And he replied,

"God bless you, daughter, for this last kindness is yet greater than your first, for
11 you have not gone after the young men, poor or rich. Now, daughter, do not be
afraid. I shall do all that you ask, for all within my people's gate know well, that
12 you are a woman of great strength. And I am indeed a redeemer to you, but there
13 is a redeemer still closer than me. Carry on lying here tonight, and in the morning if he would redeem you, good: let him redeem. And if he cares not to redeem
you, I shall redeem you myself, as the Lord lives – lie on here until morning."

14 And so she lay at his feet until morning, and left before one man could recognize
15 another. "Let not a soul know there was a woman in the shed," said he. And
then, "Give me the wrap that you are wearing, hold it out –" and he measured
six measures of barley into it; he gave them to her, and she went out into the city.
16 She came to her mother-in-law; "Who are you, my daughter?" she said. And
17 Ruth told her all that the man had done for her. "He gave me these six measures of barley," she said, "saying, 'Do not go back to your mother-in-law
18 empty-handed.'" Said Naomi, "Sit down now, daughter, until you find out how
the matter will fall. For that man will not rest today until it is settled."

4 1 Boaz went up to the City Gate and sat down. And the very redeemer of whom
he had spoken passed by: "Such-and-such," said Boaz, "come here and be
2 seated," and he came and sat down. Then Boaz took ten men from among the
3 elders of the city; "Be seated here," he said, and they too sat. And then he said
to the redeemer, "Naomi, coming back from the land of Moab, must sell the
4 field-plot of our kinsman Elimelekh. And I told her I would let you know of
it, inviting you to buy it, in front of those sitting here, in front of the elders of
this city. If you would like to redeem this: redeem; and if you will not redeem
it, tell me: let me know, for there is none but you to redeem, and I am next in
line to you." "I shall redeem," he said.

5 "On the day you buy that field from Naomi," said Boaz, "and from Ruth the
Moabitess – you will have bought the wife of a dead man with it, to restore
the dead man's name on his estate."

6 Said the redeemer: "Such a redemption I could not perform; it would be the
ruin of my own estate. You redeem in my place, I cannot redeem."

7 In those long-ago days in Israel, a redemption or exchange – anything to be
officially enacted – was completed as follows. One man would take off his
shoe, and would hand it to the other: that was the bond then recognized

ט וַיִּלָּפֵת וְהִנֵּה אִשָּׁה שֹׁכֶבֶת מַרְגְּלֹתָיו׃ וַיֹּאמֶר מִי־אָתְּ וַתֹּאמֶר אָנֹכִי
י רוּת אֲמָתֶךָ וּפָרַשְׂתָּ כְנָפֶךָ עַל־אֲמָתְךָ כִּי גֹאֵל אָתָּה׃ וַיֹּאמֶר בְּרוּכָה
אַתְּ לַיהוָה בִּתִּי הֵיטַבְתְּ חַסְדֵּךְ הָאַחֲרוֹן מִן־הָרִאשׁוֹן לְבִלְתִּי־לֶכֶת
יא אַחֲרֵי הַבַּחוּרִים אִם־דַּל וְאִם־עָשִׁיר׃ וְעַתָּה בִּתִּי אַל־תִּירְאִי כֹּל
אֲשֶׁר־תֹּאמְרִי אֶעֱשֶׂה־לָּךְ כִּי יוֹדֵעַ כָּל־שַׁעַר עַמִּי כִּי אֵשֶׁת חַיִל אָתְּ׃
יב יג וְעַתָּה כִּי אָמְנָם כִּי אם גֹאֵל אָנֹכִי וְגַם יֵשׁ גֹּאֵל קָרוֹב מִמֶּנִּי׃ לִינִי
הַלַּיְלָה וְהָיָה בַבֹּקֶר אִם־יִגְאָלֵךְ טוֹב יִגְאָל וְאִם־לֹא יַחְפֹּץ לְגָאֳלֵךְ
יד וּגְאַלְתִּיךְ אָנֹכִי חַי־יְהוָה שִׁכְבִי עַד־הַבֹּקֶר׃ וַתִּשְׁכַּב מַרְגְּלוֹתָו עַד־
הַבֹּקֶר וַתָּקָם בטרום יַכִּיר אִישׁ אֶת־רֵעֵהוּ וַיֹּאמֶר אַל־יִוָּדַע כִּי־בָאָה בְּטֶרֶם
טו הָאִשָּׁה הַגֹּרֶן׃ וַיֹּאמֶר הָבִי הַמִּטְפַּחַת אֲשֶׁר־עָלַיִךְ וְאֶחֳזִי־בָהּ וַתֹּאחֶז
טז בָּהּ וַיָּמָד שֵׁשׁ־שְׂעֹרִים וַיָּשֶׁת עָלֶיהָ וַיָּבֹא הָעִיר׃ וַתָּבוֹא אֶל־חֲמוֹתָהּ
וַתֹּאמֶר מִי־אַתְּ בִּתִּי וַתַּגֶּד־לָהּ אֵת כָּל־אֲשֶׁר עָשָׂה־לָהּ הָאִישׁ׃
יז וַתֹּאמֶר שֵׁשׁ־הַשְּׂעֹרִים הָאֵלֶּה נָתַן לִי כִּי אָמַר אַל־תָּבוֹאִי רֵיקָם אֵלַי
יח אֶל־חֲמוֹתֵךְ׃ וַתֹּאמֶר שְׁבִי בִתִּי עַד אֲשֶׁר תֵּדְעִין אֵיךְ יִפֹּל דָּבָר כִּי לֹא
ד א יִשְׁקֹט הָאִישׁ כִּי אִם־כִּלָּה הַדָּבָר הַיּוֹם׃ וּבֹעַז עָלָה הַשַּׁעַר וַיֵּשֶׁב שָׁם
וְהִנֵּה הַגֹּאֵל עֹבֵר אֲשֶׁר דִּבֶּר־בֹּעַז וַיֹּאמֶר סוּרָה שְׁבָה־פֹּה פְּלֹנִי אַלְמֹנִי
ב וַיָּסַר וַיֵּשֵׁב׃ וַיִּקַּח עֲשָׂרָה אֲנָשִׁים מִזִּקְנֵי הָעִיר וַיֹּאמֶר שְׁבוּ־פֹה וַיֵּשֵׁבוּ׃
ג וַיֹּאמֶר לַגֹּאֵל חֶלְקַת הַשָּׂדֶה אֲשֶׁר לְאָחִינוּ לֶאֱלִימֶלֶךְ מָכְרָה נָעֳמִי
ד הַשָּׁבָה מִשְּׂדֵה מוֹאָב׃ וַאֲנִי אָמַרְתִּי אֶגְלֶה אָזְנְךָ לֵאמֹר קְנֵה נֶגֶד
הַיֹּשְׁבִים וְנֶגֶד זִקְנֵי עַמִּי אִם־תִּגְאַל גְּאָל וְאִם־לֹא יִגְאַל הַגִּידָה לִּי
ה וְאֵדַע כִּי אֵין זוּלָתְךָ לִגְאוֹל וְאָנֹכִי אַחֲרֶיךָ וַיֹּאמֶר אָנֹכִי אֶגְאָל׃ וַיֹּאמֶר
בֹּעַז בְּיוֹם־קְנוֹתְךָ הַשָּׂדֶה מִיַּד נָעֳמִי וּמֵאֵת רוּת הַמּוֹאֲבִיָּה אֵשֶׁת־
ו הַמֵּת קניתי לְהָקִים שֵׁם־הַמֵּת עַל־נַחֲלָתוֹ׃ וַיֹּאמֶר הַגֹּאֵל לֹא אוּכַל קָנִיתָ
לגאול־לִי פֶּן־אַשְׁחִית אֶת־נַחֲלָתִי גְּאַל־לְךָ אַתָּה אֶת־גְּאֻלָּתִי כִּי לִגְאָל־
ז לֹא־אוּכַל לִגְאֹל׃ וְזֹאת לְפָנִים בְּיִשְׂרָאֵל עַל־הַגְּאוּלָּה וְעַל־הַתְּמוּרָה
לְקַיֵּם כָּל־דָּבָר שָׁלַף אִישׁ נַעֲלוֹ וְנָתַן לְרֵעֵהוּ וְזֹאת הַתְּעוּדָה בְּיִשְׂרָאֵל׃

8 among Israel. And now this redeemer said to Boaz, "Take possession." And
he took off his shoe.

9 "You bear witness on this day," said Boaz to the elders and to all the people
present, "that I take possession of all that was Elimelekh's, and all that was
10 Kilyon's and Maḥlon's, from Naomi's hand. And with it I take Ruth the
Moabitess, Maḥlon's wife, to be mine, to rebuild the name of the dead on his
estate. And the dead man's name will not be cut off from among his brothers,
from the gate of his home town – you are my witnesses this day."

11 And all the people at the gate, and the elders, said, "We bear witness. May the
Lord make the woman who is joining your house like Rachel and like Leah,
who together built the house of Israel; may you go from strength to strength
12 in Efrata, and your name be ever spoken in Bethlehem. And may your house
be as the house of Peretz, whom Tamar bore to Judah, growing from the seed
that the Lord will give you from this young woman."

13 And so it was that Boaz took Ruth, and she became his wife, and he came to
14 her; the Lord granted her conception, and she bore a son. And the women
said to Naomi, "Blessed be the Lord, who has not withheld your redeemer
15 on this day – may the child's name be spoken in all Israel. And may he restore
your spirit, and sustain your old age, for your daughter-in-law, who loves you,
she has borne him: she who is better to you than seven sons could be."

16 17 Naomi took the child and fed him in her bosom, and became his nurse. And
her neighbors named him, saying, "A son is born for Naomi!" They called him
Oved. And that was Oved the father of Jesse, the father of David.

18 19 This is the line of Peretz: Ḥetzron was born to Peretz. Ram was born to
20 Ḥetzron; Aminadav was born to Ram. Naḥshon was born to Aminadav;
21 Salma was born to Naḥshon. Boaz was born to Salma; Oved was born to Boaz.
22 And Jesse was born to Oved – and to Jesse, David was born.

Continue with Removing the Torah from the Ark on page 498.

ח ט וַיֹּאמֶר הַגֹּאֵל לְבֹעַז קְנֵה־לָךְ וַיִּשְׁלֹף נַעֲלוֹ: וַיֹּאמֶר בֹּעַז לַזְּקֵנִים וְכָל־
הָעָם עֵדִים אַתֶּם הַיּוֹם כִּי קָנִיתִי אֶת־כָּל־אֲשֶׁר לֶאֱלִימֶלֶךְ וְאֵת כָּל־
י אֲשֶׁר לְכִלְיוֹן וּמַחְלוֹן מִיַּד נָעֳמִי: וְגַם אֶת־רוּת הַמֹּאֲבִיָּה אֵשֶׁת מַחְלוֹן
קָנִיתִי לִי לְאִשָּׁה לְהָקִים שֵׁם־הַמֵּת עַל־נַחֲלָתוֹ וְלֹא־יִכָּרֵת שֵׁם־
יא הַמֵּת מֵעִם אֶחָיו וּמִשַּׁעַר מְקוֹמוֹ עֵדִים אַתֶּם הַיּוֹם: וַיֹּאמְרוּ כָּל־
הָעָם אֲשֶׁר־בַּשַּׁעַר וְהַזְּקֵנִים עֵדִים יִתֵּן יהוה אֶת־הָאִשָּׁה הַבָּאָה
אֶל־בֵּיתֶךָ כְּרָחֵל ׀ וּכְלֵאָה אֲשֶׁר בָּנוּ שְׁתֵּיהֶם אֶת־בֵּית יִשְׂרָאֵל וַעֲשֵׂה־
יב חַיִל בְּאֶפְרָתָה וּקְרָא־שֵׁם בְּבֵית לָחֶם: וִיהִי בֵיתְךָ כְּבֵית פֶּרֶץ אֲשֶׁר־
יָלְדָה תָמָר לִיהוּדָה מִן־הַזֶּרַע אֲשֶׁר יִתֵּן יהוה לְךָ מִן־הַנַּעֲרָה הַזֹּאת:
יג וַיִּקַּח בֹּעַז אֶת־רוּת וַתְּהִי־לוֹ לְאִשָּׁה וַיָּבֹא אֵלֶיהָ וַיִּתֵּן יהוה לָהּ הֵרָיוֹן
יד וַתֵּלֶד בֵּן: וַתֹּאמַרְנָה הַנָּשִׁים אֶל־נָעֳמִי בָּרוּךְ יהוה אֲשֶׁר לֹא הִשְׁבִּית
טו לָךְ גֹּאֵל הַיּוֹם וְיִקָּרֵא שְׁמוֹ בְּיִשְׂרָאֵל: וְהָיָה לָךְ לְמֵשִׁיב נֶפֶשׁ וּלְכַלְכֵּל
אֶת־שֵׂיבָתֵךְ כִּי כַלָּתֵךְ אֲשֶׁר־אֲהֵבַתֶךְ יְלָדַתּוּ אֲשֶׁר־הִיא טוֹבָה לָךְ
טז מִשִּׁבְעָה בָּנִים: וַתִּקַּח נָעֳמִי אֶת־הַיֶּלֶד וַתְּשִׁתֵהוּ בְחֵיקָהּ וַתְּהִי־לוֹ
יז לְאֹמֶנֶת: וַתִּקְרֶאנָה לוֹ הַשְּׁכֵנוֹת שֵׁם לֵאמֹר יֻלַּד־בֵּן לְנָעֳמִי וַתִּקְרֶאנָה
שְׁמוֹ עוֹבֵד הוּא אֲבִי־יִשַׁי אֲבִי דָוִד:

יח יט וְאֵלֶּה תּוֹלְדוֹת פָּרֶץ פֶּרֶץ הוֹלִיד אֶת־חֶצְרוֹן: וְחֶצְרוֹן הוֹלִיד אֶת־
כ רָם וְרָם הוֹלִיד אֶת־עַמִּינָדָב: וְעַמִּינָדָב הוֹלִיד אֶת־נַחְשׁוֹן וְנַחְשׁוֹן
כא הוֹלִיד אֶת־שַׂלְמָה: וְשַׂלְמוֹן הוֹלִיד אֶת־בֹּעַז וּבֹעַז הוֹלִיד אֶת־עוֹבֵד:
כב וְעֹבֵד הוֹלִיד אֶת־יִשָׁי וְיִשַׁי הוֹלִיד אֶת־דָּוִד:

Continue with הוצאת ספר תורה *on page 499.*

EIKHA

1 1 How the city that flocked with people sits alone; she is like a widow. She
2 who was great among nations, princess of states, now a bonded colony. She
weeps, weeps through the nights; on her cheek, tears. Of all her friends there
is none to console her; all her lovers have betrayed her, become enemies to
3 her. Oppression has exiled Judah, oppression and the harshness of her labor.
She sits among nations, finds no resting place; all her pursuers have caught
4 her, among the narrow spaces. The streets of Zion are grieving – festive times,
but no one comes. All her gates are desolate, her priests are groaning, her
5 young girls are sorrowful, and she – her life is bitter. Her foes are the head of
this beast now, her enemies tranquil, for the LORD has brought her sorrow
for all her crimes. Her infants walked off captive before foes.

6 It is gone from daughter Zion – all her honor gone. Her princes have become
7 like deer that find no pasture, walking without strength before pursuers. She
remembers, Jerusalem, in her days of oppression and wandering, all the ones
she treasured, who once were, then; how her people fell at the foes' hands
with none to help her. They see her now, these enemies, and laugh at what
8 has ceased in her. She has sinned – Jerusalem sinned, and so she is become
an outcast. All who once respected her abase her: they have seen her naked;
9 now she too is groaning, and sits apart. Her impurity stains her skirts; she
forgot what her end would be. Her fall was startling; none console her. "LORD,
witness this oppression; the enemy grew strong."

10 A foe has spread his hand over all her treasured ones. The nations saw her,
they came to her Temple – those that You commanded must never come
11 among Your people. All her nation groans: they are seeking bread. They gave
up their treasured ones for food, to restore their souls – "See this, LORD, look
on – I am abased.

12 "May this never come to you, all you who cross my path. Look on now and
see – is there any pain like mine? Like that, which was done to me, the sorrow
13 the LORD sent me, on the day His rage burned? From above He sent down
fire, through my bones, and broke them all. He spread the net at my feet, sent
me backwards. He rendered me desolate, all the day, ailing.

14 "The yoke of my crimes was bound together, the ropes twisted in His hand,
were raised to my neck, brought down my strength. The LORD has given
15 me over to the hands of one I cannot rise from. He cast all my heroes aside –
the LORD in my midst. He called together the forces primed to break my
young men. The LORD trod red the wine-press of the virgin daughter Judah.

איכה

א* אֵיכָ֣ה ׀ יָשְׁבָ֣ה בָדָ֗ד הָעִיר֙ רַבָּ֣תִי עָ֔ם הָיְתָ֖ה כְּאַלְמָנָ֑ה רַבָּ֣תִי בַגּוֹיִ֗ם

ב שָׂרָ֙תִי֙ בַּמְּדִינ֔וֹת הָיְתָ֖ה לָמַֽס׃ בָּכ֨וֹ תִבְכֶּ֜ה בַּלַּ֗יְלָה וְדִמְעָתָהּ֙ עַ֣ל לֶֽחֱיָ֔הּ

אֵֽין־לָ֥הּ מְנַחֵ֖ם מִכָּל־אֹהֲבֶ֑יהָ כָּל־רֵעֶ֙יהָ֙ בָּ֣גְדוּ בָ֔הּ הָ֥יוּ לָ֖הּ לְאֹיְבִֽים׃

ג גָּֽלְתָ֨ה יְהוּדָ֤ה מֵעֹ֙נִי֙ וּמֵרֹ֣ב עֲבֹדָ֔ה הִ֚יא יָשְׁבָ֣ה בַגּוֹיִ֔ם לֹ֥א מָצְאָ֖ה מָנ֑וֹחַ

ד כָּל־רֹדְפֶ֥יהָ הִשִּׂיג֖וּהָ בֵּ֥ין הַמְּצָרִֽים׃ דַּרְכֵ֤י צִיּוֹן֙ אֲבֵל֔וֹת מִבְּלִי֙ בָּאֵ֣י

מוֹעֵ֔ד כָּל־שְׁעָרֶ֙יהָ֙ שֽׁוֹמֵמִ֔ין כֹּהֲנֶ֖יהָ נֶאֱנָחִ֑ים בְּתוּלֹתֶ֥יהָ נּוּג֖וֹת וְהִ֥יא

ה מַר־לָֽהּ׃ הָי֨וּ צָרֶ֤יהָ לְרֹאשׁ֙ אֹיְבֶ֣יהָ שָׁל֔וּ כִּֽי־יְהוָ֥ה הוֹגָ֖הּ עַ֣ל רֹב־פְּשָׁעֶ֑יהָ

ו עֽוֹלָלֶ֛יהָ הָלְכ֥וּ שְׁבִ֖י לִפְנֵי־צָֽר׃ וַיֵּצֵ֥א מן־בת־צִיּ֖וֹן כָּל־הֲדָרָ֑הּ הָי֣וּ שָׂרֶ֗יהָ

ז כְּאַיָּלִים֙ לֹא־מָצְא֣וּ מִרְעֶ֔ה וַיֵּלְכ֥וּ בְלֹא־כֹ֖חַ לִפְנֵ֥י רוֹדֵֽף׃ זָכְרָ֣ה יְרוּשָׁלִַ֗ם

יְמֵ֤י עָנְיָהּ֙ וּמְרוּדֶ֔יהָ כֹּ֚ל מַחֲמֻדֶ֔יהָ אֲשֶׁ֥ר הָי֖וּ מִ֣ימֵי קֶ֑דֶם בִּנְפֹ֧ל עַמָּ֣הּ

ח בְּיַד־צָ֗ר וְאֵ֤ין עוֹזֵר֙ לָ֔הּ רָא֣וּהָ צָרִ֔ים שָׂחֲק֖וּ עַל־מִשְׁבַּתֶּֽהָ׃ חֵ֤טְא

חָֽטְאָה֙ יְר֣וּשָׁלִַ֔ם עַל־כֵּ֖ן לְנִידָ֣ה הָיָ֑תָה כָּֽל־מְכַבְּדֶ֤יהָ הִזִּיל֙וּהָ֙ כִּי־רָא֣וּ

ט עֶרְוָתָ֔הּ גַּם־הִ֥יא נֶאֶנְחָ֖ה וַתָּ֥שָׁב אָחֽוֹר׃ טֻמְאָתָ֣הּ בְּשׁוּלֶ֗יהָ לֹ֤א זָֽכְרָה֙

אַֽחֲרִיתָ֔הּ וַתֵּ֣רֶד פְּלָאִ֔ים אֵ֥ין מְנַחֵ֖ם לָ֑הּ רְאֵ֤ה יְהוָה֙ אֶת־עָנְיִ֔י כִּ֥י הִגְדִּ֖יל

י אוֹיֵֽב׃ יָדוֹ֙ פָּ֣רַשׂ צָ֔ר עַ֖ל כָּל־מַחֲמַדֶּ֑יהָ כִּֽי־רָאֲתָ֣ה גוֹיִ֗ם בָּ֚אוּ מִקְדָּשָׁ֔הּ

יא אֲשֶׁ֣ר צִוִּ֔יתָה לֹא־יָבֹ֥אוּ בַקָּהָ֖ל לָֽךְ׃ כָּל־עַמָּ֤הּ נֶאֱנָחִים֙ מְבַקְשִׁ֣ים לֶ֔חֶם

נָתְנ֧וּ מַחֲמ֛וֹדֵּיהֶ֖ם בְּאֹ֣כֶל לְהָשִׁ֣יב נָ֑פֶשׁ רְאֵ֤ה יְהוָה֙ וְֽהַבִּ֔יטָה כִּ֥י הָיִ֖יתִי

יב זוֹלֵלָֽה׃ ל֣וֹא אֲלֵיכֶם֮ כָּל־עֹ֣בְרֵי דֶרֶךְ֒ הַבִּ֣יטוּ וּרְא֔וּ אִם־יֵ֤שׁ מַכְאוֹב֙

יג כְּמַכְאֹבִ֔י אֲשֶׁ֥ר עוֹלַ֖ל לִ֑י אֲשֶׁר֙ הוֹגָ֣ה יְהוָ֔ה בְּי֖וֹם חֲר֥וֹן אַפּֽוֹ׃ מִמָּר֧וֹם

שָֽׁלַח־אֵ֛שׁ בְּעַצְמֹתַ֖י וַיִּרְדֶּ֑נָּה פָּרַ֨שׂ רֶ֤שֶׁת לְרַגְלַי֙ הֱשִׁיבַ֣נִי אָח֔וֹר נְתָנַ֙נִי֙

יד שֹֽׁמֵמָ֔ה כָּל־הַיּ֖וֹם דָּוָֽה׃ נִשְׂקַ֞ד עֹ֤ל פְּשָׁעַי֙ בְּיָד֔וֹ יִשְׂתָּ֣רְג֔וּ עָל֖וּ עַל־צַוָּארִ֑י

טו הִכְשִׁ֥יל כֹּחִ֖י נְתָנַ֣נִי אֲדֹנָ֑י בִּידֵ֖י לֹא־אוּכַ֥ל קֽוּם׃ סִלָּ֨ה כָל־אַבִּירַ֤י ׀

מבת

מַחֲמַדֵּיהֶ֖ם

16 For these things I weep, my eye, my eye streams water; for the one who could
console me is far away from me, the one who would restore my soul to me.
My children became desolate when the enemy mastered."

17 Zion spreads her hands – there is none to console her. The LORD commanded
18 enemies to Jacob all around, Jerusalem an outcast among them, bleeding. She
says, "The LORD is just: I had refused His word.

"Listen, please, all peoples, see this pain. My young girls and youths have gone
19 off in captivity. I called out to my suitors: they have deceived me. My priests
and my elders have starved in the city, they sought bread for themselves, to
20 restore their souls. See, LORD, I am anguished. My stomach churns. My heart
turns over in me, for I have refused You. Outside the sword bereaves me; at
home it is like death.

21 "Hear me – I am groaning, there is none to console me. My enemies heard
of my suffering, all – they rejoiced: You have done this. When You bring the
22 day You called for, then they shall be like me. Let all their evil come before
You and do to them all that You have done to me for all my crimes. My groans
are grown many, and my heart is ailing."

2 1 How, in His rage, the LORD darkens the skies of daughter Zion. He has flung
from Heaven down to earth all of Israel's splendor. He had no thought for
2 His footstool on the day of His rage. The LORD devoured, showed no mercy
for the sheepfolds of Jacob, devoured, in His great rage, daughter Judah's
fortresses – down they came to earth – and brought low kingdom, princes.
3 With burning rage He hacked off the horn of Israel's glory, and held His
right hand back, to let the enemy come. He burnt like flames of fire in Jacob,
4 consuming on all sides. He trod His bow like the enemy, like a foe His right
hand rose, and He killed all those the eye treasured.

5 In the tent of daughter Zion, He poured out rage like fire. It is as if He were
the enemy; the LORD devoured Israel, devoured all her palaces, razed her
6 fortresses; in daughter Judah grew much moaning, mourning. He stripped
His Shelter like a garden, destroyed His Sanctuary of meeting. The LORD has
made forgotten in Zion, such things as feast and Sabbath. He debased, in His
7 flaming rage, king and priest. The LORD shunned His altar, renounced His
own Temple, gave over the walls of her palaces to the enemy's hand. They
called out in the LORD's House as if it were a feast day.

8 The LORD planned demolition for the walls of daughter Zion. He stretched
out the ruling line, devoured, did not hold back. Now boundary and wall are

אֲדֹנָי בְּקִרְבִּי קָרָא עָלַי מוֹעֵד לִשְׁבֹּר בַּחוּרָי גַּת דָּרַךְ אֲדֹנָי לִבְתוּלַת
טז בַּת־יְהוּדָה: עַל־אֵלֶּה ׀ אֲנִי בוֹכִיָּה עֵינִי ׀ עֵינִי יֹרְדָה מַּיִם כִּי־רָחַק
יז מִמֶּנִּי מְנַחֵם מֵשִׁיב נַפְשִׁי הָיוּ בָנַי שׁוֹמֵמִים כִּי גָבַר אוֹיֵב: פֵּרְשָׂה צִיּוֹן
בְּיָדֶיהָ אֵין מְנַחֵם לָהּ צִוָּה יְהוָה לְיַעֲקֹב סְבִיבָיו צָרָיו הָיְתָה יְרוּשָׁלִַם
יח לְנִדָּה בֵּינֵיהֶם: צַדִּיק הוּא יְהוָה כִּי פִיהוּ מָרִיתִי שִׁמְעוּ־נָא כָל־עַמִּים הָעַמִּים
יט וּרְאוּ מַכְאֹבִי בְּתוּלֹתַי וּבַחוּרַי הָלְכוּ בַשֶּׁבִי: קָרָאתִי לַמְאַהֲבַי הֵמָּה
רִמּוּנִי כֹּהֲנַי וּזְקֵנַי בָּעִיר גָּוָעוּ כִּי־בִקְשׁוּ אֹכֶל לָמוֹ וְיָשִׁיבוּ אֶת־נַפְשָׁם:
כ רְאֵה יְהוָה כִּי־צַר־לִי מֵעַי חֳמַרְמָרוּ נֶהְפַּךְ לִבִּי בְּקִרְבִּי כִּי מָרוֹ מָרִיתִי
כא מִחוּץ שִׁכְּלָה־חֶרֶב בַּבַּיִת כַּמָּוֶת: שָׁמְעוּ כִּי נֶאֱנָחָה אָנִי אֵין מְנַחֵם
לִי כָּל־אֹיְבַי שָׁמְעוּ רָעָתִי שָׂשׂוּ כִּי אַתָּה עָשִׂיתָ הֵבֵאתָ יוֹם־קָרָאתָ
כב וְיִהְיוּ כָמוֹנִי: תָּבֹא כָל־רָעָתָם לְפָנֶיךָ וְעוֹלֵל לָמוֹ כַּאֲשֶׁר עוֹלַלְתָּ לִי עַל
כָּל־פְּשָׁעָי כִּי־רַבּוֹת אַנְחֹתַי וְלִבִּי דַוָּי:

ב א אֵיכָה יָעִיב בְּאַפּוֹ ׀ אֲדֹנָי אֶת־בַּת־צִיּוֹן הִשְׁלִיךְ מִשָּׁמַיִם אֶרֶץ תִּפְאֶרֶת
ב יִשְׂרָאֵל וְלֹא־זָכַר הֲדֹם־רַגְלָיו בְּיוֹם אַפּוֹ: בִּלַּע אֲדֹנָי לֹא חָמַל אֵת וְלֹא
כָּל־נְאוֹת יַעֲקֹב הָרַס בְּעֶבְרָתוֹ מִבְצְרֵי בַת־יְהוּדָה הִגִּיעַ לָאָרֶץ חִלֵּל
ג מַמְלָכָה וְשָׂרֶיהָ: גָּדַע בָּחֳרִי־אַף כֹּל קֶרֶן יִשְׂרָאֵל הֵשִׁיב אָחוֹר יְמִינוֹ
ד מִפְּנֵי אוֹיֵב וַיִּבְעַר בְּיַעֲקֹב כְּאֵשׁ לֶהָבָה אָכְלָה סָבִיב: דָּרַךְ קַשְׁתּוֹ
כְּאוֹיֵב נִצָּב יְמִינוֹ כְּצָר וַיַּהֲרֹג כֹּל מַחֲמַדֵּי־עָיִן בְּאֹהֶל בַּת־צִיּוֹן שָׁפַךְ
ה כָּאֵשׁ חֲמָתוֹ: הָיָה אֲדֹנָי ׀ כְּאוֹיֵב בִּלַּע יִשְׂרָאֵל בִּלַּע כָּל־אַרְמְנוֹתֶיהָ
ו שִׁחֵת מִבְצָרָיו וַיֶּרֶב בְּבַת־יְהוּדָה תַּאֲנִיָּה וַאֲנִיָּה: וַיַּחְמֹס כַּגַּן שֻׂכּוֹ שִׁחֵת
מֹעֲדוֹ שִׁכַּח יְהוָה ׀ בְּצִיּוֹן מוֹעֵד וְשַׁבָּת וַיִּנְאַץ בְּזַעַם־אַפּוֹ מֶלֶךְ וְכֹהֵן:
ז זָנַח אֲדֹנָי ׀ מִזְבְּחוֹ נִאֵר מִקְדָּשׁוֹ הִסְגִּיר בְּיַד־אוֹיֵב חוֹמֹת אַרְמְנוֹתֶיהָ
ח קוֹל נָתְנוּ בְּבֵית־יְהוָה כְּיוֹם מוֹעֵד: חָשַׁב יְהוָה ׀ לְהַשְׁחִית חוֹמַת בַּת־
צִיּוֹן נָטָה קָו לֹא־הֵשִׁיב יָדוֹ מִבַּלֵּעַ וַיַּאֲבֶל־חֵל וְחוֹמָה יַחְדָּו אֻמְלָלוּ:

9 grieving, laid pitiful together. Her gates are now sunk into the earth, their bars
gone and broken. Her king and ministers are gone among the nations; there
10 is no counsel. Even her prophets find no vision of the LORD. The elders in
daughter Zion sit on the ground and are silent. They lift dust up upon their
heads, wrap themselves in sacks; the young girls of Jerusalem lower their
11 heads to the ground. My eyes are wept away, my stomach churns, my marrow
is poured out to the earth over my maiden nation's breaking; as infants, little
12 ones, faint in the squares of the town; (they say to their mothers, "Where are
grain and wine?") as they faint away like the fallen in city squares; as their
souls are poured out from them into their mothers' laps.

13 How can I bear witness, to what can I liken you, daughter Jerusalem? What
can I compare you to and comfort you, o virgin daughter Zion? Your breaking
14 as vast as the ocean, who will heal you? Your prophets brought you visions –
empty, meaningless – and did not uncover your sin, to bring your fortunes
15 back. They saw empty burdens for you, misled you. All who cross your path
clap their hands now in dismay. They whistle and shake their heads over
daughter Jerusalem. "Can this really be that city that was called *Perfect Beauty,
the Delight of all the world*?"

16 All your enemies gape their snarling mouths at you. They whistle and grate
their teeth; they say, "We have devoured them: this is the very day we hoped
17 for – we have done it, seen it." The LORD has done what He planned to do.
He has performed His word, His command of long ago. He destroyed and
showed no mercy, brought the enemy joy over you; He raised the horn of
18 your foes' power. The heart cries out towards the LORD. O wall of daughter
Zion, bring down tears like a stream; day and night, do not allow yourself rest,
19 let your eyes never be silent. Get up, give voice in the night, as every watch
begins. Pour out your heart like water in the presence of the LORD. Lift up
your palms to Him over the souls of your infants, who faint for very hunger
at the end of every street.

20 LORD, see, look on – to whom have You done this? Can women eat their own
children, the little ones they nurtured? Can priest and prophet be murdered
21 in the Temple of the LORD? Lying down on the earth of streets – youths,
old men. My own young girls and youths have fallen to the sword. You have
22 killed on the day of Your rage; slaughtered, shown no compassion. You call
those living around to come, as if it were a feast day. There is no refugee or
remnant on the day of the LORD's rage. All those I nurtured and raised – my
enemy disposed of.

3 1 2 I am the man who has seen oppression at the staff of His rage. It is I that He

ט טָבְעוּ בָאָרֶץ שְׁעָרֶיהָ אִבַּד וְשִׁבַּר בְּרִיחֶיהָ מַלְכָּהּ וְשָׂרֶיהָ בַגּוֹיִם אֵין
י תּוֹרָה גַּם־נְבִיאֶיהָ לֹא־מָצְאוּ חָזוֹן מֵיְהוָה: יֵשְׁבוּ לָאָרֶץ יִדְּמוּ זִקְנֵי
בַת־צִיּוֹן הֶעֱלוּ עָפָר עַל־רֹאשָׁם חָגְרוּ שַׂקִּים הוֹרִידוּ לָאָרֶץ רֹאשָׁן
יא בְּתוּלֹת יְרוּשָׁלָםִ: כָּלוּ בַדְּמָעוֹת עֵינַי חֳמַרְמְרוּ מֵעַי נִשְׁפַּךְ לָאָרֶץ
יב כְּבֵדִי עַל־שֶׁבֶר בַּת־עַמִּי בֵּעָטֵף עוֹלֵל וְיוֹנֵק בִּרְחֹבוֹת קִרְיָה: לְאִמֹּתָם
יֹאמְרוּ אַיֵּה דָּגָן וָיָיִן בְּהִתְעַטְּפָם כֶּחָלָל בִּרְחֹבוֹת עִיר בְּהִשְׁתַּפֵּךְ נַפְשָׁם
יג אֶל־חֵיק אִמֹּתָם: מָה־אֲעוֹדֵךְ מָה אֲדַמֶּה־לָּךְ הַבַּת יְרוּשָׁלַםִ מָה אֲעִידֵךְ
אַשְׁוֶה־לָּךְ וַאֲנַחֲמֵךְ בְּתוּלַת בַּת־צִיּוֹן כִּי־גָדוֹל כַּיָּם שִׁבְרֵךְ מִי יִרְפָּא־
יד לָךְ: נְבִיאַיִךְ חָזוּ לָךְ שָׁוְא וְתָפֵל וְלֹא־גִלּוּ עַל־עֲוֺנֵךְ לְהָשִׁיב שְׁבִיתֵךְ שְׁבוּתֵךְ
טו וַיֶּחֱזוּ לָךְ מַשְׂאוֹת שָׁוְא וּמַדּוּחִים: סָפְקוּ עָלַיִךְ כַּפַּיִם כָּל־עֹבְרֵי דֶרֶךְ
שָׁרְקוּ וַיָּנִעוּ רֹאשָׁם עַל־בַּת יְרוּשָׁלָםִ הֲזֹאת הָעִיר שֶׁיֹּאמְרוּ כְּלִילַת יֹפִי
טז מָשׂוֹשׂ לְכָל־הָאָרֶץ: פָּצוּ עָלַיִךְ פִּיהֶם כָּל־אוֹיְבַיִךְ שָׁרְקוּ וַיַּחַרְקוּ־שֵׁן
יז אָמְרוּ בִּלָּעְנוּ אַךְ זֶה הַיּוֹם שֶׁקִּוִּינֻהוּ מָצָאנוּ רָאִינוּ: עָשָׂה יְהוָה אֲשֶׁר
זָמָם בִּצַּע אֶמְרָתוֹ אֲשֶׁר צִוָּה מִימֵי־קֶדֶם הָרַס וְלֹא חָמָל וַיְשַׂמַּח עָלַיִךְ
יח אוֹיֵב הֵרִים קֶרֶן צָרָיִךְ: צָעַק לִבָּם אֶל־אֲדֹנָי חוֹמַת בַּת־צִיּוֹן הוֹרִידִי
כַנַּחַל דִּמְעָה יוֹמָם וָלַיְלָה אַל־תִּתְּנִי פוּגַת לָךְ אַל־תִּדֹּם בַּת־עֵינֵךְ:
יט קוּמִי ׀ רֹנִּי בַלַּיְל לְרֹאשׁ אַשְׁמֻרוֹת שִׁפְכִי כַמַּיִם לִבֵּךְ נֹכַח פְּנֵי אֲדֹנָי
שְׂאִי אֵלָיו כַּפַּיִךְ עַל־נֶפֶשׁ עוֹלָלַיִךְ הָעֲטוּפִים בְּרָעָב בְּרֹאשׁ כָּל־
כ חוּצוֹת: רְאֵה יְהוָה וְהַבִּיטָה לְמִי עוֹלַלְתָּ כֹּה אִם־תֹּאכַלְנָה נָשִׁים
כא פִּרְיָם עֹלְלֵי טִפֻּחִים אִם־יֵהָרֵג בְּמִקְדַּשׁ אֲדֹנָי כֹּהֵן וְנָבִיא: שָׁכְבוּ
לָאָרֶץ חוּצוֹת נַעַר וְזָקֵן בְּתוּלֹתַי וּבַחוּרַי נָפְלוּ בֶחָרֶב הָרַגְתָּ בְּיוֹם אַפֶּךָ
כב טָבַחְתָּ לֹא חָמָלְתָּ: תִּקְרָא כְיוֹם מוֹעֵד מְגוּרַי מִסָּבִיב וְלֹא הָיָה בְּיוֹם
אַף־יְהוָה פָּלִיט וְשָׂרִיד אֲשֶׁר־טִפַּחְתִּי וְרִבִּיתִי אֹיְבִי כִלָּם:
ג א ב אֲנִי הַגֶּבֶר רָאָה עֳנִי בְּשֵׁבֶט עֶבְרָתוֹ: אוֹתִי נָהַג וַיֹּלַךְ חֹשֶׁךְ וְלֹא־אוֹר:

3 led, that He guided, to darkness and not light. It is to me alone that He returns,
4 and turns His hand against me all the day. He has made my flesh and skin
5 decay; He broke my bones. He built a siege-wall round me, of wormwood and
6 of hardship. He sat me in down in darkness, like those forever dead.

7 He fenced me around – no escape; made heavy the bronze that holds me.
8 9 Even as I cry out to be saved – He has blocked my prayer. He fenced across
10 my way with hewn stone and made my paths twisted. He is a bear lying in
11 wait for me, a lion in hiding. He turns my paths from me, gashes me, renders
12 me desolate. He has trod His bow and made me stand, the target to His arrow.
13 His quiver's load shot into my very marrow.

14 I am the laughing-stock of all my people, their mocking song all the day.
15 16 He has glutted me with bitterness, and quenched me with wormwood. He
17 crushed my teeth in grit, drove my head into the ashes. My soul shuns peace-
18 fulness – I have forgotten what goodness is. I said, "My endurance is lost, and
19 my hope, of the Lord." Keep in mind my affliction and wandering, worm-
20 21 wood, venom. Keep, keep in mind, my soul, bowed low. I make this reply to
my heart; and so I wait by:

22 23 The Lord's kindness – it is not finished; His compassion is not gone. New
24 with each new morning, so great is His faithfulness. I said to myself, The
25 Lord is what is mine; and so I shall yet wait for Him. The Lord is good to
26 those who hope; to souls that seek Him out. To hope is good, in silence, for
27 the Lord to come, and save. It is good, for a man, to bear the yoke in his
28 29 youth. He should sit alone and be silent: this was inflicted on him. Let him
sink his teeth into the dust – perhaps there is hope.

30 Let him offer his cheek to the one who beats him. Let him be glutted with
31 32 insult. For the Lord will not shun for all eternity. For if He brings sorrow, He
33 must, in His great kindness, have compassion. He does not oppress on His
34 heart's impulse to bring man's children sorrow, to trample underfoot all the
35 captives of this earth; to bend a man's claim before the highest Judgement;
36 37 to let one's case be twisted – and the Lord not see it all. Who ever *spoke and*
38 *it was so* without the word of the Lord? Do not all evils and good emerge
39 from the speech of the Most High? What has a living man to protest; why
40 should he protest his own sins? Let us seek out our ways, understand them,
41 and come back to the Lord. Let us place our hearts in the palms of our hands,
and raise them to God in Heaven:

42 43 "We rebelled and refused You – but You did not forgive." You covered us in rage
44 and pursued us. You killed, showed no compassion. You covered Yourself in

ג ד אַךְ בִּי יָשֻׁב יַהֲפֹךְ יָדוֹ כָּל־הַיּוֹם: בִּלָּה בְשָׂרִי וְעוֹרִי שִׁבַּר עַצְמוֹתָי:
ה ו בָּנָה עָלַי וַיַּקַּף רֹאשׁ וּתְלָאָה: בְּמַחֲשַׁכִּים הוֹשִׁיבַנִי כְּמֵתֵי עוֹלָם:
ז ח גָּדַר בַּעֲדִי וְלֹא אֵצֵא הִכְבִּיד נְחָשְׁתִּי: גַּם כִּי אֶזְעַק וַאֲשַׁוֵּעַ שָׂתַם
ט י תְּפִלָּתִי: גָּדַר דְּרָכַי בְּגָזִית נְתִיבֹתַי עִוָּה: דֹּב אֹרֵב הוּא לִי אריה
יא יב בְּמִסְתָּרִים: דְּרָכַי סוֹרֵר וַיְפַשְּׁחֵנִי שָׂמַנִי שֹׁמֵם: דָּרַךְ קַשְׁתּוֹ וַיַּצִּיבֵנִי אֲרִי
יג יד כַּמַּטָּרָא לַחֵץ: הֵבִיא בְּכִלְיוֹתָי בְּנֵי אַשְׁפָּתוֹ: הָיִיתִי שְּׂחֹק לְכָל־עַמִּי
טו טז נְגִינָתָם כָּל־הַיּוֹם: הִשְׂבִּיעַנִי בַמְּרוֹרִים הִרְוַנִי לַעֲנָה: וַיַּגְרֵס בֶּחָצָץ
יז יח שִׁנָּי הִכְפִּישַׁנִי בָּאֵפֶר: וַתִּזְנַח מִשָּׁלוֹם נַפְשִׁי נָשִׁיתִי טוֹבָה: וָאֹמַר אָבַד
יט כ נִצְחִי וְתוֹחַלְתִּי מֵיהוה: זְכָר־עָנְיִי וּמְרוּדִי לַעֲנָה וָרֹאשׁ: זָכוֹר תִּזְכּוֹר
כא כב ותשיח עָלַי נַפְשִׁי: זֹאת אָשִׁיב אֶל־לִבִּי עַל־כֵּן אוֹחִיל: חַסְדֵי יהוה וְתָשׁוּחַ
כג כִּי לֹא־תָמְנוּ כִּי לֹא־כָלוּ רַחֲמָיו: חֲדָשִׁים לַבְּקָרִים רַבָּה אֱמוּנָתֶךָ:
כד כה חֶלְקִי יהוה אָמְרָה נַפְשִׁי עַל־כֵּן אוֹחִיל לוֹ: טוֹב יהוה לְקֹוָו לְנֶפֶשׁ
כו כז תִּדְרְשֶׁנּוּ: טוֹב וְיָחִיל וְדוּמָם לִתְשׁוּעַת יהוה: טוֹב לַגֶּבֶר כִּי־יִשָּׂא
כח כט עֹל בִּנְעוּרָיו: יֵשֵׁב בָּדָד וְיִדֹּם כִּי נָטַל עָלָיו: יִתֵּן בֶּעָפָר פִּיהוּ אוּלַי יֵשׁ
ל לא תִּקְוָה: יִתֵּן לְמַכֵּהוּ לֶחִי יִשְׂבַּע בְּחֶרְפָּה: כִּי לֹא יִזְנַח לְעוֹלָם אֲדֹנָי:
לב לג כִּי אִם־הוֹגָה וְרִחַם כְּרֹב חֲסָדָו: כִּי לֹא עִנָּה מִלִּבּוֹ וַיַּגֶּה בְּנֵי־אִישׁ:
לד לה לְדַכֵּא תַּחַת רַגְלָיו כֹּל אֲסִירֵי אָרֶץ: לְהַטּוֹת מִשְׁפַּט־גָּבֶר נֶגֶד פְּנֵי
לו לז עֶלְיוֹן: לְעַוֵּת אָדָם בְּרִיבוֹ אֲדֹנָי לֹא רָאָה: מִי זֶה אָמַר וַתֶּהִי אֲדֹנָי
לח לט לֹא צִוָּה: מִפִּי עֶלְיוֹן לֹא תֵצֵא הָרָעוֹת וְהַטּוֹב: מַה־יִּתְאוֹנֵן אָדָם
מ חָי גֶּבֶר עַל־חֲטָאָו: נַחְפְּשָׂה דְרָכֵינוּ וְנַחְקֹרָה וְנָשׁוּבָה עַד־יהוה:
מא מב נִשָּׂא לְבָבֵנוּ אֶל־כַּפָּיִם אֶל־אֵל בַּשָּׁמָיִם: נַחְנוּ פָשַׁעְנוּ וּמָרִינוּ אַתָּה
מג מד לֹא סָלָחְתָּ: סַכּוֹתָה בָאַף וַתִּרְדְּפֵנוּ הָרַגְתָּ לֹא חָמָלְתָּ: סַכֹּתָה בֶעָנָן

45 cloud beyond the reach of prayers. You have made us filth and loathing among
46 47 nations. They gaped snarling mouths at us, all our enemies. Terror and snare
48 were with us; devastation, breaking. Rivers of water ran from my eyes, over my
49 50 maiden nation's breaking. My eye pours out and will not stop, no respite, until
51 the LORD shall look down, and see us from His Heaven. My eye torments my
52 soul over all the daughters of my city. He hunted me down like a bird, my enemy,
53 for no cause. They closed off my life in a pit, and then brandished a stone above
54 me. The waters came up over my head; I said, "I am condemned."

55 56 LORD, I called Your name from the very lowest of pits. You have heard my
57 voice – do not close off Your ears, to my need, to my pleading. You once were
58 close when I called You, You would tell me, "Do not fear." You would fight my
59 fight, my LORD – redeem my life. You see, LORD, this twisted justice: judge
60 61 my case. Witness all their vengefulness, all that they think to do to me. Hear
62 their insults, LORD, and all their thoughts of me, my attackers' mouths, all
63 they mutter against me, all the day. Watch their sitting and rising, see – I am
64 their mocking song. LORD, return them payment, for all that they have done.
65 66 Bring them the heart's dirge, Your curse upon them. Pursue them with rage
and annihilate them from under the skies of the LORD.

4 1 How dull gold has become; how that finest gilt has changed. The sacred
2 stones poured out at the end of every street. Precious children of Zion, worth
their very weight of gold – how they are considered now as cheap clay jugs –
the work of Potter's hands.

3 Even jackals bring out udders, give their cubs to suck. The daughter of my
4 people is cruel, like desert ostriches. The tongues of little ones have clung to
their mouths' rooves with thirst. Infants ask for bread – none break it for them.
5 Those who once ate the finest foods, stand desolate in the streets. Those
brought up in clothes of scarlet now embrace the trash heaps.

6 The sin of my people is greater even than that of Sedom, which was turned
7 over all in a moment: no hand touched it. Jerusalem's nazirites were cleaner
than snow, once; brighter than milk, glowing warm from within more than
8 rubies, hewn finely as sapphires. Now they are darker than pitch, not recog-
9 nized on the streets, with skin shriveled against bones, dry as wood. Better
to be killed by the sword than killed by hunger. The slain at least seep at their
10 wounds; do not starve for the yield of meadows. The hands of loving women
have cooked their own children. These have become their nourishment: the
breaking, of my maiden nation's fast.

11 The LORD burned all His anger; poured out all his flaming rage. He set fire
12 blazing in Zion; and it consumed all her foundations. The kings of the world

מה מו לָךְ מֵעֲבוֹר תְּפִלָּה: סְחִי וּמָאוֹס תְּשִׂימֵנוּ בְּקֶרֶב הָעַמִּים: פָּצוּ עָלֵינוּ
מז מח פִּיהֶם כָּל־אֹיְבֵינוּ: פַּחַד וָפַחַת הָיָה לָנוּ הַשֵּׁאת וְהַשָּׁבֶר: פַּלְגֵי־מַיִם
מט תֵּרַד עֵינִי עַל־שֶׁבֶר בַּת־עַמִּי: עֵינִי נִגְּרָה וְלֹא תִדְמֶה מֵאֵין הֲפֻגוֹת:
נ נא עַד־יַשְׁקִיף וְיֵרֶא יהוה מִשָּׁמָיִם: עֵינִי עוֹלְלָה לְנַפְשִׁי מִכֹּל בְּנוֹת עִירִי:
נב נג נד צוֹד צָדוּנִי כַּצִּפּוֹר אֹיְבַי חִנָּם: צָמְתוּ בַבּוֹר חַיָּי וַיַּדּוּ־אֶבֶן בִּי: צָפוּ־מַיִם
נה נו עַל־רֹאשִׁי אָמַרְתִּי נִגְזָרְתִּי: קָרָאתִי שִׁמְךָ יהוה מִבּוֹר תַּחְתִּיּוֹת: קוֹלִי
נז שָׁמָעְתָּ אַל־תַּעְלֵם אָזְנְךָ לְרַוְחָתִי לְשַׁוְעָתִי: קָרַבְתָּ בְּיוֹם אֶקְרָאֶךָּ
נח נט אָמַרְתָּ אַל־תִּירָא: רַבְתָּ אֲדֹנָי רִיבֵי נַפְשִׁי גָּאַלְתָּ חַיָּי: רָאִיתָה יהוה
ס עַוָּתָתִי שָׁפְטָה מִשְׁפָּטִי: רָאִיתָה כָּל־נִקְמָתָם כָּל־מַחְשְׁבֹתָם לִי:
סא סב שָׁמַעְתָּ חֶרְפָּתָם יהוה כָּל־מַחְשְׁבֹתָם עָלָי: שִׂפְתֵי קָמַי וְהֶגְיוֹנָם עָלַי
סג סד כָּל־הַיּוֹם: שִׁבְתָּם וְקִימָתָם הַבִּיטָה אֲנִי מַנְגִּינָתָם: תָּשִׁיב לָהֶם גְּמוּל
סה סו יהוה כְּמַעֲשֵׂה יְדֵיהֶם: תִּתֵּן לָהֶם מְגִנַּת־לֵב תַּאֲלָתְךָ לָהֶם: תִּרְדֹּף
בְּאַף וְתַשְׁמִידֵם מִתַּחַת שְׁמֵי יהוה:
ד א אֵיכָה יוּעַם זָהָב יִשְׁנֶא הַכֶּתֶם הַטּוֹב תִּשְׁתַּפֵּכְנָה אַבְנֵי־קֹדֶשׁ בְּרֹאשׁ
ב כָּל־חוּצוֹת: בְּנֵי צִיּוֹן הַיְקָרִים הַמְסֻלָּאִים בַּפָּז אֵיכָה נֶחְשְׁבוּ לְנִבְלֵי־
ג חֶרֶשׂ מַעֲשֵׂה יְדֵי יוֹצֵר: גַּם־תַּנִּין חָלְצוּ שַׁד הֵינִיקוּ גּוּרֵיהֶן בַּת־עַמִּי תַּנִּים
ד לְאַכְזָר כִּי עֵנִים בַּמִּדְבָּר: דָּבַק לְשׁוֹן יוֹנֵק אֶל־חִכּוֹ בַּצָּמָא עוֹלָלִים כַּיְעֵנִים
ה שָׁאֲלוּ לֶחֶם פֹּרֵשׂ אֵין לָהֶם: הָאֹכְלִים לְמַעֲדַנִּים נָשַׁמּוּ בַּחוּצוֹת
ו הָאֱמֻנִים עֲלֵי תוֹלָע חִבְּקוּ אַשְׁפַּתּוֹת: וַיִּגְדַּל עֲוֹן בַּת־עַמִּי מֵחַטַּאת
ז סְדֹם הַהֲפוּכָה כְמוֹ־רָגַע וְלֹא־חָלוּ בָהּ יָדָיִם: זַכּוּ נְזִירֶיהָ מִשֶּׁלֶג צַחוּ
ח מֵחָלָב אָדְמוּ עֶצֶם מִפְּנִינִים סַפִּיר גִּזְרָתָם: חָשַׁךְ מִשְּׁחוֹר תָּאֳרָם לֹא
ט נִכְּרוּ בַּחוּצוֹת צָפַד עוֹרָם עַל־עַצְמָם יָבֵשׁ הָיָה כָעֵץ: טוֹבִים הָיוּ
י חַלְלֵי־חֶרֶב מֵחַלְלֵי רָעָב שֶׁהֵם יָזוּבוּ מְדֻקָּרִים מִתְּנוּבֹת שָׂדָי: יְדֵי
נָשִׁים רַחֲמָנִיּוֹת בִּשְּׁלוּ יַלְדֵיהֶן הָיוּ לְבָרוֹת לָמוֹ בְּשֶׁבֶר בַּת־עַמִּי:
יא כִּלָּה יהוה אֶת־חֲמָתוֹ שָׁפַךְ חֲרוֹן אַפּוֹ וַיַּצֶּת־אֵשׁ בְּצִיּוֹן וַתֹּאכַל
יב יְסוֹדֹתֶיהָ: לֹא הֶאֱמִינוּ מַלְכֵי־אֶרֶץ וכל יֹשְׁבֵי תֵבֵל כִּי יָבֹא צַר וְאוֹיֵב כֹּל

did not believe it – not anyone living on earth – that a foe and enemy would
13 come and cross Jerusalem's gates. For the sins of her prophets, the offences of
14 her priests, who within her midst pour out the blood of righteous people. The
blind shift through the streets, disgusting with blood; no one could possibly
15 touch those clothes. "Keep away, impure," they cry out to them, "away, away,
do not touch." Floating, shifting away.

16 It is said among the nations, "They may stop no longer here. It is the Lord's face
that divides them; He shall look on them no more." They bore priests no honor,
17 and elders no mercy. As for us, our eyes still watch for our mirage of assistance.
18 In our wistfulness we wait for a nation that does not save. They stalked our very
steps; stopped us walking across our squares. Our end comes close, the fullness
19 of our day, our end is come. Our pursuers came swifter than eagles of the sky.
20 They spied us from the mountains, in the desert they set ambush. The breath
of our mouths, the Lord's anointed, was caught up in our slaughter; the one
whose shade we said we would live in among nations.

21 Rejoice, be merry, daughter Edom, sitting there in the Land of Utz. The cup
22 will come to you in turn; you will get drunk, and be laid bare. Your offences
are done with, daughter Zion, He will exile you no further. Your offences are
noted, daughter Edom. Your sins have been exposed.

5 1 2 Remember, Lord, what has come to us. Look on, witness our abjection; our
3 inheritance turned over to strangers, and our homes to foreign men. We are
4 orphans now, fatherless, our mothers like widows. We pay to drink our water;
5 our wood comes at a price. At our throats they chase us, we labor, they give
6 7 no respite. We put out a hand to Egypt, to Assyria, for bread. Our fathers
8 sinned – they are not; we bear their offences. Slaves now rule over us; none
9 will tear us from their hands. We lay down our souls for bread before the sword
10 11 of desertlands. Our skin burns like an oven with the fevers of starvation. They
12 raped women in Zion – virgin girls in the towns of Judah. Princes were hung up
13 by their hands, no regard was shown to elders. Young men bear the millstone,
14 boys stumble under loads of wood. No more elders at the gates, or young men
15 lost in song. No more delight in our hearts; our dance has turned to mourning.
16 The crown of our heads is fallen. Hear, please, our anguish: we have sinned.

17 18 For these things our hearts are ailing; for this our eyes grow dark. For Mount
19 Zion, desolate – foxes wander there. You, Lord, rule forever – Your throne over
20 all generations. Why would You forever forget us, desert us, as long as there
21 are days? Bring us back to You, Lord, and we will come. Renew our days, to
22 be as they once were; even if You leave and loathe us, and rage against us with
great passion.

Bring us back to You, Lord, and we will come.
Renew our days, to be as they once were.

יג בְּשַׁעֲרֵי יְרוּשָׁלָֽםִ׃ מֵחַטֹּאת נְבִיאֶיהָ עֲוֺנֹת כֹּהֲנֶיהָ הַשֹּׁפְכִים בְּקִרְבָּהּ דַּם
יד צַדִּיקִֽים׃ נָעוּ עִוְרִים בַּחוּצוֹת נְגֹֽאֲלוּ בַּדָּם בְּלֹא יֽוּכְלוּ יִגְּעוּ בִּלְבֻשֵׁיהֶֽם׃
טו סוּרוּ טָמֵא קָרְאוּ לָמוֹ סוּרוּ סוּרוּ אַל־תִּגָּעוּ כִּי נָצוּ גַּם־נָעוּ אָמְרוּ בַּגּוֹיִם
טז לֹא יוֹסִפוּ לָגֽוּר׃ פְּנֵי יהוה חִלְּקָם לֹא יוֹסִיף לְהַבִּיטָם פְּנֵי כֹהֲנִים לֹא
יז נָשָׂאוּ זקנים לֹא חָנָֽנוּ׃ עודינה תִּכְלֶינָה עֵינֵינוּ אֶל־עֶזְרָתֵנוּ הָבֶל וּזְקֵנִים
יח בְּצִפִּיָּתֵנוּ צִפִּינוּ אֶל־גּוֹי לֹא יוֹשִֽׁעַ׃ צָדוּ צְעָדֵינוּ מִלֶּכֶת בִּרְחֹבֹתֵינוּ עוֹדֵינוּ
יט קָרַב קִצֵּנוּ מָלְאוּ יָמֵינוּ כִּי־בָא קִצֵּֽנוּ׃ קַלִּים הָיוּ רֹדְפֵינוּ מִנִּשְׁרֵי שָׁמָיִם
כ עַל־הֶהָרִים דְּלָקֻנוּ בַּמִּדְבָּר אָרְבוּ לָֽנוּ׃ רוּחַ אַפֵּינוּ מְשִׁיחַ יהוה נִלְכַּד
כא בִּשְׁחִיתוֹתָם אֲשֶׁר אָמַרְנוּ בְּצִלּוֹ נִחְיֶה בַגּוֹיִֽם׃ שִׂישִׂי וְשִׂמְחִי בַּת־אֱדוֹם
כב יושבתי בְּאֶרֶץ עוּץ גַּם־עָלַיִךְ תַּעֲבָר־כּוֹס תִּשְׁכְּרִי וְתִתְעָרִֽי׃ תַּם־עֲוֺנֵךְ יוֹשֶׁבֶת
בַּת־צִיּוֹן לֹא יוֹסִיף לְהַגְלוֹתֵךְ פָּקַד עֲוֺנֵךְ בַּת־אֱדוֹם גִּלָּה עַל־חַטֹּאתָֽיִךְ׃
ה א ב זְכֹר יהוה מֶה־הָיָה לָנוּ הַבִּיט וּרְאֵה אֶת־חֶרְפָּתֵֽנוּ׃ נַחֲלָתֵנוּ נֶֽהֶפְכָה
ג לְזָרִים בָּתֵּינוּ לְנָכְרִֽים׃ יְתוֹמִים הָיִינוּ אין אָב אִמֹּתֵינוּ כְּאַלְמָנֽוֹת׃ וְאֵין
ד ה מֵימֵינוּ בְּכֶסֶף שָׁתִינוּ עֵצֵינוּ בִּמְחִיר יָבֹֽאוּ׃ עַל צַוָּארֵנוּ נִרְדָּפְנוּ יָגַעְנוּ לא וְלֹא
ו ז הֽוּנַח־לָֽנוּ׃ מִצְרַיִם נָתַנּוּ יָד אַשּׁוּר לִשְׂבֹּעַ לָֽחֶם׃ אֲבֹתֵינוּ חָטְאוּ אינם וְאֵינָם
ח ט אנחנו עֲוֺנֹתֵיהֶם סָבָֽלְנוּ׃ עֲבָדִים מָשְׁלוּ בָנוּ פֹּרֵק אֵין מִיָּדָֽם׃ בְּנַפְשֵׁנוּ וַאֲנַחְנוּ
י נָבִיא לַחְמֵנוּ מִפְּנֵי חֶרֶב הַמִּדְבָּֽר׃ עוֹרֵנוּ כְּתַנּוּר נִכְמָרוּ מִפְּנֵי זַלְעֲפוֹת
יא יב רָעָֽב׃ נָשִׁים בְּצִיּוֹן עִנּוּ בְּתֻלֹת בְּעָרֵי יְהוּדָֽה׃ שָׂרִים בְּיָדָם נִתְלוּ פְּנֵי
יג יד זְקֵנִים לֹא נֶהְדָּֽרוּ׃ בַּחוּרִים טְחוֹן נָשָׂאוּ וּנְעָרִים בָּעֵץ כָּשָֽׁלוּ׃ זְקֵנִים
טו מִשַּׁעַר שָׁבָתוּ בַּחוּרִים מִנְּגִינָתָֽם׃ שָׁבַת מְשׂוֹשׂ לִבֵּנוּ נֶהְפַּךְ לְאֵבֶל
טז יז מְחֹלֵֽנוּ׃ נָֽפְלָה עֲטֶרֶת רֹאשֵׁנוּ אֽוֹי־נָא לָנוּ כִּי חָטָֽאנוּ׃ עַל־זֶה הָיָה
יח דָוֶה לִבֵּנוּ עַל־אֵלֶּה חָֽשְׁכוּ עֵינֵֽינוּ׃ עַל הַר־צִיּוֹן שֶׁשָּׁמֵם שׁוּעָלִים
יט כ הִלְּכוּ־בֽוֹ׃ אַתָּה יהוה לְעוֹלָם תֵּשֵׁב כִּסְאֲךָ לְדֹר וָדֽוֹר׃ לָמָּה לָנֶצַח
כא תִּשְׁכָּחֵנוּ תַּֽעַזְבֵנוּ לְאֹרֶךְ יָמִֽים׃ הֲשִׁיבֵנוּ יהוה ׀ אֵלֶיךָ וְנָשׁוּבָ חַדֵּשׁ
כב יָמֵינוּ כְּקֶֽדֶם׃ כִּי אִם־מָאֹס מְאַסְתָּנוּ קָצַפְתָּ עָלֵינוּ עַד־מְאֹֽד׃

השיבנו יהוה אליך ונשובה חדש ימינו כקדם

KOHELET

1 1 2 The sayings of Kohelet son of David, King of Israel in Jerusalem: Shallowest
3 breath, said Kohelet; the shallowest breath, it is all but breath. What profit
4 remains of all the labor one toils over beneath the sun? One age departs,
5 another comes; the earth stands still forever. The sun rises, the sun sets. It
6 heaves towards its place, and there it rises. Blowing south, turning north,
turning then turning blows the wind, and back upon its turnings, the wind
7 returns. All streams flow into the sea. The sea is still not full. Into the place
8 where the streams flow, they turn to flow again. Everything is tiresome.
One can say nothing, the eye can never see enough, the ear is never filled
9 with hearing. What is to be – is what has been already, what is to be done
10 is what is done, and there is nothing new at all beneath the sun. Something
may make a person say, "Look at this: new!" – It has been here already, in all
11 the eternities that came before us. The earliest left no memory behind; and
those who are to come will still leave no memorial with the last ones who
will be.

12 13 I, Kohelet, was king of Israel in Jerusalem. And I gave my mind over to
searching and exploring with Wisdom, all that is done beneath the sky.
A wretched occupation, this, given by God to mortal man, with which
14 to be oppressed. I saw everything that is done beneath the sun. It is
15 nothing but fleeting breath, but courting the wind. What is crooked can
16 never be straightened; what is lost can never be counted. I said to my
mind, I have built up and gathered more wisdom than anyone who has
ruled over Jerusalem before, and my mind has seen much wisdom and
17 insight. And I gave my mind over to understand wisdom; and to under-
18 stand delirium and folly. I know that too is but courting the wind. For in
great wisdom lies great bitterness; and one who gathers insight gathers
pain.

2 1 I said to my mind, Come, let me try you with joy, come and see good liv-
2 ing. I found that too to be but shallow breath. Delirium, I called laughter;
3 told joy, What comes of this? And so I explored on, through my mind,
steeping my body in wine, and my mind at the helm remained wise – that I
might catch hold of folly, and finally see what is good for mortal man to do

קהלת

א א ב דִּבְרֵי קֹהֶלֶת בֶּן־דָּוִד מֶלֶךְ בִּירוּשָׁלִָם: הֲבֵל הֲבָלִים אָמַר קֹהֶלֶת
ג הֲבֵל הֲבָלִים הַכֹּל הָבֶל: מַה־יִּתְרוֹן לָאָדָם בְּכָל־עֲמָלוֹ שֶׁיַּעֲמֹל תַּחַת
ד ה הַשָּׁמֶשׁ: דּוֹר הֹלֵךְ וְדוֹר בָּא וְהָאָרֶץ לְעוֹלָם עֹמָדֶת: וְזָרַח הַשֶּׁמֶשׁ
ו וּבָא הַשָּׁמֶשׁ וְאֶל־מְקוֹמוֹ שׁוֹאֵף זוֹרֵחַ הוּא שָׁם: הוֹלֵךְ אֶל־דָּרוֹם
וְסוֹבֵב אֶל־צָפוֹן סוֹבֵב ׀ סֹבֵב הוֹלֵךְ הָרוּחַ וְעַל־סְבִיבֹתָיו שָׁב הָרוּחַ:
ז כָּל־הַנְּחָלִים הֹלְכִים אֶל־הַיָּם וְהַיָּם אֵינֶנּוּ מָלֵא אֶל־מְקוֹם שֶׁהַנְּחָלִים
ח הֹלְכִים שָׁם הֵם שָׁבִים לָלָכֶת: כָּל־הַדְּבָרִים יְגֵעִים לֹא־יוּכַל אִישׁ לְדַבֵּר
ט לֹא־תִשְׂבַּע עַיִן לִרְאוֹת וְלֹא־תִמָּלֵא אֹזֶן מִשְּׁמֹעַ: מַה־שֶּׁהָיָה הוּא
שֶׁיִּהְיֶה וּמַה־שֶּׁנַּעֲשָׂה הוּא שֶׁיֵּעָשֶׂה וְאֵין כָּל־חָדָשׁ תַּחַת הַשָּׁמֶשׁ:
י יֵשׁ דָּבָר שֶׁיֹּאמַר רְאֵה־זֶה חָדָשׁ הוּא כְּבָר הָיָה לְעֹלָמִים אֲשֶׁר הָיָה
יא מִלְּפָנֵנוּ: אֵין זִכְרוֹן לָרִאשֹׁנִים וְגַם לָאַחֲרֹנִים שֶׁיִּהְיוּ לֹא־יִהְיֶה לָהֶם
זִכָּרוֹן עִם שֶׁיִּהְיוּ לָאַחֲרֹנָה:
יב יג אֲנִי קֹהֶלֶת הָיִיתִי מֶלֶךְ עַל־יִשְׂרָאֵל בִּירוּשָׁלִָם: וְנָתַתִּי אֶת־לִבִּי
לִדְרוֹשׁ וְלָתוּר בַּחָכְמָה עַל כָּל־אֲשֶׁר נַעֲשָׂה תַּחַת הַשָּׁמָיִם הוּא ׀ עִנְיַן
יד רָע נָתַן אֱלֹהִים לִבְנֵי הָאָדָם לַעֲנוֹת בּוֹ: רָאִיתִי אֶת־כָּל־הַמַּעֲשִׂים
טו שֶׁנַּעֲשׂוּ תַּחַת הַשָּׁמֶשׁ וְהִנֵּה הַכֹּל הֶבֶל וּרְעוּת רוּחַ: מְעֻוָּת לֹא־יוּכַל
טז לִתְקֹן וְחֶסְרוֹן לֹא־יוּכַל לְהִמָּנוֹת: דִּבַּרְתִּי אֲנִי עִם־לִבִּי לֵאמֹר אֲנִי
הִנֵּה הִגְדַּלְתִּי וְהוֹסַפְתִּי חָכְמָה עַל כָּל־אֲשֶׁר־הָיָה לְפָנַי עַל־יְרוּשָׁלִָם
יז וְלִבִּי רָאָה הַרְבֵּה חָכְמָה וָדָעַת: וָאֶתְּנָה לִבִּי לָדַעַת חָכְמָה וְדַעַת
יח הֹלֵלוֹת וְשִׂכְלוּת יָדַעְתִּי שֶׁגַּם־זֶה הוּא רַעְיוֹן רוּחַ: כִּי בְּרֹב חָכְמָה
ב א רָב־כָּעַס וְיוֹסִיף דַּעַת יוֹסִיף מַכְאוֹב: אָמַרְתִּי אֲנִי בְּלִבִּי לְכָה־נָּא
ב אֲנַסְּכָה בְשִׂמְחָה וּרְאֵה בְטוֹב וְהִנֵּה גַם־הוּא הָבֶל: לִשְׂחוֹק אָמַרְתִּי
ג מְהוֹלָל וּלְשִׂמְחָה מַה־זֹּה עֹשָׂה: תַּרְתִּי בְלִבִּי לִמְשׁוֹךְ בַּיַּיִן אֶת־בְּשָׂרִי
וְלִבִּי נֹהֵג בַּחָכְמָה וְלֶאֱחֹז בְּסִכְלוּת עַד אֲשֶׁר־אֶרְאֶה אֵי־זֶה טוֹב

4 beneath the sky, for as long as he should live. I amassed a great estate. I built
5 houses for myself, planted myself vineyards, acquired gardens and orchards
6 for myself, and planted them with every kind of fruit tree. I ordered pools
7 of water, to irrigate a forest burgeoning forth with trees. I bought slaves
and maidservants, and others were born in my house; I had livestock also,
cattle and flock, more than anyone else who came before me in Jerusalem.
8 I collected silver and gold, and the treasures of kings and provinces; I called
for singers, male and female, and all the delights of mankind, took women,
many women.

9 I grew great and gathered more than anyone who had come before me in
10 Jerusalem, and my wisdom too stood by me. I withheld from my eyes nothing that they sought after. I did not withhold any joy from myself. For my
mind rejoiced in the fruits of my labor; and that was my share for all my toil.
11 And then I turned to look at all my works, at the work of my hands, at all that
I had labored to achieve – and this is what I saw: it is nothing but fleeting
breath, but courting the wind, and there is no true profit beneath the sun.
12 And I turned to look at wisdom and delirium and folly; for who is the man
13 who will come after the king, when he has done what he has done? And I saw
that there is some advantage to wisdom over foolishness, like the advantage
14 of light over darkness. For the wise man has eyes in his head, while the fool
walks in darkness; and still I know: the same fate awaits them both.

15 I said to myself, the fate of the fool awaits me also; why then should I be
16 wiser? And I told myself that this too is empty breath. For the wise man, like
the fool, leaves no memory forever. As soon as the coming days arrive, all are
17 forgotten. How can it be that the wise man dies like the fool? I hated life; this
work that is done beneath the sun is evil to me. Nothing but fleeting breath,
but courting the wind.

18 And I hated all the toil of my labor beneath the sun; all to be left to one who
19 will come after me. Who knows whether he will be wise or a fool; but he
will lord over all that labor, over all that I toiled for wisely beneath the sun;
20 making that too as empty as breath. And I turned to despair over all the labor
21 I had toiled over beneath the sun. For so often one labors with wisdom and
insight and skill – and then gives all his share to one who has not labored;
22 this too is empty as breath, and a great evil. For what remains to one of all
the labor and of all one's mind's pursuits, for which one has toiled beneath

לִבְנֵי הָאָדָם אֲשֶׁר יַעֲשׂוּ תַּחַת הַשָּׁמַיִם מִסְפַּר יְמֵי חַיֵּיהֶם: הִגְדַּלְתִּי ד
מַעֲשָׂי בָּנִיתִי לִי בָּתִּים נָטַעְתִּי לִי כְּרָמִים: עָשִׂיתִי לִי גַּנּוֹת וּפַרְדֵּסִים ה
וְנָטַעְתִּי בָהֶם עֵץ כָּל־פֶּרִי: עָשִׂיתִי לִי בְּרֵכוֹת מָיִם לְהַשְׁקוֹת מֵהֶם ו
יַעַר צוֹמֵחַ עֵצִים: קָנִיתִי עֲבָדִים וּשְׁפָחוֹת וּבְנֵי־בַיִת הָיָה לִי גַּם מִקְנֶה ז
בָקָר וָצֹאן הַרְבֵּה הָיָה לִי מִכֹּל שֶׁהָיוּ לְפָנַי בִּירוּשָׁלִָם: כָּנַסְתִּי לִי ח
גַּם־כֶּסֶף וְזָהָב וּסְגֻלַּת מְלָכִים וְהַמְּדִינוֹת עָשִׂיתִי לִי שָׁרִים וְשָׁרוֹת
וְתַעֲנוּגֹת בְּנֵי הָאָדָם שִׁדָּה וְשִׁדּוֹת: וְגָדַלְתִּי וְהוֹסַפְתִּי מִכֹּל שֶׁהָיָה ט
לְפָנַי בִּירוּשָׁלִָם אַף חָכְמָתִי עָמְדָה לִּי: וְכֹל אֲשֶׁר שָׁאֲלוּ עֵינַי לֹא י
אָצַלְתִּי מֵהֶם לֹא־מָנַעְתִּי אֶת־לִבִּי מִכָּל־שִׂמְחָה כִּי־לִבִּי שָׂמֵחַ מִכָּל־
עֲמָלִי וְזֶה־הָיָה חֶלְקִי מִכָּל־עֲמָלִי: וּפָנִיתִי אֲנִי בְּכָל־מַעֲשַׂי שֶׁעָשׂוּ יָדַי יא
וּבֶעָמָל שֶׁעָמַלְתִּי לַעֲשׂוֹת וְהִנֵּה הַכֹּל הֶבֶל וּרְעוּת רוּחַ וְאֵין יִתְרוֹן
תַּחַת הַשָּׁמֶשׁ: וּפָנִיתִי אֲנִי לִרְאוֹת חָכְמָה וְהוֹלֵלוֹת וְסִכְלוּת כִּי ׀ מֶה יב
הָאָדָם שֶׁיָּבוֹא אַחֲרֵי הַמֶּלֶךְ אֵת אֲשֶׁר־כְּבָר עָשׂוּהוּ: וְרָאִיתִי אָנִי יג
שֶׁיֵּשׁ יִתְרוֹן לַחָכְמָה מִן־הַסִּכְלוּת כִּיתְרוֹן הָאוֹר מִן־הַחֹשֶׁךְ: הֶחָכָם יד
עֵינָיו בְּרֹאשׁוֹ וְהַכְּסִיל בַּחֹשֶׁךְ הוֹלֵךְ וְיָדַעְתִּי גַם־אָנִי שֶׁמִּקְרֶה אֶחָד
יִקְרֶה אֶת־כֻּלָּם: וְאָמַרְתִּי אֲנִי בְּלִבִּי כְּמִקְרֵה הַכְּסִיל גַּם־אֲנִי יִקְרֵנִי טו
וְלָמָּה חָכַמְתִּי אֲנִי אָז יֹתֵר וְדִבַּרְתִּי בְלִבִּי שֶׁגַּם־זֶה הָבֶל: כִּי אֵין זִכְרוֹן טז
לֶחָכָם עִם־הַכְּסִיל לְעוֹלָם בְּשֶׁכְּבָר הַיָּמִים הַבָּאִים הַכֹּל נִשְׁכָּח וְאֵיךְ
יָמוּת הֶחָכָם עִם־הַכְּסִיל: וְשָׂנֵאתִי אֶת־הַחַיִּים כִּי רַע עָלַי הַמַּעֲשֶׂה יז
שֶׁנַּעֲשָׂה תַּחַת הַשָּׁמֶשׁ כִּי־הַכֹּל הֶבֶל וּרְעוּת רוּחַ: וְשָׂנֵאתִי אֲנִי יח
אֶת־כָּל־עֲמָלִי שֶׁאֲנִי עָמֵל תַּחַת הַשָּׁמֶשׁ שֶׁאַנִּיחֶנּוּ לָאָדָם שֶׁיִּהְיֶה
אַחֲרָי: וּמִי יוֹדֵעַ הֶחָכָם יִהְיֶה אוֹ סָכָל וְיִשְׁלַט בְּכָל־עֲמָלִי שֶׁעָמַלְתִּי יט
וְשֶׁחָכַמְתִּי תַּחַת הַשָּׁמֶשׁ גַּם־זֶה הָבֶל: וְסַבּוֹתִי אֲנִי לְיַאֵשׁ אֶת־לִבִּי כ
עַל כָּל־הֶעָמָל שֶׁעָמַלְתִּי תַּחַת הַשָּׁמֶשׁ: כִּי־יֵשׁ אָדָם שֶׁעֲמָלוֹ בְּחָכְמָה כא
וּבְדַעַת וּבְכִשְׁרוֹן וּלְאָדָם שֶׁלֹּא עָמַל־בּוֹ יִתְּנֶנּוּ חֶלְקוֹ גַּם־זֶה הֶבֶל
וְרָעָה רַבָּה: כִּי מֶה־הֹוֶה לָאָדָם בְּכָל־עֲמָלוֹ וּבְרַעְיוֹן לִבּוֹ שֶׁהוּא עָמֵל כב

23 the sky? All your days are pain, your occupation bitterness, and even at night
your mind does not rest, and this too is empty breath.
24 There is no good for man to find, but that he eat and drink and show him-
25 self some good of all his labor; this I saw to be a gift from God. For who
26 will eat, who will hasten after my craving if not I? He gave wisdom and
insight and joy to those who are satisfied with what they have; and to sinners He gave a preoccupation with gathering and collecting, only to give it
all to the one who pleases God. This too is shallow breath; but courting the
wind.

3 1 Everything has its moment; a time for every deed beneath the sky.
2 A time for birth, a time for death;
a time to plant and a time to uproot what is planted.
3 A time to kill, a time to heal;
a time to tear down and a time to build up.
4 A time to weep, a time to laugh;
a time for eulogy and a time for dance.
5 A time to cast away stones, a time to gather up stones;
a time to embrace and a time to hold back from embracing.
6 A time to seek, a time to lose;
a time to keep and a time to cast aside.
7 A time to sever, a time to sew;
a time to be silent and a time to speak.
8 A time to love, a time to hate;
a time of war and a time for peace.

9 10 What profit has the one who works, from all his labor? I have seen the
11 occupation that God gave mortal man to torment himself with. He made
everything right in its proper time, He placed eternity in their minds;
and no man ever fathoms what it is that God is working from beginning
12 to end. And so I know that there is no good for them but to be joyful
13 and to do what is good in their lifetime. And if any man eats and drinks
14 and sees some good of all his labor – that is a gift from God. And I know

כג תַּחַת הַשָּׁמֶשׁ: כִּי כָל־יָמָיו מַכְאֹבִים וָכַעַס עִנְיָנוֹ גַּם־בַּלַּיְלָה לֹא־שָׁכַב
כד לִבּוֹ גַּם־זֶה הֶבֶל הוּא: אֵין־טוֹב בָּאָדָם שֶׁיֹּאכַל וְשָׁתָה וְהֶרְאָה אֶת־
כה נַפְשׁוֹ טוֹב בַּעֲמָלוֹ גַּם־זֹה רָאִיתִי אָנִי כִּי מִיַּד הָאֱלֹהִים הִיא: כִּי מִי
כו יֹאכַל וּמִי יָחוּשׁ חוּץ מִמֶּנִּי: כִּי לְאָדָם שֶׁטּוֹב לְפָנָיו נָתַן חָכְמָה וְדַעַת
וְשִׂמְחָה וְלַחוֹטֶא נָתַן עִנְיָן לֶאֱסֹף וְלִכְנוֹס לָתֵת לְטוֹב לִפְנֵי הָאֱלֹהִים
ג א גַּם־זֶה הֶבֶל וּרְעוּת רוּחַ: לַכֹּל זְמָן וְעֵת לְכָל־חֵפֶץ תַּחַת הַשָּׁמָיִם:
ב עֵת לָלֶדֶת וְעֵת לָמוּת
עֵת לָטַעַת וְעֵת לַעֲקוֹר נָטוּעַ:
ג עֵת לַהֲרוֹג וְעֵת לִרְפּוֹא
עֵת לִפְרוֹץ וְעֵת לִבְנוֹת:
ד עֵת לִבְכּוֹת וְעֵת לִשְׂחוֹק
עֵת סְפוֹד וְעֵת רְקוֹד:
ה עֵת לְהַשְׁלִיךְ אֲבָנִים וְעֵת כְּנוֹס אֲבָנִים
עֵת לַחֲבוֹק וְעֵת לִרְחֹק מֵחַבֵּק:
ו עֵת לְבַקֵּשׁ וְעֵת לְאַבֵּד
עֵת לִשְׁמוֹר וְעֵת לְהַשְׁלִיךְ:
ז עֵת לִקְרוֹעַ וְעֵת לִתְפּוֹר
עֵת לַחֲשׁוֹת וְעֵת לְדַבֵּר:
ח עֵת לֶאֱהֹב וְעֵת לִשְׂנֹא
עֵת מִלְחָמָה וְעֵת שָׁלוֹם:
ט, י מַה־יִּתְרוֹן הָעוֹשֶׂה בַּאֲשֶׁר הוּא עָמֵל: רָאִיתִי אֶת־הָעִנְיָן אֲשֶׁר נָתַן
יא אֱלֹהִים לִבְנֵי הָאָדָם לַעֲנוֹת בּוֹ: אֶת־הַכֹּל עָשָׂה יָפֶה בְעִתּוֹ גַּם אֶת־
הָעֹלָם נָתַן בְּלִבָּם מִבְּלִי אֲשֶׁר לֹא־יִמְצָא הָאָדָם אֶת־הַמַּעֲשֶׂה אֲשֶׁר־
יב עָשָׂה הָאֱלֹהִים מֵרֹאשׁ וְעַד־סוֹף: יָדַעְתִּי כִּי אֵין טוֹב בָּם כִּי אִם־
יג לִשְׂמוֹחַ וְלַעֲשׂוֹת טוֹב בְּחַיָּיו: וְגַם כָּל־הָאָדָם שֶׁיֹּאכַל וְשָׁתָה וְרָאָה
יד טוֹב בְּכָל־עֲמָלוֹ מַתַּת אֱלֹהִים הִיא: יָדַעְתִּי כִּי כָּל־אֲשֶׁר יַעֲשֶׂה

that whatever God does will be forever. There is no adding to it, there
15 is no taking away; and God has made quite sure that He be feared. That
which has been is already here, and that which is to be has already been.
16 And God is seeking after the pursued. Another thing that I saw beneath
the sun: In a place of judgment – there are the evils. In a place of justice –
17 evil is there. I said to my mind: God will judge both the righteous and
the wicked, for the time comes for every deed, for all that is done, there.
18 And I said to my mind of the sons of man: God set them apart, to find
19 that they are nothing but cattle. For the fate of man is the fate of cattle;
the same fate awaits them both, the death of one is like the death of the
other, and their spirits are the same, and the pre-eminence of man over
20 beast is nothing, for it is all but shallow breath. All end in the same place;
21 all emerge from dust and all go back to dust. Who can say that the spirit
22 of a man rises up while the spirit of a beast sinks into the ground? I saw
that there is no good at all but for man to take pleasure in his works; for
that is his share. For who will bring him to see what will become of it all
when he is gone?

4 1 But I turned again and saw all those made victims beneath the sun. There
they were: the victims' tears and none to console them; power at the hands
2 of their oppressors, and none to console them. And I thought the dead
3 more fortunate, who have died already, than the living who yet live. But
better than either are those who are yet to be, for they have seen none of
the evil that is wrought beneath the sun.

4 And I saw all the labor that is performed, all the skill – saw that it is all but
one man's jealousy for another; this too is shallow breath and courting the
5 6 wind. The fool crosses his hands and eats his own flesh. Better a handful of
peace than two hands full of labor and courting the wind.

7 8 I turned again and saw shallow breath beneath the sun. It happens that a
man may be alone, with no fellow, no child even, or brother, and there may
be no end to all his labor. His eye, too, will never see enough of riches; and
who, after all, am I laboring for, and starving my spirit of good? This too is
9 shallow breath and a wretched business. Two are better than one, for they
10 have some good return for all their labor. For if they fall down, they will help
each other rise. But pity the one who falls alone, for who will ever raise him?
11 Two people lying down together are warm; but how can one ever be warm

הָאֱלֹהִים הוּא יִהְיֶה לְעוֹלָם עָלָיו אֵין לְהוֹסִיף וּמִמֶּנּוּ אֵין לִגְרֹעַ
טו וְהָאֱלֹהִים עָשָׂה שֶׁיִּרְאוּ מִלְּפָנָיו: מַה־שֶּׁהָיָה כְּבָר הוּא וַאֲשֶׁר לִהְיוֹת
טז כְּבָר הָיָה וְהָאֱלֹהִים יְבַקֵּשׁ אֶת־נִרְדָּף: וְעוֹד רָאִיתִי תַּחַת הַשָּׁמֶשׁ
יז מְקוֹם הַמִּשְׁפָּט שָׁמָּה הָרֶשַׁע וּמְקוֹם הַצֶּדֶק שָׁמָּה הָרָשַׁע: אָמַרְתִּי
אֲנִי בְּלִבִּי אֶת־הַצַּדִּיק וְאֶת־הָרָשָׁע יִשְׁפֹּט הָאֱלֹהִים כִּי־עֵת לְכָל־חֵפֶץ
יח וְעַל כָּל־הַמַּעֲשֶׂה שָׁם: אָמַרְתִּי אֲנִי בְּלִבִּי עַל־דִּבְרַת בְּנֵי הָאָדָם לְבָרָם
יט הָאֱלֹהִים וְלִרְאוֹת שְׁהֶם־בְּהֵמָה הֵמָּה לָהֶם: כִּי מִקְרֶה בְנֵי־הָאָדָם
וּמִקְרֶה הַבְּהֵמָה וּמִקְרֶה אֶחָד לָהֶם כְּמוֹת זֶה כֵּן מוֹת זֶה וְרוּחַ אֶחָד
כ לַכֹּל וּמוֹתַר הָאָדָם מִן־הַבְּהֵמָה אָיִן כִּי הַכֹּל הָבֶל: הַכֹּל הוֹלֵךְ אֶל־
כא מָקוֹם אֶחָד הַכֹּל הָיָה מִן־הֶעָפָר וְהַכֹּל שָׁב אֶל־הֶעָפָר: מִי יוֹדֵעַ רוּחַ
בְּנֵי הָאָדָם הָעֹלָה הִיא לְמָעְלָה וְרוּחַ הַבְּהֵמָה הַיֹּרֶדֶת הִיא לְמַטָּה
כב לָאָרֶץ: וְרָאִיתִי כִּי אֵין טוֹב מֵאֲשֶׁר יִשְׂמַח הָאָדָם בְּמַעֲשָׂיו כִּי־הוּא
ד א חֶלְקוֹ כִּי מִי יְבִיאֶנּוּ לִרְאוֹת בְּמֶה שֶׁיִּהְיֶה אַחֲרָיו: וְשַׁבְתִּי אֲנִי וָאֶרְאֶה
אֶת־כָּל־הָעֲשֻׁקִים אֲשֶׁר נַעֲשִׂים תַּחַת הַשָּׁמֶשׁ וְהִנֵּה ׀ דִּמְעַת
הָעֲשֻׁקִים וְאֵין לָהֶם מְנַחֵם וּמִיַּד עֹשְׁקֵיהֶם כֹּחַ וְאֵין לָהֶם מְנַחֵם:
ב וְשַׁבֵּחַ אֲנִי אֶת־הַמֵּתִים שֶׁכְּבָר מֵתוּ מִן־הַחַיִּים אֲשֶׁר הֵמָּה חַיִּים
ג עֲדֶנָה: וְטוֹב מִשְּׁנֵיהֶם אֵת אֲשֶׁר־עֲדֶן לֹא הָיָה אֲשֶׁר לֹא־רָאָה אֶת־
ד הַמַּעֲשֶׂה הָרָע אֲשֶׁר נַעֲשָׂה תַּחַת הַשָּׁמֶשׁ: וְרָאִיתִי אֲנִי אֶת־כָּל־עָמָל
וְאֵת כָּל־כִּשְׁרוֹן הַמַּעֲשֶׂה כִּי הִיא קִנְאַת־אִישׁ מֵרֵעֵהוּ גַּם־זֶה הֶבֶל
ה ו וּרְעוּת רוּחַ: הַכְּסִיל חֹבֵק אֶת־יָדָיו וְאֹכֵל אֶת־בְּשָׂרוֹ: טוֹב מְלֹא כַף
ז נַחַת מִמְּלֹא חָפְנַיִם עָמָל וּרְעוּת רוּחַ: וְשַׁבְתִּי אֲנִי וָאֶרְאֶה הֶבֶל תַּחַת
ח הַשָּׁמֶשׁ: יֵשׁ אֶחָד וְאֵין שֵׁנִי גַּם בֵּן וָאָח אֵין־לוֹ וְאֵין קֵץ לְכָל־עֲמָלוֹ
גַּם־עיניו לֹא־תִשְׂבַּע עֹשֶׁר וּלְמִי ׀ אֲנִי עָמֵל וּמְחַסֵּר אֶת־נַפְשִׁי מִטּוֹבָה עֵינוֹ
ט גַּם־זֶה הֶבֶל וְעִנְיַן רָע הוּא: טוֹבִים הַשְּׁנַיִם מִן־הָאֶחָד אֲשֶׁר יֵשׁ־לָהֶם
י שָׂכָר טוֹב בַּעֲמָלָם: כִּי אִם־יִפֹּלוּ הָאֶחָד יָקִים אֶת־חֲבֵרוֹ וְאִילוֹ הָאֶחָד
יא שֶׁיִּפּוֹל וְאֵין שֵׁנִי לַהֲקִימוֹ: גַּם אִם־יִשְׁכְּבוּ שְׁנַיִם וְחַם לָהֶם וּלְאֶחָד אֵיךְ

12 alone? If one man should assault another, then two can stand against him;
and a three-stranded thread is not readily broken.
13 Better a poor and clever child, than an old and foolish king, who does not
14 know how to take heed any more. For he may come straight out of prison
15 to rule; and in his reign too, a poor child will be born. Yes, I saw all of life
moving about beneath the sun, with the next child born to rise up after the
16 last. There is no end to this people, to all that came before them; and those
who come after them also, will not rejoice in him. This too: shallow breath;
17 courting the wind. Watch your steps when you walk to the House of God.
Better to take heed than to bring a fool's offering; for they know not what
doing wrong means.

5 1 Do not hasten your lips, do not hurry your heart, to bring forth words in the
presence of God; for God is in heaven, and you are here on earth; and so let
2 your words be few. For as dreams come of too much preoccupation, so is a
fool's voice known by too many words.

3 If you make a vow to God, do not delay to fulfill it; for there is no use being
4 a fool – whatever you vow, fulfill. Better not to vow, than to vow and not
5 fulfill. Do not let your mouth bring your flesh to punishment; and do not
tell the messenger that it was a mistake; why should you have God rage at
6 your words, and destroy the work of your hands? For so many dreams and
so much shallow breath, so many words – better only to fear God.

7 If you see oppression of a poor person, or any perversion of law and justice
in the province – do not wonder at the fact; for every watchman has a watch-
8 man over him, and there are higher ones yet above. Yet the earth below has
the advantage over all; even a king is enslaved to the field.

9 One who loves money will never be satisfied with money; nor one who loves
10 abundance, with produce. That too is fleeting breath. As goodness multiplies,
so do those who would consume it; and what gain does it bring its master but
11 longing eyes? The sleep of a worker is sweet, whether he eats much or little,
but the rich man's fullness will not let him sleep in peace.

12 There is a sickly evil I have seen beneath the sun: wealth hoarded up for its
13 owner, only to harm him. That wealth may be destroyed by some evil event,
14 and a child is born to him with not the smallest thing to his name. Naked as
he emerged from his own mother's womb, just so will he return. And not the
slightest thing will he hold from all his labor to bring with him.

15 This too is a sickly evil; just as one comes, so shall one leave again. And what
16 profit does one gain for toiling after the wind? All his days he eats in darkness,
and with great bitterness, and sickness, and fury.

יב יֵחָם׃ וְאִם־יִתְקְפוֹ הָאֶחָד הַשְּׁנַיִם יַעַמְדוּ נֶגְדּוֹ וְהַחוּט הַמְשֻׁלָּשׁ לֹא
יג בִמְהֵרָה יִנָּתֵק׃ טוֹב יֶלֶד מִסְכֵּן וְחָכָם מִמֶּלֶךְ זָקֵן וּכְסִיל אֲשֶׁר לֹא־יָדַע
יד לְהִזָּהֵר עוֹד׃ כִּי־מִבֵּית הָסוּרִים יָצָא לִמְלֹךְ כִּי גַּם בְּמַלְכוּתוֹ נוֹלַד
טו רָשׁ׃ רָאִיתִי אֶת־כָּל־הַחַיִּים הַמְהַלְּכִים תַּחַת הַשָּׁמֶשׁ עִם הַיֶּלֶד הַשֵּׁנִי
טז אֲשֶׁר יַעֲמֹד תַּחְתָּיו׃ אֵין־קֵץ לְכָל־הָעָם לְכֹל אֲשֶׁר־הָיָה לִפְנֵיהֶם גַּם
יז הָאַחֲרוֹנִים לֹא יִשְׂמְחוּ־בוֹ כִּי־גַם־זֶה הֶבֶל וְרַעְיוֹן רוּחַ׃ שְׁמֹר רגליך רַגְלְךָ
כַּאֲשֶׁר תֵּלֵךְ אֶל־בֵּית הָאֱלֹהִים וְקָרוֹב לִשְׁמֹעַ מִתֵּת הַכְּסִילִים זָבַח
ה א כִּי־אֵינָם יוֹדְעִים לַעֲשׂוֹת רָע׃ אַל־תְּבַהֵל עַל־פִּיךָ וְלִבְּךָ אַל־יְמַהֵר
לְהוֹצִיא דָבָר לִפְנֵי הָאֱלֹהִים כִּי הָאֱלֹהִים בַּשָּׁמַיִם וְאַתָּה עַל־הָאָרֶץ
ב עַל־כֵּן יִהְיוּ דְבָרֶיךָ מְעַטִּים׃ כִּי בָּא הַחֲלוֹם בְּרֹב עִנְיָן וְקוֹל כְּסִיל
ג בְּרֹב דְּבָרִים׃ כַּאֲשֶׁר תִּדֹּר נֶדֶר לֵאלֹהִים אַל־תְּאַחֵר לְשַׁלְּמוֹ כִּי אֵין
ד חֵפֶץ בַּכְּסִילִים אֵת אֲשֶׁר־תִּדֹּר שַׁלֵּם׃ טוֹב אֲשֶׁר לֹא־תִדֹּר מִשֶּׁתִּדּוֹר
ה וְלֹא תְשַׁלֵּם׃ אַל־תִּתֵּן אֶת־פִּיךָ לַחֲטִיא אֶת־בְּשָׂרֶךָ וְאַל־תֹּאמַר לִפְנֵי
הַמַּלְאָךְ כִּי שְׁגָגָה הִיא לָמָּה יִקְצֹף הָאֱלֹהִים עַל־קוֹלֶךָ וְחִבֵּל אֶת־
ו מַעֲשֵׂה יָדֶיךָ׃ כִּי בְרֹב חֲלֹמוֹת וַהֲבָלִים וּדְבָרִים הַרְבֵּה כִּי אֶת־
ז הָאֱלֹהִים יְרָא׃ אִם־עֹשֶׁק רָשׁ וְגֵזֶל מִשְׁפָּט וָצֶדֶק תִּרְאֶה בַמְּדִינָה
אַל־תִּתְמַהּ עַל־הַחֵפֶץ כִּי גָבֹהַּ מֵעַל גָּבֹהַּ שֹׁמֵר וּגְבֹהִים עֲלֵיהֶם׃
ח ט וְיִתְרוֹן אֶרֶץ בַּכֹּל הִיא מֶלֶךְ לְשָׂדֶה נֶעֱבָד׃ אֹהֵב כֶּסֶף לֹא־יִשְׂבַּע כֶּסֶף הוּא
י וּמִי־אֹהֵב בֶּהָמוֹן לֹא תְבוּאָה גַּם־זֶה הָבֶל׃ בִּרְבוֹת הַטּוֹבָה רַבּוּ
יא אוֹכְלֶיהָ וּמַה־כִּשְׁרוֹן לִבְעָלֶיהָ כִּי אִם־רְאִית עֵינָיו׃ מְתוּקָה שְׁנַת רְאוּת
הָעֹבֵד אִם־מְעַט וְאִם־הַרְבֵּה יֹאכֵל וְהַשָּׂבָע לֶעָשִׁיר אֵינֶנּוּ מַנִּיחַ לוֹ
יב לִישׁוֹן׃ יֵשׁ רָעָה חוֹלָה רָאִיתִי תַּחַת הַשָּׁמֶשׁ עֹשֶׁר שָׁמוּר לִבְעָלָיו
יג לְרָעָתוֹ׃ וְאָבַד הָעֹשֶׁר הַהוּא בְּעִנְיַן רָע וְהוֹלִיד בֵּן וְאֵין בְּיָדוֹ מְאוּמָה׃
יד כַּאֲשֶׁר יָצָא מִבֶּטֶן אִמּוֹ עָרוֹם יָשׁוּב לָלֶכֶת כְּשֶׁבָּא וּמְאוּמָה לֹא־יִשָּׂא
טו בַעֲמָלוֹ שֶׁיֹּלֵךְ בְּיָדוֹ׃ וְגַם־זֹה רָעָה חוֹלָה כָּל־עֻמַּת שֶׁבָּא כֵּן יֵלֵךְ וּמַה־
טז יִּתְרוֹן לוֹ שֶׁיַּעֲמֹל לָרוּחַ׃ גַּם כָּל־יָמָיו בַּחֹשֶׁךְ יֹאכֵל וְכָעַס הַרְבֵּה וְחָלְיוֹ

17 This is what I have seen that is good: the beauty of eating and drinking and
seeing some good of all the labor one toils over beneath the sun, all the days
18 of the life God has given one – for this is one's share. For if God gives any man
wealth and belongings, and grants him the power to eat of them, to take hold
19 of what is his, to take pleasure in his labors – that is a gift from God. For he will
not think too much about the days of his life; for God has given him the joy of
his heart to be occupied with.

6 1 There is an evil I have seen beneath the sun, and it is rife among men. There
2 will be a man to whom God gives wealth and possessions and honor, so that
he lacks nothing his heart desires. And then God will not grant him the power
to partake of it, and a stranger will consume it all; this is shallow breath and
an evil sickness.

3 And a man may have a hundred children and live for many years, and as many
as his years may be, his soul will never be satisfied with all that goodness;
though he may not receive even a burial, I say a stillborn child is better off
4 than he. For he came at a breath and leaves in darkness, and in darkness is his
5 name covered over. That child will never see sunlight and never know; and yet
6 he has more peace than such a man. If one lives a thousand years twice over,
and sees no goodness – well, do we not all go to the same place in the end?

7 All of man's labor is only for his mouth; his soul will never be filled. What
8 advantage does a wise man hold over a fool? And what does an oppressed man
9 profit from knowing how to walk with life? Better what the eyes can see than
what the soul goes walking after. Both are empty breath and courting the wind.

10 Whatever has been was called forth by name – and it is known by now that
11 this is but a man, who cannot contend with one more powerful than he. There
are so many things, such proliferation of empty breath, and what profit do
12 they bring to man? For who knows what is good for a man in his lifetime;
during the numbered days of his breath, that he lives as a shadow; for who
can tell what his fate will be beneath the sun?

7 1 Better a good name than fine oil. Better the day of death than of birth. Better
2 to frequent a house of mourning than a feast; for that is the end of all men,
3 and the living had better keep that in mind. Better bitterness than laughter,
4 for while the face is troubled, the mind is bettering itself. A wise man's heart
5 is in the house of mourning, and a fool's is in the house of celebration. Better
6 to heed the rebuke of the wise than to hear the song of fools. For those fools'
cackling is like the crackling of thorns under the pot. And that too is empty
7 breath. For oppression turns a wise man delirious, and bribery comes at the
cost of one's mind.

יז וָקָצֶף: הִנֵּה אֲשֶׁר־רָאִיתִי אָנִי טוֹב אֲשֶׁר־יָפֶה לֶאֱכוֹל־וְלִשְׁתּוֹת וְלִרְאוֹת
טוֹבָה בְּכָל־עֲמָלוֹ ׀ שֶׁיַּעֲמֹל תַּחַת־הַשֶּׁמֶשׁ מִסְפַּר יְמֵי־חַיָּו אֲשֶׁר־נָתַן־
יח לוֹ הָאֱלֹהִים כִּי־הוּא חֶלְקוֹ: גַּם כָּל־הָאָדָם אֲשֶׁר נָתַן־לוֹ הָאֱלֹהִים
עֹשֶׁר וּנְכָסִים וְהִשְׁלִיטוֹ לֶאֱכֹל מִמֶּנּוּ וְלָשֵׂאת אֶת־חֶלְקוֹ וְלִשְׂמֹחַ
יט בַּעֲמָלוֹ זֹה מַתַּת אֱלֹהִים הִיא: כִּי לֹא הַרְבֵּה יִזְכֹּר אֶת־יְמֵי חַיָּיו כִּי
ו א הָאֱלֹהִים מַעֲנֶה בְּשִׂמְחַת לִבּוֹ: יֵשׁ רָעָה אֲשֶׁר רָאִיתִי תַּחַת הַשָּׁמֶשׁ
ב וְרַבָּה הִיא עַל־הָאָדָם: אִישׁ אֲשֶׁר יִתֶּן־לוֹ הָאֱלֹהִים עֹשֶׁר וּנְכָסִים
וְכָבוֹד וְאֵינֶנּוּ חָסֵר לְנַפְשׁוֹ ׀ מִכֹּל אֲשֶׁר־יִתְאַוֶּה וְלֹא־יַשְׁלִיטֶנּוּ
הָאֱלֹהִים לֶאֱכֹל מִמֶּנּוּ כִּי אִישׁ נָכְרִי יֹאכְלֶנּוּ זֶה הֶבֶל וָחֳלִי רָע הוּא:
ג אִם־יוֹלִיד אִישׁ מֵאָה וְשָׁנִים רַבּוֹת יִחְיֶה וְרַב ׀ שֶׁיִּהְיוּ יְמֵי־שָׁנָיו וְנַפְשׁוֹ
לֹא־תִשְׂבַּע מִן־הַטּוֹבָה וְגַם־קְבוּרָה לֹא־הָיְתָה לּוֹ אָמַרְתִּי טוֹב מִמֶּנּוּ
ד ה הַנָּפֶל: כִּי־בַהֶבֶל בָּא וּבַחֹשֶׁךְ יֵלֵךְ וּבַחֹשֶׁךְ שְׁמוֹ יְכֻסֶּה: גַּם־שֶׁמֶשׁ
ו לֹא־רָאָה וְלֹא יָדָע נַחַת לָזֶה מִזֶּה: וְאִלּוּ חָיָה אֶלֶף שָׁנִים פַּעֲמַיִם
ז וְטוֹבָה לֹא רָאָה הֲלֹא אֶל־מָקוֹם אֶחָד הַכֹּל הוֹלֵךְ: כָּל־עֲמַל הָאָדָם
ח לְפִיהוּ וְגַם־הַנֶּפֶשׁ לֹא תִמָּלֵא: כִּי מַה־יּוֹתֵר לֶחָכָם מִן־הַכְּסִיל מַה־
ט לֶּעָנִי יוֹדֵעַ לַהֲלֹךְ נֶגֶד הַחַיִּים: טוֹב מַרְאֵה עֵינַיִם מֵהֲלָךְ־נָפֶשׁ גַּם־זֶה
י הֶבֶל וּרְעוּת רוּחַ: מַה־שֶּׁהָיָה כְּבָר נִקְרָא שְׁמוֹ וְנוֹדָע אֲשֶׁר־הוּא אָדָם
יא וְלֹא־יוּכַל לָדִין עִם שהתקיף מִמֶּנּוּ: כִּי יֵשׁ־דְּבָרִים הַרְבֵּה מַרְבִּים שֶׁתַּקִּיף
יב הָבֶל מַה־יֹּתֵר לָאָדָם: כִּי מִי־יוֹדֵעַ מַה־טּוֹב לָאָדָם בַּחַיִּים מִסְפַּר
יְמֵי־חַיֵּי הֶבְלוֹ וְיַעֲשֵׂם כַּצֵּל אֲשֶׁר מִי־יַגִּיד לָאָדָם מַה־יִּהְיֶה אַחֲרָיו
ז א תַּחַת הַשָּׁמֶשׁ: טוֹב שֵׁם מִשֶּׁמֶן טוֹב וְיוֹם הַמָּוֶת מִיּוֹם
ב הִוָּלְדוֹ: טוֹב לָלֶכֶת אֶל־בֵּית־אֵבֶל מִלֶּכֶת אֶל־בֵּית מִשְׁתֶּה בַּאֲשֶׁר
ג הוּא סוֹף כָּל־הָאָדָם וְהַחַי יִתֵּן אֶל־לִבּוֹ: טוֹב כַּעַס מִשְּׂחוֹק כִּי־בְרֹעַ
ד פָּנִים יִיטַב לֵב: לֵב חֲכָמִים בְּבֵית אֵבֶל וְלֵב כְּסִילִים בְּבֵית שִׂמְחָה:
ה ו טוֹב לִשְׁמוֹעַ גַּעֲרַת חָכָם מֵאִישׁ שֹׁמֵעַ שִׁיר כְּסִילִים: כִּי כְקוֹל הַסִּירִים
ז תַּחַת הַסִּיר כֵּן שְׂחֹק הַכְּסִיל וְגַם־זֶה הָבֶל: כִּי הָעֹשֶׁק יְהוֹלֵל חָכָם

8 The end of a thing is better than its beginning. Patience is better than pride.
9 10 Do not be so quick to anger, for anger lies in the lap of the fool. Do not say,
"What went wrong, that times gone by were better than these?" It is not
wisdom that brings you to ask.

11 12 Wisdom is better with an estate, though it profits all who see the sun. For
a man in the shade of wisdom is in the shade of money too; and the profit
of understanding is greater, for wisdom brings life to those who master it.
13 Look at the word of God; for nobody can straighten what He has made
14 crooked. On a good day, live goodness, and on a bad day look and see:
God has made both things, one alongside the other; and no man can find
fault with Him after.

15 I have seen it all in the days of my shallow breath; righteous men who die
in their righteousness, and wicked ones who live long in their wickedness.
16 So do not be too righteous, do not be so much wiser; for why should
17 you become desolate? Do not be too wicked, and never be a fool, for
18 why should you die before your time? Better to hold the one part, never
loosening your hand upon the other; for a God-fearing man will escape
19 both dangers. Wisdom gives the wise man more power than ten rulers in
a city.

20 Yes, there is no one in this world so righteous that he does good and never
21 sins. Do not take to heart all the words you hear said; do not overhear it
22 when your slave insults you. For many times, as your heart well knows, you
yourself have insulted others.

23 I tried all this with my wisdom. I said, "I shall be wiser"; but it was far away
24 25 from me. All that has been is far away, deep, deep beyond fathoming. I turned,
I and my mind, to understand and to explore and seek wisdom and reason;
26 and to know the wickedness of foolishness, to know folly and delirium. And
this is what I found: woman is more bitter than death, for she is all traps, with
nets laid in her heart; her arms are a prison; one favored by God escapes her,
27 while a sinner becomes entrapped. See what I found, said Kohelet, searching
28 one by one to find by reason. This too my soul sought and did not find: one
29 man in a thousand I found; but even one such woman I did not. Yes, all that
I found is this; that God created man straightforward; but they go seeking
endless inventions.

8 1 Who is like a wise man, able to see meaning? The wisdom a person has
2 lights up his face, and the pride in his face is changed. Obey the king's word,

ח וִיאַבֵּד אֶת־לֵב מַתָּנָה: טוֹב אַחֲרִית דָּבָר מֵרֵאשִׁיתוֹ טוֹב אֶרֶךְ־רוּחַ
ט מִגְּבַהּ־רוּחַ: אַל־תְּבַהֵל בְּרוּחֲךָ לִכְעוֹס כִּי כַעַס בְּחֵיק כְּסִילִים יָנוּחַ:
י אַל־תֹּאמַר מֶה הָיָה שֶׁהַיָּמִים הָרִאשֹׁנִים הָיוּ טוֹבִים מֵאֵלֶּה כִּי לֹא
יא מֵחׇכְמָה שָׁאַלְתָּ עַל־זֶה: טוֹבָה חׇכְמָה עִם־נַחֲלָה וְיֹתֵר לְרֹאֵי הַשָּׁמֶשׁ:
יב כִּי בְּצֵל הַחׇכְמָה בְּצֵל הַכָּסֶף וְיִתְרוֹן דַּעַת הַחׇכְמָה תְּחַיֶּה בְעָלֶיהָ:
יג יד רְאֵה אֶת־מַעֲשֵׂה הָאֱלֹהִים כִּי מִי יוּכַל לְתַקֵּן אֵת אֲשֶׁר עִוְּתוֹ: בְּיוֹם
טוֹבָה הֱיֵה בְטוֹב וּבְיוֹם רָעָה רְאֵה גַּם אֶת־זֶה לְעֻמַּת־זֶה עָשָׂה
טו הָאֱלֹהִים עַל־דִּבְרַת שֶׁלֹּא יִמְצָא הָאָדָם אַחֲרָיו מְאוּמָה: אֶת־הַכֹּל
רָאִיתִי בִּימֵי הֶבְלִי יֵשׁ צַדִּיק אֹבֵד בְּצִדְקוֹ וְיֵשׁ רָשָׁע מַאֲרִיךְ בְּרָעָתוֹ:
טז יז אַל־תְּהִי צַדִּיק הַרְבֵּה וְאַל־תִּתְחַכַּם יוֹתֵר לָמָּה תִּשּׁוֹמֵם: אַל־תִּרְשַׁע
יח הַרְבֵּה וְאַל־תְּהִי סָכָל לָמָּה תָמוּת בְּלֹא עִתֶּךָ: טוֹב אֲשֶׁר תֶּאֱחֹז בָּזֶה
יט וְגַם־מִזֶּה אַל־תַּנַּח אֶת־יָדֶךָ כִּי־יְרֵא אֱלֹהִים יֵצֵא אֶת־כֻּלָּם: הַחׇכְמָה
כ תָּעֹז לֶחָכָם מֵעֲשָׂרָה שַׁלִּיטִים אֲשֶׁר הָיוּ בָּעִיר: כִּי אָדָם אֵין צַדִּיק
כא בָּאָרֶץ אֲשֶׁר יַעֲשֶׂה־טּוֹב וְלֹא יֶחֱטָא: גַּם לְכׇל־הַדְּבָרִים אֲשֶׁר יְדַבֵּרוּ
כב אַל־תִּתֵּן לִבֶּךָ אֲשֶׁר לֹא־תִשְׁמַע אֶת־עַבְדְּךָ מְקַלְלֶךָ: כִּי גַּם־פְּעָמִים
כג רַבּוֹת יָדַע לִבֶּךָ אֲשֶׁר גַּם־אַתָּ קִלַּלְתָּ אֲחֵרִים: כׇּל־זֹה נִסִּיתִי בַחׇכְמָה
כד אָמַרְתִּי אֶחְכָּמָה וְהִיא רְחוֹקָה מִמֶּנִּי: רָחוֹק מַה־שֶּׁהָיָה וְעָמֹק ׀ עָמֹק
כה מִי יִמְצָאֶנּוּ: סַבּוֹתִי אֲנִי וְלִבִּי לָדַעַת וְלָתוּר וּבַקֵּשׁ חׇכְמָה וְחֶשְׁבּוֹן
כו וְלָדַעַת רֶשַׁע כֶּסֶל וְהַסִּכְלוּת הוֹלֵלוֹת: וּמוֹצֶא אֲנִי מַר מִמָּוֶת אֶת־
הָאִשָּׁה אֲשֶׁר־הִיא מְצוֹדִים וַחֲרָמִים לִבָּהּ אֲסוּרִים יָדֶיהָ טוֹב לִפְנֵי
כז הָאֱלֹהִים יִמָּלֵט מִמֶּנָּה וְחוֹטֵא יִלָּכֶד בָּהּ: רְאֵה זֶה מָצָאתִי אָמְרָה
כח קֹהֶלֶת אַחַת לְאַחַת לִמְצֹא חֶשְׁבּוֹן: אֲשֶׁר עוֹד־בִּקְשָׁה נַפְשִׁי וְלֹא
מָצָאתִי אָדָם אֶחָד מֵאֶלֶף מָצָאתִי וְאִשָּׁה בְכׇל־אֵלֶּה לֹא מָצָאתִי:
כט לְבַד רְאֵה־זֶה מָצָאתִי אֲשֶׁר עָשָׂה הָאֱלֹהִים אֶת־הָאָדָם יָשָׁר וְהֵמָּה
ח א בִקְשׁוּ חִשְּׁבֹנוֹת רַבִּים: מִי כְּהֶחָכָם וּמִי יוֹדֵעַ פֵּשֶׁר דָּבָר חׇכְמַת אָדָם
ב תָּאִיר פָּנָיו וְעֹז פָּנָיו יְשֻׁנֶּא: אֲנִי פִּי־מֶלֶךְ שְׁמוֹר וְעַל דִּבְרַת שְׁבוּעַת

3 I say; and the word of your oath to God. Do not take flight; walk clear away;
do not be present when evil is brewing, for a king will do what it pleases
4 him to do. For a king's word is rule, and who can say to him, "What is it
5 you do?" One who heeds the command will know no harm; and a wise
6 mind will know justice in its time. For every deed has its time and its
7 judgment – for great is the evil man must suffer – for man cannot know
8 what will be; for who would tell him what may be? Man has no power over
the wind, he cannot cage up the wind; no one rules on the day of death,
and no one will take your place in battle, and evil will not save those who
perform it.

9 All this have I seen, and I took it to heart; all that is done here beneath the
10 sun, wherever man wields power over man to harm him. As I observed, I
saw wicked men buried honorably, processed away from a holy place;
while those who acted with decency are forgotten from the town – here
11 again: shallow breath. For it is not soon that judgment is passed after evil,
12 and so a person's mind is filled with thoughts of doing evil. A sinner does
a hundred evils and is granted long years for it. Yes, I know that good will
13 come to those who fear God, for fearing Him. And good will not come
to an evil man, and he will not live long – he passes like a shadow, for he
does not fear God.

14 Yet see this thing of breath that happens on this earth: the righteous to
whom the same arrives as to the wicked; and the wicked to whom the same
15 as the righteous comes – and I say: Here again is empty breath. And so I
praise joy – for there is no good for man beneath the sun, but to eat and
drink and be joyful. This is what he has to accompany him in his labors,
16 through that life that God has given him beneath the sun. When I set
my mind to knowing wisdom; to seeing what it is that is done upon this
17 earth – and all day, all night, no sleep do one's eyes see – I saw all the work
of God; saw that no man can fathom out the work that is done beneath
the sun. One labors to seek it out and will never find it; if a wise man says
he knows – no; and never will he be able to find out.

9 1 All this I took into my mind, trying to understand, all this: that the righteous
and the wise and all their actions – all are in the hand of God. Their love,
2 their hate, none of it is known; it is all just placed before them. All is as it is

ג אֱלֹהִים׃ אַל־תִּבָּהֵל מִפָּנָיו תֵּלֵךְ אַל־תַּעֲמֹד בְּדָבָר רָע כִּי כָּל־אֲשֶׁר
ד יַחְפֹּץ יַעֲשֶׂה׃ בַּאֲשֶׁר דְּבַר־מֶלֶךְ שִׁלְטוֹן וּמִי יֹאמַר־לוֹ מַה־תַּעֲשֶׂה׃
ה ו שׁוֹמֵר מִצְוָה לֹא יֵדַע דָּבָר רָע וְעֵת וּמִשְׁפָּט יֵדַע לֵב חָכָם׃ כִּי לְכָל־
ז חֵפֶץ יֵשׁ עֵת וּמִשְׁפָּט כִּי־רָעַת הָאָדָם רַבָּה עָלָיו׃ כִּי־אֵינֶנּוּ יֹדֵעַ מַה־
ח שֶּׁיִּהְיֶה כִּי כַּאֲשֶׁר יִהְיֶה מִי יַגִּיד לוֹ׃ אֵין אָדָם שַׁלִּיט בָּרוּחַ לִכְלוֹא
אֶת־הָרוּחַ וְאֵין שִׁלְטוֹן בְּיוֹם הַמָּוֶת וְאֵין מִשְׁלַחַת בַּמִּלְחָמָה וְלֹא־
ט יְמַלֵּט רֶשַׁע אֶת־בְּעָלָיו׃ אֶת־כָּל־זֶה רָאִיתִי וְנָתוֹן אֶת־לִבִּי לְכָל־
מַעֲשֶׂה אֲשֶׁר נַעֲשָׂה תַּחַת הַשָּׁמֶשׁ עֵת אֲשֶׁר שָׁלַט הָאָדָם בְּאָדָם
י לְרַע לוֹ׃ וּבְכֵן רָאִיתִי רְשָׁעִים קְבֻרִים וָבָאוּ וּמִמְּקוֹם קָדוֹשׁ יְהַלֵּכוּ
יא וְיִשְׁתַּכְּחוּ בָעִיר אֲשֶׁר כֵּן־עָשׂוּ גַּם־זֶה הָבֶל׃ אֲשֶׁר אֵין־נַעֲשָׂה פִתְגָם
מַעֲשֵׂה הָרָעָה מְהֵרָה עַל־כֵּן מָלֵא לֵב בְּנֵי־הָאָדָם בָּהֶם לַעֲשׂוֹת
יב רָע׃ אֲשֶׁר חֹטֶא עֹשֶׂה רָע מְאַת וּמַאֲרִיךְ לוֹ כִּי גַּם־יוֹדֵעַ אָנִי אֲשֶׁר
יג יִהְיֶה־טּוֹב לְיִרְאֵי הָאֱלֹהִים אֲשֶׁר יִירְאוּ מִלְּפָנָיו׃ וְטוֹב לֹא־יִהְיֶה
יד לָרָשָׁע וְלֹא־יַאֲרִיךְ יָמִים כַּצֵּל אֲשֶׁר אֵינֶנּוּ יָרֵא מִלִּפְנֵי אֱלֹהִים׃ יֶשׁ־
הֶבֶל אֲשֶׁר נַעֲשָׂה עַל־הָאָרֶץ אֲשֶׁר ׀ יֵשׁ צַדִּיקִים אֲשֶׁר מַגִּיעַ אֲלֵהֶם
כְּמַעֲשֵׂה הָרְשָׁעִים וְיֵשׁ רְשָׁעִים שֶׁמַּגִּיעַ אֲלֵהֶם כְּמַעֲשֵׂה הַצַּדִּיקִים
טו אָמַרְתִּי שֶׁגַּם־זֶה הָבֶל׃ וְשִׁבַּחְתִּי אֲנִי אֶת־הַשִּׂמְחָה אֲשֶׁר אֵין־טוֹב
לָאָדָם תַּחַת הַשֶּׁמֶשׁ כִּי אִם־לֶאֱכוֹל וְלִשְׁתּוֹת וְלִשְׂמוֹחַ וְהוּא יִלְוֶנּוּ
טז בַעֲמָלוֹ יְמֵי חַיָּיו אֲשֶׁר־נָתַן־לוֹ הָאֱלֹהִים תַּחַת הַשָּׁמֶשׁ׃ כַּאֲשֶׁר נָתַתִּי
אֶת־לִבִּי לָדַעַת חָכְמָה וְלִרְאוֹת אֶת־הָעִנְיָן אֲשֶׁר נַעֲשָׂה עַל־הָאָרֶץ
יז כִּי גַם בַּיּוֹם וּבַלַּיְלָה שֵׁנָה בְּעֵינָיו אֵינֶנּוּ רֹאֶה׃ וְרָאִיתִי אֶת־כָּל־מַעֲשֵׂה
הָאֱלֹהִים כִּי לֹא יוּכַל הָאָדָם לִמְצוֹא אֶת־הַמַּעֲשֶׂה אֲשֶׁר נַעֲשָׂה
תַחַת־הַשֶּׁמֶשׁ בְּשֶׁל אֲשֶׁר יַעֲמֹל הָאָדָם לְבַקֵּשׁ וְלֹא יִמְצָא וְגַם אִם־
ט א יֹאמַר הֶחָכָם לָדַעַת לֹא יוּכַל לִמְצֹא׃ כִּי אֶת־כָּל־זֶה נָתַתִּי אֶל־לִבִּי
וְלָבוּר אֶת־כָּל־זֶה אֲשֶׁר הַצַּדִּיקִים וְהַחֲכָמִים וַעֲבָדֵיהֶם בְּיַד הָאֱלֹהִים
ב גַּם־אַהֲבָה גַם־שִׂנְאָה אֵין יוֹדֵעַ הָאָדָם הַכֹּל לִפְנֵיהֶם׃ הַכֹּל כַּאֲשֶׁר

for all. The same fate awaits the righteous and the wicked, the good and the
pure and the impure, the one who brings offerings and the one who does
not. For a good man just as for a sinner; the one who swears falsely with the
3 one who fears his oath. This is the evil in all that is done beneath the sun: the
same fate attends everyone. And the hearts of man are weighed down with
evil; delirium clouds their minds all their lives – and then they go to the dead.

4 For one who is still bound to life has something to rely upon: Better to be
5 a living dog than a dead lion. For the living know at least that they must
die; while the dead know nothing. No more reward for their actions; their
6 names are forgotten. Their love, their hate, their passions – all are already
lost. And they have no more share, no longer; no part in what is done
7 beneath the sun. Go, eat your bread in joy, and drink your wine with a joy-
8 ful heart, for God has accepted your deeds. Let your clothes at all times be
9 white; let your head never lack anointing oil. Live well, with the woman
you love, all the days of the shallow breath He has given you here beneath
the sun, for this is your share in life, and in all the toil over which you labor
10 beneath the sun. Whatever you find it in your hands to do – do that with all
your strength. For there is no work or reason, no understanding or wisdom,
in the grave to which you are going.

11 Then I turned again and saw beneath the sun – that the race is not given
to the swift, nor the war to the mighty; bread is not promised to the wise,
nor to the understanding, wealth; no more to the knowing, favor; for time,
12 for misfortune, comes to them all. And man never knows when his time
will come: as fish are entrapped in the deadly net, as birds are trapped in
the snare, so too are people caught, at just that time of harm that will fall
upon them without warning.

13 This too I saw of wisdom beneath the sun, great beyond my understand-
14 ing. A small town. Few people in it. A great king came and surrounded it
15 and built great siege-walls all around. And one poor wise man was there
to be found, able to save the whole town by his wisdom; and not a soul
16 remembered that poor man. And I said: Wisdom is better than might; but
the wisdom of a poor man is scorned, his words unheeded.

17 The quiet words of the wise are heeded more than the shout of a ruler among
18 fools. Better wisdom than weaponry – yet one lone sinner can destroy much
good.

10 1 Dead flies ferment and putrefy perfumer's oils. More costly than wisdom,

לכל מקרה אחד לצדיק ולרשע לטוב ולטהור ולטמא ולזבח
ג ולאשר איננו זבח כטוב כחטא הנשבע כאשר שבועה ירא: זה
רע בכל אשר־נעשה תחת השמש כי־מקרה אחד לכל וגם לב
בני־האדם מלא־רע והוללות בלבבם בחייהם ואחריו אל־המתים:
ד כי־מי אשר יבחר אל כל־החיים יש בטחון כי־לכלב חי הוא טוב יְחֻבַּר
ה מן־האריה המת: כי החיים יודעים שימתו והמתים אינם יודעים
ו מאומה ואין־עוד להם שכר כי נשכח זכרם: גם אהבתם גם־שנאתם
גם־קנאתם כבר אבדה וחלק אין־להם עוד לעולם בכל אשר־
ז נעשה תחת השמש: לך אכל בשמחה לחמך ושתה בלב־טוב יינך
ח כי כבר רצה האלהים את־מעשיך: בכל־עת יהיו בגדיך לבנים
ט ושמן על־ראשך אל־יחסר: ראה חיים עם־אשה אשר־אהבת
כל־ימי חיי הבלך אשר נתן־לך תחת השמש כל ימי הבלך כי הוא
י חלקך בחיים ובעמלך אשר־אתה עמל תחת השמש: כל אשר
תמצא ידך לעשות בכחך עשה כי אין מעשה וחשבון ודעת וחכמה
יא בשאול אשר אתה הלך שמה: שבתי וראה תחת־השמש כי לא
לקלים המרוץ ולא לגבורים המלחמה וגם לא לחכמים לחם וגם
לא לנבנים עשר וגם לא לידעים חן כי־עת ופגע יקרה את־כלם:
יב כי גם לא־ידע האדם את־עתו כדגים שנאחזים במצודה רעה
ולצפרים האחזות בפח כהם יוקשים בני האדם לעת רעה כשתפול
יג עליהם פתאם: גם־זה ראיתי חכמה תחת השמש וגדולה היא אלי:
יד עיר קטנה ואנשים בה מעט ובא־אליה מלך גדול וסבב אתה ובנה
טו עליה מצודים גדלים: ומצא בה איש מסכן חכם ומלט־הוא את־
טז העיר בחכמתו ואדם לא זכר את־האיש המסכן ההוא: ואמרתי
אני טובה חכמה מגבורה וחכמת המסכן בזויה ודבריו אינם
יז נשמעים: דברי חכמים בנחת נשמעים מזעקת מושל בכסילים:
יח י א טובה חכמה מכלי קרב וחוטא אחד יאבד טובה הרבה: זבובי

2 than honor – is one small dose of foolishness. A wise man's mind is to his
3 right hand; and the mind of a fool to his left. Even as he walks along the way,
a fool's mind is missing, telling every passerby that he is a fool.

4 If a ruler's spirit turns against you, do not leave your place, for appease-
5 ment can lay great sins to rest. Here is an evil I have seen beneath the sun,
6 like an error coming forth from the ruler's mouth: fools are raised to the
7 greatest heights, while rich men sit in the gutter. I have seen slaves riding
on horseback, and princes walking like slaves on the ground.

8 He who digs the pit may fall into it, and he who tears down walls – a snake
9 may bite him. He who quarries the stone will come to grief by it; and he
10 who chops the tree may by that tree be harmed. If the axe grows blunt and
is not polished, then the one who wields it must add force; for skill yields
11 profit only through wisdom. If the snake that cannot be charmed bites,
12 there is no profit to the charmer then. The words of the wise bring favor,
13 while the lips of a fool will swallow him up. His speech begins with fool-
14 ishness, and ends with evil delirium. Yet the fool speaks on and on. Man
does not know what will be; yes, who may tell him what will come after?
15 The labor of fools exhausts them; they know not even the way to the city.

16 I pity you, the land whose king is a boy, whose princes feast in the morning.
17 Happy the land whose king is a nobleman, and whose princes eat at the right
18 time, strong, without drunkenness. The roof caves in for much laziness; and
19 hands laid down spring leaks in the house. Feasts are made for laughter, and
wine fills life with joy – and money will answer for everything.

20 Never curse a king, not even in your mind, nor a rich man, even in your
innermost room. For a bird of the sky will carry that voice; a winged creature will repeat the word.

11 1 Cast your bread out onto the waters, for in the long passage of days you will
2 find it again. Give of what is yours to seven, to eight, for on this earth you
3 cannot know what evil may yet come. If the clouds fill with rain, they must
empty it onto the earth. If a tree falls to the south, to the north – wherever
4 that tree falls, there it will lie. One who watches for the wind will never sow;
5 one who gazes at the clouds will never reap. And just as you know not the
way of the wind, nor what frame fills a pregnant woman's womb, so you
6 cannot know the work of God; and everything is His work. Sow your seeds
in the morning, and by evening do not lay your hands down – for you do
not know which will prove fit, these seeds or those, or whether the two are

ב מות יבאיש יביע שמן רוקח יקר מחכמה מכבוד סכלות מעט: לב
ג חכם לימינו ולב כסיל לשמאלו: וגם־בדרך כשהסכל הלך לבו כשסכל
ד חסר ואמר לכל סכל הוא: אם־רוח המושל תעלה עליך מקומך
ה אל־תנח כי מרפא יניח חטאים גדולים: יש רעה ראיתי תחת
ו השמש כשגגה שיצא מלפני השליט: נתן הסכל במרומים רבים
ז ועשירים בשפל ישבו: ראיתי עבדים על־סוסים ושרים הלכים
ח כעבדים על־הארץ: חפר גומץ בו יפול ופרץ גדר ישכנו נחש:
ט י מסיע אבנים יעצב בהם בוקע עצים יסכן בם: אם־קהה הברזל
יא והוא לא־פנים קלקל וחילים יגבר ויתרון הכשיר חכמה: אם־ישך
יב הנחש בלוא־לחש ואין יתרון לבעל הלשון: דברי פי־חכם חן
יג ושפתות כסיל תבלענו: תחלת דברי־פיהו סכלות ואחרית פיהו
יד הוללות רעה: והסכל ירבה דברים לא־ידע האדם מה־שיהיה
טו ואשר יהיה מאחריו מי יגיד לו: עמל הכסילים תיגענו אשר לא־
טז ידע ללכת אל־עיר: אי־לך ארץ שמלכך נער ושריך בבקר יאכלו:
יז אשריך ארץ שמלכך בן־חורים ושריך בעת יאכלו בגבורה ולא
יח יט בשתי: בעצלתים ימך המקרה ובשפלות ידים ידלף הבית: לשחוק
כ עשים לחם ויין ישמח חיים והכסף יענה את־הכל: גם במדעך מלך
אל־תקלל ובחדרי משכבך אל־תקלל עשיר כי עוף השמים יוליך
יא א את־הקול ובעל הכנפים יגיד דבר: שלח לחמך על־פני המים כי־ כנפים
ב ברב הימים תמצאנו: תן־חלק לשבעה וגם לשמונה כי לא תדע
ג מה־יהיה רעה על־הארץ: אם־ימלאו העבים גשם על־הארץ יריקו
ד ואם־יפול עץ בדרום ואם בצפון מקום שיפול העץ שם יהוא: שמר
ה רוח לא יזרע וראה בעבים לא יקצור: כאשר אינך יודע מה־דרך
הרוח כעצמים בבטן המלאה ככה לא תדע את־מעשה האלהים
ו אשר יעשה את־הכל: בבקר זרע את־זרעך ולערב אל־תנח ידך
כי אינך יודע אי זה יכשר הזה או־זה ואם־שניהם כאחד טובים:

7 as good as one another. There is a sweetness in the light; it is good for the
8 eyes to see the sun. And should a man live many years he should rejoice in
all of them, remembering, too, the days of darkness, for there will be many.
All that comes is but a breath.

9 Young man, rejoice now in your youth; let your heart ease you while you are
young. Follow your heart where it leads you, your eyes where they allure
10 you – and know that God will bring you into judgment for all this. So clear
your heart of bitterness and free your flesh of pain, for youth and dark-haired
days pass by like breath.

12 1 And remember your Creator in these days of your youth; before the days of
despair, before years come when you shall say: There is nothing here that
2 I desire. Before the sun is darkened and the light, the moon and stars, and
3 clouds return again after the rain. The day when the guards of the house will
shake, and the soldiers buckle; when the grinders sit idle, grown few, and
4 the women at the windows sit in darkness. When all the doors in the street
are closed, as the mill-stone falls silent, and a man starts up at the sound of a
5 bird, but the singing girls' voices drop low. And one lives in terror of heights,
and all the pitfalls on the road. The almond blossoms, the grasshopper
bears its burden, the caper fruit breaks asunder, but man is departing for his
6 eternal home, and the mourners turn about around the streets. Remember –
before the silver cord snaps, and the golden bowl is shattered, and the jug
7 is broken beside the spring, and the basin is smashed against the well, the
dust returns to the earth where it began, and the spirit returns to God who
8 gave it. Shallowest breath, says Kohelet. It is all but shallow breath.

9 Kohelet's wisdom went further than this; he taught the people understanding always, and weighed and explored and assembled many wise sayings.
10 Kohelet sought out choicest words, and wrote words of truth honestly.
11 The words of the wise are like goads; like pointed nails are the scholars'
12 sayings. One Shepherd gave them all. And further than this, my child,
take heed; there is no end to the making of many books, and much study
wearies the flesh.

13 The final word: it has all been said. Hold God in awe, and heed His com-
14 mands, for that is all man has. And all that is done – God shall bring it to
judgment; all that is hidden, the good and the bad.

The final word: it has all been said.
Hold God in awe, and heed His commands, for that is all man has.

Continue with Removing the Torah from the Ark on page 498.

ז ח וּמָתוֹק הָאוֹר וְטוֹב לַעֵינַיִם לִרְאוֹת אֶת־הַשָּׁמֶשׁ: כִּי אִם־שָׁנִים הַרְבֵּה
יִחְיֶה הָאָדָם בְּכֻלָּם יִשְׂמָח וְיִזְכֹּר אֶת־יְמֵי הַחֹשֶׁךְ כִּי־הַרְבֵּה יִהְיוּ כָּל־
ט שֶׁבָּא הָבֶל: שְׂמַח בָּחוּר בְּיַלְדוּתֶךָ וִיטִיבְךָ לִבְּךָ בִּימֵי בְחוּרוֹתֶךָ וְהַלֵּךְ
בְּדַרְכֵי לִבְּךָ וּבְמַרְאֵי עֵינֶיךָ וְדָע כִּי עַל־כָּל־אֵלֶּה יְבִיאֲךָ הָאֱלֹהִים וּבְמַרְאֵה
י בַּמִּשְׁפָּט: וְהָסֵר כַּעַס מִלִּבֶּךָ וְהַעֲבֵר רָעָה מִבְּשָׂרֶךָ כִּי־הַיַּלְדוּת
יב א וְהַשַּׁחֲרוּת הָבֶל: וּזְכֹר אֶת־בּוֹרְאֶיךָ בִּימֵי בְּחוּרֹתֶיךָ עַד אֲשֶׁר לֹא־
ב יָבֹאוּ יְמֵי הָרָעָה וְהִגִּיעוּ שָׁנִים אֲשֶׁר תֹּאמַר אֵין־לִי בָהֶם חֵפֶץ: עַד
אֲשֶׁר לֹא־תֶחְשַׁךְ הַשֶּׁמֶשׁ וְהָאוֹר וְהַיָּרֵחַ וְהַכּוֹכָבִים וְשָׁבוּ הֶעָבִים
ג אַחַר הַגָּשֶׁם: בַּיּוֹם שֶׁיָּזֻעוּ שֹׁמְרֵי הַבַּיִת וְהִתְעַוְּתוּ אַנְשֵׁי הֶחָיִל וּבָטְלוּ
ד הַטֹּחֲנוֹת כִּי מִעֵטוּ וְחָשְׁכוּ הָרֹאוֹת בָּאֲרֻבּוֹת: וְסֻגְּרוּ דְלָתַיִם בַּשּׁוּק
ה בִּשְׁפַל קוֹל הַטַּחֲנָה וְיָקוּם לְקוֹל הַצִּפּוֹר וְיִשַּׁחוּ כָּל־בְּנוֹת הַשִּׁיר: גַּם
מִגָּבֹהַּ יִרָאוּ וְחַתְחַתִּים בַּדֶּרֶךְ וְיָנֵאץ הַשָּׁקֵד וְיִסְתַּבֵּל הֶחָגָב וְתָפֵר
הָאֲבִיּוֹנָה כִּי־הֹלֵךְ הָאָדָם אֶל־בֵּית עוֹלָמוֹ וְסָבְבוּ בַשּׁוּק הַסֹּפְדִים:
ו עַד אֲשֶׁר לֹא־ירחק חֶבֶל הַכֶּסֶף וְתָרֻץ גֻּלַּת הַזָּהָב וְתִשָּׁבֶר כַּד עַל־ יֵרָתֵק
ז הַמַּבּוּעַ וְנָרֹץ הַגַּלְגַּל אֶל־הַבּוֹר: וְיָשֹׁב הֶעָפָר עַל־הָאָרֶץ כְּשֶׁהָיָה
ח וְהָרוּחַ תָּשׁוּב אֶל־הָאֱלֹהִים אֲשֶׁר נְתָנָהּ: הֲבֵל הֲבָלִים אָמַר הַקּוֹהֶלֶת
ט הַכֹּל הָבֶל: וְיֹתֵר שֶׁהָיָה קֹהֶלֶת חָכָם עוֹד לִמַּד־דַּעַת אֶת־הָעָם וְאִזֵּן
י וְחִקֵּר תִּקֵּן מְשָׁלִים הַרְבֵּה: בִּקֵּשׁ קֹהֶלֶת לִמְצֹא דִּבְרֵי־חֵפֶץ וְכָתוּב
יא יֹשֶׁר דִּבְרֵי אֱמֶת: דִּבְרֵי חֲכָמִים כַּדָּרְבֹנוֹת וּכְמַשְׂמְרוֹת נְטוּעִים בַּעֲלֵי
יב אֲסֻפּוֹת נִתְּנוּ מֵרֹעֶה אֶחָד: וְיֹתֵר מֵהֵמָּה בְּנִי הִזָּהֵר עֲשׂוֹת סְפָרִים
יג הַרְבֵּה אֵין קֵץ וְלַהַג הַרְבֵּה יְגִעַת בָּשָׂר: סוֹף דָּבָר הַכֹּל נִשְׁמָע אֶת־
יד הָאֱלֹהִים יְרָא וְאֶת־מִצְוֺתָיו שְׁמוֹר כִּי־זֶה כָּל־הָאָדָם: כִּי אֶת־כָּל־
מַעֲשֶׂה הָאֱלֹהִים יָבִא בְמִשְׁפָּט עַל כָּל־נֶעְלָם אִם־טוֹב וְאִם־רָע:

סוף דבר הכל נשמע
את האלהים ירא ואת מצותיו שמור
כי זה כל האדם

Continue with הוצאת ספר תורה *on page 499.*

ESTHER

It is customary for the congregation to say aloud the passages marked by arrows, followed by the Reader.

1 1 It happened in the days of Ahasuerus; Ahasuerus who ruled a hundred and
2 twenty-seven provinces – from India to Ethiopia. At that time, when King
3 Ahasuerus sat upon his royal throne in the imperial city of Shushan, in the
third year of his rule, he made a feast for all his ministers and courtiers, the
military men of Persia and Medea, the noblemen and the ministers of the
4 provinces, all coming before him. And there, for many days together, one
hundred and eighty days in all, he displayed all the wealth of his noble reign,
and the glory of his dazzling greatness.

5 When that time had passed, the king held a feast for all the men of the
imperial city, Shushan, from the greatest to the lowliest, in the courtyard
6 of the king's palace garden. There were swathes of fine white fabric there, of
precious cotton and sky blue wool, all corded with strands of the finest linen
and scarlet, and draped over silver bars and columns of marble; and there
were couches of gold and silver, arranged on a terrace paved with alabaster
7 and marble, with mother of pearl and black onyx. And the guests were served
their drink in vessels of gold – vessels unlike any other – royal wine, abundant
8 as the king's largesse. And the drinking was strictly without duress; for so
the king had instructed all the overseers of his home: to honor the wishes
of each and every man.

9 Meanwhile, Vashti the queen made a feast of her own; a women's feast, in
10 King Ahasuerus' royal palace. And on the seventh day of the feasts, when the
king had grown merry with wine, he instructed Mehuman, Bizta, Ḥarvona,
Bigta and Avagta, Zeitar and Karkas – the seven eunuchs who attended the
11 king, Ahasuerus – to bring Vashti the queen before the king in her royal
crown, to show the peoples and the ministers her charms, for she was beauti-
12 ful indeed. But the queen, Vashti, refused to come at the word the king had
conveyed through the eunuchs. And fury engulfed the king, and his rage
blazed up within him.

13 Now the king addressed the wise men, who knew how to read the times –
for it was the king's practice to consult with those who knew the statutes
14 and the law. And the men of his closest circle, those who came freely into
the king's presence and occupied the first position in the realm, were seven
ministers of Persia and Media named Karshena, Shetar, Admata, Tarshish,

אסתר

It is customary for the קהל *to say aloud the passages marked by arrows, followed by the* קורא.

א א וַיְהִי בִּימֵי אֲחַשְׁוֵרוֹשׁ הוּא אֲחַשְׁוֵרוֹשׁ הַמֹּלֵךְ מֵהֹדּוּ וְעַד־כּוּשׁ שֶׁבַע
ב וְעֶשְׂרִים וּמֵאָה מְדִינָה: בַּיָּמִים הָהֵם כְּשֶׁבֶת ׀ הַמֶּלֶךְ אֲחַשְׁוֵרוֹשׁ עַל
ג כִּסֵּא מַלְכוּתוֹ אֲשֶׁר בְּשׁוּשַׁן הַבִּירָה: בִּשְׁנַת שָׁלוֹשׁ לְמָלְכוֹ עָשָׂה
מִשְׁתֶּה לְכָל־שָׂרָיו וַעֲבָדָיו חֵיל ׀ פָּרַס וּמָדַי הַפַּרְתְּמִים וְשָׂרֵי הַמְּדִינוֹת
ד לְפָנָיו: בְּהַרְאֹתוֹ אֶת־עֹשֶׁר כְּבוֹד מַלְכוּתוֹ וְאֶת־יְקָר תִּפְאֶרֶת גְּדוּלָּתוֹ
ה יָמִים רַבִּים שְׁמוֹנִים וּמְאַת יוֹם: וּבִמְלוֹאת ׀ הַיָּמִים הָאֵלֶּה עָשָׂה
הַמֶּלֶךְ לְכָל־הָעָם הַנִּמְצְאִים בְּשׁוּשַׁן הַבִּירָה לְמִגָּדוֹל וְעַד־קָטָן
ו מִשְׁתֶּה שִׁבְעַת יָמִים בַּחֲצַר גִּנַּת בִּיתַן הַמֶּלֶךְ: חוּר ׀ כַּרְפַּס וּתְכֵלֶת
אָחוּז בְּחַבְלֵי־בוּץ וְאַרְגָּמָן עַל־גְּלִילֵי כֶסֶף וְעַמּוּדֵי שֵׁשׁ מִטּוֹת ׀
ז זָהָב וָכֶסֶף עַל רִצְפַת בַּהַט־וָשֵׁשׁ וְדַר וְסֹחָרֶת: וְהַשְׁקוֹת בִּכְלֵי זָהָב
ח וְכֵלִים מִכֵּלִים שׁוֹנִים וְיֵין מַלְכוּת רָב כְּיַד הַמֶּלֶךְ: וְהַשְּׁתִיָּה כַדָּת
אֵין אֹנֵס כִּי־כֵן ׀ יִסַּד הַמֶּלֶךְ עַל כָּל־רַב בֵּיתוֹ לַעֲשׂוֹת כִּרְצוֹן אִישׁ־
ט וָאִישׁ: גַּם וַשְׁתִּי הַמַּלְכָּה עָשְׂתָה מִשְׁתֵּה נָשִׁים בֵּית
י הַמַּלְכוּת אֲשֶׁר לַמֶּלֶךְ אֲחַשְׁוֵרוֹשׁ: בַּיּוֹם הַשְּׁבִיעִי כְּטוֹב לֵב־הַמֶּלֶךְ
בַּיָּיִן אָמַר לִמְהוּמָן בִּזְּתָא חַרְבוֹנָא בִּגְתָא וַאֲבַגְתָא זֵתַר וְכַרְכַּס
יא שִׁבְעַת הַסָּרִיסִים הַמְשָׁרְתִים אֶת־פְּנֵי הַמֶּלֶךְ אֲחַשְׁוֵרוֹשׁ: לְהָבִיא
אֶת־וַשְׁתִּי הַמַּלְכָּה לִפְנֵי הַמֶּלֶךְ בְּכֶתֶר מַלְכוּת לְהַרְאוֹת הָעַמִּים
יב וְהַשָּׂרִים אֶת־יָפְיָהּ כִּי־טוֹבַת מַרְאֶה הִיא: וַתְּמָאֵן הַמַּלְכָּה וַשְׁתִּי
לָבוֹא בִּדְבַר הַמֶּלֶךְ אֲשֶׁר בְּיַד הַסָּרִיסִים וַיִּקְצֹף הַמֶּלֶךְ מְאֹד וַחֲמָתוֹ
יג בָּעֲרָה בוֹ: וַיֹּאמֶר הַמֶּלֶךְ לַחֲכָמִים יֹדְעֵי הָעִתִּים כִּי־כֵן
יד דְּבַר הַמֶּלֶךְ לִפְנֵי כָּל־יֹדְעֵי דָּת וָדִין: וְהַקָּרֹב אֵלָיו כַּרְשְׁנָא שֵׁתָר
אַדְמָתָא תַרְשִׁישׁ מֶרֶס מַרְסְנָא מְמוּכָן שִׁבְעַת שָׂרֵי ׀ פָּרַס וּמָדַי רֹאֵי

15 Meres, Marsena and Memukhan. "What," he asked, "would the law have us
do with Vashti the queen, for refusing to obey the king's word, conveyed to
her by the eunuchs?"

16 And Memukhan replied, before the king and the ministers: "It is not only
the king that Vashti the queen has wronged, but all the ministers and all the
17 peoples in all King Ahasuerus' provinces. For this tale of the queen will go
out to all the women, casting their husbands into their contempt, as they say,
'King Ahasuerus commanded Queen Vashti to be brought before him – but
18 she did not come!' Yes, this very day, all the ministers' wives of Persia and
Medea who heard what the queen did will tell all the king's ministers, and
there will be no end to the contempt and the fury.

19 "If, then, it so please the king, let a royal declaration be sent out from him,
and be written among the laws of Persia and Medea, that it never be revoked –
that Vashti shall come no more before King Ahasuerus; and the king shall
give her rule over to some other woman; to one who is better than she.
20 And the king's decree shall be heeded and obeyed in all his empire, great
as it is: that all women must honor their husbands, from the greatest to the
lowliest."

21 The suggestion pleased the king and the ministers, and the king did just as
22 Memukhan had said. He sent scrolls to all the king's provinces, province
by province, each in its script, and people by people, each in its language –
ruling that each man be master in his home, speaking the language of his
own people.

2 1 Some time later, when King Ahasuerus' fury had subsided – he remembered
2 Vashti and what she had done, and what had been decreed against her. The
king's pages, those who attended him daily, said, "Let beautiful young virgins
3 be sought out for the king; let the king appoint officers in all the provinces of
his realm, to gather every beautiful young virgin to the imperial city, Shushan,
to the harem, into the charge of Hegai the king's eunuch, the keeper of the
4 women, to be given their ointments there. And whichever young woman the
king likes best – let her become queen in Vashti's place!"

The suggestion pleased the king, and that is what he did.

5 ▸Now there was a Jewish man in the imperial city of Shushan, and his name
6 was Mordekhai, son of Yair, son of Kish, of the tribe of Benjamin. ◂ He had
been exiled from Jerusalem, among the exile expelled with Jehoiachin, king of
7 Judah, who was exiled by Nebuchadnezzar, king of Babylon. And Mordekhai

טו פְּנֵי הַמֶּלֶךְ הַיֹּשְׁבִים רִאשֹׁנָה בַּמַּלְכוּת׃ כְּדָת מַה־לַּעֲשׂוֹת בַּמַּלְכָּה
וַשְׁתִּי עַל ׀ אֲשֶׁר לֹא־עָשְׂתָה אֶת־מַאֲמַר הַמֶּלֶךְ אֲחַשְׁוֵרוֹשׁ בְּיַד
טז הַסָּרִיסִים׃ וַיֹּאמֶר מומכן לִפְנֵי הַמֶּלֶךְ וְהַשָּׂרִים לֹא עַל־ מְמוּכָן
הַמֶּלֶךְ לְבַדּוֹ עָוְתָה וַשְׁתִּי הַמַּלְכָּה כִּי עַל־כָּל־הַשָּׂרִים וְעַל־כָּל־הָעַמִּים
יז אֲשֶׁר בְּכָל־מְדִינוֹת הַמֶּלֶךְ אֲחַשְׁוֵרוֹשׁ׃ כִּי־יֵצֵא דְבַר־הַמַּלְכָּה עַל־
כָּל־הַנָּשִׁים לְהַבְזוֹת בַּעְלֵיהֶן בְּעֵינֵיהֶן בְּאָמְרָם הַמֶּלֶךְ אֲחַשְׁוֵרוֹשׁ
יח אָמַר לְהָבִיא אֶת־וַשְׁתִּי הַמַּלְכָּה לְפָנָיו וְלֹא־בָאָה׃ וְהַיּוֹם הַזֶּה
תֹּאמַרְנָה ׀ שָׂרוֹת פָּרַס־וּמָדַי אֲשֶׁר שָׁמְעוּ אֶת־דְּבַר הַמַּלְכָּה לְכֹל
יט שָׂרֵי הַמֶּלֶךְ וּכְדַי בִּזָּיוֹן וָקָצֶף׃ אִם־עַל־הַמֶּלֶךְ טוֹב יֵצֵא דְבַר־מַלְכוּת
מִלְּפָנָיו וְיִכָּתֵב בְּדָתֵי פָרַס־וּמָדַי וְלֹא יַעֲבוֹר אֲשֶׁר לֹא־תָבוֹא וַשְׁתִּי
לִפְנֵי הַמֶּלֶךְ אֲחַשְׁוֵרוֹשׁ וּמַלְכוּתָהּ יִתֵּן הַמֶּלֶךְ לִרְעוּתָהּ הַטּוֹבָה מִמֶּנָּה׃
כ וְנִשְׁמַע פִּתְגָם הַמֶּלֶךְ אֲשֶׁר־יַעֲשֶׂה בְּכָל־מַלְכוּתוֹ כִּי רַבָּה הִיא וְכָל־
כא הַנָּשִׁים יִתְּנוּ יְקָר לְבַעְלֵיהֶן לְמִגָּדוֹל וְעַד־קָטָן׃ וַיִּיטַב הַדָּבָר בְּעֵינֵי
כב הַמֶּלֶךְ וְהַשָּׂרִים וַיַּעַשׂ הַמֶּלֶךְ כִּדְבַר מְמוּכָן׃ וַיִּשְׁלַח סְפָרִים אֶל־כָּל־
מְדִינוֹת הַמֶּלֶךְ אֶל־מְדִינָה וּמְדִינָה כִּכְתָבָהּ וְאֶל־עַם וָעָם כִּלְשׁוֹנוֹ
לִהְיוֹת כָּל־אִישׁ שֹׂרֵר בְּבֵיתוֹ וּמְדַבֵּר כִּלְשׁוֹן עַמּוֹ׃ אַחַר ב א
הַדְּבָרִים הָאֵלֶּה כְּשֹׁךְ חֲמַת הַמֶּלֶךְ אֲחַשְׁוֵרוֹשׁ זָכַר אֶת־וַשְׁתִּי וְאֵת
ב אֲשֶׁר־עָשָׂתָה וְאֵת אֲשֶׁר־נִגְזַר עָלֶיהָ׃ וַיֹּאמְרוּ נַעֲרֵי־הַמֶּלֶךְ מְשָׁרְתָיו
ג יְבַקְשׁוּ לַמֶּלֶךְ נְעָרוֹת בְּתוּלוֹת טוֹבוֹת מַרְאֶה׃ וְיַפְקֵד הַמֶּלֶךְ פְּקִידִים
בְּכָל־מְדִינוֹת מַלְכוּתוֹ וְיִקְבְּצוּ אֶת־כָּל־נַעֲרָה־בְתוּלָה טוֹבַת מַרְאֶה
אֶל־שׁוּשַׁן הַבִּירָה אֶל־בֵּית הַנָּשִׁים אֶל־יַד הֵגֶא סְרִיס הַמֶּלֶךְ שֹׁמֵר
ד הַנָּשִׁים וְנָתוֹן תַּמְרוּקֵיהֶן׃ וְהַנַּעֲרָה אֲשֶׁר תִּיטַב בְּעֵינֵי הַמֶּלֶךְ תִּמְלֹךְ
ה תַּחַת וַשְׁתִּי וַיִּיטַב הַדָּבָר בְּעֵינֵי הַמֶּלֶךְ וַיַּעַשׂ כֵּן׃ · אִישׁ
יְהוּדִי הָיָה בְּשׁוּשַׁן הַבִּירָה וּשְׁמוֹ מָרְדֳּכַי בֶּן יָאִיר בֶּן־שִׁמְעִי בֶּן־קִישׁ
ו אִישׁ יְמִינִי׃ · אֲשֶׁר הָגְלָה מִירוּשָׁלַיִם עִם־הַגֹּלָה אֲשֶׁר הָגְלְתָה עִם
ז יְכָנְיָה מֶלֶךְ־יְהוּדָה אֲשֶׁר הֶגְלָה נְבוּכַדְנֶאצַּר מֶלֶךְ בָּבֶל׃ וַיְהִי אֹמֵן

had brought up Hadassa – Esther, that is – his uncle's daughter, for she had
no father or mother; and the girl was lovely, and beautiful, and when her
father and mother had died, Mordekhai had adopted her as his own child.
8 And when the king's word and his ruling were heard, and vast numbers of
young women were gathered in to the imperial city, Shushan, and into the
charge of Hegai – Esther too was taken to the king's palace, into the charge
of Hegai, the keeper of the women.

9 And the young woman pleased him, and she carried kindness with her, and
he hastened to her all her ointments and meals, and the seven young maids
to whom she was entitled, from the king's palace; and he treated her with
10 especial care, her and her maids, all the time that she was in the harem. Esther,
meanwhile, made no mention of her people or her birth, for Mordekhai had
11 bid her strictly not to tell. And every single day, Mordekhai would walk about
before the harem courtyard, to find out whether Esther was well, and what
was being done with her.

12 As each young woman's turn would arrive to come before King Ahasuerus,
after twelve months following her beauty regime (for that was how long
the days of their ointments lasted: six months in myrrh oil and six months
13 in perfumes and the women's ointments) – then the young woman would
come before the king: and all that she asked for would be given her, to bring
14 with her from the harem to the palace of the king. She would go in the evening, and in the morning would return to the harem again, into the charge
of Sha'ashgaz, the king's eunuch, keeper of the concubines. And then she
would come no more before the king, unless he desired her, and she was
called for by name.

15 And when the time came for Esther, daughter of Mordekhai's uncle, Aviḥayil,
whom Mordekhai had adopted as his own child, to come before the king –
she did not ask for anything, except for what Hegai the king's eunuch, keeper
of the women, told her to bring. And Esther carried grace in the eyes of
all who saw her.

16 Esther was taken to King Ahasuerus, to his royal palace, in the tenth month,
17 the month of Tevet, that is, in the seventh year of his reign. And the king loved
Esther more than all the other women, and she pleased him and carried grace
and kindness with her in his eyes, more so than all the other virgins, and he
placed a royal crown upon her head, and made her queen in Vashti's place.
18 And the king made a great feast for all his ministers and courtiers: the feast
of Esther. And he granted the provinces a remission of their dues, and gifts
as great as the king's largesse.

אֶת־הֲדַסָּה הִיא אֶסְתֵּר בַּת־דֹּדוֹ כִּי אֵין לָהּ אָב וָאֵם וְהַנַּעֲרָה יְפַת־
תֹּאַר וְטוֹבַת מַרְאֶה וּבְמוֹת אָבִיהָ וְאִמָּהּ לְקָחָהּ מָרְדֳּכַי לוֹ לְבַת׃
ח וַיְהִי בְּהִשָּׁמַע דְּבַר־הַמֶּלֶךְ וְדָתוֹ וּבְהִקָּבֵץ נְעָרוֹת רַבּוֹת אֶל־שׁוּשַׁן
הַבִּירָה אֶל־יַד הֵגָי וַתִּלָּקַח אֶסְתֵּר אֶל־בֵּית הַמֶּלֶךְ אֶל־יַד הֵגַי שֹׁמֵר
ט הַנָּשִׁים׃ וַתִּיטַב הַנַּעֲרָה בְעֵינָיו וַתִּשָּׂא חֶסֶד לְפָנָיו וַיְבַהֵל אֶת־
תַּמְרוּקֶיהָ וְאֶת־מָנוֹתֶהָ לָתֵת לָהּ וְאֵת שֶׁבַע הַנְּעָרוֹת הָרְאֻיוֹת לָתֶת־
י לָהּ מִבֵּית הַמֶּלֶךְ וַיְשַׁנֶּהָ וְאֶת־נַעֲרוֹתֶיהָ לְטוֹב בֵּית הַנָּשִׁים׃ לֹא־
הִגִּידָה אֶסְתֵּר אֶת־עַמָּהּ וְאֶת־מוֹלַדְתָּהּ כִּי מָרְדֳּכַי צִוָּה עָלֶיהָ אֲשֶׁר
יא לֹא־תַגִּיד׃ וּבְכָל־יוֹם וָיוֹם מָרְדֳּכַי מִתְהַלֵּךְ לִפְנֵי חֲצַר בֵּית־הַנָּשִׁים
יב לָדַעַת אֶת־שְׁלוֹם אֶסְתֵּר וּמַה־יֵּעָשֶׂה בָּהּ׃ וּבְהַגִּיעַ תֹּר נַעֲרָה וְנַעֲרָה
לָבוֹא ׀ אֶל־הַמֶּלֶךְ אֲחַשְׁוֵרוֹשׁ מִקֵּץ הֱיוֹת לָהּ כְּדָת הַנָּשִׁים שְׁנֵים
עָשָׂר חֹדֶשׁ כִּי כֵּן יִמְלְאוּ יְמֵי מְרוּקֵיהֶן שִׁשָּׁה חֳדָשִׁים בְּשֶׁמֶן הַמֹּר
יג וְשִׁשָּׁה חֳדָשִׁים בַּבְּשָׂמִים וּבְתַמְרוּקֵי הַנָּשִׁים׃ וּבָזֶה הַנַּעֲרָה בָּאָה
אֶל־הַמֶּלֶךְ אֵת כָּל־אֲשֶׁר תֹּאמַר יִנָּתֵן לָהּ לָבוֹא עִמָּהּ מִבֵּית הַנָּשִׁים
יד עַד־בֵּית הַמֶּלֶךְ׃ בָּעֶרֶב ׀ הִיא בָאָה וּבַבֹּקֶר הִיא שָׁבָה אֶל־בֵּית הַנָּשִׁים
שֵׁנִי אֶל־יַד שַׁעַשְׁגַז סְרִיס הַמֶּלֶךְ שֹׁמֵר הַפִּילַגְשִׁים לֹא־תָבוֹא עוֹד
טו אֶל־הַמֶּלֶךְ כִּי אִם־חָפֵץ בָּהּ הַמֶּלֶךְ וְנִקְרְאָה בְשֵׁם׃ וּבְהַגִּיעַ תֹּר־אֶסְתֵּר
בַּת־אֲבִיחַיִל ׀ דֹּד מָרְדֳּכַי אֲשֶׁר לָקַח־לוֹ לְבַת לָבוֹא אֶל־הַמֶּלֶךְ לֹא
בִקְשָׁה דָּבָר כִּי אִם אֶת־אֲשֶׁר יֹאמַר הֵגַי סְרִיס־הַמֶּלֶךְ שֹׁמֵר הַנָּשִׁים
טז וַתְּהִי אֶסְתֵּר נֹשֵׂאת חֵן בְּעֵינֵי כָּל־רֹאֶיהָ׃ וַתִּלָּקַח אֶסְתֵּר אֶל־הַמֶּלֶךְ
אֲחַשְׁוֵרוֹשׁ אֶל־בֵּית מַלְכוּתוֹ בַּחֹדֶשׁ הָעֲשִׂירִי הוּא־חֹדֶשׁ טֵבֵת
יז בִּשְׁנַת־שֶׁבַע לְמַלְכוּתוֹ׃ וַיֶּאֱהַב הַמֶּלֶךְ אֶת־אֶסְתֵּר מִכָּל־הַנָּשִׁים
וַתִּשָּׂא־חֵן וָחֶסֶד לְפָנָיו מִכָּל־הַבְּתוּלוֹת וַיָּשֶׂם כֶּתֶר־מַלְכוּת בְּרֹאשָׁהּ
יח וַיַּמְלִיכֶהָ תַּחַת וַשְׁתִּי׃ וַיַּעַשׂ הַמֶּלֶךְ מִשְׁתֶּה גָדוֹל לְכָל־שָׂרָיו וַעֲבָדָיו
אֵת מִשְׁתֵּה אֶסְתֵּר וַהֲנָחָה לַמְּדִינוֹת עָשָׂה וַיִּתֵּן מַשְׂאֵת כְּיַד הַמֶּלֶךְ׃

19 As the virgins were gathered in for a second time, Mordekhai was sitting
20 at the King's Gate. And Esther had not told of her birth or of her people,
just as Mordekhai had bid her; for Esther still heeded Mordekhai's words,
21 just as she had when she had lived under his care. And as Mordekhai sat at
the King's Gate at that time, a fury engulfed Bigtan and Teresh, two of the
king's eunuchs, guards of the threshold, and they plotted to lay their hands
22 upon King Ahasuerus. But Mordekhai learned of the plot, and conveyed the
knowledge to Queen Esther, and Esther told the king in Mordekhai's name.
23 The matter was investigated and found to be true, and the two men were
hung up dead on a post; and the story was written down before the king in
the Scroll of the Chronicles.

3 1 Some time after this, King Ahasuerus ennobled Haman, son of Hamedata the
Agagite, and promoted him to a seat above those of all his fellow ministers.
2 And all the king's courtiers, serving at the King's Gate, would kneel and bow
before Haman, for so had the king instructed – but Mordekhai would neither
3 kneel nor bow down. And so the king's courtiers would ask Mordekhai, as
they served at the King's Gate, "Why do you not obey the king's command?"

4 When, day after day, they said this to him and he took no heed, they reported
this to Haman, interested to see whether Mordekhai's word would stand – for
5 he had explained that he was a Jew. After that Haman noticed that Mordekhai,
indeed, did not kneel or bow down before him – and it filled Haman with rage.
6 It seemed beneath his contempt to lay his hands only on Mordekhai, for they
had told him who Mordekhai's people were. No: Haman's wish was to wipe
out all the Jews, all of Mordekhai's people, across all of Ahasuerus' empire.

7 And so in the first month, the month of Nisan, of the twelfth year of King
Ahasuerus' reign, a *pur* – lots, that is – were drawn before Haman; day for day
and month for month – and fell to the twelfth month: the month of Adar.

8 Haman then spoke to King Ahasuerus. "There is one people, scattered and
dispersed across all the provinces of your realm, whose laws are different
from those of all the other peoples, and who do not obey the king's own laws –
9 and it really is not worth the king's while to leave them so. If so it please the
king, let it be decreed in writing to destroy them – and I shall weigh out ten
thousand talents of silver, into the hands of the bureaucrats, to be delivered
to the king's treasury."

יט כ וּבְהִקָּבֵץ בְּתוּלוֹת שֵׁנִית וּמָרְדֳּכַי יֹשֵׁב בְּשַׁעַר־הַמֶּלֶךְ׃ אֵין אֶסְתֵּר
מַגֶּדֶת מוֹלַדְתָּהּ וְאֶת־עַמָּהּ כַּאֲשֶׁר צִוָּה עָלֶיהָ מָרְדֳּכָי וְאֶת־מַאֲמַר
כא מָרְדֳּכַי אֶסְתֵּר עֹשָׂה כַּאֲשֶׁר הָיְתָה בְאָמְנָה אִתּוֹ׃ בַּיָּמִים
הָהֵם וּמָרְדֳּכַי יֹשֵׁב בְּשַׁעַר־הַמֶּלֶךְ קָצַף בִּגְתָן וָתֶרֶשׁ שְׁנֵי־סָרִיסֵי
כב הַמֶּלֶךְ מִשֹּׁמְרֵי הַסַּף וַיְבַקְשׁוּ לִשְׁלֹחַ יָד בַּמֶּלֶךְ אֲחַשְׁוֵרֹשׁ׃ וַיִּוָּדַע
הַדָּבָר לְמָרְדֳּכַי וַיַּגֵּד לְאֶסְתֵּר הַמַּלְכָּה וַתֹּאמֶר אֶסְתֵּר לַמֶּלֶךְ בְּשֵׁם
כג מָרְדֳּכָי׃ וַיְבֻקַּשׁ הַדָּבָר וַיִּמָּצֵא וַיִּתָּלוּ שְׁנֵיהֶם עַל־עֵץ וַיִּכָּתֵב בְּסֵפֶר
ג א דִּבְרֵי הַיָּמִים לִפְנֵי הַמֶּלֶךְ׃ אַחַר ׀ הַדְּבָרִים הָאֵלֶּה גִּדַּל
הַמֶּלֶךְ אֲחַשְׁוֵרוֹשׁ אֶת־הָמָן בֶּן־הַמְּדָתָא הָאֲגָגִי וַיְנַשְּׂאֵהוּ וַיָּשֶׂם אֶת־
ב כִּסְאוֹ מֵעַל כָּל־הַשָּׂרִים אֲשֶׁר אִתּוֹ׃ וְכָל־עַבְדֵי הַמֶּלֶךְ אֲשֶׁר־בְּשַׁעַר
הַמֶּלֶךְ כֹּרְעִים וּמִשְׁתַּחֲוִים לְהָמָן כִּי־כֵן צִוָּה־לוֹ הַמֶּלֶךְ וּמָרְדֳּכַי לֹא
ג יִכְרַע וְלֹא יִשְׁתַּחֲוֶה׃ וַיֹּאמְרוּ עַבְדֵי הַמֶּלֶךְ אֲשֶׁר־בְּשַׁעַר הַמֶּלֶךְ
ד לְמָרְדֳּכָי מַדּוּעַ אַתָּה עוֹבֵר אֵת מִצְוַת הַמֶּלֶךְ׃ וַיְהִי באמרם אֵלָיו יוֹם כְּאָמְרָם
וָיוֹם וְלֹא שָׁמַע אֲלֵיהֶם וַיַּגִּידוּ לְהָמָן לִרְאוֹת הֲיַעַמְדוּ דִּבְרֵי מָרְדֳּכַי
ה כִּי־הִגִּיד לָהֶם אֲשֶׁר־הוּא יְהוּדִי׃ וַיַּרְא הָמָן כִּי־אֵין מָרְדֳּכַי כֹּרֵעַ
ו וּמִשְׁתַּחֲוֶה לוֹ וַיִּמָּלֵא הָמָן חֵמָה׃ וַיִּבֶז בְּעֵינָיו לִשְׁלֹחַ יָד בְּמָרְדֳּכַי לְבַדּוֹ
כִּי־הִגִּידוּ לוֹ אֶת־עַם מָרְדֳּכָי וַיְבַקֵּשׁ הָמָן לְהַשְׁמִיד אֶת־כָּל־הַיְּהוּדִים
ז אֲשֶׁר בְּכָל־מַלְכוּת אֲחַשְׁוֵרוֹשׁ עַם מָרְדֳּכָי׃ בַּחֹדֶשׁ הָרִאשׁוֹן הוּא־
חֹדֶשׁ נִיסָן בִּשְׁנַת שְׁתֵּים עֶשְׂרֵה לַמֶּלֶךְ אֲחַשְׁוֵרוֹשׁ הִפִּיל פּוּר הוּא
הַגּוֹרָל לִפְנֵי הָמָן מִיּוֹם ׀ לְיוֹם וּמֵחֹדֶשׁ לְחֹדֶשׁ שְׁנֵים־עָשָׂר הוּא־
ח חֹדֶשׁ אֲדָר׃ וַיֹּאמֶר הָמָן לַמֶּלֶךְ אֲחַשְׁוֵרוֹשׁ יֶשְׁנוֹ עַם־אֶחָד
מְפֻזָּר וּמְפֹרָד בֵּין הָעַמִּים בְּכֹל מְדִינוֹת מַלְכוּתֶךָ וְדָתֵיהֶם שֹׁנוֹת
מִכָּל־עָם וְאֶת־דָּתֵי הַמֶּלֶךְ אֵינָם עֹשִׂים וְלַמֶּלֶךְ אֵין־שֹׁוֶה לְהַנִּיחָם׃
ט אִם־עַל־הַמֶּלֶךְ טוֹב יִכָּתֵב לְאַבְּדָם וַעֲשֶׂרֶת אֲלָפִים כִּכַּר־כֶּסֶף אֶשְׁקוֹל
י עַל־יְדֵי עֹשֵׂי הַמְּלָאכָה לְהָבִיא אֶל־גִּנְזֵי הַמֶּלֶךְ׃ וַיָּסַר הַמֶּלֶךְ אֶת־

10 The king took the ring from his finger, and gave it to Haman son of Hamedata,
11 the Agagite, enemy of the Jews. And the king said to Haman, "The money is
yours, and so is the people; do with it as you will."

12 The king's scribes were called on the thirteenth day of the first month, and
they wrote all that Haman commanded the king's viceroys, the administrators of every single province and the ministers of every single people, to
each province in its language and to each people in its tongue, written in the
13 name of King Ahasuerus and sealed with the king's ring. Scrolls were sent
out with the runners, to all the provinces of the king – ruling that they wipe
out, kill and destroy all the Jews, young and old, children and women alike,
all in one day: the thirteenth [day] of the twelfth month, which is the month
14 of Adar – leaving their wealth for plunder. The text of that letter was to lay
down law in each and every province, displayed for every people to see, that
15 they should make themselves ready for that day. The runners bolted out at the
king's word, and the law was laid down in the imperial city, Shushan; and the
king and Haman sat down to drink – and the town of Shushan stood aghast
in horror.

4 1 Mordekhai understood all that had happened, and he tore his clothes, and
dressed himself in sackcloth and ash; and he walked out across the town,
2 crying out, a great and bitter cry. He came as far as the entrance to the
3 King's Gate – for no one enters the King's Gate dressed in sackcloth. And
in every single province, wherever the king's word and law extended, deep
mourning prevailed among the Jews, and fasting and weeping and grief,
the multitudes lying down upon sackcloth and ash.

4 Esther's young maids and her eunuchs came and told her of this – and the
queen's whole body shook. And she sent clothes for Mordekhai to put on,
5 to lay aside the sackcloth he was wearing – but he would not accept them. So
Esther called Hatakh, the king's eunuch employed for her service; and she
bid him go and speak to Mordekhai, to find out what all this was, and why.
6 Hatakh went out to Mordekhai, to the town square just before the King's
7 Gate; and Mordekhai told him all that had happened to him, and all about
the money that Haman had promised to have weighed out to the king's
8 treasury in return for the Jews, to destroy them. And he gave him the text
of the decree that had been issued in Shushan to have them wiped out,
telling him to show it to Esther and to speak to her, bidding her strictly

טַבַּעְתּוֹ מֵעַל יָדוֹ וַיִּתְּנָהּ לְהָמָן בֶּן־הַמְּדָתָא הָאֲגָגִי צֹרֵר הַיְּהוּדִים׃
יא וַיֹּאמֶר הַמֶּלֶךְ לְהָמָן הַכֶּסֶף נָתוּן לָךְ וְהָעָם לַעֲשׂוֹת בּוֹ כַּטּוֹב בְּעֵינֶיךָ׃
יב וַיִּקָּרְאוּ סֹפְרֵי הַמֶּלֶךְ בַּחֹדֶשׁ הָרִאשׁוֹן בִּשְׁלוֹשָׁה עָשָׂר יוֹם בּוֹ וַיִּכָּתֵב
כְּכָל־אֲשֶׁר־צִוָּה הָמָן אֶל אֲחַשְׁדַּרְפְּנֵי־הַמֶּלֶךְ וְאֶל־הַפַּחוֹת אֲשֶׁר ׀
עַל־מְדִינָה וּמְדִינָה וְאֶל־שָׂרֵי עַם וָעָם מְדִינָה וּמְדִינָה כִּכְתָבָהּ וְעַם
וָעָם כִּלְשׁוֹנוֹ בְּשֵׁם הַמֶּלֶךְ אֲחַשְׁוֵרֹשׁ נִכְתָּב וְנֶחְתָּם בְּטַבַּעַת הַמֶּלֶךְ׃
יג וְנִשְׁלוֹחַ סְפָרִים בְּיַד הָרָצִים אֶל־כָּל־מְדִינוֹת הַמֶּלֶךְ לְהַשְׁמִיד לַהֲרֹג
וּלְאַבֵּד אֶת־כָּל־הַיְּהוּדִים מִנַּעַר וְעַד־זָקֵן טַף וְנָשִׁים בְּיוֹם אֶחָד
בִּשְׁלוֹשָׁה עָשָׂר לְחֹדֶשׁ שְׁנֵים־עָשָׂר הוּא־חֹדֶשׁ אֲדָר וּשְׁלָלָם לָבוֹז׃
יד פַּתְשֶׁגֶן הַכְּתָב לְהִנָּתֵן דָּת בְּכָל־מְדִינָה וּמְדִינָה גָּלוּי לְכָל־הָעַמִּים
טו לִהְיוֹת עֲתִדִים לַיּוֹם הַזֶּה׃ הָרָצִים יָצְאוּ דְחוּפִים בִּדְבַר הַמֶּלֶךְ וְהַדָּת
נִתְּנָה בְּשׁוּשַׁן הַבִּירָה וְהַמֶּלֶךְ וְהָמָן יָשְׁבוּ לִשְׁתּוֹת וְהָעִיר שׁוּשָׁן
ד א נָבוֹכָה׃ וּמָרְדֳּכַי יָדַע אֶת־כָּל־אֲשֶׁר נַעֲשָׂה וַיִּקְרַע מָרְדֳּכַי
אֶת־בְּגָדָיו וַיִּלְבַּשׁ שַׂק וָאֵפֶר וַיֵּצֵא בְּתוֹךְ הָעִיר וַיִּזְעַק זְעָקָה גְדֹלָה
ב וּמָרָה׃ וַיָּבוֹא עַד לִפְנֵי שַׁעַר־הַמֶּלֶךְ כִּי אֵין לָבוֹא אֶל־שַׁעַר הַמֶּלֶךְ
ג בִּלְבוּשׁ שָׂק׃ וּבְכָל־מְדִינָה וּמְדִינָה מְקוֹם אֲשֶׁר דְּבַר־הַמֶּלֶךְ וְדָתוֹ
מַגִּיעַ אֵבֶל גָּדוֹל לַיְּהוּדִים וְצוֹם וּבְכִי וּמִסְפֵּד שַׂק וָאֵפֶר יֻצַּע לָרַבִּים׃
ד ותבואינה נַעֲרוֹת אֶסְתֵּר וְסָרִיסֶיהָ וַיַּגִּידוּ לָהּ וַתִּתְחַלְחַל הַמַּלְכָּה וַתָּבוֹאנָה
מְאֹד וַתִּשְׁלַח בְּגָדִים לְהַלְבִּישׁ אֶת־מָרְדֳּכַי וּלְהָסִיר שַׂקּוֹ מֵעָלָיו וְלֹא
ה קִבֵּל׃ וַתִּקְרָא אֶסְתֵּר לַהֲתָךְ מִסָּרִיסֵי הַמֶּלֶךְ אֲשֶׁר הֶעֱמִיד לְפָנֶיהָ
ו וַתְּצַוֵּהוּ עַל־מָרְדֳּכָי לָדַעַת מַה־זֶּה וְעַל־מַה־זֶּה׃ וַיֵּצֵא הֲתָךְ אֶל־
ז מָרְדֳּכָי אֶל־רְחוֹב הָעִיר אֲשֶׁר לִפְנֵי שַׁעַר־הַמֶּלֶךְ׃ וַיַּגֶּד־לוֹ מָרְדֳּכַי אֵת
כָּל־אֲשֶׁר קָרָהוּ וְאֵת ׀ פָּרָשַׁת הַכֶּסֶף אֲשֶׁר אָמַר הָמָן לִשְׁקוֹל עַל־גִּנְזֵי
ח הַמֶּלֶךְ ביהודיים לְאַבְּדָם׃ וְאֶת־פַּתְשֶׁגֶן כְּתָב־הַדָּת אֲשֶׁר־נִתַּן בְּשׁוּשָׁן בַּיְּהוּדִים
לְהַשְׁמִידָם נָתַן לוֹ לְהַרְאוֹת אֶת־אֶסְתֵּר וּלְהַגִּיד לָהּ וּלְצַוּוֹת עָלֶיהָ

to go to the king and plead with him, to entreat with him on her people's
9 10 behalf. Hatakh came and told Esther what Mordekhai had said. Esther
11 told Hatakh, bidding him repeat it to Mordekhai, "All the king's courtiers,
and all the people of his provinces know, that there is only one law for
any man or woman who comes before the king, into the inner courtyard,
without being called: to be killed. Unless, that is, the king extends the
golden scepter towards him, that he live on. And as for me – I have not
12 been called to come before the king these thirty days past." And Mordekhai
was told what Esther had said.

13 Mordekhai sent back reply to Esther – "Do not imagine that you can escape
14 to the king's palace from the fate of all the Jews. For if you keep your silence
at this time, relief and salvation will come forth for the Jews from some
other place – but you and your father's house will be lost forever. And
who can say; could it not be for just such a time as this that you came into
royalty?"

15 16 Esther sent back word to Mordekhai – "Go. Gather all the Jews in Shushan,
and fast for me, do not eat and do not drink for three whole days, day or
night; I and my maids shall fast also. And so shall I come before the king, in
defiance of the law – and if I am lost – I am lost."

17 Then Mordekhai walked on, and did all that Esther had bid him.

5 1 On the third day, Esther dressed herself in royalty, and came to stand in
the inner courtyard of the king's palace, facing the palace, while the king
sat upon his royal throne in the great hall, facing the palace entrance.
2 And when the king noticed Queen Esther standing in the courtyard,
she carried grace in his eyes, and the king extended the golden scepter
in his hand towards Esther, and Esther came forward and touched the
3 scepter's end. And the king said to her, "What brings you, Esther my
queen? And what would you ask? Be it even half my kingdom, it shall be
yours."

4 Esther said, "If it so please Your Majesty, may the king come today, with
Haman, to the feast that I have prepared for him."

5 And the king called out, "Hurry – fetch Haman to carry out Esther's word!"

6 So the king and Haman come to the feast that Esther had prepared. And
at that drinking feast, the king said to Esther, "What is your desire, then?
It shall be yours. And what would you ask? Be it even half my kingdom, it
shall be done."

ט לָב֥וֹא אֶל־הַמֶּ֛לֶךְ לְהִֽתְחַנֶּן־ל֥וֹ וּלְבַקֵּ֛שׁ מִלְּפָנָ֖יו עַל־עַמָּֽהּ׃ וַיָּב֖וֹא הֲתָ֑ךְ
י וַיַּגֵּ֣ד לְאֶסְתֵּ֔ר אֵ֖ת דִּבְרֵ֥י מָרְדֳּכָֽי׃ וַתֹּ֤אמֶר אֶסְתֵּר֙ לַהֲתָ֔ךְ וַתְּצַוֵּ֖הוּ אֶל־
יא מָרְדֳּכָֽי׃ כָּל־עַבְדֵ֣י הַ֠מֶּלֶךְ וְעַ֨ם מְדִינ֜וֹת הַמֶּ֗לֶךְ יֽוֹדְעִים֒ אֲשֶׁ֣ר כָּל־אִ֣ישׁ
וְאִשָּׁ֡ה אֲשֶׁ֣ר יָבֽוֹא־אֶל־הַמֶּלֶךְ֩ אֶל־הֶחָצֵ֨ר הַפְּנִימִ֜ית אֲשֶׁ֣ר לֹֽא־יִקָּרֵ֗א
אַחַ֤ת דָּתוֹ֙ לְהָמִ֔ית לְ֠בַד מֵֽאֲשֶׁ֨ר יֽוֹשִׁיט־ל֥וֹ הַמֶּ֛לֶךְ אֶת־שַׁרְבִ֥יט הַזָּהָ֖ב
יב וְחָיָ֑ה וַאֲנִ֗י לֹ֤א נִקְרֵ֙אתִי֙ לָב֣וֹא אֶל־הַמֶּ֔לֶךְ זֶ֖ה שְׁלוֹשִׁ֥ים יֽוֹם׃ וַיַּגִּ֣ידוּ
יג לְמָרְדֳּכָ֔י אֵ֖ת דִּבְרֵ֥י אֶסְתֵּֽר׃ וַיֹּ֥אמֶר מָרְדֳּכַ֖י לְהָשִׁ֣יב אֶל־אֶסְתֵּ֑ר אַל־
יד תְּדַמִּ֣י בְנַפְשֵׁ֔ךְ לְהִמָּלֵ֥ט בֵּית־הַמֶּ֖לֶךְ מִכָּל־הַיְּהוּדִֽים׃ כִּ֣י אִם־הַחֲרֵ֣שׁ
תַּחֲרִ֘ישִׁי֮ בָּעֵ֣ת הַזֹּאת֒ רֶ֣וַח וְהַצָּלָ֞ה יַעֲמ֤וֹד לַיְּהוּדִים֙ מִמָּק֣וֹם אַחֵ֔ר
וְאַ֥תְּ וּבֵית־אָבִ֖יךְ תֹּאבֵ֑דוּ וּמִ֣י יוֹדֵ֔עַ אִם־לְעֵ֣ת כָּזֹ֔את הִגַּ֖עַתְּ לַמַּלְכֽוּת׃
טו טז וַתֹּ֥אמֶר אֶסְתֵּ֖ר לְהָשִׁ֥יב אֶֽל־מָרְדֳּכָֽי׃ לֵךְ֩ כְּנ֨וֹס אֶת־כָּל־הַיְּהוּדִ֜ים
הַנִּמְצְאִ֣ים בְּשׁוּשָׁ֗ן וְצ֣וּמוּ עָ֠לַי וְאַל־תֹּאכְל֨וּ וְאַל־תִּשְׁתּ֜וּ שְׁלֹ֤שֶׁת יָמִים֙
לַ֣יְלָה וָי֔וֹם גַּם־אֲנִ֥י וְנַעֲרֹתַ֖י אָצ֣וּם כֵּ֑ן וּבְכֵ֞ן אָב֤וֹא אֶל־הַמֶּ֙לֶךְ֙ אֲשֶׁ֣ר
יז לֹֽא־כַדָּ֔ת וְכַאֲשֶׁ֥ר אָבַ֖דְתִּי אָבָֽדְתִּי׃ וַיַּעֲבֹ֖ר מָרְדֳּכָ֑י וַיַּ֕עַשׂ כְּכֹ֛ל אֲשֶׁר־
ה א צִוְּתָ֥ה עָלָ֖יו אֶסְתֵּֽר׃ וַיְהִ֣י ׀ בַּיּ֣וֹם הַשְּׁלִישִׁ֗י וַתִּלְבַּ֤שׁ אֶסְתֵּר֙ מַלְכ֔וּת
וַֽתַּעֲמֹ֞ד בַּחֲצַ֤ר בֵּית־הַמֶּ֙לֶךְ֙ הַפְּנִימִ֔ית נֹ֖כַח בֵּ֣ית הַמֶּ֑לֶךְ וְהַמֶּ֜לֶךְ יוֹשֵׁ֨ב
ב עַל־כִּסֵּ֤א מַלְכוּתוֹ֙ בְּבֵ֣ית הַמַּלְכ֔וּת נֹ֖כַח פֶּ֥תַח הַבָּֽיִת׃ וַיְהִי֩ כִרְא֨וֹת
הַמֶּ֜לֶךְ אֶת־אֶסְתֵּ֣ר הַמַּלְכָּ֗ה עֹמֶ֙דֶת֙ בֶּֽחָצֵ֔ר נָשְׂאָ֥ה חֵ֖ן בְּעֵינָ֑יו וַיּ֨וֹשֶׁט
הַמֶּ֜לֶךְ לְאֶסְתֵּ֗ר אֶת־שַׁרְבִ֤יט הַזָּהָב֙ אֲשֶׁ֣ר בְּיָד֔וֹ וַתִּקְרַ֣ב אֶסְתֵּ֔ר וַתִּגַּ֖ע
ג בְּרֹ֥אשׁ הַשַּׁרְבִֽיט׃ וַיֹּ֤אמֶר לָהּ֙ הַמֶּ֔לֶךְ מַה־לָּ֖ךְ אֶסְתֵּ֣ר הַמַּלְכָּ֑ה וּמַה־
ד בַּקָּשָׁתֵךְ֙ עַד־חֲצִ֥י הַמַּלְכ֖וּת וְיִנָּ֥תֵֽן לָֽךְ׃ וַתֹּ֣אמֶר אֶסְתֵּ֔ר אִם־עַל־הַמֶּ֖לֶךְ
ה ט֑וֹב יָב֨וֹא הַמֶּ֤לֶךְ וְהָמָן֙ הַיּ֔וֹם אֶל־הַמִּשְׁתֶּ֖ה אֲשֶׁר־עָשִׂ֥יתִי לֽוֹ׃ וַיֹּ֣אמֶר
הַמֶּ֔לֶךְ מַהֲרוּ֙ אֶת־הָמָ֔ן לַעֲשׂ֖וֹת אֶת־דְּבַ֣ר אֶסְתֵּ֑ר וַיָּבֹ֤א הַמֶּ֙לֶךְ֙ וְהָמָ֔ן
ו אֶל־הַמִּשְׁתֶּ֖ה אֲשֶׁר־עָשְׂתָ֥ה אֶסְתֵּֽר׃ וַיֹּ֨אמֶר הַמֶּ֤לֶךְ לְאֶסְתֵּר֙ בְּמִשְׁתֵּ֣ה
הַיַּ֔יִן מַה־שְּׁאֵלָתֵ֖ךְ וְיִנָּ֣תֵֽן לָ֑ךְ וּמַה־בַּקָּשָׁתֵ֛ךְ עַד־חֲצִ֥י הַמַּלְכ֖וּת וְתֵעָֽשׂ׃

7 8 So Esther answered and replied, "This is my desire and my request: if I am
pleasing to the king, and if it so please the king, to grant what I desire, to give
me my request – let the king and Haman come again to the feast that I shall
prepare for them. And tomorrow I shall do whatever the king asks."

9 Haman went out on that day, happy and buoyant of heart. But when he saw
Mordekhai at the King's Gate, and the latter did not stand up and did not
10 tremble in his presence, Haman was filled with rage against Mordekhai. Yet
Haman restrained himself until he reached his home, and there he sent for
11 all his friends and his wife, Zeresh. And Haman told them of his glorious
wealth and the great number of his sons, and all the ways the king had elevated him, and raised him above all the ministers and the courtiers of the king.
12 And finally Haman said, "And Esther brought no one else with the king to her
13 feast but me, and tomorrow too I am invited to her along with the king. Yet
all this is worth nothing to me, whenever I see that Jew Mordekhai, sitting
there at the King's Gate."

14 Zeresh, his wife, replied, with all his friends: "Let a post be erected, full fifty
cubits high. And in the morning, just say the word to the king and Mordekhai
shall be hung up on it, and then you will go happy with the king to the feast."
The idea pleased Haman, and he erected the post.

6 1 The king slept fitfully that night. And he called for the scroll of the records,
the Chronicles of the Realm, to be brought to him, to be read out before the
2 king. There it was found written that Mordekhai had reported Bigtan and
Teresh, two of the king's eunuchs, guards of the threshold, who had planned
3 to lay hands upon King Ahasuerus. The king said, "What honor or greatness
has been granted Mordekhai for doing this?" and the king's pages, those who
were attending him, said, "Nothing has been done for him at all."

4 "Who is in the courtyard?" asked the king. And Haman had come to the outer
courtyard of the king's palace, to speak to the king about hanging Mordekhai
5 on the post he had prepared for him. The king's pages said to him, "Ah, there
is Haman standing in the courtyard," and the king said, "Show him in!"

6 In came Haman, and the king asked him, "What should be done for a man
the king wishes to honor?" Said Haman to himself, "Who could the king
wish to honor more than me?"

7 8 So Haman told the king, "The man the king wishes to honor – well, let the
clothes of royalty be brought forth, clothes that the king himself has worn,
and a horse on which the king has ridden, with a royal crown placed upon

ז ח וַתַּעַן אֶסְתֵּר וַתֹּאמַר שְׁאֵלָתִי וּבַקָּשָׁתִי׃ אִם־מָצָאתִי חֵן בְּעֵינֵי הַמֶּלֶךְ
וְאִם־עַל־הַמֶּלֶךְ טוֹב לָתֵת אֶת־שְׁאֵלָתִי וְלַעֲשׂוֹת אֶת־בַּקָּשָׁתִי יָבוֹא
הַמֶּלֶךְ וְהָמָן אֶל־הַמִּשְׁתֶּה אֲשֶׁר אֶעֱשֶׂה לָהֶם וּמָחָר אֶעֱשֶׂה כִּדְבַר
ט הַמֶּלֶךְ׃ וַיֵּצֵא הָמָן בַּיּוֹם הַהוּא שָׂמֵחַ וְטוֹב לֵב וְכִרְאוֹת הָמָן אֶת־
מָרְדֳּכַי בְּשַׁעַר הַמֶּלֶךְ וְלֹא־קָם וְלֹא־זָע מִמֶּנּוּ וַיִּמָּלֵא הָמָן עַל־מָרְדֳּכַי
י חֵמָה׃ וַיִּתְאַפַּק הָמָן וַיָּבוֹא אֶל־בֵּיתוֹ וַיִּשְׁלַח וַיָּבֵא אֶת־אֹהֲבָיו וְאֶת־
יא זֶרֶשׁ אִשְׁתּוֹ׃ וַיְסַפֵּר לָהֶם הָמָן אֶת־כְּבוֹד עָשְׁרוֹ וְרֹב בָּנָיו וְאֵת כָּל־
יב אֲשֶׁר גִּדְּלוֹ הַמֶּלֶךְ וְאֵת אֲשֶׁר נִשְּׂאוֹ עַל־הַשָּׂרִים וְעַבְדֵי הַמֶּלֶךְ׃ וַיֹּאמֶר
הָמָן אַף לֹא־הֵבִיאָה אֶסְתֵּר הַמַּלְכָּה עִם־הַמֶּלֶךְ אֶל־הַמִּשְׁתֶּה אֲשֶׁר־
יג עָשָׂתָה כִּי אִם־אוֹתִי וְגַם־לְמָחָר אֲנִי קָרוּא־לָהּ עִם־הַמֶּלֶךְ׃ וְכָל־
זֶה אֵינֶנּוּ שֹׁוֶה לִי בְּכָל־עֵת אֲשֶׁר אֲנִי רֹאֶה אֶת־מָרְדֳּכַי הַיְּהוּדִי יוֹשֵׁב
יד בְּשַׁעַר הַמֶּלֶךְ׃ וַתֹּאמֶר לוֹ זֶרֶשׁ אִשְׁתּוֹ וְכָל־אֹהֲבָיו יַעֲשׂוּ־עֵץ גָּבֹהַּ
חֲמִשִּׁים אַמָּה וּבַבֹּקֶר ׀ אֱמֹר לַמֶּלֶךְ וְיִתְלוּ אֶת־מָרְדֳּכַי עָלָיו וּבֹא
עִם־הַמֶּלֶךְ אֶל־הַמִּשְׁתֶּה שָׂמֵחַ וַיִּיטַב הַדָּבָר לִפְנֵי הָמָן וַיַּעַשׂ
וא הָעֵץ׃ בַּלַּיְלָה הַהוּא נָדְדָה שְׁנַת הַמֶּלֶךְ וַיֹּאמֶר לְהָבִיא
ב אֶת־סֵפֶר הַזִּכְרֹנוֹת דִּבְרֵי הַיָּמִים וַיִּהְיוּ נִקְרָאִים לִפְנֵי הַמֶּלֶךְ׃ וַיִּמָּצֵא
כָתוּב אֲשֶׁר הִגִּיד מָרְדֳּכַי עַל־בִּגְתָנָא וָתֶרֶשׁ שְׁנֵי סָרִיסֵי הַמֶּלֶךְ
ג מִשֹּׁמְרֵי הַסַּף אֲשֶׁר בִּקְשׁוּ לִשְׁלֹחַ יָד בַּמֶּלֶךְ אֲחַשְׁוֵרוֹשׁ׃ וַיֹּאמֶר הַמֶּלֶךְ
מַה־נַּעֲשָׂה יְקָר וּגְדוּלָּה לְמָרְדֳּכַי עַל־זֶה וַיֹּאמְרוּ נַעֲרֵי הַמֶּלֶךְ מְשָׁרְתָיו
ד לֹא־נַעֲשָׂה עִמּוֹ דָּבָר׃ וַיֹּאמֶר הַמֶּלֶךְ מִי בֶחָצֵר וְהָמָן בָּא לַחֲצַר בֵּית־
הַמֶּלֶךְ הַחִיצוֹנָה לֵאמֹר לַמֶּלֶךְ לִתְלוֹת אֶת־מָרְדֳּכַי עַל־הָעֵץ אֲשֶׁר־
ה הֵכִין לוֹ׃ וַיֹּאמְרוּ נַעֲרֵי הַמֶּלֶךְ אֵלָיו הִנֵּה הָמָן עֹמֵד בֶּחָצֵר וַיֹּאמֶר
ו הַמֶּלֶךְ יָבוֹא׃ וַיָּבוֹא הָמָן וַיֹּאמֶר לוֹ הַמֶּלֶךְ מַה־לַּעֲשׂוֹת בָּאִישׁ אֲשֶׁר
הַמֶּלֶךְ חָפֵץ בִּיקָרוֹ וַיֹּאמֶר הָמָן בְּלִבּוֹ לְמִי יַחְפֹּץ הַמֶּלֶךְ לַעֲשׂוֹת יְקָר
ז יוֹתֵר מִמֶּנִּי׃ וַיֹּאמֶר הָמָן אֶל־הַמֶּלֶךְ אִישׁ אֲשֶׁר הַמֶּלֶךְ חָפֵץ בִּיקָרוֹ׃
ח יָבִיאוּ לְבוּשׁ מַלְכוּת אֲשֶׁר לָבַשׁ־בּוֹ הַמֶּלֶךְ וְסוּס אֲשֶׁר רָכַב עָלָיו

9 its head; and let these clothes and the horse be entrusted to one of the king's
noble ministers, to dress the man whom the king has a wish to honor. And
let him lead that man, riding on the horse, across the town square, crying
out before him as they go, *'This is what is done for the man the king wishes to
honor!'"*

10 "Hurry now!" said the king to Haman; "Take the clothes and the horse as
you have said, and do just that for Mordekhai the Jew, who sits at the King's
Gate – let no detail fall short of what you have described!"

11 So Haman took the clothes and the horse and dressed Mordekhai, and led
him across the town square, crying out before him as they went, *"This is what
is done for the man the king wishes to honor!"*

12 And then Mordekhai returned to the King's Gate, and Haman bolted back to
13 his house, grief-stricken, covering his face. Haman told his wife, Zeresh, and
all his friends, all that had happened to him, and his wise men, with his wife,
Zeresh, said to him, "If this Mordekhai you have begun to fall before is of
Jewish blood, you will not overcome him; you will fall, must fall before him –"

14 But they were still speaking when the king's eunuchs arrived, to fetch Haman,
with terrible haste, to the feast that Esther had prepared.

7 1 2 So the king and Haman arrived to drink with Queen Esther. And on that
second day also, at the drinking feast, the king said to Esther, "What is your
desire, Esther my queen? It shall be yours. And what would you ask? Be it
even half my kingdom, it shall be done."

3 And Queen Esther answered: "If I have your favor, my king," she said, "and if
so it please your majesty – let me have my life at my desire; my people at my
4 request. For we have been sold – I and my people – to be wiped out, killed
and destroyed. Had we but been sold away as slaves and bondwomen, I would
have kept my silence; for that anguish is not worth any loss to the king."

5 And King Ahasuerus spoke: he said to Esther the queen, "Who is this and
where is he, who has put it into his heart to do such a thing?"

6 "It is a foe, an enemy," said Esther, "this vicious man, Haman!" And Haman
7 was suddenly terrified before the king and queen. The king rose up in his
fury and left the wine feast for the palace garden, as Haman stood up to
entreat for his life with Esther the queen, for he saw that the king was already
8 set upon his downfall. By the time the king came back from the palace
garden to the feasting chamber, Haman had thrown himself onto Esther's

ט הַמֶּ֜לֶךְ וַאֲשֶׁ֥ר נִתַּ֛ן כֶּ֥תֶר מַלְכ֖וּת בְּרֹאשֽׁוֹ׃ וְנָת֨וֹן הַלְּב֜וּשׁ וְהַסּ֗וּס עַל־
יַד־אִ֞ישׁ מִשָּׂרֵ֤י הַמֶּ֙לֶךְ֙ הַֽפַּרְתְּמִ֔ים וְהִלְבִּ֙שׁוּ֙ אֶת־הָאִ֔ישׁ אֲשֶׁ֥ר הַמֶּ֖לֶךְ
חָפֵ֣ץ בִּיקָר֑וֹ וְהִרְכִּיבֻ֤הוּ עַל־הַסּוּס֙ בִּרְח֣וֹב הָעִ֔יר וְקָרְא֣וּ לְפָנָ֔יו כָּ֚כָה
י יֵעָשֶׂ֣ה לָאִ֔ישׁ אֲשֶׁ֥ר הַמֶּ֖לֶךְ חָפֵ֥ץ בִּיקָרֽוֹ׃ וַיֹּ֨אמֶר הַמֶּ֜לֶךְ לְהָמָ֗ן מַ֠הֵר
קַ֣ח אֶת־הַלְּב֤וּשׁ וְאֶת־הַסּוּס֙ כַּאֲשֶׁ֣ר דִּבַּ֔רְתָּ וַֽעֲשֵׂה־כֵן֙ לְמָרְדֳּכַ֣י הַיְּהוּדִ֔י
יא הַיּוֹשֵׁ֖ב בְּשַׁ֣עַר הַמֶּ֑לֶךְ אַל־תַּפֵּ֣ל דָּבָ֔ר מִכֹּ֖ל אֲשֶׁ֥ר דִּבַּֽרְתָּ׃ וַיִּקַּ֤ח הָמָן֙
אֶת־הַלְּב֣וּשׁ וְאֶת־הַסּ֔וּס וַיַּלְבֵּ֖שׁ אֶֽת־מָרְדֳּכָ֑י וַיַּרְכִּיבֵ֙הוּ֙ בִּרְח֣וֹב הָעִ֔יר
יב וַיִּקְרָ֣א לְפָנָ֔יו כָּ֚כָה יֵעָשֶׂ֣ה לָאִ֔ישׁ אֲשֶׁ֥ר הַמֶּ֖לֶךְ חָפֵ֥ץ בִּיקָרֽוֹ׃ וַיָּ֥שָׁב
מָרְדֳּכַ֖י אֶל־שַׁ֣עַר הַמֶּ֑לֶךְ וְהָמָן֙ נִדְחַ֣ף אֶל־בֵּית֔וֹ אָבֵ֖ל וַחֲפ֥וּי רֹֽאשׁ׃
יג וַיְסַפֵּ֨ר הָמָ֜ן לְזֶ֤רֶשׁ אִשְׁתּוֹ֙ וּלְכָל־אֹ֣הֲבָ֔יו אֵ֖ת כָּל־אֲשֶׁ֣ר קָרָ֑הוּ וַיֹּ֣אמְרוּ
ל֣וֹ חֲכָמָ֞יו וְזֶ֣רֶשׁ אִשְׁתּ֗וֹ אִ֣ם מִזֶּ֣רַע הַיְּהוּדִ֡ים מָרְדֳּכַ֞י אֲשֶׁר֩ הַחִלּ֨וֹתָ
יד לִנְפֹּ֤ל לְפָנָיו֙ לֹא־תוּכַ֣ל ל֔וֹ כִּֽי־נָפ֥וֹל תִּפּ֖וֹל לְפָנָֽיו׃ עוֹדָם֙ מְדַבְּרִ֣ים עִמּ֔וֹ
וְסָרִיסֵ֥י הַמֶּ֖לֶךְ הִגִּ֑יעוּ וַיַּבְהִ֙לוּ֙ לְהָבִ֣יא אֶת־הָמָ֔ן אֶל־הַמִּשְׁתֶּ֖ה אֲשֶׁר־
ז א עָשְׂתָ֥ה אֶסְתֵּֽר׃ וַיָּבֹ֤א הַמֶּ֙לֶךְ֙ וְהָמָ֔ן לִשְׁתּ֖וֹת עִם־אֶסְתֵּ֥ר הַמַּלְכָּֽה׃
ב וַיֹּאמֶר֩ הַמֶּ֨לֶךְ לְאֶסְתֵּ֜ר גַּ֣ם בַּיּ֤וֹם הַשֵּׁנִי֙ בְּמִשְׁתֵּ֣ה הַיַּ֔יִן מַה־שְּׁאֵלָתֵ֛ךְ
אֶסְתֵּ֥ר הַמַּלְכָּ֖ה וְתִנָּ֣תֵֽן לָ֑ךְ וּמַה־בַּקָּשָׁתֵ֛ךְ עַד־חֲצִ֥י הַמַּלְכ֖וּת וְתֵעָֽשׂ׃
ג וַתַּ֨עַן אֶסְתֵּ֤ר הַמַּלְכָּה֙ וַתֹּאמַ֔ר אִם־מָצָ֨אתִי חֵ֤ן בְּעֵינֶ֙יךָ֙ הַמֶּ֔לֶךְ וְאִם־
ד עַל־הַמֶּ֖לֶךְ ט֑וֹב תִּנָּֽתֶן־לִ֤י נַפְשִׁי֙ בִּשְׁאֵ֣לָתִ֔י וְעַמִּ֖י בְּבַקָּשָׁתִֽי׃ כִּ֤י נִמְכַּ֙רְנוּ֙
אֲנִ֣י וְעַמִּ֔י לְהַשְׁמִ֖יד לַהֲר֣וֹג וּלְאַבֵּ֑ד וְ֠אִלּוּ לַעֲבָדִ֨ים וְלִשְׁפָח֤וֹת נִמְכַּ֙רְנוּ֙
ה הֶחֱרַ֔שְׁתִּי כִּ֣י אֵ֥ין הַצָּ֛ר שֹׁוֶ֖ה בְּנֵ֥זֶק הַמֶּֽלֶךְ׃ וַיֹּ֙אמֶר֙ הַמֶּ֣לֶךְ
אֲחַשְׁוֵר֔וֹשׁ וַיֹּ֖אמֶר לְאֶסְתֵּ֣ר הַמַּלְכָּ֑ה מִ֣י ה֥וּא זֶה֙ וְאֵי־זֶ֣ה ה֔וּא אֲשֶׁר־
ו מְלָא֥וֹ לִבּ֖וֹ לַעֲשׂ֥וֹת כֵּֽן׃ וַתֹּ֣אמֶר אֶסְתֵּ֔ר אִ֚ישׁ צַ֣ר וְאוֹיֵ֔ב הָמָ֥ן הָרָ֖ע הַזֶּ֑ה
ז וְהָמָ֣ן נִבְעַ֔ת מִלִּפְנֵ֥י הַמֶּ֖לֶךְ וְהַמַּלְכָּֽה׃ וְהַמֶּ֜לֶךְ קָ֤ם בַּחֲמָתוֹ֙ מִמִּשְׁתֵּ֣ה
הַיַּ֔יִן אֶל־גִּנַּ֖ת הַבִּיתָ֑ן וְהָמָ֣ן עָמַ֗ד לְבַקֵּ֤שׁ עַל־נַפְשׁוֹ֙ מֵאֶסְתֵּ֣ר הַמַּלְכָּ֔ה
ח כִּ֣י רָאָ֔ה כִּֽי־כָלְתָ֥ה אֵלָ֛יו הָרָעָ֖ה מֵאֵ֥ת הַמֶּֽלֶךְ׃ וְהַמֶּ֜לֶךְ שָׁ֨ב מִגִּנַּ֜ת הַבִּיתָ֗ן

couch – "What!" said the king, "Would you take the queen too, and with me in the palace?" And the servants stepped forward to cover Haman's face.

9 And one of the eunuchs, Ḥarvona, said to the king, "You know, the post Haman prepared for Mordekhai, who spoke up well for the king, is standing now in Haman's house, fifty cubits high…" And the king said, "Hang him upon it!"

10 Thus was Haman hung up, on the very post he had prepared for Mordekhai; and the king's fury subsided.

8 1 On that day, King Ahasuerus granted Queen Esther the estate of Haman,
enemy of the Jews; and Mordekhai came before the king, for Esther had
2 finally revealed what he was to her. The king took off the very ring that he
had once given over to Haman, and gave it instead to Mordekhai; and Esther
appointed Mordekhai over Haman's estate.

3 But then Esther spoke to the king again, falling down at his feet, weeping
and pleading with him to overturn the wickedness of Haman the Agagite,
4 and the plot that he had thought up against the Jews. The king extended his
golden scepter to Esther, and Esther raised herself up and stood before the
5 king. And she said, "If so it please the king, and if I have his favor, and if it
seems right to the king and I am pleasing in his eyes – let the decree be written to revoke the scrolls that were the plot of Haman, son of Hamedata the
Agagite, who wrote to destroy all the Jews that are in all the king's provinces.
6 For how can I live to see the evil that will come upon my people; how can I
live to see the loss of those I am born of?"

7 King Ahasuerus said to Queen Esther and to Mordekhai the Jew, "Look, I
have given Haman's house to Esther, and he has been hung up on the post
8 for putting out his hand against the Jews. Now, write whatever you like about
the Jews in the king's name, and seal it with the king's ring – but no writing
that has been written in the name of the king and sealed with the king's seal
can ever be revoked."

9 And so, at that time, the king's scribes were called – on the twenty-third day of the third month, the month of Sivan, that is – and they wrote down all that Mordekhai dictated, to the Jews and to the viceroys, the

אֶל־בֵּית ׀ מִשְׁתֵּה הַיַּיִן וְהָמָן נֹפֵל עַל־הַמִּטָּה אֲשֶׁר אֶסְתֵּר עָלֶיהָ
וַיֹּאמֶר הַמֶּלֶךְ הֲגַם לִכְבּוֹשׁ אֶת־הַמַּלְכָּה עִמִּי בַּבָּיִת הַדָּבָר יָצָא
ט מִפִּי הַמֶּלֶךְ וּפְנֵי הָמָן חָפוּ׃ וַיֹּאמֶר חַרְבוֹנָה אֶחָד מִן־הַסָּרִיסִים
לִפְנֵי הַמֶּלֶךְ גַּם הִנֵּה־הָעֵץ אֲשֶׁר־עָשָׂה הָמָן לְמָרְדֳּכַי אֲשֶׁר דִּבֶּר־
טוֹב עַל־הַמֶּלֶךְ עֹמֵד בְּבֵית הָמָן גָּבֹהַּ חֲמִשִּׁים אַמָּה וַיֹּאמֶר הַמֶּלֶךְ
י תְּלֻהוּ עָלָיו׃ וַיִּתְלוּ אֶת־הָמָן עַל־הָעֵץ אֲשֶׁר־הֵכִין לְמָרְדֳּכָי וַחֲמַת
ח א הַמֶּלֶךְ שָׁכָכָה׃ בַּיּוֹם הַהוּא נָתַן הַמֶּלֶךְ אֲחַשְׁוֵרוֹשׁ לְאֶסְתֵּר
הַמַּלְכָּה אֶת־בֵּית הָמָן צֹרֵר היהודיים וּמָרְדֳּכַי בָּא לִפְנֵי הַמֶּלֶךְ הַיְּהוּדִים
ב כִּי־הִגִּידָה אֶסְתֵּר מַה הוּא־לָהּ׃ וַיָּסַר הַמֶּלֶךְ אֶת־טַבַּעְתּוֹ אֲשֶׁר
הֶעֱבִיר מֵהָמָן וַיִּתְּנָהּ לְמָרְדֳּכָי וַתָּשֶׂם אֶסְתֵּר אֶת־מָרְדֳּכַי עַל־בֵּית
ג הָמָן׃ וַתּוֹסֶף אֶסְתֵּר וַתְּדַבֵּר לִפְנֵי הַמֶּלֶךְ וַתִּפֹּל לִפְנֵי רַגְלָיו
וַתֵּבְךְּ וַתִּתְחַנֶּן־לוֹ לְהַעֲבִיר אֶת־רָעַת הָמָן הָאֲגָגִי וְאֵת מַחֲשַׁבְתּוֹ
ד אֲשֶׁר חָשַׁב עַל־הַיְּהוּדִים׃ וַיּוֹשֶׁט הַמֶּלֶךְ לְאֶסְתֵּר אֵת שַׁרְבִט הַזָּהָב
ה וַתָּקָם אֶסְתֵּר וַתַּעֲמֹד לִפְנֵי הַמֶּלֶךְ׃ וַתֹּאמֶר אִם־עַל־הַמֶּלֶךְ טוֹב
וְאִם־מָצָאתִי חֵן לְפָנָיו וְכָשֵׁר הַדָּבָר לִפְנֵי הַמֶּלֶךְ וְטוֹבָה אֲנִי בְּעֵינָיו
יִכָּתֵב לְהָשִׁיב אֶת־הַסְּפָרִים מַחֲשֶׁבֶת הָמָן בֶּן־הַמְּדָתָא הָאֲגָגִי
ו אֲשֶׁר כָּתַב לְאַבֵּד אֶת־הַיְּהוּדִים אֲשֶׁר בְּכָל־מְדִינוֹת הַמֶּלֶךְ׃ כִּי
אֵיכָכָה אוּכַל וְרָאִיתִי בָּרָעָה אֲשֶׁר־יִמְצָא אֶת־עַמִּי וְאֵיכָכָה אוּכַל
ז וְרָאִיתִי בְּאָבְדַן מוֹלַדְתִּי׃ וַיֹּאמֶר הַמֶּלֶךְ אֲחַשְׁוֵרֹשׁ לְאֶסְתֵּר
הַמַּלְכָּה וּלְמָרְדֳּכַי הַיְּהוּדִי הִנֵּה בֵית־הָמָן נָתַתִּי לְאֶסְתֵּר וְאֹתוֹ תָּלוּ
ח עַל־הָעֵץ עַל אֲשֶׁר־שָׁלַח יָדוֹ ביהודיים׃ וְאַתֶּם כִּתְבוּ עַל־הַיְּהוּדִים בַּיְּהוּדִים
כַּטּוֹב בְּעֵינֵיכֶם בְּשֵׁם הַמֶּלֶךְ וְחִתְמוּ בְּטַבַּעַת הַמֶּלֶךְ כִּי־כְתָב אֲשֶׁר־
ט נִכְתָּב בְּשֵׁם־הַמֶּלֶךְ וְנַחְתּוֹם בְּטַבַּעַת הַמֶּלֶךְ אֵין לְהָשִׁיב׃ וַיִּקָּרְאוּ
סֹפְרֵי־הַמֶּלֶךְ בָּעֵת־הַהִיא בַּחֹדֶשׁ הַשְּׁלִישִׁי הוּא־חֹדֶשׁ סִיוָן בִּשְׁלוֹשָׁה
וְעֶשְׂרִים בּוֹ וַיִּכָּתֵב כְּכָל־אֲשֶׁר־צִוָּה מָרְדֳּכַי אֶל־הַיְּהוּדִים וְאֶל

administrators and the ministers of all the provinces from India to Ethiopia,
one hundred and twenty-seven provinces, to each province in its script and
to each people in its language, and to the Jews also, in their script and in
10 their language. It was written in the name of King Ahasuerus and sealed
with the king's seal, and the scrolls were sent with the horseback runners,
11 riding the swift horses of the royal stable, young of the royal mares – to
convey that the king had granted the Jews in every single town the right
to come together to stand up and defend their lives, to wipe out, kill and
destroy all the armed hordes of the peoples and provinces who threat-
ened them, even their children and women, and to loot their plunder,
12 all on one day, the thirteenth day of the twelfth month – the month of
13 Adar, that is – in all the provinces of King Ahasuerus. The text of that
decree was to lay down law in every single province, displayed for every
people to see, that the Jews should make themselves ready for that day, to
14 wreak vengeance on their enemies. The runners, riding the swift horses of
the royal service, bolted out at great speed, spurred on at the king's word,
and the law was laid down in the imperial city, Shushan.

15 ▸ So Mordekhai left the king's presence in royal clothes of sky-blue wool
and fine white fabric, wearing a great coronet of gold, and a mantle of finest
linen and scarlet; and the town of Shushan was filled with jubilation and
16 happiness. ◂ ▸ And the Jews basked in light and happiness, joy and great
17 honor. ◂ And in each and every province, in each and every town, as far
as the king's word and law reached, happiness and joy touched the Jews,
feasting, a holiday; and many of the local people joined with the Jews, for
a terror of the Jews had fallen upon them.

9 1 And on the thirteenth day of the twelfth month, the month of Adar, when
the king's word and his law were to come into effect: on the day when the
Jews' enemies had hoped to overcome them – it was all turned over, for
2 the Jews themselves overcame those who hated them. For the Jews came
together in their cities, throughout the provinces of King Ahasuerus, to lay
hands upon those who sought their harm; and no man could stand before
3 them, for their terror had fallen upon all the nations. And the ministers of
the provinces, the viceroys and the administrators, and the bureaucrats of
the king's court, all supported the Jews, for a fear of Mordekhai had fallen
4 on them. For Mordekhai was great now, in the king's palace, and word
of him was spreading to all the provinces: the man, this Mordekhai, was
becoming ever greater.

הָאֲחַשְׁדַּרְפְּנִים וְהַפַּחוֹת וְשָׂרֵי הַמְּדִינוֹת אֲשֶׁר ׀ מֵהֹדּוּ וְעַד־כּוּשׁ שֶׁבַע
וְעֶשְׂרִים וּמֵאָה מְדִינָה מְדִינָה וּמְדִינָה כִּכְתָבָהּ וְעַם וָעָם כִּלְשֹׁנוֹ
י וְאֶל־הַיְּהוּדִים כִּכְתָבָם וְכִלְשׁוֹנָם׃ וַיִּכְתֹּב בְּשֵׁם הַמֶּלֶךְ אֲחַשְׁוֵרֹשׁ
וַיַּחְתֹּם בְּטַבַּעַת הַמֶּלֶךְ וַיִּשְׁלַח סְפָרִים בְּיַד הָרָצִים בַּסּוּסִים רֹכְבֵי
יא הָרֶכֶשׁ הָאֲחַשְׁתְּרָנִים בְּנֵי הָרַמָּכִים׃ אֲשֶׁר נָתַן הַמֶּלֶךְ לַיְּהוּדִים ׀ אֲשֶׁר ׀
בְּכָל־עִיר וָעִיר לְהִקָּהֵל וְלַעֲמֹד עַל־נַפְשָׁם לְהַשְׁמִיד וְלַהֲרֹג וּלְאַבֵּד
יב אֶת־כָּל־חֵיל עַם וּמְדִינָה הַצָּרִים אֹתָם טַף וְנָשִׁים וּשְׁלָלָם לָבוֹז׃ בְּיוֹם
אֶחָד בְּכָל־מְדִינוֹת הַמֶּלֶךְ אֲחַשְׁוֵרוֹשׁ בִּשְׁלוֹשָׁה עָשָׂר לְחֹדֶשׁ שְׁנֵים־
יג עָשָׂר הוּא־חֹדֶשׁ אֲדָר׃ פַּתְשֶׁגֶן הַכְּתָב לְהִנָּתֵן דָּת בְּכָל־מְדִינָה וּמְדִינָה
גָּלוּי לְכָל־הָעַמִּים וְלִהְיוֹת היהודיים עתודים לַיּוֹם הַזֶּה לְהִנָּקֵם (הַיְּהוּדִים עֲתִידִים)
יד מֵאֹיְבֵיהֶם׃ הָרָצִים רֹכְבֵי הָרֶכֶשׁ הָאֲחַשְׁתְּרָנִים יָצְאוּ מְבֹהָלִים וּדְחוּפִים
טו בִּדְבַר הַמֶּלֶךְ וְהַדָּת נִתְּנָה בְּשׁוּשַׁן הַבִּירָה׃ וּמָרְדֳּכַי יָצָא ׀
מִלִּפְנֵי הַמֶּלֶךְ בִּלְבוּשׁ מַלְכוּת תְּכֵלֶת וָחוּר וַעֲטֶרֶת זָהָב גְּדוֹלָה
טז וְתַכְרִיךְ בּוּץ וְאַרְגָּמָן וְהָעִיר שׁוּשָׁן צָהֲלָה וְשָׂמֵחָה׃ לַיְּהוּדִים
יז הָיְתָה אוֹרָה וְשִׂמְחָה וְשָׂשֹׂן וִיקָר׃ וּבְכָל־מְדִינָה וּמְדִינָה וּבְכָל־עִיר
וָעִיר מְקוֹם אֲשֶׁר דְּבַר־הַמֶּלֶךְ וְדָתוֹ מַגִּיעַ שִׂמְחָה וְשָׂשׂוֹן לַיְּהוּדִים
מִשְׁתֶּה וְיוֹם טוֹב וְרַבִּים מֵעַמֵּי הָאָרֶץ מִתְיַהֲדִים כִּי־נָפַל פַּחַד־
ט א הַיְּהוּדִים עֲלֵיהֶם׃ וּבִשְׁנֵים עָשָׂר חֹדֶשׁ הוּא־חֹדֶשׁ אֲדָר בִּשְׁלוֹשָׁה
עָשָׂר יוֹם בּוֹ אֲשֶׁר הִגִּיעַ דְּבַר־הַמֶּלֶךְ וְדָתוֹ לְהֵעָשׂוֹת בַּיּוֹם אֲשֶׁר
שִׂבְּרוּ אֹיְבֵי הַיְּהוּדִים לִשְׁלוֹט בָּהֶם וְנַהֲפוֹךְ הוּא אֲשֶׁר יִשְׁלְטוּ
ב הַיְּהוּדִים הֵמָּה בְּשֹׂנְאֵיהֶם׃ נִקְהֲלוּ הַיְּהוּדִים בְּעָרֵיהֶם בְּכָל־מְדִינוֹת
הַמֶּלֶךְ אֲחַשְׁוֵרוֹשׁ לִשְׁלֹחַ יָד בִּמְבַקְשֵׁי רָעָתָם וְאִישׁ לֹא־עָמַד לִפְנֵיהֶם
ג כִּי־נָפַל פַּחְדָּם עַל־כָּל־הָעַמִּים׃ וְכָל־שָׂרֵי הַמְּדִינוֹת וְהָאֲחַשְׁדַּרְפְּנִים
וְהַפַּחוֹת וְעֹשֵׂי הַמְּלָאכָה אֲשֶׁר לַמֶּלֶךְ מְנַשְּׂאִים אֶת־הַיְּהוּדִים
ד כִּי־נָפַל פַּחַד־מָרְדֳּכַי עֲלֵיהֶם׃ כִּי־גָדוֹל מָרְדֳּכַי בְּבֵית הַמֶּלֶךְ
ה וְשָׁמְעוֹ הוֹלֵךְ בְּכָל־הַמְּדִינוֹת כִּי־הָאִישׁ מָרְדֳּכַי הוֹלֵךְ וְגָדוֹל׃ וַיַּכּוּ

5 The Jews dealt all their enemies a terrible blow, of sword and of slaughter and
6 destruction; they did whatever they pleased to those who hated them. And in
the imperial city of Shushan the Jews killed and destroyed ▸ five hundred men;
7 and they killed Parshandata and
Dalfon, and
8 Aspata, and
Porata, and
Adaliya and
9 Aridata, and
Parmashta, and
Arisai, and
Aridai, and
10 Vayzata, the ten ◂
sons of Haman, son of Hamedata, enemy of the Jews – but they did not even
touch the plunder.

11 On that same day, the number of those killed in the imperial city, Shushan,
12 was brought to the king, and the king said to Queen Esther, "The Jews have
killed five hundred men in the imperial city of Shushan, alone, as well as
Haman's ten sons – what must they have done in the rest of the king's provinces? And now – what is your desire? It shall be yours. And what would you
13 ask further? It shall be done." And Esther said, "If so it please the king, may
the Jews of Shushan be granted tomorrow also, to do as they did today. And
14 let Haman's ten sons be hung up on the post." And thus the king commanded;
the law was laid down in the imperial city, Shushan, and Haman's ten sons
15 were hung up. And the Jews of Shushan gathered on the fourteenth day of
Adar also, and killed three hundred men in Shushan, never once touching
the plunder.

16 Meanwhile, the rest of the Jews in the king's provinces, having come together
and stood up to defend their lives, found rest from their enemies, killing
seventy-five thousand of those who hated them, though they did not touch
17 the plunder. That was on the thirteenth day of the month – and on the fourteenth they rested, and made it a day of feasting and happiness.

הַיְּהוּדִים בְּכׇל־אֹיְבֵיהֶם מַכַּת־חֶרֶב וְהֶרֶג וְאַבְדָן וַיַּעֲשׂוּ בְשֹׂנְאֵיהֶם
ו כִּרְצוֹנָם׃ וּבְשׁוּשַׁן הַבִּירָה הָרְגוּ הַיְּהוּדִים וְאַבֵּד · חֲמֵשׁ מֵאוֹת
ז אִישׁ׃ וְאֵת ׀
פַּרְשַׁנְדָּתָא וְאֵת ׀
דַּלְפוֹן וְאֵת ׀
ח אַסְפָּתָא׃ וְאֵת ׀
פּוֹרָתָא וְאֵת ׀
אֲדַלְיָא וְאֵת ׀
ט אֲרִידָתָא׃ וְאֵת ׀
פַּרְמַשְׁתָּא וְאֵת ׀
אֲרִיסַי וְאֵת ׀
אֲרִדַי וְאֵת ׀
י וַיְזָתָא׃ עֲשֶׂרֶת ·
בְּנֵי הָמָן בֶּן־הַמְּדָתָא צֹרֵר הַיְּהוּדִים הָרָגוּ וּבַבִּזָּה לֹא שָׁלְחוּ אֶת־יָדָם׃
יא יב בַּיּוֹם הַהוּא בָּא מִסְפַּר הַהֲרוּגִים בְּשׁוּשַׁן הַבִּירָה לִפְנֵי הַמֶּלֶךְ׃ וַיֹּאמֶר
הַמֶּלֶךְ לְאֶסְתֵּר הַמַּלְכָּה בְּשׁוּשַׁן הַבִּירָה הָרְגוּ הַיְּהוּדִים וְאַבֵּד חֲמֵשׁ
מֵאוֹת אִישׁ וְאֵת עֲשֶׂרֶת בְּנֵי־הָמָן בִּשְׁאָר מְדִינוֹת הַמֶּלֶךְ מֶה עָשׂוּ
יג וּמַה־שְּׁאֵלָתֵךְ וְיִנָּתֵן לָךְ וּמַה־בַּקָּשָׁתֵךְ עוֹד וְתֵעָשׂ׃ וַתֹּאמֶר אֶסְתֵּר
אִם־עַל־הַמֶּלֶךְ טוֹב יִנָּתֵן גַּם־מָחָר לַיְּהוּדִים אֲשֶׁר בְּשׁוּשָׁן לַעֲשׂוֹת
יד כְּדָת הַיּוֹם וְאֵת עֲשֶׂרֶת בְּנֵי־הָמָן יִתְלוּ עַל־הָעֵץ׃ וַיֹּאמֶר הַמֶּלֶךְ
טו לְהֵעָשׂוֹת כֵּן וַתִּנָּתֵן דָּת בְּשׁוּשָׁן וְאֵת עֲשֶׂרֶת בְּנֵי־הָמָן תָּלוּ׃ וַיִּקָּהֲלוּ
היהודיים אֲשֶׁר־בְּשׁוּשָׁן גַּם בְּיוֹם אַרְבָּעָה עָשָׂר לְחֹדֶשׁ אֲדָר וַיַּהַרְגוּ הַיְּהוּדִים
טז בְשׁוּשָׁן שְׁלֹשׁ מֵאוֹת אִישׁ וּבַבִּזָּה לֹא שָׁלְחוּ אֶת־יָדָם׃ וּשְׁאָר הַיְּהוּדִים
אֲשֶׁר בִּמְדִינוֹת הַמֶּלֶךְ נִקְהֲלוּ ׀ וְעָמֹד עַל־נַפְשָׁם וְנוֹחַ מֵאֹיְבֵיהֶם וְהָרוֹג
יז בְּשֹׂנְאֵיהֶם חֲמִשָּׁה וְשִׁבְעִים אָלֶף וּבַבִּזָּה לֹא שָׁלְחוּ אֶת־יָדָם׃ בְּיוֹם־
שְׁלוֹשָׁה עָשָׂר לְחֹדֶשׁ אֲדָר וְנוֹחַ בְּאַרְבָּעָה עָשָׂר בּוֹ וְעָשֹׂה אֹתוֹ יוֹם

18 And the Jews who were in Shushan came together both on the thirteenth
and on the fourteenth, and rested on the fifteenth, and made that a day of
19 feasting and happiness. Thus it came about that provincial Jews, living in
unwalled towns, make the fourteenth day of the month of Adar a day of
happiness, of feasting and festivity, and of sending one another good things
to eat.

20 Mordekhai wrote all this down, and sent scrolls to all the Jews in all the
21 provinces of King Ahasuerus, near and far, to establish among them that
they should mark the fourteenth and fifteenth days of Adar every single
22 year: the days when the Jews rested from their enemies – the month that
was turned over for them from sorrow to happiness, from mourning to
celebration – to make them days of feasting and happiness, and for sending
23 one another good things to eat, and giving gifts to the poor. And so the Jews
accepted upon themselves what they had already begun to perform, just as
Mordekhai had written.

24 For Haman, son of Hamedata the Agagite, enemy of all the Jews, had plotted
against the Jews to destroy them, and had drawn the *pur* – the lot, that is – to
25 consume and to destroy them. And when Esther came before the king, he
declared, by the scroll, that the evil plot Haman had hatched against the Jews
must come down upon his own head – and he and his sons must be hung up
26 on the post. And so these days were named Purim, after the *pur*. So, following
the words of the letter, and what they had seen, and what had befallen them,
27 they established and accepted, for themselves and for their children, and for
all who would ever come to join their ranks, never to be neglected – that they
keep these two days as they are prescribed and in their right times, every single
28 year. And indeed, these days are remembered and marked in every single
generation, family by family, province upon province, town upon town; nor
will these days of Purim ever be neglected by the Jews, nor their memory ever
cease to be among their children.

29 And Esther, daughter of Aviḥayil, the queen, together with Mordekhai the
Jew, wrote with all their authority, for this second letter of Purim to be
30 confirmed. And they sent out scrolls to all the Jews, across one hundred
and twenty-seven provinces, all of Ahasuerus' realm – words of peace and

יח מִשְׁתֶּה וְשִׂמְחָה: והיהודיים אֲשֶׁר־בְּשׁוּשָׁן נִקְהֲלוּ בִּשְׁלוֹשָׁה עָשָׂר וְהַיְּהוּדִים
בּוֹ וּבְאַרְבָּעָה עָשָׂר בּוֹ וְנוֹחַ בַּחֲמִשָּׁה עָשָׂר בּוֹ וְעָשֹׂה אֹתוֹ יוֹם מִשְׁתֶּה
יט וְשִׂמְחָה: עַל־כֵּן הַיְּהוּדִים הפרוזים הַיֹּשְׁבִים בְּעָרֵי הַפְּרָזוֹת עֹשִׂים הַפְּרָזִים
אֵת יוֹם אַרְבָּעָה עָשָׂר לְחֹדֶשׁ אֲדָר שִׂמְחָה וּמִשְׁתֶּה וְיוֹם טוֹב וּמִשְׁלֹחַ
כ מָנוֹת אִישׁ לְרֵעֵהוּ: וַיִּכְתֹּב מָרְדֳּכַי אֶת־הַדְּבָרִים הָאֵלֶּה וַיִּשְׁלַח סְפָרִים
אֶל־כָּל־הַיְּהוּדִים אֲשֶׁר בְּכָל־מְדִינוֹת הַמֶּלֶךְ אֲחַשְׁוֵרוֹשׁ הַקְּרוֹבִים
כא וְהָרְחוֹקִים: לְקַיֵּם עֲלֵיהֶם לִהְיוֹת עֹשִׂים אֵת יוֹם אַרְבָּעָה עָשָׂר לְחֹדֶשׁ
כב אֲדָר וְאֵת יוֹם־חֲמִשָּׁה עָשָׂר בּוֹ בְּכָל־שָׁנָה וְשָׁנָה: כַּיָּמִים אֲשֶׁר־נָחוּ
בָהֶם הַיְּהוּדִים מֵאֹיְבֵיהֶם וְהַחֹדֶשׁ אֲשֶׁר נֶהְפַּךְ לָהֶם מִיָּגוֹן לְשִׂמְחָה
וּמֵאֵבֶל לְיוֹם טוֹב לַעֲשׂוֹת אוֹתָם יְמֵי מִשְׁתֶּה וְשִׂמְחָה וּמִשְׁלֹחַ מָנוֹת
כג אִישׁ לְרֵעֵהוּ וּמַתָּנוֹת לָאֶבְיֹנִים: וְקִבֵּל הַיְּהוּדִים אֵת אֲשֶׁר־הֵחֵלּוּ
כד לַעֲשׂוֹת וְאֵת אֲשֶׁר־כָּתַב מָרְדֳּכַי אֲלֵיהֶם: כִּי הָמָן בֶּן־הַמְּדָתָא הָאֲגָגִי
צֹרֵר כָּל־הַיְּהוּדִים חָשַׁב עַל־הַיְּהוּדִים לְאַבְּדָם וְהִפִּל פּוּר הוּא הַגּוֹרָל
כה לְהֻמָּם וּלְאַבְּדָם: וּבְבֹאָהּ לִפְנֵי הַמֶּלֶךְ אָמַר עִם־הַסֵּפֶר יָשׁוּב מַחֲשַׁבְתּוֹ
הָרָעָה אֲשֶׁר־חָשַׁב עַל־הַיְּהוּדִים עַל־רֹאשׁוֹ וְתָלוּ אֹתוֹ וְאֶת־בָּנָיו
כו עַל־הָעֵץ: עַל־כֵּן קָרְאוּ לַיָּמִים הָאֵלֶּה פוּרִים עַל־שֵׁם הַפּוּר עַל־כֵּן
עַל־כָּל־דִּבְרֵי הָאִגֶּרֶת הַזֹּאת וּמָה־רָאוּ עַל־כָּכָה וּמָה הִגִּיעַ אֲלֵיהֶם:
כז קִיְּמוּ וְקִבְּלֻ הַיְּהוּדִים ׀ עֲלֵיהֶם ׀ וְעַל־זַרְעָם וְעַל כָּל־הַנִּלְוִים עֲלֵיהֶם
וְלֹא יַעֲבוֹר לִהְיוֹת עֹשִׂים אֶת־שְׁנֵי הַיָּמִים הָאֵלֶּה כִּכְתָבָם וְכִזְמַנָּם
כח בְּכָל־שָׁנָה וְשָׁנָה: וְהַיָּמִים הָאֵלֶּה נִזְכָּרִים וְנַעֲשִׂים בְּכָל־דּוֹר וָדוֹר
מִשְׁפָּחָה וּמִשְׁפָּחָה מְדִינָה וּמְדִינָה וְעִיר וָעִיר וִימֵי הַפּוּרִים הָאֵלֶּה לֹא
כט יַעַבְרוּ מִתּוֹךְ הַיְּהוּדִים וְזִכְרָם לֹא־יָסוּף מִזַּרְעָם: וַתִּכְתֹּב
אֶסְתֵּר הַמַּלְכָּה בַת־אֲבִיחַיִל וּמָרְדֳּכַי הַיְּהוּדִי אֶת־כָּל־תֹּקֶף לְקַיֵּם
ל אֵת אִגֶּרֶת הַפֻּרִים הַזֹּאת הַשֵּׁנִית: וַיִּשְׁלַח סְפָרִים אֶל־כָּל־הַיְּהוּדִים
אֶל־שֶׁבַע וְעֶשְׂרִים וּמֵאָה מְדִינָה מַלְכוּת אֲחַשְׁוֵרוֹשׁ דִּבְרֵי שָׁלוֹם

31 truth. The scrolls were to confirm these days of Purim in their times, just as
Mordekhai the Jew and Esther the queen had fixed them; and, indeed, as
they had all fixed their fast days and entreaties, for themselves and for their
32 children. And so, Esther's word confirmed this practice of Purim; and it was
written down in the scroll.
10 1 As for King Ahasuerus, he levied a tribute from the people of all the land and
2 of the islands of the sea. And the full account of his authority and might, and
all the greatness of Mordekhai, whom the king exalted – are they not already
3 written in the Scroll of the Chronicles of the Kings of Medea and Persia? ▸ For
Mordekhai the Jew was second-in-command to King Ahasuerus, and revered
too among the Jews – beloved of all the multitudes of his brothers, working
for the good of his people, and speaking words of peace for all his children. ◂

Continue with the Service for Purim on page 902.

לא וֶאֱמֶת׃ לְקַיֵּם אֶת־יְמֵי הַפֻּרִים הָאֵלֶּה בִּזְמַנֵּיהֶם כַּאֲשֶׁר קִיַּם עֲלֵיהֶם
מָרְדֳּכַי הַיְּהוּדִי וְאֶסְתֵּר הַמַּלְכָּה וְכַאֲשֶׁר קִיְּמוּ עַל־נַפְשָׁם וְעַל־זַרְעָם
לב דִּבְרֵי הַצּוֹמוֹת וְזַעֲקָתָם׃ וּמַאֲמַר אֶסְתֵּר קִיַּם דִּבְרֵי הַפֻּרִים הָאֵלֶּה
י א וְנִכְתָּב בַּסֵּפֶר׃ וַיָּשֶׂם הַמֶּלֶךְ אחשרש ׀ מַס עַל־הָאָרֶץ אֲחַשְׁוֵרוֹשׁ
ב וְאִיֵּי הַיָּם׃ וְכָל־מַעֲשֵׂה תָקְפּוֹ וּגְבוּרָתוֹ וּפָרָשַׁת גְּדֻלַּת מָרְדֳּכַי אֲשֶׁר
גִּדְּלוֹ הַמֶּלֶךְ הֲלוֹא־הֵם כְּתוּבִים עַל־סֵפֶר דִּבְרֵי הַיָּמִים לְמַלְכֵי מָדַי
ג וּפָרָס׃ כִּי ׀ מָרְדֳּכַי הַיְּהוּדִי מִשְׁנֶה לַמֶּלֶךְ אֲחַשְׁוֵרוֹשׁ וְגָדוֹל לַיְּהוּדִים
וְרָצוּי לְרֹב אֶחָיו דֹּרֵשׁ טוֹב לְעַמּוֹ וְדֹבֵר שָׁלוֹם לְכָל־זַרְעוֹ׃

Continue with סדר קריאת המגילה *on page 903.*

PIYUTEI GEULA – BERAḤ DODI

GEULA FOR THE FIRST DAY OF PESAḤ

A unique feature of the Yotzerot for Pesaḥ is the Piyutei Geula, which precede the blessing "who redeemed Israel."

Hasten, my Beloved, before the time comes for our youthful love;
have compassion for us once more, for the kings of the evil Edom,
our captors and tormentors, have almost destroyed us:
break them and uproot them from our midst!
Rebuild Your Temple, and let our offspring make music within.
"Here He stands behind our wall!" *Song. 2*

Hasten, my Beloved, before the envisioned time blows by;
hurry, and let the shadows fly away from our midst.
The once despised [Messiah] shall be exalted, lofty, raised high;
he shall prosper; he shall reprove and preach to many nations.
Bare Your arm as we call out:
"The voice of my Beloved – I hear Him coming!" *Song. 2*

Hasten, my Beloved, and be like a gazelle; *Song. 8*
reveal and bring near my time of redemption;
draw me out of my captivity
to be a crown of glory.
We are despised, and long for the beautiful [Temple] Mount,
but there is neither leader nor prophet,
no [Elijah the] Tishbite to straighten my path or restore me;
so plead my cause,
erase my debt and my suffering,
let my enemy see it and be put to shame. Then shall I respond to my scorner, saying:
"This is my Beloved, my closest Redeemer,
my Companion and Cherished One, God, the God of my father!"

For the sake of the ancestors, redeem the descendants,
bringing salvation to their children's children.
Blessed are You, Lord, who redeemed Israel.

Continue with the Amida on page 770.

פיוטי גאולה – ברח דודי

גאולה ליום טוב ראשון של פסח

A unique feature of the יוצרות *for* פסח *is the* פיוטי גאולה*,*
which precede the blessing גָּאַל יִשְׂרָאֵל

בְּרַח דוֹדִי עַד שֶׁתָּפֵחַ אַהֲבַת כְּלוּלֵינוּ
שׁוּב לְרַחֵם, כִּי כָלִינוּ
מַלְכֵי אֱדוֹם הָרְשָׁעָה, שׁוֹבֵינוּ, תוֹלָלֵינוּ
הָרֵס וְקַעְקַע בִּצְתָם מִתְּלֵנוּ
הָקֵם טוּרָךְ, נֶגֶן שְׁתִילֵינוּ   הִנֵּה־זֶה עוֹמֵד אַחַר כָּתְלֵנוּ: שיר השירים ב

בְּרַח דוֹדִי עַד שֶׁיָּפוּחַ קֵץ מַחֲזֶה
חִישׁ וְנָסוּ הַצְּלָלִים מִזֶּה
יָרוּם וְנִשָּׂא, וְגָבֹהַּ נִבְזֶה
יַשְׂכִּיל וְיוֹכִיחַ, וְגוֹיִם רַבִּים יַזֶּה
חֲשֹׂף זְרוֹעֲךָ, קְרָא כָּזֶה   קוֹל דּוֹדִי הִנֵּה־זֶה: שיר השירים ב

בְּרַח דוֹדִי וּדְמֵה־לְךָ לִצְבִי: / יָגֵל, יִגַּשׁ, קֵץ קִצְבִי שיר השירים ח
דַּלּוֹתִי מִשְּׁבִי / לַעֲטֶרֶת צְבִי
תְּעוּבִים, תְּאֵבִים הַר צְבִי / וְאֵין מֵבִיא וְנָבִיא
וְלֹא תַשְׁבִּי / מְשׁוּי, מְשִׁיבִי
רִיבָה רִיבִי / הָסֵר חוֹבִי וּכְאֵבִי
וְיֵרָא וְיֵבוֹשׁ אוֹיְבִי / וְאָשִׁיבָה חוֹרְפִי בְּנִיבִי
זֶה דוֹדִי, גּוֹאֲלִי, קְרוֹבִי / רֵעִי וַאֲהוּבִי / אֵל אֱלֹהֵי אָבִי.

בִּגְלַל אָבוֹת תּוֹשִׁיעַ בָּנִים, וְתָבִיא גְאֻלָּה לִבְנֵי בְנֵיהֶם
בָּרוּךְ אַתָּה יהוה, גָּאַל יִשְׂרָאֵל.

Continue with the עמידה *on page 771.*

GEULA FOR THE SECOND DAY OF PESAḤ

Hasten, my Beloved, to the place You made for Your dwelling,
and though we have violated Your covenant,
please recall Your betrothal love for us.
Affirm the truth of Your word;
rebuild the city of Your joy,
and set her above Your highest joy!

Hasten, my Beloved, to Your tabernacle in Shalem [Jerusalem],
and though we have strayed from Your path,
please gaze out from Your gap,
and save a destitute, oppressed nation;
calm Your wrath against them,
and let them find everlasting shelter under Your wing.

Hasten, my Beloved, to the place Your eyes and heart are set upon,
and though we have neglected Your goodly Law,
please listen to the roar of Your enemies and their tumult.
Let their blood soak the earth;
may the dust be saturated by their fats,
and may the stench of their corpses rise.

Hasten, my Beloved, to Your lofty Home of old,
and though we have betrayed by denying Your word,
please, listen to the outpouring of our whispered prayers.
Draw me out of the sinking mire;
save those You hold close as the reflection in Your eye,
as You once did [in Egypt], in [Nisan,] the first month.

For the sake of the ancestors,
redeem the descendants,
bringing salvation to their children's children.
Blessed are You, Lord, who redeemed Israel.

Continue with the Amida on page 770.

גאולה ליום טוב שני של פסח

בְּרַח דוֹדִי אֶל מְכוֹן לְשִׁבְתָּךְ
וְאִם עָבַרְנוּ אֶת בְּרִיתָךְ
אָנָּא זְכֹר אִוּוּי חֻפָּתָךְ
הָקֵם קֶשֶׁט מַלְכוּתָךְ / כּוֹנֵן מְשׂוֹשׂ קִרְיָתָךְ
הַעֲלוֹתָהּ עַל רֹאשׁ שִׂמְחָתָךְ

בְּרַח דוֹדִי אֶל שָׁלֵם סֻכָּךְ
וְאִם תָּעִינוּ מִדַּרְכָּךְ
אָנָּא הָצֵץ מֵחֲרַכָּךְ
וְתוֹשִׁיעַ עַם עָנִי וּמֻתְכָּךְ / חֲמָתְךָ מֵהֶם לְשַׁכָּךְ
וּבְאֶבְרָתְךָ סֶלָה לְהִסְתּוֹכָךְ

בְּרַח דוֹדִי אֶל לִבָּךְ וְעֵינֶיךָ שָׁם
וְאִם זָנַחְנוּ טוֹב מֵרֹשֶׁם
אָנָּא שְׁמַע שַׁאֲגַת קוֹל צוֹרְרֶיךָ וָרֶגֶשׁ
רַוֵּה מִדָּם גּוּשָׁם / וַעֲפָרָם מֵחֵלֶב יְדֻשָּׁם
וּפִגְרֵיהֶם, יַעֲלֶה בָאשָׁם

בְּרַח דוֹדִי אֶל מָרוֹם מֵרִאשׁוֹן
וְאִם בָּגַדְנוּ בְּכַחְשׁוֹן
אָנָּא סֻכּוֹת צָקוּן לַחֲשׁוֹן
דְּלוּתִי מִטְּבוֹעַ רִפְשׁוֹן / גְּאֹל נְצוּרֵי כְּאִישׁוֹן
כְּאָז בַּחֹדֶשׁ הָרִאשׁוֹן.

בִּגְלַל אָבוֹת תּוֹשִׁיעַ בָּנִים, וְתָבִיא גְאֻלָּה לִבְנֵי בְנֵיהֶם
בָּרוּךְ אַתָּה יהוה, גָּאַל יִשְׂרָאֵל.

Continue with the עמידה *on page 771.*

GEULA FOR SHABBAT ḤOL HAMO'ED

In years in which the first and eighth days of Pesaḥ fall on Shabbat, and there is no Shabbat Ḥol HaMo'ed, the following is said on the eighth day.

Hasten, my Beloved, to Your peaceful abode! / And though we have wearied You with our corrupted ways, / behold, we have suffered every sort of pain; / and You, LORD, are our Stronghold and Hope. / For You we wait all the day, / for You to redeem us, and make us like a watered garden.

Hasten, my Beloved, to the site of our Sanctuary! / And though our iniquity has gone beyond our heads, / behold, our bodies have been bound in iron chains; / and You, LORD, are our Light, our Holy One. / It is to You that we pour out our whispered prayers / that You, from Your holy abode, might redeem us and set us free.

Hasten, my Beloved, to our City of Righteousness! / And though we did not heed the voice of our Vindicator, / behold, our destroyers have devoured us with open mouths; / and You, LORD, are our Judge, our Lawgiver. / It is upon You that we cast our burden, / that You redeem us, supporting us in tranquility and safety.

Hasten, my Beloved, to the Tent of Meeting, Your Lofty Abode! / And though we were unwilling to burden ourselves with Your yoke, / behold, they have afflicted us with all methods of abuse;but You, LORD, bring joy to the aggrieved.It is You we await, to loosen our bindings,to redeem us, making us great beyond our borders.

Hasten, my Beloved, to the most exalted mountain!And though we have acted arrogantly, unrestrained, / behold, we have been overtaken by many terrible evils; / and You, LORD, are a God of salvation. / It is You we beseech when we cry out in prayer, / that You might redeem us, and adorn us with the delight of salvation.

For the sake of the ancestors, redeem the descendants,
bringing salvation to their children's children.
Blessed are You, LORD, who redeemed Israel.

On Shabbat Ḥol HaMo'ed, say the Amida on page 480.
On Yom Tov, say the Amida on page 770.

גאולה לשבת חול המועד פסח

In years in which the first and eighth days of פסח *fall on* שבת*, and there is no* שבת חול המועד*, the following is said on the eighth day.*

בְּרַח דּוֹדִי אֶל שַׁאֲנָן נָוֶה   אִם הֶלְאֵינוּ דֶּרֶךְ הַעֲוֵה
הִנֵּה לָקִינוּ בְּכָל מַדְוֶה   וְאַתָּה יהוה מָעוֹז וּמִקְוֶה
עָלֶיךָ כָּל הַיּוֹם נְקַוֶּה   לְגָאֳלֵנוּ וּלְשִׁיתֵנוּ כְּגַן רָוֶה.

בְּרַח דּוֹדִי אֶל מְקוֹם מִקְדָּשֵׁנוּ   אִם עֲוֹנוֹת עָבְרוּ רֹאשֵׁנוּ
הִנֵּה בַּרְזֶל בָּאָה נַפְשֵׁנוּ   וְאַתָּה יהוה אוֹרֵנוּ, קְדוֹשֵׁנוּ
עָלֶיךָ נִשְׁפֹּךְ שִׂיחַ רַחֲשֵׁנוּ   לְגָאֳלֵנוּ מִמְּעוֹן קָדְשְׁךָ לְהַחְפִּישֵׁנוּ.

בְּרַח דּוֹדִי אֶל עִיר צִדְקֵנוּ   אִם לֹא שָׁמַעְנוּ לְקוֹל מַצְדִּיקֵנוּ
הִנֵּה אֲכָלוּנוּ בְּכָל פֶּה מְדַקְּקֵינוּ   וְאַתָּה יהוה שׁוֹפְטֵנוּ, מְחוֹקְקֵנוּ
עָלֶיךָ נַשְׁלִיךְ יְהַב חֶלְקֵנוּ   לְגָאֳלֵנוּ בְּהַשְׁקֵט וּבְבִטְחָה לְהַחֲזִיקֵנוּ.

בְּרַח דּוֹדִי אֶל וַעַד הַזְּבוּל   עִם עֻלְּךָ סָבַלְנוּ בְּלִי סָבוּל
הִנֵּה שִׁחֲתוּנוּ בְּכָל מִינֵי חִבּוּל   וְאַתָּה יהוה מְשַׂמֵּחַ אָבוּל
עָלֶיךָ נַסְבִּיר לְהַתִּיר כָּבוּל   לְגָאֳלֵנוּ לְהִתְגַּדֵּל מֵעַל גְּבוּל.

בְּרַח דּוֹדִי אֶל נִשָּׂא מִגְּבָעוֹת   אִם זֵדְנוּ בְּפֶרַע פְּרָעוֹת
הִנֵּה הִשִּׂיגוּנוּ צָרוֹת רַבּוֹת וְרָעוֹת   וְאַתָּה יהוה אֵל לְמוֹשָׁעוֹת
עָלֶיךָ נִתְחַנֵּן שִׂיחַ שְׁוָעוֹת   לְגָאֳלֵנוּ וּלְעַטְּרֵנוּ נֹעַם יְשׁוּעוֹת.

בִּגְלַל אָבוֹת תּוֹשִׁיעַ בָּנִים
וְתָבִיא גְאֻלָּה לִבְנֵי בְנֵיהֶם
בָּרוּךְ אַתָּה יהוה, גָּאַל יִשְׂרָאֵל.

On שבת חול המועד*, say the* עמידה *on page 481.*
On יום טוב*, say the* עמידה *on page 771.*

GEULA FOR THE SEVENTH DAY OF PESAḤ

The day the depths turned to dry land,
the redeemed ones sang a new song of praise.

The day You were glorified through our oppressor, / You demonstrated Your love for me, / establishing Your praise
out of the mouths of babes.

Cunningly, You caused / the Anamite daughter's [Egypt's] feet to sink, / while the footsteps of the beloved Shulamite [Israel]
remained lovely in their sandals.

All those who saw me sang / when they witnessed Your glory: / "There is none like the God of Israel"
– so shall our enemies testify.

May You raise my banner as You did then / over the remnants of my people, / and gather the dispersed
like one who gleans grain.

Those who have forged with You / a covenant with Your seal, / and from the womb,
are circumcised for Your name's sake.

They display their signs / for all to see; / to the corners of their garments
they have attached fringes.

For whom was this Torah written? / Please acknowledge the truth! / Whose is the seal
and whose are the threads?

Betroth her once more, / never to be banished again, / and let her rise as the sun
making all the shadows flee.

Your beloved nation exalted You / greeting You with song: / Who is like You
among the mighty, O LORD?

For the sake of the ancestors,
redeem the descendants,
bringing salvation to their children's children.
Blessed are You, LORD, who redeemed Israel.

Continue with the Amida on page 770.

גאולה לשביעי של פסח

יוֹם לְיַבָּשָׁה נֶהֶפְכוּ מְצוּלִים
שִׁירָה חֲדָשָׁה שִׁבְּחוּ גְאוּלִים.

יוֹם בְּצַר נִכְבַּדְתָּ / וְאֵלַי נֶחְמַדְתָּ / וְלָךְ עֹז יִסַּדְתָּ
מִפִּי עוֹלָלִים.
הִטְבַּעְתָּ בְּתַרְמִית / רַגְלֵי בַּת עֲנָמִית / וּפַעֲמֵי שׁוּלַמִּית
יָפוּ בַּנְּעָלִים.
וְכָל רוֹאַי יְשׁוּרוּן / בְּעֵת הוֹדְךָ יְשֻׁרוּן / אֵין כָּאֵל יְשֻׁרוּן
וְאוֹיְבֵינוּ פְּלִילִים.
דְּגָלֵי כֵּן תָּרִים / עַל הַנִּשְׁאָרִים / וּתְלַקֵּט נִפְזָרִים
כִּמְלַקֵּט שִׁבֳּלִים.
הַבָּאִים עִמְּךָ / בִּבְרִית חוֹתָמְךָ / וּמִבֶּטֶן לְשִׁמְךָ
הֵמָּה נִמּוֹלִים.
הֶרְאוּ אוֹתוֹתָם / לְכָל רוֹאֶה אוֹתָם / וְעַל כַּנְפֵי כְסוּתָם
עָשׂוּ גְּדִילִים.
לְמִי זֹאת נִרְשֶׁמֶת / הַכֶּר נָא דְּבַר אֱמֶת / לְמִי הַחוֹתֶמֶת
וּלְמִי הַפְּתִילִים.
וְשׁוּב שֵׁנִית לְקַדְּשָׁהּ / וְאַל תּוֹסֵף לְגָרְשָׁהּ / וְהַעֲלֵה אוֹר שִׁמְשָׁהּ
וְנָסוּ הַצְּלָלִים.
יְדִידִים רוֹמְמוּךָ / בְּשִׁירָה קִדְּמוּךָ / מִי כָמֹכָה
יהוה בָּאֵלִים.

בִּגְלַל אָבוֹת תּוֹשִׁיעַ בָּנִים
וְתָבִיא גְאֻלָּה לִבְנֵי בְנֵיהֶם
בָּרוּךְ אַתָּה יהוה גָּאַל יִשְׂרָאֵל.

Continue with the עמידה *on page 771.*

הלכות תפילה

GATES TO PRAYER

The text (*nusaḥ*) of the siddur that we use today is based on the siddur of the Geonim, primarily *Seder Rav Amram Gaon* from the ninth century. The *nusaḥ* we call "*Nusaḥ Ashkenaz*" refers to the prayer texts and customs of Ashkenazi Jewry, which included the Jews of Germany and northern France. When Ashkenazi Jews moved eastward, they brought their practices with them to Poland and Russia, as well as Lithuania, Bohemia, Moravia, Austro-Hungary, Romania and the Balkans. Similarly, Ashkenazi Jews moved westward to Switzerland, France, Belgium, Holland, Northern Italy, England and, lastly, to Israel and America.

There is no single, authoritative version of *Nusaḥ Ashkenaz*. Certain differences in *nusaḥ* developed between the Jews of western Germany and eastern Germany (known today as *Minhag Polin*). For the most part, *Minhag Polin* is what Ashkenazi Jews follow today. But not exclusively. In the eighteenth century, Ḥasidic Jews adopted a new *nusaḥ* based on the Ari (R. Isaac Luria, 1534–1572), which strongly resembles the *nusaḥ* of Sephardi Jewry. As a result, many Jews of Ashkenazi descent now follow what is called "*Nusaḥ Sepharad*." Another variation on *Nusaḥ Ashkenaz* was developed by the Vilna Gaon (R. Eliyahu b. Shelomo, 1720–1797) and is called "*Minhag HaGra*." Students of the Vilna Gaon who moved to Israel in the nineteenth century brought *Minhag HaGra* with them, and it is the dominant Ashkenazi practice in Israel today.

In this Siddur we have tried to present *Nusaḥ Ashkenaz* as it is typically practiced in Ashkenazi congregations in the United States and Israel, with the differences noted in the instructions. Some practices referred to as "Israeli" are also followed by select congregations in the United States. In the pages below, we also note certain practices of *Nusaḥ Sepharad* which have become more common in Ashkenazi circles.

Rabbi Eli D. Clark

GUIDE TO THE JEWISH YEAR

ELUL

1 Beginning on the first day of Elul (the second day of Rosh Ḥodesh) and for the entire month of Elul, it is customary to say לְדָוִד, יהוה אוֹרִי (page 193) in the evening at the end of Ma'ariv and in the morning after saying the Psalm of the Day [אשי ישראל, פמ״ה:ג].

2 In addition, four shofar blasts are sounded at the end of weekday morning prayers, prior to (or following) recitation of לְדָוִד, יהוה אוֹרִי [רמ״א או״ח, תקפא:א].

Pre-Rosh HaShana Customs

3 On the Motza'ei Shabbat prior to Rosh HaShana, the congregation gathers at midnight to say *Seliḥot*. This is often preceded by a sermon from the rabbi. If Rosh HaShana falls on Monday or Tuesday, the first recitation of *Seliḥot* is moved back to the preceding Motza'ei Shabbat [רמ״א או״ח, תקפא:א].

4 The congregation says *Seliḥot* each weekday thereafter through Erev Yom Kippur. Although the original custom was to say *Seliḥot* every night after midnight and before dawn, most congregations today say them prior to Shaḥarit; some say them during the preceding evening [ערוה״ש שם, ב–ד].

5 The *Shaliaḥ Tzibbur* chosen to lead the *Seliḥot* should preferably be distinguished in Torah scholarship and personal virtue, over the age of thirty and married [רמ״א או״ח, תקפא:א].

6 One who is praying alone is permitted to say *Seliḥot* without a *minyan*, provided one omits the י״ג מידות ("Thirteen Attributes of Mercy") and the Aramaic passages [תקפא:ד]. However, one who is alone may read the י״ג מידות with *ta'amei hamikra* [שו״ע או״ח תקסה:ה].

Erev Rosh HaShana (29th of Elul)

7 The recitation of *Seliḥot* (the longest of the year) precedes regular Shaḥarit for weekdays. The congregation omits *Taḥanun* and shofar blowing [שו״ע ורמ״א או״ח, תקפא: ג].

8 It is customary to say the formula of התרת נדרים, the Annulment of Vows (page 875), in front of three adult males after Shaḥarit [חיי אדם, קלח: ח]. The formula may be said at any time of the day [שו״ע יו״ד, רלד: נו] and may be said any day prior to Yom Kippur.

9 Some have the custom to immerse in the mikveh. Other customs include fasting and visiting the graves of departed relatives [שו״ע או״ח, תקפא: ב; רמ״א, שם: ד].

10 When Rosh HaShana falls on Thursday and Friday, each household must prepare an *Eiruv Tavshilin* (page 759); this makes it permissible to prepare food on Friday for the Shabbat meals [שו״ע או״ח, תקכז].

TISHREI

Rosh HaShana (1st–2nd of Tishrei)

▸ LAWS OF ROSH HASHANA EVE

11 Candle lighting: Two blessings are said: (1) לְהַדְלִיק נֵר שֶׁל יוֹם טוֹב ("to light the festival light") and (2) שֶׁהֶחֱיָנוּ ("Who has given us life…"). When Rosh HaShana eve falls on Friday night, the conclusion of the first blessing is: לְהַדְלִיק נֵר שֶׁל שַׁבָּת וְשֶׁל יוֹם טוֹב ("to light the Shabbat and Festival light") (page 305).

12 Ma'ariv: for Shabbat and Yom Tov. Before saying the Amida for Rosh HaShana, most congregations say תִּקְעוּ בַחֹדֶשׁ שׁוֹפָר (Ps. 81:4–5). After the Amida, the Ark is opened and the *Shaliaḥ Tzibbur* and congregation say responsively Psalm 24, לְדָוִד מִזְמוֹר, לַיהוה הָאָרֶץ וּמְלוֹאָהּ. This is followed by Full Kaddish (some say Psalm 24 after the Full Kaddish), *Aleinu*, Mourner's Kaddish, Psalm 27 and Mourner's Kaddish. It is customary to conclude with the singing of Adon Olam or Yigdal.

13 Changes to the Kaddish: It is customary to replace the phrase לְעֵלָּא מִן כָּל ("beyond any") with לְעֵלָּא לְעֵלָּא מִכָּל ("above and beyond any") [משנ״ב, נו: ב] and to change the phrase עֹשֶׂה שָׁלוֹם ("He who makes peace") to עֹשֶׂה הַשָּׁלוֹם ("He who makes the peace") [ערוה״ש או״ח, תקפב: ח]. One who forgets either of these changes is not required to repeat the Kaddish.

14 Special additions to the Amida: On Rosh HaShana and Yom Kippur, additional phrases are added to the Amida: זָכְרֵנוּ לְחַיִּים is added in the first blessing; מִי כָמְוֹךָ in the second; four paragraphs are added to the third, and the ending is changed to הַמֶּלֶךְ הַקָּדוֹשׁ; וּכְתֹב is added in the penultimate blessing; and בְּסֵפֶר חַיִּים is added to the final blessing, and the ending is changed to עוֹשֵׂה הַשָּׁלוֹם (some do not change the ending of the blessing). One who forgets to say any of these passages is not required to repeat the Amida with the forgotten additions [שו״ע ורמ״א או״ח, תקפב:ה]. However, one who forgets to change the ending of the third blessing to הַמֶּלֶךְ הקדוש must repeat the Amida from the beginning, unless one corrects the error תוך כדי דיבור (see source in the *Shulḥan Arukh* for a discussion of this rule.) [שו״ע או״ח, תקפא:ג].

15 When Rosh HaShana eve falls on Friday night, Ma'ariv is preceded by the last two psalms of Kabbalat Shabbat: מִזְמוֹר שִׁיר לְיוֹם הַשַּׁבָּת and יהוה מָלָךְ, גֵּאוּת לָבֵשׁ (page 325). בַּמֶּה מַדְלִיקִין is omitted. The Amida is said with additions for Shabbat. After the Amida, before saying Psalm 24 the congregation says וַיְכֻלּוּ הַשָּׁמַיִם, and the *Shaliaḥ Tzibbur* says the abbreviated Repetition of the Amida as is customary on Shabbat eve [שו״ע או״ח, תרי״ט:ג].

16 On the eve of Rosh HaShana, it is customary to greet one another with wishes for inscription for a good new year: "לשנה טובה תיכתב ותחתם" [רמ״א או״ח, תקפב:ט].

17 Upon returning home, one says the Kiddush for Rosh HaShana. When Rosh HaShana eve falls on Friday night, the additions for Shabbat are said (page 879).

18 On the first night of Rosh HaShana, after eating the *ḥalla*, it is customary to say the blessing on fruit, eat a slice of apple dipped in honey, then say a prayer for a sweet new year [רמ״א או״ח, תקפג:א]. יַעֲלֶה וְיָבוֹא is added to *Birkat HaMazon* (page 985).

19 Shaḥarit: *Pesukei DeZimra* for Shabbat and Yom Tov is said. The *Shaliaḥ Tzibbur* for Shaḥarit begins from the words הַמֶּלֶךְ יוֹשֵׁב. After *Yishtabaḥ*, the Ark is opened and the congregation says Psalm 130 responsively. (Some say Psalm 130 before נִשְׁמַת כָּל חַי.)

20 After *Barekhu*, the congregation says הַמֵּאִיר לָאָרֶץ or, if it is Shabbat, הַכֹּל יוֹדוּךָ. The Amida for Rosh HaShana is said; if also Shabbat, one says the additions for Shabbat. The *Shaliaḥ Tzibbur* repeats the Amida, adding *piyutim* before the *Kedusha*. The congregation says *Avinu Malkenu*, but not on Shabbat [רמ״א או״ח, תקפד:א]. (Some congregations say at this point the Daily Psalm and Psalm 27, followed by the Mourner's Kaddish.) When the Torah is taken from the Ark, most congregations say the "Thirteen Attributes of Mercy" and a special supplication, except on Shabbat.

21 Torah Reading: first day – Gen. 21: 1–34; second day – Gen. 22:1–24. Five men

are called up, seven on Shabbat. Maftir (both days): Num. 29:1–6. Haftara: first day – 1 Sam. 1:1–2:10; second day – Jer. 31:1–19 [שו״ע או״ח, תקפד: ב; שם, תרא: א].

22 The Haftara is followed by (*Yekum Purkan* on Shabbat, then) the prayers for the government and the State of Israel. It is customary for the rabbi to deliver a sermon prior to the sounding of the shofar. If there is a Brit Mila, it takes place before the shofar blowing.

▸ LAWS OF SHOFAR BLOWING

23 Hearing the sound of the shofar is an affirmative mitzva from the Torah. A deaf person is exempt from this mitzva, but a blind person is not; consequently, a blind person may blow the shofar for others, but a deaf person may not. Women are exempt from this mitzva, but a woman is permitted to blow shofar for herself and other women. If a man is blowing shofar for one or more women, the women should say the blessings for themselves [שו״ע ורמ״א או״ח, תקפט: ג].

24 The first thirty shofar blasts sounded prior to Musaf represent the minimum number of shofar sounds that one is required to hear [שו״ע או״ח, תקץ: א]. However, it is customary to blow a hundred blasts. The Ashkenazi custom is to blow thirty before Musaf, thirty during the Repetition of the Amida and forty more in sets of thirty and ten during the Full Kaddish after Musaf [משנ״ב, תקצב: ד]. Some congregations follow the Sephardi custom of blowing the shofar during the silent Amida, rather than the Repetition (see law 34).

25 The person blowing the shofar is required to stand; the congregation is permitted to sit during the first set of shofar sounds, although the custom is to stand [שו״ע או״ח, תקפה: א; משנ״ב, שם: ב].

26 Two blessings are said by the person blowing the shofar: (1) לִשְׁמֹעַ קוֹל שׁוֹפָר, and (2) שֶׁהֶחֱיָנוּ [שו״ע או״ח, תקפה: ב].

27 To prevent distractions while performing the mitzva of hearing the shofar, the congregation is, until completion of the first thirty shofar blasts, forbidden to speak about matters unrelated to shofar and, until completion of the hundredth blast, forbidden to speak about matters unrelated to prayer [שו״ע או״ח, תקצב: ג].

28 The rabbis ruled that we do not blow the shofar when Rosh HaShana falls on Shabbat [ראש השנה, כט:; שו״ע או״ח, תקפח: ה].

29 After the shofar is blown, *Ashrei* is said and the Torah scrolls are returned to the Ark. The *Shaliaḥ Tzibbur* for Musaf says a special prefatory prayer, הִנְנִי הֶעָנִי מִמַּעַשׂ ("Here am I, poor of deeds"), and Half Kaddish.

30 Musaf for Rosh HaShana: Unique among the Amidot said on Shabbat and

Yom Tov, the Musaf for Rosh HaShana comprises nine blessings, rather than seven. Instead of one blessing devoted to the Festival, there are three extended blessings dedicated to three separate Rosh HaShana themes: Kingship, Remembrance and the Shofar [שו״ע או״ח, תקצא: א; שם: ד].

31 Before *Kedusha*, *piyutim* are said, culminating with וּנְתַנֶּה תֹּקֶף.

32 The fourth blessing in the Repetition of the Amida contains *Aleinu*. The Ark is opened, and the *Shaliaḥ Tzibbur* (and, in most communities, the entire congregation) kneels in prostration at the words וַאֲנַחְנוּ כּוֹרְעִים. Because one is forbidden to touch one's head against the bare stone floor when kneeling, one should place a piece of cloth or paper between one's head and the floor [רמ״א או״ח, קלא: ח].

33 Upon completion by the *Shaliaḥ Tzibbur* of each of the three middle blessings of the Amida, ten shofar blasts are sounded, and the congregation says הַיּוֹם הֲרַת עוֹלָם and אֲרֶשֶׁת שְׂפָתֵינוּ. If Rosh HaShana falls on Shabbat, the shofar is not sounded and אֲרֶשֶׁת שְׂפָתֵינוּ is omitted. The Kohanim say *Birkat Kohanim*.

34 After Musaf, the *Shaliaḥ Tzibbur* says Full Kaddish. Forty more shofar blasts are sounded, in sets of thirty and ten [רמ״א או״ח, תקצו: א; פמ״ג, שם]. Some congregations pause during the Full Kaddish to blow the thirty blasts and sound the last ten after the completion of the Full Kaddish; others sound the thirty after the completion of the Full Kaddish and the last ten prior to *Aleinu*. This is followed by *Ein Keloheinu*; the Rabbis' Kaddish; *Aleinu*; Mourner's Kaddish; the Daily Psalm; Psalm 27; Mourner's Kaddish; *Anim Zemirot*; Mourner's Kaddish and Adon Olam.

35 Minḥa: for Shabbat and Yom Tov. When Rosh HaShana falls on Shabbat, the beginning of *Ha'azinu* is read. The Amida is identical to that said during Shaḥarit, except that it is preceded by the verse beginning כִּי שֵׁם יהוה אֶקְרָא (Deut. 32:3), and, for the final blessing, the paragraph שָׁלוֹם רָב ("Great peace") substitutes for the paragraph שִׂים שָׁלוֹם ("Grant peace"). After the *Shaliaḥ Tzibbur* repeats the Amida, the congregation says *Avinu Malkenu*, except when Rosh HaShana falls on Shabbat.

36 After Minḥa, it is customary to say *Tashlikh* (page 883) beside a source of running water. If the first day of Rosh HaShana falls on Shabbat, *Tashlikh* is said on the second day [רמ״א או״ח, תקפג: ב] or on any weekday prior to Yom Kippur.

Rosh HaShana – Second Day (2nd of Tishrei)

37 Eve of second day: Candle lighting and preparations for the meal must be performed after nightfall. If the first day of Rosh HaShana fell on Shabbat, the congregation adds the paragraph וַתּוֹדִיעֵנוּ in the middle section of the Amida. Similarly,

in Kiddush, the two blessings for Havdala are inserted prior to the blessing שֶׁהֶחֱיָנוּ (page 881); thus the order of blessings is: wine, Kiddush, flame, Havdala, שֶׁהֶחֱיָנוּ.

38 On the second night of Rosh HaShana, it is customary to eat a new fruit or wear a new garment. However, one says שֶׁהֶחֱיָנוּ during Kiddush even if there is no new fruit or garment [שו״ע או״ח, תר:ב]. Similarly, שֶׁהֶחֱיָנוּ is said before blowing shofar on the second day, even if the shofar was blown on the first day [שם:ג].

39 Ma'ariv, Shaḥarit and Minḥa: Except as noted above, the prayers for the second day of Rosh HaShana parallel the prayers for the first.

40 Motza'ei Rosh HaShana: Ma'ariv for weekdays is said. In the fourth blessing of the Amida, the paragraph of אַתָּה חוֹנַנְתָּנוּ is said (page 261). Havdala is said over a cup of wine or grape juice; no blessing is made over spices or a flame [שו״ע או״ח, תרא:א].

Laws of Aseret Yemei Teshuva (the Ten Days of Repentance)

41 Changes to the Kaddish: see law 13.

42 During the morning prayers, it is customary, after *Yishtabaḥ*, to open the Ark and say Psalm 130 responsively (page 87) [משנ״ב או״ח, נד:ד]. Some say Psalm 130 before *Yishtabaḥ*.

43 Additions to the Amida: See law 14. One should also change the ending of the eleventh blessing of the Amida from מֶלֶךְ אוֹהֵב צְדָקָה וּמִשְׁפָּט to הַמֶּלֶךְ הַמִּשְׁפָּט [שו״ע או״ח, תקפא:ג], but one who forgets to do so is not required to repeat the Amida [רמ״א או״ח, קיח:א].

44 In Shaḥarit and Minḥa, after the Amida, the Ark is opened and the congregation says *Avinu Malkenu*. This is omitted on Friday afternoon and Shabbat [רמ״א או״ח, תרב:א].

Fast of Gedalya (3rd of Tishrei)

45 This fast commemorates the slaying of Gedalya ben Aḥikam by Yishmael ben Netanya, at the behest of Ba'alis, the king of Amon (circa 586 BCE). Shortly after the Babylonian conquest of Jerusalem, Gedalya was appointed governor of Judea. His assassination just months after the appointment spelled the end of Jewish self-government in the land of Israel in that era and led to the dispersion of the Jews who remained in the land of Israel after the destruction of the First Temple [II Kings 25:22–26; Jer. 40:4–41:18].

46 If the 3rd of Tishrei falls on Shabbat, the fast is postponed to Sunday.

47 The fast begins at dawn [שו״ע או״ח, תקנ:ב]. One is permitted to wake before dawn

to eat and drink, but only if one had the intention to do so before going to sleep [שו״ע או״ח, תקסד:א].

48 Eating and drinking are forbidden, but other activities (bathing, wearing leather shoes) are permitted [שו״ע או״ח, תקנ:ב]. Pregnant and nursing women are exempt from fasting [רמ״א, שם:א].

49 Shaharit: The recitation of *Selihot* precedes Shaharit for weekdays. The additions for *Aseret Yemei Teshuva* are said. During the Repetition of the Amida, the *Shaliah Tzibbur* says the paragraph עֲנֵנוּ between the seventh and eighth blessings (page 117) [שו״ע או״ח, תקסו:א]. This is followed by *Avinu Malkenu* and *Tahanun*.

50 Torah Reading (page 1112): The Torah is read only if at least six people (according to some: three people) are fasting. Only people who are fasting are called up. It is customary for the congregation to say the following passages aloud: the last seven words of Ex. 32:12: שׁוּב מֵחֲרוֹן אַפֶּךָ, וְהִנָּחֵם עַל־הָרָעָה לְעַמֶּךָ, the "Thirteen Attributes of Mercy": יהוה יהוה אֵל רַחוּם וְחַנּוּן אֶרֶךְ אַפַּיִם וְרַב־חֶסֶד וֶאֱמֶת: נֹצֵר חֶסֶד לָאֲלָפִים נֹשֵׂא עָוֹן וָפֶשַׁע וְחַטָּאָה וְנַקֵּה, and the last four words of Ex. 34:9: "וְסָלַחְתָּ לַעֲוֹנֵנוּ וּלְחַטָּאתֵנוּ וּנְחַלְתָּנוּ" [משנ״ב, שם (ג)].

51 Minha: After *Ashrei* and Half Kaddish, the Torah is read. The reading is the same as that of the morning. The third *oleh* reads the Haftara (page 1112) [רמ״א, שם]. After the Torah is returned to the Ark, the *Shaliah Tzibbur* says Half Kaddish, and Minha Amida for weekdays is said.

52 During the silent recitation of the Amida, those who are fasting say the paragraph עֲנֵנוּ as part of the sixteenth blessing, שׁוֹמֵעַ תְּפִלָּה (page 223); during the Repetition of the Amida, the *Shaliah Tzibbur* says עֲנֵנוּ between the seventh and eighth blessings, as in the morning (page 217). After the blessing הַטּוֹב שִׁמְךָ וּלְךָ נָאֶה לְהוֹדוֹת, the *Shaliah Tzibbur* says the paragraph relating to *Birkat Kohanim* (page 229). For the final blessings of the Amida, שִׂים שָׁלוֹם is said instead of שָׁלוֹם רָב. After the Amida, the congregation says *Avinu Malkenu*. This is followed by *Tahanun*, Full Kaddish and *Aleinu*.

Shabbat Shuva

53 Shabbat Shuva is named for the first word of the Haftara, *Shuva*. It is sometimes referred to as Shabbat Teshuva, "Shabbat of Repentance."

54 *Kabbalat Shabbat*: If Shabbat Shuva falls on the 3rd of Tishrei, Ma'ariv is preceded only by the last two psalms of Kabbalat Shabbat: מִזְמוֹר שִׁיר לְיוֹם הַשַּׁבָּת and יהוה מָלָךְ, גֵּאוּת לָבֵשׁ (page 325). בַּמֶּה מַדְלִיקִין is omitted. Ma'ariv Amida for Shabbat is said with additions for the *Aseret Yemei Teshuva*. Similarly, when the *Shaliah*

Tzibbur says the paragraph מָגֵן אָבוֹת, he says הַמֶּלֶךְ הַקָּדוֹשׁ instead of הָאֵל הַקָּדוֹשׁ (page 359) [שו״ע או״ח, תקפב: ג].

55 Shaḥarit: for Shabbat. The congregation says Psalm 130 responsively before *Yishtabaḥ* (some say Psalm 130 before נִשְׁמַת כָּל חַי). Amida for Shabbat is said with additions for *Aseret Yemei Teshuva*. The Haftara is Hosea 14:2–10; Joel 2:15–27.

56 It is customary for the rabbi to deliver a sermon relating to repentance.

57 It is customary not to say *Kiddush Levana* until after Yom Kippur [רמ״א או״ח, תרב: א].

Erev Yom Kippur (9th of Tishrei)

58 It is a mitzva to eat and drink on the day before Yom Kippur [שו״ע או״ח, תרד: א].

59 Every person should ask forgiveness from others, because Yom Kippur atones for sins against one's fellows only if the wronged individual has offered his or her forgiveness [שו״ע או״ח, תרו: א].

60 It is customary to say *Kaparot* (page 885) [רמ״א או״ח, תרה: א], and for males to immerse in the mikveh [שו״ע ורמ״א או״ח, תרו: ד].

61 In the morning, an abbreviated *Seliḥot* is said, followed by Shaḥarit for weekdays. During *Pesukei DeZimra,* the congregation omits Psalm 100. Similarly, *Avinu Malkenu, Taḥanun* and לַמְנַצֵּחַ (Psalm 20) are omitted. However, if Erev Yom Kippur falls on Friday, the congregation does not omit *Avinu Malkenu* [שו״ע ורמ״א או״ח, תרד: ב].

62 Minḥa: Most communities schedule an early recitation of Minḥa, to allow time for the congregants to return home and eat a final meal (*Se'uda Mafseket*) prior to the fast. Minḥa for weekdays is said with additions for *Aseret Yemei Teshuva*. Before saying the paragraph אֱלֹהַי, נְצֹר at the conclusion of the Amida, each individual says *Viduy* (page 887) [שו״ע או״ח, תרז: א]. *Viduy* is not said by the *Shaliaḥ Tzibbur* during the Repetition of the Amida. As in the morning, both *Avinu Malkenu* and *Taḥanun* are omitted.

63 The *Se'uda Mafseket* (final meal) must be finished a few minutes before sunset [שו״ע או״ח, תרח: א]. It is customary for parents to say a special blessing for their children after the meal [חיי אדם, קמד: יט].

64 Candle lighting: Two blessings are said: (1) לְהַדְלִיק נֵר שֶׁל יוֹם הַכִּפּוּרִים, and (2) שֶׁהֶחֱיָנוּ. When Yom Kippur eve falls on Friday night, the conclusion of the first blessing is: לְהַדְלִיק נֵר שֶׁל שַׁבָּת וְשֶׁל יוֹם הַכִּפּוּרִים (page 305) [שו״ע ורמ״א או״ח, תרי: א–ב].

65 One should also light a candle that will burn at least 25 hours, such as a *yahrzeit* candle, from which to light the Havdala candle after the conclusion of Yom Kippur.

Yom Kippur (10th of Tishrei)

66 Yom Kippur Eve: Many individuals say *Tefilla Zaka* ("Pure Prayer") prior to *Kol Nidrei* [משנ״ב או״ח, תרז:א]. It is customary for married men to put on their tallit before *Kol Nidrei*; many also wear a *kittel* [רמ״א או״ח, תרי: ד]. The Ark is opened, and two leaders of the congregation each bear a Torah scroll to the *bima*, where they stand on either side of the *Shaliaḥ Tzibbur*, while he chants *Kol Nidrei*. At the conclusion, the entire congregation says the blessing שֶׁהֶחֱיָנוּ (except women who said the blessing when lighting candles), and the scrolls are returned to the Ark [שו״ע או״ח, תריט:א].

67 Ma'ariv: for Shabbat and Yom Tov. When saying Shema, the congregation pronounces בָּרוּךְ שֵׁם כְּבוֹד מַלְכוּתוֹ לְעוֹלָם וָעֶד out loud [שו״ע או״ח, תריט:ב]. Before the Yom Kippur Amida, many say the verse כִּי בַיּוֹם הַזֶּה... (Lev. 16:30). After the Amida (with additions – see law 14), the *Shaliaḥ Tzibbur* leads the congregation in saying *Seliḥot* and *Viduy*. After *Viduy*, the Ark is opened and the congregation says *Avinu Malkenu* (unless Yom Kippur falls on Shabbat) and Psalm 24. This is followed by Full Kaddish, *Aleinu*, Mourner's Kaddish, Psalm 27 and Mourner's Kaddish. It is customary to conclude with the singing of Adon Olam or Yigdal. Some congregations also say Psalms 1–4, *Shir HaYiḥud* and *Anim Zemirot*.

68 When Yom Kippur eve falls on Friday night, Ma'ariv is preceded by the last two psalms of Kabbalat Shabbat: מִזְמוֹר שִׁיר לְיוֹם הַשַּׁבָּת and יהוה מָלָךְ, גֵּאוּת לָבֵשׁ (page 325). בַּמֶּה מַדְלִיקִין is omitted. The Amida is said with additions for Shabbat. After the Amida, the congregation says וַיְכֻלּוּ הַשָּׁמַיִם, and the *Shaliaḥ Tzibbur* says the abbreviated Repetition of the Amida as is customary on Shabbat eve [שו״ע או״ח, תריט:ג].

69 Shaḥarit: Many have the custom to wear a *kittel* under their tallit. The Daily Psalm is said after putting on the tallit. *Pesukei DeZimra* for Shabbat and Yom Tov is said. The *Shaliaḥ Tzibbur* for Shaḥarit begins from the words הַמֶּלֶךְ יוֹשֵׁב ("The King – enthroned..."). After *Yishtabaḥ*, the Ark is opened and the congregation says Psalm 130 responsively (some say Psalm 130 before נִשְׁמַת כָּל חַי).

70 After *Barekhu*, the congregation says הַמֵּאִיר לָאָרֶץ or, if it is also Shabbat, הַכֹּל יוֹדוּךָ. The Amida for Yom Kippur is said; if also Shabbat, one says the additions for Shabbat. The *Shaliaḥ Tzibbur* repeats the Amida, adding *piyutim* before *Kedusha*. In all the services of the day, the *Kedusha* of Musaf (נַעֲרִיצְךָ) is said. In the fourth blessing, the congregation says זְכוֹר רַחֲמֶיךָ and *Viduy*.

71 The congregation says *Avinu Malkenu*, but not on Shabbat [רמ״א או״ח, תקפד:א]. This is followed by Full Kaddish. When the Torah is taken from the Ark, most

congregations say the "Thirteen Attributes of Mercy" and a special supplication, except on Shabbat.

72 Torah reading: Lev. 16:1–34. Six men are called up, seven on Shabbat. Maftir: Num. 29:7–11. Haftara: Is. 57:14–58:14 [שו״ע או״ח, תרכא: א].

73 The Haftara is followed by (*Yekum Purkan* on Shabbat, then) the prayers for the government and the State of Israel and *Yizkor*. It is customary for the rabbi to deliver a sermon prior to *Yizkor*. Some have the custom to leave the synagogue for *Yizkor*, if both their parents are still alive [גשר החיים, לא: ב]. One who is praying alone may still say *Yizkor* [גשר החיים, לב: א].

74 After *Yizkor*, the congregation says אַב הָרַחֲמִים and *Ashrei*, and the Torah scrolls are returned to the Ark. The *Shaliaḥ Tzibbur* for Musaf says a special prefatory prayer, הִנְנִי הֶעָנִי מִמַּעַשׂ ("Here am I, poor of deeds") and Half Kaddish.

75 If there is a Brit Mila, it takes place before *Ashrei* [משנ״ב, תרכא: ז], and the cup of wine or grape juice is given to one who need not fast and the infant [רמ״א או״ח, תרכא: ג].

76 Musaf: During the Repetition of the Amida, *piyutim* are said before *Kedusha*, culminating with וּנְתַנֶּה תֹּקֶף.

77 The fourth blessing in the Repetition of the Amida contains *Aleinu*. The Ark is opened, and the *Shaliaḥ Tzibbur* (and, in most communities, the entire congregation) kneels in prostration at the words וַאֲנַחְנוּ כּוֹרְעִים. This is followed by *piyutim* describing the Yom Kippur Temple service (in which the congregation's kneeling is repeated three or four additional times), reenacting the High Priest's public pronunciation of the ineffable name of God. Because one is forbidden to touch one's head against the bare stone floor when kneeling, one should place a piece of cloth or paper between one's head and the floor [רמ״א או״ח, קלא: ח].

78 The Kohanim say *Birkat Kohanim*.

79 After Musaf, the *Shaliaḥ Tzibbur* says Full Kaddish. *Ein Keloheinu* and *Aleinu* are not said.

80 Minḥa: Neither *Ashrei* nor וּבָא לְצִיּוֹן is said; rather, Minḥa commences with taking the Torah from the Ark [רמ״א או״ח, תרכב: א]. Torah reading: Lev. 18:1–30. The third *oleh* reads the Haftara – the book of Jonah, and Micah 7:18–20 [שו״ע או״ח, תרכב: ב]. After returning the Torah to the Ark, the *Shaliaḥ Tzibbur* says Half Kaddish. The Amida is identical to that of Shaḥarit, except that it is preceded by the verse beginning כִּי שֵׁם יהוה אֶקְרָא (Deut. 32:3). The Repetition of the Amida by the *Shaliaḥ Tzibbur* includes the *Kedusha* starting with נַעֲרִיצְךָ, *Viduy* and the paragraph relating to *Birkat Kohanim*. *Avinu Malkenu* is said, unless Yom Kippur

falls on Shabbat or time is running short, as the *Shaliaḥ Tzibbur*'s Repetition of *Ne'ila* must begin before sunset [משנ״ב, שם:יב].

81 *Ne'ila*: The congregation prays a fifth service on Yom Kippur, called *Ne'ila* ("Closing"), beginning shortly before sunset. The service commences as Minḥa for Shabbat and Yom Tov: *Ashrei*, וּבָא לְצִיּוֹן, Half Kaddish [רמ״א או״ח, תרכג:א]. The congregation says the Amida for *Ne'ila*; in the Amida the term כָּתְבֵנוּ ("inscribe us") in all its conjugations is changed to חָתְמֵנוּ ("seal us") [רמ״א או״ח, תרכג:ב]. In the last blessing, שִׂים שָׁלוֹם is said. In *Viduy*, instead of עַל חֵטְא, a long, heartfelt supplication is said.

82 The Ark is opened for the entire Repetition of the Amida, which includes the *Kedusha* starting with נַעֲרִיצְךָ, *Seliḥot*, an abridged form of *Viduy* and the paragraph relating to *Birkat Kohanim*.

83 *Avinu Malkenu* is said, even when Yom Kippur falls on Shabbat; again the term כָּתְבֵנוּ is changed to חָתְמֵנוּ.

84 At the conclusion of *Ne'ila*, the *Shaliaḥ Tzibbur* leads the congregation in the responsive chanting of several verses, followed by Full Kaddish, and the sounding of the shofar [רמ״א, שם:ו]. It is customary to conclude with the singing of לְשָׁנָה הַבָּאָה בִּירוּשָׁלָיִם ("Next Year in Jerusalem").

85 Ma'ariv: as for weekdays. In the fourth blessing of the Amida, the paragraph of אַתָּה חוֹנַנְתָּנוּ (page 261) is said [שו״ע או״ח, תרכד:א]. Havdala is said over a cup of wine or grape juice, and the Havdala candle is lit from the flame that was lit before Yom Kippur began. No blessing is made over spices (unless it is also Motza'ei Shabbat) [שו״ע או״ח, תרכד:ד].

86 There is a custom to begin construction of the sukka on the night following Yom Kippur [רמ״א, שם:ה, ותרכה:א].

87 *Taḥanun* is not said between Yom Kippur and Sukkot [שו״ע או״ח, קלא:ז].

Erev Sukkot (14th of Tishrei)

88 The construction and decoration of the sukka should be completed before Sukkot begins. Likewise, the myrtle (*hadasim*) and willow (*aravot*) should be bound to the lulav before the holiday begins [שו״ע או״ח, תרנא:א].

89 When Sukkot falls on Thursday and Friday, each household must prepare an *Eiruv Tavshilin* (page 759); this makes it permissible to prepare food on Friday for the Shabbat meals [שו״ע או״ח, תקכז].

First days of Sukkot (15th–16th of Tishrei)

90 Candle lighting: Two blessings are said: (1) לְהַדְלִיק נֵר שֶׁל יוֹם טוֹב and (2) שֶׁהֶחֱיָנוּ. When Sukkot eve falls on Friday night, the conclusion of the first blessing is: לְהַדְלִיק נֵר שֶׁל שַׁבָּת וְשֶׁל יוֹם טוֹב (page 305).

91 Ma'ariv: for Shabbat and Yom Tov (page 335). Many congregations say the special verse for Yom Tov (וַיְדַבֵּר מֹשֶׁה), before saying the Amida for Yom Tov (page 771). This is followed by Full Kaddish, *Aleinu*, Mourner's Kaddish, Psalm 27 and Mourner's Kaddish. It is customary to conclude with the singing of Adon Olam or Yigdal.

92 When Sukkot eve falls on Friday night, Ma'ariv for Shabbat is preceded by the last two psalms of Kabbalat Shabbat: מִזְמוֹר שִׁיר לְיוֹם הַשַּׁבָּת and יהוה מָלָךְ, גֵּאוּת לָבֵשׁ (page 325). בַּמֶּה מַדְלִיקִין is omitted. וְשָׁמְרוּ (page 345) precedes the Yom Tov Amida, which is said with additions for Shabbat. After the Amida, the congregation says וַיְכֻלּוּ הַשָּׁמַיִם, and the *Shaliaḥ Tzibbur* says the abbreviated Repetition of the Amida as is customary on Shabbat eve [שו״ע או״ח, תרמב:א].

93 When the eve of the second day falls on Motza'ei Shabbat, the congregation adds the paragraph וַתּוֹדִיעֵנוּ in the middle section of the Amida.

94 Upon returning home, one enters the sukka. Some say the *Ushpizin* (page 767). When saying the Kiddush for Yom Tov on the first night, the blessing לֵישֵׁב בַּסֻּכָּה ("to dwell in the sukka") precedes the blessing שֶׁהֶחֱיָנוּ. On the second night, the blessing שֶׁהֶחֱיָנוּ is said prior to the blessing לֵישֵׁב בַּסֻּכָּה [שו״ע או״ח, תרסא:א]; some say the blessings in the same order as on the first night. [משנ״ב, שם:ב] When Sukkot eve falls on Friday night, Kiddush is said with additions for Shabbat. When the second night of Sukkot falls on Motza'ei Shabbat, the two blessings for Havdala are inserted prior to the blessing שֶׁהֶחֱיָנוּ; thus the order of blessings is: wine, Kiddush, flame, Havdala, שֶׁהֶחֱיָנוּ, sukka (pages 761–763) [שו״ע או״ח, תרמג:א]. In *Birkat HaMazon*, one adds יַעֲלֶה וְיָבוֹא (page 985).

95 Shaḥarit: for Shabbat and Yom Tov (page 399). The *Shaliaḥ Tzibbur* for Shaḥarit begins from the words הָאֵל בְּתַעֲצוּמוֹת עֻזֶּךָ (page 449). After *Barekhu*, the congregation says הַמֵּאִיר לָאָרֶץ or, if it is also Shabbat, הַכֹּל יוֹדוּךָ. The Amida for Yom Tov is said (page 771); if also Shabbat, one says the additions for Shabbat.

96 After the *Shaliaḥ Tzibbur* repeats the Amida, the congregation takes the lulav and says the blessing עַל נְטִילַת לוּלָב. On the first day the lulav is taken, the blessing שֶׁהֶחֱיָנוּ is also said (page 731). On Shabbat, one does not take the lulav [שו״ע או״ח, תרמד:א; שם, תרסב:א–ב]. Hallel is said, and some congregations say *Hoshanot* after Hallel. This is followed by Full Kaddish and taking the Torah from the Ark.

Some congregations precede taking the Torah from the Ark with the Daily Psalm and Psalm 27, followed by the Mourner's Kaddish. Most congregations say the "Thirteen Attributes of Mercy" and a special supplication (page 501), except on Shabbat.

97 Torah Reading: first day and second day – page 1126. Maftir and Haftarot – pages 1152–1154 [שו״ע או״ח, תרנט: א, תרסב: ג].

98 The Haftara is followed by (*Yekum Purkan* on Shabbat, then) the prayers for the government and the State of Israel. The *Shaliaḥ Tzibbur* says יָהּ אֵלִי וְגוֹאֲלִי (page 805) (except when Sukkot falls on Shabbat), the congregation says *Ashrei*, and the Torah scrolls are returned to the Ark. The *Shaliaḥ Tzibbur* says Half Kaddish.

99 Musaf: for Festivals (page 807). If also Shabbat, one says the additions for Shabbat. During the Repetition of the Amida, the Kohanim say *Birkat Kohanim.* After the Repetition, the congregation takes the lulav, the Ark is opened and one Torah scroll is taken out. The *Shaliaḥ Tzibbur* leads the congregation in saying the *Hoshanot,* while making a circuit around the *bima* (page 853) [שו״ע או״ח, תרס: א]. On Shabbat, the Ark is opened, and the special *Hoshanot* for Shabbat, אוֹם נְצוּרָה and כְּהוֹשַׁעְתָּ אָדָם (page 857), are said [שו״ע, שם: ג]. The Torah scroll is returned to the Ark, and the *Shaliaḥ Tzibbur* says Full Kaddish. This is followed by *Ein Keloheinu,* the Rabbis' Kaddish, *Aleinu,* Mourner's Kaddish, the Daily Psalm, Psalm 27, Mourner's Kaddish, *Anim Zemirot,* Mourner's Kaddish and Adon Olam.

100 Minḥa: for Shabbat and Yom Tov. When Sukkot falls on Shabbat, the Torah is taken from the Ark and the beginning of וְזֹאת הַבְּרָכָה (page 1110) is read. After returning the Torah to the Ark, the *Shaliaḥ Tzibbur* says Half Kaddish, and the congregation says the Amida for Yom Tov (page 771), with additions for Shabbat.

Ḥol HaMo'ed Sukkot

101 During Shaḥarit, Minḥa and Ma'ariv, יַעֲלֶה וְיָבוֹא is added to the seventeenth blessing of the Amida (רְצֵה). It is also added during *Birkat HaMazon* (page 985) [שו״ע או״ח, תצ: ב]. If one forgets to say יַעֲלֶה וְיָבוֹא in its proper place, see law 422.

102 The traditional Ashkenazi practice is to wear tefillin during Shaḥarit until the recitation of Hallel. However, some congregations follow the Sephardi custom, in which tefillin are not worn on Ḥol HaMo'ed; this is also the practice in Israel [שו״ע ורמ״א או״ח, לא: ב].

103 First Evening of Ḥol HaMo'ed: Ma'ariv for weekdays (page 243). אַתָּה חוֹנַנְתָּנוּ is added in the fourth blessing of the Amida. Havdala is said in the sukka (unless Ḥol HaMo'ed begins on Friday night). No blessing is made over spices or a flame

(unless Ḥol HaMo'ed begins on Saturday night), but one says the blessing לֵישֵׁב בַּסֻּכָּה before drinking (page 725).

104 Shaharit: for weekdays. After the *Shaliaḥ Tzibbur* repeats the Amida, the congregation takes the lulav and says the blessing עַל נְטִילַת לוּלָב [שו״ע או״ח, תרסב: א]. Hallel is said, and some congregations say *Hoshanot* after Hallel instead of after Musaf. This is followed by Full Kaddish.

105 Torah Reading: Pages 1155–1157. Four men are called up. Each day's reading is nine verses long. For each of the first three *aliyot,* one reads three verses. The fourth *oleh* goes back to the beginning and reads the first six verses a second time [רמ״א או״ח, תרסג: א].

106 After the Torah reading, Half Kaddish is said, the Torah is returned to the Ark, and *Ashrei* and וּבָא לְצִיּוֹן are said. The *Shaliaḥ Tzibbur* then says Half Kaddish.

107 Musaf: for Festivals (page 807). The *Kedusha* for weekdays is said; no *Birkat Kohanim* is said. After the Repetition of the Amida, the congregation takes the lulav, the Ark is opened and one Torah scroll is taken out. The *Shaliaḥ Tzibbur* leads the congregation in saying the *Hoshanot* of the day (see table on page 853), while making a circuit around the *bima.* The Torah scroll is returned to the Ark, and the *Shaliaḥ Tzibbur* says Full Kaddish. This is followed by *Aleinu* (page 181), and the conclusion of the weekday service.

Shabbat Ḥol HaMo'ed Sukkot

108 Ma'ariv for Shabbat is preceded by Psalms 92 and 93: מִזְמוֹר שִׁיר לְיוֹם הַשַּׁבָּת and יהוה מָלָךְ, גֵּאוּת לָבֵשׁ (page 325). בַּמֶּה מַדְלִיקִין is not said. The Amida for Shabbat is said with the addition of יַעֲלֶה וְיָבוֹא [שו״ע או״ח, תרסג: ב]. The conclusion of Ma'ariv is as for Shabbat (pages 359–371).

109 Shaharit: for Shabbat (page 399). The Amida for Shabbat is said with the addition of יַעֲלֶה וְיָבוֹא [שם]. Hallel is said, and some congregations say *Hoshanot* after Hallel instead of after Musaf. This is followed by Full Kaddish, the reading of *Kohelet* (page 1203) and Mourner's Kaddish [רמ״א או״ח, תצ: ט].

110 Torah Reading: page 1159. Maftir: Reading for the fourth *aliya* of the appropriate day (pages א1155–1159). Haftara: page א1159 [שו״ע או״ח, תרסג: ג]. In the concluding blessing after the Haftara, one says מְקַדֵּשׁ הַשַּׁבָּת וְיִשְׂרָאֵל וְהַזְּמַנִּים [משנ״ב, שם: ט].

111 The Haftara is followed by (*Yekum Purkan* on Shabbat, then) the prayers for the government and the State of Israel. *Ashrei* is said and the Torah scrolls are returned to the Ark. The *Shaliaḥ Tzibbur* says Half Kaddish.

112 Musaf: for Festivals, with additions for Shabbat (page 807). However, אַדִּיר אַדִּירֵנוּ

is not added to *Kedusha*, and *Birkat Kohanim* is not said. After the Repetition of the Amida, the Ark is opened, no Torah scroll is taken out, and the special *Hoshanot* for Shabbat, אוֹם נְצוּרָה and כְּהוֹשַׁעְתָּ אָדָם (page 857), are said. The Ark is closed, and the *Shaliaḥ Tzibbur* says Full Kaddish. This is followed by *Ein Keloheinu* (page 557) and the conclusion of Musaf, as for Shabbat.

113 Minḥa: for Shabbat (page 595). The Torah is taken from the Ark and the beginning of וְזֹאת הַבְּרָכָה (page 1161) is read. After returning the Torah to the Ark, the *Shaliaḥ Tzibbur* says Half Kaddish, and the congregation says the Amida for Shabbat with the addition of יַעֲלֶה וְיָבוֹא.

114 Motza'ei Shabbat: Ma'ariv for Motza'ei Shabbat is said. After the Amida, וִיהִי נֹעַם is omitted, and the *Shaliaḥ Tzibbur* says Full Kaddish. וְיִתֶּן לְךָ (page 703) is said [רמ״א אר״ח, רצה:ט].

Hoshana Raba (21st of Tishrei)

115 Shaḥarit: It is customary for the *Shaliaḥ Tzibbur* to wear a *kittel*. *Pesukei DeZimra* for Shabbat and Yom Tov is said, including Psalm 100 (מִזְמוֹר לְתוֹדָה, page 411). After אָז יָשִׁיר־מֹשֶׁה (page 441), prayers continue with Shaḥarit for weekdays (page 85) [שו״ע ורמ״א אר״ח, תרסד:א]. Some have the custom to open the Ark after *Yishtabaḥ*, and say Psalm 130 responsively (some say Psalm 130 before *Yishtabaḥ*). After the *Shaliaḥ Tzibbur* repeats the Amida, the congregation takes the lulav and says the blessing עַל נְטִילַת לוּלָב. Hallel is said, and some congregations say *Hoshanot* after Hallel instead of after Musaf. This is followed Full Kaddish.

116 While the Torah is taken from the Ark, the congregation says *Ein Kamokha* (page 499) [רמ״א, שם]. Most congregations say the "Thirteen Attributes of Mercy" and a special supplication (page 501). Torah Reading: page 1158. Some have the custom to read in the melody of *Yamim Nora'im*.

117 After the Torah reading, Half Kaddish is said, the Torah is returned to the Ark, and *Ashrei* and וּבָא לְצִיּוֹן are said. The *Shaliaḥ Tzibbur* says Half Kaddish.

118 Musaf: for Festivals (page 807). It is customary for the *Shaliaḥ Tzibbur* to wear a *kittel* [רמ״א, שם]. The *Kedusha* for Yom Tov is said, but *Birkat Kohanim* is not. After the Repetition of the Amida, the congregation takes the lulav, the Ark is opened and seven Torah scrolls are taken out to the *bima*. Many congregations have the custom of taking out all the Torah scrolls [רמ״א אר״ח, תרס:א]. The *Shaliaḥ Tzibbur* leads the congregation in saying the *Hoshanot* while making seven circuits around the *bima* (page 859) [רמ״א אר״ח, תרסד:א]. These are followed by special *piyutim* asking for rain. Then five willow branches (*aravot*) are taken

and beaten five times before the Torah scrolls are returned to the Ark (page 873). Some have the custom of beating the *aravot* after the *Shaliaḥ Tzibbur* says the Full Kaddish [רמ״א, שם:ו]. This is followed by *Ein Keloheinu,* Rabbis' Kaddish, *Aleinu,* Mourner's Kaddish, the Daily Psalm, Psalm 27 and Mourner's Kaddish.

Shemini Atzeret (22nd of Tishrei)

119 Candle lighting: Two blessings are said: (1) לְהַדְלִיק נֵר שֶׁל יוֹם טוֹב, and (2) שֶׁהֶחֱיָנוּ. When Shemini Atzeret eve falls on Friday night, the conclusion of the first blessing is: לְהַדְלִיק נֵר שֶׁל שַׁבָּת וְשֶׁל יוֹם טוֹב.

120 Ma'ariv: for Shabbat and Yom Tov. Many congregations say the special verse for Yom Tov (וַיְדַבֵּר מֹשֶׁה), before saying the Amida for Yom Tov (page 771). This is followed by Full Kaddish, *Aleinu,* Mourner's Kaddish, Psalm 27 and Mourner's Kaddish. It is customary to conclude with the singing of Adon Olam or Yigdal.

121 When Shemini Atzeret eve falls on Friday night, Ma'ariv is preceded by the last two psalms of Kabbalat Shabbat: מִזְמוֹר שִׁיר לְיוֹם הַשַּׁבָּת and יהוה מָלָךְ, גֵּאוּת לָבֵשׁ (page 325). בַּמֶּה מַדְלִיקִין is omitted. וְשָׁמְרוּ (page 345) precedes the Yom Tov Amida, which is said with additions for Shabbat. After the Amida, the congregation says וַיְכֻלּוּ הַשָּׁמַיִם, and the *Shaliaḥ Tzibbur* says the abbreviated Repetition of the Amida as is customary on Shabbat eve.

122 When Shemini Atzeret eve falls on Friday night, Kiddush for Yom Tov is said with additions for Shabbat.

123 Outside Israel the traditional Ashkenazi practice is to sit in the sukka on Shemini Atzeret, without saying the blessing לֵישֵׁב בַּסֻּכָּה [שו״ע או״ח, תרסח:א]. However, some follow the Ḥasidic custom, according to which Kiddush is said in the sukka on Shemini Atzeret eve, while the rest of the meals are eaten in the house.

124 Shaḥarit: for Shabbat and Yom Tov (page 399). The *Shaliaḥ Tzibbur* for Shaḥarit begins from the words הָאֵל בְּתַעֲצוּמוֹת עֻזֶּךָ (page 449). After *Barekhu,* the congregation says הַמֵּאִיר לָאָרֶץ or, if it is also Shabbat, הַכֹּל יוֹדוּךָ. The Amida for Yom Tov is said (page 771); if also Shabbat, one says the additions for Shabbat. The Repetition of the Amida is followed by Hallel and Full Kaddish. On Shabbat, *Kohelet* (page 1203) is read, followed by the Mourner's Kaddish.

125 While the Torah is taken from the Ark, most congregations say the "Thirteen Attributes of Mercy" and a special supplication (page 501), except on Shabbat.

126 Torah Reading: page 1143. Maftir and Haftara: page 1160 [שו״ע או״ח, תרסח:ב].

127 The Haftara is followed by (*Yekum Purkan* on Shabbat, then) the prayers for the government and the State of Israel, *Yizkor* (page 797), and אַב הָרַחֲמִים [משנ״ב, שם:טו].

The congregation says *Ashrei* (page 529), and the Torah scrolls are returned to the Ark. The *Shaliaḥ Tzibbur* says Half Kaddish.

128 Musaf for Festivals (page 807) is said. If also Shabbat, one says the additions for Shabbat. It is customary for the *Shaliaḥ Tzibbur* to wear a *kittel*. In most congregations, the announcement to begin saying מַשִּׁיב הָרְוּחַ וּמוֹרִיד הַגֶּשֶׁם precedes the silent recitation of the Amida [רמ״א או״ח, קיד:ב]. The Repetition of the Amida begins with the opening of the Ark, and the *Shaliaḥ Tzibbur* says the Prayer for Rain (page 847). The Kohanim say *Birkat Kohanim*. After the Repetition, the service continues with Full Kaddish, and the conclusion of the service is as for Shabbat and Yom Tov (page 555).

▸ LAWS OF מַשִּׁיב הָרְוּחַ

129 One begins saying מַשִּׁיב הָרְוּחַ in Musaf of Shemini Atzeret and continues until Musaf of the first day of Pesaḥ [שו״ע או״ח, קיד:א].

130 If one forgets to say מַשִּׁיב הָרְוּחַ in its proper place but realizes before beginning the words of the blessing מְחַיֵּה הַמֵּתִים, one should immediately say מַשִּׁיב הָרְוּחַ and continue with the rest of the blessing. If one realizes the omission immediately after completing the blessing מְחַיֵּה הַמֵּתִים, one should say מַשִּׁיב הָרְוּחַ and continue with the following blessing. If one realizes the omission after beginning the words אַתָּה קָדוֹשׁ, one must repeat the Amida from the beginning [שו״ע או״ח, קיד:ו].

131 If one forgets to say מַשִּׁיב הָרְוּחַ but says מוֹרִיד הַטָּל (as is the custom in Israel, and that of *Nusaḥ Sepharad*, in the spring and summer months), one need not repeat the Amida [שו״ע או״ח, קיד:ה]. If there is doubt whether one said מַשִּׁיב הָרְוּחַ, the presumption is as follows: within the first thirty days from *Shemini Atzeret*, one should assume that one forgot to say מַשִּׁיב הָרְוּחַ. After thirty days, one should assume that one said מַשִּׁיב הָרְוּחַ [שו״ע או״ח, קיד:ח].

132 Minḥa: for Shabbat and Yom Tov. When Shemini Atzeret falls on Shabbat, the Torah is taken from the Ark and the beginning of וְזֹאת הַבְּרָכָה (page 1110) is read. After returning the Torah to the Ark, the *Shaliaḥ Tzibbur* says Half Kaddish, and the congregation says the Amida for Yom Tov (page 771).

Simḥat Torah (23rd of Tishrei)

133 Candle lighting: Two blessings are said: (1) לְהַדְלִיק נֵר שֶׁל יוֹם טוֹב, and (2) שֶׁהֶחֱיָנוּ.

134 Ma'ariv: as for Shabbat and Yom Tov. Many congregations say the special verse for Yom Tov (וַיְדַבֵּר מֹשֶׁה), before saying the Amida for Yom Tov (page 771). If Shemini Atzeret fell on Shabbat, the congregation adds the paragraph וַתּוֹדִיעֵנוּ in the middle section of the Amida.

135 After Full Kaddish, the verses of אַתָּה הָרְאֵתָ are said responsively (page 789). The ark is opened, all of the Torah scrolls are taken from the Ark, and the seven *Hakafot* are performed amid joyous singing and dancing. After completion of seven *Hakafot*, all of the Torah scrolls except one are returned to the Ark. The *Shaliaḥ Tzibbur* takes the remaining scroll, and leads the congregation in saying שְׁמַע יִשְׂרָאֵל and the rest of the ceremony for taking the Torah from the Ark (page 503) [רמ״א או״ח, תרסט: א].

136 Torah reading: Customs differ. Most congregations read the beginning of וְזֹאת הַבְּרָכָה (page 1110) and three (in some congregations, five) are called up. It is customary for the Reader to use the melody of *Yamim Nora'im*. After the completion of the reading, the Torah is returned to the Ark (page 531). This is followed by *Aleinu* (page 563), and Mourner's Kaddish. It is customary to conclude with the singing of Adon Olam or Yigdal.

137 Kiddush for Yom Tov (page 761) is said. If Shemini Atzeret fell on Shabbat, the two blessings for Havdala (page 763) are inserted prior to the blessing שֶׁהֶחֱיָנוּ.

138 Shaḥarit: for Shabbat and Yom Tov. The *Shaliaḥ Tzibbur* for Shaḥarit begins from the words הָאֵל בְּתַעֲצוּמוֹת עֻזֶּךָ. After *Barekhu*, the congregation says הַמֵּאִיר לָאָרֶץ. The Amida for Yom Tov is said (page 771). During the Repetition of the Amida, the Kohanim say *Birkat Kohanim*. This is followed by Hallel and Full Kaddish. The Ark is opened and the verses of אַתָּה הָרְאֵתָ (page 789) are said responsively. All of the Torah scrolls are taken from the Ark, and the seven *Hakafot* are performed amid joyous singing and dancing.

139 Torah Reading: pages 1161–1167. The Torah reading is repeated, in cycles of five *aliyot*, until all males over thirteen have received an *aliya* [רמ״א או״ח, תרסט: א]. It is customary for children under 13 years to participate in an *aliya*, known as *Kol HaNe'arim*, in which multiple tallitot are spread to form a canopy over the children and the *oleh*. This is followed by the calling up of the *Ḥatan Torah*, for whom the final verses of the Torah are read. After the completion of the reading, it is customary that *Hagbaha* is performed with arms crossed, so that when the Torah is raised and the arms uncrossed, the lettering on the scroll faces outward toward the congregation. A second scroll is opened; the *Ḥatan Bereshit* is called up and the first verses of *Bereshit* are read [שו״ע ורמ״א או״ח, תרסט: א]. It is customary to pause in the reading for the congregation to read aloud וַיְהִי־עֶרֶב וַיְהִי בֹקֶר for each day of Creation, and to read aloud the last three verses, starting with וַיְכֻלּוּ הַשָּׁמַיִם. This is followed by Half Kaddish. A third scroll is opened for Maftir. The Haftara is the beginning of the book of Joshua (page 1166) [שם].

140 After the Haftara, the prayers for the government and the State of Israel are

said. The congregation says *Ashrei*, and the Torah scrolls are returned to the Ark. The *Shaliaḥ Tzibbur* says Half Kaddish.

141 Musaf: for Festivals (page 807). The Kohanim do not say *Birkat Kohanim*, because they are assumed to have drunk alcohol. The Repetition of the Amida is followed by Full Kaddish, and the conclusion of the service is as for Shabbat and Yom Tov (page 555).

142 Minḥa: for Shabbat and Yom Tov.

Motza'ei Sukkot (24th of Tishrei)

143 Ma'ariv: for weekdays. In the fourth blessing of the Amida, the paragraph of אַתָּה חוֹנַנְתָּנוּ is said (page 261). Havdala is said over a cup of wine or grape juice; no blessing is made over spices or a flame [שו״ע או״ח, תרצ״א:א].

Shabbat Bereshit (Mevarkhim Ḥodesh Marḥeshvan)

144 On the Shabbat preceding Rosh Ḥodesh Marḥeshvan (and each subsequent Rosh Ḥodesh), *Birkat HaḤodesh* (page 527) is said after the prayers for the government and the State of Israel. This is followed immediately by *Ashrei*. אַב הָרַחֲמִים is generally omitted on the Shabbat preceding Rosh Ḥodesh, except those preceding Rosh Ḥodesh Iyar and Sivan.

145 Minḥa: It is customary to say Psalm 104 (בָּרְכִי נַפְשִׁי) and the fifteen Songs of Ascents (page 629) after Minḥa on Shabbat, from *Shabbat Bereshit* until before *Shabbat HaGadol* [רמ״א או״ח, רצב:ב].

MARḤESHVAN

▸ LAWS OF BAHAB (בה״ב)

146 Some have the custom to say special *Seliḥot* after the Repetition of the Amida of Shaḥarit on the first Monday, the first Thursday and the second Monday of Marḥeshvan. Historically, these days were dedicated to fasting to atone for overstepping halakhic limits during the celebration of the Yom Tov. This custom is also observed on the first Monday, the first Thursday and the second Monday of Iyar [שו״ע ורמ״א או״ח, תצב:א].

KISLEV

4th–5th of December

147 In most years, during Ma'ariv on the evening of the 4th of December, one begins to say וְתֵן טַל וּמָטָר לִבְרָכָה in the ninth blessing of the Amida. In the year preceding a civil leap year, one begins to say וְתֵן טַל וּמָטָר לִבְרָכָה one day later, on the night of the 5th of December [שו״ע או״ח, קיז: א].

148 If one forgets to say וְתֵן טַל וּמָטָר לִבְרָכָה in its proper place but realizes before saying God's name in the ninth blessing (מְבָרֵךְ הַשָּׁנִים), one should immediately say וְתֵן טַל וּמָטָר לִבְרָכָה and continue with the rest of the blessing. If one realizes the omission after completing the blessing מְבָרֵךְ הַשָּׁנִים, one should say וְתֵן טַל וּמָטָר לִבְרָכָה prior to the words כִּי אַתָּה שׁוֹמֵעַ in the sixteenth blessing (שׁוֹמֵעַ תְּפִלָּה). If one realizes the omission after beginning the seventeenth blessing (רְצֵה), one must repeat the Amida from the beginning of the ninth blessing (מְבָרֵךְ הַשָּׁנִים). If one realizes the omission after completing the Amida, one must repeat the entire Amida [שו״ע או״ח, קיז: ה].

149 If there is doubt whether one properly said וְתֵן טַל וּמָטָר לִבְרָכָה, the presumption is as follows: within the first thirty days from December 4th (or 5th), one should assume that one forgot to say וְתֵן טַל וּמָטָר לִבְרָכָה. After thirty days, one should assume that one said וְתֵן טַל וּמָטָר לִבְרָכָה.

Ḥanukka (25th of Kislev–2nd of Tevet)

150 On Ḥanukka, עַל הַנִּסִּים is added to the Amida in Ma'ariv, Shaḥarit and Minḥa, as well as the second blessing of *Birkat HaMazon*. If one forgets to say עַל הַנִּסִּים, one does not repeat the Amida or *Birkat HaMazon* [שו״ע או״ח, תרפב: א].

151 It is customary to light Ḥanukka lights in the synagogue, either before or after Ma'ariv of each evening of Ḥanukka. The procedure is identical to that of lighting in the home, as described below, except that the lights should be placed along the southern wall of the synagogue.

152 After Ma'ariv, Ḥanukka lights are lit in the home. On the first night, three blessings are said: (1) לְהַדְלִיק נֵר שֶׁל חֲנֻכָּה, (2) שֶׁעָשָׂה נִסִּים ("Who performed miracles") and (3) שֶׁהֶחֱיָנוּ (page 897). On subsequent nights, only the first two blessings are said [שו״ע או״ח, תרעו: א]. When adding lights each night, the new light is always added to the left. The newest candle is lit first, and one then lights the rest of the lights from left to right.

153 The lights must burn for at least half an hour after nightfall [שו״ע או״ח, תרעב: ב; משנ״ב, שם: ד]. If one did not light during this time, one is permitted to light any time before daybreak. In such a case, one says the appropriate blessings when lighting, but only if other household members are awake [שו״ע, שם; משנ״ב, שם: יא].

154 Most have the custom for each member of the household to light separately, but the head of household may light one menora for the entire family [שו״ע ורמ״א או״ח, תרעא: ב].

155 Women are obligated to light Ḥanukka lights [שו״ע או״ח, תרעה: ג]. Hence, a woman can light for herself, on behalf of her household, and on behalf of an adult male [משנ״ב, שם: ט].

156 The menora is generally lit indoors, but near a window, so that the lights are visible to the general public as well [שו״ע או״ח, תרעה: ז].

157 After the lighting, it is customary to sing הַנֵּרוֹת הַלָּלוּ and מָעוֹז צוּר (pages 899–901) [שו״ע או״ח, תרעו: ד].

158 Shaḥarit: It is customary to light the menora in the synagogue without a blessing before the prayers begin. Shaḥarit for weekdays is said. עַל הַנִּסִּים is added to the Amida, as discussed above. After the Repetition of the Amida, *Taḥanun* is omitted and the *Shaliaḥ Tzibbur* leads the congregation in saying Full Hallel (page 733) [שו״ע או״ח, תרפג: א]. This is followed by Half Kaddish and taking the Torah from the Ark (page 159).

159 Torah reading: pages 1116–1121. Three men are called up [שו״ע או״ח, תרפד: א]. The Torah is returned to the Ark, *Ashrei* and וּבָא לְצִיּוֹן are said, but לַמְנַצֵּחַ is omitted, and the *Shaliaḥ Tzibbur* says Full Kaddish. This is followed by *Aleinu*, Mourner's Kaddish, the Daily Psalm, Psalm 30 (page 59), and Mourner's Kaddish.

▸ SHABBAT ḤANUKKA

160 Ḥanukka lights are lit at home prior to lighting the Shabbat candles. Care must be taken that the lights, though lit prior to sunset, will burn for at least half an hour after dark [שו״ע או״ח, תרעט: א]. Ḥanukka lights are lit in the synagogue after Minḥa [משנ״ב, שם: ג].

161 Ma'ariv: for Shabbat and Yom Tov. עַל הַנִּסִּים is added to the Amida (see law 150).

162 Shaḥarit: for Shabbat and Yom Tov. The Repetition of the Amida is followed by Hallel [שו״ע או״ח, תרפג: א]. Two Torah scrolls are taken from the Ark, three if Shabbat falls on Rosh Ḥodesh Tevet.

163 Torah Reading: Seven men are called up for the portion of the week (usually מִקֵּץ). Maftir: The appropriate day's reading from pages 1116–1121. Haftara: Zech.

2:14–4:7. If there are two Shabbatot during Ḥanukka, on the second Shabbat the Haftara is 1 Kings 7:40–50 [שו״ע או״ח, תרפד:ב]. If Shabbat falls on Rosh Ḥodesh Tevet, three Torah scrolls are taken from the Ark. Six men are called up for the portion of the week, and the seventh reads the Musaf offerings for Shabbat and Rosh Ḥodesh (page 1111) from the second scroll [שו״ע, שם:ג]. Half Kaddish is said. For Maftir, the portion for Ḥanukka is read from the third scroll.

164 The rest of the service continues as for Shabbat, except that אַב הָרַחֲמִים is omitted and עַל הַנִּסִּים is added to the Musaf Amida [שו״ע או״ח, תרפב:ב; תרפג:א].

165 Minḥa: עַל הַנִּסִּים is added to the Amida for Minḥa, and צִדְקָתְךָ is omitted [שם].

▸ MOTZA'EI SHABBAT ḤANUKKA

166 Ma'ariv: for weekdays. In the fourth blessing of the Amida, the paragraph of אַתָּה חוֹנַנְתָּנוּ (page 261) is said. עַל הַנִּסִּים is added to the eighteenth blessing of the Amida. In the synagogue, the Ḥanukka lights are lit prior to making Havdala [שו״ע או״ח, תרפא:ב]. In the home, Havdala is made first [ערוה״ש, שם:ב].

TEVET

Rosh Ḥodesh Tevet

167 On a weekday, Shaharit for weekdays is said. יַעֲלֶה וְיָבוֹא and עַל הַנִּסִּים are added to the Amida. After the Repetition of the Amida, *Taḥanun* is omitted and the *Shaliaḥ Tzibbur* leads the congregation in saying Hallel. This is followed by Full Kaddish.

168 Torah reading: Two scrolls are removed from the Ark. Three men are called up to the first scroll, and Num. 28:1–15 (page 1111) is read. A fourth man is called up to the second scroll, from which the appropriate day's reading from Num. 7:42–53 (page 1119) is read. The *Shaliaḥ Tzibbur* then says Half Kaddish. Prayers continue as on a regular Rosh Ḥodesh, except that עַל הַנִּסִּים is added to the Amida of Musaf.

169 On Shabbat Rosh Ḥodesh Tevet, Shaḥarit for Shabbat and Yom Tov is said. יַעֲלֶה וְיָבוֹא and עַל הַנִּסִּים are added to the Amida. The recitation of Hallel is followed by Full Kaddish.

170 Torah reading: See law 163. Prayers continue as on a regular Shabbat Rosh Ḥodesh, except that עַל הַנִּסִּים is added to the Amida of Musaf.

Asara B'Tevet (10th of Tevet)

171 This fast commemorates the besieging of Jerusalem by Nebuchadnezzar, which led to the capture of the city and the destruction of the First Temple (Ezek. 24:1–2).

172 The fast begins at dawn (see laws 47–48) [שו״ע או״ח, תקנ:ב].

173 Shaḥarit: for weekdays. During the Repetition of the Amida, the *Shaliaḥ Tzibbur* says עֲנֵנוּ between the seventh and eighth blessings (page 117) [שו״ע או״ח, תקסו:א]. This is followed by *Seliḥot, Avinu Malkenu* and *Taḥanun* [ערוה״ש או״ח, תקסו:ח].

174 Torah Reading: page 1112 (see law 50) [שו״ע או״ח, תקסו:א].

175 Minḥa: for weekdays, except that after *Ashrei* and Half Kaddish, the Torah is read. The reading is the same as that of the morning. The third *oleh* reads the Haftara (page 1112) [רמ״א, שם]. After the Torah is returned to the Ark, the *Shaliaḥ Tzibbur* says Half Kaddish, and continues with the rest of Minḥa for weekdays.

176 During the silent recitation of the Amida, those who are fasting say עֲנֵנוּ as part of the sixteenth blessing, שׁוֹמֵעַ תְּפִלָּה (page 223). During the Repetition of the Amida, the *Shaliaḥ Tzibbur* says עֲנֵנוּ between the seventh and eighth blessings, as in the morning (page 217). After the eighteenth blessing (מודים), the *Shaliaḥ Tzibbur* says the paragraph relating to *Birkat Kohanim* (page 229). For the final blessing of the Amida, שִׂים שָׁלוֹם is said instead of שָׁלוֹם רָב. After the Amida, the congregation says *Avinu Malkenu*. This is followed by *Taḥanun*, Full Kaddish and *Aleinu*. If the fast falls on Friday, *Avinu Malkenu* and *Taḥanun* are omitted [משנ״ב, תקנ:יא].

SHEVAT

Tu BiShevat (15th of Shevat)

177 *Taḥanun* is omitted [שו״ע או״ח, קלא:ו].

178 It is customary to eat many different fruits, especially fruits that are among the Seven Species associated with the land of Israel, namely, grapes, figs, pomegranates, olives and dates [משנ״ב, שם:לא].

Shabbat Parashat Shekalim (Mevarkhim Ḥodesh Adar)

179 Torah reading: On the Shabbat preceding Rosh Ḥodesh Adar (in a leap year,

Rosh Ḥodesh Adar II), a second Torah scroll is taken from the Ark. From it, *Parashat Shekalim*, the first of four special Maftir-Haftara units (ארבע פרשיות), is read. Maftir: Ex. 30:11–16. Haftara: II Kings 12:1–17 [שו״ע או״ח, תרפה: א]. אב הָרַחֲמִים is omitted.

180 When Rosh Ḥodesh Adar (in a leap year, Rosh Ḥodesh Adar II) falls on Shabbat, three Torah scrolls are taken from the Ark. Six men are called up to the first scroll and the portion of the week is read. A seventh man is called to the second scroll for the reading of Num. 28:9–15. Half Kaddish is said. Maftir (Ex. 30:11–16) is read from the third scroll. Haftara is II Kings 12:1–17 [שם]. אַב הָרַחֲמִים is omitted.

ADAR

Purim Katan (14th–15th of Adar I)

181 In a leap year, on the dates during Adar I corresponding to Purim and Shushan Purim, both *Taḥanun* and לַמְנַצֵּחַ are omitted [שו״ע או״ח, תרצז: א].

Shabbat Parashat Zakhor (Shabbat preceding Purim)

182 There is an affirmative Torah obligation to recall the actions of Amalek, in attacking the children of Israel after the exodus from Egypt [שו״ע או״ח, קלו: ו]. This mitzva is fulfilled on the Shabbat preceding Purim, when a second Torah scroll is taken from the Ark, from which *Parashat Zakhor* (Deut. 25:17–19), the second of the four special Maftir-Haftara units (ארבע פרשיות), is read. Haftara: I Sam. 15:2–34 [שו״ע או״ח, תרפה: ב]. אַב הָרַחֲמִים is omitted.

183 Because men and women are equally obligated to perform this *mitzva*, many congregations organize an additional reading of *Parashat Zakhor* for those who missed the first reading.

Fast of Esther (13th of Adar)

184 This fast commemorates Esther's fast prior to going to see King Ahasuerus without an invitation (Esther 4:15–16). Unlike other fast days, the fast of Esther is considered a custom, and anyone who experiences serious discomfort is permitted to eat or drink [רמ״א או״ח, תרפו: ב].

185 If the 13th of Adar falls on Shabbat, the fast is observed on the preceding Thursday [שו״ע, שם].

186 The fast begins at dawn (see laws 47–48).

187 Prayers as for the 10th of Tevet (see laws 173–176), except that *Avinu Malkenu* and *Taḥanun* are not said during Minḥa. However, if the 13th of Adar falls on Shabbat and the fast is moved back to Thursday, *Avinu Malkenu* and *Taḥanun* are said.

Purim (14th of Adar)

188 On Purim, עַל הַנִּסִּים is added to the Amida in Ma'ariv, Shaharit and Minḥa, as well as the second blessing of *Birkat HaMazon*. If one forgets to say עַל הַנִּסִּים, one does not repeat the Amida or *Birkat HaMazon* [שו״ע או״ח, תרצג:ב].

189 Ma'ariv: for weekdays. After recitation of the Amida, the *Shaliaḥ Tzibbur* says the Full Kaddish. The Reader of the Megilla says three blessings: (1) עַל מִקְרָא מְגִלָּה ("about reading the Megilla"), (2) שֶׁעָשָׂה נִסִּים ("Who performed miracles") and (3) שֶׁהֶחֱיָנוּ (page 903). The Megilla (page 1225) is read and the concluding blessing, הָרָב אֶת רִיבֵנוּ is said. The congregation says אֲשֶׁר הֵנִיא and concludes with a joyous singing of שׁוֹשַׁנַּת יַעֲקֹב. The *Shaliaḥ Tzibbur* leads the congregation in saying וְאַתָּה קָדוֹשׁ (page 697). On Motza'ei Shabbat, this is preceded by וִיהִי נֹעַם (page 695) [שו״ע או״ח, תרצג:א]. This is followed by Full Kaddish (omitting the sentence beginning תִּתְקַבַּל), and *Aleinu* [משנ״ב, שם:א]. On Motza'ei Shabbat, however, וְיִתֶּן לְךָ (page 703) and Havdala precede *Aleinu* [ערוה״ש, שם:ג].

190 Women are obligated to hear the reading of the Megilla [שו״ע או״ח, תרפט:א].

191 Shaharit: for weekdays. After the Repetition of the Amida, the *Shaliaḥ Tzibbur* says Half Kaddish and the Torah is taken from the Ark. The Torah reading (page 1122) is followed by Half Kaddish and returning the Torah to the Ark [שו״ע או״ח, תרצג:ד]. The Megilla reading (page 1225) is repeated, with the introductory blessings and the concluding blessing. אֲשֶׁר הֵנִיא is not said a second time, but שׁוֹשַׁנַּת יַעֲקֹב is. The congregation says *Ashrei* and וּבָא לְצִיּוֹן, followed by Full Kaddish, *Aleinu*, the Daily Psalm and Mourner's Kaddish.

192 On Purim day, one is commanded to fulfill the mitzvot of מתנות לאביונים (gifts to the poor – *tzedaka* given to at least two poor people) [שו״ע או״ח, תרצד:א]; משלוח מנות (sending at least two portions of food to one person) [שם, תרצה:ד]; and סעודת פורים (the Purim feast), at which one should drink "until he cannot distinguish between 'Cursed be Haman' and 'Blessed be Mordekhai'" [שם, תרצה:ב].

Shushan Purim (15th of Adar)

193 Both *Taḥanun* and לַמְנַצֵּחַ are omitted [שו״ע או״ח, תרצז:א].

Shabbat Parashat Para
(*Shabbat preceding Shabbat Parashat HaḤodesh*)

194 On the penultimate Shabbat of the month of Adar (Adar II in a leap year), a second Torah scroll is taken from the Ark, from which *Parashat Para* (Num. 19:1–22), the third of the four special Maftir-Haftara units, is read. Haftara: Ezek. 36:16–38 [שו״ע או״ח, תרפה: ג]. אַב הָרַחֲמִים is omitted.

Shabbat Parashat HaḤodesh (*Mevarkhim Ḥodesh Nisan*)

195 On the Shabbat preceding Rosh Ḥodesh Nisan, a second Torah scroll is taken from the Ark, from which *Parashat HaḤodesh* (Ex. 12:1–20), the fourth of the four special Maftir-Haftara units, is read. Haftara: Ezek. 45:16–46:18 [שו״ע או״ח, תרפה: ד]. אַב הָרַחֲמִים is omitted.

196 When Rosh Ḥodesh Nisan falls on Shabbat, three Torah scrolls are taken from the Ark. Six men are called up to the first scroll and the portion of the week is read. A seventh man is called to the second scroll for the reading of Num. 28:9–15. Half Kaddish is said. Maftir (Ex. 12:1–20) is read from the third scroll. Haftara is Ezek. 45:16–46:18. אַב הָרַחֲמִים is omitted.

NISAN

197 During the month of Nisan, *Taḥanun* is omitted on weekdays, and אַב הָרַחֲמִים (page 529) and צִדְקָתְךָ (page 623) are omitted on Shabbat [שו״ע ורמ״א או״ח, תכט: ב].

198 Many have the custom not to eat matza from Rosh Ḥodesh Nisan [משנ״ב, שם: יב]. Some refrain from eating matza from Purim.

199 One may not eat matza on Erev Pesaḥ [רמ״א או״ח, תעא: ב]. On Erev Pesaḥ it is permissible to eat certain kinds of matza which are not considered proper matza, such as matza made with juice instead of water, or which was cooked or fried after it was baked [שו״ע או״ח תעא, ב].

Shabbat HaGadol (*Shabbat preceding Pesaḥ*)

200 The Shabbat preceding Pesaḥ is known as *Shabbat HaGadol* [שו״ע או״ח, תל: א]. A special Haftara is said: Mal. 3:4–24. It is customary for the rabbi to deliver a sermon relating to Pesaḥ.

Erev Pesaḥ (14th of Nisan)

▸ **LAWS OF BEDIKAT ḤAMETZ**

201 As soon as possible after dark, one is required to do *Bedikat Ḥametz* in one's home (page 759) [שו״ע או״ח, תלא: א]. It is customary for a household member to hide ten pieces of *ḥametz* to be found during the search [רמ״א או״ח, תלב: ב]. Before beginning the search one says the blessing עַל בִּעוּר חָמֵץ [שו״ע או״ח, תלב: א]. The custom is to conduct the search at night by the light of a candle, but use of a flashlight is also permitted. If Pesaḥ falls on Motza'ei Shabbat, the search is made on Thursday night. Those who plan to be away on Pesaḥ should conduct the search the night before their departure, but without making a blessing. After completion of the search, one says כָּל חֲמִירָא (page 759), an Aramaic formula disclaiming one's ownership of any *ḥametz* the whereabouts of which are unknown.

202 Shaḥarit: for weekdays. מִזְמוֹר לְתוֹדָה and לַמְנַצֵּחַ are omitted [רמ״א או״ח, נא: ט].

203 First born males are required to fast (תענית בכורות), unless they attend a *siyum* (celebratory meal to mark the completion of a unit of Torah study), which is traditionally held immediately following Shaḥarit [שו״ע או״ח, תע: א].

204 One is forbidden from eating *ḥametz* from the end of the first third of the day [שו״ע או״ח, תמג: א]. There is a dispute between halakhic authorities whether the day is measured from daybreak to nightfall (Magen Avraham), or from sunrise to sunset (Vilna Gaon). One should follow local communal practice in this regard.

205 One is forbidden from owning *ḥametz* from the end of the first 5/12 of the day, by which time one should burn or otherwise destroy any *ḥametz* remaining in one's possession [שם]. One should say כָּל חֲמִירָא (page 759) a second time before the end of the first 5/12 of the day [שו״ע או״ח, תלד: ב].

206 If the first day of Pesaḥ falls on Thursday, each household must prepare an *Eiruv Tavshilin* (page 759); this makes it permissible to prepare food on Friday for the Shabbat meals [שו״ע או״ח, תקכז].

207 After Minḥa, some have the custom to say the biblical verses describing the sacrifice of the Pesaḥ lamb (Ex. 12:1–13) [משנ״ב או״ח, תעא: כב].

208 If Pesaḥ eve falls on Motza'ei Shabbat, the Fast of the Firstborn is held on the preceding Thursday [שו״ע ורמ״א או״ח, תע: ב]. *Bedikat Ḥametz* is done on Thursday night, and the *ḥametz* is burned (see law 205) on Friday morning without saying כָּל חֲמִירָא, while leaving enough *ḥametz* for Shabbat. On Shabbat morning, after eating the last of one's *ḥametz*, any leftovers must be given to a non-Jew or made inedible (e.g. by flushing it down the toilet), by the end of the first 5/12 of the day [שו״ע או״ח, תמד: ב].

209 If Erev Pesaḥ falls on Shabbat, for *Se'uda Shelishit* one can eat neither *ḥametz* nor matza (see laws 199, 204). Several solutions have been suggested: to eat matza which is not forbidden (see law 199) [שו״ע או״ח, תמד: א]; to eat the meal without bread [רמ״א, שם]; or to divide the morning meal in two, pausing in the middle and saying *Birkat HaMazon* in between [משנ״ב, שם: ח בשם הגר״א]. Some congregations hold morning services early, in order to allow ample time to eat the morning meal and destroy any *ḥametz* which is left.

Pesaḥ (15th–16th of Nisan)

210 Candle lighting: Two blessings are said: (1) לְהַדְלִיק נֵר שֶׁל יוֹם טוֹב, and (2) שֶׁהֶחֱיָנוּ. When Pesaḥ eve falls on Friday night, the conclusion of the first blessing is: לְהַדְלִיק נֵר שֶׁל שַׁבָּת וְשֶׁל יוֹם טוֹב.

211 Ma'ariv: for Shabbat and Yom Tov. The congregation says the special verse for Yom Tov (וַיְדַבֵּר מֹשֶׁה), before saying the Amida for Yom Tov (page 771). In some congregations Hallel is said after the Amida [שו״ע ורמ״א או״ח, תפז: ד]. This is followed by Full Kaddish, *Aleinu*, and Mourner's Kaddish. Kiddush is not said in the synagogue. It is customary to conclude with the singing of Adon Olam or Yigdal.

212 On the second night of Pesaḥ, one begins counting the Omer (page 285) [שו״ע או״ח, תפט: א]. Some have the custom to count the first night of the Omer at the second Seder. (See laws 221–224.)

213 When Pesaḥ eve falls on Friday night, Ma'ariv for Shabbat is preceded by the last two psalms of Kabbalat Shabbat: מִזְמוֹר שִׁיר לְיוֹם הַשַּׁבָּת and יהוה מָלָךְ, גֵּאוּת לָבֵשׁ (page 325). בַּמֶּה מַדְלִיקִין is omitted. וְשָׁמְרוּ and the special verse for Yom Tov (וַיְדַבֵּר מֹשֶׁה) (page 345) precede the Yom Tov Amida, which is said with additions for Shabbat. After the Amida, the congregation says וַיְכֻלּוּ הַשָּׁמַיִם, but the *Shaliaḥ Tzibbur* does not say the abbreviated Repetition of the Amida [שו״ע או״ח, תפז: א].

214 If either of the first two nights of Pesaḥ falls on Motza'ei Shabbat, the congregation adds the paragraph וַתּוֹדִיעֵנוּ in the middle section of the Amida on that night.

215 Shaḥarit: for Shabbat and Yom Tov (page 399). The *Shaliaḥ Tzibbur* for Shaḥarit begins from the words הָאֵל בְּתַעֲצֻמוֹת עֻזֶּךָ (page 449). After *Barekhu*, the congregation says הַמֵּאִיר לָאָרֶץ or, if it is also Shabbat, הַכֹּל יוֹדוּךָ. The Amida for Yom Tov is said (page 771); if also Shabbat, one says the additions for Shabbat. This is followed by Hallel, Full Kaddish and taking the Torah from the Ark. Most congregations say the "Thirteen Attributes of Mercy" and a special supplication (page 501), except on Shabbat.

216 Torah Reading: first day – page 1123; second day – page 1126. Five men are called up, seven on Shabbat. Maftir: page 1124. Haftara: first day – page 1125; second day – page 1128 [שו״ע או״ח, תפח: ג; שם, תצ: א].

217 The Haftara is followed by (*Yekum Purkan* on Shabbat, then) the prayers for the government and the State of Israel. The congregation says *Ashrei*, and the Torah scrolls are returned to the Ark. The *Shaliaḥ Tzibbur* says Half Kaddish.

218 Musaf: for Festivals (page 807). On Shabbat, one says the additions for Shabbat. It is customary for the *Shaliaḥ Tzibbur* to wear a *kittel*. The Repetition of the Amida begins with the opening of the Ark, and the *Shaliaḥ Tzibbur* says תפילת טל (page 841). From this point on, מַשִּׁיב הָרוּחַ is no longer said. The Kohanim say *Birkat Kohanim*. After the Repetition of the Amida, the *Shaliaḥ Tzibbur* says Full Kaddish, and the conclusion of the service is as for Shabbat and Yom Tov (page 555).

219 One ceases to say מַשִּׁיב הָרוּחַ in Musaf [שו״ע או״ח, תפח: ג]. Some have the custom to say it in the silent Amida [משנ״ב, תפח: יא]. If one erroneously says מַשִּׁיב הָרוּחַ in the spring and summer months, one must repeat the Amida. If one realizes the error after completing the blessing מְחַיֵּה הַמֵּתִים, one must repeat the Amida from the beginning [שו״ע או״ח, קיד: ג].

220 Minḥa: for Shabbat and Yom Tov. When Pesaḥ falls on Shabbat, the Torah is taken from the Ark and the beginning of the portion of the week is read. After returning the Torah to the Ark, the *Shaliaḥ Tzibbur* says Half Kaddish, and the congregation says the Amida for Yom Tov (page 771).

▸ LAWS OF SEFIRAT HAOMER

221 One counts the Omer for a given day after nightfall. The custom is to count standing up [שו״ע או״ח, תפט: א].

222 One who forgets to count at night may count prior to nightfall of the following day, although no blessing is said when counting during daylight hours [שם: ז].

223 One who forgets to count for an entire 24-hour period continues counting the Omer from the following day, but without the blessing [שם: ח].

224 Regarding customary practices during the Omer counting period, see law 251 below.

Ḥol HaMo'ed Pesaḥ

225 During Shaḥarit, Minḥa and Ma'ariv, יַעֲלֶה וְיָבוֹא is added to the seventeenth blessing of the Amida (רְצֵה). It is also added to *Birkat HaMazon* (page 985) [שו״ע או״ח, תצ: ב]. If יַעֲלֶה וְיָבוֹא is forgotten in the Amida, one should repeat the Amida, but if forgotten in *Birkat HaMazon*, one need not repeat it [שם].

226 The traditional Ashkenazi practice is to wear tefillin during Shaḥarit until the recitation of Hallel. However, some congregations follow the Sephardi custom,

in which tefillin are not worn on Ḥol HaMo'ed; this is also the practice in Israel [שו״ע ורמ״א או״ח, לא:ב].

227 First Evening of Ḥol HaMo'ed: Ma'ariv for weekdays (page 243) is said. In the fourth blessing of the Amida, the paragraph of אַתָּה חוֹנַנְתָּנוּ (page 261) is said. In the ninth blessing of the Amida (ברכת השנים), one begins to say וְתֵן בְּרָכָה, a practice which will continue until December 4th (or, in some years, December 5th) (see law 147). If one erroneously says וְתֵן טַל וּמָטָר לִבְרָכָה in the spring and summer months, one must repeat the Amida. If one realizes the error before completing the Amida, one must repeat the Amida from the beginning of ברכת השנים [שו״ע או״ח, קיז:ג]. In the seventeenth blessing of the Amida (רְצֵה), יַעֲלֶה וְיָבוֹא is added.

228 The Omer is counted prior to *Aleinu*. Havdala is said over a cup of wine or grape juice; no blessing is made over spices or a flame (except on Motza'ei Shabbat).

229 Shaḥarit: for weekdays. מִזְמוֹר לְתוֹדָה is omitted. After the Repetition of the Amida, the congregation says Half Hallel [שו״ע או״ח, תצ:ד]. The *Shaliaḥ Tzibbur* says Full Kaddish, and two Torah scrolls are taken from the Ark.

230 Torah Reading: pages 1129–1134. Four men are called up, the fourth *aliya* is read from the second scroll [שו״ע או״ח, תצ:ד–ה]. If the first day of Pesaḥ falls on Shabbat or Sunday, such that there is no Shabbat Ḥol HaMo'ed, the readings are as listed on pages 1129–1134. Otherwise, the portions of the first, second and fourth day are read on the weekdays of Ḥol HaMo'ed, as the portion for the third day is included in the reading for Shabbat Ḥol HaMo'ed.

231 After the Torah reading, Half Kaddish is said, the Torah is returned to the Ark, and *Ashrei* and וּבָא לְצִיּוֹן are said. The *Shaliaḥ Tzibbur* says Half Kaddish.

232 Musaf: for Festivals (page 807). The *Kedusha* for weekdays is said; *Birkat Kohanim* is omitted. After the Repetition of the Amida, the *Shaliaḥ Tzibbur* says Full Kaddish. This is followed by *Aleinu*, Mourner's Kaddish, the Daily Psalm, and Mourner's Kaddish.

Shabbat Ḥol HaMo'ed Pesaḥ

233 Ma'ariv for Shabbat is preceded by the last two psalms of Kabbalat Shabbat: מִזְמוֹר שִׁיר לְיוֹם הַשַּׁבָּת and יהוה מָלָךְ, גֵּאוּת לָבֵשׁ (page 325). בַּמֶּה מַדְלִיקִין is not said. The Amida for Shabbat is said with the addition of יַעֲלֶה וְיָבוֹא [שו״ע או״ח, תרסג:ב]. The rest of Ma'ariv is as for Shabbat (pages 359–371), with the counting of the Omer before *Aleinu*.

234 Shaḥarit: for Shabbat and Yom Tov (page 399). The Amida for Shabbat is said with the addition of יַעֲלֶה וְיָבוֹא. The Repetition of the Amida is followed by Half

Hallel, Full Kaddish, the reading of שיר השירים (page 1171) and Mourner's Kaddish [רמ״א או״ח, תצ:ט].

235 Torah Reading: Pages 1134–1136. Seven men are called up. Maftir: page 1134. Haftara: page 1136.

236 After the Haftara, the congregation says *Yekum Purkan*. This is followed by the prayers for the government and the State of Israel. *Ashrei* is said and the Torah scrolls are returned to the Ark. The *Shaliaḥ Tzibbur* says Half Kaddish.

237 Musaf: for Festivals with additions for Shabbat (page 807). However, אַדִּיר אַדִּירֵנוּ is not added to *Kedusha*, and *Birkat Kohanim* is not said. After the Repetition of the Amida, the *Shaliaḥ Tzibbur* says Full Kaddish. This is followed by *Ein Keloheinu* (page 557) and the conclusion of Musaf, as for Shabbat.

238 Minha: for Shabbat and Yom Tov (page 595). The Torah is removed from the Ark and the beginning of the portion of the week is read. After returning the Torah to the Ark, the *Shaliaḥ Tzibbur* says Half Kaddish, and the congregation says the Amida for Shabbat with the addition of יַעֲלֶה וְיָבוֹא.

239 Motza'ei Shabbat – Ma'ariv: After the Amida, וִיהִי נֹעַם is omitted, and the *Shaliaḥ Tzibbur* says Full Kaddish. וְיִתֶּן לְךָ (page 703) is said [רמ״א או״ח, רצה:ט].

Seventh and Eighth Days of Pesaḥ (21st–22nd of Nisan)

240 If the seventh day of Pesaḥ falls on Thursday, each household must prepare an *Eiruv Tavshilin* (page 759); this makes it permissible to prepare food on Friday for the Shabbat meals [שו״ע או״ח, תקכז].

241 Candle lighting: One blessing is said: לְהַדְלִיק נֵר שֶׁל יוֹם טוֹב (שֶׁהֶחֱיָנוּ is not said) [שו״ע או״ח, תצ:ו]. When Pesaḥ eve falls on Friday night, the conclusion of the first blessing is: לְהַדְלִיק נֵר שֶׁל שַׁבָּת וְשֶׁל יוֹם טוֹב.

242 Ma'ariv: for Shabbat and Yom Tov (page 335). The congregation says the special verse for Yom Tov (וַיְדַבֵּר מֹשֶׁה), before saying the Amida for Yom Tov (page 771). This is followed by Full Kaddish, the counting of the Omer, *Aleinu*, and Mourner's Kaddish. It is customary to conclude with the singing of Adon Olam or Yigdal.

243 When the eve of the seventh or eighth day falls on Friday night, Ma'ariv is preceded by the last two psalms of Kabbalat Shabbat: מִזְמוֹר שִׁיר לְיוֹם הַשַּׁבָּת and יהוה מָלָךְ, גֵּאוּת לָבֵשׁ (page 325). בַּמֶּה מַדְלִיקִין is omitted. וְשָׁמְרוּ (page 345) precedes the Yom Tov Amida, which is said with additions for Shabbat. After the Amida, the congregation says וַיְכֻלּוּ הַשָּׁמַיִם, and the *Shaliaḥ Tzibbur* says the abbreviated Repetition of the Amida as is customary on Shabbat eve [שו״ע או״ח, תרמב:א].

244 When the eve of the eighth day falls on Motza'ei Shabbat, the congregation adds the paragraph וַתּוֹדִיעֵנוּ in the middle section of the Amida. Similarly, in Kiddush, the two blessings for Havdala are inserted; thus the order of blessings is: wine, Kiddush, flame, Havdala (page 763).

245 Shaḥarit: for Shabbat and Yom Tov (page 399). The *Shaliaḥ Tzibbur* for Shaḥarit begins from the words הָאֵל בְּתַעֲצוּמוֹת עֻזֶּךָ (page 449). After *Barekhu*, the congregation says הַמֵּאִיר לָאָרֶץ or, if it is also Shabbat, הַכֹּל יוֹדוּךָ. The Amida for Yom Tov is said (page 771); if also Shabbat, one says the additions for Shabbat. This is followed by Half Hallel, Full Kaddish and, if also Shabbat, the reading of *Shir HaShirim* (page 1171) and the Mourner's Kaddish. Two Torah scrolls are removed from the Ark. Most congregations say the "Thirteen Attributes of Mercy" and a special supplication (page 501), except on Shabbat.

246 Torah Reading: seventh day – page 1137; eighth day – page 1144 (on Shabbat, begin on page 1143). Five men are called up, seven on Shabbat. Maftir: page 1140. Haftara, seventh day: page 1140; eighth day: page 1145.

247 The Haftara is followed by (*Yekum Purkan* on Shabbat, then) the prayers for the government and the State of Israel. On the eighth day, *Yizkor* (page 797) is said, followed by אַב הָרַחֲמִים. The *Shaliaḥ Tzibbur* says יָהּ אֵלִי וְגוֹאֲלִי (although most omit this if *Yizkor* was said), the congregation says *Ashrei*, and the Torah scrolls are returned to the Ark. The *Shaliaḥ Tzibbur* says Half Kaddish.

248 Musaf: for Festivals (page 807). If also Shabbat, one says the additions for Shabbat. The Kohanim say *Birkat Kohanim*. The *Shaliaḥ Tzibbur* says Full Kaddish. This is followed by *Ein Keloheinu* (page 557) and the conclusion of the service is as for Shabbat.

249 Minḥa: for Shabbat and Yom Tov. When the seventh or eighth day falls on Shabbat, the Torah is taken from the Ark and the beginning of the portion of the week is read. After the Torah is returned to the Ark, the *Shaliaḥ Tzibbur* says Half Kaddish, and the congregation says the Amida for Yom Tov (page 771).

Motza'ei Pesaḥ (23rd of Nisan)

250 Ma'ariv: for weekdays. In the fourth blessing of the Amida (page 261) אַתָּה חוֹנַנְתָּנוּ is said. Havdala is said, preferably over a cup of wine or grape juice (although some have a custom to say Havdala over beer); no blessing is made over spices or a flame (unless it is Motza'ei Shabbat) [שו״ע או״ח, תצא:א].

▸ LAWS OF THE SEFIRAT HAOMER PERIOD

251 During the period of counting the Omer, certain mourning rituals are observed:

one does not cut one's hair, shave, listen to music, or hold weddings and other parties [שו״ע ורמ״א או״ח, תצג א–ג]. Some permit shaving during this period. These practices commemorate a plague that killed twelve thousand pairs of students of Rabbi Akiva who, the Talmud says, did not honor one another properly. The Ashkenazi community intensified these mourning customs in the wake of the pogroms of the First Crusade, which took place in Iyar and Sivan in the year 1096 (4856).

252 Different communities observe these customs during different periods: (1) from the end of Pesaḥ to the 18th of Iyar (Lag BaOmer), (2) from the 1st of Iyar until the 3rd of Sivan, (3) during the entire period from the end of Pesaḥ until the 3rd of Sivan.

253 Beginning on the first Shabbat after Pesaḥ, it is customary, after Shabbat Minḥa, to study a single chapter of *Pirkei Avot* (pages 641–683). This practice continues through the Shabbat before Rosh HaShana [רמ״א או״ח רצב, ב].

254 On the Shabbat preceding Rosh Ḥodesh Iyar, אַב הָרַחֲמִים is said (see law 144).

IYAR

▸ LAWS OF BAHAB (בה״ב)

255 Some have the custom to say special *Seliḥot* on the first Monday, the first Thursday and the second Monday of Iyar (see law 146). If one of these days falls on Yom HaAtzma'ut or Pesaḥ Sheni, no *Seliḥot* are said.

Yom HaZikaron (4th of Iyar)

256 This day commemorates the Jews who gave their lives in defense of the Jewish settlement in the land of Israel, including soldiers of the Israel Defense Forces killed in the line of duty and civilians murdered in acts of terror. On Yom HaZikaron eve, a *yahrzeit* candle is lit and the Mourner's Kaddish is said by a bereaved parent, spouse or child. At the end of Shaharit, some congregations say special prayers (see pages 907–909).

257 Many communities hold special memorial ceremonies after Minḥa. These are generally planned to end at nightfall, when the celebrations of Yom HaAtzma'ut begin.

Yom HaAtzma'ut (5th of Iyar)

258 If the 5th of Iyar falls on Friday or Shabbat, Yom HaAtzma'ut is moved back to the preceding Thursday. If the 5th of Iyar falls on a Monday, Yom HaAtzma'ut is postponed to Tuesday.

259 On Yom HaAtzma'ut, the mourning customs of *Sefirat HaOmer* are suspended. It is permissible to cut one's hair, shave, attend parties, celebrate weddings and bar/bat mitzvas, and listen to music. The custom is to permit shaving and cutting one's hair before nightfall in honor of the holiday.

260 Ma'ariv: Customs differ (see pages 911–919). The service adopted by the Israeli Chief Rabbinate is as follows: selections from Psalms and other readings precede Ma'ariv for weekdays. It is customary for the *Shaliaḥ Tzibbur* to lead Ma'ariv using melodies associated with Yom Tov. After the Amida, the *Shaliaḥ Tzibbur* says Full Kaddish. Responsive readings and Psalm 126 to the tune of "*HaTikva*" follow. The service concludes with the counting of the Omer, *Aleinu*, Mourner's Kaddish and communal singing of אֲנִי מַאֲמִין.

261 Shaharit: *Pesukei DeZimra* as for Shabbat and Yom Tov, with the addition of מִזְמוֹר לְתוֹדָה (page 411). נִשְׁמַת is not said. After אָז יָשִׁיר (page 443), prayers continue with Shaharit for weekdays (page 85). The Repetition of the Amida by the *Shaliaḥ Tzibbur* is followed by Hallel and Half Kaddish. On a Thursday (see law 258,) the Torah is taken from the Ark and the appropriate section of the Torah is read. After the Torah reading, Half Kaddish is said. Haftara is said without blessings (page 921). The Prayer for the State of Israel (page 523) is said, followed by the Memorial Prayer for fallen soldiers (page 909). Shaharit continues as for weekdays (page 171). At the end of the service, the congregation sings אֲנִי מַאֲמִין (page 923).

262 *Taḥanun* is omitted during Shaharit and Minḥa on the 5th of Iyar, even if Yom HaAtzma'ut is celebrated on a different day.

Pesaḥ Sheni (14th of Iyar)

263 *Taḥanun* is omitted during Shaharit and Minḥa but not on Minha of the preceding day.

Lag BaOmer (18th of Iyar)

264 The mourning customs of *Sefirat HaOmer* are suspended. It is permissible to cut one's hair, shave, attend parties, celebrate weddings and bar/bat mitzvas, and listen to music [שו״ע ורמ״א או״ח, תצג: ב].

265 For some communites, the mourning period that started at Pesaḥ, ends after Lag BaOmer. For others, it continues until three days before Shavuot [שם] (see law 252).

266 When Lag BaOmer falls on Sunday, shaving and cutting one's hair are permitted on the preceding Friday, in honor of Shabbat.

267 *Taḥanun* is omitted during Shaḥarit and Minḥa [משנ״ב אורח, תצג:ט].

Yom Yerushalayim (28th of Iyar)

268 The mourning customs of *Sefirat HaOmer* are suspended. It is permissible to cut one's hair, shave, attend parties, celebrate weddings and bar/bat mitzvas, and listen to music.

269 Shaḥarit: *Pesukei DeZimra* as for Shabbat and Yom Tov, with the addition of מִזְמוֹר לְתוֹדָה (page 411). נִשְׁמַת is not said. After אָז יָשִׁיר (page 443), prayers continue with Shaḥarit as for weekdays (page 85). The Repetition of the Amida is followed by Hallel and Half Kaddish. On Monday or Thursday, the Torah is taken from the Ark and the appropriate section of the Torah is read. After the Torah reading, Half Kaddish is said, followed by the Prayer for the State of Israel. On Monday or Thursday, the Torah is returned to the Ark. *Ashrei* and וּבָא לְצִיּוֹן are said, followed by Full Kaddish, *Aleinu*, Mourner's Kaddish, the Daily Psalm, and Mourner's Kaddish.

270 *Taḥanun* is omitted during Shaḥarit and Minḥa.

271 On the Shabbat preceding Rosh Ḥodesh Sivan, אַב הָרַחֲמִים is said (see law 144).

SIVAN

272 From Rosh Ḥodesh Sivan until the day after Shavuot, *Taḥanun* is omitted in Shaḥarit and Minḥa [רמ״א אורח, תצד:ג].

Sheloshet Yemei Hagbala (3rd–5th of Sivan)

273 The three days prior to Shavuot commemorate the three days before the Torah was given at Sinai, when the Jewish people were enjoined to prepare themselves for the Divine Revelation.

274 For those who observe the customs of mourning after Lag BaOmer, the mourning period ends on the 3rd of Sivan.

Shavuot (6th–7th of Sivan)

275 When Shavuot falls on Friday, each household must prepare an *Eiruv Tavshilin* (page 759); this makes it permissible to prepare food on Friday for the Shabbat meals [שו״ע או״ח, תקכז].

276 Candle lighting: Two blessings are said: (1) לְהַדְלִיק נֵר שֶׁל יוֹם טוֹב, and (2) שֶׁהֶחֱיָנוּ. On Friday night, the conclusion of the first blessing is: לְהַדְלִיק נֵר שֶׁל שַׁבָּת וְשֶׁל יוֹם טוֹב.

277 There is a widespread custom to decorate the synagogue with flowers or plants [רמ״א או״ח, תצד:ג].

278 Ma'ariv: for Shabbat and Yom Tov. The custom is to begin Ma'ariv after nightfall [משנ״ב או״ח, תצד:א]. Many congregations say the special verse for Yom Tov (וַיְדַבֵּר מֹשֶׁה), before saying the Amida for Yom Tov (page 771). This is followed by Full Kaddish, *Aleinu* and Mourner's Kaddish. It is customary to conclude with the singing of Adon Olam or Yigdal.

279 When Shavuot eve falls on Friday night, Ma'ariv is preceded by the last two psalms of Kabbalat Shabbat: מִזְמוֹר שִׁיר לְיוֹם הַשַּׁבָּת and יהוה מָלָךְ, גֵּאוּת לָבֵשׁ (page 325). בַּמֶּה מַדְלִיקִין is omitted. וְשָׁמְרוּ and the special verse for Yom Tov (וַיְדַבֵּר מֹשֶׁה) (page 345) precede the Yom Tov Amida, which is said with additions for Shabbat. After the Amida, the congregation says וַיְכֻלּוּ הַשָּׁמַיִם, and the *Shaliaḥ Tzibbur* says the abbreviated Repetition of the Amida as is customary on Shabbat eve [שו״ע או״ח, תרי״ט:ג]. When Shavuot eve falls on Motza'ei Shabbat, the congregation adds the paragraph וַתּוֹדִיעֵנוּ in the middle section of the Amida. Similarly, in Kiddush, the two blessings for Havdala are inserted prior to the blessing שֶׁהֶחֱיָנוּ; thus the order of blessings is: wine, Kiddush, flame, Havdala, שֶׁהֶחֱיָנוּ (page 763).

280 When Shavuot eve falls on Friday night, Kiddush is said with additions for Shabbat.

281 The ארי״ (Rabbi Isaac Luria) instituted the custom to stay awake all night and to say the *Tikkun Leil Shavuot*. Today most people who stay awake spend the night engaged in Torah study [משנ״ב או״ח, תצד:א].

282 Shaḥarit: for Shabbat and Yom Tov (page 399). The *Shaliaḥ Tzibbur* for Shaḥarit begins from the words הָאֵל בְּתַעֲצוּמוֹת עֻזֶּךָ (page 449). After *Barekhu*, the congregation says הַמֵּאִיר לָאָרֶץ or, if it is also Shabbat, הַכֹּל יוֹדוּךָ. The Amida for Yom Tov is said (page 771); if also Shabbat, one says the additions for Shabbat. The Repetition of the Amida is followed by Hallel and Full Kaddish. On the second day of Shavuot, *Megillat Rut* (page 1181) is read, followed by Mourner's Kaddish.

283 While the Torah is taken from the Ark, most congregations say the "Thirteen

Attributes of Mercy" and a special supplication (page 501), except on Shabbat. After the Kohen has been called up, אַקְדָּמוּת are said (page 793) [משנ״ב או״ח, תצד:ב].

284 Torah Reading: first day – page 1146; second day – page 1143. Five men are called up, seven on Shabbat. Many congregations stand during the reading of the Ten Commandments (page 1147). Maftir (both days): page 1149. Haftara: first day – page 1149; second day – page 1151 [שו״ע או״ח, תצד: א–ב]. By custom, an Aramaic poem, יְצִיב פִּתְגָם, is said after the first two verses of the Haftara of the second day.

285 The Haftara is followed by (*Yekum Purkan* on Shabbat, then) the prayers for the government and the State of Israel. On the first day, the *Shaliaḥ Tzibbur* says יָהּ אֵלִי וְגוֹאֲלִי (page 805). On the second day, *Yizkor* (page 797) is said, followed by אַב הָרַחֲמִים. On both days, the congregation says *Ashrei*, and the Torah scrolls are returned to the Ark. The *Shaliaḥ Tzibbur* says Half Kaddish.

286 Musaf: for Festivals (page 807). If also Shabbat, one says the additions for Shabbat. During the Repetition of the Amida, the Kohanim say *Birkat Kohanim*. The *Shaliaḥ Tzibbur* says Full Kaddish. This is followed by *Ein Keloheinu* (page 557) and the conclusion of Musaf, as for Shabbat.

287 Minḥa: for Shabbat and Yom Tov. When Shavuot falls on Shabbat, the Torah is taken from the Ark and the beginning of the portion of the week is read. The Torah is returned to the Ark and the *Shaliaḥ Tzibbur* says Half Kaddish. The congregation says the Amida for Yom Tov (page 771).

TAMMUZ

Shiva Asar BeTammuz (17th of Tammuz)

288 According to the Mishna (*Ta'anit* 4:6), the fast of the 17th of Tammuz commemorates five calamities that befell the Jewish people on that date: (1) Moses broke the tablets, (2) the daily *Tamid* sacrifice was interrupted (in Second Temple times), (3) the walls of Jerusalem were breached by Titus, (4) Apostemus burned the Torah, and (5) an idol was introduced to the Temple.

289 The fast begins at dawn (see laws 47–48) [שו״ע או״ח, תקסד:א]. If the 17th of Tammuz falls on Shabbat, the fast is postponed to Sunday [שו״ע או״ח תקנ, ג].

290 Shaharit: for weekdays. During the Repetition of the Amida, the *Shaliaḥ Tzibbur* says עֲנֵנוּ between the seventh and eighth blessings (page 117) [שו״ע או״ח, תקסו:א]. This is followed by *Seliḥot, Avinu Malkenu* and *Taḥanun* [ערוה״ש או״ח, תקסו: ח].

291 Torah Reading: Page 1112 (see law 50).

292 Minḥa: for weekdays, except that after *Ashrei* and Half Kaddish, the Torah is read. The reading is the same as that of the morning. The third *oleh* reads the Haftara (page 1112) [רמ״א, או״ח, תקסו: א]. After the Torah is returned to the Ark, the *Shaliaḥ Tzibbur* says Half Kaddish, and Minḥa continues as for weekdays.

293 During the silent Amida, those who are fasting say עֲנֵנוּ as part of the sixteenth blessing, שׁוֹמֵעַ תְּפִלָּה (page 223). During the Repetition of the Amida, the *Shaliaḥ Tzibbur* says עֲנֵנוּ between the seventh and eighth blessings, as in the morning (page 217). After the eighteenth blessing (מוֹדִים), the *Shaliaḥ Tzibbur* says the paragraph relating to *Birkat Kohanim* (page 229). For the final blessing of the Amida, שִׂים שָׁלוֹם is said instead of שָׁלוֹם רָב. After the Amida, the congregation says *Avinu Malkenu.* This is followed by *Taḥanun*, Full Kaddish and *Aleinu.*

294 From the 17th of Tammuz until Tisha B'Av (the "Three Weeks"), certain mourning rituals are observed: one does not cut one's hair, shave, listen to music, buy new things, or hold weddings and other parties [שו״ע או״ח תקנא, א]. Some permit shaving during this period.

AV

295 From Rosh Ḥodesh Av through Tisha B'Av (the "Nine Days") additional mourning rituals are observed: one abstains from eating meat or drinking wine, clothes are not laundered or pressed, and one generally minimizes joyful activities [שו״ע ורמ״א או״ח, תקנא].

Shabbat Ḥazon (Shabbat preceding Tisha B'Av)

296 The Shabbat preceding Tisha B'Av is known as *Shabbat Ḥazon*, named for the first word of the Haftara, חֲזוֹן. On Friday night, many congregations sing *Lekha Dodi* to the melody of אֱלִי צִיּוֹן. The special Haftara (Is. 1:1–27) is read to the tune of *Eikha*.

297 On Motza'ei Shabbat, *Kiddush Levana* is not said [רמ״א או״ח, תקנא: ח].

Erev Tisha B'Av (8th of Av)

298 *Taḥanun* is omitted from Minḥa.

299 The *Se'uda Mafseket* (final meal) is eaten after Minḥa. The custom is to eat no more than one cooked item. Three adult males should not eat together, so that

no *zimmun* is said. Some have the custom to sit on the floor and eat eggs with ashes [שו״ע ורמ״א או״ח, תקנב].

300 When the final meal is eaten on Shabbat afternoon, these restrictions do not apply; however, the meal must be finished before sunset [שם: י].

Tisha B'Av (9th of Av)

301 According to the Mishna (*Ta'anit* 4:6), the fast of the 9th of Av commemorates five calamities that befell the Jewish people on that date: (1) God decreed that the children of Israel would not be allowed to enter the land of Israel, (2) the First Temple was destroyed, (3) the Second Temple was destroyed, (4) Beitar was captured, and (5) Jerusalem was plowed over.

302 The fast begins at sunset. In addition to eating and drinking, one is prohibited from washing and anointing oneself and from wearing leather shoes. Marital relations are likewise forbidden. One abstains from Torah study, except for topics such as mourning laws, *Eikha*, Job, and the unhappy portions of Jeremiah [שו״ע או״ח, תקנד: א–ב]. One does not greet other people or inquire after their welfare [שם: כ].

303 Ma'ariv: for weekdays. The Amida is followed by Full Kaddish, the reading of *Eikha* (page 1191) and the recitation of *Kinot*. The congregation says וְאַתָּה קָדוֹשׁ (page 697), followed by Full Kaddish (omitting the line beginning תִּתְקַבַּל), *Aleinu* (page 701), and Mourner's Kaddish. When Tisha B'Av falls on Motza'ei Shabbat, וְיִתֶּן לְךָ is omitted.

304 If the fast falls (or is observed) on Motza'ei Shabbat, וִיהִי נֹעַם is omitted, and Havdala is not said. The blessing בּוֹרֵא מְאוֹרֵי הָאֵשׁ is said on a flame [שו״ע או״ח, תקנו: א].

305 Shaharit: Neither tallit nor tefillin is worn in the morning [שו״ע או״ח, תקנה: א]. During the Repetition of the Amida, the *Shaliah Tzibbur* says עֲנֵנוּ between the seventh and eighth blessings (page 117). *Tahanun* is omitted.

306 Torah Reading: page 1113. Three men are called up. The third *oleh* reads the Haftara: page 1114 [רמ״א או״ח תקנד, ד]. Afterwards, the first three blessings following the Haftara (page 515) are said. After the Torah is returned to the Ark, *Kinot* are said. This is followed by *Ashrei*, וּבָא לְצִיּוֹן (omitting the verse וַאֲנִי זֹאת בְּרִיתִי, see page 175), Full Kaddish (omitting the line beginning תִּתְקַבַּל), *Aleinu*, and Mourner's Kaddish.

307 During Minha both tallit and tefillin are worn.

308 Minha starts with the Daily Psalm (pages 185–191), *Ashrei* and Half Kaddish. The Torah is read: page 1112. Three men are called up; the third reads the

Haftara: page 1112. After the Torah is returned to the Ark, the *Shaliaḥ Tzibbur* says Half Kaddish.

309 During the silent recitation of the Amida (page 211), the congregation says נַחֵם as part of the fourteenth blessing (בּוֹנֵה יְרוּשָׁלָיִם), עֲנֵנוּ as part of the sixteenth blessing (שׁוֹמֵעַ תְּפִלָּה) (unless one is not fasting), and שִׂים שָׁלוֹם in place of שָׁלוֹם רָב (page 229). During the Repetition of the Amida, the *Shaliaḥ Tzibbur* says עֲנֵנוּ between the seventh (גּוֹאֵל יִשְׂרָאֵל) and eighth (רוֹפֵא חוֹלֵי עַמּוֹ יִשְׂרָאֵל) blessings, נַחֵם as part of the fourteenth blessing, the paragraph relating to *Birkat Kohanim* [שו״ע ורמ״א או״ח, תקנו: א], and שִׂים שָׁלוֹם. Minḥa ends with Full Kaddish and *Aleinu*.

310 After Ma'ariv, *Kiddush Levana* is said (page 715). When Tisha B'Av begins on Motza'ei Shabbat, Havdala is said on Sunday night, preferably over a cup of wine or grape juice; no blessing is made over spices or a flame.

311 Although the fast is broken after nightfall, it is customary to continue the other mourning customs until midday of the 10th of Av. However, if the 10th of Av falls on Friday, one is permitted to bathe and otherwise prepare for Shabbat prior to midday [רמ״א או״ח, תקנח: א].

Shabbat Naḥamu (Shabbat following Tisha B'Av)

312 Named for the first word of the Haftara, נַחֲמוּ. The first of the seven Shabbatot (שבע דנחמתא) between Tisha B'Av and Rosh HaShana, on which a Haftara is read from Isaiah containing words of consolation.

Tu B'Av (15th of Av)

313 According to the Mishna (*Ta'anit* 4:8), on the 15th of Av, the young women of Jerusalem would put on borrowed white dresses and dance together in the vineyards. Young men would come out to watch them, and the women would urge the men not to be swayed by beauty, but to be drawn to women of good family.

314 *Taḥanun* is omitted during Shaḥarit and Minḥa. If it falls on Shabbat, אַב הָרַחֲמִים is omitted during Shaḥarit, and צִדְקָתְךָ during Minḥa.

DAILY PRAYER

ON WAKING

315 The custom is to say מוֹדֶה אֲנִי immediately on waking, even before washing hands [משנ״ב או״ח, א:ח].

Laws of Washing Hands; בִּרְכַּת אֲשֶׁר יָצַר; אֱלֹהַי נְשָׁמָה

316 Upon waking, one is obligated to wash hands [שבת, קח:]. Some hold that one should not walk four *amot* (around six feet) prior to washing hands [משנ״ב או״ח, א:ב (בשם הזוהר)].

317 According to some authorities, there is a separate obligation to wash hands prior to prayer [ערוה״ש או״ח, ד:ה]. One who washes and says the blessing of עַל נְטִילַת יָדָיִם after waking, does not repeat the blessing when washing prior to prayer [רמ״א או״ח, ו:ב].

318 Hands should preferably be washed using a cup, but a cup is not required [שו״ע ורמ״א, או״ח: ד, ז]. The custom is to pour water from the cup onto the right hand, then the left, and repeat a total of three times [משנ״ב, שם: י]. Where water is unavailable, one may clean one's hands using any appropriate material; in that case, the blessing is changed to עַל נְקִיוּת יָדָיִם [שו״ע או״ח, ד:כב].

319 The blessing of עַל נְטִילַת יָדָיִם may be said before drying one's hands or afterward [משנ״ב, ד:ב].

320 A number of reasons have been offered for washing hands upon waking. The Gemara states that, during the night, hands are enveloped by an "evil vapor," רוח רעה, which is removed by washing one's hands [שבת, קח:]. In addition, there is a concern that, while sleeping, one's hands may have touched an unclean part of

the body [רא"ש ברכות, פ"ט:כג]. Finally, it is noted that a person who wakes is like a newborn; therefore, one needs to sanctify oneself by washing [שו"ת רשב"א ח"א, קצא].

321 The blessing of אֲשֶׁר יָצַר should be said each time after relieving oneself. It is recommended that one should go to the bathroom immediately after washing hands, then say the blessings of עַל נְטִילַת יָדַיִם followed by אֲשֶׁר יָצַר. However, even if one does not relieve oneself, one is permitted to say אֲשֶׁר יָצַר after washing hands [רמ"א או"ח, ד:א]. One should not postpone going to the bathroom [שו"ע או"ח, ג:יז].

322 According to the Gemara, the blessing of אֱלֹהַי נְשָׁמָה should be said upon waking [ברכות, ס:]. The contemporary custom is to say אֱלֹהַי נְשָׁמָה immediately after אֲשֶׁר יָצַר [משנ"ב, שם:יב]. However, some rule that one who stays up all night should not say אֱלֹהַי נְשָׁמָה and the blessing הַמַּעֲבִיר שֵׁנָה מֵעֵינַי, and should instead hear them from others [משנ"ב, מו:כד].

323 The custom is to say the *Birkhot HaTorah* after אֲשֶׁר יָצַר, because one should not read or recite Torah verses before making the requisite blessings on Torah study [שו"ע ורמ"א, או"ח: מו, ט].

Laws of Tzitzit

324 Putting on a four-cornered garment with tzitzit attached fulfills an affirmative mitzva from the Torah. The obligation applies only during the daytime [מנחות, מג.]. Since wearing tzitzit is a time-bound mitzva, women are exempt [שו"ע או"ח, יז:ב].

325 The accepted practice is to wear a *tallit katan* all day long and to wear a *tallit gadol* during Shaharit [שו"ע או"ח, כד:א]. The dominant Ashkenazi custom is to begin wearing a *tallit gadol* when one marries [משנ"ב, יז:י], but Jews of German and Sephardi descent begin wearing the *tallit gadol* at an earlier age. Nevertheless, the custom is to wear a *tallit gadol* – even if unmarried – when acting as *Shaliaḥ Tzibbur*, reading from or being called up to the Torah, opening the Ark or performing *hagbaha* or *gelila*.

326 One should put on the *tallit katan* immediately upon dressing. One should first examine the strings of the tzitzit to ensure that they are not torn [שו"ע או"ח, ח:ט]. Then, while standing [שו"ע או"ח, ח:א], one should say the blessing of עַל מִצְוַת צִיצִית and immediately put on the garment [רמ"א או"ח, ח:ו]. One does not say the blessing if (a) one is about to put on a *tallit gadol*, and (b) one will have in mind the *tallit katan* when saying the blessing on the *tallit gadol*. On the other hand, if there is a substantial interruption between the time one puts on the *tallit katan* and one puts on the *tallit gadol*, one should say the separate blessing on the *tallit katan* [שו"ע או"ח, ח:יג].

327 The blessing on tzitzit may be said at daybreak, but not before [רמ״א או״ח, יח:ג].

328 Similarly with the *tallit gadol,* one should first examine the strings, then while standing, say the blessing לְהִתְעַטֵּף בְּצִיצִית and put on the *tallit gadol.* The word לְהִתְעַטֵּף means to wrap oneself; one should initially wrap the *tallit gadol* around to cover one's head and face for a few moments, after which it is sufficient that it cover the torso [מג״א, ח:ב].

329 If one removes the *tallit gadol* for any reason, one should repeat the blessing when putting the tallit back on [שו״ע או״ח, ח:יד]. The blessing is not repeated if the *tallit gadol* is put back on soon after taking it off, and either (a) one was wearing a *tallit katan* all along, or (b) one's original intention was to put the tallit back on shortly [משנ״ב, שם:לו].

330 If one's head is otherwise covered, there is no requirement to cover one's head with the *tallit gadol* [ט״ז או״ח, ח:ג]. Some authorities nevertheless require married men to cover their heads with the *tallit gadol* throughout Shaḥarit, because it promotes reverence in prayer [בה״ט או״ח, ח:ג (בשם הרדב״ז)]. Others have the custom to cover their heads during the Amida only, or from *Barekhu* through the end of the Amida. Unmarried persons should not wear the *tallit gadol* over their heads [קידושין, כט:].

Laws of Tefillin

331 Putting on tefillin fulfills an affirmative mitzva from the Torah. The obligation applies only on weekdays [שו״ע או״ח, לא]. Since wearing tefillin is a time-bound mitzva, women are exempt [שו״ע או״ח, לח:ג].

332 One puts on tefillin after the tallit, because the former are more sacred, and we follow the principle of "ascending in sanctity" (מעלין בקודש) [שו״ע או״ח, כה:א].

333 The *tefillin shel yad* is worn on the weaker arm, meaning that right-handed people wear it on the left arm, and left-handed people wear it on the right arm [שו״ע או״ח, כז:ו].

334 The *tefillin shel yad* is put on first, by placing the box on the biceps near the elbow joint, angled toward the heart, and saying the blessing לְהָנִיחַ תְּפִלִּין. One then tightens the strap around the muscle and wraps the strap around the forearm seven times. Without speaking or otherwise becoming distracted [שו״ע או״ח, כה:ט–י], one places the *tefillin shel rosh* on the head above the hairline, centered over the nose, and says the blessing עַל מִצְוַת תְּפִלִּין. One then adjusts the straps, so that the knot rests at the base of the skull and the two straps hang down the front of one's chest, and says בָּרוּךְ שֵׁם כְּבוֹד מַלְכוּתוֹ לְעוֹלָם וָעֶד [רמ״א או״ח, כה:ה].

Finally, one wraps the strap of the *tefillin shel yad* around the fingers, while saying וְאֵרַשְׂתִּיךְ (See page 17).

335 The box of the *tefillin shel yad* and the *tefillin shel rosh* must rest directly on the arm and head respectively, without any barrier between them [שו״ע או״ח, כז: ד]. This rule does not apply to the straps of the tefillin [רמ״א, שם].

336 One should regularly touch first the *tefillin shel yad*, then the *tefillin shel rosh*, so as to remain conscious that one is wearing them. In particular, one should touch the appropriate tefillin when saying the relevant verses of the Shema [שו״ע או״ח, כח: א] (see law 354). It is also customary to touch them when saying the verse פּוֹתֵחַ אֶת־יָדֶךָ during *Ashrei*.

337 At a minimum, tefillin should be worn while saying the Shema and the Amida [שו״ע או״ח, כה: ד]. The custom is to keep them on until one has heard the *Kedusha* three times and Kaddish four times [רמ״א, שם: יג], which means that one should not remove the tefillin until after the Mourner's Kaddish following *Aleinu* [משנ״ב, שם: נו]. In theory, one should wear tefillin all day. The custom, however, is to take the tefillin off after praying, because it is difficult to maintain a constant awareness of the tefillin and the requisite purity of mind and body throughout the day [שו״ע או״ח, לז: ב].

338 The order in which one removes tefillin is the reverse of the order in which they were put on. Thus, one first unwinds the strap of the *tefillin shel yad* from one's fingers, then removes the *tefillin shel rosh* and wraps it in its case. One then unwinds the *tefillin shel yad* from the arm, removes the box from the muscle and wraps the tefillin in its case [שו״ע או״ח, כח: ב]. This entire process should be performed standing up [משנ״ב, כח: ו].

SERVICES

Laws of Birkhot HaShaḥar and Pesukei DeZimra

339 According to the Gemara [ברכות, ס:], *Birkhot HaShaḥar* (Morning Blessings) were originally said separately, in conjunction with the performance of the associated activity. Thus, upon dressing one would say the blessing of מַלְבִּישׁ עֲרֻמִּים, and upon standing up one would say the blessing of זוֹקֵף כְּפוּפִים. However, the custom now is to say all of the blessings together in the synagogue [שו״ע או״ח, מו: ב].

340 The insertion of the verse (or verses) of Shema after *Birkhot HaShaḥar* was not meant to satisfy the individual's obligation to say the Shema every morning [רמ״א, שם:ט]. However, as discussed in further detail in law 347, the three paragraphs of Shema must be said within the first half of the morning (measured as ¼ of the time from daybreak to nightfall). Since some congregations hold Shaḥarit services late, especially on Shabbat, and as such the communal recitation of the Shema in Shaḥarit may take place too late to fulfill the halakhic obligation, under such circumstances it is recommended to say all three paragraphs of Shema after *Birkhot HaShaḥar* [משנ״ב, שם:לא].

341 One should say the biblical verses describing the קרבן תמיד (page 45), preferably with the congregation [רמ״א או״ח, מח]. Some authorities require one to stand [משנ״ב, שם:ב].

342 The fifth chapter of מסכת זבחים and the ברייתא דרבי ישמעאל were added after the biblical passages regarding sacrifices to institutionalize the daily study of Scripture, Mishna and Gemara [שו״ע או״ח, נ:א].

343 Saying Kaddish, *Barekhu* or *Kedusha* requires the presence of a *minyan* (ten adult males) [שו״ע או״ח, נה:א].

344 One should not utter idle speech from the beginning of the words בָּרוּךְ אַתָּה יהוה in *Barukh SheAmar* until one completes the Amida [שו״ע או״ח, נא:ד]. Certain responses are permitted, as detailed in the chart on pages 1329–1331.

345 If one comes late to the synagogue, one may skip all, or portions, of *Pesukei DeZimra*, as follows:

- **a** If there is sufficient time, say *Barukh SheAmar*, Psalms 145–150, and *Yishtabaḥ*.
- **b** If there is less time, say *Barukh SheAmar*, Psalms 145, 148, 150, and *Yishtabaḥ*.
- **c** If there is less time, say *Barukh SheAmar*, Psalm 145, and *Yishtabaḥ*.
- **d** If there is less time, omit *Pesukei DeZimra* altogether. Complete the rest of the service with the congregation, then say *Pesukei DeZimra* privately, omitting *Barukh SheAmar* and *Yishtabaḥ* [רמ״א ושו״ע או״ח, נב].

Morning Shema – קריאת שמע של שחרית

346 Saying the three paragraphs of the Shema each morning and each night fulfills an affirmative mitzva from the Torah. Since saying the Shema is a time-bound mitzva, women are exempt [שו״ע או״ח, ע:א]. Nevertheless, women are required to say the first verse to express their acceptance of עול מלכות שמים ("the yoke of the kingdom of Heaven") [ב״ח, שם]. Women are permitted to say the Shema and its preceding and following blessings [משנ״ב, שם:ב].

347 There is a set time period every morning during which the Shema may be said. The optimal time is immediately before sunrise, when there is assumed to be sufficient light to recognize an acquaintance from a distance of four *amot* (around 6 feet). If necessary, the Shema may be said from daybreak [שו״ע או״ח, נח:ג]. After sunrise, the earlier the Shema is said, the better [שם:ב]. At the latest, the Shema must be said during the first quarter of the day (in halakhic terminology, three halakhic "hours," where each hour represents 1⁄12 of the day; regarding the measure of a "day," see law 204) [שם:א]. After that time, one is permitted to say the Shema with the blessings during the fourth halakhic "hour," that is, until the end of the first third of the day. After that, the Shema may be said without the blessings, but this does not fulfill the mitzva [שם:ו].

348 If one says the Shema without its preceding and following blessings, one has still fulfilled the mitzva. However, one should say the blessings afterward, preferably repeating the Shema as well [שו״ע או״ח, ס:ב].

349 The Shema must be said with concentration and awe [שו״ע או״ח, סא:א]. Each word and syllable should be pronounced correctly and carefully, without slurring consonants [שו״ע או״ח, סא:טו–כא].

350 Some authorities ruled that one should say the Shema with *Ta'amei HaMikra*. Today, however, most people do not do so [שו״ע ורמ״א, שם:כד].

351 The custom is to cover the eyes with the right hand while saying the first verse, so as not look at anything that might disturb one's concentration [שו״ע או״ח, סא:ה].

352 It is customary to draw out one's pronunciation of the letters ח and ד in the word אֶחָד to emphasize God's sovereignty over creation [שו״ע או״ח, סא:ו].

353 The sentence בָּרוּךְ שֵׁם כְּבוֹד מַלְכוּתוֹ לְעוֹלָם וָעֶד is said quietly, because it does not appear in the biblical text of the Shema [שו״ע שם:יג; משנ״ב, שם:ל].

354 As discussed in law 336 above, the custom is to touch the *tefillin shel yad* when saying וּקְשַׁרְתָּם לְאוֹת עַל־יָדֶךָ and to touch the *tefillin shel rosh* when saying וְהָיוּ לְטֹטָפֹת בֵּין עֵינֶיךָ [שו״ע או״ח, כח:א].

355 If one enters the synagogue and hears the congregation about to begin saying the Shema, one is required to say the first verse of the Shema together with the congregation [שו״ע או״ח, סה:ב].

Laws of the Shaḥarit Amida

356 There is a set time period every morning during which the Amida may be said. In general, the Amida should be said at or after sunrise. At the latest, the Amida should be said during the first third of the day, (four halakhic "hours"; regarding

the measure of a "day," see law 204). If the Amida was said between daybreak and sunrise, the mitzva has been fulfilled. If necessary, it is permissible to say the Amida after the first third of the day, but before midday [שו״ע או״ח, פט: א].

357 One who must leave for work (or a journey) before sunrise is permitted to say the Amida from daybreak [שו״ע שם סע׳ ח]. If one did not say the Shaharit Amida prior to midday, one should say the Minha Amida twice [משנ״ב, שם: ס״ק ז].

358 One should not eat or drink before saying the Amida, although drinking water is permitted. Moreover, anyone who needs to eat or drink in order to concentrate on his prayers is permitted to do so [שו״ע או״ח, פט: ג–ד].

359 The Amida is said facing the site of the Temple in Jerusalem. Thus, outside Israel, one faces the land of Israel; inside Israel, one faces Jerusalem; and inside Jerusalem, one faces the Temple Mount [שו״ע או״ח, צד: א]. If one is praying in a synagogue, one should pray facing the Ark [משנ״ב, שם: ס״ק י].

360 The Amida is said standing with feet together in imitation of the angels who, according to tradition, present the appearance of having only one leg [ברכות, י:, רש״י, ד״ה ״ותלתיהם״]. One should bow one's head and imagine one is standing in the Temple, like a servant before his master [שו״ע או״ח, צה: א–ב].

361 One who is traveling in a vehicle should, if possible, say the Amida standing; if this is not possible, one is permitted to sit [שו״ע או״ח, צד: ה].

362 When saying the Shaharit Amida, one may not allow any interruption or disruption between the conclusion of the blessing גָּאַל יִשְׂרָאֵל and the introductory words to the Amida [שו״ע או״ח, סו: ח; שם, קיא: א]. This includes not responding to Kaddish, *Barekhu*, *Kedusha* or *Modim*, although on Shabbat one may do so [רמ״א, שם]. One may also answer "Amen" if one hears someone else concluding the blessing גָּאַל יִשְׂרָאֵל [רמ״א או״ח, סו: ז].

Laws of Havinenu

363 When circumstances require, one is permitted to substitute a special paragraph (*Havinenu*, page 1005) for the thirteen middle blessings of the Amida. This is only permitted in exceptional cases, such as when one is incapable of concentrating during a full-length Amida or expects interruptions. One says this abbreviated form of the Amida while standing, and one does not need to repeat the full-length Amida afterward. *Havinenu* is not said during the winter months or on Motza'ei Shabbat [שו״ע או״ח, קי: א].

Laws of חזרת הש״ץ

364 During the Repetition of the Amida, the congregation is required to listen attentively to the blessings and respond "Amen" [שו״ע או״ח, קכד: ד].

365 In order to begin the Repetition of the Amida, at least nine men are required to be listening attentively [שם].

366 Some require the congregation to stand during the Repetition of the Amida [רמ״א, שם].

367 Under extenuating circumstances, the *Shaliaḥ Tzibbur* may begin saying the Amida aloud, while the congregation says the Amida quietly along with him. The *Kedusha* is said aloud in the customary fashion and, after the *Shaliaḥ Tzibbur* finishes the blessing הָאֵל הַקָּדוֹשׁ, he and the congregation continue saying the Amida quietly [רמ״א, שם: ב].

368 At the conclusion of the Repetition of the Amida, it is recommended that the *Shaliaḥ Tzibbur* say quietly the verse יִהְיוּ לְרָצוֹן אִמְרֵי־פִי, except when Full Kaddish immediately follows the Repetition of the Amida [משנ״ב קכג: כא]. Some also say this verse during the individual's silent Amida.

Laws of Kedusha

369 There are different customs regarding what the congregation says during the *Kedusha*: (1) The congregation says only the biblical verses (...קָדוֹשׁ; ...בָּרוּךְ; ...יִמְלֹךְ) [שו״ע או״ח, קכה: א]; (2) The congregation says every word of the *Kedusha*, with the *Shaliaḥ Tzibbur* repeating each sentence [ב״ה״ט, שם (בשם האר״י)]; (3) The congregation says נְקַדֵּשׁ and all the biblical verses [ערוה״ש, שם: ב].

Laws of Birkat Kohanim

370 The Kohen has an affirmative obligation from the Torah to bless the congregation, provided there are at least ten males aged 13 or over (including the Kohen himself) [שו״ע או״ח, קכח: א–ב].

371 The Kohen is required to wash his hands (without a blessing) before saying *Birkat Kohanim*. It is customary for a Levi to pour the water [שם, ו]. If there is no water, or if the Kohen did not have enough time to wash, he may say *Birkat Kohanim*, provided that: (a) he washed his hands before Shaḥarit, and (b) since washing for Shaḥarit he has not touched anything unclean, even his own shoes [משנ״ב, שם: כ].

372 Each Kohen removes his shoes before ascending to say *Birkat Kohanim* [שם, ה]. When the *Shaliaḥ Tzibbur* begins רְצֵה, the Kohanim ascend to the Ark and

stand with their backs to the congregation [שם, ח:ו-י]. After the congregation answers "Amen" to the blessing הַטּוֹב שִׁמְךָ וּלְךָ נָאֶה לְהוֹדוֹת, if there is more than one Kohen, the *Shaliaḥ Tzibbur* calls out "Kohanim," and they turn around and say the blessing. If only one Kohen has ascended to the Ark, he starts the blessing without being prompted [שם: י-יא]. The *Shaliaḥ Tzibbur* does not answer "Amen" at the end of the blessing [משנ"ב, שם: עא].

373 The *Shaliaḥ Tzibbur* reads each word of *Birkat Kohanim* and the Kohanim repeat it in unison. At the end of each verse, the congregation answers "Amen" [שו"ע ורמ"א, שם: יג]. The *Shaliaḥ Tzibbur* does not answer "Amen" at the end of each verse [שו"ע, שם: יט].

374 If the *Shaliaḥ Tzibbur* is himself a Kohen, some rule that he should not say the blessing, unless no other Kohanim are in the synagogue [שו"ע, שם: יט]. However, the custom today is for the *Shaliaḥ Tzibbur* to participate in the blessing [משנ"ב, שם: עה].

375 During *Birkat Kohanim*, the congregation should stand silently with eyes lowered and concentrate on the words of the Kohanim. One should not look at the faces or hands of the Kohanim [שו"ע, שם: כג].

376 In most congregations in Israel, *Birkat Kohanim* is said every day in Shaḥarit and, where applicable, in Musaf, as well as in *Ne'ila* on Yom Kippur. It is also said in Minḥa on a fast day [שו"ע או"ח, קכט: א]. *Birkat Kohanim* is not said in Shaḥarit of Tisha B'Av or in a mourner's house [משנ"ב, קכא: ו], although in Jerusalem, the custom is to say *Birkat Kohanim* even in a mourner's house [גשר החיים, כ: ה]. On those occasions and when no Kohen is present, the *Shaliaḥ Tzibbur* says אֱלֹהֵינוּ וֵאלֹהֵי אֲבוֹתֵינוּ (page 133).

377 The custom outside Israel and in certain northern Israeli congregations, is for the *Shaliaḥ Tzibbur* to say אֱלֹהֵינוּ וֵאלֹהֵי אֲבוֹתֵינוּ instead of the Kohanim saying *Birkat Kohanim*, except in Musaf of Yom Tov [רמ"א או"ח, קכח: מד].

Laws of Taḥanun

378 נפילת אפיים ("Lowering the Head," pages 153/233) is said immediately after the Shaharit Amida on Sundays, Tuesdays, Wednesdays and Fridays, and after the Minḥa Amida on every weekday except for Friday. In Shaḥarit on Mondays and Thursdays, *Taḥanun* begins with page 145 (וְהוּא רַחוּם), and יהוה אֱלֹהֵי יִשְׂרָאֵל (page 153) is added.

379 On fast days (except on Tisha B'Av, when neither *Avinu Malkenu* nor *Taḥanun* is said) and during the *Aseret Yemei Teshuva, Avinu Malkenu* (page 139) is said before *Taḥanun*.

380 One should not speak between the Amida and נפילת אפיים [שו"ע או"ח, קלא: א].

381 נפילת אפיים should be said while sitting [שם: ב], with one's head lowered against one's weaker forearm. If one is wearing tefillin however, one lays one's head against the arm lacking tefillin [שו״ע ורמ״א, שם: א]. The head is lowered only where there is a Sefer Torah [רמ״א, שם: ב], except in Jerusalem, where the custom is to lower the head in any case [שו״ת אגרות משה יו״ד ח״ג, קכט (ב)].

382 For days on which *Taḥanun* is not said, see list on page 145 [שו״ע ורמ״א או״ח, קלא: ד; משנ״ב, שם: כו].

Laws of Torah Reading

383 To ensure that the Torah is read at least once every three days, Moses established the public reading of the Torah on Shabbat, Yom Tov, Ḥol HaMo'ed, Rosh Ḥodesh, and Monday and Thursday mornings. Ezra added the public reading in Shabbat Minḥa [רמב״ם הלכות תפילה פי״ב ה״א].

384 On weekdays and Shabbat Minḥa, three people are called up [שו״ע או״ח, קלה: א]. On Shabbat morning, seven are called up, though additional individuals (*hosafot*) may also be called [שו״ע או״ח, רפב: א]. On Yom Kippur morning, six are called up, five on Yom Tov, and four on Ḥol HaMo'ed and Rosh Ḥodesh.

385 If a Kohen is present, he is called up first. If a Levi is also present, he is called up second; for subsequent *aliyot*, one calls up a Yisrael [שו״ע או״ח, קלה: ג]. If a Kohen is present but a Levi is not, the same Kohen is called up for the first two *aliyot* [שם: ח]. If a Levi is present and a Kohen is not, the Levi need not be called up, but if the Levi is called up, he should be first [שו״ע ורמ״א או״ח, קלה: ו].

386 The custom is to avoid calling up a Kohen after a Yisrael, except for Maftir and, in some communities, for אחרון, provided it is a *hosafa* [רמ״א, שם: י].

387 Other individuals who are given priority for an *aliya* include: a bridegroom on his wedding day and the Shabbat preceding and following the wedding; a Bar Mitzva; the father of a newborn baby; one commemorating a parent's *yahrzeit*; and a person obligated to say *Birkat HaGomel* [בה״ל, קלו: ד״ה ״בשבת״].

388 It is considered bad luck to call up two brothers or a father and son one after the other [שו״ע או״ח, קמא: ו]. While the custom is to avoid the practice, if one is called up after one's brother or father, one should accept the *aliya*.

389 One who is called up to the Torah should take the shortest route to the *bima* [שו״ע, שם: ז]. He should open the scroll to locate where the *aliya* begins. Still holding the handle, he should say the blessing, taking care to look away from the Torah (or close the scroll or his eyes), so as not to appear to be reading the blessing from the scroll itself [שו״ע ורמ״א או״ח, קלט: ד].

390 If, after the blessing is said, the *ba'al koreh* discovers that the blessing was said over the wrong passage of the Torah, the scroll is rolled to the correct location and the *oleh* repeats the blessing. The blessing does not need to be repeated if the correct passage was visible when the blessing was said [שו״ע או״ח, קמ:ג; משנ״ב, שם:ט].

391 The Torah is read standing [שו״ע או״ח, קמא:א]. The *oleh* is also required to stand. The rest of the congregation is not obligated to stand, but it is proper to do so [ערוה״ש, שם:ב].

392 The *oleh* should read the words quietly along with the *ba'al koreh* [שו״ע או״ח, קמא:ב].

393 If the *ba'al koreh* makes an error that affects the meaning of the words, he needs to reread the Torah portion from the location of the error [שו״ע ורמ״א או״ח, קמב:א].

394 If an error is found in the Torah scroll, the reading is stopped, a new scroll is brought out, and the reading is continued from the location of the error [שו״ע או״ח, קמג:ד]. It is not required to call up all of the *aliyot* a second time to read from the new scroll, but if the remainder of the reading can be divided into the appropriate number of *aliyot* for that day, it is preferable to do so [משנ״ב, שם:טז].

395 It is customary to say a prayer for a sick person (מִי שֶׁבֵּרַךְ, page 509) at the conclusion of the Torah reading, or between *aliyot*.

396 On the Shabbat before a *yahrzeit*, it is customary to say a prayer for the deceased relative (אֵל מָלֵא רַחֲמִים, page 801), usually after the Shabbat Minḥa Torah reading.

397 After completing the reading from a Torah scroll, the open scroll is raised and displayed to the entire congregation. The congregation says וְזֹאת הַתּוֹרָה (page 165) [שו״ע ורמ״א או״ח, קלד:ב].

Laws of Birkat HaGomel

398 After being saved from mortal danger, one should say *Birkat HaGomel* [שו״ע או״ח, ריט:א,ו–ט; משנ״ב, שם:לב] (see page 507 and commentary on page 506). The blessing should be said no later than three days after the event [שו״ע, שם:ו]. *Birkat HaGomel* is said only in the presence of a *minyan*; the custom is to say the blessing after the Torah reading [שם:ג]. If one will not be in the presence of *minyan* within three days, one is permitted to say the blessing without a *minyan* [משנ״ב, שם:ח].

399 A husband may say *Birkat HaGomel* for his wife, or a father for his children [משנ״ב, שם:יז]. But, according to most authorities, it is preferable that a woman say *Birkat HaGomel* for herself in the presence of a *minyan*.

Laws of Mourner's Kaddish

400 The Mourner's Kaddish is generally said after specific chapters of Psalms at the

beginning and end of a service. It is said by one who is either (a) in mourning for a relative, or (b) commemorating the *yahrzeit* of a relative. When no such person is present, the Mourner's Kaddish is generally omitted, except after *Aleinu* at the end of Shaḥarit [רמ״א או״ח, קלב:ב], when it is said by one whose parents have died or whose parents do not object to their child saying the Mourner's Kaddish [שם].

401 Historically, the Mourner's Kaddish was said by one individual. A set of rules developed for allocating among different mourners the various opportunities for saying it [ביאור הלכה, שם; קונטרס מאמר קדישין, י]. Today, most congregations allow group recitation of the Mourner's Kaddish. In such cases, they should say the words in unison [סידור יעב״ץ].

Laws of the Minḥa Amida

402 There is a set time period every afternoon during which the Minḥa Amida may be said. At the earliest, one may say the Amida one half of a halakhic "hour" from midday (a halakhic hour is 1/12 of the day measured from daybreak to nightfall). At the latest, the Amida must be said before nightfall. It is preferable to say the Amida at least 3½ halakhic "hours" after midday [שו״ע או״ח, רלג:א].

403 One should wash hands before saying Minḥa, even if they are not dirty; but if no water is available, one need not wash [שו״ע או״ח, רלג:ב]. No blessing is said on the hand-washing.

Laws of the Evening Shema and Ma'ariv

404 There is a set time period every night during which the Shema may be said. At the earliest, one may say the Shema from nightfall [שו״ע או״ח, רלה:א]. It is preferable to say the Shema before midnight (measured from nightfall to daybreak), but one is permitted to say the Shema until daybreak [שם:ג].

405 Some congregations hold Ma'ariv services early, with the result that the communal recitation of the Shema in Ma'ariv may take place too early to fulfill the halakhic obligation. Under such circumstances, one should repeat all three paragraphs of Shema after nightfall [שו״ע, שם:א].

406 If one enters the synagogue and hears the congregation about to begin saying the Amida, one should say the Amida together with the congregation, then afterward say the Shema with its preceding and following blessings [שו״ע או״ח, רלו:ג].

407 After the blessings of the Shema, the congregation says בָּרוּךְ יהוה לְעוֹלָם (page 253), except in Israel. One who begins Ma'ariv late should omit בָּרוּךְ יהוה לְעוֹלָם in order

to say the Amida with the congregation, then say בָּרוּךְ יהוה לְעוֹלָם after Ma'ariv, without the final blessing [משנ״ב, שם: יא].

Laws of Keri'at Shema al HaMita (the Shema Before Sleep at Night)

408 *Keri'at Shema al HaMita* should be said before retiring, when one is feeling sleepy [משנ״ב או״ח, רלט: ג], after which one should not eat, drink or speak [רמ״א, שם: א].

LAWS OF HAND-WASHING, HAMOTZI AND BIRKAT HAMAZON

409 Before eating bread, one is required to wash one's hands [שו״ע או״ח, קנח: א]. After washing but before drying the hands, one says the blessing עַל נְטִילַת יָדַיִם; however, if one forgot, one may say the blessing after one's hands are dry [רמ״א, שם: יא]. One should dry one's hands carefully before touching the bread [שו״ע, שם: יב].

410 Hands should be washed using a cup or other container that holds at least a *revi'it* (about 4.4 ounces) of liquid [שו״ע או״ח, קנט: א]. Holding one's hands under flowing water is not valid [שו״ע, שם: ז].

411 One should wash each hand up to the wrist, although the minimum requirement is to wash the fingers up to the knuckle furthest from the nail [שו״ע או״ח, קסא: ד]. Hands should be free of dirt or other material that one normally removes. In addition, rings should be removed before washing [שם: א–ג].

412 If the hands are clean, it is sufficient to pour water once on each hand [שו״ע או״ח, קסב: ב], but twice on each hand is preferable [מ״ב שם, כא].

413 After washing, one should take care not to allow one's wet hands to touch the unwashed hands of another. If they do so, one must dry them and wash them again [שו״ע שם, ד].

414 If one makes the blessing הַמּוֹצִיא לֶחֶם מִן הָאָרֶץ on bread, no blessing need be said on foods that are part of the meal. If one eats foods that are not eaten with bread or are not part of the meal, such as fruit eaten as dessert, they require a separate blessing [שו״ע, קעז: א].

415 If wine is served during the meal, the blessing בּוֹרֵא פְּרִי הַגָּפֶן must be said, as the blessing on bread does not cover wine [שו״ע או״ח, קעד: א]. But if wine is drunk before the meal (or as part of Kiddush), the blessing need not be repeated when drinking wine during the meal [שם: ד].

416 One should not remove bread from the table until after *Birkat HaMazon* is said [שו״ע או״ח, קפ:א].

417 Prior to saying *Birkat HaMazon,* one should wash the grime off one's fingers with *mayim aḥaronim* [שו״ע או״ח, קפא:א]. Some have the custom not to wash with *mayim aḥaronim,* because the original reasons for the practice no longer apply [שם, י; משנ״ב שם, כב], but a fastidious person who washes after a meal should wash with *mayim aḥaronim* before *Birkat HaMazon* [שו״ע שם].

418 Women are obligated to say *Birkat HaMazon* [שו״ע או״ח, קפו:א].

419 *Birkat HaMazon* should be said where one ate. If one forgot to say *Birkat HaMazon* and went elsewhere, one should return to the site of the meal to say *Birkat HaMazon.* If one cannot return to the site of the meal, one is permitted to say *Birkat HaMazon* as soon as one remembers to do so [שו״ע ורמ״א או״ח, קפד:א; משנ״ב, שם:ז].

420 If one forgets to say *Birkat HaMazon* at the end of the meal, it must be said afterward, so long as one does not feel hungry [שו״ע או״ח, קפד:ד]. If one wants to eat again, one may wash hands and say הַמּוֹצִיא again; the subsequent *Birkat HaMazon* then covers the first meal as well [רמ״א או״ח, קעח:ב].

421 On Ḥanukka or Purim, one adds עַל הַנִּסִּים (page 981) to the second blessing. If one forgets עַל הַנִּסִּים, one is not required to repeat *Birkat HaMazon* [שו״ע או״ח, תרפב:א; שו״ע ורמ״א או״ח, תרצה:ג].

422 On Shabbat, one adds רְצֵה (page 983) to the third blessing. On Rosh Ḥodesh, Yom Tov and Ḥol HaMo'ed, one adds יַעֲלֶה וְיָבוֹא (page 985) to the third blessing; if it is also Shabbat, one says רְצֵה, then יַעֲלֶה וְיָבוֹא. If one forgets to say the required addition on Shabbat or Yom Tov, one repeats the entire *Birkat HaMazon.* Alternatively, if one remembers before beginning the fourth blessing, one may say a special blessing in honor of Shabbat or the appropriate Yom Tov [שו״ע או״ח, קפח:ה–ו]. If one forgets the required addition on Rosh Ḥodesh or Ḥol HaMo'ed, one is not required to repeat *Birkat HaMazon* [שם:ז].

423 If one started eating while it was Shabbat, Rosh Ḥodesh or other days on which additions to *Birkat HaMazon* are said, and continued the meal after sunset, one still says the additions to *Birkat HaMazon* [שם:י] (see laws 421–422 above).

424 If three adult males eat a meal together, they are required to preface *Birkat HaMazon* with *zimmun* (page 977). If women are present, they are required to join in the *zimmun* as well. Three adult females may also form a *zimmun,* but are not obligated to do so. If ten or more males are present, the word אֱלֹהֵינוּ is added to the formula [שו״ע או״ח, קצב:א].

425 *Zimmun* is required if all three participants ate bread. If only two participants ate bread, but a third person either eats a *kezayit* (about 1.5 ounces) of any food, or drinks a *revi'it* (about 4.4 ounces) of any beverage (other than water), the three should say *zimmun* [שו״ע או״ח, קצו:ג; משנ״ב, שם:כב].

426 Even if the participants are not sitting together, as long as some of the participants can see each other, they can join together in a *zimmun* [שו״ע או״ח, קצה:א].

427 If one of the three participants said *Birkat HaMazon* by himself, he may still join the other two to make a *zimmun*, but if two of them (or all three) said *Birkat HaMazon* by themselves, then no *zimmun* may be said [שו״ע או״ח, קצד:א].

428 At a *Sheva Berakhot* meal, a special addition is made to the *zimmun* (page 1043) [שו״ע אבה״ע, סב:יג; ערוה״ש, שם:יח], and the *Sheva Berakhot* (page 1041) are said after *Birkat HaMazon* [שו״ע, שם:ז].

429 At the meal after a Brit Mila, a special *zimmun* (page 1021) is said, and a series of prayers (pages 1023–1025) is added before the end of *Birkat HaMazon*.

430 At a meal in a house of mourning, a special addition is made to the *zimmun*, and the third and fourth blessings are changed (page 1069) [ערוה״ש יו״ד, שעט:א–ב].

PRAYER IN A HOUSE OF MOURNING

431 The following prayers are omitted when praying in a house of mourning during the days of *shiva*:

- **a** *Korbanot* (Offerings) – omitted only by the mourners themselves [משנ״ב או״ח, א:יז]
- **b** *Taḥanun* [שו״ע או״ח, קלא:ד]
- **c** Hallel, except when Rosh Ḥodesh falls on Shabbat [משנ״ב, שם:כ]. On Ḥanukka, those who are not mourning should say Hallel on returning home.
- **d** אֵל אֶרֶךְ אַפַּיִם [משנ״ב, שם:לה]
- **e** Psalm 20 (לַמְנַצֵּחַ) [שם]
- **f** *Pirkei Avot* or *Barekhi Nafshi* on Shabbat – omitted only by the mourners themselves [אשי ישראל, לו:צז]
- **g** *Birkat Kohanim* in Israel (see law 376)

432 In a house of mourning, it is customary to say Psalm 49 after the Daily Psalm; on days on which no *Taḥanun* is said, Psalm 16 is said instead (page 1061).

ROSH ḤODESH PRAYER

433 On Rosh Ḥodesh, יַעֲלֶה וְיָבוֹא is added to the seventeenth blessing of the Amida (רְצֵה) in Ma'ariv, Shaḥarit and Minḥa [שו״ע או״ח, תכב:א], and to the third blessing of *Birkat HaMazon* (page 985) [שם, תכד:א].

434 If one forgets to say יַעֲלֶה וְיָבוֹא in its proper place in the Amida, but realizes before beginning the blessing הַמַּחֲזִיר שְׁכִינָתוֹ לְצִיּוֹן, one should immediately say יַעֲלֶה וְיָבוֹא and continue with the rest of the blessing. If one realizes the omission immediately after completing the blessing הַמַּחֲזִיר שְׁכִינָתוֹ לְצִיּוֹן, one should say יַעֲלֶה וְיָבוֹא and continue with the following blessing. If one realizes the omission after beginning the words מוֹדִים אֲנַחְנוּ לָךְ, one must repeat the Amida from the beginning of the seventeenth blessing (from the word רְצֵה). If one realizes the omission after completing the Amida, one must repeat the Amida from the beginning [שו״ע או״ח, תכב:א].

435 If one forgets to say יַעֲלֶה וְיָבוֹא in Ma'ariv, one does not repeat the Amida [שם].

436 Shaḥarit: as for weekdays, although one adds special verses for Rosh Ḥodesh in the *Korbanot* (page 51) [שו״ע או״ח, תכא:א]. יַעֲלֶה וְיָבוֹא is added to the Amida (see laws 433–434). After the Repetition of the Amida, *Taḥanun* is omitted, and the congregation says Half Hallel [שו״ע או״ח, תכב:ב], followed by Full Kaddish.

437 Torah reading: page 1111. Four men are called up [שו״ע או״ח, תכג:א]. Note that the second *aliya* begins by repeating the last verse of the first *aliya* [שו״ע או״ח, תכב:ג]. Half Kaddish is said before the Torah is returned to the Ark. The service continues with *Ashrei*, וּבָא לְצִיּוֹן and Half Kaddish. The tefillin are then removed [שו״ע או״ח, תכג:ד], and the congregation says Musaf for Rosh Ḥodesh. This is followed by *Aleinu*, Mourner's Kaddish, the Daily Psalm, Psalm 104 (בָּרְכִי נַפְשִׁי), and Mourner's Kaddish.

Laws of Hallel

438 Hallel is said standing [שו״ע או״ח, תכב:ז]. On Rosh Ḥodesh and the last six days of Pesaḥ, the abridged form, Half Hallel, is said [שו״ע או״ח, תכב:ב; תצ, ד], omitting the first halves of Psalm 115 (לֹא לָנוּ) and Psalm 116 (אָהַבְתִּי, כִּי־יִשְׁמַע).

439 At the beginning of Psalm 118 (הוֹדוּ לַיהוה כִּי־טוֹב, page 739), it is customary for the *Shaliaḥ Tzibbur* to say each of the four verses out loud, and the congregation responds with הוֹדוּ לַיהוה כִּי־טוֹב, כִּי לְעוֹלָם חַסְדּוֹ [משנ״ב תכב, כ]. Some advise the congregation to quietly say each verse with the *Shaliaḥ Tzibbur*.

SHABBAT PRAYER

EREV SHABBAT

440 Minḥa: as for weekdays. *Taḥanun* is omitted [שו״ע או״ח, רסז:א].

SHABBAT EVE

441 Candle lighting: At least two candles are lit [שו״ע או״ח, רסג:א]. There is a custom to light one candle for each member of the household. After lighting, one says the blessing לְהַדְלִיק נֵר שֶׁל שַׁבָּת [שו״ע ורמ״א או״ח, רסג:ה]. It is customary to cover one's eyes when saying the blessing [רמ״א, שם].

442 The custom is to light Shabbat candles 18 minutes prior to sunset. In any case, the candles must be lit before sunset, at which time all labor must cease [שו״ע ורמ״א או״ח, רסא:א]. After lighting the candles, one may not perform any labor, even if one lit prior to sunset, unless one's intention to perform necessary labor before sunset is articulated explicitly prior to lighting [רמ״א או״ח, רסג:י; משנ״ב, שם:מב].

443 The candles must be lit in a location where one will benefit from the light before the candles burn out [שו״ע, שם:ט].

444 If one is not eating at home on Friday night, one should still light candles at home [שו״ע, שם:ו]. If one is not sleeping at home on Friday night, one should light where one sleeps or make a nominal payment to one's host, so as to participate in the host's candle lighting. This is not required if a family member is at home and lights candles with one in mind [שו״ע, שם:ז].

445 Kabbalat Shabbat: Many congregations sing *Yedid Nefesh* before Kabbalat Shabbat. Because Kabbalat Shabbat is not considered part of Ma'ariv, it is customary for the *Shaliaḥ Tzibbur* to stand at the *bima*, rather than at the front of the synagogue [אשי ישראל, לו: יד]. For the same reason, it is permissible for a male under the age of 13 to lead Kabbalat Shabbat.

446 When saying the last stanza of *Lekha Dodi*, the custom is to stand facing the door or the rear, which is usually the western side, of the synagogue [משנ״ב או״ח, רסב: י].

447 By custom, mourners who are sitting *shiva* remain outside the synagogue for Kabbalat Shabbat, entering when the congregation finishes *Lekha Dodi*. As they enter, the congregation calls out in unison הַמָּקוֹם יְנַחֵם אֶתְכֶם בְּתוֹךְ שְׁאָר אֲבֵלֵי צִיּוֹן וִירוּשָׁלָיִם (page 323) [ערוה״ש יו״ד, ת: ה].

448 The congregation says the last two psalms of Kabbalat Shabbat, מִזְמוֹר שִׁיר לְיוֹם הַשַּׁבָּת (Ps. 92) and יהוה מָלָךְ (Ps. 93). This is followed by the Mourner's Kaddish and the second chapter of Mishna *Shabbat* (בַּמֶּה מַדְלִיקִין) [שו״ע או״ח, ער: א]. Some congregations outside Israel say בַּמֶּה מַדְלִיקִין after Full Kaddish at the end of Ma'ariv instead [משנ״ב, שם: ב].

449 Ma'ariv for Shabbat and Yom Tov: וְהוּא רַחוּם is omitted [טור או״ח, רסז]. The *Shaliaḥ Tzibbur* moves to the front of the synagogue to say *Barekhu*. It is preferable for Ma'ariv to begin after nightfall. If it does not, the congregation needs to repeat the Shema after nightfall [משנ״ב או״ח, רסז: ג]. The conclusion of הַשְׁכִּיבֵנוּ is different from the weekday formula, and בָּרוּךְ יהוה לְעוֹלָם is omitted [שו״ע שם, ג]. If one erroneously concludes הַשְׁכִּיבֵנוּ with the weekday blessing, one should say the correct blessing, provided one remembers immediately. If not, one does not repeat the blessing [משנ״ב, שם: ט]. It is customary to say וְשָׁמְרוּ (page 345) before the Amida [משנ״ב, שם]. If it is also Yom Tov, one adds the verse relating to the Festival (וַיְדַבֵּר מֹשֶׁה, page 345).

450 The Shabbat Ma'ariv Amida is said (page 347). On Rosh Ḥodesh, יַעֲלֶה וְיָבוֹא is added in the fifth blessing (page 353). On Ḥanukka, עַל הַנִּסִּים is added in the sixth blessing (page 355).

451 If one begins to say the Amida for weekdays on Shabbat and remembers in the middle of the Amida, one should complete the blessing already started, then begin the fourth blessing for the appropriate Shabbat Amida [שו״ע או״ח, רסח: ב]. If one remembers after completing the Amida, the correct Amida should be said from the beginning [שם: ד].

452 One who says the Amida for the wrong Shabbat service (e.g., saying the Amida for Shaḥarit during Minḥa), does not repeat the Amida. The exception is one who says the wrong Amida during Musaf, or the Musaf Amida during a different

service, in which case the Amida must be repeated [שם:ו]. If, however, one remembers during the Amida, one goes back to the beginning of the fourth blessing of the correct Amida [משנ״ב, שם:טו].

453 After the Amida, the *Shaliaḥ Tzibbur* and congregation say וַיְכֻלּוּ (page 359) [שו״ע או״ח, רסח:ז]. The *Shaliaḥ Tzibbur* says the abbreviated Repetition of the Amida, unless prayers are said in a location where (a) services are not held in a regular fashion, or (b) there is no Torah scroll [משנ״ב, שם:כד]. The *Shaliaḥ Tzibbur* says the Full Kaddish. Some congregations say בַּמֶּה מַדְלִיקִין (page 329) at this point. From Shabbat Ḥol HaMo'ed Pesaḥ until Shavuot, the Omer is counted (page 285). The congregation says *Aleinu*, followed by the Mourner's Kaddish. From the 1st of Elul through Shemini Atzeret, Psalm 27 (page 369) is said. It is customary to conclude with the singing of Yigdal or Adon Olam.

454 Some congregations have the custom to say Kiddush in the synagogue prior to *Aleinu*. However, since Kiddush should generally be said where the Shabbat meal is eaten, where possible, the Kiddush wine should be drunk by a child (or children) under the age of bar/bat mitzva. If this is not possible, the person making Kiddush may drink the wine [שו״ע או״ח, רסט:א].

455 Upon returning home, the custom is to say (or sing) a number of traditional songs and prayers. Some have the custom to bless their children. The Kiddush for Shabbat is an affirmative mitzva from the Torah. By custom, one person says Kiddush and the others listen attentively, fulfilling their obligation by proxy (based on the principle of שומע כעונה – "one who hears is as one who says"). Women are obligated in this mitzva, and a woman is permitted to say Kiddush for herself and others [שו״ע או״ח, רעא:ב]. It is customary to punctuate the meal with *Zemirot*. After the meal, one adds רְצֵה to the third blessing of *Birkat HaMazon* (page 983). On Rosh Ḥodesh, יַעֲלֶה וְיָבוֹא (page 985) is added after רְצֵה [שו״ע או״ח, קפח:ה].

SHABBAT DAY

456 One does not put on tefillin. Prayers begin as on weekdays, although one adds special verses for Shabbat in the section of *Korbanot* (page 51) [שו״ע ורמ״א או״ח, מח:א]. *Pesukei DeZimra*: as for Shabbat and Yom Tov (page 399) [שו״ע או״ח, נא:ט]. After אָז יָשִׁיר, the congregation says *Nishmat*. The *Shaliaḥ Tzibbur* for Shaḥarit begins from the words שׁוֹכֵן עַד.

457 Shaharit: as for Shabbat and Yom Tov. After *Barekhu*, the congregation says הַכֹּל יוֹדוּךָ (page 457). The Shabbat Amida is said. On Rosh Ḥodesh, יַעֲלֶה וְיָבוֹא is added in the fifth blessing (page 487). On Ḥanukka, עַל הַנִּסִּים is added in the sixth blessing (page 491). After the Repetition of the Amida, on Rosh Ḥodesh, the congregation says Half Hallel [שו״ע או״ח, תכב: ב]. The *Shaliaḥ Tzibbur* then says Full Kaddish. Some congregations follow the Sephardi custom of saying at this point the Daily Psalm (Ps. 92) and, if applicable, Ps. 104 or 27 (see law 460), followed by the Mourner's Kaddish.

458 Torah Reading: see laws 383–397. Seven are called up, though additional individuals may also be called up [שו״ע או״ח, רפב: א]. After completing the final *aliya*, the *Ba'al Koreh* says Half Kaddish. The Maftir is called up, and the appropriate portion is read, followed by the Haftara. After the Haftara and its blessings, the congregation says *Yekum Purkan* and the blessing for the congregation (page 517) [רמ״א או״ח, רפד: ז]. This is followed by the prayers for the government and the State of Israel. On a Shabbat immediately preceding Rosh Ḥodesh, *Birkat HaḤodesh* is said (page 527), except on the Shabbat preceding Tishrei.

459 The congregation says אַב הָרַחֲמִים, except (a) on days when *Taḥanun* is omitted, (b) when *Birkat HaḤodesh* is said (except for the months of Iyar and Sivan), and (c) on *Shabbat Shekalim, Zakhor, Para* and *HaḤodesh* [רמ״א או״ח, רפד: ז]. *Ashrei* is said, the Torah is returned to the Ark, and the *Shaliaḥ Tzibbur* says Half Kaddish.

460 Musaf for Shabbat: On Rosh Ḥodesh, the entire fourth blessing follows a special formula (אַתָּה יָצַרְתָּ, page 543); on Ḥanukka, עַל הַנִּסִּים (page 551) is added in the sixth blessing. The *Shaliaḥ Tzibbur* repeats the Amida. This is followed by Full Kaddish, *Ein Keloheinu*, the Rabbis' Kaddish, *Aleinu*, Mourner's Kaddish, and the Daily Psalm (Ps. 92). On Rosh Ḥodesh, Psalm 104, *Barekhi Nafshi* (page 191), is added; from the 1st of Elul to Shemini Azeret, Psalm 27 is added (page 569). Mourner's Kaddish, *Anim Zemirot* (page 571), Mourner's Kaddish, and Adon Olam.

461 The time for saying Musaf is immediately after Shaḥarit. Musaf should be said no later than the seventh halakhic "hour" of the day, which is 7⁄12 of the period from daybreak to nightfall. However, if one said Musaf at any time before sunset, one has fulfilled the obligation [שו״ע או״ח, רפו: א].

462 Shabbat Morning Kiddush should be said where one eats the Shabbat meal [שו״ע או״ח, רפט: א]. If no wine or grape juice is available, one may say Kiddush over a cup of liquor or other beverage, but not over water or bread [שם: ב].

463 Minḥa: After *Ashrei* and וּבָא לְצִיּוֹן, the *Shaliaḥ Tzibbur* says Half Kaddish, the congregation says וַאֲנִי תְפִלָּתִי־לְךָ (page 601), and the Torah is taken from the Ark [שו״ע

[ורמ"א או"ח, רצב: א]. Three are called up, and the beginning of the following week's Torah portion is read. Half Kaddish is not said. After the Torah is returned to the Ark, the *Shaliaḥ Tzibbur* says Half Kaddish, and the congregation says the Shabbat Minḥa Amida. On Rosh Ḥodesh, יַעֲלֶה וְיָבוֹא is added in the fifth blessing (page 615). On Ḥanukka, עַל הַנִּסִּים is added in the sixth blessing (page 617). After the Repetition of the Amida, the congregation says צִדְקָתְךָ, except on a day when *Taḥanun* is omitted [שם: ב]. This is followed by Full Kaddish, *Aleinu* and Mourner's Kaddish.

464 Some congregations say Psalm 104 (בָּרְכִי נַפְשִׁי) and the fifteen psalms beginning שִׁיר הַמַּעֲלוֹת, Ps. 120–34 (pages 629–639) after Shabbat Minḥa, from *Shabbat Bereshit* until *Shabbat HaGadol* [רמ"א, שם].

465 It is customary to read a chapter of the Ethics of the Fathers (*Pirkei Avot*, page 641) after Shabbat Minḥa, from the Shabbat after Pesaḥ to the Shabbat before Rosh HaShana [שם].

466 One should have a third meal (*Se'uda Shelishit*) on Shabbat [שו"ע או"ח, רצא: א]. Women are also obligated to eat *Se'uda Shelishit* [שם: ו]. The meal should begin with bread, unless one is too full to eat bread [שם: ה]. After the meal, one adds רְצֵה (page 983) to *Birkat HaMazon*, even if the meal extends past nightfall.

MOTZA'EI SHABBAT

467 In some congregations, Psalms 144 and 67 (pages 693–695) are sung before Ma'ariv.

468 Ma'ariv: as for weekdays (page 243). In the fourth blessing of the Amida, אַתָּה חוֹנַנְתָּנוּ (page 261) is added [שו"ע או"ח, רצד: א]. On Rosh Ḥodesh, יַעֲלֶה וְיָבוֹא (page 269) is added in the seventeenth blessing. If one forgets either of these additions, one does not repeat the Amida [שם]. After the silent Amida, unless Yom Tov falls in the following week, the *Shaliaḥ Tzibbur* says Half Kaddish and the congregation says וִיהִי נֹעַם and וְאַתָּה קָדוֹשׁ (pages 695–699) [רמ"א או"ח, רצה: א]. The *Shaliaḥ Tzibbur* then says Full Kaddish. From the second day of Pesaḥ until Shavuot, the Omer is counted (page 285). Some have the custom to say וְיִתֶּן לְךָ (page 703) [שם]. In most congregations, the *Shaliaḥ Tzibbur* says Havdala [שו"ע, שם]. The congregation says *Aleinu*, followed by Mourner's Kaddish. From the 1st of Elul to Shemini Azeret, Psalm 27 is said (page 715).

469 After nightfall, one may not perform labor until one says Havdala or hears it said. If one says אַתָּה חוֹנַנְתָּנוּ in Ma'ariv (page 261), one may perform labor after nightfall prior to Havdala [רמ״א או״ח, רצט: י].

470 Each month, one says Kiddush Levana (page 715) on seeing the New Moon at night. Kiddush Levana may be said from the eve of the fourth day of the new month until the middle day of the month. By custom, it is said on the first Motza'ei Shabbat that falls within the time span, preferably outdoors with a *minyan*. [שו״ע ורמ״א או״ח, תכו].

471 Havdala is said at home if (a) one did not say אַתָּה חוֹנַנְתָּנוּ or hear Havdala in the synagogue; (b) one said אַתָּה חוֹנַנְתָּנוּ or heard Havdala, but intended not to fulfill one's obligation; or (c) someone at home did not yet hear Havdala [שו״ע או״ח, רצו: ז; משנ״ב, שם: לב]. Women may say Havdala for themselves [משנ״ב, שם: לה–לו]. If one forgets to say Havdala on Motza'ei Shabbat, one may say it as late as Tuesday night.

472 After Shabbat, one should eat a meal, the *Melaveh Malka*, as a way of marking the end of Shabbat [שו״ע או״ח, ש: א].

A HALAKHIC GUIDE TO PRAYER FOR VISITORS TO ISRAEL

GENERAL RULES
PUBLIC VS. PRIVATE CONDUCT

473 For halakhic purposes, the definition of "visitor" is one who intends to return to his place of origin within one year [משנ״ב, קיז: ה]. Unmarried students may be considered visitors as long as they are supported by their parents [שו״ת אגרות משה או״ח ח״ב, קא].

474 In general, a visitor to Israel should continue to follow his or her customs in private. In public, however, one should avoid conduct that deviates from local practice [שו״ע או״ח, תסח: ד; משנ״ב, שם: יד]. Hence, a visitor to Israel should generally pray in accordance with his non-Israeli customs. This rule is limited, however, to one's private prayers.

475 If one is serving as *Shaliaḥ Tzibbur*, one is required to pray in accordance with the local Israeli custom. This includes, for example, repeating the Amida according to Israeli practice: saying מוֹרִיד הַטָּל in the summer, saying וְתֵן טַל וּמָטָר לִבְרָכָה from the 7th of Marḥeshvan onward, and saying שִׂים שָׁלוֹם during Minḥa on Shabbat (page 619). This also includes saying *Ein Keloheinu* at the end of weekday Shaḥarit (page 195).

476 If one is serving as *Shaliaḥ Tzibbur* for Musaf on Yom Tov in a congregation of Israelis, in the silent Amida one should say the *Korbanot* as said outside Israel, but when repeating the Amida, say them following the Israeli practice [יום טוב שני כהלכתו, א (בשם שערי יצחק)].

477 In Israel (and in some congregations outside Israel), *Taḥanun* is not said from *Isru Ḥag* of Simḥat Torah until Rosh Ḥodesh Marḥeshvan, and from *Isru Ḥag* of Shavuot until the 12th of Sivan.

478 Even if one is not serving as *Shaliaḥ Tzibbur*, a visitor praying with Israelis should say the following prayers, because of their public nature, following local Israeli custom:

- **a** Many Israeli congregations (some daily, others only on Mondays and Thursdays) adopt the Sephardi custom of saying *Viduy* and the י״ג מידות (the Thirteen Attributes of Mercy) prior to *Taḥanun* in Shaḥarit (page 137). One who prays in such a congregation must say at least the י״ג מידות [שו״ת אגרות משה או״ח ח״ג, פט].
- **b** *Birkat Kohanim* is said daily in Shaḥarit and Musaf, in Minḥa on fast days and *Ne'ila* on Yom Kippur, although not in certain communities in northern Israel.
- **c** *Birkat HaḤodesh* concludes with the extended version of יְחַדְּשֵׁהוּ (page 527).
- **d** *Barekhu* is said at the end of weekday Shaḥarit (except on Mondays and Thursdays) and at the end of Ma'ariv.
- **e** In the Rabbis' Kaddish, the word קַדִּישָׁא is added after the words דִּי בְאַתְרָא.

Laws of Tefillin on Ḥol HaMo'ed

479 The custom in Israel is not to put on tefillin on Ḥol HaMo'ed. One whose custom is to put on tefillin on Ḥol HaMo'ed may, when visiting Israel, put on tefillin in private, but should not do so when praying with a congregation [שו״ת אגרות משה או״ח ח״ד, קה: ה].

Laws of וְתֵן טַל וּמָטָר לִבְרָכָה

480 If one is visiting Israel on the 7th of Marḥeshvan, when Israeli residents begin saying וְתֵן טַל וּמָטָר לִבְרָכָה, and one intends to remain in Israel until after the 4th (or 5th) of December, when nonresidents of Israel begin saying וְתֵן טַל וּמָטָר לִבְרָכָה, one should also begin to say וְתֵן טַל וּמָטָר לִבְרָכָה. If, however, one intends to leave Israel before then, there are two opinions: (a) while one remains in Israel one should say וְתֵן טַל וּמָטָר לִבְרָכָה, but upon leaving Israel one need not continue saying it [בה״ט או״ח, קיז: ד], and (b) while one remains in Israel one should add וְתֵן טַל וּמָטָר לִבְרָכָה to the blessing of שׁוֹמֵעַ תְּפִלָּה [אשי ישראל, כג: לו (בשם רשז״א אויערבאך)].

481 If, between the 7th of Marḥeshvan and the 4th (or 5th) of December, one forgets to say וְתֵן טַל וּמָטָר לִבְרָכָה, one need not repeat the Amida [שו״ת בצל החכמה ח״א, סב].

Laws of Second Day Yom Tov – יום טוב שני של גלויות

482 Most authorities require a visitor to Israel to celebrate two days of Yom Tov [משנ״ב, תצו: יג]. Some hold that one should not publicly celebrate the second day, but say the festival prayers in private [שם]. Others permit organizing a public service for visitors on the second day of Yom Tov, and this has become the accepted practice. If, however, there are fewer than ten visitors, they should pray privately, rather than recruit Israeli residents to complete a *minyan* [אשי ישראל, טו: יח (בשם רשז״ו אויערבאך)].

483 Some authorities rule that a visitor to Israel should celebrate only one day of Yom Tov, but, on the next day (Yom Tov outside Israel, but either Ḥol HaMo'ed or *Isru Ḥag* in Israel), one should abstain from labor and perform the מצוות עשה דאורייתא associated with Yom Tov [עיר הקודש והמקדש ח״ג, פ: יא]:

a On the second day of Sukkot, one says Ḥol HaMo'ed prayers rather than those of Yom Tov, but refrains from performing any labor.

b On the day after Shemini Atzeret (Simḥat Torah outside Israel, *Isru Ḥag* in Israel), one abstains from labor, but says weekday prayers (putting on tefillin in the morning).

c On the second night of Pesaḥ, one should say (or listen to) Kiddush, eat a *kezayit* of matza (without saying עַל אֲכִילַת מַצָּה) and read the Haggada (without the final blessings), because all of these are affirmative mitzvot from the Torah. One should refrain from performing labor, but say Ḥol HaMo'ed prayers, rather than those of Yom Tov.

d On the eighth day of Pesaḥ, one abstains from labor and eating *ḥametz*, but prays the weekday prayers (putting on tefillin in the morning, if applicable).

484 Some authorities rule that a visitor to Israel should celebrate only one day of Yom Tov. According to this view, the visitor should follow local Israeli practice without deviation [שו״ת חכם צבי, קסז].

485 If the second day of Yom Tov outside Israel falls on Shabbat, a visitor to Israel may be called to the Torah, even though the portion being read is for Shabbat, not Yom Tov [אשי ישראל, לח: ל (בשם רשז״ו אויערבאך)].

486 On a day when *Yizkor* is said in Israel, a visitor should not join, but should say *Yizkor the following day* with a *minyan* of visitors. If such a *minyan* will not be available, some rule that one should join with the Israelis [שו״ת רבבות אפרים ח״א, שמב: ב]; others rule that *Yizkor* be said in private the following day [שו״ת בצל החכמה ח״ד, קב: א].

Laws of קריאת התורה

487 When the eighth day of Pesaḥ or the second day of Shavuot falls on Shabbat, congregations in Israel will read the appropriate weekly Torah portion, while congregations outside Israel will read the special portion for Yom Tov. As a result, a person traveling to or from Israel may hear the same Torah reading two weeks in a row or miss an entire Torah portion. One who misses the reading of a Torah portion may (some say, should) organize a *minyan* for the reading of that portion for oneself [אשי ישראל לח, כט: פח].

Laws of Purim

488 In Jerusalem, Purim is celebrated on the 15th of Adar (Shushan Purim). Outside Jerusalem, Purim is celebrated on the 14th of Adar. For a resident of Jerusalem, the day of Purim is an ordinary day: one performs none of the obligations relating to Purim and one says the regular weekday prayers, although one omits *Taḥanun*.

489 One is considered a resident of Jerusalem for these purposes if one is present in Jerusalem at dawn on the morning of the 15th of Adar. Similarly, one is considered a non-resident of Jerusalem for these purposes if one is outside Jerusalem at dawn on the 14th of Adar. There is, however, an opinion that the determining factor is one's intention on the preceding evening [משנ״ב, תרפח: יג].

490 As a practical matter, a person who stays overnight outside Jerusalem on Purim eve, but stays overnight in Jerusalem on Shushan Purim eve, is obligated to celebrate Purim twice – first on the 14th of Adar, along with non-residents of Jerusalem, and then on the 15th of Adar, along with residents of Jerusalem. Conversely, a person who stays overnight in Jerusalem on Purim eve but stays overnight outside Jerusalem on Shushan Purim eve would have no obligation to celebrate Purim at all.

491 Special rules apply to residents of Jerusalem when Shushan Purim falls on Shabbat, a situation known as *Purim Meshulash*. On Thursday night and Friday morning (14th Adar), the Megilla (page 1225) is read, as is the practice outside Jerusalem. On Friday one also performs the mitzva of מתנות לאביונים (gifts to the poor). On Shabbat one adds עַל הַנִּסִּים to both the Amida and *Birkat HaMazon*. For Maftir one reads the Torah portion for Purim (page 1122). The Haftara is as for Shabbat Zakhor: 1 Sam. 15:2–34. On Sunday one performs the mitzva of משלוח מנות (sending food portions) and סעודת פורים (the Purim feast), but one does not add עַל הַנִּסִּים to the Amida or *Birkat HaMazon* [שו״ע או״ח, תרפח: ו].

TEXTUAL VARIANTS

Note: The text of this Siddur reflects the accumulation of centuries of debate and deliberation on matters of meaning, syntax and grammar. Below is a table which compares, with respect to selected passages, the text of this Siddur with alternate readings that are also endorsed by practice or noted halakhic authorities.

Page	*Koren Text*	*Alternate Text*
25, 371	הנו אדון עולם, וְכָל נוֹצָר... Behold He is Master of the Universe; and every creature…	הנו אדון עולם לְכָל נוֹצָר... Behold He is Master of the Universe; to every creature…
39	...הַמְקַדֵּשׁ את שְׁמוֹ ברבים. … who sanctifies His name among the multitudes.	...מְקַדֵּשׁ את שִׁמְךָ ברבים. … who sanctifies Your name among the multitudes.
Kaddish	יתגַּדַּל ויתקַדַּשׁ... Magnified and sanctified… (Aramaic)	יתגַּדֵּל ויתקַדֵּשׁ... Magnified and sanctified… (Hebrew)
Kaddish	לעלא לְעלא... above and beyond…	לעלא ולעלא above and beyond…
Kaddish	עשה הַשָּׁלוֹם... May He who makes the peace…	עשה שָׁלוֹם... May He who makes peace…
Rabbis' Kaddish	...**יעשה ברחמיו** שלום … in His compassion make peace	...**ברחמיו יעשה** שלום … in His compassion make peace
65, 405	...המהלל **בְּפִי** עמו … extolled by the mouth of His people	...המהלל **בְּפֶה** עמו … extolled by the mouth of His people
93, 465	בשפה ברורה ובנעימה, **קְדֻשָּׁה** כולם כאחד … in pure speech and sweet melody. All as one proclaim His holiness…	בשפה ברורה, ובנעימה **קְדוֹשָׁה**, כולם כאחד … in pure speech and sweet and holy melody. All as one proclaim…
Amida	משיב הרוח ומוריד הַגֶּשֶׁם He makes the wind blow and the rain fall.	משיב הרוח ומוריד הַגָּשֶׁם He makes the wind blow and the rain fall.
Amida	...ושבענו מטוּבָהּ … and from its goodness satisfy us	...ושבענו מטוּבֶךָ … and from Your goodness satisfy us
Amida	...וכל **אוֹיְבֵי עַמְּךָ** … all Your people's enemies	...וכל **אוֹיְבֶיךָ** … all Your enemies…
Amida	ושים חלקנו עמהם, **וּלְעוֹלָם לא** נבוש... Set our lot with them, so that we may never be ashamed…	ושים חלקנו עמהם **לְעוֹלָם, וְלֹא** נבוש... Set our lot with them forever, so that we may not be ashamed…
Amida	והשב את העבודה לדביר ביתך, **ואשי ישראל ותפלתם** באהבה תקבל ברצון. Restore the service to Your most holy House, and accept in love and favor the fire-offerings of Israel and their prayer.	והשב את העבודה לדביר ביתך **ואשי ישראל. ותפלתם באהבה** תקבל ברצון. Restore the service and the fire-offerings of Israel to Your most holy House, and in love and favor accept their prayer.

Page	*Koren Text*	*Alternate Text*
Amida	על הנסים... For the miracles...	וְעל הנסים... And for the miracles...
Amida	...ברכנו בברכה המשלשת **בתורה**, הכתובה... bless us with the threefold blessing in the Torah, written...	...ברכנו בברכה המשלשת, **בתורה** הכתובה... bless us with the threefold blessing, written in the Torah...
139	...זכרנו **בְּזִכְרוֹן** טוב לפניך. ...remember us with a memory of favorable deeds before You.	...זכרנו **בְּזִכָּרוֹן** טוב לפניך. ...remember us with a favorable memory before You.
245, 335	אל חי **וקיים תמיד**, ימלך עלינו May the living and forever enduring God rule over us...	אל חי וקיים, **תמיד ימלך** עלינו... May the living and enduring God rule over us for ever...
255	המלך **בכבודו תמיד**, ימלך עלינו... the King who in His constant glory will reign over us...	המלך בכבודו, **תמיד ימלך** עלינו... the King who in His glory will constantly reign over us...
285–293	היום __ ימים **בָּ**עמר. Today is the __ day of the Omer.	היום __ ימים **לָ**עמר. Today is the __ day of the Omer.
543, 813	...מפני היד **שנשתלחה** במקדשך. ...because of the hand that was stretched out against Your Sanctuary.	...מפני היד **הַשְׁלוּחָה** במקדשך. ...because of the hand stretched out against Your Sanctuary.
615	והנחילנו... **שבתות** קדשך ...grant us as our heritage Your holy Sabbaths	והנחילנו... **שַׁבַּת** קדשך ...grant us as our heritage Your holy Sabbath
749	זכרון לכולם **יִהְיוּ, וּתְשׁוּעַת** נפשם... May it serve as a remembrance for them all, and a deliverance...	זכרון לכולם **הָיוּ, תְּשׁוּעַת** נפשם... It served as a remembrance for them all, and a deliverance...
863	אני והו הושיעה נא Please save us, me and him	אני והו הושיעה נא Please save us, Ani vaHo
905	...ברוכים כל **ישראל**. ...blessed be all Israel.	...ברוכים כל **הַצַּדִּיקִים**. ...blessed be all the righteous.
905	ארורים כל הרשעים, ברוכים כל ישראל. Cursed be all the wicked; blessed be all Israel.	אין Omitted
985	...כי אל רחום וחנון אתה. ...because You are God, gracious and compassionate.	...כי אל **מֶלֶךְ** רחום וחנון אתה. ...because You are God, gracious and compassionate King.
985	...בונה **ברחמיו** ירושלים אמן. ...who in His compassion will rebuild Jerusalem.	...בונה ירושלים אמן. ...who will rebuild Jerusalem.
1019	אל חי... **צִוָּה** להציל ידידות שארנו משחת. the Living God...did order deliverance from destruction for the beloved of our flesh.	אל חי... **צַוֵּה** להציל ידידות שארנו משחת. the Living God...order deliverance from destruction for the beloved of our flesh.

TABLE OF PERMITTED RESPONSES

	Pesukei DeZimra (from Barukh SheAmar to Yishtabaḥ)	*Within a paragraph of the Shema or the preceding blessings*[1]	*Between the paragraphs of the Shema or the preceding blessings*	*Between concluding the blessing גָּאַל יִשְׂרָאֵל and beginning the Amida*[2]
אָמֵן יְהֵא שְׁמֵהּ רַבָּא; אָמֵן following דַּאֲמִירָן בְּעָלְמָא[3]	Permissible	Permissible	Permissible	Forbidden [שו״ע או״ח סו, ט; משנ״ב נא, ח]
אָמֵן following any blessing	Permissible	Forbidden	Permissible	Forbidden[4]
בָּרוּךְ הוּא וּבָרוּךְ שְׁמוֹ; בְּרִיךְ הוּא	Forbidden[5]	Forbidden	Forbidden	Forbidden
Tallit	Put on the tallit, but say the blessing between paragraphs [משנ״ב נג, ה]	Put on the tallit, but say the blessing after the Amida [שו״ע ורמ״א או״ח סו, ב]	Put on the tallit, but say the blessing after the Amida	Forbidden [שו״ע או״ח סו, ח]
Tefillin	Put on the tefillin, but say the blessings between sections [משנ״ב נג, ה]	Before the Shema: forbidden; within the Shema, put on the tefillin and say the blessing [משנ״ב סו, טו]	Permissible	Put on the tefillin, but say the blessings after the Amida [שו״ע או״ח סו, ח]

---

1. The paragraphs are as follows: from the blessing יוֹצֵר אוֹר to יוֹצֵר הַמְּאוֹרוֹת; from אַהֲבָה רַבָּה or אַהֲבַת עוֹלָם to Shema; from Shema to וּבִשְׁעָרֶיךָ; from וְהָיָה אִם שָׁמֹעַ to עַל־הָאָרֶץ; from וַיֹּאמֶר to גָּאַל יִשְׂרָאֵל [שו״ע או״ח סו, ה]. Responses permitted within a paragraph are also permissible within a verse, though it is preferable to respond only at the end of a thought.
2. Some rule that on Shabbat one may respond to Kaddish, *Barekhu*, *Kedusha* or *Modim* [רמ״א או״ח קיא, א]. See law 362.
3. Only these are required responses; the other responses of אָמֵן in Kaddish are only a custom [משנ״ב סו, יז].
4. One may answer אָמֵן if one hears another concluding the blessing גָּאַל יִשְׂרָאֵל [רמ״א או״ח סו, ז].
5. These responses are only a custom, as they are not mentioned in the Gemara [משנ״ב נא, ח].

	Pesukei DeZimra (from Barukh SheAmar to Yishtabaḥ)	*Within a paragraph of the Shema or the preceding blessings*[1]	*Between the paragraphs of the Shema or the preceding blessings*	*Between concluding the blessing גָּאַל יִשְׂרָאֵל and beginning the Amida*[2]
Barekhu[6]	Permissible	Permissible	Permissible	Forbidden
Shema	Say the first verse with the congregation [משנ״ב סה, יא]	Forbidden, except to close one's eyes and sing the melody of the Shema	Forbidden, except to close one's eyes and sing the melody of the Shema[7] [שו״ע או״ח סה, ב]	Forbidden
Kedusha	Permissible[8] [משנ״ב נא, ח]	Say only the verses beginning קָדוֹשׁ and בָּרוּךְ	Say only the verses beginning קָדוֹשׁ and בָּרוּךְ	Forbidden [משנ״ב סו, יז]
אָמֵן after הָאֵל הַקָּדוֹשׁ and שׁוֹמֵעַ תְּפִלָּה	Permissible	Permissible	Permissible	Forbidden [רמ״א או״ח סו, ג]
Modim DeRabanan	Permissible	Say only the words מוֹדִים אֲנַחְנוּ לָךְ	Say only the words מוֹדִים אֲנַחְנוּ לָךְ	Forbidden [משנ״ב סו, כ]
Being called up to the Torah[9]	Permissible	Permissible – but not in the middle of the first verse of the Shema or בָּרוּךְ שֵׁם כְּבוֹד מַלְכוּתוֹ לְעוֹלָם וָעֶד	Permissible	Forbidden [משנ״ב סו, כו]

6. Whether before the blessings of the Shema or before the Reading of the Torah. The blessings said by the עוֹלֶה are like any other blessing [משנ״ב סו, יח].
7. If the congregation is saying *Aleinu*, one should stand and bow with them [ערוה״ש או״ח סה, ו].
8. Say only the biblical verses [אשי ישראל פט״ו, לא; see law 369].
9. The Gabba'im should not call up to the Torah one who is in the middle of prayer; however, if only one Kohen is present, he may be called up. Likewise, if only one person knows how to read the Torah, he may interrupt his prayers in order to be the *ba'al koreh* [משנ״ב סו, כו].

	Pesukei DeZimra (from Barukh SheAmar to Yishtabaḥ)	*Within a paragraph of the Shema or the preceding blessings*[1]	*Between the paragraphs of the Shema or the preceding blessings*	*Between concluding the blessing* גָּאַל יִשְׂרָאֵל *and beginning the Amida*[2]
אֲשֶׁר יָצַר	Say the blessing between paragraphs [בה״ל, נא ד״ה צריך]	Wash one's hands, but say the blessing after the Amida	Wash one's hands, but say the blessing after the Amida	Wash one's hands, but say the blessing after the Amida [משנ״ב סו, כג]
Blessing on thunder or lightning	Permissible	Forbidden	Permissible, if the opportunity may not recur	Forbidden [משנ״ב סו, יט]

GENERAL RULES

MA'ARIV

The rules regarding responses are identical to those of Shaḥarit. After the blessing שׁוֹמֵר עַמּוֹ יִשְׂרָאֵל לָעַד until Half Kaddish, is considered to be between paragraphs, even in the middle of בָּרוּךְ יהוה לְעוֹלָם אָמֵן וְאָמֵן [ביאור הלכה סו ד״ה ואלו].

HALLEL

The laws regarding responses during Hallel are identical to those of the Shema [שו״ע או״ח תפח, א]. If a Lulav is brought in the middle of Hallel, one should say the blessing between paragraphs of Hallel [משנ״ב תרמד, ז].

REMOVING A CRYING CHILD

One should remove a crying child from the synagogue even while saying the Amida, in order to avoid disturbing others who are praying [אשי ישראל פל״ב, יג (בשם החזון איש)].

KADDISH DURING PESUKEI DEZIMRA

A mourner is permitted to say Kaddish during *Pesukei DeZimra,* if he will be unable to say it afterwards [אשי ישראל פט״ו הערה קט].

PSALMS FOR SPECIAL OCCASIONS

The following Psalms may be said on special occasions:

On the day of one's wedding	Ps. 19 on page 411
On the birth of a child	Ps. 20 on page 173 and Ps. 139 on page 1045
For someone who is ill	Ps. 23, page 1045; Ps. 121, page 633; Ps. 130, page 637; and Ps. 139 on page 1045
For safety in Israel	Ps. 20 on page 173; Ps. 120 on page 633; Ps. 121 on page 633 and Ps. 125 on page 635
On recovery from illness	Ps. 6 on page 153; Ps. 30 on page 399 and Ps. 103 on page 1045
Thanksgiving	Ps. 95 on page 311; Ps. 116 on page 737
For guidance	Ps. 139 on page 1045
For success	Ps. 121 on page 633
For repentance	Ps. 90 on page 417
For help in difficult times	Ps. 20 on page 173; Ps. 130 on page 637
When traveling	Ps. 91 on page 695
In thanksgiving for being saved	Ps. 124 on page 635

JEWISH LEAP YEARS

The words וּלְכַפָּרַת פָּשַׁע *are added in the* מוסף עמידה *of* ראש חודש *during the months of* מרחשון *to* אדר שני *in Jewish leap years.*

JEWISH YEAR	CIVIL YEAR
5779	2018–2019
5782	2021–2022
5784	2023–2024
5787	2026–2027
5790	2029–2030
5793	2032–2033
5795	2034–2035
5798	2037–2038

RABBIS' KADDISH

Mourner: Yitgadal ve-yitkadash shemeh raba. (*Cong:* Amen)
Be-alema di vera khir'uteh, ve-yamlikh malkhuteh,
be-ḥayyeikhon, uv-yomeikhon,
uv-ḥayyei de-khol beit Yisrael,
ba-agala uvi-zman kariv,
ve-imru Amen. (*Cong:* Amen)

All: Yeheh shemeh raba mevarakh le'alam ul-alemei alemaya.

Mourner: Yitbarakh ve-yishtabaḥ ve-yitpa'ar ve-yitromam ve-yitnaseh
ve-yit-hadar ve-yit'aleh ve-yit-hallal
shemeh dekudsha, berikh hu. (*Cong:* Berikh hu)
Le-ela min kol birkhata
/*Between Rosh HaShana & Yom Kippur:* Le-ela le-ela mi-kol birkhata/
ve-shirata, tushbeḥata ve-neḥemata, da-amiran be-alema,
ve-imru, Amen. (*Cong:* Amen)

Al Yisrael, ve-al rabanan,
ve-al talmideihon, ve-al kol talmidei talmideihon,
ve-al kol man de-asekin be-oraita
di be-atra (*In Israel:* kadisha) ha-dein ve-di be-khol atar va-atar,
yeheh lehon ul-khon shelama raba,
ḥina ve-ḥisda, ve-raḥamei,
ve-ḥayyei arikhei, um-zonei re-viḥei,
u-furkana min kodam avuhon di vish-maya,
ve-imru Amen. (*Cong:* Amen)

Yeheh shelama raba min shemaya
ve-ḥayyim (tovim) aleinu ve-al kol Yisrael,
ve-imru Amen. (*Cong:* Amen)

Bow, take three steps back, as if taking leave of the Divine Presence, then bow, first left, then right, then center, while saying:
Oseh shalom/*Between Rosh HaShana & Yom Kippur:* ha-shalom/
bim-romav,
hu ya'aseh ve-raḥamav shalom aleinu, ve-al kol Yisrael,
ve-imru Amen. (*Cong:* Amen)

MOURNER'S KADDISH

Mourner: Yitgadal ve-yitkadash shemeh raba. (*Cong:* Amen)
Be-alema di vera khir'uteh, ve-yamlikh malkhuteh,
be-ḥayyeikhon, uv-yomeikhon,
uv-ḥayyei de-khol beit Yisrael,
ba-agala uvi-zman kariv,
ve-imru Amen. (*Cong:* Amen)

All: Yeheh shemeh raba mevarakh le'alam ul-alemei alemaya.

Mourner: Yitbarakh ve-yishtabaḥ ve-yitpa'ar ve-yitromam ve-yitnaseh
ve-yit-hadar ve-yit'aleh ve-yit-hallal
shemeh dekudsha, berikh hu. (*Cong:* Berikh hu)
Le-ela min kol birkhata
/*Between Rosh HaShana & Yom Kippur:* Le-ela le-ela mi-kol birkhata/
ve-shirata, tushbeḥata ve-neḥemata, da-amiran be-alema,
ve-imru, Amen. (*Cong:* Amen)

Yeheh shelama raba min shemaya
ve-ḥayyim aleinu ve-al kol Yisrael,
ve-imru Amen. (*Cong:* Amen)

Bow, take three steps back, as if taking leave of the Divine Presence, then bow, first left, then right, then center, while saying:

Oseh shalom/*Between Rosh HaShana & Yom Kippur:* ha-shalom/
bim-romav,
hu ya'aseh shalom aleinu, ve-al kol Yisrael,
ve-imru Amen. (*Cong:* Amen)

קורן ירושלים